D0934505

THE WORLD'S BEST ESSAYS

David J. Brewer
Editor

Edward A. Allen & William Schuyler
Associate Editors

Volumes 6 - 10

Mini-Print® Corporation
Metuchen, N.J.   1971

OHIO STATE UNIVERSITY
LIMA BRANCH LIBRARY

The World's Best Essays
was originally published
in 10 volumes by
Ferd. P. Kaiser, St. Louis
c. 1900, 1902

ISBN 0-8108-0394-1

TABLE OF CONTENTS
VOLUME VI

HENRY HALLAM

(1777-1859)

HALLAM'S "Literary Essays and Characters," published in 1852, are made up of selections from his "Introduction to the Literature of Europe in the Fifteenth, Sixteenth, and Seventeenth Centuries,"—a work which, until Taine's "History of English Literature" appeared, held the first place among books of its class. Hallam's style is as unlike Taine's as possible and his method is the antithesis of Taine's, but he preceded, if he did not instruct, Taine in the classical method of dividing and subdividing a great subject into essays forming its topical units, so that each topic is presented in its wholeness, as well as in its connection with the larger whole. Hallam's "Literature of Europe"—which the general public has accepted as his masterpiece—becomes, as a result of this method, a true sequence of essays, each of which has an individuality of its own, while in many of them this individuality is so well defined that they are fully as capable of standing alone, outside of their connection, as any detached literary essay of De Quincey or Macaulay. As an essayist, Hallam deals in facts to a much greater extent than Macaulay or any of those essayists who formed their style as critical reviewers. His work represents original research, wide and deep. Professor Edward Robinson says that "in science and theology, mathematics and poetry, metaphysics and law, he is a competent and always a fair, if not a profound, critic," and adds that "the great qualities displayed in his work, conscientiousness, accuracy, and enormous reading, have been universally acknowledged." This is especially true of the "History of European Literature," which shows a range of reading equaled only by Gibbon. Hallam's "View of the Middle Ages" and his "Constitutional History of England" trace the development of modern England from the Feudal system to its present form of aristocratic constitutional government. It lacks the general interest which Blackstone knows how to give to even the most abstract subject, but it has become a recognized authority among English lawyers and public men, and if it is seldomer read than the "History of European Literature," it is not less widely distributed in England and America. In both countries, Hallam holds his place on the shelves with Gibbon, as he deserves to do because of a faculty of amassing and using details in which Gibbon alone surpasses him.

Hallam was born at Windsor, England, in 1777. After taking his degree at Christ Church, Oxford, in 1799, he studied at the Inner Temple and was called to the bar; but although his knowledge of the principles of law was profound, he never practiced his profession. His life was devoted to literature and to the historical research which appears so unmistakably in his three great works: "A View of the State of Europe during the Middle Ages," 1818; "The Constitutional History of England," 1827; and the "Introduction to the Literature of Europe," eleven years later. His eldest son, Arthur Henry Hallam, a young man of brilliant promise, died at the age of twenty-one, and was immortalized by Tennyson's "In Memoriam." In 1834 Hallam published "The Remains in Prose and Verse of Arthur Henry Hallam, with a Sketch of His Life." The "Literary Essays and Characters" already referred to followed this as the last of his important publications. He died January 21st, 1859, surviving all the great Whigs of the first half of the century except Macaulay, who died in December of the same year, and Brougham, who lingered in second childhood until 1868. Although Hallam took no direct part in politics, he was himself one of the "great Whigs" of his generation, but his Whiggery involved no leaning towards Democracy. He believed in the English constitution as an evolution of national character and in Aristocracy as a part of it, but he had the genuine Whig hatred of despotism. His death and that of Macaulay in the same year left the potent Whig idea of the eighteenth century without adequate representation in the literature of England during the second half of the nineteenth century. Old school Whiggery was succeeded by a quarter of a century of "Liberalism" which, as its logic worked out at the close of the century, has demonstrated itself as something far less masculine than the political idea, which from the days of Chatham to the middle of the nineteenth century was so decisive a factor in the progress of the world.   W. V. B.

THE FIRST BOOKS PRINTED IN EUROPE

ABOUT the end of the fourteenth century we find a practice of taking impressions from engraved blocks of wood; sometimes for playing cards, which were not generally used long before that time, sometimes for rude cuts of saints. The latter were frequently accompanied by a few lines of letters cut in the block. Gradually entire pages were impressed in this manner; and thus began what are called block books, printed in fixed characters, but never exceeding a very few leaves. Of these

there exist nine or ten, often reprinted, as it is generally thought, between 1400 and 1440. In using the word Printed, it is of course not intended to prejudice the question as to the real art of printing. These block books seem to have been all executed in the Low Countries. They are said to have been followed by several editions of the short grammar of Donatus. These also were printed in Holland. This mode of printing from blocks of wood has been practiced in China from time immemorial.

The invention of printing, in the modern sense, from movable letters, has been referred by most to Gutenberg, a native of Mentz, but settled at Strasburg. He is supposed to have conceived the idea before 1440, and to have spent the next ten years in making attempts at carrying it into effect, which some assert him to have done in short fugitive pieces, actually printed from his movable wooden characters before 1450. But of the existence of these, there seems to be no evidence. Gutenberg's priority is disputed by those who deem Lawrence Costar of Haarlem the real inventor of the art. According to a tradition, which seems not to be traced beyond the middle of the sixteenth century, but resting afterwards upon sufficient testimony to prove its local reception, Costar substituted movable for fixed letters as early as 1430; and some have believed that a book called "Speculum Humanæ Salvationis," of very rude wooden characters, proceeded from the Haarlem press before any other that is generally recognized. The tradition adds that an unfaithful servant, having fled with the secret, set up for himself at Strasburg or Mentz; and this treachery was originally ascribed to Gutenberg or Fust, but seems, since they have been manifestly cleared of it, to have been laid on one Gensfleisch, reputed to be the brother of Gutenberg. The evidence, however, as to this is highly precarious; and even if we were to admit the claims of Costar, there seems no fair reason to dispute that Gutenberg might also have struck out an idea, which surely did not require any extraordinary ingenuity, and left the most important difficulties to be surmounted, as they undeniably were, by himself and his coadjutors.

It is agreed by all that about 1450 Gutenberg, having gone to Mentz, entered into partnership with Fust, a rich merchant of that city, for the purpose of carrying the invention into effect, and that Fust supplied him with considerable sums of money. The subsequent steps are obscure. According to a passage in the "Annales Hirsargienses" of Trithemius, written sixty years after-

wards, but on the authority of a grandson of Peter Schæffer, their assistant in the work, it was about 1452 that the latter brought the art to perfection, by devising an easier mode of casting types. This passage has been interpreted, according to a lax construction, to mean that Schæffer invented the method of casting types in a matrix; but seems more strictly to intimate that we owe to him the great improvement in letter casting, namely, the punches of engraved steel, by which the matrices or molds are struck, and without which, independent of the economy of labor, there could be no perfect uniformity of shape. Upon the former supposition Schæffer may be reckoned the main inventor of the art of printing; for movable wooden letters, though small books may possibly have been printed by means of them, are so inconvenient, and letters of cut metal so expensive, that few great works were likely to have passed through the press till cast types were employed. Van Praet, however, believes the Psalter of 1457 to have been printed from wooden characters; and some have conceived letters of cut metal to have been employed both in that and in the first Bible. Lambinet, who thinks "the essence of the art of printing is in the engraved punch," naturally gives the chief credit to Schæffer; but this is not the more usual opinion.

The earliest book, properly so called, is now generally believed to be the Latin Bible, commonly called the Mazarin Bible, a copy having been found, about the middle of the last century, in Cardinal Mazarin's library at Paris. It is remarkable that its existence was unknown before; for it can hardly be called a book of very extraordinary scarcity, nearly twenty copies being in different libraries, half of them in those of private persons in England. No date appears in this Bible, and some have referred its publication to 1452, or even to 1450, which few, perhaps, would at present maintain; while others have thought the year 1455 rather more probable. In a copy belonging to the Royal Library at Paris an entry is made importing that it was completed in binding and illuminating at Mentz, on the Feast of the Assumption (Aug. 15), 1456. But Trithemius, in the passage above quoted, seems to intimate that no book had been printed in 1452; and, considering the lapse of time that would naturally be employed in such an undertaking during the infancy of the art, and that we have no other printed book of the least importance to fill up the interval till 1457, and also that the binding and illuminating the above-mentioned copy is likely to have followed the publication at no great length of time, we may not err in placing its appearance in the year 1455, which will secure its hitherto unimpeached priority in the records of bibliography.

It is a very striking circumstance that the high-minded inventors of this great art tried at the very outset so bold a flight as the printing an entire Bible, and executed it with astonishing success. It was Minerva leaping on earth in her divine strength and radiant armor, ready at the moment of her nativity to subdue and destroy her enemies. The Mazarin Bible is printed, some copies on vellum, some on paper of choice quality, with strong, black, and tolerably handsome characters, but with some want of uniformity, which has led, perhaps unreasonably, to a doubt whether they were cast in a matrix. We may see in imagination this venerable and splendid volume leading up the crowded myriads of its followers, and imploring, as it were, a blessing on the new art, by dedicating its first fruits to the service of heaven.

A metrical exhortation, in the German language, to take arms against the Turks, dated in 1454, has been retrieved in the present century. If this date unequivocally refers to the time of printing, which does not seem a necessary consequence, it is the earliest loose sheet that is known to be extant. It is said to be in the type of what is called the Bamberg Bible, which we shall soon have to mention. Two editions of Letters of indulgence from Nicolas V., bearing the date of 1454, are extant in single printed sheets, and two more editions of 1455; but it has justly been observed that even if published before the Mazarin Bible, the printing of the great volume must have commenced long before. An almanac for the year 1457 has also been detected; and as fugitive sheets of this kind are seldom preserved, we may justly conclude that the art of printing was not dormant so far as these light productions are concerned. A Donatus, with Schæffer's name, but no date, may or may not be older than a Psalter published in 1457 by Fust and Schæffer (the partnership with Gutenberg having been dissolved in November, 1455, and having led to a dispute and litigation), with a colophon, or notice, subjoined in the last page, in these words:—

«Psalmorum codex venustate capitalium decoratus, rubricationibusque sufficienter distinctus, adinventione artificiosa imprimendi ac caracterizandi, absque calami ulla exaratione sic effigiatus, et ad eusebiam Dei industrie est

VI—129

summatus. Per Johannem Fust, civem Moguntinum, et Petrum Schæffer de Gernsheim, anno Domini millesimo cccclvii. In vigilia Assumptionis.»

A colophon, substantially similar, is subjoined to several of the Fustine editions. And this seems hard to reconcile with the story that Fust sold his impressions at Paris, as late as 1463, for manuscripts.

Another Psalter was printed by Fust and Schæffer with similar characters in 1459; and, in the same year, "Durandi Rationale," a treatise on the liturgical offices of the church; of which Van Praet says that it is perhaps the earliest with cast types to which Fust and Schæffer have given their name and date. The two Psalters he conceives to have been printed from wood. But this would be disputed by other eminent judges. In 1460 a work of considerable size, the "Catholicon" of Balbi, came out from an opposition press established at Mentz by Gutenberg. The Clementine Constitutions, part of the canon law, were also printed by him in the same year.

These are the only monuments of early typography acknowledged to come within the present decennium. A Bible without a date, supposed by most to have been printed by Pfister at Bamberg, though ascribed by others to Gutenberg himself, is reckoned by good judges certainly prior to 1462, and perhaps as early as 1460. Daunou and others refer it to 1461. The antiquities of typography, after all the pains bestowed upon them, are not unlikely to receive still further elucidation in the course of time.

From "Introduction to the Literature of
Europe," Chap. iii.

POETS WHO MADE SHAKESPEARE POSSIBLE

"IN THE latter end of King Henry the Eighth's reign," says Puttenham in his "Art of Poesie," "sprung up a new company of courtly makers, of whom Sir Thomas Wyatt the elder and Henry, Earl of Surrey were the two chieftains, who having travailed into Italy, and there tasted the sweet and stately measures and style of the Italian poesie, as novices newly crept out of the schools of Dante, Ariosto, and Petrarch, they greatly polished our rude and homely manner of vulgar poesie, from that it had been before. and for that cause may justly be said the first reformers

of our English metre and style. In the same time or not long after was the Lord Nicolas Vaux, a man of much facility in vulgar makings." The poems of Sir Thomas Wyatt, who died in 1544, and of the Earl of Surrey, executed in 1547, were first published in 1557, with a few by other hands, in a scarce little book called "Tottel's Miscellanies." They were, however, in all probability, known before; and it seems necessary to mention them in this period, as they mark an important epoch in English literature.

Wyatt and Surrey, for we may best name them in the order of time, rather than of civil or poetical rank, have had recently the good fortune to be recommended by an editor of extensive acquaintance with literature, and of still superior taste. It will be a gratification to read the following comparison of the two poets, which I extract the more willingly that it is found in a publication somewhat bulky and expensive for the mass of readers:—

"They were men whose minds may be said to have been cast in the same mold, for they differ only in those minuter shades of character which always must exist in human nature,—shades of difference so infinitely varied, that there never were and never will be two persons in all respects alike. In their love of virtue and their instinctive hatred and contempt of vice, in their freedom from personal jealousy, in their thirst after knowledge and intellectual improvement, in nice observation of nature, promptitude to action, intrepidity and fondness for romantic enterprise, in magnificence and liberality, in generous support of others and high-spirited neglect of themselves, in constancy in friendship, and tender susceptibility of affections of a still warmer nature, and in everything connected with sentiment and principle, they were one and the same; but when those qualities branch out into particulars, they will be found in some respects to differ.

"Wyatt had a deeper and more accurate penetration into the characters of men than Surrey had; hence arises the difference in their satires. Surrey, in his satire against the citizens of London, deals only in reproach; Wyatt, in his, abounds with irony, and those nice touches of ridicule which make us ashamed of our faults, and therefore often silently effect amendment. Surrey's observation of nature was minute; but he directed it towards the words of nature in general, and the movements of the passions, rather than to the foibles and characters of men; hence it is that he excels in the description of rural objects, and is always tender and pathetic. In Wyatt's "Complaint" we hear a strain of manly grief which commands attention,

and we listen to it with respect, for the sake of him that suffers. Surrey's distress is painted in such natural terms that we make it our own, and recognize in his sorrows emotions which we are conscious of having felt ourselves.

"In point of taste and perception of propriety in composition, Surrey is more accurate and just than Wyatt; he therefore seldom either offends with conceits or wearies with repetition, and when he imitates other poets he is original as well as pleasing. In his numerous translations from Petrarch he is seldom inferior to his master; and he seldom improves upon him. Wyatt is almost always below the Italian, and frequently degrades a good thought by expressing it so that it is hardly recognizable. Had Wyatt attempted a translation of Virgil, as Surrey did, he would have exposed himself to unavoidable failure."

To remarks so delicate in taste and so founded in knowledge, I should not venture to add much of my own. Something, however, may generally be admitted to modify the ardent panegyrics of an editor. Those who, after reading this brilliant passage, should turn for the first time to the poems either of Wyatt or of Surrey, might think the praise too unbounded, and, in some respects perhaps, not appropriate. It seems to be now ascertained, after sweeping away a host of foolish legends and traditionary prejudices, that the Geraldine of Surrey, Lady Elizabeth Fitzgerald, was a child of thirteen, for whom his passion, if such it is to be called, began several years after his own marriage. But in fact there is more of the conventional tone of amorous song, than of real emotion, in Surrey's poetry. The

"Easy sighs, such as men draw in love,"

are not like the deep sorrows of Petrarch, or the fiery transports of the Castilians.

The taste of this accomplished man is more striking than his poetical genius. He did much for his own country and his native language. The versification of Surrey differs very considerably from that of his predecessors. He introduced, as Dr. Nott says, a sort of involution into his style, which gives an air of dignity and remoteness from common life. It was, in fact, borrowed from the license of Italian poetry, which our own idiom has rejected. He avoids pedantic words, forcibly obtruded from the Latin, of which our earlier poets, both English and Scotch, had been ridiculously fond. The absurd epithets of Hoccleve, Lydgate, Dunbar, and Douglas are applied equally to the most different things, so as to show that they annexed no meaning to them. Surrey rarely lays an unnatural stress on final syllables, merely as such, which they would not receive in ordinary pronunciation,—another usual trick of the school of Chaucer. His words are well chosen and well arranged.

Surrey is the first who introduced blank verse into our English poetry. It has been doubted whether it had been previously employed in Italian, save in tragedy; for the poems of Alamanni and Rucellai were not published before many of our noble poet's compositions had been written. Dr. Nott, however, admits that Boscan and other Spanish poets had used it. The translation by Surrey of the second book of the "Æneid," in blank verse, is among the chief of his productions. No one had, before his time, known how to translate or imitate with appropriate expression. But the structure of his verse is not very harmonious, and the sense is rarely carried beyond the line.

If we could rely on a theory, advanced and ably supported by his editor, Surrey deserves the still more conspicuous praise of having brought about a great revolution in our poetical numbers. It had been supposed to be proved by Tyrwhitt that Chaucer's lines are to be read metrically, in ten or eleven syllables, like the Italian, and, as I apprehend, the French of his time. For this purpose it is necessary to presume that many terminations, now mute, were syllabically pronounced; and where verses prove refractory after all our endeavors, Tyrwhitt has no scruple in declaring them corrupt. It may be added that Gray, before the appearance of Tyrwhitt's essay on the versification of Chaucer, had adopted without hesitation the same hypothesis. But, according to Dr. Nott, the verses of Chaucer, and of all his successors down to Surrey, are merely rhythmical, to be read by cadence, and admitting of considerable variety in the number of syllables, though ten may be the more frequent. In the manuscripts of Chaucer the line is always broken by a cæsura in the middle, which is pointed out by a virgule; and this is preserved in the early editions down to that of 1532. They come near, therefore, to the short Saxon line, differing chiefly by the alternate rhyme, which converts two verses into one. He maintains that a great many lines of Chaucer cannot be read metrically, though harmonious as verses of cadence. This rhythmical measure he proceeds to show in Hoccleve, Lydgate, Hawes, Barclay, Skelton, and

even Wyatt; and thus concludes that it was first abandoned by Surrey, in whom it very rarely occurs.

This hypothesis, it should be observed, derives some additional plausibility from a passage in Gascoyne's "Notes of Instruction concerning the Making of Verse or Rhyme in English," printed in 1575:—

"Whosoever do peruse and well consider his [Chaucer's] works, he shall find that, although his lines are not always of one self-same number of syllables, yet, being read by one that hath understanding, the longest verse, and that which hath most syllables in it, will fall (to the ear) correspondent unto that which hath fewest syllables; and likewise that which hath fewest syllables shall be found yet to consist of words that have such natural sound as may seem equal in length to a verse which hath many more syllables of lighter accents."

A theory so ingeniously maintained, and with so much induction of examples, has naturally gained a good deal of credit. I cannot, however, by any means concur in the extension given to it. Pages may be read in Chaucer, and still more in Dunbar, where every line is regularly and harmoniously decasyllabic; and though the cæsura may perhaps fall rather more uniformly than it does in modern verse, it would be very easy to find exceptions, which could not acquire a rhythmical cadence by any artifice of the reader. The deviations from the normal type, or decasyllable line, were they more numerous than, after allowance for the license of pronunciation, as well as the probable corruption of the text, they appear to be, would not, I conceive, justify us in concluding that it was disregarded. For these aberrant lines are much more common in the dramatic blank verse of the seventeenth century. They are, doubtless, vestiges of the old rhythmical forms; and we may readily allow that English versification had not, in the fifteenth or even sixteenth centuries, the numerical regularity of classical or Italian metre. In the ancient ballads, Scotch and English, the substitution of the anapest for the iambic foot is of perpetual recurrence, and gives them a remarkable elasticity and animation; but we never fail to recognize a uniformity of measure, which the use of nearly equipollent feet cannot, on the strictest metrical principles, be thought to impair.

If we compare the poetry of Wyatt and Surrey with that of Barclay or Skelton, about thirty or forty years before, the difference must appear wonderful. But we should not, with Dr. Nott,

attribute this wholly to superiority of genius. It is to be remembered that the later poets wrote in a court, and in one which, besides the aristocratic manners of chivalry, had not only imbibed a great deal of refinement from France and Italy, but a considerable tinge of ancient literature. Their predecessors were less educated men, and they addressed a more vulgar class of readers. Nor was this polish of language peculiar to Surrey and his friend. In the short poems of Lord Vaux, and of others about the same time, even in those of Nicolas Grimoald, a lecturer at Oxford, who was no courtier, but had acquired a classical taste, we find a rejection of obsolete and trivial phrases, and the beginnings of what we now call the style of our older poetry.

From "Introduction to the Literature of Europe,"
Part I., Chap. viii.

PHILIP GILBERT HAMERTON

(1834-1894)

THE "Intellectual Life," by Philip Gilbert Hamerton, is a series of essays written in the form of letters to imaginary correspondents who are supposed to have consulted the writer on some subject of literature or art. Hamerton was a landscape painter and etcher of ability, and among his most notable publications were "Etching and Etchers," "The Graphic Arts," and "Contemporary French Painters," volumes which are treasured because of his admirably etched illustrations. He was born in Lancashire, England, September 10th, 1834. His taste for rural life was marked, and some of his best books are impregnated with it. His autobiography, left incomplete at his death (November 5th, 1894), was published by his widow, with a supplement. His works include several novels, a number of books of art criticism, and his essays on the "Intellectual Life," —the latter his most popular production.

WOMEN AND MARRIAGE

THE subject of marriage is one concerning which neither I nor anybody else can have more than an infinitesimally small atom of knowledge. Each of us knows how his or her own marriage has turned out; but that, in comparison with a knowledge of marriage generally, is like a single plant in comparison with the flora of the globe. The utmost experience on this subject to be found in this country extends to about three trials or experiments. A man may become twice a widower, and then marry a third time, but it may be easily shown that the variety of his experience is more than counterbalanced by its incompleteness in each instance. For the experiment to be conclusive even as to the wisdom of one decision, it must extend over half a lifetime. A true marriage is not a mere temporary arrangement, and although a young couple are said to be married as soon as the lady has changed her name, the truth is that the real marriage is a long slow intergrowth, like that of two trees planted quite close together in the forest.

The subject of marriage generally is one of which men know less than they know of any other subject of universal interest. People are almost always wrong in their estimates of the marriages of others, and the best proof how little we know the real tastes and needs of those with whom we have been most intimate is our unfailing surprise at the marriages they make. Very old and experienced people fancy they know a great deal about younger couples, but their guesses, there is good reason to believe, never exactly hit the mark.

Ever since this idea, that marriage is a subject we are all very ignorant about, had taken root in my own mind, many little incidents were perpetually occurring to confirm it; they proved to me, on the one hand, how often I had been mistaken about other people, and, on the other hand, how mistaken other people were concerning the only marriage I profess to know anything about, namely, my own.

Our ignorance is all the darker that few men tell us the little that they know, that little being too closely bound up with that innermost privacy of life which every man of right feeling respects in his own case, as in the case of another. The only instances which are laid bare to the public view are the unhappy marriages, which are really not marriages at all. An unhappy alliance bears exactly the same relation to a true marriage that disease does to health, and the quarrels and misery of it are the crises by which nature tries to bring about either the recovery of happiness, or the endurable peace of a settled separation.

All that we really know about marriage is that it is based upon the most powerful of all our instincts, and that it shows its own justification in its fruits, especially in the prolonged and watchful care of children. But marriage is very complex in its effects, and there is one set of effects resulting from it, to which remarkably little attention has been paid hitherto,—I mean its effects upon the intellectual life. Surely they deserve consideration by all who value culture.

I believe that for an intellectual man only two courses are open; either he ought to marry some simple, dutiful woman who will bear him children, and see to the household matters, and love him in a trustful spirit without jealousy of his occupations; or else, on the other hand, he ought to marry some highly intelligent lady, able to carry her education far beyond school experiences, and willing to become his companion in the arduous paths

of intellectual labor. The danger in the first of the two cases is that pointed out by Wordsworth in some verses addressed to lake tourists who might feel inclined to buy a peasant's cottage in Westmoreland. The tourist would spoil the little romantic spot if he bought it; the charm of it is subtly dependent upon the poetry of a simple life, and would be brushed away by the influence of the things that are necessary to people in the middle class. I remember dining in a country inn with an English officer whose ideas were singularly unconventional. We were waited upon by our host's daughter, a beautiful girl, whose manners were remarkable for their natural elegance and distinction. It seemed to us both that no lady of rank could be more distinguished than she was; and my companion said that he thought a gentleman might do worse than ask that girl to marry him, and settle down quietly in that quiet mountain village, far from the cares and vanities of the world. That is a sort of dream which has occurred no doubt to many an honorable man. Some men have gone so far as to try to make the dream a reality, and have married the beautiful peasant. But the difficulty is that she does not remain what she was; she becomes a sort of make-belief lady, and then her ignorance, which in her natural condition was a charming naïveté, becomes an irritating defect. If, however, it were possible for an intellectual man to marry some simple-hearted peasant girl, and keep her carefully in her original condition, I seriously believe that the venture would be less perilous to his culture than an alliance with some woman of our Philistine classes, equally incapable of comprehending his pursuits, but much more likely to interfere with them. I once had a conversation on this subject with a distinguished artist, who is now a widower, and who is certainly not likely to be prejudiced against marriage by his own experience, which had been an unusually happy one. His view was that a man devoted to art might marry either a plain-minded woman, who would occupy herself exclusively with household matters and shield his peace by taking these cares upon herself, or else a woman quite capable of entering into his artistic life; but he was convinced that a marriage which exposed him to unintelligent criticism and interference would be dangerous in the highest degree. And of the two kinds of marriage which he considered possible he preferred the former, that with the entirely ignorant and simple person from whom no interference was to be apprehended. He considered the first Madame Ingres the

true model of an artist's wife, because she did all in her power to guard her husband's peace against the daily cares of life and never herself disturbed it, acting the part of a breakwater which protects a space of calm, and never destroys the peace that it has made. This may be true for artists whose occupation is rather æsthetic than intellectual, and does not get much help or benefit from talk; but the ideal marriage for a man of great literary culture would be one permitting some equality of companionship, or, if not equality, at least interest. That this ideal is not a mere dream, but may consolidate into a happy reality, several examples prove; yet these examples are not so numerous as to relieve me from anxiety about your chances of finding such companionship. The different education of the two sexes separates them widely at the beginning; and to meet on any common ground of culture, a second education has to be gone through. It rarely happens that there is resolution enough for this.

The want of thoroughness and reality in the education of both sexes, but especially in that of women, may be attributed to a sort of policy which is not very favorable to companionship in married life. It appears to be thought wise to teach boys things which women do not learn, in order to give women a degree of respect for men's attainments, which they would not be so likely to feel if they were prepared to estimate them critically; whilst girls are taught arts and languages which until recently were all but excluded from our public schools, and won no rank at our universities. Men and women had consequently scarcely any common ground to meet upon, and the absence of serious mental discipline in the training of women made them indisposed to submit to the irksomeness of that earnest intellectual labor which might have remedied the deficiency. The total lack of accuracy in their mental habits was then, and is still for the immense majority of women, the least easily surmountable impediment to culture. The history of many marriages which have failed to realize intellectual companionship is comprised in a sentence which was actually uttered by one of the most accomplished of my friends: "She knew nothing when I married her. I tried to teach her something; it made her angry, and I gave it up."

Letter I. on Woman and Marriage complete.
From "Intellectual Life."

TO A LADY OF HIGH CULTURE

I THINK that the greatest misfortune in the intellectual life of women is that they do not hear the truth from men.

All men in cultivated society say to women as much as possible that which they may be supposed to wish to hear, and women are so much accustomed to this that they can scarcely hear without resentment an expression of opinion which takes no account of their personal and private feeling. The consideration for the feelings of women gives an agreeable tone to society, but it is fatal to the severity of truth. Observe a man of the world whose opinions are well known to you,—notice the little pause before he speaks to a lady. During that little pause he is turning over what he has to say, so as to present it in the manner that will please her best; and you may be sure that the integrity of truth will suffer in the process. If we compare what we know of the man with that which the lady hears from him, we perceive the immense disadvantages of her position. He ascertains what will please her, and that is what he administers. He professes to take a deep interest in things which he does not care for in the least, and he passes lightly over subjects and events which he knows to be of the most momentous importance to the world. The lady spends an hour more agreeably than if she heard opinions which would irritate, and prognostics which would alarm her, but she has missed an opportunity for culture, she has been confirmed in feminine illusions. If this happened only from time to time, the effect would not tell so much on the mental constitution; but it is incessant, it is continual. Men disguise their thoughts for women as if to venture into the feminine world were as dangerous as traveling in Arabia, or as if the thoughts themselves were criminal.

There appeared two or three years ago in Punch a clever drawing which might have served as an illustration to this subject. A fashionable doctor was visiting a lady in Belgravia who complained that she suffered from debility. Cod-liver oil being repugnant to her taste, the agreeable doctor, wise in his generation, blandly suggested as an effective substitute a mixture of cream and curaçoa. What that intelligent man did for his patient's physical constitution, all men of politeness do for the intellectual constitution of ladies. Instead of administering the truth which would strengthen, though unpalatable, they administer intellectual cream and curaçoa.

The primary cause of this tendency to say what is most pleasing to women is likely to be as permanent as the distinction of sex itself. It springs directly from sexual feelings, it is hereditary and instinctive. Men will never talk to women with that rough frankness which they use between themselves. Conversation between the sexes will always be partially insincere. Still I think that the more women are respected, the more men will desire to be approved by them for what they are in reality, and the less they will care for approval which is obtained by dissimulation. It may be observed already that, in the most intellectual society of great capitals, men are considerably more outspoken before women than they are in the provincial middle classes. Where women have most culture, men are most open and sincere. Indeed, the highest culture has a direct tendency to command sincerity in others, both because it is tolerant of variety in opinion, and because it is so penetrating that dissimulation is felt to be of no use. By the side of an uncultivated woman, a man feels that if he says anything different from what she has been accustomed to, she will take offense; whilst if he says anything beyond the narrow range of her information, he will make her cold and uncomfortable. The most honest of men, in such a position, finds it necessary to be very cautious, and can scarcely avoid a little insincerity. But with a woman of culture equal to his own, these causes for apprehension have no existence, and he can safely be more himself.

These considerations lead me to hope that as culture becomes more general women will hear truth more frequently. Whenever this comes to pass, it will be, to them, an immense intellectual gain.

Letter VIII. on Women and Marriage complete.
From "Intellectual Life."

ALEXANDER HAMILTON

(1757–1804)

ALEXANDER HAMILTON, the celebrated founder of the Federalist party, was born in the West Indies, January 11th, 1757. He came to the United States in 1772, and entered actively into politics before attaining his majority. The talent for political writing, which had such marked effect when he displayed it through the Federalist after the Constitution had been framed, attracted attention in 1774-75, and when he entered the army he became a favorite member of Washington's staff. After serving with distinction he was elected to the Continental Congress, and in 1787 to the convention which submitted the Federal Constitution to the states. In the New York convention, called to pass upon the Federal constitution, he met powerful opposition ably represented, and defeated it by a force and flexibility of intellect which had not been shown before in American public affairs. From October, 1787, to April, 1788, he co-operated with Jay and Madison in writing the Federalist essays, which appeared serially in the Independent Journal of New York. They owe their form to the Whig Examiner of Addison's time, and their spirit to strong Anglican conservatism and repugnance to everything French. The contest between English ideals and those of eighteenth-century France was waged in America with bitterness during the decade which preceded the actual hostilities of the Revolution, when Otis, Samuel Adams, and Jefferson represented the extreme of opposition to what was afterwards called Federalism. Otis seems first to have promulgated in America the doctrine of "Individual Sovereignty," which was held by Virginia "Jacobins" with Jefferson, and afterwards by New England "Radicals" with Ralph Waldo Emerson,—who in his "English Traits" pronounces it the only distinctive "American idea." Otis died in 1783, however, and during the time of Hamilton's greatest successes, Jefferson was absent in France. Returning and finding how his followers and friends had been overmatched, Jefferson became embittered against Hamilton and began organizing the country for his overthrow. In his "Anas" Jefferson writes characteristically of the beginning of this contest, and the passage, while it cannot be fairly described, except as an exasperated attack, is vital for an understanding of Hamilton's career and of the next half-century of American history.

"The want of some authority which should procure justice to the public creditors," Jefferson writes, "and an observance of treaties with foreign nations, produced . . . the call of a convention of the states at Annapolis. Although, at this meeting, a difference of opinion was evident on the question of a republican or kingly government, yet so general through the states was the sentiment in favor of the former, that the friends of the latter confined themselves to a course of obstruction only, and delay, to everything proposed; they hoped that nothing being done, and all things going from bad to worse, a kingly government might be usurped, and submitted to by the people, as better than anarchy and wars internal and external, the certain consequences of the present want of a general government. The effect of their manœuvres, with the defective attendance of Deputies from the states, resulted in the measure of calling a more general convention, to be held at Philadelphia. At this the same party exhibited the same practices, and with the same views of preventing a government of concord, which they foresaw would be republican, and of forcing through anarchy their way to monarchy. But the mass of that convention was too honest, too wise, and too steady, to be baffled and misled by their manœuvres. One of these was a form of government proposed by Col. Hamilton, which would have been in fact a compromise between the two parties of royalism and republicanism. According to this, the executive and one branch of the legislature were to be during good behavior, i. e., for life, and the governors of the states were to be named by these two permanent organs. This, however, was rejected; on which Hamilton left the convention, as desperate, and never returned again until near its final conclusion. These opinions and efforts, secret or avowed, of the advocates for monarchy had begotten great jealousy through the states generally; and this jealousy it was which excited the strong opposition to the conventional constitution,—a jealousy which yielded at last only to a general determination to establish certain amendments as barriers against a government either monarchical or consolidated. In what passed through the whole period of these conventions, I have gone on the information of those who were members of them, being absent myself on my mission to France.

"I returned from that mission in the first year of the new government, having landed in Virginia in December, 1789, and proceeded to New York in March, 1790, to enter on the office of Secretary of State. Here, certainly, I found a state of things which, of all I had ever contemplated, I the least expected. I had left France in the first year of her revolution, in the fervor of natural rights, and zeal for reformation. My conscientious devotion to these rights could not be heightened, but it had been aroused and excited by daily exercise. The President received me cordially, and my colleagues and the circle of principal citizens apparently with welcome. The courtesies of dinner parties given me, as a stranger newly arrived among them, placed me at once in their familiar society. But I cannot describe the wonder and mortification with which the table conversation filled me. Politics were the chief topic, and a preference of kingly over republican government was evidently the favorite sentiment. An apostate I could not be, nor yet a hypocrite; and I found myself, for the most part, the only advocate on the republican side of the question, unless among the guests there chanced to be some member of that

party from the legislative houses. Hamilton's financial system had then passed. It had two objects: first, as a puzzle, to exclude popular understanding and inquiry; second, as a machine for the corruption of the legislature,—for he avowed the opinion that man could be governed by one of two motives only, force or interest; force, he observed, in this country was out of the question, and the interests, therefore, of the members must be laid hold of, to keep the legislative in unison with the executive. And with grief and shame it must be acknowledged that his machine was not without effect; that even in this, the birth of our government, some members were found sordid enough to bend their duty to their interests, and to look after personal rather than public good."

This defines the partisan issue on which the Federalist party was defeated and disorganized in 1800. Hamilton, who had been Secretary of the Treasury from 1789 to 1795, was appointed Commander in Chief of the army in 1799, and he was the real leader of the Federalist party in the struggle which seemed to result in the complete repudiation of his ideas. This appearance was delusive, however, for his ideas represent the inevitable tendencies of all parties when they are in administration; and regardless of party names and individual preferences, the Hamiltonian idea came back under Jefferson's own administration and developed until it resulted in John Quincy Adams. Briefly stated, it was that governments are founded to do everything which, in their own opinion, promote the general welfare. Jefferson's theory was that their object is the exercise of granted powers as trustees acting under instructions from the grantors. The Embargo and the purchase of Louisiana without waiting for the constitutional amendment which Jefferson said was necessary to authorize it, were in full accord with Hamilton's ideal of government, and but for Burr's bullet he might have lived to indorse as ideal Republicanism that for favoring which he himself had been so hotly denounced as a disguised monarchist. John Adams, who represented with Hamilton the Federalistic idea in the campaign of 1800, did live to renew toward Jefferson the esteem which had characterized their association in the early days of the struggle against England. Every party in opposition must become more or less Jeffersonian to succeed, while the whole tendency of power is to make every party in administration Hamiltonian. Perhaps this is logic in which reason ought never to acquiesce, but it is the logic of events; and except as it is checked by reason, it controls.

W. V. B.

ON WAR BETWEEN THE STATES OF THE UNION

Assuming it as an established truth that in case of disunion the several states, or such combinations of them as might happen to be formed out of the wreck of the general confederacy, would be subject to those vicissitudes of peace and war, of friendship and enmity with each other, which have fallen to the lot of all neighboring nations not united under one government, let us enter into a concise detail of some of the consequences that would attend such a situation.

War between the states, in the first periods of their separate existence, would be accompanied with much greater distresses than it commonly is in those countries where regular military establishments have long obtained. The disciplined armies always kept on foot on the continent of Europe, though they bear a malignant aspect to liberty and economy, have, notwithstanding, been productive of the signal advantage of rendering sudden conquests impracticable, and of preventing that rapid desolation which used to mark the progress of war prior to their introduction. The art of fortification has contributed to the same ends. The nations of Europe are encircled with chains of fortified places, which mutually obstruct invasion. Campaigns are wasted in reducing two or three frontier garrisons, to gain admittance into an enemy's country. Similar impediments occur at every step, to exhaust the strength, and delay the progress of an invader. Formerly an invading army would penetrate into the heart of a neighboring country, almost as soon as intelligence of its approach could be received; but now, a comparatively small force of disciplined troops, acting on the defensive, with the aid of posts, is able to impede, and finally to frustrate the enterprises of one much more considerable. The history of war, in that quarter of the globe, is no longer a history of nations subdued, and empires overturned; but of towns taken and retaken — of battles that decide nothing — of retreats more beneficial than victories — of much effort and little acquisition.

In this country the scene would be altogether reversed. The jealousy of military establishments would postpone them as long as possible. The want of fortifications, leaving the frontiers of one state open to another, would facilitate inroads. The populous states would, with little difficulty, overrun their less populous

VI—130

neighbors. Conquests would be as easy to be made, as difficult to be retained. War, therefore, would be desultory and predatory. Plunder and devastation ever march in the train of irregulars. The calamities of individuals would make the principal figure in the events which would characterize our military exploits.

This picture is not too highly wrought; though, I confess, it would not long remain a just one. Safety from external danger is the most powerful director of national conduct. Even the ardent love of liberty will, after a time, give way to its dictates. The violent destruction of life and property incident to war, the continual effort and alarm attendant on a state of continual danger, will compel nations the most attached to liberty to resort for repose and security to institutions which have a tendency to destroy their civil and political rights. To be more safe, they at length become willing to run the risk of being less free.

The institutions chiefly alluded to are standing armies, and the correspondent appendages of military establishment. Standing armies, it is said, are not provided against in the new constitution; and it is thence inferred that they would exist under it. This inference, from the very form of the proposition, is, at best, problematical and uncertain. But standing armies, it may be replied, must inevitably result from a dissolution of the confederacy. Frequent war, and constant apprehension, which require a state of as constant preparation, will infallibly produce them. The weaker states or confederacies would first have recourse to them, to put themselves upon an equality with their more potent neighbors. They would endeavor to supply the inferiority of population and resources by a more regular and effective system of defense, by disciplined troops, and by fortifications. They would, at the same time, be obliged to strengthen the executive arm of government; in doing which, their constitutions would acquire a progressive direction towards monarchy. It is of the nature of war to increase the executive at the expense of the legislative authority.

The expedients which have been mentioned would soon give the states or confederacies that made use of them a superiority over their neighbors. Small states, or states of less natural strength, under vigorous governments, and with the assistance of disciplined armies, have often triumphed over large states, or states of greater natural strength, which have been destitute of

these advantages. Neither the pride nor the safety of the more important states or confederacies would permit them long to submit to this mortifying and adventitious superiority. They would quickly resort to means similar to those by which it had been effected, to reinstate themselves in their lost pre-eminence. Thus we should, in a little time, see established in every part of this country, the same engines of despotism which have been the scourge of the Old World. This, at least, would be the natural course of things; and our reasonings will be likely to be just, in proportion as they are accommodated to this standard.

These are not vague inferences, deduced from speculative defects in a constitution, the whole power of which is lodged in the hands of the people, or their representatives and delegates; they are solid conclusions drawn from the natural and necessary progress of human affairs.

It may perhaps be asked by way of objections, why did not standing armies spring up out of the contentions which so often distracted the ancient republics of Greece? Different answers, equally satisfactory, may be given to this question. The industrious habits of the people of the present day, absorbed in the pursuits of gain, and devoted to the improvements of agriculture and commerce, are incompatible with the condition of a nation of soldiers, which was the true condition of the people of those republics. The means of revenue, which have been so greatly multiplied by the increase of gold and silver, and of the arts of industry, and the science of finance, which is the offspring of modern times, concurring with the habits of nations, have produced an entire revolution in the system of war, and have rendered disciplined armies, distinct from the body of citizens, the inseparable companion of frequent hostility.

There is a wide difference, also, between military establishments in a country which, by its situation, is seldom exposed to invasions, and in one which is often subject to them, and always apprehensive of them. The rulers of the former can have no good pretext, if they are even so inclined, to keep on foot armies so numerous as must of necessity be maintained in the latter. These armies being, in the first case, rarely, if at all, called into activity for interior defense, the people are in danger of being broken to military subordination. The laws are not accustomed to relaxations in favor of military exigencies; the civil state remains in full vigor, neither corrupted nor confounded with the

principles or propensities of the other state. The smallness of the army forbids competition with the natural strength of the community, and the citizens, not habituated to look up to the military power for protection, or to submit to its oppressions, neither love nor fear the soldiery: they view them with a spirit of jealous acquiescence in a necessary evil, and stand ready to resist a power which they suppose may be exerted to the prejudice of their rights.

The army, under such circumstances, though it may usefully aid the magistrate to suppress a small faction, or an occasional mob or insurrection, will be utterly incompetent to the purpose of enforcing encroachments against the united efforts of the great body of the people.

But in a country where the perpetual menacings of danger oblige the government to be always prepared to repel it, her armies must be numerous enough for instant defense. The continual necessity for his services enhances the importance of the soldier, and proportionably degrades the condition of the citizen. The military state becomes elevated above the civil. The inhabitants of territories, often the theatre of war, are unavoidably subjected to frequent infringements on their rights, which serve to weaken their sense of those rights; and by degrees, the people are brought to consider the soldiery not only as their protectors, but as their superiors. The transition from this disposition to that of considering them as masters is neither remote nor difficult, but it is very difficult to prevail upon a people under such impressions to make a bold or effectual resistance to usurpations, supported by the military power.

The kingdom of Great Britain falls within the first description. An insular situation and a powerful marine, guarding it in a great measure against the possibility of foreign invasion, supersede the necessity of a numerous army within the kingdom. A sufficient force to make head against a sudden descent till the militia could have time to rally and embody is all that has been deemed requisite. No motive of national policy has demanded, nor would public opinion have tolerated a larger number of troops upon its domestic establishment. This peculiar felicity of situation has, in a great degree, contributed to preserve the liberty which that country to this day enjoys, in spite of the prevalent venality and corruption. If Britain had been situated on the continent, and had been compelled, as she would have been by that situation, to make her military establishments at home coextensive with those of the other great powers of Europe, she, like them, would, in all probability, at this day be a victim to the absolute power of a single man. It is possible, though not easy, for the people of that island to be enslaved from other causes; but it cannot be by the prowess of an army so inconsiderable as that which has been usually kept up within the kingdom.

If we are wise enough to preserve the union, we may for ages enjoy an advantage similar to that of an insulated situation. Europe is at a great distance from us. Her colonies in our vicinity will be likely to continue too much disproportioned in strength to be able to give us any dangerous annoyance. Extensive military establishments cannot, in this position, be necessary to our security. But if we should be disunited, and the integral parts should either remain separated, or, which is most probable, should be thrown together into two or three confederacies, we should be, in a short course of time, in the predicament of the continental powers of Europe. Our liberties would be a prey to the means of defending ourselves against the ambition and jealousy of each other.

This is an idea not superficial nor futile, but solid and weighty. It deserves the most serious and mature consideration of every prudent and honest man, of whatever party. If such men will make a firm and solemn pause, and meditate dispassionately on its vast importance; if they will contemplate it in all its attitudes, and trace it to all its consequences, they will not hesitate to part with trivial objections to a constitution, the rejection of which would, in all probability, put a final period to the Union. The airy phantoms that now flit before the distempered imaginations of some of its adversaries would then quickly give place to the more substantial prospects of dangers, real, certain, and extremely formidable.

Number VIII. complete. From
the Federalist.

J. C. AND A. W. HARE
(1795–1855; 1792–1834)

"GUESSES at Truth," a series of charming essays by Julius Charles and Augustus William Hare, was published as their joint work in 1827. The authors were brothers and both clergymen of the Church of England. Julius Charles Hare, who became Archdeacon of Lewes in 1840, was celebrated as a pulpit orator and as the author of several books on divinity and ecclesiastical subjects. His sermons often present examples of melodious "concords of sweet sounds," which make them almost unique in the pulpit oratory of the English language. "Guesses at Truth," however, is the work by which he is best remembered.

THAT IT IS BETTER TO LAUGH THAN TO CRY

RIDENTEM dicere verum quid vetat? In the first place all the sour faces in the world, stiffening into a yet more rigid asperity at the least glimpse of a smile. I have seen faces, too, which so long as you let them lie in their sleepy torpor, unshaken and unstirred, have a creamy softness and smoothness, and might beguile you into suspecting their owners of being gentle; but if they catch the sound of a laugh, it acts on them like thunder, and they also turn sour. Nay, strange as it may seem, there have been such incarnate paradoxes as would rather see their fellow-creatures cry than smile.

But is not this in exact accordance with the spirit which pronounces a blessing on the weeper, and a woe on the laugher?

Not in the persons I have in view. That blessing and woe are pronounced in the knowledge how apt the course of this world is to run counter to the kingdom of God. They who weep are declared to be blessed, not because they weep, but because they shall laugh; and the woe threatened to the laughers is in like manner, that they shall mourn and weep. Therefore, they who have this spirit in them will endeavor to forward the blessing and to avert the woe. They will try to comfort the mourner, so

as to lead him to rejoice; and they will warn the laugher, that he may be preserved from the mourning and weeping, and may exchange his passing for lasting joy. But there are many who merely indulge in the antipathy, without opening their hearts to the sympathy. Such is the spirit found in those who have cast off the bonds of the lower earthly affections, without having risen as yet into the freedom of heavenly love — in those who have stopped short in the state of transition between the two lives, like so many skeletons stripped of their earthly, and not yet clothed with a heavenly body. It is the spirit of stoicism, for instance, in philosophy, and of vulgar fatalism, which in so many things answers to stoicism in religion. They who feel the harm they have received from worldly pleasures are prone at first to quarrel with pleasure of every kind altogether; and it is one of the strange perversities of our self-will to entertain anger, instead of pity, towards those whom we fancy to judge are at less wisely than ourselves. This, however, is only while the scaffolding is still standing around the edifice of their Christian life, so that they cannot see clearly out of the windows, and their view is broken up into disjointed parts. When the scaffolding is removed, and they look abroad without hindrance, they are readier than any to delight in all the beauty and true pleasure around them. They feel that it is their blessed calling, not only to rejoice always themselves, but likewise to rejoice with all who do rejoice in innocence of heart. They feel that this must be well-pleasing to him who has filled his universe with ever-bubbling springs of gladness; so that whithersoever we turn our eyes, through earth and sky as well as sea, we behold the ἀνήριθμον γέλασμα of nature. On the other hand, it is the harshness of an irreligious temper clothing itself in religious zeal, and not seldom exhibiting symptoms of mental disorganization, that looks scowlingly on every indication of happiness and mirth.

Moreover, there is a large class of people who deem the business of life far too weighty and momentous to be made light of; who would leave merriment to children, and laughter to idiots; and who hold that a joke would be as much out of place on their lips as on a gravestone or in a ledger. Wit and wisdom being sisters, not only are they afraid of being indicted for bigamy were they to wed them both, but they shudder at such a union as incestuous. So, to keep clear of temptation, and to preserve their faith where they have plighted it, they turn the

younger out of doors; and if they see or hear of anybody taking her in, they are positive he can know nothing of the elder. They would not be witty for the world. Now, to escape being so is not very difficult for those whom nature has so favored that wit with them is always at zero, or below it. Or, as to their wisdom, since they are careful never to overfeed her, she jogs leisurely along the turnpike road, with lank and meagre carcass, displaying all her bones, and never getting out of her own dust. She feels no inclination to be frisky, but if a coach or wagon passes her, is glad, like her rider, to run behind a thing so big. Now, all these people take grievous offense if any one comes near them better mounted, and they are in a tremor lest the neighing and snorting and prancing should be contagious.

Surely, however, ridicule implies contempt; and so the feeling must be condemnable, subversive of gentleness, incompatible with kindness?

Not necessarily so, or universally; far from it. The word ridicule, it is true, has a narrow, one-sided meaning. From our proneness to mix up personal feelings with those which are more purely objective and intellectual, we have in great measure restricted the meaning of ridicule, which would properly extend over the whole region of the ridiculous, the laughable, where we may disport ourselves innocently, without any evil emotion; and we have narrowed it, so that in common usage it mostly corresponds to derision, which does indeed involve personal and offensive feelings. As the great business of Wisdom in her speculative office is to detect and reveal the hidden harmonies of things, those harmonies which are the sources and the ever-flowing emanations of law, the dealings of wit, on the other hand, are with incongruities. And it is the perception of incongruity, flashing upon us, when unaccompanied, as Aristotle observes (Poet., Chap. v.), by pain, or by any predominant moral disgust, that provokes laughter and excites the feeling of the ridiculous. But it no more follows that the perception of such an incongruity must breed or foster haughtiness or disdain than that the perception of anything else that may be erroneous or wrong should do so. You might as well argue that a man must be proud and scornful because he sees that there is such a thing as sin, or such a thing as folly, in the world. Yet, unless we blind our eyes, and gag our ears, and hoodwink our minds, we shall seldom pass through a day without having some form of evil brought in one way or other before us. Besides, the perception of incongruity may exist, and may awaken laughter, without the slightest reprobation of the object laughed at. We laugh at a pun, surely without a shade of contempt either for the words punned upon or for the punster; and if a very bad pun be the next best thing to a very good one, this is not from its flattering any feeling of superiority in us, but because the incongruity is broader and more glaring. Nor when we laugh at a droll combination of imagery do we feel any contempt, but often admiration at the ingenuity shown in it, and an almost affectionate thankfulness toward the person by whom we have been amused, such as is rarely excited by any other display of intellectual power, as those who have ever enjoyed the delight of Professor Sedgwick's society will bear witness.

It is true, an exclusive attention to the ridiculous side of things is hurtful to the character and destructive of earnestness and gravity. But no less mischievous is it to fix our attention exclusively, or even mainly, on the vices and other follies of mankind. Such contemplations, unless counteracted by wholesomer thoughts, harden or rot the heart, deaden the moral principle, and make us hopeless and reckless. The objects toward which we should turn our minds habitually are those which are great, and good, and pure; the throne of virtue, and she who sits upon it; the majesty of truth, the beauty of holiness. This is the spiritual sky through which we should strive to mount, "springing from crystal step to crystal step," and bathing our souls in its living, life-giving ether. These are the thoughts by which we should whet and polish our swords for the warfare against evil, that the vapors of the earth may not rust them. But in a warfare against evil, under one or other of its forms, we are all of us called to engage; and it is a childish dream to fancy that we can walk about among mankind without perpetual necessity of remarking that the world is full of many worse incongruities besides those which make us laugh.

Nor do I deny that a laugher may often be a scoffer and a scorner. Some jesters are fools of a worse breed than those who used to wear the cap. Sneering is commonly found along with a bitter splenetic misanthrophy; or it may be a man's mockery at his own hollow heart, venting itself in mockery at others. Cruelty will try to season or to palliate its atrocities by derision. The hyena grins in its den; most wild beasts over their prey.

But though a certain kind of wit, like other intellectual gifts, may coexist with moral depravity, there has often been a playfulness in the best and greatest men,—in Phocion, in Socrates, in Luther, in Sir Thomas More,—which, as it were, adds a bloom to the severer graces of their character, shining forth with amaranthine brightness when storms assail them, and springing up in fresh blossoms under the ax of the executioner. How much is our affection for Hector increased by his tossing his boy in his arms, and laughing at his childish fears! Smiles are the language of love; they betoken the complacency and delight of the heart in the object of its contemplation. Why are we to assume that there must needs be bitterness or contempt in them, when they enforce a truth or reprove an error? On the contrary, some of those who have been richest in wit and humor have been among the simplest and kindest-hearted of men. I will only instance Fuller, Bishop Earle, La Fontaine, Matthias Claudius, Charles Lamb. *Le méchant n'est jamais comique* is wisely remarked by De Maistre, when canvassing the pretensions of Voltaire (Soirées, i. 273); and the converse is equally true: *Le comique, le vrai comique, n'est jamais méchant.* A laugh, to be joyous, must flow from a joyous heart; but without kindness there can be no true joy. And what a dull, plodding, tramping, clanking would the ordinary intercourse of society be without wit to enliven and brighten it! When two men meet they seem to be kept at bay through the estranging effects of absence, until some sportive sally opens their hearts to each other. Nor does anything spread cheerfulness so rapidly over a whole party, or an assembly of people, however large. Reason expands the soul of the philosopher; imagination glorifies the poet, and breathes a breath of spring through the young and genial; but if we take into account the numberless glances and gleams whereby wit lightens our every-day life, I hardly know what power ministers so bountifully to the innocent pleasures of mankind.

Surely, too, it cannot be requisite to a man's being in earnest that he should wear a perpetual frown. Or is there less of sincerity in Nature during her gambols in spring than during the stiffness and harshness of her wintry gloom? Does not the bird's blithe carolling come from the heart quite as much as the quadruped's monotonous cry? And is it then altogether impossible to take up one's abode with Truth, and to let all sweet homely feelings grow about it and cluster around it, and to smile

upon it as on a kind father or mother, and to sport with it, and hold light and merry talk with it, as with a loved brother or sister; and to fondle it, and play with it, as with a child? No otherwise did Socrates and Plato commune with Truth; no otherwise Cervantes and Shakespeare. This playfulness of Truth is beautifully represented by Landor, in the conversation between Marcus Cicero and his brother, in an allegory which has the voice and the spirit of Plato. On the other hand, the outcries of those who exclaim against every sound more lively than a bray or a bleat, as derogatory to truth, are often prompted, not so much by their deep feeling of the dignity of the truth in question, as of the dignity of the person by whom that truth is maintained. It is our vanity, our self-conceit, that makes us so sore and irritable. To a grave argument we may reply gravely, and fancy that we have the best of it; but he who is too dull or too angry to smile cannot answer a smile, except by fretting and fuming. Olivia lets us into the secret of Malvolio's distaste for the Clown.

For the full expansion of the intellect, moreover, to preserve it from that narrowness and partial warp which our proneness to give ourselves up to the sway of the moment is apt to produce, its various faculties, however opposite, should grow and be trained up side by side—should twine their arms together, and strengthen each other by love wrestles. Thus will it be best fitted for discerning and acting upon the multiplicity of things which the world sets before it. Thus, too, will something like a balance and order be upheld, and our minds preserved from that exaggeration on the one side, and depreciation on the other side, which are the sure results of exclusiveness. A poet, for instance, should have much of the philosopher in him; not, indeed, thrusting itself forward at the surface—this would only make a monster of his work, like the Siamese twins, neither one thing nor two—but latent within; the spindle should be out of sight, but the web should be spun by the Fates. A philosopher, on the other hand, should have much of the poet in him. A historian cannot be great without combining the elements of the two minds. A statesman ought to unite those of all the three. A great religious teacher, such as Socrates, Bernard, Luther, Schleiermacher, needs the statesman's practical power of dealing with men and things, as well as the historian's insight into their growth and purpose. He needs the philosopher's ideas, impregnated and impersonated by the imagination of the poet. In like manner, our

graver faculties and thoughts are much chastened and bettered by a blending and interfusion of the lighter, so that "the sable cloud" may "turn her silver lining on the night"; while our lighter thoughts require the graver to substantiate them and keep them from evaporating. Thus Socrates is said, in Plato's "Banquet," to have maintained that a great tragic poet ought likewise to be a great comic poet—an observation the more remarkable, because the tendency of the Greek mind, as at once manifested in their Polytheism, and fostered by it, was to insulate all their ideas; and, as it were, to split up the intellectual world into a cluster of Cyclades, leading to confusion, is the characteristic of modern times. The combination, however, was realized in himself, and in his great pupil; and may, perhaps, have been so to a certain extent in Æschylus, if we may judge from the fame of his satiric dramas. At all events the assertion, as has been remarked more than once—for instance by Coleridge ("Remains," ii. 12),—is a wonderful prophetical intuition, which has received its fulfillment in Shakespeare. No heart would have been strong enough to hold the woe of Lear and Othello, except that which had the unquenchable elasticity of Falstaff and the "Midsummer Night's Dream." He, too, is an example that the perception of the ridiculous does not necessarily imply bitterness and scorn. Along with his intense humor, and his equally intense piercing insight into the darkest, most fearful depths of human nature, there is still a spirit of universal kindness, as well as universal justice, pervading his works; and Ben Jonson has left us a precious memorial of him, where he calls him "My gentle Shakespeare." This one epithet sheds a beautiful light on his character; its truth is attested by his wisdom, which could never have been so perfect unless it had been harmonized by the gentleness of the dove. A similar union of the graver and lighter powers is found in several of Shakespeare's contemporaries, and in many others among the greatest poets of the modern world: in Boccaccio, in Cervantes, in Chaucer, in Goethe, in Tieck; so was it in Walter Scott.

Complete. From "Guesses at Truth."

JAMES HARRINGTON

(1611-1677)

THE COMMONWEALTH OF OCEANA," by James Harrington, has been called the most curious book in existence, but without attempting to contest its claims to uniqueness, the discriminating reader will remember that Swedenborg and Fourier have written, each in his own way, on the same subjects with which "Oceana" deals. It embodies Harrington's ideas of how model men would live in a model commonwealth. Many of the essays on morals and government in it are in the form of speeches supposed to be delivered in the political discussions of "Oceana." The most distinctive and practical feature of the work is the "Rotation in Office," on which Harrington insists for áll executive officers. The attempt at "Rotation" in the United States was made, undoubtedly, as a result of this suggestion.

Harrington was born in Northamptonshire, England, in January, 1611. At Oxford, he had Chillingworth for a tutor, and while still a young man enjoyed the friendship of the Prince of Orange and the Queen of Bohemia. His strong Republican ideas did not lose him the confidence of Charles I., and he was one of the friends who accompanied the deposed king to the scaffold. "Oceana" displeased Cromwell, and he ordered its suppression while it was in the printer's hands; but Harrington won him over, and when the book appeared in 1656 it was with a dedication to the Lord Protector, who then, if not always, was as far removed from Republican ideas as Charles I. himself. Under Charles II., Harrington was imprisoned until his health was broken and his intellectual powers impaired. He died September 11th, 1677.

OF A FREE STATE

IF THE liberty of a man consists in the empire of his reason, the absence whereof would betray him to the bondage of his passions, then the liberty of a commonwealth consists in the empire of her laws, the absence whereof would betray her to the lust of tyrants. And these I conceive to be the principles upon

reason; seeing they who debate, and they who resolve, be but men. And as often as reason is against a man, so often will a man be against reason.

From "Oceana."

THE PRINCIPLES OF GOVERNMENT

ALL government is founded upon overbalance, in propriety, power, or ownership.

If one man hold the overbalance unto the whole people in propriety, his propriety causeth absolute monarchy.

If the few hold the overbalance unto the whole people in propriety, their propriety causeth aristocracy, or mixed monarchy.

If the whole people be neither overbalanced by the propriety of one, nor of a few, the propriety of the people or of the many causeth democracy, or popular government.

The government of one against the balance is tyranny.

The government of a few against the balance is oligarchy.

The government of the many (or attempt of the people to govern) against the balance is rebellion or anarchy.

Where the balance of propriety is equal, it causeth a state of war.

To hold that government may be founded upon community is to hold that there may be a black swan, or a castle in the air, or that what thing soever is as imaginable, as what hath been in practice, must be as practicable as what hath been in practice.

If the overbalance of propriety be in one man, it necessitateth the form of government to be like that of Turkey.

If the overbalance of propriety be in the few, it necessitateth the form of government to be like that of king, lords, and commons.

If the people be not overbalanced by one or a few, they are not capable of any other form of government than that of a senate and a popular assembly.

From "Oceana."

which Aristotle and Livy (injuriously accused by Leviathan for not writing out of nature) have grounded their assertion that a commonwealth is an empire of laws, and not of men. But they must not carry it so. For, says he, the liberty, whereof there is so frequent and honorable mention in the history and philosophy of the ancient Greeks and Romans, and the writings and discourses of those that from them have received all their learning in the politics, is not the liberty of particular men, but the liberty of the commonwealth. He might as well have said that the estates of particular men in a commonwealth are not the riches of particular men, but the riches of the commonwealth; for equality of estates causes equality of power, and equality of power is the liberty not only of the commonwealth, but of every man. But sure a man would never be thus irreverent with the greatest authors, and positive against all antiquity, without some certain demonstration of truth; and, what is it? Why, there is written on the turrets of the city of Lucca in great characters at this day the word Libertas; yet no man can thence infer that a particular man has more liberty or immunity from the service of the commonwealth there than in Constantinople. Whether a commonwealth be monarchical or popular, the freedom is the same. The mountain has brought forth, and we have a little equivocation! for to say that a Lucchese has no more liberty or immunity from the laws of Lucca than a Turk has from those of Constantinople; and to say that a Lucchese has no more liberty or immunity by the laws of Lucca than a Turk has by those of Constantinople, are pretty different speeches. The first may be said of all governments alike; the second scarce of any two; much less of these, seeing it is known that whereas the greatest Basha is a tenant, as well of his head as of his estate, at the will of his lord, the meanest Lucchese that has land is a freeholder of both, and not to be controlled but by the law, and that framed by every private man to no other end (or they may thank themselves) than to protect the liberty of every private man, which by that means comes to be the liberty of the commonwealth.

But seeing they that make the laws of the commonwealth are but men, the main question seems to be, how a commonwealth comes to be an empire of laws and not of men, or how the debate or result of a commonwealth is so sure to be according to

FREDERIC HARRISON

(1831-)

FREDERIC HARRISON'S essay "On the Choice of Books," which appeared in 1886, is one of the most notable literary essays of the generation to which its author belongs. It was widely discussed and, it may be imagined, with some asperity by the generation which it characterized as reading Zola's seventeenth romance and listening to "Pinafore" for three hundred nights. Such a generation, according to Mr. Harrison, will read critical observations on the sublime and the beautiful, but will neither recognize them nor care for them. He speaks in a striking way of the "nausea which idle culture seems to produce" for what is best in literature. The symptoms he thus describes undoubtedly existed to a marked extent and they were undoubtedly diseased, but they belong as naturally to every transition state resulting from the diffusion of knowledge, as measles and similar disagreeable eruptions do to childish growth.

Harrison was born in London, October 18th, 1831. He graduated at Oxford, studied law, and began his literary career as an essayist on legal and ethical subjects. Among his works are "The Weaving of History," "Order and Progress," "Social Statics," "Oliver Cromwell," and "The Annals of an Old Manor House."

ON THE CHOICE OF BOOKS

IT IS the fashion for those who have any connection with letters, in the presence of thoughtful men and women, eager for knowledge, and anxious after all that can be gotten from books, to expatiate on the infinite blessings of literature, and the miraculous achievements of the press; to extol, as a gift above price, the taste for study and the love of reading. Far be it from me to gainsay the inestimable value of good books, or to discourage any man from reading the best; but I often think that we forget that other side to this glorious view of literature:— the misuse of books, the debilitating waste of life in aimless promiscuous vapid reading, or even, it may be, in the poisonous inhalation óf mere literary garbage and bad men's worst thoughts.

For what can a book be more than the man who wrote it? The brightest genius, perhaps, never puts the best of his own soul into his printed page; and some of the most famous men have certainly put the worst of theirs. Yet are all men desirable companions, much less teachers, fit to be listened to, able to give us advice, even of those who get reputation and command a hearing? Or, to put out of the question that writing which is positively bad, are we not, amidst the multiplicity of books and of writers, in continual danger of being drawn off by what is stimulating rather than solid, by curiosity after something accidentally notorious, by what has no intelligible thing to recommend it, except that it is new? Now, to stuff our minds with what is simply trivial, simply curious, or that which at best has but a low nutritive power, this is to close our minds to what is solid and enlarging, and spiritually sustaining. Whether our neglect of the great books comes from our not reading at all, or from an incorrigible habit of reading the little books, it ends in just the same thing. And that thing is ignorance of all the greater literature of the world. To neglect all the abiding parts of knowledge for the sake of the evanescent parts is really to know nothing worth nothing. It is in the end the same thing, whether we do not use our minds for serious study at all, or whether we exhaust them by an impotent voracity for idle and desultory "information," as it is called — a thing as fruitful as whistling. Of the two plans I prefer the former. At least, in that case, the mind is healthy and open. It is not gorged and enfeebled by excess in that which cannot nourish, much less enlarge and beautify our nature.

But there is much more than this. Even to those who resolutely avoid the idleness of reading what is trivial, a difficulty is presented, a difficulty every day increasing by virtue even of our abundance of books. What are the subjects, what are the class of books we are to read, in what order, with what connection, to what ultimate use or object? Even those who are resolved to read the better books are embarrassed by a field of choice practically boundless. The longest life, the greatest industry, the most powerful memory, would not suffice to make us profit from a hundredth part of the world of books before us. If the great Newton said that he seemed to have been all his life gathering a few shells on the shore, whilst a boundless ocean of truth still lay beyond and unknown to him, how much more to each of us

must the sea of literature be a pathless immensity beyond our powers of vision or of reach, — an immensity in which industry itself is useless without judgment, method, discipline; where it is of infinite importance what we can learn and remember, and of utterly no importance what we may have once looked at or heard of. Alas! the most of our reading leaves as little mark even in our own education as the foam that gathers round the keel of a passing boat! For myself, I am inclined to think the most useful part of reading is to know what we should not read, what we can keep out from that small cleared spot in the overgrown jungle of "information," the corner which we can call our ordered patch of fruit-bearing knowledge. Is not the accumulation of fresh books a fresh hindrance to our real knowledge of the old? Does not the multiplicity of volumes become a bar upon our use of any? In literature especially does it hold — that we cannot see the wood for the trees.

A man of power, who has got more from books than most of his contemporaries, has lately said: "Form a habit of reading, do not mind what you read, the reading of better books will come when you have a habit of reading the inferior." I cannot agree with him. I think a habit of reading idly debilitates and corrupts the mind for all wholesome reading; I think the habit of reading wisely is one of the most difficult habits to acquire, needing strong resolution and infinite pains; and I hold the habit of reading for mere reading's sake, instead of for the sake of the stuff we gain from reading, to be one of the worst and commonest and most unwholesome habits we have. Why do we still suffer the traditional hypocrisy about the dignity of literature, — literature, I mean, in the gross, which includes about equal parts of what is useful and what is useless? Why are books as books, writers as writers, readers as readers, meritorious and honorable, apart from any good in them, or anything that we can get from them? Why do we pride ourselves on our powers of absorbing print, as our grandfathers did on their gifts in imbibing port, when we know that there is a mode of absorbing print which makes it impossible we can ever learn anything good out of books?

Our stately Milton said in a passage which is one of the watchwords of the English race, "As good almost kill a Man as kill a good Book." But has he not also said that he would "have a vigilant eye how Bookes demeane themselves as well as

men, and do sharpest justice on them as malefactors"? . . . Yes! they do kill the good book who deliver up their few and precious hours of reading to the trivial book; they make it dead for them; they do what lies in them to destroy "the precious lifeblood of a master spirit, embalm'd and treasured up on purpose to a life beyond life"; they "spill that season'd life of man preserv'd and stor'd up in Bookes." For in the wilderness of books most men, certainly all busy men, must strictly choose. If they saturate their minds with the idler books, the "good book," which Milton calls "an immortality rather than a life," is dead to them: it is a book sealed up and buried.

It is most right that in the great republic of letters there should be a freedom of intercourse and a spirit of equality. Every reader who holds a book in his hand is free of the inmost minds of men past and present; their lives both within and without the pale of their uttered thoughts are unveiled to him; he needs no introduction to the greatest; he stands on no ceremony with them; he may, if he be so minded, scribble "doggerel" on his Shelley, or he may kick Lord Byron, if he please, into a corner. He hears Burke perorate, and Johnson dogmatize, and Scott tell his border tales, and Wordsworth muse on the hillside, without the leave of any man, or the payment of any toll. In the republic of letters there are no privileged orders or places reserved. Every man who has written a book, even the diligent Mr. Whitaker, is in one sense an author; "a book's a book although there's nothing in't"; and every man who can decipher a penny journal is, in one sense, a reader. And your "general reader," like the gravedigger in "Hamlet," is hail-fellow with all the mighty dead; he pats the skull of the jester; batters the cheek of lord, lady, or courtier; and uses "imperious Cæsar" to teach boys the Latin declensions.

But this noble equality of all writers — of all writers and of all readers — has a perilous side to it. It is apt to make us indiscriminate in the books we read, and somewhat contemptuous of the mighty men of the past. Men who are most observant as to the friends they make, or the conversation they join in, are carelessness itself as to the books to whom they intrust themselves and the printed language with which they saturate their minds. Yet can any friendship or society be more important to us than that of the books which form so large a part of our minds and even of our characters? Do we in real life take any pleasant

fellow to our homes and chat with some agreeable rascal by our firesides, we who will take up any pleasant fellow's printed memoirs, we who delight in the agreeable rascal when he is cut up into pages and bound in calf?

I have no intention to moralize or to indulge in a homily against the reading of what is deliberately evil. There is not so much need for this now, and I am not discoursing on the whole duty of man. I take that part of our reading which is by itself no doubt harmless, entertaining, and even gently instructive. But of this enormous mass of literature, how much deserves to be chosen out, to be preferred to all the great books of the world, to be set apart for those precious hours which are all that the most of us can give to solid reading? The vast proportion of books are books that we shall never be able to read. A serious percentage of books are not worth reading at all. The really vital books for us we also know to be a very trifling portion of the whole. And yet we act as if every book were as good as any other, as if it were merely a question of order which we take up first, as if any book were good enough for us, and as if all were alike honorable, precious, and satisfying. Alas! books cannot be more than the men who write them, and as a large proportion of the human race now write books, with motives and objects as various as human activity, books as books are entitled *a priori*, until their value is proved, to the same attention and respect as houses, steam engines, pictures, fiddles, bonnets, and other thoughtful or ornamental products of human industry. In the shelves of those libraries which are our pride, — libraries public or private, circulating or very stationary, — are to be found those great books of the world *rari nantes in gurgite vasto*, those books which are truly "the precious lifeblood of a master spirit." But the very familiarity which their mighty fame has bred in us makes us indifferent; we grow weary of what every one is supposed to have read, and we take down something which looks a little eccentric, or some author on the mere ground that we never heard of him before.

Thus the difficulties of literature are in their way as great as those of the world, the obstacles to finding the right friends are as great, the peril is as great of being lost in a babel of voices and an everchanging mass of beings. Books are not wiser than men, the true books are not easier to find than the true men, the bad books or the vulgar books are not less obtrusive and not less ubiquitous than the bad or vulgar everywhere; the art of right reading is as long and difficult to learn as the art of right living. Those who are on good terms with the first author they meet run as much risk as men who surrender their time to the first passer in the street, for to be open to every book is for the most part to gain as little as possible from any. A man aimlessly wandering about in a crowded city is of all men the most lonely; so he who takes up only the books that he "comes across," is pretty certain to meet but few that are worth knowing.

Now this danger is one to which we are specially exposed in this age. Our high-pressure life of emergencies, our whirling industrial organization or disorganization, have brought us in this (as in most things) their peculiar difficulties and drawbacks. In almost everything vast opportunities and gigantic means of multiplying our products bring with them new perils and troubles which are often at first neglected. Our huge cities, where wealth is piled up and the requirements and appliances of life extended beyond the dreams of our forefathers, seem to breed in themselves new forms of squalor, disease, blights, or risks to life, such as we are yet unable to cope with. So the enormous multiplicity of modern books is not altogether favorable to the knowing of the best. I listen with mixed satisfaction to the pæans that they chant over the works that issue from the press each day, how the books poured forth from Paternoster Row might in a few years be built into a pyramid that would fill the dome of St. Paul's. How in this mountain of literature am I to find the really useful book? How, when I have found it, and found its value, am I to get others to read it? How am I to keep my head clear in the torrent and din of works, all of which distract my attention, most of which promise me something, whilst so few fulfill that promise? The Nile is the source of the Egyptian's bread, and without it he perishes of hunger. But the Nile may be rather too liberal in his flood, and then the Egyptian runs imminent risk of drowning.

And thus there never was a time, at least during the last two hundred years, when the difficulties in the way of making an efficient use of books were greater than they are to-day, when the obstacles were more real between readers and the right books to read, when it was practically so troublesome to find out that which it is of vital importance to know; and that not by the dearth, but by the plethora of printed matter. For it comes to nearly the same thing whether we are actually debarred by physical impossi-

bility from getting the right book into our hand, or whether we are choked off from the right book by the obtrusive crowd of the wrong books; so that it needs a strong character and a resolute system of reading to keep the head cool in the storm of literature around us. We read nowadays in the market place—I would rather say in some large steam factory of letterpress, where damp sheets of new print whirl round us perpetually—if it be not rather some noisy book fair where literary showmen tempt us with performing dolls, and the gongs of rival booths are stunning our ears from morn till night. Contrast with this pandemonium of Leipsic and Paternoster Row the sublime picture of our Milton in his early retirement at Horton, when, musing over his coming flight to the epic heaven, practicing his pinions, as he tells Diodati, he consumed five years of solitude in reading over the whole of the ancient writers:—

" Et totum rapiunt, me, mea vita, libri."

Who now reads the whole of the ancient writers? Who systematically reads the great writers, be they ancient or modern, whom the consent of ages has marked out as classics; typical, immortal, peculiar teachers of our race? Alas! the "Paradise Lost" is lost again to us beneath an inundation of graceful academic verse, sugary stanzas of ladylike prettiness, and ceaseless explanations in more or less readable prose of what John Milton meant or did not mean, or what he saw or did not see, or why Adam or Satan is like that, or unlike the other. We read a perfect library about the "Paradise Lost," but the "Paradise Lost" itself we do not read.

I am not presumptuous enough to assert that the larger part of modern literature is not worth reading in itself, that the prose is not readable, entertaining, one may say highly instructive. Nor do I pretend that the verses which we read so zealously in place of Milton's are not good verses. On the contrary, I think them sweetly conceived, as musical and as graceful as the verse of any age in our history. I say it emphatically, a great deal of our modern literature is such that it is exceedingly difficult to resist it, and it is undeniable that it gives us real information. It seems perhaps unreasonable to many, to assert that a decent readable book which gives us actual instruction can be otherwise than a useful companion and a solid gain. I dare say many people are ready to cry out upon me as an obscurantist for ventur-

ing to doubt a genial confidence in all literature simply as such. But the question which weighs upon me with such really crushing urgency is this: What are the books that in our little remnant of reading time it is most vital for us to know? For the true use of books is of such sacred value to us that to be simply entertained is to cease to be taught, elevated, inspired by books; merely to gather information of a chance kind is to close the mind to knowledge of the urgent kind.

Every book that we take up without a purpose is an opportunity lost of taking up a book with a purpose—every bit of stray information which we cram into our heads without any sense of its importance is for the most part a bit of the most useful information driven out of our heads and choked off from our minds. It is so certain that information, i. e., the knowledge, the stored thoughts and observations of mankind, is now grown to proportions so utterly incalculable and prodigious, that even the learned whose lives are given to study can but pick up some crumbs that fall from the table of truth. They delve and tend but a plot in that vast and teeming kingdom, whilst those, whom active life leaves with but a few cramped hours of study, can hardly come to know the very vastness of the field before them, or how infinitesimally small is the corner they can traverse at the best. We know all is not of equal value. We know that books differ in value as much as diamonds differ from the sand on the seashore, as much as our living friend differs from a dead rat. We know that much in the myriad-peopled world of books—very much in all kinds—is trivial, enervating, inane, even noxious. And thus, where we have infinite opportunities of wasting our efforts to no end, of fatiguing our minds without enriching them, of clogging the spirit without satisfying it, there, I cannot but think, the very infinity of opportunities is robbing us of the actual power of using them. And thus I come often, in my less hopeful moods, to watch the remorseless cataract of daily literature which thunders over the remnants of the past, as if it were a fresh impediment to the men of our day in the way of systematic knowledge and consistent powers of thought: as if it were destined one day to overwhelm the great inheritance of mankind in prose and verse.

I remember when I was a very young man at college, that a youth, in no spirit of paradox, but out of plenary conviction, undertook to maintain before a body of serious students, the astounding proposition that the invention of printing had been one

of the greatest misfortunes that had ever befallen mankind. He argued that exclusive reliance on printed matter had destroyed the higher method of oral teaching, the dissemination of thought by the spoken word to the attentive ear. He insisted that the formation of a vast literary class looking to the making of books as a means of making money, rather than as a social duty, had multiplied books for the sake of the writers rather than for the sake of the readers; that the reliance on books as a cheap and common resource had done much to weaken the powers of memory; that it destroyed the craving for a general culture of taste, and the need of artistic expression in all the surroundings of life. And he argued lastly, that the sudden multiplication of all kinds of printed matter had been fatal to the orderly arrangement of thought, and had hindered a system of knowledge and a scheme of education.

I am far from sharing this immature view. Of course I hold the invention of printing to have been one of the most momentous facts in the whole history of man. Without it universal social progress, true democratic enlightenment, and the education of the people would have been impossible, or very slow, even if the cultured few, as is likely, could have advanced the knowledge of mankind without it. We place Gutenberg amongst the small list of the unique and special benefactors of mankind, in the sacred choir of those whose work transformed the conditions of life, whose work, once done, could never be repeated. And no doubt the things which our ardent friend regarded as so fatal a disturbance of society were all inevitable and necessary, part of the great revolution of mind through which men grew out of the mediæval incompleteness to a richer conception of life and of the world.

Yet there is a sense in which this boyish anathema against printing may be true to us by our own fault. We may create for ourselves these very evils. For this I hold that the art of printing has not been a gift wholly unmixed with evils; that it must be used wisely if it is to be a boon to man at all; that it entails on us heavy responsibilities, resolution to use it with judgment and self-control, and the will to resist its temptations and its perils. Indeed, we may easily so act that we may make it a clog on the progress of the human mind, a real curse and not a boon. The power of flying at will through space would probably extinguish civilization and society, for it would release us from the wholesome bondage of localities. The power of hearing every word that had ever been uttered on this planet would annihilate thought, as the power of knowing all recorded facts by the process of turning a handle would annihilate true science. Our human faculties and our mental forces are not enlarged simply by multiplying our materials of knowledge and our facilities for communication. Telephones, microphones, pantoscopes, steam presses, and ubiquity engines in general may, after all, leave the poor human brain panting and throbbing under the strain of its appliances, and get no bigger and no stronger than the brains of the men who heard Moses speak, and saw Aristotle and Archimedes pondering over a few worn rolls of crabbed manuscript. Until some new Newton or Watt can invent a machine for magnifying the human mind, every fresh apparatus for multiplying its work is a fresh strain on the mind, a new realm for it to order and to rule.

And so, I say it most confidently, the first intellectual task of our age is rightly to order and make serviceable the vast realm of printed material which four centuries have swept across our path. To organize our knowledge, to systematize our reading, to save, out of the relentless cataract of ink, the immortal thoughts of the greatest — this is a necessity unless the productive ingenuity of man is to lead us at last to a measureless and pathless chaos. To know anything that turns up is, in the infinity of knowledge, to know nothing. To read the first book we come across, in the wilderness of books, is to learn nothing. To turn over the pages of ten thousand volumes is to be practically indifferent to all that is good.

But this warns me that I am entering on a subject which is far too big and solemn for us to touch now. I have no pretension to deal with it as it needs. It is plain, I think, that to organize our knowledge, even to systematize our reading, to make a working selection of books for general study, really implies a complete scheme of education. A scheme of education ultimately implies a system of philosophy, a view of man's duty and powers as a moral and social being — a religion, in fact. Before a problem so great as this, on which a general audience has such different ideas and wants, and differs so profoundly on the very premises from which we start, — before such a problem as a general theory of education, I prefer to retire. I will keep silence even from good words. I have chosen my own part, and adopted

my own teacher. But to ask men to adopt the education of Auguste Comte is almost to ask them to adopt Positivism itself.

Nor will I enlarge on the matter for thought, for foreboding, almost for despair, that is presented to us by the fact of our familiar literary ways and our recognized literary profession. That things infinitely trifling in themselves; men, events, societies, phenomena, in no way otherwise more valuable than the myriad other things which flit around us like the sparrows on the housetop, should be glorified, magnified, and perpetuated, set under a literary microscope and focused in the blaze of a literary magic lantern — not for what they are in themselves, but solely to amuse and excite the world by showing how it can be done — all this is to me so amazing, so heart-breaking, that I forbear now to treat it, as I cannot say all that I would.

I pass from all systems of education — from thought of social duty, from meditation on the profession of letters — to more general and lighter topics. I will deal now only with the easier side of reading, with matter on which there is some common agreement in the world. I am very far from meaning that our whole time spent with books is to be given to study. Far from it. I put the poetic and emotional side of literature as the most needed for daily use. I take the books that seek to rouse the imagination, to stir up feeling, touch the heart; the books of art, of fancy, of ideals, such as reflect the delight and aroma of life. And here how does the trivial, provided it is the new, that which stares at us in the advertising columns of the day, crowd out the immortal poetry and pathos of the human race, vitiating our taste for those exquisite pieces which are a household word, and weakening our mental relish for the eternal works of genius! Old Homer is the very fountain head of pure poetic enjoyment, of all that is spontaneous, simple, native, and dignified in life. He takes us into the ambrosial world of heroes, of human vigor, of purity, of grace. Now Homer is one of the few poets the life of whom can be fairly preserved in a translation. Most men and women can say that they have read Homer, just as most of us can say that we have studied Johnson's Dictionary. But how few of us take him up, time after time, with fresh delight! How few have even read the entire "Iliad" and "Odyssey" through! Whether in the resounding lines of the old Greek, as fresh and ever-stirring as the waves that tumble on the seashore, filling the soul with satisfying silent wonder at its restless unison;

whether in the quaint lines of Chapman, or the clarion couplets of Pope, or the closer versions of Cowper, Lord Derby, of Philip Worsley, or even in the new prose version of the "Odyssey," Homer is always fresh and rich. And yet how seldom does one find a friend spellbound over the Greek Bible of antiquity, whilst they wade through torrents of magazine quotations from a petty versifier of to-day, and in an idle vacation will graze, as contentedly as cattle in a fresh meadow, through the chopped straw of a circulating library. A generation which will listen to "Pinafore" for three hundred nights, and will read M. Zola's seventeenth romance, can no more read Homer than it could read a cuneiform inscription. It will read about Homer just as it will read about a cuneiform inscription, and will crowd to see a few pots which probably came from the neighborhood of Troy. But to Homer and the primeval type of heroic man in his beauty, and his simpleness, and joyousness, the cultured generation is really dead, as completely as some spoiled beauty of the ball-room is dead to the bloom of the heather or the waving of the daffodils in a glade.

It is a true psychological problem, this nausea which idle culture seems to produce for all that is manly and pure in heroic poetry. One knows — at least every schoolboy has known — that a passage of Homer, rolling along in the hexameter or trumped out by Pope, will give one a hot glow of pleasure and raise a finer throb in the pulse; one knows that Homer is the easiest, most artless, most diverting of all poets; that the fiftieth reading rouses the spirit even more than the first — and yet we find ourselves (we are all alike) painfully pshaw-ing over some new and uncut barley sugar in rhyme, which a man in the street asked us if we had read, or it may be some learned lucubration about the site of Troy by some one we chanced to meet at dinner. It is an unwritten chapter in the history of the human mind, how this literary prurience after new print unmans us for the enjoyment of the old songs chanted forth in the sunrise of human imagination. To ask a man or woman who spends half a lifetime in sucking magazines and new poems to read a book of Homer would be like asking a butcher's boy to whistle "Adelaida." The noises and sights and talk, the whirl and volatility of life around us, are too strong for us. A society which is forever gossiping in a sort of perpetual "drum" loses the very faculty of caring for anything but "early copies" and the last

tale out. Thus, like the tares in the noble parable of the Sower, a perpetual chatter about books chokes the seed which is sown in the greatest books in the world.

I speak of Homer, but fifty other great poets and creators of eternal beauty would serve my argument as well. Take the latest perhaps in the series of the world-wide and immortal poets of the whole human race — Walter Scott. We all read Scott's romances, as we have all read Hume's "History of England," but how often do we read them, how zealously, with what sympathy and understanding? I am told that the last discovery of modern culture is that Scott's prose is commonplace; that the young men at our universities are far too critical to care for his artless sentences and flowing descriptions. They prefer Mr. Swinburne, Mr. Mallock, and the euphuism of young Oxford, just as some people prefer a Dresden shepherdess to the Caryatides of the Erechtheum, pronounce Fielding to be low, and Mozart to be *passé*. As boys love lollipops, so these juvenile fops love to roll phrases about under the tongue, as if phrases in themselves had a value apart from thoughts, feelings, great conceptions, or human sympathy. For Scott is just one of the poets (we may call poets all the great creators in prose or in verse) of whom one never wearies, just as one can listen to Beethoven or watch the sunrise or the sunset day by day with new delight. I think I can read the "Antiquary," or the "Bride of Lammermoor," "Ivanhoe," "Quentin Durward," and "Old Mortality," at least once a year afresh. Now Scott is a perfect library in himself. A constant reader of romances would find that it needed months to go through even the best pieces of the inexhaustible painter of eight full centuries and every type of man, and he might repeat the process of reading him ten times in a lifetime without a sense of fatigue or sameness. The poetic beauty of Scott's creations is almost the least of his great qualities. It is the universality of his sympathy that is so truly great, the justice of his estimates, the insight into the spirit of each age, his intense absorption of self in the vast epic of human civilization. What are the old almanacs that they so often give us as histories beside these living pictures of the ordered succession of ages? As in Homer himself, we see in this prose "Iliad" of modern history the battle of the old and the new, the heroic defense of ancient strongholds, the long impending and inevitable doom of mediæval life. Strong men and proud women struggle against the destiny of modern society, unconsciously working out its ways, undauntedly defying its power. How just is our island Homer! Neither Greek nor Trojan sways him; Achilles is his hero; Hector is his favorite; he loves the councils of chiefs and the palace of Priam; but the swineherd, the charioteer, the slave girl, the hound, the beggar, and the herdsman, all glow alike in the harmonious coloring of his peopled epic. We see the dawn of our English nation, the defense of Christendom against the Koran, the grace and the terror of feudalism, the rise of monarchy out of baronies, the rise of parliaments out of monarchy, the rise of industry out of serfage, the pathetic ruin of chivalry, the splendid death struggle of Catholicism, the sylvan tribes of the mountain (remnants of our prehistoric forefathers) beating themselves to pieces against the hard advance of modern industry; we see the grim heroism of the Bible martyrs, the catastrophe of feudalism overwhelmed by a practical age which knew little of its graces and almost nothing of its virtues. Such is Scott, who, we may say, has done for the various phases of modern history what Shakespeare has done for the manifold types of human character. And this glorious and most human and most historical of poets, without whom our very conception of human development would have ever been imperfect, this manliest and truest and widest of romancers we neglect for some hothouse hybrid of psychological analysis, for the wretched imitators of Balzac and the jackanapes phrasemongering of some Osric of the day, who assures us that Scott is an absolute Philistine.

In speaking with enthusiasm of Scott, as of Homer, or of Shakespeare, or of Milton, or of any of the accepted masters of the world, I have no wish to insist dogmatically upon any single name, or two or three in particular. Our enjoyment and reverence of the great poets of the world is seriously injured nowadays by the habit we get of singling out some particular quality, some particular school of art for intemperate praise or, still worse, for intemperate abuse. Mr. Ruskin, I suppose, is answerable for the taste for this one-sided and spasmodic criticism; and every young gentleman who has the trick of a few adjectives will languidly vow that Marlowe is supreme, or Murillo foul. It is the mark of rational criticism as well as of healthy thought to maintain an evenness of mind in judging of great works, to recognize great qualities in due proportion, to feel that defects are made up by beauties, and beauties are often balanced by weak-

ness. The true judgment implies a weighing of each work and each workman as a whole, in relation to the sum of human cultivation and the gradual advance of the movement of ages. And in this matter we shall usually find that the world is right, the world of the modern centuries and the nations of Europe together. It is unlikely, to say the least of it, that a young person who has hardly ceased making Latin verses will be able to reverse the decisions of the civilized world; and it is even more unlikely that Milton and Molière, Fielding and Scott, will ever be displaced by a poet who has unaccountably lain hid for one or two centuries. I know that in the style of to-day I ought hardly to venture to address you about poetry unless I am prepared to unfold to you the mysterious beauties of some unknown genius who has recently been unearthed by the Children of Light and Sweetness. I confess I have no such discovery to announce. I prefer to dwell in Gath and to pitch my tents in Ashdod; and I doubt the use of the sling as a weapon in modern war. I decline to go into hyperbolic eccentricities over unknown geniuses, and a single quality or power is not enough to arouse my enthusiasm. It is possible that no master ever painted a buttercup like this one, or the fringe of a robe like that one; that this poet has a unique subtlety, and that an undefinable music. I am still unconvinced, though the man who cannot see it, we are told, should at once retire to the place where there is wailing and gnashing of teeth.

I am against all gnashing of teeth, whether for or against a particular idol. I stand by the men, and by all the men, who have moved mankind to the depths of their souls, who have taught generations, and formed our life. If I say of Scott, that to have drunk in the whole of his glorious spirit is a liberal education in itself, I am asking for no exclusive devotion to Scott, to any poet, or any school of poets, or any age, or any country, to any style or any order of poet, one more than another. They are as various, fortunately, and as many-sided as human nature itself. If I delight in Scott, I love Fielding, and Richardson, and Sterne, and Goldsmith, and Defoe. Yes, and I will add Cooper and Marryat, Miss Edgeworth and Miss Austen — to confine myself to those who are already classics, to our own country, and to one form of art alone, and not to venture on the ground of contemporary romance in general. What I have said of Homer, I would say in a degree, but somewhat lower, of those great Ancients who

are the most accessible to us in English — Æschylus, Aristophanes, Virgil, and Horace. What I have said of Shakespeare I would say of Calderon, of Molière, of Corneille, of Racine, of Voltaire, of Alfieri, of Goethe, of those dramatists, in many forms, and with genius the most diverse, who have so steadily set themselves to idealize the great types of public life and of the phases of human history. Let us all beware lest worship of the idiosyncrasy of our peerless Shakespeare blind us to the value of the great masters who in a different world and with different aims have presented the development of civilization in a series of dramas, where the unity of a few great types of man and of society is made paramount to subtlety of character or brilliancy of language. What I have said of Milton, I would say of Dante, of Ariosto, of Petrarch, and of Tasso; nor less would I say it of Boccaccio and Chaucer, of Camoens and Spenser, of Rabelais and of Cervantes, of Gil Blas and the Vicar of Wakefield, of Byron and of Shelley, of Goethe and of Schiller. Nor let us forget those wonderful idealizations of awakening thought and primitive societies, the pictures of other races and types of life removed from our own: all those primeval legends, ballads, songs, and tales, those proverbs, apologues, and maxims, which have come down to us from distant ages of man's history — the old idyls and myths of the Hebrew race; the tales of Greece, of the Middle Ages of the East; the fables of the Old and the New World; the songs of the Nibelungs; the romances of early feudalism; the "Morte d'Arthur"; the "Arabian Nights"; the ballads of the early nations of Europe.

I protest that I am devoted to no school in particular: I condemn no school; I reject none. I am for the school of all the great men; and I am against the school of the smaller men. I care for Wordsworth as well as for Byron, for Burns as well as Shelley, for Boccaccio as well as for Milton, for Bunyan as well as Rabelais, for Cervantes as much as for Dante, for Corneille as well as for Shakespeare, for Goldsmith as well as for Goethe. I stand by the sentence of the world; and I hold that in a matter so human and so broad as the highest poetry the judgment of the nations of Europe is pretty well settled, at any rate, after a century or two of continuous reading and discussing. Let those who will assure us that no one can pretend to culture unless he swear by Fra Angelico and Sandro Botticelli, by Arnolpho the son of Lapo, or the Lombardic bricklayers, by Martini and Galuppi

(all, by the way, admirable men of the second rank); and so, in literature and poetry, there are some who will hear of nothing but Webster or Marlowe; Blake, Herrick or Keats; William Langland or the Earl of Surrey; Heine or Omar Khayyám. All of these are men of genius, and each with a special and inimitable gift of his own. But the busy world, which does not hunt poets as collectors hunt for curios, may fairly reserve these lesser lights for the time when they know the greatest well.

So, I say, think mainly of the greatest, of the best known, of those who cover the largest area of human history and man's common nature. Now when we come to count up these names accepted by the unanimous voice of Europe, we have some thirty or forty names, and amongst them are some of the most voluminous of writers. I have been running over but one department of literature alone, the poetic. I have been naming those only, whose names are household words with us, and the poets for the most part of modern Europe. Yet even here we have a list which is usually found in not less than a hundred volumes at least. Now poetry and the highest kind of romance are exactly that order of literature, which not only will bear to be read many times, but that of which the true value can only be gained by frequent, and indeed habitual reading. A man can hardly be said to know the twelfth Mass or the ninth Symphony, by virtue of having once heard them played ten years ago; he can hardly be said to take air and exercise because he took a country walk once last autumn. And so he can hardly be said to know Scott, or Shakespeare, Molière, or Cervantes, when he once read them since the close of his school days, or amidst the daily grind of his professional life. The immortal and universal poets of our race are to be read and re-read till their music and their spirit are a part of our nature; they are to be thought over and digested till we live in the world they created for us; they are to be read devoutly, as devout men read their Bibles and fortify their hearts with psalms. For as the old Hebrew singer heard the heavens declare the glory of their Maker, and the firmament showing his handiwork, so in the long roll of poetry we see transfigured the strength and beauty of humanity, the joys and sorrows, the dignity and struggles, the long life-history of our common kind.

I have said but little of the more difficult poetry, and the religious meditations of the great idealists in prose and verse, whom it needs a concentrated study to master. Some of these are hard to all men, and at all seasons. The "Divine Comedy," in its way, reaches as deep in its thoughtfulness as Descartes himself. But these books, if they are difficult to all, are impossible to the gluttons of the circulating library. To these munchers of vapid memoirs and monotonous tales, such books are closed indeed. The power of enjoyment and of understanding is withered up within them. To the besotted gambler on the turf the lonely hillside glowing with heather grows to be as dreary as a prison; and so, too, a man may listen nightly to burlesques, till "Fidelio" inflicts on him intolerable fatigue. One may be a devourer of books, and be actually incapable of reading a hundred lines of the wisest and most beautiful. To read one of such books comes only by habit, as prayer is impossible to one who habitually dreads to be alone.

In an age of steam it seems almost idle to speak of Dante, the most profound, the most meditative, the most prophetic of all poets, in whose epic the panorama of mediæval life, of feudalism at its best and Christianity at its best, stands, as in a microcosm, transfigured, judged, and measured. To most men, the "Paradise Lost," with all its mighty music and its idyllic pictures of human nature, of our first-child parents in their naked purity and their awakening thought, is a serious and ungrateful task—not to be ranked with the simple enjoyments; it is a possession to be acquired only by habit. The great religious poets, the imaginative teachers of the heart, are never easy reading. But the reading of them is a religious habit, rather than an intellectual effort. I pretend not now to be dealing with a matter so deep and high as religion, or indeed with education in the fuller sense. I will say nothing of that side of reading which is really hard study, an effort of duty, matter of meditation and reverential thought. I need speak not now of such reading as that of the Bible; the moral reflections of Socrates, of Aristotle, of Confucius; the "Confessions" of St. Augustine and the "City of God"; the discourses of St. Bernard, of Bossuet, of Bishop Butler, of Jeremy Taylor; the vast philosophical visions that were opened to the eyes of Bacon and Descartes; the thoughts of Pascal and Vauvenargues, of Diderot and Hume, of Condorcet and de Maistre; the problem of man's nature as it is told in the "Excursion," or in "Faust," in "Cain," or in the "Pilgrim's Progress"; the unsearchable outpouring of the heart in the great mystics, of

VI—132

many ages and many races; be the mysticism that of David or of John, of Mahomet or of Buddha; of Fénelon or of Shelley.

I pass by all these. For I am speaking now of the use of books in our leisure hours. I will take the books of simple enjoyment, books that one can laugh over and weep over; and learn from, and laugh and weep again; which have in them humor, truth, human nature in all its sides, pictures of the great phases of human history; and withal sound teaching in honesty, manliness, gentleness, patience. Of such books, I say, books accepted by the voice of all mankind as matchless and immortal, there is a complete library at hand for every man, in his every mood, whatever his tastes or his acquirements. To know merely the hundred volumes or so of which I have spoken would involve the study of years. But who can say that these books are read as they might be, that we do not neglect them for something in a new cover, or which catches our eye in a library? It is not merely to the idle and unreading world that this complaint holds good. It is the insatiable readers themselves who so often read to the least profit. Of course they have read all these household books many years ago, read them, and judged them, and put them away forever. They will read infinite dissertations about these authors; they will write you essays on their works; they will talk most learned criticism about them. But it never occurs to them that such books have a daily and perpetual value, such as the devout Christian finds in his morning and evening psalm; that the music of them has to sink into the soul by continual renewal; that we have to live with them and in them, till their ideal world habitually surrounds us in the midst of the real world; that their great thoughts have to stir us daily anew, and their generous passion has to warm us hour by hour; just as we need each day to have our eyes filled by the light of heaven, and our blood warmed by the glow of the sun. I vow that when I see men forgetful of the perennial poetry of the world, muck-raking in a litter of fugitive refuse, I think of that wonderful scene in the "Pilgrim's Progress," where the Interpreter shows the wayfarers the old man raking in the straw and dust, whilst he will not see the Angel who offers him a crown of gold and precious stones.

This gold, refined beyond the standard of the goldsmith, these pearls of great price, the united voice of mankind has assured us are found in those immortal works of every age and of every race whose names are household words throughout the world.

And we shut our eyes to them for the sake of the straw and litter of the nearest library or bookshop. A lifetime will hardly suffice to know, as they ought to be known, these great masterpieces of man's genius. How many of us can name ten men who may be said entirely to know (in the sense in which a thoughtful Christian knows the Psalms and the Epistles) even a few of the greatest poets? I take them almost at random, and I name Homer, Æschylus, Aristophanes, Virgil, Dante, Ariosto, Shakespeare, Cervantes, Calderon, Corneille, Molière, Milton, Fielding, Goethe, Scott. Of course every one has read these poets, but who really knows them, the whole of them, the whole meaning of them? They are too often taken "as read," as they say in the railway meetings.

Take of this immortal choir the liveliest, the easiest, the most familiar, take for the moment the three—Cervantes, Molière, Fielding. Here we have three poets who unite the profoundest insight into human nature with the most inimitable wit: "Penseroso" and "L'Allegro" in one; "sober, steadfast, and demure," and yet with "Laughter holding both his sides." And in all three, different as they are, is an unfathomable pathos, a brotherly pity for all human weakness, spontaneous sympathy with all human goodness. To know "Don Quixote," that is to follow out the whole mystery of its double world, is to know the very tragicomedy of human life, the contrast of the ideal with the real, of chivalry with good sense, of heroic failure with vulgar utility, of the past with the present, of the impossible sublime with the possible commonplace. And yet to how many reading men is "Don Quixote" little more than a book to laugh over in boyhood! So Molière is read or witnessed; we laugh and we praise. But how little do we study with insight that elaborate gallery of human character; those consummate types of almost every social phenomenon; that genial and just judge of imposture, folly, vanity, affectation, and insincerity; that tragic picture of the brave man born out of his time, too proud and too just to be of use in his age! Was ever truer word said than that about Fielding as "the prose Homer of human nature"? And yet how often do we forget in "Tom Jones" the beauty of unselfishness, the wellspring of goodness, the tenderness, the manly healthiness and heartiness underlying its frolic and its satire, because we are absorbed, it may be, in laughing at its humor, or are simply irritated by its grossness! Nay, "Robinson Crusoe" contains (not for boys,

but for men) more religion, more philosophy, more psychology, more political economy, more anthropology, than are found in many elaborate treatises on these special subjects. And yet, I imagine, grown men do not often read "Robinson Crusoe" as the article has it, "for instruction of life and ensample of manners." The great books of the world we have once read; we take them as read; we believe that we read them; at least, we believe that we know them. But to how few of us are they daily mental food! For once that we take down our Milton, and read a book of that "voice," as Wordsworth says, "whose sound is like the sea," we take up fifty times a magazine with something about Milton, or about Milton's grandmother, or a book stuffed with curious facts about the houses in which he lived, and the juvenile ailments of his first wife.

And whilst the roll of the great men yet unread is to all of us so long, whilst years are not enough to master the very least of them, we are incessantly searching the earth for something new or strangely forgotten. Brilliant essays are forever extolling some minor light. It becomes the fashion to grow rapturous about the obscure Elizabethan dramatists; about the note of refinement in the lesser men of Queen Anne; it is pretty to swear by Lyly's "Euphues" and Sidney's "Arcadia"; to vaunt Lovelace and Herrick, Marvell and Donne, Robert Burton and Sir Thomas Browne. All of them are excellent men, who have written delightful things, that may very well be enjoyed when we have utterly exhausted the best. But when one meets bevies of hyperesthetic young maidens, in lackadaisical gowns, who simper about Greene and John Ford (authors, let us trust, that they never have read), one wonders if they all know "Lear" or ever heard of "Alceste." Since to nine out of ten of the "general readers" the very best is as yet more than they have managed to assimilate, this fidgeting after something curious is a little premature and perhaps artificial.

For this reason I stand amazed at the lengths of fantastic curiosity to which persons far from learned have pushed the mania for collecting rare books, or prying into out-of-the-way holes and corners of literature. They conduct themselves as if all the works attainable by ordinary diligence were to them sucked as dry as an orange. Says one, "I came across a very curious book mentioned in a parenthesis in the 'Religio Medici.' Only one other copy exists in this country." I will not mention the work to-night, because I know that, if I did, to-morrow morning at least fifty libraries would be ransacked for it, which would be unpardonable waste of time. "I am bringing out," says another, quite simply, "'The Lives of the Washerwomen of the Queens of England.'" And when it comes out we shall have a copious collection of washing books some centuries old, and at length understand the mode of ironing a ruff in the early mediæval period. A very learned friend of mine thinks it perfectly monstrous that a public library should be without an adequate collection of works in Dutch, though I believe he is the only frequenter of it who can read that language. Not long ago I procured for a Russian scholar a manuscript copy of a very rare work by Greene, the contemporary of Shakespeare. Greene's "Funeralls" is, I think, as dismal and worthless a set of lines as one often sees; and as it has slumbered for nearly three hundred years, I should be willing to let it be its own undertaker. But this unsavory carrion is at last to be dug out of its grave, for it is now translated into Russian and published in Moscow (to the honor and glory of the Russian professor) in order to delight and inform the Muscovite public, where perhaps not ten in a million can as much as read Shakespeare. This or that collector again, with the labor of half a lifetime and by means of half his fortune, has amassed a library of old plays, every one of them worthless in diction, in plot, in sentiment, and in purpose; a collection far more stupid and uninteresting in fact than the burlesques and pantomimes of the last fifty years. And yet this insatiable student of old plays will probably know less of Molière and Alfieri than Molière's housekeeper or Alfieri's valet, and possibly he has never looked into such poets as Calderon and Vondel.

Collecting rare books and forgotten authors is perhaps of all the collecting manias the most foolish in our day. There is much to be said for rare china and curious beetles. The china is occasionally beautiful, and the beetles at least are droll. But rare books now are, by the nature of the case, worthless books, and their rarity usually consists in this: that the printer made a blunder in the text, or that they contain something exceptionally nasty or silly. To affect a profound interest in neglected authors and uncommon books is a sign, for the most part, not that a man has exhausted the resources of ordinary literature, but that he has no real respect for the greatest productions of the greatest

men in the world. This bibliomania seizes hold of rational beings and so perverts them, that in the sufferer's mind the human race exists for the sake of the books, and not the books for the sake of the human race. There is one book they might read to good purpose — the doings of a great book collector who once lived in La Mancha. To the collector, and sometimes to the scholar, the book becomes a fetich or idol, and is worthy of the worship of mankind, even if it cannot be the slightest use to anybody. As the book exists, it must have the compliment paid it of being invited to the shelves. The "library is imperfect without it," although the library will, so to speak, stink when it has got it. The great books are of course the common books, and these are treated by collectors and librarians with sovereign contempt. The more dreadful an abortion of a book the rare volume may be, the more desperate is the struggle of libraries to possess it. Civilization in fact has evolved a complete apparatus, an order of men and a code of ideas for the express purpose, one may say, of degrading the great books. It suffocates them under mountains of little books, and give the place of honor to that which is plainly literary carrion.

Now I suppose, at the bottom of all this lies that rattle and restlessness of life which belongs to the industrial maelstrom wherein we ever revolve. And connected therewith comes also that literary dandyism which results from the pursuit of letters without any social purpose or any systematic faith. To read from the pricking of some cerebral itch rather than from a desire of forming judgments; to get, like an Alpine club stripling, to the top of some unscaled pinnacle of culture; to use books as a sedative, as a means of exciting a mild intellectual titillation, instead of as a means of elevating the nature; to dribble on in a perpetual literary gossip in order to avoid the effort of bracing the mind to think — such is our habit in an age of utterly chaotic education. We read, as the bereaved poet made rhymes —

> "For the unquiet heart and brain,
> A use in measured language lies;
> The sad mechanic exercise,
> Like dull narcotics, numbing pain."

We, for whom steam and electricity have done almost everything except give us bigger brains and hearts, who have a new inven-

tion ready for every meeting of the Royal Institution, who want new things to talk about faster than children want new toys to break, we cannot take up the books we have seen about us since our childhood: Milton, or Molière, or Scott. It feels like donning knee breeches and buckles, to read what everybody has read, that everybody can read, and which our very fathers thought good entertainment scores of years ago. Hard-worked men and overwrought women crave an occupation which shall free them from their thoughts and yet not take them from their world. And thus it comes that we need at least a thousand new books every season, whilst we have rarely a spare hour left for the greatest of all. But I am getting into a vein too serious for our purpose: education is a long and thorny topic. I will cite but the words, on this head, of the great Bishop Butler: "The great number of books and papers of amusement which, of one kind or another, daily come in one's way, have in part occasioned, and most perfectly fall in with and humor, this idle way of reading and considering things. By this means time, even in solitude, is happily got rid of, without the pain of attention; neither is any part of it more put to the account of idleness, one can scarce forbear saying, is spent with less thought than great part of that which is spent in reading." But this was written exactly a century and a half ago, in 1729; since which date, let us trust, the multiplicity of print and the habits of desultory reading have considerably abated.

A philosopher with whom I hold (but with whose opinion I have no present intention of troubling you) has proposed a method of dealing with this indiscriminate use of books, which I think is worthy of attention. He has framed a short collection of books for constant and general reading. He put it forward "with the view of guiding the more thoughtful minds among the people in their choice for constant use." He declares that, "both the intellect and the moral character suffer grievously at the present time from irregular reading." It was not intended to put a bar upon other reading, or to supersede special study. It is designed as a type of a healthy and rational syllabus of essential books, fit for common teaching and daily use. It presents a working epitome of what is best and most enduring in the literature of the world. The entire collection would form, in the shape in which books now exist in modern libraries, something like five hundred volumes. They embrace books both of ancient and modern times, in all the

five principal languages of modern Europe. It is divided into four sections: poetry, science, history, religion.

The principles on what it is framed are these: First it collects the best in all the great departments of human thought, so that no part of education shall be wholly wanting. Next it puts together the greatest books, of universal and permanent value, and the greatest and the most enduring only. Next it measures the greatness of books not by their brilliancy, or even their learning, but by their power of presenting some typical chapter in thought, some dominant phase of history; or else it measures them by their power of idealizing man and nature, or of giving harmony to our moral and intellectual activity. Lastly, the test of the general value of books is the permanent relation they bear to the common civilization of Europe.

Some such firm foothold in the vast and increasing torrent of literature it is certainly urgent to find, unless all that is great in literature is to be borne away in the flood of books. With this we may avoid an interminable wandering over a pathless waste of waters. Without it, we may read everything and know nothing; we may be curious about anything that chances, and indifferent to everything that profits. Having such a catalogue before our eyes, with its perpetual warning, — *non multa sed multum*, — we shall see how with our insatiable consumption of print we wander, like unclassed spirits, round the outskirts only of these Elysian fields where the great dead dwell and hold high converse. As it is we hear but in a faint echo that voice which cries: —

> "*Onorate l'altissimo Poeta:*
> *L'ombra sua torna, ch'era dipartita.*"

We need to be reminded every day how many are the books of inimitable glory, which, with all our eagerness after reading, we have never taken in our hands. It will astonish most of us to find how much of our very industry is given to the books which leave no mark, how often we rake in the litter of the printing press, whilst a crown of gold and rubies is offered us in vain.

Complete. From the original text as it was read before the London Institution and published in the Fortnightly Review, April 1st, 1879.

JOHN HAWKESWORTH

(c. 1715-1773)

HE Adventurer, which gave Hawkesworth his place among classical English essayists, was founded by him in 1752. He had Johnson, Bathurst, and Warton for coadjutors, but of the one hundred and forty numbers which appeared, seventy-six are attributed to Hawkesworth himself. He is highly praised by the author of the "Readers' Handbook," and in his own generation the Archbishop of Canterbury made him a LL.D. for his essays. A single one of them, however, will be sufficient to illustrate both the Johnsonian style and the moral ideas of the others. Hawkesworth was born in London about 1715. He began life as apprentice to a clockmaker, but getting a similar place in an attorney's office, he found opportunity to develop his taste for books. When in 1744 Dr. Johnson ceased compiling (or composing) his remarkable parliamentary reports for the Gentleman's Magazine, Hawkesworth succeeded him. In 1761 he edited Swift's works and published a volume of "Fairy Tales." In 1773 he published three volumes of the papers of Captain Cook, for editing which the English government paid him £6,000. His work was severely criticized, however, and it is said that his death (November 17th, 1773) was hastened by his abnormal sensitiveness.

ON GOSSIP AND TATTLING

Μισω μνημονα Συμποτην.
—*Greek Proverb.*

"Far from my table be the telltale guest."

IT HAS been remarked that men are generally kind in proportion as they are happy; and it is said even of the devil, that he is good-humored when he is pleased. Every act, therefore, by which another is injured, from whatever motive, contracts more guilt and expresses great malignity, if it is committed in those seasons which are set apart to pleasantry and good-humor, and brightened with enjoyments peculiar to rational and social beings.

presence of each other are become obdurate in guilt and insensible to infamy.

Reverence thyself, is one of the sublime precepts of that amiable philosopher, whose humanity alone was an incontestible proof of the dignity of his mind. Pythagoras, in his idea of virtue, comprehended intellectual purity; and he supposed that by him who reverenced himself those thoughts would be suppressed by which a being capable of virtue is degraded. This divine precept evidently presupposes a reverence of others, by which men are restrained from more gross immoralities; and with which he hoped a reverence of self would also co-operate as an auxiliary motive.

The great Duke of Marlborough, who was perhaps the most accomplished gentleman of his age, would never suffer any approaches to obscenity in his presence; and it was said by the late Lord Cobham, that he did not reprove it as an immorality in the speaker, but resented it as an indignity to himself: and it is evident that to speak evil of the absent, to utter lewdness, blasphemy, or treason, must degrade not only him who speaks, but those who hear; for surely that dignity of character which a man ought always to sustain is in danger when he is made the confidant of treachery, detraction, impiety, or lust: for he, who in conversation displays his own vices, imputes them; as he who boasts to another of a robbery presupposes that he is a thief.

It should be a general rule never to utter anything in conversation which would justly dishonor us if it should be reported to the world. If this rule could be always kept, we should be secure in our own innocence against the craft of knaves and parasites, the stratagems of cunning, and the vigilance of envy.

But after all the bounty of nature, and all the labor of virtue, many imperfections will be still discerned in human beings, even by those who do not see with all the perspicacity of human wisdom; and he is guilty of the most aggravated detraction, who reports the weakness of a good mind discovered in an unguarded hour; something which is rather the effect of negligence than design; rather a folly than a fault; a sally of vanity rather than an eruption of malevolence. It has therefore been a maxim inviolably sacred among good men, never to disclose the secrets of private conversation; a maxim, which though it seems to arise from the breach of some other, does yet imply that general rectitude, which is produced by a consciousness of virtuous dignity, and a regard to that reverence which is due to ourselves and

Detraction is among those vices, which the most languid virtue has sufficient force to prevent; because, by detraction, that is not gained which is taken away: "He who filches from me my good name," says Shakespeare, "enriches not himself, but makes me poor indeed": as nothing, therefore, degrades human nature more than detraction, nothing more disgraces conversation. The detractor, as he is the lowest moral character, reflects greater dishonor upon his company than the hangman; and he whose disposition is a scandal to his species should be more diligently avoided than he who is scandalous only by his office.

But for this practice, however vile, some have dared to apologize, by contending that the report by which they injured an absent character was true: this, however, amounts to no more than that they have not complicated malice with falsehood, and that there is some difference between detraction and slander. To relate all the ill that is true of the best man in the world would probably render him the object of suspicion and distrust; and if this practice were universal, mutual confidence and esteem, the comforts of society, and the endearments of friendship would be at an end.

There is something unspeakably more hateful in those species of villainy by which the law is evaded than in those by which it is violated and defied. Courage has sometimes preserved rapacity from abhorrence, as beauty has been thought to apologize for prostitution; but the injustice of cowardice is universally abhorred, and, like the lewdness of deformity, has no advocate. Thus hateful are the wretches who detract with caution; and while they perpetrate the wrong, are solicitous to avoid the reproach: they do not say that Chloe forfeited her honor to Lysander, but they say that such a report has been spread, they know not how true. Those who propagate these reports frequently invent them, and it is no breach of charity to suppose this to be always the case, because no man who spreads detraction would have scrupled to produce it, and he who should diffuse poison in a brook would scarce be acquitted of a malicious design, though he should allege that he received it of another who is doing the same elsewhere.

Whatever is incompatible with the highest dignity of our nature should indeed be excluded from our conversation. As companions, not only that which we owe to ourselves, but to others, is required of us; and they who can indulge any vice in the

others: for to conceal any immoral purpose, which to disclose is to disappoint; any crime, which to hide is to countenance; or any character, which to avoid is to be safe; as it is incompatible with virtue, and injurious to society, can be a law only among those who are enemies to both.

Among such, indeed, it is a law which there is some degree of obligation to fulfill; and the secrets even of their conversation are, perhaps, seldom disclosed, without an aggravation of their guilt; it is the interest of society, that the veil of taciturnity should be drawn over the mysteries of drunkenness and lewdness; and to hide even the machinations of envy, ambition, or revenge, if they happen to mingle in these orgies among the rites of Bacchus, seems to be the duty of the initiated, though not of the profane.

If he who has associated with robbers, who has reposed and accepted a trust, and whose guilt is a pledge of his fidelity, should betray his associates for hire; if he is urged to secure himself, by the anxiety of suspicion, or the terrors of cowardice, or to punish others by the importunity of resentment and revenge; though the public receive benefit from his conduct, and may think it expedient to reward him, yet he has only added to every other species of guilt that of treachery to his friends: he has demonstrated that he is so destitute of virtue as not to possess even those vices which resemble it; and that he ought to be cut off as totally unfit for human society, but that, as poison is an antidote to poison, his crimes are a security against the crimes of others.

It is, however, true that if such an offender is stung with remorse, if he feels the force of higher obligations than those of an iniquitous compact, and if urged by a desire to atone for the injury which he has done to society, he gives in his information and delivers up his associates, with whatever reluctance, to the laws; by this sacrifice he ratifies his repentance, he becomes again the friend of his country, and deserves not only protection, but esteem: for the same action may be either virtuous or vicious, and may deserve either honor or infamy, as it may be performed upon different principles; and indeed no action can be morally classed or estimated without some knowledge of the motive by which it is produced.

But as there is seldom any other clue to the motives of particular actions than the general tenor of his life by whom they are performed; and as the lives of those who serve their country by bringing its enemies to punishment are commonly flagitious in the highest degree; the ideas of this service, and the most sordid villainy are so connected that they always recur together: if only this part of a character is known, we immediately infer that the whole is infamous; and it is, therefore, no wonder that the name by which it is expressed, especially when it is used to denominate a profession, should be odious; or that a good man should not always have sufficient fortitude to strike away the mask of dissimulation, and direct the sword of justice.

But whatever might be thought of those who discharge their obligations to the public by treachery to their companions, it cannot be pretended that he to whom an immoral design is communicated by inadvertence or mistake is under any private obligation to conceal it; the charge which devolves upon him, he must instantly renounce: for while he hesitates, his virtue is suspended: and he who communicates such design to another, not by inadvertence or mistake, but upon presumption of concurrence, commits an outrage upon his honor, and defies his resentment.

Let none, therefore, be encouraged to profane the rites of conversation, much less of friendship, by supposing there is any law which ought to restrain the indignation of virtue, or deter repentance from reparation.

From the Adventurer complete.

NATHANIEL HAWTHORNE

(1804–1864)

F NATHANIEL HAWTHORNE had not been one of the best story-tellers of modern times, he might have been the greatest American essayist. As it is, he has left only a few idyls to suggest what he might have done as an essayist, if he had loved to express his thoughts directly as well as he does to involve them in allegory. In the subtlety with which he conceals a deep allegorical meaning under what is seemingly a story told for its own sake, he often approaches the "Odyssey" itself, and perhaps among Moderns he is only approached by De la Motte Fouqué. He was born in Salem, Massachusetts, July 4th, 1804. At Bowdoin College, where he was graduated in 1825, he had John S. C. Abbott and Longfellow for classmates. And in 1837, when his "Twice-Told Tales" appeared, Longfellow noticed them favorably in the North American Review. It was not until 1839, however, that Hawthorne's genius was officially recognized by his appointment as "weigher and gauger" in the Federal customs service,— a position he owed to the good offices of the historian Bancroft, then collector of customs at Boston. From 1846 to 1850 Hawthorne was himself "surveyor of the port" of Salem, and during this period he found leisure to write "The Scarlet Letter," an immortal work which if it be thus the result of the favoritism of President Polk for a fellow-Democrat, is the one result of his administration for which posterity will thank him more than for all the rest. In accounting for it, it is worth remembering that one of Hawthorne's own ancestors was a Puritan magistrate, a witch-finder and a persecutor of Quakers. After taking up his residence in the "Manse" at Concord, Hawthorne enjoyed the friendship of Emerson and Thoreau, to whom, in nearly everything, he was as unlike as possible. He died — or perhaps we should say, his avatar ended — May 19th, 1864. His was a mind which took hold on the supernatural as part of its own essence. Among the story-tellers of all ages, no higher or sweeter soul has come on earth to give human nature assurance of its divine possibilities. It is the consciousness of such divinity which sounds in the minor chords of Hawthorne's harmonies. His feeling for eternal things saddened him with the things of time, but his sadness is a manifestation of his highest hope, — a part of that pain which the genius of Edmund Burke has recognized as inevitably incident to consciousness of the sublime.

THE HALL OF FANTASY

IT HAS happened to me on various occasions to find myself in a certain edifice which would appear to have some of the characteristics of a public exchange. Its interior is a spacious hall, with a pavement of white marble. Overhead is a lofty dome, supported by long rows of pillars of fantastic architecture, the idea of which was probably taken from the Moorish ruins of the Alhambra, or perhaps from some enchanted edifice in the Arabian tales. The windows of this hall have a breadth and grandeur of design and an elaborateness of workmanship that have nowhere been equaled, except in the Gothic cathedrals of the Old World. Like their prototypes, too, they admit the light of heaven only through stained and pictured glass, thus filling the hall with many-colored radiance and painting its marble floor with beautiful or grotesque designs; so that its inmates breathe, as it were, a visionary atmosphere, and tread upon the fantasies of poetic minds. These peculiarities, combining a wilder mixture of styles than even an American architect usually recognizes as allowable,— Grecian, Gothic, Oriental, and nondescript,— cause the whole edifice to give the impression of a dream, which might be dissipated and shattered to fragments by merely stamping the foot upon the pavement. Yet, with such modifications and repairs as successive ages demand, the Hall of Fantasy is likely to endure longer than the most substantial structure that ever cumbered the earth.

It is not at all times that one can gain admittance into this edifice, although most persons enter it at some period or other of their lives; if not in their waking moments, then by the universal passport of a dream. At my last visit I wandered thither unawares while my mind was busy with an idle tale, and was startled by the throng of people who seemed suddenly to rise up around me.

"Bless me! Where am I?" cried I, with but a dim recognition of the place.

"You are in a spot," said a friend who chanced to be near at hand, "which occupies in the world of fancy the same position which the Bourse, the Rialto, and the Exchange do in the commercial world. All who have affairs in that mystic region, which lies above, below, or beyond the actual, may here meet and talk over the business of their dreams."

"It is a noble hall," observed I.

"Yes," he replied. "Yet we see but a small portion of the edifice. In its upper stories are said to be apartments where the inhabitants of earth may hold converse with those of the moon; and beneath our feet are gloomy cells, which communicate with the infernal regions, and where monsters and chimeras are kept in confinement and fed with all unwholesomeness."

In niches and on pedestals around about the hall stood the statues or busts of men who in every age have been rulers and demigods in the realms of imagination and its kindred regions. The grand old countenance of Homer; the shrunken and decrepit form, but vivid face of Æsop; the dark presence of Dante; the wild Ariosto; Rabelais's smile of deep-wrought mirth; the profound, pathetic humor of Cervantes; the all-glorious Shakespeare; Spenser, meet guest for an allegoric structure; the severe divinity of Milton; and Bunyan, molded of homeliest clay, but instinct with celestial fire,— were those that chiefly attracted my eye. Fielding, Richardson, and Scott occupied conspicuous pedestals. In an obscure and shadowy niche was deposited the bust of our countryman, the author of "Arthur Mervyn."

"Besides these indestructible memorials of real genius," remarked my companion, "each century has erected statues of its own ephemeral favorites in wood."

"I observe a few crumbling relics of such," said I. "But ever and anon, I suppose, Oblivion comes with her huge broom and sweeps them all from the marble floor. But such will never be the fate of this fine statue of Goethe."

"Nor of that next to it,— Emanuel Swedenborg," said he. "Were ever two men of transcendent imagination more unlike?"

In the centre of the hall springs an ornamental fountain, the water of which continually throws itself into new shapes and snatches the most diversified hues from the stained atmosphere around. It is impossible to conceive what a strange vivacity is imparted to the scene by the magic dance of this fountain, with its endless transformations, in which the imaginative beholder may discern what form he will. The water is supposed by some to flow from the same source as the Castilian spring, and is extolled by others as uniting the virtues of the Fountain of Youth with those of many other enchanted wells long celebrated in tale and song. Having never tasted it, I can bear no testimony to its quality.

"Did you ever drink this water?" I inquired of my friend.

"A few sips now and then," answered he. "But there are men here who make it their constant beverage,— or, at least, have the credit of doing so. In some instances it is known to have intoxicating qualities."

"Pray, let us look at these water drinkers," said I.

So we passed among the fantastic pillars till we came to a spot where a number of persons were clustered together in the light of one of the great stained windows, which seemed to glorify the whole group as well as the marble that they trod on. Most of them were men of broad foreheads, meditative countenances, and thoughtful, inward eyes; yet it required but a trifle to summon up mirth, peeping out from the very midst of grave and lofty musings. Some strode about, or leaned against the pillars of the hall, alone and in silence; their faces wore a rapt expression, as if sweet music were in the air around them, or as if their inmost souls were about to float away in song. One or two, perhaps, stole a glance at the bystanders, to watch if their poetic absorption were observed. Others stood talking in groups, with a liveliness of expression, a ready smile, and a light, intellectual laughter, which showed how rapidly the shafts of wit were glancing to and fro among them.

A few held higher converse, which caused their calm and melancholy souls to beam moonlight from their eyes. As I lingered near them,—for I felt an inward attraction towards these men, as if the sympathy of feeling, if not of genius, had united me to their order,—my friend mentioned several of their names. The world has likewise heard those names; with some it has been familiar for years; and others are daily making their way deeper into the universal heart.

"Thank Heaven," observed I to my companion, as we passed to another part of the hall, "we have done with this techy, wayward, shy, proud unreasonable set of laurel gatherers. I love them in their works, but have little desire to meet them elsewhere."

"You have adopted an old prejudice, I see," replied my friend, who was familiar with most of these worthies, being himself a student of poetry, and not without the poetic flame. "But, so far as my experience goes, men of genius are fairly gifted with the social qualities; and in this age there appears to be a fellowfeeling among them which had not heretofore been devel-

VI—133

oped. As men, they ask nothing better than to be on equal terms with their fellowmen; and as authors, they have thrown aside their proverbial jealousy, and acknowledge a generous brotherhood."

"The world does not think so," answered I. "An author is received in general society pretty much as we honest citizens are in the Hall of Fantasy. We gaze at him as if he had no business among us, and question whether he is fit for any of our pursuits."

"Then it is a very foolish question," said he. "Now, here are a class of men whom we may daily meet on 'Change. Yet what poet in the hall is more a fool of fancy than the sagest of them?"

He pointed to a number of persons, who, manifest as the fact was, would have deemed it an insult to be told that they stood in the Hall of Fantasy. Their visages were traced into wrinkles and furrows, each of which seemed the record of some actual experience in life. Their eyes had the shrewd, calculating glance which detects so quickly and so surely all that it concerns a man of business to know about the characters and purposes of his fellowmen. Judging them as they stood, they might be honored and trusted members of the Chamber of Commerce, who had found the genuine secret of wealth and whose sagacity gave them the command of fortune. There was a character of detail and matter of fact in their talk which concealed the extravagance of its purport, insomuch that the wildest schemes had the aspect of every-day realities. Thus the listener was not startled at the idea of cities to be built, as if by magic, in the heart of pathless forests; and of streets to be laid out where now the sea was tossing; and of mighty rivers to be stayed in their courses in order to turn the machinery of a cotton mill. It was only by an effort, and scarcely then, that the mind convinced itself that such speculations were as much matter of fantasy as the old dream of Eldorado, or as Mammon's Cave, or any other vision of gold ever conjured up by the imagination of needy poet or romantic adventurer.

"Upon my word," said I, "it is dangerous to listen to such dreamers as these. Their madness is contagious."

"Yes," said my friend, "because they mistake the Hall of Fantasy for actual brick and mortar, and its purple atmosphere for unsophisticated sunshine. But the poet knows his where-

about, and therefore is less likely to make a fool of himself in real life."

"Here again," observed I, as we advanced a little further, "we see another order of dreamers, peculiarly characteristic, too, of the genius of our country."

These were the inventors of fantastic machines. Models of their contrivances were placed against some of the pillars of the hall, and afforded good emblems of the result generally to be anticipated from an attempt to reduce daydreams to practice. The analogy may hold in morals as well as physics; for instance, here was the model of a railroad through the air and a tunnel under the sea. Here was a machine — stolen, I believe — for the distillation of heat from moonshine; and another for the condensation of morning mist into square blocks of granite, wherewith it was proposed to rebuild the entire Hall of Fantasy. One man exhibited a sort of lens whereby he had succeeded in making sunshine out of a lady's smile; and it was his purpose wholly to irradiate the earth by means of this wonderful invention.

"It is nothing new," said I; "for most of our sunshine comes from woman's smile already."

"True," answered the inventor; "but my machine will secure a constant supply for domestic use, whereas hitherto it has been very precarious."

Another person had a scheme for fixing the reflections of objects in a pool of water, and thus taking the most lifelike portraits imaginable; and the same gentleman demonstrated the practicability of giving a permanent dye to ladies' dresses, in the gorgeous clouds of sunset. There were at least fifty kinds of perpetual motion, one of which was applicable to the wits of newspaper editors and writers of every description. Professor Espy was here, with a tremendous storm in a gum-elastic bag. I could enumerate many more of these Utopian inventions; but, after all, a more imaginative collection is to be found in the Patent Office at Washington.

Turning from the inventors, we took a more general survey of the inmates of the hall. Many persons were present whose right of entrance appeared to consist in some crotchet of the brain, which, so long as it might operate, produced a change in their relation to the actual world. It is singular how very few there are who do not occasionally gain admittance on such a score,

either in abstracted musings, or momentary thoughts, or bright anticipations, or vivid remembrances; for even the actual becomes ideal, whether in hope or memory, and beguiles the dreamer into the Hall of Fantasy. Some unfortunates make their whole abode and business here, and contract habits which unfit them for all the real employments of life. Others — but these are few — possess the faculty, in their occasional visits, of discovering a purer truth than the world can impart among the lights and shadows of these pictured windows.

And with all its dangerous influences, we have reason to thank God that there is such a place of refuge from the gloom and chillness of actual life. Hither may come the prisoner, escaping from his dark and narrow cell and cankerous chain, to breathe free air in this enchanted atmosphere. The sick man leaves his weary pillow, and finds strength to wander hither, though his wasted limbs might not support him even to the threshold of his chamber. The exile passes through the Hall of Fantasy to revisit his native soil. The burden of years rolls down from the old man's shoulders the moment that the door uncloses. Mourners leave their heavy sorrows at the entrance, and here rejoin the lost ones whose faces would else be seen no more, until thought shall have become the only fact. It may be said, in truth, that there is but half a life — the meaner and earthlier half — for those who never find their way into the hall. Nor must I fail to mention that in the observatory of the edifice is kept that wonderful perspective-glass, through which the shepherds of the Delectable Mountains showed Christian the far-off gleam of the Celestial City. The eye of Faith still loves to gaze through it.

"I observe some men here," said I to my friend, "who might set up a strong claim to be reckoned among the most real personages of the day."

"Certainly," he replied. "If a man be in advance of his age, he must be content to make his abode in this hall until the lingering generations of his fellowmen come up with him. He can find no other shelter in the universe. But the fantasies of one day are the deepest realities of a future one."

"It is difficult to distinguish them apart amid the gorgeous and bewildering light of this hall," rejoined I. "The white sunshine of actual life is necessary in order to test them. I am rather apt to doubt both men and their reasonings till I meet them in that truthful medium."

"Perhaps your faith in the ideal is deeper than you are aware," said my friend. "You are at least a democrat; and methinks no scanty share of such faith is essential to the adoption of that creed."

Among the characters who had elicited these remarks were most of the noted reformers of the day, whether in physics, politics, morals, or religion. There is no surer method of arriving at the Hall of Fantasy than to throw oneself into the current of a theory; for, whatever landmarks of fact may be set up along the stream, there is a law of nature that impels it thither. And let it be so; for here the wise head and capacious heart may do their work; and what is good and true becomes gradually hardened into fact, while error melts away and vanishes among the shadows of the hall. Therefore may none who believe and rejoice in the progress of mankind be angry with me because I recognized their apostles and leaders amid the fantastic radiance of those pictured windows. I love and honor such men as well as they.

It would be endless to describe the herd of real or self-styled reformers that peopled this place of refuge. They were the representatives of an unquiet period, when mankind is seeking to cast off the whole tissue of ancient custom like a tattered garment. Many of them had got possession of some crystal fragment of truth, the brightness of which so dazzled them that they could see nothing else in the wide universe. Here were men whose faith had embodied itself in the form of a potato; and others whose long beards had a deep spiritual significance. Here was the abolitionist, brandishing his one idea like an iron flail. In a word, there were a thousand shapes of good and evil, faith and infidelity, wisdom and nonsense,—a most incongruous throng.

Yet, withal, the heart of the stanchest conservative, unless he abjured his fellowship with man, could hardly have helped throbbing in sympathy with the spirit that pervaded these innumerable theorists. It was good for the man of unquickened heart to listen even to their folly. Far down beyond the fathom of the intellect the soul acknowledged that all these varying and conflicting developments of humanity were united in one sentiment. Be the individual theory as wild as fancy could make it, still the wiser spirit would recognize the struggle for a better and purer life than had yet been realized on earth. My faith revived even while I rejected all their schemes. It could

or how the universe will be wiser or better for our existence and destruction."

"We cannot tell what mighty truths may have been embodied in act through the existence of the globe and its inhabitants," rejoined my companion. "Perhaps it may be revealed to us after the fall of the curtain over our catastrophe; or not impossibly, the whole drama, in which we are involuntary actors, may have been performed for the instruction of another set of spectators. I cannot perceive that our own comprehension of it is at all essential to the matter. At any rate, while our view is so ridiculously narrow and superficial it would be absurd to argue the continuance of the world from the fact that it seems to have existed hitherto in vain."

"The poor old earth," murmured I. "She has faults enough, in all conscience; but I cannot bear to have her perish."

"It is no great matter," said my friend. "The happiest of us has been weary of her many a time and oft."

"I doubt it," answered I, pertinaciously; "the root of human nature strikes down deep into this earthly soil, and it is but reluctantly that we submit to be transplanted, even for a higher cultivation in heaven. I query whether the destruction of the earth would gratify any one individual, except perhaps some embarrassed man of business whose notes fall due a day after the day of doom."

Then methought I heard the expostulating cry of a multitude against the consummation prophesied by Father Miller. The lover wrestled with Providence for his foreshadowed bliss. Parents entreated that the earth's span of endurance might be prolonged by some seventy years, so that their newborn infant should not be defrauded of his lifetime. A youthful poet murmured because there would be no posterity to recognize the inspiration of his song. The reformers, one and all, demanded a few thousand years to test their theories, after which the universe might go to wreck. A mechanician, who was busied with an improvement of the steam engine, asked merely time to perfect his model. A miser insisted that the world's destruction would be a personal wrong to himself, unless he should first be permitted to add a specified sum to his enormous heap of gold. A little boy made dolorous inquiry whether the last day would come before Christmas, and thus deprive him of his anticipated dainties. In short, nobody seemed satisfied that this mortal scene of things

not be that the world should continue forever what it has been; a soil where Happiness is so rare a flower and Virtue so often a blighted fruit; a battlefield where the good principle, with its shield flung above its head, can hardly save itself amid the rush of adverse influences. In the enthusiasm of such thoughts I gazed through one of the pictured windows, and behold! the whole external world was tinged with the dimly glorious aspect that is peculiar to the Hall of Fantasy, insomuch that it seemed practicable at that very instant to realize some plan for the perfection of mankind. But, alas! if reformers would understand the sphere in which their lot is cast, they must cease to look through pictured windows. Yet they not only use this medium, but mistake it for the whitest sunshine.

"Come," said I to my friend, starting from a deep reverie, "let us hasten hence, or I shall be tempted to make a theory, after which there is little hope of any man."

"Come hither, then," answered he. "Here is one theory that swallows up and annihilates all others."

He led me to a distant part of the hall where a crowd of deeply attentive auditors were assembled round an elderly man of plain, honest, trustworthy aspect. With an earnestness that betokened the sincerest faith in his own doctrine, he announced that the destruction of the world was close at hand.

"It is Father Miller himself!" exclaimed I.

"No less a man," said my friend; "and observe how picturesque a contrast between his dogma and those of the reformers whom we have just glanced at. They look for the earthly perfection of mankind, and are forming schemes which imply that the immortal spirit will be connected with a physical nature for innumerable ages of futurity. On the other hand, here comes good Father Miller, and with one puff of his relentless theory scatters all their dreams like so many withered leaves upon the blast."

"It is, perhaps, the only method of getting mankind out of the various perplexities into which they have fallen," I replied. "Yet I could wish that the world might be permitted to endure until some great moral shall have been evolved. A riddle is propounded. Where is the solution? The sphinx did not slay herself until her riddle had been guessed. Will it not be so with the world? Now, if it should be burned to-morrow morning, I am at a loss to know what purpose will have been accomplished,

should have its close just now. Yet, it must be confessed, the motives of the crowd for desiring its continuance were mostly so absurd that unless Infinite Wisdom had been aware of much better reasons, the solid earth must have melted away at once.

For my own part, not to speak of a few private and personal ends, I really desired our old mother's prolonged existence for her own dear sake.

"The poor old earth!" I repeated. "What I should chiefly regret in her destruction would be that very earthliness which no other sphere or state of existence can renew or compensate. The fragrance of flowers and of new-mown hay; the genial warmth of sunshine, and the beauty of a sunset among clouds; the comfort and cheerful glow of the fireside; the deliciousness of fruits and of all good cheer; the magnificence of mountains, and seas, and cataracts, and the softer charm of rural scenery; even the fast-falling snow and the gray atmosphere through which it descends,—all these and innumerable other enjoyable things of earth must perish with her. Then the country frolics; the homely humor; the broad, open-mouthed roar of laughter, in which body and soul conjoin so heartily! I fear that no other world can show us anything just like this. As for purely moral enjoyments, the good will find them in every state of being. But where the material and the moral exist together, what is to happen then? And then our mute four-footed friends and the winged songsters of our woods! Might it not be lawful to regret them, even in the hallowed groves of Paradise?"

"You speak like the very spirit of earth, imbued with a scent of freshly turned soil," exclaimed my friend.

"It is not that I so much object to giving up these enjoyments on my own account," continued I, "but I hate to think that they will have been eternally annihilated from the list of joys."

"Nor need they be," he replied. "I see no real force in what you say. Standing in this Hall of Fantasy, we perceive what even the earth-clogged intellect of man can do in creating circumstances which, though we call them shadowy and visionary, are scarcely more so than those that surround us in actual life. Doubt not, then, that man's disembodied spirit may re-create time and the world for itself, with all their peculiar enjoyments, should there still be human yearnings amid life eternal and infinite. But I doubt whether we shall be inclined to play such a poor scene over again."

"Oh, you are ungrateful to our mother earth!" rejoined I. "Come what may, I never will forget her! Neither will it satisfy me to have her exist merely in idea. I want her great, round, solid self to endure interminably, and still to be peopled with the kindly race of man, whom I uphold to be much better than he thinks himself. Nevertheless, I confide the whole matter to Providence, and shall endeavor so to live that the world may come to an end at any moment without leaving me at a loss to find foothold somewhere else."

"It is an excellent resolve," said my companion, looking at his watch. "But come; it is the dinner hour. Will you partake of my vegetable diet?"

A thing so matter of fact as an invitation to dinner, even when the fare was to be nothing more substantial than vegetables and fruit, compelled us forthwith to remove from the Hall of Fantasy. As we passed out of the portal we met the spirits of several persons who had been sent thither in magnetic sleep. I looked back among the sculptured pillars and at the transformations of the gleaming fountain, and almost desired that the whole of life might be spent in that visionary scene where the actual world, with its hard angles, should never rub against me, and only be viewed through the medium of pictured windows. But for those who waste all their days in the Hall of Fantasy, good Father Miller's prophecy is already accomplished, and the solid earth has come to an untimely end. Let us be content, therefore, with merely an occasional visit, for the sake of spiritualizing the grossness of this actual life, and prefiguring to ourselves a state in which the Idea shall be all in all.

Complete. From "Mosses from an Old Manse."

A RILL FROM THE TOWN PUMP

(Scene—The corner of two principal streets. The Town Pump talking through its nose.)

NOON, by the north clock! Noon, by the east! High noon, too, by these hot sunbeams, which fall, scarcely aslope, upon my head, and almost make the water bubble and smoke in the trough under my nose. Truly we public characters have a tough time of it! And among all the town officers,

chosen at March meeting, where is he that sustains, for a single year, the burden of such manifold duties as are imposed, in perpetuity, upon the Town Pump? The title of "town treasurer" is rightfully mine, as guardian of the best treasure that the town has. The overseers of the poor ought to make me their chairman, since I provide bountifully for the pauper, without expense to him that pays taxes. I am at the head of the fire department, and one of the physicians to the Board of Health. As a keeper of the peace, all water drinkers will confess me equal to the constable. I perform some of the duties of the town clerk, by promulgating public notices, when they are pasted on my front. To speak within bounds, I am the chief person of the municipality, and exhibit, moreover, an admirable pattern to my brother officers, by the cool, steady, upright, downright, and impartial discharge of my business, and the constancy with which I stand to my post. Summer or winter, nobody seeks me in vain; for all day long I am seen at the busiest corner, just above the market, stretching out my arms to rich and poor alike; and at night, I hold a lantern over my head, both to show where I am and to keep people out of the gutters.

At this sultry noontide I am cupbearer to the parched populace, for whose benefit an iron goblet is chained to my waist. Like a dramseller on the mall, at muster day, I cry aloud to all and sundry in my plainest accents, and at the very tiptop of my voice: Here it is, gentlemen! Here is the good liquor! Walk up, walk up, gentlemen, walk up, walk up! Here is the superior stuff! Here is the unadulterated ale of father Adam—better than Cognac, Hollands, Jamaica, strong beer, or wine of any price, here it is by the hogshead or the single glass, and not a cent to pay! Walk up, gentlemen, walk up, and help yourselves.

It were a pity if all this outcry should draw no customers. Here they come. A hot day, gentlemen! Quaff, and away again, so as to keep yourselves in a nice cool sweat. You, my friend, will need another cupful, to wash the dust out of your throat, if it be as thick there as it is on your cowhide shoes. I see that you have trudged half a score of miles to-day; and, like a wise man, have passed by the taverns, and stopped at the running brooks and well curbs. Otherwise, betwixt heat without and a fire within, you would have been burnt to a cinder, or melted down to nothing at all, in the fashion of a jellyfish. Drink, and make room for that other fellow, who seeks my aid to quench the

fiery fever of last night's potations, which he drained from no cup of mine. Welcome, most rubicund sir! You and I have been great strangers hitherto; nor, to express the truth, will my nose be anxious for a closer intimacy, till the fumes of your breath be a little less potent. Mercy on you, man! the water absolutely hisses down your red-hot gullet, and is converted quite to steam in the miniature Tophet which you mistake for a stomach. Fill again, and tell me on the word of an honest toper, did you ever, in cellar, tavern, or any kind of a dramshop, spend the price of your children's food for a swig half so delicious? Now, for the first time these ten years, you know the flavor of cold water. Good-bye; and, whenever you are thirsty, remember that I keep a constant supply at the old stand. Who next? Oh, my little friend, you are let loose from school, and come hither to scrub your blooming face, and drown the memory of certain taps of the ferule, and other schoolboy troubles, in a draught from the Town Pump. Take it, pure as the current of your young life. Take it, and may your heart and tongue never be scorched with a fiercer thirst than now! There, my dear child, put down the cup and yield your place to this elderly gentleman, who treads so tenderly over the stones, that I suspect he is afraid of breaking them. What! he limps by without so much as thanking me, as if my hospitable offers were meant only for people who have no wine cellars. Well, well, sir,—no harm done, I hope! Go, draw the cork, tip the decanter; but when your great toe shall set you a-roaring, it will be no affair of mine. If gentlemen love the pleasant titillation of the gout, it is all one to the Town Pump. This thirsty dog, with his red tongue lolling out, does not scorn my hospitality, but stands on his hind legs, and laps eagerly out of the trough. See how lightly he capers away again. Jowler, did your worship ever have the gout?

Are you all satisfied? Then wipe your mouths, my good friends; and while my spout has a moment's leisure, I will delight the town with a few historical reminiscences. In far antiquity, beneath a darksome shadow of venerable boughs, a spring bubbled out of the leaf-strown earth, in the very spot where you now behold me on the sunny pavement. The water was as bright and clear, and deemed as precious as liquid diamonds. The Indian Sagamores drank of it from time immemorial, till the fearful deluge of fire water burst upon the red men, and swept their whole race away from the cold fountains. Endicott and his followers

came next, and often knelt down to drink, dipping their long beards in the spring. The richest goblet then was of birch bark. Governor Winthrop, after a journey afoot from Boston, drank here, out of the hollow of his hand. The elder Higginson here wet his palm, and laid it on the brow of the first town-born child. For many years it was the watering place, and, as it were, the washbowl of the vicinity—whither all decent folks resorted, to purify their visages and gaze at them afterwards—at least the pretty maidens did—in the mirror which it made. On Sabbath days, whenever a babe was to be baptized, the sexton filled his basin here, and placed it on the communion table of the humble meetinghouse, which partly covered the site of yonder stately brick one. Thus one generation after another was consecrated to heaven by its waters, and cast their waxing and waning shadows into its glassy bosom, and vanished from the earth as if mortal life were but a flitting image in a fountain. Finally, the fountain vanished also. Cellars were dug on all sides, and cartloads of gravel flung upon its source, whence oozed a turbid stream, forming a mud puddle at the corner of two streets. In the hot months, when its refreshment was most needed, the dust flew in clouds over the forgotten birthplace of the waters, now their grave. But, in the course of time, a town pump was sunk into the source of the ancient spring; and when the first decayed, another took its place—and then another, and still another—till here stand I, gentlemen and ladies, to serve you with my iron goblet. Drink, and be refreshed! The water is pure and cold as that which slaked the thirst of the red Sagamore beneath the aged boughs, though now the gem of the wilderness is treasured under these hot stones, where no shadow falls but from the brick buildings. And be it the moral of my story, that, as the wasted and long-lost fountain is now known and prized again, so shall the virtues of cold water, too little valued since your fathers' days, be recognized by all.

Your pardon, good people; I must interrupt my stream of eloquence and spout forth a stream of water, to replenish the trough for this teamster and his two yoke of oxen, who have come from Topsfield, or somewhere along that way. No part of my business is pleasanter than the watering of cattle. Look! how rapidly they lower the watermark on the sides of the trough, till their capacious stomachs are moistened with a gallon or two apiece, and they can afford time to breathe it in, with sighs of calm enjoyment. Now they roll their quiet eyes around the brim of their monstrous drinking vessel. An ox is your true toper.

But I perceive, my dear auditors, that you are impatient for the remainder of my discourse. Impute it, I beseech you, to no defect of modesty, if I insist a little longer on so fruitful a topic as my own multifarious merits. It is altogether for your good. The better you think of me the better men and women will you find yourselves. I shall say nothing of my all-important aid on washing days; though, on that account alone, I might call myself the household god of a hundred families. Far be it from me also to hint, my respectable friends, at the show of dirty faces which you would present without my pains to keep you clean. Nor will I remind you how often, when the midnight bells make you tremble for your combustible town, you have fled to the Town Pump, and found me always at my post, firm amid the confusion, and ready to drain my vital current in your behalf. Neither is it worth while to lay much stress on my claims to a medical diploma, as the physician whose simple rule of practice is preferable to all the nauseous lore which has found men sick, or left them so, since the days of Hippocrates. Let us take a broader view of my beneficial influence on mankind.

No; these are trifles compared with the merits which wise men concede to me—if not in my single self, yet as the representative of a class—of being the grand reformer of the age. From my spout, and such spouts as mine, must flow the stream that shall cleanse our earth of the vast portion of its crime and anguish, which has gushed from the fiery fountains of the still. In this mighty enterprise the cow shall be my great confederate. Milk and water! The Town Pump and the Cow! Such is the glorious copartnership that shall tear down the distilleries and brewhouses, uproot the vineyards, shatter the cider presses, ruin the tea and coffee trade, and finally monopolize the whole business of quenching thirst. Blessed consummation! Then, Poverty shall pass away from the land, find no hovel so wretched, where her squalid form may shelter itself. Then Disease, for lack of other victims, shall gnaw her own heart, and die. Then Sin, if she do not die, shall lose half her strength. Until now, the frenzy of hereditary fever has raged in the human blood, transmitted from sire to son, and rekindled, in every generation, by

fresh draughts of liquid flame. When that inward fire shall be extinguished, the heat of passion cannot but grow cool, and war —the drunkenness of nations—perhaps will cease. At least, there will be no war of households. The husband and wife, drinking deep of peaceful joy—a calm bliss of temperate affections—shall pass hand and hand through life, and lie down, not reluctantly, at its protracted close. To them, the past will be no turmoil of mad dreams, nor the future an eternity of such moments as follow the delirium of the drunkard. Their dead faces shall express what their spirits were, and are to be, by a lingering smile of memory and hope.

Ahem! Dry work, this speechifying; especially to an unpracticed orator. I never conceived, till now, what toil the temperance lecturers undergo for my sake. Hereafter, they shall have the business to themselves. Do, some kind Christian, pump a stroke or two, just to wet my whistle. Thank you, sir! My dear hearers, when the world shall have been regenerated by my instrumentality, you will collect your useless vats and liquor casks into one great pile, and make a bonfire in honor of the Town Pump. And when I shall have decayed, like my predecessors, then, if you revere my memory, let a marble fountain, richly sculptured, take my place upon the spot. Such monuments should be erected everywhere, and inscribed with the names of the distinguished champions of my cause. Now, listen; for something very important is to come next.

There are two or three honest friends of mine—and true friends I know they are—who, nevertheless, by their fiery pugnacity in my behalf, do put me in fearful hazard of a broken nose, or even a total overthrow upon the pavement, and the loss of the treasure which I guard. I pray you, gentlemen, let this fault be amended. Is it decent, think you, to get tipsy with zeal for temperance, and take up the honorable cause of the Town Pump, in the style of a toper fighting for his brandy bottle? Or can the excellent qualities of cold water be no otherwise exemplified than by plunging, slap dash, into hot water, and woefully scalding yourself and other people? Trust me, they may. In the moral warfare which you are to wage—and indeed in the whole conduct of your lives—you cannot choose a better example than myself, who have never permitted the dust and sultry atmosphere, the turbulent and manifold disquietudes of the world

around me, to reach that deep calm well of purity, which may be called my soul. And whenever I pour out that soul, it is to cool earth's fever, or cleanse its stains.

One o'clock! Nay, then, if the dinner bell begins to speak, I may as well hold my peace. Here comes a pretty young girl of my acquaintance, with a large stone pitcher for me to fill. May she draw a husband, while drawing her water, as Rachel did of old! Hold out your vessel, my dear! There it is, full to the brim; so now run home, peeping at your sweet image in the pitcher as you go; and forget not, in a glass of my own liquor, to drink "Success to the Town Pump!"

Complete. From "Twice-Told Tales."

WILLIAM HAZLITT

(1778–1830)

AZLITT was born in Kent, England, April 10th, 1778. His tastes as a young man led him to join the study of metaphysics to that of painting. When he went to London, it was to develop what he conceived to be his faculties for these antagonistic modes of intellectual activity. Naturally, he failed in both, but he established himself as a literary critic and popular essayist. It is said that he had Leigh Hunt, Charles Lamb, and Thomas Moore for friends, and that he quarreled with them all. His nerves were too sensitive for the protracted literary work he attempted and the reaction from it gave him the irritability which, as it is said to characterize all "the race of poets," is perhaps no less liable to attack those who make a profession of criticizing them. This Hazlitt did with such success that though he is under the sweeping condemnation of some, who accuse him of habitual "cramming," others praise him as one of the first to demonstrate that Shakespeare's apparent simplicity is due to the highest art. He died September 18th, 1830, after a life which was far from happy. Among his most notable works are his "Lectures on English Poetry," "Lectures on the English Comic Writers," "Characters of Shakespeare's Plays," "Table Talk," "Original Essays," and "Political Essays." "Other men have been said to speak like books," writes Richard Garnett, "Hazlitt's books speak like men."

ON THE PERIODICAL ESSAYISTS

"The proper study of mankind is man."

I NOW come to speak of that sort of writing which has been so successfully cultivated in this country by our Periodical Essayists, and which consists in applying the talents and resources of the mind to all that mixed mass of human affairs, which, though not included under the head of any regular art, science, or profession, falls under the cognizance of the writer, and "comes home to the business and bosoms of men." *Quicquid agunt homines nostri farrago libelli*, is the general motto of this department of literature. It does not treat of minerals or fossils, of the virtues of plants, or the influence of planets; it does not meddle with forms of belief, or systems of philosophy, nor launch into the world of spiritual existences; but it makes familiar with the world of men and women, records their actions, assigns their motives, exhibits their whims, characterizes their pursuits in all their singular and endless variety, ridicules their absurdities, exposes their inconsistencies, "holds the mirror up to nature, and shows the very age and body of the time, its form and pressure"; takes minutes of our dress, air, looks, words, thoughts, and actions; shows us what we are, and what we are not; plays the whole game of human life over before us, and by making us enlightened spectators of its many-colored scenes, enables us (if possible) to become tolerably reasonable agents in the one in which we have to perform a part. "The act and practic part of life is thus made the mistress of our theorique." It is the best and most natural course of study. It is in morals and manners what the experimental is in natural philosophy, as opposed to the dogmatical method. It does not deal in sweeping clauses of proscription and anathema, but in nice distinctions and liberal constructions. It makes up its general accounts from details, its few theories from many facts. It does not try to prove all black or all white as it wishes, but lays on the intermediate colors (and most of them not unpleasing ones), as it finds them blended with "the web of our life, which is of a mingled yarn, good and ill together." It inquires what human life is and has been, to show what it ought to be. It follows it into courts and camps, into town and country, into rustic sports or learned disputations, into the various shades of prejudice or ignorance, of refinement or barbarism, into its private haunts or public pageants, into its weaknesses and littlenesses, its professions and its practices — before it pretends to distinguish right from wrong, or one thing from another. How, indeed, should it do so otherwise?

> "*Quid sit pulchrum, quid turpe, quid utile, quid non,*
> *Plenius et melius Chrysippo et Crantore dicit.*"

The writers I speak of are, if not moral philosophers, moral historians, and that's better: or if they are both, they found the one character upon the other; their premises precede their conclusions; and we put faith in their testimony, for we know that it is true.

Montaigne was the first person who in his "Essays" led the way to this kind of writing among the Moderns. The great merit of Montaigne then was, that he may be said to have been the first who had the courage to say as an author what he felt as a man. And as courage is generally the effect of conscious strength, he was probably led to do so by the richness, truth, and force of his own observations on books and men. He was, in the truest sense, a man of original mind, that is, he had the power of looking at things for himself, or as they really were, instead of blindly trusting to, and fondly repeating what others told him that they were. He got rid of the go-cart of prejudice and affectation, with the learned lumber that follows at their heels, because he could do without them. In taking up his pen he did not set up for a philosopher, wit, orator, or moralist, but he became all these by merely daring to tell us whatever passed through his mind, in its naked simplicity and force, that he thought always worth communicating. He did not, in the abstract character of an author, undertake to say all that could be said upon a subject, but what in his capacity as an inquirer after truth he happened to know about it. He was neither a pedant nor a bigot. He neither supposed that he was bound to know all things, nor that all things were bound to conform to what he had fancied or would have them to be. In treating of men and manners, he spoke of them as he found them, not according to preconceived notions and abstract dogmas; and he began by teaching us what he himself was. In criticizing books he did not compare them with rules and systems, but told us what he saw to like or dislike in them. He did not take his standard of excellence "according to an exact scale" of Aristotle, or fall out with a work that was good for anything, because "not one of the angles at the four corners was a right one." He was, in a word, the first author who was not a bookmaker, and who wrote, not to make converts of others to established creeds and prejudices, but to satisfy his own mind of the truth of things. In this respect we know not which to be most charmed with, the author or the man. There is an inexpressible frankness and sincerity, as well as power, in what he writes. There is no attempt at imposition or concealment, no juggling tricks or solemn mouthings, no labored attempts at proving himself always in the right, and everybody

else in the wrong; he says what is uppermost, lays open what floats at the top or the bottom of his mind, and deserves Pope's character of him, where he professes to —

> "——— pour out all as plain
> As downright Shippen, or as old Montaigne."

He does not converse with us like a pedagogue with his pupil, whom he wishes to make as great a blockhead as himself, but like a philosopher and friend who has passed through life with thought and observation, and is willing to enable others to pass through it with pleasure and profit. A writer of this stamp, I confess, appears to me as much superior to a common bookworm as a library of real books is superior to a mere bookcase, painted and lettered on the outside with the names of celebrated works. As he was the first to attempt this new way of writing, so the same strong natural impulse which prompted the undertaking, carried him to the end of his career. The same force and honesty of mind which urged him to throw off the shackles of custom and prejudice would enable him to complete his triumph over them. He has left little for his successors to achieve in the way of just and original speculation on human life. Nearly all the thinking of the two last centuries of that kind which the French denominate *morale observatrice* is to be found in Montaigne's "Essays": there is a germ, at least, and generally much more. He sowed the seed and cleared away the rubbish, even where others have reaped the fruit, or cultivated and decorated the soil to a greater degree of nicety and perfection. There is no one to whom the old Latin adage is more applicable than to Montaigne, *Pereant isti qui ante nos nostra dixerunt.* There has been no new impulse given to thought since his time. Among the specimens of criticisms on authors which he has left us, are those on Virgil, Ovid, and Boccaccio, in the account of books which he thinks worth reading, or (which is the same thing) which he finds he can read in his old age, and which may be reckoned among the few criticisms which are worth reading at any age.

Montaigne's "Essays" were translated into English by Charles Cotton, who was one of the wits and poets of the age of Charles II.; and Lord Halifax, one of the noble critics of that day, declared it to be "the book in the world he was the best pleased with." This mode of familiar essay-writing, free from

the trammels of the schools and the airs of professed authorship, was successfully imitated, about the same time, by Cowley and Sir William Temple in their miscellaneous essays, which are very agreeable and learned talking upon paper. Lord Shaftesbury, on the contrary, who aimed at the same easy, *degagé* mode of communicating his thoughts to the world, has quite spoiled his matter, which is sometimes valuable, by his manner, in which he carries a certain flaunting, flowery, figurative, flirting style of amicable condescension to the reader, to an excess more tantalizing than the most starched and ridiculous formality of the age of James I. There is nothing so tormenting as the affectation of ease and freedom from affectation.

The ice being thus thawed, and the barrier that kept authors at a distance from common sense and feeling broken through, the transition was not difficult from Montaigne and his imitators to our Periodical Essayists. These last applied the same unrestrained expression of their thoughts to the more immediate and passing scenes of life, to temporary and local matters; and in order to discharge the invidious office of *Censor Morum* more freely, and with less responsibility, assumed some fictitious and humorous disguise, which, however, in a degree, corresponded to their own peculiar habits and character. By thus concealing their own name and person under the title of the Tatler, Spectator, etc., they were enabled to inform us more fully of what was passing in the world, while the dramatic contrast and ironical point of view to which the whole is subjected, added a greater liveliness and piquancy to the descriptions. The philosopher and wit here commences newsmonger, makes himself master of "the perfect spy o' th' time," and from his various walks and turns through life, brings home little curious specimens of the humors, opinions, and manners of his contemporaries, as the botanist brings home different plants and weeds, or the mineralogist different shells and fossils, to illustrate their several theories, and be useful to mankind.

The first of these papers that was attempted in this country was set up by Steele in the beginning of the last century; and of all our Periodical Essayists, the Tatler (for that was the name he assumed) has always appeared to me the most accomplished and agreeable. Montaigne, whom I have proposed to consider as the father of this kind of personal authorship among the Moderns, in which the reader is admitted behind the curtain, and sits down with the writer in his gown and slippers, was a most magnanimous and undisguised egotist; but Isaac Bickerstaff, Esq., was the more disinterested gossip of the two. The French author is contented to describe the peculiarities of his own mind and person, which he does with a most copious and unsparing hand. The English journalist good-naturedly lets you into the secret both of his own affairs and those of his neighbors. A young lady, on the other side of Temple Bar, cannot be seen at her glass for half a day together, but Mr. Bickerstaff takes due notice of it; and he has the first intelligence of the symptoms of the *belle passion* appearing in any young gentleman at the west end of the town. The departures and arrivals of widows with handsome jointures, either to bury their grief in the country, or to procure a second husband in town, are regularly recorded in his pages. He is well acquainted with the celebrated beauties of the preceding age at the court of Charles II.; and the old gentleman (as he feigns himself) often grows romantic in recounting "the disastrous strokes which his youth suffered" from the glances of their bright eyes, and their unaccountable caprices. In particular he dwells with a secret satisfaction on the recollection of one of his mistresses, who left him for a richer rival, and whose constant reproach to her husband, on occasion of any quarrel between them, was "I, that might have married the famous Mr. Bickerstaff, to be treated in this manner!" The club at the Trumpet consists of a set of persons almost as well worth knowing as himself. The cavalcade of the justice of the peace, the knight of the shire, the country squire, and the young gentleman, his nephew, who came to wait on him at his chambers, in such form and ceremony, seem not to have settled the order of their precedence to this hour; and I should hope that the upholsterer and his companions, who used to sun themselves in the Green Park, and who broke their rest and fortunes to maintain the balance of power in Europe, stand as fair a chance for immortality as some modern politicians. Mr. Bickerstaff himself is a gentleman and a scholar, a humorist and a man of the world, with a great deal of nice, easy *naïveté* about him. If he walks out and is caught in a shower of rain, he makes amends for this unlucky accident by a criticism on the shower in Virgil, and concludes with a burlesque copy of verses on a city shower. He entertains us, when he dates from his own apartment, with a quotation from Plutarch, or a moral reflection; from the Grecian coffeehouse with politics, and from Will's, or the

Temple, with the poets and players, the beaux and men of wit and pleasure about town. In reading the pages of the Tatler, we seem as if suddenly carried back to the age of Queen Anne, of toupees and full-bottomed periwigs. The whole appearance of our dress and manners undergoes a delightful metamorphosis. We are surprised with the rustling of hoops, and the glittering of paste buckles. The beaux and the belles are of a quite different species from what they are at present; we distinguish the dappers, the smarts, and the pretty fellows, as they pass by Mr. Lily's shop windows in the Strand; we are introduced to Betterton and Mrs. Oldfield behind the scenes; are made familiar with the persons and performances of Mr. Penkethman and Mr. Bullock; we listen to a dispute at a tavern on the merits of the Duke of Marlborough, or Marshal Turenne; or are present at the first rehearsal of a play by Vanbrugh, or the reading of a new poem by Mr. Pope. The privilege of thus virtually transporting ourselves to past times is even greater than that of visiting distant places in reality. London a hundred years ago would be much better worth seeing than Paris at the present moment.

It may be said that all this is to be found, in the same or a greater degree, in the Spectator. For myself, I do not think so; or, at least, there is in the last work a much greater proportion of commonplace matter. I have on this account always preferred the Tatler to the Spectator. Whether it is owing to my having been earlier or better acquainted with the one than the other, my pleasure in reading these two admirable works is not at all in proportion to their comparative reputation. The Tatler contains only half the number of volumes, and, I will venture to say, at least an equal quantity of sterling wit and sense. "The first sprightly runnings" are there—it has more of the original spirit, more of the freshness and stamp of nature. The indications of character and strokes of humor are more true and frequent; the reflections that suggest themselves arise more from the occasion, and are less spun out into regular dissertations. They are more like the remarks which occur in sensible conversation, and less like a lecture. Something is left to the understanding of the reader. Steele seems to have gone into his closet chiefly to set down what he observed out of doors. Addison seems to have spent most of his time in his study, and to have spun out and wire-drawn the hints, which he borrowed from Steele, or took from nature, to the utmost. I am far from wish-

ing to depreciate Addison's talents, but I am anxious to do justice to Steele, who was, I think, upon the whole, a less artificial and more original writer. The humorous descriptions of Steele resemble loose sketches, or fragments of a comedy; those of Addison are rather comments, or ingenious paraphrases, on the genuine text. The characters of the club not only in the Tatler, but in the Spectator, were drawn by Steele. That of Sir Roger de Coverley is among the number. Addison has, however, gained himself immortal honor by his manner of filling up this last character. Who is there that can forget, or be insensible to, the inimitable, nameless graces, and varied traits of nature and of old English character, in it—to his unpretending virtues and amiable weaknesses—to his modesty, generosity, hospitality, and eccentric whims—to the respect of his neighbors, and the affection of his domestics—to his wayward, hopeless, secret passion for his fair enemy, the widow, in which there is more of real romance and true delicacy than in a thousand tales of knight-errantry—(we perceive the hectic flush of his cheek, the faltering of his tongue in speaking of her bewitching airs and "the whiteness of her hand")—to the havoc he makes among the game in his neighborhood—to his speech from the bench, to show the Spectator what is thought of him in the country—to his unwillingness to be put up as a signpost, and his having his own likeness turned into the Saracen's head—to his gentle reproof of the baggage of a gipsy that tells him "he has a widow in his line of life"—to his doubts as to the existence of witchcraft, and protection of reputed witches—to his account of the family pictures, and his choice of a chaplain—to his falling asleep at church, and his reproof of John Williams, as soon as he recovered from his nap, for talking in sermon time. The characters of Will Wimble and Will Honeycomb are not a whit behind their friend, Sir Roger, in delicacy and felicity. The delightful simplicity and good-humored officiousness in the one are set off by the graceful affectation and courtly pretension in the other. How long since I first became acquainted with these two characters in the Spectator! What old-fashioned friends they seem, and yet I am not tired of them, like so many other friends, nor they of me! How airy these abstractions of the poet's pen stream over the dawn of our acquaintance with human life! How they glance their fairest colors on the prospect before us! How pure they remain in it to the last, like the rainbow in the even-

ing cloud, which the rude hand of time can neither soil nor dissipate! What a pity that we cannot find the reality, and yet if we did, the dream would be over. I once thought I knew a Will Wimble, and a Will Honeycomb, but they turned out but indifferently: the originals in the Spectator still read word for word, the same that they always did. We have only to turn to the page, and find them where we left them! Many of the most exquisite pieces in the Tatler, it is to be observed, are Addison's, as the "Court of Honor" and the "Personification of Musical Instruments," with almost all those papers that form regular sets or series. I do not know whether the picture of the family of an old college acquaintance, in the Tatler, where the children run to let Mr. Bickerstaff in at the door, and where the one that loses the race that way turns back to tell the father that he is come; with the nice gradation of incredulity in the little boy, who is got into "Guy of Warwick," and the "Seven Champions," and who shakes his head at the improbability of "Æsop's Fables," is Steele's or Addison's, though I believe it belongs to the former. The account of the two sisters, one of whom held up her head higher than ordinary, from having on a pair of flowered garters, and that of the married lady who complained to the Tatler of the neglect of her husband, with her answers to some home questions that were put to her, are unquestionably Steele's. If the Tatler is not inferior to the Spectator as a record of manners and character, it is very superior to it in the interest of many of the stories. Several of the incidents related there by Steele have never been surpassed in the heartrending pathos of private distress. I might refer to those of the lover and his mistress, when the theatre, in which they were, caught fire; of the bridegroom, who by accident kills his bride on the day of their marriage; the story of Mr. Eustace and his wife; and the fine dream about his own mistress when a youth. What has given its superior reputation to the Spectator is the greater gravity of its pretensions, its moral dissertations and critical reasonings, by which I confess myself less edified than by other things, which are thought more lightly of. Systems and opinions change, but nature is always true. It is the extremely moral and didactic tone of the Spectator which makes us apt to think of Addison (according to Mandeville's sarcasm) as "a parson in a tiewig." Many of his moral essays are, however, exquisitely beautiful and happy. Such are the reflections on cheerfulness, those in Westminster Abbey, on the Royal Exchange, and particularly some very affecting ones on the death of a young lady in the fourth volume. These, it must be allowed, are the perfection of elegant sermonizing. His critical essays are not so good. I prefer Steele's occasional selection of beautiful poetical passages, without any affectation of analyzing their beauties, to Addison's fine-spun theories. The best criticism in the Spectator, that on the Cartoons of Raphael, of which Mr. Fuseli has availed himself with great spirit in his lectures, is by Steele. I owed this acknowledgment to a writer who has so often put me in good-humor with myself, and everything about me, when few things else could, and when the tomes of casuistry and ecclesiastical history, with which the little duodecimo volumes of the Tatler were overwhelmed and surrounded, in the only library to which I had access when a boy, had tried their tranquillizing effects upon me in vain. I had not long ago in my hands, by favor of a friend, an original copy of the quarto edition of the Tatler, with a list of the subscribers. It is curious to see some names there which we should hardly think of (that of Sir Isaac Newton is among them), and also to observe the degree of interest excited by those of the different persons, which is not determined according to the rules of the Herald's College. One literary name lasts as long as a whole race of heroes and their descendants! The Guardian, which followed the Spectator, was, as may be supposed, inferior to it.

The dramatic and conversational turn which forms the distinguishing feature and greatest charm of the Spectator and Tatler is quite lost in the Rambler, by Dr. Johnson. There is no reflected light thrown on human life from an assumed character, nor any direct one from a display of the author's own. The Tatler and Spectator are, as it were, made up of notes and memorandums of the events and incidents of the day, with finished studies after nature, and characters fresh from the life, which the writer moralizes upon, and turns to account as they come before him. The Rambler is a collection of moral essays, or scholastic theses, written on set subjects, and of which the individual characters and incidents are merely artificial illustrations, brought in to give a pretended relief to the dryness of didactic discussion. The Rambler is a splendid and imposing commonplace book of general topics, and rhetorical declamation

on the conduct and business of human life. In this sense, there is hardly a reflection that had been suggested on such subjects which is not to be found in this celebrated work, and there is, perhaps, hardly a reflection to be found in it which had not been already suggested and developed by some other author, or in the common course of conversation. The mass of intellectual wealth here heaped together is immense, but it is rather the result of gradual accumulation, the produce of the general intellect, laboring in the mine of knowledge and reflection, than dug out of the quarry, and dragged into the light by the industry and sagacity of a single mind. I am not here saying that Dr. Johnson was a man without originality, compared with the ordinary run of men's minds, but he was not a man of original thought or genius, in the sense in which Montaigne or Lord Bacon was. He opened no new vein of precious ore, nor did he light upon any single pebbles of uncommon size and unrivaled lustre. We seldom meet with anything to "give us pause"; he does not set us thinking for the first time. His reflections present themselves like reminiscences; do not disturb the ordinary march of our thoughts; arrest our attention by the stateliness of their appearance, and the costliness of their garb, but pass on and mingle with the throng of our impressions. After closing the volumes of the Rambler, there is nothing that we remember as a new truth gained to the mind, nothing indelibly stamped upon the memory; nor is there any passage that we wish to turn to as embodying any known principle or observation, with such force and beauty that justice can only be done to the idea in the author's own words. Such, for instance, are many of the passages to be found in Burke, which shine by their own light, belong to no class, have neither equal nor counterpart, and of which we say that no one but the author could have written them! There is neither the same boldness of design nor mastery of execution in Johnson. In the one, the spark of genius seems to have met with its congenial matter; the shaft is sped: the forked lightning dresses up the face of nature in ghastly smiles, and the loud thunder rolls far away from the ruin that is made. Dr. Johnson's style, on the contrary, resembles rather the rumbling of mimic thunder at one of our theatres; and the light he throws upon a subject is like the dazzling effect of phosphorus, or an *ignis fatuus* of words. There is a wide difference, however, between perfect originality and perfect commonplace: neither ideas

nor expressions are trite or vulgar because they are not quite new. They are valuable, and ought to be repeated, if they have not become quite common; and Johnson's style, both of reasoning and imagery, holds the middle rank between startling novelty and vapid commonplace. Johnson has as much originality of thinking as Addison; but then he wants his familiarity of illustration, knowledge of character, and delightful humor. What most distinguishes Dr. Johnson from other writers is the pomp and uniformity of his style. All his periods are cast in the same mold, are of the same size and shape, and consequently have little fitness to the variety of things he professes to treat of. His subjects are familiar, but the author is always upon stilts. He has neither ease nor simplicity, and his efforts at playfulness, in part, remind one of the lines in Milton: —

> "————— The elephant
> To make them sport wreath'd his proboscis lithe."

His "Letters from Correspondents," in particular, are more pompous and unwieldy than what he writes in his own person. This want of relaxation and variety of manner, has, I think, after the first effects of novelty and surprise were over, been prejudicial to the matter. It takes from the general power, not only to please, but to instruct. The monotony of style produces an apparent monotony of ideas. What is really striking and valuable is lost in the vain ostentation and circumlocution of the expression; for when we find the same pains and pomp of diction bestowed upon the most trifling as upon the most important parts of a sentence or discourse, we grow tired of distinguishing between pretension and reality, and are disposed to confound the tinsel and bombast of the phraseology with want of weight in the thoughts. Thus, from the imposing and oracular nature of the style, people are tempted at first to imagine that our author's speculations are all wisdom and profundity: till having found out their mistake in some instances, they suppose that there is nothing but commonplace in them, concealed under verbiage and pedantry; and in both they are wrong. The fault of Dr. Johnson's style is, that it reduces all things to the same artificial and unmeaning level. It destroys all shades of difference, the association between words and things. It is a perpetual paradox and innovation. He condescends to the familiar till we are ashamed of our interest in it;

he expands the little till it looks big. "If he were to write a fable of little fishes," as Goldsmith said of him, "he would make them speak like great whales." We can no more distinguish the most familiar objects in his description of them than we can a well-known face under a huge painted mask. The structure of his sentences, which was his own invention, and which has been generally imitated since his time, is a species of rhyming in prose, where one clause answers to another in measure and quantity, like the tagging of syllables at the end of a verse; the close of the period follows as mechanically as the oscillation of a pendulum, the sense is balanced with the sound; each sentence, revolving round its centre of gravity, is contained within itself like a couplet, and each paragraph forms itself into a stanza. Dr. Johnson is also a complete balance-master in the topics of morality. He never encourages hope, but he counteracts it by fear; he never elicits a truth, but he suggests some objection in answer to it. He seizes and alternately quits the clew of reason, lest it should involve him in the labyrinths of endless error: he wants confidence in himself and his fellows. He dares not trust himself with the immediate impressions of things, for fear of compromising his dignity; or follow them into their consequences, for fear of committing his prejudices. His timidity is the result, not of ignorance, but of morbid apprehension. "He turns the great circle, and is still at home." No advance is made by his writings in any sentiment, or mode of reasoning. Out of the pale of established authority and received dogmas, all is skeptical, loose, and desultory: he seems in imagination to strengthen the dominion of prejudice, as he weakens and dissipates that of reason; and round the rock of faith and power, on the edge of which he slumbers blindfold and uneasy, the waves and billows of uncertain and dangerous opinion roar and heave forevermore. His "Rasselas" is the most melancholy and debilitating moral speculation that ever was put forth. Doubtful of the faculties of his mind, as of his organs of vision, Johnson trusted only to his feelings and his fears. He cultivated a belief in witches as an outguard to the evidences of religion; and abused Milton, and patronized Lauder, in spite of his aversion to his countrymen, as a step to secure the existing establishment in Church and State. This was neither right feeling nor sound logic.

The most triumphant record of the talents and character of Johnson is to be found in Boswell's life of him. The man was superior to the author. When he threw aside his pen, which he regarded as an encumbrance, he became not only learned and thoughtful, but acute, witty, humorous, natural, honest; hearty and determined, "the king of good fellows and wale of old men." There are as many smart repartees, profound remarks, and keen invectives to be found in Boswell's "inventory of all he said," as are recorded of any celebrated man. The life and dramatic play of his conversation forms a contrast to his written works. His natural powers and undisguised opinions were called out in convivial intercourse. In public he practiced with the foils; in private, he unsheathed the sword of controversy, and it was "the Ebro's temper." The eagerness of opposition roused him from his natural sluggishness and acquired timidity; he returned blow for blow; and whether the trial were of argument or wit, none of his rivals could boast much of the encounter. Burke seems to have been the only person who had a chance with him; and it is the unpardonable sin of Boswell's work, that he has purposely omitted their combats of strength and skill. Goldsmith asked, "Does he wind into a subject like a serpent, as Burke does?" And when exhausted with sickness, he himself said, "If that fellow Burke were here now, he would kill me." It is to be observed that Johnson's colloquial style was as blunt, direct, and downright, as his style of studied composition was involved and circuitious. As when Topham, Beauclerc, and Langton knocked him up at his chambers at three in the morning, and he came to the door with the poker in his hand, but, seeing them, exclaimed, "What! is it you, my lads? then I'll have a frisk with you!" and he afterwards reproaches Langton, who was a literary milksop, for leaving them to go to an engagement "with some *un-idead* girls." What words to come from the mouth of the great moralist and lexicographer! His good deeds were as many as his good sayings. His domestic habits, his tenderness to servants, and readiness to oblige his friends; the quantity of strong tea that he drank to keep down sad thoughts; his many labors reluctantly begun, and irresolutely laid aside; his honest acknowledgment of his own, and indulgence to the weaknesses of others; his throwing himself back in the post chaise with Boswell, and saying, "Now I think I am a good-humored fellow," though nobody thought him so, and yet he was; his quitting the society of Garrick and his actresses, and his reason for it; his dining with Wilkes, and his kindness to Goldsmith; his sitting with the young

ladies on his knee at the Mitre, to give them good advice, in which situation, if not explained, he might be taken for Falstaff; and last and noblest, his carrying the unfortunate victim of disease and dissipation on his back up through Fleet Street (an act which realizes the parable of the good Samaritan) — all these, and innumerable others, endear him to the reader, and must be remembered to his lasting honor. He had faults, but they lie buried with him. He had his prejudices and his intolerant feelings, but he suffered enough in the conflict of his own mind with them; for if no man can be happy in the free exercise of his reason, no wise man can be happy without it. His were not time-serving, heartless, hypocritical prejudices; but deep, inwoven, not to be rooted out but with life and hope, which he found from old habit necessary to his own peace of mind, and thought so to the peace of mankind. I do not hate, but love him for them. They were between himself and his conscience, and should be left to that higher tribunal

"Where they in trembling hope repose,
The bosom of his father and his God."

In a word, he has left behind him few wiser or better men.

The herd of his imitators showed what he was by their disproportionate effects. The Periodical Essayists that succeeded the Rambler are, and deserve to be, little read at present. The Adventurer, by Hawkesworth, is completely trite and vapid, aping all the faults of Johnson's style, without anything to atone for them. The sentences are often absolutely unmeaning; and one-half of each might regularly be left blank. The World and Connoisseur, which followed, are a little better; and in the last of these there is one good idea, that of a man in indifferent health who judges of every one's title to respect from their possession of this blessing, and bows to a sturdy beggar with sound limbs and a florid complexion, while he turns his back upon a lord who is a valetudinarian.

Goldsmith's Citizen of the World, like all his works, bears the stamp of the author's mind. It does not "go about to cozen reputation without the stamp of merit." He is more observing, more original, more natural and picturesque than Johnson. His work is written on the model of the "Persian Letters," and contrives to give an abstracted and somewhat perplexing view of

things, by opposing foreign prepossessions to our own, and thus stripping objects of their customary disguises. Whether truth is elicited in this collision of contrary absurdities, I do not know; but I confess the process is too ambiguous and full of intricacy to be very amusing to my plain understanding. For light summer reading it is like walking in a garden full of traps and pitfalls. It necessarily gives rise to paradoxes, and there are some very bold ones in the "Essays," which would subject an author less established to no very agreeable sort of *censura literaria*. Thus the Chinese philosopher exclaims very unadvisedly: "The bonzes and priests of all religions keep up superstition and imposture; all reformations begin with the laity." Goldsmith, however, was stanch in his practical creed, and might bolt speculative extravagances with impunity. There is a striking difference in this respect between him and Addison, who, if he attacked authority, took care to have common sense on his side, and never hazarded anything offensive to the feelings of others, or on the strength of his own discretional opinion. There is another inconvenience in this assumption of an exotic character and tone of sentiment, that it produces an inconsistency between the knowledge which the individual has time to acquire and which the author is bound to communicate. Thus the Chinese has not been in England three days before he is acquainted with the characters of the three countries which compose this kingdom, and describes them to his friend at Canton by extracts from the newspapers of each metropolis. The nationality of Scotchmen is thus ridiculed: —

Edinburgh — We are positive when we say that Sanders Macregor, lately executed for horse stealing, is not a native of Scotland, but born at Carrickfergus.

Now this is very good; but how should our Chinese philosopher find it out by instinct? Beau Tibbs, a prominent character in this little work, is the best comic sketch since the time of Addison; unrivaled in his finery, his vanity, and his poverty.

I have only to mention the names of the Lounger and the Mirror, which are ranked by the author's admirers with Sterne for sentiment, and with Addison for humor. I shall not enter into that; but I know that the story of "La Roche" is not like the story of "Le Fevre," nor one hundredth part so good. Do I say this from prejudice to the author? No; for I have read his

novels. Of "The Man of the World" I cannot think so favorably as some others, nor shall I here dwell on the picturesque and romantic beauties of "Julia de Roubigne," the early favorite of the author of "Rosamond Gray"; but of the "Man of Feeling" I would speak with grateful recollections, nor is it possible to forget the sensitive, irresolute, interesting Harley, and that lone figure of Miss Walton in it, that floats in the horizon, dim and ethereal, the daydream of her lover's youthful fancy, — better, far better, than all the realities of life!

Complete. Letter V. on "English Literature."

GEORG WILHELM FRIEDRICH HEGEL

(1770–1831)

HEGEL had all the qualities necessary to make him one of the greatest philosophers since Plato. The one quality in which he was most deficient as a writer every essayist must have if he is not to lose the essay in the treatise. This is the power of self-limitation which enables him to separate his subject from the universal whole and treat it in its own completeness. This quality, Bacon, as great in another way as Hegel, had in an eminent degree. But Hegel's mind was differently constituted. He does not amplify by diffusing his ideas, but by vast generalizations supported by continuity of details which accumulate until the reader is in danger of being so overwhelmed by them that he will lose sight of the governing thought. If technically Hegel is hardly to be classed among essayists, he had a vision of truth so clear that he cannot be passed over because of a mere matter of form. The idea that the spiritual or supernatural object of human society in all its forms, and of all the forces of the visible universe, is to develop individuality and to multiply to the utmost possible extent individuals of the highest possible fitness,—this thought, which if it be not wholly Hegel's as it is here expressed, is yet his by the implication of his system, and it unifies with itself the highest truths both of religion and of science.

Hegel was born at Stuttgart, August 27th, 1770. He studied theology at Tübingen; and in 1793, when he received his certificate, he was described as "of good abilities, but of middling industry and knowledge, and especially deficient in philosophy." Most great men have been misunderstood by their teachers, but at that time Hegel may have deserved something of this faint praise. His first great intellectual awakening seems to have been largely due to his association with Schelling, to whom as a fellow-student of philosophy he wrote in 1795: "Let reason and freedom remain our watchword and our point of union the Church invisible." With this watchword during the excitement of the French Revolution and the Napoleonic wars, Hegel devoted himself to the search for truth. His achievements are too great for cursory review, but without attempting to discuss the metaphysical part of his work as it concerns the operations of mind in and upon itself, we may accept without risk the judgment of those

VI—135

who declare that at his death, November 14th, 1831, he left behind him at least four of the greatest intellectual creations of the nineteenth century,—"Philosophy of History," "Æsthetics," "Philosophy of Religion," and "History of Philosophy."

HISTORY AS THE MANIFESTATION OF SPIRIT

THE true sphere of the history of the world is spiritual. The world comprises in itself both the physical and the psychical nature; physical nature plays a large part in the history of the world. But spirit, with the course of its development, is the substance of it. Nature is not here to be considered, so far as it is in itself, as it were, a system of reason, exhibited in a special and peculiar element, but only as it stands related to spirit. Spirit, however, in the theatre of the world's history, exists in its most concrete form, comes to its most real manifestations. In order to understand its connections with history, we must make some preliminary and abstract statements respecting the nature of spirit.

The nature of spirit may be easily understood by comparison with that which is the entire opposite of it,—that is, matter. The substance of matter is weight, which is only this, that it is heavy; the substance, the essence of spirit, on the contrary, is freedom. Every one finds it immediately credible that spirit, among other attributes, also possesses freedom; but philosophy teaches us that all the attributes of spirit exist only through freedom, that they all are only the means of which freedom makes use, that this alone is what they all seek for and produce. The speculative philosophy recognizes this fact, that freedom is the only truth of spirit. Matter shows that it is weight, by its tendency to one centre of gravity; it is essentially made up of parts, which parts exist separate from, and external to, each other; and it is ever seeking their unity, and thus seeks to abolish itself,—seeks the opposite of what it really is. If it attained this unity, it were no longer matter, it were destroyed; it strives to realize an idea, for in unity it is merely ideal. Spirit, on the other hand, is just this, that it has its centre in itself; its unity is not outside of itself, but it has found it; it is in itself and with itself. Matter has its substance out of itself; spirit consists in being with itself. This is freedom; for when I am dependent, I refer myself to something else which is not

myself; I cannot be without something external; but I am free when I am with myself. This is self-consciousness, the consciousness of oneself. Two things are here to be distinguished: first, that I know or am conscious; second, what I know or am conscious of. In self-consciousness, the two come together, for spirit knows itself; it judges of its own nature.

In this sense, we may say that the history of the world is the exhibition of the process by which spirit comes to the consciousness of that which it really is,—of the significancy of its own nature. And as the seed contains in itself the whole nature of the tree, even to the taste and form of the fruit, so do the first traces of spirit virtually contain the whole of history.

The Oriental world did not know that spirit, man as such, is of himself free. Since they knew it not, they were not free; they only knew that one is free: but just on this account their freedom was only arbitrariness, wildness, obtuse passion; or, if not so, yet a mildness and tameness of the passions, which is nothing but an accident or caprice of nature. This one is, therefore, only a despot, not a free man. Among the Greeks, the consciousness of freedom first arose, and therefore they were free; but they, as the Romans also, only knew that some are free, not that man, as such, is free. Even Plato and Aristotle did not know this. Hence, the Greeks not only held slaves, and had their life and the continuance of their fair freedom bound thereby, but their freedom itself was partly only an accidental and perishable flower, and partly a hard servitude of the human and humane. The German nations, under the influence of Christianity, first came to the consciousness that man, as man, is free,—that freedom of soul constitutes his own proper nature. This consciousness came first into existence in religion,—in the deepest religion of the spirit. But to fashion the world after this principle was a further problem; the solution and application of which demanded a severe and long labor. With the reception of the Christian religion, for example, slavery did not at once come to an end, still less did freedom at once become predominant in the States; their governments and constitutions were not immediately organized in a rational manner, or even based upon the principle of freedom. This application of the principle to the world at large, this thorough penetration and reformation of the condition of the world by means of it, is the long process which the history of the nations brings before our eyes. I have already called attention to the difference between a

principle, as such, and its application,—that is, the introduction of it into the actual operations of spirit and life, and carrying it through all of them; this is a fundamental position in our science, and it is essential that we hold it fast in our thoughts. Here we have brought it out distinctly, in respect to the Christian principle of self-consciousness of freedom; but it is no less essential in respect to the principle of freedom in general. The history of the world is the progress in the consciousness of freedom,—a progress which we shall have to recognize in its necessity.

What we have now said, in general terms, upon the difference in the knowledge of freedom which we find in different ages of the world, gives us, also, the true division of the history of the world, and the mode in which we shall proceed to its discussion. The scheme is this: the Oriental world only knew that one is free; the Greek and Roman world knew that some are free; but we know that all men, in their true nature, are free,—that man, as man, is free.

From "Philosophy of History."

THE RELATION OF INDIVIDUALS TO THE WORLD'S HISTORY

IN THE history of the world something else is generally brought out by means of the actions of individual men than they themselves aim at or attain, than they directly know of or will; they achieve their own ends, but something further is brought to pass in connection with their acts, which also lies therein, but which did not lie in their consciousness and purposes. As an analogous example we cite the case of a man, who out of revenge, which may have been justly excited, that is, by an unjust injury, goes to work and sets fire to the house of another man. Even in doing this, there is a connection made between the direct act and other, although themselves merely external circumstances, which do not belong to this act, taken wholly and directly by itself. This act, as such, is the holding perhaps of a small flame to a small spot of a wooden beam. What is not yet accomplished by this act goes on and is done of itself; the part of the beam that was set on fire is connected with other parts of the same beam, this too with the rafters and joists of the whole house, this house with other houses, and a widespread conflagration ensues, which destroys the property and goods of many other men besides the one against whom the revenge was directed, and even costs many men their lives. All this lay not in the general act, nor in the intention of him who began it all. But, still further, this action has another general character and destination: in the purpose of the actor it was only revenge against an individual by means of the destruction of his property; but it is also a crime, and this involves, further, a punishment. This may not have been included in the consciousness, and still less in the will of the doer, but still such is his act in itself, the general character, the very substance of it, that which is achieved by it. In this example all that we would hold fast is, that in the immediate action there can lie something more than what was in the will and consciousness of the actor. The substance of the action, and thereby the act itself, here turns round against the doer; it becomes a return blow against him, which ruins him. We have not here to lay any emphasis upon the action considered as a crime; it is intended only as an analogous example, to show that in the definite action there may be something more than the end directly willed.

One other case may be adduced which will come up later in its own place, and which, being itself historical, contains, in the special form which is essential to our purpose, the union of the general with the particular, of an end necessary in itself with an aim which might seem accidental. It is that of Cæsar, in danger of losing the position he had obtained, if not of superiority over, yet of equality with, the other man who stood at the head of the Roman state, and of submitting to those who were upon the point of becoming his enemies. These enemies, who at the same time had their own personal ends in view, had on their side the formal constitution of the state and the power of seeming legality. Cæsar fought to maintain his own position, honor, and safety, and the victory over his opponents was at the same time the conquest of the whole kingdom; and thus he became, leaving only the forms of the constitution of the state, the sole possessor of power. The carrying out of his own at first negative purpose got for him the supremacy in Rome; but this was also in its true nature a necessary element in the history of Rome and of the world, so that it was not his own private gain merely, but an instinct which consummated that which, considered by itself, lay in the times themselves. Such are the great men of history

—those whose private purposes contain the substance of that which is the will of the spirit of the world. This substance constitutes their real power; it is contained in the general and unconscious instinct of men; they are inwardly impelled thereto, and have no ground on which they can stand in opposing the man who has undertaken the execution of such a purpose in his own interest. The people assemble around his banner; he shows to them, and carries out that which is their own immanent destiny.

Should we, further, cast a look at the fate of these world-historical individuals, we see that they have had the fortune to be the leaders to a consummation which marks a stage in the progress of the general mind. That reason makes use of these instruments we might call its craft; for it lets them carry out their own aims with all the rage of passion, and not only keeps itself unharmed, but makes itself dominant. The particular is for the most part too feeble against the universal; the individuals are sacrificed. Thus the world's history presents itself as the conflict of individuals, and in the field of their special interests all goes on very naturally. In the animal world the preservation of life is the aim and instinct of each individual, and yet reason or general laws prevail, and the individuals fall; thus is it also in the spiritual world. Passions destroy each other; reason alone watches, pursues its end, and makes itself authoritative.

LAW AND LIBERTY

LAW, considered as freedom determining itself, is the objectivity of spirit: hence that alone is true volition, the will in the truth of it, which obeys law, for it then obeys only itself; it is then with itself and free; this is the freedom in the State for which the citizen is active, and which fills his soul. In that the state, the fatherland, constitutes a community of existence,—in that the subjective will of man becomes subject to the laws, the opposition between freedom and necessity vanishes. The rational, that which we have recognized as law, is necessary; and we are free when we follow what is rational; the objective and subjective will are thus reconciled. The ethics of the state are not to be regarded as the same thing with mere morality, are not the

mere result of reflection, are not dependent upon private convictions alone; this is the system of morals familiar to the modern world, while the true and ancient system was based on this, that each man stood to his duty. A citizen of Athens did as it were by instinct what belonged to him to do; but if I reflect upon the object of my actions, I must then have the consciousness that my own will is first to come in as an essential element. But the true ethics consists in duty, in conformity with right, with law which has a real, substantial existence; it has been justly called the second nature, for the first nature of man is his primitive, animal existence.

From «History of Philosophy.»

RELIGION, ART, AND PHILOSOPHY

ALL spiritual action has for its aim and result the production of the consciousness of the union of the objective and the subjective; in this is freedom. This union appears to be produced by the thinking subject, and to go out from it. Religion stands at the head of the forms of this union. Here the existing spirit, the spirit belonging to this world, becomes conscious of the Absolute Spirit; and in this consciousness of a being existing in and for itself, the will of man renounces its particular for private interests: in devotion, he puts this aside, for here he can have nothing to do with what is merely personal to himself. If he is truly penetrated with devotion, he knows that his particular interests are subordinate. This concentration of soul shows itself as feeling, but it also passes over into reflection; the *cultus*, meaning by this all forms of outward worship, is a manifestation of such reflection; the only destination and significancy of these externals is to produce that internal union,—to lead the spirit thereto. By sacrifices, man expresses his willingness to give up his own possessions, his own will, his own particular feelings. Thus Religion is the first form of the union of the objective and subjective. The second shape it takes is Art: this comes more directly into the world of sense than religion; in its worthiest bearing its object is to exhibit, not, indeed, God as spirit, but the different visible representations which the different religions give of God; and, then, what is divine and spir-

itual in general. Art is intended to make what is divine more clear; it presents it to the imagination and contemplation in visible shapes. Truth, finally, appears not only in the form of feeling and of mental images of things, as in religion; not only in visible shapes, as in art; but it is also elaborated by the thinking spirit. Thus we attain the third mode of the union of the objective and subjective, and that is philosophy. This is the highest, freest, and purest shape which it assumes.

From «Philosophy of History.»

upon the bank, and piously listened there when Monsieur Le Grand told of the warlike feats of the great Emperor, beating meanwhile the marches which were drummed during the deeds, so that I saw and heard all to the life. I saw the passage over the Simplon—the Emperor in advance and his brave grenadiers climbing on behind him, while the scream of frightened birds of prey sounded around, and avalanches thundered in the distance; I saw the Emperor with flag in hand on the bridge of Lodi; I saw the Emperor in his gray cloak at Marengo; I saw the Emperor mounted in the battle of the Pyramids—naught around save powder, smoke, and Mamelukes; I saw the Emperor in the battle of Austerlitz—ha! how the bullets whistled over the smooth, icy road; I saw, I heard the battle of Jena—*dum, dum, dum;* I saw, I heard the battles of Eylau, of Wagram—no, I could hardly stand it! Monsieur Le Grand drummed so that I nearly burst my own sheepskin.

But what were my feelings when I first saw with highly blest (and with my own) eyes him, Hosannah! the Emperor!

It was exactly in the avenue of the Court Garden at Düsseldorf. As I pressed through the gaping crowd, thinking of the doughty deeds and battles which Monsieur Le Grand had drummed to me, my heart beat the "general march"—yet at the same time I thought of the police regulation that no one should dare, under penalty of five dollars fine, ride through the avenue. And the Emperor with his cortége rode directly down the avenue. The trembling trees bowed towards him as he advanced, the sun rays quivered, frightened, yet curiously through the green leaves, and in the blue heaven above there swam visibly a golden star. The Emperor wore his invisible green uniform and the little world-renowned hat. He rode a white palfrey which stepped with such calm pride, so confidently, so nobly—had I then been Crown Prince of Prussia I would have envied him that horse. The Emperor sat carelessly, almost lazily, holding with one hand his rein, and with the other good-naturedly patting the neck of the horse. It was a sunny marble hand, a mighty hand,—one of the pair which bound fast the many-headed monster of Anarchy, and reduced to order the war of races,—and it good-naturedly patted the neck of the horse. Even the face had that hue which we find in the marble Greek and Roman busts, the traits were as nobly proportioned as in the antiques, and on that countenance was plainly written, "Thou shalt have no gods before me!" A smile, which

warmed and tranquillized every heart, flitted over the lips—and yet all knew that those lips needed but to whistle—*et la Prusse n'existait plus;* those lips needed but to whistle—and the entire clergy would have stopped their ringing and singing; those lips needed but to whistle—and the entire holy Roman realm would have danced. It was an eye, clear as heaven, it could read the hearts of men, it saw at a glance all things at once, and as they were in this world, while we ordinary mortals see them only one by one and by their shaded hues. The brow was not so clear, the phantoms of future battles were nestling there, and there was a quiver which swept over the brow, and those were the creative thoughts, the great seven-mile-boots thoughts, wherewith the spirit of the Emperor strode invisibly over the world—and I believe that every one of those thoughts would have given to a German author full material wherewith to write, all the days of his life.

The Emperor is dead. On a waste island in the Indian Sea lies his lonely grave, and he for whom the world was too narrow lies silently under a little hillock, where five weeping willows hang their green heads, and a gentle little brook, murmuring sorrowfully, ripples by. There is no inscription on his tomb; but Clio, with unerring pen, has written thereon invisible words, which will resound, like spirit tones, through thousands of years.

Britannia! the sea is thine. But the sea hath not water enough to wash away the shame with which the death of that Mighty One hath covered thee. Not thy windy Sir Hudson—no, thou thyself wert the Sicilian bravo with whom perjured kings bargained, that they might revenge on the man of the people that which the people had once inflicted on one of themselves. And he was thy guest, and had seated himself by thy hearth.

Until the latest times the boys of France will sing and tell of the terrible hospitality of the Bellerophon; and when those songs of mockery and tears resound across the strait, there will be a blush on the cheeks of every honorable Briton. But a day will come when this song will ring thither, and there will be no Britannia in existence—when the people of pride will be humbled to the earth, when Westminster's monuments will be broken, and when the royal dust which they inclosed will be forgotten. And St. Helena is the Holy Grave, whither the races of the East and of the West will make their pilgrimage in ships, with pennons of many a hue, and their hearts will grow strong with great memories of the

deeds of the worldly savior, who suffered and died under Sir Hudson Lowe, as it is written in the evangelists, Las Casas, O'Meara, and Antommarchi.

Strange! A terrible destiny has already overtaken the three greatest enemies of the Emperor. Londonderry has cut his throat, Louis XVIII. has rotted away on his throne, and Professor Saalfeld is still, as before, professor in Göttingen.

From "Pictures of Travel."

HERMAN LUDWIG FERDINAND VON HELMHOLTZ

(1821-1894)

THOUGH chiefly celebrated for his discoveries in optics and acoustics, and for his invention of the ophthalmoscope, Von Helmholtz is much esteemed for his essays on scientific and educational topics. His lectures to his classes abound in eloquent passages, but he made beauty of style a minor consideration and the definition of principle his object. He was born August 31st, 1821, at Potsdam, where in 1843 he began his professional life as an army physician. From 1849 to 1855, he was professor of Physiology at Königsberg. He taught Physiology at Heidelberg from 1858 to 1871, and held the chair of Physics at Berlin during the latter part of his life, dying at Berlin, September 8th, 1894. Among his works are "The Conservation of Energy," "The Doctrine of Tone Sensation," and "The Manual of Physiological Optics."

UNIVERSITIES, ENGLISH, FRENCH, AND GERMAN

WHILE the English universities give but little for the endowment of the positions of approved scientific teachers, and do not logically apply even that little for this object, they have another arrangement which is apparently of great promise for scientific study, but which has hitherto not effected much; that is, the institution of Fellowships. Those who have passed the best examinations are elected as Fellows of their college, where they have a home, and along with this, a respectable income, so that they can devote the whole of their leisure to scientific pursuits. Both Oxford and Cambridge have each more than five hundred such fellowships. The Fellows may, but need not act as tutors for the students. They need not even live in the university town, but may spend their stipends where they like, and in many cases may retain the Fellowship for an indefinite period. With some exceptions, they only lose it in case they marry, or are elected to certain offices. They are the real successors of the old corporation of students, by and for which the university was founded and endowed. But however beautiful this plan may seem, and notwithstanding the enormous sums devoted to it, in the opinion of all unprejudiced Englishmen it does but little for science; manifestly because most of these young men, although they are the pick of the students, and in the most favorable conditions possible for scientific work, have in their student career not come sufficiently in contact with the living spirit of inquiry, to work on afterward on their own account, and with their own enthusiasm.

In certain respects the English universities do a great deal. They bring up their students as cultivated men, who are expected not to break through the restrictions of their political and ecclesiastical party, and, in fact, do not thus break through. In two respects we might well endeavor to imitate them. In the first place, together with a lively feeling for the beauty and youthful freshness of antiquity, they develop in a high degree a sense for delicacy and precision in writing which shows itself in the way in which they handle their mother tongue. I fear that one of the weakest sides in the instruction of German youth is in this direction. In the second place, the English universities, like their schools, take greater care of the bodily health of their students. They live and work in airy, spacious buildings, surrounded by lawns and groves of trees; they find much of their pleasure in games which excite a passionate rivalry in the development of bodily energy and skill, and which, in this respect, are far more efficacious than our gymnastic and fencing exercises. It must not be forgotten that the more young men are cut off from fresh air and from the opportunity of vigorous exercise, the more induced will they be to seek an apparent refreshment in the misuse of tobacco and of intoxicating drinks. It must also be admitted that the English universities accustom their students to energetic and accurate work, and keep them up to the habits of educated society. The moral effect of the more rigorous control is said to be rather illusory.

The Scotch universities and some smaller English foundations of more recent origin,— University College and King's College in London, and Owens College in Manchester,— are constituted more on the German and Dutch model.

The development of French universities has been quite different, and indeed almost in the opposite direction. In accordance with the tendency of the French to throw overboard

everything of historic development to suit some rationalistic theory, their faculties have logically become purely institutes for instruction — special schools, with definite regulations for the course of instruction, developed and quite distinct from those institutions which are to further the progress of science, such as the Collège de France, the Jardin des Plantes, and the École des Études Supérieures. The faculties are entirely separated from one another, even when they are in the same town. The course of study is definitely prescribed, and is controlled by frequent examinations. French teaching is confined to that which is clearly established, and transmits this in a well-arranged, well-worked-out manner, which is easily intelligible, and does not excite doubt nor the necessity for deeper inquiry. The teachers need only possess good receptive talents. Thus in France it is looked upon as a false step when a young man of promising talent takes a professorship in a faculty in the provinces. The method of instruction in France is well adapted to give pupils, of even moderate capacity, sufficient knowledge for the routine of their calling. They have no choice between different teachers, and they swear in verba magistri; this gives a happy self-satisfaction and freedom from doubts. If the teacher has been well chosen, this is sufficient in ordinary cases, in which the pupil does what he has seen his teacher do. It is only unusual cases that test how much actual insight and judgment the pupil has acquired. The French people are, moreover, gifted, vivacious, and ambitious, and this corrects many defects in their system of teaching.

A special feature in the organization of French universities consists in the fact that the position of the teacher is quite independent of the favor of his hearers; the pupils who belong to his faculty are generally compelled to attend his lectures, and the far from inconsiderable fees which they pay flow into the chest of the minister of education; the regular salaries of the university professors are defrayed from this source; the state gives but an insignificant contribution toward the maintenance of the university. When, therefore, the teacher has no real pleasure in teaching, or is not ambitious of having a number of pupils, he very soon becomes indifferent to the success of his teaching, and is inclined to take things easily.

Outside the lecture rooms, the French students live without control, and associate with young men of other callings, without any special esprit de corps or common feeling. The development

of the German universities differs characteristically from these two extremes. Too poor in their own possessions not to be compelled, with increasing demands for the means of instruction, eagerly to accept the help of the state, and too weak to resist encroachments upon their ancient rights in times in which modern states attempt to consolidate themselves, the German universities have had to submit themselves to the controlling influence of the state. Owing to this latter circumstance the decision in all important university matters has in principle been transferred to the state, and in times of religious or political excitement this supreme power has occasionally been unscrupulously exerted. But in most cases the states which were working out their own independence were favorably disposed toward the universities; they required intelligent officials, and the fame of their country's university conferred a certain lustre upon the government. The ruling officials were, moreover, for the most part, students of the university; they remained attached to it. It is very remarkable how among wars and political changes in the states fighting with the decaying empire for the consolidation of their young sovereignties, while almost all other privileged orders were destroyed, the universities of Germany saved a far greater nucleus of their internal freedom and of the most valuable side of this freedom, than in conscientious, conservative England, and than in France with its wild chase after freedom.

We have retained the old conception of students, as that of young men responsible to themselves, striving after science of their own free will, and to whom it is left to arrange their own plan of studies as they think best. If attendance on particular lectures was enjoined for certain callings,— what are called "compulsory lectures,"— these regulations were not made by the university, but by the state, which was afterward to admit candidates to these callings. At the same time the students had, and still have, perfect freedom to migrate from one German university to another, from Dorpat to Zurich, from Vienna to Gratz; and in each university they had free choice among the teachers of the same subject, without reference to their position as ordinary or extraordinary professors, or as private docents. The students are, in fact, free to acquire any part of their instruction from books; it is highly desirable that the works of great men of past times should form an essential part of study.

Outside the university there is no control over the proceedings of the students, so long as they do not come in collision with the guardians of public order. Beyond these cases the only control to which they are subject is that of their colleagues, which prevents them from doing anything which is repugnant to the feeling of honor of their own body. The universities of the Middle Ages formed definite close corporations, with their own jurisdiction, which extended to the right over life and death of their own members. As they lived for the most part on foreign soil, it was necessary to have their own jurisdiction, partly to protect the members from the caprices of foreign judges, partly to keep up that degree of respect and order, within the society, which was necessary to secure the continuation of the rights of hospitality on a foreign soil; and partly, again, to settle disputes among the members. In modern times the remains of this academic jurisdiction have by degrees been completely transferred to the ordinary courts, or will be so transferred; but it is still necessary to maintain certain restrictions on a union of strong and spirited young men, which guarantee the peace of their fellow-students and that of the citizens. In cases of collision this is the object of the disciplinary power of the university authorities. This object, however, must be mainly attained by the sense of honor of the students; and it must be considered fortunate that German students have retained a vivid sense of corporate union, and of what is intimately connected therewith, a requirement of honorable behavior in the individual. I am by no means prepared to defend every individual reputation in the Codex of students' honor; there are many Middle-Age remains among them which were better swept away,— but that can only be done by the students themselves.

For most foreigners the uncontrolled freedom of German students is a subject of astonishment; the more so as it is usually some obvious excrescences of this freedom which first meet their eyes; they are unable to understand how young men can be so left to themselves without the greatest detriment. The German looks back to his student life as to his golden age; our literature and our poetry are full of expressions of this feeling. Nothing of this kind is but even faintly suggested in the literature of other European peoples. The German student alone has this perfect joy in the time, in which, in the first delight in youthful responsibility, and freed more immediately from having to work for extraneous interests, he can devote himself to the task of striving after the best and noblest which the human race has hitherto been able to attain in knowledge and in speculation, closely joined in friendly rivalry with a large body of associates of similar aspirations, and in daily mental intercourse with teachers from whom he learns something of the workings of the thoughts of independent minds.

When I think of my own student life, and of the impression which a man like Johannes Müller, the physiologist, made upon us, I must place a very high value upon this latter point. Any one who has once come in contact with one or more men of the first rank must have had his whole mental standard altered for the rest of his life. Such intercourse is, moreover, the most interesting that life can offer.

From an address at the Frederick William
University of Berlin 1877.

SIR ARTHUR HELPS
(1813–1875)

SIR ARTHUR HELPS was born in Surrey, England, July 10th, 1813. After occupying various positions in the English Civil Service, he became clerk of the privy council, a position in which he won the friendship of Queen Victoria and found leisure to write lives of Las Casas, Columbus, Cortez, and Pizarro, as well as several romances and his later volumes of essays. The essays to which he owes his celebrity, however, appeared in 1847 and 1851, as "Friends in Council,"—a series of discussions among "Milverton," "Ellesmere," and "Dunsford," three friends who read essays to each other and comment upon them. Their dialogue has been universally rejected in extracting from this book, but such essays as "The Art of Living with Others" will continue to be printed and reprinted as long as men are human enough to need the help of those who know their weakness because of sharing it. Helps died at London, March 7th, 1875.

ON THE ART OF LIVING WITH OTHERS

THE "Iliad" for war; the "Odyssey" for wandering; but where is the great domestic epic? Yet it is but commonplace to say that passions may rage round a tea table, which would not have misbecome men dashing at one another in war chariots; and evolutions of patience and temper are performed at the fireside, worthy to be compared with the Retreat of the Ten Thousand. Men have worshiped some fantastic being for living alone in a wilderness; but social martyrdoms place no saints upon the calendar.

We may blind ourselves to it if we like, but the hatreds and disgusts that there are behind friendship, relationship, service, and, indeed, proximity of all kinds, is one of the darkest spots upon earth. The various relations of life, which bring people together, cannot, as we know, be perfectly fulfilled except in a state where there will, perhaps, be no occasion for any of them. It is no harm, however, to endeavor to see whether there are

any methods which may make these relations in the least degree more harmonious now.

In the first place, if people are to live happily together, they must not fancy, because they are thrown together now, that all their lives have been exactly similar up to the present time, that they started exactly alike, and that they are to be for the future of the same mind. A thorough conviction of the difference of men is the great thing to be assured of in social knowledge; it is to life what Newton's law is to astronomy. Sometimes men have a knowledge of it with regard to the world in general; they do not expect the outer world to agree with them in all points, but are vexed at not being able to drive their own tastes and opinions into those they live with. Diversities distress them. They will not see that there are many forms of virtue and wisdom. Yet we might as well say, "Why all these stars; why this difference; why not all one star?"

Many of the rules for people living together in peace follow from the above. For instance, not to interfere unreasonably with others, not to ridicule their tastes, not to question and requestion their resolves, and not to indulge in perpetual comment on their proceedings, and to delight in their having other pursuits than ours, are all based upon a thorough perception of the simple fact that they are not we.

Another rule for living happily with others is to avoid having stock subjects of disputation. It mostly happens, when people live much together, that they come to have certain set topics, around which, from frequent dispute, there is such a growth of angry words, mortified vanity, and the like, that the original subject of difference becomes a standing subject for quarrel; and there is a tendency in all minor disputes to drift down to it.

Again, if people wish to live well together, they must not hold too much to logic, and suppose that everything is to be settled by sufficient reason. Dr. Johnson saw this clearly with regard to married people, when he said, "Wretched would be the pair above all names of wretchedness, who should be doomed to adjust by reason every morning all the minute detail of a domestic day." But the application should be much more general than he made it. There is no time for such reasonings, and nothing that is worth them. And when we recollect how two lawyers, or two politicians, can go on contending, and that there is no end of one-sided reasoning on any subject, we shall not be sure that such contention

is the best mode for arriving at truth. But certainly it is not the way to arrive at good temper.

If you would be loved as a companion avoid unnecessary criticism upon those with whom you live. The number of people who have taken out judges' patents for themselves is very large in any society. Now it would be hard for a man to live with another who was always criticizing his actions, even if it were kindly and just criticism. It would be like living between the glasses of a microscope. But these self-elected judges, like their prototypes, are very apt to have the persons they judge brought before them in the guise of culprits.

One of the most provoking forms of the criticism above alluded to is that which may be called criticism over the shoulder. "Had I been consulted," "Had you listened to me," "But you always will," and such short scraps of sentences may remind many of us of dissertations which we have suffered and inflicted, and of which we cannot call to mind any soothing effect.

Another rule is, not to let familiarity swallow up all courtesy. Many of us have a habit of saying to those with whom we live such things as we say about strangers behind their backs. There is no place, however, where real politeness is of more value than where we mostly think it would be superfluous. You may say more truth, or rather speak out more plainly, to your associates, but not less courteously than you do to strangers.

Again, we must not expect more from the society of our friends and companions than it can give, and especially must not expect contrary things. It is something arrogant to talk of traveling over other minds (mind being, for what we know, infinite); but still we become familiar with the upper views, tastes, and tempers of our associates. And it is hardly in man to estimate justly what is familiar to him. In traveling along at night, as Hazlitt says, we catch a glimpse into cheerful-looking rooms with light blazing in them, and we conclude involuntarily how happy the inmates must be. Yet there is heaven and hell in those rooms—the same heaven and hell that we have known in others.

There are two great classes of promoters of social happiness—cheerful people and people who have some reticence. The latter are more secure benefits to society even than the former. They are nonconductors of all the heats and animosities around them. To have peace in a house, or a family, or any social circle, the members of it must beware of passing on hasty and uncharitable speeches, which, the whole of the context seldom being told, is often not conveying, but creating mischief. They must be very good people to avoid doing this; for let human nature say what it will, it likes sometimes to look on at a quarrel, and that not altogether from ill-nature, but from a love of excitement, for the same reason that Charles II. liked to attend the debates in the Lords, because they were "as good as a play."

We come now to the consideration of temper, which might have been expected to be treated first. But to cut off the means and causes of bad temper is, perhaps, of as much importance as any direct dealing with the temper itself. Besides, it is probable that in small social circles there is more suffering from unkindness than ill-temper. Anger is a thing that those who live under us suffer more from than those who live with us. But all the forms of ill-humor and sour-sensitiveness, which especially belong to equal intimacy (though, indeed, they are common to all), are best to be met by impassiveness. When two sensitive persons are shut up together, they go on vexing each other with a reproductive irritability. But sensitive and hard people get on well together. The supply of temper is not altogether out of the usual laws of supply and demand.

Intimate friends and relations should be careful when they go out into the world together, or admit others to their own circle, that they do not make a bad use of the knowledge which they have gained of each other by their intimacy. Nothing is more common than this, and did it not mostly proceed from mere carelessness, it would be superlatively ungenerous. You seldom need wait for the written life of a man to hear about his weaknesses, or what are supposed to be such, if you know his intimate friends, or meet him in company with them.

Lastly, in conciliating those we live with, it is most surely done, not by consulting their interests, nor by giving way to their opinions, so much as by not offending their tastes. The most refined part of us lies in this region of taste, which is perhaps a result of our whole being rather than a part of our nature, and, at any rate, is the region of our most subtle sympathies and antipathies.

It may be said that if the great principles of Christianity were attended to, all such rules, suggestions, and observations as the above would be needless. True enough! Great principles are at the bottom of all things; but to apply them to daily life, many little rules, precautions, and insights are needed. Such things hold a middle place between real life and principles, as form does between matter and spirit, molding the one and expressing the other.

Complete. From "Friends in Council."

GREATNESS

You cannot substitute any epithet for great, when you are talking of great men. Greatness is not general dexterity carried to any extent, nor proficiency in any one subject of human endeavor. There are great astronomers, great scholars, great painters, even great poets who are very far from great men. Greatness can do without success and with it. William is greater in his retreats than Marlborough in his victories. On the other hand, the uniformity of Cæsar's success does not dull his greatness. Greatness is not in the circumstances, but in the man.

What does this greatness then consist in? Not in a nice balance of qualities, purposes, and powers. That will make a man happy, a successful man, a man always in his right depth. Nor does it consist in absence of errors. We need only glance back at any list that can be made of great men, to be convinced of that. Neither does greatness consist in energy, though often accompanied by it. Indeed, it is rather the breadth of the waters than the force of the current that we look to, to fulfill our idea of greatness. There is no doubt that energy acting upon a nature endowed with the qualities that we sum up in the word Cleverness, and directed to a few clear purposes, produces a great effect, and may sometimes be mistaken for greatness. If a man is mainly bent upon his own advancement, it cuts many a difficult knot of policy for him, and gives a force and distinctness to his mode of going on which looks grand. The same happens if he has one pre-eminent idea of any kind, even though it should be a narrow one. Indeed, success in life is mostly gained by unity of purpose; whereas greatness often fails by reason of its having manifold purposes, but it does not cease to be greatness on that account.

If greatness can be shut up in qualities, it will be found to consist in courage and in openness of mind and soul. These qualities may not seem at first to be so potent. But see what growth

there is in them. The education of a man of open mind is never ended. Then, with openness of soul, a man sees some way into all other souls that come near him, feels with them, has their experience, is in himself a people. Sympathy is the universal solvent. Nothing is understood without it. The capacity of a man, at least for understanding, may almost be said to vary according to his powers of sympathy. Again, what is there that can counteract selfishness like sympathy? Selfishness may be hedged in by minute watchfulness and self-denial, but it is counteracted by the nature being encouraged to grow out and fix its tendrils upon foreign objects.

The immense defect that want of sympathy is may be strikingly seen in the failure of the many attempts that have been made in all ages to construct the Christian character, omitting sympathy. It has produced numbers of people walking up and down one narrow plank of self-restraint, pondering over their own merits and demerits, keeping out, not the world exactly, but their fellow-creatures from their hearts, and caring only to drive their neighbors before them on this plank of theirs, or to push them headlong. Thus, with many virtues, and much hard work at the formation of character, we have had splendid bigots or censorious small people.

But sympathy is warmth and light, too. It is, as it were, the moral atmosphere connecting all animated natures. Putting aside, for a moment, the large differences that opinions, language, and education make between men, look at the innate diversity of character. Natural philosophers were amazed when they thought they had found a new-created species. But what is each man but a creature such as the world has not before seen? Then think how they pour forth in multitudinous masses, from princes delicately nurtured to little boys on scrubby commons, or in dark cellars. How are these people to be understood, to be taught to understand each other, but by those who have the deepest sympathies with all? There cannot be a great man without large sympathy. There may be men who play loud-sounding parts in life without it, as on the stage, where kings and great people sometimes enter who are only characters of secondary import — deputy great men. But the interest and the instruction lie with those who have to feel and suffer most.

Add courage to this openness we have been considering, and you have a man who can own himself in the wrong, can forgive, can trust, can adventure, can, in short, use all the means that insight and sympathy endow him with.

I see no other essential characteristics in the greatness of nations than there are in the greatness of individuals. Extraneous circumstances largely influence nations as individuals, and make a larger part of the show of the former than of the latter; as we are wont to consider no nation great that is not great in extent or resources, as well as in character. But of two nations, equal in other respects, the superiority must belong to the one which excels in courage and openness of mind and soul.

Again, in estimating the relative merits of different periods of the world, we must employ the same tests of greatness that we use to individuals. To compare, for instance, the present and the past. What astounds us most in the past is the wonderful intolerance and cruelty: a cruelty constantly turning upon the inventors; an intolerance provoking ruin to the thing it would foster. The most admirable precepts are thrown from time to time upon this caldron of human affairs, and oftentimes they only seem to make it blaze the higher. We find men devoting the best part of their intellects to the invariable annoyance and persecution of their fellows. You might think that the earth brought forth with more abundant fruitfulness in the past than now, seeing that men found so much time for cruelty, but that you read of famines and privations which these latter days cannot equal. The recorded violent deaths amount to millions. And this is but a small part of the matter. Consider the modes of justice; the use of torture, for instance. What must have been the blinded state of the wise persons (wise for their day) who used torture? Did they ever think themselves, "What should we not say if we were subjected to this?" Many times they must really have desired to get at the truth; and such was their mode of doing it. Now, at the risk of being thought a "laudator" of time present, I would say here is the element of greatness we have made progress in. We are more open in mind and soul. We have arrived (some of us at least) at the conclusion that men may honestly differ without offense. We have learned to pity each other more. There is a greatness in modern toleration which our ancestors knew not.

Then comes the other element of greatness, courage. Have we made progress in that? This is a much more dubious question. The subjects of terror vary so much in different times that it is difficult to estimate the different degrees of courage shown in resisting them. Men fear public opinion now as they did in former times the Star Chamber; and those awful goddesses, Appearances, are to us what the Fates were to the Greeks. It is hardly possible to measure the courage of a Modern against that of an Ancient; but I am unwilling to believe but that enlightenment must strengthen courage.

The application of the tests of greatness, as in the above instance, is a matter of detail and of nice appreciation, as to the results of which men must be expected to differ largely: the tests themselves remain invariable — openness of nature to admit the light of love and reason, and courage to pursue it.

Complete. From "Friends in Council."

HOW HISTORY SHOULD BE READ

I SUPPOSE that many who now connect the very word History with the idea of dullness, would have been fond and diligent students of history if it had had fair access to their minds. But they were set down to read histories which were not fitted to be read continuously, or by any but practiced students. Some such works are mere framework, a name which the author of the "Statesman" applies to them; very good things, perhaps, for their purpose, but that is not to invite readers to history. You might almost as well read dictionaries with a hope of getting a succinct and clear view of language. When, in any narration, there is a constant heaping up of facts, made about equally significant by the way of telling them, a hasty delineation of characters, and all the incidents moving on as in the fifth act of a confused tragedy, the mind and memory refuse to be so treated; and the reading ends in nothing but a very slight and inaccurate acquaintance with the mere husk of the history. You cannot epitomize the knowledge that it would take years to acquire into a few volumes that may be read in as many weeks.

The most likely way of attracting men's attention to historical subjects will be by presenting them with small portions of history, of great interest, thoroughly examined. This may give them the habit of applying thought and criticism to historical matters.

VI—137

and science at the different periods treated of. The text of civil history requires a context of this knowledge in the mind of the reader. For the same reason, some of the main facts of the geography of the countries in question should be present to him. If we are ignorant of these aids to history, all history is apt to seem alike to us. It becomes merely a narrative of men of our own time, in our own country; and then we are prone to expect the same views and conduct from them that we do from our contemporaries. It is true that the heroes of antiquity have been represented on the stage in bagwigs, and the rest of the costume of our grandfathers; but it was the great events of their lives that were thus told — the crisis of their passions — and when we are contemplating the representation of great passions and their consequences, all minor imagery is of little moment. In a long-drawn narrative, however, the more we have in our minds of what concerned the daily life of the people we read about, the better. And in general it may be said that history, like traveling, gives a return in proportion to the knowledge that a man brings to it

Complete. Number II., on "History," from "Friends in Council."

For, as it is, how are people interested in history, and how do they master its multitudinous assemblage of facts? Mostly, perhaps, in this way. A man cares about some one thing, or person, or event, and plunges into its history, really wishing to master it. This pursuit extends; other points of research are taken up by him at other times. His researches begin to intersect. He finds a connection in things. The texture of his historic acquisitions gradually attains some substance and color; and so at last he begins to have some dim notions of the myriads of men who came, and saw, and did not conquer — only struggled on as they best might, some of them — and are not.

When we are considering how history should be read, the main thing perhaps is, that the person reading should desire to know what he is reading about, not merely to have read the books that tell of it. The most elaborate and careful historian must omit, or pass lightly over, many points of his subject. He writes for all readers, and cannot indulge private fancies. But history has its particular aspect for each man; there must be portions which he may be expected to dwell upon. And everywhere, even where the history is most labored, the reader should have something of the spirit of research which was needful for the writer, — if only so much as to ponder well the words of the writer. That man reads history, or anything else, at great peril of being thoroughly misled, who has no perception of any truthfulness except that which can be fully ascertained by reference to facts; who does not in the least perceive the truth, or the reverse, of a writer's style, of his epithets, of his reasoning, of his mode of narration. In life, our faith in any narration is much influenced by the personal appearance, voice, and gesture of the person narrating. There is some part of all these things in his writing; and you must look into that well before you can know what faith to give him. One man may make mistakes in names, and dates, and references, and yet have a real substance of truthfulness in him, a wish to enlighten himself and then you. Another may not be wrong in his facts, but have a declamatory or sophistical vein in him, much to be guarded against. A third may be both inaccurate and untruthful, caring not so much for anything as to write his book. And if the reader cares only to read it, sad work they make between them of the memories of former days.

In studying history, it must be borne in mind that a knowledge is necessary of the state of manners, customs, wealth, arts,

JOHANN GOTTFRIED VON HERDER

(1744–1803)

HERDER'S greatest work was in making Goethe possible. Germany of the eighteenth century despised its own simplicity, and stood shamed before the pseudo-classicism of the decadent French monarchy. Herder taught German youth to look for the highest literary excellence, not in triolets and rondeaus, or even in tragedies written in lilting twelve-syllabled iambics supposed to represent the Athenian masters, but in the treasured ballads and songs of the common people, in Shakespeare, in Homer, in the Psalms of David, and in the book of Job. He taught Germany to understand the merits of the Scotch heroic ballads, which are the finest in the literature of Europe and are so nearly German that when "Bonny George Campbell" was translated into German, Longfellow mistook it for a German "lied" and retranslated it into admirable English verse — not very far removed from the original Scotch. By cultivating the taste for the strong and natural simplicities of primitive literature, Herder educated the generation of German singers who, with Goethe and Schiller at their head, taught Longfellow to avoid the stiffness of the English "classical" school. So great was Herder's activity and so wide its range, that at his death, December 18th, 1803, he left material which, when collected in the Stuttgart edition of his works (1827–30), made sixty volumes. Those who cannot afford to read them all should by no means miss his "Stimmen der Völker in Liedern" (Folk Songs), and his essays on the "Spirit of Hebrew Poetry."

THE SUBLIMITY OF PRIMITIVE POETRY

(Euthyphron and Alcephron converse on the poetry of Job)

EUTHYPHRON — Every age must make its poetry consistent with its ideas of the great system of being, or if not, must at least be assured of producing a greater effect by its poetical fictions than systematic truth could secure to it. And may not this often be the case? I have no doubt that from the systems of Copernicus and Newton, of Buffon and Priestley, as elevated as poetry may be made, as from the most simple and childlike views of nature.

But why have we no such poetry? Why is it, that the simple pathetic fables of ancient or unlearned tribes always affect us more than these mathematical, physical, and metaphysical niceties? Is it not because the people of those times wrote poetry with more lively apprehensions, because they conceived ideas of all things, including God himself, under analogous forms, reduced the universe to the shape of a house, and animated all that it contains with human passions, with love and hatred? The first poet, who can do the same in the universe of Buffon and Newton, will, if he is so disposed, produce with truer, at least with more comprehensive ideas, the effect which they accomplished with their limited analogies and poetic fables. Would that such a poet were already among us! But so long as that is not the case, let us not turn to ridicule the genuine beauties in the poetry of ancient nations, because they understood not our systems of natural philosophy and metaphysics. Many of their allegories and personifications contain more imaginative power, and more sensuous truth, than voluminous systems — and the power of touching the heart speaks for itself.

Alcephron — This power of producing emotion, however, seems to me not to belong in so high a degree to the poetry of nature.

E. — The more gentle and enduring sentiments of poetry at least are produced by it, and more even than by any other. Can there be any more beautiful poetry than God himself has exhibited to us in the works of creation? Poetry, which he spreads fresh and glowing before us with every revolution of days and of seasons? Can the language of poetry accomplish anything more affecting than with brevity and simplicity to unfold to us in its measure what we are and what we enjoy? We live and have our being in this vast temple of God; our feelings and thoughts, our sufferings and our joys are all from this as their source. A species of poetry that furnishes me with eyes to perceive and contemplate the works of creation and myself, to consider them in their order and relation, and to discover through all the traces of infinite love, wisdom, and power, to shape the whole with the eye of fancy, and in words suited to their purpose — such a poetry is holy and heavenly. What wretch, in the greatest tumult of his passions, in walking under a starry heaven, would not experience imperceptibly and even against his will a soothing influence from the elevating contemplation of its silent,

unchangeable, and everlasting splendors? Suppose at such a moment there occurs to his thoughts the simple language of God, "Canst thou bind together the bands of the Pleiades," — is it not as if God himself addressed the words to him from the starry firmament? Such an effect has the true poetry of nature, the fair interpreter of the nature of God. A hint, a single word, in the spirit of such poetry, often suggests to the mind extended scenes; nor does it merely bring their quiet pictures before the eye in their outward lineaments, but brings them home to the sympathies of the heart, especially, when the heart of the poet himself is tender and benevolent, and it can hardly fail to be so.

A. — Will the heart of the poet of nature always exhibit this character?

E. — Of the great and genuine poet undoubtedly, otherwise he may be an acute observer, but could not be a refined and powerful expositor of nature. Poetry, that concerns itself with the deeds of men, often in a high degree debasing and criminal, that labors, with lively and affecting apprehensions, in the impure recesses of the heart, and often for no very worthy purpose, may corrupt as well the author as the reader. The poetry of divine things can never do this. It enlarges the heart, while it expands the view; renders this serene and contemplative, that energetic, free, and joyous. It awakens a love, an interest, and a sympathy for all that lives. It accustoms the understanding to remark on all occasions the laws of nature, and guides our reason to the right path. This is especially true of the descriptive poetry of the Orientals.

A. — Do you apply the remark to the chapter of Job, of which we were speaking?

E. — Certainly. It would be childish to hunt for the system of physics implied in the individual representations of poetry, or to aim at reconciling it with the system of our own days, and thus show that Job had already learned to think like our natural philosophers; yet the leading idea, that the universe is the palace of the Divine Being, where he is himself the director and disposer, where everything is transacted according to unchangeable and eternal laws, with a providence, that continually extends to the minutest concern, with benevolence and judgment — this, I say, we must acknowledge to be great and ennobling. It is set forth, too, by examples, in which everything

manifests unity of purpose, and subordination to the combined whole. The most wonderful phenomena come before us, as the doings of an ever-active and provident father of his household. Show me a poem which exhibits our system of physics, our discoveries and opinions respecting the formation of the world, and the changes that it undergoes, under as concise images, as animated personifications, with as suitable expositions, and a plan comprising as much unity and variety for the production of effect. But do not forget the three leading qualities, of which I have spoken, animation in the objects for awakening the senses, interpretation of nature, for the heart, a plan in the poem, as there is in creation, for the understanding. The last requisite altogether fails in most of our descriptive poets.

A. — You require, I fear, what is impossible. How little plan are we able to comprehend in the scenes of nature? The kingdom of the all-powerful mother of all things is so vast, her progress so slow, her prospective views so endless —

E. — That therefore a human poem must be so vast, so slow in progress, and so incomprehensible? Let him, to whom nature exhibits no plan, no unity of purpose, hold his peace, nor venture to give her expression in the language of poetry. Let him speak, for whom she has removed the veil and displayed the true expression of her features. He will discover in all her works connection, order, benevolence, and purpose. His own poetical creation, too, like that creation which inspires his imagination, will be a true Kosmos, a regular work, with plan, outlines, meaning, and ultimate design, and commend itself to the understanding as a whole, as it does to the heart by its individual thoughts and interpretations of nature, and to the sense by the animation of its objects. In nature, all things are connected, and for the view of man are connected by their relation to what is human. The periods of time, as days and years, have their relation to the age of man. Countries and climates have a principle of unity in the one race of man, ages and worlds in the one eternal cause, one God, one Creator. He is the eye of the universe, giving expression to its otherwise boundless void, and combining in a harmonious union the expression of all its multiplied and multiform features. Here we are brought back again to the East, for the Orientals, in their descriptive poetry, however poor or rich it may be judged, secure, first of all, that unity, which the understanding

demands. In all the various departments of nature they behold the God of the heavens and of the earth. This no Greek, nor Celt, nor Roman has ever done, and how far in this respect is Lucretius behind Job and David!

From the "Spirit of Hebrew Poetry,"
translated by J. Marsh.

MARRIAGE AS THE HIGHEST FRIENDSHIP

How truly said one of his friend, "Thy love to me surpassed the love of women!" Creation knows nothing nobler than two voluntarily and indissolubly united hands, — two hearts and lives that have voluntarily become one. It matters not whether these two hands are male or female, or of both sexes. It is a proud but irrational prejudice on the part of men, that only they are capable of friendship. Woman is often tenderer, truer, firmer, more golden-pure in that relation, than many a weak, unfeeling, impure, masculine soul. Where there is want of truth, — where there is vanity, rivalry, heedlessness, there friendship in either sex is impossible. Marriage, likewise, should be friendship; and woe! if it is not, if it is only love and desire. To a noble woman, it is sweet to suffer for her husband, as well as to rejoice with him, to feel that she is honored, esteemed, and happy in him and he in her. The common education of their children is the beautiful, leading aim of their friendship, which sweetly rewards them both, even in gray old age. They stand there, and will continue to stand like two trees with branches interlocked, begirt with a garland of youthful green, — saplings and twigs. In all cases, a life, in common, is the marrow of true friendship. Mutual unlocking and sharing of hearts, intense joy in each other, sympathy in each other's sufferings, counsel, consolation, effort, mutual aid, — these are its diagnostics, its delights, its interior recompense. What delicate secrets in friendship! Refinements of feeling, as if the soul of the one were directly conscious of the soul of the other, and, anticipating, discerned the thoughts of that soul as clearly as its own! And, assuredly, the soul has sometimes power thus to discern thoughts and to dwell immediately and intimately in the heart of another. There are moments of sympathy, even in thoughts without the slightest external occasion, which indeed no psychology can explain, but which experience teaches and confirms. There are mutual, simultaneous recollections of one another — even at a distance — on the part of absent friends, which are often of the most wonderful, overpowering kind. And, indeed, if ever the soul possesses the mysterious power to act directly, without organs, on another soul, where would such action be more natural than in the case of friends? This relation is purer, and therefore, assuredly, mightier also than love. For if love will lift itself up to the strength and duration of eternity, it must first purify itself from coarse sensuality, and become true and genuine friendship. How seldom does it arrive at this! It destroys itself or destroys its object with penetrating, devouring flames; and both the loving and the loved lie there, as it were, a heap of ashes. But the glow of friendship is pure, refreshing, human warmth. The two flames upon one altar play into each other, and as in sport, lift and bear one another aloft, and often, in the melancholy hour of separation, they soar rejoicing, and united, and victorious, upward to the land of the purest union, of truest, inseparable friendship.

From "Love and Self."

SIR JOHN HERSCHEL

(1792–1871)

IR JOHN FREDERICK WILLIAM HERSCHEL was born near Windsor, England, March 7th, 1792. He became one of the most celebrated astronomers of modern times, overcoming what is perhaps the greatest possible disadvantage a young man can have,— that of having a father so great that it seems at once absurd and irreverent to attempt to equal him. Yet the younger Herschel did his work so well that when the achievements of the elder are summed up, it is said, "As an explorer of the heavens he had only one rival — his son!" Besides his technical works on astronomy and physics, Sir John Herschel wrote a volume of "Familiar Letters on Scientific Subjects" (1866), which are frequently admirable in manner, as well as in matter. He died at Collingwood, England, May 11th, 1871.

SCIENCE AS A CIVILIZER

THE difference of the degrees in which the individuals of a great community enjoy the good things of life has been a theme of declamation and discontent in all ages; and it is doubtless our paramount duty, in every state of society, to alleviate the pressure of the purely evil part of this distribution as much as possible, and, by all the means we can devise, secure the lower links in the chain of society from dragging in dishonor and wretchedness; but there is a point of view in which the picture is at least materially altered in its expression. In comparing society on its present immense scale with its infant or less developed state, we must at least take care to enlarge every feature in the same proportion. If, on comparing the very lowest states in civilized and savage life, we admit a difficulty in deciding to which the preference is due, at least in every superior grade, we cannot hesitate a moment; and if we institute a similar comparison in every different stage of its progress, we cannot fail to be struck with the rapid rate of dilatation which every degree upward of the scale, so to speak, exhibits, and which, in

an estimate of averages, gives an immense preponderance to the present over every former condition of mankind, and, for aught we can see to the contrary, will place succeeding generations in the same degree of superior relation to the present that this holds to those passed away. Or, we may put the same proposition in other words, and, admitting the existence of every inferior grade of advantage in a higher state of civilization which subsisted in the preceding, we shall find, first, that, taking state for state, the proportional numbers of those who enjoy the higher degrees of advantage increases with a constantly accelerated rapidity as society advances; and, second, that the superior extremity of the scale is constantly enlarging by the addition of new degrees. The condition of a European prince is now as far superior, in the command of real comforts and conveniences, to that of one in the Middle Ages, as that to the condition of one of his own dependants.

The advantages conferred by the augmentation of our physical resources through the medium of increased knowledge and improved art have this peculiar and remarkable property — that they are in their nature diffusive, and cannot be enjoyed in any exclusive manner by a few. An Eastern despot may extort the riches and monopolize the art of his subjects for his own personal use; he may spread around him an unnatural splendor and luxury, and stand in strange and preposterous contrast with the general penury and discomfort of his people; he may glitter in jewels of gold and raiment of needlework; but the wonders of well contrived and executed manufacture which we use daily, and the comforts which have been invented, tried, and improved upon by thousands, in every form of domestic convenience, and for every ordinary purpose of life, can never be enjoyed by him. To produce a state of things in which the physical advantages of civilized life can exist in a high degree, the stimulus of increasing comforts and constantly elevated desires must have been felt by millions; since it is not in the power of a few individuals to create that wide demand for useful and ingenious applications, which alone can lead to great and rapid improvements, unless backed by that arising from the speedy diffusion of the same advantages among the mass of mankind.

If this be true of physical advantages, it applies with still greater force to intellectual. Knowledge can neither be ade-

quately cultivated nor adequately enjoyed by a few; and although the conditions of our existence on earth may be such as to preclude an abundant supply of the physical necessities of all who may be born, there is no such law of nature in force against that of our intellectual and moral wants. Knowledge is not, like food, destroyed by use, but rather augmented and perfected. It requires not, perhaps, a greater certainty, but at least a confirmed authority and a probable duration, by universal assent; and there is no body of knowledge so complete but that it may acquire accession, or so free from error but that it may receive correction in passing through the minds of millions. Those who admire and love knowledge for its own sake ought to wish to see its elements made accessible to all, were it only that they may be the more thoroughly examined into, and more effectually developed in their consequences, and receive that ductility and plastic quality which the pressure of minds of all descriptions, constantly molding them to their purposes, can alone bestow. But to this end it is necessary that it should be divested, as far as possible, of artificial difficulties, and stripped of all such technicalities as tend to place it in the light of a craft and a mystery, inaccessible without a kind of apprenticeship. Science, of course, like everything else, has its own peculiar terms, and, so to speak, its idioms of language; and these it would be unwise, were it even possible, to relinquish: but everything that tends to clothe it in a strange and repulsive garb, and especially everything that, to keep up an appearance of superiority in its professors over the rest of mankind, assumes an unnecessary guise of profundity and obscurity, should be sacrificed without mercy. Not to do this is deliberately to reject the light which the natural unencumbered good sense of mankind is capable of throwing on every subject, even in the elucidation of principles; but where principles are to be applied to practical uses, it becomes absolutely necessary; as all mankind have then an interest in their being so familiarly understood, that no mistakes shall arise in their application.

The same remark applies to arts. They cannot be perfected till their whole processes are laid open, and their language simplified and rendered universally intelligible. Art is the application of knowledge to a practical end. If the knowledge be merely accumulated experience, the art is empirical; but if it be experience reasoned upon and brought under general principles, it assumes a higher character, and becomes a scientific art. In the progress of mankind from barbarism to civilized life, the arts necessarily precede science. The wants and cravings of our animal constitution must be satisfied; the comforts and some of the luxuries of life must exist. Something must be given to the vanity of show, and more to the pride of power; the round of baser pleasures must have been tried and found insufficient before intellectual ones can gain a footing; and when they have obtained it, the delights of poetry and its sister arts still take precedence of contemplative enjoyments, and the severer pursuits of thought; and when these in time begin to charm from their novelty, and sciences begin to arise, they will at first be those of pure speculation. The mind delights to escape from the trammels which had bound it to earth, and luxuriates in its newly-found powers. Hence, the abstractions of geometry—the properties of numbers—the movements of the celestial spheres—whatever is abstruse, remote, and extramundane—become the first objects of infant science. Applications come late; the arts continue slowly progressive, but their realm remains separated from that of science by a wide gulf which can only be passed by a powerful spring. They form their own language and their own conventions, which none but artists can understand. The whole tendency of empirical art is to bury itself in technicalities, and to place its pride in particular short cuts and mysteries known only to adepts; to surprise and astonish by results, but conceal processes. The character of science is the direct contrary. It delights to lay itself open to inquiry; and is not satisfied with its conclusions till it can make the road to them broad and beaten; and in its applications it preserves the same character; its whole aim being to strip away all technical mystery, to illuminate every dark recess, with a view to improve them on rational principles. It would seem that a union of two qualities almost opposite to each other—a going forth of the thoughts in two directions, and a sudden transfer of ideas from a remote station in one to an equally distant one in the other—is required to start the first idea of applying science. Among the Greeks this point was attained by Archimedes, but attained too late, on the eve of that great eclipse of science which was destined to continue for nearly eighteen centuries, till Galileo in Italy, and Bacon in England, at once dispelled the darkness; the one by his inventions and

discoveries, the other by the irresistible force of his arguments and eloquence.

Finally, the improvement effected in the condition of mankind by advances in physical science as applied to the useful purposes of life, is very far from being limited to their direct consequences in the more abundant supply of their physical wants, and the increase of our comforts. Great as these benefits are, they are yet but steps to others of a still higher kind. The successful results of our experiments and reasonings in natural philosophy, and the incalculable advantages which experience, systematically consulted and dispassionately reasoned on, has conferred in matters purely physical, tend of necessity to impress something of the well-weighed and progressive character of science on the more complicated conduct of our social and moral relations. It is thus that legislation and politics become gradually regarded as experimental sciences, and history, not, as formerly, the mere record of tyrannies and slaughters, which, by immortalizing the execrable actions of one age, perpetuates the ambition of committing them in every succeeding one, but as the archive of experiments, successful and unsuccessful, gradually accumulating towards the solution of the grand problem—how the advantages of government are to be secured with the least possible inconvenience to the governed. The celebrated apothegm, that nations never profit by experience, becomes yearly more and more untrue. Political economy, at least, is found to have sound principles, founded in the moral and physical nature of man, which, however lost sight of in particular measures—however even temporarily controverted and borne down by clamor—have yet a stronger and stronger testimony borne to them in each succeeding generation, by which they must, sooner or later, prevail. The idea once conceived and verified, that great and noble ends are to be achieved, by which the condition of the whole human species shall be permanently bettered, by bringing into exercise a sufficient quantity of sober thoughts, and by a proper adaptation of means, is of itself sufficient to set us earnestly on reflecting what ends are truly great and noble, either in themselves, or as conducive to others of a still loftier character; because we are not now, as heretofore, hopeless of attaining them. It is not now equally harmless and insignificant, whether we are right or wrong, since we are no longer supinely and helplessly carried down the

stream of events, but feel ourselves capable of buffeting at least with its waves, and perhaps of riding triumphantly over them: for why should we despair that the reason which has enabled us to subdue all nature to our purposes should (if permitted and assisted by the providence of God) achieve a far more difficult conquest, and ultimately find some means of enabling the collective wisdom of mankind to bear down those obstacles which individual short-sightedness, selfishness, and passion, oppose to all improvements, and by which the highest hopes are continually blighted, and the fairest prospects marred?

From a «Discourse on the Study of
Natural Philosophy.»

THE TASTE FOR READING

IF I WERE to pray for a taste which should stand me in stead under every variety of circumstances, and be a source of happiness and cheerfulness to me through life, and a shield against its ills, however things might go amiss, and the world frown upon me, it would be a taste for reading. I speak of it, of course, only as a wordly advantage, and not in the slightest degree as superseding or derogating from the higher office and surer and stronger panoply of religious principles—but as a taste, an instrument, and a mode of pleasurable gratification. Give a man this taste, and the means of gratifying it, and you can hardly fail of making a happy man, unless, indeed, you put into his hands a most perverse selection of books. You place him in contact with the best society in every period of history—with the wisest, the wittiest—with the tenderest, the bravest, and the purest characters that have adorned humanity. You make him a denizen of all nations—a contemporary of all ages. The world has been created for him. It is hardly possible but the character should take a higher and better tone from the constant habit of associating in thought with a class of thinkers, to say the least of it, above the average of humanity. It is morally impossible but that the manners should take a tinge of good breeding and civilization from having constantly before one's eyes the way in which the best-bred and the best-informed men have talked and conducted themselves in their intercourse with each

other. There is a gentle but perfectly irresistible coercion in a habit of reading, well-directed, over the whole tenor of a man's character and conduct, which is not the less effectual because it works insensibly, and because it is really the last thing he dreams of. It cannot, in short, be better summed up than in the words of the Latin poet,—

«*Emollit mores, nec sinit esse feros.*»

It civilizes the conduct of men—and suffers them not to remain barbarous.

KARL HILLEBRAND

(1829–1884)

KARL HILLEBRAND, one of the expatriated revolutionists of 1848, to whom the civilization of Germany and the world is so largely indebted, was born at Giessen, Germany, September 17th, 1829. Imprisoned at the age of twenty for taking part in the Baden movement against absolutism, he escaped to France, where he continued his studies and graduated at the Sorbonne. In 1863 he was appointed professor of Foreign Languages at Douai. He became a master of French and wrote several of his works in it, but when the Franco-Prussian War began he found that his exile had not made him a Frenchman. He solved the problem of choice between his native and his adopted country by removing to Italy where he lived until his death, October 19th, 1884. Among his works are "Lectures on German Thought," "On Good Comedy," "Contemporary Prussia," "Times, People, and Men," and a "History of France from the Accession of Louis Philippe to the Fall of Napoleon III."

GOETHE'S VIEW OF ART AND NATURE

MAN is the last and highest link in nature; his task is to understand what she aims at in him and then to fulfill her intentions. This view of Herder was Goethe's starting point in the formation of his "Weltanschauung," or general view of things.

All the world (says one of the characters in "Wilhelm Meister") lies before us, like a vast quarry before the architect. He does not deserve the name, if he does not compose with these accidental natural materials an image whose source is in his mind, and if he does not do it with the greatest possible economy, solidity, and perfection. All that we find outside of us, nay, within us, is object-matter; but deep within us lives also a power capable of giving an ideal form to this matter. This creative power allows us no rest till we have produced that ideal form in one or the other way, either without us in finished works, or in our own life.

VI—138

KARL HILLEBRAND 2195

mism disappear at once as well as fatalism; the highest and most refined intellect again accepts the world, as children and ignorant toilers do, as a given necessity. He does not even think the world could be otherwise, and within its limits he not only enjoys and suffers, but also works gaily, trying, like Horace, to subject things to himself, but resigned to submit to them, when they are invincible. Thus the simple Hellenic existence which, contrary to Christianity, but according to nature, accepted the present without ceaselessly thinking of death and another world, and acted in that present and in the circumstances allotted to each by fate, without wanting to overstep the boundaries of nature, would revive again in our modern world, and free us forever from the torment of unaccomplished wishes and of vain terrors.

The sojourn in Italy during which Goethe lived outside the struggle for life, outside the competition and contact of practical activity, in contemplation of nature and art, developed this view — the spectator's view, which will always be that of the artist and of the thinker, strongly opposed to that of the actor on the stage of human life. "Iphigenia," "Torquato Tasso," "Wilhelm Meister," are the fruits and the interpreters of this conception of the moral world. What ripened and perfected it, so as to raise it into a general view, not only of morality, but also of the great philosophical questions which man is called upon to answer, was his study of nature, greatly furthered during his stay in Italy. The problem which lay at the bottom of all the vague longing of his generation for nature he was to solve. It became his incessant endeavor to understand the coherence and unity of nature.

"You are forever searching for what is necessary in nature," Schiller wrote to him once, "but you search for it in the most difficult way. You take the whole of nature in order to obtain light on the particular case; you look into the totality for the explanation of the individual existence. From the simplest organism in nature, you ascend step by step to the more complicated, and finally construct the most complicated of all, man, out of the materials of the whole of nature. In thus creating man anew under the guidance of nature, you penetrate into his mysterious organism."

And, indeed, as there is a wonderful harmony with nature in Goethe, the poet and the man, so there is the same harmony in Goethe, the savant and the thinker; nay, even science he practiced as a poet. As one of the greatest physicists of our days, Helmholtz, has said of him: "He did not try to translate nature into

Here we already have in germ Schiller's idea that life ought to be a work of art. But how do we achieve this task, continually impeded as we are by circumstances and by our fellow-creatures, who will not always leave us in peace to develop our individual characters in perfect conformity with nature? In our relations with our neighbor, Goethe (like Lessing and Wieland, Kant and Herder, and all the great men of his and the preceding age, in England and France as well as in Germany) recommended absolute toleration not only of opinions, but also of individualities, particularly those in which Nature manifests herself "undefiled." As to circumstances, which is only another name for fate, he preached and practiced resignation. At every turn of our life, in fact, we meet with limits; our intelligence has its frontiers which bar its way; our senses are limited, and can only embrace an infinitely small part of nature; few of our wishes can be fulfilled; privation and sufferings await us at every moment. "Privation is thy lot, privation! That is the eternal song which resounds at every moment, which, our whole life through, each hour sings hoarsely to our ears!" laments Faust. What remains then for man? "Everything cries to us that we must resign ourselves." "There are few men, however, who, conscious of the privations and sufferings in store for them in life, and desirous to avoid the necessity of resigning themselves anew in each particular case, have the courage to perform the act of resignation once for all"; who say to themselves that there are eternal and necessary laws to which we must submit, and that we had better do it without grumbling; who "endeavor to form principles which are not liable to be destroyed, but are rather confirmed by contact with reality." In other words, when man has discovered the laws of nature, both moral and physical, he must accept them as the limits of his actions and desires; he must not wish for eternity of life or inexhaustible capacities of enjoyment, understanding, and acting, any more than he wishes for the moon. For rebellion against these laws must needs be an act of impotency as well as of deceptive folly. By resignation, the human soul is purified; for thereby it becomes free of selfish passions and arrives at that intellectual superiority in which the contemplation and understanding of things give sufficient contentment, without making it needful for man to stretch out his hands to take possession of them: a thought which Goethe's friend, Schiller, has magnificently developed in his grand philosophical poems. Optimism and pessi-

abstract conceptions, but takes it as a complete work of art, which must reveal its contents spontaneously to an intelligent observer." Goethe never became a thorough experimentalist; he did not want "to extort the secret from nature by pumps and retorts." He waited patiently for a voluntary revelation, i. e., until he could surprise that secret by an intuitive glance; for it was his conviction that if you live intimately with Nature, she will sooner or later disclose her mysteries to you. If you read his "Songs," his "Werther," his "Die Wahlverwandtschaften," you feel that extraordinary intimacy — I had almost said identification — with nature, present everywhere. Werther's love springs up with the blossom of all nature; he begins to sink and nears his self-made tomb, while autumn, the death of nature, is in the fields and woods. So does the moon spread her mellow light over his garden, as "the mild eye of a true friend over his destiny." Never was there a poet who humanized nature or naturalized human feeling, if I might say so, to the same degree as Goethe. Now, this same love of nature he brought into his scientific researches.

He began his studies of nature early, and he began them as he was to finish them, — with geology. Buffon's great views on the revolutions of the earth had made a deep impression upon him, although he was to end as the declared adversary of that vulcanism which we can trace already at the bottom of Buffon's theory — naturally enough, when we think how uncongenial all violence in society and nature was to him, how he looked everywhere for slow, uninterrupted evolution. From theoretical study he had early turned to direct observation; and when his administrative functions obliged him to survey the mines of the little Dukedom, ample opportunity was offered for positive studies. As early as 1778, in a paper on "Granite," he wrote: "I do not fear the reproach that a spirit of contradiction draws me from the contemplation of the human heart — this most mobile, most mutable, and fickle part of the creation — to the observation of (granite) the oldest, firmest, deepest, most immovable son of Nature. For all natural things are in connection with each other." It was his life's task to search for the links of this coherence in order to find that unity which he knew to be in the moral as well as material universe.

From "Lectures on the History of German Thought."

THOMAS HOBBES

(1588–1679)

HOMAS HOBBES (born in Wiltshire, England, April 5th, 1588) is chiefly celebrated for his "Leviathan," a curious argument against political liberty in all its forms. He was the author of a number of philosophical works, notably of "Liberty and Necessity," which appeared in 1654 and gave occasion for the title of "leader of modern rationalism," with which he has been brevetted. His methods, however, have nothing to do with the processes through which modern science has reached positive results. In his own politics, he was not specially consistent, for he lived as a Cromwellian under Cromwell and as an advocate of absolutism under Charles II. He died December 4th, 1679. He had a clear understanding of the vices of human nature, but he seems to have had no conception of the idea of evolution,—of educating and developing the good in all nature, including human nature, as the only possible way of overcoming the evil.

"THE DESIRE AND WILL TO HURT"

THE cause of mutual fear consists partly in the natural equality of men, partly in their mutual will of hurting; whence it comes to pass that we can neither expect from others, nor promise to ourselves, the least security. For if we look on men full-grown, and consider how brittle the frame of our human body is, which perishing, all its strength, vigor, and wisdom itself perisheth with it; and how easy a matter it is, even for the weakest man to kill the strongest: there is no reason why any man, trusting to his own strength, should conceive himself made by nature above others. They are equals, who can do equal things one against the other; but they who can do the greatest thing, viz., kill, can do equal things. All men, therefore, among themselves are by nature equal; the inequality we now discern hath its spring from the civil law.

All men in the state of nature have a desire and will to hurt, but not proceeding from the same cause, neither equally to be condemned. For one man, according to that natural equality which is among us, permits as much to others as he assumes to himself; which is an argument of a temperate man, and one that rightly values his power. Another, supposing himself above others, will have a license to do what he lists, and challenges respect and honor, as due to him before others; which is an argument of a fiery spirit. This man's will to hurt ariseth from vainglory, and the false esteem he hath of his own strength; the other's from the necessity of defending himself, his liberty, and his goods, against this man's violence.

Furthermore, since the combat of wits is the fiercest, the greatest discords which are must necessarily arise from this contention. For in this case it is not only odious to contend against, but also not to consent. For not to approve of what a man saith is no less than tacitly to accuse him of an error in that thing which he speaketh: as in very many things to dissent is as much as if you accounted him a fool whom you dissent from. Which may appear hence, that there are no wars so sharply waged as between sects of the same religion, and factions of the same commonweal, where the contestation is either concerning doctrines or politic prudence. And since all the pleasure and jollity of the mind consist in this, even to get some, with whom comparing, it may find somewhat wherein to triumph and vaunt itself; it is impossible, but men must declare sometimes some mutual scorn and contempt, either by laughter, or by words, or by gesture, or some sign or other; than which there is no greater vexation of mind, and than from which there cannot possibly arise a greater desire to do hurt.

But the most frequent reason why men desire to hurt each other ariseth hence, that many men at the same time have an appetite to the same thing; which yet very often they can neither enjoy in common, nor yet divide it; whence it follows that the strongest must have it, and who is strongest must be decided by the sword.

From "Philosophical Elements of a
True Citizen."

BRUTALITY IN HUMAN NATURE

IT MAY seem strange to some man that has not well weighed these things, that nature should dissociate, and render men apt to invade and destroy one another: and he may therefore, not trusting to this inference made from the passions, desire perhaps to have the same confirmed by experience. Let him therefore consider with himself, when taking a journey, he arms himself, and seeks to go well accompanied; when going to sleep, he locks his doors; when even in his house, he locks his chests; and this when he knows there be laws, and public officers, armed, to revenge all injuries which shall be done him; what opinion he has of his fellow-subjects, when he rides armed; of his fellow-citizens, when he locks his doors; and of his children and servants, when he locks his chests. Does he not there as much accuse mankind by his actions as I do by my words? But neither of us accuse man's nature in it. The desires and other passions of man are in themselves no sin. No more are the actions that proceed from those passions, till they know a law that forbids them; which, till laws be made, they cannot know: nor can any law be made till they have agreed upon the person that shall make it.

It may, peradventure, be thought there was never such a time nor condition of war as this; and I believe it was never generally so over all the world, but there are many places where they live so now. For the savage people in many places of America, except the government of small families, the concord whereof dependeth on natural lust, have no government at all, and live at this day in a brutish manner. . . . Howsoever, it may be perceived what manner of life there would be, where there were no common power to fear, by the manner of life which men that have formerly lived under a peaceful government used to degenerate into, in a civil war.

But though there had never been any time wherein particular men were in a condition of war one against another, yet in all times, kings and persons of sovereign authority, because of their independency, are in continual jealousies, and in the state and posture of gladiators, having their weapons pointing, and their eyes fixed on one another: that is, their forts, garrisons, and guns upon the frontiers of their kingdoms; and continual spies upon their neighbors; which is a posture of war. But, because they uphold thereby the industry of their subjects, there does not follow from it that misery which accompanies the liberty of particular men.

To this war of every man against every man, this also is consequent, that nothing can be unjust. The notions of right and wrong, justice and injustice, have there no place. Where there is no common power, there is no law; where no law, no injustice. Force and fraud are in war the two cardinal virtues. Justice and injustice are none of the faculties neither of the body nor mind. If they were, they might be in a man that were alone in the world, as well as his senses and passions. They are qualities that relate to men in society, not in solitude. It is consequent also to the same condition, that there be no propriety, no dominion, no mine and thine distinct; but only that to be every man's, that he can get; and for so long, as he can keep it. And thus much for the ill condition, which man by mere nature is actually placed in; though with a possibility to come out of it, consisting partly in the passions, partly in his reason.

From the "Leviathan."

OLIVER WENDELL HOLMES

(1809–1894)

"THE Autocrat of the Breakfast-Table" appeared first as a series of essays in the Atlantic Monthly at a time (1858–59) when current American humor consisted almost wholly of the broadest and most farcical burleque. Irving had written and had been much admired on English authority that he represented literary excellence of a high order, but the general circulation of his works consequent on the expiration of copyrights had not then begun. Popular taste was crude, and it was fed with crudity. A "Cyclopedia of Humor" of several hundred pages, published by one of the leading houses of the country in the year in which the "Autocrat of the Breakfast-Table" appeared, has in it hardly an example of American humor which rises above the taste of the circus ring-master. It is not strange under such circumstances that Dr. Holmes won immediate celebrity. He represented literary excellence, and, at the same time, much more of the real American spirit than is to be found in Irving's imitation of Addison. Such poems as that in which Holmes tells the history of the "One-Hoss Shay" interspersed the prose in a way which has proven popular ever since it was invented several thousand years ago in Persia; and in these, as well as in the prose, was a "benignant vein of wit" delicate enough to be pleasing to the most refined, and yet broad enough to impress itself on those who require burnt cork with their humor and red fire with their tragedy. Dr. Holmes became thus the first real American humorist with an assured standing in good literature. He followed his first great success by "The Professor at the Breakfast-Table" and "The Poet at the Breakfast-Table," as well as by poems, novels, and miscellaneous essays, all admirable in their way, but not capable singly or in mass of displacing him from the public mind in his original rôle of "Autocrat." He had a true and fine ear for melody and all his verse shows it, but he will be remembered by his ode on "The Chambered Nautilus" when all the rest is forgotten. Born at Cambridge, Massachusetts, August 29th, 1809, he adopted medicine as a profession and followed it usefully until his death, October 7th, 1894, but his highest usefulness was in curing bad humor. New England has produced many greater propagandists and a number of greater thinkers, but no one

whom the Americans of the coming century, north and south, east and west, are likely to love better as the representative of all that is best in New England good-nature.

W. V. B.

MY FIRST WALK WITH THE SCHOOLMISTRESS

THIS is the shortest way,—she said, as we came to a corner. —Then we won't take it,—said I.—The schoolmistress laughed a little, and said she was ten minutes early, so she could go around.

We walked around Mr. Paddock's row of English elms. The gray squirrels were out looking for their breakfasts, and one of them came towards us in light, soft, intermittent leaps, until he was close to the rail of the burial ground. He was on a grave with a broad blue slate-stone at its head, and a shrub growing on it. The stone said this was the grave of a young man who was the son of an Honorable gentleman, and who died a hundred years ago and more. Oh, yes, died,—with a small triangular mark in one breast, and another smaller opposite, in his back, where another young man's rapier had slid through his body; and so he lay down out there on the Common, and was found cold the next morning, with the night dews and the death dews mingled on his forehead.

Let us have one look at poor Benjamin's grave,—said I.— His bones lie where his body was laid so long ago, and where the stone says they lie,—which is more than can be said of most of the tenants of this and several other burial grounds.

[The most accursed act of vandalism ever committed within my knowledge was the uprooting of the ancient gravestones in three, at least, of our city burial grounds, and one, at least, just outside the city, and planting them in rows to suit the taste for symmetry of the perpetrators. Many years ago, when this disgraceful process was going on under my eyes, I addressed an indignant remonstrance to a leading journal. I suppose it was deficient in literary elegance, or too warm in its language; for no notice was taken of it, and the hyena-horror was allowed to complete itself in the face of daylight. I have never got over it. The bones of my own ancestors, being entombed, lie beneath

their own tablet; but the upright stones have been shuffled about like chessmen, and nothing short of the Day of Judgment will tell whose dust lies beneath any of these records, meant by affection to mark one small spot as sacred to some cherished memory. Shame! shame! shame!—that is all I can say. It was on public thoroughfares, under the eye of authority, that this infamy was enacted. The red Indians would have known better; the selectmen of an African kraal village would have had more respect for their ancestors. I should like to see the gravestones which have been disturbed all removed, and the ground leveled, leaving the flat tombstones; epitaphs were never famous for truth, but the old reproach of "Here lies" never had such a wholesome illustration as in these outraged burial places, where the stone does lie above, and the bones do not lie beneath.]

Stop before we turn away, and breathe a woman's sigh over poor Benjamin's dust. Love killed him, I think. Twenty years old, and out there fighting another young fellow on the common, in the cool of that old July evening;—yes, there must have been love at the bottom of it.

The schoolmistress dropped a rosebud she had in her hand through the rails, upon the grave of Benjamin Woodbridge. That was all her comment upon what I told her.—How women love Love! said I;—but she did not speak.

We came opposite the head of a place or court running eastward from the main street.—Look down there,—I said,—my friend, the Professor, lived in that house, at the left hand, next the further corner, for years and years. He died out of it, the other day.—Died?—said the schoolmistress.—Certainly,—said I. —We die out of houses, just as we die out of our bodies. A commercial smash kills a hundred men's homes for them, as a railroad crash kills their mortal frames and drives out the immortal tenants. Men sicken of houses until at last they quit them, as the soul leaves its body when it is tired of its infirmities. The body has been called "the house we live in"; the house is quite as much the body we live in. Shall I tell you some things the Professor said the other day?—Do!—said the schoolmistress.

A man's body,—said the Professor,—is whatever is occupied by his will and his sensibility. The small room down there, where I wrote those papers you remember reading, was much more a part of my body than a paralytic's senseless and motionless arm or leg is of his.

The soul of a man has a series of concentric envelopes around it, like the core of an onion, or the innermost of a nest of boxes. First, he has his natural garment of flesh and blood. Then, his artificial integuments, with their true skin of solid stuffs, their cuticle of lighter tissues, and their variously tinted pigments. Third, his domicile, be it a single chamber or a stately mansion. And then, the whole visible world, in which Time buttons him up as in a loose outside wrapper.

You shall observe,—the Professor said,—for like Mr. John Hunter and other great men, he brings in that "shall" with great effect sometimes,—you shall observe that a man's clothing or series of envelopes after a certain time mold themselves upon his individual nature. We know this of our hats, and are always reminded of it when we happen to put them on wrong side foremost. We soon find that the beaver is a hollow cast of the skull, with all its irregular bumps and depressions. Just so all that clothes a man, even to the blue sky which caps his head,—a little loosely,—shapes itself to fit each particular being beneath it. Farmers, sailors, astronomers, poets, lovers, condemned criminals, all find it different, according to the eyes with which they severally look.

But our houses shape themselves palpably on our inner and outer natures. See a householder breaking up and you will be sure of it. There is a shellfish which builds all manner of smaller shells into the walls of its own. A house is never a home until we have crusted it with the spoils of a hundred lives besides those of our own past. See what these are, and you can tell what the occupant is.

I had no idea,—said the Professor,—until I pulled up my domestic establishment the other day, what an enormous quantity of roots I had been making the years I was planted there. Why, there wasn't a nook or a corner that some fibre had not worked its way into; and when I gave the last wrench, each of them seemed to shriek like a mandrake, as it broke its hold and came away.

There is nothing that happens, you know, which must not inevitably, and which does not actually, photograph itself in every conceivable aspect and in all dimensions. The infinite galleries of the Past await but one brief process, and all their pictures will be called out and fixed forever. We had a curious illustration of the great fact on a very humble scale. When a certain bookcase, long standing in one place, for which it was built, was removed, there was the exact image on the wall of the whole, and of many of its portions. But in the midst of this picture was another,—the precise outline of a map which hung on the wall before the bookcase was built. We had all forgotten everything about the map until we saw its photograph on the wall. Then we remembered it, as some day or other we may remember a sin which has been built over and covered up, when this lower universe is pulled away from the wall of Infinity, where the wrongdoing stands, self-recorded.

The Professor lived in that house a long time—not twenty years, but pretty near it. When he entered that door, two shadows glided over the threshold; five lingered in the doorway when he passed through it for the last time,—and one of the shadows was claimed by its owner to be longer than his own. What changes he saw in that quiet place! Death rained through every roof but his; children came into life, grew to maturity; wedded, faded away, threw themselves away; the whole drama of life was played in that stock company's theatre of a dozen houses, one of which was his, and no deep sorrow or severe calamity ever entered his dwelling. Peace be to those walls forever,—the Professor said,—for the many pleasant years he has passed within them.

The Professor has a friend, now living at a distance, who has been with him in many of his changes of place, and who follows him in imagination with tender interest wherever he goes.— In that little court, where he lived in gay loneliness so long,— in his autumnal sojourn by the Connecticut, where it comes loitering down from its mountain fastnesses like a great lord, swallowing up the small proprietary rivulets very quietly as it goes, until it gets proud and swollen and wantons in huge luxurious oxbows about the fair Northampton meadows, and at last overflows the oldest inhabitant's memory in profligate freshets at Hartford and all along its lower shores,—up in that caravansary on the banks of the stream where Ledyard launched his log canoe, and the jovial old Colonel used to lead the commencement processions,—where blue Ascutney looked down from the far distance, and the hills of Beulah, as the Professor always called them, rolled up the opposite horizon in soft climbing masses, so suggestive of the Pilgrim's Heavenward Path that he used to look through his old "Dollond" to see if the Shining Ones were not within range of sight,—sweet visions, sweetest in those Sunday

walks that carried them by the peaceful common, through the solemn village lying in cataleptic stillness under the shadows of the rod of Moses, to the terminus of their harmless stroll,—the "patulous fage," in the Professor's classic dialect,—the spreading beech, in more familiar phrase,—[stop and breathe here a moment, for the sentence is not done yet, and we have another long journey before us.]

—and again once more up among those other hills that shut in the amber-flowing Housatonic,—dark stream, but clear, like the lucid orbs that shine beneath the lids of auburn-haired, sherry-wine-eyed demiblondes,—in the home overlooking the winding stream and the smooth, flat meadow; looked down upon by wild hills, where the tracks of bears and catamounts may yet sometimes be seen upon the winter snow; facing the twin summits which rise in the far North, the highest waves of the great land storm in this billowy region,—suggestive to mad fancies of the breasts of a half-buried Titaness, stretched out by a stray thunderbolt and hastily hidden away beneath the leaves of the forest,— in that home where seven blessed summers were passed, which stand in memory like the seven golden candlesticks in the beatific vision of the holy dreamer,—

—in that modest dwelling we were just looking at, not glorious, yet not unlovely in the youth of its drab and mahogany,— full of great and little boys' playthings from top to bottom,— in all these summer or winter nests, he was always at home and always welcome.

This long articulated sigh of reminiscences,—this calenture which shows me the maple-shadowed plains of Berkshire and the mountain-circled green of Grafton beneath the salt waves that come feeling their way along the wall at my feet, restless and soft-touching as blind men's busy fingers,—is for that friend of mine who looks into the waters of the Patapsco and sees beneath them the same visions that paint themselves for me in the green depths of the Charles.

Did I talk all this off to the schoolmistress?—Why, no—of course not. I have been talking with you, the reader, for the last ten minutes. You don't think I should expect any woman to listen to such a sentence as that long one, without g.ving her a chance to put in a word?

What did I say to the schoolmistress?—Permit me one moment. I don't doubt your delicacy and good-breeding; but in

this particular case, as I was allowed the privilege of walking alone with a very interesting young woman, you must allow me to remark, in the classic version of a familiar phrase, used by our Master Benjamin Franklin, it is *nullum tui negotii*.

When the schoolmistress and I reached the schoolroom door, the damask roses I spoke of were so much heightened in color by exercise that I felt sure it would be useful to her to take a stroll like this every morning, and made up my mind I would ask her to let me join her again.

Complete. From «The Autocrat of the
Breakfast-Table.»

EXTRACTS FROM MY PRIVATE JOURNAL

(To be burned unread)

I AM afraid I have been a fool; for I have told as much of myself to this young person as if she were of that ripe and discreet age which invites confidence and expansive utterance. I have been low spirited and listless lately,—it is coffee, I think,—(I observe that which is bought ready ground never affects the head),— and I notice that I tell my secrets too easily when I am downhearted.

There are inscriptions on our hearts, which, like that on Dighton Rock, are never to be seen except at dead-low tide.

There is a woman's footstep on the sand at the side of my deepest ocean-buried inscription.

—Oh, no, no! a thousand times, no! Yet, what is this which has been shaping itself in my soul?—is it a thought?—is it a dream?—is it a passion?—Then I know what comes next.

The asylum stood on a bright and breezy hill; those glazed corridors are pleasant to walk in, in bad weather. But there are iron bars to all the windows. When it is fair, some of us can stroll outside that very high fence. But I never see much life in the groups I sometimes meet; and then the careful man watches them so closely! How I remember that sad company I used to pass on fine mornings, when I was a schoolboy!—B., with his arms full of yellow weeds,—ore from the gold mines which he discovered long before we heard of California,—Y., born to millions, crazed by too much plum cake (the boys said), dogged, explosive,—made a Polyphemus of my weak-eyed schoolmaster by

a vicious flirt with a stick,—(the multimillionaires sent him a trifle, it was said, to buy another eye with; but boys are jealous of rich folks, and I don't doubt the good people made him easy for life),—how I remember them all!

I recollect, as all do, the story of the Hall of Eblis, in "Vathek," and how each shape, as it lifted its hand from its breast, showed its heart,—a burning coal. The real Hall of Eblis stands on yonder summit. Go there on the next visiting day, and ask that figure crouched in the corner, huddled up like those Indian mummies and skeletons found buried in the sitting posture, to lift its hand,—look upon its heart, and behold, not fire, but ashes.—No, I must not think of such an ending! Dying would be a much more gentlemanly way of meeting the difficulty. Make a will and leave her a house or two and some stocks, and other little financial conveniences to take away her necessity for keeping school.—I wonder what nice young man's feet would be in my French slippers before six months were over! Well, what then? If a man really loves a woman, of course he wouldn't marry her for the world if he were not quite sure that he was the best person that she could by any possibility marry.

It is odd enough to read over what I have just been writing. —It is the merest fancy that ever was in the world. I shall never be married. She will; and if she is as pleasant as she has been so far, I will give her a silver teaset, and go and take tea with her and her husband sometimes. No coffee, I hope, though, —it depresses me sadly. I feel very miserably; they must have been grinding it at home.—Another morning walk will be good for me, and I don't doubt the schoolmistress will be glad of a little fresh air before school.

Complete. From «The Autocrat of the
Breakfast-Table.»

MY LAST WALK WITH THE SCHOOLMISTRESS

(A parenthesis)

I CAN'T say just how many walks she and I had taken together before this one. I found the effect of going out every morning was decidedly favorable on her health. Two pleasing dimples, the places for which were just marked when she came, played, shadowy, in her freshening cheeks when she smiled and nodded good-morning to me from the schoolhouse steps.

I am afraid I did the greater part of the talking. At any rate, if I should try to report all that I said during the first half-dozen walks we took together, I fear that I might receive a gentle hint from my friends the publishers, that a separate volume, at my own risk and expense, would be the proper method of bringing them before the public.

I would have a woman as true as Death. At the first real lie which works from the heart outward, she should be tenderly chloroformed into a better world, where she can have an angel for a governess, and feed on strange fruits which will make her all over again, even to her bones and marrow.—Whether gifted with the accident of beauty or not, she should have been molded in the rose-red clay of Love, before the breath of life made a moving mortal of her. Love capacity is a congenital endowment; and I think, after a while, one gets to know the warm-hued natures it belongs to from the pretty pipe-clay counterfeits of it.—Proud she may be, in the sense of respecting herself; but pride, in the sense of contemning others less gifted than herself, deserves the two lowest circles of a vulgar woman's Inferno, where the punishments are Smallpox and Bankruptcy.—She who nips off the end of a brittle courtesy, as one breaks the tip of an icicle, to bestow upon those whom she ought cordially and kindly to recognize, proclaims the fact that she comes not merely of low blood, but of bad blood. Consciousness of unquestioned position makes people gracious in proper measure to all; but if a woman puts on airs with her real equals, she has something about herself or her family she is ashamed of, or ought to be. Middle, and more than middle-aged people, who know family histories, generally see through it. An official of standing was rude to me once. Oh, that is the maternal grandfather,—said a wise old friend to me,—he was a boor.—Better too few words, from the woman we love, than too many: while she is silent, Nature is working for her; while she talks, she is working for herself.—Love is sparingly soluble in the words of men; therefore they speak much of it; but one syllable of woman's speech can dissolve more of it than a man's heart can hold.

Whether I said any or all of these things to the schoolmistress or not,—whether I stole them out of Lord Bacon,—whether I cribbed them from Balzac,—whether I dipped them from the

VI—139

ocean of Tupperian wisdom,—or whether I have just found them in my head, laid there by that solemn fowl, Experience (who, according to my observation, cackles oftener than she drops real, live eggs),—I cannot say. Wise men have said more foolish things,—and foolish men, I don't doubt, have said as wise things. Anyhow, the schoolmistress and I had pleasant walks and long talks, all of which I do not feel bound to report.

You are a stranger to me, Ma'am.—I don't doubt you would like to know all I said to the schoolmistress.—I shan't do it;—I had rather get the publishers to return the money you have invested in this. Besides, I have forgotten a good deal of it. I shall tell only what I like of what I remember.

My idea was, in the first place, to search out the picturesque spots which the city affords a sight of, to those who have eyes. I know a good many, and it was a pleasure to look at them in company with my young friend. There were the shrubs and flowers in the Franklin Place front-yards or borders; commerce is just putting his granite foot upon them. Then there are certain small seraglio gardens, into which one can get a peep through the crevices of high fences,—one in Myrtle Street, or backing on it,—here and there one at the North and South Ends. Then the great elms in Essex Street. Then the stately horse-chestnuts in that vacant lot in Chambers Street, which hold their outspread hands over your head (as I said in my poem the other day), and look as if they were whispering, "May grace, mercy, and 'peace be with you!" and the rest of that benediction. Nay, there are certain patches of ground, which, having lain neglected for a time, Nature, who always has her pockets full of seeds, and holes in all her pockets, has covered with hungry plebeian growths, which fight for life with each other, until some of them get broad-leaved and succulent, and you have a coarse vegetable tapestry which Raphael would not have disdained to spread over the fore-ground of his masterpiece. The Professor pretends that he found such a one in Charles Street, which, in its dare-devil impudence of rough-and-tumble vegetation, beat the pretty-behaved flower beds of Public Garden as ignominiously as a group of young tatterdemalions playing pitch-and-toss beats a row of Sunday School boys with their teacher at their head.

But then the Professor has one of his burrows in that region, and puts everything in high colors relating to it. That is his way about everything.—I hold any man cheap,—he said,—of

whom nothing stronger can be uttered than that all his geese are swans.— How is that, Professor? said I;—I should have set you down for one of that sort. —Sir, said he, I am proud to say that Nature has so far enriched me, that I cannot own so much as a duck without seeing in it as pretty a swan as ever swam the basin in the garden of Luxembourg. And the Professor showed the whites of his eyes devoutly, like one returning thanks after a dinner of many courses.

I don't know anything sweeter than this leaking in of Nature through all the cracks in the walls and floors of cities. You heap up a million tons of hewn rocks on a square mile or two of earth which was green once. The trees look down from the hillsides and ask each other, as they stand on tiptoe, "What are these people about?" And the small herbs at their feet look up and whisper back, "We will go and see." So the small herbs pack themselves up in the least possible bundles, and wait until the wind steals to them at night, and whispers,—"Come with me." Then they go softly with it into the great city,—one to a cleft in the pavement, one to a spout on the roof, one to a seam in the marbles over a rich gentleman's bones, and one to the grave without a stone where nothing but a man is buried,—and there they grow, looking down on the generations of men from moldy roofs, looking up from between the less-trodden pavements, looking out through iron cemetery railings. Listen to them, when there is only a light breath stirring, and you will hear them saying to each other, "Wait awhile!" The words run along the telegraph of the narrow green lines that border the roads leading from the city, until they reach the slope of the hills, and the trees repeat in low murmurs to each other, "Wait awhile!" By and by the flow of life in the streets ebbs, and the old leafy inhabitants— the smaller tribes always in front—saunter in, one by one, very careless seemingly, but very tenacious, until they swarm so that the great stones gape from each other with the crowding of their roots, and the feldspar begins to be picked out of the granite to find them food. At last the trees take up their solemn line of march, and never rest until they have encamped in the market place. Wait long enough and you will find an old doting oak hugging a huge worn block in its yellow underground arms; that was the corner stone of the statehouse. Oh, so patient she is, this imperturbable Nature!

—Let us cry!—

But all this has nothing to do with my walks and talks with the schoolmistress. I did not say that I would not tell you something about them. Let me alone, and I shall talk to you more than I ought to, probably. We never tell our secrets to people that pump for them.

Books we talked about, and education. It was her duty to know something of these, and of course she did. Perhaps I was somewhat more learned than she, but I found that the difference between her reading and mine was like that of a man's and a woman's dusting a library. The man flaps about with a bunch of feathers; the woman goes to work softly with a cloth. She does not raise half the dust, nor fill her own eyes and mouth with it,—but she goes into all the corners and attends to the leaves as much as the covers. Books are the negative pictures of thought, and the more sensitive the mind that receives their images, the more nicely the finest lines are reproduced. A woman (of the right kind), reading after a man, follows him as Ruth followed the reapers of Boaz, and her gleanings are often the finest of the wheat.

But it was in talking of life that we came most nearly together. I thought I knew something about that,—that I could speak or write about it somewhat to the purpose.

To take up this fluid earthly being of ours as a sponge sucks up water,—to be steeped and soaked in its realities as a hide fills its pores lying seven years in a tan pit,—to have winnowed every wave of it as a mill wheel works up the stream that runs through the flume upon its float boards,—to have curled up in the keenest spasms and flattened out in the laxest languors of this breathing sickness which keeps certain parcels of matter uneasy for three or four score years,—to have fought all the devils and clasped all the angels of its delirium, and then, just at the point when the white-hot passions have cooled down to cherry red, plunge our experience into the ice-cold stream of some human language or other, one might think would end in a rhapsody with something of spring and temper in it. All this I thought my power and province.

The schoolmistress had tried life too. Once in a while one meets with a single soul greater than all the living pageant that passes before it. As the pale astronomer sits in his study, with sunken eyes and thin fingers, and weighs Uranus or Neptune as in a balance, so there are meek, slight women who have weighed all this planetary life can offer, and hold it like a bauble in the palm of their slender hands. This was one of them. Fortune had left her, sorrow had baptized her; the routine of labor and the loneliness of almost friendless city life were before her. Yet, as I looked upon her tranquil face, gradually regaining a cheerfulness that was often sprightly, as she became interested in the various matters we talked about and places we visited, I saw that eye and lip and every shifting lineament were made for love, —unconscious of their sweet office as yet, and meeting the cold aspect of Duty with the natural graces which were meant for the reward of nothing less than the Great Passion.

I never spoke one word of love to the schoolmistress in the course of these pleasant walks. It seemed to me that we talked of everything but love on that particular morning. There was, perhaps, a little more timidity and hesitancy on my part than I have commonly shown among our people at the boarding house. In fact, I considered myself the master at the breakfast-table; but, somehow, I could not command myself just then so well as usual. The truth is, I had secured a passage to Liverpool in the steamer which was to leave at noon, with the condition, however, of being released in case circumstances occurred to detain me. The schoolmistress knew nothing about all this, of course, as yet.

It was on the Common that we were walking. The mall, or boulevard of our Common, you know, has various branches leading from it in different directions. One of these runs downward from opposite Joy Street southward across the whole length of the Common to Boylston Street. We called it the long path, and were fond of it.

I felt very weak, indeed (though of a tolerably robust habit), as we came opposite the head of this path on that morning. I think I tried to speak twice without making myself distinctly audible. At last I got out the question,—Will you take the long path with me?—Certainly,—said the schoolmistress,—with much pleasure.—Think,—I said,—before you answer; if you take the long path with me now, I shall interpret it that we are to part no more!—The schoolmistress stepped back with a sudden movement, as if an arrow had struck her.

One of the long granite blocks used as seats was hard by,— the one you may still see close by the Gingko-tree.— Pray, sit down,—I said.— No, no,— she answered, softly; I will walk the long path with you!

The old gentleman who sits opposite met us walking, arm in arm, about the middle of the long path, and said very charmingly, " Good-morning, my dears!"

Complete. From "The Autocrat of the Breakfast-Table."

ON DANDIES

DANDIES are not good for much, but they are good for something. They invent or keep in circulation those conversational blank checks or counters, which intellectual capitalists may sometimes find it worth their while to borrow of them. They are useful, too, in keeping up the standard of dress, which, but for them, would deteriorate, and become, what some old fools would have it, a matter of convenience, not of taste and art. Yes, I like dandies well enough,— on one condition.

What is that, sir?— said the divinity student.

That they have pluck. I find that lies at the bottom of all true dandyism. A little boy dressed up very fine, who puts his finger in his mouth and takes to crying, if other boys make fun of him, looks very silly. But if he turns red in the face and knotty in the fists, and makes an example of the biggest of his assailants, throwing off his fine Leghorn and his thickly-buttoned jacket, if necessary, to consummate the act of justice, his small toggery takes on the splendors of the crested helmet that frightened Astyanax. You remember that the Duke said his dandy officers were his best officers. The "Sunday blood," the supersuperb sartorial equestrian of our annual fast day, is not imposing or dangerous. But such fellows as Brummel and D'Orsay and Byron are not to be snubbed quite so easily. Look out for "la main de fer sous le gant de velours" (which I printed in English the other day without quotation marks, thinking whether any *scarabæus criticus* would add this to his globe and roll in glory with it into the newspapers,— which he didn't do it, in the charming pleonasm of the London language, and therefore I claim the sole merit of exposing the same). A good many powerful and dangerous people have had a decided dash of dandyism about them. There was Alcibiades, the "curled son of Clinias," an accomplished young man, but what would be called a "swell" in these days. There was Aristoteles, a very distinguished writer,

of whom you have heard,— a philosopher in short, whom it took centuries to learn, centuries to unlearn, and is now going to take a generation or more to learn over again. Regular dandy, he was. So was Marcus Antonius; and though he lost his game, he played for big stakes, and it wasn't his dandyism that spoiled his chance. Petrarca was not to be despised as a scholar or a poet, but he was one of the same sort. So was Sir Humphry Davy, so was Lord Palmerston, formerly, if I am not forgetful. Yes, —a dandy is good for something as such; and dandies such as I was just speaking of have rocked this planet like a cradle,— aye, and left it swinging to this day.

From "The Autocrat of the Breakfast-Table."

ON "CHRYSO-ARISTOCRACY"

WE ARE forming an aristocracy, as you may observe, in this country,— not a *gratia-Dei*, nor a *jure-divino* one,— but a *de-facto* upper stratum of being, which floats over the turbid waves of common life like the iridescent film you may have seen spreading over the water about our wharves,— very splendid, though its origin may have been tar, tallow, train oil, or other such unctuous commodities. I say, then, we are forming an aristocracy; and, transitory as its individual life often is, it maintains itself tolerably, as a whole. Of course, money is its corner stone. But now observe this. Money kept for two or three generations transforms a race—I don't mean merely in manners and hereditary culture, but in blood and bone. Money buys air and sunshine, in which children grow up more kindly, of course, than in close, back streets, it buys country places to give them happy and healthy summers, good nursing, good doctoring, and the best cuts of beef and mutton. When the spring chickens come to market— I beg your pardon,— that is not what I was going to speak of. As the young females of each successive season come on, the finest specimens among them, other things being equal, are apt to attract those who can afford the expensive luxury of beauty. The physical character of the next generation rises in consequence. It is plain that certain families have in this way acquired an elevated type of face and figure, and that in a small circle of city connections one may sometimes find models of both sexes which one of the rural counties would

find it hard to match from all its townships put together. Because there is a good deal of running down, of degeneration and waste of life, among the richer classes, you must not overlook the equally obvious fact I have just spoken of,— which in one or two generations more will be, I think, much more patent than just now.

The weak point in our chryso-aristocracy is the same I have alluded to in connection with cheap dandyism. Its thorough manhood, its high-caste gallantry, are not so manifest as the plate glass of its windows and the more or less legitimate heraldry of its coach panels. It is very curious to observe of how small account military folks are held among our Northern people. Our young men must gild their spurs, but they need not win them. The equal division of property keeps the younger sons of rich people above the necessity of military service. Thus the army loses an element of refinement, and the moneyed upper class forgets what it is to count heroism among its virtues. Still I don't believe in any aristocracy, without pluck as its backbone. Ours may show it when the time comes, if it ever does come. These United States furnish the greatest market for intellectual green fruit of all the places in the world. I think so, at any rate. The demand for intellectual labor is so enormous and the market so far from nice, that young talent is apt to fair like unripe gooseberries,— get plucked to make a fool of. Think of a country which buys eighty thousand copies of the " Proverbial Philosophy," while the author's admiring countrymen have been buying twelve thousand! How can one let his fruit hang in the sun until it gets fully ripe, while there are eighty thousand such hungry mouths ready to swallow it and proclaim its praises? Consequently, there never was such a collection of crude pippins and half-grown windfalls as our native literature displays among its fruits. There are literary greengroceries at every corner, which will buy anything, from a button-pear to a pineapple. It takes long apprenticeship to train a whole people to reading and writing. The temptation of money and fame is too great for young people. Do I not remember that glorious moment when the late Mr. ——, we won't say who,— editor of the ——, we won't say what, offered me the sum of fifty cents per double-columned quarto page for shaking my young boughs over his foolscap apron? Was it not an intoxicating vision of gold and glory? I should doubtless have reveled in its wealth and splendor, but for learning the fact that the fifty cents was to be considered a rhetorical embellishment and by no means a literal expression of past fact or present intention.

Beware of making your moral staple consist of the negative virtues. It is good to abstain, and teach others to abstain, from all that is sinful or hurtful. But making a business of it leads to emaciation of character, unless one feed largely also on the more nutritious diet of active sympathetic benevolence.

From « The Autocrat of the Breakfast-
Table.»

THOMAS HOOD

(1798–1845)

THOMAS HOOD, the most inveterate of all punsters and the most pathetic of English poets, was born in London, May 23d, 1798. He was intended for an engraver, and before giving up the idea of following that trade he had developed a faculty for drawing caricatures which almost spoiled him as an essayist. As a result of it, he illustrated his sketches and finally came into a totally depraved habit of writing sketches for his illustrations — as when he would construct a disquisition on « Van Diemen's Land » in order to introduce a picture of an immigrant family, with « demons » swarming around them. If he wrote of Shakespeare it would be to introduce a picture of a matron of severe and menacing aspect, armed with the forces of maternity and explained by the quotation: " An eye like Ma's (Mars) to threaten and command." This is so characteristic of the prose of " Hood's Own " that it is not worth while to attempt to detach the text from the punning pictures. It is on such jests, some of them forced when he was exceedingly sorrowful, that Hood's reputation as a humorist chiefly depends. As a poet, he is one of the truest and tenderest who have ever written English. He died May 3d, 1845. His last lingering illness was glorified by the production of " The Bridge of Sighs," written, it has been said, when he was already more than half in heaven.

AN UNDERTAKER

AN UNDERTAKER is an ill-willer to the human race. He is by profession an enemy to his Species, and can no more look kindly at his fellows than the Sheriff's officer; for why? — his profit begins with an arrest for the Debt of Nature! As the Bailiff looks on a failing man, so doth he, and with the same hope, namely, to take the body.

Hence hath he little sympathy with his kind, small pity for the poor, and least of all for the widow and the orphans, whom he regards, Planter like, but as so many blacks on his estate. If he have any community of Feeling, it is with the Sexton, who

has likewise a percentage on the bills of mortality, and never sees a picture of health but he longs to engrave it. Both have the same quick ear for a churchyard cough, and both the same relish for the same music, to wit, the toll of Saint Sepulchre. Moreover both go constantly in black, — howbeit 'tis no mourning suit, but a livery, — for he grieves no more for the defunct than the bird of the same plumage that is the undertaker to a dead horse.

As a neighbor he is to be shunned. To live opposite to him is to fall under the evil eye. Like the witch that forespeaks other cattle, he would rot you as soon as look at you, if it could be done at a glance; but that magic being out of date, he contents himself with choosing the very spot on the house front that shall serve for a hatchment. Thenceforward he watches your going out and your coming in; your rising up and your lying down, and all your domestic imports of drink and victual, so that the veriest she gossip in the parish is not more familiar with your modes and means of living, nor knows so certainly whether the Visitor, that calls daily in his chariot, is a mere friend or a physician. Also he knows your age to a year, and your height to an inch, for he has measured you with his eye for a coffin, and your ponderosity to a pound, for he hath an interest in the dead weight, and hath so far inquired into your fortune as to guess with what equipage you shall travel on your last journey. For, in professional curiosity, he is truly a Pall Pry. Wherefore to dwell near him is as melancholy as to live in view of a churchyard; to be within sound of his hammering is to hear the knocking at Death's door.

To be friends with an undertaker is as impossible as to be the crony of a crocodile. He is by trade a hypocrite, and deals of necessity in mental reservations and equivoques. Thus he drinks to your good health, but hopes, secretly, it will not endure. He is glad to find you so hearty — as to be apoplectic; and rejoices to see you so stout — with a short neck. He bids you beware of your old gout — and recommends a quack doctor. He laments the malignant fever so prevalent — and wishes you may get it. He compliments your complexion — when it is blue or yellow; admires your upright carriage — and hopes it will break down. Wishes you good day, but means everlasting night; and commends his respects to your father and mother — but hopes you do not

honor them. In short, his good wishes are treacherous; his inquiries are suspicious; and his civilities are dangerous; as when he proffereth the use of his coach — or to see you home.

For the rest, he is still at odds with humanity; at constant issue with its Naturalists, and its philanthropists, its sages, its counselors, and its legislators. For example, he praises the weather — with the wind at east; and rejoices in a wet Spring and Fall, for Death and he reap with one sickle, and have a good or a bad harvest in common. He objects not to bones in bread (being as it were his own diet), nor to ill drugs in beer, nor to sugar of lead or arsenical finings in wine, nor to ardent spirits, nor to interment in churches. Neither doth he discountenance the sitting on infants; nor the swallowing of plum stones; nor of cold ices at hot balls; nor the drinking of embrocations, nay he hath been known to contend that the wrong dose was the right one. He approves, contra the Physicians, of a damp bed and wet feet — of a hot head and cold extremities, and lends his own countenance to the natural smallpox, rather than encourage vaccination — which he calls flying in the face of Providence. Add to these a free trade in poisons, whereby the Oxalic crystals may currently become proxy for the epsom ones; and the corrosive sublimate as common as salt in porridge. To the same end he would give unto every cockney a privilege to shoot, within ten miles around London, without a taxed license, and would never concur in a fine or deodand for fast driving, except the vehicle were a hearse. Thus, whatever the popular cry he runs counter; a heretic in opinion, and a hypocrite in practice, as when he pretends to be sorrowful at a Funeral; or, what is worse, affects to pity the ill-paid poor, and yet helpeth to screw them down.

To conclude, he is a personage of ill presage to the house of life; a raven on the chimney pot — a dead watch in the wainscot. — a winding sheet in the candle. To meet with him is ominous. His looks are sinister; his dress is lugubrious; his speech is prophetic; and his touch is mortal. Nevertheless, he hath one merit, and in this our world, and in these our times, it is a main one; namely, that whatever he undertakes he performs.

Complete.

THE MORNING CALL

I CANNOT conceive any prospect more agreeable to a weary traveler than the approach to Bedfordshire. Each valley reminds him of Sleepy Hollow; the fleecy clouds seem like blankets; the lakes and ponds are clean sheets; the setting sun looks like a warming pan. He dreams of dreams to come. His traveling cap transforms to a nightcap; the coach lining feels softlier squabbed; the guard's horn plays "Lullaby." Every flower by the roadside is a poppy. Each jolt of the coach is but a drowsy stumble upstairs. The lady opposite is the chambermaid; the gentleman beside her is Boots. He slides into imaginary slippers; he winks and nods flirtingly at Sleep, so soon to be his own. Although the wheels may be rattling into vigilant Wakefield, it appears to him to be sleepy Ware, with its great bed, a whole county of down, spread "all before him where to choose his place of rest."

It was in a similar mood, after a long, dusty, droughty dogday's journey, that I entered the Dolphin at Bedhampton. I nodded in at the door; winked at the lights; blinked at the company in the coffeeroom; yawned for a glass of negus; swallowed it with my eyes shut, as though it had been "a pint of nappy"; surrendered my boots; clutched a candlestick; and blundered, slipshod, up the stairs to number nine.

Blessed be the man, says Sancho Panza, who first invented sleep; and blessed be heaven that he did not take out a patent and keep his discovery to himself. My clothes dropped off me; I saw through a drowsy haze the likeness of a four-poster; "Great Nature's second course" was spread before me; and I fell to without a long grace!

> Here's a body — there's a bed!
> There's a pillow — here's a head!
> There's a curtain — here's a light!
> There's a puff — and so Good-Night!

It would have been gross improvidence to waste more words on the occasion, for I was to be roused up again at four o'clock the next morning to proceed by the early coach. I determined, therefore, to do as much sleep within the interval as I could; and in a minute, short measure, I was with that mandarin, Morpheus, in his Land of Nod.

How intensely we sleep when we are fatigued! Some as sound as tops, others as fast as churches. For my own part I must have slept as fast as a Cathedral,— as fast as Young Rapid wished his father to slumber;— nay, as fast as the French veteran who dreams over again the whole Russian campaign while dozing in his sentry box. I must have slept as fast as a fast post coach in my four-poster — or rather I must have slept "like winkin," for I seemed hardly to have closed my eyes when a voice cried, "Sleep no more!"

It was that of Boots, calling and knocking at the door, whilst through the keyhole a ray of candlelight darted into my chamber.

"Who's there?"

"It's me, your honor, I humbly ax pardon — but somehow I've overslept myself, and the coach be gone by!"

"The devil it is!— then I have lost my place!"

"No, not exactly, your honor. She stops a bit at the Dragon, t'other end of the town; and if your honor wouldn't object to a bit of a run —"

"That's enough — come in. Put down the light — and take up that bag — my coat over your arm — and waistcoat with it — and that cravat."

Boots acted according to orders. I jumped out of bed — pocketed my nightcap — screwed on my stockings — plunged into my trousers — rammed my feet into wrong right and left boots — tumbled down the back stairs — burst through a door, found myself in the fresh air of the stable yard holding a lantern, which, in sheer haste, or spleen, I pitched into the horsepond. Then began the race, during which I completed my toilet, running and firing a verbal volley at Boots, as often as I could spare breath for one.

"And you call this waking me up — for the coach?— My waistcoat!— Why I could wake myself — too late — without being called. Now my cravat — and be hanged to you!— Confound that stone!— and give me my coat. A nice road for a run.— I suppose you keep it — on purpose. How many gentlemen — may you do a week? — I'll tell you what. If I — run — a foot — further —"

I paused for wind, while Boots had stopped of his own accord. We had turned a corner into a small square; and on the opposite side certainly stood an inn with the sign of the Dragon, but without any sign of a coach at the door. Boots stood beside me, aghast, and surveying the house from the top to the bottom; not a wreath

of smoke came from the chimney; the curtains were closed over every window, and the door was closed and shuttered. I could hardly contain my indignation when I looked at the infernal somnolent visage of the fellow, hardly yet broad awake — he kept rubbing his black-lead eyes with his hands, as if he would have rubbed them out.

"Yes, you may well look — you have overslept yourself with a vengeance. The coach must have passed an hour ago — and they have all gone to bed again!"

"No, there be no coach, sure enough," soliloquized Boots, slowly raising his eyes from the road, where he had been searching for the track of recent wheels, and fixing them with a deprecating expression on my face. "No, there's no coach — I ax a thousand pardons, your honor — but you see, sir, what with waiting on her, and talking on her, and expecting on her, and giving notice on her, every night of my life, your honor — why I sometimes dreams on her — and that's the case as is now!"

Complete.

THEODORE HOOK

(1788–1841)

THEODORE EDWARD HOOK, one of the great "wits" of the times of the Georges, left little that belongs to permanent literature. His celebrity rests largely on his "improvisations," but in his essays, sketches, and novels there are frequent flashes of the brilliancy which made him such a favorite at court that he was appointed Governor of Mauritius, where he remained from 1812 to 1817. As a result of a defalcation for which he may not have been responsible, he was recalled to England and imprisoned. Some of his best work was done in jail; and he would have been fortunate had he remained there, as on his release he spent the rest of his life largely in the attempt to work all day and drink all night,— dying as a result of it, August 24th, 1841, "done up in purse, in mind, and in body too," as he said of himself just before his death. It is said that he is the original of Thackeray's "Mr. Wagg."

ON CERTAIN ATROCITIES OF HUMOR

THERE is one class of people who, with a depravity of appetite not excelled by that of the celebrated Anna Maria Schurman, who rejoiced in eating spiders, thirst after puns. If you fall in with these, you have no resource but to indulge them to their hearts' content; but, in order to rescue yourself from the imputation of believing punning to be wit, quote the definition of Swift, and be, like him, as inveterate a punster as you possibly can, immediately after resting everything, and hazarding all, upon the principle that the worse the pun the better.

In order to be prepared for this sort of *punic* war (for the disorder is provocative and epidemic), the moment any one gentleman or lady has, as they say in Scotland, "let a pun," everybody else in the room who can, or cannot do the same, sets to work to endeavor to emulate the example. From that period all rational conversation is at an end, and a jargon of nonsense succeeds, which lasts till the announcement of coffee, or supper, or the carriages, puts a happy termination to the riot.

Addison says, "One may say of a pun as the countryman described his nightingale, that it is *vox et præterea nihil*, a sound, and nothing but a sound"; and in another place he tells us that "the greatest authors in their most serious works make frequent use of puns; the sermons of Bishop Andrews, and the tragedies of Shakespeare are full of them; if a sinner was punned into repentance as in the latter, nothing is more usual than to see a hero weeping and grumbling for a dozen lines together"; but he also says, "it is indeed impossible to kill a weed which the soil has a natural disposition to produce. The seeds of punning are in the minds of all men, and though they may be subdued by reason, reflection, and good sense, they will be very apt to shoot up in the greatest genius that is not broken and cultivated by the rules of art."

Here is something like a justification of the enormity; and, as the pupil is to mix in all societies, he may as well be prepared.

Puns may be divided into different classes; they may be made in different ways, introduced by passing circumstances, or by references to bygone events; they may be thrown in anecdotically, or conundrumwise. It is to be observed that feeling, or pity, or commiseration, or grief are not to stand in the way of a pun — that personal defects are to be made available, and that sense, so as the sound answers, has nothing to do with the business.

If a man is pathetically describing the funeral of his mother, or sister, or wife, it is quite allowable to call it a "black-*burying* party," or to talk of a "fit of *coffin*"; a weeping relative struggling to conceal his grief may be likened to a commander of "*private tears*"; throw in a joke about the phrase of "funerals *performed*," and a re-*hearsal;* and wind up with the anagram *real-fun*, funeral.

I give this instance first, in order to explain that nothing, however solemn the subject, is to stand in the way of a pun.

It is allowable, when you have run a subject dry in English, to hitch in a bit of any other language which may sound to your liking. For instance, on a fishing party. You say fishing is out of your *line;* yet, if you did not keep *a float*, you would deserve a *rod;* and if anybody affects to find fault with your joke, exclaim, "Oh, vous *bête!*" There you have *line, rod, float,*

VI—140

and *bait* ready to your hand. Call two noodles from the city in a punt, endeavoring to catch small fry, "*East Angles*"; or, if you please, observe that "the *punters* are losing the fish," "catching nothing but a cold," or that "the fish are too deep for them." Call the Thames a "*tidy*" river; but say you prefer the *Isis* in hot weather.

Personal deformities or constitutional calamities are always to be laid hold of. If anybody tells you that a dear friend has lost his sight, observe that it will make him more hospitable than ever, since now he would be glad *to see anybody*. If a clergyman break his leg, remark that he is no longer a clergyman, but a *lame man*. If a poet is seized with apoplexy, affect to disbelieve it, although you know it to be true, in order to say: —

"*Poeta nascitur non 'fit'*";

and then, to carry the joke one step further, add, "that it is not a *fit* subject for a jest." A man falling into a tanpit you may call "sinking in the *sublime*"; a climbing boy suffocated in a chimney meets with a *sootable* death; and a pretty girl having caught the smallpox is to be much *pitted*. On the subject of the ear and its defects, talk first of something in which *a cow sticks*, and end by telling the story of the man who, having taken great pains to explain something to his companion, at last got into a rage at his apparent stupidity, and exclaimed: "Why, my dear sir, don't you comprehend? The thing is as plain as A, B, C." "I dare say it is," said the other; "but I am D, E, F."

It may be as well to give the beginner something of a notion of the use he may make of the most ordinary words for the purposes of quibbleism. For instance, in the way of observation: — The loss of a hat is always *felt;* if you don't like sugar, you may *lump* it; a glazier is a *panes*-taking man; candles are burnt because *wick*-ed things always come to *light;* a lady who takes you home from a party is kind in her *carriage*, and you say *nunc est ridendum* when you step into it; if it happen to be a chariot, she is a *charitable* person; birds' nests and king-killing are synonymous, because they are *high trees on;* a Bill for building a bridge should be sanctioned by the Court of *Arches* as well as the House of *Piers;* when a man is dull, he goes to the seaside to *Brighton;* a Cockney lover, when sentimental, should

live in *Heigh Hoburn;* the greatest fibber is the man most to *re-lie* upon; a dean expecting a bishopric looks *for lawn;* a suicide kills pigs, and not himself; a butcher is a gross man, but a fig seller is a *grocer;* Joshua never had a father or mother, because he was the son of *Nun;* your grandmother and your great-grandmother were your *aunt's sisters;* a leg of mutton is better than Heaven, because nothing is better than Heaven, and a leg of mutton is better than nothing.

Races are matters of *course*. An ass never can be a horse, although he may be a *mayor;* the Venerable Bede was the mother of Pearl; a baker makes bread when he *kneads* it; a doctor cannot be a doctor all at once, because he comes to it by *degrees;* a man hanged at Newgate has taken a *drop* too much; the *bridle* day is that on which a man leads a woman to the *halter;* never mind the aspirate; punning's all fair, as the archbishop said in the dream.

Puns interrogatory are at times serviceable. You meet a man carrying a hare: ask him if it is his own *hare*, or a wig? — there you stump him. Why is Parliament Street like a compendium? Because it goes to *a bridge*. Why is a man murdering his mother in a garret a worthy person? Because he is above, committing a crime. Instances of this kind are innumerable; and if you want to render your question particularly pointed, you are, after asking it once or twice, to say, "D'ye give it up?" — then favor your friends with the solution.

Puns scientific are effective whenever a scientific man or men are in company, because, in the first place, they invariably hate puns, especially those which are capable of being twisted into jokes which have no possible relation to the science of which the words to be joked upon are terms; and because, in the next place, dear, laughing girls, who are wise enough not to be sages, will love you for disturbing the self-satisfaction of the philosophers, and raising a laugh or titter at their expense.

Where there are three or four geologists of the party, if they talk of their scientific tours made to collect specimens, call the old ones "ninny-hammers," and the young ones "chips of the old block"; and then inform them that claret is the best specimen of *quartz* in the world. If you fall in with a botanist who is holding forth, talk of the quarrels of flowers as a sequel to the loves of the plants, and say they decide their differences with

pistols. In short, sacrifice everything to the pursuit of punning, and, in the course of time, you will acquire such a reputation for waggery, that the whole company will burst into an immoderate fit of laughing if you only ask the servants for bread, or say "No" to the offer of a cutlet.

Complete.

RICHARD HOOKER

(c. 1553–1600)

HOOKER was once esteemed and studied as a great theologian, but his prose is now valued chiefly as a model of style. It moves with a graceful and easy rhythm, the cadences of which are governed by such a melodious tone succession as is found only in the masters of language. He was born in Exeter, England, c. 1553, and educated for the Church at Oxford, where he obtained a Fellowship in 1577. His most celebrated work, « Of the Laws of Ecclesiastical Polity,» is not intended to be entertaining, but it has much in it that is stimulating to the mind and delightful to the ear of all who love beauty of thought and language. Hooker died at Bishopsbourne, England, November 2d, 1600.

THE LAW WHICH ANGELS DO WORK BY

BUT now that we may lift up our eyes (as it were) from the footstool to the throne of God, and leaving these natural, consider a little the state of heavenly and divine creatures; touching angels, which are spirits immaterial and intellectual, the glorious inhabitants of those sacred palaces, where nothing but light and blessed immortality, no shadow of matter for tears, discontentments, griefs, and uncomfortable passions to work upon, but all joy, tranquillity, and peace, even forever and ever doth dwell; as in number and order they are huge, mighty, and royal armies, so likewise in perfection of obedience unto that law, which the Highest, whom they adore, love, and imitate, hath imposed upon them, such observants they are thereof, that our Savior himself being to set down the perfect idea of that which we are to pray and wish for on earth, did not teach to pray or wish for more than only that here it might be with us, as with them it is in heaven. God, which moveth more natural agents as an efficient only, doth otherwise move intellectual creatures, and especially his holy angels; for beholding the face of God, in admiration of so great excellency they all adore him; and being

---

rapt with the love of his beauty, they cleave inseparably forever unto him. Desire to resemble him in goodness maketh them unweariable and even unsatiable in their longing to do by all means all manner of good unto all the creatures of God, but especially unto the children of men; in the countenance of whose nature, looking downward, they behold themselves beneath themselves; even as upward, in God, beneath whom themselves are, they see that character which is nowhere but in themselves and us resembled. Thus far even the painims have approached; thus far they have seen into the doings of the angels of God; Orpheus confessing that the fiery throne of God is attended on by those most industrious angels, careful how all things are performed amongst men; and the mirror of human wisdom plainly teaching that God moveth angels, even as that thing doth stir man's heart, which is thereinto presented amiable. Angelical actions may therefore be reduced unto these three general kinds: first, most delectable love arising from the visible apprehension of the purity, glory, and beauty of God, invisible saving only unto spirits that are pure; second, adoration grounded upon the evidence of the greatness of God, on whom they see how all things depend; third, imitation bred by the presence of his exemplary goodness, who ceaseth not before them daily to fill heaven and earth with the rich treasures of most free and undeserved grace.

Of angels we are not to consider only what they are and do in regard of their own being, but that also which concerneth them as they are linked into a kind of corporation amongst themselves, and of society or fellowship with men. Consider angels each of them severally in himself, and their law is that which the prophet David mentioneth, « All ye his angels praise him.» Consider the angels of God associated, and their law is that which disposeth them as an army, one in order and degree above another. Consider finally the angels as having with us that communion which the Apostle to the Hebrews noteth, and in regard whereof angels have not disdained to profess themselves our « fellow-servants »; from hence there springeth up a third law, which bindeth them to works of ministerial employment. Every one of which, their several functions, are by them performed with joy.

A part of the angels of God, notwithstanding (we know), have fallen, and that their fall hath been through the voluntary breach

---

of that law, which did require at their hands continuance in the exercise of their high and admirable virtue. Impossible it was that ever their will should change or incline to remit any part of their duty, without some object having force to avert their conceit from God, and to draw it another way; and that they attained that high perfection of bliss, wherein now the elect angels are without possibility of falling. Of anything more than of God they could not by any means like, as long as whatsoever they knew besides God they apprehended it not in itself without dependency upon God; because so long God must needs seem infinitely better than anything which they could so apprehend. Things beneath them could not in such sort be presented unto their eyes, but that therein they must needs see always how those things did depend on God. It seemeth, therefore, that there was no other way for angels to sin, but by reflex of their understanding upon themselves; when being held with admiration of their own sublimity and honor, the memory of their subordination unto God and their dependency on him was drowned in this conceit; whereupon their adoration, love, and imitation of God could not choose but be also interrupted. The fall of angels therefore was pride. Since their fall their practices have been the clean contrary unto those before mentioned. For being dispersed, some in the air, some on the earth, some in the water, some among the minerals, dens, and caves, that are under the earth; they have by all means labored to effect a universal rebellion against the laws, and as far as in them lieth utter destruction of the works of God. These wicked spirits the heathen honored instead of gods, both generally under the name of dii inferi, « gods infernal,» and particularly some in oracles, some in idols, some as household gods, some as nymphs; in a word, no foul and wicked spirit which was not one way or other honored of men as God, till such time as light appeared in the world and dissolved the works of the Devil. Thus much, therefore, may suffice for angels, the next unto whom in degree are men.

« Of the Laws of Ecclesiastical Polity,»
Book I., Chap. iv. Complete.

EDUCATION AS A DEVELOPMENT OF THE SOUL

IN THE matter of knowledge, there is between the angels of God and the children of men this difference; angels already have full and complete knowledge in the highest degree that can be imparted unto them; men, if we view them in their spring, are at the first without understanding or knowledge at all. Nevertheless from this utter vacuity they grow by degrees, till they come at length to be even as the angels themselves are. That which agreeth to the one now, the other shall attain unto in the end; they are not so far disjoined and severed but that they come at length to meet. The soul of man being therefore at the first as a book, wherein nothing is and yet all things may be imprinted, we are to search by what steps and degrees it riseth unto perfection of knowledge.

Unto that which hath been already set down concerning natural agents this we must add, that albeit therein we have comprised as well creatures living as void of life, if they be in degree of nature beneath men, nevertheless a difference we must observe between those natural agents that work altogether unwittingly, and those which have, though weak, yet some understanding what they do, as fishes, fowls, and beasts have. Beasts are in sensible capacity as ripe even as men themselves, perhaps more ripe. For as stones, though in dignity of nature inferior unto plants, yet exceed them in firmness of strength or durability of being; and plants, though beneath the excellency of creatures endued with sense, yet exceed them in the faculty of vegetation and of fertility; so beasts, though otherwise behind men, may, notwithstanding, in actions of sense and fancy go beyond them; because the endeavors of nature, when it hath a higher perfection to seek, are in lower the more remiss, not esteeming thereof so much as those things do, which have no better proposed unto them.

The soul of man, therefore, being capable of a more divine perfection, hath (besides the faculties of growing unto sensible knowledge which is common unto us with beasts) a further ability, whereof in them there is no show at all, the ability of reaching higher than unto sensible things. Till we grow to some ripeness of years, the soul of man doth only store itself with conceits of things of inferior and more open quality, which afterwards do serve as instruments unto that which is greater; in the meanwhile above the reach of meaner creatures it ascendeth not. When once it comprehendeth anything above this, as the differences of time, affirmations, negations, and contradictions in speech, we then count it to have some use of natural reason. Whereunto if afterwards there might be added the right helps of true art and learning (which helps, I must plainly confess, this age of the world, carrying the name of a learned age, doth neither much know nor greatly regard), there would, undoubtedly, be almost as great difference in maturity of judgment between men therewith inured, and that which now men are, as between men that are now and innocents. Which speech if any condemn, as being over hyperbolical, let them consider but this one thing: no art is at the first finding out so perfect as industry may after make it; yet the very first man that to any purpose knew the way we speak of and followed it hath alone thereby performed more very near in all parts of natural knowledge than sithence in any one part thereof the whole world besides hath done.

In the poverty of that other new devised aid, two things there are notwithstanding singular. Of marvelous quick dispatch it is, and doth show them that have it as much almost in three days as if it dwell threescore years with them. Again, because the curiosity of man's wit doth many times with peril wade further in the search of things than were convenient, the same is thereby restrained into such generalities as everywhere offering themselves are apparent unto men of the weakest conceit what need be. So as following the rules and precepts thereof, we may define it to be an art which teacheth the way of speedy discourse, and restraineth the mind of man that it may not wax otherwise.

Education and instruction are the means, the one by use, the other by precept, to make our natural faculty of reason both the better and the sooner able to judge rightly between truth and error, good and evil. But at what time a man may be said to have attained so far forth the use of reason, as sufficeth to make him capable of those laws, whereby he is then bound to guide his actions, this is a great deal more easy for common sense to discern than for any man by skill and learning to determine; even as it is not in philosophers, who best know the nature both of fire and of gold, to teach what degree of the one will serve to purify the other, so well as the artisan who doth this by fire discerneth by sense when the fire hath that degree of heat which sufficeth for his purpose.

"Of the Laws of Ecclesiastical Polity,"
Book I., Chap. vi. Complete.

JOHN HUGHES
(1677–1720)

JOHN HUGHES, a frequent contributor to the Spectator, Tatler, and Guardian, was born in Wiltshire, England, January 29th, 1677. He wrote much both in prose and verse, and was so well thought of that he had Johnson for a biographer. In later times, however, he has been forgotten even by the makers of encyclopædias, justifying the opinions of Swift and Pope in his own day. His "Poems on Several Occasions, with Select Essays in Prose" appeared in 1735. The book is long out of print, but as a pupil of Addison and a contributor to the Spectator, Hughes cannot be overlooked by students of the literature of Queen Anne's reign. He wrote a number of plays which did not succeed, and when on February 17th, 1720, his "Siege of Damascus" was being warmly applauded at Drury Lane Theatre, where it had "made a hit," he was dying. "What he wanted in genius he made up as an honest man," Pope said of him.

THE WONDERFUL NATURE OF EXCELLENT MINDS

——*Tentanda via est, quâ me quoque possim*
Tollere humo, victorque virum volitare per ora.
— *Virg.* Georg., III. 9.

New ways I must attempt, my groveling name
To raise aloft, and wing my flight to fame.
— *Dryden.*

IT is a remark, made, as I remember, by a celebrated French author, that no man ever pushed his capacity as far as it was able to extend. I shall not inquire whether this assertion be strictly true. It may suffice to say that men of the greatest application and acquirements can look back upon many vacant spaces, and neglected parts of time, which have slipped away from them unemployed; and there is hardly any one considering person in the world but is apt to fancy with himself, at some time or other, that if his life were to begin again he could fill it up better.

The mind is most provoked to cast on itself this ingenuous reproach, when the examples of such men are presented to it as have far outshot the generality of their species in learning, arts, or any valuable improvements.

One of the most extensive and improved geniuses we have had any instance of in our own nation, or in any other, was that of Sir Francis Bacon, Lord Verulam. This great man, by an extraordinary force of nature, compass of thought, and indefatigable study, had amassed to himself such stores of knowledge as we cannot look upon without amazement. His capacity seemed to have grasped all that was revealed in books before his time; and, not satisfied with that, he began to strike out new tracks of science, too many to be traveled over by any one man in the compass of the longest life. These, therefore, he could only mark down, like imperfect coastings on maps, or supposed points of land, to be further discovered and ascertained by the industry of after ages, who should proceed upon his notices or conjectures.

The excellent Mr. Boyle was the person who seems to have been designed by nature to succeed to the labors and inquiries of that extraordinary genius I have just mentioned. By innumerable experiments, he in a great measure filled up those plans and outlines of science which his predecessor had sketched out. His life was spent in the pursuit of nature through a great variety of forms and changes, and in the most rational as well as devout adoration of its Divine Author.

It would be impossible to name many persons who have extended their capacities so far as these two, in the studies they pursued; but my learned readers on this occasion will naturally turn their thoughts to a third, who is yet living, and is likewise the glory of our own nation. The improvements which others had made in natural and mathematical knowledge have so vastly increased in his hands as to afford at once a wonderful instance how great the capacity is of a human soul, and inexhaustible the subject of its inquiries; so true is that remark in Holy Writ that "though a wise man seek to find out the works of God from the beginning to the end, yet shall he not be able to do it."

I cannot help mentioning here one character more of a different kind, indeed, from these, yet such an one as may serve to show the wonderful force of nature and of application, and is the most singular instance of an universal genius I have ever met with. The person I mean is Leonardo da Vinci, an Italian painter,

---

descended from a noble family in Tuscany, about the beginning of the sixteenth century. In his profession of history painting he was so great a master, that some have affirmed he excelled all who went before him. It is certain that he raised the envy of Michael Angelo, who was his contemporary, and that from the study of his works Raphael himself learned his best manner of designing. He was a master, too, in sculpture and architecture, and skillful in anatomy, mathematics, and mechanics. The aqueduct from the river Adda to Milan is mentioned as a work of his contrivance. He had learned several languages, and was acquainted with the studies of history, philosophy, poetry, and music. Though it is not necessary to my present purpose, I cannot but take notice that all who have writ of him mention likewise his perfection of body. The instances of his strength are almost incredible. He is described to have been of a well-formed person, and a master of all genteel exercises. And, lastly, we are told that his moral qualities were agreeable to his natural and intellectual endowments, and that he was of an honest and generous mind, adorned with great sweetness of manners. I might break off the account of him here, but I imagine it will be an entertainment to the curiosity of my readers, to find so remarkable a character distinguished by as remarkable a circumstance at his death. The fame of his works having gained him an universal esteem, he was invited to the court of France, where, after some time, he fell sick; and Francis I. coming to see him, he raised himself in his bed to acknowledge the honor which was done him by that visit. The king embraced him, and Leonardo, fainting in the same moment, expired in the arms of that great monarch.

It is impossible to attend to such instances as these without being raised into a contemplation on the wonderful nature of a human mind, which is capable of such progressions in knowledge, and can contain such a variety of ideas without perplexity or confusion. How reasonable is it from hence to infer its divine original! And whilst we find unthinking matter endued with a natural power to last forever, unless annihilated by Omnipotence, how absurd would it be to imagine that a being so much superior to it should not have the same privilege!

At the same time it is very surprising when we remove our thoughts from such instances as I have mentioned, to consider those we so frequently meet with in the accounts of barbarous nations among the Indians; where we find numbers of people who scarce show the first glimmerings of reason, and seem to have few ideas above those of sense and appetite. These, methinks, appear like large wilds, or vast uncultivated tracts of human nature; and when we compare them with men of the most exalted characters in arts and learning, we find it difficult to believe that they are creatures of the same species.

Some are of opinion that the souls of men are all naturally equal, and that the great disparity we so often observe arises from the different organization or structure of the bodies to which they are united. But whatever constitutes this first disparity, the next great difference which we find between men in their several acquirements is owing to accidental differences in their education, fortunes, or course of life. The soul is a kind of rough diamond, which requires art, labor, and time to polish it. For want of which many a good natural-genius is lost, or lies unfashioned, like a jewel in the mine.

One of the strongest incitements to excel in such arts and accomplishments as are in the highest esteem among men is the natural passion which the mind of man has for glory; which, though it may be faulty in the excess of it, ought by no means to be discouraged. Perhaps some moralists are too severe in beating down this principle, which seems to be a spring implanted by nature to give motion to all the latent powers of the soul, and is always observed to exert itself with the greatest force in the most generous dispositions. The men whose characters have shone the brightest among the ancient Romans appear to have been strongly animated by this passion. Cicero, whose learning and services to his country are so well known, was inflamed by it to an extravagant degree, and warmly presses Lucceius, who was composing a history of those times, to be very particular and zealous in relating the story of his consulship; and to execute it speedily, that he might have the pleasure of enjoying in his lifetime some part of the honor which he foresaw would be paid to his memory. This was the ambition of a great mind; but he is faulty in the degree of it, and cannot refrain from soliciting the historian upon this occasion to neglect the strict laws of history, and, in praising him, even to exceed the bounds of truth. The younger Pliny appears to have had the same passion for fame, but accompanied with greater chasteness and modesty. His ingenious manner of owning it to a friend, who had prompted him to undertake some great work, is exquisitely beau-

tiful, and raises him to a certain grandeur above the imputation of vanity. "I must confess," says he, "that nothing employs my thoughts more than the desire I have of perpetuating my name; which in my opinion is a design worthy of a man, at least of such an one, who, being conscious of no guilt, is not afraid to be remembered by posterity."

I think I ought not to conclude without interesting all my readers in the subject of this discourse: I shall therefore lay it down as a maxim, that though all are not capable of shining in learning or the politer arts, yet every one is capable of excelling in something. The soul has in this respect a certain vegetative power which cannot lie wholly idle. If it is not laid out and cultivated into a regular and beautiful garden, it will of itself shoot up in weeds or flowers of a wilder growth.

Complete. Number 554 of the
Spectator.

VICTOR HUGO

(1802-1885)

VICTOR MARIE HUGO was born at Besançon, France, February 26th, 1802. He died at Paris, May 22d, 1885, and into his eighty-three years he crowded so much of emotion and effort that the temptation to call him the most representative product of the nineteenth century is hard to resist. He was certainly the greatest Frenchman of the century. France has produced no greater poet in any age. As a political orator he was surpassed among Frenchmen only by Mirabeau,—if, indeed, it be true that Mirabeau himself surpassed him. As a dramatist, he ranks with Voltaire, and there is good ground for the claim of his admirers that his «Les Miserables» is the "greatest novel ever written." As an essayist, he works chiefly through his novels. The greatness of idea which makes «Les Miserables» what it is is not developed wholly through the plot, but to a degree through essays with which it is interspersed. In some English translations these essays are nearly all omitted, without seeming to affect the value of the story. But Hugo wished to make the book something more than a mere story. To him it is an expression of the great tragedy of human life and, to develop it, he uses the art not merely of the novelist, but of the epic poet, the orator, and the philosopher.

The essays of his «Choses Vues» take a wholly different form. They are graphic sketches in which he projects his ideas as objectively as if they were thrown on a screen by a magic lantern. The natural mode of expression always pleased him best. Like all great artists, he was repelled by the merely abstract. To him abstraction seemed to lead, not towards truth, but away from it. To escape negation he sought to reveal truth as it is revealed in nature,—in an infinite diversity of object lessons, each harmonized with the rest by a subtle law of all-pervading unity. He was vain and often theatrical, but he loved what was noble and hated what was base so deeply that when examples of heroic courage as a manifestation of the intellectual life are sought for, his name will not be forgotten while that of Alcæus is remembered.

W. V. B.

THE END OF TALLEYRAND'S BRAIN

IN THE Rue Saint-Florentin there are a palace and a sewer.

The palace, which is of a rich, handsome, and gloomy style of architecture, was long called Hotel de l'Infantado; nowadays may be seen on the frontal of its principal doorway Hotel Talleyrand. During the forty years that he resided in this street, the last tenant of this palace never, perhaps, cast his eyes upon this sewer.

He was a strange, redoubtable, and important personage; his name was Charles Maurice de Perigord; he was of noble descent like Machiavelli, a priest like Gondi, unfrocked like Fouché, witty like Voltaire, and lame like the devil. It might be averred that everything in him was lame like himself; the nobility which he had placed at the service of the Republic, the priesthood which he had dragged through the parade ground, then cast into the gutter, the marriage which he had broken off through a score of exposures and a voluntary separation, the understanding which he disgraced by acts of baseness.

This man, nevertheless, had grandeur; the splendors of the two régimes were united in him; he was Prince de Vaux in the kingdom of France, and a Prince of the French Empire. During thirty years, from the interior of his palace, from the interior of his thoughts, he had almost controlled Europe. He had permitted himself to be on terms of familiarity with the Revolution, and had smiled upon it; ironically, it is true, but the Revolution had not perceived this. He had come in contact with, known, observed, penetrated, influenced, set in motion, fathomed, bantered, inspired all the men of his time, all the ideas of his time, and there had been moments in his life when, holding in his hand the four or five great threads which moved the civilized universe, he had for his puppet Napoleon I., Emperor of the French, King of Italy, Protector of the Confederation of the Rhine, Mediator of the Swiss Confederation. That is the game which was played by this man.

After the Revolution of July, the old race, of which he was the high chamberlain, having fallen, he found himself once more on his feet, and said to the people of 1830, seated bare-armed upon a heap of paving stones, "Make me your embassador!"

He received the confession of Mirabeau and the first confidence of Thiers. He said of himself that he was a great poet, and that he had composed a trilogy in three dynasties: Act I., the Empire of Bonaparte; Act II., the House of Bourbon; Act III., the House of Orleans.

He did all this in his palace, and in this palace, like a spider in his web, he allured and caught in succession, heroes, thinkers, great men, conquerors, kings, princes, emperors, Bonaparte, Sieyès, Madame de Stael, Châteaubriand, Benjamin Constant, Alexander of Russia, William of Prussia, Francis of Austria, Louis XVIII., Louis Philippe, all the gilded and glittering flies who buzz through the history of the last forty years. All this glistening throng, fascinated by the penetrating eye of this man, passed in turn under that gloomy entrance bearing upon the architrave the inscription Hotel Talleyrand.

Well, the day before yesterday, May 17th, 1838, this man died. Doctors came and embalmed the body. To do this they, like the Egyptians, removed the bowels from the stomach and the brain from the skull. The work done, after having transformed the Prince de Talleyrand into a mummy, and nailed down this mummy in a coffin, lined with white satin, they retired leaving upon a table the brain — that brain which had thought so many things, inspired so many men, erected so many buildings, led two revolutions, duped twenty kings, held the world. The doctors being gone, a servant entered; he saw what they had left; Hulloa! they have forgotten this. What was to be done with it? It occurred to him that there was a sewer in the street; he went there, and threw the brain into the sewer.

Complete. From "Things Seen."

THE DEATH OF BALZAC

ON THE eighteenth of August, 1850, my wife, who had been during the day to see Mme. de Balzac, told me that Balzac was dying. I hurried to him.

M. de Balzac had been suffering for eighteen months from hypertrophy of the heart. After the revolution of February he went to Russia, and there married. Some days before his departure I met him in the boulevard. He was then complaining, and breathing noisily. In May, 1850, he returned to France, married, rich, and dying! When he arrived his legs were already swollen. Four doctors held a consultation. One of them, M. Louis, told

VI—141

me on the sixth of July, "He has not six weeks to live." It is the same disease that killed Frederic Soulie.

On August 18th my uncle, General Louis Hugo, was dining with me. As soon as the table was cleared I left, and took a cab to the Avenue Fortunee (No. 14), in the Quartier Beaujon, where M. de Balzac lived. He had purchased what remained of the mansion of M. de Beaujon, some portion having escaped demolition. He had furnished it magnificently, and made it a very pretty little house, having a carriage entrance in the Avenue Fortunee, and for garden a long and narrow court, in which the pavement was here and there cut into flower beds.

I rang. The moon was up, but obscured by clouds. The street was deserted. No one came. I rang again. The door opened. A servant appeared with a candle. "What do you want, sir?" she asked. She was crying.

I told her my name. She ushered me into a room on the ground floor, in which, on a console opposite the chimney-piece, was a colossal bust of Balzac by David. A wax candle was burning upon a splendid table in the centre of the salon, and which had for feet six statuettes, gilt with the purest gold.

Another woman, who was also crying, came and said, "He is dying. Madame has gone to her own room. The doctors have not been here since yesterday. He has a wound in the left leg. Gangrene has set in. The doctors do not know what to do; they say that dropsy is a continuous dropsy, an infiltration. That is what they call it; that the skin and the flesh are like lard, and that it is impossible to tap him. Last month, when going to bed, master ran against a decorated piece of furniture and tore the skin of his leg, and all the water in the body ran out. The doctors were much astonished, and since then they have made puncturations. They said, 'Imitate nature.' But an abscess of the limb has supervened. M. Roux operated. Yesterday they removed the dressing; the wound, instead of having suppurated, was red, dry, and burning. Then they said, 'He is lost,' and they have never returned. Four or five have been sent for in vain. Every one said, 'It is no use.' He had a bad night This morning at nine Monsieur could not speak. Madame sent for a priest; he came, and has given Monsieur extreme unction. One hour after he shook the hand of his sister, Madame de Surville. Since eleven o'clock the rattle has been in his throat, and he can see no longer. He will not live through the night. If

you wish, sir, I will go and look for M. de Surville, who has not yet retired."

The woman left me. I waited for some minutes. The candle scarcely lighted the room, its splendid furniture and fine pictures by Porbus and Holbein. The marble bust showed vaguely in the gloom like the spectre of the man who was dying. A corpse-like smell pervaded the house.

M. de Surville entered and confirmed all that the servant had said. I requested to see M. de Balzac.

We proceeded along a corridor, ascended a staircase covered with red carpet and laden with objects of art — vases, statues, pictures, credence tables — and then another corridor, and I perceived an open door. I heard a loud and sinister rattling noise. I was in the death chamber of Balzac.

A bed stood in the middle of the room, a mahogany bedstead having a suspensory arrangement at the head and foot for the convenience of moving the invalid. M. de Balzac was in this bed, his head supported on a pile of pillows, to which had been added the red damask cushions from the sofa. His face was purple, almost black, and drawn to the right side; his beard untrimmed, his gray hair cut short, his eyes fixed and open. I saw him in profile, and thus he resembled the Emperor.

An old woman, — the nurse, — and a man servant stood at each side of the bed; a candle was burning behind the head of the bed upon a table, another upon the drawers near the door. A silver vase was placed on the night table. This man and this woman stood silent in fear, and listened to the death rattle of the invalid.

The candle behind the bed lighted up brightly the portrait of a young man, ruddy and smiling, hanging near the fireplace.

An insupportable smell issued from the bed. I lifted the counterpane and took the hand of Balzac. It was clammy. I pressed it. He did not respond to the pressure.

This was the same room in which I had come to see him a month previously. He was then cheerful, full of hope, having no doubt of his recovery, showing his swelled limb, and laughing. We had a long conversation and a political dispute. He called me his demagogue. He was a Legitimist. He said to me, "How have you so quietly renounced the title of Peer of France, the best after that of King of France?" He also said: "I have the house of M. de Beaujon without the garden, but with the

seat in the little church at the corner of the street. A door in my staircase opens into this church, one turn of the key and I can hear mass. I think more of the seat than of the garden." When I was about to leave him he conducted me to this staircase with difficulty, and showed me the door, and then he called out to his wife, "Mind you show Hugo all my pictures."

The nurse said to me, "He will die at daybreak."

I came down stairs again, bearing in mind the livid face. Crossing the dining room, I found the bust immovable, impassible, haughty, vaguely radiant, and I compared death with immortality.

When I reached home it was Sunday. I found many people awaiting me, among others Riza-Bey, the Turkish Chargé d'Affaires; Navarette, the Spanish poet; and the Count Arrivabene, the exiled Italian. I said to them, "Gentlemen, Europe is on the point of losing a great soul."

He died in the night. He was fifty-one years old.

They buried him on Wednesday.

He lay first in the Beaujon Chapel, and he was carried thither by the door, the key of which was more precious to him than all the beautiful gardens of the former "Fermier General."

Giraud took his portrait on the very day of his death. They wished to mold his mask, but could not; decomposition was too rapid. The day after his death, in the morning, the modelers who came found his face deformed and the nose fallen upon the cheek. They put him in an oak and lead coffin.

The service was performed at Saint-Philippe du Roule. As I stood by the coffin I remembered that there my second daughter had been baptized, and I had not been in the church since. In our memories death touches birth.

The Minister of the Interior, Baroche, came to the funeral. He was seated by me in church, near the bier, and from time to time he spoke to me. He said, "He was a distinguished man." I replied, "He was a genius."

The procession traversed Paris and went by way of the boulevard to Père La Chaise. A few drops of rain fell when we were leaving the church and when we reached the cemetery. It was one of those days on which it seems that the heavens must shed tears.

We walked all the way. I proceeded in front of the coffin, holding one of the silver tassels of the pall; Alexander Dumas was on the other side.

When we came to the grave, which was some distance up the hill, we found an immense crowd. The road was rough and narrow; the horses had some difficulty in pulling the hearse, which rolled back again. I found myself imprisoned between a wheel and a tomb, and was very nearly crushed. The spectators who were standing on the tomb helped me up.

The coffin was lowered into the grave, which is close to those of Charles Nodier and of Casimir Delavigne. The priest said the last prayer, and I spoke a few words. As I was speaking the sun set. All Paris appeared in the distance enveloped in the splendid haze of the setting orb. The earth began to fall into the grave almost at my feet, and I was interrupted by the dull sound of the clods dropping on the coffin.

Complete. From "Things Seen."

A RETROSPECT

I HAVE had for friends and allies, I have seen successively pass before me, and according to the changes and chances of destiny, I have received into my house, sometimes in intimacy, chancellors, peers, dukes, Pasquier, Pontécoulant, Montalembert, Bellune; and celebrated men, Lamennais, Lamartine, Châteaubriand; Presidents of the Republic, Manin; leaders of revolution, Louis Blanc, Montanelli, Arago, Heliade; leaders of the people, Garibaldi, Mazzini, Kossuth, Mieroslawski; artists, Rossini, David d'Angers, Pradier, Meyerbeer, Eugène Delacroix; marshals, Soult, Mackau; sergeants, Boni, Heurtebise; bishops, the Cardinal of Besançon, M. de Rohan, the Cardinal of Bordeaux, M. Donnet; and comedians, Frédéric Lemaître, Mlle. Rachel, Mlle. Mars, Mme. Dorval, Macready; ministers and embassadors, Molé, Guizot, Thiers, Lord Palmerston, Lord Normanby, M. de Ligne; and of peasants, Charles Durand; princes, Imperial and Royal Highnesses and plain Highnesses, such as the Duke of Orleans, Ernest of Saxe-Coburg, the Princess of Canino, Louis Charles Pierre, and Napoleon Bonaparte; and of shoemakers, Guay; of kings and emperors, Jerome of Westphalia, Max of Bavaria, the Emperor of Brazil; and of thorough revolutionists, Bourillon. I have had sometimes in my hands the gloved and white palm of the upper class and the heavy black hand of the lower class, and have recognized that both are but men. After all these have

passed before me, I say that Humanity has a synonym — Equality; and that under heaven there is but one thing we ought to bow to — Genius; and only one thing before which we ought to kneel — Goodness.

Complete. From "Things Seen."

WATERLOO — "QUOT LIBRAS IN DUCE"

THE battle of Waterloo is an enigma as obscure for those who gained it as for him who lost it. To Napoleon it is a panic; Blucher sees nothing in it but fire; Wellington does not understand it at all. Look at the reports: the bulletins are confused; the commentaries are entangled; the latter stammer, the former stutter. Jomini divides the battle of Waterloo into four moments; Muffling cuts it into three acts; Charras, although we do not entirely agree with him in all his appreciations, has alone caught with his haughty eye the characteristic lineaments of this catastrophe of human genius contending with divine chance. All the other historians suffer from a certain bedazzlement in which they grope about. It was a flashing day, in truth the overthrow of the military monarchy which, to the great stupor of the kings, has dragged down all kingdoms, the downfall of strength and the rout of war.

In this event, which bears the stamp of superhuman necessity, men play but a small part; but if we take Waterloo from Wellington and Blucher, does that deprive England and Germany of anything? No. Neither illustrious England nor august Germany is in question in the problem of Waterloo, for, thank heaven! nations are great without the mournful achievements of the sword. Neither Germany, nor England, nor France is held in a scabbard; at this day when Waterloo is only a clash of sabres, Germany has Goethe above Blucher, and England Byron above Wellington. A mighty dawn of ideas is peculiar to our age; and in this dawn England and Germany have their own magnificent flash. They are majestic because they think; the high level they bring to civilization is intrinsic to them; it comes from themselves, and not from an accident. Any aggrandizement the nineteenth century may have cannot boast of Waterloo as its fountain head; for only barbarous nations grow suddenly after a victory — it is the transient vanity of torrents swollen by a storm. Civilized nations, espe-

cially at the present day, are not elevated or debased by the good or evil fortune of a captain, and their specific weight in the human family results from something more than a battle. Their honor, dignity, enlightenment, and genius, are not numbers which those gamblers, heroes, and conquerors can stake in the lottery of battles. Very often a battle lost is progress gained, and less of glory, more of liberty. The drummer is silent and reason speaks; it is the game of who loses wins. Let us, then, speak of Waterloo coldly from both sides, and render to chance the things that belong to chance, and to God what is God's. What is Waterloo — a victory? No; a quine in the lottery, won by Europe, and paid by France; it was hardly worth while erecting a lion for it.

Waterloo, by the way, is the strangest encounter recorded in history; Napoleon and Wellington are not enemies, but contraries. Never did God, who delights in antitheses, produce a more striking contrast, or a more extraordinary confrontation. On one side precision, foresight, geometry, prudence, a retreat assured, reserves prepared, an obstinate coolness, an imperturbable method, strategy profiting by the ground, tactics balancing battalions, carnage measured by a plumb line, war regulated watch in hand, nothing left voluntarily to accident, old classic courage and absolute correctness. On the other side we have intuition, divination, military strangeness, superhuman instinct, a flashing glance; something that gazes like the eagle and strikes like lightning, all the mysteries of a profound mind, association with destiny; the river, the plain, the forest, and the hill summoned, and to some extent, compelled to obey, the despot going so far as even to tyrannize over the battlefield; faith in a star, blended with strategic science, heightening, but troubling it. Wellington was the Bareme of war, Napoleon was its Michael Angelo, and this true genius was conquered by calculation. On both sides somebody was expected; and it was the exact calculator who succeeded. Napoleon waited for Grouchy, who did not come; Wellington waited for Blucher, and he came.

Wellington is the classical war taking its revenge; Bonaparte, in his dawn, had met it in Italy, and superbly defeated it — the old owl fled before the young vulture. The old tactics had been not only overthrown, but scandalized. Who was this Corsican of six and twenty years of age? What meant this splendid ignoramus, who, having everything against him, nothing for him, with-

out provisions, ammunition, guns, shoes, almost without an army, with a handful of men against masses, dashed at allied Europe, and absurdly gained impossible victories? Who was this new comer of war who possessed the effrontery of a planet? The academic military school excommunicated him, while bolting, and hence arose an implacable rancor of the old Cæsarism against the new, of the old sabre against the flashing sword, and of the chessboard against genius. On June 18th, 1815, this rancor got the best; and beneath Lodi, Montebello, Montenotte, Mantua, Marengo, and Arcola, it wrote — Waterloo. It was a triumph of Mediocrity, sweet to majorities, and destiny consented to this irony. In his decline, Napoleon found a young Suvarov before him, — in fact, it is only necessary to blanch Wellington's hair in order to have a Suvarov. Waterloo is a battle of the first class, gained by a captain of the second.

What must be admired in the battle of Waterloo is England, the English firmness, the English resolution, the English blood, and what England had really superb in it, is (without offense) herself; it is not her captain, but her army. Wellington, strangely ungrateful, declares in his dispatch to Lord Bathurst, that his army, the one which fought on June 18th, 1815, was a "detestable army." What does the gloomy pile of bones buried in the trenches of Waterloo think of this? England has been too modest to herself in her treatment of Wellington, for making him so great is making herself small. Wellington is merely a hero, like any other man. The Scotch Grays, the Life Guards, Maitland and Mitchell's regiments, Pack and Kempt's infantry, Ponsonby and Somerset's cavalry, the Highlanders playing the bagpipes, under the shower of canister, Ryland's battalions, the fresh recruits who could hardly manage a musket, and yet held their ground against the old bands of Essling and Rivoli — all this is grand. Wellington was tenacious; that was his merit, and we do not deny it to him, but the lowest of his privates and his troopers was quite as solid as he, and the iron soldier is as good as the iron duke. For our part, all our glorification is offered to the English soldier, the English army, the English nation; and if there must be a trophy, it is to England that this trophy is owing. The Waterloo column would be more just, if, instead of the figure of a man, it raised to the clouds the statue of a people.

But this great England will be irritated by what we are writing here; for she still has feudal illusions, after her 1688, and the French 1789. This people believes in inheritance and hierarchy, and while no other excels it in power and glory, it esteems itself as a nation and not as a people. As a people, it readily subordinates itself, and takes a lord as its head; the workman lets himself be despised; the soldier puts up with flogging. It will be remembered that, at the battle of Inkermann, a sergeant who, as it appears, saved the British army, could not be mentioned by Lord Raglan, because the military hierarchy does not allow any hero below the rank of officer to be mentioned in dispatches. What we admire before all, in an encounter like Waterloo, is the prodigious skill of chance. The night raid, the wall of Hougomont, the hollow way of Chain, Grouchy deaf to the cannon, Napoleon's guide deceiving him, Bulow's guide enlightening him — all this cataclysm is marvelously managed.

Altogether, we will assert, there is more of a massacre than of a battle in Waterloo. Waterloo, of all pitched battles, is the one which had the smallest front for such a number of combatants. Napoleon's three-quarters of a league. Wellington's half a league, and seventy-two thousand combatants on either side. From this density came the carnage. The following calculation has been made and proportion established: loss of men, at Austerlitz, French, fourteen per cent.; Russian, thirty per cent.; Austrian, forty-four per cent.: at Wagram, French, thirteen per cent.; Austrian, fourteen per cent.: at Moskova, French, thirty-seven per cent.; Russian, forty-four per cent.: at Bautzen, French, thirteen per cent.; Russian and Prussian, fourteen per cent.: at Waterloo, French, fifty-six per cent.; allies, thirty-one per cent.: — total for Waterloo, forty-one per cent., or out of one hundred and forty-four thousand fighting men, sixty thousand killed.

The field of Waterloo has at the present day that calmness which belongs to the earth, and resembles all plains; but at night, a sort of visionary mist rises from it, and if any traveler walk about it, and listen and dream, like Virgil on the mournful plain of Philippi, the hallucination of the catastrophe seizes upon him. The frightful June 18th lives again, the false monumental hill is leveled, the wondrous lion is dissipated, the battlefield resumes its reality, lines of infantry undulate on the plain; furious galloping crosses the horizon; the startled dreamer sees the flash of sabres, the sparkle of bayonets, the red light of shells, the monstrous collision of thunderbolts; he hears, like a death groan from the tomb, the vague clamor of the phantom battle. These

shadows are grenadiers; these flashes are cuirassiers; this skeleton is Napoleon; this skeleton is Wellington; all this is nonexistent, and yet still combats, and the ravines are stained purple, and the trees rustle, and there is fury even in the clouds and in the darkness, while all the stern heights, Mont St. Jean, Hougomont, Frischemont, Papelotte, and Plancenoit, seem confusedly crowned by hosts of spectres exterminating one another.

Chapter xv. complete. From « Cosette »
in « Les Miserables. »

ALEXANDER VON HUMBOLDT

FRIEDRICH HEINRICH ALEXANDER BARON VON HUMBOLDT

(1769–1859)

HUMBOLDT was past seventy when he set himself seriously to the completion of the greatest work of his life, — his « Cosmos, » and he succeeded so well that the world at once accepted it as one of the greatest masterpieces of civilization. It has not lost in reputation with the passage of time. The severity of thought required to follow Humboldt's reasoning does not make an intellectual diversion of reading the « Cosmos, » but Humboldt had neither the desire to be entertaining nor the faculty of being so. In 1794 he wrote for Schiller's « Die Horen, » an allegorical essay, « The Rhodian Genius, » in what is an unmistakable attempt at high literary form. It is, perhaps, the only one Humboldt ever made, and it will not detract from his great reputation as a scientific teacher to confess the melancholy nature of its failure.

He was born at Berlin, September 14th, 1769. After study at Frankfort on the Oder, Göttingen, and other universities, he began a systematic attempt to acquire a juster and more comprehensive view of nature than was exhibited in the writings of the scientists and philosophers who had preceded him. The natural German tendency to lofty metaphysical exploration of the unseen universe, he steadfastly resisted. The « Cosmos » he explored was the humble world of the visible, and he counted nothing in it too low to be without infinite significance. When at last he realized his idea in the « Cosmos, » not only Germany, but all Europe, honored him as no scientific investigator had been honored since Newton. He deserved it, for if he made no astonishing actual discovery, he discovered new continents of possible achievement for those who were to carry on his work after him.

MAN

THE general picture of nature which I have endeavored to delineate would be incomplete if I did not venture to trace a few of the most marked features of the human race, considered with reference to physical gradations — to the geographical distribution of cotemporaneous types — to the influence exercised upon man by the forces of nature, and the reciprocal, although weaker action which he, in his turn, exercises on these natural forces. Dependent, although in a lesser degree than plants and animals, on the soil, and on the meteorological processes of the atmosphere with which he is surrounded — escaping more readily from the control of natural forces, by activity of mind and the advance of intellectual cultivation, no less than by his wonderful capacity of adapting himself to all climates — man everywhere becomes most essentially associated with terrestrial life. It is by these relations that the obscure and much-contested problem of the possibility of one common descent enters into the sphere embraced by a general physical cosmography. The investigation of this problem will impart a nobler, and, if I may so express myself, more purely human interest to the closing pages of this section of my work.

The vast domain of language, in whose varied structure we see mysteriously reflected the destinies of nations, is most intimately associated with the affinity of races; and what even slight differences of races may effect is strikingly manifested in the history of the Hellenic nations in the zenith of their intellectual cultivation. The most important questions of the civilization of mankind are connected with the ideas of races, community of language, and adherence to one original direction of the intellectual and moral faculties.

As long as attention was directed solely to the extremes in varieties of color and of form, and to the vividness of the first impression of the senses, the observer was naturally disposed to regard races rather as originally different species than as mere varieties. The permanence of certain types in the midst of the most hostile influences, especially of climate, appeared to favor such a view, notwithstanding the shortness of the interval of time from which the historical evidence was derived. In my opinion, however, more powerful reasons can be advanced in support of the theory of the unity of the human race, as, for instance, in the many intermediate gradations in the color of the skin and in the form of the skull, which have been made known to us in recent times by the rapid progress of geographical knowledge — the analogies presented by the varieties in the species of many wild and domesticated animals — and the more correct observations collected regarding the limits of fecundity in hybrids. The greater number of the contrasts which were formerly supposed to exist have disappeared before the laborious researches of Tiedemann on the brain of negroes and of Europeans, and the anatomical investigations of Vrolik and Weber on the form of the pelvis. On comparing the dark-colored African nations, on whose physical history the admirable work of Prichard has thrown so much light, with the races inhabiting the islands of the South Indian and West Australian archipelago, and with the Papuas and Alfourous (Haroforas, Endamenes), we see that a black skin, woolly hair, and a negro-like cast of countenance are not necessarily connected together. So long as only a small portion of the earth was known to the Western nations, partial views necessarily predominated, and tropical heat and a black skin consequently appeared inseparable. "The Ethiopians," said the ancient tragic poet Theodectes of Phaselis, "are colored by the near sun god in his course with a sooty lustre, and their hair is dried and crisped with the heat of his rays." The campaigns of Alexander, which gave rise to so many new ideas regarding physical geography, likewise first excited a discussion on the problematical influence of climate on races. "Families of animals and plants," writes one of the greatest anatomists of the day, Johannes Müller, in his noble and comprehensive work, "Physiologie des Menschen," "undergo, within certain limitations peculiar to the different races and species, various modifications in their distribution over the surface of the earth, propagating these variations as organic types of species. The present races of animals have been produced by the combined action of many different internal as well as external conditions, the nature of which cannot in all cases be defined, the most striking varieties being found in those families which are capable of the greatest distribution over the surface of the earth. The different races of mankind are forms of one sole species, by the union of two of whose members descendants are propagated. They are not different species of a genus, since in that case their hybrid descendants would remain unfruitful. But whether the human races

have descended from several primitive races of men, or from one alone, is a question that cannot be determined from experience."

Geographical investigations regarding the ancient seat, the so-called cradle of the human race, are not devoid of a mythical character. "We do not know," says Wilhelm von Humboldt, in an unpublished work, "On the Varieties of Languages and Nations," "either from history or from authentic tradition, any period of time in which the human race has not been divided into social groups. Whether the gregarious condition was original, or of subsequent occurrence, we have no historic evidence to show. The separate mythical relations found to exist independently of one another in different parts of the earth appear to refute the first hypothesis, and concur in ascribing the generation of the whole human race to the union of one pair. The general prevalence of this myth has caused it to be regarded as a traditionary record transmitted from the primitive man to his descendants. But this very circumstance seems rather to prove that it has no historical foundation, but has simply arisen from an identity in the mode of intellectual conception, which has everywhere led man to adopt the same conclusion regarding identical phenomena; in the same manner as many myths have doubtlessly arisen, not from any historical connection existing between them, but rather from an identity in human thought and imagination. Another evidence in favor of the purely mythical nature of this belief is afforded by the fact that the first origin of mankind — a phenomenon which is wholly beyond the sphere of experience — is explained in perfect conformity with existing views, being considered on the principle of the colonization of some desert island or remote mountainous valley at a period when mankind had already existed for thousands of years. It is in vain that we direct our thoughts to the solution of the great problem of the first origin, since man is too intimately associated with his own race and with the relations of time to conceive of the existence of an individual independently of a preceding generation and age. A solution of those difficult questions, which cannot be determined by inductive reasoning or by experience — whether the belief in this presumed traditional condition be actually based on historical evidence, or whether mankind inhabited the earth in gregarious associations from the origin of the race — cannot, therefore, be determined from philological data, and yet its elucidation ought not to be sought from other sources."

The distribution of mankind is, therefore, only a distribution into varieties, which are commonly designated by the somewhat indefinite term races. As in the vegetable kingdom, and in the natural history of birds and fishes, a classification into many small families is based on a surer foundation than where large sections are separated into a few but large divisions, so it also appears to me that in the determination of races a preference should be given to the establishment of small families of nations. Whether we adopt the old classification of my master, Blumenbach, and admit five races (the Caucasian, Mongolian, American, Ethiopian, and Malayan), or that of Prichard, into seven races (the Iranian, Turanian, American, Hottentots and Bushmen, Negroes, Papuas, and Alfourous), we fail to recognize any typical sharpness of definition, or any general or well-established principle in the division of these groups. The extremes of form and color are certainly separated, but without regard to the races, which cannot be included in any of these classes, and which have been alternately termed Scythian and Allophyllic. Iranian is certainly a less objectionable term for the European nations than Caucasian; but it may be maintained generally that geographical denominations are very vague when used to express the points of departure of races, more especially where the country which has given its name to the race, as, for instance, Turan (Mawerannahr), has been inhabited at different periods by Indo-Germanic and Finnish, and not by Mongolian tribes.

Languages, as intellectual creations of man, and as closely interwoven with the development of mind, are, independently of the national form which they exhibit, of the greatest importance in the recognition of similarities or differences in races. This importance is especially owing to the clew which a community of descent affords in treading that mysterious labyrinth in which the connection of physical powers and intellectual forces manifests itself in a thousand different forms. The brilliant progress made within the last half-century, in Germany, in philosophical philology, has greatly facilitated our investigations into the national character of languages and the influence exercised by descent. But here, as in all domains of ideal speculation, the dangers of deception are closely linked to the rich and certain profit to be derived.

Positive ethnographical studies, based on a thorough knowledge of history, teach us that much caution should be applied in

entering into these comparisons of nations, and of the languages employed by them at certain epochs. Subjection, long association, the influence of a foreign religion, the blending of races, even when only including a small number of the more influential and cultivated of the immigrating tribes, have produced, in both continents, similarly recurring phenomena; as, for instance, in introducing totally different families of languages among one and the same race, and idioms, having one common root, among nations of the most different origin. Great Asiatic conquerors have exercised the most powerful influence on phenomena of this kind.

But language is a part and parcel of the history of the development of mind; and, however happily the human intellect, under the most dissimilar physical conditions, may unfettered pursue a self-chosen track, and strive to free itself from the dominion of terrestrial influences, this emancipation is never perfect. There ever remains, in the natural capacities of the mind, a trace of something that has been derived from the influences of race or of climate, whether they be associated with a land gladdened by cloudless azure skies, or with the vapory atmosphere of an insular region. As, therefore, richness and grace of language are unfolded from the most luxuriant depths of thought, we have been unwilling wholly to disregard the bond which so closely links together the physical world with the sphere of intellect and of the feelings by depriving this general picture of nature of those brighter lights and tints which may be borrowed from considerations, however slightly indicated, of the relations existing between races and languages.

While we maintain the unity of the human species, we at the same time repel the depressing assumption of superior and inferior races of men. There are nations more susceptible of cultivation, more highly civilized, more ennobled by mental cultivation than others, but none in themselves nobler than others. All are in like degree designed for freedom; a freedom which, in the ruder conditions of society, belongs only to the individual, but which, in social states enjoying political institutions, appertains as a right to the whole body of the community. "If we would indicate an idea which, throughout the whole course of history, has ever more and more widely extended its empire, or which, more than any other, testifies to the much-contested and still more decidedly misunderstood perfectibility of the whole human race, it is that of establishing our common humanity — of striving to remove the barriers which prejudice and limited views of every kind have erected among men, and to treat all mankind, without reference to religion, nation, or color, as one fraternity, one great community, fitted for the attainment of one object, the unrestrained development of the physical powers. This is the ultimate and highest aim of society, identical with the direction implanted by nature in the mind of man toward the indefinite extension of his existence. He regards the earth in all its limits, and the heavens as far as his eye can scan their bright and starry depths, as inwardly his own, given to him as the objects of his contemplation, and as a field for the development of his energies. Even the child longs to pass the hills or the seas which inclose his narrow home; yet, when his eager steps have borne him beyond those limits, he pines, like the plant, for his native soil; and it is by this touching and beautiful attribute of man — this longing for that which is unknown, and this fond remembrance of that which is lost — that he is spared from an exclusive attachment to the present. Thus deeply rooted in the innermost nature of man, and even enjoined upon him by his highest tendencies, the recognition of the bond of humanity becomes one of the noblest leading principles in the history of mankind.»

With these words, which draw their charm from the depths of feeling, let a brother be permitted to close this general description of the natural phenomena of the universe. From the remotest nebulæ and from the revolving double stars, we have descended to the minutest organisms of animal creation, whether manifested in the depths of ocean or on the surface of our globe, and to the delicate vegetable germs which clothe the naked declivity of the ice-crowned mountain summit; and here we have been able to arrange these phenomena according to partially known laws; but other laws of a more mysterious nature rule the higher spheres of the organic world, in which is comprised the human species in all its varied conformation, its creative intellectual power, and the languages to which it has given existence. A physical delineation of nature terminates at the point where the sphere of intellect begins, and a new world of mind is opened to our view. It marks the limit, but does not pass it.

From Humboldt's «Cosmos.»

VI—142

DAVID HUME   2259

OF THE DIGNITY OR MEANNESS OF HUMAN NATURE

THERE are certain sects which secretly form themselves in the learned world as well as factions in the political; and though sometimes they come not to an open rupture, they give a different turn to the ways of thinking of those who have taken part on either side. The most remarkable of this kind are the sects founded on the different sentiments with regard to the dignity of human nature; which is a point that seems to have divided philosophers and poets as well as divines from the beginning of the world to this day. Some exalt our species to the skies, and represent man as a kind of human demigod, who derives his origin from heaven, and retains evident marks of his lineage and descent. Others insist upon the blind sides of human nature, and can discover nothing, except vanity, in which man surpasses the other animals, whom he affects so much to despise. If an author possess the talent of rhetoric and declamation, he commonly takes part with the former; if his turn lie towards irony and ridicule, he naturally throws himself into the other extreme.

I am far from thinking that all those who have depreciated our species have been enemies to virtue, and have exposed the frailties of their fellow-creatures with any bad intention. On the contrary, I am sensible that a delicate sense of morals, especially when attended with a splenetic temper, is apt to give a man a disgust of the world, and to make him consider the common course of human affairs with too much indignation. I must, however, be of opinion that the sentiments of those who are inclined to think favorably of mankind are more advantageous to virtue than the contrary principles, which give us a mean opinion of our nature. When a man is prepossessed with a high notion of his rank and character in the creation, he will naturally endeavor to act up to it, and will scorn to do a base or vicious action, which might sink him below that figure which he makes in his own imagination. Accordingly we find that all our polite and fashionable moralists insist upon this topic, and endeavor to represent vice as unworthy of man, as well as odious in itself.

We find few disputes that are not founded on some ambiguity in the expression; and I am persuaded that the present dispute,

DAVID HUME
(1711–1776)

HUME'S expectation of popularity from his "Essays" seems to have been modest, while from his "Treatise on Human Nature" he anticipated success which would make him at once one of the dictators of philosophical thought. To his intense disappointment, no one noticed the "Treatise," while the "Essays" gave him immediate reputation. It was so with nearly all the rest of what he esteemed his great works. His "Enquiry Concerning the Human Understanding" and his "Natural History of Religion" failed to reward him with the applause he expected, while his "History of England" was immediately accepted at a valuation at least as high as he himself had put upon it. He had, to a remarkable degree, what Sidney Smith called the Scotch love of "metapheesics," and if it brought him little besides opprobrium from his own generation, it has caused him to be studied by all subsequent generations with Locke and Berkeley as one of the few British philosophers whose opinions, right or wrong, are too important to be left out of consideration.

He was born in Edinburgh, April 26th, 1711. He studied at the university of his native city, but he owed his education more to himself than to scholastic training. His means were always limited and his life regular. He made a deliberate and successful attempt to suppress everything in himself which threatened to interfere with his work. His writings need not be defended against the attacks made upon them during his lifetime and since. But as far as he taught the scientific "skepticism," which means "looking" into all the phenomena of nature as the revelation of unity of purpose, he is entitled to be classed with those whose work made possible the educated scientific intellect of which the locomotive, the telegraph, and the electric motor are manifestations.

concerning the dignity or meanness of human nature, is not more exempt from it than any other. It may, therefore, be worth while to consider what is real and what is only verbal in this controversy.

That there is a natural difference between merit and demerit, virtue and vice, wisdom and folly, no reasonable man will deny; yet it is evident that in affixing the term, which denotes either our approbation or blame, we are commonly more influenced by comparison than by any fixed unalterable standard in the nature of things. In like manner, quantity and extension and bulk are by every one acknowledged to be real things; but when we call any animal great or little, we always form a secret comparison between that animal and others of the same species; and it is that comparison which regulates our judgment concerning its greatness. A dog and a horse may be of the very same size, while the one is admired for the greatness of its bulk and the other for the smallness. When I am present, therefore, at any dispute, I always consider with myself whether it be a question of comparison or not that is the subject of the controversy; and if it be, whether the disputants compare the same objects together, or talk of things that are widely different.

In forming our notions of human nature, we are apt to make a comparison between men and animals, the only creatures endowed with thought that fall under our senses. Certainly this comparison is favorable to mankind. On the one hand, we see a creature, whose thoughts are not limited by any narrow bounds, either of place or time; who carries his researches into the most distant regions of this globe, and beyond this globe, to the planets and heavenly bodies; looks backward to consider the first origin, at least, the history of the human race; casts his eye forward to see the influence of his action upon posterity, and the judgments which will be formed of his character a thousand years hence; a creature, who traces causes and effects to a great length and intricacy; extracts general principles from particular appearances; improves upon his discoveries; corrects his mistakes; and makes his very errors profitable. On the other hand, we are presented with a creature the very reverse of this; limited in its observations and reasonings to a few sensible objects which surround it; without curiosity, without foresight; blindly conducted by instinct, and attaining, in a short time, its utmost perfection, beyond which it is never able to advance a single step. What a wide difference is there between these creatures! And how exalted a notion must we entertain of the former, in comparison of the latter!

There are two means commonly employed to destroy this conclusion: 1. By making an unfair representation of the case, and insisting only upon the weaknesses of human nature. And, 2. By forming a new and secret comparison between man and beings of the most perfect wisdom. Among the other excellencies of man, this is one, that he can form an idea of perfections much beyond what he has experience of in himself; and is not limited in his conception of wisdom and virtue. He can easily exalt his notions, and conceive a degree of knowledge, which, when compared to his own, will make the latter appear very contemptible, and will cause the difference between that and the sagacity of animals, in a manner, to disappear and vanish. Now this being a point, in which all the world is agreed, that human understanding falls infinitely short of perfect wisdom, it is proper we should know when this comparison takes place, that we may not dispute where there is no real difference in our sentiments. Man falls much more short of perfect wisdom, and even of his own ideas of perfect wisdom, than animals do of man; yet the latter difference is so considerable, that nothing but a comparison with the former can make it appear of little moment.

It is also usual to compare one man with another; and finding very few whom we can call wise or virtuous, we are apt to entertain a contemptible notion of our species in general. That we may be sensible of the fallacy of this way of reasoning, we may observe that the honorable appellations of wise and virtuous are not annexed to any particular degree of those qualities of wisdom and virtue, but arise altogether from the comparison we make between one man and another. When we find a man, who arrives at such a pitch of wisdom as is very uncommon, we pronounce him a wise man: so that to say there are few wise men in the world is really to say nothing, since it is only by their scarcity that they merit that appellation. Were the lowest of our species as wise as Tully, or Lord Bacon, we should still have reason to say that there are few wise men. For in that case we should exalt our notions of wisdom, and should not pay a singular honor to any one, who was not singularly distinguished by his talents. In like manner, I have heard it observed by thoughtless

people, that there are few women possessed of beauty in comparison of those who want it, not considering that we bestow the epithet of "beautiful" only on such as possess a degree of beauty that is common to them with few. The same degree of beauty in a woman is called deformity, which is treated as real beauty in one of our sex.

As it is usual, in forming a notion of our species, to compare it with the other species above or below it, or to compare the individuals of the species among themselves, so we often compare together the different motives or actuating principles of human nature, in order to regulate our judgment concerning it. And, indeed, this is the only kind of comparison which is worth our attention, or decides anything in the present question. Were our selfish and vicious principles so much predominant above our social and virtuous, as is asserted by some philosophers, we ought undoubtedly to entertain a contemptible notion of human nature.

There is much of a dispute of words in all this controversy. When a man denies the sincerity of all public spirit or affection to a country and community, I am at a loss what to think of him. Perhaps he never felt this passion in so clear and distinct a manner as to remove all his doubts concerning its force and reality. But when he proceeds afterwards to reject all private friendship, if no interest or self-love intermix itself, I am then confident that he abuses terms, and confounds the ideas of things; since it is impossible for any one to be so selfish, or rather so stupid, as to make no difference between one man and another, and give no preference to qualities which engage his approbation and esteem. Is he also, say I, as insensible to anger as he pretends to be to friendship? And does injury and wrong no more affect him than kindness or benefits? Impossible. He does not know himself. He has forgotten the movements of his heart; or, rather, he makes use of a different language from the rest of his countrymen, and calls not things by their proper names. "What say you of natural affection?" I subjoin. "Is that also a species of self-love?" "Yes; all is self-love. Your children are loved only because they are yours. Your friend for a like reason. And your country engages you only so far as it has a connection with yourself. Were the idea of self removed, nothing would affect you. You would be altogether inactive and insensible. Or if you ever give yourself any movement, it would only be from vanity, and a desire of fame and reputation to this

same self." "I am willing," reply I, "to receive your interpretation of human actions, provided you admit the facts. That species of self-love, which displays itself in kindness to others, you must allow to have great influence over human actions, and even greater, on many occasions, than that which remains in its original shape and form. For how few are there, who, having a family, children, and relations, do not spend more on the maintenance and education of these than on their own pleasures? This, indeed, you justly observe, may proceed from their self-love, since the prosperity of their family and friends is one, or the chief, of their pleasures, as well as their chief honor. Be you also one of these selfish men, and you are sure of every one's good opinion and good-will; or, not to shock your ears with these expressions, the self-love of every one, and mine among the rest, will then incline us to serve you and speak well of you."

In my opinion, there are two things which have led astray those philosophers that have insisted so much on the selfishness of man. 1. They found that every act of virtue or friendship was attended with a secret pleasure; whence they concluded that friendship and virtue could not be disinterested. But the fallacy of this is obvious. The virtuous sentiment or passion produces the pleasure, and does not arise from it. I feel a pleasure in doing good to my friend, because I love him; but do not love him for the sake of that pleasure.

2. It has always been found that the virtuous are far from being indifferent to praise; and therefore they have been represented as a set of vainglorious men, who have nothing in view but the applauses of others. But this also is a fallacy. It is very unjust in the world, when they find any tincture of vanity in a laudable action to depreciate it upon that account, or ascribe it entirely to that motive. The case is not the same with vanity as with other passions. Where avarice or revenge enters into any seemingly virtuous action, it is difficult for us to determine how far it enters, and it is natural to suppose it the sole actuating principle. But vanity is so closely allied to virtue, and to love the fame of laudable actions approaches so near the love of laudable actions for their own sake, that these passions are more capable of mixture than any other kinds of affection; and it is almost impossible to have the latter without some degree of the former. Accordingly, we find that this passion for glory is always warped and varied according to the particular taste or disposition

of the mind on which it falls. Nero had the same vanity in driving a chariot that Trajan had in governing the empire with justice and ability. To love the glory of virtuous deeds is a sure proof of the love of virtue.

Complete.

OF THE FIRST PRINCIPLES OF GOVERNMENT

NOTHING appears more surprising to those who consider human affairs with a philosophical eye than the easiness with which the many are governed by the few; and the implicit submission with which men resign their own sentiments and passions to those of their rulers. When we inquire by what means this wonder is effected, we shall find that as Force is always on the side of the governed, the governors have nothing to support them but opinion. It is, therefore, on opinion only that government is founded; and this maxim extends to the most despotic and most military governments, as well as to the most free and most popular. The soldan of Egypt, or the emperor of Rome, might drive his harmless subjects, like brute beasts, against their sentiments and inclination; but he must, at least, have led his mamelukes, or pretorian bands, like men, by their opinions.

Opinion is of two kinds, to wit, opinion of interest, and opinion of right. By opinion of interest, I chiefly understand the sense of the general advantage which is reaped from government, together with the persuasion that the particular government, which is established, is equally advantageous with any other that could easily be settled. When this opinion prevails among the generality of a state, or among those who have the force in their hands, it will give great security to any government.

Right is of two kinds, right to Power and right to Property. What prevalence opinion of the first kind has over mankind may easily be understood by observing the attachment which all nations have to their ancient government, and even to those names which have had the sanction of antiquity. Antiquity always begets the opinion of right; and whatever disadvantageous sentiments we may entertain of mankind, they are always found to be prodigal both of blood and treasure in the maintenance of public justice. There is, indeed, no particular, in which, at first sight, there may appear a greater contradiction in the frame of the human mind than the present. When men act in a faction, they are apt, without shame or remorse, to neglect all the ties of honor and morality, in order to serve their party; and yet when a faction is formed upon a point of right or principle, there is no occasion, where men discover a greater obstinacy, and a more determined sense of justice and equity. The same social disposition of mankind is the cause of these contradictory appearances.

It is sufficiently understood that the opinion of right to property is of moment in all matters of government. A noted author has made property the foundation of all government; and most of our political writers seem inclined to follow him in that particular. This is carrying the matter too far; but still it must be owned that the opinion of right to property has a great influence in this subject.

Upon these three opinions, therefore, of public interest, of right to power, and of right to property, are all governments founded, and all authority of the few over the many. There are, indeed, other principles, which add force to these, and determine, limit, or alter their operation,—such as self-interest, fear, and affection; but still we may assert that these other principles can have no influence alone, but suppose the antecedent influence of those opinions above mentioned. They are, therefore, to be esteemed the secondary, not the original principles of government.

For, first, as to self-interest, by which I mean the expectation of particular rewards, distinct from the general protection which we receive from government, it is evident that the magistrate's authority must be antecedently established, at least be hoped for, in order to produce this expectation. The prospect of reward may augment his authority with regard to some particular persons; but can never give birth to it, with regard to the public. Men naturally look for the greatest favors from their friends and acquaintance; and, therefore, the hopes of any considerable number of the state would never centre in any particular set of men, if these men had no other title to magistracy, and had no separate influence over the opinions of mankind. The same observation may be extended to the other two principles of fear and affection. No man would have any reason to fear the fury of a tyrant, if he had no authority over any but from fear; since, as a single man, his bodily force can reach but a small way, and all the further power he possesses must be founded either on our own opinion, or on the presumed opinion of others. And though affection to wisdom and virtue in a sovereign extends very far,

and has great influence, yet he must antecedently be supposed invested with a public character, otherwise the public esteem will serve him in no stead, nor will his virtue have any influence beyond a narrow sphere.

A government may endure for several ages, though the balance of power and the balance of property do not coincide. This chiefly happens where any rank or order of the state has acquired a large share in the property; but, from the original constitution of the government, has no share in the power. Under what pretense would any individual of that order assume authority in public affairs? As men are commonly much attached to their ancient government, it is not to be expected that the public would ever favor such usurpations. But where the original constitution allows any share of power, though small, to an order of men, who possess a large share of the property, it is easy for them gradually to stretch their authority, and bring the balance of power to coincide with that of property. This has been the case with the House of Commons in England.

Most writers that have treated of the British government have supposed that, as the Lower House represents all the commons of Great Britain, its weight in the scale is proportioned to the property and power of all whom it represents. But this principle must not be received as absolutely true. For though the people are apt to attach themselves more to the House of Commons than to any other member of the constitution, the House being chosen by them as their representatives, and as the public guardians of their liberty, yet are there instances where the House, even when in opposition to the crown, has not been followed by the people; as we may particularly observe of the tory House of Commons in the reign of King William. Were the members obliged to receive instructions from their constituents, like the Dutch deputies, this would entirely alter the case; and if such immense power and riches, as those of all the commons of Great Britain, were brought into the scale, it is not easy to conceive that the crown could either influence that multitude of people, or withstand that balance of property. It is true the crown has great influence over the collective body in the elections of members; but were this influence, which at present is only exerted once in seven years, to be employed in bringing over the people to every vote, it would soon be wasted, and no skill, popularity, or revenue, could support it. I must, therefore,

be of opinion that an alteration in this particular would introduce a total alteration in our government, and would soon reduce it to a pure republic,—and, perhaps, to a republic of no inconvenient form. For though the people, collected in a body like the Roman tribes, be quite unfit for government, yet, when dispersed in small bodies, they are more susceptible both of reason and order; the force of popular currents and tides is, in a great measure, broken; and the public interest may be pursued with some method and constancy. But it is needless to reason any further concerning a form of government which is never likely to have place in Great Britain, and which seems not to be the aim of any party amongst us. Let us cherish and improve our ancient government as much as possible without encouraging a passion for such dangerous novelties.

Complete.

OF INTEREST

Lowness of interest is generally ascribed to plenty of money. But money, however plentiful, has no other effect, if fixed, than to raise the price of labor. Silver is more common than gold; and therefore you receive a greater quantity of it for the same commodities. But do you pay less interest for it? Interest in Batavia and Jamaica is at ten per cent., in Portugal at six; though these places, as we may learn from the prices of everything, abound more in gold and silver than either London or Amsterdam.

Were all the gold in England annihilated at once, and one and twenty shillings substituted in the place of every guinea, would money be more plentiful, or interest lower? No, surely; we should only use silver instead of gold. Were gold rendered as common as silver, and silver as common as copper, would money be more plentiful or interest lower? We may assuredly give the same answer. Our shillings would then be yellow, and our halfpence white; and we should have no guineas. No other difference would ever be observed,—no alteration on commerce, manufactures, navigation, or interest,—unless we imagine that the color of the metal is of any consequence.

Now, what is so visible in these greater variations of scarcity or abundance in the precious metals must hold in all inferior changes. If the multiplying of gold and silver fifteen times makes no difference, much less can the doubling or tripling them. All

augmentation has no other effect than to heighten the price of labor and commodities; and even this variation is little more than that of a name. In the progress towards these changes, the augmentation may have some influence, by exciting industry; but after the prices are settled, suitably to the new abundance of gold and silver, it has no manner of influence.

An effect always holds proportion with its cause. Prices have risen near four times since the discovery of the Indies, and it is probable gold and silver have multiplied much more; but interest has not fallen much above half. The rate of interest, therefore, is not derived from the quantity of the precious metals.

Money having chiefly a fictitious value, the greater or less plenty of it is of no consequence, if we consider a nation within itself; and the quantity of specie, when once fixed, though ever so large, has no other effect than to oblige every one to tell out a greater number of those shining bits of metal, for clothes, furniture, or equipage, without increasing any one convenience of life. If a man borrow money to build a house, he then carries home a greater load; because the stone, timber, lead, glass, etc., with the labor of the masons and carpenters, are represented by a greater quantity of gold and silver. But as these metals are considered chiefly as representations, there can no alteration arise, from their bulk or quantity, their weight or color, either upon their real value or their interest. The same interest, in all cases, bears the same proportion to the sum. And if you lent me so much labor and so many commodities; by receiving five per cent. you always receive proportional labor and commodities, however represented, whether by yellow or white coin, whether by a pound or an ounce. It is in vain, therefore, to look for the cause of the fall or rise of interest in the greater or less quantity of gold and silver, which is fixed in any nation.

High interest arises from three circumstances: a great demand for borrowing; little riches to supply that demand; and great profits arising from commerce: and the circumstances are a clear proof of the small advance of commerce and industry, not of the scarcity of gold and silver. Low interest, on the other hand, proceeds from the three opposite circumstances: a small demand for borrowing; great riches to supply that demand; and small profits arising from commerce,—and these circumstances are all connected together, and proceed from the increase of industry and commerce not of gold and silver.

From his "Essays."

LEIGH HUNT

(1784-1859)

EIGH HUNT was a genius when he wrote "Abou Ben Adhem" if never before or afterwards, but he was always a man of talent and an agreeable writer both of prose and verse. His "Italian Poets," while not profoundly critical, is very useful as an introduction to the best Italian literature, and the brief essays of his "Table-Talk" are in every respect so commendable that all sorts and conditions of readers thank him for the prudent foresight which led him to report in writing what he might have said orally at table had he had a Boswell to slip behind the door and make memoranda of it for posterity. He was born at Southgate, England, October 19th, 1784, and he lived to the ripe age of seventy-five, dying August 28th, 1859. The chief incident of his life was his two-years' imprisonment for writing disrespectfully of the Prince Regent in the Examiner, but the "exquisite taste" in which he furnished his cell did not tend to establish his position as a martyr. He was the associate of two generations of famous literary men. Byron patronized him, and he wrote "Recollections of Byron," which was received with marked disfavor by the poet's friends and without indorsement by his enemies. He wrote several plays and novels, but his best work was done as a poet and essayist.

"THE WITTIEST OF ENGLISH POETS"

BUTLER is the wittiest of English poets, and at the same time he is one of the most learned, and, what is more, one of the wisest. His "Hudibras," though naturally the most popular of his works from its size, subject, and witty excess, was an accident of birth and party compared with his "Miscellaneous Poems"; yet both abound in thoughts as great and deep as the surface is sparkling; and his genius altogether, having the additional recommendation of verse, might have given him a fame greater than Rabelais, had his animal spirits been equal to the rest of his qualifications for a universalist. At the same time, though not

most extraordinary license is assumed as a matter of course; the accentuation jerked out of its place with all the indifference and effrontery of a reason "sufficing unto itself." The poem is so peculiar in this respect, the laughing delight of the reader so well founded, and the passages so sure to be accompanied with a full measure of wit and knowledge, that I have retained its best rhymes throughout, and thus brought them together for the first time.

Butler, like the great wit of the opposite party, Marvel, was an honest man, fonder of his books than of worldly success, and superior to party itself in regard to final principles. He wrote a satire on the follies and vices of the court, which is most likely the reason why it is doubted whether he ever got anything by "Hudibras"; and he was so little prejudiced in favor of the scholarship he possessed that he vindicated the born poet above the poet of books, and would not have Shakespeare tried by a Grecian standard.

Complete.

CHARLES LAMB

LAMB was a humanist, in the most universal sense of the term. His imagination was not great, and he also wanted sufficient heat and music to render his poetry as good as his prose; but as a prose writer, and within the wide circuit of humanity, no man ever took a more complete range than he. He had felt, thought, and suffered so much, that he literally had intolerance for nothing; and he never seemed to have it, but when he supposed the sympathies of men, who might have known better, to be imperfect. He was a wit and an observer of the first order, as far as the world around him was concerned, and society in its existing state; for, as to anything theoretical or transcendental, no man ever had less care for it, or less power. To take him out of habit and convention, however tolerant he was to those who could speculate beyond them, was to put him into an exhausted receiver, or to send him naked, shivering, and driven to shatters, through the regions of space and time. He was only at his ease in the old arms of humanity; and humanity loved and comforted him like one of its wisest though weakest children. His life had experienced great and peculiar sorrows; but he kept up a balance between those and his consolations, by the goodness of his heart,

abounding in poetic sensibility, he was not without it. He is author of the touching simile,—

> "True as the dial to the sun,
> Although it be not shin'd upon."

The following is as elegant as anything in Lovelace or Waller:—

> "—What security's too strong
> To guard that gentle heart from wrong
> That to its friend is glad to pass
> Itself away, and all it has,
> And, like an anchorite, gives over
> This world for the heaven of a lover!"

And this, if read with the seriousness and singleness of feeling that become it, is, I think, a comparison full of as much grandeur as cordiality,—

> "Like Indian widows, gone to bed,
> In flaming curtains to the dead."

You would sooner have looked for it in one of Marvel's poems than in "Hudibras."

Butler has little humor. His two heroes, Hudibras and Ralph, are not so much humorists as pedants. They are as little like their prototypes, Don Quixote and Sancho, as two dreary puppets are unlike excesses of humanity. They are not even consistent with their other prototypes, the Puritans, or with themselves, for they are dull fellows unaccountably gifted with the author's wit. In this respect, and as a narrative, the poem is a failure. Nobody ever thinks of the story, except to wonder at its inefficiency; or of Hudibras himself, except as described at his outset. He is nothing but a ludicrous figure. But considered as a banter issuing from the author's own lips, on the wrong side of Puritanism, and, indeed, on all the pedantic and hypocritical abuses of human reason, the whole production is a marvelous compound of wit, learning, and felicitous execution. The wit is pure and incessant; the learning as quaint and out of the way as the subject; the very rhymes are echoing scourges, made of the peremptory and the incongruous. This is one of the reasons why the rhymes have been so much admired. They are laughable, not merely in themselves, but from the masterly will and violence with which they are made to correspond to the absurdities they lash. The

and the ever-willing sociality of his humor; though, now and then, as if he would cram into one moment the spleen of years, he would throw out a startling and morbid subject for reflection,— perhaps in no better shape than a pun, for he was a great punster. It was a levity that relieved the gravity of his thoughts and kept them from falling too heavily earthward.

Lamb was under the middle size, and of fragile make, but with a head as fine as if it had been carved on purpose. He had a very weak stomach. Three glasses of wine would put him in as lively a condition as can only be wrought in some men by as many bottles,—which subjected him to mistakes on the part of the inconsiderate.

Lamb's essays, especially those collected under the signature of "Elia," will take their place among the daintiest productions of English wit-melancholy,—an amiable melancholy being the groundwork of them, and serving to throw out their delicate flowers of wit and character with the greater nicety. Nor will they be liked the less for a sprinkle of old language, which was natural in him by reason of his great love of the old English writers. Shakespeare himself might have read them, and Hamlet have quoted them.

Complete. From "Table-Talk."

LIGHT AND COLOR

LIGHT is, perhaps, the most wonderful of all visible things; that is to say, it has the least analogy to other bodies, and is the least subject to secondary explanations. No object of sight equals it in tenuity, in velocity, in beauty, in remoteness of origin, and closeness of approach. It has "no respect of persons." Its beneficence is most impartial. It shines equally on the jewels of an Eastern prince and on the dust in the corner of a warehouse. Its delicacy, its power, its utility, its universality, its lovely essence, visible and yet intangible, make up something godlike to our imaginations; and, though we acknowledge divinities more divine, we feel that ignorant as well as wise fault may be found with those who have made it an object of worship.

One of the most curious things with regard to light is, that it is a body, by means of which we become sensible of the existence of other bodies. It is a substance; it exists as much in the space between our eyes and the object it makes known to us as it does in any other instance; and yet we are made sensible of that object by means of the very substance intervening. When our inquiries are stopped by perplexities of this kind, no wonder that some awe-stricken philosophers have thought further inquiry forbidden; and that others have concluded, with Berkeley, that there is no such thing as substance but in idea, and that the phenomena of creation exist but by the will of the Great Mind, which permits certain apparent causes and solutions to take place, and to act in a uniform manner. Milton doubts whether he ought to say what he felt concerning light:—

> "Hail, holy Light, offspring of Heaven first-born,
> Or of the eternal co-eternal beam,
> May I express thee unblamed? since God is light,
> And never but in an unapproached light
> Dwelt from eternity, dwelt there in thee,
> Bright effluence of bright essence increate."

And then he makes that pathetic complaint, during which we imagine him sitting with his blind eyes in the sun, feeling its warmth upon their lids, while he could see nothing:—

> "——Thee I revisit safe,
> And feel thy sovran vital lamp; but thou
> Revisit'st not these eyes, that roll in vain
> To find thy piercing ray, and find no dawn."

As color is imparted solely by the different rays of light with which they are acted upon, the sun literally paints the flowers. The hues of the pink and rose literally come, every day, direct from heaven.

Complete. From "Table-Talk."

PETRARCH AND LAURA

THERE is plenty of evidence in her lover's poetry to show that Laura portioned out the shade and sunshine of her countenance in a manner that had the instinctive effect of artifice, though we do not believe there was any intention to practice it. And this is a reasonable conclusion, warranted by the experience of the world. It is not necessary to suppose Laura a

VI—143

think it is Ugo Foscolo who remarks that Petrarch has given evidence of passion felt in solitude, amounting even to the terrible. His temperament partook of that morbid cast which makes people haunted by their ideas, and which, in men of genius, subjects them sometimes to a kind of delirium of feeling, without destroying the truth of their perceptions. Petrarch more than once represents himself in these sonnets as struggling with a propensity to suicide; nor do we know anything more affecting in the record of a man's struggles with unhappiness than the one containing a prayer of humiliation to God on account of his passion, beginning:—

> *"Padre del ciel, dopo i perduti giorni"*—

> "Father of heaven, after the lost days."

The commentators tell us that it was written on a Good Friday, exactly eleven years from the commencement of his love.

Complete. From "Table-Talk."

MORAL AND PERSONAL COURAGE

IN ALL moral courage there is a degree of personal; personal is sometimes totally deficient in moral. The reason is that moral courage is a result of the intellectual perceptions and of conscience, whereas a man totally deficient in those may have nerves or gall enough to face any danger which his body feels itself competent to oppose. When the physically courageous man comes into the region of mind and speculation, or when the question is purely one of right or wrong, he is apt to feel himself in the condition of the sailor who confessed that he was afraid of ghosts, because he "did not understand their tackle." When moral courage feels that it is in the right, there is no personal daring of which it is incapable.

Complete. From "Table-Talk."

perfect character, in order to excite the love of so imaginative a heart as Petrarch's. A good half or two-thirds of the love may have been assignable to the imagination. Part of it was avowedly attributable to the extraordinary fidelity with which she kept her marriage vow to a disagreeable husband, in a city so licentious as Avignon, and, therefore, partook of that not very complimentary astonishment and that willingness to be at an unusual disadvantage, which make chastity cut so remarkable a figure amid the rakeries of Beaumont and Fletcher. Furthermore, Laura may not have understood the ethercalities of Petrarch. It is possible that less homage might have had a greater effect upon her; and it is highly probable (as Petrarch, though he speaks well of her natural talents, says she had not been well educated) that she had that instinctive misgiving of the fine qualities attributed to her, which is produced even in the vainest of women by flights to which they are unaccustomed. It makes them resent their incompetency upon the lover who thus strangely reminds them of it. Most women, however, would naturally be unwilling to lose such an admirer, especially as they found the admiration of him extend in the world; and Laura is described by her lover as manifestly affected by it. Upon the whole, I should guess her to have been a very beautiful, well-meaning, woman, far from insensible to public homage of any sort (she was a splendid dresser, for instance), and neither so wise nor so foolish as to make her seriously responsible for any little coquetries she practiced, or wanting in sufficient address to practice them well. Her history is a lofty comment upon the line in "The Beggar's Opera":—

> "By keeping men off, you keep them on."

As to the sonnets with which this great man immortalized his love, and which are full of the most wonderful beauties, small and great (the versification being surprisingly various and charming, and the conceits of which they have been accused being for the most part as natural and delightful as anything in them, from a propensity which a real lover has to associate his mistress with everything he sees), justice has been done to their gentler beauties, but not, I think to their intensity and passion. Romeo should have written a criticism on Petrarch's sonnets. He would have done justice both to their "conceits" and their fervor. I

THOMAS HENRY HUXLEY

(1825–1895)

THOMAS HENRY HUXLEY was born in Ealing, England, May 4th, 1825. Educated at Ealing School and at Charing Cross Hospital in London, he spent the first four years of his professional life (1846–50) as assistant surgeon on an English man-of-war. In 1855 he became Fullerian professor of Physiology at the Royal Institution, and it was as a physiologist and biologist that he achieved his greatest successes. He was a pupil of Darwin, and he had what Darwin wholly lacked — a combative disposition and a keen enjoyment of controversy. He seldom found an opponent intellectually able to cope with him, even when he was wrong; and as he was frequently right, he won many controversial victories which seemed to give him a high degree of satisfaction. But if he owed much of his reputation with his contemporaries to the public's love of intellectual prize-fighting, his permanent reputation rests on a long list of essays and studies as a biologist and physiologist. Among the most popular of these are "Science and Culture," "Lay Sermons," and "Evolution and Ethics." He died June 29th, 1895. His essay "On the Method of Zadig" stands at the head of its class, unsurpassed among the popular scientific essays of the century.

ON THE METHOD OF ZADIG

("Retrospective Prophecy as a Function of Science")

IT is a usual and commendable practice to preface the discussion of the views of a philosophic thinker by some account of the man and of the circumstances which shaped his life and colored his way of looking at things; but, though Zadig is cited in one of the most important chapters of Cuvier's greatest work, little is known about him, and that little might perhaps be better authenticated than it is.

It is said that he lived at Babylon in the time of King Moabdar, but the name of Moabdar does not appear in the list of Babylonian sovereigns brought to light by the patience and the industry of the decipherers of cuneiform inscriptions in these later years; nor, indeed, am I aware that there is any other authority for his existence than that of the biographer of Zadig, one Arouet de Voltaire, among whose more conspicuous merits strict historical accuracy is perhaps hardly to be reckoned.

Happily Zadig is in the position of a great many other philosophers. What he was like when he was in the flesh, indeed whether he existed at all, are matters of no great consequence. What we care about in a light is that it shows the way, not whether it is lamp or candle, tallow or wax. Our only real interest in Zadig lies in the conceptions of which he is the putative father; and his biographer has stated these with so much clearness and vivacious illustration that we need hardly feel a pang, even if critical research should prove King Moabdar and all the rest of the story to be unhistorical, and reduce Zadig himself to the shadowy condition of a solar myth.

Voltaire tells us that, disenchanted with life by sundry domestic misadventures, Zadig withdrew from the turmoil of Babylon to a secluded retreat on the banks of the Euphrates, where he beguiled his solitude by the study of nature. The manifold wonders of the world of life had a particular attraction for the lonely student; incessant and patient observation of the plants and animals about him sharpened his naturally good powers of observation and of reasoning; until, at length, he acquired a sagacity which enabled him to perceive endless minute differences among objects which, to the untutored eye, appeared absolutely alike.

It might have been expected that this enlargement of the powers of the mind and of its store of natural knowledge could tend to nothing but the increase of a man's own welfare and the good of his fellowmen. But Zadig was fated to experience the vanity of such expectations.

"One day, walking near a little wood, he saw, hastening that way, one of the queen's chief eunuchs, followed by a troop of officials, who appeared to be in the greatest anxiety, running hither and thither like men distraught in search of some lost treasure.

"'Young man,' cried the eunuch, 'have you seen the queen's dog?' Zadig answered modestly, 'A bitch, I think, not a dog.' 'Quite right,' replied the eunuch; and Zadig continued, 'A very small spaniel who has lately had puppies; she limps with the left

foreleg, and has very long ears.' 'Ah, you have seen her then!' said the breathless eunuch. 'No,' answered Zadig, 'I have not seen her, and I really was not aware that the queen possessed a spaniel.'

"By an odd coincidence, at the very same time, the handsomest horse in the king's stables broke away from his groom in the Babylonian plains. The grand huntsman and all his staff were seeking the horse with as much anxiety as the eunuch and his people the spaniel, and the grand huntsman asked Zadig if he had not seen the king's horse go that way.

"'A first-rate galloper, small-hoofed, five feet high; tail three feet and a half long; cheek pieces of the bit of twenty-three carat gold, shoes silver?' said Zadig.

"'Which way did he go? Where is he?' cried the grand huntsman.

"'I have not seen anything of the horse, and I never heard of him before,' replied Zadig.

"The grand huntsman and the chief eunuch made sure that Zadig had stolen both the king's horse and the queen's spaniel, so they haled him before the High Court of Desterham, which at once condemned him to the knout and transportation for life to Siberia. But the sentence was hardly pronounced when the lost horse and spaniel were found. So the judges were under the painful necessity of reconsidering their decision; but they fined Zadig four hundred ounces of gold for saying he had seen that which he had not seen.

"The first thing was to pay the fine; afterward Zadig was permitted to open his defense to the court, which he did in the following terms:—

"'Stars of justice, abysses of knowledge, mirrors of truth, whose gravity is as that of lead, whose inflexibility is as that of iron, who rival the diamond in clearness, and possess no little affinity with gold; since I am permitted to address your august assembly, I swear by Ormuzd that I have never seen the respectable lady dog of the queen, nor beheld the sacrosanct horse of the king of kings.

"'This is what happened. I was taking a walk toward the little wood near which I subsequently had the honor to meet the venerable chief eunuch and the most illustrious grand huntsman. I noticed the track of an animal in the sand, and it was easy to see that it was that of a small dog. Long faint streaks upon

the little elevations of sand between the footmarks convinced me that it was a she dog with pendent dugs — showing that she must have had puppies not many days since. Other scrapings of the sand, which always lay close to the marks of the forepaws, indicated that she had very long ears; and as the imprint of one foot was always fainter than those of the other three, I judged that the lady dog of our august queen was, if I may venture to say so, a little lame.

"'With respect to the horse of the king of kings, permit me to observe that, wandering through the paths which traverse the wood, I noticed the marks of horseshoes. They were all equidistant. "Ah!" said I, "this is a famous galloper." In a narrow alley, only seven feet wide, the dust upon the trunks of the trees was a little disturbed at three feet and a half from the middle of the path. "This horse," said I to myself, "had a tail three feet and a half long, and, lashing it from one side to the other, he has swept away the dust." Branches of the trees met overhead at the height of five feet, and under them I saw newly fallen leaves; so I knew that the horse had brushed some of the branches, and was therefore five feet high. As to his bit, it must have been made of twenty-three karat gold, for he had rubbed it against a stone, which turned out to be a touchstone, with the properties of which I am familiar by experiment. Lastly, by the marks which his shoes left upon pebbles of another kind, I was led to think that his shoes were of fine silver.'

"All the judges admired Zadig's profound and subtle discernment, and the fame of it reached even the king and the queen. From the anterooms to the presence chamber Zadig's name was in everybody's mouth; and although many of the magi were of opinion that he ought to be burned as a sorcerer, the king commanded that the four hundred ounces of gold which he had been fined should be restored to him. So the officers of the court went in state with the four hundred ounces,—only they retained three hundred and ninety-eight for legal expenses, and their servants expected fees."

Those who are interested in learning more of the fateful history of Zadig must turn to the original; we are dealing with him only as a philosopher, and this brief excerpt suffices for the exemplification of the nature of his conclusions and of the method by which he arrived at them.

These conclusions may be said to be of the nature of retrospective prophecies; though it is perhaps a little hazardous to employ phraseology which perilously suggests a contradiction in terms — the word "prophecy" being so constantly in ordinary use restricted to "foretelling." Strictly, however, the term "prophecy" as much applies to outspeaking as to foretelling; and even in the restricted sense of "divination," it is obvious that the essence of the prophetic operation does not lie in its backward or forward relation to the course of time, but in the fact that it is the apprehension of that which lies out of the sphere of immediate knowledge, the seeing of that which to the natural sense of the seer is invisible.

The foreteller asserts that, at some future time, a properly situated observer will witness certain events; the clairvoyant declares that, at this present time, certain things are to be witnessed a thousand miles away; the retrospective prophet (Would that there were such a word as "backteller"!) affirms that so many hours or years ago, such and such things were to be seen. In all these cases it is only the relation to time which alters; the process of divination beyond the limits of possible direct knowledge remains the same.

No doubt it was their instinctive recognition of the analogy between Zadig's results and those obtained by authorized inspiration which inspired the Babylonian magi with the desire to burn the philosopher. Zadig admitted that he had never either seen or heard of the horse of the king or of the spaniel of the queen; and yet he ventured to assert in the most positive manner that animals answering to their description did actually exist, and ran about the plains of Babylon. If his method was good for the divination of the course of events ten hours old, why should it not be good for those of ten years or ten centuries past; nay, might it not extend to ten thousand years, and justify the impious in meddling with the traditions of Oannes and the fish, and all the sacred foundations of Babylonian cosmogony?

But this was not the worst. There was another consideration which obviously dictated to the more thoughtful of the magi the propriety of burning Zadig out of hand. His defense was worse than his offense. It showed that his mode of divination was fraught with danger to magianism in general. Swollen with the pride of human reason, he had ignored the established canons of magian lore; and, trusting to what, after all, was mere carnal common sense, he professed to lead men to a deeper insight into nature than magian wisdom, with all its lofty antagonism to everything common, had ever reached. What, in fact, lay at the foundation of all Zadig's arguments, but the coarse, commonplace assumption, upon which every act of our daily lives is based, that we may conclude from an effect to the pre-existence of a cause competent to produce that effect?

The tracks were exactly like those which dogs and horses leave; therefore they were the effects of such animals as causes. The marks at the sides of the fore prints of the dog's track were exactly such as would be produced by long trailing ears; therefore the dog's long ears were the causes of these marks—and so on. Nothing can be more hopelessly vulgar, more unlike the majestic development of a system of grandly unintelligible conclusions from sublimely inconceivable premises, such as delights the magian heart. In fact, Zadig's method was nothing but the method of all mankind. Retrospective prophecies, far more astonishing for their minute accuracy than those of Zadig, are familiar to those who have watched the daily life of nomadic people.

From freshly broken twigs, crushed leaves, disturbed pebbles, and imprints hardly discernible by the untrained eye, such graduates in the university of nature will divine, not only the fact that a party has passed that way, but its strength, its composition, the course it took, and the number of hours or days which have elapsed since it passed. But they are able to do this because, like Zadig, they perceive endless minute differences where untrained eyes discern nothing; and because the unconscious logic of common sense compels them to account for these effects by the causes which they know to be competent to produce them.

And such mere methodized savagery was to discover the hidden things of nature better than à priori deductions from the nature of Ormuzd—perhaps to give a history of the past, in which Oannes would be altogether ignored! Decidedly it were better to burn this man at once.

If instinct, or an unwonted use of reason, led Moabdar's magi to this conclusion two or three thousand years ago, all that can be said is that subsequent history has fully justified them. For the rigorous application of Zadig's logic to the results of accurate and long-continued observation has founded all those sciences which have been termed historical or palætiological, because they

are retrospectively prophetic and strive toward the reconstruction in human imagination of events which have vanished and ceased to be.

History, in the ordinary acceptation of the word, is based upon the interpretation of documentary evidence; and documents would have no evidential value unless historians were justified in their assumption that they have come into existence by the operation of causes similar to those of which documents are, in our present experience, the effects. If a written history can be produced otherwise than by human agency, or if the man who wrote a given document was actuated by other than ordinary human motives, such documents are of no more evidential value than so many arabesques.

Archæology, which takes up the thread of history beyond the point at which documentary evidence fails us, could have no existence, except for our well-grounded confidence that monuments and works of art, or artifice, have never been produced by causes different in kind from those to which they now owe their origin. And geology, which traces back the course of history beyond the limits of archæology, could tell us nothing except for the assumption that, millions of years ago, water, heat, gravitation, friction, animal and vegetable life caused effects of the same kind as they do now. Nay, even physical astronomy, in so far as it takes us back to the uttermost point of time which palætiological science can reach, is founded upon the same assumption. If the law of gravitation ever failed to be true, even to the smallest extent, for that period, the calculations of the astronomer have no application.

The power of prediction, of prospective prophecy, is that which is commonly regarded as the great prerogative of physical science. And truly it is a wonderful fact that one can go into a shop and buy for small price a book, the "Nautical Almanac," which will foretell the exact position to be occupied by one of Jupiter's moons six months hence; nay more, that, if it were worth while, the Astronomer Royal could furnish us with as infallible a prediction applicable to 1980 or 2980.

But astronomy is not less remarkable for its power of retrospective prophecy.

Thales, oldest of Greek philosophers, the dates of whose birth and death are uncertain, but who flourished about 600 B. C., is

said to have foretold an eclipse of the sun which took place in his time during a battle between the Medes and the Lydians. Sir George Airy has written a very learned and interesting memoir in which he proves that such an eclipse was visible in Lydia on the afternoon of the twenty-eighth of May in the year 585 B. C.

No one doubts that, on the day and at the hour mentioned by the Astronomer Royal, the people of Asia Minor saw the face of the sun totally obscured. But though we implicitly believe this retrospective prophecy, it is incapable of verification. It is impossible even to conceive any means of ascertaining directly whether the eclipse of Thales happened or not. All that can be said is, that the prospective prophecies of the astronomer are always verified; and that, inasmuch as his retrospective prophecies are the result of following backward the very same method as that which invariably leads to verified results when it is worked forward, there is as much reason for placing full confidence in the one as in the other. Retrospective prophecy is therefore a legitimate function of astronomical science; and if it is legitimate for one science it is legitimate for all; the fundamental axiom on which it rests, the constancy of the order of nature, being the common foundation of all scientific thought. Indeed, if there can be grades in legitimacy, certain branches of science have the advantage over astronomy, in so far as their retrospective prophecies are not only susceptible of verification, but are sometimes strikingly verified.

Such a science exists in that application of the principles of biology to the interpretation of the animal and vegetable remains imbedded in the rocks which compose the surface of the globe, which is called palæontology.

At no very distant time the question whether these so-called "fossils" were really the remains of animals and plants was hotly disputed. Very learned persons maintained that they were nothing of the kind, but a sort of concretion or crystallization which had taken place within the stone in which they are found; and which simulated the forms of animal and vegetable life, just as frost on a window pane imitates vegetation. At the present day it would probably be impossible to find any sane advocate of this opinion; and the fact is rather surprising that among the people from whom the circle squarers, perpetual motioners, flat-earth men and the like, are recruited, to say nothing of table

turners and spirit rappers, somebody has not perceived the easy avenue to nonsensical notoriety open to any one who will take up the good old doctrine that fossils are all lusus naturæ.

The position would be impregnable, inasmuch as it is quite impossible to prove the contrary. If a man choose to maintain that a fossil oyster shell, in spite of its correspondence, down to every minutest particular, with that of an oyster fresh taken out of the sea, was never tenanted by a living oyster, but is a mineral concretion, there is no demonstrating his error. All that can be done is to show him that, by a parity of reasoning, he is bound to admit that a heap of oyster shells outside a fishmonger's door may also be "sports of nature," and that a mutton bone in a dust bin may have had the like origin. And when you cannot prove that people are wrong, but only that they are absurd, the best course is to let them alone.

The whole fabric of palæontology, in fact, falls to the ground unless we admit the validity of Zadig's great principle, that like effects imply like causes; and that the process of reasoning from a shell, or a tooth, or a bone, to the nature of the animal to which it belonged, rests absolutely on the assumption that the likeness of this shell, or tooth, or bone to that of some animal with which we are already acquainted, is such that we are justified in inferring a corresponding degree of likeness in the rest of the two organisms. It is on this very simple principle, and not upon imaginary laws of physiological correlation, about which, in most cases, we know nothing whatever, that the so-called restorations of the palæontologist are based.

Abundant illustrations of this truth will occur to every one who is familiar with palæontology; none is more suitable than the case of the so-called belemnites. In the early days of the study of fossils, this name was given to certain elongated stony bodies, ending at one extremity in a conical point, and truncated at the other, which were commonly reputed to be thunderbolts, and as such to have descended from the sky. They are common enough in some parts of England; and, in the condition in which they are ordinarily found, it might be difficult to give satisfactory reasons for denying them to be merely mineral bodies.

They appear, in fact, to consist of nothing but concentric layers of carbonate of lime, disposed in subcrystalline fibres, or prisms, perpendicular to the layers. Among a great number of specimens of these belemnites, however, it was soon observed that some showed a conical cavity at the blunt end; and in still better preserved specimens this cavity appeared to be divided into chambers by delicate saucer-shaped partitions, situated at regular intervals one above the other. Now there is no mineral body which presents any structure comparable to this, and the conclusion suggested itself that the belemnites must be the effects of causes other than those which are at work in inorganic nature. On close examination, the saucer-shaped partitions were proved to be all perforated at one point, and the perforations being situated exactly in the same line, the chambers were seen to be traversed by a canal, or siphuncle, which thus connected the smallest or apical chamber with the largest. There is nothing like this in the vegetable world; but an exactly corresponding structure is met with in the shells of two kinds of existing animals, the pearly nautilus and the spirula, and only in them. These animals belong to the same division — the cephalopoda — as the cuttlefish, the squid, and the octopus. But they are the only existing members of the group which possess chambered, siphunculated shells; and it is utterly impossible to trace any physiological connection between the very peculiar structural characters of a cephalopod and the presence of a chambered shell. In fact, the squid has, instead of any such shell, a horny "pen"; the cuttlefish has the so-called "cuttle bone"; and the octopus has no shell at all, or a mere rudiment of one.

Nevertheless, seeing that there is nothing in nature at all like the chambered shell of the belemnite, except the shells of the nautilus and of the spirula, it was legitimate to prophesy that the animal from which the fossil proceeded must have belonged to the group of the cephalopoda. Nautilus and spirula are both very rare animals, but the progress of investigation brought to light the singular fact that, though each has the characteristic cephalopodous organization, it is very different from the other. The shell of nautilus is external, that of spirula internal; nautilus has four gills, spirula two; nautilus has multitudinous tentacles, spirula has only ten arms beset with horny rimmed suckers; spirula, like the squids and cuttlefishes, which it closely resembles, has a bag of ink which it squirts out to cover its retreat when alarmed; nautilus has none.

No amount of physiological reasoning could enable any one to say whether the animal which fabricated the belemnite was more like nautilus or more like spirula. But the accidental discovery of belemnites in due connection with black elongated masses which were certainly fossilized ink bags, inasmuch as the ink could be ground up and used for painting as well as if it were recent sepia, settled the question; and it became perfectly safe to prophesy that the creature which fabricated the belemnite was a two-gilled cephalopod with suckers on its arms, and with all the other essential features of our living squids, cuttlefishes, and spirulæ. The palæontologist was, by this time, able to speak as confidently about the animal of the belemnite as Zadig was respecting the queen's spaniel. He could give a very fair description of its external appearance, and even enter pretty fully into the details of its internal organization, and yet could declare that neither he nor any one else had ever seen one. And as the queen's spaniel was found, so happily has the animal of the belemnite; a few exceptionally preserved specimens having been discovered which completely verify the retrospective prophecy of those who interpreted the facts of the case by due application of the method of Zadig.

These belemnites flourished in prodigious abundance in the seas of the Mesozoic or secondary age of the world's geological history; but no trace of them has been found in any of the tertiary deposits, and they appear to have died out toward the close of the Mesozoic epoch. The method of Zadig, therefore, applies in full force to the events of a period which is immeasurably remote, which long preceded the origin of the most conspicuous mountain masses of the present world and the deposition, at the bottom of the ocean, of the rocks which form the greater part of the soil of our present continents. The Euphrates itself, at the mouth of which Oannes landed, is a thing of yesterday compared with a belemnite; and even the liberal chronology of magian cosmogony fixes the beginning of the world only at a time when other applications of Zadig's method afford convincing evidence that, could we have been there to see, things would have looked very much as they do now. Truly the magi were wise in their generation; they foresaw rightly that this pestilent application of the principles of common sense inaugurated by Zadig would be their ruin.

But it may be said that the method of Zadig, which is simple reasoning from analogy, does not account for the most striking feats of modern palæontology, — the reconstruction of entire ani-

mals from a tooth or perhaps a fragment of a bone; and it may be justly urged that Cuvier, the great master of this kind of investigation, gave a very different account of the process which yielded such remarkable results.

Cuvier is not the first man of ability who has failed to make his own mental processes clear to himself, and he will not be the last. The matter can be easily tested. Search the eight volumes of the "Recherches sur les Ossemens Fossiles" from cover to cover, and no reasoning from physiological necessities — nothing but the application of the method of Zadig pure and simple — will be found.

There is one well-known case which may represent all. It is an excellent illustration of Cuvier's sagacity, and he evidently takes some pride in telling his story about it. A split slab of stone arrived from the quarries of Montmartre, the two halves of which contained the greater part of the skeleton of a small animal. On careful examinations of the characters of the teeth and of the lower jaw, which happened to be exposed, Cuvier assured himself that they presented such a very close resemblance to the corresponding parts in the living opossum that he at once assigned the fossil to that genus.

Now the opossums are unlike most mammals in that they possess two bones attached to the fore part of the pelvis, which are commonly called "marsupial bones." The name is a misnomer, originally conferred because it was thought that these bones have something to do with the support of the pouch, or marsupium, with which some, but not all, of the opossums are provided. As a matter of fact, they have nothing to do with the support of the pouch, and they exist as much in those opossums which have no pouches as in those which possess them. In truth, no one knows what the use of these bones may be, nor has any valid theory of their physiological import yet been suggested. And if we have no knowledge of the physiological importance of the bones themselves, it is obviously absurd to pretend that we are able to give physiological reasons why the presence of these bones is associated with certain peculiarities of the teeth and of the jaws. If any one knows why four molar teeth and an inflected angle of the jaw are almost always found along with marsupial bones, he has not yet communicated that knowledge to the world.

If, however, Zadig was right in concluding from the likeness of the hoof prints which he observed to a horse's that the creature which made them had a tail like that of a horse, Cuvier, seeing that the teeth and jaw of his fossil were just like those of an opossum, had the same right to conclude that the pelvis would also be like an opossum's; and so strong was his conviction that this retrospective prophecy about an animal which he had never seen before, and which had been dead and buried for millions of years, would be verified that he went to work upon the slab which contained the pelvis in confident expectation of finding and laying bare the "marsupial bones," to the satisfaction of some persons whom he had invited to witness their disinterment. As he says: "*Cette opération se fit en présence de quelques personnes à qui j'en avais annoncé d'avance le résultat, dans l'intention de leur prouver par le fait la justice de nos théories zoologiques; puis que le vrai cachet d'une théorie est sans contredit la faculté qu'elle donne de prévoir les phénomènes.*"

In the "Ossemens Fossiles," Cuvier leaves his paper just as it first appeared in the "Annales du Muséum," as "a curious monument of the force of zoölogical laws and of the use which may be made of them."

Zoölogical laws truly, but not physiological laws. If one sees a live dog's head, it is extremely probable that a dog's tail is not far off, though nobody can say why that sort of head and that sort of tail go together; what physiological connection there is between the two. So, in the case of the Montmartre fossil, Cuvier, finding a thorough opossum's head, concluded that the pelvis also would be like an opossum's. But, most assuredly, the most advanced physiologist of the present day could throw no light on the question why these are associated, or could pretend to affirm that the existence of the one is necessarily connected with that of the other. In fact, had it so happened that the pelvis of the fossil had been originally exposed, while the head lay hidden, the presence of the "marsupial bones," however like they might have been to an opossum's, would by no means have warranted the prediction that the skull would turn out to be that of the opossum. It might just as well have been like that of some other marsupial; or even like that of the totally different group of monotremes, of which the only living representatives are the echidna and the ornithorhynchus.

For all practical purposes, however, the empirical laws of co-ordination of structures which are embodied in the generalizations of morphology may be confidently trusted, if employed with due caution, to lead to a just interpretation of fossil remains; or, in other words, we may look for the verification of the retrospective prophecies which are based upon them.

And if this be the case, the late advances which have been made in palæontological discovery open out a new field for such prophecies. For it has been ascertained with respect to many groups of animals, that, as we trace them back in time, their ancestors gradually cease to exhibit those special modifications which at present characterize the type, and more nearly embody the general plan of the group to which they belong.

Thus, in the well-known case of the horse, the toes which are suppressed in the living horse are found to be more and more complete in the older members of the group, until, at the bottom of the tertiary series of America, we find an equine animal which has four toes in front and three behind. No remains of the horse tribe are at present known from any Mesozoic deposit. Yet who can doubt that, whenever a sufficiently extensive series of lacustrine and fluviatile beds of that age becomes known, the lineage which has been traced thus far will be continued by equine quadrupeds with an increasing number of digits, until the horse type merges in the five-toed form toward which these gradations point?

But the argument which holds good for the horse, holds good, not only for all mammals, but for the whole animal world. And as the study of the pedigrees or lines of evolution to which at present we have access brings to light, as it assuredly will do, the laws of that process, we shall be able to reason from the facts with which the geological record furnishes us to those which have hitherto remained, and many of which, perhaps, may forever remain, hidden. The same method of reasoning which enables us, when furnished with a fragment of an extinct animal, to prophesy the character which the whole organism exhibited, will, sooner or later, enable us, when we know a few of the later terms of a genealogical series to predict the nature of the earlier terms.

In no very distant future the method of Zadig, applied to a greater body of facts than the present generation is fortunate enough to handle, will enable the biologist to reconstruct the

VI—144

scheme of life from its beginning, and to speak as confidently of the character of long extinct living beings, no trace of which has been preserved, as Zadig did of the queen's spaniel and the king's horse. Let us hope that they may be better rewarded for their toil and their sagacity than was the Babylonian philosopher; for perhaps, by that time, the magi also may be reckoned among the members of a forgotten fauna, extinguished in the struggle for existence against their great rival common sense.

Complete.

JOHN JAMES INGALLS

(1833–1900)

JOHN JAMES INGALLS, one of the most brilliant political orators of the second half of the nineteenth century, was born in Middleton, Massachusetts, December 29th, 1833. Graduating at Williams College in 1855, and fitting himself for the bar, he removed in 1858 to Atchison, Kansas, and until his death in 1900 he was closely identified with the political history of that State. From 1873 to 1891 he represented Kansas in the United States Senate. After his retirement he devoted himself chiefly to his law practice and to literary work. His celebrated essay on "Blue Grass," which appeared in the Kansas Magazine in 1872, shows that he had the native capacity for achieving the highest rank in literature. The Civil War and the virulent partisanship which followed it are sufficient to account for the fact that he did not realize his possibilities as a writer. With Irving, Cooper, Hawthorne, Longfellow, Emerson, Poe, Holmes, and Lowell, not to mention half a hundred meritorious writers of a lower grade, American literature during the first half of the nineteenth century had in it the promise of that pre-eminence in the literature of the world which it will finally realize. The crudity and passion of the Civil War, which interrupted its steady evolution during a full generation, turned such brilliant intellects as that of Ingalls to the ephemeral work of partisan contention. Their creativeness was not wholly destroyed, but in all sections it was so greatly impeded that it is only with the opening of the twentieth century that the hope of a national American literature, full of the spirit of the people and governed by an adequate sense of the high realities of art, returns with a prospect of progressive and uninterrupted realization. The essay on "Blue Grass," as it is given here, certainly belongs to this American literature, and it is not less certainly a characteristic Kansas product. W. V. B.

BLUE GRASS

ATTRACTED by the bland softness of an afternoon in my primeval winter in Kansas, I rode southward through the dense forest that then covered the bluffs of the North Fork of the Wildcat. The ground was sodden with the ooze of melting snow. The dripping trees were as motionless as granite. The last year's leaves, tenacious lingerers, loath to leave the scene of their brief bravery, adhered to the gray boughs like fragile bronze. There were no visible indications of life, but the broad, wintry landscape was flooded with that indescribable splendor that never was on sea or shore—a purple and silken softness, that half veiled, half disclosed the alien horizon, the vast curves of the remote river, the transient architecture of the clouds, and filled the responsive soul with a vague tumult of emotions, pensive and pathetic, in which regret and hope contended for the mastery. The dead and silent globe, with all its hidden kingdom, seemed swimming like a bubble, suspended in an ethereal solution of amethyst and silver, compounded of the exhaling whiteness of the snow, the descending glory of the sky. A tropical atmosphere brooded upon an Arctic scene, creating the strange spectacle of summer in winter, June in January, peculiar to Kansas, which unseen cannot be imagined, but once seen can never be forgotten. A sudden descent into the sheltered valley revealed an unexpected crescent of dazzling verdure, glittering like a meadow in early spring, unreal as an incantation, surprising as the sea to the soldiers of Xenophon as they stood upon the shore and shouted "Thalatta!" It was Blue Grass, unknown in Eden, the final triumph of nature, reserved to compensate her favorite offspring in the new Paradise of Kansas for the loss of the old upon the banks of the Tigris and Euphrates.

Next in importance to the divine profusion of water, light, and air, those three great physical facts which render existence possible, may be reckoned the universal beneficence of grass. Exaggerated by tropical heats and vapors to the gigantic cane congested with its saccharine secretion, or dwarfed by polar rigors to the fibrous hair of northern solitudes, embracing between these extremes the maize with its resolute pennons, the rice plant of southern swamps, the wheat, rye, barley, oats, and other cereals, no less than the humbler verdure of hillside, pasture, and prairie in the temperate zone, grass is the most widely distributed of all vegetable beings, and is at once the type of our life and the emblem of our mortality. Lying in the sunshine among the buttercups and dandelions of May, scarcely higher in intelligence than the minute tenants of that mimic wilderness, our earliest recollections are of grass; and when the fitful fever is ended, and the foolish wrangle of the market and forum is closed, grass heals over the scar which our descent into the bosom of the earth has made, and the carpet of the infant becomes the blanket of the dead.

As he reflected upon the brevity of human life, grass has been the favorite symbol of the moralist, the chosen theme of the philosopher. "All flesh is grass," said the prophet; "My days are as the grass," sighed the troubled patriarch; and the pensive Nebuchadnezzar, in his penitential mood, exceeded even these, and, as the sacred historian informs us, did eat grass like an ox.

Grass is the forgiveness of nature,—her constant benediction. Fields trampled with battle, saturated with blood, torn with the ruts of cannon, grow green again with grass, and carnage is forgotten. Streets abandoned by traffic become grass-grown like rural lanes, and are obliterated. Forests decay, harvests perish, flowers vanish, but grass is immortal. Beleaguered by the sullen hosts of winter, it withdraws into the impregnable fortress of its subterranean vitality, and emerges upon the first solicitation of spring. Sown by the winds, by wandering birds, propagated by the subtle horticulture of the elements which are its ministers and servants, it softens the rude outline of the world. Its tenacious fibres hold the earth in its place, and prevent its soluble components from washing into the wasting sea. It invades the solitude of deserts, climbs the inaccessible slopes and forbidding pinnacles of mountains, modifies climates, and determines the history, character, and destiny of nations. Unobtrusive and patient, it has immortal vigor and aggression. Banished from the thoroughfare and the field, it bides its time to return, and when vigilance is relaxed, or the dynasty has perished, it silently resumes the throne from which it has been expelled, but which it never abdicates. It bears no blazonry of bloom to charm the senses with fragrance or splendor, but its homely hue is more enchanting than the lily or the rose. It yields no fruit in earth or air, and yet, should its harvest fail for a single year, famine would depopulate the world.

One grass differs from another grass in glory. One is vulgar and another patrician. There are grades in its vegetable nobility. Some varieties are useful. Some are beautiful. Others combine utility and ornament. The sour, reedy herbage of the swamps is base born. Timothy is a valuable servant. Redtop and clover are a degree higher in the social scale. But the king of them all, with genuine blood royal, is Blue Grass. Why it is called blue, save that it is most vividly and intensely green, is inexplicable; but had its unknown priest baptized it with all the hues of the prism, he would not have changed its hereditary title to imperial superiority over all its humble kin.

Taine, in his incomparable "History of English Literature," has well said that the body of man in every country is deeply rooted in the soil of nature. He might properly have declared that men were wholly rooted in the soil, and that the character of nations, like that of forests, tubers and grains, is entirely determined by the climate and soil in which they germinate. Dogmas grow like potatoes. Creeds and carrots, catechisms and cabbages, tenets and turnips, religions and ruta-bagas, governments and grasses, all depend upon the dew point and the thermal range. Give the philosopher a handful of soil, the mean annual temperature and rainfall, and his analysis would enable him to predict with absolute certainty the characteristics of the nation.

Calvinism transplanted to the plains of the Ganges would perish of inanition. Webster is as much an indigenous product of New England as its granite and its pines. Napoleon was possible only in France; Cromwell in England; Christ, and the splendid invention of immortality, alone in Palestine. Moral causes and qualities exert influences far beyond their nativity, and ideas are transplanted and exported to meet the temporary requirements of the tastes or necessities of man; as we see exotic palms in the conservatories of Chatsworth, russet apples at Surinam, and oranges in Atchison. But there is no growth,—nothing but change of location. The phenomena of politics exhibit the operations of the same law. Contrast the enduring fabric of our federal liberties with the abortive struggles of Mexico and the Central American republics. The tropics are inconsistent with democracy. Tyranny is alien to the temperate zone.

The direct agency upon which all these conditions depend, and through which these forces operate, is food. Temperature, humidity, soil, sunlight, electricity, vital force, express themselves

primarily in vegetable existence that furnishes the basis of that animal life which yields sustenance to the human race. What a man, a community, a nation can do, think, suffer, imagine, or achieve, depends upon what it eats. Bran eaters and vegetarians are not the kings of men. Rice and potatoes are the diet of slaves. The races that live on beef have ruled the world, and the better the beef the greater the deeds they have done. Mediæval Europe, the Vandals, and Huns, and Goths, ate the wild hog, whose brutal ferocity was repeated in their truculent valor, and whose loathsome protoplasm bore the same relation to that barbarous epoch that a rosy steak from a short-horned Durham does to the civilization of the nineteenth century. A dim consciousness of the intimate connection between regimen and religion seems to have dawned upon the intellectual horizon of those savage tribes who eat the missionaries which a misguided philanthropy has sent to save their souls from perdition. . . .

The primary form of food is grass. Grass feeds the ox; the ox nourishes man; man dies and goes to grass again; and so the tide of life, with everlasting repetition, in continuous circles, moves endlessly on and upward, and in more senses than one, all flesh is grass. But all flesh is not Blue Grass. If it were, the devil's occupation would be gone.

There is a portion of Kentucky known as the "Blue-Grass Region," and it is safe to say that it has been the arena of the most magnificent intellectual and physical development that has been witnessed among men or animals upon the American continent, or perhaps upon the whole face of the world. In corroboration of this belief, it is necessary only to mention Henry Clay, the orator, and the horse, Lexington, both peerless, electric, immortal. The ennobling love of the horse has extended to all other races of animals. Incomparable herds of high-bred cattle graze the tranquil pastures, their elevating protoplasm supplying a finer force to human passions, brains, and will. Hog artists devote their genius to shortening the snouts and swelling the hams of their grunting brethren. The reflex of this solicitude appears in the muscular, athletic vigor of the men, and the voluptuous beauty of the women who inhabit this favored land. Palaces, temples, forests, peaceful institutions, social order, spring like exhalations from the congenial soil.

All these marvels are attributable as directly to the potential influence of Blue Grass as day and night to the revolution of the

earth. Eradicate it, substitute for it the scrawny herbage of impoverished barrens, and in a single generation man and beast would alike degenerate into a common decay. . . .

The typical Kansas has not yet appeared. Our population is composed of more alien and conflicting elements than were ever assembled under one political organization, each mature, each stimulated to abnormal activity. It is not yet fused and welded into a homogeneous mass, and we must therefore consult the oracles of analogy to ascertain in what garb our Coming Man will arrive. His lineaments and outline will be controlled by the abode we fashion, and the food that we prepare for him when he comes.

Though our State is embryonic and fetal at present, it is not difficult to perceive certain distinctive features indigenous to our limits. The social order is anomalous. Our politics have been exceptional, violent, personal, convulsive. The appetite of the community demands the stimulus of revolution. It is not content with average results in morals. It hungers for excitement. Its favorite apostles and prophets have been the howling dervishes of statesmanship and religion. Every new theory seeks Kansas as its tentative point, sure of partisans and disciples. Our life is intense in every expression. We pass instantaneously from tremendous energy to the most inert and sluggish torpor. There is no golden mean. We act first and think afterwards. These idiosyncrasies are rapidly becoming typical, and, unless modified by the general introduction of Blue Grass, may be rendered permanent. Nature is inconstant, and molds us to her varying moods.

Kansas is all antithesis. It is the land of extremes. It is the hottest, coldest, driest, wettest, thickest, thinnest country of the world. The stranger who crossed our borders for the first time at Wyandotte and traveled by rail to White Cloud would, with consternation, contrast that uninterrupted Sierra of rugose and oak-clad crags with the placid prairies of his imagination. Let him ride along the spine of any of those lateral "divides" or watersheds whose

"Level leagues forsaken lie,
A grassy waste, extending to the sky,"

and he would be oppressed by the same melancholy monotony which broods over those who pursue the receding horizon over the fluctuating plains of the sea. And let his discursion be whither it would, if he listened to the voice of experience he would not start upon his pilgrimage at any season of the year without an overcoat, a fan, a lightning rod, and an umbrella.

The newcomer, alarmed by the traditions of "the drought of '60," when, in the language of one of the varnished rhetoricians of that epoch, "acorns were used for food and the bark of trees for clothing," views with terror the long succession of dazzling early summer days, days without clouds and nights without dew, days when the effulgent sun floods the dome with fierce and blinding radiance, days of glittering leaves and burnished blades of serried ranks of corn, days when the transparent air, purged of all earthly exhalation and alloy, seems like a pure, powerful lens, revealing a remoter horizon and a profounder sky.

But his apprehensions are relieved by the unheralded appearance of a cloud no bigger than a man's hand, in the northwest. A huge bulk of purple and ebony vapor, preceded by a surging wave of pallid smoke, blots out the sky. Birds and insects disappear, and cattle abruptly stand agaze. An appalling silence, an ominous darkness, fill the atmosphere: A continuous roll of muffled thunder, increasing in volume, shakes the solid earth. The air suddenly grows chill, and smells like an unused cellar. A fume of yellow dust conceals the base of the meteor. The jagged scimiter of the lightning, drawn from its cloudy scabbard, is brandished for a terrible instant in the abyss, and thrust into the affrighted city with a crash, as if the rafters of the world had fallen. The wind, hitherto concealed, leaps from its ambush and lashes the earth with scourges of rain. The broken cisterns of the clouds can hold no water, and rivers run in the atmosphere. Dry ravines become turbid torrents, bearing cargoes of drift and rubbish on their swift descent. Confusion and chaos hold undisputed sway. In a moment the turmoil ceases. A gray veil of rain stands like a wall of granite in the eastern sky. The trailing banners of the storm hang from the frail bastions. The routed squadrons of mist, gray on violet, terrified fugitives, precipitately fly beneath the triumphal arch of a rainbow, whose airy and insubstantial glory dies with the dying sun.

For days the phenomenon is repeated. Water oozes from the air. The strands of rain are woven with the inconstant sunbeam. Reeds and sedges grow in the fields, and all nature tends to fins, web feet, and amphibiousness.

Oppressed by the sedate monotony of the horizon, and tortured by the alternating hopes and fears which such a climate excites, the prairie dweller becomes sombre and grave in his conversation and demeanor. Upon that illimitable expanse, and beneath that silent and cloudless sky, mirth and levity are impossible. Meditation becomes habitual. Fortitude and persistence succumb under the careless husbandry induced by the generous soil. The forests, ledges, and elevations which serve to identify other localities and make them conspicuous, are wanting here. Nature furnishes farms ready made, like clothing in a slopshop; and as we relinquish without pain what we acquire without toil, the denizen has no local attachments, and daunted by slight obstacles, or discontented by trivial discomforts, becomes migratory and follows the coyote and the bison. The pure stimulus of the air brings his nerves into unnatural sensitiveness and activity. His few diseases are brief and fatal. Rapid evaporation absorbs the juices of his body, and he grows cachectic. Hospitality is formal. Life assumes its most serious aspect. In religion he is austere; in debauchery violent and excessive, but irregular.

The thoughtful observer cannot fail to conclude that Kansas is to be the theatre of some extraordinary development in the future. Our history, soil, climate, and population have all been exceptional, and they all point to an anomalous destiny. Our position is focal. Energy accumulates here. Our material advancement indicates a concentration of force, such as no State in its infancy has ever witnessed. Every citizen is impressed with the belief that he has a special mission to perform. Every immigrant immediately catches the contagion and sleeps no more. He rushes to the frontier, stakes out a town without an inhabitant, builds a hotel without a guest, starts a newspaper without a subscriber, organizes railroad companies for direct connections with New York, San Francisco, Hudson's Bay, and the Gulf of Mexico. When two or three are gathered together they vote a million dollars of ten per cent. bonds, payable in London, and before the prairie dogs have had time to secure a new location the bonds are sold, locomotives are heard screaming in the distance, a strange population assembles from the four quarters of the globe, and an impassioned orator rises in the next State convention and demands the nomination of the Honorable Ajax Agamemnon of Marathon, to represent that ancient constituency in the halls of the national congress. In a year, or a month, it may be, the excitement subsides, corner

lots can be bought for less than the price of quarter sections, "jimson weed" starts up in the streets, second-hand clothing men purchase the improvements for a tenth of their cost, and the volcano breaks out again in some other part of the State.

The names of dead Kansas newspapers outnumber the living; her acts of incorporation for forgotten cities, towns, railroads, ferries, colleges, cemeteries, banks, fill ponderous volumes; the money that has been squandered in these chimerical schemes would build the Capitol of polished marble, and cover its dome with beaten gold.

But, notwithstanding this random and spasmodic activity, our solid progress has been without parallel. No community in the world can show a corresponding advancement in the same time and under similar circumstances. Guided by reflection, directed by prudence, controlled by calm reason, upon what higher eminence these intense forces might have placed us can hardly be conjectured. But such a career, however fortunate it might have been, our physical surroundings have rendered impossible. The sudden release of the accumulated energy so long imprisoned in the useless soil, the prodigious store of electricity in the atmosphere, and the resentment which Nature always exhibits at the invasion of her solitudes, all contributed to induce a social disorder as intemperate as their own. But an improvement in our physical conditions is already perceptible. The introduction of the metals in domestic and agricultural implements, jewelry, railroads, and telegraphs, has, to a great extent, restored the equilibrium, and by constantly conducting electricity to the earth, prevents local congestion and a recurrence of the tempests and tornadoes of early days. The rains which were wont to run from the trampled pavement of the sod suddenly into the streams are now absorbed into the cultivated soil, and gradually restored to the air by solar evaporation, making the alternation of the seasons less violent, and continued droughts less probable. Under these benign influences, prairie grass is disappearing. The various breeds of cattle, hogs, and horses are improving. The culture of orchards and vineyards yields more certain returns. A richer, healthier, and more varied diet is replacing the side meat and corn pone of antiquity. Blue Grass is marching into the bowels of the land without impediment. Its perennial verdure already clothes the bluffs and uplands along the streams, its spongy sward retaining the moisture of the earth, preventing the

annual scarification by fire, promoting the growth of forests, and elevating the nature of man.

Supplementing this material improvement is an evident advance in manners and morals. The little log schoolhouse is replaced by magnificent structures furnished with every educational appliance. Churches multiply. The commercial element has disappeared from politics. The intellectual standard of the press has advanced, and with the general diffusion of Blue Grass we may reasonably anticipate a career of unexampled and enduring prosperity.

The drama has opened with a stately procession of historic events. No ancient issues confuse the theme. No buried nations sleep in the untainted soil, vexing the present with their phantoms, retarding progress with the burden of their outworn creeds, depressing enthusiasm by the silent reproof of their mighty achievements. Heirs of the greatest results of time, we are emancipated from all allegiance to the past. Unincumbered by precedents, we stand in the vestibule of a future which is destined to disclose upon this arena time's noblest offspring,— the perfected flower of American manhood.

From the Kansas Magazine
September, 1872

WASHINGTON IRVING

(1783–1859)

NEXT to Addison himself, Washington Irving is the most thorough master of Addison's prose style. Indeed, it is not a paradox to say that at times he writes the Addisonian essay better than Addison himself, for he has a delicacy of touch in portrait drawing and character sketching which he does not lose even when he is most serious; while Addison's tender humor is far from being a characteristic of all his Spectator essays. This in Addison is not an indication of inferiority, but an incident of that solidity of judgment and loftiness of thought which are as characteristic of him at his very best as parody and burlesque are of Irving when he throws off the restraints of his classical training. Addison could not have written the Knickerbocker "History of New York," nor could Irving have written Addison's essay "On the Message of the Stars" in the Spectator of August 22d, 1712. We can see, too, that Irving's best characters in "Bracebridge Hall" are the near relations of Sir Roger de Coverley's family and friends. But if Irving takes pleasure in openly imitating the manner of the Spectator, he succeeds to an eminent degree in doing what no one else has been able to do at all,—in giving new vitality and a distinct individuality to everything he borrows from the masters of Queen Anne's reign.

Irving differs from the Spectator school much more in character than in style. To them the essay was to be the means of reforming a depraved generation. They had a deep consciousness of a serious mission, and as a result they often cease to amuse in their anxiety to instruct. Irving has little of the reformer in him. He saw the inconsistencies and incongruities of human character and of the history which grows out of them; but instead of preaching, he laughed. He is, by nature a story-teller rather than a "Vates," as Addison was, and all his essays tend to become stories. In the "Alhambra," the essay and the tale are so blended that it is impossible to separate them. So in his masterpieces, "Rip Van Winkle" and "The Legend of Sleepy Hollow," Irving, though he is still a pupil of Addison, is no longer an essayist at all, but a story-teller, illustrating a highly developed faculty of inventing plots of which Addison shows only a rudimentary trace. Charming as he is in essay writing, Irving's great strength lies in easy narrative. This he understood so thoroughly that when his

extensive writings are analyzed they are found to be nearly all narrative. Even his lightest sketches have a tendency to develop a plot. His portraits will not stay upon his easel. They "come to life," step down and begin to act in the most animated manner before they are more than half drawn. In this he resembles Hawthorne, and it is this chiefly which differentiates him from the "wits" of Queen Anne's reign. We believe in Sir Roger de Coverley—as the most admirable literary portrait ever painted. But we accept Rip Van Winkle, with all his improbabilities, as one of the high realities of a supernatural world,—not a portrait, but an absolute illogical necessity, who, when once created by Irving, is as much alive as we are. What this means we can the better realize by remembering that the difficulty of presenting Sir Roger on the stage would be as insuperable as that of keeping Rip Van Winkle off.

Irving was born at New York, April 3d, 1783. His father, William Irving, was an Englishman, and Irving at early maturity had none of the prejudice against English manners and institutions which often characterized young Americans of that time. In 1804, when he went abroad for two years for his health, he received the first impulse towards a mode of writing in which he excels,—that of describing the customs of other countries in such sketches and essays as those of "Bracebridge Hall" and the "Alhambra." In 1815 he went abroad again, and "Bracebridge Hall," which appeared seven years later, made him a great favorite with the aristocratic party in England. His Knickerbocker "History of New York," which appeared in 1809, had made him famous in America. "The Sketch Book" appeared in parts in 1819, and was published in book form in 1820. Until his death, November 28th, 1859, he continued to write one volume after another of sketches, biographies, and histories with hardly a dull line in them. It is not necessary and it would be ungrateful to complain that he lacks depth, while no doubt it is true that no other author of his generation has written so voluminously and so entertainingly on such a wide range of subjects.

W. V. B.

BRACEBRIDGE HALL

The ancientest house, and the best for housekeeping, in this county or the next; and though the master of it write but Squire, I know no lord like him.—"Merry Beggars."

THE reader, if he has perused the volumes of "The Sketch Book," will probably recollect something of the Bracebridge family, with which I once passed a Christmas. I am now on another visit at the Hall, having been invited to a wedding which is shortly to take place. The Squire's second son, Guy, a fine, spirited young captain in the army, is about to be married to his father's ward. the fair Julia Templeton. A gathering of relations and friends has already commenced, to celebrate the joyful occasion; for the old gentleman is an enemy to quiet, private weddings. "There is nothing," he says, "like launching a young couple gayly, and cheering them from the shore; a good outset is half the voyage."

Before proceeding any further, I would beg that the Squire might not be confounded with that class of hard-riding, fox-hunting gentlemen so often described, and, in fact, so nearly extinct in England. I use this rural title partly because it is his universal appellation throughout the neighborhood, and partly because it saves me the frequent repetition of his name, which is one of those rough old English names at which Frenchmen exclaim in despair.

The Squire is, in fact, a lingering specimen of the old English country gentleman; rusticated a little by living almost entirely on his estate, and something of a humorist, as Englishmen are apt to become when they have an opportunity of living in their own way. I like his hobby passing well, however, which is a bigoted devotion to old English manners and customs; it jumps a little with my own humor, having as yet a lively and unsated curiosity about the ancient and genuine characteristics of my "fatherland."

There are some traits about the Squire's family, also, which appear to me to be national. It is one of those old aristocratical families, which, I believe, are peculiar to England, and scarcely understood in other countries; that is to say, families of the ancient gentry. who, though destitute of titled rank, maintain a high

ancestral pride; who look down upon all nobility of recent creation, and would consider it a sacrifice of dignity to merge the venerable name of their house in a modern title.

This feeling is very much fostered by the importance which they enjoy on their hereditary domains. The family mansion is an old manor house, standing in a retired and beautiful part of Yorkshire. Its inhabitants have been always regarded, through the surrounding country, as "the great ones of the earth"; and the little village near the Hall looks up to the Squire with almost feudal homage. An old manor house, and an old family of this kind, are rarely to be met with at the present day; and it is probably the peculiar humor of the Squire that has retained this secluded specimen of English housekeeping in something like the genuine old style.

I am again quartered in the paneled chamber, in the antique wing of the house. The prospect from my window, however, has quite a different aspect from that which it wore on my winter visit. Through the early month of April, yet a few warm, sunshiny days have drawn forth the beauties of the spring, which, I think, are always most captivating on their first opening. The parterres of the old-fashioned garden are gay with flowers; and the gardener has brought out his exotics, and placed them along the stone balustrades. The trees are clothed with green buds and tender leaves. When I throw open my jingling casement, I smell the odor of mignonette, and hear the hum of the bees from the flowers against the sunny wall, with the varied song of the throstle, and the cheerful notes of the tuneful little wren.

While sojourning in this stronghold of old fashions, it is my intention to make occasional sketches of the scenes and characters before me. I would have it understood, however, that I am not writing a novel, and have nothing of intricate plot or marvelous adventure to promise the reader. The Hall of which I treat has, for aught I know, neither trapdoor, nor sliding panel, nor donjon keep; and, indeed, appears to have no mystery about it. The family is a worthy well-meaning family, that, in all probability, will eat and drink, and go to bed, and get up regularly, from one end of my work to the other; and the Squire is so kind-hearted that I see no likelihood of his throwing any kind of distress in the way of the approaching nuptials. In a word, I cannot foresee a single extraordinary event that is likely to occur in the whole term of my sojourn at the Hall.

I tell this honestly to the reader, lest, when he finds me dallying along, through every-day English scenes, he may hurry ahead, in hopes of meeting with some marvelous adventure further on. I invite him, on the contrary, to ramble gently on with me, as he would saunter out into the fields, stopping occasionally to gather a flower, or listen to a bird, or admire a prospect, without any anxiety to arrive at the end of his career. Should I, however, in the course of my wanderings about this old mansion see or hear anything curious, that might serve to vary the monotony of this every-day life, I shall not fail to report it for the reader's entertainment:—

> "For freshest wits I know will soon be wearie
> Of any book, how grave soe'er it be,
> Except it have odd matter, strange and merrie,
> Well sauc'd with lies and gláréd all with glee."

Complete. From "Bracebridge Hall."

THE BUSY MAN

A decayed gentleman who lives most upon his own mirth and my master's means, and much good do him with it. He does hold my master up with his stories, and songs, and catches, and such tricks and jigs, you would admire — he is with him now.
—"A JOVIAL CREW."

By no one has my return to the Hall been more heartily greeted than by Mr. Simon Bracebridge, or Master Simon, as the Squire most commonly calls him. I encountered him just as I entered the park, where he was breaking a pointer, and he received me with all the hospitable cordiality with which a man welcomes a friend to another one's house. I have already introduced him to the reader as a brisk, old, bachelor-looking little man; the wit and superannuated beau of a large family connection, and the Squire's factotum. I found him, as usual, full of bustle, with a thousand petty things to do, and persons to attend to, and in chirping good humor; for there are few happier beings than a busy idler,—that is to say, a man who is eternally busy about nothing.

I visited him, the morning after my arrival, in his chamber, which is in a remote corner of the mansion, as he says he likes

VI—145

to be to himself, and out of the way. He has fitted it up in his own taste, so that it is a perfect epitome of an old bachelor's notions of convenience and arrangement. The furniture is made up of odd pieces from all parts of the house, chosen on account of their suiting his notions, or fitting some corner of his apartment; and he is very eloquent in praise of an ancient elbow chair, from which he takes occasion to digress into a censure on modern chairs, as having degenerated from the dignity and comfort of high-backed antiquity.

Adjoining to his room is a small cabinet, which he calls his study. Here are some hanging shelves, of his own construction, on which are several old works on hawking, hunting, and farriery, and a collection or two of poems and songs of the reign of Elizabeth, which he studies out of compliment to the Squire; together with the Novelist's Magazine, the Sporting Magazine, the Racing Calendar, a volume or two of the Newgate Calendar, a book of the peerage, and another of heraldry.

His sporting dresses hang on pegs in a small closet; and about the walls of his apartment are hooks to hold his fishing tackle, whips, spurs, and a favorite fowling piece, curiously wrought and inlaid, which he inherits from his grandfather. He has, also, a couple of old single-keyed flutes, and a fiddle which he has repeatedly patched and mended himself, affirming it to be a veritable Cremona; though I have never heard him extract a single note from it that was not enough to make one's blood run cold. From this little nest his fiddle will often be heard, in the stillness of midday, drowsily sawing some long-forgotten tune; for he prides himself on having a choice collection of good old English music, and will scarcely have anything to do with modern composers. The time, however, at which his musical powers are of most use is now and then of an evening, when he plays for the children to dance in the hall, and he passes among them and the servants for a perfect Orpheus.

His chamber also bears evidence of his various avocations: there are half-copied sheets of music; designs for needlework; sketches of landscapes, very indifferently executed; a camera lucida; a magic lantern, for which he is endeavoring to paint glasses; in a word, it is the cabinet of a man of many accomplishments, who knows a little of everything, and does nothing well.

After I had spent some time in his apartments, admiring the ingenuity of his small inventions, he took me about the establish-

ment to visit the stables, dog kennel, and other dependencies, in which he appeared like a general visiting the different quarters of his camp; as the Squire leaves the control of all these matters to him, when he is at the Hall. He inquired into the state of the horses; examined their feet; prescribed a drench for one, and bleeding for another; and then took me to look at his own horse, on the merits of which he dwelt with great prolixity, and which, I noticed, had the best stall in the stable.

After this I was taken to a new toy of his and the Squire's, which he termed the falconry, where there were several unhappy birds in durance, completing their education. Among the number was a fine falcon, which Master Simon had in especial training, and he told me that he would show me, in a few days, some rare sport of the good old-fashioned kind. In the course of our round, I noticed that the grooms, gamekeeper, whippers-in, and other retainers, seemed all to be on somewhat of a familiar footing with Master Simon, and fond of having a joke with him, though it was evident they had great deference for his opinion in matters relating to their functions.

There was one exception, however, in a testy old huntsman, as hot as a peppercorn; a meagre, wiry old fellow, in a threadbare velvet jockey cap, and a pair of leather breeches, that, from much wear, shone as though they had been japanned. He was very contradictory and pragmatical and apt, as I thought, to differ from Master Simon now and then, out of mere captiousness. This was particularly the case with respect to the treatment of the hawk, which the old man seemed to have under his peculiar care, and, according to Master Simon, was in a fair way to ruin; the latter had a vast deal to say about casting, and imping, and gleaming, and enseaming, and giving the hawk the rangle, which I saw was all heathen Greek to old Christy; but he maintained his point notwithstanding, and seemed to hold all this technical lore in utter disrespect.

I was surprised at the good humor with which Master Simon bore his contradictions, till he explained the matter to me afterwards. Old Christy is the most ancient servant in the place, having lived among dogs and horses the greater part of a century, and had been in the service of Mr. Bracebridge's father. He knows the pedigree of every horse on the place, and has bestrode the great great-grandsires of most of them. He can give a circumstantial detail of every fox hunt for the last sixty or

seventy years, and has a history for every stag's head about the house and for every hunting trophy nailed to the door of the dog kennel.

All the present race have grown up under his eye, and humor him in his old age. He once attended the Squire to Oxford, when he was student there, and enlightened the whole university with his hunting lore. All this is enough to make the old man opinionated, since he finds, on all these matters of first-rate importance, he knows more than the rest of the world. Indeed, Master Simon had been his pupil, and acknowledges that he derived his first knowledge in hunting from the instructions of Christy; and I much question whether the old man does not still look upon him as rather a greenhorn.

On our return homewards, as we were crossing the lawn in front of the house, we heard the porter's bell ring at the lodge, and shortly afterwards a kind of cavalcade advanced slowly up the avenue. At sight of it my companion paused, considered it for a moment, and then, making a sudden exclamation, hurried away to meet it. As it approached I discovered a fair, fresh-looking elderly lady, dressed in an old-fashioned riding habit, with a broad-brimmed white beaver hat, such as may be seen in Sir Joshua Reynolds' paintings. She rode a sleek white pony, and was followed by a footman in rich livery, mounted on an over-fed hunter. At a little distance in the rear came an ancient cumbrous chariot, drawn by two very corpulent horses, driven by as corpulent a coachman, beside whom sat a page dressed in a fanciful green livery. Inside of the chariot was a starched prim personage, with a look somewhat between a lady's companion and a lady's maid, and two pampered curs, that showed their ugly faces, and barked out of each window.

There was a general turning out of the garrison to receive this newcomer. The squire assisted her to alight, and saluted her affectionately; the fair Julia flew into her arms, and they embraced with the romantic fervor of boarding-school friends; she was escorted into the house by Julia's lover, towards whom she showed distinguished favor; and a line of the old servants, who had collected in the Hall, bowed most profoundly as she passed.

I observed that Master Simon was most assiduous and devout in his attentions upon this old lady. He walked by the side of her pony up the avenue; and, while she was receiving the salutations of the rest of the family, he took occasion to notice the fat coachman, to pat the sleek carriage horses, and, above all, to say a civil word to my lady's gentlewoman, the prim, sour-looking vestal in the chariot.

I had no more of his company for the rest of the morning. He was swept off in the vortex that followed in the wake of this lady. Once, indeed, he paused for a moment, as he was hurrying on some errand of the good lady, to let me know that this was Lady Lillycraft, a sister of the Squire, of large fortune, which the captain would inherit, and that her estate lay in one of the best sporting counties in all England.

Complete. From « Bracebridge Hall.»

GENTILITY

—— True Gentrie standeth in the trade
Of virtuous life, not in the fleshly line;
For blood is knit, but Gentrie is divine.
—« Mirror for Magistrates.»

I HAVE mentioned some peculiarities of the Squire in the education of his sons; but I would not have it thought that his instructions were directed chiefly to their personal accomplishments. He took great pains also to form their minds, and to inculcate what he calls good old English principles, such as are laid down in the writings of Peachem and his contemporaries. There is one author of whom he cannot speak without indignation, which is Chesterfield. He avers that he did much, for a time, to injure the true national character, and to introduce, instead of open manly sincerity, a hollow perfidious courtliness. « His maxims,» he affirms, « were calculated to chill the delightful enthusiasm of youth, and to make them ashamed of that romance which is the dawn of generous manhood, and to impart to them a cold polish and a premature worldliness.» « Many of Lord Chesterfield's maxims would make a young man a mere man of pleasure; but an English gentleman should not be a mere man of pleasure. He has no right to such selfish indulgence. His ease, his leisure, his opulence, are debts due to his country, which he must ever stand ready to discharge. He should be a man at all points; simple, frank, courteous, intelligent, accomplished, and informed; upright, intrepid, and disinterested; one who can mingle among

freemen; who can cope with statesmen; who can champion his country and its rights either at home or abroad. In a country like England, where there is such free and unbounded scope for the exertion of intellect, and where opinion and example have such weight with the people, every gentleman of fortune and leisure should feel himself bound to employ himself in some way towards promoting the prosperity or glory of the nation. In a country where intellect and action are trammeled and restrained men of rank and fortune may become idlers and triflers with impunity; but an English coxcomb is inexcusable; and this, perhaps, is the reason why he is the most offensive and insupportable coxcomb in the world.»

The Squire, as Frank Bracebridge informs me, would often hold forth in this manner to his sons when they were about leaving the paternal roof; one to travel abroad, one to go to the army, and one to the university. He used to have them with him in the library, which is hung with the portraits of Sydney, Surrey, Raleigh, Wyat, and others. « Look at those models of true English gentlemen, my sons,» he would say with enthusiasm; « those were men that wreathed the graces of the most delicate and refined taste around the stern virtues of the soldier; that mingled what was gentle and gracious with what was hardy and manly; that possessed the true chivalry of spirit, which is the exalted essence of manhood. They are the lights by which the youth of the country should array themselves. They were the patterns and idols of their country at home; they were the illustrators of its dignity abroad. 'Surrey,' says Camden, 'was the first nobleman that illustrated his high birth with the beauty of learning. He was acknowledged to be the gallantest man, the politest lover, and the completest gentleman of his time.' And as to Wyat, his friend Surrey most amiably testifies of him, that his person was majestic and beautiful, his visage 'stern and mild'; that he sang, and played the lute with remarkable sweetness; spoke foreign languages with grace and fluency, and possessed an inexhaustible fund of wit. And see what a high commendation is passed upon these illustrious friends: 'They were the two chieftains, who, having traveled into Italy, and there tasted the sweet and stately measures and style of the Italian poetry, greatly polished our rude and homely manner of vulgar poetry from what it had been before, and therefore may be justly called the reformers of our English poetry and style.' And Sir Philip

Sydney, who has left us such monuments of elegant thought and generous sentiment, and who illustrated his chivalrous spirit so gloriously in the field. And Sir Walter Raleigh, the elegant courtier, the intrepid soldier, the enterprising discoverer, the enlightened philosopher, the magnanimous martyr. These are the men for English gentlemen to study. Chesterfield, with his cold and courtly maxims, would have chilled and impoverished such spirits. He would have blighted all the budding romance of their temperaments. Sydney would never have written his 'Arcadia,' nor Surrey have challenged the world in vindication of the beauties of his 'Geraldine.' These are the men, my sons,» the Squire will continue, « that show to what our national character may be exalted, when its strong and powerful qualities are duly wrought up and refined. The solidest bodies are capable of the highest polish; and there is no character that may be wrought to a more exquisite and unsullied brightness than that of the true English gentleman.»

When Guy was about to depart for the army, the Squire again took him aside, and gave him a long exhortation. He warned him against that affectation of cold-blooded indifference, which he was told was cultivated by the young British officers, among whom it was a study to « sink the soldier» in the mere man of fashion. « A soldier,» said he, « without pride and enthusiasm in his profession, is a mere sanguinary hireling. Nothing distinguishes him from the mercenary bravo but a spirit of patriotism or a thirst for glory. It is the fashion nowadays, my son,» said he, « to laugh at the spirit of chivalry; when that spirit is really extinct, the profession of a soldier becomes a mere trade of blood.» He then set before him the conduct of Edward the Black Prince, who is his mirror of chivalry; valiant, generous, affable, humane; gallant in the field; but when he came to dwell on his courtesy toward his prisoner, the king of France,— how he received him in his tent, rather as a conqueror than as a captive,— attended on him at table like one of his retinue,— rode uncovered beside him on his entry into London, mounted on a common palfrey, while his prisoner was mounted in state on a white steed of stately beauty,— the tears of enthusiasm stood in the old gentleman's eyes.

Finally, on taking leave, the good Squire put in his son's hands, as a manual, one of his favorite old volumes, the « Life of the Chevalier Bayard,» by Godefroy; on a blank page of which he had written an extract from the « Morte d'Arthur,» containing the

eulogy of Sir Ector over the body of Sir Launcelot of the Lake, which the Squire considers as comprising the excellencies of a true soldier. « Ah, Sir Launcelot! thou wert head of all Christian knights; now there thou liest; thou wert never matched of none earthly knights-hands. And thou wert the curtiest knight that ever bare shield. And thou wert the truest friend to thy lover that ever bestrood horse; and thou wert the truest lover of a sinful man that ever loved woman. And thou wert the kindest man that ever strook with sword; and thou wert the goodliest person that ever came among the presse of knights. And thou wert the meekest man and the gentlest that ever ate in hall among ladies. And thou wert the sternest knight to thy mortal foe that ever put spear in rest.»

Complete. From « Bracebridge Hall.»

FORTUNE TELLING

Each city, each town, and every village,
Afford us either an alms or pillage;
And if the weather be cold and raw,
Then in a barn we tumble on straw.
If warm and fair, by yea-cock and nay-cock,
The fields will afford us a hedge or a hay-cock.
—« Merry Beggars.»

A S I was walking one evening with the Oxonian, Master Simon, and the General, in a meadow not far from the village, we heard the sound of a fiddle, rudely played, and, looking in the direction whence it came, we saw a thread of smoke curling up from among the trees. The sound of music is always attractive; for, wherever there is music, there is good humor, or good will. We passed along a footpath, and had a peep, through a break in the hedge, at the musician and his party, when the Oxonian gave us a wink, and told us that if we would follow him we should have some sport.

It proved to be a gipsy encampment, consisting of three or four little cabins, or tents, made of blankets and sail cloth, spread over hoops stuck in the ground. It was on one side of a green lane, close under a hawthorn hedge, with a broad beech tree spreading above it. A small rill tinkled along close by, through the fresh sward that looked like a carpet.

A teakettle was hanging by a crooked piece of iron over a fire made from dry sticks and leaves, and two old gipsies in red cloaks sat crouched on the grass, gossiping over their evening cup of tea; for these creatures, though they live in the open air, have their ideas of fireside comforts. There were two or three children sleeping on the straw with which the tents were littered; a couple of donkeys were grazing in the lane, and a thievish-looking dog was lying before the fire. Some of the younger gipsies were dancing to the music of a fiddle played by a tall, slender stripling in an old frock coat, with a peacock's feather stuck in his hatband.

As we approached, a gipsy girl with a pair of fine roguish eyes came up and, as usual, offered to tell our fortunes. I could not but admire a certain degree of slattern elegance about the baggage. Her long, black silken hair was curiously plaited in numerous small braids, and negligently put up in a picturesque style that a painter might have been proud to have devised. Her dress was of figured chintz, rather ragged, and not over-clean, but of a variety of most harmonious and agreeable colors; for these beings have a singularly fine eye for colors. Her straw hat was in her hand, and a red cloak thrown over one arm.

The Oxonian offered at once to have his fortune told, and the girl began with the usual volubility of her race; but he drew her on one side, near the hedge, as he said he had no idea of having his secrets overheard. I saw he was talking to her instead of she to him, and, by his glancing towards us now and then, that he was giving the baggage some private hints. When they returned to us, he assumed a very serious air. "Zounds!" said he, "it's very astonishing how these creatures come by their knowledge; this girl has told me some things that I thought no one knew but myself!"

The girl now assailed the General: "Come, your honor," said she, "I see by your face you're a lucky man; but you're not happy in your mind; you're not, indeed, sir; but have a good heart, and give me a good piece of silver, and I'll tell you a nice fortune."

The General had received all her approaches with a banter, and had suffered her to get hold of his hand; but at the mention of the piece of silver, he hemmed, looked grave, and, turning to us, asked if we had not better continue our walk. "Come, my master," said the girl, archly, "you'd not be in such a hurry, if you knew all that I could tell you about a fair lady that has a

notion for you. Come, sir, old love burns strong; there's many a one comes to see weddings that go away brides themselves!"— Here the girl whispered something in a low voice, at which the General colored up, was a little fluttered, and suffered himself to be drawn aside under the hedge, where he appeared to listen to her with great earnestness, and at the end paid her half a crown with the air of a man that has got the worth of his money.

The girl next made her attack upon Master Simon, who, however, was too old a bird to be caught, knowing that it would end in an attack upon his purse, about which he is a little sensitive. As he has a great notion, however, of being considered a royster, he chuckled her under the chin, played her off with rather broad jokes, and put on something of the rakehelly air, that we see now and then assumed on the stage, by the sad-boy gentle-men of the old school. "Ah, your honor," said the girl, with a malicious leer, "you were not in such a tantrum last year, when I told you about the widow you know who; but if you had taken a friend's advice, you'd never have come away from Doncaster races with a flea in your ear!"

There was a secret sting in this speech that seemed quite to disconcert Master Simon. He jerked away his hand in a pet, smacked his whip, whistled to his dogs, and intimated that it was high time to go home. The girl, however, was determined not to lose her harvest. She now turned upon me, and, as I have a weakness of spirit where there is a pretty face concerned, she soon wheedled me out of my money, and, in return, read me a fortune, which, if it prove true,—and I am determined to believe it,—will make me one of the luckiest men in the chronicles of Cupid.

I saw that the Oxonian was at the bottom of all this oracular mystery, and was disposed to amuse himself with the General, whose tender approaches to the widow had attracted the notice of the wag. I was a little curious, however, to know the mean-ing of the dark hints which had so suddenly disconcerted Master Simon; and took occasion to fall in the rear with the Oxonian on our way home, when he laughed heartily at my questions, and gave me ample information on the subject.

The truth of the matter is, that Master Simon has met with a sad rebuff since my Christmas visit to the Hall. He used at that time to be joked about a widow, a fine dashing woman, as he privately informed me. I had supposed the pleasure he

betrayed on these occasions resulted from the usual fondness of old bachelors for being teased about getting married, and about flirting, and being fickle and false-hearted. I am assured, however, that Master Simon had really persuaded himself the widow had a kind-ness for him; in consequence of which he had been at some ex-traordinary expense in new clothes, and had actually got Frank Bracebridge to order him a coat from Stultz. He began to throw out hints about the importance of a man's settling himself in life before he grew old; he would look grave whenever the widow and matrimony were mentioned in the same sentence; and privately asked the opinion of the Squire and parson about the prudence of marrying a widow with a rich jointure, but who had several children.

An important member of a great family connection cannot harp much upon the theme of matrimony without its taking wind; and it soon got buzzed about that Mr. Simon Bracebridge was actually gone to Doncaster races, with a new horse; but that he meant to return in a curricle with a lady by his side. Master Simon did, indeed, go to the races, and that with a new horse; and the dash-ing widow did make her appearance in her curricle,—but it was unfortunately driven by a strapping young Irish dragoon, with whom even Master Simon's self-complacency would not allow him to venture into competition, and to whom she was married shortly afterwards.

It was a matter of sore chagrin to Master Simon for several months, having never before been fully committed. The dullest head in the family had a joke upon him; and there is no one that likes less to be bantered than an absolute joker. He took refuge for a time at Lady Lillycraft's, until the matter should blow over; and occupied himself by looking over her accounts, regulat-ing the village choir, and inculcating loyalty into a pet bullfinch, by teaching him to whistle "God Save the King."

He has now pretty nearly recovered from the mortification; holds up his head, and laughs as much as any one; again affects to pity married men, and is particularly facetious about widows, when Lady Lillycraft is not by. His only time of trial is when the General gets hold of him, who is infinitely heavy and perse-vering in his waggery, and will interweave a dull joke through the various topics of a whole dinner time. Master Simon often parries these attacks by a stanza from his old work of "Cupid's Solicitor for Love":—

"'Tis in vain to woo a widow over long,
  In once or twice her mind you may perceive;
Widows are subtle, be they old or young,
  And by their wiles young men they will deceive."
                          Complete. From "Bracebridge Hall."

LOVE CHARMS

—— Come, do not weep, my girl;
Forget him, pretty pensiveness; there will
Come others, every day, as good as he.
                          —Sir J. Suckling.

THE approach of a wedding in a family is always an event of great importance, but particularly so in a household like this in a retired part of the country. Master Simon, who is a pervading spirit, and, through means of the butler and house-keeper, knows everything that goes forward, tells me that the maidservants are continually trying their fortunes, and that the servants' hall has of late been quite a scene of incantation.

It is amusing to notice how the oddities of the head of a family flow down through all the branches. The Squire, in the in-dulgence of his love of everything which smacks of old times, has held so many grave conversations with the parson at table, about popular superstitions and traditional rites, that they have been carried from the parlor to the kitchen by the listening domestics, and, being apparently sanctioned by such high authority, the whole house has become infected by them.

The servants are all versed in the common modes of trying luck and the charms to insure constancy. They read their for-tunes by drawing strokes in the ashes, or by repeating a form of words and looking in a pail of water. St. Mark's Eve, I am told, was a busy time with them,—being an appointed night for certain mystic ceremonies. Several of them sowed hemp seed to be reaped by their true lovers; and they even ventured upon the solemn and fearful preparation of the dumb cake. This must be done fasting, and in silence. The ingredients are handed down in traditional form. "An eggshell full of salt an eggshell full of malt, and an eggshell full of barley meal." When the cake is ready, it is put upon a pan over the fire, and the future husband will appear, turn the cake, and retire; but if a word is spoken, or a fast is broken, during this awful ceremony, there is no knowing what horrible consequences would ensue.

The experiments, in the present instance, came to no result; they that sowed the hemp seed forgot the magic rhyme that they were to pronounce, so the true lover never appeared; and as to the dumb cake, what between the awful stillness they had to keep, and the awfulness of the midnight hour, their hearts failed them when they had put the cake in the pan; so that, on the striking of the great house-clock in the servants' hall, they were seized with a sudden panic, and ran out of the room, to which they did not return until morning, when they found the mystic cake burned to a cinder.

The most persevering at these spells, however, is Phœbe Wilkins, the housekeeper's niece. As she is a kind of privileged personage, and rather idle, she has more time to occupy herself with these matters. She has always had her head full of love and matrimony. She knows the dream book by heart, and is quite an oracle among the little girls of the family, who always come to her to interpret their dreams in the mornings.

During the present gayety of the house, however, the poor girl has worn a face full of trouble; and, to use the housekeeper's words, "has fallen into a sad, hystericky way lately." It seems that she was born and brought up in the village, where her father was parish clerk, and she was an early playmate and sweetheart of young Jack Tibbets. Since she has come to live at the Hall, however, her head has been a little turned. Being very pretty, and naturally genteel, she has been much noticed and indulged; and being the housekeeper's niece, she has held an equivocal station between a servant and a companion. She has learned something of fashions and notions among the young ladies, which has effected quite a metamorphosis; insomuch that her finery at church on Sundays has given mortal offense to her former intimates in the village. This has occasioned the misrepresentations which have awakened the implacable family pride of Dame Tibbets. But what is worse, Phœbe, having a spice of coquetry in her disposition, showed it on one or two occasions to her lover, which produced a downright quarrel; and Jack, being very proud and fiery, has absolutely turned his back upon her for several successive Sundays.

The poor girl is full of sorrow and repentance, and would fain make up with her lover; but he feels his security and stands aloof. In this he is doubtless encouraged by his mother, who is

continually reminding him what he owes to his family; for this same family pride seems doomed to be the eternal bane of lovers.

As I hate to see a pretty face in trouble, I have felt quite concerned for the luckless Phœbe ever since I heard her story. It is a sad thing to be thwarted in love at any time, but particularly so at this tender season of the year, when every living thing, even to the very butterfly, is sporting with its mate; and the green fields, and the budding groves, and the singing of the birds, and the sweet smell of the flowers are enough to turn the head of a love-sick girl. I am told that the coolness of young Ready Money lies very heavy at poor Phœbe's heart. Instead of singing about the house as formerly, she goes about pale and sighing, and is apt to break into tears when her companions are full of merriment.

Mrs. Hannah, the vestal gentlewoman of my Lady Lillycraft, has had long talks and walks with Phœbe, up and down the avenue, of an evening; and has endeavored to squeeze some of her own verjuice into the other's milky nature. She speaks with contempt and abhorrence of the whole sex, and advises Phœbe to despise all the men as heartily as she does. But Phœbe's loving temper is not to be curdled; she has no such thing as hatred or contempt for mankind in her whole composition. She has all the simple fondness of heart of poor, weak, loving woman; and her only thoughts at present are how to conciliate and reclaim her wayward swain.

The spells and love charms, which are matters of sport to the other domestics, are serious concerns with this love-stricken damsel. She is continually trying her fortune in a variety of ways. I am told that she has absolutely fasted for six Wednesdays and three Fridays successively, having understood that it was a sovereign charm to insure being married to one's liking within the year. She carries about, also, a lock of her sweetheart's hair, and a riband he once gave her, being a mode of producing constancy in a lover. She even went so far as to try her fortune by the moon, which has always had much to do with lovers' dreams and fancies. For this purpose she went out in the night of the full moon, knelt on a stone in the meadow, and repeated the old traditional rhyme:—

> "All hail to thee, moon, all hail to thee;
> I pray thee, good moon, now show to me
> The youth who my future husband shall be."

When she came back to the house she was faint and pale, and went immediately to bed. The next morning she told the porter's wife that she had seen some one close by the hedge in the meadow, which she was sure was young Tibbets; at any rate, she had dreamed of him all night,—both of which, the old dame assured her, were most happy signs. It has since turned out that the person in the meadow was old Christy, the huntsman, who was walking his nightly rounds with the great stag hound; so that Phœbe's faith in the charm is completely shaken.

Complete. From "Bracebridge Hall."

THE BROKEN HEART

> I never heard
> Of any true affection, but 'twas nipt
> With care, that, like the caterpillar, eats
> The leaves of the spring's sweetest book, the rose.
> —*Middleton.*

IT IS a common practice with those who have outlived the susceptibility of early feeling, or have been brought up in the gay heartlessness of dissipated life, to laugh at all love stories, and to treat the tales of romantic passion as mere fictions of novelists and poets. My observations on human nature have induced me to think otherwise. They have convinced me that however the surface of the character may be chilled and frozen by the cares of the world, or cultivated into mere smiles by the arts of society, still there are dormant fires lurking in the depths of the coldest bosom, which, when once enkindled, become impetuous, and are sometimes desolating in their effects. Indeed, I am a true believer in the blind deity, and go to the full extent of his doctrines. Shall I confess it?—I believe in broken hearts, and the possibility of dying of disappointed love! I do not, however, consider it a malady often fatal to my own sex; but I firmly believe that it withers down many a lovely woman into an early grave.

Man is the creature of interest and ambition. His nature leads him forth into the struggle and bustle of the world. Love is but the embellishment of his early life, or a song piped in the intervals of the acts. He seeks for fame, for fortune, for space in the world's thought, and dominion over his fellowmen. But a woman's

whole life is a history of the affections. The heart is her world; it is there her ambition strives for empire,—it is there her avarice seeks for hidden treasures. She sends forth her sympathies on adventure; she embarks her whole soul in the traffic of affection; and if shipwrecked, her case is hopeless,—for it is a bankruptcy of the heart.

To a man the disappointment of love may occasion some bitter pangs; it wounds some feelings of tenderness,—it blasts some prospects of felicity; but he is an active being; he may dissipate his thoughts in the whirl of varied occupation, or may plunge into the tide of pleasure; or, if the scene of disappointment be too full of painful associations, he can shift his abode at will, and taking, as it were, the wings of the morning, can "fly to the uttermost parts of the earth, and be at rest."

But woman's is comparatively a fixed, a secluded, and a meditative life. She is more the companion of her own thoughts and feelings; and if they are turned to ministers of sorrow, where shall she look for consolation? Her lot is to be wooed and won; and if unhappy in her love, her heart is like some fortress that has been captured, and sacked, and abandoned, and left desolate.

How many bright eyes grow dim,—how many soft cheeks grow pale,—how many lovely forms fade away into the tomb, and none can tell the cause that blighted their loveliness! As the dove will clasp its wings to its side, and cover and conceal the arrow that is preying on its vitals,—so is it the nature of woman to hide from the world the pangs of wounded affection. The love of a delicate female is always shy and silent. Even when fortunate, she scarcely breathes it to herself; but when otherwise, she buries it in the recesses of her bosom, and there lets it cower and brood among the ruins of her peace. With her, the desire of her heart has failed,—the great charm of existence is at an end. She neglects all the cheerful exercises which gladden the spirit, quicken the pulse, and send the tide of life in healthful currents through the veins. Her rest is broken,—the sweet refreshment of sleep is poisoned by melancholy dreams,— "dry sorrow drinks her blood," until her enfeebled frame sinks under the slightest external injury. Look for her, after a little while, and you find friendship weeping over her untimely grave, and wondering that one, who but lately glowed with all the radiance of health and beauty, should so speedily be brought down to "darkness and the worm." You will be told of some wintry chill, some casual indisposition, that laid her low,—but no one knows the mental malady that previously sapped her strength, and made her so easy a prey to the spoiler.

She is like some tender tree, the pride and beauty of the grove; graceful in its form, bright in its foliage, but with the worm preying at its heart. We find it suddenly withering, when it should be most fresh and luxuriant. We see it drooping its branches to the earth, and shedding leaf by leaf; until, wasted and perished away, it falls even in the stillness of the forest; and as we muse over the beautiful ruin, we strive in vain to recollect the blast or thunderbolt that could have smitten it with decay.

I have seen many instances of women running to waste and self-neglect, and disappearing gradually from the earth, almost as if they had been exhaled to heaven; and have repeatedly fancied that I could trace their deaths through the various declensions of consumption, cold, debility, languor, melancholy, until I reached the first symptom of disappointed love. But an instance of the kind was lately told to me; the circumstances are well known in the country where they happened, and I shall but give them in the manner in which they were related.

Every one must recollect the tragical story of young E——, the Irish patriot; it was too touching to be soon forgotten. During the troubles in Ireland he was tried, condemned, and executed, on a charge of treason. His fate made a deep impression on public sympathy. He was so young,—so intelligent,—so generous,—so brave,—so everything that we are apt to like in a young man. His conduct under trial, too, was so lofty and intrepid. The noble indignation with which he repelled the charge of treason against his country,—the eloquent vindication of his name,—and his pathetic appeal to posterity, in the hopeless hour of condemnation,—all these entered deeply into every generous bosom, and even his enemies lamented the stern policy that dictated his execution.

But there was one heart, whose anguish it would be impossible to describe. In happier days and fairer fortunes he had won the affections of a beautiful and interesting girl, the daughter of a late celebrated Irish barrister. She loved him with the disinterested fervor of a woman's first and early love. When every

worldly maxim arrayed itself against him; when blasted in fortune, and disgrace and danger darkened around his name, she loved him the more ardently for his very sufferings. If, then, his fate could awaken the sympathy even of his foes, what must have been the agony of her, whose whole soul was occupied by his image? Let those tell who have had the portals of the tomb suddenly closed between them and the being they most loved on earth—who have sat at its threshold, as one shut out in a cold and lonely world, from whence all that was most lovely and loving had departed.

But then the horrors of such a grave!—so frightful, so dishonored! There was nothing for memory to dwell on that could soothe the pang of separation,—none of those tender, though melancholy circumstances, that endear the parting scene,—nothing to melt sorrow into those blessed tears, sent, like the dews of heaven, to revive the heart in the parting hour of anguish.

To render her widowed situation more desolate, she had incurred her father's displeasure by her unfortunate attachment, and was an exile from the paternal roof. But could the sympathy and kind offices of friends have reached a spirit so shocked and driven in by horror, she would have experienced no want of consolation, for the Irish are a people of quick and generous sensibilities. The most delicate and cherishing attentions were paid her by families of wealth and distinction. She was led into society, and they tried by all kinds of occupation and amusement to dissipate her grief, and wean her from the tragical story of her loves. But it was all in vain. There are some strokes of calamity that scathe and scorch the soul,—that penetrate to the vital seat of happiness,—and blast it, never again to put forth bud or blossom. She never objected to frequent the haunts of pleasure, but she was as much alone there as in the depths of solitude. She walked about in a sad reverie, apparently unconscious of the world around her. She carried with her an inward woe that mocked at all the blandishments of friendship, and "heeded not the song of the charmer, charm he never so wisely."

The person who told me her story had seen her at a masquerade. There can be no exhibition of far-gone wretchedness more striking and painful than to meet it in such a scene. To find it wandering like a spectre, lonely and joyless, where all around is gay,—to see it dressed out in the trappings of mirth, and looking so wan and woe-begone, as if it had tried in vain to cheat

the poor heart into a momentary forgetfulness of sorrow. After strolling through the splendid rooms and giddy crowd with an air of utter abstraction, she sat herself down on the steps of an orchestra, and looking about for some time with a vacant air, that showed her insensibility to the garish scene, she began, with the capriciousness of a sickly heart, to warble a little plaintive air. She had an exquisite voice; but on this occasion it was so simple, so touching,—it breathed forth such a soul of wretchedness,—that she drew a crowd, mute and silent, around her, and melted every one into tears.

The story of one so true and tender could not but excite great interest in a country remarkable for enthusiasm. It completely won the heart of a brave officer, who paid his addresses to her, and thought that one so true to the dead could not but prove affectionate to the living. She declined his attentions, for her thoughts were irrecoverably engrossed by the memory of her former lover. He, however, persisted in his suit. He solicited not her tenderness, but her esteem. He was assisted by her conviction of his worth, and her sense of her own destitute and dependent situation, for she was existing on the kindness of friends. In a word, he at length succeeded in gaining her hand, though with the solemn assurance that her heart was unalterably another's.

He took her with him to Sicily, hoping that a change of scene might wear out the remembrance of early woes. She was an amiable and exemplary wife, and made an effort to be a happy one; but nothing could cure the silent and devouring melancholy that had entered into her very soul. She wasted away in a slow, but hopeless decline, and at length sunk into the grave, the victim of a broken heart.

It was on her that Moore, the distinguished Irish poet, composed the following lines:—

She is far from the land where her young hero sleeps,
    And lovers around her are sighing:
But coldly she turns from their gaze, and weeps,
    For her heart in his grave is lying.

She sings the wild song of her dear native plains,
    Every note which he loved awaking—
Ah! little they think, who delight in her strains,
    How the heart of the minstrel is breaking!

He had lived for his love — for his country he died,
    They were all that to life had entwined him —
Nor soon shall the tears of his country be dried,
    Nor long will his love stay behind him!

Oh! make her a grave where the sunbeams rest,
    When they promise a glorious morrow;
They'll shine o'er her sleep, like a smile from the west,
    From her own loved island of sorrow!

Complete. From "The Sketch Book."

STRATFORD-ON-AVON

Thou soft flowing Avon, by thy silver stream
Of things more than mortal sweet Shakespeare would dream;
The fairies by moonlight dance round his green bed,
For hallowed the turf is which pillowed his head.
                                        —Garrick.

TO A homeless man, who has no spot on this wide world which he can truly call his own, there is a momentary feeling of something like independence and territorial consequence, when, after a weary day's travel, he kicks off his boots, thrusts his feet into slippers, and stretches himself before an inn fire. Let the world without go as it may; let kingdoms rise or fall; so long as he has the wherewithal to pay his bill, he is, for the time being, the very monarch of all he surveys. The armchair is his throne, the poker his sceptre, and the little parlor, of some twelve feet square, his undisputed empire. It is a morsel of certainty, snatched from the midst of the uncertainties of life; it is a sunny moment gleaming out kindly on a cloudy day; and he who has advanced some way on the pilgrimage of existence, knows the importance of husbanding even morsels and moments of enjoyment. "Shall I not take mine ease in mine inn?" thought I, as I gave the fire a stir, lolled back in my elbowchair, and cast a complacent look about the little parlor of the Red Horse, at Stratford-on-Avon.

The words of sweet Shakespeare were just passing through my mind as the clock struck midnight from the tower of the church in which he lies buried. There was a gentle tap at the door, and a pretty chambermaid, putting in her smiling face, inquired, in a hesitating air, whether I had rung. I understood it as a modest hint that it was time to retire. My dream of absolute dominion was at an end; so abdicating my throne, like a prudent potentate, to avoid being deposed, and putting the Stratford Guidebook under my arm, as a pillow companion, I went to bed and dreamed all night of Shakespeare, the Jubilee, and David Garrick.

The next morning was one of those quickening mornings which we sometimes have in early spring, for it was about the middle of March. The chills of a long winter had suddenly given way; the north wind had spent its last gasp; and a mild air came stealing from the west, breathing the breath of life into nature, and wooing every bud and flower to burst forth into fragrance and beauty.

I had come to Stratford on a poetical pilgrimage. My first visit was to the house where Shakespeare was born, and where, according to tradition, he was brought up to his father's craft of wool combing. It is a small, mean-looking edifice of wood and plaster, a true nestling place of genius, which seems to delight in hatching its offspring in bycorners. The walls of its squalid chambers are covered with names and inscriptions in every language, by pilgrims of all nations, ranks, and conditions, from the prince to the peasant; and present a simple, but striking instance of the spontaneous and universal homage of mankind to the great poet of nature.

The house is shown by a garrulous old lady, with a frosty red face, lighted up by a cold blue anxious eye, and garnished with artificial locks of flaxen hair, curling from under an exceedingly dirty cap. She was peculiarly assiduous in exhibiting the relics with which this, like all other celebrated shrines, abounds. There was the shattered stock of the very matchlock with which Shakespeare shot the deer on his poaching exploits. There, too, was his tobacco box; which proves that he was a rival smoker of Sir Walter Raleigh; the sword also with which he played Hamlet; and the identical lantern with which Friar Lawrence discovered Romeo and Juliet at the tomb! There was an ample supply also of Shakespeare's mulberry tree, which seems to have as extraordinary powers of self-multiplication as the wood of the true cross; of which there is enough extant to build a ship of the line.

The most favorite object of curiosity, however, is Shakespeare's chair. It stands in the chimney nook of a small gloomy chamber, just behind what was his father's shop. Here he may many a time have sat when a boy, watching the slowly revolving spit

with all the longing of an urchin; or of an evening, listening to the crones and gossips of Stratford, dealing forth churchyard tales and legendary anecdotes of the troublesome times of England. In this chair it is the custom of every one who visits the house to sit; whether this be done with the hope of imbibing any of the inspiration of the bard, I am at a loss to say,—I merely mention the fact; and my hostess privately assured me that, though built of solid oak, such was the fervent zeal of devotees that the chair had to be new bottomed at least once in three years. It is worthy of notice also, in the history of this extraordinary chair, that it partakes something of the volatile nature of the Santa Casa of Loretto, or the flying chair of the Arabian enchanter; for though sold some few years since to a Northern princess, yet, strange to tell, it has found its way back again to the old chimney corner.

I am always of easy faith in such matters, and am very willing to be deceived, where the deceit is pleasant and costs nothing. I am therefore a ready believer in relics, legends, and local anecdotes of goblins and great men; and would advise all travelers who travel for their gratification to be the same. What is it to us whether these stories be true or false so long as we can persuade ourselves into the belief of them, and enjoy all the charm of the reality? There is nothing like resolute good-humored credulity in these matters; and on this occasion I went even so far as willingly to believe the claims of mine hostess to a lineal descent from the poet, when, unluckily for my faith, she put into my hands a play of her own composition, which set all belief in her consanguinity at defiance.

From the birthplace of Shakespeare a few paces brought me to his grave. He lies buried in the chancel of the parish church, a large and venerable pile, moldering with age, but richly ornamented. It stands on the banks of the Avon, on an embowered point, and separated by adjoining gardens from the suburbs of the town. Its situation is quiet and retired; the river runs murmuring at the foot of the churchyard, and the elms which grow upon its banks droop their branches into its clear bosom. An avenue of limes, the boughs of which are curiously interlaced, so as to form in summer an arched way of foliage, leads up from the gate of the yard to the church porch. The graves are overgrown with grass; the gray tombstones, some of them nearly sunk into the earth, are half covered with moss, which has likewise tinted the reverend old building. Small birds have built

their nests among the cornices and fissures of the walls, and keep up a continual flutter and chirping; and rooks are sailing and cawing about its lofty gray spire.

In the course of my rambles I met with the gray-headed sexton, and accompanied him home to get the key of the church. He had lived in Stratford, man and boy, for eighty years, and seemed still to consider himself a vigorous man, with the trivial exception that he had nearly lost the use of his legs for a few years past. His dwelling was a cottage, looking out upon the Avon and its bordering meadows; and was a picture of that neatness, order, and comfort, which pervade the humblest dwellings in this country. A low whitewashed room, with a stone floor, carefully scrubbed, served for parlor, kitchen, and hall. Rows of pewter and earthen dishes glittered along the dresser. On an old oaken table, well rubbed and polished, lay the family Bible and prayer book, and the drawer contained the family library, composed of about half a score of well-thumbed volumes. An ancient clock, that important article of cottage furniture, ticked on the opposite side of the room; with a bright warming pan hanging on one side of it, and the old man's horn-handled Sunday cane on the other. The fireplace, as usual, was wide and deep enough to admit a gossip knot within its jambs. In one corner sat the old man's granddaughter sewing, a pretty blue-eyed girl, —and in the opposite corner was a superannuated crony, whom he addressed by the name of John Ange, and who, I found, had been his companion from childhood. They had played together in infancy; they had worked together in manhood; they were now tottering about and gossiping away the evening of life; and in a short time they will probably be buried together in the neighboring churchyard. It is not often that we see two streams of existence running thus evenly and tranquilly side by side; it is only in such quiet "bosom scenes" of life that they are to be met with.

I had hoped to gather some traditionary anecdotes of the bard from these ancient chroniclers; but they had nothing new to impart. The long interval, during which Shakespeare's writings lay in comparative neglect, has spread its shadow over history; and it is his good or evil lot, that scarcely anything remains to his biographers but a scanty handful of conjectures.

The sexton and his companion had been employed as carpenters, on the preparations for the celebrated Stratford jubilee,

and they remembered Garrick, the prime mover of the fête, who superintended the arrangements, and who, according to the sexton, was "a short punch man, very lively and bustling." John Ange had assisted also in cutting down Shakespeare's mulberry tree, of which he had a morsel in his pocket for sale; no doubt a sovereign quickener of literary conception.

I was grieved to hear these two worthy wights speak very dubiously of the eloquent dame who shows the Shakespeare house. John Ange shook his head when I mentioned her valuable and inexhaustible collection of relics, particularly her remains of the mulberry tree; and the old sexton even expressed a doubt as to Shakespeare having been born in her house. I soon discovered that he looked upon her mansion with an evil eye, as a rival to the poet's tomb,—the latter having comparatively but few visitors. Thus it is that historians differ at the very outset, and mere pebbles make the stream of truth diverge into different channels, even at the fountain head.

We approached the church through the avenue of limes, and entered by a Gothic porch, highly ornamented with carved doors of massive oak. The interior is spacious, and the architecture and embellishments superior to those of most country churches. There are several ancient monuments of nobility and gentry, over some of which hang funeral escutcheons, and banners dropping piecemeal from the walls. The tomb of Shakespeare is in the chancel. The place is solemn and sepulchral. Tall elms wave before the pointed windows, and the Avon, which runs at a short distance from the walls, keeps up a low, perpetual murmur. A flat stone marks the spot where the bard is buried. There are four lines inscribed on it, said to have been written by himself, and which have in them something extremely awful. If they are indeed his own, they show that solicitude about the quiet of the grave which seems natural to fine sensibilities and thoughtful minds:—

> "Good friend, for Jesus' sake, forbear
> To dig the dust inclosed here.
> Blest be he that spares these stones,
> And curst be he that moves my bones."

Just over the grave, in a niche of the wall, is a bust of Shakespeare, put up shortly after his death, and considered as a resemblance. The aspect is pleasant and serene, with a finely arched forehead; and I thought I could read in it clear indications of that cheerful, social disposition by which he was as much characterized among his contemporaries as by the vastness of his genius. The inscription mentions his age at the time of his decease — fifty-three years; an untimely death for the world: for what fruit might not have been expected from the golden autumn of such a mind, sheltered as it was from the stormy vicissitudes of life, and flourishing in the sunshine of popular and royal favor!

The inscription on the tombstone has not been without its effect. It has prevented the removal of his remains from the bosom of his native place to Westminster Abbey, which was at one time contemplated. A few years since also, as some laborers were digging to make an adjoining vault, the earth caved in, so as to leave a vacant space almost like an arch, through which one might have reached into his grave. No one, however, presumed to meddle with the remains so awfully guarded by a malediction, and lest any of the idle or the curious, or any collector of relics should be tempted to commit depredations, the old sexton kept watch over the place for two days, until the vault was finished and the aperture closed again. He told me that he had made bold to look in at the hole, but could see neither coffin nor bones; nothing but dust. It was something, I thought, to have seen the dust of Shakespeare.

Next to this grave are those of his wife, his favorite daughter Mrs. Hall, and others of his family. On a tomb close by, also, is a full-length effigy of his old friend John Combe, of usurious memory, on whom he is said to have written a ludicrous epitaph. There are other monuments around, but the mind refuses to dwell on anything that is not connected with Shakespeare. His idea pervades the place — the whole pile seems but as his mausoleum. The feelings, no longer checked and thwarted by doubt, here indulge in perfect confidence; other traces of him may be false or dubious, but here is palpable evidence and absolute certainty. As I trod the sounding pavement there was something intense and thrilling in the idea that in very truth the remains of Shakespeare were moldering beneath my feet. It was a long time before I could prevail upon myself to leave the place; and as I passed through the churchyard I plucked a branch from one of the yew trees, — the only relic that I have brought from Stratford.

From "Stratford on Avon," in the "Sketch Book."

ANNA BROWNELL JAMESON

(1794–1860)

RS. JAMESON, whose "Characteristics of Women" has become a classic, was born in Dublin, May 17th, 1794. Her father, D. Brownell Murphy, was a miniature-painter, no wealthier than artists generally are, and his daughter began life at the age of sixteen as a governess in the family of the Marquis of Winchester. In 1825 she married Robert Jameson, a lawyer, with whom she did not live long. He went as a judge to Jamaica, while she remained at home to pursue her career as an authoress. Her "Characteristics of Women" appeared in 1832, her "Sacred and Legendary Art" from 1848 to 1852, and her "Miscellaneous Essays" in 1846. She wrote also "Celebrated Female Sovereigns" and a number of other works which were once widely read. She died in Middlesex, England, March 17th, 1860.

OPHELIA, POOR OPHELIA

OPHELIA — poor Ophelia! O far too soft, too good, too fair, to be cast among the briers of this working-day world, and fall and bleed upon the thorns of life! What shall be said of her? for eloquence is mute before her! Like a strain of sad sweet music, which comes floating by us on the wings of night and silence, and which we rather feel than hear — like the exhalation of the violet dying even upon the sense it charms — like the snowflake dissolved in air before it has caught a stain of earth — like the light surf severed from the billow, which a breath disperses — such is the character of Ophelia; so exquisitely delicate, it seems as if a touch would profane it; so sanctified in our thoughts by the last and worst of human woes, that we scarcely dare to consider it too deeply. The love of Ophelia, which she never once confesses, is like a secret which we have stolen from her, and which ought to die upon our hearts as upon her own. Her sorrow asks not words, but tears; and her madness has precisely the same effect that

would be produced by the spectacle of real insanity, if brought before us: we feel inclined to turn away and veil our eyes in reverential pity and too painful sympathy.

Beyond every character that Shakespeare has drawn (Hamlet alone excepted) that of Ophelia makes us forget the poet in his own creation. Whenever we bring it to mind it is with the same exclusive sense of her real existence, without reference to the wondrous power which called her into life. The effect (and what an effect!) is produced by means so simple, by strokes so few, and so unobtrusive, that we take no thought of them. It is so purely natural and unsophisticated, yet so profound in its pathos, that, Hazlitt observes, it takes us back to the old ballads — we forget that, in its perfect artlessness, it is the supreme and consummate triumph of art.

The situation of Ophelia in the story is that of a young girl who, at an early age, is brought from a life of privacy into the circle of the court — a court such as we read of in those early times, at once rude, magnificent, and corrupted. She is placed immediately about the person of the queen, and is apparently her favorite attendant. The affection of the wicked queen for this gentle and innocent creature is one of those beautiful redeeming touches, one of those penetrating glances into the secret springs of natural and feminine feeling, which we find only in Shakespeare. Gertrude, who is not so wholly abandoned but that there remains within her heart some sense of the virtues she has forfeited, seems to look with a kind yet melancholy complacency on the lovely being she has destined for the bride of her son; and the scene in which she is introduced as scattering flowers on the grave of Ophelia is one of those effects of contrast in poetry, in character, and in feeling, at once natural and unexpected which fill the eye and make the heart swell and tremble within itself; — like the nightingales singing in the grove of the Furies, in Sophocles.

Again, in the father of Ophelia, the Lord Chamberlain Polonius — the shrewd, wary, subtle, pompous, garrulous old courtier — have we not the very man who would send his son into the world to see all, learn all it could teach of good and evil, but keep his only daughter as far as possible from every taint of that world he knew so well? So that when she is brought to the court she seems in her loveliness and perfect purity like a seraph that had wandered out of bounds, and yet breathed on

earth the air of paradise. When her father and her brother find it necessary to warn her simplicity, give her lessons of worldly wisdom, and instruct her "to be scanter of her maiden presence"; for that Hamlet's vows of love "but breathe like sanctified and pious bonds, the better to beguile"; we feel at once that it comes too late: for from the moment she appears on the scene amid the dark conflict of crime and vengeance, and supernatural terrors, we know what must be her destiny. Once at Murano, I saw a dove caught in a tempest; perhaps it was young, and either lacked strength of wing to reach its home, or the instinct which teaches to shun the brooding storm; but so it was — and I watched it, pitying, as it flitted, poor bird! hither and thither, with its silver pinions shining against the black thundercloud, till, after a few giddy whirls, it fell blinded, affrighted, and bewildered into the turbid wave beneath, and was swallowed up forever. It reminded me then of the fate of Ophelia; and now when I think of her, I see again before me that poor dove, beating with weary wing, bewildered amid the storm. It is the helplessness of Ophelia, arising merely from her innocence, and pictured without any indication of weakness, which melts us with such profound pity. She is so young, that neither her mind nor her person have attained maturity; she is not aware of the nature of her own feelings; they are prematurely developed in their full force before she has strength to bear them, and love and grief together rend and shatter the frail texture of her existence, like the burning fluid poured into a crystal vase. She says very little, and what she does say seems rather intended to hide than to reveal the emotions of her heart; yet in those few words we are made as perfectly acquainted with her character, and with what is passing in her mind, as if she had thrown forth her soul with all the glowing eloquence of Juliet. Passion with Juliet seems innate, a part of her being, "as dwells the gathered lightning in the cloud"; and we never fancy her but with the dark splendid eyes and Titian-like complexion of the south. While in Ophelia we recognize as distinctly the pensive, fair-haired, blue-eyed daughter of the north, whose heart seems to vibrate to the passion she has inspired, more conscious of being loved than of loving; and yet, alas! loving in the silent depths of her young heart, far more than she is loved. . . .

When the heathen would represent their Jove as clothed in all his Olympian terrors, they mounted him on the back of an eagle, and armed him with the lightnings; but when in Holy Writ the Supreme Being is described as coming in his glory, he is upborne on the wings of cherubim, and his emblem is the dove. Even so our blessed religion, which has revealed deeper mysteries in the human soul than ever were dreamed of by Philosophy till she went hand in hand with Faith, has taught us to pay that worship to the symbols of purity and innocence which in darker times was paid to the manifestations of power; and therefore do I think that the mighty intellect, the capacious, soaring, penetrating genius of Hamlet, may be represented without detracting from its grandeur, as reposing upon the tender virgin innocence of Ophelia, with all that deep delight with which a superior nature contemplates the goodness which is at once perfect in itself, and of itself unconscious. That Hamlet regards Ophelia with this kind of tenderness,—that he loves her with a love as intense as can belong to a nature in which there is (I think) much more of contemplation and sensibility than action or passion,—is the feeling and conviction with which I have always read the play of "Hamlet."

As to whether the mind of Hamlet be or be not touched with madness—this is another point at issue among critics, philosophers, aye, and physicians. To me it seems that he is not so far disordered as to cease to be a responsible human being; that were too pitiable: but rather that his mind is shaken from its equilibrium, and bewildered by the horrors of his situation,—horrors, which his fine and subtle intellect, his strong imagination, and his tendency to melancholy, at once exaggerate, and take from him the power either to endure, or "by opposing, end them." We do not see him as a lover, nor as Ophelia first beheld him; for the days when he importuned her with love were before the opening of the drama—before his father's spirit revisited the earth; but we behold him at once in a sea of troubles, of perplexities, of agonies, of terrors; without remorse, he endures all its horrors; without guilt, he endures all its shame. A loathing of the crime he is called on to revenge, which revenge is again abhorrent to his nature, has set him at strife with himself; the supernatural visitation has perturbed his soul to its inmost depths; all things else, all interests, all hopes, all affections, appear as futile, when the majestic shadow comes lamenting from its place of torment "to shake him with thoughts beyond the reaches of his soul!" His love for Ophelia is then ranked by

himself among those trivial, fond records which he has deeply sworn to erase from his heart and brain. He has no thought to link his terrible destiny with hers; he cannot marry her; he cannot reveal to her, young, gentle, innocent as she is, the terrific influences which have changed the whole current of his life and purposes. In his distraction, he overacts the painful part to which he had tasked himself; he is like that judge of the Areopagus who, being occupied with graver matters, flung from him the little bird which had sought refuge in his bosom, and with such angry violence, that unwittingly he killed it.

In the scene with Hamlet in which he madly outrages and upbraids himself, Ophelia says very little; there are two short sentences in which she replies to his wild, abrupt discourse—

Hamlet—I did love you once.
Ophelia—Indeed, my lord, you made me believe so.
Hamlet—You should not have believed me: for virtue cannot so inoculate our old stock, but we shall relish of it. I loved you not.
Ophelia—I was the more deceived.

Those who ever heard Mrs. Siddons read the play of "Hamlet" cannot forget the world of meaning, of love, of sorrow, of despair, conveyed in these two simple phrases. Here, and in the soliloquy afterwards, where she says,—

> "And I of ladies most deject and wretched,
> That sucked the honey of his music vows,"

are the only allusions to herself and her own feelings in the course of the play; and these, uttered almost without consciousness on her own part, contain the revelation of a life of love, and disclose the secret burthen of a heart bursting with its own unuttered grief. She believes Hamlet crazed; she is repulsed, she is forsaken, she is outraged, where she had bestowed her young heart, with all its hopes and wishes; her father is slain by the hand of her lover, as it is supposed, in a paroxysm of insanity; she is entangled inextricably in a web of horrors which she cannot even comprehend, and the result seems inevitable.

Of her subsequent madness what can be said? What an affecting—what an astonishing picture of a mind utterly, hopelessly wrecked!—past hope—past cure! There is the frenzy of excited passions—there is the madness caused by intense and continued thought—there is the delirium of fevered nerves: but

Ophelia's madness is distinct from these; it is not the suspension, but the utter destruction of the reasoning powers; it is the total imbecility which, as medical people well know, too frequently follows some terrible shock to the spirits. Constance is frantic; Lear is mad; Ophelia is insane. Her sweet mind lies in fragments before us—a pitiful spectacle! Her wild, rambling fancies; her aimless, broken speeches; her quick transitions from gayety to sadness—each equally purposeless and causeless; her snatches of old ballads, such as perhaps her nurse sang her to sleep with in her infancy—are all so true to the life, that we forget to wonder, and can only weep. It belonged to Shakespeare alone so to temper such a picture that we can endure to dwell upon it—

> "Thought and affliction, passion, hell itself,
> She turns to favor and to prettiness."

That in her madness she should exchange her bashful silence for empty babbling, her sweet maidenly demeanor for the impatient restlessness that spurns at straws, and say and sing precisely what she never would or could have uttered had she been in possession of her reason, is so far from being an impropriety, that it is an additional stroke of nature. It is one of the symptoms of this species of insanity, as we are assured by physicians. I have myself known one instance in the case of a young Quaker girl, whose character resembled that of Ophelia, and whose malady arose from a similar cause.

The whole action of this play sweeps past us like a torrent which hurries along in its dark and resistless course all the personages of the drama towards a catastrophe which is not brought about by human will, but seems like an abyss ready dug to receive them, where the good and wicked are whelmed together. As the character of Hamlet has been compared, or rather contrasted, with the Greek Orestes, being, like him, called on to avenge a crime by a crime, tormented by remorseful doubts, and pursued by distraction; so to me the character of Ophelia bears a certain relation to that of the Greek Iphigenia, with the same strong distinction between the classical and the romantic conception of the portrait. Iphigenia led forth to sacrifice, with her unresisting tenderness, her mournful sweetness, her virgin innocence, is doomed to perish by that relentless power which has linked her destiny with crimes and contests in which she has no part but

as a sufferer; and even so, poor Ophelia, "divided from herself and her fair judgment," appears here like a spotless victim offered up to the mysterious and inexorable fates.

"For it is the property of crime to extend its mischiefs over innocence, as it is of virtue to extend its blessings over many that deserve them not, while frequently the author of one or the other is not, as far as we can see, either punished or rewarded." But there's a heaven above us!

From "Characteristics of Women."

JOHN JAY

(1745-1829)

OHN JAY, the associate of Hamilton and Madison in writing the essays of the Federalist, was born in New York city, December 12th, 1745. He was a lawyer of much ability, and became prominent as a patriot leader in the early troubles with England. From 1774 to 1779 he represented New York in Congress. In 1780 he went as minister to Spain, and while abroad served as one of the peace commissioners at Paris in 1782. From 1784 to 1789 he was a member of the Cabinet, holding the portfolio of foreign affairs. When the Supreme Court of the United States was organized in 1789, he became its first Chief-Justice. In 1794 he was sent abroad as minister to England, and on his return was elected Governor of New York, serving from 1795 to 1801. He died May 17th, 1829.

CONCERNING DANGERS FROM FOREIGN FORCE AND INFLUENCE

WHEN the people of America reflect that the question now submitted to their determination is one of the most important that has engaged, or can well engage, their attention, the propriety of their taking a comprehensive, as well as a very serious view of it, must be evident.

Nothing is more certain than the indispensable necessity of government; and it is equally undeniable that whenever and however it is instituted, the people must cede to it some of their natural rights, in order to vest it with requisite powers. It is well worthy of consideration, therefore, whether it would conduce more to the interest of the people of America, that they should, to all general purposes, be one nation under one federal government, than that they should divide themselves into separate confederacies, and give to the head of each the same kind of powers which they are advised to place in one national government.

It has until lately been a received and uncontradicted opinion that the prosperity of the people of America depended on their

---

continuing firmly united; and the wishes, prayers, and efforts, of our best and wisest citizens, have been constantly directed to that object. But politicians now appear, who insist that this opinion is erroneous, and that, instead of looking for safety and happiness in union, we ought to seek it in a division of the states into distinct confederacies or sovereignties. However extraordinary this new doctrine may appear, it, nevertheless, has its advocates; and certain characters who were formerly much opposed to it are at present of the number. Whatever may be the arguments or inducements which have wrought this change in the sentiments and declarations of these gentlemen, it certainly would not be wise in the people at large to adopt these new political tenets, without being fully convinced that they are founded in truth and sound policy.

It has often given me pleasure to observe that independent America was not composed of detached and distant territories, but that one connected, fertile, widespreading country, was the portion of our Western sons of liberty. Providence has in a particular manner blessed it with a variety of soils and productions, and watered it with innumerable streams, for the delight and accommodation of its inhabitants. A succession of navigable waters forms a kind of chain round its borders, as if to bind it together; while the most noble rivers in the world, running at convenient distances, present them with highways for the easy communication of friendly aids, and the mutual transportation and exchange of their various commodities.

With equal pleasure I have as often taken notice that Providence has been pleased to give this one connected country to one united people; and a people descended from the same ancestors, speaking the same language, professing the same religion, attached to the same principles of government, very similar in their manners and customs; and who, by their joint counsels, arms, and efforts, fighting side by side, throughout a long and bloody war, have nobly established their general liberty and independence.

This country and this people seem to have been made for each other; and it appears as if it was the design of Providence that an inheritance so proper and convenient for a band of brethren, united to each other by the strongest ties, should never be split into a number of unsocial, jealous, and alien sovereignties.

Similar sentiments have hitherto prevailed among all orders

---

and denominations of men among us. To all general purposes we have uniformly been one people. Each individual citizen everywhere enjoying the same national rights, privileges, and protection. As a nation we have made peace and war; as a nation, we have vanquished our common enemies; as a nation, we have formed alliances, and made treaties, and entered into various compacts and conventions with foreign states.

A strong sense of the value and blessings of union induced the people at a very early period to institute a federal government to preserve and perpetuate it. They formed it almost as soon as they had a political existence; nay, at a time when their habitations were in flames, when many of them were bleeding in the field; and when the progress of hostility and desolation left little room for those calm and mature inquiries and reflections which must ever precede the formation of a wise and well-balanced government for a free people. It is not to be wondered at that a government, instituted in times so inauspicious, should on experiment be found greatly deficient and inadequate to the purpose it was intended to answer.

This intelligent people perceived and regretted these defects. Still continuing no less attached to union than enamored of liberty, they observed the danger which immediately threatened the former and more remotely the latter; and being persuaded that ample security for both could only be found in a national government more wisely framed they, as with one voice, convened the late Convention at Philadelphia, to take that important subject under consideration.

This Convention, composed of men who possessed the confidence of the people, and many of whom had become highly distinguished by their patriotism, virtue, and wisdom, in times which tried the souls of men, undertook the arduous task. In the mild season of peace, with minds unoccupied by other subjects, they passed many months in cool, uninterrupted, and daily consultations. And, finally, without having been awed by power, or influenced by any passion, except love for their country, they presented and recommended to the people the plan produced by their joint and very unanimous counsels.

Admit, for so is the fact, that this plan is only recommended, not imposed; yet, let it be remembered that it is neither recommended to blind approbation, nor to blind reprobation; but to that sedate and candid consideration, which the magnitude and

---

importance of the subject demand, and which it certainly ought to receive. But, as has been already remarked, it is more to be wished than expected that it may be so considered and examined. Experience on a former occasion teaches us not to be too sanguine in such hopes. It is not yet forgotten that well-grounded apprehensions of imminent danger induced the people of America to form the memorable Congress of 1774. That body recommended certain measures to their constituents, and the event proved their wisdom; yet it is fresh in our memories how soon the press began to teem with pamphlets and weekly papers against those very measures. Not only many of the officers of government who obeyed the dictates of personal interest, but others from a mistaken estimate of consequences, from the undue influence of ancient attachments, or whose ambition aimed at objects which did not correspond with the public good, were indefatigable in their endeavors to persuade the people to reject the advice of that patriotic Congress. Many, indeed, were deceived and deluded, but the great majority reasoned and decided judiciously; and happy they are in reflecting that they did so.

They considered that the Congress was composed of many wise and experienced men. That being convened from different parts of the country, they brought with them and communicated to each other a variety of useful information. That in the course of the time they passed together in inquiring into and discussing the true interest of their country, they must have acquired very accurate knowledge on that head. That they were individually interested in the public liberty and prosperity, and therefore that it was not less their inclination than their duty, to recommend such measures only, as after the most mature deliberation they really thought prudent and advisable.

These and similar considerations then induced the people to rely greatly on the judgment and integrity of the Congress; and they took their advice, notwithstanding the various arts and endeavors used to deter and dissuade them from it. But if the people at large had reason to confide in the men of that Congress, few of whom had then been fully tried or generally known, still greater reason have they now to respect the judgment and advice of the Convention; for it is well known that some of the most distinguished members of that Congress, who have been since tried and justly approved for patriotism and abilities, and who have grown old in acquiring political information, were also members of this Convention, and carried into it their accumulated knowledge and experience.

It is worthy of remark, that not only the first, but every succeeding Congress, as well as the late Convention, have invariably joined with the people in thinking that the prosperity of America depended on its Union. To preserve and perpetuate it was the great object of the people in forming that Convention; and it is also the great object of the plan which the Convention has advised them to accept. With what propriety, therefore, or for what good purposes, are attempts at this particular period made by some men, to depreciate the importance of the Union? or why is it suggested that three or four confederacies would be better than one? I am persuaded in my own mind that the people have always thought right on this subject, and that their universal and uniform attachment to the cause of the Union rests on great and weighty reasons.

They who promote the idea of substituting a number of distinct confederacies in the room of the plan of the Convention, seem clearly to foresee that the rejection of it would put the continuance of the Union in the utmost jeopardy; that certainly would be the case; and I sincerely wish that it may be as clearly foreseen by every good citizen, that whenever the dissolution of the Union arrives, America will have reason to exclaim, in the words of the poet, " Farewell! A Long Farewell, to all my Greatness! "

PUBLIUS.

Complete. Number 2 of the Federalist.

RICHARD CLAVERHOUSE JEBB

(1841–)

RICHARD CLAVERHOUSE JEBB, Regius Professor of Greek at Cambridge University, and member of Parliament, was born at Dundee, Scotland, August 27th, 1841. He is a graduate of Trinity College, Cambridge, and the list of his degrees and honors from other institutions is a long one. Among his publications are "The Characters of Theophrastus," "The Attic Orators," "Introduction to Homer," "Lectures on Greek Poetry," "Humanism in Education," "Greek Literature," and "Modern Greece."

HOMER AND THE EPIC

THE Homeric poems give us the earliest sketch of certain political principles which may be traced through every branch of the Indo-European family of nations. Homeric political life has three great elements — King, Council, and Assembly,— the germs of Monarchy, Aristocracy, Democracy. The Homeric king (*Basileus*) leads his people in war, he is supreme judge, and he takes the chief part in public sacrifices to the gods,— but only as the head of the family does in a private sacrifice: the king is not a priest. He rules by divine right. The gods have given to his house that sceptre which he received from his father, and which he will hand on to his son. But his power is limited in three ways. Firstly, he must obey certain customs and traditions of his people, which form a body of unwritten yet positive law (*themistes*), and are the basis on which public justice is administered. Secondly, he must consult his Council (*Boulê*) of nobles and elders. Thirdly, his proposed measures must have the sanction of his whole people in their Assembly (*Agora*). The commoners who make up this Assembly cannot originate or discuss measures; they can only vote Aye or No. The saucy Thersites in the "Iliad" attempts to make a blustering speech, but sits down whimpering with a red weal on his back from the staff of Odysseus. In the "Odyssey" we see the beginning of a time when the Assembly was beginning to play more than this passive

---

part, and when, on the other hand, the king's successor was not necessarily his son or heir, but might be one of the nobles who were now more nearly on a level with him.

Homeric manners are the social side of Homeric politics. The public life is monarchical. The social life is patriarchal. As the king cares for his subjects, so the patriarch cares for his dependants. The intercourse of the chiefs is marked by the courtesy of a noble warrior caste, strangely mingled with brutal ferocity. Achilles is the model of Greek knighthood. His reception of King Priam is worthy of a knight. Yet even then Achilles feels the wild beast within him; he dreads lest, at some rash word, his fury should leap out, and he should slay his helpless old guest. A tie of hospitality (*xenia*) or hereditary friendship is held to exist between men whose fathers have entertained each other, and this claim insures a welcome. Hospitality to all wayfarers is recognized as a duty, since "strangers and beggars are sent by Zeus"; but a man who really "welcomed all comers" is named in the "Iliad" as if his virtue were memorable. Women have a higher position and more freedom than in the later historical age of Greece. Polygamy is unknown among Greeks, and there are few exceptions to the sanctity of marriage. The home life of King Alcinous and Queen Arêtê in the "Odyssey" is like a modern picture of fireside happiness, and no image of girlhood more noble or charming than Nausicaa can be found in poetry. A touch in the "Iliad" shows real feeling for the pathos of a lonely woman's life — the mention of the "true-hearted toiler," working all day long "to win a scanty wage for her children."

The amusements of a chief's country life are hunting, farming, or gardening, playing at games, such as throwing the javelin or quoit, or, after a solid but temperate dinner, listening to the minstrel's song. The mistress of the house weaves or embroiders among her handmaids. Queen Arêtê had made the robe which Nausicaa gave to Odysseus; and the princess helped her mother in household matters, being in sole charge of the washing. Slaves were often of gentle birth and nurture, having been taken in war or kidnaped in childhood; the latter was the case with Eumæus, the trusty swineherd of Odysseus; and we see here how intimate might be the confidence between master and old retainer. The "Iliad" gives us some bright glimpses of simple, joyous life: the patriarchal chief standing silent, glad at

---

heart, among his reapers, while food is being made ready under the trees; the troop of vintagers bearing the baskets of grapes with dance and song from the vineyard; the bridal procession, with the marriage hymn sounding and the bridegroom's friends dancing to flute and harp, while the women stand at their doors to see it pass; the maidens, with their fine linen robes and fair diadems, the youths with glossy tunics and golden swords slung by silver belts, dancing to the minstrel's music, while a delighted crowd looks on.

One test of civilization is the material of which men make their implements. Stone comes before metal. But the metal age itself has periods. In the first period, men use the metals separately, or hammer them together, but do not know how to smelt or fuse or solder them. The Homeric poems belong to the end of this first period. The next step is usually the smelting of copper with tin, so as to make bronze. The metals named come thus in Homeric order of value:— (1) gold; (2) silver; (3) tin; (4) "cyanus" (a dark metal, perhaps bronze, hardly blue steel); (5) iron; (6) copper (*chalcus*, certainly not "brass," *i. e.*, copper + zinc); (7) lead. Fine works in metal are usually of Phœnician workmanship,— as armor (cuirass, shield, helmet),— bowls and vases,— ornamental baskets,— clasps, brooches, necklaces, etc. There is no money. A fine can be paid in gold and copper; "two talents' weight of gold" are once mentioned as a gift of honor; but oxen are the only regular measure of value. A mad bargain is to exchange armor worth 100 oxen for armor worth 9; a precious daughter is one "who brings oxen" (to her parents, in dower from her suitor). There is no certain allusion to writing; in "Iliad," VII. 172, the heroes scratch their marks on their lots, and in VI. 172 the "signs" on the "folded tablet" need not be alphabetical. It does not necessarily follow that the poet could not write himself. In the "Odyssey" we hear of "professional men"—physicians, soothsayers, minstrels, heralds, artificers in wood and metal.

The earth is imagined as a sort of flat oval, with the river Oceanus flowing round it. The poet of the "Iliad" knows the coasts of Asia Minor and their islands, but describes no scenery in Greece Proper, and knows the lands to east and south only from hearsay. The poet of the "Odyssey" had probably never seen Ithaca or its neighboring islands, but knew the Peloponnesus and the eastern parts of Greece Proper. Cyprus (whence "copper") is mentioned in both poems. The Nile is "the river Egypt." Egyptian Thebes is the type of a rich and glorious place — ranking with Orchomenus in Bœotia and (for wealth) with Delphi. Its old greatness under Rameses was long past; Memphis was the capital when these poets sang: but Thebes had been embellished by Sesonchis, founder of the twenty-second Egyptian dynasty, and the fame of his march into Syria may have reached Ionian poets of 930–900 B. C. Sidon, capital and seaport of Phœnicia, is famous for embroidery and metal work. Tyre is never named.

The Greeks themselves, and all men till the end of the last century, were nearly unanimous in believing the "Iliad" and the "Odyssey" to be the work of one poet, Homer. Homer is named in a spurious fragment of Hesiod, but the earliest authentic mention is in the philosopher and poet Xenophanes, who flourished about 510 B. C. The name Homêrus means "fitted together," and was the ordinary word for a hostage, i. e., a pledge agreed upon between two parties. But nothing was accurately known about his life or date. Most opinions placed Homer either in the time when the Ionian colonies in Asia Minor were founded (about 1044 B. C.), or within a century later. The philosopher Aristotle, who wrote on Homer, and the Homeric critic Aristarchus seem to have put him about 1044 B. C. The historian Herodotus (440 B. C.), differing probably from most of his own contemporaries, made Homer, along with Hesiod, live as late as 850 B. C. According to a Greek epigram, Homer was claimed as son by Smyrna, Chios, Colophon, Ithaca, Pylus, Argos, Athens. But all the best evidence connects Homer with Smyrna, an originally Æolian city which afterwards became Ionian. An ancient epithet for him is Melesigenes, "son of Meles," the name of a stream which flowed through old Smyrna, on the border between Æolis and Ionia. This is significant when we remember that the "Iliad" is an Ionian poem on Æolian themes. The unknown author of the "Homeric" hymn to Apollo of Delos speaks of himself as a blind old man living in Chios; the Ancients thought that this hymn was by Homer, and thus the tradition of Homer's blindness was perpetuated. The little island Ios, one of the Cyclades, claimed to have Homer's grave. The Homeridæ, "sons of Homer," who claimed to be descendants of the poet, lived in the Ionian island of Chios. The art of epic poetry was hereditary in their house, as poetry and music and other arts often were in Greek families.

village still hang on the lips of him who recites one of the great Indian epics help us to imagine the passionate sympathy, the tears, the rapture, with which a Greek crowd heard it told how the king of Troy knelt to Achilles in his tent by night, or how the dying hound in the courtyard of Odysseus just lived to give a feeble welcome to the wanderer whom no one else knew.

The Homeric poems were to the Greeks more than national poems have ever been to any people. Every other people, as it has grown older, has turned away from the poetry of its youth, or has even allowed it to perish. Cicero mourns the loss of the early Roman lays; the English ballads in Percy's collection are mere gleanings of a once great harvest; Walter Scott was only in time to save relics from the minstrelsy of the Border. But the Homeric poems were simple and strong enough to be popular early, and mature enough in art to please an age of ripe culture. Boys learned Homer by heart at school, priests quoted him touching the gods, moralists went to him for maxims, statesmen for arguments, cities for claims to territory or alliance, noble houses for the title deeds of their fame. From about 450 B. C., "civic" or "public" editions were prepared by various cities for their own use at public festivals. There was the "edition of Massilia," "of Chios," "of Sinôpê," "of Argos," "of Cyprus," "of Crete." "Private editions," the work of individual revisers, were also numerous. The most famous of these was that prepared by Aristotle for his pupil Alexander, — known as the "Edition of the Casket" from the jeweled case in which Alexander is said to have carried it about with him in the East.

The learned study of Homer at Alexandria reached its highest point in Aristarchus (156 B. C.), whose revision of the text became the standard one, and is mainly the basis of our own. The Alexandrian scholars had no text as old as Pisistratus, and knew little of what his commission had done; they used the editions of the cities, especially Massilia, Chios, and Argos. The division of "Iliad" and "Odyssey" into twenty-four books each is usually ascribed to Aristarchus, but may have been as old as 350 B. C.; before the poems had been divided by "rhapsodies" or short cantos; thus our Book I. of the "Iliad" contained two cantos, "The Anger" and "The Plague." Aristarchus founded a school of Homeric criticism which continued productive till about 200 A. D. All this work is now known only from scanty notices.

Both "Iliad" and "Odyssey" had their first origin on the Ionian coast of Asia Minor, and came thence to Greece Proper. The Spartans said that their lawgiver Lycurgus first brought to Greece a complete copy of the poems, which he had got from the Creophylidæ, a family of poets in Samos. Athens was of small account when the "Iliad" was first sung; the poem mentions it only once, as "a well-built town," and the only one of Athenian warriors who is mentioned by name is quite obscure. But it was at Athens, not at Sparta, that loving care for the poems was first shown in Greece Proper. The traditions of this care refer to the sixth century B. C., and connect themselves with three names, the lawgiver Solon, the tyrant Pisistratus, and his son Hipparchus. Pisistratus, in the last period of his rule (537–527 B. C.) is said to have commissioned some learned men, of whom the poet Onomacritus was the chief, to collect the poems of Homer. It is now generally believed that an "Iliad" and an "Odyssey" already existed in writing at that time, but that the text had become much deranged, especially through the practice of reciting short passages without regard to their context. Besides these two poems, many other epic poems or fragments of the Ionian school went under Homer's name. The great task of the commission was to collect all these "poems of Homer" into one body. From this general stock, they may have supplied what they thought wanting in the "Iliad" and "Odyssey." Their work cannot, in any case, have been critical in a modern sense. But it can hardly be doubted that some systematic attempt to preserve "the poems of Homer" was made in the reign of Pisistratus. And one fact is certain. In the sixth century B. C. reciters of "Homeric poems" regularly competed for a prize at the greatest of Athenian festivals, the Panathenæa, held in every fourth year.

These reciters were called Rhapsodists. "Rhapsodist" means literally "a stitcher of songs"; hence one who weaves a long, smoothly flowing chant, i. e., an epic poet, as chanting his poem in a flowing recitative. The characters of poet and reciter were always united, — first in the early minstrel; then in the hereditary poets, such as the Homeridæ; and then in the free guild of poets, the rhapsodists, to whom the name of Homeridæ was extended. But the early minstrel sang to the harp; the later "rhapsodist" merely chanted, with a branch of laurel, the symbol of poetry, in his hand. Those who tell how the people in an Indian

Our oldest and best manuscript of either poem, the *Venetus* A of the "Iliad" is of the tenth century, and was found at Venice late in the last century, along with some *scholia* or commentaries which are of value as preserving remarks of Aristarchus and other Alexandrian scholars. Hitherto it had been thought that the text of Homer had come down to us from about 1000 B. C. It was now seen that our text was not older than the Alexandrian age. The first printed edition of Homer, revised by the Byzantine Demetrius Chalkondyles (1430–1510), was published at Florence in 1488; the first Aldine Edition at Venice in 1504.

The belief that Homer composed both "Iliad" and "Odyssey" was unquestioned until about 170 B. C. a grammarian Hellanicus, and one Xenon asserted that Homer was the author of the "Iliad," but not of the "Odyssey." They and their followers were called the Separaters (*chôrizontes*), because they separated the "Iliad," in its origin, from the "Odyssey." As to their grounds, we only know that one of these was the style, and this implies literary study. Old Greece was uncritical, and believed strongly in one author for both poems. The mere fact that a double authorship should have been mooted shows that there were good grounds for a natural doubt. But the doubt found little acceptance. Aristarchus wrote against "the paradox of Xenon," and the Roman Seneca, writing on "the shortness of life," regards this as a question for which life is too short.

Early in the last century Vico, a Neapolitan (1668–1744), in his "Principles of New Knowledge," maintained that the names of great lawgivers and poets of the Old World are symbols; thus "Homer" is Greek Epic Poetry; "Homer's poems" were made by a series of poets, and not written down at first; and the "Odyssey" is at least a century younger than the "Iliad." But Vico had no proofs. These were first offered by F. A. Wolf in his "Prolegomena" (1795) or introduction to his edition of Homer. Neither the "Iliad" nor the "Odyssey," he says, was originally made as one poem. Each has been put together from many small unwritten poems. These, by different authors, had no common plan. The "Iliad" and "Odyssey" were first framed from these, and first written down, by the Commission of Pisistratus. Wolf's theory — as throwing light on the origin of popular poetry generally — roused enthusiasm in Germany, which was then in literary revolt from art to nature.

The result of Homeric study since Wolf has been, not to prove any precise theory, but to gain wider assent for certain propositions which narrow the scope of the question.

From « Greek Literature. »

RICHARD JEFFERIES

(1848–1887)

HE art in which Richard Jefferies excelled is called in German « Tonkunst. » It has been so little practiced among English writers that there is no English name for it except « word painting, » which is inadequate. It is the art of describing natural objects and of presenting ideas in symphonies and harmonies of tone. It need not be said that while poetry depends upon it for all its forms of expression, it belongs to prose only when it is employed by a master great enough in his art, not to sacrifice sense to sound or sound to sense. No recent writer has illustrated the possibilities of this art better than Jefferies has done in his descriptions of nature.

He was born in Wiltshire, England, November 6th, 1848. His love of nature and the keenness of his vision for the infinite art it manifests appeared in his work from the first, but « Wild Life in a Southern Country, » which appeared in 1879, is the first of his important nature studies. He wrote novels and tales, which were received with some favor, but the sketches of life in the woods and fields which he continued to write until his death (August 14th, 1887) give him his claim to enduring reputation. As an observer of nature, he is entitled to be classed with John Burroughs in America.

A ROMAN BROOK

THE brook has forgotten me, but I have not forgotten the brook. Many faces have been mirrored since in the flowing water, many feet have waded in the sandy shallow. I wonder if any one else can see it in a picture before the eyes as I can, bright and vivid as the trees suddenly shown at night by a great flash of lightning. All the leaves and branches and the birds at roost are visible during the flash. It is barely a second; it seems much longer. Memory, like the lightning, reveals the pictures in the mind. Every curve, and shore, and shallow is as familiar now as when I followed the winding stream so often. When the mowing grass was at its height you could not walk far beside the bank; it grew so thick and strong and full of umbelliferous

plants as to weary the knees. The life, as it were, of the meadows seemed to crowd down toward the brook in summer to reach out and stretch toward the life-giving water. There the buttercups were taller and closer together, nails of gold driven so thickly that the true surface was not visible. Countless rootlets drew up the richness of the earth like miners in the darkness, throwing their petals of yellow ore broadcast above them. With their fullness of leaves the hawthorn bushes grow larger — the trees extend further — and thus overhung with leaf and branch, and closely set about by grass and plant, the brook disappeared only a little way off, and could not have been known from a mound and hedge. It was lost in the plain of meads — the flowers alone saw its sparkle.

Hidden in those bushes and tall grasses, high in the trees and low on the ground, there were the nests of happy birds. In the hawthorns blackbirds and thrushes built, often overhanging the stream, and the fledgelings fluttered out into the flowery grass. Down among the stalks of the umbelliferous plants, where the grasses were knotted together, the nettle-creeper concealed her treasure, having selected a hollow by the bank so that the scythe should pass over. Up in the pollard ashes and willows, here and there, wood pigeons built. Doves cooed in the little wooden inclosures where the brook curved almost round upon itself. If there was a hollow in the oak a pair of starlings chose it, for there was no advantageous nook that was not seized on. Low beside the willow stoles the sedge reedlings built; on the ledges of the ditches, full of flags, moor hens made their nests. After the swallows had coursed long miles over the meads to and fro, they rested on the tops of the ashes and twittered sweetly. Like the flowers and grass, the birds were drawn toward the brook. They built by it, they came to it to drink; in the evening a grasshopper lark trilled in a hawthorn bush. By night, crossing the footbridge, a star sometimes shone in the water under foot. At morn and even the peasant girls came down to dip; their path was worn through the mowing grass, and there was a flat stone let into the bank as a step to stand on. Though they were poorly habited, without one line of form or tint of color that could please the eye, there is something in dipping water that is Greek — Homeric — something that carries the mind home to primitive times. Always the little children came with them; they too loved the brook like the grass and the birds. They wanted to see the

fishes dart away and hide in the green flags; they flung daisies and buttercups into the stream to float and catch awhile at the flags, and float again and pass away, like the friends of our boyhood, out of sight. Where there was pasture roan cattle came to drink, and horses, restless horses, stood for hours by the edge under the shade of ash trees. With what joy the spaniel plunged in, straight from the bank out among the flags — you could mark his course by seeing their tips bend as he brushed them in swimming. All life loved the brook.

Far down away from the roads and hamlets there was a small orchard on the very bank of the stream, and just before the grass grew too high to walk through I looked in the inclosure to speak to its owner. He was busy with his spade at a strip of garden, and grumbled that the hares would not let it alone, with all that stretch of grass to feed on. Nor would the rooks, and the moor hens ran over it, and the water rats burrowed; the wood pigeons would have the peas, and there was no rest from them all. While he talked and talked, far from the object in hand, as aged people will, I thought how the apple tree in blossom before us cared little enough who saw its glory. The branches were in bloom everywhere, at the top as well as at the side, — at the top where no one could see them but the swallows. They did not grow for human admiration: that was not their purpose; that is our affair only — we bring the thought to the tree. On a short branch low down the trunk there hung the weather-beaten and broken handle of an earthenware vessel; the old man said it was a jug, one of the old folk's jugs, — he often dug them up. Some were cracked, some nearly perfect; lots of them had been thrown out to mend the lane. There were some chips among the heap of weeds yonder. These fragments were the remains of Anglo-Roman pottery. Coins had been found — half a gallon of them — the children had had most. He took one from his pocket, dug up that morning; they were of no value, — they would not ring. The laborers tried to get some ale for them, but could not; no one would take the little brass things. That was all he knew of the Cæsars: the apples were in fine bloom now, weren't they?

Fifteen centuries before there had been a Roman station at the spot where the lane crossed the brook. There the centurions rested their troops after their weary march across the downs, for the lane, now bramble-grown and full of ruts, was then a Roman road. There were villas, and baths, and fortifications; these things you may read about in books. They are lost now in the hedges, under the flowering grass, in the ash copses, all forgotten in the lane, and along the footpath where the June roses will bloom after the apple blossom has dropped. But just where the ancient military way crosses the brook, there grow the finest, the largest, the bluest, and most lovely forget-me-nots that ever lover gathered for his lady.

The old man, seeing my interest in the fragments of pottery, wished to show me something of a different kind lately discovered. He led me to a spot where the brook was deep, and had somewhat undermined the edge. A horse trying to drink there had pushed a quantity of earth into the stream and exposed a human skeleton lying within a few inches of the water. Then I looked up the stream and remembered the buttercups and tall grasses, the flowers that crowded down to the edge; I remembered the nests, and the dove cooing; the girls that came down to dip, the children who cast their flowers to float away. The wind blew the loose apple bloom and it fell in showers of painted snow. Sweetly the greenfinches were calling in the trees; afar the voice of the cuckoo came over the oaks. By the side of the living water, the water that all things rejoiced in, near to its gentle sound, and the sparkle of sunshine on it, had lain this sorrowful thing.

Complete. From "Bits of Oak Bark."

VI—148

THOMAS JEFFERSON
(1743-1826)

JEFFERSON wrote several essays in the artistic form Aristotle insists on for a poem—with a beginning, a middle, and an end. But it was an accident. He was a great artist in the construction of state papers. The Declaration of Independence has no equal as a piece of composition among the state papers of any other country. In America its only rival is Washington's Farewell Address and its only superior Jefferson's own First Inaugural Address. As a writer of political letters, Jefferson is so easily first that he has no good second. He had an almost incomparable genius for working through others, and he made letter writing the means of exercising it. His letters mount from the hundreds into the thousands, and the style he gets from his correspondence appears in his more formal writing. In his "Notes on Virginia," however, he frequently approximates the essay, and once or twice achieves it in due form. But in everything except his state papers, he is obviously careless of form; while over and above the form in whatever he writes are the ideas which have worked in all the ferment of eighteenth and nineteenth century politics.

TRUTH AND TOLERATION AGAINST ERROR

THE first settlers in this country were emigrants from England, of the English Church, just at a point of time when it was flushed with complete victory over the religious of all other persuasions. Possessed, as they became, of the powers of making, administering, and executing the laws, they showed equal intolerance in this country with their Presbyterian brethren, who had emigrated to the northern government. The poor Quakers were flying from persecution in England. They cast their eyes on these new countries as asylums of civil and religious freedom; but they found them free only for the reigning sect. Several acts of the Virginia Assembly of 1659, 1662, and 1693, had made it penal in parents to refuse to have their children baptized; had prohibited the unlawful assembling of Quakers; had

made it penal for any master of a vessel to bring a Quaker into the State; had ordered those already here, and such as should come thereafter, to be imprisoned till they should abjure the country; provided a milder punishment for their first and second return, but death for their third; had inhibited all persons from suffering their meetings in or near their houses, entertaining them individually, or disposing of books which supported their tenets. If no execution took place here, as did in New England, it was not owing to the moderation of the Church, or spirit of the legislature, as may be inferred from the law itself; but to historical circumstances which have not been handed down to us. The Anglicans retained full possession of the country about a century. Other opinions began then to creep in, and the great care of the government to support their own church having begotten an equal degree of indolence in its clergy, two-thirds of the people had become dissenters at the commencement of the present revolution. The laws, indeed, were still oppressive on them, but the spirit of the one party had subsided into moderation, and of the other had risen to a degree of determination which commanded respect.

The present state of our laws on the subject of religion is this. The convention of May, 1776, in their declaration of rights, declared it to be a truth, and a natural right, that the exercise of religion should be free; but when they proceeded to form on that declaration the ordinance of government, instead of taking up every principle declared in the bill of rights, and guarding it by legislative sanction, they passed over that which asserted our religious rights, leaving them as they found them. The same convention, however, when they met as a member of the general assembly in October, 1776, repealed all acts of parliament which had rendered criminal the maintaining any opinions in matters of religion, the forbearing to repair to church, and the exercising any mode of worship; and suspended the laws giving salaries to the clergy, which suspension was made perpetual in October, 1779. Statutory oppressions in religion being thus wiped away, we remain at present under those only imposed by the common law, or by our own acts of assembly. At the common law, heresy was a capital offense, punishable by burning. Its definition was left to the ecclesiastical judges, before whom the conviction was, till the statute of the First Elizabeth, c., 1, circumscribed it, by declaring that nothing should be deemed heresy, but what had been so

determined by authority of the canonical Scriptures, or by one of the first four general councils, or by other council, having for the grounds of their declaration the express and plain words of the Scriptures. Heresy, thus circumscribed, being an offense against the common law, our act of assembly, of October, 1777, c. 17, gives cognizance of it to the general court, by declaring that the jurisdiction of that court shall be general in all matters at the common law. The execution is by the writ *De hæretico comburendo*. By our own act of assembly of 1705, c. 30, if a person brought up in the Christian religion denies the being of a God, or the Trinity, or asserts there are more gods than one, or denies the Christian religion to be true, or the Scriptures to be of divine authority, he is punishable on the first offense by incapacity to hold any office or employment ecclesiastical, civil, or military; on the second by disability to sue, to take any gift or legacy, to be guardian, executor, or administrator, and by three years' imprisonment without bail. A father's right to the custody of his own children being founded in law on his right of guardianship, this being taken away, they may of course be severed from him, and put by the authority of a court into more orthodox hands. This is a summary view of that religious slavery under which a people have been willing to remain, who have lavished their lives and fortunes for the establishment of their civil freedom. The error seems not sufficiently eradicated, that the operations of the mind, as well as the acts of the body, are subject to the coercion of the laws. But our rulers can have no authority over such natural rights, only as we have submitted to them. The rights of conscience we never submitted, we could not submit. We are answerable for them to our God. The legitimate powers of government extend to such acts only as are injurious to others. But it does me no injury for my neighbor to say there are twenty Gods, or no God. It neither picks my pocket nor breaks my leg. If it be said his testimony in a court of justice cannot be relied on, reject it then, and be the stigma on him. Constraint may make him worse by making him a hypocrite, but it will never make him a truer man. It may fix him obstinately in his errors, but will not cure them. Reason and free inquiry are the only effectual agents against error. Give loose to them, they will support the true religion by bringing every false one to their tribunal, to the test of their investigation. They are the natural enemies of error, and of error only. Had not the Roman government permitted free inquiry, Christianity could never have been introduced. Had not free inquiry been indulged at the era of the Reformation, the corruptions of Christianity could not have been purged away. If it be restrained now, the present corruptions will be protected, and new ones encouraged. Was the government to prescribe to us our medicine and diet, our bodies would be in such keeping as our souls are now. Thus in France the emetic was once forbidden as a medicine, and the potato as an article of food. Government is just as infallible, too, when it fixes systems in physics. Galileo was sent to the Inquisition for affirming that the earth was a sphere; the government had declared it to be as flat as a trencher, and Galileo was obliged to abjure his error. This error, however, at length prevailed, the earth became a globe, and Descartes declared it was whirled round its axis by a vortex. The government in which he lived was wise enough to see that this was no question of civil jurisdiction, or we should all have been involved by authority in vortices. In fact, the vortices have been exploded, and the Newtonian principle of gravitation is now more firmly established, on the basis of reason, than it would be were the government to step in, and to make it an article of necessary faith. Reason and experiment have been indulged, and error has fled before them. It is error alone which needs the support of government. Truth can stand by itself. Subject opinion to coercion: whom will you make your inquisitors? Fallible men; men governed by bad passions, by private as well as public reasons. And why subject it to coercion? To produce uniformity. But is uniformity of opinion desirable? No more than of face and stature. Introduce the bed of Procrustes then, and as there is danger that the large men may beat the small, make us all of a size, by lopping the former and stretching the latter. Difference of opinion is advantageous in religion. The several sects perform the office of a *censor morum* over each other. Is uniformity attainable? Millions of innocent men, women, and children, since the introduction of Christianity have been burned, tortured, fined, imprisoned; yet we have not advanced one inch towards uniformity. What has been the effect of coercion? To make one-half the world fools, and the other half hypocrites. To support roguery and error all over the earth. Let us reflect that it is inhabited by a thousand millions of people. That these profess probably a thousand different systems of religion. That ours is but one of that thousand.

That if there be but one right, and ours that one, we should wish to see the nine hundred and ninety-nine wandering sects gathered into the fold of truth. But against such a majority we cannot effect this by force. Reason and persuasion are the only practicable instruments. To make way for these, free inquiry must be indulged; and how can we wish others to indulge it while we refuse it ourselves. But every State, says an inquisitor, has established some religion. No two, say I, have established the same. Is this a proof of the infallibility of establishments? Our sister States of Pennsylvania and New York, however, have long subsisted without any establishment at all. The experiment was new and doubtful when they made it. It has answered beyond conception. They flourish infinitely. Religion is well supported; of various kinds, indeed, but all good enough; all sufficient to preserve peace and order; or if a sect arises, whose tenets would subvert morals, good sense has fair play, and reasons and laughs it out of doors, without suffering the state to be troubled with it. They do not hang more malefactors than we do. They are not more disturbed with religious dissensions. On the contrary, their harmony is unparalleled, and can be ascribed to nothing but their unbounded tolerance, because there is no other circumstance in which they differ from every nation on earth. They have made the happy discovery that the way to silence religious disputes is to take no notice of them. Let us too give this experiment fair play, and get rid, while we may, of those tyrannical laws. It is true we are as yet secured against them by the spirit of the times. I doubt whether the people of this country would suffer an execution for heresy, or a three years' imprisonment for not comprehending the mysteries of the Trinity. But is the spirit of the people an infallible, a permanent reliance? Is it government? Is this the kind of protection we receive in return for the rights we give up? Besides, the spirit of the times may alter, will alter. Our rulers will become corrupt, our people careless. A single zealot may commence persecutor, and better men be his victims. It can never be too often repeated that the time for fixing every essential right on a legal basis is while our rulers are honest, and ourselves united. From the conclusion of this war we shall be going down hill. It will not then be necessary to resort every moment to the people for support. They will be forgotten therefore, and their rights disregarded. They will forget themselves but in the sole

faculty of making money, and will never think of uniting to effect a due respect for their rights. The shackles, therefore, which shall not be knocked off at the conclusion of this war, will remain on us long, will be made heavier and heavier, till our rights shall revive or expire in a convulsion.

Complete. From Jefferson's «Notes on Virginia.»

LORD FRANCIS JEFFREY

(1773-1850)

FRANCIS JEFFREY, one of the founders of the Edinburgh Review, was born in Edinburgh, October 23d, 1773, and educated for the bar. He began practice in 1794, but the claims of his business as a young advocate left him ample leisure and he joined with Brougham, Sidney Smith, and others, in establishing the Edinburgh Review, the first number of which (October 10th, 1802) was edited by Sidney Smith and the next three by Jeffrey, with Brougham as the principal political contributor. The Review which remained chiefly under the editorship of Jeffrey, was a success from the beginning, and it made all its principal contributors famous. But Jeffrey never wholly recovered from the *ex cathedra* style which the critical reviewer of that period used as an indispensable part of his offensive armament. In 1829 he gave up the editorship of the Review to become Dean of the Faculty of Advocates, and the rest of his life was largely devoted to law and public affairs. He became Lord Rector of Glasgow University in 1820, Lord Advocate in 1830, Member of Parliament in 1832, and Judge of the Court of Sessions in 1834. He died January 26th, 1850. He had a strong and active intellect, and it appears in his essays, saving many of them from the deserved oblivion which has overtaken most of the overbearing geniuses of that period of talented and insolent reviewers. Of his best essay—his Obituary of Watt—it is at once simple justice and the highest possible praise to say that it is worthy of the subject.

WATT AND THE WORK OF STEAM

MR. JAMES WATT, the great improver of the steam engine, died on the twenty-fifth of August, 1819, at his seat of Heathfield, near Birmingham, in the eighty-fourth year of his age. This name fortunately needs no commemoration of ours, for he that bore it survived to see it crowned with undisputed and unenvied honors; and many generations will probably pass away before it shall have gathered «all its fame.» We have said that Mr. Watt was the great improver of the steam engine, but, in truth, as to all that is admirable in its structure, or vast in its utility, he should rather be described as its inventor. It was by his inventions that its action was so regulated as to make it capable of being applied to the finest and most delicate manufacturers, and its power so increased as to set weight and solidity at defiance. By his admirable contrivance it has become a thing stupendous alike for its force and its flexibility,—for the prodigious power which it can exert, and the ease, and precision, and ductility with which that power can be varied, distributed, and applied. The trunk of an elephant that can pick up a pin or rend an oak is as nothing to it. It can engrave a seal and crush masses of obdurate metal before it—draw out, without breaking, a thead as fine as gossamer, and lift a ship of war like a bauble in the air. It can embroider muslin and forge anchors, cut steel into ribands, and impel loaded vessels against the fury of the winds and waves.

It would be difficult to estimate the value of the benefits which these inventions have conferred upon this country. There is no branch of industry that has not been indebted to them; and, in all the most material, they have not only widened most magnificently the field of its exertions, but multiplied a thousand-fold the amount of its productions. It was our improved steam engine, in short, that fought the battles of Europe, and exalted and sustained, through the late tremendous contest, the political greatness of our land. It is the same great power which now enables us to pay the interest of our debt, and to maintain the arduous struggle in which we are still engaged (1819), with the skill and capital of countries less oppressed with taxation. But these are poor and narrow views of its importance. It has increased indefinitely the mass of human comforts and enjoyments; and rendered cheap and accessible, all over the world, the materials of wealth and prosperity. It has armed the feeble hand of man, in short, with a power to which no limits can be assigned; completed the dominion of mind over the most refractory qualities of matter; and laid a sure foundation for all those future miracles of mechanic power which are to aid and reward the labors of after generations. It is to the genius of one man, too, that all this is mainly owing! And certainly no man ever bestowed such a gift on his kind. The blessing is not only universal, but unbounded; and the fabled inventors of the plow and the loom, who were deified by the erring gratitude of their

rude cotemporaries, conferred less important benefits on mankind than the inventor of our present steam engine.

This will be the fame of Watt with future generations. And it is sufficient for his race and his country. But to those to whom he more immediately belonged, who lived in his society and enjoyed his conversation, it is not, perhaps, the character in which he will be most frequently recalled—most deeply lamented —or even most highly admired. Independently of his great attainments in mechanics, Mr. Watt was an extraordinary, and in many respects a wonderful man. Perhaps no individual in his age possessed so much and such varied and exact information,— had read so much, or remembered what he had read so accurately and well. He had infinite quickness of apprehension, a prodigious memory, and a certain rectifying and methodizing power of understanding, which extracted something precious out of all that was presented to it. His stores of miscellaneous knowledge were immense,—and yet less astonishing than the command he had at all times over them. It seemed as if every subject that was casually started in conversation with him had been that which he had been last occupied in studying and exhausting;— such was the copiousness, the precision, and the admirable clearness of the information which he poured out upon it, without effort or hesitation. Nor was this promptitude and compass of knowledge confined in any degree to the studies connected with his ordinary pursuits. That he should have been minutely and extensively skilled in chemistry and the arts, and in most of the branches of physical science, might perhaps have been conjectured; but it could not have been inferred from his usual occupations, and probably is not generally known, that he was curiously learned in many branches of antiquity, metaphysics, medicine, and etymology, and perfectly at home in all the details of architecture, music, and law. He was well acquainted too with most of the modern languages, and familiar with their most recent literature. Nor was it at all extraordinary to hear the great mechanician and engineer detailing and expounding, for hours together, the metaphysical theories of the German logicians, or criticizing the measures or the matter of the German poetry.

His astonishing memory was aided, no doubt, in a great measure, by a still higher and rarer faculty—by his power of digesting and arranging in its proper place all the information he received, and of casting aside and rejecting, as it were instinc-

tively, whatever was worthless or immaterial. Every conception that was suggested to his mind seemed instantly to take its proper place among its other rich furniture; and to be condensed into the smallest and most convenient form. He never appeared, therefore, to be at all encumbered or perplexed with the verbiage of the dull books he perused, or the idle talk to which he listened; but to have at once extracted, by a kind of intellectual alchemy, all that was worthy of attention, and to have reduced it, for his own use, to its true value and to its simplest form. And thus it often happened that a great deal more was learned from his brief and vigorous account of the theories and arguments of tedious writers than an ordinary student could ever have derived from the most painful study of the originals,—and that errors and absurdities became manifest from the mere clearness and plainness of his statement of them, which might have deluded and perplexed most of his hearers without that invaluable assistance.

It is needless to say that with those vast resources his conversation was at all times rich and instructive in no ordinary degree. But it was, if possible, still more pleasing than wise, and had all the charms of familiarity, with all the substantial treasures of knowledge. No man could be more social in his spirit, less assuming or fastidious in his manners, or more kind and indulgent towards all who approached him. He rather liked to talk—at least in his latter years. But though he took a considerable share of the conversation, he rarely suggested the topics on which it was to turn, but readily and quietly took up whatever was presented by those around him, and astonished the idle and barren propounders of an ordinary theme, by the treasures which he drew from the mine they had unconsciously opened. He generally seemed, indeed, to have no choice or predilection for one subject of discourse rather than another; but allowed his mind, like a great cyclopædia, to be opened at any letter his associates might choose to turn up, and only endeavored to select, from his inexhaustible stores, what might be best adapted to the taste of his present hearers. As to their capacity he gave himself no trouble; and, indeed, such was his singular talent for making all things plain, clear, and intelligible, that scarcely any one could be aware of such a deficiency in his presence. His talk, too, though overflowing with information, had no resemblance to lecturing or solemn discoursing, but, on the con-

trary, was full of colloquial spirit and pleasantry. He had a certain quiet and grave humor, which ran through most of his conversation, and a vein of temperate jocularity, which gave infinite zest and effect to the condensed and inexhaustible information which formed its main staple and characteristic. There was a little air of affected testiness too, and a tone of pretended rebuke and contradiction, with which he used to address his younger friends, that was always felt by them as an endearing mark of his kindness and familiarity,—and prized accordingly, far beyond all the solemn compliments that ever proceeded from the lips of authority. His voice was deep and powerful— though he commonly spoke in a low and somewhat monotonous tone, which harmonized admirably with the weight and brevity of his observations; and set off to the greatest advantage the pleasant anecdotes, which he delivered with the same grave brow, and the same calm smile playing soberly on his lips. There was nothing of effort indeed, or impatience, any more than of pride or levity, in his demeanor; and there was a finer expression of reposing strength and mild self-possession in his manner than we ever recollect to have met with in any other person. He had in his character the utmost abhorrence for all sorts of forwardness, parade, and pretensions; and, indeed, never failed to put all such impostures out of countenance, by the manly plainness and honest intrepidity of his language and deportment.

In his temper and dispositions he was not only kind and affectionate, but generous and considerate of the feelings of all around him; and gave the most liberal assistance and encouragement to all young persons who showed any indications of talent, or applied to him for patronage or advice. His health, which was delicate from his youth upwards, seemed to become firmer as he advanced in years; and he preserved up almost to the last moment of his existence, not only the full command of his extraordinary intellect, but all the alacrity of spirit, and the social gayety which had illumined his happiest days. His friends in this part of the country never saw him more full of intellectual vigor and colloquial animation,—never more delightful or more instructive,—than in his last visit to Scotland in the autumn of 1817. Indeed, it was after that time that he applied himself, with all the ardor of early life, to the invention of a machine for mechanically copying all sorts of sculpture and statuary;— and distributed among his friends some of its earliest performances, as the productions of "a young artist, just entering on his eighty-third year!"

This happy and useful life came at last to a gentle close. He had suffered some inconvenience through the summer, but was not seriously indisposed till within a few weeks from his death. He then became perfectly aware of the event which was approaching, and with his usual tranquillity and benevolence of nature seemed only anxious to point out to the friends around him the many sources of consolation which were afforded by the circumstances under which it was about to take place. He expressed his sincere gratitude to Providence for the length of days with which he had been blessed, and his exemption from most of the infirmities of age, as well as for the calm and cheerful evening of life that he had been permitted to enjoy, after the honorable labors of the day had been concluded. And thus, full of years and honors, in all calmness and tranquillity, he yielded up his soul, without pang or struggle, — and passed from the bosom of his family to that of his God.

Complete. From the Edinburgh Review. Published on the death of Watt.

ON GOOD AND BAD TASTE

IF THINGS are not beautiful in themselves, but only as they serve to suggest interesting conceptions to the mind, then everything which does, in point of fact suggest such a conception to any individual is beautiful to that individual; and it is not only quite true that there is no room for disputing about tastes, but that all tastes are equally just and correct in so far as each individual speaks only of his own emotions. When a man calls a thing beautiful, however, he may indeed mean to make two very different assertions: he may mean that it gives him pleasure by suggesting to him some interesting emotion; and, in this sense, there can be no doubt that, if he merely speak the truth, the thing is beautiful; and that it pleases him precisely in the same way that all other things please those to whom they appear beautiful. But if he mean further to say that the thing possesses some quality which should make it appear beautiful to every other person, and that it is owing to some prejudice or defect in them if it appear otherwise, then he is as unreasonable and absurd as he would think those who should attempt to convince him that he felt no emotion of beauty.

All tastes, then, are equally just and true, in so far as concerns the individual whose taste is in question; and what a man feels distinctly to be beautiful is beautiful to him, whatever other people may think of it. All this follows clearly from the theory now in question; but it does not follow from it that all tastes are equally good or desirable, or that there is any difficulty in describing that which is really the best and the most to be envied. The only use of the faculty of taste is to afford an innocent delight, and to aid the cultivation of a finer morality; and that man certainly will have the most delight from this faculty, who has the most numerous and the most powerful perception of beauty. But if beauty consist in the reflection of our affections and sympathies, it is plain that he will always see the most beauty whose affections are warmest and most exercised, whose imagination is most powerful, and who has most accustomed himself to attend to the objects by which he is surrounded. In so far as mere feeling and enjoyment are concerned, therefore, it seems evident that the best taste must be that which belongs to the best affections, the most active fancy, and the most attentive habits of observation. It will follow pretty exactly, too, that all men's perceptions of beauty will be nearly in proportion to the degree of their sensibility and social sympathies; and that those who have no affections towards sentient beings will be just as insensible to beauty in external objects, as he who cannot hear the sound of his friend's voice must be deaf to its echo.

In so far as the sense of beauty is regarded as a mere source of enjoyment, this seems to be the only distinction that deserves to be attended to; and the only cultivation that taste should ever receive, with a view to the gratification of the individual, should be through the indirect channel of cultivating the affections and powers of observation. If we aspire, however, to be creators as well as observers of beauty, and place any part of our happiness in ministering to the gratification of others, as artists, or poets, or authors of any sort, then, indeed, a new distinction of tastes, and a far more laborious system of cultivation will be necessary. A man who pursues only his own delight will be as much charmed with objects that suggest powerful emotions, in consequence of personal and accidental associations, as with those that introduce similar emotions by means of associations that are universal and indestructible. To him all objects of the former class

are really as beautiful as those of the latter; and for his own gratification, the creation of that sort of beauty is just as important an occupation. But if he conceive the ambition of creating beauties for the admiration of others, he must be cautious to employ only such objects as are the natural signs, or the inseparable concomitants of emotions, of which the greater part of mankind are susceptible; and his taste will then deserve to be called bad and false, if he obtrude upon the public, as beautiful, objects that are not likely to be associated in common minds with any interesting impressions.

For a man himself, then, there is no taste that is either bad or false; and the only difference worthy of being attended to is that between a great deal and a very little. Some who have cold affections, sluggish imaginations, and no habits of observation, can with difficulty discern beauty in anything; while others, who are full of kindness and sensibility, and who have been accustomed to attend to all the objects around them, feel it almost in everything. It is no matter what other people may think of the objects of their admiration; nor ought it to be any concern of theirs that the public would be astonished or offended, if they were called upon to join in that admiration. So long as no such call is made, this anticipated discrepancy of feeling need give them no uneasiness; and the suspicion of it should produce no contempt in any other persons. It is a strange aberration indeed of vanity that makes us despise persons for being happy, for having sources of enjoyment in which we cannot share; and yet this is the true account of the ridicule, which is so generally poured upon individuals who seek only to enjoy their peculiar tastes unmolested. For if there be any truth in the theory we have been expounding, no taste is bad for any other reason than because it is peculiar, as the objects in which it delights must actually serve to suggest to the individual those common emotions and universal affections upon which the sense of beauty is everywhere founded. The misfortune is, however, that we are apt to consider all persons who make known their peculiar relishes, and especially all who create any objects for their gratification, as in some measure dictating to the public, and setting up an idol for general adoration; and hence this intolerant interference with almost all peculiar perceptions of beauty, and the unsparing derision that pursues all deviations from acknowledged standards. This intolerance, we admit, is often provoked by

something of a spirit of proselytism and arrogance in those who mistake their own casual associations for natural or universal relations; and the consequence is, that mortified vanity dries up the fountain of their peculiar enjoyment, and disenchants, by a new association of general contempt or ridicule, the scenes that had been consecrated by some innocent but accidental emotion.

As all men must have some peculiar associations, all men must have some peculiar notions of beauty, and, of course, to a certain extent, a taste that the public would be entitled to consider as false or vitiated. For those who make no demands on public admiration, however, it is hard to be obliged to sacrifice this source of enjoyment; and even for those who labor for applause, the wisest course, perhaps, if it were only practicable, would be to have two tastes; one to enjoy, and one to work by; one founded upon universal associations, according to which they finished those performances for which they challenged universal praise, and another guided by all casual and individual associations, through which they looked fondly upon nature, and upon the objects of their secret admiration.

From the essay on "Beauty."

JEROME K. JEROME
(1859–)

EROME KLAPKA JEROME was born at Walsall, England, May 2d, 1859. He is the son of a clergyman, and in a sketch of his life, which he is supposed to have revised for the press, it is said in summing up his work that he has been "clerk, schoolmaster, actor, and journalist." He has edited To-Day and the Idler, and published a notable list of books, chief among which stands "Idle Thoughts of an Idle Fellow," 1889,—a work which is so full of good nature, and so entirely free from unnecessary seriousness that the world will not willingly let it die. Among his latest works are "Sketches in Lavender," "Letters to Clorinda," and "Second Thoughts of an Idle Fellow."

ON GETTING ON IN THE WORLD

NOT exactly the sort of thing for an idle fellow to think about, is it? But outsiders, you know, often see most of the game; and sitting in my arbor by the wayside, smoking my hookah of contentment, and eating the sweet lotus leaves of indolence, I can look out musingly upon the whirling throng that rolls and tumbles past me on the great highroad of life.

Never-ending is the wild procession. Day and night you can hear the quick tramp of the myriad feet—some running, some walking, some halting and lame; but all hastening, all eager in the feverish race, all straining life and limb and heart and soul to reach the ever-receding horizon of success.

Mark them as they surge along—men and women, old and young, gentle and simple, fair and foul, rich and poor, merry and sad—all hurrying, bustling, scrambling. The strong pushing aside the weak; the cunning creeping past the foolish; those behind elbowing those before; those in front kicking, as they run, at those behind. Look close, and see the flitting show. Here is an old man panting for breath; and there a timid maiden, driven by a hard and sharp-faced matron; here is a studious youth, read-

VI—149

grows sick, and the eyes grow blurred and a gurgling groan tells those behind they may close up another space.

And yet in spite of the killing pace and the stony track, who but the sluggard or the dolt can hold aloof from the course? Who—like the belated traveler that stands watching fairy revels till he snatches and drains the goblin cup, and springs into the whirling circle—can view the mad tumult, and not be drawn into its midst? Not I, for one. I confess to the wayside arbor, the pipe of contentment, and the lotus leaves being altogether unsuitable metaphors. They sounded very nice and philosophical, but I'm afraid I am not the sort of person to sit in arbors, smoking pipes, when there is any fun going on outside. I think I more resemble the Irishman, who, seeing a crowd collecting, sent his little girl out to ask if there was going to be a row—"'Cos, if so, father would like to be in it."

I love the fierce strife. I like to watch it. I like to hear of people getting on in it—battling their way bravely and fairly—that is, not slipping through by luck or trickery. It stirs one's old-Saxon fighting blood, like the tales of "knights who fought 'gainst fearful odds" that thrilled us in our schoolboy days.

And fighting the battle of life is fighting against fearful odds too. There are giants and dragons in this nineteenth century, and the golden casket that they guard is not so easy to win as it appears in the storybooks. There, Algernon takes one long, last look at the ancestral hall, dashes the teardrop from his eye, and goes off—to return in three years' time, rolling in riches. The authors do not tell us "how it's done," which is a pity, for it would surely prove exciting.

But then not one novelist in a thousand ever does tell us the real story of his hero. They linger for a dozen pages over a tea party, but sum up a life's history with "he had become one of our merchant princes," or, "he was now a great artist, with the whole world at his feet." Why, there is more real life in one of Gilbert's patter songs than in half the biographical novels ever written. He relates to us all the various steps by which his office boy rose to be the "ruler of the Queen's navee," and explains to us how the briefless barrister managed to become a great and good judge, "ready to try this breach of promise of marriage." It is in the petty details, not in the great results, that the interest of existence lies.

ing "How to Get On in the World," and letting everybody pass him as he stumbles along with his eyes on his book; here is a bored-looking man, with a fashionably dressed woman jogging his elbow; here a boy gazing wistfully back at the sunny village that he never again will see; here, with a firm and easy step, strides a broad-shouldered man; and here, with a stealthy tread, a thin-faced, stooping fellow dodges and shuffles upon his way; here, with gaze fixed always on the ground, an artful rogue carefully works his way from side to side of the road, and thinks he is going forward; and here a youth with a noble face stands, hesitating as he looks from the distant goal to the mud beneath his feet.

And now into the sight comes a fair girl, with her dainty face growing more wrinkled at every step; and now a careworn man, and now a hopeful lad.

A motley throng—a motley throng! Prince and beggar, sinner and saint, butcher and baker and candlestick maker, tinkers and tailors, and plowboys and sailors—all jostling along together. Here the counsel in his wig and gown, and here the old Jew clothesman under his dingy tiara; here the soldier in scarlet, and here the undertaker's mute in streaming hatband and worn cotton gloves; here the musty scholar, fumbling his faded leaves, and here the scented actor, dangling his showy seals. Here the glib politician, crying his legislative panaceas; and here the peripatetic Cheap-Jack, holding aloft his quack cures for human ills. Here the sleek capitalist, and there the sinewy laborer; here the man of science, and here the shoeblack; here the poet, and here the water-rate collector; here the cabinet minister, and there the ballet dancer. Here a red-nosed publican, shouting the praises of his vats, and here a temperance lecturer at fifty pounds a night; here a judge, and there a swindler; here a priest, and there a gambler. Here a jeweled duchess, smiling and gracious; here a thin lodging-house keeper, irritable with cooking; and here a wabbling, strutting thing, tawdry in paint and finery.

Cheek by cheek they struggle onward. Screaming, cursing, and praying, laughing, singing, and moaning, they rush past side by side. Their speed never slackens, the race never ends. There is no wayside rest for them, no halt by cooling fountains, no pause beneath green shades. On, on, on—on through the heat and the crowd and the dust—on, or they will be trampled down and lost—on, with throbbing brain and tottering limbs—on, till the heart

What we really want is a novel showing us all the hidden undercurrent of an ambitious man's career—his struggles, and failures, and hopes, his disappointments and victories. It would be an immense success. I am sure the wooing of Fortune would prove quite as interesting a tale as the wooing of any flesh-and-blood maiden, though, by the way, it would read extremely similar; for Fortune is, indeed, as the Ancients painted her, very like a woman—not quite so unreasonable and inconsistent, but nearly so—and the pursuit is much the same in one case as in the other. Ben Jonson's couplet—

"Court a mistress, she denies you;
Let her alone, she will court you"

puts them both in a nutshell. A woman never thoroughly cares for her lover until he has ceased to care for her; and it is not until you have snapped your fingers in Fortune's face, and turned on your heel, that she begins to smile upon you.

But by that time you do not much care whether she smiles or frowns. Why could she not have smiled when her smiles would have thrilled you with ecstasy? Everything comes too late in this world.

Good people say that it is quite right and proper that it should be so, and that it proves ambition is wicked.

Bosh! Good people are altogether wrong. (They always are, in my opinion. We never agree on any single point.) What would the world do without ambitious people, I should like to know? Why, it would be as flabby as a Norfolk dumpling. Ambitious people are the leaven which raises into wholesome bread. Without ambitious people the world would never get up. They are busybodies who are about early in the morning, hammering, shouting, and rattling the fire irons, and rendering it generally impossible for the rest of the house to remain in bed.

Wrong to be ambitious, forsooth! The men wrong, who, with bent back and sweating brow, cut the smooth road over which Humanity marches forward from generation to generation! Men wrong, for using the talents that their Master has intrusted to them—for toiling while others play!

Of course they are seeking their reward. Man is not given that God-like unselfishness that thinks only of others' good. But in working for themselves they are working for us all. We are so bound together that no man can labor for himself alone.

Each blow he strikes in his own behalf helps to mold the Universe. The stream, in struggling onward, turns the mill wheel; the coral insect, fashioning its tiny cells, joins continents to each other; and the ambitious man, building a pedestal for himself, leaves a monument to posterity. Alexander and Cæsar fought for their own ends, but, in doing so, they put a belt of civilization half round the earth. Stephenson, to win a fortune, invented the steam engine; and Shakespeare wrote his plays in order to keep a comfortable home for Mrs. Shakespeare and the little Shakespeares.

Contented, unambitious people are all very well in their way. They form a neat, useful background for great portraits to be painted against; and they make a respectable, if not particularly intelligent audience for the active spirits of the age to play before. I have not a word to say against contented people so long as they keep quiet. But do not, for goodness' sake, let them go strutting about, as they are so fond of doing, crying out that they are the true models for the whole species. Why, they are the deadheads, the drones in the great hive, the street crowds that lounge about, gaping at those who are working.

And let them not imagine either — as they are also fond of doing — that they are very wise and philosophical, and that it is a very artful thing to be contented. It may be true that "a contented mind is happy anywhere," but so is a Jerusalem pony, and the consequence is that both are put anywhere and are treated anyhow. "Oh, you need not bother about him," is what is said; "he is very contented as he is, and it would be a pity to disturb him." And so your contented party is passed over, and the discontented man gets his place.

If you are foolish enough to be contented, don't show it, but grumble with the rest; and if you can do with a little, ask for a great deal. Because if you don't you won't get any. In this world, it is necessary to adopt the principle pursued by the plaintiff in an action for damages, and to demand ten times more than you are ready to accept. If you can feel satisfied with a hundred, begin by insisting on a thousand; if you start by suggesting a hundred, you will only get ten.

It was by not following this simple plan that poor Jean Jacques Rousseau came to such grief. He fixed the summit of his earthly bliss at living in an orchard with an amiable woman and a cow, and he never attained even that. He did get as far as

the orchard, but the woman was not amiable, and she brought her mother with her, and there was no cow. Now, if he had made up his mind for a large country estate, a houseful of angels, and a cattle show, he might have lived to possess his kitchen garden and one head of live stock, and even possibly have come across that *rara avis* — a really amiable woman.

What a terribly dull affair, too, life must be for contented people! How heavy the time must hang upon their hands, and what on earth do they occupy their thoughts with, supposing that they have any? Reading the paper and smoking seems to be the intellectual food of the majority of them, to which the more energetic add playing the flute and talking about the affairs of the next-door neighbor.

They never know the excitement of expectation, nor the stern delight of accomplished effort, such as stir the pulse of the man who has objects, and hopes, and plans. To the ambitious man, life is a brilliant game, — a game that calls forth all his tact, and energy, and nerve, — a game to be won in the long run, by the quick eye and the steady hand, and yet having sufficient chance about its working out to give it all the glorious zest of uncertainty. He exults in it, as the strong swimmer in the heaving billows, as the athlete in the wrestle, as the soldier in the battle.

And if he be defeated, he wins the grim joy of fighting; if he lose the race, he, at least, has had a run. Better to work and fail than to sleep one's life away.

So, walk up, walk up, walk up. Walk up, ladies and gentlemen! walk up, boys and girls! Show your skill and try your strength; brave your luck, and prove your pluck. Walk up! The show is never closed, and the game is always going. The only genuine sport in all the fair, gentlemen — highly respectable and strictly moral — patronized by the nobility, clergy, and gentry. Established in the year one, gentlemen, and been flourishing ever since! — walk up. Walk up, ladies and gentlemen, and take a hand. There are prizes for all, and all can play. There is gold for the man and fame for the boy; rank for the maiden and pleasure for the fool. So walk up, ladies and gentlemen, walk up! — all prizes, and no blanks; for some few win, and as to the rest, why —

"The rapture of pursuing
Is the prize the vanquished gain."

Complete.

DOUGLAS JERROLD

(1803–1857)

OUGLAS WILLIAM JERROLD, author of Mrs. Caudle's immortal "Curtain Lectures," was born in London, January 3d, 1803. He was the eldest son of an actor, Samuel Jerrold, who introduced him to stage life at a very early age. Not fancying the stage, he left it at the age of sixteen and entered the navy as a midshipman. After two years' service, he returned to London and began his literary career as apprentice to a printer, working in the shop and using his leisure to write contributions for the magazines. In 1829 "Black-Eyed Susan," his first successful play, was produced, and several years later he attempted the management of the Strand Theatre. Not succeeding, he returned to writing for the magazines, and in 1841, when Punch appeared, he became one of its favorite contributors. His articles signed "Q." continued to appear in it, until his death, June 8th, 1857. He wrote a large number of plays as well as essays, sketches, and stories. Next to "Mrs. Caudle's Curtain Lectures," his "Story of a Feather" is the most widely circulated of his works.

BARBARISM IN BIRDCAGE WALK

MAY we ask the reader to behold with us a melancholy show — a saddening, miserable spectacle? We will not take him to prison, a workhouse, a Bedlam, where human nature expiates its guiltiness, its lack of worldly goods, its most desolate perplexity; but we will take him to a wretchedness, first contrived by wrong and perpetrated by folly. We will show him the embryo mischief that in due season shall be born in the completion of its terror, and shall be christened with a sounding name, — Folly and Wickedness standing its sponsors.

We are in St. James's Park. The royal standard of England burns in the summer air — the Queen is in London. We pass the Palace, and in a few paces are in Birdcage Walk. There, reader, is the miserable show we promised you. There are some fifty recruits, drilled by a sergeant to do homicide, killingly,

handsomely. In Birdcage Walk Glory sits upon her eggs, and hatches eagles!

How very beautiful is the sky above us! What a blessing comes with the fresh, quick air! The trees, drawing their green beauty from the earth, quicken our thoughts of the bounteousness of this teeming world. Here in this nook, this patch, where we yet feel the vibrations of surrounding London — even here Nature, constant in her beauty, blooms and smiles, uplifting the heart of man — if the heart be his to own her.

Now, look aside and contemplate God's image with a musket. Your bosom duly expanding with gratitude to Nature for the blessings she has heaped about you, behold the crowning glory of God's work managed, like a machine, to slay the image of God — to stain the teeming earth with homicidal blood — to fill the air with howling anguish! Is not yonder row of clowns a melancholy sight? Yet are they the sucklings of Glory — the baby mighty ones of a future Gazette. Reason beholds them with a deep pity. Imagination magnifies them into fiends of wickedness. There is carnage about them — carnage, and the pestilential vapor of the slaughtered. What a fine-looking thing is war! Yet dress it as we may, dress and feather it, daub it with gold, huzza it and sing swaggering songs about it — what is it, nine times out of ten — but murder in uniform? Cain taking the sergeant's shilling?

And now we hear the fifes and drums of her Majesty's grenadiers. They pass on the other side; and a crowd of idlers, their hearts jumping to the music, their eyes dazzled, and their feelings perverted, hang about the march and catch the infection — the love of glory! And true wisdom thinks of the world's age, and sighs at its slow advance in all that really dignifies man, — the truest dignity being the truest love for his fellow. And then hope, and faith in human progress, contemplate the pageant, its real ghastliness disguised by outward glare and frippery, and know the day will come when the symbols of war will be as the sacred beasts of old Egypt — things to mark the barbarism of bygone war; melancholy records of the past perversity of human nature.

We can imagine the deep-chested laughter — the look of scorn which would annihilate, and then the smile of compassion — of the man of war at this, the dream of folly and the wanderings of an inflamed brain. Yet, O man of war! at this very moment are you shrinking, withering like an aged giant. The fingers of Opinion have been busy at your plume—you are not the feathered thing you were; and then that little tube, the goose quill, has sent its silent shot into your huge anatomy; and the corroding ink, even whilst you look at it, and think it shines so brightly, is eating with a tooth of rust into your sword.

That a man should kill a man and rejoice in the deed—nay, gather glory from it—is the act of a wild animal. The force of muscle and the dexterity of limb which make the wild man a conqueror are deemed, in savage life, man's highest attributes. The creature whom, in the pride of our Christianity, we call heathen and spiritually desolate, has some personal feeling in the strife—he kills his enemy, and then, making an oven of hot stones, bakes his dead body, and, for crowning satisfaction, eats it. His enemy becomes a part of him; his glory is turned to nutriment; and he is content. What barbarism! Field marshals sicken at the horror; nay, troopers shudder at the tale, like a fine lady at a toad.

In what, then, consists the prime evil? In the murder, or in the meal? Which is the most hideous deed—to kill a man, or to cook and eat the man when killed?

But, softly, there is no murder in the case. The craft of man has made a splendid ceremony of homicide—has invested it with dignity. He slaughters with flags flying, drums beating, trumpets braying. He kills according to method, and has worldly honors for his grim handiwork. He does not, like the unchristian savage, carry away with him mortal trophies from the skulls of his enemies. No, the alchemy and magic of authority turn his well-won scalps into epaulets, or hang them in stars and crosses at his buttonhole; and then, the battle over, the dead not eaten but carefully buried—and the maimed and mangled howling and blaspheming in hospitals—the meek Christian warrior marches to church, and reverently folding his sweet and spotless hands, sings Te Deum. Angels wave his fervent thanks to God, to whose footstool—in his own faith—he has so lately sent his shuddering thousands. And this spirit of destruction working within him is canonized by the craft and ignorance of man and worshiped as glory!

And this religion of the sword—this dazzling heathenism, that makes a pomp of wickedness—seizes and distracts us even on the threshold of life. Swords and drums are our baby play-

things; the types of violence and destruction are made the petty pastimes of our childhood; and as we grow older, the outward magnificence of the ogre Glory—his trappings and his trumpets, his privileges, and the songs that are shouted in his praise—ensnare the bigger baby to his sacrifice. Hence slaughter becomes an exalted profession; the marked, distinguished employment of what in the jargon of the world is called a gentleman.

But for this craft operating upon this ignorance, who—in the name of outraged God—would become the hireling of the sword? Hodge, poor fellow, enlists. He wants work; or he is idle, dissolute. Kept, by the injustice of the world, as ignorant as the farmyard swine, he is the better instrument for the world's craft. His ear is tickled with the fife and drum; or he is drunk; or the sergeant—the lying valet of glory—tell a good tale, and already Hodge is a warrior in the rough. In a fortnight's time you may see him at Chatham; or, indeed, he was one of those we marked in Birdcage Walk. Day by day the sergeant works at the block plowman, and, chipping and chipping, at length carves out a true, handsome soldier of the line. What knew Hodge of the responsibility of man? What dreams had he of the self-accountability of the human spirit? He is become the lackey of carnage, the liveried footman, at a few pence per day, of fire and blood. The musket stock, which for many an hour he hugs—hugs in sulks and weariness—was no more a party to its present use than was Hodge. That piece of walnut is the fragment of a tree that might have given shade and fruit for another century; homely, rustic people gathering under it. Now it is the instrument of wrong and violence, the working tool of slaughter. Tree and man, are not their destinies as one?

And is Hodge alone of benighted mind? Is he alone deficient of that knowledge of moral right and wrong, which really and truly crowns the man king of himself? When he surrenders up his nature, a mere machine with human pulses to do the bidding of war, has he taken counsel with his own reflection—does he know the limit of the sacrifice? He has taken his shilling, and knows the facings of his uniform!

When the born and bred gentleman, to keep to coined and current terms, pays down his thousand pounds or so for his commission, what incites to the purchase? It may be the elegant idleness of the calling; it may be the bullion and glitter of the regimentals; or, devout worshiper, it may be an unquenchable

thirst for glory. From the moment when his name stars the Gazette, what does he become? The bond servant of war! Instantly he ceases to be a judge between moral right and moral injury. It is his duty not to think, but to obey. He has given up, surrendered to another the freedom of his soul; he has dethroned the majesty of his own will. He must be active in wrong, and see not the injustice; shed blood for craft and usurpation, calling bloodshed valor. He may be made, by the iniquity of those who use him, a burglar and a brigand; but glory calls him pretty names for his prowess, and the wicked weakness of the world shouts and acknowledges him. And is this the true condition of reasonable man? Is it by such means that he best vindicates the greatness of his mission here? Is he when he most gives up the free motions of his own soul—is he then most glorious?

A few months ago chance showed us a band of ruffians who, as it afterwards appeared, were intent upon most desperate mischief. They spread themselves over the country, attacking, robbing, and murdering all who fell into their hands. Men, women, and children all suffered alike. Nor were the villains satisfied with this. In their wanton ruthlessness they set fire to cottages, and tore up and destroyed plantations. Every footpace of their march was marked with blood and desolation.

Who were these wretches? you ask. What place did they ravage? Were they not caught and punished?

They were a part of the army of Africa; valorous Frenchmen, bound for Algiers to cut Arab throats; and, in the name of glory, and for the everlasting glory of France, to burn, pillage, and despoil; and all for national honor—all for glory!

But Glory cannot dazzle Truth. Does it not at times appear no otherwise than a highwayman with a pistol at a nation's breast? a burglar with a crowbar entering a kingdom? Alas! in this world there is no Old Bailey for nations, otherwise where would have been the crowned heads that divided Poland? Those felon monarchs anointed to—steal? It is true the historian claps the cutpurse conqueror in the dock, and he is tried by the jury of posterity. He is past the verdict, yet is not its damnatory voice lost upon generations? For thus is the world taught—albeit slowly taught—true glory; when that which passed for virtue is truly tested to be vile; when the hero is hauled from the car and fixed forever in the pillory.

But war brings forth the heroism of the soul; war tests the magnanimity of man. Sweet is the humanity that spares a fallen foe; gracious the compassion that tends his wounds, that brings even a cup of water to his burning lips. Granted. But is there not a heroism of a grander mold—the heroism of forbearance? Is not the humanity that refuses to strike a nobler virtue than the late pity born of violence? Pretty is it to see the victor with salve and lint to his bloody trophy—a maimed and agonized fellowman; but surely it had been better to withhold the blow than to have first been mischievous, to be afterwards humane.

That nations professing a belief in Christ should couple glory with war is monstrous blasphemy. Their faith, their professing faith, is—"Love one another"; their practice is to—cut throats; and more, to bribe and hoodwink men to the wickedness, the trade of blood is magnified into a virtue. We pray against battle, and glorify the deeds of death. We say beautiful are the ways of peace, and then cocker ourselves upon our perfect doings in the art of manslaying. Let us then cease to pay the sacrifice of admiration to the demon—War; let us not acknowledge him as a mighty and majestic principle, but at the very best a grim and melancholy necessity.

But there always has been—there always will be—war. It is inevitable; it is a part of the condition of human society. Man has always made glory to himself from the destruction of his fellow; so it will continue. It may be very pitiable; would it were otherwise! But so it is, and there is no helping it.

Happily we are slowly killing this destructive fallacy. A long breathing time of peace has been fatal to the dread magnificence of glory. Science and philosophy—*povera e nuda filosofia*—have made good their claims, inducing man to believe that he may vindicate the divinity of his nature otherwise than by perpetrating destruction. He begins to think there is a better glory in the communication of triumphs of the mind than in the clash of steel and the roar of artillery. At the present moment a society, embracing men of distant nations—"natural enemies," as the old wicked cant of the old patriotism had it—is at work plucking the plumes from Glory, unbracing his armor, and divesting the ogre of all that dazzled foolish and unthinking men, showing the rascal in his natural hideousness, in all his base deformity. Some, too, are calculating the cost of Glory's table; some showing what an appetite the demon has, devouring at a meal the substance of these thousand sons of industry — yea, eating up the wealth of kingdoms. And thus by degrees are men beginning to look upon this god Glory as no more than a finely trapped Sawney Bean — a monster and a destroyer — a nuisance — a noisy lie.

Complete. From the «Handbook of Swindling.»

SAMUEL JOHNSON
(1709–1784)

IT IS as unpardonable not to know Samuel Johnson in his various moods as an essayist as it would be to pretend to love his prose style as we may love that of Addison or Irving, Earle or Fuller. He was a great man, and in the eighteenth century a great writer. He will always remain a great man — virile, full of *virtus*, daring to be himself at any cost, including the actual experience of misery verging close on starvation; fierce in the assertion of his right to count for a unit in creation and not to be overborne by any one, gentle or common, noble or ignoble; yet under this fierceness so tender that from the depths of his sympathy for the suffering of others we may judge how deeply he himself must have suffered under —

> «The insolence of office and the spurns
> That patient merit of the unworthy takes.»

We can see his sensibility still more plainly when he writes Lord Chesterfield: «The notice which you have been pleased to take of my labors, had it been early, had been kind.» That rebuke, the proudest which struggling merit ever administered to the vanity of fashionable culture, we could not wish to have been other than it was. From the time Homer learned to describe the insolence of the suitors of Penelope at meals, by his own experience in living on scraps from lordly tables, to the Augustan Age when Horace and Virgil were obliged to buy permission to become immortal at the price of the meanest sycophancy to power; — from the very beginning of literature until Teutonic individuality met the pride of aristocratic power in the Teutoburgerwald and with naked breast bore it backward, — there was never the match of that reply from this plebeian «son of John» to his lord. When in the time of Tacitus, the German ancestors of the remote and unknown English «John,» who begot the original «Johnson,» waded the Rhine bare-legged through broken ice, making their way towards Rome, they were preparing the world for the coming of this heroic soul, fitted by the anguish of deep and long-continued humiliation for the pride of this answer. To be «humble with the humble and haughty with the proud» is the highest of the merely human virtues, but it is truly assumed in the mythology of the race which produced the «Johnsons» that human virtues belong to «Midgard,» — the «middle yard,» — a condition of

soul in which the celestial and infernal powers are forever blent, — not in harmony, but in the keen struggle of hand-to-hand fighting. We would be above or below humanity not to love Johnson for the pride of his poverty, but no genius of Carlyle, Taine, or Macaulay can change by eulogy the law under which the human soul acts in doing its creative work. Complete self-forgetfulness, the absorption of the artist in his art, is the first necessity of great creative work, and for Dr. Samuel Johnson, whether in Grub Street poverty or as the flattered author of the Dictionary and the «Great Cham of Literature» in his day, complete self-forgetfulness was never possible. The panoplied dignity he asserted against Chesterfield stiffens his essays and robs them of the grace which, if they only had it, would make them the great intellectual masterpieces of the eighteenth century. Among the great intellects of England in that century, none was stronger than Samuel Johnson, but in the Kingdom of Heaven in literature where the sweetness of Addison and the tender love of Thackeray for all goodness are the highest, he that is least is greater than he. Yet when we see this uncouth and almost absurd figure coming from the wilderness of Grub Street garrets, in the rusty camel's-hair of his threadbare coat, shambling towards the twentieth century, mumbling to himself and making strange gestures as he approaches, we would be unworthy, indeed, of his sacrifices, if we did not uncover and do him the deepest reverence as to the John the Baptist of a new dispensation in literature — a dispensation which the journalist Franklin illustrated when at table he pledged the trade lords of Philadelphia in water gruel and told them that those who could live on it needed no man's patronage. Samuel Johnson made that possible. To realize what it means to literature, we have only to read Dryden's prefaces and the average «dedication» of the seventeenth and eighteenth centuries. In modern times no greater work has been done for the world than that which accomplished the revolution from such conditions. It made Truth possible for genius, and set so high a standard of manhood in literature, that no man of real intellect dares now to be openly the sycophant of Vanity, Folly and Falsehood — even when these hold all the avenues of preferment, and demand subservience as the price of advancement.

Owing this and more to Samuel Johnson, we ought to thank Heaven for him and to read his Rambler and Idler essays, his «Rasselas,» his poems, his biographies, and his Dictionary too, to learn what manner of man he was in the realities back of the unequaled portrait Boswell has left.

When once or twice in a century heaven sends a Man on earth to show us what manhood means, we cannot learn too much of him. And Samuel Johnson was a Man.   W. V. B.

OMAR, THE SON OF HASSAN

OMAR, the son of Hassan, had passed seventy-five years in honor and prosperity. The favor of three successive caliphs had filled his house with gold and silver; and whenever he appeared, the benedictions of the people proclaimed his passage.

Terrestrial happiness is of short continuance. The brightness of the flame is wasting its fuel; the fragrant flower is passing away in its own odors. The vigor of Omar began to fail, the curls of beauty fell from his head, strength departed from his hands, and agility from his feet. He gave back to the caliph the keys of trust and the seals of secrecy; and sought no other pleasure for the remains of life than the converse of the wise, and the gratitude of the good.

The powers of his mind were yet unimpaired. His chamber was filled by visitants, eager to catch the dictates of experience, and officious to pay the tribute of admiration. Caled, the son of the viceroy of Egypt, entered every day early, and retired late. He was beautiful and eloquent; Omar admired his wit and loved his docility. Tell me, said Caled, thou to whose voice nations have listened, and whose wisdom is known to the extremities of Asia, tell me how I may resemble Omar the prudent. The arts by which you have gained power and preserved it are to you no longer necessary or useful; impart to me the secret of your conduct, and teach me the plan upon which your wisdom has built your fortune.

Young man, said Omar, it is of little use to form plans of life. When I took my first survey of the world, in my twentieth year, having considered the various conditions of mankind, in the hour of solitude I said thus to myself, leaning against a cedar which spread its branches over my head: — Seventy years are allowed to man; I have yet fifty remaining: ten years I will allot to the attainment of knowledge, and ten I will pass in foreign countries; I shall be learned, and therefore shall be honored; every city will shout at my arrival, and every student will solicit my friendship. Twenty years thus passed will store my mind with images which I shall be busy through the rest of my life in combining and comparing. I shall revel in inexhaustible accumulations of intellectual riches; I shall find new pleasures for every moment, and shall never more be weary of myself. I will, however, not deviate too far from the beaten track of life, but will try what can be found in female delicacy. I will marry a wife beautiful as the Houries, and wise as Zobeide; with her I will live twenty years within the suburbs of Bagdad, in every pleasure that wealth can purchase and fancy can invent. I will then retire to a rural dwelling, pass my last days in obscurity and contemplation, and lie silently down on the bed of death. Through my life it shall be my settled resolution that I will never depend upon the smile of princes; that I will never stand exposed to the artifices of courts; I will never pant for public honors, nor disturb my quiet with the affairs of state. Such was my scheme of life, which I impressed indelibly upon my memory.

The first part of my ensuing time was to be spent in search of knowledge; and I know not how I was diverted from my design. I had no visible impediments without, nor any ungovernable passions within. I regarded knowledge as the highest honor and the most engaging pleasure; yet day stole upon day, and month glided after month, till I found that seven years of the first ten had vanished, and left nothing behind them. I now postponed my purpose of traveling; for why should I go abroad while so much remained to be learned at home? I immured myself for four years, and studied the laws of the empire. The fame of my skill reached the judges; I was found able to speak upon doubtful questions, and was commanded to stand at the footstool of the caliph. I was heard with attention, I was consulted with confidence, and the love of praise fastened on my heart.

I still wished to see distant countries, listened with rapture to the relations of travelers, and resolved some time to ask my dismission that I might feast my soul with novelty; but my presence was always necessary, and the stream of business hurried me along. Sometimes I was afraid lest I should be charged with ingratitude; but I still proposed to travel, and therefore would not confine myself by marriage.

In my fiftieth year I began to suspect that the time of traveling was past, and thought it best to lay hold on the felicity yet in my power, and indulge myself in domestic pleasures. But at fifty no man easily finds a woman beautiful as the Houries, and wise as Zobeide. I inquired and rejected, consulted and deliberated, till the sixty-second year made me ashamed of gazing upon girls. I had now nothing left but retirement, and for

VI—150

retirement I never found a time, till disease forced me from public employment.

Such was my scheme, and such has been its consequence. With an insatiable thirst for knowledge, I trifled away the years of improvement; with a restless desire of seeing different countries, I have always resided in the same city; with the highest expectation of connubial felicity, I have lived unmarried; and with unalterable resolutions of contemplative retirement, I am going to die within the walls of Bagdad.

Complete. Number 101 of
the Idler.

DIALOGUE IN A VULTURE'S NEST

MANY naturalists are of opinion that the animals which we commonly consider as mute have the power of imparting their thoughts to one another. That they can express general sensations is very certain: every being that can utter sounds has a different voice for pleasure and for pain. The hound informs his fellows when he scents his game; the hen calls her chickens to their food by her cluck, and drives them from danger by her scream.

Birds have the greatest variety of notes; they have, indeed, a variety, which seems almost sufficient to make a speech adequate to the purposes of a life which is regulated by instinct, and can admit little change or improvement. To the cries of birds curiosity or superstition has been always attentive; many have studied the language of the feathered tribes, and some have boasted that they understood it.

The most skillful or most confident interpreters of the sylvan dialogues have been commonly found among the philosophers of the East, in a country where the calmness of the air and the mildness of the seasons allow the student to pass a great part of the year in groves and bowers. But what may be done in one place by peculiar opportunities may be performed in another by peculiar diligence. A shepherd of Bohemia has, by long abode in the forests, enabled himself to understand the voice of birds; at least he relates with great confidence a story, of which the credibility is left to be considered by the learned:—

As I was sitting (said he) within a hollow rock, and watching my sheep that fed in the valley, I heard two vultures inter-

changeably crying on the summit of a cliff. Both voices were earnest and deliberate. My curiosity prevailed over the care of the flock; I climbed slowly and silently from crag to crag, concealed among the shrubs, till I found a cavity where I might sit and listen without suffering, or giving disturbance.

I soon perceived that my labor would be well repaid, for an old vulture was sitting on a naked prominence, with her young about her, whom she was instructing in the arts of a vulture's life, and preparing, by the last lecture, for their final dismission to the mountains and the skies.

My children, said the old vulture, you will the less want my instructions, because you have had my practice before your eyes; you have seen me snatch from the farm the household fowl, you have seen me seize the leveret in the bush, and the kid in the pasturage; you know how to fix your talons, and how to balance your flight when you are laden with your prey. But you remember the taste of more delicious food. I have often regaled you with the flesh of man. Tell us, said the young vultures, where man may be found, and how he may be known; his flesh is surely the natural food of a vulture. Why have you never brought a man in your talons to the nest? He is too bulky, said the mother; when we find a man we can only tear away his flesh, and leave his bones upon the ground. Since man is so big, said the young ones, how do you kill him? You are afraid of the wolf and of the bear, by what power are vultures superior to man? Is man more defenseless than a sheep? We have not the strength of man, returned the mother, and I am sometimes in doubt whether we have the subtilty; and the vultures would seldom feast upon his flesh, had not nature, that devoted him to our uses, infused into him a strange ferocity, which I have never observed in any other being that feeds upon the earth. Two herds of men will often meet and shake the earth with noise, and fill the earth with fire. When you hear noise, and see fire, with flashes along the ground, hasten to the place with your swiftest wing, for men are surely destroying one another; you will then find the ground smoking with blood and covered with carcasses, of which many are dismembered, and mangled for the convenience of the vulture. But when men have killed their prey, said the pupil, why do they not eat it? When the wolf has killed a sheep, he suffers not the vulture to touch it till he has satisfied himself. Is not man another kind of wolf? Man,

said the mother, is the only beast who kills that which he does not devour, and this quality makes him so much a benefactor to our species. If men kill our prey, and lay it in our way, said the young one, what need shall we have of laboring for ourselves? Because man will sometimes, replied the mother, remain for a long time quiet in his den. The old vultures will tell you when you are to watch his motions. When you see men in great numbers moving close together, like a flight of storks, you may conclude that they are hunting, and that you will soon revel in human blood. But still, said the young one, I would gladly know the reason of this mutual slaughter. I could never kill what I could not eat. My child, said the mother, this is a question which I cannot answer, though I am reckoned the most subtle bird of the mountain. When I was young, I used frequently to visit the aerie of an old vulture, who dwelt upon the Carpathian rocks; he had made many observations; he knew the places that afforded prey round his habitation, as far in every direction as the strongest wing can fly between the rising and setting of the summer sun; he had fed year after year on the entrails of men. His opinion was that men had only the appearance of animal life, being really vegetables with the power of motion; and that as the boughs of an oak are dashed together by the storm, that swine may fatten upon the fallen acorns, so men are by some unaccountable power driven one against another, till they lose their motion, that vultures may be fed. Others think they have observed something of contrivance and policy among these mischievous beings; and those that hover more closely round them pretend that there is in every herd one that gives directions to the rest and seems to be more eminently delighted with a wide carnage. What it is that entitles him to such pre-eminence we know not; he is seldom the biggest or the swiftest, but he shows by his eagerness and diligence that he is, more than any of the others, a friend to the vultures.

Complete. Number 22 of the Idler.

ON THE ADVANTAGES OF LIVING IN A GARRET

Ὄσσαν ἐπ' Οὐλύμπῳ μέμασαν θέμεν αὐτὰρ ἐπ' Ὄσσῃ
Πήλιον εἰνοσίφυλλον, ἵν' οὐρανὸς ἀμβατὸς εἴη.
— *Homer.*

The gods they challenge, and affect the skies:
Heaved on Olympus, tottering Ossa stood;
On Ossa, Pelion nods with all his wood.
— *Pope.*

To the Rambler

Sir: —

NOTHING has more retarded the advancement of learning than the disposition of vulgar minds to ridicule and vilify what they cannot comprehend. All industry must be excited by hope; and as the student often proposes no other reward to himself than praise, he is easily discouraged by contempt and insult. He who brings with him into a clamorous multitude the timidity of recluse speculation, and has never hardened his front in public life, or accustomed his passions to the vicissitudes and accidents, the triumphs and defeats of mixed conversation, will blush at the stare of petulant incredulity, and suffer himself to be driven, by a burst of laughter, from the fortresses of demonstration. The mechanist will be afraid to assert before hardy contradictions the possibility of tearing down bulwarks with a silkworm's thread; and the astronomer of relating the rapidity of light, the distance of the fixed stars, and the height of the lunar mountains.

If I could by any efforts have shaken off this cowardice, I had not sheltered myself under a borrowed name, nor applied to you for the means of communicating to the public the theory of a garret; a subject which, except some slight and transient strictures, has been hitherto neglected by those who were best qualified to adorn it, either for want of leisure to prosecute the various researches in which a nice discussion must engage them, or because it requires such diversity of knowledge, and such extent of curiosity, as is scarcely to be found in any single intellect; or perhaps others foresaw the tumults which would be raised against them, and confined their knowledge to their own breasts, and abandoned prejudice and folly to the direction of chance.

That the professors of literature generally reside in the highest stories has been immemorially observed. The wisdom of the

Ancients was well acquainted with the intellectual advantages of an elevated situation; why else were the Muses stationed on Olympus, or Parnassus, by those who could with equal right have raised them bowers in the vale of Tempe, or erected their altars among the flexures of Meander? Why was Jove himself nursed upon a mountain? or why did the goddesses, when the prize of beauty was contested, try the cause upon the top of Ida? Such were the fictions by which the great masters of the earlier ages endeavored to inculcate to posterity the importance of a garret, which, though they had been long obscured by the negligence and ignorance of succeeding times, were well enforced by the celebrated symbol of Pythagoras, ἀνεμῶν πνεόντων τὴν ἠχὼ προσκύνει; "when the wind blows, worship its echo." This could not but be understood by his disciples as an inviolable injunction to live in a garret, which I have found frequently visited by the echo and the wind. Nor was the tradition wholly obliterated in the age of Augustus, for Tibullus evidently congratulates himself upon his garret, not without some allusion to the Pythagorean precept: —

Quem juvat immites ventos audire cubantem —
Aut, gelidas hybernus aquas cum fuderit auster,
Securum somnos, imbre juvante, sequi!

How sweet in sleep to pass the careless hours,
Lull'd by the beating winds and dashing showers!

And it is impossible not to discover the fondness of Lucretius, an early writer, for a garret, in his description of the lofty towers of serene learning, and of the pleasure with which a wise man looks down upon the confused and erratic state of the world moving below him: —

Sed nil dulcius est, bene quam munita tenere
Edita doctrina sapientum templa serena;
Despicere unde queas alios, passimque videre
Errare, atque viam palanteis quærere vitæ.

————'Tis sweet thy laboring steps to guide
To virtue's heights, with wisdom well supplied,
And all the magazines of learning fortified:
From thence to look below on human kind,
Bewilder'd in the maze of life, and blind.
— *Dryden.*

The institution has, indeed, continued to our own time; the garret is still the usual receptacle of the philosopher and poet; but this, like many ancient customs, is perpetuated only by an accidental imitation, without knowledge of the original reason for which it was established: —

Causa latet: res est notissima.

The cause is secret, but th' effect is known.
— *Addison.*

Conjectures have, indeed, been advanced concerning these habitations of literature, but without much satisfaction to the judicious inquirer. Some have imagined that the garret is generally chosen by the wits as most easily rented; and concluded that no man rejoices in his aërial abode, but on the days of payment. Others suspect that a garret is chiefly convenient, as it is remoter than any other part of the house from the outer door, which is often observed to be infested by visitants, who talk incessantly of beer, or linen, or a coat, and repeat the same sounds every morning, and sometimes again in the afternoon, without any variation, except that they grow daily more importunate and clamorous, and raise their voices in time from mournful murmurs to raging vociferations. This eternal monotony is always detestable to a man whose chief pleasure is to enlarge his knowledge, and vary his ideas. Others talk of freedom from noise, and abstraction from common business or amusements; and some, yet more visionary, tell us that the faculties are enlarged by open prospects, and that the fancy is more at liberty when the eye ranges without confinement.

These conveniences may perhaps all be found in a well-chosen garret; but surely they cannot be supposed sufficiently important to have operated invariably upon different climates, distant ages, and separate nations. Of a universal practice, there must still be presumed a universal cause, which, however recondite and abstruse, may be perhaps reserved to make me illustrious by its discovery, and you by its promulgation.

It is universally known that the faculties of the mind are invigorated or weakened by the state of the body, and that the body is in a great measure regulated by the various compressions of the ambient element. The effects of the air in the production or cure of corporal maladies have been acknowledged from

the time of Hippocrates; but no man has yet sufficiently considered how far it may influence the operations of the genius, though every day affords instances of local understanding, of wits and reasoners, whose faculties are adapted to some single spot, and who, when they are removed to any other place, sink at once into silence and stupidity. I have discovered by a long series of observations that invention and elocution suffer great impediments from dense and impure vapors, and that the tenuity of a defecated air at a proper distance from the surface of the earth accelerates the fancy and sets at liberty those intellectual powers which were before shackled by too strong attraction, and unable to expand themselves under the pressure of a gross atmosphere. I have found dullness to quicken into sentiment in a thin ether, as water, though not very hot, boils in a receiver partly exhausted; and heads, in appearance empty, have teemed with notions upon rising ground, as the flaccid sides of a football would have swelled out into stiffness and extension.

For this reason I never think myself qualified to judge decisively of any man's faculties, whom I have only known in one degree of elevation; but take some opportunity of attending him from the cellar to the garret, and try upon him all the various degrees of rarefaction and condensation, tension and laxity. If he is neither vivacious aloft, nor serious below, I then consider him as hopeless; but as it seldom happens that I do not find the temper to which the texture of his brain is fitted, I accommodate him in time with a tube of mercury, first marking the point most favorable to his intellects, according to rules which I have long studied, and which I may perhaps reveal to mankind in a complete treatise of barometrical pneumatology.

Another cause of the gayety and sprightliness of the dwellers in garrets is probably the increase of that vertiginous motion, with which we are carried round by the diurnal revolution of the earth. The power of agitation upon the spirits is well known; every man has felt his heart lightened in a rapid vehicle, or on a galloping horse; and nothing is plainer than that he who towers to the fifth story is whirled through more space by every circumrotation, than another that grovels upon the ground floor. The nations between the tropics are known to be fiery, inconstant, inventive, and fanciful, because, living at the utmost length of the earth's diameter, they are carried about with more swiftness than those whom nature has placed nearer to the poles; and, therefore, as it becomes a wise man to struggle with the inconveniences of his country, whenever celerity and acuteness are requisite, we must actuate our languor by taking a few turns round the centre in a garret.

If you imagine that I ascribe to air motion and effects which they cannot produce, I desire you to consult your own memory, and consider whether you have never known a man acquire reputation in his garret, which, when fortune or a patron had placed him upon the first floor, he was unable to maintain; and who never recovered his former vigor of understanding till he was restored to his original situation. That a garret will make every man a wit I am very far from supposing; I know there are some who would continue blockheads even on the summit of the Andes, or on the peak of Teneriffe. But let not any man be considered as unimprovable till this potent remedy has been tried; for perhaps he was formed to be great only in a garret, as the joiner of Aretæus was rational in no other place but in his own shop.

I think a frequent removal to various distances from the centre, so necessary to a just estimate of intellectual abilities, and consequently of so great use in education, that if I hoped that the public could be persuaded to so expensive an experiment, I would propose that there should be a cavern dug, and a tower erected, like those which Bacon describes in Solomon's house, for the expansion and concentration of understanding, according to the exigence of different employments or constitutions. Perhaps some that fume away in meditations upon time and space in the tower might compose tables of interest at a certain depth; and he that upon level ground stagnates in silence, or creeps in narrative, might at the height of half a mile ferment into merriment, sparkle with repartee, and froth with declamation.

Addison observes that we may find the heat of Virgil's climate in some lines of his "Georgics": so when I read a composition, I immediately determine the height of the author's habitation. As an elaborate performance is commonly said to smell of the lamp, my commendation of a noble thought, a sprightly sally, or a bold figure, is to pronounce it fresh from the garret; an expression which would break from me upon the perusal of most of your papers, did I not believe that you sometimes quit the garret, and ascend into the cock loft.   HYPERTATUS.

Complete. Number 117 of the Rambler.

need not wonder to find Hector quoting Aristotle, when we see the loves of Theseus and Hippolyta combined with the Gothic mythology of fairies. Shakespeare, indeed, was not the only violator of chronology, for in the same age Sidney, who wanted not the advantages of learning, has, in his "Arcadia," confounded the pastoral with the feudal times; the days of innocence, quiet, and security, with those of turbulence, violence, and adventure.

In his comic scenes he is seldom very successful when he engages his characters in reciprocations of smartness and contests of sarcasm; their jests are commonly gross, and their pleasantry licentious; neither his gentlemen nor his ladies have much delicacy, nor are sufficiently distinguished from his clowns by any appearance of refined manners. Whether he represented the real conversation of his time is not easy to determine: the reign of Elizabeth is commonly supposed to have been a time of stateliness, formality, and reserve; yet perhaps the relaxations of that severity were not very elegant. There must, however, have been always some modes of gayety preferable to others, and a writer ought to choose the best.

In tragedy his performance seems constantly to be worse, as his labor is more. The effusions of passion which exigence forces out are for the most part striking and energetic; but whenever he solicits his invention, or strains his faculties, the offspring of his throes is tumor, meanness, tediousness, and obscurity.

In narration he affects a disproportionate pomp of diction, and a wearisome train of circumlocution, and tells the incident imperfectly in many words, which might have been more plainly delivered in few. Narration in dramatic poetry is naturally tedious, as it is unanimated and inactive, and obstructs the progress of the action; it should therefore always be rapid, and enlivened by frequent interruption. Shakespeare found it an incumbrance, and instead of lightening it by brevity, endeavored to recommend it by dignity and splendor.

His declamations or set speeches are commonly cold and weak, for his power was the power of nature; when he endeavored, like other tragic writers, to catch opportunities of amplification, and instead of inquiring what the occasion demanded, to show how much his stores of knowledge could supply, he seldom escapes without the pity or resentment of his reader.

It is incident to him to be now and then entangled with an unwieldy sentiment, which he cannot well express, and will not

SOME OF SHAKESPEARE'S FAULTS

SHAKESPEARE with his excellencies has likewise faults, and faults sufficient to obscure and overwhelm any other merit. I shall show them in the proportion in which they appear to me, without envious malignity or superstitious veneration. No question can be more innocently discussed than a dead poet's pretensions to renown; and little regard is due to that bigotry which sets candor higher than truth.

His first defect is that to which may be imputed most of the evil in books or in men. He sacrifices virtue to convenience, and is so much more careful to please than to instruct, that he seems to write without any moral purpose. From his writings, indeed, a system of social duty may be selected, for he that thinks reasonably must think morally; but his precepts and axioms drop casually from him; he makes no just distribution of good or evil, nor is always careful to show in the virtuous a disapprobation of the wicked; he carries his persons indifferently through right and wrong, and at the close dismisses them without further care, and leaves their examples to operate by chance. This fault the barbarity of his age cannot estimate; for it is always a writer's duty to make the world better, and justice is a virtue independent of time or place.

The plots are often so loosely formed that a very slight consideration may improve them, and so carelessly pursued that he seems not always fully to comprehend his own design. He omits opportunities of instructing or delighting, which the train of his story seems to force upon him, and apparently rejects those exhibitions which would be more affecting, for the sake of those which are more easy.

It may be observed that in many of his plays the latter part is evidently neglected. When he found himself near the end of his work, and in view of his reward, he shortened the labor to snatch the profit. He therefore remits his efforts where he should most vigorously exert them, and his catastrophe is improbably produced or imperfectly represented.

He had no regard to distinction of time or place, but gives to one age or nation, without scruple, the customs, institutions, and opinions of another, at the expense not only of likelihood, but of possibility. These faults Pope has endeavored, with more zeal than judgment, to transfer to his imagined interpolators. We

reject; he struggles with it awhile, and, if it continues stubborn, comprises it in words such as occur, and leaves it to be disentangled and solved by those who have more leisure to bestow upon it.

Not that always where the language is intricate the thought is subtle, or the image always great where the line is bulky; the equality of words to things is very often neglected, and trivial sentiments and vulgar ideas disappoint the attention, to which they are recommended by sonorous epithets and swelling figures.

But the admirers of this great poet have most reason to complain when he approaches nearest to his highest excellence, and seems fully resolved to sink them in dejection, and mollify them with tender emotions by the fall of greatness, the danger of innocence, or the crosses of love. What he does best, he soon ceases to do. He is not soft and pathetic without some idle conceit, or contemptible equivocation. He no sooner begins to move than he counteracts himself; and terror and pity, as they are rising in the mind, are checked and blasted by sudden frigidity. A quibble is to Shakespeare what luminous vapors are to the traveler; he follows it at all adventures; it is sure to lead him out of his way, and sure to engulf him in the mire. It has some malignant power over his mind, and its fascinations are irresistible. Whatever be the dignity or profundity of his disposition, whether he be enlarging knowledge or exalting affection, whether he be amusing attention with incidents, or enchaining it in suspense, let but a quibble spring up before him, and he leaves his work unfinished. A quibble is the golden apple for which he will always turn aside from his career, or stoop from his elevation. A quibble, poor and barren as it is, gave him such delight that he was content to purchase it, by the sacrifice of reason, propriety, and truth. A quibble was to him the fatal Cleopatra for which he lost the world, and was content to lose it.

It will be thought strange that in enumerating the defects of this writer, I have not yet mentioned his neglect of the unities; his violation of those laws which have been instituted and established by the joint authority of poets and critics.

For his other deviations from the art of writing, I resign him to critical justice, without making any other demand in his favor than that which must be indulged to all human excellence: that his virtues be rated with his failings: but from the censure which this irregularity may bring upon him, I shall, with due reverence to that learning which I must oppose, adventure to try how I can defend him.

His histories, being neither tragedies nor comedies, are not subject to any of their laws; nothing more is necessary to all the praise which they expect than that the changes of action be so prepared as to be understood; that the incidents be various and affecting, and the characters consistent, natural, and distinct. No other unity is intended, and therefore none is to be sought.

In his other works he has well enough preserved the unity of action. He has not, indeed, an intrigue regularly perplexed and regularly unraveled; he does not endeavor to hide his design only to discover it, for this is seldom the order of real events, and Shakespeare is the poet of nature; but his plan has commonly, what Aristotle requires, a beginning, a middle, and an end; one event is concatenated with another, and the conclusion follows by easy consequence. There are perhaps some incidents that might be spared, as in other poets there is much talk that only fills up time upon the stage; but the general system makes gradual advances, and the end of the play is the end of expectation.

To the unities of time and place he has shown no regard; and perhaps a nearer view of the principles on which they stand will diminish their value, and withdraw from them the veneration which, from the time of Corneille, they have very generally received, by discovering that they have given more trouble to the poet than pleasure to the auditor. . . .

Our author's plots are generally borrowed from novels; and it is reasonable to suppose that he chose the most popular, such as were read by many, and related by more; for his audience could not have followed him through the intricacies of the drama, had they not held the thread of the story in their hands.

The stories, which we now find only in remoter authors, were in his time accessible and familiar. The fable of "As You Like It," which is supposed to be copied from Chaucer's "Gamelyn," was a little pamphlet of those times; and old Mr. Cibber remembered the tale of "Hamlet" in plain English prose, which the critics have now to seek in Saxo Grammaticus. His English histories he took from English chronicles and English ballads; and as the ancient writers were made known to his countrymen by version, they supplied him with new objects; he dilated some of Plutarch's "Lives" into plays, when they had been translated by North.

His plots, whether historical or fabulous, are always crowded with incidents, by which the attention of a rude people was more easily caught than by sentiment or argumentation; and such is the power of the marvelous, even over those who despise it, that every man finds his mind more strongly seized by the tragedies of Shakespeare than of any other writer; others please us by particular speeches, but he always makes us anxious for the event, and has perhaps excelled all but Homer in securing the first purpose of a writer, by exciting restless and unquenchable curiosity, and compelling him that reads his work to read it through.

The shows and bustle with which his plays abound have the same original. As knowledge advances, pleasure passes from the eye to the ear, but returns, as it declines, from the ear to the eye. Those to whom our author's labors were exhibited had more skill in pomps or processions than in poetical language, and perhaps wanted some visible and discriminating events, as comments on the dialogue. He knew how he should most please; and whether his practice is more agreeable to nature, or whether his example has prejudiced the nation, we still find that on our stage something must be done as well as said, and inactive declamation is very coldly heard, however musical or elegant, passionate or sublime.

From the preface to "Shakespeare."

PARALLEL BETWEEN POPE AND DRYDEN

POPE professed to have learned his poetry from Dryden, whom, whenever an opportunity was presented, he praised through his whole life with unvaried liberality; and perhaps his character may receive some illustration, if he be compared with his master.

Integrity of understanding and nicety of discernment were not allotted in a less proportion to Dryden than to Pope. The rectitude of Dryden's mind was sufficiently shown by the dismission of his poetical prejudices, and the rejection of unnatural thoughts and rugged numbers. But Dryden never desired to apply all the judgment that he had. He wrote, and professed to write, merely for the people; and when he pleased others he contented himself. He spent no time in struggles to rouse latent powers: he never

attempted to make that better which was already good, nor often to mend what he must have known to be faulty. He wrote, as he tells us, with very little consideration; when occasion or necessity called upon him, he poured out what the present moment happened to supply, and, when once it had passed the press, ejected it from his mind; for when he had no pecuniary interest, he had no further solicitude.

Pope was not content to satisfy; he desired to excel, and therefore always endeavored to do his best: he did not court the candor, but dared the judgment of his reader, and expecting no indulgence from others, he showed none to himself. He examined lines and words with minute and punctilious observation, and retouched every part with indefatigable diligence, till he had left nothing to be forgiven.

For this reason he kept his pieces very long in his hands, while he considered and reconsidered them. The only poems which can be supposed to have been written with such regard to the times as might hasten their publication, were the two satires of "Thirty-eight," of which Dodsley told me that they were brought to him by the author, that they might be fairly copied. "Almost every line," he said, "was then written twice over; I gave him a clean transcript, which he sent sometime afterwards to me for the press with almost every line written twice over a second time."

His declaration that his care for his works ceased at their publication was not strictly true. His parental attention never abandoned them; what he found amiss in the first edition, he silently corrected in those that followed. He appears to have revised the "Iliad," and freed it from some of its imperfections; and the "Essay on Criticism" received many improvements after its first appearance. It will seldom be found that he altered without adding clearness, elegance, or vigor.

Pope had perhaps the judgment of Dryden, but Dryden certainly wanted the diligence of Pope.

In acquired knowledge, the superiority must be allowed to Dryden, whose education was more scholastic, and who, before he became an author, had been allowed more time for study with better means of information. His mind has a larger range, and he collects his images and illustrations from a more extensive circumference of science. Dryden knew more of man in his general nature, and Pope in his local manners. The notions of Dry-

den were formed by comprehensive speculation, and those of Pope by minute attention. There is more dignity in the knowledge of Dryden, and more certainty in that of Pope.

Poetry was not the sole praise of either, for both excelled likewise in prose; but Pope did not borrow his prose from his predecessor. The style of Dryden is capricious and varied, that of Pope is cautious and uniform. Dryden obeys the motions of his own mind, Pope constrains his mind to his own rules of composition. Dryden is sometimes vehement and rapid, Pope is always smooth, uniform, and gentle. Dryden's page is a natural field, rising into inequalities, and diversified by the varied exuberance of abundant vegetation; Pope's is a velvet lawn, shaven by the scythe, and leveled by the roller.

Of genius, that power which constitutes a poet, that quality without which judgment is cold and knowledge is inert, that energy which collects, combines, amplifies, and animates, the superiority must, with some hesitation, be allowed to Dryden. It is not to be inferred that of this poetical vigor Pope had only a little, because Dryden had more; for every other writer since Milton must give place to Pope; and even of Dryden it must be said that if he has brighter paragraphs, he has not better poems. Dryden's performances were always hasty, either excited by some external occasion, or extorted by domestic necessity; he composed without consideration, and published without correction. What his mind could supply at call, or gather in one excursion, was all that he sought and all that he gave. The dilatory caution of Pope enabled him to condense his sentiments, to multiply his images, and to accumulate all that study might produce or chance might supply. If the flights of Dryden, therefore, are higher, Pope continues longer on the wing. If of Dryden's fire the blaze is brighter, of Pope's the heat is more regular and constant. Dryden often surpasses expectation, and Pope never falls below it. Dryden is read with frequent astonishment, and Pope with perpetual delight.

This parallel will, I hope, when it is well considered, be found just; and if the reader should suspect me, as I suspect myself, of some partial fondness for the memory of Dryden, let him not too hastily condemn me, for meditation and inquiry may, perhaps, show him the reasonableness of my determination.

From "Lives of the Poets."

BEN JONSON

(c. 1573-1637)

EN JONSON'S "Discoveries Made upon Men and Matter" are not essays in the same sense with Bacon's. He is a quaint and entertaining prose writer, and it frequently happens that in rambling from subject to subject over the wide range of things which interest him, he finds something which results in an essay as complete in form as could be desired. Quite frequently, however, he prefers to gossip pleasantly, changing the subject as soon as he is tired of it, without regard to whether he has reached the end of it or not. In his lyric poems, he shows the artistic sense which belonged to his seasons of concentrated effort. His ode to the moon,—

> "Queen and huntress chaste and fair,
> Now the sun is laid to sleep,"

is scarcely surpassed in its art by any other lyric in the language, and it represents him well on the too infrequent occasions when he subjected himself to the strain of doing his best.

He was born at Westminster, England, about the year 1573, from obscure parentage. His stepfather was a bricklayer, but he was sent to school first to St. Martins-in-the-Fields, and afterwards to Westminster. In 1597 he is found working in London as a player and writer of plays. In 1598 his "Every Man in His Humor" was put on the stage at the Globe Theatre, and it is said that Shakespeare appeared as one of the actors in it. Jonson was popular as a playwright, and so great a favorite at court that he had a pension of £200 a year. He knew and valued Shakespeare, but, as one of the passages in his "Discoveries" shows, his admiration was not undiscriminating. In 1637, when Jonson died, the court was engaged in preparing for the life-and-death struggle which was to come with Cromwell's Ironsides. The poet was forgotten after his burial in Westminster Abbey, until one of his admirers, Sir John Young, caused to be cut upon the tomb the celebrated epitaph, "O Rare Ben Jonson."

VI—151

ON SHAKESPEARE—ON THE DIFFERENCE OF WITS

I REMEMBER the players have often mentioned it as an honor to Shakespeare, that in his writing, whatsoever he penned, he never blotted out a line. My answer hath been, "Would he had blotted a thousand," which they thought a malevolent speech. I had not told posterity this, but for their ignorance who chose that circumstance to commend their friend by wherein he most faulted; and to justify mine own candor, for I loved the man, and do honor his memory on this side idolatry as much as any. He was, indeed, honest, and of an open and free nature; had an excellent phantasy, brave notions, and gentle expressions, wherein he flowed with that facility, that sometimes it was necessary he should be stopped. *Sufflaminandus erat*, as Augustus said of Haterius. His wit was in his own power: would the rule of it had been so too. Many times he fell into those things which could not escape laughter, as when he said in the person of Cæsar, one speaking to him, "Cæsar, thou dost me wrong." He replied, "Cæsar did never wrong but with just cause"; and such like, which were ridiculous. But he redeemed his vices with his virtues. There was ever more in him to be praised than to be pardoned.

In the difference of wits I have observed there are many notes; and it is a little maistry to know them, to discern what every nature, every disposition will bear; for before we sow our land we should plough it. There are no fewer forms of minds than of bodies amongst us. The variety is incredible, and therefore we must search. Some are fit to make divines, some poets, some lawyers, some physicians, some to be sent to the plow, and trades.

There is no doctrine will do good where nature is wanting. Some wits are swelling and high; others low and still; some hot and fiery; others cold and dull; one must have a bridle, the other a spur.

There be some that are forward and bold; and these will do every little thing easily. I mean that is hard by and next them, which they will utter unretarded without any shamefacedness. These never perform much, but quickly. They are what they are on the sudden; they show presently like grain that, scattered on the top of the ground, shoots up, but takes no root; has a yellow blade, but the ear empty. They are wits of good promise

at first, but there is an *ingenistitium;* they stand still at sixteen, they get no higher.

You have others that labor only to ostentation; and are ever more busy about the colors and surface of a work than in the matter and foundation, for that is hid, the other is seen.

Others that in composition are nothing but what is rough and broken. *Quæ per salebras, altaque saxa cadunt.* And if it would come gently, they trouble it of purpose. They would not have it run without rubs, as if that style were more strong and manly that struck the ear with a kind of unevenness. These men err not by chance, but knowingly and willingly; they are like men that affect a fashion by themselves; have some singularity in a ruff, cloak, or hatband; or their beards specially cut to provoke beholders, and set a mark upon themselves. They would be reprehended while they are looked on. And this vice, one that is authority with the rest, loving, delivers over to them to be imitated; so that ofttimes the faults which he fell into, the others seek for. This is the danger, when vice becomes a precedent.

Others there are that have no composition at all; but a kind of tuning and rhyming fall in what they write. It runs and slides, and only makes a sound. Women's poets they are called, as you have women's tailors.

> "They write a verse as smooth, as soft as cream,
> In which there is no torrent, nor scarce stream."

You may sound these wits and find the depth of them with your middle finger. They are cream-bowl, or but puddle-deep.

Some that turn over all books, and are equally searching in all papers; that write out of what they presently find or meet, without choice. By which means it happens that what they have discredited and impugned in one week, they have before or after extolled the same in another. Such are all the essayists, even their master Montaigne. These, in all they write, confess still what books they have read last, and therein their own folly so much that they bring it to the stake raw and undigested; not that the place did need it neither, but that they thought themselves furnished and would vent it.

Some again who, after they have got authority, or, which is less, opinion, by their writings, to have read much, dare presently to feign whole books and authors, and lie safely. For what never was will not easily be found, not by the most curious.

And some, by a cunning protestation against all reading, and false vendition of their own naturals, think to divert the sagacity of their readers from themselves, and cool the scent of their own fox-like thefts; when yet they are so rank, as a man may find whole pages together usurped from one author; their necessities compelling them to read for present use, which could not be in many books; and so come forth more ridiculously and palpably guilty than those who, because they cannot trace, they yet would slander their industry.

But the wretcheder are the obstinate contemners of all helps and arts; such as presuming on their own naturals (which, perhaps, are excellent), dare deride all diligence, and seem to mock at the terms when they understand not the things; thinking that way to get off wittily with their ignorance. These are imitated often by such as are their peers in negligence, though they cannot be in nature; and they utter all they can think with a kind of violence and indisposition, unexamined, without relation either to person, place, or any fitness else; and the more willful and stubborn they are in it the more learned they are esteemed of the multitude, through their excellent vice of judgment, who think those things the stronger that have no art; as if to break were better than to open, or to rend asunder gentler than to loose.

It cannot but come to pass that these men who commonly seek to do more than enough may sometimes happen on something that is good and great; but very seldom: and when it comes it doth not recompense the rest of their ill. For their jests, and their sentences (which they only and ambitiously seek for) stick out and are more eminent because all is sordid and vile about them; as lights are more discerned in a thick darkness than a faint shadow. Now, because they speak all they can (however unfitly), they are thought to have the greater copy; where the learned use ever election and a mean, they look back to what they intended at first, and make all an even and proportioned body. The true artificer will not run away from Nature as he were afraid of her, or depart from life and the likeness of truth, but speak to the capacity of his hearers. And though his language differ from the vulgar somewhat, it shall not fly from all humanity, with the Tamerlanes and Tamer-chams of the late age, which had nothing in them but the scenical strutting and furious vociferation to warrant them to the ignorant gapers. He knows it is his only art so to carry it as none but artificers perceive it. In the meantime, perhaps, he is called barren, dull, lean, a poor writer, or by what contumelious word can come in their cheeks, by these men who, without labor, judgment, knowledge, or almost sense, are received or preferred before him. He gratulates them and their fortune. Another age, or juster men, will acknowledge the virtues of his studies, his wisdom in dividing, his subtlety in arguing, with what strength he doth inspire his readers, with what sweetness he strokes them; in inveighing, what sharpness; in jest, what urbanity he uses; how he doth reign in men's affections; how invade and break in upon them, and makes their minds like the thing he writes. Then in his elocution to behold what word is proper, which hath ornaments, which height, what is beautifully translated, where figures are fit, which gentle, which strong, to show the composition manly; and how he hath avoided faint, obscure, obscene, sordid, humble, improper, or effeminate phrase; which is not only praised of the most, but commended (which is worse), especially for that it is naught.

Complete. From «Timber; or, Discoveries Made upon Men and Matter.»

ON MALIGNANCY IN STUDIES

THERE be some men are born only to suck out the poison of books: *Habent venenum pro victu; imo, pro deliciis.* And such are they that only relish the obscene and foul things in poets; which makes the profession taxed. But by whom? Men that watch for it; and (had they not had this hint) are so unjust valuers of letters, as they think no learning good but what brings in gain. It shows they themselves would never have been of the professions they are, but for the profits and fees. But if another learning well used can instruct to good life, inform manners, no less persuade and lead men, than they threaten and compel, and have no reward: is it therefore the worse study? I could never think the study of wisdom confined only to the philosopher; or of piety to the divine; or of state to the politic: but that he which can feign a commonwealth (which is the poet) can govern it with counsels, strengthen it with laws, correct it with judgments, inform it with religion and morals is all these. We

do not require in him mere elocution, or an excellent faculty in verse, but the exact knowledge of all virtues, and their contraries, with ability to render the one loved, the other hated, by his proper embattling them. The philosophers did insolently, to challenge only to themselves that which the greatest generals and gravest counselors never durst. For such had rather do, than promise the best things.

Complete. From «Timber; or, Discoveries Made upon Men and Matter.»

OF GOOD AND EVIL

A GOOD man will avoid the spot of any sin. The very aspersion is grievous; which makes him choose his way in his life as he would in his journey. The ill man rides through all confidently; he is coated and booted for it. The oftener he offends, the more openly; and the fouler, the fitter in fashion. His modesty, like a riding coat, the more it is worn, is the less cared for. It is good enough for the dirt still, and the ways he travels in. An innocent man needs no eloquence; his innocence is instead of it; else I had never come off so many times from these precipices, whither men's malice hath pursued me. It is true, I have been accused to the lords, to the king, and by great ones: but it happened my accusers had not thought of the accusation with themselves; and so were driven, for want of crimes, to use invention, which was found slander: or too late (being entered so far) to seek starting holes for their rashness, which were not given them. And then they may think what accusation that was like to prove, when they that were the engineers feared to be the authors. Nor were they content to feign things against me, but to urge things feigned by the ignorant against my profession; which though, from their hired and mercenary impudence, I might have passed by, as granted to a nation of barkers, that let out their tongues to lick others' sores, yet I durst not leave myself undefended, having a pair of ears unskillful to hear lies, or have those things said of me, which I could truly prove of them. They objected making of verses to me, when I could object to most of them, their not being able to read them, but as worthy of scorn. Nay, they would offer to urge mine own writings against me, but by pieces (which was an excellent way of

malice): as if any man's context might not seem dangerous and offensive, if that which was knit to what went before were defrauded of his beginning; or that things by themselves uttered might not seem subject to calumny, which, read entire, would appear most free. At last they upbraided my poverty: I confess she is my domestic; sober of diet, simple of habit, frugal, painful, a good counselor to me, that keeps me from cruelty, pride, or other more delicate impertinences, which are the nurse children of riches. But let them look over all the great and monstrous wickednesses, they shall never find those in poor families. They are the issue of the wealthy giants, and the mighty hunters: whereas no great work, worthy of praise or memory, but came out of poor cradles. It was the ancient poverty that founded commonweals, built cities, invented arts, made wholesome laws, armed men against vices, rewarded them with their own virtues, and preserved the honor and state of nations, till they betrayed themselves to riches.

Complete. From «Timber; or, Discoveries Made upon Man and Matter.»

«JUNIUS»

SIR PHILIP FRANCIS (?)

(1740-1818)

AMONG the letters of «Junius,»—each a masterpiece of vituperation,—that of July 8th, 1769, to the Duke of Grafton is unapproachable. It is as hard to read it without feeling that its victim must have deserved it as it is to escape regret at the necessity of even suspecting the depths of infamy possible for those who aspire to control others by force and fraud. Of all who have studied politics since Machiavelli showed scoundrels how to make a public policy of their worst villainy, Junius alone has adequately expressed the indignant contempt every honest man who knows such politics must feel for such politicians. Swift, who approaches Junius in knowledge of the subject, broke his heart and died, wrecked in mind and body, by the «cruel indignation» which alone could have endowed the author of the «Junius» letters with the transcendent ability he displays in attacking the great criminals of the commercial and political combination which was then using the power of the oppressed English people to rob the people of India. To appreciate the full significance of the domestic politics which provoked the letters of «Junius,» the reader who has the letter to the Duke of Grafton fresh in mind, must take up Burke's speech opening the bribery charges against Hastings and read on until he has learned how the imposts laid on Hindoo farmers by the allies and agents of the British East India Company were collected by the use of torture. If, as Macaulay supposes, Sir Philip Francis wrote the letters of «Junius,» he had ample opportunity to realize abroad the meaning of the corruption he had denounced at home, for he was in India from 1774 to 1780 as a member of the council appointed to check Hastings. He was born at Dublin, October 22d, 1740, his father, Rev. Philip Francis, being the author of a celebrated translation of Horace which, in spite of some pardonable pedantry, remains still the English masterpiece of its class. With this family tradition of ability, the younger Francis developed in his own right, talent of a high order. From being a junior clerk in the office of the Secretary of State in 1756, he rose in 1774 to be one of the Council for India. On his return from the East, he was elected to Parliament (1784) where, as in his writings, he showed himself a formidable opponent of those he considered opponents of justice and progress. He died December 23d, 1818. The argument for his authorship of "Junius" has been repeatedly made and often controverted. Macaulay's statement of the evidence in his essay on Warren Hastings is an interesting one and as nearly convincing, no doubt, as can be made where the evidence is wholly circumstantial.

W. V. B.

TO THE DUKE OF GRAFTON

July 8th, 1769.

My Lord:—

IF NATURE had given you an understanding qualified to keep pace with the wishes and principles of your heart, she would have made you perhaps the most formidable minister that ever was employed under a limited monarch to accomplish the ruin of a free people. When neither the feelings of shame, the reproaches of conscience, nor the dread of punishment, form any bar to the designs of a minister, the people would have too much reason to lament their condition if they did not find some resource in the weakness of his understanding. We owe it to the bounty of Providence, that the completest depravity of the heart is sometimes strangely united with a confusion of the mind which counteracts the most favorite principles, and makes the same man treacherous without art and a hypocrite without deceiving. The measures, for instance, in which your Grace's activity has been chiefly exerted, as they were adopted without skill, should have been conducted with more than common dexterity. But truly, my lord, the execution has been as gross as the design. By one decisive step you have defeated all the arts of writing. You have fairly confounded the intrigues of opposition and silenced the clamor of faction. A dark, ambiguous system might require and furnish the materials of ingenious illustration; and, in doubtful measures, the virulent exaggeration of party must be employed to rouse and engage the passions of the people. You have now brought the merits of your administration to an issue on which every Englishman of the narrowest capacity may determine for himself. It is not an alarm to the passions, but a calm appeal to the judgment of the people upon their own most essential interests. A more experienced minister would

not have hazarded a direct invasion of the first principles of the constitution before he had made some progress in subduing the spirit of the people. With such a cause as yours, my lord, it is not sufficient that you have the court at your devotion, unless you can find means to corrupt or intimidate the jury. The collective body of the people form that jury, and from their decision there is but one appeal.

Whether you have talents to support you at a crisis of such difficulty and danger should long since have been considered. Judging truly of your disposition, you have perhaps mistaken the extent of your capacity. Good faith and folly have so long been received as synonymous terms that the reverse of the proposition has grown into credit, and every villain fancies himself a man of abilities. It is the apprehension of your friends, my lord, that you have drawn some hasty conclusion of this sort, and that a partial reliance upon your moral character has betrayed you beyond the depth of your understanding. You have now carried things too far to retreat. You have plainly declared to the people what they are to expect from the continuance of your administration. It is time for your grace to consider what you also may expect in return from their spirit and their resentment.

Since the accession of our most gracious sovereign to the throne, we have seen a system of government which may well be called a reign of experiments. Parties of all denominations have been employed and dismissed. The advice of the ablest men in this country has been repeatedly called for and rejected; and when the royal displeasure has been signified to a minister, the marks of it have usually been proportioned to his abilities and integrity. The spirit of the favorite had some apparent influence upon every administration; and every set of ministers preserved an appearance of duration as long as they submitted to that influence. But there were certain services to be performed for the favorite's security, or to gratify his resentments, which your predecessors in office had the wisdom or the virtue not to undertake. The moment this refractory spirit was discovered, their disgrace was determined. Lord Chatham, Mr. Grenville, and Lord Rockingham have successively had the honor to be dismissed for preferring their duty as servants of the public to those compliances which were expected from their station. A submissive administration was at last gradually collected from the deserters of all parties, interests, and connections; and nothing remained but to

find a leader for these gallant, well-disciplined troops. Stand forth, my lord; for thou art the man. Lord Bute found no resource of dependence or security in the proud, imposing superiority of Lord Chatham's abilities, the shrewd, inflexible judgment of Mr. Grenville,. nor in the mild but determined integrity of Lord Rockingham. His views and situation required a creature void of all these properties; and he was forced to go through every division, resolution, composition, and refinement of political chemistry before he happily arrived at the *caput mortuum* of vitriol in your grace. Flat and insipid in your retired state; but, brought into action, you become vitriol again. Such are the extremes of alternate indolence or fury which governed your whole administration. Your circumstances with regard to the people soon becoming desperate, like other honest servants, you determined to involve the best of masters in the same difficulties with yourself. We owe it to your grace's well-directed labors that your sovereign has been persuaded to doubt of the affections of his subjects, and the people to suspect the virtues of their sovereign at a time when both were unquestionable. You have degraded the royal dignity into a base, dishonorable competition with Mr. Wilkes; nor had you abilities to carry even this last contemptible triumph over a private man without the grossest violation of the fundamental laws of the constitution and rights of the people. But these are rights, my lord, which you can no more annihilate than you can the soil to which they are annexed. The question no longer turns upon points of national honor and security abroad, or on the degrees of expedience and propriety of measures at home. It was not inconsistent that you should abandon the cause of liberty in another country, which you had persecuted in your own; and, in the common arts of domestic corruption, we miss no part of Sir Robert Walpole's system except his abilities. In this humble imitative line you might long have proceeded safe and contemptible. You might probably never have risen to the dignity of being hated, and even have been despised with moderation. But it seems you meant to be distinguished; and to a mind like yours there was no other road to fame but by the destruction of a noble fabric, which you thought had been too long the admiration of mankind. The use you have made of the military force introduced an alarming change in the mode of executing the laws. The arbitrary appointment of Mr. Luttrell invades the foundation of the laws

themselves, as it manifestly transfers the right of legislation from those whom the people have chosen to those whom they have rejected. With a succession of such appointments we may soon see a House of Commons collected, in the choice of which the other towns and counties of England will have as little share as the devoted county of Middlesex.

Yet I trust your grace will find that the people of this country are neither to be intimidated by violent measures nor deceived by refinements. When they see Mr. Luttrell seated in the House of Commons by mere dint of power, and in direct opposition to the choice of a whole county, they will not listen to those subtleties by which every arbitrary exertion of authority is explained into the law and privilege of parliament. It requires no persuasion of argument, but simply the evidence of the senses to convince them that to transfer the right of election from the collective to the representative body of the people contradicts all those ideas of a House of Commons which they have received from their forefathers, and which they have already, though vainly perhaps, delivered to their children. The principles on which this violent measure has been defended have added scorn to injury, and forced us to feel that we are not only oppressed, but insulted.

With what force, my lord, with what protection are you prepared to meet the united detestation of the people of England? The city of London has given a generous example to the kingdom in what manner a king of this country ought to be addressed; and I fancy, my lord, it is not yet in your courage to stand between your sovereign and the addressed of his subjects. The injuries you have done this country are such as demand not only redress, but vengeance. In vain shall you look for protection to that venal vote which you have already paid for: another must be purchased; and, to save a minister, the House of Commons must declare themselves not only independent of their constituents, but the determined enemies of the constitution. Consider, my lord, whether this be an extremity to which their fears will permit them to advance; or, if their protection should fail you, how far you are authorized to rely upon the sincerity of those smiles which a pious court lavishes without reluctance upon a libertine by profession. It is not, indeed, the least of the thousand contradictions which attend you, that a man marked to the world by the grossest violation of all ceremony and decorum should be the first servant of a court in which prayers are morality, and kneeling is religion.

Trust not too far to appearances, by which your predecessors have been deceived, though they have not been injured. Even the best of princes may at last discover that this is a contention in which everything may be lost, but nothing can be gained; and as you became minister by accident, were adopted without choice, trusted without confidence, and continued without favor, be assured that whenever an occasion presses you will be discarded without even the forms of regret. You will then have reason to be thankful if you are permitted to retire to that seat of learning which in contemplation of the system of your life, the comparative purity of your manners, with those of their highsteward, and a thousand other recommending circumstances, has chosen you to encourage the growing virtue of their youth, and to preside over their education. Whenever the spirit of distributing prebends and bishoprics shall have departed from you, you will find that learned seminary perfectly recovered from the delirium of an installation, and, what in truth it ought to be, once more a peaceful scene of slumber and thoughtless meditation. The venerable tutors of the university will no longer distress your modesty by proposing you for a pattern to their pupils. The learned dullness of declamation will be silent; and even the venal muse, though happiest in fiction, will forget your virtues. Yet for the benefit of the succeeding age I could wish that your retreat might be deferred until your morals shall happily be ripened to that maturity of corruption at which the worst examples cease to be contagious.

Complete. From Woodfall's "Junius."

IMMANUEL KANT

(1724–1804)

IN the "Canon of Pure Reason" as in the entire "Critique," of which it is a part, Kant attempts to define the laws of the mind's operation. As his style is obscure and his reasoning abstruse, the practical usefulness of his work is sometimes questioned. When, however, we get beyond metaphysics to the common problems of life and of the experimental science which aims at efficiency, we can see that if the "Canon of Reason" were really ascertained and clearly defined, it would be of the greatest possible advantage. If, for example, the mind operates now as it did at the origin of language, then we have only our own lack of intellectual activity to blame that there is not a true "science of language." So of "anthropology" in all its phases; so of the higher science of civilization which so many great minds have attempted to create. In the conclusion of the "Canon of Reason," Kant repudiates the idea that he is attempting to transcend what may be understood as a result of the general experience. "Nature," he says, "in respect of that which affects all men without distinction, has not to be charged with any partial distribution of its gifts; . . . the highest philosophy in respect of the essential ends of human nature cannot advance any further than the guide which nature likewise conferred upon the most common understanding."

Kant was born at Königsberg, Prussia, April 22d, 1724. His father was a saddler of limited means, who managed, nevertheless, to secure him early educational advantages, which enabled him to enter the university and take his degree. He had supported himself meanwhile by work as a tutor, and a year after his graduation he secured employment in the royal library at Königsberg. Four years later he became professor of Logic and Metaphysics in Königsberg University, a position he held until his death February 12th, 1804. His career was thus identified with his native city, and it is said that he was never more than thirty miles away from it in his life. The "Critique of Pure Reason" (Kritik der Reinen Vernunft), his greatest philosophical work, appeared in 1781. It was followed in 1788 by the "Critique of Practical Reason," and in 1790 by the "Critique of the Power of Judgment." Among his other works are "Dreams of a Ghost-Seer," "Observations on the Sense of the Beautiful and Sublime,"

"Metaphysical Elements of Legal Science," and the "Foundation of the Metaphysics of Ethics." His "Critique of Pure Reason" is often called the most important work of modern philosophy.

THE CANON OF PURE REASON

OPINION (the "Holding-to-be-True") is an event in our understanding which may repose upon objective grounds, but requires also subjective causes in the mind of him who then judges. If it be valid for every one, so far as it has only reason, the ground thereof is then objectively sufficient, and the holding of a thing for true is then termed Conviction. If it have only its foundation in the particular quality of the subject, it is then termed persuasion.

Persuasion is a mere appearance, since the ground of the judgment which lies in the subject only is held to be objective. Consequently, such a judgment has also only private (individual) validity, and the holding of a thing for true cannot be imparted. But Truth reposes upon the accordance with the object, in respect of which, consequently, the judgments of every understanding must be accordant. The touchstone of the holding a thing for true, whether it be conviction or merely persuasion, is, therefore, externally, the possibility of imparting it and of finding this holding for true, valid for the reason of every man; for then it is at least a presumption that the ground of the accordance of all judgments, notwithstanding the difference of subjects with one another, will repose upon the common foundation, namely, the object with which they, consequently, will all accord, and thereby prove the truth of the judgment.

Hence persuasion cannot certainly be distinguished subjectively from conviction, if the subject have before its eyes the holding for true merely as a phenomenon of its own mind: but the experiment which we make with the grounds of this, which are valid for us, as to another understanding, whether they operate the selfsame effect upon this other reason as upon ours is, nevertheless, a means, although only a subjective one, not assuredly for operating conviction, but, nevertheless, for disclosing the merely private validity of the judgment, that is to say, something in it, which is mere persuasion.

If, moreover, we can develop the subjective causes of the judgment, which we take for its objective grounds, and, conse-

quently, explain the deceptive holding for true, as an event in our mind, without having need for this of the quality of the object, we thus expose the appearance, and are thereby no longer deceived, although we still are always in a certain degree cajoled, if the subjective cause of the appearance belong to our nature.

I can maintain nothing (that is, declare it as a necessarily valid judgment for every man), except what produces conviction. Persuasion I can retain for myself, if I am content with it, but I cannot wish, and ought not to wish to make it valid beyond myself.

The holding for true, or the subjective validity of the judgment, in reference to conviction (which at the same time is objectively valid) has the three following degrees: Opining, Believing, and Knowing. Opining is an insufficient holding for true with consciousness, subjectively equally as objectively. If this last (holding for true) is only sufficient, subjectively, and is at the same time held to be insufficient, objectively, it is then termed Believing. Lastly, the sufficient holding for true, subjectively equally as well as objectively, is termed Knowledge. The subjective sufficiency is termed Conviction (as to myself), the objective certainty (as to every one). I shall not stop for the explanation of such comprehensible conceptions.

I must never venture to opine without at least knowing something, by means of which the merely problematical judgment in itself receives a connection with truth, which connection, although not complete, is still more than arbitrary fiction. The law, moreover, of such a connection must be certain. For if I in respect of the law have also nothing but opinion, then everything is only a play of the imagination, without the least reference to truth. In judgments from pure reason, it is not at all permitted to opine. For since they are not supported upon reasons of experience, but everything is to be cognized a priori, where everything is necessary, the principle of connection thus requires universality — as otherwise no guide at all to truth is met with. It is, therefore, absurd to opine in pure mathematics; we must know, or abstain from all judgment. The case is just the same with the principles of morality, as we must not hazard an action upon the mere opinion that something is permitted, but we must know it.

In the transcendental use of reason, on the other hand, to opine is certainly too little, but to know is likewise too much.

With mere speculative intention we cannot, therefore, at all judge in this case, since subjective grounds of holding for true, such as those which can effect belief, deserve no approbation in speculative questions, because they do not sustain themselves free of all empirical assistance, nor are imparted to others in equal measure.

But the theoretical insufficient holding for true may be termed generally belief, merely in practical reference. Now this practical intention is either that of ability, or of morality,—the first for arbitrary and contingent ends, but the second for those absolutely necessary.

If once an end be proposed, the conditions for its attainment are thus hypothetically necessary. The necessity is subjective, but still only comparatively sufficient, if I know no other conditions at all by which the end was to be attained; but it is absolute and sufficient for every one, if I know certainly that no one can be acquainted with other conditions that lead to the proposed end. In the first case, my presupposition and the holding for true of certain conditions, is mere contingent belief, but in the second case, a necessary one. The physician is compelled to do something for his patient who is in danger; but he is not acquainted with the disease. He looks at symptoms, and judges, since he knows nothing better, that it is a phthisis. His belief in his own judgment even is merely contingent; another perhaps might better hit upon it. I term such belief contingent, but what lies at the foundation of the real use of means for certain actions is the pragmatical belief.

The usual touchstone, whether something is mere persuasion, or at least subjective conviction, that is, firm belief, which a certain one maintains, is Wagering. Frequently a man states his propositions with such confident and inflexible defiance that he seems wholly to have laid aside all apprehension of error. A wager startles him. Sometimes it appears that he certainly possesses enough persuasion as may be estimated at a ducat in value, but not at ten. For as to the first ducat he, indeed, stakes readily, but at ten he is then for the first time aware, which previously he had not remarked, namely, that it is nevertheless very possible he is in error. Provided we represented to our mind that we were to wager the happiness of a whole life upon this, our exulting judgment would then give way very much and we should be exceedingly alarmed, and so discover for the first time that our belief did not extend thus far. The prag-

VI—152

matic belief has in this way only a degree, which, according to the difference of interest that is at stake therein, may be great or yet small.

But as, although in relation to an object we can undertake nothing at all, and therefore the holding for true is merely theoretical, still in many cases we may embrace and imagine to ourselves in thought an undertaking for which we fancy we possess sufficient grounds, provided there is a means for constituting certainty of the thing, so there is, in mere theoretical judgments, an analogon of what is practical, the holding of which for true, the word Believing suits, and which we may term Doctrinal Belief. If it were possible to decide through an experience, so might I very well wager, as to this point, all that is mine, that, at least in some one of the planets that we see, there were inhabitants. Consequently, I say it is not mere opinion but a firm belief (as to the correctness of which I would, to begin with, hazard many advantages in life) that there are also inhabitants of other worlds.

Now we must confess that the doctrine of the existence of God belongs to doctrinal belief. For, although in respect of theoretical cognition of the world, I have nothing to arrange which necessarily presupposes this idea, as the condition of my explanations of the phenomena of the world, but rather am compelled so to make use of my reason as if everything were merely nature, still, the unity conformable to its end is so great a condition of the application of reason to nature, that since experience moreover furnishes me freely with examples of it, I cannot at all pass it by. But for this unity I know no other condition which it made to me, as a clew for my investigation of nature, but when I presuppose that a supreme intelligence has thus ordered everything according to the wisest ends. Consequently, it is a condition, certainly of a casual, but yet not unimportant intention, namely, in order to have a guide in the investigation of nature, to presuppose a wise Creator of the world. The result of my researches, likewise, so frequently confirms the utility of this presupposition, and nothing can decidedly be adduced in opposition, that I say much too little, if I desire to term my holding for true, merely an opining, for it may even be said in this theoretic relationship, that I firmly believe in God — but this belief, however, in strict signification, is then, nevertheless, not practical, but must be termed a doctrinal belief, which the

theology of nature (physico-theology) must everywhere necessarily operate. In respect of this selfsame wisdom, in regard of the excellent endowment of human nature, and the shortness of life so badly adapted to it, an equally satisfactory cause for a doctrinal belief in the future life of the human soul may be met with.

The expression of belief is in such cases an expression of modesty as to objective intention, but, at the same time, of the firmness of confidence as to subjective. If I wished to term here the mere theoretical holding for true (hypothesis only), which I was justified in admitting, I should thereby already find myself pledged to have a conception, more as to the quality of a cause of the world and of another world than I really can show — for what I assume likewise only as hypothesis, of this must I, according to its properties, at least, still know so much, that I must not invent its conception, but only its existence. But the word Belief refers only to the guide which an idea gives me, and to the subjective influence upon the advancement of my actions of reason, which keeps me fast to the same guide, although as to this I am not in a state to give an account with a speculative view.

But the mere doctrinal belief has something unsteady about it; one is often turned from this, through difficulties which present themselves in speculation, although we certainly always infallibly return back again thereto.

It is quite otherwise with moral belief. For there it is absolutely necessary that something must happen, namely, that I should in all points fulfill the moral law. The object is here indispensably established, and there is only one single condition, according to my introspection, possible, under which this end coheres with all ends together, and thereby possesses objective validity, namely, that there is a God and a future world:— I also know quite certainly that no one is acquainted with other conditions that lead to this unity of ends under the moral law. But as the moral precept, therefore, is at the same time my maxim (as reason then commands that it is to be so), I shall thus infallibly believe the existence of God and a future life, and I am sure that nothing can render this belief vacillating, since thereby my moral principles themselves would be subverted, which I cannot relinquish without being detestable in my own eyes.

In such a way there still remains to us enough, after the disappointment of all the ambitious views of a reason wandering about beyond the limits of experience, that we have cause to be satisfied therewith in a practical point of view. Certainly, no one is able to boast that he knows there is a God, and that there is a future life, for if he knows this, he is then exactly the man whom I long have sought after. All knowing (if it concern an object of pure reason) can be imparted, and I should likewise, therefore, be able to hope through his instruction to see my knowledge extended in so wonderful a manner. But no, the conviction is not logical but moral certitude, and as it reposes upon subjective grounds (moral sentiment), so must I not ever state that it is morally certain there is a God, etc., but that I am morally certain. That is, the belief in a God and another world is so interwoven with my moral sentiment, that as little as I run the danger of losing the first, just so little do I fear that the second can ever be torn from me.

The only difficulty which is met with in this case is that this reason-belief is founded upon the presupposition of moral sentiments. If we depart from this, and adopt a belief that would be quite indifferent as to moral laws, the question then which reason proposes becomes merely a problem for speculation, and may then certainly be still supported by strong grounds from analogy, but never by those to which the stubbornest skepticism must surrender. But in these questions no man is free from all interest. For although he might be severed from the moral one by the want of good sentiments, still there yet remains enough besides, in this case, in order to cause that he should fear a divine existence and a futurity. For nothing further is required for this purpose than that he is not able to plead certainty, that no such being and no future life is to be met with; for which effect, inasmuch as this must be shown through mere reason,—consequently, apodeictically,—he would have to demonstrate the impossibility of both, which certainly no rational being can undertake. This would be a negative belief, which certainly could not produce morality and good sentiments, but yet the analogon of the same, that is, could restrain powerfully the outbreak of what is bad.

But it will be said, is this all which Pure Reason executes in opening out views beyond the limits of experience? Nothing more than two articles of belief? The common understanding without, as to this, consulting philosophers, would have been able also, in fact, to execute as much!

I will not here boast of the merit which philosophy has, as to human reason, by means of the laborious effort of its critique — though it be granted that such merit also in the result were to be found merely negative; for as to this, something more will appear in the following section. But do you require, then, that a cognition which concerns all men should transcend the common understanding, and should only be discovered to you by philosophers? That very thing which you blame is the best confirmation of the correctness of the previous assertions, since it discovers what in the beginning we could not foresee, namely, that nature in respect of that which affects all men without distinction has not to be charged with any partial distribution of its gifts, and that the highest philosophy, in respect of the essential ends of human nature, cannot advance any further than the guide which nature likewise conferred upon the most common understanding.

Complete. From the «Critique of Pure Reason.»
Haywood's translation.

THOMAS KEIGHTLEY

(1789–1872)

THE essays of Keightley's «Fairy Mythology,» which appeared in 1828, are the beginning of the serious attempt to make a science of Folklore; but they are not too serious or too scientific to be delightful reading for people of all ages. Its author, who wrote nothing else to compare with it, was born in Ireland, in 1789, and educated at Trinity College, Dublin. From 1824 to his death in 1872, he lived in England, occupied chiefly with the preparation of educational text-books.

ON MIDDLE-AGE ROMANCE

Ecco quei che le carte empion di sogni,
Lancilotto, Tristano e gli altri erranti,
Onde conven che il volgo errante agogni.
—Petrarca.

FEW will now endeavor to trace romantic and marvelous fiction to any individual source. An extensive survey of the regions of fancy and their productions will incline us rather to consider the mental powers of man as having a uniform operation under every sky, and under every form of political existence, and to acknowledge that identity of invention is not more to be wondered at than identity of action. It is strange how limited the powers of the imagination are. Without due consideration of the subject, it might be imagined that her stores of materials and powers of combination are boundless; yet reflection, however slight, will convince us that here also "there is nothing new," and charges of plagiarism will, in the majority of cases, be justly suspected to be devoid of foundation. The finest poetical expressions and similes of occidental literature meet us when we turn our attention to the East, and a striking analogy pervades the tales and fictions of every region. The reason is, the materials presented to the inventive faculties are scanty. The power of combination is therefore limited to a narrow compass, and similar combinations must hence frequently occur.

Yet still there is a high degree of probability in the supposition of the luxuriant fictions of the East having through Spain and Syria operated on European fancy. The poetry and romance of the Middle Ages are notoriously richer in detail, and more gorgeous in invention than the more correct and chaste strains of Greece and Latium; the island of Calypso, for example, is in beauty and variety left far behind by the retreats of the fairies of romance. Whence arises this difference? No doubt—

" When ancient chivalry display'd
The pomp of her heroic games,
And crested knights and tissued dames
Assembled at the clarion's call,
In some proud castle's high-arch'd hall "—

that a degree of pomp and splendor met the eye of the minstrel and romancer on which the bards of the simple republics of ancient times had never gazed, and this might account for the difference between the poetry of ancient and of middle-age Europe. Yet, notwithstanding, we discover such an Orientalism in the latter as would induce us to acquiesce in the hypothesis of the fictions and the manner of the East having been early transmitted to the West; and it is highly probable that along with more splendid habits of life entered a more lavish use of the gorgeous stores laid open to the plastic powers of fiction. The tales of Arabia were undoubtedly known in Europe from a very early period. The romance of «Cléomadès and Claremonde,» which was written in the thirteenth century, not merely resembles, but actually is the story of the Enchanted Horse in the «Thousand and One Nights.» Another tale in the same collection, the two sisters who envied their younger sister, may be found in Straparola, and is also a popular story in Germany; and in the «Pentameron» and other collections of tales published long before the appearance of M. Galland's translation of the Eastern ones, numerous traces of an Oriental origin may be discerned. The principal routes they came by may also be easily shown. The necessities of commerce and the pilgrimage to Mecca occasioned a constant intercourse between the Moors of Spain and their fellow-sectaries of the East; and the Venetians, who were the owners of Candia, carried on an extensive trade with Syria and Egypt. It is worthy of notice that the «Notti Piacevoli» of Straparola were first published in Venice, and that Basile the author of the «Pentameron,»

---

spent his youth in Candia, and was afterwards a long time at Venice. Lastly, pilgrims were notorious narrators of marvels, and each, as he visited the Holy Land, was anxious to store his memory with those riches, the diffusal of which procured him attention and hospitality at home.

We think, therefore, that European romance may be indebted, though not for the name, yet for some of the attributes and exploits of its' fairies to Asia. This is more especially the case with the romances composed or turned into prose in the fourteenth, fifteenth, and sixteenth centuries; for in the earlier ones the «Fairy Mythology» is much more sparingly introduced.

From «Fairy Mythology.»

ARABIAN ROMANCE

THE Prophet is the centre round which everything connected with Arabia revolves. The period preceding his birth is regarded and designated as the times of ignorance, and our knowledge of the ancient Arabian mythology comprises little more than he has been pleased to transmit to us. The Arabs, however, appear at no period of their history to have been a people addicted to fanciful invention. Their minds are acute and logical, and their poetry is that of the heart rather than of the fancy. They dwell with fondness on the joys and pains of love, and with enthusiasm describe the courage and daring deeds of warriors, or in moving strains pour forth the plaintive elegy; but for the description of gorgeous palaces and fragrant gardens, or for the wonders of magic, they are indebted chiefly to their Persian neighbors.

What classes of beings the popular creed may have recognized before the establishment of Islam, we have no means of ascertaining. The Suspended Poems, and Antar, give us little or no information; we know only that the tales of Persia were current among them, and were listened to with such avidity as to rouse the indignation of the Prophet. We must, therefore, quit the tents of the Bedoween, and the valleys of "Araby the Blest," and accompany the khaleefehs to their magnificent capital on the Tigris, whence emanated all that has thrown such a halo of splendor around the genius and language of Arabia. It is in this seat of empire that we must look to meet with the origin of the marvels of Arabian literature.

Transplanted to a rich and fertile soil, the sons of the desert speedily abandoned their former simple mode of life; and the court of Bagdad equaled or surpassed in magnificence anything that the East has ever witnessed. Genius, whatever its direction, was encouraged and rewarded, and the musician and the story-teller shared with the astronomer and historian the favor of the munificent khaleefehs. The tales which had amused the leisure of the Shapoors and Yezdejirds were not disdained by the Haroons and Almansoors. The expert narrators altered them so as to accord with the new faith. And it was thus, probably, that the delightful " Thousand and One Nights " were gradually produced and modified.

As the Genii or Jinn are prominent actors in these tales, where they take the place of the Persian Peries and Deevs, we will here give some account of them.

According to Arabian writers, there is a species of beings named Jinn or Jan (Jinnee m., Jinniyeh f. sing.), which were created and occupied the earth several thousand years before Adam. A tradition from the Prophet says that they were formed of " smokeless fire," i. e., the fire of the wind Simoom. They were governed by a succession of forty, or, as others say, seventy-two monarchs, named Suleyman, the last of whom, called Jan-ibn-Jan, built the Pyramids of Egypt. Prophets were sent from time to time to instruct and admonish them; but on their continued disobedience, an army of angels appeared, who drove them from the earth to the regions of the islands, making many prisoners, and slaughtering many more. Among the prisoners was a young Jinnee, named Âzazeel, or El-Harith (afterwards called Iblees, from his despair), who grew up among the angels, and became at last their chief. When Adam was created, God commanded the angels to worship him; and they all obeyed except Iblees, who, for his disobedience, was turned into a Sheytan or Devil, and he became the father of the Sheytans.

The Jinn are not immortal; they are to survive mankind, but to die before the general resurrection. Even at present many of them are slain by other Jinn, or by men; but chiefly by shooting stars hurled at them from heaven. The fire of which they were created circulates in their veins instead of blood, and when they receive a mortal wound it bursts forth and consumes them to ashes. They eat and drink, and propagate their species. Sometimes they unite with human beings, and the offspring partakes

of the nature of both parents. Some of the Jinn are obedient to the will of God, and believers in the Prophet, answering to the Peries of the Persians; others are like the Deevs, disobedient and malignant. Both kinds are divided into communities, and ruled over by princes. They have the power to make themselves visible and invisible at pleasure. They can assume the form of various animals, especially those of serpents, cats, and dogs. When they appear in the human form, that of the good Jinnee is usually of great beauty; that of the evil one, of hideous deformity and sometimes of gigantic size.

When the Zoba'ah, a whirlwind that raises the sand in the form of a pillar of tremendous height, is seen sweeping over the desert, the Arabs, who believe it to be caused by the flight of the evil Jinnee, cry, Iron! Iron! (Hadeed! Hadeed!) or Iron! thou unlucky one! (Hadeed! ya meshoom!) of which metal the Jinn are believed to have a great dread. Or else they cry, God is most great! (Allahu akbar!) They do the same when they see a water spout at sea; for they assign the same cause to its origin.

The chief abode of the Jinn of both kinds is the mountains of Kaf. But they also are dispersed through the earth, and they occasionally take up their residence in baths, wells, latrinæ, ovens, and ruined houses. They also frequent the sea and rivers, crossroads, and market places. They ascend at times to the confines of the lowest heaven, and by listening there to the conversation of the angels they obtain some knowledge of futurity, which they impart to those men who, by means of talismans or magic arts, have been able to reduce them to obedience.

The following are anecdotes of the Jinn, given by historians of eminence: —

It is related, says El-Kasweenee, by a certain narrator of traditions, that he descended into a valley with his sheep, and a wolf carried off a ewe from among them; and he arose and raised his voice, and cried: "O inhabitant of the valley!" whereupon he heard a voice saying, "O wolf, restore him his sheep!" and the wolf came with the ewe and left her, and departed.

Ben Shohnah relates that in the year 456 of the Hejgira, in the reign of Kaiem, the twenty-sixth khaleefeh of the house of Abbas, a report was raised in Bagdad, which immediately spread throughout the whole province of Irak, that some Turks being out hunting saw in the desert a black tent, beneath which there was a

number of people of both sexes who were beating their cheeks, and uttering loud cries, as is the custom in the East when any one is dead. Amidst their cries they heard these words — The great king of the Jinn is dead, woe to this country! and then there came out a great troop of women, followed by a number of other rabble, who proceeded to a neighboring cemetery, still beating themselves in token of grief and mourning.

The celebrated historian Ebn Athir relates that when he was at Mosul on the Tigris, in the year 600 of the Hejgira, there was in that country an epidemic disease of the throat; and it was said that a woman of the race of the Jinn having lost her son, all those who did not condole with her on account of his death were attacked with that disease; so that to be cured of it men and women assembled, and with all their strength cried out, O mother of Ankood, excuse us! Ankood is dead, and we did not mind it!

Complete. From " Fairy Mythology."

HOW TO READ OLD-ENGLISH POETRY

Our forefathers, like their Gotho-German kindred, regulated their verse by the number of accents, not of syllables. The foot, therefore, as we term it, might consist of one, two, three, or even four syllables, provided it had only one strongly marked accent. Further, the accent of a word might be varied, chiefly by throwing it on the last syllable, as nature for náture, honoúr for hónour, etc. (the Italians, by the way, throw it back when two accents come into collision, as, Il Pástor Fido); they also sounded what the French call the feminine e of their words, as, In oldè dayès of the King Artoúr; and so well known seems this practice to have been, that the copyists did not always write this e, relying on the skill of the reader to supply it. There was only one restriction, namely, that it was never to come before a vowel, unless where there was a pause. In this way the poetry of the Middle Ages was just as regular as that of the present day; and Chaucer, when properly read, is fully as harmonious as Pope. But the editors of our ancient poems, with the exception of Tyrwhitt, seem to have been ignorant or regardless of this principle; and in the " Canterbury Tales " alone is the verse properly arranged.

From " Fairy Mythology."

THOMAS À KEMPIS

(c. 1380-1471)

Thomas À Kempis, the greatest devotional writer since apostolic times, was born at Kempen, in Rhenish Prussia, about 1380. His father, whose name was " Hammerken," was a poor peasant, but his mother (" sparing in her words, and modest in her actions," as he tells us she was), was well enough educated to teach the village school for young children. To her influence, no doubt, the world owes the " De Imitatione Christi," which " has been translated into more languages than any other book except the Bible." After leaving his mother's school, Thomas became a pupil of Radewyn at Kempen, and took the name of the school instead of that of his family. Joining the Augustinian order, he entered the convent of Mount St. Agnes, where he remained until his death at the age of ninety-one (August 8th, 1471). He was first subprior and then prior of the convent; but after his promotion to the priorship, he was reduced to subprior again, as having too little shrewdness for business management. His authorship of the " Imitation of Christ " has been questioned, and the controversy over it is likely to continue. The arguments which would make his authorship of so remarkable a work incredible, because of his simplicity of mind, would apply even more strongly against St. John's authorship of the Fourth Gospel. The " De Imitatione Christi " is not a work of talent, but of that inspired genius which has taken hold on the central realities of life through its own suffering.

OF WISDOM AND PROVIDENCE IN OUR ACTIONS

We must not give ear to every saying or suggestion, but ought warily and leisurely to ponder things according to the will of God.

But alas! such is our weakness that we often rather believe and speak evil of others than good.

Those that are perfect men do not easily give credit to everything told them; for they know that human frailty is prone to evil, and very subject to fail in words.

It is great wisdom not to be rash in thy proceedings, nor to stand stiffly in thine own conceits;

As also not to believe everything which thou hearest, nor presently to relate again to others what thou hast heard or dost believe.

Consult with him that is wise and conscientious, and seek to be instructed by a better than thyself, rather than to follow thine own inventions.

A good life maketh a man wise according to God, and giveth him experience in many things.

The more humble a man is in himself, and the more subject and resigned unto God, so much the more prudent shall he be in all his affairs, and enjoy greater peace and quiet of heart.

Complete. «Imitation of Christ,»
Chap. iv.

OF THE PROFIT OF ADVERSITY

IT is good that we have sometimes some troubles and crosses; for they often make a man enter into himself, and consider that he is here in banishment, and ought not to place his trust in any worldly thing.

It is good that we be sometimes contradicted, and that there be an evil or a lessening conceit had of us; and this, although we do and intend well.

These things help often to the attaining of humility, and defend us from vainglory; for then we chiefly seek God for our inward witness, when outwardly we be condemned by men, and when there is no credit given unto us.

And therefore a man should settle himself so fully in God that he need not to seek many comforts of men with evil thougths; then he understandeth better the great need he hath of God, without whom he perceiveth he can do nothing that is good.

Then also he sorroweth, lamenteth, and prayeth, by reason of the miseries he suffereth.

Then he is weary of living longer, and wisheth that death would come, that he might be dissolved and be with Christ.

Then also he well perceiveth that perfect security and full peace cannot be had in this world.

Complete. «Imitation of Christ,»
Chap. xii.

Without charity the exterior work profiteth nothing; but whatsoever is done of charity, be it never so little and contemptible in the sight of the world, it becomes wholly fruitful.

For God weigheth more with how much love a man worketh, than how much he doeth. He doeth much that loveth much.

He doeth much that doeth a thing well.

He doeth well that rather serveth the community than his own will.

Oftentimes it seemeth to be charity, and it is rather carnality, because natural inclination, self-will, hope of reward, and desire of our own interest, will seldom be away.

He that hath true and perfect charity seeketh himself in nothing, but only desireth in all things that the glory of God should be exalted.

He also envieth none, because he affecteth no private good; neither will he rejoice in himself, but wisheth above all things to be made happy in the enjoyment of God.

He attributeth nothing that is good to any man, but wholly referreth it unto God; from whom as from the fountain all things proceed; in whom finally all the saints do rest as in their highest fruition.

Oh! he that hath but one spark of true charity would certainly discern that all earthly things be full of vanity.

Complete. «Imitation of Christ,»
Chap. xv.

OF BEARING WITH THE DEFECTS OF OTHERS

THOSE things that a man cannot amend in himself or in others, he ought to suffer patiently, until God order things otherwise.

Think that perhaps it is better so for thy trial and patience, without which all our good deeds are not much to be esteemed.

Thou oughtest to pray, notwithstanding, when thou hast such impediments, that God would vouchsafe to help thee, and that thou mayest bear them kindly.

If one that is once or twice warned will not give over, contend not with him, but commit all to God, that his will may be fulfilled, and his name honored in all his servants, who well knoweth how to turn evil into good.

OF AVOIDING RASH JUDGMENT

TURN thine eyes unto thyself, and beware thou judge not the deeds of other men. In judging of others a man laboreth in vain, often erreth, and easily sinneth; but in judging and discussing of himself, he always laboreth fruitfully.

We often judge of things according as we fancy them; for private affection bereaves us easily of true judgment.

If God were always the pure intention of our desire, we should not be so easily troubled, through the repugnance of our carnal mind.

But oftentimes something lurketh within, or else occurreth from without, which draweth us after it.

Many secretly seek themselves in their actions, and know it not.

They seem also to live in good peace of mind, when things are done according to their will and opinion; but if things happen otherwise than they desire, they are straightway troubled and much vexed.

The diversities of judgments and opinions cause oftentimes dissensions between friends and countrymen, between religious and devout persons.

An old custom is hardly broken, and no man is willing to be led further than he himself can see.

If thou dost more rely upon thine own reason or industry than upon that power which brings thee under the obedience of Jesus Christ, it will be long before thou become illuminated; for God will have us perfectly subject unto him, that, being inflamed with his love, we may transcend the narrow limits of human reason.

Complete. «Imitation of Christ,»
Chap. xiv.

OF WORKS DONE IN CHARITY

FOR no worldly thing, nor for the love of any man, is any evil to be done; but yet for the profit of one that standeth in need, a good work is sometimes to be intermitted without any scruple, or changed also for a better.

For by doing this, a good work is not lost, but changed into a better.

Endeavor to be patient in bearing with the defects and infirmities of others, of what sort soever they be; for that thou thyself also hast many failings which must be borne with by others.

If thou canst not make thyself such a one as thou wouldst, how canst thou expect to have another in all things to thy liking?

We would willingly have others perfect, and yet we amend not our own faults.

We will have others severely corrected, and will not be corrected ourselves.

The large liberty of others displeaseth us, and yet we will not have our own desires denied us.

We will have others kept under by strict laws, but in no sort will ourselves be restrained.

And thus it appeareth how seldom we weigh our neighbor in the same balance with ourselves.

If all men were perfect, what should we have to suffer of our neighbor for God?

But now God hath thus ordered it, that we may learn to bear one another's burdens; for no man is without fault; no man but hath his burden; no man sufficient of himself; no man wise enough of himself; but we ought to bear with one another, comfort one another, help, instruct, and admonish one another.

Occasions of adversity best discover how great virtue or strength each one hath.

For occasions do not make a man frail, but they show what he is.

Complete. «Imitation of Christ,»
Chap. xvi.

OF A RETIRED LIFE

THOU must learn to break thy own will in many things, if thou wilt have peace and concord with others.

It is no small matter to dwell in a religious community and to converse therein without complaint, and to persevere therein faithfully unto death.

Blessed is he that hath there lived well, and ended happily.

If thou wilt persevere in grace as thou oughtest, and profit in virtue, esteem thyself as a banished man, and a pilgrim upon earth.

Thou must be contented for Christ's sake to be esteemed as a fool in this world, if thou desire to lead a holy life.

The wearing of a religious habit, and shaving of the crown, do little profit; but change of manners, and perfect mortification of passions, make a true religious man.

He that seeketh anything else but God, and the salvation of his soul, shall find nothing but tribulation and sorrow.

Neither can he remain long in peace, that laboreth not to be the least, and subject unto all.

Thou camest to serve, not to rule. Know that thou wast called to suffer and to labor, not to be idle, or to spend thy time in talk.

Here, therefore, men are proved as gold in the furnace.

Here no man can stand, unless he humble himself with his whole heart for the love of God.

Complete. "Imitation of Christ," Chap. xvii.

VI—153

CHARLES KINGSLEY
(1819–1875)

KINGSLEY'S "Prose Idyls" are unique among his productions for their restful quality. His career in literature and in the ministry of the Church of England was inspired by the spirit of unrest which makes progress possible. He was not content to accept anything as a substitute for the best unless it were the best possible, and as he failed to find that in the religious, social, commercial, or political life of his time, he did his best to bring it about. Born in Devonshire, January 12th, 1819, he graduated at Cambridge, and entering the ministry of the English Established Church, became Canon first of Middleham, then of Chester, and finally of Westminster. The "agnostic" spirit of science moved him to write "Hypatia, or Old Foes with New Faces,"—a very remarkable historical study, more widely read, no doubt, than "Yeast" and "Alton Locke," two novels with a sociological motive which preceded it. His "Water Babies" is a child's book with a concealed motive of protest against theories he did not approve. He died January 23d, 1875.

A CHARM OF BIRDS

Is IT merely a fancy that we English, the educated people among us at least, are losing that love for spring which among our old forefathers rose almost to worship? That the perpetual miracle of the budding leaves and the returning song birds awakes no longer in us the astonishment which it awoke yearly among the dwellers in the Old World, when the sun was a god who was sick to death each winter, and returned in spring to life, and health, and glory; when the death of Adonis, at the autumnal equinox, was wept over by the Syrian women, and the death of Baldur, in the colder north, by all living things, even to the dripping trees, and the rocks furrowed by the autumn rains; when Freya, the goddess of youth and love, went forth over the earth each spring, while the flowers broke forth under her tread over the brown moors, and the birds welcome her with song; when, according to Olaus Magnus, the Goths and South Swedes had, on

the return of spring, a mock battle between summer and winter, and welcomed the returning splendor of the sun with dancing and mutual feasting, rejoicing that a better season for fishing and hunting was approaching? To those simpler children of a simpler age, in more direct contact with the daily and yearly facts of nature, and more dependent on them for their bodily food and life, winter and spring were the two great facts of existence; the symbols, the one of death, the other of life; and the battle between the two—the battle of the sun with darkness, of winter with spring, of death with life, of bereavement with love—lay at the root of all their myths and all their creeds. Surely a change has come over our fancies. The seasons are little to us now. We are nearly as comfortable in winter as in summer, or in spring. Nay, we have begun, of late, to grumble at the two latter as much as at the former, and talk (and not without excuse at times) of "the treacherous month of May," and of "summer having set in with its usual severity." We work for the most part in cities and towns, and the seasons pass by us unheeded. May and June are spent by most educated people anywhere rather than among birds and flowers. They do not escape into the country till the elm hedges are growing black, and the song birds silent, and the hay cut, and all the virgin bloom of the country has passed into a sober and matronly ripeness—if not into the sere and yellow leaf. Our very landscape painters, till Creswick arose and recalled to their minds the fact that trees were sometimes green, were wont to paint few but brown autumnal scenes. As for the song of birds, of which in the Middle Age no poet could say enough, our modern poets seem to be forgetting that birds ever sing.

It was not so of old. The climate, perhaps, was more severe than now; the transition from winter to spring more sudden, like that of Scandinavia now. Clearage of forests and drainage of land have equalized our seasons, or rather made them more uncertain. More broken winters are followed by more broken springs; and May-day is no longer a marked point to be kept as a festival by all childlike hearts. The merry month of May is merry only in stage songs. The May garlands and dances are all but gone; the borrowed plate, and the milkmaids who borrowed it, gone utterly. No more does Mrs. Pepys go to "lie at Woolwich, in order to a little ayre and to gather May-dew" for her complexion, by Mrs. Turner's advice. The Maypole is gone

likewise; and never more shall the Puritan soul of a Stubbs be aroused in indignation at seeing "against Maie, every parish, towne, and village assemble themselves together, both men, women, and children, old and young, all indifferently, and goe into the woodes and groves, hilles and mountaines, where they spend the night in pastyme and in the morning they returne, bringing with them birch bowes and braunches of trees to deck their assembly withal. . . . They have twentie or fourtie yoke of oxen, every oxe having a sweete nosegay of flowers tyed on the tippe of his hornes, and these draw home this Maypole (this stincking idol rather) which is covered all over with flowers and hearbes with two or three hundred men, women, and children following it with great devotion. . . . And then they fall to banquet and feast, daunce and leap about it, as the heathen people did at the dedication of their idols, whereof this is a perfect pattern, or a thing itself."

This, and much more, says poor Stubbs, in his "Anatomie of Abuses," and had, no doubt, good reason enough for his virtuous indignation at May-day scandals. But people may be made dull without being made good; and the direct and only effect of putting down May games and such like was to cut off the dwellers in towns from all healthy communion with nature, and leave them to mere sottishness and brutality.

Yet perhaps the May games died out, partly because the feelings which had given rise to them died out before improved personal comforts. Of old, men and women fared hardly, and slept cold; and were thankful to Almighty God for every beam of sunshine which roused them out of their long hybernation; thankful for every flower and every bird which reminded them that joy was stronger than sorrow, and life than death. With the spring came not only labor, but enjoyment:—

"In the spring, the young man's fancy lightly turned to thoughts of love,"

as lads and lassies, who had been pining for each other by their winter firesides, met again, like Daphnis and Chloe, by shauw and lea; and learned to sing from the songs of birds, and to be faithful from their faithfulness.

Then went out troops of fair damsels to seek spring garlands in the forest, as Scheffel has lately sung once more in his "Frau Aventiure": and while the dead leaves rattled beneath their feet, hymned "La Regine Avrillouse" to the music of some Minnesinger, whose song was as the song of birds; to whom the birds were friends, fellow-lovers, teachers, mirrors of all which he felt within himself of joyful and tender, true and pure; friends to be fed hereafter (as Walther von der Vogelweide had them fed) with crumbs upon his grave.

True melody, it must be remembered, is unknown, at least at present, in the tropics, and peculiar to the races of those temperate climes, into which the song birds come in spring. It is hard to say why. Exquisite songsters, and those, strangely, of an European type, may be heard anywhere in tropical American forests; but native races whose hearts their song can touch are either extinct or yet to come. Some of the old German Minnelieder, on the other hand, seem actually copied from the songs of birds. "Tanderadei" does not merely ask the nightingale to tell no tales; it repeats, in its cadences, the nightingale's song, as the old Minnesinger heard when he nestled beneath the lime tree with his love. They are often almost as inarticulate, these old singers, as the birds from whom they copied their notes; the thinnest chain of thought links together some bird-like refrain; but they make up for their want of logic and reflection by the depth of their passion, the perfectness of their harmony with nature. The inspired Swabian, wandering in the pine forest, listens to the blackbird's voice till it becomes his own voice; and he breaks out, with the very carol of the blackbird —

> "*Vogele im Tannenwald pfeifet so hell.*
> *Pfeifet de Wald aus und ein, wo wird mein Schatze sein?*
> *Vogele im Tannenwald pfeifet so hell.*"

And he has nothing more to say. That is his whole soul for the time being; and, like a bird, he sings it over and over again, and never tires.

Another, a Nieder-Rheinischer, watches the moon rise over the Lowenburg, and thinks upon his love within the castle hall till he breaks out in a strange, sad, tender melody — not without stateliness and manly confidence in himself and his beloved — in the true strain of the nightingale: —

> "*Verstohlen geht der Mond auf,*
> *Blau, blau, Blumelein,*
> *Durch Silberwolkchen fuhrt sein Lauf.*
> *Rosen im Thal, Madel im Saal, O schonste Rosa!* . . ."

> *Und siehst du mich,*
> *Und siehst du sie,*
> *Blau, blau, Blumelein,*
> *Zwei treu're Herzen sah'st du nie;*
> *Rosen im Thal u. s. w.*"

There is little sense in the words, doubtless, according to our modern notions of poetry; but they are like enough to the long, plaintive notes of the nightingale to say all that the poet has to say, again and again through all his stanzas.

Thus the birds were, to the mediæval singers, their orchestra, or rather their chorus; from the birds they caught their melodies; the sounds which the birds gave them they rendered into words.

And the same bird keynote surely is to be traced in the early English and Scotch songs and ballads, with their often meaningless refrains, sung for the mere pleasure of singing: —

> "Binnorie, O Binnorie."

Or —

> "With a hey lillelu and a how lo lan,
> And the birk and the broom blooms bonnie."

Or —

> "She sat down below a thorn,
> Fine flowers in the valley,
> And there has she her sweet babe born,
> And the green leaves they grow rarely."

Or even those "fal-la-las," and other nonsense refrains, which, if they were not meant to imitate bird notes, for what were they meant?

In the old ballads, too, one may hear the bird keynote. He who wrote (and a great rhymer he was)

> "As I was walking all alane,
> I heard twa corbies making a mane,"

had surely the "mane" of the "corbies" in his ears before it shaped itself into words in his mind; and he had listened to many a "woodwele" who first thrummed on harp, or fiddled on crowd, how —

> In summer, when the shawes be shene
> And leaves be large and long,
> It is full merry in fair forest
> To hear the fowles' song.

> "The woodwele sang, and wolde not cease
> Sitting upon the spray;
> So loud it wakened Robin Hood
> In the greenwood where he lay."

And Shakespeare — are not his scraps of song saturated with these same bird notes? "Where the bee sucks," "When daisies pied," "Under the greenwood tree," "It was a lover and his lass," "When daffodils begin to peer," "Ye spotted snakes," have all a ring in them which was caught not in the roar of London, or babble of the Globe Theatre, but in the woods of Charlcote and along the banks of Avon, from

> "The ouzel-cock so black of hue,
> With orange-tawny bill;
> The throstle with his note so true;
> The wren with little quill;
> The finch, the sparrow, and the lark,
> The plain-song cuckoo gray" —

and all the rest of the birds of the air.

Why is it, again, that so few of our modern songs are truly songful, and fit to be set to music? Is it not that the writers of them — persons often of much taste and poetic imagination — have gone for their inspiration to the intellect, rather than to the ear? That (as Shelley does by the skylark, and Wordsworth by the cuckoo), instead of trying to sing like the birds, they only think and talk about the birds, and therefore, however beautiful and true the thoughts and words may be, they are not song? Surely they have not, like the mediæval songsters, studied the speech of the birds, the primeval teachers of melody; nor even melodies already extant, round which, as round a framework of pure music, their thoughts and images might crystallize themselves, certain thereby of becoming musical likewise. The best modern song writers, Burns and Moore, were inspired by their old national airs; and followed them, Moore at least, with a reverent fidelity, which has had its full reward. They wrote words to music; and not, as modern poets are wont, wrote the words

first, and left others to set music to the words. They were right; and we are wrong. As long as song is to be the expression of pure emotion, so long it must take its key from music, — which is already pure emotion, untranslated into the grosser medium of thought and speech — often (as in the case of Mendelssohn's "Songs without Words") not to be translated into it at all.

And so it may be, that in some simpler age, poets may go back, like the old Minnesingers, to the birds of the forest, and learn of them to sing.

From "Prose Idyls." Macmillan & Co.

PRINCE KRAPOTKIN

(1842-)

PETER KRAPOTKIN, scientist and nihilist, was born at Moscow, Russia, in 1842. His family belongs to the oldest and highest nobility of Russia, and he himself was bred at the imperial court, and, after completing his studies at the university, was appointed Chamberlain to the Czarina. His standing in science was attested by his appointment as Secretary of the Russian Geographical Society, but when he adopted the "individualistic" views taught by Ralph Waldo Emerson and the Concord School of Philosophy in America, the Russian government arrested him. After three years' imprisonment, he escaped in 1876 to France, where he was again imprisoned. Since his release by the French authorities, he has lived chiefly in England, supporting himself by writing on scientific, literary, and political topics for the reviews and newspapers. His views of "individual sovereignty" do not seem to be as extreme as those held at one time by Emerson and William Lloyd Garrison. He leans rather to the idea that if all central power of taxation and coercion were abolished, production could be carried on most effectively under municipal organization. Among extremists in political theorizing, he may be considered representing the extreme of opposition to the theories of Karl Marx.

THE COURSE OF CIVILIZATION

THROUGHOUT the whole history of our civilization, two traditions, two opposed tendencies, have been in conflict: the Roman tradition and the popular tradition; the imperial tradition and the federalist tradition; the authoritarian one and the libertarian one. . . .

History has not been an uninterrupted evolution. At different intervals evolution has been broken in a certain region, to begin again elsewhere. Egypt, Asia, the banks of the Mediterranean, Central Europe, have in turn been the scene of historical development. But in every case, the first phase of the evolution has been the primitive tribe, passing on into a village commune, then into that of the free city, and finally dying out when it reached the phase of the state.

In Egypt civilization began by the primitive tribe. It reached the village community phasis, and later on the period of free cities; still later that of the state, which, after a flourishing period, resulted in the death of the country.

The evolution began again in Assyria, in Persia, in Palestine. Again it traversed the same phasis: the tribe, the village community, the free city, the all-powerful state, and finally the result was — death!

A new civilization then sprang up in Greece. Always beginning by the tribe, it slowly reached the village commune, then the period of republican cities. In these cities civilization reached its highest summits. But the East brought to them its poisoned breath, its traditions of despotism. Wars and conquests created Alexander's empire of Macedonia. The state enthroned itself, the bloodsucker grew, killed all civilization, and then came — death!

Rome in its turn restored civilization. Again we find the primitive tribe at its origin; then the village commune; then the free city. At that stage it reached the apex of its civilization. But then came the state, the empire, and then — death!

On the ruins of the Roman Empire, Celtic, Germanic, Slavonian, and Scandinavian tribes began civilization anew. Slowly the primitive tribe elaborated its institutions and reached the village commune. It remained at that stage till the twelfth century. Then rose the republican cities which produced the glorious expansion of the human mind, attested by the monuments of architecture, the grand development of arts, the discoveries that laid the basis of natural sciences. But then came the state. . . .

Will it again produce death? Of course it will, unless we reconstitute society on a libertarian and anti-imperial basis. Either the state will be destroyed and a new life will begin in thousands of centres, on the principle of an energetic initiative of the individual, of groups, and of free agreement; or else the state must crush the individual and local life, it must become the master of all the domains of human activity; must bring with it its wars and internal struggles for the possession of power, its surface revolutions which only change one tyrant for another, and inevitably, at the end of this evolution, — death!

Choose yourselves which of the two issues you prefer.

From "The State: Its Historic Rôle."

JEAN DE LA BRUYÈRE

(1645-1696)

JEAN DE LA BRUYÈRE translated Theophrastus and published his own "Characters" with his translations from the Greek in 1688. ("Les Caractères de Théophraste avec les Caractères et les Mœurs de ce Siècle." Michallet. Paris.) As Sir Thomas Overbury's little volume of "Characters," suggested by those of Theophrastus, appeared seventy-four years (1614) before the date of the first edition of La Bruyère's, the greater celebrity of the French wit scarcely entitles him to be called "the founder of the modern school of Theophrastus." His own countrymen, however, will not admit the claim of any one else to rank with him in his class. In wit and sententiousness he is superior to Overbury, Earle, Fuller, and Felltham, the leading English exponents of the methods of Theophrastus, but the circumstance to which chiefly he owed his celebrity with his own generation is not an advantage in his work as it appeals to posterity. He sketched "Characters," not as types of human nature, but as portraits of actual men and women, his friends, his enemies, or his rivals in the Parisian world of letters and politics. While the age in which he wrote was that of Bossuet, Fénelon, Boileau, Racine, Corneille, Fontenelle, the great Condé, and others scarcely less famous, those whose traits he described without naming them did not become typical under his pen. Thus while to Frenchmen this part of his work has an enduring antiquarian interest, it does not appeal to the general reader outside of France, as do his biting epigrams on the faults and foibles of common humanity. He seems to have set down his thoughts as they came into his mind, without attempting to give them any other connection than that of an underlying idea. He will condense a page of thought into a three-line epigram, or expand three lines into an essay of a page, at his own pleasure, without asking the reader's consent. The result is pleasing, and though he deals too seldom with the good in human nature, the subtle quality of the wit with which he discovers and displays the evil prevents him from being classed either as a cynic or a scold.

It is said that he was the master of Addison in literature; but if Addison learned from him subtlety in the display of wit, he did not learn the sarcasm which above everything else is characteristic of whatever La Bruyère writes in dealing with human nature. He lacks

Addison's good fellowship, but he is keener and more pungent than any writer of the Spectator school.

He was born at Paris in August, 1645, and trained for the bar, but he supported himself chiefly by work in the government revenue service and as a tutor in the family of the Prince of Condé, with whom he was a favorite. When the first edition of the "Caractères" appeared in 1688, they were only three hundred and eighty-six in number; but as their popularity was immediate, he added to them in successive editions until in the ninth, which was in press at the time of his death (May 10th, 1696), they had been increased to over a thousand. The names of those he satirized were not given, but some were easily identified by their friends, and others maliciously by their enemies, so that La Bruyère's increase in celebrity was at the expense of his popularity. He had a long struggle with his enemies in the academy before he finally gained admission. They voted him down three times in a single year, and on one occasion reduced the number of his supporters to seven. As Boileau, Bossuet, and Racine were among the seven who upheld him in his claim to a place among the "Immortals," there is no room to complain that the judgment of posterity on him was not adequately represented in the contest.

W. V. B.

ON THE CHARACTER OF MANKIND

LET us not be angry with men when we see them cruel, ungrateful, unjust, proud, egotists, and forgetful of others; they are made so; it is their nature; we might just as well quarrel with a stone for falling to the gound, or with a fire when the flames ascend.

In one sense men are not fickle, or only in trifles; they change their habits, language, outward appearance, their rules of propriety, and sometimes their taste; but they always preserve their bad morals, and adhere tenaciously to what is ill and to their indifference for virtue.

Stoicism is a mere fancy, a fiction, like Plato's "Republic." The Stoics pretend a man may laugh at poverty; not feel insults, ingratitude, loss of property, relatives, and friends; look unconcernedly on death, and regard it as a matter of indifference which ought neither to make him merry nor melancholy; nor let pleasure or pain conquer him; be wounded or burned without breathing the slightest sigh or shedding a single tear; and this phantasm of courage and imaginary firmness they are pleased to call a philosopher. They have left man with the same faults they found in him, and did not blame his smallest foible. Instead of depicting vice as something terrible or ridiculous, which might have corrected him, they have limned an idea of perfection and heroism of which man is not capable, and they exhorted him to aim at what is impossible. Thus, the philosopher that is to be, but will never exist except in imagination, finds himself naturally, and without any exertions of his own, above all events and all ills; the most excruciating fit of the gout, the most severe attack of colic, cannot draw from him the least complaint; heaven and earth may be overturned, without dragging him along in their downfall; and he remains calm and collected amidst the ruins of the universe, whilst a man really beside himself utters loud exclamations, despairs, looks fierce, and is in an agony for the loss of a dog or for a china dish broken into pieces. . . .

Power, favor, genius, riches, dignity, nobility, force, industry, capacity, virtue, vice, weakness, stupidity, poverty, impotence, plebeianism, and servility generally are combined in men in endless variety. These qualities mixed together in a thousand various manners, and compensating one another in many ways, form the different states and conditions of human life. Moreover, people who are acquainted with each other's strength and weakness act reciprocally, for they believe it their duty; they know their equals, are conscious that some men are their superiors, and that they are superior to some others; and hence familiarity, respect or deference, pride or contempt. This is the reason why, in places of public resort, we see each moment some persons we wish to accost or bow to, and others we pretend not to know, and still less desire to meet; and why we are proud of being with the first and ashamed of the others. Hence it even happens that the very person with whom you think it an honor to be seen, and with whom you are desirous to converse, deems you troublesome and leaves you; and that often the very person who blushes when he meets others receives the same treatment when others meet him, and that a man who treated others with contempt is himself disdained, for it is common enough to despise those who despise us. How wretched is such a behavior; and since it is certain that in this strange interchange we gain on one side what we lose on another, should we not do better to abandon all haughtiness and pride, qualities so unsuited

to frail humanity, and make an arrangement to treat one another with mutual kindness, by which we should at once gain the advantage of never being mortified ourselves, and the happiness, which is just as great, of never mortifying others?

Instead of being frightened, or even ashamed, at being called a philosopher, everybody in this world ought to have a strong tincture of philosophy; it suits every one; its practice is useful to people of all ages, sexes, and conditions; it consoles us for the happiness of others, for the promotion of those whom we think undeserving, for failures, and the decay of strength and beauty; it steels us against poverty, age, sickness, and death, against fools and buffoons; it will help us to pass away our life without a wife, or to bear with the one with whom we have to live.

Men are one hour overjoyed at trifles, and the next overcome with grief for a mere disappointment; nothing is more unequal and incoherent than the emotions stirring their hearts and minds in so short a time. If they would set no higher value on the things of this world than they really deserve, this evil would be cured.

It is as difficult to find a vain man who believes himself as happy as he deserves, as a modest man who believes himself too unhappy.

When I contemplate the fortune of princes and of their ministers, which is not mine, I am prevented from thinking myself unhappy by considering, at the same time, the fate of the vine dresser, the soldier, and the stonecutter.

There is but one real misfortune which can befall a man, and that is to find himself at fault, and to have something to reproach himself with.

The generality of men are more capable of great efforts to obtain their ends than of continuous perseverance; their occupation and inconstancy deprives them of the fruits of the most promising beginnings; they are often overtaken by those who started some time after them, and who walk slowly, but without intermission.

I almost dare affirm that men know better how to plan certain measures than to pursue them, how to resolve what they must needs do and say than to do or to say what is necessary. A man is firmly determined not to mention a certain subject when negotiating some business; and afterwards, either through passion, garrulity, or in the heat of conversation, it is the first thing which escapes him.

Men are indolent in what is their particular duty, while they think it very deserving, or rather while it pleases their vanity to busy themselves about those things which do not concern them, nor suit their condition of life or character.

There is as much difference between a heterogeneous character a man adopts and his real character as there is between a mask and a countenance of flesh and blood.

Telephus has some intelligence, but ten times less, if rightly computed, than he imagines he has; therefore, in everything he says, does, meditates, and projects, he goes ten times beyond his capacity, and thus always exceeds the true measure of his intellectual power and grasp. And this argument is well founded. He is limited by a barrier, as it were, and should be warned not to pass it; but he leaps over it, launches out of his sphere, and though he knows his own weakness, always displays it; he speaks about what he does not understand, or badly understands; attempts things above his power, and aims at what is too much for him; he thinks himself the equal of the very best men ever seen. Whatever is good and commendable in him is obscured by an affectation of doing something great and wonderful; people can easily see what he is not, but have to guess what he really is. He is a man who never measures his ability, and does not know himself; his true character is not to be satisfied with the one that suits him, and which is his own.

The intelligence of a highly cultivated man is not always the same, and has its ebbs and flows; sometimes he is full of animation, but cannot keep it up; then, if he be wise, he will say little, not write at all, and not endeavor either to draw upon his imagination, or try to please. Does a man sing who has a cold; and should he not rather wait till he recover his voice?

A blockhead is an automaton, a piece of machinery moved by springs and weights, always turning him about in one direction; he always displays the same equanimity, is uniform, and never alters; if you have seen him once you have seen him as he ever was, and will be; he is at best but like a lowing ox or a whistling blackbird; I may say he acts according to the persistence and doggedness of his nature and species. What you see least is his torpid soul, which is never stirring, but always dormant.

A blockhead never dies; or if, according to our manner of speaking, he dies at one time or other, I may truly say he gains by it, and that, when others die, he begins to live. His mind then

thinks, reasons, draws inferences and conclusions, judges, foresees, and does everything it never did before; it finds itself released from a lump of flesh in which it seemed buried without having anything to do, and without any motion, or at least any worthy of that name; I should almost say it blushes to have lodged in such a body, as well as for its own crude and imperfect organs, to which it has been shackled so long, and with which it could only produce a blockhead or a fool. Now it is equal to the greatest of those minds which animated the bodies of the cleverest or the most intellectual men, and the mind of the merest clodhopper is no longer to be distinguished from those of Condé, Richelieu, Pascal, and Lingendes. . . .

Timon, or the misanthrope, may have an austere and savage mind, but outwardly he is polite, and even ceremonious; he does not lose all command over himself, and does not become familiar with other men; on the contrary, he treats them politely and gravely, and in a manner that does not encourage any freedom to be taken; he does not desire to be better acquainted with them nor to make friends of them, and is somewhat like a lady visiting another lady.

Reason is ever allied to truth, and is almost identical with it; only one way leads to it, but a thousand roads can lead us astray. The study of wisdom is not so extensive as that of fools and coxcombs; he who has seen none but polite and reasonable men, either does not know men, or knows them only by halves. Whatever difference may be noticed in disposition and manners, intercourse with the world and politeness produce the same appearance in all, and externally make men resemble one another in some way which mutually pleases, and, being common to all, leads us to believe that everything else is in the same proportion. A man on the contrary, who mixes with the common people, or retires into the country, will, if he has eyes, in a short time make some strange discoveries, and see things which are new to him, and which he never before imagined existed; gradually and by experience he increases his knowledge of humanity, and almost calculates in how many different ways man may become unbearable.

After having maturely considered mankind and found out the insincerity of their thoughts, opinions, inclinations, and affections, we are compelled to acknowledge that stubbornness does them more harm than inconstancy.

How many weak, effeminate, careless minds exist without any extraordinary faults, and who yet are proper subjects for satire! How many various kinds of ridicule are disseminated amongst the whole human race, which by their very eccentricity are of little consequence, and are not ameliorated by instruction or morality. Such vices are individual and not contagious, and are rather personal than belonging to humanity in general.

From « Characters. »

ON HUMAN NATURE IN WOMANKIND

THE male and female sex seldom agree about the merits of a woman, as their interests vary too much. Women do not like those same charms in one another which render them agreeable to men; many ways and means which kindle in the latter the greatest passions raise among them aversion and antipathy.

There exists among some women an artificial grandeur depending on a certain way of moving their eyes, tossing their heads, and on their manner of walking, which does not go further; it is like a dazzling wit which is deceptive, and is only admired because it is superficial. In a few others is to be found an ingenuous natural greatness, not beholden to gestures and motion, which springs from the heart, and is, as it were, the result of their noble birth; their merit, as unruffled as it is efficient, is accompanied by a thousand virtues, which, in spite of all their modesty, break out and display themselves to all who can discern them.

I have heard some people say that they should like to be a girl, and a handsome girl, too, from thirteen to two and twenty, and after that age again to become a man.

Some young ladies are not sensible of the advantages of a happy disposition, and how beneficial it would be to them to give themselves up to it; they enfeeble these rare and fragile gifts which heaven has given them by affectation and by bad imitation; their very voice and gait are affected; they fashion their looks, adorn themselves, consult their looking-glasses to see whether they have sufficiently changed their own natural appearance, and take some trouble to make themselves less agreeable.

VI—154

For a woman to paint herself red or white is, I admit, a smaller crime than to say one thing and think another; it is also something less innocent than to disguise herself or to go masquerading, if she does not pretend to pass for what she seems to be, but only thinks of concealing her personality and of remaining unknown; it is an endeavor to deceive the eyes, to wish to appear outwardly what she is not; it is a kind of « white lie. »

We should judge of a woman without taking into account her shoes and headdress, and, almost as we measure a fish, from head to tail.

If it be the ambition of women only to appear handsome in their own eyes and to please themselves, they are, no doubt, right in following their own tastes and fancies as to how they should beautify themselves, as well as in choosing their dress and ornaments; but if they desire to please men, if it is for them they paint and besmear themselves, I can tell them that all men, or nearly all, have agreed that white and red paint makes them look hideous and frightful; that red paint alone ages and disguises them; and that these men hate as much to see white lead on their countenances as to see false teeth in their mouths or balls of wax to plump out their cheeks; that they solemnly protest against all artifices women employ to make themselves look ugly; that they are not responsible for it to heaven, but, on the contrary, that it seems the last and infallible means to reclaim men from loving them.

If women were by nature what they make themselves by art; if they were to lose suddenly all the freshness of their complexions, and their faces to become as fiery and leaden as they make them with the red and the paint they besmear themselves with, they would consider themselves the most wretched creatures on earth.

A coquette is a woman who never yields to the passion she has for pleasing, nor to the good opinion she entertains for her own beauty; she regards time and years only as things that wrinkle and disfigure other women, and forgets that age is written on her face. The same dress, which formerly enhanced her beauty when she was young, now disfigures her, and shows the more the defects of old age; winning manners and affectation cling to her even in sorrow and sickness; she dies dressed in her best, and adorned with gay-colored ribbons.

From « Characters. »

TABLE OF CONTENTS

VOLUME VII

CHARLES LAMB

(1775-1834)

ETWEEN the ages of forty-five and fifty years,—having suffered and renounced whatever was necessary to educate him for so high a mission,—Charles Lamb wrote the "Essays of Elia." It is hard to think of an angel with a stoop and a bad habit of stuttering. We do not usually imagine that the garments of the Seraphim smell of stale tobacco smoke, or that the ministers of grace are liable to make puns without provocation. Still of such supernatural souls as Lamb it has been written:—

> "Through all the world heaven's angels walk obscure,
> With radiance hidden from our darkened eyes
> By forms of humblest clay, whose mean disguise
> May veil celestial light more rare and pure
> Than we with purblind sight could dare endure."

If there is anything in evidence, Lamb in a London tavern, stuttering out his jokes through thick clouds of tobacco smoke, was even then an inhabitant of the same heaven in which Thomas à Kempis wrote the "Imitatio Christi,"—the heaven which belongs to the pure in heart. "St. Charles," Coleridge called him, after having known him from the time they were Blue-Coat boys together in Christ's Hospital School. Nothing short of saintliness would have made him the great humorist he is. His life was a long tragedy. An innocent victim of a hereditary taint, he was confined in a madhouse at twenty-one. Only a few months after his release, his sister Mary, in a violent paroxysm of insanity, killed her mother and was committed to a lunatic asylum, with the prospect of life imprisonment among the insane. Her brother, scarcely more than a boy and with "the means of a day laborer," pledged himself to the authorities to nurse and care for her if they would make him her guardian, and it was to this martyrdom that he devoted himself, sacrificing his hopes of happiness with Alice Winterton, and remaining a bachelor all his life. He lived with his sister as her guardian and nurse, watching for the recurrence of the symptoms of her madness, and when they appeared, going with her to the asylum that she might be confined until restored to herself. Out of this touching love between the brother and sister came the "Tales from Shakespeare" and "Poetry for Children," "by

prosing himself, he is reputed to have furnished frequent texts to Coleridge—who did both. "I think, Charles," said Coleridge, "you never heard me preach." "I ne-ne-never heard you do anything else," replied Lamb with severe gravity, and no doubt with a deliberately protracted stutter.

Lamb's antecedents were anything but patrician. His father, who was "engaged in his youth in domestic service," never rose higher than a clerkship for a bencher in the Inner Temple. Seven years in the Blue-Coat School of Christ's Hospital was all the scholastic education Charles ever had. In 1789 he became a clerk in the South Sea House, and in 1792 in the India House, where he worked until his fiftieth year. He was then retired on a pension of £400 a year, but he wrote little after this and lived to enjoy his moneyed ease for only nine years. He died December 27th, 1834, and when Professor Morley tells us that on that date he "entered into his heavenly rest," we will not think of questioning it. But as for the kind of a heaven it is he entered, we can only guess that there will be a London in it with no fogs, and many clubrooms, inhabited exclusively by people who are fit to associate with the author of "The Complaint of the Decay of Beggars." W. V. B.

A COMPLAINT OF THE DECAY OF BEGGARS IN THE METROPOLIS

THE all-sweeping besom of societarian reformation—your only modern Alcides' club to rid the time of its abuses—is uplift with many-handed sway to extirpate the last fluttering tatters of the bugbear mendicity from the metropolis. Scrips, wallets, bags—staves, dogs, and crutches—the whole mendicant fraternity with all their baggage, are fast posting out of the purlieus of this eleventh persecution. From the crowded crossing, from the corners of streets and turnings of alleys, the parting Genius of Beggary is "with sighing sent."

I do not approve of this wholesale going to work, this impertinent crusado, or *bellum ad exterminationem*, proclaimed against a species. Much good might be sucked from these Beggars.

They were the oldest and the honorablest form of pauperism. Their appeals were to our common nature; less revolting to an ingenuous mind than to be a suppliant to the particular humors or caprice of any fellow-creature, or set of fellow-

Charles and Mary Lamb,"—joint productions which make it evident that Lamb sought to inspire his sister with his own spirit of hope and cheerfulness. That the "Tales from Shakespeare," which will be read with delight by children as long as the language in which they are written remains intelligible, could have been the result of the struggle for self-possession of two supersensitive minds under the constant dread of the recurrence of madness, is one of those miracles of contradiction which glorify human nature and human sanity in the teeth of Lombroso and all others who, having discovered that "genius is a neurosis," imagine that it is nothing more.

In Lamb it was the fruit of ripening manliness in that form which is called "Virtue,"—the quality of the "Vir," or fighting man, who can stand at the front in the first rank, stooped down behind his shield, but unyielding when the lines are broken and every one else is retreating. "Certa tanquam miles bonus!" writes Thomas à Kempis of such a one as Lamb. "Fight like a good soldier!" So does the metaphor of struggle endured and of blows taken without shrinking inhere in the meaning of such patient virtue as this—virtue which makes manliness divine even in its weakness.

Lamb's humor is clearly a result of consciousness of his own infirmities and of the clear perception such self-knowledge gives him of the infirmities of others. Grote, Gibbon, and Macaulay, Locke, Descartes, and Plato, the historians, and the philosophers know much and tell much of human nature, but those who know more than they care or dare to tell do not write history or philosophy. They write such fairy tales as those of De la Motte Fouqué, and Hans Christian Andersen, and such essays as those of Lamb. The tenderness of Andersen and the playfulness of Lamb are marks of the acute sensitiveness of physical organization which must accompany the responsiveness of the body to the control of mind. One of the marks of self-mastery in the physical suffering such responsiveness entails is humor. All humor is the result of a reaction. It may grow more and more brutal as the brutal nature is strengthened by reaction against the higher; but in Lamb it grows more and more tender and delicate as he ripens for translation to some heaven where—let us hope—reactions are no more; where there are no headaches in unlimited punches, and no dryness of tongue after such long nights of innumerable pipes as preceded the "Renunciation" in which Lamb wrote:—

> "For thy sake, tobacco, I
> Would do anything—but die!"

Delightful as is the secret wisdom of Lamb's essays, it is said that his conversation was even more so. Never preaching and never

creatures, parochial or societarian. Theirs were the only rates uninvidious in the levy, ungrudged in the assessment.

There was a dignity springing from the very depth of their desolation; as to be naked is to be so much nearer to the being a man than to go in livery.

The greatest spirits have felt this in their reverses; and when Dionysius from king turned schoolmaster, do we feel anything towards him but contempt? Could Vandyke have made a picture of him, swaying a ferula for a sceptre, which would have affected our minds with the same heroic pity, the same compassionate admiration, with which we regard his Belisarius begging for an obolus? Would the moral have been more graceful, more pathetic?

The Blind Beggar in the legend,—the father of pretty Bessy,—whose story doggerel rhymes and alehouse signs cannot so degrade or attenuate but that some sparks of a lustrous spirit will shine through the disguisements—this noble Earl of Cornwall (as indeed he was) and memorable sport of fortune, fleeing from the unjust sentence of his liege lord, stripped of all, and seated on the flowering green of Bethnal, with his more fresh and springing daughter by his side, illumining his rags and his beggary—would the child and parent have cut a better figure, doing the honors of a counter, or expiating their fallen condition upon the three-foot eminence of some sempstering shopboard?

In tale or history your Beggar is ever the just antipode to your king. The poets and romancical writers (as dear Margaret Newcastle would call them) when they would most sharply and feelingly paint a reverse of fortune, never stop till they have brought down their hero in good earnest to rags and the wallet. The depth of the descent illustrates the height he falls from. There is no medium which can be presented to the imagination without offense. There is no breaking the fall. Lear, thrown from his palace, must divest him of his garments, till he answer "mere nature"; and Cressid, fallen from a prince's love, must extend her lazar arms, pale with other whiteness than of beauty, supplicating lazar alms with bell and clap-dish.

The Lucian wits knew this very well; and, with a converse policy, when they would express scorn of greatness without the pity, they show us an Alexander in the shades cobbling shoes, or a Semiramis getting up foul linen.

How would it sound in song, that a great monarch had declined his affections upon the daughter of a baker! yet do we feel the imagination at all violated when we read the "true ballad," where King Cophetua wooes the beggar maid?

"Pauperism," "pauper," "poor man," are expressions of pity, but pity alloyed with contempt. No one properly contemns a beggar. Poverty is a comparative thing, and each degree of it is mocked by its "neighbor grice." Its poor rents and comings-in are soon summed up and told. Its pretenses to property are almost ludicrous. Its pitiful attempts to save excite a smile. Every scornful companion can weigh his trifle-bigger purse against it. Poor man reproaches poor man in the streets with impolitic mention of his condition, his own being a shade better, while the rich pass by and jeer at both. No rascally comparative insults a Beggar, or thinks of weighing purses with him. He is not in the scale of comparison. He is not under the measure of property. He confessedly hath none, any more than a dog or a sheep. No one twitteth him with ostentation above his means. No one accuses him of pride, or unbraideth him with mock humility. None jostle with him for the wall, or pick quarrels for precedency. No wealthy neighbor seeketh to eject him from his tenement. No man sues him. No man goes to law with him. If I were not the independent gentleman that I am, rather than I would be a retainer to the great, a led captain, or a poor relation, I would choose, out of the delicacy and true greatness of my mind, to be a Beggar.

Rags, which are the reproach of poverty, are the Beggar's robes, and graceful insignia of his profession, his tenure, his full dress, the suit in which he is expected to show himself in public. He is never out of the fashion, or limpeth awkwardly behind it. He is not required to put on court mourning. He weareth all colors, fearing none. His costume hath undergone less change than the Quaker's. He is the only man in the universe who is not obliged to study appearances. The ups and downs of the world concern him no longer. He alone continueth in one stay. The price of stock or land affecteth him not. The fluctuations of agricultural or commercial prosperity touch him not, or at worst but change his customers. He is not expected to become bail or surety for any one. No man troubleth him with questioning his religion or politics. He is the only free man in the universe.

Fixit inoffenso gressu; gelidumque sedile
In nudo nactus saxo, qua prætereuntium
Unda frequens confluxit, ibi miserisque tenebras
Lamentis, noctemque oculis ploravit abortam.
Ploravit nec frustra; obolum dedit alter et alter,
Queis corda et mentem indiderat natura benignam.
Ad latus interea jacui sopitus herile,
Vel mediis vigil in somnis; ad herilia jussa
Auresque atque animum arrectus, seu frustula amicè
Porrexit sociasque dapes, seu longa diei
Tædia perpessus, reditum sub nocte parabat.
    Hi mores, hæc vita fuit, dum fata sinebant,
Dum neque languebam morbis, nec inerte senectâ;
Quæ tandem obrepsit, veterique satellite cæcum
Orbavit dominum: prisci sed gratia facti
Ne tota intereat, longos delecta per annos,
Exiguum hunc Irus tumulum de cespite fecit,
Etsi inopis, non ingratæ, munuscula dextræ;
Carmine signavitque brevi, dominumque canemque
Quod memoret, fidumque canem dominumque benignum."

"Poor Irus's faithful wolf-dog here I lie,
That wont to tend my old blind master's steps,
His guide and guard: nor, while my service lasted,
Had he occasion for that staff, with which
He now goes picking out his path in fear
Over the highways and crossings; but would plant,
Safe in the conduct of my friendly string,
A firm foot forward still, till he had reach'd
His poor seat on some stone, nigh where the tide
Of passers-by in thickest confluence flow'd:
To whom with loud and passionate laments
From morn to eve his dark estate he wail'd.
Nor wail'd to all in vain: some here and there,
The well-disposed and good, their pennies gave.
I meantime at his feet obsequious slept;
Not all-asleep in sleep, but heart and ear
Prick'd up at his least motion; to receive
At his kind hand my customary crumbs,
And common portion in his feast of scraps;
Or when night warn'd us homeward, tired and spent
With our long day and tedious beggary.
    These were my manners, this my way of life,
Till age and slow disease me overtook,
And sever'd from my sightless master's side.
But lest the grace of so good deeds should die,

The Mendicants of this great city were so many of her sights, her lions. I can no more spare them than I could the Cries of London. No corner of a street is complete without them. They are as indispensable as the Ballad Singer; and in their picturesque attire as ornamental as the Signs of Old London. They were the standing morals, emblems, mementoes, dial mottoes, the spital sermons, the books for children, the salutary checks and pauses to the high and rushing tide of greasy citizenry—

———"Look
Upon that poor and broken bankrupt there."

Above all, those old blind Tobits that used to line the wall of Lincoln's, Inn Garden, before modern fastidiousness had expelled them, casting up their ruined orbs to catch a ray of pity, and (if possible) of light, with their faithful dog guide at their feet,—whither are they fled? or into what corners, blind as themselves, have they been driven, out of the wholesome air and sun warmth? Immured between four walls, in what withering poorhouse do they endure the penalty of double darkness, where the chink of the dropped half-penny no more consoles their forlorn bereavement, far from the sound of the cheerful and hopestirring tread of the passenger? Where hang their useless staves? and who will farm their dogs? Have the overseers of St. L—— caused them to be shot? or were they tied up in sacks, and dropped into the Thames, at the suggestion of B——, the mild rector of ——?

Well fare the soul of unfastidious Vincent Bourne, most classical and, at the same time, most English, of the Latinists!—who has treated of this human and quadrupedal alliance, this dog and man friendship in the sweetest of his poems, the "Epitaphium in Canem," or "Dog's Epitaph." Reader, peruse it; and say, if customary sights, which could call up such gentle poetry as this, were of a nature to do more harm or good to the moral sense of the passengers through the daily thoroughfares of a vast and busy metropolis.

"Pauperis hic Iri requiesco Lyciscus, herilis,
Dum vixi, tutela vigil columenque senectæ,
Dux cæco fidus: nec, me ducente, solebat,
Prætenso hinc atque hinc baculo, per iniqua locorum
Incertam explorare viam; sed fila secutus,
Quæ dubios regerent passus, vestigia tuta

Through tract of years in mute oblivion lost,
This slender tomb of turf hath Irus reared,
Cheap monument of no ungrudging hand,
And with short verse inscribed it, to attest,
In long and lasting union to attest,
The virtues of the Beggar and his Dog."

These dim eyes have in vain explored for some months past a well-known figure or part of the figure, of a man, who used to glide his comely upper half over the pavements of London, wheeling along with most ingenious celerity upon a machine of wood; a spectacle to natives, to foreigners, and to children. He was of a robust make, with a florid sailor-like complexion, and his head was bare to the storm and sunshine. He was a natural curiosity, a speculation to the scientific, a prodigy to the simple. The infant would stare at the mighty man brought down to his own level. The common cripple would despise his own pusillanimity, viewing the hale stoutness and hearty heart of this half-limbed giant. Few but must have noticed him; for the accident, which brought him low, took place during the riots of 1780, and he has been a groundling so long. He seemed earth-born, an Antæus, and to suck in fresh vigor from the soil which he neighbored. He was a grand fragment; as good as an Elgin marble. The nature which should have recruited his left legs and thighs was not lost, but only retired into his upper parts, and he was half a Hercules. I heard a tremendous voice thundering and growling, as before an earthquake, and casting down my eyes it was this mandrake reviling a steed that had started at his portentous appearance. He seemed to want but his just statue to have rent the offending quadruped in shivers. He was as the man part of a Centaur, from which the horse half had been cloven in some dire Lapithan controversy. He moved on as if he could have made shift with yet half of the body portion which was left him. The *os sublime* was not wanting; and he threw out yet a jolly countenance upon the heavens. Forty-and-two years had he driven this out-of-door trade, and now that his hair is grizzled in the service, but his good spirits no way impaired, because he is not content to exchange his free air and exercise for the restraints of a poorhouse, he is expiating his contumacy in one of those houses (ironically christened) of Correction.

Was a daily spectacle like this to be deemed a nuisance, which called for legal interference to remove; or not rather a salutary and a touching object, to the passers-by in a great city?

Among her shows, her museums, and supplies for ever-gaping curiosity (and what else but an accumulation of sights—endless sights—is a great city; or for what else is it desirable?) was there not room for one *Lusus* (not *Naturæ*, indeed, but) *Accidentium?* What if in forty-and-two years' going about the man had scraped together enough to give a portion to his child (as the rumor ran) of a few hundreds—whom had he injured? whom had he imposed upon? The contributors had enjoyed their sight for their pennies. What if after being exposed all day to the heats, the rains, and the frosts of heaven—shuffling his ungainly trunk along in an elaborate and painful motion—he was enabled to retire at night to enjoy himself at a club of his fellow-cripples over a dish of hot meat and vegetables, as the charge was gravely brought against him by a clergyman deposing before a House of Commons' committee—was this, or was his truly paternal consideration, which (if a fact) deserved a statue rather than a whipping post, and is inconsistent at least with the exaggeration of nocturnal orgies which he has been slandered with—a reason that he should be deprived of his chosen, harmless, nay edifying, way of life, and be committed in hoary age for a sturdy vagabond?

There was a Yorick once, whom it would not have shamed to have sat down at the cripples' feast, and to have thrown in his benediction, aye, and his mite too, for a companionable symbol. "Age, thou hast lost thy breed."

Half of these stories about the prodigious fortunes made by begging are (I verily believe) misers' calumnies. One was much talked of in the public papers some time since, and the usual charitable inferences deduced. A clerk in the Bank was surprised with the announcement of a five-hundred-pound legacy left him by a person whose name he was a stranger to. It seems that in his daily morning walks from Peckham (or some village thereabouts) where he lived, to his office, it had been his practice for the last twenty years to drop his half-penny duly into the hat of some blind Bartimeus, that sat begging alms by the wayside in the borough. The good old beggar recognized his daily benefactor by the voice only; and, when he died, left all the amassings of his alms (that had been half a century perhaps in the accumulating) to his old Bank friend. Was this a story to purse up people's hearts, and pennies, against giving an alms to the blind?—or not rather a beautiful moral of well-directed charity on the one part, and noble gratitude upon the other?

I sometimes wish I had been that Bank clerk.

I seem to remember a poor old grateful kind of creature, blinking and looking up with his no eyes in the sun.

Is it possible I could have steeled my purse against him?

Perhaps I had no small change.

Reader, do not be frightened at the hard words, imposition, imposture—give and ask no questions. Cast thy bread upon the waters. Some have unawares (like this Bank clerk) entertained angels.

Shut not **thy** purse strings always against painted distress. Act a charity sometimes. When a poor creature (outwardly and visibly such) comes before thee, do not stay to inquire whether the "seven small children," in whose name he implores thy assistance, have a veritable existence. Rake not into the bowels of unwelcome truth, to save a half-penny. It is good to believe him. If he be not all that he pretendeth, give, and under a personate father of a family think (if thou pleasest) that thou hast relieved an indigent bachelor. When they come with their counterfeit looks, and mumping tones, think them players. You pay your money to see a comedian feign these things, which, concerning these poor people, thou canst not certainly tell whether they are feigned or not.

"Pray God, your honor, relieve me," said a poor beadswoman to my friend L—— one day: "I have seen better days." "So have I, my good woman," retorted he, looking up at the welkin, which was just then threatening a storm—and the jest (he will have it) was as good to the beggar as a tester. It was, at all events, kinder than consigning her to the stocks, or the parish beadle.

But L—— has a way of viewing things in rather a paradoxical light on some occasions.

P. S.—My friend Hume (not M. P.) has a curious manuscript in his possession, the original draft of the celebrated "Beggar's Petition" (who cannot say by heart the "Beggar's Petition"?) as it was written by some school usher (as I remember), with corrections interlined from the pen of Oliver Goldsmith. As a specimen of the Doctor's improvement, I recollect one most judicious alteration,

"A pamper'd menial drove me from the door."

It stood originally —

"A livery servant drove me," etc.

Here is an instance of poetical or artificial language properly substituted for the phrase of common conversation; against Wordsworth, I think I must get H. to send it to the London as a corollary to the foregoing.

Complete. From the London Magazine, June, 1822.

A DISSERTATION UPON ROAST PIG

MANKIND, says a Chinese manuscript, which my friend M. was obliging enough to read and explain to me, for the first seventy thousand ages ate their meat raw, clawing or biting it from the living animal, just as they do in Abyssinia to this day. This period is not obscurely hinted at by their great Confucius in the second chapter of his "Mundane Mutations," where he designates a kind of golden age by the term Cho-fang, literally the Cooks' holiday. The manuscript goes on to say that the art of roasting, or rather broiling (which I take to be the elder brother) was accidentally discovered in the manner following. The swineherd, Ho-ti, having gone out into the woods one morning, as his manner was, to collect mast for his hogs, left his cottage in the care of his eldest son Bo-bo, a great lubberly boy, who being fond of playing with fire, as younkers of his age commonly are, let some sparks escape into a bundle of straw, which kindling quickly spread the conflagration over every part of their poor mansion, till it was reduced to ashes. Together with the cottage (a sorry antediluvian makeshift of a building, you may think it), what was of much more importance, a fine litter of new-farrowed pigs, no less than nine in number, perished. China pigs have been esteemed a luxury all over the East from the remotest periods that we read of. Bo-bo was in the utmost consternation, as you may think, not so much for the sake of the tenement, which his father and he could easily build up again with a few dry branches, and the labor of an hour or two, at any time, as for the loss of the pigs. While he was thinking what he should say to his father, and wringing his hands over the smoking remnants of one of those untimely sufferers, an odor assailed his nostrils, unlike any scent which he had before experienced. What could it proceed from?—not from the burnt cottage—he had smelt that smell before—indeed

this was by no means the first accident of the kind which had occurred through the negligence of this unlucky young firebrand. Much less did it resemble that of any known herb, weed, or flower. A premonitory moistening at the same time overflowed his nether lip. He knew not what to think. He next stooped down to feel the pig, if there were any signs of life in it. He burnt his fingers, and to cool them he applied them in his booby fashion to his mouth. Some of the crumbs of the scorched skin had come away with his fingers, and for the first time in his life (in the world's life indeed, for before him no man had known it) he tasted—crackling! Again he felt and fumbled at the pig. It did not burn him so much now, still he licked his fingers from a sort of habit. The truth at length broke into his slow understanding that it was the pig that smelt so, and the pig that tasted so delicious; and, surrendering himself up to the new-born pleasure, he fell to tearing up whole handfuls of the scorched skin with the flesh next it, and was cramming it down his throat in his beastly fashion, when his sire entered amid the smoking rafters, armed with a retributory cudgel, and, finding how affairs stood, began to rain blows upon the young rogue's shoulders as thick as hailstones, which Bo-bo heeded not any more than if they had been flies. The tickling pleasure which he experienced in his lower regions had rendered him quite callous to any inconveniences he might feel in those remote quarters. His father might lay on, but he could not beat him from his pig till he had fairly made an end of it, when, becoming a little more sensible of his situation, something like the following dialogue ensued:—

"You graceless whelp, what have you got there devouring? Is it not enough that you have burnt me down three houses with your dog's tricks, and be hanged to you, but you must be eating fire, and I know not what—what have you got there, I say?"

Oh, father, the pig, the pig, do come and taste how nice the burnt pig eats!"

The ears of Ho-ti tingled with horror. He cursed his son, and he cursed himself that ever he should beget a son that should eat burnt pig.

Bo-bo, whose scent was wonderfully sharpened since morning, soon raked out another pig, and fairly rending it asunder, thrust the lesser half by main force into the fists of Ho-ti, still shouting out, "Eat, eat, eat the burnt pig, father, only taste—O Lord!"—with such like barbarous ejaculations, cramming all the while as if he would choke.

Ho-ti trembled in every joint while he grasped the abominable thing, wavering whether he should not put his son to death for an unnatural young monster, when the crackling scorching his fingers, as it had done his son's, and applying the same remedy to them, he, in his turn, tasted some of its flavor, which, make what sour mouths he would for a pretense, proved not altogether displeasing to him. In conclusion (for the manuscript here is a little tedious) both father and son fairly sat down to the mess, and never left off till they had despatched all that remained of the litter.

Bo-bo was strictly enjoined not to let the secret escape, for the neighbors would certainly have stoned them for a couple of abominable wretches, who could think of improving upon the good meat which God had sent them. Nevertheless, strange stories got about. It was observed that Ho-ti's cottage was burnt down now more frequently than ever. Nothing but fires from this time forward. Some would break out in broad day, others in the nighttime. As often as the sow farrowed, so sure was the house of Ho-ti to be in a blaze; and Ho-ti himself, which was the more remarkable, instead of chastising his son, seemed to grow more indulgent to him than ever. At length they were watched, the terrible mystery discovered, and father and son summoned to take their trial at Pekin, then an inconsiderable as-size town. Evidence was given, the obnoxious food itself produced in court, and verdict about to be pronounced, when the foreman of the jury begged that some of the burnt pig, of which the culprits stood accused, might be handed into the box. He handled it, and they all handled it, and burning their fingers as Bo-bo and his father had done before them, and nature prompting to each of them the same remedy, against the face of all the facts, and the clearest charge which judge had ever given,—to the surprise of the whole court, townsfolk, strangers, reporters, and all present—without leaving the box, or any manner of consultation whatever, they brought in a simultaneous verdict of Not Guilty.

The judge, who was a shrewd fellow, winked at the manifest iniquity of the decision; and, when the court was dismissed, went privily, and bought up all the pigs that could be had for love or

money. In a few days his lordship's town house was observed to be on fire. The thing took wing, and now there was nothing to be seen but fires in every direction. Fuel and pigs grew enormously dear all over the district. The insurance offices one and all shut up shop. People built slighter and slighter every day, until it was feared that the very science of architecture would in no long time be lost to the world. Thus this custom of firing houses continued, till in process of time, says my manuscript, a sage arose, like our Locke, who made a discovery that the flesh of swine, or, indeed, of any other animal, might be cooked (burnt as they called it) without the necessity of consuming a whole house to dress it. Then first began the rude form of a gridiron. Roasting by the string, or spit, came in a century or two later, I forget in whose dynasty. By such slow degrees, concludes the manuscript, do the most useful, and seemingly the most obvious arts, make their way among mankind.

Without placing too implicit faith in the account above given, it must be agreed that if a worthy pretext for so dangerous an experiment as setting houses on fire (especially in these days) could be assigned in favor of any culinary object, that pretext and excuse might be found in roast pig.

Of all the delicacies in the whole *mundus edibilis*, I will maintain it to be the most delicate—*princeps obsoniorum*.

I speak not of your grown porkers—things between pig and pork—those hobbydehoys—but a young and tender suckling—under a moon old—guiltless as yet of the sty—with no original speck of the *amor immunditiæ*, the hereditary failing of the first parent, yet manifest—his voice as yet not broken, but something between a childish treble and a grumble—the mild forerunner, or *præludium*, of a grunt.

He must be roasted. I am not ignorant that our ancestors ate them seethed, or boiled—but what a sacrifice of the exterior tegument!

There is no flavor comparable, I will contend, to that of the crisp, tawny, well-watched, not over-roasted crackling, as it is well called—the very teeth are invited to their share of the pleasure at this banquet in overcoming the coy, brittle resistance—with the adhesive oleaginous—oh, call it not fat—but an indefinable sweetness growing up to it—the tender blossoming of fat—fat cropped in the bud—taken in the shoot—in the first innocence—the cream and quintessence of the child-pig's yet pure

food—the lean, no lean, but a kind of animal manna—or, rather, fat and lean (if it must be so) so blended and running into each other that both together make but one ambrosian result, or common substance.

Behold him, while he is doing—it seemeth rather a refreshing warmth than a scorching heat that he is so passive to. How equably he twirleth round the string!—Now he is just done. To see the extreme sensibility of that tender age, he hath wept out his pretty eyes—radiant jellies—shooting stars!

See him in the dish, his second cradle, how meek he lieth!—wouldst thou have had this innocent grow up to the grossness and indocility which too often accompany maturer swinehood? Ten to one he would have proved a glutton, a sloven, an obstinate, disagreeable animal—wallowing in all manner of filthy conversation! From these sins he is happily snatched away—

"Ere sin could blight, or sorrow fade,
Death came with timely care"—

his memory is odoriferous—no clown curseth, while his stomach half rejecteth, the rank bacon—no coal heaver bolteth him in reeking sausages—he hath a fair sepulchre in the grateful stomach of the judicious epicure—and for such a tomb might be content to die.

He is the best of sapors. Pineapple is great. She is, indeed, almost too transcendent—a delight, if not sinful, yet so like to sinning, that really a tender-conscienced person would do well to pause—too ravishing for mortal taste, she woundeth and excoriateth the lips that approach her—like lovers' kisses, she biteth—she is a pleasure bordering on pain from the fierceness and insanity of her relish—but she stoppeth at the palate—she meddleth not with the appetite—and the coarsest hunger might barter her consistently for a mutton chop.

Pig—let me speak his praise—is no less provocative of the appetite than he is satisfactory to the criticalness of the censorious palate. The strong man may batten on him, and the weakling refuseth not his mild juices.

Unlike to mankind's mixed characters, a bundle of virtues and vices, inexplicably intertwisted, and not to be unraveled without hazard, he is—good throughout. No part of him is better or worse than another. He helpeth, as far as his little means

extend, all around. He is the least envious of banquets. He is all neighbors' fare.

I am one of those who freely and ungrudgingly impart a share of the good things of this life which fall to their lot (few as mine are in this kind) to a friend. I protest I take as great an interest in my friend's pleasures, his relishes, and proper satisfactions, as in mine own. "Presents," I often say, "endear Absents." Hares, pheasants, partridges, snipes, barn-door chickens (those "tame villatic fowl"), capons, plovers, brawn, barrels of oysters, I dispense as freely as I receive them. I love to taste them, as it were, upon the tongue of my friend. But a stop must be put somewhere. One would not, like Lear, "give everything." I make my stand upon pig. Methinks it is an ingratitude to the Giver of all good flavors, to extra-domiciliate, or send out of the house, slightingly (under pretext of friendship, or I know not what), a blessing so particularly adapted, predestined, I may say, to my individual palate. It argues an insensibility.

I remember a touch of conscience in this kind at school. My good old aunt, who never parted from me at the end of a holiday without stuffing a sweetmeat, or some nice thing into my pocket, had dismissed me one evening with a smoking plum cake, fresh from the oven. On my way to school (it was over London Bridge) a gray-headed old beggar saluted me (I have no doubt at this time of day that he was a counterfeit). I had no pence to console him with, and in the vanity of self-denial, and the very coxcombry of charity, schoolboy-like, I made him a present of—the whole cake! I walked on a little, buoyed up, as one is on such occasions, with a sweet soothing of self-satisfaction; but before I had got to the end of the bridge my better feelings returned and I burst into tears, thinking how ungrateful I had been to my good aunt, to go and give her good gift away to a stranger that I had never seen before, and who might he a bad man for aught I knew; and then I thought of the pleasure my aunt would be taking in thinking that I—I myself, and not another—would eat her nice cake—and what should I say to her the next time I saw her—how naughty I was to part with her pretty present—and the odor of that spicy cake came back upon my recollection, and the pleasure and the curiosity I had taken in seeing her make it, and her joy when she sent it to the oven, and how disappointed she would feel that I had never had a bit of it in my mouth at last—and I blamed my impertinent spirit of almsgiving, and out-of-place hypocrisy of goodness, and, above all, I wished never to see the face again of that insidious, good-for-nothing, old gray impostor.

Our ancestors were nice in their method of sacrificing the tender victims. We read of pigs whipped to death with something of a shock, as we hear of any other obsolete custom. The age of discipline is gone by, or it would be curious to inquire (in a philosophical light merely) what effect this process might have towards intenerating and dulcifying a substance, naturally so mild and dulcet as the flesh of young pigs. It looks like refining a violet. Yet we should be cautious, while we condemn the inhumanity, how we censure the wisdom of the practice. It might impart a gusto.

I remember an hypothesis, argued upon by the young students, when I was at St. Omer's, and maintained with much learning and pleasantry on both sides, "Whether supposing that the flavor of a pig who obtained his death by whipping (*per flagellationem extremam*) superadded a pleasure upon the palate of a man more intense than any possible suffering we can conceive in the animal, is man justified in using that method of putting the animal to death?" I forget the decision.

His sauce should be considered. Decidedly, a few bread crumbs, done up with his liver and brains, and a dash of mild sage. But, banish, dear Mrs. Cook, I beseech you, the whole onion tribe. Barbecue your whole hogs to your palate, steep them in shallots, stuff them out with plantations of the rank and guilty garlic; you cannot poison them, or make them stronger than they are— but consider, he is a weakling—a flower.

Complete. From the London Magazine, September, 1822.

NEW YEAR'S EVE

EVERY man hath two birthdays: two days at least, in every year, which set him upon revolving the lapse of time, as it affects his mortal duration. The one is that which in an especial manner he termeth "his." In the gradual desuetude of old observances, this custom of solemnizing our proper birthday hath nearly passed away, or is left to children, who reflect nothing at all about the matter, nor understand anything in it beyond cake and orange. But the birth of a New Year is of an

In a degree beneath manhood, it is my infirmity to look back upon those early days. Do I advance a paradox when I say that, skipping over the intervention of forty years, a man may have leave to love himself, without the imputation of self-love?

If I know aught of myself, no one whose mind is introspective —and mine is painfully so—can have a less respect for his present identity than I have for the man Elia. I know him to be light, and vain, and humorsome; a notorious . . . ; addicted to . . . ; averse from counsel, neither taking it, nor offering it;— . . . besides; a stammering buffoon; what you will; lay it on, and spare not; I subscribe to it all, and much more, than thou canst be willing to lay at his door—but for the child Elia—that "other me," there, in the background—I must take leave to cherish the remembrance of that young master—with as little reference, I protest, to this stupid changeling of five-and-forty, as if it had been a child of some other house, and not of my parents. I can cry over its patient smallpox at five, and rougher medicaments. I can lay its poor fevered head upon the sick pillow at Christ's, and wake with it in surprise at the gentle posture of maternal tenderness hanging over it, that unknown had watched its sleep. I know how it shrank from any the least color of falsehood.—God help thee, Elia, how art thou changed! Thou art sophisticated.—I know how honest, how courageous (for a weakling) it was; how religious, how imaginative, how hopeful! From what have I not fallen, if the child I remember was indeed myself,—and not some dissembling guardian, presenting a false identity, to give the rule to my unpracticed steps, and regulate the tone of my moral being!

That I am fond of indulging, beyond a hope of sympathy, in such retrospection, may be the symptom of some sickly idiosyncrasy. Or is it owing to another cause; simply, that being without wife or family, I have not learned to project myself enough out of myself; and having no offspring of my own to dally with, I turn back upon memory, and adopt my own early idea, as my heir and favorite? If these speculations seem fantastical to thee, reader—(a busy man, perchance), if I tread out of the way of thy sympathy, and am singularly conceited only, I retire impenetrable to ridicule, under the phantom cloud of Elia.

The elders, with whom I was brought up, were of a character not likely to let slip the sacred observance of any old institution; and the ringing out of the Old Year was kept by them with

interest too wide to be pretermitted by king or cobbler. No one ever regarded the First of January with indifference. It is that from which all date their time, and count upon what is left. It is the nativity of our common Adam.

Of all sound of all bells—(bells, the music nighest bordering upon heaven)—most solemn and touching is the peal which rings out the Old Year. I never hear it without a gathering up of my mind to a concentration of all the images that have been diffused over the past twelvemonth; all I have done or suffered, performed or neglected—in that regretted time. I begin to know its worth, as when a person dies. It takes a personal color; nor was it a poetical flight in a contemporary, when he exclaimed:—

"I saw the skirts of the departing Year."

It is no more than what in sober sadness every one of us seems to be conscious of, in that awful leave-taking. I am sure I felt it, and all felt it with me, last night; though some of my companions affected rather to manifest an exhilaration at the birth of the coming year, than any very tender regrets for the decease of its predecessor. But I am none of those who—

"Welcome the coming, speed the parting guest."

I am naturally, beforehand, shy of novelties; new books, new faces, new years,—from some mental twist which makes it difficult in me to face the prospective. I have almost ceased to hope; and am sanguine only in the prospects of other (former) years. I plunge into foregone visions and conclusions. I encounter pell-mell with past disappointments. I am armor proof against old discouragements. I forgive, or overcome in fancy, old adversaries. I play over again for love, as the gamesters phrase it, games, for which I once paid so dear. I would scarce now have any of those untoward accidents and events of my life reversed. I would no more alter them than the incidents of some well-contrived novel. Methinks it is better that I should have pined away seven of my goldenest years, when I was thrall to the fair hair, and fairer eyes, of Alice W——n, than that so passionate a love adventure should be lost. It was better that our family should have missed that legacy, which old Dorrell cheated us of, than that I should have at this moment two thousand pounds *in banco*, and be without the idea of that specious old rogue.

circumstances of peculiar ceremony. In those days the sound of those midnight chimes, though it seemed to raise hilarity in all around me, never failed to bring a train of pensive imagery into my fancy. Yet I then scarce conceived what it meant, or thought of it as a reckoning that concerned me. Not childhood alone, but the young man till thirty, never feels practically that he is mortal. He knows it indeed, and, if need were, he could preach a homily on the fragility of life; but he brings it not home to himself, any more than in a hot June we can appropriate to our imagination the freezing days of December. But now, shall I confess a truth?—I feel these audits but too powerfully. I begin to count the probabilities of my duration, and to grudge at the expenditure of moments and shortest periods, like misers' farthings. In proportion as the years both lessen and shorten, I set more count upon their periods and would fain lay my ineffectual finger upon the spoke of the great wheel. I am not content to pass away "like a weaver's shuttle." Those metaphors solace me not, nor sweeten the unpalatable draught of mortality. I care not to be carried with the tide, that smoothly bears human life to eternity; and reluct at the inevitable course of destiny. I am in love with this green earth; the face of town and country; the unspeakable rural solitudes, and the sweet security of streets. I would set up my tabernacle here. I am content to stand still at the age to which I am arrived; I, and my friends: to be no younger, no richer, no handsomer. I do not want to be weaned by age; or drop like mellow fruit, as they say, into the grave. Any alteration on this earth of mine, in diet or in lodging, puzzles and discomposes me. My household gods plant a terribly fixed foot, and are not rooted up without blood. They do not willingly seek Lavinian shores. A new state of being staggers me.

Sun, and sky, and breeze, and solitary walks, and summer holidays, and the greenness of fields, and the delicious juices of meats and fishes, and society, and the cheerful glass, and candle-light, and fireside conversations, and innocent vanities, and jests, and irony itself—do these things go out with life?

Can a ghost laugh, or shake his gaunt sides, when you are pleasant with him?

And you, my midnight darlings, my Folios! must I part with the intense delight of having you (huge armfuls) in my embraces? Must knowledge come to me, if it come at all, by some awkward experiment of intuition, and no longer by this familiar process of reading?

Shall I enjoy friendships there, wanting the smiling indications which point me to them here,—the recognizable face—the "sweet assurance of a look"—?

In winter this intolerable disinclination to dying—to give it its mildest name—does more especially haunt and beset me. In a genial August noon, beneath a sweltering sky, death is almost problematic. At those times do such poor snakes as myself enjoy an immortality. Then we expand and burgeon. Then are we as strong again, as valiant again, as wise again, and a great deal taller. The blast that nips and shrinks me puts me in thoughts of death. All things allied to the insubstantial wait upon that master feeling; cold, numbness, dreams, perplexity; moonlight itself, with its shadowy and spectral appearances,—that cold ghost of the sun, or Phœbus's sickly sister, like that innutritious one denounced in the Canticles:—I am none of her minions—I hold with the Persian.

Whatsoever thwarts, or puts me out of my way, brings death into my mind. All partial evils, like humors, run into that capital plague sore. I have heard some profess an indifference to life. Such hail the end of their existence as a port of refuge; and speak of the grave as of some soft arms, in which they may slumber as on a pillow. Some have wooed death—but out upon thee, I say, thou foul, ugly phantom! I detest, abhor, execrate, and (with Friar John) give thee to sixscore thousand devils, as in no instance to be excused or tolerated, but shunned as a universal viper; to be branded, proscribed, and spoken evil of! In no way can I be brought to digest thee, thou thin, melancholy privation, or more frightful and confounding positive!

Those antidotes prescribed against the fear of thee are altogether frigid and insulting, like thyself. For what satisfaction hath a man that he shall "lie down with kings and emperors in death," who in his lifetime never greatly coveted the society of such bedfellows?—or, forsooth, that "so shall the fairest face appear?"—why, to comfort me, must Alice W——n be a goblin? More than all, I conceive disgust at those impertinent and misbecoming familiarities inscribed upon your ordinary tombstones. Every dead man must take upon himself to be lecturing me with his odious truism, that "such as he now is, I must

shortly be." Not so shortly, friend, perhaps as thou imaginest. In the meantime I am alive. I move about. I am worth twenty of thee. Know thy betters! Thy New Years' Days are past. I survive, a jolly candidate for 1821. Another cup of wine—and while that turncoat bell that just now mournfully chanted the obsequies of 1820 departed, with changed notes lustily rings in a successor, let us attune to its peal the song made on a like occasion, by hearty, cheerful Mr. Cotton:—

THE NEW YEAR

HARK! the cock crows, and yon bright star
Tells us, the day himself's not far;
And see where, breaking from the night,
He gilds the western hills with light.
With him old Janus doth appear,
Peeping into the future year,
With such a look as seems to say,
The prospect is not good that way.
Thus do we rise ill sights to see,
And 'gainst ourselves to prophesy;
When the prophetic fear of things
A more tormenting mischief brings,
More full of soul-tormenting gall
Than direst mischiefs can befall.
But stay! but stay! methinks my sight,
Better inform'd by clearer light,
Discerns sereneness in that brow
That all contracted seem'd but now.
His reversed face may show distaste,
And frown upon the ills are past;
But that which this way looks is clear,
And smiles upon the Newborn Year.
He looks too from a place so high,
The Year lies open to his eye;
And all the moments open are
To the exact discoverer.
Yet more and more he smiles upon
The happy revolution.
Why should we then suspect or fear
The influences of a year,
So smiles upon us the first morn,
And speaks us good so soon as born.
Plague on't! the last was ill enough,

This cannot but make better proof;
Or, at the worst, as we brush'd through
The last, why so we may this too;
And then the next in reason should
Be superexcellently good:
For the worst ills (we daily see)
Have no more perpetuity
Than the best fortunes that do fall;
Which also bring us wherewithal
Longer their being to support
Than those do of the other sort:
And who has one good year in three,
And yet repines at destiny,
Appears ungrateful in the case,
And merits not the good he has.
Then let us welcome the New Guest
With lusty brimmers of the best;
Mirth always should Good Fortune meet,
And render e'en Disaster sweet:
And though the Princess turn her back,
Let us but line ourselves with sack,
We better shall by far hold out,
Till the next Year she face about.

How say you, reader—do not these verses smack of the rough magnanimity of the old English vein? Do they not fortify like a cordial; enlarging the heart, and productive of sweet blood, and generous spirits, in the concoction? Where be those puling fears of death, just now expressed or affected? Passed like a cloud—absorbed in the purging sunlight of clear poetry—clean washed away by a wave of genuine Helicon, your only Spa for these hypochondries—And now another cup of the generous! and a merry New Year, and many of them, to you all, my masters!

Complete. From the London Magazine,
January, 1821.

MODERN GALLANTRY

IN COMPARING modern with ancient manners, we are pleased to compliment ourselves upon the point of gallantry; a certain obsequiousness, or deferential respect, which we are supposed to pay to females, as females.

I shall believe that this principle actuates our conduct, when I can forget that in the nineteenth century of the era from which we date our civility, we are but just beginning to leave off the very frequent practice of whipping females in public, in common with the coarsest male offenders.

I shall believe it to be influential, when I can shut my eyes to the fact that in England women are still occasionally—hanged.

I shall believe in it when actresses are no longer subject to be hissed off a stage by gentlemen.

I shall believe in it, when Dorimant hands a fishwife across the kennel; or assists the apple woman to pick up her wandering fruit, which some unlucky dray has just dissipated.

I shall believe in it, when the Dorimants in humbler life, who would be thought in their way notable adepts in this refinement, shall act upon it in places where they are not known, or think themselves not observed—when I shall see the traveler for some rich tradesman part with his admired box coat, to spread it over the defenseless shoulders of the poor woman who is passing to her parish on the roof of the same stagecoach with him, drenched in the rain—when I shall no longer see a woman standing up in the pit of a London theatre, till she is sick and faint with the exertion, with men about her, seated at their ease and jeering at her distress; till one that seems to have more manners or conscience than the rest significantly declares "she should be welcome to his seat, if she were a little younger and handsomer." Place this dapper warehouseman, or that rider, in a circle of their own female acquaintance, and you shall confess you have not seen a politer bred man in Lothbury.

Lastly, I shall begin to believe that there is some such principle influencing our conduct, when more than one-half of the drudgery and coarse servitude of the world shall cease to be performed by women.

Until that day comes, I shall never believe this boasted point to be anything more than a conventional fiction; a pageant got up between the sexes, in a certain rank, and at a certain time of life, in which both find their account equally.

I shall be even disposed to rank it among the salutary fictions of life, when in polite circles I shall see the same attentions paid to age as to youth, to homely features as to handsome, to coarse complexions as to clear—to the woman, as she is a woman, not as she is a beauty, a fortune, or a title.

I shall believe it to be something more than a name, when a well-dressed gentleman in a well-dressed company can advert to the topic of female old age without exciting, and intending to excite, a sneer; — when the phrases "antiquated virginity" and such a one has "overstood her market," pronounced in good company, shall raise immediate offense in man, or woman, that shall hear them spoken.

Joseph Paice, of Bread Street Hill, merchant, and one of the directors of the South Sea Company, — the same to whom Edwards, the Shakespeare commentator, has addressed a fine sonnet, — was the only pattern of consistent gallantry I have met with. He took me under his shelter at an early age, and bestowed some pains upon me. I owe to his precepts and example whatever there is of the man of business (and that is not much) in my composition. It was not his fault that I did not profit more. Though bred a Presbyterian, and brought up a merchant, he was the finest gentleman of his time. He had not one system of attention to females in the drawing-room, and another in the shop, or at the stall. I do not mean that he made no distinction. But he never lost sight of sex, or overlooked it in the casualties of a disadvantageous situation. I have seen him stand bareheaded — smile, if you please — to a poor servant girl, while she has been inquiring of him the way to some street — in such a posture of unforced civility as neither to embarrass her in the acceptance, nor himself in the offer, of it. He was no dangler, in the common acceptation of the word, after women; but he reverenced and upheld, in every form in which it came before him, womanhood. I have seen him — nay, smile not — tenderly escorting a market woman, whom he had encountered in a shower, exalting his umbrella over her poor basket of fruit, that it might receive no damage, with as much carefulness as if she had been a countess. To the reverend form of Female Eld he would yield the wall (though it were to an ancient beggar woman) with more ceremony than we can afford to show our grandams. He was the Preux Chevalier of Age; the Sir Calidore, or Sir Tristan, to those who have no Calidores or Tristans to defend them. The roses, that had long faded thence, still bloomed for him in those withered and yellow cheeks.

He was never married, but in his youth he paid his addresses to the beautiful Susan Winstanley, — old Winstanley's daughter of Clapton, — who, dying in the early days of their courtship, con-

firmed in him the resolution of perpetual bachelorship. It was during their short courtship, he told me, that he had been one day treating his mistress with a profusion of civil speeches — the common gallantries — to which kind of thing she had hitherto manifested no repugnance — but in this instance with no effect. He could not obtain from her a decent acknowledgment in return. She rather seemed to resent his compliments. He could not set it down to caprice, for the lady had always shown herself above that littleness. When he ventured on the following day, finding her a little better humored, to expostulate with her on her coldness of yesterday, she confessed, with her usual frankness, that she had no sort of dislike to his attentions; that she could even endure some high-flown compliments; that a young woman placed in her situation had a right to expect all sort of civil things said to her; that she hoped she could digest a dose of adulation, short of insincerity, with as little injury to her humility as most young women; but that — a little before he had commenced his compliments — she had overheard him by accident, in rather rough language, rating a young woman, who had not brought home his cravats quite to the appointed time, and she thought to herself, "As I am Miss Susan Winstanley, and a young lady — a reputed beauty, and known to be a fortune, — I can have my choice of the finest speeches from the mouth of this very fine gentleman who is courting me — but if I had been poor Mary Such-a-one (naming the milliner), — and had failed of bringing home the cravats to the appointed hour, — though perhaps I had sat up half the night to forward them, — what sort of compliments should I have received then? — And my woman's pride came to my assistance, and I thought that if it were only to do me honor, a female, like myself, might have received handsomer usage; and I was determined not to accept any fine speeches, to the compromise of that sex, the belonging to which was, after all, my strongest claim and title to them."

I think the lady discovered both generosity, and a just way of thinking, in this rebuke which she gave her lover; and I have sometimes imagined that the uncommon strain of courtesy which through life regulated the actions and behavior of my friend towards all of womankind indiscriminately, owed its happy origin to this seasonable lesson from the lips of his lamented mistress.

I wish the whole female world would entertain the same notion of these things that Miss Winstanley showed. Then we

should see something of the spirit of consistent gallantry; and no longer witness the anomaly of the same man — a pattern of true politeness to a wife — of cold contempt, or rudeness, to a sister — the idolater of his female mistress — the disparager and despiser of his no less female aunt, or unfortunate — still female — maiden cousin. Just so much respect as a woman derogates from her own sex, in whatever condition placed — her handmaid, or dependant — she deserves to have diminished from herself on that score; and probably will feel the diminution, when youth, and beauty, and advantages, not inseparable from sex, shall lose of their attraction. What a woman should demand of a man in courtship, or after it, is first — respect for her as she is a woman; — and next to that — to be respected by him above all other women. But let her stand upon her female character as upon a foundation; and let the attentions, incident to individual preference, be so many pretty additaments and ornaments — as many, and as fanciful, as you please — to that main structure. Let her first lesson be — with sweet Susan Winstanley — to reverence her sex.

Complete. From the London Magazine,
November, 1822.

POPULAR FALLACIES

THAT ENOUGH IS AS GOOD AS A FEAST

NOT a man, woman, or child, in ten miles round Guildhall, who really believes this saying. The inventor of it did not believe it himself. It was made in revenge by somebody who was disappointed of a regale. It is a vile cold-scrag-of-mutton sophism; a lie palmed upon the palate, which knows better things. If nothing else could be said for a feast, this is sufficient, that from the superflux there is usually something left for the next day. Morally interpreted, it belongs to a class of proverbs which have a tendency to make us undervalue money. Of this cast are those notable observations, that money is not health; riches cannot purchase everything; the metaphor which makes gold to be mere muck, with the morality which traces fine clothing to the sheep's back, and denounces pearl as the unhandsome excretion of an oyster. Hence, too, the phrase which imputes dirt to acres — a sophistry so barefaced that even the

literal sense of it is true only in a wet season. This, and abundance of similar sage saws assuming to inculcate content, we verily believe to have been the invention of some cunning borrower who had designs upon the purse of his wealthier neighbor, which he could only hope to carry by force of these verbal jugglings. Translate any one of these sayings out of the artful metonymy which envelops it, and the trick is apparent. Goodly legs and shoulders of mutton, exhilarating cordials, books, pictures, the opportunities of seeing foreign countries, independence, heart's-ease, a man's own time to himself, are not muck — however we may be pleased to scandalize with that appellation the faithful metal that provides them for us.

Complete. Number VI.

THAT THE WORST PUNS ARE THE BEST

IF BY worst be only meant the most far-fetched and startling, we agree to it. A pun is not bound by the laws which limit nicer wit. It is a pistol let off at the ear, not a feather to tickle the intellect. It is an antic which does not stand upon manners, but comes bounding into the presence, and does not show the less comic for being dragged in sometimes by the head and shoulders. What though it limp a little, or prove defective in one leg — all the better. A pun may easily be too curious and artificial. Who has not at one time or other been at a party of professors (himself perhaps an old offender in that line), where, after ringing a round of the most ingenious conceits, every man contributing his shot, and some there the most expert shooters of the day; after making a poor word run the gauntlet till it is ready to drop; after hunting and winding it through all the possible ambages of similar sounds; after squeezing and hauling and tugging at it till the very milk of it will not yield a drop further — suddenly some obscure, unthought-of fellow in a corner, who was never 'prentice to the trade, whom the company for very pity passed over, as we do by a known poor man when a money subscription is going round, no one calling upon him for his quota, has all at once come out with something so whimsical, yet so pertinent — so brazen in its pretensions, yet so impossible to be denied — so exquisitely good, and so deplorably bad at the same time — that it has proved a Robin

Hood's shot? Anything ulterior to that is despaired of; and the party breaks up, unanimously voting it to be the very worst (that is, best) pun of the evening. This species of wit is the better for not being perfect in all its parts. What it gains in completeness, it loses in naturalness. The more exactly it satisfies the critical, the less hold it has upon some other faculties. The puns which are most entertaining are those which will least bear an analysis. Of this kind is the following, recorded with a sort of stigma in one of Swift's "Miscellanies":

An Oxford scholar, meeting a porter who was carrying a hare through the streets, accosts him with this extraordinary question: "Prithee, friend, is that thy own hare, or a wig?"

There is no excusing this, and no resisting it. A man might blur ten sides of paper in attempting a defense of it against a critic who should be laughter proof. The quibble in itself is not considerable. It is only a new turn given by a little false pronunciation to a very common, though not a very courteous inquiry. Put by one gentleman to another at a dinner party, it would have been vapid; to the mistress of the house, it would have shown much less wit than rudeness. We must take in the totality of time, place, and person: the pert look of the inquiring scholar, the desponding looks of the puzzled porter; the one stopping at leisure, the other hurrying on with his burden; the innocent though rather abrupt tendency of the first member of the question, with the utter and inextricable irrelevancy of the second; the place—a public street—not favorable to frivolous investigations; the affrontive quality of the primitive inquiry (the common question) invidiously transferred to the derivative (the new turn given to it) in the implied satire; namely, that few of that tribe are expected to eat of the good things which they carry, they being in most countries considered rather as the temporary trustees than owners of such dainties—which the fellow was beginning to understand; but then the wig again comes in, and he can make nothing of it; all put together constitute a picture. Hogarth could have made it intelligible on canvas.

Yet nine out of ten critics will pronounce this a very bad pun, because of the defectiveness in the concluding member, which is its very beauty, and constitutes the surprise. The same person shall cry up for admirable the cold quibble from Virgil about the broken Cremona, because it is made out in all its parts, and leaves nothing to the imagination. We venture to call it cold;

because of thousands who have admired it, it would be difficult to find one who has heartily chuckled at it. As appealing to the judgment merely (setting the risible faculty aside) we must pronounce it a monument of curious felicity. But as some stories (applied by Swift to a lady's dress, or mantua, as it was then termed, coming in contact with one of those fiddles called Cremonas), are said to be too good to be true, it may with equal truth be asserted of this biverbal allusion, that it is too good to be natural. One cannot help suspecting that the incident was invented to fit the line. It would have been better had it been less perfect. Like some Virgilian hemistichs, it has suffered by filling up. The *nimium Vicina* was enough in conscience; the *Cremonæ* afterward loads it. It is, in fact, a double pun, and we have always observed that a superfetation in this sort of wit is dangerous. When a man has said a good thing, it is seldom politic to follow it up. We do not care to be cheated a second time; or, perhaps, the mind of man (with reverence be it spoken) is not capacious enough to lodge two puns at a time. The impression, to be forcible, must be simultaneous and undivided.

Complete. Number IX.

THAT WE SHOULD RISE WITH THE LARK

AT WHAT precise minute that little airy musician doffs his night gear, and prepares to tune up his unseasonable matins, we are not naturalists enough to determine. But for a mere human gentleman—that has no orchestra business to call him from his warm bed to such preposterous exercise—we take ten, or half after ten (eleven, of course, during this Christmas solstice), to be the very earliest hour at which he can begin to think of abandoning his pillow. To think of it, we say; for to do it in earnest requires another half hour's good consideration. Not but there are pretty sunrisings, as we are told, and such like gauds abroad in the world, in summertime especially, some hours before what we have assigned, which a gentleman may see, as they say, only for getting up. But having been tempted once or twice, in earlier life, to assist at those ceremonies, we confess our curiosity abated. We are no longer ambitious of being the sun's courtiers, to attend at his morning levees. We hold the good hours of the dawn too sacred to waste them upon

such observances; which have in them, besides, something Pagan and Persic. To say truth, we never anticipated our usual hour, or got up with the sun (as 'tis called), to go a journey, or upon a foolish whole day's pleasuring, but we suffered for it all the long hours after in listlessness and headaches; Nature herself sufficiently declaring her sense of our presumption in aspiring to regulate our frail waking courses by the measures of that celestial and sleepless traveler. We deny not that there is something sprightly and vigorous, at the outset especially, in these break-of-day excursions. It is flattering to get the start of a lazy world, to conquer death by proxy in his image. But the seeds of sleep and mortality are in us; and we pay usually, in strange qualms before night falls, the penalty of the unnatural inversion.

Therefore, while the busy part of mankind are fast huddling on their clothes, or are already up and about their occupations, content to have swallowed their sleep by wholesale, we choose to linger abed, and digest our dreams. It is the very time to recombine the wandering images which night in a confused mass presented; to snatch them from forgetfulness; to shape and mold them. Some people have no good of their dreams. Like fast feeders, they gulp them too grossly to taste them curiously. We love to chew the cud of a foregone vision; to collect the scattered rays of a brighter phantasm, or act over again, with firmer nerves, the sadder nocturnal tragedies; to drag into daylight a struggling and half-vanishing nightmare; to handle and examine the terrors or the airy solaces. We have too much respect for these spiritual communications to let them go so lightly. We are not so stupid or so careless as that imperial forgetter of his dreams, that we should need a seer to remind us of the form of them. They seem to us to have as much significance as our waking concerns; or rather to import us more nearly, as more nearly we approach by years to the shadowy world whither we are hastening. We have shaken hands with the world's business; we have done with it; we have discharged ourselves of it. Why should we get up? We have neither suit to solicit, nor affairs to manage. The drama has shut in upon us at the fourth act. We have nothing here to expect but in a short time a sickbed and a dismissal. We delight to anticipate death by such shadows as night affords. We are already half acquainted with ghosts. We were never much in the world. Disappointment

VII—156

early struck a dark veil between us and its dazzling illusions. Our spirits showed gray before our hairs. The mighty changes of the world already appear as but the vain stuff out of which dramas are composed. We have asked no more of life than what the mimic images in playhouses present us with. Even those types have waxed fainter. Our clock appears to have struck. We are superannuated. In this dearth of mundane satisfaction, we contract politic alliances with shadows. It is good to have friends at court. The abstracted media of dreams seem no ill introduction to that spiritual presence, upon which, in no long time, we expect to be thrown. We are trying to know a little of the usages of that colony; to learn the language, and the faces we shall meet with there, that we may be the less awkward at our first coming among them. We willingly call a phantom our fellow, as knowing we shall soon be of their dark companionship. Therefore we cherish dreams. We try to spell in them the alphabet of the invisible world, and think we know already how it shall be with us. Those uncouth shapes, which, while we clung to flesh and blood, affrighted us, have become familiar. We feel attenuated into their meagre essences, and have given the hand of half-way approach to incorporeal being. We once thought life to be something; but it has unaccountably fallen from us before its time. Therefore we choose to dally with visions. The sun has no purposes of ours to light us to. Why should we get up?

Complete. Number XI.

THAT WE SHOULD LIE DOWN WITH THE LAMB

WE COULD never quite understand the philosophy of this arrangement, or the wisdom of our ancestors in sending us for instruction to these woolly bedfellows. A sheep, when it is dark, has nothing to do but to shut his silly eyes, and sleep if he can. Man found out long sixes. Hail candlelight! without disparagement to sun or moon, the kindliest luminary of the three—if we may not rather style thee their radiant deputy, mild viceroy of the moon! We love to read, talk, sit silent, eat, drink, sleep, by candlelight. They are everybody's sun and moon. This is our peculiar and household planet. Wanting it, what savage unsocial nights must our ancestors have spent, wintering in caves and unillumined fastnesses! They must have lain about and grumbled at one another in the dark. What repartees could have passed, when you must have felt about for a smile, and handled a neighbor's cheek to be sure that he understood it? This accounts for the seriousness of the elder poetry. It has a sombre cast (try Hesiod or Ossian), derived from the tradition of those unlanterned nights. Jokes came in with candles. We wonder how they saw to pick up a pin, if they had any. How did they sup? What a mélange of chance carving they must have made of it! Here one had got a leg of a goat, when he wanted a horse's shoulder; there another had dipped his scooped palm in a kid skin of wild honey, when he meditated right mare's milk. There is neither good eating nor drinking in fresco. Who, even in these civilized times, has never experienced this, when at some economic table he has commenced dining after dusk, and waited for the flavor till the lights came? The senses absolutely give and take reciprocally. Can you tell pork from veal in the dark, or distinguish Sherris from pure Malaga? Take away the candle from the smoking man: by the glimmering of the left ashes, he knows that he is still smoking, but he knows it only by an inference; till the restored light, coming in aid of the olfactories, reveals to both senses the full aroma. Then how he redoubles his puffs! how he burnishes! There is absolutely no such thing as reading but by a candle. We have tried the affectation of a book at noonday in gardens, and in sultry arbors; but it was labor thrown away. Those gay motes in the beam come about you, hovering and teasing, like so many coquettes, that will have you all to themselves, and are jealous of your abstractions. By the midnight taper the writer digests his meditations. By the same light we must approach to their perusal, if we would catch the flame, the odor. It is a mockery, all that is reported of the influential Phœbus. No true poem ever owed its birth to the sun's light. They are abstracted works —

> "Things that were born when none but the still night
> And his dumb candle saw his pinching throes."

Marry, daylight — daylight might furnish the images, the crude material; but for the fine shapings, the true turning and filing (as mine author hath it), they must be content to hold their inspiration of the candle. The mild internal light, that reveals them, like fires on the domestic hearth, goes out in the sunshine. Night and silence call out the starry fancies. Milton's "Morning

Hymn in Paradise," we would hold a good wager, was penned at midnight; and Taylor's rich description of a sunrise smells decidedly of the taper. Even ourself, in these our humbler lucubrations, tune our best-measured cadences (Prose has her cadences) not unfrequently to the charm of the drowsier watchman, "blessing the doors," or the wild sweep of winds at midnight. Even now a loftier speculation than we have yet attempted courts our endeavors. We would indite something about the Solar System. — Betty, bring the candles.

Complete. Number XII.

WALTER SAVAGE LANDOR

(1775-1864)

WALTER SAVAGE LANDOR was born at Warwick, England, January 30th, 1775. He lived to be eighty-five years old, and, according to his passionate admirer, Algernon Charles Swinburne, "in the course of this long life he won for himself such a double crown of glory in verse and in prose as had been won by no other Englishman but Milton." That Landor was a man of the most highly developed intellect is unquestionable, and but for a most singular contradiction he might have been the greatest force in the literature of the nineteenth century. An extreme Republican in his politics, he was in all his literary sympathies an intellectual aristocrat of the severest and most exclusive type. By his politics he alienated the class to which he belonged by virtue of the habits of his mind, and by the haughtiness of his intellectual superiority he excluded from his circle the masses with whom he sympathized. What he stood for in the poetry of the nineteenth century was illustrated when, after publishing his poem of "Gebir" in a first edition in English, he corrected it in a second English edition, and then translated it into Latin, in order to satisfy his own sense of harmony. According to Mr. Swinburne, the Latin version "has a might and melody of line, and a power and perfection of language," by virtue of which "it must always dispute the palm of precedence with the English version." We may well believe it, and regret the more on account of it that Landor's genius was not led by the necessary study of the past to a fuller recognition of the demands of the present and the future. Of his prose writings, his "Pericles and Aspasia," published in 1836, best exhibits the fullness of his knowledge of classical subjects, while his "Imaginary Conversations" (1821-48) more nearly approximates the level of modern taste. His tragedy of "Count Julian," which appeared in 1812, is generally considered the best of his poems, and his admirers sometimes class it with Milton's "Samson Agonistes." Landor's career was erratic. He was expelled from Oxford for firing a gun at the window of a peculiarly obnoxious Tory. In 1808 he served as a volunteer against Napoleon in Spain, and in 1811 married Miss Julia Thuillier, a banker's daughter, with whom he "fell in love at first sight" and from whom he finally separated. Much of his life was spent in Italy, where he died September 17th, 1864.

ADDISON VISITS STEELE

[The time of the visit is shortly after Steele's arrest for debt caused by Addison, supposedly to give him an opportunity for sobriety.]

Addison —

DICK! I am come to remonstrate with you on the unlucky habits which have been so detrimental to your health and fortune.

Steele — Many thanks, Mr. Addison; but really my fortune is not much improved by your arresting me for the hundred pounds; nor is my health, if spirits are an indication of it, on seeing my furniture sold by auction to raise the money.

Addison — Pooh, pooh, Dick! what furniture had you about the house?

Steele — At least I had the armchair, of which you never before had dispossessed me longer than the evening; and happy should I have been to enjoy your company in it again and again, if you had left it me.

Addison — We will contrive to hire another. I do assure you, my dear Dick, I have really felt for you.

Steele — I only wish, my kind friend, you had not put out your feelers quite so far, nor exactly in this direction; and that my poor wife had received an hour's notice; she might have carried a few trinkets to some neighbor. She wanted her salts; and the bailiff thanked her for the bottle that contained them, telling her the gold head of it was worth pretty nearly half a guinea.

Addison — Lady Steele then wanted her smelling bottle? Dear me! the weather, I apprehend, is about to change. Have you any symptoms of your old gout?

Steele — My health has been long on the decline, you know.

Addison — Too well I know it, my dear friend, and I hinted it as delicately as I could. Nothing on earth beside this consideration should have induced me to pursue a measure in appearance so unfriendly. You must grow more temperate . . . you really must.

Steele — Mr. Addison, you did not speak so gravely and so firmly when we used to meet at Will's. You always drank as much as I did, and often invited and pressed me to continue, when I was weary, sleepy, and sick.

Addison — You thought so because you were drunk. Indeed, at my own house I have sometimes asked you to take another glass, in compliance with the rules of society and hospitality.

Steele — Once, it is true, you did it at your house; the only time I ever had an invitation to'dine in it. The Countess was never fond of the wit that smells of wine; her husband could once endure it.

Addison — We could talk more freely, you know, at the tavern. There we have dined together some hundred times.

Steele — Most days, for many years.

Addison — Ah, Dick! Since we first met there, several of our friends are gone off the stage.

Steele — And some are still acting.

Addison — Forbear, my dear friend, to joke and smile at infirmities or vices. Many have departed from us, in consequence, I apprehend, of indulging in the bottle! When passions are excited, when reason is disturbed, when reputation is sullied, when fortune is squandered, and when health is lost by it, a retreat is sounded in vain. Some cannot hear it, others will not profit by it.

Steele — I must do you the justice to declare that I never saw any other effect of hard drinking upon you than to make you more circumspect and silent.

Addison — If ever I urged you, in the warmth of my heart, to transgress the bounds of sobriety, I entreat you as a Christian to forgive me.

Steele — Most willingly, most cordially.

Addison — I feel confident that you will think of me, speak of me, and write of me, as you have ever done, without a diminution of esteem. We are feeble creatures; we want one another's aid and assistance; a want ordained by Providence, to show us at once our insufficiency and our strength. We must not abandon our friends from slight motives, nor let our passions be our interpreters in their own cause. Consistency is not more requisite to the sound Christian than to the accomplished politician.

Steele — I am inconsistent in my resolutions of improvement . . . no man ever was more so; but my attachments have a nerve in them neither to be deadened by ill treatment nor loosened by indulgence. A man grievously wounded knows by the acuteness of the pain that a spirit of vitality is yet in him. I know that I retain my friendship for you by what you have made me suffer.

Addison — Entirely for your own good, I do protest, if you could see it.

If ever you have remembered the anniversary of some day whereon a dear friend was lost to you, tell me whether that anniversary was not purer and even calmer than the day before. The sorrow, if there should be any left, is soon absorbed, and full satisfaction takes place of it, while you perform a pious office to Friendship, required and appointed by the ordinances of Nature. When my Tulliola was torn away from me, a thousand plans were in readiness for immortalizing her memory, and raising a monument up to the magnitude of my grief. The grief itself has done it; the tears I then shed over her assuaged it in me, and did everything that could be done for her, or hoped, or wished. I called upon Tulliola: Rome and the whole world heard me. Her glory was a part of mine, and mine of hers, and when Eternity had received her at my hands, I wept no longer. The tenderness wherewith I mentioned, and now mention her, though it suspends my voice, brings what consoles and comforts me; it is the milk and honey left at the sepulchre, and equally sweet, I hope, to the departed.

The gods, who have given us our affections, permit us rarely the uses and the signs of them. Immoderate grief, like everything else immoderate, is useless and pernicious; but if we did not tolerate and endure it; if we did not prepare for it, meet it, commune with it; if we did not even cherish it in its season,— much of what is best in our faculties, much of our tenderness, much of our generosity, much of our patriotism, much, also, of our genius, would be stifled and extinguished.

When I hear any one call upon another to be manly and restrain his tears, if they flow from the social and the kind affections, I doubt the humanity and distrust the wisdom of the counselor. Were he humane, he would be more inclined to pity and to sympathize than to lecture and reprove; and were he wise, he would consider that tears are given us by nature as a remedy to affliction, although, like other remedies, they should come to our relief in private. Philosophy, we may be told, would prevent the tears, by turning away the sources of them, and by raising up a rampart against pain and sorrow. I am of opinion that philosophy, quite pure and totally abstracted from our appetites and passions, instead of serving us the better, would do us little or no good at all. We may receive so much light as not to see, and so much philosophy as to be worse than foolish.

From « Imaginary Conversations.»

Steele — Alas! all our sufferings are so; the only mischief is that we have no organs for perceiving it.

Addison — You reason well, my worthy sir; and relying on your kindness in my favor (for every man has enemies, and those mostly who serve their friends best), I say, Dick, on these considerations, since you never broke your word with me, and since I am certain you would be sorry it were known that fourscore pounds' worth could be found in the house, I renounce for the present the twenty yet wanting. Do not beat about for an answer; say not one word; farewell.

Steele — Ah! could not that cold heart, often and long as I reposed on it, bring me to my senses! I have, indeed, been drunken; but it is hard to awaken in such heaviness as this of mine is. I shared his poverty with him; I never aimed to share his prosperity. Well, well; I cannot break old habits. I love my glass; I love Addison. Each will partake in killing me. Why cannot I see him again in the armchair, his right hand upon his heart under the fawn-colored waistcoat, his brow erect and clear as his conscience; his wig even and composed as his temper, with measurely curls and antithetical topknots, like his style; the calmest poet, the most quiet patriot; dear Addison! drunk, deliberate, moral, sentimental, foaming over with truth and virtue, with tenderness and friendship, and only the worse in one ruffle for the wine.

Complete. From «Imaginary
Conversations.»

THE PANGS OF APPROACHING THE GODS

(Cicero speaks)

I AM persuaded of the truth in what I have spoken, and yet — ah, Quintus! there is a tear that philosophy cannot dry, and a pang that will rise as we approach the gods.

Two things tend beyond all others, after philosophy, to inhibit and check our ruder passions as they grow and swell in us, and to keep our gentler in their proper play; and these two things are, seasonable sorrow and inoffensive pleasure, each moderately indulged. Nay, there is also a pleasure, humble, it is true, but graceful and insinuating, which follows close upon our very sorrows, reconciles us to them gradually, and sometimes renders us, at last, undesirous altogether of abandoning them.

ANDREW LANG

(1844–)

MOST Scotchmen are serious, but by some miracle Andrew Lang escaped the North British sense of responsibility which would have made him great instead of entertaining. No one who knows him, however, will wish him to be other than he is. He is, perhaps, at his best in his verse of the Old French school, though he is an attractive prose writer on many themes. He writes old English with great purity and clearness, as he has illustrated in his translations from Homer. His « Ballads and Verses Vain » and other poems have been widely read in America, as well as in England, and « The World's Desire,» a novel he published as joint author with Haggard, in 1890, is one of the most entertaining of all the stories of the Argive Helen. As an essayist and reviewer, Lang has long occupied a prominent place in the best English periodicals. He was born at Selkirk, Scotland, March 31st, 1844. After graduating at Oxford, he was made a Fellow of one of its colleges, and in 1888 Gifford lecturer at St. Andrew's University.

THE BERESFORD GHOST STORY

JUST as the anecdote of William Tell and the Apple occurs in various times, and among widely severed races, so, in a minor degree, does the famous Beresford ghost story present itself in mythical fashion. The Beresford tale is told at great length by Dr. F. G. Lee, in his « Glimpses of the Supernatural.» As usual, Dr. Lee does not give the names of his informants, nor trace the channels through which the legend reached them. But he calls his version of the myth, « an authentic record.» To be brief, Lord Tyrone and Miss Blank were orphans, educated in the same house « in the principles of Deism.» When they were about fourteen years of age their preceptor died, and their new guardians tried to « persuade them to embrace revealed religion.» The boy and girl, however, stuck to Deism. But they made a compact that he or she who died first should appear to the survivor « to declare what religion was most approved by the

Supreme Being." Miss Blank married Sir Martin Beresford. One day she appeared at breakfast with a pale face, and a black band round her wrist. Long afterwards, on her deathbed, she explained that this band covered shrunken sinews. The ghost of Lord Tyrone, at the hour of his death, had appeared to her, had prophesied (correctly) her future, and had touched her wrist by way of a sign.

"He struck my wrist; his hand was as cold as marble; in a moment the sinews shrank up, every nerve withered. . . . I bound a piece of black ribbon round my wrist." The black ribbon was formerly in the possession of Lady Betty Cobb, who, during her long life, was ever ready to attest the truth of this narration, as are, to the present hour, the whole of the Tyrone and Beresford families.

Nothing would induce me to dispute the accuracy of a report vouched for by Lady Betty Cobb and all the Tyrones and Beresfords. But I must be permitted to point out that Lord Tyrone merely did what many ghosts had done before in that matter of touching Lady Beresford's wrist. Thus, according to Henry More, "one" (bogie) "took a relation of Melanchthon's by the hand, and so scorched her that she bore the mark of it to her dying day." Before Melanchthon the anecdote was "improved" by Eudes de Shirton in a sermon. According to Eudes, a certain clerk, Serlon, made with a friend the covenant which Miss Blank made with Lord Tyrone. The survivor was to bring news of the next world. Well, the friend died, and punctually appeared to Serlon, "in a parchment cloak, covered with the finest writing in the world." Being asked how he fared, he said that this cloak, a punishment for his love of Logic, weighed heavier than lead, and scorched like the shirt of Nessus. Then he held out his hand and let fall a drop which burned Serlon to the bone —

"And evermore that Master wore
A covering on his wrist."

Before Eudes de Shirton, William of Malmesbury knew this anecdote, which he dates about 1060–1063, and localizes in Nantes. His characters are "two clerks," an Epicurean and a Platonist, who made the usual contract that the first to die should appear to the survivor, and state whether Plato's ideas or "Epicurus his atoms" were the correct reply to the conundrum of the universe.

The visit was to be paid within thirty days of the death. One of the philosophical pair was killed, a month passed, no news of him came. Then, when the other expected nothing less, and was busy with some ordinary matter, the dead man suddenly stood before him. The spectre explained that he had been unable to keep his appointment earlier; and, stretching out his hand, let fall three burning drops of blood, which branded, not the wrist, but the brow of the psychical inquirer. The anecdote recurs later, and is attached by certain commentators on Dante to one Siger de Brabant. Now this legend may be true about Lady Beresford, or about William of Malmesbury's two clerks, or about Siger de Brabant, or about Serlon; but the same facts of a compact, the punctual appearance of the survivor, and the physical sign which he gave, can scarcely have occurred more than once. I am inclined, therefore, to believe that the narrative vouched for by two noble families is accurate, and that the tales of William of Malmesbury, Henry More, Eudes de Shirton, and Siger de Brabant are myths —

"Or such refraction of events
As often rises ere they rise."

From "The Comparative Study
of Ghost Stories."

CELEBRATED LITERARY FORGERIES

THE most famous forgeries of the eighteenth century were those of Macpherson, Chatterton, and Ireland. Space (fortunately) does not permit a discussion of the Ossianic question. That fragments of Ossianic legend (if not of Ossianic poetry) survive in oral Gaelic traditions, seems certain. How much Macpherson knew of these, and how little he used them in the bombastic prose which Napoleon loved (and spelled "Ocean") it is next to impossible to discover. The case of Chatterton is too well known to need much more than mention. The most extraordinary poet for his years who ever lived began with the forgery of a sham feudal pedigree for Mr. Bergum, a pewterer. Ireland started on his career in much the same way, unless Ireland's "Confessions" be themselves a fraud, based on what he knew about Chatterton. Once launched in his career, Chatterton drew endless stores of poetry from "Rowley's MS." and the muni-

ment chest in St. Mary Redcliff's. Jacob Bryant believed in them and wrote an "Apology" for the credulous. Bryant, who believed in his own system of mythology, might have believed in anything. When Chatterton sent his "discoveries" to Walpole (himself somewhat of a mediæval imitator), Gray and Mason detected the imposture, and Walpole, his feelings as an antiquary injured, took no more notice of the boy. Chatterton's death was due to his precocity. Had his genius come to him later, it would have found him wiser and better able to command the fatal demon of intellect, for which he had to find work, like Michael Scott in the legend.

The end of the eighteenth century, which had been puzzled or diverted by the Chatterton and Macpherson frauds, witnessed also the great and famous Shakespearean forgeries. We shall never know the exact truth about the fabrication of the Shakespearean documents, and "Vortigern," and the other plays. We have, indeed, the confession of the culprit; habemus confitentem reum, but Mr. W. H. Ireland was a liar and a solicitor's clerk, so versatile and accomplished that we cannot always believe him, even when he is narrating the tale of his own iniquities. The temporary, but wide and turbulent success of the Ireland forgeries suggests the disagreeable reflection that criticism and learning are (or a hundred years ago were) worth very little as literary touchstones. A polished and learned society, a society devoted to Shakespeare and to the stage, was taken in by a boy of eighteen. Young Ireland not only palmed off his sham documents, most makeshift imitations of the antique, but even his ridiculous verse on the experts. James Boswell went down on his knees and thanked Heaven for the sight of them; and feeling thirsty after these devotions, drank hot brandy and water. Dr. Parr was as readily gulled, and probably the experts, like Malone, who held aloof, were as much influenced by jealousy as by science. The whole story of young Ireland's forgeries is not only too long to be told here, but forms the topic of a novel, "The Talk of the Town," on which Mr. James Payn is at present engaged. The frauds are not likely in his hands to lose either their humor or their complicated interest of plot. To be brief, then, Mr. Samuel Ireland was a gentleman extremely fond of old literature and old books. If we may trust the "Confessions" (1805) of his candid son, Mr. W. H. Ireland, a more harmless and confiding old person than Samuel never collected early English tracts.

Living in his learned society, his son, Mr. W. H. Ireland, acquired not only a passion for black letters, but a desire to emulate Chatterton. His first step in guilt was the forgery of an autograph on an old pamphlet, with which he gratified Samuel Ireland. He also wrote a sham inscription on a modern bust of Cromwell, which he presented as an authentic antique. Finding that the critics were taken in, and attributed this new bust to the old sculptor Simon, Ireland conceived a very low and not unjustifiable opinion of critical tact. Critics would find merit in anything which seemed old enough. Ireland's next achievement was the forgery of some legal documents concerning Shakespeare. Just as the bad man who deceived the guileless Mr. Shapira, forged his Deuteronomy on the blank spaces of old synagogue rolls, so young Ireland used the cut-off ends of old rent rolls. He next bought up quantities of old fly-leaves of books, and on this ancient paper he indited a sham confession of faith, which he attributed to Shakespeare. Being a strong "evangelical," young Mr. Ireland gave a very Protestant complexion to this edifying document. And still the critics gaped and wondered and believed. Ireland's method was to write in an ink made by blending various liquids used in the marbling of paper for bookbinding. This stuff was supplied to him by a bookbinder's apprentice. When people asked questions as to whence all the new Shakespeare manuscripts came, he said they were presented to him by a gentleman who wished to remain anonymous. Finally, the impossibility of producing this gentleman was one of the causes of the detection of the fraud. According to himself, Ireland performed prodigies of acuteness. Once he had forged, at random, the name of a contemporary of Shakespeare. He was confronted with a genuine signature, which, of course, was quite different. He obtained leave to consult his "anonymous gentleman," rushed home, forged the name on the model of what had been shown to him, and returned with this signature as a new gift from his benefactor. That nameless friend had informed him that there were two persons of the same name, and that both signatures were genuine. Ireland's impudence went the length of introducing an ancestor of his own, with the same name as himself, among the companions of Shakespeare. If "Vortigern" had succeeded (and it was actually put on the stage with all possible pomp), Ireland meant to have produced a series of pseudo-Shakespearean plays from William the Conqueror to Queen Elizabeth. When busy with "Vortigern" he was detected by a friend of his own age, who pounced on him while he was at work, as Lasus pounced on Onomacritus. The discoverer, however, consented to "stand in" with Ireland, and did not divulge his secret. At last, after the fiasco of "Vortigern," suspicion waxed so strong, and disagreeable inquiries for the anonymous benefactor were so numerous that Ireland fled from his father's house. He confessed all, and, according to his own account, fell under the undying wrath of Samuel Ireland. Any reader of Ireland's "Confessions" will be likely to sympathize with old Samuel as the dupe of his son. The whole story is told with a curious mixture of impudence and humor, and with great plausibility. Young Ireland admits that his "desire for laughter" was almost irresistible, when people — learned, pompous, sagacious people — listened attentively to the papers. One feels half inclined to forgive the rogue for the sake of his youth, his cleverness, his humor. But the "Confessions" are, not improbably, almost as apocryphal as the original documents. They were written for the sake of money, and it is impossible to say how far the same mercenary motive actuated Ireland in his forgeries. Dr. Ingleby, in his "Shakespeare Fabrications," takes a very rigid view of the conduct, not only of William, but of old Samuel Ireland. Sam, according to Dr. Ingleby, was a partner in the whole imposture, and the "Confessions" was only one element in the scheme of fraud. Old Samuel was the Fagan of a band of young literary Dodgers. He "positively trained his whole family to trade in forgery," and as for Mr. W. H. Ireland, he was "the most accomplished liar that ever lived," which is certainly a distinction in its way. The point of the joke is that, after the whole conspiracy exploded, people were anxious to buy examples of the forgeries. Mr. W. H. Ireland was equal to the occasion. He actually forged his own, or (according to Dr. Ingleby) his father's forgeries, and, by thus increasing the supply, he deluged the market with sham shams, with imitations of imitations. If this accusation be correct, it is impossible not to admire the colossal impudence of Mr. W. H. Ireland. Dr. Ingleby, in the ardor of his honest indignation, pursues William into his private life, which it appears was far from exemplary. But literary criticism should be content with a man's works, his domestic life is matter, as Aristotle often says, "for a separate kind of investigation."

SIDNEY LANIER

(1842–1881)

IN SUSTAINED power of description, De Quincey's "Pains of Opium" is the only essay in the English language which can be rightly classed with "On the Ocklawaha in May," by Sidney Lanier, while, as might be expected, the melody of Lanier's prose is greatly superior to that of De Quincey's. Almost wholly neglected during his lifetime, Lanier was recognized after his death as one of the greatest poets of the nineteenth century. He wrote little, but of that little nothing can be spared. His "Hymns of the Marshes" have been pronounced by his English admirers the greatest poems ever written in America; and if we take purity and sublimity as the standard by which to judge the essential element of great poetry, we need not hesitate to conclude that they are unequaled in the English verse of the nineteenth century. They show a greater intensity than Browning's and a higher lyrical faculty than Tennyson's. Lanier is not Longfellow's equal in breadth; and a life of suffering made him so intensive and introspective that, while distinctly superior to Longfellow in poetic quality, he is greatly his inferior in that most important quality by which the poet who has a message to deliver to mankind succeeds in making it intelligible to the largest possible number of people. Lanier's poetry has been growing steadily in favor with the decrease of sectional prejudices, but as a prose writer he is scarcely known at all. The prose essay by which he is best known is an examination of the fundamental principles of English verse. While it is of interest chiefly to specialists, it is a most extraordinary production. In it Lanier, who was a highly trained musician with an exquisite ear for melody, was carried by his sense of music to a realization of the fundamental principle which governs the melody of Homer and other great classical poets who practiced the Homeric mode. This may be called a coincidence, as Lanier had made no special study of classical verse, and as far as appears was unaware of the fundamental identity of principle governing the music of English verse, and that of the classical poets. But if a coincidence, it is one of governing law — not of chance. Lanier's own verse approximates the melody of the great classical poets, especially of the Horatian lyric and the Virgilian hexameter, to an extent that can never be realized except through the

closest scientific comparison. It is scientifically accurate to say that he illustrates classical modes better than any other poet of the nineteenth century, and classical melody better than any other of the century except Burns. The ear for melody which governs his verse controls every inflection of the wonderful prose of his "On the Ocklawaha in May." Whether he is in jest or earnest, whether he is listening to a deck hand's whistling, or looking at the stars, the simple unforced, thoroughly natural prose in which he expresses his own unconscious sublimity, rises and falls with the free swing of a tune played by a master of the violin expressing his own deepest feelings and highest thoughts in his music. The essay is one of a series on Florida scenery contributed by Lanier to Lippincott's Magazine in 1875. It was afterwards used with others by Florida railroads to advertise the State, and those who read it aloud in his cadences will not need to be told that neither before nor since has any State had such an advertisement. There is no pretense of fine writing or "word painting" about it. The effort which becomes evident in the highest reaches of De Quincey's descriptive writing is nowhere apparent. The reader can hardly avoid the fear that Lanier will break down before the close and lapse into the bathos which so often punishes vigorous American attempts at eloquence; but Lanier is not more vigorous in his attempt than he would be in playing the flute or the violin, and whether he is gay or sad, sublime, or witty, he goes through to the end as easily, as unostentatiously, as naturally, as if the music of his language were really that of the instruments on which he learned "the whole art of composition."

He was born at Macon, Georgia, February 3d, 1842. His father, Robert S. Lanier, was a lawyer of ability and standing; and the family had sufficient means to educate Sidney at Oglethorpe College, where he graduated in 1860. At the age of nineteen he enlisted in the Confederate Army and served until captured near the close of the war, contracting, as a result of hardship and exposure, the disease of the lungs of which, after years of suffering, he died at Lynn, North Carolina, September 7th, 1881. From 1868 to 1872 he studied and practiced law at Macon. In 1873 he removed to Baltimore where he supported himself by playing the flute at concerts, and afterwards (1879–1881) as lecturer on English Literature at Johns Hopkins University. His poems, edited by his wife, were first collected and published in 1884. They have not yet attained general circulation, and they probably will not until they can be reproduced in popular editions. But no one who reads them at all is ever likely to forget them. In such verses as —

"Ye marshes, how candid and simple and nothing-withholding and free,
Ye publish yourselves to the sky and offer yourselves to the sea!

Tolerant plains, that suffer the sea and the rains and the sun,
Ye spread and span like the Catholic man who hath mightily won
God out of knowledge and good out of infinite pain
And sight out of blindness and purity out of a stain,"—

we have a suggestion more nearly adequate than can be found in any other modern poet of the free melody of classical verse, and with it a sublimity of thought which no classical poet ever attained. Lanier's life was one of infinite pathos, and he set it to immortal music.

W. V. B.

ON THE OCKLAWAHA IN MAY

FOR a perfect journey God gave us a perfect day. The little Ocklawaha steamboat Marion — a steamboat which is like nothing in the world so much as a Pensacola gopher with a preposterously exaggerated back — had started from Pilatka some hours before daylight, having taken on her passengers the night previous; and by seven o'clock of such a May morning as no words could describe, unless words were themselves May mornings, we had made the twenty-five miles up the St. John's to where the Ocklawaha flows into that stream nearly opposite Welaka.

Just before entering the mouth of the river, our little gopher boat scrambled alongside a long raft of pine logs which had been brought in separate sections down the Ocklawaha, and took off the lumbermen to carry them back up the stream for another descent, while this raft was being towed by a tug to Jacksonville.

That man who is now stepping from the wet logs to the bow guards of the Marion,—how can he ever cut down a tree? He is a slim, melancholy native, and there is not bone enough in his whole body to make the left leg of a good English coal heaver; moreover, he does not seem to have the least suspicion that a man needs grooming. He is disheveled and wry-trussed to the last degree; his poor weasel jaws nearly touch their inner sides as they suck at the acrid ashes in his dreadful pipe; and there is no single filament of either his hair or his beard that does not look sourly and at wild angles upon its neighbors' filament. His eyes are viscidly unquiet; his nose is merely dreariness come to a point; the corners of his mouth are pendulous with that sort of suffering which involves no particular heroism, such as gnats, or waiting for the corn bread to get done, or being out of tobacco; and his—But, poor devil! I withdraw all that has been said; he has a right to look disheveled and sorrowful; for listen: "Well, sir," he says, with a dilute smile, as he wearily leans his arm against the low deck and settles himself so, though there are a dozen vacant chairs in reach, "ef we didn' have ther sentermentalest rain right thar on them logs last night, I'll be dadbusted!" He had been in it all night.

I fell to speculating on his word "sentermental," wondering by what vague associations with the idea of "centre"—e. g., a centre shot, perhaps, as a shot which beats all other shots—he had arrived at such a form of expletive, or, rather, intensive.

But not long, for presently we rounded the raft, abandoned the broad and garish highway of the St. John's and turned off to the right into the narrow lane of the Ocklawaha, the sweetest water lane in the world—a lane which runs for a hundred miles of pure delight betwixt hedgerows of oaks and cypresses and palms and magnolias and mosses and manifold vine growths; a lane clean to travel along, for there is never a speck of dust in it, save the blue dust and gold dust which the wind blows out of the flags and the lilies; a lane which is as if a typical woods ramble had taken shape, and as if God had turned into water and trees the recollection of some meditative stroll through the lonely seclusions of his own soul.

As we advanced up the stream our wee craft seemed to emit her steam in more leisurely whiffs, as one puffs one's cigar in a contemplative walk through the forest. Dick, the pole man,—a man of marvelous fine function when we shall presently come to the short narrow curves,—lay asleep on the guards, in great peril of rolling into the river over the three inches that intervened between his length and the edge; the people of the boat moved not, spoke not; the white crane, the curlew, the limpkin, the heron, the water turkey were scarcely disturbed in their several vocations as we passed, and seemed quickly to persuade themselves, after each momentary excitement of our gliding by, that we were really, after all, no monster, but only a mere daydream of a monster. The stream, which in its broader stretches reflected the sky so perfectly that it seemed a ribbon of heaven, bound in lovely doublings upon the breast of the land, now began to narrow; the blue of heaven disappeared, and the green of the overleaning trees assumed its place. The lucent current

lost all semblance of water. It was simply a distillation of many-shaded foliages, smoothly sweeping along beneath us. It was green trees fluent. One felt that a subtle amalgamation and mutual give and take had been effected between the natures of water and of leaves. A certain sense of pellucidness seemed to breathe coolly out of the woods on either side of us, while the glassy dream of a forest over which we sailed appeared to send up exhalations of balms and stimulant pungencies and odors.

"Look at that snake in the water!" said a gentleman as we sat on deck with the engineer, just come up from his watch.

The engineer smiled. "Sir, it is a water turkey," he said gently.

The water turkey is the most preposterous bird within the range of ornithology. He is not a bird; he is a Neck, with such subordinate rights, members, appurtenances, and hereditaments thereunto appertaining as seem necessary to that end. He has just enough stomach to arrange nourishment for his neck, just enough wings to fly painfully along with his neck, and just enough legs to keep his neck from dragging on the ground; and, as if his neck were not already pronounced enough by reason of its size, it is further accentuated by the circumstance that it is light colored, while the rest of him is dark.

When the water turkey saw us, he jumped up on a limb and stared. Then suddenly he dropped into the water, sank like a leaden ball out of sight, and made us think he was certainly drowned, when presently the tip of his beak appeared, then the length of his neck lay along the surface of the water, and in this position, with his body submerged, he shot out his neck, drew it back, wriggled it, twisted it, twiddled it, and spirally poked it into the east, the west, the north, and the south, with a violence of involution and a contortionary energy that made one think in the same breath of corkscrews and of lightning.

But what nonsense! All that labor and perilous asphyxiation for a beggarly sprat or a couple of inches of water snake! Yet I make no doubt this same water turkey would have thought us as absurd as we him if he could have seen us taking our breakfast a few minutes later. For as we sat there, some half-dozen men at table in the small cabin, all that sombre melancholy which comes over the average American citizen at his meals descended upon us. No man talked after the first two or three feeble sparks of conversation had gone out; each of us could hear

the other crunching his bread in faucibus, and the noise thereof seemed to me, in the ghastly stillness, like the noise of earthquakes and of crashing worlds. Even our furtive glances toward each other's plates were presently awed down to a sullen gazing of each into his own; the silence increased, the noises became intolerable, a cold sweat broke out over me. I felt myself growing insane, and rushed out to the deck with a sigh as of one saved from a dreadful death by social suffocation.

There is a certain position a man can assume on board the Marion which constitutes an attitude of perfect rest, and leaves one's body in such blessed ease that one's soul receives the heavenly influences of the voyage absolutely without physical impediment. Know, therefore, tired friends that shall hereafter ride up the Ocklawaha,—whose name I would fain call legion,—that if you will place a chair just in the narrow passageway which runs alongside the cabin, at the point where this passageway descends by a step to the open space in front of the pilot house, on the left-hand side as you face the bow, you will, as you sit down in your chair, perceive a certain slope in the railing where it descends by a gentle angle of some thirty degrees to accommodate itself to the step just mentioned; and this slope should be in such a position that your left leg unconsciously stretches itself along the same by the pure insinuating solicitations of the fitness of things, and straightway dreams itself off into Elysian tranquillity. You should then tip your chair in a slightly diagonal direction back to the side of the cabin, so that your head will rest there-against, your right arm will hang over the chair back, and your left arm will repose along the level railing. I might go further and arrange your right leg, but upon reflection I will give no specific instructions for it, because I am disposed to be liberal in this matter, and to leave some gracious scope for personal idiosyncrasies, as well as a margin of allowance for the accidents of time and place. Dispose, therefore, your right leg as your own heart may suggest, or as all the precedent forces of time and of the universe may have combined to require you.

Having secured this attitude, open wide the eyes of your body and of your soul; repulse with heavenly suavity the conversational advances of the natty drummer who fancies he might possibly sell you a bill of white goods and notions, as well as the far-off inquiries of the real-estate person, who has his little private theory that you desire to purchase a site for an orange

grove; thus sail, sail, sail, through the cypresses, through the vines, through the May day, through the floating suggestions of the unutterable that come up, that sink down, that waver and sway hither and thither; so shall you have revelations of rest, and so shall your heart forever afterward interpret Ocklawaha to mean Repose.

Some twenty miles from the mouth of the Ocklawaha, at the right-hand edge of the stream, is the handsomest residence in America. It belongs to a certain alligator of my acquaintance, a very honest and worthy saurian, of good repute. A little cove of water, dark green under the overhanging leaves, placid, pellucid, curves round at the river edge into the flags and lilies with a curve just heartbreaking for the pure beauty of the flexure of it. This house of my saurian is divided into apartments,—little subsidiary bays which are scalloped out by the lily pads according to the sinuous fantasies of their growth. My saurian, when he desires to sleep, has but to lie down anywhere; he will find marvelous mosses for his mattress beneath him; his sheets will be white lily-petals; and the green disks of the lily pads will rise above him as he sinks, and embroider themselves together for his coverlet. He never quarrels with his cook, he is not the slave of a kitchen, and his one housemaid, the stream, forever sweeps his chambers clean. His conservatories there under the glass of that water are ever and without labor filled with the enchantments of strange under-water growths; his parks and his pleasure grounds are bigger than any king's. Upon my saurian's house the winds have no power; the rains are only a new delight to him, and the snows he will never see! Regarding fire, as he does not employ its slavery, so he does not fear its tyranny. Thus, all the elements are the friends of my saurian's house. While he sleeps he is being bathed; what glory to awake sweet and clean, sweetened and cleaned in the very act of sleep! Lastly, my saurian has unnumbered mansions, and can change his dwelling as no human householder may. It is but a mere fillup of his tail, and, lo! he is established in another palace, as good as the last, ready furnished to his liking.

For many miles together the Ocklawaha is, as to its main channel, a river without banks, though not less clearly defined as a stream for that reason. The swift, deep current meanders between tall lines of forests; beyond these, on both sides, there is water also—a thousand shallow runlets lapsing past the bases of multitudes of trees. Along the immediate edges of the stream every tree trunk, sapling, stump, or other projecting coign of vantage is wrapped about with a close-growing vine. At first, like an unending procession of nuns disposed along the aisle of a church, these vine figures stand. But presently, as one journeys, this nun imagery fades out of one's mind; a thousand other fancies float with ever-new vine shapes into one's eyes. One sees repeated all the forms one has ever known, in grotesque juxtapositions. Look! here is a graceful troop of girls, with arms wreathed over their heads, dancing down into the water; here are high velvet armchairs and lovely green fauteuils of divers patterns and of softest cushionment; now the vines hang in loops, in pavilions, in columns, in arches, in caves, in pyramids, in women's tresses, in harps and lyres, in globular mountain ranges, in pagodas, domes, minarets, machicolated towers, dogs, belfries, draperies, fish, dragons; yonder is a bizarre congress — Una on her lion, Angelo's Moses, two elephants with howdahs, the Laocoon group; Arthur and Lancelot, with great brands extended aloft in combat; Adam, bent with love and grief, leading Eve out of Paradise; Cæsar shrouded in his mantle, receiving his stab; Greek chariots, locomotives, brazen shields and cuirasses, columbiads, the Twelve Apostles, the stock exchange; — it is a green dance of all things and times!

The edges of the stream are further defined by flowers and water leaves. The tall blue flags; the ineffable lilies sitting on their round lily pads like white queens on green thrones; the tiny stars and long ribbons of the water grasses; the cunning phalanxes of a species of bar net which, from a long stem that swings off down stream along the surface, sends up a hundred graceful stemlets, each bearing a shield-like disk, and holding it aloft as the antique soldiers held their bucklers to form the *testudo* in attacking, — all these border the river in infinite varieties of purfling and chasement.

The river itself has an errant fantasy and takes many shapes. Presently we came to where it seemed to branch off into four separate curves, like two opposed S's intersecting at their middle point. " Them's the winding Blades," said my raftsman.

To look down these lovely vistas is like looking down the dreams of some young girl's soul; and the gray moss-bearded trees gravely lean over them in contemplative attitudes, as if they were studying, in the way that wise old poets study, the

mysteries and sacrednesses and tender depths of some visible reverie of maidenhood.

And then after this day of glory came a night of glory. Down in these deep-shaded lanes it was dark, indeed, as night drew on. The stream, which had been all day a ribbon of beauty, sometimes blue and sometimes green, now became a black band of mystery. But presently a brilliant flame flares out overhead; they have lighted the pine knots on top of the pilot house. The fire advances up these dark sinuosities, like a brilliant god that for his mere whimsical pleasure calls the black chaos into instantaneous definite forms as he floats along the river curves. The white columns of the cypress trunks, the silver-embroidered crowns of the maples, the green and white galaxies of the lilies, — these all come in a continuous apparition out of the bosom of the darkness, and retire again; it is endless creation succeeded by endless oblivion. Startled birds suddenly flutter into the light, and, after an instant of illuminated flight, melt into the darkness. From the perfect silence of these short flights one derives a certain sense of awe. The mystery of this enormous blackness which is on either hand appears to be about to utter herself in these suddenly articulated forms, and then to change her mind and die back into mystery again.

Now there is a mighty crack and crash; limbs and leaves scrape and scrub along the deck; a bell tinkles below; we stop. In turning a short curve the boat has run her nose smack into the right bank, and a projecting stump has thrust itself sheer through the starboard side. Out, Dick! out, Henry! Dick and Henry shuffle forward to the bow, thrust forth their long white pole against a tree trunk, strain and push and bend to the deck, as if they were salaming the god of night and adversity. The bow slowly rounds into the stream, the wheel turns, and we puff quietly along.

Somewhere back yonder in the stern Dick is whistling. You should hear him! With the great aperture of his mouth and the rounding vibratory surfaces of his thick lips he gets out a mellow breadth of tone that almost entitles him to rank as an orchestral instrument. Here is what he is whistling: —

It is a genuine plagal cadence. Observe the syncopations marked in this tune; they are characteristic of negro music. I have heard negroes change a well-known air by adroitly syncopating it in this way, so as to give it a barbaric effect scarcely imaginable; and nothing illustrates the negro's natural gifts in the way of keeping a difficult tempo more clearly than his perfect execution of airs thus transformed from simple to complex times and accentuations.

Dick has changed his tune: allegro! —

Da capo, of course, and da capo indefinitely; for it ends on the dominant! The dominant is a chord of progress; there is no such thing as stopping. It is like dividing ten by nine, and carrying out the decimal remainders, — there is always one over.

Thus the negro shows that he does not like the ordinary accentuations, nor the ordinary cadences of tunes; his ear is primitive. If you will follow the course of Dick's musical reverie, — which he now thinks is solely a matter betwixt himself and the night, as he sits back there in the stern alone, — presently you will hear him sing a whole minor tune without once using a semitone; the semitone is weak, it is a dilution, it is not vigorous and large like the whole tone; and I have heard a whole congregation of negroes at night, as they were worshiping in their church with some wild song or other, and swaying to and fro with the ecstasy and the glory of it, abandon, as by one consent, the semitone that should come according to the civilized modus, and sing in its place a big lusty whole tone that would shake any man's soul. It is strange to observe that some of the most magnificent effects in advanced modern music are produced by the same method — notably in the works of Asger Hamerik of Baltimore and of Edward Grieg of Copenhagen. Any one who has heard Thomas's orchestra lately will have no difficulty in remembering his delight at the beautiful Nordische Suite by the former writer and the piano concerto by the latter.

As I sat in the cabin to note down Dick's music by the single candle therein, through the door came a slim line of dragon flies, of a small whitish species, out of the dark toward the candle flame, and proceeded incontinently to fly into the same, to get singed and to fall on the table in all varieties of melancholy mayhem, crisp-winged, no-legged, blind, aimlessly fluttering, dead. Now, it so happened that as I came down into Florida out of the North this spring, I passed just such a file of human moths flying toward their own hurt; and I could not help moralizing on it, even at the risk of voting myself a didactic prig. It was in the early April (though even in March I should have seen them all the same), and the Adam insects were all running back northward, — from the St. John's, from the Ocklawaha, from St. Augustine, from all Florida, — moving back indeed, not toward warmth, but toward a cold which equally consumes, to such a degree that its main effect is called consumption. Why should the Florida visitors run back into the catarrhal North in the early spring? What could be more unwise? In New York is not even May simultaneously warm water and iced vinegar? But in Florida May is May. Then why not stay in Florida till May?

But they would not. My route was by the "Atlantic Coast Line," which brings and carries the great mass of the Florida pilgrims. When I arrived at Baltimore there they were; you could tell them infallibly. If they did not have slat boxes with young alligators or green orange-sticks in their hands, you could at any rate discover them by the sea beans rattling against the alligator's teeth in their pockets; when I got aboard the Bay Line steamer which leaves Baltimore every afternoon at four o'clock for Portsmouth, the very officers and waiters on the steamer were talking alligator and Florida visitors. Between Portsmouth and Weldon I passed a train load of them; from Weldon to Wilmington, from Wilmington to Columbia, from Columbia to Augusta, from Augusta to Savanna, from Savanna to Jacksonville, in passenger cars, in parlor cars, in sleeping cars, they thickened as I passed. And I wondered how many of them would, in a little while, be crawling about, crippled in lung, in liver, in limbs, like these flies.

And then it was bedtime.

Let me tell you how to sleep on an Ocklawaha steamer in May. With a small bribe persuade Jim the steward to take the mattress out of your berth and lay it slanting just along the railing that incloses the lower part of the upper deck, to the left of the pilot house. Then lie flat-backed down on the same, draw your blanket over you, put your cap on your head in consideration of the night air, fold your arms, say some little prayer or other, and fall asleep with a star looking right down into your eyes!

When you awake in the morning your night will not seem any longer, any blacker, any less pure, than this perfect white blank in the page, and you will feel as new as Adam.

At sunrise, when I awoke, I found that we were lying still with the boat's nose run up against a sandy bank, which quickly rose into a considerable hill. A sandy-whiskered native came down from the pine cabin on the knoll. "How air ye?" he sang out to our skipper, with an evident expectation is his voice. "Got any freight for me?"

The skipper handed him a heavy parcel in brown wrapper. He examined it keenly with all his eyes, felt it over carefully with all his fingers; his countenance fell, and the shadow of a great despair came over it. "Look a here!" he said, "hain't you brought me no terbacker?"

"Not unless it's in that bundle," said the skipper.

"H—l!" said the native; "hit's nothin' but shot"; and he turned off toward the forest, as we shoved away, with a face like the face of the apostate Julian when the devils were dragging him down the pit.

I would have let my heart go out in sympathy to this man — for the agony of his soaked soul after "terbacker" during the week that must pass ere the Marion come again is not a thing to be laughed at — had I not believed that he was one of the vanilla gatherers. You must know that in the low grounds of the Ocklawaha grows what is called the vanilla plant, and that its leaves are much like those of tobacco. This "vanilla" is now extensively used to adulterate cheap chewing tobacco, as I am informed, and the natives along the Ocklawaha drive a considerable trade in gathering it. The process of their commerce is exceedingly simple, and the bills drawn against the consignments are primitive. The officer in charge of the Marion showed me several of the communications received at various landings during our journey, accompanying shipments of the spurious weed. They were generally about as follows: —

Deer Sir: — .

I send you one bag Verneller, pleeze fetch one par of shus numb 8 and ef enny over fetch twelve yards hoamspin.

Yrs. trly,

————   ————

The captain of the steamer takes the bags to Pilatka, barters the vanilla for the articles specified, and distributes them on the next trip up to their respective owners.

In a short time we came to the junction of Silver Spring "Run," with the Ocklawaha proper. This "run" is a river formed by the single outflow of the waters of Silver Spring, nine miles above. Here new astonishments befell. The water of the Ocklawaha, which had before seemed clear enough, now showed but like a muddy stream as it flowed side by side, unmixing, for a little distance, with this Silver Spring water.

The Marion now left the Ocklawaha and turned into the run. How shall one speak quietly of this journey over transparency? The run is in many places very deep; the white bottom is hollowed out in a continual succession of large spherical holes, whose entire contents of darting fish, of under mosses, of flowers, of submerged trees, of lily stems, of grass ribbons, revealed themselves to us through the lucid fluid as we sailed along thereover. The long series of convex bodies of water filling these great cavities impressed one like a chain of globular worlds composed of a transparent lymph. Great numbers of keen-snouted, long-bodied garfish shot to and fro in unceasing motion beneath us; it seemed as if the underworlds were filled with a multitude of crossing sword blades wielded in tireless thrust and parry by invisible arms.

The shores too had changed. They now opened into clear savannas, overgrown with broad-leafed grass to a perfect level two or three feet above the water, stretching back to the boundaries of cypress and oak; and occasionally, as we passed one of these expanses curving into the forest with a diameter of half a mile, a single palmetto might be seen in or near the centre — perfect type of that lonesome solitude which the Germans call "*Einsamkeit*" (one-some-ness.) Then, again, the palmettoes and cypresses would swarm toward the stream and line its banks.

Thus for nine miles, counting our gigantic rosary of water wonders and lonelinesses, we fared on. Then we rounded to in

the very bosom of Silver Spring itself, and came to the wharf. Here there were warehouses, a turpentine distillery, men running about with boxes of freight and crates of Florida vegetables for the Northern market, country stores with wondrous assortment of goods, — physic, fiddles, groceries, schoolbooks, what-not, — and, a little further up the shore of the spring, a tavern. I learned, in a hasty way, that Ocala was five miles distant, that I could get a very good conveyance from the tavern to that place, and that on the next day, Sunday, a stage would leave Ocala for Gainesville, some forty miles distant, being the third relay of the long stage line which runs three times a week between Tampa and Gainesville *via* Brooksville and Ocala.

Then the claims of scientific fact and of guidebook information could hold me no longer. I ceased to acquire knowledge, and got me back to the wonderful Spring, drifting over it, face downward, as over a new world. It is sixty feet deep a few feet off shore, they say, and covers an irregular space of several acres; but this sixty feet does not at all represent the actual impression of depth which one gets as one looks through the superincumbent water down to the bottom. The distinct sensation is, that, although the bottom down there is clearly seen, and although all the objects in it are about of their natural size, undiminished by any narrowing of the visual angle, yet it and they are seen from a great distance. It is as if Depth itself, that subtle abstraction, had been compressed into a crystal lymph, one inch of which would represent miles of ordinary depth.

As one rises from gazing into these quaint profundities, and glances across the broad surface of the spring, one's eye is met by a charming mosaic of brilliant hues. The water plain varies in color according to what it lies upon. Over the pure white limestone and shells of the bottom it is perfect malachite green; over the water grass it is a much darker green; over the moss it is that rich brown and green which Bodmer's forest engravings so vividly suggest; over neutral bottoms it reflects the sky's or the clouds' colors. All these hues are further varied by mixture with the manifold shades of foliage reflections cast from over-hanging boscage near the shore, and still further by the angle of the observer's eye. One would think that these elements of color variation were numerous enough, but they were not nearly all. Presently the splash of an oar in some distant part of the spring sent a succession of ripples circling over the

pool. Instantly it broke into a thousandfold prism. Every ripple was a long curve of variegated sheen; the fundamental hues of the pool when at rest were distributed into innumerable kaleidoscope flashes and brilliancies; the multitudes of fish became multitudes of animated gems, and the prismatic lights seemed actually to waver and play through their translucent bodies, until the whole spring, in a great blaze of sunlight, shown like an enormous fluid jewel that, without decreasing, forever lapsed away upward in successive exhalations of dissolving sheens and glittering colors.

Complete. From Lippincott's Magazine 1875. Reproduced by permission. Copyright, 1875, by J. B. Lippincott & Co.

JOHANN CASPAR LAVATER

(1741-1801)

JOHANN CASPAR LAVATER is chiefly celebrated for his attempt to formulate a science of physiognomy, but he was noted in his own generation as a poet and theologian. He was born at Zurich, Switzerland, November 15th, 1741, and educated there for the Church. He passed his life in his native town, and wrote there the "Swiss Songs" (1767) and "The Looks into Eternity" (1768), which gave him his first reputation. His celebrated work on "Physiognomy," to which Goethe contributed a chapter, appeared in 1775-78. While he did not reduce physiognomy to an exact science, Lavater's good qualities of mind and style so appealed to the universal wish that such a science were possible as to immortalize the book. Lavater died January 2d, 1801, as a result of protracted suffering caused by a wound received from infuriated soldiers he was attempting to appease after the taking of Zurich by the French in 1799.

ON READING CHARACTER

ALL countenances, all forms, all created beings, are not only different from each other in their classes, races, and kinds, but are also individually distinct.

Each being differs from every other being of its species. However generally known, it is a truth the most important to our purpose, and necessary to repeat, that: "There is no rose perfectly similar to another rose, no egg to an egg, no eel to an eel, no lion to a lion, no eagle to an eagle, no man to a man."

Confining this proposition to man only, it is the first, the most profound, most secure, and unshaken foundation stone of physiognomy that, however intimate the analogy and similarity of the innumerable forms of men, no two men can be found who, brought together, and accurately compared, will not appear to be very remarkably different.

Nor is it less incontrovertible that it is equally impossible to find two minds, as two countenances, which perfectly resemble each other.

This consideration alone will be sufficient to make it received as a truth, not requiring further demonstration, that there must be a certain native analogy between the external varieties of the countenance and form, and the internal varieties of the mind. Shall it be denied that this acknowledged internal variety among all men is the cause of the external variety of their forms and countenances? Shall it be affirmed that the mind does not influence the body, or that the body does not influence the mind?

Anger renders the muscles protuberant; and shall not therefore an angry mind and protuberant muscles be considered as cause and effect?

After repeated observation that an active and vivid eye and an active and acute wit are frequently found in the same person, shall it be supposed that there is no relation between the active eye and the active mind? Is this the effect of accident? Of accident! Ought it not rather to be considered as sympathy, an interchangeable and instantaneous effect, when we perceive that, at the very moment the understanding is most acute and penetrating and the wit the most lively, the motion and fire of the eye undergo, at that moment, the most visible change?

Shall the open, friendly, and unsuspecting eye and the open, friendly, and unsuspecting heart be united in a thousand instances, and shall we say the one is not the cause, the other the effect?

Shall Nature discover wisdom and order in all things; shall corresponding causes and effects be everywhere united; shall this be the most clear, the most indubitable of truths; and in the first, the most noble of the works of Nature, shall she act arbitrarily, without design, without law? The human countenance, that mirror of the Divinity, that noblest of the works of the Creator,—shall not motive and action, shall not the correspondence between the interior and the exterior, the visible and the invisible, the cause and the effect, be there apparent?

Yet this is all denied by those who oppose the truth of the science of physiognomy.

Truth, according to them, is ever at variance with itself. Eternal order is degraded to a juggler, whose purpose it is to deceive.

Calm reason revolts at the supposition that Newton or Leibnitz ever could have the countenance and appearance of an idiot, incapable of a firm step, a meditating eye; of comprehending

the least difficult of abstract propositions, or of expressing himself so as to be understood; that one of these in the brain of a Laplander conceived his Theodica; and that the other in the head of an Eskimo, who wants the power to number further than six, and affirms all beyond to be innumerable, had dissected the rays of light, and weighed worlds.

Calm reason revolts when it is asserted that the strong man may appear perfectly like the weak, the man in full health like another in the last stage of a consumption, or that the rash and irascible may resemble the cold and phlegmatic. It revolts to hear it affirmed that joy and grief, pleasure and pain, love and hatred, all exhibit themselves under the same traits; that is to say, under no traits whatever, on the exterior of man. Yet such are the assertions of those who maintain physiognomy to be a chimerical science. They overturn all that order and combination by which eternal wisdom so highly astonishes and delights the understanding. It cannot be too emphatically repeated that blind chance and arbitrary disorder constitute the philosophy of fools; and that they are the bane of natural knowledge, philosophy, and religion. Entirely to banish such a system is the duty of the true inquirer, the sage, and the divine.

All men (this is indisputable), absolutely all men, estimate all things whatever by their physiognomy, their exterior, temporary superficies. By viewing these on every occasion, they draw their conclusions concerning their internal properties.

What merchant, if he be unacquainted with the person of whom he purchases, does not estimate his wares by the physiognomy or appearance of those wares? If he purchase of a distant correspondent, what other means does he use in judging whether they are or are not equal to his expectation? Is not his judgment determined by the color, the fineness, the superficies, the exterior, the physiognomy? Does he not judge money by its physiognomy? Why does he take one guinea and reject another? Why weigh a third in his hand? Does he not determine according to its color, or impression; its outside, its physiognomy? If a stranger enter his shop, as a buyer or seller, will he not observe him? Will he not draw conclusions from his countenance? Will he not, almost before he is out of hearing, pronounce some opinion upon him, and say: "This man has an honest look," "That man has a pleasing, or forbidding, countenance"? What is it to the purpose whether his judgment be right or wrong? He

judges. Though not wholly, he depends in part upon the exterior form, and thence draws inferences concerning the mind.

How does the farmer, walking through his grounds, regulate his future expectations by the color, the size, the growth, the exterior; that is to say, by the physiognomy of the bloom, the stalk, or the ear, of his corn; the stem and shoots of his vine tree? "This ear of corn is blighted," "That wood is full of sap; this will grow, that not," affirms he, at the first or second glance. "Though these vine shoots look well, they will bear but few grapes." And wherefore? He remarks, in their appearance, as the physiognomist in the countenances of shallow men, the want of native energy. Does not he judge by the exterior?

Does not the physician pay more attention to the physiognomy of the sick than to all the accounts that are brought him concerning his patient? Zimmermann, among the living, may be brought as a proof of the great perfection at which this kind of judgment has arrived; and among the dead, Kempf, whose son has written a treatise on "Temperament."

The painter—Yet of him I will say nothing; his art too evidently reproves the childish and arrogant prejudices of those who pretend to disbelieve physiognomy.

The traveler, the philanthropist, the misanthrope, the lover, (and who not?) all act according to their feelings and decisions, true or false, confused or clear, concerning physiognomy. These feelings, these decisions, excite compassion, disgust, joy, love, hatred, suspicion, confidence, reserve, or benevolence.

Do we not daily judge of the sky by its physiognomy? No food, not a glass of wine or beer, not a cup of coffee or tea, comes to table, which is not judged by its physiognomy, its exterior, and of which we do not thence deduce some conclusion respecting its interior, good or bad properties.

Is not all nature physiognomy, superficies and contents; body and spirit; exterior effect and internal power; invisible beginning and visible ending?

What knowledge is there, of which man is capable, that is not founded on the exterior; the relation that exists between visible and invisible, the perceptible and the imperceptible?

Physiognomy, whether understood in its most extensive or confined signification, is the origin of all human decisions, efforts, actions, expectations, fears, and hopes; of all pleasing and unpleasing sensations, which are occasioned by external objects.

From the cradle to the grave, in all conditions and ages, throughout all nations, from Adam to the last existing man, from the worm we tread on to the most sublime of philosophers, (and why not to the angel, why not to the Mediator Christ?) physiognomy is the origin of all we do and suffer.

Each insect is acquainted with its friend and its foe; each child loves and fears, although it knows not why. Physiognomy is the cause; nor is there a man to be found on earth who is not daily influenced by physiognomy; not a man who cannot figure to himself a countenance which shall to him appear exceedingly lovely, or exceedingly hateful; not a man who does not, more or less, the first time he is in company with a stranger, observe, estimate, compare, and judge him, according to appearances, although he might never have heard of the word or thing called physiognomy; not a man who does not judge of all things that pass through his hands, by their physiognomy; that is, of their internal worth by their external appearance.

WILLIAM EDWARD HARTPOLE LECKY

(1838–)

WILLIAM EDWARD HARTPOLE LECKY was born near Dublin, Ireland, March 26th, 1838, and educated at Cheltenham College and at Trinity College, Dublin. His first work "The Leaders of Public Opinion in Ireland," which appeared in 1861, did not attract general attention; but "The History of the Rise and Influence of the Spirit of Rationalism in Europe," which followed four years later, made him one of the most influential historical writers of his generation. In 1869 he followed it with his "History of European Morals from Augustus to Charlemagne," which is by many considered his masterpiece. He has published numerous other works, including a volume of poems, whose extraordinary lack of merit is wholly unaccountable, in view of the extraordinary goodness of his prose style. In 1896 he was elected to Parliament as a representative of Dublin University.

MONTAIGNE AND MIDDLE-AGE SUPERSTITION

IT HAS been justly remarked by Malebranche, that Montaigne is an example of a writer who had no pretensions to be a great reasoner, but who, nevertheless, exercised a most profound and general influence upon the opinions of mankind. It is not, I think, difficult to discover the explanation of the fact. In an age which was still spellbound by the fascinations of the past, he applied to every question a judgment entirely unclouded by the imaginations of theologians, and unshackled by the dictates of authority. His originality consists not so much in his definite opinions or in his arguments, as in the general tone and character of his mind. He was the first French author who had entirely emancipated himself from the retrospective habits of thought that had so long been universal; who ventured to judge all questions by a secular standard, by the light of common sense, by the measure of probability which is furnished by daily experience. He was, no doubt, perfectly aware that "the laws of Plato, of the twelve tables, of the consuls, of the emperors, and

of all nations and legislators,—Persian, Hebrew, Greek, Latin, German, French, Italian, Spanish, English,—had decreed capital penalties against sorcerers"; he knew that "prophets, theologians, doctors, judges, and magistrates, had elucidated the reality of the crime by many thousand violent presumptions, accusations, testimonies, convictions, repentances, and voluntary confessions, persisted in to death"; but he was also sensible of the extreme fallibility of the human judgment; of the facility with which the mind discovers, in the phenomena of history, a reflection of its preconceived notions; and of the rapidity with which systems of fiction are formed in a credulous and undiscriminating age. While Catholics, Protestants, and Deists were vying with each other in their adoration of the past; while the ambition of every scholar and of every theologian was to form around his mind an atmosphere of thought that bore no relation to the world that was about him; while knowledge was made the bondslave of credulity, and those whose intellects were most shackled by prejudice were regarded as the wisest of mankind, it was the merit of Montaigne to rise, by the force of his masculine genius, into the clear world of reality; to judge the opinions of his age with an intellect that was invigorated, but not enslaved, by knowledge; and to contemplate the systems of the past, without being dazzled by the reverence that had surrounded them. He looked down upon the broad field of history, upon its clashing enthusiasms, its discordant systems, the ebb and flow of its ever-changing belief, and he drew from the contemplation a lesson widely different from his contemporaries. He did not, it is true, fully recognize those moral principles which shine with an unchanging splendor above the fluctuations of speculative opinions; he did not discover the great laws of eternal development which preside over and direct the progress of belief, infuse order into the seeming chaos, and reveal in every apparent aberration the traces of a superintending Providence; but he, at least, obtained an intense and realized perception of the fallibility of the human intellect; a keen sense of the absurdity of an absolute deference to the past, and of the danger of punishing men with death on account of opinions concerning which we can have so little assurance. These things led him to suspect that witchcraft might be a delusion. The bent and character of his mind led him to believe that witchcraft was grossly improbable. He was the first great representative of the modern secular and rationalistic spirit.

By extricating his mind from the trammels of the past, he had learned to judge the narratives of diabolical intervention by a standard and with a spirit that had been long unknown. The predisposition of the old theologians had been to believe that the phenomena of witchcraft were all produced by the Devil; and, when some manifest signs of madness or of imposture were exhibited, they attempted to accommodate them to their supernatural theory. The strong predisposition of Montaigne was to regard witchcraft as the result of natural causes; and, therefore, though he did not attempt to explain all the statements which he had heard, he was convinced that no conceivable improbability could be as great as that which would be involved in their reception. This was not the happy guess of ignorance. It was the result of a mode of thought which he applied to all theological questions. Fifty years earlier, a book embodying such conceptions would have appeared entirely incomprehensible, and its author would perhaps have been burned. At the close of the sixteenth century, the minds of men were prepared for its reception, and it flashed like a revelation upon France. From the publication of the "Essays" of Montaigne, we may date the influence of that gifted and ever-enlarging rationalistic school, which gradually effected the destruction of the belief in witchcraft, not by refuting or explaining its evidence, but simply by making men more and more sensible of its intrinsic absurdity.

From "Rationalism in Europe."

SEX AND MORAL CHARACTER

MORALLY, the general superiority of women over men is, I think, unquestionable. If we take the somewhat coarse and inadequate criterion of police statistics, we find that, while the male and female populations are nearly the same in number, the crimes committed by men are usually rather more than five times as numerous as those committed by women; and although it may be justly observed that men, as the stronger sex, and the sex upon whom the burden of supporting the family is thrown, have more temptations than women, it must be remembered, on the other hand, that extreme poverty which verges upon starvation is most common among women, whose means of livelihood are most restricted, and whose earnings are smallest and most precarious. Self-sacrifice is the most conspicuous element of a virtuous and religious character, and it is certainly far less common among men than among women, whose whole lives are usually spent in yielding to the will and consulting the pleasures of another.

There are two great departments of virtue: the impulsive, or that which springs spontaneously from the emotions, and the deliberative, or that which is performed in obedience to the sense of duty; and in both of these I imagine women are superior to men. Their sensibility is greater, they are more chaste both in thought and act, more tender to the erring, more compassionate to the suffering, more affectionate to all about them. On the other hand, those who have traced the course of the wives of the poor, and of many who, though in narrow circumstances, can hardly be called poor, will probably admit that in no other class do we so often find entire lives spent in daily persistent self-denial, in the patient endurance of countless trials, in the ceaseless and deliberate sacrifice of their own enjoyments to the well-being or the prospects of others. In active courage women are inferior to men. In the courage of endurance they are commonly their superiors; but their passive courage is not so much fortitude which bears and defies, as resignation which bears and bends. In the ethics of intellect they are decidedly inferior. To repeat an expression I have already employed, women very rarely love truth, though they love passionately what they call "the truth," or opinions they have received from others, and hate vehemently those who differ from them. They are little capable of impartiality or of doubt; their thinking is chiefly a mode of feeling; though very generous in their acts, they are rarely generous in their opinions, and their leaning is naturally to the side of restriction. They persuade rather than convince, and value belief rather as a source of consolation than as a faithful expression of the reality of things. They are less capable than men of perceiving qualifying circumstances, of admitting the existence of elements of good in systems to which they are opposed, of distinguishing the personal character of an opponent from the opinions he maintains. Men lean most to justice, and women to mercy. Men are most addicted to intemperance and brutality, women to frivolity and jealousy. Men excel in energy, self-reliance, perseverance, and magnanimity; women in humility, gentleness, modesty, and endurance. The realizing imagination which causes us to pity and

to love is more sensitive in women than in men, and it is especially more capable of dwelling on the unseen. Their religious or devotional realizations are incontestably more vivid; and it is probable that, while a father is most moved by the death of a child in his presence, a mother generally feels most the death of a child in some distant land. But though more intense, the sympathies of women are commonly less wide than those of men. Their imaginations individualize more; their affections are, in consequence, concentrated rather on leaders than on causes; and if they care for a great cause, it is generally because it is represented by a great man, or connected with some one whom they love. In politics their enthusiasm is more naturally loyalty than patriotism. In history they are even more inclined than men to dwell exclusively upon biographical incidents or characteristics as distinguished from the march of general causes. In benevolence, they excel in charity, which alleviates individual suffering, rather than in philanthropy, which deals with large masses, and is more frequently employed in preventing than in allaying calamity. It was a remark of Winckelmann, that "the supreme beauty of Greek art is rather male than female"; and the justice of this remark has been amply corroborated by the greater knowledge we have of late years attained of the works of the Phidian period, in which art achieved its highest perfection, and in which, at the same time, force, and freedom, and masculine grandeur, were its pre-eminent characteristics. A similar observation may be made of the moral ideal of which ancient art was simply the expression. In antiquity the virtues that were most admired were almost exclusively those which are distinctively masculine. Courage, self-assertion, magnanimity, and, above all, patriotism, were the leading features of the ideal type; and chastity, modesty, and charity, the gentler and the domestic virtues, which are especially feminine, were greatly undervalued.

With the single exception of conjugal fidelity, none of the virtues that were very highly prized were virtues distinctively or pre-eminently feminine. With this exception, nearly all the illustrious women of antiquity were illustrious chiefly because they overcame the natural conditions of their sex. It is a characteristic fact that the favorite female ideal of the artists appears to have been the Amazon. We may admire the Spartan mother, or the mother of the Gracchi, repressing every sign of grief when their children were sacrificed upon the altar of their country; we

may wonder at the majestic courage of a Porcia, or an Arria, but we extol them chiefly because, being women, they emancipated themselves from the frailty of their sex, and displayed a heroic fortitude worthy of the strongest and the bravest of men. We may bestow an equal admiration upon the noble devotion and charity of a St. Elizabeth of Hungary, or a Mrs. Fry, but we do not admire them because they displayed these virtues, although they were women, for we feel that their virtues were of the kind which the female nature is most fitted to produce. The change from the heroic to the saintly ideal, from the ideal of Paganism to the ideal of Christianity, was a change from a type which was essentially male to one which was essentially feminine. Of all the great schools of philosophy, no other reflected so faithfully the Roman conception of moral excellence as Stoicism, and the greatest Roman exponent of Stoicism summed up its character in a single sentence when he pronounced it to be beyond all other sects the most emphatically masculine. On the other hand, an ideal type in which meekness, gentleness, patience, humility, faith, and love are the most prominent features, is not naturally male, but female. A reason probably deeper than the historical ones which are commonly alleged, why sculpture has always been peculiarly Pagan and painting peculiarly Christian, may be found in the fact that sculpture is especially suited to represent male beauty, or the beauty of strength, and painting female beauty, or the beauty of softness; and that Pagan sentiment was chiefly a glorification of the masculine qualities of strength, and courage, and conscious virtue, while Christian sentiment is chiefly a glorification of the feminine qualities of gentleness, humility, and love. The painters whom the religious feeling of Christendom has recognized as the most faithful exponents of Christian sentiment have always been those who infused a large measure of feminine beauty even into their male characters; and we never, or scarcely ever, find that the same artist has been conspicuously successful in delineating both Christian and Pagan types. Michael Angelo, whose genius loved to expatiate on the sublimity of strength and defiance, failed signally in his representations of the Christian ideal; and Perugino was equally unsuccessful when he sought to portray the features of the heroes of antiquity. The position that was gradually assigned to the Virgin as the female ideal in the belief and the devotion of Christendom was a consecration or an expression of

the new value that was attached to the feminine virtues. The general superiority of women to men in the strength of their religious emotions, and their natural attraction to a religion which made personal attachment to its Founder its central duty, and which imparted an unprecedented dignity and afforded an unprecedented scope to their characteristic virtues, account for the very conspicuous position they assumed in the great work of the conversion of the Roman Empire.

From the "History of European Morals."

HUGH SWINTON LEGARÉ

(1789-1843)

HUGH SWINTON LEGARÉ, a distinguished scholar and essayist of South Carolina, was born at Charleston, January 2d, 1789. His attention as a writer was divided between the classical studies, of which he was fond, and politics, into which as one of the best-educated men of his State, during its formative period, he was almost necessarily drawn. He represented South Carolina in Congress from 1837 to 1839, retiring to serve as Attorney-General and Secretary of State from 1841 to his death in June, 1843. His style as a prose writer is a valuable illustration of the evolution of American prose through forms derived from oratory.

LIBERTY AND GREATNESS

THE name of Republic is inscribed upon the most imperishable monuments of the species, and it is probable that it will continue to be associated, as it has been in all past ages, with whatever is heroic in character, and sublime in genius, and elegant and brilliant in the cultivation of arts and letters. It would not have been difficult to prove that the base hirelings who, in this age of legitimacy and downfall, have so industriously inculcated a contrary doctrine, have been compelled to falsify history and abuse reason. I might have "called up antiquity from the old schools of Greece" to show that these apostles of despotism would have passed at Athens for barbarians and slaves. I might have asked triumphantly, What land had even been visited with the influences of liberty, that did not flourish like the spring? What people had ever worshiped at her altars, without kindling with a loftier spirit and putting forth more noble energies? Where she had ever acted, that her deeds had not been heroic? Where she had ever spoken, that her eloquence had not been triumphant and sublime? It might have been demonstrated that a state of society in which nothing is obtained by patronage — nothing is yielded to the accidents of birth and fortune — where those who are already distinguished must

exert themselves lest they be speedily eclipsed by their inferiors, and these inferiors are, by every motive, stimulated to exert themselves that they may become distinguished — and where, the lists being open to the whole world, without any partiality or exclusion, the champion who bears off the prize must have tasked his powers to the very uttermost, and proved himself the first of a thousand competitors — is necessarily more favorable to a bold, vigorous, and manly way of thinking and acting, than any other. I should have asked with Longinus, Who but a Republican could have spoken the Philippics of Demosthenes? and what has the patronage of despotism ever done to be compared with the spontaneous productions of the Attic, the Roman, and the Tuscan muse?

With respect to ourselves, who have been so systematically vilified by British critics — if any answer were expected to be given to their shallow and vulgar sophistry, and there was not a sufficient practical refutation of it, in the undoubted success of some of the artists and writers that are springing up in our own times — we should be perfectly safe, in resting, upon the operation of general causes and the whole analogy of history, our anticipation of the proudest success, in all the pursuits of a high and honorable ambition. That living, as we do, in the midst of a forest, we have been principally engaged in felling and improving it; and that those arts, which suppose wealth and leisure and a crowded population, are not yet so flourishing amongst us as they will be in the course of a century or two, is so much a matter of course, that, instead of exciting wonder and disgust, one is only surprised how it should even have attracted notice; but the question whether we are destitute of genius and sensibility and loftiness of character, and all the aspirings that prompt to illustrious achievements, and all the elements of national greatness and glory, is quite a distinct thing, and we may appeal, with confidence, to what we have done and to what we are, to the Revolution we are this day celebrating, to the career we have since run, to our recent exploits upon the flood and in the field, to the skill of our diplomacy, to the comprehensive views and undoubted abilities of our statesmen, to the virtues and prosperity of our people, to the exhibition on every occasion of all the talents called for by its exigencies and admitted by its nature; nay, to the very hatred — the vehement and irrepressible hatred with which these revilers themselves have so abundantly

honored us — to show that nothing can be more preposterous than the contempt with which they have sometimes affected to speak of us.

And, were there no other argument, as there are many, to prove that the character of the nation is altogether worthy of its high destinies, would it not be enough to say that we live under a form of government and in a state of society to which the world has never yet exhibited a parallel? Is it then nothing to be free? How many nations, in the whole annals of human kind have proved themselves worthy of being so? Is it nothing that we are Republicans? Were all men as enlightened, as brave, as proud as they ought to be, would they suffer themselves to be insulted with any other title? Is it nothing that so many independent sovereignties should be held together in such a confederacy as ours? What does history teach us of the difficulty of instituting and maintaining such a polity, and of the glory that, of consequence, ought to be given to those who enjoy its advantages in so much perfection and on so grand a scale? For can anything be more striking and sublime than the idea of an imperial republic, spreading over an extent of territory more immense than the empire of the Cæsars, in the accumulated conquests of a thousand years — without prefects or proconsuls or publicans — founded in the maxims of common sense — employing within itself no arms but those of reason — and known to its subjects only by the blessings it bestows or perpetuates, yet capable of directing against a foreign foe all the energies of a military despotism — a Republic in which men are completely insignificant, and principles and laws exercise throughout its vast dominion a peaceful and irresistible sway, blending in one divine harmony such various habits and conflicting opinions, and mingling in our institutions the light of philosophy with all that is dazzling in the associations of heroic achievement and extended domination, and deep-seated and formidable power!

From "Characteristics of the American
Revolution."

A MIRACULOUS PEOPLE

IT is impossible to contemplate the annals of Greek literature and art without being struck with them, as by far the most extraordinary and brilliant phenomena in the history of the human mind. The very language — even in its primitive simplicity, as it came down from the rhapsodists who celebrated the exploits of Hercules and Theseus, was as great a wonder as any it records. All the other tongues that civilized man has spoken are poor and feeble and barbarous, in comparison with it. Its compass and flexibility, its riches and its powers, are altogether unlimited. It not only expresses with precision all that is thought or known at any given period, but it enlarges itself naturally, with the progress of science, and affords, as if without an effort, a new phrase, or a systematic nomenclature whenever one is called for. It is equally adapted to every variety of style and subject — to the most shadowy subtlety of distinction, and the utmost exactness of definition, as well as to the energy and the pathos of popular eloquence — to the majesty, the elevation, the variety of the epic, and the boldest license of the dithyrambic, no less than to the sweetness of the elegy, the simplicity of the pastoral, or the heedless gayety and delicate characterization of comedy. Above all what is an unspeakable charm — a sort of naïveté is peculiar to it, which appears in all those various styles, and is quite as becoming and agreeable in a historian or a philosopher — Xenophon for instance — as in the light and jocund numbers of Anacreon. Indeed, were there no other object in learning Greek but to see to what perfection language is capable of being carried, not only as a medium of communication, but as an instrument of thought, we see not why the time of a young man would not be just as well bestowed in acquiring a knowledge of it — for all the purposes, at least, of a liberal or elementary education — as in learning algebra, another specimen of a language or arrangement of signs perfect in its kind. But this wonderful idiom happens to have been spoken, as was hinted in the preceding paragraph, by a race as wonderful. The very first monument of their genius — the most ancient relic of letters in the western world — stands to this day altogether unrivaled in the exalted class to which it belongs. What was the history of this immortal poem and of its great fellow? Was it a single individual, and who was he, that composed them? Had he any master or model? What had been his education, and what was the state of society in which he lived? These questions are full of interest to a philosophical inquirer into the intellectual history of the species, but they are especially important with a view to the subject of the present discussion. Whatever causes account for the matchless excellence of these primitive poems, and for that of the language in which they are written, will go far to explain the extraordinary circumstance, that the same favored people left nothing unattempted in philosophy, in letters, and in arts, and attempted nothing without signal, and, in some cases, unrivaled success. Winckelmann undertakes to assign some reasons for this astonishing superiority of the Greeks, and talks very learnedly about a fine climate, delicate organs, exquisite susceptibility, the full development of the human form by gymnastic exercises, etc. For our own part, we are content to explain the phenomenon after the manner of the Scottish school of metaphysicians, in which we learned the little that we profess to know of that department of philosophy, by resolving it at once in an original law of nature; in other words, by substantially, but decently, confessing it to be inexplicable.

From an essay on «Classical Learning.»

GOTTFRIED WILHELM VON LEIBNITZ

(1646–1716)

OTTFRIED WILHELM VON LEIBNITZ, one of the most celebrated philosophers and mathematicians of the seventeenth century, was born at Leipsic, Germany, July 6th, 1646. His father was professor of Law in Leipsic University, where Leibnitz himself was educated in jurisprudence and philosophy. After studying mathematics at Jena and taking a degree of Doctor of Law at Altdorf, he began life as an assistant in revising the statutes for the elector of Mainz, in whose service he remained for about six years, leaving it to reside at Hanover where for forty years he served the Brunswick family under three successive princes,— dying November 14th, 1716, in neglect due to the fact that the House of Brunswick had succeeded to the throne of England and removed its seat to London. It is said that there was only a single mourner at his grave, and an eyewitness of the interment says that he was «buried more like a robber than what he really was, the ornament of his country.» He was a man of almost universal genius, «distinguished in mathematics, natural science, philosophy, theology, history, jurisprudence, politics, and philology.» He made notable discoveries in physics, and invented a calculating machine which «added, subtracted, multiplied, divided, and extracted roots.» Among his many celebrated writings, those which continue to be most generally read are his philosophical works, a valuable translation of which has been recently made by Prof. George Martin Duncan, of Yale University.

ON THE ULTIMATE ORIGIN OF THINGS

IN ADDITION to the world or aggregate of finite things, there is some unique Being who governs, not only like the soul in me, or rather like the Ego itself in my body, but in a much higher relation. For one Being dominating the universe not only rules the world, but he creates and fashions it, is superior to the world, and, so to speak, extramundane, and by this very fact is the ultimate reason of things. For the sufficient reason of existence can be found neither in any particular thing, nor in

the whole aggregate or series. Suppose a book on the elements of geometry to have been eternal and that others had been successively copied after it, it is evident, that, although we might account for the present book by the book which was its model, we could, nevertheless, never, by assuming any number of books whatever, reach a perfect reason for them; for we may always wonder why such books have existed from all time; that is, why books are and why they are thus written. What is true of books is also true of the different states of the world, for, in spite of certain laws of transformation, a succeeding state is in a certain way only a copy of the preceding, and to whatever anterior state you may go back you will never find there a perfect reason why, forsooth, there is any world at all, and such a world as exists. For even if you imagine the world eternal, nevertheless, since you posit nothing but a succession of states, and as you find a sufficient reason for them in none of them whatsoever, and as any number of them whatever does not aid you in giving a reason for them, it is evident that the reason must be sought elsewhere. For in eternal things it must be understood that even where there is no cause there is a reason which, in perduring things, is necessity itself or essence, but in the series of changing things, if it were supposed that they succeed each other eternally, this reason would be, as will soon be seen, the prevalence of indications where the reasons are not necessitating (by an absolute or metaphysical necessity, the opposite of which would imply contradiction), but inclining. From which it follows that, by supposing the eternity of the world, an ultimate extramundane reason of things, or God, cannot be escaped.

The reasons of the world, therefore, lie hidden in something extramundane different from the chain of states or series of things the aggregate of which constitutes the world. We must, therefore, pass from physical or hypothetical necessity, which determines the posterior states of the world by the prior, to something which is absolute or metaphysical necessity, the reason for which cannot be given. For the present world is necessary, physically or hypothetically, but not absolutely or metaphysically. It being granted, indeed, that the world is such as it is, it follows that things may hereafter be such as they are. But as the ultimate origin must be in something which is metaphysically necessary, and as the reason of the existing can only be from the existing, there must exist some one being metaphysically necessary, or

whose essence is existence; and thus there exists something which differs from the plurality of beings or from the world, which, as we have recognized and shown, is not metaphysically necessary.

But in order to explain a little more clearly how, from eternal or essential or metaphysical truths, temporary, contingent, or physical truths arise, we ought first to recognize that from the very fact that something exists rather than nothing, there is in possible things, that is, in the very possibility or essence, a certain need of existence, and, so to speak, some claim to existence; in a word, that essence tends itself towards existence. Whence it further follows that all possible things, whether expressing essence or possible reality, tend by equal right toward existence, according to their quantity of essence or reality, or according to the degree of perfection which they contain, for perfection is nothing else than quantity of essence.

Hence it is most clearly understood that among the infinite combinations of possibles and possible series, that one exists by which the most of essence or of possibility is brought into existence. And, indeed, there is always in things a principle of determination which is to be taken from the greatest and the smallest, or in such a way that the greatest effect is obtained with the least, so to speak, expenditure. And here the time, place, or, as many say, the receptivity or capacity of the world may be considered as the expenditure or the ground which can be most easily built upon, whereas the varieties of forms correspond to the commodiousness of the edifice and the multiplicity and elegance of its chambers. And it is with it in this respect as with certain games where all the spaces on a table are to be filled according to determined laws. Now, unless a certain skill be employed, you will be finally excluded by unfavorable spaces and forced to leave many more places empty than you can or wish. But there is a certain very easy way of filling the most possible space. Just as, therefore, if it is resolved to make a triangle, there being no other determining reason, it commonly happens that an equilateral results; and if it is resolved to go from one point to another without any further determination as to the way, the easiest and shortest path will be chosen; so it being once posited that being is better than not being, or that there is a reason why something should be rather than nothing, or that we must pass from the possibility to the act, it follows that even in the absence of every other determination the quantity of existence is as great as possible, regard being had to the capacity of the time and of the place (or to the possible order of existence), exactly as the squares are disposed in a given area in such a way that it shall contain the greatest number of them possible. From this it is now marvelously understood how, in the very origin of things, a sort of divine mathematics or of metaphysical mechanism was employed, and how the determination of the greatest quantity of existence takes place. It is thus that from all angles the determined angle in geometry is the right angle, and that liquids placed in heterogeneous positions take that form which has the most capacity, or the spherical; but especially it is thus that in ordinary mechanics itself, when several heavy bodies strive together, the motion which results constitutes, on the whole, the greatest descent. For just as all the possibles tend by equal right to exist by reason of reality, so all weights tend by an equal right to descend by reason of their gravity; and as here a movement is produced which contains the greatest possible descent of heavy bodies, so there a world is produced in which is found realized the greatest number of possibles.

And thus we now have physical necessity from metaphysical; for, although the world be not metaphysically necessary, in the sense that its contrary implies a contradiction or a logical absurdity, it is nevertheless physically necessary, or determined in such a way that its contrary implies imperfection or moral absurdity. And as possibility is the principle of essence, so perfection or the degree of essence (through which the greatest possible number is at the same time possible) is the principle of existence. Whence at the same time it is evident that the author of the world is free, although he makes all things determinately, for he acts according to a principle of wisdom or of perfection. Indeed, indifference arises from ignorance, and the wiser one is the more determined one is to the highest degree of perfection.

But, you will say, however ingenious this comparison of a certain determining metaphysical mechanism with the physical mechanism of heavy bodies may appear, nevertheless it fails in this, that heavy bodies truly exist, whereas possibilities and essences prior to existence or outside of it are only fancies or fictions in which the reason of existence cannot be sought. I answer, that neither these essences nor these so-called eternal

truths are fictions, but that they exist in a certain region of ideas, if I may thus speak, that is, in God himself, the source of all essences and of the existence of all else. And the existence of the actual series of things shows sufficiently of itself that my assertion is not gratuitous. For since the reason is not found in this series, as we have shown above, but must be sought in metaphysical necessities or eternal truths, and since that which exists can only come from that which existed, as we have remarked above, eternal truths must have their existence in a certain subject absolutely and metaphysically necessary, that is, in God, through whom those things which otherwise would be imaginary, are, to speak barbarously but significantly, realized.

And in truth we discover that everything is done in the world according to the laws, not only geometrical, but also metaphysical, of eternal truths; that is, not only according to material necessities, but also according to formal necessities; and this is true, not only generally in that which concerns the reason, which we have just explained, of a world existing rather than nonexisting, and existing thus rather than otherwise (a reason which can only be found in the tendency of the possible to existence), but if we descend to the special we see the metaphysical laws of cause, of power, of action holding good in admirable manner in all nature, and prevailing over the purely geometrical laws themselves of matter, as I found in accounting for the laws of motion: a thing which struck me with such astonishment that, as I have explained more at length elsewhere, I was forced to abandon the law of the geometrical composition of forces which I had defended in my youth when I was more materialistic.

Thus, therefore, we have the ultimate reason of the reality, as well of essences as of existences, in a Being who is necessarily much superior and anterior to the world itself, since it is from him that not only the existences which this world contains, but also the possibles themselves derive their reality. And this reason of things can be sought only in a single source, because of the connection which they all have with one another. But it is evident that it is from this source that existing things continually emanate, that they are and have been its products, for it does not appear why one state of the world rather than another, the state of to-day rather than that of to-morrow, should come from the world itself. We see also, with the same clearness, how God acts, not only physically but freely; how the efficient

and final cause of things is in him, and how he manifests not only his greatness and his power in the construction of the machine of the world, but also his goodness and his wisdom in the creation. And in order that no one should think that we confound here moral perfection or goodness with metaphysical perfection or greatness, or that the former is denied while the latter is granted, it must be known that it follows from what has been said that the world is most perfect, not physically, or, if you prefer, metaphysically, because that series of things is produced in which there is the most reality in action, but also that it is most perfect morally, because really moral perfection is physical perfection for souls themselves. Thus the world is not only the most admirable machine, but, in so far as it is composed of souls, it is also the best republic, through which as much happiness or joy is brought to souls as is possible, in which their physical perfection consists.

But you will say, we experience the contrary in this world, for often good people are very unhappy, and not only innocent brutes, but also innocent men, are afflicted and even put to death with torture; finally, the world, if you regard especially the government of the human race, resembles a sort of confused chaos rather than the well-ordered work of a supreme wisdom. This may appear so at the first glance, I confess, but if you examine the thing more closely, it evidently appears from the things which have been alleged, that the contrary should be affirmed; that is, that all things and consequently souls attain to the highest degree of perfection possible. And in truth it is not proper to judge before having examined, as the jurisconsults say, the whole law. We know only a very small part of the eternity which extends into immensity; for the memory of the few thousands of years which history transmits to us are, indeed, a very little thing. And yet from an experience so short we dare to judge of the immense and of the eternal, like men who, born and brought up in a prison, or, if you prefer, in the subterranean salt mines of the Sarmatiæ, think that there is no other light in the world than the lamp whose feeble gleam hardly suffices to direct their steps. Let us look at a very beautiful picture, and let us cover it in such a way as to see only a very small part of it. What else will appear in it, however closely we may examine it and however near we may approach to it, except a certain confused mass of colors, without choice and with-

out art? And yet when we remove the covering and regard it from the proper point of view, we will see that what appeared thrown on the canvas at haphazard has been executed with the greatest art by the author of the work. What the eyes discover in the picture, the ears discover in music. The most illustrious composers often introduce discords into their harmonies in order to excite and pique, so to speak, the listener, who, anxious as to the outcome, is all the more pleased when soon all things are restored to order. Just as we rejoice to have passed through slight dangers and experienced small ills, whether because of a feeling of egotism, or because we find pleasure in the frightful images which tight-rope dances or leapings between swords (*sauts perilleux*) present, so we partly lose laughing children, pretending to throw them far away from us, like the ape which, having taken Christian, king of the Danes, while still an infant wrapped in swaddling clothes, carried him to the top of the roof, and, when everybody was frightened, brought him back laughing, safe and sound to his cradle. According to the same principle, it is insipid always to eat sweetmeats; we must mingle with them sharp, acid, and even bitter things, which excite the taste. He who has not tasted bitter things has not merited sweet things, and even will not appreciate them. It is the law even of joy that pleasure be not uniform, for it engenders disgust, renders us stupid and not joyous.

As to what we said, that a part may be disturbed without prejudice to the general harmony, it must not be understood as meaning that no account is made of the parts, or that it suffices that the entire world be perfect in measure, although it might happen that the human race should be unhappy, and that there should be in the universe no regard for justice, no heed taken of our lot, as some think who do not judge rightly enough of the whole of things. For it must be known that as in a well-constituted republic as much care as possible is taken of the good of the individual, so the universe cannot be perfect if individual interests are not protected as much as the universal harmony will permit. And here a better law could not be established than the very law of justice which wills that each one participate in the perfection of the universe and in a happiness of his own proportioned to his own virtue and to the good-will he entertains toward the common good, by which that which we call the charity and love of God is fulfilled, in which alone, according to the judgment of the wisest theologians, the force and power of the Christian religion itself consists. And it ought not appear astonishing that so large a part should be given to souls in the universe since they reflect the most faithful image of the supreme Author, and hold to him not only the relation of machine to artificer, but also that of citizen to prince; and they are to continue as long as the universe itself; and in a manner they express and concentrate the whole in themselves so that it can be said that souls are whole parts.

As regards especially the afflictions of good people, we must hold for certain that there results for them a greater good, and this is not only theologically, but physically true. So grain cast into the ground suffers before producing its fruit. And we may affirm, generally, that afflictions, temporarily evil, are in effect good, since they are short cuts to greater perfections. So in physics, liquors which ferment slowly take more time also to improve; whereas, those the agitation of which is greater, reject certain parts with more force and are more promptly improved.

And we might say of this that it is retreating in order the better to leap forward (*qu' on recede, pour mieux sauter*).

We should, therefore, regard these considerations not merely as agreeable and consoling, but also as most true. And, in general, I feel that there is nothing truer than happiness, and nothing happier nor sweeter than truth.

Complete. Chapter xvii. From the «Philosophical Works» of Leibnitz. Translated by Prof. George Martin Duncan, Yale University.

By permission. Copyright, 1890, by Tuttle, Morehouse & Taylor, Publishers, New Haven, Conn.

GOTTHOLD EPHRAIM LESSING

(1729–1781)

LESSING'S «Nathan the Wise» might have remained the favorite drama of Germany, if Goethe and Schiller had not written after him; and, in spite of them and of their works as critics in the same field, his «Laocoon» keeps its place above all other critical writings of modern times, occupying for modern times the same place of unquestionable pre-eminence that is conceded to Longinus «On the Sublime,» among classical writers on related subjects. Its purpose was to define the nature, the principles, and the scope of sculpture, painting, and poetry, as modes of expressing human thought and emotion. His familiarity with the great classical poets was so intimate that his knowledge of plastic and graphic art, as well as of poetic, seems to be due chiefly to their teachings or to suggestions from their principles. His illustrations are so largely based on classical verse that ideas which cannot fail to be stimulating to all can be wholly intelligible only to those who will consent to share his enthusiasm for the great masters from whom his education was so largely derived.

He was born at Kamenz, in Upper Lusatia, January 22d, 1729. His father, who was a clergyman, sent him to Leipsic to study theology; but it is said that Lessing devoted his time largely to the theatre and the drama instead of to his text-books. The result was his first comedy, «The Young Scholar,» which was produced in 1748,—giving great offense to his parents, who concluded that he was neglecting his studies and took him away from the University. He returned and took up the study of medicine, but soon afterwards left the University for Berlin, where he supported himself by writing until 1751. He then entered the University of Wittenberg to complete his studies. Taking his degree of Master and returning to Berlin, he began the brilliant career which made him one of the greatest names in the literature in Germany. As a poet he is attractive, as a writer of fables he is a friend of successive generations of the young in and out of Germany; as the author of «Minna von Barnhelm,» «Emilia Galotti,» and «Nathan the Wise,» he is secure in his place as one of the favorite dramatists of Germany, and as a critic he has given the world in his «Laocoon» a work so great that it redeems criticism from the reproach of negation and almost gives it a place as one of the

creative arts. Lessing belonged to the great period of intellectual development in Germany which rescued the country from the domination of Parisian taste in art and literature, thus making possible Goethe,—the only Gothic writer who can rank with Shakespeare. At Lessing's death, February 15th, 1781, Germany already had full assurance of Goethe as the greatest Teutonic genius of modern times; but it is no exaggeration to say that the «Faust» does not give fuller play to the genius of the Teutonic peoples for poetry than the «Laocoon» does to what is their not less characteristic genius for criticism.

W. V. B.

«LAOCOON»—ART'S HIGHEST LAW

BE IT a fable or history that Love caused the first attempt of the creative Art, thus much is certain, that it was never weary of assisting the great old Masters; for although now the scope of Painting is enlarged so as to be more especially the art which imitates bodies upon flat surfaces, yet the wise Greek placed it within much narrower limits and confined it to the imitation of beautiful bodies. His Painter painted nothing but the beautiful; even the common type of the beautiful, the beautiful of an inferior kind, was to him only an accidental object for the exercise of his practice and for his recreation. The perfection of the object itself must be the thing which enraptures him: he was too great to require of those who contemplated him that they should be content with the cold satisfaction arising from the sight of a successful resemblance, or from reflection upon the skill of the artist producing it; to his art nothing was dearer, nothing seemed to him nobler than the object and end of Art itself.

"Who would paint you when nobody will look at you?" says the old epigrammatist of a very ugly man. Many modern artists would say, "Be as ugly as it is possible to be, I will nevertheless paint you; though no one will willingly look at you, yet they will willingly look at my picture,—not because it reproduces you, but because it is a proof of my skill which can so exactly imitate so hideous an object."

In truth the connection between this extravagant boasting and a fatal dexterity, which is not ennobled by the worth of the object, is only too natural; even the Greeks have had their Pauson and their Pyreicus. They had them, but they passed severe judgment upon them. Pauson, who confined himself to the beau-

tiful of ordinary nature, whose low taste most congenially expressed the deficient and the hateful, lived in the most sordid poverty; and Pyreicus, who painted barbers' rooms, dirty workshops, donkeys, and kitchen vegetables with all the diligence of a Dutch painter, as if such things in nature had so much fascination and were so rarely seen, obtained the nickname of Ρυπαρόγραφος (the filth painter); although the rich voluptuary bought his works at extravagant prices, thus coming to the help of their utter worthlessness by impressing upon them a fictitious value. Governments themselves have not thought it unworthy of their vigilance to restrain by force the artist within his proper sphere. The law of the Thebans, which ordered the imitation of the beautiful and forbade the imitation of the ugly, is well known. It was no law against the bungler, which it was generally supposed to be, even by Junius. It condemned the Greek Ghezzi, the unworthy trick of Art to attain a likeness through an exaggeration of the uglier parts of the original—in a word, the caricature.

From the spirit of the beautiful also flowed the law of the Olympic judges. Every Olympian conqueror obtained a statue, but an Iconic was only granted to him who had been three times a conqueror. Portraits of the moderately successful were not allowed to abound among works of Art, for although even the portrait approached to the ideal, nevertheless the likeness was the dominant circumstance; it is the ideal of a certain man, not the ideal of a man generally.

We smile when we hear that with the Ancients even the Arts were subjected to civil laws; but we are not always right when we smile. Unquestionably, laws should exercise no power over sciences, for the end of science is truth. Truth is necessary for the soul, and it would be tyranny to exercise the slightest compulsion with respect to the satisfaction of this essential need.

The end of Art, on the other hand, is pleasure, and pleasure can be dispensed with; therefore, it may always depend upon the lawgiver what kind of pleasure he will allow, and what amount of each kind.

The plastic Arts especially, over and above the certain influence which they exercise upon the character of a nation, are capable of an effect which requires the vigilant supervision of the law. If beautiful men are the cause of beautiful statues, the latter, on the other hand, have reacted upon the former, and the state has to thank beautiful men.

With us the tender imagination of the mother appears to express itself only in monsters. From this point of view I believe that in certain ancient legends, which are generally thrown aside as untrue, there is some truth to be found. The mothers of Aristomenes, Aristodæmos, Alexander the Great, Scipio, Augustus, Galerius, all dreamed during their pregnancy that their husband was a snake. The snake was the sign of godhead, and the beautiful statues of a Bacchus, an Apollo, a Mercury, a Hercules, were seldom without snakes. These honorable wives had in the daytime fed their eyes on the god, and the bewildering dream awakened the form of the wild beast. This is how I read the dream, and despise the explanation which was given by the pride of sires and the shamelessness of flatterers; for certainly there must have been one cause why the adulterous fancy always took the form of a snake.

But I return to my path. My only wish has been to lay down firmly the principle that with the Ancients beauty was the highest law of the imitative Arts.

This principle being firmly established, it necessarily follows that everything else by which imitative Art can at the same time extend its influence must, if it does not harmonize with beauty, entirely give place to it, and if it does harmonize, at least be subordinate to it. Let me dwell on the consideration of Expression.

There are passions and degrees of passion which express themselves in the countenance by the most hideous distortions, and which place the whole body in such attitudes of violence that all the fine lines which mark it in a position of repose are lost. The ancient artists either abstained from these altogether and entirely, or used them in a subordinate degree, in which they were susceptible of some measure of beauty. Rage and despair do not disgrace any of their works. I dare aver that they have never created a Fury.

Wrath is diminished into severity. The Jupiter of the poet who hurls the thunderbolt is wrathful; the Jupiter of the artist is severe.

Lamentation is softened into sorrow; and when this mitigation cannot take place—if the lamentation should be equally degrading and disfiguring, what did Timanthes do? His picture of the Sacrifice of Iphigenia, in which he distributed to all the bystanders their proper share of grief, but veiled the countenance

of the father, which ought to manifest a grief surpassing that of all the others, is well known, and many clever things have been said about it. He had, said one critic, so exhausted himself in the physiognomy of sorrow that he despaired of being able to give an expression of greater sorrow to the father. He thereby confessed, said another critic, that the grief of a father in such a catastrophe was beyond all expression. I, for my part, see neither the incapacity of the artist nor the incapacity of the Art. As the degree of the affection becomes stronger, so do the corresponding features of the countenance; the highest degree has the most decided features, and nothing is easier for Art than to express them. But Timanthes knew the limits which the Graces had fixed to his Art. He knew that the grief which overcame Agamemnon as a father found expression in distortions, which are always hideous. So far as beauty and dignity could be combined with this expression, he went. He might easily have passed over or have softened what was hideous; but inasmuch as his composition did not permit him to do either, what resource remained but to veil it? What he might not paint he left to conjecture. In a word, this veiling is a sacrifice which the artist made to beauty. It is an example not how an artist can force expression beyond the limits of Art, but how an artist should subject it to the first law of Art,—the law of beauty.

Apply this observation to the Laocoon, and the reason which I seek is clear. The master strove to attain the highest beauty in given circumstances of bodily anguish. It was impossible to combine the latter in all its disfiguring vehemence with the former. It was therefore necessary to diminish it; he must soften screams into sighs, not because the screaming betrayed an ignoble soul, but because it disfigured the countenance in a hideous manner. Let any one only in thought force wide open the mouth of Laocoon and judge. Let any one make him scream and then look. It was a creation which inspired sympathy, because it exhibited beauty and suffering at the same time; now it has become a hideous horrible creation from which we gladly turn away our face, because the aspect of it excites what is unpleasant in pain without the beauty in the suffering object which can change this unpleasantness into the secret feeling of sympathy.

The mere wide-opening of the mouth—putting out of consideration how violent and disgusting the other portions of the

face distorted and displaced by it would become—is in painting a blot, and in statuary a cavity, which produces the worst effect possible. Montfaucon showed little taste when he declared an old bearded head with an open mouth to be Jupiter instructing an oracle. Must a god scream when he reveals the future? Would a pleasing curve of the mouth make his speech suspicious? Neither do I believe Valerius, that Ajax, in the picture by Timanthes already mentioned, must have been represented as screaming. Far worse masters in the time of decayed Art do not allow the wildest barbarians, when suffering terror and agony of death under the sword of the conqueror, to open their mouths so as to scream.

It is certain that this reduction of the most extreme bodily anguish to a lower scale of feeling was visible in many of the ancient works of Art. The suffering Hercules in the poisoned garment, by the hand of an unknown ancient master, was not the Hercules of Sophocles, who yelled so dreadfully that the Locrian cliffs and the Eubean promontories re-echoed with it. He was rather melancholy than mad. The Philoctetes of Pythagoras Leontinus appeared to impart his pain to the observer, an effect which the slightest feature of ugliness would have prevented. It may be asked how I know that this master had made a statue of Philoctetes?—from a passage in Pliny, which ought not to have waited for my correction, so palpably is it corrupted or mutilated.

Complete. «Laocoon,» Chap. ii.

POETRY AND PAINTING COMPARED

Does not Poetry suffer too great a loss if we take away from her all images of corporeal beauty? Who wishes to take them away? If we seek to prevent her pursuing a particular path, by which she expects to arrive at such images, while she follows the footsteps of a sister Art, but in which she painfully wanders up and down without ever reaching the same goal: do we therefore close every other path to her, even those in which Art in her turn must follow her a great distance?

Even Homer, who so carefully abstains from all detailed description of corporeal beauty, from whom we barely learn, even parenthetically, that Helen has white arms and beautiful hair, even this poet knows, nevertheless, how to give us an idea of her

beauty, which far surpasses all that art is capable of representing to us.

Let us only remember the passage in which Helen appears before the council of the Trojan elders. The venerable old men gaze on her, and one says to the other:—

> Οὐ νέμεσις Τρῶας καὶ ἐϋκνήμιδας Ἀχαιοὺς
> Τοιῇδ᾽ ἀμφὶ γυναικὶ πολὺν χρόνον ἄλγεα πάσχειν·
> Αἰνῶς ἀθανάτῃσι θεῇς εἰς ὦπα ἔοικεν.

What can convey to us a more lively idea of beauty than that cold old age should think it justified the woe which had cost so much blood and so many tears?

What Homer could not describe in detail he makes us understand by the effect: O poets! paint for us the pleasure, inclination, love, rapture, which beauty causes, and you will have painted beauty itself. Who can think that the beloved object of Sappho, at the sight of whom she confesses to have lost sense and judgment, was ugly? Who does not believe that he has seen the most beautiful and perfect form the moment he sympathizes with the emotions which only such a form can awaken?

It is not because Ovid describes the different parts of the beautiful body of his Lesbia, in the lines—

> « Quos humeros, quales vidi tetigique lacertos! » etc.,

but it is because he describes them with that inebriating voluptuousness which so readily awakens our desires, that we imagine ourselves to enjoy the sight which he enjoyed.

Another way by which poetry attains the end of painting in the description of corporeal beauty is by changing beauty into grace. Grace is beauty in motion, and therefore less within the province of the painter than the poet. The painter can only create a presumption of motion; in reality, however, his figures are without motion. Consequently, grace with him borders on grimace. But in poetry it remains what it is,—a transitory beauty which we wish to see repeated. It comes and goes; and as we can generally more easily and more vividly remember a motion than a mere form or color, it follows that grace in the same proportions will produce a stronger impression upon us than beauty. All that in the picture of Alcina pleases and excites us is grace. The impression which her eyes make is not in consequence of their being black and fiery, but because they are—

« Pietosi à riguardar, à mover parchi »;

have a look of sweetness and languor; that love flutters round them and discharges his whole quiver from them. Her mouth charms us, not because her vermilion lips disclose two rows of choice pearl; but because they form that love-inspiring smile which of itself opens paradise upon earth; because from them come those friendly words which soften the roughest heart. Her bosom enchants us less because milk and ivory and apples are the image of their whiteness and exquisite form — but rather because we see them gently undulate like the waves on the extremest edge of the shore when a playful zephyr agitates the sea.

« Due pome acerbe, e pur d'avorio fatte,
Vengono e van, come onda al primo margo
Quando piacevole aura il mar combatte.»

I am certain that such traits of grace compressed into one or two stanzas would have produced more effect than the five others, over which Ariosto has scattered them, interweaving with them cold indications of a beautiful form, in a manner far too learned to affect our feelings.

Anacreon himself preferred to err by an obvious impropriety, in requiring an impossibility from the painter, rather than not animate with grace the image of his mistress.

Τρυφεροῦ δ' ἔσω γενειου,
Περὶ λυγδίνῳ τραχήλῳ
Χάριτες πέτοιντο πᾶσαι.

« Let all the graces hover over her soft chin and her marble neck.» How did he intend this? In the most literal meaning? It was incapable of execution by the painter. The painter could give the chin its finest round — its most beautiful dimple *amoris digitulo impressum* (for the ἔσω appears to me to indicate a dimple), he could give the most beautiful carnation to the neck, but he could go no further. The movement of this beautiful neck, the play of the muscles by which the dimple became more or less visible, the special grace was beyond the reach of his power. The poet used the most forcible expressions of his art to make beauty visible to us, in order that the painter might make use of the most forcible expression of his art. A new illustration of our former remark that the poet, even when he

speaks of works of Art, is not on that account obliged to confine himself within the boundaries of Art.

Complete. « Laocoon,» Chap. xxi.

THE EDUCATION OF THE HUMAN RACE

EDUCATION has its aim with the race, not less than with the individual. That which is educated is educated for some end. The flattering prospects which are opened to the youth, the honor and affluence which are held up before him, — what are these but means by which he is educated to become a man, a man who, though these prospects of affluence and honor should fail, shall still be capable of doing his duty? Is this the aim of human education? And does the Divine education fall short of this? What art can accomplish with the individual, shall not nature accomplish with the whole? Blasphemy! Blasphemy!

No! it will come! it will surely come, the period of perfection, when, the more convinced his understanding is of an ever-better future, the less man will need to borrow from that future the motives of his actions; when he will choose the good because it is good, and not because arbitrary rewards are annexed to it which are only to fix and strengthen his wandering gaze, at first, until he is able to appreciate the interior and nobler reward of well doing. It will surely come, the period of a new, eternal gospel, which is promised us, even in the elementary books of the New Covenant. Proceed in thine imperceptible course, Eternal Providence! Only let me not despair of thee, because imperceptible. Let me not despair of thee, even though thy steps to me should seem to retrograde. It is not true that the shortest way is always a straight one. Thou hast, in thine eternal course, so much to take along with thee! So many sidelong steps to make! And what if it be now, as good as proved, that the great, slow wheel which brings the race nearer to its perfection, is put in motion, only by smaller, quicker wheels, of which each contributes its part to the same end?

Not otherwise! The path by which the race attains to its perfection, each individual man — some earlier, and some later — must first have gone over. « Must have gone over in one and the same life? Can he have been a sensual Jew and a spiritual Chris-

tian in the same life? Can he, in the same life, have overtaken both these?» Perhaps not! But why may not each individual man have existed more than once in this world? Is this hypothesis, therefore, so ridiculous, because it is the oldest? because it is the one which the human understanding immediately hit upon, before it was distracted and weakened by the sophistry of the schools? Why may not I at one time have accomplished, already here on earth, all those steps toward my perfection, which mere temporal rewards and punishments will enable man to accomplish; and, at another time, all those, in which we are so powerfully assisted by the prospect of eternal compensations. Why should I not return as often as I am able to acquire new knowledges, new talents? Is it because I carry away so much at one time as to make it not worth the while to return, or because I forget that I have been here before? It is well for me that I forget it. The remembrance of my former states would allow me to make but a poor use of the present. Besides, what I am necessitated to forget now, have I forgotten it forever? Or because, on this supposition, too much time would be lost to me? Lost? What have I then to delay? Is not the whole eternity mine?

The summing up in the essay on « The Education
of the Human Race.»

GEORGE HENRY LEWES

(1817–1878)

WHEN a history or biography makes its way by fifty years of slow growth from the full-leather binding of the gentleman's library to the paper-backed edition sold at a shilling, it is beyond the reach of negative criticism. George Henry Lewes wrote a « History of Philosophy,» which gained him the consideration of scholars. His « Studies in Animal Life » showed his sympathy with the high purposes of science. His « Aristotle » and « Life of Goethe » testified his habit of frequenting « the higher walks » of the world's literature. But only in his « Life of Robespierre » has he attained what seems to be the enduring honor of the paper back. The popularity of the book is due first to its picturesqueness, but scarcely less to the essay writer's habit of limiting himself. There is a sufficient element of completeness in the treatment of each episode to allow the book to be read, a little at a time, with satisfaction. For those who believe or feel with Dr. Johnson that « smattering » is a necessary habit of the human intellect, a result of the compulsion under which it cannot escape practicing the comparative method of scientific investigation, the essayist must always be the best historian and the most instructive biographer.

Lewes was born in London, April 18th, 1817. He lived to the age of sixty-one, dying November 30th, 1878, after a life devoted industriously and successfully to literature. It seems to be the irony of some half-mocking moral law, that such a man after such labors should be remembered chiefly as the associate of George Eliot!—the man who gave up his own uncongenial family life to seek the pleasures of intellectual sympathy. It is irony, however, which probes what seems to be the radical failing of his character,—a failing which initially was more than half a virtue,—the fineness of nerve which made all that is repulsive in life so painful to him that he shunned it, and so lost that discipline of intellectual disturbance through which moral greatness is fostered and enabled to find its readiest expression.

ROUSSEAU, ROBESPIERRE, AND THE FRENCH REVOLUTION

THE spirit which animated the Revolution was the spirit of Rousseau. From the Declaration of the Rights of Man to the formation of the Constitution in 1793, there is no important act in which the influence of the Genevese philosopher is not discernible. But beyond this Rousseau has special interest for us here, as the acknowledged teacher of Robespierre, who, of all his disciples, adhered most rigidly to his principles, and gave them the most unflinching application.

Rightly to understand Robespierre it is first indispensable that we should understand Rousseau. I shall be fulfilling, therefore, the first object of this biography in devoting a few pages to the political writings of the author of the "Social Contract."

The gayety, frivolity, wit, and elegance of France, so charming to those who lived in the salons, formed, as it were, but the graceful vine which clustered over a volcano about to burst; or, rather, let me say it was the rouge which, on a sallow, sunken cheek, simulated the ruddy glow of health. Lying deep down in the heart of society there was profound seriousness: the sadness of misery, of want, of slavery clanking its chains, of free thought struggling for empire. This seriousness was about to find utterance. The most careless observer could not fail to perceive the heavy thunderclouds which darkened the horizon of this sunny day. The court and the salons were not France; they occupied the foremost place upon the stage, but another actor was about to appear, before whom they would shrink into insignificance; that actor was the People.

The people became the fashion. Philanthrophy was *de bon ton*. The philosophers speculated about the people; the littérateurs declaimed about them. Courtiers played at being peasants. A village was constructed at Trianon; village fêtes were given at royal farms by royal peasants. Idyls were *à la mode*. Florian, Gesner, and "Paul et Virginie" were the flowers of this peasant literature. As in our own day we see some aristocratic writers joining with the most democratic in the senseless laudation of that grandiose abstraction — "The People," — so in unhappy France the warmest eulogists of the starved, uneducated, uncared-for masses were those who profited by their subjection. Restless, unbelieving, sick at heart of the existing state of things, they played at being peasants, and poetized the people!

Among the philosophic nobles, there were some who quitted their *talons rouges* to wear thick shoes; and relinquished their costume to put on that of the bourgeoisie. It was very dangerous work playing thus with their dignities, when those dignities were already tottering!

Few were in earnest, because few had convictions. At length a man arose in whom pretense grew into seriousness, paradoxes ripened into convictions: that man was Rousseau. The "Contrat Social" was the bible of the Revolution. From it orators drew their principles, their political aphorisms, their political language. As a metaphysician, and as a rhetorician, his influence was incalculable. He was the man of his epoch, and therefore was he powerful. He united the elegance and eloquence of the philosophers and littérateurs to the sadness and seriousness of the people. In his strange career we see him uneasily moving amidst the salons of Paris, dressed in his Armenian robes, creating a sensation amongst the wits and poets, the dilettanti and beauties; "among them, but not of them"; and then, sick of his uneasy position, brusquely breaking away from all society, turning misanthrope, disdaining all the elegancies of life, and endeavoring in solitude to find that peace among plants which men had denied him. A similar course is observable in his writings: he commences with a frivolous paradox to end with an extravagant conviction.

The mixture of pretense and reality in Rousseau; of willful folly, and of glorious truth; of despicable baseness, and of noble qualities, makes up the mystery and piquant charm of his character. "He was," as Carlyle finely says, "a lonely man, his life a long soliloquy." In that soliloquy may be read the heights and depths of human nature. His ideas were often noble, grand, and tender; his acts degraded. He taught mothers by his eloquence to nurse their children, and threw his own children into the foundling hospital. His sensibility led him to sympathize with whatever was beautiful; his weakness and selfishness suggested acts which have left ineffaceable stains upon his memory. He was one of that class of men whose practice springs not from their precepts; in whom the unclouded intellect discerns and honors truth, while the will is too miserably weak to act the truth. He has had his acrid antagonists, and his eloquent defenders. Are not both right — both wrong? It is possible to draw, and truly draw, a fearful picture of one-half of this man;

but such a one-sided view will never obtain general acceptance, for many will deeply sympathize with what was noble in him, and impartial men will always proclaim it.

Few read his works. That marvelous book, "The Confessions," will never, indeed, cease to find readers; but while "Émile" and "La Nouvelle Héloïse" from time to time tempt the adventurous, lured by celebrated titles, I do not believe that one student in fifty ever looks into the "Discourse on the Inequality of Conditions," or the "Social Contract." But as these were his great revolutionary works, it is to them that I must here direct attention.

The period which elapses between 1745 and 1764 is at once the most disastrous, and, in some respects, the most remarkable, in the history of France. No period offers such striking contrasts. On the one hand, France, beaten in every quarter of the globe, loses her colonies, her marine, and even her honor; on the other hand, she collects together at Paris a brilliant band of writers, whose ideas are destined to become the guiding lights of Europe. Among these Rousseau holds a foremost rank.

In the year 1750 the Academy of Dijon proposed, as the subject of its prize essay, this question: "Has the establishment of science and literature contributed to purify society?"

It was an absurd question. Absurd, because as literature is itself the expression of society, which it in turn reacts upon, you cannot separate the two, and determine either the influence of literature upon society, or what society would have been had there been no literature: in other words, what society would have been, had it not been society; for society is a complex condition, of which literature is a vital element. In rude ballads as in wealthy libraries, literature is an agent inseparable from civilization. You might as well speculate on what a man's constitution would be without a liver, as on what the constitution of society would be without literature. In this question, however, the metaphysicians of the eighteenth century saw no absurdity. Rousseau determined to answer it.

"One day, walking with Diderot at Vincennes, talking on the proposed question, 'Which side do you take?' I asked him (it is Diderot who speaks). He replied, 'The affirmative.' 'That' said I, 'is the *pons asinorum:* all the mediocre talents will take that route, and you can only utter commonplaces. Take the other side, and you will find it an open field, rich and fruitful,

for eloquence and philosophy.' 'You are right,' said he, after a few moments' reflection; 'I will follow your advice.'"

It was as a paradox which would startle rather than as a truth which might be commonplace, that Rousseau first threw down the gauntlet against civilization, proclaiming the superiority of ignorance and the greatness of savage life. There was something piquant in the idea. He confesses as much in the first page, where he asked himself, "How shall I dare to blame the sciences in the presence of one of the most learned bodies of Europe? or praise ignorance before a celebrated Academy?" But the result is more piquant still; this Academy absolutely awarded the prize to the audacious eulogist of ignorance! After this we cannot wonder if a paradox which an Academy could crown should produce an immense sensation in a frivolous society startled by the novelty, and allured by the eloquence of the Discourse. There was an air of serious conviction about Rousseau. A close and pressing logic, bold and sweeping dogmatism, and a masterly style, if they failed to convince, at least left readers in an embarrassment from whence there was no escape. No one was persuaded, yet no one could refute him. Replies abounded; even a king condescended to step into the arena; but Rousseau's antagonists did not see the absurdity of the question, and could not, therefore, see the πρωτον ψευδος of his answer.

Rousseau's position is this: Science, Art, and Literature are the produce and producers of all the vices of civilization. Man in a state of unlettered simplicity is healthy, brave, and virtuous. He loses these qualities in society. "The ebb and flow of the ocean have not been more regularly subjected to the course of the planet which illumes the night than the fate of morals and probity to the progress of science and art." This aphorism is universally accepted, and Rousseau's tactic consists in boldly, and without qualification, applying it in the sense contrary to that accepted by mankind. He thus continues: "We have seen virtue disappear, according as the light of the sciences has risen upon our horizon, and the same phenomenon has been observed in all times and in all countries." This position, so authoritatively assumed, domineers over the whole argument. He subsequently supports it by a magnificent audacity: he gives to every science a vice as its origin! "Astronomy is born from superstition; Eloquence from ambition, from hate, from flattery, from falsehood; Geometry from avarice (!); Physics from a vain curiosity; all — including Morality itself — from human pride.»

No sane man could seriously maintain such arguments, although this was not the first time they had found utterance. St. Aubain, in a now forgotten work, called «Traité de l'Opinion,» which Rousseau had studied in his youth, advanced most of the objections to be found in this «Discours.» In fact skepticism had infested every department of human inquiry, until at last men began to doubt whether all inquiry were not useless. Rousseau's paradox, therefore, although suggested by Diderot, was the legitimate product of the epoch, and hence its success.

Not merely as a protest against the science and literature of the age did this «Discours» startle France; there were tones in it of a higher strain; there were sentences of serious application. Philosophers were on thrones, were at court, were caressed in salons. Princes prided themselves on their patronage of literature. Rousseau, instead of swelling the list of eulogists who proclaimed such liberality as the great virtue of an enlightened monarch, boldly declared this patronage was adroit tyranny.

Extravagant as the leading idea of this Discourse unquestionably is, it was surpassed in his next work. Men are prone to believe in their own lies when they find others credulous, and the idea which Rousseau took up as a paradox to display his ingenuity produced so great a sensation that he began to believe he had discovered a truth. He had accidentally lighted upon a mine, and now dug vigorously onwards in search of the ore. His own unhappy life, his own unsociable temper, his consciousness of genius, and irritated self-love, all fitted him for the task of declaiming against unjust social distinctions; and while thus indulging in his vengeance, he was earning his laurels. He spat upon the society wherein he felt his false position, and the world applauded that indulgence of his wrath!

The Academy of Dijon having gained celebrity by its foolish program, grew bolder, and proposed this momentous question: «What is the origin of the inequality among men, and is it sanctioned by the law of nature?» Rousseau's famous «Discours» did not obtain the prize, but it created a greater sensation than any prize essay ever written. It is the paradox of the first «Discours,» but more seriously meditated, more powerfully stated. It is less of a caprice, and more of a conviction. It is a sombre, vehement protest against civilization, a protest in favor of the poor

against the rich, of the oppressed and degraded Many against the polished, vicious Few. This very seriousness, I suppose, prevented the prize being awarded to the «Discours.» Certain it is, that it alarmed the ingenious, frivolous society of France, and that its full success was not obtained till some years later, when the times had grown more serious.

L'homme qui médité est un animal dépravé. That is the keystone of the arch; and it is nothing more than the aphoristic formula of his first «Discours.» He admits that inequalities, physical as well as mental, exist, but these inequalities he attributes to the corrosive influence of civilization, with its luxuries, its subtleties, and its vices. In a state of nature, men's bodies, being equally exercised, become equally vigorous, and the healthy body forms the healthy mind. He paints in glowing colors the ideal state of savage life, of men without language, except a few expressive sounds such as animals employ to articulate their wants, wandering amidst boundless forests, chasing their game, reposing under trees, unperverted by the illimitable desires and unsatisfied passions of civilized men, knowing none of the subtleties of affection, taking a wife to satisfy a passing desire, and heedless of his offspring, brave, simple, truthful, and free.

«Not with blinded eyesight poring over miserable books!»

That is what man was, and what he is you are called upon to compare with that primeval state.

So far it is only another statement of his former idea, but, as he proceeds, the dangerous consequences, rigorously deduced from it, appear. Men were born equal — equal in health, in strength, in virtue, in property. The earth belonged to all, and to none. Society began with the spoliation of the many, in favor of the few; it, and its laws, are the consecration of that spoliation.

«The first man who, having inclosed a piece of land, took it into his head to say, 'This is mine,' and found people simple enough to believe him, was the real founder of civil society. What crimes, what battles, what murders, and what horrible miseries, would he have spared the human race, who should have torn down the fence, and exclaimed: 'Beware how you listen to this impostor; you are lost if you forget that the fruits belong to all, and the earth to no one!'»

This bold attack upon the very nature of property so startled the age, that even Voltaire called it the philosophy of a black-

guard who counseled the poor to plunder the rich. It was passing beyond the limits of permissible paradox, and was becoming alarming. Rousseau was serious. He met the objection naturally made, that a man having built a wall by his own labor was entitled to its benefit, by asking, «Who gave you the right to build it? How can you pretend to be repaid for a labor we, the masses, never imposed upon you? The unanimous consent of the whole human race was necessary before you could appropriate from the common funds more than was necessary for your own subsistence. You are rich! but we suffer. Your wealth is our poverty. In vain you appeal to laws. What are laws but the adroit selfishness of men, who framed maxims for the preservation of their possessions? Property is a spoliation; laws may secure, but they cannot justify it.»

This is no longer a mere audacious paradox; it is an unhappy error. It is not a caprice of speculative ingenuity, it is a vigorously deduced conclusion. It has not only logical consistency, but is strengthened by popular feeling. It is a doctrine which will fructify in Revolutions! To those who are in misery and want, it comes like a revelation of truth, responding to their sense of social injustice. To those who roll in wealth, it comes like a spectre to scare them from their possessions, — a spectre they cannot exorcise. It is a doctrine, it is a conviction, and is backed by millions, stung by a sense of injustice! Attempt not to answer it with phrases about «sacred rights of property,» «security of order,» «well-being of the state,» and so forth; it tells you plainly that these rights are un-sacred, and that this well-being of a state is the pampered indulgence of a few, wrung from the sufferings of millions!

That bold idea once thrown upon the world, the world «will not willingly let die.» France suffered from it. We, in our wealthy England, also suffer from it. In thousands of heads and hearts it works, forming the basis of a political gospel. Those who most revolt against it, find it difficult to answer. It never will be answered so long as social science continues in the hands of metaphysicians. Happily, their reign is drawing to a close!

From the «Life of Robespierre.»

JUSTUS VON LIEBIG

(1803–1873)

JUSTUS VON LIEBIG, one of the greatest chemists of the nineteenth century, was born May 12th, 1803, at Darmstadt, Germany, where his father was a «dry salter» and dealer in dye stuffs. The chemical experiments made by his father in attempting to purify his dyes are thought to have given the first impulse to the scientific genius of the son. It is said that even as a boy Justus Liebig acquired through persistent experimenting a greater knowledge of chemistry than that of «many full-grown professors of the science.» Under the impulse thus gained, he studied at Bonn and Erlangen, graduating from the latter university in 1822 and studying afterwards under Gay-Lussac at Paris. On his return to Germany he became professor of Chemistry in the University of Giessen, where he remained for twenty-five years. During this time he published his «Letters on Chemistry» and other works of the highest merit, which made him a world-wide reputation. In 1852 he left Giessen for the University of Munich, where he served as professor of Chemistry until his death, April 18th, 1873. In 1845 he had been «ennobled» as «Freiherr von Liebig,» and it is to this that he owes the title of «Baron,» by which he is frequently called. His work practically founded the science of organic chemistry, out of which some of the greatest discoveries of the age have developed. His «Letters on Chemistry» are admirable in their methods of expression. He has a faculty many scientific investigators lack, — that of making himself so clearly intelligible that he transmits to his readers no small part of his own enthusiasm for his subject.

GOLDMAKERS AND THE PHILOSOPHER'S STONE

IN ALL metals, according to the creed of the alchemists, there is contained a principle which gives to them the metallic character. This is the mercury of the adepts. To increase the proportion of this principle in the baser metals is to ennoble them. If we extract this metallic principle from any body or metal, if we increase its power by refining it, and thus produce the quintessence of all metallicity (to coin a word), we have the stone which, when made to act on base or unripe metals, matures and ennobles them. The mode of action of the philosopher's stone was considered by many as analogous to that of a ferment. " Does not yeast change the juice of plants or a solution of sugar by a new arrangement of their particles into the youth-giving and invigorating water of life? (*Aqua vitæ*, alcohol.) Does it not effect the expulsion of all impurities? Does not a ferment (sour dough) convert flour into nourishing bread?" (George Rippel, fifteenth century.)

In its utmost perfection, as the " universale," one part, according to Roger Bacon, sufficed to transmute a million parts — according to Raymond Lully, ten billions of parts — of a base metal into gold. According to Basil Valentine, the power of the philosopher's stone extends only to seventy parts; and John Price, the last alchemist and goldmaker of the eighteenth century, describes it as transmuting only from thirty to sixty parts of base metal.

For the preparation of the philosopher's stone the first requisite was the raw material, the Adamic earth, virgin earth, which is indeed to be found everywhere, but its discovery is dependent on certain conditions known to the initiated alone. " When we have once obtained this," says Isaacus Hollandus, " the preparation of the stone is a labor fit only for women, or child's play. From the *materies prima*, *cruda* or *remota*, the philosopher obtains first the mercury of the adepts, which differs from ordinary quicksilver, and is the quintessence, the first condition of the creation or procreation of all metals. To this is added philosophical gold, and the mixture is left for a long time in an incubatory or brooding furnace, which must have the form of an egg. There is thus obtained a black substance, the raven's head, or *caput corvi*, which, after long exposure to heat, is converted into a white body. This is the white swan, *cygnus albus*. After this has been long and more fiercely heated, it becomes yellow, and finally bright red, and now the great work is consummated."

Other accounts of the process for preparing the philosopher's stone are rendered, by their being mixed up with mystical views, yet darker and more mysterious. The custom, too, prevalent in those ages, of regulating divisions of time by the hours of prayer, passed, during the tenth, eleventh, and twelfth centuries, into the laboratories of the alchemists; and it is easy to perceive how, by degrees, the success of the operation came to be regarded as

essentially dependent on the efficacy of prayers, which prayers were at first used only to determine its duration. In the seventeenth century, the transformation of alchemistical ideas into religious notions had become so complete, that alchemistical expressions were frequently employed to designate religious ideas. In the writings of the mystics (for example, in those of the enthusiastic Jacob Böhme, 1624), the term " philosopher's stone " no longer signifies the substance which transmutes baser metals into gold, but " conversion "; the clay furnace is " the earthly body "; and the green lion is " the Lion of David."

Previous to the invention of printing, it was easy for an alchemist to keep secret his discoveries. He exchanged them only for the observations of other adepts. The chemical processes which they published are clearly and intelligibly described, in so far, at least, as they are not such as to lead to any practical result in reference to the chief object of their search; but they expressed their views, and described their labors, on the subject of " the grand arcanum " in figurative language and in mysterious symbols. They propounded in an unintelligible language that which, in their own minds, was only the faint dawn of an idea.

That which chiefly excites our wonder is, that the existence of the philosopher's stone should have been regarded, for so many centuries, as a truth established beyond all doubt, while yet no one possessed it, and each adept only maintained that it was in the possession of another.

Who, indeed, could entertain a doubt, after Van Helmont had declared, in 1618, that on several occasions there had been sent to him, from an unknown hand, one-fourth of a grain of the precious material, with which he had converted into pure gold eight ounces of quicksilver? Did not Helvétius, the distinguished body physician to the Prince of Orange, and the bitter opponent of alchemy, himself relate, in his " Vitulus Aureus quem Mundus Adorat et Orat " (1667), that he had obtained the most convincing proofs of the existence of the philosopher's stone? For he, the skeptic, had received, from a stranger, a fragment of the size of half a rape seed, and therewith, in presence of his wife and son, had transmuted six drams of lead into gold, which stood the tests applied to it by the warden of the mint at the Hague! Were not two pounds and a half of quicksilver converted into pure gold, of which a large medal was struck (Kopp. Geschichte der Chemie, IV. 171), with the figure of the God of Day (Sol or

gold) holding the caduceus of Mercury, to indicate the origin of the precious metal, and the legend " *Divina Metamorphosis Exhibita Pragæ*," *XV. Jan., An. MDCXLVII?* in *"Præsentia Sac. Cæs. Maj. Ferdinandi Tertü,"* etc.? Was not this done at Prague, in presence of the Emperor Ferdinand III. (1637-1657) by the Burgomaster, Count von Russ, with the aid of one grain of a red powder, which he had received from a certain Richthausen, and he again from an unknown? (According to J. F. Gmelin, this medal was still extant in 1797, in the treasury at Vienna.) The Landgrave of Hesse, Darmstadt also, Ernst Ludwig, as we are told by the alchemists, received, from an unknown hand, a packet containing red and white tincture, with directions for their use. Ducats were coined of the gold which had been made from lead by this means, and from the silver thus obtained were coined the Hessian " specie dollars " of 1717, on which is the legend, " *Sic Deo Placuit in Tribulationibus.*" (Kopp. II. 172.)

It can hardly be doubted that the amateurs of alchemy in these cases experienced something similar to that which befell the distinguished and highly deserving professor of theology, Semler, in Halle (1791), who occupied himself at one time in experiments with a then renowned universal medicine, which was offered for sale under the name of atmospheric salt (Luftsalz) by a certain Baron von Hirsch. Semler thought he had discovered that gold grew, or was produced in this salt when kept warm and moist. He sent, in 1787, a portion of the salt, with the gold grown in it to the Academy of Sciences, at Berlin. Klaproth, who examined it, found it to contain glauber salt (sulphate of soda) and sulphate of magnesia, enveloped in a " magna," and gold leaf in considerable quantity. Semler also sent to Klaproth some of the salt in which no gold had yet grown, and a liquor which " contained the germ of gold, and which impregnated the atmospheric salt in a proper warm temperature." It appeared, however, that the salt was already mixed with gold. Semler firmly believed in the production of the gold. In 1788 he wrote, " Two glasses are bearing gold. Every five or six days I remove it; each time about twelve to fifteen grains. Two or three other glasses are in progress, and the gold blooms out below." A new portion which was sent to Klaproth in leaves of from four to nine square inches proved that the gold plant had unfortunately degenerated, for it now bore adulterated gold or pinchbeck. At last the matter was cleared up. Semler's servant, who had to

take care of the hothouse, had introduced gold into the glasses, in order to give his master pleasure; but being on one occasion prevented from doing so himself, his wife undertook the business; but she was of opinion that pinchbeck leaf was much cheaper and would serve the purpose equally well. . . .

During the sixteenth century alchemists were found in the courts of all princes. The Emperor Rudolph II. and the Elector Palatine Frederick were known as patrons of alchemy. Men of all ranks studied transmutation, and strove to attain possession of the grand arcanum. Just as in the present day vast sums are expended by princes, private persons, and associations in mining enterprises for the discovery of metallic ores, of coal, or of strata of salt, so were vast sums squandered in the sixteenth and seventeenth centuries for the researches deemed necessary in order to discover the philosopher's stone. A multitude of adventurers appeared, who endeavored, at the courts of the great and mighty, to pass for adepts, that is, possessors of the secret; but this was a dangerous game, for those who at one court, or at another, succeeded, by dexterously managed transmutations, in establishing their character as adepts, and carried off honors and riches as their reward, were sure finally to fail elsewhere; and their end commonly was, to be hung in a robe covered with gold leaf on a gallows adorned in a like manner. Those, again, whose imposture could not be proved, expiated the fatal honor of being believed to possess the philosopher's stone, under the hands of covetous princes, by imprisonment and tortures. Indeed, the cruel treatment which such adventurers experienced was regarded as the strongest proof of the truth of their art.*

The great (Francis) Bacon, Benedict Spinoza, and Leibnitz believed in the philosopher's stone, and in the possibility of the transmutation of metals; and the decisions of Faculties of Jurisprudence prove how deep and how widely extended these ideas had at that period become. The Faculty of Law in Leipsic declared in 1580, in their judgment against David Beuther, that he was proved to possess the knowledge of the philosopher's stone; and the same faculty, in 1725, gave a decision in the affair of the Countess Anna Sophia von Erbach against her husband, Count Frederick Charles von Erbach. The lady had granted protection, in her castle of Frankenstein, to a fugitive, who was pursued and hunted like a wild beast; and he, who was an adept,

* Kopp.

had, to show his gratitude, converted the silver plate of the countess into gold. The count claimed the half of it, because the increase in its value had been obtained on his territory, and under coverture. But the faculty decided against him, because the object claimed had been, before its conversion into gold, the property of the countess, and she could not lose her right of property in it by the transmutation.

In our day, men are only too much disposed to regard the views of the disciples and followers of the Arabian school, and of the late alchemists, on the subject of transmutation of metals, as a mere hallucination of the human mind, and, strangely enough, to lament it. But the idea of the variable and changeable corresponds to universal experience, and always precedes that of the unchangeable. The notion of bodies, chemically simple, was first firmly established in the science by the introduction of the Daltonian doctrine, which admits the existence of solid particles, not further divisible, or atoms. But the ideas connected with this view are so little in accordance with our experience of nature, that no chemist of the present day holds the metals, absolutely, for simple, undecomposable bodies, for true elements. Only a few years since, Berzelius was firmly convinced of the compound nature of nitrogen, chlorine, bromine, and iodine; and we allow our so-called simple substances to pass for such, not because we know that they are in reality undecomposable, but because they are as yet undecomposed; that is, because we cannot yet demonstrate their decomposability, so as to satisfy the requirements of science. But we all hold it possible that this may be done to-morrow. In the year 1807, the alkalies, alkaline earths, and earths proper, were regarded as simple bodies, till Davy demonstrated that they were compounds of metals with oxygen.

In the last twenty-five years of the preceding century, many of the most distinguished philosophers believed in the transmutation of water into earth. Indeed, the belief was so widely prevalent, that Lavoisier, the greatest chemist of his day, thought it advisable, in a series of beautiful experiments, to submit to investigation the grounds on which it rested, and to point out their fallacy. Such notions as that of the production of lime during the incubation of eggs, and of iron and metallic oxides in the animal and vegetable vital processes, have found, even in the present century, acute and enthusiastic defenders.

It is the prevailing ignorance of chemistry, and especially of its history, which is the source of the very ludicrous and excessive estimation of ourselves, with which many look back on the age of alchemy; as if it were possible or even conceivable that for more than a thousand years the most learned and acute men, such as Francis Bacon, Spinoza, and Leibnitz, could have regarded as true and well-founded an opinion void of all foundation. On the contrary, must we not suppose, as a matter beyond a doubt, that the idea of the transmutability of metals stood in the most perfect harmony with all the observation and all the knowledge of that age, and in contradiction to none of these?

In the first stage of the development of science, the alchemists could not possibly have any other notions of the nature of metals than those which they actually held. No others were admissible or even possible; and their views were consequently, by natural law, inevitable. Without these ideas, chemistry would not now stand in its present perfection; and in order to call that science into existence, and in the course of fifteen hundred or two thousand years to bring it to the point which it has now reached, it would have been necessary to create the science anew. We hear it said that the idea of the philosopher's stone was an error; but all our views have been developed from errors, and that which to-day we regard as truth in chemistry, may, perhaps, before to-morrow, be recognized as a fallacy. . . .

Alchemy was never at any time anything different from chemistry. It is utterly unjust to confound it, as is generally done, with the goldmaking of the sixteenth and seventeenth centuries. Among the alchemists there was always to be found a nucleus of genuine philosophers, who often deceived themselves in their theoretical views; whereas the goldmakers, properly so called, knowingly deceived both themselves and others. Alchemy was the pure science, goldmaking included all those processes in which chemistry was technically applied. The achievements of such alchemists as Glauber, Böttger, and Kunkel, in this direction, may be boldly compared to the greatest discoveries of our century.

From « Letters on Chemistry. »

MAN AS A CONDENSED GAS

MANY of the fundamental or leading ideas of the present time appear, to him who knows not what science has already achieved, as extravagant as the notions of the alchemists. Not, indeed, the transmutation of metals, which seemed so probable to the Ancients, but far stranger things are held by us to be attainable. We have become so accustomed to wonders, that nothing any longer excites our wonder. We fix the solar rays on paper, and send our thoughts literally with the velocity of lightning to the greatest distances. We can, as it were, melt copper in cold water, and cast it into statues. We can freeze water into ice, or mercury into a solid malleable mass, in white-hot crucibles; and we consider it quite practicable to illuminate most brightly entire cities with lamps devoid of flame or fire, and to which the air has no access. We produce, artificially, ultramarine, one of the most precious minerals; and we believe that to-morrow or next day some one may discover a method of producing from a piece of charcoal a splendid diamond; from a bit of alum, sapphires or rubies; or from coal tar the beautiful coloring principle of madder, or the valuable remedies known as quinine and morphine. All these things are either as precious or more useful than gold. Every one is occupied in the attempt to discover them, and yet this is the occupation of no individual inquirer. All are occupied with these things, inasmuch as they study the laws of the changes and transformations to which matter is subject; and yet no one individual is specially engaged in these researches, inasmuch as no one, for example, devotes his life and energies to the solution of the problem of making diamonds or quinine. Did such a man exist, furnished with the necessary knowledge, and with the courage and perseverance of the old goldmakers, he would have a good prospect of being enabled to solve such problems. The latest discoveries on the constitution and production of the organic bases permit us to believe all this, without giving to any one the right to ridicule us as makers of gold.

Science has demonstrated that man, the being who performs all these wonders, is formed of condensed or solidified or liquefied gases; that he lives on condensed as well as uncondensed gases, and clothes himself in condensed gases; that he prepares his food by means of condensed gas, and, by means of the same

agent, moves the heaviest weights with the velocity of the wind. But the strangest part of the matter is, that thousands of these tabernacles formed of condensed gas, and going on two legs, occasionally, and on account of the production and supply of those forms of condensed gas which they require for food and clothing, or on account of their honor and power, destroy each other in pitched battles by means of condensed gas; and, further, that many believe the peculiar powers of the bodiless, conscious, thinking, and sensitive being, housed in this tabernacle, to be the result, simply, of its internal structure and the arrangement of its particles or atoms.

From « Letters on Chemistry. »

JOHN LINGARD

(1771-1851)

LINGARD's "History of England," which appeared in fourteen volumes between 1819 and 1831, ran through numerous editions during the author's lifetime, and was translated into French, German, and Italian. Cardinal Wiseman called it the only impartial history of England, and it is valued by students because it is, in fact, the only history which gives the material necessary for an impartial study of the evolution of English civilization during the period when the priests of the Roman Catholic Church were hanged, drawn and quartered as traitors, if they persisted in the attempt to say mass anywhere in England, Scotland, or Wales. Lingard was born at Winchester, England, February 7th, 1771, and educated in the Roman Catholic College at Douay, France. Returning to England he was ordained a priest of the Roman Catholic Church in 1795. In 1811 he took up his residence at Hornby, in Lancashire, where he spent the rest of his life in clerical and literary labors. Besides his "History of England" he wrote the "History and Antiquities of the Anglo-Saxon Church" and a considerable number of controversial tracts and essays. He died at Hornby, July 17th, 1851.

CROMWELL'S GOVERNMENT BY THE "MAILED HAND"

AT LENGTH (1653) Cromwell fixed on his plan to procure the dissolution of the parliament, and to vest for a time the sovereign authority in a council of forty persons, with himself at their head. It was his wish to effect this quietly by the votes of the parliament—his resolution to effect it by open force, if such votes were refused. Several meetings were held by the officers and members at the lodgings of the lord general in Whitehall. St. John and a few others gave their assent; the rest, under the guidance of Whitelock and Widrington, declared that the dissolution would be dangerous, and the establishment of the proposed council unwarrantable. In the meantime the house resumed the consideration of the new representative body; and several qualifications were voted, to all of which the officers

the men who had bled for them in the field, that they might gain the Presbyterians who had apostatized from the cause; and with doing all this in order to perpetuate their own power and to replenish their own purses. But their time was come; the Lord had disowned them; he had chosen more worthy instruments to perform his work. Here the orator was interrupted by Sir Peter Wentworth, who declared that he had never heard language so unparliamentary,—language, too, the more offensive, because it was addressed to them by their own servant, whom they had too fondly cherished, and whom, by their unprecedented bounty, they had made what he was. At these words Cromwell put on his hat, and, springing from his place, exclaimed, "Come, come, sir, I will put an end to your prating." For a few seconds, apparently in the most violent agitation, he paced forward and backward, and then, stamping on the floor, added, "You are no parliament; I say you are no parliament; bring them in, bring them in!" Instantly the door opened, and Colonel Worsley entered, followed by more than twenty musketeers. "This," cried Sir Henry Vane, "is not honest; it is against morality and common honesty." "Sir Henry Vane," replied Cromwell; "Oh, Sir Henry Vane! The Lord deliver me from Sir Henry Vane! He might have prevented this. But he is a juggler, and has not common honesty himself!" From Vane he directed his discourse to Whitelock, on whom he poured a torrent of abuse; then pointing to Chaloner, "There," he cried, "sits a drunkard"; next to Marten and Wentworth, "There are two whoremasters"; and afterwards, selecting different members in succession, described them as dishonest and corrupt livers, a shame and scandal to the profession of the Gospel. Suddenly, however, checking himself, he turned to the guard and ordered them to clear the house. At these words Colonel Harrison took the speaker by the hand and led him from the chair; Algernon Sidney was next compelled to quit his seat; and the other members, eighty in number, on the approach of the military, rose and moved towards the door. Cromwell now resumed his discourse. "It is you," he exclaimed, "that have forced me to do this. I have sought the Lord both day and night that he would rather slay me than put me on the doing of this work." Alderman Allan took advantage of these words to observe that it was not yet too late to undo what had been done; but Cromwell instantly charged him with peculation, and gave him into custody. When all were gone,

raised objections, but chiefly to the "admission of members," a project to strengthen the government by the introduction of the presbyterian interest. "Never," said Cromwell, "shall any of that judgment who have deserted the good cause be admitted to power." On the last meeting, held on the nineteenth of April, all these points were long and warmly debated. Some of the officers declared that the parliament must be dissolved "one way or other"; but the general checked their indiscretion and precipitancy, and the assembly broke up at midnight, with an understanding that the leading men on each side should resume the subject in the morning.

At an early hour the conference was recommenced, and, after a short time, interrupted, in consequence of the receipt of a notice by the general, that it was the intention of the house to comply with the desires of the army. This was a mistake; the opposite party had, indeed, resolved to pass a bill of dissolution; not, however, the bill proposed by the officers, but their own bill, containing all the obnoxious provisions, and to pass it that very morning, that it might obtain the force of law before their adversaries could have time to appeal to the power of the sword. While Harrison "most strictly and humbly" conjured them to pause before they took so important a step, Ingoldsby hastened to inform the lord general at Whitehall. His resolution was immediately formed, and a company of musketeers received orders to accompany him to the house. At this eventful moment, big with the most important consequences, both to himself and his country, whatever were the workings of Cromwell's mind, he had the art to conceal them from the eyes of the beholders. Leaving the military in the lobby, he entered the house and composedly seated himself on one of the outer benches. His dress was a plain suit of black cloth, with gray worsted stockings. For a while he seemed to listen with interest to the debate; but when the speaker was going to put the question, he whispered to Harrison, "This is the time; I must do it"; and rising, put off his hat to address the house. At first his language was decorous, and even laudatory. Gradually he became more warm and animated; at last he assumed all the vehemence of passion, and indulged in personal vituperation. He charged the members with self-seeking and profaneness; with the frequent denial of justice, and numerous acts of oppression; with idolizing the lawyers, the constant advocates of tyranny; with neglecting

fixing his eye on the mace, "What," said he, "shall we do with this fool's bauble? Here, carry it away." Then, taking the act of dissolution from the clerk, he ordered the doors to be locked, and, accompanied by the military, returned to Whitehall.

That afternoon the members of the council assembled in their usual place of meeting. Bradshaw had just taken the chair, when the lord general entered and told them that if they were there as private individuals they were welcome; but if as the council of state, they must know that the parliament was dissolved, and with it also the council. "Sir," replied Bradshaw, with the spirit of an ancient Roman, "we have heard what you did at the house this morning, and before many hours all England will know it. But, sir, you are mistaken to think that the parliament is dissolved. No power under heaven can dissolve them but themselves; therefore take you notice of that." After this protest they withdrew. Thus, by the parricidal hands of its own children, perished the Long Parliament, which, under a variety of forms, had, for more than twelve years, defended and invaded the liberties of the nation. It fell without a struggle or a groan, unpitied and unregretted. The members slunk away to their homes, where they sought by submission to purchase the forbearance of their new master; and their partisans, if partisans they had, reserved themselves in silence for a day of retribution, which came not before Cromwell slept in his grave. The royalists congratulated each other on an event which they deemed a preparatory step to the restoration of the king; the army and navy, in numerous addresses, declared that they would live and die, stand and fall, with the lord general; and in every part of the country the congregations of the saints magnified the arm of the Lord, which had broken the mighty, that in lieu of the sway of mortal men, the fifth monarchy, the reign of Christ might be established on earth.

From "History of England."

LIVY

(Titus Livius)

(c. 59 B.C.–17 A.D.)

IVY's prose style is essentially that of the writer of direct narrative. He is conceded to be the "most important prose writer of the Augustan Age," but if a writer's philosophy were to be judged by the moralizing he does, rather than by the view he takes of events, Livy might fairly be called the least philosophical of historians. That he was not so, however; that he did really consider events for their meaning as a part of a connected whole, rather than for their own sake as facts appealing to patriotic or individual vanity, he shows in the preface to his "History." "To the following considerations," he says, "I wish every one seriously and earnestly to attend: By what kind of men and by what sort of conduct in peace and war the empire has been both acquired and extended; then, as discipline gradually declines, let him follow in his thoughts the structure of ancient morals (at first as it were leaning aside; then sinking further and further; then beginning to fall precipitate), until he arrives at the present times, when our vices have attained to such a height of enormity that we can no longer endure either the burden of them or the sharpness of the necessary remedies. This is the great advantage to be derived from the study of history,—indeed, the only one which can make it answer any profitable and salutary purpose." This certainly is a philosophical motive of the highest order, and those who remember that Livy has defined it as the only motive which justified him in the immense labor of his "History" will acquit him of the charge of using fact and myth to glorify Rome, rather than to develop what he conceived to be the truth. The preface to his "History" is an essay of great merit and correct form. It might not be safe to say that no other such can be found in his historical works, but a search through the "History" will seldom show an interruption of the continuity of his narrative longer than half a page at a time. He stops occasionally to define his facts in a few terse sentences of comment or explanation, but nearly always he seeks to illustrate his idea of the meaning of history by the statement of fact itself rather than by comment upon it. He was born at Padua (Patavium), c. 61 B.C., and died there at the age of seventy-six. Over

forty years of his life were spent in Rome, where he wrote his "History" in one hundred and forty-two books, of which thirty-five have come down to us. He also wrote a celebrated treatise on "Oratory" in the form of dialogues, discussing the training of an orator and the secret of his success at the bar and in public life.

ON THE MAKING OF HISTORY

WHETHER, in tracing the series of the Roman history from the foundation of the city, I shall employ my time to good purpose is a question which I cannot positively determine: nor, were it possible, would I venture to pronounce such determination; for I am aware that the matter is of high antiquity, and has been already treated by many others; the latest writers always supposing themselves capable, either of throwing some new light on the subject, or, by the superiority of their talents for composition, of excelling the more inelegant writers who preceded them. However that may be, I shall, at all events, derive no small satisfaction from the reflection that my best endeavors have been exerted in transmitting to posterity the achievements of the greatest people in the world; and if, amidst such a multitude of writers, my name should not emerge from obscurity, I shall console myself by attributing it to the eminent merit of those who stand in my way in the pursuit of fame. It may be further observed that such a subject must require a work of immense extent, as our researches must be carried back through a space of more than seven hundred years; that the state has, from very small beginnings, gradually increased to such a magnitude that it is now distressed by its own bulk; and that there is every reason to apprehend that the generality of readers will receive but little pleasure from the accounts of its first origin, or of the times immediately succeeding, but will be impatient to arrive at that period, in which the powers of this overgrown state have been long employed in working their own destruction. On the other hand, this much will be derived from my labor, that, so long at least as I shall have my thoughts totally occupied in investigating the transactions of such distant ages, without being embarrassed by any of those unpleasing considerations, in respect of later days, which, though they might not have power to warp a writer's mind from the truth, would

yet be sufficient to create uneasiness, I shall withdraw myself from the sight of the many evils to which our eyes have been so long accustomed. As to the relations which have been handed down of events prior to the founding of the city, or to the circumstances that gave occasion to its being founded, and which bear the semblance rather of poetic fictions than of authentic records of history:—these, I have no intention either to maintain or refute. Antiquity is always indulged with the privilege of rendering the origin of cities more venerable, by intermixing divine with human agency; and if any nation may claim the privilege of being allowed to consider its original as sacred, and to attribute it to the operations of the gods, surely the Roman people, who rank so high in military fame, may well expect that, while they choose to represent Mars as their own parent, and that of their founder, the other nations of the world may acquiesce in this, with the same deference with which they acknowledge their sovereignty. But what degree of attention or credit may be given to these and such like matters, I shall not consider as very material.

To the following considerations, I wish every one seriously and earnestly to attend: By what kind of men, and by what sort of conduct, in peace and war, the empire has been both acquired and extended; then, as discipline gradually declines, let him follow in his thoughts the structure of ancient morals (at first as it were leaning aside; then sinking further and further; then beginning to fall precipitate), until he arrives at the present times, when our vices have attained to such a height of enormity that we can no longer endure either the burden of them or the sharpness of the necessary remedies. This is the great advantage to be derived from the study of history,—indeed, the only one which can make it answer any profitable and salutary purpose; for being abundantly furnished with clear and distinct examples of every kind of conduct, we may select for ourselves, and for the state to which we belong, such as are worthy of imitation; and, carefully noting such as, being dishonorable in their principles, are equally so in their effects, learn to avoid them. Now, either partiality to the subject of my intended work misleads me, or there never was any state either greater, or of purer morals, or richer in good examples, than this of Rome; nor was there ever any city into which avarice and luxury made their entrance so late, or where poverty and frugality were so highly

and so long held in honor; men contracting their desires in proportion to the narrowness of their circumstances. Of late years, indeed, opulence has introduced a greediness for gain, and the boundless variety of dissolute pleasures has created in many a passion for ruining themselves, and all around them. But let us, in the first stage at least of this undertaking, avoid gloomy reflections, which, when perhaps unavoidable, will not, even then, be agreeable. If it were customary with us, as it is with poets, we would more willingly begin with good omens, and vows, and prayers to the gods and goddesses, that they would propitiously grant success to our endeavors, in the prosecution of so arduous a task.

The preface to his "History" complete.

JOHN LOCKE

(1632–1704)

T IS impossible to overestimate the extent of the influence which ideas defined by John Locke have exerted on the civilization of the eighteenth and nineteenth centuries. No American of our colonial period had more to do than he did with forcing the revolution which separated the North American colonies from England and created the United States. During the Middle Ages the Schoolmen and others who were left unnoticed by their sovereigns as learned triflers discussed, with all the niceties of scholastic method, the question of whether or not one man has ever really derived from heaven the right to render its decrees for the control of others, without their consent and against their will. All the arguments which slowly accumulated on the negative side of this question Locke mastered and co-ordinated, — advancing beyond his predecessors with the confidence which belonged only to the highest genius. His treatise "Of Civil Government" and his "Letters concerning Toleration" bore their ripe fruit in the American Declaration of Independence, the constitution of the United States, and the gradual cessation of "religious" persecutions, through the use of the political machinery of the State. The worst and the almost only reproach against Locke is that when he attempted to draw a Constitution which would make his ideas practical, he was absurdly inconsistent with his own high ideals. But nothing less was to have been expected. The men who drafted and adopted the Constitution of the United States were consciously or unconsciously moved by the same ideals, but their collective wisdom in what is rightly pronounced the greatest success of its kind in history did not free it from inconsistencies so gross that radical differences of interpretation due to them resulted in the bloodiest civil war of modern times. It is not desirable to attempt to vindicate Locke against any charge of inconsistency, crudity, or absurdity which may be reasonably based on isolated facts of his life and writings. There is scarcely a page in the greatest work of Bacon which does not present similar contrasts. Every genius of the highest order becomes so by virtue of triumphing once or twice only over the iron laws of tradition and environment which govern his generation. In most things he must belong to his generation, or he could not exist in it. In a few things which con-

stitute his governing idea and are the result of the Titanic triumph of individuality in its struggle with the governing mind and impulses of the mass, he belongs to the whole past and future of the human race. This itself is an inconsistency; but only in the measure in which it exists and appears does genius exist as the governing influence in the life and work of any man. Locke's great genius showed itself most effectively and usefully in his assertion of fundamental political principles, but it is in his "Essay concerning Human Understanding" that he develops his greatest power of connected thought. It occasioned one of the most protracted controversies in the history of modern philosophy, — a controversy concerning which it needs only to be said here that in declaring "sensation" to be the "great source of most of the ideas we have," Locke stops with the "understanding" as a mode of interpreting facts. With the faith "which is the substance of things hoped for, the evidence of things unseen," he does not deal as a part of the understanding. Whatever may be the shortcomings of his philosophy, he has written, without doubt, in a single sentence, more than the majority of philosophers succeed in putting in a volume. That sentence, "Let us then suppose the mind to be, as we say, white paper void of all characters, without any ideas; how comes it to be furnished?" is one of the most celebrated and the most pregnant in the history of thought. Locke was born in Somerset, England, August 29th, 1632. His father was a lawyer who had been a captain in the Parliamentary army during the civil wars; so that Locke came in his youth directly under the control of the same influences which had educated Pym and Hampden. He completed his scholastic education at Christ's Church, Oxford, in 1656, and for some time afterwards continued to reside at the University as a lecturer on Greek and Rhetoric. He studied medicine, but did not take a degree, though when he entered the family of the Earl of Shaftesbury he served as family physician, as well as the Earl's confidential agent. It was through this connection that Locke made his celebrated failure as a constitution maker. His patron, being at that time one of the "proprietors" of the Carolinas, induced him to attempt to have a model government for the colony. After the fall of Shaftesbury, Locke was compelled to go into exile, and he lived abroad, chiefly in Holland, until 1688, when he returned to England as the favorite of William of Orange, who wished to promote him to high rank in the diplomatic service. Locke declined, however, and became Commissioner of Appeals, — a modest office with light duties, which enabled him to pursue his studies. The "Essay concerning Human Understanding" appeared in 1690, Locke receiving £30 for the copyright. Professor Fraser recalls the fact that this is almost exactly the sum that Kant received for his "Critique of Pure Reason," the only

philosophical work written since Locke's "Essay," which is generally admitted to belong to the same class with it. Locke's health began to fail in 1690, but, in spite of asthma and other infirmities, he continued to write vigorously until 1700, when his accumulating weaknesses checked, but did not suppress, his activity. His last years were spent in the study of the Gospels and the Epistles of St. Paul. He began his fourth letter on "Toleration" in 1704 and on the twenty-eighth of October in that year, leaving his work in the middle of a sentence, he declared himself "in perfect charity with all men" and died. He is buried in the parish church of High Laver in a tomb which attracts few visitors, but his mind is omnipresent as a part of the "perfect charity with all men," which, as it imperfectly governs the lives of individuals and enables them to tolerate each other, constitutes the world's civilization.

W. V. B.

"OF CIVIL GOVERNMENT"—ITS PURPOSES

IF MAN in the state of nature be so free, as has been said, if he be absolute lord of his own person and possessions, equal to the greatest, and subject to nobody, why will he part with his freedom? Why will he give up this empire, and subject himself to the dominion and control of any other power? To which it is obvious to answer, that though in the state of nature he hath such a right, yet the enjoyment of it is very uncertain, and constantly exposed to the invasions of others. For all being kings as much as he, every man his equal, and the greater part no strict observers of equity and justice, the enjoyment of the property he has in this state is very unsafe, very insecure. This makes him willing to quit this condition, which, however free, is full of fears and continual dangers; and it is not without reason that he seeks out and is willing to join in society with others, who are already united, or have a mind to unite, for the mutual preservation of their lives, liberties, and estates, which I call by the general name, Property.

The great and chief end, therefore, of men's uniting into commonwealths, and putting themselves under government, is the preservation of their property; to which in the state of nature there are many things wanting.

Firstly, there wants an established, settled, known law, received and allowed by common consent to be the standard of right and wrong, and the common measure to decide all contro-

versies between them. For though the law of nature be plain and intelligible to all rational creatures, yet men, being biased by their interest, as well as ignorant for want of study of it, are not apt to allow of it as a law binding to them in the application of it to their particular cases.

Secondly, in the state of nature there wants a known and indifferent judge, with authority to determine all differences according to the established law. For every one in that state, being both judge and executioner of the law of nature, men being partial to themselves, passion and revenge is very apt to carry them too far, and with too much heat in their own cases, as well as negligence and unconcernedness, to make them too remiss in other men's.

Thirdly, in the state of nature there often wants power to back and support the sentence when right, and to give it due execution. They who by any injustice offend will seldom fail, where they are able by force to make good their injustice; such resistance many times makes the punishment dangerous, and frequently destructive to those who attempt it.

Thus mankind, notwithstanding all the privileges of the state of nature, being but in an ill condition, while they remain in it, are quickly driven into society. Hence it comes to pass that we seldom find any number of men live any time together in this state. The inconveniences that they are therein exposed to by the irregular and uncertain exercise of the power every man has of punishing the transgressions of others makes them take sanctuary under the established laws of government, and therein seek the preservation of their property. It is this makes them so willingly give up every one his single power of punishing, to be exercised by such alone as shall be appointed to it amongst them; and by such rules as the community, or those authorized by them to that purpose, shall agree on. And in this we have the original right and rise of both the legislative and executive power, as well as of the governments and societies themselves.

For in the state of nature, to omit the liberty he has of innocent delights, a man has two powers.

The first is to do whatsoever he thinks fit for the preservation of himself, and others within the permission of the law of nature, by which law, common to them all, he and all the rest of mankind are of one community make up one society, distinct from all other creatures. And were it not for the corruption and viciousness of degenerate men there would be no need of any other, no necessity that men should separate from this great and natural community, and by positive agreements combine into smaller and divided associations.

The other power a man has in the state of nature is the power to punish the crimes committed against that law. Both these he gives up when he joins in a private, if I may so call it, or particular political society, and incorporates into any commonwealth separate from the rest of mankind.

The first power, *viz.*, of doing whatsoever he thought fit for the preservation of himself and the rest of mankind, he gives up to be regulated by laws made by the society, so far forth as the preservation of himself and the rest of that society shall require; which laws of the society in many things confine the liberty he had by the law of nature.

Secondly, the power of punishing he wholly gives up, and engages his natural force (which he might before employ in the execution of the law of nature, by his own single authority as he thought fit) to assist the executive power of the society, as the law thereof shall require. For being now in a new state, wherein he is to enjoy many conveniences, from the labor, assistance, and society of others in the same community, as well as protection from its whole strength, he has to part also with as much as his natural liberty, in providing for himself, as the good, prosperity, and safety of the society shall require; which is not only necessary but just, since the other members of the society do the like.

But though men, when they enter into society, give up the equality, liberty, and executive power they had in the state of nature into the hands of the society, to be so far disposed of by the legislative as the good of the society shall require, yet it being only with an intention in every one the better to preserve himself, his liberty, and property (for no rational creature can be supposed to change his condition with an intention to be worse), the power of the society, or legislative constituted by them, can never be supposed to extend further than the common good, but is obliged to secure every one's property by providing against those three defects above mentioned that made the state of nature so unsafe and uneasy. And so whoever has the legislative or supreme power of any commonwealth is bound to govern by established standing laws, promulgated and known to the people,

and not by extemporary decrees; by indifferent and upright judges, who are to decide controversies by those laws; and to employ the force of the community at home only in the execution of such laws, or abroad, to prevent or redress foreign injuries, and secure the community from inroads and invasion. And all this to be directed to no other end but the peace, safety, and public good of the people.

OF TYRANNY

As usurpation is the exercise of power which another has a right to, so tyranny is the exercise of power beyond right, which nobody can have a right to. And this is making use of the power any one has in his hands, not for the good of those who are under it, but for his own private separate advantage. When the governor, however entitled, makes not the law, but his will the rule, and his commands and actions are not directed to the preservation of the properties of his people, but the satisfaction of his own ambition, revenge, covetousness, or any other irregular passion.

If one can doubt this to be truth or reason, because it comes from the obscure hand of a subject, I hope the authority of a king will make it pass with him. King James I. in his speech to the parliament, 1603, tells them thus: "I will ever prefer the weal of the public and of the whole commonwealth, in making of good laws and constitutions, to any particular and private ends of mine,—thinking ever the wealth and weal of the commonwealth to be my greatest weal and worldly felicity,—a point wherein a lawful king doth directly differ from a tyrant. For I do acknowledge that the special and greatest point of difference that is between a rightful king and a usurping tyrant is this: that whereas the proud and ambitious tyrant doth think his kingdom and people are only ordained for satisfaction of his desires and unreasonable appetites, the righteous and just king doth, by the contrary, acknowledge himself to be ordained for the procuring of the wealth and property of his people." And again, in his speech to the parliament, 1609, he hath these words: "The king binds himself by a double oath to the observation of the fundamental laws of his kingdom. Tacitly, as by being a king, and so bound to protect as well the people as the laws of

his kingdom, and expressly by his oath at his coronation; so as every just king, in a settled kingdom, is bound to observe that paction made to his people, by his laws in framing his government agreeable thereunto, according to that paction which God made with Noah after the Deluge. Hereafter, seedtime and harvest, and cold and heat, and summer and winter, and day and night, shall not cease while the earth remaineth. And therefore a king governing in a settled kingdom leaves to be a king and degenerates into a tyrant, as soon as he leaves off to rule according to his laws." And a little after, "Therefore all kings that are not tyrants, or perjured, will be glad to bound themselves within the limits of their laws. And they that persuade them the contrary are vipers and pests, both against them and the commonwealth." Thus that learned king, who well understood the notions of things, makes the difference betwixt a king and a tyrant to consist only in this, that one makes the laws the bounds of his power, and the good of the public the end of his government; the other makes all give way to his own will and appetite.

It is a mistake to think this fault is proper only to monarchies; other forms of government are liable to it as well as that. For wherever the power that is put in any hands for the government of the people and the preservation of their properties is applied to other ends, and made use of to impoverish, harass, or subdue them to the arbitrary irregular commands of those that have it, there it presently becomes tyranny, whether those that thus use it are one or many. Thus we read of the thirty tyrants at Athens, as well as one at Syracuse, and the intolerable dominion of the Decemviri at Rome was nothing better.

Wherever law ends tyranny begins, if the law be transgressed to another's harm. And whosoever in authority exceeds the power given him by the law, and makes use of the force he has under his command to compass that upon the subject which the law allows, not ceases in that to be a magistrate; and, acting without authority, may be opposed as any other man who by force invades the right of another. This is acknowledged in subordinate magistrates. He that hath authority to seize my person in the street may be opposed as a thief and a robber if he endeavor to break into my house to execute a writ, notwithstanding that I know he has such a warrant and such a legal authority as will empower him to arrest me abroad. And why

this should not hold in the highest, as well as in the most inferior magistrate, I would gladly be informed. Is it reasonable that the eldest brother, because he has the greatest part of his father's estate, should thereby have a right to take away any of his younger brother's portions? Or that a rich man, who possessed a whole country, should from thence have a right to seize, when he pleased, the cottage and garden of his poor neighbor? The being rightfully possessed of great power and riches exceedingly beyond the greatest part of the sons of Adam is so far from being an excuse, much less a reason, for rapine and oppression, which the endamaging one another without authority is, that it is a great aggravation of it. For the exceeding the bounds of authority is no more a right in a great than a petty officer, no more justifiable in a king than a constable; but is so much the worse in him in that he has more trust put in him, has already a much greater share than the rest of his brethren, and is supposed, from the advantages of his education, employment, and counselors, to be more knowing in the measures of right and wrong.

May the commands then of a prince be opposed? May he be resisted as often as any one shall find himself aggrieved, and but imagine he has not a right done him? This will unhinge and overturn all polities, and, instead of government and order, leave nothing but anarchy and confusion.

To this I answer that force is to be opposed to nothing but to unjust and unlawful force; whoever makes any opposition in any other case draws on himself a just condemnation both from God and man, and so no such danger or confusion will follow, as is often suggested. For:—

Firstly, as in some countries, the person of the prince by law is sacred, and so whatever he commands or does his person is still free from all question or violence, not liable to force, or any judicial censure or condemnation. But yet opposition may be made to the illegal acts of any inferior officer, or other commissioned by him, unless he will, by actually putting himself into a state of war with his people, dissolve the government, and leave them to that defense which belongs to every one in the state of nature. For of such things who can tell what the end will be? And a neighbor kingdom has shown the world an odd example. In all other cases the sacredness of the person exempts him from all inconveniences, whereby he is secure, whilst the government stands from all violence and harm whatsoever, than which there cannot be a wiser constitution. For the harm he can do in his own person not being likely to happen often, nor to extend itself far, nor being able by his single strength to subvert the laws, nor oppress the body of the people, should any prince have so much weakness and ill nature as to be willing to do it, the inconveniency of some particular mischiefs that may happen sometimes when a heady prince comes to the throne are well recompensed by the peace of the public and security of the government in the person of the chief magistrate thus set out of the reach of danger; it being safer for the body that some few private men should be sometimes in danger to suffer than that the head of the republic should be easily and upon slight occasions exposed.

Secondly, but this privilege belonging only to the king's person, hinders not, but they may be questioned, opposed, and resisted who use unjust force, though they pretend a commission from him which the law authorizes not. As is plain in the case of him that has the king's writ to arrest a man, which is a full commission from the king, and yet he that has it cannot break open a man's house to do it, nor execute this command of the king upon certain days, nor in certain places, though this commission have no such exception in it, but they are the limitations of the law, which, if any one transgress, the king's commission excuses him not. For the king's authority being given him only by the law, he cannot empower any one to act against the law, or justify him by his commission in so doing; the commission or command of any magistrate where he has no authority being as void and insignificant as that of any private man. The difference between the one and the other being that the magistrate has some authority so far and to such ends, and the private man has none at all. For it is not the commission, but the authority, that gives the right of acting, and against the laws there can be no authority; but, notwithstanding such resistance, the king's person and authority are still both secured, and so no danger to governor or government.

Thirdly, supposing a government wherein the person of the chief magistrate is not thus sacred, yet this doctrine of the lawfulness of resisting all unlawful exercises of his power will not, upon every slight occasion, endanger him or embroil the government. For where the injured party may be relieved, and his

damages repaired by appeal to the law, there can be no pretense for force, which is only to be used where a man is intercepted from appealing to the law. For nothing is to be accounted hostile force but where it leaves not the remedy of such an appeal. And it is such force alone that puts him that uses it into a state of war, and makes it lawful to resist him. A man with a sword in his hand demands my purse in the highway, when perhaps I have not 12d. in my pocket; this man I may lawfully kill. To another I deliver £100 to hold only whilst I alight, which he refuses to restore me when I am got up again, but draws his sword to defend the possession of it by force if I endeavor to retake it. The mischief this man does me is a hundred, or possibly a thousand times more than the other perhaps intended me (whom I killed before he really did me any), and yet I might lawfully kill the one, and cannot so much as hurt the other lawfully. The reason whereof is plain, because the one using force, which threatened my life, I could not have time to appeal to the law to secure it, and when it was gone it was too late to appeal. The law could not restore life to my dead carcass. The loss was irreparable, which, to prevent the law of nature, gave me a right to destroy him who had put himself into a state of war with me, and threatened my destruction. But in the other case, my life not being in danger, I may have the benefit of appealing to the law, and have reparation for my £100 that way.

Fourthly, but if the unlawful acts done by the magistrate be maintained (by the power he has got), and the remedy which is due by law be, by the same power, obstructed, yet the right of resisting, even in such manifest acts of tyranny, will not suddenly or on slight occasions disturb the government. For if it reach no further than some private men's cases, though they have a right to defend themselves and recover by force what by unlawful force is taken from them, yet the right to do so will not easily engage them in a contest wherein they are sure to perish; it being as impossible for one or a few oppressed men to disturb the government, where the body of the people do not think themselves concerned in it, as for a raving madman or heady malcontent to overturn a well-settled state, the people being as little apt to follow the one as the other.

But if either these illegal acts have extended to the majority of the people, or if the mischief and oppression has light only on some few, but in such cases as the precedent, and conse-

quences seem to threaten all, and they are persuaded in their consciences, that their laws, and with them their estates, liberties, and lives are in danger, and perhaps their religion too, how they will be hindered from resisting illegal force used against them I cannot tell. This is an inconvenience, I confess, that attends all governments whatsoever when the governors have brought it to this pass to be generally suspected of their people; the most dangerous state which they can possibly put themselves in, wherein they are the less to be pitied, because it is so easy to be avoided,—it being impossible for a governor, if he really means the good of his people, and the preservation of them and their laws together, not to make them see and feel it, as it is for the father of a family not to let his children see he loves and takes care of them.

But if all the world shall observe pretenses of one kind and actions of another; arts used to elude the law, and trust of prerogative (which is an arbitrary power in some things left in the prince's hand to do good, not harm to the people) employed contrary to the end for which it was given. If the people shall find the ministers and subordinate magistrate chosen suitable to such ends, and favored or laid by proportionably as they promote or oppose them; if they see several experiments made of arbitrary power, and that religion underhand favored (though publicly proclaimed against) which is readiest to introduce it, and the operators in it supported as much as may be; and when that cannot be done, yet approved still, and liked the better; if a long train of actings show the councils all tending that way, how can a man any more hinder himself from being persuaded in his own mind which way things are going, or from casting about how to save himself, than he could from believing the captain of the ship he was in was carrying him and the rest of the company to Algiers when he found him always steering that course, though cross winds, leaks in his ship, and want of men and provisions did often force him to turn his course another way for some time, which he steadily returned to again as soon as the wind, weather, and other circumstances would let him?

OF THE CONDUCT OF THE UNDERSTANDING

THERE is, it is visible, great variety in men's understandings, and their natural constitutions put so wide a difference between some men in this respect, that art and industry would never be able to master; and their very natures seem to want a foundation to raise on it that which other men easily attain unto. Amongst men of equal education there is a great inequality of parts. And the woods of America, as well as the schools of Athens, produce men of several abilities in the same kind. Though this be so, yet I imagine most men come very short of what they might attain unto in their several degrees, by a neglect of their understandings. A few rules of logic are thought sufficient in this case for those who pretend to the highest improvement; whereas I think there are a great many natural defects in the understanding capable of amendment, which are overlooked and wholly neglected. And it is easy to perceive that men are guilty of a great many faults in the exercise and improvement of this faculty of the mind, which hinder them in their progress and keep them in ignorance and error all their lives. Some of them I shall take notice of, and endeavor to point out proper remedies for in the following discourse.

Besides the want of determined ideas, and of sagacity and exercise in finding out and laying in order intermediate ideas, there are three miscarriages that men are guilty of in reference to their reason, whereby this faculty is hindered in them from that service it might do and was designed for. And he that reflects upon the actions and discourses of mankind will find their defects in this kind very frequent and very observable.

The first is of those who seldom reason at all, but do and think according to the example of others, whether parents, neighbors, ministers, or who else they are pleased to make choice of to have an implicit faith in, for the saving of themselves the pains and trouble of thinking and examining for themselves.

The second is of those who put passion in the place of reason, and being resolved that shall govern their actions and arguments, neither use their own, nor hearken to other people's reason, any further than it suits their humor, interest, or party; and these, one may observe, commonly content themselves with words which have no distinct ideas to them, though, in other matters that they come with an unbiased indifferency to, they want not abilities to talk and hear reason, where they have no secret inclination that hinders them from being untractable to it.

The third sort is of those who readily and sincerely follow reason, but, for want of having that which one may call large, sound, round-about sense, have not a full view of all that relates to the question and may be of moment to decide it. We are all shortsighted, and very often see but one side of a matter; our views are not extended to all that has a connection with it. From this defect, I think, no man is free. We see but in part, and we know but in part, and therefore it is no wonder we conclude not right from our partial views. This might instruct the proudest esteemer of his own parts how useful it is to talk and consult with others, even such as came short with him in capacity, quickness, and penetration; for, since no one sees all, and we generally have different prospects of the same thing, according to our different, as I may say, positions to it, it is not incongruous to think, nor beneath any man to try, whether another may not have notions of things which have escaped him, and which his reason would make use of, if they came into his mind. The faculty of reasoning seldom or never deceives those who trust to it; its consequences from what it builds on are evident and certain; but that which it oftenest, if not only, misleads us in, is that the principles from which we conclude, the grounds upon which we bottom our reasoning, are but a part; something is left out which should go into the reckoning to make it just and exact. . . .

In this we may see the reason why some men of study and thought, that reason right, and are lovers of truth, do make no great advances in their discoveries of it. Error and truth are uncertainly blended in their minds, their decisions are lame and defective, and they are very often mistaken in their judgments. The reason whereof is, they converse but with one sort of men, they read but one sort of books, they will not come in the hearing but of one sort of notions; the truth is, they canton out to themselves a little Goshen in the intellectual world, where light shines, and, as they conclude, day blesses them; but the rest of that vast expanse they give up to night and darkness, and so avoid coming near it. They have a petty traffic with known correspondents in some little creek; within that they confine themselves, and are dexterous managers enough of the wares and prod-

ucts of that corner with which they content themselves, but will not venture out into the great ocean of knowledge, to survey the riches that nature hath stored other parts with, no less genuine, no less solid, no less useful, than what has fallen to their lot in the admired plenty and sufficiency of their own little spot, which to them contains whatsoever is good in the universe. Those who live thus mewed up within their own contracted territories, and will not look abroad beyond the boundaries that chance, conceit, or laziness has set to their inquiries, but live separate from the notions, discourses, and attainments of the rest of mankind, may not amiss be represented by the inhabitants of the Marian Islands, which, being separated by a large tract of sea from all communion with the habitable parts of the earth, thought themselves the only people of the world. And though the straitness and conveniences of life amongst them had never reached so far as to the use of fire, till the Spaniards, not many years since, in their voyages from Acapulco to Manila brought it amongst them, yet, in the want and ignorance of almost all things, they looked upon themselves, even after that the Spaniards had brought amongst them the notice of variety of nations abounding in sciences, arts, and conveniences of life, of which they knew nothing, they looked upon themselves, I say, as the happiest and wisest people in the universe. . . .

We are born with faculties and powers capable almost of anything, such at least as would carry us further than can be easily imagined; but it is only the exercise of those powers which gives us ability and skill in anything, and leads us towards perfection.

A middle-aged plowman will scarce ever be brought to the carriage and language of a gentleman, though his body be as well proportioned, and his joints as supple, and his natural parts not any way inferior. The legs of a dancing master, and the fingers of a musician, fall, as it were, naturally without thought or pains into regular and admirable motions. Bid them change their parts, and they will in vain endeavor to produce like motions in the members not used to them, and it will require length of time and long practice to attain but some degrees of a like ability. What incredible and astonishing actions do we find rope dancers and tumblers bring their bodies to! Not but that sundry in almost all manual arts are as wonderful, but I name those which the world takes notice of for such, because, on that very account, they give money to see them. All these admired motions,

beyond the reach and almost the conception of unpracticed spectators, are nothing but the mere effects of use and industry in men, whose bodies have nothing peculiar in them from those of the amazed lookers-on.

As it is in the body, so it is in the mind; practice makes it what it is; and most even of those excellencies which are looked on as natural endowments will be found, when examined into more narrowly, to be the product of exercise, and to be raised to that pitch only by repeated actions. Some men are remarked for pleasantness in raillery, others for apologues and opposite diverting stories. This is apt to be taken for the effect of pure nature, and that rather because it is not got by rules; and those who excel in either of them never purposely set themselves to the study of it as an art to be learned. But yet it is true that at first some lucky hit which took with somebody, and gained him commendation, encouraged him to try again, inclined his thoughts and endeavors that way, till at last he insensibly got a facility in it without perceiving how; and that is attributed wholly to nature, which was much more the effect of use and practice. I do not deny that natural disposition may often give the first rise to it; but that never carries a man far without use and exercise, and it is practice alone that brings the powers of the mind as well as those of the body to their perfection. Many a good poetic vein is buried under a trade, and never produces anything for want of improvement. We see the ways of discourse and reasoning are very different, even concerning the same matter, at court and in the university. And he that will go but from Westminster Hall to the Exchange will find a different genius and turn in their ways of talking; and one cannot think that all whose lot fell in the city were born with different parts from those who were bred at the university or Inns of Court.

To what purpose all this, but to show that the difference, so observable in men's understandings and parts, does not arise so much from the natural faculties as acquired habits? He would be laughed at that should go about to make a fine dancer out of a country hedger, at past fifty. And he will not have much better success who shall endeavor at that age to make a man reason well, or speak handsomely, who has never been used to it, though you should lay before him a collection of all the best precepts of logic or oratory. Nobody is made anything by hearing of rules, or laying them up in his memory; practice must settle

the habit of doing without reflecting on the rule; and you may as well hope to make a good painter or musician extempore, by a lecture and instruction in the arts of music and painting, as a coherent thinker, or strict reasoner, by a set of rules, showing him wherein right reasoning consists.

This being so, that defects and weakness in men's understandings, as well as other faculties, come from want of a right use of their own minds, I am apt to think the fault is generally mislaid upon nature, and there is often a complaint of want of parts, when the fault lies in want of a due improvement of them.

From the essay on « The Conduct of the Understanding.»

CONCERNING TOLERATION AND POLITICS IN THE CHURCHES

THE end of a religious society is the public worship of God, and, by means thereof, the acquisition of eternal life. All discipline ought therefore to tend to that end, and all ecclesiastical laws to be thereunto confined. Nothing ought nor can be transacted in this society relating to the possession of civil and worldly goods. No force is here to be made use of upon any occasion whatsoever. Force belongs wholly to the civil magistrate, and the possession of all outward goods is subject to his jurisdiction.

But it may be asked, by what means, then, shall ecclesiastical laws be established, if they must be thus destitute of all compulsive power? I answer: They must be established by means suitable to the nature of such things, whereof the external profession and observation — if not proceeding from a thorough conviction and approbation of the mind — is altogether useless and unprofitable. The arms by which the members of this society are to be kept within their duty are exhortations, admonitions, and advices. If by these means the offenders will not be reclaimed, and the erroneous convinced, there remains nothing further to be done but that such stubborn and obstinate persons, who give no ground to hope for their reformation, should be cast out and separated from the society. This is the last and utmost force of ecclesiastical authority. No other punishment can thereby be inflicted than that, the relation ceasing between the body and the member which is cut off. The person so condemned ceases to be a part of the church.

These things being thus determined, let us inquire, in the next place, how far the duty of toleration extends, and what is required from every one by it.

And, firstly, I hold that no church is bound, by the duty of toleration, to retain any such person in her bosom as, after admonition, continues obstinately to offend against the laws of the society. For these being the condition of communion and the bond of the society, if the breach of them were permitted without any animadversion the society would immediately be thereby dissolved. But, nevertheless, in all such cases care is to be taken that the sentence of excommunication, and the execution thereof, carry with it no rough usage of word or action whereby the ejected person may in any wise be damnified in body or estate. For all force (as has often been said) belongs only to the magistrate, nor ought any private persons at any time to use force, unless it be in self-defense against unjust violence. Excommunication neither does, nor can, deprive the excommunicated person of any of those civil goods that he formerly possessed. All those things belonged to the civil government, and are under the magistrate's protection. The whole force of excommunication consists only in this: that the resolution of the society in that respect being declared, the union that was between the body and some member comes thereby to be dissolved; and that relation ceasing, the participation of some certain things which the society communicated to its members, and unto which no man has any civil right, comes also to cease. For there is no civil injury done unto the excommunicated person by the church minister's refusing him that bread and wine, in the celebration of the Lord's Supper, which was not bought with his, but other men's money.

Secondly, no private person has any right in any manner to prejudice another person in his civil enjoyments because he is of another church or religion. All the rights and franchises that belong to him as a man, or as a denizen, are inviolably to be preserved to him. These are not the business of religion. No violence nor injury is to be offered him, whether he be Christian or Pagan. Nay, we must not content ourselves with the narrow measures of bare justice; charity, bounty, and liberality must be added to it. This the Gospel enjoins, this reason directs, and this that natural fellowship we are born into requires of us. If any man err from the right way, it is his own misfortune, no injury to thee; nor therefore art thou to punish him in

the things of this life because thou supposest he will be miserable in that which is to come.

What I say concerning the mutual toleration of private persons differing from one another in religion, I understand also of particular churches which stand, as it were, in the same relation to each other as private persons among themselves: nor has any one of them any manner of jurisdiction over any other; no, not even when the civil magistrate (as it sometimes happens) comes to be of this or the other communion. For the civil government can give no new right to the church, nor the church to the civil government. So that whether the magistrate join himself to any church, or separate from it, the church remains always as it was before—a free and voluntary society. It neither requires the power of the sword by the magistrate's coming to it, nor does it lose the right of instruction and excommunication by his going from it. This is the fundamental and immutable right of a spontaneous society—that it has power to remove any of its members that transgress the rules of its institution; but it cannot, by the accession of any new members, acquire any right of jurisdiction over those that are not joined with it. And therefore peace, equity, and friendship are always mutually to be observed by particular churches, in the same manner as by private persons, without any pretense of superiority or jurisdiction over one another.

That the thing may be made clearer by an example, let us suppose two churches—the one of Arminians, the other of Calvinists—residing in the city of Constantinople. Will any one say that either of these churches has right to deprive the members of the other of their estates and liberty (as we see practiced elsewhere), because of their differing from it in some doctrines and ceremonies, whilst the Turks in the meanwhile silently stand by, and laugh to see with what inhuman cruelty Christians thus rage against Christians? But if one of these churches hath this power of treating the other ill, I ask which of them it is to whom that power belongs, and by what right. It will be answered, undoubtedly, that it is the orthodox church which has the right of authority over the erroneous or heretical. This is, in great and specious words, to say just nothing at all. For every church is orthodox to itself; to others, erroneous or heretical. For whatsoever any church believes, it believes to be true; and the contrary unto those things, it pronounces to be error. So that the

controversy between these churches about the truth of their doctrines, and the purity of their worship, is on both sides equal; nor is there any judge, either at Constantinople or elsewhere upon earth, by whose sentence it can be determined. The decision of that question belongs to the Supreme Judge of all men, to whom also alone belongs the punishment of the erroneous. In the meanwhile, let those men consider how heinously they sin, who, adding injustice, if not to their error, yet certainly to their pride, do rashly and arrogantly take upon them to misuse the servants of another master, who are not at all accountable to them.

Nay, further: if it could be manifest which of these two dissenting churches were in the right, there would not accrue thereby unto the orthodox any right of destroying the other. The churches have neither any jurisdiction in worldly matters, nor are fire and sword any proper instruments wherewith to convince men's minds of error, and inform them of the truth. Let us suppose, nevertheless, that the civil magistrate inclined to favor one of them, and to put his sword into their hands, that (by his consent) they might chastise the dissenters as they pleased. Will any man say that any right can be derived unto a Christian church over its brethren from a Turkish emperor? An infidel, who has himself no authority to punish Christians for the articles of their faith, cannot confer such an authority upon any society of Christians, nor give unto them a right which he has not himself. This would be the case at Constantinople; and the reason of the thing is the same in any Christian kingdom. The civil power is the same in every place. Nor can that power, in the hands of a Christian prince, confer any greater authority upon the Church than in the hands of a heathen; which is to say, just none at all.

Nevertheless, it is worthy to be observed and lamented that the most violent of these defenders of the truth, the opposers of errors, the exclaimers against schism, do hardly ever let loose this their zeal for God, with which they are so warmed and inflamed, unless where they have the civil magistrate on their side. But so soon as ever court favor has given them the better end of the staff, and they begin to feel themselves the stronger, then presently peace and charity are to be laid aside. Otherwise they are religiously to be observed. Where they have not the power to carry on persecution and to become masters, there they desire

to live upon fair terms, and preach up toleration. When they are not strengthened with the civil power, then they can bear most patiently and unmovedly the contagion of idolatry, superstition, and heresy in their neighborhood; of which on other occasions the interest of religion makes them to be extremely apprehensive. They do not forwardly attack those errors which are in fashion at court or are countenanced by the government. Here they can be content to spare their arguments; which yet (with their leave) is the only right method of propagating truth, which has no such way of prevailing as when strong arguments and good reason are joined with the softness of civility and good usage.

Nobody, therefore, in fine, neither single persons nor churches, nay, nor even commonwealths, have any just title to invade the civil rights and worldly goods of each other upon pretense of religion. Those that are of another opinion would do well to consider with themselves how pernicious a seed of discord and war, how powerful a provocation to endless hatreds, rapines, and slaughters they thereby furnish unto mankind. No peace and security, no, not so much as common friendship, can ever be established or preserved amongst men so long as this opinion prevails, that dominion is founded in grace and that religion is to be propagated by force of arms.

In the third place, let us see what the duty of toleration requires from those who are distinguished from the rest of mankind (from the laity, as they please to call us) by some ecclesiastical character and office; whether they be bishops, priests, presbyters, ministers, or however else dignified or distinguished. It is not my business to inquire here into the original of the power or dignity of the clergy. This only I say, that whencesoever their authority he sprung, since it is ecclesiastical, it ought to be confined within the bonds of the Church, nor can it in any manner be extended to civil affairs, because the Church itself is a thing absolutely separate and distinct from the commonwealth. The boundaries on both sides are fixed and immovable. He jumbles heaven and earth together, the things most remote and opposite, who mixes these two societies, which are in their original end, business, and in everything perfectly distinct and infinitely different from each other. No man, therefore, with whatsoever ecclesiastical office he be dignified, can deprive another man that is not of his church and faith either of liberty or of any part of his worldly goods upon the account of that difference between them in religion. For whatsoever is not lawful to the whole Church cannot by any ecclesiastical right become lawful to any of its members.

But this is not all. It is not enough that ecclesiastical men abstain from violence and rapine and all manner of persecution. He that pretends to be a successor of the Apostles, and takes upon him the office of teaching, is obliged also to admonish his hearers of the duties of peace and good-will towards all men, as well towards the erroneous as the orthodox; towards those that differ from them in faith and worship as well as towards those that agree with them therein. And he ought industriously to exhort all men, whether private persons or magistrates (if any such there be in his church), to charity, meekness, and toleration, and diligently endeavor to allay and temper all that heat and unreasonable averseness of mind which either any man's fiery zeal for his own sect or the craft of others has kindled against dissenters. I will not undertake to represent how happy and how great would be the fruit, both in Church and State, if the pulpits everywhere sounded with this doctrine of peace and toleration, lest I should seem to reflect too severely upon those men whose dignity I desire not to detract from, nor would have it diminished either by others or themselves. But this I say, that thus it ought to be. And if any one that professes himself to be a minister of the Word of God, a preacher of the Gospel of Peace, teach otherwise, he either understands not or neglects the business of his calling, and shall one day give account thereof unto the Prince of Peace. If Christians are to be admonished that they abstain from all manner of revenge, even after repeated provocations and multiplied injuries, how much more ought they who suffer nothing, who have had no harm done them, forbear violence and abstain from all manner of ill usage towards those from whom they have received none! This caution and temper they ought certainly to use towards those who mind only their own business, and are solicitous for nothing but that (whatever men think of them) they may worship God in that manner which they are persuaded is acceptable to him, and in which they have the strongest hopes of eternal salvation. In private domestic affairs, in the management of estates, in the conservation of bodily health, every man may consider what suits his own convenience, and follow what course he likes best. No man com-

plains of the ill management of his neighbor's affairs. No man is angry with another for an error committed in sowing his land or in marrying his daughter. Nobody corrects a spendthrift for consuming his substance in taverns. Let any man pull down, or build, or make whatsoever expenses he pleases, nobody murmurs, nobody controls him; he has his liberty. But if any man do not frequent the church, if he do not there conform his behavior exactly to the accustomed ceremonies, or if he brings not his children to be initiated in the sacred mysteries of this or the other congregation, this immediately causes an uproar. The neighborhood is filled with noise and clamor. Every one is ready to be the avenger of so great a crime, and the zealots hardly have the patience to refrain from violence and rapine so long till the cause be heard, and the poor man be, according to form, condemned to the loss of liberty, goods, or life. Oh, that our ecclesiastical orators of every sect would apply themselves with all the strength of arguments that they are able to the confounding of men's errors! But let them spare their persons. Let them not supply their want of reasons with the instruments of force, which belong to another jurisdiction, and do ill become a churchman's hands. Let them not call in the magistrate's authority to the aid of their eloquence or learning, lest perhaps, whilst they pretend only love for the truth, this their intemperate zeal, breathing nothing but fire and sword, betray their ambition and show that what they desire is temporal dominion.

From the «Letter concerning
Toleration.»

OF IDEAS IN GENERAL, AND THEIR ORIGINAL

EVERY man being conscious to himself that he thinks, and that which his mind is applied about whilst thinking being the ideas that are there, it is past doubt that men have in their minds several ideas, such as are those expressed by the words: Whiteness, hardness, sweetness, thinking, motion, man, elephant, army, drunkenness, and others. It is in the first place, then, to be inquired how he comes by them. I know it is a received doctrine that men have native ideas and original characters stamped upon their minds in their very first being. This opinion I have, at large, examined already; and I suppose what I have said in the foregoing book will be much more easily

admitted, when I have shown whence the understanding may get all the ideas it has, and by what ways and degrees they may come into the mind; for which I shall appeal to every one's own observation and experience.

Let us then suppose the mind to be, as we say, white paper void of all characters, without any ideas; how comes it to be furnished? Whence comes it by that vast store which the busy and boundless fancy of man has painted on it, with an almost endless variety? Whence has it all the materials of reason and knowledge? To this I answer in one word, from experience; in that all our knowledge is founded, and from that it ultimately derives itself. Our observation employed either about external sensible objects, or about the internal operations of our minds, perceived and reflected on by ourselves, is that which supplies our understandings with all the materials of thinking. These two are the fountains of knowledge, from whence all the ideas we have, or can naturally have, do spring.

Firstly, our senses, conversant about particular sensible objects, do convey into the mind several distinct perceptions of things, according to those various ways wherein those objects do affect them: and thus we come by those ideas we have of yellow, white, heat, cold, soft, hard, bitter, sweet, and all those which we call sensible qualities; which, when I say the senses convey into the mind, I mean, they, from external objects, convey into the mind what produces there those perceptions. This great source of most of the ideas we have, depending wholly upon our senses, and derived by them to the understanding, I call Sensation.

Secondly, the other fountain from which experience furnisheth the understanding with ideas, is the perception of the operations of our own mind within us, as it is employed about the ideas it has got, which operations, when the soul comes to reflect on and consider, do furnish the understanding with another set of ideas, which could not be had from things without; and such are perception, thinking, doubting, believing, reasoning, knowing, willing, and all the different actings of our own minds; which we, being conscious of and observing in ourselves, do from these receive into our understandings as distinct ideas, as we do from bodies affecting our senses. This source of ideas every man has wholly in himself; and though it be not sense, as having nothing to do with external objects, yet it is very like it, and might prop-

erly enough be called internal sense. But as I call the other Sensation, so I call this, Reflection, the ideas it affords being such only as the mind gets by reflecting on its own operations within itself. By reflection, then, in the following part of this discourse, I would be understood to mean that notice which the mind takes of its own operations, and the manner of them; by reason whereof there come to be ideas of these operations in the understanding. These two, I say, viz., external material things, as the objects of sensation, and the operations of our own minds within, as the objects of reflection, are to me the only originals from whence all our ideas take their beginnings. The term Operations here I use in a large sense, as comprehending not barely the actions of the mind about its ideas, but some sort of passions arising sometimes from them, such as is the satisfaction or uneasiness arising from any thought.

The understanding seems to me not to have the least glimmering of any ideas, which it doth not receive from one of these two. External objects furnish the mind with the ideas of sensible qualities, which are all those different perceptions they produce in us; and the mind furnishes the understanding with ideas of its own operations.

From Book II. «Of Human
Understanding.»

JOHN GIBSON LOCKHART

(1794-1854)

HIEFLY remembered as the son in law and biographer of Sir Walter Scott, John Gibson Lockhart was in his own generation a literary man of great distinction. He edited the Quarterly Review from 1826 to 1853; and in his official capacity as the leading critic of England, did not hesitate to pronounce Tennyson a melancholy failure in his first attempts at poetry. Lockhart's own best work was done in verse as the translator of "Ancient Spanish Ballads," which are never likely to lose their popularity with lovers of spirited, narrative poetry. He was born at Cambusnethan, in Lanarkshire, Scotland, July 14th, 1794, and was educated for the bar. After joining the staff of Blackwoods in 1818, he never attempted to practice his profession. In 1820 he married Sir Walter Scott's eldest daughter, Sophia. His association with Sir Walter was intimate, qualifying him in every way for his principal prose work, "Memoirs of the Life of Sir Walter Scott," which appeared in seven volumes from 1837 to 1839. He died at Abbotsford, November 25th, 1854.

THE CHARACTER OF SIR WALTER SCOTT

NO MAN was a firmer or more indefatigable friend. I know not he ever lost one; and a few with whom, during the energetic middle stage of life, from political differences or other accidental circumstances, he lived less familiarly, had all gathered round him, and renewed the full warmth of early affection in his later days. There was enough to dignify the connection in their eyes; but nothing to chill it on either side. The imagination that so completely mastered him when he chose to give her the rein was kept under most determined control when any of the positive obligations of active life came into question. A high and pure sense of duty presided over whatever he had to do as a citizen and a magistrate; and as a landlord he considered his estate as an extension of his hearth.

Of his political creed, the many who hold a different one will of course say that it was the natural fruit of his political devo-

tion to the mere prejudice of antiquity; and I am quite willing to allow that this must have had a great share in the matter— and that he himself would have been as little ashamed of the word Prejudice as of the word Antiquity. Whenever Scotland could be considered as standing separate on any question from the rest of the empire, he was not only apt, but eager to embrace the opportunity of again rehoisting, as it were, the old signal of national independence; and I sincerely believe that no circumstance in his literary career gave him so much personal satisfaction as the success of "Malachi Malagrowther's Epistles." He confesses, however, in his diary, that he was aware how much it became him to summon calm reason to battle imaginative prepossessions on this score; and I am not aware that they ever led him into any serious political error. He delighted in letting his fancy run wild about ghosts and witches and horoscopes— but I venture to say, had he sat on the judicial bench a hundred years before he was born, no man would have been more certain to give juries sound direction in estimating the pretended evidence of supernatural occurrences of any sort; and I believe, in like manner, that had any anti-English faction, civil or religious, sprung up in his own time in Scotland, he would have done more than any other living man could have hoped to do, for putting it down. He was on all practical points a steady, conscientious Tory of the school of William Pitt; who, though an anti-revolutionist, was certainly anything but an anti-reformer. He rejected the innovations, in the midst of which he died, as a revival, under alarmingly authoritative auspices, of the doctrines which had endangered Britain in his youth, and desolated Europe throughout his prime of manhood. May the gloomy anticipations which hung over his closing years be unfulfilled! But should they be so, let posterity remember the warnings and the resistance of his and other powerful intellects were probably in that event the appointed means for averting a catastrophe in which, had England fallen, the whole civilized world must have been involved.

Sir Walter received a strictly religious education under the eye of parents, whose virtuous conduct was in unison with the principles they desired to instill into their children. From the great doctrines thus recommended he appears never to have swerved; but he must be numbered among the many who have incurred considerable risk of doing so, in consequence of the rigid-

ity with which Presbyterian heads of families, in Scotland, were used to enforce compliance with various relics of the puritanical observance. He took up, early in life, a repugnance to the mode in which public worship is conducted in the Scottish Establishment; and adhered to the sister Church, whose system of government and discipline he believed to be the fairest copy of the primitive polity, and whose litanies and collects he reverenced as having been transmitted to us from the age immediately succeeding that of the Apostles. The few passages in his diaries, in which he alludes to his own religious feelings and practices, show clearly the sober, serene, and elevated frame of mind in which he habitually contemplated man's relations with his Maker; the modesty with which he shrunk from indulging either the presumption of reason, or the extravagance of imagination, in the province of Faith; his humble reliance on the wisdom and mercy of God; and his firm belief that we are placed in this state of existence, not to speculate about another, but to prepare ourselves for it by active exertion of our intellectual faculties, and the constant cultivation of kindness and benevolence towards our fellowmen.

But his moral, political, and religious character has sufficiently impressed itself upon the great body of his writings. He is, indeed, one of the few great authors of modern Europe who stand acquitted of having written a line that ought to have embittered the bed of death. His works teach the practical lessons of morality and Christianity in the most captivating form — unobtrusively and unaffectedly. And I think it is not refining too far to say, that in these works, as well as in his whole demeanor as a man of letters, we may trace the happy effects — enough has already been said as to some less fortunate and agreeable ones — of his having written throughout with a view to something beyond the acquisition of personal fame. Perhaps no great poet ever made his literature so completely ancillary to the objects and purposes of practical life. However his imagination might expatiate, it was sure to rest over his home. The sanctities of domestic love and social duty were never forgotten, and the same circumstance that most ennobled all his triumphs affords also the best apology for his errors.

From "Life of Scott."

BURNS AND THE PUNDITS OF EDINBURGH

IT NEEDS no effort of imagination to conceive what the sensations of an isolated set of scholars, almost all either clergymen or professors, must have been in the presence of this bigboned, black-browed, brawny stranger, with his great flashing eyes, who, having forced his way among them from the plow-tail at a single stride, manifested in the whole strain of his bearing and conversation, a most thorough conviction that, in a society of the most eminent men of his nation, he was exactly where he was entitled to be; hardly deigned to flatter them by exhibiting even an occasional symptom of being flattered by their notice: by turns calmly measured himself against the most cultivated understandings of his time in discussion; overpowered the *bon mots* of the most celebrated convivialists by broad floods of merriment, impregnated with all the burning life of genius; astounded bosoms habitually enveloped in the thrice-piled folds of social reserve, by compelling them to tremble — nay to tremble visibly — beneath the fearless touch of natural pathos; and all this without indicating the smallest willingness to be ranked among those professional ministers of excitement, who are content to be paid in money and smiles for doing what the spectators and auditors would be ashamed of doing in their own persons, even if they had the power of doing it; and — last and probably worst of all — who was known to be in the habit of enlivening societies which they would have scorned to approach, still more frequently than their own, with eloquence no less magnificent; with wit in all likelihood still more daring; often enough, as the superiors whom he fronted without alarm might have guessed from the beginning, and had ere long no occasion to guess, with wit pointed at themselves.

The lawyers of Edinburgh, in whose wider circles Burns figured at his outset, with at least as much success as among the professional *literati*, were a very different race of men from these; they would neither, I take it, have pardoned rudeness, nor been alarmed by wit. But being, in those days, with scarcely an exception, members of the landed aristocracy of the country, and forming by far the most influential body, as indeed they still do, in the society of Scotland, they were, perhaps, as proud a set of men as ever enjoyed the tranquil pleasures of unquestioned superiority. What their haughtiness, as a body, was, may be guessed, when we know that inferior birth was reckoned a fair and legitimate ground for excluding any man from the bar. In one remarkable instance, about this very time, a man of very extraordinary talents and accomplishments was chiefly opposed in a long and painful struggle for admission, and, in reality, for no reasons but those I have been alluding to, by gentlemen who, in the sequel, stood at the very head of the Whig party in Edinburgh; and the same aristocratical prejudice has, within the memory of the present generation, kept more persons of eminent qualifications in the background, for a season, than any English reader would easily believe. To this body belonged nineteen out of twenty of those patricians, whose stateliness Burns so long remembered and so bitterly resented. It might, perhaps, have been well for him had stateliness been the worst fault of their manners. Winebibbing appears to be in most regions a favorite indulgence with those whose brains and lungs are subjected to the severe exercises of legal study and forensic practice. To this day, more traces of these old habits linger about the Inns of Court than in any other section of London. In Dublin and Edinburgh the barristers are even now eminently convivial bodies of men; but among the Scotch lawyers of the time of Burns the principle of jollity was, indeed, in its high and palmy state. He partook largely in those tavern scenes of audacious hilarity, which then soothed, as a matter of course, the arid labors of the northern *noblesse de la robe* — so they were called in "Redgauntlet" — and of which we are favored with a specimen in the High Jinks chapter of "Guy Mannering."

From "Life of Burns."

CESARE LOMBROSO

(1836–)

LOMBROSO'S essays on the "Pathology of Genius" created one of the hottest literary discussions of the last quarter of the nineteenth century. While he does not commit himself to the direct assertion that genius is a diseased as well as an abnormal condition of the human intellect, the facts and anecdotes with which he illustrated his essays all tended to leave that impression in the mind of the general public. The discussion which ensued was at all times animated and sometimes bitter, frequently subjecting Lombroso himself to severe tests by his own standards. "The Man of Genius," which appeared in 1888, summarizes his conclusions on this subject. He has made a comprehensive study of the pathology of the criminal intellect, and his works on "criminology" are valued by specialists in all civilized countries. He was born at Venice in November, 1836 (at Verona, according to other authorities). The University of Turin was his Alma Mater, and he is now professor of Psychiatry there.

ECCENTRICITIES OF FAMOUS MEN

FORGETFULNESS is one of the characteristics of genius. It is said that Newton once rammed his niece's finger into his pipe; when he left his room to seek for anything he usually returned without bringing it. Rouelle generally explained his ideas at great length, and when he had finished, he added: "But this is one of my arcana which I tell to no one." Sometimes one of his pupils rose and repeated in his ear what he had just said aloud; then Rouelle believed that the pupil had discovered the arcanum by his own sagacity, and begged him not to divulge what he had himself just told to two hundred persons. One day, when performing an experiment during a lecture, he said to his hearers: "You see, gentlemen, this caldron over the flame? Well, if I were to leave off stirring it, an explosion would at once occur which would make us all jump." While saying these words, he did not fail to forget to stir, and the pre-

diction was accomplished; the explosion took place with a fearful noise: the laboratory windows were all smashed, and the audience fled to the garden. Sir Everard Home relates that he once suddenly lost his memory for half an hour, and was unable to recognize the house and the street in which he lived; he could not recall the name of the street, and seemed to hear it for the first time. It is told of Ampère that when traveling on horseback in the country he became absorbed in a problem; then, dismounting, began to lead his horse, and finally lost it; but he did not discover his misadventure until, on arrival, it attracted the attention of his friends. Babinet hired a country house, and after making the payments returned to town; then he found that he had entirely forgotten both the name of the place and from what station he had started.

One day Buffon, lost in thought, ascended a tower and slid down by the ropes, unconscious of what he was doing, like a somnambulist. Mozart, in carving meat, so often cut his fingers, accustomed only to the piano, that he had to give up this duty to other persons. Of Bishop Munster, it is said that, seeing at the door of his own antechamber the announcement: "The master of the house is out," he remained there awaiting his own return. Of Toucherel, it is told by Arago, that he once even forgot his own name. Beethoven, on returning from an excursion in the forest, often left his coat on the grass, and often went out hatless. Once, at Neustadt, he was arrested in this condition, and taken to prison as a vagabond; here he might have remained, as no one would believe that he was Beethoven, if Herzog, the conductor of the orchestra, had not arrived to deliver his own return. Gioia, in the excitement of composition, wrote a chapter on the table of his bureau instead of on paper. The Abbé Beccaria, absorbed in his experiments, said during mass: "*Ite! experientia facta est.*" St. Dominic, in the midst of a princely repast, suddenly struck the table and exclaimed: "*Conclusum est contra Manicheos.*" It is told of Ampère that having written a formula, with which he was pre-occupied, on the back of a cab, he started in pursuit as soon as the cab went off. Diderot hired vehicles which he then left at the door and forgot, thus needlessly paying coachmen for whole days. He often forgot the hour, the day, the month, and even the person to whom he was speaking; he would then speak long monologues like a somnambulist. Rossini, conducting the orchestra at the rehearsal of his "Barbiere," which was a fiasco,

did not perceive that the public, and even the performers, had left him alone in the theatre until he reached the end of an act.

Hagen notes that originality is the quality that distinguishes genius from talent. And Jurgen-Meyer: "The imagination of talent reproduces the stated fact; the inspiration of genius makes it anew. The first disengages or repeats; the second invents or creates. Talent aims at a point which appears difficult to reach; genius aims at a point which no one perceives. The novelty, it must be understood, resides not in the elements, but in their shock." Novelty and grandeur are the two chief characters which Bettinelli attributes to genius; "for this reason," he says, "poets call themselves troubadours or trouvères." Cardan conceived the idea of the education of deaf mutes before Harriot; he caught a glimpse of the application of algebra to geometry and geometric constructions before Descartes. Giordano Bruno divined the modern theories of cosmology and of the origin of ideas. Cola di Rienzi conceived Italian unity, with Rome as capital, four hundred years before Cavour and Mazzini. Stoppani admits that the geological theory of Dante, with the regard to the formation of seas, is at all points in accordance with the accepted ideas of to-day.

Genius divines facts before completely knowing them; thus Goethe described Italy very well before knowing it; and Schiller, the land and people of Switzerland, without having been there. And it is on account of those divinations which all precede common observation, and because genius, occupied with lofty researches, does not possess the habits of the many, and because, like the lunatic and unlike the man of talent, he is often disordered, the man of genius is scorned and misunderstood. Ordinary persons do not perceive the steps which have led the man of genius to his creation, but they see the difference between his conclusions and those of others, and the strangeness of his conduct. Rossini's "Barbiere," and Beethoven's "Fidelio" were received with hisses; Boito's "Mefistofele" and Wagner's "Lohengrin" have been hissed at Milan. How many academicians have smiled compassionately at Marzolo, who has discovered a new philosophic world! Bolyai, for his invention of the fourth dimension in anti-Euclidian geometry, has been called the geometrician of the insane, and compared to a miller who wishes to make flour of sand. Every one knows the treatment accorded to Fulton and Columbus and Papin, and, in our own days, to

Piatti and Praga and Abel, and to Schliemann, who found Ilium, where no one else had dreamed of looking for it, while learned academicians laughed. "There never was a liberal idea," wrote Flaubert, "which has not been unpopular; never an act of justice which has not caused scandal; never a great man who has not been pelted with potatoes or struck by knives. 'The history of human intellect is the history of human stupidity,' as M. de Voltaire said."

In this persecution, men of genius have no fiercer or more terrible enemies than the men of academies, who possess the weapons of talent, the stimulus of vanity, and the prestige by preference accorded to them by the vulgar, and by governments which, in large part, consist of the vulgar. There are, indeed, countries in which the ordinary level of intelligence sinks so low that the inhabitants come to hate, not only genius, but even talent.

From «The Man of Genius.»

HENRY WADSWORTH LONGFELLOW

(1807–1882)

IF THE ability to express the best and most helpful thoughts that are common to humanity in all ages and countries, and to make this expression so lucid, so simple, so truthful, that those who most need to be helped by it are reached, influenced, and elevated—if to do this is the highest work of the poet, then Longfellow's sphere of usefulness in poetry is higher and more nearly universal than that of any other poet who has written English verse during the nineteenth century. In what may be classed as the peculiar qualities of genius, he may not rank with Byron, with Shelley, or even with Tennyson or Swinburne in England, or with Poe and Lanier in America. But his usefulness is incomparably greater in America than that of any other poet of his century. He is peculiarly the poet of the home and the favorite of all those who prefer for themselves, or for those they wish to influence, an assured future of quiet usefulness rather than an uncertain and feverish life of that spasmodic admiration which the world bestows only on the extraordinary or the abnormal. The quiet stream which, beginning as a cold and pellucid brook flowing from the melting snows of some lofty mountain peak, gathers volume and increasing warmth in the lowlands until, without losing its native purity and clarity, it swells at last to a noble river, fertilizing wide areas of wood and field, of orchard and garden where grain and fruit and flowers in profusion and in beauty cheer the eye and delight the heart as a result of its fructifying influences—this is the type of the usefulness of Longfellow as a poet, as a benefactor of his own country, as a friend of universal humanity.

That he was one of the greatest scholars of New England, as well as its greatest poet, is a fact which his own modesty left unasserted. But no one who attempts to follow him where his traces are obvious, through the literature of the classical, mediæval, and modern period, will doubt the extent of his industry or the thoroughness of his scholarship. As a prose writer he has an unpretentious and lucid style of direct statement which is always admirable in its spirit, and seldom at fault in its expression. His prose in the essays he has prefixed to "The Poets and Poetry of Europe," in his "Hyperion," and "Outre-Mer" ranks with the very best prose of its class written in

America, and it is essentially superior both in idea and expression to the best work of the members of Longfellow's own literary circle, who made prose writing much more a specialty that he ever attempted to do. If it were not that his use of German hexameter in his "Evangeline" is still under discussion, it might be said without danger of dispute that he did his best work in everything he attempted, and that he did even his worst work well. It is true when all is said that "Evangeline" is an admirable poem, worthy of its theme and of its author, though its mode is that of Voss rather than of Homer. When all has been admitted that can be truly said in depreciation of Longfellow, his work remains still unimpeached, to testify that there is no higher name in the American literature of the nineteenth century. He was born at Portland, Maine, February 27th, 1807. After graduating at Bowdoin College in 1825, he spent between two and three years in Europe, returning to become professor of Modern Languages at Bowdoin (1829–1835). After a second visit to Europe he became professor of Modern Languages and Belles-Lettres at Harvard, where he remained eighteen years, retiring in 1854 and continuing to reside at Cambridge, where he devoted himself to literature. His poems were widely circulated in England, and many of them have been translated into German and other continental languages. He died March 24th, 1882, after a life so placid that but for his deep sorrow at the loss of his wife it might have been redeemed wholly from that pathetic element which so frequently excites, if it does not occasion, poetic genius. The placidity of his life which re-appears in his verse has been the chief occasion for the charge of commonplaceness brought against him. But it is illogical to the last degree to confound the peaceful with the commonplace. The spirit of peace is as rare in poetry as it is in life, and it is Longfellow's greatest glory that his work expresses it.

W. V. B.

ANGLO-SAXON LANGUAGE AND POETRY

WE READ in history that the beauty of an ancient manuscript tempted King Alfred, when a boy at his mother's knee, to learn the letters of the Saxon tongue. A volume which that monarch minstrel wrote in after years now lies before me so beautifully printed that it might tempt any one to learn, not only the letters of the Saxon language, but the language also. The monarch himself is looking from the ornamental initial letter of the first chapter. He is crowned and careworn; having a beard, and long, flowing locks, and a face of majesty.

He seems to have just uttered those remarkable words, with which his preface closes: "And now he prays, and for God's name implores, every one of those whom it lists to read this book, that he would pray for him, and not blame him, if he more rightly understand it than he could; for every man must, according to the measure of his understanding, and according to his leisure, speak that which he speaks, and do that which he does."

I would fain hope that the beauty of this and other Anglo-Saxon books may lead many to the study of that venerable language. Through such gateways will they pass, it is true, into no gay palace of song; but among the dark chambers and moldering walls of an old national literature, all weather-stained and in ruins. They will find, however, venerable names recorded on those walls; and inscriptions, worth the trouble of deciphering. To point out the most curious and important of these is my present purpose; and according to the measure of my understanding, and according to my leisure, I speak that which I speak.

The Anglo-Saxon language was the language of our Saxon forefathers in England, though they never gave it that name. They called it English. Thus King Alfred speaks of translating "from book-latin into English" (*of bec Ledene on Englisc*); Abbot Ælfric was requested by Æthelward "to translate the book of Genesis from Latin into English" (*anwendan of Ledene on Englisc tha boc Genesis*); and Bishop Leofric, speaking of the manuscript he gave to the Exeter Cathedral, calls it "a great English book" (*mycel Englisc boc*). In other words, it is the old Saxon, a Gothic tongue, as spoken and developed in England. That it was spoken and written uniformly throughout the land is not to be imagined, when we know that Jutes and Angles were in the country as well as Saxons. But that it was essentially the same language everywhere is not to be doubted, when we compare pure West Saxon texts with Northumbrian glosses and books of Durham. Hickes speaks of a Dano-Saxon period in the history of the language. The Saxon kings reigned six hundred years; the Danish dynasty, twenty only. And neither the Danish boors, who were earthlings (*yrthlingas*) in the country, nor the Danish soldiers, who were dandies at the court of King Canute, could, in the brief space of twenty years, have so overlaid or interlarded the pure Anglo-Saxon with their provincialisms, as to give it a new character, and thus form a new period in its history, as was afterwards done by the Normans.

The Dano-Saxon is a dialect of the language, not a period which was passed through in its history. Down to the Norman Conquest, it existed in the form of two principal dialects; namely, the Anglo-Saxon in the South; and the Dano-Saxon, or Northumbrian, in the North. After the Norman Conquest, the language assumed a new form, which has been called, properly enough, Norman-Saxon and Semi-Saxon.

This form of the language, ever flowing and filtering through the roots of national feeling, custom, and prejudice, prevailed about two hundred years; that is, from the middle of the eleventh to the middle of the thirteenth century, when it became English. It is impossible to fix the landmarks of a language with any great precision; but only floating beacons, here and there. . . .

It is oftentimes curious to consider the far-off beginnings of great events, and to study the aspect of the cloud no bigger than one's hand. The British peasant looked seaward from his harvest field, and saw, with wondering eyes, the piratical schooner of a Saxon Viking making for the mouth of the Thames. A few years — only a few years — afterward, while the same peasant, driven from his homestead north or west, still lives to tell the story to his grandchildren, another race lords it over the land, speaking a different language and living under different laws. This important event in his history is more important in the world's history. Thus began the reign of the Saxons in England; and the downfall of one nation, and the rise of another, seem to us at this distance only the catastrophe of a stage play.

The Saxons came into England about the middle of the fifth century. They were pagans; they were a wild and warlike people; brave, rejoicing in sea storms, and beautiful in person, with blue eyes, and long flowing hair. Their warriors wore their shields suspended from their necks by chains. Their horsemen were armed with iron sledge hammers. Their priests rode upon mares, and carried into the battlefield an image of the god Irminsula; in figure like an armed man; his helmet crested with a cock; in his right hand a banner, emblazoned with a red rose; a bear carved upon his breast; and, hanging from his shoulders, a shield, on which was a lion in a field of flowers.

Not two centuries elapsed before the whole people was converted to Christianity. Ælfric, in his homily on the birthday of St. Gregory, informs us that this conversion was accomplished by the holy wishes of that good man, and the holy works of St. Augustine and other monks. St. Gregory beholding one day certain slaves set for sale in the market place of Rome, who were "men of fair countenance and nobly haired," and learning that they were heathen, and called Angles, heaved a long sigh, and said: "Well-away! that men of so fair a hue should be subjected to the swarthy devil! Rightly are they called Angles, for they have angels' beauty; and therefore it is fit that they in heaven should be companions of angels." As soon, therefore, as he undertook the popehood (*papanhad underfeng*), the monks were sent to their beloved work. In the Witena Gemot, or Assembly of the Wise, convened by King Edwin of Northumbria to consider the propriety of receiving the Christian faith, a Saxon Ealdorman arose, and spoke these noble words: "Thus seemeth to me, O king, this present life of man upon earth, compared with the time which is unknown to us; even as if you were sitting at a feast, amid your Ealdormen and Thegns in winter time. And the fire is lighted, and the hall warmed, and it rains, and snows, and storms without. Then cometh a sparrow, and flieth about the hall. It cometh in at one door, and goeth out at another. While it is within, it is not touched by the winter's storm; but that is only for a moment, only for the least space. Out of the winter it cometh, to return again into the winter eftsoon. So also this life of man endureth for a little space. What goeth before it and what followeth after, we know not. Wherefore, if this new lore bring aught more certain and more advantageous, then it is worthy that we should follow it."

Thus the Anglo-Saxons became Christians. For the good of their souls they built monasteries and went on pilgrimages to Rome. "The whole country," to use Malmesbury's phrase, "was glorious and refulgent with relics." The priests sang psalms night and day; and so great was the piety of St. Cuthbert, that, according to Bede, he forgot to take off his shoes for months together, — sometimes the whole year round; — from which Mr. Turner infers, that he had no stockings. They also copied the Evangelists, and illustrated them with illuminations; in one of which St. John is represented in a pea-green dress with red stripes. They also drank ale out of buffalo horns and wooden-

knobbed goblets. A Mercian king gave to the Monastery of Croyland his great drinking horn, that the elder monks might drink therefrom at festivals, and "in their benedictions remember sometimes the soul of the donor, Witlaf." They drank his health with that of Christ, the Virgin Mary, the Apostles, and other saints. Malmesbury says that excessive drinking was the common vice of all ranks of people. We know that King Hardicanute died in a revel; and King Edmund, in a drunken brawl at Pucklechurch, being, with all his court, much overtaken by liquor, at the festival of St. Augustine. Thus did mankind go reeling through the Dark Ages; quarreling, drinking, hunting, hawking, singing Psalms, wearing breeches, grinding in mills, eating hot bread, rocked in cradles, buried in coffins, — weak, suffering, sublime. Well might King Alfred exclaim, "Maker of all creatures! help now thy miserable mankind."

A national literature is a subject which should always be approached with reverence. It is difficult to comprehend fully the mind of a nation; even when that nation still lives, and we can visit it, and its present history, and the lives of men we know, help us to a comment on the written text. But here the dead alone speak. Voices, half understood; fragments of song, ending abruptly, as if the poet had sung no further, but died with these last words upon his lips; homilies, preached to congregations that have been asleep for many centuries; lives of saints, who went to their reward long before the world began to scoff at sainthood; and wonderful legends, once believed by men, and now, in this age of wise children, hardly credible enough for a nurse's tale; nothing entire, nothing wholly understood, and no further comment or illustration than may be drawn from an isolated fact found in an old chronicle, or, perchance, a rude illumination in an old manuscript! Such is the literature we have now to consider. Such fragments and mutilated remains has the human mind left of itself, coming down through the times of old, step by step, and every step a century. Old men and venerable accompany us through the Past; and, pausing at the threshold of the Present, they put into our hands at parting, such written records of themselves as they have. We should receive these things with reverence. We should respect old age.

> "This leaf, is it not blown about by the wind?
> Woe to it for its fate!
> Alas! it is old."

What an Anglo-Saxon glee-man was, we know from such commentaries as are mentioned above. King Edgar forbade the monks to be ale-poets (*ealascopas*); and one of his accusations against the clergy of his day was, that they entertained glee-men in their monasteries, where they had dicing, dancing, and singing till midnight. The illumination of an old manuscript shows how a glee-man looked. It is a frontispiece to the Psalms of David. The great psalmist sits upon his throne, with a harp in his hand, and his masters of sacred song around him. Below stands the glee-man; throwing three balls and three knives alternately into the air, and catching them, as they fall, like a modern juggler. But all the Anglo-Saxon poets were not glee-men. All the harpers were not hoppesteres, or dancers. The scoop, the creator, the poet, rose, at times, to higher things. He sang the deeds of heroes, victorious odes, death songs, epic poems; or sitting in cloisters, and afar from these things, converted Holy Writ into Saxon chimes.

The first thing which strikes the reader of Anglo-Saxon poetry is the structure of the verse; the short exclamatory lines, whose rhythm depends on alliteration in the emphatic syllables, and to which the general omission of the particles gives great energy and vivacity. Though alliteration predominates in all Anglo-Saxon poetry, rhyme is not wholly wanting. It had line rhymes and final rhymes; which, being added to the alliteration, and brought so near together in the short, emphatic lines, produce a singular effect upon the ear. They ring like blows of hammers on an anvil. For example: —

"Flah mah fliteth,	The strong dart flitteth,
Flan man hwiteth,	The spear man whetteth,
Burg sorg biteth,	Care the city biteth,
Bald ald thwiteth,	Age the bold quelleth,
Wraec-faec writheth,	Vengeance prevaileth,
Wrath ath smiteth."	Wrath a city assaileth.

Other peculiarities of Anglo-Saxon poetry, which cannot escape the reader's attention, are its frequent inversions, its bold transitions, and abundant metaphors. These are the things which render Anglo-Saxon poetry so much more difficult than Anglo-Saxon prose. But upon these points I need not enlarge. It is enough to have thus alluded to them.

One of the oldest and most important remains of Anglo-Saxon literature is the epic poem of "Beowulf." Its age is unknown; but it comes from a very distant and hoar antiquity; somewhere between the seventh and tenth centuries. It is like a piece of ancient armor; rusty and battered, and yet strong. From within comes a voice sepulchral, as if the ancient armor spoke, telling a simple, straightforward narrative; with here and there the boastful speech of a rough old Dane, reminding one of those made by the heroes of Homer. The style, likewise, is simple,—perhaps one should say austere. The bold metaphors, which characterize nearly all the Anglo-Saxon poems we have read, are for the most part wanting in this. The author seems mainly bent upon telling us how his Sea-Goth slew the grendel and the firedrake. He is too much in earnest to multiply epithets and gorgeous figures. At times he is tedious; at times obscure; and he who undertakes to read the original will find it no easy task.

The poem begins with a description of King Hrothgar the Scylding, in his great hall of Heort, which re-echoed with sound of harp and song. But not far off, in the fens and marshes of Jutland, dwelt a grim and monstrous giant, called Grendel, a descendant of Cain. This troublesome individual was in the habit of occasionally visiting the Scylding's palace by night, to see, as the author rather quaintly says, "how the doughty Danes found themselves after their beer carouse." On his first visit, he destroyed some thirty inmates, all asleep, with beer in their brains; and ever afterwards kept the whole land in fear of death. At length the fame of these evil deeds reached the ears of Beowulf, the Thane of Higelac, a famous Viking in those days, who had slain sea monsters, and wore a wild boar for his crest. Straightway he sailed with fifteen followers for the court of Heort; unarmed, in the great mead hall, and at midnight fought the Grendel, tore off one of his arms, and hung it up on the palace wall as a curiosity; the fiend's fingers being armed with long nails, which the author calls the hand spurs of the heathen hero (*haethenes hond-sporu hilde-rinces*). Retreating to his cave, the grim ghost (*grima gast*) departed this life; whereat there was great carousing at Heort. But at night came the Grendel's mother, and carried away one of the beer-drunken heroes of the ale-wassail (*beore druncne ofer eolwaege*). Beowulf, with a great escort, pursued her to the fen lands of the Grendel; plunged, all armed, into a dark-rolling and dreary river, that flowed from the monster's cavern; slew worms and dragons manifold; was dragged to the bottom by the old wife; and seizing a magic sword, which

lay among the treasures of that realm of wonders, with one fell blow let her heathen soul out of its bone-house (*ban-hus*). Having thus freed the land from the giants, Beowulf, laden with gifts and treasures, departed homeward, as if nothing special had happened; and, after the death of King Higelac, ascended the throne of the Scyldings. Here the poem should end, and, we doubt not, did originally end. But, as it has come down to us, eleven more cantos follow, containing a new series of adventures. Beowulf has grown old. He has reigned fifty years; and now, in his gray old age, is troubled by the devastations of a monstrous firedrake, so that his metropolis is beleaguered, and he can no longer fly his hawks and merles in the open country. He resolves, at length, to fight with this firedrake; and with the help of his attendant, Wiglaf, overcomes him. The land is made rich by the treasures found in the dragon's cave; but Beowulf dies of his wounds.

Thus departs Beowulf, the Sea-Goth, of the world-kings the mildest to men, the strongest of hand, the most clement to his people, the most desirous of glory. And thus closes the oldest epic in any modern language; written in forty-three cantos and some six thousand lines. The outline, here given, is filled up with abundant episodes and warlike details. We have ale revels, and giving of bracelets, and presents of mares, and songs of bards. The battles with the Grendel and the Firedrake are minutely described; as likewise are the dwellings and rich treasure-houses of those monsters. The fire stream flows with lurid light; the dragon breathes out flame and pestilential breath; the gigantic sword, forged by the Jutes of old, dissolves and thaws like an icicle in the hero's grasp; and the swart raven tells the eagle how he fared with the fell wolf at the death feast. Such is, in brief, the machinery of the poem. It possesses great epic merit, and in parts is strikingly graphic in its descriptions. As we read, we can almost smell the brine, and hear the sea breeze blow, and see the mainland stretch out its jutting promontories, those sea-noses (*sae-naessas*), as the poet calls them, into the blue waters of the solemn main.

In the words of Mr. Kemble, I exhort the reader "to judge this poem not by the measure of our times and creeds, but by those of the times which it describes; as a rude, but very faithful picture of an age, wanting, indeed, in scientific knowledge, in mechanical expertness, even in refinement; but brave, generous, and

right principled; assuring him of what I well know, that these echoes from the deserted temples of the past, if listened to in a sober and understanding spirit, bring with them matter both strengthening and purifying the heart."

The next work to which I would call the attention of my readers is very remarkable, both in a philological and in a poetical point of view; being written in a more ambitious style than "Beowulf." It is Cædmon's "Paraphrase of Portions of Holy Writ." Cædmon was a monk in the minster of Whitby. He died in the year 680. The only account we have of his life is that given by the Venerable Bede in his "Ecclesiastical History."

By some he is called the "father of Anglo-Saxon poetry," because his name stands first in the history of Saxon songcraft; by others, the "Milton of our forefathers," because he sang of Lucifer and the Loss of Paradise.

The poem is divided into two books. The first is nearly complete, and contains a paraphrase of parts of the Old Testament and the Apocrypha. The second is so mutilated as to be only a series of unconnected fragments. It contains scenes from the New Testament, and is chiefly occupied with Christ's descent into the lower regions; a favorite theme in old times, and well known in the history of miracle plays, as the "Harrowing of Hell." The author is a pious, prayerful monk; "an awful, reverend, and religious man." He has all the simplicity of a child. He calls his Creator the Blithe-heart King; the patriarchs, Earls; and their children, Noblemen. Abraham is a wise-heedy man, a guardian of bracelets, a mighty earl; and his wife Sarah, a woman of elfin beauty. The sons of Reuben are called Sea Pirates. A laugher is a laughter-smith (hleahtor-smith); the Ethiopians, a people brown with the hot coals of heaven (*brune leode hatum heofon-colum*).

Striking poetic epithets and passages are not, however, wanting. They are sprinkled here and there throughout the narrative. The sky is called the roof of nations, the roof adorned with stars. After the overthrow of Pharaoh and his folk, he says, the blue air was with corruption tainted, and the bursting ocean whooped a bloody storm. Nebuchadnezzar described as a naked, unwilling wanderer, a wondrous wretch and weedless. Horrid ghosts, swart and sinful,

"Wide through windy halls
Wail woeful."

And, in the sack of Sodom, we are told how many a fearful, pale-faced damsel must trembling go into a stranger's embrace; and how fell the defenders of brides and bracelets, sick with wounds. Indeed, whenever the author has a battle to describe, and hosts of arm-bearing and war-faring men draw from their sheaths the ring-hilted sword of edges doughty (*hring-maeled sweord ecgum dihtig*), he enters into the matter with so much spirit that one almost imagines he sees, looking from under that monkish cowl, the visage of no parish priest, but of a grim war wolf, as the brave were called in the days when Cædmon wrote.

The genuineness of these remains has been called in question, or, perhaps, I should say, denied, by Hickes and others. They suppose the work to belong to as late a period as the tenth century, on account of its similarity in style and dialect to other poems of that age. Besides, the fragment of the ancient Cædmon, given by Bede, describing the Creation, does not correspond exactly with the passage on the same subject in the Junian or Pseudo Cædmon; and, moreover, Hickes says he has detected so many Dano-Saxon words and phrases in it, that he "cannot but think it was written by some Northumbrian (in the Saxon sense of the word), after the Danes had corrupted their language." Mr. Thorpe replies very conclusively to all this; that the language of the poem is as pure Anglo-Saxon as that of Alfred himself; that the Danisms exist only in the "imagination of the learned author of the Thesaurus"; and that, if they were really to be found in the work under consideration, it would prove no more than that the manuscript was a copy made by a Northumbrian scribe, at a period when the language had become corrupted. As to the passage in Bede, the original of Cædmon was not given; only a Latin translation by Bede, which Alfred, in his version of the venerable historian, has retranslated into Anglo-Saxon. Hence the difference between these lines and the opening lines of the poem. In its themes the poem corresponds exactly with that which Bede informs us Cædmon wrote; and its claim to genuineness can hardly be destroyed by such objections as have been brought against it.

Such are the two great narrative poems of the Anglo-Saxon tongue. Of a third, a short fragment remains. It is a mutilated thing; a mere torso. Judith of the Apocrypha is the heroine. The part preserved describes the death of Holofernes in a fine, brilliant style, delighting the hearts of all Anglo-Saxon scholars.

The original will be found in Mr. Thorpe's "Analecta"; and translations of some passages in Turner's "History." But a more important fragment is that on the "Death of Byrhtnoth" at the battle of Maldon. This, likewise, is in Thorpe; and a prose translation is given by Conybeare in his "Illustrations." It savors of rust and antiquity, like "Old Hildebrand" in German. What a fine passage is this, spoken by an aged vassal over the dead body of the hero, in the thickest of the fight!

"Byrhtwold spoke; he was an aged vassal; he raised his shield; he brandished his ashen spear; he full boldly exhorted the warriors. 'Our spirit shall be the hardier, our heart shall be the keener, our soul shall be the greater, the more our forces diminish. Here lieth our chief all mangled; the brave one in the dust; ever may he lament his shame that thinketh to fly from this play of weapons! Old am I in life, yet will I not stir hence; but I think to lie by the side of my lord, by that much loved man!'"

Shorter than either of these fragments is a third on the "Fight of Finsborough." Its chief value seems to be, that it relates to the same action which formed the theme of one of Hrothgar's bards in "Beowulf." Mr. Conybeare has given it a place in his work. In addition to these narrative poems and fragments, two others, founded on "Lives of Saints," are mentioned, though they have never been published. They are the "Life and Passion of St. Juliana," and the "Visions of the Hermit Guthlac."

There is another narrative poem, which I must mention here on account of its subject, though of a much later date than the foregoing. It is in the "Chronicle of King Lear and His Daughters," in Norman-Saxon; not rhymed throughout, but with rhymes too often recurring to be accidental. As a poem it has no merit, but shows that the story of Lear is very old; for, in speaking of the old King's death and burial, it refers to a previous account, "as the book telleth" (ase the bock telleth). Cordelia is married to Aganippus, king of France; and, after his death, reigns over England, though Maglaudus, king of Scotland, declares that it is a "muckle shame, that a queen should be king over the land."

Besides these long, elaborate poems, the Anglo-Saxons had their odes and ballads. Thus, when King Canute was sailing by the abbey of Ely, he heard the voices of the monks chanting

their vesper hymn. Whereupon he sang, in the best Anglo-Saxon he was master of, the following rhyme:—

"Merry sang the monks in Ely,
    As King Canute was steering by;
Row, ye knights, near the land,
    And hear we these monks' song."

The best and properly speaking, perhaps the only, Anglo-Saxon odes we have, are those preserved in the "Saxon Chronicle," in recording the events they celebrate. They are five in number. "Æthelstan's Victory at Brunanburh," A. D. 938; the "Victories of Edmund Ætheling," A. D. 942; the "Coronation of King Edgar," A. D. 973; the "Death of King Edgar," A. D. 975; and the "Death of King Edward," A. D. 1065. The "Battle of Brunanburh" is already pretty well known by the numerous English versions and attempts thereat, which have been given of it. This ode is one of the most characteristic specimens of Anglo-Saxon poetry. What a striking picture is that of the lad with flaxen hair, mangled with wounds; and of the seven earls of Anlaf, and the five young kings, lying on the battlefield, lulled asleep by the sword! Indeed, the whole ode is striking, bold, graphic. The furious onslaught; the cleaving of the wall of shields; the hewing down of banners; the din of the fight; the hard hand-play; the retreat of the Northmen, in nailed ships, over the stormy sea; and the deserted dead, on the battle ground, left to the swart raven, the war hawk, and the wolf;—all these images appeal strongly to the imagination. The bard has nobly described this victory of the illustrious war smiths (wlance wig-smithas), the most signal victory since the coming of the Saxons into England; so say the books of the old wise men.

And here I would make due and honorable mention of the "Poetic Calendar," and of King Alfred's "Version of the Metres of Boethius." The "Poetic Calendar" is a chronicle of great events in the lives of saints, martyrs, and apostles, referred to the days on which they took place. At the end is a strange poem, consisting of a series of aphorisms, not unlike those that adorn a modern almanac.

In addition to these narratives and odes and didactic poems, there is a vast number of minor poems on various subjects, some of which have been published, though for the most part they still lie asleep in manuscripts,—hymns, allegories, doxologies,

proverbs, enigmas, paraphrases of the Lord's Prayer, poems on Death and the Day of Judgment, and the like. A great quantity of them is contained in the celebrated Exeter Manuscript; a folio given by Bishop Leofric to the Cathedral of Exeter in the eleventh century, and called by the donor, a "mycel Englisc boc be gehwylcum thingum on leothwisan geworht," a great English book about everything, composed in verse. A minute account of the contents of this manuscript, with numerous extracts, is given by Conybeare in his "Illustrations." Among these is the beginning of a very singular and striking poem, entitled, "The Soul's Complaint against the Body." But perhaps the most curious poem in the Exeter Manuscript is the "Rhyming Poem," to which I have before alluded.

I will close this introduction with a few remarks on Anglo-Saxon prose. At the very boundary stand two great works, like landmarks. These are the "Saxon Laws," promulgated by the various kings that ruled the land; and the "Saxon Chronicle," in which all great historic events, from the middle of the fifth to the middle of the twelfth century, are recorded by contemporary writers, mainly, it would seem, the monks of Winchester, Peterborough, and Canterbury. Setting these aside, doubtless the most important remains of Anglo-Saxon prose are the writings of King Alfred the Great.

What a sublime old character was King Alfred! Alfred, the Truth-Teller! Thus the ancient historian surnamed him, as others were surnamed the Unready, Ironside, Harefoot. The principal events of his life are known to all men,—the nine battles fought in the first year of his reign; his flight to the marshes and forests of Somersetshire; his poverty and suffering, wherein was fulfilled the prophecy of St. Neot, that he should "be bruised like the ears of wheat"; his life with the swineherd, whose wife bade him turn the cakes, that they might not be burnt, for she saw daily that he was a great eater; his successful rally; his victories, and his future glorious reign; these things are known to all men. And not only these which are events in his life, but also many more, which are traits in his character, and controlled events; as, for example, that he was a wise and virtuous man, a religious man, a learned man for that age. Perhaps they know, even, how he measured time with his six horn lanterns; also, that he was an author and wrote many books. But of these books how few persons have read even a single line! And

yet it is well worth one's while, if he wish to see all the calm dignity of that great man's character, and how in him the scholar and the man outshone the king. For example, do we not know better, and honor him more, when we hear from his own lips, as it were, such sentiments as these? "God has made all men equally noble in their original nature. True nobility is in the mind, not in the flesh. I wished to live honorably whilst I lived, and, after my life, to leave to the men who were after me my memory in good works!"

The chief writings of this royal author are his translations of Gregory's "Pastoralis," Boethius's "Consolations of Philosophy," Bede's "Ecclesiastical History," and the "History of Orosius," known in manuscripts by the mysterious title of "Hormesta." Of these works the most remarkable is the Boethius; so much of his own mind has Alfred infused into it. Properly speaking, it is not so much a translation as a gloss or paraphrase; for the Saxon king, upon his throne, had a soul which was near akin to that of the last of the Roman philosophers in his prison. He had suffered, and could sympathize with suffering humanity. He adorned and carried out still further the reflections of Boethius. He begins his task, however, with an apology, saying, "Alfred, king, was translator of this book, and turned it from book-latin into English, as he most plainly and clearly could, amid the various and manifold worldly occupations which often busied him in mind and body"; and ends with a prayer, beseeching God, "by the sign of the holy cross, and by the virginity of the blessed Mary, and by the obedience of the blessed Michael, and by the love of all the saints and their merits," that his mind might be made steadfast to the divine will and his own soul's need.

Other remains of Anglo-Saxon prose exist in the tale of "Apollonius of Tyre"; the "Bible Translations" and "Colloquies" of Abbot Ælfric; "Glosses of the Gospels," at the close of one of which the conscientious scribe has written, "Aldred, an unworthy and miserable priest, with the help of God and St. Cuthbert, overglossed it in English"; and, finally, various miscellaneous treatises, among which the most curious is a "Dialogue between Saturn and Solomon."

Hardly less curious, and infinitely more valuable, is a "Colloquy" of Ælfric, composed for the purpose of teaching boys to speak Latin. The Saxon is an interlinear translation of the

Latin. In this "Colloquy" various laborers and handicraftsmen are introduced,—plowmen, herdsmen, huntsmen, shoemakers, and others; and each has his say, even to the blacksmith, who dwells in his smithy amid iron fire sparks and the sound of beating sledge hammers and blowing bellows (*isenne fyrspearean, and swegincga beatendra slecgea, and blawendra byliga*).

Complete. From "The Poets and
Poetry of Europe."

A WALK IN PÈRE LACHAISE

Our fathers find their graves in our short memories, and sadly tell us how we may be buried in our survivors.

Oblivion is not to be hired. The greater part must be content to be as though they had not been,—to be found in the register of God, not in the record of man.

Sir Thomas Browne's "Urn Burial."

THE cemetery of Père Lachaise is the Westminster Abbey of Paris. Both are the dwellings of the dead; but in one they repose in green alleys and beneath the open sky,—in the other their resting place is in the shadowy aisle and beneath the dim arches of an ancient abbey. One is a temple of nature; the other a temple of art. In one the soft melancholy of the scene is rendered still more touching by the warble of birds and the shade of trees, and the grave receives the gentle visit of the sunshine and the shower: in the other no sound but the passing footfall breaks the silence of the place; the twilight steals in through high and dusky windows; and the damps of the gloomy vault lie heavy on the heart, and leave their stain upon the moldering tracery of the tomb.

Père Lachaise stands just beyond the Barrière d'Aulney, on a hillside looking toward the city. Numerous gravel walks, winding through shady avenues and between marble monuments, lead up from the principal entrance to a chapel on the summit. There is hardly a grave that has not its little inclosure planted with shrubbery, and a thick mass of foliage half conceals each funeral stone. The sighing of the wind, as the branches rise and fall upon it,—the occasional note of a bird among the trees, and the shifting of light and shade upon the tombs beneath have a soothing effect upon the mind; and I doubt whether any one can enter that inclosure, where repose the dust and ashes of so many

great and good men, without feeling the religion of the place steal over him, and seeing something of the dark and gloomy expression pass off from the stern countenance of Death.

It was near the close of a bright summer afternoon that I visited this celebrated spot for the first time. The first object that arrested my attention on entering was a monument in the form of a small Gothic chapel which stands near the entrance, in the avenue leading to the right hand. On the marble couch within are stretched two figures, carved in stone and dressed in the antique garb of the Middle Ages. It is the tomb of Abélard and Héloïse. The history of these two unfortunate lovers is too well known to need recapitulation; but perhaps it is not so well known how often their ashes were disturbed in the slumber of the grave. Abélard died in the monastery of St. Marcel, and was buried in the vaults of the church. His body was afterward removed to the convent of the Paraclete, at the request of Héloïse, and at her death her body was deposited in the same tomb. Three centuries they reposed together; after which they were separated to different sides of the church, to calm the delicate scruples of the lady abbess of the convent. More than a century afterward, they were again united in the same tomb; and when at length the Paraclete was destroyed, their moldering remains were transported to the church of Nogent-sur-Seine. They were next deposited in an ancient cloister at Paris, and now repose near the gateway of the cemetery of Père Lachaise. What a singular destiny was theirs! that, after a life of such passionate and disastrous love,—such sorrows, and tears, and penitence,—their very dust should not be suffered to rest quietly in the grave!—that their death should so much resemble their life in its changes and vicissitudes, its partings and its meetings, its inquietudes and its persecutions!—that mistaken zeal should follow them down to the very tomb,—as if earthly passion could glimmer, like a funeral lamp, amid the damps of the charnel house, and "even in their ashes burn their wonted fires"!

As I gazed on the sculptured forms before me, and the little chapel whose Gothic roof seemed to protect their marble sleep, my busy memory swung back the dark portals of the past, and the picture of their sad and eventful lives came up before me in the gloomy distance. What a lesson for those who are endowed with the fatal gift of genius! It would seem, indeed, that he who "tempers the wind to the shorn lamb" tempers also his

chastisements to the errors and infirmities of a weak and simple mind,—while the transgressions of him upon whose nature are more strongly marked the intellectual attributes of the Deity are followed, even upon earth, by severer tokens of the Divine displeasure. He who sins in the darkness of a benighted intellect sees not so clearly, through the shadows that surround him, the countenance of an offended God; but he who sins in the broad noonday of a clear and radiant mind, when at length the delirium of sensual passion has subsided and the cloud flits away from before the sun, trembles beneath the searching eye of that accusing Power which is strong in the strength of a godlike intellect. Thus the mind and the heart are closely linked together, and the errors of genius bear with them their own chastisement, even upon earth. The history of Abélard and Héloïse is an illustration of this truth. But at length they sleep well. Their lives are like a tale that is told; their errors are "folded up like a book"; and what mortal hand shall break the seal that death has set upon them?

Leaving this interesting tomb behind me, I took a pathway to the left, which conducted me up the hillside. I soon found myself in the deep shade of heavy foliage, where the branches of the yew and willow mingled, interwoven with the tendrils and blossoms of the honeysuckle. I now stood in the most populous part of this city of tombs. Every step awakened a new train of thrilling recollections, for at every step my eye caught the name of some one whose glory had exalted the character of his native land, and resounded across the waters of the Atlantic. Philosophers, historians, musicians, warriors, and poets slept side by side around me; some beneath the gorgeous monument, and some beneath the simple headstone. But the political intrigue, the dream of science, the historical research, the ravishing harmony of sound, the tried courage, the inspiration of the lyre,—where are they? With the living, and not with the dead! The right hand has lost its cunning in the grave; but the soul, whose high volitions it obeyed, still lives to reproduce itself in ages yet to come.

Amid these graves of genius I observed here and there a splendid monument, which had been raised by the pride of family over the dust of men who could lay no claim either to the gratitude or remembrance of posterity. Their presence seemed like an intrusion into the sanctuary of genius. What had wealth to do there? Why should it crowd the dust of the great? That

was no thoroughfare of business,—no mart of gain! There were no costly banquets there; no silken garments, nor gaudy liveries, nor obsequious attendants! "What servants," says Jeremy Taylor, "shall we have to wait upon us in the grave? what friends to visit us? what officious people to cleanse away the moist and unwholesome cloud reflected upon our faces from the sides of the weeping vaults, which are the longest weepers for our funerals?" Material wealth gives a factitious superiority to the living, but the treasures of intellect give a real superiority to the dead; and the rich man, who would not deign to walk the street with the starving and penniless man of genius, deems it an honor, when death has redeemed the fame of the neglected, to have his ashes laid beside him, and to claim with him the silent companionship of the grave.

I continued my walk through the numerous winding paths, as chance or curiosity directed me. Now I was lost in a little green hollow overhung with thick-leaved shrubbery, and then came out upon an elevation, from which, through an opening in the trees, the eye caught glimpses of the city, and the little esplanade at the foot of the hill where the poor lie buried. There poverty hires its grave and takes but a short lease of the narrow house. At the end of a few months, or at most of a few years, the tenant is dislodged to give place to another, and he in turn to a third. "Who," says Sir Thomas Browne, "knows the fate of his bones, or how often he is to be buried? Who hath the oracle of his ashes, or whither they are to be scattered?"

Yet even in that neglected corner the hand of affection had been busy in decorating the hired house. Most of the graves were surrounded with a slight wooden paling, to secure them from the passing footstep; there was hardly one so deserted as not to be marked with its little wooden cross and decorated with a garland of flowers; and here and there I could perceive a solitary mourner, clothed in black, stooping to plant a shrub on the grave, or sitting in motionless sorrow beside it.

As I passed on amid the shadowy avenues of the cemetery, I could not help comparing my own impressions with those which others have felt when walking alone among the dwellings of the dead. Are, then, the sculptured urn and storied monument nothing more than symbols of family pride? Is all I see around me a memorial of the living more than of the dead, an empty show of sorrow, which thus vaunts itself in mournful pageant and funeral parade? Is it indeed true, as some have said, that the simple wild flower which springs spontaneously upon the grave, and the rose which the hand of affection plants there, are fitter objects wherewith to adorn the narrow house? No! I feel that it is not so! Let the good and the great be honored even in the grave. Let the sculptured marble direct our footsteps to the scene of their long sleep; let the chiseled epitaph repeat their names, and tell us where repose the nobly good and wise! It is not true that all are equal in the grave. There is no equality even there. The mere handful of dust and ashes, the mere distinction of prince and beggar, of a rich winding sheet and a shroudless burial, of a solitary grave and a family vault,— were this all, then, indeed it would be true that death is a common leveler. Such paltry distinctions as those of wealth and poverty are soon leveled by the spade and mattock; the damp breath of the grave blots them out forever. But there are other distinctions which even the mace of death cannot level or obliterate. Can it break down the distinction of virtue and vice? Can it confound the good with the bad? the noble with the base? all that is truly great, and pure, and godlike, with all that is scorned, and sinful, and degraded? No! Then death is not a common leveler! Are all alike beloved in death and honored in their burial? Is that holy ground where the bloody hand of the murderer sleeps from crime? Does every grave awaken the same emotions in our hearts? And do the footsteps of the stranger pause as long beside each funeral stone? No! Then all are not equal in the grave! And as long as the good and evil deeds of men live after them, so long will there be distinctions even in the grave. The superiority of one over another is in the nobler and better emotions which it excites; in its more fervent admonitions to virtue; in the livelier recollection which it awakens of the good and the great, whose bodies are crumbling to dust beneath our feet.

If, then, there are distinctions in the grave, surely it is not unwise to designate them by the external marks of honor. Those outward appliances and memorials of respect,— the mournful urn,— the sculptured bust,— the epitaph eloquent in praise,— cannot, indeed, create these distinctions, but they serve to mark them. It is only when pride or wealth builds them to honor the slave of Mammon or the slave of appetite, when the voice from the grave rebukes the false and pompous epitaph, and the dust

and ashes of the tomb seem struggling to maintain the superiority of mere worldly rank, and to carry into the grave the baubles of earthly vanity,— it is then, and then only, that we feel how utterly worthless are all the devices of sculpture and the empty pomp of monumental brass!

After rambling leisurely about for some time, reading the inscriptions on the various monuments which attracted my curiosity, and giving way to the different reflections they suggested, I sat down to rest myself on a sunken tombstone. A winding gravel walk, overshaded by an avenue of trees, and lined on both sides with richly sculptured monuments, had gradually conducted me to the summit of the hill upon whose slope the cemetery stands. Beneath me in the distance, and dim discovered through the misty and smoky atmosphere of evening, rose the countless roofs and spires of the city. Beyond, throwing its level rays athwart the dusky landscape, sank the broad red sun. The distant murmur of the city rose upon my ear, and the toll of the evening bell came up, mingled with the rattle of the paved street and the confused sounds of labor. What an hour for meditation! What a contrast between the metropolis of the living and the metropolis of the dead! I could not help calling to my mind that allegory of mortality, written by a hand which has been many a long year cold:—

> "Earth goeth upon earth as man upon mold,
>   Like as earth upon earth never go should,
> Earth goeth upon earth as glistening gold,
>   And yet shall earth unto earth rather than he would.

> "Lo, earth on earth, consider thou may,
>   How earth cometh to earth naked alway;
> Why shall earth upon earth go stout or gay,
>   Since earth out of earth shall pass in poor array?"

Before I left the graveyard the shades of evening had fallen, and the objects around me grown dim and indistinct. As I passed the gateway, I turned to take a parting look. I could distinguish only the chapel on the summit of the hill, and here and there a lofty obelisk of snow-white marble, rising from the black and heavy mass of foliage around, and pointing upward to the gleam of the departed sun, that still lingered in the sky, and mingled with the soft starlight of a summer evening.

Complete. From "Outre-Mer."

WHEN THE SWALLOWS COME

IT WAS a sweet carol, which the Rhodian children sang of old in spring, bearing in their hands, from door to door, a swallow, as herald of the season:—

> "The swallow is come!
> The swallow is come!
> O fair are the seasons, and light
>   Are the days that she brings,
>   With her dusky wings,
> And her bosom snowy white."

A pretty carol, too, is that, which the Hungarian boys, on the islands of the Danube, sing to the returning stork in spring:—

> "Stork! stork! poor stork!
> Why is thy foot so bloody?
> A Turkish boy hath torn it;
> Hungarian boy will heal it,
> With fiddle, fife, and drum."

But what child has a heart to sing in this capricious clime of ours, where spring comes sailing in from the sea, with wet and heavy cloud-sails, and the misty pennon of the east wind nailed to the mast? Yet even here, and in the stormy month of March even, there are bright warm mornings, when we open our windows to inhale the balmy air. The pigeons fly to and fro, and we hear the whirring sound of wings. Old flies crawl out of the cracks, to sun themselves; and think it is summer. They die in their conceit; and so do our hearts within us, when the cold sea breath comes from the eastern sea; and again,—

> "The driving hail
> Upon the window beats with icy flail."

The red-flowering maple is first in blossom, its beautiful purple flowers unfolding a fortnight before the leaves. The moosewood follows, with rose-colored buds and leaves; and the dogwood, robed in the white of its own pure blossoms. Then comes the sudden rain storm; and the birds fly to and fro, and shriek. Where do they hide themselves in such storms? At what firesides dry their feathery cloaks? At the fireside of the great,

hospitable sun, to-morrow, not before,— they must sit in wet garments until then.

In all climates spring is beautiful. In the south it is intoxicating, and sets a poet beside himself. The birds begin to sing; — they utter a few rapturous notes, and then wait for an answer in the silent woods. Those green-coated musicians, the frogs, make holiday in the neighboring marshes. They, too, belong to the orchestra of nature; whose vast theatre is again opened, though the doors have been so long bolted with icicles, and the scenery hung with snow and frost, like cobwebs. This is the prelude, which announces the rising of the broad green curtain. Already the grass shoots forth. The waters leap with thrilling pulse through the veins of the earth; the sap through the veins of the plants and trees; and the blood through the veins of man. What a thrill of delight in springtime! What a joy in being and moving! Men are at work in gardens; and in the air there is an odor of the fresh earth. The leaf buds begin to swell and blush. The white blossoms of the cherry hang upon the boughs like snowflakes, and ere long our next-door neighbors will be completely hidden from us by the dense green foliage. The May flowers open their soft blue eyes. Children are let loose in the fields and gardens. They hold buttercups under each others' chins, to see if they love butter. And the little girls adorn themselves with chains and curls of dandelions; pull out the yellow leaves to see if the schoolboy loves them, and blow the down from the leafless stalk, to find out if their mothers want them at home.

And at night so cloudless and so still! Not a voice of living thing,— not a whisper of leaf or waving bough,— not a breath of wind,— not a sound upon the earth nor in the air! And overhead bends the blue sky, dewy and soft, and radiant with innumerable stars, like the inverted bell of some blue flower, sprinkled with golden dust, and breathing fragrance. Or if the heavens are overcast, it is no wild storm of wind and rain; but clouds that melt and fall in showers. One does not wish to sleep, but lies awake to hear the pleasant sound of the dropping rain.

From "Hyperion."

THE FIRST BLOOM OF SUMMER

THEY were right,—those old German minnesingers,—to sing the pleasant summer time! What a time it is! How June stands illuminated in the calendar! The windows are all wide open; only the Venetian blinds closed. Here and there a long streak of sunshine streams in through a crevice. We hear the low sound of the wind among the trees; and, as it swells and freshens, the distant doors clap to, with a sudden sound. The trees are heavy with leaves; and the gardens full of blossoms, red and white. The whole atmosphere is laden with perfume and sunshine. The birds sing. The cock struts about, and crows loftily. Insects chirp in the grass. Yellow buttercups stud the green carpet like golden buttons, and the red blossoms of the clover like rubies. The elm trees reach their long, pendulous branches almost to the ground. White clouds sail aloft; and vapors fret the blue sky with silver threads. The white village gleams afar against the dark hills. Through the meadow winds the river,— careless, indolent. It seems to love the country, and is in no haste to reach the sea. The bee only is at work,—the hot and angry bee. All things else are at play; he never plays, and is vexed that any one should.

People drive out from town to breathe, and to be happy. Most of them have flowers in their hands; bunches of apple blossoms, and still oftener lilacs. Ye denizens of the crowded city, how pleasant to you is the change from the sultry streets to the open fields, fragrant with clover blossoms! How pleasant the fresh breezy country air, dashed with brine from the meadows! How pleasant, above all, the flowers, the manifold beautiful flowers!

It is no longer day. Through the trees rises the red moon, and the stars are scarcely seen. In the vast shadow of night, the coolness and the dews descend. I sit at the open window to enjoy them; and hear only the voice of the summer wind. Like black hulks, the shadows of the great trees ride at anchor on the billowy sea of grass. I cannot see the red and blue flowers, but I know that they are there. Far away in the meadow gleams the silver Charles. The tramp of horses' hoofs sounds from the wooden bridge. Then all is still, save the continuous wind of the summer night. Sometimes I know not if it be the wind or the sound of the neighboring sea. The village clock strikes; and I feel that I am not alone.

Angelo, and Raphael, and how much would still be wanting to the completeness of her glory! How would the history of Spain look if the leaves were torn out, on which are written the names of Cervantes, Lope de Vega, and Calderon! What would be the fame of Portugal, without her Camoens; of France, without her Racine, and Rabelais, and Voltaire; or Germany, without her Martin Luther, her Goethe, and Schiller! Nay, what were the nations of old, without their philosophers, poets, and historians! Tell me, do not these men in all ages and in all places, emblazon with bright colors the armorial bearings of their country? Yes, and far more than this; for in all ages and all places they give humanity assurance of its greatness; and say, Call not this time or people wholly barbarous; for thus much, even then and there, could the human mind achieve! But the boisterous world has hardly thought of acknowledging all this. Therein it has shown itself somewhat ungrateful. Else, whence the great reproach, the general scorn, the loud derision, with which, to take a familiar example, the monks of the Middle Ages are regarded? That they slept their lives away is most untrue. For in an age when books were few,—so few, so precious, that they were often chained to their oaken shelves with iron chains, like galley slaves to their benches, these men, with their laborious hands, copied upon parchment all the lore and wisdom of the past, and transmitted it to us. Perhaps it is not too much to say that but for these monks, not one line of the classics would have reached our day. Surely, then, we can pardon something to those superstitious ages, perhaps even the mysticism of the scholastic philosophy, since, after all, we can find no harm in it, only the mistaking of the possible for the real, and the high aspirings of the human mind after a long-sought and unknown somewhat. I think the name of Martin Luther, the monk of Wittenberg, alone sufficient to redeem all monkhood from the reproach of laziness! If this will not, perhaps the vast folios of Thomas Aquinas will;—or the countless manuscripts, still treasured in old libraries, whose yellow and wrinkled pages remind one of the hands that wrote them, and the faces that once bent over them.

From «Hyperion.»

How different is it in the city! It is late and the crowd is gone. You step out upon the balcony, and lie in the very bosom of the cool dewy night, as if you folded her garments about you. The whole starry heaven is spread out overhead. Beneath lies the public walk with trees, like a fathomless, black gulf, into whose silent darkness the spirit plunges and floats away, with some beloved spirit clasped in its embrace. The lamps are still burning up and down the long street. People go by, with grotesque shadows, now foreshortened and now lengthening away into the darkness and vanishing, while a new one springs up behind the walker, and seems to pass him on the sidewalk. The iron gates of the park shut with a jangling clang. There are footsteps, and loud voices,— tumult,— a drunken brawl,— an alarm of fire;— then silence again. And now at length the city is asleep, and we can see the night. The belated moon looks over the roofs, and finds no one to welcome her. The moonlight is broken. It lies here and there in the squares, and the opening of streets,— angular, like blocks of white marble.

From «Hyperion.»

MEN OF BOOKS

WHAT a strange picture a university presents to the imagination. The lives of scholars in their cloistered stillness; — literary men of retired habits, and professors who study sixteen hours a day, and never see the world but on a Sunday. Nature has, no doubt, for some wise purpose, placed in their hearts this love of literary labor and seclusion. Otherwise, who would feed the undying lamp of thought? But for such men as these, a blast of wind through the chinks and crannies of this old world, or the flapping of a conqueror's banner, would blow it out forever. The light of the soul is easily extinguished. And whenever I reflect upon these things I become aware of the great importance, in a nation's history, of the individual fame of scholars and literary men. I fear that it is far greater than the world is willing to acknowledge; or, perhaps, I should say, than the world has thought of acknowledging. Blot out from England's history the names of Chaucer, Shakespeare, Spenser, and Milton only, and how much of her glory would you blot out with them! Take from Italy such names as Dante, Petrarch, Boccaccio, Michael

LEADERS OF HUMANITY

IT HAS become a common saying, that men of genius are always in advance of their age; which is true. There is something equally true, yet not so common; namely, that of these men of genius the best and bravest are in advance not only of their own age, but of every age. As the German prose poet says, every possible future is behind them. We cannot suppose that a period of time will ever come, when the world, or any considerable portion of it, shall have come up abreast with these great minds, so as fully to comprehend them.

And oh! how majestically they walk in history; some like the sun, with all his traveling glories round him; others wrapped in gloom, yet glorious as a night with stars. Through the else silent darkness of the past, the spirit hears their slow and solemn footsteps. Onward they pass, like those hoary elders seen in the sublime vision of an earthly paradise, attendant angels bearing golden lights before them, and, above and behind, the whole air painted with seven listed colors, as from the trail of pencils!

And yet, on earth, these men were not happy,—not all happy, in the outward circumstance of their lives. They were in want, and in pain, and familiar with prison bars, and the damp, weeping walls of dungeons! Oh, I have looked with wonder upon those, who, in sorrow and privation, and bodily discomfort, and sickness, which is the shadow of death, have worked right on to the accomplishment of their great purposes; toiling much, enduring much, fulfilling much;—and then, with shattered nerves, and sinews all unstrung, have laid themselves down in the grave, and slept the sleep of death,—and the world talks of them, while they sleep.

It would seem, indeed, as if all their sufferings had but sanctified them! As if the Death Angel, in passing, had touched them with the hem of his garment, and made them holy! As if the hand of disease had been stretched out over them only to make the sign of the cross upon their souls. And as in the sun's eclipse we can behold the great stars shining in the heavens, so in this life eclipse have these men beheld the lights of the great eternity, burning solemnly and forever!

From «Hyperion.»

THE LOOM OF LIFE

LIFE is one, and universal; its forms many and individual. Throughout this beautiful and wonderful creation there is never-ceasing motion, without rest by night or day, ever weaving to and fro. Swifter than a weaver's shuttle it flies from birth to death, from death to birth; from the beginning seeks the end, and finds it not, for the seeming end is only a dim beginning of a new outgoing and endeavor after the end. As the ice upon the mountain, when the warm breath of the summer's sun breathes upon it, melts, and divides into drops, each of which reflects an image of the sun, so life, in the smile of God's love, divides itself into separate forms, each bearing in it and reflecting an image of God's love. Of all these forms the highest and most perfect in its God likeness is the human soul. The vast cathedral of nature is full of holy scriptures, and shapes of deep, mysterious meaning; but all is solitary and silent there; no bending knee, no uplifted eye, no lip adoring, praying. Into this vast cathedral comes the human soul, seeking its Creator; and the universal silence is changed to sound, and the sound is harmonious, and has a meaning, and is comprehended and felt. It was an ancient saying of the Persians, that the waters rush from the mountains and hurry forth into all the lands to find the lord of the earth; and the flame of the fire, when it awakes, gazes no more upon the ground, but mounts heavenward to seek the lord of heaven; and here and there the earth has built the great watch towers of the mountains, and they lift their heads far up into the sky, and gaze ever upward and around, to see if the Judge of the World comes not! Thus in nature herself, without man, there lies a waiting, and hoping, a looking and yearning, after an unknown somewhat. Yes; when, above there, where the mountain lifts its head over all others, that it may be alone with the clouds and storms of heaven, the lonely eagle looks forth into the gray dawn, to see if the day comes not! when, by the mountain torrent, the brooding raven listens to hear if the chamois is returning from his nightly pasture in the valley; and when the soon uprising sun calls out the spicy odors of the thousand flowers, the Alpine flowers, with heaven's deep blue and the blush of sunset on their leaves;—then there awakes in nature, and the soul of man can see and comprehend it, an expectation and a longing for a future revelation of God's majesty. It awakens, also, when in the fullness

of life, field and forest rest at noon, and through the stillness is heard only the song of the grasshopper and the hum of the bee; and when at evening the singing lark, up from the sweet-swelling vineyards rises, or in the later hours of night Orion puts on his shining armor, to walk forth in the fields of heaven. But in the soul of man alone is this longing changed to certainty and fulfilled. For lo! the light of the sun and the stars shines through the air, and is nowhere visible and seen; the planets hasten with more than the speed of the storm through infinite space, and their footsteps are not heard, but where the sunlight strikes the firm surface of the planets, where the storm wind smites the wall of the mountain cliff, there is the one seen and the other heard. Thus is the glory of God made visible, and may be seen, where in the soul of men it meets its likeness changeless and firm-standing. Thus, then, stands man;—a mountain on the boundary between two worlds;—its foot in one, its summit far-rising into the other. From this summit the manifold landscape of life is visible, the way of the past and perishable, which we have left behind us; and, as we evermore ascend, bright glimpses of the daybreak of eternity beyond us!

From "Hyperion."

THE MODERN ROMANS

THE modern Romans are a very devout people. The Princess Doria washes the pilgrims' feet in Holy Week; every evening, foul or fair, the whole year round, there is a rosary sung before an image of the Virgin, within a stone's throw of my window; and the young ladies write letters to St. Louis Gonzaga, who in all paintings and sculpture is represented as young and angelically beautiful. I saw a large pile of these letters a few weeks ago in Gonzaga's chapel, at the church of St. Ignatius. They were lying at the foot of the altar, prettily written on smooth paper, and tied with silken ribbons of various colors. Leaning over the marble balustrade, I read the following superscription upon one of them: "*All' Angelico Giovane S. Luigi Gonzaga, Paradiso*" (To the angelic youth St. Louis Gonzaga, Paradise). A soldier with a musket kept guard over this treasure, and I had the audacity to ask him at what hour the mail went out; for which heretical impertinence he cocked his mustache at

me with the most savage look imaginable, as much as to say, "Get thee gone":—

> "*Andate,*
> *Niente pigliate,*
> *E mai ritornate.*"

The modern Romans are likewise strongly given to amusements of every description. *Panem et circenses*, says the Latin satirist, when chiding the degraded propensities of his countrymen; *Panem et circenses*,—they are content with bread and the sports of the circus. The same may be said at the present day. Even in this hot weather, when the shops are shut at noon, and the fat priests waddle about the streets with fans in their hands, the people crowd to the Mausoleum of Augustus, to be choked with the smoke of fireworks and see deformed and hump-backed dwarfs tumbled into the dirt by the masked horns of young bullocks. What a refined amusement for the inhabitants of "pompous and holy Rome!" . . .

Yonder across the square goes a *Minente* of Trastevere, a fellow who boasts the blood of the old Romans in his veins. He is a plebeian exquisite of the western bank of the Tiber, with a swarthy face and the step of an emperor. He wears a slouched hat and blue velvet jacket and breeches, and has enormous silver buckles in his shoes. As he marches along he sing a ditty in his own vulgar dialect:—

> "*Uno, due, e tre,*
> *E lo Papa non è Re.*"

Now he stops to talk with a woman with a pan of coals in her hand. What violent gestures! what expressive attitudes! Head, hands, and feet are all in motion,—not a muscle is still. It must be some interesting subject that excites him so much and gives such energy to his gestures and his language. No; he only wants to light his pipe!

It is now past midnight. The moon is full and bright, and the shadows lie so dark and massive in the street that they seem a part of the walls that cast them. I have just returned from the Coliseum, whose ruins are so marvelously beautiful by moonlight. No stranger at Rome omits this midnight visit; for though there is something unpleasant in having one's admiration forestalled, and being, as it were, romantic aforethought, yet the charm

is so powerful, the scene so surpassingly beautiful and sublime,— the hour, the silence, and the colossal ruin have such a mastery over the soul,—that you are disarmed when most upon your guard, and betrayed into an enthusiasm which perhaps you had silently resolved you would not feel.

On my way to the Coliseum I crossed the Capitoline Hill, and descended into the Roman Forum by the broad staircase that leads to the triumphal arch of Septimius Severus. Close upon my right hand stood the three remaining columns of the temple of the Thunderer and the beautiful Ionic portico of the temple of Concord, their base in shadow, and the bright moonbeam striking aslant upon the broken entablature above. Before me rose the Phocian column — an isolated shaft, like a thin vapor hanging in the air scarce visible — and far to the left the ruins of the temple of Antonio and Faustina and the three colossal arches of the temple of Peace, dim, shadowy, indistinct, seemed to melt away and mingle with the sky. I crossed the Forum to the foot of the Palatine, and, ascending the Via Sacra, passed beneath the Arch of Titus. From this point I saw below me the gigantic outline of the Coliseum, like a cloud resting upon the earth. As I descended the hillside, it grew more broad and high, more definite in its form, and yet more grand in its dimensions, till, from the vale in which it stands encompassed by three of the seven hills of Rome,—the Palatine, the Cœlian, and the Esquiline,—the majestic ruin in all its solitary grandeur "swelled vast to heaven."

A single sentinel was pacing to and fro beneath the arched gateway which leads to the interior, and his measured footsteps were the only sound that broke the breathless silence of the night. What a contrast with the scene which that same midnight hour presented, when, in Domitian's time, the eager populace began to gather at the gates, impatient for the morning sports! Nor was the contrast within less striking. Silence, and the quiet moonbeams, and the broad, deep shadows of the ruined wall! Where were the senators of Rome, her matrons, and her virgins? Where the ferocious populace that rent the air with shouts when in the hundred holidays' that marked the dedication of this imperial slaughterhouse, five thousand wild beasts from the Libyan deserts and the forests of Anatolia made the arena sick with blood? Where were the Christian martyrs, that died with prayers upon their lips amid the jeers and imprecations of their fellowmen? Where the barbarian gladiators, brought forth to the festival of blood, and "butchered to make a Roman holiday?" The awful silence answered, "They are mine!" The dust beneath me answered, "They are mine!"

I crossed to the opposite extremity of the amphitheatre. A lamp was burning in the little chapel which has been formed from what was once a den for the wild beasts of the Roman festivals. Upon the steps sat the old beadsman, the only tenant of the Coliseum, who guides the stranger by night through the long galleries of this vast pile of ruins. I followed him up a narrow wooden staircase, and entered one of the long and majestic corridors which in ancient times ran entirely round the amphitheatre. Huge columns of solid mason work, that seem the labor of Titans, support the flattened arches above; and, though the iron clamps are gone which once fastened the hewn stones together, yet the columns stand majestic and unbroken amid the ruin around them, and seem to defy "the iron tooth of time." Through the arches at the right I could faintly discern the ruins of the Baths of Titus on the Esquiline; and from the left, through every chink and cranny of the wall, poured in the brilliant light of the full moon, casting gigantic shadows around me, and diffusing a soft, silvery twilight through the long arcades. At length I came to an open space where the arches above had crumbled away, leaving the pavement an unroofed terrace high in air. From this point I could see the whole interior of the amphitheatre spread out beneath me, half in shadow, half in light, with such a soft and indefinite outline that it seemed less an earthly reality than a reflection in the bosom of a lake. The figures of several persons below were just perceptible, mingling grotesquely with their foreshortened shadows. The sound of their voices reached me in a whisper; and the cross that stands in the centre of the arena looked like a dagger thrust into the sand. I did not conjure up the past, for the past had already become identified with the present. It was before me in one of its visible and most majestic forms. The arbitrary distinctions of time, years, ages, centuries were annihilated. I was a citizen of Rome! This was the amphitheatre of Flavius Vespasian!

Mighty is the spirit of the past amid the ruins of the Eternal City!

From "Outre-Mer."

ON THE SUBLIME

You know, my dear Terentianus, that when we perused Cecilius's pamphlet "On the Sublime" together, we thought it below a subject of that magnitude, that it was entirely defective in its principal branches, and that its advantage to readers, which ought to be the principal aim of every writer, would prove very small. Besides, though in every scientific treatise two points are required: the first, that the nature of the subject treated of be fully explained; the second, I mean in order of writing, since in importance it is superior that directions be given how and by what methods the object sought may be attained: yet Cecilius, who brings ten thousand instances to show what the sublime is, as if his readers were ignorant of the matter, has somehow or other omitted, as unnecessary, the discipline that might enable us to raise our natural genius in any degree whatever to this sublime. But, perhaps, this writer is not so much to be blamed for his omissions as commended for the mere conception of the idea, and his earnest endeavors. You, indeed, have exhorted me also by all means to set down my thoughts on this sublime, on your own account; let us, then, consider whether anything can be drawn from my private studies, for the service of those who write for the world, or speak in public.

But you, my friend, will give me your judgment on whatever I advance with that exactness which is due to truth, and that sincerity which is habitual to you. For well did the sage answer the question, "In what do we most resemble the gods?" when he replied, "In doing good and speaking truth." But since I write, my friend, to you, who are thoroughly versed in polite learning, there will be little occasion to use many previous words in proving that the sublime is a certain excellence and perfection of language, and that the greatest writers, both in verse and prose, have by this alone obtained the prize of glory, and clothed their renown with immortality. For the grand not only persuades, but even transports an audience. And the admirable, by its astounding effect, is always more efficacious than that which merely persuades or delights; for in most cases it rests wholly with ourselves either to resist or yield to persuasion. But these, by the application of a sovereign power and irresistible might, get the ascendency over every hearer. Again, dex-

LONGINUS
(c. 210–273 A. D.)

THE treatise of Longinus "On the Sublime" is second in importance among the critical essays of antiquity only to the "Poetics" of Aristotle. If he cannot claim such strength of intellect as Aristotle possessed, Longinus is unquestionably his superior in taste and appreciation for the subtleties of poetry as well as inherent sympathy for its sublimity. He is, in fine, much more nearly a poet himself than Aristotle, the light from whose intellect is always as dry as it is steady. Longinus frequently flames up into a brilliancy of which there is no trace in the "Poetics." His essay "On the Sublime" has been admired by the greatest intellects of modern times. It was the model of Burke's essay "On the Sublime and Beautiful," and it seems to have been oftener in the hands of D:. Johnson than any other critical essay. The text which has come down to us is incomplete, but the treatise is made up of essays, which, though connected by a thread of well-sustained argument, have each an individuality which would make any one of them valuable, if all the rest were lost. Longinus Cassius (sometimes called also Dionysius Cassius Longinus) was a Greek, perhaps born at Emesa in Syria, where his nearest relatives are known to have resided. He was a disciple of Plato, and became celebrated not only for his own works in philosophy, but as the tutor of the equally celebrated Porphyry. The date of his birth is not known, but that of his death is fixed by the tragical circumstance that, becoming secretary to the unfortunate Zenobia, he was put to death by the Roman Emperor Aurelian because his loyalty to his queen made him hostile to Roman supremacy. The question of his authorship of the treatise "On the Sublime" has been disputed by professional critics of the classics, who have found thus some amusement for themselves without discrediting the title of Longinus to this great work, or at least without discrediting it more seriously than the title of Homer to the "Odyssey" and of Shakespeare to "Hamlet" has been discredited by similar recreations in "Higher Criticism."

W. V. B.

terity of invention, and good order and economy in composition, are not to be discerned from one or two passages, and sometimes hardly from the whole texture of a discourse; but the sublime, when uttered in good season, with the lightning's force scatters all before it in an instant, and shows at once the might of genius in a single stroke. For in these, and truths like these, experimentally conversant as you are with them, you might, my dearest Terentianus, be the instructor of others yourself.

But we ought not to advance before we clear the point whether or not there be any art in the sublime or the pathetic. For some are of opinion that they are altogether mistaken who would reduce it to the rules of art. "The sublime [say they] is born with us, and is not to be learned by precept. The only art to reach it is to have the power from Nature." And, as they reason, the productions of Nature are deteriorated and altogether enervated by the emaciating effects of artistic rules.

But I maintain that the contrary might easily appear, would they only reflect that, though Nature for the most part challenges a sovereign and uncontrollable power in the pathetic and sublime, yet she is not altogether lawless, but delights in a proper regulation. That again, though she is in every case the foundation, and the primary source, and original pattern of production, yet method is able to determine and adjust the measures, and discriminate the season in each thing, and moreover to teach the cultivation and use of them with the greatest degree of certainty. And further, that flights of grandeur are more exposed to danger when abandoned to themselves, without the aid of science, and having nothing to give them steadiness or equipoise, but left to blind impulse alone and untutored daring. For they often, indeed, want the spur, but they stand as frequently in need of the curb.

Demosthenes somewhere judiciously observes that: "In common life success is the greatest good; that the next, and no less important, is conduct, without which the other must be unavoidably of short continuance." Now the same may be asserted of composition, where Nature supplies the place of success, and art the place of conduct.

But there is one consideration which deserves particular attention, for the very fact that there is anything in eloquence which depends upon Nature alone, could not be known without that light which we receive from art. If, therefore, as I said before, he who censures them that pursue such useful literary labors as this in which I am now engaged, would give due attention to these reflections, I believe he would no longer think an investigation of this nature superfluous or useless.

> "Let them the chimney's flashing flames repel.
> Could but these eyes one lurking wretch arrest,
> I'd whirl aloft one streaming curl of flame,
> And into embers turn his crackling roof.
> But now a generous song I have not sounded."

Streaming curls of flame, spewing against heaven, and making Boreas a piper, with such-like expressions, are not tragical, but supertragical; for the diction is coarse and turbid, and the images are jumbled and tumultuous, and therefore cannot possibly adorn or raise the subject; and whenever carefully examined in the light, their show of being terrible gradually disappears, and they become contemptible and ridiculous. Tragedy will indeed, by its nature, admit of some pomp and grandiloquence, yet even in tragedy it is unpardonable to swell immoderately; much less allowable must it therefore be in prose writing, or those works which are founded in truth. Upon this account some expressions of Gorgias the Leontine are ridiculed, who styles Xerxes the Persian Jupiter, and calls vultures living sepulchres. Some expressions of Callisthenes deserve the same treatment, for they are not sublime, but inflated. And Clitarchus comes under this censure still more, who is like a tree all bark, and who blows, as Sophocles expresses it, "on small pipes, but without a mouthpiece."

Amphicrates, Hegesias, and Matris, may all be taxed with the same imperfections; for often when, in their own opinion, they are all divine, what they imagine to be inspiration proves empty froth.

Upon the whole, bombast seems to be amongst those faults which are most difficult to be avoided; for all who are naturally inclined to aim at grandeur, in shunning the censure of impotence and phlegm, are somehow or other hurried into this fault, being persuaded that

> "In great attempts 'tis glorious ev'n to fall."

But tumors in writing, like those in the human body, are certain disorders. Empty and veiled over with superficial greatness, they

only delude, and work effects contrary to those for which they were designed. "Nothing," according to the old saying, "is drier than a person distempered with a dropsy."

Now this swollen and puffed-up style endeavors to go beyond the true sublime, whereas puerilities are directly opposite to it. They are altogether low and groveling, meanly and faintly expressed, and, in a word, are the most ungenerous and unpardonable errors that an author can be guilty of.

But what do we mean by a puerility? Why, it is certainly no more than a schoolboy's thought, which by too eager a pursuit of elegance, becomes dry and insipid. And those persons commonly fail in this particular who, by an ill-managed zeal for that which is out of the common way, high-wrought, and, above all, sweet, run into trumpery and affected expressions.

To these may be added a third sort of imperfection in the pathetic, which Theodorus has named the Parenthyrse, or an ill-timed emotion. It is an attempt to work upon the passions, where there is no need of pathos; or some excess, where moderation is requisite. For some authors, as if from the effects of intoxication, fall into passionate expressions, which bear no relation at all to their subject, but are whims of their own, or borrowed from the schools. The consequence is, as might be expected, that they meet with nothing but contempt and derision from their unmoved audience,—transported themselves, whilst their hearers are calm and unexcited. But I have reserved the pathetic for another place.

Timæus abounds very much in the Frigid, the other vice I mentioned—a writer, it is true, sufficiently skilled in other points, and who sometimes reaches the genuine sublime. He was also a person of great erudition and fertility of thought, but extreme to mark the imperfections of others, and utterly blind to his own, though a fond desire of new thoughts and uncommon turns has often plunged him into shameful puerilities. The truth of these assertions I shall confirm by one or two instances alone, since Cecilius has anticipated me in most of them.

When he commends Alexander the Great, he tells us "that he conquered all Asia in fewer years than it took Isocrates to compose his panegyric on the Persian War." A wonderful parallel indeed, between the conqueror of the world and a professor of rhetoric! By your method of computation, Timæus, the Lacedæmonians fall vastly short of Isocrates in prowess, for they spent

thirty years in the siege of Messene, he only ten in writing that panegyric.

But how does he inveigh against those Athenians who were made prisoners after the defeat in Sicily, "Guilty [says he] of sacrilege against Hermes, and having defaced his images, they now suffered a just retribution, and chiefly at the hands of Hermocrates, the son of Hermon, who was paternally descended from the injured deity." Really, my Terentianus, I am surprised that he has not written of Dionysius the tyrant, "that, for his heinous impiety towards Jupiter (or Dia) and Hercules (Heraclea), he was dethroned by Dion and Heraclides."

Why should I dwell any longer upon Timæus, when even the very heroes of good writing, Xenophon and Plato, though educated in the school of Socrates, sometimes forget themselves, and transgress through an affectation of such pretty flourishes? The former, in his "Polity of the Lacedæmonians," speaks thus: "They observe an uninterrupted silence, and keep their eyes as fixed and unmoved as if they were so many statues of stone or brass. You might with reason think them more modest than the virgins in their eyes." Amphicrates might, perhaps, be allowed to use the term "modest virgins" for the pupils of the eyes; but what an indecency is it in the great Xenophon! And what a strange persuasion, that the pupils of the eyes should be in general the seats of modesty, when impudence is nowhere more visible than in the eyes of some! Homer, for instance, says of an impertinent person:—

> "Drunkard! thou dog in eye!"

Timæus, as if he had found a booty, could not pass by even this insipid turn of Xenophon without appropriating it. Accordingly he speaks thus of Agathocles: "He ravished his own cousin though married to another person, and on the very day when she was first seen by her husband without a veil,—a crime of which none but he who had prostitutes, not virgins, in his eyes could be guilty." Neither is the otherwise divine Plato to be acquitted of this failing, when he says, for instance, "After they are written, they deposit in the temples these cypress memorials," meaning the tables of the laws. And in another passage, "As to the walls, Megillus, I would join in the opinion of Sparta, to let them sleep supine on the earth, and not to rouse them up." Neither does an expression of Herodotus fall short of it, when he calls

beautiful women "the pains of the eye," though this, indeed, may admit of some excuse, since in his history it is spoken by drunken barbarians. But it is not good to incur the ridicule of posterity for a low conception, though uttered by such characters as these.

Now all such instances of the mean and poor in composition take their rise from the same original; I mean that eager pursuit of uncommon turns of thought, which most infatuates the writers of the present age, for our excellences and defects flow from the same common source. So that those elegant, sublime, and sweet expressions, which contribute so much to success in writing, are frequently made the causes and foundations of opposite failures. This is manifest in hyperboles and plurals; but the danger attending an injudicious use of these figures I shall exhibit in the sequel of this work. At present it is incumbent upon me to inquire by what means we may be enabled to avoid those vices which border so near upon, and are so easily blended with, the true sublime.

And this may be, if we first of all gain a thorough and critical insight into the nature of the true sublime, which, however, is by no means an easy acquisition. For to pass a right judgment upon composition is the last result of long experience. Not but that a power of distinguishing in these things may perhaps be acquired by attending to some such precepts as I am about to deliver.

It should be understood, my dearest friend, that as in the affairs of life nothing great which it is magnanimous to despise—as, for example, riches, honors, titles, crowns, and whatever is varnished over with an imposing exterior—can ever be regarded as worthy of preference in the opinion of a wise man, since to think lightly of such things is no ordinary excellence; for certainly the persons who have ability sufficient to acquire, but scorn them, are more admired than those who actually possess them—much in the same way also must we judge in respect of the sublime, both in poetry and prose. We must carefully examine whether some things be not tricked out with this seeming grandeur, this imposing exterior of varnish laid on thickly, which, when examined, would be found a mere delusion, meriting the contempt rather than the admiration of a truly great mind; for, somehow or other, the soul is naturally elevated by the true sublime, and, lifted up with exultation, is filled with transport and inward pride, as if what was only heard had been the product of its own invention.

He, therefore, who has a competent share of natural and acquired taste, may easily discover the value of any performance from often hearing it. If he find that it does not transport his soul, or exalt his thoughts—that it does not leave in his mind matter for more enlarged reflection than the mere sounds of the words convey, but that on attentive examination its dignity lessens and declines—he may conclude that whatever pierces no deeper than the ears can never be the true sublime. For that is truly grand and lofty, which the more we consider the greater ideas we conceive of it; whose force is hard, or, rather, impossible to withstand; which sinks deep, and makes such impressions on the mind as cannot be easily worn out or effaced. In a word, you may pronounce that sublime to be commendable and genuine, which pleases all sorts of men at all times. For when persons of different pursuits, habits of life, tastes, ages, principles, agree in the same joint approbation of any performance, then this union of assent, this combination of so many different judgments, stamps a high and indisputable value on that performance which meets with such general applause.

Now there are, if I may so express it, five very copious sources of the sublime, if we presuppose a talent for speaking as a common foundation for these five sorts; and, indeed, without it anything whatever will avail but little:—

1. The first and most potent of these is a felicitous boldness in the thoughts, as I have laid down, in my essay on Xenophon.

2. The second is a capacity of intense and enthusiastic passion; and these two constituents of the sublime are for the most part the immediate gifts of nature, whereas the remaining sources depend also upon art.

3. The third consists in a skillful molding of figures; which are twofold of sentiment and language.

4. The fourth is a noble and graceful manner of expression, which is not only to select significant and elegant words, but also to adorn the style and embellish it by the assistance of tropes.

5. The fifth source of the sublime, which embraces all the preceding, is to construct the periods with all possible dignity and grandeur.

I proceed next to consider what is comprehended in each of these sources; but must first observe that, of the five, Cecilius,

among other defects, has wholly omitted the pathetic. Now, if he thought that the grand and pathetic, as one and the same thing, were always found together, and were naturally inseparable, he was under a mistake. For some passions are far removed from grandeur and are in themselves of a lowly character; as pity, grief, fear; and, on the contrary, there are many things grand and lofty without any passion; as, among a thousand instances, we may see, from what the poet has said, with such exceeding boldness of the Aloides:—

> " To raise
> Huge Ossa on Olympus' top they strove,
> And place on Ossa Pelion with its grove;
> That heaven itself, thus climbed, might be assailed. »

But the sublimity of what he afterwards adds is yet greater:—

> " Nor would success their bold attempts have failed, » etc.

Among the orators also, all panegyrics and orations composed for pomp and show may be sublime in every way, but yet are for the most part void of passion. Whence those orators who excel in the pathetic scarcely ever succeed as panegyrists; and those whose talents lie chiefly in panegyric are very seldom able in affecting the passions. But, on the other hand, if Cecilius was of opinion that the pathetic did not contribute to the sublime, and on that account judged it not worth mentioning, he is guilty of an unpardonable error. For I might confidently aver that nothing so much raises discourse as a fine pathos seasonably applied. For it is this that causes it to breathe forth an energy and fire, resembling the intensity of madness and divine instinct, and inspires it in a manner with the present god.

Introductory essay complete. From the text of Morley.

SUBLIMITY IN THE GREAT POETS

B^{UT} though the first and most important of these divisions, I mean elevation of thought, be rather a natural than an acquired qualification, yet we ought to spare no pains to educate our souls to grandeur, and impregnate them, as it were, with generous and enlarged ideas.

"But how," it will be asked, "can this be done?" I hinted in another place that this sublimity is an echo of the inward greatness of the soul. Hence it comes to pass that a bare thought without words challenges admiration for the sake of its grandeur alone. Such is the silence of Ajax in the "Odyssey" (Book XI., v. 565), which is undoubtedly great, and far loftier than anything he could have said.

To arrive at excellence like this, then, we must needs presuppose as the primary cause of it that an orator of the true genius must have no mean and ungenerous way of thinking. For it is impossible for those who have groveling and servile ideas, or are engaged in sordid pursuits all their lives, to produce anything worthy of admiration and the praise of all posterity. But grand and sublime expressions must in reason flow from them alone whose conceptions are stored and big with greatness. And thus it is that grand thoughts are commonly found to have been uttered by men of the loftiest minds. When Parmenio cried, "I would accept these proposals if I were Alexander," Alexander replied, "And so would I if I were Parmenio." His answer showed the greatness of his mind.

So the space between heaven and earth marks out the vast reach and capacity of Homer's genius when he says:—

> "While scarce the skies her horrid head can bound,
> She stalks on earth. »

This description may with no less justice be applied to Homer's genius than to Discord.

But what disparity, what a fall there is in Hesiod's description of Melancholy, if, at least, the poem of "The Shield" may be ascribed to him:—

> "A filthy moisture from her nostrils flowed. »

He has not represented his image as terrible, but hateful. On the other hand, with what majesty and pomp does Homer exalt his deities:—

> "Far as a shepherd from some spot on high
> O'er the wide main extends his boundless eye,
> Through such a space of air, with thundering sound,
> At one long leap th' immortal coursers bound. »

He measures the leap of the horses by the extent of the world. And who is there that, considering the exceeding great-

ness of the space, would not, with good reason, cry out that, " if the steeds of the Deity were to take a second leap, the world itself would want room for it » ?

How grand, too, are those creations of the imagination in the combat of the gods:—

> " Heaven in loud thunders bids the trumpet sound,
> And wide beneath them groans the rending ground.
> Deep in the dismal regions of the dead
> Th' infernal monarch reared his horrid head.
> Leaped from his throne, lest Neptune's arm should lay
> His dark dominions open to the day,
> And pour in light on Pluto's drear abodes,
> Abhorred by men, and dreadful ev'n to gods. »

What a prospect is here, my friend! The earth laid open to its centre; Tartarus itself disclosed to view; the whole world turned upside down and rent in twain; all things at once—heaven, hell, things mortal and immortal share alike the toil and danger of that battle! These are terrific representations, but if not allegorically understood, are inapplicable to deity, and violate the laws of propriety. For Homer, in my opinion, when he relates the wounds, the seditions, the retaliations, imprisonments, and tears of the deities, with those evils of every kind under which they languish, has to the utmost of his power exalted the heroes who fought at Troy into gods, and degraded the gods into men. Nay, he makes their condition worse than human; for when man is overwhelmed with misfortunes, he has a reserve in the peaceful haven of death. But he makes the infelicity of the gods as everlasting as their nature.

But how far does he excel those descriptions of the combats of the gods, when he sets a deity in his true light, and paints him in all his majesty, purity, and perfection; as in that description of Neptune, which has been handled already by several writers:—

> " Fierce as he passed the lofty mountains nod,
> The forests shake, earth trembled as he trod,
> And felt the footsteps of the immortal god.
> His whirling wheels the glassy surface sweep;
> Th' enormous monsters, rolling o'er the deep,
> Gambol around him on the wat'ry way,
> And heavy whales in awkward measures play;
> The sea subsiding spreads a level plain,
> Exults and owns the monarch of the main:

The parting waves before his coursers fly;
The wond'ring waters leave the axle dry."

So likewise the Jewish legislator,—no ordinary person,—having conceived a just idea of the power of God, has nobly expressed it in the beginning of his law. "And God said: What? 'Let there be light,' and there was light. 'Let the earth be,' and the earth was."

I hope my friend will not think me tedious if I add another quotation from the poet, where he treats of mortal things; that you may see how he is accustomed to mount along with his heroes to heights of grandeur. A thick cloud and embarrassing darkness as of night envelops the Grecian army, and suspends the battle. Ajax, perplexed what course to take, prays thus:—

"Accept a warrior's prayer, eternal Jove;
This cloud of darkness from the Greeks remove;
Give us but light, and let us see our foes,
We'll bravely fall, though Jove himself oppose."

The feelings of Ajax are here expressed to the life: it is Ajax himself. He begs not for life; a request like that would be beneath a hero. But because in that hampering darkness he could display his valor in no illustrious exploit, and his great heart was unable to brook a sluggish inactivity in the field of action, he prays for instant light, not doubting to crown his fall with some meritorious deed, though Jove himself should oppose his efforts. Here, indeed, Homer, like a brisk and favorable gale, swells the fury of the battle; he is as warm and impetuous as his heroes, or (as he says of Hector)—

"With such a furious rage his steps advance,
As when the god of battles shakes his lance,
Or baleful flames, on some thick forest cast,
Swift marching, lay the wooded mountain waste:
Around his mouth a foamy moisture stands."

Yet Homer himself shows in the "Odyssey" (the remark I am going to add is necessary on several accounts) that when a great genius is in decline, a fondness for the fabulous clings fast to age. Many arguments may be brought to prove that this poem was written after the "Iliad"; but this especially, that in the "Odyssey" he has introduced the sequel of those calamities

which began at Troy as so many episodes of the Trojan War; and that therein he renders to his heroes the tribute of mourning and lamentations, as that which he had previously resolved to be due to them. For, in reality, the "Odyssey" is no more than the epilogue of the "Iliad"—

"There warlike Ajax, there Achilles lies,
Patroclus there, a man divinely wise;
There, too, my dearest son."

It proceeds, I suppose, from the same cause, that having written the "Iliad" in the youth and vigor of his genius, he has furnished it with continued scenes of action and combat; whereas the greatest part of the "Odyssey" consists of narrative, the characteristic of old age. So that in the "Odyssey," Homer may with justice be likened to the setting sun, whose grandeur still remains, without the meridian heat of his beams. For the style is not so grand and majestic as that of the "Iliad"; the sublimity not kept up in so uniform and sustained a manner throughout; the tides of passion flow not so copiously, nor in such rapid succession; there is not the same fertility of invention and oratorical energy; nor is it adorned with such a throng of images drawn from real life; but like the ocean when he retires within himself, and forsakes his proper bounds, so the genius of Homer still exhibits the ebbing of a mighty tide even in those fabulous and incredible ramblings of Ulysses. Not that I am forgetful of those storms which are described in several parts of the "Odyssey"; of Ulysses's adventures with the Cyclops, and some other instances of the true sublime. No; I am speaking indeed of old age, but it is the old age of Homer. However, it is evident, from the whole series of the "Odyssey," that there is far more of fiction in it than of real life.

I have digressed thus far merely for the sake of showing, as I observed, that, in the decline of their vigor, the greatest geniuses are apt to turn aside into trifles. Those stories of shutting up the winds in a bag; of the men fed by Circe like swine, whom Zoilus calls weeping porkers; of Jupiter's being nursed by doves like one of their young; of Ulysses in a wreck, when he took no sustenance for ten days; and those improbabilities about the slaughter of the suitors;—all these are undeniable instances of what I have said. Dreams, indeed, they are, but such as even Jove might dream.

Accept, my friend, in further excuse of this inquiry into the character of the "Odyssey," my desire of convincing you that a decrease of the pathetic in great orators and poets often ends in the moral kind of writing. Thus the "Odyssey," furnishing us with ethical narratives relating to that course of life which the suitors led in the palace of Ulysses, has in some degree the air of a comedy, wherein the various manners of men are described.

Let us consider next whether we cannot find out some other means to infuse sublimity into our style. Now, as there are no subjects which are not attended by certain circumstances which are always found where they exist, a judicious choice of the most suitable of these adjuncts, and a faculty of accumulating them into one body, as it were, must necessarily produce the sublime. For what by the judgment displayed in the circumstances selected, and what by the skillful combination of them, they cannot but attract the hearer.

Sappho is an instance of this; who, in portraying the characteristics of intense love, always selects her materials from its attendant circumstances, and from the passion as it really exists in nature. But in what particular has she shown her excellence? In her ability to select those circumstances which are most striking and effective, and afterwards to connect them together:—

"Blest as the immortal gods is he,
The youth who fondly sits by thee,
And hears and sees thee all the while
Softly speak and sweetly smile.

"'Twas this deprived my soul of rest,
And raised such tumults in my breast;
For while I gazed, in transport tost,
My breath was gone, my voice was lost.

"My bosom glowed; the subtle flame
Ran quick through all my vital frame;
O'er my dim eyes a darkness hung;
My ears with hollow murmurs rung.

"In dewy damps my limbs were chilled;
My blood with gentle horrors thrilled;
My feeble pulse forgot to play,
I fainted, sunk, and died away."

Are you not amazed, my friend, to find how in the same moment she is to seek for her soul, her body, her ears, her tongue,

her eyes, her color, all of them as much absent from her as if they had never belonged to her? And what contrary affections she feels together! How she glows, chills, raves, reasons; for either she is in tumults of alarm, or she is dying away. The effect of which is, that she seems not to be attacked by one alone, but by a combination of affections.

All the symptoms of this kind are true effects of love; but the excellence of this ode, as I observed before, consists in the judicious choice and connection of the most striking circumstances. And it proceeds from his due application of the most formidable incidents, that the poet excels so much in describing tempests. The author of the poem on the Arimaspians deems these things full of terror:—

"Ye powers, what madness! How on ships so frail
(Tremendous thought!) can thoughtless mortals sail?
For stormy seas they quit the pleasing plain,
Plant woods in waves, and dwell amidst the main.
Far o'er the deep, a trackless path, they go,
And wander oceans in pursuit of woe.
No ease their hearts, no rest their eyes can find,
On heaven their looks, and on the waves their mind
Sunk are their spirits, while their arms they rear,
And gods are wearied with their fruitless prayer."

But every impartial reader will discern that these lines are more florid than terrible. But how does Homer raise a description, to mention only one example amongst a thousand!—

"He bursts upon them all:
Bursts as a wave that from the cloud impends,
And swelled with tempests on the ship descends;
White are the decks with foam; the winds aloud
Howl o'er the masts, and sing through every shroud:
Pale, trembling, tired, the sailors freeze with fears,
And instant death on every wave appears."

Aratus has attempted a refinement upon the last thought, and turned it thus:—

"A slender plank preserves them from their fate."

But instead of exciting terror, he only lessens and refines it away; and besides, he sets a bound to the impending danger, by saying, "a plank preserves them," and thus removes it. But the poet does not once for all limit the danger, but paints them as all but swallowed up ever and anon by each successive wave. Nay, more, by forcing into unnatural composition propositions which ought not to be compounded, and clashing them one against another, as in ὑπἐκ θανάτοιο he has made the verse exhibit signs of agony corresponding with the calamity it represents; has modeled a striking image of it by the jarring of the words; and has all but stamped the peculiar character of the danger upon his diction. So Archilochus in describing a wreck, and Demosthenes, where he relates the confusion at Athens upon the arrival of ill news. "It was," says he, "in the evening," etc. So to speak, they reviewed their forces, and culling out the flower of them, combined them into one body, from which everything trumpery, or undignified, or puerile, was excluded. For such expressions, like unsightly bits of matter, or fissures, entirely mar the beauty of those parts which, when fitly framed together and built up coherently, constitute the sublime.

Chapters ix. and x. complete.

GREAT MASTERS OF ELOQUENCE

THE sublimity of Demosthenes is, for the most part, sudden and concise; that of Cicero, diffuse and consecutive. Again, our countryman, by reason of the force, nay the rapidity, strength, and impetuosity with which he, in a manner, burns and bears down at once all before him, may be likened to a tornado or a thunderbolt; but Cicero, to my thinking, like some widespreading conflagration, rolls on devouring on all sides, with fires exhaustless, incessant, and abiding, dealt out, now here, now there, from their own central stores, and drawing fresh vigor from successive advances. But of these matters you can better judge than I can. Now the proper season for applying a sublimity so intense as that of Demosthenes is when things are to be portrayed in the deepest colors; where vehement passion is to be expressed; and where it is expedient to strike the hearer with astonishment all at once; but the season for employing the diffuse kind is when it is required to pour a shower of gentler influences upon the hearer. For the latter is adapted to the discussion of commonplaces, the generality of perorations, digressions, all narratives and panegyrical orations, histories, physiological dissertations, and no few other kinds.

That Plato, indeed,—for I will return to him,—though his eloquence is as the noiseless lapse of a mighty river, is nevertheless sublime, you cannot be ignorant when you have read the following specimen in his "Republic": "They," says he, "that are unprincipled in the lore of wisdom and virtue, and give themselves wholly to feasting and the like, are urged, as it seems, by a downward impulse, and thus pass their whole life under a delusion. For they have never lifted up their eyes to look on Truth, nor been moved by any aspirations after her, nor have experienced the taste of durable and unpolluted pleasure, but, like the beasts, with eyes forever downward bent, stooping towards the earth and bending over tables, they feed their appetites and lusts; and to obtain a larger share of these things, so insatiable are their desires, they kick, and gore, and slay each other with horns and hoofs of iron." And this man instructs us, if we would but listen to him, that there is also some other way, besides those already mentioned, which leads to things sublime. And what way is this, and what is its nature? It is to imitate and emulate the great historians and poets of former days. And be this, my dearest friend, our fixed and steadfast aim. For many are they that are moved to a divine enthusiasm by another's spirit, in the same manner as fame records, that when the pythoness draws nigh the sacred tripod (where, as they say, the cleft earth breathes an inspiring exhalation) she is thereby impregnated with the divine influence, and forthwith breaks out in strains of prophecy, according as the Deity inspires her. Thus it is that from the sublime geniuses of the Ancients certain effluvia are wafted to the souls of those that emulate them, as from the sacred caverns; by whose inspiration, even such as are not over-gifted of Phœbus catch enthusiasm from the sublimities of others. Was Herodotus the only devoted imitator of Homer? Stesichorus was so before him, and so was Archilochus; but more than all of them, Plato, who from the famed Homeric fountain has drawn water by ten thousand by-streams to irrigate his own genius. And, perhaps, it were needful for me to point out instances, had not Ammonius and his disciples given a classified list of them. Nor is this plagiarism; but to take a hint from models of poetic fiction or works of art is as defensible as to copy good manners. Neither do I think that Plato would have displayed so much vigor in delivering his philosophical doctrines, and so often have soared to the matter and diction of poetry,

had he not strenuously entered the lists, even with Homer, and disputed the palm with him, like some undistinguished champion that matches himself with one who has already engrossed the admiration of the world. The attack was perhaps too rash, the opposition perhaps had too much the air of enmity, but yet it could not fail of some advantage, for, as Hesiod says:—

"Such brave contention works the good of men."

And, assuredly, glorious are the efforts, worthy our highest ambition the crown in this contest for pre-eminence of fame, wherein even to be worsted by the heroes of former days is unattended with dishonor.

Wherefore, whenever we, too, are engaged in a work which requires grandeur of style and exalted sentiments, it were good to raise in ourselves such reflections as these:—How in this matter would Homer, as the case may be, or Plato, or Demosthenes have raised their thoughts? Or, if it be historical, how would Thucydides? For these persons, being set before us, and appearing, as it were, in bright array, as patterns for our imitation, will in some degree raise our souls to the standard we have pictured to our imaginations. It will be yet of greater use if to the preceding reflections we add these: What would Homer or Demosthenes have thought of this piece; or how would they have been affected by it? For of a truth it is no light contest we engage in when we set before us such a tribunal and such an auditory to adjudicate upon our own performances; and are possessed with the idea, though but in imagination, that we are submitting our writings to the scrutiny of such distinguished characters, who are at once both our judges and witnesses. There is yet another motive which may yield still more powerful incitements, if we ask ourselves, "What would all posterity think of me if they heard these writings of mine recited?" But if any one, in the moments of composing, should apprehend that his performance may not be able to survive him and endure, the conceptions of a soul so affected must needs be crude and imperfect, like things born out of due season, so that they can never attain to the praise of future ages.

Chapter xiii. and xiv. complete.

LIBERTY AND GREATNESS

IN consideration of your desire for useful information, my dearest Terentianus, I shall not hesitate to add an elucidation of that remaining question which was recently proposed by a certain philosopher. "I wonder," said he, "and not I alone, but doubtless many others also, how it happens that in the age we live in there are many men eminently endowed with talents for persuasion and public speaking, remarkable for shrewdness and readiness, and, above all, expert in the arts which give grace and sweetness to language; but that there are now none at all, or very few, who are distinguished for loftiness and grandeur of style. So great and universal is the dearth of genuine eloquence that prevails in this age. Must we believe at last that there is truth in that oft-repeated observation, that democracy is the kindly nurse of sublime genius, with whose strength alone truly powerful orators flourish, and disappear as it declines? For liberty, say they, is able to supply nutriment to the lofty conceptions of great minds and feed their aspirations, and, at the same time, to foster the flame of mutual emulation and stimulate ambition for pre-eminence — nay, further, that the mental excellences of orators are whetted continually by reason of the rewards proposed in free states; that they are made, as it were, to give out fire by collision, and naturally exhibit the light of liberty in their oratorical efforts. But we of the present day," continued he, "seem to be trained from our childhood to absolute slavery, having been all but swathed in its customs and institutes, and never allowed to taste of that most copious fountain of all that is admirable and attractive in eloquence — I mean liberty — and hence it is that we turn out to be nothing but pompous flatterers." This, he said, was the cause why we see that all other attainments may be found in menials, but never yet a slave become an orator. His spirit being effectually broken, the timorous vassal will still be uppermost; the habit of subjection continually overawes and beats down his genius. For, according to Homer ("Odyssey," I. 322):—

"Jove fixed it certain that whatever day
Makes man a slave, takes half his worth away."

"As then," said he, "(if what I have heard deserves credit), the cages in which what are called pigmies are kept, not only prevent the growth of those who are inclosed in them, but contract their dimensions by reason of the confinement in which their whole bodies are placed; so slavery of every kind, even the mildest, one might declare to be the cage and common prison of the mind."

Now here I rejoined: It is easy and characteristic of human nature to find fault with the existing state of things, whatever it be; but I would have you consider whether, in some degree, this corruption of genius is not owing to the profound peace which reigns throughout the world, but much more to the well-known war which our lusts are waging within us universally; and, moreover, to those mental foes that have invaded the present age, and waste and ravage all before them. For avarice (that disease of which the whole world is sick beyond a cure), aided by voluptuousness, holds us in abject thraldrom; or, rather, if I may so express it, drowns us body and mind. For the love of money is the canker of the soul's greatness, and the love of pleasure corrodes every generous sentiment. I have, indeed, thought much upon it; but, after all, judge it impossible for them that set their hearts upon, or, to speak more truly, that deify unbounded riches, to preserve their souls from the infection of all those vices which are firmly allied to them. For riches that know no bounds and restraint bring with them profuseness, their close-leagued and, as they call it, dogging attendant; and while wealth unbars the gates of cities, and opens the doors of houses, profuseness gets in at the same time, and takes up a joint residence. And when they have remained awhile in our principles and conduct, they build their nests there (in the language of philosophy), and speedily proceeding to propagate their species, they hatch arrogance, pride, and luxury—no spurious brood, but their genuine offspring. If these children of wealth be fostered and suffered to reach maturity, they quickly engender in our souls those inexorable tyrants,—insolence, injustice, and impudence. When men are thus fallen, what I have mentioned must needs result from their depravity. They can no longer lift up their eyes to anything above themselves, nor feel any concern for reputation; but the corruption of every principle must needs be gradually accomplished by such a series of vices; and the nobler faculties of the soul decay and wither, and lose all the fire of emulation, when men neglect the cultivation of their immortal parts, and suffer the mortal and worthless to engross all their care and admiration.

For he that has received a bribe to pervert judgment is incapable of forming an unbiased and sound decision in matters pertaining to equity and honor. For it must needs be that one corrupted by gifts should be influenced by self-interest in judging of what is just and honorable. And when the whole tenor of our several lives is guided only by corruption, by a desire for the death of others, and schemes to creep into their wills; when we are ready to barter our lives for paltry gains, led captive, one and all, by the thirst for lucre—can we expect, in such a general corruption, so contagious a depravity, that there should be found one unbiased and unperverted judge that can discriminate what is truly great, or will stand the test of time, uninfluenced in his decisions by the lust of gain? But if this is the case, perhaps it is better for such as we are to be held in subjection than to be free; for, be sure, if such rapacious desires were suffered to prey upon others without restraint, like wild beasts let out of confinement, they would set the world on fire with the mischiefs they would occasion. Upon the whole, then, I have shown that the bane of true genius in the present day is that dissolution of morals which, with few exceptions, prevails universally among men, who, in all they do or undertake, seek only applause and self-gratification, without a thought of that public utility which cannot be too zealously pursued, or too highly valued.

Concluding essay, Chapter xliv. complete.

JAMES RUSSELL LOWELL

(1819–1891)

THE "Biglow Papers" of 1846–48 immortalized Lowell. Those who admire most his later work in the upper walks of literary criticism have not demonstrated to the satisfaction of the public at large—which in every such case is the court of last resort—that Lowell did not surpass himself for a lifetime in them. He was transported out of himself by the events of the decade of the Mexican War, and his hot indignation at the manner in which that weak republic was overrun drove him to humor in simple despair of doing the subject justice by serious denunciation. When he makes Mr. Biglow quote the patriotic editor of the time, we can see the white heat of Lowell's indignation under the pretense of humor in such lines as these:—

«I du believe wutever trash
   'll keep the people in blindness,—
Thet we the Mexicuns can thrash
   Right inter brotherly kindness,
Thet bombshells, grape, an' powder 'n' ball
   Air good-will's strongest magnets,
Thet peace, to make it stick at all,
   Must be druv in with bagnets.»

This whole essay, "The Pious Editor's Creed," both in its prose and in its still more effective doggerel verse, remains unsurpassed in its field, and one generation after another which hears the cant and witnesses the crimes by which greed supports rapacity, will thank Lowell that when the press and the pulpit were alike committed to the species of "civilization" which goes out "with a Bible in one hand and a revolver in the other," he had the courage and the spirit of human sympathy which transcended all restrictions of provincialism and spoke for the universal rights of mankind. Of the second series of "Biglow Papers" which he wrote when the whole country was paying the penalty for the Mexican conquest, it is unnecessary to speak. He lived to regret, as every other American of his moral plane must regret, that the prophetic indignation he felt in '48 became a part of the subconsciousness of that higher general intellect which is as enduring as the race and as inflexible in its retributions as the great principles which

control the movement of the tides and direct the course of the hurricane. Had he lived a century later, Lowell might have become a very great poet. But his sympathies with the world-struggles of his time tempted him always to use his poetical faculty as a weapon, where otherwise it might have been used as a lamp. "The Vision of Sir Launfal" is an admirable poem, but it is as far surpassed in force by the best of his political poems as his "Biglow Papers" surpass in reality the critical essays of his later years. It would be invidious and unjustifiable to say that one who had written so much and such meritorious verse is at his best in his prose, but it is certainly true that Lowell never sacrificed the critical instinct to the poetic; and of the critical faculties prose is not only the natural, but the only natural vehicle of expression.

Lowell was born at Cambridge, Massachusetts, February 22d, 1819. Graduating at Harvard College in 1838, he published three years later "A Year's Life," and followed it up in 1844 with a second book of verse. Others followed in 1848, and at intervals until 1876. "The Vision of Sir Launfal" in 1845, "A Fable for Critics" in 1848, and the "Biglow Papers" in 1846–48, had given him full assurance of an enduring reputation, and when Longfellow resigned his professorship at Harvard, Lowell became his successor. From 1857 to 1862 he edited the Atlantic Monthly, and from 1863 to 1872 the North American Review. From 1877 to 1885 he remained abroad as minister to Spain and to Great Britain. After his return he delivered a course of lectures on the "English Dramatists" at the Lowell Institute. Besides lecturing and speaking on subjects of popular interest, he continued to take the most active interest in politics until his death, August 12th, 1891. With George William Curtis and William Cullen Bryant, he gives the best illustration we have had in the United States of the power of the "Scholar in Politics." From the time he wrote the "Biglow Papers" until his death, he carried at the point of his single pen at least as much power as the greatest newspaper in the country. He made as many mistakes in using it as most men make in learning to realize their capacities and responsibilities; but it is his chief glory, as it must be of every efficient man, that he did not allow the dread of mistakes or the shame of failure to prevent him from doing his best to the top of his bent. He was essentially a New Englander, and a great New Englander. When continental America produces a man representing to itself Lowell's relation to New England, we shall certainly have a man indeed.

W. V. B.

THE PIOUS EDITOR'S CREED

[At the special instance of Mr. Biglow, I preface the following satire with an extract from a sermon preached during the past summer, from Ezekiel xxxiv. 2: "Son of man, prophesy against the shepherds of Israel." Since the Sabbath on which this discourse was delivered, the editor of the Jaalam Independent Blunderbuss has unaccountably absented himself from our house of worship.

"I KNOW of no so responsible position as that of the public journalist. The editor of our day bears the same relation to his time that the clerk bore to the age before the invention of printing. Indeed, the position which he holds is that which the clergyman should hold even now. But the clergyman chooses to walk off to the extreme edge of the world, and to throw such seed as he has clear over into that darkness which he calls the Next Life. As if next did not mean nearest, and as if any life were nearer than that immediately present one which boils and eddies all around him at the caucus, the ratification meeting, and the polls! Who taught him to exhort men to prepare for eternity, as for some future era of which the present forms no integral part? The furrow which Time is even now turning runs through the Everlasting, and in that must he plant, or nowhere. Yet he would fain believe and teach that we are going to have more of eternity than we have now. This "going" of his is like that of the auctioneer, on which "gone" follows before we have made up our minds to bid,—in which manner, not three months back, I lost an excellent copy of Chappelow on Job. So it has come to pass that the preacher, instead of being a living force, has faded into an emblematic figure at christenings, weddings, and funerals. Or, if he exercise any other function, it is as keeper and feeder of certain theologic dogmas, which, when occasion offers, he unkennels with a staboy! 'to bark and bite as it is their nature to,' whence that reproach of *odium theologicum* has arisen.

"Meanwhile, see what a pulpit the editor mounts daily, sometimes with a congregation of fifty thousand within reach of his voice, and never so much as a nodder, even, among them! And from what a Bible can he choose his text,—a Bible which needs no translation, and which no priestcraft can shut and clasp from the laity,—the open volume of the world, upon which with a pen of sunshine or destroying fire, the inspired Present is even now

writing the annals of God! Methinks the editor who should understand his calling, and be equal thereto, would truly deserve that title of ποιμὴν λαῶν, which Homer bestows upon princes. He would be the Moses of our nineteenth century, and whereas the old Sinai, silent now, is but a common mountain stared at by the elegant tourist and crawled over by the hammering geologist, he must find his tables of the new law here among factories and cities in this Wilderness of Sin (Numbers xxxiii. 12) called Progress of Civilization, and be the captain of our Exodus into the Canaan of a truer social order.

"Nevertheless, our editor will not come so far within even the shadow of Sinai as Mahomet did, but chooses rather to construe Moses by Joe Smith. He takes up the crook, not that the sheep may be fed, but that he may never want a warm woolen suit and a joint of mutton.

Immemor, O, fidei, pecorumque oblite tuorum!

For which reason I would derive the name editor not so much from *edo*, to publish, as from *edo*, to eat, that being the peculiar profession to which he esteems himself called. He blows up the flames of political discord for no other occasion than that he may thereby handily boil his own pot. I believe there are two thousand of these mutton-loving shepherds in the United States and of these how many have even the dimmest perception of their immense power, and the duties consequent thereon? Here and there, haply, one. Nine hundred and ninety-nine labor to impress upon the people the great principles of Tweedledum, and other nine hundred and ninety-nine preach with equal earnestness the gospel according to Tweedledee."—H. W.]

I du believe in Freedom's cause,
    Ez fur away ez Paris is;
I love to see her stick her claws
    In them infarnal Pharisees;
It 's wal enough agin a king
    To dror resolves an' triggers,—
But libbaty's a kind o' thing
    Thet don't agree with niggers.

I du believe the people want
    A tax on tea an' coffees,
Thet nothin' ain't extravygunt,—
    Purvidin' I'm in office;

Fer I hev loved my country sence
    My eye-teeth filled their sockets
An' Uncle Sam I reverence,
    Partic'larly his pockets.

I du believe in any plan
    O' levyin' the taxes,
Ez long ez, like a lumberman,
    I git jest wut I axes;
I go free-trade thru thick an' thin,
    Because it kind o'rouses
The folks to vote,—an' keeps us in
    Our quiet customhouses.

I du believe it's wise an' good
    To sen' out furrin missions,
Thet is, on sartin understood
    An' orthydox conditions;—
I mean nine thousan' dolls. per ann.,
    Nine thousan' more fer outfit,
An' me to recommend a man
    The place 'ould jest about fit.

I du believe in special ways
    O' prayin' an' convartin';
The bread comes back in many days,
    An' buttered, tu, fer sartin;—
I mean in preyin' till one busts
    On wut the party chooses,
An' in convartin' public trusts
    To very privit uses.

I du believe hard coin the stuff
    Fer 'lectioneers to spout on;
The people's ollers soft enough
    To make hard money out on;
Dear Uncle Sam pervides fer his,
    An' gives a good-sized junk to all,
I don't care how hard money is,
    Ez long ez mine's paid punctooal.

I du believe with all my soul
    In the gret Press's freedom,
To pint the people to the goal
    An' in the traces lead 'em;

Palsied the arm thet forges yokes
    At my fat contracts squintin',
An' withered be the nose thet pokes
    Inter the gov'ment printin'!

I du believe thet I should give
    Wut's his'n unto Cæsar,
Fer it's by him I move an' live,
    Frum him my bread an' cheese air;
I du believe thet all o' me
    Doth bear his souperscription,—
Will, conscience, honor, honesty,
    An' things o' thet description.

I du believe in prayer an' praise
    To him thet hez the grantin'
O' jobs,—in every thin' thet pays,
    But most of all in Cantin';
This doth my cup with marcies fill,
    This lays all thought o' sin to rest,—
I don't believe in princerple,
    But, O, I du in interest.

I du believe in bein' this
    Or thet, ez it may happen
One way or t'other hendiest is
    To ketch the people nappin';
It ain't by princerples nor men
    My preudunt course is steadied,—
I scent wich pays the best, an' then
    Go into it baldheaded.

I du believe thet holdin' slaves
    Comes nat'ral tu a Presidunt,
Let 'lone the rowdedow it saves
    To hev a wal-broke precedunt;
Fer any office, small or gret,
    I couldn't ax with no face,
Without I'd ben, thru dry an' wet,
    Th' unrizzest kind o' doughface.

I du believe wutever trash
    'll keep the people in blindness,—
Thet we the Mexicuns can thrash
    Right inter brotherly kindness,

Thet bombshells, grape, an' powder 'n' ball
    Air good-will's strongest magnets,
Thet peace, to make it stick at all,
    Must be druv in with bagnets.

In short, I firmly du believe
    In Humbug generally,
Fer it's a thing that I perceive
    To hev a solid vally;
This heth my faithful shepherd ben,
    In pasturs sweet heth led me,
An' this 'll keep the people green
    To feed ez they hev fed me.

[I subjoin here another passage from my before-mentioned discourse:—

"Wonderful to him that has eyes to see it rightly, is the newspaper. To me, for example, sitting on the critical front bench of the pit, in my study here in Jaalam, the advent of my weekly journal is as that of a strolling theatre, or rather of a puppet show, on whose stage, narrow as it is, the tragedy, comedy, and farce of life are played in little. Behold the whole huge earth sent to me hebdomadally in a brown paper wrapper!

"Hither to my obscure corner, by wind or steam, on horseback or dromedary back, in the pouch of the Indian runner, or clicking over the magnetic wires, troop all the famous performers from the four quarters of the globe. Looked at from a point of criticism, tiny puppets they seem all, as the editor sets up his booth upon my desk and officiates as showman. Now I can truly see how little and transitory is life. The earth appears almost as a drop of vinegar, on which the solar microscope of the imagination must be brought to bear in order to make out anything distinctly. That animalcule there, in the pea-jacket, is Louis Philippe, just landed on the coast of England. That other, in the gray surtout and cocked hat, is Napoleon Bonaparte Smith, assuring France that she need apprehend no interference from him in the present alarming juncture. At that spot, where you seem to see a speck of something in motion, is an immense mass meeting. Look sharper, and you will see a mite brandishing his mandibles in an excited manner. That is the great Mr. Soandso, defining his position amid tumultuous and irrepressible cheers. That infinitesimal creature, upon whom some score of others as minute as he are gazing in open-mouthed admiration, is a famous philosopher, expounding to a select audience their capacity for the Infinite. That scarce discernible pufflet of smoke and dust is a revolution. That speck there is a reformer, just arranging the lever with

which he is to move the world. And lo, there creeps forward the shadow of a skeleton that blows one breath between its grinning teeth, and all our distinguished actors are whisked off the slippery stage into the dark Beyond.

"Yes, the little show box has its solemner suggestions. Now and then we catch a glimpse of a grim old man, who lays down a scythe and hour glass in the corner while he shifts the scenes. There, too, in the dim background, a weird shape is ever delving. Sometimes he leans upon his mattock, and gazes, as a coach whirls by, bearing the newly married on their wedding jaunt, or glances carelessly at a babe brought home from christening. Suddenly (for the scene grows larger and larger as we look) a bony hand snatches back a performer in the midst of his part, and him, whom yesterday two infinities (past and future) would not suffice, a handful of dust is enough to cover and silence forever. Nay, we see the same fleshless fingers opening to clutch the showman himself, and guess, not without a shudder, that they are lying in wait for spectator also.

"Think of it: for three dollars a year I buy a season ticket to this great Globe Theatre, for which God would write the dramas (only that we like farces, spectacles, and the tragedies of Apollyon better), whose scene shifter is Time, and whose curtain is rung down by Death.

"Such thoughts will occur to me sometimes as I am tearing off the wrapper of my newspaper. Then suddenly that otherwise too often vacant sheet becomes invested for me with a strange kind of awe. Look! deaths and marriages, notices of inventions, discoveries, and books, lists of promotions, of killed, wounded, and missing, news of fires, accidents, of sudden wealth and as sudden poverty;——I hold in my hand the ends of myriad invisible electric conductors, along which tremble the joys, sorrows, wrongs, triumphs, hopes, and despairs of as many men and women everywhere. So that upon that mood of mind which seems to isolate me from mankind as a spectator of their puppet pranks, another supervenes, in which I feel that I, too, unknown and unheard of, am yet of some import to my fellows. For, through my newspaper here, do not families take pains to send me, an entire stranger, news of a death among them? Are not here two who would have me know of their marriage? And, strangest of all, is not this singular person anxious to have me informed that he has received a fresh supply of Dimitry Bruisgins? But to none of us does the Present (even if for a moment discerned as such) continue miraculous. We glance carelessly at the sunrise, and get used to Orion and the Pleiades. The wonder wears off, and to-morrow this sheet, in which a vision was let down to me from heaven, shall be the wrappage to a bar of soap or the platter for a beggar's broken victuals."—H. W.]

Complete. Number 6 of "Biglow Papers."

ON PARADISAICAL FASHIONS FOR WOMEN

("John" speaks)

FASHION, being the art of those who must purchase notice at some cheaper rate than that of being beautiful, loves to do rash and extravagant things. She must be forever new, or she becomes insipid. If to-day she have been courteous, she will be rude to-morrow; if to-day thinks her over-refined, to-morrow will wonder at seeing her relapsed into a semisavage state. A few years ago, certain elaborate and amorphous structures might be seen moving about the streets, in the whole of which the only symptom of animated nature to be discerned was in the movable feet and ankles which conveyed them along. Now, even that sign of vitality has vanished; the amorphous structures move about as usual, but their motive principle is as mysterious as that of Maëlzel's chess player. My own theory is that a dwarf is concealed somewhere within. They may be engines employed for economical purposes by the civic authorities, as their use has been conjectured by an ingenious foreigner, who observed our manners attentively, to be the collection of those particles of mud and dust which are fine enough to elude the birchen brooms of the police, whose duty it is to cleanse the streets. There is more plausibility in this theory, as they are actually provided with a cloth train or skirt of various colors, which seems very well adapted to this end. A city poet, remarkable for the boldness of his metaphorical imagery, has given them the name of "women," though from so nice an analogy as hitherto to have eluded my keenest researches.

("Philip" responds)

It must have been the same who gave the title of "full dress" to the half dress worn now by females of the better sort at parties, the sole object of which seems to be to prove the wearer's claim to rank with the genus *mammiferæ*. One-half of the human race, I see, is resolved to get rid of the most apparent token of our great ancestors' fall, and is rapidly receding to a paradisaical simplicity of vesture. Already have the shoulders emerged from their superstitious enthrallment, and their bold example will no doubt be rapidly followed by equally spirited demonstrations from the rest of the body impolitic. For the sake of con-

sistency we must suppose that train oil will soon elbow the ices from the supper table. But a truce to this cynical vein. It is, nevertheless, mournful, that women, who stint not in large assemblies to show that, to the eyes of strangers which the holy privacy of home is not deemed pure enough to look upon, would yet grow crimson with modest horror, through the whole vast extent of their uncovered superficies, if one but dared to call by its dear English name that which, in the loved one, is the type of all maidenhood and sweetest retirement,—in the wife, of all chastity and whitest thoughts,—and in the mother, of all that is most tender and bounteous. On such a bosom, methinks, a rose would wither, and the snowy petals of a lily drop away in silent, sorrowful reproof. We have grown too polite for what is holiest, noblest, and kindest in the social relations of life; but, alas! to blush, to conceal, to lie, to envy, to sneer, to be illiberal,—these trench not on the bounds of any modesty, human or divine. Yes, our English, which for centuries has been the mother tongue of honest frankness, and the chosen phrase of freedom, is become so slavish and emasculate, that its glorious Bacons, Taylors, and Miltons would find their outspoken and erect natures inapt to walk in its fetters, golden, indeed, and of cunningest Paris workmanship, but whose galling the soul is not nice enough to discern from that of baser metal. The wild singing brook has been civilized; the graceful rudeness of its banks has been pared away to give place to smooth-clipped turf; the bright pebbles, which would not let it pass without the tribute of some new music, have been raked out; and it has become a straight, sluggish canal.

From "Conversations on the Poets."

SOME ADVANTAGES OF POVERTY

("John" speaks)

PERHAPS actual want may be inconsistent with that serenity of mind which is needful to the highest and noblest exercise of the creative power; but I am not ready to allow that poverty is so. Few can dignify it like our so admirable prose poet, whose tales are an honor even to the illustrious language they are written in; few can draw such rich revenues of wise humbleness from it as our beloved R. C.; few can win a smile from it by his Lambish humor, and that generous courtesy which transmutes his fourpence into a bank note in the beggar's eyes, like S.; but there is none for whom it has not some kind lesson. Poverty is a rare mistress for the poet. She alone can teach him what a cheap thing delight is; to be had of every man, woman, and child he meets; to be gathered from every tree, shrub, and flower; nay, to be bought of the surly northwestern wind himself, by the easily paid installments of a cheerful, unhaggling spirit. Who knows the true taste of buns, but the boy who receives the annual godsend of one with election day? Whoever really went to the theatre, but Kit Nubbles? Who feels what a fireside is, but the little desolate barefooted Ruths, who glean the broken laths and waste splinters after the carpenters have had a full harvest? Who believes that his cup is overflowing, but he who has rarely seen anything but the dry bottom of it? Poverty is the only seasoner of felicity. Except she be the cook, the bread is sour and heavy, and the joint tough or overdone. As brisk exercise is the cheapest and warmest overcoat for the body, so is poverty for the heart. But it must be independent, and not of Panurge's mind,—that to owe is a heroic virtue. Debt is like an ingenious mechanical executioner I have read of somewhere, which presented the image of a fair woman standing upon a pedestal of three steps. When the victim mounted the first, she opened her arms; at the second, she began to close them slowly around him; and at the third, she locked him in her iron embrace forever.

On the other hand, however, poverty has its bad side. Poverty in one hour's time shall transport a man from the warm and fruitful climate of sworn brotherhood with the world into the bare, bleak, desert, and polar ice field of distant country cousinship; and the world's whole duty of man towards him becomes on a sudden the necessity of staving off asking him to dinner. Then, for the first time, he gets an insight into the efficacy of buttons, and discovers, to his great surprise, that the world has one at each pocket. This gives him an excellent hint for a sonnet to a button, comparing it to the dragon of the Hesperides, in which he gets no further than the end of the second quatrain, finding it impossible to think of anybody or anything analogous to Hercules in his victory over the monster. Besides, he now learns that there are no golden apples to be guarded, the world assuring him on its honor that it has enormous sums to pay and not a cent to meet them with. In a fit of inspired despair he

writes an elegy, for the first two stanzas of which (having learned economy) he uses up the two quatrains already adjusted for his sonnet. By employing the extremely simple process of deduction invented by the modern expounders of old myths, he finds that Hercules and Ὄτις are identical, and that the same word in the Syro-Phœnician language imports a dragon and a button. The rest of the elegy is made easy by merely assuming the other steps of the proposition, as every expounder of old myths has a clear right to do, by a rule of logic founded on the usage of the best writers in that department. He therefore considers the heart in the poetical light of a pocket or garden of Hesperides, buttoned up tight against all intruders. As Scripture is always popular, he ends by comparing it also to that box which Jehoiada set at the gate of the Temple, which had a hole in the top ample enough to admit the largest coins, though you might shake till you were tired without getting the smallest one out of it. Having now commenced author, we may as well leave him; for, at that lowest ebb of fortune, the bare, muddy flats of poverty lie exposed, and the tide must soon turn again.

(«*Philip*» replies)

That poverty may be of use to the poet, as you have said, may be granted, without allowing that it must come to the actual pinch and gripe of want with him. The man of genius surely needs it not as a spur, for his calling haunts him from childhood up. He knows that he has that to say that will make the great heart of the universe beat with a more joyous peacefulness and an evener motion. As he grows to man's estate, the sense of a duty imposed on him by nature, and of a necessary obedience to heavenly messengers, which the world neither sees nor acknowledges, grows stronger and stronger. The exceeding brightness of his countenance weaves a crown around his head out of the thick air of earth; but earthlings cannot see it. He tells his errand, and the world turns its hard face upon him and says, "Thou art a drone in my busy hive; why doest thou not something?" Alas! when the winter season comes, the world will find that he had been storing honey for it from heavenly flowers, for the famishing heart to feed upon. He must elbow through the dust and throng of the market, when he should be listening to the still, small voice of God; he must blaspheme his high nature, and harden his heart to a touchstone to ring gold upon,

when it is bursting with the unutterable agony of a heavenly errand neglected,—that bitterest feeling of having "once had wings." The world has at last acknowledged his sovereignty, and crowned him with a crown of thorns. Thomson, in one of his letters, says:—

"The great fat doctor of Bath told me that poets should be kept poor, the more to animate their genius. This is like the cruel custom of putting a bird's eyes out, that it may sing the sweeter."

The world plays the great fat doctor very well.
Milton tells us that:—

"Fame is the spur which the clear spirit doth raise
To scorn delights and live laborious days";

but the greater part of mankind, having more sympathy with the body than with its heavenly tenant, seem to derive the word "fame" from the Latin "*fames.*" They would have the alleged temperate habits of the chameleon held up to poets, as that of the busy bee is to good little Jackies and Tommies. But it may well be doubted whether a forced Pythagoreanism would lead to the same happy results as a willing one. The system has, moreover, been often exaggerated into the lamentablest fanaticism. A contempt of the body has been gradually engendered in the soul, which has sometimes overpersuaded her to break her way out, as in Chatterton,—or to carry her zeal to the extent of not eating at all, and so forcing the spirit by slowly wasting away the flesh, as in Otway and others. This species of devotion, moreover, seems to meet with the hearty approbation of the reading public, who usually commemorate such by the rather incongruous ceremony of placing a huge monument to mark the resting place of that very body whose entire subjection by sudden conquest or gradual overthrow they had regarded with so much satisfaction. In England, men of this profession seem to be erected into a distinct caste or guild and the practice of its mysteries is restrained by statute to geniuses and operatives; for an unprincipled vagrant named Cavanagh was sentenced, a few years ago, to the treadmill, for pretending to live without eating, he having no license so to do.

From «Conversations on the Poets.»

LAMB'S GOOD NATURE

THE sweet lovingness of Lamb's nature fitted him for a good critic; but there were knotty quirks in the grain of his mind, which seemed, indeed, when polished by refined studies, little less than beauties, and which we cannot help loving, but which led him to the worship of strange gods, and with the more scrupulous punctuality that the mass were of another persuasion. No field is so small or so barren but there will be grazing enough in it to keep a hobby in excellent case. Lamb's love was of too rambling and widespreading a kind to be limited by the narrow trellises which satisfy a common nature. It stretched out its feelers and twined them around everything within its reach, clipping with its tender and delicate green the fair tree and unsightly stump alike. Everything that he loved was, for the time, his ideal of loveliness. Even tobacco, when he was taking leave of it, became the very "crown of perfumes," and he affirmed:—

"Roses and violets but toys
For the greener sort of boys,
Or for greener damsels meant."

In this, and in the finer glimpses of his humor, and in the antique richness of his style in the best parts, he reminds me of Emerson; but he had not the divine eye of our American poet, nor his deep transparency and majestic simpleness of language, full of images that seem like remembrance-flowers dropped from between the pages of Bacon, or Montaigne, or Browne, or Herbert; reminding us of all felicitous seasons in our own lives, and yet infused with a congenial virtue from the magic leaves between which they had been stored.

From «Conversations on the Poets.»

PROPHETS OF THE NEW DISPENSATION

POETS are the forerunners and prophets of changes in the moral world. Driven by their fine nature to search into and reverently contemplate the universal laws of soul, they find some fragment of the broken tables of God's law, and interpret it, half conscious of its mighty import. While philosophers are wrangling, and politicians playing at snapdragon with the destinies of millions, the poet, in the silent deeps of his soul, listens to those mysterious pulses which, from one central heart, send life and beauty through the finest veins of the universe, and utters truths to be sneered at, perchance, by contemporaries, but which become religion to posterity. Not unwisely ordered is that eternal destiny which renders the seer despised of men, since thereby he is but the more surely taught to lay his head meekly upon the mother-breast of Nature, and hearken to the musical soft beating of her bounteous heart.

That Poesy, save as she can soar nearer to the blissful throne of the Supreme Beauty, is of no more use than all other beautiful things are, we are fain to grant. That she does not add to the outward wealth of the body, and that she is only so much more excellent than any bodily gift, as spirit is more excellent than matter, we must also yield. But, inasmuch as all beautiful things are direct messages and revelations of himself, given us by our Father, and as Poesy is the searcher out and interpreter of all these, tracing by her inborn sympathy the invisible nerves which bind them harmoniously together, she is to be revered and cherished. The poet has a fresher memory of Eden, and of the path leading back thereto, than other men; so that we might almost deem him to have been conceived, at least, if not born and nursed, beneath the ambrosial shadow of those dimly remembered bowers, and to have had his infant ears filled with the divine converse of angels, who then talked face to face with his sires, as with beloved younger brethren, and of whose golden words only the music remained to him, vibrating forever in his soul, and making him yearn to have all sounds of earth harmonize therewith. In the poet's lofty heart Truth hangs her aerie, and there Love flowers, scattering thence her winged seeds over all the earth with every wind of heaven. In all ages the poet's fiery words have goaded men to remember and regain their ancient freedom, and, when they had regained it, have tempered it with a love of beauty, so as that it should accord with the freedom of nature, and be as unmovably eternal as that. The dreams of poets are morning dreams, coming to them in the early dawn and daybreaking of great truths, and are surely fulfilled at last. They repeat them, as children do, and all Christendom, if it be not too busy with quarreling about the meaning of creeds, which have no meaning at all, listens with a shrug of

the shoulders and a smile of pitying incredulity; for reformers are always madmen in their own age, and infallible saints in the next.

We love to go back to the writings of our old poets, for we find in them the tender germs of many a thought which now stands like a huge oak in the inward world, an ornament and a shelter. We cannot help reading with awful interest what has been written or rudely scrawled upon the walls of this our earthly prison house, by former dwellers therein. From that which centuries have established, too, we may draw true principles of judgment for the poetry of our own day. A right knowledge and apprehension of the past teaches humbleness and self-sustainment to the present. Showing us what has been, it also reveals what can be done. Progress is Janus-faced, looking to the bygone as well as to the coming; and Radicalism should not so much busy itself with lopping off the dead or seeming dead limbs, as with clearing away that poisonous rottenness around the roots, from which the tree has drawn the principle of death into its sap. A love of the beautiful and harmonious, which must be the guide and forerunner to every onward movement of humanity, is created and cherished more surely by pointing out what beauty dwells in anything, even the most deformed (for there is something in that also, else it could not even be), than by searching out and railing at all the foulnesses in nature. Not till we have patiently studied beauty can we safely venture to look at defects, for not till then can we do it in that spirit of earnest love, which gives more than it takes away. Exultingly as we hail all signs of progress, we venerate the past also. The tendrils of the heart, like those of ivy, cling but the more closely to what they have clung to long, and even when that which they entwine crumbles beneath them, they still run greenly over the ruin, and beautify those defects which they cannot hide. The past, as well as the present, molds the future, and the features of some remote progenitor will revive again freshly in the latest offspring of the womb of time. Our earth hangs well-nigh silent now, amid the chorus of her sister orbs, and not till past and present move harmoniously together will music once more vibrate on this long silent chord in the symphony of the universe.

From an essay in the Pioneer of 1843.

LOVING AND SINGING

As LOVE is the highest and holiest of all feelings, so those songs are best in which love is the essence. All poetry must rest on love for a foundation, or it will only last so long as the bad passions it appeals to, and which it is the end of true poesy to root out. If there be not in it a love of man, there must at least be a love of nature, which lies next below it, and which, as is the nature of all beauty, will lead its convert upward to that nobler and wider sympathy. True poetry is but the perfect reflex of true knowledge, and true knowledge is spiritual knowledge, which comes only of love, and which, when it has solved the mystery of one, even the smallest effluence of the eternal beauty, which surrounds us like an atmosphere, becomes a clew leading to the heart of the seeming labyrinth. All our sympathies lie in such close neighborhood, that when music is drawn from one string, all the rest vibrate in sweet accord. As in the womb the brain of the child changes, with a steady rise, through a likeness to that of one animal and another, till it is perfected in that of man, the highest animal, so in this life, which is but as a womb wherein we are shaping to be born in the next, we are led upward from love to love till we arrive at the love of God, which is the highest love. Many things unseal the springs of tenderness in us ere the full glory of our nature gushes forth to the one benign spirit which interprets for us all mystery, and is the key to unlock all the most secret shrines of beauty. Woman was given us to love chiefly to this end, that the sereneness and strength which the soul wins from that full sympathy with one, might teach it the more divine excellence of a sympathy with all, and that it was man's heart only which God shaped in his own image, which it can only rightly emblem in an all-surrounding love. Therefore, we put first those songs which tell of love, since we see in them not an outpouring of selfish and solitary passion, but an indication of that beautiful instinct which prompts the heart of every man to turn toward its fellows with a smile, and to recognize its master even in the disguise of clay; and we confess that the sight of the rudest and simplest love verses in the corner of a village newspaper oftener brings tears of delight into our eyes than awakens a sense of the ludicrous. . . .

The songs of our great poets are unspeakably precious. In them find vent those irrepressible utterances of homely fireside humanity, inconsistent with the loftier aim and self-forgetting enthusiasm of a great poem, which preserve the finer and purer sensibilities from wilting and withering under the black frost of ambition. The faint records of flitting impulses, we light upon them sometimes imbedded round the bases of the basaltic columns of the epic or the drama, like heedless insects or tender ferns which had fallen in while those gigantic crystals were slowly shaping themselves in the molten entrails of the soul all aglow with the hidden fires of inspiration, or like the tracks of birds from far-off climes, which had lighted upon the ductile mass ere it had hardened into eternal rock. They make the lives of the masters of the lyre encouragements and helps to us, by teaching us humbly to appreciate and sympathize with, as men, those whom we should else almost have worshiped as beings of a higher order. In Shakespeare's dramas we watch with awe the struggles and triumphs and defeats, which seem almost triumphs, of his unmatched soul;—in his songs we can yet feel the beating of a simple, warm heart, the mate of which can be found under the first homespun frock you meet on the highroad. He who, instead of carefully plucking the fruit from the tree of knowledge, as others are fain to, shook down whole showers of leaves and twigs and fruit at once; who tossed down systems of morality and philosophy by the handful; who wooed nature as a superior, and who carpeted the very earth beneath the delicate feet of his fancy with such flowers of poesy as bloom but once in a hundred years,—this vast and divine genius in his songs and his unequaled sonnets (which are but epic songs, songs written, as it were, for an organ or rather ocean accompaniment), shows all the humbleness, and wavering, and self-distrust, with which the weakness of the flesh tempers souls of the boldest aspiration and most unshaken self-help, as if to remind them gently of that brotherhood to assert and dignify whose claims they were sent forth as apostles.

From the Pioneer of 1843.

POETRY AND RELIGION

" Infantine,
Familiar, clasp of things divine "

AN AUTHOR'S piety cannot be proved from the regular occurrence of certain decorums and respectabilities of religion in his works, but from a feeling which permeates the whole. I have read books in which the name of God was never once so much as alluded to, which yet irresistibly persuaded me of the writer's faith in him and childlike love of him. And I have read others, where that blessed name with a parenthetical and systematic piety, made part of every sentence, and only impressed me like the constantly recurring figures upon calico. There is no intentional piety about Chaucer, no French collar-and-wristband morality, too common in our day. Now, certain days of the week, and certain men, seem to claim a monopoly in religion. It is something quite too costly and precious to make part of every day's furniture. We must not carry it into the street or the market, lest it get soiled. We doff it and hang it up as easily as a Sunday suit. The Ancients esteemed it sacrilege to touch what was set apart for the gods. Many of our own time imitate that ethnic scrupulousness, and carefully forbear religion, yet are deemed pious men, too. In Chaucer, you will find a natural piety everywhere shining through, mildly and equably, like a lamp set in an alabaster vase. The wise man maintains a hospitable mind. He scruples not to entertain thoughts, no matter how strange and foreign they may be, and to ask news of them of realms which he has never explored. He has no fear of their stirring any treason under his own roof. Chaucer apparently acted upon this principle. He loved speculation, and, when he was running down some theological dogma, he does not mind leaping the church inclosure, and pursuing his prey till it takes refuge under the cassock of the priest himself. But, though he seems not to set much store by forms and outward observances, he is quite too near the days of wonder and belief and earnestness not to be truly religious.

The earliest poetry of all countries is sacred poetry, or that in which the idea of God predominates and is developed. The first effort at speech which man's nature makes in all tongues is, to pronounce the word "Father." Reverence is the foundation of all poetry. From reverence the spirit climbs on to love, and

thence beholds all things. No matter in what Scythian fashion these first recognitions of something above and beyond the soul are uttered, they contain the germs of psalms and prophecies. Whether, for a while, the immortal guest rests satisfied with a Fetich or an Apollo, it has already grasped the clew which leads unerringly to the very highest idea. For reverence is the most keen-eyed and exacting of all the faculties, and, if there be the least flaw in its idol, it will kneel no longer. From wood it rises to gold and ivory; from these, to the yet simpler and more majestic marble; and, planting its foot upon that, it leaps upward to the infinite and invisible. Let our external worship be paid to what gods you will, the soul is restless and dissatisfied until she has soared into the higher region of that true piety in whose presence creeds and forms become mere husks and straw. Always in her intimate recesses the soul builds an altar to the unknown God, and it is here that Poesy makes her sacrifices and officiates as authorized priestess. When I assume reverence, then, as the very primal essence and life of poetry, I claim for it a nobler stirps than it has been the fashion to allow it. Beyond Adam runs back its illustrious genealogy. It stood with Uriel in the sun, and looked down over the battlements of heaven with the angelic guards. In short, it is no other than the religious sentiment itself. That is poetry which makes sorrow lovely, and joy solemn to us, and reveals to us the holiness of things. Faith casts herself upon her neck as upon a sister's. She shows us what glimpses we get of life's spiritual face. What she looks on becomes miraculous, though it be but the dust of the wayside; and miracles become but as dust, for their simpleness. There is nothing noble without her; with her there can be nothing mean. What songs the Druids sang within the sacred circuit of Stonehenge we can barely conjecture; but those forlorn stones doubtless echoed with appeals to a higher something; and are not even now without their sanctity, since they chronicle a nation's desire after God. Whether those forest priests worshiped the strangely beautiful element of fire, or if the pilgrim Belief pitched her tent and for a night rested in some ruder and bleaker creed, there we may yet trace the light footsteps of Poesy, as she led her sister onward to fairer fields, and streams flowing nearer to the oracle of God.

From *" Conversations on the Poets."* Second Conversation, *" Chaucer."*

SIR JOHN LUBBOCK

(1834–)

SIR JOHN LUBBOCK has written a number of the most pleasantly instructive essays that could well be imagined. He is a member of the British Parliament, President of the Institute of Bankers, President of the Linnean Society of Great Britain, Trustee of the British Museum, Vice-President of the Royal Society, and the inventor of an admirable system of identifying ants by splotches of paint on their backs. A man of such diversified usefulness could not have expected to escape reproach, and Sir John can hardly have been surprised if his discoveries of the almost miraculous intelligence shown in the management of the ant hills he has kept under glass for observation, excited something of the same incredulity which rewarded Huber's discovery of the intellectual operations of ant life. Lubbock's *" Ants, Bees, and Wasps,"* published in 1882, and his book on *" The Senses, Instinct, and Intelligence of Animals,"* published six years later, made him a general favorite as a writer of popular science. But this popularity has been far surpassed by his moral essays collected and given coherency under the title of *" The Pleasures of Life."* Few moralists have equaled him in usefulness. *" The Pleasures of Life "* is still running through one edition after another, and it is doubtful if its circulation has been equaled by any novel published since it was issued,—a proof, if proof were needed, that the public is fonder of nothing than of being preached to by the right person in the right way.

A SONG OF BOOKS

" Oh for a booke and a shadie nooke,
Eyther in-a-doore or out;
With the grene leaves whispering overhede,
Or the streete cryes all about.
Where I maie reade all at my ease,
Both of the newe and olde;
For a jollie goode booke whereon to looke,
Is better to me than golde."
  —*Old English Song.*

OF ALL the privileges we enjoy in this nineteenth century, there is none, perhaps, for which we ought to be more thankful than for the easier access to books.

The debt we owe to books was well expressed by Richard de Bury, Bishop of Durham, author of " Philobiblon," published as long ago as 1473, and the earliest English treatise on the delights of literature: " These are the masters who instruct us without rods and ferules, without hard words and anger, without clothes or money. If you approach them, they are not asleep; if investigating you interrogate them, they conceal nothing; if you mistake them, they never grumble; if you are ignorant, they cannot laugh at you."

This feeling that books are real friends is constantly present to all who love reading.

" I have friends," said Petrarch, " whose society is extremely agreeable to me; they are of all ages and of every country. They have distinguished themselves both in the cabinet and in the field, and obtained high honors for their knowledge of the sciences. It is easy to gain access to them, for they are always at my service, and I admit them to my company, and dismiss them from it, whenever I please. They are never troublesome, but immediately answer every question I ask them. Some relate to me the events of past ages, while others reveal to me the secrets of nature. Some teach me how to live, and others how to die. Some by their vivacity, drive away my cares and exhilarate my spirits; while others give fortitude to my mind, and teach me the important lesson how to restrain my desires, and to depend wholly on myself. They open to me, in short, the various avenues of all the arts and sciences, and upon their information I may safely rely in all emergencies. In return for all their services, they only ask me to accommodate them with a convenient chamber in some corner of my humble habitation, where they may repose in peace; for these friends are more delighted by the tranquillity of retirement than with the tumults of society."

"He that loveth a book," says Isaac Barrow, "will never want a faithful friend, a wholesome counselor, a cheerful companion, an effectual comforter. By study, by reading, by thinking, one may innocently divert and pleasantly entertain himself, as in all weathers, so in all fortunes."

Southey took a rather more melancholy view:—

> "My days among the dead are pass'd,
> Around me I behold,
> Where'er these casual eyes are cast,
> The mighty minds of old;
> My never-failing friends are they,
> With whom I converse day by day."

Imagine, in the words of Aikin, "that we had it in our power to call up the shades of the greatest and wisest men that ever existed, and oblige them to converse with us on the most interesting topics — what an inestimable privilege should we think it! — how superior to all common enjoyments! But in a well-furnished library we, in fact, possess this power. We can question Xenophon and Cæsar on their campaigns, make Demosthenes and Cicero plead before us, join in the audiences of Socrates and Plato, and receive demonstrations from Euclid and Newton. In books we have the choicest thoughts of the ablest men in their best dress."

"Books," says Jeremy Collier, "are a guide in youth and an entertainment for age. They support us under solitude, and keep us from being a burden to ourselves. They help us to forget the crossness of men and things; compose our cares and our passions; and lay our disappointments asleep. When we are weary of the living, we may repair to the dead, who have nothing of peevishness, pride, or design in their conversation."

Cicero described a room without books as a body without a soul. But it is by no means necessary to be a philosopher to love reading.

Sir John Herschel tells an amusing anecdote illustrating the pleasure derived from a book, not assuredly of the first order.

In a certain village the blacksmith had got hold of Richardson's novel, "Pamela, or Virtue Rewarded," and used to sit on his anvil in the long summer evenings and read it aloud to a large and attentive audience. It is by no means a short book, but they fairly listened to it all. "At length, when the happy turn of fortune arrived, which brings the hero and heroine together, and sets them living long and happily, according to the most approved rules, the congregation were so delighted as to raise a great shout, and, procuring the church keys, actually set the parish bells ringing."

"The lover of reading," says Leigh Hunt, "will derive agreeable terror from Sir Bertram and the Haunted Chamber; will assent with delighted reason to every sentence in Mrs. Barbauld's Essay; will feel himself wandering into solitudes with Gray; shake honest hands with Sir Roger de Coverley; be ready to embrace Parson Adams, and to chuck Pounce out of the window instead of the hat; will travel with Marco Polo and Mungo Park; stay at home with Thomson; retire with Cowley; be industrious with Hutton; sympathizing with Gay and Mrs. Inchbald; laughing with (and at) Buncle; melancholy, and forlorn, and self-restored with the shipwrecked mariner of Defoe."

Carlyle has wisely said that a collection of books is a real university.

The importance of books has been appreciated in many quarters where we might least expect it. Among the hardy Norsemen runes were supposed to be endowed with miraculous power. There is an Arabic proverb, that "a wise man's day is worth a fool's life," and, though it rather perhaps reflects the spirit of the Califs than of the Sultans, that "the ink of science is more precious than the blood of the martyrs."

Confucius is said to have described himself as a man who "in his eager pursuit of knowledge forgot his food, who in the joy of its attainment forgot his sorrows, and did not even perceive that old age was coming on."

Yet, if this could be said by the Chinese and the Arabs, what language can be strong enough to express the gratitude we ought to feel for the advantages we enjoy! We do not appreciate, I think, our good fortune in belonging to the nineteenth century. Sometimes, indeed, one may be inclined to wish that one had not lived quite so soon, and to long for a glimpse of the books, even the school books, of one hundred years hence. A hundred years

ago not only were books extremely expensive and cumbrous, many of the most delightful books were still uncreated — such as the works of Scott, Thackeray, Dickens, Bulwer, Lytton, and Trollope, not to mention living authors. How much more interesting science has become, especially if I were to mention only one name, through the genius of Darwin! Renan has characterized this as a most amusing century; I should rather have described it as most interesting: presenting us with an endless vista of absorbing problems, with infinite opportunities; with more than the excitements, and less of the dangers, which surrounded our less fortunate ancestors.

Reading, indeed, is by no means necessarily study. Far from it. "I put," says Mr. Frederic Harrison, in his excellent article on the "Choice of Books," "I put the poetic and emotional side of literature as the most needed for daily use."

In the prologue to the "Legends of Goode Women," Chaucer says:—

> "And as for me, though that I konne but lyte,
> On bokes for to rede I me delyte,
> And to him give I feyth and ful credence,
> And in myn herte have him in reverence,
> So hertely, that ther is game noon,
> That fro my bokes maketh me to goon,
> But yt be seldome on the holy day,
> Save, certynly, when that the monthe of May
> Is comen, and that I here the foules synge,
> And that the floures gynnen for to sprynge,
> Farewel my boke, and my devocion."

But I doubt whether, if he had enjoyed our advantages, he could have been so certain of tearing himself away even in the month of May.

Macaulay, who had all that wealth and fame, rank and talents could give, yet, we are told, derived his greatest happiness from books. Sir G. Trevelyan, in his charming biography says that—"of the feelings which Macaulay entertained towards the great minds of bygone ages it is not for any one except himself to speak. He has told us how his debt to them was incalculable; how they guided him to truth; how they filled his mind with noble and graceful images; how they stood by him in all vicissitudes—comforters in sorrow, nurses in sickness, companions in solitude, the old friends who are never seen with new faces; who are the

same in wealth and in poverty, in glory and in obscurity. Great as were the honors and possessions which Macaulay acquired by his pen, all who knew him were well aware that the titles and rewards which he gained by his own works were as nothing in the balance as compared with the pleasure he derived from the works of others."

There was no society in London so agreeable that Macaulay would have preferred it at breakfast or at dinner "to the company of Sterne or Fielding, Horace Walpole or Boswell."

The love of reading which Gibbon declared he would not exchange for all the treasures of India was, in fact, with Macaulay "a main element of happiness in one of the happiest lives that it has ever fallen to the lot of the biographer to record."

"History," says Fuller, "maketh a young man to be old without either wrinkles or gray hair, privileging him with the experience of age without either the infirmities or the inconveniences thereof."

So delightful, indeed, are our books that we must be careful not to neglect other duties for them; in cultivating the mind we must not neglect the body.

To the lover of literature or science exercise often presents itself as an irksome duty, and many a one has felt like "the fair pupil of Ascham, who, while the horns were sounding and dogs in full cry, sat in the lonely oriel with eyes riveted to that immortal page which tells how meekly and bravely the first martyr of intellectual liberty took the cup from his weeping jailor."

Still, as the late Lord Derby justly observed, those who do not find time for exercise will have to find time for illness.

Books are now so cheap as to be within the reach of almost every one. This was not always so. It is quite a recent blessing. Mr. Ireland, to whose charming little "Book Lover's Enchiridion," in common with every lover of reading, I am greatly indebted, tells us that when a boy he was so delighted with White's "Natural History of Selborne," that, in order to possess a copy of his own he actually copied out the whole work.

Mary Lamb gives a pathetic description of a studious boy lingering at a bookstall:—

> "I saw a boy with eager eye
> Open a book upon a stall,
> And read, as he'd devour it all;
> Which, when the stallman did espy,

Soon to the boy I heard him call,
'You, sir, you never buy a book,
Therefore in one you shall not look.'
The boy passed slowly on, and with a sigh
He wished he never had been taught to read,
Then of the old churl's books he should have no need."

Such snatches of literature have, indeed, a special and peculiar charm. This is, I believe, partly due to the very fact of their being brief. Many readers, I think, miss much of the pleasure of reading by forcing themselves to dwell too long continuously on one subject. In a long railway journey, for instance, many persons take only a single book. The consequence is that, unless it is a story, after half an hour or an hour they are quite tired of it. Whereas, if they had two, or still better three, on different subjects, and one of them being of an amusing character, they would probably find that by changing as soon as they felt at all weary, they would come back again and again to each with renewed zest, and hour after hour would pass pleasantly away. Every one, of course, must judge for himself, but such at least is my experience.

I quite agree, therefore, with Lord Iddesleigh, as to the charm of desultory reading, but the wider the field the more important that we should benefit by the very best books in each class. Not that we need confine ourselves to them, but that we should commence with them, and they will certainly lead us on to others. There are, of course, some books which we must read, mark, learn, and inwardly digest. But these are exceptions. As regards by far the larger number, it is probably better to read them quickly, dwelling only on the best and most important passages. In this way, no doubt, we shall lose much, but we gain more by ranging over a wider field. We may, in fact, I think, apply to reading Lord Brougham's wise dictum as regards education, and say that it is well to read everything of something, and something of everything. In this way only we can ascertain the bent of our own tastes, for it is a general, though not, of course, an invariable rule, that we profit little by books which we do not enjoy.

Every one, however, may suit himself. The variety is endless. We may sit in our library and yet be in all quarters of the earth. We may travel round the world with Captain Cook or Darwin, with Kingsley or Ruskin, who will show us much more,

perhaps, than ever we should see for ourselves. The world itself has no limits for us; Humboldt and Herschel will carry us far away to the mysterious nebulæ, far beyond the sun and even the stars; time has no more bounds than space; history stretches out behind us, and geology will carry us back for millions of years before the creation of man, even to the origin of the material universe itself. We are not limited even to one plane of thought. Aristotle and Plato will transport us into a sphere none the less delightful because it requires some training to appreciate it. We may make a library, if we do but rightly use it, a true paradise on earth, a garden of Eden without its one drawback, for all is open to us, including and especially the fruit of the tree of knowledge for which we are told that our first mother sacrificed all the rest. Here we may read the most important histories, the most exciting volumes of travels and adventures, the most interesting stories, the most beautiful poems; we may meet the most eminent statesmen and poets and philosophers, benefit by the ideas of the greatest thinkers, and enjoy all the greatest creations of human genius.

Complete. From "The Pleasures of Life."

THE HAPPINESS OF DUTY

EMERSON closes his "Conduct of Life" with a striking allegory. The young Mortal enters the Hall of the Firmament. The Gods are sitting there, and he is alone with them. They pour on him gifts and blessings, and beckon him to their thrones. But between him and them suddenly appear snowstorms of illusions. He imagines himself in a vast crowd, whose behests he fancies he must obey. The mad crowd drives hither and thither, and sways this way and that. What is he that he should resist? He lets himself be carried about. How can he think or act for himself? But the clouds lift, and there are the Gods still sitting on their thrones; they alone with him alone.

"The great man," he elsewhere says, "is he who in the midst of the crowd keeps with perfect sweetness the serenity of solitude."

We may all, if we will, secure peace of mind for ourselves.

"Men seek retreats," says Marcus Aurelius, "houses in the country, seashores, and mountains; and thou too art wont to desire such things very much. But this is altogether a mark of the

most common sort of men; for it is in thy power whenever thou shalt choose to retire into thyself. For nowhere either with more quiet or more freedom from trouble does a man retire, than into his own soul, particularly when he has within him such thoughts that by looking into them he is immediately in perfect tranquillity."

Happy, indeed, is the man who has such a sanctuary in his own soul. "He who is virtuous is wise; and he who is wise is good; and he who is good is happy."

But we cannot expect to be happy if we do not lead pure and useful lives. To be good company for ourselves we must store our minds well; fill them with happy and pure thoughts; with pleasant memories of the past, and reasonable hopes for the future. We must, as far as may be, protect ourselves from self-reproach, from care, and from anxiety. We shall make our lives pure and happy by resisting evil, by placing restraint upon our appetites, and perhaps even more by strengthening and developing our tendencies to good. We must be careful, then, how we choose our thoughts. The soul is dyed by its thoughts; we cannot keep our minds pure if we allow them to dwell on detailed accounts of crime and sin. Peace of mind, as Ruskin beautifully observes, "must come in its own time, as the waters settle themselves into clearness as well as quietness; you can no more filter your mind into purity than you can compress it into calmness; you must keep it pure if you would have it pure, and throw no stones into it if you would have it quiet."

The penalty of injustice, said Socrates, is not death or stripes, but the fatal necessity of becoming more and more unjust. Few men have led a wiser or more virtuous life than Socrates himself, of whom Xenophon gives us the following description: "To me, being such as I have described him, so pious that he did nothing without the sanction of the gods; so just, that he wronged no man even in the most trifling affair, but was of service in the most important matters to those who enjoyed his society; so temperate that he never preferred pleasure to virtue; so wise, that he never erred in distinguishing better from worse; needing no counsel from others, but being sufficient in himself to discriminate between them; so able to explain and settle such questions by argument; and so capable of discerning the character of others, of confuting those who were in error, and of exhorting them to virtue and honor, he seemed to be such as the

best and happiest of men would be. But if any one disapproves of my opinion, let him compare the conduct of others with that of Socrates, and determine accordingly."

Marcus Aurelius again has drawn for us a most instructive lesson in his character of Antoninus: "Do everything as a disciple of Antoninus. Remember his constancy in every act which was conformable to reason, his evenness in all things, his piety, the serenity of his countenance, his sweetness, his disregard of empty fame, and his efforts to understand things; how he would never let anything pass without having first carefully examined it and clearly understood it; how he bore with those who blamed him unjustly without blaming them in return; how he did nothing in a hurry; how he listened not to calumnies, and how exact an examiner of manners and actions he was; not given to reproach people, nor timid, nor suspicious, nor a sophist; with how little he was satisfied, such as lodging, bed, dress, food, servants; how laborious and patient; how sparing he was in his diet; his firmness and uniformity in his friendships; how he tolerated freedom of speech in those who opposed his opinions; the pleasure that he had when any man showed him anything better, and how pious he was without superstition. Imitate all this that thou mayest have as good a conscience, when thy last hour comes, as he had."

Such peace of mind is, indeed, an inestimable boon, a rich reward of duty fulfilled. Well, then, does Epictetus ask, "Is there no reward? Do you seek a reward greater than that of doing what is good and just? At Olympia you wish for nothing more, but it seems to you enough to be crowned at the games. Does it, then, seem to you so small and worthless a thing to be good and happy?"

From "The Pleasures of Life."

LUCIAN

(c. 120–c. 200 A. D.)

LUCIAN, the most interesting of all Greek writers of prose satire, was born at Samosata, in Syria, about 120 A. D. It appears from his own account of himself that his father was poor and that when a boy he served as apprentice to a sculptor, from whom he ran away after receiving a beating. In his old age he lived in Egypt and held office as Keeper of Records or Master of the Rolls in that country. He died probably about the year 200 A. D. This is as doubtful as everything else that concerns his life. His writings which have survived in abundance are almost wholly humorous or satirical. He suggested themes for Swift and the author of "Baron Munchausen" among Moderns, as well as for many who have openly borrowed his style. He excelled in the dialogue, especially in dialogue which enabled him to put into the mouths of famous persons sarcastic or humorous comment on the follies and superstitions of the day. He saw that the polytheism which had been a popular religion in southern Europe and Egypt was decadent and near its end. In his "Dialogues of the Dead" and his "Dialogues of the Gods," he ridicules the religion of the people, while in other Dialogues he is even less merciful towards the professional philosophers who cultivated long beards and attempted to live without work on the strength of their assumed superiority. Lucian is one of the last writers of Greek prose which can be described as classical. He is sometimes criticized severely for impurities of style, but he writes with ease, and, in proof of the interest he has managed to excite and hold, his admirers can point to one hundred and twenty-four of his books and prose treatises which have survived, besides his epigrams and poems.

THAT BIBLIOMANIACS SHOULD READ THEIR OWN BOOKS

How can you be expected to distinguish those books which are old and valuable from those which are not, unless by their being thumbed and worm-eaten; for which purpose you do well to call to your aid a council of moths, otherwise no accurate judgment can ever be formed by you. But, if I should grant that you are not unacquainted with the taste of Callinus, or the

not pretend to vie in knowledge with the booksellers, because we have not so many books. Yet, if you examine them, you may possibly find some of them hardly more learned than yourself, equally ignorant, and inelegant, scarce seeing any difference between right and wrong. And yet what is your handful of authors, which you purchase of them, when compared to the multitudes, which they are handling night and day? I want to know what good reason you can assign for your conduct; unless you can believe that, when books lie on a shelf, they make the shelf as learned as themselves. Answer me a question or two, if you please. Or rather give me a nod, to show your assent or dissent, when you have heard what I am going to say. If a man unskilled in music should possess the pipes of Timotheus, or those which cost Ismenias five talents at Corinth, would that make him a piper? Being ignorant of their use, the possession of the pipes would be of no avail. Could it? You nod very properly, meaning no. For the pipe of Marsyas, or Olympus, would not enable a man to play without first learning music. The bow and arrows of a Hector would not make a Philoctetes. Do you think they would? No; you say no. For the very same reason a person ignorant of navigation, though master of the finest ship, and the best appointed, could no more direct it to a port than a man ignorant of the equestrian art can make any figure on horseback, though mounted on the finest steed in the world. You allow what I say to be true. Be candid then, and do the same by what I have further to observe; an illiterate man, like you, by purchasing a great number of books, only makes his ignorance the more conspicuous, and the more object of derision. What, no nod of assent? Can you deny it? It is a clear case, for everybody asks what a dog has to do with a bath. Not long ago there was in Asia a rich man who had the misfortune to lose his feet, in consequence, I believe, of having been obliged to travel through the snow. To remedy which loss as well as he could, he procured a pair of wooden feet, which he fastened to the stumps, and made a shift to crawl about by leaning on a servant. But the ridiculous part of the story was, that he made a point of having always the handsomest shoes, and those of the very newest fashion, to adorn his blocks,—his feet I mean. I think your conduct is not very unlike his.

From the translation of John Carr, 1779.

industrious Atticus, of what use, I pray, can those beauties be to you, which you can no more enjoy than a blind man those of his mistress? You examine some authors very carefully, even more than enough, and some you skim slightly over with a single glance of your eye. But what can it all signify, when you can be no judge of the merit or demerit of the work? when you are ignorant of the scope of the writer? what arrangement he has proposed to himself, where he has happily succeeded to a nicety, and where his diction appears vapid and adulterate? Or do you pretend to the art of criticism without any previous study? If so, you must have been presented, like the shepherd, with a branch of laurel from the Muses. But I believe you never once heard the trickling of Helicon, where the goddesses have fixed their abode. You never were a neighbor of theirs in the days of your youth, nor have the least recollection of any such beings. I do not say that the Muses have not condescended to visit a homely shepherd, sunburned, and roughly clad; but to such a person as you (Venus, the goddess of Elegance, will excuse my speaking more plainly), to such a man as you, I am confident, they will never come near. Instead of a present of laurel, you would be more likely to get a good beating with mallow. Their Holmus and their Hippocrene they would choose to keep unpolluted for thirsty flocks and the pure lips of shepherds. Impudent and audacious as you are, you will hardly presume to say that you derive any advantage from education, or have any more than outside acquaintance with authors. I have never heard the name of your schoolmaster, nor of any of your schoolfellows. But all the benefits of education, you think, may be obtained by having plenty of books. Very well; go on; collect all the manuscripts of Demosthenes, to which add the books of Thucydides, which the former is reported to have copied fairly over no less than eight times with his own hand. If you had all the books, which Sylla sent home from Athens, how much wiser, can you suppose, they would make you, even if you should sleep upon them, or wear them round your body? An ape, the proverb says, is still an ape, though decorated with a golden collar. You have always a book in your hand, and are continually reading, but what then? What are you more than the ass moving his ears at the sound of the lyre? Truly if the possession of books would make a man a scholar, they could never be sold for their worth, and we poor fellows going to market would make no figure at all. We could

MARTIN LUTHER

(1483–1546)

MARTIN LUTHER was born at Eisleben, Prussian Saxony, November 10th, 1483. His father was a slate cutter by trade, but Luther, by reason of his destination for the Church, became one of the most highly educated men of the time. After graduating at the University of Erfurt, he entered the Augustinian monastery in that town and in 1507 was consecrated a priest. A year later he became a professor of Philosophy in the University of Wittenberg. His career as a controversial theologian dates from October 31st, 1517, when he posted on the church door at Wittenberg, his ninety-five theses against indulgences. His translation of the Bible which greatly influenced the German language was completed in 1532 and finally published in 1534. Besides his sermons and theological writings, he wrote hymns and fables, as well as a number of short essays and treatises on various subjects. He died at Eisleben, February 18th, 1546, after a life of almost continuous struggle, which is still an active influence, not merely in denominational religion, but in international politics. In fact it may be pointed out as one of the most significant single facts of Luther's life that it marks the line between the international politics of the Middle Ages and of modern times.

THAT UNNECESSARY IGNORANCE IS CRIMINAL

Now if thou hast a child that is fit to receive instruction, and art able to hold him to it and dost not, but goest thy way and carest not what shall become of the secular government, its laws, its peace, etc., thou warrest against the secular government, as much as in thee lies, like the Turk, yea, like the Devil himself. For thou withholdest from the kingdom, principality, country, city, a redeemer, comfort, corner stone, helper, and savior. And on thy account the emperor loses both sword and crown; the country loses safeguard and freedom, and thou art the man through whose fault (as much as in thee lies) no man shall hold his body, wife, child, house, home, and goods in safety. Rather thou sacrificest all these without ruth in the shambles, and givest cause that men shall become mere beasts, and at last devour one another. This all thou wilt assuredly do, if thou withdraw thy child from so wholesome a condition, for the belly's sake. Now art thou not a pretty man and a useful in the world who makest daily use of the kingdom and its peace, and by way of thanks, in return, robbest the same of thy son, and deliverest him up to avarice, and laborest with all diligence to this end, that there may be no man who shall help maintain the kingdom, law, and peace; but that all may go to wreck, notwithstanding thou thyself possessest and holdest body and life, goods and honor by means of said kingdom?

I will say nothing here of how fine a pleasure it is for a man to be learned, albeit he have never an office; so that he can read all manner of things by himself at home, talk and converse with learned people, travel and act in foreign lands. For peradventure there be few who will be moved by such delights. But seeing thou art so bent upon mammon and victual, look here and see how many and how great goods God has founded upon schools and scholars, so that thou shalt no more despise learning and art by reason of poverty. Behold! emperors and kings must have chancellors and scribes, counselors, jurists, and scholars. There is no prince but he must have chancellors, jurists, counselors, scholars, and scribes; so likewise, all counts, lords, cities, castles must have syndics, city clerks, and other learned men; nay, there is not a nobleman but must have a scribe. Reckon up, now, how many kings, princes, counts, lords, cities, and towns, etc. Where will they find learned men three years hence, seeing that here and there already a want is felt? Truly I think kings will have to become jurists, and princes chancellors, counts and lords will have to become scribes, and burgomasters sacristans.

Therefore, I hold that never was there a better time to study than now; not only for the reason that the art is now so abundant and so cheap, but also because great wealth and honor must needs ensue, and they that study now will be men of price; insomuch that two princes and three cities shall tear one another for a single scholar. For look above or around thee and thou wilt find that innumerable offices wait for learned men, before ten years shall have sped; and that few are being educated for the same.

Besides honest gain, they have, also, honor. For chancellors, city clerks, jurists, and people in office, must sit with those who

are placed on high, and help counsel and govern. And they, in fact, are the lords of this world, although they are not so in respect of person, birth, and rank.

Solomon himself mentions that a poor man once saved a city, by his wisdom, against a mighty king. Not that I would have, herewith, warriors, troopers, and what belongs to strife done away, or despised and rejected. They also, where they are obedient, help to preserve peace and all things with their fist. Each has his honor before God, as well as his place and work.

On the other hand, there are found certain scratchers who conceit that the title of Writer is scarce worthy to be named or heard. Well, then, regard it not, but think on this wise: these good people must have their amusement and their jest. Leave them their jest, but remain thou, nevertheless, a writer before God and the world. If they scratch long, thou shalt see that they honor, notwithstanding, the pen above all things; that they place it upon hat and helmet, as if they would confess, by their action, that the pen is the top of the world, without which they can neither be equipped for battle nor go about in peace; much less scratch so securely. For they also have need of the peace which the emperors, preachers, and teachers (the lawyers) teach and maintain. Wherefore thou seest that they place our implement, the dear pen, uppermost. And with reason, since they gird their own implement, the sword, about the thighs; there it hangs fitly and well for their work; but it would not beseem the head; there must hover the plume. If, then, they have sinned against thee, they herewith expiate the offense, and thou must forgive them.

There be some that deem the office of a writer to be an easy and trivial office; but to ride in armor, to endure heat, cold, dust, thirst, and other inconvenience, they think to be laborious. Yea! that is the old, vulgar, daily tune; that no one sees where the shoe pinches another. Every one feels only his own troubles, and stares at the ease of others. True it is, it would be difficult for me to ride in armor; but then, on the other hand, I would like to see the rider who should sit me still the whole day long and look into a book, though he were not compelled to care for aught, to invent or think or read. Ask a chancery clerk, a preacher or an orator, what kind of work writing and haranguing is? Ask a schoolmaster what kind of work is teaching and bringing up of boys? The pen is light, it is true, and

among all trades no tool so easily furnished as that of the writing trade, for it needeth only a goose's wing, of which one shall everywhere find a sufficiency, gratis. Nevertheless, in this employment, the best piece of the human body (as the head) and the noblest member (as the tongue) and the highest work (as speech) must take part and labor most; while, in others, either the fist or the feet or the back, or members of that class alone work; and they that pursue them may sing merrily the while, and jest freely, which a writer cannot do. Three fingers do the work (so they say of writers), but the whole body and soul must co-operate.

I have heard of the worthy and beloved Emperor Maximilian, how, when the great boobies complained that he employed so many writers for missions and other purposes, he is reported to have said: "What shall I do? They will not suffer themselves to be used in this way, therefore I must employ writers." And further: "Knights I can create, but doctors I cannot create." So have I likewise heard of a fine nobleman, that he said: "I will let my son study. It is no great art to hang two legs over a steed and be a rider; he shall soon learn me that; and he shall be fine and well-spoken."

They say, and it is true, the pope was once a pupil too. Therefore despise me not the fellows who say *panem propter Deum* before the doors and sing the bread song. Thou hearest, as this psalm says, great princes and lords sing. I, too, have been one of these fellows, and have received bread at the houses, especially at Eisenach, my native city. Although, afterward, my dear father maintained me, with all love and faith, in the high school at Erfurt, and, by his sore sweat and labor, has helped me to what I have become,—still I have been a beggar at the doors of the rich, and, according to this psalm, have attained so far by means of the pen, that now I would not compound with the Turkish emperor, to have his wealth and forego my art. Yea, I would not take for it the wealth of the world many times multiplied; and yet, without doubt, I had never attained to it, had I not chanced upon a school and the writers' trade.

Therefore, let thy son study, nothing doubting, and though he should beg his bread the while, yet shalt thou give to our Lord God a fine piece of wood out of which he can whittle thee a lord. And be not disturbed that vulgar niggards contemn the art so disdainfully, and say: Aha! if my son can write German

and read and cipher, he knows enough; I will have him a merchant. They shall soon become so tame that they will be fain to dig with their fingers, ten yards deep in the earth, for a scholar. For my merchant will not be a merchant long, when law and preaching fail. That know I for certain; we theologians and lawyers must remain, or all must go down with us together. It cannot be otherwise. When theologians go, then goes the word of God, and remains nothing but the heathen, yea! mere devils. When jurists go, then goes justice together with peace, and remains only murder, robbery, outrage, force, yea! mere wild beasts. But what the merchant shall earn and win, when peace is gone, I will leave it to his books to inform him. And how much profit all his wealth shall be to him when preaching fails, his conscience, I trow, shall declare to him.

I will say briefly of a diligent, pious schoolteacher or magister, or of whomsoever it is, that faithfully brings up boys and instructs them, that such an one can never be sufficiently recompensed or paid with money; as also the heathen Aristotle says. Yet is this calling so shamefully despised among us as though it were altogether naught. And we call ourselves Christians!

And if I must or could relinquish the office of preacher and other matters, there is no office I would more willingly have than that of schoolmaster or teacher of boys. For I know that this work, next to the office of preacher, is the most profitable, the greatest, and the best. Besides, I know not even which is the best of the two. For it is hard to make old dogs tame and old rogues upright; at which task, nevertheless, the preacher's office labors, and often labors in vain. But young trees be more easily bent and trained, howbeit some should break in the effort. Beloved! count it one of the highest virtues upon earth, to educate faithfully the children of others, which so few, and scarcely any, do by their own.

From a discourse on the "Furtherance of Schools," etc.

SIR CHARLES LYELL

(1797–1875)

SIR CHARLES LYELL was born at Kinnordy, Forfarshire, Scotland, November 14th, 1797. He took his degree at Oxford in 1819 and began practice at the bar, but from his boyhood he had had a strong leaning towards scientific research which drew him under the influence of Cuvier, Humboldt, and other great investigators, who were just beginning to rid science of the limitations imposed on it by the Middle Ages. Lyell's researches in geology gave them effective support and made him one of the founders of geology as a true science. His works include "Principles of Geology," 1830–1833; "Travels in North America," 1845; "The Antiquity of Man," 1863; and "The Student's Elements of Geology," 1871. He died at London, February 22d, 1875.

THE GREAT EARTHQUAKE OF LISBON

IN NO part of the volcanic region of southern Europe has so tremendous an earthquake occurred in modern times as that which began on the first of November, 1755, at Lisbon. A sound of thunder was heard underground, and immediately afterwards a violent shock threw down the greater part of that city. In the course of about six minutes, sixty thousand persons perished. The sea first retired and laid the bar dry; it then rolled in, rising fifty feet above its ordinary level. The mountains of Arrabida, Estrella, Julio, Marvan, and Cintra, being some of the largest in Portugal, were impetuously shaken, as it were, from their very foundations; and some of them opened at their summits, which were split and rent in a wonderful manner, huge masses of them being thrown down into the subjacent valleys. Flames are related to have issued from these mountains, which are supposed to have been electric; they are also said to have smoked; but vast clouds of dust may have given rise to this appearance.

The most extraordinary circumstance which occurred at Lisbon during the catastrophe, was the subsidence of a new quay, built

entirely of marble, at an immense expense. A great concourse of people had collected there for safety, as a spot where they might be beyond the reach of falling ruins; but suddenly the quay sank down with all the people on it, and not one of the dead bodies ever floated to the surface. A great number of boats and small vessels anchored near it, all full of people, were swallowed up as in a whirlpool. No fragments of these wrecks ever rose again to the surface, and the water in the place where the quay had stood is stated, in many accounts, to be unfathomable; but Whitehurst says he ascertained it to be one hundred fathoms.

In this case, we must either suppose that a certain tract sank down into a subterranean hollow, which would cause a "fault" in the strata to the depth of six hundred feet, or we may infer, as some have done, from the entire disappearance of the substances engulfed, that a chasm opened and closed again. Yet in adopting this latter hypothesis, we must suppose that the upper part of the chasm, to the depth of one hundred fathoms, remained open after the shock. According to the observations made at Lisbon, in 1837, by Mr. Sharpe, the destroying effects of this earthquake were confined to the tertiary strata, and were most violent on the blue clay, on which the lower part of the city is constructed. Not a building, he says, on the secondary limestone or the basalt was injured.

The great area over which this Lisbon earthquake extended is very remarkable. The movement was most violent in Spain, Portugal, and the north of Africa; but nearly the whole of Europe, and even the West Indies, felt the shock on the same day. A seaport called St. Ubes, about twenty miles south of Lisbon, was engulfed. At Algiers and Fez, in Africa, the agitation of the earth was equally violent; and at the distance of eight leagues from Morocco, a village with the inhabitants, to the number of about eight or ten thousand persons, together with all their cattle, were swallowed up. Soon after, the earth closed again over them.

The shock was felt at sea on the deck of a ship to the west of Lisbon, and produced very much the same sensation as on dry land. Off St. Lucar, the captain of the ship Nancy felt his vessel so violently shaken, that he thought she had struck the ground, but, on heaving the lead, found a great depth of water. Captain Clark, from Denia, in latitude 36° 24′ N., between nine and ten in the morning, had his ship shaken and strained as if

she had struck upon a rock. Another ship forty leagues west of St. Vincent experienced so violent a concussion that the men were thrown a foot and a half perpendicularly up from the deck. In Antigua and Barbadoes, as also in Norway, Sweden, Germany, Holland, Corsica, Switzerland, and Italy, tremors and slight oscillations of the ground were felt.

The agitation of lakes, rivers, and springs in Great Britain was remarkable. At Loch Lomond, in Scotland, for example, the water, without the least apparent cause, rose against its banks, and then subsided below its usual level. The greatest perpendicular height of this swell was two feet four inches. It is said that the movement of this earthquake was undulatory, and that it traveled at the rate of twenty miles a minute. A great wave swept over the coast of Spain, and is said to have been sixty feet high at Cadiz. At Tangier, in Africa, it rose and fell eighteen times on the coast; at Funchal, in Madeira, it rose full fifteen feet perpendicular above high-water mark, although the tide, which ebbs and flows there seven feet, was then at half-ebb. Besides entering the city and committing great havoc, it overflowed other seaports in the island. At Kinsale, in Ireland, a body of water rushed into the harbor, whirled round several vessels, and poured into the market place.

It was before stated that the sea first retired at Lisbon; and this retreat of the ocean from the shore at the commencement of an earthquake, and its subsequent return in a violent wave, is a common occurrence. In order to account for the phenomenon, Michell imagined a subsidence at the bottom of the sea from the giving way of the roof of some cavity, in consequence of a vacuum produced by the condensation of steam. Such condensation, he observes, might be the first effect of the introduction of a large body of water into fissures and cavities already filled with steam, before there had been sufficient time for the heat of the incandescent lava to turn so large a supply of water into steam, which, being soon accomplished, causes a greater explosion.

JOHN LYLY

(c. 1554–1606)

"EUPHUES, OR THE ANATOMY OF WIT," by John Lyly, is responsible for the word "Euphuism" to indicate what Saintsbury calls "conceited and precious language in general." Burton's "Anatomy of Melancholy," published in 1621, more than forty years after Lyly wrote "Euphues," is another noted example of the same style. Lyly was born in Kent, England, about 1554. At Oxford, where he took his first degree in 1573, he was known as a "noted wit" whose genius, it was said, "naturally bent to the pleasant paths of poetry, as if Apollo had given him a wreath of his own bays, without snatching or struggling." Lyly wrote a number of plays and followed the "Anatomy of Wit" with his "Euphues and his England" in 1580. In 1589 he published a tract entitled, "Pappe with an Hatchet, *alias* a Figge for My Godsonne; or Crack Me This Nut; or A Countrie Cuffe," etc., as his contribution to the celebrated Martin Marprelate controversies. He died in neglect in 1606. His burial is registered on November 20th of that year at St. Bartholomew the Less, in London. His work belongs largely to the curiosities of literature; but in spite of its worst affectation, it is frequently interesting in itself, and always so as an illustration of the eccentricities of intellect which accompany such great crises in history as that which developed in the Puritan revolution against the Stuarts.

A COOLING CARD FOR ALL FOND LOVERS

IT IS a world to see how commonly we are blinded with the collusions of women, and more enticed by their ornaments being artificial than their proportion being natural. I loathe almost to think on their ointments and apothecary drugs, the sleeking of their faces, and all their slibber sauces, which bring quasiness to the stomach, and disquiet to the mind.

Take from them their periwigs, their paintings, their jewels, their roules, their bolsterings, and thou shalt soon perceive that a woman is the least part of herself. When they be once robbed of their robes, then will they appear so odious, so ugly, so monstrous, that thou wilt rather think them serpents than saints, and so like hags that thou wilt fear rather to be enchanted than enamored. Look in their closets, and there shalt thou find an apothecary's shop of sweet confections, a surgeon's box of sundry salves, a peddler's pack of new fangles. . . . If every one of these things severally be not of force to move thee, yet all of them jointly should mortify thee.

Moreover, to make thee the more stronger to strive against these sirens, and more subtle to deceive these tame serpents, my counsel is that thou have more strings to thy bow than one. It is safe riding at two anchors; a fire divided in twain burneth slower; a fountain running into many rivers is of less force; the mind enamored on two women is less affected with desire, and less infected with despair; one love expelleth another, and the remembrance of the latter quencheth the concupiscence of the first.

Yet if thou be so weak, being bewitched with their wiles, that thou hast neither will to eschew nor wit to avoid their company; if thou be either so wicked that thou wilt not, or so wedded that thou canst not, abstain from their glances, yet at the least dissemble thy grief. If thou be as hot as mount Ætna, feign thyself as cold as the hill Caucasus, carry two faces in one hood, cover thy flaming fancy with feigned ashes, show thyself sound when thou art rotten, let thy hue be merry when thy heart is melancholy, bear a pleasant countenance with a pined conscience, a painted sheath with a leaden dagger. Thus dissembling thy grief, thou mayest recur thy disease. Love creepeth in by stealth, and by stealth slideth away. . . .

Let every one loathe his lady, and be ashamed to be her servant. It is riches and ease that nourisheth affection; it is play, wine, and wantonness, that feedeth a lover as fat as a fool; refrain from all such meats as shall provoke thine appetite, and all such means as may allure thy mind to folly. Take clear water for strong wine; brown bread for fine manchet; beef and brews for quail and partridge; for ease, labor; for pleasure, pain; for surfeiting, hunger; for sleep, watching; for the fellowship of ladies, the company of philosophers. If thou say to me, Physician heal thyself, I answer that I am meetly well purged of that disease, and yet was I never more willing to cure myself than to comfort my friend. And seeing the cause that made in me so cold a devotion should make in thee also as frozen a desire, I hope thou wilt be as ready to provide a salve as thou

wast hasty in seeking a sore. And yet, Philautus, I would not that all women should take pepper in the nose, in that I have disclosed the legerdemains of a few; for well I know none will wince except they be galled, neither any be offended unless she be guilty. Therefore I earnestly desire thee that thou show this cooling card to none, except thou show also this, my defense, to them all. For although I weigh nothing the ill-will of light housewives, yet would I be loath to lose the good-will of honest matrons. Thus being ready to go to Athens, and ready there to entertain thee whensoever thou shalt repair thither, I bid thee farewell, and fly women.

From Arber's reprint, 1579.

HOW THE LIFE OF A YOUNG MAN SHOULD BE LED

THERE are three things which cause perfection in man, Nature, Reason Use. Reason I call Discipline, Use, Exercise. If any one of these branches want, certainly the tree of virtue must needs wither. For Nature without discipline is of small force, and discipline without Nature more feeble; if exercise or study be void of any of these, it availeth nothing. For as in tilling of the ground and husbandry, there is first chosen a fertile soil, then a cunning sower, then good seed, even so must we compare Nature to the fat earth, the expert husbandman to the schoolmaster, the faculties and sciences to the pure seeds. If this order had not been in our predecessors, Pythagoras, Socrates, Plato, and whosoever was renowned in Greece, for the glory of wisdom, they had never been eternized for wise men, neither canonized, as it were, for saints, among those that study sciences. It is therefore a most evident sign of God's singular favor towards him that is endowed with all these qualities without the least of which man is most miserable. But if there be any one that thinketh wit not necessary to the obtaining of wisdom, after he hath gotten the way to virtue by industry and exercise, he is a heretic in my opinion, touching the true faith of learning, for if Nature play not her part, in vain is labor, and, as I said before, if study be not employed, in vain is Nature. Sloth turneth the edge of wit; study sharpeneth the mind; a thing, be it never so easy, is hard to the (idle); a thing, be it never so hard, is easy to the wit well employed. And most plainly we may see in many things the efficacy of industry and labor.

The little drop of rain pierceth hard marble; iron with often handling is worn to nothing. Besides this, Industry showeth herself in other things: the fertile soil if it be never tilled doth wax barren, and that which is most noble by nature is made most vile by negligence. What tree if it be not topped beareth any fruit? What vine if it be not pruned bringeth forth grapes? Is not the strength of the body turned to weakness with too much delicacy; were not Milo his arms brawnfallen for want of wrestling? Moreover by labor the fierce unicorn is tamed, the wildest falcon is reclaimed, the greatest bulwark is sacked. It is well answered of that man of Thessaly, who being demanded who among the Thessalians were reputed most vile, those, said he, that live at quiet and ease, never giving themselves to martial affairs. But what should one use many words in a thing already proved? It is custom, use, and exercise that bringeth a young man to virtue, and virtue to his perfection. Lycurgus, the lawgiver of the Spartans, did nourish two whelps both of one sire and one dam. But after a sundry manner, for the one he framed to hunt, and the other to lie always in the chimney's end at the porridge pot. Afterward calling the Lacedæmonians into one assembly he said: To the attaining of virtue, ye Lacedæmonians, education, industry, and exercise is the most noblest means, the truth of which I will make manifest unto you by trial; then bringing forth the whelps, and setting down there a pot and a hare, the one ran at the hare, the other to the porridge pot. The Lacedæmonians scarce understanding this mystery, he said: Both of these be of one sire and one dam, but you see how education altereth nature.

Complete. From Arber's reprint of 1579.

LORD LYTTON

(EDWARD GEORGE EARLE LYTTON BULWER, BARON LYTTON)

(1803–1873)

AS AN orator, dramatist, poet, politician, and novelist, "Bulwer Lytton" acquitted himself with credit, winning his chief celebrity and perhaps his greatest usefulness by the long list of novels which continue to be read in spite of the disapproval of Thackeray whose usually mild temper was stirred almost to virulence by everything "Bulwig" did. But Thackeray to the contrary notwithstanding, several of these novels have already vindicated their places as classics, and at least one of them, "The Last Days of Pompeii," has taken almost as strong a hold on popular favor as the higher and more artistic fiction of Scott himself. As an essayist, Lord Lytton is at his best. He writes easily and gracefully, is always interesting and is frequently surprising in the novelty, if not in the originality, of his thought. As a poet, he lacked only a very little of high excellence; but in the useful translations of Horace, in which he attempts to represent the original rhythm of that most melodious of the Augustan lyric poets, he shows that this little is an inherent defect in his sense of time in language. Such failures at his climaxes are not altogether rare even in his prose; but in view of his excellencies, no one who follows him long will remember them against him. He was a "Conservative" in politics, and the violent animosities which some of his celebrated contemporaries wreaked upon him were largely a result of political partisanship, which his works have long ago outlived.

THE SANGUINE TEMPERAMENT

WE ARE always disposed to envy the man of a hopeful temper; but a hopeful temper, where it so predominates as to be the conspicuous attribute, is seldom accompanied with prudence, and therefore seldom attended with worldly success. It is the hopeful temper that predominates in gamblers, in speculators, in political dreamers, in enthusiasts of all kinds. Endeavoring many years ago to dissuade a friend of mine from the roulette table, I stated all the chances which calculators sum up in favor of the table against the gamester. He answered gayly, "Why look to the dark side of the question? I never do!" And so, of course, he was ruined. I observe, in reading history and biography, that the men who have been singularly unfortunate have for the most part been singularly hopeful. This was remarkably the case with Charles I. It startles one to see in Clarendon how often he is led into his most fatal actions by a sanguine belief that fate will humor the die for him. Every day a projector lays before you some ingenious device for extracting sunbeams from cucumbers with the most sanguine expectation that the age has just arrived at the certainty that his cucumber alone can enlighten it. The late Mr. Robert Owen remained to the last as sure of converting the world to his schemes for upsetting it as if he had never known a disappointment. When, a short time before his death, that amiable logician, after rejecting all the evidences of nature and all the arguments of sages in support of the soul's immortality, accepted that creed on the authority of a mahogany table, the spirit of one of George IV.'s portly brothers, evidently wishing to secure so illustrious a convert, took care to rap out "Yes" when Mr. Owen asked if he should bring his plans before parliament, and to sustain his new faith in a heaven by promising him that within a year his old hope of reforming the earth should be realized. Had his Royal Highness told him that he could never square the circle of life by a social parallelogram, I greatly fear that Mr. Owen would have remained a materialist, and declared table rapping to be a glaring imposture.

In my recollections of school and college, I remember that, as between two youths of equal ability and ambition, the odds of success in rivalry were always in favor of the one least sanguinely confident of succeeding, and obviously for this reason: He who distrusts the security of chance takes more pains to effect the safety which results from labor. To find what you seek in the road of life, the best proverb of all is that which says: "Leave no stone unturned."

As all men, however, have in their natures a certain degree of hope, so he is the wisest who husbands it with the most care. When you are engaged in any undertaking in which success depends partly on skill, partly on luck, always presuppose that the luck may go against you, for the presupposition redoubles all

your efforts to obtain the advantages that belong to skill. Hope nothing from luck, and the probability is that you will be so prepared, forewarned, and forearmed, that all shallow observers will call you lucky.

At whist, a game into which, of all games needing great skill, perhaps luck enters most, indifferent players, or even good players who have drunk too much wine, will back some run of luck upon system, and are sure to lose at the year's end. The most winning player I ever knew was a good but not a first-rate player, and, playing small stakes, though always the same stakes, he made a very handsome yearly income. He took up whist as a profession instead of the bar, saying ingenuously, "At the bar, if I devoted myself to it, I think I could make the same yearly sum with pains, which at whist I make with pleasure. I prefer pleasure to pain when the reward is equal, and I choose whist." Well, this gentleman made it a rule never to bet, even though his partner were a B. or a C. (the two finest players in England, now living since the empire of India has lost us General A.), and his adversaries any Y. Z. at the foot of the alphabet. "For," said he, "in betting on games and rubbers, chance gets an advantage over the odds in favor of skill. My object is to win at the year's end, and the player who wins at the year's end is not the man who has won the most games and rubbers, but the man who in winning has made the greatest number of points, and who in losing has lost the fewest. Now if I, playing for, say, 10 s. a point, with B. or C. for my partner, take a £5 bet on the rubber, X. and Y. may have four by honors twice running; and grant that I save two points in the rubber by skill, losing six points instead of eight points, still I have the bet of £5 to pay all the same; the points are saved by the skill of the playing, but the rubbers are lost by the chance of the cards."

Adhering to this rule, abridging the chances of the cards, concentrating his thoughts on the chances in favor of skill, this whist player, steady and safe, but without any of those inspirations which distinguish the first-rate from the second-rate player, made, I say, regularly a handsome income out of whist; and I do not believe that any first-rate whist player who takes bets can say the same, no matter what stakes he plays.

In life as in whist, hope nothing from the way cards may be dealt to you. Play the cards, whatever they be, to the best of your skill.

But, unhappily, life is not like the whist table; you have it not at your option whether to cut in or not; cut in and play your hand you must. Now, talking of proverbs, "What must be must." It is one thing to be the braggadocio of hope, and it is another thing to be the craven of fear. A good general before fighting a battle in which he cannot choose his ground — to which he is compelled, will he, nill he — makes all the provisions left in his power, and then, since "what must be must," never reveals to his soldiers any fear of the issue. Before it comes to the fight, it is mapping and planning. When the fight begins, it is "Forward, and St. George!"

An old poet, Lord Brook, has two striking lines, which I will quote and then qualify: —

> "For power is proud till it look down on fear,
> Though only safe by ever looking there."

No, not safe by ever looking there, but by looking there — at the right moment.

Before you commence anything, provide as if all hope were against you. When you must set about it, act as if there were not such a thing as fear. When you have taken all precautions as to skill in the circumstances against which you can provide, dismiss from consideration all circumstances dependent on luck which you cannot control. When you can't choose your ground, it is "Forward, and St. George!" But look for no help from St. George unless you have taken the same pains he did in training his horse and his dogs before he fought with the dragon. In short, hope warps judgment in council, but quickens energy in action.

There is a quality in man often mistaken for a hopeful temperament, though in fact it is the normal acquisition of that experience which is hope's sternest corrective, — the quality of self-confidence.

As we advance in years, hope diminishes and self-confidence increases. Trials have taught us what we can do, and trained us to calculate with serene accuracy on the probable results. Hope, which has so much to do with gaming, has nothing to do with arithmetic. And as we live on, we find that for all which really belongs to the insurance against loss, we had better consult the actuary than stake against the croupier.

"Fortune," saith a fine Latin proverb, "lends much at interest, but gives a fee simple to none." According to the security you offer to her, Fortune makes her loans easy or ruinous.

Self-confidence is not hope; it is the self-judgment of your own internal forces, in their relation to the world without, which results from the failures of many hopes, and the nonrealization of many fears; for the two classes of things that most rarely happen to us are the things we hoped for and the things we dreaded. But there is one form of hope which is never unwise, and which certainly does not diminish with the increase of knowledge. In that form it changes its name, and we call it patience. "Patience," says Vauvenargues, "is only hope prolonged." It is that kind of hope which belongs to the highest order of mind, and is so essential to the enterprise of genius that Buffon calls genius itself "a long patience," as Helvetius calls it "a sustained attention." Patience, indeed, is the soul of speculation, "and the scope of all speculation is the performance of some action or thing to be done." This is the true form of hope that remained at the bottom of Pandora's Box; the more restless images or simulacra of the consolatory sustainer must have flown away among the earliest pinions that dispersed into air at the opening of the lid.

Complete. From "Caxtoniana."

SOME OBSERVATIONS ON SHY PEOPLE

TO MORAL excellence there are two rewards, neither of which is bestowed by the loud huzzas of the populace; one within the conscience — one far out of reach, beyond the stars.

But for intellectual excellence, man asks first a test, and next a reward, in the praise of his fellowmen.

Therefore the love of human approbation is at the root of all those sustained labors by which man works out his ideal of intellectual excellence; at least so generally that we need not care to count the exceptions. During the later stages of a great career, that love of approbation, in a mind well disciplined, often ceases to be perceptible, chiefly because it has become too habitually familiar to retain distinctness. We are, then, as little acutely sensible of the pervading force of the motive, as, while in health, we are sensible of the beats of our pulse and the circulation of our blood. But there it still is, no less—there, in the pulse, in the blood. A cynic or a misanthrope may disown it; but if he have genius, and the genius urge him to address men even in vindication of misanthropy and cynicism, he is inevitably courting the approbation which he pretends to scorn. As Cicero says with quiet irony, "The authors who affect contempt for a name in the world put their names to the books which they invite the world to read." But to return to my starting point, the desire of approbation will be accompanied by that nervous susceptibility which, however well disguised, is inseparable from the vibrating oscillation between hope and fear. And this nervousness in things not made mechanically familiar by long practice will be in proportion to the height of a man's own standard of excellence, and the care with which he measures the difficulties that interpose between a cherished conception and a worthy execution of design.

Out of this nervousness comes the shyness common to all youth, where it aspires to excel and fears to fail.

It follows from what I have said that those races are the most active, have accomplished the greatest marvels of energy, and, on the whole, exhibit the highest standard of public honesty in administrative departments, to which the national character of shyness is generally accorded, distinct from its false counterfeit-pride.

For the best guarantee for honesty is a constant sense of responsibility, and that sense is rendered lively and acute by a certain anxious diffidence of self, which is—Shyness. And again, it is that diffidence which makes men take pains to win and deserve success—stimulates energy and sustains perseverance.

The Turk is proud, not shy; he walks the world, or rather lets the world walk by him, serene in his self-esteem. The Red Indian is proud, not shy; his dignity admits of no dysopia—is never embarrassed nor taken by surprise. But the Turk and the Red Indian do not improve; and when civilization approaches them, it is rather to corrupt than to enlighten. The British race are shy to a proverb. And what shore does not bear the stamp of their footstep? What boundary in the regions of intellect has yet satisfied their ardor of progress? Ascham's ideal of perfectness is in the mind of the whole nation.

To desire to do something, not only as well as it can be done, but better than we can do it—to feel to exaggeration all our

own natural deficiencies toward the doing of it—to resolve by redoubled energy and perseverance to extract from art whatever may supply those deficiencies in nature—this is the surest way to become great—this is the character of the English race—this should be the character of an English genius.

But he who thus feels, thus desires, and thus resolves, will keep free from rust those mainsprings of action—the sensibility to shame, and the yearning toward perfection. It is the elasticity of the watchspring that renders it the essential principle to the mechanism of the watch; but elasticity is only the property of solid bodies to recover, after yielding to pressure, their former shape. The mind which retains to the last youth's quick susceptibility to disgrace and to glory retains to the last the power to resume the shape that it wore in youth. Cynicism is old at twenty. Impudence has no elasticity. If you care no more than the grasshopper for the favor of gods and the reverence of men, your heart has the age of Tithonus, though your cheek have the bloom of Achilles. But if, even alone in your room or a desert, you could still blush or turn pale at the thought of a stain on your honor—if your crest still could rise, your pulse quicken, at the flash of some noble thought or brave deed—then you have the heart of Achilles, though at the age of Tithonus. There is certain august shamefacedness—the Romans called it *Pudor*—which, under hairs white as snow, preserves the aspect of youth to all personations of honor, of valor, of genius.

From "Caxtoniana."

READERS AND WRITERS

READING without purpose is sauntering, not exercise. More is got from one book on which the thought settles for definite end in knowledge than from libraries skimmed over by a wandering eye. A cottage flower gives honey to the bee, a king's garden none to the butterfly.

Youths who are destined for active careers, or ambitious of distinction in such forms of literature as require freshness of invention or originality of thought, should avoid the habit of intense study for many hours at a stretch. There is a point in all tension of the intellect beyond which effort is only waste of strength. Fresh ideas do not readily spring up within a weary

brain; and whatever exhausts the mind not only enfeebles its power, but narrows its scope. We often see men who have overread at college entering upon life as languidly as if they were about to leave it. They have not the vigor to cope with their own generation; for their own generation is young, and they have wasted the nervous energy which supplies the sinews of war to youth in its contests for fame or fortune.

Study with regularity, at settled hours. Those in the forenoon are the best, if they can be secured. The man who has acquired the habit of study, though for only one hour every day in the year, and keeps to the one thing studied till it is mastered, will be startled to see the way he has made at the end of a twelvemonth.

He is seldom overworked who can contrive to be in advance of his work. If you have three weeks before you to learn something which a man of average quickness could learn in a week, learn it the first week, and not in the third. Business dispatched is business well done, but business hurried is business ill done.

In learning what others have thought, it is well to keep in practice the power to think for oneself; when an author has added to your knowledge, pause and consider if you can add nothing to his.

Be not contented to have learned a problem by heart; try and deduce from it a corollary not in the book.

Spare no pains in collecting details before you generalize; but it is only when details are generalized that a truth is grasped. The tendency to generalize is universal with all men who achieve great success, whether in art, literature, or action. The habit of generalizing, though at first gained with care and caution, secures, by practice, a comprehensiveness of judgment and a promptitude of decision which seem to the crowd like the intuitions of genius. And, indeed, nothing more distinguishes the man of genius from the mere man of talent than the facility of generalizing the various details, each of which demands the aptitude of a special talent, but all of which can be only gathered into a single whole by the grasp of a mind which may have no special aptitude for any.

Invention implies the power of generalization, for an invention is but the combining of many details known before into a new whole, and for new results.

Upon any given point, contradictory evidence seldom puzzles the man who has mastered the laws of evidence, but he knows

little of the laws of evidence who has not studied the unwritten law of the human heart; and without this last knowledge a man of action will not attain to the practical, nor will a poet achieve the ideal.

He who has no sympathy never knows the human heart; but the obtrusive parade of sympathy is incompatible with dignity of character in a man, or with dignity of style in a writer. Of all the virtues necessary to the completion of the perfect man, there is none to be more delicately implied and less ostentatiously vaunted than that of exquisite feeling or universal benevolence.

In science, address the few; in literature, the many. In science, the few must dictate opinion to the many; in literature, the many, sooner or later, force their judgment on the few. But the few and the many are not necessarily the few and the many of the passing time; for discoverers in science have not unoften, in their own day, had the few against them, and writers the most permanently popular not unfrequently found, in their own day, a frigid reception from the many. By the few, I mean those who must ever remain the few, from whose dicta, we, the multitude, take fame upon trust; by the many, I mean those who constitute the multitude in the long run. We take the fame of a Harvey or a Newton upon trust, from the verdict of the few in successive generations; but the few could never persuade us to take poets and novelists on trust. We, the many, judge for ourselves of Shakespeare and Cervantes.

He who addresses the abstract reason addresses an audience that must forever be limited to the few; he who addresses the passions, the feelings, the humors, which we all have in common, addresses an audience that must forever compose the many. But either writer, in proportion to his ultimate renown, embodies some new truth, and new truths require new generations for cordial welcome. This much I would say meanwhile: Doubt the permanent fame of any work of science which makes immediate reputation with the ignorant multitude; doubt the permanent fame of any work of imagination which is at once applauded by a conventional clique that styles itself "the critical few."

Complete. From "Caxtoniana."

JUSTIN McCARTHY

(1830–)

McCARTHY's "History of Our Own Times," published in 1878–1880, won him an honorable place among the prose writers of his generation, and he has increased his reputation by his work as an essayist. He has been long a favorite contributor to the leading English reviews, chiefly on subjects which require historical research. He was born at Cork, Ireland, November 22d, 1830, and has been not less prominent in the politics of the Irish Home Rule movement than in literature. On the fall of Parnell in 1890, McCarthy succeeded to the leadership of the Irish Parliamentary party and acquitted himself with credit. Besides the "History of Our Own Times," he has published, among other books, the "History of the Four Georges," 1884; "The Epoch of Reform," 1882; and a number of novels, several in collaboration with Mrs. Campbell-Praed.

THE LAST OF THE NAPOLEONS

Now that the weapon of a naked savage has struck down in a nameless skirmish the last of the eldest branch of the Bonapartes, and the first of the race who ever fell upon a field of battle, men's eyes are not unnaturally turned again upon one who often commanded their gaze before, but who seemed of late days to have passed from their notice forever,— the man whom strange chance has placed at the head of the Napoleon family. It seems in keeping with the pitiless irony of fate which has always pursued the Bonaparte dynasty — a fate as stern as the fabled destiny of the Pelopids — that the death of Prince Louis Napoleon should place whatever remains of succession at the feet of the man whom neither he nor his mother loved overmuch, at the feet of the Esau or rather the Ishmael of the house, Prince Napoleon Joseph Charles Paul Bonaparte (Jérôme), better known as Prince Napoleon, better known still in the argot of history as Plon-Plon. Prince Napoleon is the son of that somewhat feather-headed king of Westphalia who is chiefly conspicuous for his

marriage with Miss Patterson of Baltimore — she who died but the other day — and for his exclamation at the battle of Waterloo: "Brother, here should perish all who bear the name of Bonaparte!" an heroic exclamation which did not prevent him from escaping from the field and living till 1860. Westphalia Jérôme was the youngest brother of the first Napoleon; but as the great Napoleon did what he liked with the succession, and set aside his other brothers when they displeased him, the year 1852 saw his son the heir presumptive to the imperial crown. The birth of the poor lad who died last June in Zululand took away from him the succession to a great and apparently firmly established empire; his death has given him the headship of a fallen house, and put him nominally in command of a powerless party.

Prince Napoleon is one of the strangest figures of modern history. His career has been one long riddle unexplained as yet. No man in Europe has been more misunderstood, and few have been more disliked; no man had better chances of success than he, and no man ever made less use of his chances. To-day finds him as much a puzzle alike to his friends and his enemies as he was thirty years ago when he first swore allegiance to a French Republic. He has been described by a witty critic as a Cæsar out of place. But the epigram would have been much truer which described him as an unemployed Antony. The marvelous capability for doing the right thing at the right time which characterized Cæsar never was the property of Prince Napoleon. He has rather been conspicuous all his life for doing the right thing at the wrong moment. And now, close to his sixtieth year, he, the strangest evolution of the race Bonaparte, remains just where he was when he started, having succeeded in convincing the world first that he was a fool, then that he was a man of genius, without winning any success either from his folly or his intellect. Among the many witty and bitter things that the Prince Napoleon has said about the members of his own family, one saying deserves especial remembrance — his epigrammatic observation that his cousin the Emperor took in the world twice: first, when he made the world believe that he was an idiot; and secondly, when he made it believe he was a statesman. The epigram would apply almost as well to its author as to its object.

This is his portrait, drawn by the hand of a bitter enemy:— "He is of a tall form, but with his neck sinking between his shoulders; his waist is fast disappearing before the irruption of

corpulency; his gait is heavy and undignified; he is short-sighted, and his glance is an oblique one. His general appearance reminds you of the elder Bonaparte, the one whom MM. Thiers and Marco Saint-Hilaire, Troplong and Havin, and likewise M. Prudhomme style 'le Grand Homme,' but it reminds you still more of Otho or Vitellius, and somewhat also of the common mask of 'Punch.'" Such a description as this gives no real idea of the appearance of the man or of the quality of character to be inferred from a study of his face. Flandrin's famous portrait gave another and a truer view of his nature. Strangely like the first Napoleon was it, so like that it would have passed in the eyes of most spectators as a picture of the Little Corporal. A more attentive observer would have assumed it to be a study of the Great Emperor after Leipsic or Waterloo, for there was stamped on the sensuous face a look of sullen discontent, of a disappointment that did not often belong to the features of the first of the Bonapartes. It was the face of a Napoleon without success, of a Napoleon who had not found his chance, who had waited too long for his Marengo. It was the face of a Napoleon compelled by strange fate to inaction; it was the face of Prince Napoleon. . . .

There can be little doubt that his genius, his far-sighted political intelligence, and his power of appreciating the relative values of nations, might have made his assistance of great service to Napoleon III., if Napoleon III. had seen fit to profit by it more often. It is true that Prince Napoleon's political judgment generally led him to different conclusions from those evolved from the Tuileries, and it must be admitted that his opinions generally ran counter to those of the majority upon most great questions; but events have almost invariably justified Prince Napoleon, and showed that his Imperial cousin would have done wiser in listening to his single voice than to any clamor of public opinion. When Prince Napoleon went over to America during the Civil War, to judge the question on its native ground, hearing the cause discussed in New York salons, in reunions of Boston Abolitionists, and in the not altogether impartial atmosphere of General Beauregard's tent, he had the sense to see that the North was sure to win in the end; and he saw this at a time when the Emperor was moving heaven and earth to induce England to aid him in supporting by arms the cause of the South and slavery. Prince Napoleon was also strongly opposed

to the Mexican intervention. He knew the temper of the American people too well to fancy that they would suffer Napoleon to carry out his dearly cherished infringement of what has come to be called the Monroe Doctrine, but which is really the doctrine suggested to and impressed upon President Monroe by George Canning. The sequel of that most disastrous undertaking thoroughly justified his views. Upon all the great European questions, too, he showed a shrewd and foreseeing mind. He believed in Italy, he supported the cause of Poland, he foresaw the downfall of Austria, and we have it on his own authority that he strongly objected to the action of the French government with regard to Rome, and attributed to that action the result of the war with Prussia. Moreover, he was a free-trader long before the Emperor could be induced to believe that the doctrine was an essential law of political economy. It may be asked why a man who showed such capacity for statesmanship as to foresee the result of all the great political crises during his time should yet have received such little honor for his prophecies, not only in his own country, but everywhere else. The truth doubtless is that Prince Napoleon's character is marred not only by his bad temper and his proverbially bitter tongue, which make it impossible, or next to impossible, for him to get on with any one or for any one to get on with him — faults which caused him to fling up the Algerian administration, and brought him back to France from so many important missions — but by a worse defect than either of these, a fatal want of energy. He lacks the proud patience which is so essential to true success, and he is disposed, when people decline to see things as he sees them, to give up in disgust, and let them learn by experience the wisdom of councils he had not himself the energy to do battle for. There is in him a great deal of the nature of Byron's Sardanapalus who, while having no small share of the stuff that heroes are made of, fritters away his life in purposeless inaction and aimless pleasures. In aimless pleasures, indeed, a good deal of Prince Napoleon's life has been passed. Witness his purposeless wanderings in his yacht all over the world, wanderings which made wits inquire if the prince was qualifying to be a teacher of geography in case of any unexpected reverse to the Napoleon family. Witness, too, his endeavor to live the life of a Roman in modern Paris. Hence the villa, Diomede, which most visitors to Paris have seen, and where, according to rumor, the

Pompeian walls saw scenes Roman enough to have satisfied the taste of the *Arbiter Elegantiæ*. But the Pompeian dwelling was not a success. The Prince attempted baths after the Roman fashion, and they made the house too damp to live in; and gradually he got tired of his toy and of playing at being a Roman, and the villa Diomede was abandoned. Those who saw the Palais Royal when it was Prince Napoleon's might well have wondered why a man with such a house should want to be anything better than a Bonaparte prince in an Orleanist palace. To do justice to the Prince, the palace showed that its temporary owner was a man of refined taste and high culture, both in art and letters. I quote an account of the Palais Royal written while the Bonaparte dynasty still swayed the fortunes of France:—

"His Palais Royal is one of the most tasteful and elegant abodes belonging to a European prince. The stranger in Paris who is fortunate enough to obtain admission to it—and, indeed, admission is easy to procure—must be sadly wanting in taste if he does not admire the treasures of art and vertu which are laid up there, and the easy graceful manner of their arrangement. Nothing of the showplace is breathed there; no rules, no conditions, no watchful, dogging lackeys or sentinels make the visitor uncomfortable. Once admitted, the stranger goes where he will, and admires and examines what he pleases. He finds there curiosities and relics, medals and statues, bronzes and stones, from every land in which history or romance takes any interest; he gazes on the latest artistic successes—Doré's magnificent lights and shadows, Gérôme's audacious nudities; he observes autograph collections of value inestimable; he notices that on the tables, here and there, lie the newest triumphs or sensations of literature,—the poem that every one is just talking of, the play that fills the theatres, George Sand's last novel, Renan's new volume, Taine's freshest criticism; he is impressed everywhere with the conviction that he is in the house of a man of high culture and active intellect, who keeps up with the progress of the world in arts, and letters and politics." . . .

Some slight solution of the enigma of the Prince's life is perhaps to be found in the following lines, written by him in the Revue des deux Mondes a few years back:—

"I have always had for the Emperor, my cousin, a thorough devotion, of which I think I have given him sufficient proofs by the frankness of my conduct, even by the very opposition I have shown to

many acts of his government—a thankless rôle, which rarely confers power and influence, and which exposes its supporter to every kind of calumny. I found my only satisfaction in the sentiment of duty accomplished. My personal rôle, sometimes effaced, sometimes preponderating, has always had the same aim,—the greatness of France, to be obtained by the alliance of the Napoleons with democratic ideas."

Prince Napoleon has always been persistently disbelieved; it never seems to have entered into the minds of his enemies that he could possibly speak the truth. Yet the course of his life has been generally in accordance with his own statements, and his declaration that the aim of his life has ever been the greatness of France, to be obtained by the union of Bonapartism and Democracy, has never been belied by any action of his career. Indeed, it is to this strange faith in an impossible combination that his unsuccess might very fairly be attributed. His Bonapartism has injured him with the Democrats, his Democracy with the Bonapartes. The result has been that want of power and influence over which his deeply disappointed ambition was compelled to utter one cry in the confession of faith we have quoted.

From the Gentleman's Magazine.

THOMAS BABINGTON MACAULAY

(BARON MACAULAY)

(1800-1859)

S AN essayist Macaulay constitutes a class of his own. He has had many imitators, but as his prose style depends for its success on the same ear for rhythm (musical time) he shows in his ballads, he can be successfully imitated only by those who, with his almost miraculous memory for detailed facts, have also the "ear" which will enable them to balance their clauses as he does in musical antithesis. What in him is a triumph over the natural becomes when others fail to achieve it, obviously disagreeable and unnatural. Whether or not we may agree with Morley that imitation of Macaulay and Carlyle has been a calamity to English literature, we cannot fail to recognize that Macaulay himself is one of the world's great masters of style. It may be denied with reason, that it is "English" style. In any strict or evolutionary sense it is not. The English of King Alfred, which is as good in its way as that of Macaulay, illustrates the genius of a language whose spirit expresses itself with greatest force in direct and independent sentences, each inclosing a single definite idea. English, however, has become very largely Latinized since Alfred's time, and it is in a Latin style that Macaulay expresses himself. He has been called the greatest nineteenth-century disciple of the school of Cicero, and he had no one to dispute the title with him except Taine, his younger contemporary and admirer. For flexibility, for capacity to marshal the largest possible number of facts, and to carry them through the most rapid military evolutions in the least possible compass, these great commanders of language have no superiors in modern times. An incident of their method is an almost irresistible tendency to sacrifice to the necessary manœuvering of their clauses much that is valued by less brilliant writers. Macaulay, himself, seems to have recognized this, for he generally takes pains to sum up the evidence against his own position with a formidable showing of impartiality; but when all is said, he remains in his essays the most brilliant, admirable, and convincing of all special pleaders. Of his "History," it is only necessary to say here that he did not cease to be

an essayist in becoming a historian, but used the same style and the same methods which he had developed as a critical reviewer. If we are to make the necessary distinction between a genuine essay and a critical review, we must look for Macaulay's essays as episodes of his reviews rather than in the completeness of the reviews themselves. Some of his most celebrated reviews consist of several essays, each complying with the Greek rule of completeness by having "a beginning, a middle, and an end," while the review itself begins nowhere in particular and ends only with the exhaustion of the space in the magazine he had to fill. Thus, if we take the review of Southey's edition of "Pilgrim's Progress," written by Macaulay for the Edinburgh Review in 1821, we have in it one of the most admirable essays in the English language or any other; but it does not begin until the fourth paragraph of the review—the whole introduction to which consists of a comment on the attractions of a particular edition of the book. Another incident of Macaulay's style as a critical reviewer is what becomes on occasion an almost intolerable insolence,—as when he showed his unquestionable superiority over the unfortunate and by no means unmeritorious Montgomery, or when, perhaps, after refreshing his own memory from the Greek grammar, he proceeded to expose Croker's unguarded pretensions to extraordinary scholarship. Such peculiarities as this, however, are peculiarities of Macaulay's time and of the profession of the critical reviewer which he followed as an amateur. His idiosyncrasies are all amiable. He is good-natured as a rule and an admirer of everything that is most admirable, a hater of cant and sham, a lover of freedom and justice. He was a great Liberal, who might have been an extreme Conservative had he been born a lord; or the greatest Radical of the century, if the English aristocracy, always quick to recognize and conciliate menacing merit, had not adopted him as a favorite. He was born at Rothley Temple in Leicestershire, October 25th, 1800. After leaving the University of Cambridge where he was educated, he was called to the bar in 1826, and four years later began a brilliant political career by entering Parliament, where he served for many years. At various times he was a member of the Supreme Council in India, Secretary-at-War in the English Cabinet, and Paymaster General. Two years before his death, which occurred December 28th, 1859, he was raised to the peerage as "Baron Macaulay." As a poet, orator, and essayist, he illustrates the extraordinary command of language which depends fundamentally on a high development, not merely of the intellectual faculties of co-ordination, but on a corresponding development of the musical sense which makes possible a knowledge of the intrinsic harmonies of language. Macaulay's ballads are closer in their music and in their form to the genuine epic style of the popular ballads he imitates than the work of almost any one else who has attempted to succeed in this difficult field. His speeches have the same simplicity of diction and the same musical movement which found its freest illustration in the ballads. The "antithesis" which he has been accused of indulging at the expense of accuracy is a development of the natural laws of the mind in language, and especially of the natural laws of poetical expression. Macaulay is at times a statesman, frequently a philosopher, and, if we except times when he is at his worst as a critical reviewer, we may say, without great danger of overstatement, that he is always essentially a poet,—the Shakespeare of the English historical essay.

W. V. B.

JOHN BUNYAN AND THE "PILGRIM'S PROGRESS"

THIS is an eminently beautiful and splendid edition of a book which well deserves all that the printer and the engraver can do for it. The life of Bunyan is, of course, not a performance which can add much to the literary reputation of such a writer as Mr. Southey; but it is written in excellent English, and, for the most part, in an excellent spirit. Mr. Southey propounds, we need not say, many opinions from which we altogether dissent; and his attempts to excuse the odious persecution to which Bunyan was subjected have sometimes moved our indignation. But we will avoid this topic. We are at present much more inclined to join in paying homage to the genius of a great man than to engage in a controversy concerning church government and toleration.

We must not pass without notice the engravings with which this beautiful volume is decorated. Some of Mr. Heath's wood cuts are admirably designed and executed. Mr. Martin's illustrations do not please us quite so well. His Valley of the Shadow of Death is not that Valley of the Shadow of Death which Bunyan imagined. At all events, it is not that dark and horrible glen which has from childhood been in our mind's eye. The valley is a cavern; the quagmire is a lake; the straight path runs zigzag; and Christian appears like a speck in the darkness of the immense vault. We miss, too, those hideous forms which make so striking a part of the description of Bunyan, and which Salvator Rosa would have loved to draw. It is with unfeigned

diffidence that we pronounce judgment on any question relating to the art of painting. But it appears to us that Mr. Martin has not of late been fortunate in his choice of subjects. He should never have attempted to illustrate the "Paradise Lost." There can be no two manners more directly opposed to each other than the manner of his painting and the manner of Milton's poetry. Those things which are mere accessories in the descriptions become the principal objects in the pictures; and those figures which are most prominent in the descriptions can be detected in the pictures only by a very close scrutiny. Mr. Martin has succeeded perfectly in representing the pillars and candelabrums of Pandemonium. But he has forgotten that Milton's Pandemonium is merely the background to Satan. In the picture, the Archangel is scarcely visible amidst the endless colonnades of his infernal palace. Milton's Paradise, again, is merely the background to his Adam and Eve. But in Mr. Martin's picture the landscape is everything. Adam, Eve, and Raphael attract much less notice than the lake and the mountains, the gigantic flowers, and the giraffes which feed upon them. We have read, we forget where, that James II. sat to Verelst, the great flower painter. When the performance was finished, his Majesty appeared in the midst of sunflowers and tulips; which completely drew away all attention from the central figure. All who looked at the portrait took it for a flower piece. Mr. Martin, we think, introduces his immeasurable spaces, his innumerable multitudes, his gorgeous prodigies of architecture and landscape, almost as unseasonably as Verelst introduced his flower pots and nosegays. If Mr. Martin were to paint Lear in the storm, the blazing sky, the sheets of rain, the swollen torrents, and the tossing forest, would draw away all the attention from the agonies of the insulted king and father. If he were to paint the death of Lear, the old man, asking the bystanders to undo his button, would be thrown into the shade by a vast blaze of pavilions, standards, armor, and herald's coats. He would illustrate the "Orlando Furioso" well, the "Orlando Innamorato" still better, the "Arabian Nights" best of all. Fairy palaces and gardens, porticoes of agate, and groves flowering with emeralds and rubies, inhabited by people for whom nobody cares, these are his proper domain. He would succeed admirably in the enchanted ground of Alcina, or the mansion of Aladdin. But he should avoid Milton and Bunyan.

The characteristic peculiarity of the "Pilgrim's Progress" is, that it is the only work of its kind which possesses a strong human interest. Other allegories only amuse the fancy. The allegory of Bunyan has been read by many thousands with tears. There are some good allegories in Johnson's works, and some of still higher merit by Addison. In these performances there is, perhaps, as much wit and ingenuity as in the "Pilgrim's Progress." But the pleasure which is produced by the "Vision of Mirza," or the "Vision of Theodore," the Genealogy of Wit, or the contest between Rest and Labor, is exactly similar to the pleasure which we derive from one of Cowley's odes, or from a canto of "Hudibras." It is a pleasure which belongs wholly to the understanding, and in which the feelings have no part whatever. Nay, even Spenser himself, though assuredly one of the greatest poets that ever lived, could not succeed in the attempt to make allegory interesting. It was in vain that he lavished the riches of his mind on the House of Pride, and the House of Temperance. One unpardonable fault, the fault of tediousness, pervades the whole of the "Faery Queene." We become sick of Cardinal Virtues and Deadly Sins, and long for the society of plain men and women. Of the persons who read the first canto, not one in ten reaches the end of the first book, and not one in a hundred perseveres to the end of the poem. Very few and very weary are those who are in at the death of the Blatant Beast. If the last six books, which are said to have been destroyed in Ireland, had been preserved, we doubt whether any heart less stout than that of a commentator would have held out to the end.

It is not so with the "Pilgrim's Progress." That wonderful book, while it obtains admiration from the most fastidious critics, is loved by those who are too simple to admire it. Doctor Johnson, all whose studies were desultory, and who hated, as he said, to read books through, made an exception in favor of the "Pilgrim's Progress." That work, he said, was one of the two or three works which he wished longer. It was by no common merit that the illiterate sectary extracted praise like this from the most pedantic of critics and the most bigoted of Tories. In the wildest parts of Scotland the "Pilgrim's Progress" is the delight of the peasantry. In every nursery the "Pilgrim's Progress" is a greater favorite than "Jack the Giant-Killer." Every reader knows the straight and narrow path as well as he knows a road in which he has gone backward and forward a hundred times. This is the highest miracle of genius

—that things which are not should be as though they were, that the imaginations of one mind should become the personal recollections of another. And this miracle the tinker has wrought. There is no ascent, no declivity, no resting place, no turnstile, with which we are not perfectly acquainted. The wicket gate, and the desolate swamp which separates it from the City of Destruction; the long line of road, as straight as a rule can make it; the Interpreter's house, and all its fair shows; the prisoner in the iron cage; the palace, at the doors of which armed men kept guard, and on the battlements of which walked persons clothed all in gold; the cross and the sepulchre; the steep hill and the pleasant arbor; the stately front of the House Beautiful by the wayside; the low green valley of Humiliation, rich with grass and covered with flocks, all are as well known to us as the sights of our own street. Then we come to the narrow place where Apollyon strode right across the whole breadth of the way, to stop the journey of Christian, and where afterwards the pillar was set up to testify how bravely the pilgrim had fought the good fight. As we advance, the valley becomes deeper and deeper. The shade of the precipices on both sides falls blacker and blacker. The clouds gather overhead. Doleful voices, the clanking of chains, and the rushing of many feet to and fro, are heard through the darkness. The way, hardly discernible in gloom, runs close by the mouth of the burning pit, which sends forth its flames, its noisome smoke, and its hideous shapes, to terrify the adventurer. Thence he goes on, amidst the snares and pitfalls, with the mangled bodies of those who have perished lying in the ditch by his side. At the end of the long dark valley, he passes the dens in which the old giants dwelt, amidst the bones and ashes of those whom they had slain.

Then the road passes straight on through a waste moor, till at length the towers of a distant city appear before the traveler; and soon he is in the midst of the innumerable multitudes of Vanity Fair. There are the jugglers and the apes, the shops and the puppet shows. There are Italian Row, and French Row, and Spanish Row, and Britain Row, with their crowds of buyers, sellers, and loungers, jabbering all the languages of the earth.

Thence we go on by the little hill of the silver mine, and through the meadow of lilies, along the bank of that pleasant river which is bordered on both sides by fruit trees. On the left side branches off the path leading to that horrible castle, the courtyard of which is paved with the skulls of pilgrims; and right onward are the sheepfolds and orchards of the Delectable Mountains.

From the Delectable Mountains, the way lies through the fogs and briers of the Enchanted Ground, with here and there a bed of soft cushions spread under a green arbor. And beyond is the land of Beulah, where the flowers, the grapes, and the songs of birds never cease, and where the sun shines night and day. Thence are plainly seen the golden pavements and streets of pearl on the other side of that black and cold river over which there is no bridge.

All the stages of the journey, all the forms which cross or overtake the pilgrims,— giants and hobgoblins, ill-favored ones and shining ones; the tall, comely, swarthy Madam Bubble, with her great purse by her side, and her fingers playing with the money; the black man in the bright vesture; Mr. Worldly-Wiseman and my Lord Hategood; Mr. Talkative and Mrs. Timorous,— are all actually existing beings to us. We follow the travelers through their allegorical progress with interest not inferior to that with which we follow Elizabeth from Siberia to Moscow, or Jeanie Deans from Edinburgh to London. Bunyan is almost the only writer that ever gave to the abstract the interest of the concrete. In the works of many celebrated authors, men are mere personifications. We have not an Othello, but jealousy; not an Iago, but perfidy; not a Brutus, but patriotism. The mind of Bunyan, on the contrary, was so imaginative, that personifications, when he dealt with them, became men. A dialogue between two qualities in his dream, has more dramatic effect than a dialogue between two human beings in most plays. In this respect the genius of Bunyan bore a great resemblance to that of a man who had very little else in common with him, Percy Bysshe Shelley. The strong imagination of Shelley made him an idolater in his own despite. Out of the most indefinite terms of a hard, cold, dark, metaphysical system, he made a gorgeous Pantheon, full of beautiful, majestic, and life-like forms. He turned atheism itself into a mythology, rich with visions as glorious as the gods that live in the marble of Phidias, or the virgin saints that smile on us from the canvas of Murillo. The Spirit of Beauty, the Principle of Good, the Principle of Evil, when he treated of them, ceased to be abstractions. They took shape and color. They were no longer mere words, but " intelligible forms";

"fair humanities"; objects of love, of adoration, or of fear. As there can be no stronger signs of a mind destitute of the poetical faculty than that tendency which was so common among the writers of the French school to turn images into abstractions,— Venus, for example, into Love, Minerva into Wisdom, Mars into War, and Bacchus into Festivity,— so there can be no stronger sign of a mind truly poetical than a disposition to reverse this abstracting process, and to make individuals out of generalities. Some of the metaphysical and ethical theories of Shelley were certainly most absurd and pernicious. But we doubt whether any modern poet has possessed in an equal degree the highest qualities of the great ancient masters. The words Bard and Inspiration, which seem so cold and affected when applied to other modern writers, have a perfect propriety when applied to him. He was not an author, but a bard. His poetry seems not to have been an art, but an inspiration. Had he lived to the full age of man, he might not improbably have given to the world some great work of the very highest rank in design and execution. But, alas!

χώ Δάφνις ἔβα ῥόον· ἔκλυσε δίνα
τὸν Μώσαις φίλον ἄνδρα, τὸν οὐ Νύμφαισιν ἀπεχθῆ

But we must return to Bunyan. The "Pilgrim's Progress" undoubtedly is not a perfect allegory. The types are often inconsistent with each other; and sometimes the allegorical disguise is altogether thrown off. The river, for example, is emblematic of death, and we are told that every human being must pass through the river. But Faithful does not pass through it. He is martyred, not in shadow, but in reality, at Vanity Fair. Hopeful talks to Christian about Esau's birthright, and about his own convictions of sin, as Bunyan might have talked with one of his own congregation. The damsels at the House Beautiful catechise Christiana's boys, as any good ladies might catechise any boys at a Sunday school. But we do not believe that any man, whatever might be his genius, and whatever his good luck, could long continue a figurative history without falling into many inconsistencies. We are sure that inconsistencies, scarcely less gross than the worst into which Bunyan has fallen, may be found in the shortest and most elaborate allegories of the Spectator and the Rambler. The "Tale of a Tub" and the "History of John Bull" swarm with similar errors, if the name of error can be properly

applied to that which is unavoidable. It is not easy to make a simile go on all fours. But we believe that no human ingenuity could produce such a centiped as a long allegory, in which the correspondence between the outward sign and the thing signified should be exactly preserved. Certainly no writer, ancient or modern, has yet achieved the adventure. The best thing, on the whole, that an allegorist can do, is to present to his readers a succession of analogies, each of which may separately be striking and happy, without looking very nicely to see whether they harmonize with each other. This Bunyan has done; and, though a minute scrutiny may detect inconsistencies in every page of his tale, the general effect which the tale produces on all persons, learned and unlearned, proves that he has done well. The passages which it is most difficult to defend are those in which he altogether drops the allegory, and puts into the mouth of his pilgrims religious ejaculations and disquisitions, better suited to his own pulpit at Bedford or Reading than to the Enchanted Ground of the Interpreter's Garden. Yet even these passages, though we will not undertake to defend them against the objections of critics, we feel that we could ill spare. We feel that the story owes much of its charm to these occasional glimpses of solemn and affecting subjects, which will not be hidden, which force themselves through the veil, and appear before us in their native aspect. The effect is not unlike that which is said to have been produced on the ancient stage, when the eyes of the actor were seen flaming through his mask, and giving life and expression to what would else have been an inanimate and uninteresting disguise.

It is very amusing and very instructive to compare the "Pilgrim's Progress" with the "Grace Abounding." The latter work is, indeed, one of the most remarkable pieces of autobiography in the world. It is a full and open confession of the fancies which passed through the mind of an illiterate man, whose affections were warm, whose nerves were irritable, whose imagination was ungovernable, and who was under the influence of the strongest religious excitement. In whatever age Bunyan had lived, the history of his feelings would, in all probability, have been very curious. But the time in which his lot was cast was the time of a great stirring of the human mind. A tremendous burst of public feeling, produced by the tyranny of the hierarchy, menaced the old ecclesiastical institutions with destruction. To the gloomy

regularity of one intolerant church had succeeded the license of innumerable sects, drunk with the sweet and heady must of their new liberty. Fanaticism, engendered by persecution and destined to engender fresh persecution in turn, spread rapidly through society. Even the strongest and most commanding minds were not proof against this strange taint. Any time might have produced George Fox and James Naylor. But to one time alone belong the frantic delusions of such a statesman as Vane, and the hysterical tears of such a soldier as Cromwell.

The history of Bunyan is the history of a most excitable mind in an age of excitement. By most of his biographers he has been treated with gross injustice. They have understood in a popular sense all those strong terms of self-condemnation which he employed in a theological sense. They have, therefore, represented him as an abandoned wretch, reclaimed by means almost miraculous; or, to use their favorite metaphor, "as a brand plucked from the burning." Mr. Ivimey calls him the depraved Bunyan, and the wicked tinker of Elstow. Surely Mr. Ivimey ought to have been too familiar with the bitter accusations which the most pious people are in the habit of bringing against themselves to understand literally all the strong expressions which are to be found in the "Grace Abounding." It is quite clear, as Mr. Southey most justly remarks, that Mr. Bunyan never was a vicious man. He married very early; and he solemnly declares that he was strictly faithful to his wife. He does not appear to have been a drunkard. He owns, indeed, that when a boy, he never spoke without an oath. But a single admonition cured him of this bad habit for life; and the cure must have been wrought early: for at eighteen he was in the Army of the Parliament; and if he had carried the vice of profaneness into that service, he would doubtless have received something more than an admonition from Sergeant Bind-their-kings-in-chains, or Captain Hew-Agag-in-pieces-before-the-Lord. Bell ringing, and playing at hockey on Sundays, seem to have been the worst vices of this depraved tinker. They would have passed for virtues with Archbishop Laud. It is quite clear that from a very early age Bunyan was a man of a strict life and of a tender conscience. "He had been," says Mr. Southey, "a blackguard." Even this we think too hard a censure. Bunyan was not, we admit, so fine a gentleman as Lord Digby; yet he was a blackguard no otherwise than as every tinker that ever lived has been a blackguard. Indeed,

Mr. Southey acknowledges this: "Such he might have been expected to be by his birth, breeding, and vocation. Scarcely, indeed, by possibility, could he have been otherwise." A man
whose manners and sentiments are decidedly below those of his
class deserves to be called a blackguard. But it is surely unfair
to apply so strong a word of reproach to one who is only what
the great mass of every community must inevitably be.

Those horrible internal conflicts which Bunyan has described
with so much power of language prove, not that he was a worse
man than his neighbors, but that his mind was constantly occupied by religious considerations, that his fervor exceeded his
knowledge, and that his imagination exercised despotic power
over his body and mind. He heard voices from heaven; he saw
strange visions of distant hills, pleasant and sunny as his own
Delectable Mountains; from those seats he was shut out, and
placed in a dark and horrible wilderness, where he wandered
through ice and snow, striving to make his way into the happy
region of light. At one time he was seized with an inclination
to work miracles. At another time he thought himself actually
possessed by the devil. He could distinguish the blasphemous
whispers. He felt his infernal enemy pulling at his clothes behind him. He spurned with his feet, and struck with his hands,
at the destroyer. Sometimes he was tempted to sell his part in
the salvation of mankind. Sometimes a violent impulse urged
him to start up from his food, to fall on his knees, and break
forth into prayer. At length he fancied that he had committed
the unpardonable sin. His agony convulsed his robust frame.
He was, he says, as if his breastbone would split; and this he
took for a sign that he was destined to burst asunder like Judas.
The agitation of his nerves made all his movements tremulous;
and this trembling, he supposed, was a visible mark of his reprobation, like that which had been set on Cain. At one time,
indeed, an encouraging voice seemed to rush in at the window,
like the noise of wind, but very pleasant, and commanded, as he
says, a great calm in his soul. At another time, a word of comfort "was spoke loud unto him; it showed a great word; it
seemed to be writ in great letters." But these intervals of ease
were short. His state, during two years and a half, was generally the most horrible that the human mind can imagine. "I
walked," says he, with his own peculiar eloquence, "to a neighboring town; and sat down upon a settle in the street, and fell

into a very deep pause about the most fearful state my sin had
brought me to; and, after long musing, I lifted up my head; but
methought I saw as if the sun that shineth in the heavens did
grudge to give me light; and as if the very stones in the streets
and tiles upon the houses did band themselves against me. Methought that they all combined together to banish me out of the
world! I was abhorred of them, and unfit to dwell among them,
because I had sinned against the Savior. Oh, how happy now
was every creature over I! for they stood fast, and kept their
station. But I was gone and lost." Scarcely any madhouse
could produce an instance of delusion so strong, or of misery so
acute.

It was through this Valley of the Shadow of Death, overhung by darkness, peopled with devils, resounding with blasphemy and lamentation, and passing amidst quagmires, snares,
and pitfalls, close by the very mouth of hell, that Bunyan jour-
neyed to that bright and fruitful land of Beulah, in which he
sojourned during the latter days of his pilgrimage. The only
trace which his cruel sufferings and temptations seem to have
left behind them, was an affectionate compassion for those who
were still in the state in which he had once been. Religion has
scarcely ever worn a form so calm and soothing as in his allegory. The feeling which predominates through the whole book
is a feeling of tenderness for weak, timid, and harassed minds.
The character of Mr. Fearing, of Mr. Feeble-Mind, of Mr. Despondency and his daughter, Miss Muchafraid; the account of
poor Littlefaith, who was robbed by the three thieves of his
spending money; the description of Christian's terror in the dungeons of Giant Despair, and in his passage through the river, all
clearly show how strong a sympathy Bunyan felt, after his own
mind had become clear and cheerful, for persons afflicted with
religious melancholy.

Mr. Southey, who has no love for the Calvinists, admits that,
if Calvinism had never worn a blacker appearance than in Bunyan's works, it would never have become a term of reproach.
In fact, those works of Bunyan with which we are acquainted,
are by no means more Calvinistic than the homilies of the
Church of England. The moderation of his opinions on the subject of predestination, gave offense to some zealous persons. We
have seen an absurd allegory, the heroine of which is named
Hephzibah, written by some raving supralapsarian preacher, who

was dissatisfied with the mild theology of the "Pilgrim's Progress." In this foolish book, if we recollect rightly, the Interpreter is called the Enlightener, and the House Beautiful is Castle
Strength. Mr. Southey tells us that the Catholics had also their
"Pilgrim's Progress" without a Giant Pope, in which the Interpreter is the Director, and the House Beautiful, Grace's Hall. It
is surely a remarkable proof of the power of Bunyan's genius,
that two religious parties, both of which regarded his opinions as
heterodox, should have had recourse to him for assistance.

There are, we think, some characters and scenes in the "Pilgrim's Progress," which can be fully comprehended and enjoyed
only by persons familiar with the history of the times through
which Bunyan lived. The character of Mr. Greatheart, the guide,
is an example. His fighting is, of course, allegorical; but the
allegory is not strictly preserved. He delivers a sermon on
imputed righteousness to his companions; and, soon after, he
gives battle to Giant Grim, who had taken upon him to back
the lions. He expounds the fifty-third chapter of Isaiah to the
household and guests of Gaius; and then sallies out to attack
Slaygood, who was of the nature of flesh eaters, in his den.
These are inconsistencies; but they are inconsistencies which add,
we think, to the interest of the narrative. We have not the
least doubt that Bunyan had in view some stout old Greatheart
of Naseby and Worcester, who prayed with his men before he
drilled them; who knew the spiritual state of every dragoon in
his troop; and who, with the praises of God in his mouth, and a
two-edged sword in his hand, had turned to flight, on many fields
of battle, the swearing, drunken bravoes of Rupert and Lunsford.

Every age produces such men as By-ends. But the middle
of the seventeenth century was eminently prolific of such men.
Mr. Southey thinks that the satire was aimed at some particular
individual; and this seems by no means improbable. At all
events, Bunyan must have known many of those hypocrites who
followed religion only when religion walked in silver slippers,
when the sun shone, and when the people applauded. Indeed,
he might have easily found all the kindred of By-ends among
the public men of his time. He might have found among the
peers, my Lord Turn-about, my Lord Time-server, and my Lord
Fair-speech; in the House of Commons, Mr. Smooth-man, Mr.
Anything, and Mr. Facing-both-ways; nor would "the parson
of the parish, Mr. Two-tongues," have been wanting. The town

of Bedford probably contained more than one politician, who,
after contriving to raise an estate by seeking the Lord during
the reign of the saints, contrived to keep what he had got by
persecuting the saints during the reign of the strumpets; and
more than one priest who, during repeated changes in the discipline and doctrines of the church, had remained constant to
nothing but his benefice.

One of the most remarkable passages in the "Pilgrim's Progress," is that in which the proceedings against Faithful are described. It is impossible to doubt that Bunyan intended to
satirize the mode in which state trials were conducted under
Charles II. The license given to the witnesses for the prosecution, the shameless partiality and ferocious insolence of the judge,
the precipitancy and the blind rancor of the jury, remind us of
those odious mummeries which, from the Restoration to the
Revolution, were merely forms preliminary to hanging, drawing,
and quartering. Lord Hategood performs the office of counsel
for the prisoners as well as Scroggs himself could have performed it:—

"*Judge*—Thou runagate, heretic, and traitor, hast thou heard
what these honest gentlemen have witnessed against thee?

"*Faithful*—May I speak a few words in my own defense?

"*Judge*—Sirrah, Sirrah! thou deservest to live no longer, but to
be slain immediately upon the place; yet, that all men may see our
gentleness to thee, let us hear what thou, vile runagate, hast to say."

No person who knows the state trials can be at a loss for
parallel cases. Indeed, write what Bunyan would, the baseness and
cruelty of the lawyers of those times "sinned up to it still," and
even went beyond it. The imaginary trial of Faithful before a
jury composed of personified vices, was just and merciful, when
compared with the real trial of Lady Alice Lisle before that tribunal where all the vices sat in the person of Jeffries.

The style of Bunyan is delightful to every reader, and invaluable as a study to every person who wishes to obtain a wide
command over the English language. The vocabulary is the
vocabulary of the common people. There is not an expression,
if we except a few technical terms of theology, which would
puzzle the rudest peasant. We have observed several pages
which do not contain a single word of more than two syllables.
Yet no writer has said more exactly what he meant to say. For

magnificence, for pathos, for vehement exhortation, for subtle disquisition, for every purpose of the poet, the orator, and the divine, this homely dialect, the dialect of plain workingmen, was perfectly sufficient. There is no book in our literature on which we could so readily stake the fame of the old unpolluted English language; no book which shows so well how rich that language is in its own proper wealth, and how little it has been improved by all that it has borrowed.

Cowper said, forty or fifty years ago, that he dared not name John Bunyan in his verse, for fear of moving a sneer. To our refined forefathers, we suppose, Lord Roscommon's " Essay on Translated Verse," and the Duke of Buckinghamshire's " Essay on Poetry," appeared to be compositions infinitely superior to the allegory of the preaching tinker. We live in better times; and we are not afraid to say that, though there were many clever men in England during the latter half of the seventeenth century, there were only two great creative minds. One of those minds produced the " Paradise Lost," the other the " Pilgrim's Progress."

Complete. From the Edinburgh Review, 1831. On Southey's edition of the
" Pilgrim's Progress."

THE IMPEACHMENT OF WARREN HASTINGS

ON THE thirteenth of February, 1788, the sittings of the Court commenced. There have been spectacles more dazzling to the eye, more gorgeous with jewelry and cloth of gold, more attractive to grown-up children, than that which was then exhibited at Westminster; but, perhaps, there never was a spectacle so well calculated to strike a highly cultivated, a reflecting, an imaginative mind. All the various kinds of interest which belong to the near and to the distant, to the present and to the past, were collected on one spot and in one hour. All the talents and all the accomplishments which are developed by liberty and civilization were now displayed, with every advantage that could be derived both from co-operation and from contrast. Every step in the proceedings carried the mind either backward, through many troubled centuries, to the days when the foundations of the constitution were laid; or far away, over boundless seas and deserts, to dusky nations living under strange stars, worshiping strange gods, and writing strange characters from

right to left. The High Court of Parliament was to sit, according to forms handed down from the days of the Plantagenets, on an Englishman accused of exercising tyranny over the lord of the holy city of Benares, and the ladies of the princely house of Oude.

The place was worthy of such a trial. It was the great hall of William Rufus; the hall which had resounded with acclamations at the inauguration of thirty kings; the hall which had witnessed the just sentence of Bacon and the just absolution of Somers; the hall where the eloquence of Strafford had for a moment awed and melted a victorious party inflamed with just resentment; the hall where Charles had confronted the High Court of Justice with the placid courage which has half redeemed his fame. Neither military nor civil pomp was wanting. The avenues were lined with grenadiers. The streets were kept clear by cavalry. The peers, robed in gold and ermine, were marshaled by the heralds under the Garter King-at-arms. The judges, in their vestments of state, attended to give advice on points of law. Near a hundred and seventy lords, three-fourths of the Upper House, as the Upper House then was, walked in solemn order from their usual place of assembling to the tribunal. The junior baron present led the way — Lord Heathfield, recently ennobled for his memorable defense of Gibraltar against the fleets and armies of France and Spain. The long procession was closed by the Duke of Norfolk, Earl Marshal of the realm, by the great dignitaries, and by the brothers and sons of the king. Last of all came the Prince of Wales, conspicuous by his fine person and noble bearing. The gray old walls were hung with scarlet. The long galleries were crowded by such an audience as has rarely excited the fears or the emulation of an orator. There were gathered together, from all parts of a great, free, enlightened, and prosperous realm, grace and female loveliness, wit and learning, the representatives of every science and of every art. There were seated around the queen the fair-haired young daughters of the house of Brunswick. There the ambassadors of great kings and commonwealths gazed with admiration on a spectacle which no other country in the world could present. There Siddons, in the prime of her majestic beauty, looked with emotion on a scene surpassing all the imitations of the stage. There the historian of the Roman empire thought of the days when Cicero pleaded the cause of Sicily against Verres; and

when, before a senate which had still some show of freedom, Tacitus thundered against the oppressor of Africa. There were seen, side by side, the greatest painter and the greatest scholar of the age. The spectacle had allured Reynolds from that easel which has preserved to us the thoughtful foreheads of so many writers and statesmen, and the sweet smiles of so many noble matrons. It had induced Parr to suspend his labors in that dark and profound mine from which he had extracted a vast treasure of erudition; a treasure too often buried in the earth, too often paraded with injudicious and inelegant ostentation, but still precious, massive, and splendid. There appeared the voluptuous charms of her to whom the heir of the throne had in secret plighted his faith. There, too, was she, the beautiful mother of a beautiful race, the Saint Cecilia, whose delicate features, lighted up by love and music, art has rescued from the common decay. There were the members of that brilliant society which quoted, criticised, and exchanged repartees, under the rich peacock hangings of Mrs. Montague. And there the ladies whose lips, more persuasive than those of Fox himself, had carried the Westminster election against palace and treasury, shone round Georgiana, Duchess of Devonshire.

The sergeants made proclamation. Hastings advanced to the bar, and bent his knee. The culprit was, indeed, not unworthy of that great presence. He had ruled an extensive and populous country, had made laws and treaties, had sent forth armies, had set up and pulled down princes. And in his high place he had so borne himself that all had feared him, that most had loved him, and that hatred itself could deny him no title to glory, except virtue. He looked like a great man, and not like a bad man. A person small and emaciated, yet deriving dignity from a carriage which, while it indicated deference to the court, indicated also habitual self-possession and self-respect; a high and intellectual forehead; a brow pensive, but not gloomy; a mouth of inflexible decision; a face pale and worn, but serene, on which was written, as legibly as under the great picture in the Council Chamber at Calcutta, *Mens æqua in arduis:* such was the aspect with which the great proconsul presented himself to his judges.

His counsel accompanied him, men all of whom were afterwards raised by their talents and learning to the highest posts in their profession: the bold and strong-minded Law, afterwards

Chief Justice of the King's Bench; the more humane and eloquent Dallas, afterwards Chief Justice of the Common Pleas; and Plomer, who, nearly twenty years later, successfully conducted in the same high court the defense of Lord Melville, and subsequently became Vice Chancellor and Master of the Rolls.

But neither the culprit nor his advocates attracted so much notice as the accusers. In the midst of the blaze of red drapery, a space had been fitted up with green benches and tables for the Commons. The managers, with Burke at their head, appeared in full dress. The collectors of gossip did not fail to remark that even Fox, generally so regardless of his appearance, had paid to the illustrious tribunal the compliment of wearing a bag and sword. Pitt had refused to be one of the conductors of the impeachment; and his commanding, copious, and sonorous eloquence was wanting to that great muster of various talents. Age and blindness had unfitted Lord North for the duties of a public prosecutor; and his friends were left without the help of his excellent sense, his tact, and his urbanity. But, in spite of the absence of these two distinguished members of the Lower House, the box in which the managers stood contained an array of speakers such as perhaps had not appeared together since the great age of Athenian eloquence. There stood Fox and Sheridan, the English Demosthenes and the English Hyperides. There was Burke, — ignorant, indeed, or negligent of the art of adapting his reasonings and his style to the capacity and taste of his hearers, but in aptitude of comprehension and richness of imagination superior to every orator, ancient or modern. There, with eyes reverentially fixed on Burke, appeared the finest gentleman of the age, his form developed by every manly exercise, his face beaming with intelligence and spirit — the ingenious, the chivalrous, the high-souled Windham. Nor, though surrounded by such men, did the youngest manager pass unnoticed. At an age when most of those who distinguished themselves in life are still contending for prizes and fellowships at college, he had won for himself a conspicuous place in parliament. No advantage of fortune or connection was wanting that could set off to the height his splendid talents and his unblemished honor. At twenty-three he had been thought worthy to be ranked with the veteran statesmen who appeared as the delegates of the British Commons, at the bar of the British nobility. All who stood at that bar, save him alone, are gone, —

culprit, advocates, accusers. To the generation which is now in the vigor of life, he is the sole representative of a great age which has passed away. But those who, within the last ten years, have listened with delight, till the morning sun shone on the tapestries of the House of Lords, to the lofty and animated eloquence of Charles Earl Grey, are able to form some estimate of the powers of a race of men among whom he was not the foremost.

The charges and the answers of Hastings were first read. This ceremony occupied two whole days, and was rendered less tedious than it would otherwise have been, by the silver voice and just emphasis of Cowper, the clerk of the court, a near relation of the amiable poet. On the third day Burke rose. Four sittings of the court were occupied by his opening speech, which was intended to be a general introduction to all the charges. With an exuberance of thought and a splendor of diction which more than satisfied the highly-raised expectation of the audience, he described the character and institutions of the natives of India; recounted the circumstances in which the Asiatic empire of Britain had originated; and set forth the constitution of the company and of the English presidencies. Having thus attempted to communicate to his hearers an idea of Eastern society, as vivid as that which existed in his own mind, he proceeded to arraign the administration of Hastings, as systematically conducted in defiance of morality and public law. The energy and pathos of the great orator extorted expressions of unwonted admiration even from the stern and hostile chancellor; and, for a moment, seemed to pierce even the resolute heart of the defendant. The ladies in the galleries, unaccustomed to such displays of eloquence, excited by the solemnity of the occasion, and perhaps not unwilling to display their taste and sensibility, were in a state of uncontrollable emotion. Handkerchiefs were pulled out; smelling bottles were handed round; hysterical sobs and screams were heard; and Mrs. Sheridan was carried out in a fit. At length the orator concluded. Raising his voice till the old arches of Irish oak resounded — "Therefore," said he, "hath it with all confidence been ordered by the Commons of Great Britain, that I impeach Warren Hastings of high crimes and misdemeanors. I impeach him in the name of the Commons House of Parliament, whose trust he has betrayed. I impeach him in the name of the English nation, whose ancient honor he has sullied. I impeach him in the name of the people of India, whose rights

he has trodden under foot, and whose country he has turned into a desert. Lastly, in the name of human nature itself, in the name of both sexes, in the name of every age, in the name of every rank, I impeach the common enemy and oppressor of all!"

When the deep murmur of various emotions had subsided, Mr. Fox rose to address the lords respecting the course of proceeding to be followed. The wish of the accuser was, that the court would bring to a close the investigation of the first charge before the second was opened. The wish of Hastings and his counsel was, that the managers should open all the charges, and produce all the evidence for the prosecution, before the defense began. The lords retired to their own house, to consider the question. The chancellor took the side of Hastings. Lord Loughborough, who was now in opposition, supported the demand of the managers. The division showed which way the inclination of the tribunal leaned. A majority of near three to one decided in favor of the course for which Hastings contended.

When the court sat again, Mr. Fox, assisted by Mr. Grey, opened the charge respecting Cheyte Sing, and several days were spent in reading papers and hearing witnesses. The next article was that relating to the Princesses of Oude. The conduct of this part of the case was intrusted to Sheridan. The curiosity of the public to hear him was unbounded. His sparkling and highly-finished declamation lasted two days; but the hall was crowded to suffocation during the whole time. It was said that fifty guineas had been paid for a single ticket. Sheridan, when he concluded, contrived, with a knowledge of stage effect which his father might have envied, to sink back, as if exhausted, into the arms of Burke, who hugged him with the energy of generous admiration!

June was now far advanced. The session could not last much longer, and the progress which had been made in the impeachment was not very satisfactory. There were twenty charges. On two only of these had even the case for the prosecution been heard; and it was now a year since Hastings had been admitted to bail.

The interest taken by the public in the trial was great when the court began to sit, and rose to the height when Sheridan spoke on the charge relating to the Begums. From that time the excitement went down fast. The spectacle had lost the attraction of novelty. The great displays of rhetoric were over.

What was behind was not of a nature to entice men of letters from their books in the morning, or to tempt ladies who had left the masquerade at two, to be out of bed before eight. There remained examinations and cross-examinations. There remained statements of accounts. There remained the reading of papers, filled with words unintelligible to English ears,—with lacs and crores, zemindars and aumils, sunnuds and perwannahs, jaghires and nuzzurs. There remained bickerings, not always carried on with the best taste or with the best temper, between the managers of the impeachment and the counsel for the defense, particularly between Mr. Burke and Mr. Law. There remained the endless marches and countermarches of the peers between their house and the hall; for as often as a point of law was to be discussed their lordships retired to discuss it apart; and the consequence was, as the late Lord Stanhope wittily said, that the judges walked and the trial stood still.

It is to be added, that in the spring of 1788, when the trial commenced, no important question, either of domestic or foreign policy, excited the public mind. The proceeding in Westminster Hall, therefore, naturally excited most of the attention of parliament and of the public. It was the one great event of that season. But in the following year, the king's illness, the debates on the regency, the expectation of a change of ministry, completely diverted public attention from Indian affairs; and within a fortnight after George III. had returned thanks in St. Paul's for his recovery, the States-general of France met at Versailles. In the midst of the agitation produced by those events, the impeachment was for a time almost forgotten.

The trial in the hall went on languidly. In the session of 1788, when the proceedings had the interest of novelty, and when the peers had little other business before them, only thirty-five days were given to the impeachment. In 1789, the Regency Bill occupied the Upper House till the session was far advanced. When the king recovered, the circuits were beginning. The judges left town; the lords waited for the return of the oracles of jurisprudence; and the consequence was, that during the whole year only seventeen days were given to the case of Hastings. It was clear that the matter would be protracted to a length unprecedented in the annals of criminal law.

In truth, it is impossible to deny that impeachment, though it is a fine ceremony, and though it may have been useful in the

seventeenth century, is not a proceeding from which much good can now be expected. Whatever confidence may be placed in the decisions of the peers on an appeal arising out of ordinary litigation, it is certain that no man has the least confidence in their impartiality, when a great public functionary, charged with a great state crime, is brought to their bar. They are all politicians. There is hardly one among them, whose vote on an impeachment may not be confidently predicted before a witness has been examined; and even were it possible to rely on their justice, they would still be quite unfit to try such a cause as that of Hastings. They sit only during half the year. They have to transact much legislative and much judicial business. The law lords, whose advice is required to guide the unlearned majority, are employed daily in administering justice elsewhere. It is impossible, therefore, that during a busy session, the Upper House should give more than a few days to an impeachment. To expect that their lordships would give up partridge shooting, in order to bring the greatest delinquent to speedy justice, or to relieve accused innocence by speedy acquittal, would be unreasonable indeed. A well constituted tribunal, sitting regularly six days in the week, and nine hours in the day, would have finished the trial of Hastings in less than three months. The lords had not finished their work in seven years.

The result ceased to be a matter of doubt, from the time when the lords resolved that they would be guided by the rules of evidence which are received in inferior courts of the realm. Those rules, it is well known, exclude much information which would be quite sufficient to determine the conduct of any reasonable man, in the most important transactions of private life. Those rules, at every assizes, save scores of culprits, whom judges, jury, and spectators, firmly believed to be guilty. But when those rules were rigidly applied to offenses committed many years before, at the distance of many thousand miles, conviction was, of course, out of the question. We do not blame the accused and his counsel for availing themselves of every legal advantage in order to obtain an acquittal. But it is clear that an acquittal so obtained cannot be pleaded in bar of the judgment of history.

Several attempts were made by the friends of Hastings to put a stop to the trial. In 1789 they proposed a vote of censure upon Burke, for some violent language which he had used respecting the death of Nuncomar, and the connection between Hastings and Impey. Burke was then unpopular in the last degree both with the House and with the country. The asperity and indecency of some expressions which he had used during the debates on the Regency had annoyed even his warmest friends. The vote of censure was carried, and those who had moved it hoped that the managers would resign in disgust. Burke was deeply hurt. But his zeal for what he considered as the cause of justice and mercy triumphed over his personal feelings. He received the censure of the House with dignity and meekness, and declared that no personal mortification or humiliation should induce him to flinch from the sacred duty which he had undertaken.

In the following year, the parliament was dissolved; and the friends of Hastings entertained a hope that the new House of Commons might not be disposed to go on with the impeachment. They began by maintaining that the whole proceeding was terminated by the dissolution. Defeated on this point, they made a direct motion that the impeachment should be dropped; but they were defeated by the combined forces of the government and the opposition. It was, however, resolved that, for the sake of expedition, many of the articles should be withdrawn. In truth, had not some such measure been adopted, the trial would have lasted till the defendant was in his grave.

At length, in the spring of 1795, the decision was pronounced, nearly eight years after Hastings had been brought by the sergeant-at-arms of the Commons to the bar of the lords. On the last day of this great procedure, the public curiosity, long suspended, seemed to be revived. Anxiety about the judgment there could be none; for it had been fully ascertained that there was a great majority for the defendant. But many wished to see the pageant, and the hall was as much crowded as on the first day. But those, who having been present on the first day, now bore a part in the proceedings of the last, were few, and most of those few were altered men.

As Hastings himself said, the arraignment had taken place before one generation, and the judgment was pronounced by another. The spectator could not look at the woolsack, or at the red benches of the peers, or at the green benches of the Commons, without seeing something that reminded him of the instability of all human things;— of the instability of power, and

fame, and life, of the more lamentable instability of friendship. The great seal was borne before Lord Loughborough, who, when the trial commenced, was a fierce opponent of Mr. Pitt's government, and who was now a member of that government; while Thurlow, who presided in the court when it first sat, estranged from all his old allies, sat scowling among the junior barons. Of a hundred and sixty nobles who walked in the procession on the first day, sixty had been laid in their family vaults. Still more affecting must have been the sight of the managers' box. What had become of that fair fellowship, so closely bound together by public and private ties, so resplendent with every talent and accomplishment? It had been scattered by calamities more bitter than the bitterness of death. The great chiefs were still living, and still in the full vigor of their genius. But their friendship was at an end. It had been violently and publicly dissolved with tears and stormy reproaches. If those men, once so dear to each other, were now compelled to meet for the purpose of managing the impeachment, they met as strangers whom public business had brought together, and behaved to each other with cold and distant civility. Burke had in his vortex whirled away Windham. Fox had been followed by Sheridan and Grey.

Only twenty-nine peers voted. Of these only six found Hastings guilty, on the charges relating to Cheyte Sing and to the Begums. On other charges the majority in his favor was still greater. On some he was unanimously absolved. He was then called to the bar, informed from the woolsack that the lords had acquitted him, and solemnly discharged. He bowed respectfully, and retired.

From the review of Gleig's "Life of Hastings."
Edinburgh Review, 1841.

SAMUEL JOHNSON IN GRUB STREET

NEVER, since literature became a calling in England, had it been a less gainful calling than at the time when Johnson took up his residence in London. In the preceding generation a writer of eminent merit was sure to be munificently rewarded by the government. The least that he could expect was a pension or a sinecure place; and, if he showed any aptitude for politics, he might hope to be a member of parliament, a lord of the

treasury, an ambassador, a secretary of state. It would be easy, on the other hand, to name several writers of the nineteenth century of whom the least successful has received forty thousand pounds from the booksellers. But Johnson entered on his vocation in the most dreary part of the dreary interval which separated two ages of prosperity. Literature had ceased to flourish under the patronage of the great, and had not begun to flourish under the patronage of the public. One man of letters, indeed, Pope, had acquired by his pen what was then considered as a handsome fortune, and lived on a footing of equality with nobles and ministers of state. But this was a solitary exception. Even an author whose reputation was established, and whose works were popular, such an author as Thomson, whose "Seasons" were in every library, such an author as Fielding, whose "Pasquin" had had a greater run than any drama since "The Beggar's Opera," was sometimes glad to obtain, by pawning his best coat, the means of dining on tripe at a cook shop underground, where he could wipe his hands after his greasy meal, on the back of a Newfoundland dog. It is easy, therefore, to imagine what humiliations and privations must have awaited the novice who had still to earn a name. One of the publishers to whom Johnson applied for employment measured with scornful eye that athletic though uncouth frame, and exclaimed, " You had better get a porter's knot, and carry trunks." Nor was the advice bad; for a porter was likely to be as plentifully fed, and as comfortably lodged, as a poet.

Some time appears to have elapsed before Johnson was able to form any literary connection from which he could expect more than bread for the day which was passing over him. He never forgot the generosity with which Hervey, who was now residing in London, relieved his wants during this time of trial. " Harry Hervey," said the old philosopher many years later, " was a vicious man; but he was very kind to me. If you call a dog Hervey I shall love him." At Hervey's table Johnson sometimes enjoyed feasts which were made more agreeable by contrast. But in general he dined, and thought that he dined well, on six pennyworth of meat, and a pennyworth of bread, at an alehouse near Drury Lane.

The effect of the privations and sufferings which he endured at this time was discernible to the last in his temper and his deportment. His manners had never been courtly. They now became almost savage. Being frequently under the necessity of

wearing shabby coats and dirty shirts, he became a perfect sloven. Being often very hungry when he sat down to his meals, he contracted a habit of eating with ravenous greediness. Even to the end of his life, and even at the tables of the great, the sight of food affected him as it affects wild beasts and birds of prey. His taste in cookery, formed in subterranean ordinaries and alamode beef shops, was far from delicate. Whenever he was fortunate to have near him a hare that had been kept too long, or meat pie made with rancid butter, he gorged himself with such violence that his veins swelled, and the moisture broke out on his forehead. The affronts which his poverty emboldened stupid and lowminded men to offer to him would have broken a mean spirit into sycophancy, but made him rude even to ferocity. Unhappily the insolence which, while it was defensive, was pardonable, and in some sense respectable, accompanied him into societies where he was treated with courtesy and kindness. He was repeatedly provoked into striking those who had taken liberties with him. All the sufferers, however, were wise enough to abstain from talking about their beatings, except Osborne, the most rapacious and brutal of booksellers, who proclaimed everywhere that he had been knocked down by the huge fellow whom he had hired to puff the Harleian Library.

About a year after Johnson had begun to reside in London, he was fortunate enough to obtain regular employment from Cave, an enterprising and intelligent bookseller, who was proprietor and editor of the Gentleman's Magazine. That journal, just entering on the ninth year of its long existence, was the only periodical work in the kingdom which then had what would now be called a large circulation. It was, indeed, the chief source of parliamentary intelligence. It was not then safe, even during recess, to publish an account of the proceedings of either House, without some disguise. Cave, however, ventured to entertain his readers with what he called "Reports of the Debates of the Senate of Lilliput." France was Blefuscu; London was Milendo; pounds were sprugs; the Duke of Newcastle was the Nardac Secretary of State; Lord Hardwicke was the Hurgo Hickrad; and William Pulteney was Wingul Pulnub. To write the speeches was, during several years, the business of Johnson. He was generally furnished with notes, meagre, indeed, and inaccurate, of what had been said; but sometimes he had to find arguments and eloquence both for the ministry and for opposition. He was himself a Tory, not from rational conviction—for his serious opinion was that one form of government was just as good or as bad as another—but from mere passion, such as inflamed the Capulets against the Montagues, or the Blues of the Roman circus against the Greens. In his infancy he had heard so much talk about the villainies of the Whigs, and the dangers of the Church, that he had become a furious partisan when he could scarcely speak. Before he was three he had insisted on being taken to hear Sacheverell preach at Lichfield Cathedral, and had listened to the sermon with as much respect, and probably with as much intelligence, as any Staffordshire squire in the congregation. The work which had been begun in the nursery had been completed by the university. Pembroke, when Johnson resided there, was one of the most Jacobital colleges in Oxford. The prejudices which he brought up to London were scarcely less absurd than those of his own Tom Tempest. Charles II. and James II. were two of the best kings that ever reigned. Laud, a poor creature who never did, said, or wrote anything indicating more than the ordinary capacity of an old woman, was a prodigy of parts and learning over whose tomb Art and Genius still continued to weep. Hampden deserved no more honorable name than that of "the zealot of rebellion." Even the ship money, condemned not less decidedly by Falkland and Clarendon than by the bitterest Roundheads, Johnson would not pronounce to have been an unconstitutional impost. Under a government, the mildest that had ever been known in the world,—under a government which allowed to the people an unprecedented liberty of speech and action,—he fancied that he was a slave; he assailed the ministry with obloquy which refuted itself, and regretted the lost freedom and happiness of those golden days in which a writer who had taken but one-tenth part of the license allowed to him would have been pilloried, mangled with shears, whipped at the cart's tail, and flung into a noisome dungeon to die. He hated dissenters and stockjobbers, the excise and the army, septennial parliaments, and continental connections. He long had an aversion to the Scotch, an aversion which he could not remember the commencement, but which, he owned, had probably originated in his abhorrence of the conduct of the nation during the Great Rebellion. It is easy to guess in what manner debates on great party questions were likely to be reported by a man whose judgment was so much disordered by party spirit.

A show of fairness was indeed necessary to the prosperity of the magazine. But Johnson long afterwards owned that, though he had saved appearances, he had taken care that the Whig dogs should not have the best of it; and, in fact, every passage which has lived, every passage which bears the marks of his higher faculties, is put into the mouth of some member of the opposition.

A few weeks after Johnson had entered on these obscure labors, he published a work which at once placed him high among the writers of the age. It is probable that what he had suffered during his first year in London had often reminded him of some parts of that noble poem in which Juvenal had described the misery and degradation of a needy man of letters, lodged among the pigeons' nests in the tottering garrets which overhung the streets of Rome. Pope's admirable imitations of Horace's "Satires" and "Epistles" had recently appeared, were in every hand, and were by many readers thought superior to the originals. What Pope had done for Horace, Johnson aspired to do for Juvenal. The enterprise was bold, and yet judicious, for between Johnson and Juvenal there was much in common, much more certainly than between Pope and Horace.

Johnson's "London" appeared without his name in May, 1738. He received only ten guineas for this stately and vigorous poem: but the sale was rapid, and the success complete. A second edition was required within a week. Those small critics who are always desirous to lower established reputations ran about proclaiming that the anonymous satirist was superior to Pope in Pope's own peculiar department of literature. It ought to be remembered, to the honor of Pope, that he joined heartily in the applause with which the appearance of a rival genius was welcomed. He made inquiries about the author of "London." Such a man, he said, could not long be concealed. The name was soon discovered; and Pope, with great kindness, exerted himself to obtain an academical degree and the mastership of a grammar school for the poor young poet. The attempt failed; and Johnson remained a bookseller's hack.

It does not appear that these two men, the most eminent writer of the generation which was going out, and the most eminent writer of the generation which was coming in, ever saw each other. They lived in very different circles, one surrounded by dukes and earls, the other by starving pamphleteers and index makers. Among Johnson's associates at this time may be

mentioned Boyse, who, when his shirts were pledged, scrawled Latin verses sitting up in bed with his arms through two holes in his blanket; who composed very respectable sacred poetry when he was sober; and who was at last run over by a hackney coach when he was drunk: Hoole, surnamed the metaphysical tailor, who, instead of attending to his measures, used to trace geometrical diagrams on the board where he sat crosslegged: and the penitent impostor, George Psalmanazar, who, after poring all day, in a humble lodging, on the folios of Jewish rabbis and Christian fathers, indulged himself at night with literary and theological conversation at an alehouse in the city. But the most remarkable of the persons with whom at this time Johnson consorted was Richard Savage, an earl's son, a shoemaker's apprentice, who had seen life in all its forms, who had feasted among blue ribands in St. James's Square, and who had lain with fifty pounds' weight of iron on his legs in the condemned ward of Newgate. This man had, after many vicissitudes of fortune, sunk at last into abject and hopeless poverty. His pen had failed him. His patrons had been taken away by death, or estranged by the riotous profusion with which he squandered their bounty, and the ungrateful insolence with which he rejected their advice. He now lived by begging. He dined on venison and champagne whenever he had been so fortunate as to borrow a guinea. If his questing had been unsuccessful, he appeased the rage of hunger with some scraps of broken meat, and lay down to rest under the piazza of Covent Garden in warm weather, and, in cold weather, as near as he could get to the furnace of a glasshouse. Yet, in his misery, he was still an agreeable companion. He had an inexhaustible store of anecdotes about that gay and brilliant world from which he was now an outcast. He had observed the great men of both parties in hours of careless relaxation, had seen the leaders of opposition without the mask of patriotism, and had heard the prime minister roar with laughter and tell stories not over decent. During some months Savage lived in the closest familiarity with Johnson; and then the friends parted, not without tears. Johnson remained in London to drudge for Cave. Savage went to the west of England, lived there as he had lived everywhere, and, in 1743, died, penniless and heartbroken, in Bristol jail.

Extract from Samuel Johnson, in the Encyclopedia Britannica, December, 1856.
Reprinted in Macaulay's "Miscellaneous Writings."

ADDISON AND HIS FRIENDS

To the influence which Addison derived from his literary talents, was added all the influence which arises from character. The world, always ready to think the worst of needy political adventurers, was forced to make one exception. Restlessness, violence, audacity, laxity of principle, are the vices ordinarily attributed to that class of men. But faction itself could not deny that Addison had, through all changes of fortune, been strictly faithful to his early opinions, and to his early friends; that his integrity was without stain; that his whole deportment indicated a fine sense of the becoming; that, in the utmost heat of controversy, his zeal was tempered by a regard for truth, humanity, and social decorum; that no outrage could ever provoke him to retaliation unworthy of a Christian and a gentleman; and that his only faults were a too sensitive delicacy, and a modesty which amounted to bashfulness.

He was undoubtedly one of the most popular men of his time; and much of his popularity he owed, we believe, to that very timidity which his friends lamented. That timidity often prevented him from exhibiting his talents to the best advantage. But it propitiated Nemesis. It averted that envy which would otherwise have been excited by fame so splendid, and by so rapid an elevation. No man is so great a favorite with the public as he who is at once an object of admiration, of respect, and of pity; and such were the feelings which Addison inspired. Those who enjoyed the privilege of hearing his familiar conversation, declared with one voice that it was superior even to his writings. The brilliant Mary Montagu said that she had known all the wits, and that Addison was the best company in the world. The malignant Pope was forced to own that there was a charm in Addison's talk which could be found nowhere else. Swift, when burning with animosity against the Whigs, could not but confess to Stella, that, after all, he had never known any associate so agreeable as Addison. Steele, an excellent judge of lively conversation, said, that the conversation of Addison was at once the most polite, and the most mirthful, that could be imagined;—that it was Terence and Catullus in one, heightened by an exquisite something which was neither Terence nor Catullus, but Addison alone. Young, an excellent judge of serious conversation, said, that when Addison was at his ease, he went on in a noble strain of thought and language, so as to chain the attention of every hearer. Nor were his great colloquial powers more admirable than the courtesy and softness of heart which appeared in his conversation. At the same time, it would be too much to say that he was wholly devoid of the malice which is, perhaps, inseparable from a keen sense of the ludicrous. He had one habit which both Swift and Stella applauded, and which we hardly know how to blame. If his first attempts to set a presuming dunce right were ill received, he changed his tone, "assented with civil leer," and lured the flattered coxcomb deeper and deeper into absurdity. That such was his practice we should, we think, have guessed from his works. The Tatler's criticisms on Mr. Softly's sonnet, and the Spectator's dialogue with the politician, who is so zealous for the honor of Lady Q–p–t–s, are excellent specimens of this innocent mischief.

Such were Addison's talents for conversation. But his rare gifts were not exhibited to crowds or to strangers. As soon as he entered a large company, as soon as he saw an unknown face his lips were sealed, and his manners became constrained. None who met him only in great assemblies, would have been able to believe that he was the same man who had often kept a few friends listening and laughing round a table, from the time when the play ended, till the clock of St. Paul's in Covent Garden struck four. Yet, even at such a table, he was not seen to the best advantage. To enjoy his conversation in the highest perfection, it was necessary to be alone with him, and to hear him, in his own phrase, think aloud. "There is no such thing," he used to say, "as real conversation, but between two persons."

This timidity, a timidity surely neither ungraceful nor unamiable, led Addison into the two most serious faults which can with justice be imputed to him. He found that wine broke the spell which lay on his fine intellect, and was therefore too easily seduced into convivial excess. Such excess was in that age regarded, even by grave men, as the most venial of all peccadillos; and was so far from being a mark of ill breeding that it was almost essential to the character of a fine gentleman. But the smallest speck is seen on a white ground; and almost all the biographers of Addison have said something about this failing. Of any other statesman or writer of Queen Anne's reign, we should no more think of saying that he sometimes took too much wine, than that he wore a long wig and a sword.

To the excessive modesty of Addison's nature, we must ascribe another fault which generally arises from a very different cause. He became a little too fond of seeing himself surrounded by a small circle of admirers to whom he was as a king or rather as a god. All these men were far inferior to him in ability, and some of them had very serious faults. Nor did those faults escape his observation; for, if ever there was an eye which saw through and through men, it was the eye of Addison. But with the keenest observation, and the finest sense of the ridiculous, he had a large charity. The feeling with which he looked on most of his humble companions was one of benevolence, slightly tinctured with contempt. He was at perfect ease in their company; he was grateful for their devoted attachment; and he loaded them with benefits. Their veneration for him appears to have exceeded that with which Johnson was regarded by Boswell, or Warburton by Hurd. It was not in the power of adulation to turn such a head, or deprave such a heart as Addison's. But it must in candor be admitted, that he contracted some of the faults which can scarcely be avoided by any person who is so unfortunate as to be the oracle of a small literary coterie.

One member of this little society was Eustace Budgell, a young templar of some literature, and a distant relation of Addison. There was at this time no stain on the character of Budgell, and it is not improbable that his career would have been prosperous and honorable, if the life of his cousin had been prolonged. But when the master was laid in the grave, the disciple broke loose from all restraint; descended rapidly from one degree of vice and misery to another; ruined his fortune by follies; attempted to repair it by crimes; and at length closed a wicked and unhappy life by self-murder. Yet, to the last, the wretched man, gambler, lampooner, cheat, forger, as he was, retained his affection and veneration for Addison; and recorded those feelings in the last lines which he traced before he hid himself from infamy under London Bridge.

Another of Addison's favorite companions was Ambrose Philips, a good Whig and a middling poet, who had the honor of bringing into fashion a species of composition which has been called after his name, "Namby-Pamby." But the most remarkable members of the little senate, as Pope long afterwards called it, were Richard Steele and Thomas Tickell.

Steele had known Addison from childhood. They had been together at the Charter House and at Oxford; but circumstances

had then, for a time, separated them widely. Steele had left college without taking a degree, had been disinherited by a rich relation, had led a vagrant life, had served in the army, had tried to find the philosopher's stone, and had written a religious treatise and several comedies. He was one of those people whom it is impossible either to hate or to respect. His temper was sweet, his affections warm, his spirits lively, his passions strong, and his principles weak. His life was spent in sinning and repenting; in inculcating what was right, and doing what was wrong. In speculation, he was a man of piety and honor; in practice, he was much of the rake and a little of the swindler. He was, however, so good-natured that it was not easy to be seriously angry with him, and that even rigid moralists felt more inclined to pity than to blame him, when he diced himself into a spunging house, or drank himself into a fever. Addison regarded Steele with kindness not unmingled with scorn,—tried, with little success, to keep him out of scrapes, introducing him to the great, procured a good place for him, corrected his plays, and, though by no means rich, lent him large sums of money. One of these loans appears, from a letter dated in August, 1708, to have amounted to a thousand pounds. These pecuniary transactions probably led to frequent bickerings. It is said that, on one occasion, Steele's negligence, or dishonesty, provoked Addison to repay himself by the help of a bailiff. We cannot join with Miss Aikin in rejecting this story. Johnson heard it from Savage, who heard it from Steele. Few private transactions which took place a hundred and twenty years ago are proved by stronger evidence than this. But we can by no means agree with those who condemn Addison's severity. The most amiable of mankind may well be moved to indignation, when what he has earned hardly, and lent with great inconvenience to himself, for the purpose of relieving a friend in distress, is squandered with insane profusion. We will illustrate our meaning by an example, which is not the less striking because it is taken from fiction. Dr. Harrison, in Fielding's "Amelia," is represented as the most benevolent of human beings; yet he takes in execution, not only the goods, but the person of his friend Booth. Dr. Harrison resorts to this strong measure because he has been informed that Booth, while pleading poverty as an excuse for not paying just debts, has been buying fine jewelry, and setting up a coach. No person who is well acquainted with Steele's life and correspond-

ence, can doubt that he behaved quite as ill to Addison as Booth was accused of behaving to Dr. Harrison. The real history, we have little doubt, was something like this: A letter comes to Addison, imploring help in pathetic terms, and promising reformation and speedy repayment. Poor Dick declares that he has not an inch of candle, or a bushel of coals, or credit with the butcher for a shoulder of mutton. Addison is moved. He determines to deny himself some medals which are wanting to his series of the Twelve Cæsars; to put off buying the new edition of "Bayle's Dictionary," and to wear his old sword and buckles another year. In this way he manages to send a hundred pounds to his friend. The next day he calls on Steele, and finds scores of gentlemen and ladies assembled. The fiddles are playing. The table is groaning under champagne, Burgundy, and pyramids of sweetmeats. Is it strange that a man whose kindness is thus abused, should send sheriff's officers to reclaim what is due to him?

From the Edinburgh Review, 1843.

MILTON AND DANTE

POETRY, which relates to the beings of another world, ought to be at once mysterious and picturesque. That of Milton is so. That of Dante is picturesque, indeed, beyond any that was ever written. Its effect approaches to that produced by the pencil or the chisel. But it is picturesque to the exclusion of all mystery. This is a fault indeed on the right side, a fault inseparable from the plan of his poem, which, as we have already observed, rendered the utmost accuracy of description necessary. Still it is a fault. His supernatural agents excite an interest; but it is not the interest which is proper to supernatural agents. We feel that we could talk with his ghosts and demons without any emotions of unearthly awe. We could, like Don Juan, ask them to supper, and eat heartily in their company. His angels are good men with wings. His devils are spiteful, ugly executioners. His dead men are merely living men in strange situations. The scene which passes between the poet and Facinata is justly celebrated. Still, Facinata in the burning tomb is exactly what Facinata would have been at an *auto da fé*. Nothing can be more touching than the first interview of Dante and Beatrice. Yet what is it, but a lovely woman chiding, with sweet austere composure, the lover for whose affections she is grateful, but whose vices she reprobates? The feelings which give the passage its charm would suit the streets of Florence, as well as the summit of the Mount of Purgatory.

The Spirits of Milton are unlike those of almost all other writers. His fiends, in particular, are wonderful creations. They are not metaphysical abstractions. They are not wicked men. They are not ugly beasts. They have no horns, no tails, none of the fee-faw-fum of Tasso and Klopstock. They have just enough in common with human nature to be intelligible to human beings. Their characters are, like their forms, marked by a certain dim resemblance to those of men, but exaggerated to gigantic dimensions and veiled in mysterious gloom.

Perhaps the gods and demons of Æschylus may best bear a comparison with the angels and devils of Milton. The style of the Athenian had, as we have remarked, something of the vagueness and tenor of the Oriental character; and the same peculiarity may be traced in his mythology. It has nothing of the amenity and elegance which we generally find in the superstitions of Greece. All is rugged, barbaric, and colossal. His legends seem to harmonize less with the fragrant groves and graceful porticoes, in which his countrymen paid their vows to the God of Light and Goddess of Desire, than with those huge and grotesque labyrinths of eternal granite, in which Egypt enshrined her mystic Osiris, or in which Hindostan still bows down to her seven-headed idols. His favorite gods are those of the elder generations,—the sons of heaven and earth, compared with whom Jupiter himself was a stripling and an upstart,—the gigantic Titans and the inexorable Furies. Foremost among his creations of this class stands Prometheus, half fiend, half redeemer, the friend of man, the sullen and implacable enemy of heaven. He bears undoubtedly a considerable resemblance to the Satan of Milton. In both we find the same impatience of control, the same ferocity, the same unconquerable pride. In both characters also are mingled, though in very different proportions, some kind and generous feelings. Prometheus, however, is hardly superhuman enough. He talks too much of his chains and his uneasy posture. He is rather too much depressed and agitated. His resolution seems to depend on the knowledge which he possesses, that he holds the fate of his torturer in his hands, and that the hour of his release will surely come. But Satan is a creature of another sphere.

The might of his intellectual nature is victorious over the extremity of pain. Amidst agonies which cannot be conceived without horror, he deliberates, resolves, and even exults. Against the sword of Michael, against the thunder of Jehovah, against the flaming lake and the marl burning with solid fire, against the prospect of an eternity of unintermitent misery, his spirit bears up unbroken, resting on its own innate energies, requiring no support from anything external, nor even from hope itself!

To return for a moment to the parallel which we have been attempting to draw between Milton and Dante, we would add, that the poetry of these great men has, in a considerable degree, taken its character from their moral qualities. They are not egotists. They rarely obtrude their idiosyncrasies on their readers. They have nothing in common with those modern beggars for fame, who extort a pittance from the compassion of the inexperienced, by exposing the nakedness and sores of their minds. Yet it would be difficult to name two writers whose works have been more completely, though undesignedly, colored by their personal feelings.

The character of Milton was peculiarly distinguished by loftiness of thought; that of Dante by intensity of feeling. In every line of the "Divine Comedy" we discern the asperity which is produced by pride struggling with misery. There is, perhaps, no work in the world so deeply and uniformly sorrowful. The melancholy of Dante was no fantastic caprice. It was not, as far as at this distance of time can be judged, the effect of external circumstances. It was from within. Neither love nor glory, neither the conflicts of the earth nor the hope of heaven could dispel it. It twined every consolation and every pleasure into its own nature. It resembled that noxious Sardinian soil of which the intense bitterness is said to have been perceptible even in its honey. His mind was, in the noble language of the Hebrew poet, "a land of darkness, as darkness itself, and where the light was as darkness!" The gloom of his character discolors all the passions of men and all the face of nature, and tinges with its own livid hue the flowers of Paradise and the glories of the Eternal Throne! All the portraits of him are singularly characteristic. No person can look on the features, noble even to ruggedness, the dark furrows of the cheek, the haggard and woful stare of the eye, the sullen and contemptuous curve of the lip,

and doubt that they belonged to a man too proud and too sensitive to be happy.

Milton was, like Dante, a statesman and a lover; and, like Dante, he had been unfortunate in ambition and in love. He had survived his health and his sight, the comforts of his home and the prosperity of his party. Of the great men, by whom he had been distinguished at his entrance into life, some had been taken away from the evil to come; some had carried into foreign climates their unconquerable hatred of oppression; some were pining in dungeons; and some had poured forth their blood on scaffolds. That hateful proscription, facetiously termed the Act of Indemnity and Oblivion, had set a mark on the poor, blind, deserted poet, and held him up by name to the hatred of a profligate court and an inconstant people! Venal and licentious scribblers, with just sufficient talent to clothe the thoughts of a pander in the style of a bellman, were now the favorite writers of the sovereign and the public. It was a loathsome herd — which could be compared to nothing so fitly as to the rabble of "Comus," grotesque monsters, half bestial, half human, dropping with wine, bloated with gluttony, and reeling in obscene dances. Amidst these his Muse was placed, like the chaste lady of the Masque, lofty, spotless, and serene—to be chatted at, and pointed at, and grinned at, by the whole rabble of Satyrs and Goblins. If ever despondency and asperity could be excused in any man, it might have been excused in Milton. But the strength of his mind overcame every calamity. Neither blindness, nor gout, nor age, nor penury, nor domestic afflictions, nor political disappointments, nor abuse, nor proscription, nor neglect, had power to disturb his sedate and majestic patience. His spirits do not seem to have been high, but they were singularly equable. His temper was serious, perhaps stern; but it was a temper which no sufferings could render sullen or fretful. Such as it was, when, on the eve of great events, he returned from his travels, in the prime of health and manly beauty, loaded with literary distinctions and glowing with patriotic hopes, such it continued to be—when, after having experienced every calamity which is incident to our nature, old, poor, sightless, and disgraced, he retired to his hovel to die!

From the review of Sumner's translation of Milton's "Treatise on Christian Doctrine." Edinburgh Review, 1825.

THE GENIUS OF MIRABEAU

WE HAVE never met with so vivid and interesting a picture of the National Assembly as that which M. Dumont has set before us. His Mirabeau, in particular, is incomparable. All the former Mirabeaus were daubs in comparison. Some were merely painted from the imagination, others were gross caricatures; this is the very individual, neither god nor demon, but a man, a Frenchman, a Frenchman of the eighteenth century, with great talents, with strong passions, depraved by bad education, surrounded by temptations of every kind, made desperate at one time by disgrace, and then again intoxicated by fame. All his opposite and seemingly inconsistent qualities are in this representation so blended together as to make up a harmonious and natural whole. Till now, Mirabeau was to us, and, we believe, to most readers of history, not a man, but a string of antitheses. Henceforth he will be a real human being, a remarkable and eccentric being indeed, but perfectly conceivable.

He was fond, M. Dumont tells us, of giving odd compound nicknames. Thus, M. de Lafayette was Grandison-Cromwell; the King of Prussia was Alaric-Cottin; D'Espremenil was Crispin-Catiline. We think that Mirabeau himself might be described, after his own fashion, as a Wilkes-Chatham. He had Wilkes's sensuality, Wilkes's levity, Wilkes's insensibility to shame. Like Wilkes, he had brought on himself the censure even of men of pleasure by the peculiar grossness of his immorality, and by the obscenity of his writings. Like Wilkes, he was heedless, not only of the laws of morality, but of the laws of honor. Yet he affected, like Wilkes, to unite the character of the demagogue to that of the fine gentleman. Like Wilkes, he conciliated, by his good-humor and his high spirits, the regard of many who despised his character. Like Wilkes, he was hideously ugly; like Wilkes, he made a jest of his own ugliness; and, like Wilkes, he was, in spite of his ugliness, very attentive to his dress, and very successful in affairs of gallantry.

Resembling Wilkes in the lower and grosser parts of his character, he had, in his higher qualities, some affinities to Chatham. His eloquence, as far as we can judge of it, bore no inconsiderable resemblance to that of the great English minister. He was not eminently successful in long set speeches. He was not, on the other hand, a close and ready debater. Sudden bursts, which seemed to be the effect of inspiration; short sentences, which came like lightning, dazzling, burning, striking down everything before them; sentences which, spoken at critical moments, decided the fate of great questions; sentences which at once became proverbs; sentences which everybody still knows by heart; in these chiefly lay the oratorical power both of Chatham and of Mirabeau. There have been far greater speakers and far greater statesmen than either of them; but we doubt whether any men have, in modern times, exercised such vast personal influence over stormy and divided assemblies. The power of both was as much moral as intellectual. In true dignity of character, in private and public virtue, it may seem absurd to institute any comparison between them; but they had the same haughtiness and vehemence of temper. In their language and manner there was a disdainful self-confidence, an imperiousness, a fierceness of passion, before which all common minds quailed. Even Murray and Charles Townshend, though intellectually not inferior to Chatham, were always cowed by him. Barnave, in the same manner, though the best debater in the National Assembly, flinched before the energy of Mirabeau. Men, except in bad novels, are not all good or all evil. It can scarcely be denied that the virtue of Lord Chatham was a little theatrical. On the other hand, there was in Mirabeau, not indeed anything deserving the name of virtue, but that imperfect substitute for virtue which is found in almost all superior minds, a sensibility to the beautiful and the good, which sometimes amounted to sincere enthusiasm, and which, mingled with the desire of admiration, sometimes gave to his character a lustre resembling the lustre of true goodness; as the " faded splendor wan " which lingered round the fallen archangel, resembled the exceeding brightness of those spirits who had kept their first estate.

From a review of Dumont's " Recollections of
Mirabeau." Edinburgh Review, 1843.

HISTORY AS AN EVOLUTION

Bishop Watson compares a geologist to a gnat mounted on an elephant, and laying down theories as to the whole internal structure of the vast animal, from the phenomena of the hide. The comparison is unjust to the geologists; but it is very

applicable to those historians who write as if the body politic were homogeneous, who look only on the surface of affairs, and never think of the mighty and various organization which lies deep below.

In the works of such writers as these, England at the close of the Seven Years' War, is in the highest state of prosperity. At the close of the American war, she is in a miserable and degraded condition; as if the people were not on the whole as rich, as well governed, and as well educated, at the latter period as at the former. We have read books called histories of England, under the reign of George II., in which the rise of Methodism is not even mentioned. A hundred years hence this breed of authors will, we hope, be extinct. If it should still exist, the late ministerial interregnum will be described in terms which will seem to imply that all government was at an end; that the social contract was annulled, and that the hand of every man was against his neighbor, until the wisdom and virtue of the new cabinet educed order out of the chaos of anarchy. We are quite certain that misconceptions as gross prevail at this moment, respecting many important parts of our annals.

The effect of historical reading is analogous in many respects, to that produced by foreign travel. The student, like the tourist, is transported into a new state of society. He sees new fashions. He hears new modes of expression. His mind is enlarged by contemplating the wide diversities of laws, of morals, and of manners. But men may travel far, and return with minds as contracted as if they had never stirred from their own market town. In the same manner, men may know the dates of many battles, and the genealogies of many royal houses, and yet be no wiser. Most people look at past times, as princes look at foreign countries. More than one illustrious stranger has landed on our island amidst the shouts of a mob, has dined with the king, has hunted with the master of the staghounds, has seen the guards reviewed, and a knight of the garter installed; has cantered along Regent Street; has visited St. Paul's, and noted down its dimensions, and has then departed, thinking that he has seen England. He has, in fact, seen a few public buildings, public men, and public ceremonies. But of the vast and complex system of society, of the fine shades of national character, of the practical operation of government and laws, he knows nothing. He who would understand these things rightly must not confine his observations to palaces and solemn days. He must see ordinary men as they

appear in their ordinary business and in their ordinary pleasures. He must mingle in the crowds of the exchange and the coffeehouse. He must obtain admittance to the convivial table and the domestic hearth. He must bear with vulgar expressions. He must not shrink from exploring even the retreats of misery. He who wishes to understand the condition of mankind in former ages, must proceed on the same principle. If he attend only to public transactions, to wars, congresses, and debates, his studies will be as unprofitable as the travels of those imperial, royal, and serene sovereigns, who form their judgment of our island from having gone in state to a few fine sights, and from having held formal conferences with a few great officers.

The perfect historian is he in whose work the character and spirit of an age is exhibited in miniature. He relates no fact, he attributes no expression to his characters, which is not authenticated by sufficient testimony. But by judicious selection, rejection, and arrangement, he gives to truth those attractions which have been usurped by fiction. In his narrative, a due subordination is observed; some transactions are prominent, others retire. But the scale on which he represents them is increased or diminished, not according to the dignity of the persons concerned in them, but according to the degree in which they elucidate the condition of society and the nature of man. He shows us the court, the camp, and the senate. But he shows us also the nation. He considers no anecdote, no peculiarity of manner, no familiar saying, as too insignificant for his notice, which is not too insignificant to illustrate the operation of laws, of religion, and of education, and to mark the progress of the human mind. Men will not merely be described, but will be made intimately known to us. The changes of manners will be indicated, not merely by a few general phrases, or a few extracts from statistical documents, but by appropriate images presented in every line.

If a man, such as we are supposing, should write the history of England, he would assuredly not omit the battles, the sieges, the negotiations, the seditions, the ministerial changes. But with these he would intersperse the details which are the charm of historical romances. At Lincoln Cathedral there is a beautiful painted window, which was made by an apprentice out of the pieces of glass which had been rejected by his master. It is so far superior to every other in the church, that, according to the tradition, the vanquished artist killed himself from mortification.

Sir Walter Scott, in the same manner, has used those fragments of truth which historians have scornfully thrown behind them, in a manner which may well excite their envy. He has constructed out of their gleanings works which, even considered as histories, are scarcely less valuable than theirs. But a truly great historian would reclaim those materials which the novelist has appropriated. The history of the government and the history of the people would be exhibited in that mode in which alone they can be exhibited justly, in inseparable conjunction and intermixture. We should not then have to look for the wars and votes of the Puritans in Clarendon, and for their phraseology in " Old Mortality "; for one half of King James in Hume, and for the other half in " The Fortunes of Nigel."

The early part of our imaginary history would be rich with coloring from romance, ballad, and chronicle. We should find ourselves in the company of knights such as those of Froissart, and of pilgrims such as those who rode with Chaucer from the Tabard. Society would be shown from the highest to the lowest —from the royal cloth of state to the den of the outlaw; from the throne of the legate to the chimney corner where the begging friar regaled himself. Palmers, minstrels, crusaders—the stately monastery, with the good cheer in its refectory, and the high mass in its chapel—the manor house, with its hunting and hawking—the tournament, with the heralds and ladies, the trumpets and the cloth of gold—would give truth and life to the representation. We should perceive, in a thousand slight touches, the importance of the privileged burgher, and the fierce and haughty spirit which swelled under the collar of the degraded villain. The revival of letters would not merely be described in a few magnificent periods. We should discern, in innumerable particulars, the fermentation of mind, the eager appetite for knowledge, which distinguished the sixteenth from the fifteenth century. In the Reformation we should see, not merely a schism which changed the ecclesiastical constitution of England, and the mutual relations of the European powers, but a moral war which raged in every family, which set the father against the son, and the son against the father, the mother against the daughter, and the daughter against the mother. Henry would be painted with the skill of Tacitus. We should have the change of his character from his profuse and joyous youth to his savage and imperious old age. We should perceive the gradual progress of selfish and tyrannical passions, in a mind not naturally insensible or ungenerous; and to the last we should detect some remains of that open and noble temper which endeared him to a people whom he oppressed, struggling with the hardness of despotism and the irritability of disease. We should see Elizabeth in all her weakness, and in all her strength, surrounded by the handsome favorites whom she never trusted, and the wise old statesmen, whom she never dismissed, uniting in herself the most contradictory qualities of both her parents — the coquetry, the caprice, the petty malice of Anne — the haughty and resolute spirit of Henry. We have no hesitation in saying, that a great artist might produce a portrait of this remarkable woman, at least as striking as that in the novel of Kenilworth, without employing a single trait not authenticated by ample testimony.* In the meantime, we should see arts cultivated, wealth accumulated, the conveniences of life improved. We should see the keeps, where nobles, insecure themselves, spread insecurity around them, gradually giving place to the halls of peaceful opulence, to the oriels of Longleat, and the stately pinnacles of Burleigh. We should see towns extended, deserts cultivated, the hamlets of fishermen turned into wealthy havens, the meal of the peasant improved, and his hut more commodiously furnished. We should see those opinions and feelings which produced the great struggle against the house of Stuart, slowly growing up in the bosom of private families, before they manifested themselves in parliamentary debates. Then would come the civil war. Those skirmishes, on which Clarendon dwells so minutely, would be told, as Thucydides would have told them, with perspicuous conciseness. They are merely connecting links. But the great characteristics of the age, the loyal enthusiasm of the brave English gentry, the fierce licentiousness of the swearing, dicing, drunken reprobates, whose excesses disgraced the royal cause — the austerity of the Presbyterian Sabbaths in the city, the extravagance of the Independent preachers in the camp, the precise garb, the severe countenance, the petty scruples, the affected accent, the absurd names and phrases which marked the Puritans — the valor, the policy, the public spirit, which lurked beneath these ungraceful disguises, the dreams of the raving Fifth Monarchyman, the dreams, scarcely less wild, of the philosophic republican — all these would enter into the representation, and render it at once more exact and more striking.

* See the portrait by Green elsewhere in this work.

The instruction derived from history thus written would be of a vivid and practical character. It would be received by the imagination as well as by the reason. It would be not merely traced on the mind, but branded into it. Many truths, too, would be learned, which can be learned in no other manner. As the history of states is generally written, the greatest and most momentous revolutions seem to come upon them like supernatural inflictions, without warning or cause. But the fact is, that such revolutions are almost always the consequences of moral changes, which have gradually passed on the mass of the community, and which ordinarily proceed far before their progress is indicated by any public measure. An intimate knowledge of the domestic history of nations is therefore absolutely necessary to the prognosis of political events. A narrative, defective in this respect, is as useless as a medical treatise which should pass by all the symptoms attendant on the early stage of a disease, and mention only what occurs when the patient is beyond the reach of remedies.

From a review of Neele's "Romance of History."
Edinburgh Review, 1828.

MONTGOMERY'S SATAN.

THE Day of Judgment is to be described, — and a roaring cataract of nonsense is poured forth upon this tremendous subject. Earth, we are told, is dashed into Eternity. Furnace blazes wheel round the horizon, and burst into bright wizard phantoms. Racing hurricanes unroll and whirl quivering fire clouds. The white waves gallop. Shadowy worlds career around. The red and raging eye of Imagination is then forbidden to pry further. But further Mr. Robert Montgomery persists in prying. The stars bound through the airy roar. The unbosomed deep yawns on the ruin. The billows of Eternity then begin to advance. The world glares in fiery slumber. A car comes forward driven by living thunder.

"Creation shudders with sublime dismay,
And in a blazing tempest whirls away."

And this is fine poetry! This is what ranks its writer with the master-spirits of the age! This is what has been described over and over again, in terms which would require some qualification if used respecting "Paradise Lost!" It is too much that

this patchwork, made by stitching together old odds and ends of what, when new, was, for the most part, but tawdry frippery, is to be picked off the dunghill on which it ought to rot, and to be held up to admiration as an inestimable specimen of art. And what must we think of a system, by means of which verses like those which we have quoted — verses fit only for the poet's corner of the Morning Post — can produce emolument and fame? The circulation of this writer's poetry has been greater than that of Southey's "Roderick," and beyond all comparison greater than that of Carey's "Dante," or of the best works of Coleridge. Thus encouraged, Mr. Robert Montgomery has favored the public with volume after volume. We have given so much space to the examination of his first and most popular performance, that we have none to spare for his "Universal Prayer," and his smaller poems, which, as the puffing journals tell us, would alone constitute a sufficient title to literary immortality. We shall pass at once to his last publication, entitled "Satan."

This poem was ushered into the world with the usual roar of acclamation. But the thing was now past a joke. Pretensions so unfounded, so impudent, and so successful, had aroused a spirit of resistance. In several magazines and reviews, accordingly, "Satan" has been handled somewhat roughly, and the arts of the puffers have been exposed with good sense and spirit. We shall, therefore, be very concise.

Of the two poems, we rather prefer that on the "Omnipresence of the Deity," for the same reason which induced Sir Thomas More to rank one bad book above another. "Marry, this is somewhat. This is rhyme. But the other is neither rhyme nor reason." "Satan" is a long soliloquy, which the Devil pronounces in five or six thousand lines of blank verse, concerning geography, politics, newspapers, fashionable society, theatrical amusements, Sir Walter Scott's novels, Lord Byron's poetry, and Mr. Martin's pictures. The new designs for Milton have, as was natural, particularly attracted the attention of a personage who occupies so conspicuous a place in them. Mr. Martin must be pleased to learn, that, whatever may be thought of those performances on earth, they give full satisfaction in Pandemonium, and that he is there thought to have hit off the likenesses of the various thrones and dominions very happily.

The motto to the poem of "Satan" is taken from the Book of Job: "Whence comest thou? From going to and fro in the

earth, and walking up and down in it." And certainly, Mr. Robert Montgomery has not failed to make his hero go to and fro, and walk up and down. With the exception, however, of this propensity to locomotion, "Satan" has not one Satanic quality. Mad Tom had told us, that "the prince of darkness is a gentleman"; but we had yet to learn that he is a respectable and pious gentleman, whose principal fault is, that he is something of a twaddle, and far too liberal of his good advice. That happy change in his character which Origen anticipated, and of which Tillotson did not despair, seems to be rapidly taking place. Bad habits are not eradicated in a moment. It is not strange, therefore, that so old an offender should now and then relapse for a short time into wrong dispositions. But to give him his due, as the proverb recommends, we must say, that he always returns, after two or three lines of impiety, to his preaching tone. We would seriously advise Mr. Montgomery to omit, or alter, about a hundred lines in different parts of this large volume, and to republish it under the name of "Gabriel." The reflections of which it consists would come less absurdly, as far as there is a more and a less in extreme absurdity, from a good than from a bad angel.

We can afford room only for a single quotation. We give one taken at random — neither worse nor better, as far as we can perceive, than any other equal number of lines in the book. The Devil goes to the play, and moralizes thereon as follows:—

Music and pomp their mingling spirit shed
Around me; beauties in their cloud-like robes
Shine forth, — a scenic paradise, it glares
Intoxication through the reeling sense
Of flushed enjoyment. In the motley host
Three prime gradations may be ranked: the first,
To mount upon the wings of Shakespeare's mind,
And win a flash of his Promethean thought, —
To smile and weep, to shudder and achieve
A round of passionate omnipotence,
Attend: the second, are a sensual tribe,
Convened to hear romantic harlots sing,
On forms to banquet a lascivious gaze,
While the bright perfidy of wanton eyes
Through brain and spirit darts delicious fire:
The last, a throng most pitiful! who seem,
With their corroded figures, rayless glance

And death-like struggle of decaying age,
Like painted skeletons in charnel pomp
Set forth to satirize the human kind!—
How fine a prospect for demoniac view!
'Creatures whose souls outbalance worlds awake!'
Methinks I hear a pitying angel cry."

Here we conclude. If our remarks give pain to Mr. Robert Montgomery, we are sorry for it. But, at whatever cost of pain to individuals, literature must be purified of this taint. And, to show that we are not actuated by any feelings of personal enmity towards him, we hereby give notice, that, as soon as any book shall, by means of puffing, reach a second edition, our intention is, to do unto the writer of it as we have done unto Mr. Robert Montgomery.

From a review of Montgomery's poems.
Edinburgh Review, 1830.

ON GLADSTONE'S «CHURCH AND STATE»

WE THINK that government, like every other contrivance of human wisdom, from the highest to the lowest, is likely to answer its main end best when it is constructed with a single view to that end. Mr. Gladstone, who loves Plato, will not quarrel with us for illustrating our proposition, after Plato's fashion, from the most familiar objects. Take cutlery, for example. A blade which is designed both to shave and to carve will certainly not shave so well as a razor or carve so well as a carving knife. An academy of painting, which should also be a bank, would in all probability exhibit very bad pictures and discount very bad bills. A gas company, which should also be an infant school society, would, we apprehend, light the streets ill, and teach the children ill. On the principle, we think that government should be organized solely with a view to its main end; and that no part of its efficiency for that end should be sacrificed in order to promote any other end, however excellent.

But does it follow from hence that governments ought never to promote any other end than their main end? In no wise. Though it is desirable that every institution should have a main end, and should be so formed as to be in the highest degree efficient for that main end; yet if, without any sacrifice of its efficiency for that end, it can promote any other good end, it ought to do

so. Thus, the end for which a hospital is built is the relief of the sick, not the beautifying of the street. To sacrifice the health of the sick to splendor of architectual effect—to place the building in a bad air only that it may present a more commanding front to a great public place—to make the wards hotter or cooler than they ought to be, in order that the columns and windows of the exterior may please the passers-by, would be monstrous. But if, without any sacrifice of the chief object, the hospital can be made an ornament to the metropolis, it would be absurd not to make it so.

In the same manner, if a government can, without any sacrifice of its main end, promote any other good end, it ought to do so. The encouragement of the fine arts, for example, is by no means the main end of government; and it would be absurd, in constituting a government, to bestow a thought on the question whether it would be a government likely to train Raphaels and Domenichinos. But it by no means follows that it is improper for a government to form a national gallery of pictures. The same may be said of patronage bestowed on learned men—of the publication of archives—of the collecting of libraries, menageries, plants, fossils, antiques—of journeys and voyages for purposes of geographical discovery or astronomical observation. It is not for these ends that government is constituted. But it may well happen that a government may have at its command resources which will enable it, without any injury to its main end, to serve these collateral ends far more effectually than any individual or any voluntary association could do. If so, government ought to serve these collateral ends.

It is still more evidently the duty of government to promote—always in subordination to its main end—everything which is useful as a means for the attaining of that main end. The improvement of steam navigation, for example, is by no means a primary object of government. But as steam vessels are useful for the purpose of national defense, and for the purpose of facilitating intercourse between distant provinces, and thereby consolidating the force of the empire, it may be the bounden duty of government to encourage ingenious men to perfect an invention which so directly tends to make the State more efficient for its great primary end.

Now, on both these grounds, the instruction of the people may with propriety engage the care of the government. That

the people should be well educated is in itself a good thing; and the State ought therefore to promote this object, if it can do so without any sacrifice of its primary object. The education of the people, conducted on those principles of morality which are common to all the forms of Christianity, is highly valuable as a means of promoting the main end for which government exists; and is on this ground an object well deserving the attention of rulers. We will not at present go into the general question of education, but will confine our remarks to the subject which is more immediately before us, namely, the religious instruction of the people.

We may illustrate our view of the policy which governments ought to pursue with respect to religious instruction, by recurring to the analogy of a hospital. Religious instruction is not the main end for which a hospital is built; and to introduce into a hospital any regulations prejudicial to the health of the patients, on the plea of promoting their spiritual improvement—to send a ranting preacher to a man who has just been ordered by the physician to lie quiet and try to get a little sleep—to impose a strict observance of Lent on a convalescent who has been advised to eat heartily of nourishing food—to direct, as the bigoted Pius V. actually did, that no medical assistance should be given to any person who declined spiritual attendance—would be the most extravagant folly. Yet it by no means follows that it would not be right to have a chaplain to attend the sick, and to pay such a chaplain out of the hospital funds. Whether it will be proper to have such a chaplain at all, and of what religious persuasion such a chaplain ought to be, must depend on circumstances. There may be a town in which it would be impossible to set up a good hospital without the help of people of different opinions. And religious parties may run so high that, though people of different opinions are willing to contribute for the relief of the sick, they will not concur in the choice of any one chaplain. The High Churchmen insist that, if there is a paid chaplain, he shall be a High Churchman. The Evangelicals stickle for an Evangelical. Here it would evidently be absurd and cruel to let a useful and humane design, about which all are agreed, fall to the ground, because all cannot agree about something else. The governors must either appoint two chaplains, and pay them both, or they must appoint none; and every one of them must, in his individual capacity, do what he can for the purpose of providing the sick with such religious

instruction and consolation as will, in his opinion, be most useful to them.

We should say the same of government. Government is not an institution for the propagation of religion any more than St. George's Hospital is an institution for the propagation of religion. And the most absurd and pernicious consequences would follow, if government should pursue, as its primary end, that which can never be more than its secondary end; though intrinsically more important than its primary end. But a government which considers the religious instruction of the people as its secondary end, and follows out that principle faithfully, will, we think, be likely to do much good, and little harm.

We will rapidly run over some of the consequences to which this principle leads, and point out how it solves some problems which, on Mr. Gladstone's hypothesis, admit of no satisfactory solution.

All persecution directed against the persons or property of men is, on our principle, obviously indefensible. For the protection of the persons and property of men being the primary end of government, and religious instruction only a secondary end, to secure the people from heresy by making their lives, their limbs, or their estates insecure, would be to sacrifice the primary end to the secondary end. It would be as absurd as it would be in the governors of a hospital to direct that the wounds of all Arian and Socinian patients should be dressed in such a way as to make them fester.

Again, on our principles, all civil disabilities on account of religious opinions are indefensible. For all such disabilities make government less efficient for its main end; they limit its choice of able men for the administration and defense of the State; they alienate from it the hearts of the sufferers; they deprive it of a part of its effective strength in all contests with foreign nations. Such a course is as absurd as it would be in the governors of a hospital to reject an able surgeon because he is a Universal Restitutionist, and to send a bungler to operate because he is perfectly orthodox.

Again, on our principles, no government ought to press on the people religious instruction, however sound, in such a manner as to excite among them discontents dangerous to public order. For here again government would sacrifice its primary end to an end intrinsically, indeed, of the highest importance, but still only a secondary end of government, as government. This rule at once disposes of the difficulty about India—a difficulty of which Mr. Gladstone can get rid only by putting in an imaginary discharge in order to set aside an imaginary obligation. There is assuredly no country where it is more desirable that Christianity should be propagated. But there is no country in which the government is so completely disqualified for the task. By using our power in order to make proselytes, we should produce the dissolution of society, and bring utter ruin on all those interests for the protection of which government exists. Here the secondary end is, at present, inconsistent with the primary end, and must therefore be abandoned. Christian instruction given by individuals and voluntary societies may do much good. Given by the government, it would do unmixed harm. At the same time, we quite agree with Mr. Gladstone in thinking that the English authorities in India ought not to participate in any idolatrous rite; and, indeed, we are fully satisfied that all such participation is not only unchristian, but also unwise and most undignified.

Supposing the circumstances of a country to be such that the government may with propriety, on our principles, give religious instruction to a people, the next question is, what religion shall be taught? Bishop Warburton answers, The religion of the majority. And we so far agree with him, that we can scarcely conceive any circumstances in which it would be proper to establish, as the one exclusive religion of the State, the religion of the minority. Such a preference could hardly be given without exciting most serious discontent, and endangering those interests the protection of which is the first object of government. But we never can admit that a ruler can be justified in assisting to spread a system of opinions solely because that system is pleasing to the majority. On the other hand, we cannot agree with Mr. Gladstone, who would, of course, answer that the only religion which a ruler ought to propagate is the religion of his own conscience. In truth, this is an impossibility. And, as we have shown, Mr. Gladstone himself, whenever he supports a grant of money to the Church of England, is really assisting to propagate, not the precise religion of his own conscience, but some one or more, he knows not how many or which, of the innumerable religions which lie between the confines of Pelagianism and those of Antinomianism, and between the confines of Popery and those of Presby-

terianism. In our opinion, that religious instruction which the ruler ought, in his public capacity, to patronize, is the instruction from which he, in his conscience, believes that the people will learn most good with the smallest mixture of evil. And thus it is not necessarily his own religion that he will select. He will, of course, believe that his own religion is unmixedly good. But the question which he has to consider is, not how much good his religion contains, but how much good the people will learn, if instruction is given them in that religion. He may prefer the doctrines and government of the Church of England to those of the Church of Scotland. But if he knows that a Scotch congregation will listen with deep attention and respect while an Erskine or a Chalmers set before them the fundamental doctrines of Christianity, and that the glimpse of a cassock or a single line of a liturgy would be the signal for hooting and riot, and would probably bring stools and brickbats about the ears of the minister, he acts wisely if he conveys religious knowledge to the Scotch rather by means of that imperfect Church, as he may think it, from which they will learn much, than by means of that perfect Church, from which they will learn nothing. The only end of teaching is, that men may learn; and it is idle to talk of the duty of teaching truth in ways which only cause men to cling more firmly to falsehood.

On these principles we conceive that a statesman, who might be far, indeed, from regarding the Church of England with the reverence which Mr. Gladstone feels for her, might yet firmly oppose all attempts to destroy her. Such a statesman may be far too well acquainted with her origin to look upon her with superstitious awe. He may know that she sprang from a compromise huddled up between the eager zeal of reformers and the selfishness of greedy, ambitious, and time-serving politicians. He may find in every page of her annals ample cause for censure. He may feel that he could not, with ease to his conscience, subscribe to all her articles. He may regret that all the attempts which have been made to open her gates to large classes of nonconformists should have failed. Her episcopal polity he may consider as of purely human institution. He cannot defend her on the ground that she possesses the apostolical succession; for he does not know whether that succession may not be altogether a fable. He cannot defend her on the ground of her unity; for he knows that her frontier sects are much more remote from each other than

one frontier is from the Church of Rome, or the other from the Church of Geneva. But he may think that she teaches more truth with less alloy of error than would be taught by those who, if she were swept away, would occupy the vacant space. He may think that the effect produced by her beautiful services and by her pulpits on the national mind, is, on the whole, highly beneficial. He may think that her civilizing influence is usefully felt in remote districts. He may think that, if she were destroyed, a large portion of those who now compose her congregations would neglect all religious duties; and that a still larger part would fall under the influence of spiritual mountebanks, hungry for gain or drunk with fanaticism. While he would with pleasure admit that all the qualities of Christian pastors are to be found in large measure within the existing body of dissenting ministers, he would perhaps be inclined to think that the standard of intellectual and moral character among that exemplary class of men may have been raised to its present high point and maintained there by the indirect influence of the Establishment. And he may be by no means satisfied that, if the Church were at once swept away, the place of our Sumners and Whateleys would be supplied by Doddridges and Halls. He may think that the advantages which we have described are obtained, or might, if the existing system were slightly modified, be obtained, without any sacrifice of the paramount objects which all governments ought to have chiefly in view. Nay, he may be of opinion that an institution, so deeply fixed in the hearts and minds of millions, could not be subverted without loosening and shaking all the foundations of civil society. With at least equal ease he would find reason for supporting the Church of Scotland. Nor would he be under the necessity of resorting to any contract to justify the connection of two religious establishments with one government. He would think scruples on that head frivolous in any person who is zealous for a Church, of which both Dr. Herbert Marsh and Dr. Daniel Wilson are bishops. Indeed, he would gladly follow out his principles much further. He would have been willing to vote in 1825 for Lord Francis Egerton's resolution, that it is expedient to give a public maintenance to the Catholic clergy of Ireland; and he would deeply regret that no such measure was adopted in 1829.

In this way, we conceive, a statesman might, on our principles, satisfy himself that it would be in the highest degree inex-

pedient to abolish the Church, either of England or of Scotland.

But if there were, in any part of the world, a national church regarded as heretical by four-fifths of the nation committed to its care—a Church established and maintained by the sword—a Church producing twice as many riots as conversions—a Church which, though possessing great wealth and power, and though long backed by persecuting laws, had, in the course of many generations, been found unable to propagate its doctrines, and barely able to maintain its ground—a Church so odious, that fraud and violence, when used against its clear rights of property, were generally regarded as fair play—a Church whose ministers were preaching to desolate walls, and with difficulty obtaining their lawful subsistence by the help of bayonets—such a Church, on our principles, could not, we must own, be defended. We should say that the State which allied itself with such a Church, postponed the primary end of government to the secondary; and that the consequences had been such as any sagacious observer would have predicted. Neither the primary nor the secondary end is attained. The temporal and spiritual interests of the people suffer alike. The minds of men, instead of being drawn to the Church, are alienated from the State. The magistrate, after sacrificing order, peace, union, all the interests which it is his first duty to protect, for the purpose of promoting pure religion, is forced, after the experience of centuries, to admit that he has really been promoting error. The sounder the doctrines of such a Church—the more absurd and noxious the superstition by which those doctrines are opposed—the stronger are the arguments against the policy which has deprived a good cause of its natural advantages. Those who preach to rulers the duty of employing power to propagate truth would do well to remember that falsehood, though no match for truth alone, has often been found more than a match for truth and power together.

A statesman, judging on our principles, would pronounce without hesitation that a Church, such as we have last described, never ought to have been set up. Further than this we will not venture to speak for him. He would doubtless remember that the world is full of institutions which, though they never ought to have been set up, yet having been set up, ought not to be rudely pulled down; and that it is often wise in practice to be content with the mitigation of an abuse which, looking at it in the abstract, we might feel impatient to destroy.

We have done; and nothing remains but that we part from Mr. Gladstone with the courtesy of antagonists who bear no malice. We dissent from his opinions, but we admire his talents; we respect his integrity and benevolence; and we hope that he will not suffer political avocations so entirely to engross him as to leave him no leisure for literature and philosophy.

From a review of Gladstone's "The State; Its Relations with the Church," 1839.

MACHIAVELLI

WE DOUBT whether any name in literary history be so generally odious as that of the man whose character and writings we now propose to consider. The terms in which he is commonly described would seem to import that he was the Tempter, the Evil Principle, the discoverer of ambition and revenge, the original inventor of perjury; that, before the publication of his fatal "Prince," there had never been a hypocrite, a tyrant, or a traitor, a simulated virtue or a convenient crime. One writer gravely assures us, that Maurice of Saxony learned all his fraudulent policy from that execrable volume. Another remarks, that since it was translated into Turkish, the Sultans have been more addicted than formerly to the custom of strangling their brothers. Our own foolish Lord Lyttleton charges the poor Florentine with the manifold treasons of the House of Guise, and the massacre of St. Bartholomew. Several authors have hinted that the Gunpowder Plot is to be primarily attributed to his doctrines, and seem to think that his effigy ought to be substituted for that of Guy Fawkes, in those processions by which the ingenuous youth of England annually commemorate the preservation of the Three Estates. The Church of Rome has pronounced his works accursed things. Nor have our own countrymen been backward in testifying their opinion of his merits. Out of his surname they have coined an epithet for a knave — and out of his Christian name a synonym for the devil.

It is indeed scarcely possible for any person, not well acquainted with the history and literature of Italy, to read, without horror and amazement, the celebrated treatise which has brought so much obloquy on the name of Machiavelli. Such a display of wickedness, naked, yet not ashamed, such cool, judicious, scien-

tific atrocity, seem rather to belong to a fiend than to the most depraved of men. Principles which the most hardened ruffian would scarcely hint to his most trusted accomplice, or avow, without the disguise of some palliating sophism, even to his own mind, are professed without the slightest circumlocution, and assumed as the fundamental axioms of all political science.

It is not strange that ordinary readers should regard the author of such a book as the most depraved and shameless of human beings. Wise men, however, have always been inclined to look with great suspicion on the angels and demons of the multitude; and in the present instance, several circumstances have led even superficial observers to question the justice of the vulgar decision. It is notorious that Machiavelli was, through life, a zealous republican. In the same year in which he composed his manual of Kingcraft, he suffered imprisonment and torture in the cause of public liberty. It seems inconceivable that the martyr of freedom should have designedly acted as the apostle of tyranny. Several eminent writers have, therefore, endeavored to detect, in this unfortunate performance, some concealed meaning more consistent with the character and conduct of the author than that which appears at the first glance.

One hypothesis is, that Machiavelli intended to practice on the young Lorenzo de Medici a fraud, similar to that which Sunderland is said to have employed against our James II., — that he urged his pupil to violent and perfidious measures, as the surest means of accelerating the moment of deliverance and revenge. Another supposition, which Lord Bacon seems to countenance is, that the treatise was merely a piece of grave irony, intended to warn nations against the arts of ambitious men. It would be easy to show that neither of these solutions is consistent with many passages in "The Prince" itself. But the most decisive refutation is that which is furnished by the other works of Machiavelli. In all the writings which he gave to the public, and in all those which the research of editors has, in the course of three centuries, discovered — in his comedies, designed for the entertainment of the multitude — in his comments on Livy, intended for the perusal of the most enthusiastic patriots of Florence — in his "History," ascribed to one of the most amiable and estimable of the popes — in his public dispatches — in his private memoranda, the same obliquity of moral principle for which "The Prince" is so severely censured, is more or less dis-

cernible. We doubt whether it would be possible to find, in all the many volumes of his compositions, a single expression indicating that dissimulation and treachery had ever struck him as discreditable.

After this it may seem ridiculous to say, that we are acquainted with few writings which exhibit so much elevation of sentiment, so pure and warm a zeal for the public good, or so just a view of the duties and rights of citizens, as those of Machiavelli. Yet so it is. And even from "The Prince" itself we could select many passages in support of this remark. To a reader of our age and country this inconsistency is, at first, perfectly bewildering. The whole man seems to be an enigma, — a grotesque assemblage of incongruous qualities, — selfishness and generosity, cruelty and benevolence, craft and simplicity, abject villainy and romantic heroism. One sentence is such as a veteran diplomatist would scarcely write in cipher for the direction of his most confidential spy; the next seems to be extracted from a theme composed by an ardent schoolboy on the death of Leonidas. An act of dexterous perfidy, and an act of patriotic self-devotion, call forth the same kind and the same degree of respectful admiration. The moral sensibility of the writer seems at once to be morbidly obtuse and morbidly acute. Two characters altogether dissimilar are united in him. They are not merely joined, but interwoven. They are the warp and the woof of his mind; and their combination, like that of the variegated threads in shot silk, gives to the whole texture a glancing and ever-changing appearance. The explanation might have been easy, if he had been a very weak or a very affected man. But he was evidently neither the one nor the other. His works prove beyond all contradiction, that his understanding was strong, his taste pure, and his sense of the ridiculous exquisitely keen.

This is strange — and yet the strangest is behind. There is no reason whatever to think, that those amongst whom he lived saw anything shocking or incongruous in his writings. Abundant proofs remain of the high estimation in which both his works and his person were held by the most respectable among his contemporaries. Clement VII. patronized the publication of those very books which the council of Trent, in the following generation, pronounced unfit for the perusal of Christians. Some members of the democratical party censured the secretary for

dedicating "The Prince" to a patron who bore the unpopular name of Medici. But to those immoral doctrines, which have since called forth such severe reprehensions, no exception appears to have been taken. The cry against them was first raised beyond the Alps — and seems to have been heard with amazement in Italy. The earliest assailant, as far as we are aware, was a countryman of our own, Cardinal Pole. The author of the "Anti-Machiavelli" was a French Protestant.

It is, therefore, in the state of moral feeling among the Italians of those times, that we must seek for the real explanation of what seems most mysterious in the life and writings of this remarkable man. . . .

Every age and every nation has certain characteristic vices, which prevail almost universally, which scarcely any person scruples to avow, and which even rigid moralists but faintly censure. Succeeding generations change the fashion of their morals, with their hats and their coaches; take some other kind of wickedness under their patronage, and wonder at the depravity of their ancestors. Nor is this all. Posterity, that high court of appeal which is never tired of eulogizing its own justice and discernment, acts, on such occasions, like a Roman dictator after a general mutiny. Finding the delinquents too numerous to be all punished, it selects some of them at hazard to bear the whole penalty of an offense in which they are not more deeply implicated than those who escape. Whether decimation be a convenient mode of military execution, we known not; but we solemnly protest against the introduction of such a principle into the philosophy of history.

In the present instance, the lot has fallen on Machiavelli: a man whose public conduct was upright and honorable, whose views of morality, where they differed from those of the persons around him, seem to have differed for the better, and whose only fault was, that, having adopted some of the maxims then generally received, he arranged them more luminously, and expressed them more forcibly than any other writer.

From the review of Perier's Edition of "Machiavelli."
Edinburg Review, 1827.

NICCOLO MACHIAVELLI

(1469-1527)

MACHIAVELLI, whose "Prince" is one of the most celebrated books in the prose literature of Europe was born at Florence, Italy, May 3d, 1469. His family was noble, and though it had fallen into decay and poverty, he was educated as liberally as the times allowed. He was a classical scholar of extensive attainment, a poet and historian as well as an essayist. Had he not written "The Prince" his name might be held in high repute, as indeed it might at any rate if several of the chapters which make that work deservedly infamous could have been cut out of it before its publication. In "The Prince" in. giving his views of the proper political management of a state he justifies as a rule of conduct the common political practices of his day. It has been said in excusing him that he represented the manners of his age, but it is quite true, and notorious as it is true, that what he recommends with such flagrancy is practiced in modern politics even beyond the flagrancy of his recommendation. It is as inevitable in politics as embezzlement is in the circulation of money and robbery in the exchange of commodities; but while civilization will recognize and deal with its existence as a fact, the whole object of civilization is to minimize its power for evil and if possible to eradicate it. In the measure in which civilization fails of this, it degenerates into an expression of that mere barbaric desire to take all possible advantage which as it expresses itself in the fraud which precedes violence is often called "Machiavellism." Morally unsound and on this point intellectually defective, Machiavelli had great powers of mind and as he used them in politics for the unification of Italy he has come into greatly increased favor with his countrymen during the second half of the nineteenth century. He died at Florence, June 22d, 1527. His principal works besides "The Prince" are a "History of Florence," a treatise on the "Art of War" and "Discourses" on Livy and on government.

appearance of craft, and thoroughly to understand the art of feigning and dissembling; for men are generally so simple and so weak, that he who wishes to deceive easily finds dupes.

One example, taken from the history of our own times, will be sufficient. Pope Alexander VI. played during his whole life a game of deception; and notwithstanding his faithless conduct was extremely well known, his artifices always proved successful. Oaths and protestations cost him nothing; never did a prince so often break his word or pay less regard to his engagements. This was because he so well understood this chapter in the art of government.

It is not necessary, however, for a prince to possess all the good qualities I have enumerated, but it is indispensable that he should appear to have them. I will even venture to affirm, that it is sometimes dangerous to use, though it is always useful to seem to possess them. A prince should earnestly endeavor to gain the reputation of kindness, clemency, piety, justice, and fidelity to his engagements. He ought to possess all these good qualities, but still retain such power over himself as to display their opposites whenever it may be expedient. I maintain that a prince, and especially a new prince, cannot with impunity exercise all the virtues, because his own self-preservation will often compel him to violate the laws of charity, religion, and humanity. He should habituate himself to bend easily to the various circumstances which may from time to time surround him. In a word, it will be as useful to him to persevere in the path of rectitude, while he feels no inconvenience in doing so, as to know how to deviate from it when circumstances dictate such a course. He should make it a rule above all things, never to utter anything which does not breathe of kindness, justice, good faith, and piety; this last quality it is most important for him to appear to possess, as men in general judge more from appearance than from reality. All men have eyes, but few have the gift of penetration. Every one sees your exterior, but few can discern what you have in your heart; and those few dare not oppose the voice of the multitude, who have the majesty of their prince on their side. Now, in forming a judgment of the minds of men, and more especially of princes, as we cannot recur to any tribunal, we must attend only to results. Let it then be the prince's chief care to maintain his authority; the means he employes, be what they may, will, for this purpose, always appear

WHETHER PRINCES OUGHT TO BE FAITHFUL TO THEIR ENGAGEMENTS

IT IS unquestionably very praiseworthy in princes to be faithful to their engagements; but among those of the present day, who have been distinguished for great exploits, few indeed have been remarkable for this virtue, or have scrupled to deceive others who may have relied on their good faith.

It should, therefore, be known, that there are two ways of deciding any contest; the one by laws, the other by force. The first is peculiar to men, the second to beasts; but when laws are not sufficiently powerful, it is necessary to recur to force; a prince ought therefore to understand how to use both these descriptions of arms. This doctrine is admirably illustrated to us by the ancient poets in the allegorical history of the education of Achilles, and many other princes of antiquity, by the centaur Chiron, who, under the double form of man and beast, taught those who were destined to govern, that it was their duty to use by turns the arms adapted to both these natures, seeing that one without the other, cannot be of any durable advantage. Now, as a prince must learn how to act the part of a beast sometimes, he should make the fox and the lion his patterns. The first can but feebly defend himself against the wolf, and the latter readily falls into such snares as are laid for him. From the fox, therefore, a prince will learn dexterity, in avoiding snares; and from the lion, how to employ his strength to keep the wolves in awe. But they who entirely rely upon the lion's strength, will not always meet with success; in other words a prudent prince cannot and ought not to keep his word, except when he can do it without injury to himself, or when the circumstances under which he contracted the engagement still exist.

I should be cautious in inculcating such a precept if all men were good; but as the generality of mankind are wicked, and ever ready to break their words, a prince should not pique himself in keeping his more scrupulously, especially as it is always easy to justify a breach of faith on his part. I could give numerous proofs of this, and show numberless engagements and treaties which have been violated by the treachery of princes, and that those who enacted the part of the fox, have always succeeded best in their affairs. It is necessary, however, to disguise the

honorable and meet applause; for the vulgar are ever caught by appearances, and judge only by the event. And as the world is chiefly composed of such as are called the vulgar, the voice of the few is seldom or never heard or regarded.

There is a prince now alive (whose name it may not be proper to mention) who ever preaches the doctrines of peace and good faith; but if he had observed either the one or the other, he would long ago have lost both his reputation and dominions.

Complete. From "The Prince," chap. xviii.

HOW FAR FORTUNE INFLUENCES THE THINGS OF THIS WORLD, AND HOW FAR SHE MAY BE RESISTED

IKNOW that several have thought, and many still are of the opinion, that all sublunary events are governed either by Divine Providence or by chance, in such a manner that human wisdom has no share in their direction; and hence they infer that man should abstain from interfering with their course, and leave everything to its natural tendency.

The revolutions which in our times are of such frequent recurrence, seem to support this doctrine, and I own, that I, myself, am almost inclined to favor such opinions, particularly when I consider how far those events surpass all human conjecture; yet, as we confessedly possess a free will, it must, I think, be allowed, that chance does not so far govern the world as to leave no province for the exercise of human prudence.

For my own part, I cannot help comparing the blind power of chance to a rapid river, which, having overflowed its banks, inundates the plain, uproots trees, carries away houses and lands, and sweeps all before it in its destructive progress; everybody flies possessing neither resolution nor power to oppose its fury. But this should not discourage us, when the river has returned within its natural limits from constructing dikes and banks to prevent a recurrence of similar disasters. It is the same with Fortune; she exercises her power when we oppose no barrier to her progress.

If we cast our eyes on Italy, which has been the theatre of these revolutions, and consider the causes by which they have been provoked, we shall find it to be a defenseless country. If she had been properly fortified like Germany, Spain, or France, such inundations of foreigners would never have happened, or at least their irruptions would have been attended with less devastation.

Let this suffice in general concerning the necessity of opposing fortune. But to descend to particulars. It is no uncommon thing to see a prince fall from prosperity to adversity, without our being able to attribute his fate to any change in conduct or character; for, as I have already shown at large, he who relies solely on Fortune, must be ruined inevitably whenever she abandons him.

Those princes who adapt their conduct to circumstances are rarely unfortunate. Fortune is only changeable to those who cannot conform themselves to the varying exigencies of the times; for we see different men take different courses to obtain the end they have in view; for instance, in pursuit of riches or glory, one prosecutes his object at random, the other with caution and prudence; one employs art, the other force; one is impetuosity itself, the other all patience; means by which each may severally succeed. It also happens that of two who follow the same route, one may arrive at his destination, and the other fail; and that if two other persons, whose dispositions are diametrically opposite, pursue the same object by wholly different means, yet both shall equally prosper; which is entirely owing to the temper of the times, which always prove favorable or adverse, according as men conform to them.

Circumstances also frequently decide whether a prince conducts himself well or ill on any particular occasion. There are times when an extraordinary degree of prudence is necessary, there are others when the prince should know how to trust some things to chance; but there is nothing more difficult than suddenly to change his conduct and character, sometimes from inability to resist his old habits and inclinations, at others, from want of resolution to quit a course in which he had always been successful.

Julius II., who was of a fiery and violent disposition, succeeded in all his enterprises; doubtless, because a prince of such a character was best adapted to the circumstances under which the church was then governed by this pontiff. Witness his first invasion of the territory of Bologna, in the life of John Bentivoglio, which gave great umbrage to the Venetians and the kings of France and Spain, but none of them dared to interfere. The

first, because they did not feel themselves strong enough to cope with a pontiff of his character; Spain, because she was engaged in the conquest of Naples; and France, besides having an interest in keeping fair with Julius, wished still to humble the Venetians, so that she, without hesitation, granted the pope all the assistance he required.

Julius II., therefore, by a precipitate mode of proceeding, succeeded in an enterprise which could not have been accomplished by cool and deliberate measures. He would unquestionably have failed had he given Spain and the Venetians time to reflect on his designs, and if he had allowed France the opportunity of amusing him by excuses and delays.

Julius II. displayed in all his enterprises the same character of violence, and his successes have in that respect fully justified; but he did not, perhaps, live long enough to experience the inconstancy of fortune, for had an occasion unexpectedly occurred in which it would have been necessary to act with prudence and circumspection, he would infallibly have been ruined, in consequence of that impetuosity and inflexibility of character which wholly governed him.

From all these circumstances we may conclude, that those who cannot change their system when occasion requires it, will no doubt continue prosperous as long as they glide with the stream of Fortune; but when that turns against them, they are ruined, from not being able to follow that blind goddess, through all her variations.

Besides, I think that it is better to be bold than too circumspect; because Fortune is of a sex that likes not a tardy wooer, and repulses all who are not ardent; she declares also, more frequently, in favor of those who are young, because they are bold and enterprising.

Complete. From «The Prince,» chap. **xxv.**

HENRY MACKENZIE

(1745–1831)

HE LOUNGER, edited by Henry Mackenzie, has the distinction of being among the first of British periodicals to recognize the genius of Robert Burns. Mackenzie is an essayist of the school of Steele and Addison, and although some of his critics have been at unnecessary pains to say that he is "in no wise a great writer," he is often entertaining and frequently useful. He wrote, besides his essays, several novels, including "The Man of the World," "Julia de Boubigné," and "The Man of Feeling." The latter work became celebrated and is still remembered. Mackenzie was born at Edinburgh, Scotland, in August, 1745. He died there January 14th, 1831.

AN OLD COUNTRYHOUSE AND AN OLD LADY

I HAVE long cultivated a talent very fortunate for a man of my disposition, that of traveling in my easy-chair; of transporting myself, without stirring from my parlor, to distant places and to absent friends; of drawing scenes in my mind's eye, and of peopling them with the groups of fancy, or the society of remembrance. When I have sometimes lately felt the dreariness of the town, deserted by my acquaintance; when I have returned from the coffeehouse, where the boxes were unoccupied, and strolled out from my accustomed walk, which even the lame beggar had left, I was fain to shut myself up in my room, order a dish of my best tea (for there is a sort of melancholy which disposes one to make much of oneself), and calling up the powers of memory and imagination, leave the solitary town for a solitude more interesting, which my younger days enjoyed in the country, which I think, and if I am wrong I do not wish to be undeceived, was the most Elysian spot in the world.

'Twas at an old lady's, a relation and godmother of mine, where a particular incident occasioned my being left during the vacation of two successive seasons. Her house was formed out of the remains of an old Gothic castle, of which one tower was

still almost entire; it was tenanted by kindly daws and swallows. Beneath, in a modernized part of the house, resided the mistress of the mansion. The house was skirted by a few majestic elms and beeches, and the stumps of several others showed that once they had been more numerous. To the west a clump of firs covered a rugged rocky dell, where the rooks claimed a prescriptive seigniory. Through this a dashing rivulet forced its way, which afterwards grew quiet in its progress, and gurgling gently through a piece of downy meadow ground, crossed the bottom of the garden, where a little rustic paling inclosed a washing green, and a wicker seat, fronting the south, was placed for the accommodation of the old lady, whose lesser tour, when her fields did not require a visit, used to terminate in this spot. Here, too, were ranged the hives for her bees, whose hum, in a still warm sunshine, soothed the good old lady's indolence, while their proverbial industry was sometimes quoted for the instruction of her washers. The brook ran brawling through some underwood on the outside of the garden, and soon after formed a little cascade, which fell into the river that winded through a valley in front of the house. When haymaking or harvest was going on, my godmother took her long stick in her hand, and overlooked the labors of the mowers or reapers; though I believe there was little thrift in the superintendency, as the visit generally cost her a draught of beer or a dram, to encourage their diligence.

Within doors she had so able an assistant, that her labor was little. In that department an old manservant was her minister, the father of my Peter, who serves me not the less faithfully that we have gathered nuts together in my godmother's hazel bank. This old butler (I call him by his title of honor, though in truth he had many subordinate offices) had originally enlisted with her husband, who went into the army a youth (though he afterwards married and became a country gentleman), had been his servant abroad, and attended him during his last illness at home. His best hat, which he wore on Sundays, with a scarlet waistcoat of his master, had still a cockade in it.

Her husband's books were in a room at the top of a screw staircase, which had scarce been opened since his death; but her own library, for Sabbath or rainy days, was ranged in a little book press in the parlor. It consisted, so far as I can remember, of several volumes of sermons, a Concordance, Thomas à Kempis, Antoninus's "Meditations," the works of the author of the

"Whole Duty of Man," and a translation of Boethius; the original editions of the Spectator and Guardian, Cowley's "Poems" (of which I had lost a volume soon after I first came about her house), Baker's "Chronicle," Burnet's "History of His Own Times," Lamb's "Royal Cookery," Abercromby's "Scots Warriors," and Nisbet's "Heraldry."

The subject of the last-mentioned book was my godmother's strong ground; and she could disentangle a point of genealogy beyond any one I ever knew. She had an excellent memory for anecdotes, and her stories, though sometimes long, were never tiresome; for she had been a woman of great beauty and accomplishment in her youth, and had kept such company as made the drama of her stories respectable and interesting. She spoke frequently of such of her own family as she remembered when a child, but scarcely ever of those she had lost, though one could see that she thought of them often. She had buried a beloved husband and four children. Her youngest, Edward, "her beautiful, her brave," fell in Flanders, and was not entombed with his ancestors. His picture, done when a child, an artless red and white portrait, smelling at a nosegay, but very like withal, hung at her bedside, and his sword and gorget were crossed under it. When she spoke of a soldier, it was in a style above her usual simplicity; there was a sort of swell in her language, which sometimes a tear (for her age had not lost the privilege of tears) made still more eloquent. She kept her sorrows, like her devotions that solaced them, sacred to herself. They threw nothing of gloom over her deportment; a gentle shade only, like the fleckered clouds of summer, that increase, not diminish, the benignity of the season.

She had few neighbors, and still fewer visitors; but her reception of such as did visit her was cordial in the extreme. She pressed a little too much, perhaps; but there was so much heart and good-will in her importunity, as made her good things seem better than those of any other table. Nor was her attention confined only to the good fare of her guests, though it might have flattered her vanity more than that of most exhibitors of good dinners, because the cookery was generally directed by herself. Their servants lived as well in her hall, and their horses in her stable. She looked after the airing of their sheets, and saw their fires mended if the night was cold. Her old butler, who rose betimes, would never suffer anybody to mount his horse fasting.

The parson of the parish was her guest every Sunday, and said prayers in the evening. To say truth, he was no great genius, nor much of a scholar. I believe my godmother knew rather more of divinity than he did; but she received from him information of another sort,—he told her who were the poor, the sick, the dying of the parish, and she had some assistance, some comfort for them all.

I could draw the old lady at this moment! dressed in gray, with a clean white hood nicely plaited (for she was somewhat finical about the neatness of her person), sitting in her straight-backed elbowchair, which stood in a large window, scooped out of the thickness of the ancient wall. The middle panes of the window were of painted glass—the story of Joseph and his brethren. On the outside waved a honeysuckle tree, which often threw its shade across her book or her work; but she would not allow it to be cut down. "It has stood there many a day," said she, "and we old inhabitants should bear with one another." Methinks I see her thus seated, her spectacles on, but raised a little on her brow for a pause of explanation, their shagreen case laid between the leaves of a silver-clasped family Bible. On one side, her bell and snuffbox; on the other, her knitting apparatus in a blue damask bag. Between her and the fire an old Spanish pointer, that had formerly been her son Edward's, teased, but not teased out of his gravity, by a little terrier of mine. All this is before me, and I am a hundred miles from town, its inhabitants, and its business. In town I may have seen such a figure; but the country scenery around, like the tasteful frame of an excellent picture, gives it a heightening, a relief, which it would lose in any other situation.

Some of my readers, perhaps, will look with little relish on the portrait. I know it is an egotism in me to talk of its value; but over this dish of tea, and in such a temper of mind, one is given to egotism. It will be only adding another to say that when I recall the rural scene of the good old lady's abode, her simple, her innocent, her useful employments, the afflictions she sustained in this world, the comforts she drew from another, I feel a serenity of soul, a benignity of affections, which I am sure confer happiness, and, I think, must promote virtue.

Complete. From the Lounger.

SIR JAMES MACKINTOSH

(1765–1832)

IR JAMES MACKINTOSH was born at Aldourie, Scotland, October 24th, 1765. He was educated for the bar, and in 1795 began the practice of his profession in London. In 1803 he went to India in the government service, and in 1806 became Judge of the Court of Vice-Admiralty at Bombay. Returning to England, he entered Parliament, where he rendered civilization the distinguished service of contributing to shape the policy under which England abandoned the coercive ideas of Lord North in her treatment of Canada and Australia, and virtually erected them into independent states, voluntarily recognizing English sovereignty. Mackintosh died in 1832. Among his more celebrated works are the "Vindiciæ Gallicæ," which he published in 1791 as a reply to Burke's "Reflections on the French Revolution"; his "Dissertation on the Progress of Ethical Philosophy," which appeared in the seventh edition of the Encyclopædia Britannica; his "History of the Revolution in England in 1688," and his "Essays" which are written with much strength and dignity. He was not only a philosopher, historian, essayist, and publicist, but also a most effective orator; and his speech in defense of Peltier is one of the most celebrated of British forensic orations.

ON THE GENIUS OF BACON

"HISTORY," says Lord Bacon, "is natural, civil or ecclesiastical, or literary; whereof of the first three I allow as extant, the fourth I note as deficient. For no man hath propounded to himself the general state of learning, to be described and represented from age to age, as many have done the works of nature, and the state civil and ecclesiastical; without which the history of the world seemeth to me to be as the statue of Polyphemus with his eye out; that part being wanting which doth most show the spirit and life of the person. And yet I am not ignorant that in divers particular sciences, as of the jurisconsults, the mathematicians, the rhetoricians, the philosophers, there are set down some small memorials of the schools, — of authors of books; so likewise some barren relations touching the invention of arts

or usages. But a just story of learning, containing the antiquities and originals of knowledges, and their sects, their inventions, their traditions, their divers administrations and managings, their oppositions, decays, depressions, oblivions, removes, with the causes and occasions of them, and all other events concerning learning throughout the ages of the world, I may truly affirm to be wanting. The use and end of which work I do not so much design for curiosity, or satisfaction of those who are lovers of learning, but chiefly for a more serious and grave purpose, which is this, in few words, 'that it will make learned men wise in the use and administration of learning.'"

Though there are passages in the writings of Lord Bacon more splendid than the above, few, probably, better display the union of all the qualities which characterized his philosophical genius. He has in general inspired a fervor of admiration which vents itself in indiscriminate praise, and is very adverse to a calm examination of the character of his understanding, which was very peculiar, and on that account described with more than ordinary imperfection, by that unfortunately vague and weak part of language which attempts to distinguish the varieties of mental superiority. To this cause it may be ascribed, that perhaps no great man has been either more ignorantly censured, or more uninstructively commended. It is easy to describe his transcendent merit in general terms of commendation; for some of his great qualities lie on the surface of his writings. But that in which he most excelled all other men was the range and compass of his intellectual view and the power of contemplating many and distant objects together without indistinctness or confusion, which he himself has called the "discursive" or "comprehensive" understanding. This wide-ranging intellect was illuminated by the brightest Fancy that ever contented itself with the office of only ministering to Reason; and from this singular relation of the two grand faculties of man, it has resulted that his philosophy, though illustrated still more than adorned by the utmost splendor of imagery, continues still subject to the undivided supremacy of Intellect. In the midst of all the prodigality of an imagination which, had it been independent, would have been poetical, his opinions remained severely rational

It is not so easy to conceive, or at least to describe, other equally essential elements of his greatness, and conditions of his success. His is probably a single instance of a mind which, in philosophizing, always reaches the point of elevation whence the whole prospect is commanded, without ever rising to such a distance as to lose a distinct perception of every part of it. It is, perhaps, not less singular, that his philosophy should be founded at once on disregard for the authority of men, and on reverence for the boundaries prescribed by nature to human inquiry; that he who thought so little of what man had done hoped so highly of what he could do; that so daring an innovator in science should be so wholly exempt from the love of singularity or paradox; and that the same man who renounced imaginary provinces in the empire of science, and withdrew its landmarks within the limits of experience, should also exhort posterity to push their conquests to its utmost verge, with a boldness which will be fully justified only by the discoveries of ages from which we are yet far distant.

No man ever united a more poetical style to a less poetical philosophy. One great end of his discipline is to prevent mysticism and fanaticism from obstructing the pursuit of truth. With a less brilliant fancy, he would have had a mind less qualified for philosophical inquiry. His fancy gave him that power of illustrative metaphor, by which he seemed to have invented again the part of language which respects philosophy; and it rendered new truths more distinctly visible even to his own eye, in their bright clothing of imagery. Without it, he must, like others, have been driven to the fabrication of uncouth technical terms, which repel the mind, either by vulgarity or pedantry, instead of gently leading it to novelties in science, through agreeable analogies with objects already familiar. A considerable portion, doubtless, of the courage with which he undertook the reformation of philosophy, was caught from the general spirit of his extraordinary age, when the mind of Europe was yet agitated by the joy and pride of emancipation from long bondage. The beautiful mythology, and the poetical history of the ancient world,—not yet become trivial or pedantic,—appeared before his eyes in all their freshness and lustre. To the general reader they were then a discovery as recent as the world disclosed by Columbus. The ancient literature, on which his imagination looked back for illustration, had then as much the charm of novelty as that rising philosophy through which his reason dared to look onward to some of the last periods in its unceasing and resistless course.

In order to form a just estimate of this wonderful person, it is essential to fix steadily in our minds, what he was not,—what

he did not do,—and what he professed neither to be, nor to do. He was not what is called a metaphysician: his plans for the improvement of science were not inferred by abstract reasoning from any of those primary principles to which the philosphers of Greece struggled to fasten their systems. Hence he has been treated as empirical and superficial by those who take to themselves the exclusive name of profound speculators. He was not, on the other hand, a mathematician, an astronomer, a physiologist, a chemist. He was not eminently conversant with the particular truths of any of those sciences which existed in his time. For this reason he was underrated even by men themselves of the highest merit, and by some who had acquired the most just reputation, by adding new facts to the stock of certain knowledge. It is not, therefore, very surprising to find that Harvey, "though the friend as well as physician of Bacon, though he esteemed him much for his wit and style, would not allow him to be a great philosopher"; but said to Aubrey, "He writes philosophy like a Lord Chancellor,"—"in derision,"—as the honest biographer thinks fit expressly to add. On the same ground, though in a manner not so agreeable to the nature of his own claims on reputation, Mr. Hume has decided that Bacon was not so great a man as Galileo, because he was not so great an astronomer. The same sort of injustice to his memory has been more often committed than avowed, by professors of the exact and the experimental sciences, who are accustomed to regard, as the sole test of service to Knowledge, a palpable addition to her store. It is very true that he made no discoveries; but his life was employed in teaching the method by which discoveries are made. This distinction was early observed by that ingenious poet and amiable man on whom we, by our unmerited neglect, have taken too severe a revenge, for the exaggerated praises bestowed on him by our ancestors:—

"Bacon, like Moses, led us forth at last,
    The barren wilderness he passed
    Did on the very border stand
    Of the blest promised land;
    And from the mountain top of his exalted wit,
    Saw it himself, and showed us it."

The writings of Bacon do not even abound with remarks so capable of being separated from the mass of previous knowledge and reflection, that they can be called new. This, at least, is

very far from their greatest distinction; and where such remarks occur, they are presented more often as examples of his general method than as important on their own separate account. In physics, which presented the principal field for discovery, and which owe all that they are, or can be, to his method and spirit, the experiments and observations which he either made or registered, form the least valuable part of his writings, and have furnished some cultivators of that science with an opportunity for an ungrateful triumph over his mistakes. The scattered remarks, on the other hand, of a moral nature, where absolute novelty is precluded by the nature of the subject, manifest most strongly both the superior force and the original bent of his understanding. We more properly contrast than compare the experiments in the "Natural History" with the moral and political observations which enrich the "Advancement of Learning," the speeches, the letters, the "History of Henry VII.," and, above all, the "Essays," a book which, though it has been praised with equal fervor by Voltaire, Johnson, and Burke, has never been characterized with such exact justice and such exquisite felicity of expression as in the discourse of Mr. Stewart. It will serve still more distinctly to mark the natural tendency of his mind, to observe that his moral and political reflections relate to these practical subjects, considered in their most practical point of view; and that he has seldom or never attempted to reduce to theory the infinite particulars of that "civil knowledge," which, as he himself tells us, is, "of all others, most immersed in matter, and hardliest reduced to axiom."

His mind, indeed, was formed and exercised in the affairs of the world; his genius was eminently civil. His understanding was peculiarly fitted for questions of legislation and of policy; though his character was not an instrument well qualified to execute the dictates of his reason. The same civil wisdom which distinguishes his judgments on human affairs may also be traced through his reformation of philosophy. It is a practical judgment applied to science. What he effected was reform in the maxims of state,—a reform which had always before been unsuccessfully pursued in the republic of letters. It is not derived from metaphysical reasoning, nor from scientific detail, but from a species of intellectual prudence, which, on the practical ground of failure and disappointment in the prevalent modes of pursuing knowledge, builds the necessity of alteration, and inculcates

the advantage of administering the sciences on other principles. It is an error to represent him either as imputing fallacy to the syllogistic method, or as professing his principle of induction to be a discovery. The rules and forms of argument will always form an important part of the art of logic; and the method of induction, which is the art of discovery, was so far from being unknown to Aristotle, that it was often faithfully pursued by that great observer. What Bacon aimed at, he accomplished; which was, not to discover new principles, but to excite a new spirit, and to render observation and experiment the predominant characteristics of philosophy. It is for this reason that Bacon could not have been the author of a system or the founder of a sect. He did not deliver opinions; he taught modes of philosophizing. His early immersion in civil affairs fitted him for this species of scientific reformation. His political course, though in itself unhappy, probably conduced to the success, and certainly influenced the character, of the contemplative part of his life. Had it not been for his active habits, it is likely that the pedantry and quaintness of his age would have still more deeply corrupted his significant and majestic style. The force of the illustrations which he takes from his experience of ordinary life is often as remarkable as the beauty of those which he so happily borrows from his study of antiquity. But if we have caught the leading principle of his intellectual character, we must attribute effects still deeper and more extensive, to his familiarity with the active world. It guarded him against vain subtlety and against all speculation that was either visionary or fruitless. It preserved him from the reigning prejudices of contemplative men, and from undue preference to particular parts of knowledge. If he had been exclusively bred in the cloister or the schools, he might not have had courage enough to reform their abuses. It seems necessary that he should have been so placed as to look on science in the free spirit of an intelligent spectator. Without the pride of professors, or the bigotry of their followers, he surveyed from the world the studies which reigned in the schools; and, trying them by their fruits, he saw that they were barren, and therefore pronounced that they were unsound. He himself seems, indeed, to have indicated as clearly as modesty would allow, in a case that concerned himself, and where he departed from an universal and almost natural sentiment, that he regarded scholastic seclusion, then more unsocial and rigorous than it now can be, as a hindrance in the pursuit of knowledge. In one of the noblest passages of his writings, the conclusion of the "Interpretation of Nature," he tells us that: "There is no composition of estate or society, nor order or quality of persons, which have not some point of contrariety towards true knowledge; that monarchies incline wits to profit and pleasure; commonwealths to glory and vanity; universities to sophistry and affectation; cloisters to fables and unprofitable subtlety; study at large to variety; and that it is hard to say whether mixture of contemplations with an active life, or retiring wholly to contemplations, do disable or hinder the mind more."

But, though he was thus free from the prejudices of a science, a school, or a sect, other prejudices of a lower nature, and belonging only to the inferior class of those who conduct civil affairs, have been ascribed to him by encomiasts as well as by opponents. He has been said to consider the great end of science to be the increase of the outward accommodations and enjoyments of human life; we cannot see any foundation for this charge. In laboring, indeed, to correct the direction of study, and to withdraw it from these unprofitable subtleties, it was necessary to attract it powerfully towards outward acts and works. He no doubt duly valued "the dignity of this end, the endowment of man's life with new commodities"; and he strikingly observes that the most poetical people of the world had admitted the inventors of the useful and manual arts among the highest beings in their beautiful mythology. Had he lived to the age of Watt and Davy, he would not have been of the vulgar and contracted mind of those who cease to admire grand exertions of intellect, because they are useful to mankind; but he would certainly have considered their great works rather as tests of the progress of knowledge than as parts of its highest end. His important questions to the doctors of his time were: "Is truth ever barren? Are we the richer by one poor invention, by reason of all the learning that hath been these many hundred years?" His judgment, we may also hear from himself: "Francis Bacon thought in this manner. The knowledge whereof the world is now possessed, especially that of nature, extendeth not to magnitude and certainty of works." He found knowledge barren; he left it fertile. He did not underrate the utility of particular inventions; but it is evident that he valued them most,

as being themselves among the highest exertions of superior intellect,—as being monuments of the progress of knowledge,—as being the bands of that alliance between action and speculation, wherefrom spring an appeal to experience and utility, checking the proneness of the philosopher to extreme refinements, while teaching men to revere, and exciting them to pursue science by these splendid proofs of its beneficial power. Had he seen the change in this respect, which, produced chiefly in his own country by the pirit of his own philosophy, has made some degree of science almost necessary to the subsistence and fortune of large bodies of men, he would assuredly have regarded it as an additional security for the future growth of the human understanding. He taught, as he tells us, the means, not of the "amplification of the power of one man over his country, nor of the amplification of the power of that country over other nations, but the amplification of the power and kingdom of mankind over the world,"—"a restitution of man to the sovereignty of nature,"—"and the enlarging the bounds of human empire to the effecting all things possible."—From the enlargement of reason, he did not separate the growth of virtue, for he thought that "truth and goodness were one, differing but as the seal and the print; for truth prints goodness."

As civil history teaches statesmen to profit by the faults of their predecessors, he proposes that the history of philosophy should teach, by example, "learned men to become wise in the administration of learning." Early immersed in civil affairs, and deeply imbued with their spirit, his mind in this place contemplates science only through the analogy of government, and considers principles of philosophizing as the easiest maxims of policy for the guidance of reason. It seems also that in describing the objects of a history of philosophy, and the utility to be derived from it, he discloses the principle of his own exertions in behalf of knowledge;—whereby a reform in its method and maxims, justified by the experience of their injurious effects, is conducted with a judgment analogous to that civil prudence which guides a wise lawgiver. If (as may not improperly be concluded from this passage) the reformation of science was suggested to Lord Bacon by a review of the history of philosophy, it must be owned that his outline of that history has a very important relation to the general character of his philosophical genius. The smallest circumstances attendant on that outline

serve to illustrate the powers and habits of thought which distinguished its author. It is an example of his faculty of anticipating,—not insulated facts or single discoveries,—but (what from its complexity and refinement seem much more to defy the power of prophecy) the tendencies of study, and the modes of thinking, which were to prevail in distant generations, that the parts which he had chosen to unfold or enforce in the Latin versions are those which a thinker of the present age would deem both most excellent and most arduous in a history of philosophy;—"the causes of literary revolutions; the study of contemporary writers, not merely as the most authentic sources of information, but as enabling the historian to preserve in his own description the peculiar color of every age, and to recall its literary genius from the dead." This outline has the uncommon distinction of being at once original and complete. In this province, Bacon had no forerunner; and the most successful follower will be he who most faithfully observes his precepts.

Here, as in every province of knowledge, he concludes his review of the performances and prospects of the human understanding, by considering their subservience to the grand purpose of improving the condition, the faculties, and the nature of man, without which, indeed, science would be no more than a beautiful ornament, and literature would rank no higher than a liberal amusement. Yet it must be acknowledged that he rather perceived than felt the connection of Truth and Good. Whether he lived too early to have sufficient experience of the moral benefit of civilization, or his mind had early acquired too exclusive an interest in science to look frequently beyond its advancement; or whether the infirmities and calamities of his life had blighted his feelings, and turned away his eyes from the active world;—to whatever cause we may ascribe the defect, certain it is that his works want one excellence of the highest kind, which they would have possessed if he had habitually represented the advancement of knowledge as the most effectual means of realizing the hopes of benevolence for the human race.

Complete. From the Edinburgh Review, Vol. XXVI.

JAMES MADISON

(1751–1836)

AMES MADISON, fourth President of the United States, was born at Port Conway, Virginia, March 16th, 1751. His place as an essayist is determined by the fact that he was associated with Hamilton and Jay in writing the papers of the Federalist (1787–88). Twenty-nine of the eighty-five essays in the series are by Madison, five by Jay, and the rest by Hamilton. Madison's style is clear and forcible. He had no intention of attempting to be entertaining, and no one is likely to read many of the Federalist essays merely for amusement; but Madison did through these essays more than was done by any other writer, except Hamilton, to bring about the adoption of the Federal Constitution, and they will always be studied by those who wish to have a definite understanding of the principles underlying American institutions. Madison was a man of thorough intellectual training and wide reading. He graduated at Princeton College in 1771 and was almost immediately drawn into the movement which culminated in the Revolution. He was a member of the Continental Congress, of the Constitutional Convention of 1787, and of the Federal Congress from 1789 to 1797. The Virginia Resolutions of 1798, which represented a sharply defined issue with the views of the Federalist, were drawn by him; but as Madison interpreted them they did not trouble him with any sense of inconsistency, and he resented a subsequent attempt to base the theory of Nullification upon them. His authorship of them led to his choice as Secretary of State under Jefferson, and to his election to the Presidency as Jefferson's successor (1809–17). He died at Montpelier, Orange County, Virginia, June 28th, 1836.

GENERAL VIEW OF THE POWERS PROPOSED TO BE VESTED IN THE UNION

THE constitution proposed by the convention may be considered under two general points of view. The first relates to the sum or quantity of power which it vests in the government, including the restraints imposed on the states. The second, to the particular structure of the government, and the distribution of this power among its several branches.

Under the first view of the subject, two important questions arise: 1. Whether any part of the powers transferred to the general government be unnecessary or improper. 2. Whether the entire mass of them be dangerous to the portion of jurisdiction left in the several states.

Is the aggregate power of the general government greater than ought to have been vested in it? This is the first question.

It cannot have escaped those, who have attended with candor to the arguments employed against the extensive powers of the government, that the authors of them have very little considered how far these powers were necessary means of attaining a necessary end. They have chosen rather to dwell on the inconveniences which must be unavoidably blended with all political advantages; and on the possible abuses which must be incident to every power or trust, of which a beneficial use can be made. This method of handling the subject cannot impose on the good sense of the people of America. It may display the subtlety of the writer; it may open a boundless field for rhetoric and declamation; it may inflame the passions of the unthinking. But cool and candid people will at once reflect that the purest of human blessings must have a portion of alloy in them; that the choice must always be made, if not of the lesser evil, at least of the greater, not the perfect good; and that in every political institution, a power to advance the public happiness involves a discretion which may be misapplied and abused. They will see, therefore, that in all cases where power is to be conferred, the point first to be decided is whether such a power be necessary to the public good; as the next will be, in case of an affirmative decision, to guard as effectually as possible against a perversion of the power to the public detriment.

That we may form a correct judgment on this subject, it will be proper to review the several powers conferred on the government of the union; and that this may be more conveniently done, they may be reduced into different classes, as they relate to the following different objects: 1. Security against foreign danger; 2. Regulation of the intercourse with foreign nations; 3. Maintenance of harmony and proper intercourse among the states; 4. Certain miscellaneous objects of general utility; 5. Restraint of the states from certain injurious acts; 6. Provisions for giving due efficacy to all these powers.

The powers falling within the first class are those of declaring war and granting letters of marque, of providing armies and fleets, of regulating and calling forth the militia, of levying and borrowing money.

Security against foreign danger is one of the primitive objects of civil society. It is an avowed and essential object of the American union. The powers requisite for attaining it must be effectually confided to the federal councils.

Is the power of declaring war necessary? No man will answer this question in the negative. It would be superfluous, therefore, to enter into a proof of the affirmative. The existing confederation establishes this power in the most ample form.

Is the power of raising armies and equipping fleets necessary? This is involved in the foregoing power. It is involved in the power of self-defense.

But was it necessary to give an indefinite power of raising troops, as well as providing fleets; and of maintaining both in peace, as well as in war?

The answer to these questions has been too far anticipated, in another place, to admit an extensive discussion of them in this place. The answer, indeed, seems to be so obvious and conclusive as scarcely to justify such a discussion in any place. With what color of propriety could the force necessary for defense be limited, by those who cannot limit the force of offense? If a federal constitution could chain the ambition, or set bounds to the exertions of all other nations, then, indeed, might it prudently chain the discretion of its own government, and set bounds to the exertions for its own safety.

How could a readiness for war in time of peace be safely prohibited, unless we could prohibit, in like manner, the preparations and establishments of every hostile nation? The means of security can only be regulated by the means and the danger of attack. They will, in fact, be ever determined by these rules, and by no other. It is in vain to oppose constitutional barriers to the impulse of self-preservation. It is worse than in vain, because it plants in the constitution itself necessary usurpations of power, every precedent of which is a germ of unnecessary and multiplied repetitions. If one nation maintains constantly a disciplined army, ready for the service of ambition or revenge, it obliges the most pacific nations, who may be within the reach of its enterprises, to take corresponding precautions. The fifteenth century was the

unhappy epoch of military establishments in time of peace. They were introduced by Charles VII. of France. All Europe has followed, or been forced into the example. Had the example not been followed by other nations, all Europe must long ago have worn the chains of a universal monarch. Were every nation, except France, now to disband its peace establishment, the same event might follow. The veteran legions of Rome were an overmatch for the undisciplined valor of all other nations, and rendered her mistress of the world.

Not less true is it that the liberties of Rome proved the final victim to her military triumphs, and that the liberties of Europe, as far as they ever existed, have, with few exceptions, been the price of her military establishments. A standing force, therefore, is a dangerous, at the same time that it may be a necessary, provision. On the smallest scale it has its inconveniences. On an extensive scale its consequences may be fatal. On any scale, it is an object of laudable circumspection and precaution. A wise nation will combine all these considerations; and whilst it does not rashly preclude itself from any resource which may become essential to its safety, will exert all its prudence in diminishing both the necessity and the danger of resorting to one, which may be inauspicious to its liberties.

The clearest marks of this prudence are stamped on the proposed constitution. The union itself, which it cements and secures, destroys every pretext for a military establishment which could be dangerous. America united, with a handful of troops, or without a single soldier, exhibits a more forbidding posture, to foreign ambition, than America disunited, with a hundred thousand veterans ready for combat. It was remarked, on a former occasion, that the want of this pretext had saved the liberties of one nation in Europe. Being rendered, by her insular situation, and her maritime resources, impregnable to the armies of her neighbors, the rulers of Great Britain have never been able, by real or artificial dangers, to cheat the public into an extensive peace establishment. The distance of the United States from the powerful nations of the world gives them the same happy security. A dangerous establishment can never be necessary or plausible, so long as they continue a united people. But let it never for a moment be forgotten that they are indebted for this advantage to their union alone. The moment of its dissolution will be the date of a new order of things. The

fears of the weaker or the ambition of the stronger states or confederacies will set the same example in the New as Charles VII. did in the Old World. The example will be followed here, from the same motives which produced universal imitation there. Instead of deriving from our situation the precious advantage which Great Britain has derived from hers, the face of America will be but a copy of that of the continent of Europe. It will present liberty everywhere crushed between standing armies and perpetual taxes. The fortunes of disunited America will be even more disastrous than those of Europe. The sources of evil in the latter are confined to her own limits. No superior powers of another quarter of the globe, intrigue among her rival nations, inflame their mutual animosities, and render them the instruments of foreign ambition, jealousy, and revenge. In America the miseries springing from her internal jealousies, contentions, and wars, would form a part only of her lot. A plentiful addition of evils would have their source in that relation in which Europe stands to this quarter of the earth, and which no other quarter of the earth bears to Europe.

This picture of the consequences of disunion cannot be too highly colored, or too often exhibited. Every man who loves peace, every man who loves his country, every man who loves liberty, ought to have it ever before his eyes, that he may cherish in his heart a due attachment to the union of America, and be able to set a due value on the means of preserving it.

From the Federalist.

SIR HENRY JAMES SUMNER MAINE

(1822–1888)

IR HENRY MAINE, one of the ablest legal essayists of the nineteenth century, was especially noted for his lectures and essays on International Law. He was born August 15th, 1822, and educated at Cambridge University, where he became Regius Professor of Civil Law in 1847. This position he held for seven years. From 1869 to 1878 he was Corpus Professor of Jurisprudence at Oxford. In 1887 he returned to Cambridge as Whewell Professor of International Law, but his usefulness was cut short by his death the next year (February 3d, 1888). Among his most notable works are "Ancient Law," "Village Communities," "Popular Government," "Early History of Institutions," and "International Law,"—the latter, published in 1888, being his last work.

THE LAW OF NATIONS

THERE has been a difference of opinion among writers concerning the foundation of the Law of Nations. It has been considered by some as a mere system of positive institutions, founded upon consent and usage; while others have insisted that it was essentially the same as the Law of Nature, applied to the conduct of nations, in the character of moral persons, susceptible of obligations and laws. We are not to adopt either of these theories as exclusively true. The most useful and practical part of the Law of Nations is, no doubt, instituted or positive law, founded on usage, consent, and agreement. But it would be improper to separate this law entirely from natural jurisprudence, and not to consider it as deriving much of its force and dignity from the same principles of right reason, the same views of the nature and constitution of man, and the same sanction of Divine revelation, as those from which the science of morality is deduced. There is a natural and a positive Law of Nations. By the former every state, in its relations with other states, is bound to conduct itself with justice, good faith, and benevolence; and this application of the Law of Nature has been called by Vattel the neces-

sary Law of Nations, because nations are bound by the Law of Nature to observe it; and it is termed by others the internal Law of Nations, because it is obligatory upon them in point of conscience. We ought not, therefore, to separate the science of public law from that of ethics, nor encourage the dangerous suggestion that governments are not so strictly bound by the obligations of truth, justice, and humanity, in relation to other powers, as they are in the management of their own local concerns.

States, or bodies politic, are to be considered as moral persons, having a public will, capable and free to do right and wrong, inasmuch as they are collections of individuals, each of whom carries with him into the service of the community the same binding law of morality and religion which ought to control his conduct in private life. The Law of Nations is a complex system, composed of various ingredients. It consists of general principles of right and justice, equally suitable to the government of individuals in a state of natural equality, and to the relations and conduct of nations; of a collection of usages, customs, and opinions, the growth of civilization and commerce; and of a code of positive law.

In the absence of these latter regulations, the intercourse and conduct of nations are to be governed by principles fairly to be deduced from the rights and duties of nations, and the nature of moral obligation; and we have the authority of the lawyers of antiquity, and of some of the first masters in the modern school of public law, for placing the moral obligation of nations and of individuals on similar grounds, and for considering individual and national morality as parts of one and the same science. The Law of Nations, so far as it is founded on the principles of Natural Law, is equally binding in every age and upon all mankind. But the Christian nations of Europe, and their descendants on this side of the Atlantic, by the vast superiority of their attainments in arts, and science, and commerce, as well as in policy and government; and, above all, by the brighter light, the more certain truths, and the more definite sanction which Christianity has communicated to the ethical jurisprudence of the Ancients, have established a Law of Nations peculiar to themselves. They form together a community of Nations united by religion, manners, morals, humanity, and science, and united also by the mutual advantages of commercial intercourse, by the habit of forming alliances and treaties with each other, of interchanging

embassadors, and of studying and recognizing the same writers and systems of public law.

This *Jus Gentium* of the Imperial jurisconsults is identical with the Law of Nature, or Natural Law, of many modern ethical and juridical writers; and both are, in fact, the law of God, made known somewhat dimly to the whole human race at all times, and set forth with unmistakable certainty and transcendent power in his revealed will. This is, in truth, the highest law by which moral beings can be governed; highest in its Lawgiver, who is omnipotent over each individual man, as well as over societies and states; highest in the absolute perfection of the rules which it contains; highest in the absolute cogency of the commands which it utters; highest in the absolute obligation of duties which it enforces; highest in the absolute certainty and irresistible coercive power of the sanctions which it wields, and which operate upon the deepest spiritual nature of every human being. . . .

In more ancient times, and to a great extent even at this day, in that Eastern portion of the world in which so much of the usages of earlier mankind still survive, systems of religion and systems of morals, generally drawing with them some system of laws, gain currency by their own moral influence; certain minds being naturally predisposed to receive them acquiesce in them even with enthusiasm. Mr. Justice Stephen, in the controversial work which he calls "Liberty, Equality, and Fraternity," has an eloquent passage on the subject. "The sources of religion lie hid from us. All that we know is, that now and again in the course of ages some one sets to music the tune which is haunting millions of ears. It is caught up here and there, and repeated till the chorus is thundered out by a body of singers able to drown all discords and to force the vast unmusical mass to listen to them. Such results as these come not by observation, but when they do come they carry away as with a flood and hurry in their own direction all the laws and customs of those whom they affect." What is here said of religion is true to a certain extent of morality. In the East a body of new moral ideas is sure in time to produce a string of legal rules; and it is said by those who know India and its natives well that the production of what for want of a better name we must call a Code is a favorite occupation with learned and active minds, though of course in a country which nowadays follows to a great

extent the morality (though not the faith) of Christian Europe, and receives new laws from a regularly constituted Legislature, the enthusiasm for new moral doctrines is ever growing feebler and the demand for legal rules accommodated to them is becoming less. Now, International Law was a Code in the same sense in which many Eastern collections of rules were Codes. It was founded on a new morality, that which had been discovered in the supposed Law of Nature, and in some minds it excited unbounded enthusiasm.

The same process had previously been followed in Europe as regards Roman Civil Law. We may not quite understand the admiration which the technical part of the Roman Law inspired, but of the fact there is no doubt. This process by which laws extended themselves out had not quite died out when the international jurists appeared, and in point of fact their system of rules was received by the world very much as a system of law founded on morals is received to this day in the East. No doubt it fell on soil prepared for it. The literate classes, the scholars, great parts of the clergy, and the sovereigns and statesmen of Europe accepted it, and the result was an instant decay of the worst atrocities of war. Indeed, it is only necessary to look at the earliest authorities on International Law, in the "De Jure Belli et Pacis" of Grotius for example, to see that the Law of Nations is essentially a moral, and, to some extent, a religious, system. The appeal of Grotius is almost as frequent to morals and religion as to precedent, and no doubt it is these portions of the book, which to us have become almost commonplace or which seem irrelevant, which gained for it much of the authority which it ultimately obtained.

From Lecture II. of "International Law."

PAUL HENRI MALLET

(1730–1807)

ALLET'S "Northern Antiquities," which was translated into English by Bishop Percy in 1770, gave the general public its first idea of the rich treasures of the Scandinavian Sagas and Eddas. The mythology of the Northern tribes, preserved chiefly in Icelandic, is second only to the myths of Greece in beauty, while in strength it frequently surpasses them. Mallet lived before mythology became a science, and he is sometimes sharply criticized by those who are more ready to express critical opinion than they are to appreciate merit; but he undoubtedly has great merit both as a scholar and a writer, and his works on Scandinavian myths and customs are never likely to be wholly out of date. He was born at Geneva, Switzerland, in 1730, and educated there. In 1752 he became professor of Literature in the Academy at Copenhagen, and in 1755 published his introduction to the "History of Denmark," following it in 1756 with a second part entitled "Monuments of the Mythology and the Poetry of the Celts, and More Particularly of the Ancient Scandinavians." This is the work which, as translated by Bishop Percy under the title of "Northern Antiquities," has become an English classic, largely through its own intrinsic merit, but to a considerable extent, no doubt, through the excellence of Percy's style. In 1760 Mallet returned to Geneva and became professor of History there. He was strongly opposed to the French Revolutionists, and in 1792 was obliged to leave Geneva on account of political persecutions which kept him in exile until 1801. He returned in that year and died at Geneva, February 8th, 1807.

CIVILIZATION AND THE EARLIEST LITERATURE

MANKIND, everywhere essentially the same, have been always led to poetical composition prior to that of prose. This seems at present the reverse of the natural order; but we think so either through our prejudices, or for want of putting ourselves in the place of a people who are ignorant of the art of writing. Pleasing sounds and the attractions of harmony would strike at first every ear; but song could not long subsist without

poetry. No sooner was it observed how these two united powers fixed and impressed those images on the mind, which the memory was desirous of retaining, than they acquired a new degree of esteem, especially among such as aspired to a lasting fame. Verse was made use of to preserve the memory of remarkable events and great actions. The laws of a people, their religious ceremonies and rural labors were also recorded in numbers, because these are subjects which, consisting of a great variety of particulars, might easily fall into oblivion. Hence it was that Greece could already boast of a Homer, a Hesiod, and of many other poets, several ages before Pherecydes had written in prose. Hence among the Gauls and other Celtic nations there were poems composed on all subjects from the earliest ages, which the Druids, who were appointed to educate the youth, frequently employed twenty years in teaching them to repeat. This custom, rendered sacred by its high antiquity, which ever commands respect from the people, was in force many ages after the art of writing had pointed out a more perfect method of preserving the memorials of human knowledge. In like manner the Scandinavians for a long time applied their Runic letters only to the senseless purposes above mentioned; nor did they, during so many years, ever think of committing to writing those verses with which their memories were loaded; and it is probable that they only wrote down a small quantity of them at last. The idea of making a book never entered into the heads of those fierce warriors, who knew no medium between the violent exercises and fatigues of war or hunting and a stupid lethargic state of inaction. Among the innumerable advantages which accrued to the Northern nations from the introduction of the Christian religion, that of teaching them to apply the knowledge of letters to useful purposes is not the least valuable. Nor could a motive less sacred have eradicated that habitual and barbarous prejudice which caused them to neglect so admirable a secret. The churches and monasteries were at least so many asylums where this secret was preserved, while the ferocity of manners which prevailed in the Dark Ages tended again to consign it to oblivion.

So long as paganism prevailed in the North, the use of letters being very limited, it is no paradox to say that verse was a necessary medium of knowledge, and the poet an essential officer of the state. And if it requires a peculiar and uncommon

genius to excel in this art, the professors of it would, of course, acquire a very high degree of esteem and respect. All the historical monuments of the North are full of the honors paid this order of men, both by princes and people; nor can the annals of poetry produce any age or country which reflects more glory and lustre upon it. The ancient chronicles constantly represent the kings of Denmark, Norway, and Sweden, as attended by one or more Skalds; for this was the name they gave their poets. They were more especially honored and caressed at the courts of those princes who distinguished themselves by their great actions and passion for glory. Harold Harfagr, for instance, placed them at his feasts above all the officers of his court. Many princes intrusted them both in peace and war with commissions of the utmost importance. They never set out on any considerable expedition without some of them in their train. Hakon, Earl of Norway, had five celebrated Skalds along with him in that famous battle, when warriors of Jomsburg were defeated; and history records that they sung each an ode to animate the soldiers before they engaged. But they enjoyed another advantage, which would be more the envy of the poets of these days. They were rewarded for the poems they composed in honor of the kings and heroes with magnificent presents; we never find the Skald singing his verses at the courts of princes without being recompensed with golden rings, glittering arms, and rich apparel. Their respect for this order of men often extended so far as to remit the punishment of crimes they had committed, on condition they sued out their pardon in verse. In a word, the poetic art was held in such high estimation that great lords and even kings did not disdain to cultivate it with the utmost pains themselves. Ragnvald, earl of the Orkney Islands, passed for a very able poet; he boasts himself in a song of his which is still extant, that he knew how to compose verses on all subjects. Ragnar Lodbrok was no less distinguished for his skill in poetry than in war and navigation. Many of his poems were long preserved in the North, and may be found inserted in the history of his life; and it is well known that he died no less like a poet than a hero.

The respect, however, which the Northern nations paid to their Skalds was not owing to the nobility of their extraction. A people whose object was glory could not fail of showing a great deference to those who both published it abroad and consigned it to futurity, let their origin be what it would. A prince

or illustrious warrior oftentimes exposed his life with so much intrepidity, only to be praised by his Skald, who was both the witness and judge of his bravery. It is affirmed that this kind of men, although poets, were never guilty of flattery, and never lavished their praises on heroes and kings themselves, unless their gallant exploits were quite incontestable. Hence arose the custom of always bringing them into the scene of action: Olaf, king of Norway, placing three of them one day around him in battle, cried out with spirit: "You shall not relate what you have only heard, but what you are eyewitnesses of yourselves!" The same poets usually recited their verses themselves at solemn festivals and in great assemblies. But the subject of these poems was not confined to one single event, such as a victory or some generous action; it was frequently a genealogical history of all the kings of the country, deduced down from the gods to the reigning prince, who always derived his origin from them. These poems were, according to Tacitus, the only annals of the Germans. They had great numbers of them, which were not wholly forgotten in the eighth century; since Einhard relates that Charlemagne caused them to be committed to writing. "And even learnt himself," adds the historian, "the rude and ancient songs in which the exploits and the wars of the first princes were celebrated." In poems of the same kind consisted for many ages all the history of the Scandinavians. A bard named Thiodolf celebrated in his verses the exploits of Harold and thirty of his predecessors; another called Eyvind composed an historical poem which went back as far as Odin. Such are the sources whence Saxo drew his materials for the first six or seven books of his "History," and he might doubtless have derived great assistance from them, if he had not happened to live in an age wholly destitute of that exact skill in criticism which knows how to separate facts from the fictions with which they are blended.

The necessity there was for poets, the natural attractions of the art itself, and those it derived from the manners of the age, greatly multiplied the number of Skalds. An ancient Icelandic manuscript has preserved a list of all such as distinguished themselves in the three northern kingdoms, from the reign of Ragnar Lodbrok to that of Valdemar II. They are in number two hundred and thirty, among whom we find more than one crowned head. But what is not less remarkable is, that the greatest part of them are natives of Iceland. The reader has, doubtless, by this time, observed that we are indebted to that island for almost all the historical monuments of the northern nations now remaining. It cannot easily be accounted for how it came to pass that a people, disjoined from the rest of the world, few in number, depressed by poverty, and situated in so unfavorable a climate, should be capable, in those Dark Ages, of manifesting such a taste for literature, and should even rise to the perception of the more refined mental pleasures. While they were heathen, the Icelandic annalists were always deemed the best in the North. After they had embraced the Christian faith, they were the first who thought of unraveling the chaos of ancient history, who collected the old poems, digested the chronicles into a regular form, and applied themselves to rescue from oblivion the traditions of their pagan theology. Were we better informed of certain particulars relating to the state of the North during those remote ages, we might possibly find the cause of this phenomenon either in the poverty of the inhabitants of Iceland, which drove them to seek their fortune at the neighboring courts, or in the success of their first bards, which excited their emulation, and at the same time prepossessed strangers in their favor; or lastly, in the nature of their republican government, in which the talent of oratory and the reputation of superior sense and capacity are the direct roads to respect and preferment.

The style of these ancient poems is very enigmatical and figurative, very remote from the common language, and for that reason, grand, but tumid; sublime, but obscure. If it be the character of poetry to have nothing in common with prose, if the language of the gods ought to be quite different from that of men, if everything should be expressed by imagery, figures, hyperboles, and allegories, the Scandinavians may rank in the highest class of poets; nor is this unaccountable. The soaring flights of fancy may possibly more peculiarly belong to a rude and uncultivated than to a civilized people. The great objects of nature strike more forcibly on rude imaginations. Their passions are not impaired by the constraint of laws and education. The paucity of their ideas and the barrenness of their language oblige them to borrow from all nature images fit to clothe their conceptions in. How should abstract terms and reflex ideas, which so much enervate our poetry, be found in theirs? They could seldom have been met with in their most familiar conversations. The

moment the soul, reflecting on its own operations, recurs inwards, and detaches itself from exterior objects, the imagination loses its energy, the passions their activity, the mind becomes severe, and requires ideas rather than sensations; language then becomes precise and cautious, and poetry, being no longer the child of pure passion, is able to affect but feebly. If it be asked what is become of that magic power which the Ancients attributed to this art, it may be well said to exist no more. The poetry of the modern languages is nothing more than reasoning in rhyme, addressed to the understanding, but very little to the heart. No longer essentially connected with religion, politics, or morality, it is at present, if I may so say, a mere private art, an amusement that attains its end when it has gained the cold approbation of a few select judges.

From «Northern Antiquities.»

THOMAS ROBERT MALTHUS

(1766–1834)

THE first chapter of Malthus's work on the «Principle of Population» is perhaps the most celebrated essay ever written on an economic topic. In it he defines his famous theory of «The Ratios of the Increase of Population and Food,»—a theory which is severely logical from its premises,—which omits, however, the most important of all premises in dealing with human affairs,—the fact that the human intellect operates at its best, under its highest tension, when subjected to its supremest necessities, and that the possibilities of its efficient activities are indefinable, if not absolutely limitless. While no one has found a vitiating flaw in the Malthusian ratios, considered merely as a piece of logic, the activity of the creative intellect has been such in the century since he published his «Essay on Population,» that though the increase of population throughout the civilized world has been far greater than it ever was since statistics began to be kept, «world politics» at the close of the century depend largely on finding a satisfactory means of distributing a so-called «surplus» of bread stuffs, which is sure to result in years when modern machinery applied to agriculture is favored by average conditions of heat and moisture. It was impossible for Malthus to include in his calculation of ratios such phenomena as the steam plow, the improved reaper and binder, and all the machinery of production and distribution which depends upon steam and electricity; but while his logic too largely ignored the beneficent spirit of the really educated human intellect and ignored altogether the creative results of this spirit manifesting itself in scientific discovery and invention, the same moral and intellectual impulses which controlled him in reaching his conclusions are still always a potent and frequently the decisive factor in government and in trade. He was born near Guildford, Surrey, February 17th, 1766. After graduating at Cambridge, he took orders in the English Established Church and settled as a curate in Surrey, where he wrote his first essay on the «Principle of Population» (1798). In 1803 he followed it with a revised and amended version, under the title of an «Essay on Population.» This work became immediately popular with the English Conservatives, though Malthus himself was a Whig. He wrote also «The Nature and Progress of Rent» (1815), and «Political Economy» (1820). His death occurred at St. Catharine's, near Bath, December 23d, 1834.   W. V. B.

RATIOS OF THE INCREASE OF POPULATION AND FOOD

IN AN inquiry concerning the improvement of society, the mode of conducting the subject which naturally presents itself, is:

1. To investigate the causes that have hitherto impeded the progress of mankind towards happiness; and,

2. To examine the probability of the total or partial removal of these causes in future.

To enter fully into this question, and to enumerate all the causes that have hitherto influenced human improvement, would be much beyond the power of an individual. The principal object of the present essay is to examine the effects of one great cause intimately united with the very nature of man; which, though it has been constantly and powerfully operating since the commencement of society, has been little noticed by the writers who have treated this subject. The facts which establish the existence of this cause have, indeed, been repeatedly stated and acknowledged; but its natural and necessary effects have been almost totally overlooked; though probably among these effects may be reckoned a very considerable portion of that vice and misery, and of that unequal distribution of the bounties of nature, which it has been the unceasing object of the enlightened philanthropist in all ages to correct.

The cause to which I allude is the constant tendency in all animated life to increase beyond the nourishment prepared for it.

It is observed by Dr. Franklin that there is no bound to the prolific nature of plants or animals but what is made by their crowding and interfering with each other's means of subsistence. Were the face of the earth, he says, vacant of other plants, it might be gradually sowed and overspread with one kind only, as for instance with fennel; and were it empty of other inhabitants, it might in a few ages be replenished from one nation only, as for instance with Englishmen.

This is incontrovertibly true. Through the animal and vegetable kingdoms Nature has scattered the seeds of life abroad with the most profuse and liberal hand; but has been comparatively sparing in the room and the nourishment necessary to rear them. The germs of existence contained in this earth, if they could freely develop themselves, would fill millions of worlds in the course of a few thousand years. Necessity, that imperious, all-pervading law of nature, restrains them within the prescribed bounds. The race of plants and the race of animals shrink under this great restrictive law; and man cannot by any efforts of reason escape from it.

In plants and irrational animals, the view of the subject is simple. They are all impelled by a powerful instinct to the increase of their species; and this instinct is interrupted by no doubts about providing for their offspring. Wherever therefore there is liberty, the power of increase is exerted; and the superabundant effects are repressed afterwards by want of room and nourishment.

The effects of this check on man are more complicated. Impelled to the increase of his species by an equally powerful instinct, reason interrupts his career, and asks him whether he may not bring beings into the world for whom he cannot provide the means of support. If he attend to this natural suggestion, the restriction too frequently produces vice. If he hear it not, the human race will be constantly endeavoring to increase beyond the means of subsistence. But as, by that law of our nature which makes food necessary to the life of man, population can never actually increase beyond the lowest nourishment capable of supporting it, a strong check on population, from the difficulty of acquiring food, must be constantly in operation. This difficulty must fall somewhere, and must necessarily be severely felt in some or other of the various forms of misery, or the fear of misery, by a large portion of mankind.

That population has this constant tendency to increase beyond the means of subsistence, and that it is kept to its necessary level by these causes, will sufficiently appear from a review of the different states of society in which man has existed. But before we proceed to this review, the subject will, perhaps, be seen in a clearer light, if we endeavor to ascertain what would be the natural increase of population, if left to exert itself with perfect freedom; and what might be expected to be the rate of increase in the productions of the earth, under the most favorable circumstances of human industry.

It will be allowed that no country has hitherto been known where the manners were so pure and simple, and the means of subsistence so abundant, that no check whatever has existed to early marriages from the difficulty of providing for a family, and that no waste of the human species has been occasioned by

vicious customs, by towns, by unhealthy occupations, or too severe labor. Consequently, in no state that we have yet known has the power of population been left to exert itself with perfect freedom.

Whether the law of marriage be instituted or not, the dictate of nature and virtue seems to be an early attachment to one woman; and where there were no impediments of any kind in the way of a union to which such an attachment would lead, and no causes of depopulation afterwards, the increase of the human species would be evidently much greater than any increase which has been hitherto known.

In the northern states of America, where the means of subsistence have been more ample, the manners of the people more pure, and the checks to early marriages fewer, than in any of the modern states of Europe, the population has been found to double itself, for above a century and a half successively, in less than twenty-five years. Yet even during these periods, in some of the towns, the deaths exceeded the births,—a circumstance which clearly proves that in those parts of the country which supplied this deficiency the increase must have been much more rapid than the general average.

In the back settlements, where the sole employment is agriculture, and vicious customs and unwholesome occupations are little known, the population has been found to double itself in fifteen years. Even this extraordinary rate of increase is probably short of the utmost power of population. Very severe labor is requisite to clear a fresh country; such situations are not in general considered as particularly healthy; and the inhabitants, probably, are occasionally subject to the incursions of the Indians, which may destroy some lives, or at any rate diminish the fruits of their industry.

According to a table of Euler, calculated on a mortality of 1 in 36, if the births be to the deaths in the proportion of 3 to 1, the period of doubling will be only 12 years and 4-5ths. And this proportion is not only a possible supposition, but has actually occurred for short periods in more countries than one.

Sir William Petty supposes a doubling possible in so short a time as ten years.

But to be perfectly sure that we are far within the truth, we will take the slowest of these rates of increase, a rate in which all concurring testimonies agree, and which has been repeatedly ascertained to be from procreation only.

It may safely be pronounced, therefore, that population, when unchecked, goes on doubling itself every twenty-five years, or increases in a geometrical ratio.

The rate according to which the productions of the earth may be supposed to increase, it will not be so easy to determine. Of this, however, we may be perfectly certain, that the ratio of their increase must be totally of a different nature from the ratio of the increase of population. A thousand millions are just as easily doubled every twenty-five years by the power of population as a thousand. But the food to support the increase from the greater number will by no means be obtained with the same facility. Man is necessarily confined in room. When acre has been added to acre till all the fertile land is occupied, the yearly increase of food must depend upon the amelioration of the land already in possession. This is a fund, which, from the nature of all soils, instead of increasing, must be gradually diminishing. But population, could it be supplied with food, would go on with unexhausted vigor; and the increase of one period would furnish the power of a greater increase the next, and this without any limit.

From the accounts we have of China and Japan, it may be fairly doubted whether the best-directed efforts of human industry could double the produce of these countries even once in any number of years. There are many parts of the globe, indeed, hitherto uncultivated, and almost unoccupied; but the right of exterminating, or driving into a corner where they must starve, even the inhabitants of these thinly peopled regions, will be questioned in a moral view. The process of improving their minds and directing their industry would necessarily be slow; and during this time, as population would regularly keep pace with the increasing produce, it would rarely happen that a great degree of knowledge and industry would have to operate at once upon rich unappropriated soil. Even where this might take place, as it does sometimes in new colonies, a geometrical ratio increases with such extraordinary rapidity, that the advantage could not last long. If the United States of America continue increasing, which they certainly will do, though not with the same rapidity as formerly, the Indians will be driven further and further back into the country, till the whole race is ultimately exterminated, and the territory is incapable of further extension.

These observations are, in a degree, applicable to all the parts of the earth, where the soil is imperfectly cultivated. To exter-

minate the inhabitants of the greatest part of Asia and Africa is a thought that could not be admitted for a moment. To civilize and direct the industry of the various tribes of Tartars and Negroes would certainly be a work of considerable time, and of variable and uncertain success.

Europe is by no means so fully peopled as it might be. In Europe there is the fairest chance that human industry may receive its best direction. The science of agriculture has been much studied in England and Scotland; and there is still a great portion of uncultivated land in these countries. Let us consider at what rate the produce of this island might be supposed to increase under circumstances the most favorable to improvement.

If it be allowed that by the best possible policy, and great encouragements to agriculture, the average produce of the island could be doubled in the twenty-five years, it will be allowing, probably, a greater increase than could with reason be expected.

In the next twenty-five years it is impossible to suppose that the produce could be quadrupled. It would be contrary to all our knowledge of the properties of land. The improvement of the barren parts would be a work of time and labor; and it must be evident to those who have the slightest acquaintance with agricultural subjects, that in proportion as cultivation extended, the additions that could yearly be made to the former average produce must be gradually and regularly diminishing. That we may be the better able to compare the increase of population and food, let us make a supposition, which, without pretending to accuracy, is clearly more favorable to the power of production in the earth than any experience we have had of its quantities will warrant.

Let us suppose that the yearly additions which might be made to the former average produce, instead of decreasing, which they certainly would do, were to remain the same; and that the produce of this island might be increased every twenty-five years by a quantity equal to what it at present produces. The most enthusiastic speculator cannot suppose a greater increase than this. In a few centuries it would make every acre of land in the island like a garden.

If this supposition be applied to the whole earth, and if it be allowed that the subsistence for man which the earth affords might be increased every twenty-five years by a quantity equal to what it at present produces, this will be supposing a rate of increase much greater than we can imagine that any possible exertions of mankind could make it.

It may be fairly pronounced, therefore, that, considering the present average state of the earth, the means of subsistence, under circumstances the most favorable to human industry, could not possibly be made to increase faster than in an arithmetical ratio.

The necessary effects of these two different rates of increase, when brought together, will be very striking. Let us call the population of this island eleven millions; and suppose the present produce equal to the easy support of such a number. In the first twenty-five years the population would be twenty-two millions, and the food being also doubled, the means of subsistence would be equal to this increase. In the next twenty-five years, the population would be forty-four millions, and the means of subsistence only equal to the support of thirty-three millions. In the next period the population would be eighty-eight millions, and the means of subsistence just equal to the support of half of that number. And, at the conclusion of the first century, the population would be a hundred and seventy-six millions, and the means of subsistence only equal to the support of fifty-five millions, leaving a population of a hundred and twenty-one millions totally unprovided for.

Taking the whole earth, instead of this island, emigration would, of course, be excluded; and, supposing the present population equal to a thousand millions, the human species would increase as the numbers 1, 2, 4, 8, 16, 32, 64, 128, 256, and subsistence as 1, 2, 3, 4, 5, 6, 7, 8, 9. In two centuries the population would be to the means of subsistence as 256 to 9; in three centuries as 4096 to 13, and in two thousand years the difference would be almost incalculable.

In this supposition no limits whatever are placed to the produce of the earth. It may increase forever, and be greater than any assignable quantity; yet still the power of population being in every period so much superior, the increase of the human species can only be kept down to the level of the means of subsistence by the constant operation of the strong law of necessity, acting as a check upon the greater power.

Chapter i. in "Essay on the Principle of Population" complete.

SIR JOHN MANDEVILLE

(Fourteenth Century)

SIR JOHN MANDEVILLE'S "Travels" (1357-71) occupies an important place in English prose literature, because it makes the connection clear between modern English and those Middle-English dialects which resulted from the influence of the Danish and Norman invasions. Where Mandeville was born is not known and it has not been decided that such a person really existed at all; but if the name is a pseudonym, no trace of the real name of the author of this remarkable book has been found. According to Mandeville's own account, he was "born and bred in England of the town of St. Albans." His "Travels" began in 1322 and included Turkey, Armenia, Tartary, Persia, Syria, Arabia, Egypt, India, and other countries, such as the "Realms of Prester John," which may be described best as not accurately identified. Mandeville's reputation for veracity has helped to bring all other "traveler's tales" under suspicion, but he is often far more interesting than more accurate cosmographers, while his "Travels" is so firmly established as a necessary part of every antiquarian's library, and as a book of general interest to all who love the quaint and improbable that it may fairly be described as beyond the reach of criticism.

A MOHAMMEDAN ON CHRISTIAN VICES

I SHALL tell you what the Soudan told me upon a day, in his chamber. He let voiden out of his chamber all manner of men, lords, and other; for he would speak with me in counsel. And there he asked me how the Christian men governed 'em in our country. And I said [to] him, "Right well, thonked be God." And he said [to] me, "Truly nay, for ye Christian men ne reckon right not how untruly to serve God. Ye should given ensample to the lewed people for to do well, and ye given 'em ensample to don evil. For the commons, upon festival days, when they shoulden go to church to serve God, then gon they to taverns, and ben there in gluttony all the day and all night, and eaten and drinken, as beasts that have no reason, and wit not when they have enow. And therewithal they ben so proud, that they knowen not how to ben clothed; now long, now short,

---

now strait, now large, now sworded, now daggered, and in all manner guises. They shoulden ben simple, meek, and true, and full of alms-deed, as Jesu was, in whom they trow; but they ben all the contrary, and ever inclined to the evil, and to don evil. And they been so covetous, that for a little silver they sellen 'eir daughters, 'eir sisters, and 'eir own wives, to putten 'em to lechery. And one withdraweth the wife of another; and none of 'em holdeth faith to another, but they defoulen 'eir law, that Jesu Christ betook 'em keep for 'eir salvation. And thus for 'eir sins, han [have] they lost all this lond that we holden. For 'eir sins here, hath God taken 'em in our honds, not only by strength of ourself, but for 'eir sins. For we knowen well in very sooth, that when ye serve God, God will help you; and when he is with you, no man may be against you. And that know we well by our prophecies, that Christian men shall winnen this lond again out of our honds, when they serven God more devoutly. But as long as they ben of foul and unclean living (as they ben now), we have no dread of 'em in no kind; for here God will not helpen 'em in no wise."

And then I asked him how he knew the state of Christian men. And he answered me, that he knew all the state of the commons also by his messengers, that he sent to all londs, in manner as they were merchants of precious stones, of cloths of gold, and of other things, for to knowen the manner of every country amongs Christian men. And then he let clepe in all the lords that he made voiden first out of his chamber; and there he showed me four that were great lords in the country, that tolden me of my country, and of many other Christian countries, as well as if they had been of the same country; and they spak French right well, and the Soudan also, whereof I had great marvel. Alas, that it is great slander to our faith and to our laws, when folk that ben withouten law shall reproven us, and undernemen us of our sins. And they that shoulden ben converted to Christ and to the law of Jesu, by our good example and by our acceptable life to God, ben through our wickedness and evil living, far fro us; and strangers fro the holy and very belief shall thus appellen us and holden us for wicked levirs and cursed. And truly they say sooth. For the Saracens ben good and faithful. For they keepen entirely the commandment of the holy book Alcoran, that God sent 'em by his messager Mahomet; to the which, as they sayen, St. Gabriel, the angel, oftentime told the will of God.

From his "Travels."

THE DEVIL'S HEAD IN THE VALLEY PERILOUS

BESIDE that isle of Mistorak, upon the left side, nigh to the river Phison, is a marvellous thing. There is a vale between the mountains, that dureth nigh a four mile. And some clepen it the Vale Enchanted, some clepen it the Vale of Devils, and some clepen it the Vale Perilous; in that vale hearen men oftentime great tempests and thunders, and great murmurs and noises, all day and nights; and great noise as it were sound of tabors and of nakeres and trumps, as though it were of a great feast. This vale is all full of devils, and hath been always. And men say there, that it is one of the entries of hell. In that vale is plenty of gold and silver; wherefore many misbelieving men, and many Christian men also, gon in oftentime, for to have of the treasure that there is, but few comen again; and namely, of the misbelieving men, ne of the Christian men nouther, for they ben anon strangled of devils. And in mid place of that vale, under a rock, is an head of the visage of the devil bodily, full horrible and dreadful to see; and it showeth not but the head, to the shoulders. But there is no man in the world so hardy, Christian man ne other, but that he would ben adrad for to behold it; and that it would seemen him to die for dread; so is it hideous for to behold. For he beholdeth every man so sharply with dreadful eyen that ben evermore moving and sparkling as fire, and changeth and steereth so often in divers manner, with so horrible countenance, that no man dare not nighen towards him. And fro him cometh smoke and stink, and fire, and so much abomination, that unethe no man may there endure. But the good Christian men, that been stable in the faith, entren well withouten peril: for they will first shriven 'em, and marken hem with the token of the Holy Cross; so that the fiends ne han no power over 'em. But albeit that they ben withouten peril, zit natheles ne ben they not withouten dread, when that they seen the devils visibly and bodily all about 'em, that maken full many divers assauts and menaces in air and in earth, and agasten 'em with strokes of thunder-blasts and of tempests. And the most dread is, that God will taken vengeance then, of that men han misdone again his will. And ye should understand that when my fellows and I weren in that vale, we weren in great thought whether that we dursten putten our bodies in aventure, to gon in or non, in the protection of God. And some of our fellows accordeden to enter, and some noght.

So there were with us two worthy men, friars minors that were of Lombardy, that said, that if any man would enter, they would go in with us. And when they had said so, upon the gracious trust of God and of 'em, we let sing mass; and made every man to be shriven and housel'd; and then we entered fourteen persons; but at our going out, we were but nine. And so we wisten never, whether that our fellows were lost, or elles turned again for dread; but we ne saw them never after; and tho were two men of Greece and three of Spain; and our other fellows that would not go in with us, they went by another coast to ben before us, and so they were. And thus we passed that perilous vale, and found therein gold and silver, and precious stones, and rich jewels great plenty, both here and there, as us seemed; but whether that it was, as us seemed, I wot nere; for I touched none, because that the devils be so subtle to make a thing to seem otherwise than it is, for to deceive mankind; and therefore I touched none; and also because that I would not be put out of my devotion: for I was more devout than ever I was before or after, and all for the dread of fiends, that I saw in divers figures; and also for the great multitude of dead bodies that I saw there lying by the way, by all the vale, as though there had been a battle between two kings, and the mightiest of the country, and that the greater part had been discomfitted and slain. And I trow that unethe should any country have so much people within him, as lay slain in that vale, as us thought; the which was an hideous sight to seen. And I marvelled much, that there were so many, and the bodies all whole withouten rotting. But I trow that fiends made them seem to be so whole, withouten rotting. But that might not be to my avys, that so many should have entered so newly, ne so many newly slain, without stinking and rotting. And many of them were in habit of Christian men; but I trow well that it were of such that went in for covetyse of the treasure that was there, and had overmuch feebleness in faith; so that their hearts ne might not endure in the belief for dread. And therefore were we the more devout a great deal; and yet we were cast down, and beaten down many times to the hard earth, by winds and thunders, and tempests; but evermore, God, of his grace, helped us. And so we passed that perilous vale, without peril, and without incumbrance. Thanked be Almighty God.

From his "Travels."

AMMIANUS MARCELLINUS

(c. 330–c. 395 A. D.)

THE "History of Rome," written by Ammianus Marcellinus, consisted of thirty-one books beginning with the period of the accession of Nerva and extending to the death of Valens. The eighteen books which survive begin with the seventeenth year of the reign of Constantine and do not go beyond the year 378. Gibbon calls Marcellinus an "accurate and faithful guide who composed the history of his own time without indulging the prejudices and passion which usually affect the mind of a contemporary"—certainly a high compliment which few historians have deserved. Marcellinus was born at Antioch in Syria and began life as a soldier, entering the service of the Emperor Constantius in the year 350, and serving under him several campaigns. He also accompanied the expedition of the Emperor Julian into Persia. After leaving the army he went to Rome and devoted the rest of his life chiefly to his "History." Little or nothing is known of him beyond this, except that he was still living as late as the year 380 A. D. The dates of his birth and death are both conjectural.

LUXURY OF ROMAN DECADENCE

THE greatness of Rome was founded on the rare and almost incredible alliance of virtue and of fortune. The long period of her infancy was employed in a laborious struggle against the tribes of Italy, the neighbors and enemies of the rising city. In the strength and ardor of youth she sustained the storms of war, carried her victorious arms beyond the seas and mountains, and brought home triumphant laurels from every country of the globe. At length, verging towards old age, and sometimes conquering by the terror only of her name, she sought the blessings of ease and tranquillity. The venerable city, which had trampled on the necks of the fiercest nations, and established a system of laws, the perpetual guardians of justice and freedom, was content, like a wise and wealthy parent, to devolve on the Cæsars, her favorite sons, the care of governing her ample patri-

mony. A secure and profound peace, such as had been once enjoyed in the reign of Numa, succeeded to the tumults of a republic; while Rome was still adored as the queen of the earth; and the subject nations still reverenced the name of the people and the majesty of the senate. But this native splendor is degraded and sullied by the conduct of some nobles, who, unmindful of their own dignity and of that of their country, assume an unbounded license of vice and folly. They contend with each other in the empty vanity of titles and surnames; and curiously select or invent the most lofty and sonorous appellations. Reburrus or Fabunius, Pagonius or Tarrasius, which may impress the ears of the vulgar with astonishment and respect. From a vain ambition of perpetuating their memory, they affect to multiply their likeness in statues of bronze and marble; nor are they satisfied unless those statues are covered with plates of gold; an honorable distinction first granted to Acilius the consul, after he had subdued, by his arms and counsels, the power of King Antiochus. The ostentation of displaying, or magnifying perhaps, the rent roll of the estates which they possess in all the provinces, from the rising to the setting sun, provokes the just resentment of every man who recollects that their poor and invincible ancestors were not distinguished from the meanest of the soldiers by the delicacy of their food or the splendor of their apparel. But the modern nobles measure their rank and consequence according to the loftiness of their chariots and the weighty magnificence of their dress. Their long robes of silk and purple float in the wind; and as they are agitated, by art or accident, they occasionally discover the under garments, and rich tunics, embroidered with the figures of various animals. Followed by a train of fifty servants, and tearing up the pavement, they move along the streets with the same impetuous speed as if they traveled with post horses; and the example of the senators is boldly imitated by the matrons and ladies, whose covered carriages are continually driving round the immense space of the city and suburbs. Whenever these persons of high distinction condescend to visit the public baths, they assume, on their entrance, a tone of loud and insolent command, and appropriate to their own use the conveniences which were designed for the Roman people. · If, in these places of mixed and general resort, they meet any of the infamous ministers of their pleasures, they express their affection by a tender embrace; while they proudly decline the salutations

of their fellow-citizens, who are not permitted to aspire above the honor of kissing their hands or their knees. As soon as they have indulged themselves in the refreshment of the bath, they resume their rings and the other ensigns of their dignity; select from their private wardrobe of the finest linen such as might suffice for a dozen persons, the garments the most agreeable to their fancy, and maintain till their departure the same haughty demeanor, which perhaps might have been excused in the great Marcellus, after the conquest of Syracuse. Sometimes, indeed, these heroes undertake more arduous achievements; they visit their estates in Italy, and procure themselves, by the toil of servile hands, the amusements of the chase. If at any time, but more especially on a hot day, they have courage to sail, in their painted galleys, from the Lucrine lake to their elegant villas on the seacoast of Puteoli and Cayeta, they compare their own expeditions to the marches of Cæsar and Alexander. Yet, should a fly presume to settle on the silken folds of their gilded umbrellas, should a sunbeam penetrate through some unguarded and imperceptible chink, they deplore their intolerable hardships, and lament, in affected language, that they were not born in the land of the Cimmerians, the regions of eternal darkness. In these journeys into the country the whole body of the household march with their master. In the same manner as the cavalry and infantry, the heavy and light-armed troops, the advanced guard and the rear, are marshaled by the skill of their military leaders; so the domestic officers, who bear a rod as an ensign of authority, distribute and arrange the numerous train of slaves and attendants. The baggage and wardrobe move in the front, and are immediately followed by a multitude of cooks and inferior ministers, employed in the service of the kitchens and of the table. The main body is composed of a promiscuous crowd of slaves, increased by the accidental concourse of idle or independent plebeians. The rear is closed by the favorite band of eunuchs, distributed from age to youth, according to the order of seniority. Their numbers and their deformity excite the horror of the indignant spectators. In the exercise of domestic jurisdiction, the nobles of Rome express an exquisite sensibility for any personal injury, and a contemptuous indifference to the rest of the human species. When they have called for warm water, if a slave has been tardy in his obedience, he is instantly chastised with three hundred lashes; but should the same slave commit a willful murder, the master will mildly observe that he is a worthless fellow, but that, if he repeats the offense, he shall not escape punishment. Hospitality was formerly the virtue of the Romans, and every stranger who could plead either merit or misfortune was relieved or rewarded by their generosity. At present, if a foreigner, perhaps of no contemptible rank, is introduced to one of the proud and wealthy senators, he is welcomed, indeed, in the first audience, with such warm professions, and such kind inquiries, that he retires enchanted with the affability of his illustrious friend, and full of regret that he had so long delayed his journey to Rome, the native seat of manners as well of empire. Secure of a favorable reception, he repeats his visit the ensuing day, and is mortified by the discovery that his person, his name, and his country are already forgotten. If he still has resolution to persevere, he is gradually numbered in the train of dependents, and obtains the permission to pay his assiduous and unprofitable court to a haughty patron, incapable of gratitude or friendship, who scarcely deigns to remark his presence, his departure, or his return. Whenever the rich prepare a solemn and popular entertainment; whenever they celebrate, with profuse and pernicious luxury, their private banquets, the choice of the guests is the subject of anxious deliberation. The modest, the sober, and the learned are seldom preferred; and the recommendators, who are commonly swayed by interested motives, have the address to insert, in the list of invitations, the obscure names of the most worthless of mankind. But the frequent and familiar companions of the great are those parasites who practice the most useful of all arts, the art of flattery; who eagerly applaud each word and every action of their immortal patron; gaze with rapture on his marble columns and variegated pavements; and strenuously praise the pomp and elegance, which he is taught to consider as a part of his personal merit. At the Roman tables, the birds, the squirrels, or the fish, which appear of an uncommon size, are contemplated with curious attention; a pair of scales is accurately applied to ascertain their real weight; and, while the more rational guests are disgusted by the vain and tedious repetition, notaries are summoned to attest, by an authentic record, the truth of such a marvelous event. Another method of introduction into the houses and society of the great is derived from the profession of gaming, or, as it is more politely styled, of play. The confederates are united by a strict and indissoluble

bond of friendship, or rather of conspiracy; a superior degree of skill in the Tesserarian art (which may be interpreted the game of dice and tables) is a sure road to wealth and reputation. A master of that sublime science, who in a supper, or assembly, is placed below a magistrate, displays in his countenance the surprise and indignation which Cato might be supposed to feel when he was refused the pretorship by the votes of a capricious people. The acquisition of knowledge seldom engages the curiosity of the nobles, who abhor the fatigue and disdain the advantages of study; and the only books which they peruse are the "Satires" of Juvenal and the verbose and fabulous histories of Marius Maximus. The libraries which they have inherited from their fathers are secluded, like dreary sepulchres, from the light of day. But the costly instruments of the theatre, flutes, and enormous lyres, and hydraulic organs, are constructed for their use; and the harmony of vocal and instrumental music is incessantly repeated in the palaces of Rome. In those palaces, sound is preferred to sense, and the care of the body to that of the mind. It is allowed, as a salutary maxim, that the light and frivolous suspicion of a contagious malady is of sufficient weight to excuse the visits of the most intimate friends; and even the servants, who are despatched to make the decent inquiries, are not suffered to return home till they have undergone the ceremony of a previous ablution. Yet this selfish and unmanly delicacy occasionally yields to the more imperious passion of avarice. The prospect of gain will urge a rich and gouty senator as far as Spoleto; every sentiment of arrogance and dignity is subdued by the hopes of an inheritance, or even of a legacy; and a wealthy childless citizen is the most powerful of the Romans. The art of obtaining the signature of a favorable testament, and sometimes of hastening the moment of its execution, is perfectly understood, and it has happened that, in the same house, though in different apartments, a husband and a wife, with the laudable design of overreaching each other, have summoned their respective lawyers, to declare, at the same time, their mutual but contradictory intentions. The distress which follows, and chastises extravagant luxury, often reduces the great to the use of the most humiliating expedients; when they desire to borrow, they employ the base and supplicating style of the slave in the comedy; but when they are called upon to pay, they assume the royal and tragic declamation of the grandsons of Hercules. If the demand

is repeated, they readily procure some trusty sycophant, instructed to maintain a charge of poison, or magic, against the insolent creditor, who is seldom released from prison till he has signed a discharge of the whole debt. These vices, which degrade the moral character of the Romans, are mixed with a puerile superstition that disgraces their understanding. They listen with confidence to the predictions of haruspices, who pretend to read, in the entrails of victims, the signs of future greatness and prosperity; and there are many who do not presume either to bathe, or to dine, or to appear in public, till they have diligently consulted, according to the rules of astrology, the situation of Mercury and the aspect of the moon. It is singular enough that this vain credulity may often be discovered among the profane skeptics, who impiously doubt or deny the existence of a celestial power.

HARRIET MARTINEAU

(1802–1876)

ARRIET MARTINEAU was one of the most noted of the intellectual women of England who flourished during the first half of the nineteenth century. She was one of the first English women to attempt the career of a professional writer on political and economic subjects,—a field in which she became noted both in England and America at the too heavy expense of losing the permanent popularity she might have won had she devoted her really remarkable intellect to subjects which would not have tended so strongly to develop her aggressiveness at the expense of her amiability. She was born at Norwich, England, June 12th, 1802. In her youth she was greatly influenced by the writings of Dr. Priestley, and later on she came within the sphere of Malthus, Ricardo, and Mill, whose theories she illustrated in a series of tales. As she entitled these, "Illustrations of Political Economy," they were naturally viewed with distrust by publishers, but when finally she secured a publisher on terms very disadvantageous to herself, the sale of her stories is described as having been "enormous." This success encouraged a new series as, "Illustrations of Taxation." In 1834 she visited the United States, and after her return published two books on the subject of American manners, which did not increase her popularity in this country. One of her critics, speaking with much reserve, says that in these books she does not show "her usual calmness and judicial common sense." No such reserve was shown in contemporaneous American resentment of her opinions of Americans as she saw them. She wrote a number of novels and a considerable number of essays, besides translating and condensing the "Philosophy" of Comte. She died in Westmoreland, June 27th, 1876,—her celebrated brother, Rev. James Martineau, who was only three years her junior, surviving her until the very close of the century (1900). Miss Martineau's ability is unquestionable, and perhaps her severity, when it grows excessive, is to be accounted for by the subconsciousness of her physical infirmities. She never possessed the senses of taste and smell, and as she became very deaf at the age of sixteen, she was compelled to depend on her single sense of sight in the exercise of her human sympathies.

WALTER SAVAGE LANDOR

WE MAY be called paradoxical ourselves if we say (but it is true) that never was anything more of a piece than the mind and life, the surroundings, the utterances, and the acts of this wonderfully sane yet thoroughly inconsistent being. His tall, broad, muscular, active frame was characteristic; and so was his head, with the strange elevation of the eyebrows, which expresses self-will as strongly in some cases as astonishment in others. Those eyebrows, mounting up till they comprehended a good portion of the forehead, have been observed in many more paradoxical persons than one. Then there was the retreating but broad forehead, showing the deficiency of reasoning and speculative power, with the preponderance of imagination, and a huge passion for destruction. The massive self-love and self-will carried up his head to something more than a dignified bearing — even to one of arrogance. His vivid and quick eye, and the thoughtful mouth, were fine, and his whole air was that of a man distinguished in his own eyes certainly, but also in those of others. Tradition reports that he was handsome in his youth. In age he was more. The first question about him usually was why, with his frame, and his courage, and his politics, and his social position, he was not in the army. One reply might be that he could neither obey nor co-operate; another was that his godfather, General Powell, wished it, and Landor therefore preferred something else. As for that something else — his father offered him £400 a year to study law, and reside in the Temple for that purpose, whereas he would give him only £150 if he would not; and of course he took the £150, and went as far as he well could from the Temple, — that is, to Swansea. Warwick was his native place. He was born in the best house in the city, where the fine old garden, with its noble elms and horse-chestnuts, might have influenced his imagination, so as to have something to do possibly with his subsequent abode in Italy. His mother was of the ancient family of Savage; and hereditary estates lay about him in Staffordshire and Warwickshire, which had been in the possession of the family for nearly seven centuries. These he sold to shift himself to Wales; and nowhere did his spirit of destructive waywardness break out more painfully than in the sale of those

old estates, and his treatment of the new. He employed many scores of laborers on his Welsh estates, made roads and planted, and built a house which cost him £8,000. He set his heart upon game preserving (of all pursuits for a democratic republican), and had at times twenty keepers out upon the hills at night, watching his grouse; but, with twelve thousand acres of land, he never saw a grouse on his table. His tenants cheated him, he declared, and destroyed his plantations; and, though he got rid of them, he left, not only Wales but Great Britain, in wrath. Then the steward in charge of his house cheated him, when he not only got rid of the steward, but had his splendid new house pulled down — out of consideration, he declared, for his son's future ease and convenience, in being rid of so vexatious a property. His flatterers called this an act of characteristic indignation. To others it appeared that his republican and self-governing doctrines came rather strangely from one who could not rule his own affairs and his own people; and who, finding his failure, could do nothing better than lay waste the whole scene.

He had obtained some of his scholarship at Rugby, and somewhat more at Oxford, — where, however, his stay was short. Having fired a gun in the quadrangle of his college, he was rusticated; and, instead of returning, published a volume of poems, when he was only eighteen. While at Swansea he studied and wrote "Gebir." On the invasion of Spain, he determined to be a soldier on his own account, raised a small troop at his own expense, and was the first Englishman who landed in aid of the Spaniards. He was rewarded for this aid, and for a gift of money, by the thanks of the Supreme Junta, and by the rank of Colonel on his return to England; but he sent back his commission and the record of thanks when Ferdinand set aside the Constitution. Among many good political acts, perhaps none was better than this. At thirty-six years of age he married a French lady of good family; and a few years after, in 1818, fixed his residence in Italy, — first in the Palazzo Medici, in Florence, and when obliged to leave it, in a charming villa two miles off. That Villa Gherardesca was built by Michael Angelo. Few British travelers in Italy fail to go and see Fiesole; and while Landor lived there, he was the prey of lion hunters, — as he vehemently complained on occasion of the feud between him and N. P. Willis, the American, who lost a MS. confided to him for his opinion. Such a subordination of the full, ripe scholar and discourser to

the shallow, flippant sketcher by the wayside might seem to deserve such a result; but it did not tend to reconcile Landor to lion hunters. While in Italy, he sent to English newspapers, and especially to the Examiner, frequent comments on passing events in the political world, in the form of letters or of verse. He was collecting pictures all the while; and when he returned to England to pass the rest of his days, as he supposed, he left the bulk of his collection in his villa, for his son's benefit, bringing only a few gems wherewith to adorn such a modest residence as he now intended to have in his own country. That residence was in St. James's Square, Bath, where he became an octogenarian, living for awhile in peace and quiet — still commenting on men and measures through the Liberal papers, and putting forth, in his eightieth year, the little volume called "Last Fruit from an Old Tree." The spectacle of a vigorous, vivid, undaunted old age, true to the aims and convictions of youth, is always a fine one; and it was warmly felt to be so in Landor's case. His prejudices mattered less, when human affairs went on maturing themselves in spite of them; and many of his complaints were silenced in the best possible way, — by the reform of the abuses which he, with some unnecessary violence, denounced. He, for his part, talked less about killing kings; and his steady assertion of the claims of the humble fell in better with the spirit of the time, after years had inaugurated the works of peace. About many matters of political principle and practice he was right, while yet the majority of society were wrong; and it would be too much to require that he should be wholly right in doctrine and fact, or very angelic in his way of enforcing his convictions. Nature did not make him a logician, and if we were ever disappointed at not finding him one, the fault was our own. She made him brave, though wayward; an egotist in his method, but with the good of mankind for his aim. He was passionate and prejudiced, but usually in some great cause, and on the right side of it; though there was a deplorable exception to that general rule in the particular instance of defamation which broke up the repose and dignity of his latter days, and caused his self-exile from England for the remnant of his life. This brief notice of the painful fact is enough for truth and justice. As for the rest, he was of aristocratic birth, fortune, and education, with democracy for his political aim, and poverty and helplessness for his clients. All this would have made Walter

Savage Landor a remarkable man in his generation, apart from his services to literature; but when we recall some of his works — such pictures as that of the English officer shot at the Pyramids — such criticisms as in his "Pentameron" — and discourses so elevating and so heart-moving as some which he has put into the mouths of heroes, sages, scholarly and noble women, and saintly and knightly men, we feel that our cumulative obligations to him are very great, and that his death is a prominent incident of the time.

From "Biographical Sketches."

KARL MARX

(1818–1883)

KARL MARX, perhaps the most celebrated of the German socialistic economists, whose writings so powerfully exaggerated the tendencies of the last quarter of the nineteenth century towards centralization, was born at Treves, in Prussia, May 5th, 1818. At the universities of Bonn and Berlin he studied history, jurisprudence, and philosophy; and it was not until 1843, after he had been expelled from Germany for his revolutionary tendencies, that he began his systematic study of sociology and political economy. After his exile from Germany in 1843, he took up his residence in Paris; but the German government had sufficient influence to secure his expulsion from France, and he lived in Brussels until 1848. In that year he returned to Germany to take part in the revolutionary movement of "Young Germany," on the failure of which he went again into exile, settling finally in London, where he died March 14th, 1883. His chief work is "Capital" ("Das Kapital"), 1867.

THE BUYING AND SELLING OF LABOR-POWER

THE change of value that occurs in the case of money intended to be converted into capital cannot take place in the money itself, since in its function of means of purchase and of payment it does no more than realize the price of the commodity it buys or pays for; and, as hard cash, it is value petrified, never varying. Just as little can it originate in the second act of circulation, the resale of the commodity, which does no more than transform the article from its bodily form back again into its money-form. The change must, therefore, take place in the commodity bought by the first act, M—C, but not in its value, for equivalents are exchanged, and the commodity is paid for at its full value. We are, therefore, forced to the conclusion that the change originates in the use-value, as such, of the commodity; i. e., in its consumption. In order to be able to extract value from the consumption of the commodity, our friend Moneybags must be so lucky as to find within the sphere of circulation in the

market a commodity whose use-value possesses the peculiar property of being a source of value whose actual consumption, therefore, is itself an embodiment of labor, and consequently a creation of value. The possessor of money does find on the market such a special commodity in capacity for labor or labor-power.

By labor-power or capacity for labor is to be understood the aggregate of those mental and physical capabilities existing in a human being, which he exercises whenever he produces a use-value of any description.

But, in order that our owner of money may be able to find labor-power offered for sale as a commodity, various conditions must first be fulfilled. The exchange of commodities of itself implies no other relations of dependence than those which result from its own nature. On this assumption labor-power can appear upon the market as a commodity, only if, and so far as, its possessor, the individual whose labor-power it is, offers it for sale or sells it as a commodity. In order that he may be able to do this, he must have at his disposal, must be the untrammeled owner of his capacity for labor; i. e., of his person. He and the owner of money meet in the market and deal with each other as on the basis of equal rights, with this difference alone — that one is buyer, the other seller; both, therefore, equal in the eyes of the law. The continuance of this relation demands that the owner of the labor-power should sell it only for a definite period; for if he were to sell it rump and stump, once for all, he would be selling himself, converting himself from a free man into a slave, from an owner of a commodity into a commodity. He must constantly look upon his labor-power as his own property, his own commodity; and this he can only do by placing it at the disposal of the buyer temporarily, for a definite period of time. By this means alone can he avoid renouncing his rights of ownership over it.

The second essential condition to the owner of money finding labor-power in the market as a commodity is this: that the laborer, instead of being in the position to sell commodities in which his labor is incorporated, must be obliged to offer for sale as a commodity that very labor-power which exists only in his living self.

In order that a man may be able to sell commodities other than labor-power, he must, of course, have the means of production, as raw material, implements, etc. No boots can be made

without leather. He requires also the means of subsistence. Nobody, not even "a musician of the future," can live upon future products, or upon use-values in an unfinished state; and, ever since the first moment of his appearance on the world's stage, man always has been, and must still be, a consumer both before and while he is producing. In a society where all products assume the form of commodities, these commodities must be sold after they have been produced; it is only after their sale that they can serve in satisfying the requirements of their producer. The time necessary for their sale is superadded to that necessary for their production.

For the conversion of his money into capital, therefore, the owner of money must meet in the market with the free laborer — free in the double sense: that as a free man he can dispose of his labor-power as his own commodity, and that, on the other hand, he has no other commodity for sale, is short of everything necessary for the realization of his labor-power. . . .

The minimum limit of the value of labor-power is determined by the value of the commodities, without the daily supply of which the laborer cannot renew his vital energy, consequently by the value of those means of subsistence that are physically indispensable. If the price of labor-power fall to this minimum it falls below its value, since under such circumstances it can be maintained and developed only in a crippled state. But the value of every commodity is determined by the labor-time requisite to turn it out so as to be of normal quality.

It is a very cheap sort of sentimentality which declares this method of determining the value of labor-power — a method prescribed by the very nature of the case — to be a brutal method, and which wails with Rossi that "to comprehend capacity for labor (*puissance de travail*) at the same time that we make abstraction from the means of subsistence of the laborers during the process of production, is to comprehend a phantom (*être de raison*). When we speak of labor, or capacity for labor, we speak at the same time of the laborer and his means of subsistence, of laborer and wages." When we speak of capacity for labor, we do not speak of labor any more than when we speak of capacity for digestion we speak of digestion. The latter process requires something more than a good stomach. When we speak of capacity for labor, we do not abstract from the necessary means of subsistence. On the contrary, their value is expressed in its

value. If his capacity for labor remains unsold, the laborer derives no benefit from it; but rather he will feel it to be a cruel, nature-imposed necessity that this capacity has cost for its production a definite amount of the means of subsistence, and that it will continue to do so for its reproduction. He will then agree with Sismondi, "that capacity for labor . . . is nothing unless it is sold."

From "Capitalist Production."

FREDERICK DENISON MAURICE

(1805–1872)

REDERICK DENISON MAURICE, professor of English Literature
and History in King's College, and afterwards of Moral Philosophy at Cambridge, was born in England in 1805. He
studied both at Cambridge and Oxford, and began life as a curate in
the Church of England. His most notable work, however, was done
in literature and in education. He held the chair of Theology, as well
as of Literature, at King's College. Queen's College was founded by
him, and he was also largely instrumental in founding the Workingmen's College of London. He became professor of Moral Philosophy
at Cambridge in 1866, and died in 1872. Besides his essays he wrote
a number of philosophical works and treatises.

THE FRIENDSHIP OF BOOKS

I HAVE proposed to speak to you this evening on the Friendship
of Books. I have some fear that an age of reading is not
always favorable to the cultivation of this friendship. I do
not mean that we are in any special danger of looking upon them
as enemies. That is no doubt the temptation of some persons.
I have known both boys and men who have looked at books
with a kind of rage and hatred, as if they were the natural foes
of the human species. I am far from thinking that these were
bad boys or bad men; nor were they stupid. Some of them I
have found very intelligent, and have learned much from them.
I could trace the dislike in some cases to a cause which I thought
honorable. The dogs and horses which they did care about, and
were always on good terms with, they regarded as living creatures, who could receive affection, and in some measure could return it. Their horses could carry them over hills and moors;
their dogs had been out with them from morning till night, and
took interest in the pursuit that was interesting them. Books
seemed to them dead things in stiff bindings, that might be patted or caressed ever so much, and would take no notice, that

a folio — I mean, of course, to those who are not going themselves to be cut up in it, but only to have the pleasure of seeing their friends and neighbors cut up. Moreover, the writer of
the newspaper or magazine or review commonly assumes an off-
hand, dashing air. He has a number of colloquial phrases and
stock jests which seem intended to put us at our ease. He
speaks in a loud, rattling tone, like one who wishes to shake
hands the first time you meet him. But then, when you stretch
out your hand, what is it you meet? Not that of a man, but of
a shadow, of something that calls itself "We." Be friends with
a "We!" How is that possible? If the mist is scattered, if we
discover that there is an actual human being there, then the case
is altered altogether. If Lord Jeffrey, or Mr. Macaulay, or Sir
James Stephen publishes articles which he has written in a review, with his name affixed to them, or if a "Times correspondent" whom, in our superstition, we had supposed to be one of
the fairies or genii that descend from some other world to our
planet, appears with an ordinary name, and dressed like a mortal,
why, then we feel we are on fair terms. A person is presenting
himself to us, one who may have a right to judge us, but who
is willing to be tried himself by his peers. That, you see, is because the We has become an I. All his apparent dignity is dissolved; we can recognize him as a fellow-creature.

Now, I do not say this the least in condemnation of reviewers,
or of any person who, for any reasons whatever, thinks it
better to call himself We than I. I only say that there is no
friendship under such conditions as this; that we never can
make any book our friend until we look upon it as the work of an
I. It is the principle which I hope to maintain throughout this
lecture, and therefore I begin with stating it at once. I want
to speak to you about a few books which exhibit very trans-
parently, I think, what sort of a person he was who wrote them,
which show him to us. I think we shall find that there is the
charm of the book, the worth of the book. He may be writing
about a great many things, but there is a man who writes, and
when you get acquainted with that man you get acquainted with
the book. It is no more a collection of letters and leaves; it is
a friend.

I mean to speak entirely, or almost entirely, of English books.
And I shall begin with a writer who seems to offer a great
exception to the remark I have just made. If I thought he was

knew nothing of toil or pleasure, of hill or stubble field, of sunrise or sunsetting, of the earnest chase or the feast after it. Was
it not better to leave them on the shelves which seemed to be
made for them? Was it not treating them most respectfully not
to finger or soil them, but to secure the services of a housemaid
who should occasionally dust them?

I frankly own that I have great sympathy with these feelings,
and with those who entertain them. If books are only dead
things, if they do not speak to one, or answer one when one
speaks to them, if they have nothing to do with the common
things that we are busy with,—with the sky over our head, and
the ground under our feet,—I think that they had better stay on
the shelves; I think any horse or dog, or tree or flower, is a better companion for human beings than they are. And therefore I
say again, it is not with those who count them enemies that
I find fault. They have much to say for themselves; if their
premises are right, they are right in their conclusions. What I
regret is, that many of us spend much of our time in reading
books, and in talking of books—that we like nothing worse
than the reputation of being indifferent to them, and nothing
better than the reputation of knowing a great deal about them;
and yet that, after all, we do not know them in the same way as
we know our fellow-creatures, not even in the way we know any
dumb animal that we walk with or play with. This is a great
misfortune, in my opinion, and one which I am afraid is increasing as what we call "the taste for literature" increases. I cannot enter into all the different reasons which lead me to think
so, nor can I trace the evil to its source. But I will mention
one characteristic of the reading in our times, which must have
much to do with it.

A large part of our reading is given to reviews and magazines and newspapers. Now I am certain that these must have
a very important use. We should all of us be trying to find out
what the use of them is, because it is clear that we are born
into an age in which they exercise great power; and that fact
must bring a great responsibility not only upon those who wield
the power, but upon us who have to see that it does us good,
and not hurt. But whatever good effects works of this kind
may have produced, we certainly are not able to make them our
friends. Perhaps you will wonder that I should say that a newspaper or a review is a much less awful thing than a quarto or

really an exception I should be much puzzled, or rather I should
give up my position altogether. For since he is the greatest and
the best known of all English authors, for him to be an instance
against me would be a clear proof that I was wrong. We continually hear this observation: "William Shakespeare is not to be
found in any of his plays." It is his great and wonderful distinction that he is not. Othello speaks his word, Hamlet his,
Bottom, the weaver, his; Desdemona, Imogen, Portia, each her
word. But Shakespeare does not intrude himself into any of
their places; he does not want us to know what he thought about
this matter or that. If you look into one corner or another for
him, he is not there. It would appear, then, according to my
maxim, as if Shakespeare could never be his reader's friend. It
would appear as if he were the great precedent for all newspaper writers and reviewers, as if he were overlooking mankind
just as they do, and had the best possible right to describe himself as a We, and not as an I.

Well, that sounds very plausible, and, like everything that
sounds plausible, there is a truth at the bottom of it. But that
the truth is not this, I think the feeling and judgment of the
people of England (I might say of the continents of Europe and
of America) might convince you without any arguments of mine.
For they have been so sure that there was a William Shakespeare, they were so certain that he had a local habitation and a
name, that they have rummaged parish registers, hunted Doctors'
Commons for wills, made pilgrimages to Stratford-upon-Avon, put
together traditions about old houses and shops, that they might
make, if possible, some clear image of him in their minds. I do
not know that they have succeeded very well. The facts of his
biography are few. A good deal of imagination has been needed
to put them together, and to fill up the blanks in them. I do
not suppose registers, or wills, or old houses, will give many
more answers concerning him. But that only shows, I think,
how very clear a witness his own works give, even when the
outward information is ever so scanty, of the man that he was,
and of the characteristics which distinguished him from his fellows. If you ask me how I reconcile this assertion with the
undoubted fact that he does not put himself forward as other
dramatists do, and give his own opinions instead of allowing the
persons of his drama to utter theirs, I should answer: Have you
found that the man who is in the greatest hurry to tell you all

that he thinks about all possible things is the friend that is best worth knowing? Have you found that the one who talked most about himself and his own doings is the most worth knowing? Do you not generally become rather exhausted with men of his kind? Do not you say sometimes, in Shakespeare's own words, or rather in Falstaff's, "I do see to the bottom of this same Justice Shallow; he has told me all he has to tell. There is no reserve in him, nothing that is worth searching after"? On the other hand, have you not met with some men who very rarely spoke about their own impressions and thoughts, who seldom laid down the law, and yet who you were sure had a fund of wisdom within, and who made you partakers of it by the light which they threw on the earth in which they were dwelling, especially by the kindly, humorous, pathetic way in which they interested you about your fellowmen, and made you acquainted with them? I do not say that this is the only class of friends which one would wish for. One likes to have some who in quiet moments are more directly communicative about their own sufferings and struggles. But certainly you would not say that men of the other class are not very pleasant and very profitable. Of this class Shakespeare is the most remarkable specimen. Instead of being a reviewer who sits above the universe, and applies his own narrow rules to the members of it, he throws himself with the heartiest and most genial sympathy into the feelings of all, he understands their position and circumstances, he perceives how each must have been affected by them. Instead of being a big, imaginary We, he is so much of a man himself that he can enter into the manhood of people who are the furthest off from him, and with whom he has the least to do. And so, I believe, his books may become most valuable friends to us — to us especially who ought to be acquainted with what is going on with all kinds of people. Every now and then, I think (especially, perhaps, in the characters of Hamlet and of Prospero), one discovers signs how Shakespeare as an individual man had fought and suffered. I quite admit, however, that his main work is not to do this, but to help us in knowing ourselves — the past history of our land, the people we are continually meeting. And any book that does this is surely a friend.

Before I leave Shakespeare, I would speak of the way in which he made friends with books. Perhaps I can do it best by comparing his use of them with the use which was made of them by

a very clever and accomplished contemporary of his. Ben Jonson, though he was the son of a bricklayer, made himself a thoroughly good Latin and Greek scholar. He read the best Latin books, and the commentaries which illustrated them; he wrote two plays on subjects taken from Roman history. Very striking subjects they were. The hero of one was Catiline, who tried to overthrow the social order of the republic; the hero of the other was Sejanus, who represents, by his grandeur and his fall, the very character and spirit of the empire in the days of Tiberius. In dealing with these subjects Ben Jonson had the help of two of the greatest Roman authors, both of them possessing remarkable powers of narration, one of them a man of earnest character, subtle insight, deep reflection. Though few men in his day understood these authors, and the government and circumstances of Rome, better than Jonson, though he was a skillful and experienced playwriter, most readers are glad when they have got Catiline and Sejanus fairly done with. They do not find that they have received any distinct impressions from them of Roman life; to learn what it was they must go to the authors whom he has copied. Shakespeare wrote three plays on Roman subjects: "Coriolanus," "Julius Cæsar," "Antony and Cleopatra." He knew very little of Latin, and the materials he had to work with were a tolerable translation of Livy's "History," and a capital one of Plutarch's "Lives." With no aid but these, and his knowledge of Warwickshire peasants and London citizens, he has taught us more of the Romans, he has made us more at home in their city, and at their fireside, than the best historians who lived upon the soil are able to do. Jonson studied their books; Shakespeare made friends of them. He did just the same with our old chronicles. He read of King John, of Richard II., of John of Gaunt, of Harry of Lancaster, of Hotspur and Owen Glendower, of the good Humphrey of Gloucester, and the dark Cardinal Beaufort, of Wolsey and Catherine. He read of them, and they stood up before him, real armed men, or graceful, sorrowing women. Instead of being dead letters, they all became living persons; not appearing in solitary grandeur, but forming groups; not each with a fixed, immovable nature, but acted upon and educated by all the circumstances of their times; not dwelling in an imaginary world, but warmed by the sun of Italy, or pinched by the chilly nights of Denmark — essentially men such as are to be found in all countries and in all ages, and therefore

exhibiting all the varieties of temperament and constitution which belong to each age and to each country.

Shakespeare's mind was formed in an age when men were at work, and when they wanted books to explain and illustrate their work. He lived on into another, when men began to value books for their own sakes. James I., who was called a Solomon (and who would have deserved that name if Solomon had not considered that his wisdom was given him that he might rule his subjects well, and if James had not supposed that his was given for every purpose except that), was the great promoter of this worship of books. But they did not speak to Englishmen of that which was going on around them as they had done in Elizabeth's time. Learned people drew a line about themselves, and signified to common people who had business that they must keep their distance. Still there were many influences which counteracted this tendency. One man, who was not free from it by any means, helped to check it by opening to his fellows a new and real world. Lord Bacon found that they knew the secrets of nature only through books, that they did not come freely and directly into contact with them; he showed them how they might converse with the things they saw, how they might know them as they were in themselves, instead of only seeing them distorted by their spectacles. That was a great work to do; and as I said, it was never more wanted than just at this time, when men were in danger of falling so much in love with the letters in books as to forget into what a universe of mysteries God had put his creature man that he might search them out. Bacon reverenced the study of nature more than he did the study of man; and no wonder! For he found out what a beautiful order there was in nature; and though I believe he looked for an order in human affairs too, and sometimes discerned, and always wished for it, yet there is no denying that he had a keen eye for the disorders and wrongdoings of his fellowmen, and that he rather reconciled himself to them than sought to remedy them. I refer to him, because I fancy that many have a notion of his books on the interpretation of nature as very valuable for scientific men, and his books on morals and politics as very wise for statesmen and men of the world, but not as friends. They form this notion because they suppose that the more we knew of Bacon himself, the less sympathy we should have with him. I should be sorry to hold this opinion, because I owe him immense gratitude; and I could

not cherish it if I thought of him, even as the sagest of bookmakers, and not as a human being. I should be sorry to hold it, because if I did not find in him a man who deserved reverence and love, I should not feel either the indignation or the sorrow which I desire to feel for his misdoings. Niebuhr said of Cicero that he knew his faults as well as anybody, but that he felt as much grieved when people spoke of them as if he were his brother. That is the right way to feel about great men who are departed, and I do not think that an Englishman should feel otherwise about Bacon. It is hard to measure the exact criminality of his acts; one of the truest sentences ever passed on them was his own. His words are faithful transcripts of both his strength and weakness. There are some, especially of his dedications, which one cannot read without a sense of burning shame; there are passages in the very treatises which those dedications introduce that it does one's heart good to remember, and which we are inwardly sure must have come from the heart of him who put them into language. He does not give us at all the genial impressions of other men which Shakespeare gives, but he detects very shrewd tricks which we practice upon ourselves. His worldly wisdom is what we have most to dread, lest he should make us contented with the wrong in ourselves and in the society about us, and should teach us to admire low models. But if we apply to our moral pursuits the zeal for truth, and the method of seeking it and of escaping from our own conceits, which he imparts to us in his physical lessons, if we consider his own errors, and his punishment for tolerating and embracing the base maxims of his time, we shall find him all the safer as a guide because we have felt with him as a friend. When we do that we can always appeal from the man to himself; we can say: "Thank you heartily for what you have said to me; but there were clouds about you when you were here; you did not always walk with straight feet, and with your eyes turned to the light. Now you know better, and I will make use of what you tell me, as well as of all that I can learn about your doings, as warnings to keep me from wandering to the right or to the left."

I might speak of other books in this bookish time of James I., which many of us have found valuable and genial friends; as, for instance, the poems of George Herbert, which nobody that ever reads them can think of merely as poems; they are so completely the utterances of the heart of an affectionate, faithful, earnest man, they speak so directly to whatever is best in ourselves, and give us such friendly and kindly admonitions about what is worst. But I must go on to the next period, which was a period of action and strife, when men could no more regard writing books, or even reading them, as an amusement; when the past must be studied for the sake of the present, or not at all. John Milton belongs to that time. He was the most learned of all our poets, the one who from his childhood upwards was a devourer of Greek and Latin books, of the romances of the Middle Ages, of French and Italian poetry, above all of the Hebrew scriptures. All these became his friends; for all of them connected themselves with the thoughts that occupied men in his own time, with the deep religious and political controversies which were about to bring on a civil war. Many persons think that the side which he took in that war must hinder us from making his books our friends; that we may esteem him as a great poet, but that we cannot meet him cordially as a man. No one is more likely to entertain that opinion than an English clergyman, for Milton dealt his blows unsparingly enough, and we come in for at least our full share of them. I know all that, and yet I must confess that I have found him a friend, and a very valuable friend, even when I have differed from him most and he has made me smart most. It does not strike me that on the whole we profit most by the friends who flatter us. We may be stirred up to the recollection of our duty by those who speak stern and terrible words of us, and of our class. If we are persuaded that they are utterly wrong in condemning the institutions to which we are attached, we may often admit that they are very right in condemning us for the sins which hinder men from seeing the worth of those institutions. I do not know any one who makes us feel more than Milton does the grandeur of the ends which we ought to keep always before us, and therefore our own pettiness and want of courage and nobleness in pursuing them. I believe he failed to discern many of the intermediate relations which God has established between himself and us; but I know no one who teaches us more habitually that disobedience to the Divine Will is the seat of all misery to men. I would rather converse with him as a friend than talk of him as a poet; because then we put ourselves into a position to receive the best wisdom which he has to give us, and that wisdom helps to purge away whatever dross is mingled with it; whereas if we merely contemplate him at a dis-

tance as a great genius, we shall receive some powerful influence from him, but we shall not be in a condition to compare one thing that he says to us with another. And to say the truth, I do not know what genius is, except it be that which begets some life in those who come in contact with it, which kindles some warmth in them. If there is genius in a poem, it must have been first in the poet; and if it was in the poet, it must have been because he was not a stock or a stone, but a breathing and suffering man. And there is no writer whose books more force upon us the thought of him as a person than Milton's. There are few passages in his prose writings, full as they are of gorgeous passages, more beautiful than that in which he defends himself from the charge of entering from choice or vanity into controversies, by alleging the far different object and kind of writing to which from his youth upwards he had desired to devote himself. And in his latest poem of "Samson Agonistes," where what he had learned from the playwriters of Greece is wonderfully raised, and mellowed, and interpreted by what he had learned from the Old Testament, he himself speaks to us in every line. He transfers himself to the prison of Samson in Gaza; he is the blind, downcast, broken man whom God appears to have cast off. The thought of God as the Deliverer gives him a consolation which nothing else can give; he looks forward to some triumph which God will give to his race, as the only hope for himself.

I have dwelt some time upon these "friends," because Shakespeare, Bacon, Milton, are the greatest names in our literature, and therefore it was important for my purpose to show you that their books do fulfill the purpose which I have said all books ought to fulfill. I might very fairly have gone back, and spoken to you of older writers than these. I might have spoken of the time of our Edward III., and have given you some proofs that our first poet, Chaucer, was a cordial, genial, friendly man, who could tell us a great many things which we want to know about his own time, and could also break down the barrier between his time and ours, and make us feel that, though our dress may be very much unlike theirs, and our houses a good deal better, and our language a little less French, yet that on the whole our fathers worked at much the same trades as we do, fell into the same kind of sins, looked up at the same skies, had the same wants in their hearts, and required that they should be satisfied in the same way. I might have spoken to you also of some of

the men who flourished at the time of the Reformation — of Latimer for instance, whose broad, simple, humorous sermons address themselves to all the common sympathies of Englishmen, and are as free from starch and buckram as any one could wish. I might have spoken to you also of some of Shakespeare's contemporaries, especially of that delightful and instructive companion, Spenser's "Faery Queene," which makes us feel that without stepping a yard from our native English ground, or deserting any of our common occupations, we may be, aye, and must be, engaged in a great fight with invisible enemies, and that we have invisible champions on our side. But as I have not time to speak of many books to-night, I have passed over these and have begun at once with those which, for one reason or another, people are most likely to think of as having claims upon their respect rather than upon their friendship. That must be my reason too for not dwelling upon a book belonging to Milton's time, which many people would at once recognize as a delightful friend; I mean Izaak Walton's "Angler." Knowing nothing of his craft, I should only betray my ignorance by entering upon it, and should lessen the pleasure which some of you, I dare say, have received from its quiet descriptions and devout reflections. But I am glad to remember that there is such a book in our libraries, even if I understand very little of it, because it is one of the links between the life of the woods and streams and the life of the study, which it would be a great misfortune for us to lose.

A link between this age and the one that follows it is found in Thomas Fuller, one of the liveliest, and yet, in the inmost heart of him, one of the most serious writers one can meet with. I speak of this writer partly because there is no one who is so resolute that we should treat him as a friend, and not as a solemn dictator. By some unexpected jest, or comical turn of expression, he disappoints your purpose of receiving his words as if they were fixed in print, and asserts his right to talk with you, and convey his subtle wisdom in his own quaint and peculiar dialect. Fuller uses his wit to make his reader a friend. The writers of Charles II.'s court used their wit to prove that there could be no such thing as friendship with either books or men, that it was altogether a ridiculous obsolete sentiment. They established their point so far as they themselves were concerned; one has no right to ask of them what they had not to give. But their punishment is a singular one. They wished to pass for men of the

world, and not for vulgar bookwrights. We are obliged to regard them as bookwrights simply, and not as men at all. There is one exception. John Dryden stands apart from the men whose vices infected him, not merely because his style in prose and verse was immeasurably more vigorous than theirs, but because his confused life and his evil companions did not utterly destroy his heart. I do not know that one could make the writings of John Dryden friends; so many of the very cleverest of them are bitter satires, containing a great deal of shrewd observation, sometimes just, as well as severe, but certainly not binding us by any strong ties of affection to their author. Yet there is such a tragedy in the history of a mind so full of power as his, and so unable to guide itself amidst the shoals and quicksands of his time, that I believe we need not, and that we cannot, speak of him merely with the admiration which is due to his gifts; we must feel for him somewhat of the pity that is akin to love. Mr. Macaulay charges Dryden with changing his religion chiefly that he might get a pension from James II. I do not believe that was his motive, or that the lesson from his life would be worth as much as it is if it had been. If we compare his "Religio Laici," which he wrote in his former, with his "Hind and Panther," which expressed his later opinions, I think we may perceive that his mind was unhinged, that he found nothing fixed or certain in heaven or earth, and that he drifted naturally wherever the tide of events carried him. That is the fate which may befall many who have no right to be described as mercenary time-servers.

However, one is glad to escape from this age, which had become a very detestable one, and to find ourselves in one which, though not exemplary for goodness, produced books of which we can very well make friends. If you take up the Spectator, or the Guardian, your first feeling is that the writers in it wish to cultivate your friendship. They have thrown off the stiff manners of those who reckon it their chief business to write books; at the same time they do not affect to be men of the world despising books. Their object is to bring books and people of the world into a good understanding with each other; to make fine ladies and gentlemen somewhat wiser and better behaved by feeding them with good and wholesome literature; to show the student what things are going on about him, that he may not be a mere pedant and recluse. I do not mean that this was the deliberate purpose of Addison and Steele. It was the natural effect of their position that they took this course. They had been educated as scholars; they entered into civil life, and became members of parliament. The two characters were mixed in them; and when they wrote books they could not help showing that they knew something of men. The two men were well fitted to work together. Addison had the calmer and clearer intellect; he had inherited a respect for English faith and morality. Steele, with a more wavering conduct, had perhaps even more reverence in his inmost heart for goodness. Between them they appeared just formed to give a turn to the mind of their age; not presenting to society a very heroical standard, but raising it far above the level to which it had sunk, and is apt to sink.

The Spectator and the Guardian have sometimes been called the beginning of our periodical literature. Perhaps they are; but they are very unlike what we describe by that name in our day. There is no We in them. Though the papers have letters of the alphabet, and not names, put to them, and though they profess to be members of a club, each writer calls himself I. You can hardly conceive what a difference it would make in the pleasure with which you read any paper, if the singular pronoun were changed for the plural. The good humor of the writing would evaporate immediately. You would no longer find that you were in the presence of a kindly, friendly observer, who was going about with you and pointing out to you this folly of the town, and that pleasant characteristic of a country gentleman's life. All would be the dry, hard criticism of some distant being, who did not take you into his counsels at all, but merely told you what you were to think or not to think. And with the good humor, what we call the humor when we do not prefix the adjective to it would also disappear. Mr. Thackeray, the most competent person possible for such a task, has introduced Addison and Steele among the humorists of England, and has shown very clearly both how the humor of the one differed from that of the other, and how unlike both were to Dean Swift, who is the best and most perfect specimen of ill humor — that is to so to say, of a man of the keenest intellect and the most exquisite clearness of expression, who is utterly out of sorts with the world and with himself. Addison is on good terms with both. He amuses himself with people, not because he dislikes them, but because he likes them, and is not discomposed by their

absurdities. He does not go very far down into the hearts of them; he never discovers any of the deeper necessities which there are in human beings. But everything that is upon the surface of their lives, and all the little cross-currents which disturb them, no one sees so accurately, or describes so gracefully. In certain moods of our mind, therefore, we have here a most agreeable friend, one who tasks us to no great effort, who does not set us on encountering any terrible evils, or carrying forward any high purpose, but whom one must always admire for his quietness and composure; who can teach us to observe a multitude of things that we should else pass by, and reminds us that in man's life, as in nature, there are days of calm and sunshine as well as of storm.

But though one may have a very pleasant and useful conversation with this kind-hearted Spectator now and then, I do not think that such conversation would brace one to the hard work of life, or would enable one to sympathize with those who are engaged in it. We must remember that a very considerable majority of the world do not ride in coaches, as nearly all those we read of in the Spectator do: that to earn bread by the sweat of the brow is the common heritage of the sons of Adam, and that it is a great misfortune not to understand that necessity, even if circumstances have exempted us from it. For that reason some of us may welcome another friend, far less happy and genial than Addison, often very rough and crossgrained, with rude inward affection. Old Samuel Johnson had none of Addison's soft training. He had nothing to do with the House of Commons, except as a contraband reporter; he had not the remotest chance of being a secretary of state even if he had not been a fierce Tory, and in the reign of George II. all but a Jacobite. With only booksellers for his patrons, obliged to seek his bread from hand to mouth by writing for them what they prescribed, with a bad digestion, a temper anything but serene, a faith certainly as earnest as Addison's, but which contemplated its objects on the dark and not on the sunny side, he offers the greatest contrast one can conceive to the happy well-conditioned man of whom I have just been speaking. The opposition between them is all the more remarkable because the Rambler was formed on the model of the Spectator, and because Johnson as much as Addison belongs to what ought to be called the club period of English literature. I do not suppose any one will be bold enough

to vindicate that name, be it good or evil, for our day, merely because gentlemen are now able to eat solitary dinners, hear news, and sleep over newspapers and magazines, in very magnificent houses in Pall Mall. The genuine club, though its locality might be in some dark alley out of Fleet Street, was surely that in which men of different occupations after the toil of the day met to exchange thoughts. In that world Johnson flourished even more than Addison. The latter is accused by Pope of giving his little senate laws; but Johnson's senate contained many great men who yet listened to his oracles with reverence. And those oracles were not delivered in sentences of three clauses ending in a long word in "tion," like those papers in the Rambler which are so well parodied in the "Rejected Addresses." I think that young men ought, undoubtedly, to be early warned of these pompous sentences, not because it is worse to imitate this style than any other,—for we have no business to imitate any (our style must be our own, or it is worth nothing),—but because it is particularly easy to catch this habit of writing, and to fancy there is substance when there is only wind. But I cannot admit that Johnson's most inflated sentences contain mere wind. He had something to put into them: they did express what he felt, and what he was, better than simpler, more English, more agreeable ones would have done. He adopted them naturally; they are part of himself; if we want to be acquainted with him, we must not find fault with them. And when he is describing scenes as in "Rasselas, Prince of Abyssinia," he is often quite free and picturesque; when he is writing about business, as in his "Falkland Island," he does not let his eloquence, which in that book is often very splendid, hinder him from being pointed and direct in his blows. He falls into what some people call King Cambyses' vein chiefly when he is moralizing on the condition of the world, and the disappointment of all man's hopes and projects in it. In his club, no one could speak with more straightness, wasting no words, but bringing out the thing he wants to say in the strongest and most distinct dress that could be found. One may not agree in half of the opinions he expresses, and may think that he delivers them very dogmatically. If one looked either at his writings or at Boswell's life of him merely as books, one would go away very discontented and very angry; but when one thinks of both as exhibiting to us a man, the case becomes altogether different. We are all greatly indebted, I think, to Mr. Carlyle for having determined

mined that we should contemplate Johnson in this way, and not chiefly as a critic or a lexicographer. We may judge of him in those characters very differently; but in himself Mr. Carlyle has shown most clearly that he deserves our sympathy and our reverence.

There were two members of Johnson's club to each of whom he was sincerely attached, and who were attached to each other, though in their habits, occupations, talents, modes of thinking, they were as unlike him, and unlike each other, as any two men could be. They had, indeed, a common origin — Oliver Goldsmith and Edmund Burke were both Irishmen. But Goldsmith carried his country about with him wherever he went; he was always blundering, and reckless, and good-natured. Burke only showed where he had been born by his zeal for the improvement of his country whenever her affairs came under discussion. I believe that these two men, with the vast differences that there are between them, may both become our friends, and that we shall not thoroughly enjoy the "Deserted Village," or the "Vicar of Wakefield," or the "Speeches on American Taxation," or the "Reflections on the French Revolution," unless they do. All Goldsmith's friends were always scolding him, laughing at him, and learning from him. They found that he had a fund of knowledge which he had picked up they could not tell how, but apparently by sympathizing with all the people that he came into contact with, and so getting to be really acquainted with them. He compiled histories without much learning about the people he was writing of: yet he did not make them false or foolish, because he had more notion than many diligent historians have of what men must be like in any latitudes. In his poetry he never goes out of his depth; he speaks of things which he has seen and felt himself, and so it tells us of him if it does not tell us of much else. In spite of all his troubles, he is as good-natured as Addison; only he mixed with a different class of people from Addison, and can tell us of country vicars and their wives and daughters, though he may not know much of a Sir Roger de Coverley. His books, I think, must be always pleasant, as well as profitable friends, provided we do not expect from them, as we ought not to expect from any friend, more than they profess to give.

Burke is a friend of another order. Johnson said of him that if you met him under a gateway in a shower of rain, you must perceive that he was a remarkable man. I do not think we can take up the most insignificant fragment of the most insignificant speech or pamphlet he ever put forth without arriving at the same conviction. But he does what is better than make us acknowledge him as a remarkable man. He makes us acknowledge that we are small men, that we have talked about subjects of which we had little knowledge, and the principles of which we had imperfectly sounded.

He told the electors of Bristol, that they might reject him if they pleased, but that he should maintain his position as an English statesman, and an honest man. They did reject him, of course, but his speech remains as a model for all true men to follow, as a warning to all who adopt another course, that they may make friends for the moment, but that they will not have a friend in their own conscience, and that their books, if they leave any, will be no friends to those who read them in the times to come.

Away from the club in which Johnson, Burke, and Goldsmith were wont to meet, in a little village in Buckinghamshire, dwelt another poet, who was not uninterested in their doings, and who had in his youth mixed with London wits. William Cowper inspired much friendship among men, and still more among women, during his lifetime; they found him the pleasantest of all companions in his bright hours, and they did not desert him in his dark hours. His books have been friends to a great many since he left the earth, because they exhibit him very faithfully in both; some of his letters and some of his poems being full of mirth and quiet gladness, some of them revealing awful struggles and despair. Whatever estimate may be formed of his poetry in comparison with that of earlier or later writers, every one must feel that his English is that of a scholar and a gentleman—that he had the purest enjoyment of domestic life, and of what one may call the domestic or still life of nature. One is sure, also, that he had the most earnest faith, which he cherished for others when he could find no comfort in it for himself. These would be sufficient explanations of the interest which he has awakened in so many simple and honest readers who turn to books for sympathy and fellowship, and do not like a writer at all the worse because he also demands their sympathy with him. Cowper is one of the strongest instances and proofs how much more qualities of this kind affect Englishmen than any others. The gentleness of his life might lead some to suspect him of effeminacy; but the old Westminster schoolboy and cricketer comes out in the midst of his «Meditation on Sofas»; and the deep tragedy

which was at the bottom of his whole life, and which grew more terrible as the shadows of evening closed upon him, shows that there may be unutterable struggles in those natures which seem least formed for the rough work of the world. In one of his later poems he spoke of himself as one—

> «Who, tempest-tossed, and wrecked at last,
> Comes home to port no more.»

But his nephew, who was with him on his deathbed, says that there was a look of holy surprise on his features after his eyes were closed, as if there were very bright visions for him behind the veil that was impenetrable to him here.

I have thus given you a few hints about the way in which books may be friends. I have taken my examples from the books which are most likely to come in our way; and I have chosen them from different kinds of authors, that I may not impose my own tastes upon other people. I purposely avoid saying anything about more recent writers, who have lately left the world or are in it still, because private notions and prejudices for or against the men are likely to mingle with our thoughts of their books. I do not mean that this is not the case with the older writers too. I think I have shown you that I have no wish to forget the men in the books—that my great desire is that we should connect them together. But if we have known anything about the writers, or our fathers have known anything about them, if we have heard their acts and words gossiped about, they are not such good tests of the way in which we may discern them in their books, and learn what they are from their books. But as I began this lecture with some animadversions upon the tendency of one part of our popular literature to weaken our feeling that books are our friends, I ought to say that I am very far, indeed, from thinking that this is the effect which the more eminent writers among us produce. In their different ways, I believe most of them have addressed themselves to our human sympathies, and have claimed a place for their books, not upon our shelves, but in our hearts. Of some, both prose writers and poets, this is eminently true. Perhaps, from feeling the depressing influence of the We-teaching upon all our minds, they have taken even overmuch pains to show that each one of them comes before us as an I, and will not meet us upon any other terms. Many, I hope, who have established this intercourse with

us will keep it with our children and our children's children, and will leave books that will be regarded as friends as long as the English language lasts, and in whatever regions of the earth it may be spoken.

It is very pleasant to think in what distant parts of the earth it is spoken, and that in all those parts these books which are friends of ours are acknowledged as friends. And there is a living and productive power in them. They have produced an American literature, which is coming back to instruct us. They will produce by and by an Australian literature, which will be worth all the gold that is sent to us from the diggings.

American books have of late asserted very strongly their right to be reputed as our friends, and we have very generally and very cordially responded to the claim. I refer to one book now —Mrs. Stowe's «Dred,» though I did not mean to notice any contemporary book at all—for the sake of certain passages in it which I think that none that have read them can have forgotten. They are those in which the authoress describes the effects which were produced upon a very simple-hearted and brave negro—whose whole life had been one of zealous self-devotion to some white children, but who had had no book-teaching whatsoever—by the stories which were read to him out of the Old and New Testaments. We are told with great simplicity and with self-evident truth, how every one of these stories started to life in his mind, how every person who is spoken of in them came forth before the hearer as an actual living being, how his inmost soul confessed the book as a reality and as a friend. No lesson, I think, is more suited to our purpose. It shows us what injury we do to the Book of Books when we regard it as a book of letters, and not as a book of life; none can bear a stronger witness to us how it may come forth as the Book of Life, to save all others from sinking into dryness and death. I have detained you far too long in endeavoring to show you how every true book exhibits to us some man from whose mind its thoughts have issued, and with whom it brings us acquainted. May I add this one word in conclusion?—that I believe all books may do that for us, because there is one Book which, besides bringing into clearness and distinctness a number of men of different ages from the creation downwards, brings before us one Friend, the chief and centre of all, who is called there the Son of Man.

From his Lectures.

MATTHEW FONTAINE MAURY

(1806–1873)

MATTHEW FONTAINE MAURY, one of the greatest scientific investigators of America, was born in Spottsylvania County, Virginia, January 14th, 1806. He was educated for the United States naval service, and after serving his apprenticeship at sea was stationed at Washington for a number of years as superintendent of the Hydrographical Office and National Observatory (1844–61). During this period he practically invented the science of Meteorology. He says in one of his letters that his first idea of the laws governing the circulation of air and water was given him by the passage in Ecclesiastes, "All the rivers run into the sea, yet the sea is not full," etc. The modern signal-service system grew out of his work, and his investigation of the bed of the Atlantic Ocean made it possible to lay the Atlantic Cable successfully. His most noted work, "Physical Geography of the Sea," was published in 1855. It sustained, and perhaps increased, his already great reputation for discoveries, which had brought him honor from the principal governments and learned societies of the world. At the beginning of the Civil War he "went with his State" and became a Commodore in the Confederate navy. After the close of the war he spent several years in Mexico and Europe, returning to become professor of Physics in the Virginia Military Institute at Lexington, where he died February 1st, 1873.

THE SEA AND ITS SUBLIME LAWS

THE inhabitants of the ocean are as much the creatures of climate as are those of the dry land; for the same Almighty Hand which decked the lily and cares for the sparrow, fashioned also the pearl and feeds the great whale, and adapted each to the physical conditions by which his providence has surrounded it. Whether of the land or the sea, the inhabitants are all his creatures, subjects of his laws, and agents in his economy. The sea, therefore, we may safely infer, has its offices and duties to perform; so may we infer, has its currents, and so, too, its inhabitants; consequently, he who undertakes to study its phenomena must cease to regard it as a waste of waters. He must look upon it as a part of that exquisite machinery by which the harmonies of nature are preserved, and then he will begin to perceive the developments of order and the evidences of design; these make it a most beautiful and interesting subject for contemplation.

To one who has never studied the mechanism of a watch, its mainspring or the balance wheel is a mere piece of metal. He may have looked at the face of the watch, and, while he admires the motion of its hands, and the time it keeps, or the tune it plays, he may have wondered in idle amazement as to the character of its machinery which is concealed within. Take it to pieces, and show him each part separately; he will recognize neither design, nor adaptation, nor relation between them; but put them together, set them to work, point out the offices of each spring, wheel, and cog, explain their movements, and then show him the result; now he perceives that it is all one design,—that, notwithstanding the number of parts, their diverse forms and various offices, and the agents concerned, the whole piece is of one thought, the expression of one idea. He now rightly concludes that when the mainspring was fashioned and tempered, its relation to all the other parts must have been considered,—that the cogs on this wheel are cut and regulated—adapted—to the ratchets on that, etc.; and his final conclusion will be, that such a piece of mechanism could not have been produced by chance; for the adaptation of the parts is such as to show it to be according to design, and obedience to the will of one intelligence. So, too, when one looks out upon the face of this beautiful world, he may admire its lovely scenery, but his admiration can never grow into adoration unless he will take the trouble to look behind and study, in some of its details at least, the exquisite system of machinery by which such beautiful results are brought about. To him who does this, the sea, with its physical geography, becomes as the mainspring of a watch; its waters, and its currents, and its salts, and its inhabitants, with their adaptations, as balance wheels, cogs and pinions, and jewels. Thus he perceives that they, too, are according to design; that they are the expression of One Thought, a unity with harmonies which One Intelligence, and One Intelligence alone, could utter. And when he has arrived at this point, then he feels that the study of the sea, in its physical aspect, is truly sublime. It elevates the mind and ennobles the man. The Gulf Stream is now no longer, therefore, to be regarded by such a one merely as an immense current of warm water running across the ocean, but as a balance wheel—a part of that grand machinery by which air and water are adapted to each other, and by which this earth itself is adapted to the well-being of its inhabitants — of the flora which decks, and the fauna which enlivens its surface.

Let us now consider the influence of the Gulf Stream upon the meteorology of the ocean. To use a sailor expression, the Gulf Stream is the great "weather breeder" of the north Atlantic Ocean. The most furious gales of winds sweep along with it; and the fogs of Newfoundland, which so much endanger navigation in winter, doubtless owe their existence to the presence, in that cold sea, of immense volumes of warm water brought by the Gulf Stream. Sir Philip Brooke found the air on each side of it at the freezing point, while that of its waters was 80°. "The heavy, warm, damp air over the current produced great irregularities in his chronometers." The excess of heat daily brought into such a region by the waters of the Gulf Stream would, if suddenly stricken from them, be sufficient to make the column of superincumbent atmosphere hotter than melted iron.

With such an element of atmospherical disturbance in its bosom, we might expect storms of the most violent kind to accompany it in its course. Accordingly, the most terrific that rage on the ocean have been known to spend their fury within or near its borders.

Our nautical works tell us of a storm which forced this stream back to its sources, and piled up the waters in the Gulf to the height of thirty feet. The "Ledbury Snow" attempted to ride it out. When it abated she found herself high up on the dry land, and discovered that she had let go her anchor among the tree tops on Elliott's Key. The Florida Keys were inundated many feet, and it is said the scene presented in the Gulf Stream was never surpassed in awful sublimity on the ocean. The water thus dammed up is said to have rushed out with wonderful velocity against the fury of the gale, producing a sea that beggared description.

The "great hurricane" of 1780 commenced at Barbados. In it the bark was blown from the trees, and the fruits of the earth destroyed; the very bottom and depths of the sea were uprooted, and the waves rose to such a height that forts and castles

were washed away, and their great guns carried about in the air like chaff; houses were razed, ships were wrecked, and the bodies of men and beasts lifted up in the air and dashed to pieces in the storm. At the different islands, not less than twenty thousand persons lost their lives on shore, while further to the north the "Sterling Castle" and the "Dover Castle," men of war, went down at sea, and fifty sail were driven on shore at the Bermudas.

Several years ago the British admiralty set on foot inquiries as to the cause of the storms in certain parts of the Atlantic, which so often rage with disastrous effects to navigation. The result may be summed up in the conclusion to which the investigation led: that they are occasioned by the irregularity between the temperature of the Gulf Stream and the neighboring regions, both in the air and water.

The habitual dampness of the climate of the British Islands, as well as the occasional dampness of that along the Atlantic coasts of the United States when easterly winds prevail, is attributable also to the Gulf Stream. These winds come to us loaded with vapors gathered from its warm and smoking waters. The Gulf Stream carries the temperature of summer, even in the dead of winter, as far north as the Grand Banks of Newfoundland.

From "Physical Geography of the Sea."

TABLE OF CONTENTS

VOLUME VIII

GIUSEPPE MAZZINI

(1805–1872)

IUSEPPE MAZZINI was one of the most remarkable men of the nineteenth century, and though his work as the creator of United Italy has overshadowed his achievement as a writer, there is no question but that his writings alone would have perpetuated his memory, were they the sole monument of his extraordinary genius. It is true, however, and it must not be forgotten in connection with them, that his essays, and indeed whatever else he has written, are incidents of the moral force and intellectual activity which made him one of the great agencies in compelling the progress of Europe in spite of the strong reactionary tendencies of the second half of the nineteenth century. A man of action whose whole life was that of the leaven which disturbs while it renovates the lump, he wrote not for the sake of artistic expression, but rather to express what he conceived to be the purposes of a broader humanity and a higher civilization.

He was born at Genoa in June, 1805. His father, Giacomo Mazzini, a reputable physician of that city, was able to give him a university education, and in 1826 Mazzini graduated in law after having completed his course in literature. He joined the Carbonari society at an early age, but became dissatisfied with its methods and was on the point of organizing a new association when he was arrested (1830) and imprisoned for six months in the fortress of Savona. There he conceived what he called his "Apostolate," and on his release he began the serious work of his life,—nothing less than the enfranchisement of Italy and Europe. He purposed to organize the young men of Italy and other European countries to check centralization and to substitute self-governing republics of free people for the great military empires which were then beginning to threaten. Taking refuge at Marseilles, and when driven from Marseilles working from Geneva and London, he organized the "Young Europe Association" of 1834, and was largely instrumental in organizing the movement of 1847 and 1848, which resulted in the German Revolution. As a result of this movement, during which the Roman republic of 1849 collapsed almost immediately after it was proclaimed, he spent much of his life not merely an exile, but a hunted exile, with a sentence of death hanging over his head. He continued his agitation until, with the help of Garibaldi and Cavour, Italian unity had been secured; but

unity at the expense of monarchy, Mazzini would not accept. When the monarchy was proclaimed he declared that he sorrowfully recognized the national will; "but monarchy," he added, "will never number me among its servants or followers." He refused to take office when elected to the Italian parliament, and when a pardon was decreed for him he refused to be thus relieved from the sentence of death which had been decreed against him "for having loved Italy above all earthly things." He returned to Geneva and resumed the work of organizing the most daring among European Liberals into societies for the support of republican institutions, and in 1869 the Italian government rewarded his services by securing his expulsion from Switzerland. After visiting England he landed in Sicily and was imprisoned for several months. After his release his activity was cut short by failing health, and he died at Pisa, March 10th, 1872. Much of his best prose was written and published in London, but English literature has no claim upon it. It belongs to Italy which alone could have produced Mazzini. He had the spirit of Dante, softened and made more nearly divine by love. The "cruel indignation" against wrong, which tortured Dante, ceased to be a fire in the soul of Mazzini and became light, making his whole life incandescent with love of liberty and humanity. The nineteenth century produced no loftier character. He was in the old Hebrew sense a prophet, not the mere soothsayer who predicts events, but the maker of destiny who prophesies for (that is speaks for) those who cannot speak for themselves. "Whom shall I send?" God said to Isaiah when the cause of progress and civilization seemed lost. And when the same call came to Mazzini in the nineteenth century which came to Isaiah "in the year that King Uzziah died," the Italian prophet answered as the Hebrew prophet had answered before him, "Send me!"

W. V. B.

ON THE FRENCH REVOLUTION

IDEAS rule the world and its events. A revolution is the passage of an idea from theory to practice. Whatever men have said, material interests never have caused, and never will cause, a revolution. Extreme poverty, financial ruin, oppressive or unequal taxation, may provoke risings that are more or less threatening or violent, but nothing more. Revolutions have their origin in the mind, in the very root of life; not in the body, in the material organism. A religion or a philosophy lies at the base of every revolution. This is a truth that can be proved from the whole historical tradition of humanity.

Now, what were the ruling ideas in the period immediately preceding the revolution? What were the doctrines that hovered over its cradle? What was it that inspired and baptized its development and the various parties that promoted it? Did they go beyond the confines of the age of the individual and his rights? Did they initiate the age of duty; and of association, the only means of fulfilling duty?

Three men, Voltaire, Rousseau, Montesquieu, comprehended the whole intellectual movement of the eighteenth century, and exercised a visible and predominant influence on the development of the Revolution; Montesquieu, on the ideas of the Constituent Assembly; Rousseau, on the men of the Convention; Voltaire, on the beginnings of the movement and certain general tendencies that reappear intermittently to recall his name, and the indefatigable war he waged for fifty years against the traditions of the Church and the caprice of despotism.

Voltaire's genius was quick, subtle, acute, analytic, encyclopedic, but not profound; he was moved by good and philanthropic instincts rather than by strong and reasoned moral beliefs; a warrior rather than an apostle; a hater of evil rather than a worshiper of good; too much extolled by some, too much depreciated by others, Voltaire founded no doctrine, but, as I have said, popularized tendencies,—tendencies that existed already, and were almost innate in the French genius, but to which he gave new force and clothed in noble language,—tendencies which leak out in a number of the events of the Revolution, and, excepting the more rigid puritans of the Mountain, from Camille Desmoulins to Barras, influence, one might say, every actor of the period. They were philanthropic tendencies, inspired by momentary impulses of kindness rather than by a conception of life, and of its law,—tendencies of a vague, sterile, superficial deism, that relegated God to heaven and sundered his undying connection with the world, and which was merely a compromise between the tradition still extant in the popular mind, and the skepticism that, however covertly, dominated Voltaire and his followers,—tendencies of antagonism to every imposed authority, to every form of superstition and fanaticism, but born rather of a sense of rebellion natural to one who thinks than of faith in the destinies of those who have yet to learn to think,—tendencies that worshiped the rights of reason, but only for those individuals who by good fortune and education

can share in them, and which were mingled with some spirit of contempt for the masses, a spirit which afterwards founded the fatal distinction between the popular and the bourgeois classes, —tendencies of equality, but confined, as in the philosophy of the Ancients, to one order of men, regardless of the rest. I have mentioned the bourgeois class, and Voltaire was, in fact, consciously or unconsciously, the teacher and master of the bourgeoisie, and his influence was all-powerful in the acts that, in the period just before the Revolution, traced the first lines of a division that has been more recently organized into a system, by Guizot and the French eclectic school. The bourgeoisie of the two Bourbon revolutions idolized him. A man of impulses, of intuitions, rapid but short-lived, of enthusiasm, intellectual rather than moral, Voltaire, who displayed rare humanity in his efforts to clear the memory of Calas and the Sirven family, was flatterer at once of the Empress Catherine and King Frederic of Prussia. He sanctified their crimes; he burlesqued, in low comic verse, the heroic resistance of the Poles to the dismemberment of their Fatherland. An apostle of toleration in religious matters, he was the type of intolerance towards all his enemies, and capable of using any weapon, even calumny, to their prejudice. He waged a relentless, rabid war against catholicism, and when threatened with death wrote a declaration of catholic faith and repentance. I write this as a debt to my own conscience, and because I see arising among our young men, who have neither studied all his works nor his life, an intemperate and dangerous admiration for him; but it is more important to my present purpose to note how Voltaire destroyed prejudices and errors, but neither built nor cared for the future. He had no perception (his historical works and his theory that great events depend upon little causes prove this) of a law dominating the life of humanity, no perception of progress, of a human mission, of duty, of association, or of anything that constitutes the end and the method of the new era that we invoke. He recognized no standard of good except in the rights of the individual. And like all who start from the idea of right alone, he could not help being forced to give the preference to rights already existing and recognized. He declared that "A State being a collection of lands and houses, those who possessed neither land nor house ought not to have any deliberative voice in the management of public affairs." In one of the most beautiful moments of his long life, he gave full expression to the idea that guided him, when he uttered, under guise of a blessing on Franklin's young son, the sacred but insufficient words — God and Liberty; a formula that opens the way to a possible initiative, but does not itself initiate. Liberty is a mere instrument of good or evil according to the path it chooses.

Montesquieu, a more profound thinker than Voltaire, though less profound than some say, was the chief of a political school that had for its disciples, in the first period of the Revolution, Monnier, Malouet, and many others in the Assembly; Rivarol, Bergasse, Mallet Dupan, and others in the periodical press. The influence of the ideas he expounded in the Esprit des Lois is visible in the acts of the Constituent Assembly.

His influence lay in his historical studies of antiquity, that would be thought superficial at the present day, but then appeared vast and almost unique. His intellect was acute, and swift in seizing the salient points of things; his aspirations were advanced; the expression of his thoughts vigorous. Montesquieu was at times unconsciously impelled, by his native logic, near to the unknown confines of the new age; but he was hindered by his lack of any religious conception of the life of humanity, by the prevailing theory of the ebb and flow of nations, perhaps, too, by the inevitable influences of a semi-patrician birth and the conditions of office; and so he retreated ever more and more towards the old age, and never, even in his most daring flights, crossed the limits of a period that began the transition. For an instant he caught a glimpse of the true definition of liberty, when he said that it consisted "in being able to do what one ought to will, and in not being constrained to do what one ought not to will." But this was a momentary flash, an isolated saying, whose consequences he was unable to deduce. He suspected the existence of a general end, common to humanity, and a special end, belonging to each nation; but he was incapable of rising from that glimpse of an idea to the conception of a providential mission. He notes "that the object of Rome was aggrandizement; of Lacedæmonia, war; of the Judaic laws, religion; of Marseilles, commerce; of the barbarians, natural liberty"; but he never saw that those facts were only means to reach the end, and that the appointed end is general progressive civilization, the slow formation of a collective human unity. It is clear from twenty passages that he feels in his soul the superiority of the Republican form

of government to all others; and yet, finding no body of principles that convert the intuition of the moment into a demonstrated truth, he concludes by laboring to teach how a monarchy may be durably established. He too, in all his researches, starts only from the individual, and so, like all who have no other criterion of truth, he can only grasp the notion of right. For him, as for the other philosophic thinkers of the time, there are rights consecrated by the fact of their existence, by prolonged possession; and the political program is reduced to efforts to find a place for them in the social organism, and to seek an impossible equilibrium that shall preserve the peace among them, and prevent one right from doing violence to another. Placed between a monarchy that said "France is mine," an aristocracy powerful by past domination and an exclusive influence over the monarchy, and the first threatening murmurings of the Tiers État, Montesquieu did not pretend to pass judgment on those three forces, or ascertain the sum of vitality that existed in each, and which was doomed to early death, which destined to long life in the future. They existed, and he accepted them, consecrating the labor of his intellect to co-ordinate their existence and functions in the organization of the State. His ideal was the English system, the result, not of any conception of political philosophy, but of a unique historical development of causes and effects which existed nowhere else. His theory is that which we have seen in practice for more than half a century under the name of constitutional monarchy, where the search for an equilibrium between the three elements of Crown, and Nobility, and Commons, has everywhere condemned the peoples to alternate between stagnation, reaction, and periodic revolution.

The problem, therefore, in the Esprit des Lois is vitiated by a fundamental error. Montesquieu labors heavily about the distinction between the three powers, legislative, executive, and judiciary, and makes this the cardinal point of the whole question; he thus, by exaggerating this distinction, destroys the conception of national unity. The real, the sole, the vital question should be, for him as for us all, the question of sovereignty; what is its origin, and where its interpretation is to be sought with the least uncertainty and the greatest probability.

There does not, and ought not to exist more than one law; it is its application to the diverse branches of social life that implies a distinction in the higher branches of the administration

between the different functions delegated to provide for its execution. Just as the exaggeration of the triple aspect of life in God changed little by little the three different aspects of divine action into Three Persons, and founded a Tri-theism in religion opposed to the conception of Unity, so the theory of rights, and hence of acquired rights, impelled Montesquieu to discover powers where they did not exist, and found a political Tri-theism which has survived even to this day, and impairs every conception of national organization. Having raised these social elements to powers, he confers on them attributes which suffice to break up the harmony of the State. He was confronted by the danger, either of antagonism between the three powers, or compulsory stagnation; but he replied with superficial carelessness, "that, as they were urged forward by the necessary movement of things, they would be constrained to move in unison."

Montesquieu abounds in false ideas respecting the hereditary nature of the aristocracy, the function of the monarchy, the rights conceded to the executive over the legislative, and many other questions. But it is not my task to notice them. It is sufficient for my purpose to have reminded my readers of the thought that dominates his conceptions. He has no criterion outside that of the individual. He reaches no formula of political organization beyond that of rights. He has no scope, no mission to suggest for the State, except liberty, and by liberty he understands, in the general course of his work, nothing more than "the citizen's consciousness of his own safety, and of having nothing to fear from any other citizen." Political science is therefore narrowed to a science of limits, of mutual defense. And the government deprived of any other mission is to use the force of society to watch that those limits are not overstepped by violence. A religious conception, the law of progress, duty, association, the end assigned to humanity and to each people, collective education, and the office of the press to gradually promote the unity of the human family, everything, in short, that is characteristic of the age we call for, is unknown to the man who inspired the Constituent Assembly.

Montesquieu was neither inspirer nor prophet of an age. He summarized, with singular acumen, the conditions and consequences of political laws as he found them, incomplete or in partial activity, in the period in which he lived. He sketched in outline, not always, but frequently exact, the existing tradition,

but nothing more. When we point to him, at the present time, as the master of future legislation, we commit the same error as when we make poor Machiavelli the guardian of the cradle of reborn Italy — Machiavelli, who anatomized the dead body of old Italy and showed the wounds that caused her death; when we take Adam Smith — who was but the wise exponent of the laws that governed the economic phenomena of his time — and make him the founder of an immutable science, the teacher of an age in which the economic relations between class and class are hastening to an inevitable change.

Rousseau, the inspirer of the Convention, followed another road, but without passing the confines of the age that France was preparing to summarize. A poor plebeian, without deep study of the past, abhorring the times in the consciousness of his own superiority, and for the exaggerated demands of society as he found it, he, on the great political questions of the day, questioned only his own intelligence and the intuitions of the heart. His intelligence was more powerful than that of Montesquieu; his heart was led astray by a leaven of egotism that too often soured his natural inclination to good; and both together drove him to the principle that takes its birth, if not its consecration, from him — the principle of popular sovereignty. A true principle, if considered as the best method of interpreting a supreme moral law which a nation has accepted as its guide, which is solemnly declared in its contract and transmitted by national education; but a false and anarchical principle if proclaimed in the name of force, or in the name of a convention, and abandoned to the caprice of majorities, uneducated, and corrupted by a false conception of life.

For Rousseau, the popular sovereignty remained in these last terms, uncertain, ineffective, shifting. He, too, had no conception of the collective life of humanity, of its tradition, of the law of progress appointed for the generations, of a common end towards which we ought to strive, of association that can alone attain it step by step. Starting from the philosophy of the *ego* end of individual liberty, he robbed that principle of fruit by basing it, not on a duty common to all, not on a definition of man as an essentially social creature, not on the conception of a divine authority and a providential design, not on the bond that unites the individual to humanity of which he is a factor, but on a simple convention, avowed or understood. All Rousseau's teaching proceeds from the assertion "that social right is not derived from nature, but is based upon conventions." He drives this doctrine so far as to comprehend the family itself within it. "Sons," he says, "do not remain united to their fathers except so long as they have need of them for their preservation. . . . From that time forth the family is only maintained in virtue of a convention."

From the doctrine that recognizes the rights of the contracting individuals as the only source of social life, nothing could result but a political system capable of protecting, within the limits of a narrow possibility, the liberty and equality of each citizen; and Rousseau has no other program. "The aim of every system of legislation"—these are his very words—"reduces itself to two principal objects, liberty and equality; and to find a form of society that shall defend and protect with all the collective forces the person and the property of each associate, and in which each one, uniting himself to all, shall obey only himself and remain as free as he was before; this is the fundamental problem." Stated in these terms, the problem contains neither the elements of normal progress, nor the possibility of solving the social economic question that is so prominently agitating men's minds in our time. An isolated sentence in the book seems to lay down the principle that "no citizen ought to be rich enough to be in a position to buy another; none poor enough to be constrained to sell himself"; this is just, but it does not connect itself with the general bearing of the principles he expounds, nor is there any indication how it may be reduced to fact. It is of little importance that in many particulars he is superior to every other thinker of that period. The Society of Rousseau, like that of Montesquieu, is a mutual insurance society, and nothing more.

That first statement, the key of the whole system, is by now proven to be false; and, because false, fatal to the development of the principle of popular sovereignty. It is not by the force of conventions or of aught else, but by a necessity of our nature, that societies are founded and grow. Each of us is a part of humanity, each of us lives its life, each is called upon to live for it, to aid the attainment of the end assigned to it, to realize, as far as possible in each one of us, the ideal type, the divine thought that guides it. Law is one and the same for individual and collective life, both of which are the expression of a single universal phenomenon, differently modified by space and time.

And life, we know now, is progress. If you throw over moral authority, our natural tendencies, our mission, and substitute the merely human authority of conventions as the source of social development, you risk arresting that development, or subjecting it to arbitrary caprice. And since you need the consent of all the contracting parties to dissolve these conventions and make a change for the better, you are threatened, on the one hand by the power of every minority, logically indeed of every individual, to stop you; on the other hand, inasmuch as the prolonged existence of a fact pre-supposes, at all events, a tacit convention, you are threatened by the necessity of perpetuating rights and powers that are not founded on justice, or conducive to the common good. No "man" has, you say, "natural authority over his fellows; might cannot create right; therefore conventions are left as the only basis of legitimate authority." But is there not an authority higher than any man, in the True, the Just, the end which we have set before us and which we are bound above all things to discover? Is not some of that authority passed on to the people or to that fraction of the people which is its best interpreter? And, to discover that end, do we not possess the double criterion supplied when the tradition of humanity and the conscience of our times both harmonize? And for a method of practical verification, can we not examine whether this item of discovered truth profits or not the common progress? Rousseau believed in God, but in his study of human phenomena he continually forgot him.

Rousseau believed in God. He believed—and it is well to remind of this those republican materialists who venerate the "Contrat Social"—that a State could not be established without having religion for its foundation. And he pushed this belief to the fanaticism of intolerance, declaring that the sovereign power could exile from the State all who disbelieved in God and immortality, and condemn any citizen to death who, after publicly confessing his belief in those dogmas, by his subsequent conduct convicted himself of deliberate falsehood. But he confined himself within a narrow deism that placed God far off in heaven, and never understood his universal, never-dying life manifested in creation; he was ignorant of the law of progress—the sole but potent and living mediator between God and humanity; he was fettered by the individualist's philosophy; he had no glimpse of any religion besides Christianity, and so he was incapable of

deducing and applying the logical consequences of his faith to society.

Like Voltaire and Montesquieu, Rousseau was not the intellectual herald of the age. His conception, though more daring, more explicit, more advanced than theirs, never passes the limits of the individualist world, elaborated by the Pagan-Christian age. The influence of the three schools with which these names are associated could not push the Revolution beyond those limits to the world of progress and association for which we are now fighting.

Complete.

MENCIUS (MENG-TSE)

(c. 372–289 B. C.)

MENCIUS, who is generally ranked as the greatest of the disciples of Confucius, is in a most important respect greater than his master. Confucius saw that civilization would develop of itself, if men would merely refrain from oppression, each making his own feelings the test of what he ought not to do to others. Mencius went beyond this to search for the efficient cause through which civilization develops when oppression ceases. He found it in the spirit of mutual helpfulness made operative through love. His definitions, as we have them in Doctor Legge's translation, represent intellect on its highest plane. Plato himself did not reach a higher. Indeed, no higher system of ethics is conceivable by the human intellect than that which would necessarily develop from a genuine attempt to put in practice the principles of the chapters on "Universal Love" by Mencius; but as he says with remarkable insight it is "the most difficult thing in the world" because "the scholars and superior men do not understand the advantageousness of the law, and to conduct their reasonings upon that." Mencius, whose real name was Meng or Mang ("Meng-tse" the Master Meng) was born, according to some authorities, in 372 B. C., while others place his birth in the year 385. He was an ardent admirer and deep student of Confucius, like whom he went from court to court as a political and ethical reformer, hoping to find a ruler who would attempt to base government on right principles. Like Confucius he failed, but after his death his countrymen erected statues and temples to him and they still honor his spirit as that of one of their tutelary demigods. "The great man," he said, "is he who does not lose his child heart," —paralleling in this the Christian Gospels in a most striking way, as he does in making love "the fulfilling of the law" of civilization.

UNIVERSAL LOVE

IT IS the business of the sages to effect the good government of the empire. They must know, therefore, whence disorder and confusion arise, for without this knowledge their object cannot be effected. We may compare them to a physician who undertakes to cure a man's disease:—he must ascertain whence the disease has arisen, and then he can assail it with effect, while, without such knowledge, his endeavors will be in vain. Why should we except the case of those who have to regulate disorder from this rule? They must know whence it has arisen, and then they can regulate it.

It is the business of the sages to effect the good government of all under heaven. They must examine therefore into the cause of disorder; and when they do so, they will find that it arises from want of mutual love. When a minister and a son are not filial to their sovereign and their father, this is what is called disorder. A son loves himself, and does not love his father;—he therefore wrongs his father and advantages himself: a younger brother loves himself, and does not love his elder brother;—he therefore wrongs his elder brother, and advantages himself: a minister loves himself, and does not love his sovereign;—he therefore wrongs his sovereign, and advantages himself:—all these are cases of what is called disorder. Though it be the father who is not kind to his son, or the elder brother who is not kind to his younger brother, or the sovereign who is not gracious to his minister:—the case comes equally under the general name of disorder. The father loves himself, and does not love his son;—he therefore wrongs his son, and advantages himself: the elder brother loves himself, and does not love his younger brother;—he therefore wrongs his younger brother, and advantages himself: the sovereign loves himself, and does not love his minister;—he therefore wrongs his minister, and advantages himself. How do these things come to pass? They all arise from the want of mutual love. Take the case of any thief or robber:—it is just the same with it. The thief loves his own house, and does not love his neighbor's house;—he therefore steals from his neighbor's house to advantage his own: the robber loves his own person, and does not love his neighbor;—he therefore does violence to his neighbor to advantage himself. How is this? It all arises from the want of mutual love. Come to the case of great officers throwing each other's families into confusion, and of princes attacking one another's States:—it is just the same with them. The great officer loves his own family, and does not love his neighbor's;—he therefore throws his neighbor's family into disorder to advantage his own: the prince loves his own State, and does not love his neighbor's;

—he therefore attacks his neighbor's State to advantage his own. All disorder in the empire has the same explanation. When we examine into the cause of it, it is found to be the want of mutual love.

Suppose that universal mutual love prevailed throughout the kingdom;—if men loved others as they love themselves, disliking to exhibit what was unfilial. . . . would there be those who were unkind? Looking on their sons, younger brothers, and ministers as themselves, and disliking to exhibit what was unkind . . . the want of filial duty would disappear. And would there be thieves and robbers? When every man regarded his neighbor's house as his own, who would be found to steal? When every one regarded his neighbor's person as his own, who would be found to rob? Thieves and robbers would disappear. And would there be great officers throwing one another's families into confusion, and princes attacking one another's States? When officers regarded the families of others as their own, what one would make confusion? When princes regarded other States as their own, what one would begin an attack? Great officers throwing one another's families into confusion, and princes attacking one another's States, would disappear. If, indeed, universal mutual love prevailed throughout the kingdom; one State not attacking another, and one family not throwing another into confusion; thieves and robbers nowhere existing; rulers and ministers, fathers and sons, all being filial and kind:—in such a condition the kingdom would be well governed. On this account, how many sages, whose business it is to effect the good government of the kingdom, do other than prohibit hatred and advise to love? On this account it is affirmed that universal mutual love throughout the kingdom will lead to its happy order, and that mutual hatred leads to confusion. This was what our Master, the philosopher Mih, meant, when he said, "We must not but advise to the love of others."

Chapter iii. of "The Works of Mencius" complete.
Translated by James Legge.

THE MOST DIFFICULT THING IN THE WORLD

OUR Master, the philosopher Mih, said, "That which benevolent men consider to be incumbent on them as their business is to stimulate and promote all that will be advantageous to the kingdom, and to take away all that is injurious to it. This is what they consider to be their business."

And what are the things advantageous to the kingdom, and the things injurious to it? Our Master said, "The mutual attacks of State on State; the mutual usurpations of family on family; the mutual robberies of man on man; the want of kindness on the part of the sovereign and of loyalty on the part of the minister; the want of tenderness and filial duty between father and son:—these, and such as these, are the things injurious to the empire."

And from what do we find, on examination, that these injurious things are produced? Is it not from the want of mutual love?

Our Master said, "Yes, they are produced by the want of mutual love. Here is a prince who only knows to love his own State, and does not love his neighbor's;—he therefore does not shrink from raising all the power of his State to attack his neighbor. Here is the chief of a family who only knows to love it, and does not love his neighbor's;—he therefore does not shrink from raising all his powers to seize on that other family. Here is a man who only knows to love his own person, and does not love his neighbor's;—he therefore does not shrink from using all his strength to rob his neighbor. Thus it happens that the princes, not loving one another, have their battlefields; and the chiefs of families, not loving one another, have their mutual usurpations; and men, not loving one another, having their mutual robberies; and sovereigns and ministers, not loving one another, become unkind and disloyal; and fathers and sons, not loving one another, lose their affection and filial duty; and brothers, not loving one another, contract irreconcilable enmities. Yea, men in general not loving one another, the strong make prey of the weak; the rich do despite to the poor; the noble are insolent to the mean; and the deceitful impose upon the stupid. All the miseries, usurpations, enmities, and hatreds in the world, when traced to their origin, will be found to arise from the want of mutual love. On this account, the benevolent condemn it."

They may condemn it; but how shall they change it?

Our Master said, "They may change it by universal mutual love, and by the interchange of mutual benefits."

How will this law of universal mutual love and the interchange of mutual benefits accomplish this?

Our Master said, "(It would lead) to the regarding another kingdom as one's own; another family as one's own; another person as one's own. That being the case, the princes, loving one another, would have no battlefields; the chiefs of families, loving one another, would attempt no usurpations; men, loving one another, would commit no robberies; rulers and ministers, loving one another, would be gracious and loyal; fathers and sons, loving one another, would be kind and filial; brothers, loving one another, would be harmonious and easily reconciled. Yea, men in general loving one another, the strong would not make prey of the weak; the many would not plunder the few; the rich would not insult the poor; the noble would not be insolent to the mean; and the deceitful would not impose upon the simple. The way in which all the miseries, usurpations, enmities, and hatreds in the world may be made not to arise, is universal love. On this account, the benevolent value and praise it." Yes; but the scholars of the empire and superior men say, "True; if there were this universal love, it would be good. It is, however, the most difficult thing in the world."

Our Master said, "This is because the scholars and superior men simply do not understand the advantageousness (of the law), and to conduct their reasonings upon that."

From Chapter ii. of "Universal Love."

MOSES MENDELSSOHN

(1729-1786)

OSES MENDELSSOHN, the prototype of Lessing's "Nathan the Wise," was born at Dessau, Germany, September 6th, 1729. His father taught a small school, educating children in the Jewish law to which the family adhered. Moses was of delicate constitution, and he became early in life a victim of the spinal disease which sometimes accompanies, if it does not exaggerate, abnormal intellectual activity. Leaving Dessau at twenty-four to seek his fortune in Berlin, he underwent great hardships while attempting to fit himself for a literary career. Herder, Wieland, Lavater, and Lessing finally found him out and gave him the opportunity he needed. One of his papers won a prize from the Berlin Academy against Kant himself, and he soon came to be known as the "German Socrates." His plea for toleration and moral liberty show that he was above the level of either the eighteenth or the nineteenth century. He died January 4th, 1786, after a life of usefulness so lofty in its simplicity and unselfishness, that the *Judenfresser* of Germany has never since been able to recover the ground from which it forced him to retreat.

THE HISTORICAL ATTITUDE OF JUDAISM

PURSUANT to the principles of my religion, I am not to seek to convert any one who is not born according to our laws. This proneness to conversion, the origin of which some would fain tack on the Jewish religion, is, nevertheless, diametrically opposed to it. Our rabbins unanimously teach that the written and oral laws, which form conjointly our revealed religion, are obligatory on our nation only. "Moses commanded us a law, even the inheritance of the congregation of Jacob." We believe that all other nations of the earth have been directed by God to adhere to the laws of nature and to the religion of the patriarchs. Those who regulate their lives according to the precepts of this religion of nature and of reason are called virtuous men of other nations, and are the children of eternal salvation.

I am so fortunate as to count among my friends many a worthy man who is not of my faith. We love each other sincerely, notwithstanding we presume, or take for granted, that, in matters of belief, we differ widely in opinion. I enjoy the delight of their society, which both improves and solaces me. Never yet has my heart whispered, "Alas! for this excellent man's soul!" He who believes that no salvation is to be found out of the pale of his own church must often feel such sighs rise in his bosom.

It is true, every man is naturally bound to diffuse knowledge and virtue among his fellow-creatures, and to eradicate error and prejudice as much as lies in his power. It might therefore be concluded that it is a duty publicly to fling the gauntlet at every religious opinion which one deems erroneous. But all prejudices are not equally noxious. Certainly, there are some which strike directly at the happiness of the human race; their effect on morality is obviously deleterious, and we cannot expect even a casual benefit from them. These must be unhesitatingly assailed by the philanthropist. To grapple with them, at once, is indisputably the best mode, and all delay, from circuitous measures, unwarrantable. Of this kind are those errors and prejudices which disturb man's own, and his fellow-creatures' peace and happiness, and canker, in youth, the germ of benevolence and virtue, before it can shoot forth. Fanaticism, ill-will, and a spirit of persecution, on the one side; levity, epicureanism, and boasting infidelity, on the other.

Yet the opinions of my fellow-creatures, erroneous as they may appear to my conviction, do sometimes belong to the higher order of theoretical principles, and are too remote from practice to become immediately pernicious; they constitute, however, from their generality, the basis on which the people who entertain them have raised their system of morality and social order; and so they have casually become of great importance to that portion of mankind. To attack such dogmas openly, because they appear prejudices, would be like sapping the foundation of an edifice, for the purpose of examining its soundness and stability, without first securing the superstructure against a total downfall. He who values the welfare of mankind more than his own fame will bridle his tongue on prejudices of this description, and beware of seeking to reform them prematurely and precipitately, lest he should overset what he thinks a defective theory of morality

Our rabbins are so remote from Proselytomania, that they enjoin us to dissuade, by forcible remonstrances, every one who comes forward to be converted. We are to lead him to reflect that, by such a step, he is subjecting himself needlessly to a most onerous burthen; that, in his present condition, he has only to observe the precepts of a Noachide, to be saved; but the moment he embraces the religion of the Israelites, he subscribes gratuitously to all the rigid rites of that faith, to which he must then strictly conform, or await the punishment which the legislator has denounced on their infraction. Finally, we are to hold up to him a faithful picture of the misery, tribulation, and obloquy, in which the nation is now living, in order to guard him from a rash act, which he might ultimately repent.

Thus, you see, the religion of my fathers does not wish to be extended. We are not to send missions to both the Indies, or to Greenland, to preach our doctrine to those remote people. The latter, in particular, who, by all accounts, observe the law of nature stricter, alas! than we do, are, in our religious estimation, an enviable race. Whoever is not born conformable to our laws has no occasion to live according to them. We alone consider ourselves bound to acknowledge their authority; and this can give no offense to our neighbors. Let our notions be held ever so absurd, still there is no need to cavil about them, and others are certainly at liberty to question the validity of laws, to which they are, by our own admission, not amenable; but whether they are acting humanely, socially, and charitably, in ridiculing these laws, must be left to their consciences. So long as we do not tamper with their opinions, wrangling serves no purpose whatsoever.

Suppose there were amongst my contemporaries a Confucius or a Solon, I could consistently with my religious principles love and admire the great man, but I should never hit on the extravagant idea of converting a Confucius or a Solon. What should I convert him for? As he does not belong to the congregation of Jacob, my religious laws were not legislated for him; and on doctrines we should soon come to an understanding. Do I think there is a chance of his being saved? I certainly believe that he who leads mankind on to virtue in this world cannot be damned in the next. And I need not now stand in awe of any reverend college, that would call me to account for this opinion, as the Sorbonne did honest Marmontel.

before his fellow-creatures are firm in the perfect one, which he means to substitute.

Therefore, there is nothing inconsistent in my thinking myself bound to remain neutral, under the impression of having detected national prejudices and religious errors amongst my fellow-citizens,—provided these errors and prejudices do not subvert, directly, either their religion or the laws of nature, and that they have a tendency to promote, casually, that which is good and desirable. The morality of our actions, when founded in error, it is true, scarcely deserves that name; and the advancement of virtue will be always more efficaciously and permanently effected through the medium of truth, where truth is known, than through that of prejudice or error. But where truth is not known, where it has not become national, so as to operate as powerfully on the bulk of the people as deep-rooted prejudice — there prejudice will be held almost sacred by every votary of virtue.

How much more imperative, then, does this discretion become, when the nation, which in our opinion fosters such prejudices, has rendered itself otherwise estimable through wisdom and virtue, when it contains numbers of eminent men, who rank with the benefactors of mankind! The human errors of such a noble portion of our species ought to be deferentially overlooked by one, who is liable to the same; he should dwell on its excellences only, and not insidiously prowl to pounce upon it, where he conceives it to be vulnerable.

These are the reasons which my religion and my philosophy suggest to me for scrupulously avoiding polemical controversy.

From a letter to J. C. Lavater.

SHAKESPEARE AS A MASTER OF THE SUBLIME

NO ONE is more happy in taking advantage of the commonest circumstances and making them sublime, by a fortunate turn, than Shakespeare. The effect of this species of the sublime must necessarily be stronger the more unexpectedly it surprises us and the less prepared we are to anticipate such weighty and tragic consequences from such trivial causes. I will give one or two examples of this out of "Hamlet." The King institutes public entertainments in order to dissipate the melancholy of the Prince. Plays are performed. Hamlet has seen the tragedy of "Hecuba." He appears to be in good humor. The company leaves him; and now mark with astonishment the tragic consequence which Shakespeare knows how to draw from these trivial common circumstances. The prince soliloquizes:—

"Oh! what a rogue and peasant slave am I!
Is it not monstrous that this player here,
But in a fiction, in a dream of passion,
Could force his soul so to his own conceit,
That from her working all his visage wanned;
Tears in his eyes, distraction in 's aspect,
A broken voice and his whole function suiting
With forms to his conceit! And all for nothing!
For Hecuba!
What 's Hecuba to him or he to Hecuba,
That he should weep for her? What would he do
Had he the motive and the cue for passion
That I have?"

What a master trait! Experience teaches that pers s afflicted with melancholy find unexpectedly in every occasion, even in entertainments, a transition to the prevailing idea of their grief; and the more it is attempted to divert them from it, the more suddenly they fall back. This experience guided the genius of Shakespeare wherever he had to depict melancholy. His "Hamlet" and his "Lear" are full of these unexpected transitions causing terror to the spectator.

In the third act, Guildenstern, a former confidant of Hamlet, at the instigation of the king endeavors to sound him and to ascertain the secret cause of his melancholy. The prince detects his purpose and resents it.

Guild.—O my lord! if my duty be too bold, my love is too unmannerly.

Ham.—I do not well understand that. Will you play upon this pipe?

Guild.—My lord, I cannot.

Ham.—I pray you.

Guild.—Believe me I cannot.

Ham.—I do beseech you.

Guild.—I know no touch of it, my lord.

Ham.—'Tis as easy as lying. Govern these ventages with your finger and thumb, give it breath with your mouth, and it will discourse most eloquent music. Look you, these are the stops.

Guild.—But these cannot I command to any utterance of harmony; I have not the skill.

Ham.—Why, look you now, how unworthy a thing do you make of me! You would play upon me; you would seem to know my stops; you would sound me from my lowest note to the top of my compass: and there is much music, excellent voice in this little organ; yet cannot you make it speak. 'S blood! do you think I am easier to be played on than a pipe! Call me what instrument you will, though you can fret me you cannot play upon me.

None but Shakespeare must venture to introduce such common matters upon the stage, for no one but he possesses the art to use them. Must not the spectator, in this case, be as much amazed as Guildenstern, who feels the superior address of the Prince, and withdraws, covered with shame?

If the artist wishes to give us, in his work, a clear and sensible proof of those perfections which he possesses in the highest degree, he must direct his attention to the highest beauties which can animate his description. The little touches of the pencil, it is true, attest the finishing hand of the master, his diligence and his care to please. But it is not in them, certainly, that we are to look for the sublime which deserves our admiration. Admiration is a tribute which we owe to extraordinary gifts of mind. These are what we call genius in the strictest sense. Accordingly, wherever, in a work of art, there are found sensible marks of genius, there we are ready to accord to the artist the admiration which is his due. But the unimportant adjuncts, the last finish—that which belongs indeed to the picture, but does not constitute an essential part of the picture—exhibits too plainly the diligence and the care which it has cost the artist; and we are accustomed to deduct so much from genius as we ascribe to diligence.

From the essay on the "Sublime and
Naïve in Belles-Lettres."

2881

JULES MICHELET

(1798–1874)

JULES MICHELET, an eminent French historian, was born at Paris, August 21st, 1798. His education began at the case in his father's printing office, and was continued under the direction of a friendly dealer in old books until he had prepared himself for college. Carrying off the highest honors of his university, he began life as professor of History in the Collège Rollin. His first works were chronological studies of history, and he wrote on law, ethics, and philosophy, before giving to the world his great work, "The History of France," which is one of the most interesting histories ever written—made so by the brilliant picturesqueness of the subsidiary essays which develop its most important topics. He died February 9th, 1874.

THE DEATH OF JEANNE D'ARC

THE great English people, with so many good and solid qualities, is infected by one vice, which corrupts these very qualities themselves. This rooted, all-poisoning vice is pride; a cruel disease, but which is, nevertheless, the principle of English life, the explanation of its contradictions, the secret of its acts. With them, virtue or crime is almost ever the result of pride; even their follies have no other source. This pride is sensitive, and easily pained in the extreme; they are great sufferers from it, and again make it a point of pride to conceal these sufferings. Nevertheless, they will have vent. The two expressive words, Disappointment and Mortification, are peculiar to the English language.

This self-adoration, this internal worship of the creature for its own sake, is the sin by which Satan fell; the height of impiety. This is the reason that with so many of the virtues of humanity, with their seriousness and sobriety of demeanor, and with their biblical turn of mind, no nation is further off from grace. They are the only people who have been unable to claim the authorship of the "Imitation of Jesus": a Frenchman might

write it, a German, an Italian, never an Englishman. From Shakespeare to Milton, from Milton to Byron, their beautiful and sombre literature is skeptical, Judaical, satanic,—in a word, antichristian. "As regards law," as a jurist well says, "the English are Jews, the French Christians." A theologian might express himself in the same manner as regards faith. The American Indians, with that penetration and originality they so often exhibit, expressed this distinction in their fashion. "Christ," said one of them, "was a Frenchman whom the English crucified in London; Pontius Pilate was an officer in the service of Great Britain."

The Jews never exhibited the rage against Jesus which the English did against the Pucelle. It must be owned that she had wounded them cruelly in the most sensible part—in the simple but deep esteem they have for themselves. At Orléans, the invincible men-at-arms, the famous archers, Talbot at their head, had shown their backs; at Jargeau, sheltered by the good walls of a fortified town, they had suffered themselves to be taken; at Patay, they had fled as fast as their legs would carry them,—fled before a girl. . . . This was hard to be borne, and these taciturn English were forever pondering over the disgrace. . . . They had been afraid of a girl, and it was not very certain but that, chained as she was, they felt fear of her still, . . . though, seemingly, not of her, but of the Devil, whose agent she was. At least, they endeavored both to believe and to have it believed so. . . .

It was nine o'clock, she was dressed in female attire, and placed on a cart. On one side of her was brother Martin l'Advenu; the constable, Massieu, was on the other. The Augustine monk, brother Isambart, who had already displayed such charity and courage, would not quit her. It is stated that the wretched Loyseleur also ascended the cart to ask her pardon; but for the Earl of Warwick, the English would have killed him.

Up to this moment the Pucelle had never despaired, with the exception, perhaps, of her temptation in the Passion week. While saying, as she at times would say, "These English will kill me," she in reality did not think so. She did not imagine that she could ever be deserted. She had faith in her king, in the good people of France. She had said expressly, "There will be some disturbance either in prison or at the trial, by which I shall be delivered,—greatly, victoriously delivered." But though king and people deserted her, she had another source of aid, and a far more powerful and certain one, from her friends above, her kind and dear saints. When she was assaulting Saint-Pierre, and deserted by her followers, her saints sent an invisible army to her aid. How could they abandon their obedient girl, they who had so often promised her safety and deliverance?

What then must her thoughts have been when she saw that she must die; when, carried in a cart, she passed through a trembling crowd, under the guard of eight hundred Englishmen armed with sword and lance? She wept and bemoaned herself, yet reproached neither her king nor her saints. She was only heard to utter, "O Rouen, Rouen! must I then die here?"

The term of her sad journey was the old market place, the fish market. Three scaffolds had been raised: on one was the Episcopal and royal chair, the throne of the Cardinal of England, surrounded by the stalls of his prelates; on another were to figure the principal personages of the mournful drama, the preacher, the judges, and the bailli, and, lastly, the condemned one; apart was a large scaffolding of plaster, groaning under a weight of wood—nothing had been grudged the stake, which struck terror by its height alone. This was not only to add to the solemnity of the execution, but was done with the intent that from the height to which it was reared, the executioner might not get at it save at the base, and that to light it only, so that he would be unable to cut short the torments and relieve the sufferer as he did with others, sparing them the flames. On this occasion, the important point was that justice should not be defrauded of her due, or a dead body be committed to the flames; they desired that she should be really burned alive, and that placed on the summit of this mountain of wood, and commanding the circle of lances and of swords, she might be seen from every part of the market place. There was reason to suppose that being slowly, tediously burned before the eyes of a curious crowd, she might at last be surprised into some weakness, that something might escape her which could be set down as a disavowal, at the least some confused words which might be interpreted at pleasure,—perhaps low prayers, humiliating cries for mercy, such as proceed from a woman in despair. . . .

The frightful ceremony began with a sermon. Master Nicolas Midy, one of the lights of the University of Paris, preached

upon the edifying text: "When one limb of the Church is sick, the whole Church is sick." This poor Church could only be cured by cutting off a limb. He wound up with the formula: "Jeanne, go in peace, the Church can no longer defend thee."

The ecclesiastical judge, the Bishop of Beauvais, then benignly exhorted her to take care of her soul and to recall all her misdeeds, in order that she might awaken to true repentance. The assessors had ruled that it was the law to read over her abjuration to her; the bishop did nothing of the sort. He feared her denials, her disclaimers. But the poor girl had no thoughts of so chicaning away life: her mind was fixed on far other subjects. Even before she was exhorted to repentance, she had knelt down and invoked God, the Virgin, St. Michael, and St. Catherine, pardoning all and asking pardon, saying to the bystanders, "Pray for me!" In particular, she besought the priests to say each a mass for her soul. And all this so devoutly, humbly, and touchingly, that sympathy becoming contagious, no one could any longer contain himself; the Bishop of Beauvais melted into tears, the Bishop of Boulogne sobbed, and the very English cried and wept as well, Winchester with the rest.

Might it be in this moment of universal tenderness, of tears, of contagious weakness, that the unhappy girl softened, and, relapsing into the mere woman, confessed that she saw clearly she had erred, and that apparently she had been deceived when promised deliverance. This is a point on which we cannot implicitly rely on the interested testimony of the English. Nevertheless, it would betray scant knowledge of human nature to doubt, with her hopes so frustrated, her having wavered in her faith. Whether she confessed to this effect in words is uncertain; but I will confidently affirm that she owned it in thought.

Meanwhile the judges, for a moment put out of countenance, had recovered their usual bearing, and the Bishop of Beauvais, drying his eyes, began to read the act of condemnation. He reminded the guilty one of all her crimes, of her schism, idolatry, invocation of demons, how she had been admitted to repentance, and how, "seduced by the prince of lies, she had fallen, O grief! like the dog which returns to his vomit. Therefore, we pronounce you to be a rotten limb, and as such to be lopped off from the Church. We deliver you over to the secular power, praying it at the same time to relax its sentence, and to spare you death and the mutilation of your members."

Deserted thus by the Church, she put her whole trust in God. She asked for the cross. An Englishman handed her a cross which he made out of a stick; she took it, rudely fashioned as it was, with not less devotion, kissed it, and placed it under her garments next to her skin. But what she desired was the crucifix belonging to the Church, to have it before her eyes till she breathed her last. The good huissier Massieu and brother Isambart, interfered with such effect that it was brought her from St. Sauveur's. While she was embracing this crucifix, and brother Isambart was encouraging her, the English began to think all this exceedingly tedious; it was now noon at least; the soldiers grumbled and the captains called out, "What's this, priest; do you mean us to dine here?" Then, losing patience, and without waiting for the order from the bailli, who alone had authority to dismiss her to death, they sent two constables to take her out of the hands of the priests. She was seized at the foot of the tribunal by the men-at-arms, who dragged her to the executioner with the words, "Do thy office." The fury of the soldiery filled all present with horror; and many there, even of the judges, fled the spot that they might see no more.

When she found herself brought down to the market place, surrounded by English, laying rude hands on her, nature asserted her rights, and the flesh was troubled. Again she cried out, "O Rouen, thou art then to be my last abode?" She said no more, and, in this hour of fear and trouble, did not sin with her lips.

She accused neither her king nor her holy ones. But when she set foot on the top of the pile, on viewing this great city, this motionless and silent crowd, she could not refrain from exclaiming, "Ah! Rouen, Rouen, much do I fear you will suffer from my death!" She who had saved the people, and whom that people deserted, gave voice to no other sentiment when dying (admirable sweetness of soul!) than that of compassion for it.

She was made fast under the infamous placard, mitred with a mitre on which was read: "Heretic, relapser, apostate, idolater." And then the executioner set fire to the pile. She saw this from above and uttered a cry. Then as the brother who was exhorting her paid no attention to the fire, forgetting herself in her fear for him, she insisted on his descending. . . .

Meanwhile the flames rose. When they first seized her, the unhappy girl shrieked for holy water—this must have been the cry of fear. But soon recovering, she called only on God, on

her angels and her saints. She bore witness to them: "Yes, my voices were from God, my voices have not deceived me." The fact that all her doubts vanished at this trying moment must be taken as a proof that she accepted death as the promised deliverance; that she no longer understood her salvation in the Judaic and material sense, as until now she had done; that at length she saw clearly; and that rising above all shadows, her gifts of illumination and of sanctity were at the final hour made perfect unto her. . . .

"Ten thousand men wept." A few of the English alone laughed, or endeavored to laugh. One of the most furious among them had sworn that he would throw a fagot on the pile. Just as he brought it, she breathed her last. He was taken ill. His comrades led him to a tavern to recruit his spirits by drink, but he was beyond recovery. "I saw," he exclaimed, in his frantic despair, "I saw a dove fly out of her mouth with her last sigh." Others had read in the flames the word "Jesus," which she so often repeated. The executioner repaired in the evening to brother Isambart, full of consternation, and confessed himself; but felt persuaded that God would never pardon him. . . . One of the English king's secretaries said aloud, on returning from the dismal scene, "We are lost; we have burned a saint."

Though these words fell from an enemy's mouth, they are not the less important, and will live, uncontradicted by the future. Yes, whether considered religiously or patriotically, Jeanne d'Arc was a saint. . . .

There have been many martyrs; history shows us numberless ones, more or less pure, more or less glorious. Pride has had its martyrs; so have hate and the spirit of controversy. No age has been without martyrs militant, who no doubt died with a good grace when they could no longer kill. Such fanatics are irrelevant to our subject. The sainted girl is not of them; she had a sign of her own — goodness, charity, sweetness of soul.

She had the sweetness of the ancient martyrs, but with a difference. The first Christians remained gentle and pure only by shunning action, by sparing themselves the struggles and the trials of the world. Jeanne was gentle in the roughest struggle, good amongst the bad, pacific in war itself; she bore into war (that triumph of the devil) the spirit of God.

She took up arms, when she knew "the pity for the kingdom of France." She could not bear to see "French blood flow."

This tenderness of heart she showed towards all men. After a victory she would weep and would attend to the wounded English.

Purity, sweetness, heroic goodness—that this supreme beauty of the soul should have centred in a daughter of France may surprise foreigners who choose to judge of our nation by the levity of its manners alone. We may tell them (and without partiality, as we speak of circumstances so long since past) that under this levity, and in the midst of its follies and its very vices, old France was not styled without reason the most Christian people. They were certainly the people of love and of grace; and whether we understand this humanly or Christianly, in either sense it will ever hold good.

The savior of France could be no other than a woman. France herself was woman; having her nobility, but her amiable sweetness likewise, her prompt and charming pity; at the least, possessing the virtue of quickly-excited sympathies. And though she might take pleasure in vain elegances and external refinements, she remained at bottom closer to nature. The Frenchman, even when vicious, preserved, beyond the man of every other nation, good sense and goodness of heart.

May new France never forget the saying of old France: "Great hearts alone understand how much glory there is in being good!" To be and to keep so, amidst the injuries of man and the severity of Providence, is not the gift of a happy nature alone, but it is strength and heroism. To preserve sweetness and benevolence in the midst of so many bitter disputes, to pass through a life's experiences without suffering them to touch this internal treasure—is divine. They who persevere, and so go on to the end, are the true elect. And though they may even at times have stumbled in the difficult path of the world, amidst their falls, their weaknesses and their infancies, they will not the less remain children of God!

From the "History of France."

JOHN STUART MILL
(1806–1873)

IN WHAT he writes of "Liberty," John Stuart Mill is most concerned to demonstrate that the right object of social order is to foster the development of character and to create higher types of individual manhood. With Herbert Spencer he represented during the nineteenth century the evolution of those eighteenth-century ideals of higher freedom and usefulness for the individual, out of which grew the American Constitution. From the time of Alfred the Great to that of John, and from John at Runnymede to Charles I. at the block, England slowly developed the idea of government for the man in opposition to the long-accepted theory that man exists by divine ordinance for government. That men may be, may do, may grow, with no other restriction than the equal right of each to equal opportunity—this is the fundamental principle of liberty as it has grown out of the long struggle of English-speaking peoples against arbitrary power. For this Mill stood with boldness in his generation, and it will be long before succeeding generations cease to feel his influence.

He was born in London, May 20th, 1806. His "Logic," which appeared in 1843, gave him standing as one of the foremost thinkers of England, and his reputation was further increased by his "Political Economy" in 1848. "Liberty," which is perhaps his masterpiece, appeared in 1859. He wrote also "On the Subjection of Women," "Auguste Comte and Positivism," "England and Ireland," "On the Irish Land Question," and on allied topics of philosophy and political economy. He died at Avignon, France, May 8th, 1873.

ON LIBERTY

THE subject of this essay is not the so-called Liberty of the Will, so unfortunately opposed to the misnamed doctrine of Philosophical Necessity; but Civil or Social Liberty: the nature and limits of the power which can be legitimately exercised by society over the individual. A question seldom stated, and hardly ever discussed, in general terms, but which profoundly influences the practical controversies of the age by its

latent presence, and is likely soon to make itself recognized as the vital question of the future! It is so far from being new, that, in a certain sense, it has divided mankind, almost from the remotest ages; but in the stage of progress into which the more civilized portions of the species have now entered, it presents itself under new conditions, and requires a different and more fundamental treatment.

The struggle between Liberty and Authority is the most conspicuous feature in the portions of history with which we are earliest familiar, particularly in that of Greece, Rome, and England. But in old times this contest was between subjects, or some classes of subjects, and the government. By liberty, was meant protection against the tyranny of the political rulers. The rulers were conceived (except in some of the popular governments of Greece) as in a necessarily antagonistic position to the people whom they ruled. They consisted of a governing One, or a governing tribe or caste, who derived their authority from inheritance or conquest; who, at all events, did not hold it at the pleasure of the governed, and whose supremacy men did not venture, perhaps did not desire, to contest, whatever precautions might be taken against its oppressive exercise. Their power was regarded as necessary, but also as highly dangerous; as a weapon which they would attempt to use against their subjects, no less than against external enemies. To prevent the weaker members of the community from being preyed upon by innumerable vultures, it was needful that there should be an animal of prey stronger than the rest, commissioned to keep them down. But as the king of the vultures would be no less bent upon preying on the flock than any of the minor harpies, it was indispensable to be in a perpetual attitude of defense against his beak and claws. The aim, therefore, of patriots was to set limits to the power which the ruler should be suffered to exercise over the community; and this limitation was what they meant by liberty. It was attempted in two ways. First, by obtaining a recognition of certain immunities, called political liberties or rights, which it was to be regarded as a breach of duty in the ruler to infringe, and which, if he did infringe, specific resistance, or general rebellion, was held to be justifiable. A second, and generally a later expedient, was the establishment of constitutional checks; by which the consent of the community, or of a body of some sort supposed to represent

its interests, was made a necessary condition to some of the more important acts of the governing power. To the first of these modes of limitation, the ruling power, in most European countries, was compelled, more or less, to submit. It was not so with the second; and to attain this, or when already in some degree possessed, to attain it more completely, became everywhere the principal object of the lovers of liberty. And so long as mankind were content to combat one enemy by another, and to be ruled by a master, on condition of being guaranteed more or less efficaciously against his tyranny, they did not carry their aspirations beyond this point.

A time, however, came, in the progress of human affairs, when men ceased to think it a necessity of nature that their governors should be an independent power, opposed in interest to themselves. It appeared to them much better that the various magistrates of the State should be their tenants or delegates, revocable at their pleasure. In that way alone, it seemed, could they have complete security that the powers of government would never be abused to their disadvantage. By degrees, this new demand for elective and temporary rulers became the prominent object of the exertions of the popular party, wherever any such party existed; and superseded, to a considerable extent, the previous efforts to limit the power of rulers. As the struggle proceeded for making the ruling power emanate from the periodical choice of the ruled, some persons began to think that too much importance had been attached to the limitation of the power itself. That (it might seem) was a resource against rulers whose interests were habitually opposed to those of the people. What was now wanted was, that the rulers should be identified with the people; that their interest and will should be the interest and will of the nation. The nation did not need to be protected against its own will. There was no fear of its tyrannizing over itself. Let the rulers be effectually responsible to it, promptly removable by it, and it could afford to trust them with power of which it could itself dictate the use to be made. Their power was but the nation's own power, concentrated, and in a form convenient for exercise. This mode of thought, or rather perhaps of feeling, was common among the last generation of European liberalism, in the continental section of which it still apparently predominates. Those who admit any limit to what a government may do, except in the case of such governments as they think ought not to exist, stand out as brilliant exceptions among the political thinkers of the continent. A similar tone of sentiment might by this time have been prevalent in our own country, if the circumstances which for a time encouraged it had continued unaltered.

But, in political and philosophical theories, as well as in persons, success discloses faults and infirmities which failure might have concealed from observation. The notion that the people have no need to limit their power over themselves might seem axiomatic, when popular government was a thing only dreamed about, or read of as having existed at some distant period of the past. Neither was that notion necessarily disturbed by such temporary aberrations as those of the French Revolution, the worst of which were the work of a usurping few, and which, in any case, belonged, not to the permanent working of popular institutions, but to a sudden and convulsive outbreak against monarchical and aristocratic despotism. In time, however, a democratic republic came to occupy a large portion of the earth's surface, and made itself felt as one of the most powerful members of the community of nations; and elective and responsible government became subject to the observations and criticisms which wait upon a great existing fact. It was now perceived that such phrases as "self-government" and "the power of the people over themselves" do not express the true state of the case. The "people" who exercise the power are not always the same people with those over whom it is exercised, and the "self-government" spoken of is not the government of each by himself, but of each by all the rest. The will of the people, moreover, practically means the will of the most numerous or the most active part of the people; the majority, or those who succeed in making themselves accepted as the majority: the people, consequently, may desire to oppress a part of their number; and precautions are as much needed against this as against any other abuse of power. The limitation, therefore, of the power of government over individuals loses none of its importance when the holders of power are regularly accountable to the community, that is, to the strongest party therein. This view of things, recommending itself equally to the intelligence of thinkers and to the inclination of those important classes in European society to whose real or supposed interests democracy is adverse, has had no difficulty in establishing itself; and in political specula-

tions "the tyranny of the majority" is now generally included among the evils against which society requires to be on its guard.

Like other tyrannies, the tyranny of the majority was at first, and is still vulgarly, held in dread, chiefly as operating through the acts of the public authorities. But reflecting persons perceived that when society is itself the tyrant — society collectively, over the separate individuals who compose it — its means of tyrannizing are not restricted to the acts which it may do by the hands of its political functionaries. Society can and does execute its own mandates; and if it issues wrong mandates instead of right, or any mandates at all in things with which it ought not to meddle, it practices a social tyranny more formidable than many kinds of political oppression, since, though not usually upheld by such extreme penalties, it leaves fewer means of escape, penetrating much more deeply into the details of life, and enslaving the soul itself. Protection, therefore, against the tyranny of the magistrate is not enough; there needs protection also against the tyranny of the prevailing opinion and feeling; against the tendency of society to impose, by other means than civil penalties, its own ideas and practices as rules of conduct on those who dissent from them; to fetter the development, and, if possible, prevent the formation, of any individuality not in harmony with its ways, and compel all characters to fashion themselves upon the model of its own. There is a limit to the legitimate interference of collective opinion with individual independence; and to find that limit, and maintain it against encroachment, is as indispensable to a good condition of human affairs, as protection against political despotism.

But though this proposition is not likely to be contested in general terms, the practical question, where to place the limit — how to make the fitting adjustment between individual independence and social control — is a subject on which nearly everything remains to be done. All that makes existence valuable to any one depends on the enforcement of restraints upon the actions of other people. Some rules of conduct, therefore, must be imposed, by law in the first place, and by opinion on many things which are not fit subjects for the operation of law. What these rules should be is the principal question in human affairs; but if we except a few of the most obvious cases, it is one of those which least progress has been made in resolving. No two ages, and scarcely any two countries, have decided it alike; and

the decision of one age or country is a wonder to another. Yet the people of any given age and country no more suspect any difficulty in it than if it were a subject on which mankind had always been agreed. The rules which obtain among themselves appear to them self-evident and self-justifying. This all but universal illusion is one of the examples of the magical influence of custom, which is not only, as the proverb says, a second nature, but is continually mistaken for the first. The effect of custom in preventing any misgiving respecting the rules of conduct which mankind impose on one another is all the more complete because the subject is one on which it is not generally considered necessary that reasons should be given, either by one person to others, or by each to himself. People are accustomed to believe, and have been encouraged in the belief by some who aspire to the character of philosophers, that their feelings, on subjects of this nature, are better than reasons, and render reasons unnecessary. The practical principle which guides them to their opinions on the regulation of human conduct is the feeling in each person's mind that everybody should be required to act as he, and those with whom he sympathizes, would like them to act. No one, indeed, acknowledges to himself that his standard of judgment is his own liking; but an opinion on a point of conduct, not supported by reasons, can only count as one person's preference; and if the reasons, when given, are a mere appeal to a similar preference felt by other people, it is still only many people's liking instead of one. To an ordinary man, however, his own preference, thus supported, is not only a perfectly satisfactory reason, but the only one he generally has for any of his notions of morality, taste, or propriety, which are not expressly written in his religious creed; and his chief guide in the interpretation even of that. Men's opinions, accordingly, on what is laudable or blamable, are affected by all the multifarious causes which influence their wishes in regard to the conduct of others, and which are as numerous as those which determine their wishes on any other subject. Sometimes their reason — at other times their prejudices or superstitions; often their social affections, not seldom their antisocial ones, their envy or jealousy, their arrogance or contemptuousness; but most commonly, their desires or fears for themselves — their legitimate or illegitimate self-interest. Wherever there is an ascendant class, a large portion of the morality of the country emanates from its class interests, and its

feelings of class superiority. The morality between Spartans and Helots, between planters and negroes, between princes and subjects, between nobles and roturiers, between men and women, has been for the most part the creation of these class interests and feelings: and the sentiments thus generated react in turn upon the moral feelings of the members of the ascendant class, in their relations among themselves. Where, on the other hand, a class, formerly ascendant, has lost its ascendancy, or where its ascendancy is unpopular, the prevailing moral sentiments frequently bear the impress of an impatient dislike of superiority. Another grand determining principle of the rules of conduct, both in act and forbearance, which have been enforced by law or opinion, has been the servility of mankind towards the supposed preferences or aversions of their temporal masters, or of their gods. This servility, though essentially selfish, is not hypocrisy; it gives rise to perfectly genuine sentiments of abhorrence; it made men burn magicians and heretics. Among so many baser influences, the general and obvious interests of society have of course had a share, and a large one, in the direction of the moral sentiments; less, however, as a matter of reason, and on their own account, than as a consequence of the sympathies and antipathies which grew out of them; and sympathies and antipathies which had little or nothing to do with the interests of society, have made themselves felt in the establishment of moralities with quite as great force.

The likings and dislikings of society, or of some powerful portion of it, are thus the main thing which has practically determined the rules laid down for general observance, under the penalties of law or opinion. And in general those who have been in advance of society in thought and feeling have left this condition of things unassailed in principle, however they may have come into conflict with it in some of its details. They have occupied themselves rather in inquiring what things society ought to like or dislike than in questioning whether its likings or dislikings should be a law to individuals. They preferred endeavoring to alter the feelings of mankind on the particular points on which they were themselves heretical rather than make common cause in defense of freedom with heretics generally. The only case in which the higher ground has been taken on principle and maintained with consistency by any but an individual here and there is that of religious belief: a case instructive in many ways, and not least so as forming a most striking instance of the fallibility of what is called the moral sense; for the *odium theologicum*, in a sincere bigot, is one of the most unequivocal cases of moral feeling. Those who first broke the yoke of what called itself the Universal Church were in general as little willing to permit difference of religious opinion as that Church itself. But when the heat of the conflict was over, without giving a complete victory to any party, and each church or sect was reduced to limit its hopes to retaining possession of the ground it already occupied; minorities seeing that they had no chance of becoming majorities were under the necessity of pleading to those whom they could not convert, for permission to differ. It is accordingly on this battlefield, almost solely, that the rights of the individual against society have been asserted on broad grounds of principle, and the claim of society to exercise authority over dissentients openly controverted. The great writers to whom the world owes what religious liberty it possesses have mostly asserted freedom of conscience as an indefeasible right, and denied absolutely that a human being is accountable to others for his religious belief. Yet so natural to mankind is intolerance in whatever they really care about, that religious freedom has hardly anywhere been practically realized, except where religious indifference, which dislikes to have its peace disturbed by theological quarrels, has added its weight to the scale. In the minds of almost all religious persons, even in the most tolerant countries, the duty of toleration is admitted with tacit reserves. One person will bear with dissent in matters of church government, but not of dogma; another can tolerate everybody, short of a Papist or a Unitarian; another, every one who believes in revealed religion; a few extend their charity a little further, but stop at the belief in a God and in a future state. Wherever the sentiment of the majority is still genuine and intense, it is found to have abated little of its claim to be obeyed.

In England, from the peculiar circumstances of our political history, though the yoke of opinion is perhaps heavier, that of law is lighter than in most other countries of Europe; and there is considerable jealousy of direct interference, by the legislative or the executive power with private conduct; not so much from any just regard for the independence of the individual, as from the still subsisting habit of looking on the government as representing an opposite interest to the public. The majority have

not yet learned to feel the power of the government their power, or its opinions their opinions. When they do so, individual liberty will probably be as much exposed to invasion from the government as it already is from public opinion. But, as yet, there is a considerable amount of feeling ready to be called forth against any attempt of the law to control individuals in things in which they have not hitherto been accustomed to be controlled by it; and this with very little discrimination as to whether the matter is, or is not, within the legitimate sphere of legal control; insomuch that the feeling, highly salutary on the whole, is perhaps quite as often misplaced as well grounded in the particular instances of its application. There is, in fact, no recognized principle by which the propriety or impropriety of government interference is customarily tested. People decide according to their personal preferences. Some, whenever they see any good to be done, or evil to be remedied, would willingly instigate the government to undertake the business; while others prefer to bear almost any amount of social evil rather than add one to the departments of human interests amenable to governmental control. And men range themselves on one or the other side in any particular case, according to this general direction of their sentiments; or according to the degree of interest which they feel in the particular thing which it is proposed that the government should do; or according to the belief they entertain that the government would, or would not, do it in the manner they prefer; but very rarely on account of any opinion to which they consistently adhere, as to what things are fit to be done by a government. And it seems to me that, in consequence of this absence of rule or principle, one side is at present as often wrong as the other; the interference of government is, with about equal frequency, improperly invoked and improperly condemned.

The object of this essay is to assert one very simple principle, as entitled to govern absolutely the dealings of society with the individual in the way of compulsion and control, whether the means used be physical force in the form of legal penalties, or the moral coercion of public opinion. That principle is, that the sole end for which mankind are warranted, individually or collectively, in interfering with the liberty of action of any of their number, is self-protection. That the only purpose for which power can be rightfully exercised over any member of a civilized

community, against his will, is to prevent harm to others. His own good, either physical or moral, is not a sufficient warrant. He cannot rightfully be compelled to do or forbear because it will be better for him to do so, because it will make him happier, because, in the opinions of others, to do so would be wise, or even right. These are good reasons for remonstrating with him, or reasoning with him, or persuading him, or entreating him, but not for compelling him, or visiting him with any evil, in case he do otherwise. To justify that, the conduct from which it is desired to deter him must be calculated to produce evil to some one else. The only part of the conduct of any one, for which he is amenable to society, is that which concerns others. In the part which merely concerns himself, his independence is, of right, absolute. Over himself, over his own body and mind, the individual is sovereign.

It is, perhaps, hardly necessary to say that this doctrine is meant to apply only to human beings in the maturity of their faculties. We are not speaking of children, or of young persons below the age which the law may fix as that of manhood or womanhood. Those who are still in a state to require being taken care of by others must be protected against their own actions as well as against external injury. For the same reason we may leave out of consideration those backward states of society in which the race itself may be considered as in its nonage. The early difficulties in the way of spontaneous progress are so great that there is seldom any choice of means for overcoming them; and a ruler full of the spirit of improvement is warranted in the use of any expedients that will attain an end, perhaps otherwise unattainable. Despotism is a legitimate mode of government in dealing with barbarians, provided the end be their improvement, and the means justified by actually effecting that end. Liberty, as a principle, has no application to any state of things anterior to the time when mankind have become capable of being improved by free and equal discussion. Until then there is nothing for them but implicit obedience to an Akbar or a Charlemagne, if they are so fortunate as to find one. But as soon as mankind have attained the capacity of being guided to their own improvement by conviction or persuasion (a period long since reached in all nations with whom we need here concern ourselves), compulsion, either in the direct form or in that of pains and penalties for noncompliance, is no longer admissible as

a means to their own good, and justifiable only for the security of others.

It is proper to state that I forego any advantage which could be derived to my argument from the idea of abstract right, as a thing independent of utility. I regard utility as the ultimate appeal on all ethical questions; but it must be utility in the largest sense, grounded on the permanent interests of man as a progressive being. Those interests, I contend, authorize the subjection of individual spontaneity to external control, only in respect to those actions of each, which concern the interest of other people. If any one does an act hurtful to others, there is a *prima facie* case for punishing him, by law, or, where legal penalties are not safely applicable, by general disapprobation. There are also many positive acts for the benefit of others, which he may rightfully be compelled to perform: such as, to give evidence in a court of justice; to bear his fair share in the common defense, or in any other joint work necessary to the interest of the society of which he enjoys the protection; and to perform certain acts of individual beneficence, such as saving a fellow-creature's life, or interposing to protect the defenseless against ill usage, things which, whenever it is obviously a man's duty to do, he may rightfully be made responsible to society for not doing. A person may cause evil to others not only by his actions, but by his inaction; and in either case he is justly accountable to them for the injury. The latter case, it is true, requires a much more cautious exercise of compulsion than the former. To make any one answerable for doing evil to others is the rule; to make him answerable for not preventing evil is, comparatively speaking, the exception. Yet there are many cases clear enough and grave enough to justify that exception. In all things which regard the external relations of the individual, he is *de jure* amenable to those whose interests are concerned, and, if need be, to society as their protector. There are often good reasons for not holding him to the responsibility; but these reasons must arise from the special expediencies of the case: either because it is a kind of case in which he is on the whole likely to act better, when left to his own discretion, than when controlled in any way in which society have it in their power to control him; or because the attempt to exercise control would produce other evils greater than those which it would prevent. When such reasons as these preclude the enforcement of responsibility, the conscience of the agent himself should step into the vacant judgment seat, and protect those interests of others which have no external protection; judging himself all the more rigidly, because the case does not admit of his being made accountable to the judgment of his fellow-creatures.

But there is a sphere of action in which society, as distinguished from the individual, has, if any, only an indirect interest; comprehending all that portion of a person's life and conduct which affects only himself, or, if it also affects others, only with their free, voluntary, and undeceived consent and participation. When I say only himself, I mean directly, and in the first instance, for whatever affects himself may affect others through himself, and the objection which may be grounded on this contingency will receive consideration in the sequel. This, then, is the appropriate region of human liberty. It comprises, first, the inward domain of consciousness; demanding liberty of conscience, in the most comprehensive sense; liberty of thought and feeling; absolute freedom of opinion and sentiment on all subjects, practical or speculative, scientific, moral, or theological. The liberty of expressing and publishing opinions may seem to fall under a different principle, since it belongs to that part of the conduct of an individual which concerns other people; but, being almost of as much importance as the liberty of thought itself, and resting in great part on the same reasons, is practically inseparable from it. Secondly, the principle requires liberty of tastes and pursuits; of framing the plan of our life to suit our own character; of doing as we like, subject to such consequences as may follow; without impediment from our fellow-creatures, so long as what we do does not harm them, even though they should think our conduct foolish, perverse, or wrong. Thirdly, from this liberty of each individual follows the liberty, within the same limits, of combination among individuals; freedom to unite, for any purpose not involving harm to others: the persons combining being supposed to be of full age, and not forced or deceived.

No society in which these liberties are not, on the whole, respected, is free, whatever may be its form of government; and none is completely free in which they do not exist absolute and unqualified. The only freedom which deserves the name is that of pursuing our own good in our own way, so long as we do not attempt to deprive others of theirs, or impede their efforts to obtain it. Each is the proper guardian of his

Apart from the peculiar tenets of individual thinkers, there is also in the world at large an increasing inclination to stretch unduly the powers of society over the individual, both by the force of opinion and even by that of legislation; and as the tendency of all the changes taking place in the world is to strengthen society, and diminish the power of the individual, this encroachment is not one of the evils which tend spontaneously to disappear, but, on the contrary, to grow more and more formidable. The disposition of mankind, whether as rulers or as fellow-citizens, to impose their own opinions and inclinations as a rule of conduct on others, is so energetically supported by some of the best and by some of the worst feelings incident to human nature, that it is hardly ever kept under restraint by anything but want of power; and as the power is not declining, but growing, unless a strong barrier of moral conviction can be raised against the mischief, we must expect, in the present circumstances of the world, to see it increase.

It will be convenient for the argument, if, instead of at once entering upon the general thesis, we confine ourselves in the first instance to a single branch of it, on which the principle here stated is, if not fully, yet to a certain point, recognized by the current opinions. This one branch is the Liberty of Thought, from which it is impossible to separate the cognate liberty of speaking and of writing. Although these liberties, to some considerable amount, form part of the political morality of all countries which profess religious toleration and free institutions, the grounds, both philosophical and practical, on which they rest, are perhaps not so familiar to the general mind, nor so thoroughly appreciated by many even of the leaders of opinions, as might have been expected. Those grounds, when rightly understood, are of much wider application than to only one division of the subject, and a thorough consideration of this part of the question will be found the best introduction to the remainder. Those to whom nothing which I am about to say will be new may, therefore, I hope, excuse me, if on a subject which for now three centuries has been so often discussed, I venture on one discussion more.

From "Liberty." The introductory essay complete.

own health, whether bodily, or mental and spiritual. Mankind are greater gainers by suffering each other to live as seems good to themselves than by compelling each to live as seems good to the rest.

Though this doctrine is anything but new, and, to some persons, may have the air of a truism, there is no doctrine which stands more directly opposed to the general tendency of existing opinion and practice. Society has expended fully as much effort in the attempt (according to its lights) to compel people to conform to its notions of personal, as of social excellence. The ancient commonwealths thought themselves entitled to practice, and the ancient philosophers countenanced, the regulation of every part of private conduct by public authority, on the ground that the State had a deep interest in the whole bodily and mental discipline of every one of its citizens; a mode of thinking which may have been admissible in small republics surrounded by powerful enemies, in constant peril of being subverted by foreign attack or internal commotion, and to which even a short interval of relaxed energy and self-command might so easily be fatal, that they could not afford to wait for the salutary permanent effects of freedom. In the modern world, the greater size of political communities, and, above all, the separation between the spiritual and temporal authority (which placed the direction of men's consciences in other hands than those which controlled their wordly affairs), prevented so great an interference by law in the details of private life; but the engines of moral repression have been wielded more strenuously against divergence from the reigning opinion in self-regarding than even in social matters; religion, the most powerful of the elements which have entered into the formation of moral feeling, having almost always been governed either by the ambition of a hierarchy, seeking control over every department of human conduct, or by the spirit of Puritanism. And some of those modern reformers who have placed themselves in strongest opposition to the religions of the past have been no way behind either churches or sects in their assertion of the right of spiritual domination,— M. Comte, in particular, whose social system as unfolded in his "Système de Politique Positive" aims at establishing (though by moral more than by legal appliances) a despotism of society over the individual, surpassing anything contemplated in the political ideal of the most rigid disciplinarian among the ancient philosophers.

JOHN MILTON

(1608–1674)

F MILTON's prose is frequently rugged and disconnected, it never loses the essential qualities which distinguish the work of a master; and from time to time it rises above mere dignity to the sublimity he illustrates in his verse. In his verse he is primarily an artist, writing to gratify his sense of beauty through the expression of truth. In his prose he makes the expression of truth the object and art the mere incident of its attainment. His mind was severe, his thoughts weighty, his earnestness intense. His prose expresses all these qualities, and when he is writing on points of politics or theology which have lost their interest, it is hard to follow him with pleasure. When, however, he is dealing with enduring principles, he can at once fire the imagination and convince the judgment. "Eikonoklastes," one of the most famous of his political pamphlets, appeared in 1649 as an answer to the royalist "Eikon Basilike," and until his death, November 8th, 1674, he continued to write in Latin and English against the "divine right of kings" to control Church and State. In his prose he was a pamphleteer rather than an essayist; and although his pamphlets are seldom read except for the sake of the history they made, they were one of the great liberalizing forces of the seventeenth century.

THE STRONGEST THING IN THE WORLD

IT HAPPENED once, as we find in Esdras and Josephus, authors not less believed than any under sacred, to be a great and solemn debate in the court of Darius what thing was to be counted strongest of all other. He that could resolve this, in reward of his excellent wisdom, should be clad in purple, drink in gold, sleep on a bed of gold, and sit next Darius. None but they, doubtless, who were reputed wise had the question propounded to them; who after some respite given them by the king to consider, in full assembly of all his lords and gravest counselors, returned severally what they thought. The first held that wine was strongest; another, that the king was strongest; but Zorobabel, prince of the captive Jews, and heir to the crown of Judah, being one of them, proved women to be stronger than the king, for that he himself had seen a concubine take his crown from off his head to set it upon her own; and others beside him have likewise seen the like feat done, and not in jest. Yet he proved on, and it was so yielded by the king himself, and all his sages, that neither wine, nor women, nor the king, but truth of all other things was the strongest.

For me, though neither asked, nor in a nation that gives such rewards to wisdom, I shall pronounce my sentence somewhat different from Zorobabel, and shall defend that either truth and justice are all one (for truth is but justice in our knowledge, and justice is but truth in our practice), and he, indeed, so explains himself, in saying that with truth is no accepting of persons, which is the property of justice, or else if there be any odds, that justice, though not stronger than truth, yet by her office, is to put forth and exhibit more strength in the affairs of mankind. For truth is properly no more than contemplation, and her utmost efficiency is but teaching; but justice in her very essence is all strength and activity, and hath a sword put into her hand to use against all violence and oppression on the earth. She it is most truly, who accepts no person, and exempts none from the severity of her stroke. She never suffers injury to prevail, but when falsehood first prevails over truth; and that also is a kind of justice done on them who are so deluded. Though wicked kings and tyrants counterfeit her sword, as some did that buckler fabled to fall from heaven into the capitol, yet she communicates her power to none but such as, like herself, are just, or at least will do justice. For it were extreme partiality and injustice, the flat denial and overthrow of herself, to put her own authentic sword into the hand of an unjust and wicked man, or so far to accept and exalt one mortal person above his equals, that he alone shall have the punishing of all other men transgressing, and not receive like punishment from men, when he himself shall be found the highest transgressor.

We may conclude, therefore, that justice, above all other things, is and ought to be the strongest; she is the strength, the kingdom, the power, and majesty of all ages. Truth herself would subscribe to this, though Darius and all the monarchs of the world should deny. And if by sentence thus written it were my happiness to set free the minds of Englishmen from longing to return poorly under that captivity of kings from which the

strength and supreme sword of justice hath delivered them, I shall have done a work not much inferior to that of Zorobabel; who, by well-praising and extolling the force of truth, in that contemplative strength conquered Darius, and freed his country and the people of God from the captivity of Babylon. Which I shall yet not despair to do, if they in this land, whose minds are yet captive, be but as ingenuous to acknowledge the strength and supremacy of justice as that heathen king was to confess the strength of truth; or let them but, as he did, grant that, and they will soon perceive that truth resigns all her outward strength to justice; justice therefore must needs be strongest, both in her own and in the strength of truth. But if a king may do among men whatsoever is his will and pleasure, and notwithstanding be unaccountable to men, then, contrary to his magnified wisdom of Zorobabel, neither truth nor justice, but the king, is strongest of all other things, which that Persian monarch himself, in the midst of all his pride and glory, durst not assume.

Let us see, therefore, what this king hath to affirm, why the sentence of justice, and the weight of that sword, which she delivers into the hands of men, should be more partial to him offending than to all others of human race. First, he pleads that "no law of God or man gives to subjects any power of judicature without or against him." Which assertion shall be proved in every part to be most untrue. The first express law of God given to mankind was that to Noah, as a law, in general, to all the sons of men. And by that most ancient and universal law, "Whosoever sheddeth man's blood, by man shall his blood be shed," we find here no exception. If a king therefore do this, to a king, and that by men also, the same shall be done. This in the law of Moses, which came next, several times is repeated, and in one place remarkably, Numbers xxxv. "Ye shall take no satisfaction for the life of a murderer, but he shall surely be put to death: the land cannot be cleansed of the blood that is shed therein, but by the blood of him that shed it." This is so spoken as that which concerned all Israel, not one man alone, to see performed; and if no satisfaction were to be taken, then certainly no exception. Nay, the king, when they should set up any, was to observe the whole law, and not only to see it done, but to "do it; that his heart might not be lifted up above his brethren"; to dream of vain and useless prerogatives or exemptions, whereby the law itself must needs be founded in unrighteousness.

And were that true, which is most false, that all kings are the Lord's anointed, it were yet absurd to think that the anointment of God should be, as it were, a charm against law, and give them privilege, who punish others, to sin themselves unpunishably. The high-priest was the Lord's anointed as well as any king, and with the same consecrated oil; yet Solomon had put to death Abiathar, had it not been for other respects than that anointment. If God himself say to kings, "Touch not mine anointed," meaning his chosen people, as is evident in that Psalm, yet no man will argue thence that he protects them from civil laws if they offend; then certainly, though David, as a private man, and in his own cause, feared to lift his hand against the Lord's anointed, much less can this forbid the law, or disarm justice from having legal power against any king. No other supreme magistrate, in what kind of government soever, lays claim to any such enormous privilege; wherefore then should any king, who is but one kind of magistrate, and set over the people for no other end than they?

From "Eikonoklastes."

ON HIS READING IN YOUTH

HE who would not be frustrate of his hope to write well hereafter in laudable things ought himself to be a true poem; that is, a composition and pattern of the best and honorablest things; not presuming to sing high praises of heroic men, or famous cities, unless he have in himself the experience and the practice of all that which is praiseworthy. These reasonings, together with a certain niceness of nature, an honest haughtiness, and self-esteem either of what I was, or what I might be (which let envy call pride), and lastly that modesty, whereof, though not in the title-page, yet here I may be excused to make some beseeming profession; all these uniting the supply of their natural aid together kept me still above those low descents of mind, beneath which he must deject and plunge himself, that can agree to salable and unlawful prostitutions.

Next (for hear me out now, readers), that I may tell ye whither my younger feet wandered; I betook me among those lofty fables and romances, which recount in solemn cantos the deeds of knighthood founded by our victorious kings, and from hence had in renown over all Christendom. There I read it in

the oath of every knight, that he should defend to the expense of his best blood, or of his life, if it so befell him, the honor and chastity of virgin or matron; from whence even then I learned what a noble virtue chastity sure must be, to the defense of which so many worthies, by such a dear adventure of themselves, had sworn. And if I found in the story afterward, any of them, by word or deed, breaking that oath, I judged it the same fault of the poet, as that which is attributed to Homer, to have written indecent things of the gods. Only this my mind gave me, that every free and gentle spirit, without that oath, ought to be born a knight, nor needed to expect the gilt spur, or the laying of a sword upon his shoulder to stir him up both by his counsel and his arms, to secure and protect the weakness of any attempted chastity. So that even these books, which to many others have been the fuel of wantonness and loose living, I cannot think how, unless by divine indulgence, proved to me so many incitements, as you have heard, to the love and steadfast observation of that virtue which abhors the society of bordelloes.

Thus, from the laureate fraternity of poets, riper years and the ceaseless round of study and reading led me to the shady spaces of philosophy; but chiefly to the divine volumes of Plato, and his equal Xenophon: where, if I should tell ye what I learned of chastity and love, (I mean that which is truly so, whose charming cup is only virtue, which she bears in her hand to those who are worthy—the rest are cheated with a thick intoxicating potion, which a certain sorceress, the abuser of love's name, carries about); and how the first and chiefest office of love begins and ends in the soul, producing those happy twins of her divine generation, knowledge and virtue.

From the "Apology for Smectymnuus."

ON GIVING DESPOTS A FAIR TRIAL

CERTAINLY if men, not to speak of heathen, both wise and religious, have done justice upon tyrants what way they could soonest, how much more mild and humane then is it to give them fair and open trial; to teach lawless kings, and all who so much adore them, that not mortal man, or his imperious will, but justice, is the only true sovereign and supreme majesty upon earth? Let men cease therefore, out of faction and hypocrisy, to make outcries and horrid things of things so just and honorable. Though perhaps till now, no protestant state or kingdom can be alleged to have openly put to death their king, which lately some have written, and imputed to their great glory; much mistaking the matter. It is not, neither ought to be, the glory of a protestant state, never to have put their king to death; it is the glory of a protestant king never to have deserved death. And if the parliament and military council do what they do without precedent, if it appear their duty, it argues the more wisdom, virtue, and magnanimity, that they know themselves able to be a precedent to others; who perhaps in future ages, if they prove not too degenerate, will look up with honor, and aspire towards these exemplary and matchless deeds of their ancestors, as to the highest top of their civil glory and emulation; which heretofore, in the pursuance of fame and foreign dominion, spent itself vain-gloriously abroad; but henceforth may learn a better fortitude, to dare execute highest justice on them that shall by force of arms endeavor the oppressing and bereaving of religion and their liberty at home,— that no unbridled potentate or tyrant, but to his sorrow, for the future may presume such high and irresponsible license over mankind, to havoc and turn upside down whole kingdoms of men, as though they were no more in respect of his perverse will than a nation of pismires.

From « Tenure of Kings.»

RAGGED NOTIONS AND BABBLEMENTS IN EDUCATION

SEEING every nation affords not experience and tradition enough for all kind of learning, therefore we are chiefly taught the languages of those people who have at any time been most industrious after wisdom; so that language is but the instrument conveying to us things useful to be known. And though a linguist should pride himself to have all the tongues that Babel cleft the world into, yet, if he have not studied the solid things in them, as well as the words and lexicons, he were nothing so much to be esteemed a learned man as any yeoman or tradesmen competently wise in his mother dialect only. Hence appear the many mistakes which have made learning generally so unpleasing and so unsuccessful: first, we do amiss to spend seven or eight years merely in scraping together so much miserable

Latin and Greek as might be learned otherwise easily and delightfully in one year.

And that which casts our proficiency therein so much behind is our time lost partly in too oft idle vacancies given both to schools and universities; partly in a preposterous exaction, forcing the empty wits of children to compose themes, verses, and orations, which are the acts of ripest judgment, and the final work of a head filled by long reading and observing, with elegant maxims and copious invention. These are not matters to be wrung from poor striplings, like blood out of the nose, or the plucking of untimely fruit; besides the ill habit which they get of wretched barbarizing against the Latin and Greek idiom, with their untutored Anglicisms, odious to be read, yet not to be avoided without a well-continued and judicious conversing among pure authors digested, which they scarce taste; whereas, if after some preparatory grounds of speech by their certain forms got into memory, they were lead to the praxis thereof in some chosen short book lessoned thoroughly to them, they might then forthwith proceed to learn the substance of good things and arts in due order, which would bring the whole language quickly into their power. This I take to be the most rational and most profitable way of learning languages, and whereby we may best hope to give account to God of our youth spent herein.

And for the usual method of teaching arts, I deem it to be an old error of universities, not yet well recovered from the scholastic grossness of barbarous ages, that instead of beginning with arts most easy (and those be such as are most obvious to the sense), they present their young unmatriculated novices at first coming with the most intellective abstractions of logic and metaphysics, so that they having but newly left those grammatic flats and shallows where they stuck unreasonably to learn a few words with lamentable construction, and now on the sudden transported under another climate, to be tossed and turmoiled with their unballasted wits in fathomless and unquiet deeps of controversy, do for the most part grow into hatred and contempt of learning, mocked and deluded all this while with ragged notions and babblements, while they expected worthy and delightful knowledge; till poverty or youthful years call them importunately their several ways, and hasten them, with the sway of friends, either to an ambitious and mercenary, or ignorantly zealous divinity; some allured to the trade of law, grounding their pur-

poses not on the prudent and heavenly contemplation of justice and equity, which was never taught them, but on the promising and pleasing thoughts of litigious terms, fat contentions, and flowing fees; others betake them to state affairs, with souls so unprincipled in virtue and true generous breeding, that flattery and courtshifts, and tyrannous aphorisms, appear to them the highest points of wisdom; instilling their barren hearts with a conscientious slavery; if, as I rather think, it be not feigned. Others, lastly, of a more delicious and airy spirit, retire themselves (knowing no better) to the enjoyments of ease and luxury, living out their days in feasts and jollity; which, indeed, is the wisest and the safest course of all these, unless they were with more integrity undertaken. And these are the errors, and these are the fruits of misspending our prime youth at schools and universities as we do, either in learning mere words, or such things chiefly as were better unlearned.

I shall detain you now no longer in the demonstration of what we should not do, but straight conduct you to a hillside, where I will point you out the right path of a virtuous and noble education; laborious, indeed, at the first ascent, but else so smooth, so green, so full of goodly prospect and melodious sounds on every side, that the harp of Orpheus was not more charming. I doubt not but ye shall have more ado to drive our dullest and laziest youth, our stocks and stubs, from the infinite desire of such a happy nurture, than we have now to hale and drag our choicest and hopefullest wits to that asinine feast of sow thistles and brambles which is commonly set before them, as all the food and entertainment of their tenderest and most docile age.

I call, therefore, a complete and generous education that which fits a man to perform justly, skillfully, and magnanimously, all the offices, both private and public, of peace and war.

From « Tractate of Education.›

DONALD GRANT MITCHELL

(1822–)

DONALD GRANT MITCHELL, better known perhaps as "Ik Marvel," was born at Norwich, Connecticut, in April, 1822. "Reveries of a Bachelor," by which he first became known, appeared serially in 1850, and he followed it in 1851 by "Dream Life," in the same vein. These remain his most popular books, though he has written since: "My Farm at Edgewood"; "Seven Stories with Basement and Attic"; "Wet Days at Edgewood"; "Rural Studies"; and a number of other books, including "Doctor Johns," a novel.

SPRING

THE old chroniclers made the year begin in the season of frosts; and they have launched us upon the current of the months, from the snowy banks of January. I love better to count time from spring to spring; it seems to me far more cheerful to reckon the year by blossoms than by blight.

Bernardin de Saint-Pierre, in his sweet story of Virginia, makes the bloom of the cocoa tree, or the growth of the banana, a yearly and a loved monitor of the passage of her life. How cold and cheerless in the comparison would be the icy chronology of the North: So many years have I seen the lakes locked, and the foliage die!

The budding and blooming of spring seem to belong properly to the opening of the months. It is the season of the quickest expansion, of the warmest blood, of the readiest growth; it is the boy age of the year. The birds sing in chorus in the spring — just as children prattle; the brooks run full — like the overflow of young hearts; the showers drop easily — as young tears flow; and the whole sky is as capricious as the mind of a boy.

Between tears and smiles the year, like the child, struggles into the warmth of life. The old year,— say what the chronologists will,—lingers upon the very lap of spring, and is only fairly gone when the blossoms of April have strewn their pall of glory upon his tomb, and the bluebirds have chanted his requiem.

It always seems to me as if an access of life came with the melting of the winter's snows; and as if every rootlet of grass that lifted its first green blade from the matted débris of the old year's decay bore my spirit upon it, nearer to the largess of heaven.

I love to trace the break of spring step by step; I love even those long rain storms that sap the icy fortresses of the lingering winter,—that melt the snows upon the hills, and swell the mountain brooks;—that make the pools heave up their glassy cerements of ice, and hurry down the crashing fragments into the wastes of ocean.

I love the gentle thaws that you can trace, day by day, by the stained snowbanks, shrinking from the grass; and by the gentle drip of the cottage eaves. I love to search out the sunny slopes by a southern wall, where the reflected sun does double duty to the earth, and where the frail anemone, or the faint blush of the arbutus, in the midst of the bleak March atmosphere, will touch your heart, like a hope of heaven, in a field of graves! Later come those soft, smoky days, when the patches of winter grain show green under the shelter of leafless woods, and the last snowdrifts, reduced to shrunken skeletons of ice, lie upon the slope of northern hills, leaking away their life.

Then the grass at your door grows into the color of the sprouting grain, and the buds upon the lilacs swell, and burst. The peaches bloom upon the wall, and the plums wear bodices of white. The sparkling oriole picks string for his hammock on the sycamore, and the sparrows twitter in pairs. The old elms throw down their dingy flowers, and color their spray with green; and the brooks, where you throw your worm or the minnow, float down whole fleets of the crimson blossoms of the maple. Finally, the oaks step into the opening quadrille of spring, with grayish tufts of a modest verdure, which, by and by, will be long and glossy leaves. The dogwood pitches his broad, white tent, in the edge of the forest; the dandelions lie along the hillocks, like stars in a sky of green; and the wild cherry, growing in all the hedgerows, without other culture than God's, lifts up to him, thankfully, its tremulous white fingers.

Amid all this, come the rich rains of spring. The affections of a boy grow up with tears to water them; and the year blooms with showers. But the clouds hover over an April sky, timidly—like shadows upon innocence. The showers come gently, and drop daintily to the earth,—with now and then a glimpse of sunshine to make the drops bright—like so many tears of joy.

The rain of winter is cold, and it comes in bitter scuds that blind you; but the rain of April steals upon you coyly, half reluctantly,—yet lovingly,—like the steps of a bride to the altar.

It does not gather like the storm clouds of winter, gray and heavy along the horizon, and creep with subtle and insensible approaches (like age) to the very zenith; but there are a score of white-winged swimmers afloat, that your eye has chased, as you lay fatigued with the delicious languor of an April sun;—nor have you scarce noticed that a little bevy of those floating clouds had grouped together in a sombre company. But presently you see across the fields the dark gray streaks stretching like lines of mists, from the green bosom of the valley to that spot of sky where the company of clouds is loitering; and with an easy shifting of the helm, the fleet of swimmers come drifting over you, and drop their burden into the dancing pools, and make the flowers glisten, and the eaves drip with their crystal bounty.

The cattle linger still, cropping the new-come grass; and childhood laughs joyously at the warm rain;—or, under the cottage roof, catches with eager ear the patter of its fall.

And with that patter on the roof,—so like to the patter of childish feet,—my story of boyish dreams shall begin.

Complete. Introduction to "Dreams of Boyhood."

A REVERIE OF HOME

I T IS a strange force of the mind and of the fancy that can set the objects which are closest to the heart far down the lapse of time. Even now, as the fire fades slightly, and sinks slowly towards the bar, which is the dial of my hours, I seem to see that image of love which has played about the fire-glow of my grate—years hence. It still covers the same warm, trustful, religious heart. Trials have tried it; afflictions have weighed upon it; danger has scared it; and death is coming near to subdue it; but still it is the same.

The fingers are thinner; the face has lines of care and sorrow crossing each other in a web work that makes the golden tissue of humanity. But the heart is fond and steady; it is the same dear heart, the same self-sacrificing heart, warming, like a fire, all around it. Affliction has tempered joy; and joy adorned affliction. Life and all its troubles have become distilled into a holy incense, rising ever from your fireside,—an offering to your household gods.

Your dreams of reputation, your swift determination, your impulsive pride, your deep-uttered vows to win a name, have all sobered into affection—have all blended into that glow of feeling, which finds its centre, and hope, and joy in Home. From my soul I pity him whose soul does not leap at the mere utterance of that name.

A home!—it is the bright, blessed, adorable phantom which sits highest on the sunny horizon that girdeth Life! When shall it be reached? When shall it cease to be a glittering daydream, and become fully and fairly yours?

It is not the house, though that may have its charms; nor the fields carefully tilled, and streaked with your own footpaths;—nor the trees, though their shadow be to you like that of a great rock in a weary land;—nor yet is it the fireside, with its sweet blaze play;—nor the pictures which tell of loved ones, nor the cherished books,—but more far than all these—it is the Presence. The Lares of your worship are there; the altar of your confidence there; the end of your worldly faith is there; and adorning it all, and sending your blood in passionate flow, is the ecstasy of the conviction, that there at least you are beloved; that there you are understood; that there your errors will meet ever with gentlest forgiveness; that there your troubles will be smiled away; that there you may unburden your soul, fearless of harsh, unsympathizing ears; and that there you may be entirely and joyfully—yourself!

There may be those of coarse mold—and I have seen such even in the disguise of women—who will reckon these feelings puling sentiment. God pity them!—as they have need of pity.

That image by the fireside, calm, loving, joyful, is there still; it goes not, however my spirit tosses, because my wish, and every will, keep it there, unerring.

The fire shows through the screen, yellow and warm, as a harvest sun. It is in its best age, and that age is ripeness.

A ripe heart!—now I know what Wordsworth meant, when he said:—

> "The good die first,
> And they whose hearts are dry as summer dust,
> Burn to the socket!"

The town clock is striking midnight. The cold of the night wind is urging its way in at the door and window-crevice; the fire has sunk almost to the third bar of the grate. Still my dream tires not, but wraps fondly round that image,—now in the far-off, chilling mists of age, growing sainted. Love has blended into reverence; passion has subsided into joyous content.

And what if age comes, said I, in a new flush of excitation,—what else proves the wine? What else gives inner strength, and knowledge, and a steady pilot-hand, to steer your boat out boldly upon that shoreless sea, where the river of life is running? Let the white ashes gather; let the silver hair lie, where lay the auburn; let the eye gleam further back, and dimmer; it is but retreating toward the pure sky-depths, an usher to the land where you will follow after.

From "Reveries of a Bachelor."

MARY RUSSELL MITFORD

(1786–1855)

MARY RUSSELL MITFORD, author of "Our Village," was born in Hampshire, England, December 16th, 1786. Her father was a physician, liberally educated and wealthy, but he squandered his fortune and finally came to rely for support on the money earned by his daughter's pen. In 1797, when only ten years of age, she drew a lottery prize of £20,000, but in 1820 this, too, had been squandered and the family was virtually destitute. To support herself and her father, she wrote a number of tragedies which were received with favor. "Rienzi," which is described as the best of them, contains passages of great force. In 1819 she began to publish in the Lady's Magazine sketches and essays describing life in a quiet village and in the woods and fields around it. These when republished under the title of "Our Village" have done most for her reputation, but she wrote poems, fiction, and reminiscences, as well as essays and dramas. She died January 10th, 1855.

THE TALKING LADY

BEN JONSON has a play called "The Silent Woman," who turns out, as might be expected, to be no woman at all—nothing, as Master Slender said, but "a great lubberly boy"; thereby, as I apprehend, discourteously presuming that a silent woman is a nonentity. If the learned dramatist, thus happily prepared and predisposed, had happened to fall in with such a specimen of female loquacity as I have just parted with, he might perhaps have given us a pendant to his picture in the Talking Lady. Pity but he had! He would have done her justice, which I could not at any time, least of all now: I am too much stunned; too much like one escaped from a belfry on a coronation day. I am just resting from the fatigue of four days' hard listening; four snowy, sleety, rainy days—days of every variety of falling weather, all of them too bad to admit the possibility that any petticoated thing, were she as hardy as a Scotch fir, should stir out,—four days chained by "sad civility" to that fireside, once

so quiet, and again—cheering thought! again I trust to be so, when the echo of that visitor's incessant tongue shall have died away.

The visitor in question is a very excellent and respectable elderly lady, upright in mind and body, with a figure that does honor to her dancing master, a face exceedingly well preserved, wrinkled and freckled, but still fair, and an air of gentility over her whole person, which is not the least affected by her out-of-fashion garb. She could never be taken for anything but a woman of family, and perhaps she could as little pass for any other than an old maid. She took us in her way from London to the west of England; and being, as she wrote, "not quite well, not equal to much company, prayed that no other guest might be admitted, so that she might have the pleasure of our conversation all to herself" (Ours! as if it were possible for any of us to slide in a word edgewise!)—"and especially enjoy the gratification of talking over old times with the master of the house, her countryman." Such was the promise of her letter, and to the letter it has been kept. All the news and scandal of a large county forty years ago, and a hundred years before, and ever since, all the marriages, deaths, births, elopements, law suits, and casualties of her own times, her father's, grandfather's, great-grandfather's, nephew's, and grand-nephew's, has she detailed with a minuteness, an accuracy, a prodigality of learning, a profuseness of proper names, a pedantry of locality, which would excite the envy of a county historian, a king-at-arms, or even a Scotch novelist. Her knowledge is astonishing; but the most astonishing part of all is how she came by that knowledge. It should seem, to listen to her, as if, at some time of her life, she must have listened herself; and yet her countryman declares that in the forty years he has known her, no such event has occurred; and she knows new news too! It must be intuition.

The manner of her speech has little remarkable. It is rather old fashioned and provincial, but perfectly lady-like, low and gentle, and not seeming so fast as it is; like the great pedestrians she clears her ground easily, and never seems to use any exertion; yet, "I would my horse had the speed of her tongue, and so good a continuer." She will talk you sixteen hours a day for twenty days together, and not deduct one poor five minutes for halts and baiting time. Talking, sheer talking, is meat and drink and sleep

to her. She likes nothing else. Eating is a sad interruption. For the tea table she has some toleration; but dinner, with its clatter of plates and jingle of knives and forks, dinner is her abhorrence. Nor are the other common pursuits of life more in her favor. Walking exhausts the breath that might be better employed. Dancing is a noisy diversion, and singing is worse; she cannot endure any music, except the long, grand, dull concerto, which nobody thinks of listening to. Reading and chess she classes together as silent barbarisms, unworthy of a social and civilized people. Cards, too, have their faults; there is a rivalry, a mute eloquence in those four aces, that leads away the attention; besides, partners will sometimes scold; so she never plays at cards; and upon the strength of this abstinence had very nearly passed for serious, till it was discovered that she could not abide a long sermon. She always looks out for the shortest preacher, and never went to above one Bible meeting in her life. "Such speeches!" quoth she, "I thought the men never meant to have done. People have great need of patience." Plays, of course, she abhors; and operas, and mobs, and all things that will be heard, especially children; though for babies, particularly when asleep, for dogs and pictures, and such silent intelligences as serve to talk of and talk to, she has a considerable partiality; and an agreeable and gracious flattery to the mammas and other owners of these pretty dumb things is a very usual introduction to her miscellaneous harangues. The matter of these orations is inconceivably various. Perhaps the local and genealogical anecdotes, the sort of supplement to the history of ————shire, may be her strongest point; but she shines almost as much in medicine and housewifery. Her medical dissertations savor a little of that particular branch of the science called quackery. She has a specific against almost every disease to which the human frame is liable; and is terribly prosy and unmerciful in her symptoms. Her cures kill. In housekeeping, her notions resemble those of other verbal managers; full of economy and retrenchment, with a leaning towards reform, though she loves so well to declaim on the abuses in the cook's department, that I am not sure that she would very heartily thank any radical who should sweep them quite away. For the rest, her system sounds very fine in theory, but rather fails in practice. Her recipes would be capital, only that some way or other they do not eat well; her preserves seldom keep; and her sweet wines are sure to turn sour. These are

certainly her favorite topics; but any one will do. Allude to some anecdote of the neighborhood, and she forthwith treats you with as many parallel passages as are to be found in an air with variations. Take up a new publication, and she is equally at home there; for though she knows little of books, she has, in the course of an up-and-down life, met with a good many authors, and teases and provokes you by telling of them precisely what you do not care to hear, the maiden names of their wives, and the Christian names of their daughters, and into what families their sisters and cousins married, and in what towns they have lived, what streets, and what numbers. Boswell himself never drew up the table of Dr. Johnson's Fleet-Street courts with greater care than she made out to me the successive residences of P. P., Esq., author of a tract on the French Revolution, and a pamphlet on the Poor Laws. The very weather is not a safe subject. Her memory is a perpetual register of hard frosts, and long droughts, and high winds, and terrible storms, with all the evils that followed in their train, and all the personal events connected with them, so that if you happen to remark that clouds are come up, and you fear it may rain, she replies, "Aye, it is just such a morning as three and thirty years ago, when my poor cousin was married—you remember my cousin Barbara—she married so and so, the son of so and so"; and then comes the whole pedigree of the bridegroom; the amount of the settlements, and the reading and signing them over night; a description of the wedding dresses, in the style of Sir Charles Grandison, and how much the bride's gown cost per yard; the names, residences, and a short subsequent history of the bridemaids and men, the gentleman who gave the bride away, and the clergyman who performed the ceremony, with a learned antiquarian digression relative to the church; then the setting out in procession; the marriage; the kissing; the crying; the breakfasting; the drawing the cake through the ring; and finally, the bridal excursion, which brings us back again at an hour's end to the starting post, the weather, and the whole story of the sopping, the drying, the clothes-spoiling, the cold-catching, and all the small evils of a summer shower. By this time it rains, and she sits down to a pathetic seesaw of conjectures on the chance of Mrs. Smith's having set out for her daily walk, or the possibility that Dr. Brown may have ventured to visit his patients in his gig, and the certainty that Lady Green's new housemaid would come from London on the outside of the coach.

With all this intolerable prosing, she is actually reckoned a pleasant woman! Her acquaintance in the great manufacturing town where she usually resides is very large, which may partly account for the misnomer. Her conversation is of a sort to bear dividing. Besides, there is, in all large societies, an instinctive sympathy which directs each individual to the companion most congenial to his humor. Doubtless her associates deserve the old French compliment, "*Ils ont tous un grand talent pour le silence.*" Parceled out amongst some seventy or eighty, there may even be some savor in her talk. It is the tête-à-tête that kills, or the small fireside circle of three or four, where only one can speak and all the rest must seem to listen — seem! did I say? — must listen in good earnest. Hotspur's expedient in a similar situation of crying "Hem! go to," and marking not a word, will not do here; compared to her, Owen Glendower was no conjurer. She has the eye of a hawk, and detects a wandering glance, an incipient yawn, the slightest movement of impatience. The very needle must be quiet. If a pair of scissors do but wag, she is affronted, draws herself up, breaks off in the middle of a story, of a sentence, of a word, and the unlucky culprit must, for civility's sake, summon a more than Spartan fortitude, and beg the torturer to resume her torments — "That that is the unkindest cut of all!" I wonder, if she had happened to have married, how many husbands she would have talked to death. It is certain that none of her relations are long-lived after she comes to reside with them. Father, mother, uncle, sister, brother, two nephews, and one niece, all these have successively passed away, though a healthy race, and with no visible disorder — except — but we must not be uncharitable. They might have died, though she had been born dumb: — "It is an accident that happens every day." Since the decease of her last nephew, she attempted to form an establishment with a widow lady, for the sake, as they both said, of the comfort of society. But — strange miscalculation! she was a talker too! They parted in a week.

And we also have parted. I am just returning from escorting her to the coach, which is to convey her two hundred miles westward; and I have still the murmur of her adieus resounding in my ears, like the indistinct hum of the air on a frosty night. It was curious to see how, almost simultaneously, these mournful adieux shaded into cheerful salutations of her new comrades, the passengers in the mail. Poor souls! Little does the civil young

lad who made way for her, or the fat lady, his mamma, who with pains and inconvenience made room for her, or the grumpy gentleman in the opposite corner, who, after some dispute, was at length won to admit her dressing box, — little do they suspect what is to befall them. Two hundred miles! and she never sleeps in a carriage! Well, patience be with them, and comfort and peace! A pleasant journey to them! And to her all happiness! She is a most kind and excellent person, one for whom I would do anything in my poor power — aye, even were it to listen to her another four days.

Complete. From "Our Village."

ST. GEORGE MIVART

(1827–1900)

PERHAPS the most animated religious controversy of the last quarter of the nineteenth century was precipitated by the appearance of St. George Mivart's article on "Happiness in Hell," published in 1892. Peculiar interest was lent to it by the fact that Dr. Mivart was a pronounced Roman Catholic and also a pronounced evolutionist of the Darwinian school. The ground of the essay is that hell is primarily a moral state developing into an intellectual condition in which those who impose it on themselves find pleasure; and that because of the pleasure it gives them, they seek to realize it, turning thought to action and from the invisible hell within creating a corresponding hell, outward and visible. While Mivart was not strongly attacked on the main point, he found opponents resisting at all points his assumption that those who choose their own hell to suit their peculiar condition can find happiness in it.

He was born in London, November 30th, 1827, and educated for the bar. Giving up law for science, he became a naturalist of great attainment and international reputation. The Pope was pleased with his argument that Catholic "dogma" and scientific truth are not antagonistic, and Mivart is himself authority for the statement that the degree of Doctor conferred on him by the Church was on this account. He was by no means satisfied, however, with the "orthodox" support given him on his theories of future punishment. His worst hell is virtually identical with that described by Plutarch in his wonderful passages on "The Delay of the Deity." Mivart died April 1st, 1900.

HAPPINESS IN HELL

"*Per me si va nella citta dolente,*
Per me si va nell' eterno dolore,
Per me si va tra la perduta gente.

.   .   .   .   .

Lasciate ogni speranza, voi che entrate."

"Leave every hope behind, O ye who enter here!"

DANTE's terrible words truly express what was the almost universal belief of Christians for many centuries. The mental agony of despair, in addition to extreme physical torture, was recognized as the inevitable lot of the multitude of lost souls. It was also of the essence of this belief that the agony should be eternal, and known to be eternal by the wretched inmates — the "*perduta gente*" — of that "*citta dolente,*" that city of despair.

But the modern mind has come to feel an abhorrence for beliefs which were viewed with complacency or accepted without difficulty for so many ages. And not only the sentiment of our day, but what we take to be its more highly evolved moral perceptions, are shocked beyond expression at the doctrine that countless multitudes of mankind will burn forever in hell fire, out of which there is no possible redemption. Our experience shows that not a few persons have abandoned Christianity on account of this dogma, which also constitutes the very greatest difficulty for many who desire to obtain a rational religious belief and to accept the Church's teaching.

Is, then, the doctrine against which so strong a repugnance is felt really one essential to Christianity; and, if so, can it be a belief reconcilable with right reason, the highest morality, and the greatest benevolence? . . .

As to the nature of damnation, there are two affirmations we think it well to quote. One is by an anonymous theologian, who represents it as a necessary result of universal law. He says: —

"Hell is a law. Just as it is a law that pent-up water, when its weight and force have reached a certain point, breaks its barriers and sweeps down upon the region below it, so it is a law that sin, or unrighteousness, or willful aversion from God, if it reach the boundary, death, unreformed, will go on forever so, and will bring eternal separation from God, and separation in a spiritual nature means misery. Thus punishment is but the necessary effect of the laws which God has instituted. He crushes evil with the absolute calm wherewith an avalanche grinds rocks to dust, and the evil-doer constructs his own Gehenna.»

In a similar vein Mr. Oxenham asks: —

«What, then, is meant by the dogma of eternal damnation? It means, in one word, leaving the sinner to himself. 'Ephraim is joined to idols; let him alone.' It is no arbitrary infliction of a vengeful Deity!»

Let us now further address ourselves directly to the consideration of what Christian authoritative teaching affirms and permits us to believe with respect to hell. We have already seen how benevolent its teaching is with respect to those who die in a state of mere nature without deliberately committing grave sins the gravity of which they fully recognize.

Let us imagine a man in perfect health of mind and body, intelligent, amiable, and wealthy, enjoying the universal esteem of all who know him, the devoted affection of his family, the peace of a good conscience, and the happiness of a natural love of and union with God. Let us further suppose that all his wishes are gratified, and that he has a full and certain knowledge that this great felicity will exist unimpaired and be unceasingly enjoyed by him for all eternity. Yet such a being will be in hell. Such at least (according to Catholic teaching) will be the lot of the immense multitude of mankind who, from before the formation of the earliest flint implement to the present day, have died unbaptized and free from deliberate mortal sin, understood to be such. They are subjects, indeed, of the *pœna damni*, (penalty of loss), but that is no cause of regret to them. Not having had the "light of glory" (*i. e.*, been raised to the order of grace) they have no aptitude or faculty for the supernatural, without which its possession (were it possible) would rather be torture than happiness. Perfectly happy according to their nature, they could no more desire the supernatural state than fishes can desire to become birds, or oysters sigh because they are not butterflies.

A singular consequence follows from the above consideration. Since the inexpressibly higher condition, according to the Church, carries with it fearful risks and responsibilities, there is, on

Church principles, small reason to regret the late advent and limited diffusion of Christianity or the falling away from the Church of masses of Christians. In consequence thereof, the diminution of risk and responsibility to multitudes of mankind — unfavorably placed to fulfill higher claims — is so great, that God alone can know whether the apparent loss is not a real gain.

As to the nonbaptized who lead abandoned lives knowingly and willingly, their lot must be light indeed, compared with those who, having been called to the higher state, have voluntarily outraged its privileges. And thus we come at last to the one great difficulty, the real crux of the whole matter: what are we to say to the state of baptized Christians who lead bad lives and depart from the world in their sins — what are we to say of them from the Catholic point of view?

Now, in the first place, we must never forget the mitigating circumstances as regards heredity and environment, to which we have before referred. Multitudes of sins which are "mortal" according to the letter of the Christian code are, owing to such circumstances, but "venial" in fact; so that their perpetrators, if condemned by "law," must be absolved by "equity." Secondly, we must also remember what has been already said about the need of advertence and deliberate volition, in order that any sinful act should be a mortal one.

But those who knowingly and with malice sin mortally and so persist till death, obstinately turning a deaf ear to all good influences, are, the Church tells us, really condemned to hell, there to suffer, not only the state of loss, but the *pœna sensus* also.

Nevertheless, their state is declared to be most unequal, and to vary with their demerits. Also the existence of the very worst is felt by him to be preferable to his nonexistence. He does not, like so many poor wretches on earth, even desire the cessation of his being. May we not therefore believe that his suffering is not so great as theirs? It seems also that, in spite of Dante, hope may still be his if a process of evolution does, as some theologians teach, take place in hell.

But we cannot think that right reason demands the belief that no one in hell suffers severely, even compared with life on earth. For although we may judge no man, and although reason tells us how almost impossible it is for us fairly to judge even ourselves, yet men do seem, now and again, to give evidence of extreme malice and of a positive hatred of God; so that it would

ill become us to represent hell as being in no case an object of just fear, nay of prudent, reasonable terror. The poignancy of persistent regret for a misspent past, and for actions to recall which life would be willingly surrendered, are states of mind by no means unknown in our present existence. It may well be that the clearer mental vision of a future day as to what might have been may give rise to a wretchedness which it is beyond our power to imagine.

But for the multitude of even the positively damned, besides the possible consciousness of their state and the also possible consolations of a hoped-for amelioration, we are not, so far as we know, forbidden to think that as they have by their actions constructed their own hell, they may therein find a certain kind of harmony with their own mental condition. It may be they seek and meet with the society of souls like minded with themselves, and, as it were, together hug their chains, esteeming as preferable these lower mental activities and desires which had been their choice and solace upon earth. We read in the New Testament the words: —

«He that is unjust, let him be unjust still; and he that is filthy, let him be filthy still.»

But to have the will persistently averted from what is best must entail suffering; nor can it be denied that (according to the teaching of the Church) some positive suffering will never cease for those who have voluntarily and deliberately cast away from them their supreme beatitude.

The reader will naturally ask how, if such views as some of those which have been here brought forward be tenable views, can those teachers be pardoned who have represented hell in the uniformly terrible and revolting way they have represented it.

The answer to this question reposes upon the joint consideration of God's perfection and man's intellectual limitation.

As to the former, it is simply beyond, infinitely beyond, all our powers of conception, and the same must therefore be said of the supernatural happiness it is in his power to bestow — the happiness of a nature endowed by "the light of glory," with a capacity for the Beatific Vision. This is what "eye hath not seen, nor ear heard, nor hath it entered into the heart of man to conceive."

Such being the case, the limitation of our nature necessitates what Cardinal Newman has called "economies" in making known

facts concerning the life hereafter. We are reduced to symbols so inadequate that words cannot adequately express their inadequacy. The result is that in order to convey to the mind as practically serviceable an image as may be of what such bliss and glory are, the only possible course has been to endeavor to depict them by contrast. In order to bring home to men what their loss will be should they by vice and malice forfeit so inconceivable a beatitude, it has been necessary to represent that loss by means of such symbols as may, least inadequately and most effectively, strike the imaginations of the greatest multitude of mankind.

If a painter has to depict, as best he may, a brightness which no pigment can approach, he is reduced to attempt it by deepening shadows as much as his palette will permit — regretting all the time that he has no sables nearly black enough to convey, by contrast, a due appreciation of that unrepresentable brightness.

Just as we saw that the contrast between Christianity and Paganism was only most imperfectly and inadequately represented by its earliest advocates when they spoke of the heathen gods as demons, so the bliss of heaven was only most imperfectly and inadequately represented by those who described hell as a place of all the horrors their imagination could possibly depict.

So to have represented it has not caused the least practical error or misled any one by one jot or tittle.

Thus, on the presumption that heaven is what the Church declares it to be, the author of "Hell Opened to Christians" only speaks the words of truth and soberness when he says: "Do not suppose I have exaggerated anything; I have failed, indeed, in the opposite way."

The horrors of that book multiplied a thousandfold could not give the faintest conception of the real difference which exists between the attainment of heaven and its loss, even though the lost ones had an eternal existence of the most extreme natural beatitude far exceeding all we can possibly imagine on earth.

The loss of heaven is an infinite loss, and therefore no symbols can represent it adequately.

Thus the preachers and writers of the Church, her sculptors and her painters, have barely done their duty in seeking to portray the contrast between such loss and gain by the most practically serviceable symbols which were at their disposal. The teaching of theologians (very unlike that of Rousseau) deals not with imaginary human beings, but with living men and women with all their vivid passions and keen temptations, seeking to make them apprehend, least inadequately and most forcibly, what it is impossible adequately to express.

The limitation of our faculties, even as regards the natural world, often compels us to make use of different means with respect to one and the same sense, and it is frequently impossible to gain an accurate perception of one object without thereby simultaneously obtaining a quite inaccurate perception of another object.

We shall vainly seek with a field glass to observe Jupiter's satellites or the rings of Saturn; and if when observing with a high power we so adjust a microscope as to bring a deeper stratum of some object into focus, we are, by that very act, presented with an inaccurate image of the higher stratum we may have correctly seen before.

Thus while the most startling symbols are applicable for depicting the difference between the final loss of grace (hell) and life in heaven, they altogether fail if they are taken to depict existence in hell as compared with life on earth. It is, indeed, absolutely certain that in the latter case they are and must be altogether false; for the difference between what is divine and aught else is an infinite difference, and infinitely greater than any other contrast and distinction whatsoever it may be. Therefore, what is most proper approximately to represent the former cannot properly represent the latter also.

Thus it seems that the objections of our own day against the Catholic doctrine of hell altogether fall to the ground.

When it is said that the belief in eternal tortures really comparable with the pains of our present life, and enormously exceeding them is "a horrible doctrine, worse than atheism," the reply that such symbols are not comparable with life on earth appears to us to be a completely satisfactory one.

If our estimate of the value and significance of the most authoritative and dogmatic Christian teaching be correct (and we have sought the most skilled advice), then, while it permits of the most practically effective appeals being truthfully addressed to the multitude, it none the less proclaims nothing which is not reconcilable with the most benevolent ethical conceptions.

Its teaching, as we understand it, may be briefly summed up as follows: God has with infinite benevolence, but with

inscrutable purposes, created human beings, the overwhelming majority of whom, being incapable of grave sin, attain to an eternity of unimaginable natural happiness — the utmost of which their nature is capable and which includes a natural knowledge and love of God. Another multitude undergo a certain probation on earth and attain to a future state exactly proportioned to their merits or demerits, which may equal or fall short of the natural happiness of those incapable of sin.

God has further endowed a certain number of mankind with faculties whereby they are rendered capable of a supernatural union with him — a bliss which, in life, they can neither imagine nor really desire, though they may aspire to it as to a good beyond their power to picture.

This privilege carries with it a dread risk of failure, resulting in the loss of such supernatural happiness. But this failure may be of all degrees, with corresponding divergencies of conditions. Yet for the very worst, in spite of the positive and unceasing suffering before referred to, existence is acceptable and is by them preferred to nonexistence; while we are permitted to believe in an eternal upward progress, though never attaining to the supernatural state which would be most unwelcome and repugnant to such souls. They are left to themselves in those various inferior conditions which they have made theirs by their own choice and which they have led themselves to persist in and prefer. Thus the hell even of the positively damned, who have forfeited grace bestowed, may yet be regarded as a place which God has from all eternity prepared for those who will not accept the higher good offered by him for their acceptance.

Nevertheless, if we consider how impossible it is for us to understand, on the one hand, our own real responsibility (our full relations with our environment) and, on the other, our knowledge of our own individual demerits, there is plenty of reason for anxiety and apprehension concerning those two final states, one of which must, the Church teaches, be the lot of every one of us. Yet when the variety of conditions of reprobation and their nature, as here put forward, are pondered over, it appears to us that the eternal duration of such a hell may well result from the creative action of God's benevolence and justice combined. In the words of Dante: "*Fecemi la divina Potestate, la somma Sapienza e il primo Amore.*" Nothing, in fact, has been

defined by the Church on the subject of hell which does not accord with right reason, the highest morality, and the greatest benevolence.

According to it no one in the next life suffers the deprivation of any happiness which he can imagine or desire, or which is congruous with his nature and faculties, save by his conscious and deliberate choice. According to it, also, God has refused to no man who fully obeys the voice of conscience, heathen though he be, the full beatitude of the light of glory and the Beatific Vision.

Hell in its widest sense — namely, as including all those blameless souls who do not enjoy that vision — must be considered as, for them, an abode of happiness transcending all our most vivid anticipations, so that man's natural capacity for happiness is there gratified to the very utmost; nor is it even possible for the Catholic theologian of the most severe and rigid school to deny that, thus considered, there is, and there will for all eternity be, a real and true happiness in hell.

From the Nineteenth Century.

VIII—184

LADY MARY WORTLEY MONTAGU

(1689–1762)

LADY MARY WORTLEY MONTAGU, whose "Letters" have given her an enduring reputation, was born in 1689 (baptized May 26th of that year). Her father was the fifth earl of Kingston, and she was an intimate friend of a number of noble English ladies to whom her "Letters" have given celebrity. The Princess of Wales (afterwards Queen Caroline) was fond of her, and in 1716 Edward Wortley Montagu, whom she had privately married in 1712, was sent as embassador to Constantinople. She accompanied him, and during her two years in the East wrote some of the most noted of her "Letters." She died in England, August 21st, 1762. The first series of her "Letters" appeared in 1763; the second in 1767. One of the most celebrated episodes in her life was her quarrel with Pope, who was at one time her warm admirer. He satirized her under the name of "Sappho."

IN PRAISE OF ORIENTAL LIFE

I AM extremely pleased with hearing from you, and my vanity [the darling frailty of her (*sic*) mankind] not a little flattered by the uncommon questions you ask me, though I am utterly incapable of answering them. And, indeed, were I as good a mathematician as Euclid himself, it requires an age's stay to make just observations on the air and vapors. I have not been yet a full year here, and am on the point of removing. Such is my rambling destiny. This will surprise you, and can surprise nobody so much as myself.

Perhaps you will accuse me of laziness, or dullness, or both together, that can leave this place without giving you some account of the Turkish court. I can only tell you that if you please to read Sir Paul Rycaut, you will there find a full and true account of the viziers, the beglerbegs, the civil and spiritual government, the officers of the seraglio, etc., things that 'tis very easy to procure lists of, and therefore may be depended on; though other stories, God knows—I say no more—everybody is at liberty to write their own remarks; the manners of people may change or some of them escape the observation of travelers, but 'tis not the same of the government; and for that reason, since I can tell you nothing new, I will tell nothing of it.

In the same silence shall be passed over the arsenal and seven towers; and for mosques, I have already described one of the noblest to you very particularly. But I cannot forbear taking notice to you of a mistake of Gemelli (though I honor him in a much higher degree than any other voyage writer): he says there are no remains of Calcedon; this is certainly a mistake; I was there yesterday, and went across the canal in my galley, the sea being very narrow between that city and Constantinople. 'Tis still a large town, and has several mosques in it: The Christians still call it Calcedonia, and the Turks give it a name I forgot, but which is only a corruption of the same word. I suppose this an error of his guide, which his short stay hindered him from rectifying; for I have in other matters a very just esteem for his veracity. Nothing can be pleasanter than the canal; and the Turks are so well acquainted with its beauties, all their pleasure seats are built on its banks, where they have at the same time the most beautiful prospects in Europe and Asia; there are near one another some hundreds of magnificent palaces.

Human grandeur being here yet more unstable than anywhere else, 'tis common for the heirs of a great three-tailed pasha not to be rich enough to keep in repair the house he built; thus, in a few years, it falls to ruin. I was yesterday to see that of the late Grand Vizier, who was killed at Peterwaradin. It was built to receive his royal bride, daughter of the present Sultan, but he did not live to see her there. I have a great mind to describe it to you; but I check that inclination, knowing very well that I cannot give you, with my best description, such an idea of it as I ought. It is situated on one of the most delightful parts of the canal, with a fine wood on the side of a hill behind it. The extent of it is prodigious; the guardian assured me that there are eight hundred rooms in it; I will not answer for that number, since I did not count them; but 'tis certain that the number is very large, and the whole adorned with a profusion of marble, gilding, and the most exquisite painting of fruit and flowers. The windows are all sashed with the finest crystalline

glass brought from England; and all the expensive magnificence that you can suppose in a palace founded by a vain young luxurious man, with the wealth of a vast empire at his command. But no part of it pleased me better than the apartment destined for the bagnios. There are two built exactly in the same manner, answering to one another; the baths, fountains, and pavements, all of white marble, the roofs gilt, and the walls covered with Japan china; but adjoining to them, two rooms, the upper part of which is divided into a sofa; in the four corners are falls of water from the very roof, from shell to shell, of white marble, to the lower end of the room, where it falls into a large basin, surrounded with pipes, that throw up water as high as the room. The walls are in the nature of lattices; and, on the outside of them, vines and woodbines planted, that form a sort of green tapestry, and give an agreeable obscurity to these delightful chambers.

I should go on and let you into some of the other apartments (all worthy your curiosity), but 'tis yet harder to describe a Turkish palace than any other, being built entirely irregular. There is nothing which can be properly called front or wings; and though such a confusion is, I think, pleasing to the sight, yet it would be very unintelligible in a letter. I shall only add that the chamber destined for the Sultan, when he visits his daughter, is wainscoted with mother-of-pearl fastened with emeralds like nails. There are others of mother-of-pearl and olive wood inlaid, and several of Japan china. The galleries, which are numerous and very large, are adorned with jars of flowers, and porcelain dishes of fruit of all sorts, so well done in plaster, and colored in so lively a manner, that it has an enchanting effect. The garden is suitable to the house, where arbors, fountains and walks, are thrown together in an agreeable confusion. There is no ornament wanting, except that of statues. Thus, you see, sir, these people are not so unpolished as we represent them. 'Tis true their magnificence is of a different taste from ours, and perhaps of a better. I am almost of opinion they have a right notion of life; while they consume it in music, gardens, wine, and delicate eating, we are tormenting our brains with some scheme of politics, or studying some science to which we can never attain, or, if we do, cannot persuade people to set that value upon it we do ourselves. 'Tis certain what we feel and see is properly (if anything is properly) our own; but the good of fame, the folly

of praise, hardly purchased, and, when obtained, a poor recompense for loss of time and health. We die or grow old and decrepid before we can reap the fruit of our labors. Considering what short-lived weak animals men are, is there any study so beneficial as the study of present pleasure? I dare not pursue this theme; perhaps I have already said too much; but I depend upon the true knowledge you have of my heart. I don't expect from you the insipid railleries I should suffer from another in answer to this letter. You know how to divide the idea of pleasure from that of vice, and they are only mingled in the heads of fools. But I allow you to laugh at me for the sensual declaration that I had rather be a rich effendi with all his ignorance than Sir Isaac Newton with all his knowledge.

Complete. To the Abbé Conti. Dated from Constantinople, May 19th, 1718.

ON MATRIMONIAL HAPPINESS

IF WE marry, our happiness must consist in loving one another; 'tis principally my concern to think of the most probable method of making that love eternal. You object against living in London; I am not fond of it myself, and readily give it up to you, though I am assured there needs more art to keep a fondness alive in solitude, where it generally preys upon itself. There is one article absolutely necessary — to be ever beloved one must be ever agreeable. There is no such thing as being agreeable without a thorough good-humor, a natural sweetness of temper, enlivened by cheerfulness. Whatever natural funds of gayety one is born with, 'tis necessary to be entertained with agreeable objects. Anybody capable of tasting pleasure, when they confine themselves to one place, should take care 'tis the place in the world the most agreeable. Whatever you may now think (now, perhaps, you have some fondness for me), though your love should continue in its full force, there are hours when the most beloved mistress would be troublesome. People are not forever (nor is it in human nature that they should be) disposed to be fond; you would be glad to find in me the friend and the companion. To be agreeably the last, it is necessary to be gay and entertaining. A perpetual solitude, in a place where you see nothing to raise your spirits, at length wears them out, and conversation

insensibly falls into dullness and insipidity. When I have no more to say to you, you will like me no longer. How dreadful is that view! You will reflect, for my sake you have abandoned the conversation of a friend that you liked, and your situation in a country where all things would have contributed to make your life pass in (the true *volupté*) a smooth tranquillity. I shall lose the vivacity which should entertain you, and you will have nothing to recompense you for what you have lost. Very few people that have settled entirely in the country but have grown at length weary of one another. The lady's conversation generally falls into a thousand impertinent effects of idleness; and the gentleman falls in love with his dogs and his horses, and out of love with everything else. I am not now arguing in favor of the town; you have answered me as to that point. In respect of your health, 'tis the first thing to be considered, and I shall never ask you to do anything injurious to that. But 'tis my opinion, 'tis necessary to be happy, that we neither of us think any place more agreeable than that where we are.

From a "Letter" to E. W. Montagu.

ON TRAINING YOUNG GIRLS

PEOPLE commonly educate their children as they build their houses, according to some plan they think beautiful, without considering whether it is suited to the purposes for which they are designed. Almost all girls of quality are educated as if they were to be great ladies, which is often as little to be expected as an immoderate heat of the sun in the north of Scotland. You should teach yours to confine their desires to probabilities, to be as useful as is possible to themselves, and to think privacy (as it is) the happiest state of life. I do not doubt your giving them all the instructions necessary to form them to a virtuous life: but 'tis a fatal mistake to do this without proper restrictions. Vices are often hid under the name of virtues, and the practice of them followed by the worst of consequences. Sincerity, friendship, piety, disinterestedness, and generosity are all great virtues; but pursued without discretion become criminal. I have seen ladies indulge their own ill-humor by being very rude and impertinent, and think they deserved approbation by saying I love to speak truth. One of your acquaintance made a ball the day after her

mother died, to show she was sincere. I believe your own reflection will furnish you with but too many examples of the ill
effects of the rest of the sentiments I have mentioned, when too
warmly embraced. They are generally recommended to young
people without limits or distinction, and this prejudice hurries
them into great misfortunes, while they are applauding themselves
in the noble practice (as they fancy) of very eminent virtues.

From a "Letter" to the Countess of Bute.

MICHEL EYQUEM DE MONTAIGNE

(1533-1592)

MONTAIGNE was the first great essayist of modern times, and,
except in Bacon, modern times have scarcely produced a
greater. His master was Plutarch, whose amiable discursiveness he reproduces in all its charm as Bacon does the intensity
of Aristotle in all its severity. In the great art of digression Montaigne is unrivaled, far surpassing Plutarch, who alone could have
suggested to him its possibilities. Although he frequently devotes
no inconsiderable attention to what he professes to be talking about,
his professions are still more frequently mere pretexts which conceal
his real purpose of digressing into a hundred subjects on which he is
well assured that he knows something worth saying. His essay on
"Certain Verses of Virgil" not only illustrates this habit, but also the
attractive egotism which enabled him to put so much of himself into
his work. We learn thus, much that is of singular interest concerning him. He was the product of an educational system. His father
began experimenting on him from the cradle, intending to make a
great man of him. Thus he was taught Latin as one of his "mother
tongues" and much of what is usually considered "higher education,"
and difficult of attainment, he learned as a child without having opportunity to suspect its difficulty. In addition to this home education, he graduated from the college at Bordeaux and studied law.
From 1559, when he went to the court of Francis II., until 1580, when
his "Essays" appeared at Bordeaux, he amused himself, traveled, or
idled, and wrote in retirement on his estate. The second volume of
the "Essays" appeared in 1588. In 1581, when in Rome, he was
summoned to France by the news of his election as Mayor of Bordeaux. He did not make a bad mayor as appears from the fact
that he was elected for a second term, but he made no pretense of
being enthusiastic in the public service. He defined the object of his
"Essays" as self-expression, without regard to utility or reputation. He
wished to express what he had in himself with its flaws unconcealed.
His life seems to have had the same purpose as his "Essays," and in
this he does not seem to have differed in principle from Goethe, who
had much the same theory of the object of existence. Montaigne,
however, had nothing of Goethe's concentrated power and intensity.

He went through the world as an inquisitive but well-trained child
goes through a strange flower garden, examining every flower with
earnest curiosity, but plucking none. Emerson chooses him as the
type of the "skeptic," but his was not the skepticism of mere negation and unfaith. He examined all things for the pleasure the examination gave him, but he was not an agnostic and he had a
singularly clear conception of the difference between the rational and
the absurd. In him is drawn for the first time a clearly defined line
between the mediæval and the modern. He may be called with
justice the first great writer of modern prose, and he might be called
the first great modern thinker but for his persistent habit of avoiding conclusions. He meditates, studies, reflects, and reasons, but think
he does not,—that is, if we are to understand by "thought" that concentrated and determined effort in which every faculty of the mind
co-operates to co-ordinate its knowledge and through co-ordination to
reach a conclusion. Montaigne's knowledge was vast, uncoördinated,
vague, centrifugal, tending always to lose itself in the Infinite to
which he so manifestly belongs. If any one else had written much
of what is his, we might wish it changed for the better! Yet who
could change Montaigne except for the worse?

W. V. B.

OF BOOKS*

I MAKE no doubt, but that I oft happen to speak of things that
are much better, and more truly handled by those who are
masters of the trade. This here is purely an essay of my
natural parts, and not of those acquir'd: and whoever shall take
me tripping in my ignorance will not in any sort displease me;
for I should be very unwilling to become responsible to another
for my writings, who am not so to my self, nor satisfied with
them. Whoever goes in quest of knowledge, let him fish for it
where it is to be found; there is nothing I so little profess.
These are fancies of my own, by which I do not pretend to discover things, but to lay open my self: they may, peradventure,
one day be known to me, or have formerly been, according as
my fortune has been able to bring me in place where they have
been explained; but I have utterly forgot them: and if I am a
man of some reading, I am a man of no retention: so that I
can promise no certainty, if not to make known to what certain

* In using Cotton's translation his spelling has been retained as far as
possible.

mark the knowledge I now have does rise. Therefore let no
body insist upon the matter I write, but my method in writing.
Let them observe in what I borrow, if I have known how to
chuse what is proper to raise, or relieve the invention, which is
always my own: for I make others say for me, what, either for
want of language, or want of sense, I cannot my self well express. I do not number my borrowings, I weigh them. And
had I design'd to raise their estimate by their number, I had
made them twice as many. They are all, or within a very few,
so fam'd and ancient authors, that they seem, methinks,
themselves sufficiently to tell who they are, without giving me
the trouble. In reasons, comparisons, and arguments, if I trans-
plant any into my own soil, and confound them amongst my
own, I purposely conceal the author to awe the temerity of those
precipitous censures, that fall upon all sorts of writings; particularly the late ones, of men yet living, and in the vulgar tongue,
which put every one into a capacity of censuring, and which seem
to convince the authors themselves of vulgar conception and design.
I will have them wound Plutarch through my sides, and rail
against Seneca when they think they rail at me. I must shelter
my own weakness under these great reputations; I shall love
any one that can plume me, that is, by clearness of understanding and judgment, and by the sole distinction of the force and
beauty of discourse. For I, who, for want of memory, am at
every turn at a loss to pick them out of their national livery,
am yet wise enough to know, by the measure of my own abilities, that my soil is incapable of producing any of those rich
flowers, that I there find set, and growing; and that all the
fruits of my own growth are not worth any one of them. For
this, indeed, I hold my self very responsible, tho' the confession makes against me; if there be any vanity and vice in my
writings, which I do not of my self perceive, nor can discern,
when pointed out to me by another; for many faults escape the
eye, but the infirmity of judgment consists in not being able to
discern them, when, by another, laid open to us. Knowledge
and truth may be in us without judgment, and judgment also
without them; but the confession of ignorance is one of the
fairest and surest testimonies of judgment that I know; I have
no other officer to put my writings in rank and file, but only
fortune. As things come into my head, I heap them one upon
another, which sometimes advance in whole bodies, sometimes

in single files: I am content that every one should see my nat- ural and ordinary pace as ill as it is. I suffer my self to jog on at my own rate and ease. Neither are these subjects, which a man is not permitted to be ignorant in, or casually, and at a venture, to discourse of. I could wish to have a more perfect knowledge of things, but I will not buy it so dear as it will cost. My design is to pass over easily, and not laboriously, the remainder of my life. There is nothing that I will cudgel my brains about; no, not knowledge, of what price soever. I seek, in the reading of books, only to please my self by an irre- proachable diversion: or if I study, it is for no other science than what treats of the knowledge of my self, and instructs me how to die, and live well. I do not bite my nails about the difficulties I meet with in my reading; after a charge or two, I give them over. Should I insist upon them, I should both lose my self, and time; for I have an impatient understanding that must be satisfied at first: what I do not discern at first is, by persistency, rendered more obscure. I do nothing without gayety; continuation, and a too obstinate endeavour, darkens, stupefies, and tires my judgment. My sight is confounded, and dissipated with poring; I must withdraw it, and refer my dis- covery to new attempts: just, as to judge rightly of the lustre scarlet, we are taught to pass it lightly with the eye, in running it over at several suddain and reiterated views and glances. If one book do not please me, I take another, and never meddle with any, but at such times as I am weary of doing nothing. I care not much for new ones, because the old seem fuller, and of stronger reason; neither do I much tamper with Greek authors, my knowledge in that language being too little to read them with any delight. Amongst those that are simply pleasant, of the Moderns, Boccace his "Decamerone," Rabelais, and the "Basia" of Johannes Secundus (if those may be ranged under that title) are worth reading. As to "Amadis de Gaul," and such kind of stuff, they had not the credit to take me, so much as in my childish years. And I will moreover say (whether boldly, or rashly) that this old, heavy soul of mine is now no longer de- lighted with Ariosto; no, nor with Ovid; and that his facility and invention, with which I was formerly so ravished, are now of no more relish, and I can hardly have the patience to read him. I speak my opinion freely of all things, even of those that, perhaps, exceed my capacity, and that I do not conceive

to be in any wise under my jurisdiction. And, accordingly, the judgment I deliver is to show the measure of my own sight, and not of the things I make so bold to censure: when I find myself disgusted with Plato's "Axiochus," as with a work (with due respect to such an author be it spoken) without force my judgment does not believe it self: it is not so arrogant as to op- pose the authority of so many other famous judgments of antiq- uity, which it considers as its regents and masters, and with whom it is rather content to err. In such a case it condemns it self, either for stopping at the outward bark, nor being able to penetrate to the heart, or for considering it by some false light, and is content with securing it self from trouble and error only; and, as to its own weakness, does frankly acknowledge and con- fess it. It thinks it gives a just interpretation, according to the appearances, by its conceptions presented to it; but they are weak and imperfect. Most of the fables of Æsop have in them several senses and meanings, of which the mythologists chose some one that quadrates well to the fable; but, for the most part, 'tis but the first face that presents it self, and is superficial only, there yet remain others more lively, essential, and pro- found, into which they have not been able to penetrate; and just so I do.

But, to pursue the business of this essay, I have always thought that in poesie, Virgil, Lucretius, Catullus, and Horace do many degrees excel the rest; and signally, Virgil in his "Geor- gics," which I look upon for the most accomplished piece of poetry; and, in comparison of which, a man may easily discern that there are some places in his "Æneids" to which the author would have given a little more of the file had he had leisure: and the fifth book of his "Æneids" seems to me the most per- fect. I also love Lucan, and willingly read him; not so much for his stile, as for his own worth, and the truth and solidity of his opinions and judgments. As for Terence, I find the quaint- ness and eloquencies of the Latin tongue so admirable lively to represent our manners, and the movements of the soul, that our actions throw me, at every turn, upon him; and cannot read him so oft, that I do not still discover some new grace and beauty. Such as lived near Virgil's time were scandaliz'd that some should compare him with Lucretius. I am, I confess, of opinion that the comparison is, in truth, very unequal; a belief that, nevertheless, I have much ado to assure my self in, when I meet

with some excellent passages in Lucretius: but if they were so angry at this comparison, what would they have said of the brutish and barbarous stupidity of those who, at this hour, com- pare him with Ariosto? Or would not Ariosto himself say?—

O Sæclum insipiens, et infacetum! — *Catul.* Epig. 40.

I think the Ancients had more reason to be angry with those who compared Plautus with Terence, than Lucretius with Virgil. It makes much for the estimation and preference of Terence, that the father of the Roman eloquence has him so often in his mouth; and the sentence that the best judge of Roman poets has passed upon the other. I have often observed that those of our times who take upon them to write comedies (in imitation of the Italians, who are happy enough in that way of writing) take in three or four arguments of those of Plautus, or Terence, to make one of theirs, and crowd five or six of Boccace his novels, into one single comedy. And that which makes them so load them- selves with matter is the diffidence they have of being able to support themselves with their own strength. They must find out something to lean to; and having not of their own where- with to entertain the audience, bring in the story, to supply the defect of language. It is quite otherwise with my author; the elegancy and perfection of his way of speaking makes us lose the appetite of his plot. His fine expression, elegancy, and quaintness is every where taking: he is so pleasant throughout.

Liquidus, puroque simillimus amni. — *Hor.* Lib. II., Epis. 2.

"Liquid, and like a crystal running stream."

And does so possess the soul with his graces, that we forget those of his fable. This very consideration carries me further: I observe that the best and most ancient poets have avoided the affectation, and hunting after, not only of fantastick Spanish, and Petrarchick elevations, but even the softest, and most gentle touches, which are the only ornaments of succeeding poesie. And yet there is no good judgment that will condemn this in the Ancients, and that does not incomparably more admire the equal politeness, and that perpetual sweetness, and flourishing beauty, that appears in Catullus his epigrams, than all the stings with which Martial arms the tails of his. This is by the same reason that I gave before, and as Martial says of himself: "*Minus illi*

ingenio laborandum fuit, in cujus locum materia successerat.» — *Mart.* Prœlib. 8. These first, without being mov'd, or making themselves angry, make themselves sufficiently felt; they have matter enough of laughter throughout, they need not tickle them- selves: the others have need of foreign assistance, as they have the less wit, they must have the more body; they mount on horseback, because they are not able to stand on their own legs. As in our balls, those mean fellows that teach to dance, not being able to represent the presence and decency of our nobleness, are fain to supply it with dangerous leaps and other strange motions, and fantastick tricks. And the ladies are less put to it in dances, where there are several coupees, changes, and quick motions of body, than in some other of a more solemn kind, where they are only to move a natural pace, and to represent their ordinary grace and presence. And, as I have also seen good tumblers, when in their own every-day-cloaths, and with the same face they always wear, give us all the pleasure of their art, when their apprentices, not yet arrived to such a pitch of perfection, are fain to meal their faces, put themselves into ridiculous disguises, and make a hundred mimick faces, to prepare us for laughter. This conception of mine is no where more demonstrable than in com- paring the "Æneid" with "Orlando Furioso"; of which, we see the first, by dint of wing, flying in a brave and lofty place, and always following his point; the latter, fluttering and hopping from tale to tale, as from branch to branch, not daring to trust his wings but in very short flights, and perching at every turn, lest his breath and force should fail.

Excursusque breves tentat. — *Virg.* Georg. 4.

These then, as to this sort of subjects, are the authors that best please me. As to what concerns my other reading that mixes a little more profit with the pleasure, and from whence I learn how to marshal my opinions and qualities, the books that serve me to this purpose are Plutarch (since translated into French) and Seneca: both of which have this great convenience suited to my humor, that the knowledge I there seek is discoursed in loose pieces, that do not engage me in any great trouble of read- ing long, of which I am impatient. Such are the "Opusculums" of the first, and the "Epistles" of the latter, which are also the best, and most profiting of all their writings. 'Tis no great at- tempt to take one of them in hand, and I give over at pleasure;

for they have no sequel or dependance upon one another. These authors, for the most part, concur in useful and true opinions; and there is this parallel betwixt them, that fortune brought them into the world about the same age; they were both tutors to two Roman emperors; both sought out from foreign countries; both rich, and both great men. Their instruction is the cream of philosophy, and deliver'd after a plain and pertinent manner. Plutarch is more uniform and constant; Seneca more various and waving. The last toil'd, set himself, and bent his whole force to fortifie vertue against frailty, fear, and vicious appetites; the other seems more to slight their power, and to disdain to alter his pace, and to stand upon his guard. Plutarch's opinions are Platonick, sweet, and accommodated to civil society; those of the other are stoical and epicurean, more remote from the common usance, but, in my opinion, more especially proper, and more firm. Seneca seems to lean a little to the tyranny of the emperors of his time, and only seems; for I take it for granted that he spake against his judgment, when he condemns the generous action of those who assassinated Cæsar. Plutarch is frank throughout. Seneca abounds with brisk touches and sallies; Plutarch with things that heat and move you more; this contents and pays you better. This guides us, the other pushes us on. As to Cicero, those of his works that are more useful to my design are they that treat of philosophy, especially moral: but boldly to confess the truth, his way of writing, and that of all other long-winded authors, appears to me very tedious: for his prefaces, definitions, divisions, and etymologies take up the greatest part of his work: whatever there is of life and marrow is smother'd and lost in the preparation. When I have spent an hour in reading him (which is a great deal for me) and recollect what I have thence extracted of juice and substance; for the most part I find nothing but wind; for he is not yet come to the arguments that serve to his purpose, and the reasons that should properly help to loose the knot I would untie. For me, who only desire to become more wise, not more learned or eloquent, these logical or Aristotelian dispositions of parts are of no use. I would have a man begin with the main proposition; and that wherein the force of the argument lies: I know well enough what death and pleasure are; let no man give himself the trouble to anatomize them to me; I look for good and solid reasons at the first dash to instruct me how to stand the shock, and resist them; to which

purpose, neither grammatical subtleties, nor the quaint contexture of words and argumentations are of any use at all: I am for discourses that give the first charge into the heart of the doubt; his languish about his subjects, and delay our expectation. Those are proper for the schools, for the bar, and for the pulpit, where we have leisure to nod, and may awake a quarter of an hour after time enough to find again the thread of the discourse. It is necessary to speak after this manner to judges, whom a man has a design, right or wrong, to incline to favor his cause, to children and common people; to whom a man must say all he can, and try what effects his eloquence can produce. I would not have an author make it his business to render me attentive. Or that he should cry out fifty times, "Oh, yes," as the clerks and heralds do. The Romans, in their religious exercises, began with "*hoc age,*" as we in ours do with "*sursum corda,*" which are so many words lost to me; I come thither already fully prepared for my chamber; I need no allurement, no invitation, no sauce; I eat the meat raw, so that, instead of whetting my appetite by these preparatives, they tire and pall it. Will the license of the time excuse the sacrilegious boldness to censure the dialogisms of Plato himself, for as dull and heavy as the other before nam'd, whilst he too much stifles his matter? And to lament so much time lost by a man who had so many better things to say, in so many long and needless preliminary interlocutions? My ignorance will better excuse me in that I understand not Greek so well, as to discern the beauty of his language. I would generally chuse books that use sciences not such as only lead to them. The two first, and Pliny, and their like, have nothing of this *hoc age*; they will have to do with men already instructed; or if they have, 'tis a substantial *hoc age*, and that has a body by it self. I also delight in reading his Epistles, *ad Atticum;* not only because they contain a great deal of history, and the affairs of his time, but much more because I therein discover much of his own private humour; for I have a singular curiosity (as I have said elsewhere) to pry into the souls, and the natural and true judgments of the authors with whom I converse. A man may, indeed, judge of their parts, but not of their manners, nor of themselves, by the writings they expose upon the theatre of the world. I have a thousand times lamented the loss of the treatise Brutus writ upon Vertue; for it is best learning the theory of those who best know the practick. But seeing the thing

preached, and the preacher are different things, I would as willingly see Brutus in Plutarch as in a book of his own. I would rather choose to be certainly inform'd of the conference he had in his tent with some particular friend of his the night before a battle than of the harangue he made the next day to his army; and of what he did in his closet and his chamber than what he did in the publick place and in the senate. As to Cicero, I am of the common opinion that (learning excepted) he had no great natural parts. He was a good citizen, of an affable nature, as all fat, heavy men, such as he was, usually are; but given to ease, and had a mighty share of vanity and ambition. Neither do I know how to excuse him for thinking his poetry fit to be publish'd. 'Tis no great imperfection to make ill verses; but it is an imperfection not to be able to judge how unworthy his verses were of the glory of his name. For what concerns his eloquence, that is totally out of comparison, and I believe it will never be equall'd. The younger Cicero, who resembled his father in nothing but in name, whilst commanding in Asia, had several strangers one day at his table, and amongst the rest, Cæstius seated at the lower end, as men often intrude to the open tables of the great: Cicero ask'd one of the waiters who that man was, who presently told him his name; but he, as one that had his thoughts taken up with something else, and that had forgot the answer made him, asking three or four times, over, and over again, the same question, the fellow, to deliver himself from so many questions, and to make him know him by some particular circumstance: "'Tis that Cæstius," said he, "of whom it was told you that he makes no great account of your father's eloquence in comparison of his own." At which, Cicero being suddenly nettled, commanded poor Cæstius presently to be seiz'd, and caus'd him to be very well whipt in his own presence: a very discourteous entertainer! Yet even amongst those, who, all things considered, have reputed his eloquence incomparable, there have been some, however, who have not stuck to observe some faults in his writing: as that great Brutus, his friend for example, who said 'twas a broken and feeble eloquence, "*fractam et elumbem.*" The orators also nearest to the age wherein he liv'd, reprehended in him the care he had of a certain long cadence in his periods, and particularly took notice of these words, *esse videatur,* which he there so oft makes use of. For my part, I better approve of a shorter stile, and that comes more roundly

off. He does, though sometimes, shuffle his parts more briskly together, but 'tis very seldom. I have myself taken notice of this one passage, "*Ego vero me minus diu senem mallem, quam esse senem, antequam essem.*" The historians are my true province, for they are pleasant and easie; where immediately man in general, the knowledge of whom I hunt after, does there appear more lively and intire than any where besides: the variety and truth of his internal qualities, in gross and piecemeal, the diversity of means by which he is united and knit, and the accidents that threaten him. Now, those that write lives, by reason they insist more upon counsels than events, more upon what sallies from within than upon that which happens without, are the most proper for my reading; and therefore, above all others, Plutarch is the man for me. I am very sorry we have not a dozen Laertii, or that he was not further extended, and better understood; for I am equally curious to know the lives and fortunes of these great instructors of the world, as to know the diversities of their doctrines and opinions. In this kind of study (the reading of histories) a man must tumble over, without distinction, all sorts of authors, both antique and modern; as well barbarous and obsolete, as those of current language, there to know the things of which they variously treat: but Cæsar, in my opinion, particularly deserves to be studied, not for the knowledge of the history only, but for himself, so great an excellence and perfection he has above all the rest, though Sallust be one of the number. In earnest, I read this author with more reverence and respect than is usually allow'd to human writings; one while considering him in his person, by his actions and miraculous greatness, and another in the purity and inimitable neatness of his language and stile, wherein he not only excels all other historians, as Cicero confesses, but, peradventure, even Cicero himself; speaking of his enemies with so much sincerity in his judgment, that the false colors with which he strives to palliate his ill cause, and the ordure of his pestilent ambition excepted, I think there is no fault to be objected against him, saving this, that he speaks too sparingly of himself, seeing so many great things could not have been perform'd under his conduct, but that his own personal valor must necessarily have had a greater share in the execution than he attributes to himself. I love historians, who are either very sincere, or very excellent. The sincere who have nothing of their own to mix with it, and who only make it their business to make a faithful collection of all that comes to their knowledge, and faithfully to record all things without choice or prejudice, leaving to us the entire judgment of discerning the truth of things. Such, for example amongst others, as honest Froissart, who has proceeded in his undertaking with so frank a plainness, that having committed an error, he is not asham'd to confess, and correct it in the place where the finger has been laid, and who represents to us even the variety of rumors that were then spread abroad, and the different reports that were made to him; which is the naked and unaffected matter of history, and of which every one may make his profit, according to his proportion of understanding. The more excellent sort of historians have judgment to pick out what is most worthy to be known; and of two reports, to examine which is the most likely to be true: from the condition of princes, and their humors, they conclude the counsels, and attribute to them words proper for the occasion; and such have title to assume the authority of regulating our belief to what they themselves believe; but, certainly, this privilege belongs not to every one. For the middle sort of historians (of which the most part are) they spoil all; they will chew our meat for us, they take upon them to judge of, and, consequently, to incline the history to their own liking; for if the judgment partially lean to one side, a man cannot avoid wresting and writhing his narrative to that byass. They undertake to chuse things worthy to be known, and yet very oft conceal from us such a word, such a private action, as would much better instruct us; omit, as incredible, such things as they do not understand, and peradventure some, because they cannot express them well in good French or Latin. Let them, in God's name, display their eloquence, and judge according to their own fancy; but let them, withal, leave us something to judge of after them, and neither alter, nor disguise, by their abridgments, and at their own choice, any thing of the substance of the matter; but deliver it to us pure and entire in all its dimensions. For the most part, and especially in these latter ages, persons are cull'd out for this work, from amongst the common people, upon the sole consideration of well-speaking, as if we were to learn grammar from thence; and the men so chosen have also reason, being hired for no other end, and pretending to nothing but babble, not to be very solicitous of any part but that, and so, with a fine jingle of

words, prepare us a pretty contexture of reports, they pick up in the streets. The only good histories are those that have been writ by the persons themselves who commanded in the affairs whereof they write, or who have participated in the conduct of them, or, at least, who have had the conduct of others of the same nature. Such almost are all the Greek and Roman: for several eyewitnesses having writ of the same subject (in the time when grandeur and learning frequently met in the same person) if there happen to be an errour, it must of necessity be a very slight one, and upon a very doubtful accident. What can a man expect from a physician, who will undertake to write of war; or from a meer scholar, treating upon the designs of princes? If we could take notice how religious the Romans were in this, there would need but this example: Asinius Pollio found in the history of Cæsar himself, something misreported; a mistake occasioned, either by reason he could not have his eye in all parts of his army at once, and had given credit to some particular person, who had not delivered him a very true account; or else, for not having had too perfect notice given him by his lieutenants, of what they had done in his absence. By which we may see, whether the inquisition after truth be not very delicate, when a man cannot believe the report of a battle from the knowledge of him who there commanded, nor from the soldiers who were engaged in it, unless, after the method of a judicatory information, the witnesses be confronted, and the challenges received upon the proof of the punctilios of every accident. In good earnest, the knowledge we have of our own private affairs is much more obscure; but that has been sufficiently handled by Bodin, and according to my own sentiment. A little to relieve the weakness of my memory (so extream, that it has happen'd to me more than once, to take books again into my hand for new, and unseen, that I had carefully read over a few years before, and scribled with my notes) I have taken a custom of late, to fix at the end of every book (that is, of those I never intended to read again) the time when I made an end on't, and the judgment I had made of it, to the end that that might, at least, represent to me the air and general idea I had conceived of the author in reading it; and I will here transcribe some of those annotations. I writ this, some ten years agoe, in my Guicciardin (of what language soever my books speak to me in, I always speak to them in my own):

"He is a diligent historiographer, and from whom, in my opinion, a man may learn the truth of affairs of his time, as exactly as from any other; in the most of which he was himself also a personal actor, and in honorable command. 'Tis not to be imagined that he should have disguised any thing, either upon the account of hatred, favor, or vanity; of which, the liberal censures he passes upon the great ones; and particularly, those by whom he was advanced, and employed in commands of great trust and honor (as Pope Clement VII.), give ample testimony. As to that part, which he thinks himself the best at, namely, his digressions and discourses, he has, indeed, very good ones, and enriched with fine expressions; but he is too fond of them: for to leave nothing unsaid, having a subject so plain, ample, and almost infinite, he degenerates into pedantry, and relishes a little of the scholastick prattle. I have also observed this in him, that of so many souls, and so many effects; so many motives, and so many counsels as he judges of, he never attributes any one to virtue, religion, or conscience; as if all those were utterly extinct in the world: and of all the actions how brave in outward shew soever they appear in themselves, he always throws the cause and motive upon some vicious occasion, or some prospect of profit. It is impossible to imagine but that amongst such an infinite number of actions as he makes mention of, there must be some one produced by the way of reason. No corruption could so universally have infected men, that some one would not have escaped the contagion: which makes me suspect that his own taste was vicious; from whence it might happen that he judged other men by himself." In my "Philip de Comines," there is this written: "You will here find the language sweet and delightful, of a native simplicity, the narration pure, and wherein the veracity of the author does evidently shine; free from vanity, when speaking of himself; and from affection or envy, when speaking of others: his discourses and exhortations more accompanied with zeal and truth than with any exquisite sufficiency; and throughout, with authority and gravity, which speak him a man of extraction, and nourished up in great affairs." Upon the "Memoirs" of Monsieur du Bellay, I find this: "'Tis always pleasant to read things writ by those that have experimented how they ought to be carried on; but withal, it cannot be deny'd but there is a manifest decadence in these two lords from the freedom and liberty of writing, that shines in the

ancient historians: such as the Sire de Joinville, a domestick to St. Louis; Eginard, chancellor to Charlemain; and, of latter date, in "Philip de Comines." This here is rather an apology for King Francis against the Emperor Charles V. than a history. I will not believe that they have falsified any thing, as to matter of fact; but they make a common practice of wresting the judgment of events (very often contrary to reason) to our advantage, and of omitting whatsoever is nice to be handl'd in the life of their master; witness the relation of Messieurs de Montmorency and De Brion, which were here omitted: nay, so much as the very name of Madame d'Estampes is not here to be found. Secret actions an historian may conceal; but to pass over in silence what all the world knows, and things that have drawn after them publick consequences, is an inexcusable defect. In fine, whoever has a mind to have a perfect knowledge of King Francis, and the revolutions of his reign, let him seek it elsewhere, if my advice may prevail. The only profit a man can reap from hence is, from the particular narrative of battels, and other exploits of war, wherein these gentlemen were personally engaged; some words and private actions of the princes of their time, and the practices and negotiations carried on by the Seigneur de Lancay; where, indeed, there are, every where, things worthy to be known, and discourses above the vulgar strain."

Complete.

THAT MEN ARE NOT TO JUDGE OF OUR HAPPINESS TILL AFTER DEATH

—— scilicet ultima semper
Expectanda dies homini est, dicique beatus,
Ante obitum nemo supremaque funera debet.
— Ovid. Met., 1. 3.

EVERY one is acquainted with the story of King Crœsus to this purpose, who being taken prisoner by Cyrus, and by him condemn'd to die, as he was going to execution, cry'd out, O Solon, Solon! which being presently reported to Cyrus, and he sending to enquire what it meant, Crœsus gave him to understand that he now found the advertisement Solon had formerly given him true to his cost, which was, "That men, however fortune may smile upon them, could never be said to be happy, till they had been seen to pass over the last day of their lives, by reason of the uncertainty and mutability of human things, which upon very light and trivial occasions are subject to be totally chang'd into a quite contrary condition.» And therefore it was, that Agesilaus made answer to one that was saying, «What a happy young man the king of Persia was, to come so young to so mighty a kingdom»; «'Tis true [said he], but neither was Priam unhappy at his years.» In a short time, of kings of Macedon, successors to that mighty Alexander, were made joyners and scriveners at Rome; of a tyrant of Sicily, a pedant at Corinth; of a conqueror of one-half of the world, and general of so many armies, a miserable suppliant to the rascally officers of a king of Ægypt. So much the prolongation of five or six months of life cost the great and noble Pompey, and no longer since than our fathers' days, Ludovico Forza, the tenth duke of Milan, whom all Italy had so long truckled under, was seen to die a wretched prisoner at Loches, but not till he had lived ten years in captivity, which was the worst part of his fortune. The fairest of all queens, (Mary, Queen of Scots) widow to the greatest king in Europe, did she not come to die by the hand of an executioner? Unworthy and barbarous cruelty! and a thousand more examples there are of the same kind; for it seems that as storms and tempests have a malice to the proud, and overtow'ring heights of our lofty buildings, there are also spirits above that are envious of the grandeurs here below.

Usque adeo res humanas vis abdita quædam
Obterit, et pulchros fasces, sævasque secures
Proculcare, ac ludibrio sibi habere videtur.
—Lucret., l. 5.

And it should seem also that Fortune sometimes lies in wait to surprise the last hour of our lives, to shew the power she has in a moment to overthrow what she was so many years in building, making us cry out with Laborius, «*Nimirum hac die una plus vixi mihi quam vivendum fuit.*» —Macrob., l. 2., c. 2. «I have liv'd longer by this one day than I ought to have done.» And in this sense, this good advice of Solon may reasonably be taken; but he being a philosopher, with which sort of men the favors and disgraces of fortune stand for nothing, either to the making a man happy or unhappy, and with whom grandeurs and powers, accidents of quality, are upon the matter indifferent: I am apt

ous designs had nothing in them so high and great as their interruption; and he arrived without compleating his course, at the place to which his ambition pretended with greater glory than he could himself either hope or desire, and anticipated by his fall the name and power to which he aspir'd, by perfecting his career. In the judgment I make of another man's life, I always observe how he carried himself at his death; and the principal concern I have for my own is that I may die handsomely, that is patiently and without noise.

Complete.

OF LIBERTY OF CONSCIENCE

'TIS usual to see good intentions, if carried on without moderation, push men on to very vicious effects. In this dispute, which has at this time engag'd France in a civil war, the better and the soundest cause, no doubt, is that which maintains the ancient religion and government of the kingdom. Nevertheless, amongst the good men of that party (for I do not speak of those that only make a pretence, either to execute their own particular revenges, or to gratifie their avarice, or to pursue the favor of princes; but of those who engage in the quarrel out of true zeal to religion, and a vertuous affection to maintain the peace and government of their country) of these, I say, we see many whom passion transports beyond the bounds of reason, and sometimes inspires them with counsels that are unjust and violent, and moreover inconsiderate and rash. It is true, that in those first times when our religion began to gain authority with the laws, zeal arm'd many against all sorts of Pagan books, by which the learned suffer'd an exceeding great loss. A disorder that I conceive did more prejudice to letters than all the flames of the barbarians. Of this Cornelius Tacitus is a very good testimony; for though the Emperour Tacitus, his kinsman, had by express order furnish'd all the libraries in the world with it, nevertheless one entire copy could not escape the curious examination of those who desir'd to abolish it, for only five or six idle clauses that were contrary to our belief. They had also the trick easily to lend undue praises to all the emperours who did any thing for us, and universally to condemn all the actions of those who were our adversaries, as is evidently manifest in the Emperour Julian, surnamed the Apostate; who was in truth a very great

to think that he had some further aim, and that his meaning was that the very felicity of life it self, which depends upon the tranquillity and contentment of a well-descended spirit, and the resolution and assurance of a well-order'd soul, ought never to be attributed to any man, till he has first been seen to play the last, and doubtless the hardest act of his part, because there may be disguise and dissimulation in all the rest, where these fine philosophical discourses are only put on; and where accidents do not touch us to the quick, they give us leisure to maintain the same sober gravity; but in this last scene of death, there is no more counterfeiting, we must speak plain, and must discover what there is of pure and clean in the bottom.

Nam veræ voces tum demum pectore ab imo
Ejiciuntur, et eripitur persona, manet res.
—Lucret., l. 3.

«Then that at last truth issues from the heart,
The vizor's gone, we act our own true part.»

Wherefore at this last all the other actions of our life ought to be try'd and sifted. 'Tis the master-day, 'tis the day that is judge of all the rest, 'tis the day (says one of the Ancients) that ought to judge of all my foregoing years. To death do I refer the essay of the fruit of all my studies. We shall then see whether my discourses came only from my mouth or from my heart. I have seen many by their death give a good or an ill repute to their whole life. Scipio, the father-in-law of Pompey the Great, in dying well, wip'd away the ill opinion that till then every one had conceiv'd of him. Epaminondas being ask'd which of the three he had in the greatest esteem, Chabrias, Iphicrates, or himself; «You must first see us die (said he) before that question can be resolv'd»: and, in truth, he would infinitely wrong that great man, who would weigh him without the honor and grandeur of his end. God Almighty has order'd all things as it has best pleased him; but I have in my time seen three of the most execrable persons that ever I knew in all manners of abominable living, and the most infamous to boot, who all dy'd a very regular death, and in all circumstances compos'd even to perfection. There are brave, and fortunate deaths. I have seen death cut the thread of the progress of a prodigious advancement, and in the height and flower of its encrease of a certain person, with so glorious an end, that in my opinion his ambitious and gener-

and rare man, a man in whose soul philosophy was imprinted in the best characters, by which he profess'd to govern all his actions; and in truth there is no sort of vertue of which he has not left behind him very notable examples. In chastity (of which the whole course of his life has given manifest proof) we read the same of him, that was said of Alexander and Scipio, that being in the flower of his age, for he was slain by the Parthians at one and thirty, of a great many very beautiful captives, he would not so much as look upon one. As to his justice, he took himself the pains to hear the parties, and although he would out of curiosity enquire what religion they were of, nevertheless the hatred he had to ours never gave any counterpoise to the balance. He made himself several good laws, and cut off a great part of the subsidies and taxes impos'd and levied by his predecessors. We have two good historians who were eyewitnesses of his actions; one of which, Marcellinus, in several places of his "History," sharply reproves an edict of his whereby he interdicted all Christian rhetoricians and grammarians to keep school, or to teach, and says he could wish that act of his had been buried in silence. It is very likely that had he done any more severe things against us, he, so affectionate as he was to our party, would not have pass'd it over in silence. He was, indeed, sharp against us, but yet no cruel enemy: for our own people tell this story of him, that one day, walking about the city of Chalcedon, Maris, bishop of the place, was so bold as to tell him that he was impious, and an enemy to Christ, at which, say they, therein affecting a philosophical patience, he was no further mov'd, than to reply, «Go wretch, and lament the loss of thy eyes,» to which the bishop reply'd again, «I thank Jesus Christ for taking away my sight, that I may not see thy impudent face.» So it is that this action of his savours nothing of the cruelty that he is said to have exercis'd towards us. «He was» (says Eutropius, my other witness) «an enemy to Christianity, but without putting his hand to blood.» And to return to his justice, there is nothing in that whereof he can be accus'd, the severity excepted he practis'd in the beginning of his reign against those who had follow'd the party of Constantius, his predecessor. As to his sobriety, he liv'd always a souldier's kind of life; and kept a table in the most profound peace, like one that prepar'd and inur'd himself to the austerities of war. His vigilancy was such, that he divided the night into three or four parts, of which, always the least was dedicated to sleep, the rest was spent either in visiting the estate of his army and guards, in person, or in study, for, amongst other rare qualities, he was very excellent in all sorts of learning. 'Tis said of Alexander the Great, that being in bed, for fear lest sleep should divert him from his thoughts and studies, he had always a basin set by his bedside, and held one of his hands out with a ball of copper in it, to the end, that beginning to fall asleep, and his fingers leaving their hold, the ball by falling into the basin might awake him. But the other had his mind so bent upon what he had a mind to do, and so little disturb'd with fumes, by reason of his singular abstinence, that he had no need of any such invention. As to his military experience, he was excellent in all the qualities of a great captain, as it was likely he should, being almost all his life in a continual exercise of war, and most of that time with us in France, against the Germans and Francks: we hardly read of any man that ever saw more dangers, or that made more frequent proofs of his personal valour. His death has something in it parallel with that of Epaminondas, for he was wounded with an arrow, and try'd to pull it out, and had done it, but that being edg'd, it cut and disabl'd his hand. He incessantly call'd out, that they would carry him again in this condition into the heat of the battel to encourage his souldiers, who very bravely disputed the battel without him, till night parted the armies. We stood oblig'd to his philosophy for the singular contempt he had for his life, and all human things. He had a firm belief of the immortality of the soul. In matter of religion, he was vicious throughout, and was surnam'd the Apostate, for having relinquish'd ours; though, methinks, 'tis more likely that he had never thoroughly embrac'd it, but had dissembled out of obedience to the laws, till he came to the empire. He was in his own so superstitious, that he was laugh'd at for it by those of the same opinion of his own time, who jeeringly said that had he got the victory over the Parthians, he had destroy'd the breed of oxen in the world to supply his sacrifices: he was more over besotted with the art of divination, and gave authority to all sorts of predictions. He said, amongst other things, at his death, that he was oblig'd to the gods, and thank'd them, in that they would not cut him off by surprise, having long before advertis'd him of the place and hour of his death, nor by a mean and unmanly death, more becoming lazy and delicate people, nor by a death that was languishing, long, and painful; and that they had thought him worthy to die after that noble manner, in the progress of his

victories, in the flower of his age, and in the height of his glory. He had a vision like that of Marcus Brutus, that first threatened him in Gaul, and afterward appear'd to him in Persia just before his death. These words, that some make him say when he felt himself wounded, "Thou hast overcome, Nazarene," or as others, "Content thyself, Nazarene," would hardly have been omitted, had they been believ'd by my witnesses, who, being present in the army, have set down to the least motions and words of his end, no more than certain other miracles that are recorded of him. And to return to my subject, he long nourish'd, says Marcellinus, paganism in his heart; but all his army being Christians, he durst not own it. But in the end, seeing himself strong enough to dare to discover himself, he caus'd the temples of the gods to be thrown open, and did his utmost to set on foot and to encourage idolatry: which the better to effect, having at Constantinople found the people disunited, and also the prelates of the Church divided amongst themselves, having conven'd them all before him, he gravely and earnestly admonish'd them to calm those civil dissensions, and that every one might freely and without fear follow his own religion. Which he did the more sedulously solicit, in hope that this license would augment the schisms and faction of their division, and hinder the people from reuniting, and consequently fortifying themselves against him by their unanimous intelligence and concord; having experimented by the cruelty of some Christians, that there is no beast in the world so much to be fear'd by man, as man. These are very near his words, wherein this is very worthy of consideration, that the Emperour Julian made use of the same receipt of liberty of conscience to inflame the civil dissensions, that our kings do to extinguish them. So that a man may say on one side, that to give the people the reins to entertain every man his own opinion is to scatter and sow division, and, as it were, to lend a hand to augment it, there being no sence nor correction of law to stop and hinder their career; but, on the other side, a man may also say that to give the people the reins to entertain every man his own opinion is to mollifie and appease them by facility and toleration, and dull the point which is whetted and made sharper by variety, novelty, and difficulty. And I think it is better for the honour of the devotion of our kings, that not having been able to do what they would, they have made a shew of being willing to do what they could.

Complete.

THAT WE TASTE NOTHING PURE

THE imbecility of our condition is such, that things cannot in their natural simplicity and purity fall into our use; the elements that we enjoy are chang'd, even metals themselves, and gold must in some sort be debas'd to fit it for our service. Neither has vertue, so simple as that which Aristo, Pyrrho, and also the Stoicks have made the principal end of life; nor the Cerenaick and Aristippick pleasure been without mixture useful to it. Of the pleasure and goods that we enjoy, there is not one exempt from some mixture of ill and inconvenience. Our extreamest pleasure has some air of groaning and complaining in't. Would you not say that it is dying of pain? Nay, when we forge the image of it, we stuff it with sickly and painful epithets, languor, softness, feebleness, faintness, morbidezza, a great testimony of their consanguinity and consubstantiality. The most profound joy has more of severity than gayety in it. The most extream and most full contentment more of the grave and temperate than of the wanton. "*Ipsa felicitas, se nisi temperat premit.*" — *Sen.* Ep. 74. "Even felicity, unless it moderate it self, oppresseth." Delight chews and grinds us; according to the old Greek verse, which says that "the gods sell us all the goods they give us," that is to say, that they give us nothing pure and perfect, and that we do not purchase them but at the price of some evil. Labour and pleasure, very unlike in nature, associate, nevertheless, by I know not what natural conjunction. Socrates says that "some god try'd to mix in one mass, and confound pain and pleasure, but not being able to do it, he unbethought him, at least to couple them by the tail." Metrodorus said that: "In sorrow there is some mixture of pleasure." I know not whether or no he intended any thing else by that saying; but for my part, I am of opinion that there is design, consent, and complacency in giving a man's self up to melancholy. I say, that besides ambition, which may also have a stroke in the business, there is some shadow of delight and delicacy which smiles upon and flatters us even in the very lap of melancholy. Are there not some complexions that feed upon it?

We find apples that have a sweet tartness. Nature discovers this confusion to us. Painters hold that the same motions and screwings of the face that serve for weeping serve for laughter

too; and, indeed, before the one or the other be finish'd, do but observe the painter's manner of handling, as you will be in doubt to which of the two the design does tend. And the extremity of laughter does at last bring tears. "*Nullum sine auctore mente malum est.*" — *Sen.* Ep. 70. "No evil is without its compensation." When I the most strictly and religiously confess my self, I find that the best vertue I have has in it some tincture of vice; and am afraid that Plato, in his purest vertue (I who am as sincere and perfect a lover of vertue of that stamp as any other whatever), if he had listen'd, and laid his ear close to himself (as he did so), he would have heard some jarring sound of human mixture; but faint and remote, and only to be perceiv'd by himself. Man is wholly and throughout but patcht and motly. Even the laws of justice themselves cannot subsist without mixture of injustice; insomuch that Plato says, "They undertake to cut off the Hydra's head, who pretend to clear the law of all inconvenience." "*Omne magnum exemplum habet aliquid ex iniquo, quod contra singulos utilitate publica rependitur.*" — *Tac.* Annal., Lib. XIV. "Every great example has in it some mixture of injustice, which recompenses the wrong done to particular men by the publick utility." It is likewise true, that for the usage of life, and the service of publick commerce, there may be some excesses in the purity and perspicacity of our minds; that penetrating light has in it too much of subtlety and curiosity; we must a little stupefy and blunt and abate them, to render them more obedient to example and practice; and a little veil and obscure them, the better to proportion them to this dark and earthy life. And yet common and less speculative souls are found to be more proper and more successful in the management of affairs; and the elevated and exquisite opinions of philosophy more unfit for business. This sharp vivacity of soul, and the supple and restless volubility attending it, disturb our negotiations. We are to manage human enterprises more superficially and rudely, and leave a great part to fortune. It is not necessary to examine affairs with so much subtlety, and so deep; a man loses himself in the consideration of so many contrary lustres, and so many various forms. "*Voluntatibus res inter se pugnantes, obturbaverant animi.*" — *Livy.* "Whilst they consider'd of things so indifferent in themselves, they were astonish'd and knew not what to do." 'Tis what the Ancients say of Simonides, that by reason his imagination suggested to him, upon the question King Hiero had put to him (to answer which he had had many days to meditate in), several witty and subtle considerations, whilst he doubted which was the most likely, he totally despair'd of the truth. Who dives into, and in his inquisition comprehends all circumstances and consequences, hinders his election; a little engine well handled is sufficient for executions of less or greater weight and moment. The best husbands are those who can worst give account how they are so; and the greatest talkers for the most part do nothing to purpose. I know one of this sort of men, and the most excellent director in all sorts of good husbandry, who has miserably let an hundred thousand livres yearly revenue slip through his hands. I know another, who says that he is able to give better advice than any of his counsel; and there is not in the world a fairer show of a soul, and of greater understanding, than he has; nevertheless, when he comes to the test, his servants find him quite another thing.

Complete.

OF THUMBS AND POLTROONS

TACITUS reports that amongst certain barbarian kings, their manner was, when they would make a firm obligation, to joyn their hands close to one another, and twist their thumbs, and when by force of straining the blood it appear'd in the ends, they lightly pricked them with some sharp instrument, and mutually suck'd them. Physicians say that the thumbs are the master fingers of the hand, and that their Latin etymology is derived from *pollere*. The Greeks call'd them ἀντιχεῖρ, as who should say, another hand. And it seems that the Latins also sometimes take it in this sense for the whole hand. It was at Rome a signification of favor to depress and clap in the thumbs, and of disfavor to elevate and thrust them outward.

The Romans exempted from war all such as were maim'd in the thumbs, as having no more sufficient strength to hold their arms. Augustus confiscated the estate of a Roman knight, who had maliciously cut off the thumbs of two young children he had, to excuse them from going into the armies: and before him, the Senate, in the time of the Italick war, had condemn'd Cajus Valienus to perpetual imprisonment, and confiscated all his goods, for having purposely cut off the thumb of his left hand, to exempt himself from that expedition. Some one, I have forgot who, having won a naval battel, cut off the thumbs of all his

vanquish'd enemies, to render them incapable of fighting, and of handling the oar. And in Lacedæmonia, pedagogues chastis'd their scholars by biting their thumbs.

Complete.

OF THE VANITY OF WORDS

A RHETORICIAN of times past said that to make little things appear great was his profession. This is a shooe-maker, who can make a great shooe for a little foot. They would in Sparta have sent such a fellow to be whipp'd, for making profession of a lying and deceitful art: and I fancie that Archidamus, who was king of that country, was a little surpris'd at the answer of Thucydides, when enquiring of him, which was the better wrestler, Pericles, or he, he reply'd that it was hard to affirm; "for when I have thrown him," said he, "he always perswades the spectators that he had no fall, and carries away the prize." They who paint, pounce, and plaister up the ruins of women, filling up their wrinckles and deformities, are less to blame; because it is no great matter, whether we see them in their natural complexions, or no. Whereas these make it their business to deceive not our sight only, but our judgments, and to adulterate and corrupt the very essence of things. The republicks that have maintain'd themselves in a regular and well modell'd government, such as those of Lacedæmon and Crete, had orators in no very great esteem. Aristo did wisely define Rhetorick to be a science to perswade the people; Socrates and Plato, an art to flatter and deceive. And those who deny it in the general description, verifie it throughout in their precepts. The Mahometans will not suffer their children to be instructed in it, as being useless, and the Athenians perceiving of how pernicious consequence the practice of it was, it being in their city of universal esteem, order'd the principal part, which is to move affections, with their exordiums and perorations, to be taken away. 'Tis an engine invented, to manage and govern a disorderly and tumultuous rabble, and that never is made use of, but like physick to the sick, in the paroxysms of a discompos'd estate. In those, where the vulgar, or the ignorant, or both together, have been all-powerful, and able to give the law, as in those of Athens, Rhodes, and Rome, and where the publick affairs have been in a continual tempest of commotion, to such places

have the orators always repair'd. And in truth, we shall find few persons in those republicks, who have push'd their fortunes to any great degree of eminence, without the assistance of elocution: Pompey, Cæsar, Crassus, Lucullus, Lentulus, and Metellus, have thence taken their chiefest spring to mount to that degree of authority to which they did at last arrive: making it of greater use to them, than arms, contrary to the opinion of better times. For L. Volumnius speaking publickly in favour of the election of Q. Fabius, and Pub. Decius, to the consular dignity: "These are men," said he, "born for war, and great in execution, in the combat of the tongue altogether to seek; spirits truly consular. The subtle, eloquent, and learned are only good for the city, to make pretors of, to administer justice." Eloquence flourished most at Rome, when the publick affairs were in the worst condition, and the republick most disquieted with intestine commotions, as a rank and untill'd soil bears the worst weeds. By which it should seem that a monarchical government has less need of it than any other; for the brutality, and facility, natural to the common people, and that render them subject to be turn'd and twin'd, and led by the ears, by this charming harmony of words, without weighing or considering the truth and reality of things by the force of reason: this facility, I say, is not easily found in a single person, and it is also more easie by good education and advice, to secure him from the impression of this poison. There was never any famous orator known to come out of Persia or Macedon.

I have enter'd into this discourse upon the occasion of an Italian I lately receiv'd into my service and who was clerk of the kitchen to the late Cardinal Caraffa till his death. I put this fellow upon an account of his office: where he fell to discourse of this palate science, with such a settled countenance, and magisterial gravity, as if he had been handling some profound point of divinity. He made a learned distinction of the several sorts of appetites, of that a man has before he begins to eat, and of those after the second and third service: the means simply to satisfie the first, and then to raise and actuate the other two: the ordering of the sauces, first in general, and then proceeded to the qualities of the ingredients, and their effects: the differences of sallets according to their seasons, which aught to be serv'd up hot, and which cold: the manner of their garnishment and decoration, to render them yet more acceptable to the eye.

After which he enter'd upon the order of the whole service, full of weighty and important considerations.

And all this set out with lofty and magnifick words; the very same we make use of, when we discourse of the regiment of an empire.

And yet even the Greeks themselves did very much admire, and highly applaud the order and disposition that Paulus Æmilius observ'd in the feast he made them at his return from Macedon; but I do not here speak of effects, I speak of words only. I do not know whether it may have the same operation upon other men that it has upon me; but when I hear our architects thunder out their bombast words of pilasters, architraves, and cornices, of the Corinthian and Dorick orders, and such like stuff, my imagination is presently possess'd with the palace of Apollidonius in "Amadis de Gaul"; when after all, I find them but the paltry pieces of my own kitchen door. And to hear men talk of metonymies, metaphors, and allegories, and other grammar words, would not a man think they signified some rare and exotick form of speaking? And this other is a gullery of the same stamp, to call the offices of our kingdom by the lofty titles of the Romans, though they have no similitude of function, and yet less authority and power. And this also, which I doubt will one day turn to the reproach of this age of ours, unworthily and indifferently to confer upon any we think fit the most glorious sirnames with which antiquity honor'd but one or two persons in several ages. Plato carried away the sirname of Divine, by so universal a consent, that never any one repin'd at it, or attempted to take it from him; and yet the Italians, who pretend, and with good reason, to more sprightly wits, and sounder discourses, than the other nations of their times, have lately honour'd Aretine with the same title; in whose writings, save a tumid phrase, set out with smart periods,—ingenious indeed, but far fetch'd and fantastick,—and eloquence (be it what it will) I see nothing above the ordinary writers of his time,—so far is he from approaching the ancient divinity. And we make nothing of giving the sirname of Great to princes, that have nothing in them above a popular grandeur.

Complete.

THAT THE INTENTION IS JUDGE OF OUR ACTIONS

'T is a saying, " that death discharges us of all our obligations." However, I know some who have taken it in another sense. Henry VII., king of England, articled with Don Philip, son to Maximilian the Emperour, and father to the Emperour Charles V., when he had him upon English ground, that the said Philip should deliver up the Duke of Suffolk of the White Rose, his mortal enemy, who was fled into the Low Countries, into his hands; which Philip (not knowing how to evade it) accordingly promis'd to do, but upon condition, nevertheless, that Henry should attempt nothing against the life of the said duke, which during his own life he perform'd; but coming to die, in his last will, commanded his son to put him to death immediately after his decease. And lately, in the tragedy, that the Duke of Alva presented to us in the persons of the two counts, Egmont and Horne, at Brussels, there were very remarkable passages, and one amongst the rest, that the said Count Egmont (upon the security of whose word and faith Count Horne had come and surrendered himself to the Duke of Alva) earnestly entreated that he might first mount the scaffold, to the end that death might disengage him from the obligation he had pass'd to the other. In which case, methinks death did not acquit the former of his promise, and the second was satisfied in the good intention of the other, even though he had not died with him; for we cannot be oblig'd beyond what we are able to perform, by reason that the effects and intentions of what we promise are not at all in our power, and that, indeed, we are masters of nothing but the will, in which, by necessity, all the rules and whole duty of mankind is founded and establish'd. And therefore Count Egmont, conceiving his soul and will bound and indebted to the promise, although he had not the power to make it good, had doubtless been absolv'd of his duty, even though he had outliv'd the other; but the king of England willfully and premeditately breaking his faith was no more to be excused for deferring the execution of his infidelity till after his death, than Herodotus his mason, who having inviolably, during the time of his life, kept the secret of the treasure of the king of Ægypt his master, at his death discover'd it to his children. I have taken notice of several in my time, who, convinc'd by their consciences of unjustly detaining the goods of another, have endeavour'd to make amends by their will, and after their decease; but they had as good do nothing as delude themselves both in taking so much time in so pressing an affair, and also in going about to repair an injury with so little demonstration of resentment and concern. They owe over and above something of their own, and by how much their payment is more strict and incommodious to themselves, by so much is their restitution more perfect, just, and meritorious; for penitency requires penance: but they yet do worse than these, who reserve the declaration of a mortal animosity against their neighbour to the last gasp, having conceal'd it all the time of their lives before, wherein they declare to have little regard of their own honour whilst they irritate the party offended against their memory; and less to their conscience, not having the power, even out of respect to death it self, to make their malice die with them; but extending the life of their hatred even beyond their own. Unjust judges, who defer judgment to a time wherein they can have no knowledge of the cause! For my part, I shall take care, if I can, that my death discover nothing that my life has not first openly manifested and publickly declar'd.

Complete.

OF IDLENESS

A s we see some grounds that have long lain idle, and untill'd, when grown rank and fertile by rest, to abound with, and spend their vertue in the product of innumerable sorts of weeds, and wild herbs, that are unprofitable, and of no wholesome use, and that to make them perform their true office we are to cultivate and prepare them for such seeds as are proper for our service. And as we see women that without the knowledge of men do sometimes of themselves bring forth inanimate and formless lumps of flesh, but that to cause a natural and perfect generation they are to be husbanded with another kind of seed; even so it is with wits, which if not apply'd to some certain study that may fix and restrain them, run into a thousand extravagancies, and are eternally roving here and there in the inextricable labyrinth of restless imagination.

> Like as the quivering reflection
> Of fountain waters, when the morning sun

> Darts on the bason, or the moon's pale beam
> Gives light and colour to the captive stream,
> Whips with fantastick motion round the place,
> And walls and roof strikes with its trembling rays.
> —*Æn.*, l. 8.

In which wild and irregular agitation, there is no folly nor idle fancy they do not light upon:—

> "Like sick men's dreams, that from a troubled brain
> Phantasms create, ridiculous and vain.
> —*Hor.* Arts Poet.

The soul that has no establish'd limit to circumscribe it loses it self, as the epigrammatist says:—

> "He that lives every where does no where live."

When I lately retir'd my self to my own house, with a resolution, as much as possibly I could, to avoid all manner of concern in affairs, and to spend in privacy and repose the little remainder of time I have to live, I fancy'd I could not more oblige my mind than to suffer it at full leisure to entertain and divert itself, which I also now hop'd it might the better be entrusted to do, as being by time and observation become more settled and mature; but I find,

> "———— Even in the most retir'd estate
> Leisure it self does various thoughts create.
> —*Lucan.*, l. 4.

that, quite contrary, it is like a horse that has broke from his rider, who voluntarily runs into a much more violent career than any horseman would put him to, and creates me so many chimæra's and fantastick monsters one upon another, without order or design, that, the better at leisure to contemplate their strangeness and absurdity, I have begun to commit them to writing, hoping in time to make them asham'd of themselves.

Complete.

OF "LYARS"

T here is not a man living, whom it would so little become to speak of memory as my self, for I have none at all; and do not think that the world has again another so treacherous as mine. My other faculties are all very ordinary and mean; but in this I think my self very singular, and to such a degree of excellence, that (besides the inconvenience I suffer by it, which merits something) I deserve methinks, to be famous for it, and to have more than a common reputation: though, in truth, the necessary use of memory consider'd, Plato had reason when he call'd it a great and powerful goddess. In my country, when they would decypher a man that has no sense, they say, such a one has no memory; and when I complain of mine, they seem not to believe I am in earnest, and presently reprove me, as tho I accus'd myself for a fool, not discerning the difference betwixt memory and understanding; wherein they are very wide of my intention, and do me wrong: experience rather daily shewing us, on the contrary, that a strong memory is commonly coupled with infirm judgment; and they do me, moreover (who am so perfect in nothing as the good friend), at the same time a greater wrong in this, that they make the same words which accuse my infirmity represent me for an ingrateful person; wherein they bring my integrity and good-nature into question upon the account of my memory, and from a natural imperfection unjustly derive a defect of conscience. He has forgot, says one, this request, or that promise; he no more remembers his friends, he has forgot, to say or do, or to conceal such and such a thing for my sake. And truly, I am apt enough to forget many things, but to neglect any thing my friend has given me in charge I never do it. And it should be enough, methinks, that I feel the misery and inconvenience of it, without branding me with malice, a vice so much a stranger, and so contrary to my nature. However, I derive these comforts from my infirmity; first, that it is an evil from which principally I have found reason to correct a worse, that would easily enough have grown upon me,—namely, ambition; this defect being intolerable in those who take upon them the negotiations of the world, an employment of the greatest honor and trust among men. Secondly, that (as several like examples in the progress of nature demonstrate to us) she has fortify'd me in my other faculties, proportionally as she has unfurnish'd me in this: I should otherwise have been apt implicitly to have repos'd my wit and judgment upon the bare report of other men, without ever setting them to work upon any inquisition whatever, had the strange inventions and opinions of the authors I have read been ever present with me by the benefit of memory; thirdly, that by this means I am not so talkative, for the magazine of the memory is ever better furnish'd with matter than that of the invention; and had mine been faithful to me, I had ere this, deaf'd all my friends with my eternal babble, the subjects themselves rousing and stirring up the little faculty I have of handling, and applying them, heating and extending my discourse. 'Tis a great imperfection, and what I have observ'd in several of my intimate friends, who, as their memories supply them with a present and entire review of things, derive their narratives from so remote a fountain, and crowd them with so many impertinent circumstances, that though the story be good in itself, they make a shift to spoil it; and if otherwise, you are either to curse the strength of their memory, or the weakness of their judgment: And it is a hard thing to close up a discourse, and to cut it short, when you are once in, and have a great deal more to say. Neither is there anything wherein the force and readiness of a horse is so much seen, as in a round, graceful, and sudden stop; and I see even those who are pertinent enough, who would, but cannot stop short in their career; for whilst they are seeking out a handsome period to conclude the sense, they talk at random, and are so perplex'd, and entangl'd in their own eloquence, that they know not what they say. But above all, old men, who yet retain the memory of things past, and forget how often they have told them, are the most dangerous company for this fault; and I have known stories from the mouth of a man of very great quality, otherwise very pleasant in themselves, becoming very troublesome, by being a hundred times repeated over and over again. The fourth obligation I have to this infirm memory of mine is, that by this means I less remember the injuries I have receiv'd; insomuch, that (as the Ancient said) I should have a protocol, a register of injuries, or a prompter, like Darius, who, that he might not forget the offence he had receiv'd from those of Athens, so oft as he sat down to dinner, order'd one of his pages three times to whoop in his ear, "Sir, remember the Athenians": and also, the places which I revisit, and the books I read over again, still smile upon me with a fresh novelty. It is not without good reason said that he who has not a good memory should never take upon him the trade of lying. I know very well that the grammarians distinguish betwixt an untruth and a lye, and say that to tell an untruth is to tell a thing that is false, but that we our selves believe to be true; and that to lye is to tell a thing that we know in our conscience to be utterly false and untrue; and it is of this

last sort of lyars only that I now speak. Now these do either wholly contrive and invent the untruths they utter, or so alter and disguise a true story, that it always ends in a lye; and when they disguise and often alter the same story according to their own fancy, 'tis very hard for them at one time or another to escape being trapp'd by reason that the real truth of the thing having first taken possession of the memory, and being there lodg'd, and imprinted by the way of knowledge and science, it will be ever ready to present it self to the imagination, and to shoulder out any falsehood of their own contriving, which cannot there have so sure and settled a footing as the other; and the circumstances of the first true knowledge evermore running in their minds will be apt to make them forget those that are illegitimate, and only forg'd by their own fancy. In what they wholly invent, forasmuch as there is no contrary impression to justle their invention, there seems to be less danger of tripping; and yet even this also, by reason it is a vain body, and without any other foundation than fancy only, is very apt to escape the memory, if they be not careful to make themselves very perfect in their tale. Of which I have had very pleasant experience, at the expense of such as profess only to form, and accommodate their speech to the affair they have in hand, or to the humour of the person with whom they have to do; for the circumstances to which these men stick not to enslave their consciences, and their faith being subject to several changes, their language must accordingly vary; from whence it happens that of the same thing they tell one man, that it is this, and another that it is that, giving it several forms, and colours; which men, if they once come to confer notes, and find out the cheat, what becomes of this fine art? To which may be added, that they must of necessity very often ridiculously trap themselves; for what memory can be sufficient to retain so many different shapes as they have forg'd upon one and the same subject? I have known many in my time, very ambitious of the repute of this fine piece of discretion; but they do not see that if there be a reputation of being wise, there is really no prudence in it. In plain truth, lying is a hateful and an accursed vice. We are not men, nor have other tye upon one another, but our word. If we did but discover the horror and ill consequences of it, we should pursue it with fire and sword, and more justly than other crimes. I see that parents commonly, and with indiscretion enough, correct their children

for little innocent faults, and torment them for wanton childish tricks, that have neither impression, nor tend to any consequence; whereas, in my opinion, lying only, and (what is of something a lower form) stomach, are the faults which are to be severely whipp'd out of them, both in the infancy and progress of the vices, which will otherwise grow up and increase with them; and after a tongue has once got the knack of lying, 'tis not to be imagin'd how impossible almost it is to reclaim it. Whence it comes to pass, that we see some, who are otherwise very honest men, so subject to this vice. I have an honest lad to my taylor, whom I never knew guilty of one truth, no not when it had been to his advantage. If falsehood had, like truth, but one face only, we should be upon better terms; for we should then take the contrary to what the lyar says for certain truth; but the reverse of truth has an hundred thousand figures, and a field indefinite without bound or limit. The Pythagoreans make good to be certain and finite, and evil infinite and uncertain; there are a thousand ways to miss the white, there is only one to hit it. For my own part, I have this vice in so great horror, that I am not sure I could prevail with my conscience to secure myself from the most manifest and extream danger, by an impudent and solemn lye. An ancient father says, "that a dog we know is better company than a man whose language we do not understand."—*Plin. Nat. Hist., Lib. VII., Cap. i. Ut externus non alieno sit hominis vice.* As a foreigner, to one that understands not what he says, cannot be said to supply the place of a man, because he can be no company. And how much less sociable is false speaking than silence. King Francis I. bragg'd that he had, by this means, nonpluss'd Francisco Taverna, the embassadour of Francisco Sforza, Duke of Milan, a man very famous for his eloquence in those days. This gentleman had been sent to excuse his master to his Majesty about a thing of very great consequence; which was this: King Francis, to maintain ever more some intelligence in Italy, out of which he had lately been driven, and particularly in the dutchy of Milan, had thought it (to that end) convenient to have evermore a gentleman on his behalf to lie leiger in the court of that duke: an embassadour in effect, but in outward appearance no other than a private person who pretended to reside there upon the single account of his own particular affairs; which was so carried, by reason that the duke, much more depending upon the emperour, especially at a time when he was in a treaty of a mar-

riage with his neece, daughter to the king of Denmark, and since dowager of Lorrain, could not own any friendship or intelligence with us, but very much to his own prejudice. For this commission then one Merveille, a Milanois gentleman, and equerry to the king, being thought very fit, he was accordingly dispatch'd thither with private letters of credence, his instructions of embassadour, and other letters of recommendation to the duke about his own private concerns, the better to colour the business; and so long continued in that court, that the emperour at last had some inkling of his real employment there, and complain'd of it to the duke, which was the occasion of what follow'd after, as we suppose; which was, that under pretence of a murther by him committed, his tryal was in two days dispatch'd, and his head in the night struck off in prison. Signior Francisco then being upon this account come to the court of France, and prepared with a long counterfeit story to excuse a thing of so dangerous example, (for the king had apply'd himself to all the princes of Christendom, as well as to the duke himself, to demand satisfaction for this outrage upon the person of his minister) had his audience at the morning council; where, after he had for the support of his cause, in a long-premeditated oration, laid open several plausible justifications of the fact, he concluded that the duke his master had never look'd upon this Merveille for other than a private gentleman, and his own subject, who was there only in order to his own business, neither had he ever liv'd after any other manner; absolutely disowning that he had ever heard he was one of the king's domestic servants, or that his Majesty so much as knew him, so far was he from taking him for an embassadour. When having made an end, and the king pressing him with several objections and demands, and sifting him on all hands, gravell'd him at last, by asking, why then the execution was perform'd by night, and, as it were, by stealth. At which the poor confounded embassadour, the more handsomely to disengage himself, made answer, that the duke would have been very loath, out of respect to his Majesty, that such an execution should have been perform'd in the face of the sun. Any one may guess if he was not well schooled when he came home, for having so grossly tripp'd in the presence of a prince of so delicate a nostril as King Francis. Pope Julius II., having sent an embassadour to the king of England to animate him against King Francis, the embassadour having had his audience, and the king, before he would give a positive answer, insisting upon the difficulties he found in setting on foot so great a preparation as would be necessary to attack so potent a king, and urging some reasons to that effect, the embassadour very unseasonably reply'd, that he had also himself consider'd the same difficulties, and had represented as much to the pope. From which saying of his, so directly opposite to the thing propounded, and the business he came about, which was immediately to incite him to war, the king first deriv'd argument (which also he afterwards found to be true) that this embassadour, in his own private bosom, was a friend to the French; of which having advertis'd the pope, his estate at his return home was confiscate, and himself very narrowly escap'd the losing of his head.

Complete.

OF QUICK OR SLOW SPEECH

« Once ne fut à tous toutes graces donnees.»

«All graces by all-liberal heaven
Were never yet to all men given.»

As we see in the gift of eloquence, wherein some have such a facility and promptness, and that which we call a present wit, so easie, that they are ever ready upon all occasions, and never to be surpris'd: and others more heavy and slow, never venture to utter any thing but what they have long premeditated, and taken great care and pains to fit and prepare. Now, as we teach young ladies those sports and exercises which are most proper to set out the grace and beauty of those parts wherein their chiefest ornament and perfection lie: so in these two advantages of eloquence, to which the lawyers and preachers of our age seem principally to pretend. If I were worthy to advise, the slow speaker, methinks, should be more proper for the pulpit, and the other for the bar; and that because the employment of the first does naturally allow him all the leisure he can desire to prepare himself, and besides his career is perform'd in an even and unintermitted line, without stop or interruption; whereas, the pleader's business and interest compels him to enter the lists upon all occasions, and the unexpected objections and replies of his adverse party justle him out of his course, and put him upon the instant, to pump for new and extempore answers and defences. Yet, at the interview betwixt Pope Clement and

King Francis at Marseilles, it happen'd quite contrary, that Monsieur de Poyet, a man bred up all his life at the bar, and in the highest repute for eloquence, having the charge of making the harangue to the pope committed to him, and having so long meditated on it beforehand, as (it was said) to have brought it ready made along with him from Paris; the very day it was to have been pronounc'd, the pope, fearing some thing might be said that might give offence to the other princes' embassadours who were there attending on him, sent to acquaint the king with the argument which he conceiv'd most suiting to the time and place, but by chance quite another thing to that Monsieur de Poyet had taken so much pains about: so that the fine speech he had prepared was of no use, and he was upon the instant to contrive another; which finding himself unable to do, Cardinal Bellay was constrain'd to perform that office. The pleader's part is, doubtless, much harder than that of the preacher; and yet in my opinion we see more passable lawyers than preachers. It should seem that the nature of wit is, to have its operation prompt and sudden, and that of judgment to have it more deliberate and more slow; but he who remains totally silent for want of leisure to prepare himself to speak well, and he also whom leisure does no ways benefit to better speaking, are equally unhappy. 'Tis said of Severus (Cassius) that he spoke best extempore, that he stood more oblig'd to fortune, than his own diligence, that it was an advantage to him to be interrupted in speaking, and that his adversaries were afraid to nettle him, lest his anger should redouble his eloquence. I know experimentally, a disposition so impatient of a tedious and elaborate premeditation, that if it do not go frankly and gayly to work, can perform nothing to purpose. We say of some compositions, that they stink of oyl, and smell of the lamp, by reason of a certain rough harshness that the laborious handling imprints upon those where great force has been employ'd: but besides this, the solicitude of doing well, and a certain striving and contending of a mind too far strain'd, and over-bent upon its undertaking, breaks, and hinders it self, like water, that, by force of its own pressing violence and abundance, cannot find a ready issue through the neck of a bottle, or a narrow sluice. In this condition of nature, of which I was now speaking, there is this also, that it would not be disorder'd, and stimulated with such a passion as the fury of Cassius; for such a motion would be too violent and rude: it would not be justled,

but solicited, and would be rouz'd and heated by unexpected, sudden, and accidental occasions. If it be left to itself, it flags and languishes, agitation only gives it grace and vigour. I am always worst in my own possession, and when wholly at my own disposal. Accident has more title to any thing that comes from me, than I; occasion, company, and even the very rising and falling of my own voice, extract more from my fancy than I can find when I examine and employ it by my self; by which means, the things I say are better than those I write, if either were to be preferr'd where neither are worth any thing. This also befalls me, that I am at a loss, when I seek, and light upon things more by chance, than by any inquisition of my own judgment. I perhaps sometimes hit upon some thing when I write that seems quaint and spritely to me, but will appear dull and heavy to another. But let us leave this subject. Every one talks thus of himself according to his talent. For my part, I am already so lost in it, that I know not what I was about to say, and in such cases a stranger often finds it out before me. If I should always carry my razor about me, to use so oft as this inconvenience befalls me, I should make clean work; but some occurrence or other may at some other time lay it as visible to me as the light, and make me wonder what I should stick at.

Complete.

THAT THE SOUL DISCHARGES HER PASSIONS UPON FALSE OBJECTS WHERE THE TRUE ARE WANTING

A gentleman of my country, who was very often tormented with the gout, being importun'd by his physicians totally to reclaim his appetite from all manner of salt meats, was wont presently to reply that he must needs have some thing to quarrel with in the extremity of his fits, and that he fancy'd that railing at and cursing one while the Bolognia sawsages, and another the dry'd tongues and the hams, was some mitigation to his pain. And in good earnest, as the arm when it is advanced to strike, if it fail of meeting with that upon which it was design'd to discharge the blow, and spends it self in vain, does offend the striker himself; and as also, that to make a pleasant prospect the sight should not be lost and dilated in a vast extent of empty air, but have some bounds to limit and circumscribe it at a reasonable distance: —

"As winds do lose their strength, unless withstood
By some dark grove of strong opposing wood."

So it appears that the soul being transported and discompos'd, turns its violence upon it self, if not supply'd with some thing to oppose it, and therefore always requires an enemy as an object on which to discharge its fury and resentment. Plutarch says very well of those who are delighted with little dogs and monkeys, that the amorous part which is in us, for want of a legitimate object, rather than lie idle, does after that manner forge, and create one frivolous and false; as we see that the soul in the exercise of its passions inclines rather to deceive itself, by creating a false and fantastical subject, even contrary to its own relief, than not to have something to work upon. And after this manner brute beasts direct their fury to fall upon the stone or weapon that has hurt them, and with their teeth even execute their revenge upon themselves, for the injury they have receiv'd from another.

So the fierce bear, made fiercer by the smart
Of the bold Lybian's mortal guided dart,
Turns round upon the wound, and the tough spear
Contorted o'er her breast does flying bear
Down. . . . — *Claudian.*

What causes of the misadventures that befall us do we not invent? What is it that we do not lay the fault to right or wrong, that we may have something to quarrel with? Those beautiful tresses, young lady, you may so liberally tear off, are no way guilty, nor is it the whiteness of those delicate breasts you so unmercifully beat, that with an unlucky bullet has slain your beloved brother: quarrel with something else. Livy, Dec. 3, l. 5., speaking of the Roman army in Spain, says that for the loss of two brothers, who were both great captains, *"Flere omnes repente, et offensare capita,"* that they all wept, and tore their hair. 'Tis the common practice of affliction. And the philosopher Bion said pleasantly of the king, who by handfuls pull'd his hair off his head for sorrow, "Does this man think that baldness is a remedy for grief?" Who has not seen peevish gamesters worry the cards with their teeth, and swallow whole bales of dice in revenge for the loss of their money? Xerxes whipp'd the sea, and writ a challenge to Mount Athos; Cyrus employ'd a whole army several days at work, to revenge himself of the river Gnidus, for the fright it had put him into in passing over; and Caligula demolish'd a very beautiful palace for the pleasure his mother had once enjoy'd there. I remember there was a story current, when I was a boy, that one of our neighbouring kings having receiv'd a blow from the hand of God, swore he would be reveng'd, and in order to it, made proclamation that for ten years to come no one should pray to him, or so much as mention him throughout his dominions; by which we are not so much to take measure of the folly, as the vainglory of the nation of which this tale was told. They are vices that, indeed, always go together; but such actions as these have in them more of presumption than want of wit. Augustus Cæsar, having been tost with a tempest at sea, fell to defying Neptune, and in the pomp of the Circensian games, to be reveng'd, depos'd his statue from the place it had amongst the other deities. Wherein he was less excusable than the former, and less than he was afterwards, when having lost a battle under Quintilius Varus in Germany, in rage and despair he went running his head against the walls, and crying out, O Varus! give me my men again! for this exceeds all folly, forasmuch as impiety is joined with it, invading God himself, or at least Fortune, as if she had ears that were subject to our batteries; like the Thracians, who, when it thunders, or lightens, fall to shooting against heaven with Titanian madness, as if by flights of arrows they intended to reduce God Almighty to reason. Though the ancient poet in Plutarch tells us,

"We must not quarrel heaven in our affairs."

But we can never enough decry nor sufficiently condemn the senseless and ridiculous sallies of our unruly passions.

Complete.

OF THE INEQUALITY AMONGST US

PLUTARCH says somewhere, that he does not find so great a difference betwixt beast and beast as he does betwixt man and man. Which is said in reference to the internal qualities and perfections of the soul. And, in truth, I find (according to my poor judgment) so vast a distance betwixt Epaminondas, and some that I know (who are yet men of common sense), that I could willingly enhance upon Plutarch, and say that there is more difference betwixt such and such a man, than there is betwixt such a man and such a beast:—

Why, in giving your estimate of a man, do you prize him wrapp'd and muffled up in cloaths? He then discovers nothing to you but such parts as are not in the least his own; and conceals those by which alone one may rightly judge of his value. 'Tis the price of the blade that you inquire into, and not of the scabbard; you would not, peradventure, bid a farthing for him, if you saw him stripp'd. You are to judge him by himself, and not by what he wears. And as one of the Ancients very pleasantly said, "Do you know why you repute him tall? You reckon withal the height of his chepines, whereas the pedestal is no part of the statue." Measure him without his stilts, let him lay aside his revenues, and his titles, let him present himself in his shirt, then examine if his body be sound and spritely, active and dispos'd to perform its functions? What soul has he? Is she beautiful, capable, and happily provided of all her faculties? Is she rich of what is her own, or of what she has borrowed? Has fortune no hand in the affair? Can she, without winking, stand the lightning of swords; is she indifferent, whether her life expire by the mouth, or through the throat? Is she settled, even, and content? This is what is to be examin'd, and by that you are to judge of the vast differences betwixt man and man. Is he—

———— sapiens, sibique imperiosus
Quem neque pauperies, neque mors, neque vincula terrent,
Responsare cupidinibus, contemnere honores
Fortis, et in seipso totus teres atque rotundus,
Externi nequid valeat per læve morari,
In quem manca ruit semper fortuna?
—Hor. Lib. II., Sat. 7.

"Wise, and commanding o'er his appetite,
One whom, nor want, nor death, nor bonds, can fright,
To check his lusts, and honours scorn, so stout,
And in himself so round and clear throughout,
That no external thing can stop his course,
And on whom fortune vainly tries her force,"—

such a man is rais'd five hundred fathoms above kingdoms and dutchies, he is an absolute monarch in and to himself.

Sapiens pol ipse fingit fortunam sibi.
—Plaut. Tri., Act. ii., Sc. 2.

"The wise man his own fortune makes.
What remains for him to covet, or desire?"

Heu vir viro quid præstat!—Ter. For. Act. ix., Sc. 3.

————How much alas,
One man another doth surpass!

And that there are as many and innumerable degree of wits, as there are cubits betwixt this and heaven. But as touching the estimate of men, 'tis strange that, our selves excepted, no other creature is esteem'd beyond its proper qualities. We commend a horse for his strength, and sureness of foot,

————volucrem
Sic laudamus equum, facili cui plurima palm.
Fervet, et exultat rauco victoria circo.
—Juv. Sat. 8.

"So we commend the horse for being fleet,
Who many palms by breath and speed does get,
And which the trumpets in the circle grace,
With their hoarse clangours for his well-run race."

and not for his rich caparisons; a greyhound for his share of heels, not for his fine collar; a hawk for her wing, not for her gesses and bells. Why, in like manner, do we not value a man for what is properly his own? He has a great train, a beautiful palace, so much credit, so many thousand pounds a year, and all these are about him, but not in him. You will not buy a pig in a poke; if you cheapen a horse, you will see him stripp'd of his housing-cloaths, you will see him naked and open to your eye; or if he be cloath'd, as they anciently were wont to present them to princes to sell, 'tis only on the less important parts, that you may not so much consider the beauty of his color, or the breadth of his crupper, as principally to examine his limbs, eyes, and feet, which are the members of greatest use:—

Regibus hic mos est, ubi equos mercantur, opertos
Suspiciunt, ne si facies, ut sæpe, decora
Molli fulta pede est, emptorem inducat hiantem,
Quod pulchræ clunes, breve quod caput, ardua cervix.
—Hor. Lib. I., Sat. 2.

"When kings' steeds cloath'd, as 'tis their manner, buy,
They straight examine very curiously,
Lest a short head, a thin and well-rais'd crest,
A broad-spread buttock, and an ample chest,
Should all be propt with an old beaten hoof,
To gull the buyer, when they come to proof."

Compare with such a one the common rabble of mankind, stupid and mean spirited, servile, instable, and continually floating with the tempest of various passions, that tosses and tumbles them to and fro, and all depending upon others, and you will find a greater distance than betwixt heaven and earth; and yet the blindness of common usage is such, that we make little or no account of it. Whereas, if we consider a peasant, and a king, a nobleman, and a villain, a magistrate, and a private man, a rich man, and a poor, there appears a vast disparity, though they differ no more (as a man may say) than in their breeches. In Thrace, the king was distinguish'd from his people, after a very pleasant manner; he had a religion by himself, a god of his own, and which his subjects were not to presume to adore, which was Mercury, whilst, on the other side, he disdain'd to have any thing to do with theirs, Mars, Bacchus, and Diana. And yet they are no other than pictures, that make no essential dissimilitude; for as you see actors in a play, representing the person of a duke, or an emperour, upon the stage, and immediately after, in the tiring room, return to their true and original condition, so the emperour, whose pomp and lustre, does so dazzle you in publick,—

Silicet, et grandes viridi cum luce smaragdi
Auro includuntur, teriturque Thalassina vestis
Assidue, et veneris sudorem exercita petat.
—Luc., l. 4.

"Great emeralds richly are in gold enchast,
To dart green lustre, and the sea-green vest
Continually is worn and rubb'd to frets,
Whilst it imbibes the juice that Venus sweats."

do but peep behind the curtain, and you'll see nothing more than an ordinary man and, peradventure, more contemptible than the meanest of his subjects. "Ille beatus introrsum est, istius bracteata felicitas est."—Sen. Ep. 115. "True happiness lies within, the other is but a counterfeit felicity." Cowardice, irresolution, ambition, spite, and envy are as predominant in him as in another.

Non enim gazæ, neque consularis
Mentis, et curas laqueata circum
Summovet lictor miseros tumultus
Tecta volantes.
—Hor. Lib. II., Ode 16.

"For neither wealth, honours, nor offices,
    Can the wild tumults of the mind appease,
    Nor chase those cares, that with unweary'd wings
    Hover about the palaces of kings."

Nay, solitude and fear attack him even in the centre of his battalions. Do fevers, gouts, and apoplexies, spare them any more than one of us? When old age hangs heavy upon a prince's shoulders, can the yeomen of his guard ease him of the burthen? When he is astonish'd with the apprehension of death, can the gentlemen of his bedchamber comfort and assure him? When jealousie, or any other capricio swims in his brain, can our compliments and ceremonies restore him to his good-humour? The canopy embroider'd with pearl and gold, he lies under, has no vertue against a violent fit of the stone or cholick.   .   .   .

In Anacharsis his opinion, the happiest estate of government would be, where all other things being equal, precedency should be measur'd out by the vertues, and repulses by the vices of men. When King Pyrrhus prepar'd for his expedition into Italy, his wise counsellor Cyneas, to make him sensible of the vanity of his ambition; "Well, sir, (said he), to what end do you make all this mighty preparation?" "To make myself master of Italy," (reply'd the king). "And what after that is done?" (said Cyneas.) "I will pass over into Gaul and Spain," said the other. "And what then?" "I will then go to subdue Africk; and lastly, when I have brought the whole world to my subjection, I will sit down and rest content at my own ease." For God's sake, sir, (reply'd Cyneas), tell me what hinders, that you may not, if you please, be now in the condition you speak of? Why do you not now at this instant, settle yourself in the state you seem to aim at, and spare the labour and hazard you interpose?"

Nimirum quia non bene norat quæ esset habendi
Finis, et omnino quoad crescat vera voluptas.
        —*Lucret.*, l. 5.

"The end of being rich he did not know;
    Nor to what pitch felicity should grow."

I will conclude with an old versicle, that I think very pat to the purpose:—

Mores cuique sui fingunt fortunam.
        —*Corn.* Nep. in vit. A. Hici.

"Himself, not fortune, ev'ry one must blame,
    Since men's own manners do their fortunes frame."

OF GLORY AND THE LOVE OF PRAISE

Is it reasonable that the life of a wise man should depend upon the judgment of fools? "*An quidquam stultius, quam quos singulos contemnas, eos aliquid putare esse universos?*"— *Elian. Varro.* "Can any thing be more foolish than to think that those you despise single, can be any other when join'd together?" He that makes it his business to please them will have enough to do, and never have done: 'tis a mark that never is to be reach'd or hit. "*Nil tam inæstimabile est, quam animi multitudinis.*" "Nothing is to be so little esteem'd as the minds of the multitude." Demetrius pleasantly said of the voice of the people, that he made no more account of that which came from above than of that which fum'd from below. Cicero says more, "*Ego hoc judico, si quando turpe non sit, tamen non esse non turpe, quum id à multitudine laudatur.*"—*Cic.* de Fin. "I am of opinion, that though a thing be not foul in itself, yet it cannot but become so when commended by the multitude." No art, no activity of wit could conduct our steps so as to follow so wandering and so irregular a guide. In this windy confusion of the noise of vulgar reports and opinions that drive us on, no way worth any thing can be chosen. Let us not purpose to ourselves so floating and wavering an end; let us follow constantly after reason, let the publick approbation follow us there, if it will, and it wholly depending upon fortune, we have no reason sooner to expect it by any other way than that. Though I would not follow the right way because it is right, I should, however, follow it for having experimentally found that at the end of the reckoning 'tis commonly the most happy, and of greatest utility. "*Dedit hoc providentia hominibus munus, ut honesta magis juvarent.*" "This gift providence has given to man, that honest things should be the most delightful." The mariner said thus to Neptune, "O god, thou mayest save me if thou wilt, and if thou wilt thou mayest destroy me; but, however, I will steer my rudder true." I have seen a thousand men of ambiguous natures, and that no one doubted but they were more worldly wise than I, throw themselves away, where I have sav'd one.

Risi successus posse carere dolos.
        — *Ovid.* Ep. Penult.

"I have laught, I must confess,
    To see cunning want success."

Paulus Æmylius, going in the glorious expedition of Macedonia, above all things charg'd the people of Rome not to speak of his actions during his absence. Oh, the license of judgments is a great disturbance to great affairs! Forasmuch as every one has not the constancy of Fabius against common, adverse, and injurious ways: who rather suffer'd his authority to be dissected by the vain fancies of man than to go less in his charge with a favourable reputation and the popular applause. There is, I know not what natural sweetness in hearing a man's self commended; but we are a great deal too fond of it.

I care not so much what I am in the opinions of others, as what I am in my own. I would be rich of myself, and not by borrowing. Strangers see nothing but events and outward apparences; every body can set a good face on the matter, when they have trembling and terror within. They do not see my heart, they see but by my countenance. 'Tis with good reason that men decry the hypocrite that is in war; for what is more easie to an old souldier than to shift in a time of danger, and to counterfeit the brave when he has no more heart than a chicken? There are so many ways to avoid hazarding a man's own person that we have deceiv'd the world a thousand times before we come to be engag'd in a real danger; and even then, finding ourselves in an inevitable necessity of doing some thing, we can make shift for that time to conceal our apprehensions with setting a good face on the business, though the heart beats within; and whoever had the use of the Platonick ring, which renders those invisible that wear it, if turn'd inward towards the palm of the hand, a great many would hide themselves when they ought most to appear, and would repent being plac'd in so honourable a post, where necessity must make them brave.

Thus we see how all the judgments that are founded upon external apparences are marvellously incertain and doubtful; and that there is no certain testimony as every one is to himself. In these other, how many powder monkeys are made companions of our glory? He that stands firm in an open trench, what does he in that do more than fifty poor pioneers, who open him the way, and cover it with their own bodies for five pence a day pay, have done before him?

The dispersing and scattering our names into many mouths, we call making them more great; we will have them there well receiv'd, and that this increase turn to their advantage, which

is all that can be excusable in this design; but the excess of this disease proceeds so far, that many covet to have a name, be it what it will. Trogus Pompeius says of Herostratus, and Titus Livius of Manlius Capitolinus, "that they were more ambitious of a great reputation than a good one." This vice is very common. We are more solicitous that men speak of us, than how they speak; and 'tis enough for us that our names are often mention'd, be it after what manner it will. It should seem that to be known is in some sort to have a man's life and its duration in another's keeping. I for my part hold that I am not but in my self, and of that other life of mine which lies in the knowledge of my friends, to consider it naked and simply in it self. I know very well that I am sensible of no fruit nor enjoyment, but by the vanity of a fantastick opinion; and when I shall be dead, I shall be much less sensible of it; and shall withal absolutely lose the use of those real advantages that sometimes accidently follow it; I shall have no more handle whereby to take hold of reputation: neither shall it have any whereby to take hold of, or to cleave to me. For, to expect that my name should be advanc'd by it, in the first place, I have no name that is enough my own; of two that I have, one is common to all my race, and even to others also. There are two families at Paris and Montpellier, whose sirname is Montaigne, another in Brittany, and another Montaigne in Xaintonge. The transposition of one syllable only is enough to ravel our affairs, so that I shall, peradventure, share in their glory, and they shall partake of my shame; and, moreover, my ancestors have formerly been sirnam'd Eyquem, a name wherein a family well known in England is at this day concern'd. As to my other name, every one may take it that will. And so perhaps I may honour a porter in my own stead. And besides, though I had a particular distinction by my self, what can it distinguish when I am no more? Can it favour inanity? But of this I have spoken else where. As to what remains, in a great battel where ten thousand men are maim'd or kill'd, there are not fifteen that are taken notice of. It must be some very eminent greatness, or some consequence of great importance, that fortune has added to it, that must signalize a private action, not of a harquebuser only, but of a great captain; for to kill a man, or two, or ten, to expose a man's self bravely to the utmost peril of death, is, indeed, something in every one of us, because we there hazard all; but for the world's concern they are things so ordinary, and so many of them are every day seen, and there must of necessity be so many of the same kind to produce any notable effect, that we cannot expect any particular renown.

Of so many thousands of valiant men that have died within these fifteen years in France, with their swords in their hands, not a hundred have come to our knowledge. The memory, not of the commanders only, but of battels and victories, is buried and gone. The fortunes of above half of the world, for want of a record, stir not from their place, and vanish without duration. If I had unknown events in my possession, I should think with great ease to outdo those that are recorded in all sorts of examples. Is it not strange, that even of the Greeks and Romans, amongst so many writers and witnesses, and so many rare and noble exploits, so few are arriv'd at our knowledge?

Ad nos vix tenuis famæ perlabitur aura.—Æn., 1. 7.

«An obscure rumor scarce is hither come.»

From the essay on «Glory.»

OF PRESUMPTION AND MONTAIGNE'S OWN MODESTY

THERE is another sort of glory, which is the having too good an opinion of our own worth. 'Tis an inconsiderate affection with which we flatter our selves, and that represents us to our selves other than we truly are. Like the passion of love, that lends beauties and graces to the person it does embrace; and that makes those who are caught with it, with a deprav'd and corrupt judgment, consider the thing they love, other and more perfect than it is. I would not, nevertheless, for fear of failing on the other side, that a man should not know him self aright, or think him self less than he is, the judgment ought in all things to keep it self upright and just: 'tis all the reason in the world he should discern in him self, as well as in others, what truth sets before him; if he be Cæsar, let him boldly think him self the greatest captain in the world. We are nothing but ceremony; ceremony carries us away, and we leave the substance of things; we hold by the branches and quit the trunk. Ceremony forbids us to express by words things that are lawful and natural, and we obey it; reason forbids us to do things unlawful and ill, and no

body obeys it. I find my self here fetter'd by the laws of ceremony; for it neither permits a man to speak well of him self nor ill. We will leave it there for this time. They whom Fortune (call it good or ill) has made to pass their lives in some eminent degree may by their publick actions manifest what they are; but they whom she has only employed in the crowd, and of whom nobody will say a word unless they speak them selves, are to be excus'd, if they take the boldness to speak of them selves to such whose interest it is to know them. . . .

Methinks philosophy has never so fair a game to play as when it falls upon our vanity and presumption; when it most lays open their irresolution, weakness, and ignorance. I look upon the too good opinion that man has of him self to be the nursing mother of all the most false, both publick and private opinions. Those people who ride astride upon the Epicycle of Mercury, who see so far into the heavens, are worse to me than a tooth drawer that comes to draw my teeth: for in my study, the subject of which is man, finding so great a variety of judgments, so great a labyrinth of difficulties one upon another; so great diversity and uncertainty, even in the school of wisdom it self, you may judge, seeing those people could not resolve upon the knowledge of them selves, and their own condition, which is continually before their eyes, and within them, seeing they do not know, how that moves which they them selves move, nor how to give us a description of the springs they them selves govern and make use of; how can I believe them about the ebbing and flowing of the Nile. The curiosity of knowing things has been given to man for a scourge, says the Holy Scripture. But to return to what concerns my self: I think it very hard that any other should have a meaner opinion of him self, nay, that any other should have a meaner opinion of me, than I have of my self. I look upon my self as one of the common sort, saving in this, that I have no better an opinion of my self; guilty of the meanest and most popular defects, but not disown'd or excus'd, and do not value my self upon any other account than because I know my own value. If there be any glory in the case, 'tis superficially infus'd into me by the treachery of my complexion, and has no body that my judgment can discern. I am sprinkled, but not tincted. For in truth, as to the effects of the mind, there is no part of me, be it what it will, with which I am satisfied; and the approbation of others makes me not think the bet-

ter of my self; my judgment is tender and fickle, especially in things that concern my self; I feel my self float and waver by reason of my weakness. I have nothing of my own that satisfies my judgment; my sight is clear and regular enough, but in opening it, it is apt to dazzle; as I most manifestly find in poesie. I love it infinitely, and am able to give a tolerable judgment of other men's works; but in good earnest, when I apply my self to it, I play the child, and am not able to endure my self. A man may play the fool in every thing else, but not in poetry. I would to God the sentence was writ over the doors of all our printers, to forbid the entrance of so many rhymers.

Why have not we such people? Dionysius the father valu'd him self so much upon nothing as his poetry. At the Olympick games, with chariots surpassing the others in magnificence, he sent also poets and musicians to present his verses with tents and pavilions royally gilt and hung with tapistry. When his verses came to be recited, the excellency of the pronunciation did at first attract the attention of the people; but when they afterwards came to poise the meanness of the composition, they first enter'd in to disdain, and continuing to nettle their judgments, presently proceeded to fury, and ran to pull down, and tear to pieces all his pavilions; and in that his chariots neither perform'd any thing to purpose in the course; and that the ship which brought back his people fail'd of making Sicily, and was by the tempest driven and wrack'd upon the coast of Tarentum, they did certainly believe, was through the anger of the gods, incens'd, as they them selves were, against that paltry poem; and even the mariners who escap'd from the wrack seconded this opinion of the people. To which also the Oracle, that foretold his death, seem'd to subscribe; which was, «That Dionysius should be near his end when he should have overcome those who were better than him self,» which he interpreted of the Carthaginians, who surpass'd him in power; and having war with them, often declin'd the victory, not to incur the sense of this perdition. But he understood it ill; for the god pointed at the time of the advantage that by favour and injustice he obtain'd at Athens over the tragick poets, better than him self, having caus'd his own play call'd the «Leineicus» to be acted in emulation. Presently after which victory he died, and partly of the excessive joy he conceiv'd at the success. What I find tolerable of mine is not so really, and in it self; but in comparison of other worse things,

that I see are well enough receiv'd. I envy the happiness of those that can please and hug them selves in what they do, for 'tis a very easie thing to be so pleas'd, because a man extracts that pleasure from him self, especially if he be constant in his self-conceit. I know a poet, against whom both the intelligent and the ignorant, abroad and at home, both heaven and earth, exclaim, that he understands very little in it; and yet for all that, he has never a whit the worse opinion of him self; but is always falling upon some new piece, always contriving some new invention, and still persists; by so much the more obstinate, as it only concerns him to stand up in his own defence. My works are so far from pleasing me, that as oft as I review them they disgust me.

I have always an idea in my soul, which presents me a better form than that I have made use of; but I cannot catch it, nor fit it to my purpose; and yet even that idea is but of the meaner sort, by which I conclude that the productions of those great souls of former times, as very much beyond the utmost stretch of my imagination, or my wish; their writings do not only satisfie and fill me, but they astonish me, and ravish me with admiration. I judge of their beauty, I see it, if not to the utmost, yet so far at least as 'tis possible for me to aspire. Whatever I undertake, I owe a sacrifice to the Graces, as Plutarch says of some one, to make a return for their favour.

From the essay on «Presumption.»

OF FRIENDSHIP AND LOVE

WE ARE not here to bring the love we bear to women, though it be an act of our own choice, into comparison; nor rank it with the others; the fire of which I confess—

Neque enim est Dea nescia nostri
Quæ dulcem curis miscet amaritiem.
—Catullus.

«Nor is my goddess ign'rant what I am,
Who pleasing sorrows mixes with my flame.»

is more active, more eager, and more sharp; but withal, 'tis more precipitous, fickle, moving, and inconstant: a fever subject to intermission, and paroxysms, that has seiz'd but on one part, one cor-ncr of the building; whereas in friendship, 'tis a general and universal fire, but temperate, and equal, a constant establish'd heat, all easie, and smooth, without poignancy or roughness. Moreover, in love, 'tis no other than frantick desire, to that which flies from us.

> *«Com segue la lepre il cacciatore*
> *Al fredo, al caldo, alla montagna, al litto:*
> *Ne piu l'estima poi, che presa vede,*
> *Et sol dietro a chi fugge affretta il piede.»*

> « Like hunters, that the flying hare pursue
> O'er hill, and dale, through heat, and morning dew,
> Which being ta'en, the quarry they despise,
> Being only pleas'd in following that which flies. »

So soon as ever they enter into terms of friendship, that is to say, into a concurrence of desires, it vanishes, and is gone, fruition destroys it. Friendship, on the contrary, is enjoy'd proportionably, as it is desir'd, and only grows up, is nourish'd and improves by enjoyment, as being of it self spiritual, and the soul growing still more perfect by practice. Under, and subsellious to this perfect friendship, I cannot deny but that the other vain affections, have, in my younger years, found some place in my thoughts that I may say nothing of him, who him self confesses but too much in his verses; so that I had both these passions, but always so, that I could myself well enough distinguish them, and never in any degree of comparison with one another. The first maintaining its flight in so lofty and so brave a place, as with disdain to look down, and see the other flying at a far humbler pitch below. As concerning marriage, besides, that it is a covenant, the entrance into which, is only free, but the continuance in it, forc'd and compell'd, having another dependance than that of our own free will, and a bargain commonly contracted to other ends, there almost always happens a thousand intricacies in it, to unravel enough to break the thread, and to divert the current of a lively affection: whereas friendship has no manner of business or traffick with any but it self.

From the essay on « Friendship.»

OF PRAYERS AND THE JUSTICE OF GOD

I KNOW not if, or no, I am deceiv'd; but since by a particular favour of the divine bounty, a certain form of prayer has been prescrib'd and dictated to us, word by word, from the mouth of God him self, I have ever been of opinion that we ought to have it in more frequent use than we yet have, and if I were worthy to advise, at the sitting down to, and rising from our tables, at our rising, and going to bed, and in every particular action wherein prayer is requir'd, I would that Christians always make use of the Lord's Prayer, if not alone, yet at least always. The church may lengthen, or alter prayers, according to the necessity of our instruction, for I know very well that it is always the same in substance, and the same thing; but yet such a preference ought to be given to that prayer, that the people should have it continually in their mouths; for it is most certain, that all necessary petitions are comprehended in it, and that it is infinitely proper for all occasions. 'Tis the only prayer I use in all places and conditions, and what I still repeat instead of changing; whence it also happens, that I have no other by heart, but that only. It just now comes into my mind, from whence we should derive that errour of having recourse to God in all our designs and enterprises, to call him to our assistance in all sorts of affairs, and in all places where our weakness stands in need of support without considering whether the occasion be just, or otherwise, and to invoke his name and power, in what estate soever we are, or action we are engag'd in, how vicious soever: he is, indeed, our sole and only protector, and can do all things for us: but though he is pleas'd to honour us with his paternal care, he is, notwithstanding, as just as he is good and mighty, and does ofter exercise his justice than his power, and favours us according to that, and not according to our petitions. Plato, in his laws, makes three sorts of belief injurious to the gods; that there is none; that they concern not them selves about human affairs; and that they never reject or deny any thing to our vows, offerings, and sacrifices. The first of these errours (according to his opinion) did never continue rooted in any man, from his infancy to his old age; the other two, he confesses, men might be obstinate in. God's justice and his power are inseparable, and therefore in vain we invoke his power in an unjust cause: we are to have

---

our souls pure and clean, at that moment at least, wherein we pray to him, and purified from all vicious passions, otherwise we our selves present him the rods wherewith to chastise us. Instead of repairing any thing we have done amiss, we double the wickedness and the offence, whilst we offer to him to whom we are to sue for pardon an affection full of irreverence and hatred. Which makes me not very apt to applaud those whom I observe to be so frequent on their knees, if the actions nearest of kin to prayer do not give me some evidence of reformation. . . .

A man whose whole meditation is continually working upon nothing but impurity, which he knows to be so odious to Almighty God, what can he say when he comes to speak to him? He reforms, but immediately falls into a relapse. If the object of the divine justice, and the presence of his maker, did, as he pretends, strike and chastise his soul, how short soever the repentance might be, the very fear of offending that infinite majesty would so often present itself to his imagination, that he would soon see himself master of those vices that are most natural and habitual in him. But what shall we say of those who settle their whole course of life upon the profit and emolument of sins, which they know to be mortal? How many trades of vocations have we admitted and countenanc'd amongst us, whose very essence is vicious? And he that confessing himself to me, voluntarily told me that he had all his lifetime profess'd and practis'd a religion, in his opinion damnable, and contrary to that he had in his heart, only to preserve his credit, and the honor of his employments, how could his courage suffer so infamous a confession? What can men say to the divine justice upon this subject? Their repentance consisting in a visible and manifest reformation and restitution, they lose the colour of alleging it both to God and man. Are they so impudent as to sue for remission, without satisfaction, and without penitency or remorse?

From the essay on « Prayers.»

MONTESQUIEU

(CHARLES LOUIS DE SECONDAT, BARON DE LA BREDE ET DE MONTESQUIEU)

(1689-1755)

MONTESQUIEU's "Spirit of the Laws," which appeared in 1748, is one of the most remarkable books of the eighteenth century, and perhaps no other book written during the century has equaled it in influence. It inspired Beccaria in Italy and Bentham in England, and it has helped in so many ways to make history, that its importance to the student of history can hardly be over-estimated. The style in which it is written is much more nearly Attic than Parisian. Montesquieu deals point by point with every subordinate phase of his subject. As if each were of primary importance, he makes his treatment of it a complete essay, while at the same time he keeps it within an allotted limit and subordinates it to the whole. The lack of ability to do this is the worst of the negative faults of the prose of the nineteenth century, and on this account Montesquieu would be worth serious study even if he were not a great thinker. Of the status of the book in literature, Professor Saintsbury writes: " It is an assemblage of the most fertile, original, and inspiriting views on legal and political subjects put in language of singular suggestiveness and vigor, illustrated by examples which are always apt and luminous, permeated by the spirit of temperate and tolerant desire for human improvement and happiness, and almost unique in its entire freedom at once from doctrinairism, from visionary enthusiasm, from egotism, and from an undue spirit of system.»

Though Montesquieu is chiefly remembered by this great work, he was already famous when it appeared, as it was preceded by his " Persian Letters » (1721) and his « Considerations on the Causes of the Grandeur and Decadence of the Romans.»

He was born from a patrician family at the Château de la Brède, near Bordeaux, France, January 18th, 1689. He was educated carefully in literature and law; and when his hereditary position made him president of the Bordeaux parliament, he was well fitted for the place. Knowing himself better fitted for literature, however, he withdrew from public life, and devoted himself to a life of study, relieved chiefly by travel. When he died, February 10th, 1755, his generation had recognized him as one of its greatest men, and posterity has sustained its judgment.

OF THE LIBERTIES AND PRIVILEGES OF EUROPEAN WOMEN

("Rica to Ibben at Smyrna." Dated "Paris 26th of the Moon 1713.")

WHETHER it is better to deprive women of their liberty or to permit it them, is a great question among men: it appears to me that there are good reasons for and against this practice. If the Europeans urge that there is a want of generosity in rendering those persons miserable whom we love, our Asiatics answer that it is meanness in men to renounce the empire which nature has given them over women. If they are told that a great number of women, shut up, are troublesome, they reply that ten women in subjection are less troublesome than one who is refractory. But they object, in their turn, that the Europeans cannot be happy who are faithless to them, they reply that this fidelity, of which they boast so much, does not hinder that disgust which always follows the gratification of the passions; that our women are too much ours; that a possession so easily obtained leaves nothing to be wished or feared; that a little coquetry provokes desire, and prevents disgust. Perhaps a man wiser than myself would be puzzled to decide this question; for if the Asiatics do find out proper means to calm their uneasiness, the Europeans also do as well to have uneasiness. After all, say they, though we should be unhappy as husbands, we should always find means to recompense ourselves as lovers. For that a man might have reason to complain of the infidelity of his wife, it must be that there should be but three persons in the world; they will always be at even hands when there are four. Another question among the learned is, whether the law of nature subjects the women to the men. No, said a gallant philosophers to me the other day, nature never dictated such a law. The empire we have over them is real tyranny, which they only suffer us to assume, because they have more good-nature than we, and, in consequence, more humanity and reason. These advantages, which ought to have given them the superiority, had we acted reasonably, have made them lose it, because we have not the same advantages. But if it is true that the power we have over women is only tyrannical, it is no less so that they have over us a natural empire, that of beauty, which nothing can resist. Our power extends not to all countries; but that of beauty is universal. Wherefore then do we hear of this privilege? Is

it because we are strongest? But this is really injustice. We employ every kind of means to reduce their spirits. Their abilities would be equal with ours, if their education was the same. Let us examine them in those talents which education hath not enfeebled, and we shall see if ours are as great. It must be acknowledged, though it is contrary to our custom, that among the most polite people the women have always had the authority over their husbands; it was established among the Egyptians in honor of Isis, and among the Babylonians in honor of Semiramis. It is said of the Romans, that they commanded all nations, but obeyed their wives. I say nothing of the Sauromates, who were in perfect slavery to their sex; they were too barbarous to be brought for an example. Thou seest, my dear Ibben, that I have contracted the fashion of this country, where they are fond of defending extraordinary opinions, and reducing everything to a paradox. The prophet hath determined the question, and settled the rights of each sex; the women, says he, must honor their husbands, and the men their wives; but the husbands are allowed one degree of honor more.

Complete. Number 38 of the "Persian Letters."

RELATION OF LAWS TO DIFFERENT BEINGS

LAWS, in their most general signification, are the necessary relations arising from the nature of things. In this sense all beings have their laws; the Deity his laws, the material world its laws, the intelligences superior to man their laws, the beasts their laws, man his laws.

They who assert that a blind fatality produced the various effects we behold in this world talk very absurdly; for can any thing be more unreasonable than to pretend that a blind fatality could be productive of intelligent beings?

There is, then, a primitive reason; and laws are the relations subsisting between it and different beings, and the relations of these to one another.

God is related to the universe, as Creator and Preserver; the laws by which he created all things are those by which he preserves them. He acts according to these rules, because he knows them; he knows them, because he made them; and he made them, because they are relative to his wisdom and power.

Since we observe that the world, though formed by the motion of matter, and void of understanding, subsists through so long a succession of ages, its motions must certainly be directed by invariable laws; and could we imagine another world, it must also have constant rules, or it would inevitably perish.

Thus the creation, which seems an arbitrary act, supposes laws as invariable as those of the fatality of the Atheists. It would be absurd to say that the Creator might govern the world without those rules, since without them it could not subsist.

These rules are a fixed and variable relation. In bodies moved, the motion is received, increased, diminished, lost, according to the relations of the quantity of matter and velocity; each diversity is uniformity, each change is constancy.

Particular intelligent beings may have laws of their own making, but they have some likewise which they never made. Before they were intelligent beings, they were possible; they had therefore possible relations, and consequently possible laws. Before laws were made, there were relations of possible justice. To say that there is nothing just or unjust but what is commanded or forbidden by positive laws is the same as saying that before the describing of a circle all the radii were not equal.

We must therefore acknowledge relations of justice antecedent to the positive law by which they are established: as for instance, that if human societies existed it would be right to conform to their laws; if there were intelligent beings that had received a benefit of another being, they ought to show their gratitude; if one intelligent being had created another intelligent being, the latter ought to continue in its original state of dependence; if one intelligent being injures another, it deserves a retaliation; and so on.

But the intelligent world is far from being so well governed as the physical. For though the former has also its laws, which of their own nature are invariable, it does not conform to them so exactly as the physical world. This is, because, on the one hand, particular intelligent beings are of a finite nature, and consequently liable to error; and on the other, their nature requires them to be free agents. Hence they do not steadily conform to their primitive laws; and even those of their own instituting they frequently infringe.

Whether brutes be governed by the general laws of motion, or by a particular movement, we cannot determine. Be that as it may, they have not a more intimate relation to God than the rest of the material world; and sensation is of no other use to them than in the relation they have either to other particular beings or to themselves.

By the allurements of pleasure they preserve the individual, and by the same allurements they preserve their species. They have natural laws, because they are united by sensation; positive laws they have none, because they are not connected by knowledge. And yet they do not invariably conform to their natural laws; these are better observed by vegetables, that have neither understanding nor sense.

Brutes are deprived of the high advantages which we have; but they have some which we have not. They have not our hopes, but they are without our fears; they are subject like us to death, but without knowing it; even most of them are more attentive than we to self-preservation, and do not make so bad a use of their passions.

Man, as a physical being, is like other bodies, governed by invariable laws. As an intelligent being, he incessantly transgresses the laws established by God, and changes those of his own instituting. He is left to his private direction, though a limited being, and subject, like all finite intelligencies, to ignorance and error; even his imperfect knowledge he loses; and as a sensible creature, he is hurried away by a thousand impetuous passions. Such a being might every instant forget his Creator; God has therefore reminded him of his duty by the laws of religion. Such a being is liable every moment to forget himself; philosophy has provided against this by the laws of morality. Formed to live in society, he might forget his fellow-creatures; legislators have therefore by political and civil laws confined him to his duty

Complete. "The Spirit of Laws," Chap. i.

EDUCATION IN A REPUBLICAN GOVERNMENT

IT is in a republican government that the whole power of education is required. The fear of despotic governments naturally arises of itself amidst threats and punishments; the honor of monarchies is favored by the passions, and favors them in its turn;

but virtue is a self-renunciation, which is ever arduous and painful.

This virtue may be defined, the love of the laws and of our country. As such love requires a constant preference of public to private interest, it is the source of all private virtues; for they are nothing more than this very preference itself.

This love is peculiar to democracies. In these alone the government is intrusted to private citizens. Now government is like everything else; to preserve it, we must love it.

Has it ever been heard that kings were not fond of monarchy, or that despotic princes hated arbitrary power?

Everything therefore depends on establishing this love in a republic; and to inspire it ought to be the principle of education: but the surest way of instilling it into children is, for parents to set them an example. People have it generally in their power to communicate their ideas to their children; but they are still better able to transfuse their passions.

If it happens otherwise, it is because the impressions made at home are effaced by those they have received abroad.

It is not the young people that degenerate; they are not spoiled till those of maturer age are already sunk into corruption.

Complete. "The Spirit of Laws,"
Book IV., Chap. v.

CONQUESTS MADE BY A REPUBLIC

IT is contrary to the nature of things that in a confederate government one state should make any conquest over another, as in our days we have seen in Switzerland. In mixed confederate republics, where the association is between petty republics and monarchies, of a small extent, this is not so absurd.

Contrary it is also to the nature of things, that a democratical republic should conquer towns, which cannot enter into the sphere of its democracy. It is necessary that the conquered people should be capable of enjoying the privileges of sovereignty, as was settled in the very beginning among the Romans. The conquest ought to be limited to the number of citizens fixed for the democracy.

If a democratical republic subdues a nation in order to govern them as subjects, it exposes its own liberty; because it intrusts

too great a power to those who are appointed to the command of the conquered provinces.

How dangerous would have been the situation of the republic of Carthage, had Hannibal made himself master of Rome? What would not he have done in his own country, had he been victorious,—he who caused so many revolutions in it after his defeat?

Hanno could never have dissuaded the senate from sending succors to Hannibal had he used no other arguments than his own jealousy. The Carthaginian senate, whose wisdom is so highly extolled by Aristotle (and which has been evidently proved by the prosperity of that republic), could never have been determined by other than solid reasons. They must have been stupid not to see that an army at the distance of three hundred leagues would necessarily be exposed to losses which required reparation.

Hanno's party insisted that Hannibal should be delivered up to the Romans. They could not at that time be afraid of the Romans; they were therefore apprehensive of Hannibal.

It was impossible, some will say, for them to imagine that Hannibal had been so successful. But how was it possible for them to doubt of it? Could the Carthaginians, a people spread over all the earth, be ignorant of what was transacting in Italy? No; they were sufficiently acquainted with it, and for that reason they did not care to send supplies to Hannibal.

Hanno became more resolute after the battle of Trebia, after the battle of Thrasimenus, after that of Cannæ; it was not his incredulity that increased, but his fear.

Complete. "The Spirit of Laws,"
Book X., Chap. vi.

OF PUBLIC DEBTS

SOME have imagined that it was for the advantage of a state to be indebted to itself; they thought that this multiplied riches, by increasing the circulation.

Those who are of this opinion have, I believe, confounded a circulating paper which represents money, or a circulating paper which is the sign of the profits that a company has, or will make by commerce, with a paper which represents a debt. The two first are extremely advantageous to the state; the last can never

be so; and all that we can expect from it is, that individuals have a good security from the government for their money. But let us see the inconveniences which result from it:—

1. If foreigners possess much paper which represents a debt, they annually draw out of the nation a considerable sum for interest.

2. A nation that is thus perpetually in debt ought to have the exchange very low.

3. The taxes raised for the payment of the interest of the debt are a hurt to the manufacturers, by raising the price of the artificer's labor.

4. It takes the true revenue of the state from those who have activity and industry, to convey it to the indolent; that is, it gives the conveniences for labor to those who do not labor, and clogs with difficulties the industrious artist.

These are its inconveniences; I know of no advantages. Ten persons have each a yearly income of a thousand crowns, either in land or trade; this raises to the nation, at five per cent., a capital of two hundred thousand crowns. If these ten persons employed the half of their income, that is, five thousand crowns, in paying the interest of a hundred thousand crowns, which they had borrowed of others, that would be only to the state, as two hundred thousand crowns; that is, in the language of the Algebraists, 200,000 crowns — 100,000 crowns + 100,000 crowns = 200,000.

People are thrown, perhaps, into this error, by reflecting that the paper which represents the debt of a nation is the sign of riches; for none but a rich state can support such paper without falling into decay. And if it does not fall, it is a proof that the state has other riches besides. They say that it is not an evil, because there are resources against it; and that it is an advantage, since these resources surpass the evil.

Complete. From "The Spirit of Laws."

A PARADOX OF MR. BAYLE

MR. BAYLE has pretended to prove that it is better to be an Atheist than an Idolater; that is, in other words, that it is less dangerous to have no religion at all, than a bad one. "I had rather," said he, "it should be said of me that I had no existence, than that I am a villain." This is only a sophism

founded on this, that it is of no importance to the human race to believe that a certain man exists; whereas it is extremely useful for them to believe the existence of a God. From the idea of his nonexistence immediately follows that of our independence; or, if we cannot conceive this idea, that of disobedience. To say that religion is not a restraining motive, because it does not always restrain, is equally absurd as to say that the civil laws are not a restraining motive. It is a false way of reasoning against religion to collect, in a large work, a long detail of the evils it has produced, if we do not give, at the same time, an enumeration of the advantages which have flowed from it. Were I to relate all the evils that have arisen in the world from civil laws, from monarchy, and from republican government, I might tell of frightful things. Were it of no advantage for subjects to have religion, it would still be of some, if princes had it, and if they whitened with foam the only rein which can restrain those who fear not human laws.

A prince who loves and fears religion is a lion, who stoops to the hand that strokes, or to the voice that appeases him. He who fears and hates religion is like the savage beast that growls and bites the chain, which prevents his flying on the passenger. He who has no religion at all is that terrible animal, who perceives his liberty only when he tears in pieces, and when he devours.

The question is not to know whether it would be better that a certain man, or a certain people, had no religion, than to abuse what they have; but to know what is the least evil, that religion be sometimes abused, or that there be no such restraint as religion on mankind.

To diminish the horror of atheism, they lay too much to the charge of idolatry. It is far from being true that when the Ancients raised altars to a particular vice they intended to show that they loved the vice; this signified, on the contrary, that they hated it. When the Lacedæmonians erected a temple to Fear, it was not to show that this warlike nation desired that he would in the midst of battle possess the hearts of the Lacedæmonians. They had deities to whom they prayed not to inspire them with guilt; and others whom they besought to shield them from it.

Complete. "The Spirit of Laws,"
Book XXIV., Chap. ii.

SUMPTUARY LAWS IN A DEMOCRACY

WE HAVE observed that in a republic, where riches are equally divided, there can be no such thing as luxury; and as we have shown in the fifth book, that this equal distribution constitutes the excellency of a republican government: hence it follows that the less luxury there is in a republic, the more it is perfect. There was none among the old Romans, none among the Lacedæmonians; and in republics where this equality is not quite lost, the spirit of commerce, industry, and virtue renders every man able and willing to live on his own property, and consequently prevents the growth of luxury.

The laws concerning the new division of lands, insisted upon so eagerly in some republics, were of the most salutary nature. They are dangerous, only as they are subitaneous. By reducing instantly the wealth of some, and increasing that of others, they form a revolution in each family, and must produce a general one in the state.

In proportion as luxury gains ground in a republic, the minds of the people are turned towards their particular interests. Those who are allowed only what is necessary have nothing but their own reputation and their country's glory in view. But a soul depraved by luxury has many other desires, and soon becomes an enemy to the laws that confine it. The luxury in which the garrison of Rhegio began to live was the cause of their massacring the inhabitants.

No sooner were the Romans corrupted, than their desires became boundless and immense. Of this we may judge by the price they set on things. A pitcher of Falernian wine was sold for a hundred denarii; a barrel of salt meat from the kingdom of Pontus cost four hundred; a good cook four talents; and for boys, no price was reckoned too great. When the whole world, impelled by the force of corruption, is immersed in voluptuousness, what must then become of virtue?

Complete. "The Spirit of Laws," Book VII., Chap. vii.

PARTICULAR CAUSE OF THE CORRUPTION OF THE PEOPLE

GREAT success, especially when chiefly owing to the people, intoxicates them to such a degree that it is impossible to contain them within bounds. Jealous of their magistrates, they soon become jealous likewise of the magistracy; enemies to those who govern, they soon prove enemies also to the constitution. Thus it was that the victory over the Persians in the straits of Salamis corrupted the republic of Athens; and thus the defeat of the Athenians ruined the republic of Syracuse.

Marseilles never experienced those great transitions from lowness to grandeur; this was owing to the prudent conduct of that republic, who always preserved her principles.

Complete. "The Spirit of Laws," Book VIII., Chap. iv.

HANNAH MORE

(1745-1833)

HANNAH MORE, perhaps the most influential of all female moralists, was born in Gloucestershire, England, February 2d, 1745. Her father, Jacob More, was a schoolmaster, who educated her carefully, and she began life as a teacher in a boarding school for young ladies, established by herself and sisters, at Bristol, in 1757. It was for the young ladies of this school that her first play, "The Search for Happiness," was written. Her writings attracted the attention of Garrick and she became a favorite with him and his friends, including Doctor Johnson himself. After writing plays, poems, essays, and tales, she began (1795-98) writing "tracts" for circulation among the working classes. By this work she hoped to check the growth of infidelity, and she so far succeeded that she may be called one of the chief inventors of the modern tract society's system of work. It is said that two million of her sketches written for this purpose were circulated in a single year.

She lived to be eighty-seven years old, dying at Clifton, September 7th, 1833. Among the most noted of her stories are "The Shepherd of Salisbury Plain" and "Cœlebs in Search of a Wife." Her "Moriana" is a series of short essays and epigrammatic sayings arranged alphabetically by title. They represent her at her best as an essayist.

"MORIANA"

ACCOMPLISHMENTS

IT is superfluous to decorate woman highly for early youth; youth is itself a decoration. We mistakingly adorn most that part of life which least requires it, and neglect to provide for that which will want it most. It is for that sober period, when life has lost its freshness, the passions their intenseness, and the spirits their hilarity, that we should be preparing. Our wisdom would be, to anticipate the wants of middle life, to lay in a store of notions, ideas, principles, and habits, which may preserve, or transfer to the mind, that affection which was at first partly attracted by the person. But to add a vacant mind to a

form which has ceased to please, to provide no subsidiary aid to beauty while it lasts, and especially no substitute when it is departed, is to render life comfortless, and marriage dreary.

Let such women as are disposed to be vain of their comparatively petty attainments look up with admiration to those two contemporary shining examples, the venerable Elizabeth Carter and the blooming Elizabeth Smith. I knew them both, and to know was to revere them. In them let our young ladies contemplate profound and various learning, chastised by true Christian humility. In them let them venerate acquirements which would have been distinguished in a university, meekly softened and beautifully shaded by the gentle exertion of every domestic virtue, by the unaffected exercise of every feminine employment.

Complete.

APPLAUSE

HUMAN applause is, by a worldly man, reckoned not only among the luxuries of life, but among articles of the first necessity.

An undue desire to obtain it has certainly its foundation in vanity, and it is one of our grand errors to reckon vanity a trivial fault. An over-estimation of character, and an anxious wish to conciliate all suffrages, is an infirmity from which even worthy men are not exempt; nay, it is a weakness from which, if they are not governed by a strict religious principle, worthy men are in most danger. Reputation being in itself so very desirable a good, those who actually possess it, and in some sense deserve to possess it, are apt to make it their standard, and to rest in it as their supreme aim and end.

We are as fond of the applauses even of the upper gallery as the dramatic poet. Like him, we affect to despise the mob, considered as individual judges, yet, as a mass, we court their applause. Like him, we feel strengthened by the number of voices in our favor, and are less anxious about the goodness of the work than about the loudness of the acclamation. Success is merit in the eyes of both.

Complete.

AUTHORS

IF WE resolve never to read a work of instruction because the author had faults, Lord Bacon's inexhaustible mine of intellectual wealth might still have been unexplored. Luther, the man to whom the Protestant world owes more than to any other uninspired being, might remain unread, because he is said to have wanted the meekness of Melanchthon. Even the divine instructions in the book of Ecclesiastes would have been written in vain.

Evil in the man would not invalidate the truths he has been teaching. Balaam, though a bad man, prophesied truly. Erasmus, whose piety is almost as doubtful as his wit and learning were unquestionable, yet, by throwing both into the right scale, was a valuable instrument in effecting the great work in which he was concerned. Erasmus powerfully assisted the Reformation, though it is not quite so clear that the Reformation essentially benefited Erasmus.

If, then, the writer advances unanswerable arguments in the cause of truth, if he impressively enforces its practical importance, his character, even if defective, should not invalidate his reasoning. Though we allow that even to the reader it is far more satisfactory when the life illustrates the writing, yet we must never bring the conduct of the man as any infallible test of the truth of his doctrine. Allow this, and the reverse of the proposition will be pleaded against us. Take the opposite case. Do we ever produce certain moral qualities which Hobbes, Bayle, Hume, and other sober skeptics possessed, as arguments for adopting their opinions? Do we infer, as a necessary consequence, that their sentiments are sound, because their lives were not flagitious?

It would be the highest degree of unfairness to prefer a charge of injustice, hypocrisy, or inconsistency against an author, because his life, in some respects, falls short of the strictness of his writings. It is a disparity almost inseparable from this state of frail mortality. He may have fallen into errors, and yet deserve to have no heavier charges brought against him than he has brought against others. Infirmity of temper, inequality of mind, a heart, though fearing to offend God, yet not sufficiently dead to the world,—these are the lingering effects of sin imperfectly subdued, in a heart which yet longs, prays, and labors, for a complete deliverance from all its corruptions.

While we are discussing events, they cease to be; while we are criticizing customs, they become obsolete; while we are adopting fashions, they vanish; while we are condemning or defending parties, they change sides. While we are contemplating feuds, opposing factions, or deploring revolutions, they are extinct. Of created things, mutability is their character at the best, brevity their duration at the longest. But "the word of the Lord endureth forever."

The Bible never warns us against imaginary evils, nor courts us to imaginary good.

Young persons should read the Scriptures, unaltered, unmutilated, unabridged. If parents do not make a point of this, the peculiarities of sacred language will become really obsolete to the next generation.

Complete.

BOOKS

FOR those who have much business and little time, it is a great and necessary art to learn to extract the essential spirit of an author from the body of his work; to know how to seize on the vital parts; to discern where his strength lies; and to separate it from those portions of the work which are superfluous, collateral, or merely ornamental.

In avoiding books which excite the passions, it would seem strange to include even some devotional works. Yet such as merely kindle warm feelings are not always the safest. Let us rather prefer those which, while they tend to raise a devotional spirit, awaken the affections without disordering them; which, while they elevate the desires, purify them; which show us our own nature, and lay open its corruptions. Such as show us the malignity of sin, the deceitfulness of our hearts, the feebleness of our best resolutions; such as teach us to pull off the mask from the fairest appearance, and discover every hiding place where some lurking evil would conceal itself; such as show us not what we appear to others, but what we really are; such as, co-operating with our interior feelings, and showing us our natural state, point out our absolute need of a Redeemer, lead us to seek for him for pardon from a conviction that there is no other refuge, no other salvation. Let us be conversant with such writings as teach us that while we long to obtain the

Of two evils, had not an author better be tedious than superficial? From an overflowing vessel you may gather more, indeed, than you want, but from an empty one you can gather nothing.

Complete.

THE BIBLE

THE sacred volume was composed by a vast variety of writers, men of every different rank and condition, of every diversity of character and turn of mind; the monarch and the plebeian, the illiterate and the learned, the foremost in talent and the moderately gifted in natural advantages, the historian and the legislator, the orator and the poet,—each had his immediate vocation, each his peculiar province: some prophets, some apostles, some evangelists, living in ages remote from each other, under different modes of civil government, under different dispensations of the Divine economy, filling a period of time which reached from the first dawn of heavenly light to its meridian radiance.

The Old Testament and the New, the Law and the Gospel; the prophets predicting events, and the evangelists recording them; the doctrinal yet didactic epistolary writers, and he who closed the sacred canon in the apocalyptic vision;—all these furnished their respective portions, and yet all tally with a dovetailed correspondence: all the different materials are joined with a completeness the most satisfactory, with an agreement the most incontrovertible.

This instance of uniformity without design, of agreement without contrivance; this consistency maintained through a long series of ages, without a possibility of the ordinary methods for conducting such a plan; these unparalleled congruities, these unexampled coincidences—form altogether a species of evidence, of which there is no other instance in the history of all the other books in the world.

Our Divine Teacher does not say Read, but Search the Scriptures. The doctrines of the Bible are of everlasting interest. All the great objects of history lose their value, as through the lapse of time they recede further from us; but those of the book of God are commensurate with the immortality of our nature. All existing circumstances, as they relate to this world merely, lose their importance as they lose their novelty; they even melt in air, as they pass before us.

remission of our transgressions, we must not desire the remission of our duties. Let us seek for such a Savior as will not only deliver us from the punishment of sin, but from the domination also.

The "Arabian Nights" and other Oriental books of fable, though loose and faulty in many respects, yet have always a reference to the religion of the country. Nothing is introduced against the law of Mahomet; nothing subversive of the opinions of a Mussulman. I do not quarrel with books for having no religion, but for having a false religion. A book which in nothing opposes the principles of the Bible I would be far from calling a bad book, though the Bible was never named in it.

It is not sufficient to avoid reading pernicious books, care should be taken to prevent their circulation. This duty, however, it is to be feared, is too little regarded even by those who are sincere in religious profession.

When the French Revolution had brought to light the fatal consequences of some of Voltaire's writings, some half-scrupulous persons, no longer willing to afford his fourscore volumes a place in their library, sold them at a low price. This measure, though it "stayed the plague" in their own houses, caused the infection to spread wider. The Ephesian magicians made no such compromise; they burned theirs.

We have too many elementary books. They are read too much and too long. The youthful mind, which was formerly sick from inanition, is now in danger from a plethora. Much, however, will depend on capacity and disposition. A child of slower parts may be indulged till nine years old with books which a lively genius will look down upon at seven. A girl of talents will read. To her, no excitement is wanting. The natural appetite is a sufficient incentive. The less brilliant child requires the allurement of lighter books. She wants encouragement as much as the other requires restraint.

Complete.

CALAMITIES

MOST of the calamities of human life originate with ourselves. Even sickness, shame, pain, and death were not originally the infliction of God. But out of many evils, whether sent us by his immediate hand, or brought on us by our own faults, much eventual good is educed by him who, by turning our suffering to our benefit, repairs by grace the evils produced by sin. Without being the author of evil, the bare suggestion of which is blasphemy, he converts it to his own glory, by causing the effects of it to promote our good. If the virtuous suffer from the crimes of the wicked, it is because their imperfect goodness stood in need of chastisement. Even the wicked, who are suffering by their own sins, or the sins of each other, are sometimes brought back to God by mutual injuries, the sense of which awakens them to compunction for their own offenses. God makes use of the faults even of good men to show them their own insufficiency, to abase them in their own eyes, to cure them of vanity and self-dependence. He makes use of their smaller failings to set them on the watch against great ones; of their imperfections, to put them on their guard against sins; of their faults of inadvertence, to increase their dread of such as are willful. This superinduced vigilance teaches them to fear all the resemblances, and to shun all the approaches to sin. It is a salutary fear, which keeps them from using all the liberty they have; it leads them to avoid, not only whatever is decidedly wrong, but to stop short of what is doubtful, to keep clear of what is suspicious; well knowing the thin partitions which separate danger from destruction. It teaches them to watch the buddings and germinations of evil, to anticipate the pernicious fruit in the opening blossom.

As no calamity is too great for the power of Christianity to mitigate, so none is too small to experience its beneficial results.

Complete.

CHRISTIANITY

CHRISTIANITY is not merely a religion of authority; the soundest reason embraces most confidently what the most explicit revelation has taught, and the deepest inquirer is usually the most convinced Christian. The reason of philosophy is a disputing reason, that of Christianity an obeying reason. The glory of the pagan religion consisted in virtuous sentiments; the glory of the Christian in the pardon and the subjugation of sin. The humble Christian may say with one of the ancient fathers, "I will not glory because I am righteous, but because I am redeemed."

EDUCATION

WE OFTEN hear of the necessity of being qualified for the world; and this is the grand object in the education of our children, overlooking the difficult duty of qualifying them for retirement. But if part of the immense pains which are taken to fit them for the company of others were employed in fitting them for their own company, in teaching them the duties of solitude as well as of society, this earth would be a happier place than it is; a training suitable to a world of such brief duration would be a better preparatory study for a world which will have no end.

VIII—189

Complete.

Christianity has no by-laws, no particular exemptions, no individual immunities. That there is no appropriate way of attaining salvation for a prince or a philosopher is probably one reason why greatness and wisdom have so often rejected it. But if rank cannot plead its privileges, genius cannot claim its distinctions. That Christianity did not owe its success to the arts of rhetoric, or the sophistry of the schools, but that God intended by it "to make foolish the wisdom of this world," actually explains why the "disputers of this world" have always been its enemies.

Christianity was a second creation. It completed the first order of things, and introduced a new one of its own, not subversive, but perfective of the original. It produced an entire revolution in the condition of men, and accomplished a change in the state of the world, which all its confederated power, wit, and philosophy, not only could not effect, but could not even conceive. It threw such a preponderating weight into the scale of morals, by the superinduction of the new principle of faith in a Redeemer, as rendered the hitherto insupportable trials of the afflicted comparatively light. It gave strength to weakness, spirit to action, motive to virtue, certainty to doubt, patience to suffering, light to darkness, life to death.

Complete.

DUTY

BUSINESS must have its period as well as devotion. We were sent into this world to act as well as to pray; active duties must be performed as well as devout exercises. Even relaxation must have its interval: only let us be careful that the indulgence of the one does not destroy the effect of the other; that our pleasures do not encroach on the time, or deaden the spirit of our devotions; let us be careful that our cares, occupations, and amusements, may be always such that we may not be afraid to implore the divine blessings on them; this is the criterion of their safety, and of our duty. Let us endeavor that in each, in all, one continually growing sentiment and feeling of loving, serving, and pleasing God maintain its predominant station in the heart.

Complete.

SIR THOMAS MORE

(1478-1535)

SIR THOMAS MORE, one of the best men and best writers of his age, was born in London, February 7th, 1478. He was the son of Sir John More, a London barrister; but his education was influenced perhaps more by Thomas Morton, Archbishop of Canterbury, than by his father. He entered the Archbishop's service at the age of thirteen, and, after studying at Oxford, thought seriously of becoming a monk. Changing his mind, he devoted himself to politics, entering Parliament in 1504 and increasing in reputation until 1518, when he was made Master of Bequests and Privy Councilor to Henry VIII. That arbitrary despot knighted him, and promoted him from one position to another, until on October 25th, 1829, he succeeded Wolsey as Chancellor. After six years of this precarious greatness, he was decapitated on Tower Hill (July 6th, 1535) for refusing to coincide in the matrimonial and theological views of his master. More was the friend of Erasmus and the opponent of Luther's innovations. He is credited with suggesting to Henry VIII. the defense of the Papacy which won for English royalty the title of "Defender of the Faith" it has not yet abandoned. He wrote dialogues, epigrams, meditations, and controversial treatises, but the work by which he will always be remembered is his "Utopia,"—a semi-romantic treatise, dealing with what he looked upon as the ideal commonwealth.

OF THEIR TRADES AND MANNER OF LIFE IN UTOPIA

AGRICULTURE is that which is so universally understood among them that no person, either man or woman, is ignorant of it; they are instructed in it from their childhood, partly by what they learn at school, and partly by practice, they being led out often into the fields about the town, where they not only see others at work, but are likewise exercised in it themselves. Besides agriculture, which is so common to them all, every man has some peculiar trade to which he applies himself; such as the manufacture of wool or flax, masonry, smith's work, or carpenter's work; for there is no sort of trade that is in great esteem among them. Throughout the island they wear the same sort of clothes, without any other distinction except what is necessary to distinguish the two sexes and the married and unmarried. The fashion never alters, and as it is neither disagreeable nor uneasy, so it is suited to the climate, and calculated both for their summers and winters. Every family makes their own clothes; but all among them, women as well as men, learn one or other of the trades formerly mentioned. Women, for the most part, deal in wool and flax, which suit best with their weakness, leaving the ruder trades to the men. The same trade generally passes down from father to son, inclinations often following descent; but if any man's genius lies another way, he is, by adoption, translated into a family that deals in the trade to which he is inclined, and when that is to be done, care is taken, not only by his father, but by the magistrate, that he may be put to a discreet and good man; and if, after a person has learned one trade, he desires to acquire another, that is also allowed, and is managed in the same manner as the former. When he has learned both, he follows that which he likes best, unless the public has more occasion for the other.

The chief, and almost the only, business of the Syphogrants is to take care that no man may live idle, but that every one may follow his trade diligently; yet they do not wear themselves out with perpetual toil from morning to night, as if they were beasts of burden, which as it is, indeed, a heavy slavery, so it is everywhere the common course of life amongst all mechanics except the Utopians: but they, dividing the day and night into twenty-four hours, appoint six of these for work, three of which are before dinner and three after; they then sup, and at eight o'clock, counting from noon, go to bed and sleep eight hours: the rest of their time, besides that taken up in work, eating, and sleeping, is left to every man's discretion; yet they are not to abuse that interval to luxury and idleness, but must employ it in some proper exercise, according to their various inclinations, which is, for the most part, reading. It is ordinary to have public lectures every morning before daybreak, at which none are obliged to appear but those who are marked out for literature; yet a great many, both men and women, of all ranks, go to hear lectures of one sort or other, according to their inclinations. But if others that are not made for contemplation, choose rather to employ themselves at that time in their trades, as many of them do, they are not hindered, but are rather commended, as men that

take care to serve their country. After supper they spend an hour in some diversion, in summer in their gardens, and in winter in the halls where they eat, where they entertain each other either with music or discourse. They do not so much as know dice, or any such foolish and mischievous games. They have, however, two sorts of games not unlike our chess: the one is between several numbers, in which one number, as it were, consumes another; the other resembles a battle between the virtues and the vices, in which the enmity in the vices among themselves, and their agreement against virtue, is not unpleasantly represented, together with the special opposition between the particular virtues and vices, as also the methods by which vice either openly assaults or secretly undermines virtue; and virtue, on the other hand, resists it. But the time appointed for labor is to be narrowly examined, otherwise you may imagine that since there are only six hours appointed for work, they may fall under a scarcity of necessary provisions: but it is so far from being true that this time is not sufficient for supplying them with plenty of all things, either necessary or convenient, that it is rather too much; and this you will easily apprehend if you consider how great a part of all other nations is quite idle. First, women generally do little, who are the half of mankind; and if some few women are diligent, their husbands are idle: then consider the great company of idle priests, and of those that are called religious men; add to these all rich men, chiefly those that have estates in land, who are called noblemen and gentlemen, together with their families, made up of idle persons, that are kept more for show than use; add to these all those strong and lusty beggars that go about pretending some disease in excuse for their begging; and upon the whole account you will find that the number of those by whose labors mankind is supplied is much less than you perhaps imagined: then consider how few of those that work are employed in labors that are of real service, for we, who measure all things by money, give rise to many trades that are both vain and superfluous, and serve only to support riot and luxury: for if those who work were employed only in such things as the conveniences of life require, there would be such an abundance of them that the prices of them would so sink that tradesmen could not be maintained by their gains; if all those who labor about useless things were set to more profitable employments, and if all they that languish out their lives in sloth and idleness (every one of whom

consumes as much as any two of the men that are at work) were forced to labor, you may easily imagine that a small proportion of time would serve for doing all that is either necessary, profitable, or pleasant to mankind, especially while pleasure is kept within its due bounds: this appears very plainly in Utopia; for there, in a great city, and in all the territory that lies round it, you can scarce find five hundred, either men or women, by their age and strength capable of labor, that are not engaged in it. Even the Syphogrants, though excused by the law, yet do not excuse themselves, but work, that by their examples they may excite the industry of the rest of the people; the like exemption is allowed to those who, being recommended to the people by the priests, are, by the secret suffrages of the Syphogrants, privileged from labor, that they may apply themselves wholly to study; and if any of these fall short of those hopes that they seemed at first to give, they are obliged to return to work; and sometimes a mechanic that so employs his leisure hours as to make a considerable advancement in learning is eased from being a tradesman and ranked among their learned men. Out of these they choose their embassadors, their priests, their Tranibors, and the Prince himself, anciently called their Barzenes, but is called of late their Ademus.

And thus from the great numbers among them that are neither suffered to be idle nor to be employed in any fruitless labor, you may easily make the estimate how much may be done in those few hours in which they are obliged to labor. But besides all that has been already said, it is to be considered that the needful arts among them are managed with less labor than anywhere else. The building or the repairing of houses among us employs many hands, because often a thriftless heir suffers a house that his father built to fall into decay, so that his successor must, at a great cost, repair that which he might have kept up with a small charge; it frequently happens that the same house which one person built at a vast expense is neglected by another, who thinks he has a more delicate sense of the beauties of architecture, and he, suffering it to fall to ruin, builds another at no less charge. But among the Utopians all things are so regulated that men very seldom build upon a new piece of ground, and are not only very quick in repairing their houses, but show their foresight in preventing their decay, so that their buildings are preserved very long with but very little labor, and thus the

builders, to whom that care belongs, are often without employment, except the hewing of timber and the squaring of stones, that the materials may be in readiness for raising a building very suddenly where there is any occasion for it. As to their clothes, observe how little work is spent on them; while they are at labor they are clothed with leather and skins, cast carelessly about them, which will last seven years, and when they appear in public they put on an upper garment which hides the other; and these are all of one color, and that is the natural color of the wool. As they need less woolen cloth than is used anywhere else, so that which they make use of is much less costly; they use linen cloth more, but that is prepared with less labor, and they value cloth only by the whiteness of the linen or the cleanness of the wool, without much regard to the fineness of the thread. While in other places four or five upper garments of woolen cloth of different colors, and as many vests of silk, will scarce serve one man, and while those that are nicer think ten too few, every man there is content with one, which very often serves him two years; nor is there anything that can tempt a man to desire more, for if he had them he would neither be the warmer nor would he make one jot the better appearance for it. And thus, since they are all employed in some useful labor, and since they content themselves with fewer things, it falls out that there is a great abundance of all things among them; so that it frequently happens that, for want of other work, vast numbers are sent out to mend the highways; but when no public undertaking is to be performed, the hours of working are lessened. The magistrates never engage the people in unnecessary labor, since the chief end of the constitution is to regulate labor by the necessities of the public, and to allow the people as much time as is necessary for the improvement of their minds, in which they think the happiness of life consists.

From Morley's text.

JOHN MORLEY

(1838–)

JOHN MORLEY, one of the leading English prose writers of the last quarter of the nineteenth century, was born in Lancashire, England, December 24th, 1838. He was graduated from Oxford in 1859 and called to the bar in the same year, but his life has been devoted chiefly to literature, diversified by politics. He has been editor of the Fortnightly, of the Pall Mall Gazette, and of Macmillan's Magazine, as well as of various "series" of sketches and biographies of celebrated men. Among his own best-known works are biographies or character studies of Machiavelli, Cobden, Voltaire, Rousseau, Emerson, and Diderot. Since 1883 he has been a member of Parliament and one of the chief props of the Liberal party.

GEORGE ELIOT AND HER TIMES

THE period of George Eliot's productions was from 1856, the date of her first stories, down to 1876, when she wrote, not under her brightest star, her last novel of "Daniel Deronda." During this time the great literary influences of the epoch immediately preceding had not, indeed, fallen silent, but the most fruitful seed had been sown. Carlyle's "Sartor Resartus" (1833–34), and his "Miscellaneous Essays" (collected 1839), were in all hands; but he had fallen into the terrible slough of his Prussian history (1858–65), and the last word of his evangel had gone forth to all whom it concerned. "In Memoriam," whose noble music and deep-browed thought awoke such new and wide response in men's hearts, was published in 1850. The second volume of "Modern Painters," of which I have heard George Eliot say, as of "In Memoriam" too, that she owed much and very much to it, belongs to an earlier date still (1846), and when it appeared, though George Eliot was born in the same year as its author, she was still translating Strauss at Coventry. Mr. Browning, for whose genius she had such admiration, and who was always so good a friend, did indeed produce during this period some work which

the adepts find as full of power and beauty as any that ever came from his pen. But Mr. Browning's genius has moved rather apart from the general currents of his time, creating character and working out motives from within, undisturbed by transient shadows from the passing questions and answers of the day.

The romantic movement was then upon its fall. The great Oxford movement, which besides its purely ecclesiastical effects, had linked English religion once more to human history, and which was itself one of the unexpected outcomes of the romantic movement, had spent its original force, and no longer interested the stronger minds among the rising generation. The hour had sounded for the scientific movement. In 1859 was published the "Origin of Species," undoubtedly the most far-reaching agency of the time, supported, as it was, by a volume of new knowledge which came pouring in from many sides. The same period saw the important speculations of Mr. Spencer, whose influence on George Eliot had from their first acquaintance been of a very decisive kind. Two years after the "Origin of Species" came Maine's "Ancient Law," and that was followed by the accumulations of Mr. Tylor and others, exhibiting order and fixed correlation among great sets of facts which had hitherto lain in that cheerful chaos of general knowledge which has been called general ignorance. The excitement was immense. Evolution, development, heredity, adaptation, variety, survival, natural selection, were so many patent pass-keys that were to open every chamber.

George Eliot's novels, as they were the imaginative application of this great influx of new ideas, so they fitted in with the moods which those ideas had called up. "My function," she said "is that of the æsthetic, not the doctrinal teacher — the rousing of the nobler emotions which make mankind desire the social right, not the prescribing of special measures, concerning which the artistic mind, however strongly moved by social sympathy, is often not the best judge." Her influence in this direction over serious and impressionable minds was great indeed. The spirit of her art exactly harmonized with the new thoughts that were shaking the world of her contemporaries. Other artists had drawn their pictures with a strong ethical background, but she gave a finer color and a more spacious air to her ethics, by showing the individual passions and emotions of her characters, their adventures and their fortunes, as evolving themselves from long series of antecedent causes, and bound up with many widely operating forces and dis-

tant events. Here, too, we find ourselves in the full stream of evolution, hereditary, survival, and fixed inexorable law.

This scientific quality of her work may be considered to have stood in the way of her own aim. That the nobler emotions roused by her writings tend to "make mankind desire the social right" is not to be doubted; that we are not sure that she imparts peculiar energy to the desire. What she kindles is not a very strenuous, aggressive, and operative desire. The sense of the iron limitations that are set to improvement in present and future by inexorable forces of the past is stronger in her than any intrepid resolution to press on to whatever improvement may chance to be within reach if we only make the attempt. In energy, in inspiration, in the kindling of living faith in social effort, George Sand, not to speak of Mazzini, takes a far higher place.

It was certainly not the business of an artist to form judgments in the sphere of practical politics, but George Eliot was of far too humane a nature not to be deeply moved by momentous events as they passed. Yet her observations, at any rate after 1848, seldom show that energy of sympathy of which we have been speaking, and these observations illustrate our point. We can hardly think that anything was ever said about the great Civil War in America, so curiously far-fetched as the following reflection: "My best consolation is that an example on so tremendous a scale of the need for the education of mankind through the affections and sentiments as a basis for true development will have a strong influence on all thinkers, and be a check to the arid narrow antagonism which in some quarters is held to be the only form of liberal thought."

In 1848, as we have said, she felt the hopes of the hour in all their fullness. To a friend she writes:—

"You and Carlyle (Have you seen his article in last week's Examiner?) are the only two people who feel just as I would have them — who can glory in what is actually great and beautiful, without putting forth any cold reservations and incredulities to save their credit for wisdom. I am all the more delighted with your enthusiasm because I didn't expect it. I feared that you lacked revolutionary ardor. But no — you are just as *sans-culottish* and rash as I would have you. You are not one of those sages whose reason keeps so tight a rein on their emotions that they are too constantly occupied in calculating consequences to rejoice

in any great manifestation of the forces that underlie our everyday existence.

"I thought we had fallen on such evil days that we were to see no really great movement — that ours was what St. Simon calls a purely critical epoch, not at all an organic one; but I begin to be glad of my date. I would consent, however, to have a year clipped off my life for the sake of witnessing such a scene as that of the men of the barricades bowing to the image of Christ, 'who first taught fraternity to men.' One trembles to look into every fresh newspaper lest there should be something to mar the picture; but hitherto even the scoffing newspaper critics have been compelled into a tone of genuine respect for the French people and the Provisional Government. Lamartine can act a poem, if he cannot write one of the very first order. I hope that beautiful face given to him in the pictorial newspaper is really his; it is worthy of an aureole. I have little patience with people who can find time to pity Louis Philippe and his moustachioed sons. Certainly our decayed monarchs should be pensioned off: we should have a hospital for them, or a sort of zoölogical garden, where these worn-out humbugs may be preserved. It is but justice that we should keep them, since we have spoiled them for any honest trade. Let them sit on soft cushions, and have their dinner regularly, but, for heaven's sake, preserve me from sentimentalizing over pampered old man, when the earth has its millions of unfed souls and bodies. Surely he is not so Ahab-like as to wish that the revolution had been deferred till his son's days; and I think the shades of the Stuarts would have some reason to complain if the Bourbons, who are so little better than they had been allowed to reign much longer."

The hopes of '48 were not very accurately fulfilled, and in George Eliot they never came to life again. Yet in social things we may be sure that undying hope is the secret of vision.

There is a passage in Coleridge's "Friend," which seems to represent the outcome of George Eliot's teaching on most, and not the worst, of her readers: "The tangle of delusions," says Coleridge, "which stifled and distorted the growing tree of our well-being has been torn away; the parasite weeds that fed on its very roots have been plucked up with a salutary violence. To us there remain only quiet duties, the constant care, the gradual improvement, the cautious and unhazardous labors of the industrious though contented gardener — to prune, to strengthen, to engraft, and one by one to remove from its leaves and fresh shoots the slug and the caterpillar." Coleridge goes further than George Eliot, when he adds the exhortation, " Far be it from us to undervalue with light and senseless detraction the conscientious hardihood of our predecessors, or even to condemn in them that vehemence to which the blessings it won for us leave us now neither temptation nor pretext."

George Eliot disliked vehemence more and more as her work advanced. The word "crudity," so frequently on her lips, stood for all that was objectionable and distasteful. The conservatism of an artistic moral nature was shocked by the seeming peril to which priceless moral elements of human character were exposed by the energumens of progress. Their impatient hopes for the present appeared to her rather unscientific; their disregard of the past, very irreverent and impious. Mill had the same feeling when he disgusted his father by standing up for Wordsworth, on the ground that Wordsworth was helping to keep alive in human nature elements which utilitarians and innovators would need when their present and particular work was done. Mill, being free from the exaltations that make the artist, kept a truer balance. His famous pair of essays on " Bentham " and " Coleridge " were published (for the first time, so far as our generation was concerned) in the same year as "Adam Bede," and I can vividly remember how the " Coleridge " first awoke in many of us, who were then youths at Oxford, that sense of truth having many mansions, and that desire and power of sympathy with the past, with the positive bases of the social fabric, and with the value of Permanence in States, which form the reputable side of all conservatisms. This sentiment and conviction never took richer or more mature form than in the best work of George Eliot, and her stories lighted up with a fervid glow the truths that minds of another type had just brought to the surface. It was this that made her a great moral force at that epoch, especially for all who were capable by intellectual training of standing at her point of view. We even, as I have said, tried hard to love her poetry, but the effort has ended less in love than in a very distant homage to the majestic in intention and the sonorous in execution. In fiction, too, as the years go by, we begin to crave more fancy, illusion, enchantment, than the quality of her genius allowed. But the loftiness of her character is abiding, and it

passes nobly through the ordeal of an honest biography. " For the lessons," says the fine critic already quoted, " most imperatively needed by the mass of men, the lessons of deliberate kindness, of careful truth, of unwavering endeavor, — for these plain themes one could not ask a more convincing teacher than she whom we are commemorating now. Everything in her aspect and presence was in keeping with the bent of her soul. The deeply-lined face, the too marked and massive features, were united with an air of delicate refinement, which in one way was the more impressive because it seemed to proceed so entirely from within. Nay, the inward beauty would sometimes quite transform the external harshness; there would be moments when the thin hands that entwined themselves in their eagerness, the earnest figure that bowed forward to speak and hear, the deep gaze moving from one face to another with a grave appeal, — all these seemed the transparent symbols that showed the presence of a wise, benignant soul." As a wise, benignant soul, George Eliot will still remain for all right-judging men and women.

From a review of " George Eliot's Life,"
by J. W. Cross.

WILLIAM MORRIS

(1834-1896)

WILLIAM MORRIS, author of " The Earthly Paradise " and of numerous prose studies and essays, was born near London in 1834, and educated at Oxford University. There he met Burne-Jones, and through intimacy with him became one of the chief factors in the æsthetic movement which so greatly influenced England during the last quarter of the nineteenth century. Morris had hopes of re-creating society through his ideals of order and beauty, and he unquestionably did much to improve typography and decorating in general through work done under his direction. " The Earthly Paradise " is a poem conceived on an elevated plane, and it lacks nothing of the first rank in its class, save sustained musical expression. He wrote other poems of merit, and his essays, collected under the title of " Hopes and Fears for Art," are admirable examples of the best English prose. He died at Hammersmith near London, October 3d, 1896.

THE BEAUTY OF LIFE

WHEN you hear of the luxuries of the Ancients, you must remember that they were not like our luxuries, they were rather indulgence in pieces of extravagant folly than what we to-day call luxury, — which perhaps you would rather call comfort; well, I accept the word, and say that a Greek or a Roman of the luxurious time would stare astonished could he be brought back again and shown the comforts of a well-to-do middle-class house.

But some, I know, think that the attainment of these very comforts is what makes the difference between civilization and uncivilization, — that they are the essence of civilization. Is it so indeed? Farewell my hope then! — I had thought that civilization meant the attainment of peace and order and freedom, of good-will between man and man, of the love of truth, and the hatred of injustice, and by consequence the attainment of the good life which these things breed, a life free from craven fear,

but full of incident; that was what I thought it meant, not more stuffed chairs and more cushions, and more carpets and gas, and more dainty meat and drink — and therewithal more and sharper differences between class and class.

If that be what it is, I for my part wish I were well out of it, and living in a tent in the Persian desert, or a turf hut on the Iceland hillside. But however it be, and I think my view is the true view, I tell you that art abhors that side of civilization; she cannot breath in the houses that lie under its stuffy slavery.

Believe me if we want art to begin at home, as it must, we must clear our houses of troublesome superfluities that are forever in our way; conventional comforts that are no real comforts, and do but make work for servants and doctors. If you want a golden rule that will fit everybody, this is it: " Have nothing in your houses that you do not know to be useful, or believe to be beautiful."

And if we apply that rule strictly, we shall in the first place show the builders and such-like servants of the public what we really want. We shall create a demand for real art, as the phrase goes; and in the second place, we shall surely have more money to pay for decent houses.

Perhaps it will not try your patience too much if I lay before you my idea of the fittings necessary to the sitting room of a healthy person; a room, I mean, which he would not have to cook in much, or sleep in generally, or in which he would not have to do any very litter-making manual work.

First, a bookcase with a great many books in it; next a table that will keep steady when you write or work at it; then several chairs that you can move, and a bench that you can sit or lie upon; next a cupboard with drawers; next, unless either the bookcase or the cupboard be very beautiful with painting or carving, you will want pictures or engravings, such as you can afford, only not stop-gaps, but real works of art on the wall; or else the wall itself must be ornamented with some beautiful and restful pattern; we shall also want a vase or two to put flowers in, which latter you must have sometimes, especially if you live in a town. Then there will be the fireplace, of course, which in our climate is bound to be the chief object in the room.

That is all we shall want, especially if the floor be good; if it be not, as, by the way, in a modern house it is pretty certain not to be, I admit that a small carpet which can be bundled out of the room in two minutes will be useful, and we must also take care that it is beautiful, or it will annoy us terribly.

Now, unless we are musical, and need a piano (in which case, as far as beauty is concerned, we are in a bad way), that is quite all we want; and we can add very little to these necessaries without troubling ourselves, and hindering our work, our thought, and our rest.

If these things were done at the least cost for which they could be done well and solidly, they ought not to cost much; and they are so few, that those that could afford to have them at all could afford to spend some trouble to get them fitting and beautiful; and all those who care about art ought to take trouble to do so, and to take care that there be no sham art amongst them, nothing that it has degraded a man to make or to sell. And I feel sure, that if all who care about art were to take this pains, it would make a great impression upon the public.

This simplicity you may make as costly as you please or can, on the other hand; you may hang your walls with tapestry in stead of whitewash or paper; or you may cover them with mosaic, or have them frescoed by a great painter; all this is not luxury, if it be done for beauty's sake, and not for show; it does not break our golden rule: "Have nothing in your houses which you do not know to be useful or believe to be beautiful."

All art starts from this simplicity; and the higher the art rises, the greater the simplicity. I have been speaking of the fittings of a dwelling house,—a place in which we eat and drink, and pass familiar hours; but when you come to places which people want to make more specially beautiful because of the solemnity or dignity of their uses, they will be simpler still, and have little in them save the bare walls made as beautiful as they may be. St. Mark's at Venice has very little furniture in it, much less than most Roman Catholic churches; its lovely and stately mother, St. Sophia of Constantinople, had less still, even when it was a Christian church; but we need not go either to Venice or Stamboul to take note of that; go into one of our own mighty Gothic naves (do any of you remember the first time you did so?) and note how the huge free space satisfies and elevates you, even now when window and wall are stripped of ornament; then think of the meaning of simplicity, and absence of encumbering gewgaws.

Now, after all, for us who are learning art, it is not far to seek what is the surest way to further it; that which most breeds art is art; every piece of work that we do which is well done is so much help to the cause; every piece of pretense and half-heartedness is so much hurt to it; most of you who take to the practice of art can find out in no very long time whether you have any gifts for it or not: if you have not, throw the thing up, or you will have a wretched time of it yourselves, and will be damaging the cause by laborious pretense; but if you have gifts of any kind you are happy, indeed, beyond most men, for your pleasure is always with you, nor can you be intemperate in the enjoyment of it; and as you use it, it does not lessen, but grows; if you are by chance weary of it at night, you get up in the morning eager for it; or if perhaps in the morning it seems folly to you for awhile, yet presently, when your hand has been moving a little in its wonted way, fresh hope has sprung up beneath it and you are happy again. While others are getting through the day like plants thrust into the earth, which cannot turn this way or that but as the wind blows them, you know what you want, and your will is on the alert to find it, and you, whatever happens, whether it be joy or grief, are at least alive.

From "Hopes and Fears for Art."

JOHN LOTHROP MOTLEY

(1814–1877)

JOHN LOTHROP MOTLEY, the historian of the Dutch Republic, was born in Dorchester, Massachusetts, April 15th, 1814. He studied at Harvard, Berlin, and Göttingen, and began life as an attorney. His mind was soon diverted, however, to his true vocation,—that of the historian. The best faculties of his intellect and the best years of his life were given to the painstaking study of history, the result being "Rise of the Dutch Republic" (1856), "History of the United Netherlands" (1860–68), and "Life and Death of John of Barneveld" (1874),—works which fixed his place in the front rank of the prose writers of the nineteenth century. From 1861 to 1867 he was United States Minister to Austria, and to Great Britain from 1869 to 1870. He died in Dorset, England, May 29th, 1877.

WILLIAM THE SILENT

IN PERSON, Orange was above the middle height, perfectly well made and sinewy, but rather spare than stout. His eyes, hair, beard, and complexion were brown. His head was small, symmetrically shaped, combining the alertness and compactness characteristic of the soldier, with the capacious brow furrowed prematurely with the horizontal lines of thought, denoting the statesman and the sage. His physical appearance was, therefore, in harmony with his organization, which was of antique model. Of his moral qualities, the most prominent was his piety. He was more than anything else a religious man. From his trust in God, he ever derived support and consolation in the darkest hours. Implicitly relying upon Almighty wisdom and goodness, he looked danger in the face with a constant smile, and endured incessant labors and trials with a serenity which seemed more than human. While, however, his soul was full of piety, it was tolerant of error. Sincerely and deliberately himself a convert to the Reformed Church, he was ready to extend freedom of worship to Catholics on the one hand and to Anabaptists on the other, for no man ever felt more keenly than he

that the reformer who becomes in his turn a bigot is doubly odious.

His firmness was allied to his piety. His constancy in bearing the whole weight of struggle as unequal as men have ever undertaken was the theme of admiration even to his enemies. The rock in the ocean, "tranquil amid raging billows," was the favorite emblem by which his friends expressed their sense of his firmness. From the time when, as a hostage in France, he first discovered the plan of Philip to plant the Inquisition in the Netherlands, up to the last moment of his life, he never faltered in his determination to resist that iniquitous scheme. This resistance was the labor of his life. To exclude the Inquisition, to maintain the ancient liberties of his country, was the task which he appointed to himself when a youth of three-and-twenty. Never speaking a word concerning a heavenly mission, never deluding himself or others with the usual phraseology of enthusiasts, he accomplished the task through danger, amid toils, and with sacrifices such as few men have ever been able to make on their country's altar;—for the disinterested benevolence of the man was as prominent as his fortitude. A prince of high rank and with royal revenues, he stripped himself of station, wealth, almost at times of the common necessaries of life, and became, in his country's cause, nearly a beggar as well as an outlaw. Nor was he forced into his career by an accidental impulse from which there was no recovery. Retreat was ever open to him. Not only pardon, but advancement, was urged upon him again and again. Officially and privately, directly and circuitously, his confiscated estates, together with indefinite and boundless favors in addition, were offered to him on every great occasion. On the arrival of Don John, at the Breda negotiations, at the Cologne conferences, we have seen how calmly these offers were waved aside, as if their rejection was so simple that it hardly required many words for its signification, yet he had mortgaged his estates so deeply that his heirs hesitated at accepting their inheritance, for fear it should involve them in debt. Ten years after his death, the account between his executors and his brother John amounted to one million four hundred thousand florins due to the count, secured by various pledges of real and personal property, and it was finally settled upon this basis. He was besides largely indebted to every one of his powerful relatives, so that the payment of the incumbrances upon his estate very nearly justified the fears of his children. While on the one hand, therefore, he poured out these enormous sums like water, and firmly refused a hearing to the tempting offers of the royal government, upon the other hand he proved the disinterested nature of his services by declining, year after year, the sovereignty over the provinces; and by only accepting, in the last days of his life, when refusal had become almost impossible, the limited, constitutional supremacy over that portion of them which now makes the realm of his decendants. He lived and died, not for himself, but for his country: "God pity this poor people!" were his dying words.

His intellectual faculties were various and of the highest order. He had the exact, practical, and combining qualities which make the great commander, and his friends claimed that, in military genius, he was second to no captain in Europe. This was, no doubt, an exaggeration of partial attachment, but it is certain that the Emperor Charles had an exalted opinion of his capacity for the field. His fortification of Philippeville and Charlemont, in the face of the enemy—his passage of the Meuse in Alva's sight—his unfortunate but well-ordered campaign against that general—his sublime plan of relief, projected and successfully directed at last from his sick bed, for the besieged city of Leyden—will always remain monuments of his practical military skill.

Of the soldier's great virtues—constancy in disaster, devotion to duty, hopefulness in defeat—no man ever possessed a larger share. He arrived, through a series of reverses, at a perfect victory. He planted a free commonwealth under the very battery of the Inquisition, in defiance of the most powerful empire existing. He was therefore a conqueror in the loftiest sense, for he conquered liberty and a national existence for a whole people. The contest was long, and he fell in the struggle, but the victory was to the dead hero, not to the living monarch. It is to be remembered, too, that he always wrought with inferior instruments. His troops were usually mercenaries, who were but too apt to mutiny upon the eve of battle, while he was opposed by the most formidable veterans of Europe, commanded successively by the first captains of the age. That, with no lieutenant of eminent valor or experience, save only his brother, Louis, and with none at all after that chieftain's death, William of Orange should succeed in baffling the efforts of Alva, Requesens, Don John of

Austria, and Alexander Farnese—men whose names are among the most brilliant in the military annals of the world—is in itself sufficient evidence of his warlike ability. At the period of his death he had reduced the number of obedient provinces to two; only Artois and Hainault acknowledging Philip, while the other fifteen were in open revolt, the greater part having solemnly forsworn their sovereign.

The supremacy of his political genius was entirely beyond question. He was the first statesman of the age. The quickness of his perception was only equaled by the caution which enabled him to mature the results of his observations. His knowledge of human nature was profound. He governed the passions and sentiments of a great nation as if they had been but the keys and chords of one vast instrument; and his hand rarely failed to evoke harmony even out of the wildest storms. The turbulent city of Ghent, which could obey no other master, which even the haughty Emperor could only crush without controlling, was ever responsive to the master hand of Orange. His presence scared away Imbize and his bat-like crew confounded the schemes of John Casimir, frustrated the wiles of Prince Chimay, and while he lived Ghent was what it ought always to have remained, the bulwark, as it had been the cradle, of popular liberty. After his death it became its tomb.

Ghent, saved thrice by the policy, the eloquence, the self-sacrifices of Orange, fell within three months of his murder into the hands of Parma. The loss of this most important city, followed in the next year by the downfall of Antwerp, sealed the fate of the Southern Netherlands. Had the Prince lived, how different might have been the country's fate! If seven provinces could dilate, in so brief a space, into the powerful commonwealth which the Republic soon became, what might not have been achieved by the united seventeen—a confederacy which would have united the adamantine vigor of the Batavian and Frisian races with the subtler, more delicate, and more graceful national elements in which the genius of the Frank, the Roman, and the Romanized Celt were so intimately blended? As long as the Father of the country lived, such a union was possible. His power of managing men was so unquestionable, that there was always a hope, even in the darkest hour, for men felt implicit reliance, as well in his intellectual resources as on his integrity.

This power of dealing with his fellowmen he manifested in the various ways in which it has been usually exhibited by statesmen. He possessed a ready eloquence—sometimes impassioned, oftener argumentative, always rational. His influence over his audience was unexampled in the annals of that country or age; yet he never condescended to flatter the people. He never followed the nation, but always led her in the path of duty and of honor, and was much more prone to rebuke the vices than to pander to the passions of his hearers. He never failed to administer ample chastisement to parsimony, to jealousy, to insubordination, to intolerance, to infidelity, wherever it was due, nor feared to confront the states or the people in their most angry hours, and to tell them the truth to their faces. This commanding position he alone could stand upon, for his countrymen knew the generosity which had sacrificed all for them, the self-denial which had eluded rather than sought political advancement, whether from king or people, and the untiring devotion which had consecrated a whole life to toil and danger in the cause of their emancipation. While, therefore, he was ever ready to rebuke, and always too honest to flatter, he at the same time possessed the eloquence which could convince or persuade. He knew how to reach both the mind and the heart of his hearers. His orations, whether extemporaneous or prepared—his written messages to the states-general, to the provincial authorities, to the municipal bodies—his private correspondence with men of all ranks, from emperors and kings down to secretaries, and even children—all show an easy flow of language, a fullness of thought, a power of expression rare in that age, a fund of historical allusion, a considerable power of imagination, a warmth of sentiment, a breadth of view, a directness of purpose—a range of qualities, in short, which would in themselves have stamped him as one of the master minds of his century, had there been no other monument to his memory than the remains of his spoken or written eloquence. The bulk of his performances in this department was prodigious. Not even Philip was more industrious in the cabinet. Not even Granvelle held a more facile pen. He wrote and spoke equally well in French, German, or Flemish; and he possessed, besides, Spanish, Italian, Latin. The weight of his correspondence alone would have almost sufficed for the common industry of a lifetime, and although many volumes of his speeches and letters

have been published, there remain in the various archives of the Netherlands and Germany many documents from his hand which will probably never see the light. If the capacity for unremitted intellectual labor in an honorable cause be the measure of human greatness, few minds could be compared to the "large composition" of this man. The efforts made to destroy the Netherlands by the most laborious and painstaking of tyrants were counteracted by the industry of the most indefatigable of patriots.

Thus his eloquence, oral or written, gave him almost boundless power over his countrymen. He possessed, also, a rare perception of human character, together with an iron memory which never lost a face, a place, or an event, once seen or known. He read the minds, even the faces of men, like printed books. No man could overreach him, excepting only those to whom he gave his heart. He might be mistaken where he had confided, never where he had been distrustful or indifferent. He was deceived by Renneberg, by his brother-in-law, Van den Berg, by the Duke of Anjou. Had it been possible for his brother Louis or his brother John to have proved false, he might have been deceived by them. He was never outwitted by Philip, or Granvelle, or Don John, or Alexander of Parma. Anna of Saxony was false to him, and entered into correspondence with the royal governors and with the King of Spain; Charlotte of Bourbon or Louisa de Coligny might have done the same had it been possible for their natures also to descend to such depths of guile.

As for the Aerschots, the Havres, the Chimays, he was never influenced either by their blandishments or their plots. He was willing to use them when their interest made them friendly, or to crush them when their intrigues against his policy rendered them dangerous. The adroitness with which he converted their schemes in behalf of Matthias, of Don John, of Anjou, into so many additional weapons for his own cause can never be too often studied. It is instructive to observe the wiles of the Machiavelian school employed by a master of the craft, to frustrate, not to advance, a knavish purpose. This character, in a great measure, marked his whole policy. He was profoundly skilled in the subtleties of Italian statesmanship, which he had learned as a youth at the Imperial court, and which he employed in his manhood in the service, not of tyranny, but of liberty. He fought the Inquisition with its own weapons. He dealt with Philip on his own ground. He excavated the earth beneath the

King's feet by a more subtle process than that practiced by the most fraudulent monarch that ever governed the Spanish empire, and Philip, chain-mailed as he was in complicated wiles, was pierced to the quick by a keener policy than his own.

Ten years long the King placed daily his most secret letters in hands which regularly transmitted copies of the correspondence to the Prince of Orange, together with a key to the ciphers and every other illustration which might be required. Thus the secrets of the King were always as well known to Orange as to himself; and the Prince being as prompt as Philip was hesitating, the schemes could often be frustrated before their execution had been commenced. The crime of the unfortunate clerk, John de Castillo, was discovered in the autumn of the year 1651, and he was torn to pieces by four horses. Perhaps his treason to the monarch whose bread he was eating, while he received a regular salary from the King's most determined foe, deserved even this horrible punishment; but casuists must determine how much guilt attaches to the Prince for his share in the transaction. This history is not the eulogy of Orange, although, in discussing his character, it is difficult to avoid the monotony of panegyric. Judged by a severe moral standard, it cannot be called virtuous or honorable to suborn treachery or any other crime, even to accomplish a lofty purpose; yet the universal practice of mankind in all ages has tolerated the artifices of war, and no people has ever engaged in a holier or more mortal contest than did the Netherlands in their great struggle with Spain. Orange possessed the rare quality of caution, a characteristic by which he was distinguished from his youth. At fifteen he was the confidential counselor, as at twenty-one he became the general-in-chief, to the most politic, as well as the most warlike potentate of his age, and if he at times indulged in wiles which modern statesmanship, even while it practices condemns, he ever held in his hand the clew of an honorable purpose to guide him through the tortuous labyrinth.

It is difficult to find any other characteristic deserving of grave censure, but his enemies have adopted a simpler process. They have been able to find few flaws in his nature, and therefore have denounced it in gross. It is not that his character was here and there defective, but that the eternal jewel was false. The patriotism was counterfeit. He was governed only by ambition — by a desire of personal advancement. They never attempted to deny

his talents, his industry, his vast sacrifices of wealth and station; but they ridiculed the idea that he could have been inspired by any but unworthy motives. God alone knows the heart of man. He alone can unweave the tangled skein of human motives, and detect the hidden springs of human action, but as far as can be judged by a careful observation of undisputed facts, and by a diligent collation of public and private documents, it would seem that no man — not even Washington — has ever been inspired by a purer patriotism. At any rate, the charge of ambition and self-seeking can only be answered by a reference to the whole picture which these volumes have attempted to portray. The words, the deeds of the man are there. As much as possible, his inmost soul is revealed in his confidential letters, and he who looks in a right spirit will hardly fail to find what he desires.

Whether originally of a timid temperament or not, he was certainly possessed of perfect courage at last. In siege and battle — in the deadly air of pestilential cities — in the long exhaustion of mind and body which comes from unduly protracted labor and anxiety — amid the countless conspiracies of assassins — he was daily exposed to death in every shape. Within two years, five different attempts against his life had been discovered. Rank and fortune were offered to any malefactor who would compass the murder. He had already been shot through the head, and almost mortally wounded. Under such circumstances even a brave man might have seen a pitfall at every step, a dagger in every hand, and poison in every cup. On the contrary, he was ever cheerful, and hardly took more precaution than usual. " God in his mercy," said he, with unaffected simplicity, " will maintain my innocence and my honor during my life and in future ages. As to my fortune and my life, I have dedicated both, long since, to his service. He will do therewith what pleases him for his glory and my salvation." Thus suspicions were not even excited by the ominous face of Gerard, when he first presented himself at the dining-room door. The Prince laughed off his wife's prophetic apprehension at the sight of his murderer, and was as cheerful as usual to the last.

He possessed, too, that which to the heathen philosopher seemed the greatest good, — the sound mind in the sound body. His physical frame was after death found so perfect that a long life might have been in store for him, notwithstanding all which he

had endured. The desperate illness of 1574, the frightful gunshot wound inflicted by Jaureguy in 1582, had left no traces. The physicians pronounced that his body presented an aspect of perfect health. His temperament was cheerful. At table, the pleasures of which, in moderation, were his only relaxation, he was always animated and merry, and this jocoseness was partly natural, partly intentional. In the darkest hours of his country's trial, he affected a serenity which he was far from feeling, so that his apparent gayety at momentous epochs was even censured by dullards, who could not comprehend its philosophy nor applaud the flippancy of William the Silent.

He went through life bearing the load of a people's sorrows upon his shoulders with a smiling face. Their name was the last word upon his lips, save the simple affirmative with which the soldier who had been battling for the right all his lifetime commended his soul in dying " to his great captain, Christ." The people were grateful and affectionate, for they trusted the character of their " Father William," and not all the clouds which calumny could collect ever dimmed to their eyes the radiance of that lofty mind to which they were accustomed, in their darkest calamities, to look for light. As long as he lived, he was the guiding star of a whole brave nation, and when he died the little children cried in the streets.

From the " Rise of the Dutch Republic."

LOUISE CHANDLER MOULTON

(1835-)

BOTH in her essays and in her poems Mrs. Moulton represents the highest ideals of loveliness of character and purity of thought. Whatever things are pure and of good report and loveworthy through their innate qualities of truth and beauty, attract her and inspire her to expression. The common things of life as she treats them develop a charm of which those who know them best would be least likely to suspect them. Living in an age when to many life seemed worth living only for those who showed themselves capable of the strange, the extraordinary, the surprising, she calmly irradiated her sphere of influence with the white light of her womanly goodness of nature and goodness of intellect. Those who read the essays in " Ourselves and Our Neighbors " will know from them that neither fanaticism nor faddism can cheat the American woman of her future. That usefulness is better than excellence, that sympathy is more nearly divine than superiority, that it is better to be worthy of love than to excite wonder — all this Mrs. Moulton teaches by example in writings full of the genius of womanly sanity. The best women are not the equals but the superiors of the best men, in all the qualities which redeem life from loss and corruption, giving it the heaven which Goethe denies to the highest masculine intellect, except as it is educated by what he calls " the Eternal Feminine." Mrs. Moulton's work is full of that true womanliness which Goethe thought the truest and highest thing in human nature. Her essays will be valued for their truth, simplicity, and grace, long after nine-tenths of the pretentious productions which found temporary favor with the nineteenth century have been swept into the kitchen middens of the twentieth.

YOUNG BEAUX AND OLD BACHELORS

THE line of demarcation between " eligibles " and " detrimentals " is not so sharply drawn in America as in England, for the very good reason that the " detrimental " of this year is quite likely to become the " eligible " of the next. In England a younger son who has no fortune of his own, and who has manifested no remarkable genius in any direction, is considered decidedly a "detrimental." He is an alarming neighbor, at whose approach all wise mammas gather in their pretty daughters as a hen gathers her chickens under her wings, unless, indeed, he be the younger son of a noble house. In that case his good blood and good breeding have a decided market value in certain directions, and the father of many a pretty girl will be glad to pay for them a large part of the fortune he himself has made in brewing or baking.

In America what is most in demand is capacity. Most American fathers value the evident capacity to succeed in business and to make a fortune quite as highly as they do an inherited competence; and the young man who has shown that he can get on and who has already made for himself a place is not regarded as a "detrimental." In the Eastern States, at least, where in Massachusetts alone there are thirty thousand more women than men, the position of a prosperous and unmarried young man is a very pleasant one. He is as welcome everywhere as flowers are in January.

He is a joy forever, whether he is a thing of beauty or not; and if he is handsome and distinguished looking, his life is as surrounded by pleasant things, and he is as much sought and courted as any pretty girl of them all. He is in request for parties, he must lead the german, and beauty wears for him her brightest smiles and her prettiest gowns.

This is his danger. The mocking bird, who sings every other bird's song so well, has no song of its own; and the fine young man who suns himself in so many smiles now and then forgets to choose, and finds himself, before he knows it, getting to be an old beau, with the habit of society upon him and the habit of home unformed. The handsome and prosperous young man in society is perhaps the happiest of human creatures. He is better off than his pretty sister, because he has the privilege of choice, and, like the prince in the fairy story, can say "Come thou along with me" to whomever he will. But I believe that for the young man of society to become an old beau is just as sad a thing as for the prettiest rosebud to feel that she is overblown.

The perception of his lessening social value is longer in coming to him, no doubt; but he sees it, at last, in the inattentive glance that roves beyond him when he comes nigh the beauty of the season; in the occasional omission of his name from a party of young people; even in the greater freedom with which

winning in a double sense of the word. He is full of pleasant surprises for his acquaintances; he gives the most charming of little parties; he takes one friend for a drive; he finds a long-sought book for another; he always manages to do the right thing at the right time. I have even known him to chance to bring the loveliest hothouse flowers to a country dinner party in December, and thus enchant the hostess who was grieving over the nonfulfillment of her own order to a city florist. He has the supreme good fortune to know how to make himself agreeable; and, instead of pitying him because his fireside is lonely, his friends are selfishly a little rejoiced at it because they can, by reason of that loneliness, lure him more frequently to their own.

But I am speaking of a very rare man,—scholar and gentleman, the very pink of courtesy and a fellow of infinite jest. To be all this, and therefore perennially acceptable, would scarcely be so easy of achievement to most men as to marry, and thus secure for themselves a family circle, of which, as Artemus Ward observed, they may be "it, principally."

It must be an exceptionally fine man, or an exceptionally charming and attractive woman, who can pass middle age unmarried and escape that flippant pity, that toleration consciously kind, which wounds while it strives to heal. But the world is gentler to our misfortunes than to our follies; and Dr. Holmes laughed his cynical and yet not ungenial laugh at his maiden aunt, not because her curls were wintry, but because she twined them still "in such a spring-like way." To be a young bachelor in society is to be the king of the hour, and to hold the cup of life to one's lips bubbling with pleasure and beaded with success; to be an old beau — an elderly man about town — is to have drunk off the bubbles, indeed, and to have reached the dregs. But if, instead of an old beau, a man elects to step aside from the ranks of those who wait on woman's favor to be the friend of his peers, the counselor of the young fellows who come after him, the faithful knight in whom all womanhood finds its champion,—to him the world is full of noble uses and serene joys; and if he has missed the keenest bliss of youth, he may possess the noblest serenity of age, and at least rejoice that what he has never won he cannot lose.

Complete. From "Ourselves and Our Neighbors." By permission of Messrs. Little, Brown & Co., Boston, successors to Roberts Brothers. Copyright by Roberts Brothers 1887.

girls are confided to his care, as if he were no longer dangerous. Then is his soul filled with bitterness, and he begins to say to himself that the seasons have grown cold, and his heart is lonely.

Perhaps he honestly tries to fall in love and finds it impossible; and that is a far more pathetic thing than even to love in vain. To have flitted so long from flower to flower, that rose and lily and pink have each an equal charm, and not one can hold his fancy more than another, that is a sad fate for a bee who should long ago have begun to store up honey for his life's winter.

The old beau looks about him and sees his contemporaries buying houses and leading their children by the hand, and he scoffs a little perhaps, and tries to think that he is glad not thus to be bored and burdened. But his laughter is hollow, and when he goes home at night and sits before his lonesome fire, he sees in the firelight glow the long-lost Spanish castle, of which he threw away the key in his youth, and fancies what might have been if youth had but known.

"Is there any moral to that?" asks the sauciest young voice over my shoulder; and I am awake again, for I too had begun to dream.

Yes, my infant, a moral there is. Roses belong to June, and you cannot gather them under the skies of November.

Since I believe a happy domestic life to be this world's best gift, I do not believe that the old beau can have the best of life, unless by some rare chance he find the four-leaved clover of luck and love growing out of season and gather it. But if he is contented to wear his bachelor's button frankly and easily, and take the goods the gods still provide him, he may yet be a very agreeable member of society. The man who at fifty believes himself to be twenty-five is as incongruous and uncomfortable a spectacle as the woman who at forty appears to have forgotten that she is more than eighteen; but there is nothing undignified in the position of the spinster who has frankly accepted her single life, or of the bachelor who takes his middle-aged pleasures cheerfully, and no longer aspires to lead the german or to break hearts. I have one such example in my mind, and with —

"A merrier man,
Within the limits of becoming mirth,
I never spent an hour's talk withal."

He likes his game of whist, and he is a winning and delightful partner to the women who are old enough to play well,—

MOTIVES FOR MARRIAGE

I HAVE been turning over the leaves of an old book, written before I was born, and which was familiar to my childhood, and I have come upon the following extremely sensible remark:—

"What a pity it is that the thousandth chance of a gentleman's becoming your lover should deprive you of the pleasure of a free, unembarrassed, intellectual intercourse with the single men of your acquaintance."

The pity of it is that the Girl of the Period so often has no desire for this unembarrassed and sensible friendship, and values the men she knows only in proportion as they minister to her pleasure or her vanity. And this superficial and unreal valuation prevents her from getting honestly and thoroughly acquainted with any man,—from seeing him as he is seen by his own womankind, or as he would show himself in the stress and strain of real life, with its vital interests and stern realities, when the heydey and playday of youth should be over.

That any other motives should enter into marriage than that noble and well-founded love which can safely promise to be faithful unto death — because to be unfaithful would be as impossible to it as for a mother's heart to turn from her child — is one of the saddest features of our boasted civilization; but we see interested and mercenary marriages every day, and it would be idle to say they were the rare exception. If all girls and all young men could be impressed, not only with the sacredness of marriage, but with a profound sense of its importance in the growth of character, its influence, for good or evil, on their whole natures and their whole careers, they would be less ready to enter into its obligations carelessly, and we should see less of the frivolity of flirtation, the vulgarity of husband seeking.

To my thinking, Love is the most sacred of heaven's gifts, and should be waited for as reverently as the descent of the Holy Ghost. Matrimony may, indeed, be a means of grace, even when it is as unhappy as was the marriage of that pair on whose tombstone, in a New Hampshire churchyard, appreciative neighbors sculptured, for epitaph:—

"Their Warfare Is Over."

but surely matrimony should never be entered into as a means of livelihood. The woman who deliberately marries for money has something to boast over her "unclassed" sisters of the demi-monde in propriety, but little in principle.

Some blunders will, of course, be made in the purest good faith. Plenty of foolish girls will mistake for love their own enjoyment of admiration and pleasure in being loved, and plenty of young men will mistake for something sacred and eternal the transient stir of fancy awakened by a pretty face or a taking manner. If marriages are born of these delusions, the error is to be pitied and not despised; yet from the lifelong penalty of such a blunder can no man or woman hope wholly to escape. Though the best joys of life may thus have been lost, its burdens can still be borne with dignity, while self-respect remains unchallenged. But can that girl respect herself who deliberately, and of set purpose, tries to attract a man simply because he is a good match; or that young man who seeks a girl because through her he hopes to add to his own resources by some gain in family, or wealth, or political influence?

It is to the "marriage of true minds" that Shakespeare bids us to "admit no impediments"; and it is only such a marriage — born, on either side, of the perception of and love for the inmost soul of the real human creature to whom one is drawn by force of spiritual and mental attraction — that has any claim on our admiration, however we may accord to a more imperfect bond our pardon or our pity.

Were this lofty ideal of marriage constantly kept before the minds of young people as the only desirable thing, I think society would be immeasurably dignified by it. A girl with Una-like purity and that sensitive perception of truth and refinement which belongs to purity would never be sufficiently attracted by a false and evil man to be in danger of harm from the association; and the young man, however unskilled in the world's wiles, who held in his heart a shy and sacred worship for that "not impossible she," who could really command the homage of his mind and soul, would be as safe as Sir Galahad from any Fay Vivian of them all.

But what of the undeveloped and unaspiring minds and souls who have hardly discovered that they have any mental or spiritual needs, but who know very well that they have human hearts to need comfort, human longings to fulfill? Shall they be

shut out from love and marriage because they cannot talk about ethics, and are hardly aware that they have any intellects at all?

By no means. As Browning says in "Evelyn Hope," "delayed it may be for more lives yet, ere the time be come" for them to live completely, but at least it is in their power to live sincerely. They know the difference between love and interest; they know whether this woman or this man is honestly nearer and dearer than all the rest of the world; whether they are seeking a mate by reason of absolute, inherent attraction, or for any worldly, and therefore unworthy, motive whatever. There have been noble and honorable and faithful marriages often enough among people who could not write their own names, but whose hearts were absolutely loyal and sound to the core.

Marriage, it seems to me, should be waited for, not sought. Who knows round what corner his destiny may be hiding, — at what unexpected turn he may come upon the face above all the faces for him? To put aside as far as possible the thought of marriage until compelled to think of it by some strong and special attraction toward some special person is wiser than to be seeking in every chance acquaintance the possible husband or wife. "We shall meet the people who are coming to meet us," no matter in what far-off land their journey toward us begins.

Perhaps parents are more to blame for worldly marriages than we are apt to think. How constantly we hear the term "married well" applied, not to character or congeniality or true fitness, but to a comfortable income. And yet there is something to be said for "the stern parent" of the novels, with his "hard facts." The old adage that "when Poverty comes in at the door Love flies out of the window" is true only of small and poor natures, — natures incapable of a great love; but it is nevertheless true that to be loved it is necessary to be lovely, and that it is far more difficult to be lovely when we are hard pressed by want and rendered fretful by care and overwork. Human creatures cannot build their nests as inexpensively as the birds do; and not even the scant hospitality of homestead eaves or orchard boughs awaits their fledglings. To marry for money, or for any object whatever save and except immortal and all-powerful Love, is to perjure and debase the human heart; but to marry without some provision for the future, such as money, or money's worth

in a well-furnished mind and a capacity for skilled labor, is to defy common sense and invoke the evil fates.

Complete. From "Ourselves and Our Neighbors." By permission of Messrs. Little, Brown & Co., Boston, successors to Roberts Brothers. Copyright by Roberts Brothers 1887.

ENGAGEMENTS

I HAVE spoken of the only true and right motive for marriage, and venture to air my own opinion that marriage should not be too eagerly sought by either sex, but rather waited for until the certainty has come that one loves worthily and well. I mean that for a man to say to himself, in cold blood, that it is time he should marry, and for that reason to look about for a wife, — instead of being aware that he loves and therefore desires to marry the one beloved woman, — is to my thinking as unwise and in almost as poor taste as for a girl to discover that it is time she were settled in life, and in consequence to set about trying to attract a husband. In neither case is happiness in marriage likely to be the result of such a quest.

But let us suppose that a man's heart has really been touched, and he honestly believes that he has seen the one woman who could insure his happiness and make his life complete, — then I think he may still be in danger of imperiling his success by too great rashness. It is true that a girl does not like a timid or cowardly wooer; but if she be the "perfect woman, nobly planned," whom the poets have taught us to desire, she is not to be taken by storm, and a man must give her time to know her own mind. She must have found in her own girlish heart the "yes" he craves before he question her too rudely; or he may receive, instead, a "no" which might have ripened into "yes" under fostering and delaying suns.

There is no danger that he will not show what he feels without direct words, even were he ever so much resolved to keep silence. There is an atmosphere about love which makes itself felt. "All the world loves a lover," wrote Emerson; and, by the way, no one has more fully expressed the beauty and mystery of love than this same philosopher of Concord, who stands to so many for a sort of severe incarnation of abstract thought, instead of what he was, — a lofty human soul instinct with the fullest life of humanity. "All the world loves a lover"; and our lover,

whose lips are still silent, speaks none the less eloquently in a thousand varying ways.

As a rule, a delicate woman does not think of a man as a lover, or even know whether she could care for him in that capacity or not, until she has received some impression of his special interest in her. Then she begins to consider him. Does a long talk with him bore or delight her? Does she find herself talking to him freely, or entertaining him with an effort? Is the festive occasion from which he is absent robbed of some portion of its brightness? Does she "see his face, all faces among" — catch his voice, though a dozen are speaking? Then, unconsciously, do her cheeks begin to glow at his coming. In her eyes smiles a welcome, timid yet sweet; and the reverent, waiting lover may speak safely, for his time has come.

He has a theory, perhaps, that he should first ask her father's consent to address her, but it is one of those theories mostly kept for show and seldom acted upon. The man who really loves is most likely to be surprised by some unexpected opportunity, — to speak before he quite knows what words are on his tongue. Then, should fortune have favored his suit, he goes to the dreaded paternal interview strengthened for the ordeal — the bad half-hour that it means to most men — by the knowledge that he is beloved.

It is a debatable question how far a father has a right to refuse his consent to a prayer to which his daughter has said Amen. If she is too young to know her own mind, he may, surely, insist on delay. If there is anything really wrong and ignoble in a suitor's character, he will point it out and use his influence and even his authority — so far as authority in such a case can avail — to prevent the marriage. But if it is a mere question of personal prejudice or of worldly policy, and a girl is old enough to be quite sure of herself, it seems to me that a parent has hardly a right to interfere, and that a daughter is not compelled to accept a decision based upon prejudice or ambition.

On the other hand, a girl cannot too carefully consider the objections made by her father. It is not probable that a parent who has filled his daughter's life with proofs of love and devotion will seek to cross her in the dearest wish of her heart, without what seem to him good reasons; and to an unprejudiced mind it seems quite possible that a man of fifty should be as good a judge of character and of mutual suitability and the chances for happiness as a girl of twenty.

Yet, when all has been said, "the soul has certain inalienable rights, and the first of these is love"; and where love is true and strong, I do not believe that any parent has a right to cross it save on account of some grave defect of moral character. "Gods and men" would justify a father who should refuse his daughter to a gambler or a drunkard, or a man of known evil life in any direction. She herself would doubtless live to be grateful; or if she died, it were better to die unstained by such an association.

Let us consider the happier cases, in which the course of true love meets with no such formidable obstacles, where parents have consented and friends approved and all goes merry as a marriage bell.

Then let the betrothed pair beware lest love should become what a French cynic has called it,—"selfishness for two." Surely the influence of a great and holy joy should be to enlarge the heart and ennoble the life. Surely to be very happy should make one more tender to the sorrowful. There is a great temptation to lovers to withdraw themselves from other interests, to make the parents and brothers and sisters who have loved a girl all her life feel that they are no longer necessary to her; that her heart is gone from them while her presence is in their midst. But it would be a nobler love, and one that, to my thinking, would promise more for future happiness, which should only hold the old ties more nearly and dearly because of this new one dearer than them all; which would be sedulous to spare the home circle any slight, any sense of loss, beyond the inevitable one of parted presence. Love is the best gift of God, but it should be crowned with honor,—a sovereign who exalts his subjects, not a tyrant who debases them. If I were a man I would prefer to marry a girl who would be careful in no least thing to hurt or slight the home hearts she was leaving, who could afford to wait a little even for her happiness rather than grasp it with unseemly eagerness.

I am old fashioned, you think? Nó, even now I know of such a love in two young lovers for whom every wind blows good fortune, yet who pause on the threshold of the new, bright life to leave tender memories of their sweet thoughtfulness in the life behind them.

Complete. From "Ourselves and Our Neighbors." By permission of Messrs. Little, Brown & Co., Boston, successors to Roberts Brothers. Copyright by Roberts Brothers 1887.

MAX MÜLLER   3045

reach them. If anywhere it is in language that we may say, We are what we have been. In language everything that is new is old, and everything that is old is new. That is true evolution, true historical continuity. A man who knows his language, and all that is implied by it, stands on a foundation of ages. He feels the past under his feet, and feels at home in the world of thought, a loyal citizen of the oldest and widest republic.

It is this historical knowledge of language, and not of language only, but of everything that has been handed down to us by an uninterrupted tradition from father to son, it is that kind of knowledge which I hold that our universities and schools should strive to maintain. It is the historical spirit with which they should try to inspire every new generation. As we trace the course of a mighty river back from valley to valley, as we mark its tributaries, and watch its meanderings till we reach its source, or, at all events, the watershed from which its sources spring, in the same manner the historical school has to trace every current of human knowledge from century to century back to its fountain head, if that is possible, or, at all events, as near to it as the remaining records of the past will allow. The true interest of all knowledge lies in its growth. The very mistakes of the past form the solid ground on which the truer knowledge of the present is founded. Would a mathematician be a mathematician who had not studied his Euclid? Would an astronomer be an astronomer who did not know the Ptolemaic system of astronomy, and had not worked his way through its errors to the truer views of Copernicus? Would a philosopher be a philosopher who had never grappled with Plato and Aristotle? Would a lawyer be a lawyer who had never heard of Roman law? There is but one key to the present—that is the past. There is but one way to understand the continuous growth of the human mind and to gain a firm grasp of what it has achieved in any department of knowledge—that is to watch its historical development.

No doubt, it will be said, there is no time for all this in the hurry and flurry of our modern life. There are so many things to learn that students must be satisfied with results, without troubling themselves how these results were obtained by the labors of those who came before us. This really would mean that our modern teaching must confine itself to the surface, and keep aloof from what lies beneath. Knowledge must be what is called cut and dry, if it is to prove serviceable in the open market.

MAX MÜLLER

(1823–1900)

FRIEDRICH MAXIMILIAN MÜLLER, one of the most celebrated philologists of the nineteenth century, died in the closing year of the century, full of years and honors. He was born in Dessau, Germany, December 6th, 1823. His father was Wilhelm Müller, the well-known German poet, from whom no doubt he inherited the faculties which made him a great linguist. After studying at Leipsic, Berlin, and Paris, he settled in England, becoming a Professor at Oxford, and remaining there until his death. From 1868 to 1900 he was professor of Comparative Philology at Oxford, and by such works as "Chips from a German Workshop" he succeeded in popularizing the science of language as it never had been popularized before. The list of his learned works is a long one and his essays, contributed to the reviews and as yet uncollected, would make an important volume.

LANGUAGE SCIENCE AND HISTORY

WITH the light which the study of the antiquity of language has shed on the past, the whole world has been changed. We know now not only what we are, but whence we are. We know our common Aryan home. We know what we carried away from it, and how our common intellectual inheritance has grown and grown from century to century till it has reached a wealth, unsurpassed anywhere, amounting in English alone to two hundred and fifty thousand words. What does it matter whether we know the exact latitude and longitude of that Aryan home, though among reasonable people there is, I believe, very little doubt as to its whereabouts "somewhere in Asia." The important point is that we know that there was such a home, and that we can trace the whole intellectual growth of the Aryan family back to roots which sprang from a common soil. And we can do this not by mere guesses only, or theoretically, but by facts, that is, historically. Take any word or thought that now vibrates through our mind, and we know now how it was first struck in countries far away, and in times so distant that hardly any chronology can

My experience is the very opposite. The cut and dry knowledge which is acquired from the study of manuals or from so-called crammers is very apt to share the fate of cut flowers. It makes a brilliant show for one evening, but it fades and leaves nothing behind. The only knowledge worth having, and which lasts us for life, must not be cut and dry, but, on the contrary, it should be living and growing knowledge, knowledge of which we know the beginning, the middle, and the end, knowledge of which we can produce the title deeds whenever they are called for. That knowledge may be small in appearance, but, remember, the knowledge required for life is really very small.

We learn, no doubt, a great many things, but what we are able to digest, what is converted *in succum et sanguinem*, into our very lifeblood, and gives us strength and fitness for practical life, is by no means so much as we imagine in our youth. There are certain things which we must know, as if they were part of ourselves. But there are many other things which we simply put into our pockets, which we can find there whenever we want them, but which we do not know as we must know, for instance, the grammar of a language. It is well to remember this distinction between what we know intuitively, and what we know by a certain effort of memory only, for our success in life depends greatly on this distinction—on our knowing what we know, and knowing what we do not know, but what, nevertheless, we can find if wanted.

It has often been said that we only know thoroughly what we can teach, and it is equally true that we can only teach what we know thoroughly.

From "Some Lessons of Antiquity."

WOMEN IN MOHAMMED'S PARADISE

IT HAS often been said that a religion must be false which teaches what the Koran teaches about a future life. I do not think so. In every religion we must make allowances for anthropomorphic imagery, nor would it be possible to describe the happiness of Paradise except in analogy with human happiness. Why, then, exclude the greatest human happiness, companionship with friends, of either sex, if sex there be in the next world? Why assume the pharisaical mien of contempt for what has been our greatest blessing in this life, while yet we speak in very human imagery of the city of Holy Jerusalem, twelve thousand furlongs in length, in breadth and height, and the walls thereof one hundred and forty-four cubits, and the building of the wall of jasper and the city of pure gold, and the foundations of the wall garnished with all manner of precious stones, jasper, sapphire, chalcedony, emerald, sardonyx, sardius, chrysolite, chrysoprasus, jacinth, and amethyst? If such childish delights as that of women in certain so-called precious stones are admitted in the life to come, why should the higher joys of life be excluded from the joys of heaven? If Mohammed placed the loveliness of women above the loveliness of gold and amethyst, why should he be blamed for it? People seem to imagine that Mohammed knew no other joys of heaven, and represented Paradise as a kind of heavenly harem. Nothing can be more mistaken. In many places when he speaks of Paradise the presence of women is not even mentioned, and where they are mentioned, they are generally mentioned as wives or friends. Thus we read, " Verily the fellows of Paradise upon that day shall be employed in enjoyment, they and their wives, in shade upon thrones, reclining; therein they shall have fruits, and they shall have what they may call for, Peace, a speech from the merciful God." Or, " For these shall enter Paradise, and shall not be wronged at all, gardens of Eden, which the Merciful has promised to his servants in the unseen; verily, this promise ever comes to pass." Is it so very wrong, then, that saints are believed to enter Paradise with their wives, as when we read, " O my servants, enter ye into paradise, ye and your wives, happy " ?

In this and similar ways the pure happiness of the next life is described in the Koran, and if, in a few passages, not only wives but beautiful maidens also are mentioned among the joys of heaven, why should this rouse indignation? True, it shows a less spiritual conception of the life to come than a philosopher would sanction, but, however childish, there is nothing indelicate or impure in the description of the Houris.

The charge of sensuality is a very serious charge in the Western world, and it is difficult for us to make allowances for the different views on the subject among Oriental people. From our point of view, Mohammed himself would certainly be called a sensualist. He sanctioned polygamy, and he even allowed himself a larger number of wives and slaves than to his followers.

Mohammedans, however, as I was informed, take a different view. They admire him for having remained for twenty-five years faithful to one wife, a wife a good deal older than himself. They consider his marrying other wives as an act of benevolence, in granting them his protection while others were " averse from marrying orphan women." Mohammedans look upon polygamy as a remedy for many social evils, and they are not far wrong. We must not forget that Mohammed had to give laws to barbarous and degenerate tribes, with whom a woman was no more than a chattel, carried off, like a camel or a horse, by whoever was strong enough to defy his rivals. In Arabia, as elsewhere, women were more numerous than men, and the only protection for a woman, particularly an orphan woman, was a husband. Much worse than polygamy was female slavery; still even that was better than what existed before.

From " Mohammedanism and Christianity."

CARDINAL NEWMAN

(1801–1890)

OHN HENRY NEWMAN (created Cardinal Newman, May 12th, 1879) was born in London, February 21st, 1801. After taking his degree at Oxford and becoming a Fellow of Oriel College, he was associated with Dr. Pusey in what was called the "High-Church movement." Many of the "Oxford tracts," which excited world-wide attention, were written by him. The bent of his mind towards fixed authority as a refuge from the restlessness of skepticism carried him into the Roman Catholic Church, which gave him its highest honors. His hymn, "Lead, Kindly Light," is one of the best lyrics of modern times. He died August 11th, 1890, leaving this hymn as his most enduring movement, but he was a prose writer of no mean rank. Besides his purely theological writings, he wrote a number of popular essays on religious subjects, which are as yet uncollected. Of these, his article on "Inspiration and Higher Criticism" is an excellent example.

INSPIRATION AND HIGHER CRITICISM

THE Psalms are inspired; but when David, in the outpouring of his deep contrition, disburdened himself before his God in the words of the "Miserere," could he, possibly, while uttering them, have been directly conscious that every word he uttered was not simply his, but another's? Did he not think that he was personally asking forgiveness and spiritual help?

Doubt again seems incompatible with a consciousness of being inspired. But Father Patrizi, while reconciling two Evangelists in a passage of their narratives, says, if I understand him rightly, that though we admit that there were some things about which inspired writers doubted, this does not imply that inspiration allowed them to state what is doubtful as certain, but only it did not hinder them from stating things with a doubt on their minds about them; but how can the All-knowing Spirit doubt? or how can an inspired man doubt, if he is conscious of his inspiration?

And, again, how can a man whose hand is guided by the Holy Spirit, and who knows it, make apologies for his style of writing, as if deficient in literary exactness and finish? If then the writer of Ecclesiasticus, at the very time that he wrote his Prologue, was not only inspired but conscious of his inspiration, how could he have entreated his readers to "come with benevolence," and to make excuse for his "coming short in the composition of words"? Surely, if at the very time he wrote he had known it, he would, like other inspired men, have said, "Thus saith the Lord," or what was equivalent to it.

The same remark applies to the writer of the Second Book of Machabees, who ends his narrative by saying, "If I have done well, it is what I desired, but if not so perfectly, it must be pardoned me." What a contrast to St. Paul, who, speaking of his inspiration (I. Cor. vii. 40) and of his "weakness and fear" (id. ii. 4), does so in order to boast that his "speech was, not in the persuasive words of human wisdom, but in the showing of the Spirit and the power." The historian of the Machabees would have surely adopted a like tone of "glorying," had he had at the time a like consciousness of his divine gift.

Again, it follows from there being two agencies, divine grace and human intelligence, co-operating in the production of the Scriptures, that, whereas, if they were written, as in the Decalogue by the immediate finger of God, every word of them must be his and his only; on the contrary, if they are man's writing, informed and quickened by the presence of the Holy Ghost, they admit, should it so happen, of being composed of outlying materials, which have passed through the minds and from the fingers of inspired penmen, and are known to be inspired, on the ground that those who were the immediate editors, as they may be called, were inspired.

For an example of this we are supplied by the writer of the Second Book of Machabees, to which reference has already been made. " All such things," says the writer, " as have been comprised in five books by Jason of Cyrene, we have attempted to abridge in one book." Here we have the human aspect of an inspired work. Jason need not, the writer of the Second Book of Machabees must, have been inspired.

Again, St. Luke's gospel is inspired, as having gone through and come forth from an inspired mind; but the extrinsic sources of his narrative were not necessarily all inspired any more than was Jason of Cyrene; yet such sources there were, for, in contrast with the testimony of the actual eyewitnesses of the events which he records, he says of himself that he wrote after a careful inquiry, "according as they delivered them to us, who from the beginning were eyewitnesses and ministers of the word"; as to himself, he had but "diligently attained to all things from the beginning." Here it was not the original statements, but his edition of them, which needed to be inspired.

Hence we have no reason to be surprised, nor is it against the faith to hold, that a canonical book may be composed, not only from, but even of, pre-existing documents, it being always borne in mind, as a necessary condition, that an inspired mind has exercised a supreme and an ultimate judgment on the work, determining what was to be selected and embodied in it, in order to its truth in all "matters of faith and morals pertaining to the edification of Christian doctrine," and its unadulterated truth.

Thus Moses may have incorporated in his manuscript as much from foreign documents as is commonly maintained by the critical school; yet the existing Pentateuch, with the miracles which it contains, may still (from that personal inspiration which belongs to a prophet) have flowed from his mind and hand on to his composition. He new made and authenticated what till then was no matter of faith.

This being considered, it follows that a book may be, and may be accepted as, inspired, though not a word of it is an original document. Such is almost the case with the First Book of Esdras. A learned writer in a publication of the day says: "It consists of the contemporary historical journals, kept from time to time by the prophets or other authorized persons, who were eyewitnesses for the most part of what they record, and whose several narratives were afterward strung together, and either abridged or added to, as the case required, by a later hand, of course an inspired hand."

And in like manner the Chaldee and Greek portions of the Book of Daniel, even though not written by Daniel, may be, and we believe are, written by penmen inspired in matters of faith and morals; and so much, and nothing beyond, does the Church "oblige" us to believe.

I have said that the Chaldee, as well as the Hebrew portion of Daniel, requires, in order to its inspiration, not that it should be Daniel's writing, but that its writer, whoever he was, should

be inspired. This leads me to the question whether inspiration requires and implies that the book inspired should in its form and matter be homogeneous, and all its parts belong to each other. Certainly not. The Book of Psalms is the obvious instance destructive of any such idea. What it really requires is an inspired editor,—that is, an inspired mind, authoritative in faith and morals, from whose fingers the sacred text passed. I believe it is allowed generally, that at the date of the captivity and under the persecution of Antiochus, the books of Scripture and the sacred text suffered much loss and injury. Originally the Psalms seem to have consisted of five books; of which, only a portion, perhaps the first and second, were David's. That arrangement is now broken up, and the Council of Trent was so impressed with the difficulty of their authorship, that, in its formal decree respecting the Canon, instead of calling the collection "David's Psalms," as was usual, they called it the "Psalterium Davidicum," thereby meaning to imply, that, although canonical and inspired and in spiritual fellowship and relationship with those of "the choice Psalmist of Israel," the whole collection is not therefore necessarily the writing of David.

And as the name of David, though not really applicable to every Psalm, nevertheless protected and sanctioned them all, so the appendices which conclude the Book of Daniel, Susanna, and Bel, though not belonging to the main history, come under the shadow of that Divine Presence, which primarily rests on what goes before.

And so again, whether or not the last verses of St. Mark's, and two portions of St. John's Gospel, belong to those evangelists respectively, matters not as regards their inspiration; for the Church has recognized them as portions of that sacred narrative which precedes or embraces them.

Nor does it matter whether one or two Isaiahs wrote the book which bears that Prophet's name; the Church, without settling this point, pronounces it inspired in respect of faith and morals, both Isaiahs being inspired; and, if this be assured to us, all other questions are irrelevant and unnecessary.

Nor do the councils forbid our holding that there are interpolations or additions in the sacred text, say, the last chapter of the Pentateuch, provided they are held to come from an inspired penman, such as Esdras, and are thereby authoritative in faith and morals.

From "The Inspiration of Scripture."

BARTHOLD GEORG NIEBUHR

(1776-1831)

BARTHOLD GEORG NIEBUHR, one of the painstaking historical students whose work has revolutionized the modern historical method, was born at Copenhagen, August 27th, 1776; but he is more closely identified with Germany than with Denmark. In 1806 he left the civil service of his native country for that of Prussia. He served as Prussian ambassador at Rome (1816-23), but the great work of his life, his "History of Rome," was more directly due to the demands of his work as a university lecturer at Berlin and Bonn. The first volume of the "History" was published in 1811 and the last in 1832, a year after the author's death, which occurred January 2d, 1831. His miscellaneous writings were collected and published,—the last volumes in 1843.

THE IMPORTANCE OF ROMAN HISTORY

THE importance of the history of Rome is generally acknowledged, and will probably never be disputed. There may be persons who, in regard to ancient history in general, entertain fanciful opinions and underrate its value; but they will never deny the importance of Roman history. For many sciences it is indispensable as an introduction or a preparation. As long as the Roman law retains the dignified position which it now occupies, so long Roman history cannot lose its importance for the student of the law in general. A knowledge of the history of Rome, her laws and institutions, is absolutely necessary to a theologian who wishes to make himself acquainted with ecclesiastical history. There are indeed sciences which are in no such direct relation to Roman history, and to which it cannot therefore be of the same importance; but it is important in the history of human life in general, and whoever wishes, for instance, to acquire a knowledge of the history of diseases, must be intimately acquainted with Roman history, for without it many things will remain utterly obscure to him. Its immense importance to a philologer requires no explanation. If philologers are

principally occupied with Roman literature, the Roman classics in all their detail must be as familiar to them as if they were their contemporaries; and even those whose attention is chiefly engaged by the literature of the Greeks cannot dispense with Roman history, or else they will remain one-sided, and confine themselves within such narrow limits as to be unable to gain a free point of view. Let Greek philology be ever so much a man's real element, still he must know in what manner the Greeks ended, and what was their condition under the Roman dominion. The consequence of this necessity having never yet been duly recognized is, that the later periods of the history of Greece are still much neglected. If, on the other hand, we look at the history of a country by itself, as a science which, independently of all others, possesses sufficient intrinsic merits of its own, the history of Rome is not surpassed by that of any other country. The history of all nations of the ancient world ends in that of Rome, and that of all modern nations has grown out of that of Rome. Thus, if we compare history with history, that of Rome has the highest claims to our attention. It shows us a nation which was in its origin small like a grain of corn; but this originally small population waxed great, transferred its character to hundreds of thousands, and became the sovereign of nations from the rising to the setting sun. The whole of western Europe adopted the language of the Romans, and its inhabitants looked upon themselves as Romans. The laws and institutions of the Romans acquired such a power and durability, that even at the present moment they still continue to maintain their influence upon millions of men. Such a development is without parallel in the history of the world. Before this star all others fade and vanish. In addition to this, we have to consider the greatness of the individuals and their achievements, the extraordinary character of the institutions which formed the ground work of Rome's grandeur, and those events which in greatness surpass all others: all this gives to Roman history importance and durability. Hence we find, that in the Middle Ages, when most branches of knowledge were neglected, the history of Rome, although in an imperfect form, was held in high honor. Whatever eminent men appear during the Middle Ages, they all show a certain knowledge of Roman history, and an ardent love of Roman literature. The Revival of Letters was not a little promoted by this disposition in the minds of men: it was through the medium of Roman literature that sciences were revived in Europe, and the first restorers were distinguished for their enthusiastic love of Roman history and literature. Dante and Petrarch felt as warmly for Rome as the ancient Romans did. Throughout the Middle Ages, Valerius Maximus was considered the most important book next to the Bible; it was the mirror of virtues, and was translated into all the languages of Europe. Rienzi, the tribune, is said to have read all the works of the Ancients. At the tables of the German knights stories used to be read aloud, which alternately related the events of the Old Testament and the heroic deeds of the Romans. This partiality for Roman history continued after the Revival of Letters; and although it was often studied in an unprofitable manner, still every one had a dim notion of its surpassing importance and instructive character.

Complete. Lecture XII. of Introductory Lectures
on Rome.

NIZAMI

(ABU MOHAMMED BEN YUSUF SHEIKH NIZAM EDDIN)

(1141–1202)

ALTHOUGH Nizami is, in his own right and his own language, a poet and not an essayist, the English translations in essay form made from his works, by Sir William Jones, belong to the literature of the English essay, as they helped to give an Oriental tinge to the essays of the latter part of the eighteenth century. Nizami, who was one of the greatest poets of Persia, was born in 1141 A.D. His productive capacity was immense, as his «Divan» alone contains twenty-eight thousand distichs, and it is only one of six of his chief productions. Of these «Laila and Majnun» is best known to Occidental readers. Nizami died in 1202 A.D.

ON TRUTH

THERE was a king who oppressed his subjects: in his fondness of false evidence he had the manners of Hejjaj (a tyrant of Basrah).

Whatever in the nighttime was born (or conceived) from the morning was repeated in his palace at early dawn.

One morning a person went to the king, more apt to disclose secrets than the orb of the moon,

Who from the moon acquired nightly stratagems, and from the dawn learned the art of an informer.

He said: "A certain old man in private has called thee a disturber, and a tyrant, and bloodthirsty."

The king was enraged by this speech: he said, "Even now I put him to death."

He spread a cloth, and scattered sand on it: (to catch the blood) the devil himself fled from his madness.

A youth went, like the wind, to the face of the old man: he said, "The king is ill disposed towards thee.

"Before this evil-minded tyrant has pronounced thy doom, arise, go to him, that thou mayst bring him to his right state of mind."

The sage performed his ablution; took his shroud; went before the king, and took up his discourse.

The dark-minded monarch clapped his hands together; and, from a desire of revenge, his eye was bent back towards the heel of his foot.

He said, "I have heard that thou hast given loose to thy speech; thou hast called me revengeful and mad-headed.

"Art thou apprised of my monarchy like that of Soliman? Dost thou call me in this manner an oppressive demon?"

The old man said to him, "I have not been sleeping: I have said worse of thee than what thou repeatest.

"Old and young are in peril from thy act; town and village are injured by thy ministry.

"I, who am thus enumerating thy faults, am holding a mirror to thee both for bad and good.

"When the mirror shows thy blemishes truly, break thyself: it is a crime to break the mirror.

"See my truth, and apply thy understanding to me; and if it be not so, kill me on a gibbet."

When the sage made a confession with truth, the veracity of the old man had an effect on him.

When the king saw that veracity of his before him, he perceived his rectitude, his own crookedness.

He said, "Take away his spices and his shroud; bring in my sweet odors, and robe of honor."

He went back from the height of injustice; he became a just prince, cherishing his subjects.

No virtuous man has kept his truth concealed; for a true speech no man has been injured.

Bring truth (rasti) forward, that thou mayst be saved (rastigar). Truth from thee is victory from the Creator.

Though true words were all pearls, yet they would be harsh, very harsh, for "truth is bitter."

Complete. Translation of Sir William Jones.

ON THE PRIDE OF WEALTH

WHEN the period of the Khalafet came to Harun, the standard of Abbas extended over the world.

One midnight he turned his back on the partner of his bed, and turned his face to the enjoyment of the warm bath.

A barber, who was shaving his head, cutting hair by hair, dispelled his sorrow,

Saying, "O thou, who hast been apprised of my pre-eminence, connect me to thee this day by making me thy son-in-law:

"Publish the discourse of thy marriage; make thy daughter betrothed to thy servant."

The temper of the Khalifah grew a little warm; but became again inclined to lenity.

He said, "My dominion has turned his liver; he has gotten wild stupidity though my amazing grandeur.

"His being beside himself has made him a talker of such nonsense; if not, he would not have made this request and demand to me."

The next day he tried him better: the same impression was on the coin of his heart.

Thus he made trial of him several times: the habit of the man departed not from its fixed place.

Since a want of clearness carried the matter from light, the king carried the story to a consultation with his Vezir,

Saying, "From the rough pen of a hair cutter has this event, written on my forehead by destiny, fallen on my head.

"He must have the rank of being my son-in-law! See what a want of good breeding suggests to him.

"Whenever he comes, like fate, upon my head, he throws stones upon me and upon my gems.

"In his mouth is a poniard, and in his hand a sword, I will give him the edge of the sabre without fail."

The Vezir said, "Thou art secure from any design of his: perhaps his foot is on the top of a treasure.

"When the simple man shall come towards thy head, say, 'Turn aside from the place, where thy foot first stood.'

"If he be refractory, strike off his neck; if not, dig up the place where he stepped first."

The man with obedience, from the desire of compliance which he had, changed his place in the manner that was directed.

When he separated his foot from the first station, the manner of the barber was different.

While his foot was on the head of a treasure, the figure of royalty was in his mirror.

When he saw his foot devoid of the treasure, he saw again the cottage of his barber's business.

Having sewed up his mouth, he saw the propriety of little speech; he had taught good breeding to his eye and tongue.

They soon dug up the place where he stood, and found a treasure under his foot.

Whoever sets his foot on the head of a treasure, by his own speech opens the door of the treasury.

The treasure of Nizami, who has thrown down the talisman which concealed it, is a clear bosom and an enlightened heart.

Complete. Translation of Sir William Jones.

"NOVALIS"

(FRIEDRICH VON HARDENBERG)

(1772–1801)

"NOVALIS" died at the age of twenty-nine, after having hinted rather than shown himself to be one of the most extraordinary geniuses of modern times. The volume of his writings in prose and verse is not large, and much of it is not specially remarkable. Some of it, however, is almost supernatural. His was the only genius among the poets of Germany with a higher flight than that of Goethe. It was impossible for such elevation of intellect to be sustained, and so "Novalis" died one of the minor poets of Germany. His name in real life (to which he did not belong) was Friedrich von Hardenberg and he was born at Wiederstedt, May 2d, 1772. After studying jurisprudence at Jena, Leipsic, and Wittenberg, he filled a minor judicial position in Thuringia, but he was not fitted for it and he left it as soon as possible. At his death, March 25th, 1801, he left behind him a novel, a volume of lyric poems, a number of miscellaneous sketches and apothegms, and his "Hymns to the Night," an extraordinary series of "prose poems," occasioned by the death of his betrothed, Sophie von Kühn. "Novalis" did his best work at the close of the eighteenth century, and he has sometimes put into his lines more of the real higher mind of humanity than has gone to vivify volumes from the pens of some of the celebrated critical writers of the diffusive school of the last half of the nineteenth.

THE HOLY MYSTERY OF NIGHT

BEFORE all the wondrous shows of the widespread space around him, what living, sentient thing loves not the all-joyous light, with its colors, its rays and undulations, its gentle omnipresence in the form of the wakening Day? The giant world of the unresting constellations inhales it as the innermost soul of life and floats dancing in its azure flood; and the sparkling, ever-tranquil stone, the thoughtful, imbibing plant, and the

wild, burning, multiform beast-world inhales it; but more than all, the lordly stranger with the meaning eyes; the swaying walk, and the sweetly closed, melodious lips. Like a king over earthly nature, it rouses every force to countless transformations, binds and unbinds innumerable alliances, hangs its heavenly form around every earthly substance. Its presence alone reveals the marvelous splendor of the kingdoms of the world.

Aside I turn to the holy, unspeakable, mysterious Night. Afar lies the world, sunk in a deep grave; waste and lonely is its place In the chords of the bosom blows a deep sadness. I am ready to sink away in drops of dew, and mingle with the ashes. The distances of memory, the wishes of youth, the dreams of childhood, the brief joys and vain hopes of a whole long life, arise in gray garments, like an evening vapor after the sunset. In other regions the light has pitched its joyous tents: what if it should never return to its children, who wait for it with the faith of innocence?

What springs up all at once so sweetly boding in my heart, and stills the soft air of sadness? Dost thou also take a pleasure in us, dusky Night? What holdest thou under thy mantle, that with hidden power affects my soul? Precious balm drips from thy hand out of its bundle of poppies Thou upliftest the heavy-laden pinions of the soul. Darkly and inexpressibly are we moved: joy-startled, I see a grave countenance that, tender and worshipful, inclines toward me, and, amid manifold entangled locks, reveals the youthful loveliness of the Mother. How poor and childish a thing seems to me now the light! how joyous and welcome the departure of the day! Didst thou not only therefore, because the Night turns away from thee thy servants, strew in the gulfs of space those flashing globes, to proclaim, in seasons of thy absence, thy omnipotence and thy return?

More heavenly than those glittering stars we hold the eternal eyes which the Night hath opened within us. Further they see than the palest of those countless hosts. Needing no aid from the light, they penetrate the depths of a loving soul that fills a loftier region with bliss ineffable. Glory to the queen of the world, to the great prophetess of holier worlds, to the foster mother of blissful love! she sends thee to me, thou tenderly beloved, the gracious sun of the Night. Now am I awake, for now am I thine and mine. Thou hast made me know the Night, and brought her to me to be my life: thou hast made of me a man.

Consume my body with the ardor of my soul, that I, turned to finer air, may mingle more closely with thee, and then our bridal night endure forever.

Complete. From "Hymns to the Night."

SLEEP

MUST the morning always return? Will the despotism of the earthly never cease? Unholy activity consumes the angel visit of the Night. Will the time never come when Love's hidden sacrifice shall burn eternally? To the Light a season was set; but everlasting and boundless is the dominion of the Night. Endless is the duration of sleep. Holy Sleep, gladden not too seldom in this earthly day-labor, the devoted servant of the Night. Fools alone mistake thee, knowing naught of sleep but the shadow which, in the gloaming of the real night, thou pitifully castest over us. They feel thee not in the golden flood of the grapes, in the magic oil of the almond tree, and the brown juice of the poppy. They know not that it is thou who hauntest the bosom of the tender maiden, and makest a heaven of her lap; never suspect it is thou, the portress of heaven, that steppest to meet them out of ancient stories, bearing the key to the dwellings of the blessed, silent messenger of secrets infinite.

Complete. From "Hymns to the Night."

ETERNITY

ONCE when I was shedding bitter tears, when, dissolved in pain, my hope was melting away, and I stood alone by the barren hillock, which in its narrow dark bosom hid the vanished form of my life, lonely as never yet was lonely man, driven by anguish unspeakable, powerless, and no longer aught but a conscious misery;—as there I looked about me for help, unable to go on or turn back, and clung to the fleeting, extinguished life with an endless longing: then, out of the blue distances, from the hills of my ancient bliss, came a shiver of twilight, and at once snapped the bond of birth, the fetter of the Light. Away fled the glory of the world, and with it my mourning; the sadness flowed together into a new, unfathomable world. Thou, soul of the Night, heavenly Slumber, didst come upon me; the region gently upheaved itself, and over it hovered my unbound, newborn spirit. The hillock became a cloud of dust, and through the cloud I saw the glorified face of my beloved. In her eyes eternity reposed. I laid hold of her hands, and the tears became a sparkling chain that could not be broken. Into the distance swept by, like a tempest, thousands of years. On her neck I welcomed the new life with ecstatic tears. Never was such another dream; then first and ever since I hold fast an eternal, unchangeable faith in the heaven of the Night, and its sun, the Beloved.

Complete. From «Hymns to the Night.»

THE TRANSPORTS OF DEATH

Now I know when will come the last morning: when the Light no more scares away Night and Love; when sleep shall be without waking, and but one continuous dream. I feel in me a celestial exhaustion. Long and weariful was my pilgrimage to the holy grave, and crushing was the cross. The crystal wave, which, imperceptible to the ordinary sense, springs in the dark bosom of the hillock against whose foot breaks the flood of the world, he who has tasted it, who has stood on the mountain frontier of the world, and looked across into the new land, into the abode of the Night, verily he turns not again into the tumult of the world, into the land where dwells the Light in ceaseless unrest.

On whose heights he builds for himself tabernacles — tabernacles of peace; there longs and loves and gazes across, until the welcomest of all hours draws him down into the waters of the spring. Afloat above remains what is earthly, and is swept back in storms; but what became holy by the touch of Love runs free through hidden ways to the region beyond, where, like odors, it mingles with love asleep. Still wakest thou, cheerful Light, the weary man to his labor, and into me pourest gladsome life; but thou wilst me not away from Memory's moss-grown monument. Gladly will I bestir the deedy hands, everywhere behold where thou hast need of me; bepraise the rich pomp of thy splendor; pursue unwearied the lovely harmonies of thy skilled handicraft; gladly contemplate the thoughtful pace of thy mighty radiant clock; explore the balance of the forces and the laws of the wondrous play of countless worlds and their seasons; but true

to the Night remains my secret heart, and to creative Love, her daughter. Canst thou show me a heart eternally true? Has thy sun friendly eyes that know me? Do thy stars lay hold of my longing hand? Do they return me the tender pressure and the caressing word? Was it thou didst bedeck them with colors and a flickering outline? Or was it she who gave to thy jewels a higher, a dearer significance? What delight, what pleasure offers thy life, to outweigh the transports of Death? Wears not everything that inspirits us the livery of the Night? Thy mother, it is she who brings thee forth, and to her thou owest all thy glory. Thou wouldst vanish into thyself, thou wouldst dissipate in boundless space, if she did not hold thee fast, if she swaddled thee not, so that thou grewest warm, and, flaming, gavest birth to the universe. Verily I was before thou wast; the mother sent me with my sisters to inhabit thy world, to sanctify it with love that it might be an ever-present memorial, to plant it with flowers unfading. As yet they have not ripened, these thoughts divine; as yet there is small trace of our coming apocalypse. One day thy clock will point to the end of Time, and then thou shalt be as one of us, and shalt, full of ardent longing, be extinguished and die. I feel in me the close of thy activity, I taste heavenly freedom, and happy restoration. With wild pangs I recognize thy distance from our home, thy feud with the ancient lordly heaven. Thy rage and thy raving are in vain. Inconsumable stands the cross, victory-flag of our race.

> Over I journey
> Where every pain,
> Zest only of pleasure,
> Shall one day remain.
> Yet a few moments
> Then free am I,
> And intoxicated
> In Love's lap lie.
> Life everlasting
> Lifts, wave-like, at me:
> I gaze from its summit
> Down after thee.
> O Sun, thou must vanish
> Yon hillock beneath;
> A shadow will bring thee
> Thy cooling wreath.
> Oh, draw at my heart, love,

> Draw till I'm gone;
> That, fallen asleep, I
> Still may love on!
> I feel the flow of
> Death's youth-giving flood;
> To balsam and ether it
> Changes my blood!
> I live all the daytime
> In faith and in might:
> In holy rapture
> I die every night.

Complete. From «Hymns to the Night.» All the preceding are from the translation of George Macdonald. Longmans, Green & Co., London.

STAR DUST

Where no gods are, spectres rule.

———

The best thing that the French achieved by their Revolution was a portion of Germanism.

———

Germanism is genuine popularity, and therefore an ideal.

———

Where children are, there is the golden age.

———

Spirit is now active here and there: when will Spirit be active in the whole? When will mankind, in the mass, begin to consider?

———

Nature is pure Past, foregone freedom; and therefore, throughout, the soil of history.

———

The antithesis of body and spirit is one of the most remarkable and dangerous of all antitheses. It has played an important part in history.

———

Only by comparing ourselves, as men, with other rational beings, could we know what we truly are, what position we occupy.

The history of Christ is as surely poetry as it is history. And, in general, only that history is history which might also be fable.

———

The Bible begins gloriously with Paradise, the symbol of youth, and ends with the everlasting kingdom, with the holy city. The history of every man should be a Bible.

———

Prayer is to religion what thinking is to philosophy. To pray is to make religion.

———

The more sinful man feels himself, the more Christian he is.

———

Christianity is opposed to science, to art, to enjoyment in the proper sense.
It goes forth from the common man. It inspires the great majority of the limited on earth.
It is the germ of all democracy, the highest fact in the domain of the popular.

———

Light is the symbol of genuine self-possession. Therefore, light, according to analogy, is the action of the self-contact of matter. Accordingly, day is the consciousness of the planet, and while the sun, like a god, in eternal self-action, inspires the centre, one planet after another closes one eye for a longer or shorter time, and with cool sleep refreshes itself for new life and contemplation. Accordingly, here, too, there is religion. For is the life of the planets aught else but sun worship?

———

The Holy Ghost is more than the Bible. This should be our teacher of religion, not the dead, earthly, equivocal letter.

———

All faith is miraculous, and worketh miracles.

———

Sin is, indeed, the real evil in the world. All calamity proceeds from that. He who understands sin, understands virtue and Christianity, himself and the world.

———

The greatest of miracles is a virtuous act.

If a man could suddenly believe, in sincerity, that he was moral, he would be so.

———

We need not fear to admit that man has a preponderating tendency to evil. So much the better is he by nature, for only the unlike attracts.

———

Everything distinguished (peculiar) deserves ostracism. Well for it if it ostracizes itself. Everything absolute must quit the world.

———

A time will come, and that soon, when all men will be convinced that there can be no king without a republic, and no republic without a king; that both are as inseparable as body and soul. The true king will be a republic, the true republic a king.

———

In cheerful souls there is no wit. Wit shows a disturbance of the equipoise.

———

Most people know not how interesting they are, what interesting things they really utter. A true representation of themselves, a record and estimate of their sayings, would make them astonished at themselves, would help them to discover in themselves an entirely new world.

———

Man is the Messiah of Nature.

———

The soul is the most powerful of all poisons. It is the most penetrating and diffusible stimulus.

———

Every sickness is a musical problem; the cure is the musical solution.

———

Inoculation with death, also, will not be wanting in some future universal therapia.

———

The idea of a perfect health is interesting only in a scientific point of view. Sickness is necessary to individualization.

If God could be man, he can also be stone, plant, animal, element, and perhaps, in this way, there is a continuous redemption in nature.

———

Life is a disease of the spirit, a passionate activity. Rest is the peculiar property of the spirit. From the spirit comes gravitation.

———

As nothing can be free, so, too, nothing can be forced, but spirit.

———

A space-filling individual is a body, a time-filling individual is a soul.

———

It should be inquired whether nature has not essentially changed with the progress of culture.

———

All activity ceases when knowledge comes. The state of knowing is eudemonism, blest repose of contemplation, heavenly quietism.

———

Miracles, as contradictions of nature, are unmathematical. But there are no miracles in this sense. What we so term is intelligible precisely by means of mathematics; for nothing is miraculous to mathematics.

———

In music, mathematics appears formally, as revelation, as creative idealism. All enjoyment is musical, consequently mathematical. The highest life is mathematics.

———

There may be mathematicians of the first magnitude who cannot cipher. One can be a great cipherer without a conception of mathematics.

———

Instinct is genius in Paradise, before the period of self-abstraction (self-recognition).

———

The fate which oppresses us is the sluggishness of our spirit. By enlargement and cultivation of our activity, we change our-

selves into fate. Everything appears to stream in upon us, because we do not stream out. We are negative, because we choose to be so; the more positive we become, the more negative will the world around us be, until, at last, there is no more negative, and we are all in all. God wills gods.

———

All power appears only in transition. Permanent power is substance.

———

Every act of introversion — every glance into our interior — is at the same time ascension, going up to heaven, a glance at the veritable outward.

———

Only so far as a man is happily married to himself, is he fit for married life and family life generally.

———

One must never confess that one loves oneself. The secret of this confession is the life principle of the only true and eternal love.

———

We conceive God as personal, just as we conceive ourselves personal. God is just as personal and as individual as we are; for what we call I is not our true I, but only its off glance.

From «The Fragments.»

"MAX O'RELL"

(PAUL BLOUET)

(1848–)

THE author of "John Bull and His Island" has done his work too well as "Max O'Rell" ever to be known by the name of "Paul," given him on or soon after March 2d, 1848,—the date of his birth into the Blouet family of Brittany, France. "John Bull and His Island," his first and greatest success, has been followed by "Jonathan and His Continent" and others in the same vein, all meritorious and all the easiest of easy reading. He is a genuine Frenchman, but blended with the "attic wit" * of the intellectual products of Parisian literary garrets, there is a dash of the true Celtic, which entitles him to the O' of his pseudonym. He is still living to delight the newspaper and magazine readers of two continents.

JOHN BULL AND HIS MORAL MOTIVES

THE French fight for glory; the Germans for a living; the Russians to divert the attention of the people from home affairs; but John Bull is a reasonable, moral, and reflecting character: he fights to promote trade, to maintain peace and order on the face of the earth, and the good of mankind in general. If he conquers a nation, it is to improve its condition in this world and secure its welfare in the next: a highly moral aim, as you perceive. "Give me your territory, and I will give you the Bible." Exchange no robbery.

John is so convinced of his intentions being pure and his mission holy, that when he goes to war and his soldiers get killed, he does not like it. In newspaper reports of battles, you may see at the head of the telegrams: "Battle of . . . So many of the enemy killed, so many British massacred."

During the Zulu war, the savages one day surprised an English regiment, and made a clean sweep of them. Next day, all the papers had: "Disaster at Isandula; Massacre of British troops;

* Souvestre's pun.

Barbarous perfidy of the Zulus." Yet these excellent Zulus were not accused of having decoyed the English into a trap; no, they had simply neglected to send their cards to give notice of their arrival, as gentlemen should have done. That was all. It was cheating. As a retaliatory measure, there was a general demand in London for the extermination of the enemy to the last man. After all, these poor fellows were only defending their own invaded country. The good sense of England prevailed, however, and they were treated as worsted belligerents. England, at heart, is generous; when she has conquered a people, she freely says to them: "I forgive you." Above all things she is practical. When she has achieved the conquest of a nation, she sets to work to organize it; she gives it free institutions; allows it to govern itself; trades with it; enriches it, and endeavors to make herself agreeable to her new subjects. There are always thousands of Englishmen ready to go and settle in such new pastures, and fraternize with the natives. When England gave her colonies the right of self-government, there were not wanting people to prophesy that the ruin of the empire must be the result. Contrary to their expectation, however, the effect of this excellent policy has been to bind but closer the ties which held the colonies to the mother country. If England relied merely upon her bayonets to guard her empire, that empire would collapse like a house of cards; it is a moral force, something far more powerful than bayonets, that keeps it together.

England's way of utilizing her colonies is not our way. To us they are mere military stations for the cultivation of the science of war. To her they are stores, branch shops of the firm "John Bull & Co." Go to Australia—that is, to the antipodes of London—you will, it is true, see people eating strawberries and wearing straw hats at Christmas; setting aside this difference, you will easily be able to fancy yourself in England.

The Spaniards once possessed nearly the whole of the New World; but their only aim being to enrich themselves at the expense of their colonies, they lost them all. You cannot with impunity suck a colony's blood to the last drop.

It is not given to everyone to be a colonist.

John Bull is a colonist, if ever there was one. This he owes to his singular qualities,—nay, even to defects which are peculiarly his own.

From "John Bull and His Island."

DEGRADATION IN LONDON

"HELL is a city much like London," said the great poet Shelley. London is, indeed, an ignoble mixture of beer and Bible; of gin and gospel; of drunkenness and hypocrisy; of unheard-of squalor and unbridled luxury; of misery and prosperity; of poor, abject, shivering, starving creatures, and people insolent with happiness and wealth, whose revenues would appear to us a colossal fortune.

Except at the East End, the poor are not confined to any special quarter of the capital; you may see them everywhere clothed in rags and degradation. In this free country, the most abject human beings seem to go about clothed with a covering that resembles in form the vestures of the upper classes, just to parade their misery in the open street, as a constant reproach to the indifference and contempt of the rich. A celebrated author commits a serious error—an error which only his short stay in England can account for—when he says that there are no beggars or low people to be seen in the parks of London. These places swarm with them, and so do Regent Street, Oxford Street, and all the great arteries of the town.

Let us take a look at the public promenades.

Hyde Park is a kind of large field badly kept in order, and situated in the midst of London. There may be seen by day the richest aristocracy in the world, on horseback, or in their carriages, going round and round the graveled drives. At nightfall, Hyde Park becomes a resort for cutthroats, a huge *lupanar* at sixpence a head, that an Englishman will advise you to carefully avoid; the vilest scum of the streets meet there to wallow in the mire to their hearts' content; the gates are left open purposely by night. The policemen who stand at the entrance could easily cleanse this hotbed of vice; but they have express orders not to meddle in that which, it would appear, is not their business. The London populace is a malignant one; it is best not to meddle with it. . . .

The drunkenness in the streets is indescribable. On Saturday nights it is a general witches' sabbath. The women drink to almost as great an extent as the men. In Scotland they equal them. In Ireland they surpass them. My authority is an official report made to the English government in 1877. I find the following advertisement in the Christian World: "The wife of a

clergyman of the Church of England wishes to recommend to a Christian family a cook formerly given to drinking, but who has taken a firm resolution of leading a better life." Dear good lady! Why does she not take her herself? Ah! I will tell you why. The worthy lady is not selfish; clergyman's wife though she be, she does not wish to monopolize all the opportunities of doing good; she leaves some for you; you should be grateful to her.

The Englishman is only noisy when he is drunk; then he becomes combative and wicked. One-half the murders one hears of are committed under the influence of drink. It is not so very long since a gentleman was not ashamed to be seen tipsy in the street. At the beginning of the century they went to parliament in this state; it was rather good form. There is a story which says that Pitt one day went to the House of Commons leaning upon the arm of an honorable friend. They were both of them drunk. "I say, Pitt," cried the great statesman's friend, "How is it? I can't see the speaker."

"That's funny! I—see—two," replied Pitt.

I remember hearing a drunkard one day in Cannon Street station—it was at the time when a war between England and Russia appeared imminent—challenging loudly the latter country. "Come on, Russia, I'll manage you," he shouted. As Russia did not make her appearance: "Well, then, come on, Turkey; Russia or Turkey, I don't care which it is." The same silence on the part of the Turk. "Well, then, come on, Russia, Turkey, England, I'll fight the b—— lot of you." He was got into a carriage somehow. I pity his poor wife if he reached home without having slaked his thirst for battle upon one of the European powers.

The saddest spectacle that man, in his degradation, has yet given to the world, is a file of sandwiches. Two boards are slung over the sandwich man's neck, one on his chest, the other on his back, and he is sent about the streets placarded with the strangest, most grotesque advertisements. For the meagre pay of a few pence, he has, all day long, in all the samples of weather that this cold, damp climate affords, to pace along the gutters of the principal streets. I say in the gutter, for he is not allowed to leave it, lest he should intercept the traffic, either of the road or the pavement. I have seen these poor wretches dragging one tired foot after the other, and encased in great

square trunks, that covered them from knee to neck. Only their head and arms were free, and even the arms were not at liberty altogether, for they had to distribute to the passers-by the circulars of a trunk-making firm. Our *chiffonniers* are princes in comparison with these poor beasts of burden:—

"Plutot souffrir que mourir
C'est la devise des hommes."

You will not have gone a hundred paces along the street with a valise or bag in your hand, without having a band of street boys and loafers at your heels. They are all on the lookout for a chance of earning a penny, if you confide your luggage to them to carry, or of disappearing round the corner with it, if you turn your back an instant. If you require to cross the road, a beggar in rags will step in front of you and sweep away the mud out of your path with his broom. You will come across these poor devils in the most fashionable quarters: in Piccadilly, in Regent Street, at Hyde Park Corner, under the very windows of Buckingham Palace even.

The most flourishing businesses in London, and the only ones that are really substantial, are those of beer and old clothes. No credit for the poor man: to get his glass of beer he must come down with his three halfpence. The publican and the pawnbroker are the princes of English trade. The one is the consequence of the other. Each is the best friend of the other.

In England the government does not interfere in these matters; it does not monopolize any industry, does not undertake to supply the taxpayer with brimstone matches that will not light, and threepenny fireproof cigars.

The needy person applies to the pawnbroker. The manner in which these gentry, whom I have heard magistrates plainly call receivers of stolen goods, carry on business, favors and encourages theft. *Ma tante*, who, in France, corresponds to my uncle on this side of the Channel, is obliged by law to pay the person who pledges or sells any object of value in that person's own residence. This, at any rate, is a slight guarantee. Here, you may give the pawnbroker the first name and address that occur to your mind, and he pays you. He lends at the rate of thirty per cent. and advances as little as he can, because he takes all articles at his own risk; if they have been stolen and are subsequently identified by their rightful owner, he is obliged to restore them.

The language of the streets is beyond everything that any French dictionary places at the disposal of the translator; all idea of conveying a notion of it must be renounced. Just as choice, euphemistic, and free from objectionable expressions as is the language of the well-educated classes, just so crude and obscene is that of the lower orders. These latter seem to have but one adjective at their disposition, the adjective bl——y. This word, which corresponds to our oath *sacré*, makes one shudder in England. To French ears it can only sound ridiculous. An English workman will say, for instance, " I told my —— master that he only gave me a—— sovereign every —— week, and that I wanted five—— shillings more. He said he had not the—— time to listen to my—— complaints," etc. And so on all the while. This word, however, which happens to be now spelled like the synonym of sanguinary is, we believe, no other than a corruption of the expression " by'r lady" (by our lady) which we come across several times in Shakespeare.

Cock-fighting and dog-fighting, so famous in former days, are now forbidden by law. Boxers themselves have ceased to be an attraction; they are liable to prosecution, and only meet for a match clandestinely. These remnants of barbarism are fast disappearing. These combats were terrible. The Englishman hits a blow that would knock your head off your shoulders. This is a curious thing: even when these savages fight in earnest, they never kick each other; it is contrary to the national spirit. The kick is reserved strictly for the weaker sex, who enjoy the whole and sole monopoly of it.

From " John Bull and His Island."

to choose the good and to reject the evil. It is worthy of remark how often men allow themselves to be deceived by a name. We frequently call the past ages, "the olden times," and our ancestors "the Ancients," and we fancy that we thus pay particular respect to their age and their wisdom. But what are called the " ancient days" were exactly the " young days" of the human race; mankind is now older and more experienced than it was in past ages; but we should not pride ourselves on that, for our descendants will be still better and more experienced than we are. Let us only endeavor to leave behind us the remembrance that we have not disgraced the time in which we lived.

Valor was the virtue most usually met with among our ancestors. Exactly because men were less enlightened they were more easily roused into a dispute, and tempted by rapacity; and since countries at that time rarely enjoyed good governments and wise regulations, people lived in continual warfare. Each petty lord could wage war against his neighbor; and several petty lords, when united, were able to join against their sovereign. They therefore recognized no virtue but valor, which they constantly strove for. In our days the passions of men are more curbed by reason, and, above all, internal peace is better protected by laws and good regulations. We are also more cautious than formerly about commencing a war, by which the lives and welfare of so many men are at stake. Yet, notwithstanding this, when war has been waged in modern times, we have seen great actions performed, which might fairly take their place beside those of former days.

The praise which is bestowed upon the honor of ancient days has far less foundation than that bestowed upon their valor. If we do not limit ourselves to reading certain modern books, which blindly praise the past ages, but if we rather read older writings, which are composed by men who have seen the events with their own eyes, or heard them related by men who have themselves experienced them, we learn that promises were often broken, that even perjury was not uncommon, and that near relations frequently deceived one another. We also find, in the old writings, that they treated one another with what we should now think a very exaggerated distrust. The petty kings, who swarmed in the North, before each country was subject to its own king, covertly attacked each other, although they did not come to open war. When heroes feasted one another, they were at the same moment

HANS CHRISTIAN ÖRSTED

(1777–1851)

ANS CHRISTIAN ÖRSTED, the celebrated Danish scientist, was born at Rudkjöbing, Denmark, August 14th, 1777. His studies in Electro-Magnetism resulted in discoveries which, when complemented by those of Arago and given a practical application by Morse, resulted in the electric telegraph. He died March 9th, 1851, after publishing scientific works of enduring importance. He was an essayist of ability, and his essays, mostly on scientific and philosophical themes, have been extensively read in and out of Denmark.

ARE MEN GROWING BETTER?

WE SEE that in what concerns material things, the state of man is not worse, but better than it was in former ages. The question now only remains, whether the case is not different with spiritual things. I know that many speak of the ancient times of the world as if they were replete with virtue, and as if the men of the present day had shamefully degenerated from their fathers. This commendation of past times has even less foundation than what is said about the size of the body, its strength, and its health; but I should act unadvisedly, were I not previously to explain why our ancestors must have been inferior to us in many good qualities. They were, namely, less enlightened, which was natural; for as every ordinary man grows wiser with age, it is the same with the whole human race. Every year we experience something new, and we invent something new; the son learns from the father, and the young generally from the old. In this way an increasing treasure of knowledge is constantly collected in the world, which cannot be lost, unless men so entirely surrender themselves to folly and vice, that they do not even endeavor to learn anything good and useful. It is easy to conceive that men, in all well-regulated states, must improve, and be better instructed, and that their understanding is more disposed

ready for each other's destruction. It is true they were heathen, but in Christian times the great lords in these kingdoms continued, for many centuries, to act almost as badly; and certainly in none of the succeeding centuries was artifice so much detested as it is in our days.

Men of the present day should not fear a comparison with those of past ages, with respect to their probity and their love of truth; but they might well fear of blushing before posterity, if they do not earnestly strive to excel their ancestors far more than they have hitherto done. It might be supposed that Christianity itself would imbue the most ignorant among its followers with a horror of all vices, and it will not fail to do so, when man devotes himself to it with his whole heart. But we should not forget that the imperfection of human nature makes it in various ways difficult for us to receive the simple comprehension of the great truths of Christianity as clearly and purely as is intended. The enlightenment of the understanding is the real way to expel the animal part of our nature, which allows the wild desires and appetites to govern, and which is also frequently led astray by false ideas. If we consider the path of Divine Providence in the distribution of Christianity, we see with admiration how everything is so arranged as to oblige man to acquire knowledge, to use his powers of reflection, and to advance in enlightenment. I do not, however, deny that men, in their endeavors towards enlightenment, have frequently fallen into great and detrimental errors; but if many honest men strive after truth, they will be gradually corrected.

We may here be contented to see how much good has already been derived from the enlightenment of the understanding.

Superstition is one of the most pernicious errors which prevailed in less enlightened times, and which has not yet entirely lost its power. In the Dark Ages, an extraordinary confidence was placed in astrologers, who foretold by the stars portentous events and the destinies of man. It was but slowly perceived that these prophecies consisted in mere imagination or deception, for only two hundred years ago most people still believed in them. Equal faith was placed in the power of magic. There were many at that time who willingly allowed the people to believe that they understood the diabolical art; indeed, some few put faith in it themselves; namely, they had learned from wicked men some secret means of injuring others, and did not themselves understand the matter; therefore they easily believed that it proceeded from the devil. Some also learned a peculiar way of preparing stupefying drinks, which caused a kind of intoxication, and afterwards a sleep, in which people had singular visions, and fancied that they had been in distant countries, although their bodies had remained in the same spot. It is now well known to us how all this can be done, but its practice would at the present day be as much ridiculed as it would be shunned by all reasonable people. Must we not shrink from the idea that not only in the Dark Ages, but even whole centuries after the revival of learning, people yielded to such foolish notions; and, above all, that so many both in the upper and lower classes could seek advice and assistance from men whose wisdom and power proceeded, as they believed, from the devil? The enlightenment of the understanding has here paved the way for Christianity; for as soon as we perceive that evil is folly, it is held in the greatest contempt. Future enlightenment will gradually bring more and more people to the clear knowledge that all that is wicked is also foolish; and he who constantly keeps this truth in view, which is taught both by religion and by reason, cannot but feel himself through it strengthened in virtue.

Enlightenment contributes powerfully to extinguish revenge, cruelty, and pride, among mankind. Christianity condemns these vices in the strongest manner, and exhorts us with all its power towards love. We must be mentally blind, if in reading the events of the world we do not see the great effect it has thus exercised on the numerous nations who have been received into the Christian church. But an attentive perusal of these events proves to us, again, that enlightenment has accompanied Christianity. The more Christians became enlightened, so much the more they were obliged to fulfill the commandment of love and humility. The two commandments are more intimately connected than at first sight would appear; for he who thinks a great deal of himself, and but slightly of others, is strongly tempted to forget love; indeed, to undervalue others so disproportionately is of itself a proof of a want of love. I need not say much of the contempt with which those formerly in power treated the common people, and especially their own subjects; the case is sufficiently well known. A great many bad usages are connected with it; the pride of the master usually demanded the greatest humility from those beneath him. It is delightful to see what

a great change has been introduced by the increase of enlightenment. As the upper classes became more enlightened, they found less delight in seeing their fellow-creatures humble themselves before them in the dust; and as the lower classes became more enlightened, their superiors found that they could both demand as well as deserve better treatment. . . .

Before I conclude, I must guard against a misinterpretation of what I have here said. I should be greatly misunderstood if it were supposed to be my opinion, that much good did not happen in past ages, and that many pious and noble men had not then lived. That would be at variance with clear truth. I should as little believe that great improvements are not wanted in our days. My intention was only to show that the world, taken altogether, is advancing towards a better condition, and to point out the way by which man has approached a more desirable state, in order that we may pursue our path so much the more courageously in future, and that every one may promote in his own circle the distribution of useful knowledge, as much by the instruction of the young as by the enlightenment of the old.

From «Ancient and Modern Times.» Translation of James B. Horner (revised.)

3081

«OUIDA»

(LOUISE DE LA RAMÉE)

(1840–)

UIDA'S» essays are distinctively of the school which has been characterized as *fin de siécle*,—a school which expressed the spirit of protest observable in the last decade of the nineteenth century. As they were collected and published in America («Critical Studies by Ouida,» Cassell & Co., Limited, 1900, New York), they are probably the last collection of essays published during the nineteenth century and certainly the last collection of the century sufficiently notable to be generally noticed by the American press. Their celebrated author is of French extraction, but she was born at Bury St. Edmunds, England, in 1840. Among her best-known novels are «Strathmore,» «Chandos,» «Idalia,» «Tricotrin,» «Pascarel,» «Moths,» and «Princess Napraxine.» As an essayist, she shows great fire and force. Her feelings are intense, and her command of language is adequate for their expression. She is unconfined by conventionality or by respect for prejudice, but her motives are a deep-seated hatred of baseness and a sympathy for goodness such as Tennyson has described as «the hate of hate, the scorn of scorn, the love of love.» She is generally Latin, however, rather than English in her intellectual habits, and at times too she is Latin in her ethics.

THE UGLINESS OF MODERN LIFE

EVERY invention of what is called science takes the human race further and further from nature, nearer and nearer to an artificial, unnatural, and dependent state. One seems to hear the laugh of Goethe's Mephistopheles behind the hiss of steam; and in the tinkle of the electric bell there lurks the chuckle of glee with which the tempter sees the human fools take as a boon and a triumph the fatal gifts he has given.

What shall it profit a man if he gain the whole world and lose his own soul? What shall it profit the world to put a girdle about its loins in forty minutes when it shall have become a desert of stone, a wilderness of streets, a treeless waste, a

songless city, where man shall have destroyed all life except his own, and can hear no echo of his heart's pulsation save in the throb of an iron piston?

The engine tearing through the disemboweled mountain, the iron and steel houses towering against a polluted sky, the huge cylinders generating electricity and gas, the network of wires cutting across the poisoned air, the overgrown cities spreading like scurvy, devouring every green thing like locusts; haste instead of leisure; neurasthenia instead of health, mania instead of sanity, egotism and terror instead of courage and generosity,—these are the gifts which the modern mind creates for the world. It can chemically imitate every kind of food and drink; it can artificially produce every form of disease and suffering; it can carry death in a needle and annihilation in an odor; it can cross an ocean in five days; it can imprison the human voice in a box; it can make a dead man speak from a paper cylinder; it can transmit thoughts over hundreds of miles of wire; it can turn a handle and discharge scores of death-dealing tubes at one moment as easily as a child can play a tune on a barrel organ; it can pack death and horror up in a small tin case which has served for sardines or potted herrings, and leave it on a window sill; and cause by it towers to fall, and palaces to crumble, and flames to upleap to heaven, and living men to change to calcined corpses; all this it can do, and much more. But it cannot give back to the earth, or to the soul, «the sweet, wild freshness of morning.» And when all is said of its great inventions and their marvels and mysteries, are they more marvelous or more mysterious than the changes of chrysalis and caterpillar and butterfly, or the rise of the giant oak from the tiny acorn, or the flight of swallow and nightingale over ocean and continent?

Man has created for himself in the iron beast a greater tyrant than any Nero or Caligula. And what is the human child of the iron beast; what is the typical, notable, most conspicuous creation of the iron beast's epoch?

It is the Cad, vomited forth from every city and town in hundreds, thousands, millions, with every holy day and holy-day. The chief creation of modern life is the Cad; he is an exclusively modern manufacture, and it may safely be said that the poorest slave in Hellas, the meanest fellah in Egypt, the humblest pariah in Asia, was a gentleman beside him. The Cad is the entire epitome, the complete blossom and fruit in one, of what we are told is an age of culture. Behold him in the velodrome as he yells insanely after his kind as they tear along on their tandem machines in a match, and then ask yourself candidly, O my reader, if any age before this in all the centuries of earth ever produced any creature so utterly low and loathsome, so physically, mentally, individually, and collectively hideous. The helot of Greece, the gladiator of Rome, the swashbuckler of mediæval Europe, nay, the mere pimp and pander of Elizabethan England, of the France of the Valois, of the Spain of Velasquez, were dignity, purity, courage in person beside the Cad of this breaking dawn of the twentieth century; the Cad rushing on with his shrill scream of laughter as he knocks down the feeble woman or the yearling child, and making life and death and all eternity seem ridiculous by the mere existence of his own intolerable fatuity and bestiality.

From "Critical Studies," Chap. x.

THE QUALITY OF MERCY

THE desire for excitement is the most conspicuous feature, and the most dangerous disease of the age; anything which provides it is welcome; people are bored despite their incessant search of distraction, and anything which will exorcise the spectre of boredom is eagerly received; and, after all, it would be absurd if persons who go to see steeple chases pretended to be too squeamish to cry the "Habet"! Let the managers of Olympia obtain permission for gladiatorial games (death being guaranteed), and I will promise them that "all London" in the most fashionable sense of those words will crowd from April to August to see the sport.

If the ladies could be allowed to descend into the arena, to touch the dying bodies, as Nero used to like to do, to see the faint life still lingering shrink and writhe, this success would be still greater; and Nero was but a primitive creature, he had but a heated iron wand, whereas my ladies could be provided by their favorite scientist with the much more excruciating torment of electricity. Imagine what exquisite little jeweled instruments of torture, made to fasten on to a bracelet, or hide within a ring, would fill the shops in Bond Street and Piccadilly. "We are going electrolyzing!" would be heard from all the pretty lips

If she were told that she is a more barbaric creature than the squaw of the poor Indian trapper who poisoned the parrakeets, she would be equally astonished and offended.

Let us now look at her next-door neighbor; he is a very wealthy person and seldom refuses a subscription, thinks private charity pernicious and pauperizing, attends his church regularly, and votes in the House of Commons in favor of pigeon shooting and spurious sports. If any one asks him if he "likes animals," he answers cheerily, "Oh, dear me, yes. Poor creatures, why not?" But it does not disturb him that the horse in the hansom cab, which he has called to take him to the city, has weals all over its loins, and a bit that fills its mouth with blood and foam; nor does he notice the over-driven and half-starved condition of a herd of cattle being taken from Cannon Street to Smithfield, but only curses them heartily for blocking the traffic.

He eats a capon, drives behind a gelding, warms himself at a hearth of which the coal has been procured by untold sufferings of man and beast, has his fish crimped, and his lobsters scalded to death in his kitchens, relishes the green fat cut from a living turtle, reads with approbation his head keeper's account of the last pair of owls on his estate having been successfully trapped, writes to that worthy to turn down two thousand more young pheasants for the autumn shooting, orders his agent to have his young cattle on his home farm dishorned, and buys as a present for his daughters a cardcase made from the shell of a tortoise which was roasted alive, turned on its back on the fire, to give the ruddy glow to its shell. Why not? His favorite preacher and his popular scientist alike assure him that all the subject races are properly sacrificed to man. It is obviously wholly impossible to convince such a person that he is cruel; he merely studies his own convenience, and he has divine and scientific authority for considering that he is perfectly right in doing so. He is quite comfortable, both for time and for eternity. It were easier to change the burglar of the slums, the brigand of the hills, than to change this self-complacent and pachydermatous householder who represents nine-tenths of the ruling classes.

Let us not mistake; he is not personally a cruel man; he would not himself hurt anything, except in sport which he thinks is legitimate, and in science which he is told is praiseworthy; he is amiable, good-natured, perhaps benevolent, but he is wrapped up in habits, customs, facts, egotisms, tyrannies, which all

of the leaders of society; and they would cease to care for their bicycles, and autocars, and even for the discussion of actresses' new gowns. "How many dead 'uns did you knock off last night?" their most intimate friend would ask, as he would lean over the rails in Rotten Row, sucking the crook of his cane.

Does this appear exaggerated and libelous? Well, let us look at the example given by a London leader of fashion and politics as she goes down at election time to shed sweetness and light around her in Poplar or Shoreditch.

In her bonnet is, of course, an osprey aigret; she knows it was torn from a living creature, but then that was done far away in some Asiatic or American creek or forest, and so really does not matter. Her suède gloves fit like her skin; they were the skin of a kid, and were probably stripped from its living body, as this lends suppleness to the skin. The jacket she carries on her arm is lined with Astrakhan fur, which was taken from an unborn lamb to give to the fur that curl and kink which pleases her; it has been cut from its mother's ripped-up womb. Her horses, as they wait for her at the corner of the street, have their heads fixed in air, and the muscles of their necks cramped by immovable bearing reins. Her Japanese pug runs after her, shaking his muzzle-tortured nose. She has a telegram in her pocket which has momentarily vexed her. She sent her sable collie to the dog exhibition at Brussels, and the excitement, or the crush, or the want of water, or something, has brought on heat apoplexy, and they wire that he is dead,—poor old nervous Ossian! She really has no luck, for her Java sparrows died too at the bird show in Edinburgh, because the footman, sent with them, forgot to fill their water glass when it got dry on the journey; a great many people send birds to shows with nobody at all to take care of them, so she feels that she was not to blame in the very least.

"Why will you show?" says her husband, who is vexed about Ossian; "you don't want to win and you don't want to sell."

"Oh, everybody does it," she answers.

He goes into his study to console himself with a new model of a pole-trap; and she, her canvassing done, runs upstairs to see her gown for the May drawing-room. The train is of quite a new design, embroidered with orchids in natural colors, and fringed with the feathers of the small green parrakeet, a beautiful little bird which has been poisoned by hundreds in the jungles of New Guianea to make the border to this *manteau de cour*.

seem to him to be good, indeed to be essential His horse is a thing to him like his mail phaeton; his dog is a dummy like his umbrella stand; his cattle are wealth-producing stores like his timber or wheat; he uses them all as he requires, as he uses his hats and gloves. He sees no more unkindness in doing away with any of them than in discarding his old boots, and he passes the most atrocious laws and by-laws for animal torment as cheerfully as he signs a check payable to self.

His ears are wadded by prejudice, his eyes are blinded by formula, his character is steeped in egotism; you might as well try, I repeat, to touch the heart of the Sicilian brigand or the London crib cracker as to alter his views and opinions; you would speak to him in a language which is as unintelligible to his world as Etruscan to the philologist.

The majority of his friends, like himself, lead their short, bustling bumptious, and frequently wholly useless lives, purblind always and entirely deaf where anything except their own interests is concerned. They think but very rarely of anything except themselves, and the competitions, ambitions, or jealousies which occupy them. But in their pastimes cruelty is to them acceptable; it is an outlet for the barbarian who sleeps in them, heavily drugged, but not dead; the sight of blood titillates agreeably their own slow circulation.

Between them and the cad who breaks the back of the bagged rabbit, there is no difference except in the degree of power to indulge the slaughter lust.

Alas! it were easier "to quarry the granite rock with razors" than to touch the feelings of such as this man, or this woman, where their vanities, or their mere sheep-like love of doing as others do, are in question.

From "Critical Studies."

SIR THOMAS OVERBURY

(1581-1613)

IR THOMAS OVERBURY's permanent place in English literature is due to the fact that he is the founder of what may be called the English school of Theophrastus. His character studies, imitated from Theophrastus, are among the earliest, if they are not the earliest, of the essays of this class in English. He has decided merit as a writer, but it is impaired by his love for "conceits" and by the licentiousness of his time. He was born in Warwickshire, in 1581. After completing his studies at Oxford and the Temple, he began life at Court as the friend of Robert Carr, Viscount Rochester,* a corrupt favorite of James I., and the lover of the still more corrupt Lady Essex. Having incurred her enmity by warning her lover against her, Overbury was thrown into the Tower as a result of her plottings, where she and Carr caused him to be poisoned. He died September 15th, 1613, and his murderers were brought to bar and proven guilty, but royal favor shielded them from the punishment they deserved. Besides his "Characters," Overbury wrote "Crumms Fall'n from King James' Table," and "The Wife," a poem which contains several striking lines, notably the famous ones:—

> "In part to blame is she
> Which hath without consent bin only tride;
> He comes too near who comes to be denied."

A GOOD WIFE

A GOOD wife is a man's best movable, a scion incorporate with the stock, bringing sweet fruit, one who to her husband is more than a friend, less than trouble, an equal with him in the yoke. Calamities and troubles she shares alike, nothing pleases her that doth not him. She is relative in all, and he without her, but half himself. She is his absent hands, eyes, ears, and mouth, his present and absent all; she frames her nature into his howsoever, the hyacinth follows not the sun more willingly, stubbornness and obstinacy are herbs that grow not in

* Afterwards Earl of Somerset.

her garden. She leaves tattling to the gossips of the town, and is more seen than heard; her household is her charge, her care to that makes her seldom nonresident. Her pride is but to be cleanly, and her thrift not to be prodigal. By her discretion she hath children not wantons; a husband without her is a misery in man's apparel; none but she hath an aged husband, to whom she is both a staff and a chair. To conclude, she is both wise and religious, which makes her all this.

Complete. From "Characters."

A USURER

A USURER is sowed as cumin or hempseed, with curses, and thinks he thrives the better; he is better read in the penal statutes than the Bible, and his evil angel persuades him he shall no sooner be saved by them. He can be no man's friend, for all men he hath most interest in he undoes; and a double dealer he is certainly, for by his good-will he ever takes the forfeit. He puts his money to the unnatural act of generation, and his scrivener is the supervivor bawd to it; good deeds he loves none, but sealed and delivered; nor doth he wish anything to thrive in the country, but beehives, for they make him wax rich. He hates all but law Latin, yet thinks he might be drawn to love a scholar, could he reduce the year to a shorter compass, that his use-money might come in the faster; he seems to be the son of a tailor, for all his estate is most heavy and cruel bonds. He doth not give, but sell days of payments, and those at the rate of a man's undoing; he doth only fear that the day of judgment should fall sooner than the payment of some great sum of money due to him; he removes his lodging when a subsidy comes, and if he be found out, and pay it, he grumbles treason, but it is in such a deformed silence, as witches raise their spirits in; . . . and it seems, he was at Tilbury camp, for you must not tell him of a Spaniard. He is a man of no conscience; for, like the farmer that swooned with going into Bucklersbury, he falls into a cold sweat, if he but look into the Chancery; he thinks it his religion,—we are in the right for everything if that were abolished; he hides his money as if he thought to find it again at the last day, and then begin his old trade with it; his clothes plead prescription, and whether they or his body are more rotten, is a question; yet should he live to be hanged in them, this good they would do him, the very

hangman would pity his case; the table he keeps is able to starve twenty tall men; his servants have not their living, but their dying from him, and that is of hunger; a spare diet he commends in all men but himself; he comes to cathedrals only for love of the singing boys, because they look hungry; he likes our religion best, because 'tis best cheap, yet would fain allow of purgatory, because 'twas of his trade, and brought in so much money; his heart closes with the same snaphance his purse doth, 'tis seldom open to any man; friendship he accounts but a word without any signification; nay, he loves all the world so little, that if it were possible, he would make himself his own executor; for certain he is made administrator to his own good name, while he is in perfect memory, for that dies long before him, but he is so far from being at the charge of a funeral for it, that he lets it stink above ground. In conclusion, for neighborhood you were better dwell by a contentious lawyer; and for his death, 'tis rather surfeit, or despair; for seldom such as he die of God's making, as honest men should do.

From "Characters."

AN INGROSSER OF CORN

THERE is no vermin in the land like him; he slanders both heaven and earth with pretended dearths, when there's no cause of scarcity. His hoarding in a dear year is like Erisicthon's bowels in Ovid, *"quodque urbibus esse; quodque satis poterat populo, non sufficit uni."* He prays daily for more inclosures, and knows no reasons in his religion why we should call our forefathers' days the time of ignorance, but only because they sold wheat for twelve pence a bushel. He wishes that Dantzick were at the Mollocco's, and had rather be certain of some foreign invasion than of the setting up the stilyard. When his barns and granaries are full, if it be a time of dearth, he will buy half a bushel in the market to serve his household, and winnows his corn in the night, lest as the chaff thrown upon the water showed plenty in Egypt, so his, carried by the wind, should proclaim his abundance. No painting pleases him so well as Pharaoh's dream of the seven lean kine that ate up the fat ones; that he has in his parlor, which he will describe to you like a motion, and his comment ends with a smothered prayer for the like scarcity. He cannot away with tobacco, for he is persuaded,

and not much amiss, that it is a sparer of bread,—corn, which he could find in his heart to transport without license, but weighing the penalty, he grows mealy mouthed, and dares not; sweet smiles he cannot abide,—wishes that the pure air were generally corrupted,—nay, that the spring had lost her fragrancy forever, or we our superfluous sense of smelling, as he terms it, that his corn might not be found musty. The poor he accounts the justices' intelligencers and cannot abide them; he complains of our negligence of discovering new parts of the world, only to rid them from our climate. His son, by a certain kind of instinct, he binds apprentice to a tailor, who all the term of his indenture hath a dear year in his belly, and ravins bread extremely when he comes to be a freeman; if it be a dearth, he marries him to a baker's daughter.

Complete.

THE TINKER

A TINKER is a movable, for he hath no abiding in one place; by his motion he gathers heat, thence his choleric nature. He seems to be very devout, for his life is a continual pilgrimage; and sometimes in humility goes barefoot, therein making necessity a virtue. His house is as ancient as Tubal Cain's, and so is a renegade by antiquity; yet he proves himself a gallant, for he carries all his wealth upon his back; or a philosopher, for he bears all his substance about him. From his art was music first invented, and therefore is he always furnished with a song, to which his hammer, keeping tune, proves that he was the first founder of the kettledrum. Note that where the best ale is, there stands his music most upon crotchets. The companion of his travels is some foul sunburnt quean; that, since the terrible statute, recanted gipsyism, and is turned peddleress. So marches he all over England with his bag and baggage; his conversation is irreprovable, for he is ever mending. He observes truly the statutes, and therefore had rather steal than beg, in which he is irremovably constant, in spite of whips or imprisonment; and so strong an enemy to idleness, that, in mending one hole, he had rather make three than want work; and when he hath done, he throws the wallet of his faults behind him. He embraceth naturally ancient customs, conversing in open fields and lowly cottages; if he visit cities or towns, 'tis but to deal upon the imperfections of our weaker vessels. His tongue is very voluble, which, with canting, proves him a linguist. He is entertained in every place, but enters no further than the door, to avoid suspicion. Some would take him to be a coward, but, believe it, he is a lad of mettle; his valor is commonly three or four yards long, fastened to a pike in the end for flying off. He is very provident, for he will fight with but one at once, and then also he had rather submit than be counted obstinate. To conclude, if he 'scape Tyburn and Banbury, he dies a beggar

THE FAIR AND HAPPY MILKMAID

IS A country wench that is so far from making herself beautiful by art, that one look of hers is able to put all face-physic out of countenance. She knows a fair look is but a dumb orator to commend virtue, therefore minds it not. All her excellences stand in her so silently, as if they had stolen upon her without her knowledge. The lining of her apparel, which is herself, is far better than outsides of tissue; for though she be not arrayed in the spoil of the silkworm, she is decked in innocence, a far better wearing. She doth not, with lying long in bed, spoil both her complexion and conditions. Nature hath taught her, too, immoderate sleep is rust to the soul; she rises, therefore, with Chanticleer, her dame's cock, and at night makes the lamb her curfew. In milking a cow, and straining the teats through her fingers, it seems that so sweet a milk-press makes the milk whiter or sweeter; for never came almond-glore or aromatic ointment on her palm to taint it. The golden ears of corn fall and kiss her feet when she reaps them, as if they wished to be bound and led prisoners by the same hand that felled them. Her breath is her own, which scents all the year long of June, like a new-made haycock. She makes her hand hard with labor, and her heart soft with pity; and when winter evenings fall early, sitting at her merry wheel, she sings defiance to the giddy wheel of fortune. She doth all things with so sweet a grace, it seems ignorance will not suffer her to do ill, being her mind is to do well. She bestows her year's wages at next fair; and in choosing her garments, counts no bravery in the world like decency. The garden

holds them no relics of Popery. He is not so inquisitive after news derived from the privy-closet, when the finding an aerie of hawks in his own ground, or the foaling of a colt come of a good strain, are tidings more pleasant and more profitable. He is lord paramount within himself, though he hold by never so mean a tenure, and dies the more contentedly (though he leave his heir young), in regard he leaves him not liable to a covetous guardian. Lastly, to end him, he cares not when his end comes; he needs not fear his audit, for his quietus is in heaven.

Complete.

and beehive are all her physic and surgery, and she lives the longer for it. She dares go alone and unfold sheep in the night, and fears no manner of ill, because she means none; yet, to say truth, she is never alone, but is still accompanied with old songs, honest thoughts, and prayers, but short ones; yet they have their efficacy, in that they are not palled with ensuing idle cogitations. Lastly, her dreams are so chaste that she dare tell them; only a Friday's dream is all her superstition; that she conceals for fear of danger. Thus lives she, and all her care is, she may die in the springtime, to have store of flowers stuck upon her winding sheet

Complete.

A FRANKLIN

HIS outside is an ancient yeoman of England, though his inside may give arms (with the best gentleman) and never see the herald. There is no truer servant in the house than himself. Though he be master, he says not to his servants, "Go to field," but "Let us go," and with his own eye doth both fatten his flock, and set forward all manner of husbandry. He is taught by nature to be contented with a little; his own fold yields him both food and raiment; he is pleased with any nourishment God sends, whilst curious gluttony ransacks, as it were, Noah's ark for food, only to feed the riot of one meal. He is never known to go to law; understanding to be law-bound among men, is like to be hide-bound among his beasts; they thrive not under it, and that such men sleep as unquietly as if their pillows were stuffed with lawyers' penknives. When he builds, no poor tenant's cottage hinders his prospects; they are, indeed, his alms-houses, though there be painted on them no such superscription. He never sits up late, but when he hunts the badger, the vowed foe of his lambs; nor uses he any cruelty, but when he hunts the hare; nor subtlety, but when he setteth snares for the snipe, or pitfalls for the blackbird; nor oppression, but when in the month of July he goes to the next river and shears his sheep. He allows of honest pastime, and thinks not the bones of the dead anything bruised, or the worse for it, though the country lasses dance in the churchyard after evensong. Rock-Monday, and the wake in summer, shrovings, the wakeful catches on Christmas eve, the hoky, or seedcake, these he yearly keeps, yet

THOMAS PAINE

(c. 1737–1809)

PAINE'S "Rights of Man" (1791–92) was one of the most influential political treatises of the eighteenth century. His "Common Sense," published in 1776 in America, had been one of the chief factors in uniting the doubtful and conservative element of the Colonists with the Radicals who from the first had determined to overthrow the power of England in North America. Paine, the son of a Quaker stay-maker, was born in Norfolk, England, January 29th, 1737, and came to America in 1774, attracted perhaps by the hope of finding opportunity for his remarkable talents as an agitator and political controversialist. In 1787, after the close of the Revolution, in which he had been one of the most important factors, he returned to England and threw himself into the struggle which the Republicans of France were forcing to an issue against Royalty. The "Rights of Man," for which Paine was at once prosecuted by the English government, was received with satisfaction by not a few influential Whigs, and when Paine was prosecuted, Erskine, who afterwards appeared for the prosecution in the case against the "Age of Reason," made one of his most celebrated appeals in behalf of free speech. In 1793 Paine, who had taken up his residence in Paris, was elected to the Assembly, and his course there caused him to be imprisoned by the Terrorists. His "Age of Reason" had made him bitter enemies in the United States, and his former political associates were so slow in coming to his assistance that he suspected them of a desire to see him guillotined as the easiest way to avoid recognizing his services. When finally released he returned to the United States (1802), but was received with great caution by his former friends; and when he died at New York, June 8th, 1809, it was in obscurity and poverty.

THE RIGHTS OF MAN

REASON and ignorance, the opposites of each other, influence the great bulk of mankind. If either of these can be rendered sufficiently extensive in a country, the machinery of government goes easily on. Reason shows itself, and ignorance submits to whatever is dictated to it.

The two modes of government which prevail in the world are: First, government by election and representation; second, government by hereditary succession. The former is generally known by the name of republic; the latter by that of monarchy and aristocracy.

Those two distinct and opposite forms erect themselves on the two distinct and opposite bases of reason and ignorance. As the exercise of government requires talents and abilities, and as talents and abilities cannot have hereditary descent, it is evident that hereditary succession requires a belief from man, to which his reason cannot subscribe, and which can only be established upon his ignorance; and the more ignorant any country is, the better it is fitted for this species of government.

On the contrary, government in a well-constituted republic requires no belief from man beyond what his reason authorizes. He sees the *rationale* of the whole system, its origin, and its operation; and as it is best supported when best understood, the human faculties act with boldness, and acquire, under this form of government, a gigantic manliness.

As, therefore, each of those forms acts on a different basis, the one moving freely by the aid of reason, the other by ignorance, we have next to consider what it is that gives motion to that species of government which is called mixed government, or, as it is sometimes ludicrously styled, a government of this, that, and t'other.

The moving power in this species of government is, of necessity, corruption. However imperfect election and representation may be in mixed governments, they still give exertion to a greater portion of reason than is convenient to the hereditary part; and therefore it becomes necessary to buy the reason up. A mixed government is an imperfect everything, cementing and soldering the discordant parts together, by corruption, to act as a whole. Mr. Burke appears highly disgusted that France, since she had resolved on a revolution, did not adopt what he calls "a British constitution"; and the regret which he expresses on this occasion implies a suspicion that the British constitution needed something to keep its defects in countenance.

In mixed governments there is no responsibility; the parts cover each other till responsibility is lost; and the corruption which moves the machine contrives at the same time its own escape. When it is laid down as a maxim that a king can do

no wrong, it places him in a state of similar security with that of idiots and persons insane, and responsibility is out of the question, with respect to himself. It then descends upon the minister, who shelters himself under a majority in parliament, which, by places, pensions, and corruption, he can always command; and that majority justifies itself by the same authority with which it protects the minister. In this rotary motion, responsibility is thrown off from the parts, and from the whole.

When there is a part in a government which can do no wrong, it implies that it does nothing; and is only the machine of another power, by whose advice and direction it acts. What is supposed to be the king, in mixed governments, is the cabinet; and as the cabinet is always a part of the parliament, and the members justifying in one character what they act in another, a mixed government becomes a continual enigma, entailing upon a country, by the quantity of corruption necessary to solder the parts, the expense of supporting all the forms of government at once, and finally resolving itself into a government by committee; in which the advisers, the actors, the approvers, the justifiers, the persons responsible, and the persons not responsible, are the same person.

By this pantomimical contrivance, and change of scene and character, the parts help each other out in matters, which, neither of them singly, would presume to act. When money is to be obtained, the mass of variety apparently dissolves, and a profusion of parliamentary praises passes between the parts. Each admires, with astonishment, the wisdom, the liberality, and disinterestedness of the other; and all of them breathe a pitying sigh at the burdens of the nation.

But in a well-conditioned republic, nothing of this soldering, praising, and pitying, can take place; the representation being equal throughout the country, and complete in itself, however it may be arranged into legislative and executive, they have all one and the same natural source. The parts are not foreigners to each other, like democracy, aristocracy, and monarchy. As there are no discordant distinctions, there is nothing to corrupt by compromise, nor confound by contrivance. Public measures appeal of themselves to the understanding of the nation, and, resting on their own merits, disown any flattering application to vanity. The continual whine of lamenting the burden of taxes, however successfully it may be practiced in mixed governments,

is inconsistent with the sense and spirit of a republic. If taxes are necessary, they are, of course, advantageous; but if they require an apology, the apology itself implies an impeachment. Why, then, is man thus imposed upon, or why does he impose upon himself?

When men are spoken of as kings and subjects, or when government is mentioned under distinct or combined heads of monarchy, aristocracy, and democracy, what is it that reasoning man is to understand by the terms? If there really existed in the world two more distinct and separate elements of human power, we should then see the several origins to which those terms would descriptively apply; but as there is but one species of man, there can be but one element of human power, and that element is man himself. Monarchy, aristocracy, and democracy are but creatures of imagination; and a thousand such may be contrived as well as three.

From the revolutions of America and France, and the symptoms that have appeared in other countries, it is evident that the opinion of the world is changing with respect to systems of government, and that revolutions are not within the compass of political calculations. The progress of time and circumstances, which men assign to the accomplishment of great changes, is too mechanical to measure the force of the mind, and the rapidity of reflection, by which revolutions are generated; all the old governments have received a shock from those that already appear, and which were once more improbable, and are a greater subject of wonder, than a general revolution in Europe would be now.

When we survey the wretched condition of man, under the monarchical and hereditary systems of government, dragged from his home by one power, or driven by another, and impoverished by taxes more than by enemies, it becomes evident that those systems are bad, and that a general revolution in the principle and construction of governments is necessary.

What is government more than the management of the affairs of a nation? It is not, and from its nature cannot be, the property of any particular man or family, but of the whole community at whose expense it is supported; and though by force or contrivance it has been usurped into an inheritance, the usurpation cannot alter the right of things. Sovereignty as a matter of right appertains to the nation only, and not to any individual; and a nation has at all times an inherent, indefeasible right to

abolish any form of government it finds inconvenient, and establish such as accords with its interest, disposition, and happiness. The romantic and barbarous distinctions of men into kings and subjects, though it may suit the condition of courtiers cannot that of citizens; and is exploded by the principle upon which governments are now founded. Every citizen is a member of the sovereignty, and as such can acknowledge no personal subjection; and his obedience can be only to the laws.

When men think of what government is, they must necessarily suppose it to possess a knowledge of all the objects and matters upon which its authority is to be exercised. In this view of government, the republican system, as established by America and France, operates to embrace the whole of a nation; and the knowledge necessary to the interest of all the parts is to be found in the centre, which the parts by representation form; but the old governments are on a construction that excludes knowledge as well as happiness; government by monks, who know nothing of the world beyond the walls of a convent, is as consistent as government by kings.

What were formerly called revolutions were little more than a change of persons, or an alteration of local circumstances. They rose and fell like things of course, and had nothing in their existence or their fate that could influence beyond the spot that produced them. But what we now see in the world, from the revolutions of America and France, are a renovation of the natural order of things, a system of principles as universal as truth and the existence of man, and combining moral with political happiness and national prosperity.

"I. Men are born, and always continue, free and equal, in respect to their rights. Civil distinctions, therefore, can be founded only on public utility.

"II. The end of all political associations is the preservation of the natural and imprescriptible rights of man, and these rights are liberty, property, security, and resistance of oppression.

"III. The nation is essentially the source of all sovereignty; nor can any individual, or any body of men, be entitled to any authority which is not expressly derived from it."

In these principles there is nothing to throw a nation into confusion, by inflaming ambition. They are calculated to call forth wisdom and abilities, and to exercise them for the public good, and not for the emolument or aggrandizement of particular descriptions of men or families. Monarchical sovereignty, the enemy of mankind and the source of misery, is abolished; and sovereignty itself is restored to its natural and original place, the nation. Were this the case throughout Europe, the cause of wars would be taken away.

It is attributed to Henry IV. of France, a man of an enlarged and benevolent heart, that he proposed, about the year 1620, a plan for abolishing war in Europe. The plan consisted in constituting a European congress, or, as the French authors style it, a pacific republic; by appointing delegates from the several nations, who were to act, as a court of arbitration, in any disputes that might arise between nation and nation.

Had such a plan been adopted at the time it was proposed, the taxes of England and France, as two of the parties, would have been at least ten millions sterling annually, to each nation, less than they were at the commencement of the French Revolution.

To conceive a cause why such a plan has not been adopted (and that instead of a congress for the purpose of preventing war, it has been called only to terminate a war, after a fruitless expense of several years), it will be necessary to consider the interest of governments as a distinct interest to that of nations.

Whatever is the cause of taxes to a nation becomes also the means of revenue to a government. Every war terminates with an addition of taxes, and, consequently, with an addition of revenue; and in any event of war, in the manner they are now commenced and concluded, the power and interest of governments are increased. War, therefore, from its productiveness, as it easily furnishes the pretense of necessity for taxes and appointments to places and offices, becomes the principal part of the system of old governments; and to establish any mode to abolish war, however advantageous it might be to nations, would be to take from such government the most lucrative of its branches. The frivolous matters upon which war is made show the disposition and avidity of governments to uphold the system of war, and betray the motives upon which they act.

Why are not republics plunged into war, but because the nature of their government does not admit of an interest distinct from that of the nation? Even Holland, though an ill-constructed republic, and with a commerce extending over the world, existed nearly a century without war; and the instant the form of government was changed in France, the republican principles of peace, and domestic prosperity and economy, arose with the new

government; and the same consequences would follow the same causes in other nations.

As war is the system of government on the old construction, the animosity which nations reciprocally entertain is nothing more than what the policy of their governments excite, to keep up the spirit of the system. Each government accuses the other of perfidy, intrigue, and ambition, as a means of heating the imagination of their respective nations, and incensing them to hostilities. Man is not the enemy of man, but through the medium of a false system of government. Instead, therefore, of exclaiming against the ambition of kings, the exclamation should be directed against the principle of such governments; and instead of seeking to reform the individual, the wisdom of a nation should apply itself to reform the system.

Whether the forms and maxims of governments which are still in practice were adapted to the condition of the world at the period they were established is not in this case the question. The older they are the less correspondence can they have with the present state of things. Time, and change of circumstances and opinions, have the same progressive effect in rendering modes of government obsolete as they have upon customs and manners. Agriculture, commerce, manufactures, and the tranquil arts, by which the prosperity of nations is best promoted, require a different system of government, and a different species of knowledge to direct its operations, to what might have been the former condition of the world.

As it is not difficult to perceive, from the enlightened state of mankind, that the hereditary governments are verging to their decline, and that revolutions on the broad basis of national sovereignty, and government by representation, are making their way in Europe, it would be an act of wisdom to anticipate their approach, and produce revolutions by reason and accommodation, rather than commit them to the issue of convulsions.

From what we now see, nothing of reform in the political world ought to be held improbable. It is an age of revolutions, in which everything may be looked for. The intrigue of courts, by which the system of war is kept up, may provoke a confederation of nations to abolish it; and a European congress to patronize the progress of free government and promote the civilization of nations with each other is an event nearer in probability than once were the revolutions and alliance of France and America.

Complete. Concluding essay of Part I.

BLAISE PASCAL

(1623–1662)

PASCAL was a man of genius so high that it cannot be accounted for by the known laws of mental physiology. While still a child he developed a faculty for mathematics so extraordinary that his friends endeavored to check it, fearing his health would be destroyed by the incessant activity of his mind. Deprived of books, the boy of twelve began an independent investigation of the principles of mathematics and it is said that he "invented geometry anew." In 1640, at the age of seventeen, he produced a famous "Treatise on Conic Sections," and as long as he devoted his mind to mathematics no problem appeared too difficult for him. While still a youth, he seems to have thought out for himself the sum total of possible human achievement and to have been influenced by his conclusions to devote his mind to preparation for a more satisfactory existence. He became a devotee, and through at first he had occasional lapses into dissipation, he finally gave up the world and devoted his genius wholly to religion. Joining the Port Royalists, he wrote his famous "Provincial Letters" against the Jesuits. The greatness of his intellect does not fully appear, however, except in his "Penseés" first published in 1670. Out of these, it seems that he intended to construct a great theological work, but it is probably fortunate for the world that he did not do so. His "Thoughts" created a class for themselves in modern literature and they stand at the head of it. Sometimes the sudden flashes of genius in them have almost the force of a revelation. Pascal was born at Clermont-Ferrand, France, June 19th, 1623. He died at the age of thirty-nine, apparently exhausted by the incessant activity of his intellect. Such genius as his may be, as some suppose in spite of Lombroso, an approximation to the true race norm of intellectual sanity, but it is often fatal when its possessor gives it free rein at the expense of a body as sensitive and responsive as Pascal's seems to have been.

W. V. B.

VOCATIONS

THE sweetness of glory is so great that join it to what we will, even to death, we love it.

Evil is easy, and its forms are infinite; good is almost unique. But a certain kind of evil is as difficult to find as what is called good; and often on this account this particular kind of evil gets passed off as good. There is even needed an extraordinary greatness of soul to attain to it as well as to good.

We are so presumptuous that we would fain be known by the whole world, even by those who shall come after, when we are no more. And we are such triflers that the esteem of five or six persons about us diverts and contents us.

Vanity is so anchored in the heart of man that a soldier, a camp-follower, a cook, a porter makes his boasts, and is for having his admirers; even philosophers wish for them. Those who write against it, yet desire the glory of having written well as those who read their works wish a reputation for reading; I who write this have, may be, this desire and perhaps those will who read it.

In towns through which we pass we care not whether men esteem us, but we do care if we have to live there any time. How long is needed? A time in proportion to our vain and fleeting life.

The condition of man: inconstancy, weariness, unrest.

Whoever will know fully the vanity of man has but to consider the causes and the effects of love. The cause is an unknown quantity, and the effects are terrible. This unknown quantity, so small a matter that we cannot recognize it, moves a whole country, princes, armies, and all the world.

Cleopatra's nose: had it been shorter, the face of the world had been changed.

Nothing better shows the frivolity of men than to consider what are the causes and what the effects of love, for all the universe is changed by them.

From "Thoughts."

SELFISHNESS

SELF is hateful. You Milton, conceal self, but do not thereby destroy it; therefore you are still hateful.

Not so, for in acting as we do, to oblige everybody, we give no reason for hating us.—True, if we only hated in self the vexation which it causes us.

But if I hate it because it is unjust, and because it makes itself the centre of all, I shall always hate it.

In one word Self has two qualities: it is unjust in its essence because it makes itself the centre of all; it is inconvenient to others, in that it would bring them into subjection, for each "I" is the enemy, and would fain be the tyrant of all others. You take away the inconvenience, but not the injustice, and thus you do not render it lovable to those who hate injustice; you render it lovable only to the unjust, who find in it an enemy no longer. Thus you remain unjust and can please none but the unjust.

OF SELF-LOVE.—The nature of self-love and of this human "I" is to love self only, and consider self only. But what can it do? It cannot prevent the object it loves from being full of faults and miseries; man would fain be great and sees that he is little; would fain be happy, and sees that he is miserable; would fain be perfect, and sees that he is full of imperfections; would fain be the object of the love and esteem of men, and sees that his faults merit only their aversion and contempt. The embarrassment wherein he finds himself produces in him the most unjust and criminal passion imaginable. For he conceives a mortal hatred against that truth which blames him and convinces him of his faults. Desiring to annihilate it, yet unable to destroy it in its essence, he destroys it as much as he can in his own knowledge, and in that of others; that is to say, he devotes all his care to the concealment of his faults, both from others and from himself, and he can neither bear that others should show them to him, nor that they should see them.

It is no doubt an evil to be full of faults, but it is a greater evil to be full of them, yet unwilling to recognize them, because that is to add the further fault of a voluntary illusion. We do not like others to deceive us, we do not think it just in them to require more esteem from us than they deserve; it is therefore unjust that we should deceive them, desiring more esteem from them than we deserve.

Thus if they discover no more imperfections and vices in us than we really have, it is plain they do us no wrong, since it is not they who cause them; but rather they who do us a service, since they help us to deliver ourselves from an evil, the ignorance of these imperfections. We ought not to be troubled that they know our faults and despise us, since it is but just they should know us as we are, and despise us if we are despicable.

Such are the sentiments which would arise in a heart full of equity and justice. What should we say then of our own heart, finding in it a wholly contrary disposition? For is it not true that we hate truth, and those who tell us it, and that we would wish them to have an erroneously favorable opinion of us, and to esteem us other than indeed we are?

One proof of this fills me with dismay. The Catholic religion does not oblige us to tell out our sins indiscriminately to all; it allows us to remain hidden from men in general; but she excepts one alone, to whom she commands us to open the very depths of our hearts, and to show ourselves to him as we are. There is but this one man in the world whom she orders us to undeceive; she binds him to an inviolable secrecy, so that this knowledge is to him as though it were not. We can imagine nothing more charitable and more tender. Yet such is the corruption of man, that he finds even this law harsh, and it is one of the main reasons which has set a large portion of Europe in revolt against the Church.

How unjust and unreasonable is the human heart which finds it hard to be obliged to do in regard to one man what in some degree it were just to do to all men. For is it just that we should deceive them?

There are different degrees in this dislike to the truth, but it may be said that all have it in some degree, for it is inseparable from self-love. This false delicacy causes those who must needs reprove others to choose so many windings and modifications in order to avoid shocking them. They must needs lessen

our faults, seem to excuse them, mix praises with their blame, give evidences of affection and esteem. Yet this medicine is always bitter to self-love, which takes as little as it can, always with disgust, often with a secret anger against those who administer it.

Hence it happens that if any desire our love, they avoid doing us a service which they know to be disagreeable; they treat us as we would wish to be treated: we hate the truth, and they hide it from us; we wish to be flattered, they flatter us; we love to be deceived, they deceive us.

Thus each degree of good fortune which raises us in the world removes us further from truth, because we fear most to wound those whose affection is most useful, and whose dislike is most dangerous. A prince may be the byword of all Europe, yet he alone know nothing of it. I am not surprised; to speak the truth is useful to whom it is spoken, but disadvantageous to those who speak it, since it makes them hated. Now those who live with princes love their own interests more than that of the prince they serve, and thus they take care not to benefit him so as to do themselves a disservice.

This misfortune is, no doubt, greater and more common in the higher classes, but lesser men are not exempt from it, since there is always an interest in making men love us. Thus human life is but a perpetual illusion, an interchange of deceit and flattery. No one speaks of us in our presence as in our absence. The society of men is founded on this universal deceit; few friendships would last if every man knew what his friend said of him behind his back, though he then spoke in sincerity and without passion.

Man is, then, only disguise, falsehood, and hypocrisy, both in himself and with regard to others. He will not be told the truth; he avoids telling it to others; and all these tendencies, so far removed from justice and reason, have their natural roots in his heart.

From "Thoughts."

SKEPTICISM

ALL things here are true in part, and false in part. Essential truth is not thus, it is altogether pure and true. This mixture dishonors and annihilates it. Nothing is purely true, and therefore nothing is true, understanding by that pure truth.

You will say it is true that homicide is an evil; yes, for we know well what is evil and false. But what can be named as good? Chastity? I say no, for then the world would come to an end. Marriage? No, a celibate life is better. Not to kill? No, for lawlessness would be horrible, and the wicked would kill all the good. To kill then? No, for that destroys nature. Goodness and truth are therefore only partial, and mixed with what is evil and false.

Were we to dream the same thing every night, this would affect us as much as the objects we see every day, and were an artisan sure to dream every night, for twelve hours at a stretch, that he was a king, I think he would be almost as happy as a king who should dream every night for twelve hours at a stretch that he was an artisan.

Should we dream every night that we were pursued by enemies, and harassed by these painful phantoms, or that we were passing all our days in various occupations, as in traveling, we should suffer almost as much as if the dream were real, and should fear to sleep, as now we fear to wake when we expect in truth to enter on such misfortunes. And, in fact, it would bring about nearly the same troubles as the reality.

But since dreams are all different, and each single dream is diversified, what we see in them affects us much less than what we see when awake, because that is continuous, not indeed so continuous and level as never to change, but the change is less abrupt, except occasionally, as when we travel, and then we say, "I think I am dreaming," for life is but a little less inconstant dream.

From "Thoughts."

THOUGHTS ON STYLE

ELOQUENCE is an art of saying things in such a manner, first, that those to whom we speak can hear them without pain, and with pleasure; second, that they feel themselves interested, so that self-love leads them more willingly to reflect upon what is said. It consists therefore in a correspondence which we endeavor to establish between the mind and the heart of those to whom we speak on the one hand, and, on the other, the thoughts and the expressions employed; this supposes that we have thoroughly studied the heart of man so as to know all its springs, and to find at last the true proportions of the discourse we wish to suit to it. We should put ourselves in the place of those who are to listen to us, and make experiment on our own heart of the turn we give to our discourse, to see whether one is made for the other, and whether we can be sure that our auditor will be, as it were, forced to yield. So far as possible we must confine ourselves to what is natural and simple, not aggrandize that which is little, or belittle that which is great. It is not enough that a phrase be beautiful, it must be fitted to the subject, and not have in it excess or defect.

Eloquence is painted thought, and thus those who, after having painted it add somewhat more, make a picture, not a portrait.

———

We need both what is pleasing and what is real, but that which pleases must itself be drawn from the true.

Eloquence, which persuades by gentleness, not by empire, as a king, not as a tyrant.*

There is a certain pattern of charm and beauty which consists in a certain relation between our nature, such as it is, whether weak or strong, and the thing which pleases us.

Whatever is formed on this pattern delights us, whether house, song, discourse, verse, prose, woman, birds, rivers, trees, rooms, dresses, etc.

Whatever is not made on this pattern displeases those who have good taste.

And as there is a perfect relation between a song and a house which are made on a good pattern, because they are like this unique pattern, though each after its kind, there is also a perfect relation between things made on a bad pattern. Not that the bad is unique, for there are many; but every bad sonnet, for instance, on whatever false pattern it is constructed, is exactly like a woman dressed on that pattern.

Nothing makes us understand better the absurdity of a false sonnet than to consider nature and the pattern, and then to imagine a woman or a house constructed on that pattern.

When a natural discourse paints a passion or an effect, we feel in our mind the truth of what we read, which was there be-

* The disconnected nature of these sentences illustrates the character of the "Pensée" in the original. They are often mere disconnected jottings intended to be rewritten.

fore, though we did not know it, and we are inclined to love him who makes us feel it. For he has not made a display of his own riches, but of ours, and thus this benefit renders him pleasant to us, besides that such a community of intellect necessarily inclines the heart to love.

All the false beauties which we blame in Cicero have their admirers and in great number.

The last thing we decide on in writing a book is what shall be the first we put in it.

———

LANGUAGES.— We ought not to turn the mind from one thing to another save for relaxation, at suitable times, and no other, for he that diverts us out of season wearies, and he who wearies us out of season repels us, and we simply turn away. So much it pleases our wayward lust to do the exact contrary of what those seek to obtain from us who gives us no pleasure,— the coin for which we will do whatever we are asked.

When we meet with a natural style, we are charmed and astonished, for we looked for an author, and we found a man. But those who have good taste, and who seeing a book expect to find a man, are altogether surprised to find an author: *plus poetice quam humane locutus es*. Those pay great honor to Nature, who show her that she is able to discourse on all things, even on theology.

Languages are ciphers, where letters are not changed into letters, but words into words, so that an unknown language can be deciphered.

When in a discourse we find words repeated, and in trying to correct them find we cannot change them for others without manifest disadvantage, we must let them stand, for this is the true test; our criticism came of envy which is blind, and does not see that repetition is not in this place a fault, for there is no general rule.

Those who force words for the sake of an antithesis are like those who make false windows for symmetry.

Their rule is not to speak accurately, but in accurate form.

To put a mask on Nature and disguise her. No more king, pope, bishop, but sacred majesty; no more Paris, but the capital of the kingdom.

There are places in which we should call Paris, Paris, and others in which we ought to call it the capital of the kingdom.

There are those who speak well and write ill, because the place and the audience warm them and draw from their minds more than would have been produced without that warmth.

———

MISCELLANEOUS EXAMPLES OF JOTTINGS BY PASCAL.— A figure of speech, "I should have wished to apply myself to that."

The aperitive virtue of a key, the attractive virtue of a crook.

To guess. The part that I take in your sorrow. The cardinal did not choose to be guessed.

My mind is disquieted within me. I am disquieted is better.

To extinguish the torch of sedition, too luxuriant.

The restlessness of his genius. Two striking words too much.

A coach upset or overturned, according to the meaning.

Spread abroad, or upset, according to the meaning.

The argument by force of M. le M. over the friar.

Symmetry. Is what we see at one glance. Founded on the fact that there is no reason for any difference. And founded also on the face of man.

Whence it comes that symmetry is only wanted in breadth, not in height or depth.

Skeptic, for obstinate.

Descartes useless and uncertain.

No one calls another a courtier but he who is not one himself, a pedant save a pedant, a provincial but a provincial, and I would wager it was the printer who put it on the title of "Letters to a Provincial."

The chief talent, that which rules all others.

If the lightning were to strike low-lying places, etc., poets, and those whose only reasonings are on things of that nature would lack proofs.

———

POETICAL BEAUTY.— As we talk of poetical beauty, so ought we to talk of mathematical beauty and medical beauty; yet we do not use those terms, because we know perfectly the object of mathematics, that it consists in proofs, and the object of medicine, that it consists in healing, but we do not understand wherein consists charm which is the object of poetry. We do not know what is the natural model to be imitated, and for want of that knowledge we invent a set of extravagant terms, "the golden age, the wonder of our times, fatal," etc., and call this jargon poetic beauty.

But if we imagine a woman on that pattern, which consists in saying little things in great words, we shall see a pretty girl bedecked with mirrors and chains absurd to our taste, because we know better wherein consists the charm of woman than the charm of verse. But those who do not know would admire her in such trimmings, and in many villages she would be taken for the queen, wherefore sonnets made on such a pattern have been called the Village Queens.

Those who judge of a work without rule are in regard to others as those who possess a watch are in regard to others. One says, "It was two hours ago"; another, "It is only three-quarters of an hour." I look at my watch and say to the one, "You are weary of us," and to the other, "Time flies fast with you, for it is only an hour and a half." And I laugh at those who say that time goes slowly with me, and that I judge by fancy. They do not know that I judge by my watch.

From "Thoughts." All the foregoing are from the translation of C. Keegan Paul. (Keegan Paul, Trench & Co., London.)

WALTER PATER

(1839–1894)

WALTER PATER'S novel, "Marius the Epicurean" (1885), gave him an international reputation as a writer of the highest class of fiction. Among scholars he had already become well known from his studies of Plato and his philosophical essays. He differs from many modern students of Plato in the depth of his actual appreciation of his master. His Platonism means something more than mere metaphysics for display or discussion. He gets at the human purpose of the Platonic philosophy, and in presenting it to modern readers strips away the shell of artificial strangeness, which is due to accidental differences of time, country, language, and habits, rather than to anything essentially abnormal or supernormal in the thoughts of Plato. Pater's "Appreciations," published in 1889, have found marked favor with the reading public. He died at Oxford, July 30th, 1894.

THE GENIUS OF PLATO

TO TRACE that thread of physical color, entwined throughout, and multiplied sometimes into large tapestried figures, is the business, the enjoyment, of the student of the Dialogues, as he reads them. For this or that special literary quality, indeed, we may go safely by preference to this or that particular Dialogue; to the "Gorgias," for instance, for the readiest Attic wit, and a manly practical sense in the handling of philosophy; to the "Charmides," for something like the effect of sculpture in modeling a person; to the "Timæus," for certain brilliant chromatic effects. Yet who that reads the "Theætetus," or the "Phædrus," or the seventh book of the "Republic," can doubt Plato's gift in precisely the opposite direction; his gift of sounding by words the depths of thought, a plastic power literally, molding to term and phrase what might have seemed in its very nature too impalpable and abstruse to lend itself, in any case, to language? He gives names to the invisible acts, processes, creations, of abstract mind, as masterfully, as efficiently, as Adam

abstract language, he gave an illusive air of reality or substance to the mere nonentities of metaphysic hypothesis,—of a mind trying to feed itself on its own emptiness.

Just there,—in the situation of one shaped, by combining nature and circumstance into a seer who has a sort of sensuous love of the unseen,—is the paradox of Plato's genius, and therefore, always, of Platonism, of the Platonic temper. His aptitude for things visible, his gift of words, empower him to express, as if for the eyes, what, except to the eye of the mind, is strictly invisible,—what an acquired asceticism induces him to rank above, and sometimes, in terms of harshest dualism, oppose to, the sensible world. Plato is to be interpreted not merely by his antecedents, by the influence upon him of those who preceded him, but by his successors, by the temper, the intellectual alliances, of those who directly or indirectly have been sympathetic with him. Now it is noticeable that, at first sight somewhat incongruously, a certain number of Manicheans have always been of his company; people who held that matter was evil. Pointing significantly to an unmistakable vein of Manichean, or Puritan, sentiment actually there in the Platonic Dialogues, these rude companions or successors of his carry us back to his great predecessor, to Socrates, whose personal influence had so strongly enforced on Plato the severities moral and intellectual alike, of Parmenides, and of the Pythagoreans. The cold breath of a harshly abstract, a too incorporeal, philosophy, had blown, like an east wind, on that last depressing day in the prison cell of Socrates; and the venerable commonplaces then put forth, in which an overstrained pagan sensuality seems to be reacting, to be taking vengeance, on itself, turned now sick and suicidal, will lose none of their weight with Plato:—That "all who rightly touch philosophy, study nothing else than to die, and to be dead." That "the soul reasons best, when, as much as possible, it comes to be alone with itself, bidding good-by to the body, and, to the utmost of its power, rejecting communion with it, with the very touch of it, aiming at what is." It was, in short, as if for the soul to have come into a human body at all had been the seed of disease in it, the beginning of its own proper death.

As for any adornments or provision for this body, the master had declared that a true philosopher as such would make as little of them as possible. To those young hearers, the words of Socrates may well have seemed to anticipate, not the visible

himself to the visible living creations of old. As Plato speaks of them, we might say those abstractions too become visible living creatures. We read the speculative poetry of Wordsworth or Tennyson; and we may observe that a great metaphysical force has come into language which is by no means purely technical or scholastic; what a help such language is to the understanding, to a real hold over the things, the thoughts, the mental processes, those words denote; a vocabulary to which thought freely commits itself, trained, stimulated, raised, thereby, toward a high level of abstract conception, surely to the increase of our general intellectual powers. That, of course, is largely due to Plato's successor, to Aristotle's lifelong labor of analysis and definition, and to his successors the Schoolmen, with their systematic culture of a precise instrument for the registration, by the analytic intellect, of its own subtlest movements. But then, Aristotle, himself the first of the Schoolmen, had succeeded Plato, and did but formulate, as a terminology "of art," as technical language, what for Plato is still vernacular, original, personal, the product in him of an instinctive imaginative power,—a sort of visual power, but causing others also to see what is matter of original intuition for him.

From the first, in fact, our faculty of thinking is limited by our command of speech. Now it is straight from Plato's lips, as if in natural conversation, that the language came, in which the mind has ever since been discoursing with itself concerning itself, in that inward dialogue, which is the "active principle" of the dialectic method as an instrument for the attainment of truth. For the essential, or dynamic, dialogue is ever that dialogue of the mind with itself, which any converse with Socrates or Plato does but promote. The very words of Plato, then, challenge us straightway to larger and finer apprehension of the processes of our own minds; are themselves a discovery in the sphere of mind. 'Twas he made us freemen of those solitary places, so trying yet so attractive; so remote and high, they seem, yet are naturally so close to us; he peopled them with intelligible forms. Nay, more! By his peculiar gift of verbal articulation he anticipated the mere hollow spaces which a knowledge, then merely potential, and an experience still to come, would one day occupy. And so, those who cannot admit his actual speculative results, precisely his report on the invisible theoretic world, have been to the point sometimes, in that their objection, by sheer effectiveness of

world he had then delineated in glowing color as if for the bodily eye, but only the chilling influence of the hemlock; and it was because Plato was only half convinced of the Manichean or Puritan element in his master's doctrine, or rather was in contact with it on one side only of his complex and genial nature, that Platonism became possible, as a temper for which, in strictness, the opposition of matter to spirit has no ultimate or real existence. Not to be "pure" from the body, but to identify it, in its utmost fairness, with the fair soul, by a gymnastic "fused in music," became, from first to last, the aim of education as he conceived it. That the body is but "a hindrance to the attainment of philosophy, if one takes it along with one as a companion in one's search," a notion which Christianity, at least in its later though wholly legitimate developments, will correct, —can hardly have been the last thought of Plato himself on quitting it. He opens his door indeed to those austere monitors. They correct the sensuous richness of his genius, but could not suppress it. The sensuous lover becomes a lover of the invisible, but still a lover, after his earlier pattern, carrying into the world of intellectual vision, of θεωρία, all the associations of the actual world of sight. Some of its invisible realities he can all but see with the bodily eye: the absolute Temperance, in the person of the youthful Charmides; the absolute Righteousness, in the person of the dying Socrates. Yes, truly! all true knowledge will be like the knowledge of a person, of living persons, and truth, for Plato, in spite of his Socratic asceticism, to the last, something to look at. The eyes which had noted physical things, so finely, vividly, continuously, would be still at work; and, Plato, thus qualifying the Manichean or Puritan element in Socrates by his own capacity for the world of sense, Platonism has contributed largely, has been an immense encouragement toward the redemption of matter of the world of sense, by art, by all right education, by the creeds and worship of the Christian Church,—toward the vindication of the dignity of the body.

It was doubtless because Plato was an excellent scholar that he did not begin to teach others till he was more than forty years old,—one of the great scholars of the world, with Virgil and Milton: by which is implied that, possessed of the inborn genius, of those natural powers, which sometimes bring with them a certain defiance of rule, of the intellectual habits of others, he acquires, by way of habit and rule, all that can be taught and learned; and what is thus derived from others by docility and discipline, what is *rangé*, comes to have in him, and in his work, an equivalent weight with what is unique, impulsive, underivable. Raphael,—Raphael as you see him in the Blenheim "Madonna," is a supreme example of such scholarship in the sphere of art. Born of a romantically ancient family, understood to be the descendant of Solon himself, Plato had been in early youth a writer of verse. That he turned to a more vigorous, though pedestrian mode of writing, was perhaps an effect of his corrective intercourse with Socrates, through some of the most important years of his life,— from twenty to twenty-eight.

He belonged to what was just then the discontented class, and might well have taken refuge from active political life in political ideals, or in a kind of self-imposed exile. A traveler, adventurous for that age, he certainly became. After the *Lehrjahre*, the *Wander-jahre!*—all round the Mediterranean coasts as far west as Sicily. Think of what all that must have meant just then, for eyes which could see. If those journeys had begun in angry flight from home, it was for purposes of self-improvement they were continued: the delightful fruit of them is evident in what he writes; and finding him in friendly intercourse with Dionysius the elder, with Dio, and Dionysius the younger, at the polished court of Syracuse, we may understand they were a search also for "the philosophic king," perhaps for the opportune moment of realizing "the ideal state." In that case, his quarrels with those capricious tyrants show that he was disappointed. For the future he sought no more to pass beyond the charmed theoretic circle, "speaking wisdom," as was said of Pythagoras, only "among the perfect." He returns finally to Athens; and there, in the quiet precincts of the Acadêmus, which has left a somewhat dubious name to places where people come to be taught or to teach, founds, not a state, not even a brotherhood, but only the first college, with something of a common life, of communism on that small scale, with Aristotle for one of its scholars, with its chapel, its gardens, its library with the authentic text of his "Dialogues" upon the shelves: we may just discern the sort of place, through the scantiest notices. His reign was, after all, to be in his writings. Plato himself does nothing in them to retard the effacement which mere time brings to persons and their abodes; and there had been that, moreover, in his own temper, which promotes self-effacement. Yet as he left it,

the place remained for centuries, according to his will, to its original use. What he taught through the remaining forty years of his life, the method of that teaching, whether it was less or more esoteric than the teaching of the extant "Dialogues," is but matter of surmise. Writers, who in their day might still have said much we should have liked to hear, give us little but old, quasi-supernatural stories, told as if they had been new ones, about him. The year of his birth fell, according to some, in the very year of the death of Pericles (a significant date!) but is not precisely ascertainable: nor is the year of his death, nor its manner. "*Scribens est mortuus*," says Cicero: after the manner of a true scholar, "he died pen in hand."

From the Contemporary Review.

PETRARCH

(FRANCESCO PETRARCA, OR PETRACCO)

(1304–1374)

FRANCESCO PETRARCA, son of a Florentine notary, who had been exiled to Arezzo, was one of the greatest scholars of the Middle Ages and one of the greatest lyric poets of any age. He is chiefly known by his sonnets to Laura, but the same wonderful ear for the melody of language they illustrate made him a great linguist, and his mastery of Homer and the classical poets of the Homeric school fitted him for leadership in forcing the revival of learning which made modern times possible. The "Laura" to whom the sonnets were addressed was "the daughter of Audibert de Noves and the wife of Hugues de Sade." It is said that she was an entirely decorous matron, the mother of a numerous family of children. Petrarch's admiration for her was Platonic, and he seems to have used her for poetical purposes as a peg to hang his sonnets on, with much the same reality and unreality of passion Don Quixote felt towards Dulcinea del Toboso, after adopting her as a necessary part of the outfit of a knight-errant. It is hard for the modern mind to enter into the mediæval idea of romantic or chivalric love. It is much easier to appreciate Petrarch's intellectual dignity when we turn from his sonnets to his work as a "humanist." Among his essays and prose treatises written in Latin are those "On the Contempt of the World," "On Solitude," "On True Wisdom," and "On Illustrious Men." He also wrote a Latin poem, "Africa," which he himself valued highly, though it has found few readers since his death. His "Treatise on the Remedies of Good and Bad Fortune" (De Remediis Utriusque Fortunæ") was dedicated to his friend Azzo da Correggio. In it Petrarch declares that "our distresses arise chiefly from ourselves," and as a remedy for them he proposed, as did Goethe, development of the true self. To that end, he studied the great classical poets and the great fathers of the Christian Church, valuing Homer and St. Augustine if not equally, yet alike as masters. His mildness and his catholic sympathy gave him a popularity in his own generation which was denied to the sterner and sublimer Dante. On April 8th, 1341, he was crowned at Rome as the Poet Laureate of the "Holy Roman Empire." His house at Vaucluse was bought in

1337 and much of his later life was spent there, but he had princes and great nobles among his friends and they frequently called on him for services in diplomacy and politics. He died at Arquà on July 18th or 19th, 1374, holding then, as he does still, a place next to Dante among Italian poets. He had as a lyric poet the same ear for "time" and melody which immortalized Horace, and the study of his sonnets can do much to elucidate the important and almost wholly misapprehended laws of "quantity" on which Horatian verse depends.

W. V. B.

CONCERNING GOOD AND BAD FORTUNE

WHEN I consider the instability of human affairs, and the variations of fortune, I find nothing more uncertain or restless than the life of man. Nature has given to animals an excellent remedy under disasters, which is the ignorance of them. We seem better treated in intelligence, foresight, and memory. No doubt these are admirable presents; but they often annoy more than they assist us. A prey to unuseful or distressing cares, we are tormented by the present, the past, and the future; and, as if we feared we should not be miserable enough, we join to the evil we suffer the remembrance of a former distress and the apprehension of some future calamity. This is the Cerberus with three heads we combat without ceasing. Our life might be gay and happy if we would; but we eagerly seek subjects of affliction to render it irksome and melancholy. We pass the first years of this life in the shades of ignorance, the succeeding ones in pain and labor, the latter part in grief and remorse, and the whole in error; nor do we suffer ourselves to possess one bright day without a cloud.

Let us examine this matter with sincerity, and we shall agree that our distresses chiefly arise from ourselves. It is virtue alone which can render us superior to Fortune; we quit her standard, and the combat is no longer equal. Fortune mocks us; she turns us on her wheel: she raises and abases us at her pleasure, but her power is founded on our weakness. This is an old-rooted evil, but it is not incurable: there is nothing a firm and elevated mind cannot accomplish. The discourse of the wise and the study of good books are the best remedies I know of; but to these we must join the consent of the soul, without which the best advice will be useless. What gratitude do we not owe to those great men who, though dead many ages before us, live with us by their works, discourse with us, are our masters and guides, and serve us as pilots in the navigation of life, where our vessel is agitated without ceasing by the storms of our passions! It is here that true Philosophy brings us to a safe port, by a sure and easy passage; not like that of the schools, which, raising us in its airy and deceitful wings, and causing us to hover on the clouds of frivolous dispute, lets us fall without any light or instruction in the same place where she took us up.

Dear friend, I do not attempt to exhort you to the study I judge so important. Nature has given you a taste for all knowledge, but Fortune has denied you the leisure to acquire it; yet, whenever you could steal a moment from public affairs, you sought the conversation of wise men; and I have remarked that your memory often served you instead of books. It is therefore unnecessary to invite you to do what you have always done; but, as we cannot retain all we hear or read, it may be useful to furnish your mind with some maxims that may best serve to arm you against the assaults of misfortune. The vulgar, and even philosophers, have decided that adverse fortune was most difficult to sustain. For my own part I am of a different opinion, and believe it more easy to support adversity than prosperity; and that fortune is more treacherous and dangerous when she caresses than when she dismays. Experience has taught me this, not books or arguments. I have seen many persons sustain great losses, poverty, exile, tortures, death, and even disorders that were worse than death, with courage; but I have seen none whose heads have not been turned by power, riches, and honors. How often have we beheld those overthrown by good fortune, who could never be shaken by bad! This made me wish to learn how to support a great fortune. You know the short time this work has taken. I have been less attentive to what might shine than to what might be useful on this subject. Truth and virtue are the wealth of all men; and shall I not discourse on these with my dear Azon? I would prepare for you, as in a little portable box, a friendly antidote against the poison of good and bad fortune. The one requires a rein to repress the sallies of a transported soul; the other a consolation to fortify the overwhelmed and afflicted spirit.

Nature gave you, my friend, the heart of a king, but she gave you not a kingdom, of which therefore Fortune could not deprive

you. But I doubt whether our age can furnish an example of worse or better treatment from her than yourself. In the first part of your life you were blessed with an admirable constitution and astonishing health and vigor: some years after we beheld you thrice abandoned by the physicians who despaired of your life. The heavenly Physician, who was your sole resource, restored your health, but not your former strength. You were then called iron-footed, for your singular force and agility; you are now bent, and lean upon the shoulders of those whom you formerly supported. Your country beheld you one day its governor, the next an exile. Princes disputed for your friendship, and afterwards conspired your ruin. You lost by death the greatest part of your friends; the rest, according to custom, deserted you in calamity. To these misfortunes was added a violent disease, which attacked you when destitute of all succors, at a distance from your country and family, in a strange land, invested by the troops of your enemies; so that those two or three friends whom fortune had left you could not come near to relieve you. In a word, you have experienced every hardship but imprisonment and death. But what do I say? You have felt all the horrors of the former, when your faithful wife and children were shut up by your enemies; and even death followed you, and took one of those children, for whose life you would willingly have sacrificed your own.

In you have been united the fortunes of Pompey and Marius; but you were neither arrogant in prosperity as the one, nor discouraged in adversity as the other. You have supported both in a manner that has made you loved by your friends and admired by your enemies. There is a peculiar charm in the serene and tranquil air of virtue, which enlightens all around it, in the midst of the darkest scenes, and the greatest calamities. My ancient friendship for you has caused me to quit everything for you to perform a work, in which, as in a glass, you may adjust and prepare your soul for all events; and be able to say, as Æneas did to the Sibyl, "Nothing of this is new to me; I have foreseen, and am prepared for it all." I am sensible that, in the disorders of the mind, as well as those of the body, discourses are not thought the most efficacious remedies; but I am persuaded also that the malady of the soul ought to be cured by spiritual applications.

If we see a friend in distress, and give him all the consolation we are able, we perform the duties of friendship, which pays

more attention to the disposition of the heart than the value of the gift. A small present may be the testimony of a great love. There is no good I do not wish you, and this is all I can offer toward it. I wish this little treatise may be of use to you. If it should not answer my hopes, I shall, however, be secure of pardon from your friendship. It presents you with the four great passions: Hope and Joy, the daughters of Prosperity; Fear and Grief, the offspring of Adversity; who attack the soul, and launch at it all their arrows. Reason commands in the citadel to repulse them; your penetration will easily perceive which side will obtain the victory.

From "Treatise on the Remedies of Good and Bad Fortune."

VIII—196

PLATO

(c. 429–347 B. C.)

PLATO'S "Dialogues" are not strictly essays in their form. The discursiveness of the "Socratic method" of developing a thought through leading questions which involve the idea of the response to them is antagonistic to the true method of the essayist as it was defined and developed by Plato's great pupil, Aristotle. But if Aristotle is the master to whom we owe the Baconian essay, Plutarch, who was Plato's pupil and Montaigne's master, has transmitted the amiable Platonic discursiveness to modern times, so that we have the schools of Plato, of Aristotle, of Theophrastus, and of Cicero all clearly defined in modern essay writing. It is remarkable that Plato, Aristotle, and Theophrastus all belong to the school of Socrates, and are explainable as results of his inspiration. Theophrastus who was taught by Aristotle as the latter was by Plato is the best representative of Socratic humor, as Plato is of Socratic thought. Among philosophical writers on "the higher life," Plato has not been surpassed in ancient or modern times. It is impossible to guess how much of all he attributes to Socrates he really owed to him. There can be no question, however, of his own genius or his own originality. To the Greek world and to the classical Pagan world everywhere, what he wrote of the soul, of death, of the future life, and of the Divinity had the effect of a revelation. We may imagine, if we cannot realize, the strength of his influence then by the admiration and even love he still excites in students of his writings. He is the great master of all philosophical idealists, and of those who go beyond philosophical idealism to the faith that the only true "realism" concerns itself with the enduring realities of a life of which the present life is a transitory phase. What Aristotle did to prepare the way for science Plato did to make it ready for the Christianity of the Gospels.

He was born at Ægina 427 (perhaps 429) B. C. His parents were of patrician descent, and in his youth he was much like other well-bred Greeks. He wrestled, went to the wars, and wrote verse. Several short poems still extant are attributed to him, and one of them is a remarkably artistic example of the vowel symphony constructed according to the Homeric mode in melody. After he became a pupil of Socrates, however, it is said that he burned as many of his poems as he could collect,—perhaps because they were chiefly erotic lyrics of a most unphilosophical kind. After the death of Socrates, whom he had constantly attended, he left Athens, traveling in Egypt, Sicily, and Magna Græcia. During this tour, it is said that he offended Dionysius, tyrant of Syracuse, who sold him as a slave. On being ransomed, he returned to Athens and began teaching in the "Academy," a school which he founded and taught for nearly fifty years until his death in 347 B.C.* His most popular works are perhaps "Crito" and "Phædo," in which he deals with the imprisonment and death of Socrates, but his "The Banquet" and "Republic" are also widely read by those who are not professional students of philosophy. Among other dialogues scarcely less noted are "Phædrus," "Gorgias," "Theætetus," "Timæus," "Politicus," "Critias," and "Ion."

No one who reads half a dozen pages of Plato will need to be told he is a great thinker. Of his style, except as we can see his discursive tendencies, it would be presumptuous to speak. He has been called "a prose poet," but the melody of the Greek language cannot be translated into any other and we do not read Greek prose with its own rhythms; but before the close of the twentieth century, the learned world will probably so far revive the quantities of the Greek language and revitalize it into a living tongue, that it will be possible to decide whether the sense of music shown in the verse, attributed to Plato, governs in his prose also. If so, he will take rank among the world's greatest masters of melodious prose.

W. V. B.

CRITO;—"OF WHAT WE OUGHT TO DO"

[*Socrates and Crito converse while Socrates is under sentence of death.*]

Socrates — What is the occasion of your coming here so soon, Crito? As I take it, it is very early.

Crito — Indeed, it is.

Socrates — What o'clock may it be then?

Crito — A little before the break of day.

Socrates — I wonder that the jailer permitted you to come in.

Crito — He is one I know very well. I have been with him here frequently; and he is in some measure obliged to me.

Socrates — Are you but just come? Or is it long since you came?

Crito — I have been here a good while.

* These statements are nearly all more or less controverted.

Socrates — Why did you not awaken me then when you came in?

Crito — Pray God forbid, Socrates. For my own part, I would gladly shake off the cares and anxiety that keep my eyes from shutting. But when I entered this room, I wondered to find you so sound asleep, and was loath to awaken you, that I might not deprive you of those happy minutes. Indeed, Socrates, ever since I became acquainted with you, I have been always delighted with your patience and calm temper; but in a distinguishing manner in this juncture, since, in the circumstances you are in, your eye looks so easy and unconcerned.

Socrates — Indeed, Crito, it would be very unbecoming in one of my age to be fearful of death.

Crito — Aye! And how many do we see every day, under the like misfortunes, whom age does not free from those dreads?

Socrates — That is true. But after all what made you come hither so early?

Crito — I came to tell you a perplexing piece of news, which, though it may not seem to affect you, yet it overwhelms both me and your relations and friends with insupportable grief. In short, I bring the most terrible news that ever could be brought.

Socrates — What news? Is the ship arrived from Delos, upon whose return I am to die?

Crito — It is not yet arrived; but doubtless it will be here this day, according to the intelligence we have from some persons that came from Sunium, and left it there. For at that rate it cannot fail of being here to-day; and to-morrow you must unavoidably die.

Socrates — Why not, Crito? Be it so, since 'tis the will of God. However, I do not think that the vessel will arrive this day.

Crito — What do you ground that conjecture upon?

Socrates — I'll tell you: I am not to die till the day after the arrival of the vessel.

Crito — At least those who are to execute the sentence say so.

Socrates — That vessel will not arrive till to-morrow, as I conjecture from a certain dream I had this night about a minute ago. And it seems to me a pleasure that you did not awaken me.

Crito — Well, what is this dream?

Socrates — I thought I saw a very gentle comely woman, dressed in white, come up to me, who, calling me by name, said: "In three days thou shalt be in the fertile Phthia."

Crito — That is a very remarkable dream, Socrates.

Socrates — 'Tis a very significant one, Crito.

Crito — Yes, without doubt. But for this time, prithee, Socrates, take my advice, and make your escape. For my part, if you die, besides the irreparable loss of a friend, which I shall ever bewail, I am afraid that numbers of people, who are not well acquainted either with you or me, will believe that I have forsaken you, in not employing my interest for promoting your escape, now that it is in my power. Is there anything more base than to lie under the disrepute of being wedded to my money more than to my friend? For, in fine, the people will never believe that 'twas you who refused to go from hence, when we urged you to be gone.

Socrates — My dear Crito, why should we be so much concerned for the opinion of the people? Is it not enough that the more sensible part, who are the only men we ought to regard, know how the case stands?

Crito — But you see, Socrates, there's a necessity of being concerned for the noise of the mob, for your example is sufficient instance that they are capable of doing, not only small, but the greatest of injuries, and display their passion in an outrageous manner against those who are once run down by the vulgar opinion.

Socrates — I wish, Crito, that the people were able to do the greatest of injuries. Were it so, they would likewise be capable of doing the greatest good. That would be a great happiness. But neither the one nor the other is possible. For they cannot make men either wise men or fools.

Crito — I grant it. But pray answer me: Is it out of tenderness to me and your other friends that you will not stir from hence? Is it fear lest upon your escape we should be troubled, and charged with carrying you off, and by that means be obliged to quit our possession, or pay a large sum of money, or else suffer something more fatal than either? If that be your fear, shake it off, Socrates, in the name of the gods. Is not it highly reasonable that we should purchase your escape at the rate of exposing ourselves to these dangers, and greater ones, if there be occasion? Once more, my dear Socrates, believe me, and go along with me.

Socrates — I own, Crito, that I have such thoughts, and several others besides in my view.

Crito — Fear nothing, I entreat you; for, in the first place, they require no great sum to let you out. And on the other hand, you see what a pitiful condition those are in who probably might arraign us. A small sum of money will stop their mouths: my estate alone will serve for that. If you scruple to accept of my offer, here are a great many strangers who desire nothing more than to furnish you with what money you want. Simmias the Theban himself has brought up very considerable sums. Cebes is capable of doing as much, and so are several others. Let not your fears then stifle the desire of making your escape. And as for what you told me the other day, in court, that if you made your escape, you should not know how to live — pray let not that trouble you. Whithersoever you go, you'll be beloved in all parts of the world. If you'll go to Thessaly, I have friends there who will honor you according to your merit, and think themselves happy in supplying you with what you want, and covering you from all occasions of fear in their country. Besides, Socrates, without doubt you are guilty of a very unjust thing in delivering up yourself, while 'tis in your power to make your escape, and promoting what your enemies so passionately wish for. For you not only betray yourself, but likewise your children by abandoning them, when you might make a shift to maintain and educate them. You are not at all concerned at what may befall them, though at the same time they are like to be in as dismal a condition as ever poor orphans were. A man ought either to have no children, or else to expose himself to the care and trouble of breeding them. You seem to me to act the softest and most insensible part in the world; whereas you ought to take up a resolution worthy of a generous soul; above all, you who boast that you pursued nothing but virtue all the days of your life. I tell you, Socrates, I am ashamed upon the account of you and your relations, since the world will believe 'twas owing to our cowardliness that you did not get off. In the first place, they will charge you with standing a trial that you might have avoided; then they will censure your conduct in making your defenses; and at last, which is the most shameful of all, they will upbraid us with forsaking you through fear or cowardice, since we did not accomplish your escape. Pray consider of it, my dear Socrates; if you do not prevent the approaching evil, you'll bear a part in the shame that will cover us all. Pray advise with yourself quickly. But now I think on it, there is not time for advising, there's no choice left, all must be put in execution.

Socrates — My dear Crito, your good-will is very commendable, provided it agree with right reason; but if it swerve from that, the stronger it is, the more is it blameworthy. The first thing to be considered is, whether we ought to do as you say, or not. For you know, 'tis not of yesterday that I've accustomed myself only to follow the reasons that appear most just after a mature examination. Though fortune frown upon me, yet I'll never part with the principles I have all along professed. These principles appear always the same, and I esteem them equally at all times. So if your advice be not backed by the strongest reasons, assure yourself I will never comply, not if all the power of the people should arm itself against me, or offer to frighten me like a child by laying on fresh chains, and threatening to deprive me of the greatest good, and oblige me to suffer the cruellest death.

Crito — Now, how shall we manage this inquiry justly?

Socrates — To be sure, the fairest way is to resume what you have been saying of the vulgar opinions; that is, to inquire whether there are some reports that we ought to regard, and others that are to be slighted; or whether the saying so is only a groundless and childish proposition. I have a strong desire, upon this occasion, to try, in your presence, whether this principle will appear to me in different colors from what it did while I was in other circumstances, or whether I shall always find it the same, in order to determine me to compliance or refusal.

If I mistake not, 'tis certain that several persons, who thought themselves men of sense, have often maintained in this place, that of all the opinions of men, some are to be regarded and others to be slighted. In the name of the gods, Crito, do not you think that was well said? In all human appearance you are in no danger of dying to-morrow; and therefore 'tis presumed that the fear of the present danger cannot work any change upon you. Wherefore, pray consider it well: do not you think they spoke justly who said that all the opinions of men are not always to be regarded, but only some of them; and those not of all men, but only of some? What do you say? Do not you think 'tis very true?

Crito — Very true.

Socrates — At any rate, then, ought not we to esteem the good opinions and slight the bad ones?

Crito — Aye, doubtless.

Socrates — Are not the good opinions then those of wise men, and the bad ones those of fools?

Crito — It cannot be otherwise.

Socrates — Let us see, then, how you will answer this. When a man who makes his exercises, and comes to have his lesson, should he regard the commendation or censure of whoever comes first, or only of him that is either a physician or a master?

Crito — Of the last, to be sure.

Socrates — Then he ought to fear the censure and value the commendation of that man alone, and slight what comes from others.

Crito — Without doubt.

Socrates — For that reason this young man must neither eat nor drink, nor do anything, without the orders of that master, that man of sense, and he is not at all to govern himself by the caprices of others.

Crito — That is true.

Socrates — Let us fix upon that, then. But suppose he disobeys this master, and disregards his applause or censure, and suffers himself to be blinded by the caresses and applauses of the ignorant mob, will not he come to some harm by this means?

Crito — How is it possible it should be otherwise?

Socrates — But what will be the nature of this harm that will accrue to him thereupon? Where will it terminate? And what part of him will it affect?

Crito — His body, without doubt; for by that means he'll ruin himself.

Socrates — Very well, but is not the case the same all over? Upon the point of justice or injustice, honesty or dishonesty, good or evil, which at present are the subject of our dispute, shall we rather refer ourselves to the opinion of the people than to that of an experienced wise man, who justly challenges more respect and deference from us than all the world besides? And if we do not act conformably to the opinion of this one man, is it not certain that we shall ruin ourselves, and entirely lose that which only lives and gains new strength by justice, and perishes only through injustice? Or must we take all that for a thing of no account?

Crito — I am of your opinion.

Socrates — Take heed, I entreat you; if, by following the opinions of the ignorant, we destroy that which is only preserved by health and wasted by sickness, can we survive the corruption of that, whether it be our body or somewhat else?

Crito — That's certain.

Socrates — Can one live then after the corruption and destruction of the body?

Crito — No, to be sure.

Socrates — But can one survive the corruption of that which lives only by justice, and dies only through injustice? Or is this thing (whatever it be) that has justice or injustice for its object to be less valued than the body?

Crito — Not at all.

Socrates — What, is it much more valuable then?

Crito — A great deal more.

Socrates — Then, my dear Crito, we ought not to be concerned at what the people say, but what he says, who knows what is just and unjust; and that alone is nothing else but the truth. Thus you see you established false principles at first, in saying that we ought to pay a deference to the opinions of the people upon what is just, good, honest, and its contraries. Some, perhaps, will object that the people are able to put us to death.

Crito — To be sure they will start that objection.

Socrates — 'Tis also true. But that does not alter the nature of what we were saying; that is still the same. For you must still remember that 'tis not life, but a good life, that we ought to court.

Crito — That is a certain truth.

Socrates — But is it not likewise certain that this good life consists in nothing else but honesty and justice?

Crito — Yes.

Socrates — Now, before we go further, let us examine, upon the principles you have agreed to, whether my departure from hence, without the permission of the Athenians, is just or unjust. If it be found just, we must do our utmost to bring it about; but if it be unjust, we must lay aside the design. For as to the considerations you alleged just now of money, reputation, and family, these are only the thoughts of the baser mob, who put innocent persons to death, and would afterwards bring them to life if 'twere possible. But as for us who bend our thoughts another way, all that we are to mind is whether we do a just

---

thing in giving money, and lying under an obligation to those who promote our escape; or whether both we and they do not commit a piece of injustice in so doing. If this be an unjust thing, we need not reason much upon the point, since 'tis better to abide here and die than to undergo somewhat more terrible than death.

Crito — You are in the right, Socrates; let us see then how it will fall.

Socrates — We shall go hand in hand in the inquiry. If you have anything of weight to answer, pray do it when I have spoken, that so I may comply; if not, pray forbear any further to press me to go hence without the consent of the Athenians. I shall be infinitely glad if you can persuade me to do it; but I cannot do it without being first convinced. Take notice then whether my way of pursuing this inquiry satisfies you, and do your utmost to make answer to my questions.

Crito — I will.

Socrates — Is it true that we ought not to do an unjust thing to any man? Or is it lawful in any measure to do it to one when we are forbidden to do it to another? Or is it not absolutely true that all manner of injustice is neither good nor honest, as we were saying but now? Or, in fine, are all these sentiments which we formerly entertained, vanished in a few days? And is it possible, Crito, that those of years, our most serious conferences, should resemble those of children, and we at the same time not be sensible that 'tis so? Ought not we rather to stand to what we have said, as being a certain truth, that all injustice is scandalous and fatal to the person that commits it, let men say what they will, and let our fortune be never so good or bad?

Crito — That's certain.

Socrates — Then must we avoid the least measure of injustice?

Crito — Most certainly.

Socrates — Since we are to avoid the least degree of it, then we ought not to do it to those who are unjust to us, notwithstanding that this people think it lawful.

Crito — So I think.

Socrates — But what! Ought we to do evil or not?

Crito — Without doubt we ought not.

Socrates — But is it justice to repay evil with evil, pursuant to the opinion of the people, or is it unjust?

Crito — 'Tis highly unjust.

Socrates — Then there's no difference between doing evil and being unjust?

Crito — I own it.

Socrates — Then we ought not to do the least evil or injustice to any man, let him do by us as he will. But take heed, Crito, that by this concession you do not speak against your own sentiments. For I know very well there are few that will go this length; and 'tis impossible for those who vary in their sentiments upon this point to agree well together. Nay, on the contrary, the contempt of one another's opinions leads them to a reciprocal contempt of one another's persons. Consider well then if you are of the same opinion with me; and let us ground our reasonings upon this principle, that we ought not to do evil for evil, or treat those unjustly who are unjust to us. For my part, I never did, nor ever will, entertain any other principle. Tell me then if you have changed your mind; if not, give ear to what follows.

Crito — I give ear.

Socrates — Well: a man that has made a just promise, ought he to keep it, or to break it?

Crito — He ought to keep it.

Socrates — If I go hence without the consent of the Athenians, shall not I injure some people, and especially those who do not deserve it? Or shall we in this follow what we think equally just to everybody?

Crito — I cannot answer you, for I do not understand you.

Socrates — Pray take notice; when we put ourselves in a way of making our escape, or going hence, or how you please to call it, suppose the law and the republic should present themselves in a body before us, and accost us in this manner: "Socrates, what are you going to do? To put in execution what you now design were wholly to ruin the laws and the state. Do you think a city can subsist when justice has not only lost its force, but is likewise perverted, overturned, and trampled under foot by private persons?" What answer could we make to such and many other questions? For what is it that an orator cannot say upon the overturning of that law which provides that sentences once pronounced shall not be infringed? Shall we answer that the republic has judged amiss and passed an unjust sentence upon us? Shall that be our answer?

much greater." What shall we answer to all this, Crito? Shall we acknowledge the truth of what the laws advance?

Crito — How can we avoid it?

Socrates — "Do you see, then, Socrates," continue they, "what reason we have to brand your enterprise against us as unjust? Of us you hold your birth, your maintenance, your education; in fine, we have done you all the good we are capable of, as well as the other citizens. Indeed, we do not fail to make public proclamation, that 'tis lawful for every private man, if he does not find his account in the laws and customs of our republic, after a mature examination, to retire with all his effects whither he pleases. And if any of you cannot comply with our customs, and desires to remove and live elsewhere, not one of us shall hinder him, he may go where he pleases. But on the other hand, if any one of you continues to live here, after he has considered our way of administering justice, and the policy observed in the state, then we say he is in effect obliged to obey all our commands, and we maintain that his disobedience is unjust on a threefold account: for not obeying those to whom he owes his birth; for trampling under foot those that educated him; and for violating his faith after he engaged to obey us, and not taking the pains to make remonstrances to us, if we happen to do any unjust thing. For notwithstanding that we only propose things without using any violence to procure obedience, and give every man his choice whether to obey us, or reclaim us by his counsel or remonstrances, yet he does neither the one nor the other. And we maintain, Socrates, that if you execute what you are now about, you will stand charged with all these crimes, and that in a much higher degree than if another private man had committed the same injustice." If I asked them the reason, without doubt they would stop my mouth by telling me that I submitted myself in a distinguishing manner to all these conditions. "And we," continue they, "have great evidence that you were always pleased with us and the republic; for if this city had not been more agreeable to you than any other, you had never continued in it, no more than the other Athenians. None of the shows could ever tempt you to go out of the city, except once, that you went to see the games at the Isthmus; you never went anywhere else, excepting your military expeditions, and never undertook a voyage, as others are wont to do. You never had the curiosity to visit other cities, or inquire after other laws, as

Crito — Ah, without any scruple, Socrates.

Socrates — What will the laws say then? "Socrates, is it not true that you agreed with us to submit yourself to a public trial?" And if we should seem to be surprised at such language, they'll continue, perhaps, "Be not surprised, Socrates, but make an answer, for you yourself used to insist upon question and answer. Tell then what occasion you have to complain of the republic and of us, that you are so eager upon destroying it? Are not we the authors of your birth? Is it not by our means that your father married her who brought you forth? What fault can you find with the laws we have established as to marriage?" "Nothing at all," should I answer. "As to the nourishing and bringing up of children, and the manner of your education, are not the laws just that we enacted upon that head, by which we obliged your father to bring you up to music and the exercises?" "Very just," I'd say. "Since you were born, brought up, and educated under our influence, durst you maintain that you are not our nursed child and subject as well as your father? And if you are, do you think to have equal power with us, as if it were lawful for you to inflict upon us all we enjoin you to undergo? But since you cannot lay claim to any such right against your father or your master, so as to repay evil for evil, injury for injury, how can you think to obtain that privilege against your country and the laws, insomuch that if we endeavor to put you to death, you'll counteract us by endeavoring to prevent us and to ruin your country and its laws? Can you call such an action just, you that are an inseparable follower of true virtue? Are you ignorant that your country is more considerable, and more worthy of respect and veneration before God and man than your father, mother, and all your relations together? That you ought to honor your country, yield to it, and humor it more than an angry father? That you must either reclaim it by your counsel, or obey its injunctions, and suffer without grumbling all that it imposes upon you? If it orders you to be whipped, or laid in irons, if it sends you to the wars, there to spend your blood, you ought to do it without demurring; you must not shake off the yoke, or flinch or quit your post; but in the army, in prison, and everywhere else, ought equally to obey the orders of your country, or else assist it with wholesome counsel. For if offering violence to a father or mother be a piece of grand impiety, to put force upon one's country is a

being contented with us and our republic. You always made a distinguishing choice of us, and on all occasions testified that you submitted with all your heart to live according to our maxims. Besides, your having had children in this city is an infallible evidence that you like it. In fine, in this very last juncture you might have been sentenced to banishment if you would, and might then have done, with the consent of the republic, what you now attempt without their permission. But you were so stately, so unconcerned at death, that in your own terms you preferred death to banishment. But now you have no regard to these fine words, you are no further concerned for the laws, since you are going to overturn them. You do just what a pitiful slave would offer to do, by endeavoring to make your escape contrary to the laws of the treaty you have signed, by which you obliged yourself to live according to our rules. Pray answer us: Did not we say right in affirming that you agreed to this treaty, and submitted yourself to these terms, not only in words, but in deeds?" What shall we say to all this, Crito? And what can we do else but acknowledge that 'tis so?

Crito — How can we avoid it, Socrates?

Socrates — "What else then," continue they, "is this action of yours but a violation of that treaty, and all its terms? That treaty that you were not made to sign either by force or surprise, not without time to think on it: for you had the whole course of seventy years to have removed in, if you had been dissatisfied with us, or unconvinced of the justice of our proposals. You neither pitched upon Lacedæmon nor Crete, notwithstanding that you always cried up their laws; nor any of the other Grecian cities, or strange countries. You have been less out of Athens than the lame and the blind; which is an invincible proof that the city pleased you in a distinguishing manner, and consequently that we did, since a city never can be agreeable if its laws are not such. And yet at this time you counteract the treaty. But, if you will take our advice, Socrates, we would have you to stand to your treaty, and not expose yourself to be ridiculed by the citizens, by stealing out from hence. Pray consider what advantage can redound either to you or your friends by persisting in that goodly design. Your friends will infallibly be either exposed to danger or banished their country, or have their estates forfeited. And as for yourself, if you retire to any neighboring city, such as Thebes or Megara, which are admirably well governed, you'll there be looked upon as an enemy. All that have any love for their country will look upon you as a corrupter of the laws. Besides, you'll fortify in them the good opinion they have of your judges, and move them to approve the sentence given against you; for a corrupter of the law will at any time pass for a debaucher of the youth, and of the vulgar people. What, will you keep out of these well-governed cities, and these assemblies of just men? But pray will you have enough to live upon in that condition? Or will you have the face to go and live with them? And pray what will you say to them, Socrates? Will you preach to them, as you did here, that virtue, justice, the laws and ordinances ought to be reverenced by men? Do you not think that this will sound very ridiculous in their ears? You ought to think so. But perhaps you'll quickly leave those well-governed cities, and go to Thessaly, to Crito's friends, where there is less order, and more licentiousness; and doubtless in that country they'll take a singular pleasure in hearing you relate in what equipage you made your escape from this prison, that is, covered with some old rags, or a beast's skin, or disguised some other way, as fugitives are wont to be. Everybody will say, 'This old fellow, that has scarce any time to live, had such a strong passion for living, that he did not stand to purchase his life by trampling under foot the most sacred laws.' Such stories will be bandied about of you at a time when you offend no man; but upon the least occasion of complaint, they'll tease you with a thousand other reproaches unworthy of you. You'll spend your time in sneaking and insinuating yourself into the favor of all men, one after another, and owning an equal subjection to them all. For what can you do? Will you feast perpetually in Thessaly, as if the good cheer had drawn you thither? But what will become then of all your fine discourses upon justice and virtue? Besides, if you design to preserve your life for the sake of your children, that cannot be in order to bring them up in Thessaly, as if you could do them no other service but make them strangers. Or if you design to leave them here, do you imagine that during your life they'll be better brought up here, in your absence, under the care of your friends? But will not your friends take the same care of them after your death that they would do in your absence? You ought to be persuaded that all those who call themselves your friends will at all times do them all the service they can. To conclude, Socrates, submit yourself

to our reasons, follow the advice of those who brought you up, and do not put your children, your life, or anything whatsoever, in the balance with justice; to the end that when you come before the tribunal of Pluto, you may be able to clear yourself before your judges. For do not deceive yourself: if you perform what you now design, you will neither better your own cause, nor that of your party; you will neither enlarge its justice nor sanctity either here or in the regions below. But if you die bravely, you owe your death to the injustice, not of the laws, but of men; whereas if you make your escape by repulsing so shamefully the injustice of your enemies, by violating at once both your own faith and our treaty, and injuring so many innocent persons as yourself, your friends, and your country, together with us, we will still be your enemies as long as you live; and when you are dead, our sisters, the laws in the other world, will certainly afford you no joyful reception, as knowing that you endeavored to ruin us. Wherefore do not prefer Crito's counsel to ours."

I think, my dear Crito, I hear what I have now spoken, just as the priests of Cybele imagine they hear the cornets and flutes; and the sound of these words makes so strong an impression in my ears, that it stops me from hearing anything else. These are the sentiments I like; and all you can say to take me off them will be in vain. However, if you think to succeed, I do not prevent you from speaking.

Crito—I have nothing to say, Socrates.

Socrates—Then be quiet, and let us courageously run this course, since God calls and guides us to it.

Complete. From Morley's text.

SOCRATES DRINKS THE HEMLOCK

CRITO said· "I think, Socrates, the sun is still upon the mountains, and has not yet set. I have known persons who have drunk the poison late in the evening, who after the announcement was made to them supped well and drank well, and enjoyed the society of their dearest friends. Do not act in haste. There is yet time."

"Probably," said Socrates, "those who did as you say thought that it was a gain to do so, and I have equally good reasons for not doing so. I shall gain nothing by drinking the poison a little

later except to make myself ridiculous to myself, as if I were so fond of life that I would cling to it when it is slipping away. But go," said he "do as I say, and no otherwise."

On this, Crito made a sign to the servant who stood by; and he, going out after some time, brought in the man who was to administer the poison, which he brought prepared in a cup. And Socrates, seeing the man, said:—

"Well, my excellent friend, you are skillful in this matter: what am I to do?"

"Nothing," said he; "but when you have drunk it, walk about till your legs feel heavy, and then lie down. The drink will do the rest"; and at the same time he offered the cup to Socrates.

And he, taking it, said very calmly (I assure you, Echecrates, without trembling or changing color or countenance, but, as his wont was, looking with protruded brow at the man), "Tell me," said he, "about this beverage: is there any to spare for a libation, or is that not allowable?"

And he replied:—

"We prepare so much, Socrates, as we think to be needed for the potion."

"I understand," said he; "but at least it is allowable and it is right to pray to the gods that our passage from hence to that place may be happy. This I pray, and so may it be"; and as he said this he put the cup to his lips and drank it off with the utmost serenity and sweetness.

Up to this time the greater part of us were able to restrain our tears; but when we saw him drink the potion and take the cup from his lips, we could refrain no longer. For my part, in spite of myself, my tears flowed so abundantly that I drew my mantle over my head and wept to myself, not grieving for Socrates, but for my own loss of such a friend.

And Crito had risen up and gone away already, being unable to restrain his tears. Apollodorus, even before this, had been constantly weeping, and now burst into a passion of grief, wailing and sobbing, so that every one was moved to tears except Socrates himself. And he said:—

"O my friends, what are you doing? On this account mainly I sent the women away, that they might not behave so unwisely; for I have heard that we ought to die with good words in our ears. Be silent, then, and be brave."

And we at hearing this were ashamed, and refrained ourselves from weeping. And he, walking about, when he said his legs felt heavy, lay down on his back; for so the man directed. And the man who gave him the poison came near him, and after a time examined his feet and legs, and, squeezing his foot strongly, asked him if he felt anything; and he said he did not. And then he felt his legs, and so upward, and showed us that they were cold and stiff. And, feeling them himself, he said that when the cold reached his heart he would depart. And now the lower part of the body was already cold, and he, uncovering his face,—for he had covered it,—said the last words that he spoke.

"Crito," said he, "we owe a cock to Æsculapius: discharge it, and do not neglect it."

"It shall be done," said Crito.

To this he made no reply, but after a little time there was a movement in the body, and the man uncovered him, and his eyes were set. And hereupon Crito closed his mouth and his eyes. This was the end, Echecrates, of our friend—of all the men whom we have known, the best, the wisest, and the most just.

From "Phædo." Whewell's translation.

THE IMMORTALITY OF THE SOUL

(Socrates, Cebes and Simmias.)

SOCRATES—"During the conjunction of body and soul, nature orders the one to obey and be a slave, and the other to command and hold the empire. Which of these two characters is most suitable to the Divine Being, and which to what is mortal? Are not you sensible that the divine is only capable of commanding and ruling, and that mortal is only worthy of obedience and slavery?"

"Sure enough."

"Which of these two, then, agrees best with the soul?"

"'Tis evident, Socrates, that our soul resembles what is divine, and our body what is mortal."

"You see, then, my dear Cebes, the necessary result of all is, that our soul bears a strict resemblance to what is divine, immortal, intellectual, simple, indissolvable; and is always the same, and always like, and that our body does perfectly resemble what is human, mortal, sensible, compounded, dissolvable, always changing, and never like itself. Can anything be alleged to destroy that consequence or to make out the contrary?"

"No, surely, Socrates."

"Does not it, then, suit with the body to be quickly dissolved, and with the soul to be always indissolvable, or something very near it?"

"That is a standing truth."

"Accordingly you see every day, when a man dies, his visible body, that continues exposed to our view, and which we call the corpse, that alone admits of dissolution, alteration, and dissipation; this, I say, does not immediately undergo any of these accidents, but continues a pretty while in its entire form, or in its flower, if I may so speak, especially in this season. Bodies embalmed after the manner of those in Egypt remain entire for an infinity of years, and even in those that corrupt there are always some parts, such as the bones, nerves, and the like, that continue in a manner immortal. Is not this true?"

"Very true."

"Now as for the soul, which is an invisible being, that goes to a place like itself, marvelous, pure, and invisible, in the infernal world; and returns to a God full of goodness and wisdom, which I hope will be the fate of my soul in a minute, if it please God. Shall a soul of this nature, and created with all these advantages, be dissipated and annihilated, as soon as it parts from the body, as most men believe? No such thing, my dear Simmias, and my dear Cebes. I'll tell you what will rather come to pass, and what we ought to believe steadily. If the soul retain its purity without any mixture of filth from the body, as having entertained no voluntary correspondence with it, but, on the contrary, having always avoided it, and recollected itself within itself in continual meditations; that is, in studying the true philosophy, and effectually learning to die,—for philosophy is a preparation to death: I say, if the soul departs in this condition, it repairs to a being like itself, a being that's divine, immortal, and full of wisdom; in which it enjoys an inexpressible felicity, as being freed from its errors, its ignorance, its fears, its amours, that tyrannized over it, and all the other evils pertaining to human nature: and as 'tis said of those who have been initiated into holy mysteries, it truly passes a whole course of eternity with the gods? Ought not this to be the matter of our belief?"

"Sure enough, Socrates."

"But if the soul depart full of uncleanness and impurity, as having been all along mingled with the body, always employed in its service, always possessed by the love of it, wheedled and charmed by its pleasures and lusts, insomuch that it is believed there was nothing real or true beyond what is corporeal, what may be seen, touched, drank, or eaten, or what is the object of carnal pleasures, that it hated, dreaded, and avoided what the eyes of the body could not descry, and all that is intelligible, and can only be enjoyed by philosophy. Do you think, I say, that a soul in this condition can depart pure and simple from the body?"

"No, surely, Socrates, that's impossible."

"On the contrary, it departs stained with corporeal pollution, which was rendered natural to it by its continual commerce and too intimate union with the body, at a time when it was its constant companion, and was still employed in serving and gratifying it. . . . Were death the dissolution of the whole man, it would be a great advantage to the wicked after death to be rid at once of their body, their soul, and their vices. But forasmuch as the soul is immortal, the only way to avoid those evils and obtain salvation is to become good and wise: for it carries nothing along with it but its good or bad actions, and its virtues or vices, which are the cause of its eternal happiness or misery, commencing from the first minute of its arrival in the other world. And 'tis said that after the death of every individual person, the Demon or Genius, that was partner with it and conducted it during life, leads it to a certain place, where all the dead are obliged to appear, in order to be judged, and from thence are conducted by a guide to the world below. And after they have there received their good or bad deserts, and continued there their appointed time, another conductor brings them back to this life, after several revolutions of ages. Now this road is not a plain united road, else there would be no occasion for guides, and nobody would miss their way; but there are several by-ways and cross-ways, as I conjecture from the method of our sacrifices and religious ceremonies. So that a temperate, wise soul follows its guide, and is not ignorant of what happens to it; but the soul that's nailed to its body, as I said just now, that is inflamed with the love of it, and has been long its slave, after much struggling and suffering in this visible world, is at last

dragged along against its will by the Demon allotted for its guide. And when it arrives at that rendezvous of all souls, if it has been guilty of any impurity, or polluted with murder, or has committed any of those atrocious crimes that desperate and lost souls are commonly guilty of, the other souls abhor it, and avoid its company; it finds neither companion nor guide, but wanders in a fearful solitude and horrible desert, till after a certain time necessity drags it into the mansions it deserves; whereas the temperate and pure soul has the gods themselves for its guides and conductors, and goes to cohabit with them in the mansions of pleasure prepared for it."

From "Phædo," Morley's text.

PLATONIC ANALECTS

WISDOM

THAT alone—I mean wisdom—is the true and unalloyed coin, for which we ought to exchange all these things; for this, and with this, everything is in reality bought and sold—fortitude, temperance and justice; and, in a word, true virtue subsists with wisdom.

From "Phædo."

THE FALSEHOODS OF SENSE

THIS life is a road that's apt to mislead us and our reason in our inquiries, because, while we have a body, and while our soul is drowned in so much corruption, we shall never attain the object of our wishes, *i. e.*, truth. The body throws a thousand obstacles and crosses in our way, by demanding necessary food; and then the diseases that ensue do quite disorder our inquiry. Besides, it fills us with love, desires, fears, and a thousand foolish imaginations, insomuch that there is nothing truer than the common saying, "That the body will never conduct us to wisdom." What is it that gives rise to wars, and occasions seditions and dueling? Is it not the body and its desires? In effect, all wars take rise from the desire of riches, which we are forced to heap up for the sake of our body, in order to supply its wants, and serve it like slaves. 'Tis this that cramps our application to philosophy. And the greatest of all our evils is that when it has given us some respite, and we are set upon

meditation, it steals in and interrupts our meditation all of a sudden. It cumbers, troubles, and surprises us in such a manner that it hinders us from descrying the truth. Now we have made it out, that in order to trace the purity and truth of anything, we should lay aside the body, and only employ the soul to examine the objects we pursue. So that we can never arrive at the wisdom we court till after death. Reason is on our side. For if it is impossible to know anything purely while we are in the body, one of these two things must be true: either the truth is never known, or it is known after death; because at that time the soul will be left to itself, and freed of its burden, and not before. And while we are in this life, we can only approach to the truth in proportion to our removing from the body, and renouncing all correspondence with it that is not of mere necessity, and keeping ourselves clear from the contagion of its natural corruption, and all its filth, till God himself comes to deliver us. Then, indeed, being freed from all bodily folly, we shall converse, in all probability, with men that enjoy the same liberty, and shall know within ourselves the pure essence of things, which perhaps is nothing but the truth. But he who is not pure is not allowed to approach to purity itself.

From "Phædo."

HEAVENLY AND EARTHLY LOVE

SIMPLY to praise Love, O Phædrus, seems to me too bounded a scope for our discourse. If Love were one, it would be well. But since Love is not one, I will endeavor to distinguish which is the Love whom it becomes us to praise, and having thus discriminated one from the other, will attempt to render him who is the subject of our discourse the honor due to his divinity. We all know that Venus is never without Love; and if Venus were one, Love would be one; but since there are two Venuses, of necessity also must there be two Loves. For assuredly are there two Venuses: one, the elder, the daughter of Uranus, born without a mother, whom we call the Uranian; the other younger, the daughter of Jupiter and Dione, whom we call the Pandemian;—of necessity must there also be two Loves, the Uranian and Pandemian companions of these goddesses. It is becoming to praise all the gods, but the attributes which fall to the lot of each may be distinguished and selected. For any particular action whatever in itself is neither good nor evil; what we are now doing—drinking, singing, talking, none of these things are good in themselves, but the mode in which they are done stamps them with its own nature; and that which is done well is good, and that which is done ill is evil. Thus, not all love, nor every mode of love is beautiful, or worthy of commendation, but that alone which excites us to love worthily.

From « The Banquet.» Shelley's translation.

MISANTHROPY

MISANTHROPY arises from a man trusting another without having a sufficient knowledge of his character, and, thinking him to be truthful, sincere, and honorable, finds a little afterwards that he is wicked, faithless; and then he meets with another of the same character. When a man experiences this often, and, more particularly, from those whom he considered his most dear and best friends,—at last, having frequently made a slip, he hates the whole world, and thinks that there is nothing sound at all in any of them.

From « Phædo.»

THE EFFECT OF LOVE

IT is love that causes peace among men, a calm on the sea, a lulling of the winds, sweet sleep on joyless beds. It is he who takes from us the feeling of enmity, and fills us with those of friendship; who establishes friendly meetings, being the leader in festivals, dances, and sacrifices, giving mildness and driving away harshness; the beneficent bestower of good-will, the nongiver of enmity; gracious to the good, looked up to by the wise, admired by the gods; envied by those who have no lot in life, possessed by those who have; the parent of luxury, of tenderness, of elegance, of grace, of desire, and regret; careful of the good, regardless of the bad; in labor, in fear, in wishes, and in speech, the pilot, the defender, the bystander, and best savior; of gods and men, taken altogether, the ornament; a leader the most beautiful and best, in whose train it becomes every man to follow, hymning well his praise, and bearing a part in that sweet song which he sings himself, when soothing the mind of every god and man

From « The Banquet.»

THE PHILOSOPHER

WHETHER a man dwelling in the city is nobly or ignobly born, whether some unfortunate event has taken place to one of his ancestors, man or woman, is equally unknown to him as the number of measures of water in the sea, as the proverb goes. And he is not aware of his own ignorance; nor does he keep aloof from such things from mere vanity, but, in reality, his body only dwells in the city and sojourns there, while his mind, regarding all such things as trivial, and of no real moment, despising them, is carried about everywhere, as Pindar says, measuring things under the earth and upon its surface, raising his eyes to the stars in heaven, and examining into the nature of everything in the whole universe, never stooping to anything near at hand.

From « Theætetus.»

EVIL

IT is not possible, Theodorus, to get rid of evil altogether; for there must always be something opposite to good; nor can it be placed among the gods, but must of necessity circulate round this mortal nature and world of ours. Wherefore we ought to fly hence as soon as possible to that upper region; but this flight is our resembling the Divinity as much as we are able, and this resemblance is that we should be just, and holy, and wise.

From « Theætetus.»

GOD AND MAN

GOD is in nowise in the least unjust, but is as just as possible; and there is no one more like to him than the man among us who has become as just as possible. It is on this that the real excellence of a man depends, and his nothingness and worthlessness

From « Theætetus.»

HEAVEN'S PERFECT GIFTS

TELL me, therefore, what benefits the gods derive from the gifts they receive from us; for the advantage derived from what they bestow is evident to every one; for there is no perfect gift which they do not bestow; but how are they bene-

fited by what they get from us? Have we so much advantage in this traffic, that we receive everything good from them, and they nothing from us?

From « Euthyphron.»

EXPERIENCE

THERE are many arts among men, the knowledge of which is acquired bit by bit by experience. For it is experience that causes our life to move forward by the skill we acquire, while want of experience subjects us to the effects of chance.

From « Gorgias.»

PLINY THE YOUNGER

(CAIUS PLINIUS CÆCILIUS SECUNDUS)

(62-113 A. D.)

PLINY THE YOUNGER, nephew of the celebrated naturalist of the same name, was born at Como, Italy, 62 A. D. His «Epistles» are among the most famous prose epistles written in classical Latin. He seems to have written them chiefly for the pleasure he derived from euphony, but they illustrate the operations of a well-stored and well-trained intellect. Pliny was bred to the bar, and he was proud of his talents as an orator. His «Eulogy of Trajan» has been preserved, and while it is interesting as a specimen of his oratory, it is not so generally admired as are his Letters. For a number of years he was Consul, and afterwards Governor of Bithynia and Pontica. He died 113 A. D.

THE DESTRUCTION OF POMPEII

YOUR request that I would send you an account of my uncle's death,* in order to transmit a more exact relation of it to posterity, deserves my acknowledgments; for if this accident shall be celebrated by your pen, the glory of it, I am well assured, will be rendered forever illustrious. And notwithstanding he perished by a misfortune, which, as it involved at the same time a most beautiful country in ruins, and destroyed so many populous cities, seems to promise him an everlasting remembrance,—notwithstanding he has himself composed many and lasting works,— yet I am persuaded the mentioning of him in your immortal writings will greatly contribute to eternalize his name. Happy I esteem those to whom Providence has distinguished with the abilities either of doing such actions as are worthy of being related, or of relating them in a manner worthy of being read; but doubly happy are they who are blessed with both these uncommon talents; in the number of which my uncle—as his own writings

* Pliny the Elder perished in the eruption which destroyed Pompeii.

and your history will evidently prove — may justly be ranked. It is with extreme willingness, therefore, I execute your commands, and should, indeed, have claimed the task if you had not enjoined it. He was at that time with the fleet under his command at Misenum. On the twenty-third of August, about one in the afternoon, my mother desired him to observe a cloud which appeared of a very unusual size and shape. He had just returned from taking the benefit of the sun, and after bathing himself in cold water, and taking a slight repast, was retired to his study; he immediately rose and went out upon an eminence from whence he might more distinctly view this very uncommon appearance. It was not at that distance discernible from what mountain this cloud issued, but it was found afterwards to ascend from Mount Vesuvius. I cannot give a more exact description of its figure than by comparing it to a pine tree, for it shot up to a great height in the form of a trunk, which extended itself at the top into a sort of branches; occasioned, I imagine, either by a sudden gust of air that impelled it, the force of which decreased as it advanced upwards, or the cloud itself, being pressed back again by its own weight, expanded in this manner; it appeared sometimes bright and sometimes dark and spotted, as if it was either more or less impregnated with earth and cinders. This extraordinary phenomenon excited my uncle's philosophical curiosity to take a nearer view of it. He ordered a light vessel to be got ready, and gave me the liberty, if I thought proper, to attend him. I rather chose to continue my studies, for, as it happened, he had given me an employment of that kind. As he was coming out of the house he received a note from Rectina, the wife of Bassus, who was in the utmost alarm at the imminent danger which threatened her, — for her villa being situated at the foot of Mount Vesuvius, there was no way to escape but by sea; she earnestly entreated him, therefore, to come to her assistance. He accordingly changed his first design, and what he began with a philosophical, he pursued with an heroical, turn of mind. He ordered the galleys to put to sea, and went himself on board with an intention of assisting not only Rectina, but several others, for the villas stand extremely thick upon that beautiful coast. When hastening to the place whence others fled with the utmost terror, he steered his direct course to the point of danger, and with so much calmness and presence of mind as to be able to make and dictate his observations upon the motion and figure of that dreadful scene.

He was now so nigh the mountain that the cinders, which grew thicker and hotter the nearer he approached, fell into the ships, together with pumice stones and pieces of burning rock; they were likewise in danger not only of being aground by the sudden retreat of the sea, but also from the vast fragments which rolled down from the mountain and obstructed all the shore. Here he stopped to consider whether he should return back again, to which the pilot advising him, "Fortune," said he, "befriends the brave; carry me to Pomponianus." Pomponianus was then at Stabiæ, separated by a gulf which the sea, after several insensible windings, forms upon that shore. He had already sent his baggage on board; for though he was not at that time in actual danger, yet being within the view of it, and indeed extremely near, if it should in the least increase, he was determined to put to sea as soon as the wind should change. It was favorable, however, for carrying my uncle to Pomponianus, whom he found in the greatest consternation: he embraced him with tenderness, encouraging and exhorting him to keep up his spirits, and, the more to dissipate his fears, he ordered, with an air of unconcern, the baths to be got ready; when, after having bathed, he sat down to supper with great cheerfulness, or at least (what is equally heroic) with all the appearance of it. In the meanwhile the eruption from Mount Vesuvius flamed out in several places with much violence, which the darkness of the night contributed to render still more visible and dreadful. But my uncle, in order to soothe the apprehensions of his friend, assured him it was only the burning of the villages which the country people had abandoned to the flames; after this he retired to rest, and it is most certain he was so little discomposed as to fall into a deep sleep; for being pretty fat and breathing hard, those who attended without actually heard him snore. The court which led to his apartment being now almost filled with stones and ashes, if he had continued there any time longer it would have been impossible for him to have made his way out; it was thought proper, therefore, to awaken him. He got up and went to Pomponianus and the rest of his company, who were not unconcerned enough to think of going to bed. They consulted together whether it would be most prudent to trust to the houses, which now shook from side to side with frequent and violent concussions, or fly to the open fields, where the calcined stones and cinders, though light indeed, yet fell in large showers, and threatened destruction. In this distress they

resolved for the fields as the less dangerous situation of the two; a resolution which, while the rest of the company were hurried into it by their fears, my uncle embraced upon cool and deliberate consideration. They went out then, having pillows tied upon their heads with napkins; and this was their whole defense against the storm of stones that fell around them. Though it was now day everywhere else, with them it was darker than the most obscure night, excepting only what light proceeded from the fire and flames. They thought proper to go down further upon the shore to observe if they might safely put out to sea, but they found the waves still run extremely high and boisterous. There my uncle, having drunk a draught or two of cold water, threw himself down upon a cloth which was spread for him, when immediately the flames and a strong smell of sulphur which was the forerunner of them, dispersed the rest of the company, and obliged him to rise. He raised himself up with the assistance of two of his servants, and instantly fell down dead, — suffocated, as I conjecture, by some gross and noxious vapor, having always had weak lungs, and frequently subjected to a difficulty of breathing. As soon as it was light again, which was not till the the third day after this melancholy accident, his body was found entire, and without any marks of violence upon it, exactly in the same posture that he fell, and looking more like a man asleep than dead. During all this time my mother and I, who were at Misenum —— but as this has no connection with your history, so your inquiry went no further than concerning my uncle's death; with that, therefore, I will put an end to my letter; — suffer me only to add that I have faithfully related to you what I was either an eye-witness of myself or received immediately after the accident happened, and before there was time to vary the truth. You will choose out of this narrative such circumstances as shall be most suitable to your purpose; for there is a great difference between what is proper for a letter and a history, between writing to a friend and writing to the public. Farewell.

To Cornelius Tacitus.

A ROMAN FOUNTAIN

HAVE you ever seen the source of the river Clitumnus?* As I never heard you mention it, I imagine not; let me therefore advise you to do so immediately. It is but lately, indeed, I had that pleasure, and I condemn myself for not having seen it sooner. At the foot of a little hill, covered with venerable and shady cypress trees, a spring issues out, which, gushing in different and unequal streams, forms itself, after several windings, into a spacious basin, so extremely clear that you may see the pebbles and the little pieces of money which are thrown into it, as they lie at the bottom. From thence it is carried off not so much by the declivity of the ground, as by its own strength and fullness. It is navigable almost as soon as it has quitted its source, and wide enough to admit a free passage for vessels to pass by each other, as they sail with or against the stream. The current runs so strong, though the ground is level, that the large barges which go down the river have no occasion to make use of their oars; while those which ascend find it difficult to advance, even with the assistance of oars and poles; and this vicissitude of labor and ease is exceedingly amusing when one sails up and down merely for pleasure. The banks on each side are shaded with the verdure of great numbers of ash and poplar trees, as clearly and distinctly seen in the stream, as if they were actually sunk in it. The water is cold as snow, and as white too. Near it stands an ancient and venerable temple, wherein is placed the river god Clitumnus, clothed in a robe whose immediate presence the prophetic oracles here delivered sufficiently testify. Several little chapels are scattered round, dedicated to particular gods, distinguished by different names, and some of them too presiding over different fountains. For, besides the principal one, which is as it were the parent of all the rest, there are several other lesser streams, which, taking their rise from various sources, lose themselves in the river: over which a bridge is built, that separates the sacred part from that which lies open to common use. Vessels are allowed to come above this bridge, but no person is permitted to swim except below it. The Hispalletes, to whom Augustus gave this

*Now called Clitumno. It rises a little below the village of Campello in Ombria.

place, furnish a public bath, and likewise entertain all strangers at their own expense. Several villas, attracted by the beauty of this river, are situated upon its borders. In short, every object that presents itself will afford you entertainment. You may also amuse yourself with numberless inscriptions, that are fixed upon the pillars and walls by different persons, celebrating the virtues of the fountain, and the divinity that presides over it. There are many of them you will greatly admire, as there are some that will make you laugh; but I must correct myself when I say so: you are too humane, I know, to laugh upon such an occasion. Farewell.

To Romanus. Complete.

PLUTARCH
(c. 46 A. D.— ?)

LUTARCH'S "Lives" carried the art of the biographer to its climax, and in his "Morals" this remarkable artist invented the modern essay as it comes to us through Montaigne. He is sometimes called a "historian," and it is possible that he should be so described. But if he is sometimes a historian, he is always an artist. Perhaps no other man of his time had studied so deeply the history, the philosophy, and the poetry of the "Divine age" of his country; but we can never be sure that the men whose portraits he draws with such loving and careful art, are not in their heroic essence the product of art. They existed certainly, and the actions he attributes to them are not of his invention. His whole "plot" is historical, but under his pen human nature is transformed as it is under Doré's brush. The Greeks who followed Alexander to overthrow the Persian Empire were probably as much below the physical standard of the Teutonic races as Cæsar's legionaries were; but when Doré shows them surrounding the dying Darius, we recognize them as conquerors of the world by the subtle suggestion of an etherealized, superhuman, superiority of physique he puts into every line with which he draws their bodies. They are men, but we could not mistake them for mere men. They are Doré's men. So Plutarch's heroes who were once men—perhaps mere men—became "Plutarch's men,"—a glorious race who inspire all after times to emulation of their heroic virtues. An idealist and a philosopher, one of the greatest of the later disciples of Plato, Plutarch expressed his own ideals by bringing into strong relief all he most admired in the characters he described. His "Morals," which are not so much read as his "Lives," are a series of essays and disquisitions on almost every imaginable subject. He is the only ancient writer on the Homeric mode in verse who seems to have had an adequate conception of the high and careful art underlying the apparent simplicities of Homeric technique. He goes much beyond Aristotle in this respect, and it will be a great gain to higher education when the whole of his treatise on Homeric verse is adequately translated and studied in the universities. From Homeric prosody he could shift without visible effort to a discussion of the man in the moon, or the causes of the apparent delay of the gods in punishing the wicked. This latter

essay contains passages as remarkable as are to be found in literature. It would be hard for the most ardent admirer of Plato to find in his works anything to surpass Plutarch's demonstrations that the kingdom of hell, like that of heaven, is an interior reality before it becomes an exterior phenomenon.

Plutarch was born at Chæronea, in Bœotia, about 46 A. D. Little is known of his life, except that the better part of it is immortal in works whose influence on modern times is too great to be estimated. It has been said that if the cabin of the typical American frontiersman of the first quarter of the nineteenth century contained half a dozen books, Plutarch's "Lives" was almost sure to be one of them. Axmen and riflemen who read almost no other book but the Bible, read the "Lives" and named their sons after Epaminondas, Leonidas, and Miltiades. And though Plutarch might have smiled at the incongruity of the blending of Greek and English names, thus brought about, he would not have needed to blush for many things done in nineteenth-century America, under his inspiration.

W. V. B.

CONCERNING THE DELAY OF THE DEITY

IT is said that the fly called Cantharides by a certain contradiction contains within itself the remedy of the harm it does; but wickedness doeth not so, producing within itself its own torment and punishment in the very act of the crime itself—even as every malefactor when he is punished is made to bear upon his own body the cross on which he is to suffer. Wickedness thus is a marvelous artificer of an unhappy life which she produceth out of herself—a constant torture which is inflicted in agitations, in baseness, with frequent terrors, with carking cares, with remorse and everlasting burning as though of a fire. Still we have among us those who are so like children that when they see the wicked in the theatre in their gold-embroidered tunics and with their purple cloaks, crowned and dancing as if they were happy, are stupefied in admiration and envy until they see them tortured with whips, torn with punishment, and at last, as it were, with flame bursting out from under their painted and sumptuous garments. Thus, indeed, there are often wicked men surrounded by numerous households, high in office, and splendid in their wealth, whom we do not understand to be malefactors until we have seen them punished or brought as it were to the very place of execution—things which cannot be so well called

the punishment itself as the consummation and ending of punishment. For as Plato relates that Herodicus the Selymbrian, who fell into a lingering and mortal disease, was the first who joined gymnastic exercises and medicine as a remedy, protracting in doing so the tediousness of inevitable death for himself and all others so diseased,—thus the wicked who seem to have escaped punishment for the time being are really enduring their punishment, not after a longer time, but for a longer time. Nor are they punished when they are old merely, but they grow old under the anguish of their punishments. I speak of time as "long" as length of time appears to us; for to the gods, indeed, the whole space of human life is a nothing, a mere moment of present time. To them a reprieve of thirty years in the punishment of a criminal is as though we should debate whether the condemned malefactor should be brought to the scaffold or the torture in the morning or the afternoon,—especially as men are committed to life in custody as prisoners are committed to a jail, whence they cannot go out or escape, although while prisoners we may transact business, enjoy society, be promoted to honors and divert ourselves with amusement,—even as prisoners in the jail may play at checkers or dice while they are waiting to be hanged. What reason, therefore, have we to say that prisoners in chains awaiting execution are not punished until the ax has fallen, or that one who has drunk the deadly hemlock and can still keep his feet and walk is not punished until he falls senseless because of the coagulation of his blood and the loss of his senses,—if indeed we look upon the last moment of punishment as the punishment itself, leaving out of consideration the perturbation, the trepidation, the expectation, the remorse, and all the tortures of mind with which every wicked man is punished through his own very wickedness. It is as if we should reason that a fish which has swallowed a hook is not caught until we see him cut up and boiled by the cook. For the penalty of his wickedness incubates for every malefactor in the wickedness itself which he has swallowed as a sweet bait. His conscience tears him and he is lacerated—

> "As the hooked tunny tugs against the line
> Which rends its jaws and draws it from the brine."

For, indeed, the audacity and ferocity of perverseness remains daring and full of hardiness until the wicked deed is done, but soon, as a tempest ceases its violence, it grows abject and blood-less, surrendering itself to all manner of fears and superstition. Hence it seems that the Stesichorus composed the "Dream of Clytemnestra" as a parable of life and truth (when to the wicked dreamer)—

"There came a dragon with a human head
With grume and blood besmeared as though
The King Plisthenides had thus appeared."

*Inceder'est visus draco cui humanum caput esset
Rex hinc Plisthenidas obtulit sese oculis.*

. . . .

Hence if the mind ceaseth to exist when fatal law is accomplished, if death is the end of reward and punishment, we might say that the Deity is too remiss and too merciful if he should suddenly give death as a penalty for wickedness. For even if we should say that there is no evil in the life and career of the wicked, still it is evident that wickedness is sterile and unpleasing, bearing nothing good or worthy of being desired out of its many and great agonies, while the very feeling of them subverts the mind. It is a tradition that Lysimachus when violently affected by thirst, surrendered his person and his army to the Scythians that he might drink as a captive. "Alas, then," he said, "what a wretch I am, who for so fleeting a pleasure have deprived myself of so great a kingdom!" How hard it is for a man to resist the impulses of his animal instincts; but when a man either to gratify such instincts or for the sake of political reputation and power has committed some base and atrocious crime in the reaction from which his fury leaves him while the foul and terrible perturbations of his crime remain and he gains from it nothing useful or gratifying for his life, is it not probable that he is forced to think for what an empty glory or barren and sordid pleasure he has overthrown the most noble and sublime principles of life, covering, in doing so, his own life with trouble and with shame?

Simonides was accustomed to say that the box he kept for his cash was always full, but that which he kept for his gratitude was always empty So knaves when they contemplate their own wickedness find it void of good, but full of fears, sorrows, odious memories, suspicion of the future, and distrust of the

present. So Ino is introduced in the theatre complaining in her remorse:—

"Dear friends, I pray you tell me with what face
I can return with Athamus to dwell,
As though I were not criminal and base."

Is it not likely, then, that the mind of every depraved man reacts upon itself thus, seeking if it can find a way to escape the memory of its wickedness, that freed from the consciousness of its crime it may begin life afresh? For in evil those who follow it can find neither confidence nor stability nor endurance, or otherwise they would be forced to say that the wicked alone are wise. Wherever the thirst for money, wherever burning passion, wherever impotent envy, has its home with wickedness, there, if you search, you will find superstition, languor in labor, fear of death, a succession of violent passion and the thirst after undeserved honor gaping in its own insolence. Such men fear those who condemn them and condemn those who praise as if the praise itself were a trick. And above everything, they are bitter enemies of the base because they commend willingly those who have the appearance of probity. But the hardness of wickedness, like that of faulty iron, is itself the cause of its breaking, and thus in passage of time when they explore their own state of mind, they grieve, they are angry, they repudiate their former course of life. If, indeed, we see a wicked man who restores what has been pledged with him or becomes security for a friend or does a patriotic act through ambition, very soon he repents and is ashamed of his action, if only because of the fickleness of his inclination which is incident to the depravity of his mind; when we see some men when they are applauded in the theatres sigh soon afterwards, because of the avarice of their ambition, we cannot believe that men like Apollodorus who sacrifice human life in their conspiracies and tyrannies or rob their own friends of property, as did Glaucus, the son of Epicides,—we cannot believe that such men as these do not repent and abhor themselves in the torment of their own wickedness. So if it be not wrong to say I believe for my part that there is no occasion for the interference of either gods or men to punish the wicked, since the whole life of such men, subverted and convulsed as it is by their vices, suffices for their punishment.

From the version of Hermann Cruserius (1580), revised by the version of Philips

APOTHEGMS

HOMER ON THE METHODS OF GOD

IN surprising and startling actions, where the supernatural and the assistance of the Divinity may be required, Homer does not introduce the Supreme Being as taking away the freedom of the will, but merely as influencing it. The Divine Power is not represented as causing the resolution, but only thoughts and ideas which naturally lead to the resolution. In this way the act cannot be called altogether involuntary, since God is the moving cause to the voluntary, and thus gives confidence and good hope. For we must either banish entirely the Supreme Being from all casuality and influence over our actions, or what other way is there in which he can assist and co-operate with men? for it is impossible to suppose that he fashions our corporeal organs, or directs the motions of our hands and feet, to accomplish what he intends; but it is by suggesting certain motives, and predisposing the mind, that he excites the active powers of the will, or restrains them.

From Coriolanus.

FAMILY HEREDITY

UNLESS the foundations of a family be properly prepared and laid, those who are sprung from it must necessarily be unfortunate.

De Lib. Educ., cap. ii.

THE EVIL DEEDS OF PARENTS

THERE is no one, however high-spirited he may be, that does not quail when he thinks of the evil deeds of his parents.

De Lib. Educ., cap. ii.

NATURE, LEARNING, AND TRAINING

NATURE without learning is like a blind man; learning without nature is like the maimed; practice without both these is incomplete. As in agriculture a good soil is first sought for,

then a skillful husbandman, and then good seed; in the same way nature corresponds to the soil; the teacher to the husbandman; precepts and instruction to the seed.

De Lib. Educ., cap. iv.

MOTHERS AND CHILDREN

IN my opinion mothers ought to bring up and nurse their own children; for they bring them up with greater affection and with greater anxiety, as loving them from the heart, and, so to speak, every inch of them. But the love of a nurse is spurious and counterfeit, as loving them only for hire.

De Lib. Educ., cap. v.

TEACHERS AND THEIR PUPILS

TEACHERS ought to be sought who are of blameless lives, not liable to be found fault with, and distinguished for learning; for the source and root of a virtuous and honorable life is to be found in good training. And as husbandmen underprop plants, so good teachers, by their precepts and training, support the young, that their morals may spring up in a right and proper way.

De Lib. Educ., cap. vii.

THE EYE OF THE MASTER FATTENS THE HORSE

IN this place we may very properly insert the saying of the groom, who maintained that there was nothing which served to fatten a horse so much as the eye of its master.

De Lib. Educ., cap. xiii.

GARRULITY

THE talkative listen to no one, for they are ever speaking. And the first evil that attends those who know not how to be silent is, that they hear nothing.

De Garrulitate, cap. i.

MAN

MAN is a plant, not fixed in the earth, nor immovable, but heavenly, whose head, rising as it were from a root upwards, is turned towards heaven

De Exilio, cap. v.

EDGAR ALLAN POE

(1809–1849)

EDGAR ALLAN POE, the most musical of all American poets, was born in Boston, January 19th, 1809. His father was an actor, and the temporary residence of the family in Boston was an incident of his professional work. While very young, Poe was adopted by Mr. John Allan, a wealthy resident of Richmond, Virginia, who sent him to school for several years in England, and afterwards to the University of Virginia. Poe learned with the rapidity of genius, but was fickle in his ardor for study. After remaining a short time at the university, he left it to make his fortune as a poet. In 1827 he published "Tamerlane and Other Poems," which, as a matter of course, failed to bring him a living, and he was forced to enlist as a private in the United States army. Under the *alias* of "Edward A. Perry," he rose to be Sergeant Major, and his foster father secured his admission to West Point. Poe disliked the school, and it is said "contrived to get himself dismissed." He was dismissed, at any rate, and as Mr. Allan repudiated further responsibility for him, he was left wholly destitute and dependent on literature for support. After working for some time in Baltimore, he became associate editor, first of the Southern Literary Messenger and afterwards of the Gentleman's Magazine. He also edited Graham's Magazine and assisted N. P. Willis on the Mirror, increasing steadily in reputation, but with no corresponding increase of fortune. "The Raven," which made him famous, was published in 1845, when he was already disheartened and despondent. He died four years later in a Baltimore hospital, where he was carried after having been found delirious on the street. The stories of his wild and protracted dissipation seem to be without foundation, but he illustrated the central fact of the physiology of genius,—that its highly organized physique is apt to be disorganized rapidly by what for the average man is a moderate indulgence in the enjoyments of sense. Poe's theory of verse divorced it from truth and confined its province to the expression of beauty. This incapacitated him for attaining the highest rank as a poet, but did not affect his extraordinary genius as a musician. No other poet of the century in America has equaled him as composer of tone harmonies in words. He approaches the "*Tonkunst*" of Homer. His prose tales have founded a "school" of their own, but he has found his disciples chiefly in France. As a reviewer and

critical essayist, his perceptions were keen, but his prejudices intense and his judgment frequently inoperative. His life was distorted and sad, chiefly because he lacked "the much-enduring mind," without which the life of every man of great genius must become an inferno of intellectual and spiritual disorder.

W. V. B.

THE PLEASURES OF RHYME

THE effect derivable from well-managed rhyme is very imperfectly understood. Conventionally "rhyme" implies merely close similarity of sound at the ends of verse, and it is really curious to observe how long mankind have been content with their limitation of the idea. What, in rhyme, first and principally pleases, may be referred to the human sense or appreciation of equality — the common element, as might be easily shown, of all the gratification we derive from music in its most extended sense — very especially in its modifications of metre and rhythm. We see, for example, a crystal, and are immediately interested by the equality between the sides and angles of one of its faces — but, on bringing to view a second face, in all respects similar to the first, our pleasure seems to be squared — on bringing to view a third, it appears to be cubed, and so on: I have no doubt, indeed, that the delight experienced, if measurable, would be found to have exact mathematical relations, such, or nearly such, as I suggest,— that is to say, as far as a certain point, beyond which there would be a decrease, in similar relations. Now here, as the ultimate result of analysis, we reach the sense of mere equality, or rather the human delight in this sense; and it was an instinct, rather than a clear comprehension of this delight as a principle, which, in the first instance, led the poet to attempt an increase of the effect arising from the mere similarity (that is to say equality) between two sounds — led him, I say, to attempt increasing this effect by making a secondary equalization, in placing the rhymes at equal distances — that is, at the ends of lines of equal length. In this manner, rhyme and the termination of the line grew connected in men's thoughts — grew into a conventionalism — the principle being lost sight of altogether. And it was simply because Pindaric verses had, before this epoch, existed — *i. e.*, verses of unequal length — that rhymes were subsequently found at unequal distances. It was for this reason solely, I say, — for none more profound. Rhyme had come to be regarded as

of right appertaining to the end of verse — and here we complain that the matter has finally rested. But it is clear that there was much more to be considered. So far, the sense of equality alone entered the effect; or if this equality was slightly varied, it was varied only through an accident — the accident of the existence of Pindaric metres. It will be seen that the rhymes were always anticipated. The eye, catching the end of a verse, whether long or short, expected, for the ear, a rhyme. The great element of unexpectedness was not dreamed of — that is to say, of novelty — of originality. "But," says Lord Bacon (how justly!) "there is no exquisite beauty without some strangeness in the proportions." Take away this element of strangeness — of unexpectedness — of novelty — of originality — call it what we will — and all that is ethereal in loveliness is lost at once. We lose — we miss the unknown — the vague — the uncomprehended because offered before we have time to examine and comprehend. We lose, in short, all that assimilates the beauty of earth with what we dream of the beauty of heaven. Perfection of rhyme is attainable only in the combination of the two elements, Equality and Unexpectedness. But as evil cannot exist without good, so unexpectedness must arise from expectedness. We do not contend for mere arbitrariness of rhyme. In the first place, we must have equidistant or regularly recurring rhymes, to form the basis, expectedness, out of which arises the element, unexpectedness, by the introduction of rhymes, not arbitrarily, but with an eye to the greatest amount of unexpectedness. We should not introduce them, for example, at such points that the entire line is a multiple of the syllables preceding the points. When, for instance, I write —

And the silken, sad, uncertain rustling of each purple curtain.

I produce more, to be sure, but not remarkably more than the ordinary effect of rhymes regularly recurring at the ends of lines; for the number of syllables in the whole verse is merely a multiple of the number of syllables preceding the rhyme introduced at the middle, and there is still left, therefore, a certain degree of expectedness. What there is of the element, unexpectedness, is addressed, in fact, to the eye only — for the ear divides the verse into two ordinary lines, thus:—

And the silken, sad, uncertain
Rustling of each purple curtain.

I obtain, however, the whole effect of unexpectedness, when I write—

Thrilled me, filled me with fantastic terrors never felt before.

N. B.—It is very commonly supposed that rhyme, as it now ordinarily exists, is of modern invention—but see the "Clouds" of Aristophanes. Hebrew verse, however, did not include it,—the terminations of the lines, where most distinct, never showing anything of the kind.

Complete. From "Marginalia."

IMAGINATION

THE pure Imagination chooses, from either beauty or deformity, only the most combinable things hitherto uncombined; the compound, as a general rule, partaking, in character, of beauty, or sublimity, in the ratio of the respective beauty or sublimity of the things combined,—which are themselves still to be considered as atomic,—that is to say, as previous combinations. But as often analogously happens in physical chemistry, so not unfrequently does it occur in this chemistry of the intellect, that the admixture of two elements results in a something that has nothing of the qualities of one of them, or even nothing of the qualities of either. . . . Thus, the range of Imagination is unlimited. Its materials extend throughout the universe. Even out of deformities it fabricates that Beauty which is at once its sole object and its inevitable test. But, in general, the richness or force of the matters combined; the facility of discovering combinable novelties worth combining; and, especially, the absolute "chemical combination" of the completed mass—are the particulars to be regarded in our estimate of Imagination. It is this thorough harmony of an imaginative work which so often causes it to be undervalued by the thoughtless, through the character of obviousness which is superinduced. We are apt to find ourselves asking why it is that these combinations have never been imagined before.

Complete. From "Marginalia."

THE FATE OF THE VERY GREATEST

I HAVE sometimes amused myself by endeavoring to fancy what would be the fate of an individual gifted, or rather accursed, with an intellect very far superior to that of his race. Of course, he would be conscious of his superiority; nor could he (if otherwise constituted as man is) help manifesting his consciousness. Thus he would make himself enemies at all points. And since his opinions and speculations would widely differ from those of all mankind—that he would be considered a madman is evident. How horribly painful such a condition! Hell could invent no greater torture than that of being charged with abnormal weakness on account of being abnormally strong.

In like manner, nothing can be clearer than that a very generous spirit—truly feeling what all merely profess—must inevitably find itself misconceived in every direction—its motives misinterpreted. Just as extremeness of intelligence would be thought fatuity, so excess of chivalry could not fail of being looked upon as meanness in its last degree:—and so on with other virtues. This subject is a painful one, indeed. That individuals have so soared above the plane of their race is scarcely to be questioned; but, in looking back through history for traces of their existence, we should pass over all biographies of "the good and the great," while we search carefully the slight records of wretches who died in prison, in Bedlam, or upon the gallows.

Complete. From "Marginalia."

THE ART OF CONVERSING WELL

TO CONVERSE well, we need the cool tact of talent—to talk well, the glowing abandon of genius. Men of very high genius, however, talk at one time very well, at another very ill: well, when they have full time, full scope, and a sympathetic listener; ill, when they fear interruption and are annoyed by the impossibility of exhausting the topic during that particular talk. The partial genius is flashy—scrappy. The true genius shudders at incompleteness—imperfection—and usually prefers silence to saying the something which is not everything that should be said. He is so filled with his theme that he is dumb, first, from not knowing how to begin, where there seems eternally

beginning behind beginning, and, second, from perceiving his true end at so infinite a distance. Sometimes, dashing into a subject, he blunders, hesitates, stops short, sticks fast, and because he has been overwhelmed by the rush and multiplicity of his thoughts, his hearers sneer at his inability to think. Such a man finds his proper element in those "great occasions" which confound and prostrate the general intellect.

Nevertheless, by his conversation, the influence of the conversationist upon mankind in general is more decided than that of the talker by his talk; the latter invariably talks to best purpose with his pen. And good conversationists are more rare than respectable talkers. I know many of the latter; and of the former only five or six,—among whom I can call to mind, just now, Mr. Willis; Mr. J. T. S. Sullivan, of Philadelphia; Mr. W. M. R., of Petersburg, Va.; and Mrs. S——d, formerly of New York. Most people, in conversing, force us to curse our stars that our lot was not cast among the African nation mentioned by Eudoxus,—the savages who, having no mouths, never opened them, as a matter of course. And yet, if denied mouth, some persons whom I have in my eye would contrive to chatter on still—as they do now—through the nose.

Complete. From "Marginalia."

THE GENIUS OF SHELLEY

IF EVER mortal "wreaked his thoughts upon expression," it was Shelley. If ever poet sang—as a bird sings—earnestly—impulsively—with utter abandonment—to himself solely—and for the mere joy of his own song—that poet was the author of "The Sensitive Plant." Of art—beyond that which is instinctive with genius—he either had little or disdained all. He really disdained that Rule which is an emanation from Law, because his own soul was Law in itself. His rhapsodies are but the rough notes—the stenographic memoranda of poems—memoranda which, because they were all-sufficient for his own intelligence, he cared not to be at the trouble of writing out in full for mankind. In all his works we find no conception thoroughly wrought. For this reason he is the most fatiguing of poets. Yet he wearies in saying too little rather than too much. What in him seems the diffuseness of one idea is the conglomerate

concision of many; and this species of concision it is which renders him obscure. With such a man, to imitate was out of the question. It would have served no purpose; for he spoke to his own spirit alone, which would have comprehended no alien tongue. Thus he was profoundly original. His quaintness arose from intuitive perception of that truth to which Bacon alone has given distinct utterance: "There is no exquisite Beauty which has not some strangeness in its proportions." But whether obscure, original, or quaint, Shelley had no affectations. He was at all times sincere.

From his ruins, there sprang into existence, affronting the heavens, a tottering and fantastic pagoda, in which the salient angles, tipped with mad jangling bells, were the idiosyncratic faults of the original—faults which cannot be considered such in view of his purposes, but which are monstrous when we regard his works as addressed to mankind. A "school" arose—if that absurd term must still be employed—a school—a system of rules upon the basis of the Shelley who had none. Young men innumerable, dazzled with the glare and bewildered by the bizarrerie of the lightning that flickered through the clouds of "Alastor" had no trouble whatever in heaping up imitative vapors, but, for the lightning, were forced to be content with its spectrum, in which the bizarrerie appeared without the fire. Nor were mature minds unimpressed by the contemplation of a greater and more mature; and thus, gradually, into this school of all lawlessness—of obscurity, quaintness, and exaggeration—were interwoven the out-of-place didacticism of Wordsworth, and the more anomalous metaphysicianism of Coleridge. Matters were now fast verging to their worst; and at length, in Tennyson, poetic inconsistency attained its extreme. But it was precisely this extreme (for the greatest truth and the greatest error are scarcely two points in a circle) which, following the law of all extremes, wrought in him (Tennyson) a natural and inevitable revulsion; leading him first to contemn, and secondly to investigate, his early manner, and finally to winnow, from its magnificent elements, the truest and purest of all poetical styles. But not even yet is the process complete; and for this reason in part, but chiefly on account of the mere fortuitousness of that mental and moral combination which shall unite in one person (if ever it shall) the Shelleyan abandon and the Tennysonian poetic sense with the most profound Art (based both in Instinct

and Analysis) and the sternest Will properly to blend and rigorously to control all — chiefly, I say, because such combination of
seeming antagonisms will be only a "happy chance" — the world
has never yet seen the noblest poem which, possibly, can be
composed.

Complete. From "Marginalia."

ALEXANDER POPE

(1688–1744)

OPE'S best essays were written in verse, but the prose essays
he contributed to the Guardian are by no means the worst
in that collection, and they are no doubt the best specimens
of Pope's prose style. It is curious to see how much less intense he
is in his prose than his verse. While his prose contains frequent
quotable phrases, they do not follow each other as they do in the
"Essay on Man," the "Moral Essays," the "Imitations of Horace," and
other verse to which some nineteenth-century critics denied the name
of poetry, — seemingly on no other ground than that it had too much
common sense in it to be really poetical. It may as well be admitted that though Pope's prose is better than that of his great
pupil, Byron, he never satisfies himself or his reader in it as he does
when he is rhyming. In facility as a versifier he has not been surpassed by any English poet, and Byron alone has equaled him. And
without attempting to enter into the dispute of what constitutes a
poet, it may be safely asserted that he has said in memorable verse
more things worth remembering than any other English poet except
Shakespeare.

He was born in Lombard Street, London, May 21st, 1688. His
father was a linen draper, and he had little or no scholastic training.
He educated himself, however, until he became fit to make what still
remains the most popular, if not the only popular, English translation
of Homer's "Iliad." He was of a very delicate physique and his work
was done in spite of constant suffering, which ended only with his
death May 30th, 1744. Much has been written of his moral weakness, but out of it he developed the strength of genius which could
use a frail and almost worthless body to accomplish painfully the
enduring purposes of an immortal spirit.

HOW TO MAKE AN EPIC POEM

Docebo
Unde parentur opes; quid alat formetque poetam.
— *Hor.* Ars Poet., ver. 306.

I will teach to write,
Tell what the duty of a poet is,
Wherein his wealth and ornament consist,
And how he may be form'd, and how improv'd.
— *Roscommon.*

IT IS no small pleasure to me, who am zealous in the interests
of learning, to think I may have the honor of leading the
town into a very new and uncommon road of criticism. As
that kind of literature is at present carried on, it consists only in
a knowledge of mechanic rules which contribute to the structure
of different sorts of poetry, as the receipts of good housewives do
to the making puddings of flour, oranges, plums, or any other
ingredients. It would, methinks, make these my instructions
more easily intelligible to ordinary readers, if I discoursed of
these matters in the style in which ladies learned in economics
dictate to their pupils for the improvement of the kitchen and
larder.

I shall begin with epic poetry, because the critics agree it is
the greatest work human nature is capable of. I know the
French have already laid down many mechanical rules for compositions of this sort, but at the same time they cut off almost
all undertakers from the possibility of ever performing them; for
the first qualification they unanimously require in a poet is a
genius. I shall here endeavor (for the benefit of my countrymen) to make it manifest that epic poems may be made "without a genius," nay, without learning, or much reading. This
must necessarily be of great use to all those poets who confess
they never read, and of whom the world is convinced they never
learn. What Molière observes of making a dinner, that any man
can do it with money, and if a professed cook cannot without,
he has his art for nothing, the same may be said of making a
poem, — it is easily brought about by him that has a genius, but
the skill lies in doing it without one. In pursuance of this
end, I shall present the reader with a plain and certain receipt,

by which even sonneteers and ladies may be qualified for this
grand performance.

I know it will be objected that one of the chief qualifications
of an epic poet is to be knowing in all arts and sciences But
this ought not to discourage those that have no learning, as long
as indexes and dictionaries may be had, which are the compendium of all knowledge. Besides, since it is an established rule
that none of the terms of those arts and sciences are to be made
use of, one may venture to affirm our poet cannot impertinently
offend in this point. The learning which will be more particularly necessary to him is the ancient geography of towns,
mountains, and rivers; for this let him take Culverius, value
fourpence.

Another quality required is a complete skill in languages. To
this I answer that it is notorious persons of no genius have
been often times great linguists. To instance in the Greek, of
which there are two sorts; the original Greek, and that from
which our modern authors translate. I should be unwilling to
promise impossibilities; but modestly speaking, this may be
learned in about an hour's time with ease. I have known one who
became a sudden professor of Greek, immediately upon application of the left-hand page of the Cambridge Homer to his eye.
It is in these days with authors as with other men, the well bred
are familiarly acquainted with them at first sight; and as it is
sufficient for a good general to have surveyed the ground he is
to conquer, so it is enough for a good poet to have seen the
author he is to be master of. But to proceed to the purpose of
this paper.

A RECEIPT TO MAKE AN EPIC POEM

FOR THE FABLE. — Take out of any old poem, history book,
romance, or legend (for instance, Geoffrey of Monmouth, or Don
Belianis of Greece), those parts of story which afford most scope
for long descriptions. Put these pieces together, and throw all
the adventures you fancy into one tale. Then take a hero you
may choose for the sound of his name, and put him into the
midst of these adventures. There let him work for twelve
books; at the end of which you may take him out ready prepared to conquer, or to marry; it being necessary that the conclusion of an epic poem be fortunate.

To Make an Episode. — Take any remaining adventure of your former collection, in which you could no way involve your hero; or any unfortunate accident that was too good to be thrown away; and it will be of use applied to any other person, who may be lost and evaporate in the course of the work, without the least damage to the composition.

For the Moral and Allegory. — These you may extract out of the fable afterwards, at your leisure. Be sure you strain them sufficiently.

For the Manners. — For those of the hero, take all the best qualities you can find in all the celebrated heroes of antiquity; if they will not be reduced to a consistency, lay them all on a heap upon him. But be sure they are qualities which your patron would be thought to have; and, to prevent any mistake which the world may be subject to, select from the alphabet those capital letters that compose his name, and set them at the head of a dedication before your poem. However, do not absolutely observe the exact quantity of these virtues, it not being determined whether or no it be necessary for the hero of a poem to be an honest man. For the under characters, gather them from Homer and Virgil, and change the names as occasion serves.

For the Machines. — Take of deities, male and female, as many as you can use. Separate them into two equal parts, and keep Jupiter in the middle. Let Juno put him in a ferment, and Venus mollify him. Remember on all occasions to make use of volatile Mercury. If you have need of devils, draw them out of Milton's Paradise, and extract your spirits from Tasso. The use of these machines is evident; for since no epic poem can possibly subsist without them, the wisest way is to reserve them for your greatest necessities. When you cannot extricate your hero by any human means, or yourself by your own wits, seek relief from heaven, and the gods will do your business very readily. This is according to the direct prescription of Horace in his "Art of Poetry," verse 191: —

Nec deus intersit, nisi dignus vindice Nodus
Inciderit———

Never presume to make a god appear,
But for a business worthy of a god.
— *Roscommon.*

ing too much fire in their works. I should advise rather to take their warmest thoughts, and spread them abroad upon paper; for they are observed to cool before they are read.

Complete. From the Guardian.

CRUELTY AND CARNIVOROUS HABITS

———*Primâque è cæde ferarum*
Incaluisse putem maculatum sanguine ferrum.
— *Ovid.* Met., Lib. XV. 106.

Th' essay of bloody feasts on brutes began,
And after forg'd the sword to murder man.
— *Dryden.*

I CANNOT think it extravagant to imagine that mankind are no less in proportion accountable for the ill use of their dominion over creatures of the lower rank of beings than for the exercise of tyranny over their own species. The more entirely the inferior creation is submitted to our power, the more answerable we should seem for our mismanagement of it; and the rather, as the very condition of nature renders these creatures incapable of receiving any recompense in another life for their ill treatment in this.

It is observable of those noxious animals, which have qualities most powerful to injure us, that they naturally avoid mankind, and never hurt us unless provoked or necessitated by hunger. Man, on the other hand, seeks out and pursues even the most inoffensive animals, on purpose to persecute and destroy them.

Montaigne thinks it some reflection upon human nature itself, that few people take delight in seeing beasts caress or play together, but almost every one is pleased to see them lacerate and worry one another. I am sorry this temper is become almost a distinguishing character of our own nation, from the observation which is made by foreigners of our beloved pastimes, bear baiting, cockfighting, and the like. We should find it hard to vindicate the destroying of anything that has life, merely out of wantonness; yet in this principle our children are bred up, and one of the first pleasures we allow them is the license of inflicting pain upon poor animals; almost as soon as we are sensible what life is ourselves, we make it our sport to take it from other creatures. I cannot but believe a very good use might be made

That is to say, a poet should never call upon the gods for their assistance, but when he is in great perplexity.

For the Descriptions

For a Tempest. — Take Eurus, Zephyr, Auster, and Boreas, and cast them together in one verse. Add to these of rain, lightning, and of thunder (the loudest you can) *quantum sufficit*. Mix your clouds and billows well together until they foam, and thicken your description here and there with a quicksand. Brew your tempest well in your head, before you set it a-blowing.

For a Battle — Pick a large quantity of images and descriptions from Homer's "Iliad," with a spice or two of Virgil, and if there remain any overplus you may lay them by for a skirmish. Season it well with similes, and it will make an excellent battle.

For Burning a Town. — If such a description be necessary, because it is certain there is one in Virgil, Old Troy is ready burnt to your hands. But if you fear that would be thought borrowed, a chapter or two of the Theory of the Conflagration, well circumstanced, and done into verse, will be a good succedaneum.

As for Similes and Metaphors, they may be found all over the creation; the most ignorant may gather them, but the danger is in applying them. For this advise with your bookseller.

For the Language

(I mean the diction). Here it will do well to be an imitator of Milton, for you will find it easier to imitate him in this than anything else. Hebraisms and Grecisms are to be found in him, without the trouble of learning the languages. I knew a painter, who (like our poet) had no genius, make his daubings to be thought originals by setting them in the smoke. You may in the same manner give the venerable air of antiquity to your piece by darkening it up and down with Old English. With this you may be easily furnished upon any occasion by the dictionary commonly printed at the end of Chaucer.

I must not conclude without cautioning all writers without genius in one material point, which is, never to be afraid of hav·

of the fancy which children have for birds and insects. Mr. Locke takes notice of a mother who permitted them to her children, but rewarded or punished them as they treated them well or ill. This was no other than entering them betimes into a daily exercise of humanity, and improving their very diversion to a virtue.

I fancy, too, some advantage might be taken of the common notion, that it is ominous or unlucky to destroy some sorts of birds, as swallows or martins; this opinion might possibly arise from the confidence these birds seem to put in us by building under our roofs, so that it is a kind of violation of the laws of hospitality to murder them. As for robin redbreasts in particular, it is not improbable they owe their security to the old ballad of the "Children in the Wood." However it be, I do not know, I say, why this prejudice, well improved and carried as far as it would go, might not be made to conduce to the preservation of many innocent creatures, which are now exposed to all the wantonness of an ignorant barbarity.

There are other animals that have the misfortune, for no manner of reason, to be treated as common enemies wherever found. The conceit that a cat has nine lives has cost at least nine lives in ten of the whole race of them. Scarce a boy in the streets but has in this point outdone Hercules himself, who was famous for killing a monster that had but three lives. Whether the unaccountable animosity against this useful domestic may be any cause of the general persecution of owls (who are a sort of feathered cats), or whether it be only an unreasonable pique the Moderns have taken to a serious countenance, I shall not determine, though I am inclined to believe the former, since I observe the sole reason alleged for the destruction of frogs is because they are like toads. Yet amidst all the misfortunes of these unfriended creatures, it is some happiness that we have not yet taken a fancy to eat them; for should our countrymen refine upon the French never so little, it is not to be conceived to what unheard-of torments owls, cats, and frogs may be yet reserved.

When we grow up to men, we have another succession of sanguinary sports; in particular hunting. I dare not attack a diversion which has such authority and custom to support it; but must have leave to be of opinion that the agitation of that exercise, with the example and number of the chasers, not a little contribute to resist those checks, which compassion would naturally suggest in behalf of the animal pursued. Nor shall I say with Monsieur Fleury, that this sport is a remain of the Gothic barbarity. But I must animadvert upon a certain custom yet in use with us, and barbarous enough to be derived from the Goths, or even the Scythians; I mean that savage compliment our huntsmen pass upon ladies of quality, who are present at the death of a stag, when they put the knife in their hands to cut the throat of a helpless, trembling, and weeping creature.

«————*Questuque cruentus,*
Atque imploranti similis.»——

«———— That lies beneath the knife,
Looks up, and from her butcher begs her life.»

But if our sports are destructive, our gluttony is more so, and in a more inhuman manner. Lobsters roasted alive, pigs whipped to death, fowls sewed up, are testimonies of our outrageous luxury. Those who (as Seneca expresses it) divide their lives betwixt an anxious conscience and a nauseated stomach have a just reward of their gluttony in the diseases it brings with it; for human savages, like other wild beasts, find snares and poison in the provisions of life, and are allured by their appetite to their destruction. I know nothing more shocking or horrid than the prospect of one of their kitchens covered with blood, and filled with the cries of creatures expiring in tortures. It gives one an image of a giant's den in a romance, bestrewed with the scattered heads and mangled limbs of those who were slain by his cruelty.

The excellent Plutarch (who has more strokes of good-nature in his writings than I remember in any author) cites a saying of Cato to this effect, "That it is no easy task to preach to the belly, which has no ears." "Yet if," says he, "we are ashamed to be so out of fashion as not to offend, let us at least offend with some discretion and measure. If we kill an animal for our provision, let us do it with the meltings of compassion, and without tormenting it. Let us consider that it is in its own nature cruelty to put a living creature to death; we at least destroy a soul that has sense and perception." — In the life of Cato the Censor, he takes occasion, from the severe disposition of that man, to discourse in this manner: "It ought to be esteemed a happiness to mankind, that our humanity has a wider sphere to exert itself in

than bare justice. It is no more than the obligation of our very birth to practice equity to our own kind; but humanity may be extended through the whole order of creatures, even to the meanest. Such actions of charity are the overflowings of a mild good-nature on all below us. It is certainly the part of a well-natured man to take care of his horses and dogs, not only in expectation of their labor while they are foals and whelps, but even when their old age has made them incapable of service."

History tells us of a wise and polite nation, that rejected a person of the first quality, who stood for a judiciary office, only because he had been observed in his youth to take pleasure in tearing and murdering of birds; and of another that expelled a man out of the senate for dashing a bird against the ground which had taken shelter in his bosom. Every one knows how remarkable the Turks are for their humanity in this kind. I remember an Arabian author, who has written a treatise to show how far a man, supposed to have subsisted in a desert island, without any instruction, or so much as the sight of any other man, may, by the pure light of nature, retain the knowledge of philosophy and virtue. One of the first things he makes him observe is, that universal benevolence of nature in the protection and preservation of its creatures. In imitation of which the first act of virtue he thinks his self-taught philosopher would of course fall into is to relieve and assist all the animals about him in their wants and distresses.

Ovid has some very tender and pathetic lines applicable to this occasion:—

Quid meruistis, oves, placidum pecus, inque tegendos
Natum homines, pleno quæ fertis in ubere nectar?
Mollia quæ nobis vestras velamina lanas
Præbetis; vitâque magis quàm morte juvatis.
Quid meruere boves, animal sine fraude dolisque,
Innocuum, simplex, natum tolerare labores?
Immemor est demum, nec frugum munere dignus,
Qui potuit, curvi dempto modo pondere aratri,
Ruricolam mactare suum ——

—*Met. Lib.* xv. 116.

Quàm malè consuevit, quàm se parat ille cruori
Impius humano, vituli qui guttura cultro
Rumpit, et immotas præbet mugitibus aures!

Aut qui vagitus similes puerilibus hædum
Edentem jugulare potest! ——

—*Ib.*, ver. 463.

The sheep was sacrific'd on no pretense,
But meek and unresisting innocence.
A patient, useful creature, born to bear
The warm and woolly fleece, that clothed her murderer;
And daily to give down the milk she bred,
A tribute for the grass on which she fed.
Living, both food and raiment she supplies,
And is of least advantage when she dies.
How did the toiling ox his death deserve;
A downright simple drudge, and born to serve?
O tyrant! with what justice canst thou hope
The promise of the year, a plenteous crop;
When thou destroy'st thy lab'ring steer, who till'd,
And plough'd with pains, thy else ungrateful field!
From his yet reeking neck to draw the yoke,
That neck, with which the surly clods he broke:
And to the hatchet yield thy husbandman,
Who finish'd autumn, and the spring began?

What more advance can mortals make in sin
So near perfection, who with blood begin?
Deaf to the calf that lies beneath the knife,
Looks up, and from her butcher begs her life:
Deaf to the harmless kid, that ere he dies,
All methods to procure thy mercy tries,
And imitates in vain the children's cries.

—*Dryden.*

Perhaps that voice or cry so nearly resembling the human, with which Providence has endued so many different animals, might purposely be given them to move our pity, and prevent those cruelties we are too apt to inflict on our fellow-creatures.

There is a passage in the Book of Jonas when God declares his unwillingness to destroy Nineveh, where methinks that compassion of the Creator, which extends to the meanest rank of his creatures, is expressed with wonderful tenderness: "Should I not spare Nineveh, that great city, wherein are more than six score thousand persons — and also much cattle?" And we have in Deuteronomy a precept of great good-nature of this sort, with a blessing in form annexed to it, in those words: "If thou shalt

find a bird's nest in the way, thou shalt not take the dam with the young But thou shalt in any wise let the dam go; that it may be well with thee, and that thou may'st prolong thy days."

From the Guardian.

ON SHAKESPEARE

IT is not my design to enter into a criticism upon this author, though to do it effectually and not superficially would be the best occasion that any just writer could take, to form the judgment and taste of our nation. For of all English poets Shakespeare must be confessed to be the fairest and fullest subject for criticism, and to afford the most numerous, as well as most conspicuous instances, both of beauties and faults of all sorts. But this far exceeds the bounds of a preface, the business of which is only to give an account of the fate of his works, and the disadvantages under which they have been transmitted to us. We shall hereby extenuate many faults which are his, and clear him from the imputation of many which are not; a design which, though it can be no guide to future critics to do him justice in one way, will at least be sufficient to prevent their doing him an injustice in the other.

I cannot, however, but mention some of his principal and characteristic excellencies, for which (notwithstanding his defects) he is justly and universally elevated above all other dramatic writers. Not that this is the proper place of praising him, but because I would not omit any occasion of doing it.

If ever any author deserved the name of an original, it was Shakespeare. Homer himself drew not his art so immediately from the fountains of Nature; it proceeded through Egyptian strainers and channels, and came to him not without some tincture of the learning, or some cast of the models, of those before him. The poetry of Shakespeare was inspiration indeed; he is not so much an imitator as an instrument of Nature; and it is not so just to say that he speaks from her as that she speaks through him.

His characters are so much Nature herself, that 'tis a sort of injury to call them by so distant a name as copies of her. Those of other poets have a constant resemblance, which shows that they received them from one another, and were but multipliers of the same image; each picture, like a mock rainbow, is but the reflection of a reflection. But every single character in Shakespeare is as much an individual as those in life itself; it is impossible to find any two alike; and such as from their relation or affinity in any respect appear most to be twins, will upon comparison be found remarkably distinct. To this life and variety of character we must add the wonderful preservation of it, which is such throughout his plays, that, had all the speeches been printed without the very names of the persons, I believe one might have applied them with certainty to every speaker.

The power over our passions was never possessed in a more eminent degree, or displayed in so many different instances. Yet all along there is seen no labor, no pains to raise them; no preparation to guide our guess to the effect, or be perceived to lead toward it; but the heart swells, and the tears burst out, just at the proper places. We are surprised the moment we weep; and yet upon reflection find the passion so just, that we should be surprised if we had not wept, and wept at that very moment.

How astonishing it is, again, that the passions directly opposite to these, laughter and spleen, are no less at his command! That he is not more a master of the great than of the ridiculous in human nature; of our noblest tendernesses than of our vainest foibles; of our strongest emotions than of our idlest sensations!

Nor does he only excel in the passion; in the coolness of reflection and reasoning he is full as admirable. His sentiments are not only in general the most pertinent and judicious upon every subject; but by a talent very peculiar, something between penetration and felicity, he hits upon that particular point on which the bent of every argument turns, or the force of each motive depends. This is perfectly amazing, from a man of no education or experience in those great and public scenes of life which are usually the subject of his thoughts: so that he seems to have known the world by intuition, to have looked through human nature at one glance, and to be the only author that gives ground for a very new opinion, that the philosopher, and even the man of the world, may be born, as well as the poet.

It must be owned that with all these great excellencies, he has almost as great defects; and that as he has certainly written better, so he has perhaps written worse, than any other. But I think I can in some measure account for these defects, from several causes and accidents; without which it is hard to imagine that so large and so enlightened a mind should ever have been

susceptible of them. That all these contingencies should unite to his disadvantage seems to me almost as singularly unlucky, as that so many various (nay contrary) should meet in one man, was happy and extraordinary.

It must be allowed that stage poetry, of all other, is more particularly leveled to please the populace, and its success more immediately depending on the common suffrage. One cannot therefore wonder if Shakespeare, having at his first appearance no other aim in his writings than to procure a subsistence, directed his endeavors solely to hit the taste and humor that then prevailed. The audience was generally composed of the meaner sort of people; and therefore the images of life were to be drawn from those of their own rank: accordingly we find that not our author's only, but almost all the old comedies, have their scene amongst tradesmen and mechanics; and even their historical plays strictly follow the common old stories or vulgar traditions of that kind of people. In tragedy, nothing was so sure to surprise and cause admiration as the most strange, unexpected, and consequently most unnatural events and incidents: the most pompous rhymes, and thundering versification. In comedy, nothing was so sure to please as mean buffoonery, vile ribaldry, and unmannerly jests of fools and clowns. Yet even in these our author's wit buoys up, and is borne above his subject; his genius in these low parts is like some prince of a romance in the disguise of a shepherd or peasant; a certain greatness and spirit now and then break out, which manifest his higher extraction and qualities.

It may be added, that only the common audience had no notion of the rules of writing, but few even of the better sort piqued themselves upon any great degree of knowledge or nicety that way, till Ben Johnson, getting possession of the stage, brought critical learning into vogue. And that this was not done without difficulty may appear from those frequent lessons (and, indeed, almost declamations) which he was forced to prefix to his first plays, and put into the mouth of his actors, the Grex, Chorus, etc., to remove the prejudices, and inform the judgment of his hearers. Till then, our authors had no thoughts of writing on the model of the Ancients: their tragedies were only histories in dialogue; and their comedies followed the thread of any novel as they found it, no less implicitly than if it had been true history.

To judge therefore of Shakespeare by Aristotle's rules is like trying a man by the laws of one country, who acted under those of another. He writ to the people, and writ* at first without patronage from the better sort, and therefore without aims of pleasing them; without assistance or advice from the learned, as without the advantage of education or acquaintance among them; without that knowledge of the best models, the Ancients, to inspire him with an emulation of them,—in a word, without any views of reputation, and of what poets are pleased to call immortality: some or all of which have encouraged the vanity, or animated the ambition of other writers.

Yet it must be observed that when his performances had merited the protection of his prince, and when the encouragement of the court had succeeded to that of the town, the works of his riper years are manifestly raised above those of his former. The dates of his plays sufficiently evidence that his productions improved, in proportion to the respect that he had for his auditors. And I make no doubt this observation would be found true in every instance, were but editions extant from which we might learn the exact time when every piece was composed, and whether writ for the town or the court.

Another cause (and no less strong than the former) may be deduced from our author being a player, and forming himself first upon the judgments of that body of men whereof he was a member. They have ever had a standard to themselves, upon other principles than those of Aristotle. As they live by the majority, they know no rule but that of pleasing the present humor, and complying with the wit in fashion; a consideration which brings all their judgment to a short point. Players are just such judges of what is right as tailors are of what is graceful. And in this view it will be but fair to allow that most of our author's faults are less to be ascribed to his wrong judgment as a poet than to his right judgment as a player.

By these men it was thought a praise to Shakespeare that he scarce ever blotted a line. This they industriously propagated, as appears from what we are told by Ben Jonson in his "Discoveries," and from the preface of Heminges and Condell to the first folio edition. But in reality (however it has prevailed) there never was a more groundless report, or to the contrary of which

*"Writ" is good Queen Anne English.

there are more undeniable evidences—as to the comedy of the "Merry Wives of Windsor," which he entirely new writ, the "History of Henry VI.," which was first published under the title of the "Contention of York and Lancaster"; and that of "Henry V.," extremely improved; that of "Hamlet," enlarged to almost as much again as at first, and many others. I believe the common opinion of his want of learning proceeded from no better ground. This, too, might be thought a praise by some, and to this his errors have as injudiciously been ascribed by others. For, 'tis certain, were it true, it could concern but a small part of them; the most are such as are not properly defects, but superfœtations; and arise not from want of learning or reading, but from want of thinking or judging: or rather (to be more just to our author) from a compliance to those wants in others. As to a wrong choice of the subject, a wrong conduct of the incidents, false thoughts, forced expressions, etc., if these are not to be ascribed to the aforesaid accidental reasons, they must be charged upon the poet himself and there is no help for it. But I think the two disadvantages which I have mentioned (to be obliged to please the lowest of people, and to keep the worst of company), if the consideration be extended as far as it reasonably may, will appear sufficient to mislead and depress the greatest genius upon earth. Nay the more modesty with which such a one is endued, the more he is in danger of submitting and conforming to others, against his own better judgment.

From the Preface to Shakespeare.

THOUGHTS ON VARIOUS SUBJECTS

PARTY ZEAL

THERE never was any party, faction, sect, or cabal whatsoever, in which the most ignorant were not the most violent; for a bee is not a busier animal than a blockhead. However, such instruments are necessary to politicians; and perhaps it may be with states as with clocks, which must have some dead weight hanging at them, to help and regulate the motion of the finer and more useful parts.

ACKNOWLEDGMENT OF ERROR

A MAN should never be ashamed to own he has been in the wrong, which is but saying, in other words, that he is wiser to-day than he was yesterday.

DISPUTATION

WHAT Tully says of war may be applied to disputing: it should be always so managed as to remember that the only true end of it is peace; but generally true disputants are like true sportsmen, their whole delight is in the pursuit; and a disputant no more cares for the truth than the sportsman for the hare.

CENSORIOUS PEOPLE

SUCH as are still observing upon others are like those who are always abroad at other men's houses, reforming everything there, while their own runs to ruin.

HOW TO BE REPUTED A WISE MAN

A SHORT and certain way to obtain the character of a reasonable and wise man is, whenever any one tells you his opinion, to comply with him.

AVARICE

THE character of covetousness is what a man generally acquires more through some niggardliness or ill grace in little and inconsiderable things, than in expenses of any consequence. A very few pounds a year would ease that man of the scandal of avarice.

WILLIAM HICKLING PRESCOTT

(1796–1859)

WILLIAM HICKLING PRESCOTT, whose brilliant studies of Spanish and Spanish-American history are an enduring monument of his genius, wrote also a number of critical studies and miscellaneous essays of a high order of merit. He was born at Salem, Massachusetts, May 4th, 1796, and educated at Harvard where, as the result of an accident, he became nearly blind. His far-reaching historical researches were carried on chiefly through the aid of secretaries and readers. His first notable work was "The Reign of Ferdinand and Isabella," published in 1838. It was followed by the "Conquest of Mexico" and the "Conquest of Peru," both of which surpassed it in popularity. Prescott died January 28th, 1859, leaving his "History of the Reign of Philip II." unfinished.

DON QUIXOTE AND HIS TIMES

"DON QUIXOTE" is too familiar to the reader to require any analysis; but we will enlarge on a few circumstances attending its composition but little known to the English scholar, which may enable him to form a better judgment for himself. The age of chivalry, as depicted in romances, could never, of course, have had any real existence; but the sentiments which are described as animating that age have been found more or less operative in different countries and different periods of society. In Spain, especially, this influence is to be discerned from a very early date. Its inhabitants may be said to have lived in a romantic atmosphere, in which all the extravagances of chivalry were nourished by their peculiar situation. Their hostile relations with the Moslem kept alive the full glow of religious and patriotic feeling. Their history is one interminable crusade. An enemy always on the borders invited perpetual displays of personal daring and adventure. The refinement and magnificence of the Spanish Arabs throw a lustre over these contests such as could not be reflected from the rude skirmishes with their Christian neighbors. Lofty sentiments, embellished by

the softer refinements of courtesy, were blended in the martial bosom of the Spaniard, and Spain became emphatically the land of romantic chivalry.

The very laws themselves, conceived in this spirit, contributed greatly to foster it. The ancient code of Alfonso X., in the thirteenth century, after many minute regulations for the deportment of the good knight, enjoins on him to "invoke the name of his mistress in the fight, that it may infuse new ardor into his soul and preserve him from the commission of unknightly actions." Such laws were not a dead letter. The history of Spain shows that the sentiment of romantic gallantry penetrated the nation more deeply and continued longer than in any other quarter of Christendom.

Foreign chroniclers, as well as domestic, of the fifteenth and sixteenth centuries, notice the frequent appearance of Spanish knights in different courts of Europe, whither they had traveled, in the language of an old writer, "to seek honor and reverence" by their feats of arms. In the "Paston Letters," written in the time of Henry VI. of England, we find a notice of a Castilian knight who presented himself before the court, and, with his mistress's favor around his arm, challenged the English cavaliers "to run a course of sharp spears with him for his sovereign lady's sake." Pulgar, a Spanish chronicler of the close of the sixteenth century, speaks of this roving knight-errantry as a thing of familiar occurrence among the young cavaliers of his day; and Oviedo, who lived somewhat later, notices the necessity under which every true knight found himself of being in love, or feigning to be so, in order to give a suitable lustre and incentive to his achievements. But the most singular proof of the extravagant pitch to which these romantic feelings were carried in Spain occurs in the account of the jousts appended to the fine old chronicle of Alvaro de Luna, published by the Academy in 1784. The principal champion was named Sueño de Quenones, who, with nine companions in arms, defended a pass at Orbigo, not far from the shrine of Compostella, against all comers, in the presence of King John II. and his court. The object of this passage of arms, as it was called, was to release the knight from the obligation imposed on him by his mistress of publicly wearing an iron collar round his neck every Thursday. The jousts continued for thirty days, and the doughty champions fought without shield or target, with weapons bearing points of Milan

steel. Six hundred and twenty-seven encounters took place, and one hundred and sixty-six lances were broken, when the emprise was declared to be fairly achieved. The whole affair is narrated, with becoming gravity, by an eyewitness, and the reader may fancy himself perusing the adventures of a Launcelot or an Amadis. The particulars of this tourney are detailed at length in Mills's "Chivalry" (Vol. II., chap. v.), where, however, the author has defrauded the successful champions of their full honors by incorrectly reporting the number of lances broken as only sixty-six.

The taste for these romantic extravagancies naturally fostered a corresponding taste for the perusal of tales of chivalry. Indeed, they acted reciprocally on each other. These chimerical legends had once, also, beguiled the long evenings of our Norman ancestors, but, in the progress of civilization, had gradually given way to other and more natural forms of composition. They still maintained their ground in Italy, whither they had passed later, and where they were consecrated by the hand of genius. But Italy was not the true soil of chivalry, and the inimitable fictions of Bojardo, Pulci, and Ariosto were composed with that lurking smile of half-suppressed mirth which, far from a serious tone, could raise only a corresponding smile of incredulity in the reader.

In Spain, however, the marvels of romance were all taken in perfect good faith. Not that they were received as literally true; but the reader surrendered himself up to the illusion, and was moved to admiration by the recital of deeds which, viewed in any other light than as a wild frolic of imagination, would be supremely ridiculous; for these tales had not the merit of a seductive style and melodious versification to relieve them. They were, for the most part, an ill-digested mass of incongruities, in which there was as little keeping and probability in the characters as in the incidents, while the whole was told in that stilted "Hercles' vein" and with that licentiousness of allusion and imagery which could not fail to debauch both the taste and the morals of the youthful reader. The mind, familiarized with these monstrous, over-colored pictures, lost all relish for the chaste and sober productions of art. The love of the gigantic and the marvelous indisposed the reader for the simple delineations of truth in real history. . . .

Cervantes brought forward a personage, in whom were embodied all those generous virtues which belong to chivalry; disinterestedness, contempt of danger, unblemished honor, knightly courtesy, and those aspirations after ideal excellence which, if empty dreams, are the dreams of a magnanimous spirit. They are, indeed, represented by Cervantes as too ethereal for this world, and are successively dispelled as they come in contact with the coarse realities of life. It is this view of the subject which has led Sismondi, among other critics, to consider that the principal end of the author was "the ridicule of enthusiasm,—the contrast of the heroic with the vulgar,"—and he sees something profoundly sad in the conclusions to which it leads. This sort of criticism appears to be over-refined. It resembles the efforts of some commentators to allegorize the great epics of Homer and Virgil, throwing a disagreeable mistiness over the story by converting mere shadows into substances, and substances into shadows.

The great purpose of Cervantes was, doubtless, that expressly avowed by himself, namely, to correct the popular taste for romances of chivalry. It is unnecessary to look for any other in so plain a tale, although, it is true, the conduct of the story produces impressions on the reader, to a certain extent, like those suggested by Sismondi. The melancholy tendency, however, is in a great degree counteracted by the exquisitely ludicrous character of the incidents. Perhaps after all, if we are to hunt for a moral as the key of the fiction, we may with more reason pronounce it to be the necessity of proportioning our undertakings to our capacities.

The mind of the hero, Don Quixote, is an ideal world into which Cervantes has poured all the rich stores of his own imagination, the poet's golden dreams, high romantic exploit, and the sweet visions of pastoral happiness; the gorgeous chimeras of the fancied age of chivalry, which had so long entranced the world; splendid illusions, which, floating before us like the airy bubbles which the child throws off from his pipe, reflect, in a thousand variegated tints, the rude objects around, until, brought into collision with these, they are dashed in pieces and melt into air. These splendid images derive tenfold beauty from the rich antique coloring of the author's language, skillfully imitated from the old romances, but which necessarily escapes in the translation into a foreign tongue. Don Quixote's insanity operates both in mistaking the ideal for the real, and the real for the ideal. Whatever he has found in romances he believes to exist in the

world; and he converts all he meets with in the world into the visions of his romances. It is difficult to say which of the two produces the most ludicrous results.

For the better exposure of these mad fancies, Cervantes has not only put them into action in real life, but contrasted them with another character which may be said to form the reverse side of his hero's. Honest Sancho represents the material principle as perfectly as his master does the intellectual or ideal. He is of the earth, earthy. Sly, selfish, sensual, his dreams are not of glory, but of good feeding. His only concern is for his carcass. His notions of honor appear to be much the same with those of his jovial contemporary Falstaff, as conveyed in his memorable soliloquy. In the sublime night-piece which ends with the fulling-mills—truly sublime until we reach the dénouement—Sancho asks his master: "Why need you go about this adventure? It is main dark, and there is never a living soul sees us; we have nothing to do but to sheer off and get out of harm's way. Who is there to take notice of our flinching?" Can anything be imagined more exquisitely opposed to the true spirit of chivalry? The whole compass of fiction nowhere displays the power of contrast so forcibly as in these two characters; perfectly opposed to each other, not only in their minds and general habits, but in the minutest details of personal appearance.

It was a great effort of art for Cervantes to maintain the dignity of his hero's character in the midst of the whimsical and ridiculous distresses in which he has perpetually involved him. His infirmity leads us to distinguish between his character and his conduct, and to absolve him from all responsibility for the latter. The author's art is no less shown in regard to the other principal figure in the piece, Sancho Panza, who, with the most contemptible qualities, contrives to keep a strong hold on our interest by the kindness of his nature and his shrewd understanding. He is far too shrewd a person, indeed, to make it natural for him to have followed so crack-brained a master unless bribed by the promise of a substantial recompense. He is a personification, as it were, of the popular wisdom,—a "bundle of proverbs," as his master somewhere styles him; and proverbs are the most compact form in which the wisdom of a people is digested. They have been collected into several distinct works in Spain, where they exceed in number those of any other, if not every other, country in Europe. As many of them are of great

antiquity, they are of inestimable price with the Castilian jurists, as affording rich samples of obsolete idioms and the various mutations of the language.

The subordinate portraits in the romance, though not wrought with the same care, are admirable studies of national character. In this view, the Don Quixote may be said to form an epoch in the history of letters, as the original of that kind of composition, the Novel of Character, which is one of the distinguishing peculiarities of modern literature. When well executed, this sort of writing rises to the dignity of history itself, and may be said to perform no insignificant part of the functions of the latter. History describes men less as they are than as they appear, as they are playing a part on the great political theatre,—men in masquerade. It rests on state documents, which too often cloak real purposes under an artful veil of policy, or on the accounts of contemporaries blinded by passion or interest. Even without these deductions, the revolutions of states, their wars, and their intrigues do not present the only aspect, nor, perhaps, the most interesting, under which human nature can be studied. It is man in his domestic relations, around his own fireside, where alone his real character can be truly disclosed; in his ordinary occupations in society, whether for purposes of profit or pleasure; in his every-day manner of living, his tastes and opinions, as drawn out in social intercourse; it is, in short, under all those forms which make up the interior of society that man is to be studied, if we would get the true form and pressure of the age,—if, in short, we would obtain clear and correct ideas of the actual progress of civilization.

But these topics do not fall within the scope of the historian. He cannot find authentic materials for them. They belong to the novelist, who, indeed, contrives his incidents and creates his characters, but who, if true to his art, animates them with the same tastes, sentiments, and motives of action which belong to the period of his fiction. His portrait is not the less true because no individual has sat for it. He has seized the physiognomy of the times. Who is there that does not derive a more distinct idea of the state of society and manners in Scotland from the "Waverley Novels" than from the best of its historians? Of the condition of the Middle Ages from the single romance of "Ivanhoe" than from the volumes of Hume or Hallam? In like manner, the pencil of Cervantes has given a far more distinct and a

richer portraiture of life in Spain in the sixteenth century than can be gathered from a library of monkish chronicles.

From "Biographical and Critical
Miscellanies."

ISABELLA AND ELIZABETH

IT IS in the amiable qualities of her sex that Isabella's superiority becomes most apparent over her illustrious namesake, Elizabeth of England, whose history presents some features parallel to her own. Both were disciplined in early life by the teachings of that stern nurse of wisdom, adversity. Both were made to experience the deepest humiliation at the hands of their nearest relative, who should have cherished and protected them. Both succeeded in establishing themselves on the throne after the most precarious vicissitudes. Each conducted her kingdom, through a long and triumphant reign, to a height of glory which it had never before reached. Both lived to see the vanity of all earthly grandeur, and to fall the victims of an inconsolable melancholy; and both left behind an illustrious name, unrivaled in the subsequent annals of the country.

But with these few circumstances of their history, the resemblance ceases. Their characters afford scarcely a point of contact. Elizabeth, inheriting a large share of the bold and bluff King Harry's temperament, was haughty, arrogant, coarse, and irascible; while with these fiercer qualities she mingled deep dissimulation and strange irresolution. Isabella, on the other hand, tempered the dignity of royal station with the most bland and courteous manners. Once resolved, she was constant in her purposes; and her conduct in public and private life was characterized by candor and integrity. Both may be said to have shown that magnanimity which is implied by the accomplishment of great objects in the face of great obstacles. But Elizabeth was desperately selfish; she was incapable of forgiving, not merely a real injury, but the slightest affront to her vanity; and she was merciless in exacting retribution. Isabella, on the other hand, lived only for others,—was ready at all times to sacrifice self to considerations of public duty; and, far from personal resentments, showed the greatest condescension and kindness to those who had most sensibly injured her; while her benevolent heart sought every means to mitigate the authorized severities of the law, even toward the guilty.

Both possessed rare fortitude. Isabella, indeed, was placed in situations which demanded more frequent and higher displays of it than her rival; but no one will doubt a full measure of this quality in the daughter of Henry VIII. Elizabeth was better educated, and every way more highly accomplished than Isabella. But the latter knew enough to maintain her station with dignity; and she encouraged learning by a munificent patronage. The masculine powers and passions of Elizabeth seemed to divorce her in a great measure from the peculiar attributes of her sex; at least from those which constitute its peculiar charm; for she had abundance of its foibles—a coquetry and love of admiration which age could not chill; a levity most careless, if not criminal; and a fondness for dress and tawdry magnificence of ornament, which was ridiculous, or disgusting, according to the different periods of life in which it was indulged. Isabella, on the other hand, distinguished through life for decorum of manners and purity beyond the breath of calumny, was content with the legitimate affection which she could inspire within the range of her domestic circle. Far from a frivolous affectation of ornament or dress, she was most simple in her own attire, and seemed to set no value on her jewels, but as they could serve the necessities of the state; when they could be no longer useful in this way, she gave them away to her friends.

Both were uncommonly sagacious in the selection of their ministers; though Elizabeth was drawn into some errors in this particular by her levity, as was Isabella by religious feeling. It was this, combined with her excessive humility, which led to the only grave errors in the administration of the latter. Her rival fell into no such errors; and she was a stranger to the amiable qualities which led to them. Her conduct was certainly not controlled by religious principle; and, though the bulwark of the Protestant faith, it might be difficult to say whether she were at heart most a Protestant or a Catholic. She viewed religion in its connection with the State, in other words, with herself; and she took measures for enforcing conformity to her own views, not a whit less despotic, and scarcely less sanguinary, than those countenanced for conscience' sake by her more bigoted rival.

This feature of bigotry, which has thrown a shade over Isabella's otherwise beautiful character, might lead to a disparage-

ment of her intellectual power compared with that of the English queen. To estimate this aright, we must contemplate the results of their respective reigns. Elizabeth found all the materials of prosperity at hand, and availed herself of them most ably to build up a solid fabric of national grandeur. Isabella created these materials. She saw the faculties of her people locked up in a deathlike lethargy, and she breathed into them the breath of life for those great and heroic enterprises which terminated in such glorious consequences to the monarchy. It is when viewed from the depressed position of her early days, that the achievements of her reign seem scarcely less than miraculous. The masculine genius of the English queen stands out relieved beyond its natural dimensions by its separation from the softer qualities of her sex; while her rival's, like some vast, but symmetrical edifice, loses in appearance somewhat of its actual grandeur from the perfect harmony of its proportions.

The circumstances of their deaths, which were somewhat similar, displayed the great dissimilarity of their characters. Both pined amidst their royal state, a prey to incurable despondency rather than any marked bodily distemper. In Elizabeth it sprung from wounded vanity, a sullen conviction that she had outlived the admiration on which she had so long fed,—and even the solace of friendship and the attachment of her subjects. Nor did she seek consolation, where alone it was to be found, in that sad hour. Isabella, on the other hand, sunk under a too acute sensibility to the sufferings of others. But, amidst the gloom which gathered around her, she looked with the eye of faith to the brighter prospects which unfolded of the future; and when she resigned her last breath, it was amidst the tears and universal lamentations of her people.

From "Ferdinand and Isabella."

3193

RICHARD A. PROCTOR

(1834–1888)

RICHARD ANTHONY PROCTOR, one of the most popular scientific essayists of the second half of the nineteenth century, was born at Chelsea, England, March 23d, 1834. Ater studying at King's College, London, and St. John's College, Cambridge, he devoted himself to astronomy, with notable success. His scientific tastes were too catholic to be confined by a specialty, however, and he wrote on almost every imaginable subject from the physiology of the Cambridge rowing stroke to the flight of Florida buzzards in its bearing on aërial navigation. During the latter part of his life he lived in the United States, making his home for a number of years at St. Joseph, Missouri. He died September 12th, 1888.

THE DUST WE BREATHE

A MICROSCOPIST (Mr. Dancer, F. R. A. S.) has been examining the dust of our cities. The results are not pleasing. We had always recognized city dust as a nuisance, and had supposed that it derived the peculiar grittiness and flintiness of its structure from the constant macadamizing of city roads. But it now appears that the effects produced by dust, when, as is usual, it finds its way to our eyes, our nostrils, and our throats, are as nothing compared with the mischief it is calculated to produce in a more subtle manner. In every specimen examined by Mr. Dancer, animal life was abundant. But the amount of "molecular activity"—such is the euphuism under which what is exceedingly disagreeable to contemplate is spoken about—is variable according to the height at which the dust is collected. And of all heights which these molecular wretches could select for the display of their activity, the height of five feet is that which has been found to be the favorite. Just at the average height of the foot-passenger's mouth these moving organisms are always waiting to be devoured and to make us ill. And this is not all. As if animal abominations were insufficient, a large proportion of vegetable matter also disports itself in the light dust of our

streets. The observations show that in thoroughfares where there are many animals engaged in the traffic, the greater part of the vegetable matter thus floating about "consists of what has passed through the stomachs of animals," or has suffered decomposition in some way or other. This unpleasing matter, like the "molecular activity," floats about at a height of five feet, or thereabouts.

After this one begins to recognize the manner in which some diseases propagate themselves. What had been mysterious in the history of plagues and pestilences seems to receive at least a partial solution. Take cholera, for example. It has been shown by the clearest and most positive evidence that this disease is not propagated in any way save one—that is, by the actual swallowing of the cholera poison. In Prof. Thudichum's masterly paper on the subject, in the Monthly Microscopical Journal, it is stated that doctors have inhaled a full breathing from a person in the last stage of this terrible malady without any evil effects. Yet the minutest atom of the cholera poison received into the stomach will cause an attack of cholera. A small quantity of this matter drying on the floor of the patient's room, and afterward caused to float about in the form of dust, will suffice to prostrate a houseful of people. We can understand, then, how matter might be flung into the streets, and, after drying, its dust be wafted through a whole district, causing the death of hundreds. One of the lessons to be learned from these interesting researches of Mr. Dancer is clearly this—that the watering cart should be regarded as one of the most important of our hygienic institutions. Supplemented by careful scavengering, it might be effective in dispossessing many a terrible malady which now holds sway from time to time over our towns.

Complete. From the London Daily News.

PHOTOGRAPHIC GHOSTS

ON THE outskirts of the ever-widening circle lighted up by science there is always a borderland wherein superstition holds sway. The arts and sciences may drive away the vulgar hobgoblin of darker days, but they bring with them new sources of illusion. The ghosts of old could only gibber; the spirits of our days can read and write, and play on divers instruments, and quote Shakespeare and Milton. It is not, therefore, altogether surprising to learn that they can take photographs also. You go to have your photograph taken, we will suppose, desiring only to see your own features depicted in the carte; and lo! the spirits have been at work, and a photographic phantom makes its appearance beside you. It is true this phantom is of a hazy and dubious aspect; the "dull mechanic ghost" is indistinct, and may be taken for any one. Still, it is not difficult for the eye of fancy to trace in it the lineaments of some departed friend, who, it is to be assumed, has come to be photographed along with you. In fact, photography, according to the Spiritualist, resembles what Byron called

"The lightning of the mind,
Which, out of things familiar, undesigned,
When least we deem of such, calls up to view
The spectres whom no exorcism can bind."

The phenomena of spiritual photography were first observed some years since, and a set of carte photographs were sent from America to Dr. Walker, of Edinburgh, in which photographic phantoms were very obviously, however indistinctly, discernible. More recently an English photographer noticed a yet stranger circumstance, though he was too sensible to seek for a supernatural interpretation of it. When he took a photograph with a particular lens, there could be seen not only the usual portrait of the sitter, but at some little distance a faint "double," exactly resembling the principal image. Superstitious minds might find this result even more distressing than the phantom photographic friend. To be visited by the departed through the medium of a lens is at least not more unpleasing than to hold converse with spirits through an ordinary "rapping" medium. But the appearance of a "double" or "fetch," has ever been held by the learned in ghostly lore to signify approaching death.

Fortunately, both one and the other appearance can be very easily accounted for without calling in the aid of the supernatural. At a recent meeting of the Photographical Society it was shown that an image may often be so deeply impressed on the glass that the subsequent cleaning of the plate, even with strong acids, will not completely remove the picture. When the plate is used for receiving another picture, the original image makes its reappearance, and as it is too faint to be recognizable, a highly

susceptible imagination may readily transform it into the image of a departed friend. The "double" is generated by the well-known property of double refraction obtained by a lens under certain circumstances of unequal pressure, or sometimes by inequalities in the process of annealing. So vanish two ghosts which might have been more or less troublesome to those who are ready to see the supernatural in commonplace phenomena. Will the time ever come when no more such phantoms will remain to be exorcised?

Complete. From the London Daily News.

MIRACLES WITH FIGURES

OF THE effect of practice in some arithmetical processes curious evidence was afforded by the feats of a Chinese who visited America in 1875. He was simply a trained computer, asserting that hundreds in China were trained to equal readiness in arithmetical processes, and that among those thus trained those of exceptional abilities far surpassed himself in dexterity. Among the various tests applied during a platform exhibition of his powers was one of the following nature. About thirty numbers of four digits each were named to him, as fast as a quick writer could take them down. When all had been given he was told to add them, mentally, while a practiced arithmetician was to add them on paper. "It is unnecessary for me to add them," he said, "I have done that as you gave them to me; the total is — so-and-so." It presently appeared that the total thus given was quite correct.

At first sight such a feat seems astounding. Yet in reality it is but a slight modification of what many bankers' clerks can readily accomplish. They will take an array of numbers, each of four or five figures, and cast them up in one operation. Grant them only the power of as readily adding a number named as a number seen to a total already obtained, and their feat would be precisely that of the Chinese arithmetician. There can be no doubt that, with a very little practice, nine-tenths, if not all of the clerks who can achieve one feat would be able to achieve the other feat also.

I do not know how clerks who add at once a column of four-figured numbers together accomplish the task. That is to say, I

do not know the mental process they go through in obtaining their final result. It may be that they keep the units, tens, hundreds, and thousands apart in their mind, counting them properly at the end of the summation; or, on the other hand, they may treat each successive number as a whole, and keep the gradually growing total as a whole. Or some may follow one plan, and some the other. When I heard of the Chinese arithmetician's feats, my explanation was that he adopted the former plan. I should myself, if I wanted to acquire readiness in such processes, adopt that plan, applying it after a fashion suggested by my method of computing when I was a boy. I should picture the units, tens, hundreds, and thousands as objects of different sorts. Say the units as dots, the tens as lines, the hundreds as discs, the thousands as squares. When a number of four digits was named to me, I should see so many squares, discs, lines, and dots. When the next number of four digits was named, I should see my sets of squares, discs, lines, and dots correspondingly increased. When a new number was named these sets would be again correspondingly increased. And so on, until there were several hundreds of squares, of discs, of lines, and of dots. These (when the last number had been named) could be at once transmuted into a number, which would be the total required.

Take for instance the numbers, 7234, 9815, 9127, 4183. When the first was named the mind's eye would picture 7 squares, 2 discs, 3 lines, and 4 dots. When the second (9815) was named there would be seen 16 squares, 10 discs, 4 lines, and 9 dots. After the third (9127), there would be 25 squares, 11 discs, 6 lines, and 16 dots; after the fourth (4183), there would be 29 squares, 12 discs, 14 lines, and 19 dots. This being all, the total is at once run off from the units' place; the 19 dots give 9 for the units, one 10 to add to the 14 lines (each representing ten), making 15, so that 5 is the digit in the tens' place, while 100 is added to the 12 discs or hundreds, giving 13 or 3 in the hundreds' place, and 1,000 to add to the 29 squares or thousands, making 30, or for the total 30,359. The process has taken many words in describing, but each part of it is perfectly simple, the mental picturing of the constantly increasing numbers of squares, discs, lines, and dots being almost instantaneous (in the case, of course, of those only who possess the power of forming these mental pictures). The final process is equally simple, and would

be so even if the number of squares, discs, lines, and dots were great. Thus, suppose there were 324 squares, 411 discs, 391 lines, and 433 dots. We take 3 for units, carrying 43 lines or 434 in all, whence 4 for the tens, carrying 43 discs, or 444 in all, whence 4 for the hundreds, carrying 44 squares or 468 in all, whence finally 468,443 is the total required.

We can understand then how easy to Bidder must have been the summation of the fifteen products of cross-multiplication to the carried remainder — they would be added consecutively in far less time than the quickest penman could write them down. Probably they would be obtained as well as added in less time than they could be written down. Thus digit after digit of the result of what appears a tremendous sum in multiplication would be obtained with that rapidity which to many seemed almost miraculous. We must further take into account a circumstance pointed out by Mr. G. Bidder. "The faculty of rapid operation," he says, speaking of his father's wonderful feats in this respect, "was no doubt congenital, but it was developed by incessant practice, and by the confidence thereby acquired. I am certain," he proceeds, "that unhesitating confidence is half the battle. In mental arithmetic, it is most true that 'he who hesitates is lost.' When I speak of incessant practice, I do not mean deliberate drilling of set purpose; but with my father, as with myself, the mental handling of numbers or playing with figures afforded a positive pleasure and constant occupation of leisure moments. Even up to the last year of his life (his age was seventy-two) my father took delight in working out long and difficult arithmetical problems." [*]

[*] Mr. G. Bidder's powers as a mental arithmetician would be considered astonishing if the achievements of his father and others were not known. "I myself," he says, "can perform pretty extensive arithmetical operations mentally, but I cannot pretend to approach even distantly to the rapidity and accuracy with which my father worked. I have occasionally multiplied 15 figures by 15 in my head, but it takes me a long time, and I am liable to occasional errors. Last week, after speaking to Prof. Elliot, I tried the following sum to see if I could still do it:—

378,201,969,513,825
199,631,057,265,413

and I got, in my head, the answer, 75,576,299,427,512,145,197,597,834,725: in which, I think, if you will take the trouble to work it out, you will find 4 figures out of the 29 are wrong." I have only run through the cross multiplication far enough to detect the first error, which is in the digit representing thousands of millions. This should be 4 not 7.

We must always remember, in considering such feats as Bidder and other "calculating boys" accomplished, that the power of mentally picturing numbers is in their case far greater than we are apt to imagine such a power can possibly be. Precisely as the feats of a Morphy seem beyond belief till actually witnessed, and even then (especially to those who know what his chess play meant) almost miraculous, so the mnemonic powers of some arithmeticians would seem incredible if they had not been tested, and even as witnessed seem altogether marvelous. Colburn tells us that a notorious freethinker who had seen his arithmetical achievements at the age of six, "went home much disturbed, passed a sleepless night, and ever afterwards renounced infidel opinions." "And this," says the writer in the Spectator, from whom I have already quoted, "was only one illustration of the vague feeling of awe and open-mouthed wonder, which his performances excited. People came to consult him about stolen spoons; and he himself evidently thought that there was something decidedly uncanny, something supernatural, about his gift."

But so far as actual mnemonic arithmetical power is concerned, the feats of Colburn, and even of Bidder, have been surpassed. Consider, for instance, the following instances of the strong power of abstraction possessed by Dr. Wallis: "December 22d, 1669.— In a dark night in bed," he says in a letter to his friend, Mr. Thomas Smith, B. D., Fellow of Magdalen College, "without pen, ink, or paper, or anything equivalent, I did by memory extract the square root of 30000,00000,00000,00000,00000,00000,00000,00000, which I found to be 1,77205,08075,68077,29353, *ferè*, and did the next day commit it to writing."

And again: "February 18th, 1670.—Johannes Georgius Pelshower (Regiomontanus Borussus) giving me a visit, and desiring an example of the like, I did that night propose to myself in the dark, without help to my memory, a number in 53 places: 24681357910-12141113151618201719212242628302325272931, of which I extracted the square root in 27 places: 15710301687148280581715217 *proxime;* which numbers I did not commit to paper till he gave me another visit, March following, when I did from memory dictate them to him." Mr. E. W. Craigie, commenting on these feats, says that they "are not perhaps as difficult as multiplying 15 figures by 15, for while of course it is easy to remember such a number as three thousand billion trillions, being nothing but noughts, so also it may be noticed that there is a certain order in the row

of 53 figures; the numbers follow each other in little sets of arithmetical progression (2, 4, 6, 8), (1, 3, 5, 7, 9), (10, 12, 14), (11, 13, 15), (16, 18, 20), and so on; not regularly, but still enough to render it an immense assistance to a man engaged in a mental calculation. A row of 53 figures set down at hazard would have been much more difficult to remember, like Foote's famous sentence with which he puzzled the quack mnemonician; but still we must give the doctor the credit for remembering the answer." Mr. Craigie seems to overlook the circumstance that remembering the original number, and remembering the answer, in cases of this kind, are utterly unimportant feats compared with the work of obtaining the answer. If any one will be at the pains to work out the problem of extracting the square root of any number in 53 places, he will see that it would be a very small help indeed to have the original number written down before him, if the solution was to be worked out mnemonically. Probably in both cases Wallis took easily remembered numbers, not to help him at the time, but so that if occasion required he might be able to recall the problem months or years after he had solved it. Any one who could work out in his mind such a problem as the second of those given above would have no difficulty in remembering an array of two or three hundred figures set down entirely at random.

I have left small space in which to consider the singular evidence given by Prof. Elliot and Mr. G. Bidder respecting the transmission in the Bidder family of that special mental quality on which the elder Bidder's arithmetical power was based. Hereafter I may take occasion to discuss this evidence more at length, and with particular reference to its bearing on the question of hereditary genius. Let it suffice to mention here that, although Mr. G. Bidder and other members of the family have possessed in large degree the power of dealing mentally with large numbers, yet in other cases, though the same special mental quality involved has been present, the way in which that quality has shown itself has been altogether different. Thus Mr. G. Bidder states that his father's eldest brother, "who was a Unitarian minister, was not remarkable as an arithmetician, but he had an extraordinary memory for biblical texts, and could quote almost any text in the Bible, and give chapter and verse." A granddaughter of G. P. Bidder's once said to Prof. Elliot, "Isn't it strange: when I hear anything remarkable said or read to me, I think I see it

in print?" Mr. G. Bidder "can play two games of chess simultaneously," Prof. Elliot mentions, "without seeing the board." "Several of Mr. G. P. Bidder's nephews and grandchildren," he adds, "possess also very remarkable powers. One of his nephews at an early age showed a degree of mechanical ingenuity beyond anything I had ever seen in a boy. The summer before last, to test the calculating powers of some of his grandchildren (daughters of Mr. G. Bidder, the barrister), I gave them a question which I scarcely expected any of them to answer. I asked them, 'At what point in the scale do Fahrenheit's thermometer and the Centigrade show the same number at the same temperature?' The nature of the two scales had to be explained, but after that they were left to their own resources. The next morning one of the younger ones (about ten years old) came to tell me it was at 40 degrees below zero. This was the correct answer; she had worked it out in bed."

From "Belgravia."

"FATHER PROUT"

(FRANCIS MAHONY)

(c. 1804–1866)

"FATHER PROUT" is inimitable and unequaled among modern humorous essayists, but unfortunately he wrote chiefly for masters of not less than six languages. When it is necessary to be an expert in Greek as well as in French, Italian, Latin, and ancient Irish to see the point of a joke, there are those of us who will admire Prout from a respectful distance without attempting to realize the niceties of his humor. He was no pretender to learning, however, and no mere pedant. It is doubtful if the nineteenth century produced a greater linguist, but he used his mastery of ancient and modern languages chiefly to amuse himself at the expense of the learned false pretenses of his friends and of contemporary celebrities who probably wished for as little as possible of such friendship as his. His real name was Francis Mahony, and he was born at Cork, Ireland, about 1804. He was educated for the priesthood at Paris and Rome, and the latter part of his life was passed in a monastery; but from 1834 to 1864, he was one of the literary celebrities of Great Britain. His "Reliques of Father Prout" were originally contributed to Fraser's Magazine. As a versifier he has a nice ear for melody, and but for a defective sense of "time," he might have become a lyric poet of the highest rank. His possibilities appear in "The Bells of Shandon" and in many of his translations. He died at Paris, May 18th, 1866.

THE ROGUERIES OF TOM MOORE

THE Blarney stone in my neighborhood has attracted hither many an illustrious visitor; but none has been so assiduous a pilgrim in my time as Tom Moore. While he was engaged in his best and most unexceptionable work on the melodious ballads of his country, he came regularly every summer, and did me the honor to share my humble roof repeatedly. He knows well how often he plagued me to supply him with original songs which I had picked up in France among the merry troubadours and carol-loving inhabitants of that once happy land, and to what extent he has transferred these foreign inventions into the "Irish Melodies." Like the robber Cacus, he generally dragged the plundered cattle by the tail, so as that, moving backwards in his cavern of stolen goods, the foot tracks might not lead to detection. Some songs he would turn upside down, by a figure in rhetoric called ὕστερον πρότερον; others he would disguise in various shapes; but he would still worry me to supply him with the productions of the Gallic muse; "for, d'ye see, old Prout," the rogue would say,

> "The best of all ways
> To lengthen our lays,
> Is to steal a few thoughts from the French, 'my dear.'"

Now I would have let him enjoy unmolested the renown which these "Melodies" have obtained for him, but his last treachery to my round-tower friend [O'Brien] has raised my bile, and I shall give evidence of the unsuspected robberies.

> "*Abstractæque boves abjuratæque rapinæ*
> *Cælo ostendentur.*"

It would be easy to point out detached fragments and stray metaphors which he has scattered here and there in such gay confusion that every page has within its limits a mass of felony and plagiarism sufficient to hang him. For instance, I need only advert to his "Bard's Legacy." Even on his dying bed this "dying bard" cannot help indulging his evil pranks; for, in bequeathing his "heart" to his "mistress dear," and recommending her to "borrow" balmy drops of port wine to bathe the relic, he is all the while robbing old Clement Marot, who thus disposes of his remains: —

> "*Quand je suis mort, je veux qu'on m'entère*
> *Dans la cave où est le vin;*
> *Le corps sous un tonneau de Madére,*
> *Et la bouche sous le robin.*"

But I won't strain at a gnat when I can capture a camel — a huge dromedary laden with pilfered soil; for would you believe it if you had never learned it from Prout, the very opening and foremost song of the collection,

> "Go where glory waits thee,"

Quand de la famille	And at night when gazing
L'antique foyer brille,	On the gay hearth blazing,
Pense encore à moi!	Oh, then remember me!
Et si de la chanteuse	Then, should music, stealing
La voix melodieuse	All the soul of feeling,
Berce ton âme heureuse	To thy heart appealing,
Et ravit tes sens,	Draw one tear from thee;
Pense à l'air que chante	Then let memory bring thee
Pour toi ton amante —	Strains I used to sing thee —
Tant aimés accens!	Oh, then remember me!

Any one who has the slightest tincture of French literature must recognize the simple and unsophisticated style of a genuine love song in the above, the language being that of the century in which Clement Marot and Maitre Adam wrote their incomparable ballads, and containing a kindly mixture of gentleness and sentimental delicacy, which no one but a "ladye" and a loving heart could infuse into the composition. Moore has not been infelicitous in rendering the charms of the wondrous original into English lines adapted to the measure and tune of the French. The air is plaintive and exquisitely beautiful; but I recommend it to be tried first on the French words, as it was sung by the charming lips of the Countess of Châteaubriand to the enraptured ear of the gallant Francis I. . . . .

Everything was equally acceptable in the way of a song to Tommy; and provided I brought grist to his mill he did not care where the produce came from — even the wild oats and the thistles of native growth on Watergrasshill — all was good provender for his Pegasus. There was an old Latin song of my own, which I made when a boy, smitten with the charms of an Irish milkmaid, who crossed by the hedge school occasionally, and who used to distract my attention from "Corderius" and "Erasmi Colloquia." I have often laughed at my juvenile gallantry when my eye has met the copy of verses in overhauling my papers. Tommy saw it, grasped it with avidity; and I find he has given it, word for word, in an English shape, in his "Irish Melodies." Let the intelligent reader judge if he has done common justice to my young muse.

is but a literal and servile translation of an old French ditty, which is among my papers, and which I believe to have been composed by that beautiful and interesting "ladye," Françoise de Foix, Comtesse de Châteaubriand, born in 1491, and the favorite of Francis I., who soon abandoned her; indeed, the lines appear to anticipate his infidelity. They were written before the battle of Pavia.

CHANSON	TOM MOORE
De la Comtesse de Châteaubriand	*Translation of this song in the "Irish*
a François I.	*Melodies"*
Va où la gloire t'invite;	Go where glory waits thee;
Et quand d'orgueil palpite	But while fame elates thee,
Ce Cœur, qu'il pense à moi!	Oh, still remember me!
Quand l'éloge enflamme	When the praise thou meetest
Toute l'ardeur de ton âme,	To thine ear is sweetest,
Pense encore à moi!	Oh, then remember me!
Autres charmes peut-être	Other arms may press thee,
Tu voudras connaître,	Dearer friends caress thee —
Autre amour en maître	All the joys that bless thee
Regnera sur toi;	Dearer far may be;
Mais quand ta lèvre presse	But when friends are dearest,
Celle qui te caresse,	And when joys are nearest,
Méchant, pense à moi!	Oh, then remember me!
Quand au soir tu erres	When at eve thou rovest
Sous l'astre des bergères,	By the star thou lovest,
Pense aux doux instans	Oh, then remember me!
Lorsque cette étoile,	Think, when home returning,
Qu'un beau ciel dévoile,	Bright we've seen it burning —
Guida deux amans!	Oh, then remember me!
Quand la fleur, symbole	Oft as summer closes,
D'été qui s'envole,	When thy eye reposes
Penche sa tête molle,	On its lingering roses,
S'exhalant à l'air,	Once so loved by thee,
Pense á la guirlande,	Think of her who wove them —
De ta mie l'offrande —	Her who made thee love them
Don qui fut si cher!	Oh, then remember me!
Quand la feuille d'automme	When around thee, dying,
Sous tes pas resonne,	Autumn leaves are lying,
Pense alors à moi!	Oh, then remember me!

IN PULCHRAM LACTIFERAM	TO A BEAUTIFUL MILKMAID
Carmen, Auctore Prout	*A Melody by Thomas Moore*
Lesbia semper hinc et inde	Lesbia hath a beaming eye,
Oculorum tela movit;	But no one knows for whom
	it beameth;
Captat omnes, sed deinde	Right and left its arrows fly,
Quis ametur nemo novit.	But what they aim at, no one
	dreameth.
Palpebrarum, Nora cara,	Sweeter 'tis to gaze upon
Lux tuarum non est foris,	My Nora's lid, that seldom rises;
Flamma micat ibi rara,	Few her looks, but every one
Sed sinceri lux amoris.	Like unexpected light surprises,
Nora Creina sit regina,	Oh, my Nora Creina dear!
Vultu, gressu tam modesto!	My gentle, bashful Nora Creina!
Hæc, puellas inter bellas,	Beauty lies
Jure omnium dux esto!	In many eyes —
	But love's in thine, my Nora
	Creina!
Lesbia vestes auro graves	Lesbia wears a robe of gold;
Fert, et gemmis, juxta normam;	But all so tight the nymph hath
	laced it,
Gratiæ sed, eheu! suaves	Not a charm of beauty's mold
Cinctam reliquere formam.	Presumes to stay where nature
	placed it.
Noræ tunicam præferres,	Oh, my Nora's gown for me,
Flante zephyro volantem;	That floats as wild as mountain
	breezes,
Oculis et raptis erres	Leaving every beauty free
Contemplando ambulantem!	To sink or swell as Heaven pleases.
Vesta Nora tam decora	Yes, my Nora Creina dear!
Semper indui memento,	My simple, graceful Nora Creina!
Semper puræ sic naturæ	Nature's dress
Ibis tecta vestimento.	Is loveliness —
	The dress you wear, my Nora
	Creina!
Lesbia mentis præfert lumen	Lesbia hath a wit refined;
Quod coruscat perlibenter;	But when its points are gleam-
	ing round us,
Sed quis optet hoc acumen,	Who can tell if they're design'd
Quando acupuncta dentur?	To dazzle merely, or to wound us?

Noræ sinu cum recliner,
  Dormio luxuriose
Nil corrugat hoc pulvinar,
  Nisi crispæ ruga rosæ.
Nora blanda, lux amanda,
  Expers usque tenebrarum,
Tu cor mulces per tot dulces
  Dotes, fons illecebrarum!

Pillow'd on my Nora's heart,
  In safer slumber Love reposes —
Bed of peace, whose roughest part
  Is but the crumpling of the roses.
Oh, my Nora Creina dear!
  My mild, my artless Nora Creina!
    Wit, though bright,
    Hath not the light
  That warms your eyes, my Nora
    Creina!

It will be seen by these specimens that Tom Moore can eke
out a tolerably fair translation of any given ballad; and, indeed,
to translate properly, retaining all the fire and spirit of the original, is a merit not to be sneezed at—it is the next best thing to
having a genius of one's own; for he who can execute a clever
forgery, and make it pass current, is almost as well off as the
capitalist who can draw a substantial check on the bank of sterling genius; so, to give the devil his due, I must acknowledge
that in terseness, point, pathos, and elegance, Moore's translations
of these French and Latin trifles are very near as good as the
primary compositions themselves.* He has not been half so lucky
in hitting off Anacreon; but he was a young man then, and a
"wild fellow," since which time it is thought that he has got to
that climacteric in life to which few poets attain, *viz.*, the years of
discretion. A predatory sort of life, the career of a literary free-
booter, has had great charms for him from his cradle; and I am
afraid he will pursue it on to final impenitence. He seems to
care little about the stern reception he will one day receive from
that inflexible judge, Rhadamanthus, who will make him confess
all his rogueries,—"*Castigatque dolos, subigitque fateri,*"— our bard
being of that epicurean and careless turn of mind so strikingly
expressed in these lines of "Lalla Rookh"—

"Oh! if there be an Elysium on earth,
  It is this! it is this!"

Which verses, by the by, are alone enough to convict him of
downright plagiarism and robbery; for they are (as Tommy knows
right well) to be seen written in large letters in the Mogul lan-

* The French and Latin "trifles" are of course Prout's own "forgeries"
for the occasion.

were very fine; but there is nothing, after all, like the associations which early infancy attaches to the well-known and long-
remembered chimes of our own parish steeple; and no magic
can equal the effect on our ear when returning after long absence in foreign, and perhaps happier countries. As we perfectly
coincided in the truth of this observation, I added, that long ago,
while at Rome, I had thrown my ideas into the shape of a song,
which I would sing him to the tune of the "Groves."

THE BELLS OF SHANDON

Sabbata Pango,
Funera Plango,
Solemnia Clango.
  —*Inscription on an old bell.*

WITH deep affection
  And recollection
I often think of
  Those Shandon bells,
Whose sounds so wild would,
In days of childhood,
Fling round my cradle
  Their magic spells.
On this I ponder
Where'er I wander,
And thus grow fonder,
  Sweet Cork, of thee;
With thy bells of Shandon,
That sound so grand on
The pleasant waters
  Of the River Lee.

I've heard bells chiming
Full many a clime in,
Tolling sublime in
  Cathedral shrine;
While at a glib rate
Brass tongues would vibrate,
But all their music
  Spoke naught like thine;
For memory, dwelling
On each proud swelling
Of the belfry, knelling

guage over the audience chamber of the king of Delhi; in fact,
to examine and overhaul his "Lalla Rookh" would be a most diverting task, which I may one day undertake. He will be found
to have been a chartered pirate in the Persian Gulf, as he was a
highwayman in Europe—"*spoliis Orientis onustum.*" . . .

A simple hint was sometimes enough to set his Muse at work;
and he not only was, to my knowledge, an adept in translating
accurately, but he could also string together any number of lines
in any given measure, in imitation of a song or ode which casually came in his way. This is not such arrant robbery as what
I have previously stigmatized; but it is a sort of quasi-pilfering,
a kind of petty larceny, not to be encouraged. There is, for instance, his "National Melody," or jingle, called in the early edition of his poems, "Those Evening Bells, a Petersburg Air,"
of which I could unfold the natural history. It is this: In
one of his frequent visits to Watergrasshill, Tommy and I spent
the evening in talking of our continental travels, and more particularly of Paris and its mirabilia; of which he seemed quite
enamored. The view from the tower of the central church,
Notre Dame, greatly struck his fancy; and I drew the conversation to the subject of the simultaneous ringing of all the bells
in all the steeples of that vast metropolis on some feast day, or
public rejoicing. The effect, he agreed with me, is most enchanting, and the harmony most surprising. At that time Victor Hugo
had not written his glorious romance, the "Hunchback Quasi-
modo"; and, consequently, I could not have read his beautiful
description: "In an ordinary way, the noise issuing from Paris
in the daytime is the talking of the city; at night, it is the
breathing of the city; in this case, it is the singing of the city.
Lend your ear to this opera of steeples. Diffuse over the whole
the buzzing of half a million of human beings, the eternal murmur of the river, the infinite piping of the wind, the grave and
distant quartet of the four forests, placed like immense organs
on the four hills of the horizon; soften down as with a demitint
all that is too shrill and too harsh in the central mass of sound,
—and say if you know anything in the world more rich, more
gladdening, more dazzling, than that tumult of bells—than that
furnace of music—than those ten thousand brazen tones, breathed
all at once from flutes of stone three hundred feet high—than
that city which is but one orchestra—than that symphony rushing and roaring like a tempest." All these matters, we agreed,

  Its bold notes free,
Made the bells of Shandon
Sound far more grand on
  The pleasant waters
    Of the River Lee.

I've heard the bells tolling
Old Adrian's Mole in,
Their thunder rolling
  From the Vatican,
And cymbals glorious,
Swinging uproarious
In the gorgeous turrets
  Of Notre Dame;
But thy sounds were sweeter
Than the dome of Peter
Flings o'er the Tiber,
  Pealing solemnly.
Oh! the bells of Shandon
Sound far more grand on
The pleasant waters
  Of the River Lee.

There's a bell in Moscow,
While on tower and kiosk, O!
In Saint Sophia
  The Turkman gets,
And loud in air
Calls men to prayer
From the tapering summit
  Of tall minarets.
Such empty phantom
I freely grant them;
But there's an anthem
  More dear to me,—
'Tis the bells of Shandon,
That sound so grand on
The pleasant waters
  Of the River Lee.

Shortly afterwards Moore published his "Evening Bells, a
Petersburg Air." But any one can see that he only rings a few
changes on my Roman ballad, cunningly shifting the scene as
far north as he could, to avoid detection. He deserves richly to
be sent on a hurdle to Siberia.

I do not feel so much hurt at this nefarious "belle's strata- gem" regarding me as at his wickedness towards the man of the round towers; and to this matter I turn in conclusion.

"Oh, blame not the bard!" some folks will no doubt exclaim, and perhaps think that I have been over-severe on Tommy, in my vindication of O'B. I can only say, that if the poet of all circles and the idol of his own, as soon as this posthumous re- buke shall meet his eye, begins to repent him of his wicked at- tack on my young friend, and, turning him from his evil ways, betakes him to his proper trade of ballad-making, then shall he experience the comfort of living at peace with all mankind, and old Prout's blessing shall fall as a precious ointment on his head. In that contingency if (as I understand it to be his intention) he should happen to publish a fresh number of his "Melodies," may it be eminently successful; and may Power of the Strand, by some more sterling sounds than the echoes of fame, be convinced of the power of song—

> "For it is not the magic of streamlet or hill;
> Oh, no! it is something that sounds in the 'till!'"

My humble patronage, it is true, cannot do much for him in fashionable circles; for I never mixed much in the *beau monde* (at least in Ireland), during my lifetime, and can be of no serv- ice, of course, when I'm dead; nor will his "Melodies," I fear, though well adapted to mortal pianofortes, answer the purposes of that celestial choir in which I shall then be an obscure but cheerful vocalist. But as I have touched on this great topic of mortality, let Moore recollect that his course here below, how- ever harmonious in the abstract, must have a finale; and at his last hour let him not treasure up for himself the unpleasant ret- rospect of young genius nipped in the bud by the frost of his criticism, or glad enthusiasm's early promise damped by inconsid- erate sneers. O'Brien's book can, and will, no doubt, afford much matter for witticism and merriment to the superficial, the unthinking, and the profane; but to the eye of candor it ought to have presented a page richly fraught with wondrous research —redolent with all the perfumes of Hindoostan; its leaves, if they failed to convince, should, like those of the mysterious lotus, have inculcated silence; and if the finger of meditation did not rest on every line, and pause on every period, the volume, at least, should not be indicated to the vulgar by the finger of scorn.

Let Moore, then, vent his indignation and satiate his voracity on the proper objects of a volatile of prey; but he will find in his own province of imaginative poetry a kindlier element, a purer atmosphere, for his winged excursions. Long, long may we be- hold the gorgeous bird soaring through the regions of inspira- tion, distinguished in his loftier as in his gentler flights, and combining, by a singular miracle of ornithology, the voice of the turtledove, the eagle's eye and wing, with the plumage of the "bird of Paradise."

From "Reliques of Father Prout."

Even granting that there were in the book some errors of fancy, of judgment, or of style, which of us is without reproach in our juvenile productions? and though I myself am old, I am the more inclined to forgive the inaccuracies of youth. Again, when all is dark, who would object to a ray of light, merely because of the faulty or flickering medium by which it is transmitted? And if these round towers have been hitherto a dark puzzle and a mys- tery, must we scare away O'Brien because he approaches with a rude and unpolished, but serviceable lantern? No; forbid it, Diogenes; and though Tommy may attempt to put his extin- guisher on the towers and their historian, there is enough of good sense in the British public to make common cause with O'Brien the enlightener. Moore should recollect that knowledge conveyed in any shape will ever find a welcome among us; and that, as he himself beautifully observes in his "Loves of the Angels"—

> "Sunshine broken in the rill,
> Though turn'd aside, is sunshine still."

For my own part, I protest to heaven, that were I, while wan- dering in a gloomy forest, to meet on my dreary path the small, faint, glimmering light even of a glow worm, I should shudder at the thought of crushing with my foot that dim speck of bril- liancy; and were it only for its being akin to brighter rays, hon- oring it for its relationship to the stars, I would not harm the little lamplighter as I passed along in the woodland shade.

If Tommy is rabidly bent on satire, why does he not fall foul of Dr. Lardner, who has got the clumsy machinery of a whole cyclopædia at work, grinding that nonsense which he calls "Useful Knowledge"? Let the poet mount his Pegasus, or his Rosinante, and go tilt a lance against the doctor's windmill. It was unworthy of him to turn on O'Brien after the intimacy of private correspondence; and if he was inclined for battle, he might have found a seemlier foe. Surely my young friend was not the quarry on which the vulture should delight to pounce, when there are so many literary reptiles to tempt his beak and glut his maw! Heaven knows, there is fair game and plentiful carrion on the plains of Bœotia. In the poet's picture of the pursuits of a royal bird, we find such sports alluded to—

> "*In reluctantes dracones*
> *Egit amor dapis atque pugnæ.*"

QUINTILIAN

(MARCUS FABIUS QUINTILIANUS)

(c. 35 – c. 96 A. D.)

QUINTILIAN, whose "Institutes of Oratory" rank with the simi- lar treatises of Aristotle and Cicero, was born at Calagurris in Spain, "not later than 35 A. D." His father taught rhet- oric at Rome; and for twenty years under Galba, Quintilian himself was the head of the leading Roman school of oratory. His reputa- tion as a teacher was so great that Vespasian endowed his school with a gift of public money. He was an orator of celebrity and a success- ful practitioner in the courts. He died at an uncertain date in the last decade of the first century. His "Institutes of Oratory" are the production of an accomplished scholar, a master of style, and an inde- pendent thinker.

ADVANTAGES OF READING HISTORY AND SPEECHES

As we are treating of the first rudiments of rhetoric, I should not omit, I think, to observe how much the professor would contribute to the advancement of his pupils, if, as the ex- planation of the poets is required from teachers of grammar, so he, in like manner, would exercise the pupils under his care in the reading of history, and even still more in that of speeches; a practice which I myself have adopted in the case of a few pupils, whose age required it, and whose parents thought it would be serviceable to them. But though I then deemed it an excellent method, two circumstances were obstructions to the practice of it; that long custom had established a different mode of teaching, and that they were mostly full-grown youths, who did not require that exercise, that were forming themselves on my model. But though I should make a new discovery ever so late, I should not be ashamed to recommend it for the future. I know, however, that this is now done among the Greeks, but chiefly by assistant masters, since the time would seem hardly sufficient, if the pro- fessors were always to lecture to each pupil as he read. Such lecturing, indeed, as is given, that boys may follow the writing of an author easily and distinctly with their eyes, and such even as explains the meaning of every word at all uncommon that occurs, is to be regarded as far below the profession of a teacher of rhetoric.

But to point out the beauties of authors, and, if occasion ever present itself, their faults, is eminently consistent with that profession and engagement, by which he offers himself to the public as a master of eloquence, especially as I do not require such toil from teachers, that they should call their pupils to their lap, and labor at the reading of whatever book each of them may fancy. For to me it seems easier, as well as far more advantageous, that the master, after calling for silence, should appoint some one pupil to read (and it will be best that this duty should be imposed on them by turns), that they may thus accustom themselves to clear pronunciation; and then, after explaining the cause for which the oration was composed (for so that which is said will be better understood), that he should leave nothing unnoticed which is important to be remarked, either in the thought or the language; that he should observe what method is adopted in the exordium for conciliating the judge; what clearness, brevity, and apparent sincerity, is displayed in the statement of facts; what design there is in certain passages, and what well-concealed artifice (for that is the only true art in pleading which cannot be perceived except by a skillful pleader); what judgment appears in the division of the matter; how subtle and urgent is the argumentation; with what force the speaker excites, with what amenity he soothes; what severity is shown in his invectives, what urbanity in his jests; how he commands the feelings, forces a way into the understanding, and makes the opinions of the judges coincide with what he asserts. In regard to the style, too, he should notice any expression that is peculiarly appropriate, elegant, or sublime; when the amplification deserves praise; what quality is opposed to it, what phrases are happily metaphorical, what figures of speech are used, what part of the composition is smooth and polished, and yet manly and vigorous.

Nor is it without advantage, indeed, that inelegant and faulty speeches, yet such as many, from depravity of taste, would admire, should be read before boys, and that it should be shown how many expressions in them are inappropriate, obscure, tumid, low, mean, affected, or effeminate; expressions which,

however, are not only extolled by many readers, but, what is worse, are extolled for the very reason that they are vicious, for straightforward language, naturally expressed, seems to some of us to have nothing of genius; but whatever departs, in any way, from the common course, we admire as something exquisite; as, with some persons, more regard is shown for figures that are distorted, and in any respect monstrous, than for such as have lost none of the advantages of ordinary conformation. Some, too, who are attracted by appearance, think that there is more beauty in men who are depilated and smooth, who dress their locks, hot from the curling irons, with pins, and who are radiant with a complexion not their own, than unsophisticated nature can give; as if beauty of person could be thought to spring from corruption of manners.

Nor will the preceptor be under the obligation merely to teach these things, but frequently to ask questions upon them, and try the judgment of his pupils. Thus carelessness will not come upon them while they listen, nor will the instructions that shall be given fail to enter their ears; and they will at the same time be conducted to the end which is sought in this exercise, namely that they themselves may conceive and understand. For what object have we in teaching them, but that they may not always require to be taught?

I will venture to say that this sort of diligent exercise will contribute more to the improvement of students than all the treatises of all the rhetoricians that ever wrote; which doubtless, however, are of considerable use, but their scope is more general; and how, indeed, can they go into all kinds of questions that arise almost every day? So, though certain general precepts are given in the military art, it will yet be of far more advantage to know what plan any leader has adopted wisely or imprudently, and in what place or at what time; for in almost every art precepts are of much less avail than practical experiments. Shall a teacher declaim that he may be a model to his hearers, and will not Cicero and Demosthenes, if read, profit them more? Shall a pupil, if he commits faults in declaiming, be corrected before the rest, and will it not be more serviceable to him to correct the speech of another? Indisputably, and even more agreeable; for every one prefers that others' faults should be blamed rather than his own. Nor are there wanting more arguments for me to offer; but the advan-

tage of this plan can escape the observation of no one, and I wish that there may not be so much unwillingness to adopt it as there will be pleasure in having adopted it.

If this method be followed there will remain a question not very difficult to answer, which is, what authors ought to be read by beginners. Some have recommended inferior writers, as they thought them easier of comprehension; others have advocated the more florid kind of writers, as being better adapted to nourish the minds of the young. For my part, I would have the best authors commenced at once, and read always; but I would choose the clearest in style, and most intelligible; recommending Livy, for instance, to be read by boys rather than Sallust, who, however, is the greater historian, but to understand him there is need of some proficiency. Cicero, as it seems to me, is agreeable even to beginners, and sufficiently intelligible, and may not only profit, but even be loved; and next to Cicero (as Livy advises), such authors as most resemble Cicero.

There are two points in style on which I think that the greatest caution should be used in respect to boys: one is that no master, from being too much an admirer of antiquity, should allow them to harden, as it were, in the reading of the Gracchi, Cato, and other like authors; for they would thus become uncouth and dry; since they cannot, as yet, understand their force of thought, and, content with adopting their style, which, at the time it was written, was doubtless excellent, but is quite unsuitable to our day, they will appear to themselves to resemble those eminent men. The other point, which is the opposite of the former, is, lest, being captivated with the flowers of modern affectation, they should be so seduced by a corrupt kind of pleasure, as to love that luscious manner of writing which is the more agreeable to the minds of youth in proportion as it has more affinity with them. When their taste is formed, however, and out of danger of being corrupted, I should recommend them to read not only the Ancients (from whom if a solid and manly force of thought be adopted, while the rust of a rude age is cleared off, our present style will receive additional grace), but also the writers of the present day, in whom there is much merit. For nature has not condemned us to stupidity, but we ourselves have changed our mode of speaking, and have indulged our fancies more than we ought; and thus the Ancients did not excel us so much in genius as in severity of manner. It will be pos-

sible, therefore, to select from the Moderns many qualities for imitation, but care must be taken that they be not contaminated with other qualities with which they are mixed. Yet that there have been recently, and are now, many writers whom we may imitate entirely, I would not only allow (for why should I not?), but even affirm. But who they are it is not for everybody to decide. We may even err with greater safety in regard to the Ancients; and I would therefore defer the reading of the Moderns, that imitation may not go before judgment.

From "Institutes of Oratory."

MADAME DE RÉMUSAT

(Claire Elisabeth Jeanne Gravier de Vergennes Comtesse de Rémusat)

(1780–1821)

REFIXED to Madame de Rémusat's "Memoirs" is one of the most searching studies of the character of Napoleon in print. She had a keenly critical intellect and she probes mercilessly the vital weaknesses of his character. Her husband, who was Napoleon's chamberlain, became disaffected, and after the Restoration took office under the Bourbons. Born in 1780, and married to the Comte de Rémusat when very young, Madame de Rémusat became one of Josephine's court ladies and was greatly admired for her talents. The extent of her abilities was not suspected, however, until after her death (1821), when one of her essays was "crowned" by the French Academy. More than fifty years later (1879) her son published her "Memoirs," which at once became famous. She was a most extraordinary woman in many respects, but perhaps most remarkable for her lack of reserve in estimating character and in recording incident and anecdote illustrating it.

THE CHARACTER OF NAPOLEON BONAPARTE

BEFORE I enter upon my own recollections, I think it well to make some preliminary observations on the Emperor and the various members of his family. By doing so the difficult task I am about to undertake will be facilitated, and I shall be assisted in recalling the impressions of the last twelve years. I will begin with Bonaparte himself. I do not pretend that he always appeared to me in the light in which I see him now; my opinions have altered, even as he has altered: but I am so far from being influenced by personal feeling, that I am certain I shall not for a moment deviate from the exact truth.

Napoleon Bonaparte is of low stature, and ill made; the upper part of his body is too long in proportion to his legs. He has thin chestnut hair; his eyes are grayish blue; and his skin, which was yellow whilst he was slight, has become of late years a dead

white without any color. His forehead, the setting of his eye, the line of his nose — are all beautiful, and remind one of an antique medallion; his mouth, which is thin-lipped, becomes pleasant when he laughs; the teeth are regular; his chin is short, and his jaw heavy and square; he has well-formed hands and feet, — I mention them particularly, because he thought a good deal of them.

He has a habitual slight stoop; his eyes are dull, giving to his face a melancholy and meditative expression when in repose. When he is angry his looks are fierce and menacing. Laughter becomes him; it makes him look more youthful, and less formidable. When he laughs, his countenance improves. He was always simple in his dress, and generally wore the uniform of his own guard. He was cleanly rather from habit than from a liking for cleanliness; he bathed often, sometimes in the middle of the night, because he thought the practice good for his health. Otherwise, the precipitation with which he did everything did not admit of his clothes being put on carefully; and on gala days and full-dress occasions, his attendants were obliged to consult together as to when they might snatch a moment to dress him.

He could not endure the wearing of ornaments; the slightest constraint was insupportable to him. He would tear off or break anything that gave him the least annoyance, and the poor valet who had occasioned him a passing inconvenience would receive violent proofs of his anger. I have said there was fascination in the smile of Bonaparte; but, during all the time when I was in the habit of seeing him constantly, he rarely put forth that charm. Gravity was at the bottom of his character; not the gravity of a dignified and noble manner, but that which arises from profound thought. In his youth he was a dreamer, later in life he became a moody, and, later still, a habitually ill-tempered man. When I first began to know him well, he was exceedingly fond of all that leads to reverie, — of Ossian, of the twilight, of melancholy music. I have seen him enraptured by the murmur of the wind, I have heard him talk with enthusiasm of the moaning of the sea, and he was tempted sometimes to believe that nocturnal apparitions were not beyond the bounds of possibility; in fact, he had a leaning towards superstition. When, on leaving his study in the evening, he went into Madame Bonaparte's drawing-room, he would sometimes have the candles shaded, desire us to keep profound silence, and amuse himself by telling or listening

to ghost stories; or he would have soft, sweet music executed by Italian singers, and accompanied only by a few instruments lightly touched. Then he would fall into a reverie which we all respected, no one venturing to stir, or to change his or her place. When he aroused himself from that state, which seemed to procure him a sort of repose, he was generally more serene and communicative. He liked to talk at such times about the sensations he had experienced. He would explain the effect music had upon him; he always preferred that of Paisiello, because he said it was monotonous, and that only impressions which repeat themselves take possession of us. The geometrical turn of his mind disposed him to analyze even his emotions. No man has ever meditated more deeply than Bonaparte on the "wherefore" that rules human actions. Always aiming at something, even in the least important acts of his life, always assigning a secret motive for each of them to himself, he could never understand that natural carelessness which leads some persons to act without a project and without an aim. He judged others by himself, and was often mistaken his conclusions and the actions which ensued upon them alike proving erroneous.

Bonaparte was deficient in education and in manners; it seemed as if he must have been destined either to live in a tent where all men are equal, or upon a throne where everything is permitted. He did not know how either to enter or to leave a room; he did not know how to make a bow, how to rise, or how to sit down. His questions were abrupt, and so also was his manner of speech. Spoken by him, Italian loses all its grace and sweetness. Whatever language he speaks, it always sounds like a foreign tongue; he appears to force it to express his thoughts. And, as any rigid rule becomes an insupportable annoyance to him, and every liberty which he takes pleases him as though it were a victory, he would never yield to grammar. He used to say that in his youth he had liked reading romances as well as studying the exact sciences; and probably he was influenced by so incongruous a mixture. Unfortunately, he had met with the worst of the former kind of books, and retained so keen and pleasant a remembrance of them, that when he married the Archduchess Marie Louise, he gave her "Hippolyte, Comte de Douglas," and "Les Contemporains," so that, as he said, she might form an idea of refined feeling, and also of the customs of society.

In trying to depict Bonaparte, it would be necessary, if one were to follow the analytical forms of which he was so fond, to separate into three distinct parts his soul, his heart, and his mind, for no one of these ever blended completely with the others. Although remarkable for certain intellectual qualities, no man, it must be allowed, was ever less lofty of soul. There was no generosity, no true greatness in him. I have never known him to admire, I have never known him to comprehend, a fine action. He always regarded every indication of a good feeling with suspicion; he did not value sincerity, and he did not hesitate to say that he recognized the superiority of a man by the greater or less dexterity with which he practiced the art of lying. On the occasion of his saying this, he added, with great complacency, that when he was a child, one of his uncles had predicted of him that he should govern the world, because he was a habitual liar. "M. de Metternich," he added, "approaches to being a statesman — he lies very well."

Bonaparte's methods of government were all selected from among those which have a tendency to debase men. He dreaded the ties of affection; he endeavored to isolate every one; he never sold a favor without awakening a sense of uneasiness, for he held that the true way to attach the recipient to himself was by compromising him, and often even by blasting him in public opinion. He could not pardon virtue until he had succeeded in weakening its effect by ridicule. He cannot be said to have truly loved glory, for he never hesitated to prefer success; thus, although he was audacious in good fortune, and pushed it to its utmost limits, he was timid and troubled when threatened with reverses. Of generous courage he was not capable; and, indeed, on that head one would hardly venture to tell the truth so plainly as he has told it himself, by an admission recorded in an anecdote which I have never forgotten. One day, after his defeat at Leipsic, and when, as he was about to return to Paris, he was occupied in collecting the remains of his army for the defense of our frontiers, he was talking to M. de Talleyrand of the ill success of the Spanish war, and of the difficulty in which it had involved him. He spoke openly of his own position, not with the noble frankness that does not fear to own a fault, but with that haughty sense of superiority which releases one from the necessity of dissimulation. In the midst of this plain speaking, M. de Talleyrand said to him suddenly: "But how is this? You consult me as if you and I had not quarreled."

Bonaparte answered: "Ah, circumstances! circumstances! Let us leave the past and the future alone. I want to hear what you think of the present moment."

"Well," replied M. de Talleyrand, "there is only one thing you can do. You have made a mistake: you must say so; try to say so nobly. Proclaim, therefore, that being a king by the choice of the people, elected by the nation, it has never been your design to set yourself against them. Say that when you began the war with Spain, you believed you were about to deliver the people from the yoke of an odious minister, who was encouraged by the weakness of his prince; but that perceiving, on closer observation, that the Spaniards, although aware of the faults of their king, are none the less attached to his dynasty, you are about to restore it to them, so that it may not be said you have opposed a national aspiration. After that proclamation, restore King Ferdinand to liberty, and withdraw your troops. Such an avowal, made in a lofty tone, and when the enemy are yet hesitating on our frontier, can only do you honor, and you are still too strong for it to be regarded as a cowardly act."

"A cowardly act!" replied Bonaparte; "what does that matter to me? Understand that I should not fail to commit one, if it were useful to me. In reality, there is nothing really noble or base in this world; I have in my character all that can contribute to secure my power, and to deceive those who think they know me. Frankly, I am base, essentially base. I give you my word that I should feel no repugnance to commit what would be called by the world a dishonorable action; my secret tendencies, which are, after all, those of nature, apart from certain affectations of greatness which I have to assume, give me infinite resources with which to baffle every one. Therefore, all I have to do now is to consider whether your advice agrees with my present policy, and to try and find out besides," added he, with a satanic smile, "whether you have not some private interest in urging me to take this step."

From the Introduction to the "Memoirs."

JOSEPH ERNEST RENAN
(1823–1892)

JOSEPH ERNEST RENAN, perhaps the most celebrated French representative of what is sometimes called "higher criticism," was born at Tréguier, France, January 27th, 1823. When he left his native town to complete his studies in Paris, he had a strong bent towards theology, which controlled his later writings; but his attention was distracted from theology to philology, and it was for philology chiefly that he educated himself and took his university degree. He published in 1857 "Studies of Religious History" and the next year studies "On the Origin of Language." These works suggest at once his method and the scope of his life work. He applied the modern critical philological method to theology and made an international reputation by works which were accepted as representing the highest reaches of scientific criticism. Renan was a man of genius and a most attractive writer; but as a philologist, he belonged to what may be called, without inaccuracy, the Romantic school, swift in assumption and daring in generalization. He was a great essayist rather than a great scientist. Among his noted works are "Essays Moral and Critical," "The Life of Jesus," "St. Paul and His Mission," "Marcus Aurelius and the End of the Ancient World," and "History of the Origins of Christianity." He died at Paris, October 2d, 1892.

STATE OF THE WORLD AT THE TIME OF CHRIST

THE political state of the world was of the saddest kind. All authority was concentrated at Rome and in the legions. There occurred the most shameful and degrading scenes. The Roman aristocracy, which had conquered the world, and which, in short, had alone governed under the Cæsars, delivered itself up to the most frightful Saturnalia of crime which the world has ever seen. Cæsar and Augustus, in establishing the aristocracy, had seen with perfect accuracy the necessities of their times. The world was so low in the political sense that no other government was possible. Since Rome had conquered provinces

innumerable, the ancient constitution, founded on the privileges of patrician families, a species of obstinate and malevolent Tories, could not subsist. But Augustus had failed in all the duties of true policy in that he left the future to chance. Without regular hereditary succession, without fixed rules of adoption, without electoral laws, without constitutional limitations, Cæsarism was like a colossal weight on the deck of a ship without ballast. The most terrible shocks were inevitable. Thrice in a century, under Caligula, under Nero, and under Domitian, the greatest power which had ever existed fell into the hands of execrable or extravagant men. Hence, horrors, which have scarcely been exceeded by the monsters of the Mongal dynasties. In that fatal series of sovereigns we are reduced almost to excusing a Tiberius, who was absolutely wicked only towards the close of his life! a Claudius, who was simply eccentric, awkward, and surrounded by evil advisers. Rome became a school of vice and cruelty. It must be added that the evil came especially from the East, from those flatterers of low rank, from these infamous men whom Egypt and Syria sent to Rome, where, profiting by the oppression of the true Romans, they felt themselves all powerful with the scoundrels who governed them. The most shocking ignominies of the Empire, such as the apotheosis of the Emperor, his deification, when alive, came from the East, and especially from Egypt, which was then one of the most corrupt countries in the universe.

The true Roman spirit, in effect, still survived. Human nobility was far from being extinct. A great tradition of pride and of virtue was kept up in some families, which came to power with Nerva, and made the splendor of the century of the Antonines of which Tacitus has been the eloquent interpreter. A time, which was that of minds so profoundly honest as Quintilian, Pliny the Younger, and Tacitus, is not a time of which we need despair. The disturbance of the surface did not affect the great basis of honesty and of seriousness which underlay good society in Rome; some families still afforded models of valor, of devotion to duty, of concord, of solid virtue. There were in the noble houses admirable wives, admirable sisters. Was there ever a more touching fate than that of the young and chaste Octavia, daughter of Claudius, and wife of Nero, pure amidst so many infamies, killed at twenty-two years of age, before she had had time to enjoy her life? The women described in the inscriptions

as *Castissimæ, univiræ* are not rare. Wives accompanied their husbands in exile; others shared their noble deaths. The old Roman simplicity was not lost; the education of children was grave and careful. The noblest women labored with their hands at wool work; the cares of the toilet were almost unknown in good families.

The excellent statesmen who sprang up under Trajan were not improvised. They had served under preceding reigns; only they had had little influence, cast into the shade as they were by the freedmen and the basest favorites of the Emperor. Men of the highest character thus occupied exalted positions under Nero. The skeleton was good, the accession of the bad emperors to power, disastrous though it was, did not suffice to change the general course of affairs and the principles of the State. The Empire, far from being in decadence, was in all the force of the most robust youth. The decadence was coming, but that would be two centuries later, and, strange to say, under the least evil of the sovereigns. Looked at from the political point of view, the situation was analogous to that of France, which, for want of an invariable rule since the Revolution as to the succession of powers, has gone through the most perilous adventures, without its internal organization and national force suffering too much. From the moral point of view we may compare the time of which we speak with the eighteenth century, an epoch which we might fancy to be altogether corrupt, if we judged by the memories, the manuscript literature, the collection of anecdotes of the times, yet, in which houses maintained a great severity of morals.

Philosophy has allied itself with the honest Roman families, and resisted nobly. The Stoic school produced the great characters of Cremastius Cordus, of Thraseas, of Arria, of Helvidius Priscus, of Annæus Cornelius, of Musonius Rufus,—admirable masters of aristocratic virtue. The stiffness and the exaggerations of this school arose from the horrible cruelty of the government of the Cæsars. The perpetual thought of the good man was how he might best endure tortures and prepare for death. Lucan, with bad taste, Persius, with greater talents, expressed the highest sentiments of a great soul. Seneca the philosopher, Pliny the Elder, Papirius Fabianus, maintained an elevated tradition of science and philosophy. Every one did not yield; there were still wise men. But too often they had no other resource than death. The ignoble parts of humanity were at times in the ascendant. The spirit of vertigo and cruelty then overflowed and turned Rome into a veritable hell.

This government, so frightfully unequal at Rome, was much better in the provinces. Few of the disorders which shocked the capital were felt there. In spite of its defects the Roman administration was much better than the royalties and republics which the conquest had suppressed. The time of the sovereign municipalities had gone by for centuries. These little states had destroyed themselves by their egotism, their jealous spirit, their ignorance, or their little care for private liberties. The ancient Greek life, all struggles, all exterior, satisfied no one. It had been charming in its day, but this brilliant Olympus of a democracy of demigods having lost its freshness, had become something dry, cold, insignificant, vain, superficial, for want of goodness and of solid honesty. This it was which constituted the legitimacy of the Macedonian domination, then of the Roman administration. The Empire did not yet know the excess of centralization. Until the time of Diocletian, it left much liberty to the provinces and cities. Kingdoms, almost independent, existed in Palestine, in Syria, in Asia Minor, in little Armenia, in Thrace, under the protection of Rome. These kingdoms became dangers only in the days of Caligula, because the rules of the great and profound political policy of Augustus were neglected. The free cities, and they were numerous, governed themselves according to their own laws; they had the legislative power and all the magistracy of an autonomous state; until the third century, municipal decrees began with the formula, "The senate and the people. . . ." The theatres served, not only for the pleasures of the stage, they were the centres of opinion and of movement. The majority of the towns were under various names, little republics. The municipal spirit was very strong in them; they had not lost the right of declaring war,—a melancholy right which had turned the world into a field of carnage. "The benefits conferred by the Roman people on the human race" were the theme of declamations which were sometimes adulatory, but the sincerity of which cannot always be denied with justice. The worship of the "Roman peace," the idea of a great democracy organized under the protection of Rome was at the bottom of all thoughts. A Greek orator exhibited vast erudition in proving that the glory of Rome ought to be gathered amongst all the branches of the Hellenic race as a sort of common patri-

mony. In what concerned Syria, Asia Minor, Egypt, it may be said that the Roman Conquest destroyed no liberty. These countries had long been dead to the political life which they had never had.

In short, notwithstanding the exactions of the governors, and the violence, inseparable from an absolute government, the world in many respects had never yet been so happy. An administration coming from a distant centre was so great an advantage that even the plunderings of the Pretors in the last days of the Republic had not been sufficient to make it odious. The Julian law, besides, had greatly narrowed the field of abuse and of collusions. The follies or the cruelties of the Emperor, except under Nero, affected only the Roman aristocracy and the immediate surroundings of the Prince. There never was a time when a man who did not meddle in politics could live more comfortably. The republics of antiquity, in which every one was forced to occupy himself with the quarrels of parties, were exceedingly uncomfortable places of abode. People were incessantly upset or proscribed. Now the time seemed expressly fitted for large proselytisms above the quarrels of the little towns and the rivalries of dynasties. Such attempts against liberty as there were, arose out of what was still left of independence in provinces or communities much more than from the Roman administration. We have had, and we shall still have, numerous instances of this kind of thing to remark.

In those of the conquered countries in which political necessities had not existed for centuries, and where the people were deprived only of the right to tear each other to pieces by continual wars, the Empire was a period of prosperity and of wellbeing, such as had never been known, we may even add without paradox, of liberty. On the one hand, freedom of trade and of industry, of which the Greek republics had no idea, became possible. On the other, liberty of thought could only gain by the new system. That liberty is always stronger when it has to deal with a king or a prince than when it has to negotiate with a narrow and jealous citizen. The ancient republics did not possess it. The Greeks did without it in great things, thanks to the incomparable strength of their genius, but it ought not to be forgotten that Athens had her inquisition. The inquisition was the archon king; the holy office was the Royal Porch, whither were taken accusations of "impiety." Accusations of that kind were

very numerous; it is concerning cases of this description that most of the great Attic orations were delivered. Not merely philosophical crimes, such as denying God or Providence, but the slightest blow struck at the municipal worship, the preaching of foreign religions, the most childish infractions of the scrupulous legislation of the mysteries, were crimes which might be punished with death. The gods whom Aristophanes mocked at on the stage, killed sometimes. They killed Socrates, they wanted to kill Alcibiades. Anaxagoras, Protagoras, Theodorus the atheist, Diagoras of Melos, Prodicus of Ceos, Stilpo, Aristotle, Theophrastus, Aspasia, Euripides, were more or less seriously disquieted. Liberty of thought was, in short, the fruit of the royalties which sprang out of the Macedonian conquest. It was the Attali, the Ptolemies, who first gave to thinkers the facilities that none of the old republics had ever offered to them. The Roman Empire continued the same tradition. There was, under the empire, more than one arbitrary act against the philosophers, but they arose always, through their interfering with politics. We may seek in vain in the list of Roman laws before Constantine for a text against the liberty of thought, in the history of the emperors for a process against abstract doctrine. Not one scholar was disturbed. Men who would have been burned in the Middle Ages, such as Galen, Lucian, Plotinus, live on in peace, protected by the law. The Empire inaugurated a period of liberty, inasmuch as it extinguished the absolute sovereignty of the family, of the city, of the tribe, and replaced or tempered these sovereignties by that of the State. Now an absolute power becomes more vexatious in proportion to the narrowness of the limits within which it is exercised. The ancient republics, feudality, tyrannized over the individual much more than the State did. We must admit that the Roman Empire at certain periods persecuted Christianity cruelly, but, at least, it did not stop it. Now the republics would have rendered it impossible; Judaism, if it had not submitted to the pressure of Roman authority, would have been sufficient to stifle it. The Pharisees were prevented from crushing out Christianity only by the Roman magistrates.

Large ideas of universal brotherhood springing for the most part out of stoicism, a sort of general sentiment of humanity, were the fruits of the less narrow system and of the less exclusive education to which the individual was subjected. There

were dreams of a new era and of new worlds. The public wealth was great, and, notwithstanding the imperfection of the economic doctrines of the times, wealth was widely spread. Morals were not what they have often been imagined to be. At Rome, it is true, all the vices were displayed with a revolting cynicism; the spectacles, especially, had introduced a frightful corruption. Certain countries, like Egypt, have thus sunk into the lowest depths. But there was, in most of the provinces, a middle class, where goodness, conjugal faith, the domestic virtues, probity, were sufficiently spread out. Is there anywhere an idea of family life in a world of honest citizens of small towns, more charming than that which Plutarch has left us? What bonhomie! What gentleness of manners! What chaste and amiable simplicity! Chæronea was evidently not the only place where life was so pure and so innocent.

Customs even outside Rome were still to a certain extent cruel, it may be through the memory of antique manners; everywhere rather sanguinary, it may be through the special influence of Roman hardness. But there was progress even in this respect. What soft and pure sentiment, what impression of tender melancholy had not found its tenderest expression by the pen of Virgil or Tibullus? The world grew more yielding, lost its antique rigor, acquired gentleness and susceptibility. Maxims of humanity grew common; equality, the abstract idea of the rights of man, was loudly preached by stoicism. Woman, thanks to the dowry system of the Roman law, became more and more her own mistress; precepts on the manner of treating slaves improved, — Seneca ate with his. The slave was no longer of necessity that grotesque and malicious being whom Latin comedy introduced to provoke outbursts of laughter, and whom Cato recommended to be treated as a beast of burden. The times have now greatly changed. The slave is morally the equal of his master; it is admitted that he is capable of virtue, of fidelity, of devotion, and he has given proofs that he is so. Prejudices as to nobility of birth are dying out. Many very humane and very just laws are enacted even under the worst of the emperors. Tiberius was an able financier; he founded upon an excellent basis an establishment of the nature of a land bank. Nero brought to the system of taxation, until then iniquitous and barbarous, improvements which put our own times to the blush. The progress of legislation was considerable, though the punishment of death was stupidly frequent.   Love of the poor, sympathy for all, almsgiving, became virtues.

The theatre was one of the most insupportable scandals to honest people, and was one of the first causes of the antipathy of Jews and Judaizers of every class against the profane civilization of the time.   These gigantic circles appeared to them the sewer in which all the vices festered.   Whilst the front ranks applauded, repulsion and horror alone were produced on the upper benches.   The spectacles of gladiators were established in the provinces only with difficulty.   The Greek countries at least objected to them, and clung more often to their ancient Greek exercises.   The sanguinary games preserved always in the East a very pronounced mark of their Roman origin.   The Athenians, in emulation of the Corinthians, having one day deliberated as to imitating these barbarous games, a philosopher is said to have risen and moved that before this was done, the altar of Pity should be overthrown.   The horror of the theatre, of the stadium, of the gymnasium, that is to say, of the public places, and of what constituted essentially a Greek or a Roman city, was thus one of the deepest sentiments of the Christian, and one of those which produced the greatest results.   Ancient civilization was a public civilization; everything was done in the open air, before the assembled citizens.   It was the reverse of our societies, where life is altogether private and closed within the compass of the house.   The theatre was the heir of the agora and of the forum.   The anathema uttered against the theatre rebounded upon all society.   A profound rivalry was established between the Church on the one hand, the public games on the other.   The slave, driven from the games, betook himself to the Church.   I never sit down in these mournful arenas, which are always the best-preserved ruins of an ancient city, without seeing there in the spirit the struggle of the two worlds—here the honest poor man, already half a Christian, sitting in the last rank, veiling his face, and going out indignant—there a philosopher rising suddenly and reproaching the crowd with its baseness.   These examples were rare in the first century, but the protest began to make itself heard.   The theatre began to fall into evil repute.   .   .   .

To sum up: The middle of the first century is one of the worst epochs of ancient history.   Greek and Roman society show themselves in decadence after what has gone before, and much behindhand with respect to what is to follow.   But the grandeur

of the crisis revealed clearly some strange and sacred formation. Life appeared to have lost its motive: suicides were multiplied. Never had a century presented such a struggle between good and evil.   The evil was a powerful despotism, which put the world into the hands of men, who were either criminals or lunatics; it was the corruption of morals, the result of introducing into Rome the vices of the East; it was the absence of a good religion, and of a serious public instruction.

From «History of the Origins of
Christianity.»

SIR JOSHUA REYNOLDS

(1723–1792)

HREE of the essays in Dr. Johnson's Idler were written by Sir Joshua Reynolds, and the collection would not have suffered either in style or interest had the number been indefinitely increased.   He is better known, however, for his «Discourses» before the Royal Academy than he is as a miscellaneous writer.   He was born in Devonshire, England, July 16th, 1723.   His father, a clergyman and schoolmaster, trained him so carefully that his scholarship does not suffer by comparison with that of the greatest «wits» of his time. Most of these, including Dr. Johnson, Garrick, and Goldsmith, became his friends after he had settled in London, where he went in 1766 to begin work as a portrait painter.   Except the years spent abroad in study, he lived the rest of his life in London, growing in celebrity as an artist until his death February 23d, 1792.   He was one of the most famous of modern portrait painters.   He helped to organize the Royal Academy, and in 1768 became its first president. Among his most notable paintings are portraits of Johnson, Garrick, Goldsmith, Sterne, and Mrs. Siddons.

EASY POETRY

EASY poetry is universally admired; but I know not whether any rule has yet been fixed by which it may be decided when poetry can be properly called easy.   Horace has told us that it is such as «every reader hopes to equal, but after long labor finds unattainable.»   This is a very loose description, in which only the effect is noted; the qualities which produce this effect remain to be investigated.

Easy poetry is that in which natural thoughts are expressed without violence to the language.   The discriminating character of ease consists principally in the diction; for all true poetry requires that the sentiments be natural.   Language suffers violence by harsh or by daring figures, by transposition, by unusual acceptations of words, and by any license which would be avoided by a writer of prose.   Where any artifice appears in the construc-

tion of the verse, that verse is no longer easy.   Any epithet which can be ejected without diminution of the sense, any curious iteration of the same word, and all unusual, though not ungrammatical structure of speech, destroy the grace of easy poetry.

The first lines of Pope's «Iliad» afford examples of many licenses which an easy writer must decline:—

> « Achilles' wrath, to Greece the direful spring
> Of woes unnumber'd heavenly goddess sing,
> The wrath which hurl'd to Pluto's gloomy reign
> The souls of mighty chiefs untimely slain.»

In the first couplet the language is distorted by inversions, clogged with superfluities, and clouded by a harsh metaphor; and in the second there are two words used in an uncommon sense, and two epithets inserted only to lengthen the line; all these practices may in a long work easily be pardoned, but they always produce some degree of obscurity and ruggedness.

Easy poetry has been so long excluded by ambition of ornament, and luxuriance of imagery, that its nature seems now to be forgotten.   Affectation, however opposite to ease, is sometimes mistaken for it; and those who aspire to gentle elegance, collect female phrases and fashionable barbarisms, and imagine that style to be easy which custom has made familiar.   Such was the idea of the poet who wrote the following verses to a countess cutting paper:—

> « Pallas grew vap'rish once and odd,
>   She would not do the least right thing
> Either for goddess or for god,
>   Nor work, nor play, nor paint, nor sing.
>
> « Jove frowned, and 'Use,' he cried, 'those eyes
>   So skillful, and those hands so taper;
> Do something exquisite and wise.'—
>   She bow'd, obey'd him, and cut paper.
>
> « This vexing him who gave her birth,
>   Thought by all heaven a burning shame,
> What does she next, but bids on earth
>   Her Burlington do just the same!
>
> « Pallas, you give yourself strange airs;
>   But sure you'll find it hard to spoil
> The sense and taste of one that bears
>   The name of Saville and of Boyle.

« Alas! one bad example shown,
　How quickly all the sex pursue!
See, Madam! see the arts o'erthrown
　Between John Overton and you.»

It is the prerogative of easy poetry to be understood as long as the language lasts; but modes of speech, which owe their prevalence only to modish folly, or to the eminence of those that use them, die away with their inventors, and their meaning in a few years is no longer known.

Easy poetry is commonly sought in petty compositions upon minute subjects; but ease, though it excludes pomp, will admit greatness. Many lines in Cato's soliloquy are at once easy and sublime:—

« The divinity that stirs within us;
'Tis heaven itself that points out an hereafter,
And intimates eternity to man.
　　　　　—If there is a power above us,
And that there is all Nature cries aloud
Thro' all her works, he must delight in virtue,
And that which he delights in must be happy.»

Nor is ease more contrary to wit than to sublimity; the celebrated stanza of Cowley, on a lady elaborately dressed, loses nothing of its freedom by the spirit of the sentiment:—

« Th' adorning thee with so much art
Is but a barbarous skill,
'Tis like the pois'ning of a dart,
Too apt before to kill.»

Cowley seems to have possessed the power of writing easily beyond any other of our poets; yet his pursuit of remote thoughts led him often into harshness of expression. Waller often attempted, but seldom attained it; for he is too frequently driven into transpositions. The poets, from the time of Dryden, have gradually advanced in embellishment, and consequently departed from simplicity and ease.

To require from any author many pieces of easy poetry would be, indeed, to oppress him with too hard a task. It is less difficult to write a volume of lines swelled with epithets, brightened by figures, and stiffened by transpositions, than to produce a few couplets graced only by naked elegance and simple purity, which

requires so much care and skill, that I doubt whether any of our authors have yet been able, for twenty lines together, nicely to observe the true definition of easy poetry.

Complete. From the Idler.

GENIUS AND RULES

WE ARE very sure that the beauty of form, the expression of the passions, the art of composition, even the power of giving a general air of grandeur to a work, is at present very much under the dominion of rules. These excellencies were heretofore considered merely as the effects of Genius; and justly, if Genius is not taken for inspiration, but as the effect of close observation and experience.

He who first made any of these observations, and digested them, so as to form an invariable principle for himself to work by, had that merit, but probably no one went very far at once; and generally the first who gave the hint did not know how to pursue it steadily and methodically; at least, not in the beginning. He himself worked on it, and improved it; others worked more and improved further; until the secret was discovered, and the practice made as general as refined practice can be made. How many more principles may be fixed and ascertained we cannot tell; but as criticism is likely to go hand in hand with the art which is its subject, we may venture to say that as that art shall advance, its powers will be still more and more fixed by rules.

But, by whatever strides criticism may gain ground, we need be under no apprehension that invention will ever be annihilated or subdued; or intellectual energy be brought entirely within the restraint of written law. Genius will still have room enough to expatiate, and keep always at the same distance from narrow comprehension and mechanical performance.

What we now call Genius, begins, not where rules, abstractedly taken, end, but where known vulgar and trite rules have no longer any place. It must of necessity be, that even works of Genius, like every other effect, as they must have their cause, must likewise have their rules; it cannot be by chance that excellences are produced with any constancy or any certainty, for this is not the nature of chance; but the rules by which men of

extraordinary parts, and such as are called men of Genius, work, are either such as they discover by their own peculiar observations, or of such a nice texture as not easily to admit being expressed in words; especially as artists are not very frequently skillful in that mode of communicating ideas. Unsubstantial, however, as these rules may seem, and difficult as it may be to convey them in writing, they are still seen and felt in the mind of the artist; and he works from them with as much certainty as if they were embodied, as I may say, upon paper. It is true these refined principles cannot be always made palpable, like the more gross rules of art; yet it does not follow, but that the mind may be put in such a train, that it shall perceive, by a kind of scientific sense, that propriety, which words, particularly words of unpracticed writers, such as we are, can but very feebly suggest.

Invention is one of the great marks of Genius; but if we consult experience we shall find that it is by being conversant with the inventions of others that we learned to invent, as by reading the thoughts of others we learn to think.

From « Discourses on Art.»

MICHAEL ANGELO, «THE HOMER OF PAINTING»

AMONGST the painters and the writers on painting, there is one maxim universally admitted, and continually inculcated. Imitate nature is the invariable rule, but I know none who have explained in what manner this rule is to be understood; the consequence of which is, that every one takes it in the most obvious sense, that objects are represented naturally when they have such relief that they seem real. It may appear strange, perhaps, to hear this sense of the rule disputed; but it must be considered that, if the excellence of a painter consisted only in this kind of imitation, painting must lose its rank, and be no longer considered as a liberal art, and sister to poetry, this imitation being merely mechanical, in which the slowest intellect is always sure to succeed best; for the painter of genius cannot stoop to drudgery, in which the understanding has no part; and what pretense has the art to claim kindred with poetry, but by its powers over the imagination? To this power the painter of genius directs his aim; in this sense he studies nature, and often arrives at his end, even by being unnatural in the confined sense of the word.

The grand style of painting requires this minute attention to be carefully avoided, and must be kept as separate from it as the style of poetry from that of history. Poetical ornaments destroy that air of truth and plainness which ought to characterize history; but the very being of poetry consists in departing from this plain narration, and adopting every ornament that will warm the imagination. To desire to see the excellencies of each style united, to mingle the Dutch with the Italian school, is to join contrarieties which cannot subsist together, and which destroy the efficacy of each other. The Italian attends only to the invariable, the great and general ideas which are fixed and inherent in universal nature; the Dutch, on the contrary, to literal truth, and a minute exactness in the detail, as I may say of nature modified by accident. The attention to these petty peculiarities is the very cause of this naturalness, so much admired in the Dutch pictures, which, if we suppose it to be a beauty, is certainly of a lower order, which ought to give place to a beauty of a superior kind, since one cannot be obtained but by departing from the other.

If my opinion were asked concerning the works of Michael Angelo, whether they would receive any advantage from possessing this mechanical merit, I should not scruple to say that they would not only receive no advantage, but would lose, in a great measure, the effect which they now have on every mind susceptible of great and noble ideas. His works may be said to be all genius and soul; and why should they be loaded with heavy matter, which can only counteract his purpose by retarding the progress of the imagination?

If this opinion should be thought one of the wild extravagancies of enthusiasm, I shall only say that those who censure it are not conversant in the works of the great masters. It is very difficult to determine the exact degree of enthusiasm that the arts of painting and poetry may admit. There may perhaps be too great an indulgence, as well as too great a restraint of imagination; and if the one produces incoherent monsters, the other produces what is full as bad, lifeless insipidity. An intimate knowledge of the passions, and good sense, but not common sense, must at last determine its limits. It has been thought, and I believe with reason, that Michael Angelo sometimes transgressed those limits; and I think I have seen figures of him of which it was very difficult to determine whether they were in the highest degree sublime or extremely ridiculous. Such faults may be said to be the ebullitions of genius; but at least he had this merit, that he never was insipid, and whatever passion his works may excite, they will always escape contempt.

What I have had under consideration is the sublimest style, particularly that of Michael Angelo, the Homer of painting. Other kinds may admit of this naturalness, which of the lowest kind is the chief merit; but in painting, as in poetry, the highest style has the least of common nature.

One may very safely recommend a little more enthusiasm to the modern painters; too much is certainly not the vice of the present age. The Italians seem to have been continually declining in this respect from the time [of Michael Angelo to that of Carlo Maratti, and from thence to the very bathos of insipidity to which they are now sunk; so that there is no need of remarking that where I mentioned the Italian painters in opposition to the Dutch, I mean not the Moderns, but the heads of the old Roman and Bolognian schools; nor did I mean to include in my idea of an Italian painter, the Venetian school, which may be said to be the Dutch part of the Italian genius. I have only to add a word of advice to the painters, that however excellent they may be in painting naturally, they would not flatter themselves very much upon it; and to the connoisseurs, that when they see a cat or fiddle painted so finely that, as the phrase is, "It looks as if you could take it up," they would not for that reason immediately compare the painter to Raphael and Michael Angelo.

Complete. From the Idler.

DAVID RICARDO

(1772–1823)

D AVID RICARDO, one of the most celebrated economists of modern times, was born in London, April 19th, 1772. His father, a stock broker of Hebrew ancestry, wished to educate his son for business, but Ricardo preferred science, and his admiration for Adam Smith made him a political economist. His "Principles of Political Economy and Taxation" appeared in 1817 and soon took rank as one of the notable books of the century. It was preceded and followed by a long list of essays, treatises, and elaborate works on similar topics. Ricardo's theory that exchange value is determined by labor cost has been taken into account by all his successors, as has also his theory of rent. He died September 11th, 1823.

THE INFLUENCE OF DEMAND AND SUPPLY ON PRICES

I T is the cost of production which must ultimately regulate the price of commodities, and not, as has been often said, the proportion between the supply and demand. The proportion between supply and demand may, indeed, for a time, affect the market value of a commodity, until it is supplied in greater or less abundance, according as the demand may have increased or diminished; but this effect will be only of temporary duration.

Diminish the cost of production of hats, and their price will ultimately fall to their new natural price, although the demand should be doubled, trebled, or quadrupled. Diminish the cost of subsistence of men by diminishing the natural price of the food and clothing by which life is sustained, and wages will ultimately fall, notwithstanding that the demand for laborers may very greatly increase.

The opinion that the price of commodities depends solely on the proportion of supply to demand, or demand to supply, has become almost an axiom in political economy, and has been the source of much error in that science. It is this opinion which

has made Mr. Buchanan maintain that wages are not influenced by a rise or fall in the price of provisions, but solely by the demand and supply of labor; and that a tax on the wages of labor would not raise wages, because it would not alter the proportion of the demand of laborers to the supply.

The demand for a commodity cannot be said to increase if no additional quantity of it be purchased or consumed; and yet, under such circumstances, its money value may rise. Thus, if the value of money were to fall, the price of every commodity would rise, for each of the competitors would be willing to spend more money than before on its purchase; but though its price rose ten or twenty per cent., if no more were bought than before, it would not, I apprehend, be admissible to say that the variation in the price of the commodity was caused by the increased demand for it. Its natural price, its money cost of production, would be really altered by the altered value of money; and without any increase of demand, the price of the commodity would be naturally adjusted to that new value.

"We have seen," says M. Say, "that the cost of production determines the lowest price to which things can fall: the price below which they cannot remain for any length of time, because production would then be either entirely stopped or diminished." Vol. II., p. 26.

He afterwards says that the demand for gold having increased in a still greater proportion than the supply, since the discovery of the mines, "its price in goods, instead of falling in the proportion of ten to one, fell only in the proportion of four to one"; that is to say, instead of falling in proportion as its natural price had fallen, fell in proportion as the supply exceeded the demand.—"The value of every commodity rises always in a direct ratio to the demand, and in an inverse ratio to the supply."

The same opinion is expressed by the Earl of Lauderdale:— "With respect to the variations in value, of which everything valuable is susceptible, if we could for a moment suppose that any substance possessed intrinsic and fixed value, so as to render an assumed quantity of it constantly, under all circumstances, of an equal value, then the degree of value of all things, ascertained by such a fixed standard, would vary according to the proportion betwixt the quantity of them and the demand for them, and every commodity would, of course, be subject to a variation in its value, from four different circumstances:—

"1. It would be subject to an increase of its value, from a diminution of its quantity.

"2. To a diminution of its value, from an augmentation of its quantity.

"3. It might suffer an augmentation in its value, from the circumstance of an increased demand.

"4. Its value might be diminished by a failure of demand.

"As it will, however, clearly appear that no commodity can possess fixed and intrinsic value, so as to qualify it for a measure of the value of other commodities, mankind are induced to select, as a practical measure of value, that which appears the least liable to any of these four sources of variations, which are the sole causes of alteration of value.

"When, in common language, therefore, we express the value of any commodity, it may vary at one period from what it is at another, in consequence of eight different contingencies:—

"1. From the four circumstances above stated, in relation to the commodity of which we mean to express the value.

"2. From the same four circumstances, in relation to the commodity we have adopted as a measure of value."

This is true of monopolized commodities, and, indeed, of the market price of all other commodities for a limited period. If the demand for hats should be doubled, the price would immediately rise, but that rise would be only temporary, unless the cost of production of hats or their natural price were raised. If the natural price of bread should fall fifty per cent. from some great discovery in the science of agriculture, the demand would not greatly increase, for no man would desire more than would satisfy his wants, and as the demand would not increase, neither would the supply; for a commodity is not supplied merely because it can be produced, but because there is a demand for it. Here, then, we have a case where the supply and demand have scarcely varied, or, if they have increased, they have increased in the same proportion; and yet the price of bread will have fallen fifty per cent., at a time, too, when the value of money had continued invariable.

Commodities which are monopolized, either by an individual or a company, vary according to the law which Lord Lauderdale has laid down; they fall in proportion as the sellers augment their quantity, and rise in proportion to the eagerness of the buyers to purchase them; their price has no necessary connection with their natural value; but the prices of commodities which are subject to competition, and whose quantity may be increased in any moderate degree, will ultimately depend, not on the state of demand and supply, but on the increased or diminished cost of their production.

From «Principles of Political Economy and Taxation.» Chapter XXX. complete.

SAMUEL RICHARDSON
(1689–1761)

ONE of the early editors of the Rambler, anonymously unkind, says of the essay on Woman, contributed by Richardson, that "although mean and hackneyed in style and sentiment, it was the only paper which had a great sale during the publication of the Rambler in its original form." Between this criticism and the judgment of the London public in the eighteenth century, let twentieth-century readers decide. Richardson, who disputes with Fielding the title of "Inventor of the Modern Novel," was born in Derbyshire, England, in 1689. In 1706 he began life as an apprentice in a London printing office. "Pamela, or Virtue Rewarded" was published in three volumes in 1741 and 1742. It was successful, and he followed it by "Clarissa Harlowe" and "The History of Sir Charles Grandison." He died at London, July 4th, 1761. It was by "Pamela" that Fielding was drawn into novel writing, as he began "Joseph Andrews" as a parody on it.

A RAMBLER ESSAY ON WOMAN

Fœcunda culpæ secula nuptias
Primum inquinavere, et genus, et domos.
Hoc fonte derivata clades
In patriam populumque fluxit.
—Horace.

Fruitful of crimes, this age first stain'd
Their hapless offspring, and profaned
The nuptial bed; from whence the woes,
Which various and unnumber'd rose
From this polluted fountain head,
O'er Rome and o'er the nations spread.
—Francis.

The reader is indebted for this day's entertainment to an author from whom the age has received greater favors, who has enlarged the knowledge of human nature, and taught the passions to move at the command of virtue.
— Introductory note by the
« Rambler.»

To the Rambler

Sir:—

WHEN the Spectator was first published in single papers, it gave me so much pleasure that it is one of my favorite amusements of my age to recollect it; and when I reflect on the foibles of those times, as described in that useful work, and compare them with the vices now reigning among us, I cannot but wish that you would oftener take cognizance of the manners of the better half of the human species, that if your precepts and observations be carried down to posterity, the Spectators may show to the rising generation what were the fashionable follies of their grandmothers, the Rambler of their mothers, and that from both they may draw instruction and warning.

When I read those Spectators which took notice of the misbehavior of young women at church, by which they vainly hope to attract admirers, I used to pronounce such forward young women Seekers, in order to distinguish them by a mark of infamy from those who had patience and decency to stay till they were sought.

But I have lived to see such a change in the manners of women, that I would now be willing to compound with them for that name, although I then thought it disgraceful enough, if they would deserve no worse; since now they are too generally given up to negligence of domestic business, to idle amusements, and to wicked rackets, without any settled view at all out of squandering time.

In the time of the Spectator, excepting sometimes in appearance in the ring, sometimes at a good and chosen play, sometimes on a visit at the house of a grave relation, the young ladies contented themselves to be found employed in domestic duties; for then routs, drums, balls, assemblies, and such-like markets for women were not known.

Modesty and diffidence, gentleness and meekness, were looked upon as the appropriate virtues and characteristic graces of the sex. And if a forward spirit pushed itself into notice, it was exposed in print as it deserved.

The churches were almost the only places where single women were to be seen by strangers. Men went thither expecting to see them, and perhaps too much for that only purpose.

But some good often resulted, however improper might be their motives. Both sexes were in the way of their duty. The

man must be abandoned, indeed, who loves not goodness in another; nor were the young fellows of that age so wholly lost to a sense of right, as pride and conceit have since made them affect to be. When therefore they saw a fair one, whose decent behavior and cheerful piety showed her earnest in her first duties, they had the less doubt, judging politically only, that she would have a conscientious regard to her second.

With what ardor have I watched for the rising of a kneeling beauty; and what additional charms has devotion given to her recommunicated features!

The men were often the better for what they heard. Even a Saul was once found prophesying among the prophets whom he had set out to destroy. To a man thus put into good humor by a pleasing object, religion itself looked more amiable. The men Seekers of the Spectator's time loved the holy place for the object's sake, and loved the object for her suitable behavior in it.

Reverence mingled with their love, and they thought that a young lady of such good principles must be addressed only by the man who at least made a show of good principles, whether his heart was quite right or not.

Nor did the young lady's behavior, at any time of the service, lessen this reverence. Her eyes were her own, her ears the preacher's. Women are always most observed when they seem themselves least to observe, or to lay out for observation. The eye of a respectful lover loves rather to receive confidence from the withdrawn eye of the fair one, than to find itself obliged to retreat.

When a young gentleman's affection was thus laudably engaged, he pursued its natural dictates; keeping then was a rare, at least a secret and scandalous vice, and a wife was the summit of his wishes. Rejection was now dreaded, and pre-engagement apprehended. A woman whom he loved, he was ready to think must be admired by all the world. His fears, his uncertainties, increased his love.

Every inquiry he made into the lady's domestic excellence, which, when a wife is to be chosen, will surely not be neglected, confirmed him in his choice. He opens his heart to a common friend, and honestly discovers the state of his fortune. His friend applies to those of the young lady, whose parents, if they approve his proposals, disclose them to their daughter.

She, perhaps, is not an absolute stranger to the passion of the young gentleman. His eyes, his assiduities, his constant attendance at a church, whither, till 'of late, he used seldom to come, and a thousand little observances that he paid her, had very probably first forced her to regard, and then inclined her to favor, him.

That a young lady should be in love, and the love of the young gentleman undeclared, is a heterodoxy which prudence, and even policy, must not allow. But thus applied to, she is all resignation to her parents. Charming resignation, which inclination opposes not!

Her relations applaud her for her duty; friends meet; points are adjusted; delightful perturbations, and hopes, and a few lover's fears fill up the tedious space till an interview is granted; for the young lady had not made herself cheap at public places.

The time of interview arrives. She is modestly reserved; he is not confident. He declares his passion; the consciousness of her own worth, and his application to her parents, take from her any doubt of his sincerity; and she owns herself obliged to him for his good opinion. The inquiries of her friends into his character have taught her that his good opinion deserves to be valued.

She tacitly allows of his future visits; he renews them; the regard of each for the other is confirmed; and when he presses for the favor of her hand, he receives a declaration of an entire acquiescence with her duty, and a modest acknowledgment of esteem for him.

He applies to her parents therefore for a near day; and thinks himself under obligation to them for the cheerful and affectionate manner with which they receive his agreeable application.

With this prospect of future happiness, the marriage is celebrated. Gratulations pour in from every quarter. Parents and relations on both sides, brought acquainted in the course of the courtship, can receive the happy couple with countenances illumined and joyful hearts.

The brothers, the sisters, the friends of one family, are the brothers, the sisters, the friends of the other. Their two families, thus made one, are the world to the young couple.

Their home is the place of their principal delight, nor do they ever occasionally quit it but they find the pleasure of returning to it augmented in proportion to the time of their absence from it.

even these wretches marry to enjoy the conversation of those who render their company so cheap?

And what, after all, is the benefit which the gay coquette obtains by her flutters? As she is approachable by every man without requiring, I will not say incense or adoration, but even common complaisance, every fop treats her as upon the level, looks upon her light airs as invitations, and is on the watch to take the advantage: she has companions, indeed, but no lovers,— for love is respectful, and timorous; and where among all her followers will she find a husband?

Set, dear sir, before the youthful, the gay, the inconsiderate, the contempt as well as the danger to which they are exposed. At one time or other, women not utterly thoughtless will be convinced of the justice of your censure, and the charity of your instruction.

But should your expostulations and reproofs have no effect upon those who are far gone in fashionable folly, they may be retailed from their mouths to their nieces (marriage will not often have entitled these to daughters), when they, the meteors of a day, find themselves elbowed off the stage of vanity by other flutterers; for the most admired women cannot have many Tunbridge, many Bath seasons to blaze in, since even fine faces, often seen, are less regarded than new faces,—the proper punishment of showy girls, for rendering themselves so impoliticly cheap.

Complete. From the Rambler.

VIII—204

Oh, Mr. Rambler! forgive the talkativeness of an old man! When I courted and married my Lætitia, then a blooming beauty, everything passed just so! But how is the case now? The ladies, maidens, wives, and widows, are engrossed by places of open resort and general entertainment, which fill every quarter of the metropolis, and being constantly frequented, make home irksome. Breakfasting places, dining places, routs, drums, concerts, balls, plays, operas, masquerade for the evening, and even for all night; and lately, public sales of the goods of broken housekeepers, which the general dissoluteness of manners has contributed to make very frequent, come in as another seasonable relief to these modern time-killers.

In the summer there are in every country-town assemblies; Tunbridge, Bath, Cheltenham, Scarborough! What expense of dress and equipage is required to qualify the frequenters for such emulous appearance!

By the natural infection of example, the lowest people have places of sixpenny resort, and gaming tables for pence. Thus servants are now induced to fraud and dishonesty, to support extravagance, and supply their losses.

As to the ladies who frequent those public places, they are not ashamed to show their faces wherever men dare go, nor blush to try who shall stare most impudently, or who shall laugh loudest on the public walks.

The men who would make good husbands, if they visit those places, are frighted at wedlock, and resolve to live single, except they are bought at a very high price. They can be spectators of all that passes, and, if they please, more than spectators, at the expense of others. The companion of an evening, and the companion for life, require very different qualifications.

Two thousand pounds in the last age, with a domestic wife, would go further than ten thousand in this. Yet settlements are expected, that often, to a mercantile man especially, sink a fortune into uselessness: and pin money is stipulated for, which makes a wife independent, and destroys love, by putting it out of a man's power to lay any obligation upon her, that might engage gratitude, and kindle affection. When to all this the card tables are added, how can a prudent man think of marrying?

And when the worthy men know not where to find wives, must not the sex be left to the foplings, the coxcombs, the libertines of the age, whom they help to make such? And need

JEAN PAUL FRIEDRICH RICHTER

(1763–1825)

JEAN PAUL FRIEDRICH RICHTER, one of the most famous humorists and essayists of Germany, was born at Wunsiedel, Bavaria, March 21st, 1763. His father was a pastor and teacher who accumulated no property, and his death left the boy Jean Paul to support himself as best he could. Going to Leipsic in the hope of making a living as a tutor, he began in 1783 the literary career which made him a favorite wherever German is read. The eccentricity of his style, which so greatly influenced that of Carlyle, is clearly imitated from Rabelais. In his "Flower, Fruit, and Thorn Pieces," he often ceases to be intelligible except to those who are experts in his methods as a humorist. As it was a part of his method, however, to become on occasion as profoundly unintelligible as possible, this is not to be wondered at nor seriously complained of. He wrote "Selections from the Papers of the Devil"; "Flower, Fruit, and Thorn Pieces"; "The Invisible Lodge"; "Hesperus"; "Quintus Fixlein"; "Preparatory Course in Æsthetics"; "Levana, or the Theory of Education"; and an unmentionable number of other essays, pamphlets, and literature of all kinds, to the total number of sixty volumes in the Berlin edition of 1879. He died at Bayreuth, November 14th, 1825.

LOVE AND MARRIAGE

TO GIRLS love is the sun's propinquity—yes, it is the transition of every such Venus through the sun of the ideal world.

In this period of the higher style of their souls they love all that we love—even science—and the whole better world within the bosom; and they despise what we despise—even clothes and news. In the spring, these nightingales sing up to the time of the summer solstice. The wedding day is their longest day. Then the devil fetches away, not everything, indeed, but every day a little bit. The bass bond of marriage ties the poetical wings; and the marriage bed is for the imagination an Engelsburg and a prison with bread-and-water allowance. I have often followed the poor bird of paradise, or peacock of Psyche, in the honeymoon, and in this molting season picked up the glorious feathers of the wings and tail, which the bird scattered abroad; and afterwards, when the husband thinks he has married a naked crow, I show him the bunch of feathers. How explain this? Thus: Marriage overspreads the poetical world with the rind of the real world; as, according to Descartes, our earthly sphere is a sun overlaid with a dirty bark. The hands of labor are awkward, hard, and full of callosities, and find it difficult to continue to hold or draw the fine thread of the ideal woof; therefore, among the higher ranks, where women in lieu of work rooms have only work baskets, where they turn the little spinning wheels on their laps with the finger, and where love still endures in marriage — frequently even towards the husband himself — the marriage ring is not so often as among the lower orders a Gyges-ring, which renders books, and all the arts of music, poetry, painting, and dancing, invisible. Upon heights, plants and flowers of all kinds, especially female plants, become stronger and more spicy. A woman is not able, like a man, to protect her inner castles of air and magic on the outer side exposed to the weather. To what, then, is the wife to cling? To her husband. The husband must always stand near the liquid silver of the female spirit with a spoon, and continually skim off the scum which covers it, that the silver glance of the ideal may continue to glitter.

But there are two species of husbands — Arcadians, or lyric poets of life, who love forever, like Rousseau, even with gray hairs. Such are not to be controlled or comforted when, in the female "flower wreath," bound with gilt edges, on turning over the little work, leaf by leaf, they no longer see any of the gold, as is the case with all gilt-edged books.

Secondly, there are shepherd swains and pastors of itchy sheep — I mean master minstrels, or men of business, who thank God when the enchantress, like other sorceresses, is at length transformed into a grumbling house cat, which destroys the vermin.

No one has more ennui and fear (and therefore some day I will direct the compassion of my readers to the circumstance in a comic biography) than a fat, pompous, weighty bass singer of a man of business, who, like the Roman elephants in former times, is forced to dance on the slack rope of love, and whose

loving gestures and play of features I find most perfectly imaged in the marmot, who, when first awakened from his winter's sleep by the warmth of the room, finds it so difficult to get into the way of moving. With widows alone, who are less desirous of being loved than of being married, a heavy man of business can begin his romance at the point where all romance writers terminate theirs, namely, upon the step of the marriage altar. Such a man, built in the simplest style, would have a load taken from his heart, if any one would love his shepherdess for him, in his name, so long until he had nothing else to do in the affair but to celebrate the wedding; and no one would have more pleasure in relieving them of this burden or cross than myself. I wanted to advertise myself in the public papers (but was afraid it might be taken for a joke), and announce that I was willing to swear platonic eternal love to all endurable girls whom a man of business has not even the time to love — to make them the necessary declarations of love as plenipotentiary of the husband; and, in short, to lead them, as *substitutus sine spe succedendi*, or as company cavalier, on my arm, through the whole uneven land of love, until, on the borders, I should be able to deliver over my charge, ready prepared, to the *sponsus* (bridegroom). This would then be a love-making, rather than a marriage, by embassadors If, in accordance with such a *systema assistentiæ*, any one would wish to employ the writer of this article as feoffee and principal commissary even in the honeymoon itself, as some love also occurs at this period, he must be man of sense enough to make the condition beforehand, that —*

From "Flower, Fruit, and Thorn Pieces."

HIS VIEW OF GOETHE

AN OPINION concerning Herder, Wieland, or Goethe, is as much contested as any other. Who would believe that the three watchtowers of our literature avoid and dislike each other? I will never again bend myself anxiously before any great man, but only before the virtuous. Under this impression, I went timidly to meet Goethe. Every one had described him as cold to everything upon the earth. Madame von Kalb said, "He no

* This ending is characteristic of Richter. Having said all he cared to say on the subject he stops in the middle of a sentence.

longer admires anything, not even himself. Every word is ice. Curiosities, merely, warm the fibres of his heart." Therefore I asked Knebel to petrify or incrust me by some mineral spring, that I might present myself to him like a statue or a fossil. Madame von Kalb advised me, above all things, to be cold and self-possessed, and I went without warmth, merely from curiosity. His house, palace rather, pleased me; it is the only one in Weimar in the Italian style, — with such steps! a Pantheon full of pictures and statues. Fresh anxiety oppressed my breast. At last the god entered, cold, one-syllabled, without accent. "The French are drawing towards Paris," said Knebel. "Hm!" said the god. His face is massive and animated, his eye a ball of light. But, at last, the conversation led from the campaign to art, publications, etc., and Goethe was himself. His conversation is not so rich and flowing as Herder's, but sharp-toned, penetrating, and calm. At last he read, that is, played for us, an unpublished poem, in which his heart impelled the flame through the outer crust of ice, so that he pressed the hand of the enthusiastic Jean Paul. (It was my face, not my voice; for I said not a word.) He did it again when we took leave, and pressed me to call again. By Heaven! we will love each other! He considers his poetic course as closed. His reading is like deep-toned thunder, blended with soft, whispering raindrops. There is nothing like it.

From an account of a visit to Goethe quoted by Longfellow in "Poets and Poetry of Europe" 1849.

A DREAM UPON THE UNIVERSE

I HAD been reading an excellent dissertation of Krüger's upon the old vulgar error which regards the space from one earth and sun to another as empty. Our sun, together with all its planets, fills only the 31,419,460,000,000,000th part of the whole space between itself and the next solar body. Gracious Heavens! thought I, in what an unfathomable abyss of emptiness were this universe swallowed up and lost, if all were void and utter vacuity except the few shining points of dust which we call a planetary system! To conceive of our earthly ocean as the abode of death and essentially incapable of life, and of its populous islands as being no greater than snail shells, would be a

far less error in proportion to the compass of our planet than that which attributes emptiness to the great mundane spaces; and the error would be far less if the marine animals were to ascribe life and fullness exclusively to the sea, and to regard the atmospheric ocean above them as empty and untenanted. According to Herschel, the most remote of the galaxies which the telescope discovers lie at such a distance from us, that their light, which reaches us at this day, must have set out on its journey two millions of years ago; and thus by optical laws it is possible that whole squadrons of the starry hosts may be now reaching us with their beams, which have themselves perished ages ago. Upon this scale of computation for the dimensions of the world, what heights and depths and breadths must there be in this universe — in comparison of which the positive universe would be itself a nihility, were it crossed, pierced, and belted about by so illimitable a wilderness of nothing! But is it possible that any man can for a moment overlook those vast forces which must pervade these imaginary deserts with eternal surges of flux and reflux, to make the very paths to those distant starry coasts voyageable to our eyes? Can you lock up in a sun or in its planets their reciprocal forces of attraction! Does not the light stream through the immeasurable spaces between our earth and the nebula which is furthest removed from us? And in this stream of light there is as ample an existence of the positive, and as much a home for the abode of a spiritual world, as there is a dwelling-place for thy own spirit in the substance of the brain. To these and similar reflections succeeded the following dream: —

Methought my body sank down in ruins, and my inner form stepped out appareled in light; and by my side there stood another form which resembled my own, except that it did not shine like mine, but lightened unceasingly. "Two thoughts," said the Form, "are the wings with which I move: the thought of Here, and the thought of There. And, behold! I am yonder," — pointing to a distant world. "Come, then, and wait on me with thy thoughts and with thy flight, that I may show to thee the universe under a veil." And I flew along with the Form. In a moment our earth fell back, behind our consuming flight, into an abyss of distance; a faint gleam only was reflected from the summits of the Cordilleras, and a few moments more reduced the sun to a little star; and soon there remained nothing visible of our system except a comet which was traveling from our sun with angelic speed in the direction of Sirius. Our flight now carried us so rapidly through the flocks of solar bodies — flocks past counting, unless to their heavenly Shepherd — that scarcely could they expand themselves before us into the magnitude of moons, before they sank behind us into pale nebular gleams; and their planetary earths could not reveal themselves for a moment to the transcendent rapidity of our course. At length Sirius and all the brotherhood of our constellations and the galaxy of our heavens stood far below our feet as a little nebula amongst other yet more distant nebulæ. Thus we flew on through the starry wildernesses: one heaven after another unfurled its immeasurable banners before us, and then rolled up behind us; galaxy behind galaxy towered up into solemn altitudes before which the spirit shuddered; and they stood in long array through which the Infinite Being might pass in progress. Sometimes the Form that lightened would outfly my weary thoughts; and then it would be seen far off before me like a coruscation amongst the stars — till suddenly I thought again to myself the thought of There, and then I was at its side. But, as we were thus swallowed up by one abyss of stars after another, and the heavens above our heads were not emptier, neither were the heavens below them fuller; and as suns without intermission fell into the solar ocean like waterspouts of a storm which fall into the ocean of waters: then at length the human heart within me was overburdened and weary, and yearned after some narrow cell or quiet oratory in this metropolitan cathedral of the universe. And I said to the Form at my side, "O Spirit! has then this universe no end?" And the Form answered and said, "Lo! it has no beginning."

Suddenly, however, the heavens above us appeared to be emptied, and not a star was seen to twinkle in the mighty abyss; no gleam of light to break the unity of the infinite darkness. The starry hosts behind us had all contracted into an obscure nebula: and at length that also had vanished. And I thought to myself, "At last the universe has ended": and I trembled at the thought of the illimitable dungeon of pure, pure darkness which here began to imprison the creation: I shuddered at the dead sea of nothing, in whose unfathomable zone of blackness the jewel of the glittering universe seemed to be set and buried forever; and through the night in which we moved I saw the Form which still lightened as before, but left all around it unillumi-

nated. Then the Form said to me in my anguish — "Oh! creature of little faith! Look up! the most ancient light is coming!" I looked; and in a moment came a twilight — in the twinkling of an eye a galaxy — and then with a choral burst rushed in all the company of stars. For centuries gray with age, for millennia hoary with antiquity, had the starry light been on its road to us; and at length out of heights inaccessible to thought it had reached us. Now then, as through some renovated century, we flew through new cycles of heavens. At length again came a starless interval; and far longer it endured, before the beams of a starry host again had reached us.

As we thus advanced forever through an interchange of nights and solar heavens, and as the interval grew still longer and longer before the last heaven we had quitted contracted to a point, and as once we issued suddenly from the middle of thickest night into an Aurora Borealis, the herald of an expiring world, and we found throughout this cycle of solar systems that a day of judgment had indeed arrived; the suns had sickened, and the planets were heaving — rocking, yawning in convulsions, the subterraneous waters of the great deeps were breaking up, and lightnings that were ten diameters of a world in length ran along — from east to west — from Zenith to Nadir; and here and there, where a sun should have been, we saw instead through the misty vapor a gloomy, ashy, leaden corpse of a solar body, that sucked in flames from the perishing world, but gave out neither light nor heat; and as I saw, through a vista which had no end, mountain towering above mountain, and piled up with what seemed glittering snow from the conflict of solar and planetary bodies; then my spirit bent under the load of the universe, and I said to the Form, "Rest, rest; and lead me no further: I am too solitary in the creation itself; and in its deserts yet more so: the full world is great, but the empty world is greater; and with the universe increase its Zaarahs."

Then the Form touched me like the flowing of a breath, and spoke more gently than before: "In the presence of God there is no emptiness: above, below, between, and round about the stars, in the darkness and in the light, dwelleth the true and very universe, the sum and fountain of all that is. But thy spirit can bear only earthly images of the unearthly; now then I cleanse thy sight with euphrasy; look forth, and behold the images." Immediately my eyes were opened; and I looked, and I saw as

it were an interminable sea of light, — sea immeasurable, sea unfathomable, sea without a shore. All spaces between all heavens were filled with happiest light; and there was a thundering of floods: and there were seas above the seas, and seas below the seas; and I saw all the trackless regions that we had voyaged over; and my eye comprehended the furthest and the nearest; and darkness had become light, and the light darkness; for the deserts and wastes of the creation were now filled with the sea of light, and in this sea the suns floated like ash-gray blossoms, and the planets like black grains of seed. Then my heart comprehended that immortality dwelled in the spaces between the worlds, and death only amongst the worlds. Upon all the suns there walked upright shadows in the form of men; but they were glorified when they quitted these perishable worlds, and when they sank into the sea of light; and the murky planets, I perceived, were but cradles for the infant spirits of the universe of light. In the Zaarahs of the creation I saw — I heard — I felt — the glittering — the echoing — the breathing of life and creative power. The suns were but as spinning wheels, the planets no more than weavers' shuttles, in relation to the infinite web which composes the veil of Isis, — which veil is hung over the whole creation, and lengthens as any finite being attempts to raise it. And in sight of this immeasurability of life, no sadness could endure; but only joy that knew no limit, and happy prayers.

But in the midst of this great vision of the universe the Form that lightened eternally had become invisible, or had vanished to its home in the unseen world of spirits: I was left alone in the centre of a universe of life, and I yearned after some sympathizing being. Suddenly from the starry deeps there came floating through the ocean of light a planetary body; and upon it there stood a woman whose face was as the face of a Madonna; and by her side there stood a child, whose countenance varied not, neither was it magnified as he drew nearer. This child was a king, for I saw that he had a crown upon his head, but the crown was a crown of thorns. Then also I perceived that the planetary body was our unhappy earth; and, as the earth drew near, this child who had come forth from the starry deeps to comfort me threw upon me a look of gentlest pity and of unutterable love, so that in my heart I had a sudden rapture of joy such as passes all understanding, and I awoke in the tumult of my happiness.

I awoke: but my happiness survived my dream; and I exclaimed — Oh! how beautiful is death, seeing that we die in a world of life and of creation without end, and I blessed God for my life upon earth, but much more for the life in those unseen depths of the universe which are emptied of all but the Supreme Reality, and where no earthly life nor perishable hope can enter.

Complete. De Quincey's translation.

ANALECTS

COMPLAINT OF THE BIRD IN A DARKENED CAGE

"AH!" SAID the imprisoned bird, "how unhappy were I in my eternal night, but for those melodious tones which sometimes make their way to me like beams of light from afar, and cheer my gloomy day. But I will myself repeat these heavenly melodies like an echo, until I have stamped them in my heart; and then I shall be able to bring comfort to myself in my darkness!" Thus spoke the little warbler, and soon had learned the sweet airs that were sung to it with voice and instrument. That done, the curtain was raised; for the darkness had been purposely contrived to assist in its instruction. O man! how often dost thou complain of overshadowing grief and of darkness resting upon thy days! And yet what cause for complaint, unless indeed thou hast failed to learn wisdom from suffering? For is not the whole sum of human life a veiling and an obscuring of the immortal spirit of man? Then first, when the fleshly curtain falls away, may it soar upwards into a region of happier melodies!

ON THE DEATH OF YOUNG CHILDREN

EPHEMERA die all at sunset, and no insect of this class has ever sported in the beams of the morning sun. Happy are ye, little human ephemera! Ye played only in the ascending beams, and in the early dawn, and in the eastern light; ye drank only of the prelibations of life, hovered for a little space over a world of freshness and of blossoms, and fell asleep in innocence before yet the morning dew was exhaled!

THE PROPHETIC DEWDROPS

A DELICATE child, pale and prematurely wise, was complaining on a hot morning that the poor dewdrops had been too hastily snatched away, and not allowed to glitter on the flowers like other happier dewdrops that live the whole night through, and sparkle in the moonlight and through the morning onwards to noonday. "The sun," said the child, "has chased them away with his heat, or swallowed them in his wrath." Soon after came rain and a rainbow; whereupon his father pointed upwards: "See," said he, "there stand thy dewdrops gloriously reset — a glittering jewelry — in the heavens; and the clownish foot tramples on them no more. By this, my child, thou art taught that what withers upon earth blooms again in heaven." Thus the father spoke, and knew not that he spoke prefiguring words: for soon after the delicate child, with the morning brightness of his early wisdom, was exhaled, like a dewdrop, into heaven.

ON DEATH

WE SHOULD all think of death as a less hideous object, if it simply untenanted our bodies of a spirit, without corrupting them; secondly, if the grief which we experience at the spectacle of our friends' graves were not by some confusion of the mind blended with the image of our own; thirdly, if we had not in this life seated ourselves in a warm domestic nest, which we are unwilling to quit for the cold blue regions of the unfathomable heavens; finally, if death were denied to us. Once in dreams I saw a human being of heavenly intellectual faculties, and his aspirations were heavenly; but he was chained (methought) eternally in the earth. The immortal old man had five great wounds in his happiness — five worms that gnawed forever at his heart: he was unhappy in springtime, because that is a season of hope, and rich with phantoms of far happier days than any which this aceldama of earth can realize. He was unhappy at the sound of music, which dilates the heart of man into its whole capacity for the infinite, and he cried aloud — "Away! away! Thou speakest of things which throughout my endless life I have found not, and shall not find!" He was unhappy at the remembrance of earthly affections and dissevered hearts; for love is a plant which may

bud in this life, but it must flourish in another. He was unhappy under the glorious spectacle of the starry host, and ejaculated forever in his heart — "So then I am parted from you to all eternity by an impassable abyss: the great universe of suns is above, below, and round about me; but I am chained to a little ball of dust and ashes." He was unhappy before the great ideas of Virtue, of Truth, and of God; because he knew how feeble are the approximations to them which a son of earth can make. But this was a dream: God be thanked, that in reality there is no such craving and asking eye directed upwards to heaven, to which death will not one day bring an answer!

IMAGINATION UNTAMED BY REALITIES

HAPPY is every actor in the guilty drama of life, to whom the higher illusion within supplies or conceals the external illusion; to whom, in the tumult of his part and its intellectual interest, the bungling landscapes of the stage have the bloom and reality of nature, and whom the loud parting and shocking of the scenes disturb not in his dream!

ON REVIEWERS

IN SUABIA, in Saxony, in Pomerania, are towns in which are stationed a strange sort of officers — valuers of author's flesh, something like our old market-lookers in this town. They are commonly called tasters (or *Prægustatores*) because they eat a mouthful of every book beforehand, and tell the people whether its flavor be good. We authors, in spite, call them reviewers; but I believe an action of defamation would lie against us for such bad words. The tasters write no books themselves; consequently they have the more time to look over and tax those of other people. Or, if they do sometimes write books, they are bad ones; which again is very advantageous to them, for who can understand the theory of badness in other people's books so well as those who have learned it by practice in their own? They are reputed the guardians of literature and the literati for the same reason that St. Nepomuk is the patron saint of bridges and of all who pass over them, *viz.*, because he himself once lost his life from a bridge.

FEMALE TONGUES

HIPPEL, the author of the book "Upon Marriage," says, "A woman that does not talk must be a stupid woman." But Hippel is an author whose opinions it is more safe to admire than to adopt. The most intelligent women are often silent among women; and again the most stupid and the most silent are often neither one nor the other except among men. In general the current remark upon men is valid also with respect to women — that those for the most part are the greatest thinkers who are the least talkers; as frogs cease to croak when light is brought to the water edge. However, in fact, the disproportionate talking of women arises out of the sedentariness of their labors: sedentary artisans, as tailors, shoemakers, weavers, have this habit as well as hypochondriacal tendencies in common with women. Apes do not talk, as savages say, that they may not be set to work; but women often talk double their share — even because they work.

FORGIVENESS

NOTHING is more moving to man than the spectacle of reconciliation: our weaknesses are thus indemnified and are not too costly, — being the price we pay for the hour of forgiveness; and the archangel, who has never felt anger, has reason to envy the man who subdues it. When thou forgivest — the man who has pierced thy heart stands to thee in the relation of the sea worm that perforates the shell of the mussel, which straightway closes the wound with a pearl.

NAMELESS HEROES

THE graves of the best of men, of the noblest martyrs, are, like the graves of the Herrnhuters (the Moravian brethren), level and undistinguishable from the universal earth; and if the earth could give up her secrets, our whole globe would appear a Westminster Abbey laid flat. Ah! what a multitude of tears, what myriads of bloody drops have been shed in secrecy about the three corner trees of earth — the tree of life, the tree of knowledge, and the tree of freedom — shed, but never reckoned! It

is only great periods of calamity that reveal to us our great men, as comets are revealed by total eclipses of the sun. Not merely upon the field of battle, but also upon the consecrated soil of virtue, and upon the classic ground of truth, thousands of nameless heroes must fall and struggle to build up the footstool from which history surveys the one hero, whose name is embalmed, bleeding — conquering — and resplendent. The grandest of heroic deeds are those which are performed within four walls and in domestic privacy. And, because History records only the self-sacrifices of the male sex, and because she dips her pen only in blood, therefore is it that in the eyes of the unseen spirit of the world our annals appear doubtless far more beautiful and noble than in our own.

THE GRANDEUR OF MAN IN HIS LITTLENESS

MAN upon this earth would be vanity and hollowness, dust and ashes, vapor and a bubble, were it not that he felt himself to be so. That it is possible for him to harbor such a feeling — this, by implying a comparison of himself with something higher in himself, this is it which makes him the immortal creature that he is.

NIGHT

THE earth is every day overspread with the veil of night, for the same reason as the cages of birds are darkened — *viz.*, that we may the more readily apprehend the higher harmonies of thought in the hush and quiet of darkness. Thoughts, which day turns into smoke and mist, stand about us in the night as lights and flames: even as the column which fluctuates above the crater of Vesuvius, in the daytime appears a pillar of cloud, but by night a pillar of fire.

THE STARS

LOOK up, and behold the eternal fields of light that lie round about the throne of God. Had no star ever appeared in the heavens, to man there would have been no heavens; and he would have laid himself down to his last sleep, in a spirit of anguish, as upon a gloomy earth vaulted over by a material arch — solid and impervious.

MARTYRDOM

To die for truth — is not to die for one's country, but to die for the world. Truth, like the Venus de Medici, will pass down in thirty fragments to posterity; but posterity will collect and recompose them into a goddess. Then also thy temple, O eternal truth! that now stands half below the earth, made hollow by the sepulchres of its witnesses, will raise itself in the total majesty of its proportions; and will stand in monumental granite; and every pillar on which it rests will be fixed in the grave of a martyr.

THE QUARRELS OF FRIENDS

Why is it that the most fervent love becomes more fervent by brief interruption and reconciliation? and why must a storm agitate our affections before they can raise the highest rainbow of peace? Ah! for this reason it is — because all passions feel their object to be as eternal as themselves, and no love can admit the feeling that the beloved object should die. And under this feeling of imperishableness it is that we hard fields of ice shock together so harshly, whilst all the while under the sunbeams of a little space of seventy years we are rapidly dissolving.

DREAMING

But for dreams, that lay mosaic worlds tesselated with flowers and jewels before the blind sleeper, and surround the recumbent living with the figures of the dead in the upright attitude of life, the time would be too long before we are allowed to rejoin our brothers, parents, friends: every year we should become more and more painfully sensible of the desolation made around us by death, if sleep — the antechamber of the grave — were not hung by dreams with the busts of those who live in the other world.

TWO DIVISIONS OF PHILOSOPHIC MINDS

There are two very different classes of philosophic heads, which, since Kant has introduced into philosophy the idea of positive and negative quantities, I shall willingly classify by means

of that distinction. The positive intellect is, like the poet, in conjunction with the outer world, the father of an inner world; and, like the poet, also, holds up a transforming mirror in which the entangled and distorted members as they are seen in our actual experience enter into new combinations which compose a fair and luminous world: the hypothesis of Idealism (*i. e.*, the Fichtéan system), the Monads and the Pre-established Harmony of Leibnitz — and Spinozism are all births of a genial moment, and not the wooden carving of logical toil. Such men, therefore, as Leibnitz, Plato, Herder, etc., I call positive intellects, because they seek and yield the positive; and because their inner world, having raised itself higher out of the water than in others, thereby overlooks a larger prospect of island and continents. A negative head, on the other hand, discovers by its acuteness — not any positive truths, but the negative (*i. e.*, the errors) of other people. Such an intellect, as for example, Bayle, one of the greatest of that class — appraises the funds of others, rather than brings any fresh funds of his own. In lieu of the obscure ideas which he finds he gives us clear ones: but in this there is no positive accession to our knowledge; for all that the clear idea contains in development exists already by implication in the obscure idea. Negative intellects of every age are unanimous in their abhorrence of everything positive. Impulse, feeling, instinct — everything, in short, which is incomprehensible, they can endure just once — that is, at the summit of their chain of arguments, as a sort of hook on which they may hang them, but never afterwards.

THE DIGNITY OF MAN IN SELF-SACRIFICE

That for which man offers up his blood or his property must be more valuable than they. A good man does not fight with half the courage for his own life that he shows in the protection of another's. The mother, who will hazard nothing for herself, will hazard all in defense of her child; in short, only for the nobility within us, only for virtue, will man open his veins and offer up his spirit: but this nobility, this virtue, presents different phases: with the Christian martyr it is faith; with the savage it is honor; with the republican it is liberty.

All the foregoing are from De Quincey's
translation.

TABLE OF CONTENTS

VOLUME IX

———

MADAME ROLAND

(Manon Jeanne Phlipon Roland de la Platière)

(1754–1793)

N INTELLECT, Madame Roland was one of the most remarkable women of the eighteenth century, and in the romantic interest of her life, she is second among the heroines of the French Revolution only to Charlotte Corday. Her "Philosophical and Literary Essays," published soon after her death and republished in London in 1800, fully sustain the historical and traditional theory of her ability. It was the remarkable power of her intellect which energized her husband and enabled the Girondist party to keep a foothold in the stormy politics of the Revolution at a time when to be accused of moderation was almost equivalent to a conviction of capital crime. Gratien Phlipon, Madame Roland's father, was an engraver by profession and it is from him that she seems to have received the speculative impulses which enabled her to break away from the political conventionality of her time and become a leader in revolution. Her earliest reading was of the great classical writers from whom she imbibed the republican principles which animated her work for the overthrow of the royalty in France. In M. Roland, whom she married in 1781, she found a kindred spirit. He was nearly twenty-two years her senior and no doubt greatly her superior in thoroughness, but he lacked her quickness of intellect and was always ready to rely rather upon the intuitions of her genius than on his own common sense. When they appeared together at Paris in 1791, they soon became one of the potent influences against royalty. Roland became a member of the Jacobin Club and acted with them until their radicalism resulted in the formation of a more conservative party,—the Girondists,—which in the crisis of 1792 made him Minister of the Interior. He used this position to force issues with the king. A letter written by Madame Roland, and addressed by her husband to the king, led to a Cabinet crisis and to the dismissal of Roland. This was the prelude to the overthrow of royalty, but instead of being the Aspasia of a great and world-reforming republic as she had hoped, Madame Roland found herself at first the sport and then the victim of forces too violent to be checked or directed by any power of intellect or of combination. After the death of the king and the September massacres, the Girondists fearlessly devoted themselves to

IX—205

inevitable destruction. Hated alike by Royalists and Jacobins, they had no refuge except in honorable death; and this, with Vergniaud and Roland at their head, they challenged by impeaching Robespierre when he was at the height of his power. On June 1st, 1793, Madame Roland was arrested, and on November 8th, 1793, was carried to the guillotine in the Place de la Revolution, where the scaffold was overlooked by a statue of Liberty, which she addressed in her celebrated apostrophe, "O Liberty, what crimes are committed in thy name!" On hearing of her death, her husband, then at Rouen, pinned on his breast a paper declaring his unwillingness to survive her, and killed himself by falling on the point of the stiletto he carried in his walking cane.

LIBERTY—ITS MEANING AND ITS COST

INSULATED and tranquil, in the stillness of the night and in that of the passions, I dare think, I dare write, without presumption and without fear. Silence, son of repose, it is in thy profound bosom that my wandering ideas are heaped up and collected. The shades spread on the theatre of illusion stop its prestiges; all is confounded; all is silent . . . even to my heart: this is the moment when victorious reason commands, and acts with liberty. What have I said? What implies that great name, whose imposing and confused object by turns astonishes, misleads, and inflames the imagination? What is liberty?*

I cannot consider it so generally; I distinguish, liberty of the will, that of the mind. I doubt whether the first exists; the second appears to me very uncommon, and the third belongs but to sages. Metaphysical liberty is a problem on which I endeavor to exercise my ideas; political liberty is a blessing the image and utility of which I love to recall to mind; philosophical liberty, the only liberty, perhaps, that it is my province to know, is a treasure which I wish to acquire.

Political liberty, for each individual of a society, consists in doing everything that he judges proper for his own happiness, in what does not injure others. It is the power of being happy, without doing harm to any one. Is there an advantage that can be compared to it? Nothing in the world can supply its place: delicious fruit of the laws, it gives the human soul all the energy of which it is susceptible.

* This paragraph follows exactly the text of 1800 as do all the articles by Madame Roland here given.

The reign of the general will is the only reign that maintains public felicity; from the moment when power secures independence to some parts of the state, corruption introduces itself, and soon becomes manifest by the misery of the oppressed.

Slavery and virtue are incompatible. Slavery breaks all the ties that connect man with his fellow-creature; it relaxes and destroys the two springs that contribute most to the development of our faculties, the esteem of ourselves, and glory, which is only the result of public esteem; it suffers nothing to subsist but odious force and degrading fear.

Tyranny equally debases him who exercises it and those whom it enslaves; with it all lose the sentiment of truth, the idea of justice, and the taste of good.

It is to him who knows the extent and the limits of his rights, that we may look for a respect for those of others, a generous intrepidity in their defense, and the noble care of their preservation.

True courage belongs only to the free man. Of what can those be capable who are nothing except by the will of the master? And to what obligations would he believe himself restricted, who must fancy himself of a nature superior to that of the people he commands?

The enjoyment and the inviolability of the first rights of social man,—personal safety and property,—with the power of claiming them in case of an accidental injury, properly constitute the essence of liberty. This is the masterpiece of legislation; but so many things prevent its being carried into execution, or counteract its being brought to perfection and concur in its ruin, that very seldom is it seen to subsist, even for a short time, unimpaired.

All nations are not capable of enjoying liberty; the same nation cannot support it equally at all times.

The climate, the soil, and the species of its productions, the situation of the places, their extent, etc., pave the way to it or estrange it from its inhabitants, according to the spirit, the wants, and the resources which it affords them. Liberty is for the most part the companion of poverty; the fertility of a country abounding in superfluities, stifles it in a manner by its richness. And, indeed, it is pretty generally true, that the finest countries are those which have the worst governments.

Bare competence, or comfort acquired by labor, makes men honest and the state happy; in this, it is with the nation as with

the individual, too many wants excite cupidity and engender corruption.

The English are said to be free, and I believe they are so more than their neighbors,—more than most of the nations of Europe, except the Swiss; but commerce and the love of gain, riches, and luxury, by weakening their morals, insensibly sap their constitution, or render useless a great part of its effects.

People are often mistaken respecting the word liberty. I give not this name to the anarchy into which fell again certain republics; such, for instance, as Syracuse, after the death or expulsion of the tyrants who had governed them by intrigue or by violence, and whom they had given themselves through weakness. Liberty suits none but simple men, who have few wants. When we consider the infinite care, the continual vigilance, which the maintenance of the laws demand in a free state, the time required for the acts of sovereignty which regard each of the citizens, we are sensible how few of them remain for other occupations. If we reflect, besides, that industry and the arts open the first door to inequality, insulate those who profess them by affording them extraordinary means of acquiring property, and offering them resources independent of the common good, we shall perceive how great was the wisdom of the legislators who banished them from their states.

The Lacedæmonians were nothing else than husbandmen and soldiers; but they had helots? It would be very astonishing if, in the same government, the slavery of one part of the species should be absolutely necessary to the perfect happiness of the other. This idea makes me shudder; I dare not investigate it.

I hasten to arrive at what suits me much better; I leave metaphysical reveries and political speculations to the more able; I prefer what more nearly concerns action, and I think that is my element. I understand by liberty of mind, not only that sound view of an enlightened judgment which is not disturbed by prejudices or by passions, but also that firm and tranquil temper of a strong soul, superior to events. I call it philosophy, because it is the fruit of wisdom and one of its most unequivocal proofs; it is under these titles that I regard it as a treasure. I add that I am determined to labor to acquire it; nothing is more true nor more easy. With reason sufficient to appreciate things at what they are worth, we may suffer ourselves to be affected too warmly by some of them, for want of having contracted the habit of conquering ourselves by courageous and daily exercise. The same vivacity of feeling which on many occasions elevates us above ourselves, often sinks us again below our level by the frequent revolutions of which it renders us the sport.

The empire over ourselves is the finest of empires, that of which the conquest costs us most, and the possession of which is the sweetest. We think we have done much when we have familiarized ourselves with austerity,—let us speak more correctly, with grief; it seems that it is it which, acting on our organs in the most immediate manner, must principally disturb the liberty of the mind. Yet if it be true that the value which we attach to things makes almost their whole importance, and that the force of ideas and the power of imagination are capable of diverting us from the actual impressions which they make on our senses, it must be acknowledged that physical evils are not the most dangerous for an elevated and delicate soul. It is not precisely in undergoing such and such trials that our courage is manifested, but it is in supporting the loss of what is dearest to us, and this, too, is where it generally fails. Alas! we are so constituted for pain, that all the efforts employed to bear us up against it, serve only to render it more acute in certain parts. The better we have known the variety of those things which fix the desires of the misled vulgar, and the more we have diminished the objects of our esteem, the more, too, do we remain violently attached to those which we preserve and which we think we ought to distinguish. Reason, virtue, everything draws these ties the closer; if cruel necessity chance to break them, what dreadful torments! the disorder of the body is nothing; the rigors of fate scarcely deserved to be mentioned; but in the pains which proceed from the heart, or which strike at it, I can do no more than wrap up my head and waste away in silence. O sensibility! delight and torment of our days, how much do thy sacrifices exercise and fatigue our philosophy! it is with the greatest justice that has been established, as the first principle of happiness, that secret enjoyment of virtue, which consists in the recollection of having done well, and in the resolution of continuing to do so; beyond that, every thing is full of illusions and falsehoods, and the sweetest accessories to this first pleasure are crossed by poignant and bitter afflictions. Where is the man who has learned to content himself with this satisfaction and dispense with every other? His felicity

not affected in a warm and touching manner. Such never wrote but from the want of something to divert his mind: how many others would have thought little had not active grief unfolded their faculties?

Complete.

DOING GOOD

BENEFICENCE has this peculiarity, that the more we exercise it, the more pleasure we find in its exercise. We attach ourselves to the unfortunate object that we relieve, and the assistance we give him becomes a want to those by whom it is administered.

He who has once caused the tears of gratitude to flow, and who can afterwards seek a pleasure sweeter than that, is not worthy of feeling all the charm of doing good.

Complete.

BORROWED IDEAS

IT is useful to borrow the ideas of others; but the habit of consulting them, makes the mind contract a sort of sloth and dullness, which renders it incapable of ever determining by its own powers. Reading extends the judgment; to form it, is the province of meditation.

There are some people who are stupid from dint of science; so many names, facts, and experiences are heaped up in their head, that natural genius has been smothered by them; their conversation is a repertory of what they have read, without ever being the expression of what they have reasoned upon; it does very well to make use of them as of a dictionary, but the thinking, contemplative being must be sought for elsewhere.

Too much reading overloads the memory, and dulls the imagination; meditation, on the contrary, carried to excess, heats, exalts, and leads to madness.

Complete.

is independent and unchangeable; that is the true sage and my hero; he alone can preserve perfect liberty of mind.

We have so perverted the use of the blessings bestowed on us by nature, that we have reduced ourselves no longer to find, but in their voluntary privation, the peace that ought to accompany them.

We must love mankind sufficiently to concern ourselves about their welfare, and esteem them so little as not to expect any return on their part.

Judgment appears to me to consist in discovering that we can accomplish our own happiness only in laboring at that of others; reason seems to me the firm resolution of acting always agreeably to this principle; the highest degree of virtue is to do good with enthusiasm, because it is honorable and delightful. Sublime delirium, by which the exalted soul finds unheard-of strength, and puts itself on a footing with the gods! Happy he who knows its transports and renders himself worthy of ever enjoying them! Exact calculation and cold reasoning never make us capable of doing so; it belongs to feelings alone to inspire us with them. Reflection sometimes damps the ardor of our efforts, as repose cools courage; in point of morals, as soon as we are certain of having adopted the best, we must follow them blindfold. But it is to the fascination, to the enchantment of virtue alone, that it is allowable to subject the liberty of the mind.

I touch lightly on these subjects; how many things concerning each of them do I perceive confusedly in my mind, and which a little application would draw forth! But I will not labor: I rapidly sketch the most prominent ideas, and I wait for the others to become clear.

Complete. From the works of Mme. Roland.
London, 1800.

PENSÉES

ON HAPPINESS

HAPPINESS! . . . every one talks of it, few know it, and those who feel it, waste not their time in describing it. I, who am meditating on it I enjoy it not at this moment.

Feeling fills the soul; every enjoyment absorbs profound reflections; he, whose mind discusses matters coolly, is certainly

THE GIFT OF SILENCE

I HAVE often remarked, that the persons who passed for the most discreet were not the most happy in the choice of their confidants.

There is a strength of mind, by no means common, in burying in silence what strongly affects us. Yet prudence imposes on us a law almost equal, to conceal the secrets of others and our own violent feelings; the passions mislead us to such a degree, that, blushing, after their crisis is over, at the blindness into which they have plunged us, we almost always regret our having communicated the opinions with which they inspired us. Besides, an excessive reserve, at least with friends, bespeaks a mistrust of ourselves, and a fear of examination, which are not very honorable to him who entertains them. Honest souls are unreserved; dissimulation, on the contrary, serves as a mask to bad intentions; it is the cloak of the courtier and the virtue of intrigue.

In affairs, there must be inviolable secrecy; in the ordinary commerce of life, a prudent reserve; and in the connections of the heart, an unlimited confidence.

The last part of my precept is not without inconvenience, I know; but for myself, I rather choose to run the risk of its observation, than to deprive myself of the pleasures that must thence result.

Complete.

VIRTUE AN INSPIRATION

VIRTUE is not to be demonstrated, it is calculated to be felt; we must inspire it, and not preach it up; it is by far the best thing in the world, but it is for those who love it. Some one has said, with a deal of justness, that we attach ourselves still less to virtue from the charms that we find in it, than from the sacrifices that we make to it. I like this idea; it touches, flatters, and penetrates me.

In a constitution of things where natural order is perverted, where consequence, esteem, distinctions,—exterior advantages, in short,—are the reward of factitious merit, it would be a very improper idea to wish to cause virtue to be adopted because it is useful; we must cause it to be cherished, because it is amiable;

it belongs to those who possess it, to know all its utility, and to congratulate themselves on their choice.

Our morals are such, that it amounts almost to audacity, to undertake to rear new citizens; we must hope for many circumstances, and rely still more on the example that we feel ourselves capable of affording.

Complete.

CHARACTER AND ASSOCIATION

THE commerce of the world affords us the facility of expressing ourselves readily and gracefully concerning the objects which present themselves; but it cannot contribute to improve the judgment, except of those who have theirs already well formed.

Men, in general, lose part of their natural character by being in continual company, and we are never less ourselves than in living much with others. It is hardly anywhere but in solitude that we learn to think strongly; there it is that the mind is improved and enlightened, that the ideas are extended and strengthened, that the feelings become refined and fortified, that the moral man acquires a consistency, and assumes those qualities which he afterwards exercises among his fellows.

There are persons who cannot endure solitude; and it is so much the worse for them; I know some of these; I see only the more reason to pity them.

We may cherish solitude without becoming misanthropes; none are less susceptible of attachment than dissipated people; feeling souls withdraw from the crowd.

I am tired of those amphibious beings whom we cannot define, who do not know themselves, and whom we find everywhere dragging their incapacity; they make me impatient for retirement.

Complete.

INTELLECT AND PROGRESS

IF WE understand by thinking, the action of the mind, inasmuch as it considers its own ideas, combines and rectifies them, I state it as a fact that the most contemplative man has not thought the quarter of his life.

JEAN JACQUES ROUSSEAU

(1712–1778)

PERHAPS if an impartial jury were called upon to decide on the evidence what thousand words of modern prose have made the most history, the verdict would be for (or against!) the sixth chapter of Rousseau's first book on the "Social Contract." It is the most definite formulation made, prior to 1776, of the idea that "all men are created equal; that they are endowed by the Creator with certain unalienable rights; that among these are Life, Liberty, and the Pursuit of Happiness; that to secure these rights governments are instituted among men, deriving their just powers from the consent of the governed." The problem of government, as Rousseau stated it, is "to find a form of association which may defend and protect with the whole force of the community the person and property of every associate, and by means of which each, coalescing with all, may, nevertheless, obey only himself and remain as free as before."

John Locke in England and Rousseau in France, gave the intellectual impulse to the movement which resulted in the two great revolutions of the eighteenth century. The Republic of America and the Republic of France might have come without them through evolution, had it been possible for evolution to do its work against the obstructive forces of eighteenth-century "Toryism." With the eighteenth century as it was, however, nothing might have been accomplished except through the power of great intellects moved to radicalism by such uncompromising analyses of fundamental principles as those in which Rousseau swept away the claim that one class of men can rightly assert a title from Heaven to rule. Since the "Social Contract" appeared, "Divine Right," as a title to govern, has been abandoned by all publicists who make any serious pretension to logic. When "Higher Civilization" is substituted for "Divine Right" in later times, Rousseau's definition is evaded rather than combated. Indeed, the corollary from his definition, "that governments are instituted to secure rights rather than to support privilege," and that "they derive their just powers from the governed," has not been met with any other logic than that of the *status quo ante*, in the presence of which it remains still to the minds of many practical-minded men what it was called by Rufus Choate,—"a glittering gen-

Our wants are so numerous, the necessity of satisfying them occurs so frequently, engages so much of our attention,—continued sensations occupying us in such a manner, by the mere images of objects, or tyrannizing over us so much by their presence, that it is still surprising that we can employ ourselves about so many things. What a considerable portion of time lost to the mind! In representing to ourselves the species as a great individual being, ought we to be astonished at the slowness of its progress in every way, and at the almost eternal infancy in which it seems to remain? I am frightened at the immensity of time that has been required to bring us only where we are.

Enter into details: see every man, always confused by varied and successive impressions,—he acquires without enjoying, adopts without examining, and judges mechanically. Inattention and habit maintain and encourage ignorance and error; every thing counteracts the discovery of truth, and dilatory experience cannot cause it to be admitted but in the process of time.

Complete.

erality." It is one of those definitions, however, which, when once formulated, become to thousands who do not possess the power of analysis in their own intellectual right, as sacred as a religious creed. The American Revolution of 1776, the French Revolution which followed it, and the American Civil War, alike testify the terrible power of a definition which first and finally reduces a great, world-moving idea to its simplest terms. Had Rousseau not impregnated the mind of civilization with the idea that "just government" must be representative in order to be just, the plea that American slavery made the slave contented and happy might have been accepted by the public opinion of the world,—which, however, could not entertain it when Rousseau was represented in the nineteenth century by Garrison and Lincoln, as he had been in the eighteenth by Jefferson, Danton, and Wilberforce. It is singular that this remarkable man should not only dominate thus the politics of the eighteenth and nineteenth centuries, but that the theories of education which he formulated in his "Émile" should, at the opening of the twentieth century, still remain the governing impulse in all that is most distinctively modern in the training of youth for citizenship. He inspired Fröbel in Germany, as he did the founders of the public school system in America. It is hard to find in history any one who, by purely intellectual force, has exerted a power over the course of events which can be compared to that attributable with certainty to Rousseau. It is impossible to account for his possession of it on any other theory than that his genuine benevolence overcame weaknesses and vices which otherwise would have vitiated his influence and nullified his work. No life was ever more unequal to the demand of a great intellect than his. The highest benevolence seemed not incompatible in him with moral weakness verging close on depravity,—as when, while writing on Virtue and Philosophy, he sent his own children one after another to the foundling asylum. Perhaps what often verges on "moral idiocy" in him may be accounted for to a very great extent by the circumstances of his birth and early education. At Geneva, where he was born (June 28th, 1712), his father was without social standing, and, as his mother died in giving him birth, he was left without the training which gives intellectual power its stimulus and complement of moral force. His father "mended watches and taught dancing" for a living, and Jean Jacques himself "was successively an engraver's apprentice, a lackey, a student in a seminary, a clerk, a private tutor, and a music copyist," before he became a great author. Where the least said about his morals is the soonest mended, this, perhaps, is sufficient to suggest the lack of stability of character which seems to be the radical infirmity of his nature. The astonishing versatility of his genius, the powerful analytical faculty which characterized his intellect, and the incessant activity of his mind,—these are rather to be wondered at than accounted for. Of the scores of books and pamphlets he left behind, his «Confessions» and the «New Héloïse» are the most generally read, while the «Social Contract» and the «Émile» are the most influential. Of the great power both these works have exerted for progress there can be no question. There is a reasonable question, however, if writing in the spirit which comes only of a virtuous life, Rousseau might not have accomplished far greater results through the same intellectual energy exerted in modes which would have made those he influenced more willing to trust the power of demonstrated truth, than to triumph suddenly and violently at the expense of those whose weakness or selfishness made them its opponents.

W. V. B.

THAT MEN ARE BORN FREE

MAN is born free, and everywhere he is in chains. Many a one believes himself the master of others, and yet he is a greater slave than they. How has this change come about? I do not know. What can render it legitimate? I believe that I can settle this question.

If I considered only force and the results that proceed from it, I should say that so long as a people is compelled to obey and does obey, it does well; but that, so soon as it can shake off the yoke and does shake it off, it does better; for, if men recover their freedom by virtue of the same right by which it was taken away, either they are justified in resuming it, or there was no justification for depriving them of it. But the social order is a sacred right which serves as a foundation for all others. This right, however, does not come from nature. It is, therefore, based on conventions. The question is to know what these conventions are.

«Social Contract,» Book I., Chap. i.

THE SOCIAL CONTRACT

I ASSUME that men have reached a point at which the obstacles that endanger their preservation in the state of nature overcome by their resistance the forces which each individual can exert with a view to maintaining himself in that state. Then

this primitive condition can no longer subsist, and the human race would perish unless it changed its mode of existence.

Now, as men cannot create any new forces, but only combine and direct those that exist, they have no other means of self-preservation than to form by aggregation a sum of forces which may overcome the resistance, to put them in action by a single motive power, and to make them work in concert.

The sum of forces can be produced only by the combination of many; but the strength and freedom of each man being the chief instruments of his preservation, how can he pledge them without injuring himself, and without neglecting the cares which he owes to himself? This difficulty, applied to my subject, may be expressed in these terms:—

"To find a form of association which may defend and protect, with the whole force of the community, the person and property of every associate, and by means of which each, coalescing with all, may, nevertheless, obey only himself, and remain as free as before." Such is the fundamental problem of which the social contract furnishes the solution.

The clauses of this contract are so determined by the nature of the act that the slightest modification would render them vain and ineffectual; so that, although they have never perhaps been formally enunciated, they are everywhere the same, everywhere tacitly admitted and recognized, until, the social pact being violated, each man regains his original rights and recovers his natural liberty, whilst losing the conventional liberty for which he renounced it.

These clauses, rightly understood, are reducible to one only, *viz.*, the total alienation to the whole community of each associate with all his rights; for, in the first place, since each gives himself up entirely, the conditions are equal for all; and, the conditions being equal for all, no one has any interest in making them burdensome to others.

Further, the alienation being made without reserve, the union is as perfect as it can be, and an individual associate can no longer claim anything; for, if rights were left to individuals, since there would be no common superior who could judge between them and the public, each, being on some point his own judge, would soon claim to be so on all; the state of nature would still subsist, and the association would necessarily become tyrannical or useless.

In short, each giving himself to all, gives himself to nobody; and as there is not one associate over whom we do not acquire the same rights which we concede to him over ourselves, we gain the equivalent of all that we lose, and more power to preserve what we have.

If, then, we set aside what is not of the essence of the social contract, we shall find that it is reducible to the following terms: "Each of us puts in common his person and his whole power under the supreme direction of the general will; and in return we receive every member as an indivisible part of the whole."

Forthwith, instead of the individual personalities of all the contracting parties, this act of association produces a moral and collective body, which is composed of as many members as the assembly has voices, and which receives from this same act its unity, its common self (*moi*), its life, and its will. This public person, which is thus formed by the union of all the individual members, formerly took the name of city, and now takes that of republic or body politic, which is called by its members state when it is passive, sovereign when it is active, power when it is compared to similar bodies. With regard to the associates, they take collectively the name of people, and are called individually citizens, as participating in the sovereign power, and subjects, as subjected to the laws of the state. But these terms are often confused and are mistaken for one another; it is sufficient to know how to distinguish them when they are used with complete precision.

Complete. «Social Contract,» Book I., Chap. vi.

NATURE AND EDUCATION

EVERYTHING is perfect, coming from the hands of the Creator; everything degenerates in the hands of man. He forces a spot of ground to nourish the productions of a foreign soil; or a tree to bear fruit by the insition of another; he mixes and confounds climates, elements, seasons; he mutilates his dog, his horse, his slave; he inverts the nature of things, only to disfigure them; he is fond of deformity and monstrous productions; he is pleased with nothing, as it is framed by nature, not even with man; we must break him to his mind, like a managed

horse; we must fashion him to his taste, like the trees or plants of his garden.

Were it not for this culture, things would still be worse; for our species will not bear being fashioned by halves. In the present constitution of things, man abandoned from his birth to his own guidance among the rest of society, would be a monstrous animal. Prejudices, authority, necessity, example, and all the social institutions with which we are surrounded, would stifle the voice of nature, and substitute nothing else in its place. Nature would be to him like a plant or shrub, that shoots up spontaneously in the highway, but is soon trodden down and destroyed by travelers.

To thee do I therefore address my discourse, O fond and careful mother, whose sense has led thee out of the common tract, and taught thee to preserve the tender plant from the injurious blast of human opinions! Be sure to water the young sprig before it dies; it will one day yield such fruit as must afford thee infinite delight. Take care to erect an early enclosure around the infant's mind; others may mark out the circumference, but to thee alone it belongs to fix the barrier.

Plants are fashioned by culture, and men by education. Were man to be born of full size and strength, these would avail him nought, till he learnt to make use of them; nay, they would rather resound to his prejudice, by preventing others from lending him assistance; so that, being left to himself, he would die miserably before he knew his wants. We are apt to complain of the state of infancy; not reflecting, that if man had not commenced an infant, the human species must have perished.

We are all brought into the world feeble and weak, yet we stand in need of strength; we are destitute of everything, yet we want assistance; we are senseless and stupid, yet we have occasion for judgment. All that we have not at our birth, and that we stand in need of at the years of maturity, is the gift of education.

Education is either from nature, from men, or from things. The developing of our faculties and organs, is the education of nature; that of men, is the application we learn to make of this very developing; and that of things is the experience we acquire in regard to the different objects by which we are affected.

Mankind are all formed by three sorts of masters. The pupil, in whom their instructions contradict each other, is ill-educated, and will never be self-consistent. He, in whom they all coincide on the same point, and tend to the same end, he alone may be said to hit his aim, and to live consistently. In short, he alone is well educated.

Now, of those three different educations, that of nature is independent in us; that of things depends on us only in particular respects, and this in a hypothetical sense; for who can pretend to direct every word and action of those who have the care of an infant?

No sooner, therefore, does education become an art, than it is almost impossible it should succeed; since the concurrence of circumstances necessary for its success is in no man's power. All that we can possibly do, by dint of care, is to come near the mark, more or less; but he must be very fortunate indeed who hits it.

But what mark is this? you will say; the very same that nature has in view. This we have just now proved; for since the concurrence of the three educations is necessary for their completion, the other two must be directed towards that which is no way subject to our control. But, perhaps, the word nature may bear, on this occasion, to indeterminate a sense; we shall, therefore, endeavor to fix it.

Nature, you will say, is nothing more than a habit. But what do you mean by that? Are not habits contracted by mere force, which cannot be said, however, to stifle nature? Such, for instance, is the habit of plants, constrained in their vertical direction. Restored to their liberty, they still retain the direction they have been forced to assume; yet the sap has not changed its original impression; and if the plant continues to vegetate, its prolongation once more becomes vertical. It is the same in regard to human inclinations. So long as we continue in the same state, we may retain such inclinations as result from habit, and are least natural to us; but as soon as the situation changes, the habit ceases, and nature revives. Education surely is nothing more than habit. And yet are there not some people who altogether forget, and others who retain, their education? Whence this difference? If we are to confine the word nature to habits conformable to nature, surely we may spare ourselves the trouble of this nonsensical expression.

We are all born with a certain degree of sensibility, and from the very first instant of our existence we are differently affected

IX—206

by the objects that surround us. As soon as we acquire, if I may so speak, a consciousness of our sensations, we are disposed either to pursue or to flee from the objects that produce them; at first, as they are agreeable or displeasing to us; in the next place, in proportion to the agreement or disagreement we find between ourselves and the objects; and lastly, pursuant to the judgment we form of them, from the idea of happiness or perfection acquired by reason. These dispositions are enlarged and strengthened, in proportion as we become more sensible and intelligent; but restrained by habit, they are altered more or less by opinion. Before this alteration, they are what I distinguish in man by the name of nature.

To these primitive dispositions every thing must, therefore, be referred; and this might easily be done, were the three sorts of education no more than different; but what are we to do, when they happen to be opposite? When, instead of educating a man for himself, you want to educate him for others, the harmony or agreement is then impossible. Being obliged either to combat nature or social institutions, you must make your option, whether you are to form the man or the citizen; for you cannot do both.

Every partial society, when it is close and compact, deviates greatly from the general link; great lovers of their country are rude and uncivil to strangers; they look upon them only in the common light as men, and as unworthy of their regard. This inconveniency is inevitable, but of no great consequence. The point is, to behave kindly towards our fellow-subjects. Abroad, the Spartans were ambitious, avaricious, and unjust; while disinterestedness, equity, and concord reigned within their walls. Beware of those cosmopolites who pore over old books in search of duties, which they neglect to fulfill within their own communities. Thus you will see a philosopher admiring the Tartars, in order to be excused from loving his neighbors.

Man in his natural state is all for himself; he is the numerical unit or the absolute integer, that refers only to himself, or to his likeness. Man in the civil state is a fractionary unit, who depends on the denominator, and whose value consists in his relation to the integer, namely, the body politic. Among social institutions, those are the best, which are best adapted for divesting man of his natural state; for depriving him of his absolute, to give him a relative, existence; in short, for transferring self to a common unit; to the end, that each individual may no

longer consider himself as one, but as part of a unit, and have no sense or feeling but in conjunction with the whole. A Roman citizen was neither Caius nor Lucius,—he was a Roman; but he loved his country exclusive of himself. Regulus pretended to be a Carthaginian, as he was become the property of his masters. In the quality of a stranger, he refused to take his seat in the Roman senate; and before he would comply, he insisted upon receiving orders from a Carthaginian. With indignation he beheld the endeavors used to save his life. He carried his point, and returned triumphant to Carthage, to resign his last breath amidst the most exquisite tortures. Here we behold a man of quite a different stamp from those of the present age.

From «Émile.» Translated by N. Nugent.

CHRIST AND SOCRATES

I WILL confess that the majesty of the Scriptures strikes me with admiration, as the purity of the Gospel hath its influence on my heart. Peruse the works of our philosophers with all their pomp of diction: how mean, how contemptible are they compared with the Scriptures! Is it possible that a book, at once so simple and sublime, should be merely the work of man? Is it possible that the sacred personage, whose history it contains, should be himself a mere man? Do we find that he assumed the tone of an enthusiast or ambitious sectary? What sweetness, what purity in his manner! What an affecting gracefulness in his delivery! What sublimity in his maxims! what profound wisdom in his discourses! What presence of mind, what subtlety, what truth in his replies! How great the command over his passions! Where is the man, where the philosopher, who could so live, and so die, without weakness, and without ostentation? When Plato described his imaginary good man loaded with all the shame of guilt, yet meriting the highest rewards of virtue, he describes exactly the character of Jesus Christ: the resemblance was so striking, that all the Fathers perceived it.

What prepossession, what blindness must it be to compare the son of Sophronicus to the son of Mary! What an infinite disproportion there is between them! Socrates dying without pain or ignominy, easily supported his character to the last; and if his death, however easy, had not crowned his life, it might have

been doubted whether Socrates, with all his wisdom, was anything more than a vain sophist. He invented, it is said, the theory of morals. Others, however, had before put them in practice; he had only to say, therefore, what they had done, and to reduce their examples to precepts. Aristides had been just before Socrates defined justice; Leonidas had given up his life for his country before Socrates declared patriotism to be a duty; the Spartans were a sober people before Socrates recommended sobriety; before he had even defined virtue, Greece abounded in virtuous men. But where could Jesus learn, among his competitors, that pure and sublime morality, of which he only hath given us both precept and example? The greatest wisdom was made known amongst the most bigoted fanaticism, and the simplicity of the most heroic virtues did honor to the vilest people on earth. The death of Socrates, peaceably philosophizing with his friends, appears the most agreeable that could be wished for; that of Jesus, expiring in the midst of agonizing pains, abused, insulted, and accused by a whole nation, is the most horrible that could be feared. Socrates, in receiving the cup of poison, blessed, indeed, the weeping executioner who administered it; but Jesus, in the midst of excruciating torments, prayed for his merciless tormentors. Yes, if the life and death of Socrates were those of a sage, the life and death of Jesus are those of a God. Shall we suppose the evangelic history a mere fiction? Indeed, my friend, it bears not the marks of fiction; on the contrary, the history of Socrates, which nobody presumes to doubt, is not so well attested as that of Jesus Christ. Such a supposition, in fact, only shifts the difficulty without obviating it: it is more inconceivable that a number of persons should agree to write such a history, than that one only should furnish the subject of it. The Jewish authors were incapable of the diction, and strangers to the morality, contained in the Gospel, the marks of whose truth are so striking and inimitable, that the inventor would be a more astonishing character than the hero.

JOHN RUSKIN

(1819-1900)

AMONG English prose writers of the second half of the nineteenth century, John Ruskin was scarcely equaled in the attractiveness of his style, and he was not equaled at all in the range of his thought and the variety of his productions. He is peculiarly identified with the second half of the century, for, with the exception of the first and minor edition of his "Modern Painters," nearly all his great works were published between 1849 and 1900. As an "art critic," he has had no equal among English writers. But it is with "art" as the expression of the whole idea impressed on humanity by nature that he deals, rather than with art in the limited sense in which it is generally understood. Students of any single art, as of painting or sculpture, are apt to dissent from his conclusions and to question the practical usefulness of his methods; and in the sense in which a professional painter criticizes technique, Ruskin is hardly to be classed as an art critic at all. He represents in England more nearly than any one else the larger view of art which Hegel in Germany did so much to make possible. It was from Carlyle, however, rather than from any German master, that Ruskin received his most potent inspiration. He may be called Carlyle's greatest pupil. Indeed in many things he is Carlyle's superior. His prose style shows traces of Carlyle's mannerisms, but it is more fluent, more melodious, and more persuasive, than that of Carlyle, whose intensity of expression is often more apt to excite admiration than to carry conviction. Like Carlyle, Ruskin was, in his political views, distrustful of freedom as a mode of progress. He defined his distrust in the assertion that men are only fit for freedom in the inverse ratio of their desire for it. In his later life, he developed an ideal of æsthetic culture for the masses, depending on socialism as a mode of aristocratic control and tutelage. He was deeply moved by beauty in art and nature. The old Greek "beauty worship" has had no greater disciple than he. He himself looked on beauty as a revelation of divine goodness. And his message was one of reverence for the good and true not less than for the beautiful. He seems not to have considered, however, that physiological laws which made the Greeks what they were, operate against substituting the Greek for the Puritan ideal among "Anglo-Saxons." Pericles and Aspasia, listening to a recitation from Homer with an "ear" which enabled

them to co-ordinate perfectly the relation of every vowel to every other in a period of melody as easily as a trained composer does in listening to his own opera,— such finely-organized beings as these were not fitted to serve as saints of progress for the race which produced John Milton and John Bunyan,— which in their spirit must seek its salvation by pressing through the "Valley of the Shadow of Death," with the smoke of hell coming up through the grass-roots and a leather-winged Apollyon hovering over it. "Sin" was something the Greeks knew nothing about, and when Phidias worked, the self-consciousness of the world had not advanced far enough to make possible the conception of a Devil as it is present in the subconsciousness of English-speaking peoples. The world of the old Saxons was a "Midgard"— a "middle enclosure," with heaven on one side and hell on the other. The world of the primitive Greeks was thronged with genially human gods and demigods. Heaven was no further away than the top of Mount Olympus, and the idea of hell, of the progressive and finally climacteric punitive reactions of evil, was not sufficiently developed to cause alarm. Neither Ruskin nor any other prophet of art could have transferred to nineteenth-century England the artistic cult developed by such conditions as these. But Ruskin in attempting it, achieved all that was possible.

He was born in London, February 8th, 1819. His father was a wine merchant who had accumulated a large fortune. On his death it descended to Ruskin, who was thus enabled to gratify without great sacrifices the desire for the study of art, which early in life became his ruling passion. After graduating from Christ Church College, Oxford, in 1842, he studied painting under Copley Fielding, and Harding, and afterwards spent much of his time in Italy,— especially in Venice where he found everything he most needed to inspire him. He held professorships both at Cambridge and Oxford, and utilized his lectures as material for a number of the remarkable volumes which during the last twenty-five years of his life he published with such astonishing rapidity. The completion of his "Modern Painters" established his standing as the leading English authority on the philosophy of art, and, in consequence, the public demands on his energies were incessant and remorseless. In endeavoring to meet them, he wrecked his nervous system and for several years before he died (January 20th, 1900) he was insane. His life was a tragedy. The beautiful woman whom he loved and married did not love him. Finding that she did love his friend, the painter, Millais, Ruskin secured a divorce for her and brought about her marriage to Millais. Deprived thus of domestic happiness, he devoted himself wholly to his work, and in it found "every good and perfect gift" except that consummation and sum of all, without which all is fruitless—peace.

W. V. B.

THE SKY

IT is a strange thing how little in general people know about the sky. It is the part of creation in which nature has done more for the sake of pleasing man — more for the sole and evident purpose of talking to him, and teaching him — than in any other of her works; and it is just the part in which we least attend to her. There are not many of her other works in which some more material or essential purpose than the mere pleasing of man is not answered by every part of their organization; but every essential purpose of the sky might, so far as we know, be answered if once in three days, or thereabouts, a great, ugly, black rain cloud were brought up over the blue, and everything well watered, and so all left blue again till next time, with perhaps a film of morning and evening mist for dew — and instead of this, there is not a moment of any day of our lives, when nature is not producing scene after scene, picture after picture, glory after glory, and working still upon such exquisite and constant principles of the most perfect beauty, that it is quite certain * it is all done for us, and intended for our perpetual pleasure. And every man, wherever placed, however far from other sources of interest or of beauty, has this doing for him constantly. The noblest scenes of the earth can be seen and known but by few; it is not intended that man should live always in the midst of them; he injures them by his presence, he ceases to feel them if he is always with them; but the sky is for all: bright as it is, it is not

> "too bright nor good
> For human nature's daily food";

it is fitted in all its functions for the perpetual comfort and exalting of the heart,— for soothing it, and purifying it from its dross and dust. Sometimes gentle, sometimes capricious, sometimes awful — never the same for two moments together; almost human in its passions, almost spiritual in its tenderness, almost divine in its infinity, its appeal to what is immortal in us is as distinct as its ministry of chastisement or of blessing to what is

---

* At least, I thought so, when I was four-and-twenty. At five-and-twenty I fancy that it is just possible there may be other creatures in the universe, to be pleased, or,—it may be,—displeased by the weather.

J. R.

mortal is essential. And yet we never attend to it, we never make it a subject of thought, but as it has to do with our animal sensations, we look upon all by which it speaks to us more clearly than to brutes, upon all which bears witness to the intention of the Supreme that we are to receive more from the covering vault than the light and the dew which we share with the weed and the worm, only as a succession of meaningless and monotonous accident, too common and too vain to be worthy of a moment of watchfulness, or a glance of admiration. If in our moments of utter idleness and insipidity, we turn to the sky as a last resource, which of its phenomena do we speak of? One says, it has been wet; and another, it has been windy; and another, it has been warm. Who among the whole chattering crowd can tell me of the forms and the precipices of the chain of tall white mountains that girded the horizon at noon yesterday? Who saw the narrow sunbeam that came out of the south, and smote upon their summits until they melted and moldered away in the dust of blue rain? Who saw the dance of the dead clouds where the sunlight left them last night, and the west wind blew them before it like withered leaves? All has passed unregretted as unseen; or if the apathy be ever shaken off even for an instant, it is only by what is gross, or what is extraordinary. And yet it is not in the broad and fierce manifestations of the elemental energies, nor in the clash of the hail, nor the drift of the whirlwind, that the highest characters of the sublime are developed. God is not in the earthquake, nor in the fire, but in the still small voice. They are but the blunt and the low faculties of our nature, which can only be addressed through lampblack and lightning. It is in quiet and unsubdued passages of unobtrusive majesty, the deep and the calm, and the perpetual; that which must be sought ere it is seen, and loved ere it is understood; things which the angels work out for us daily, and yet vary eternally; which are never wanting, and never repeated, which are to be found always, yet each found but once; it is through these that the lesson of devotion is chiefly taught, and the blessing of beauty given.

We habitually think of the rain cloud only as dark and gray; not knowing that we owe to it perhaps the fairest, though not the most dazzling, of the hues of heaven. Often in our English mornings, the rain clouds in the dawn form soft, level fields, which melt imperceptibly into the blue; or, when of less extent, gather into apparent bars, crossing the sheets of broader clouds above; and all these bathed throughout in an unspeakable light of pure rose-color, and purple, and amber, and blue; not shining, but misty-soft; the barred masses, when seen nearer, composed of clusters or tresses of cloud, like floss silk; looking as if each knot were a little swathe or sheaf of lighted rain.

Aqueous vapor or mist, suspended in the atmosphere, becomes visible exactly as dust does in the air of a room. In the shadows, you not only cannot see the dust itself, because unillumined, but you can see other objects through the dust, without obscurity; the air being thus actually rendered more transparent by a deprivation of light. Where a sunbeam enters, every particle of dust becomes visible, and a palpable interruption to the sight; so that a transverse sunbeam is a real obstacle to the vision—you cannot see things clearly through it. In the same way, wherever vapor is illuminated by transverse rays, there it becomes visible as a whiteness more or less affecting the purity of the blue, and destroying it exactly in proportion to the degree of illumination. But where vapor is in shade, it has very little effect on the sky, perhaps making it a little deeper and grayer than it otherwise would be, but not, itself, unless very dense, distinguishable, or felt as mist.

Has the reader any distinct idea of what clouds are?

That mist which lies in the morning so softly in the valley, level and white, through which the tops of the trees rise as if through an inundation—why is it so heavy, and why does it lie so low, being yet so thin and frail that it will melt away utterly into splendor of morning when the sun has shone on it but a few moments more? Those colossal pyramids, huge and firm, with outlines as of rocks, and strength to bear the beating of the high sun full on their fiery flanks,—why are they so light, their bases high over our heads, high over the heads of Alps? Why will these melt away, not as the sun rises, but as he descends, and leave the stars of twilight clear; while the valley vapor gains again upon the earth, like a shroud? Or that ghost of a cloud, which steals by yonder clump of pines; nay, which does not steal by them, but haunts them, wreathing yet round them, and yet, —and yet,—slowly; now falling in a fair waved line like a woman's veil; now fading, now gone; we look away for an instant, and look back, and it is again there. What has it to do with that clump of pines, that it broods by them, and waves itself among their branches, to and fro? Has it hidden a cloudy

treasure among the moss at their roots, which it watches thus? Or has some strong enchanter charmed it into fond returning, or bound it fast within those bars of bough? And yonder filmy crescent, bent like an archer's bow above the snowy summit, the highest of all the hills—that white arch which never forms but over the supreme crest,—how it is stayed there, repelled apparently from the snow,—nowhere touching it, the clear sky seen between it and the mountain edge, yet never leaving it—poised as a white bird hovers over its nest! Or those war clouds that gather on the horizon, dragon-crested, tongued with fire,—how is their barbed strength bridled? What bits are those they are champing with their vaporous lips, flinging off flakes of black foam? Leagued leviathans of the Sea of Heaven,—out of their nostrils goeth smoke, and their eyes are like the eyelids of the morning; the sword of him that layeth at them cannot hold the spear, the dart, nor the habergeon. Where ride the captains of their armies? Where are set the measures of their march? Fierce murmurers, answering each other from morning until evening—what rebuke is this which has awed them into peace;—what hand has reined them back by the way in which they came?

I know not if the reader will think at first that questions like these are easily answered. So far from it, I rather believe that some of the mysteries of the clouds never will be understood by us at all. "Knowest thou the balancing of the clouds?" Is the answer ever to be one of pride? The wondrous works of him, which is perfect in knowledge? Is our knowledge ever to be so?

For my own part, I enjoy the mystery, and perhaps the reader may. I think he ought. He should not be less grateful for summer rain, or see less beauty in the clouds of morning, because they come to prove him with hard questions; to which, perhaps, if we look close at the heavenly scroll, we may find also a syllable or two of answer, illuminated here and there.

And though the climates of the south and east may be comparatively clear, they are no more absolutely clear than our own northern air. Intense clearness, whether in the north, after or before rain, or in some moments of twilight in the south, is always, as far as I am acquainted with natural phenomena, a notable thing. Mist of some sort, or mirage, or confusion of light or of cloud, are the general facts; the distance may vary in different climates at which the effects of mist begin, but they are

always present; and therefore, in all probability, it is meant that we should enjoy them. . . . We surely need not wonder that mist and all its phenomena have been made delightful to us, since our happiness as thinking beings must depend on our being content to accept only partial knowledge even in those matters which chiefly concern us. If we insist upon perfect intelligibility and complete declaration in every moral subject, we shall instantly fall into misery of unbelief. Our whole happiness and power of energetic action depend upon our being able to breathe and live in the cloud; content to see it opening here, and closing there; rejoicing to catch through the thinnest films of it glimpses of stable and substantial things; but yet perceiving a nobleness even in the concealment, and rejoicing that the kindly veil is spread where the untempered light might have scorched us, or the infinite clearness wearied. And I believe that the resentment of this interference of the mist is one of the forms of proud error which are too easily mistaken for virtues. To be content in utter darkness and ignorance is indeed unmanly, and therefore we think that to love light and find knowledge must always be right. Yet (as in all matters before observed), wherever pride has any share in the work, even knowledge and light may be ill pursued. Knowledge is good, and light is good; yet man perished in seeking knowledge, and moths perish in seeking light; and if we, who are crushed before the moth, will not accept such mystery as is needful to us, we shall perish in like manner. But, accepted in humbleness, it instantly becomes an element of pleasure; and I think that every rightly constituted mind ought to rejoice, not so much in knowing anything clearly, as in feeling that there is infinitely more which it cannot know. None but proud or weak men would mourn over this, for we may always know more if we choose by working on; but the pleasure is, I think, to humble people, in knowing that the journey is endless, the treasure inexhaustible,—watching the cloud still march before them with its summitless pillar, and being sure that, to the end of time, and to the length of eternity, the mysteries of its infinity will still open further and further, their dimness being the sign and necessary adjunct of their inexhaustibleness. I know there are an evil mystery and a deathful dimness,—the mystery of a great Babylon—the dimness of the sealed eye and soul; but do not let us confuse these with the glorious mystery of the things which the angels "desire to look

into," or with the dimness which, even before the clear eye and open soul, still rests on sealed pages of the eternal volume.

On some isolated mountain at daybreak,* when the night mists first rise from off the plain, watch their white and lake-like fields, as they float in level bays, and winding gulfs about the islanded summits of the lower hills, untouched yet by more than dawn, colder and more quiet than a windless sea under the moon of midnight; watch when the first sunbeam is sent upon the silver channels, how the foam of their undulating surface parts, and passes away, and down under their depths the glittering city and green pasture lie like Atlantas, between the white paths of winding rivers; the flakes of light falling every moment faster and broader among the starry spires, as the wreathed surges break and vanish above them, and the confused crests and ridges of the dark hills shorten their gray shadows upon the plain. Wait a little longer, and you shall see those scattered mists rallying in the ravines, and floating up towards you, along the winding valleys, till they couch in quiet masses, iridescent with the morning light, upon the broad breasts of the higher hills, whose leagues of massy undulation will melt back, back into that robe of material light, until they fade away, and set in its lustre, to appear again above in the serene heaven like a wild, bright, impossible dream, foundationless, and inaccessible, their very base vanishing in the unsubstantial, and making blue of the deep lake below. Wait yet a little longer, and you shall see those mists gather themselves into white towers, and stand like fortresses along the promontories, massy and motionless, only piled with every instant higher and higher into the sky, and casting longer shadows athwart the rocks; and out of the pale blue of the horizon you will see forming and advancing a troop of narrow, dark, pointed vapors, which will cover the sky, inch by inch, with their gray network, and take the light off the landscape with an eclipse which will stop the singing of the birds, and the motion of the leaves, together;—and then you will see horizontal bars of black shadow forming under them, and lurid

* I forget now what all this is about. It seems to be a recollection of the Rigi, with assumption that the enthusiastic spectator is to stand for a day and night in observation; to suffer the effects of a severe thunder storm, and to get neither breakfast nor dinner. I have seen such a storm on the Rigi, however, and more than one such sunrise; and I much doubt if its present visitors by rail will see more.

                 J. R.

wreaths create themselves, you know not how, among the shoulders of the hills; you never see them form, but when you look back to a place which was clear an instant ago, there is a cloud on it, hanging by the precipice as a hawk pauses over his prey; — and then you will hear the sudden rush of the awakened wind, and you will see those watchtowers of vapor swept away from their foundations, and waving curtains of opaque rain let down to the valley, swinging from the burdened clouds in black bending fringes, or, pacing in pale columns along the lake level, grazing its surface into foam as they go. And then as the sun sinks you shall see the storm drift for an instant from off the hills, leaving their broad sides smoking and loaded yet with snow-white, torn, steam-like rags of capricious vapor, now gone, now gathered again,—while the smoldering sun, seeming not far away, but burning like a red hot-ball beside you, and as if you could reach it, plunges through the rushing wind and rolling cloud with headlong fall, as if it meant to rise no more, dyeing all the air about it with blood;—and then you shall hear the fainting tempest die in the hollow of the night, and you shall see a green halo kindling on the summit of the eastern hills, brighter, brighter yet, till the large white circle of the slow moon is lifted up among the barred clouds, step by step, line by line; star after star she quenches with her kindling light, setting in their stead an army of pale, penetrable fleecy wreaths in the heaven, to give light upon the earth, which move together hand in hand, company by company, troop by troop, so measured in their unity of motion that the whole heaven seems to roll with them, and the earth to reel under them. And then wait yet for one hour, until the east again becomes purple, and the heaving mountains, rolling against it in darkness, like waves of a wild sea, are drowned one by one in the glory of its burning; watch the white glaciers blaze in their winding paths about the mountains, like mighty serpents with scales of fire; watch the columnar peaks of solitary snow, kindling downwards chasm by chasm, each in itself a new morning—their long avalanches cast down in keen streams brighter than the lightning, sending each his tribute of driven snow, like altar smoke up to heaven, the rose light of their silent domes flushing that heaven about them, and above them, piercing with purer light through its purple lines of lifted cloud, casting a new glory on every wreath, as it passes by, until the whole heaven one scarlet canopy is interwoven with

a roof of waving flame, and tossing vault beyond vault, as with the drifted wings of many companies of angels: and then when you can look no more for gladness, and when you are bowed down with fear and love of the Maker and Doer of this, tell me who has best delivered this his message unto men!

*The account given of the stages of creation in the first chapter of Genesis is in every respect clear and intelligible to the simplest reader, except in the statement of the work of the second day. I suppose that this statement is passed over by careless readers without any endeavor to understand it, and contemplated by simple and faithful readers as a sublime mystery which was not intended to be understood. But there is no mystery in any other part of the chapter, and it seems to me unjust to conclude that any was intended here. And the passage ought to be peculiarly interesting to us, as being the first in the Bible in which the heavens are named, and the only one in which the word "heaven," all important as that word is to our understanding of the most precious promises of Scripture, receives a definite explanation. Let us therefore see whether, by a little careful comparison of the verse with other passages in which the word occurs, we may not be able to arrive at as clear an understanding of this portion of the chapter as of the rest. In the first place the English word "firmament" itself is obscure and useless; because we never employ it but as a synonym of heaven, it conveys no other distinct idea to us; and the verse, though from our familiarity with it we imagine that it possesses meaning, has in reality no more point nor value than if it were written, "God said, Let there be a something in the midst of the waters, and God called the something, Heaven." But the marginal reading, "Expansion," has definite value; and the statement that God said, Let there be an expansion in the midst of the waters, and "God called the expansion, Heaven," has an apprehensible meaning. Accepting this expression as the one intended, we have next to ask what expansion there is, between two waters, describable by the term "heaven." Milton adopts the term "expanse," but he understands it of the whole volume of the air which surrounds the earth. Whereas, so far as we can tell, there is no water be-

* This passage, to the end of the section, is one of the last, and best, which I wrote in the temper of my youth; and I can still ratify it, thus far, that the texts referred to in it must either be received as it explains them, or neglected altogether.

J. R.

yond the air, in the fields of space; and the whole expression of division of waters from waters is thus rendered valueless. Now with respect to this whole chapter, we must remember always that it is intended for the instruction of all mankind, not for the learned reader only; and that therefore the most simple and natural interruption is the likeliest in general to be the true one. An unscientific reader knows little about the manner in which the volume of the atmosphere surrounds the earth; but I imagine that he could hardly glance at the sky when rain was falling in the distance, and see the level line of the bases of the clouds from which the shower descended, without being able to attach an instant and easy meaning to the words, "expansion in the midst of the waters"; and if, having once seized this idea, he proceeded to examine it more accurately, he would perceive at once, if he had ever noticed anything of the nature of clouds, that the level line of their bases did indeed most severely and stringently divide "waters from waters"—that is to say, divide water in its collective and tangible state, from water in its aërial state; or the waters which fall and flow, from those which rise and float. Next, if we try this interpretation in the theological sense of the word Heaven, and examine whether the clouds are spoken of as God's dwelling place, we find God going before the Israelites in a pillar of cloud; revealing himself in a cloud on the mercy seat, filling the temple of Solomon with the cloud when its dedication is accepted; appearing in a great cloud to Ezekiel; ascending into a cloud before the eyes of the disciples on Mount Olivet; and in like manner returning to judgment: "Behold he cometh with clouds, and every eye shall see him." "Then shall they see the Son of Man coming in the clouds of heaven, with power and great glory." While further the "clouds" and "heavens" are used as interchangeable words in those Psalms which most distinctly set forth the power of God: "He bowed the heavens also, and came down; he made darkness pavilions round about him, dark waters, and thick clouds of the skies." And again, "Thy mercy, O Lord, is in the heavens, and thy faithfulness reacheth unto the clouds." And again, "His excellency is over Israel, and his strength is in the clouds." And again, "The clouds poured out water, the skies sent out a sound, the voice of thy thunder was in the heaven." Again, "Clouds and darkness are round about him, righteousness and judgment are the habitation of his throne; the heavens declare his righteousness, and all the people see his glory." In all

these passages the meaning is unmistakable if they possess definite meaning at all. We are too apt to take them merely for sublime and vague imagery, and therefore gradually to lose the apprehension of their life and power. The expression, "He bowed the heavens," for instance, is, I suppose, received by most readers as a magnificent hyperbole, having reference to some peculiar and fearful manifestation of God's power to the writer of the Psalm in which the words occur. But the expression either has plain meaning, or it has no meaning. Understand by the term "heavens" the compass of infinite space around the earth, and the expression "bowed the heavens," however sublime, is wholly without meaning: infinite space cannot be bent or bowed. But understand by the "heavens" the veil of clouds above the earth, and the expression is neither hyperbolical nor obscure; it is pure, plain, accurate truth, and it describes God, not as revealing himself in any peculiar way to David, but doing what he is still doing before our own eyes, day by day. By accepting the words in their simple sense, we are thus lead to apprehend the immediate presence of the Deity, and his purpose of manifesting himself as near us whenever the storm cloud stoops upon its course; while by our vague and inaccurate acceptance of the words, we remove the idea of his presence far from us, into a region which we can neither see nor know: and gradually, from the close realization of a living God, who "maketh the clouds his chariot," we define and explain ourselves into dim and distant suspicion of an inactive God inhabiting inconceivable places, and fading into the multitudinous formalisms of the laws of nature. All errors of this kind—and in the present day we are in constant and grievous danger of falling into them—arise from the originally mistaken idea that man can, "by searching, find out God—find out the Almighty to perfection"—that is to say, by help of courses of reasoning and accumulations of science, apprehend the nature of the Deity, in a more exalted and more accurate manner than in a state of comparative ignorance; whereas it is clearly necessary, from the beginning to the end of time, that God's way of revealing himself to his creatures should be a simple way, which all those creatures may understand. Whether taught or untaught, whether of mean capacity or enlarged, it is necessary that communion with their Creator should be possible to all; and the admission to such communion must be rested, not on their having a knowledge of astronomy, but on their having a human soul. In order to render this communion possible, the Deity has stooped from his throne, and has, not only in the person of the Son, taken upon him the veil of our human flesh, but, in the person of the Father, taken upon him the veil of our human thoughts, and permitted us, by his own spoken authority, to conceive him simply and clearly as a loving father and friend; a being to be walked with and reasoned with, to be moved by our entreaties, angered by our rebellion, alienated by our coldness, pleased by our love, and glorified by our labor; and finally to be beheld in immediate and active presence in all the powers and changes of creation. This conception of God, which is the child's, is evidently the only one which can be universal, and, therefore, the only one which for us can be true. The moment that, in our pride of heart, we refuse to accept the condescension of the Almighty, and desire him, instead of stooping to hold our hands, to rise up before us into his glory, we, hoping that, by standing on a grain of dust or two of human knowledge higher than our fellows, we may behold the Creator as he rises,—God takes us at our word. He rises, into his own invisible and inconceivable majesty; he goes forth upon the ways which are not our ways, and retires into the thoughts which are not our thoughts; and we are left alone. And presently we say in our vain hearts, "There is no God."

I would desire, therefore, to receive God's account of his own creation as under the ordinary limits of human knowledge and imagination it would be received by a simple-minded man; and finding that the "heavens and the earth" are spoken of always as having something like equal relation to each other ("Thus the heavens and the earth were finished, and all the host of them"), I reject at once all idea of the term "heavens" being intended to signify the infinity of space inhabited by countless worlds; for between those infinite heavens and the particle of sand, which not the earth only, but the sun itself, with all the solar system, is, in relation to them, no relation of equality or comparison could be inferred. But I suppose the heavens to mean that part of creation which holds equal companionship with our globe; I understand the "rolling of these heavens together as a scroll," to be an equal and relative destruction with the melting of the elements in fervent heat; and I understand the making of the firmament to signify that, so far as man is concerned, most magnificent ordinance of the clouds;—the ordinance

IX—207

that as the great plain of waters was formed on the face of the earth, so also a plain of waters should be stretched along the height of air, and the face of the cloud answer the face of the ocean; and that this upper and heavenly plain should be of waters, as it were, glorified in their nature, no longer quenching the fire, but now bearing fire in their own bosoms; no longer murmuring only when the winds raise them or rocks divide, but answering each other with their own voices, from pole to pole; no longer restrained by established shores, and guided through unchanging channels; but going forth at their pleasure like the armies of the angels, and choosing their encampments upon the heights of the hills; no longer hurried downwards forever, moving but to fall, nor lost in the lightless accumulation of the abyss, but covering the east and west with the waving of their wings, and robing the gloom of the further infinite with a vesture of diverse colors, of which the threads are purple and scarlet, and the embroideries flame.

This, I believe, is the ordinance of the firmament; and it seems to me that in the midst of the material nearness of these heavens, God means us to acknowledge his own immediate presence as visiting, judging, and blessing us: "The earth shook, the heavens also dropped at the presence of God." "He doth set his bow in the clouds," and thus renews, in the sound of every drooping swathe of rain, his promises of everlasting love. "In them he hath set a tabernacle for the sun"; whose burning ball, which, without the firmament, would be seen but as an intolerable and scorching circle in blackness of vacuity, is by that firmament surrounded with gorgeous service, and tempered by mediatorial ministries: by the firmament of clouds the temple is built, for his presence to fill with light at noon; by the firmament of clouds the purple veil is closed at evening, round the sanctuary of his rest; by the mists of the firmament his implacable light is divided, and its separated fierceness appeased into the soft blue that fills the depth of distance with its bloom, and the flush with which the mountains burn, as they drink the overflowing of the dayspring. And in this tabernacling of the unendurable sun with men, through the shadows of the firmament, God would seem to set forth the stooping of his own Majesty to men, upon the throne of the firmament. As the Creator of all the worlds, and the Inhabiter of eternity, we cannot behold him; but as the Judge of the earth and the Preserver of men, those heavens are

indeed his dwelling place: "Swear not, neither by heaven, for it is God's throne; nor by the earth, for it is his footstool!" And all of those passings to and fro of fruitful showers and grateful shade, and all those visions of silver palaces built about the horizon, and voices of moaning winds and threatening thunders, and glories of colored robe and cloven ray, are but to deepen in our hearts the acceptance, and distinctness, and dearness, of the simple words, "Our Father, which art in heaven."

Complete as edited from "Modern Painters"
in "Frondes Agrestes."

PRINCIPLES OF ART

PERFECT taste is the faculty of receiving the greatest possible pleasure from those material sources which are attractive to our moral nature in its purity and perfection; but why we receive pleasure from some forms and colors and not from others is no more to be asked or answered than why we like sugar and dislike wormwood.

The temper by which right taste is formed is characteristically patent. It dwells upon what is submitted to it. It does not trample upon it,—lest it should be pearls, even though it look like husks. It is good ground, penetrable, retentive; it does not send up thorns of unkind thoughts, to choke the weak seed; it is hungry and thirsty too, and drinks all the dew that falls on it. It is an honest and good heart, that shows no too ready springing before the sun be up, but fails not afterwards; it is distrustful of itself, so as to be ready to believe and to try all things, and yet so trustful of itself, that it will neither quit what it has tried, nor take anything without trying. And the pleasure which it has in things that it finds true and good is so great, that it cannot possibly be led aside by any tricks of fashion, or diseases of vanity; it cannot be cramped in its conclusions by partialities and hypocrisies; its visions and its delights are too penetrating,—too living,—for any whitewashed object or shallow fountain long to endure or supply. It clasps all that it loves so hard that it crushes it if it be hollow.

It is the common consent of men that whatever branch of any pursuit ministers to the bodily comforts, and regards material uses, is ignoble, and whatever part is addressed to the mind only, is noble; and that geology does better in reclothing dry bones

and revealing lost creations, than in tracing veins of lead and beds of iron; astronomy better in opening to us the houses of heaven than in teaching navigation; botany better in displaying structure than in expressing juices; surgery better in investigating organization than in setting limbs. Only it is ordained that, for our encouragement, every step we make in the more exalted range of science adds something also to its practical applicabilities; that all the great phenomena of nature, the knowledge of which is desired by the angels only, by us partly, as it reveals to further vision the being and the glory of him in whom they rejoice and we live, dispense yet such kind influences and so much of material blessing as to be joyfully felt by all inferior creatures, and to be desired by them with such single desire as the imperfection of their nature may admit; that the strong torrents, which, in their own gladness, fill the hills with hollow thunder, and the vales with winding light, have yet their bounden charge of field to feed, and barge to bear; that the fierce flames to which the Alp owes its upheaval and the volcano its terror, temper for us the metal vein, and warm the quickening spring; and that for our excitement, I say, not our reward,—for knowledge is its own reward,—herbs have their healing, stones their preciousness, and stars their times.

Had it been ordained by the Almighty * that the highest pleasures of sight should be those most difficult attainment, and that to arrive at them it should be necessary to accumulate gilded palaces, tower over tower, and pile artificial mountains around insinuated lakes, there would never have been a direct contradiction between the unselfish duties and the inherent desires of every individual. But no such contradiction exists in the system of Divine Providence; which, leaving it open to us if we will, as creatures in probation, to abuse this sense like every other, and pamper it with selfish and thoughtless vanities, as we pamper the palate with deadly meats, until the appetite of tasteful cruelty is lost in its sickened satiety, incapable of pleasure, unless, Caligula like, it concentrates the labor of a million of lives into the sensation of an hour, leaves it also open to us,—by hum-

---

* The reader must observe that, having been thoroughly disciplined in the evangelical schools, I supposed myself, at four-and-twenty, to know all about the ordinances of the Almighty. Nevertheless, the practical contents of the sentence are good if only they are intelligible, which I doubt.

J. R.

ble and loving ways, to make ourselves susceptible of deep delight, which shall not separate us from our fellows, nor require the sacrifice of any duty or occupation, but which shall bind us closer to men and to God, and be with us always, harmonized with every action, consistent with every claim, unchanging and eternal.

A great idealist never can be egotistic. The whole of his power depends upon his losing sight and feeling of his own existence, and becoming a mere witness and mirror of truth, and a scribe of visions — always passive in sight, passive in utterance, lamenting continually that he cannot completely reflect nor clearly utter all he has seen — not by any means a proud state for a man to be in. But the man who has no invention is always setting things in order,* and putting the world to rights, and mending, and beautifying, and pluming himself on his doings, as supreme in all ways.

So far as education does indeed tend to make the senses delicate, and the perceptions accurate, and thus enables people to be pleased with quiet instead of gaudy color; and with graceful instead of coarse form; and by long acquaintance with the best things, to discern quickly what is fine from what is common — so far acquired taste is an honorable faculty, and it is true praise of anything to say, it is "in good taste." But so far as this higher education has a tendency to narrow the sympathies and harden the heart, diminishing the interest of all beautiful things by familiarity, until even what is best can hardly please, and what is brightest hardly entertain — so far as it fosters pride, and leads men to found the pleasure they take in anything, not on the worthiness of the thing, but on the degree in which it indicates some greatness of their own (as people build marble porticoes, and inlay marble floors, not so much because they like the colors of marble, or find it pleasant to the foot, as because such porches and floors are costly, and separated in all human eyes from plain entrances of stone and timber), — so far as it leads people to prefer gracefulness of dress, manner, and aspect, to value of substance and heart, liking a well-said thing better than a true thing, and a well-trained manner better than a sincere one, and a delicately-formed face better than a good-

---

*I am now a comic illustration of this sentence, myself. I have not a ray of invention in all my brains; but am intensely rational and orderly, and have resolutely begun to set the world to rights.

J. R.

natured one — and in all other ways and things setting custom and semblance above everlasting truth — so far, finally, as it induces a sense of inherent distinction between class and class, and causes everything to be more or less despised which has no social rank, so that the affection, pleasure, or grief of a clown are looked upon as of no interest compared with the affection and grief of a well-bred man — just so far in all these several ways, the feeling induced by what is called "a liberal education" is utterly adverse to the understanding of noble art.

He who habituates himself in his daily life to seek for the stern facts in whatever he hears or sees will have these facts again brought before him by the involuntary imaginative power, in their noblest associations; and he who seeks for frivolities and fallacies will have frivolities and fallacies again presented to him in his dreams.*

All the histories of the Bible are yet waiting to be painted. Moses has never been painted; Elijah never; David never (except as a mere ruddy stripling); Deborah never; Gideon never; Isaiah never.† What single example does the reader remember of painting which suggested so much as the faintest shadow of their deeds? Strong men in armor, or aged men with flowing beards, he may remember, who, when he looked at his Louvre or Uffizii catalogue, he found were intended to stand for David or Moses. But does he suppose that, if these pictures had suggested to him the feeblest image of the presence of such men, he would have passed on, as he assuredly did, to the next picture representing, doubtless, Diana and Actæon, or Cupid and the Graces, or a gambling quarrel in a pothouse — with no sense of pain or surprise? Let him meditate over the matter, and he will find ultimately that what I say is true, and that religious art at once complete and sincere never yet has existed.

---

*Very good. Few people have any idea how much more important the government of the mind is than the force of its exertion. Nearly all the world flog their horses, without ever looking where they are going.

J. R.

†I knew nothing, when I wrote this passage, of Luini, Filippo Lippi, or Sandro Botticelli; and had not capacity to enter into the deeper feelings even of the men whom I was chiefly studying, — Tintoret and Fra Angelico. But the British public is at present as little acquainted with the greater Florentines as I was then, and the passage, for them, remains true.

J. R.

Complete as edited in "Frondes Agrestes" from "Modern Painters." The notes are Ruskin's own.

WORK

WISE work is, briefly, work with God. Foolish work is work against God. And work done with God, which he will help, may be briefly described as "Putting in Order," — that is, enforcing God's law of order, spiritual and material, over men and things. The first thing you have to do, essentially; the real "good work" is, with respect to men, to enforce justice, and, with respect to things, to enforce tidiness and fruitfulness. And against these two great human deeds, justice and order, there are perpetually two great demons contending, — the devil of iniquity, or inequity, and the devil of disorder, or of death; for death is only consummation of disorder. You have to fight these two fiends daily. So far as you don't fight against the fiend of iniquity, you work for him. You "work iniquity," and the judgment upon you, for all your "Lord, Lord's," will be "Depart from me, ye that work iniquity." And so far as you do not resist the fiend of disorder, you work disorder, and you yourself do the work of Death, which is sin, and has for its wages, Death himself.

Observe, then, all wise work is mainly threefold in character. It is honest, useful, and cheerful.

It is honest. I hardly know anything more strange than that you recognize honesty in play, and you do not in work. In your lightest games, you have always some one to see what you call "fair play." In boxing you must hit fair; in racing, start fair. Your English watchword is Fair play; your English hatred, Foul play. Did it ever strike you that you wanted another watchword also, Fair work, and another hatred also, Foul work? Your prize fighter has some honor in him yet; and so have the men in the ring round him: they will judge him to lose the match, by foul hitting. But your prize merchant gains his match by foul selling, and no one cries out against that. You drive a gambler out of the gambling room who loads dice, but you leave a tradesman in flourishing business who loads scales! For observe, all dishonest dealing is loading scales. What does it matter whether I get short weight, adulterate substance, or dishonest fabric? The fault in the fabric is incomparably the worst of the two. Give me short measure of food, and I only lose by you; but give me adulterate food, and I die by you. Here, then, is your chief duty, you workmen and tradesmen — to be true to

yourselves, and to us who would help you. We can do nothing for you, nor you for yourselves, without honesty. Get that, you get all; without that, your suffrages, your reforms, your free-trade measures, your institutions of science, are all in vain. It is useless to put your heads together, if you can't put your hearts together. Shoulder to shoulder, right hand to right hand, among yourselves, and no wrong hand to anybody else, and you'll win the world yet.

Then, secondly, wise work is useful. No man minds, or ought to mind, its being hard, if only it comes to something: but when it is hard and comes to nothing; when all our bees' business turns to spiders', and for honeycomb we have only resultant cobweb, blown away by the next breeze — that is the cruel thing for the worker. Yet do we ever ask ourselves, personally, or even nationally, whether our work is coming to anything or not? We don't care to keep what has been nobly done; still less do we care to do nobly what others would keep; and, least of all, to make the work itself useful instead of deadly to the doer, so as to use his life indeed, but not to waste it. Of all wastes the greatest waste that you can commit is the waste of labor. If you went down in the morning into your dairy, and you found that your youngest child had got down before you, and that he and the cat were at play together, and that he had poured out all the cream on the floor for the cat to lap up, you would scold the child and be sorry the milk was wasted. But if, instead of wooden bowls with milk in them, there are golden bowls with human life in them, and instead of the cat to play with — the devil to play with; and you yourself the player; and instead of leaving that golden bowl to be broken by God at the fountain, you break it in the dust yourself, and pour the human blood out on the ground for the fiend to lick up — that is no waste! What! you perhaps think, "to waste the labor of men is not to kill them." Is it not? I should like to know how you could kill them more utterly — kill them with second deaths? It is the slightest way of killing to stop a man's breath. Nay, the hunger, and the cold, and the little whistling bullets — our love messengers between nation and nation — have brought pleasant messages from us to many a man before now; orders of sweet release, and leave at last to go where he will be most welcome and most happy. At the worst you do but shorten his life, you do not corrupt his life. But if you put him to base labor, if you bind his thoughts, if you blind his eyes, if you blunt his hopes, if you steal his joys, if you stunt his body, and blast his soul, and at last leave him not so much as to reap the poor fruit of his degradation, but gather that for yourself, and dismiss him to the grave, when you have done with him, having, so far as in you lay, made the walls of that grave everlasting (though, indeed, I fancy the goodly bricks of some of our family vaults will hold closer in the resurrection day than the sod over the laborer's head), this you think is no waste, and no sin!

Then, lastly, wise work is cheerful, as a child's work is. And now I want you to take one thought home with you, and let it stay with you.

Everybody in this room has been taught to pray daily, "Thy kingdom come." Now, if we hear a man swear in the streets, we think it very wrong, and say he "takes God's name in vain." But there's a twenty times worse way of taking his name in vain than that. It is to ask God for what we don't want. He doesn't like that sort of prayer. If you don't want a thing, don't ask for it; such asking is the worst mockery of your King you can mock him with; the soldiers striking him on the head with the reed was nothing to that. If you do not wish for his kingdom, don't pray for it. But if you do, you must do more than pray for it; you must work for it. And, to work for it, you must know what it is: we have all prayed for it many a day without thinking. Observe, it is a kingdom that is to come to us; we are not to go to it. Also, it is not to be a kingdom of the dead, but of the living. Also, it is not to come all at once, but quietly: nobody knows how: "the kingdom of God cometh not with observation." Also, it is not to come outside of us, but in the hearts of us: "the kingdom of God is within you." And being within us, it is not a thing to be seen, but to be felt; and though it brings all substance of good with it, it does not consist in that: "the kingdom of God is not meat and drink, but righteousness, peace, and joy in the Holy Ghost,"—joy, that is to say, in the holy, healthful, and helpful Spirit. Now, if we want to work for this kingdom, and to bring it, and enter into it, there's just one condition to be first accepted. You must enter it as children, or not at all; "Whosoever will not receive it as a little child shall not enter therein." And again, "Suffer little children to come unto me, and forbid them not, for of such is the kingdom of heaven."

Of such, observe. Not of children themselves, but of such as children. I believe most mothers who read that text think that all heaven is to be full of babies. But that's not so. There will be children there, but the hoary head is the crown. "Length of days, and long life and peace," that is the blessing, not to die in babyhood. Children die but for their parents' sins; God means them to live, but he can't let them always; then they have their earlier place in heaven, and the little child of David, vainly prayed for;—the little child of Jeroboam, killed by its mother's step on its own threshold,—they will be there. But weary old David, and weary old Barzillai, having learned children's lessons at last, will be there too; and the one question for us all, young or old, is, Have we learned our child's lesson? It is the character of children we want, and must gain at our peril; let us see, briefly, in what it consists.

The first character of right childhood is that it is Modest. A well-bred child does not think it can teach its parents, or that it knows everything. It may think its father and mother know everything,—perhaps that all grown-up people know everything; very certainly it is sure that it does not. And it is always asking questions, and wanting to know more. Well, that is the first character of a good and wise man at his work. To know that he knows very little;—to perceive that there are many above him far wiser than he; and to be always asking questions, wanting to learn, not to teach. No one ever teaches well who wants to teach, or governs well who wants to govern; it is an old saying (Plato's, but I know not if his first), and as wise as old.

Then, the second character of right childhood is to be Faithful. Perceiving that its father knows best what is good for it, and having found always, when it has tried its own way against his, that he was right and it was wrong, a noble child trusts him at last wholly, gives him its hand, and will walk blindfold with him, if he bids it. And that is the true character of all good men also, as obedient workers, or soldiers under captains. They must trust their captains;—they are bound for their lives to choose none but those whom they can trust. Then, they are not always to be thinking that what seems strange to them, or wrong in what they are desired to do, is strange or wrong. They know their captain: where he leads they must follow, what he bids they must do; and without this trust and faith, without this captainship and soldiership, no great deed, no great salvation, is

possible to man. Among all the nations it is only when this faith is attained by them that they become great; the Jew, the Greek, and the Mahometan agree at least in testifying to this. It was a deed of this absolute trust which made Abraham the father of the faithful; it was the declaration of the power of God as captain over all men, and the acceptance of a leader appointed by him as commander of the faithful, which laid the foundation of whatever national power yet exists in the East; and the deed of the Greeks, which has become the type of unselfish and noble soldiership to all lands, and to all times, was commemorated, on the tomb of those who gave their lives to do it, in the most pathetic, so far as I know, or can feel, of all human utterances: "O stranger, go and tell our people that we are lying here, having obeyed their words."

Then the third character of right childhood is to be Loving and Generous. Give a little love to a child, and you get a great deal back. It loves everything near it, when it is a right kind of child—would hurt nothing, would give the best it has away, always, if you need it—does not lay plans for getting everything in the house for itself, and delights in helping people; you cannot please it so much as by giving it a chance of being useful, in ever so little a way.

And because of all these characters, lastly, it is Cheerful. Putting its trust in its father, it is careful for nothing—being full of love to every creature, it is happy always, whether in its play or in its duty. Well, that's the great worker's character also. Taking no thought for the morrow; taking thought only for the duty of the day; trusting somebody else to take care of to-morrow; knowing, indeed, what labor is, but not what sorrow is; and always ready for play,—beautiful play,—for lovely human play is like the play of the Sun. There's a worker for you. He, steady to his time, is set as a strong man to run his course, but, also, he rejoiceth as a strong man to run his course. See how he plays in the morning, with the mists below, and the clouds above, with a ray here and a flash there, and a shower of jewels everywhere;—that's the Sun's play; and great human play is like his—all various—all full of light and life, and tender, as the dew of the morning.

So then, you have the child's character in these four things: Humility, Faith, Charity, and Cheerfulness. That's what you have got to be converted to. "Except ye be converted and become as little children"—You hear much of conversion nowa-

days; but people always seem to think you have got to be made wretched by conversion,—to be converted to long faces. No, friends, you have got to be converted to short ones; you have to repent into childhood, to repent into delight, and delightsomeness. You can't go into a conventicle but you'll hear plenty of talk of backsliding. Backsliding, indeed! I can tell you, on the ways most of us go, the faster we slide back the better. Slide back into the cradle, if going on is into the grave—back, I tell you; back—out of your long faces, and into your long clothes. It is among children only, and as children only, that you will find medicine for your healing and true wisdom for your teaching. There is poison in the counsels of the man of this world; the words they speak are all bitterness, "the poison of asps is under their lips," but "the sucking child shall play by the hole of the asp." There is death in the looks of men. "Their eyes are privily set against the poor"; they are as the uncharmable serpent, the cockatrice, which slew by seeing. But "the weaned child shall lay his hand on the cockatrice den." There is death in the steps of men; "their feet are swift to shed blood; they have compassed us in our steps like the lion that is greedy of his prey, and the young lion lurking in secret places," but, in that kingdom, the wolf shall lie down with the lamb, and the fatling with the lion, and "a little child shall lead them." There is death in the thoughts of men; the world is one wide riddle to them, darker and darker as it draws to a close; but the secret of it is known to the child, and the Lord of heaven and earth is most to be thanked in that "he has hidden these things from the wise and prudent, and has revealed them unto babes." Yes, and there is death—infinitude of death in the principalities and powers of men. As far as the east is from the west, so far are our sins are—not set from us, but multiplied around us: the Sun himself, think you he now "rejoices" to run his course, when he plunges westward to the horizon, so widely red, not with clouds, but blood? And it will be red more widely yet. Whatever drought of the early and latter rain may be, there will be none of that red rain. You fortify yourselves against it in vain; the enemy and avenger will be upon you also, unless you learn that it is not out of the mouths of the knitted gun, or the smoothed rifle, but "out of the mouths of babes and sucklings" that the strength is ordained, which shall "still the enemy and avenger."

From "The Crown of Wild Olives."
Conclusion of the first lecture.

SIBYLLINE LEAVES

WANT OF SELF-KNOWLEDGE

HALF the evil in this world comes from people not knowing what they do like, not deliberately setting themselves to find out what they really enjoy. All people enjoy giving away money, for instance: they don't know that,—they rather think they like keeping it; and they do keep it under this false impression, often to their great discomfort. Everybody likes to do good; but not one in a hundred finds this out.

THE RESPONSIBILITY OF A RICH MAN

A RICH man ought to be continually examining how he may spend his money for the advantage of others; at present, others are continually plotting how they may beguile him into spending it apparently for his own. The aspect which he presents to the eyes of the world is generally that of a person holding a bag of money with a stanch grasp, and resolved to part with none of it unless he is forced, and all the people about him are plotting how they may force him; that is to say, how they may persuade him that he wants this thing or that; or how they may produce things that he will covet and buy. One man tries to persuade him that he wants perfumes; another that he wants jewelry; another that he wants sugarplums; another that he wants roses at Christmas. Anybody who can invent a new want for him is supposed to be a benefactor to society; and thus the energies of the poorer people about him are continually directed to the production of covetable, instead of serviceable things; and the rich man has the general aspect of a fool, plotted against by all the world. Whereas the real aspect which he ought to have is that of a person wiser than others, intrusted with the management of a larger quantity of capital, which he administers for the profit of all, directing each man to the labor which is most healthy for him, and most serviceable for the community.

ART AND DECADENCE

WE DON'T want either the life or the decorations of the thirteenth century back again; and the circumstances with which you must surround your workmen are those simply of happy modern English life, because the designs you have now to ask for from your workmen are such as will make modern English life beautiful. All that gorgeousness of the Middle Ages, beautiful as it sounds in description, noble as in many respects it was in reality, had, nevertheless, for foundation and for end, nothing but the pride of life—the pride of the so-called superior classes; a pride which supported itself by violence and robbery, and led in the end to the destruction both of the arts themselves and the States in which they flourished.

The great lesson of history is, that all the fine arts hitherto—having been supported by the selfish power of the nobless, and never having extended their range to the comfort or the relief of the mass of the people—the arts, I say, thus practiced, and thus matured, have only accelerated the ruin of the States they adorned; and at the moment when, in any kingdom, you point to the triumphs of its greatest artists, you point also to the determined hour of the kingdom's decline.

INFINITY

THAT which we foolishly call vastness is, rightly considered, not more wonderful, not more impressive, than that which we insolently call littleness, and the infinity of God is not mysterious, it is only unfathomable, not concealed, but incomprehensible; it is a clear infinity, the darkness of the pure unsearchable sea.

THE SOCIETY OF NATURE

TO THE mediæval knight, from Scottish moor to Syrian sand, the world was one great exercise ground, or field of adventure; the stanch pacing of his charger penetrated the pathlessness of outmost forest, and sustained the sultriness of the most secret desert. Frequently alone,—or if accompanied,

for the most part only by retainers of lower rank, incapable of entering into complete sympathy with any of his thoughts,—he must have been compelled often to enter into dim companionship with the silent nature around him, and must assuredly sometimes have talked to the wayside flowers of his love, and to the fading clouds of his ambition.

ALL CARVING AND NO MEAT

THE divisions of a church are much like the divisions of a sermon; they are always right so long as they are necessary to edification, and always wrong when they are thrust upon the attention as divisions only. There may be neatness in carving when there is richness in feasting; but I have heard many a discourse, and seen many a church wall, in which it was all carving and no meat.

MODERN GREATNESS

THE simple fact, that we are, in some strange way, different from all the great races that have existed before us, cannot at once be received as the proof of our own greatness; nor can it be granted, without any question, that we have a legitimate subject of complacency in being under the influence of feelings, with which neither Miltiades nor the Black Prince, neither Homer nor Dante, neither Socrates nor St. Francis, could for an instant have sympathized.

Whether, however, this fact be one to excite our pride or not, it is assuredly one to excite our deepest interest. The fact itself is certain. For nearly six thousand years the energies of man have pursued certain beaten paths, manifesting some constancy of feeling throughout all that period, and involving some fellowship at heart, among the various nations who by turns succeeded or surpassed each other in the several aims of art or policy. So that, for these thousands of years, the whole human race might be to some extent described in general terms. Man was a creature separated from all others by his instinctive sense of an Existence superior to his own, invariably manifesting this sense of the being of a God more strongly in proportion to his

own perfectness of mind and body; and making enormous and self-denying efforts, in order to obtain some persuasion of the immediate presence or approval of the Divinity.

THE CORONATION OF THE WHIRLWIND

MUCH of the love of mystery in our romances, our poetry, our art, and, above all, in our metaphysics, must come under that definition so long ago given by the great Greek, " speaking ingeniously concerning smoke." And much of the instinct, which, partially developed in painting, may be now seen throughout every mode of exertion of mind,—the easily encouraged doubt, easily excited curiosity, habitual agitation, and delight in the changing and the marvelous, as opposed to the old quiet serenity of social custom and religious faith, is again deeply defined in those few words, the " dethroning of Jupiter," the " coronation of the whirlwind."

SACRIFICES THAT MAKE ASHAMED

THE vain and haughty projects of youth for future life; the giddy reveries of insatiable self-exaltation; the discontented dreams of what might have been or should be, instead of the thankful understanding of what is; the casting about for sources of interest in senseless fiction, instead of the real human histories of the people round us; the prolongation from age to age of romantic historical deceptions instead of sifted truth; the pleasures taken in fanciful portraits of rural or romantic life in poetry and on the stage, without the smallest effort to rescue the living rural population of the world from its ignorance or misery; the excitement of the feelings by labored imagination of spirits, fairies, monsters, and demons, issuing in total blindness of heart and sight to the true presences of beneficent or destructive spiritual powers around us; in fine, the constant abandonment of all the straightforward paths of sense and duty, for fear of losing some of the enticement of ghostly joys, or trampling somewhat " sopra lor vanità, che par persona"; all these various forms of false idealism have so entangled the modern mind, often called, I suppose ironically, practical, that truly I believe there never yet was idolatry of stock or staff so utterly unholy as this our idolatry of shadows; nor can I think that, of those who burnt incense under oaks, and poplars, and elms, because "the shadow thereof was good," it could in any wise be more justly or sternly declared than of us—"The wind hath bound them up in her wing, and they shall be ashamed because of their sacrifices."

OPPRESSION UNDER THE SUN

You cannot but have noticed how often in those parts of the Bible which are likely to be oftenest opened when people look for guidance, comfort, or help in the affairs of daily life, namely, the Psalms and Proverbs, mention is made of the guilt attaching to the Oppression of the poor. Observe: not the neglect of them, but the Oppression of them; the word is as frequent as it is strange. You can hardly open either of those books, but somewhere in their pages you will find a description of the wicked man's attempts against the poor, such as, "He doth ravish the poor when he getteth him into his net."

"His mouth is full of deceit and fraud; in the secret places doth he murder the innocent."

"They are corrupt, and speak wickedly concerning oppression."

"Their poison is like the poison of a serpent. Ye weigh the violence of your hands in the earth."

Yes: "Ye weigh the violence of your hands"; weigh these words as well. The last things we usually think of weighing are Bible words. We like to dream and dispute over them, but to weigh them and see what their true contents are—anything but that! Yet weigh them; for I have purposely taken these verses, perhaps more strikingly in this connection, than separately in their places out of the Psalms, because, for all people belonging to the Established Church of this country these Psalms are appointed lessons, portioned out to them by their clergy to be read once through every month. Presumably, therefore, whatever portions of Scripture we may pass by or forget, these, at all events, must be brought continually to our observance as useful for the direction of daily life. Now, do we ever ask ourselves what the real meaning of these passages may be, and who these wicked people are, who are "murdering the innocent"? You know it is rather singular language this!—rather strong

IX—208

language, we might, perhaps, call it—hearing it for the first time. Murder! and murder of innocent people!—nay, even a sort of cannibalism. Eating people,—yes, and God's people, too—eating my people as if they were bread! swords drawn, bows bent, poison of serpents mixed! violence of hands weighed, measured, and trafficked with as so much coin! where is all this going on? Do you suppose it was only going on in the time of David, and that nobody but Jews ever murder the poor? If so, it would surely be wiser not to mutter and mumble for our daily lessons what does not concern us; but if there be any chance that it may concern us, and if this description, in the Psalms, of human guilt is at all generally applicable, as the descriptions in the Psalms of human sorrow are, may it not be advisable to know wherein this guilt is being committed round about us, or by ourselves? And when we take the words of the Bible into our mouths in a congregational way, to be sure whether we mean sincerely to chant a piece of melodious poetry relating to other people (we know not exactly whom)—or to assert our belief in facts bearing somewhat astringently on ourselves and our daily business. And if you make up your minds to do this no longer, and take pains to examine into the matter, you will find that these strange words, occurring as they do, not in a few places only, but almost in every alternate Psalm, and every alternate chapter of Proverbs or Prophecy, with tremendous reiteration, were not written for one nation or one time only, but for all nations and languages, for all places and all centuries; and it is as true of the wicked man now as ever it was of Nabal or Dives, that "his eyes are set against the poor."

MERCANTILE PANICS

No MERCHANT deserving the name ought to be more liable to a "panic" than a soldier should; for his name should never be on more paper than he could at any instant meet the call of, happen what will. I do not say this without feeling at the same time how difficult it is to mark, in existing commerce, the just limits between the spirit of enterprise and of speculation. Something of the same temper which makes the English soldier do always all that is possible, and attempt more than is possible, joins its influence with that of mere avarice in tempting the

English merchant into risks which he cannot justify, and efforts which he cannot sustain; and the same passion for adventure which our travelers gratify every summer on perilous snow wreaths and cloud-encompassed precipices surrounds with a romantic fascination the glittering of a hollow investment, and gilds the clouds that curl round gulfs of ruin. Nay, a higher and a more serious feeling frequently mingles in the motley temptation; and men apply themselves to the task of growing rich as to a labor of providential appointment, from which they cannot pause without culpability, nor retire without dishonor. Our large trading cities bear to me very nearly the aspect of monastic establishments in which the roar of the mill wheel and the crane takes the place of other devotional music, and in which the worship of Mammon and Moloch is conducted with a tender reverence and an exact propriety: the merchant rising to his Mammon matins with the self-denial of an anchorite, and expiating the frivolities into which he may be beguiled in the course of the day by late attendance at Mammon vespers. But, with every allowance that can be made for these conscientious and romantic persons, the fact remains the same, that by far the greater number of the transactions which lead to these times of commercial embarrassment may be ranged simply under two great heads,—gambling and stealing; and both of these in their most culpable form, namely, gambling with money which is not ours, and stealing from those who trust us. I have sometimes thought a day might come, when the nation would perceive that a well-educated man who steals a hundred thousand pounds, involving the entire means of subsistence of a hundred families, deserves, on the whole, as severe a punishment as an ill-educated man who steals a purse from a pocket, or a mug from a pantry.

IMMORTALITY OF THE BIBLE

You are not philosophers of the kind who suppose that the Bible is a superannuated book; neither are you of those who think the Bible is dishonored by being referred to for judgment in small matters. The very divinity of the Book seems to me, on the contrary, to justify us in referring everything to it, with respect to which any conclusion can be gathered from its pages. Assuming, then, that the Bible is neither super-

annuated now, nor ever likely to be so, it will follow that the illustrations which the Bible employs are likely to be clear and intelligible illustrations to the end of time. I do not mean that everything spoken of in the Bible histories must continue to endure for all time, but that the things which the Bible uses for illustration of eternal truths are likely to remain eternally intelligible illustrations.

DISSECTORS AND DREAMERS

All experience goes to teach us, that among men of average intellect the most useful members of society are the dissectors, not the dreamers. It is not that they love nature or beauty less, but that they love result, effect, and progress more; and when we glance broadly along the starry crowd of benefactors to the human race, and guides of human thought, we shall find that this dreaming love of natural beauty—or at least its expression—has been more or less checked by them all, and subordinated either to hard work or watching of human nature.

THE USE OF BEAUTY

Beauty has been appointed by the Deity to be one of the elements by which the human soul is continually sustained; it is therefore to be found more or less in all natural objects, but in order that we may not satiate ourselves with it, and weary of it, it is rarely granted to us in its utmost degrees. When we see it in those utmost degrees, we are attracted to it strongly, and remember it long, as in the case of singularly beautiful scenery, or a beautiful countenance. On the other hand, absolute ugliness is admitted as rarely as perfect beauty; but degrees of it more or less distinct are associated with whatever has the nature of death and sin, just as beauty is associated with what has the nature of virtue and of life.

RESPECTABILITY OF ART

I BELIEVE that there is no chance of art truly flourishing in any country, until you make it a simple and plain business, providing its masters with an easy competence, but rarely with anything more. And I say this, not because I despise the great painter, but because I honor him; and I should no more think of adding to his respectability or happiness by giving him riches, than, if Shakespeare or Milton were alive, I should think we added to their respectability, or were likely to get better work from them, by making them millionaires.

OPINIONS

IN MANY matters of opinion, our first and last coincide, though on different grounds; it is the middle stage which is furthest from the truth. Childhood often holds a truth with its feeble fingers, which the grasp of manhood cannot retain,—which it is the pride of utmost age to recover.

THE NECESSITY OF WORK

BY FAR the greater part of the suffering and crime which exist at this moment in civilized Europe arises simply from people not understanding this truism,—not knowing that produce or wealth is eternally connected by the laws of heaven and earth with resolute labor; but hoping in some way to cheat or abrogate this everlasting law of life, and to feed where they have not furrowed, and be warm where they have not woven.

I repeat, nearly all our misery and crime result from this one misapprehension. The law of nature is, that a certain quantity of work is necessary to produce a certain quantity of good, of any kind whatever. If you want knowledge, you must toil for it; if food, you must toil for it; and if pleasure, you must toil for it. But men do not acknowledge this law, or strive to evade it, hoping to get their knowledge, and food, and pleasure for nothing; and in this effort they either fail of getting them, and remain ignorant and miserable, or they obtain them by making other men work for their benefit; and then they are tyrants and robbers. Yes, and worse than robbers. I am not one who in

the least doubts or disputes the progress of this century in many things useful to mankind; but it seems to me a very dark sign respecting us that we look with so much indifference upon dishonesty and cruelty in the pursuit of wealth. In the dream of Nebuchadnezzar it was only the feet that were part of iron and part of clay; but many of us are now getting so cruel in our avarice, that it seems as if, in us, the heart were part of iron, and part of clay.

ON WAR

WHEREVER there is war, there must be injustice on one side or the other, or on both. There have been wars which were little more than trials of strength between friendly nations, and in which the injustice was not to each other, but to the God who gave them life. But in a malignant war of these present ages there is injustice of ignobler kind, at once to God and man, which must be stemmed for both their sakes.

BASE CRITICISM

IT MAY perhaps be said that I attach too much importance to the evil of base criticism; but those who think so have never rightly understood its scope, nor the reach of that stern saying of Johnson's (Idler, No. 3, April 29th, 1758): "Little does he (who assumes the character of a critic) think how many harmless men he involves in his own guilt, by teaching them to be noxious without malignity, and to repeat objections which they do not understand." And truly not in this kind only, but in all things whatsoever, there is not, to my mind, a more woeful or wonderful matter of thought than the power of a fool. In the world's affairs there is no design so great or good but it will take twenty wise men to help it forward a few inches, and a single fool can stop it; there is no evil so great or so terrible but that, after a multitude of counselors have taken means to avert it, a single fool will bring it down. Pestilence, famine, and the sword are given into the fool's hand as the arrows into the hand of the giant and if he were fairly set forth in the right motley, the web of it should be sackcloth and sable; the bells on his cap, passing bells; his badge, a bear robbed of her whelps; and his bauble, a sexton's spade.

EDUCATION

THE most helpless and sacred work which can at present be done for humanity is to teach people (chiefly by example, as all best teaching must be done) not how to "better themselves," but how to "satisfy themselves." It is the curse of every evil nature and creature to eat and not be satisfied. The words of blessing are, that they shall eat and be satisfied; and as there is only one kind of water which quenches all thirst, so there is only one kind of bread which satisfies all hunger,—the bread of justice or righteousness, which, hungering after, men shall always be filled, that being the bread of heaven; but hungering after the bread of wages of unrighteousness shall not be filled, that being the bread of Sodom. And in order to teach men how to be satisfied, it is necessary fully to understand the art of joy and humble life—this, at present, of all arts or sciences, being the one most needing study. Humble life, that is to say, proposing to itself no future exaltation, but only a sweet continuance; not excluding the idea of foresight, but wholly of fore-sorrow, and taking no troublous thought for coming days; so also not excluding the idea of providence or provision, but wholly of accumulation;—the life of domestic affection and domestic peace, full of sensitiveness to all elements of costless and kind pleasure; —therefore, chiefly to the loveliness of the natural world.

CHARLES AUGUSTIN SAINTE-BEUVE

(1804-1869)

CHARLES AUGUSTIN SAINTE-BEUVE, one of the most admired critical essayists of France, was born at Boulogne-sur-Mer, December 23d, 1804. He began life as a physician, but he had been carefully educated in general literature, and his tastes drew him away from his profession. He began writing critical essays, chiefly book reviews, which soon brought him reputation. He became a contributor to La Revue de Paris, La Revue des Deux Mondes, and other leading periodicals. He published several volumes of poems between 1829 and 1837, and in 1832 "Volupté," a novel. His "Literary Portraits" and "Portraits of Women" appeared between 1832 and 1844, and his "Causeries du Lundi" from 1851 to 1857. He was elected to the French Academy in 1845, and to the Senate in 1865. He interested himself in education as well as in literature and politics. Besides lecturing in the smaller French cities, he taught in the Collège de France as professor of Latin Poetry, and from 1857 to 1861 was a lecturer in the École Normale. He died at Paris, October 13th, 1869.

A TYPICAL MAN OF THE WORLD

EACH epoch has produced its treatise intended for the formation of the polite man, the man of the world, the courtier, when men only lived for courts, and the accomplished gentleman. In these various treatises on knowledge of life and politeness, if opened after a lapse of ages, we at once see portions which are as antiquated as the cut and fashion of our forefathers' coats; the model has evidently changed. But looking into it carefully as a whole, if the book has been written by a sensible man with a true knowledge of mankind, we shall still find profit in studying those models which have been placed before preceding generations. The letters that Lord Chesterfield wrote to his son, and which contain a whole school of *savoir vivre* and worldly science, are interesting in this particular, that there has been no idea of forming a model for imitation, but they are simply intended to bring up a pupil in the closest intimacy. They are confidential letters, which, suddenly produced in the light of day, have betrayed all the secrets and ingenious artifices of paternal solicitude. If, in reading them nowadays, we are struck with the excessive importance attached to accidental and promiscuous circumstances, with pure details of costume, we are not less struck with the durable part, with that which belongs to human observation in all ages; and this last part is much more considerable than at a superficial glance would be imagined. In applying himself to the formation of his son as a polite man in society, Lord Chesterfield has not given us a treatise on duty as Cicero has; but he has left letters which, by their mixture of justness and lightness, by certain lightsome airs which insensibly mingle with the serious graces, preserve the medium between the "Mémoires of the Chevalier de Grammont" and "Télémaque."

Before going into detail, it will be necessary to know a little about Lord Chesterfield, one of the most brilliant English wits of his time, and one most closely allied to France. Philip Dormer Stanhope, Earl of Chesterfield, was born in London, on the twenty-second of September, 1694, the same year as Voltaire. The descendant of an illustrious race, he knew the value of birth, and wished to sustain its honor; nevertheless, it was difficult for him not to laugh at genealogical pretensions when carried too far. To keep himself from this folly, he had placed amongst the portraits of his ancestors two old figures of a man and woman; beneath one was written, "Adam de Stanhope," and beneath the other, "Eve de Stanhope." Thus, while upholding the honor of race, he put his veto upon chimerical vanities arising from it.

His father paid no attention whatever to his education; he was placed under the care of his grandmother, Lady Halifax. From a very early age he manifested a desire to excel in everything, a desire which later he did his utmost to excite in the breast of his son, and which for good or ill is the principle of all that is great. Like himself in his early youth, he was without guidance, he was deceived more than once in the objects of his emulation, and followed some ridiculous chimera. He confesses that at one period of inexperience he gave himself up to wine, and other excesses, for which he was not at all inclined by nature, but it flattered his vanity to hear himself cited as a man of pleasure. In this way he plunged into play (which he

considered a necessary ingredient in the composition of a young man of fashion), at first without passion, but afterwards without being able to withdraw himself from it, and by that means compromised his fortune for years. "Take warning by my conduct," said he to his son, "choose your own pleasures, and do not let others choose them for you."

This desire to excel and to distinguish himself did not always lead him astray, and he often applied it rightly; his first studies were the best. Placed at the University of Cambridge, he studied all that was there taught, civil law and philosophy; he attended the mathematical classes of Saunderson, the blind professor. He read Greek fluently, and sent accounts of his progress in French to his old tutor, M. Jouneau, a French clergyman and refugee. Lord Chesterfield had, when a child, learned our tongue from a Norman nurse who attended him. When he visited Paris the last time, in 1744, M. de Fontenelle having remarked a slight Norman accent in his pronunciation, spoke of it to him, and asked him if he had not first been taught French by a person from Normandy,—which turned out to be the case.

After two years of university life, he made his continental tour, according to the custom of young Englishmen. He visited Holland, Italy, and France. He wrote from Paris to M. Jouneau, on the seventh of December, 1714, as follows:—

"I shall not tell you what I think of the French, because I am being often taken for a Frenchman, and more than one of them has paid me the highest possible compliment, by saying: 'Monsieur, you are quite one of ourselves.' I shall only tell you that I am impudent; that I talk a great deal very loudly, and with an air of authority; that I sing; that I dance in my walk; and, finally, that I spend immense sums in powder, feathers, white gloves, etc."

In this extract one recognizes the mocking, satirical, and slightly insolent wit, who makes his mark for the first time at the expense of the French; he will do justice later to our serious qualities. In his letters to his son, he has pictured himself the first day he made his entrée into good society, still covered with the rust of Cambridge, shamefaced, embarrassed, silent; and, finally, forcing his courage with both hands to say to a beautiful woman near him, "Madame, don't you find it very warm to-day?" But Lord Chesterfield told his son that to encourage him, and to show what it is necessary to pass through. He

makes himself an example to embolden him, and to draw the boy more readily to him. I shall be careful not to take his word for this anecdote. If he was for a moment embarrassed in the world, the moment was assuredly very short, nor was he much concerned with it.

Immediately on the death of Queen Anne, Chesterfield hailed the accession of the House of Hanover, of which he became an avowed champion. He had at first a seat in the House of Commons, and made his début there with fair credit. But a circumstance, in appearance frivolous, kept him, it is said, in check, and in some measure paralyzed his eloquence. One of the members of the House, who was distinguished by no talent of a superior order, had that of imitating and counterfeiting to perfection the orators to whom he replied. Chesterfield was afraid of ridicule; it was one of his weaknesses, and he kept silence more than he otherwise would have done for fear of giving occasion for the exercise of his colleague and opponent's talent. He inherited a large property on the death of his father, and was raised to the Upper House, which was, perhaps, a better setting for the grace, finish, and urbanity of his eloquence. He found no comparison between the two scenes with regard to the importance of the debates and the political influence to be acquired.

"It is surprising," he said later of Pitt, at the time when that great orator consented to enter the Upper House as Lord Chatham, "it is surprising that a man in the plenitude of his power, at the very moment when his ambition has obtained the most complete triumph, should leave the House which procured him that power, and which alone could ensure its maintenance, to retire into that Hospital for Incurables, the House of Lords."

It is not my intention here to estimate the political career of Lord Chesterfield. Nevertheless, if I hazarded a judgment upon it as a whole, I should say that his ambition was never wholly satisfied, and that the brilliant distinctions with which his public life was filled, covered, at bottom, many lost desires and the decay of many hopes. Twice, in the two decisive circumstances of his political life, he failed. Young, and in the first heat of ambition, he took an early opportunity of staking his odds on the side of the heir presumptive to the throne, who became George II. He was one of those who, at the accession of that prince, counted most surely upon his favor, and upon enjoying a share of power. But this clever man, wishing to turn himself to the rising sun,

knew not how to accomplish it with perfect justice; he had played court to the prince's mistress, believing in her destined influence, and he had neglected the legitimate wife, the future queen, who alone had the real power. Queen Caroline never pardoned him, and this was the first check in the political fortune of Lord Chesterfield, then thirty-three years old, and in the full flush of hope. He was in too great a hurry and took the wrong road. Robert Walpole, less active, and with less apparent skill, took his measures and made his calculations better.

Thrown with eclat into the opposition, especially from 1732, the time when he had to cease his court duties, Lord Chesterfield worked with all his might for ten years for the downfall of Walpole, which did not take place until 1742. But even then he inherited none of his power, and he remained out of the new ministries. When two years afterwards, in 1744, he became one of the administration, first as embassador to The Hague and Viceroy of Ireland, then as Secretary of State and member of the Cabinet (1746–48), the honor was more nominal than real. In a word, Lord Chesterfield, at all times a noted politician in his own country, whether as one of the chiefs of the opposition, or as a clever diplomatist, was never a powerful, or even a very influential minister.

In politics he certainly possessed that far-sightedness and those glimpses into the future which belong to very wide intelligence, but he possessed those qualities to a much greater degree than the patient perseverance and constant practical firmness that are so necessary to the members of a government. It may truly be said of him, as of Rochefoucauld, that politics served to make an accomplished moralist of the imperfect man of action.

In 1744, when he was only fifty years of age, his political ambition seemed, in part, to have died out, and the indifferent state of his health left him to choose a private life. And then the object of his secret ideal and his real ambition we know now. Before his marriage he had, about the year 1732, by a French lady (Mdme. du Bouchet) whom he met in Holland, a natural son, to whom he was tenderly attached. He wrote to this son, in all sincerity, "From the first day of your life, the dearest object of mine has been to make you as perfect as the weakness of human nature will allow." Towards the education of this son all his wishes, all his affectionate and worldly predilections tended. And whether Viceroy of Ireland or Secretary of

State in London, he found time to write long letters full of minute details to him to instruct him in small matters and to perfect him in mind and manner.

The Chesterfield, then, that we love especially to study is the man of wit and experience, who knew all the affairs and passed through all phases of political and public life only to find out its smallest resources, and to tell us the last mot; he who from his youth was the friend of Pope and Bolingbroke, the introducer into England of Montesquieu and Voltaire, the correspondent of Fontenelle and Mdme. de Teucin, he whom the Academy of Inscriptions placed among its members, who united the wit of the two nations, and who, in more than one intellectual essay, but particularly in his letters to his son, shows himself to us as a moralist as amiable as he is consummate, and one of the masters of life. It is the Rochefoucauld of England of whom we speak. Montesquieu, after the publication of L'Esprit des Lois, wrote to the Abbé de Guasco, who was then in England — " Tell my Lord Chesterfield that nothing is so flattering to me as his approbation; but that, though he is reading my work for the third time, he will only be in a better position to point out to me what wants correcting and rectifying in it; nothing could be more instructive to me than his observations and his critique." It was Chesterfield who, speaking to Montesquieu one day of the readiness of the French for revolutions, and their impatience at slow reforms, spoke this sentence, which is a résumé of our whole history: "You French know how to make barricades, but you never raise barriers."

Lord Chesterfield certainly appreciated Voltaire; he remarked, à propos of the "Siècle de Louis XIV.," "Lord Bolingbroke had taught me how to read history, Voltaire teaches me how it should be written." But, at the same time, with that practical sense which rarely abandons men of wit on the other side of the straits, he felt the imprudences of Voltaire, and disapproved of them. When he was old, and living in retirement, he wrote to a French lady on the subject thus:—

"Your good authors are my principal resource: Voltaire especially charms me, with the exception of his impiety, with which he cannot help seasoning all that he writes, and which he would do better carefully to suppress, for one ought not to disturb established order. 'Let every one think as he will, or rather as he can, but let him not communicate his ideas if they are of a nature to trouble the peace of society.'"

What he said then, in 1768, Chesterfield had already said more than twenty years previously, writing to the younger Crébillon, a singular correspondent and a singular confidant in point of morality. Voltaire was under consideration, on account of his tragedy of "Mahomet," and the daring ideas it contains:—

"What I do not pardon him for, and that which is not deserving of pardon in him," wrote Chesterfield to Crébillon, "is his desire to propagate a doctrine as pernicious to domestic society as contrary to the common religion of all countries. I strongly doubt whether it is permissible for a man to write against the worship and belief of his country, even if he be fully persuaded of its error, on account of the trouble and disorder it might cause; but I am sure that it is in no wise allowable to attack the foundations of true morality, and to break necessary bonds which are already too weak to keep men in the path of duty."

Chesterfield, in speaking thus, was not mistaken as to the great inconsistency of Voltaire. His inconsistency, in a few words, was this: Voltaire, who looked upon men as fools or children, and who could never laugh at them enough, at the same time put loaded firearms into their hands, without troubling himself as to the use they would put them to.

Lord Chesterfield himself, in the eyes of the Puritans of his country, has been accused, I should state here, of a breach of morality in the letters addressed to his son. The strict Johnson, who was not impartial on the subject, and who thought he had cause of complaint against Chesterfield, said, when the letters were published, that "they taught the morals of a courtesan, and the manners of a dancing master."

Such a judgment is supremely unjust, and if Chesterfield, in particular instances, insists upon graces of manner at any price, it is because he has already provided for the more solid parts of education, and because his pupil is not in the least danger of sinning on the side which makes man respectable, but rather on that which renders him agreeable. Although more than one passage in these letters may seem very strange, coming from a father to a son, the whole is animated with a true spirit of tenderness and wisdom. If Horace had had a son, I imagine he would not have written to him very differently.

The letters begin with the A B C of education and instruction. Chesterfield teaches his son in French the rudiments of mythology and history. I do not regret the publication of these

first letters. He lets slip some very excellent advice in those early pages. The little Stanhope is no more than eight years old when his father suits a little rhetoric to his juvenile understanding, and tries to show him how to use good language, and to express himself well. He especially recommends to him attention in all that he does, and he gives the word its full value. It is attention alone, he says, which fixes objects in the memory. "There is no surer mark of a mean and meagre intellect in the world than inattention. All that is worth the trouble of doing at all deserves to be done well, and nothing can be well done without attention." This precept he incessantly repeats, and varies the application of it as his pupil grows, and is in a condition to comprehend it to its fullest extent. Whether pleasure or study, everything one does must be well done, done entirely and at its proper time, without allowing any distraction to intervene. "When you read Horace pay attention to the accuracy of his thoughts, to the elegance of his diction, and to the beauty of his poetry, and do not think of the 'De Homine et Cive' of Puffendorf; and when you read Puffendorf do not think of Mdme. de St. Germain; nor of Puffendorf when you speak to Mdme. de St. Germain." But this strong and easy subjugation of the order of thought to the will only belongs to great or very good intellects. M. Royer-Collard used to say that "what was most wanting in our day was respect in the moral disposition, and attention in the intellectual." Lord Chesterfield, in a less grave manner, might have said the same thing. He was not long in finding out what was wanting in this child whom he wished to bring up; whose bringing up was, indeed, the end and aim of his life. "On sounding your character to its very depths," he said to him, "I have not, thank God, discovered any vice of heart or weakness of head so far; but I have discovered idleness, inattention, and indifference, defects which are only pardonable in the aged, who, in the decline of life, when health and spirits give way, have a sort of right to that kind of tranquillity. But a young man ought to be ambitious to shine and excel." And it is precisely this sacred fire, this lightning, that makes the Achilles, the Alexanders, and the Cæsars to be the first in every undertaking, this motto of noble hearts and of eminent men of all kinds, that nature had primarily neglected to place in the honest but thoroughly mediocre soul of the younger Stanhope: "You appear to want," said his father, "that vivida

vis animi which excites the majority of young men to please, to strive, and to outdo others." "When I was your age," he says again, "I should have been ashamed for another to know his lesson better, or to have been before me in a game, and I should have had no rest till I had regained the advantage." All this little course of education by letters offers a sort of continuous dramatic interest; we follow the efforts of a fine distinguished energetic nature as Lord Chesterfield's was, engaged in a contest with a disposition honest but indolent, with an easy and dilatory temperament, from which it would, at any expense, form a masterpiece accomplished, amiable, and original, and with which it only succeeded in making a sort of estimable copy. What sustains and almost touches the reader in this strife, where so much art is used, and where the inevitable counsel is the same beneath all metamorphoses, is the true fatherly affection which animates and inspires the delicate and excellent master, as patient as he is full of vigor, lavish in resources and skill, never discouraged, untiring in sowing elegances and graces on this infertile soil. Not that this son, the object of so much culture and zeal, was in any way unworthy of his father. It has been pretended that there could be no one duller or more sullen than he was, and Johnson is quoted in support of the statement. There are caricatures which surpass the truth. It appears from the best authorities, that Mr. Stanhope, without being a model of grace, had the air of a man who had been well brought up, and was polite and agreeable. But do you not think that that is the most grievous part of all? It would have been better worth while, almost, to have totally failed, and to have only succeeded in making an original in the inverse sense, rather than with so much care and expense to have produced nothing more than an ordinary and insignificant man of the world, one of those about whom it suffices to say, there is nothing to be said of them; he had cause to be truly grieved and pity himself for his work, if he were not a father.

Lord Chesterfield had early thought of France to polish his son, and to give him that courtesy which cannot be acquired late in life. In private letters written to a lady at Paris, whom I believe to be Mdme. de Monconseil, we see that he had thought of sending him to France from his childhood.

"I have a boy," he wrote to this friend, "who is now thirteen years old: I freely confess to you that he is not legitimate; but his mother was well born and was kinder to me than I deserved. As to the boy, perhaps it is partiality, but I think him amiable: he has a pretty face; he has much sprightliness, and I think intelligence, for his age. He speaks French perfectly; he knows a good deal of Latin and Greek, and he has ancient and modern history at his fingers' ends. He is at school at present, but as they never dream here of forming the manners of young people, and they are almost all foolish, awkward, and unpolished, in short such as you see them when they come to Paris at the age of twenty or twenty-one, I do not wish my boy to remain here to acquire such bad habits; for this reason, when he is fourteen I think of sending him to Paris. As I love the child dearly, and have set myself to make something good of him, as I believe he has the stuff in him, my idea is to unite in him what has never been found in one person before—I mean the best qualities of the two nations."

And he enters into the details of his plan, and the means he thinks of using; a learned Englishman every morning, a French teacher after dinner, but above all the help of the fashionable world and good society. The war which broke out between France and England postponed this plan, and the young man did not make his début in Paris until 1751, when he was nineteen years old, and had finished his tour through Switzerland, Germany, and Italy.

Everything has been arranged by the most attentive of fathers for his success and well-being upon this novel scene. The young man is placed at the Academy with M. de la Guérinière; the morning he devotes to study, and the rest of the time is to be consecrated to the world. "Pleasure is now the last branch of your education," this indulgent father writes; "it will soften and polish your manners, it will incite you to seek and finally to acquire graces." Upon this last point he is exacting, and shows no quarter. Graces! he returns continually to them, for without them all effort is vain. "If they are not natural to you, cultivate them," he cries. He indeed speaks confidently; as if to cultivate graces, it is not necessary to have them already!

Three ladies, friends of his father, are especially charged to watch over and guide the young man at his début; they are his *gouvernantes;* Mdme. de Monconseil, Lady Hervey, and Mdme. du Bocage. But these introducers appear essential for the first time only; the young man must afterwards depend upon himself, and

choose some charming and more familiar guide. Upon this delicate subject of woman, Lord Chesterfield breaks the ice: "I shall not talk to you on this subject like a theologian, or a moralist, or a father," he says: "I set aside my age, and only take yours into consideration. I wish to speak to you as one man of pleasure would to another if he has taste and spirit." And he expresses himself in consequence, stimulating the young man as much as possible towards polite arrangements and delicate pleasures, to draw him from common and coarse habits. His principle is that "a polite arrangement becomes a gallant man." All his morality on this point is summed up in a line of Voltaire:—

« Il n'est jamais de mal en bonne compagnie.»

It is at these sentences more especially that the modesty of the grave Johnson is put to the blush; ours is content to smile at them.

The serious and frivolous are perpetually mingling in these letters. Marcel, the dancing master, is very often recommended; Montesquieu no less. The Abbé de Guasco, a sort of toady to Montesquieu, is a useful personage for introductions. "Between you and me," writes Chesterfield, "he has more knowledge than genius; but a clever man knows how to make use of everything, and every man is good for something. As to the Président of Montesquieu, he is in all respects a precious acquaintance; he has genius, with the most extensive reading in the world. Drink of this fountain as much as possible."

Of authors, those whom Chesterfield particularly recommends at this time, and those whose names occur most frequently in his counsels, are La Rochefoucauld and La Bruyère. "If you read some of La Rochefoucauld's maxims in the morning, consider them, examine them well, and compare them with the originals you meet in the evening. Read La Bruyère in the morning, and see in the evening if his portraits are correct." But these guides, excellent as they are, have no other use by themselves than that of a map. Without personal observation and experience, they would be useless, and would even be conducive to error, as a map might be if one thought to get from it a complete knowledge of towns and provinces. Better read one man than ten books. "The world is a country that no one has ever known by means of descriptions; each of us must traverse it in person to be thoroughly initiated into its ways."

Here are some precepts or remarks which are worthy of those masters of human morality:—

"The most essential of all knowledge, I mean the knowledge of the world, is never acquired without great attention, and I know a great many aged persons who, after having had an extensive acquaintance, are still mere children in the knowledge of the world."

"Human nature is the same all over the world; but its operations are so varied by education and custom that we ought to see it in all its aspects to get an intimate knowledge of it."

"Almost all men are born with every passion to some extent, but there is hardly a man who has not a dominant passion to which the others are subordinate. Discover this governing passion in every individual; search into the recesses of his heart, and observe the different effects of the same passion in different people. And when you have found the master passion of a man, remember never to trust to him where that passion is concerned."

"If you wish particularly to gain the good graces and affection of certain people, men or women, try to discover their most striking merit, if they have one, and their dominant weakness, for every one has his own, then do justice to the one, and a little more than justice to the other."

"Women, in general, have only one object, which is their beauty, upon which subject hardly any flattery can be too gross to please them."

"The flattery which is most pleasing to really beautiful or decidedly ugly women, is that which is addressed to the intellect."

On the subject of women, again, if he seems disdainful now and then, he makes reparation elsewhere; and, above all, whatever he thinks of them, he never allows his son to slander them too much. "You appear to think that from the days of Eve to the present time they have done much harm: as regards that lady I agree with you; but from her time history teaches you that men have done more harm in the world than women; and to speak truly, I would warn you not to trust either sex more than is absolutely necessary. But what I particularly advise you is this; never to attack whole bodies, whatever they may be."

"Individuals occasionally forgive, but bodies and societies never do."

In general, Chesterfield counsels his son to be circumspect and to preserve a sort of prudent neutrality, even in the case of

the knaves and fools with which the world abounds. "After their friendship there is nothing more dangerous than to have them for enemies." It is not the morality of Cato nor of Zeno, but that of Alcibiades, of Aristippus, or Atticus.

Upon religion he shall speak, in reply to some trenchant opinions that his son had expressed: "The reason of every man is and ought to be his guide; and I should have as much right to expect every man to be of my height and temperament as to wish that he should reason precisely as I do."

In everything he is of the opinion that the good and the best should be known and loved, but that it is not necessary to make oneself a champion for or against everything. One must know even in literature how to tolerate the weaknesses of others: "Let them enjoy quietly their errors both in taste and religion." Oh! how far from such wisdom is the bitter trade of criticism, as we do it!

He does not, however, advise lying; he is precise in this particular. His precept always runs thus, do not tell all, but never tell a lie. "I have always observed," he frequently repeats, "that the greatest fools are the greatest liars. For my part, I judge of the truth of a man by the extent of his intellect."

We see how easily he mixes the useful and the agreeable. He is perpetually demanding from the intellect something resolute and subtle, sweetness in the manner, energy at bottom.

Lord Chesterfield thoroughly appreciated the serious state of France and the dread events that the eighteenth century brought to light. According to him, Duclos, in his "Reflections," is right when he says that "a germ of reason is beginning to appear in France." "What I can confidently predict," adds Chesterfield, "is that before the end of this century the trades of king and priest will have lost half their power."

Our revolution has been clearly predicted by him since 1750.

He warned his son from the beginning against the idea that the French are entirely frivolous. "The cold inhabitants of the North look upon the French as a frivolous people who sing and whistle and dance perpetually; this is very far from being the truth, though the army of fops seems to justify it. But these fops, ripened by age and experience, often turn into very able men." The ideal, according to him, would be to unite the merits of the two nations; but in this mixture he still seems to lean towards France: "I have said many times, and I really think, that a Frenchman who joins to a good foundation of virtue, learning, and good sense, the manners and politeness of his country, has attained the perfection of human nature." He unites sufficiently well in himself the advantages of the two nations, with one characteristic which belongs exclusively to his race, there is imagination even in his wit. Hamilton himself has this distinctive characteristic, and introduces it into French wit. Bacon, the great moralist, is almost a poet by expression, one cannot say so much of Lord Chesterfield; nevertheless, he has more imagination in his sallies and in the expression of his wit than one meets with in St. Evremond and our acute moralists in general. He resembles his friend Montesquieu in this respect.

If in the letters to his son we can, without being severe, **lay hold** of some cases of slightly damaged morality, we should have to point out, by way of compensation, some very serious and really admirable passages, where he speaks of the Cardinal de Retz, of Mazarin, of Bolingbroke, of Marlborough, and of many others. It is a rich book. One cannot read a page without finding some happy observation worthy of being remembered.

Lord Chesterfield intended this beloved son for a diplomatic life; he at first found some difficulties in the way on account of his illegitimacy. To cut short these objections, he sent his son to parliament; it was the surest method of conquering the scruples of the court. Mr. Stanhope, in his maiden speech, hesitated a moment, and was obliged to have recourse to notes. He did not make a second attempt at speaking in public. It appears that he succeeded better in diplomacy, in those second-rate places where solid merit is sufficient. He filled the post of embassador extraordinary to the court of Dresden. But his health, always delicate, failed before he was old, and his father had the misfortune to see him die before him when he was scarcely thirty-six years old (1768). Lord Chesterfield at that time lived entirely retired from the world, on account of his infirmities, the most painful of which was complete deafness. Montesquieu, whose sight failed, said to him once, "I know how to be blind." But he was not able to say as much; he did not know how to be deaf. He wrote of it to his friends, even to those in France, thus: "The exchange of letters," he remarked, "is the conversation of deaf people, and the only link which connects them with society." He found his latest consolations in his pretty country house at Blackheath, which he had called by the French name

of Babiole. He employed his time there in gardening and cultivating his melons and pineapples; he amused himself by vegetating in company with them:—

"I have vegetated here all this year," he wrote to a French friend (September, 1753), "without pleasures and without troubles; my age and deafness prevented the first; my philosophy, or rather my temperament (for one often confounds them), guaranteed me against the last. I always get as much as I can of the quiet pleasures of gardening, walking, and reading, and in the meantime I await death without desiring or fearing it."

He never undertook long works, not feeling himself sufficiently strong, but he sometimes sent agreeable essays to a periodical publication, the World. These essays are quite worthy of his reputation for skill and urbanity. Nevertheless, nothing approaches the work — which was no work to him — of those letters, which he never imagined any one would read, and which are yet the foundation of his literary success.

His old age, which was an early one, lasted a long time. His wit gave a hundred turns to this sad theme. Speaking of himself and of one of his friends, Lord Tyrawley, equally old and infirm, "Tyrawley and I," he said, "have been dead two years, but we do not wish it to be known."

Voltaire, who under the pretense of being always dying, had preserved his youth much better, wrote to him on the twenty-fourth of October, 1771, this pretty letter, signed, "*Le vieux malade de Ferney*":—

"Enjoy an honorable and happy old age, after having passed through the trials of life. Enjoy your wit and preserve the health of your body. Of the five senses with which we are provided, you have only one enfeebled, and Lord Huntingdon assures me that you have a good stomach, which is worth a pair of ears. It will be perhaps my place to decide which is the most sorrowful, to be deaf or blind, or have no digestion. I can judge of all these three conditions with a knowledge of the cause; but it is a long time since I ventured to decide upon trifles, least of all upon things so important. I confine myself to the belief that, if you have sun in the beautiful house that you have built, you will spend some tolerable moments; that is all we can hope for at our age. Cicero wrote a beautiful treatise upon old age, but he did not verify his words by deeds; his last years were very unhappy. You have lived longer and more happily than he did. You have had to do neither with perpetual dictators nor with triumvirs. Your lot has been, and still is, one of

the most desirable in that great lottery where good tickets are so scarce, and where the Great Prize of continual happiness has never been gained by any one. Your philosophy has never been upset by chimeras which have sometimes perplexed tolerably good brains. You have never been in any sense a charlatan, nor the dupe of charlatans, and that I reckon as a rare merit, which adds something to the shadow of happiness that we are allowed to taste of in this short life."

Lord Chesterfield died on the twenty-fourth of March, 1773. In pointing out his charming course of wordly education, we have not thought it out of place even in a democracy, to take lessons of *savior vivre* and politeness, and to receive them from a man whose name is so closely connected with those of Montesquieu and Voltaire, who, more than any of his countrymen in his own time, showed singular fondness for our nation; who delighted, more than was right, perhaps, in our amiable qualities; who appreciated our solid virtues, and of whom it might be said, as his greatest praise, that he was a French wit, if he had not introduced into the verve and vivacity of his sallies that inexplicable something of imagination and color that bears the impress of his race.

Complete.

GEORGE EDWARD BATEMAN SAINTSBURY

(1845-)

FOR nearly two decades past, Saintsbury has been a favorite contributor to the English reviews. Much of his work as an essayist has been in the form of literary biographies and book reviews. As a book reviewer, he is much less aggressive than the slashing critics of the first half of the century. The change of style is as marked as the improvement of literary morality which made it possible. Saintsbury was born at Southampton, England, October 23d, 1845. After graduating from Merton College, Oxford, he taught the Classics at Elizabeth College in Guernsey, and was head master of the Elgin Educational Institute (1874-76). In 1876 he began in London the work as an editor and essayist he has since continued. Among his works are "English Worthies," "History of Elizabethan Literature," and "Essays on English Literature."

ON PARTON'S "VOLTAIRE"

OF NEARLY all the events of this remarkable life Mr. Parton has given an account, sometimes faulty in form, but sufficient and complete in substance. His book, though it may give some new facts, will, of course, not materially alter the idea of Voltaire to those who have previously studied his life and his works; but to those who do not already possess much knowledge of him it furnishes a convenient means of informing themselves. A book of thirteen hundred pages, deformed by American misspelling of the English tongue, and by references to "inflationists" and such-like irrelevances, not to mention constant expressions of the author's sentiments, which are, to say the least, unimportant, may seem a formidable undertaking. But its copiousness of incident and anecdote and its abundant quotations lighten the task of reading very considerably. At the end of it he must be a somewhat thoughtless reader (if, indeed, any such be likely to reach the end) who does not endeavor to make up for himself, assisted by the critical comments of those of Mr. Parton's predecessors to whom Pallas has been more kind, some notion of the singular personality here portrayed. Mr. Parton's own notion of that personality is decided enough. In his own marvelous language he tells us that Voltaire's empty sepulchre "is vocal, it is resonant, it booms and thunders over the earth." The superstition-crusher pushes everything and everybody else aside in his estimate. I think, for my own part, that from such a standpoint it is as difficult to judge Voltaire rightly as from that of my friend who called him a wretch, from that of Johnson, or from that of George III.

The truth seems to be that Voltaire was an extremely complicated character; the wonderful diversity of his literary work only reflects this complexity in part, though the one, no doubt, is the reason of the other. As I can hardly think of any man who displayed so many different forms of the literary faculty, so I can hardly think of any man, whether of letters or of business, who united the capacity and in a way the actual performance of so many different parts. Of his varied ability in practical administrative business there is proof almost as ample as of his varied ability in literary work. If he failed anywhere in what he undertook it was in diplomacy, and it is fair to remember that he had an antagonist to contend with there by whom it was no shame to be beaten. He has not, like Wordsworth, left us explicit intimations that in his own opinion his mission was to be Prime Minister, or Archbishop of Canterbury, or Commander in Chief, or Lord Chancellor, or all of them together. But I have no doubt that if the opportunity of any or all of these posts had come in his way he would have accepted it cheerfully, and would have performed the duties on the whole very well. The complementary defect of the quality of jack of all trades is well known. Voltaire suffered from it less than most people, but he did suffer from it. In no literary style, except in that of satirical prose fiction, or allegory of the social kind, can he be said to have attained the highest mastery. In work requiring research of any kind he was rather rapid than thorough, and he carried to excess the national habit of hasty deduction from insufficiently investigated premises. His moral and intellectual character, with which we are here more specially concerned, shows inconsistencies and blemishes of all kinds. Let us try and sum up what the devil's advocates say against him. He was an unscrupulous liar; he was extraordinarily vain; he was utterly destitute of reverence; he had an impure imagination which was

not checked by the slightest sense of even external decency; he was given to filthy lucre; he was spiteful and revengeful in the extreme toward his personal enemies. This is an ugly catalogue, and it is unfortunately true that no single article in it can be struck out entirely by the most uncompromising defender who knows and respects the facts. Mitigating pleas are all that is possible. His lying, which is a very unpleasant feature to English examiners of his character, has to be taken in conjunction with the fact that it was, so to speak, official and professional lying for the most part. The absurd and iniquitous political and social system of the time and country necessitated and in a manner recognized it. It was little more than the conventional "not guilty," not so much as the equally conventional "not at home." The charge of vanity must be admitted *sans phrase*, but it is not a very damning one. The lack of reverence also is not contestable, though there are some circumstances on the other side, notably the mountain-top story, which I have not noticed in Mr. Parton, and his lifelong cult of the starry heavens. This was, however, a distinct and inevitable consequence of his peculiar faculty of ridicule, which must also excuse as far as it can (and that is not very far) the uncleanness of his writings. I shall frankly own that that uncleanness is to me the most unpleasant variety of the disease that I know, with the possible exception of Dryden's. His carrying out of the maxim *non olet* is another blot on his character. There is nothing inexcusable, though perhaps there is something rather undignified, in a poet's making money by stockbroking and money changing; but the Hirsch matter, as to which something has been said already, cannot be defended, and the persistent way in which the author of "L'Homme aux Quarante Ecus" and a hundred other protests against financial mismanagement allowed himself to profit by contracts, loans, and so forth, where the profit was due to corrupt administration, is a still greater blot. With respect to Fréron, Desfontaines, et Cie., perhaps the worst thing that can be said about Voltaire is that in point of malignity there is sometimes nothing and generally very little to choose between himself and his adversaries.

And yet I have not the least intention of admitting that Voltaire was a wretch, or anything of the kind. All the worst of his faults were emphatically the faults of his time and his education. His merits, on the other hand, were personal and his

own, a distinction which, however hackneyed it may be, is almost the only one available in this world of ours. These merits Mr. Parton's book ought to make clear to everybody who is not hopelessly prejudiced. One of the chief of them was an extraordinary kindness of heart and affection for his friends, relations, and, indeed, everybody with whom he was not brought into violent collision. Madame du Châtelet and Madame Denis, the feminine plagues of the greater part of his long life, certainly had nothing to complain of in him. Notwithstanding his occasional fits of ill temper, all his servants and dependants were fond of him, and even the passionate Collini did not find those fits intolerable. His friendship for Thieriot, a person of very doubtful merit, and not unfrequently, as in the Desfontaines affair, and in the matter of the employments which Voltaire sought to procure for him from Richelieu, a troublesome and even treacherous friend, was unwearying. No one, even of his enemies, fails to acknowledge his remarkable benevolence to oppressed or unfortunate persons of every degree of merit, from Calas and Lally to La Barre and Desfontaines. Something, perhaps, must be allowed for his love of playing the grand seigneur in estimating his good deeds at Ferney; but even when that allowance is made, a solid amount will remain to his credit. Unscrupulous as he was in some ways in the getting of money, he neither spent it unworthily nor hoarded it for the mere sake of hoarding; his object being, as has been said, the securing of independence, which in his time and country no man, who was neither a priest nor a noble, could hope for without a competent estate. These things are, of course, perfectly well known to students of French literature and French history; but the general reader is less likely to be acquainted with them. Such a reader will find in Mr. Parton's book a good deal to amuse him, and a good deal to correct and heighten his idea of Voltaire as a man. It has been hinted that the merits of the book, as a literary commentary, are hardly equal to its merits as a repository of fact. In the former respect, however, as has also been suggested, more than one *scriptor haud paulo melior quam ego aut*, Mr. Parton has supplied the deficiency in English by anticipation, and it is therefore superfluous to say any more on that score.

From a review of Parton's "Life of Voltaire."

FRIEDRICH WILHELM JOSEPH VON SCHELLING

(1775–1854)

THE "highest relation of Art and Nature," writes Schelling, "is shown in this, that Art makes Nature the medium of manifesting the soul it contains." This strongly suggests, if it does not define, the central thought of the philosophical system he attempted to elaborate, progressively, in a series of works which when collected (1856–61) make fourteen volumes. It is the idea that nature and spirit are both realities, each distinct, but that both are the correlated parts of a whole which cannot exist in its completeness without both. Spirit is not considered in this system as distinct from, but rather as the inspiration of, Nature — as its "reason for existence" (*ratio essendi*). "Art" becomes thus the mode by which the human mind expresses the correlated harmony of the mind in nature. The thought thus developed by the philosophy of Schelling will do much to make intelligible the view of art which inspired Ruskin and his school in England.

Schelling was born in Würtemberg, January 27th, 1775. Receiving his own university education at Tübingen, he became a Professor at Jena (1798) and later at Würzberg, Munich, and Berlin. His university associations brought him into close relations with Hegel and the Schlegels, by whom he was influenced as he was, perhaps to a greater extent, by Fichte. Among his more notable works are "First Plan of a System of the Philosophy of Nature," "Transcendental Idealism," "Exposition of My System of Philosophy," "Philosophy and Religion," and "Human Freedom." He died in Switzerland, August 20th, 1854.

NATURE AND ART

NATURE in her wide circumference ever exhibits the higher with the lower: creating in Man the godlike, she elaborates in all her other productions only its material and foundation, which must exist in order that in contrast with it the Essence as such may appear. And even in the higher world of Man the great mass serves again as the basis upon which the godlike that is preserved pure in the few manifests itself in legislation, government, and the establishment of Religion. So that wherever Art works with more of the complexity of Nature, it may and must display together with the highest measure of Beauty also its groundwork and raw material as it were, in distinct appropriate forms.

Here first prominently unfolds itself the difference in Nature of the forms of Art.

Plastic Art, in the more exact sense of the term, disdains to give Space outwardly to the object, but bears it within itself. This, however, narrows its field; it is compelled, indeed, to display the beauty of the Universe almost in a single point. It must therefore aim immediately at the highest, and can attain complexity only separately and in the strictest exclusion of all conflicting elements. By isolating the purely animal in human nature it succeeds in forming inferior creations too, harmonious and even beautiful, as we are taught by the beauty of numerous Fauns preserved from Antiquity; it can, indeed, parodying itself like the merry spirit of Nature, reverse its own Ideal, and for instance, in the extravagance of the Silenic figures, by light and sportive treatment, appear freed again from the pressure of matter.

But in all cases it is compelled strictly to isolate the work, in order to make it self-consistent and a world in itself; since for this form of Art there is no higher unity, in which the dissonance of particulars should be melted into harmony.

Painting, on the contrary, in the very extent of its sphere, can better measure itself with the Universe, and create with epic profusion. In an "Iliad" there is room even for a Thersites, and what does not find a place in the great epic of Nature and History!

Here the Particular scarcely counts anything by itself; the Universe takes its place, and that, which by itself would not be beautiful, becomes so in the harmony of the whole. If in an extensive painting, uniting forms by the allotted space, by light, by shade, by reflection, the highest measure of Beauty were everywhere employed, the result would be the most unnatural monotony; for, as Winckelmann says, the highest idea of Beauty is everywhere one and the same, and scarce admits of variation. The detail would be preferred to the whole, where, as in every case in which the whole is formed by multiplicity, the detail must be subordinate to it.

but cannot overflow its banks. Otherwise, this striving after moderation would resemble only those shallow moralists, who, the more readily to dispose of Man, prefer to mutilate his nature; and who have so entirely removed every positive element from actions, that the people gloat over the spectacle of great crimes, in order to refresh themselves at last with the view of something positive.

In Nature and Art the Essence strives first after actualization, or exhibition of itself in the Particular. Thus in each the utmost severity is manifested at the commencement; for without bound, the boundless could not appear; without severity, gentleness could not exist; and if unity is to be perceptible, it can only be through particularity, detachment, and opposition. In the beginning, therefore, the creative spirit shows itself entirely lost in its form, inaccessibly shut up, and even in its grandeur still harsh. But the more it succeeds in uniting its entire fullness in one product, the more it gradually relaxes from its severity; and where it has fully developed the form, so as to rest contented and self-collected in it, it seems to become cheerful, and begins to move in gentle lines. This is the period of its fairest maturity and blossom, in which the pure vessel has arrived at perfection; the spirit of Nature becomes free from its bonds, and feels its relationship to the soul. As by a gentle morning blush stealing over the whole form, the coming soul announces itself; it is not yet present, but everything prepares for its reception, by the delicate play of gentle movements; the rigid outlines melt and temper themselves into flexibility; a lovely essence, neither sensuous nor spiritual, but which cannot be grasped, diffuses itself over the form, and entwines itself with every outline, every vibration of the frame.

This essence, not to be seized, as we have already remarked, but yet perceptible to all, is what the language of the Greeks designated by the name Charis, ours as Grace.

Wherever, in a fully developed form, Grace appears, the work is complete on the side of Nature; nothing more is wanting; all demands are satisfied. Here, already, soul and body are in complete harmony; Body is Form, Grace is Soul, although not Soul in itself, but the Soul of Form, or the Soul of Nature.

Art may linger, and remain stationary at this point; for, already, on one side at least, its whole task is finished. The pure image of Beauty arrested at this point is the Goddess of Love.

In such a work, therefore, a gradation of Beauty must be observed, by which alone the full Beauty concentrated in the focus becomes visible; and from an exaggeration of particulars proceeds an equipoise of the whole. Here, then, the limited and characteristic finds its place; and theory at least should direct the painter, not so much to the narrow space in which the entire Beauty is concentrically collected, as to the characteristic complexity of Nature, through which alone he can impart to an extensive work the full measure of living significance.

Thus thought, among the founders of modern art, the noble Leonardo; thus Raphael, the master of high Beauty, who shunned not to exhibit it in smaller measure rather than to appear monotonous, lifeless, and unreal—though he understood not only how to produce it, but also how to break up uniformity by variety of expression.

For, although Character can show itself also in rest and equilibrium of form, yet it is only in action that it becomes truly alive.

By Character we understand a unity of several forces, operating constantly to produce among them a certain equipoise and determinate proportion, to which, if undisturbed, a like equipoise in the symmetry of the forms corresponds. But if this vital Unity is to display itself in act and operation, this can only be when the forces, excited by some cause to rebellion, forsake their equilibrium. Every one sees that this is the case in the Passions.

But here we are met by the well-known maxim of the theorists, which demands that Passion should be moderated as far as possible, in its actual outburst, that Beauty of Form may not be injured. But we think this maxim should rather be reversed, and read thus:—that Passion should be moderated by Beauty itself. For it is much to be feared that this desired moderation too may be taken in a negative sense—whereas, what is really requisite is, to oppose to Passion a positive force. For as Virtue consists, not in the absence of passions, but in the mastery of the spirit over them, so Beauty is preserved, not by their removal or abatement, but by the mastery of Beauty over them.

The forces of Passion must actually show themselves—it must be seen that they are prepared to rise in mutiny, but are kept down by the power of Character, and break against the forms of firmly founded Beauty, as the waves of a stream that just fills,

But the beauty of the Soul in itself, joined to sensuous Grace, is the highest apotheosis of Nature.

The spirit of Nature is only in appearance opposed to the Soul; essentially, it is the instrument of its revelation; it brings about indeed the antagonism that exists in all things, but only that the one essence may come forth, as the utmost benignity, and the reconciliation of all the forces.

All other creatures are driven by the mere force of Nature, and through it maintain their individuality; in Man alone, as the central point, arises the soul, without which the world would be like the natural universe without the sun.

The Soul in Man, therefore, is not the principle of individuality, but that whereby he raises himself above all egoism, whereby he becomes capable of self-sacrifice, and of disinterested love, and (which is the highest) of the contemplation and knowledge of the Essence of things; and thus of Art.

In him it is no longer employed about Matter, nor has to do with it immediately, but only with the spirit (as the life) of things. Even while appearing in the body, it is yet free from the body, the consciousness of which hovers in the Soul in the most beauteous shapes only as a light, undisturbing dream. It is no quality, no faculty, nor anything special of the sort; it knows not, but is Science; it is not good, but Goodness; it is not beautiful, as body even may be, but Beauty itself.

Most readily, or most immediately, indeed, in a work of art, the soul of the artist is seen as invention, in the detail, and in the total result, as the unity that hovers over it in serene stillness. But the Soul must be visible in objective representation, as the primeval energy of thought, in portraitures of human beings, altogether filled by an idea, by a noble contemplation; or as indwelling essential Goodness.

Each of these finds its distinct expression even in the completest repose, but a more living one where the Soul can reveal itself in activity and antagonism; and since it is by the passions mainly that the force of life is interrupted, it is the generally received opinion, that the beauty of the Soul shows itself especially in its quiet supremacy amid the storm of the passions.

But here an important distinction is to be made. For the Soul must not be called upon to moderate those passions which are only an outbreak of the lower spirits of Nature, nor can it be displayed in antithesis with these; for where calm considerateness is still in contention with them, the Soul has not yet appeared: they must be moderated by unassisted Nature in Man, by the might of the Spirit. But there are cases of a higher sort, in which, not a single force alone, but the intelligent Spirit itself, breaks down all barriers; cases, indeed, where the Soul is subjected by the bond that connects it with sensuous existence, to pain, which should be foreign to its divine nature; where Man feels himself invaded and attacked in the root of his existence, not by mere powers of Nature, but by moral forces; where innocent error hurries him into crime, and thus into misery; where deep-felt injustice excites to rebellion the holiest feelings of humanity.

This is the case in all situations, truly, and in a high sense, tragical, such as the Tragedy of the Ancients brings before our eyes. Where blindly passionate forces are aroused, the collected Spirit is present as the guardian of Beauty; but if the Spirit itself be hurried away, as by an irresistible might, what power shall watch over and protect sacred Beauty? Or, if the Soul participate in the struggle, how shall it save itself from pain and from desecration?

Arbitrarily to limit the power of pain, of excited feeling, would be to sin against the very meaning and aim of Art, and would betray a want of feeling and Soul in the artist himself.

Already therein, that Beauty, based on grand and firmly established forms has become Character, Art has provided the means of displaying without injury to symmetry the whole intensity of Feeling. For where Beauty rests on mighty forms, as upon immovable pillars, a slight change in its relations, scarcely touching the form, causes us to infer the great force that was necessary in order to effect it. Still more does Grace sanctify pain. It is the essential nature of Grace that it does not know itself; but not being willfully acquired, it also cannot be willfully lost. When intolerable anguish, when even madness, sent by avenging Gods, takes away consciousness and reflection, Grace stands as a protecting demon by the suffering form, and prevents it from manifesting anything unseemly, anything discordant to Humanity; but if it fall, to fall at least a pure and unspotted victim.

Not yet the Soul itself, but the prophecy of it; Grace accomplishes by natural means, what the Soul does by a divine power, in transforming pain, torpor, even death itself, into Beauty.

IX—210

Yet Grace thus preserved amid the extremest discordance would be dead, without a transfiguration by the Soul. But what expression can belong to the Soul in this situation? It delivers itself from pain, and comes forth conquering, not conquered, by relinquishing its connection with sensuous existence.

It is for the natural Spirit to exert its energies for the preservation of sensuous existence, the Soul enters not into this contest; but its presence moderates even the storms of painfully struggling life. Outward force can take away only outward goods, but not reach the Soul; it can tear asunder a temporal bond, not dissolve the eternal one of a truly divine love. Not hard and unfeeling, nor wanting in love itself, the Soul, on the contrary, displays in pain this alone, as the sentiment that outlasts sensuous existence, and thus raises itself above the ruins of outward life or fortune in divine glory.

It is this expression of the Soul that the creator of the Niobe has shown us in this statue. All the means by which Art tempers even the Terrible, are here made use of. Mightiness of form, sensuous Grace, nay, even the nature of the subject-matter itself, softens the expression, since pain, transcending all expression, annihilates itself, and Beauty, which it seemed impossible to preserve from destruction, is protected from injury by the commencing torpor.

But what would it all be without the Soul, and how shall this manifest itself?

We see on the countenance of the mother, not grief alone for the already prostrated flower of her children; not alone deadly anxiety for the preservation of those yet remaining, and of the youngest daughter, who has fled for safety to her bosom; nor resentment against the cruel deities; least of all, as is pretended, cool defiance: all these we see, indeed, but not these alone, for, through grief, anxiety, and resentment streams, like a divine light, eternal love, as that which alone remains; and in this is preserved the mother, as one who was not, but now is a mother, and who remains united with the beloved ones by an eternal bond.

Every one acknowledges that greatness, purity, and goodness of soul have also their sensuous expressions. But how is this conceivable, unless the principle that acts in Matter be itself cognate and similar to Soul?

For the representation of the Soul there are again gradations

in Art according as it is joined with the merely Characteristic, or in visible union with the Charming and Graceful.

Who perceives not, in the tragedies of Æschylus, that lofty morality already predominant, which is at home in the works of Sophocles? But in the former it is enveloped in a bitter rind, and passes less into the whole work, since the bond of sensuous Grace is yet wanting. But out of this severity, and the still terrible charms of earlier Art, could yet proceed the grace of Sophocles, and with it the complete fusion of the two elements, which leaves us doubtful whether it is more moral or sensuous Grace that enchants us in the works of this poet.

The same is true of the plastic productions of the early and severe style, in comparison with the gentleness of the later.

If Grace, besides being the transfiguration of the spirit of Nature, is also the medium of connection between moral Goodness and sensuous Appearance, it is evident how Art must tend from all points towards it as its centre. This Beauty, which results from the perfect interpenetration of moral Goodness and sensuous Grace, seizes and enchants us when we meet it, with the force of a miracle. For, whilst the spirit of Nature shows itself everywhere else independent of the Soul, and, indeed, in a measure opposed to it, here, it seems, as if by voluntary accord, and the inward fire of divine love, to melt into union with it: the remembrance of the fundamental unity of the essence of Nature and the essence of the Soul comes over the beholder with sudden clearness: the conviction that all antagonism is only apparent, that Love is the bond of all things, and pure Goodness the foundation and substance of the whole Creation.

Here Art as it were transcends itself, and becomes means only. On this summit sensuous Grace becomes in turn only the husk and body of a higher life: what was before a whole is treated as a part, and the highest relation of Art and Nature is reached in this, that Art makes Nature the medium of manifesting the soul which it contains.

From "Relations of the Plastic Arts to Nature."

JOHANN CHRISTOPH FRIEDRICH VON SCHILLER

(1759–1805)

WHEN Goethe wrote "Faust," he left no question of his pre-eminence among German poets, but it can be questioned if even the idea which inspired Faust is as lofty or as deep as Schiller's idea that the "Spieltrieb" is the impulse of higher civilization. As a hypothesis, it begins where the "agnostic" theory of the "survival of the fittest" under pressure of environment ends. The Darwinian theory shows man compelled by necessity to develop so much intelligence as will save him from destruction. The theory of Schiller shows him led by his affections to develop into the Infinity beyond Necessity. The "pressure of environment" may account for the kraal of the Kaffir, and the snow hut of the Eskimo, but Schiller's hypothesis accounts for the Parthenon and the dome of St. Peter's. He saw that men improve most by doing not what they must, but what they love best, and he found his solution of the problem of progress in Liberty and Love. Children who mold the rude image of a man from clay after a rain, or savages who scrawl a drawing into the face of a cliff, are compelled by no other necessity than that of doing their own pleasure — of the "Spieltrieb" or "play impulse," acting under perfect liberty. But in such acts, Schiller saw the beginnings of all those arts which express the higher operations of mind.

As an essayist he is greatly superior to Goethe in the power of connected and sustained statement. Few writers in or out of Germany have equaled him in this. It is as remarkable in one sense as it is regrettable, that a poet who expresses himself through verse in thronging images of sensuous beauty should, in defining in prose the high ideas which animate his verse, become abstract and severe to the last degree. In any ten lines of the essays in which he is stating his conclusions, the strongest intellect can find material for longer meditation than busy readers are generally able to give to ten pages. Hence Schiller has never been popular as an essayist, and he is never likely to become so. But those who will make a serious attempt to respond to the severe demands he makes on all who come to him for instruction are not likely either to forget him as a teacher or to cease to thank him,

He was born at Marbach, Würtemberg, November 10th,* 1759. In 1780, after concluding his studies in medicine, he became regimental surgeon at Stuttgart, where in 1781 he published his first notable work, "The Robbers." Not only was he obliged to publish it at his own expense, but when it appeared, his "suzerain" and military superior, Duke Karl Eugen, of Würtemberg, ordered him as a regimental surgeon to write no more poetry. Seeing no recourse as a poet except to disobey as a military surgeon, Schiller did so. After being sentenced to a fortnight's arrest for his contumacy, he "fled" to Mannheim and afterwards to Darmstadt and Frankfort, living under assumed names until he had made his own so famous that even Duke Karl Eugen concluded it would not be advisable to subject him to further military discipline for writing poetry. Returning to Mannheim in 1783, Schiller left it for Leipsic in 1785. Growing tired successively of Leipsic and Dresden, he removed in 1787 to Weimar, where he made his home for many years and where he died May 9th, 1805. His association with Goethe began in 1794, and it was of great advantage to both. Under the influence of the increased confidence in himself resulting from Goethe's appreciation, Schiller wrote many of his best lyrics, including "The Song of the Bell,"— no doubt the best "ode" in the German language, if the word "ode" be understood in the modern sense. As a writer of odes (*carmina*) in the ancient sense, Schiller is not the equal of Goethe or of Heine. It was not that Schiller failed intellectually of fitness for the highest possible rank in poetry; the greatest poet of any age must be also its greatest musician; and in musical power over language, Schiller, who is second only to Goethe in everything else, is inferior also to Heine. Had it been otherwise he might easily have been the greatest poet, not only of Germany but of modern times, for his power of sustained thought and coherent expression surpasses that of Goethe. It is remarkable that the poems of Schiller should be classical in nearly everything but their melody, while those of Goethe, Teutonic in their spirit, derive their supreme charm from a closer approximation to the classical mode in melody than had been made by any other German poet.

W. V. B.

MAN AND THE UNIVERSE

WHILE man, in his first physical condition, is only passively affected by the world of sense, he is still entirely identified with it; and for this reason the external world, as yet, has no objective existence for him. When he begins in his

---

* The date is also given as November 11th, but the authorities favor the 10th.

æsthetic state of mind to regard the world objectively, then only is his personality severed from it, and the world appears to him an objective reality, for the simple reason that he has ceased to form an identical portion of it.

That which first connects man with the surrounding universe is the power of reflective contemplation. Whereas desire seizes at once its object, reflection removes it to a distance and renders it inalienably her own by saving it from the greed of passion. The necessity of sense which he obeyed during the period of mere sensations, lessens during the period of reflection: the senses are for the time in abeyance; even ever-reflecting time stands still whilst the scattered rays of consciousness are gathering and shape themselves; an image of the infinite is reflected upon the perishable ground. As soon as light dawns in man, there is no longer night outside of him; as soon as there is peace within him the storm lulls throughout the universe, and the contending forces of nature find rest within prescribed limits. Hence we cannot wonder if ancient traditions allude to these great changes in the inner man as to a revolution in surrounding nature, and symbolize thought triumphing over the laws of time, by the figure of Zeus, which terminates the reign of Saturn.

As long as man derives sensations from a contact with Nature, he is her slave; but as soon as he begins to reflect upon her objects and law she becomes her lawgiver. Nature, which previously ruled him as a power, now expands before him as an object. What is objective to him can have no power over him, for in order to become objective it has to experience his own power. As far and as long as he impresses a form upon matter, he cannot be injured by its effect; for a spirit can only be injured by that which deprives it of its freedom. Whereas he proves his own freedom by giving a form to the formless; where the mass rules heavily and without shape, and its undefined outlines are forever fluctuating between uncertain boundaries, fear takes up its abode; but man rises above any natural terror as soon as he knows how to mold it, and transform it into an object of his art. As soon as he upholds his independence towards phenomenal natures he maintains his dignity toward her as a thing of power, and with a noble freedom he rises against his gods. They throw aside the mask with which they had kept him in awe during his infancy, and to his surprise his mind perceives the reflection of his own image. The divine monster of the Oriental,

which roams about changing the world with the blind force of a beast of prey, dwindles to the charming outline of humanity in Greek fable; the empire of the Titans is crushed, and boundless force is tamed by infinite form.

But whilst I have been merely searching for an issue from the material world, and a passage into the world of mind, the bold flight of my imagination has already taken me into the very midst of the latter world. The beauty of which we are in search we have left behind by passing from the life of mere sensations to the pure form and to the pure object. Such a leap exceeds the condition of human nature; in order to keep pace with the latter, we must return to the world of sense.

Beauty is indeed the sphere of unfettered contemplation and reflection; beauty conducts us into the world of ideas, without, however, taking us from the world of sense, as occurs when a truth is perceived and acknowledged. This is the pure product of a process of abstraction from everything material and accidental, a pure object free from every subjective barrier, a pure state of self-activity without any admixture of passive sensations. There is, indeed, a way back to sensation from the highest abstraction; for thought teaches the inner sensation, and the idea of logical or moral unity passes into a sensation of sensual accord. But if we delight in knowledge we separate very accurately our own conceptions from our sensations; we look upon the latter as something accidental, which might have been omitted without the knowledge being impaired thereby, without truth being less true. It would, however, be a vain attempt to suppress this connection of the faculty of feeling with the idea of beauty, consequently we shall not succeed in representing to ourselves one as the effect of the other; but we must look upon them both together and reciprocally as cause and effect. In the pleasure which we derive from knowledge we readily distinguish the passage from the active to the passive state, and we clearly perceive that the first ends when the second begins. On the contrary, from the pleasure which we take in beauty, this transition from the active to the passive is not perceivable, and reflection is so intimately blended with feeling that we believe we feel the form immediately. Beauty is then an object to us, it is true, because reflection is the condition of the feeling which we have of it; but it is also a state of our personality (our *ego*) because the feeling is the condition of the idea we conceive of it: beauty is therefore

doubtless form, because we contemplate it, but it is equally life, because we feel it. In a word, it is at once our state and our act. And precisely because it is at the same time both a state and an act, it triumphantly proves to us that the passive does not exclude the active, neither matter nor form, neither the finite nor the infinite; and that consequently the physical dependence to which man is necessarily devoted does not in any way destroy his moral liberty. This is the proof of beauty, and I ought to add that this alone can prove it. In fact, as in the possession of truth or of logical unity, feeling is not necessarily one with the thought, but follows it accidentally; it is a fact which only proves that a sensitive nature can succeed a rational nature, and *vice versa;* not that they co-exist, that they exercise a reciprocal action one over the other; and, lastly, that they ought to be united in an absolute and necessary manner. From this exclusion of feeling as long as there is thought, and of thought so long as there is feeling, we should, on the contrary, conclude that the two natures are incompatible, so that in order to demonstrate that pure reason is to be realized in humanity, the best proof given by the analysis is that this realization is demanded. But, as in the realization of beauty or in æsthetic unity, there is a real union, mutual substitution of matter and of form, of passive and of active, by this alone is proved the compatibility of the two natures, the possible realization of the infinite in the finite, and consequently, also, the possibility of the most sublime humanity.

Henceforth we need no longer be embarrassed to find a transition from dependent feeling to moral liberty, because beauty reveals to us the fact that they can perfectly co-exist, and that to show himself a spirit, man need not escape from matter. But if, on one side, he is free, even in his relation with a visible world, as the fact of beauty teaches, and if, on the other side, freedom is something absolute and supersensuous, as its idea necessarily implies, the question is no longer how man succeeds in raising himself from the finite to the absolute, and opposing himself in his thought and will to sensuality, as this has already been produced in the fact of beauty. In a word, we have no longer to ask how he passes from virtue to truth which is already included in the former, but how he opens a way for himself from vulgar reality to æsthetic reality, and from the ordinary feelings of life to the perception of the beautiful.

Complete.

THE IMPULSE TO PLAY AS THE CAUSE OF PROGRESS

I HAVE shown that it is only the æsthetic disposition of the soul that gives birth to liberty. It cannot, therefore, be derived from liberty, nor have a moral origin. It must be a gift of nature; the favor of chance alone can break the bonds of the physical state and bring the savage to duty. The germ of the beautiful will find an equal difficulty in developing itself in countries where a severe nature forbids man to enjoy himself, and in those where a prodigal nature dispenses him from all effort; where the blunted senses experience no want, and where violent desire can never be satisfied. The delightful flower of the beautiful will never unfold itself in the case of the Troglodyte hid in his cavern always alone, and never finding humanity outside himself; nor among nomads, who, traveling in great troops, only consist of a multitude, and have no individual humanity. It will only flourish in places where man converses peacefully with himself in his cottage, and with the whole race when he issues from it. In those climates where a limpid ether opens the senses to the lightest impression, whilst a life-giving warmth develops a luxuriant nature, where even in the inanimate creation the sway of inert matter is overthrown, and the victorious form ennobles even the most abject natures; in this joyful state and fortunate zone, where activity alone leads to enjoyment, and enjoyment to activity, from life itself issues a holy harmony, and the laws of order develop life, a different result takes place. When imagination incessantly escapes from reality, and does not abandon the simplicity of nature in its wanderings, then and there only the mind and the senses, the receptive force and the plastic force, are developed in that happy equilibrium which is the soul of the beautiful and the condition of humanity.

What phenomenon accompanies the initiation of the savage into humanity? However far we look back into history, the phenomenon is identical among all people who have shaken off the slavery of the animal state: the love of appearance, the inclination for dress and for games.

Extreme stupidity and extreme intelligence have a certain affinity in only seeking the real and being completely insensible to mere appearance. The former is only drawn forth by the immediate presence of an object in the senses, and the second is reduced to a quiescent state only by referring conceptions to the

facts of experience. In short, stupidity cannot rise above reality, nor the intelligence descend below truth. Thus, in as far as the want of reality and attachment to the real are only the consequence of a want and a defect, indifference to the real and an interest taken in appearances are a real enlargement of humanity and a decisive step towards culture. In the first place it is the proof of an exterior liberty, for as long as necessity commands and want solicits, the fancy is strictly chained down to the real; it is only when want is satisfied that it develops without hindrance. But it is also the proof of an internal liberty, because it reveals to us a force which, independent of an external substratum, sets itself in motion, and has sufficient energy to remove from itself the solicitations of nature. The reality of things is effected by things; the appearance of things is the work of man, and a soul that takes pleasure in appearance does not take pleasure in what it receives, but in what it makes.

It is self-evident that I am speaking of æsthetical evidence different from reality and truth, and not of logical appearance identical with them. Therefore if it is liked it is because it is an appearance, and not because it is held to be something better than it is; the first principle alone is a play, whilst the second is a deception. To give a value to the appearance of the first kind can never injure truth, because it is never to be feared that it will supplant it — the only way in which truth can be injured. To despise this appearance is to despise in general all the fine arts of which it is the essence. Nevertheless, it happens sometimes that the understanding carries its zeal for reality as far as this intolerance, and strikes with a sentence of ostracism all the arts relating to beauty in appearance, because it is only an appearance. However, the intelligence only shown this vigorous spirit when it calls to mind the affinity pointed out further back. I shall find some day the occasion to treat specially of the limits of beauty in its appearance.

It is Nature herself which raises man from reality to appearance by endowing him with two senses which only lead him to the knowledge of the real through appearance. In the eye and the ear the organs of the senses are already freed from the persecutions of nature, and the object with which we are immediately in contact through the animal senses is remoter from us. What we see by the eye differs from what we feel; for the understanding to reach objects overleaps the light which separates us

from them. In truth, we are passive to an object: in sight and hearing the object is a form we create. While still a savage, man only enjoys through touch merely aided by sight and sound. He either does not rise to perception through sight, or does not rest there. As soon as he begins to enjoy through sight, vision has an independent value, he is æsthetically free, and the instinct of play is developed.

The instinct of play likes appearance, and directly it is awakened it is followed by the formal imitative instinct which treats appearance as an independent thing. Directly man has come to distinguish the appearance from the reality, the form from the body, he can analyze; in fact he has already done so. Thus the faculty of the art of imitation is given with the faculty of form in general. The inclination that draws us to it reposes on another tendency I have not to notice here. The exact period when the æsthetic instinct, or that of art, develops, depends entirely on the attraction that mere appearance has for men.

As every real existence proceeds from nature as a foreign power, whilst every appearance comes in the first place from man as a percipient subject, he only uses his absolute sight in separating semblance from essence, and arranging according to subjective law. With an unbridled liberty he can unite what nature has severed, provided he can imagine his union, and he can separate what nature has united, provided this separation can take place in his intelligence. Here nothing can be sacred to him but his own law; the only condition imposed upon him is to respect the border which separates his own sphere from the existence of things or from the realm of nature.

This human right of ruling is exercised by man in the art of appearance, and his success in extending the empire of the beautiful, and guarding the frontiers of truth, will be in proportion with the strictness with which he separates form from substance; for if he frees appearance from reality, he must also do the converse. But man possesses sovereign power only in the world of appearance, in the unsubstantial realm of imagination, only by abstaining from giving being to appearance in theory, and by giving it being in practice. It follows that the poet transgresses his proper limits when he attributes being to his ideal, and when he gives this ideal aim as a determined existence. For he can only reach this result by exceeding his right as a poet, that of encroaching by the ideal on the field of experience, and by pretending to determine real existence in virtue of a simple possi-

bility, or else he renounces his right as a poet by letting experience encroach on the sphere of the ideal, and by restricting possibility to the conditions of reality.

It is only by being frank or disclaiming all reality, and by being independent or doing without reality, that the appearance is æsthetical. Directly it apes reality or needs reality for effect, it is nothing more than a vile instrument for material ends, and can prove nothing for the freedom of the mind. Moreover, the object in which we find beauty need not be unreal if our judgment disregards this reality, for if it regards this the judgment is no longer æsthetical. A beautiful woman, if living, would no doubt please us as much and rather more than an equally beautiful woman seen in painting; but what makes the former please men is not her being an independent appearance, she no longer pleases the pure æsthetic feeling. In the painting, life must only attract as an appearance, and reality as an idea. But it is certain that to feel in a living object only the pure appearance requires a greatly higher æsthetic culture than to do without life in the appearance.

When the frank and independent appearance is found in man separately, or in a whole people, it may be inferred they have mind, taste, and all prerogatives connected with them. In this case the ideal will be seen to govern real life, honor triumphing over fortune, thought over enjoyment, the dream of immortality over a transitory existence.

In this case public opinion will no longer be feared, and an olive crown will be more valued than a purple mantle. Impotence and perversity alone have recourse to false and paltry semblance, and individuals as well as nations who lend to reality the support of appearance, or to the æsthetic appearance the support of reality, show their moral unworthiness and their æsthetical impotence. Therefore, a short and conclusive answer can be given to this question — How far will appearance be permitted in the moral world? It will run thus in proportion as this appearance will be æsthetical, that is, an appearance that does not try to make up for reality, nor requires to be made up for by it. The æsthetical appearance can never endanger the truth of morals; wherever it seems to do so the appearance is not æsthetical. Only a stranger to the fashionable world can take the polite assurances, which are only a form, for proofs of affection, and say he has been deceived, but only a clumsy fellow in good society calls in the aid of duplicity and flatters to become amiable.

The former lacks the pure sense for independent appearance; therefore he can only give a value to appearance by truth. The second lacks reality, and wishes to replace it by appearance. Nothing is more common than to hear depreciators of the times utter the paltry complaint that all solidity has disappeared from the world, and that essence is neglected for semblance. Though I feel by no means called upon to defend this age against these reproaches, I must say that the wide application of these criticisms shows that they attach blame to the age, not only on the score of the false, but also of the frank appearance. And even the exceptions they admit in favor of the beautiful have, for their object, less the independent appearance than the needy appearance. Not only do they attack the artificial coloring that hides truth and replaces reality, but also the beneficent appearance that fills a vacuum and clothes poverty; and they even attack the ideal appearance that ennobles a vulgar reality. Their strict sense of truth is rightly offended by the falsity of manners; unfortunately, they class politeness in this category. It displeases them that the noisy and showy so often eclipse true merit, but they are no less shocked that appearance is also demanded from merit and that a real substance does not dispense with an agreeable form. They regret the cordiality, the energy, and solidity of ancient times; they would restore with them ancient coarseness, heaviness, and the old Gothic profusion. By judgments of this kind they show an esteem for the matter itself unworthy of humanity, which ought only to value the matter inasmuch as it can receive a form and enlarge the empire of ideas. Accordingly, the taste of the age need not much fear these criticisms if it can clear itself before better judges. Our defect is not to grant a value to æsthetic appearance (we do not do this enough): a severe judge of the beautiful might rather reproach us with not having arrived at pure appearance, with not having separated clearly enough existence from the phenomenon, and thus established their limits. We shall deserve this reproach so long as we cannot enjoy the beautiful in living nature without desiring it; as long as we cannot admire the beautiful in the imitative arts without having an end in view; as long as we do not grant to imagination an absolute legislation of its own; and as long as we do not inspire it with care for its dignity by the esteem we testify for its works.

Complete.

the ingenious poet must have brought his wonderful inventions before the eyes of his audience in a manner equally bold and astonishing. Even Barthelemy's description of the Grecian stage is not a little confused, and the subjoined plan extremely erroneous; in the place which he assigns for the representation of the pieces in Antigone and Ajax, for instance, he is altogether wrong. The following observations will not therefore appear the less superfluous.

The theatres of the Greeks were quite open above, and their dramas were always acted in open day, and beneath the canopy of heaven. The Romans, at an after period, endeavored by a covering to shelter the audience from the rays of the sun; but this degree of luxury was hardly ever enjoyed by the Greeks. Such a state of things appears very inconvenient to us; but the Greeks had nothing of effeminacy about them, and we must not forget, too, the beauty of their climate. When they were overtaken by a storm or a shower, the play was of course interrupted; and they would much rather expose themselves to an accidental inconvenience, than, by shutting themselves up in a close and crowded house, entirely destroy the serenity of a religious solemnity, which their plays certainly were. To have covered in the scene itself, and imprisoned gods and heroes in dark and gloomy apartments with difficulty lighted up, would have appeared still more ridiculous to them. An action which so nobly served to establish the belief of the relations with heaven could only be exhibited under an unobstructed heaven, and under the very eyes of the gods, as it were, for whom, according to Seneca, the sight of a brave man struggling with adversity is a becoming spectacle. With respect to the supposed inconvenience, which, according to the assertion of many modern critics, was felt by the poets from the necessity of always laying the scene of their pieces before houses, a circumstance that often forced them to violate probability, this inconvenience was very little felt by tragedy and the older comedy. The Greeks, like so many southern nations of the present day, lived much more in the open air than we do, and transacted many things in public which usually take place with us in houses. For the theatre did not represent the street, but a place before the house belonging to it, where the altar stood on which sacrifices to the household gods were offered up. Here the women, who lived in so retired a manner among the Greeks, even those who were unmarried, might appear with-

AUGUST WILHELM VON SCHLEGEL

(1767–1845)

AUGUST WILHELM VON SCHLEGEL, celebrated for his essays on art and poetry, as well as for his own verses, was born at Hannover, September 8th, 1767. After studying at Göttingen and teaching in Amsterdam, he became professor of Literature and Æsthetics at Jena in 1798. Leaving this position in 1801, he taught at Berlin and spent several years in travel, remaining for some time in Sweden where he was "ennobled." In 1818 he became professor of Literature and Æsthetics at Bonn and remained there until his death, May 12th, 1845. His "Lectures on Dramatic Literature," delivered in Vienna, were published between 1809 and 1811. His first volume of poems appeared in 1800, and the first of his celebrated translations from Shakespeare in 1797.

THE GREEK THEATRE

WHEN we hear the word Theatre, we naturally think of what with us bears the same name; and yet nothing can be more different from our theatre than the Grecian, in every part of its construction. If in reading the Grecian pieces we associate our own stage with them, the light in which we shall view them must be false in every respect.

The accurate mathematical dimensions of the principal part of it are to be found in Vitruvius, who also distinctly points out the great difference between the Greek and Roman theatres. But these and similar passages of the ancient writers have been most perversely interpreted by architects unacquainted with the ancient dramatists; and the philologists on the other hand, who were altogether ignorant of architecture, have also fallen into egregious errors. The ancient dramatists are still, therefore, altogether in want of that sort of illustration which relates to scenic regulation. In many tragedies I conceive that my ideas on this subject are sufficiently clear; but others again present difficulties which are not so easily solved. We find ourselves most at a loss in figuring to ourselves the representation of the pieces of Aristophanes;

out impropriety. Neither was it impossible for them to give a view of the interior of the houses; and this was effected, as we shall immediately see, by means of the encyclema.

But the principal reason for this observance was that publicity, according to the republican nations of the Greeks, was essential to a grave and important transaction. This is clearly proved by the presence of the chorus, whose remaining on many occasions, when secret transactions were going on, has been judged of according to rules of propriety inapplicable to that country, and most undeservedly censured.

The theatres of the Ancients were, in comparison with the small scale of ours, of a colossal magnitude, partly for the sake of containing the whole of the people, with the concourse of strangers who flocked to the festivals, and partly to correspond with the majesty of the dramas represented in them, which required to be seen at a respectful distance. The seats of the spectators consisted of steps, which rose backwards round the semicircle of the orchestra (called by us the pit), so that they all could see with equal convenience. The effect of distance was remedied by an artificial heightening of the subject represented to the eye and ear, produced by means of masks, and contrivances for increasing the loudness of the voice, and the size of the figures. Vitruvius speaks also of vehicles of sound, distributed throughout the building; but the commentators are very much at variance with respect to them. We may without hesitation venture to assume that the theatres of the Ancients were constructed on excellent acoustical principles.

The lowest step of the amphitheatre was still raised considerably above the orchestra, and the stage was placed opposite to it, at an equal degree of elevation. The sunk semicircle of the orchestra contained no spectators, and was destined for another purpose. It was otherwise, however, with the Romans, but we are not at present considering the distribution of their theatres.

The stage consisted of a strip which stretched from one end of the building to the other, and of which the depth bore little proportion to this breadth. This was called the logeum, in the Latin, *pulpitum*, and the usual place for persons who spoke was in the middle of it. Behind this middle part, the scene went inward in a quadrangular form, with less depth, however, than breadth. The space here comprehended was called the proscenium. The remaining part of the logeum, to the right and left of the scene, had, both before the brink which adjoined the orchestra, and behind, a wall possessing no scenical decorations, but entirely simple, or at most architecturally ornamented, which was elevated to an equal height with the uppermost steps for the audience.

The decoration was contrived in such a manner, that the principal object in front covered the background, and the prospects of distance were given at two sides, the very reverse of the mode adopted by us. This had also its rules: on the left appeared the town to which the palace, temple, or whatever occupied the middle, belonged; on the right the open country, landscape, mountains, seashore, etc. The lateral decorations were composed of triangles, which turned on an axis fastened underneath; and in this manner the change of scene was effected. In the hindmost decoration it is probable that many things were exhibited in a bodily form which are only painted with us. When a palace or temple was represented, there appeared in the proscenium an altar, which answered a number of purposes in the performance of the pieces.

The decoration was for the most part architectural, but it was also not unfrequently a painted landscape, as in Prometheus, where it represented Caucasus; or in Philoctetus, where the desert island of Lemnos, with its rocks and his cave, were exhibited. It is clear, from a passage of Plato, that the Greeks, in the deceptions of theatrical perspective, carried things much further than we might have inferred from some wretched landscapes discovered in Herculaneum.

In the back wall of this scene there was a large main entrance, and two side entrances. It has been maintained that from them it might be discovered whether an actor played a principal or under part, as in the first case he came in at the main entrance, and in the second, at the side doors. But this should be understood with the distinction, that it must have been regulated according to the nature of the piece. As the hindmost decoration was generally a palace, in which the principal characters of royal descent resided, they naturally came through the great door, while the servants resided in the wings. There were two other entrances; the one at the end of the logeum, from whence the inhabitants of the town came; the other underneath in the orchestra, which was the side for those who had to come from a distance: they ascended a staircase of the logeum

opposite to the orchestra, which could be applied to all sorts of purposes, according to circumstances. The entrance, therefore, with respect to the lateral decorations, declared the place from whence the players were supposed to come; and it might naturally happen, that the principal characters were in a situation to avail themselves with propriety of the two last-mentioned entrances. The situation of these entrances serves to explain many passages in the ancient dramas, where the persons standing in the middle see some one advancing, long before he approaches them. Beneath the seats of the spectators a stair was somewhere constructed, which was called the Charonic, and through which the shadows of the departed, without being seen by the audience, ascended into the orchestra, and then, by the stair which we formerly mentioned, made their appearance on the stage. The nearest brink of the logeum sometimes represented the seashore. The Greeks were well skilled in availing themselves even of what lay beyond the decoration, and making it subservient to scenical effect. I doubt not, therefore, that in the "Eumenides" the spectators were twice addressed as an assembled people; first, by Pythia, when she calls upon the Greeks to consult the oracle; and a second time, when Pallas, by a herald, commands silence throughout the place of judgment. The frequent addresses to heaven were undoubtedly directed to a real heaven; and when Electra, on her first appearance, exclaims: "O holy light, and thou air which fillest the expanse between earth and heaven!" she probably turned towards the rising sun. The whole of this procedure is highly deserving of praise; and though modern critics have censured the mixture of reality and imitation, as destructive of theatrical illusion, this only proves that they have misunderstood the essence of the illusion which can be produced by an artificial representation. If we are to be truly deceived by a picture, that is, if we are to believe in the reality of the object which we see, we must not perceive its limits, but look at it through an opening; the frame at once declares it for a picture. In scenical decorations we are now unavoidably compelled to make use of architectural contrivances, productive of the same effect as the frames of pictures. It is consequently much better to avoid this, and to renounce the modern illusion, though it may have its advantages, for the sake of extending the view beyond the mere decoration. It was, generally speaking, a principle of the Greeks, that everything imi-

tated on the stage should, if possible, consist of actual representation; and only where this could not be done were they satisfied with a symbolical exhibition.

The machinery for the descent of the gods through the air, or the withdrawing of men from the earth, was placed aloft behind the walls of the two sides of the scene, and consequently removed from the sight of the spectators. Even in the time of Æschylus great use was made of it, as he not only brings Oceanus through the air on a griffin, but also introduces the whole choir of ocean nymphs, at least fifteen in number, in a winged chariot. There were hollow places beneath the stage, and contrivances for thunder and lightning, for the apparent fall or burning of a house, etc.

An upper story could be added to the furthermost wall of the scene, when they wished to represent a tower with a wide prospect, or anything similar. The encyclema could be thrust behind the great middle entrance, a machine of a semicircular form within, and covered above, which represented the objects contained in it as in a house. This was used for producing a great theatrical effect, as we may see from many pieces. The side door of the entrance would naturally be then open, or the curtain which covered it withdrawn.

A stage curtain, which, we clearly see from a description of Ovid, was not dropped, but drawn upwards, is mentioned both by Greek and Roman writers, and the Latin appellation, *aulæum*, is even borrowed from the Greeks. I suspect, however, that the curtain on the Attic stage was not in use at its commencement. In the pieces of Æschylus and Sophocles the scene is evidently empty at the opening as well as the conclusion, and therefore it did not require any contrivance for preventing the view of the spectators. However, in many of the pieces of Euripides, perhaps also in the "Œdipus Tyrannus," the stage is at once filled, and represents a standing group, who could not have been first assembled under the eyes of the spectators. It must be recollected, that it was only the comparatively small proscenium, and not the logeum, which was covered by the curtain; for, from its great breadth, to have attempted to screen the logeum would have been almost impracticable, without answering any good end.

The entrances of the chorus were beneath in the orchestra, in which it generally remained, and in which also it performed its solemn dance going backwards and forwards during the choral

songs. In the front of the orchestra, opposite to the middle of the scene, there was an elevation with steps, resembling an altar, as high as the stage, which was called thymele. This was the station of the chorus when it did not sing, but merely took an interest in the action. The leader of the chorus then took his station on the top of the thymele, to see what was passing on the stage, and to communicate with the characters. For though the choral song was common to the whole, yet when it entered into the dialogue one person spoke for the rest; and hence we are to account for the shifting from "thou" to "ye" in addressing them. The thymele was situated in the very centre of the building; all the measurements were calculated from it, and the semicircle of the amphitheatre was described round that point. It was, therefore, an excellent contrivance to place the chorus, who were the ideal representatives of the spectators, in the very situation where all the radii were concentrated.

From "Lectures on Dramatic Literature."
Black's translation.

ARTHUR SCHOPENHAUER

(1788–1860)

SCHOPENHAUER was born at Dantzic, Germany, February 22d, 1788. After a short novitiate in the office of a Hamburg merchant, where he had been placed by his father, he decided that he was unfit for business and determined to become great in literature. Studying at Göttingen and beginning his literary work with the deepest problems of philosophy, he published in 1813 his monograph "On the Fourfold Root of the Principle of Sufficient Reason," and in 1819 followed it with his most celebrated work, "The World as Will and Idea." After spending several years as a tutor at the University of Berlin, he went to Frankfort-on-the-Main, where he lived from 1831 until his death, September 21st, 1860. His shorter essays, which were published in 1851, are artistically the best which have come from any professional philosopher of Germany. Schopenhauer knows how to condense his thought to the utmost possible extent without making it obscure, and to expand as much as he pleases without making it so abstract that it ceases to be intelligible. His admirers are not generally inclined to admit that he is a humorist, but there is a latent suspicion of an undertone of humor in his deepest philosophy. His "pessimism" reduces itself to the proposition that the world as men make it "must be some kind of a mistake." At another time, he compares it to "a drop of water seen through a microscope, a single drop teeming with infusoria, or a speck of cheese full of mites invisible to the naked eye." This is pessimism, but, after all, it is much less bitter than that of Swift. Indeed, Schopenhauer's view of the world as it manifests itself through selfishness, is in no essential respect different from that presented in the opening chapters of the Book of Genesis, which account for human life and for the physical and moral conditions under which it is passed as the result of degeneracy or a "Fall" into conditions which destroy the wholly unfit and force those who are fit for survival to improve. When a world controlled by the impulses of selfish struggle is said to be either "a hell or a hospital," the pessimism of the definition depends on the conclusion from it. Those who argue from it to negation must become hopeless and useless. But while St. Paul and St. John agree with the most extreme modern pessimists in conceding the weariness and uselessness

of the life natural to the world, they made this conclusion merely the premise for asserting the infinite possibility of increasing efficiency, to be achieved through Faith and Love, operating as governing motives of action. Schopenhauer's theory that the body is "the Will objectified" is related on one side to the Pythagorean idea that the Will or the soul it represents, must necessarily take such shapes in animal life as represent its moral qualities; and on the other side it seems to bear a not less distinct relation to the Darwinian hypothesis of the gradual modification of species as a result of Will determining the habits of typical individuals of the class.

W. V. B.

BOOKS AND AUTHORSHIP

THERE are, first of all, two kinds of authors: those who write for the subject's sake, and those who write for writing's sake. While the one have had thoughts or experiences which seem to them worth communicating, the others want money, and so they write for money. Their thinking is part of the business of writing. They may be recognized by the way in which they spin out their thoughts to the greatest possible length; then, too, by the very nature of their thoughts, which are only half-true, perverse, forced, vacillating; again, by the aversion they generally show to saying anything straight out, so that they may seem other than they are. Hence their writing is deficient in clearness and definiteness, and it is not long before they betray that their only object in writing at all is to cover paper. This sometimes happens with the best authors: now and then, for example, with Lessing in his "Dramaturgie," and even in many of Jean Paul's romances. As soon as the reader perceives this, let him throw the book away; for time is precious. The truth is that when an author begins to write for the sake of covering paper he is cheating the reader; because he writes under the pretext that he has something to say.

Writing for money and reservation of copyright are, at bottom, the ruin of literature. No one writes anything that is worth writing, unless he writes entirely for his subject. What an inestimable boon it would be, if in every branch of literature there were only a few books, but those excellent! This can never happen, as long as money is to be made by writing. It seems as though the money lay under a curse; for every au-

thor degenerates as soon as he begins to put pen to paper in any way for the sake of gain. The best works of the greatest men all come from the time when they had to write for nothing or for very little. And here, too, that Spanish proverb holds good, which declares that honor and money are not to be found in the same purse —"*Honray provecho no caben en un saco.*" The reason literature is in such a bad plight nowadays is simply and solely that people write books to make money. A man who is in want sits down and writes a book, and the public is stupid enough to buy it. The secondary effect of this is the ruin of language.

A great many bad writers make their whole living by that foolish mania of the public for reading nothing but what has just been printed — journalists, I mean. Truly, a most appropriate name. In plain language it is journeymen, day-laborers!

Again, it may be said that there are three kinds of authors. First come those who write without thinking. They write from a full memory, from reminiscences; it may be, even straight out of other people's books. This class is the most numerous. Then come those who do their thinking whilst they are writing. They think in order to write, — and there is no lack of them. Last of all come those authors who think before they begin to write. They are rare.

Authors of the second class, who put off their thinking until they come to write, are like a sportsman who goes forth at random and is not likely to bring very much home. On the other hand, when an author of the third or rare class writes, it is like a *battue*. Here the game has been previously captured and shut up within a very small space, from which it is afterward let out, so many at a time, into another space, also confined. The game cannot possibly escape the sportsman; he has nothing to do but aim and fire, — in other words, write down his thoughts. This is a kind of sport from which a man has something to show.

But even though the number of those who really think seriously before they begin to write is small, extremely few of them think about the subject itself: the remainder think only about the books that have been written on the subject, and what has been said by others. In order to think at all, such writers need the more direct and powerful stimulus of having other people's thoughts before them. These become their immediate theme, and the result is that they are always under their influence, and

so never, in any real sense of the word, original. But the former are roused to thought by the subject itself, to which their thinking is thus immediately directed. This is the only class that produces writers of abiding fame.

It must, of course, be understood that I am speaking here of writers who treat of great subjects; not of writers on the art of making brandy.

Unless an author takes the material on which he writes out of his own head, that is to say, from his own observation, he is not worth reading. Book manufacturers, compilers, the common run of history writers, and many others of the same class, take their material immediately out of books; and the material goes straight to their finger tips without even paying freight or undergoing examination as it passes through their heads, to say nothing of elaboration or revision. How very learned many a man would be if he knew everything that was in his own books!

.   .   .   .

A book can never be anything more than the impress of its author's thoughts; and the value of these will lie either "in the matter about which he has thought," or in the form which his thoughts take; in other words, "what it is that he has thought about it."

The matter of books is most various; and various also are the several excellences attaching to books on the score of their matter. By matter I mean everything that comes within the domain of actual experience; that is to say, the facts of history and the facts of nature, taken in and by themselves and in their widest sense. Here it is the thing treated of which gives its peculiar character to the book; so that a book can be important, whoever it was that wrote it.

But in regard to the form, the peculiar character of a book depends upon the person who wrote it. It may treat of matters which are accessible to every one and well known; but it is the way in which they are treated, what it is that is thought about them, that gives the book its value; and this comes from its author. If, then, from this point of view a book is excellent and beyond comparison, so is its author. It follows that if a writer is worth reading, his merit rises just in proportion as he owes little to his matter; therefore, the better known and the more hackneyed this is, the greater he will be. The three great tragedians of Greece, for example, all worked at the same subject-matter.

So when a book is celebrated, care should be taken to note whether it is so on account of its matter or its form; and a distinction should be made accordingly.

Books of great importance on account of their matter may proceed from very ordinary and shallow people, by the fact that they alone have had access to this matter; books, for instance, which describe journeys in distant lands, rare natural phenomena, or experiments; or historical occurrences of which the writers were witnesses, or in connection with which they have spent much time and trouble in the research and special study of original documents.

On the other hand, where the matter is accessible to every one or very well known, everything will depend upon the form; and what it is that is thought about the matter will give the book all the value it possesses. Here only a really distinguished man will be able to produce anything worth reading; for the others will think nothing but what any one else can think. They will just produce an impress of their own minds; but this is a print of which every one possesses the original.

However, the public is very much more concerned to have matter than form; and for this very reason it is deficient in any high degree of culture. The public shows its preference in this respect in the most laughable way when it comes to deal with poetry; for there it devotes much trouble to the task of tracking out the actual events or personal circumstances in the life of the poet which served as the occasion of his various works; nay, these events and circumstances come in the end to be of greater importance than the works themselves; and rather than read Goethe himself, people prefer to read what has been written about him, and to study the legend of Faust more industriously than the drama of that name. And when Bürger declared that "people would write learned disquisitions on the question, who Leonora really was," we find this literally fulfilled in Goethe's case; for we now possess a great many learned disquisitions on Faust and the legend attaching to him. Study of this kind is, and remains, devoted to the material of the drama alone. To give such preference to the matter over the form is as though a man were to take a fine Etruscan vase, not to admire its shape or coloring, but to make a chemical analysis of the clay and paint of which it is composed.

The attempt to produce an effect by means of the material employed—an attempt which panders to this evil tendency of

the public—is most to be condemned in branches of literature where any merit there may be lies expressly in the form; I mean, in poetical work. For all that, it is not rare to find bad dramatists trying to fill the house by means of the matter about which they write. For example, authors of this kind do not shrink from putting on the stage any man who is in any way celebrated, no matter whether his life may have been entirely devoid of dramatic incident; and sometimes, even, they do not wait until the persons immediately connected with him are dead.

The distinction between matter and form to which I am here alluding, also holds good of conversation. The chief qualities which enable a man to converse well are intelligence, discernment, wit, and vivacity; these supply the form of conversation. But it is not long before attention has to be paid to the matter of which he speaks; in other words, the subjects about which it is possible to converse with him—his knowledge. If this is very small, his conversation will not be worth anything, unless he possesses the above-named formal qualities in a very exceptional degree: for he will have nothing to talk about but those facts of life and nature which everybody knows. It will be just the opposite, however, if a man is deficient in these formal qualities, but has an amount of knowledge which lends value to what he says. This value will then depend entirely upon the matter of his conversation; for, as the Spanish proverb has it, "*Mas sabe el necio en su casa, que el sabio en la ageno*"—a fool knows more of his own business than a wise man of others'.

THE VANITY OF EXISTENCE

THIS vanity finds expression in the whole way in which things exist: in the infinite nature of Time and Space, as opposed to the finite nature of the individual in both; in the ever-passing present moment as the only mode of actual existence; in the interdependence and relativity of all things; in continual becoming without ever being; in constant wishing and never being satisfied; in the long battle which forms the history of life, where every effort is checked by difficulties, and stopped until they are overcome. Time is that in which all things pass away; it is merely the form under which the Will to Live—the Thing in

Itself and therefore imperishable—has revealed to it that its efforts are in vain; it is that agent by which at every moment all things in our hands become as nothing, and lose any real value they possess.

That which has been exists no more; it exists as little as that which has never been. But of everything that exists you must say, in the next moment, that it has been. Hence something of great importance now past is inferior to something of little importance now present, in that the latter is a reality, and related to the former as something to nothing.

A man finds himself, to his great astonishment, suddenly existing, after thousands and thousands of years of nonexistence: he lives for a little while; and then, again, comes an equally long period when he must exist no more. The heart rebels against this, and feels that it cannot be true. The crudest intellect cannot speculate on such a subject without having a presentiment that Time is something ideal in its nature. This ideality of Time and Space is the key to every true system of metaphysics; because it provides for quite another order of things than is to be met with in the domain of nature. This is why Kant is so great.

Of every event in our life we can say only for one moment that it is; forever after, that it was. Every evening we are poorer by a day. It might, perhaps, make us mad to see how rapidly our short span of time ebbs away, if it were not that in the furthest depths of our being we are secretly conscious of our share in the inexhaustible spring of eternity, so that we can always hope to find life in it again.

Considerations of the kind touched on above might, indeed, lead us to embrace the belief that the greatest wisdom is to make the enjoyment of the present the supreme object of life; because that is the only reality, all else being merely the play of thought. On the other hand, such a course might just as well be called the greatest folly; for that which in the next moment exists no more, and vanishes utterly, like a dream, can never be worth a serious effort.

The whole foundation on which our existence rests is the present—the ever-fleeting present. It lies, then, in the very nature of our existence to take the form of constant motion, and to offer no possibility of our ever attaining the rest for which we are always striving. We are like a man running downhill, who cannot

keep on his legs unless he runs on, and will inevitably fall if he stops; or, again, like a pole balanced on the tip of one's finger; or like a planet, which would fall into its sun the moment it ceased to hurry forward on its way. Unrest is the mark of existence.

In a world where all is unstable, and naught can endure, but is swept onward at once in the hurrying whirlpool of change; where a man, if he is to keep erect at all, must always be advancing and moving, like an acrobat on a rope—in such a world, happiness is inconceivable. How can it dwell where, as Plato says, "continual Becoming and never Being" is the sole form of existence? In the first place, a man never is happy, but spends his whole life in striving after something which he thinks will make him so; he seldom attains his goal, and when he does, it is only to be disappointed; he is mostly shipwrecked in the end, and comes into harbor with masts and rigging gone. And then, it is all one whether he has been happy or miserable; for his life was never anything more than a present moment always vanishing; and now it is over.

At the same time it is a wonderful thing that, in the world of human beings as in that of animals in general, this manifold restless motion is produced and kept up by the agency of two simple impulses—hunger and the sexual instinct; aided a little, perhaps, by the influence of boredom, but by nothing else; and that, in the theatre of life, these suffice to form the *primum mobile* of how complicated a machinery, setting in motion how strange and varied a scene!

On looking a little closer, we find that inorganic matter presents a constant conflict between chemical forces, which eventually works dissolution; and on the other hand, that organic life is impossible without continual change of matter, and cannot exist if it does not receive perpetual help from without. This is the realm of finality; and its opposite would be an infinite existence, exposed to no attack from without, and needing nothing to support it; ἀεὶ ὡσαύτως ὄν, the realm of eternal peace; οὔτε γιγνόμενον οὔτε ἀπολλύμενον, some timeless, changeless state, one and undiversified; the negative knowledge of which forms the dominant note of the Platonic philosophy. It is to some such state as this that the denial of the Will to live opens up the way.

The scenes of our life are like pictures done in rough mosaic. Looked at close, they produce no effect. There is nothing beautiful to be found in them, unless you stand some distance off. So, to gain anything we have longed for is only to discover how vain and empty it is; and even though we are always living in expectation of better things, at the same time we often repent and long to have the past back again. We look upon the present as something to be put up with while it lasts, and serving only as the way toward our goal. Hence most people, if they glance back when they come to the end of life, will find that all along they have been living *ad interim;* they will be surprised to find the very thing they disregarded and let slip by unenjoyed was just the life in the expectation of which they passed all their time. Of how many a man may it not be said that hope made a fool of him until he danced into the arms of Death!

Then, again, how insatiable a creature is man. Every satisfaction he attains lays the seeds of some new desire, so that there is no end to the wishes of each individual Will. And why is this? The real reason is simply that, taken in itself, Will is the lord of all worlds; everything belongs to it, and therefore no one single thing can ever give it satisfaction, but only the whole, which is endless. For all that, it must rouse our sympathy to think how very little the Will, this lord of the world, really gets when it takes the form of an individual; usually only just enough to keep the body together. This is why man is so very miserable.

Life presents itself chiefly as a task—the task, I mean, of subsisting at all, *ganger sa vie.* If this is accomplished, life is a burden, and then there comes the second task of doing something with that which has been won—of warding off boredom, which, like a bird of prey, hovers over us, ready to fall wherever it sees a life secure from need. The first task is to win something; the second, to banish the feeling that it has been won; otherwise it is a burden.

Human life must be some kind of mistake. The truth of this will be sufficiently obvious if we only remember that man is a compound of needs and necessities hard to satisfy; and that even when they are satisfied, all he obtains is a state of painlessness, where nothing remains to him but abandonment to boredom. This is direct proof that existence has no real value in itself; for what is boredom but the feeling of the emptiness of life? If life—the craving for which is the very essence of our being—were possessed of any positive intrinsic value, there would be no such thing as boredom at all: mere existence would satisfy us in itself, and we should want for nothing. But as it is, we take no delight in existence except when we are struggling for something; and then distance and difficulties to be overcome make our goal look as though it would satisfy us—an illusion which vanishes when we reach it; or else when we are occupied with some purely intellectual interest—where in reality we have stepped forth from life to look upon it from the outside, much after the manner of spectators at a play. And even sensual pleasure itself means nothing but a struggle and aspiration, ceasing the moment its aim is attained. Whenever we are not occupied in one of these ways, but cast upon existence itself, its vain and worthless nature is brought home to us; and this is what we mean by boredom. The hankering after what is strange and uncommon—an innate and ineradicable tendency of human nature—shows how glad we are at any interruption of that natural course of affairs which is so very tedious.

That this most perfect manifestation of the Will to live, the human organism, with the cunning and complex working of its machinery, must fall to dust and yield up itself and all its strivings to extinction—this is the naïve way in which Nature, who is always so true and sincere in what she says, proclaims the whole struggle of this Will as in its very essence barren and unprofitable. Were it of any value in itself, anything unconditioned and absolute, it could not thus end in mere nothing.

If we turn from contemplating the world as a whole, and, in particular, the generations of men as they live their little hour of mock existence and then are swept away in rapid succession; if we turn from this, and look at life in its small details, as presented, say, in a comedy, how ridiculous it all seems! It is like a drop of water seen through a microscope, a single drop teeming with infusoria, or a speck of cheese full of mites invisible to the naked eye. How we laugh as they bustle about so eagerly, and struggle with one another in so tiny a space! And whether here, or in the little span of human life, this terrible activity produces a comic effect.

It is only in the microscope that our life looks so big. It is an indivisible point, drawn out and magnified by the powerful lenses of Time and Space.

Complete.

PARABLES

The Apple Tree and the Fir

A WIDESPREADING apple tree stood in full bloom, and behind it a straight fir raised its dark and tapering head. "Look at the thousands of gay blossoms which cover me everywhere," said the apple tree; "what have you to show in comparison? Dark green needles!" "That is true," replied the fir, "but when winter comes, you will be bared of your glory; and I shall be as I am now."

Complete.

The Young Oak

ONCE, as I was botanizing under an oak, I found among a number of other plants of similar height one that was dark in color, with tightly closed leaves and a stalk that was very straight and stiff. When I touched it, it said to me in firm tones: "Let me alone; I am not for your collection, like these plants to which nature has given only a single year of life. I am a little oak."

So it is with a man whose influence is to last for hundreds of years. As a child, as a youth, often even as a full-grown man, nay, his whole life long, he goes about among his fellows, looking like them and seemingly as unimportant. But let him alone; he will not die. Time will come and bring those who know how to value him.

Complete.

The Balloon Mystery

THE man who goes up in a balloon does not feel as though he were ascending; he only sees the earth sinking deeper and deeper under him.

This is a mystery which only those will understand who feel the truth of it.

Complete.

The Varnish of Nature

NATURE covers all her works with a varnish of beauty, like the tender bloom that is breathed, as it were, on the surface of a peach or plum. Painters and poets lay themselves out to take off this varnish, to store it up, and give it us to be enjoyed at our leisure. We drink deep of this beauty long before we enter upon life itself; and when afterward we come to see the works of nature for ourselves, the varnish is gone: the artists have used it up and we have enjoyed it in advance. Thus it is that the world so often appears harsh and devoid of charm, nay, actually repulsive. It were better to leave us to discover the varnish for ourselves. This would mean that we should not enjoy it all at once and in large quantities; we should have no finished pictures, no perfect poems; but we should look at all things in the genial and pleasing light in which even now a child of nature sometimes sees them—some one who has not anticipated his æsthetic pleasures by the help of art, or taken the charms of life too early.

Complete.

The Cathedral in Mayence

THE cathedral in Mayence is so shut in by the houses that are built round about it, that there is no one spot from which you can see it as a whole. This is symbolic of everything great or beautiful in the world. It ought to exist for its own sake alone, but before very long it is misused to serve alien ends. People come from all directions wanting to find in it support and maintenance for themselves; they stand in the way and spoil its effect. To be sure, there is nothing surprising in this, for in a world of need and imperfection everything is seized upon which can be used to satisfy want. Nothing is exempt from this service, no, not even those very things which arise only when need and want are for a moment lost sight of—the beautiful and the true, sought for their own sakes.

This is especially illustrated and corroborated in the case of institutions—whether great or small, wealthy or poor, founded, no matter in what century or in what land, to maintain and advance human knowledge, and generally to afford help to those intellectual efforts which ennoble the race. Wherever these institutions may be, it is not long before people sneak up to them under the pretense of wishing to further those special ends, while they are really led on by the desire to secure the emoluments which have been left for their furtherance, and thus to satisfy certain coarse and brutal instincts of their own. Thus it is that we come to have so many charlatans in every branch of knowledge. The charlatan takes very different shapes, according to circumstances; but at bottom he is a man who cares nothing about knowledge for his own sake, and only strives to gain the semblance of it that he may use it for his own personal ends, which are always selfish and material.

Complete.

THE FATE OF SAMSON

EVERY hero is a Samson. The strong man succumbs to the intrigues of the weak and the many; and if in the end he loses all patience, he crushes both them and himself. Or he is like Gulliver at Lilliput, overwhelmed by an enormous number of little men.

Complete.

ENLIGHTENED RATIONALISTS

A MOTHER gave her children Æsop's "Fables" to read, in the hope of educating and improving their minds; but they very soon brought the book back, and the eldest, wise beyond his years, delivered himself as follows: "This is no book for us; it's much too childish and stupid. You can't make us believe that foxes and wolves and ravens are able to talk; we've got beyond stories of that kind!"

In these young hopefuls you have the enlightened Rationalists of the future.

Complete.

CO-OPERATION AMONG PORCUPINES

A NUMBER of porcupines huddled together for warmth on a cold day in winter; but, as they began to prick one another with their quills, they were obliged to disperse. However, the cold drove them together again, when just the same thing
IX—212

3379

happened. At last, after many turns of huddling and dispersing, they discovered that they would be best off by remaining at a little distance from one another. In the same way the need of society drives the human porcupines together, only to be mutually repelled by the many prickly and disagreeable qualities of their nature. The moderate distance which they at last discover to be the only tolerable condition of intercourse, in the code of politeness and fine manners; and those who transgress it are roughly told — in the English phrase — "to keep their distance." By this arrangement the mutual need of warmth is only very moderately satisfied; but then people do not get pricked. A man who has some heat in himself prefers to remain outside, where he will neither prick other people nor get pricked himself.

Complete. All the foregoing were translated by T. B. Saunders.

OLIVE SCHREINER

(c. 1863-)

THE writings of Olive Schreiner are the firstfruits which modern Africa offers to world-literature. From the fall of the Greek civilization in Egypt and of the Roman in Numidia until our own times, the "Dark Continent" has produced nothing except a few Arab songs and stories to which not even the most strained courtesy can impute literary quality. Olive Schreiner's "Dreams," however, have in them the unmistakable signs of such genius as immortalizes whatever it inspires. They are strange and fanciful, but they will not easily be forgotten. She comes of the Boer stock of Cape Colony. Her father was a Lutheran minister at Cape Town, and all her work shows the impression of this heredity. "The Story of an African Farm," which she published in 1883, was an immediate success, but it was not until "Dreams" appeared in 1890 that the full strength of her genius was evident. She left Africa for Europe in 1883, and she has since spent most of her time in England. She married Mr. Cronwright in 1894. Her latest publication, "An English South African's View of the Situation" (1899), deals with the overthrow of the Boer republics by the English "Conservatives."

IN A RUINED CHAPEL

THERE are four bare walls; there is a Christ upon the walls, in red, carrying his cross; there is a Blessèd Bambino with the face rubbed out; there is a Madonna in blue and red; there are Roman soldiers and a Christ with tied hands. All the roof is gone; overhead is the blue, blue Italian sky; the rain has beaten holes in the walls, and the plaster is peeling from it. The Chapel stands here alone upon the promontory, and by day and by night the sea breaks at its feet. Some say that it was set here by the monks from the island down below, that they might bring their sick here in times of deadly plague. Some say that it was set here that the passing monk and friars, as they hurried by upon the roadway, might stop and say their prayers here. Now no one stops to pray here, and the sick come no more to be healed.

Behind it runs the old Roman road. If you climb it and come and sit there alone on a hot sunny day you may almost hear at last the clink of the Roman soldiers upon the pavement, and the sound of that older time, as you sit there in the sun, when Hannibal and his men broke through the brushwood, and no road was.

Now it is very quiet. Sometimes a peasant girl comes riding by between her panniers, and you hear the mule's feet beat upon the bricks of the pavement; sometimes an old woman goes past with a bundle of weeds upon her head, or a brigand-looking man hurries by with a bundle of sticks in his hand; but for the rest the Chapel lies here alone upon the promontory, between the two bays and hears the sea break at its feet.

I came here one winter's day when the midday sun shone hot on the bricks of the Roman road. I was weary, and the way seemed steep. I walked into the Chapel to the broken window, and looked out across the bay. Far off, across the blue, blue water, were towns and villages, hanging white and red dots, upon the mountain sides, and the blue mountains rose up into the sky, and now stood out from it and now melted back again.

The mountains seemed calling to me, but I knew there would never be a bridge built from them to me; never, never, never! I shaded my eyes with my hand and turned away. I could not bear to look at them.

I walked through the ruined Chapel, and looked at the Christ in red carrying his cross, and the Blessèd rubbed-out Bambino, and the Roman soldiers, and the folded hands, and the rod; and I went and sat down in the open porch upon a stone. At my feet was the small bay, with its white row of houses buried among the olive trees; the water broke in a long, thin, white line of foam along the shore; and I leaned my elbows on my knees. I was tired, very tired; tired with a tiredness that seemed older than the heat of the day and the shining of the sun on the bricks of the Roman road; and I lay my head upon my knees; I heard the breaking of the water on the rocks three hundred feet below, and the rustling of the wind among the olive trees and the ruined arches, and then I fell asleep there. I had a dream.

A man cried up to God, and God sent down an angel to help him; and the angel came back and said, "I cannot help that man."

God said, "How is it with him?"

And the angel said, "He cries out continually that one has injured him; and he would forgive him and he cannot."

God said, "What have you done for him?"

The angel said, "All——. I took him by the hand, and I said, 'See, when other men speak ill of that man do you speak well of him; secretly, in ways he shall not know, serve him; if you have anything you value share it with him; so, serving him, you will at last come to feel possession in him, and you will forgive.' And he said, 'I will do it.' Afterward, as I passed by in the dark of night, I heard one crying out, 'I have done all. It helps nothing! My speaking well of him helps me nothing! If I share my heart's blood with him, is the burning within me less? I cannot forgive; I cannot forgive! Oh, God, I cannot forgive!'

"I said to him, 'See here, look back on all your past. See from your childhood all smallness, all indirectness that has been yours; look well at it, and in its light do you not see every man your brother? Are you so sinless you have a right to hate?'

"He looked, and said, 'Yes, you are right; I, too, have failed, and I forgive my fellow. Go, I am satisfied; I have forgiven'; and he laid him down peacefully and folded his hands on his breast, and I thought it was well with him. But scarcely had my wings rustled and I turned to come up here, when I heard one crying out on earth again, 'I cannot forgive! I cannot forgive! Oh, God, God, I cannot forgive! It is better to die than to hate! I cannot forgive! I cannot forgive!' And I went and stood outside his door in the dark, and I heard him cry, 'I have not sinned so, not so! If I have torn my fellow's flesh ever so little, I have kneeled down and kissed the wound with my mouth till it was healed. I have not willed that any soul should be lost through hate of me. If they have but fancied that I wronged them I have lain down on the ground before them that they might tread on me, and so, seeing my humiliation, forgive and not be lost through hating me; they have not cared that my soul should be lost; they have not willed to save me; they have not tried that I should forgive them!'

"I said to him, 'See here, be thou content; do not forgive; forget this soul and its injury; go on your way. In the next world perhaps——'

And the angel said, "What is it?"

He answered, "It is I! it is myself!" And he went forward as if he would have lain his heart against it; but the angel held him back and covered his eyes.

Now God had given power to the angel further to unclothe that soul, to take from it all those outward attributes of time and place and circumstance whereby the individual life is marked off from the life of the whole.

Again the angel uncovered the man's eyes, and he looked. He saw before him that which in its tiny drop reflects the whole universe; he saw that which marks within itself the step of the furthest star, and tells how the crystal grows under ground where no eye has seen it; that which is where the germ in the egg stirs; which moves the out-stretched fingers of the little newborn babe, and keeps the leaves of the trees pointing upward; which moves where the jellyfish sail alone on the sunny seas, and is where the lichens form on the mountain's rocks.

And the man looked.

And the angel touched him.

But the man bowed his head and shuddered. He whispered, "It is God!"

And the angel recovered the man's eyes. And when he uncovered them there was one walking from them a little way off—for the angel had reclothed the soul in its outward form and vesture—and the man knew who it was.

And the angel said, "Do you know him?"

And the man said, "I know him," and he looked after the figure.

And the angel said, "Have you forgiven him?"

But the man said, "How beautiful my brother is!"

And the angel looked into the man's eyes, and he shaded his own face with his wing from the light. He laughed softly and went up to God.

But the men were together on earth.

I awoke.

The blue, blue sky was over my head, and the waves were breaking below on the shore. I walked through the little Chapel, and I saw the Madonna in blue and red, and the Christ carrying his cross, and the Roman soldiers with the rod, and the Blessèd Bambino with its broken face; and then I walked down the slop-

"He cried, 'Go from me, you understand nothing! What is the next world to me! I am lost now, to-day. I cannot see the sunlight shine, the dust is in my throat, the sand is in my eyes! Go from me, you know nothing! Oh, once again before I die to see that the world is beautiful! Oh, God, God, I cannot live and not love. I cannot live and hate. Oh, God, God, God!' So I left him crying out and came back here."

God said, "This man's soul must be saved."

And the angel said, "How?"

God said, "Go down you, and save it."

The angel said, "What more shall I do?"

Then God bent down and whispered in the angel's ear, and the angel spread out its wings and went down to earth.

And partly I woke, sitting there upon the broken stone with my head on my knee; but I was too weary to rise. I heard the wind roam through the olive trees and among the ruined arches, and then I slept again.

The angel went down and found the man with the bitter heart and took him by the hand, and led him to a certain spot.

Now the man wist not where it was the angel would take him, nor what he would show him there. And when they came the angel shaded the man's eyes with his wing, and when he moved it, the man saw somewhat on the earth before them. For God had given it to that angel to unclothe a human soul; to take from it all those outward attributes of form and color, and age, and sex, whereby one man is known from among his fellows and is marked off from the rest, and the soul lay before them bare, as a man turning his eye inward beholds himself.

They saw its past, its childhood, the tiny life with the dew upon it; they saw its youth when the dew was melting, and the creature raised its Lilliputian mouth to drink from a cup too large for it, and they saw how the water spilt; they saw its hopes that were never realized; they saw its hours of intellectual blindness, men call sin; they saw its hours of all-radiating insight, which men call righteousness; they saw its hour of strength, when it leaped to its feet crying, "I am omnipotent"; its hour of weakness, when it fell to the earth and grasped dust only; they saw what it might have been, but never would be.

The man bent forward.

ing road to the brick pathway. The olive trees stood up on either side of the road, their black berries and pale-green leaves stood out against the sky; and the little ice plants hung from the crevices in the stone wall. It seemed to me as if it must have rained while I was asleep. I thought I had never seen the heavens and the earth look so beautiful before. I walked down the road. The old, old, old tiredness was gone.

Presently there came a peasant boy down the path leading his ass; she had two large panniers fastened to her sides; and they went down the road before me.

I had never seen him before; but I should have liked to walk by him and to have held his hand—only he would not have known why.

Complete. From "Dreams." Written at Alassio, Italy.

THE GARDENS OF PLEASURE

SHE walked upon the beds, and the sweet, rich scent arose; and she gathered her hands full of flowers. Then Duty, with his white, clear features, came and looked at her. Then she ceased from gathering, but she walked away among the flowers, smiling, and with her hands full.

Then Duty, with his still, white face, came again, and looked at her; but she,—she turned her head away from him. At last she saw his face, and she dropped the fairest of the flowers she had held, and walked silently away.

Then again he came to her. And she moaned, and bent her head low, and turned to the gate. But as she went out she looked back at the sunlight on the faces of the flowers, and wept in anguish. Then she went out and it shut behind her forever; but still in her hand she held of the buds she had gathered, and the scent was very sweet in the lonely desert.

But he followed her. Once more he stood before her with his still, white, death-like face. And she knew what he had come for; she unbent the fingers, and let the flowers drop out, the flowers she had loved so, and walked on without them, with dry, aching eyes. Then for the last time he came. And she showed him her empty hands, the hands that held nothing now. But still he looked. Then at length she opened her bosom and took out of it one small flower she had hidden there, and laid it on the sand. She had nothing more to give now, and she wandered away, and the gray sand whirled about her.

Complete. From «Dreams.»

IN A FAR-OFF WORLD

There is a world in one of the far-off stars, and things do not happen here as they happen there. In that world were a man and a woman; they had one work, and they walked together side by side on many days, and were friends — and that is a thing that happens now and then in this world also.

But there was something in that star-world that there is not here. There was a thick wood; where the trees grew closest, and the stems were interlocked, and the summer sun never shone, there stood a shrine. In the day all was quiet, but at night, when the stars shone or the moon glinted on the tree-tops, and all was quiet below, if one crept here quite alone and knelt on the steps of the stone altar, and uncovering one's breast, so wounded it that the blood fell down on the altar steps, then whatever he who knelt there wished for was granted him. And all this happens, as I said, because it is a far-off world and things often happen there as they do not happen here.

Now the man and the woman walked together; and the woman wished well to the man. One night when the moon was shining so that the leaves of all the trees glinted, and the waves of the sea were silvery, the woman walked alone to the forest. It was dark there; the moonlight fell only in little flecks on the dead leaves under her feet, and the branches were knotted tight overhead. Further in it got darker, not even a fleck of moonlight shone. Then she came to the shrine; she knelt down before it and prayed; there came no answer. Then she uncovered her breast; with a sharp two-edged stone that lay there she wounded it. The drops dripped slowly down onto the stone, and a voice cried, «What do you seek?»

She answered, «There is a man; I hold him nearer than anything. I would give him the best of all blessings.»

The voice said, «What is it?»

The girl said, «I know not, but that which is most good for him I wish him to have.»

The other artists came and said, «Where does he get his color from?» They asked him; and he smiled and said, «I cannot tell you»; and worked on with his head bent low.

And one went to the far East and bought costly pigments, and made a rare color and painted, but after a time the picture faded. Another read in the old books, and made a color rich and rare, but when he had put it on the picture it was dead.

But the artist painted on. Always the work got redder and redder, and the artist grew whiter and whiter. At last one day they found him dead before his picture, and they took him up to bury him. The other men looked about in all the pots and crucibles, but they found nothing they had not.

And when they undressed him to put his graveclothes on him, they found above his left breast the mark of a wound — it was an old, old wound, that must have been there all his life, for the edges were old and hardened; but Death, who seals all things, had drawn the edges together, and closed it up.

And they buried him. And still the people went about saying, «Where did he find his color from?»

And it came to pass that after a while the artist was forgotten — but the work lived.

Complete. From «Dreams.»

The voice said, «Your prayer is answered; he shall have it.»

Then she stood up. She covered her breast and held the garment tight upon it with her hand, and ran out of the forest, and the dead leaves fluttered under her feet. Out in the moonlight the soft air was blowing, and the sand glittered on the beach. She ran along the smooth shore, then suddenly she stood still. Out across the water there was something moving. She shaded her eyes and looked. It was a boat; it was sliding swiftly over the moonlight water out to sea. One stood upright in it; the face the moonlight did not show, but the figure she knew. It was passing swiftly; it seemed as if no one propelled it; the moonlight's shimmer did not let her see clearly, and the boat was far from shore, but it seemed almost as if there was another figure sitting in the stern. Faster and faster it glided over the water away, away. She ran along the shore; she came no nearer it. The garment she had held closed fluttered open; she stretched out her arms, and the moonlight shone on her long loose hair.

Then a voice beside her whispered, «What is it?»

She cried, «With my blood I bought the best of all gifts for him. I have come to bring it him! He is going from me!»

The voice whispered softly, «Your prayer was answered. It was given him.»

She cried, «What is it?»

The voice answered, «It is that he might leave you.»

The girl stood still.

Far out at sea the boat was lost to sight beyond the moonlight sheen.

The voice spoke softly, «Art thou contented?»

She said, «I am contented.»

At her feet the waves broke in long ripples softly on the shore.

Complete. From «Dreams.»

THE ARTIST'S SECRET

There was an artist once, and he painted a picture. Other artists had colors richer and rarer, and painted more notable pictures. He painted his with one color; there was a wonderful red glow on it; and the people went up and down, saying, «We like the picture, we like the glow.»

SIR WALTER SCOTT

(1771–1832)

Sir Walter Scott's literary biographies are not in the strictest sense essays. They are narratives rather than essays, but they belong to the literature of the English essay cycle and deserve to be studied as part of it. His incomparable gifts as a novelist were developed through a method which is incompatible with high excellence in essay writing. He was the greatest romance writer of his century and he became so because his mind expressed itself through the construction of romantic plots as naturally as Addison and Lamb expressed theirs through monologue, characterized by that kaleidoscopic shifting of topics which is the charm of the essay and the despair of the novel. Even when he is at his best as an essayist, Sir Walter is still the great novelist, with the virtue of the novelist rather than of the essayist. But the narrative style he loves rather enhances than detracts from the interest of his essays. Whatever he lacks in attention to the art of construction, he more than makes good by crowding incident on incident and anecdote on anecdote, until we forget to regret the loss of the great essayist he might have become had he not been the incomparable story-teller he is.

THE CHARACTER AND HABITS OF SWIFT

Swift was in person tall, strong, and well made, of a dark complexion, but with blue eyes, black and bushy eyebrows, nose somewhat aquiline, features which remarkably expressed the stern, haughty, and dauntless turn of his mind. He was never known to laugh, and his smiles are happily characterized by the well-known lines of Shakespeare. Indeed, the whole description of Cassius might be applied to Swift:—

«——————————— He reads much,
He is a great observer, and he looks
Quite through the deeds of men.—
Seldom he smiles, and smiles in such a sort,
As if he mock'd himself, and scorn'd his spirit
That could be mov'd to smile at any thing.»

The features of the Dean have been preserved in several paintings, busts, and medals. In youth he was reckoned handsome, Pope observed that though his face had an expression of dullness, his eyes were very particular. They were as azure, he said, as the heavens, and had an unusual expression of acuteness. In old age the Dean's countenance conveyed an expression which, though severe, was noble and impressive. He spoke in public with facility and impressive energy; and as his talents for ready reply were so well calculated for political debate, it must have increased the mortification of Queen Anne's ministers, that they found themselves unable to secure him a seat on the bench of Bishops. The government of Ireland dreaded his eloquence as much as his pen.

His manners in society were, in his better days, free, lively, and engaging, not devoid of peculiarities, but bending them so well to circumstances that his company was universally courted. When age and infirmity had impaired the elasticity of his spirits and the equality of his temper, his conversation was still valued, not only on account of the extended and various acquaintance with life and manners, of which it displayed an inexhaustible fund, but also for the shrewd and satirical humor which seasoned his observations and anecdotes. This, according to Orrery, was the last of his powers which decayed, but the Dean himself was sensible that, as his memory failed, his stories were too often repeated. His powers of conversation and of humorous repartee were in his time regarded unrivaled; but, like most who have assumed a despotic sway in conversation, he was sometimes silenced by unexpected resistance. He was very fond of puns. Perhaps the application of the line of Virgil to the lady who threw down with her mantua a Cremona fiddle is the best that ever was made:—

"Mantua, væ miseræ nimium vicina Cremonæ!"

The comfort which he gave an elderly gentleman who had lost his spectacles was more grotesque: "If this rain continues all night, you will certainly recover them in the morning betimes:

"Nocte pluit tota — redeunt spectacula mane."

His pre-eminence in more legitimate wit is asserted by many anecdotes. A man of distinction not remarkable for regularity in his private concerns, chose for his motto, *"Eques haud male*

notus." "Better known than trusted," was the Dean's translation, when someone related the circumstance.

Swift had an odd humor of making extempore proverbs. Observing that a gentleman, in whose garden he walked with some friends, seemed to have no intention to request them to eat any of the fruit, Swift observed, it was a saying of his dear grandmother,

"Always pull a peach
When it is within your reach,"

and helping himself accordingly, his example was followed by the whole company. At another time, he framed an "old saying and true" for the benefit of a person who had fallen from his horse into the mire:—

"The more dirt,
The less hurt."

The man rose much consoled; but as he was a collector of proverbs himself, he wondered he had never before heard that used by the Dean upon the occasion. He threw some useful rules into rhyming adages; and indeed, as his "Journal to Stella" proves, had a felicity in putting rhymes together on any trifling occasion, which must have added considerably to the flow and facility of his poetical compositions.

In his personal habits he was cleanly, even to scrupulousness. At one period of his life he was said to lie in bed till eleven o'clock, and think of wit for the day; but latterly he was an early riser. Swift was fond of exercise, and particularly of walking. And although modern pedestrians may smile at his proposing to journey to Chester, by walking ten miles a day, yet he is said to have taken this exercise too violently, and to a degree prejudicial to his health. He was also a tolerable horseman, fond of riding, and a judge of the noble animal, which he chose to celebrate, as the emblem of moral merit, under the name of Houyhnhnm. Exercise he pressed on his friends, particularly upon Stella and Vanessa, as a sort of duty; and scarce any of his letters conclude without allusion to it; especially as relating to the preservation of his own health, which his constitutional fits of deafness and giddiness rendered very precarious. His habit of body in other respects appears to have been indifferent, with a tendency to scrofula, which, perhaps, hastened his mental

disorder. But the immediate cause was the pressure of water upon the head, as appeared upon dissection after death.

Of his learning we have already spoken; it seems to have both been extensive and useful, but not profoundly scholastic. Of modern languages he spoke and wrote French with facility, and understood Italian. His Latin verses indicate an imperfect knowledge of prosody, and no great command of the language in which they are written. The poem called "Rupes Carberiæ," has, in particular, been severely criticized. It is seldom that Swift alludes to English literature; yet it is evident he had perused with attention those classics to which his name is now added. How carefully he had read Milton appears from his annotations on the "Paradise Lost," for the benefit of Stella. Chaucer also appears to have been his favorite, for I observe among his papers a memorandum of the oaths used in the "Canterbury Tales," classed with the personages by whom they are used. It appears from a note upon Mr. Todd's edition of Milton, that Swift was a peruser of the ancient romances of chivalry. But he never mentions the romances and plays of the period in which he lived, without expressing the most emphatic contempt. To the drama, particularly, he was so indifferent, that he never once alludes to the writings of Shakespeare, nor, wonderful to be told, does he appear to have possessed a copy of his works. After noticing this, it will scarce be held remarkable that the catalogue of his library only contains the works of three dramatic authors, Ben Jonson, Wycherley, and Rowe, the last two being presentation copies from the authors, in 1700 and 1702. History and classical authors formed the Dean's favorite studies, and, during the decay of his faculties, his reading was almost entirely confined to Clarendon.

Swift loved the country, like most men of genius, but rather practiced rural occupations than rural sports. At Quilca, Gaulstown, and Markethill, he delighted in acting as a sort of overseer or bailiff to those employed in improving the property of his friends, and he dwells fondly in his "Journal" on his plantations and canal at Laracor.

It does not appear from any part of his works, unless, perhaps, the Latin verses on the rocks of Carbery, that he was an admirer of the beautiful or romantic in landscapes; but he was a curious, though not a scientific, observer of any singular natural phenomena which came under his attention.

The humor of stubborn independence which influenced the Dean's whole character stamps it, at first examination, with a whole chain of paradoxes. A devout believer in the truths of Christianity, a constant observer of the rules of religion, and zealous even to slaying in the cause of the Church of England, Swift assumed an occasional levity of writing, speaking, and acting, which caused his being branded an infidel, a contemner of public ordinances, and a scoffer of church discipline. Nor was this all. A zealous friend of liberty in temporal politics, he acted during his whole life with the Tory party. Disliking Ireland even to virulent prejudice, he was the first and most effectual vindicator of her rights and liberties; and, charitable and benevolent to the extreme limits of a moderate revenue, he lay under the reproach of avarice and parsimony. An admirer of paradoxes, like Dr. Fuller, might have found points in his history, as well as opinions, capable of being placed in strong contrast. The first writer of his age was disgraced at college; the principal supporter of Queen Anne's last administration, whose interest had made many a prelate, was himself unable to attain that dignity; and he who in his writings exhibited a tone of the most bitter misanthropy, was in active life a steady patriot, a warm friend, and a bountiful patron. He had also this remarkable fate as a political writer, that, although his publishers were in four instances subjected to arrest and examination,—although large rewards were twice offered for the discovery of the author of works generally and truly ascribed to him,— yet he never personally felt the grasp of power;

"For not a Judas could be found,
To sell him for three hundred pound."

Many of these apparent paradoxes arose from Swift's stern and unbending pride of temper, which rather contemned and avoided public applause than studied to present his character under favorable colors to the general eye. Even his politeness assumed often a singular turn of cynicism, and much of his conduct in life reminds us of his favorite style of composition, that irony

"Which he was born to introduce,
Refined at first, and showed its use."

From the same cause he often exhibited, in his first address, a sternness and a bluntness of demeanor, which, detached from the mode in which he well knew how to repair the pain he had given, was harsh to his inferiors, and uncivil to those of higher rank. An anecdote which, though told by Mrs. Pilkington, is well attested, bears, that the last time he was in London he went to dine with the Earl of Burlington, who was then but newly married. The Earl being willing, it is supposed, to have some diversion, did not introduce him to his lady, nor mention his name. After dinner, said the Dean, "Lady Burlington, I hear you can sing; sing me a song." The lady looked on this unceremonious manner of asking a favor with distaste, and positively refused. He said, "She should sing, or he would make her. Why, madam, I suppose you take me for one of your poor English hedge parsons; sing when I bid you." As the Earl did nothing but laugh at this freedom, the lady was so vexed, that she burst into tears, and retired. His first compliment to her when he saw her again, was, "Pray, madam, are you as proud and as ill natured now as when I saw you last?" To which she answered with great humor, "No, Mr. Dean; I'll sing for you, if you please." From which time he conceived great esteem for her. The Dean received with complaisance such praise as was delicately administered; but it belonged to his character to repel whatever was extravagant or coarse. When a man professed to love Swift better than all his friends and relations, he said, "The man is a fool." And when Pope talked to him of a lady who admired him above all things, he replied, "Then I despise her heartily." In fact, he seems rather to have expected his friends to gratify him by implicit compliance with his humor, however whimsical, than by any verbal flattery disguising perhaps from himself, that such servile compliance was the grossest sort of practical adulation.

From "The Life of Swift."

LORD BYRON

AMIDST the general calmness of the political atmosphere, we have been stunned, from another quarter, by one of those death notes, which are pealed at intervals, as from an archangel's trumpet, to awaken the soul of a whole people at once. Lord Byron, who has so long and so amply filled the highest place in the public eye, has shared the lot of humanity. He died at Missolonghi, on the nineteenth of April, 1824. That mighty gen-

IX—213

tentions and kindness he was secure, had often great weight with him; but there were few who could or dared venture on a task so difficult. Reproof he endured with impatience, and reproach hardened him in his error; so that he often resembled the gallant war steed who rushes forward on the steel that wounds him. In the most painful crisis of his private life, he evinced this irritability and impatience of censure in such a degree as almost to resemble the noble victim of the bullfight, which is more maddened by the squibs, darts, and petty annoyances of the unworthy crowds beyond the lists, than by the lance of his nobler, and, so to speak, his more legitimate antagonist. In a word, much of that in which he erred, was in bravado and scorn of his censors, and was done with the motive of Dryden's despot, "to show his arbitrary power." It is needless to say that his was a false and prejudiced view of such a contest; and that if the noble bard gained a species of triumph, by compelling the world to read poetry, though mixed with baser matter, because it was his, he gave, in return, an unworthy triumph to the unworthy, besides deep sorrow to those whose applause, in his cooler moments, he most valued.

It was the same with his politics, which on several occasions assumed a tone menacing and contemptuous to the constitution of his country; while, in fact, Lord Byron was in his own heart sufficiently sensible, not only of his privileges as a Briton, but of the distinction attending his high birth and rank, and was peculiarly sensitive of those shades which constitute what is termed the manners of a gentleman. Indeed, notwithstanding his having employed epigrams, and all the petty war of wit, when such would have been much better abstained from, he would have been found, had a collision taken place between the aristocratic and democratic parties in the state, exerting all his energies in defense of that to which he naturally belonged. His own feeling on these subjects he has explained in the very last canto of "Don Juan"; and they are in entire harmony with the opinions which we have seen expressed in his correspondence, at a moment when matters appeared to approach a serious struggle in his native country. "If we are to fall," he expressed himself to this purpose, "let the independent aristocracy and gentry of England suffer by the sword of an arbitrary prince, who has been born and bred a gentleman, and will behead us after the manner of our ancestors; but do not let us suffer ourselves to be massacred by the ignoble swarms of ruffians, who are endeavoring to throttle

ius, which walked among men as something superior to ordinary mortality, and whose powers were beheld with wonder, and something approaching to terror, as if we knew not whether they were of good or of evil, is laid as soundly to rest as the poor peasant whose ideas never went beyond his daily task. The voice of just blame, and that of malignant censure, are at once silenced; and we feel almost as if the great luminary of heaven had suddenly disappeared from the sky, at the moment when every telescope was leveled for the examination of the spots which dimmed its brightness. It is not now the question, what were Byron's faults, what his mistakes; but, How is the blank which he has left in British literature to be filled up, Not, we fear, in one generation, which, among many highly gifted persons, has produced none who approached Byron in originality, the first attribute of genius. Only thirty-seven years old — so much already done for immortality — so much time remaining, as it seemed to us shortsighted mortals, to maintain and to extend his fame, and to atone for errors in conduct and levities in composition,—who will not grieve that such a race has been shortened, though not always keeping the straight path, such a light extinguished, though sometimes flaming to dazzle and bewilder? One word on this ungrateful subject ere we quit it forever.

The errors of Lord Byron arose neither from depravity of heart,—for nature had not committed the anomaly of uniting to such extraordinary talents an imperfect moral sense,—nor from feelings dead to the admiration of virtue. No man had ever a kinder heart for sympathy, or a more open hand for the relief of distress; and no mind was ever more formed for the enthusiastic admiration of noble actions, providing he was convinced that the actors had proceeded on disinterested principles. Lord Byron was totally free from the curse and degradation of literature,—its jealousies, we mean, and its envy. But his wonderful genius was of a nature which disdained restraint, even when restraint was most wholesome. When at school, the tasks in which he excelled were those only which he undertook voluntarily; and his situation as a young man of rank, with strong passions, and in the uncontrolled enjoyment of a considerable fortune, added to that impatience of strictures or coercion which was natural to him. As an author he refused to plead at the bar of criticism; as a man he would not submit to be morally amenable to the tribunal of public opinion. Remonstrances from a friend, of whose in-

their way to power." Accordingly, he expresses in the strongest terms his purpose of resisting to the last extremity the tendency to anarchy, which commercial distress had generated, and disaffection was endeavoring to turn to its own purposes. His poetry expresses similar sentiments:—

"It is not that I adulate the people;
    Without me there are demagogues enough,
And infidels to pull down every steeple,
    And set up in their stead some proper stuff,
Whether they may sow Skepticism to reap Hell,
    As is the Christian dogma rather rough,
I do not know;—I wish men to be free
    As much from mobs as kings—from you as me.
The consequence is, being of no party,
    I shall offend all parties."

We are not, however, Byron's apologists,—for now alas! he needs none. His excellences will now be universally acknowledged, and his faults (let us hope and believe) not remembered in his epitaph. It will be recollected what a part he has sustained in British literature since the first appearance of "Childe Harold," a space of nearly sixteen years. There has been no reposing under the shade of his laurels, no living upon the resource of past reputation; none of that coddling and petty precaution, which little authors call "taking care of their fame." Byron let his fame take care of itself. His foot was always in the arena, his shield hung always in the lists; and, although his own gigantic renown increased the difficulty of the struggle, since he could produce nothing, however great, which exceeded the public estimate of his genius, yet he advanced to the honorable contest again and again and again, and came always off with distinction, almost always with complete triumph. As various in composition as Shakespeare himself (this will be admitted by all who are acquainted with his "Don Juan") he has embraced every topic of human life, and sounded every string on the divine harp, and from its slightest to its most powerful and heart-astounding tones. There is scarce a passion or a situation which has escaped his pen; and he might be drawn, like Garrick, between the weeping and the laughing muse, although his most powerful efforts have certainly been dedicated to Melpomene. His genius seemed as prolific as various. The most prodigal use did not exhaust his powers, nay, seemed rather to increase their vigor. Neither "Childe Harold," nor any of the most beautiful of Byron's earlier tales, contain more exquisite morsels of poetry than are to be found scattered through the cantos of "Don Juan," amidst verses which the author appears to have thrown off with an effort as spontaneous as that of a tree resigning its leaves to the wind. But that noble tree will never more bear fruit or blossom! It has been cut down in its strength, and the past is all that remains to us of Byron. We can scarce reconcile ourselves to the idea — scarce think that the voice is silent forever, which, bursting so often on our ear, was often heard with rapturous admiration, sometimes with regret, but always with the deepest interest,—

> "All that's bright must fade,
> The brightest still the fleetest!"

With a strong feeling of awful sorrow, we take leave of the subject. Death creeps upon our most serious, as well as upon our most idle, employments; and it is a reflection solemn and gratifying that he found our Byron in no moment of levity, but contributing his fortune, and hazarding his life in behalf of a people only endeared to him by their past glories, and as fellow-creatures suffering under the yoke of a heathen oppressor.

From "Biographies."

JOHN SELDEN

(1584–1654)

JOHN SELDEN, remembered now as the author of Selden's "Table-Talk," was in his generation a man of great and varied activities. He was born in Sussex, England, December 16th, 1584, and was thus contemporary with many of the greatest men of what still remains the most remarkable age of England. Lyttleton, Herbert, Drayton, and Ben Jonson were among his intimates. He was a lawyer and jurist of reputation, and among his forgotten works are "England's Epinomis," "Janus Anglorum," and a "History of Luther," published in 1618 and suppressed. He was committed to the Tower for sedition in 1621 and seven years later he helped to draw up the Petition of Right. In 1640 he was elected to the Long Parliament, and he was a member of the committee which impeached Archbishop Laud. He died at London, November 30th, 1654.

TABLE–TALK

CHANGING SIDES

'TIS the trial of a man to see if he will change his side; and if he be so weak as to change once, he will change again.

Your country fellows have a way to try if a man be weak in the hams, by coming behind him and giving him a blow unawares; if he bend once, he will bend again.

The lords that fall from the king after they have got estates by base flattery at court and now pretend conscience, do as a vintner, that when he first sets up, you may go to his house, and carouse there; but when he grows rich, he turns conscientious, and will sell no wine upon the Sabbath Day.

Col. Goring, serving first the one side and then the other, did like a good miller that knows how to grind which way soever the wind sits.

After Luther had made a combustion in Germany about religion, he was sent to by the Pope, to be taken off, and offered any preferment in the Church that he would make choice of: Luther answered, if he had offered half as much at first, he would have accepted it; but now he had gone so far, he could not come back. In truth, he had made himself a greater thing than they could make him; the German princes courted him, he was become the author of a sect ever after to be called Lutherans. So have our preachers done that are against the bishops; they have made themselves greater with the people than they can be made the other way; and, therefore, there is the less probability of bringing them off.

Complete.

CONTRACTS

IF OUR fathers have lost their liberty, why may not we labor to regain it? Answer: We must look to the contract; if that be rightly made, we must stand to it; if we once grant we may recede from contracts upon any inconveniency that may afterwards happen, we shall have no bargain kept. If I sell you a horse and do not like my bargain, I will have my horse again.

Keep your contracts — so far a divine goes; but how to make our contracts is left to ourselves; and as we agree upon the conveying of this house or that land, so it must be. If you offer me a hundred pounds for my glove, I tell you what my glove is, a plain glove, pretend no virtue in it, the glove is my own, I profess not to sell gloves, and we agree for a hundred pounds, I do not know why I may not with a safe conscience take it. The want of that common obvious distinction of *jus præceptivum* and *jus permissivum* does much trouble men.

Lady Kent articled with Sir Edward Herbert that he should come to her when she sent for him, and stay with her as long as she would have him, to which he set his hand; then he articled with her that he should go away when he pleased, and stay away as long as he pleased, to which she set her hand. This is the epitome of all the contracts in the world betwixt man and man, betwixt prince and subject; they keep them as long as they like them, and no longer.

Complete.

EVIL SPEAKING

HE THAT speaks ill of another, commonly before he is aware, makes himself such a one as he speaks against: for if he had civility or breeding, he would forbear such kind of language.

A gallant man is above ill words; an example we have in the old Lord of Salisbury, who was a great wise man. Stone had called some lord about court, "Fool": the lord complains and has Stone whipped; Stone cries, "I might have called my Lord of Salisbury 'fool' often enough before he would have had me whipped."

Speak not ill of a great enemy, but rather give him good words, that he may use you the better if you chance to fall into his hands. The Spaniard did this when he was dying. His confessor told him (to work him to repentance) how the devil tormented the wicked that went to hell: the Spaniard, replying, called the devil "my lord": "I hope my lord the devil is not so cruel." His confessor reproved him. "Excuse me," said the Don, "for calling him so; I know not into what hands I may fall, and if I happen into his I hope he will use me the better for giving him good words."

Complete.

THE MEASURE OF THINGS

WE MEASURE from ourselves; and as things are for our use and purpose, so we approve them. Bring a pear to the table that is rotten, we cry it down, "'Tis naught"; but bring a medlar that is rotten, and "'Tis a fine thing": and yet I'll warrant you the pear thinks as well of itself as the medlar does.

We measure the excellency of other men by some excellency we conceive to be in ourselves. Nash, a poet, poor enough (as poets used to be), seeing an alderman with his gold chain, upon his great horse, by way of scorn said to one of his companions, "Do you see yon fellow, how goodly, how big he looks? Why, that fellow cannot make a blank verse!"

Nay, we measure the goodness of God from ourselves; we measure his goodness, his justice, his wisdom, by something we call just, good, or wise in ourselves; and in so doing we judge proportionally to the country fellow in the play, who said if he were a king he would live like a lord, and have peas and bacon every day, and a whip that cried, "Slash!"

Complete.

WISDOM

A WISE man should never resolve upon anything, at least never let the world know his resolution, for if he cannot arrive at that he is ashamed. How many things did the king resolve in his declaration concerning Scotland never to do, and yet did them all! A man must do according to accidents and emergencies.

Never tell your resolution beforehand; but when the cast is thrown play it as well as you can to win the game you are at. 'Tis but folly to study how to play size-ace when you know not whether you shall throw it or no.

Wise men say nothing in dangerous times. The lion, you know, called the sheep to ask her if his breath smelt: she said, "Aye"; he bit off her head for a fool. He called the wolf and asked him: he said "No"; he tore him in pieces for a flatterer. At last he called the fox and asked him: truly he had got a cold and could not smell.

Complete.

WIT

WIT and wisdom differ; wit is upon the sudden turn, wisdom is in bringing about ends.

Nature must be the groundwork of wit and art; otherwise whatever is done will prove but jack-pudding's work.

Wit must grow like fingers. If it be taken from others 'tis like plums stuck upon blackthorns; there they are for a while, but they come to nothing.

He that will give himself to all manner of ways to get money may be rich; so he that lets fly all he knows or thinks may by chance be satirically witty. Honesty sometimes keeps a man from growing rich, and civility from being witty.

Women ought not to know their own wit, because they will still be showing it, and so spoil it; like a child that will continually be showing its fine new coat, till at length it all bedaubs it with its pah hands.

Fine wits destroy themselves with their own plots, in meddling with great affairs of state. They commonly do as the ape that saw the gunner put bullets in the cannon, and was pleased with it, and he would be doing so too: at last he puts himself into the piece, and so both ape and bullet were shot away together.

Complete.

WOMEN

"LET the women have power of their heads, because of the angels." The reason of the words, "because of the angels," is this: The Greek Church held an opinion that the angels fell in love with women; an opinion grounded upon that, Genesis vi. "The sons of God saw the daughters of men that they were fair." This fancy St. Paul discreetly catches, and uses it as an argument to persuade them to modesty.

The grant of a place is not good, by the canon law, before a man be dead: upon this ground some mischief might be plotted against him in present possession, by poisoning, or some other way. Upon the same reason a contract made with a woman, during her husband's life, was not valid.

Men are not troubled to hear a man dispraised, because they know, though he be naught, there's worth in others; but women are mightily troubled to hear any of them spoken against, as if the sex itself were guilty of some unworthiness.

Women and princes must both trust somebody; and they are happy or unhappy according to the desert of those under whose hands they fall. If a man knows how to manage the favor of a lady, her honor is safe, and so is a prince's.

Complete.

LUCIUS ANNÆUS SENECA

(c. 4 B. C.–65 A. D.)

SENECA was born at Corduba, in Spain, about 4 B. C. His parents brought him to Rome and educated him thoroughly in rhetoric and philosophy. He soon became celebrated as a pleader in the courts, and his writings raised him to eminence among the Stoics at a time when the despotism of a series of the worst tyrants made the Stoic philosophy of repression the only recourse of the intellectual classes at Rome. Seneca was a man of much flexibility of intellect and he became a Senator under Caligula; but under Claudius, Messalina caused him to be banished to Corsica, where he remained until recalled to become the tutor of Nero. The promise of virtue which characterized the early years of Nero's reign was due to Seneca's teaching, but when in 65 A. D. the philosopher was compelled by his pupil to commit suicide, it is not unfair to inquire of the system whether the same flaw in it which made so great a writer and teacher as Seneca himself one of the most notorious usurers of Rome, might not have been instrumental in making Nero what he became in the later years of his reign. Seneca's chief works as a moralist and essayist are "On Anger," "On Clemency," "On Benefits," "On Providence," and "On Tranquillity." His tragedies show that he had talent as a poet and maker of maxims scarcely inferior to that of Pope among the Moderns. His tragedies are imitated from Greek originals, it is true, but this is equally true of all other Latin verse. Among writers of Latin prose, Seneca ranks with Cicero in power of synthesis, but his prose style has found few imitators, while that of Cicero has been a model for students in all succeeding generations.

W. V. B.

ON ANGER

ARISTOTLE says that "certain passions, if one makes a proper use of them, act as arms": which would be true if, like weapons of war, they could be taken up or laid aside at the pleasure of their wielder. These arms, which Aristotle assigns to virtue, fight of their own accord, do not wait to be seized by the hand, and possess a man instead of being possessed by him.

We have no need of external weapons, Nature has equipped us sufficiently by giving us reason. She has bestowed this weapon upon us, which is strong, imperishable, and obedient to our will, not uncertain or capable of being turned against its master. Reason suffices by itself not merely to take thought for the future, but to manage our affairs: what, then, can be more foolish than for reason to beg anger for protection, that is, for what is certain to beg of what is uncertain? what is trustworthy of what is faithless? what is whole of what is sick? What, indeed? since reason is far more powerful by itself even in performing those operations in which the help of anger seems especially needful: for when Reason has decided that a particular thing should be done, she perseveres in doing it; not being able to find anything better than herself to exchange with. She, therefore, abides by her purpose when it has once been formed; whereas anger is often overcome by pity: for it possesses no firm strength, but merely swells like an empty bladder, and makes a violent beginning, just like the winds which rise from the earth and are caused by rivers and marshes, which blow furiously without any continuance: anger begins with a mighty rush, and then falls away, becoming fatigued too soon: that which but lately thought of nothing but cruelty and novel forms of torture is become quite softened and gentle when the time comes for punishment to be inflicted. Passion soon cools, whereas reason is always consistent: yet even in cases where anger has continued to burn, it often happens that although there may be many who deserve to die, yet after the death of two or three it ceases to slay. Its first onset is fierce, just as the teeth of snakes when first roused from their lair are venomous, but become harmless after repeated bites have exhausted their poison. Consequently those who are equally guilty are not equally punished, and often he who has done less is punished more, because he fell in the way of anger when it was fresher. It is altogether irregular; at one time it runs into undue excess, at another it falls short of its duty: for it indulges its own feelings and gives sentence according to its caprices, will not listen to evidence, allows the defense no opportunity of being heard, clings to what it has wrongly assumed, and will not suffer its opinion to be wrested from it, even when it is a mistaken one.

Reason gives each side time to plead; moreover, she herself demands adjournment, that she may have sufficient scope for the discovery of the truth; whereas anger is in a hurry: reason wishes to give a just decision; anger wishes its decision to be thought just: reason looks no further than the matter in hand; anger is excited by empty matters hovering on the outskirts of the case: it is irritated by anything approaching to a confident demeanor, a loud voice, and unrestrained speech, dainty apparel, high-flown pleading, or popularity with the public. It often condemns a man because it dislikes his patron; it loves and maintains error even when truth is staring it in the face. It hates to be proved wrong, and thinks it more honorable to persevere in a mistaken line of conduct than to retract it. I remember Gnæus Piso, a man who was free from many vices, yet of a perverse disposition, and one who mistook harshness for consistency. In his anger he ordered a soldier to be led off to execution because he had returned from furlough without his comrade, as though he must have murdered him if he could not show him. When the man asked for time for search, he would not grant it: the condemned man was brought outside the rampart, and was just offering his neck to the ax, when suddenly there appeared his comrade who was thought to be slain. Hereupon the centurion in charge of the execution bade the guardsman sheathe his sword, and led the condemned man back to Piso, to restore to him the innocence which fortune had restored to the soldier. They were led into his presence by their fellow-soldiers amid the great joy of the whole camp, embracing one another and accompanied by a vast crowd. Piso mounted the tribunal in a fury and ordered them both to be executed, both him who had not murdered and him who had not been slain. What could be more unworthy than this? Because one was proved to be innocent, two perished. Piso even added a third: for he actually ordered the centurion, who had brought back the condemned man, to be put to death. Three men were set up to die in the same place because one was innocent. Oh, how clever is anger at inventing reasons for its frenzy! "You," it says, "I order to be executed, because you have been condemned to death; you, because you have been the cause of your comrade's condemnation; and you, because when ordered to put him to death you disobeyed your general." He discovered the means of charging them with three crimes, because he could find no crime in them.

Irascibility, I say, has this fault — it is loath to be ruled: it is angry with the truth itself, if it comes to light against its will:

it assails those whom it has marked for its victims with shouting and riotous noise and gesticulation of the entire body together with reproaches and curses. Not thus does reason act: but if it must be so, she silently and quietly wipes out whole households, destroys entire families of the enemies of the state, together with their wives and children, throws down their very dwellings, levels them with the ground, and roots out the names of those who are the foes of liberty. This she does without grinding her teeth or shaking her head, or doing anything unbecoming to a judge, whose countenance ought to be especially calm and composed at the time when he is pronouncing an important sentence. "What need is there," asks Hieronymus, "for you to bite your own lips when you want to strike some one?" What would he have said, had he seen a proconsul leap down from the tribunal, snatch the fasces from the lictor, and tear his own clothes because those of others were not torn as fast as he wished. Why need you upset the table, throw down the drinking cups, knock yourself against the columns, tear your hair, smite your thigh and your breast? How vehement do you suppose anger to be, if it thus turns back upon itself, because it cannot find vent on another as fast as it wishes? Such men, therefore, are held back by the bystanders and are begged to become reconciled with themselves. But he who while free from anger assigns to each man the penalty which he deserves does none of these things. He often lets a man go after detecting his crime, if his penitence for what he has done gives good hope for the future, if he perceives that the man's wickedness is not deeply rooted in his mind, but is only, as the saying is, skin-deep. He will grant impunity in cases where it will hurt neither the receiver nor the giver. In some cases he will punish great crimes more leniently than lesser ones, if the former were the result of momentary impulse, not of cruelty, while the latter were instinct with secret, underhand, long-practiced craftiness. The same fault, committed by two separate men, will not be visited by him with the same penalty, if the one was guilty of it through carelessness, the other with a premeditated intention of doing mischief. In all dealing with crime he will remember that the one form of punishment is meant to make bad men better, and the other to put them out of the way. In either case he will look to the future, not to the past: for, as Plato says, "no wise man punishes any one because he has sinned, but that he may sin no more: for

what is past cannot be recalled, but what is to come may be checked." Those, too, whom he wishes to make examples of the ill success of wickedness, he executes publicly, not merely in order that they themselves may die, but that by dying they may deter others from doing likewise. You see how free from any mental disturbance a man ought to be who has to weigh and consider all this, when he deals with a matter which ought to be handled with the utmost care, — I mean, the power of life and death. The sword of justice is ill placed in the hands of an angry man.

Neither ought it to be believed that anger contributes anything to magnanimity: what it gives is not magnanimity but vainglory. The increase which disease produces in bodies swollen with morbid humors is not healthy growth, but bloated corpulence. All those whose madness raises them above human considerations believe themselves to be inspired with high and sublime ideas; but there is no solid ground beneath, and what is built without foundation is liable to collapse in ruin. Anger has no ground to stand upon, and does not rise from a firm and enduring foundation, but is a windy, empty quality, as far removed from true magnanimity as foolhardiness from courage, boastfulness from confidence, gloom from austerity, cruelty from strictness. There is, I say, a great difference between a lofty and a proud mind: anger brings about nothing grand or beautiful. On the other hand, to be constantly irritated seems to me to be the part of a languid and unhappy mind, conscious of its own feebleness, like folk with diseased bodies covered with sores, who cry out at the lightest touch. Anger, therefore, is a vice which for the most part affects women and children. "Yet it affects men also." Because many men, too, have womanish or childish intellects. "But what are we to say? do not some words fall from angry men which appear to flow from a great mind?" Yes, to those who know not what true greatness is: as, for example, that foul and hateful saying, "Let them hate me, provided they fear me," which you may be sure was written in Sulla's time. I know not which was the worse of the two things he wished for, that he might be hated or that he might be feared. It occurs to his mind that some day people will curse him, plot against him, crush him: what prayer does he add to this? May all the gods curse him — for discovering a cure for hate so worthy of it. "Let them hate." How? "Provided they obey me"? No! "Provided they approve of me"? No! How

then? "Provided they fear me"! I would not even be loved upon such terms. Do you imagine that this was a very spirited saying? You are wrong: this is not greatness, but monstrosity. You should not believe the words of angry men, whose speech is very loud and menacing, while their mind within them is as timid as possible: nor need you suppose that the most eloquent of men, Titus Livius, was right in describing somebody as being "of a great rather than a good disposition." The things cannot be separated: he must either be good or else he cannot be great, because I take greatness of mind to mean that it is unshaken, sound throughout, firm and uniform to its very foundation; such as cannot exist in evil dispositions. Such dispositions may be terrible, frantic, and destructive, but cannot possess greatness; because greatness rests upon goodness, and owes its strength to it. "Yet by speech, action, and all outward show they will make one think them great." True, they will say something which you may think shows a great spirit, like Gaius Cæsar, who when angry with heaven because it interfered with his ballet dancers, whom he imitated more carefully than he attended to them when they acted, and because it frightened his revels by its thunders, surely ill directed, challenged Jove to fight, and that to the death, shouting the Homeric verse: —

"Carry me off, or I will carry thee!"

How great was his madness! He must have believed either that he could not be hurt even by Jupiter himself, or that he could hurt even Jupiter itself. I imagine that this saying of his had no small weight in nerving the minds of the conspirators for their task: for it seemed to be the height of endurance to bear one who could not bear Jupiter.

There is therefore nothing great or noble in anger, even when it seems to be powerful and to contemn both gods and men alike. Any one who thinks that anger produces greatness of mind would think that luxury produces it: such a man wishes to rest on ivory, to be clothed with purple, and roofed with gold; to remove lands, embank seas, hasten the course of rivers, suspend woods in the air. He would think that avarice shows greatness of mind: for the avaricious man broods over heaps of gold and silver, treats whole provinces as merely fields on his estate, and has larger tracts of country under the charge of single bailiffs than those which consuls once drew lots to administer. He would think that lust shows greatness of mind: for the lustful man swims across straits, castrates troops of boys, and puts himself within reach of the swords of injured husbands with complete scorn of death. Ambition, too, he would think shows greatness of mind: for the ambitious man is not content with office once a year, but, if possible, would fill the calendar of dignities with his name alone, and cover the whole world with his titles. It matters nothing to what heights or lengths these passions may proceed: they are narrow, pitiable, groveling. Virtue alone is lofty and sublime, nor is anything great which is not at the same time tranquil.

«On Anger,» Chaps. xvii., xviii., xix., xx., and xxi.,
complete. Bohn edition.

MADAME DE SÉVIGNÉ

(MARIE DE RABUTIN-CHANTAL, MARQUISE DE SÉVIGNÉ)

(1626–1696)

MADAME DE SÉVIGNÉ, perhaps the most celebrated letter writer of modern times, was born at Paris, February 6th, 1626. She was carefully educated by her family, and at eighteen was married in the usual French way to the Marquis de Sévigné, by whom she had a daughter and a son. Her husband, who did not make her happy, was killed in a duel, and his widow devoted herself to the care of her children with such success that the letters written by her to her daughter are now read all over the civilized world. She died April 18th, 1696.

A BIT OF PARISIAN GOSSIP

I AM going to tell you a thing, the most astonishing, the most surprising, the most marvelous, the most miraculous, the most magnificent, the most confounding, the most unheard-of, the most singular, the most extraordinary, the most incredible, the most unforeseen, the greatest, the least, the rarest, the most common, the most public, the most private till to-day, the most brilliant, the most enviable;—in short, a thing of which there is but one example in past ages, and that not an exact one either; a thing that we cannot believe at Paris; how, then, will it gain credence at Lyons? a thing which makes everybody cry, " Lord have mercy upon us!" a thing which causes the greatest joy to Madame de Rohan and Madame de Hauterive; a thing, in fine, which is to happen on Sunday next, when those who are present will doubt the evidence of their senses; a thing which, though it is to be done on Sunday, yet perhaps will not be finished on Monday. I cannot bring myself to tell you; guess what it is. I give you three times to do it in. What, not a word to throw at a dog? Well, then, I find I must tell you. Monsieur de Lauzun is to be married next Sunday at the Louvre, to —— pray guess to whom! I give you four times to do it in,—I give you six,—

I give you a hundred. Says Madame de Coulanges: "It is really very hard to guess; perhaps it is Madame de la Vallière." Indeed, madame, it is not. It is "Mademoiselle de Retz, then." No, nor she either; you are extremely provincial. "Lord bless me," say you, "what stupid wretches we are! it is Mademoiselle de Colbert all the while." Nay, now you are still further from the mark. "Why, then, it must certainly be Mademoiselle de Crequy." You have it not yet. Well, I find I must tell you at last. He is to be married next Sunday at the Louvre, with the king's leave, to Mademoiselle — Mademoiselle de —— Mademoiselle — guess, pray guess her name; he is to be married to Mademoiselle, the great Mademoiselle; Mademoiselle, daughter to the late Monsieur; Mademoiselle, granddaughter of Henry IV; Mademoiselle d'Eu, Mademoiselle de Dombes, Mademoiselle de Montpensier, Mademoiselle d'Orleans, Mademoiselle, the king's cousin-german,—Mademoiselle, destined to the throne,—Mademoiselle, the only match in France that was worthy of Monsieur. What glorious matter for talk! If you should burst forth like a bedlamite, say we have told you a lie, that it is false, that we are making a jest of you, and that a pretty jest it is, without wit or invention; in short, if you abuse us, we shall think you are quite in the right; for we have done just the same things ourselves. Farewell, you will find by the letters you receive this post, whether we tell you truth or not.

Monsieur de Coulanges. Paris,
December 15th, 1670.

AN ARTISTIC FUNERAL

My Dear Child:—

I MUST return to narration, it is a folly I can never resist. Prepare, therefore, for a description. I was yesterday at a service performed in honor of the Chancellor Segnier at the Oratory. Painting, sculpture, music, rhetoric,—in a word, the four liberal arts,—were at the expense of it. Nothing could exceed the beauty of the decorations; they were finely imagined, and designed by Le Brun. The mausoleum reached to the top of the dome, adorned with a thousand lamps, and a variety of figures characteristic of him in whose honor it was erected. Beneath were four figures of Death, bearing the marks of his several dignities, as having taken away his honors with his life. One of

them held his helmet, another his ducal coronet, another the ensigns of his order, another his chancellor's mace. The four sister arts, painting, music, eloquence, and sculpture, were represented in deep distress, bewailing the loss of their protector. The first representation was supported by the four virtues, fortitude, temperance, justice, and religion. Above these, four angels, or genii, received the soul of the deceased, and seemed preening their purple wings to bear their precious charge to heaven. The mausoleum was adorned with a variety of little seraphs, who supported an illuminated shrine, which was fixed to the top of the cupola. Nothing so magnificent or so well imagined was ever seen; it is Le Brun's masterpiece. The whole church was adorned with pictures, devices, and emblems, which all bore some relation to the life, or office, of the chancellor; and some of his noblest actions were represented in painting. Madame de Verneuil offered to purchase all the decoration at a great price; but it was unanimously resolved by those who had contributed to it, to adorn a gallery with it, and to consecrate it as an everlasting monument of their gratitude and magnificence. The assembly was grand and numerous, but without confusion. I sat next to Monsieur de Tulle, Madame Colbert and the Duke of Monmouth, who is as handsome as when we saw him at the *palais royal.* (Let me tell you in a parenthesis, that he is going to the army to join the king.) A young father of the Oratory came to speak the funeral oration. I desired Monsieur de Tulle to bid him come down, and to mount the pulpit in his place; since nothing could sustain the beauty of the spectacle, and the excellence of the music, but the force of his eloquence. My child, this young man trembled when he began, and we all trembled for him. Our ears were at first struck with a provincial accent; he is of Marseilles, and called Lené. But as he recovered from his confusion, he became so brilliant; established himself so well; gave so just a measure of praise to the deceased; touched with so much address and delicacy all the passages in his life where delicacy was required; placed in so true a light all that was most worthy of admiration; employed all the charms of expression, all the masterly strokes of eloquence, with so much propriety and so much grace, that every one present, without exception, burst into applause, charmed with so perfect, so finished a performance. He is twenty-eight years of age, the intimate friend of M. de Tulle, who accompanied him when he left the assembly. We were for naming him the Chevalier Mascaron, and I think he will even surpass his friend. As for the music, it was fine beyond all description. Baptiste exerted himself to the utmost, and was assisted by all the king's musicians. There was an addition made to that fine "Miserere," and there was a "Libera" which filled the eyes of the whole assembly with tears; I do not think the music in heaven could exceed it. There were several prelates present. I desired Guitaut to look for the good Bishop of Marseilles, but we could not see him. I whispered him, that if it had been the funeral oration of any person living, to whom he might have made his court by it, he would not have failed to have been there. This little pleasantry made us laugh, in spite of the solemnity of the ceremony. My dear child, what a strange letter is this! I fancy I have almost lost my senses! What is this long account to you? To tell the truth, I have satisfied my love of description.

> Written from Paris, May 6th, 1672,
> to her daughter.

TO MADAME DE GRIGNAN

WHEN we reckon without Providence, we must frequently reckon twice. I was dressed from head to foot by eight o'clock; I had drunk my coffee, heard mass, taken leave of everybody, the mules were loaded, and the tinkling of their bells gave me notice that it was time to mount my litter; my room was full of people, entreating me not to think of setting out on account of the heavy rain which had fallen incessantly for several days, and was then pouring more violently than ever; but I resisted all their arguments, resolving to abide by the promise I made you in my letter of yesterday, of being with you by Thursday, at furthest: at that very instant, in came M. de Grignan in his nightgown and slippers, and talked to me very gravely of the rashness of such an undertaking, saying that the muleteer would not be able to follow the litter; that my mules would fall into some ditch on the road; that my people would be so wet and fatigued that they would not be able to lend me assistance; so that I changed my mind in a moment, and yielded to his sage remonstrances: and now, my dear child, the trunks are brought back, the mules are unharnessed, the footmen and maids are drying themselves by the fire, for they were wet

through in only crossing the courtyard; and I dispatch you this messenger, knowing your goodness will make you uneasy, and wishing to lessen my own uneasiness, being very anxious about your health; for this man will either bring me word here, or meet one on the road. In short, my dear, he will be with you at Grignan on Thursday instead of me; and I shall set out the first moment it pleases God and M. de Grignan, who is become absolute master of me, and well knows my reasons for wishing so much to be at Grignan. I should be glad if this affair could be kept a secret from M. de la Garde, for he will take a most unmerciful pleasure in finding everything turn out as he foretold; but let him take care, and not grow vain upon this pretended gift of prophecy.

> Lambesc, 1672.

THE EARL OF SHAFTESBURY

(ANTHONY ASHLEY COOPER, THIRD EARL OF SHAFTESBURY)

(1671–1713)

ANTHONY ASHLEY COOPER, third Earl of Shaftesbury, was born in London, February 26th, 1671. He had for a teacher no less a person than John Locke, by whom he was subjected to an experimental system of education which succeeded so well that at the age of eleven Shaftesbury had already acquired the mastery of the classical languages for which he was noted. His chief work, "Characteristics of Men, Manners, Opinions, and Times," appeared in 1711. His "Inquiry concerning Virtue" and other notable essays were included in it. He died at Naples, February 15th, 1713.

DEGENERACY AND THE PASSIONS

IT HAPPENS with mankind that whilst some are by necessity confined to labor, others are provided with abundance of all things by the pains and labor of inferiors. Now, if amongst the superior and easy sort there be not something of fit and proper employment raised in the room of what is wanting in common labor and toil; if instead of an application to any sort of work, such as has a good and honest end in society (as letters, sciences, arts, husbandry, public affairs, economy, or the like), there be a thorough neglect of all duty or employment, a settled idleness, supineness, and inactivity; this of necessity must occasion a most relaxed and dissolute state; it must produce a total disorder of the passions, and break out in the strangest irregularities imaginable.

We see the enormous growth of luxury in capital cities, such as have been long the seat of empire. We see what improvements are made in vice of every kind, where numbers of men are maintained in lazy opulence, and wanton plenty. It is otherwise with those who are taken up in honest and due employment and have been well inured to it from their youth. This we may observe in the hardy remote provincials, the in-

habitants of smaller towns, and the industrious sort of common people; where it is rare to meet with any instances of those irregularities, which are known in courts and palaces, and in the rich foundations of easy and pampered priests.

Now if what we have advanced concerning an inward constitution be real and just; if it be true that Nature works by a just order and regulation as well in the passions and affections as in the limbs and organs which she forms; if it appears withal, that she has so constituted this inward part, that nothing is so essential to it as exercise; and no exercise is so essential as that of social or natural affection: it follows that where this is removed or weakened, the inward part must necessarily suffer and be impaired. Let indolence, indifference, and insensibility be studied as an art, or cultivated with the utmost care; the passions thus restrained will force their prison, and in one way or other procure their liberty, and find full employment. They will be sure to create to themselves unusual and unnatural exercise, where they are cut off from such as is natural and good. And thus in the room of orderly and natural affection, new and unnatural must be raised, and all inward order and economy destroyed.

One must have a very imperfect idea of the order of nature in the formation and structure of animals to imagine that so great a principle, so fundamental a part as that of natural affection should possibly be lost or impaired, without any inward ruin or subversion of the temper and frame of mind.

Whoever is the least versed in this moral kind of architecture will find the inward fabric so adjusted and the whole so nicely built, that the barely extending of a single passion a little too far, or the continuance of it too long, is able to bring irrecoverable ruin and misery. He will find this experienced in the ordinary case of frenzy and distraction; when the mind, dwelling too long upon one subject (whether prosperous or calamitous), sinks under the weight of it, and proves what the necessity is, of a due balance and counterpoise in the affections. He will find that in every different creature, and distinct sex, there is a different and distinct order, set, or suit of passions, proportionable to the different order of life, the different functions, and capacities assigned to each. As the operations and effects are different, so are the springs and causes in each system. The inside work is fitted to the outward action and performance. So that where habits or affections are dislodged, misplaced, or changed; where those belonging to one species are intermixed with those belonging to another, there must of necessity be confusion and disturbance within.

All this we may observe easily, by comparing the more perfect with the imperfect natures, such as are imperfect from their birth, by having suffered violence within, in their earliest form and inmost matrix. We know how it is with monsters, such as are compounded of different kinds, or different sexes. Nor are they less monsters, who are misshapen or distorted in an inward part. The ordinary animals appear unnatural and monstrous, when they lose their proper instincts, forsake their kind, neglect their offspring, and pervert those functions or capacities bestowed by nature. How wretched must it be, therefore, for Man, of all other creatures, to lose that sense and feeling, which is proper to him as a man, and suitable to his character and genius! How unfortunate must it be for a creature, whose dependence on society is greater than any other's, to lose that natural affection by which he is prompted to the good and interest of his species, and community! Such, indeed, is man's natural share of this affection, that he, of all other creatures, is plainly the least able to bear solitude. Nor is anything more apparent than that there is naturally in every man such a degree of social affection as inclines him to seek the familiarity and friendship of his fellows. It is here that he lets loose a passion, and gives reins to a desire, which can hardly by any struggle or inward violence be withheld; or if it be, is sure to create a sadness, dejection, and melancholy in the mind. For whoever is unsociable, and voluntarily shuns society, or commerce with the world, must of necessity be morose and ill-natured. He, on the other side, who is withheld by force or accident, finds in his temper the ill effects of this restraint. The inclination, when suppressed, breeds discontent; and, on the contrary, affords a healing and enlivening joy, when acting at its liberty, and with full scope: as we may see particularly, when, after a time of solitude and long absence, the heart is opened, the mind disburdened, and the secrets of the breast unfolded to a bosom friend.

This we see yet more remarkably instanced in persons of the most elevated stations; even in princes, monarchs, and those who seem by their condition to be above ordinary human commerce, and who affect a sort of distant strangeness from the rest of

mankind. But their carriage is not the same towards all men. The wiser and better sort, it is true, are often held at a distance as unfit for their intimacy or secret trust. But, to compensate this, there are others substituted in their room who, though they have the least merit, and are perhaps the most vile and contemptible of men, are sufficient, however, to serve the purpose of an imaginary friendship, and can become favorites in form. These are the subjects of humanity in the Great. For these, we see them often in concern and pain; in these, they easily confide; to these, they can with pleasure communicate their power and greatness,—be open, free, generous, confiding, bountiful; as rejoicing in the action itself: having no intention or aim beyond it; and their interest, in respect of policy, often standing a quite contrary way. But where neither the love of mankind, nor the passion for favorites prevails, the tyrannical temper fails not to show itself in its proper colors, and to the life, with all the bitterness, cruelty, and mistrust, which belong to that solitary and gloomy state of uncommunicative and unfriendly greatness. Nor needs there any particular proof from history, or present time, to second this remark.

Thus it may appear, how much natural affection is predominant; how it is inwardly joined to us, and implanted in our natures; how interwoven with our other passions; and how essential to that regular motion and course of our affections, on which our happiness and self-enjoyment so immediately depend.

And thus we have demonstrated, that as, on one side, to have the natural and good affections is to have the chief means and power of self-enjoyment, so, on the other side, to want them is certain misery and ill.

From « Inquiry concerning Virtue.»

PERCY BYSSHE SHELLEY

(1792–1822)

SHELLEY wrote a considerable number of essays which were edited by Mrs. Shelley after his death. All of them show the effects of his inclination to metaphysics, which was even stronger than that of Coleridge. His prose is often remarkable, but it does not demonstrate the genius which makes his verse unmistakably the product of one of the greatest lyric poets of modern times. Born in Sussex, England, August 4th, 1792, Shelley was schooled for six years at Eton and then sent to the University of Oxford which expelled him for writing a pamphlet on « The Necessity of Atheism.» In the year of his expulsion, he married Harriet Westbrook, a girl of sixteen, the daughter of a tavern keeper. Three years later he deserted her for Mary Wollstonecraft, whom, after the suicide of his wife in 1816, he married. In 1818 he went with her to Italy and they were living together at Spezia when Shelley was drowned, July 8th, 1822, by the capsizing of the boat in which he and his friend, Edward Williams, were sailing on the bay of Spezia. Shelley's body was recovered and burned in the presence of Byron, Leigh Hunt, and Trelawney.

BENEVOLENCE

THERE is a class of emotions which we instinctively avoid. A human being, such as is man considered in his origin, a child a month old, has a very imperfect consciousness of the existence of other natures resembling itself. All the energies of its being are directed to the extinction of the pains with which it is perpetually assailed. At length it discovers that it is surrounded by natures susceptible of sensations similar to its own. It is very late before children attain to this knowledge. If a child observes, without emotion, its nurse or its mother suffering acute pain, it is attributable rather to ignorance than insensibility. So soon as the accents and gestures, significant of pain, are referred to the feelings which they express, they awaken in the mind of the beholder a desire that they should cease. Pain is thus apprehended to be evil for its own sake, without any other

necessary reference to the mind by which its existence is perceived than such as is indispensable to its perception. The tendencies of our original sensations, indeed, all have for their object the preservation of our individual being. But these are passive and unconscious. In proportion as the mind acquires an active power, the empire of these tendencies becomes limited. Thus an infant, a savage, and a solitary beast, is selfish, because its mind is incapable of receiving an accurate intimation of the nature of pain as existing in beings resembling itself. The inhabitant of a highly civilized community will more acutely sympathize with the sufferings and enjoyments of others than the inhabitant of a society of a less degree of civilization. He who shall have cultivated his intellectual powers by familiarity with the highest specimens of poetry and philosophy will usually sympathize more than one engaged in the less refined functions of manual labor. Every one has experience of the fact that to sympathize with the sufferings of another is to enjoy a transitory oblivion of his own.

The mind thus acquires, by exercise, a habit, as it were, of perceiving and abhorring evil, however remote from the immediate sphere of sensations with which that individual mind is conversant. Imagination or mind employed in prophetically imaging forth its objects is that faculty of human nature on which every gradation of its progress, nay, every, the minutest, change depends. Pain or pleasure, if subtly analyzed, will be found to consist entirely in prospect. The only distinction between the selfish man and the virtuous man is that the imagination of the former is confined within a narrow limit, whilst that of the latter embraces a comprehensive circumference. In this sense, wisdom and virtue may be said to be inseparable, and criteria of each other. Selfishness is the offspring of ignorance and mistake; it is the portion of unreflecting infancy, and savage solitude, or of those whom toil or evil occupations have blunted or rendered torpid; disinterested benevolence is the product of a cultivated imagination, and has an intimate connection with all the arts which add ornament, or dignity, or power, or stability to the social state of man. Virtue is thus entirely a refinement of civilized life; a creation of the human mind; or, rather, a combination which it has made, according to elementary rules contained within itself, of the feelings suggested by the relations established between man and man.

All the theories which have refined and exalted humanity, or those which have been devised as alleviations of its mistakes and evils, have been based upon the elementary emotions of disinterestedness, which we feel to constitute the majesty of our nature. Patriotism, as it existed in the ancient republics, was never, as has been supposed, a calculation of personal advantages. When Mutius Scævola thrust his hand into the burning coals, and Regulus returned to Carthage, and Epicharis sustained the rack silently, in the torments of which she knew that she would speedily perish, rather than betray the conspirators to the tyrant, these illustrious persons certainly made a small estimate of their private interest. If it be said that they sought posthumous fame, instances are not wanting in history which prove that men have even defied infamy for the sake of good. But there is a great error in the world with respect to the selfishness of fame. It is certainly possible that a person should seek distinction as a medium of personal gratification. But the love of fame is frequently no more than a desire that the feelings of others should confirm, illustrate, and sympathize with our own. In this respect it is allied with all that draws us out of ourselves. It is the "last infirmity of noble minds." Chivalry was likewise founded on the theory of self-sacrifice. Love possesses so extraordinary a power over the human heart, only because disinterestedness is united with the natural propensities. These propensities themselves are comparatively impotent in cases where the imagination of pleasure to be given, as well as to be received, does not enter into the account. Let it not be objected that patriotism, and chivalry, and sentimental love, have been the fountains of enormous mischief. They are cited only to establish the proposition that, according to the elementary principles of mind, man is capable of desiring and pursuing good for its own sake.

Complete. From "Speculations on Morals."

ON GOOD AND BAD ACTIONS

THE internal influence, derived from the constitution of the mind from which they flow, produces that peculiar modification of actions which makes them intrinsically good or evil.

To attain an apprehension of the importance of this distinction, let us visit, in imagination, the proceedings of some metropolis. Consider the multitude of human beings who inhabit it,

and survey, in thought, the actions of the several classes into which they are divided. Their obvious actions are apparently uniform: the stability of human society seems to be maintained sufficiently by the uniformity of the conduct of its members, both with regard to themselves, and with regard to others. The laborer arises at a certain hour, and applies himself to the task enjoined him. The functionaries of government and law are regularly employed in their offices and courts. The trader holds a train of conduct from which he never deviates. The ministers of religion employ an accustomed language, and maintain a decent and equable regard. The army is drawn forth, the motions of every soldier are such as they were expected to be; the general commands, and his words are echoed from troop to troop. The domestic actions of men are, for the most part, undistinguishable one from the other, at a superficial glance. The actions which are classed under the general appellation of marriage, education, friendship, etc., are perpetually going on, and, to a superficial glance, are similar one to the other.

But, if we would see the truth of things, they must be stripped of this fallacious appearance of uniformity. In truth, no one action has, when considered in its whole extent, any essential resemblance with any other. Each individual who composes the vast multitude which we have been contemplating has a peculiar frame of mind, which, whilst the features of the great mass of his actions remain uniform, impresses the minuter lineaments with its peculiar hues. Thus, whilst his life, as a whole, is like the lives of other men, in detail it is most unlike, and the more subdivided the actions become; that is, the more they enter into that class which have a vital influence on the happiness of others and his own, so much the more are they distinct from those of other men.

———"Those little, nameless unremembered acts
Of kindness and of love,"

as well as those deadly outrages which are inflicted by a look, a word — or less — the very refraining from some faint and most evanescent expression of countenance; these flow from a profounder source than the series of our habitual conduct, which, it has been already said, derives its origin from without. These are the actions, and such as these, which make human life what it is, and are the fountains of all the good and evil with which

its entire surface is so widely and impartially overspread; and though they are called minute, they are called so in compliance with the blindness of those who cannot estimate their importance. It is in the due appreciating the general effects of their peculiarities, and in cultivating the habit of acquiring decisive knowledge respecting the tendencies arising out of them in particular cases, that the most important part of moral science consists. The deepest abyss of these vast and multitudinous caverns it is necessary that we should visit.

This is the difference between social and individual man. Not that this distinction is to be considered definite, or characteristic of one human being as compared with another, it denotes rather two classes of agency, common in a degree to every human being. None is exempt, indeed, from that species of influence which affects, as it were, the surface of his being, and gives the specific outline to his conduct. Almost all that is ostensible submits to that legislature created by the general representation of the past feelings of mankind — imperfect as it is from a variety of causes, as it exists in the government, the religion, and domestic habits. Those who do not nominally, yet actually, submit to the same power. The external features of their conduct, indeed, can no more escape it than the clouds can escape from the stream of the wind; and his opinion, which he often hopes he has dispassionately secured from all contagion of prejudice and vulgarity, would be found, on examination, to be the inevitable excrescence of the very usages from which he vehemently dissents. Internally all is conducted otherwise; the efficiency, the essence, the vitality of actions, derives its color from what is no way contributed to from any external source. Like the plant, which, while it derives the accident of its size and shape from the soil in which it springs, and is cankered, or distorted, or inflated, yet retains those qualities which essentially divide it from all others; so that hemlock continues to be poison, and the violet does not cease to emit its odor in whatever soil it may grow.

We consider our own nature too superficially. We look on all that in ourselves with which we can discover a resemblance in others; and consider those resemblances as the materials of moral knowledge. It is in the differences that it actually consists.

Complete. From "Speculations on Morals."

ANCIENT LITERATURE AND MODERN PROGRESS

THE modern nations of the civilized world owe the progress which they have made — as well in those physical sciences in which they have already excelled their masters, as in the moral and intellectual inquiries, in which, with all the advantage of the experience of the latter, it can scarcely be said that they have yet equaled them — to what is called the Revival of Learning; that is, the study of the writers of the age which preceded and immediately followed the government of Pericles, or of subsequent writers, who were, so to speak, the rivers flowing from those immortal fountains. And though there seems to be a principle in the modern world, which, should circumstances analogous to those which modeled the intellectual resources of the age to which we refer into so harmonious a proportion again arise, would arrest and perpetuate them, and consign their results to a more equal, extensive, and lasting improvement of the condition of man — though justice and the true meaning of human society are, if not more accurately, more generally understood; though perhaps men know more, and therefore are more, as a mass, yet this principle has never been called into action, and requires indeed a universal and almost appalling change in the system of existing things. The study of modern history is the study of kings, financiers, statesmen, and priests. The history of ancient Greece is the study of legislators, philosophers, and poets; it is the history of men, compared with the history of titles. What the Greeks were was a reality, not a promise. And what we are and hope to be is derived, as it were, from the influence and inspiration of these glorious generations.

Whatever tends to afford a further illustration of the manners and opinions of those to whom we owe so much, and who were, perhaps, on the whole, the most perfect specimens of humanity of whom we have authentic record, were infinitely valuable. Let us see their errors, their weaknesses, their daily actions, their familiar conversation, and catch the tone of their society. When we discover how far the most admirable community ever framed was removed from that perfection to which human society is impelled by some active power within each bosom to aspire, how great ought to be our hopes, how resolute our struggles. For the Greeks of the Periclean age were widely different from us. It is to be lamented that no modern writer has hitherto dared to show them precisely as they were. Barthélemi cannot be denied the praise of industry and system; but he never forgets that he is a Christian and a Frenchman. Wieland, in his delightful novels, makes, indeed, a very tolerable Pagan, but cherishes, too, many political prejudices, and refrains from diminishing the interest of his romances by painting sentiments in which no European of modern times can possibly sympathize. There is no book which shows the Greeks precisely as they were; they seem all written for children, with the caution that no practice or sentiment highly inconsistent with our present manners should be mentioned, lest those manners should receive outrage and violation. But there are many to whom the Greek language is inaccessible, who ought not to be excluded by this prudery from possessing an exact and comprehensive conception of the history of man; for there is no knowledge concerning what man has been and may be, from partaking of which a person can depart, without becoming in some degree more philosophical, tolerant, and just.

From an unfinished essay on
«Athenian Literature.»

IX—215

SIR PHILIP SIDNEY

(1554–1586)

SIR PHILIP SIDNEY, author of "Arcadia," and the "Defense of Poesy" was born in Kent, England, November 29th, 1554. After leaving the University of Oxford, he traveled several years in various European countries "to complete his education." On his return he came into such high favor with Queen Elizabeth that she called him one of the "jewels of her crown." At the age of twenty-two he was pronounced "one of the ripest statemen in Europe," by no less a judge of statesmanship than William the Silent. This early ripeness of intellect is attested by his "Arcadia," his "Sonnets," his "Defense of Poesy," and other works he left behind when he died at the early age of thirty-two, as a result of a wound received at the battle of Zutphen, September 22d, 1586. It is said by the critical that the story of his generosity in passing to a dying soldier the cup of water he was about to drink when wounded at Zutphen is not sufficiently attested to be regarded as historical, but it is one of the things which it is well to believe on the general principle that it is much easier for the critical to assert a negative than to prove it.

THE USES OF POETRY

SINCE poetry is of all human learnings the most ancient, and of most fatherly antiquity, as from whence other learnings have taken their beginnings; since it is so universal that no learned nation doth despise it, nor barbarous nation is without it; since both Roman and Greek gave such divine names unto it, the one of prophesying, the other of making, and that indeed that name of making is fit for him, considering that where all other arts retain themselves within their subject, and receive, as it were, their being from it, the poet only, only bringeth his own stuff, and doth not learn a conceit out of a matter, but maketh matter for a conceit; since neither his description nor end containeth any evil, the thing described cannot be evil; since his effects be so good as to teach goodness, and delight the learners of it; since therein (namely, in moral doctrine, the chief of all knowl-

edges) he doth not only far pass the historian, but, for instructing, is well nigh comparable to the philosopher; for moving, leaveth him behind him; since the Holy Scripture (wherein there is no uncleanness) hath whole parts in it poetical, and that even our Savior Christ vouchsafed to use the flowers of it; since all his kinds are not only in their united forms, but in their severed dissections fully commendable; I think, and think I think rightly, the laurel crown appointed for triumphant captains, doth worthily, of all other learnings, honor the poet's triumph.

But because we have ears as well as tongues, and that the lightest reasons that may be will seem to weigh greatly if nothing be put in the counterbalance, let us hear, and, as well as we can, ponder what objections may be made against this art, which may be worthy either of yielding or answering.

First, truly, I note, not only in these μισομουσοι, poet haters, but in all that kind of people who seek a praise by dispraising others, that they do prodigally spend a great many wandering words in quips and scoffs, carping and taunting at each thing, which, by stirring the spleen, may stay the brain from a thorough beholding the worthiness of the subject. Those kind of objections, as they are full of a very idle uneasiness (since there is nothing of so sacred a majesty but that an itching tongue may rub itself upon it), so deserve they no other answer, but, instead of laughing at the jest, to laugh at the jester. We know a playing wit can praise the discretion of an ass, the comfortableness of being in debt, and the jolly commodities of being sick of the plague; so of the contrary side, if we will turn Ovid's verse,—

"Ut lateat virtus proximitate mali."

"That good lies hid in nearness of the evil," Agrippa will be as merry in the showing the Vanity of Science as Erasmus was in the commending of Folly; neither shall any man or matter escape some touch of these smiling railers. But for Erasmus and Agrippa, they had another foundation than the superficial part would promise. Marry, these other pleasant fault-finders, who will correct the verb before they understand the noun, and confute others' knowledge before they confirm their own; I would have them only remember that scoffing cometh not of wisdom; so as the best title in true English they got with their merriments is to be called good fools; for so have our grave forefathers ever termed that humorous kind of jesters.

But that which giveth greatest scope to their scorning humor is rhyming and versing. It is already said, and, as I think, truly said, it is not rhyming and versing that maketh poesy; one may be a poet without versing, and a versifier without poetry. But yet, presuppose it were inseparable, as, indeed, it seemeth Scaliger judgeth truly, it were an inseparable commendation; for if "oratio" next to "ratio," speech next to reason, be the greatest gift bestowed upon mortality, that cannot be praiseless which doth most polish that blessing of speech; which considereth each word, not only as a man may say by his forcible quality, but by his best-measured quantity; carrying even in themselves a harmony; without, perchance, number, measure, order, proportion be in our time grown odious.

But lay aside the just praise it hath, by being the only fit speech for music—music, I say, the most divine striker of the senses; thus much is undoubtedly true, that if reading be foolish without remembering, memory being the only treasure of knowledge, those words which are fittest for memory are likewise most convenient for knowledge. Now, that verse far exceedeth prose in the knitting up of the memory, the reason is manifest: the words, besides their delight, which hath a great affinity to memory, being so set as one cannot be lost, but the whole work fails: which, accusing itself, calleth the remembrance back to itself, and so most strongly confirmeth it. Besides, one word so, as it were, begetting another, as, be it in rhyme or measured verse, by the former a man shall have a near guess to the follower. Lastly, even they that have taught the art of memory have showed nothing so apt for it as a certain room divided into many places, well and thoroughly known; now that hath the verse in effect perfectly, every word having his natural seat, which seat must needs make the word remembered. But what needs more in a thing so known to all men? Who is it that ever was a scholar that doth not carry away some verses of Virgil, Horace, or Cato, which in his youth he learned, and even to his old age serve him for hourly lessons? as,—

"Percontatorem fugito: nam garrulus idem est.
Dum sibi quisque placet credula turba sumus."

But the fitness it hath for memory is notably proved by all delivery of arts, wherein, for the most part, from grammar to logic, mathematics, physic, and the rest, the rules chiefly necessary to be borne away are compiled in verses. So that verse being in itself sweet and orderly, and being best for memory, the only handle of knowledge, it must be in jest that any man can speak against it.

From « Defense of Poesy.»

THE UNIVERSE NO CHANCE MEDLEY

You say, because we know not the causes of things, therefore Fear was the mother of Superstition; nay, because we know that each effect hath a cause, that hath engendered a true and lively devotion. For this goodly work of which we are, and in which we live, hath not his being by chance; on which opinion it is beyond marvel by what chance any brain could stumble. For if it be eternal, as you would seem to conceive of it, eternity and chance are things unsufferable together. For that is chanceable which happeneth; and if it happen, there was a time before it happened when it might have not happened; or else it did not happen, and so, if chanceable, not eternal. And as absurd it is to think that, if it had a beginning, his beginning was derived from chance; for chance could never make all things of nothing: and if there were substances before which by chance should meet to make up this work, thereon follows another bottomless pit of absurdities. For then those substances must needs have been from ever, and so eternal; and that eternal causes should bring forth chanceable effects is as sensible as that the sun should be the author of darkness. Again if it were chanceable, then was it not necessary; whereby you take away all consequents. But we see in all things, in some respect or other, necessity of consequence; therefore, in reason, we must needs know that the causes were necessary. Lastly, chance is variable, or else it is not to be called chance; but we see this work is steady and permanent. If nothing but chance had glued those pieces of this All, the heavy parts would have gone infinitely downward, the light infinitely upward, and so never have met to have made up this goodly body. For, before there was a heaven or earth, there was neither a heaven to stay the height of the ring, or an earth which, in respect of the round walls of heaven, should become a centre. Lastly, perfect order, perfect beauty, perfect constancy,— if these be the children of chance, let wisdom be counted the root of wickedness.

senses to witness, which can hear nor see nothing which yields not most evident evidence of the unspeakableness of that wisdom, each thing being directed to an end of preservation; so proper effects of judgment as speaking and laughing are of mankind. But what mad fury can ever so inveigle any conceit as to see our mortal and corruptible selves to have a reason, and that this universality, whereof we are but the least pieces, should be utterly devoid thereof? As if one should say that one's foot might be wise, and himself foolish. This heard I once alleged against such a godless mind as yours, who, being driven to acknowledge this beastly absurdity, that our bodies should be better than the whole world if it had the knowledge whereof the other were void, he sought, not able to answer directly, to shift it off in this sort: that, if that reason were true, then must it follow also that the world must have in it a spirit that could write and read too, and be learned, since that was in us commendable. Wretched fool! not considering that books be but supplies of defects, and so are praised because they help our want, and therefore cannot be incident to the Eternal Intelligence, which needs no recording of opinions to confirm his knowledge, no more than the sun wants wax to be the fuel of his glorious lightfulness.

This world, therefore, cannot otherwise consist but by a mind of wisdom which governs it, which whether you will allow to be the Creator thereof, as undoubtedly he is, or the soul and governor thereof, most certain it is that, whether he govern all, or make all, his power is above either his creatures or his government. And if his power be above all things, then, consequently, it must needs be infinite, since there is nothing above it to limit it; for that beyond which there is nothing must needs be boundless and infinite. If his power be infinite, then likewise must his knowledge be infinite; for else there should be an infinite proportion of power which he should not know how to use, the unsensibleness whereof I think even you can conceive; and if infinite, then must nothing, no, not the estate of flies, which you with so unsavory scorn did jest at, be unknown to him; for if there were, then were his knowledge bounded, and so not infinite. If his knowledge and power be infinite, then must needs his goodness and justice march in the same rank; for infiniteness of power and knowledge, without like measure of goodness, must necessarily bring forth destruction and ruin, and not orna-

But, you will say, it is so by nature; as much as if you said it is so because it is so. If you mean of many natures conspiring together, as in a popular government, to establish this fair estate, as if the elementish and ethereal parts should in their town-house set down the bounds of each one's office, then consider what follows: that there must needs have been a wisdom which made them concur. For their natures, being absolutely contrary, in nature rather would have sought each other's ruin than have served as well-consorted parts to such an unexpressible harmony. For that contrary things should meet to make up a perfection without force and wisdom above their powers is absolutely impossible, unless you will fly to that hissed-out opinion of chance again. But you may perhaps affirm that one universal nature, which hath been forever, is the knitting-together of these many parts to such an excellent unity. If you mean a nature of wisdom, goodness, and providence, which knows what it doth, then say you that which I seek of you, and cannot conclude those blasphemies with which you defiled your mouth and mine ears. But if you mean a nature as we speak of the fire, which goeth upward it knows not why, and of the nature of the sea, which in ebbing and flowing seems to observe so just a dance and yet understands no music, it is but still the same absurdity superscribed with another title. For this word One being attributed to that which is All is but one mingling of many, and many ones; as in a less matter when we say one kingdom which contains many cities, or one city which contains many persons; wherein the under-ones, if there be not a superior power and wisdom, cannot by nature regard any preservation but of themselves; no more we see they do, since the water willingly quenches the fire, and drowns the earth, so far are they from a conspired unity; but that a right heavenly nature, indeed, as it were unnaturing them, doth so bridle them.

Again, it is as absurd in nature that from a unity many contraries should proceed, still kept in a unity, as that from the number of contrarieties a unity should arise. I say still, if you banish both a singularity and a plurality of judgment from among them, then, if so earthly a mind can lift itself up so high, do but conceive how a thing whereto you give the highest and most excellent kind of being, which is eternity, can be of a base and vilest degree of being, and next to a not-being, which is so to be as not to enjoy his own being. I will not here call all your

ment and preservation. Since, then, there is a God, and an all-knowing God, so as he seeth into the darkness of all natural secrets, which is the heart of man, and sees therein the deepest dissembled thoughts — nay, sees the thoughts before they be thought; since he is just to exercise his might, and mighty to perform his justice, assure thyself, most wicked woman, that hast so plaguily a corrupted mind as thou canst not keep thy sickness to thyself, but must most wickedly infect others — assure thyself, I say, for what I say depends of everlasting and unremovable causes, that the time will come when thou shalt know that power by feeling it, when thou shalt see his wisdom in the manifesting thy ugly shamefulness, and shalt only perceive him to have been a Creator in thy destruction.

From « Arcadia,» Book III.

LYDIA H. SIGOURNEY

(1791–1865)

LYDIA HUNTLEY, who as Lydia H. Sigourney, became one of the most celebrated American authoresses of the first half of the nineteenth century, was born at Norwich, Connecticut, September 1st, 1791. Until her marriage in 1819 to Charles Sigourney she taught school, but when her husband's fortune became impaired she attempted professional writing in the hope of helping him, and succeeded probably much beyond her expectations. She wrote essays, poems, sketches, and stories in great numbers to supply the demand she had created. Her work was helpful to her generation and frequently has a decided literary quality. She died at Hartford, Connecticut, June 10th, 1865. Among her books are "Letters to Young Ladies," "Gleanings," "The Man of Uz and Other Poems," "Olive Leaves," and "Lucy Howard's Journal."

THE END OF ALL PERFECTION

I HAVE seen a man in the glory of his days, and in the pride of his strength. He was built like the strong oak, that strikes its root deep in the earth — like the tall cedar, that lifts its head above the trees of the forest. He feared no danger — he felt no sickness — he wondered why any should groan or sigh at pain. His mind was vigorous like his body; he was perplexed at no intricacy, he was daunted at no obstacle. Into hidden things he searched, and what was crooked he made plain. He went forth boldly upon the face of the mighty deep. He surveyed the nations of the earth. He measured the distances of the stars, and called them by their names. He gloried in the extent of his knowledge, in the vigor of his understanding, and strove to search even into what the Almighty had concealed. And when I looked upon him, I said with the poet, "What a piece of work is man! how noble in reason! how infinite in faculties! in form and moving, how express and admirable! in action how like an angel! in apprehension how like a god!"

I saw an infant, with a ruddy brow, and a form like polished ivory. Its motions were graceful, and its merry laughter made other hearts glad. Sometimes it wept, — and again it rejoiced, — when none knew why. But whether its cheek dimpled with smiles, or its blue eyes shone more brilliant through tears, it was beautiful. It was beautiful because it was innocent. And care-worn and sinful men admired, when they beheld it. It was like the first blossom which some cherished plant has put forth, whose cup sparkles with a dewdrop, and whose head reclines upon the parent stem.

Again I looked. It had become a child. The lamp of reason had beamed into its mind. It was simple, and single-hearted, and a follower of the truth. It loved every little bird that sang in the trees, and every fresh blossom. Its heart danced with joy as it looked around on this good and pleasant world. It stood like a lamb before its teachers — it bowed its ear to instruction — it walked in the way of knowledge. It was not proud, nor stubborn, nor envious, and it had never heard of the vices and vanities of the world. And when I looked upon it, I remembered our Savior's words, "Except ye become as little children, ye cannot enter into the kingdom of heaven."

I saw a man, whom the world calls honorable. Many waited for his smile. They pointed to the fields that were his, and talked of the silver and gold which he had gathered. They praised the stateliness of his domes, and extolled the honor of his family. But the secret language of his heart was, "By my wisdom have I gotten all this." So he returned no thanks to God, neither did he fear or serve him. As I passed along, I heard the complaints of the laborers, who had reaped his fields — and the cries of the poor, whose covering he had taken away. The sound of feasting and revelry was in his mansion, and the unfed beggar came tottering from his door. But he considered not that the cries of the oppressed were continually entering into the ears of the Most High. And when I knew that this man was the docile child whom I had loved, the beautiful infant on whom I had gazed with delight, I said in my bitterness, "Now have I seen an end of all perfection!" And I laid my mouth in the dust.

Complete.

I returned — but his look was no more lofty, nor his step proud. His broken frame was like some ruined tower. His hairs were white and scattered, and his eye gazed vacantly upon the passers-by. The vigor of his intellect was wasted, and of all that he had gained by study, nothing remained. He feared when there was no danger, and where was no sorrow he wept. His decaying memory had become treacherous. It showed him only broken images of the glory that had departed. His house was to him like a strange land, and his friends were counted as enemies. He thought himself strong and healthful, while his feet tottered on the verge of the grave. He said of his son, "He is my brother"; of his daughter, "I know her not." He even inquired what was his own name. And as I gazed mournfully upon him, one who supported his feeble frame, and ministered to his many wants, said to me, "Let thine heart receive instruction, for thou hast seen an end of all perfection!"

I have seen a beautiful female, treading the first stages of youth, and entering joyfully into the pleasures of life. The glance of her eye was variable and sweet, and on her cheek trembled something like the first blush of the morning. Her lips moved, and there was melody, and when she floated in the dance, her light form, like the aspen, seemed to move with every breeze.

I returned — she was not in the dance. I sought her among her gay companions, but I found her not. Her eye sparkled not there — the music of her voice was silent. She rejoiced on earth no more. I saw a train — sable and slow-paced. Sadly they bore towards an open grave what once was animated and beautiful. As they drew near, they paused, and a voice broke the solemn silence: "Man that is born of a woman is of few days and full of misery. He cometh up, and is cut down like a flower, he fleeth as it were a shadow, and never continueth in one stay." Then they let down into the deep, dark pit, that maiden whose lips but a few days since were like the half-blown rosebud. I shuddered at the sound of clods falling upon the hollow coffin. Then I heard a voice saying, "Earth to earth, ashes to ashes, dust to dust." They covered her with the damp soil, and the uprooted turf of the valley, and turned again to their own homes. But one mourner lingered to cast himself upon the tomb. And as he wept he said, "There is no beauty, nor grace, nor loveliness, but what vanisheth like the morning dew. I have seen an end of all perfection!"

JEAN CHARLES LEONARD DE SISMONDI

(1773–1842)

SISMONDI, the celebrated historian of Italy and of Italian literature, was born at Geneva, Switzerland, May 9th, 1773. His father, a village pastor, was named "Simonde," a patronymic which the son for literary and other purposes altered to the more aristocratic one of "de Sismondi." The Simonde family emigrated from Geneva during the French Revolution, and after spending a short time in England, settled at Pescia, near Lucca, in Italy, where Sismondi received the bent which resulted in his most celebrated works. His "History of the Italian Republics" appeared between 1807 and 1818, and his "Literature of the South of Europe" between 1813 and 1829. He wrote, besides, a "History of France," a number of works on Political Economy and "Julia Severa," a historical novel, which appeared in 1829. He died at Geneva, June 25th, 1842.

ROMANTIC LOVE AND PETRARCH'S POETRY

NEVER did passion burn more purely than in the love of Petrarch for Laura. Of all the erotic poets, he alone never expresses a single hope offensive to the purity of a heart which had been pledged to another. When Petrarch first beheld her, on the sixth of April, 1327, Laura was in the church of Avignon. She was the daughter of Audibert de Noves, and wife of Hugues de Sade, both of Avignon. When she died of the plague, on the sixth of April, 1348, she had been the mother of eleven children. Petrarch has celebrated, in upwards of three hundred sonnets, all the little circumstances of this attachment; those precious favors which, after an acquaintance of fifteen or twenty years, consisted at most of a kind word, a glance not altogether severe, a momentary expression of regret or tenderness at his departure, or a deeper paleness at the idea of losing her beloved and constant friend. Yet even these marks of an attachment so pure and unobtrusive, and which he had so often struggled to subdue, were repressed by the coldness of Laura, who, to preserve her lover, cautiously abstained from giving the least encouragement to his love. She avoided his presence, except at church, in the brilliant levees of the papal court, or in the country, where, surrounded by her friends, she is described by Petrarch as exhibiting the semblance of a queen, pre-eminent amongst them all in the grace of her figure, and the brilliancy of her beauty. It does not appear that, in the whole course of these twenty years, the poet ever addressed her, unless in the presence of witnesses. An interview with her alone would surely have been celebrated in a thousand verses; and, as he has left us four sonnets on the good fortune he enjoyed in having an opportunity of picking up her glove, we may fairly presume that he would not have passed over in silence so happy a circumstance as a private interview. There is no poet, in any language, so perfectly pure as Petrarch, so completely above all reproach of levity and immorality; and this merit, which is due equally to the poet and to his Laura, is still more remarkable, when we consider that the models which he followed were by no means entitled to the same praise. The verses of the Troubadours and of the Trouveres were very licentious. The court of Avignon, at which Laura lived, the Babylon of the West, as the poet himself often terms it, was filled with the most shameful corruption; and even the Popes, more especially Clement V. and Clement VI. had afforded examples of great depravity. Indeed, Petrarch himself, in his intercourse with other ladies, was by no means so reserved. For Laura he had conceived a sort of religious and enthusiastic passion; such as mystics imagine they feel towards the Deity, and such as Plato supposes to be the bond of union between elevated minds. The poets who have succeeded Petrarch have amused themselves with giving representations of a similar passion, of which, in fact, they had little or no experience.

In order to appreciate the full beauty of Petrarch's sonnets, it would be necessary to write the history of his attachment, as M. Ginguené has so ably done; and thus to assign to every sonnet the place to which its particular sentiment destines it. But it would be even more necessary that I should myself be sensible of the excellence of these poems, and that I should feel that charm which has enchanted every nation and every age. To this I must acknowledge that I am a stranger. I could have wished, in order to comprehend and to become interested in the passion of Petrarch, that there should have been a somewhat better understanding between the lovers; that they should have had a more intimate knowledge of each other; and that, by this means, we might ourselves have been better acquainted with both.

I could have wished to have seen some impression made upon the sensibility of this loving and long-loved lady; to have seen her heart, as well as her mind, enlarging itself and yielding to the constancy and the purity of true friendship, since virtue denied a more tender return. It is tiresome to find the same veil, always shading not only the figure, but the intellect and the heart of the woman who is celebrated in these monotonous verses. If the poet had allowed us a fairer view of her, he would have been less likely to fall into exaggerations, into which my imagination, at least, is unable to follow him. How desirable would it be that he should have recalled her to our minds by thought, by feeling, and by passion, rather than by a perpetual play upon the words Laura (the laurel), and l'aura (the air). The first of these conceits, more especially, is incessantly repeated, nor merely in the poems alone. Throughout Petrarch's whole life, we are in doubt whether it is of Laura or of the laurel that he is enamored; so great is the emotion which he expresses, whenever he beholds the latter; so passionately does he mention it; and so frequently has he celebrated it in his verses. Nor is that personified heart, to which Petrarch perpetually addresses himself, less fatiguing. It speaks, it answers, it argues, it is ever upon his lips, in his eyes, and yet ever at a distance. He is always absent, and we cannot avoid wishing that during his banishment, he would for once cease to speak of it. Judging from these conceits, and from the continual personification of beings which have no personal attributes, it has always appeared to me that Petrarch is by no means so great a poet as Dante, because he is less of a painter. There is scarcely one of his sonnets, in which the leading idea is not completely at variance with the principles of painting, and which does not, therefore, escape from the imagination. Poetry may be called a happy union of two of the fine arts. It has borrowed its harmonies from music, and its images from painting. But to confound the two objects which poetry has thus in view is to be equally in error; whether we attempt, by an image, to represent a coincidence in sound, as when the laurel is put for Laura; or whether we wish to call up an image by sounds, as when, neglecting the rules of harmony, we produce a discordance suited to the object we design to paint, and make the serpents of which we are speaking hiss in our verses.

From "Literature of the South of Europe."

SAMUEL SMILES

(1812-)

SAMUEL SMILES was born at Haddington, Scotland, in 1812. He began life as a physician, practicing at Haddington and in Leeds. Becoming editor of the Leeds Times, he gave up medicine for journalism and essay writing, and in such books as "Character," "Thrift," and "Self-Help," he has almost created a school of his own. His essays are characterized by a wealth of incident and anecdote which makes them interesting and entertaining even when they are most didactic. Besides his essays Smiles wrote a "History of Ireland," a "Life of George Stephenson," "Brief Biographies," and "The Huguenots in France." From 1845 to 1866 he was an officer of various English railway companies. The whole tendency of his writings is to establish a more efficient faith in honesty and persistent industry as the basis of success in life and business.

MEN WHO CANNOT BE BOUGHT

Thou must be brave thyself,
    If thou the truth would teach;
Live truly and thy life shall be
    A great and noble creed.

'Tis a very good world we live in,
To lend, or to spend, or to give in;
But to beg, or to borrow, or to get a man's own
'Tis the very worst world that ever was known.
            — *Bulwer Lytton.*

Good name in man or woman, dear my lord,
Is the immediate jewel of their souls:
Who steals my purse, steals trash: 'tis something, nothing,
'Twas mine, 'tis his, and has been slave to thousand;
But he that filches from me my good name,
Robs me of that which not enriches him,
And makes me poor indeed.
            — *Shakespeare.*

L'honneur vaut mieux que l'argent.
            — *French Proverb.*

FIRST, there are men who can be bought. There are rogues innumerable, who are ready to sell their bodies and souls for money and for drink. Who has not heard of the elections which have been made void through bribery and corruption? This is not the way to enjoy liberty or to keep it. The men who sell themselves are slaves; their buyers are dishonest and unprincipled. Freedom has its humbugs. "I'm standing on the soil of liberty," said an orator. "You ain't," replied a bootmaker in the audience. "You're standing in a pair of boots you never paid me for."

The tendency of men is ever to go with the majority — to go with the huzzas. "Majority," said Schiller, "what does that mean? Sense has ever been centred in the few. Votes should be weighed, not counted. That state must sooner or later go to ruin where numbers sway and ignorance decides."

When the secession from the Scotch Church took place, Norman Macleod said it was a great trial to the flesh to keep by the unpopular side, and to act out what conscience dictated as the line of duty. Scorn and hissing greeted him at every turn. "I saw a tomb to-day," he says, in one of his letters, "in the chapel of Holyrood, with this inscription, 'Here lies an honest man!' I only wish to live in such a way as to entitle me to the same éloge."

The ignorant and careless are at the mercy of the unprincipled; and the ignorant are as yet greatly in the majority. When a French quack was taken before the Correctional Tribunal at Paris for obstructing the Pont Neuf, the magistrate said to him, "Sirrah! how is it you draw such crowds about you, and extract so much money from them in selling your 'infallible' rubbish?" "My lord," replied the quack, "how many people do you think cross the Pont Neuf in the hour?" "I don't know," said the judge. "Then I can tell you — about ten thousand; and how many of these do you think are wise?" "Oh, perhaps a hundred!" "It is too many," said the quack; "but I leave the hundred persons to you, and take the nine thousand and nine hundred for my customers!"

Men are bribed in all directions. They have no spirit of probity, self-respect, or manly dignity. If they had, they would spurn bribes in every form. Government servants are bribed to pass goods, fit or unfit for use. Hence soldiers' half-tanned shoes give way on a march; their shoddy coats become ragged;

their tinned provisions are found rotten. Captain Nares had a sad account to give of the feeding of his sailors while in the Arctic regions. All this is accomplished by bribery and corruption in the lower quarters of the civil service.

Much is done in the way of illicit commissions. A check finds its way to a certain official, and he passes the account. Thus many a man becomes rich upon a moderate salary. After a great act of corruption had been practiced by the servant of a public company, a notice was placed over the office door to this effect: "The servants of the company are not allowed to take bribes." The cook gets a commission from the tradesman; the butler has a secret understanding with the wine merchant.

"These illicit commissions," says the Times, "do much to poison business relations. But if the vice were ever to mount from the servants' hall or the market and invade any public office, there would be an end to efficiency or confidence in public men. It is all-important that the public service should be pure, and that no suspicion should rest on the name of any official in a post of confidence. It would be an evil day if it were generally suspected that civil servants took backsheesh or *pots de vin.*"

An inventor suggested a method for registering the number of persons entering an omnibus, but the secretary was unable to entertain it. "It is of no use to us," he said; "the machine which we want is one that will make our men honest, and that, I am afraid, we are not likely to meet with." We want honest men! is the cry everywhere. The police courts too often reveal the stealing and swindling of men in whom confidence has been placed; and the result is that they are dragged down from confidence to ruin. It is trustworthy character that is most wanted. Character is reliableness; convincing other men by your acts that you can be trusted.

Abroad it is the same. Russia, Egypt, and Spain are the worst. In Russia the corruption of public servants, even of the highest grade, is most gross. You must buy your way by gold. Bribery in every conceivable form is practiced — from arrangements between furnishers and the officials who should control them, to the direct handling over of the goods — is undeniably prevalent. The excuse is that the public servants are so badly paid. The Moscow and Petersburg Railway was constructed at great expense. Vast sums were paid to engineers and workmen, and stolen by overseers and directors. Prince Mentchikoff ac-

IX—216

companied his Imperial Master in a jaunt through the capital, undertaken for the benefit of the Persian embassador, who was making a visit to the country. The Persian surveyed golden domes, granite pillars, glittering miles of shops, with true Oriental indifference. The Emperor at last bent toward his favorite and whispered with an air of vexation, "Can't we find anything that will astonish this fellow?" "Yes, your Majesty," replied the Prince; "show him the accounts of the Moscow and Petersburg Railway!" At Alexandria, in Egypt, the "leakage," as it is called, is enormous, unless bought off by gold. In Spain, every ship has to work its way into port after bribing the customs officers. The excuse is the same as in Russia; the civil servants of Spain cannot live except by taking bribes.

Even in republics men are apt and willing to be bribed. Money gets over many difficulties; it solves many problems. In America, the cream of republics, bribery is conducted in a wholesale way. The simple salary of an official is not sufficient. Even the highest in office is bribed by presents of carriages and horses, and even by hard cash. The most far-seeing and honest of American statesmen see that jobbery and corruption are fast undermining the efficiency of the administration, and debasing the standard of public virtue.

It has been the same all over the world. It does not matter what the form of government is called — whether a monarchy, an aristocracy, or a republic. It is not the form of government, but the men who administer it. Selfishly used, political power is a curse; intelligently and impartially used, it may be one of the greatest blessings to a community. If selfishness begins with the governing classes, woe to the country that is governed. The evil spreads downward, and includes all classes, even the poorest. The race of life becomes one for mere pelf and self. Principle is abandoned. Honesty is a forgotten virtue. Faith dies out, and society becomes a scramble for place and money.

Yet there are men who have refused to be bought, in all times and ages. Even the poorest, inspired by duty, have refused to sell themselves for money. Among the North American Indians a wish for wealth is considered unworthy of a brave man — so that the chief is often the poorest of his tribe. The best benefactors of the race have been poor men, among the Israelites, among the Greeks, and among the Romans. Elisha was at the plow when called to be a prophet, and Cincinnatus

was in his fields when called to lead the armies of Rome. Socrates and Epaminondas were among the poorest men in Greece. Such, too, were the Galilean fishermen, the inspired founders of our faith.

Aristides was called The Just from his unbending integrity. His sense of justice was spotless, and his self-denial unimpeachable. He fought at Marathon, at Salamis, and commanded at the battle of Platea. Though he had borne the highest offices in the state, he died poor. Nothing could buy him; nothing could induce him to swerve from his duty. It is said that the Athenians became more virtuous from contemplating his bright example. In the representation of one of the tragedies of Æschylus, a sentence was uttered in favor of moral goodness, on which the eyes of the audience turned involuntarily from the actor to Aristides.

Phocion, the Athenian general, a man of great bravery and foresight, was surnamed The Good. Alexander the Great, when overrunning Greece, endeavored to win him from his loyalty. He offered him riches, and the choice of four cities in Asia. The answer of Phocion bespoke the spotless character of the man. "If Alexander really esteems me," he said, "let him leave me my honesty."

Yet Demosthenes, the eloquent, could be bought. When Harpalus, one of Alexander's chiefs, came to Athens, the orators had an eye upon his gold. Demosthenes was one of them. What is eloquence without honesty? On his visit to Harpalus, the chief perceived that Demosthenes was much pleased with one of the king's beautifully engraved cups. He desired him to take it in his hand that he might feel its weight. "How much might it bring?" asked Demosthenes. "It will bring you twenty talents," replied Harpalus. That night the cup was sent to Demosthenes, with twenty talents in it. The present was not refused. The circumstance led to the disgrace of the orator, and he soon after poisoned himself.

Cicero, on the other hand, refused all presents from friends, as well as from the enemies of his country. Some time after his assassination Cæsar found one of his grandsons with a book of Cicero's in his hands. The boy endeavored to hide it, but Cæsar took it from him. After having run over it, he returned it to the boy, saying, "My dear child, this was an eloquent man, and a lover of his country."

Bias, when asked why he did not, like others of his countrymen, load himself with part of his property when all were obliged to fly, said, "Your wonder is without reason; I am carrying all my treasures with me."

When Diocletian had quitted the imperial purple for some time, Maximilian invited him to reassume the reins of government. Diocletian replied, "If I could show you the cabbages that I have planted with my own hands at Salona, and the fine melons that I have been ripening, and the delightful plantations I have made about my villa, I should no longer be urged to relinquish the enjoyment of happiness for the pursuit of power."

What he had worked for was his own, the fruit of his own labor and pains. He had imbibed the spirit of industry, which gives perseverance to the worker, enterprise to the warrior, and firmness to the statesman. Labor shuts up the first avenues to dishonesty; it opens a broader field for the display of every talent; and inspires with a new vigor the performance of every social and religious duty. Hence the Romans desired to call Diocletian back to his political duties.

Contentment is also better than luxury or power; indeed, it is natural wealth. Mary, sister of Elizabeth, often wished that she had been born a milkmaid instead of a queen. She would have been saved the torture of unrequited love, and the degradation of power through the hands of her ministers. Many martyrs would have been saved from burning.

Brave and honest men do not work for gold. They work for love, for honor, for character. When Socrates suffered death rather than abandon his views of right morality; when Las Casas endeavored to mitigate the tortures of the poor Indians, they had no thought of money or country. They worked for the elevation of all that thought, and for the relief of all that suffered.

When Michael Angelo was commanded by the Pope to undertake the direction of the works of St. Peter's, he consented only upon condition that he should receive no salary, but that he should labor "for the love of God alone." "Keep your money," said Wiertz of Brussels to a gentleman who wished to buy one of his pictures; "gold gives the deathblow to art." At the same time it must be confessed that Wiertz was a man of outré character.

In political life, place and money are too much in request. The gift of office, when not fairly earned by public service, proves often the corruption of morals. It is the substitution of an inferior motive for a patriotic one; and wherever it prevails from considerations of personal favoritism, it degrades politics and debases character.

Andrew Marvell was a patriot of the old Roman build. He lived in troublous times. He was born at Hull at the beginning of the reign of Charles I. When a young man, he spent four years at Trinity College, Cambridge. He afterward traveled through Europe. In Italy he met Milton, and continued his friend through life. On his return to England the civil war was raging. It does not appear that he took any part in the struggle, though he was always a defender and promoter of liberty. In 1660 he was elected member of Parliament for his native town, and during his membership he wrote to the mayor and his constituents by almost every post, telling them of the course of affairs in Parliament.

Marvell did not sympathize with Milton's antimonarchical tendencies. His biographer styles him "the friend of England, Liberty, and Magna Charta." He had no objections to a properly restricted monarchy, and therefore favored the Restoration. The people longed for it, believing that the return of Charles II. would prove the restoration of peace and loyalty. They were much mistaken. Marvell was appointed to accompany Lord Carlisle on an embassy to Russia, showing that he was not reckoned an enemy to the court. During his absence much evil had been done. The restored king was constantly in want of money. He took every method, by selling places and instituting monopolies, to supply his perpetual need. In one of Marvell's letters to his constituents he said, "The court is at the highest pitch of want and luxury, and the people are full of discontent." In a trial of two Quakers, Pen and Mead, at the Old Bailey, the recorder, among the rest, commended the Spanish Inquisition, saying "it would never be well till we had something like it."

The king continued to raise money unscrupulously, by means of his courtiers and apostate patriots. He bought them up by bribes of thousands of pounds. But Marvell was not to be bought. His satires upon the court and its parasites were published. They were read by all classes, from the king to the tradesman. The king determined to win him over. He was

threatened, he was flattered, he was thwarted, he was caressed, he was beset with spies, he was waylaid by ruffians, and courted by beauties. But no Delilah could discover the secret of his strength. His integrity was proof alike against danger and against corruption. Against threats and bribes, pride is the ally of principle. In a court which held no man to be honest, and no woman chaste, this soft sorcery was cultivated to perfection; but Marvell, revering and respecting himself, was proof against its charms.

It has been said that Lord Treasurer Danby, thinking to buy over his old schoolfellow, called upon Marvell in his garret. At parting, the lord treasurer slipped into his hand an order on the treasury for £1,000, and then went to his chariot. Marvell, looking at the paper, calls after the treasurer, "My lord, I request another moment." They went up again to the garret, and Jack, the servant boy, was called. "Jack, child, what had I for dinner yesterday?" "Don't you remember, sir? you had the little shoulder of mutton that you ordered me to bring from a woman in the market." "Very right, child. What have I for dinner to-day?" "Don't you know, sir, that you bid me lay by the blade bone to broil?" "'Tis so, very right, child, go away." "My lord," said Marvell, turning to the treasurer, "do you hear that? Andrew Marvell's dinner is provided; there's your piece of paper. I want it not. I knew the sort of kindness you intended. I live here to serve my constitutents: the ministry may seek men for their purpose; I am not one."

Marvell conducted himself nobly to the end. He remained unimpeachable in his character. He was the true representative of his constituents. Though not poor, his mode of living was simple and frugal. In July, 1678, he visited his constituents for the last time. Shortly after his return to London, without any previous illness or visible decay, he expired. Some say he died from poison. That may not be true. But certainly he died an honest man. He always preserved his purity. He ever defended the right. He was "beloved by good men; feared by bad; imitated by few; and scarce paralleled by any." These are the words on his tombstone at Hull.

Ben Jonson, like Marvell, was sturdy and plain spoken. When Charles I. sent that brave poet a tardy and slight gratuity during his poverty and sickness, Ben sent back the money, with the message, "I suppose he sends me this because I live in an alley; tell him his soul lives in an alley."

Goldsmith also was a man who would not be bought. He had known the depths of poverty. He had wandered over Europe, paying his way with his flute. He had slept in barns and under the open sky. He tried acting, ushering, doctoring. He starved amid them all. Then he tried authorship, and became a gentleman. But he never quite escaped from the clutches of poverty. He described himself as "in a garret writing for bread, and expecting to be dunned for a milk score." One day Johnson received a message from Goldsmith, stating that he was in great distress. The doctor went to see him, and found that his landlady had arrested him for his rent. The only thing he had to dispose of was a packet of manuscript. Johnson took it up, and found it to be the "Vicar of Wakefield." Having ascertained its merit, Johnson took it to a bookseller and sold it for sixty pounds.

Poor though he was then, and poor though he was at the end of his life,—for he died in debt,—Goldsmith could not be bought. He refused to do dirty political work. About £50,000 annually was then expended by Sir Robert Walpole in secret-service money. Daily scribblers were suborned to write up the acts of the administration, and to write down those of their opponents. In the time of Lord North "Junius" was in opposition. It was resolved to hire Goldsmith to baffle his terrible sarcasm. Dr. Scott, chaplain to Lord Sandwich, was deputed to negotiate with him. "I found him," says Dr. Scott, "in a miserable suite of chambers in the Temple. I told him my authority. I told how I was empowered to pay for his exertions; and, would you believe it?—he was so absurd as to say, 'I can earn as much as will supply my wants without writing for any party'; and, the assistance you offer is therefore unnecessary to me'; and so I left him in his garret!"

Thus did poor and noble Goldsmith spurn the wages of unrighteousness! He preferred using his pen to write the famous tale of "Goody Two Shoes" for the amusement of children rather than become the hack pamphleteer of political prostitutes.

Pulteney, the leader of the Opposition in the House of Commons, having in one of his speeches made a Latin quotation, was corrected by Sir Robert Walpole, who offered to wager a guinea on the inaccuracy of the lines. The bet was accepted, the classic was referred to, and Pulteney was found to be right. The minister threw a guinea across the table, and Pulteney, on taking it

up, called the house to witness that this was the first guinea of the public money he had ever put into his pocket! The very coin thus lost and won is preserved in the British Museum, as the "Pulteney Guinea."

From "Duty."

ADAM SMITH

(1723-1790)

ADAM SMITH, author of the « Wealth of Nations, » and one of the most celebrated economists of modern times, was born in Fifeshire, Scotland, June 5th, 1723. After completing his own scholastic education at Glasgow and Oxford, he taught Rhetoric and Belles-Lettres at Edinburgh, Logic at Glasgow, and finally Moral Philosophy in the latter university. In 1778 he was appointed Commissioner of Customs at Edinburgh; in 1787 was chosen Lord Rector of the University of Glasgow. His « Inquiry into the Nature and Causes of the Wealth of Nations » appeared in 1776, and his « Theory of Moral Sentiments » in 1759. He died at Edinburgh, July 17th, 1790. He wrote industriously on what seems to have been a wide range of topics, but just before his death he selected a few essays from the mass of his manuscripts and directed that all the rest should be burned. This was accordingly done, perhaps to the advantage of his reputation, but certainly to the disadvantage of posterity, as even the worst and most unpolished writing of a man of his intellectual rank may be more valuable than the masterpieces of mediocrity.

JUDGING OTHERS BY OURSELVES

WHEN the original passions of the person principally concerned are in perfect concord with the sympathetic emotions of the spectator, they necessarily appear to this last just and proper, and suitable to their objects; and, on the contrary, when, upon bringing the case home to himself, he finds that they do not coincide with what he feels, they necessarily appear to him unjust and improper, and unsuitable to the causes which excite them. To approve of the passions of another, therefore, as suitable to their objects, is the same thing as to observe that we entirely sympathize with them; and not to approve of them as such is the same thing as to observe that we do not entirely sympathize with them. The man who resents the injuries that have

very frivolous nature, because in them the judgments of mankind are less apt to be perverted by wrong systems. We may often approve of a jest, and think the laughter of the company quite just and proper, though we ourselves do not laugh, because, perhaps, we are in a grave humor, or happen to have our attention engaged with other objects. We have learned, however, from experience, what sort of pleasantry is upon most occasions capable of making us laugh, and we observe that this is one of that kind. We approve, therefore, of the laughter of the company, and feel that it is natural and suitable to its object; because, though in our present mode we cannot easily enter into it, we are sensible that upon most occasions we should very heartily join in it.

The same thing often happens with regard to all the other passions. A stranger passes by us in the street with all the marks of the deepest affliction; and we are immediately told that he has just received the news of the death of his father. It is impossible that, in this case, we should not approve of his grief. Yet it may often happen, without any defect of humanity on our part, that, so far from entering into the violence of his sorrow, we should scarce conceive the first movements of concern upon his account. Both he and his father, perhaps, are entirely unknown to us, or we happen to be employed about other things, and do not take time to picture out in our imagination the different circumstances of distress which must occur to him. We have learned, however, from experience, that such a misfortune naturally excites such a degree of sorrow, and we know that if we took time to consider his situation fully in all its parts, we should, without doubt, most sincerely sympathize with him. It is upon the consciousness of this conditional sympathy, that our approbation of his sorrow is founded, even in those cases in which that sympathy does not actually take place; and the general rules derived from our preceding experience of what our sentiments would commonly correspond with, correct upon this, as upon many other occasions, the impropriety of our present emotions.

The sentiment or affection of the heart from which any action proceeds, and upon which its whole virtue or vice must ultimately depend, may be considered under two different aspects, or in two different relations; first, in relation to the cause which excites it, or the motive which gives occasion to it; and second, in relation

been done to me, and observes that I resent them precisely as he does, necessarily approves of my resentment. The man whose sympathy keeps time to my grief cannot but admit the reasonableness of my sorrow. He who admires the same poem, or the same picture, and admires them exactly as I do, must surely allow the justness of my admiration. He who laughs at the same joke, and laughs along with me, cannot well deny the propriety of my laughter. On the contrary, the person who, upon these different occasions, either feels no such emotion as that which I feel, or feels none that bears any proportion to mine, cannot avoid disapproving my sentiments on account of their dissonance with his own. If my animosity goes beyond what the indignation of my friend can correspond to; if my grief exceeds what his most tender compassion can go along with; if my admiration is either too high or too low to tally with his own; if I laugh loud and heartily when he only smiles, or, on the contrary, only smile when he laughs loud and heartily; in all these cases, as soon as he comes from considering the object, to observe how I am affected by it, according as there is more or less disproportion between his sentiments and mine, I must incur a greater or less degree of his disapprobation: and upon all occasions his own sentiments are the standards and measures by which he judges of mine.

To approve of another man's opinions is to adopt those opinions, and to adopt them is to approve of them. If the same arguments which convince you convince me likewise, I necessarily approve of your conviction; and if they do not, I necessarily disapprove of it: neither can I possibly conceive that I should do the one without the other. To approve or disapprove, therefore, of the opinions of others is acknowledged by everybody to mean no more than to observe their agreement or disagreement with our own. But this is equally the case with regard to our approbation or disapprobation of the sentiments or passions of others.

There are, indeed, some cases in which we seem to approve without any sympathy or correspondence of sentiments, and in which, consequently, the sentiment of approbation would seem to be different from the perception of this coincidence. A little attention, however, will convince us that even in these cases our approbation is ultimately founded upon a sympathy or correspondence of this kind. I shall give an instance in things of a

to the end which it proposes, or the effect which it tends to produce.

In the suitableness or unsuitableness, in the proportion or disproportion which the affection seems to bear to the cause or object which excites it, consists the propriety or impropriety, the decency or ungracefulness of the consequent action.

In the beneficial or hurtful nature of the effects which the affection aims at, or tends to produce, consists the merit or demerit of the action, the qualities by which it is entitled to reward, or is deserving of punishment.

Philosophers have, of late years, considered chiefly the tendency of affections, and have given little attention to the relation which they stand in to the cause which excites them. In common life, however, when we judge of any person's conduct, and of the sentiments which directed it, we constantly consider them under both these aspects. When we blame in another man the excesses of love, of grief, of resentment, we not only consider the ruinous effect which they tend to produce, but the little occasion which was given for them. The merit of his favorite, we say, is not so great, his misfortune is not so dreadful, his provocation is not so extraordinary, as to justify so violent a passion. We should have indulged, we say, perhaps have approved of the violence of his emotion, had the cause been in any respect proportioned to it.

When we judge in this manner of any affection as proportioned or disproportioned to the cause which excites it, it is scarce possible that we should make use of any other rule or canon but the correspondent affection in ourselves. If, upon bringing the case home to our own breast, we find that the sentiments which it gives occasion to, coincide and tally with our own, we necessarily approve of them as proportioned and suitable to their objects; if otherwise, we necessarily disapprove of them, as extravagant and out of proportion.

Every faculty in one man is the measure by which he judges of the like faculty in another. I judge of your sight by my sight, of your ear by my ear, of your reason by my reason, of your resentment by my resentment, of your love by my love. I neither have, nor can have, any other way of judging about them.

Chap. iii., « Of Sympathy, » complete. From « Theory of Moral Sentiments. »

THE DIVISION OF LABOR

OBSERVE the accommodation of the most common artificer or day laborer in a civilized and thriving country, and you will perceive that the number of people, of whose industry a part, though but a small part, has been employed in procuring him this accommodation, exceeds all computation. The woolen coat, for example, which covers the day laborer, as coarse and rough as it may appear, is the produce of the joint labor of a great multitude of workmen. The shepherd, the sorter of the wool, the wool comber or carder, the dyer, the scribbler, the spinner, the weaver, the fuller, the dresser, with many others, must all join their different arts in order to complete even this homely production. How many merchants and carriers, besides, must have been employed in transporting the materials from some of those workmen to others, who often live in a very distant part of the country! How much commerce and navigation in particular, how many shipbuilders, sailors, sail makers, rope makers, must have been employed in order to bring together the different drugs made use of by the dyer, which often come from the remotest corners of the world! What a variety of labor, too, is necessary in order to produce the tools of the meanest of those workmen! To say nothing of such complicated machines as the ship of the sailor, the mill of the fuller, or even the loom of the weaver, let us consider only what a variety of labor is requisite in order to form that very simple machine, the shears with which the shepherd clips the wool. The miner, the builder of the furnace for smelting the ore, the feller of the timber, the burner of the charcoal to be made use of in the smelting house, the brickmaker, the bricklayer, the workmen who attend the furnace, the millwright, the forger, the smith, must all of them join their different arts in order to produce them. Were we to examine in the same manner all the different parts of his dress and household furniture, the coarse linen shirt which he wears next his skin, the shoes which cover his feet, the bed which he lies on, and all the different parts which compose it, the kitchen grate at which he prepares his victuals, the coals which he makes use of for that purpose, dug from the bowels of the earth, and brought to him, perhaps, by a long sea and a long land carriage, all the other utensils of his kitchen, all the furniture of his table,

the knives and forks, the earthen or pewter plates upon which he serves up and divides his victuals, the different hands employed in preparing his bread and his beer, the glass window which lets in the heat and the light, and keeps out the wind and the rain, with all the knowledge and art requisite for preparing that beautiful and happy invention, without which these northern parts of the world could scarce have afforded a very comfortable habitation, together with the tools of all the different workmen employed in producing those different conveniences; if we examine, I say, all these things, and consider what a variety of labor is employed about each of them, we shall be sensible that, without the assistance and co-operation of many thousands, the very meanest person in a civilized country could not be provided, even according to what we very falsely imagine the easy and simple manner in which he is commonly accommodated. Compared, indeed, with the more extravagant luxury of the great, his accommodation must, no doubt, appear extremely simple and easy; and yet it may be true, perhaps, that the accommodation of a European prince does not always so much exceed that of an industrious and frugal peasant, as the accommodation of the latter exceeds that of many an African king, the absolute master of the lives and liberties of ten thousand naked savages.

From "Wealth of Nations."

HORACE SMITH

(1779–1849)

HORACE SMITH, joint author with his brother James of the famous "Rejected Addresses," was born at London, December 31st, 1779. The "Rejected Addresses" made the brothers so celebrated that Horace found a field for indulging his inclination towards humorous essay writing. His "Gayeties and Gravities," published in three volumes in 1826, deserve to be read much more frequently than they have been since his death in 1849. The occasion of the "Rejected Addresses" was the rebuilding of Drury Lane Theatre in 1812, and the offer of a prize of £50 for an address to be recited at the dedication in October of that year. On noticing the advertisement of the prize, the Smith brothers conceived the idea of writing and publishing as having been rejected by the managers a volume of addresses which they imputed to Wordsworth, Southey, Coleridge, Crabbe, Byron, Moore, Scott, and Bowles. The parodies were so clever and the idea which inspired them so attractively comic that the "Rejected Addresses" at once took the hold on English literature which the passage of time has shown to be a permanent one.

THE DIGNITY OF A TRUE JOKE

The gravest beast is an ass; the gravest bird is an owl; the gravest fish is an oyster; and the gravest man a fool.
—*Joe Miller.*

GRAVITY, says Lord Bolingbroke, is the very essence of imposture. A quack or a pretender is generally a very grave and reverend signior; and though I would not venture to assert that the converse of this proposition is invariably true, I must confess that as I am apt to doubt the virtue of an obtrusive Puritan and rigorist, so am I marvelously prone to suspect the wisdom of your serious and solemn Precisian. While the shallow pedant endeavors to impose upon the world by a serious and pompous deportment, minds of a superior order will be often found abandoning themselves to playfulness and puerility. Plato, after discoursing philosophy with his disciples upon the promon-

tory of Sunium, frequently indulged the gayety of his heart by relaxing into a vein of the most trivial jocoseness; but once seeing a grave formalist approach in the midst of their trifling, he exclaimed, "Silence, my friends! let us be wise now; here is a fool coming." This man's race is not extinct. Reader! hast thou not sometimes encountered a starched-looking quiz, who seemed to have steeped his countenance in vinegar to preserve it from the infection of laughter?—a personage of whom it might be pronounced, as Butler said of the Duke of Buckingham, that he endures pleasures with less patience than other men do their pains?—a staid, important, dogged, square-rigged, mathematical-minded sort of an animal? Question him, and I will lay my head to yours (for I like to take the odds), that whatever tolerance he may be brought to admit for other deviations from the right line of gravity, he will profess a truculent and implacable hatred of that most kind-hearted, sociable, and urbane witticism, termed—a Pun.

Oh, the Anti-risible rogue! Oh, the jesticide—the Hilarifuge! the extinguisher of "quips and cranks and wanton wiles";—the queller of quirks, quiddets, quibbles, equivocation, and quizzing! the gagger of gigglers! the Herod of witlings, and Procrustes of full-grown Punsters! Look at his atrabilarious complexion; it is the same that Cæsar feared in Brutus and Cassius: such a fellow is indeed fit for treasons, stratagems, and plots; he has no music in his soul, for he will not let us even play upon words. Will nothing but pure wit serve thy turn, most sapient Sir? Well, then set us the example—

———"Lay on, Macduff,
And damn'd be he that first cries, Hold! enough!"

How,—dumbfounded? Not quite;—methinks I hear him quoting Dr. Johnson's stale hyperbole, "Sir, the man that would commit a pun would pick a pocket"; to which I would oppose an equally valid dictum of an illustrious quibbler, "Sir, no man ever condemned a good pun who was able to make one." I know not a more aggrieved and unjustly proscribed character in the present day than the poor painstaking punster. He is the pariah of the dining table; it is the fashion to run him down: and as every dull ass thinks that he may have a kick at the prostrate witling, may I be condemned to pass a whole week without punning (a fearful adjuration!) if I do not show that the greatest sages, poets, and philosophers of all ages have been enrolled upon this proscribed list!

Even in Holy Writ, whatever might have been the intention of the speaker, there is authority for a play upon words equivalent to a pun. When Simon Bar-Jona, for his superior faith, received the name of Peter (which in Greek signifies a stone or rock), the divine bestower of that appellation exclaimed, "I say unto thee, that thou art Peter, and upon this rock will I build my church," etc. Homer has made the wily Ulysses save his life by means of a pun. In the ninth book of the "Odyssey" that hero informs the Cyclops that his name is Noman; and when the monster, after having had his eye put out in his sleep, awakes in agony, he thus roars to his companions for assistance: —

> "Friends! No-man kills me. No-man in the hour
> Of sleep oppresses me with fraudful power.—
> If No-man hurt thee, but the hand divine
> Inflicts disease, it fits thee to resign.
> To Jove, or to thy father Neptune pray,
> The brethren cried, and instant strode away" —

a joke upon which Euripides dilates with huge delight in the drama of the "Cyclops." * It will be observed that Pope has preserved the equivoque in his translation, which attests his respect for this most ancient *jeu de mots;* while Ulysses is described as hurrying away in high glee, "pleased with the effect of conduct and of art," which is an evidence that Homer felicitated himself upon the happiness of the thought. This passage exhibits a very rude and primitive state of the art; for had any modern Cyclopses been invoked to aid their comrade, under similar circumstances, they would have seen through so flimsy a trick only with one eye.

Later Greek writers were by no means slow in following so notable an example. Plutarch has preserved several of these *Pterœnta*, or flying words, particularly King Philip's celebrated pun to the physician who attended him when his collar bone was broken; and Diogenes the Cynic made so happy an equivoque upon a damsel's eye, which the profligate Didymus undertook to cure, that Scaliger said he would rather have been author of it

* Cibber, in translating the Italian opera of "Polifemo," make Ulysses answer, "I take no name"; whereby all that followed became unintelligible, and the Greek pun was most ingeniously spoilt.　　　　H. S.

IX—217

than King of Navarre. From the comic authors a whole galaxy of similar jokes might be collected; but I reserve the specification for a new edition of Hierocles, the Joe Miller of Alexandria, which I am preparing for the press in ten volumes quarto.

The Romans, who imitated the Greeks in everything, were not likely to forget their puns, *verbaque apta joco.* Cicero informs us that Cæsar was a celebrated performer in this way. Horace in his seventh Satire, giving an account of the quarrel between Persius and Rupilius Rex, before Brutus the Pretor, makes the former exclaim, "*Per magnos, Brute, Deos te oro, qui reges consuêris tollere, cur non hunc Regem jugulas?*" thus playing upon the names of both parties. Martial was an accomplished punster; and Ovid not only quibbled upon words, but metamorphosed them into a thousand phantasies and vagaries.

The same valuable privilege formed the staple commodity of the ancient Oracles; for if the presiding deities had not been shrewd punsters, or able to inspire the Pythoness with ready equivoques, the whole establishment must speedily have been declared bankrupt. Sometimes, indeed, they only dabbled in accentuation, and accomplished their prophecies by the transposition of a stop, as in the well-known answer to a soldier inquiring his fate in the war for which he was about to embark. " *Ibis, redibis. Nunquam in bello, peribis.*" The warrior set off in high spirits upon the faith of this prediction, and fell in the first engagement, when his widow had the satisfaction of being informed that he should have put the full stop after the word " *nunquam,*" which would probably have put a full stop to his enterprise and saved his life. More commonly, however, they betook themselves to a positive pun, the double construction of which enabled them to be always right: sometimes playing upon a single word, and sometimes upon the whole clause of a sentence. When Crœsus, about to make war upon Cyrus, consulted the Delphian priestess, he was told that in crossing the river Halys he would overturn a great empire — which could hardly fail to be true; for, if he succeeded, he would subvert the Assyrian kingdom; if he failed, his own would be overwhelmed. Pyrrhus received a similar response as to the fate of his expedition against the Romans. "*Credo equidem Æacidas Romanos vincere posse*"; which might import either that the Æacides, from whom Pyrrhus was descended, would conquer the Romans, or precisely the reverse: such are the advantages of a double accusative.

Christianity, by superseding these Oracles, did not, most fortunately, extinguish quibbling, for which we have the authority of one of the earliest Popes. Some Pagan English youths of extraordinary beauty being presented to him, he exclaimed, " *Non Angli, sed Angeli forent, si essent Christiani.*"

Heraldic bearings are supposed to have been invented to distinguish the different nations, armies, and clans, that were congregated together in the Crusades; and the mottoes assumed upon this occasion, if we may judge by those of England, bore almost universally some punning allusion to the name or device of the chief. The similar epigraphs still retained by the Vernon, Fortescue, and Cavendish families, as well as by numerous others, may be viewed as so many venerable testimonies to the antiquity of punning in this our happy island.

There is not one of our sterling old English writers from whom we might not glean some specimen of this noble art; which seems to have attained its golden age in that Augustan era of our literature — the reign of our renowned Queen Elizabeth, when clergymen punned in the pulpit, judges upon the bench, and criminals in their last dying speeches. Then was it that the deer-stealing attorney's clerk fled from Stratford, and introducing whole scenes of punning into his immortal plays, eliciting quibbles not less affluently from the mouths of fools and porters, than from the dread lips of the weird sisters, "who palter with us in a double sense," established upon an imperishable basis the glory of his favorite science of Paronomasia; — a glory irradiating and reflected by the whole galaxy of dramatic talent with which he was surrounded.

Succeeding writers, though they have never equaled this splendor of quibble, have not failed to deposit occasional offerings upon the altar of Janus, the god of puns. Dryden pretended to be angry, when being in a coffeehouse with his back towards Rowe, one of his friends said to him, "You are like a waterman: you look one way and Rowe another"; but, though unwilling to be the object of a pun, he had no compunction in being the author of many, for the support of which assertion the reader may consult his dramatic works. Addison's opinion of this laugh-provoking practice may be collected from the 440th Number of the Spectator, wherein he describes a society, who had established among themselves an infirmary for the cure of all defects of temper and infractions of good manners. "After dinner a very hon-

est fellow chancing to let a pun fall from him, his neighbor cried out, 'to the infirmary!' at the same time pretending to be sick at it, as having the same natural antipathy to a pun which some have to a cat. This produced a long debate. Upon the whole, the punster was acquitted and his neighbor sent off." Pope's authority we have already cited. Gay was probably the author of the play upon his own name, when he observed that the great success of his "Beggar's Opera," whilst Rich was proprietor of the theatre, had made Gay rich and Rich gay. But what shall we say of Swift, the punster's *vade mecum,* the Hierarch, the Pontifex, Magnus Apollo of the tribe; the Alpha and Omega, the first and last of the professors of equivocation; whose mind was an ever-springing fountain of quiddets, and the thread of whose life was an unbroken string of puns from his first to his second childhood? Impossible as it is to do justice to the memory of so great a man, I feel the eulogomania swelling within me; and that I may effectually check its yearnings, I leap athwart a measureless hiatus, and revert to that lugubrious, somnolent, single-sensed, and no-witted Antipunster, whom I apostrophized in the outset.

And now, thou word measurer, thou line-and-rule mechanic, thou reasoning but not ruminating animal, now that I have produced these authorities, limited to a narrow list from the want of room, not of materials, wilt thou have the ridiculous arrogance to affect contempt for a pun? That genuine wit which thou pretendest to worship (as the Athenians built an altar to the unknown Deity), has been defined to be an assimilation of distant ideas; and what is a pun but an eliciter of remote meanings, which, though they may not always amount to a definite idea, are at all events the materials of one, and therefore ingredients in the composition of real wit? These Protean combinations are the stimulants of fancy, the titillators of the imagination, the awakeners of the risible faculties; and to condemn them because the same happy results may be produced by a more rare and difficult process is either an exemplification of the fox and the sour grapes, or the pride of mental luxury, which would quarrel with all gratifications that are cheap and accessible. The sterling commodity is scarce — let us prize it the more when we encounter it; but in the meantime let us not reject a good substitute when it is presented. Gooseberry wine is no very lofty succedaneum for sparking Champagne, but it is better than fasting. Some may not like the flavor of the beverage, but none would think of abusing the caterer who puts upon the table the best liquor that his cellar affords. These sullen stupidities are reserved for an Antipunster.

Complete. From "Gayeties and Gravities."

UGLY WOMEN

Un homme rencontre une femme, et est choqué de sa laideur; bientôt, si elle n'a pas de prétentions, sa physionomie lui fait oublier les défauts de ses traits, il la trouve aimable, et conçoit qu'on puisse l'aimer; huit jours après il a des espérances, huit jours après on les lui retire, huit jours après il est fou.— "De l'Amour."

THE ancient inhabitants of Amathus, in the island of Cyprus, were the most celebrated statuaries in the world, which they almost exclusively supplied with gods and goddesses. Every one who had a mind to be in the vogue ordered his deity from those fashionable artists: even Jupiter himself was hardly considered orthodox and worship-worthy, unless emanating from the established Pantheon of the Cypriots; and as to Juno, Venus, Minerva, and Diana, it was admitted that they had a peculiar knack in their manufacture, and it need hardly be added that they drove a thriving trade in those popular goddesses. But this monopoly was more favorable to the fortunes than to the happiness of the parties. By constantly straining above humanity, and aspiring to the representation of celestial beauty; by fostering the enthusiasm of their imaginations in the pursuit of the beau ideal,— they acquired a distaste, or at least an indifference, for mortal attractions, and turned up their noses at their fair country-women for not being Junos and Minervas. Not one of them equaled the model which had been conjured up in their minds, and not one of them, consequently, would they deign to notice. At the public games, the women were all huddled together, whispering and looking glum, while the men congregated as far from them as possible, discussing the beau ideal. Had they been prosing upon politics, you might have sworn it was an English party. Dancing was extinct, unless the ladies chose to lead out one another; the priests waxed lank and woe-begone for want of the marriage offerings; Hymen's altar was covered with as many cobwebs as a poor's box; successive moons rose and set without

a single honeymoon, and the whole island threatened to become an antinuptial colony of bachelors and old maids.

In this emergency, Pygmalion, the most eminent statuary of the place, falling in love with one of his own works, a figure of Diana, which happened to possess the beau ideal in perfection, implored Venus to animate the marble; and she, as is well known to every person conversant with authentic history, immediately granted his request. So far as this couple were concerned, one would have imagined that the evil was remedied; but, alas! the remedy was worse than the disease. The model of excellence was now among them, alive and breathing; the men were perfectly mad, beleaguering the house from morn to night to get a peep at her; all other women were treated with positive insult, and, of course, the whole female population was possessed by all the Furies. Marmorea (such was the name of the animated statue) was no Diana in the flesh, whatever she might have been in the marble: if the scandalous chronicles of those days may be believed, she had more than one favored lover; certain is it that she was the cause of constant feuds and battles in which many lives were lost, and Pygmalion himself was at last found murdered in the neighborhood of his own house. The whole island was now on the point of a civil war on account of this philanthropical Helen, when one of her disappointed wooers, in a fit of jealousy, stabbed her to the heart, and immediately after threw himself from a high rock into the sea.

Such is the tragedy which would probably be enacting at the present moment in every country of the world, but for the fortunate circumstance that we have no longer any fixed standard of beauty, real or imaginary, and by a necessary and happy consequence no determinate rule of ugliness. In fact, there are no such animals as ugly women, though we still continue to talk of them as we do of harpies, gorgons, and chimeras. There is no deformity that does not find admirers, and no loveliness that is not deemed defective. Anamaboo, the African prince, received so many attentions from a celebrated belle of London, that in a moment of tenderness, he could not refrain from laying his hand on his heart and exclaiming, "Ah! madam, if heaven had only made you a negress, you would have been irresistible!" And the same beauty, when traveling among the Swiss Cretins, heard several of the men ejaculating, "How handsome she is! what a pity that she wants a goitre!" Plain women were formerly so

common, that they were termed "ordinary," to signify the frequency of their occurrence; in these happier days the phrase, "extra-ordinary," would be more applicable. However parsimonious, or even cruel, nature may have been in other respects, they all cling to admiration by some solitary tenure that redeems them from the unqualified imputation of unattractiveness. One has an eye that, like Charity, covers a multitude of sins; another is a female Samson, whose strength consists in her hair; a third holds your affections by her teeth; a fourth is a Cinderella who wins hearts by her pretty little foot; a fifth makes an irresistible appeal from her face to her figure, and so on, to the end of the catalogue. An expressive countenance may always be claimed in the absence of any definite charm; if even this be questionable, the party generally contrives to get a reputation for great cleverness; and if that, too, be inhumanly disputed, envy itself must allow that she is "excessively amiable."

Still it must be acknowledged that however men may differ as to the details, they agree as to results, and crowd about an acknowledged beauty, influenced by some secret attraction, of which they are themselves unconscious, and of which the source has never been clearly explained. It would seem impossible that it should originate in any sexual symptoms, since we feel the impulsion without carrying ourselves, even in idea, beyond the present pleasure of gazing, and are even sensibly affected by the sight of beautiful children; yet it cannot be an abstract admiration, for it is incontestable that neither men nor women are so vehemently impressed by the contemplation of beauty in their own as in the opposite sex. This injustice towards our own half of humanity might be assigned to a latent envy, but that the same remark applies to the pleasure we derive from statues, of the proportions of which we could hardly be jealous. Ugly statues may be left to their fate without any compunctious visitings of nature; but our conduct towards women whom we conceive to be in a similar predicament is by no means entitled to the same indulgence. We shuffle away from them at parties, and sneak to the other end of the dinner table, as if their features were catching; and as to their falling in love and possessing the common feelings of their sex, we laugh at the very idea. And yet these pariahs of the drawing-room generally atone by interior talent for what they want in exterior charms; as if the Medusa's head were still destined to be carried by Minerva.

Nature seldom lavishes her gifts upon one subject: the peacock has no voice; the beautiful camellia japonica has no odor; and belles, generally speaking, have no great share of intellect. Some visionaries amuse themselves with imagining that the complacency occasioned by the possession of physical charms conduces to moral perfection.—

"Why doth not beauty, then, refine the wit,
And good complexion rectify the will?"

This is a fond conceit, unwarranted by earthly test, though destined perhaps to be realized in a happier state of existence.

What a blessing for these unhandsome damsels whom we treat still more unhandsomely by our fastidious neglect, that some of us are less squeamish in our tastes, and more impartial in our attentions! Solomon proves the antiquity of the adage, "De gustibus nil disputandum," for he compares the hair of his beloved to a flock of goats appearing from Mount Gilead, and in a strain of enamored flattery exclaims, "Thy eyes are like the fish pools in Heshbon, by the gate of Bath-rabbim; thy nose like the tower of Lebanon looking towards Damascus." Now I deem it as becoming to see a woman standing behind a good roomy nose as to contemplate a fair temple with a majestic portico; but it may be questioned whether a nose like the tower of Lebanon be not somewhat too elephantine and bordering on the proboscis. The nez retroussé is smart and piquant; the button nose, like all other diminutives, is endearing; and even the snub absolute has its admirers. Cupid can get over it, though it have no bridge, and jumps through a wall-eye like a harlequin. As to the latter feature, my taste may be singular, perhaps bad, but I confess that I have a penchant for that captivating cast, sometimes invidiously termed a squint. Its advantages are neither few nor unimportant. Like a bowl, its very bias makes it sure of hitting the jack, while it seems to be running out of the course; and it has, moreover, the invaluable property of doing execution without exciting suspicion, like the Irish guns with crooked barrels, made for shooting round a corner. Common observers admire the sun in its common state, but philosophers find it a thousand times more interesting when suffering a partial eclipse; while the lovers of the picturesque are more smitten with its rising and setting than with its meridian splendor. Such men must be enchanted with a strabismus or squint, where they may behold the ball of sight emerging from the nasal East, or setting in its Occidental depths, presenting every variety of obscuration. With regard to teeth, also, a very erroneous taste prevails. Nothing can be more stiff and barrack-like than that uniformity of shape and hue which is so highly vaunted, for the merest tyro in landscape will tell us that castellated and jagged outlines, with a pleasing variety of tints, are infinitely more pictorial and pleasing. Patches of bile in the face are by no means to be deprecated; they impart to it a rich mellow tone of autumnal coloring, which we would in vain seek in less gifted complexions: and I am most happy to vindicate the claims of a moderate beard upon the upper lip, which is as necessary to the perfect beauty of the mouth as are the thorns and moss to a rose, or the leaves to a cherry. If there be any old maids still extant, while misogynists are so rare, the fault must be attributable to themselves, and they must incur all the responsibility of their single blessedness.

In the connubial lottery ugly women possess an advantage to which sufficient importance has not been attached. It is a common observation that husband and wife frequently resemble one another; and many ingenious theorists, attempting to solve the problem by attributing it to sympathy, contemplation of one another's features, congeniality of habits and modes of life, etc., have fallen into the very common error of substituting the cause for the effect. This mutual likeness is the occasion, not the result, of marriage. Every man, like Narcissus, becomes enamored of the reflection of himself, only choosing a substance instead of a shadow. His love for any particular woman is self-love at second hand, vanity reflected, compound egotism. When he sees himself in the mirror of a female face, he exclaims, "How intelligent, how amiable, how interesting!—how admirably adapted for a wife!" and forthwith makes his proposals to the personage so expressly and literally calculated to keep him in countenance. The uglier he is, the more need he has of this consolation; he forms a romantic attachment to the "fascinating creature with the snub nose," or the "bewitching girl with the roguish leer" (Anglicè—squint), without once suspecting that he is paying his addresses to himself, and playing the innamorato before a looking glass. Take self-love from love, and very little remains: it is taking the flame from Hymen's torch and leaving the smoke. The same feeling extends to his progeny: he would rather see

them resemble himself, particularly in his defects, than be modeled after the chubbiest cherubs or cupids that ever emanated from the studio of Canova. One sometimes encounters a man of a most unqualified hideousness, who obviously considers himself an Adonis; and when such a one has to seek a congenial Venus, it is evident that her value will be in the inverse ratio of her charms. Upon this principle ugly women will be converted into belles, perfect frights will become irresistible, and none need despair of conquests if they have but the happiness to be sufficiently plain.

The best part of beauty, says Bacon, is that which a statue or painting cannot express. As to symmetry of form and superficial grace, sculpture is exquisitely perfect, but the countenance is of too subtle and intangible a character to be arrested by any modification of marble. Busts, especially where the pupil of the eye is unmarked, have the appearance of mere masks, and are representations of little more than blindness and death. Painting supplies by coloring and shade much that sculpture wants; but, on the other hand, it is deficient in what its rival possesses— fidelity of superficial form. Nothing can compensate for our inability to walk round a picture, and choose various points of view. Facility of production, meanness of material, and vulgarity of association have induced us to look down with unmerited contempt upon those waxen busts in the perfumers' shops, which, as simple representations of female nature, have attained a perfection that positively amounts to the kissable. That delicacy of tint and material which so admirably adapts itself to female beauty forms, however, but a milk-maidish representation of virility, and the men have, consequently, as epicene and androgynous an aspect as if they had just been bathing in the Salmacian fountain.

Countenance, however, is not within the reach of any of these substances or combinations. It is a species of moral beauty, as superior to mere charm of surface as mind is to matter. It is, in fact, visible spirit, legible intellect, diffusing itself over the features, and enabling minds to commune with each other by some secret sympathy unconnected with the senses. The heart has a silent echo in the face, which frequently carries to us a conviction diametrically opposite to the audible expressions of the mouth; and we see, through the eyes, into the understanding of the man, long before it can communicate with us by utterance. This emanation of character is the light of a soul destined to the

skies, shining through its tegument of clay, and irradiating the countenance, as the sun illuminates the face of nature before it rises above the earth to commence its heavenly career. Of this indefinable charm all women are alike susceptible: it is to them what gunpowder is to warriors; it levels all distinctions, and gives to the plain and the pretty, to the timid and the brave, an equal chance of making conquests. It is, in fine, one among a thousand proofs of that system of compensation, both physical and moral, by which a superior power is perpetually evincing his benignity; affording to every human being a commensurate chance of happiness, and inculcating upon all, that when they turn their faces towards heaven, they should reflect the light from above, and be animated by one uniform expression of love, resignation, and gratitude.

Complete. From "Gayeties and Gravities."

SYDNEY SMITH

(1771–1845)

YDNEY SMITH was celebrated in his generation as an orator, wit, clergyman, essayist, and philosopher, with an incidental reputation as a book reviewer, at a time when, as he himself has suggested, book reviewers did not necessarily "prejudice" themselves by acquiring in advance a knowledge of the books they were writing about. His table-talk and his humor in conversation seem to have been almost, if not quite, unrivaled in the history of English "wits," but his essays, as a rule, are far from demonstrating the humor which would be expected from his reputation. They are often characterized, however, by brilliant flashes of wit which, when the reader is least expecting it, illuminate whole pages of logic. And again they develop from what had been apparently the deepest seriousness into the most striking and effective irony. Sydney Smith was born at Woodford, England, June 3d, 1771. After beginning life as a curate in a small village on Salisbury Plain, he spent several years in Edinburgh where he helped to found the Edinburgh Review, of which he became the first editor. He lectured on moral philosophy, at the Royal Institution of London, from 1804 to 1808. In 1809 he became rector of a Yorkshire parish, where it is said there had been no clergyman before him for a century. After remaining there for twenty years he became prebend of Bristol, and in 1831 canon of St. Paul's. He died in London, February 22d, 1845. His "Plymley Letters" advocating Catholic emancipation were published in 1807 and 1808, and in 1839 his contributions to the Edinburgh Review were collected and republished. These essays, which include his best works, are generally printed in the same volume with his speeches, which include what is perhaps the most celebrated political speech of the nineteenth century,—that in which he compared Tory opposition to reform to the attempt of Mrs. Partington of Sidmouth to mop the Atlantic out of her front door during the great flood at that place in 1824.

WIT AND HUMOR

I WISH, after all I have said about wit and humor, I could satisfy myself of the good effects upon the character and disposition; but I am convinced the probable tendency of both is to corrupt the understanding and the heart. I am not speaking of wit where it is kept down by more serious qualities of mind, and thrown into the background of the picture; but where it stands out boldly and emphatically, and is evidently the master quality in any particular mind. Profound wits, though they are generally courted for the amusement they afford, are seldom respected for the qualities they possess. The habit of seeing things in a witty point of view, increases, and makes incursions from its own proper regions, upon principles and opinions which are ever held sacred by the wise and good. A witty man is a dramatic performer: in process of time, he can no more exist without applause than he can exist without air; if his audience be small, or if they are inattentive, or if a new wit defrauds him of any portion of his admiration, it is all over with him — he sickens and is extinguished. The applauses of the theatre on which he performs are so essential to him that he must obtain them at the expense of decency, friendship, and good feeling. It must always be probable, too, that a mere wit is a person of light and frivolous understanding. His business is not to discover relations of ideas that are useful, and have a real influence upon life, but to discover the more trifling relations which are only amusing; he never looks at things with the naked eye of common sense, but is always gazing at the world through a Claude Lorraine glass, — discovering a thousand appearances which are created only by the instrument of inspection, and covering every object with factitious and unnatural colors. In short, the character of a mere wit it is impossible to consider as very amiable, very respectable, or very safe. So far the world, in judging of wit where it has swallowed up all other qualities, judge aright; but I doubt if they are sufficiently indulgent to this faculty where it exists in a lesser degree, and as one out of many other ingredients of the understanding. There is an association in men's minds between dullness and wisdom, amusement and folly, which has a powerful influence in decision upon character, and is not overcome without considerable difficulty. The reason is, that the outward signs

of a dull man and a wise man are the same, and so are the outward signs of a frivolous man and a witty man; and we are not to expect that the majority will be disposed to look to much more than the outward sign. I believe the fact to be, that wit is very seldom the only eminent quality which resides in the mind of any man; it is commonly accompanied by many other talents of every description, and ought to be considered as a strong evidence of a fertile and superior understanding. Almost all the great poets, orators, and statesmen of all times have been witty. Cæsar, Alexander, Aristotle, Descartes, and Lord Bacon were witty men; so were Cicero, Shakespeare, Demosthenes, Boileau, Pope, Dryden, Fontenelle, Jonson, Waller, Cowley, Solon, Socrates, Dr. Johnson, and almost every man who has made a distinguished figure in the House of Commons. I have talked of the danger of wit: I do not mean by that to enter into commonplace declamation against faculties because they are dangerous; — wit is dangerous, eloquence is dangerous, a talent for observation is dangerous, everything is dangerous that has efficacy and vigor for its characteristics; nothing is safe but mediocrity. The business is, in conducting the understanding well, to risk something; to aim at uniting things that are commonly incompatible. The meaning of an extraordinary man is, that he is eight men, not one man; that he has as much wit as if he had no sense, and as much sense as if he had no wit; that his conduct is as judicious as if he were the dullest of human beings, and his imagination as brilliant as if he were irretrievably ruined. But when wit is combined with sense and information; when it is softened by benevolence, and restrained by strong principle; when it is in the hands of a man who can use it and despise it, who can be witty and something much better than witty, who loves honor, justice, decency, good-nature, morality, and religion ten thousand times better than wit; — wit is then a beautiful and delightful part of our nature. There is no more interesting spectacle than to see the effects of wit upon the different characters of men; than to observe it expanding caution, relaxing dignity, unfreezing coldness, — teaching age, and care, and pain, to smile, — extorting reluctant gleams of pleasure from melancholy, and charming even the pangs of grief. It is pleasant to observe how it penetrates through the coldness and awkwardness of society, gradually bringing men nearer together, and, like the combined force of wine and oil, giving every man a glad heart and shining countenance.

Genuine and innocent wit, like this, is surely the flavor of the mind! Man could direct his ways by plain reason, and support his life by tasteless food; but God has given us wit, and flavor, and brightness, and laughter, and perfumes, to enliven the days of man's pilgrimage, and to "charm his pained steps over the burning marle."

EDGEWORTH ON BULLS

WE HARDLY know what to say about this rambling, scrambling book;* but that we are quite sure the author, when he began any sentence in it, had not the smallest suspicion of what it was about to contain. We say the author, because, in spite of the mixture of sexes in the title-page, we are strongly inclined to suspect that the male contributions exceed the female in a very great degree. The essay on "Bulls" is written much with the same mind, and in the same manner, as a schoolboy takes a walk: he moves on for ten yards on the straight road, with surprising perseverance; then sets out after a butterfly, looks for a bird's nest, or jumps backwards and forwards over a ditch. In the same manner, this nimble and digressive gentleman is away after every object which crosses his mind. If you leave him at the end of a comma, in a steady pursuit of his subject, you are sure to find him, before the next full stop, a hundred yards to the right or left, frisking, capering, and grinning, in a high paroxysm of merriment and agility. Mr. Edgeworth seems to possess the sentiments of an accomplished gentleman, the information of a scholar, and the vivacity of a first-rate harlequin. He is fuddled with animal spirits, giddy with constitutional joy; in such a state he must have written on, or burst. A discharge of ink was an evacuation absolutely necessary, to avoid fatal and plethoric congestion.

The object of the book is to prove that the practice of making bulls is not more imputable to the Irish than to any other people; and the manner in which he sets about it is to quote examples of bulls produced in other countries. But this is surely a singular way of reasoning the question; for there are goitres out of Valais, extortioners who do not worship Moses, oatcakes out of the

___
* "An Essay on Irish Bulls," 1802, written by Miss Edgeworth in collaboration with her father.

Tweed, and balm beyond the precincts of Gilead. If nothing can be said to exist pre-eminently and emphatically in one country, which exists at all in another, then Frenchmen are not gay, nor Spaniards grave, nor are gentlemen of the Milesian race remarkable for their disinterested contempt of wealth in their connubial relations. It is probable there is some foundation for a character so generally diffused; though it is also probable that such foundation is extremely enlarged by fame. If there were no foundation for the common opinion, we must suppose national characters formed by chance; and that the Irish might, by accident, have been laughed at as bashful and sheepish; which is impossible. The author puzzles himself a good deal about the nature of bulls, without coming to any decision about the matter. Though the question is not a very easy one, we shall venture to say that a bull is an apparent congruity, and real incongruity, of ideas, suddenly discovered. And if this account of bulls be just, they are (as might have been supposed) the very reverse of wit; for as wit discovers real relations, that are not apparent, bulls admit apparent relations that are not real. The pleasure arising from wit proceeds from our surprise at suddenly discovering two things to be similar, in which we suspected no similarity. The pleasure arising from bulls proceeds from our discovering two things to be dissimilar, in which a resemblance might have been suspected. The same doctrine will apply to wit, and to bulls in action. Practical wit discovers connection or relation between actions, in which duller understandings discover none; and practical bulls originate from an apparent relation between two actions, which more correct understandings immediately perceive to have no relation at all.

Louis XIV. being extremely harassed by the repeated solicitations of a veteran officer for promotion, said one day, loud enough to be heard, "That gentleman is the most troublesome officer I have in my service." "That is precisely the charge," said the old man, "which your Majesty's enemies bring against me."

"An English gentleman," says Mr. Edgeworth, in a story cited from Joe Miller, "was writing a letter in a coffeehouse; and perceiving that an Irishman stationed behind him was taking that liberty which Parmenio used with his friend Alexander, instead of putting his seal upon the lips of the curious impertinent, the English gentleman thought proper to reprove the Hibernian, if not with delicacy, at least with poetical justice.

He concluded writing his letter in these words: 'I would say more, but a damned tall Irishman is reading over my shoulder every word I write.'

" 'You lie, you scoundrel,' said the self-convicted Hibernian."

The pleasure derived from the first of these stories proceeds from the discovery of the relation that subsists between the object he had in view, and the assent of the officer to an observation so unfriendly to that end. In the first rapid glance which the mind throws upon his words, he appears, by his acquiescence, to be pleading against himself. There seems to be no relation between what he says and what he wishes to effect by speaking.

In the second story, the pleasure is directly the reverse. The lie given was apparently the readiest means of proving his innocence, and really the most effectual way of establishing his guilt. There seems for a moment to be a strong relation between the means and the object; while, in fact, no irrelation can be so complete.

What connection is there between pelting stones at monkeys and gathering cocoanuts from lofty trees? Apparently none. But monkeys sit upon cocoanut trees; monkeys are imitative animals; and if you pelt a monkey with a stone, he pelts you with a cocoanut in return. This scheme of gathering cocoanuts is very witty, and would be more so, if it did not appear useful; for the idea of utility is always inimical to the idea of wit. There appears, on the contrary, to be some relation between the revenge of the Irish rebels against a banker, and the means which they took to gratify it, by burning all his notes wherever they found them; whereas they could not have rendered him a more essential service. In both these cases of bulls, the one verbal, the other practical, there is an apparent congruity and real incongruity of ideas. In both the cases of wit, there is an apparent incongruity and a real relation.

It is clear that a bull cannot depend upon mere incongruity alone; for if a man were to say that he would ride to London upon a cocked hat, or that he would cut his throat with a pound of pickled salmon, this, though completely incongruous, would not be to make bulls, but to talk nonsense. The stronger the apparent connection, and the more complete the real disconnection of the ideas, the greater the surprise and the better the bull. The less apparent, and the more complete the relations established by wit, the higher gratification does it afford. A great deal of the

IX—218

pleasure experienced from bulls proceeds from the sense of superiority in ourselves. Bulls which we invented, or knew to be invented, might please, but in a less degree, for want of this additional zest.

As there must be apparent connection, and real incongruity, it is seldom that a man of sense and education finds any form of words by which he is conscious that he might have been deceived into a bull. To conceive how the person has been deceived, he must suppose a degree of information very different from, and a species of character very heterogeneous to, his own; a process which diminishes surprise, and consequently pleasure. In the above-mentioned story of the Irishman overlooking the man writing, no person of ordinary sagacity can suppose himself betrayed into such a mistake; but he can easily represent to himself a kind of character that might have been so betrayed. There are some bulls so extremely fallacious, that any man may imagine himself to have been betrayed into them; but these are rare: and, in general, it is a poor, contemptible species of amusement; a delight in which evinces a very bad taste in wit.

Whether the Irish make more bulls than their neighbors, is, as we have before remarked, not a point of much importance; but it is of considerable importance, that the character of a nation should not be degraded; and Mr. Edgeworth has great merit in his very benevolent intention of doing justice to the excellent qualities of the Irish. It is not possible to read his book, without feeling a strong and a new disposition in their favor. Whether the imitation of the Irish manner be accurate in his little stories we cannot determine; but we feel the same confidence in the accuracy of the imitation that is often felt in the resemblance of a portrait, of which we have never seen the original. It is no very high compliment to Mr. Edgeworth's creative powers to say he could not have formed anything which was not real, so like reality; but such a remark only robs Peter to pay Paul, and gives everything to his powers of observation, which it takes from those of his imagination. In truth, nothing can be better than his imitation of the Irish manner: It is first-rate painting.

Edgeworth and Co. have another faculty in great perfection. They are eminently masters of the pathos. The Firm drew tears from us in the stories of little Dominick, and of the Irish beggar, who killed his sweetheart: Never was any grief more

natural or simple. The first, however, ends in a very foolish way;

"——formosa superne
Desinit in piscem."

We are extremely glad that our avocations did not call us from Bath to London on the day that the Bath coach conversation took place. We except from this wish the story with which the conversation terminates; for as soon as Mr. Edgeworth enters upon a story he excels.

We must confess we have been much more pleased with Mr. Edgeworth in his laughing and in his pathetic, than in his grave and reasoning, moods. He meant, perhaps, that we should; and it certainly is not very necessary that a writer should be profound on the subject of bulls. Whatever be the deficiencies of the book, they are, in our estimation, amply atoned for by its merits; by none more than that lively feeling of compassion which pervades it for the distresses of the wild, kind-hearted, blundering poor of Ireland.

Complete. From the Edinburgh
Review 1803.

TABLE-TALK

ON A HABITUAL BORE

LORD CHESTERTON we have often met with, and suffered a good deal from his lordship: a heavy, pompous, meddling peer, occupying a great share of the conversation — saying things in ten words which required only two, and evidently convinced that he is making a great impression; a large man with a large head, and a very candid manner. Knowing enough to torment his fellow-creatures, not to instruct them; the intimate of young ladies, and the natural butt and target of wit. It is easy to talk of carnivorous animals and beasts of prey; but does such a man, who lays waste a whole civilized party of beings by prosing, reflect upon the joy he spoils, and the misery he creates, in the course of his life? and that any one who listens to him through politeness, would prefer toothache or earache to his conversation? Does he consider the extreme uneasiness which ensues when the

company have discovered a man to be an extremely absurd person, at the same time that it is absolutely impossible to convey, by words or manner, the most distant suspicion of the discovery? And, then, who punishes this bore? What sessions or what assizes for him? What bill is found against him? Who indicts him? When the judges have gone their vernal and autumnal rounds, the sheepstealer disappears — the swindler gets ready for the Bay — the solid parts of the murderer are preserved in anatomical collections. But after twenty years of crime, the bore is discovered in the same house, in the same attitude, eating the same soup — untried — unpunished — undissected.

MONK LEWIS'S TRAGEDY OF "ALFONSO"

THIS tragedy delights in explosions. Alfonso's empire is destroyed by a blast of gunpowder, and restored by a clap of thunder. After the death of Cæsario, and a short exhortation to that purpose by Orsino, all the conspirators fall down in a thunderclap, ask pardon of the king and are forgiven. This mixture of physical and moral power is beautiful! How interesting a waterspout would appear among Mr. Lewis's kings and queens. We anxiously look forward, in his next tragedy, to a fall of snow, three or four feet deep, or expect a plot shall gradually unfold itself by means of a general thaw.

A DINNER PARTY

AN EXCELLENT and well-arranged dinner is a most pleasing occurrence, and a great triumph of civilized life. It is not only the descending morsel and the enveloping sauce, but the rank, wealth, wit, and beauty which surround the meats; the learned management of light and heat; the silent and rapid services of the attendants; the smiling and sedulous host, proffering gusts and relishes; the exotic bottles; the embossed plate; the pleasant remarks; the handsome dresses; the cunning artifices in fruit and farina! The hour of dinner, in short, includes everything of sensual and intellectual gratification, which a great nation glories in producing.

CLASSICAL GLORY

DR. GENGE, the celebrated Grecian, upon hearing the praises of the great king of Prussia, entertained considerable doubts whether the king, with all his victories, knew how to conjugate a Greek verb in μ.

OFFICIAL DRESS

THE Americans, we believe, are the first persons who have discarded the tailor in the administration of justice, and his auxiliary the barber,—two persons of endless importance in codes and pandects of Europe. A judge administers justice, without a calorific wig and party-colored gown, in a coat and pantaloons. He is obeyed, however; and life and property are not badly protected in the United States. We shall be denounced by the laureate as atheists and jacobins; but we must say that we have doubts whether one atom of useful influence is added to men in important situations by any color, quantity, or configuration of cloth and hair. The true progress of refinement, we conceive, is to discard all the mountebank drapery of barbarous ages. One row of gold and fur falls off after another from the robe of power, and is picked up and worn by the parish beadle and the exhibitor of wild beasts. Meantime, the afflicted wiseacre mourns over equality of garment, and wotteth not of two men, whose doublets have cost alike, how one shall command and the other obey.

PULPIT ELOQUENCE

PULPIT discourses have insensibly dwindled from speaking to reading,—a practice, of itself, sufficient to stifle every germ of eloquence. It is only by the fresh feelings of the heart, that mankind can be very powerfully affected. What can be more ludicrous than an orator delivering stale indignation, and fervor of a week old; turning over whole pages of violent passions, written out in German text; reading the tropes and apostrophes into which he is hurried by the ardor of his mind; and so affected at a preconcerted line and page, that he is unable to proceed any further!

IMPERTINENCE OF OPINION

IT IS always considered as a piece of impertinence in England, if a man of less than two or three thousand a year has any opinions at all upon important subjects.

PARASITES

NATURE descends down to infinite smallness. A great man has his parasites; and if you take a large, buzzing bluebottle fly, and look at it in a microscope, you may see twenty or thirty little ugly insects crawling about it, which, doubtless, think their fly to be the bluest, grandest, merriest, most important animal in the universe; and are convinced the world would be at an end if it ceased to buzz.

THE THEATRE

THERE is something in the word Playhouse which seems so closely connected, in the minds of some people, with sin and Satan, that it stands in their vocabulary for every species of abomination. And yet why? Where is every feeling more roused in favor of virtue than at a good play? Where is goodness so feelingly, so enthusiastically learned? What so solemn as to see the excellent passions of the human heart called forth by a great actor, animated by a great poet? To hear Siddons repeat what Shakespeare wrote? To behold the child and his mother—the noble and the poor artisan—the monarch and his subjects—all ages and all ranks convulsed with one common passion—wrung with one common anguish, and, with loud sobs and cries, doing involuntary homage to the God that made their hearts! What wretched infatuation to interdict such amusements as these! What a blessing that mankind can be allured from sensual gratification, and find relaxation and pleasure in such pursuits!

MARY FAIRFAX SOMERVILLE

(1780–1872)

MRS. SOMERVILLE, whose "Connection of the Physical Sciences" and similar works gave her high rank among the scientific essayists of the nineteenth century, was born at Jedburgh, Scotland, December 26th, 1780. Her father, Sir William George Fairfax, was an admiral in the British navy. She had, and improved to an extraordinary degree, the advantages of her education and position. After the death of her first husband, Capt. Samuel Greig, she married her cousin, Dr. William Somerville, who encouraged and assisted her in the study of the physical sciences. After translating Laplace's "Mécanique Céleste," in 1831, she published her "Connection of the Physical Sciences" four years later, and in 1848 her "Physical Geography." Her "Molecular and Microscopic Science" appeared in 1866 and her "Personal Recollections" after her death, which occurred at Naples November 28, 1872.

THE LAWS OF MUSIC

WHEN the particles of elastic bodies are suddenly disturbed by an impulse, they return to their natural position by a series of isochronous vibrations, whose rapidity, force, and permanency depend upon the elasticity, the form, and the mode of aggregation which unites the particles of the body. These oscillations are communicated to the air, and on account of its elasticity they excite alternate condensations and dilatations in the strata of the fluid nearest to the vibrating body: from thence they are propagated to a distance. A string or wire stretched between two pins, when drawn aside and suddenly let go, will vibrate till its own rigidity and the resistance of the air reduce it to rest. These oscillations may be rotatory in every plane, or confined to one plane, according as the motion is communicated. In the pianoforte, where the strings are struck by a hammer at one extremity, the vibrations probably consist of a bulge running to and fro from end to end. Different modes of vibration may be obtained from the same sonorous body. Suppose a vibrating string to give the lowest C of the pianoforte,

which is the fundamental note of the string; if it be lightly touched exactly in the middle so as to retain that point at rest, each half will then vibrate twice as fast as the whole, but in opposite directions; the ventral or bulging segments will be alternately above and below the natural position of the string, and the resulting note will be the octave above C. When a point at a third of the length of the string is kept at rest, the vibrations will be three times as fast as those of the whole string, and will give the twelfth above C. When the point of rest is one-fourth of the whole, the oscillations will be four times as fast as those of the fundamental note, and will give the double octave; and so on. These acute sounds are called the harmonics of the fundamental note. It is clear from what has been stated, that the string thus vibrating could not give these harmonics spontaneously unless it divided itself at its aliquot parts into two, three, four, or more segments in opposite states of vibration separated by points actually at rest. In proof of this, pieces of paper placed on the string at the half, third, fourth, or other aliquot points, according to the corresponding harmonic sound, will remain on it during its vibration, but will instantly fly off from any of the intermediate points. The points of rest called the nodal points of the string are a mere consequence of the law of interferences. For if a rope fastened at one end be moved to and fro at the other extremity so as to transmit a succession of equal waves along it, they will be successively reflected when they arrive at the other end of the rope by the fixed point, and in returning they will occasionally interfere with the advancing waves; and as these opposite undulations will at certain points destroy one another, the point of the rope in which this happens will remain at rest. Thus a series of nodes and ventral segments will be produced, whose number will depend upon the tension and the frequency of the alternate motions communicated to the movable end. So, when a string fixed at both ends is put in motion by a sudden blow at any point of it, the primitive impulse divides itself into two pulses running opposite ways, which are each totally reflected at the extremities, and, running back again along the whole length, are again reflected at the other ends. And thus they will continue to run backward and forward, crossing one another at each traverse, and occasionally interfering, so as to produce nodes; so that the motion of a string fastened at both ends consists of a wave or pulse, continually doubled back on itself by reflection at the fixed extremities.

Harmonics generally coexist with the fundamental sound in the same vibrating body. If one of the lowest strings of the pianoforte be struck, an attentive ear will not only hear the fundamental note, but will detect all the others sounding along with it, though with less and less intensity as their pitch becomes higher. According to the law of coexisting undulations, the whole string and each of its aliquot parts are in different and independent states of vibration at the same time; and as all the resulting notes are heard simultaneously, not only the air but the ear also vibrates in unison with each at the same instant.

Harmony consists in an agreeable combination of sounds. When two chords perform their vibrations in the same time, they are in unison. But when their vibrations are so related as to have a common period after a few oscillations, they produce concord. Thus when the vibrations of two strings bear a very simple relation to each other, as where one of them makes two, three, four, etc., vibrations in the time the other makes one; or if it accomplishes three, four, etc., vibrations while the other makes two, the result is a concord which is the more perfect the shorter the common period. In discords, on the contrary, the beats are distinctly audible, which produces a disagreeable and harsh effect, because the vibrations do not bear a simple relation to one another, as where one of two strings makes eight vibrations while the other accomplishes fifteen. The pleasure afforded by harmony is attributed by Dr. Young to the love of order, and to a predilection for a regular repetition of sensations natural to the human mind, which is gratified by the perfect regularity and rapid recurrence of the vibrations. The love of poetry and dancing he conceives to arise in some degree from the rhythm of the one and the regularity of the motions in the other.

A blast of air passing over the open end of a tube, as over the reeds in Pan's pipes; over a hole in one side, as in the flute; or through the aperture called a reed with a flexible tongue, as in the clarinet, puts the internal column of air into longitudinal vibrations by the alternate condensations and rarefactions of its particles. At the same time the column spontaneously divides itself into nodes between which the air also vibrates longitudinally, but with a rapidity inversely proportional to the length of the divisions, giving the fundamental note or one of its harmonics.

The nodes are produced on the principle of interferences by the reflection of the longitudinal undulations of the air at the ends of the pipe, as in the musical string, only that in one case the undulations are longitudinal, and in the other transverse.

A pipe either open or shut at both ends when sounded vibrates entire, or divides itself spontaneously into two, three, four, etc., segments separated by nodes. The whole column gives the fundamental note by waves or vibrations of the same length with the pipe. The first harmonic is produced by waves half as long as the tube, the second harmonic by waves a third as long, and so on. The harmonic segments in an open and shut pipe are the same in number, but differently placed. In a shut pipe the two ends are nodes, but in an open pipe there is half a segment at each extremity, because the air at these points is neither rarefied nor condensed, being in contact with that which is external. If one of the ends of the open pipe be closed, its fundamental note will be an octave lower, the air will now divide itself into three, five, seven, etc., segments,—and the wave producing its fundamental note will be twice as long as the pipe, so that it will be doubled back. All these notes may be produced separately, by varying the intensity of the blast. Blowing steadily and gently, the fundamental note will sound; when the force of the blast is increased, the note will all at once start up an octave; when the intensity of the wind is augmented, the twelfth will be heard, and by continuing to increase the force of the blast the other harmonics may be obtained, but no force of wind will produce a note intermediate between these. The harmonics of a flute may be obtained in this manner, from the lowest C or D upward, without altering the fingering, merely by increasing the intensity of the blast, and altering the form of the lips. Pipes of the same dimensions, whether of lead, glass, or wood, give the same tone as to pitch under the same circumstances, which shows that the air alone produces the sound.

Metal springs fastened at one end, when forcibly bent, endeavor to return to rest by a series of vibrations, which give very pleasing tones, as in musical boxes. Various musical instruments have recently been constructed, consisting of metallic springs thrown into vibration by a current of air. Among the most perfect of these are Mr. Wheatstone's symphonion, concertina, and æolian organ, instruments of different effects and capabilities, but all possessing considerable execution and expression.

The syren is an ingenious instrument, devised by M. Cagniard de la Tour, for ascertaining the number of pulsations in a second corresponding to each pitch; the notes are produced by jets of air passing through small apertures arranged at regular distances in a circle on the side of a box, before which a disk revolves pierced with the same number of holes. During a revolution of the disk the currents are alternately intercepted and allowed to pass as many times as there are apertures in it, and a sound is produced whose pitch depends on the velocity of rotation.

A glass or metallic rod, when struck at one end, or rubbed in the direction of its length with a wet finger, vibrates longitudinally like a column of air, by the alternate condensation and expansion of its constituent particles, producing a clear and beautiful musical note of a high pitch, on account of the rapidity with which these substances transmit sound. Rods, surfaces, and, in general, all undulating bodies, resolve themselves into nodes. But in surfaces, the parts which remain at rest during their vibrations are lines, which are curved or plane according to the substance, its form, and the mode of vibration. If a little fine dry sand be strewed over the surface of a plate of glass or metal, and if undulations be excited by drawing the bow of a violin across its edge, it will emit a musical sound, and the sand will immediately arrange itself in the nodal lines, where alone it will accumulate and remain at rest, because the segments of the surface on each side will be in different states of vibration, the one being elevated while the other is depressed; and as these two motions meet in the nodal lines, they neutralize one another. These lines vary in form and position with the part where the bow is drawn across, and the point by which the plate is held. The motion of the sand shows in what direction the vibrations take place. If they be perpendicular to the surface, the sand will be violently tossed up and down, till it finds the points of rest. If they be tangential, the sand will only creep along the surface to the nodal lines. Sometimes the undulations are oblique, or compounded of both the preceding. If a bow be drawn across one of the angles of a square plate of glass or metal held firmly by the centre, the sand will arrange itself in two straight lines parallel to the sides of the plate, and crossing in the centre so as to divide it into four equal squares, whose motions will be contrary to each other. Two of the diagonal squares will make their excursions on one side of the plate, while the other two

make their vibrations on the other side of it. This mode of vibration produces the lowest tone of the plate. If the plate be still held by the centre, and the bow applied to the middle of one of the sides, the vibrations will be more rapid, and the tone will be a fifth higher than in the preceding case; now the sand will arrange itself from corner to corner, and will divide the plate into four equal triangles, each pair of which will make their excursions on opposite sides of the plate. The nodal lines and pitch vary not only with the point where the bow is applied, but with the point by which the plate is held, which, being at rest, necessarily determines the direction of one of the quiescent lines. The forms assumed by the sand in square plates are very numerous, corresponding to all the various modes of vibration. The lines in circular plates are even more remarkable for their symmetry, and upon them the forms assumed by the sand may be classed in three systems. The first is the diametrical system, in which the figures consist of diameters dividing the circumference of the plate into equal parts, each of which is in a different state of vibration from those adjacent. Two diameters, for example, crossing at right angles, divide the circumference into four equal parts; three diameters divide it into six equal parts; four divide it into eight, and so on. In a metallic plate, these divisions may amount to thirty-six or forty. The next is the concentric system, where the sand arranges itself in circles, having the same centre with the plate; and the third is the compound system, where the figures assumed by the sand are compounded of the other two, producing very complicated and beautiful forms. Galileo seems to have been the first to notice the points of rest and motion in the sounding-board of a musical instrument; but to Chladni is due the whole discovery of the symmetrical forms of the nodal lines in vibrating plates. Prof. Wheatstone has shown in a paper read before the Royal Society, in 1833, that all Chladni's figures, and indeed all the nodal figures of vibrating surfaces, result from very simple modes of vibration, oscillating isochronously, and superposed upon each other; the resulting figure varying with the component modes of vibration, the number of the superpositions, and the angles at which they are superposed. For example, if a square plate be vibrating so as to make the sand arrange itself in straight lines parallel to one side of the plate, and if, in addition to this, such vibrations be excited as would have caused the sand to form in lines perpendicular to the first had the plate been at rest, the combined vibrations will make the sand form in lines from corner to corner. . . .

A musical string gives a very feeble sound when vibrating alone, on account of the small quantity of air set in motion. But when attached to a sounding-board, as in the harp and pianoforte, it communicates its undulations to that surface, and from thence to every part of the instrument; so that the whole system vibrates isochronously, and by exposing an extensive undulating surface, which transmits its undulations to a great mass of air, the sound is much reinforced. The intensity is greatest when the vibrations of the string or sounding body are perpendicular to the sounding-board, and least when they are in the same plane with it. The sounding-board of the pianoforte is better disposed than that of any other stringed instrument, because the hammers strike the strings so as to make them vibrate at right angles to it. In the guitar, on the contrary, they are struck obliquely, which renders the tone feeble, unless when the sides, which also act as a sounding-board, are deep. It is evident that the sounding-board and the whole instrument are agitated at once by all the superposed vibrations excited by the simultaneous or consecutive notes that are sounded, each having its perfect effect independently of the rest. A sounding-board not only reciprocates the different degrees of pitch, but all the nameless qualities of tone. This has been beautifully illustrated by Prof. Wheatstone in a series of experiments on the transmission through solid conductors of musical performances, from the harp, piano, violin, clarinet, etc. He found that all the varieties of pitch, quality, and intensity, are perfectly transmitted with their relative gradations, and may be communicated through conducting wires or rods of very considerable length, to a properly disposed sounding-board in a distant apartment. The sounds of an entire orchestra may be transmitted and reciprocated by connecting one end of a metallic rod with a sounding-board near the orchestra, so placed as to resound to all the instruments, and the other end with the sounding-board of a harp, piano, or guitar, in a remote apartment. Prof. Wheatstone observes, "The effect of this experiment is very pleasing; the sounds, indeed, have so little intensity as scarcely to be heard at a distance from the reciprocating instrument; but on placing the ear close to it, a diminutive band is heard, in which all the instruments preserve their distinctive qualities, and the pianos and fortes, the crescendos and diminu-

endos, their relative contrasts. Compared with an ordinary band heard at a distance through the air, the effect is as a landscape seen in miniature beauty through a concave lens, compared with the same scene viewed by ordinary vision through a murky atmosphere."

Every one is aware of the reinforcement of sound by the resonance of cavities. When singing or speaking near the aperture of a wide-mouthed vessel, the intensity of some one note in unison with the air in the cavity is often augmented to a great degree. Any vessel will resound, if a body vibrating the natural note of the cavity be placed opposite to its orifice, and be large enough to cover it; or at least to set a large portion of the adjacent air in motion. For the sound will be alternately reflected by the bottom of the cavity and the undulating body at its mouth. The first impulse of the undulating substance will be reflected by the bottom of the cavity, and then by the undulating body, in time to combine with the second new impulse. This reinforced sound will also be twice reflected in time to conspire with the third new impulse; and as the same process will be repeated on every new impulse, each will combine with all its echoes to reinforce the sound prodigiously. Prof. Wheatstone, to whose ingenuity we are indebted for so much new and valuable information on the theory of sound, has given some very striking instances of resonance. If one of the branches of a vibrating tuning fork be brought near the embouchure of a flute, the lateral apertures of which are stopped so as to render it capable of producing the same sound as the fork, the feeble and scarcely audible sound of the fork will be augmented by the rich resonance of the column of air within the flute, and the tone will be full and clear. The sound will be found greatly to decrease by closing or opening another aperture; for the alteration in the length of the column of air renders it no longer fit perfectly to reciprocate the sound of the fork. This experiment may be made on a concert flute with a C tuning fork. But Prof. Wheatstone observes that in this case it is generally necessary to finger the flute for B, because when blown into with the mouth the upper lip partly covers the embouchure, which renders the sound about a semitone flatter than it would be were the embouchure entirely uncovered. He has also shown, by the following experiment, that any one among several simultaneous sounds may be rendered separately audible. If two bottles be selected, and tuned

by filling them with such a quantity of water as will render them unisonant with two tuning forks which differ in pitch, on bringing both of the vibrating tuning forks to the mouth of each bottle alternately, in each case that sound only will be heard which is reciprocated by the unisonant bottle.

Several attempts have been made to imitate the articulation of the letters of the alphabet. About the year 1779 MM. Kratzenstein of St. Petersburg, and Kempelen of Vienna, constructed instruments which articulated many letters, words, and even sentences. Mr. Willis of Cambridge has recently adapted cylindrical tubes to a reed, whose length can be varied at pleasure by sliding joints. Upon drawing out a tube while a column of air from the bellows of an organ is passing through it, the vowels are pronounced in the order, *i, e, a, o, u*. On extending the tube they are repeated after a certain interval, in the inverted order, *u, o, a, e, i*. After another interval they are again obtained in the direct order, and so on. When the pitch of the reed is very high, it is impossible to sound some of the vowels, which is in perfect correspondence with the human voice, female singers being unable to pronounce *u* and *o* in their high notes. From the singular discoveries of M. Savart on the nature of the human voice, and the investigations of Mr. Willis on the mechanism of the larynx, it may be presumed that ultimately the utterance or pronunciation of modern languages will be conveyed, not only to the eye, but also to the ear of posterity. Had the Ancients possessed the means of transmitting such definite sounds, the civilized world would still have responded in sympathetic notes at the distance of many ages.

From "Connection of the Physical
Sciences."

ROBERT SOUTHEY

(1774-1843)

ROBERT SOUTHEY was born at Bristol, England, August 12th, 1774. After having been expelled from Westminster School for writing an essay on "Flogging" for the school paper, he was admitted, after considerable difficulty, to Balliol College, Oxford, where he formed associations which were decisive of his future. One of his college friends was Coleridge, with whom he was interested in the famous scheme of "pantisocracy," through which the young poets hoped to establish the millennium in the United States. The association helped to make Southey one of the Lake School of English poets. After a year of travel, and a brief term in an official position, he took up his residence in 1804 at Greta Hall, near Keswick, where he devoted himself to study with painstaking industry. Few men of his century equaled him in the range and variety of his studies. His "Commonplace Book" is astonishing. It would be hard to find anywhere else so great an amount of curious, entertaining, and generally useless information as he collected in it. He was a man of books rather than of the world, and the distinction shows in all he wrote, both of prose and verse. He became Poet Laureate of England in 1813,—an honor he owed not only to his talent, but to his conversion to "Conservatism" and his complete abandonment of "pantisocracy" and all similar millennium ideals. He died at Greta Hall, March 21st, 1843. Among his best-known prose works are his "History of Brazil," "Life of Nelson," and "The Doctor,"—the latter a collection of highly original essays which show him at his best.

FAME

GUESS, reader, where I once saw a full-sized figure of Fame, erect, tiptoe, in the act of springing to take flight, and soar aloft, her neck extended, her head raised, the trumpet at her lips, and her cheeks inflated, as if about to send forth a blast which the whole city of London was to hear? Perhaps thou mayst have seen this very figure thyself, and surely if thou hast, thou wilt not have forgotten it. It was in the Borough Road, placed above a shopboard which announced that Mr. Somebody fitted up water-closets upon a new and improved principle.

But it would be well for mankind if Fame were never employed in trumpeting anything worse. There is a certain stage of depravity in which men derive an unnatural satisfaction from the notoriety of their wickedness, and seek for celebrity " *ob magnitudinem infamiæ, cujus apud prodigos novissima voluptas est. Ils veulent faire parler d'eux,*" says Bayle, " *et leur vanité ne serait pas satisfaite s'il n'y avait quelque chose de superlatif et d'éminent dans leur mauvaise reputation. Le plus haut degré de l'infamie est le but de leurs souhaits, et il y a des choses qu'ils ne feraient pas si elles n'étaient extraordinairement odieuses.*"

Plutarch has preserved the name of Chœrephanes, who was notorious among the Ancients for having painted such subjects as Giulio Romano has the everlasting infamy of having designed for the flagitious Aretine. He has also transmitted to posterity the name of Parmeno, famous for grunting like a pig; and of Theodorus, not less famous for the more difficult accomplishment of mimicking the sound of a creaking cart-wheel. Who would wish to have his name preserved for his beggarliness, like Pauson, the painter, and Codrus, the poet? or for his rascality and wickedness, like Phrynondas? or like Callianax, the physician, for callous brutality? Our doctor used to instance these examples when he talked of "the bubble reputation," which is sometimes to be had so cheaply, and yet for which so dear a price has often been paid in vain. It amused him to think by what odd or pitiful accidents that bubble might be raised. "Whether the regular practitioner may sneer at Mr. Ching," says the historian of Cornwall, "I knew not; but the Patent Worm Lozenges have gained our Launceton apothecary a large fortune, and secured to him perpetual fame."

Would not John Dory's name have died with him, and so been long ago dead as a doornail, if a grotesque likeness to him had not been discovered in the fish, which, being called after him, has immortalized him and his ugliness? But if John Dory could have anticipated this sort of immortality when he saw his own face in the glass, he might very well have " blushed to find it fame." There would have been no other memorial of Richard Jacquett at this day than the letters of his name in an old dead and obsolete hand, now well-nigh rendered illegible by time, if he had not, in the reign of Edward VI., been lord of the manor of Tyburn, with its appurtenances, wherein the gallows was included, wherefore, from the said Jacquett, it is presumed by anti-

sented with a collection of English proverbs, and told by the author that it contained them all, 'Nay,' replied she, 'Bate me an ace, quoth Bolton!' which proverb being instantly looked for, happened to be wanting in his collection." "Who this Bolton was," Ray says, "I know not, neither is it worth inquiring." Nevertheless, I ask who was Bolton; and when echo answers, "who?" say in my heart, "*Vanitas vanitatum, omnia vanitas.*" And having said this, conscience smites me with the recollection of what Pascal has said, " *Ceux qui écrivent contre la gloire, veulent avoir la gloire d'avoir bien écrit; et ceux qui le lisent, voulent avoir la gloire de l'avoir lu; et moi qui écris ceci, j'ai peut-être cette envie, et peut-être que ceux qui le lirent l'aurent aussi.*"

Who was old Ross of Potern, who lived till all the world was weary of him? All the world has forgotten him now. Who was Jack Raker, once so well known that he was named proverbially as a scapegrace by Skelton, and in the "Ralph Roister Doister" of Nicholas Udall, that Udall who, on poor Tom Tusser's account, ought always to be called the bloody schoolmaster? Who was William Dickins, whose wooden dishes were sold so badly, that when any one lost by the sale of his wares, the said Dickins and his dishes were brought up in scornful comparison? Outroaring Dick was a strolling singer of such repute that he got twenty shillings a day by singing at Braintree Fair; but who was that desperate Dick that was such a terrible cutter at a chine of beef, and devoured more meat at ordinaries in discoursing of his frays and deep acting, of his flashing and hewing, than would serve half a dozen brewer's draymen? It is at this day doubtful whether it was Jack Drum, or Tim Drum, whose mode of entertainment no one wishes to receive;—for it was to haul a man in by the head and thrust him out by the neck and shoulders. Who was that other Dick who wore so queer a hatband, that it has ever since served as a standing comparison for all queer things? By what name besides Richard was he known? Where did he live, and when? His birth, parentage, education, life, character, and behavior, who can tell? "Nothing," said the doctor, "is remembered of him, except that he was familiarly called Dick, and that his queer hatband went nine times round and would not tie."

"O vain world's glory and unsteadfast state
Of all that lives on face of sinful earth!"

quaries that the hangman hath been ever since corruptly called Jack Ketch. A certain William Dowsing, who, during the great Rebellion, was one of the parliamentary visitors for demolishing superstitious pictures and ornaments of churches, is supposed by a learned critic to have given rise to an expression in common use among schoolboys and blackguards. For this worshipful commissioner broke so many "mighty great angels" in glass, knocked so many apostles and cherubims to pieces, demolished so many pictures and stone crosses, and boasted with so much puritanical rancor of what he had done, that it is conjectured the threat of giving any one a dowsing preserves his rascally name. So, too, while Bracton and Fleta rest on the shelves of some public library, Nokes and Stiles are living names in the courts of law; and for John Doe and Richard Roe, were there ever two litigious fellows so universally known as these eternal antagonists?

Johnson tells a story of a man who was standing in an inn kitchen with his back to the fire, and thus accosted a traveler, who stood next to him, "Do you know, sir, who I am?" "No, sir," replied the traveler, "I have not that advantage." "Sir," said the man, "I am the great Twalmley, who invented the new flood-gate iron." Who but for Johnson would have heard of the great Twalmley now? Reader, I will answer the question which thou hast already asked, and tell thee that his invention consisted in applying a sliding door, like a flood gate, to an ironing box, flat irons having till then been used, or box irons with a door and a bolt.

Who was Tom Long the carrier? when did he flourish? what road did he travel? did he drive carts or wagons, or was it in the age of pack horses? Who was Jack Robinson? not the once well-known Robinson of the treasury (for his celebrity is now like a tale that is told), but the one whose name is in everybody's mouth, because it is so easily and so soon said. Who was Magg? and what was his diversion? was it brutal, or merely boorish? the boisterous exuberance of rude and unruly mirth, or the gratification of a tyrannical temper and a cruel disposition? Who was Crop the conjuror, famous in trivial speech as Merlin in romantic lore, or Doctor Faustus in the school of German extravagance? What is remembered now of Bully Dawson? All I have read of him is that he lived three weeks on the credit of a brass shilling, because nobody would take it of him. "There goes a story of Queen Elizabeth," says Ray, "that being pre-

Who was Betty Martin, and wherefore should she so often be mentioned in connection with my precious eye or yours? Who was Ludlam, whose dog was so lazy that he leaned his head against a wall to bark? And who was Old Cole, whose dog was so proud that he took the wall of a dung cart, and got squeezed to death by the wheel? Was he the same person of whom the song says:—

"Old King Cole
Was a merry old soul,
And a merry old soul was he"?

And was his dog proud because his master was called king? Here are questions to be proposed in the examination papers of some Australian Cambridge, two thousand years hence, when the people of that part of the world shall be as reasonably inquisitive concerning our affairs as we are now concerning those of the Greeks. But the Burneys, the Parrs, and the Porsons, the Elmsleys, Monks, and Blomfields of that age will puzzle over them in vain, for we cannot answer them now.

"Who was the Vicar of Bray? I have had long chase after him," said Mr. Brome to Rawlins, in 1735. "Simon Aleyn, or Allen, was his name; he was Vicar of Bray about 1540, and died in 1588; so he held the living near fifty years. You now partake of the sport that has cost me some pains to take. And if the pursuit after such game seems mean, one Mr. Vernon followed a butterfly nine miles before he could catch him." Reader, do not refuse your belief of this fact, when I can state to you, on my own recollection, that the late Dr. Shaw, the celebrated naturalist, a librarian of the British Museum, and known by the name of the learned Shavius, from the facility and abundance of his Latin compositions, pointed out to my notice there, many years ago, two volumes written by a Dutchman, upon the wings of a butterfly. "The dissertation is rather voluminous, sir, perhaps you will think," said the doctor, with somewhat of that apologetic air, which modest science is wont occasionally to assume in her communications with ignorance, "but it is immensely important." Good-natured excellent enthusiast! fully didst thou appreciate the book, the Dutchman, and, above all, the butterfly.

"I have known a great man," says Taylor, the water poet, "very expert on the Jew's-harp; a rich heir excellent at noddy; a justice of the peace skillful at quoits; a merchant's wife a quick gamester at Irish, especially when she came to bearing of men, that she would seldom miss entering." Injurious John Taylor! thus to defraud thy friends of their fame, and leave in irremediable oblivion the proper name of that expert Jew's-harper, that person excellent at noddy, that great quoits man, and that mistress who played so masterly a game at Irish! But I thank thee for this, good John the water poet; thou hast told us that Monsieur La Ferr, a Frenchman, was the first inventor of that admirable game of double-hand, hotcockles, etc., and that Gregory Dawson, an Englishman, devised the unmatchable mystery of blindman's-buff. But who can tell me what the game of carps was, the *Ludus Carparum*, which Hearne says was used in Oxford much, and being joined with cards, and reckoned as a kind of *alea*, is prohibited in some statutes? When Thomas Hearne, who learned whatever time forgot, was uncertain what game or play it really was, and could only conjecture that perhaps it might be a kind of backgammon, what antiquary can hope to ascertain it?

"Elizabeth Canning, Mary Squires, the gipsy, and Miss Blandy," says one who remembered their days of celebrity, "were such universal topics in 1752, that you would have supposed it the business of mankind to talk only of them; yet now, in 1790, ask a young man of twenty-five or thirty a question relative to these extraordinary personages, and he will be puzzled to answer."

Who now knows the steps of that dance, or has heard the name of its author, of which in our fathers' days it was said in verse, that—

"Isaac's rigadoon shall live as long
As Raphael's paintings, or as Virgil's song"?

Nay, who reads the poem wherein those lines are found, though the author predicted for them, in self-applauding pleasantry, that—

"Whilst birds in air or fish in streams we find,
Or damsels fresh with aged partners joined,
As long as nymphs shall with attentive ear
A fiddle rather than a sermon hear,
So long the brightest eye shall oft peruse
These useful lines of my instructive muse"?

Even of the most useful of those lines the "uses are gone by." Ladies before they leave the ballroom are now no longer fortified

king of Prussia! and who's he?" The "who's he?" of this old woman might serve as a text for a notable sermon upon ambition. "Who's he?" may now be asked of men greater as soldiers in their day than Frederick and Wellington; greater as discoverers than Sir Isaac, or Sir Humphrey. Who built the pyramids? Who ate the first oyster? *Vanitas vanitatum, omnia vanitas!*

RETIREMENT

IT is neither so easy a thing, nor so agreeable a one, as men commonly expect, to dispose of leisure when they retire from the business of the world. Their old occupations cling to them even when they hope that they have emancipated themselves. Go to any seaport town, and you will see that the sea captain, who has retired upon his well-earned earnings, sets up a weather cock in full view from his window, and watches the variations of the wind as duly as when he was at sea, though no longer with the same anxiety. A tallow chandler, having amassed a fortune, disposed of his business, and took a house in the country, not far from London, that he might enjoy himself; and, after a few months' trial of a holiday life, requested permission of his successor to come into town and assist him on melting days. The keeper of a retail spirit-shop, having in like manner retired from trade, used to employ himself by having one puncheon filled with water, and measuring it off by pints into another. A butcher in a small town, for some time after he had left off business, informed his old customers that he meant to kill a lamb once a week just for amusement.

PREACHING TO THE POOR

A WOMAN in humble life was asked one day on her way back from church whether she had understood the sermon—a stranger having preached. "Wud I hae the presumption!" was her simple and contented answer.

"Well, Master Jackson," said his minister, walking homeward after service, with an industrious laborer, who was a constant attendant, "well, Master Jackson, Sunday must be a blessed day of rest for you, who work so hard all the week! And you make good use of the day, for you are always to be seen at church."

against the sudden change of temperature by a cup of generous white wine, mulled with ginger; nor is it necessary now to caution them at such times against a draught of cold small beer, because, as the poet in his own experience assured them,—

"Destruction lurks within the poisonous dose,
A fatal fever, or a pimpled nose."

From "The Doctor."

THE DOCTOR'S WISE SAYINGS

SCHOOL LEARNING

I AM sometimes inclined to think that pigs are brought up upon a wiser system than boys at a grammar school. The pig is allowed to feed upon any kind of offal, however coarse, on which he can thrive, till the time approaches when pig is to commence pork, or take a degree as bacon.

LOVERS OF LITERATURE

YOUR true lover of literature is never fastidious. I do not mean the *helluo librorum*, the swinish feeder, who thinks that every name which is to be found in a title-page, or on a tombstone, ought to be rescued from oblivion; nor those first cousins of the moth, who labor under a passion for black letter, and believe everything to be excellent which was written in the reign of Elizabeth. I mean the man of robust and healthy intellect, who gathers the harvest of literature into his barns, thrashes the straw, winnows the grain, grinds it at his own mill, bakes it in his own oven, and then eats the true bread of knowledge. If he take his loaf upon a cabbage leaf, and eat onions with his bread and cheese, let who will find fault with him for his taste — not I!

VANITY OF HUMAN FAME

AN old woman in a village of the west of England was told one day that the king of Prussia was dead, such a report having arrived when the great Frederick was in the noonday of his glory. Old Mary lifted up her great slow eyes at the news, and, fixing them in the fullness of vacancy upon her informant, replied, "Is a! is a! the Lord ha' mercy! Well, well! the

"Aye, sir," replied Jackson, "it is, indeed, a blessed day; I works hard enough all the week; and then I comes to church o' Sundays, and sets me down, and lays my legs up, and thinks o' nothing."

VOLUMINOUS TRIFLING

DR. SHAW, the naturalist, was one day showing to a friend two volumes written by a Dutchman, upon the wings of a butterfly, in the British Museum. "The dissertation is rather voluminous, perhaps you will think," said the doctor gravely, "but it is immensely important."

PARLIAMENTARY JOKES

OF WHAT use a story may be, even in the most serious debates, may be seen from the circulation of old Joes in parliament, which are as current there as their current namesakes used to be in the city some threescore years ago. A jest, though it shall be as stale as last year's newspapers, and as flat as Lord Flounder's face, is sure to be received with laughter by the collective wisdom of the nation; nay, it is sometimes thrown out like a tub to the whale, or like a trail of carrion to draw off hounds from the scent.

BOOK MADNESS

A COLLECTOR of scarce books was one day showing me his small but curious hoard. "Have you ever seen a copy of this book?" he asked, with every volume that he put into my hands; and when my reply was that I had not, he always rejoined, with a look and tone of triumphant delight, "I should have been exceedingly sorry if you had!"

ÉMILE SOUVESTRE

(1806–1854)

ÉMILE SOUVESTRE, novelist and essayist, was born in Morlaix, Brittany, April 15th, 1806. He began life with no other means of support than his daily labor, and it was only after years of struggle as bookseller's clerk, schoolmaster, and journalist, that he finally won the reputation as a writer for which he had industriously striven. He wrote novels and dramas which were more popular during his life than his essays; but while the novels are now seldom read, his «Attic Philosopher in Paris» (Un Philosophe sous les Toits) continues to go through one edition after another. It is a collection of essays in half narrative style, with just enough plot to give the characters in them vitality. Souvestre died July 5th, 1854.

MISANTHROPY AND REPENTANCE

AUGUST 3d, nine o'clock P. M.— There are days when everything appears gloomy to us; the world is, like the sky, covered by a dark fog. Nothing seems in its place; we only see misery, improvidence, and cruelty; the world seems without God, and given up to all the evils of chance.

Yesterday I was in this unhappy humor. After a long walk in the faubourgs, I returned home, sad and dispirited.

Everything I had seen seemed to accuse the civilization of which we are so proud! I had wandered into a little by-street, with which I was not acquainted, and I found myself suddenly in the middle of those dreadful abodes where the poor are born, languish, and die. I looked at those decaying walls, which time has covered with a foul leprosy; those windows, from which dirty rags hang out to dry; those fetid gutters, which coil along the fronts of the houses like venomous reptiles! I felt oppressed with grief, and hastened on.

A little further on I was stopped by the hearse of a hospital, —a dead man, nailed down in his deal coffin, was going to his last abode, without funeral pomp or ceremony, and without fol-

gardens below; here I am again leaning on my elbows by the window, inhaling the freshness and gladness of this first wakening of the day.

My eye always passes over the roofs filled with flowers, warbling and sunlight with the same pleasure; but to-day it stops at the end of a buttress which separates our house from the next. The storms have stripped the top of its plaster covering, and dust, carried by the wind, has collected in the crevices, and, being fixed there by the rain, has formed a sort of aërial terrace, where some green grass has sprung up. Amongst it rises a stalk of wheat, which to-day is surmounted by a sickly ear that droops its yellow head.

This poor stray crop on the roofs, the harvest of which will fall to the neighboring sparrows, has carried my thoughts to the rich crops which are now falling beneath the sickle; it has recalled to me the beautiful walks I took as a child through my native province, when the threshing floors at the farmhouses resounded from every part with the sound of the flail, and when the carts, loaded with golden sheaves, came in by all the roads. I still remember the songs of the maidens, the cheerfulness of the old men, the open-hearted merriment of the laborers. There was, at that time, something in their looks both of pride and feeling. The latter came from thankfulness to God; the former from the sight of the harvest, the reward of their labor. They felt indistinctly the grandeur and the holiness of their part in the general work of the world; they looked with pride upon their mountains of corn sheaves, and they seemed to say — next to God, it is we who feed the world!

What a wonderful order there is in all human labor! Whilst the husbandman furrows his land, and prepares for every one his daily bread, the town artisan, far away, weaves the stuff in which he is to be clothed; the miner seeks under ground the iron for his plow; the soldier defends him against the invader; the judge takes care that the law protects his fields; the tax comptroller adjusts his private interests with those of the public; the merchant occupies himself in exchanging his products with those of distant countries; the men of science and of art add every day a few horses to this ideal team, which draws along the material world, as steam impels the gigantic trains of our iron roads! Thus all unite together, all help one another; the toil of each one benefits himself and all the world; the work has

lowers. There was not here even that last friend of the outcast, —the dog, which a painter has introduced as the sole attendant at the pauper's burial! He whom they were preparing to commit to the earth was going to the tomb as he had lived, alone; doubtless, no one would be aware of his end. In this great battle of society, what signifies a soldier the less?

But what, then, is this human society, if one of its members can thus disappear, like a leaf carried away by the wind?

The hospital was near a barrack, at the entrance of which old men, women, and children were quarreling for the remains of the coarse bread which the soldiers had given them in charity! Thus, beings like ourselves daily wait, in destitution, on our compassion, till we give them leave to live! Whole troops of outcasts, in addition to the trials imposed on all God's children, have to endure the pangs of cold, hunger, and humiliation. Unhappy human commonwealth! where man is in a worse condition than the bee in its hive, or the ant in its subterranean city!

Ah! what then avails our reason? What is the good of so many high faculties, if we are neither the wiser nor the happier for them? Which of us would not exchange his life of labor and trouble with that of the birds of the air, to whom the whole world is a life of joy.

How well I understand the complaint of Mao, in the popular tales of the "Le Foyer Breton," who, when dying of hunger and thirst, says, as he looks at the bullfinches rifling the fruit trees,—

"Alas! those birds are happier than Christians; they have no need of inns, or butchers, or bakers, or gardeners. God's heaven belongs to them and earth spreads a continual feast before them! The tiny flies are their game, ripe grass their cornfields, and hips and haws their store of fruit. They have the right of taking everywhere, without paying or asking leave; thus comes it that the little birds are happy, and sing all the livelong day."

But the life of man in a natural state is like that of the birds; he equally enjoys nature. "The earth spreads a continual feast before him." What, then, has he gained by that selfish and imperfect association which forms a nation? Would it not be better for every one to return again to the fertile bosom of Nature, and live there upon her bounty in peace and liberty?

August 10th, four o'clock A. M.—The dawn casts a red glow on my bed curtains; the breeze brings in the fragrance of the

been apportioned among the different members of the whole of society by a tacit agreement. If, in this apportionment, errors are committed, if certain individuals have not been employed according to their capacities, these defects of detail diminish in the sublime conception of the whole. The poorest man included in this association has his place, his work, his reason for being there; each is something in the whole.

There is nothing like this for man in the state of nature; as he depends only upon himself, it is necessary that he be sufficient for everything. All creation is his property; but he finds in it as many hindrances as helps. He must surmount these obstacles with the single strength that God has given him; he cannot reckon on any other aid than chance and opportunity. No one reaps, manufactures, fights, or thinks for him; he is nothing to any one. He is a unit multiplied by the cipher of his own single powers; while the civilized man is a unit multiplied by the powers of the whole of society.

Yet, notwithstanding this, the other day, disgusted by the sight of some vices in detail, I cursed the latter, and almost envied the life of the savage.

One of the infirmities of our nature is always to mistake feeling for evidence, and to judge of the season by a cloud or a ray of sunshine.

Was the misery, the sight of which made me regret a savage life, really the effect of civilization? Must we accuse society of having created these evils, or acknowledge, on the contrary, that it has alleviated them? Could the women and children who were receiving the coarse bread from the soldier hope in the desert for more help or pity? That dead man, whose forsaken state I deplored, had he not found, by the cares of a hospital, a coffin, and the humble grave where he was about to rest? Alone, and far from men, he would have died like the wild beast in his den, and would now be serving as food for vultures! These benefits of human society are shared, then, by the most destitute. Whoever eats the bread that another has reaped and kneaded is under an obligation to his brother, and cannot say he owes him nothing in return. The poorest of us has received from society much more than his own single strength would have permitted him to wrest from nature.

But cannot society give us more? Who doubts it? Errors have been committed in this distribution of tasks and workers.

Time will diminish the number of them; with new lights a better division will arise; the elements of society go on towards perfection, like everything else; the difficulty is to know how to adapt ourselves to the slow step of time, whose progress can never be forced on without danger.

August 14th, six o'clock A. M.— My garret window rises upon the roof like a massive watchtower. The corners are covered by large sheets of lead, which run into the tiles; the successive action of cold and heat has made them rise, and so a crevice has been formed in an angle on the right side. There a sparrow has built her nest.

I have followed the progress of this aërial habitation from the first day. I have seen the bird successively bring the straw, moss, and wool designed for the construction of her abode; and I have admired the persevering skill she expended in this difficult work. At first, my new neighbor spent her days in fluttering over the poplar in the garden, and in chirping along the gutters. A fine lady's life seemed the only one to suit her; then, all of a sudden, the necessity of preparing a shelter for her brood transformed our idler into a worker: she no longer gave herself either rest or relaxation. I saw her always either flying, fetching, or carrying; neither rain nor sun stopped her. A striking example of the power of necessity! We are not only indebted to it for most of our talents, but for many of our virtues!

Is it not necessity which has given the people of less favored climates that constant activity which has placed them so quickly at the head of nations? As they are deprived of most of the gifts of nature, they have supplied them by their industry; necessity has sharpened their understanding; endurance awakened their foresight. Whilst elsewhere man, warmed by an ever brilliant sun, and loaded with the bounties of the earth, was remaining poor, ignorant and naked in the midst of gifts he did not attempt to explore, here he was forced by necessity to wrest his food from the ground, to build habitations to defend himself from the intemperance of the weather, and to warm his body by clothing himself with the wool of animals. Work makes him both more intelligent and more robust: disciplined by it, he seems to mount higher on the ladder of creation, while those more favored by nature remain on the step the nearest to the brutes.

I made these reflections while looking at the bird, whose instinct seemed to have become more acute since she had been occupied in work. At last the nest was finished; she set up her household there, and I followed her through all the phases of her new existence.

When she had sat on the eggs and the young ones were hatched, she fed them with the most attentive care. The corner of my window had become a stage of moral action which fathers and mothers might come to take lessons from. The little ones soon became great, and this morning I have seen them take their first flight. One of them, weaker than the others, was not able to clear the edge of the roof, and fell into the gutter. I caught him with some difficulty, and placed him again on the tile in front of his house, but the mother has not noticed him. Once freed from the cares of a family, she has resumed her wandering life among the trees and along the roofs. In vain I have kept away from my window, to take from her every excuse for fear; in vain the feeble little bird has called to her with plaintive cries; his bad mother has passed by, singing and fluttering with a thousand airs and graces. Once only the father came near; he looked at his offspring with contempt, and then disappeared, never to return!

I crumbled some bread before the little orphan, but he did not know how to peck it with his bill. I tried to catch him, but he escaped into the forsaken nest. What will become of him there, if his mother does not come back!

August 15th, six o'clock.— This morning, on opening my window, I found the little bird dying upon the tiles; his wounds showed me that he had been driven from the nest by his unworthy mother. I tried in vain to warm him again with my breath; I felt the last pulsations of life; his eyes were already closed, and his wings hung down! I placed him on the roof in a ray of sunshine, and I closed my window. The struggle of life against death has always something gloomy in it; it is a warning to us.

Happily I hear some one in the passage; without doubt, it is my old neighbor; his conversation will distract my thoughts.

It was my portress. Excellent woman! She wished me to read a letter from her son the sailor, and begged me to answer it for her.

I kept it to copy into my journal. Here it is:—

Dear Mother :—

This is to tell you that I have been very well ever since the last time, except that last week I was nearly drowned with the boat, which would have been a great loss, as there is not a better craft anywhere.

A gust of wind capsized us; and just as I came up above water, I saw the captain sinking. I went after him, as was my duty, and, after diving three times, I brought him to the surface, which pleased him much; for when we were hoisted on board, and he had recovered his senses, he threw his arms round my neck, as he would have done to an officer.

I do not hide from you, dear mother, that this has delighted me. But it isn't all; it seems that fishing up the captain has reminded them that I had a good character, and they have just told me that I am promoted to be a sailor of the first class. Directly I knew it, I cried out, «My mother shall have coffee twice a day!» And really, dear mother, there is nothing now to hinder you, as I shall now have a larger allowance to send you.

I conclude by begging you to take care of yourself if you wish to do me good; for nothing makes me feel so well as to think that you want for nothing.

Your son, from the bottom of my heart,
JACQUES.

This is the answer the portress dictated to me:—

My good Jacquot:—

It makes me very happy to see that your heart is still as true as ever, and that you will never shame those who have brought you up. I need not tell you to take care of your life, because you know it is the same as my own, and that without you, dear child, I should wish for nothing but the grave; but we are not bound to live, while we are bound to do our duty.

Do not fear for my health, good Jacques. I was never better! I do not grow old at all, for fear of making you unhappy. I want nothing, and I live like a lady. I even had some money over this year, and as my drawers shut very badly, I put it into the savings bank, where I have opened an account in your name. So, when you come back, you will find yourself with an income. I have also furnished your chest with new linen, and I have knitted you three new sea jackets.

All your friends are well. Your cousin is just dead, leaving his widow in difficulties. I gave her your thirty francs remittance, and

said that you had sent it to her; and the poor woman remembers you day and night in her prayers. So, you see, I have put that money in another sort of savings bank; but there it is our hearts which get the interest.

Good-bye, dear Jacquot; write to me often, and always remember the good God and your old mother.

PHROSINE MILLOT.

Good son, and worthy mother! how such examples bring us back to a love for the human race! In a fit of fanciful misanthropy, we may envy the fate of the savage, and prefer that of the bird to such as he; but impartial observation soon does justice to such paradoxes. We find, on examination, that in the mixed good and evil of human nature, the good so far abounds that we are not in the habit of noticing it, while the evil strikes us precisely on account of its being the exception. If nothing is perfect, nothing is so bad as to be without its compensation or its remedy. What spiritual riches are there in the midst of the evils of society! How much does the moral world redeem the material!

That which will ever distinguish man from the rest of creation is his power of deliberate affection and of enduring self-sacrifice. The mother who took care of her brood in the corner of my window devoted to them the necessary time for accomplishing the laws which insure the preservation of her kind; but she obeyed an instinct and not a rational choice. When she had accomplished the mission appointed her by Providence, she cast off the duty, as we get rid of a burden, and she returned again to her selfish liberty. The other mother, on the contrary, will go on with her task as long as God shall leave her here below; the life of her son will still remain, so to speak, joined to her own, and when she disappears from the earth, she will leave there that part of herself.

Thus, the affections make for our species an existence separate from all the rest of creation. Thanks to them, we enjoy a sort of terrestrial immortality; and if other beings succeed one another, man alone perpetuates himself.

Complete. «An Attic Philosopher in Paris,» Chap. viii.

HERBERT SPENCER

(1820-)

ERBERT SPENCER was born at Derby, England, April 27th, 1820. To his father, a schoolmaster at Derby, and to his father's brother, Rev. Thomas Spencer, rector at Hinton, he owed his early education and the first impulse towards the profound studies which made him the founder of "Synthetic Philosophy." He began life as an assistant in the office of a civil engineer, but in 1845 turned from engineering to the career of a writer, to which he devoted himself with remarkable industry and astonishing fertility during the remainder of the century. He worked with Darwin in elucidating the theories of evolution, but as against those who call him "a pupil of Darwin," his admirers cite the fact that in his "Principles of Psychology," published in 1855, he stated the principles of evolution four years before the appearance of "The Origin of Species." There is scarcely room for controversy on such a point, however, as only the "terminology" of the evolutionists of the nineteenth century was new. Their philosophy was itself an evolution. Spencer was really more remarkable, however, as a political essayist than in the science of which he was so fond. His determined and aggressive individualism did much to hold in check the "Collectionism" of Fourier, Marx, and Lassalle. To Spencer, society and all its institutions exist for man, not man for society. He reasoned that the only right society has to legislate for and to coerce the individual is that individuality may be the more fully developed through the establishment of a more nearly perfect justice. The only vitiating flaw in his severe logic was its consistency carried to its extreme. It made "the law of the survival of the fittest" apply against state aid, even to the helpless; and charity to the undeserving is by his theories almost criminal. It was on such consistencies as these that his opponents seized as they might have seized on the inconsistencies of a weaker intellect. They did not break his influence, however, and he became an inspiration for all who endeavor to check the tendency to restrictive legislation. The list of his works is so long and all are in one sense or another so important that it is hard to select from among them, but he himself no doubt intended to make the various volumes of his "Synthetic Philosophy" the great masterpiece of his life. His essay on "Education," his "Social Statics," "Data of Ethics,"

IX—220

"The Man versus the State," and the essay on "The Philosophy of Style" are works which have had extensive circulation among general readers.

EVOLUTION OF THE PROFESSIONS

THE saying that we cannot put old heads on young shoulders figuratively expresses, among other truths, the truth that the beliefs which in youth result from small information joined with undisciplined thought and feeling cannot, until after long years, be replaced by the beliefs which wider knowledge and better balanced mental powers produce. And while it is usually impracticable to antedate the results of mental development and culture, it is also usually impracticable to arouse, during early stages, any such distrust of convictions then formed, as should be caused by the perception that there is much more to be learned.

This general remark, trite in substance though it is, I am prompted to make à propos of the profound change which study of many peoples in many places and times causes in those ideas of social organization which are current — ideas entertained not only by the young, but also by the majority of the old, who, relatively to the subject-matter to be investigated, are also young. For patient inquiry and calm thought make it manifest that sundry institutions regarded with strong prejudices have been essential institutions; and that the development of society has everywhere been determined by agencies — especially political and ecclesiastical — of characters condemned by the higher sentiments and incongruous with an advanced social ideal.

One in whom aversion to autocratic rule is strong does not willingly recognize the truth that without autocratic rule the evolution of society could not have commenced; and one to whom the thought of priestly control is repugnant cannot, without difficulty, bring himself to see that during early stages priestly control was necessary. But contemplation of the evidence, while proving these general facts, also makes it manifest that in the nature of things groups of men out of which organized societies germinate must, in passing from the homogeneous to the heterogeneous, have first assumed the form in which one individual predominates,—a nucleus of the group serving as a centre of initiation for all subsequent steps in development. Though, as

---

fast as society advances, and especially as fast as the militant type yields place to the industrial type, a centralized and coercive control, political and ecclesiastical, becomes less needful, and plays a continually decreasing part in social evolution; yet the evidence compels us to admit that at first it was indispensable.

This generalization, which we saw variously illustrated by political institutions and ecclesiastical institutions, we now see again illustrated by professional institutions. As the foregoing chapters have shown, all the professions originate by differentiation from the agency which, beginning as political, becomes, with the apotheosis of the dead ruler, politico-ecclesiastical, and thereafter develops the professions chiefly from its ecclesiastical element. Egypt which, by its records and remains, exhibits so well the early phases of social progress, shows us how at first various governmental functions, including the professional, were mingled in the king and in the cluster of those who surrounded the king. Says Tiele:—

"A conflict between the authority of priest and king was hardly possible in earlier times, for then the kings themselves, their sons, and their principal officers of state were the chief priests, and the priestly dignities were not dissevered from nor held to be inconsistent with other and civil functions."

And again:—

"The priestly offices were state functions . . . which did not differ at all in kind from that of commander of the troops, governor of a district, architect, and chamberlain. In fact, both kinds of office were, for the most part, filled by the same persons."

And since, as Brugsch tells us, "Pharaoh's architects (the Mur-ket) . . . were often of the number of the king's sons and grandsons," we see that in the governing group the political, ecclesiastical, and professional functions were united.

No group of institutions illustrates with greater clearness the process of social evolution; and none shows more undeniably how social evolution conforms to the law of evolution at large. The germs out of which the professional agencies arise, forming at first a part of the regulative agency, differentiate from it at the same time that they differentiate from one another; and while severally being rendered more multiform by the rise

---

of subdivisions, severally become more coherent within themselves and more definitely marked off. The process parallels completely that by which the parts of an individual organism pass from their initial state of simplicity to their ultimate state of complexity.

Originally one who was believed by himself and others to have power over demons — the mystery man or medicine man — using coercive methods to expel disease-producing spirits, stood in the place of doctor; and when his appliances, at first supposed to act supernaturally, came to be understood as acting naturally, his office eventually lost its priestly character altogether: the resulting physician class, originally uniform, eventually dividing into distinguishable subclasses while acquiring a definite embodiment.

Less early, because implying more developed groups, arose those who as exhibitors of joy, now in the presence of the living ruler and now in the supposed presence of the deceased ruler, were at first simultaneously singers and dancers, and, becoming specialized from the people at large, presently became distinct from one another; whence, in course of time, two groups of professionals, whose official laudations, political or religious, extended in their range and multiplied in their kinds. And then by like steps were separated from one another vocal and instrumental musicians, and eventually composers; within which classes also there arose subdivisions.

Ovations, now to the living king and now to the dead king, while taking saltatory and musical forms, took also verbal forms, originally spontaneous and irregular, but presently studied and measured; whence, first, the unrhythmical speech of the orator, which under higher emotional excitement grew into the rhythmical speech of the priest poet, chanting verses — verses that finally became established hymns of praise. Meanwhile from accompanying rude imitations of the hero's acts, performed now by one and now by several, grew dramatic representations, which, little by little elaborated, fell under the regulation of a chief actor, who prefigured the playwright. And out of these germs, all pertaining to worship, came eventually the various professions of poets, actors, dramatists, and the subdivisions of these.

The great deeds of the hero god, recited, chanted, or sung, and mimetically rendered, naturally came to be supplemented by details, so growing into accounts of his life; and thus the priest poet gave origin to the biographer, whose narratives, being extended to less sacred personages, became secularized. Stories of the apotheosized chief or king, joined with stories of his companions and amplified by narratives of accompanying transactions, formed the first histories. And from these accounts of the doings of particular men and groups of men, partly true but passing by exaggeration into the mythical, came the wholly mythical, or fiction; which then and always preserved the biographico-historical character. Add to which that out of the criticisms and reflections scattered through this personal literature an impersonal literature slowly emerged; the whole group of these products having as their deepest root the eulogies of the priest poet.

Prompted as were the medicine men of savages and the priests of early civilized peoples to increase their influence, they were ever stimulated to acquire knowledge of natural actions and the properties of things; and, being in alleged communication with supernatural beings, they were supposed to acquire such knowledge from them. Hence, by implication, the priest became the primitive man of science; and led by his special experiences to speculate about the causes of things, thus entered the sphere of philosophy: both his science and his philosophy being pursued in the service of his religion.

Not only his higher culture, but his alleged intercourse with the gods, whose mouthpiece he was, made him the authority in cases of dispute; and being also, as historian, the authority concerning past transactions and traditional usages, or laws, he acquired in both capacities the character of judge. Moreover, when the growth of legal administration brought the advocate, he, though usually of lay origin, was sometimes clerical.

Distinguished in early stages as the learned man of the tribe or society, and especially distinguished as the possessor of that knowledge which was thought of most value — knowledge of unseen things — the priest of necessity became the first teacher. Transmitting traditional statements concerning ghosts and gods, at first to neophytes of his class only, but afterward to the cultured classes, he presently, beyond instruction in supernatural things, gave instruction in natural things; and, having been the first secular teacher, has retained a large share in secular teaching even down to our own days.

As making a sacrifice was the original priestly act, and as the building of an altar for the sacrifice was by implication a priestly

act, it results that the making of a shelter over the altar, which in its developed form became the temple, was also a priestly act. When the priest, ceasing to be himself the executant, directed the artificers, he continued to be the designer; and when he ceased to be the actual designer, the master builder or architect thereafter continued to fulfill his general directions. And then the temple and the palace in sundry early societies, being at once the residence of the apotheosized ruler and the living ruler (even now a palace usually contains a small temple), and being the first kinds of developed architecture, eventually gave origin to secular architecture.

A rudely carved or modeled image of a man placed on his grave gave origin to the sculptured representation of a god inclosed in his temple. A product of priestly skill at the outset, it continued in some cases to be such among early civilized peoples; and always thereafter, when executed by an artisan, conformed to priestly direction. Extending presently to the representation of other than divine and semidivine personages, it eventually thus passed into its secularized form.

So was it with painting. At first used to complete the carved representation of the revered or worshiped personage, and being otherwise in some tribes used by the priest and his aids for exhibiting the tribal hero's deeds, it long remained subservient to religion, either for the coloring of statues (as it does still in Roman Catholic images of saints, etc.), or for the decoration of temples, or for the portraiture of deceased persons on sarcophagi and stelæ; and when it gained independence it was long employed almost wholly for the rendering of sacred scenes, — its eventual secularization being accompanied by its subdivision into a variety of kinds and of the executant artists into correlative groups.

Thus the process of professional evolution betrays throughout the same traits. In stages like that described by Huc as still existing among the Tibetans, where "the Lama is not merely a priest, he is the painter, poet, sculptor, architect, physician," there are joined in the same individual, or group of individuals, the potentialities out of which gradually arise the specialized groups we know as professions. While out of the one primitive class there come by progressive divergences many classes, each of these classes itself undergoes a kindred change: there are formed in it subdivisions and even sub-subdivisions, which become gradually

more marked; so that, throughout, the advance is from an indefinite homogeneity to a definite heterogeneity.

In presence of the fact that the immense majority of mankind adhere pertinaciously to the creeds, political and religious, in which they are brought up; and in presence of the further fact that on behalf of their creeds, however acquired, there are soon enlisted prejudices which practically shut out adverse evidence, it is not to be expected that the foregoing illustrations, even joined with kindred illustrations previously given, will make them see that society is a growth and not a manufacture, and has its laws of evolution.

From prime ministers down to plowboys there is either ignorance or disregard of the truth that nations acquire their vital structures by natural processes and not by artificial devices. If the belief is not that social arrangements have been divinely ordered thus or thus, then it is that they have been made thus or thus by kings, or if not by kings, then by parliaments. That they have come about by small accumulated changes not contemplated by rulers is an open secret which only of late has been recognized by a few, and is still unperceived by the many, — educated as well as uneducated. Though the turning of the land into a food-producing surface, cleared, fenced, drained, and covered with farming appliances, has been achieved by men working for individual profit, not by legislative direction — though villages, towns, cities, have insensibly grown up under the desires of men to satisfy their wants — though by spontaneous co-operation of citizens have been formed canals, railways, telegraphs, and other means of communication and distribution, the natural forces which have done all this are ignored as of no account in political thinking. Our immense manufacturing system with its multitudinous inventions, supplying both home and foreign consumers, and the immense mercantile marine by which its products are taken all over the globe and other products brought back, have been naturally and not artificially originated. That transformation by which, in thousands of years, men's occupations have been so specialized that each, aiding to satisfy some small division of his fellow-citizen's needs has his own needs satisfied by the work of hundreds of others, has taken place without design and unobserved. Knowledge developing into science, which has become so vast in mass that no one can grasp a tithe of it, and which now guides productive activities at large has

resulted from the workings of individuals prompted not by the ruling agency, but by their own inclinations. So, too, has been created the still vaster mass distinguished as literature, yielding the gratifications filling so large a space in our lives. Nor is it otherwise with the literature of the hour. That ubiquitous journalism which provides satisfactions for men's more urgent mental wants has resulted from the activities of citizens severally pursuing private benefits. And supplementing these come the innumerable companies, associations, unions, societies, clubs, subserving enterprise, commerce, philanthropy, culture, art, amusement; as well as the multitudinous institutions annually receiving millions by endowments and subscriptions: all of them arising from the unforced co-operations of citizens. And yet so hypnotized are nearly all by fixedly contemplating the doings of ministers and parliaments, that they have no eyes for this marvelous organization which has been growing for thousands of years without governmental help — nay, indeed, in spite of governmental hindrances. For in agriculture, manufactures, commerce, banking, journalism, immense injuries have been done by laws, — injuries afterward healed by social forces which have thereupon set up afresh the normal courses of growth. So unconscious are men of the life of the social organism that though the spontaneous actions of its units, each seeking livelihood, generate streams of food which touch at their doors every hour — though the water for their morning bath, the lights for their rooms, the fires in their grates, the bus or tram which takes them to the city, the business they carry on (made possible by the distributing system they share in), the evening Special they glance at, the theatre or concert to which they presently go, and the cab home, all result from the unprompted workings of this organized humanity, they remain blind. Though by its vital activities capital is drafted to places where it is most wanted, supplies of commodities balanced in every locality and prices universally adjusted — all without official supervision; yet, being oblivious of the truth that these processes are socially originated without design of any one, they cannot believe that society will be bettered by natural agencies. And hence when they see an evil to be cured or a good to be achieved, they ask for legal coercion as the only possible means.

More than this is true. If, as every parliamentary debate and every political meeting show, the demands for legislation pay no attention to that beneficent social development which has done so much and may be expected to increase in efficiency, still more do they ignore the laws of that development — still less do they recognize a natural order in the changes by which society passes from its lower to its higher stages. Though, as we have seen, the process of evolution exemplified in the genesis of the professions is similar in character to the process exemplified in the genesis of political and ecclesiastical institutions and everywhere else; and though the first inquiry rationally to be made respecting any proposed measure should be whether or not it falls within the lines of this evolution, and what must be the effects of running counter to the normal course of things; yet not only is no such question ever entertained, but one who raised it would be laughed down in any popular assemblage and smiled at as a dreamer in the House of Commons: the only course thought wise in either the cultured or the uncultured gathering being that of trying to estimate immediate benefits and evils.

Nor will any argument or any accumulation of evidence suffice to change this attitude until there has arisen a different type of mind and a different quality of culture. The politician will still spend his energies in rectifying some evils and making more — in forming, reforming, and again reforming — in passing acts to amend acts that were before amended; while social schemers will continue to think that they have only to cut up society and re-arrange it after their ideal pattern and its parts will join together again and work as intended

Complete.

MEDDLESOME AND CODDLING PATERNALISM

THE enthusiastic philanthropist, urgent for some act of parliament to remedy this evil or secure the other good, thinks it a very trivial and far-fetched objection that the people will be morally injured by doing things for them instead of leaving them to do things themselves. He vividly realizes the benefit he hopes to get achieved, which is a positive and readily imaginable thing: he does not realize the diffused, invisible, and slowly accumulating effect wrought on the popular mind, and so does not believe in it; or, if he admits it, thinks it beneath consideration. Would he but remember, however, that all national

character is gradually produced by the daily action of circumstances, of which each day's result seems so insignificant as not to be worth mentioning, he would see that what is trifling when viewed in its increments, may be formidable when viewed in its sum total. Or if he would go into the nursery, and watch how repeated actions — each of them apparently unimportant, create, in the end, a habit which will affect the whole future life; he would be reminded that every influence brought to bear on human nature tells, and if continued, tells seriously. The thoughtless mother who hourly yields to the requests: "Mamma, tie my pinafore," "Mamma, button my shoe," and the like, cannot be persuaded that each of these concessions is detrimental; but the wiser spectator sees that if this policy be long pursued, and be extended to other things, it will end in hopeless dependence. The teacher of the old school who showed his pupil the way out of every difficulty did not perceive that he was generating an attitude of mind greatly militating against success in life. The modern instructor, however, induces his pupil to solve his difficulties himself; believes that in so doing he is preparing him to meet the difficulties which, when he goes into the world, there will be no one to help him through; and finds confirmation for this belief in the fact that a great proportion of the most successful men are self-made.

Well, is it not obvious that this relationship between discipline and success holds good nationally? Are not nations made of men; and are not men subject to the same laws of modification in their adult as in their early years? Is it not true of the drunkard, that each carouse adds a thread to his bonds? of the trader, that each acquisition strengthens the wish for acquisitions? of the pauper, that the more you assist him the more he wants? of the busy man, that the more he has to do the more he can do? And does it not follow that if every individual is subject to this process of adaptation to conditions, a whole nation must be so — that just in proportion as its members are little helped by extraneous power they will become self-helping, and in proportion as they are much helped they will become helpless? What folly is it to ignore these results because they are not direct, and not immediately visible. Though slowly wrought out, they are inevitable. We can no more elude the laws of human development than we can elude the law of gravitation; and so long as they hold true must these effects occur.

If we are asked in what special directions this alleged helplessness, entailed by much state superintendence, shows itself, we reply that it is seen in a retardation of all social growths requiring self-confidence in the people — in a timidity that fears all difficulties not before encountered — in a thoughtless contentment with things as they are. Let any one, after duly watching the rapid evolution going on in England, where men have been comparatively little helped by governments — or better still, after contemplating the unparalleled progress of the United States, which is peopled by self-made men, and the recent descendants of self-made men; — let such a one, we say, go on to the Continent, and consider the relatively slow advance which things are there making; and the still slower advance they would make but for English enterprise. Let him go to Holland, and see that though the Dutch early showed themselves good mechanics, and have had abundant practice in hydraulics, Amsterdam has been without any due supply of water until now that works are being established by an English company. Let him go to Berlin, and there be told that, to give that city a water supply such as London has had for generations, the project of an English firm is about to be executed by English capital, under English superintendence. Let him go to Paris, where he will find a similar lack, and a like remedy now under consideration. Let him go to Vienna, and learn that it, in common with other continental cities, is lighted by an English gas company. Let him go on the Rhone, on the Loire, on the Danube, and discover that Englishmen established steam navigation on those rivers. Let him inquire concerning the railways in Italy, Spain, France, Sweden, Denmark, how many of them are English projects, how many have been largely helped by English capital, how many have been executed by English contractors, how many have had English engineers. Let him discover, too, as he will, that where railways have been government made, as in Russia, the energy, the perseverance, and the practical talent developed in England and the United States have been called in to aid.

And then if these illustrations of the progressiveness of a self-dependent race, and the torpidity of paternally governed ones, do not suffice him, he may read Mr. Laing's successive volumes of European travel, and there study the contrast in detail. What, now, is the cause of this contrast? In the order of nature, a capacity for self-help must in every case have been brought into

existence by the practice of self-help; and, other things equal, a lack of this capacity must in every case have arisen from the lack of demand for it. Do not these two antecedents and their two consequents agree with the facts as presented in England and Europe? Were not the inhabitants of the two, some centuries ago, much upon a par in point of enterprise? Were not the English even behind, in their manufactures, in their colonization, and in their commerce? Has not the immense relative change the English have undergone in this respect been coincident with the great relative self-dependence they have been since habituated to? And is not this change proximately ascribable to this habitual self-dependence? Whoever doubts it is asked to assign a more probable cause. Whoever admits it must admit that the enervation of a people by perpetual state aids is not a trifling consideration, but the most weighty consideration. A general arrest of national growth he will see to be an evil greater than any special benefits can compensate for. And, indeed, when, after contemplating this great fact, the overspreading of the earth by the Anglo-Saxons, he remarks the absence of any parallel phenomenon exhibited by a continental race — when he reflects how this difference must depend chiefly on difference of character, and how such difference of character has been mainly produced by difference of discipline; he will perceive that the policy pursued in this matter may have a large share in determining a nation's ultimate fate.

We are not sanguine, however, that argument will change the convictions of those who put their trust in legislation. With men of a certain order of thought the foregoing reasons will have weight. With men of another order of thought they will have little or none; nor would any accumulation of such reasons affect them. The truth that experience teaches has its limits. The experiences that will teach must be experiences that can be appreciated; and experiences exceeding a certain degree of complexity become inappreciable to the majority. It is thus with most social phenomena. If we remember that for these two thousand years and more, mankind have been making regulations for commerce, which have all along been strangling some trades, and killing others with kindness; and that though the proofs of this have been constantly before their eyes, they have only just discovered that they have been uniformly doing mischief;—if we remember that even now only a small portion of them see this, we are taught that perpetually-repeated and ever-accumulating experiences will fail to teach, until there exist the mental conditions required for the assimilation of them. Nay, when they are assimilated, it is very imperfectly. The truth they teach is only half understood, even by those supposed to understand it best. For example, Sir Robert Peel, in one of his last speeches, after describing the immensely increased consumption consequent on free trade, goes on to say:—

« If, then, you can only continue that consumption—if, by your legislation, under the favor of Providence, you can maintain the demand for labor, and make your trade and manufactures prosperous, you are not only increasing the sum of human happiness, but are giving the agriculturists of this country the best chance of that increased demand which must contribute to their welfare.»—Times, February 22d, 1850.

Thus the prosperity really due to the abandonment of all legislation, is ascribed to a particular kind of legislation. "You can maintain the demand," he says; "you can make trade and manufactures prosperous"; whereas, the facts he quotes prove that they can do this only by doing nothing. The essential truth of the matter—that law had been doing immense harm, and that this prosperity resulted not from law, but from the absence of law—is missed; and his faith in legislation in general, which should, by this experience, have been greatly shaken seemingly remains as strong as ever. Here, again, is the House of Lords, apparently not yet believing in the relationship of supply and demand, adopting within these few weeks, the standing order—

« That before the first reading of any bill for making any work in the construction of which compulsory power is sought to take thirty houses or more inhabited by the laboring classes in any one parish or place, the promoters be required to deposit in the office of the clerk of the parliaments a statement of the number, description, and situation of the said houses, the number (so far as they can be estimated) of persons to be displaced, and whether any and what provision is made in the bill for remedying the inconvenience likely to arise from such displacements.»

If, then, in the comparatively simple relationships of trade, the teachings of experience remain for so many ages unperceived, and are so imperfectly apprehended when they are perceived, it

is scarcely to be hoped that where all social phenomena—moral, intellectual, and physical—are involved, any due appreciation of the truths displayed will presently take place. The facts cannot yet get recognized as facts. As the alchemist attributed his successive disappointments to some disproportion in the ingredients, some impurity, or some too great temperature, and never to the futility of his process, or the impossibility of his aim, so every failure cited to prove the impotence of state regulations the law-worshiper explains away as being caused by this trifling oversight, or that little mistake,—all which oversights and mistakes, he assures you, will in future be avoided. Eluding the facts as he does after this fashion, volley after volley of them produce no effect.

Indeed, this faith in governments is in a certain sense organic, and can diminish only by being outgrown. A subtle form of fetichism, it is as natural to the present phase of human evolution as its grosser prototype was to an earlier phase. From the time when rulers were thought demigods, there has been a gradual decline in men's estimates of their power. This decline is still in progress, and has still far to go. Doubtless, every increment of evidence furthers it in some degree, though not to the degree that at first appears. Only in so far as it modifies character does it produce a permanent effect. For while the mental type remains the same, the removal of a special error is inevitably followed by the growth of other errors of the same genus. All superstitions die hard; and we fear that this belief in government omnipotence will form no exception.

From his « Essays.»

EDUCATION—WHAT KNOWLEDGE IS OF MOST WORTH?

IT HAS been truly remarked that, in order of time, decoration precedes dress. Among people who submit to great physical suffering that they may have themselves handsomely tattooed, extremes of temperature are borne with but little attempt at mitigation. Humboldt tells us that an Orinoco Indian, though quite regardless of bodily comfort, will yet labor for a fortnight to purchase pigment wherewith to make himself admired; and that the same woman who would not hesitate to leave her hut without a fragment of clothing on, would not dare to commit

such a breach of decorum as to go out unpainted. Voyagers uniformly find that colored beads and trinkets are much more prized by wild tribes than are calicoes or broadcloths. And the anecdotes we have of the ways in which, when shirts and coats are given, they turn them to some ludicrous display, show how completely the idea of ornament predominates over that of use. Nay, there are still more extreme illustrations: witness the fact narrated by Captain Speke of his African attendants, who strutted about in their goatskin mantles when the weather was fine, but when it was wet, took them off, folded them up, and went about naked, shivering in the rain! Indeed, the facts of aboriginal life seem to indicate that dress is developed out of decorations. And when we remember that even among ourselves most think more about the fineness of the fabric than its warmth, and more about the cut than the convenience—when we see that the function is still in great measure subordinated to the appearance, we have further reason for inferring such an origin.

It is not a little curious that the like relations hold with the mind. Among mental as among bodily acquisitions, the ornamental comes before the useful. Not only in times past, but almost as much in our own era, that knowledge which conduces to personal well-being has been postponed to that which brings applause. In the Greek schools, music, poetry, rhetoric, and a philosophy which, until Socrates taught, had but little bearing upon action, were the dominant subjects; while knowledge, aiding the arts of life, had a very subordinate place. And in our own universities and schools at the present moment the like antithesis holds. We are guilty of something like a platitude when we say that throughout his after career a boy, in nine cases out of ten, applies his Latin and Greek to no practical purposes. The remark is trite that in his shop, or his office, in managing his estate or his family, in playing his part as director of a bank or a railway, he is very little aided by this knowledge he took so many years to acquire,—so little, that generally the greater part of it drops out of his memory; and if he occasionally vents a Latin quotation or alludes to some Greek myth, it is less to throw light on the topic in hand than for the sake of effect. If we inquire what is the real motive for giving boys a classical education, we find it to be simply conformity to public opinion. Men dress their children's minds as they do their bodies, in the prevailing fashion. As the Orinoco Indian puts on his paint before leaving

his hut, not with a view to any direct benefit, but because he would be ashamed to be seen without it, so a boy's drilling in Latin and Greek is insisted on, not because of their intrinsic value, but that he may not be disgraced by being found ignorant of them—that he may have "the education of a gentleman"—the badge marking a certain social position, and bringing a consequent respect.

This parallel is still more clearly displayed in the case of the other sex. In the treatment of both mind and body, the decorative element has continued to predominate in a greater degree among women than among men. Originally personal adornment occupied the attention of both sexes equally. In these latter days of civilization, however, we see that in the dress of men the regard for appearance has, in a considerable degree, yielded to the regard for comfort; while in their education the useful has of late been trenching on the ornamental. In neither direction has this change gone so far with women. The wearing of ear rings, finger rings, bracelets; the elaborate dressings of the hair; the still occasional use of paint; the immense labor bestowed in making habiliments sufficiently attractive; and the great discomfort that will be submitted to for the sake of conformity; show how greatly, in the attiring of women, the desire of approbation overrides the desire for warmth and convenience. And similarly in their education, the immense preponderance of "accomplishments" proves how here, too, use is subordinated to display. Dancing, deportment, the piano, singing, drawing—what a large space do these occupy! If you ask why Italian and German are learned, you will find that, under all the sham reasons given, the real reason is, that a knowledge of those tongues is thought ladylike. It is not that the books written in them may be utilized, which they scarcely ever are, but that Italian and German songs may be sung, and that the extent of attainment may bring whispered admiration. The births, deaths, and marriages of kings, and other like historic trivialities, are committed to memory, not because of any direct benefits that can possibly result from knowing them, but because society considers them parts of a good education—because the absence of such knowledge may bring the contempt of others. When we have named reading, writing, spelling, grammar, arithmetic, and sewing, we have named about all the things a girl is taught with a view to their direct uses in life; and even some of these have more reference to the good opinion of others than to immediate personal welfare.

Thoroughly to realize the truth that with the mind as with the body the ornamental precedes the useful, it is needful to glance at its rationale. This lies in the fact that, from the far past down even to the present, social needs have subordinated individual needs, and that the chief social need has been the control of individuals. It is not, as we commonly suppose, that there are no governments but those of monarchs, and parliaments, and constituted authorities. These acknowledged governments are supplemented by other unacknowledged ones, that grow up in all circles, in which every man or woman strives to be king or queen or lesser dignitary. To get above some and be reverenced by them, and to propitiate those who are above us, is the universal struggle in which the chief energies of life are expended. By the accumulation of wealth, by style of living, by beauty of dress, by display of knowledge or intellect, each tries to subjugate others, and so aids in weaving that ramified network of restraints by which society is kept in order. It is not the savage chief only who, in formidable war paint, with scalps at his belt, aims to strike awe into his inferiors; it is not only the belle who, by elaborate toilet, polished manners, and numerous accomplishments, strives to "make conquests"; but the scholar, the historian, the philosopher, use their acquirements to the same end. We are none of us content with quietly unfolding our own individualities to the full in all directions, but have a restless craving to impress our individualities upon others, and in some way subordinate them. And this it is which determines the character of our education. Not what knowledge is of most real worth is the consideration, but what will bring most applause, honor, respect — what will most conduce to social position and influence — what will be most imposing. As throughout life not what we are, but what we shall be thought, is the question; so in education, the question is, not the intrinsic value of knowledge, so much as its extrinsic effects on others. And this being our dominant idea, direct utility is scarcely more regarded than by the barbarian when filing his teeth and staining his nails.

If there needs any further evidence of the rude, undeveloped character of our education, we have it in the fact that the comparative worths of different kinds of knowledge have been as yet scarcely even discussed — much less discussed in a methodic way

with definite results. Not only is it that no standard of relative values has yet been agreed upon, but the existence of any such standard has not been conceived in any clear manner. And not only is it that the existence of any such standard has not been clearly conceived, but the need for it seems to have been scarcely even felt. Men read books on this topic, and attend lectures on that; decide that their children shall be instructed in these branches of knowledge, and shall not be instructed in those; and all under the guidance of mere custom, or liking, or prejudice, without ever considering the enormous importance of determining in some rational way what things are really most worth learning. It is true that in all circles we have occasional remarks on the importance of this or the other order of information. But whether the degree of its importance justifies the expenditure of the time needed to acquire it, and whether there are not things of more importance to which the time might be better devoted, are queries which, if raised at all, are disposed of quite summarily, according to personal predilections. It is true, also, that from time to time we hear revived the standing controversy respecting the comparative merits of classics and mathematics. Not only, however, is this controversy carried on in an empirical manner, with no reference to an ascertained criterion, but the question at issue is totally insignificant when compared with the general question of which it is part. To suppose that deciding whether a mathematical or a classical education is the best, in deciding what is the proper curriculum, is much the same thing as to suppose that the whole of dietetics lies in determining whether or not bread is more nutritive than potatoes!

The question, which we contend is of such transcendent moment, is not whether such or such knowledge is of worth, but what is its relative worth. When they have named certain advantages which a given course of study has secured them, persons are apt to assume that they have justified themselves, quite forgetting that the adequateness of the advantages is the point to be judged. There is, perhaps, not a subject to which men devote attention that has not some value. A year diligently spent in getting up heraldry would very possibly give a little further insight into ancient manners and morals, and into the origin of names. Any one who should learn the distances between all the towns in England might, in the course of his life, find one or two of the thousand facts he has acquired of some

slight service when arranging a journey. Gathering together all the small gossip of a county, profitless occupation as it would be, might yet occasionally help to establish some useful fact,— say, a good example of hereditary transmission. But in these cases every one would admit that there was no proportion between the required labor and the probable benefit. No one would tolerate the proposal to devote some years of a boy's time to getting such information, at the cost of much more valuable information which he might else have got. And if here the test of relative value is appealed to and held conclusive, then should it be appealed to and held conclusive throughout. Had we time to master all subjects we need not be particular. To quote the old song: —

> "Could a man be secure
> That his days would endure
> As of old, for a thousand long years,
> What things might he know!
> What deeds might he do!
> And all without hurry or cares."

"But we that have but span-long lives" must ever bear in mind our limited time for acquisition. And remembering how narrowly this time is limited, not only by the shortness of life, but also still more by the business of life, we ought to be especially solicitous to employ what time we have to the greatest advantage. Before devoting years to some subject which fashion or fancy suggests, it is surely wise to weigh with great care the worth of the results, as compared with the worth of various alternative results which the same years might bring if otherwise applied.

In education, then, this is the question of questions, which it is high time we discussed in some methodic way. The first in importance, though the last to be considered, is the problem, how to decide among the conflicting claims of various subjects on our attention. Before there can be a rational curriculum, we must settle which things it most concerns us to know; or, to use a word of Bacon, now unfortunately obsolete, we must determine the relative values of knowledges. . . .

How to live? — that is the essential question for us. Not how to live in the mere material sense only, but in the widest sense. The general problem which comprehends every special problem is the right ruling of conduct in all directions under all circum-

stances. In what way to treat the body; in what way to treat the mind; in what way to manage our affairs; in what way to bring up a family; in what way to behave as a citizen; in what way to utilize all those sources of happiness which nature supplies — how to use all our faculties to the greatest advantage of ourselves and others — how to live completely. And this being the great thing needful for us to learn, is, by consequence, the great thing which education has to teach. To prepare us for complete living is the function which education has to discharge; and the only rational mode of judging of any educational course is to judge in what degree it discharges such function.

From "Education."

BARUCH SPINOZA

(1632–1677)

ARUCH (or BENEDICT) SPINOZA was born in Amsterdam, November 24th, 1632,— John Locke, his coadjutor in the cause of free speech, being at that time an infant in arms in Somersetshire, England. Spinoza's parents were Jews, but his active mind, as it developed under the inspiration of Descartes, so exceeded the limits set by what was then considered orthodoxy, that in 1656 he was excommunicated by the synagogue at Amsterdam. His "Tractatus Theologico-Politicus," which appeared in 1670, may be due to this incident, and, if so, the modern world is fortunate because of the opposition to his theories which led him to make this notable plea for freedom of intellectual development. His "Ethics," the most celebrated modern exposition of Pantheism, was completed in 1674, but was not published until after his death, which occurred at The Hague, February 21st, 1677.

THAT IN A FREE STATE EVERY MAN MAY THINK WHAT HE LIKES AND SAY WHAT HE THINKS

IF MEN's minds were as easily controlled as their tongues, every king would sit safely on his throne, and government by compulsion would cease; for every subject would shape his life according to the intentions of his rulers, and would esteem a thing true or false, good or evil, just or unjust, in obedience to their dictates. No man's mind, however, can possibly lie wholly at the disposition of another, for no one can willingly transfer his natural right of free reason and judgment, or be compelled so to do. For this reason government which attempts to control minds is accounted tyrannical, and it is considered an abuse of sovereignty and a usurpation of the rights of subjects, to seek to prescribe what shall be accepted as true, or rejected as false, or what opinions should actuate men in their worship of God. All these questions fall within a man's natural right, which he cannot abdicate even with his own consent.

I admit that the judgment can be biased in many ways, and to an almost incredible degree, so that while exempt from the direct external control it may be so dependent on another man's words, that it may fitly be said to be ruled by him; but although this influence is carried to great lengths, it has never gone so far as to invalidate the statement, that every man's understanding is his own, and that brains are as diverse as palates.

Moses, not by fraud, but by divine virtue, gained such a hold over the popular judgment that he was accounted superhuman, and believed to speak and act through the inspiration of the Deity; nevertheless, even he could not escape murmurs and evil interpretations. How much less, then, can other monarchs avoid them! Yet such unlimited power, if it exists at all, must belong to a monarch, and least of all to a democracy, where the whole or a great part of the people wield authority collectively. This is a fact which I think every one can explain for himself.

However unlimited, therefore, the power of a sovereign may be, however implicitly it is trusted as the exponent of law and religion, it can never prevent men from forming judgments according to their intellect, or being influenced by any given emotion. It is true that it has the power to treat as enemies all men whose opinions do not, on all subjects, entirely coincide with its own; but we are not discussing its strict powers, but its proper course of action. I grant that it has the power to rule in the most violent manner, and to put citizens to death for very trivial causes, but no one supposes it can do this with the approval of sound judgment. Nay, inasmuch as such things cannot be done without extreme peril to itself, we may even deny that it has the absolute power to do them, consequently the absolute right; for the rights of the sovereign are limited by his power.

Since, therefore, no one can abdicate his freedom of judgment and feeling; since every man is by indefeasible natural right the master of his own thoughts, it follows that men thinking in diverse and contradictory fashions, cannot, without disastrous results, be compelled to speak only according to the dictates of the supreme power. Not even the most experienced, to say nothing of the multitude, know how to keep silence. Men's common failing is to confide their plans to others, though there be need for secrecy, so that a government would be most harsh which deprived the individual of his freedom of saying and teaching what he thought; and would be moderate if such freedom were granted. Still we cannot deny that authority may be as much injured by words as by actions; hence, although the freedom we are dis-

cussing cannot be entirely denied to subjects, its unlimited concession would be most baneful; we must, therefore, now inquire how far such freedom can and ought to be conceded without danger to the peace of the state, or the power of the rulers; and this is my principal object.

It follows, plainly, from the explanation given above, of the foundations of a state, that the ultimate aim of government is not to rule, or restrain, by fear, nor to exact obedience, but, contrariwise, to free every man from fear, that he may live in all possible security; in other words, to strengthen his natural right to exist and work without injury to himself or others.

No, the object of government is not to change men from rational beings into beasts or puppets, but to enable them to develop their minds and bodies in security, and to employ their reason unshackled; neither showing hatred, anger, or deceit, nor watched with the eyes of jealousy and injustice. In fact, the true aim of government is liberty.

Now we have seen that in forming a state the power of making laws must either be vested in the body of the citizens, or in a portion of them, or in one man. For, although men's free judgments are very diverse, each one thinking that he alone knows everything, and although complete unanimity of feeling and speech is out of the question, it is impossible to preserve peace, unless individuals abdicate their right of acting entirely on their own judgment. Therefore, the individual justly cedes the right of free action, though not of free reason and judgment; no one can act against the authorities without danger to the state, though his feelings and judgment may be at variance therewith; he may even speak against them, provided that he does so from rational conviction, not from fraud, anger, or hatred, and provided that he does not attempt to introduce any change on his private authority.

For instance, supposing a man shows that a law is repugnant to sound reason, and should therefore be repealed; if he submits his opinion to the judgment of the authorities (who alone have the right of making and repealing laws), and meanwhile acts in nowise contrary to that law, he has deserved well of the state, and has behaved as a good citizen should; but if he accuses the authorities of injustice, and stirs up the people against them, or if he seditiously strives to abrogate the law without their consent, he is a mere agitator and rebel.

Thus we see how an individual may declare and teach what he believes, without injury to the authority of his rulers, or to the public peace; namely, by leaving in their hands the entire power of legislation as it affects action, and by doing nothing against their laws, though he be compelled often to act in contradiction to what he believes, and openly feels, to be best.

Such a course can be taken without detriment to justice and dutifulness; nay, it is the one which a just and dutiful man would adopt. We have shown that justice is dependent on the laws of the authorities, so that no one who contravenes their accepted decrees can be just, while the highest regard for duty is exercised in maintaining public peace and tranquillity; these could not be preserved if every man were to live as he pleased; therefore it is no less than undutiful for a man to act contrary to his country's laws, for if the practice become universal the ruin of states would necessarily follow.

Hence, so long as a man acts in obedience to the laws of his rulers, he in nowise contravenes his reason, for in obedience to reason he transferred the right of controlling his actions from his own hands to theirs. This doctrine we can confirm from actual custom, for in a conference of great and small powers, schemes are seldom carried unanimously, yet all unite in carrying out what is decided on, whether they voted for or against. But I return to my proposition.

From the fundamental notions of a state, we have discovered how a man may exercise free judgment without detriment to the supreme power; from the same premises we can no less easily determine what opinions would be seditious. Evidently those which by their very nature nullify the compact by which the right of free action was ceded. For instance, a man who holds that the Supreme Power has no rights over him, or that promises ought not to be kept, or that every one should live as he pleases, or other doctrines of this nature in direct opposition to the above-mentioned contract, is seditious, not so much from his actual opinions and judgment, as from the deeds which they involve; for he who maintains such theories abrogates the contract which tacitly, or openly, he made with his rulers. Other opinions which do not involve acts violating the contract, such as revenge, anger, and the like, are not seditious, unless it be in some corrupt state, where superstitious and ambitious persons, unable to endure men of learning, are so popular with the multitude that their word is more valued than the law.

However, I do not deny that there are some doctrines which, while they are apparently only concerned with abstract truths and falsehoods, are yet propounded and published with unworthy motives. This question we have discussed and shown that reason should nevertheless remain unshackled. If we hold to the principle that a man's loyalty to the state should be judged, like his loyalty to God, from his actions only, namely, from his charity towards his neighbors, we cannot doubt that the best government will allow freedom of philosophical speculation no less than of religious belief. I confess that from such freedom inconveniences may sometimes arise, but what question was ever settled so wisely that no abuses could possibly spring therefrom? He who seeks to regulate everything by law is more likely to arouse vices than to reform them. It is best to grant what cannot be abolished, even though it be in itself harmful. How many evils spring from luxury, envy, avarice, drunkenness, and the like, yet these are tolerated — vices as they are — because they cannot be prevented by legal enactments. How much more, then, should free thought be granted, seeing that it is in itself a virtue and that it cannot be crushed! Besides, the evil results can easily be checked, as I will show, by the secular authorities, not to mention that such freedom is absolutely necessary for progress in science and the liberal arts; for no man follows such pursuits to advantage unless his judgment be entirely free and unhampered.

But let it be granted that freedom may be crushed, and men be so bound down, that they do not dare to utter a whisper, save at the bidding of their rulers; nevertheless this can never be carried to the pitch of making them think according to authority, so that the necessary consequences would be that men would daily be thinking one thing and saying another, to the corruption of good faith, that mainstay of government, and to the fostering of hateful flattery and perfidy, whence spring stratagems, and the corruption of every good art.

It is far from possible to impose uniformity of speech, for the more rulers strive to curtail freedom of speech the more obstinately are they resisted; not indeed by the avaricious, the flatterers, and other numskulls, who think supreme salvation consists in filling their stomachs and gloating over their money bags, but by those whom good education, sound morality, and virtue have ren-

dered more free. Men, as generally constituted, are most prone to resent the branding as criminal of opinions which they believe to be true, and the proscription as wicked of that which inspires them with piety towards God and man; hence they are ready to forswear the laws and conspire against the authorities, thinking it not shameful but honorable to stir up seditions and perpetrate any sort of crime with this end in view. Such being the constitution of human nature, we see that laws directed against opinions affect the generous-minded rather than the wicked, and are adapted less for coercing criminals than for irritating the upright; so that they cannot be maintained without great peril to the state.

Moreover, such laws are almost always useless, for those who hold that the opinions proscribed are sound cannot possibly obey the law; whereas those who already reject them as false, accept the law as a kind of privilege, and make such boast of it, that authority is powerless to repeal it, even if such a course be subsequently desired.

To these considerations may be added what we said in treating of the history of the Hebrews. And, lastly, how many schisms have arisen in the Church from the attempt of the authorities to decide by law the intricacies of theological controversy! If men were not allured by the hope of getting the law and the authorities on their side; of triumphing over their adversaries in the sight of an applauding multitude, and of acquiring honorable distinctions, they would not strive so maliciously, nor would such fury sway their minds. This is taught not only by reason, but by daily examples; for laws of this kind, prescribing what every man shall believe and forbidding any one to speak or write to the contrary, have often been passed, as sops or concessions to the anger of those who cannot tolerate men of enlightenment, and who, by such harsh and crooked enactments, can easily turn the devotion of the masses into fury and direct it against whom they will.

How much better would it be to restrain popular anger and fury, instead of passing useless laws, which can only be broken by those who love virtue and the liberal arts, thus paring down the state till it is too small to harbor men of talent. What greater misfortune for a state can be conceived than that honorable men should be sent like criminals into exile, because they hold diverse opinions which they cannot disguise? What, I say,

can be more hurtful than that men who have committed no crime or wickedness should, simply because they are enlightened, be treated as enemies and put to death, and that the scaffold, the terror of evil doers, should become the arena where the highest examples of tolerance and virtue are displayed to the people with all the marks of ignominy that authority can devise?

He that knows himself to be upright does not fear the death of a criminal, and shrinks from no punishment; his mind is not wrung with remorse for any disgraceful deed; he holds that death in a good cause is no punishment, but an honor, and that death for freedom is glory.

What purpose then is served by the death of such men; what example is proclaimed? The cause for which they die is unknown to the idle and the foolish, hateful to the turbulent, loved by the upright. The only lesson we can draw from such scenes is to flatter the persecutor, or else to imitate the victim.

If formal assent is not to be esteemed above conviction, and if governments are to retain a firm hold of authority and not be compelled to yield to agitators, it is imperative that freedom of judgment should be granted, so that men may live together in harmony, however diverse, or even openly contradictory their opinions may be. We cannot doubt that such is the best system of government and open to the fewest objections, since it is the one most in harmony with human nature. In a democracy, the most natural form of government, every one submits to the control of authority over his actions, but not over his judgment and reason; that is, seeing that all cannot think alike, the voice of the majority has the force of law, subject to repeal if circumstances bring about a change of opinion. In proportion as the power of free judgment is withheld, we depart from the natural condition of mankind, and consequently the government becomes more tyrannical.

In order to prove that from such freedom no inconvenience arises, which cannot easily be checked by the exercise of the sovereign power, and that men's actions can easily be kept in bounds, though their opinions be at open variance, it will be well to cite an example. Such a one is not very far to seek. The city of Amsterdam reaps the fruit of this freedom in its own great prosperity and in the admiration of all other people. For in this most flourishing state, and most splendid city, men of every nation and religion live together in the greatest harmony,

and ask no questions before trusting their goods to a fellow-citizen, save whether he be rich or poor, and whether he generally acts honestly, or the reverse. His religion and sect is considered of no importance; for it has no effect before the judges in gaining or losing a cause, and there is no sect so despised that its followers, provided that they harm no one, pay every man his due, and live uprightly, are deprived of the protection of the magisterial authority.

On the other hand, when the religious controversy between Remonstrants and Counter-Remonstrants began to be taken up by politicians and the states, it grew into a schism, and abundantly showed that laws dealing with religion and seeking to settle its controversies are much more calculated to irritate than to reform, and that they give rise to extreme license; further, it was seen that schisms do not originate in a love of truth, which is a source of courtesy and gentleness, but rather in an inordinate desire for supremacy. From all these considerations it is clearer than the sun at noonday, that the true schismatics are those who condemn other men's writings, and seditiously stir up the quarrelsome masses against their authors, rather than those authors themselves, who generally write only for the learned, and appeal solely to reason. In fact, the real disturbers of the peace are those who, in a free state, seek to curtail the liberty of judgment which they are unable to tyrannize over.

I have thus shown: I. That it is impossible to deprive men of the liberty of saying what they think. II. That such liberty can be conceded to every man without injury to the rights and authority of the sovereign power, and that every man may retain it without injury to such rights, provided that he does not presume upon it to the extent of introducing any new rights into the state, or acting in any way contrary to the existing laws. III. That every man may enjoy this liberty without detriment to the public peace, and that no inconveniences arise therefrom which cannot easily be checked. IV. That every man may enjoy it without injury to his allegiance. V. That laws dealing with speculative problems are entirely useless. VI. Lastly, that not only may such liberty be granted without prejudice to the public peace, to loyalty, and to the rights of rulers, but that it is even necessary for their preservation. For when people try to take it away, and bring to trial, not only the acts which alone are capable of offending, but also the opinions of mankind, they only succeed in surrounding their victims with an appearance of martyrdom, and raise their feelings of pity and revenge rather than of terror. Uprightness and good faith are thus corrupted, flatterers and traitors are encouraged, and sectarians triumph, inasmuch as concessions have been made to their animosity, and they have gained the state sanction for the doctrines of which they are the interpreters. Hence they arrogate to themselves the state authority and rights, and do not scruple to assert that they have been directly chosen by God, and that their laws are Divine, whereas the laws of the state are human, and should therefore yield obedience to the laws of God — in other words, to their own laws. Every one must see that this is not a state of affairs conducive to public welfare. Wherefore, the safest way for a state is to lay down the rule that religion is comprised solely in the exercise of charity and justice, and that the rights of rulers in sacred, no less than in secular matters, should merely have to do with actions, but that every man should think what he likes and say what he thinks.

I have thus fulfilled the task I set myself in this treatise. It remains only to call attention to the fact that I have written nothing which I do not most willingly submit to the examinations and approval of my country's rulers; and that I am willing to retract anything which they shall decide to be repugnant to the laws, or prejudicial to the public good. I know that I am a man, and as a man liable to error, but against error I have taken scrupulous care, and have striven to keep in entire accordance with the laws of my country, with loyalty and with morality.

Complete. Concluding chapter of the
"Tractatus Theologico-Politicus."

MADAME DE STAËL

(ANNE LOUISE GERMAINE NECKER, BARONNE DE STAËL-HOLSTEIN)

(1766–1817)

THE celebrated Necker, Minister of Finance under Louis XVI., did his best and most enduring work in the education of the daughter, who as "Madame de Staël" surpassed him in celebrity and in brilliancy. Born in Paris, April 22d, 1766, she passed her girlhood in her father's house at a time when it was frequented by some of the greatest men of the age. Buffon, Grimm, and Gibbon were among the early acquaintances who stimulated her intellect and encouraged her to effort. In 1788, two years after her marriage to the Swedish embassador, Baron de Staël-Holstein, she published her first notable essays under the title of "Letters on the Character and Writings of J. J. Rousseau." Her husband died in 1802, and for several years after his death she resided in Germany and Italy. Her celebrated novel, "Corinne," appeared in 1807 and established for her the high place in French literature she is never likely to lose. The philosophical purpose of the book is too plainly apparent to allow it to become popular with lovers of the romantic in fiction. It illustrates the fact that Madame de Staël is in all her literary instincts the essayist rather than the novelist. She has as much difficulty in expressing herself through direct narration as such writers as Irving and Hawthorne have in refraining from constructing a plot for their essays. The tendency to philosophical reflection and speculation which shows in her novels showed in her conversation also. It was one of the causes no doubt which made Napoleon detest her. He lost no opportunity of making her uncomfortable, and in 1812 his enmity drove her from France. She visited Austria, Russia, Sweden, and England, during her exile, returning to France after the fall of Napoleon, and dying at Paris, July 14th, 1817. Among her best-known works are "Germany," "Literature Considered in Its Relation to Social Institutions," "Considerations on the French Revolution," "Dramatic Essays," and "Ten Years of Exile."

OF THE GENERAL SPIRIT OF MODERN LITERATURE

IT MAY be to thought, and not to imagination, that we are indebted for the new acquisitions made to literature in the Middle Ages. Imitation, the principle of the fine arts, as I have before remarked, does not admit of unlimited perfection; the Moderns, in this respect, can never proceed further than by following the path traced out by the Ancients. But if the images of poetry and description always remain nearly the same, more eloquence is added to the passions by a new development of sensibility and a profound knowledge of character, which gives a charm to our superior specimens of literature, which cannot be attributed solely to poetical imagination.

The Ancients esteemed men as their friends, while they considered women in no other light than as slaves designed by nature for that unhappy state; and, indeed, the greater part of them were deserving of that appellation,—their minds were not furnished with a single idea that could distinguish them from the brute creation, nor were they enlightened by one generous sentiment. This circumstance, without doubt, was the cause why the Ancients represented in their tender scenes merely sensations.

The preference of the Ancients towards the softer sex was solely influenced by their beauty; but the Moderns acknowledge that superior talents and ties can alone insure their happiness or misery, in that predilection to which they owe the destiny of their lives.

Novels, those varied productions of modern genius, were almost entirely unknown to the Ancients; it is true, they composed a few pastorals in that style, at a period when the Greeks endeavored to discover some employment as a relaxation during servitude. But before women had created an interest in domestic life, there was nothing sufficiently desirable to excite the curiosity of men, whose time was almost entirely occupied by political pursuits.

A greater number of shades were perceptible in the characters of women, which their wish to obtain power, and their fear of subjection, presented to general view; but they were singularly useful in furnishing new secrets of emotion for the exercise of dramatic talents; their fear of death, their desire of life, the devotion of themselves, their resentments, and, in short, every

sentiment which they were suffered to deliver, embellished literature with new expressions. The women, it may be said, not being strictly answerable for their conduct, did not scruple to relate what their different sentiments naturally suggested. A solid understanding, with a scrutinizing discernment, may clearly perceive these developments of the human heart when it appears in a state of nature; it is for this reason that the modern moralists have, in general, so much the advantage over the Ancients in regard to their subtlety in the knowledge of mankind.

With the Ancients, those who could not acquire fame had no motive for development: but after the period when connections were formed in domestic life, the communications of the mind and the exercise of morals always existed, at least in a limited circle; the children became dearer to the parents from reciprocal tenderness, which more closely united the conjugal tie; and the different affections assumed the appearance of that divine alliance of friendship in love, of attraction and esteem, of a merited confidence and an involuntary seduction.

Advanced age that was crowned with glory and virtue, although it ceased to hope, might continue to be animated by the emotions of the heart, and was consoled with a pensive melancholy which allowed individuals to remember, to regret, and still to regard what had formerly claimed their affection. When moral reflections have been united to the violent passions of youth, they may be extended by an exalted remembrance to the termination of existence, and present the same pleasing picture through the awful variations of time.

A profound and melancholy sensibility is one of the greatest beauties perceptible in some of our modern writings; this, without doubt, is owing to the fair sex, who, being ignorant of most other things in life, except the art of pleasing, transmitted the softness of their impressions to the style of certain authors. In perusing those works which were composed since the renewal of letters, we may in every separate page remark those ideas which were wanting before they accorded to women a kind of civil equality.

Generosity, courage, and humanity have in some respects a different meaning. The Ancients founded the chief of their virtues on the love of their country; the qualities of women were exercised in a different and an independent manner:—a sympathy for misfortune, a pity for weakness, an elevation of soul, without any other aim than the enjoyment of that elevation, is much more in their nature than political virtues. The Moderns, influenced by women, easily gave way to philanthropy, and the mind acquired a more philosophical liberty when they were less under the empire of exclusive associations.

The only advantage which the writers of the last centuries have over the Ancients in their works of imagination is the talent of expressing a more delicate sensibility; and that of giving greater variety to situations and characters, from a more intimate knowledge of the human heart. But how much superior are the philosophers of the present era in the sciences, in method, in analysis, in the arrangement of ideas, and the chain of events.

Mathematical arguments resemble. the two great ideas of metaphysics, space and eternity; millions of leagues may be added and centuries multiplied; each calculation is true, yet the term remains indefinite. The wisest step ever taken by the human understanding was, to renounce all doubtful systems and adopt methods capable of demonstration.

Although modern eloquence may be deficient in the emulation of a free people, nevertheless it acquires from philosophy and a melancholy imagination a new character, which has a very powerful effect. I do not think that among the Ancients there was one composition, or a single orator, that could equal Bossuet, Rousseau, or the English, in some of their poetry, or the German in some of their phrases, in the sublime art of affecting the heart. It is to the spirituality of the Christian ideas, and to the sombre truths of philosophy, that we must attribute the art of introducing, even into private discussions, general and affecting reflections which touched the heart, awakened recollection, and induced man to consider the interest of his fellow-creatures.

The Ancients knew how to add vigor to the arguments necessary to be used on every occasion; but, at the present period, the mind, through a succession of ages, has become so indifferent to the interest of individuals and also to that of nations, that the eloquent writer finds it necessary to adopt a more pathetic style, in order to awaken the feelings which are common to all men. Without doubt, it is requisite to strike the imagination with a lively and forcible impression of the object intended to create an interest; but the appeal to pity is never irresistible, except when melancholy represents what the imagination has portrayed.

IX—222

The Moderns possess a readiness of expression, the sole aim of which is to engage the eloquence of thought; antiquity presents no model of this kind but Tacitus. Montesquieu, Pascal, and Machiavelli are eloquent by a single expression, by a striking epithet, or in a rapidity of imagery, the purpose of which is the elucidation of an idea, and the endeavor to enlarge and embellish what is intended to be explained. The impression given by this peculiar style may be compared to the effect produced by the disclosure of an important secret: it seems likewise as if a number of thoughts had preceded that which had just been expressed, and each separate idea appears connected with the most profound meditations; and that suddenly, and by a single word, we are permitted to extend our ideas to those immense regions which have been accurately traced by the efforts of genius.

The ancient philosophers exercised, so to speak, a magistracy of instruction among men; having always in view the general benefit, they enforced certain rules, and left nothing undone that was likely to enlighten mankind. The knowledge of morals must have advanced with the progress of human reason; but philosophical demonstrations are considered more applicable to that moral which is of the intellectual order. We must not compare modern virtues with those of the Ancients, as citizens; it is only in a free country where there can exist that constant duty and that generous relation between the citizens and their country. It is true that, in a despotic government, custom or prejudice may still inspire some brilliant acts of military courage; but the continued and painful attention given to civil employments and legislative virtues, added to the disinterested sacrifice of the greater part of their lives to the public, can only exist where there is a real passion for liberty: it is therefore in private qualities, sentiments of philanthropy, and in a few writings of a superior order, that we are to examine the progress of morals.

The principles of modern philosophy are much more conducive to happiness than those of the Ancients; the duties imposed by our moralists are courtesy, docility, pity, and affection. Filial reverence was holden in the highest estimation by the Ancients, and parental attachment is viewed in the same light by the Moderns; but without doubt, in the connection between father and son, it is more advantageous that the benefactor should be the individual whose tenderness is the strongest.

The Ancients could not be exceeded in their love of justice, but they did not consider benevolence as a duty; justice may be enforced by the laws, notwithstanding general opinion is the criterion of beneficence, and is sufficient to exclude from esteem the being who is insensible to the miseries of his fellow-creatures.

The Ancients only required of others to refrain from injuring them; and simply desired them not to stand in their sunshine, but that they might be left to nature and themselves. But the Moderns, endowed with softer sentiments, solicit assistance, support, and that interest which their situation inspires. They have constituted into a virtue everything that can be useful to mutual happiness; domestic ties are cemented by a rational liberty; and no one has an arbitrary power over his fellow-creature.

With the ancient people of the North, lessons of prudence, dexterity, and maxims which commanded a supernatural empire over their own afflictions, were placed among the first precepts of virtue: but the importance of duties is much better classed by the Moderns; the reciprocal obligation from man to man holds the first rank; what regards ourselves ought to be considered relatively to the influence which we may possess over the destiny of others. What each individual is to procure, to promote his own happiness, is a counsel and not an order; the strictest moral does not impute to man as a crime that grief which is natural, and which his feelings will not allow him to conceal, but that grief which he occasions to others.

In a word, that which both the Gospel and philosophy alike inculcate is the doctrine of humanity. We are taught to respect the gift of life; and the existence of man is now considered as sacred to man, and is not viewed with that political indifference which some of the Ancients believed compatible with the true principles of virtue. We now feel a sensation of horror at the sight of blood; and the warrior who is entirely indifferent to his own personal danger acquires a degree of honor when he shudders at being the necessary cause of destruction to another. If any circumstance at this period gives reason to apprehend that a condemnation has been unjust, that an innocent person has fallen a victim to a supposed justice, nations will listen with terror to the lamentations which arise from an irreparable misfortune; the sensation caused by an unmerited death is recorded from one generation to another; and even children will listen with horror to the recital of so great a grievance. When the eloquent Lally,

twenty years after the death of his father, demanded in France the re-establishment of his manes, those young men who could not have seen or known the victim whom he wished to reclaim, felt themselves violently agitated, and shed tears in abundance, as if that fatal day, when innocence was sacrificed, could never be effaced from their remembrance.

Thus ages rolled on towards the conquest of liberty, for virtue is always its herald. Alas! by what means shall we banish the painful contrast which so forcibly strikes the imagination? One crime was recollected during a long succession of years; but we have since witnessed cruelties without number committed and forgotten at the same moment! And it was under the shadow of the republic, the noblest, the most glorious, and the proudest institution of the human mind, that those execrable crimes have been committed! Ah! how difficult do we find it to repel those melancholy ideas, every time we reflect upon the destiny of man: the horrid phantom of the revolution appears before us; in vain we wish to look back on times that are past; in vain we desire to recognize in late events the constant connection of abstract combinations; if in the regions of metaphysics one word awakens recollection, the emotions of the heart resume all their empire, and, no longer supported by reflection, we are suddenly plunged into the abyss of despair.

Nevertheless, let us not yield to this despondency, but return to general observations and literary ideas,—to anything and everything, in short, that can divert our attention from personal sentiments; they are of too painful a nature to be developed. Talents may be animated by a certain degree of emotion; but long and heavy affliction stifles the genius of expression; and when sorrow is become habitual to the mind, the imagination loses even the wish to express what it feels.

Complete. « The Influence of Literature upon Society,» Chap. ix.

OF SPANISH AND ITALIAN LITERATURE

THE greatest part of the ancient manuscripts, the monuments of art, and, in short, all the remains of Roman splendor and knowledge, existed in Italy; and considerable expenses and the authority of public power were necessary in order to make the researches requisite to bring them to light. It was consequently in this country, where the sources of all scientific pursuits were to be found, that literature first made its reappearance, and commenced its career under the auspices of princes; for the different means which are indispensably necessary to the first progress, are immediately dependent upon the power and will of government.

The protection of the Italian princes greatly contributed to the revival of letters; but it must have been an obstacle to the light of philosophy, and those obstacles would have existed even if religious superstition had not, in many instances, been detrimental to the investigation of truth.

I must once more explain the meaning which I have constantly attached to the word Philosophy in the course of this work; what I mean by the use of that term is a more minute inquiry into the principles of political and religious institutions; the analysis of characters, and the events of history,—in a word, the study of the human heart and the natural rights of man. Such a philosophy imagines a state of liberty, or must necessarily lead towards it.

The men of letters in Italy were further from that independence requisite to this philosophy than any other nation; as they required pecuniary means and the approbation of princes, in order to discover those manuscripts of antiquity that were to serve them as guides.

There were in all the great cities of Italy numberless academies and universities; these associations were particularly proper for the learned researches that were to rescue from oblivion so many superior compositions of antiquity. But these public establishments, even from the nature of their institutions, were entirely under the subjection of government; and the corporations, like all other orders, classes, and sects, were extremely useful to one particular aim, but much less favorable than the efforts of individual genius to the advancement of philosophy. We must add to these general reflections, that the long and patient researches requisite for the examination of the ancient manuscripts was peculiarly adapted to a monastic life; and the monks, in fact, were the most active in the study of literature. Thus the same cause which produced the revival of letters opposed the development of natural reason. The Italians took the first steps, and pointed out the way in which the human understanding has since made such immense progress; but they were destined never to make any advance in the path which they themselves had laid open.

Principalities, whether under a federal or a theocratical government, have each of them been a prey to civil wars, parties, and factions altogether unfavorable to liberty. The minds of men were depraved by mutual hatred, instead of being enlarged by the love of their country. Even while they submitted to tyranny, they were familiar with assassination; incredulity was occasionally found the companion of fanaticism, but sound reason was never to be met with.

The Italians, notwithstanding their general incredulity and their universal professions, were much more addicted to pleasantry than reasoning,—which led them to make a jest of their own existence. When they wished to lay aside their natural talent, the comic, and attempted eloquent orations, they were always mixed with the most absurd affectation. Their recollection of past grandeur, without one idea of present greatness, must necessarily produce the stupendous. The Italians might possess dignity, if there were any mixture of the gloomy or melancholy in their characters; but when the successors of the Romans, deprived of all national splendor, and all political liberty, are yet the gayest people on earth, it shows that there is a natural want of elevation of soul.

It was perhaps from antipathy to the Italian bombast, that Machiavelli used such extreme simplicity when he analyzed tyranny. It is very probable that he wished that the horror of crimes should arise from the development of their principles; and carrying his contempt rather too far even for the appearance of declamation, he left everything to the imagination of his readers. The reflections of Machiavelli upon Titus Livy are far superior to his " Prince." These reflections may be considered as one of the works in which the human understanding has showed itself to the greatest advantage; such a production belongs entirely to the genius of the author, and has no connection with the general character of the Italian literature.

The literature of the Spaniards ought to have been more remarkable than that of the Italians; it should have united the imagination of the North with that of the East, the Oriental grandeur with the splendor of chivalry, the martial spirit which repeated wars had exalted, and the poetry which was inspired by the beauty of their climate: but regal power, which served as a prop for superstition, stifled in their birth those puerile dispositions to glory.

In Italy the imagination was intoxicated by the inimitable charms of poetry and the fine arts; but the writers in prose were, in general, neither moralists nor philosophers, and their efforts to appear eloquent produced nothing but bombast. Nevertheless, as it is in the nature of the human understanding always to improve, the Italians, to whom philosophy was interdicted, and who could not, in poetry, exceed the limit prescribed to all arts,—that of perfection,—the Italians, I say, rendered themselves illustrious by the astonishing progress which, by their perseverance, they affected in the sciences. After the century of Leo X., after Ariosto and Tasso, their poetry visibly assumed a retrograde course; but, in Galileo, Cassini, and in others still more recently, they acquired a number of useful discoveries in nature which associated them for the intellectual perfection of the human species.

Superstition made many attempts to persecute Galileo, but a number of the Italian princes came to his relief. Religious fanaticism is very inimical to the arts and sciences, as well as to philosophy; but absolute regal power, or federal aristocracy, have often protected them, and are only averse to a philosophical independence.

In a country where priesthood is predominant, every evil and every prejudice have been often found united; but the diversity of governments in Italy lightened the yoke of priesthood by creating a rivalry between those states or princes, who secured the very limited independence necessary to the arts and sciences.

After having affirmed that it was in the sciences only that the Italians advanced progressively, and furnished their tribute towards the general knowledge of the human species, let us proceed to examine into each branch of intellectual learning, into philosophy, eloquence, and poetry, with the causes of the successes and failures of the Italian literature.

The subdivision of states in the same country is, in general, very favorable to philosophy; this is what I have occasion to show in speaking of the German literature. But in Italy this subdivision did not produce its natural effect; the despotism of the priests destroyed, in a great measure, the happy results which might have arisen from a federal government; it would perhaps have been better if the whole nation had been united under one government; their recollection would have been more active, and the sentiments it inspired would have produced a retrospect favorable to virtue.

The subdivision of states, although it precluded Italy from becoming one nation, gave sufficient liberty for the study of the sciences; but the united despotism of Spain, in encouraging the active power of the Inquisition, left no pursuit for thought, no resource nor means of escaping the yoke. We may, however, judge what the Spanish literature might have been, by some essays which may yet be collected.

The romances of the Moors established in Spain borrowed their respect for the fair sex from chivalry. This respect was not to be found in the national manners of the East. The Arabs who remained in Africa did not in this instance resemble the Arabs established in Spain; the Moors inspired the Spaniards with their spirit of magnificence; and the Spaniards reciprocally taught their love and their chivalric honor to the Moors. No mixture could be more favorable to works of imagination, if literature had been encouraged in Spain. Amongst their romances, the "Cid" gives us some idea of the grandeur which would have characterized the efforts of their genius. In the poem of Camoens, which is written in the same spirit as many of the Spanish productions, we find a most beautiful fiction in the phantom which defends the entrance of the Indian seas. In the comedies of Calderoni, and of Lopez de Vega, an elevation of sentiment always shines through the cloud of faults by which their beauties are veiled. The love and jealousy of the Spaniards have quite a different character from the sentiments represented in the Italian pieces; their expressions are very subtile, though not entirely insipid; they never portray perfidy of character nor depravity of manners: it is true, they have too much pompousness of style; but while we condemn their bombast, we are convinced of the truth of their sentiments. It is not the same in Italy: if the affectation of certain works were taken away, there would remain nothing at all; while, if we could remove that of the Spaniards, they would shortly attain to the perfection of dignity, courage, and the most affecting sensibility.

It was not possible that the elements of philosophy could be improved in Spain; the invasion of the North introduced nothing but the military spirit; and the Arabians were altogether enemies to philosophy: their absolute government, and the fatality of their religion, led them to detest the light of philosophy: this hatred caused them to burn the library of Alexandria. They, however, cultivated the sciences and poetry: but they studied the former like astrologers, and the latter like warriors. They cultivated their vocal talents, merely to sing their exploits; and they studied nature only with the hopes of attaining the magic art. They had no idea of strengthening their reason: and in reality, to what use could they have applied a faculty which would have overthrown what they most respected, despotism and superstition?

The Spaniards, strangers like the Italians to the labors of philosophy, were entirely diverted from all literary emulation by the gloomy and oppressive tyranny of the Inquisition. They drew no profit from the inexhaustible sources of poetic invention which the Arabians brought with them. Italy was in possession of the ancient monuments; was also immediately connected with the Greeks of Constantinople; and drew from Spain the Oriental style, which the Moors had introduced, but which the Spaniards neglected. . . .

In Italy everything conspired to fill the life of man with the agreeable sensations which naturally arise from their fine arts and their unclouded sun; but since this country has lost the empire of the world, it seems as if its inhabitants disdained a political existence; and, according to the maxims of Cæsar, they aspired to the first rank in pleasure, rather than the second place in the annals of fame.

Dante having, as well as Machiavelli, supported a character in the civil commotions of his country, in some of his poems we observe an energy in no degree analogous to the literature of his time; but the numberless faults with which we may reproach him, belonged without doubt to the century he lived in. It is only in the time of Leo X. that we remark a decided purity in the Italian literature; the ascendency of this prince was to the Italian government what unity might have been; the rays of knowledge were collected into one focus, in which taste also might have been concentrated, and literary judgments have proceeded from the same tribunal.

After the age of the Medici, the Italian literature made no progress of any kind, either because some central point was necessary to rally all the forces of the intellect, or, principally, because philosophy was not at all cultivated in Italy. When the literature of imagination has attained to the highest possible degree of perfection, the subsequent age belongs to philosophy, in order that the human understanding may not cease in its advancement towards perfection in some way or other. After

Racine, we have seen Voltaire; because, in the eighteenth century, men were more profound thinkers than in the seventeenth. But what could have been added to the excellence of poetry after Racine?

The Italians have no romances like those of the French and English, because the love which inspired them, not being a passion of the mind capable of any long continuation, their customs and manners were too licentious to preserve any interest in this style. Their comedies were filled with that kind of buffoonery which arises from the absurdities and vices; but we do not find, if we except a few pieces of Goldoni, one striking and variegated picture of the vices of the human heart, such as are found in the French comedies. The Italians simply wished to create laughter; no serious aim can be discovered through the veil of flippancy, and their comedies are not the picture of human life, but its caricature.

The Italians, even in their theatres, have often turned their priests into ridicule, although in other respects they were entirely subjected to them; but it was not with a philosophical view that they attacked the abuses of religion; they had not, like some of our writers a wish to reform the faults they complained of; it was easy to perceive that their real opinions were totally opposite to that kind of authority to which they were compelled to submit; but this spirit of opposition incited them to nothing more than a contempt for those who commanded esteem; it was like the cunning of children to their teachers; they were willing to obey them on condition they might be permitted to make sport of them.

It follows from this that all the works of the Italians, except those which treat on physical sciences, have nothing useful in view; which is absolutely necessary in order to give a real strength and solidity to their reflections. The works of Beccaria, Filangieri, and a few others, make the only exception to what I have now advanced.

One question more remains to be decided before I close,—which is, whether the Italians have carried the dramatic art to any length in tragedy.

For myself, in spite of the charms of Metastasio, and the energy of Alfieri, I do not think they have. The Italians have a lively invention in subjects, and a brilliancy in expression; but the personages which they represent are not characterized in a

manner to leave any lasting traces on the mind; and the affliction which they portray excites but little sympathy. This may be occasioned by their moral and political situation, not allowing the mind its full display: their sensibility is not serious, their sadness is without melancholy, and their grandeur commands no respect. The Italian author was therefore obliged to have recourse entirely to himself; and, to compose a tragedy, he must not only forget all he sees, but renounce all his habitual ideas and impressions: and it is very difficult to find out the true basis of a tragedy which is so widely different from the general manners and customs of the time in which it was composed.

Vengeance is the passion which is the best described in the Italian tragedies: it is natural to their character to be suddenly roused by this sentiment in the midst of that habitual indolence in which they spent their lives; and their resentments were naturally expressed, because they really felt them.

The operas alone were followed, because at the opera was heard that enchanting music which was the glory and pleasure of Italy. The performers did not exert themselves in tragedy; fine acting would have been thrown away; they were not even heard; and it must ever be thus, when the art of touching the passions is not carried to a sufficient length to predominate over every other pleasure. The Italians did not require to be softened, and the authors for want of spectators, and the spectators for want of authors, did not give themselves up to the profound impressions of the dramatic art.

Metastasio, however, found out the secret of turning his operas almost into tragedies; and though compelled to struggle with all the difficulties imposed by the obligation of submitting to music, he still preserved many beauties of style and situation truly dramatic. It may be that there exist yet some other exceptions little known to strangers; but to draw the principal characters of any national literature, it is absolutely necessary to lay aside many details; there are no general ideas that are not contradicted by certain exemptions; but the mind would be incapable of ever forming any determination, if it were to stop at each particular instead of drawing a consequence from a collective whole.

Melancholy, that sentiment which is so fertile in works of genius, appears to have belonged almost exclusively to the people of the North. The Oriental style, which the Italians have often imitated, had a sort of melancholy of which we find some traces

in the Arabian poetry, and likewise in the Hebrew psalms; but it has a character entirely distinct from that we shall find when we analyze the literature of the North.

The people of the East, whether Jews or Mahometans, were sustained and directed by their positive reliance on their religion. It was not that uncertain and undetermined apprehension which afforded the mind a more philosophical impression; the melancholy of the Orientals was that of men who were happy from every enjoyment of nature; they simply reflected with regret upon the brevity of human life, and the rapid decay of prosperity; while the melancholy of the people of the North was that which is inspired by the sufferings of the mind, the void which the absence of sensibility makes in the existence, and that continual musing upon the calamities of this life, and the uncertainty of their destiny in a life to come.

From « The Influence of Literature
upon Society.»

SIR RICHARD STEELE

(1672-1729)

T HAPPENS often if not always to men whose high purposes and prophetic insight are accompanied by extreme weakness of will, that their "glory is given to another." It happened so to Steele. He is the real founder of the "Addisonian school" of essay writing. In the Tatler, which he founded April 12th, 1709, he developed the methods and suggested the style in which Addison peculiarly excelled. It is not too much to say of Steele that he inspired Addison and gave direction to that which posterity accepts as most characteristically "Addisonian." And it is eminently characteristic of Steele himself that he did this consciously and with good-natured contempt of his own impotence. "I fared like a distressed prince," he writes, "who calls in a powerful neighbor to his aid; I was undone by my auxiliary. When I had once called him in, I could not subsist without dependence upon him." This was written in acknowledging the papers contributed to the Tatler by Addison who began to write for it after Steele had founded it. It applies to the Spectator as fully as to the Tatler. Indeed, it suggests the relation which existed between the two friends during the epoch of their greatest creative activity. Addison had the better education in books; he also had the benevolence which ennobled Steele and was the bond of union between them; but he had what Steele lacked — what he never acquired — what was wholly incompatible with his habits of life and of work, — the calmness of habitual self-control. It may not be true that Addison, without losing his dignity, his sweetness, or his calm self-poise — without even "rumpling a ruffle," as has been said, could drink the whole of the third bottle, the half of which would make Steele uproariously forgetful of all the high purposes of his life; but even if this is picturesque exaggeration, something not unlike it is fundamentally true of the two friends. They were born in the same year, 1672, — a year in which curled, ruffled, and powdered Reactionists, with unspeakable morals of the latest Parisian fashion, were endeavoring to set back all the clocks in England to the time of Henry VIII. Steele was eleven years old when these exquisites and wits sent Algernon Sidney to the scaffold, and only thirteen when Richard Rumbold was hanged,

eviscerated, and cut into quarters for holding the belief that God is not sufficiently a respecter of persons to give one man a title from heaven to master another. It was in 1660, only twelve years before Steele's birth, that Thomas Harrison had been actually eviscerated alive in accordance with the sentence of a court controlled by the "Merry Monarch." It is not pleasant to remember such things; but if they are forgotten, it will be impossible to understand Steele or his mission. In 1701, when he began what he always considered his apostolate by writing "The Christian Hero," the morals of England were indescribably corrupt. He was at the time a captain in Lord Lucas's Fusiliers, having left Oxford without a degree to join the army as a private soldier. Debauchery and cruelty characterized the modes through which the pride of the ruling class manifested its impulses of domination. Captain Steele who wrote "The Christian Hero" in the hope that the standard of morals he thus set for others would incidentally elevate his own, was so far defeated in his purpose of shaming himself into sobriety and dignity, that in defending the ethics of "The Christian Hero," he felt obliged to fight a duel and wound dangerously one of the Wildrakes who had insulted him for advocating meekness, temperance, and soberness. In an eminently characteristic way, Steele followed this up by writing "The Funeral," "The Conscious Lover," and other comedies, with the well-defined purpose of redeeming himself from the suspicion of too much sanctity, or, as he says, "to enliven" his character. He had a deep, underlying, and governing purpose, however, which he never abandoned — drunk or sober! It was to use his pen to reform the manners of his time. The frequency of his own lapses under temptation served to make him more steadfast in this governing purpose by convincing him the more deeply of the need for his work as a means of helping to redeem others from sufferings of which his own infirmities made him aware. Thus we have illustrated in his life the remarkable contradiction of a feeble will joined to extraordinary tenacity of life purpose. In such feebleness, controlled by the inspiration of hopes of usefulness, he was one of the very "babes and sucklings" out of whose mouths is perfected the praise which belongs in fullness only to the perfect expression of the Divinely Human. Steele is often absurd, and sometimes irresistibly ludicrous in his career as a reformer and prophet. But whether he was writing essays on virtue for the Tatler and Spectator, or drunk under the table over which Addison presided with still unruffled dignity; whether he was accepting Addison's charity as the only means of escaping imprisonment for debt, or founding the Plebeian to oppose the Toryism into which he feared even Addison had lapsed, — at all times, in all the follies and mischances of his life, he had always in him the strength

of the same idea which gave greatness to Chatham and Burke, to Brougham and Macaulay. He believed in the divine right of every man to grow better, larger, and stronger; he believed also in the divine duty of attempting it, no matter how feebly; he feared and fought against that "merriness" of morals which he saw destroying the people as he felt it destroying himself. His ideal was of larger liberty and higher living for England and all the world. No man was ever weaker against temptation, but this high purpose saved and glorified him. If it did not make him an Addison, it fitted him to become at some later stage of the continuous existence throughout the eternity in which he believed the "Christian hero" he had longed to be in this life — the hero we may say with certainty that Addison never even attempted to be. For certainly though the "wit," who scarcely rumpled his ruffles when in the extremest stages of dissolute living, may reform and become a saint, — as Addison did, — there is nothing specially characteristic of the hero in him.

Steele was born in Dublin in March, 1672. He first met Addison when they were boys together at the Charterhouse School, and they were afterwards college mates at Oxford. After leaving the army with the rank of Captain, Steele, through his favor of influential Whigs, was elected to Parliament, from which he was not very long afterwards expelled for "seditious language" published in the Crisis. George I. knighted him and appointed him to various offices, because of his ability as a Whig pamphleteer. Between 1709 and 1711 he founded and edited the Tatler, and followed it up with the Spectator, in which he was associated with Addison (1711-12). He founded successively the Guardian, Town Talk, the Tea Table, Chit Chat, the Plebeian, and the Theatre, none of which were notable successes financially. Steele was usually more concerned, however, with some moral, literary, or political purpose than with money-making or with "establishing a property." When he could find no other way of exerting his influence at what seemed to him a crisis, he would found a paper (as he did the Plebeian, in which he opposed Addison) and run it, either until money failed or he had accomplished his purpose. It is hard to tell which of the two events was more apt to be fatal to his newspaper enterprises, as without a definite, moral purpose to inspire him, he seems to have been incapable of long-sustained effort. He died September 1st, 1729, leaving his memory for a jest to his lovers and his influence on English literature for a blessing to the remotest posterity.   W. V. B.

THE CHARACTER OF ISAAC BICKERSTAFF

Rura mihi placeant, riguique in vallibus amnes,
Flumina amem sylvasque inglorius —
                    —Virg. Georg. II. 485.

My next desire is, void of care and strife,
To lead a soft, secure, inglorious life:
A country cottage near a crystal flood,
A winding valley and a lofty wood.
                    —Dryden.

GRECIAN COFFEEHOUSE, November 2d.

I HAVE received this short epistle from an unknown hand.

Sir:—

I have no more to trouble you with than to desire you would in your next help me to some answer to the inclosed concerning yourself. In the meantime I congratulate you upon the increase of your fame, which you see has extended itself beyond the bills of mortality.

Sir:—

That the country is barren of news has been the excuse, time out of mind, for dropping a correspondence with our friends in London, — as if it were impossible, out of a coffeehouse, to write an agreeable letter. I am too ingenuous to endeavor at the covering of my negligence with so common an excuse. Doubtless, amongst friends, bred, as we have been, to the knowledge of books as well as men, a letter dated from a garden, a grotto, a fountain, a wood, a meadow, or the banks of a river, may be more entertaining than one from Tom's, Will's, White's, or St. James's. I promise, therefore, to be frequent for the future in my rural dates to you. But, for fear you should, from what I have said, be induced to believe I shun the commerce of men, I must inform you that there is a fresh topic of discourse lately arisen amongst the ingenious in our part of the world, and is become the more fashionable for the ladies giving into it. This we owe to Isaac Bickerstaff, who is very much censured by some, and as much justified by others. Some criticize his style, his humor, and his matter; others admire the whole man. Some pretend, from the informations of their friends in town, to decipher the author; and others confess they are lost in their guesses. For my part, I must own myself a professed admirer of the paper, and desire you to send me a complete set, together with your thoughts of the squire and his lucubrations.

There is no pleasure like that of receiving praise from the praiseworthy; and I own it a very solid happiness, that these my lucubrations are approved by a person of so fine a taste as the author of this letter, who is capable of enjoying the world in the simplicity of its natural beauties. This pastoral letter, if I may so call it, must be written by a man who carries his entertainment wherever he goes, and is, undoubtedly, one of those happy men who appear far otherwise to the vulgar. I dare say he is not envied by the vicious, the vain, the frolic, and the loud; but is continually blessed with that strong and serious delight, which flows from a well-taught and liberal mind. With great respect to country sports, I may say, this gentleman could pass his time agreeably, if there were not a hare or a fox in his county. That calm and elegant satisfaction which the vulgar call melancholy is the true and proper delight of men of knowledge and virtue. What we take for diversion, which is a kind of forgetting ourselves, is but a mean way of entertainment, in comparison of that which is considering, knowing, and enjoying ourselves. The pleasures of ordinary people are in their passions; but the seat of this delight is in the reason and understanding. Such a frame of mind raises that sweet enthusiasm, which warms the imagination at the sight of every work of nature, and turns all round you into picture and landscape. I shall be ever proud of advices from this gentleman; for I profess writing news from the learned, as well as the busy world.

As for my labors, which he is pleased to inquire after, if they can but wear one impertinence out of human life, destroy a single vice, or give a morning's cheerfulness to an honest mind; in short, if the world can be but one virtue the better, or in any degree less vicious, or receive from them the smallest addition to their innocent diversions, I shall not think my pains, or indeed my life, to have been spent in vain.

Thus far as to my studies. It will be expected I should, in the next place, give some account of my life. I shall, therefore, for the satisfaction of the present age, and the benefit of posterity, present the world with the following abridgment of it.

It is remarkable that I was bred by hand, and ate nothing but milk until I was a twelve-month old; from which time, to the eighth year of my age, I was observed to delight in pudding and potatoes; and, indeed, I retain a benevolence for that sort of food to this day. I do not remember that I distinguished

IX—223

myself in anything at those years, but by my great skill at taw, for which I was so barbarously used, that it has ever since given me an aversion to gaming. In my twelfth year I suffered very much for two or three false concords.* At fifteen I was sent to the university, and stayed there for some time; but a drum passing by, being a lover of music, I enlisted myself for a soldier. As years came on, I began to examine things, and grew discontented at the times. This made me quit the sword, and take to the study of the occult sciences, in which I was so wrapped up, that Oliver Cromwell had been buried and taken up again five years before I heard he was dead. This gave me first the reputation of a conjurer, which has been of great disadvantage to me ever since, and kept me out of all public employments. The greater part of my later years has been divided between Dick's coffeehouse, the Trumpet in Sheer-lane, and my own lodgings.

FROM MY OWN APARTMENT, November 2d.

The evil of unseasonable visits has been complained of to me with much vehemence by persons of both sexes; and I am desired to consider this very important circumstance, that men may know how to regulate their conduct in an affair which concerns no less than life itself. For to a rational creature, it is almost the same cruelty to attack his life, by robbing him of so many moments of his time, or so many drops of his blood. The author of the following letter has a just delicacy in this point, and hath put it into a very good light: —

Mr. Bickerstaff: —   October 29th.

I am very much afflicted with the gravel, which makes me sick and peevish. I desire to know of you, if it be reasonable that any of my acquaintance should take advantage over me at this time, and afflict me with long visits, because they are idle, and I am confined. Pray, sir, reform the town in this matter. Men never consider whether the sick person be disposed for company, but make their visits to

*Isaac Bickerstaff, Esq., declares that he was sixty-three in 1709; he was born, therefore, in 1646; he could only be fifteen in 1661, when the body of Cromwell was exposed. Yet he was sent to the university at fifteen;—then he was a soldier, a cadet at the battle of Coldstream; afterward he took to the study of the occult sciences, and did not hear of Cromwell's fate till five years after it happened. Kept out of all public employments, the greater part of his later years was divided between Dick's coffeehouse, a tavern, or alehouse, and his own obscure lodgings in Sheer-lane. How was such a man qualified to decide on all subjects private and public? (Steele's note.)

humor themselves. You may talk upon this topic, so as to oblige all persons afflicted with chronical distempers, among which I reckon visits. Do not think me a sour man, for I love conversation and my friends; but I think one's most intimate friend may be too familiar, and that there are such things as unseasonable wit and painful mirth.

It is with some so hard a thing to employ their time, that it is a great good fortune when they have a friend indisposed, that they may be punctual in perplexing him, when he is recovered enough to be in that state which cannot be called sickness or health; when he is too well to deny company and too ill to receive them. It is no uncommon case, if a man is of any figure or power in the world, to be congratulated into a relapse.

WILL'S COFFEEHOUSE, November 2d.

I was very well pleased this evening, to hear a gentleman express a very becoming indignation against a practice which I myself have been very much offended at. "There is nothing," said he, "more ridiculous, than for an actor to insert words of his own in the part he is to act, so that it is impossible to see the poet for the player. You will have Penkethman and Bullock helping out Beaumont and Fletcher. It puts me in mind," continued he, "of a collection of antique statues which I once saw in a gentleman's possession, who employed a neighboring stonecutter to add noses, ears, arms, or legs, to the maimed works of Phidias or Praxiteles. You may be sure this addition disfigured the statue much more than time had. I remember Venus, that, by the nose he had given her, looked like mother Shipton; and a Mercury, with a pair of legs that seemed very much swelled with the dropsy."

I thought the gentleman's observations very proper, and he told me I had improved his thought in mentioning on this occasion those wise commentators who had filled up the hemistichs of Virgil; particularly that notable poet, who, to make the "Æneid" more perfect, carried on the story to Lavinia's wedding. If the proper officer will not condescend to take notice of these absurdities, I shall myself, as a censor of the people, animadvert upon such proceedings.

Complete. From the Tatler.

BICKERSTAFF AND MARIA

FROM MY OWN APARTMENT, October 19th.

IT is my frequent practice to visit places of resort in this town where I am least known, to observe what reception my works meet with in the world, and what good effects I may promise myself from my labors, and it being a privilege asserted by Monsieur Montaigne, and others, of vainglorious memory, that we writers of essays may talk of ourselves, I take the liberty to give an account of the remarks which I find are made by some of my gentle readers upon these my dissertations.

I happened this evening to fall into a coffeehouse near the 'Change, where two persons were reading my account of the "Table of Fame."

The one of these was commenting as he read, and explaining who was meant by this and the other worthy, as he passed on. I observed the person over against him wonderfully intent and satisfied with his explanation. When he came to Julius Cæsar, who is said to have refused any conductor to the table: "No, no," said he, "he is in the right of it, he has money enough to be welcome wherever he comes"; and then whispered, "He means a certain colonel of the Trainbands." Upon reading that Aristotle made his claim with some rudeness, but great strength of reason; "Who can that be, so rough and so reasonable? It must be some Whig, I warrant you. There is nothing but party in these public papers." Where Pythagoras is said to have a golden thigh, "Aye, aye," said he, "he has money enough in his breeches; that is the alderman of our ward." You must know, whatever he read, I found he interpreted from his own way of life and acquaintance. I am glad my readers can construe for themselves these difficult points; but, for the benefit of posterity, I design, when I come to write my last paper of this kind, to make it an explanation of all my former. In that piece you shall have all I have commended with their proper names. The faulty characters must be left as they are, because we live in an age wherein vice is very general, and virtue very particular; for which reason the latter only wants explanation.

But I must turn my present discourse to what is of yet greater regard to me than the care of my writings; that is to say, the preservation of a lady's heart. Little did I think I should ever have business of this kind on my hands more; but, as little as any one who knows me would believe it, there is a lady at this time who professes love to me. Her passion and good humor you shall have in her own words:—

Mr. Bickerstaff:—

I had formerly a very good opinion of myself; but it is now withdrawn, and I have placed it upon you, Mr. Bickerstaff, for whom I am not ashamed to declare I have a very great passion and tenderness. It is not for your face, for that I never saw; your shape and height I am equally a stranger to; but your understanding charms me, and I am lost if you do not dissemble a little love for me. I am not without hopes; because I am not like the tawdry gay things that are fit only to make bone-lace. I am neither childish young, nor beldam old, but, the world says, a good, agreeable woman.

Speak peace to a troubled heart, troubled only for you; and in your next paper let me find your thoughts of me.

Do not think of finding out who I am, for, notwithstanding your interest in demons, they cannot help you either to my name, or a sight of my face; therefore, do not let them deceive you.

I can bear no discourse, if you are not the subject; and believe me, I know more of love than you do of astronomy.

Pray, say some civil things in return to my generosity, and you shall have my very best pen employed to thank you, and I will confirm it.

I am your admirer,
MARIA.

There is something wonderfully pleasing in the favor of women; and this letter has put me in so good a humor, that nothing could displease me since I received it. My boy breaks glasses and pipes, and instead of giving him a knock on the pate, as my way is, for I hate scolding at servants, I only say, " Ah, Jack! thou hast a head, and so has a pin," or some such merry expression. But, alas! how am I mortified when he is putting on my fourth pair of stockings on these poor spindles of mine! " The fair one understands love better than I astronomy!" I am sure, without the help of that art, this poor meagre trunk of mine is a very ill habitation for love. She is pleased to speak civilly of my sense, but *Ingenium malè habitat* is an invincible difficulty in cases of this nature. I had always, indeed, from a passion to please the eyes of the fair, a great pleasure in dress.

Add to this, that I have writ songs since I was sixty, and have lived with all the circumspection of an old beau, as I am. But my friend Horace has very well said, " Every year takes something from us"; and instructed me to form my pursuits and desires according to the stage of my life; therefore, I have no more to value myself upon than that I can converse with young people without peevishness, or wishing myself a moment younger. For which reason, when I am amongst them, I rather moderate than interrupt their diversions. But though I have this complacency, I must not pretend to write to a lady civil things, as Maria desires. Time was, when I could have told her, " I had received a letter from her fair hands; and that, if this paper trembled, as she read it, it then best expressed its author," or some other gay conceit. Though I never saw her, I could have told her, " that good sense and good humor smiled in her eyes; that constancy and good nature dwelt in her heart; that beauty and good breeding appeared in all her actions." When I was five-and-twenty, upon sight of one syllable, even wrong spelt, by a lady I never saw, I could tell her, " that her height was that which was fit for inviting our approach, and commanding our respect; that a smile sat on her lips, which prefaced her expressions before she uttered them, and her aspect prevented her speech. All she could say, though she had an infinite deal of wit, was but a repetition of what was expressed by her form; her form! which struck her beholders with ideas more moving and forcible than ever were inspired by music, painting, or eloquence." At this rate I panted in those days; but ah! sixty-three! I am very sorry I can only return the agreeable Maria a passion expressed rather from the head than the heart.

Dear Madam:—

You have already seen the best of me, and I so passionately love you that I desire we may never meet. If you will examine your heart, you will find that you join the man with the philosopher; and if you have that kind opinion of my sense as you pretend, I question not but you add to it complexion, air, and shape; but, dear Molly, a man in his grand climacteric is of no sex. Be a good girl, and conduct yourself with honor and virtue, when you love one younger than myself. I am, with the greatest tenderness, your innocent lover,

I. B

Complete. From the Tatler.

SIR ROGER AND THE WIDOW

——Hærent infixi pectore vultus.
—Virg. Æn. IV. 4.

" Her looks were deep imprinted in his heart."

IN MY first description of the company in which I pass most of my time, it may be remembered that I mentioned a great affliction which my friend Sir Roger had met with in his youth; which was no less than a disappointment in love. It happened this evening that we fell into a very pleasing walk at a distance from his house. As soon as we came into it, " It is," quoth the good old man, looking round him with a smile, " very hard that any part of my land should be settled upon one who has used me so ill as the perverse widow did; and yet I am sure I could not see a sprig of any bough of this whole walk of trees, but I should reflect upon her and her severity. She has certainly the finest hand of any woman in the world. You are to know, this was the place wherein I used to muse upon her; and by that custom I can never come into it, but the same tender sentiments revive in my mind, as if I had actually walked with that beautiful creature under these shades. I have been fool enough to carve her name on the bark of several of these trees; so unhappy is the condition of men in love, to attempt the removing of their passion by the methods which serve only to imprint it deeper. She has certainly the finest hand of any woman in the world."

Here she followed a profound silence; and I was not displeased to observe my friend falling so naturally into a discourse, which I had ever before taken notice he industriously avoided. After a very long pause, he entered upon an account of this great circumstance in his life, with an air which I thought raised my idea of him above what I had ever had before; and gave me the picture of that cheerful mind of his before it received that stroke which has ever since affected his words and actions. But he went on as follows:—

" I came to my estate in my twenty-second year, and resolved to follow the steps of the most worthy of my ancestors who have inhabited this spot of earth before me, in all the methods of hospitality and good neighborhood, for the sake of my fame; and in country sports and recreations, for the sake of my health. In

my twenty-third year I was obliged to serve as sheriff of the county; and in my servants, officers, and whole equipage, indulged the pleasure of a young man (who did not think ill of his own person) in taking that public occasion of showing my figure and behavior to advantage. You may easily imagine to yourself what appearance I made, who am pretty tall, rid well, and was very well dressed, at the head of a whole county, with music before me, a feather in my hat, and my horse well bitted. I can assure you, I was not a little pleased with the kind looks and glances I had from all the balconies and windows as I rode to the hall where the assizes were held. But when I came there, a beautiful creature, in a widow's habit, sat in court to hear the event of a cause concerning her dower. This commanding creature (who was born for the destruction of all who behold her) put on such a resignation in her countenance, and bore the whispers all around the court with such a pretty uneasiness, I warrant you, and then recovered herself from one eye to another, until she was perfectly confused by meeting something so wistful in all she encountered, that at last, with a murrain to her, she cast her bewitching eye upon me. I no sooner met it but I bowed like a great surprised booby; and knowing her cause was to be the first which came on, I cried, like a great captivated calf as I was, ' Make way for the defendant's witnesses.' This sudden partiality made all the county immediately see the sheriff also was become a slave to the fine widow. During the time her cause was upon trial, she behaved herself, I warrant you, with such a deep attention to her business, took opportunities to have little billets handed to her counsel, then would be in such a pretty confusion, occasioned, you must know, by acting before so much company, that not only I, but the whole court, was prejudiced in her favor; and all that the next heir to her husband had to urge was thought so groundless and frivolous, that when it came to her counsel to reply, there was not half so much said as every one besides in the court thought he could have urged to her advantage. You must understand, sir, this perverse woman is one of those unaccountable creatures that secretly rejoice in the admiration of men, but indulge themselves in no further consequences. Hence it is that she has ever had a train of admirers, and she removes from her slaves in town to those in the country, according to the seasons of the year. She is a reading lady, and far gone in the pleasures of friendship. She is always accompanied by a confidant, who is witness to her daily protestations against our sex, and consequently a bar to her first steps towards love, upon the strength of her own maxims and declarations.

"However, I must needs say this accomplished mistress of mine has distinguished me above the rest, and has been known to declare Sir Roger de Coverley was the tamest and most humane of all the brutes in the country. I was told she said so by one who thought he rallied me; but upon the strength of this slender encouragement of being thought least detestable, I made new liveries, new paired my coach horses, sent them all to town to be bitted, and taught to throw their legs well, and move altogether, before I pretended to cross the country, and wait upon her. As soon as I thought my retinue suitable to the character of my fortune and youth, I set out from hence to make my addresses. The particular skill of this lady has ever been to inflame your wishes, and yet command respect. To make her mistress of this art, she has a greater share of knowledge, wit, and good sense, than is usual even among men of merit. Then she is beautiful beyond the race of women. If you will not let her go on with a certain artifice with her eyes, and the skill of beauty, she will arm herself with her real charms, and strike you with admiration instead of desire. It is certain that if you were to behold the whole woman, there is that dignity in her aspect, that composure in her motion, that complacency in her manner, that if her form makes you hope, her merit makes you fear. But then again, she is such a desperate scholar, that no country gentleman can approach her without being a jest. As I was going to tell you, when I came to her house, I was admitted to her presence with great civility; at the same time she placed herself to be first seen by me in such an attitude as I think you call the posture of a picture, that she discovered new charms, and I at last came towards her with such an awe as made me speechless. This she no sooner observed but she made her advantage of it, and began a discourse to me concerning love and honor, as they both are followed by pretenders, and the real votaries to them. When she discussed these points in a discourse, which I verily believe was as learned as the best philosopher in Europe could possibly make, she asked me whether she was so happy as to fall in with my sentiments on these important particulars. Her confidant sat by her, and upon my being in the

last confusion and silence, this malicious aid of hers, turning to her, says, 'I am very glad to observe Sir Roger pauses upon this subject, and seems resolved to deliver all his sentiments upon the matter when he pleases to speak.' They both kept their countenances, and after I had sat half an hour meditating how to behave before such profound casuists, I rose up and took my leave. Chance has since that time thrown me very often in her way, and she as often directed a discourse to me which I do not understand. This barbarity has kept me ever at a distance from the most beautiful object my eyes ever beheld. It is thus also she deals with all mankind, and you must make love to her, as you would conquer the sphinx, by posing her. But were she like other women, and that there were any talking to her, how constant must the pleasure of that man be, who could converse with a creature—but, after all, you may be sure her heart is fixed on some one or other; and yet I have been credibly informed; but who can believe half that is said! After she had done speaking to me, she put her hand to her bosom, and adjusted her tucker. Then she cast her eyes a little down, upon my beholding her too earnestly. They say she sings excellently; her voice in her ordinary speech has something in it inexpressibly sweet. You must know I dined with her at a public table the day after I first saw her, and she helped me to some tansy in the eye of all the gentlemen in the country. She has certainly the finest hand of any woman in the world. I can assure you, sir, were you to behold her, you would be in the same condition; for as her speech is music, her form is angelic. But I find I grow irregular while I am talking of her; but, indeed, it would be stupidity to be unconcerned at such perfection. Oh, the excellent creature! she is as inimitable to all women as she is inaccessible to all men."

I found my friend begin to rave, and insensibly led him towards the house, that we might be joined by some other company; and am convinced that the widow is the secret cause of all that inconsistency which appears in some parts of my friend's discourse; though he has so much command of himself as not directly to mention her, yet according to that of Martial, which one knows not how to render into English, *Dum tacet hanc loquitur*. I shall end this paper with that whole epigram, which represents with much humor my honest friend's condition:—

Quicquid agit Rufus, nihil est, nisi Nævia Rufo,
Si gaudet, si flet, si tacet, hanc loquitur:
Cænat, propinat, poscit, negat, annuit, una est
Nævia; si non sit Nævia, mutus erit,
Scriberit hesternâ patri cum luce salutem,
Nævia lux, inquit, Nævia numen, ave.
　　　　　—Mart. Epig. LXIX., 1. i.

"Let Rufus weep, rejoice, stand, sit, or walk,
Still he can nothing but of Nævia talk;
Let him eat, drink, ask questions, or dispute,
Still he must speak of Nævia, or be mute.
He writ to his father, ending with this line,
I am, my lovely Nævia, ever thine."

　　　　　　　　Complete. From the Spectator.

THE COVERLEY FAMILY PORTRAITS

Abnormis sapiens —
　—*Hor*. Lib. II., Sat. II. 3.

"Of plain good sense, untutor'd in the schools."

I WAS this morning walking in the gallery, when Sir Roger entered at the end opposite to me, and, advancing towards me, said he was glad to meet me among his relations the De Coverleys, and hoped I liked the conversation of so much good company who were as silent as myself. I knew he alluded to the pictures, and as he is a gentleman who does not a little value himself upon his ancient descent, I expected he would give me some account of them. We were now arrived at the upper end of the gallery, when the knight faced towards one of the pictures, and as we stood before it, he entered into the matter, after his blunt way of saying things, as they occur to his imagination, without regular introduction, or care to preserve the appearance of chain of thought.

"It is," said he, "worth while to consider the force of dress; and how the persons of one age differ from those of another, merely by that only. One may observe also, that the general fashion of one age has been followed by one particular set of people in another, and by them preserved from one generation to another. Thus the vast jutting coat and small bonnet, which was the habit in Henry the Seventh's time, is kept on in the yeomen of the guard; not without a good and politic view, because

they look a foot taller, and a foot and a half broader; besides, that the cap leaves the face expanded, and consequently more terrible, and fitter to stand at the entrance of palaces.

"This predecessor of ours you see is dressed after this manner, and his cheeks would be no larger than mine, were he in a hat as I am. He was the last man that won a prize in the Tiltyard (which is now a common street before Whitehall). You see the broken lance that lies there by his right foot. He shivered that lance of his adversary all to pieces; and bearing himself, look you, sir, in this manner, at the same time he came within the target of the gentleman who rode against him, and taking him with incredible force before him on the pommel of his saddle, he in that manner rid the tournament over, with an air that showed he did it rather to perform the rule of the lists than expose his enemy; however, it appeared he knew how to make use of a victory, and with a gentle trot he marched up to a gallery, where their mistress sat (for they were rivals), and let him down with laudable courtesy and pardonable insolence. I do not know but it might be exactly where the coffeehouse is now.

"You are to know this my ancestor was not only of a military genius, but fit also for the arts of peace, for he played on the bass viol as well as any gentleman at court; you see where his viol hangs by his basket-hilt sword. The action at the Tilt-yard you may be sure won the fair lady, who was a maid of honor, and the greatest beauty of her time; here she stands the next picture. Your see, sir, my great great great grandmother has on the new-fashioned petticoat, except that the modern is gathered at the waist. My grandmother appears as if she stood in a large drum, whereas the ladies now walk as if they were in a gocart. For all this lady was bred at court, she became an excellent country wife, she brought ten children, and when I show you the library, you shall see in her own hand (allowing for the difference of the language) the best receipt now in England both for a hasty pudding and a white-pot.

"If you please to fall back a little, because it is necessary to look at the three next pictures at one view; these are three sisters. She on the right hand, who is so very beautiful, died a maid; the next to her, still handsomer, had the same fate, against her will; this homely thing in the middle had both their portions added to her own, and was stolen by a neighboring gentleman, a man of stratagem and resolution, for he poisoned three mastiffs to come at her, and knocked down two deer stealers in carrying her off. Misfortunes happen in all families. The theft of this romp, and so much money, was no great matter to our estate. But the next heir that possessed it was this soft gentleman whom you see there. Observe the small buttons, the little boots, the laces, the slashes about his clothes, and, above all, the posture he is drawn in (which, to be sure, was his own choosing), you see he sits with one hand on a desk writing and looking, as it were, another way, like an easy writer, or a sonneteer. He was one of those that had too much wit to know how to live in the world; he was a man of no justice, but great good manners; he ruined everybody that had anything to do with him, but never said a rude thing in his life; the most indolent person in the world; he would sign a deed that passed away half his estate, with his gloves on, but would not put on his hat before a lady if it were to save his country. He is said to be the first that made love by squeezing the hand. He left the estate with ten thousand pounds debt upon it; but, however, by all hands I have been informed that he was every way the finest gentleman in the world. That debt lay heavy on our house for one generation, but it was retrieved by a gift from that honest man you see there, a citizen of our name, but nothing at all akin to us. I know Sir Andrew Freeport has said behind my back that this man was descended from one of the ten children of the maid of honor I showed you above; but it was never made out. We winked at the thing, indeed, because money was wanting at that time."

Here I saw my friend a little embarrassed, and turned my face to the next portraiture.

Sir Roger went on with his account of the gallery in the following manner: "This man [pointing to him I looked at] I take to be the honor of our house. Sir Humphrey de Coverley; he was in his dealings as punctual as a tradesman, and as generous as a gentleman. He would have thought himself as much undone by breaking his word, as if it were to be followed by bankruptcy. He served his country as a knight of the shire to his dying day. He found it no easy matter to maintain an integrity in his words and actions, even in things that regarded the offices which were incumbent upon him, in the care of his own affairs and relations of life, and therefore dreaded (though he had great

talents) to go into employments of state, where he must be exposed to the snares of ambition. Innocence of life and great ability were the distinguishing parts of his character; the latter, he had often observed, had led to the destruction of the former, and he used frequently to lament that great and good had not the same signification. He was an excellent husbandman, but had resolved not to exceed such a degree of wealth; all above it he bestowed in secret bounties many years after the sum he aimed at for his own use was attained. Yet he did not slacken his industry, but to a decent old age spent the life and fortune which was superfluous to himself, in the service of his friends and neighbors."

Here we were called to dinner, and Sir Roger ended the discourse of this gentleman, by telling me, as we followed the servant, that this his ancestor was a brave man, and narrowly escaped being killed in the civil wars. "For," said he, "he was sent out of the field upon a private message the day before the battle of Worcester." The whim of narrowly escaping by having been within a day of danger, with other matters above mentioned, mixed with good sense, left me at a loss whether I was more delighted with my friend's wisdom or simplicity.

Complete. From the Spectator.

ON CERTAIN SYMPTOMS OF GREATNESS

Nimirum insanus paucis videatur, eò quòd
Maxima pars hominum morbo jactatur eodem.
    —*Hor*. Lib. II., Sat. III. 120.

By few, forsooth, a madman he is thought,
For half mankind the same disease have caught.
    — *Francis*.

FROM MY OWN APARTMENT, January 30th.

THERE is no affection of the mind so much blended in human nature, and wrought into our very constitution, as pride.

It appears under a multitude of disguises, and breaks out in ten thousand different symptoms. Every one feels it in himself, and yet wonders to see it in his neighbor. I must confess, I met with an instance of it the other day where I should very little have expected it. Who would believe the proud person I am going to speak of is a cobbler upon Ludgate-hill? This artist being naturally a lover of respect, and considering that his

circumstances are such that no man living will give it him, has contrived the figure of a beau, in wood; who stands before him in a bending posture, with his hat under his left arm, and his right hand extended in such a manner as to hold a thread, a piece of wax, or an awl, according to the particular service in which his master thinks fit to employ him. When I saw him, he held a candle in this obsequious posture. I was very well pleased with the cobbler's invention, that had so ingeniously contrived an inferior, and stood a little while contemplating this inverted idolatry, wherein the image did homage to the man. When we meet with such a fantastic vanity in one of this order, it is no wonder if we may trace it through all degrees above it, and particularly through all the steps of greatness. We easily see the absurdity of pride when it enters into the heart of a cobbler; though in reality it is altogether as ridiculous and unreasonable, wherever it takes possession of a human creature. There is no temptation to it from the reflection upon our being in general, or upon any comparative perfection, whereby one man may excel another. The greater a man's knowledge is, the greater motive he may seem to have for pride; but in the same proportion as the one rises, the other sinks, it being the chief office of wisdom to discover to us our weaknesses and imperfections.

As folly is the foundation of pride, the natural superstructure of it is madness. If there was an occasion for the experiment, I would not question to make a proud man a lunatic in three weeks' time, provided I had it in my power to ripen his frenzy with proper applications. It is an admirable reflection in Terence, where it is said of a parasite, "*Hic homines ex stultis facit insanos.*" "This fellow," says he, "has an art of converting fools into madmen." When I was in France, the region of complaisance and vanity, I have often observed that a great man who has entered a levee of flatterers humble and temperate has grown so insensibly heated by the court which was paid him on all sides, that he has been quite distracted before he could get into his coach.

If we consult the collegiates of Moor-fields, we shall find most of them are beholden to their pride for their introduction into that magnificent palace. I had, some years ago, the curiosity to inquire into the particular circumstances of these whimsical freeholders; and learned from their own mouths the condition and character of each of them. Indeed, I found that all I spoke to

were persons of quality. There were at that time five duchesses, three earls, two heathen gods, an emperor, and a prophet. There were also a great number of such as were locked up from their estates, and others who concealed their titles. A leather seller of Taunton whispered me in the ear that he was the "Duke of Monmouth," but begged me not to betray him. At a little distance from him sat a tailor's wife, who asked me, as I went, if I had seen the sword bearer, upon which I presumed to ask her who she was, and was answered, "My lady mayoress."

I was very sensibly touched with compassion towards these miserable people; and, indeed, extremely mortified to see human nature capable of being thus disfigured. However, I reaped this benefit from it, that I was resolved to guard myself against a passion which makes such havoc in the brain, and produces so much disorder in the imagination. For this reason I have endeavored to keep down the secret swellings of resentment, and stifle the very first suggestions of self-esteem; to establish my mind in tranquillity, and over-value nothing in my own or in another's possession.

For the benefit of such whose heads are a little turned, though not to so great a degree as to qualify them for the place of which I have been now speaking, I shall assign one of the sides of the college which I am erecting, for the cure of this dangerous distemper.

The most remarkable of the persons, whose disturbance arises from pride, and whom I shall use all possible diligence to cure, are such as are hidden in the appearance of quite contrary habits and dispositions. Among such, I shall, in the first place, take care of one who is under the most subtle species of pride that I have observed in my whole experience.

The patient is a person for whom I have a great respect, as being an old courtier, and a friend of mine in my youth. The man has but a bare subsistence, just enough to pay his reckoning with us at the Trumpet: but, by having spent the beginning of his life in the hearing of great men and persons of power, he is always promising to do good offices to introduce every man he converses with into the world; will desire one of ten times his substance to let him see him sometimes, and hints to him that he does not forget him. He answers to matters of no consequence with great circumspection; but, however, maintains a general civility in his words and actions, and an insolent benevolence to all whom he has to do with. This he practices with a grave tone and air; and though I am his senior by twelve years, and richer by forty pounds per annum, he had yesterday the impudence to commend me to my face, and tell me, "he should be always ready to encourage me." In a word, he is a very insignificant fellow, but exceeding gracious. The best return I can make him for his favors is to carry him myself to Bedlam and see him well taken care of.

The next person I shall provide for is of a quite contrary character, that has in him all the stiffness and insolence of quality, without a grain of sense or good-nature, to make it either respected or beloved. His pride has infected every muscle of his face; and yet, after all his endeavors to show mankind that he contemns them, he is only neglected by all that see him, as not of consequence enough to be hated.

For the cure of this particular sort of madness, it will be necessary to break through all forms with him, and familiarize his carriage by the use of a good cudgel. It may likewise be of great benefit to make him jump over a stick half a dozen times every morning.

A third, whom I have in my eye, is a young fellow, whose lunacy is such that he boasts of nothing but what he ought to be ashamed of. He is vain of being rotten, and talks publicly of having committed crimes which he ought to be hanged for by the laws of his country.

There are several others whose brains are hurt with pride, and whom I may hereafter attempt to recover; but shall conclude my present list with an old woman, who is just dropping into her grave, that talks of nothing but her birth. Though she has not a tooth in her head, she expects to be valued for the blood in her veins, which she fancies is much better than that which glows in the cheeks of Belinda, and sets half the town on fire.

Complete. From the Tatler.

HOW TO BE HAPPY THOUGH MARRIED

—— *Garrit aniles*
Ex re fabellas ——
—*Hor.* Lib. II., Sat. VI. 78.

"He tells an old wife's tale very pertinently."

IX—224

the greatness of her own passion; but I easily collected it from the representation she gave me of his. "I have everything," says she, "in Tranquillus, that I can wish for; and enjoy in him, what, indeed, you have told me were to be met with in a good husband, the fondness of a lover, the tenderness of a parent, and the intimacy of a friend." It transported me to see her eyes swimming in tears of affection when she spoke. "And is there not, dear sister," said I, "more pleasure in the possession of such a man than in all the little impertinencies of balls, assemblies, and equipage, which it cost me so much pains to make you contemn?" She answered, smiling, "Tranquillus has made me a sincere convert in a few weeks, though I am afraid you could not have done it in your whole life. To tell you truly, I have only one fear hanging upon me, which is apt to give me trouble in the midst of all my satisfactions: I am afraid, you must know, that I shall not always make the same amiable appearance in his eye that I do at present. You know, brother Bickerstaff, that you have the reputation of a conjurer; and, if you have any one secret in your art to make your sister always beautiful, I should be happier than if I were mistress of all the worlds you have shown me in a starry night." "Jenny," said I, "without having recourse to magic, I shall give you one plain rule that will not fail of making you always amiable to a man who has so great a passion for you, and is of so equal and reasonable a temper as Tranquillus. Endeavor to please, and you must please; be always in the same disposition as you are when you ask for this secret, and you may take my word, you will never want it. An inviolable fidelity, good humor, and complacency of temper outlive all the charms of a fine face, and make the decays of it invisible."

We discoursed very long upon this head, which was equally agreeable to us both; for, I must confess, as I tenderly love her, I take as much pleasure in giving her instructions for her welfare, as she herself does in receiving them. I proceeded, therefore, to inculcate these sentiments by relating a very particular passage that happened within my own knowledge.

There were several of us making merry at a friend's house in a country village, when the sexton of the parish church entered the room in a sort of surprise, and told us, "that as he was digging a grave in the chancel, a little blow of his pickax opened a decayed coffin, in which there were several written papers."

FROM MY OWN APARTMENT, December 5th.

MY BROTHER Tranquillus being gone out of town for some days, my sister Jenny sent me word she would come and dine with me, and therefore desired me to have no other company. I took care accordingly, and was not a little pleased to see her enter the room with a decent and matron-like behavior, which I thought very much became her. I saw she had a great deal to say to me, and easily discovered in her eyes, and the air of her countenance, that she had abundance of satisfaction in her heart, which she longed to communicate. However, I was resolved to let her break into her discourse her own way, and reduced her to a thousand little devices and intimations to bring me to the mention of her husband. But finding I was resolved not to name him, she began of her own accord. "My husband," said she, "gives his humble service to you," to which I only answered, "I hope he is well"; and, without waiting for a reply, fell into other subjects. She at last was out of all patience, and said, with a smile and manner that I thought had more beauty and spirit than I had ever observed in her, "I did not think, brother, you had been so ill natured. You have seen, ever since I came in, that I had a mind to talk of my husband, and you will not be so kind as to give me an occasion." "I did not know," said I, "but it might be a disagreeable subject to you. You do not take me for so old fashioned a fellow as to think of entertaining a young lady with the discourse of her husband. I know nothing is more acceptable than to speak of one who is to be so, but to speak of one who is so! indeed, Jenny, I am a better-bred man than you think me." She showed a little dislike at my raillery; and, by her bridling up, I perceived she expected to be treated hereafter not as Jenny Distaff, but Mrs. Tranquillus. I was very well pleased with this change in her humor; and, upon talking with her on several subjects, I could not but fancy I saw a great deal of her husband's way and manner in her remarks, her phrases, the tone of her voice, and the very air of her countenance. This gave me an unspeakable satisfaction, not only because I had found her a husband, from whom she could learn many things that were laudable, but also because I looked upon her imitation of him as an infallible sign that she entirely loved him. This is an observation that I never knew fail, though I do not remember that any other has made it. The natural shyness of her sex hindered her from telling me

Our curiosity was immediately raised, so that we went to the place where the sexton had been at work, and found a great concourse of people about the grave. Among the rest there was an old woman, who told us the person buried there was a lady whose name I do not think fit to mention, though there is nothing in the story but what tends very much to her honor. This lady lived several years an exemplary pattern of conjugal love, and, dying soon after her husband, who every way answered her character in virtue and affection, made it her deathbed request, "that all the letters which she had received from him, both before and after her marriage, should be buried in the coffin with her." These, I found upon examination, were the papers before us. Several of them had suffered so much by time that I could only pick out a few words; as my soul! lilies! roses! dearest angel! and the like. One of them, which was legible throughout, ran thus:—

Madam:—

If you would know the greatness of my love, consider that of your own beauty. That blooming countenance, that snowy bosom, that graceful person, return every moment to my imagination; the brightness of your eyes hath hindered me from closing mine since I last saw you. You may still add to your beauties by a smile. A frown will make me the most wretched of men, as I am the most passionate of lovers.

It filled the whole company with a deep melancholy, to compare the description of the letter with the person that occasioned it, who was now reduced to a few crumbling bones, and a little moldering heap of earth. With much ado I deciphered another letter which began with, "My dear, dear wife." This gave me a curiosity to see how the style of one written in marriage differed from one written in courtship. To my surprise, I found the fondness rather augmented than lessened, though the panegyric turned upon a different accomplishment. The words were as follows:—

Before this short absence from you, I did not know that I loved you so much as I really do; though, at the same time, I thought I loved you as much as possible. I am under great apprehension lest you should have any uneasiness whilst I am defrauded of my share in it, and cannot think of tasting any pleasures that you do not partake with me. Pray, my dear, be careful of your health, if for no other reason but because you know I could not outlive you. It is natural in absence to make professions of an inviolable constancy; but towards so much merit it is scarce a virtue, especially when it is but a bare return to that of which you have given me such continued proofs ever since our first acquaintance. I am, etc.

It happened that the daughter of these two excellent persons was by when I was reading this letter. At the sight of the coffin, in which was the body of her mother, near that of her father, she melted into a flood of tears. As I had heard a great character of her virtue, and observed in her this instance of filial piety, I could not resist my natural inclination of giving advice to young people, and therefore addressed myself to her. "Young lady," said I, "you see how short is the possession of that beauty, in which nature has been so liberal to you. You find the melancholy sight before you is a contradiction to the first letter that you heard on that subject; whereas, you may observe the second letter, which celebrates your mother's constancy, is itself, being found in this place, an argument of it. But, madam, I ought to caution you not to think the bodies that lie before you your father and your mother. Know their constancy is rewarded by a nobler union than by this mingling of their ashes, in a state where there is no danger or possibility of a second separation."

Complete. From the Tatler.

PÆTUS AND ARRIA

Quicquid agunt homines ——
—— nostri est farrago libelli.
—*Juv.* Sat. I. 85, 86.

"Whate'er men do, or say, or think, or dream,
Our motley paper seizes for its theme."

WHITE'S CHOCOLATEHOUSE, September 23d.

I HAVE taken upon me no very easy task in turning all my thoughts on panegyric, when most of the advices I receive tend to the quite contrary purpose; and I have few notices but such as regard follies and vices. But the properest way for me to treat is to keep in general upon the passions and affections of men, with as little regard to particulars as the nature of the thing will admit. However, I think there is something so passionate in the circumstances of the lovers mentioned in the fol-

lowing letter, that I am willing to go out of my way to obey what is commanded in it:—

Sir:—   LONDON, September 17th.

Your design of entertaining the town with the characters of the ancient heroes, as persons shall send an account to Mr. Morphew, encourages me and others to beg of you that, in the meantime, if it is not contrary to the method you have proposed, you would give us one paper upon the subject of the death of Pætus and his wife, when Nero sent him an order to kill himself; his wife, setting him the example, died with these words: "Pætus, it is not painful." You must know the story, and your observations upon it will oblige, sir,

Your most humble servant.

When the worst man that ever lived in the world had the highest station in it, human life was the object of his diversion; and he sent orders frequently, out of mere wantonness, to take off such and such, without so much as being angry with them. Nay frequently, his tyranny was so humorous, that he put men to death because he could not but approve of them. It came one day to his ear that a certain married couple, Pætus and Arria, lived in a more happy tranquillity and mutual love than any other persons who were then in being. He listened with great attention to the account of their manner of spending their time together, of the constant pleasure they were to each other in all their words and actions; and found, by exact information, that they were so treasonable as to be much more happy than his imperial Majesty himself. Upon which he writ Pætus the following billet:—

Pætus, you are hereby desired to despatch yourself. I have heard a very good character of you; and therefore leave it to yourself whether you will die by dagger, sword, or poison. If you outlive this order above an hour, I have given directions to put you to death by torture.

NERO.

This familiar epistle was delivered to his wife Arria, who opened it.

One must have a soul very well turned for love, pity, and indignation, to comprehend the tumult this unhappy lady was thrown into upon this occasion. The passion of love is no more to be understood by some tempers than a problem in a science

by an ignorant man; but he that knows what affection is will have, upon considering the condition of Arria, ten thousand thoughts flowing upon him, which the tongue was not formed to express; but the charming statue is now before my eyes, and Arria, in her 'unutterable sorrow, has more beauty than ever appeared in youth, in mirth, or in triumph. These are the great and noble incidents which speak the dignity of our nature, in our sufferings and distresses. Behold, her tender affection for her husband sinks her features into a countenance which appears more helpless than that of an infant; but again, her indignation shows in her visage and her bosom a resentment as strong as that of the bravest man. Long she stood in this agony of alternate rage and love; but at last composed herself for her dissolution, rather than survive her beloved Pætus. When he came into her presence, he found her with the tyrant's letter in one hand and a dagger in the other. Upon his approach to her, she gave him the order: and at the same time stabbing herself, "Pætus," says she, "it is not painful," and expired. Pætus immediately followed her example. The passion of these memorable lovers was such, that it illuded the rigor of their fortune, and baffled the force of a blow, which neither felt, because each received it for the sake of the other. The woman's part in this story is by much the more heroic, and has occasioned one of the best epigrams transmitted to us from antiquity.*

Casta suo gladium cum traderet Arria Pæto
Quem de visceribus traxerat ipsa suis;
Si qua fides, vulnus quod feci, non dolet, inquit
Sed quod tu facies hoc mihi, Pæte, dolet.
—*Mart.* Epig. I. 14.

"When the chaste Arria reached the reeking sword,
Drawn from her bosom, to her honor'd lord,
Trust me, she said, for this I do not grieve,
I die by that which Pætus must receive."

Complete. From the Tatler—No. 72.

THE RING OF GYGES

Secretosque pios, his dantem jura Catonem.
—*Virg.* Æn. VIII. 670.

Apart from these, the happy souls he draws,
And Cato's pious ghost dispensing laws.
—*Dryden,*

SHEER-LANE, February 24th.

I T IS an argument of a clear and worthy spirit in a man to be able to disengage himself from the opinions of others, so far as not to let the deference due to the sense of mankind ensnare him to act against the dictates of his own reason. But the generality of the world are so far from walking by any such maxim, that it is almost a standing rule to do as others do, or be ridiculous. I have heard my old friend, Mr. Hart, speak it as an observation among the players, "that it is impossible to act with grace, except the actor has forgot that he is before an audience." Until he is arrived at that, his motion, his air, his every step and gesture, has something in them which discovers he is under a restraint, for fear of being ill received; or if he considers himself as in the presence of those who approve his behavior, you see an affectation of that pleasure run through his whole carriage. It is as common in life, as upon the stage, to behold a man in the most indifferent action betray a sense he has of doing what he is about gracefully. Some have such an immoderate relish for applause that they expect it for things which in themselves are so frivolous that it is impossible, without this affectation, to make them appear worthy either of blame or praise. There is Will Glare, so passionately intent upon being admired, that when you see him in public places, every muscle of his face discovers his thoughts are fixed upon the consideration of what figure he makes. He will often fall into a musing posture, to attract observation; and is then obtruding himself upon the company, when he pretends to be withdrawn from it. Such little arts are the certain and infallible tokens of a superficial mind, as the avoiding observation is the sign of a great and sublime one. It is therefore extremely difficult for a man to judge even of his own actions, without forming to himself an idea of what he should act, were it in his power to execute all his desires without the observation of the rest of the world. There is an allegorical fable in Plato, which seems to admonish us that we are very little acquainted with ourselves, while we know our actions are to pass the censures of others; but, had we the power to accomplish all our wishes unobserved, we should then easily inform ourselves how far we are possessed of real and intrinsic virtue. The fable I was going to mention is that of Gyges, who is said to have had an enchanted ring, which had in it a miraculous quality, making him who wore it visible or invisible, as he turned it to or from his body. The use Gyges made of his occasional invisibility was, by the advantage of it, to violate a queen, and murder a king. Tully takes notice of this allegory, and says very handsomely, "that a man of honor who had such a ring would act just in the same manner as he would without it." It is indeed no small pitch of virtue, under the temptation of impunity, and the hopes of accomplishing all a man desires, not to transgress the rules of justice and virtue; but this is rather not being an ill man, than being positively a good one; and it seems wonderful that so great a soul as that of Tully should not form to himself a thousand worthy actions, which a virtuous mind would be prompted to by the possession of such a secret. There are certainly some parts of mankind who are guardian beings to the other. Sallust could say of Cato, "That he had rather be than appear good," but, indeed, this eulogium rose no higher than, as I just now hinted, to an inoffensiveness, rather than an active virtue. Had it occurred to the noble orator to represent, in his language, the glorious pleasures of a man secretly employed in beneficence and generosity, it would certainly have made a more charming page than any he has left behind him. How might a man, furnished with Gyges's secret, employ it in bringing together distant friends; laying snares for creating good-will in the room of groundless hatred; in removing the pangs of an unjust jealousy, the shyness of an imperfect reconciliation, and the tremor of an lawful love! Such a one could give confidence to bashful merit, and confusion to overbearing impudence.

Certain it is, that secret kindnesses done to mankind are as beautiful as secret injuries are detestable. To be invisibly good is as godlike as to be invisibly ill, diabolical. As degenerate as we are apt to say the age we live in is, there are still amongst us men of illustrious minds, who enjoy all the pleasures of good actions, except that of being commended for them. There happens, among other very worthy instances of a public spirit, one which I am obliged to discover, because I know not otherwise how to obey the commands of the benefactor. A citizen of London has given directions to Mr. Rayner, the writing master of St. Paul's school, to educate at his charge ten boys, who shall be nominated by me, in writing and accounts, until they shall be fit for any trade; I desire, therefore, such as know any proper objects for receiving this bounty, to give notice thereof to

Mr. Morphew, or Mr. Lillie; and they shall, if properly qualified, have instructions accordingly.

Actions of this kind have in them something so transcendent, that it is an injury to applaud them, and a diminution of that merit which consists in shunning our approbation. We shall therefore leave them to enjoy that glorious obscurity; and silently admire their virtue who can contemn the most delicious of human pleasures, that of receiving due praise. Such celestial dispositions very justly suspend the discovery of their benefactions, until they come where their actions cannot be misinterpreted, and receive their first congratulations in the company of angels.

ADVERTISEMENT

Whereas, Mr. Bickerstaff, by a letter bearing date this twenty-fourth of February, has received information that there are in and about the Royal Exchange a sort of people commonly known by the name of Whetters, who drink themselves into an intermediate state of being neither drunk nor sober before the hours of Exchange, or business; and in that condition buy and sell stocks, discount notes, and do many other acts of well-disposed citizens; this is to give notice that from this day forward no Whetter shall be able to give or indorse any note, or execute any other point of commerce, after the third half-pint, before the hour of one: and whoever shall transact any matter or matters with a Whetter, not being himself of that order, shall be conducted to Moor-fields upon the first application of his next of kin.

N. B. No tavern near the Exchange shall deliver wine to such as drink at the bar standing, except the same shall be three-parts of the best cider; and the master of the house shall produce a certificate of the same from Mr. Tintoret, or some other credible wine-painter.

Whereas the model of the intended Bedlam is now finished, and the edifice itself will be very suddenly begun, it is desired that all such as have relations whom they would recommend to our care would bring in their proofs with all speed, none being to be admitted, of course, but lovers, who are put into an immediate regimen. Young politicians also are received without fees or examination.

Complete. From the Tatler.

THE ART OF PLEASING

Principibus placuisse viris non ultima laus est.
                                    —*Hor.* Epist. I. 17, 35.

To please the great is not the smallest praise.
                                    —*Creech.*

THE desire of pleasing makes a man agreeable or unwelcome to those with whom he converses, according to the motive from which that inclination appears to flow. If your concern for pleasing others arises from an innate benevolence, it never fails of success; if from a vanity to excel, its disappointment is no less certain. What we call an agreeable man is he who is endowed with that natural bent to do acceptable things from a delight he takes in them merely as such; and the affectation of that character is what constitutes a fop. Under these leaders one may draw up all those who make any manner of figure, except in dumb show. A rational and select conversation is composed of persons who have the talent of pleasing with delicacy of sentiments flowing from habitual chastity of thought; but mixed company is frequently made up of pretenders to mirth, and is usually pestered with constrained, obscene, and painful witticisms. Now and then you meet with a man so exactly formed for pleasing that it is no matter what he is doing or saying—that is to say, that there need be no manner of importance in it to make him gain upon everybody who hears or beholds him. This felicity is not the gift of nature only, but must be attended with happy circumstances, which add a dignity to the familiar behavior which distinguishes him whom we call an agreeable man. It is from this that everybody loves and esteems Polycarpus. He is in the vigor of his age and the gayety of life, but has passed through very conspicuous scenes in it; though no soldier, he has shared the danger, and acted with great gallantry and generosity, on a decisive day of battle. To have those qualities which only make other men conspicuous in the world as it were supernumerary to him, is a circumstance which gives weight to his most indifferent actions; for as a known credit is ready cash to a trader, so is acknowledged merit immediate distinction, and serves in the place of equipage, to a gentleman. This renders Polycarpus graceful in mirth, important in business, and

regarded with love in every ordinary occurrence. But not to dwell upon characters which have such particular recommendations to our hearts, let us turn our thoughts rather to the methods of pleasing which must carry men through the world who cannot pretend to such advantages. Falling in with the particular humor or manner of one above you, abstracted from the general rules of good behavior, is the life of a slave. A parasite differs in nothing from the meanest servant but that the footman hires himself for bodily labor, subjected to go and come at the will of his master, but the other gives up his very soul: he is prostituted to speak, and professes to think, after the mode of him whom he courts. This servitude to a patron, in an honest nature would be more grievous than that of wearing his livery; therefore we shall speak of those methods only which are worthy and ingenuous.

The happy talent of pleasing either those above you or below you seems to be wholly owing to the opinion they have of your sincerity. This quality is to attend the agreeable man in all the actions of his life; and I think there need be no more said in honor of it than that it is what forces the approbation even of your opponents. The guilty man has an honor for the judge who, with justice, pronounces against him the sentence of death itself. The author of the sentence at the head of this paper was an excellent judge of human life, and passed his own in company the most agreeable that ever was in the world. Augustus lived amongst his friends as if he had his fortune to make in his own court. Candor and affability, accompanied with as much power as ever mortal was vested with, were what made him in the utmost manner agreeable among a set of admirable men, who had thoughts too high for ambition, and views too large to be gratified by what he could give them in the disposal of an empire, without the pleasures of their mutual conversation. A certain unanimity of taste and judgment, which is natural to all of the same order in the species, was the band of this society; and the emperor assumed no figure in it but what he thought was his due, from his private talents and qualifications, as they contributed to advance the pleasures and sentiments of the company. Cunning people, hypocrites, all who are but half virtuous or half wise, are incapable of tasting the refined pleasure of such an equal company as could wholly exclude the regard of fortune in their conversations. Horace, in the discourse from whence I take the hint of the present speculation, lays down excellent rules for conduct in conversation with men of power; but he speaks it with an air of one who had no need of such an application for anything which related to himself. It shows he understood what it was to be a skillful courtier, by just admonitions against importunity, and showing how forcible it was to speak modestly of your own wants. There is indeed something so shameless in taking all opportunities to speak of your own affairs that he who is guilty of it towards him on whom he depends, fares like the beggar who exposes his sores, which, instead of moving compassion, makes the man he begs of turn away from the object.

I cannot tell what is become of him, but I remember about sixteen years ago an honest fellow who so justly understood how disagreeable the mention or appearance of his wants would make him that I have often reflected upon him as a counterpart of Irus, whom I have formerly mentioned. This man, whom I have missed for some years in my walks, and have heard was some way employed about the army, made it a maxim that good wigs, delicate linen, and a cheerful air, were to a poor dependent the same that working tools are to a poor artificer. It was no small entertainment to me, who knew his circumstances, to see him, who had fasted two days, attribute the thinness they told him of to the violence of some gallantries he had lately been guilty of. The skillful dissembler carried this on with the utmost address; and if any suspected his affairs were narrow, it was attributed to indulging himself in some fashionable vice rather than an irreproachable poverty, which saved his credit with those on whom he depended.

The main art is to be as little troublesome as you can, and make all you hope for come rather as a favor from your patron than claim from you. But I am here prating of what is the method of pleasing so as to succeed in the world, when there are crowds who have — in city, town, court, and country — arrived to considerable acquisitions, and yet seem incapable of acting in any constant tenor of life, but have gone on from one successful error to another: therefore I think I may shorten this inquiry after the method of pleasing, and as the old beau said to his son, once for all, "Pray, Jack, be a fine gentleman," so may I to my reader abridge my instructions and finish the art of pleasing in a word, "Be rich."

Complete.

BENIGNITY

Consuetudinem benignitatis largitioni munerum longè antepono. Hæc est gravium hominum atque magnorum; illa quasi assentatorum populi, multitudinis levitatem voluptate quasi titillantium. — Cicero.

"I esteem a habit of benignity greatly preferable to munificence. The former is peculiar to great and distinguished persons; the latter belongs to flatterers of the people, who tickle the levity of the multitude with a kind of pleasure."

WHEN we consider the offices of human life, there is, methinks, something in what we ordinarily call generosity; which, when carefully examined, seems to flow rather from a loose and unguarded temper than an honest and liberal mind. For this reason it is absolutely necessary that all liberality should have for its basis and support, frugality. By this means the beneficent spirit works in a man from the convictions of reason, not from the impulses of passion. The generous man in the ordinary acceptation, without respect to the demands of his own family, will soon find upon the foot of his account that he has sacrificed to fools, knaves, flatterers, or the deservedly unhappy, all the opportunities of affording any future assistance where it ought to be. Let him therefore reflect that, if to bestow be in itself laudable, should not a man take care to secure an ability to do things praiseworthy as long as he lives? Or could there be a more cruel piece of raillery upon a man who should have reduced his fortune below the capacity of acting according to his natural temper than to say of him, "That gentleman was generous"? My beloved author therefore has, in the sentence on the top of my paper, turned his eye with a certain satiety from beholding the addresses to the people by largesses and public entertainments, which he asserts to be in general vicious, and are always to be regulated according to the circumstances of time and a man's own fortune. A constant benignity in commerce with the rest of the world, which ought to run through all a man's actions, has effects more useful to those whom you oblige, and is less ostentatious in yourself. He turns his recommendation of this virtue on commercial life; and, according to him, a citizen who is frank in his kindnesses, and abhors severity in his demands; he who, in buying, selling, lending, doing acts of good neighborhood, is just and easy; he who

appears naturally averse to disputes, and above the sense of little sufferings — bears a nobler character, and does much more good to mankind than any other man's fortune, without commerce, can possibly support. For the citizen, above all other men, has opportunities of arriving at "that highest fruit of wealth," to be liberal without the least expense of a man's own fortune. It is not to be denied but such a practice is liable to hazard; but this therefore adds to the obligation that, among traders, he who obliges is as much concerned to keep the favor a secret as he who receives it. The unhappy distinctions among us in England are so great that to celebrate the intercourse of commercial friendship, with which I am daily made acquainted, would be to raise the virtuous man so many enemies of the contrary party. I am obliged to conceal all I know of "Tom the Bounteous," who lends at the ordinary interest, to give men of less fortune opportunities of making greater advantages. He conceals, under a rough air and distant behavior, a bleeding compassion and womanish tenderness. This is governed by the most exact circumspection, that there is no industry wanting in the person whom he is to serve, and that he is guilty of no improper expenses. This I know of Tom; but who dare say it of so known a Tory? The same care I was forced to use some time ago in the report of another's virtue, and said fifty instead of a hundred, because the man I pointed at was a Whig. Actions of this kind are popular, without being invidious; for every man of ordinary circumstances looks upon a man who has this known benignity in his nature as a person ready to be his friend upon such terms as he ought to expect it; and the wealthy who may envy such a character can do no injury to its interests but by the imitation of it, in which the good citizens will rejoice to be rivaled. I know not how to form to myself a greater idea of human life than in what is the practice of some wealthy men whom I could name, that make no step to the improvement of their own fortunes wherein they do not also advance those of other men who would languish in poverty without that munificence. In a nation where there are so many public funds to be supported, I know not whether he can be called a good subject who does not embark some part of his fortune with the state, to whose vigilance he owes the security of the whole. This certainly is an immediate way of laying an obligation upon many, and extending your benignity the furthest a man can possibly

who is not engaged in commerce. But he who trades, besides giving the state some part of this sort of credit he gives his banker, may, in all the occurrences of his life, have his eye upon removing want from the door of the industrious, and defending the unhappy upright man from bankruptcy. Without this benignity, pride or vengeance will precipitate a man to choose the receipt of half his demands from one whom he has undone, rather than the whole from one to whom he has shown mercy. This benignity is essential to the character of a fair trader, and any man who designs to enjoy his wealth with honor and self-satisfaction; nay, it would not be hard to maintain that the practice of supporting good and industrious men would carry a man further even to his profit than indulging the propensity of serving and obliging the fortunate. My author argues on this subject in order to incline men's minds to those who want them most, after this manner: "We must always consider the nature of things, and govern ourselves accordingly. The wealthy man, when he has repaid you, is upon a balance with you; but the person whom you favored with a loan, if he be a good man, will think himself in your debt after he has paid you. The wealthy and the conspicuous are not obliged by the benefits you do them; they think they conferred a benefit when they received one. Your good offices are always suspected, and it is with them the same thing to expect their favor as to receive it. But the man below you, who knows, in the good you have done him, you respected himself more than his circumstances, does not act like an obliged man only to him from whom he has received a benefit, but also to all who are capable of doing him one. And whatever little offices he can do for you, he is so far from magnifying it that he will labor to extenuate it in all his actions and expressions. Moreover, the regard to what you do to a great man at best is taken notice of no further than by himself or his family; but what you do to a man of a humble fortune, provided always that he is a good and a modest man, raises the affections towards you of all men of that character, of which there are many, in the whole city."

There is nothing gains a reputation to a preacher so much as his own practice; I am therefore casting about what act of benignity is in the power of a spectator. Alas! that lies but in a very narrow compass; and I think the most immediately under my patronage are either players, or such whose circumstances bear an affinity with theirs. All, therefore, I am able to do at this time of this kind is to tell the town that on Friday, the eleventh of this instant, April, there will be performed, in York Buildings, a concert of vocal and instrumental music, for the benefit of Mr. Edward Keen, the father of twenty children; and that this day the haughty George Powell hopes all the good-natured part of the town will favor him, whom they applauded in "Alexander," "Timon," "Lear," and "Orestes," with their company this night, when he hazards all his heroic glory for their approbation in the humbler condition of honest Jack Falstaff.

Complete.

THE DREAM OF FAME

Hic manus ob patriam pugnando vulnera passi, —
Quique pii vates, et Phœbo digna locuti;
Inventas aut qui vitam excoluere per artes,
Quique sui memores alios fecere merendo.
—*Virg. Æn. VI. 660.*

Here patriots live, who, for their country's good,
In fighting fields were prodigal of blood;
Here poets worthy their inspiring god,
And of unblemish'd life, make their abode:
And searching wits, of more mechanic parts,
Who grac'd their age with new-invented arts:
Those who to worth their bounty did extend;
And those who knew that bounty to commend.
—*Dryden.*

FROM MY OWN APARTMENT, October 14th.

THERE are two kinds of immortality; that which the soul really enjoys after this life, and that imaginary existence by which men live in their fame and reputation. The best and greatest actions have proceeded from the prospect of the one or the other of these; but my design is to treat only of those who have chiefly proposed to themselves the latter, as the principal reward of their labors. It was for this reason that I excluded from my Tables of Fame all the great founders and votaries of religion; and it is for this reason also, that I am more than ordinary* anxious to do justice to the persons of whom I am now going to speak; for, since fame was the only end of all their

* Steele is above modern rules of syntax.

IX—225

enterprises and studies, a man cannot be too scrupulous in allotting them their due proportion of it. It was this consideration which made me call the whole body of the learned to my assistance; to many of whom I must own my obligations for the catalogues of illustrious persons, which they have sent me in upon this occasion. I yesterday employed the whole afternoon in comparing them with each other; which made so strong an impression upon my imagination, that they broke my sleep for the first part of the following night, and at length threw me into a very agreeable vision, which I shall beg leave to describe in all its particulars.

I dreamed that I was conveyed into a wide and boundless plain that was covered with prodigious multitudes of people, which no man could number. In the midst of it there stood a mountain, with its head above the clouds. The sides were extremely steep, and of such a particular structure that no creature which was not made in a human figure could possibly ascend it. On a sudden there was heard from the top of it a sound like that of a trumpet, but so exceeding sweet and harmonious, that it filled the hearts of those who heard it with raptures, and gave such high and delightful sensations, as seemed to animate and raise human nature above itself. This made me very much amazed to find so very few in that innumerable multitude who had ears fine enough to hear or relish this music with pleasure; but my wonder abated when, upon looking round me, I saw most of them attentive to three sirens, clothed like goddesses, and distinguished by the names of Sloth, Ignorance, and Pleasure. They were seated on three rocks, amidst a beautiful variety of groves, meadows, and rivulets, that lay on the borders of the mountain. While the base and groveling multitude of different nations, ranks, and ages were listening to these delusive deities, those of a more erect aspect and exalted spirit separated themselves from the rest, and marched in great bodies towards the mountain from whence they heard the sound, which still grew sweeter the more they listened to it.

On a sudden methought this select band sprang forward, with a resolution to climb the ascent, and follow the call of that heavenly music. Every one took something with him that he thought might be of assistance to him in his march. Several had their swords drawn, some carried rolls of paper in their hands, some had compasses, others quadrants, others telescopes, and

others pencils. Some had laurels on their heads, and others buskins on their legs; in short, there was scarce any instrument of a mechanic art, or liberal science, which was not made use of on this occasion. My good demon, who stood at my right hand during the course of this whole vision, observing in me a burning desire to join that glorious company, told me, "he highly approved that generous ardor with which I seemed transported; but, at the same time, advised me to cover my face with a mask all the while I was to labor on the ascent." I took his counsel without inquiring into his reasons. The whole body now broke into different parties, and began to climb the precipice by ten thousand different paths. Several got into little alleys, which did not reach far up the hill, before they ended, and led no further; and I observed that most of the artisans, which considerably diminished our number, fell into these paths.

We left another considerable body of adventurers behind us, who thought they had discovered byways up the hill, which proved so very intricate and perplexed that, after having advanced in them a little, they were quite lost among the several turns and windings; and though they were as active as any in their motions, they made but little progress in the ascent. These, as my guide informed me, were men of subtle tempers, and puzzled politics, who would supply the place of real wisdom with cunning and artifice. Among those who were far advanced in their way, there were some that by one false step fell backward and lost more ground in a moment than they had gained for many hours, or could be ever able to recover. We were now advanced very high, and observed that all the different paths which ran about the sides of the mountain began to meet in two great roads; which insensibly gathered the whole multitude of travelers into two great bodies. At a little distance from the entrance of each road there stood a hideous phantom that opposed our further passage. One of these apparitions had his right hand filled with darts, which he brandished in the face of all who came up that way. Crowds ran back at the appearance of it, and cried out, Death. The spectre that guarded the other road was Envy. She was not armed with weapons of destruction, like the former; but by dreadful hissings, noises of reproach, and a horrid distracted laughter, she appeared more frightful than Death itself, insomuch that abundance of our company were discouraged from passing any further, and some

appeared ashamed of having come so far. As for myself, I must confess, my heart shrunk within me at the sight of these ghastly appearances; but, on a sudden, the voice of the trumpet came more full upon us, so that we felt a new resolution reviving in us; and in proportion as this resolution grew, the terrors before us seemed to vanish. Most of the company, who had swords in their hands, marched on with great spirit, and an air of defiance, up the road that was commanded by Death; while others, who had thought and contemplation in their looks, went forward in a more composed manner up the road possessed by Envy. The way above these apparitions grew smooth and uniform, and was so delightful, that the travelers went on with pleasure, and in a little time arrived at the top of the mountain. They here began to breathe a delicious kind of ether, and saw all the fields about them covered with a kind of purple light, that made them reflect with satisfaction on their past toils; and diffused a secret joy through the whole assembly, which showed itself in every look and feature. In the midst of these happy fields there stood a palace of very glorious structure. It had four great folding doors, that faced the four several quarters of the world. On the top of it was enthroned the goddess of the mountain, who smiled upon her votaries, and sounded the silver trumpet which had called them up, and cheered them in their passage to her palace. They had now formed themselves into several divisions,—a band of historians taking their stations at each door, according to the persons whom they were to introduce.

On a sudden, the trumpet, which had hitherto sounded only a march, or a point of war, now swelled all its notes into triumph and exultation. The whole fabric shook, and the doors flew open. The first who stepped forward was a beautiful and blooming hero, and as I heard by the murmurs round me, Alexander the Great. He was conducted by a crowd of historians. The person who immediately walked before him was remarkable for an embroidered garment, who, not being well acquainted with the place, was conducting him to an apartment appointed for the reception of fabulous heroes. The name of this false guide was Quintus Curtius. But Arrian and Plutarch, who knew better the avenues of this palace, conducted him into the great hall, and placed him at the upper end of the first table. My good demon, that I might see the whole ceremony, conveyed me to a corner of this room, where I might perceive all that passed, without being seen myself. The next who entered was a charming virgin, leading in a venerable old man that was blind. Under her left arm she bore a harp, and on her head a garland. Alexander, who was very well acquainted with Homer, stood up at his entrance, and placed him on his right hand. The virgin, who it seems was one of the nine sisters that attended on the goddess of Fame, smiled with an ineffable grace at their meeting, and retired.

Julius Cæsar was now coming forward; and, though most of the historians offered their service to introduce him, he left them at the door, and would have no conductor but himself.

The next who advanced was a man of a homely but cheerful aspect, and attended by persons of greater figure than any that appeared on this occasion. Plato was on his right hand, and Xenophon on his left. He bowed to Homer, and sat down by him. It was expected that Plato would himself have taken a place next to his master, Socrates; but on a sudden there was heard a great clamor of disputants at the door, who appeared with Aristotle at the head of them. That philosopher, with some rudeness, but great strength of reason, convinced the whole table that a title to the fifth place was his due, and took it accordingly.

He had scarce sat down, when the same beautiful virgin that had introduced Homer, brought in another, who hung back at the entrance, and would have excused himself, had not his modesty been overcome by the invitation of all who sat at the table. His guide and behavior made me easily conclude it was Virgil. Cicero next appeared and took his place. He had inquired at the door for one Lucceius to introduce him; but, not finding him there, he contented himself with the attendance of many other writers, who all, except Sallust, appeared highly pleased with the office.

We waited some time in expectation of the next worthy, who came in with a great retinue of historians whose names I could not learn, most of them being natives of Carthage. The person thus conducted, who was Hannibal, seemed much disturbed, and could not forbear complaining to the board of the affronts he had met with among the Roman historians, "who attempted," says he, "to carry me into the subterraneous apartment; and perhaps would have done it, had it not been for the impartiality of this gentleman," pointing to Polybius, "who was the only

person, except my own countrymen, that was willing to conduct me hither."

The Carthaginian took his seat, and Pompey entered with great dignity in his own person, and preceded by several historians. Lucan the poet was at the head of them, who, observing Homer and Virgil at the table, was going to sit down himself, had not the latter whispered him that whatever pretense he might otherwise have had, he forfeited his claim to it, by coming in as one of the historians. Lucan was so exasperated with the repulse, that he muttered something to himself; and was heard to say, "that since he could not have a seat among them himself, he would bring in one who alone had more merit than their whole assembly," upon which he went to the door, and brought in Cato of Utica. That great man approached the company with such an air that showed he contemned the honor which he laid a claim to. Observing the seat opposite to Cæsar was vacant, he took possession of it, and spoke two or three smart sentences upon the nature of precedency, which, according to him, consisted not in place, but in intrinsic merit; to which he added, "that the most virtuous man, wherever he was seated, was always at the upper end of the table." Socrates, who had a great spirit of raillery with his wisdom, could not forbear smiling at a virtue which took so little pains to make itself agreeable. Cicero took the occasion to make a long discourse in praise of Cato, which he uttered with much vehemence. Cæsar answered him with a great deal of seeming temper; but, as I stood at a great distance from them, I was not able to hear one word of what they said. But I could not forbear taking notice, that, in all the discourse which passed at the table, a word or nod from Homer decided the controversy.

After a short pause, Augustus appeared, looking round him with a serene and affable countenance upon all the writers of his age, who strove among themselves which of them should show him the greatest marks of gratitude and respect. Virgil rose from the table to meet him; and though he was an acceptable guest to all, he appeared more such to the learned than the military worthies.

The next man astonished the whole table with his appearance. He was slow, solemn, and silent in his behavior, and wore a raiment curiously wrought with hieroglyphics. As he came into the middle of the room, he threw back the skirt of it, and dis-

covered a golden thigh. Socrates, at the sight of it, declared against keeping company with any who were not made of flesh and blood; and, therefore, desired Diogenes the Laertian to lead him to the apartment allotted for fabulous heroes, and worthies of dubious existence. At his going out, he told them, "that they did not know whom they dismissed; that he was now Pythagoras, the first of philosophers, and that formerly he had been a very brave man at the siege of Troy." "That may be very true," said Socrates; "but you forget that you have likewise been a very great harlot in your time." This exclusion made way for Archimedes, who came forward with a scheme of mathematical figures in his hand, among which I observed a cone and a cylinder.

Seeing this table full, I desired my guide, for variety, to lead me to the fabulous apartment, the roof of which was painted with gorgons, chimeras, and centaurs, with many other emblematical figures, which I wanted both time and skill to unriddle. The first table was almost full: at the upper end sat Hercules, leaning an arm upon his club; on his right hand were Achilles and Ulysses, and between them Æneas; on his left were Hector, Theseus, and Jason; the lower end had Orpheus, Æsop, Phalaris, and Musæus. The ushers seemed at a loss for a twelfth man, when, methought, to my great joy and surprise, I heard some at the lower end of the table mention Isaac Bickerstaff; but those of the upper end received it with disdain, and said, "if they must have a British worthy, they would have Robin Hood." While I was transported with the honor that was done me, and burning with envy against my competitor, I was awakened by the noise of the cannon which were then fired for the taking of Mons. I should have been very much troubled at being thrown out of so pleasing a vision on any other occasion; but thought it an agreeable change to have my thoughts diverted from the greatest among the dead and fabulous heroes to the most famous among the real and the living.

Complete. From the Tatler.

OF PATRIOTISM AND PUBLIC SPIRIT

———*Fuit hæc sapientia quondam
Publica privatis secernere.*
—Hor. Ars Poet. 396.

"Our sage forefathers wisely understood
To sep'rate public from the private good."

FROM MY OWN APARTMENT, June 9th.

WHEN men look into their own bosoms, and consider the generous seeds which are there planted, that might, if rightly cultivated, ennoble their lives, and make their virtue venerable to futurity; how can they, without tears, reflect on the universal degeneracy from that public spirit, which ought to be the first and principal motive of all their actions? In the Grecian and Roman nations, they were wise enough to keep up this great incentive, and it was impossible to be in the fashion without being a patriot. All gallantry had its first source from hence; and to want a warmth for the public welfare was a defect so scandalous that he who was guilty of it had no pretense to honor or manhood. What makes the depravity among us in this behalf the more vexatious and irksome to reflect upon is that the contempt of life is carried as far amongst us as it could be in those memorable people; and we want only a proper application of the qualities which are frequent among us, to be as worthy as they. There is hardly a man to be found who will not fight upon any occasion which he thinks may taint his own honor. Were this motive as strong in everything that regards the public as it is in this our private case, no man would pass his life away without having distinguished himself by some gallant instance of his zeal towards it in the respective incidents of his life and profession. But it is so far otherwise, that there cannot at present be a more ridiculous animal than one who seems to regard the good of others. He, in civil life, whose thoughts turn upon schemes which may be of general benefit, without further reflection, is called a projector; and the man whose mind seems intent upon glorious achievements, a knight-errant. The ridicule among us runs strong against laudable actions; nay, in the ordinary course of things, and the common regards of life, negligence of the public is an epidemic vice. The brewer in his excise, the merchant in his customs, and, for aught we know, the soldier in his muster rolls, think never the worse of themselves for being guilty of their respective frauds towards the public. This evil is come to such a fantastical height that he is a man of a public spirit, and heroically affected to his country, who can go so far as even to turn usurer with all he has in her funds. There is not a citizen in whose imagination such a one does not appear in the same light of glory as Codrus, Scævola, or any other great name in old Rome. Were it not for the heroes of so much per cent. as have regard enough for themselves and their nation to trade with her with their wealth, the very notion of public love would long before now have vanished from among us. But however general custom may hurry us away in the stream of a common error, there is no evil, no crime, so great as that of being cold in matters which relate to the common good. This is in nothing more conspicuous than in a certain willingness to receive anything that tends to the diminution of such as have been conspicuous instruments in our service. Such inclinations proceed from the most low and vile corruption, of which the soul of man is capable. This effaces not only the practice, but the very approbation of honor and virtue; and has had such an effect that, to speak freely, the very sense of public good has no longer a part even of our conversations. Can then the most generous motive of life, the good of others, be so easily banished the breast of man? Is it possible to draw all our passions inward? Shall the boiling heat of youth be sunk in pleasures, the ambition of manhood in selfish intrigues? Shall all that is glorious, all that is worth the pursuit of great minds, be so easily rooted out? When the universal bent of a people seems diverted from the sense of their common good and common glory, it looks like a fatality, and crisis of impending misfortune.

The generous nations we just now mentioned understood this so very well that there was hardly an oration ever made which did not turn upon this general sense, "That the love of their country was the first and most essential quality in an honest mind." Demosthenes, in a cause wherein his fame, reputation, and fortune, were embarked, puts his all upon this issue; "Let the Athenians," says he, "be benevolent to me, as they think I have been zealous for them." This great and discerning orator knew there was nothing else in nature could bear him up against his adversaries, but this one quality of having shown himself willing or able to serve his country. This certainly is the test of merit; and the first foundation for deserving goodwill is having it yourself. The adversary of this orator at that time was Æschines, a man of wily arts and skill in the world, who could, as occasion served, fall in with a national start of passion, or sullenness of humor; which a whole nation is sometimes taken with as well as a private man, and by that means divert them from their common sense, into an aversion for

receiving anything in its true light. But when Demosthenes had awakened his audience with that one hint of judging by the general tenor of his life towards them, his services bore down his opponent before him, who fled to the covert of his mean arts, until some more favorable occasion should offer against the superior merit of Demosthenes.

It were to be wished that love of their country were the first principle of action in men of business, even for their own sakes; for, when the world begins to examine into their conduct, the generality, who have no share in, or hopes of any part in power or riches, but what is the effect of their own labor or property, will judge of them by no other method than that of how profitable their administration has been to the whole. They who are out of the influence of men's fortune or favor will let them stand or fall by this one only rule; and men who can bear being tried by it are always popular in their fall. Those who cannot suffer such a scrutiny are contemptible in their advancement.

But I am here running into shreds of maxims from reading Tacitus this morning, that has driven me from my recommendation of public spirit, which was the intended purpose of this lucubration. There is not a more glorious instance of it than in the character of Regulus. This same Regulus was taken prisoner by the Carthaginians, and was sent by them to Rome, in order to demand some Punic noblemen, who were prisoners, in exchange for himself; and was bound by an oath, that he would return to Carthage if he failed in his commission. He proposes this to the senate, who were in suspense upon it, which Regulus observing, without having the least notion of putting the care of his own life in competition with the public good, desired them to consider that he was old and almost useless; that those demanded in exchange were men of daring tempers, and great merit in military affairs; and wondered they would make any doubt of permitting him to go back to the short tortures prepared for him at Carthage, where he should have the advantage of ending a long life both gloriously and usefully. This generous advice was consented to; and he took his leave of his country and his weeping friends, to go to certain death, with that cheerful composure, as a man, after the fatigue of business in a court or a city, retires to the next village for the air.

Complete. From the Tatler.

OF MEN WHO ARE NOT THEIR OWN MASTERS

Stultitia patiuntur opes.
— *Hor.* Lib. I., Epist. XVIII. 29.

"Their folly pleads the privilege of wealth."

FROM MY OWN APARTMENT, June 2d.

I HAVE received a letter which accuses me of partiality in the administration of the censorship; and says that I have been very free with the lower part of mankind, but extremely cautious in representations of matters which concern men of condition. This correspondent takes upon him also to say, the upholsterer was not undone by turning politician, but became bankrupt by trusting his goods to persons of quality; and demands of me that I should do justice upon such as brought poverty and distress upon the world below them, while they themselves were sunk in pleasures and luxury, supported at the expense of those very persons whom they treated with negligence, as if they did not know whether they dealt with them or not. This is a very heavy accusation, both of me, and such as the man aggrieved accuses me of tolerating. For this reason I resolved to take this matter into consideration; and upon very little meditation could call to my memory many instances which made this complaint far from being groundless. The root of this evil does not always proceed from injustice in the men of figure, but often from a false grandeur which they take upon them in being unacquainted with their own business; not considering how mean a part they act, when their names and characters are subjected to the little arts of their servants and dependants. The overseers of the poor are a people who have no great reputation for the discharge of their trust; but are much less scandalous than the overseers of the rich. Ask a young fellow of a great estate who was that odd fellow that spoke to him in a public place, he answers, "one that does my business." It is, with many, a natural consequence of being a man of fortune that they are not to understand the disposal of it; and they long to come to their estates, only to put themselves under new guardianship. Nay, I have known a young fellow, who was regularly bred an attorney, and was a very expert one until he had an estate fallen to him. The moment that happened, he, who could

before prove the next land he cast his eye upon his own, and was so sharp that a man at first sight would give him a small sum for a general receipt, whether he owed him anything or not; such a one, I say, have I seen, upon coming to an estate, forget all his diffidence of mankind, and become the most manageable thing breathing. He immediately wanted a stirring man to take upon him his affairs, to receive and pay, and do everything which he himself was now too fine a gentleman to understand. It is pleasant to consider that he who would have got an estate, had he not come to one, will certainly starve because one fell to him; but such contradictions are we to ourselves, and any change of life is insupportable to some natures.

It is a mistaken sense of superiority to believe a figure or equipage gives men precedence to their neighbors. Nothing can create respect from mankind, but laying obligations upon them; and it may very reasonably be concluded that if it were put into a due balance, according to the true state of the account, many who believe themselves in possession of a large share of dignity in the world must give place to their inferiors. The greatest of all distinctions in civil life is that of debtor and creditor; and there needs no great progress in logic to know which, in that case, is the advantageous side. He who can say to another, "Pray, master," or, "Pray, my lord, give me my own," can as justly tell him, "It is a fantastical distinction you take upon you to pretend to pass upon the world for my master or lord, when, at the same time that I wear your livery, you owe me wages; or, while I wait at your door, you are ashamed to see me until you have paid my bill."

The good old way among the gentry of England, to maintain their pre-eminence over the lower rank, was by their bounty, munificence, and hospitality; and it is a very unhappy change, if at present, by themselves or their agents, the luxury of the gentry is supported by the credit of the trader. This is what my correspondent pretends to prove out of his own books, and those of his whole neighborhood. He has the confidence to say that there is a mughouse near Longacre, where you may every evening hear an exact account of distresses of this kind. One complains that such a lady's finery is the occasion that his own wife and daughter appear so long in the same gown. Another, that all the furniture of her visiting apartment are no more hers than the scenery of a play are the proper goods of the actress. Nay, at the lower end of the same table, you may hear a butcher and poulterer say that, at their proper charge, all that family has been maintained since they last came to town.

The free manner in which people of fashion are discoursed on at such meetings is but a just reproach of their failures in this kind; but the melancholy relations of the great necessities tradesmen are driven to, who support their credit in spite of the faithless promises which are made them, and the abatement which they suffer when paid by the extortion of upper servants, is what would stop the most thoughtless man in the career of his pleasures, if rightly represented to him.

If this matter be not very speedily amended, I shall think fit to print exact lists of all persons who are not at their own disposal, though above the age of twenty-one; and as the trader is made bankrupt for absence from his abode, so shall the gentleman for being at home, if, when Mr. Morphew calls, he cannot give an exact account of what passes in his own family. After this fair warning, no one ought to think himself hardly dealt with, if I take upon me to pronounce him no longer master of his estate, wife, or family, than he continues to improve, cherish, and maintain them upon the basis of his own property, without incursions upon his neighbor in any of these particulars.

According to that excellent philosopher, Epictetus, we are all but acting parts in a play; and it is not a distinction in itself to be high or low, but to become the parts we are to perform. I am by my office prompter on this occasion; and shall give those who are a little out in their parts such soft hints as may help them to proceed, without letting it be known to the audience they were out; but if they run quite out of character, they must be called off the stage, and receive parts more suitable to their genius. Servile complaisance shall degrade a man from his honor and quality, and haughtiness be yet more debased. Fortune shall no longer appropriate distinctions, but nature direct us in the disposition both of respect and discountenance. As there are tempers made for command, and others for obedience, so there are men born for acquiring possessions, and others incapable of being other than mere lodgers in the houses of their ancestors, and have it not in their very composition to be proprietors of anything. These men are moved only by the mere effects of impulse: then good-will and disesteem are to be regarded equally; for neither is the effect of their judgment. This loose temper is

that which makes a man, what Sallust so well remarks to happen frequently in the same person, to be covetous of what is another's, and profuse of what is his own. This sort of men is usually amiable to ordinary eyes; but, in the sight of reason, nothing is laudable but what is guided by reason. The covetous prodigal is of all others the worst man in society. If he would but take time to look into himself, he would find his soul all over gashed with broken vows and promises; and his retrospect on his actions would not consist of reflections upon those good resolutions after mature thought, which are the true life of a reasonable creature, but the nauseous memory of imperfect pleasures, idle dreams, and occasioned amusements. To follow such dissatisfying pursuits, is it possible to suffer the ignominy of being unjust? I remember in Tully's "Epistle," in the recommendation of a man to an affair which had no manner of relation to money, it is said, "You may trust him, for he is a frugal man." It is certain he who has not regard to strict justice in the commerce of life can be capable of no good action in any other kind; but he who lives below his income lays up, every moment of life, armor against a base world, that will cover all his frailties while he is so fortified, and exaggerate them when he is naked and defenseless.

ADVERTISEMENT

A stagecoach sets out exactly at six from Nando's coffeehouse to Mr. Tiptoe's dancing school, and returns at eleven every evening, for one shilling and fourpence.

N. B. Dancing shoes, not exceeding four inches height in the heels, and periwigs, not exceeding three feet in length, are carried in the coach box gratis.

Complete. From the Tatler.

SIR JAMES STEPHEN

(1789-1859)

SIR JAMES STEPHEN, one of the noted essayists of the Edinburgh Review, was born in London, January 3d, 1789. He was a graduate of Cambridge University, and a successful lawyer, author of a volume of "Essays," a "History of France," and "Desultory and Systematic Reading," a lecture published in 1853. He served for some time as Undersecretary for the Colonies, and on his retirement was made Knight Commander of the Bath. In 1849 he became Regius Professor of Modern History at Cambridge. The appointment is credited to the influence of his essays in the Edinburgh Review, which were collected and republished under the title of "Essays on Ecclesiastical Biography and Other Subjects." He died at Coblenz September 15th, 1859.

CHRISTIANITY AND PROGRESS

IF SCIPIO had his dream of colloquies after death with the wise and good of all ages, the Eskimo has his heaven where sealskins may be procured in placid seas, and undying lamps are fed with inexhaustible supplies of the odorous grease of bears. Mahomet promised his Arabian converts "rivers of incorruptible water and rivers of milk, the taste whereof changeth not; gardens planted with shady trees, in each of which shall be two flowing fountains; couches, the linings whereof shall be of thick silk interwoven with gold, and beautous damsels, refraining their eyes from beholding any but their spouses, having complexions like rubies and pearls, and fine black eyes." The stream can rise no higher than the fountain. Our ideas of immortal good are but amplifications of our mortal enjoyments. To sublimate our conceptions of felicity, by associating together all innocent and not incompatible delights, and by subtracting from them every alloy of pain, satiety, and languor, is to create for ourselves the only heaven with the contemplation of which hope can be sustained and activity invigorated. He who carefully surveys the Elysium which reason or imagination has laid out and

planted for him in the next world will acquire far better acquaintance with the "happy gardens" to which choice or fortune has directed him in this. Judged by this standard, and giving him credit for having made his public confessions with entire candor, the author of the "Theory of a Future Life" may be esteemed a wise and happy man—wise, because he has no fear of acknowledging to himself or to others the dependence of his spiritual on his animal economy, and affects no superhuman disdain of mere bodily gratifications; and happy, because his felicity consists in bringing the body into that unresisting servitude to the mind, without which freedom and serenity are but empty words. Such as is his paradise in the highest conceivable degree, such in the highest attainable degree must be his earthly Eden. Dismiss it if you will as a midsummer night's dream; yet must it be confessed that it is such a dream as could visit no slumbers but those of one whose fancy was pure from sensual defilement, and whose intellect had been trained to active exercise and to close self-observation. Or, give the theorist credit for nothing more than having skillfully selected the most alluring possibilities of future good from the many celestial schemes with which the poetry and the poetical prose of all ages abounds, and still it will be true that the choice has been guided by opinions such as every one would wish to adopt, and by tastes which in our better moments we should all desire to gratify. The time subtracted, for such visions, from the scarcely more substantial delights among which we are living, will send us back to the cares of life, not less fitted resolutely to endure them; and to the pleasures of life, not less prepared wisely to enjoy them. . . .

There is in Christianity an expansive power, sometimes repressed, but never destroyed; and that latent energy the Christian strives to draw forth into life and action. Those mysteries which shroud the condition and the prospects of our race, however inscrutable to the slaves of appetite, are not absolutely impervious to a soul purified by devout contemplation; and to these empyreal heights he aspires at once to point and to lead the way. To him whose foot is firmly planted on the eternal verities of heaven, there belong motives of such force, and a courage so undaunted, as should burst through all resistance; and he calls on those who enjoy this high privilege to assert their native supremacy above the sordid ambition, the frivolities, and the virulence of the lower world. The voice thus raised in expostulation will die away, not unheeded by the interior circle he addresses, nor unblessed by a meet recompense; but unrewarded, we fear, by the accomplishment of these exalted purposes. Eloquent as is the indignation with which our anonymous monitor regards the low level to which divine and human literature has fallen amongst us, and mean as is his estimate of the pursuits with which the men of his own days are engaged, a hope may perhaps, without presumption, be indulged, that less fastidious and not less capable judges will pronounce a more lenient sentence on us and on our doings.

In the great cycle of human affairs there are many stages, each essential to the consummation of the designs of Providence, and each separated by broad distinctions from the rest. They whose province it is to censure, and they whose desire it is to improve their age, will never find their sacred fires extinct from the mere want of fuel. History and theory are always at hand with humiliating contrasts to the times we live in. That men have been better or might be better than they are has been true since the first fathers of our race returned to their native dust, and will still be true as long as our planet shall be inhabited by their descendants. But below the agitated surface of the ocean, under currents are silently urging forward, on their destined path, the waters of the mighty deep, themselves impelled by that Power which none may question or resist. Human society obeys a similar influence. Laws as anomalous in appearance, as uniform in reality, as those which direct the planetary movements, determine the present state, and regulate the progress of commonwealths, whether political, literary, or religious. Christianity demands the belief, and experience justifies the hope, that their ultimate tendency is towards the universal dominion of piety and virtue. But it is neither pious nor rational to suppose that this consummation can be attained by any sequence of identical causes constantly working out similar effects. The best generations, like the best men, are those which possess an individual and distinctive character. A chain of splendid biographies constitutes the history of past centuries. Whoever shall weave the chronicles of our own must take for his staple statistics illuminated by a skillful generalization. Once every eye was directed to the leaders of the world; now all are turned to the masses of which it is composed. Instead of Newtons presiding over royal societies, we have Dr. Birkbecks lecturing at mechanics' institutes. If no Wolseys arise to found colleges like that of Christ Church, Joseph

IX—226

Lancaster and William Bell have emulated each other in works not less momentous at the Borough Road and Baldwin's Gardens. We people continents, though we have ceased to discover them. We abridge folios for the many, though we no longer write them for the few. . . .

We know not how to regret that Genius has from the moment abdicated her austere supremacy, and stooped to be popular and plain. Mackintosh surrendered his philosophy to the compilation of a familiar history of England. Faithless to his Peris and Glendowers, Mr. Moore is teaching the commonalty of the realm the sad tale of the woes inflicted on the land of his birth. No longer emulous of Porson, the Bishop of London devotes his learned desire to preparing cheap and easy lessons for the householders of his diocese. Lord Brougham arrests the current of his eloquence to instruct mechanics in the principles of the sciences which they are reducing to daily practice. Tracts for the times are extorted from the depositories of ecclesiastical tradition, obedient to the general impulse which they condemn, and constrained to render the Church argumentative, that they may render her oracular. Nay, the author of the « Natural History of Enthusiasm » himself, despite his own protests, yields at length to the current, and has become the periodical writer of monthly tracts, where, in good round controversial terms, the superficial multitude are called to sit in judgment on the claims of the early fathers to sound doctrine, good morals, and common sense. Let who will repine at what has passed, and at what is passing, if they will allow us to rejoice in what is to come. If we witness the growth of no immortal reputations, we see the expansion of universal intelligence. The disparities of human understanding are much the same in all times; but it is when the general level is the highest that the mighty of the earth rise to the most commanding eloquence.

From a review of « Physical Theory of Another Life.»

LAURENCE STERNE

(1713–1768)

THE author of « Tristram Shandy » and the « Sentimental Journey » was as incapable of writing an essay according to rule as he was of telling a story with a plot or a purpose. The « Chapter on Sleep » in « Tristram Shandy » is an essay, to be sure, complete in itself, and in every way admirable. It is one of the best in the English language, but it is accidental as far as Sterne is concerned. It was his deliberate and lifelong habit to begin nowhere in particular and never to end at all. This with his extensive and curious learning (which he is unkindly charged with borrowing in a great measure from Burton's « Anatomy of Melancholy ») constitutes his peculiar excellence and his greatest charm. Time was when the « Sentimental Journey » and « Tristram Shandy » were considered improper books for family reading, but they have come to be « classics,» and it is well known that all classics are not only safe but necessary *virginibus puerisque.* It must be noted also that whoever sets out to get his morals corrupted by Sterne will have much labor for his pains,—for it is a « Shandean » habit to tantalize the reader with fifty pages of curious philosophy as the price of getting at the suspicion of a doubtful jest. And moreover, though nothing is more delightful than five minutes of « Tristram Shandy,» nothing could be more calculated to break the spirit than five hours of it. This, however, is not to Sterne's discredit. He is deliberately disconnected, writing in defiance of all the known laws of the mind's operation and still succeeding in impressing himself on the English literature of all time. He is not « purely original,» for he followed Rabelais; but while Rabelais has found many imitators, Sterne himself has defied all. He was the first and last representative of a school of English humor of which the world needs nothing more than he has given it,—though of that it could spare nothing. He was born at Clonmel, Ireland, November 24th, 1713. His father was an English officer whose regiment was stationed at Clonmel, and Sterne, after remaining with the regiment until his tenth year, was then sent to school in England. He graduated at Cambridge in 1736, and took orders in the English Established Church, in the ministry of which he remained until his death, March 18th, 1768. His « Sermons » and several volumes of his letters are included with « Tristram Shandy » and the « Sentimental Journey » to make up the total of his works. The « Sermons » are described as

« Shandean » in their style, and when first published they were very popular. His best sermon, however, is the story of Le Fevre, in consideration of which he may fairly have asked the recording angel to shed tears enough over the unclerical parts of « Tristram Shandy » to allow its author to pass into heaven in full canonicals without the formality of a trial.

W. V. B.

A CHAPTER ON SLEEP

I WISH I could write a chapter upon sleep.

A fitter occasion could never have presented itself than what this moment offers, when all the curtains of the family are drawn, the candles put out, and no creature's eyes are open but a single one — for the other has been shut these twenty years — of my mother's nurse.

It is a fine subject.

And yet, as fine as it is, I would undertake to write a dozen chapters upon buttonholes, both quicker and with more fame, than a single chapter upon this.

Buttonholes! there is something lively in the very idea of 'em; and trust me, when I get amongst 'em, you gentry with great beards, look as grave as you will, I'll make merry work with my buttonholes — I shall have 'em all to myself,—'tis a maiden subject — I shall run foul of no man's wisdom or fine saying in it.

But for sleep, I know I shall make nothing of it before I begin; I am no dab at your fine sayings, in the first place; and in the next, I cannot for my soul set a grave face upon a bad matter, and tell the world 'tis the refuge of the unfortunate, the enfranchisement of the prisoner, the downy lap of the hopeless, the weary, and the broken-hearted; nor could I set out with a lie in my mouth, by affirming that of all the soft and delicious functions of our nature, by which the great Author of it, in his bounty, has been pleased to recompense the sufferings wherewith his justice and his good pleasure has wearied us, that this is the chiefest (I know pleasures worth ten of it); or what a happiness it is to man, after the anxieties and passions of the day are over, and he lies down upon his back, that his soul shall be so seated within him, that whichever way she turns her eyes, the heavens shall look calm and sweet above her; no desire, or fear, or doubt, that troubles the air; nor any difficulty, past, present, or to come, that the imagination may not pass over without offense, in that sweet secession.

"God's blessing," said Sancho Panza, "be upon the man who first invented this self-same thing called Sleep; it covers a man all over like a cloak." Now there is more to me in this, and it speaks warmer to my heart and affections than all the dissertations squeezed out of the heads of the learned together upon the subject.

Not that I altogether disapprove of what Montaigne advances upon it; 'tis admirable in its way. I quote by memory.

The world enjoys other pleasures, says he, as they do that of sleep, without tasting or feeling it as it slips and passes by. We should study and ruminate upon it, in order to render proper thanks to him who grants it to us. For this end, I cause myself to be disturbed in my sleep, that I may the better and more sensibly relish it; and yet I see few, says he again, who live with less sleep, when need requires. My body is capable of a firm, but not of a violent and sudden agitation; I evade of late all violent exercises, I am never weary with walking, but from my youth I never liked to ride upon pavements. I love to lie hard and alone, and even without my wife. This last word may stagger the faith of the world; but remember, "*La Vraisemblance*" (as Bayle says in the affair of Liceti) "*n'est pas toujours du Cote de la Verite*." And so much for sleep.

Complete. "Life and Opinions of Tristram Shandy," Book IV., Chap. xv.

A PEASANT'S PHILOSOPHY

A SHOE coming loose from the forefoot of the thill horse, at the beginning of the ascent of Mount Taurira, the postilion dismounted, twisted the shoe off, and put it in his pocket. As the ascent was of five or six miles, and that horse our main dependence, I made a point of having the shoe fastened on again as well as we could; but the postilion had thrown away the nails, and the hammer in the chaise box being of no great use without them, I submitted to go on. He had not mounted half a mile higher, when, coming to a flinty piece of road, the poor devil lost a second shoe, and from off his other forefoot. I then got out of the chaise in good earnest; and seeing a house about a quarter

now and then a little to the tune, then intermitted, and joined her old man again as their children and grandchildren danced before them.

It was not till the middle of the second dance, when, for some pauses in the movement, wherein they all seemed to look up, I fancied I could distinguish an elevation of spirit different from that which is the cause or the effect of simple jollity. In a word, I thought I beheld Religion mixing in the dance; but as I had never seen her so engaged, I should have looked upon it now as one of the illusions of an imagination which is eternally misleading me, had not the old man, as soon as the dance ended, said that this was their constant way; and that all his life long he had made it a rule, after supper was over, to call out his family to dance and rejoice; believing, he said, that a cheerful and contented mind was the best sort of thanks to Heaven that an illiterate peasant could pay. Or a learned prelate either, said I.

From the "Sentimental Journey."

of a mile to the left hand, with a great deal to do I prevailed upon the postilion to turn up to it. The look of the house, and of everything about it, as we drew nearer, soon reconciled me to the disaster. It was a little farmhouse, surrounded with about twenty acres of vineyard, and about as much corn; and close to the house on one side was a *potagerie* of an acre and a half, full of everything which could make plenty in a French peasant's house; and on the other side was a little wood, which furnished wherewithal to dress it. It was about eight in the evening when I got to the house; so I left the postilion to manage his point as he could,—and for mine, I walked directly into the house.

The family consisted of an old gray-headed man and his wife, with five or six sons and sons in law and their several wives, and a joyous genealogy out of them. They were all sitting down together to their lentil soup; a large wheaten loaf was in the middle of the table; and a flagon of wine at each end of it promised joy through the stages of the repast; 'twas a feast of love. The old man rose up to meet me, and with a respectful cordiality would have me sit down at the table; my heart was set down the moment I entered the room, so I sat down at once like a son of the family; and to invest myself in the character as speedily as I could, I instantly borrowed the old man's knife, and, taking up the loaf, cut myself a hearty luncheon; and as I did it, I saw a testimony in every eye, not only of an honest welcome, but of a welcome mixed with thanks that I had not seemed to doubt it. Was it this,—or tell me, Nature, what else it was,—that made this morsel so sweet; and to what magic I owe it, that the draught I took of their flagon was so delicious with it, that they remain upon my palate to this hour? If the supper was to my taste, the grace which followed it was much more so.

When supper was over, the old man gave a knock upon the table with the haft of his knife, to bid them prepare for the dance. The moment the signal was given, the women and girls ran all together into a back apartment to tie up their hair, and the young men to the door to wash their faces and change their sabots; and in three minutes every soul was ready, upon a little esplanade before the house, to begin. The old man and his wife came out last, and, placing me betwixt them, sat down upon a sofa of turf by the door. The old man had some fifty years ago been no mean performer upon the vielle; and at the age he was then of, touched it well enough for the purpose. His wife sung

ROBERT LOUIS STEVENSON

(1850–1894)

AFTER the death of Thackeray and Dickens, English prose fiction tended more and more towards "the novel with a purpose," and in the last quarter of the century, when Stevenson first made himself felt, the reading public was wholly under the power of fiction, which was properly classed as "degenerate." Much of it was radically unhealthy. It is no exaggeration to say that tons of fair, white paper were desecrated by "studies" of problems of physiology and psychology on which no healthy mind will wish to dwell—if for no other reason than that their existence as "problems" does not become evident except through abnormality in its most diseased and generally its most contagious form. Stevenson brought about a strong reaction. His "Doctor Jekyll and Mr. Hyde," the prose masterpiece of the nineteenth century, was in some sense a "problem book," but it deals with the whole problem of human life as a struggle between good and evil. Stevenson, who saw things, as he expresses it, "bare to the buff," felt this struggle in himself, and saw it everywhere in the world outside of himself. The expression he gives it in "Doctor Jekyll and Mr. Hyde" verges on the supernatural. In this book at least, Scott's greatest pupil is greater than his master. The romantic novel and the prose allegory found their perfect union and their climax in this book, which stands quite unique in English literature, since Stevenson himself never approached it afterwards. His other stories and novels show, however, a great and compelling genius for narration. In some of them it is almost too great to be endurable. "Treasure Island," for instance, is professedly a book for boys, but any one of any age who surrenders himself to it is apt to feel an effect from it comparable to nothing less violent than that of brandy. This intensity appears in all Stevenson's work. He had an extraordinary power of focusing all his energies,—a power as dangerous as it is unusual. It belongs only to genius and it cannot be exercised except at the expense of vitality. What Landor knew of "the pangs of approaching the gods," Stevenson felt as he gradually burned his life away in the brilliant flame of his own powers. He welcomed death with joy, as the reward of one who had done his best without sparing himself. There is nothing more pathetic in literature than the stanza he wrote for his own epitaph:—

"Under the wide and starry sky,
Dig me a grave and let me lie;
Glad did I live and gladly I die
And I laid me down with a will.

"This be the verse you grave for me:
'Here he lies where he longed to be;
Home is the sailor, home from the sea,
And the hunter home from the hill.'"

No one who reads this will need to be told that its author was a poet capable of attaining the highest reaches of poetical expression. But Stevenson sang only in snatches. In some of these, he is more musical than Burns at his best. In such verses as:—

"It is ill to break the bonds which God decreed to bind;
Still will we be the children of the heather and the wind,"

we hear echoes of such melody as the world had not known for eighteen hundred years. It appears from them, unmistakably, that Stevenson as a poet might have surpassed his highest successes in prose. Why he did not do so it is idle to inquire, but the cause is probably closely involved with the painful reactions which brought him his untimely death (Apia, Samoa, December 3d, 1894).

He was born at Edinburgh, November 13th, 1850. His father was a lighthouse engineer, a son of Robert Stevenson, and the family represented a Scottish ancestral tradition which inspired Stevenson's best work. He had all possible advantages of early training, including education at Edinburgh University and for the bar. After his first literary successes, he went to live in London, but, except in his deep love for Scotland, he was a cosmopolitan. He found his wife in America, and from 1889 he lived, or rather slowly died, in Samoa, where he had gone, that in spite of increasing weakness due to consumption, he might gain strength to complete his work. When he had completed it, the objection that remains against it, is that he did himself too little justice as a poet while putting into his novels the full intensity of a genius which in prose narrative is frequently too close to the intoxicating to be entirely healthy for those who indulge it without reserve. As an essayist, however, no such objection lies against him. Had he attempted his greatest success in essay writing instead of in fiction, he might have become easily first among the essayists of the nineteenth century. In delicacy, he is equaled only by Lamb, while he has the strength of Thackeray. But even when he is gayest or most commonplace, he never ceases to be unearthly. In his essays as in his poems and his fiction, he is the dying man who, having already awakened to realities beyond the earthly, is waiting for death as a deliverance and working for it as a reward. W. V. B.

EL DORADO

IT SEEMS as if a great deal were attainable in a world where there are so many marriages and decisive battles, and where we all, at certain hours of the day, and with great gusto and dispatch, stow a portion of victuals finally and irretrievably into the bag which contains us. And it would seem also, on a hasty view, that the attainment of as much as possible was the one goal of man's contentious life. And yet, as regards the spirit, this is but a semblance. We live in an ascending scale when we live happily, one thing leading to another in an endless series. There is always a new horizon for onward-looking men, and although we dwell on a small planet, immersed in petty business and not enduring beyond a brief period of years, we are so constituted that our hopes are inaccessible, like stars, and the term of hoping is prolonged until the term of life. To be truly happy is a question of how we begin and not of how we end, of what we want and not of what we have. An aspiration is a joy forever, a possession as solid as a landed estate, a fortune which we can never exhaust and which gives us year by year a revenue of pleasurable activity. To have many of these is to be spiritually rich. Life is only a very dull and ill-directed theatre unless we have some interests in the piece; and to those who have neither art nor science, the world is a mere arrangement of colors, or a rough footway where they may very well break their shins. It is in virtue of his own desires and curiosities that any man continues to exist with even patience, that he is charmed by the look of things and people, and that he wakens every morning with a renewed appetite for work and pleasure. Desire and curiosity are the two eyes through which he sees the world in the most enchanted colors: it is they that make women beautiful or fossils interesting; and the man may squander his estate and come to beggary, but if he keeps these two amulets he is still rich in the possibilities of pleasure. Suppose he could take one meal so compact and comprehensive that he should never hunger any more; suppose him, at a glance, to take in all the features of the world and allay the desire for knowledge; suppose him to do the like in any province of experience — would not that man be in a poor way for amusement ever after?

One who goes touring on foot with a single volume in his knapsack reads with circumspection, pausing often to reflect, and

often laying the book down to contemplate the landscape or the prints in the inn parlor; for he fears to come to an end of his entertainment, and be left companionless on the last stages of his journey. A young fellow recently finished the works of Thomas Carlyle, winding up, if we remember aright, with the ten notebooks upon Frederick the Great. "What!" cried the young fellow, in consternation, "is there no more Carlyle? Am I left to the daily papers?" A more celebrated instance is that of Alexander, who wept bitterly because he had no more worlds to subdue. And when Gibbon had finished the "Decline and Fall," he had only a few moments of joy; and it was with a "sober melancholy" that he parted from his labors.

Happily we all shoot at the moon with ineffectual arrows; our hopes are set on an inaccessible El Dorado; we come to an end of nothing here below. Interests are only plucked up to sow themselves again, like mustard. You would think, when the child was born, there would be an end to trouble; and yet it is only the beginning of fresh anxieties; and when you have seen it through its teething and its education, and at last its marriage, alas! it is only to have new fears, new quivering sensibilities, with every day; and the health of your children's children grows as touching a concern as that of your own. Again, when you have married your wife, you would think you were got upon a hilltop, and might begin to go downward by an easy slope. But you have only ended courting to begin marriage. Falling in love and winning love are often difficult tasks to overbearing and rebellious spirits; but to keep in love is also a business of some importance, to which both man and wife must bring kindness and good-will. The true love story commences at the altar, when there lies before the married pair a most beautiful contest of wisdom and generosity, and a life-long struggle towards an unattainable ideal. Unattainable? Aye, surely unattainable, from the very fact that there are two instead of one.

"Of making books there is no end," complained the preacher; and did not perceive how highly he was praising letters as an occupation. There is no end, indeed, to making books or experiments, or to travel, or to gathering wealth. Problem gives rise to problem. We may study forever, and we are never as learned as we would be. We have never made a statue worthy of our dreams. And when we have discovered a continent, or crossed a chain of mountains, it is only to find another ocean or

another plain upon the further side. In the infinite universe there is room for our swiftest diligence and to spare. It is not like the works of Carlyle, which can be read to an end. Even in a corner of it, in a private park, or in the neighborhood of a single hamlet, the weather and the seasons keep so deftly changing that although we walk there for a lifetime there will be always something new to startle and delight us.

There is only one wish realizable on the earth; only one thing that can be perfectly attained: Death. And from a variety of circumstances we have no one to tell whether it be worth attaining. A strange picture we make on our way to our chimeras, ceaselessly marching, grudging ourselves the time for rest; indefatigable, adventurous pioneers. It is true that we shall never reach the goal; it is even more than probable that there is no such place; and if we lived for centuries and were endowed with the powers of a god, we should find ourselves not much nearer what we wanted at the end. O toiling hands of mortals! O unwearied feet, traveling ye know not whither! Soon, soon, it seems to you, you must come forth on some conspicuous hilltop, and but a little way further, against the setting sun, descry the spires of El Dorado. Little do ye know your own blessedness; for to travel hopefully is a better thing than to arrive, and the true success is to labor.

Complete. From "Virginibus Puerisque."

OLD MORTALITY

BOOKS AND TOMBSTONES

THERE is a certain graveyard, looked upon on the one side by a prison, on the other by the windows of a quiet hotel; below, under a steep cliff, it beholds the traffic of many lines of rail, and the scream of the engine and the shock of meeting buffers mount to it all day long. The aisles are lined with the inclosed sepulchres of families, door beyond door, like houses in a street; and in the morning the shadow of the prison turrets, and of many tall memorials, fall upon the graves. There, in the hot fits of youth, I came to be unhappy. Pleasant incidents are woven with my memory of the place. I here made friends with a certain plain old gentleman, a visitor on sunny mornings, gravely cheerful, who, with one eye upon the place that awaited him, chirped about his youth like winter sparrows; a beautiful housemaid of the hotel once, for some days together, humbly flirted with me from a window and kept my wild heart flying; and once—she possibly remembers—the wise Eugenia followed me to that austere inclosure. Her hair came down, and in the shelter of the tomb my trembling fingers helped her to repair the braid. But for the most part I went there solitary and, with irrevocable emotion, pored on the names of the forgotten. Name after name, and to each the conventional attributions and the idle dates; a regiment of the unknown that had been the joy of mothers, and had thrilled with the illusions of youth, and at last, in the dim sick room, wrestled with the pangs of old mortality. In that whole crew of the silenced there was but one of whom my fancy had received a picture; and he, with his comely, florid countenance, bewigged and habited in scarlet, and in his day combining fame and popularity, stood forth, like a taunt, among that company of phantom appellations. It was then possible to leave behind us something more explicit than these severe, monotonous, and lying epitaphs; and the thing left, the memory of a painted picture and what we call the immortality of a name, was hardly more desirable than mere oblivion. Even David Hume, as he lay composed beneath that "circular idea," was fainter than a dream; and when the housemaid, broom in hand, smiled and beckoned from the open window, the fame of that bewigged philosopher melted like a raindrop in the sea.

And yet in soberness I cared as little for the housemaid as for David Hume. The interests of youth are rarely frank; his passions, like Noah's dove, come home to roost. The fire, sensibility, and volume of his own nature, that is all that he has learned to recognize. The tumultuary and gray tide of life, the empire of routine, the unrejoicing faces of his elders, fill him with contemptuous surprise; there also he seems to walk among the tombs of spirits; and it is only in the course of years, and after much rubbing with his fellowmen, that he begins by glimpses to see himself from without and his fellows from within; to know his own for one among the thousand undenoted countenances of the city street, and to divine in others the throb of human agony and hope. In the meantime he will avoid the hospital doors, the pale faces, the cripple, the sweet whiff of chloroform—for there, on the most thoughtless, the pains of others are burned home; but he will continue to walk, in a divine self-pity,

the aisles of the forgotten graveyard. The length of man's life, which is endless to the brave and busy, is scorned by his ambitious thought. He cannot bear to have come for so little, and to go again so wholly. He cannot bear, above all, in that brief scene, to be still idle, and, by way of cure, neglects the little that he has to do. The parable of the talent is the brief epitome of youth. To believe in immortality is one thing, but it is first needful to believe in life. Denunciatory preachers seem not to suspect that they may be taken gravely and in evil part; that young men may come to think of time as of a moment, and with the pride of Satan wave back the inadequate gift. Yet here is a true peril; this it is that sets them to pace the graveyard alleys, and to read, with strange extremes of pity and derision, the memorials of the dead.

Books were the proper remedy: books of vivid human import, forcing upon their minds the issues, pleasures, business, importance, and immediacy of that life in which they stand; books of smiling or heroic temper, to excite or to console; books of a large design, shadowing the complexity of that game of consequences to which we all sit down, the hanger-back not least. But the average sermon flees the point, disporting itself in that eternity of which we know, and need to know, so little; avoiding the bright, crowded, and momentous fields of life where destiny awaits us. Upon the average book a writer may be silent; he may set it down to his ill-hap that when his own youth was in the acrid fermentation, he should have fallen and fed upon the cheerless fields of Obermann. Yet to Mr. Arnold, who led him to these pastures, he still bears a grudge. The day is perhaps not far off when people will begin to count "Moll Flanders," aye, or "The Country Wife," more wholesome and more pious diet than these guide books to consistent egoism.

But the most inhuman of boys soon wearies of the inhumanity of Obermann. And even while I still continued to be a haunter of the graveyard, I began insensibly to turn my attention to the gravediggers, and was weaned out of myself to observe the conduct of visitors. This was dayspring, indeed, to a lad in such great darkness. Not that I began to see men, or to try to see them, from within, nor to learn charity and modesty and justice from the sight; but still stared at them externally from the prison windows of my affectation. Once I remember to have observed two workingwomen with a baby halting by a grave;

there was something monumental in the grouping, one upright carrying the child, the other with bowed face crouching by her side. A wreath of immortelles under a glass dome had thus attracted them; and, drawing near, I overheard their judgment on that wonder. "Eh! what extravagance!" To a youth afflicted with the callosity of sentiment, this quaint and pregnant saying appeared merely base.

My acquaintance with gravediggers, considering its length, was unremarkable. One, indeed, whom I found plying his spade in the red evening, high above Allan Water and in the shadow of Dunblane Cathedral, told me of his acquaintance with the birds that still attended on his labors; how some would even perch about him, waiting for their prey; and in a true Sexton's Calendar, how the species varied with the season of the year. But this was the very poetry of the profession. The others whom I knew were somewhat dry. A faint flavor of the gardner hung about them, but sophisticated and disbloomed. They had engagements to keep, not alone with the deliberate series of the seasons, but with mankind's clocks and hour-long measurement of time. And thus there was no leisure for the relishing pinch, or the hour-long gossip, foot on spade. They were men wrapped up in their grim business; they liked well to open long-closed family vaults, blowing in the key and throwing wide the grating; and they carried in their minds a calendar of names and dates. It would be "in fifty-twa" that such a tomb was last opened for "Miss Jemimy." It was thus they spoke of their past patients—familiarly, but not without respect, like old family servants. Here is indeed a servant, whom we forget that we possess; who does not wait at the bright table, or run at the bell's summons, but patiently smokes his pipe beside the mortuary fire, and in his faithful memory notches the burials of our race. To suspect Shakespeare in his maturity of a superficial touch savors of paradox; yet he was surely in error when he attributed insensibility to the digger of the grave. But perhaps it is on Hamlet that the charge should lie; or perhaps the English sexton differs from the Scotch. The "goodman delver," reckoning up his years of office, might have at least suggested other thoughts. It is a pride common among sextons. A cabinetmaker does not count his cabinets, nor even an author his volumes, save when they stare upon him from the shelves; but the gravedigger numbers his graves. He would indeed be something different from

human if his solitary open-air and tragic labors left not a broad mark upon his mind. There, in his tranquil aisle, apart from city clamor, among the cats and robins and the ancient effigies and legends of the tomb, he waits the continual passage of his contemporaries, falling like minute drops into eternity. As they fall, he counts them; and this enumeration, which was at first perhaps appalling to his soul, in the process of years, and by the kindly influence of habit, grows to be his pride and pleasure. There are many common stories telling how he piques himself on crowded cemeteries. But I will rather tell of the old gravedigger of Monkton, to whose unsuffering bedside the minister was summoned. He dwelt in a cottage built into the wall of the churchyard; and through a bull's-eye pane above his bed he could see, as he lay dying, the rank grasses and the upright and recumbent stones. Dr. Laurie was, I think, a Moderate: 'tis certain, at least, that he took a very Roman view of deathbed dispositions, for he told the old man that he had lived beyond man's natural years, that his life had been easy and reputable, that his family had all grown up and been a credit to his care, and that it now behooved him unregretfully to gird his loins and follow the majority. The gravedigger heard him out; then he raised himself upon one elbow, and with the other hand pointed through the window to the scene of his lifelong labors. "Doctor," he said, "I ha'e laid three hunner and fower-score in that kirkyaird; an' it had been his wull," indicating Heaven, "I would ha'e likit weel to ha'e made out the fower hunner." But it was not to be; this tragedian of the fifth act had now another part to play, and the time had come when others were to gird and carry him.

THE HAUNTER OF GRAVES

I WOULD fain strike a note that should be more heroical; but the ground of all youth's suffering, solitude, hysteria, and haunting of the grave, is nothing else than naked, ignorant selfishness. It is himself that he sees dead; those are his virtues that are forgotten; his is the vague epitaph. Pity him but the more, if pity be your cue; for where a man is all pride, vanity, and personal aspiration, he goes through fire unshielded. In every part and corner of our life, to lose oneself is to be gainer; to forget oneself is to be happy; and this poor, laughable and tragic fool has not yet learned the rudiments; himself, giant Prometheus, is still ironed on the peaks of Caucasus. But by and by his truant interests will leave that tortured body, slip abroad and gather flowers. Then shall death appear before him in an altered guise; no longer as a doom peculiar to himself, whether fate's crowning injustice or his own last vengeance upon those who fail to value him; but now as a power that wounds him far more tenderly, not without solemn compensations, taking and giving, bereaving and yet storing up.

The first step for all is to learn to the dregs our own ignoble fallibility. When we have fallen through story after story of our vanity and aspiration, and sit rueful among the ruins, then it is that we begin to measure the stature of our friends: how they stand between us and our own contempt, believing in our best; how, linking us with others, and still spreading wide the influential circle, they weave us in and in with the fabric of contemporary life; and to what petty size they dwarf the virtues and the vices that appeared gigantic in our youth. So that at the last, when such a pin falls out — when there vanishes in the least breath of time one of those rich magazines of life on which we drew for our supply — when he who had first dawned upon us as a face among the faces of the city, and, still growing, came to bulk on our regard with those clear features of the loved and living man, falls in a breath to memory and shadow, there falls along with him a whole wing of the palace of our life.

THE HEAVEN OF NOBLE FAILURE

ONE such face I now remember; one such blank some half a dozen of us labor to dissemble. In his youth he was most beautiful in person; most serene and genial by disposition; full of racy words and quaint thoughts. Laughter attended on his coming. He had the air of a great gentleman, jovial and royal with his equals, and to the poorest student gentle and attentive. Power seemed to reside in him exhaustless; we saw him stoop to play with us, but held him marked for higher destinies; we loved his notice; and I have rarely had my pride more gratified than when he sat at my father's table, my acknowledged

IX—227

railing on the rose leaves in our princely bed of life, and he would patiently give ear and wisely counsel; and it was only upon some return of our own thoughts that we were reminded what manner of man this was to whom we disembosomed: a man, by his own fault, ruined; shut out of the garden of his gifts; his whole city of hope both ploughed and salted; silently awaiting the deliverer. Then something took us by the throat; and to see him there, so gentle, patient, brave, and pious, oppressed but not cast down, sorrow was so swallowed up in admiration that we could not dare to pity him. Even if the old fault flashed out again, it but awoke our wonder that, in that lost battle, he should have still the energy to fight. He had gone to ruin with a kind of kingly abandon, like one who condescended; but once ruined, with the lights all out, he fought as for a kingdom. Most men, finding themselves the authors of their own disgrace, rail the louder against God or destiny. Most men, when they repent, oblige their friends to share the bitterness of that repentance. But he had held an inquest and passed sentence: *mene, mene;* and condemned himself to smiling silence. He had given trouble enough; had earned misfortune amply, and foregone the right to murmur.

Thus was our old comrade, like Samson, careless in his days of strength; but on the coming of adversity, and when that strength was gone that had betrayed him,—"for our strength is weakness,"— he began to blossom and bring forth. Well, now, he is out of the fight: the burden that he bore thrown down before the great deliverer. We —

> "in the vast cathedral leave him;
> God accept him,
> Christ receive him!"

THE DOOR OF IMMORTALITY

IF WE go now and look on these innumerable epitaphs, the pathos and the irony are strangely fled. They do not stand merely to the dead, these foolish monuments; they are pillars and legends set up to glorify the difficult but not desperate life of man. This ground is hallowed by the heroes of defeat.

I see the indifferent pass before my friend's last resting place; pause, with a shrug of pity, marveling that so rich an argosy had

friend. So he walked among us, both hands full of gifts, carrying with nonchalance the seeds of a most influential life.

The powers and the ground of friendship are a mystery; but, looking back, I can discern that, in part, we love the thing he was, for some shadow of what he was to be. For with all his beauty, power, breeding, urbanity, and mirth, there was in those days something soulless in our friend. He would astonish us by sallies, witty, innocent, and inhumane; and by a misapplied Johnsonian pleasantry, demolish honest sentiment. I can still see and hear him, as he went his way along the lamplit streets, "*Là ci darem la mano*" on his lips, a noble figure of a youth, but following vanity and incredulous of good; and sure enough, somewhere on the high seas of life, with his health, his hopes, his patrimony, and his self-respect, miserably went down.

From this disaster, like a spent swimmer, he came desperately ashore, bankrupt of money and consideration; creeping to the family he had deserted; with broken wing, never more to rise. But in his face there was a light of knowledge that was new to it. Of the wounds of his body he was never healed; died of them gradually, with clear-eyed resignation; of his wounded pride, we knew only from his silence. He returned to that city where he had lorded it in his ambitious youth; lived there alone, seeing few; striving to retrieve the irretrievable; at times still grappling with that mortal frailty that had brought him down; still joying in his friend's successes; his laugh still ready but with kindlier music; and over all his thoughts the shadow of that unalterable law which he had disavowed and which had brought him low. Lastly, when his bodily evils had quite disabled him, he lay a great while dying, still without complaint, still finding interests; to his last step gentle, urbane, and with the will to smile.

The tale of this great failure is, to those who remain true to him, the tale of a success. In his youth he took thought for no one but himself; when he came ashore again, his whole armada lost, he seemed to think of none but others. Such was his tenderness for others, such his instinct of fine courtesy and pride, that of that impure passion of remorse he never breathed a syllable; even regret was rare with him, and pointed with a jest. You would not have dreamed, if you had known him then, that this was that great failure, that beacon to young men, over whose fall a whole society had hissed and pointed fingers. Often have we gone to him, red-hot with our own hopeful sorrows,

sunk. A pity, now that he is done with suffering,— a pity most uncalled for, and an ignorant wonder. Before those who loved him, his memory shines like a reproach; they honor him for silent lessons; they cherish his example; and in what remains before them of their toil, fear to be unworthy of the dead. For this proud man was one of those who prospered in the valley of humiliation;— of whom Bunyan wrote that, "Though Christian had the hard hap to meet in the valley with Apollyon, yet I must tell you that in former times men have met with angels here; have found pearls here; and have in this place found the words of life."

Complete. From "Memories and Portraits."

BALFOUR STEWART

(1828-1887)

BALFOUR STEWART, a noted essayist on scientific subjects, was born at Edinburgh, Scotland, November 1st, 1828. After studying at St. Andrews and Edinburgh Universities, he went to Australia, remaining there seven years and returning in 1853. In 1858 he published his work on "Radiant Heat," and in 1859 became director of Kew Observatory. In 1870 he was appointed professor of Physics at Owens College, Manchester, and in the next three years published "Elementary Lessons in Physics," "An Elementary Treatise on Heat," "Physics Primer," and "The Conservation of Energy." The latter work, no doubt the most important of his life, appeared in 1873. He was joint author with Prof. Tait of "The Unseen Universe," which was published in 1875. He died December 19th, 1887, near Drogheda, Ireland.

THE CONSERVATION OF ENERGY

MATHEMATICIANS inform us that if matter consists of atoms or small parts, which are actuated by forces depending only upon the distances between these parts, and not upon the velocity, then it may be demonstrated that the law of conservation of energy will hold good. Thus we see that conceptions regarding atoms and their forces are allied to conceptions regarding energy. A medium of some sort pervading space seems also necessary to our theory. In fine, a universe composed of atoms, with some sort of medium between them, is to be regarded as the machine, and the laws of energy as the laws of working of this machine. It may be that a theory of atoms of this sort, with a medium between them, is not, after all, the simplest, but we are probably not yet prepared for any more general hypothesis. Now, we have only to look to our own solar system, in order to see on a large scale an illustration of this conception, for there we have the various heavenly bodies attracting one another, with forces depending only on the distances between them, and independent of the velocities; and we have

likewise a medium of some sort, in virtue of which radiant energy is conveyed from the sun to the earth. Perhaps we shall not greatly err if we regard a molecule as representing on a small scale something analogous to the solar system, while the various atoms which constitute the molecule may be likened to the various bodies of the solar system. The short historical sketch which we are about to give will embrace, therefore, along with energy, the progress of thought and speculation with respect to atoms, and also with respect to a medium, inasmuch as these subjects are intimately connected with the doctrines of energy.

Heraclitus, who flourished at Ephesus, 500 B. C., declared that fire was the great cause, and that all things were in a perpetual flux. Such an expression will no doubt be regarded as very vague in these days of precise physical statements; and yet it seems clear that Heraclitus must have had a vivid conception of the innate restlessness and energy of the universe, a conception allied in character to and only less precise than that of modern philosophers, who regard matter as essentially dynamical.

Democritus, who was born 470 B. C., was the originator of the doctrine of atoms, a doctrine which, in the hands of John Dalton, has enabled the human mind to lay hold of the laws which regulate chemical changes, as well as to picture to itself what is there taking place. Perhaps there is no doctrine that has nowadays a more intimate connection with the industries of life than this of atoms, and it is probable that no intelligent director of chemical industry among civilized nations fails to picture to his own mind, by means of this doctrine, the inner nature of the changes which he sees with his eyes. Now, it is a curious circumstance that Bacon should have lighted upon this very doctrine of atoms, in order to point one of his philosophical morals.

"Nor is it less an evil," says he, "that in their philosophies and contemplations men spend their labor in investigating and treating of the first principles of things, and the extreme limits of nature, when all that is useful and of avail in operation is to be found in what is intermediate. Hence it happens that men continue to abstract Nature till they arrive at potential and unformed matter; and again they continue to divide Nature, until they have arrived at the atom; things which, even if true, can be of little use in helping on the fortunes of men."

Surely we ought to learn a lesson from these remarks of the great father of experimental science, and be very cautious before we dismiss any branch of knowledge or train of thought as essentially unprofitable.

As regards the existence of a medium, it is remarked by Whewell that the Ancients also caught a glimpse of the idea of a medium, by which the qualities of bodies, as colors and sounds, are perceived, and he quotes the following from Aristotle: "In a void there could be no difference of up and down; for, as in nothing there are no differences, so there are none in a privation or negation."

Upon this the historian of science remarks, "It is easily seen that such a mode of reasoning elevates the familiar forms of language, and the intellectual connections of terms, to a supremacy over facts."

Nevertheless, may it not be replied that our conceptions of matter are deduced from the familiar experience, that certain portions of space affect us in a certain manner; and, consequently, are we not entitled to say there must be something where we experience the difference of up or down? Is there, after all, a very great difference between this argument and that of modern physicists in favor of a plenum, who tell us that matter cannot act where it is not?

Aristotle seems also to have entertained the idea that light is not any body, or the emanation of any body (for that, he says, would be a kind of body), and that therefore light is an energy or act.

These quotations render it evident that the Ancients had, in some way, grasped the idea of the essential unrest and energy of things. They had also the idea of small particles or atoms, and, finally, of a medium of some sort. And yet these ideas were not prolific — they gave rise to nothing new.

Now, while the historian of science is unquestionably right in his criticism of the Ancients, that their ideas were not distinct and appropriate to the facts, yet we have seen that they were not wholly ignorant of the most profound and deeply-seated principles of the material universe. In the great hymn chanted by Nature, the fundamental notes were early heard, but yet it required long centuries of patient waiting for the practiced ear of the skilled musician to appreciate the mighty harmony aright. Or, perhaps, the attempts of the Ancients were as the sketches of

a child who just contrives to exhibit, in a rude way, the leading outlines of a building; while the conceptions of the practiced physicist are more allied to those of the architect, or at least, of one who has realized, to some extent, the architect's views.

The Ancients possessed great genius and intellectual power, but they were deficient in physical conceptions, and, in consequence, their ideas were not prolific. It cannot indeed be said that we of the present age are deficient in such conceptions; nevertheless, it may be questioned whether there is not a tendency to rush into the opposite extreme, and to work physical conceptions to an excess. Let us be cautious that in avoiding Scylla we do not rush into Charybdis. For the universe has more than one point of view, and there are possibly regions which will not yield their treasures to the most determined physicists, armed only with kilograms and metres and standard clocks.

In modern times Descartes, author of the vertical hypothesis, necessarily presupposed the existence of a medium in interplanetary spaces, but, on the other hand, he was one of the originators of that idea which regards light as a series of particles shot out from a luminous body. Newton likewise conceived the existence of a medium, although he became an advocate of the theory of emission. It is to Huyghens that the credit belongs of having first conceived the undulatory theory of light with sufficient distinctness to account for double refraction. After him, Young, Fresnel, and their followers, have greatly developed the theory, enabling it to account for the most complicated and wonderful phenomena.

With regard to the nature of heat, Bacon, whatever may be thought of his arguments, seems clearly to have recognized it as a species of motion. He says, "From these instances, viewed together and individually, the nature of which heat is the limitation seems to be motion"; and again he says, "But when we say of motion that it stands in the place of a genus to heat, we mean to convey, not that heat generates motion or motion heat (although even both may be true in some cases), but that essential heat is motion and nothing else."

Nevertheless it required nearly three centuries before the true theory of heat was sufficiently rooted to develop into a productive hypothesis.

In a previous chapter we have already detailed the labors in respect of heat of Davy, Rumford, and Joule. Galileo and Newton, if they did not grasp the dynamical nature of heat, had yet a clear conception of the functions of a machine. The former saw that what we gain in power we lose in space; while the latter went further, and saw that a machine, if left to itself, is strictly limited in the amount of work which it can accomplish, although its energy may vary from that of motion to that of position, and back again, according to the geometric laws of the machine.

There can, we think, be no question that the great development of industrial operations in the present age has indirectly furthered our conceptions regarding work. Humanity invariably strives to escape as much as possible from hard work. In the days of old those who had the power got slaves to work for them; but even then the master had to give some kind of equivalent for the work done. For at the very lowest a slave is a machine, and must be fed, and is moreover apt to prove a very troublesome machine if not properly dealt with. The great improvements in the steam engine, introduced by Watt, have done as much, perhaps, as the abolition of slavery to benefit the workingman. The hard work of the world has been put upon iron shoulders, that do not smart; and, in consequence, we have had an immense extension of industry, and a great amelioration in the position of the lower classes of mankind. But if we have transferred our hard work to machines, it is necessary to know how to question a machine — how to say to it, At what rate can you labor? How much work can you turn out in a day? It is necessary, in fact, to have the clearest possible idea of what work is.

Our readers will see from all this that men are not likely to err in their method of measuring work. The principles of measurement have been stamped as it were with a brand into the very heart and brain of humanity. To the employer of machinery or of human labor, a false method of measuring work simply means ruin; he is likely, therefore, to take the greatest possible pains to arrive at accuracy in his determination.

Now, amid the crowd of workers smarting from the curse of labor, there rises up every now and then an enthusiast, who seeks to escape by means of an artifice from this insupportable tyranny of work. Why not construct a machine that will go on giving you work without limit, without the necessity of being fed in any way. Nature must have some weak point in her armor; there must surely be some way of getting round her; she is only

tyrannous on the surface, and in order to stimulate our ingenuity, but will yield with pleasure to the persistence of genius.

Now, what can the man of science say to such an enthusiast? He cannot tell him that he is intimately acquainted with all the forces of Nature, and can prove that perpetual motion is impossible; for, in truth, he knows very little of these forces. But he does think that he has entered into the spirit and design of Nature, and therefore he denies at once the possibility of such a machine. But he denies it intelligently, and works out this denial of his into a theory which enables him to discover numerous and valuable relations between the properties of matter — produces, in fact, the laws of energy and the great principle of conservation.

We have thus endeavored to give a short sketch of the history of energy, including its allied problems, up to the dawn of the strictly scientific period. We have seen that the unfruitfulness of the earlier views was due to a want of scientific clearness in the conceptions entertained, and we have now to say a few words regarding the theory of conservation.

Here also the way was pointed out by two philosophers, namely, Grove in this country, and Mayer on the continent, who showed certain relations between the various forms of energy; the name of Seguin ought likewise to be mentioned. Nevertheless, to Joule belongs the honor of establishing the theory on an incontrovertible basis; for, indeed, this is pre-eminently a case where speculation has to be tested by unimpeachable experimental evidence. Here the magnitude of the principle is so vast, and its importance is so great, that it requires the strong fire of genius, joined to the patient labors of the scientific experimentalist, to forge the rough ore into a good weapon that will cleave its way through all obstacles into the very citadel of Nature, and into her most secret recesses.

Following closely upon the labors of Joule, we have those of William and James Thomson, Helmholtz, Rankine, Clausius, Tait, Andrews, Maxwell, who, along with many others, have advanced the subject; and while Joule gave his chief attention to the laws which regulate the transmutation of mechanical energy into heat, Thomson, Rankine, and Clausius gave theirs to the converse problem, or that which relates to the transmutation of heat into mechanical energy. Thomson, especially, has pushed forward so resolutely from this point of view that he has succeeded in grasping a principle scarcely inferior in importance to that of the con-

servation of energy itself, and of this principle it behooves us now to speak.

Joule, we have said, proved the law according to which work may be changed into heat; and Thomson and others, that according to which heat may be changed into work. Now, it occurred to Thomson that there was a very important and significant difference between these two laws, consisting in the fact that, while you can with the greatest ease transform work into heat, you can by no method in your power transform all the heat back again into work. In fact, the process is not a reversible one; and the consequence is that the mechanical energy of the universe is becoming every day more and more changed into heat.

It is easily seen that if the process were reversible, one form of a perpetual motion would not be impossible. For, without attempting to create energy by a machine, all that would be needed for a perpetual motion would be the means of utilizing the vast stores of heat that lie in all the substances around us, and converting them into work. The work would, no doubt, by means of friction and otherwise, be ultimately reconverted into heat; but if the process be reversible, the heat could again be converted into work, and so on forever. But the irreversibility of the process puts a stop to all this. In fact, I may convince myself by rubbing a metal button on a piece of wood how easily work can be converted into heat, while the mind completely fails to suggest any method by which this heat can be reconverted into work.

Now, if this process goes on, and always in one direction, there can be no doubt about the issue. The mechanical energy of the universe will be more and more transformed into universally diffused heat, until the universe will no longer be a fit abode for living beings. . . .

Although, therefore, in a strictly mechanical sense, there is a conservation of energy, yet, as regards usefulness or fitness for living beings, the energy of the universe is in process of deterioration. Universally diffused heat forms what we may call the great waste heap of the universe, and this is growing larger year by year. At present it does not sensibly obtrude itself, but who knows that the time may not arrive when we shall be practically conscious of its growing bigness?

It will be seen that we have regarded the universe, not as a collection of matter, but rather as an energetic agent,—in fact,

as a lamp. Now, it has been well pointed out by Thomson, that, looked at in this light, the universe is a system that had a beginning and must have an end; for a process of degradation cannot be eternal. If we could view the universe as a candle not lit, then it is perhaps conceivable to regard it as having been always in existence; but if we regard it rather as a candle that has been lit, we become absolutely certain that it cannot have been burning from eternity, and that a time will come when it will cease to burn. We are led to look to a beginning in which the particles of matter were in a diffuse chaotic state, but endowed with the power of gravitation, and we are led to look to an end in which the whole universe will be one equally heated inert mass, and from which everything like life or motion or beauty will have utterly gone away.

From «The Conservation of Energy.»

SNORRE STURLESON

(c. 1179–1241)

SNORRE STURLESON, the author of the "Heimskringla" and the "Younger," or "Prose Edda," is the best representative of the early prose literature native to Northern Europe. In his writings, and especially in the "Younger Edda," we see the first beginnings of the coherent development of the Teutonic prose essay as distinct from the Latin. In the change of form which takes place between the "Elder" and the "Younger Edda," we see how the essay originated as a vehicle for the traditional thought of primitive peoples. The "Elder Edda" stands for the expression of religious myth, or primitive science, philosophy, and ethics, in its natural form—the poetical. In the "Younger Edda," a later age translates the archaic poetical form into the first phase of the essay—a prose paraphrase of the verse, relieved by frequent quotations from the verse itself. Sometimes these quotations are exact; oftener they are paraphrased to please the taste of the later editor. We see in Persian literature the same phenomenon which is presented by the far North. The parallel is so close that if we were wholly ignorant of the laws of the parallel development of mind under pressure of related circumstances, we would be forced to the erroneous conclusion that the early Icelandic and the classical Persian writers had necessarily a common model, or were governed by some common tradition of style. The Homeric tradition undoubtedly influenced Iceland as it did Persia; but beyond the scope of its influence, we can see the effects of the natural laws of the mind working out in .the literature of both countries. Comparisons of this kind have only to be made sufficiently comprehensive to force the conclusion that in all countries style itself is a product of natural causes, with an underlying unity governing in all its diversities.

Snorre (spelled also "Snorri," and "Snorro"; "Sturlason," "Sturleson," and "Sturluson") was born at Hvamm in Iceland in 1178 or 1179. He was a man of the highest Icelandic culture at a time when the literary culture of Iceland was the most remarkable native growth of Northern Europe. He visited Norway twice and was in favor at the Norwegian court. In his own country he served as "lawman," as well as the historian, poet, and prophet of his people. He met the usual reward of prophets at the last, for his great talents and his

patriotism necessarily forced him into political leadership, and as he took sides against the Norwegian court influence, his assassination was instigated as a measure of court policy, and he was killed September 23d, 1241, by his own kinsman and friends. He is, in his own right, one of the greatest men produced by the primitive culture of Northern Europe. As a historian he has been compared to Thucydides, and in the "Younger Edda" he has left an immortal work of genius. His knowledge of poetical composition belongs to a time when the art of poetry was still consciously a part of the art of music, and what he has written on the subject has a high value as material for scientific investigation in the comparative study of the "Iliad," the "Odyssey," and the early poetry of Palestine and Persia. The most important philological discoveries of the twentieth century are likely to be made along lines of research which will show how great is the scientific importance of the unconsidered knowledge in which this thirteenth-century poet and philosopher was superior to the nineteenth.

W. V. B.

GEFJON'S PLOUGHING

KING GYLFI ruled over the land which is now called Svithiod (Sweden). It is related of him that he once gave a wayfaring woman, as a recompense for her having diverted him, as much land in his realm as she could plough with four oxen in a day and a night. This woman was, however, of the race of the Æsir, and was called Gefjon. She took four oxen from the North, out of Jotunheim (but they were the sons she had had with a giant), and set them before a plow. Now the plow made such deep furrows that it tore up the land, which the oxen drew westward out to sea until they came to a sound. There Gefjon fixed the land, and called it Saelund. And the place where the land had stood became water, and formed a lake which is now called "The Water" (Laugur), and the inlets of this lake correspond exactly with the headlands of Saelund. As Skald Bragi the Old saith:—

> "Gefjon drew from Gylfi,
> Rich in stored-up treasure,
> The land she joined to Denmark.
> Four heads and eight eyes bearing,
> While hot sweat trickled down them,
> The oxen dragged the reft mass
> That formed this winsome island."

GYLFI'S JOURNEY TO ASGARD

KING GYLFI was renowned for his wisdom and skill in magic. He beheld with astonishment that whatever the Æsir willed took place; and was at a loss whether to attribute their success to the superiority of their natural abilities, or to a power imparted to them by the mighty gods whom they worshiped. To be satisfied in this particular, he resolved to go to Asgard, and, taking upon himself the likeness of an old man, set out on his journey. But the Æsir, being too well skilled in divination not to foresee his design, prepared to receive him with various illusions. On entering the city Gylfi saw a very lofty mansion, the roof of which, as far as his eye could reach, was covered with golden shields. Thiodolf of Hvina thus alludes to Valhalla being roofed with shields.

> "Warriors all careworn,
> (Stones had poured upon them),
> On their backs let glisten
> Valhalla's golden shingles."

At the entrance of the mansion Gylfi saw a man who amused himself by tossing seven small swords in the air, and catching them as they fell, one after the other. This person having asked his name, Gylfi said that he was called Gangler, and that he came from a long journey, and begged for a night's lodging. He asked, in his turn, to whom this mansion belonged. The other told him that it belonged to their king, and added, "But I will lead thee to him, and thou shalt thyself ask him his name." So saying, he entered the hall, and as Gylfi followed the door banged to behind him. He there saw many stately rooms crowded with people, some playing, some drinking, and others fighting with various weapons. Gangler, seeing a multitude of things, the meaning of which he could not comprehend, softly pronounced the following verse (from the "Hava-mal"):—

> "Scan every gate
> Ere thou go on,
> With greatest caution;
> For hard to say 'tis
> Where foes are sitting
> In this fair mansion."

He afterwards beheld three thrones raised one above another, with a man sitting on each of them. Upon his asking what the names of these lords might be, his guide answered: "He who sitteth on the lowest throne is a king; his name is Har (the High or Lofty One); the second is Jafnhar (i. e., equal to the High); but he who sitteth on the high throne is called Thridi (the Third)." Har, perceiving the stranger, asked him what his errand was, adding that he should be welcome to eat and drink without cost, as were all those who remained in Hava Hall. Gangler said he desired first to ascertain whether there was any person present renowned for his wisdom.

"If thou art not the most knowing," replied Har, "I fear thou wilt hardly return safe. But go, stand there below, and propose thy questions; here sits one who will be able to answer them."

OF THE SUPREME DEITY

GANGLER thus began his discourse:—"Who is the first or eldest of the gods?"

"In our language," replied Har, "he is called Alfadir (All-Father, or the Father of All); but in the old Asgard he had twelve names."

"Where is this god?" said Gangler; "What is his power, and what hath he done to display his glory?"

"He liveth," replied Har, "from all ages, he governeth all realms, and swayeth all things great and small."

"He hath formed," added Jafnhar, "heaven and earth, and the air, and all things thereunto belonging."

"And what is more," continued Thridi, "he hath made man, and given him a soul which shall live and never perish though the body shall have moldered away, or have been burned to ashes. And all that are righteous shall dwell with him in the place called Gimli, or Vingolf; but the wicked shall go to Hel, and thence to Niflhel, which is below, in the ninth world."

"And where did this god remain before he made heaven and earth?" asked Gangler.

"He was then," replied Har, "with the Hrimthursar."

OF THE PRIMORDIAL STATE OF THE UNIVERSE

"BUT with what did he begin, or what was the beginning of things?" demanded Gangler.

"Hear," replied Har, "what is said in the 'Völuspá':—

"'Twas time's first dawn,
When naught yet was,
Nor sand nor sea,
Nor cooling wave;
Earth was not there
Nor heaven above.
Naught save a void
And yawning gulf,
But verdure none.'"

"Many ages before the earth was made," added Jafnhar, "was Niflheim formed, in the middle of which lies the spring called Hvergelmir, from which flow twelve rivers, Gjoll being the nearest to the gate of the abode of Death."

"But, first of all," continued Thridi, "there was in the southern region (sphere) the world called Muspell. It is a world too luminous and glowing to be entered by those who are not indigenous there. He who sitteth on its borders (or the land's end) to guard it is named Surtur. In his hand he beareth a flaming falchion, and at the end of the world shall issue forth to combat, and shall vanquish all the gods, and consume the universe with fire. As it is said in the 'Völuspá':—

"'Surtur from the south wends
With seething fire
The falchion of the mighty one
A sunlight flameth.
Mountains together dash,
Giants headlong rush,
Men tread the paths to Hel,
And Heaven in twain is rent.'"

OF THE WAY THAT LEADS TO HEAVEN

"I MUST now ask," said Gangler, "which is the path leading from earth to heaven."

"That is a senseless question," replied Har, with a smile of derision. "Hast thou not been told that the gods made a bridge from earth to heaven, and called it Bifröst? Thou must

IX—228

surely have seen it; but, perhaps, thou callest it the rainbow. It is of three hues, and is constructed with more art than any other work. But, strong though it be, it will be broken to pieces when the sons of Muspell, after having traversed great rivers, shall ride over it."

"Methinks," said Gangler, "the gods could not have been in earnest to erect a bridge so liable to be broken down, since it is in their power to make whatever they please."

"The gods," replied Har, "are not to be blamed on that account; Bifröst is of itself a very good bridge, but there is nothing in nature that can hope to make resistance when the sons of Muspell sally forth to the great combat."

"What did All-Father do after Asgard was made?" demanded Gangler.

"In the beginning," answered Har, "he appointed rulers, and bade them judge with him the fate of men, and regulate the government of the celestial city. They met for this purpose in a place called Idavoll, which is in the centre of the divine abode. Their first work was to erect a court or hall wherein are twelve seats for themselves, besides the throne which is occupied by All-Father. This hall is the largest and most magnificent in the universe, being resplendent on all sides, both within and without, with the finest gold. Its name is Gladsheim. They also erected another hall for the sanctuary of the goddesses. It is a very fair structure, and called by men Vingolf. Lastly they built a smithy, and furnished it with hammers, tongs, and anvils, and with these made all the other requisite instruments, with which they worked in metal, stone, and wood, and composed so large a quantity of the metal called gold that they made all their movables of it. Hence that age was named the Golden Age. This was the age that lasted until the arrival of the women out of Jotunheim, who corrupted it.

"Then the gods, seating themselves upon their thrones, distributed justice, and bethought them how the dwarfs had been bred in the mold of the earth, just as worms are in a dead body. It was, in fact, in Ymir's flesh that the dwarf's were engendered, and began to move and live. At first they were only maggots, but by the will of the gods they at length partook both of human shape and understanding, although they always dwell in rocks and caverns.

"Modsognir and Durin are the principal ones. As it is said in the 'Völuspá':—

"'Then went the rulers there,
All gods most holy,
To their seats aloft,
And counsel together took,
Who should of dwarfs
The race then fashion
From the livid bones
And blood of the giant.
Modsognir, chief
Of the dwarfish race,
And Durin too
Were then created.
And like to men
Dwarfs in the earth
Were formed in numbers
As Durin ordered.'"

OF THE ASH YGGDRASILL, MIMIR'S WELL, AND THE NORNS OR DESTINIES

"WHERE," asked Gangler, "is the chief or holiest seat of the gods?"

"It is under the ash Yggdrasill," replied Har, "where the gods assemble every day in council."

"What is there remarkable in regard to that place?" said Gangler.

"That ash," answered Jafnhar, "is the greatest and best of all trees. Its branches spread over the whole world, and even reach above heaven. It has three roots very wide asunder. One of them extends to the Æsir, another to the Frost-giants in that very place where was formerly Ginnungagap, and the third stands over Niflheim, and under this root, which is constantly gnawed by Nidhogg, is Hvergelmir. But under the root that stretches out towards the Frost-giants there is Mimir's well, in which wisdom and wit lie hidden. The owner of this well is called Mimir. He is full of wisdom, because he drinks the waters of the well from the horn Gjoll every morning. One day All-Father came and begged a draught of this water, which he obtained, but was obliged to leave one of his eyes as a pledge for it. As it is said in the 'Völuspá':—

"'All know I, Odin!
How thou hiddest thine eye
In Mimir's well-spring
Of limpid water.
Mead quaffs Mimir
Each morn from the pledge
Valfadir left him.
Conceive ye this or not?'"

"The third root of the ash is in heaven, and under it is the holy Urdar-fount. 'Tis here that the gods sit in judgment. Every day they ride up hither on horseback over Bifröst, which is called the Æsir Bridge. These are the names of the horses of the Æsir. Sleipnir is the best of them; he has eight legs, and belongs to Odin. The others are Gladr, Gyllir, Glaer, Skeidbrimir, Silfrintoppr, Synir, Gils, Falhofnir, Gulltoppr, and Lettfeti. Baldur's horse was burned with his master's body. As for Thor, he goes on foot, and is obliged every day to wade the rivers called Kormt and Œrmt, and two others called Kerlaung.

"Through these shall Thor wade every day, as he fares to the doomstead under Yggdrasill's ash, else the Æsir Bridge would be in flames, and boiling hot would become the holy waters."

"But tell me," said Gangler, "does fire burn over Bifröst?"

"That," replied Har, "which thou seest red in the bow is burning fire; for the Frost-giants and the Mountain-giants would go up to heaven by that bridge if it were easy for every one to walk over it. There are in heaven many goodly homesteads, and none without a celestial ward. Near the fountain, which is under the ash, stands a very beauteous dwelling, out of which go three maidens, named Urd, Verandi, and Skuld. These maidens fix the lifetime of all men, and are called Norns. But there are, indeed, many other Norns, for, when a man is born, there is a Norn to determine his fate. Some are known to be of heavenly origin, but others belong to the races of the elves and dwarfs; as it is said:—

"'Methinks the Norns were born far asunder, for they are not of the same race. Some belong to the Æsir, some to the Elves, and some are Dvalin's daughters.'"

"But if these Norns dispense the destinies of men," said Gangler, "they are, methinks, very unequal in their distribution; for some men are fortunate and wealthy, others acquire neither riches nor honors, some live to a good old age, while others are cut off in their prime."

"The Norns," replied Har, "who are of a good origin are good themselves, and dispense good destinies. But those men to whom misfortunes happen ought to ascribe them to the evil Norns."

OF THE NORNS AND THE URDAR-FOUNT

"WHAT more wonders hast thou to tell me," said Gangler, "concerning the ash?"

"What I have further to say respecting it," replied Har, "is, that there is an eagle perched upon its branches who knows many things: between his eyes sits the hawk called Vedurfolnir. The squirrel named Ratatosk runs up and down the ash, and seeks to cause strife between the eagle and Nidhogg. Four harts run across the branches of the tree, and bite the buds. They are called Dainn, Dvalinn, Duneyr, and Durathror. But there are so many snakes with Nidhogg in Hvergelmir that no tongue can recount them. As it is said:—

> "'Yggdrasill's ash
> More hardship bears
> Than men imagine;
> The hart bites above,
> At the sides it rots,
> Below gnaws Nidhogg.'

"And again:—

> "'More serpents lie
> Under Yggdrasill's ash
> Than simpletons think of;
> Goinn and Moinn,
> The sons of Grafvitnir,
> Grabak and Grafjollud,
> Ofnir and Svafnir,
> Must for aye, methinks,
> Gnaw the roots of that tree.'

"It is also said that the Norns who dwell by the Urdar-fount draw every day water from the spring, and with it and the clay

that lies around the fount sprinkle the ash, in order that its branches may not rot and wither away. This water is so holy that everything placed in the spring becomes as white as the film within an eggshell. As it is said in the 'Völuspá':—

> "'An ash know I standing,
> Named Yggdrasill,
> A stately tree sprinkled
> With water the purest;
> Thence come the dewdrops
> That fall in the dales;
> Ever blooming, it stands
> O'er the Urdar-fount.'

"The dew that falls thence on the earth men call honeydew, and it is the food of the bees. Two fowls are fed in the Urdarfount; they are called swans, and from them are descended all the birds of this species."

OF LOKI AND HIS PROGENY

"THERE is another deity," continued Har, "reckoned in the number of the Æsir, whom some call the calumniator of the gods, the contriver of all fraud and mischief, and the disgrace of gods and men. His name is Loki or Loptur. He is the son of the giant Farbauti. His mother is Laufey or Nal; his brothers are Byleist and Helblindi. Loki is handsome and well made, but of a very fickle mood, and most evil disposition. He surpasses all beings in those arts called Cunning and Perfidy. Many a time has he exposed the gods to very great perils, and often extricated them again by his artifices. His wife is called Siguna, and their son Nari."

OF THE JOYS OF VALHALLA

"IF IT be as thou hast told me," said Gangler, "that all men who have fallen in fight since the beginning of the world are gone to Odin, in Valhalla, what has he to give them to eat, for methinks there must be a great crowd there?"

"What thou sayest is quite true," replied Har, "the crowd there is indeed great, but great though it be, it will still increase, and will be thought too little when the wolf cometh. But how-

ever great the band of men in Valhalla may be, the flesh of the boar Sæhrimnir will more than suffice for their sustenance. For although this boar is sodden every morning, he becomes whole again every night. But there are few, methinks, who are wise enough to give thee, in this respect, a satisfactory answer to thy question. The cook is called Andhrimnir, and the kettle Eldhrimnir. As it is said: 'Andhrimnir cooks in Eldhrimnir, Sæhrimnir.' 'Tis the best of flesh, though few know how much is required for the Einherjar."

"But has Odin," said Gangler, "the same food as the heroes?"

"Odin," replied Har, "gives the meat that is set before him to two wolves, called Geri and Freki, for he himself stands in no need of food. Wine is for him both meat and drink. As it is said:—

> "'Geri and Freki
> Feedeth the warfaring
> Famed Father of hosts,
> For 'tis with wine only
> That Odin, in arms renowned,
> Is nourished for aye.'

"Two ravens sit on Odin's shoulders and whisper in his ear the tidings and events they have heard and witnessed. They are called Hugin and Munin. He sends them out at dawn of day to fly over the whole world, and they return at eve towards mealtime. Hence it is that Odin knows so many things, and is called the Raven's God. As it is said:—

> "'Hugin and Munin
> Each dawn take their flight
> Earth's fields over.
> I fear me for Hugin,
> Lest he come not back,
> But much more for Munin.'"

All the foregoing are from Bishop Percy's translation of the "Younger Edda."

JONATHAN SWIFT

(1667–1745)

JONATHAN SWIFT, Dean of St. Patrick's, and the most remarkable of all satirists, was born at Dublin, November 30th, 1667. In 1688, after taking his degree *speciali gratia* at Trinity College, Dublin, he went to England and became secretary to Sir William Temple, serving in this position for about a year, after which he returned to Ireland. He did not remain very long, however, for in 1696, after taking a degree at Oxford and orders in the English Church, he returned to Sir William Temple's service and remained in it until January, 1699. It was during this period that he first became attached to Esther Johnson, the "Stella" to whom it is said that he was privately married in 1716. His "Tale of a Tub" and "Battle of the Books" both appeared in 1704. "Gulliver's Travels" his greatest work,—the greatest satire ever written,—did not appear until 1726, when a long list of essays, pamphlets, poems, and miscellanies of almost every conceivable description, including the celebrated Drapier letters, had already made him one of the foremost men of letters of his generation. All his other works are so far eclipsed by "Gulliver's Travels" that, full of his genius as they are, they might be completely forgotten without jeopardizing his place in literature. He was associated intimately with Steele, Addison, Pope, Congreve, Gay, and other noted writers of his day. All of them he surpassed in force, and had it not been impaired by bitterness, it would have made him the most effective prose writer of modern times. The same bitterness, however, which finally brought him insanity and death, shows in his best work to such an extent that he fails most in persuading where he succeeds best in compelling admiration. In his political affiliations from 1710 to his death (October 19th, 1745) he was ostensibly a Tory, but he was really the greatest Radical of his day. His "Argument against Abolishing Christianity" and the frightful irony of his proposal that the starving peasantry of Ireland should relieve the English government of embarrassment by eating their own children, suggest the "cruel indignation" which almost robbed him of his reason when he saw the enormous injustices to which the helpless classes of the eighteenth century were subjected. "*Ubi sæva indignatio ulterius cor lacerare nequit*" is part of the noble epitaph over the tomb in St. Patrick's Cathedral where his body was laid to rest in the same coffin with that of "Stella." He wrote the epitaph himself:—"Here lies the body of Jonathan Swift, S. T. P., Dean of this Cathedral — where cruel indignation can lacerate his heart no longer!" The lines are an autobiography. They tell more of the reality of his life than any one else can ever put into words.

THE ART OF POLITICAL LYING

I AM prevailed on, through the importunity of friends, to interrupt the scheme I had begun in my last paper, by an essay upon the Art of Political Lying. We are told the devil is the father of lies, and was a liar from the beginning; so that, beyond contradiction, the invention is old: and, which is more, his first essay of it was purely political, employed in undermining the authority of his prince, and seducing a third part of the subjects from their obedience: for which he was driven down from heaven, where (as Milton expresses it) he had been viceroy of a great western province; and forced to exercise his talent in inferior regions among other fallen spirits, poor or deluded men, whom he still daily tempts to his own sin, and will ever do so, till he be chained in the bottomless pit.

But although the devil be the father of lies, he seems, like other great inventors, to have lost much of his reputation, by the continual improvements that have been made upon him.

Who first reduced lying into an art, and adapted it to politics, is not so clear from history, although I have made some diligent inquiries. I shall therefore consider it only according to the modern system, as it has been cultivated these twenty years past in the southern part of our own island.

The poets tell us, that after the giants were overthrown by the gods, the earth in revenge produced her last offspring which was Fame. And the fable is thus interpreted: that when tumults and seditions are quieted, rumors and false reports are plentifully spread through a nation. So that, by this account, lying is the last relief of a routed, earth-born, rebellious party in a state. But here the Moderns have made great additions, applying this art to the gaining of power and preserving it, as well as revenging themselves after they have lost it; as the same instruments are made use of by animals to feed themselves when they are hungry, and to bite those that tread upon them.

But the same genealogy cannot always be admitted for political lying; I shall therefore desire to refine upon it, by adding some circumstances of its birth and parents. A political lie is sometimes born out of a discarded statesman's head, and thence delivered to be nursed and dandled by the rabble. Sometimes it is produced a monster, and licked into shape; at other times it comes into the world completely formed, and is spoiled in the licking. It is often born an infant in the regular way, and requires time to mature it; and often it sees the light in its full growth, but dwindles away by degrees. Sometimes it is of noble birth; and sometimes the spawn of a stockjobber. Here it screams aloud at the opening of the womb; and there it is delivered with a whisper. I know a lie that now disturbs half the kingdom with its noise, which, although too proud and great at present to own its parents, I can remember its whisperhood. To conclude the nativity of this monster; when it comes into the world without a sting, it is stillborn; and whenever it loses its sting, it dies.

No wonder if an infant so miraculous in its birth should be destined for great adventures; and accordingly we see it hath been the guardian spirit of a prevailing party for almost twenty years. It can conquer kingdoms without fighting, and sometimes with the loss of a battle. It gives and resumes employments; can sink a mountain to a molehill, and raise a molehill to a mountain; hath presided for many years at committees of elections; can wash a blackmoor white; make a saint of an atheist, and a patriot of a profligate; can furnish foreign ministers with intelligence and raise or let fall the credit of the nation. This goddess flies with a huge looking-glass in her hands, to dazzle the crowd, and make them see, according as she turns it, their ruin in their interest, and their interest in their ruin. In this glass you will behold your best friends, clad in coats powdered with fleurs-de-lis, and triple crowns; their girdles hung round with chains, and beads, and wooden shoes; and your worst enemies adorned with the ensigns of liberty, property, indulgence, moderation, and a cornucopia in their hands. Her large wings, like those of a flying fish, are of no use but while they are moist; she therefore dips them in mud, and soaring aloft scatters it in the eyes of the multitude, flying with great swiftness; but at every turn is forced to stoop in dirty ways for new supplies.

I have been sometimes thinking, if a man had the art of the second sight for seeing lies, as they have in Scotland for seeing

spirits, how admirably he might entertain himself in this town, by observing the different shapes, sizes, and colors of those swarms of lies which buzz about the heads of some people, like flies about a horse's ears in summer; or those legions hovering every afternoon in Exchange alley, enough to darken the air; or over a club of discontented grandees, and thence sent down in cargoes to be scattered at elections.

There is one essential point wherein a political liar differs from others of the faculty, that he ought to have but a short memory, which is necessary, according to the various occasions he meets with every hour of differing from himself, and swearing to both sides of a contradiction, as he finds the persons disposed with whom he hath to deal. In describing the virtues and vices of mankind, it is convenient, upon every article, to have some eminent person in our eye, from whom we copy our description. I have strictly observed this rule, and my imagination this minute represents before me a certain great man famous for this talent, to the constant practice of which he owes his twenty years' reputation of the most skillful head in England, for the management of nice affairs. The superiority of his genius consists in nothing else but an inexhaustible fund of political lies, which he plentifully distributes every minute he speaks, and by an unparalleled generosity forgets, and consequently contradicts, the next half hour. He never yet considered whether any proposition were true or false, but whether it were convenient for the present minute or company to affirm or deny it; so that if you think fit to refine upon him, by interpreting everything he says, as we do dreams, by the contrary, you are still to seek, and will find yourself equally deceived whether you believe or not; the only remedy is to suppose that you have heard some inarticulate sounds, without any meaning at all; and besides, that will take off the horror you might be apt to conceive at the oaths, wherewith he perpetually tags both ends of every proposition; although, at the same time, I think he cannot with any justice be taxed with perjury, when he invokes God and Christ, because he hath often fairly given public notice to the world that he believes in neither.

Some people may think that such an accomplishment as this can be of no great use to the owner, or his party, after it has been often practiced, and is become notorious; but they are widely mistaken. Few lies carry the inventor's mark, and the

most prostitute enemy to truth may spread a thousand, without being known for the author; besides, as the vilest writer hath his readers, so the greatest liar hath his believers, and it often happens that if a lie be believed only for an hour, it hath done its work, and there is no further occasion for it. Falsehood flies, and truth comes limping after it, so that when men come to be undeceived, it is too late; the jest is over, and the tale hath had its effect: like a man, who hath thought of a good repartee when the discourse is changed, or the company parted; or like a physician, who hath found out an infallible medicine, after the patient is dead.

From the Examiner.

A MEDITATION UPON A BROOMSTICK

(According to the style and manner of the Hon. Robert Boyle's meditations.)

THIS single stick, which you now behold ingloriously lying in that neglected corner, I once knew in a flourishing state in a forest. It was full of sap, full of leaves, and full of boughs; but now in vain does the busy art of man pretend to vie with nature, by tying that withered bundle of twigs to its sapless trunk; it is now at best but the reverse of what it was, a tree turned upside down, the branches on the earth, and the root in the air; it is now handled by every dirty wench, condemned to do her drudgery, and, by a capricious kind of fate, destined to make other things clean, and be nasty itself; at length, worn to the stumps in the service of the maids, it is either thrown out of doors, or condemned to the last use — of kindling a fire. When I beheld this I sighed, and said within myself, "Surely mortal man is a broomstick!" Nature sent him into the world strong and lusty, in a thriving condition, wearing his own hair on his head, the proper branches of this reasoning vegetable, till the ax of intemperance has lopped off his green boughs, and left him a withered trunk; he then flies to art, and puts on a periwig, valuing himself upon an unnatural bundle of hairs, all covered with powder, that never grew on his head; but now should this our broomstick pretend to enter the scene, proud of those birchen spoils it never bore, and all covered with dust, through the sweepings of the finest lady's chamber, we should be apt to ridicule and despise its vanity. Partial judges that we are of our own excellencies, and other men's defaults!

But a broomstick, perhaps you will say, is an emblem of a tree standing on its head; and pray what is a man but a topsy-turvy creature, his animal faculties perpetually mounted on his rational, his head where his heels should be, groveling on the earth? And yet, with all his faults, he sets up to be a universal reformer and corrector of abuses, a remover of grievances; rakes into every slut's corner of nature, bringing hidden corruptions to the light; and raises a mighty dust where there was none before, sharing deeply all the while in the very same pollutions he pretends to sweep away. His last days are spent in slavery to women, and generally the least deserving; till, worn to the stumps, like his brother besom, he is either kicked out of doors, or made use of to kindle flames for others to warm themselves by.

Complete.

THOUGHTS ON VARIOUS SUBJECTS

WE HAVE just enough religion to make us hate, but not enough to make us love one another.

Reflect on things past, as wars, negotiations, factions, etc. We enter so little into those interests, that we wonder how men could possibly be so busy and concerned for things so transitory; look on the present times, we find the same humor, yet wonder not at all.

A wise man endeavors, by considering all circumstances, to make conjectures and form conclusions; but the smallest accident intervening (and in the course of affairs it is impossible to foresee all) does often produce such turns and changes, that at last he is just as much in doubt of events as the most ignorant and inexperienced person.

Positiveness is a good quality for preachers and orators, because he that would obtrude his thoughts and reasons upon a multitude, will convince others the more, as he appears convinced himself.

How is it possible to expect that mankind will take advice, when they will not so much as take warning?

I forget whether Advice be among the lost things which Aristo says are to be found in the moon; that and Time ought to have been there.

time; that is to say, it seldom happens to above one person in a company to be possessed with any high degree of spleen or melancholy.

I am apt to think that, in the Day of Judgment, there will be small allowance given to the wise for their want of morals, nor to the ignorant for their want of faith, because both are without excuse. This renders the advantages equal of ignorance and knowledge. But some scruples in the wise and some vices in the ignorant will perhaps be forgiven upon the strength of temptation to each.

The value of several circumstances in story lessens very much by distance of time, though some minute circumstances are very valuable; and it requires great judgment in a writer to distinguish.

It is grown a word of course for writers to say, "This critical age," as divines say, "This sinful age."

It is pleasant to observe how free the present age is in laying taxes on the next. Future ages shall talk of this; this shall be famous to all posterity. Whereas their time and thoughts will be taken up about present things, as ours are now.

The chameleon, which is said to feed upon nothing but air, hath, of all animals, the nimblest tongue.

When a man is made a spiritual peer he loses his surname; when a temporal, his Christian name.

It is in disputes as in armies, where the weaker side sets up false lights, and makes a great noise, to make the enemy believe them more numerous and strong than they really are.

Some men, under the notions of weeding out prejudices, eradicate virtue, honesty, and religion.

In all well-instituted commonwealths care has been taken to limit men's possessions; which is done for many reasons, and among the rest, for one which perhaps is not often considered: that when bounds are set to men's desires, after they have acquired as much as the laws will permit them, their private interest is at an end, and they have nothing to do but to take care of the public.

There are but three ways for a man to revenge himself of the censure of the world: to despise it, to return the like, or to endeavor to live so as to avoid it. The first of these is usually pretended, the last is almost impossible; the universal practice is for the second.

No preacher is listened to but Time, which gives us the same train and turn of thought that elder people have tried in vain to put into our heads before.

When we desire or solicit anything, our minds run wholly on the good side or circumstances of it; when it is obtained, our minds run wholly on the bad ones.

In a glasshouse the workmen often fling in a small quantity of fresh coals, which seems to disturb the fire, but very much enlivens it. This seems to allude to a gentle stirring of the passions, that the mind may not languish.

Religion seems to have grown an infant with age, and requires miracles to nurse it, as it had in its infancy.

All fits of pleasure are balanced by an equal degree of pain or languor; it is like spending this year part of the next year's revenue.

The latter part of a wise man's life is taken up in curing the follies, prejudices, and false opinions he had contracted in the former.

Would a writer know how to behave himself with relation to posterity, let him consider in old books what he finds that he is glad to know, and what omissions he most laments.

Whatever the poets pretend, it is plain they give immortality to none but themselves; it is Homer and Virgil we reverence and admire, not Achilles or Æneas. With historians it is quite the contrary; our thoughts are taken up with the actions, persons, and events we read, and we little regard the authors.

When a true genius appears in the world you may know him by this sign, that the dunces are all in confederacy against him.

Men who possess all the advantages of life are in a state where there are many accidents to disorder and discompose, but few to please them.

It is unwise to punish cowards with ignominy, for if they had regarded that they would not have been cowards; death is their proper punishment, because they fear it most.

The greatest inventions were produced in the times of ignorance, as the use of the compass, gunpowder, and printing, and by the dullest nation, as the Germans.

One argument to prove that the common relations of ghosts and spectres are generally false may be drawn from the opinion held that spirits are never seen by more than one person at a

I never heard a finer piece of satire against lawyers than that of astrologers, when they pretend by rules of art to tell when a suit will end, and whether to the advantage of the plaintiff or defendant; thus making the matter depend entirely upon the influence of the stars, without the least regard to the merits of the cause.

The expression in the Apocrypha about Tobit and his dog following him I have often heard ridiculed, yet Homer has the same words of Telemachus more than once; and Virgil says something like it of Evander. And I take the book of Tobit to be partly poetical.

I have known some men possessed of good qualities which were very serviceable to others, but useless to themselves; like a sundial on the front of a house, to inform the neighbors and passengers, but not the owner within.

If a man would register all his opinions upon love, politics, religion, learning, etc., beginning from his youth and so go on to old age, what a bundle of inconsistencies and contradictions would appear at last!

What they do in heaven we are ignorant of; what they do not we are told expressly: that they neither marry, nor are given in marriage.

It is a miserable thing to live in suspense; it is the life of a spider.

The stoical scheme of supplying our wants by lopping off our desires is like cutting off our feet when we want shoes.

Physicians ought not to give their judgment of religion, for the same reason that butchers are not admitted to be jurors upon life and death.

The reason why so few marriages are happy is because young ladies spend their time in making nets, not in making cages.

If a man will observe as he walks the streets, I believe he will find the merriest countenances in mourning coaches.

Nothing more unqualifies a man to act with prudence than a misfortune that is attended with shame and guilt.

The power of fortune is confessed only by the miserable; for the happy impute all their success to prudence or merit.

Ambition often puts men upon doing the meanest offices; so climbing is performed in the same posture with creeping.

Censure is the tax a man pays to the public for being eminent.

Although men are accused for not knowing their own weakness, yet perhaps as few know their own strength. It is in men as in soils, where sometimes there is a vein of gold which the owner knows not of.

Satire is reckoned the easiest of all wit, but I take it to be otherwise in very bad times; for it is as hard to satirize well a man of distinguished vices as to praise well a man of distinguished virtues. It is easy enough to do either to people of moderate characters.

Invention is the talent of youth, and judgment of age; so that our judgment grows harder to please, when we have fewer things to offer it. This goes through the whole commerce of life. When we are old, our friends find it difficult to please us, and are less concerned whether we be pleased or no.

No wise man ever wished to be younger.

An idle reason lessens the weight of the good ones you gave before.

The motives of the best actions will not bear too strict an inquiry. It is allowed that the cause of most actions, good or bad, may be resolved into the love of ourselves; but the self-love of some men inclines them to please others, and the self-love of others is wholly employed in pleasing themselves. This makes the great distinction between virtue and vice. Religion is the best motive of all actions, yet religion is allowed to be the highest instance of self-love.

Old men view best at a distance with the eyes of their understanding as well as with those of nature.

Some people take more care to hide their wisdom than their folly.

Anthony Henley's farmer, dying of an asthma, said, " Well, if I can get this breath once out, I'll take care it shall never get in again.»

The humor of exploding many things under the name of trifles, fopperies, and only imaginary goods, is a very false proof either of wisdom or magnanimity, and a great check to virtuous actions. For instance, with regard to fame, there is in most people a reluctance and unwillingness to be forgotten. We observe, even among the vulgar, how fond they are to have an inscription over their grave. It requires but little philosophy to discover and observe that there is no intrinsic value in all this; however, if it be founded in our nature as an incitement to virtue, it ought not to be ridiculed.

Praise is the daughter of present power.

How inconsistent is man with himself!

I have known several persons of great fame for wisdom in public affairs and counsels governed by foolish servants.

I have known great ministers, distinguished for wit and learning, who preferred none but dunces.

I have known men of great valor cowards to their wives.

I have known men of the greatest cunning perpetually cheated.

I knew three great ministers, who could exactly compute and settle the accounts of a kingdom, but were wholly ignorant of their own economy.

The preaching of divines helps to preserve well-inclined men in the course of virtue, but seldom or never reclaims the vicious.

Princes usually make wiser choices than the servants whom they trust for the disposal of places: I have known a prince, more than once, choose an able minister, but I never observed that minister to use his credit in the disposal of an employment to a person whom he thought the fittest for it. One of the greatest in this age owned and excused the matter from the violence of parties and the unreasonableness of friends.

Small causes are sufficient to make a man uneasy when great ones are not in the way. For want of a block he will stumble at a straw.

Dignity, high station, or great riches, are in some sort necessary to old men, in order to keep the younger at a distance, who are otherwise too apt to insult them upon the score of their age.

Every man desires to live long; but no man would be old.

Love of flattery in most men proceeds from the mean opinion they have of themselves; in women from the contrary.

If books and laws continue to increase as they have done for fifty years past, I am in some concern for future ages how any man will be learned, or any man a lawyer.

Kings are commonly said to have long hands; I wish they had as long ears.

Princes in their infancy, childhood, and youth are said to discover prodigious parts and wit, to speak things that surprise and astonish. Strange, so many hopeful princes, and so many shameful kings! If they happen to die young, they would have been prodigies of wisdom and virtue. If they live, they are often prodigies indeed, but of another sort.

Complaint is the largest tribute heaven receives, and the sincerest part of our devotion.

The common fluency of speech in many men, and most women, is owing to a scarcity of matter, and a scarcity of words; for whoever is a master of language, and hath a mind full of ideas, will be apt, in speaking, to hesitate upon the choice of both; whereas common speakers have only one set of ideas, and one set of words to clothe them in, and these are always ready at the mouth. So people come faster out of a church when it is almost empty than when a crowd is at the door.

Few are qualified to shine in company; but it is in most men's power to be agreeable. The reason, therefore, why conversation runs so low at present is not the defect of understanding, but pride, vanity, ill nature, affectation, singularity, positiveness, or some other vice, the effect of a wrong education.

To be vain is rather a mark of humility than pride. Vain men delight in telling what honors have been done them, what great company they have kept, and the like, by which they plainly confess that these honors were more than their due, and such as their friends would not believe if they had not been told; whereas a man truly proud thinks the greatest honors below his merit, and consequently scorns to boast. I therefore deliver it as a maxim, that whoever desires the character of a proud man ought to conceal his vanity.

Law, in a free country, is, or ought to be, the determination of the majority of those who have property in land.

One argument used to the disadvantage of Providence I take to be a very strong one in its defense. It is objected that storms and tempests, unfruitful seasons, serpents, spiders, flies, and other noxious or troublesome animals, with many more instances of the like kind, discover an imperfection in nature, because human life would be much easier without them; but the design of Providence may clearly be perceived in this proceeding. The motions of the sun and moon—in short, the whole system of the universe, as far as philosophers have been able to discover and observe—are in the utmost degree of regularity and perfection; but wherever God hath left to man the power of interposing a remedy by thought or labor, there he hath placed things in a state of imperfection, on purpose to stir up human industry, without which life would stagnate, or, indeed, rather, could not subsist at all: *Curis accuunt mortalia corda.*

Politics, as the word is commonly understood, are nothing but corruptions, and consequently of no use to a good king or a good ministry; for which reason courts are so overrun with politics.

A nice man is a man of nasty ideas.

Apollo was held the god of physic and sender of diseases. Both were originally the same trade, and still continue.

Old men and comets have been reverenced for the same reason: their long beards, and pretenses to foretell events.

A person was asked at court, what he thought of an embassador and his train, who were all embroidery and lace, full of bows, cringes, and gestures; he said it was Solomon's importation, gold and apes.

Most sorts of diversion in men, children, and other animals, is an imitation of fighting.

Augustus meeting an ass with a lucky name foretold himself good fortune. I meet many asses, but none of them have lucky names.

If a man makes me keep my distance, the comfort is, he keeps his at the same time.

Who can deny that all men are violent lovers of truth when we see them so positive in their errors, which they will maintain out of their zeal to truth, although they contradict themselves every day of their lives?

That was excellently observed say I, when I read a passage in an author, where his opinion agrees with mine. When we differ, there I pronounce him to be mistaken.

Very few men, properly speaking, live at present, but are providing to live another time.

Laws penned with the utmost care and exactness, and in the vulgar language, are often perverted to wrong meanings; then why should we wonder that the Bible is so?

Although men are accused for not knowing their weakness, yet perhaps as few know their own strength.

A man seeing a wasp creeping into a vial filled with honey, that was hung on a fruit tree, said thus: " Why, thou sottish animal, art thou mad to go into that vial, where you see many hundreds of your kind there dying in it before you?» " The reproach is just,» answered the wasp, " but not from you men, who are so far from taking example by other people's follies, that you will not take warning by your own. If after falling several times into this vial, and escaping by chance, I should fall in again, I should then but resemble you.»

An old miser kept a tame jackdaw, that used to steal pieces of money, and hide them in a hole, which the cat observing, asked why he would hoard up those round shining things that he could make no use of? "Why," said the jackdaw, "my master has a whole chest full, and makes no more use of them than I."

Men are content to be laughed at for their wit, but not for their folly.

If the men of wit and genius would resolve never to complain in their works of critics and detractors, the next age would not know that they ever had any.

After all the maxims and systems of trade and commerce, a stander-by would think the affairs of the world were most ridiculously contrived.

There are few countries which, if well cultivated, would not support double the number of their inhabitants, and yet fewer where one-third of the people are not extremely stinted even in the necessaries of life. I send out twenty barrels of corn, which would maintain a family in bread for a year, and I bring back in return a vessel of wine, which half a dozen good fellows would drink in less than a month, at the expense of their health and reason.

A man would have but few spectators, if he offered to show for threepence how he could thrust a red-hot iron into a barrel of gunpowder, and it should not take fire.

Complete.

AGAINST ABOLISHING CHRISTIANITY IN ENGLAND

I AM very sensible what a weakness and presumption it is to reason against the general humor and disposition of the world. I remember it was with great justice, and a due regard to the freedom, both of the public and the press, forbidden upon several penalties to write, or discourse, or lay wagers against the —— even before it was confirmed by parliament; because that was looked upon as a design to oppose the current of the people, which, besides the folly of it, is a manifest breach of the fundamental law, that makes this majority of opinions the voice of God. In like manner, and for the very same reasons, it may perhaps be neither safe nor prudent to argue against the abolishing of Christianity, at a juncture when all parties seem so

unanimously determined upon the point, as we cannot but allow from their actions, their discourses, and their writings. However, I know not how, whether from the affectation of singularity, or the perverseness of human nature, but so it unhappily falls out, that I cannot be entirely of this opinion. Nay, though I were sure an order were issued for my immediate prosecution by the Attorney-General, I should still confess that in the present posture of our affairs at home or abroad, I do not yet see the absolute necessity of extirpating the Christian religion from among us.

This perhaps may appear too great a paradox even for our wise and paradoxical age to endure; therefore I shall handle it with all tenderness, and with the utmost deference to that great and profound majority which is of another sentiment.

And yet the curious may please to observe how much the genius of a nation is liable to alter in half an age: I have heard it affirmed for certain by some very odd people, that the contrary opinion was even in their memories as much in vogue as the other is now; and that a project for the abolishing of Christianity would then have appeared as singular, and been thought as absurd, as it would be at this time to write or discourse in its defense.

Therefore I freely own that all appearances are against me. The system of the Gospel after the fate of other systems, is generally antiquated and exploded, and the mass or body of the common people, among whom it seems to have had its latest credit, are now grown as much ashamed of it as their betters; opinions, like fashions, always descending from those of quality to the middle sort, and thence to the vulgar, where at length they are dropped and vanish.

But here I would not be mistaken, and must therefore be so bold as to borrow a distinction from the writers on the other side, when they make a difference betwixt nominal and real Trinitarians. I hope no reader imagines me so weak to stand up in the defense of real Christianity, such as used in primitive times (if we may believe the authors of those ages) to have an influence upon men's belief and actions. To offer at the restoring of that would indeed be a wild project: it would be to dig up foundations; to destroy at one blow all the wit, and half the learning of the kingdom; to break the entire frame and constitution of things; to ruin trade, extinguish arts and sciences, with the professors of them; in short, to turn our courts, exchanges, and shops into des-

erts; and would be full as absurd as the proposal of Horace, where he advises the Romans all in a body to leave their city, and seek a new seat in some remote part of the world, by way of a cure for the corruption of their manners.

Therefore I think this caution was in itself altogether unnecessary (which I have inserted only to prevent all possibility of caviling), since every candid reader will easily understand my discourse to be intended only in defense of nominal Christianity, the other having been for some time wholly laid aside by general consent, as utterly inconsistent with all our present schemes of wealth and power.

But why we should therefore cast off the name and title of Christians, although the general opinion and resolution be so violent for it, I confess I cannot (with submission) apprehend the consequence necessary.

AGAINST BAD ENGLISH

FROM MY OWN APARTMENT, September 28th.

THE following letter has laid before me many great and manifest evils in the world of letters, which I had overlooked; but they open to me a very busy scene, and it will require no small care and application to amend errors which are become so universal. The affectation of politeness is exposed in this epistle with a great deal of wit and discernment; so that whatever discourses I may fall into hereafter upon the subjects the writer treats of, I shall at present lay the matter before the world, without the least alteration from the words of my correspondent.

TO ISAAC BICKERSTAFF, ESQ.

Sir:—

There are some abuses among us of great consequence, the reformation of which is properly your province; though, as far as I have been conversant in your papers, you have not yet considered them. These are, the deplorable ignorance that for some years hath reigned among our English writers, the great depravity of our taste, and the continual corruption of our style. I say nothing here of those who handle particular sciences, divinity, law, physic, and the like; I mean the traders in history, politics, and the Belles-Lettres; together with those by whom books are not translated, but, as the common expressions are, done out of French, Latin, or other language, and made

English. I cannot but observe to you that until of late years a Grub-Street book was always bound in sheepskin, with suitable print and paper, the price never above a shilling, and taken off wholly by common tradesmen or country peddlers; but now they appear in all sizes and shapes, and in all places. They are handed about from lapfuls in every coffeehouse to persons of quality; are shown in Westminster Hall and the Court of Requests. You may see them gilt, and in royal paper of five or six hundred pages, and rated accordingly. I would engage to furnish you with a catalogue of English books, published within the compass of seven years past, which at the first hand would cost you a hundred pounds, wherein you shall not be able to find ten lines together of common grammar or common sense.

These two evils, ignorance and want of taste, have produced a third; I mean the continual corruption of our English tongue, which, without some timely remedy, will suffer more by the false refinements of twenty years past, than it hath been improved in the foregoing hundred. And this is what I design chiefly to enlarge upon, leaving the former evils to your animadversion.

But instead of giving you a list of the late refinements crept into our language, I here send you the copy of a letter I received, some time ago, from a most accomplished person in this way of writing; upon which I shall make some remarks. It is in these terms:—

Sir:—

I cou'd n't get the things you sent for all about town —— I thôt to ha come down myself, and then I'd h' brôt 'um; but I ha'nt don't, and I believe I can't do't that's pozz —— Tom begins to gi'mself airs, because he's going with the plenipo's —— 'Tis said the French king will bamboozl us agen, which causes many speculations. The Jacks and others of that kidney are very uppish and alert upon't, as you may see by their phizz's —— Will Hazard has got the hipps, having lost to the tune of five hund'rd pound, tho' he understands play very well, nobody better. He has promis't me upon rep, to leave off play; but you know 'tis a weakness he's too apt to give into, tho' he has as much wit as any man, nobody more. He has lain incog ever since —— The mob's very quiet with us now —— I believe you thôt I banter'd you in my last, like a country put —— I shan't leave town this month, etc.

This letter is in every point an admirable pattern of the present polite way of writing; nor is it of less authority for being an epistle. You may gather every flower in it, with a thousand more of equal sweetness, from the books, pamphlets, and single papers offered us every day in the coffeehouses: and these are the beauties introduced to supply the want of wit, sense, humor, and learning, which formerly were looked upon as qualifications for a writer. If a man of wit, who died forty years ago, were to rise from the grave on purpose, how would he be able to read this letter? and after he had got through that difficulty, how would he be able to understand it? The first thing that strikes your eye is the breaks at the end of almost every sentence; of which I know not the use, only that it is a refinement, and very frequently practiced. Then you will observe the abbreviations and elisions, by which consonants of most obdurate sound are joined together, without one softening vowel to intervene; and all this only to make one syllable of two, directly contrary to the example of the Greeks and Romans, altogether of the Gothic strain, and a natural tendency towards relapsing into barbarity, which delights in monosyllables, and uniting of mute consonants, as it is observable in all the Northern languages. And this is still more visible in the next refinement, which consists in pronouncing the first syllable in a word that has many, and dismissing the rest, such as phizz, hipps, mob, pozz, rep, and many more, when we are already overloaded with monosyllables, which are the disgrace of our language. Thus we cram one syllable, and cut off the rest, as the owl fattened her mice after she had bit off their legs to prevent them from running away; and if ours be the same reason for maiming our words, it will certainly answer the end; for I am sure no other nation will desire to borrow them. Some words are hitherto but fairly split, and therefore only in their way to perfection, as incog and plenipo; but in a short time, it is to be hoped, they will be further docked to inc and plen. This reflection has made me of late years very impatient for a peace, which I believe would save the lives of many brave words, as well as men. The war has introduced abundance of polysyllables, which will never be able to live many more campaigns: speculations, operations, preliminaries, embassadors, pallisadoes, communication, circumvallation, battalions; as numerous as they are, if they attack us too frequently in our coffeehouses, we shall certainly put them to flight, and cut off the rear.

The third refinement observable in the letter I send you, consists in the choice of certain words invented by some pretty fellows, such as banter, bamboozle, country put, and kidney, as it is there applied; some of which are now struggling for the vogue, and others are in possession of it. I have done my utmost for some years past to stop the progress of mob and banter, but have been plainly borne down by numbers, and betrayed by those who promised to assist me.

In the last place, you are to take notice of certain choice phrases scattered through the letter, some of them tolerable enough, until they were worn to rags by servile imitators. You might easily find them, though they were not in a different print, and therefore I need not disturb them.

These are the false refinements in our style which you ought to correct: first, by argument and fair means; but, if those fail, I think

you are to make use of your authority as Censor, and by an annual *Index Expurgatorius* expunge all words and phrases that are offensive to good sense, and condemn those barbarous mutilations of vowels and syllables. In this last point the usual pretense is, that they spell as they speak. A noble standard for language! to depend upon the caprice of every coxcomb, who, because words are the clothing of our thoughts, cuts them out and shapes them as he pleases, and changes them oftener than his dress. I believe all reasonable people would be content that such refiners were more sparing in their words, and liberal in their syllables: and upon this head I should be glad you would bestow some advice upon several young readers in our churches, who, coming up from the university full fraught with admiration of our town politeness, will needs correct the style of their prayer books. In reading the Absolution, they are very careful to say pardons and absolves; and in the prayer for the royal family, it must be endue'um, enrich'um, prosper'um, and bring'um. Then in their sermons they use all the modern terms of art, sham, banter, mob, bubble, bully, cutting, shuffling, and palming; all which, and many more of the like stamp, as I have heard them often in the pulpit from such young sophisters, so I have read them in some of "those sermons that have made most noise of late." The design, it seems, is to avoid the dreadful imputation of pedantry; to show us that they know the town, understand men and manners, and have not been poring upon old, unfashionable books in the university.

I should be glad to see you the instrument of introducing into our style that simplicity which is the best and truest ornament of most things in life, which the politer ages always aimed at in their building and dress, *simplex munditiis*, as well as their productions of wit. It is manifest that all new-affected modes of speech, whether borrowed from the court, the town, or the theatre, are the first perishing parts in any language; and, as I could prove by many hundred instances, have been so in ours. The writings of Hooker, who was a country clergyman, and of Parsons the Jesuit, both in the reign of Queen Elizabeth, are in a style that, with very few allowances, would not offend any present reader, and are much more clear and intelligible than those of Sir Harry Wooton, Sir Robert Naunton, Osborn, Daniel the historian, and several others who writ later; but being men of the court, and affecting the phrases then in fashion, they are often either not to be understood, or appear perfectly ridiculous.

What remedies are to be applied to these evils I have not room to consider, having, I fear, already taken up most of your paper. Besides, I think it is our office only to represent abuses, and yours to redress them. I am, with great respect, sir,   Yours, etc.

Complete. From the Tatler.

ALGERNON CHARLES SWINBURNE

(1837–)

ALGERNON CHARLES SWINBURNE, a celebrated English poet and critic, was born in London, April 5th, 1837. His studies were begun in France and completed at Oxford, which he left without a degree in 1857. It is possible, however, that he did not leave a better Greek scholar behind him at the university, which failed to honor him. His love for Greek and French verse decided his career and his style. He became the most melodious versifier of his time. The English language as he employed it by joining Saxon alliteration to classical "staff rhyme" showed a capacity for melody before unsuspected. He employed this in his earlier poems and ballads (republished in America in 1866 as "Laus Veneris") to express a spirit of intense revolt against modern moral and social restrictions. This is more or less apparent throughout all his work, which in his later years shows an increasing tendency to prefer melody to meaning. In his youth he was a fierce Republican, a disciple of Landor and Hugo; but among his latest poems is a strongly patriotic ode in favor of crushing the Boers of the South African republics. He has published numerous essays, chiefly critical. Some of them have been collected in his "Prose Miscellanies," published in 1886.

W. V. B.

CHAUCER AND THE ITALIAN POETS

OF ALL whose names may claim anything like equality of rank on the roll of national poets — not even excepting Virgil — we may say that Chaucer borrowed most from abroad, and did most to improve whatever he borrowed. I believe it would be but accurate to admit that in all his poems of serious or tragic narrative we hear a French or Italian tongue speaking with a Teutonic accent through English lips. It has utterly unlearned the native tone and cadence of its natural inflections; it has perfectly put on the native tone and cadence of a stranger's; yet is it always what it was at first — *lingua romana in bocca tedesca*. It speaks not only with more vigor, but actually with more sweetness than the tongues of its teachers: but it speaks

after its own fashion no other than the lesson they have taught. Chaucer was in the main a French or Italian poet, lined thoroughly and warmly throughout with the substance of an English humorist. And with this great gift of specially English humor he combined, naturally as it were and inevitably, the inseparable twinborn gift of peculiarly English pathos. In the figures of Arcite and Grisilde he has actually outdone Boccaccio's very self for pathos; as far almost as Keats was afterward to fall short of the same great model in the same great quality. And but for the instinctive distaste and congenital repugnance of his composed and comfortable genius from its accompanying horror, he might haply have come nearer than he has cared or dared to come even to the unapproachable pathos of Dante. But it was only in the world of one who stands far higher above Dante than even Dante can on the whole be justly held to stand above Chaucer, that figures as heavenly as the figures of Beatrice and Matilda could move unspotted and undegraded among figures as earthly as those of the Reve, the Miller, and the Wife of Bath; that a wider, if not keener, pathos than Ugolino's or Francesca's could alternate with a deeper, if not richer, humor than that of Absolon and Nicholas.

It is a notable dispensation of chance that the three great typical poets of the three great representative nations of Europe during the dark and lurid lapse of the Middle Ages should each afford as complete and profound a type of a different and alien class as of a different and alien people. Vast as are the diversities of their national and personal characters, these are yet less radical than the divergences between class and class which mark off each from either of his fellows in nothing but in fame. Dante represents, at its best and highest, the upper class of the Dark Ages not less than he represents their Italy; Chaucer represents their middle class at its best and wisest not less than he represents their England; Villon represents their lower class at its worst and its best alike even more than he represents their France. And of these three the English middle class, being incomparably the happiest and the wisest, is indisputably, considering the common circumstances of their successive times, the least likely to have left us the highest example of all poetry then possible to men. And of their three legacies, precious and wonderful as it is, the Englishman's is accordingly the least wonderful and the least precious. The poet of the sensible and prosperous middle class in England had less to suffer and to sing than the theosophic aristocrat of Italy, or the hunted and hungry vagabond who first found articulate voice for the dumb longing and the blind love, as well as for the reckless appetites and riotous agonies of the miserable and terrible multitude in whose darkness lay dormant, as in a cerecloth, which was also a chrysalis, the debased and disfigured godhead which was one day to exchange the degradation of the lowest populace for the revelation of the highest people — for the world-wide apocalypse of France. The golden-tongued gallows bird of Paris is distinguished from his two more dignified compeers by a deeper difference yet — a difference, we might say, of office and of mission no less than of genius and of gift. Dante and Chaucer are wholly and solely poets of the past or present — singers, indeed, for all time, but only singers of their own; Villon, in an equivocal and unconscious fashion, was a singer also of the future; he was the first modern and the last mediæval poet. He is of us in a sense in which it cannot be said that either Chaucer or Dante is of us, or even could have been; a man of a changing and self-transforming time, not utterly held fast, though still sorely struggling, in the jaws of hell and the ages of faith.

But in happy perfection of manhood the great and fortunate Englishman almost more exceeds his great and unfortunate fellow-singers than he is exceeded by them in depth of passion and height of rapture, in ardor and intensity of vision or of sense. With the single and sublimer exception of Sophocles, he seems to me the happiest of all great poets on record; their standing type and sovereign example of noble and manly happiness. As prosperous, indeed, in their several ages and lines of life were Petrarch and Ariosto, Horace and Virgil; but one only of these impresses us in every lineament of his work with the same masculine power of enjoyment. And when Ariosto threw across the windy sea of glittering legend and fluctuant romance the broad summer lightnings of his large and jocund genius, the Dark Ages had already returned into the outer darkness where there is weeping and gnashing of teeth — the tears of Dante Alighieri and the laughter of François Villon. But the wide warm harvest field of Chaucer's husbandry was all glorious with gold of ripening sunshine, while all the world beside lay in blackness and bonds, throughout all those ages of death called ages of faith by men who can believe in nothing beyond a build-

ing or a book, outside the codified creeds of a Bible or the ecumenical structures of a church.

From «Short Notes on English Poets.»

A POET'S HAUGHTY PATIENCE

IT is the fashion of our day to look for the typical man or representative figure of the English commonwealth not so much in the poet who glorified as in the dictator who destroyed it. This is but natural and consistent in such historians as see nothing in the record of our short-lived republic worth admiration or regret but the triumph of a more harsh and earnest form of superstition over one somewhat less hellish in its cast of creed and greatly more graceful in its tone of life, accompanied by the substitution of a stern and steady system of dictatorial rule for the lax and trustless impulse of a treacherous and shifting tyranny; but those whose faith or feeling in the matter of historic patriotism lies deeper than a mere preference for competent over incompetent autocracy must perceive, or at least will believe, that the restoration which they admire as little as any military-minded Neo-Calvinist or Muscovitic imperialist of their time was not so much the doing of James Monk as the work of Oliver Cromwell: a consummation of catastrophe directly rather than indirectly due to the weakness and selfishness of the nominal and temporary protector, the actual and final destroyer of the commonwealth of England. For surely the dying hand which put into Richard Cromwell's the sceptre of its sway put by that act the crown of England into Monk's for delivery into Charles the Second's. And this, if we never have learned it from the evidence of Milton himself, we may learn with equal confidence from Landor's that Milton surely saw. "He had grown calmer at the close of life, and saw in Cromwell as a fault what he had seen before as a necessity or a virtue." And therefore is it rather in the loftier, purer, more loyal and more liberal virtue of its poet, than in the dubious and double-faced majesty of its august and imperious dictator, that we should salute the highest and most perfect type of the English republic; dragged down into his own grave by the fatal dead hand of Cromwell, yet surviving after a sort in the figure of the blind man "left upright" — in the phrase of a poet as glorious and a republican as faithful as himself — on the verge and in the shadow of her sepulchre.

In private matters, or such as belong to the range of ethics rather than of politics, the instinct of Milton seems to me as much truer and finer than the instinct of Dante as his judgment and his conscience were juster, sounder, purer than the conscience or the judgment of Cromwell. Only those disciples in whom congenital idolatry has passed into the stage of acute monomania can maintain that the quality of Dante's great work is never in any considerable degree impaired by the incessant invasion of merely personal polemics; that the reader is never or but rarely, fatigued and nauseated by the obtrusion and obsession of "verminous fellows," whom the higher muses at least should be content to leave in the native and natural shelter of that obscene obscurity which alone is proper to such animalcules as make the filth they feed on. There are others beside the "brothel lackeys" of a bastard empire who, as Victor Hugo said once, would desire us to shut our eyes, but compel us to stop our noses.

No matter what manner of offense may naturally be given by creatures whose very nature is offensive, a man who is duly and soberly conscious of any reason for self-respect will ultimately, as Milton did and Dante did not, determine that personal insolence, whether masked as Caliban or manifest as Thersites, shall draw down no further notice from his hand or foot. There are things unmentionable save by a too faithful pupil or too literal imitator of Swift, which, only for our own sake, we are careful not to spurn as we step over them. Upon such Milton did not hesitate to set his heel, when duly guarded by the thick-soled boot of prose; but, unlike Dante, he never permitted the too fetid contact of their feculence to befoul the sandal of his muse. The reddening knots of his controversial scourge fell only in cadences of prose, or at least but very rarely in brief reverberation of rhythmic numbers, on the noisome nudity exposed as in provocation of its lash by Saumaise or Du Moulin, the literary lackey of a princeling or the cryptonymous railer for his bread.

This high-souled and haughty respect for the dignity of his natural art should be duly borne in mind whenever we are tempted to dwell somewhat disapprovingly on Milton's indefatigable and fierce delight in "double-thonging" such equivocal sons of a dubious kennel; though it will not be denied that he spent more strength of arm than he need have wasted on the reso-

nant reiteration of stripes from a deserved but superfluous dog whip, too constantly sent curling about their currish flanks.

It is certainly no very dignified amusement, no very profitable expenditure of energy or time, to indulge in the easy diversion of making such curs yelp, and watching them writhe under the chastisement which an insulted superior may condescend to inflict, till their foul mouths foam over in futile and furious response, reeking and rabid with virulent froth and exhalations of raging ribaldry. Yet when, like those that swarmed at the heels of Milton, the vermin venture on all possible extremes of personal insult and imputation to which dullness may give ear or malice may give tongue, a man cannot reasonably be held to derogate from the duty and the dignity of self-respect if he spurns or scourges them out of his way. To give these rascals rope is a needless waste of hemp; a spider's thread, spun from the inner impurity of his own venomous vitals, will suffice for such a creature to hang himself.

A ground more plausible may seem to exist for a graver charge against Milton than that of a ferocious condescension to take unmerciful notice of such leprous little malignants as these; for the charge of relentless and unmitigable savagery toward the dead, whose misdoings might seem — or to us may seem at this distance — to have been amply expiated by discomfiture and death. Cheap and not over-nice chivalry — the false Florimel who assumes and degrades the appearance of true knightliness of mind and sound nobility of spirit — is ever ready, when tyrants are fallen or when traitors are degraded, to remind us in the shrillest note of reproachful impertinence that "it is ill boasting over dead men." Ill indeed, and worse than ill, it is when those who could see nothing to blame in Nero, nothing to loathe in Judas, till the moment of ruin which reduced them to suicide, begin to cast stones at the carrion which had been found worthy of their adoration when a pontiff, of their adulation when an emperor. But ill it would also be, abominable and absurd, if the "piteous and unpitied end" of either were to be held as expiation sufficient to reverse the branding judgment or silence the damning voice of history or of poetry; to bid those now be silent out of pitiable pity and hypocritical high-mindedness who did not hesitate, while some among the posthumous revilers, as well as the posthumous champions of these wretches, were prone before the vilest of all idols on their knees like the courtier or on their bellies like the serpent, to call Judas by his name of Iscariot and Nero by his name of Bonaparte.

The self-confiden and self-conscious majesty of Milton's devotion and dedication to their natural work of all the faculties assigned to him by nature has foolishly enough been objected against him as evidence of his poetic inferiority to Shakespeare. With that unapproachable name no rational man will assert the equality of Milton's; but if Shakespeare's claim to superiority rested only on the evidence of his intellectual self-effacement, his modest unconsciousness and humble-minded abnegation or ignorance of his right to put forward any claim whatever, it would be but too easy a task to convict him out of his own mouth, and prove by the avowal of his own pretensions that he can pretend to the credit of no such imbecility. No sandier foundation was ever discovered for a fallacy more futile than this. No man ever lived who had less title than Shakespeare to whatever blessing may be reserved for the poor in spirit. Not even Milton, not even Dante, had less right to say in appeal to God or man, « I am not high-minded. » No man's writings bear witness more unquestionable that he worked and waited with the haughty patience of self-assured expectation for the inevitable homage of mankind in centuries to come.

From the Fortnightly Review.

JOHN ADDINGTON SYMONDS
(1840–1893)

OHN ADDINGTON SYMONDS, an English writer, specially noted as an essayist and classical scholar, was born at Bristol, October 5th, 1840. He graduated at Oxford and won the Newdigate prize in 1860. In 1872 his «Introduction to the Study of Dante» laid the foundations of a reputation which he increased by his «Studies of the Greek Poets.» He has made many admirable translations from Greek, Latin, and Italian verse. «Italian By-Ways,» «Sketches of Study in Italy,» and a «Life of Michael Angelo» are among his more noted works. He died at Rome, April 19th, 1893.

MORNING RAMBLES IN VENICE

A STORY is told of Poussin, the French painter, that when he was asked why he would not stay in Venice, he replied, "If I stay here, I shall become a colorist!" A somewhat similar tale is reported of a fashionable English decorator. While on a visit to friends in Venice he avoided every building which contains a Tintoretto, averring that the sight of Tintoretto's pictures would injure his carefully trained taste. It is probable that neither anecdote is strictly true. Yet there is a certain epigrammatic point in both; and I have often speculated whether even Venice could have so warped the genius of Poussin as to shed one ray of splendor on his canvasses, or whether even Tintoretto could have so sublimed the prophet of Queen Anne as to make him add dramatic passion to a London drawing-room. Anyhow it is exceedingly difficult to escape from color in the air of Venice, or from Tintoretto in her buildings. Long, delightful mornings may be spent in the enjoyment of the one and the pursuit of the other by folk who have no classical or pseudo-mediæval theories to oppress them.

Tintoretto's house, though changed, can still be visited. It formed part of the Fondamenta dei Mori, so called from having been the quarter assigned to Moorish traders in Venice. A spirited carving of a turbaned Moor leading a camel charged with

merchandise remains above the water line of a neighboring building, and all about the crumbling walls sprout flowering weeds — samphire and snapdragon and the spiked campanula, which shoots a spire of sea-blue stars from chinks of Istrian stone.

The house stands opposite the Church of Santa Maria dell' Orto, where Tintoretto was buried, and where four of his chief masterpieces are to be seen. This church, swept and garnished, is a triumph of modern Italian restoration. They have contrived to make it as commonplace as human ingenuity could manage. Yet no malice of ignorant industry can obscure the treasures it contains — the pictures of Cimabue, Giovanni Bellini, Palma, and the four Tintorettos, which form its crowning glory. Here the master may be studied in four of his chief moods: as the painter of tragic passion and movement, in the huge «Last Judgment»; as the painter of impossibilities, in the «Vision of Moses upon Sinai»; as the painter of purity and tranquil pathos, in the «Miracle of St. Agnes»; as the painter of biblical history brought home to daily life, in the «Presentation of the Virgin.» Without leaving the «Madonna dell' Orto,» a student can explore his genius in all its depth and breadth; comprehend the enthusiasm he excites in those who seek, as the essentials of art, imaginative boldness and sincerity; understand what is meant by adversaries who maintain that, after all, Tintoretto was but an inspired Gustave Doré. Between that quiet canvas of the «Presentation,» so modest in its cool grays and subdued gold, and the tumult of flying, running, ascending figures in the «Judgment,» what an interval there is! How strangely the white lamb-like maiden, kneeling beside her lamb in the picture of «St. Agnes,» contrasts with the dusky gorgeousness of the Hebrew women despoiling themselves of jewels for the golden calf! Comparing these several manifestations of creative power, we feel ourselves in the grasp of a painter who was essentially a poet, one for whom his art was the medium for expressing before all things thought and passion. Each picture is executed in the manner suited to its tone of feeling, the key of its conception.

Elsewhere than in the «Madonna dell' Orto» there are more distinguished single examples of Tintoretto's realizing faculty. The «Last Supper» in San Giorgio, for instance, and the «Adoration of the Shepherds,» in the Scuola di San Rocco, illustrate his unique power of presenting sacred history in a novel, romantic framework of familiar things. The most commonplace circumstances of ordinary life have been employed to portray in the one

case a lyric of mysterious splendor; in the other an idyl of infinite sweetness. Divinity shines through the rafters of that upper chamber, where round the low large table the Apostles are assembled in a group translated from the social customs of the painter's days. Divinity is shed upon the straw-spread manger, where Christ lies sleeping in the loft, with shepherds crowding through the room beneath.

A studied contrast between the simplicity and repose of the central figure and the tumult of passions in the multitude around may be observed in the «Miracle of St. Agnes.» It is this which gives dramatic vigor to the composition. But the same effect is carried to its highest fulfillment, with even a loftier beauty, in the episode of Christ before the judgment seat of Pilate, at San Rocco. Of all Tintoretto's religious pictures that is the most profoundly felt, the most majestic. No other artist succeeded as he has here succeeded in presenting to us God incarnate. For this Christ is not merely the just man, innocent, silent before his accusers. The stationary, white-draped figure raised high above the agitated crowd, with tranquil forehead slightly bent, facing his perplexed and fussy judge, is more than man. We cannot say perhaps precisely why he is divine. But Tintoretto has made us feel that he is. In other words, his treatment of the high theme chosen by him has been adequate.

We must seek the Scuola di San Rocco for examples of Tintoretto's liveliest imagination. Without ceasing to be Italian in his attention to harmony and grace, he far exceeded the masters of his nation in the power of suggesting what is weird, mysterious, upon the borderland of the grotesque. And of this quality there are three remarkable instances in the Scuola. No one but Tintoretto could have evoked the fiend in his «Temptation of Christ.» It is an indescribable hermaphroditic genius, the genius of carnal fascination, with outspread downy rose-plumed wings, and flaming bracelets on the full, plump arms, who kneels and lifts aloft great stones, smiling entreatingly to the sad, gray Christ seated beneath a rugged penthouse of the desert. No one again but Tintoretto could have dashed the hot lights of that fiery sunset in such quivering flakes upon the golden flesh of Eve, half hidden among laurels, as she stretches forth the fruit of the Fall to shrinking Adam. No one but Tintoretto, till we come to Blake, could have imagined yonder Jonah, summoned by the beck of God from the whale's belly. The monstrous fish rolls over in the ocean, blowing portentous vapor from his trump-shaped nostril. The prophet's beard descends upon his naked breast in hoary ringlets to the girdle. He has forgotten the past peril of the deep, although the whale's jaws yawn around him. Between him and the outstretched finger of Jehovah calling him again to life there runs a spark of unseen spiritual electricity.

To comprehend Tintoretto's touch upon the pastoral idyl we must turn our steps to San Giorgio again, and pace those meadows by the running river in company with his Manna-Gatherers. Or we may seek the Accademia, and notice how he here has varied the "Temptation of Adam by Eve," choosing a less tragic motive of seduction than the one so powerfully rendered at San Rocco. Or in the Ducal Palace we may take our station, hour by hour, before the "Marriage of Bacchus and Ariadne." It is well to leave the very highest achievements of art, untouched by criticism, undescribed. And in this picture we have the most perfect of all modern attempts to realize an antique myth — more perfect than Raphael's "Galatea" or Titian's "Meeting of Bacchus with Ariadne," or Botticelli's "Birth of Venus from the Sea." It may suffice to marvel at the slight effect which melodies so powerful and so direct as these produce upon the ordinary public. Sitting, as is my wont, one Sunday morning, opposite the "Bacchus," four Germans with a cicerone sauntered by. The subject was explained to them. They waited an appreciable space of time. Then the youngest opened his lips and spake: "*Bacchus war der Weingott.*" And they all moved heavily away. *Bos locutus est.* "Bacchus was the wine god!" This, apparently, is what a picture tells to one man. To another it presents divine harmonies, perceptible indeed in nature, but here by the painter poet for the first time brought together and cadenced in a work of art. For another it is perhaps the hieroglyph of pent-up passions and desired impossibilities. For yet another it may only mean the unapproachable inimitable triumph of consummate craft.

Tintoretto, to be rightly understood, must be sought all over Venice — in the church as well as the Scuola di San Rocco; in the "Temptation of St. Anthony" at St. Trovaso no less than in the "Temptations" of Eve and Christ; in the decorative pomp of the Sala del Senato, and in the paradisal vision of the Sala del Gran Consiglio. Yet, after all, there is one of his most characteristic moods, to appreciate which fully we return to the "Madonna dell' Orto." I have called him "the painter of impos-

sibilities." At rare moments he rendered them possible by sheer imaginative force. If we wish to realize this phase of his creative power, and to measure our own subordination to his genius in its most hazardous enterprise, we must spend much time in the choir of this church. Lovers of art who mistrust this play of the audacious fancy — aiming at sublimity in supersensual regions, sometimes attaining to it by stupendous effort or authentic revelation, not seldom sinking to the verge of bathos, and demanding the assistance of interpretative sympathy in the spectator — such men will not take the point of view required of them by Tintoretto in his boldest flights, in the "Worship of the Golden Calf" and in the "Destruction of the World by Water." It is for them to ponder well the flying archangel with the scales of judgment in his hand, and the seraph-charioted Jehovah enveloping Moses upon Sinai in lightnings.

The gondola has had a long rest. Were Francesco but a little more impatient, he might be wondering what had become of the padrone. I bid him turn, and we are soon gliding into the Sacca della Misericordia. This is a protected float, where the wood which comes from Cadore and the hills of the Ampezzo is stored in spring. Yonder square white house, standing out to sea, fronting Murano and the Alps, they call the Casa degli Spiriti. No one cares to inhabit it; for here, in old days, it was the wont of the Venetians to lay their dead for a night's rest before their final journey to the graveyard of San Michele. So many generations of dead folk had made that house their inn, that it is now no fitting home for living men. San Michele is the island close before Murano, where the Lombardi built one of their most romantically graceful churches of pale Istrian stone, and where the Campo Santo has for centuries received the dead into its oozy clay. The cemetery is at present undergoing restoration. Its state of squalor and abandonment to cynical disorder makes one feel how fitting for Italians would be the custom of cremation. An island in the lagoons devoted to funeral pyres is a solemn and ennobling conception. This graveyard, with its ruinous walls, its mangy riot of unwholesome weeds, its corpses festering in slime beneath neglected slabs in hollow chambers, and the mephitic wash of poisoned waters that surround it, inspires the horror of disgust.

The morning has not lost its freshness. Antelao and Tofana, guarding the vale above Cortina, show faint streaks of snow

upon their amethyst. Little clouds hang in the still autumn sky. There are men dredging for shrimps and crabs through shoals uncovered by the ebb. Nothing can be lovelier, more resting to eyes tired with pictures than this tranquil, sunny expanse of the lagoon. As we round the point of the Bersaglio new landscapes of island and Alp and low-lying mainland move into sight at every slow stroke of the oar. A luggage train comes lumbering along the railway bridge, puffing white smoke into the placid blue. Then we strike down Cannaregio, and I muse upon processions of kings and generals and noble strangers, entering Venice by this water path from Mestre, before the Austrians built their causeway for the trains. Some of the rare scraps of fresco upon house fronts, still to be seen in Venice, are left in Cannaregio. They are chiaroscuro allegories in a bold bravura manner of the sixteenth century. From these and from a few rosy fragments on the Fondaco dei Tedeschi, the Fabbriche Nuove, and precious fading figures in a certain courtyard near San Stefano, we form some notion how Venice looked when all her palaces were painted. Pictures by Gentile Bellini, Mansueti, and Carpaccio help the fancy in this work of restoration. And here and there, in black canals, we come across colored sections of old buildings, capped by true Venetian chimneys, which for a moment seem to realize our dream.

A morning with Tintoretto might well be followed by a morning with Carpaccio or Bellini. But space is wanting in these pages. Nor would it suit the manner of this medley to hunt the Lombardi through palaces and churches, pointing out their singularities of violet and yellow pannelings in marble, the dignity of their wide-opened arches, or the delicacy of their shallow chiseled traceries in cream-white Istrian stone. It is enough to indicate the goal of many a pleasant pilgrimage; warrior angels of Vivarini and Basaiti, hidden in a dark chapel of the Frari; Fra Francesco's fantastic orchard of fruits and flowers in distant S. Francesco della Vigna; the golden Gian Bellini in San Zaccaria; Palma's majestic San Barbara in San Maria Formosa; San Giobbe's wealth of sculptured frieze and floral scroll; the Ponte di Paradiso, with its Gothic arch; the painted plates in the Museo Civico; and palace after palace, loved for some quaint piece of tracery, some molding full of mediæval symbolism, some fierce impossible Renaissance freak of fancy.

Complete. From "A Venetian Medley."

TABLE OF CONTENTS

VOLUME X

NOTED SAYINGS AND CELEBRATED PASSAGES

CORNELIUS TACITUS

(c. 55–c. 117 A. D.)

HE "Germania" of Tacitus stands first among the historical essays of Greece and Rome. It gives the first definite suggestion of the modern historical method of studying human nature in connection with all the circumstances which environ it; and though this method could not have been fully developed except as a concomitant of the scientific theory of evolution, the genius of Tacitus is so great that his work does not suffer by comparison with the best historical essays of the nineteenth century. It does not give the "Germania" undue credit to call it one of the greatest historical essays in the history of literature. If the "ten greatest" were balloted on as is sometimes done for the amusement of students, it would scarcely be omitted from any list prepared by a reader well informed in the world's literature. Its style is admirable, but it derives its greatest importance from the fact that it is a close philosophical study by one of the greatest men of the classical civilization, of the new intellectual mode out of which at last were to develop the results of modern civilization. Of course when such a man as Tacitus studies thus closely so rude a people as the Germans of his day, it is because he has recognized in them a new mode in the operations of intellect—a strange new method by which the common nature of the race had begun to manifest forces omnipotent for change and growth. When, a little earlier, it had been asserted in Jerusalem that out of material as low and unformed as the stones under the feet of "the children of Abraham," God could create a new civilization, the assertion, though it could have come only from a knowledge too far-reaching for definition, suggests the nature of the impulse which must have moved Tacitus to study the forces inherent in the race which was to create modern times. The historical value of the results of his study is too great to be estimated. Modern history, to be at all intelligible, must be studied with the "Germania" as a starting point. "Breastplates are uncommon. In a whole army, you will not see more than one or two helmets." Tacitus wrote of the men who, when art, science, literature, philosophy, and religion were all decadent, and when the degraded imperialism of Rome had made political liberty impossible under the old order, were to lead the forlorn hopes of progress. He did not miss the most vital and essential fact of their history. When

stirred to action by the subconscious race impulse which controls them, they have always been "Berserkers,"—men who fight barebreasted, throwing themselves headlong upon their opportunities and, where all depends on the force of the onset, never stopping to defend either head or breast. The supreme force of individual initiative has always been in the Gothic breed from the times of Tacitus to our own. The founders of the United States of America recognized it and trusted it when they attempted to found a republic greater than Rome, without any other force to support it than the reserve forces of the individuality which can seize the initiative at a crisis, and, though "breastplates are uncommon," use it, as it has been used at so many forgotten Sempachs, to open the way for progress.

Tacitus was born under the Emperor Claudius in the early part of the second century (about 55 A. D., according to some authorities; between 52 and 54 A. D., according to others). He held the office of questor under Vespasian (78 or 79 A. D.) and in 97 A. D., became consul. These offices, however, meant little under the empire, and the fact that Tacitus held them only made him feel the more keenly the loss of Roman liberty and the degradation of morals which resulted from political servitude. In his "Dialogue on Orators" as in his "Annals" and his "Histories," he starts always from the premise that civilization can increase and morality exist as a controlling force only in the measure in which liberty exists. He was a friend of the Younger Pliny and a son-in-law of Julius Agricola. Beyond these scanty facts, we know little of his life except that in addition to his great work as a historian and essayist, he practiced at the Roman bar and was one of the most noted orators of his time. He died near the close of the reign of Trajan, perhaps in the year 117 A. D. Brodribb says that he "ranks beyond dispute in the highest place among men of letters of all ages." If such a generalization is ever safe it is certainly safe in the case of the historian who, when political liberty was lost and political virtue had become a reproach, remained true to his high ideals and dared "to rescue merit from oblivion and to hold up the condemnation of posterity as a menace to baseness."

W. V. B.

THE GERMANIA

THE whole vast country of Germany is separated from Gaul, from Rhætia and Pannonia, by the Rhine and the Danube; from Dacia and Sarmatia, by a chain of mountains, and where the mountains subside, mutual dread forms a sufficient barrier. The rest is bounded by the ocean, embracing in its depth of water several spacious bays, and islands of prodigious

extent, whose kings and people are now, in some measure, known to us, the progress of our arms having made recent discoveries. The Rhine has its source on the steep and lofty summit of the Rhætian Alps, from which it precipitates itself, and, after winding towards the west, directs its course through a long tract of country, and falls into the Northern Ocean. The Danube, gushing down the soft and gentle declivity of the mountain Abnoba, visits several nations in its progress, and at last through six channels (the seventh is absorbed in fens and marshes), discharges itself into the Pontic Sea.

The Germans, there is reason to think, are an indigenous race, the original natives of the country, without any intermixture of adventitious settlers from other nations. In the early ages of the world, the adventurers, who issued forth in quest of new habitations, did not traverse extensive tracts of land; the first migrations were made by sea. Even at this day the Northern Ocean vast and boundless, and, as I may say, always at enmity with mariners, is seldom navigated by ships from our quarter of the world. Putting the dangers of a turbulent and unknown sea out of the case, who would leave the softer climes of Asia, Africa, or Italy, to fix his abode in Germany, where nature offers nothing but scenes of deformity; where the inclemency of the seasons never relents; where the land presents a dreary region, without form or culture, and, if we except the affection of a native for his mother country, without an allurement to make life supportable? In old songs and ballads, the only memorials of antiquity amongst them, the god Tuisto, who was born of the Earth, and Mannus, his son, are celebrated as the founders of the German race. Mannus, it is said, had three sons, from whom the Ingævones, who border on the seacoast; the Hermiones, who inhabit the midland country; and the Istævones, who occupy the remaining tract, have all respectively derived their names. Some, indeed, taking advantage of the obscurity that hangs over remote and fabulous ages, ascribe to the god Tuisto a more numerous issue, and thence trace the names of various tribes, such as the Marsians, the Gambrivians, the Suevians, and the Vandals. The ancient date and authenticity of those names are, as they contend, clearly ascertained. The word "Germany" is held to be of modern addition. In support of this hypothesis, they tell us that the people who first passed the Rhine and took possession of a canton in Gaul, though known at present by the name

of Tungrians, were, in that expedition, called Germans, and thence the title assumed by a band of emigrants, in order to spread a general terror in their progress, extended itself by degrees, and became, in time, the appellation of a whole people. They have a current tradition that Hercules visited those parts. When rushing to battle, they sing in preference to all other heroes the praises of that ancient worthy.

The Germans abound with rude strains of verse, the reciters of which, in the language of the country, are called Bards. With this barbarous poetry they inflame their minds with ardor in the day of action, and prognosticate the event from the impression which it happens to make on the minds of the soldiers, who grow terrible to the enemy, or despair of success, as the war song produces an animated or a feeble sound. Nor can their manner of chanting this savage prelude be called the tone of human organs: it is rather a furious uproar; a wild chorus of military virtue. The vociferation used upon these occasions is uncouth and harsh, at intervals interrupted by the application of their bucklers to their mouths, and by the repercussion bursting out with redoubled force. An opinion prevails among them, that Ulysses, in the course of those wanderings, which are so famous in poetic story, was driven into the Northern Ocean, and that, having penetrated into the country, he built, on the banks of the Rhine, the city of Asciburgium, which is inhabited at this day, and still retains the name given originally by the founder. It is further added that an altar dedicated to Ulysses, with the name of Laertes, his father, engraved upon it, was formerly discovered at Asciburgium. Mention is likewise made of certain monuments and tombstones, still to be seen on the confines of Germany and Rhætia, with epitaphs, or inscriptions, in Greek characters. But these assertions it is not my intention either to establish or refute; the reader will yield or withhold his assent, according to his judgment or his fancy.

I have already acceded to the opinion of those who think that the Germans have hitherto subsisted without intermarrying with other nations, a pure, unmixed, and independent race, unlike any other people, all bearing the marks of a distinct national character. Hence, what is very remarkable in such prodigious numbers, a family likeness throughout the nation; the same form and feature, stern blue eyes, ruddy hair, their bodies large and robust, but powerful only in sudden efforts. They are impatient of toil and labor; thirst and heat overcome them; but, from the nature of their soil and climate, they are proof against cold and hunger.

The face of the country, though in some parts varied, presents a cheerless scene, covered with the gloom of forests, or deformed with wide extended marshes; towards the boundaries of Gaul, moist and swampy; on the side of Noricum and Pannonia, more exposed to the fury of the winds. Vegetation thrives with sufficient vigor. The soil produces grain, but is unkind to fruit trees; well stocked with cattle, but of an undersize, and deprived by nature of the usual growth and ornament of the head. The pride of a German consists in the number of his flocks and herds; they are his only riches, and in these he places his chief delight. Gold and silver are withheld from them. Is it by the favor or the wrath of heaven? I do not mean to assert, however, that in Germany there are no veins of precious ore; for who has been a miner in those regions? Certain it is they do not enjoy the possession and use of those metals with our sensibility. There are, indeed, silver vessels to be seen amongst them, but they were presents to their chiefs or embassadors; the Germans regard them in no better light than common earthenware. It is, however, observable that near the borders of the empire, the inhabitants set a value upon gold and silver, finding them subservient to the purposes of commerce. The Roman coin is known in those parts, and some of our specie is not only current, but in request. In places more remote, the simplicity of ancient manners still prevails: commutation of property is their only traffic. Where money passes in the way of barter, our old coin is the most acceptable, particularly that which is indented at the edge, or stamped with the impression of a chariot and two horses, called the serrati and bigati. Silver is preferred to gold, not from caprice or fancy, but because the inferior metal is of more expeditious use in the purchase of low-priced commodities.

Iron does not abound in Germany, if we may judge from the weapons in general use. Swords and large lances are seldom seen. The soldier grasps his javelin, or, as it is called in their language, his Fram; an instrument tipped with a short and narrow piece of iron, sharply pointed, and so commodious that, as occasion requires, he can manage it in close engagement, or in distant combat. With this and a shield the cavalry is completely armed. The infantry have an addition of missive weapons. Each man carries a considerable number, and, being naked, or, at least,

not encumbered by his light mantle, he throws his weapon to a distance almost incredible. A German has no attention to the ornament of his person; his shield is the object of his care, and this he decorates with the liveliest colors. Breastplates are uncommon. In a whole army you will not see more than one or two helmets. Their horses have neither swiftness nor elegance of shape, nor are they trained to the various evolutions of the Roman cavalry. To advance in a direct line, or wheel suddenly to the right, is the whole of their skill, and this they perform in so compact a body, that no one is thrown out of his rank. According to the best estimate, the infantry form the national strength, and, for that reason, always fight intermixed with the cavalry. The flower of their youth, able by their vigor and activity to keep pace with the movements of the horse, are selected for this purpose, and placed in the front of the lines. The number of these is fixed and certain: each canton sends a hundred, from that circumstance called "Hundredors" by the army. The name was at first numerical only; it is now a title of honor. Their order of battle presents the form of a wedge. To give ground in the heat of action, provided you return to the charge, is military skill, not fear or cowardice. In the most fierce and obstinate engagement, even when the fortune of the day is doubtful, they make it a point to carry off their slain. To abandon the shield is a flagitious crime. The person guilty of it is interdicted from religious rites, and excluded from the assembly of the state. Many who survived their honor on the day of battle have closed a life of ignominy by a halter.

The kings in Germany owe their election to the nobility of their birth; the generals are chosen for their valor. The power of the former is not arbitrary or unlimited; the latter command more by warlike example than by their authority. To be of a prompt and daring spirit in battle, and to attack in the front of the lines, is the popular character of the chieftain; when admired for his bravery, he is sure to be obeyed. Jurisdiction is vested in the priests. It is theirs to sit in judgment upon all offenses. By them delinquents are put in irons, and chastised with stripes. The power of punishing is in no other hands. When exerted by the priests, it has neither the air of vindictive justice, nor of military execution; it is rather a religious sentence, inflicted with the sanction of the god, who, according to the German creed, attends their armies on the day of battle. To impress on their

minds the idea of a tutelar deity, they carry with them to the field certain images and banners, taken from their usual depository, the religious groves. A circumstance which greatly tends to inflame them with heroic ardor is the manner in which their battalions are formed. They are neither mustered nor embodied by chance. They fight in clans, united by consanguinity, a family of warriors. Their tenderest pledges are near them in the field. In the heat of the engagement, the soldier hears the shrieks of his wife and the cries of his children. These are the darling witnesses of his conduct, the applauders of his valor, at once beloved and valued. The wounded seek their mothers and their wives: undismayed at the sight, the women count each honorable scar, and suck the gushing blood. They are even hardy enough to mix with the combatants, administering refreshment, and exhorting them to deeds of valor.

From tradition, they have a variety of instances of armies put to rout, and by the interposition of their wives and daughters again incited to renew the charge. Their women saw the ranks give way, and, rushing forward in the instant, by the vehemence of their cries and supplication, by opposing their breasts to danger, and by representing the horrors of slavery, restored the order of the battle. To a German mind the idea of a woman led into captivity is insupportable. In consequence of this prevailing sentiment, the states, which deliver as hostages the daughters of illustrious families, are bound by the most effectual obligation. There is, in their opinion, something sacred in the female sex, and even the power of foreseeing future events. Their advice is, therefore, always heard; they are frequently consulted, and their responses are deemed oracular. We have seen, in the reign of Vespasian, the famous Veleda revered as a divinity by her countrymen. Before her time, Aurinia and others were held in equal veneration; but a veneration founded on sentiment and superstition, free from that servile adulation which pretends to people heaven with human deities.

Mercury is the god chiefly adored in Germany. On stated days they think it lawful to offer to him human victims. They sacrifice to Hercules and Mars such animals as are usually slain in honor of the gods. In some parts of the country of the Suevians, the worship of Isis is established. To trace the introduction of ceremonies, which had their growth in another part of the world, were an investigation for which I have no materials:

suffice it to say that the figure of a ship (the symbolic representation of the goddess) clearly shows that the religion was imported into the country. Their deities are not immured in temples, nor represented under any kind of resemblance to the human form. To do either were, in their opinion, to derogate from the majesty of superior beings. Woods and groves are sacred depositories; and the spot being consecrated to those pious uses, they give to that sacred recess the name of the divinity that fills the place, which is never profaned by the steps of man. The gloom fills every mind with awe; revered at a distance, and never seen but with the eye of contemplation.

Their attention to auguries, and the practice of divining by lots, is conducted with a degree of superstition not exceeded by any other nation. Their mode of proceeding by lots is wonderfully simple. The branch of a fruit tree is cut into small pieces, which, being all distinctly marked, are thrown at random on a white garment. If a question of public interest be depending, the priest of the canton performs the ceremony; if it be nothing more than a private concern, the master of the family officiates. With fervent prayers offered up to the gods, his eyes devoutly raised to heaven, he holds up three times each segment of the twig, and as the marks rise in succession, interprets the decrees of fate. If appearances prove unfavorable, there ends all consultation for that day; if, on the other hand, the chances are propitious, they require, for greater certainty, the sanction of auspices. The well-known superstition, which in other countries consults the flight and notes of birds, is also established in Germany; but to receive intimations of future events from horses is the popular credulity of the country. For this purpose a number of milk-white steeds, unprofaned by mortal labor, is constantly maintained at the public expense, and placed to pasture in the religious groves. When occasion requires, they are harnessed to a sacred chariot, and the priest, accompanied by the king or chief of the state, attends to watch the motions and the neighing of the horses. No other mode of augury is received with such implicit faith by the people, the nobility, and the priesthood. The horses, upon these solemn occasions, are supposed to be the organs of the gods, and the priests their favored interpreters. They have still another way of prying into futurity, to which they have recourse, when anxious to know the issue of an important war. They seize by any means in their power a captive from the adverse nation, and commit him in single combat with the champion selected from their own army. Each is provided with weapons after the manner of his country, and the victory, wherever it falls, is deemed a sure prognostic of the event.

In matters of inferior moment the chiefs decide; important questions are reserved for the whole community. Yet even in those cases, where all have a voice, the business is discussed and prepared by the chiefs. The general assembly, if no sudden alarm calls the people together, has its fixed and stated periods, either at the new or full moon. This is thought the season most propitious to public affairs. Their account of time differs from that of the Romans: instead of days they reckon the number of nights. Their public ordinances are so dated; and their proclamations run in the same style. The night, according to them, leads the day. Their passion for liberty is attended with this ill consequence: when a public meeting is announced, they never assemble at the stated time. Regularity would look like obedience; to mark their independent spirit, they do not convene at once, but two or three days are lost in delay. When they think themselves sufficiently numerous, the business begins. Each man takes his seat, completely armed. Silence is proclaimed by the priests, who still retain their coercive authority. The king, or chief of the community, opens the debate; the rest are heard in their turn, according to age, nobility of descent, renown in war, or fame for eloquence. No man dictates to the assembly; he may persuade, but cannot command. When anything is advanced not agreeable to the people, they reject it with a general murmur. If the proposition pleases, they brandish their javelins. This is their highest and most honorable mark of applause; they assent in a military manner, and praise by the sound of their arms.

In this council of the state accusations are exhibited, and capital offenses prosecuted. Pains and penalties are proportioned to the nature of the crime. For treason and desertion, the sentence is to be hanged on a tree: the coward, and such as are guilty of unnatural practices, are plunged under a hurdle into bogs and fens. In these different punishments the point and spirit of the law is, that crimes which affect the state may be exposed to public notoriety; infamous vice cannot be too soon buried in oblivion. He who is convicted of transgressions of an inferior

X—231

nature pays a mulct of horses or of cattle. Part of that fine goes to the king, or the community, and part to the person injured, or to his family. It is in these assemblies that princes are chosen, and chiefs elected to act as magistrates in the several cantons of the state. To each of these judicial officers assistants are appointed from the body of the people, the number of a hundred, who attend to give their advice, and strengthen the hands of justice.

A German transacts no business, public or private, without being completely armed. The right of carrying arms is assumed by no person whatever, till the state has declared him duly qualified. The young candidate is introduced before the assembly, where one of the chiefs or his father, or some near relation, provides him with a shield and javelin. This, with them, is the manly gown; the youth from that moment ranks as a citizen; till then he was considered as part of the household; he is now a member of the commonwealth. In honor of illustrious birth, and to mark the sense men entertain of the father's merit, the son, though yet of tender years, is called to the dignity of a prince or chief. Such as are grown up to manhood, and have signalized themselves by a spirit of enterprise, have always a number of retainers in their train. Where merit is conspicuous, no man blushes to be seen in the list of followers or companions. A clanship is formed in this manner, with degrees of rank and subordination. The chief judges the pretensions of all, and assigns to each man his proper station. A spirit of emulation prevails among his whole train, all struggling to be the first in favor, while the chief places all his glory in the number and intrepidity of his companions. In that consists his dignity; to be surrounded by a band of young men is the source of his power; in peace, his brightest ornament; in war, his strongest bulwark. Nor is his fame confined to his own country: it extends to foreign nations, and is then of the first importance, if he surpasses his rivals in the number and courage of his followers. He receives presents from all parts: embassadors are sent to him; and his name alone is often sufficient to decide the issue of a war.

In the field of action, it is disgraceful to the prince to be surpassed in valor by his companions; and not to vie with him in martial deeds is equally a reproach to his followers. If he dies in the field, he who survives him survives to live in infamy. All are bound to defend their leader, to succor him in the heat

of action, and to make even their own actions subservient to his renown. This is the bond of union, the most sacred obligation. The chief fights for victory; the followers for their chief. If, in the course of a long peace, the people relax into sloth and indolence, it often happens that the young nobles seek a more active life in the service of other states engaged in war. The German mind cannot brook repose. The field of danger is the field of glory. Without violence and rapine a train of dependants cannot be maintained. The chief must show his liberality, and the follower expects it. He demands at one time this warlike horse, at another that victorious lance imbrued with the blood of the enemy. The prince's table, however inelegant, must always be plentiful: it is the only pay of his followers. War and depredations are the ways and means of the chieftain. To cultivate the earth, and wait the regular produce of the seasons, is not the maxim of a German; you will more easily persuade him to attack the enemy, and provoke honorable wounds in the field of battle. In a word, to earn by the sweat of your brow what you may gain by the price of your blood is, in the opinion of a German, a sluggish principle, unworthy of a soldier.

When the state has no war to manage, the German mind is sunk in sloth. The chase does not afford sufficient employment. The time is passed in sleep and gluttony. The intrepid warrior, who in the field braved every danger, becomes in time of peace a listless sluggard. The management of his house and lands he leaves to the woman, to the old men, and to the infirm part of his family. He himself lounges in stupid repose, by a wonderful diversity of nature, exhibiting in the same man the most inert aversion to labor, and the fiercest principle of action. It is a custom established in the several states to present a contribution of corn and cattle to their chieftains. Individuals follow the example, and this bounty proves at once an honor to the prince, and his best support. Presents are also sent from the adjacent states, as well by private persons as in the name of the community. Nothing is so flattering to the pride of the chiefs as those foreign favors consisting of the best horses, magnificent armor, splendid harness, and beautiful collars. The Romans have lately taught them to receive presents of money.

The Germans, it is well known, have no regular cities, nor do they allow a continuity of houses. They dwell in separate

habitations, dispersed up and down, as a grove, a meadow, or a fountain happens to invite. They have villages, but not, in our fashion, with a series of connected buildings. Every tenement stands detached, with a vacant piece of ground round it, either to prevent accidents by fire, or for want of skill in the art of building. They neither know the use of mortar nor of tiles. They build with rude materials, regardless of beauty, order, and proportion. Particular parts are covered over with a kind of earth so smooth and shining, that the natural veins have some resemblance to the lights and shades of painting. Besides these habitations, they have a number of subterraneous caves, dug by their own labor, and carefully covered over with dung; in winter their retreat from cold, and the repository of their corn. In those recesses they not only find a shelter from the rigor of the season, but in times of foreign invasion their effects are safely concealed. The enemy lays waste the open country, but the hidden treasure escapes the general ravage; safe in its obscurity, or because the search would be attended with too much trouble.

The clothing in use is a loose mantle, made fast with a clasp, or, when that cannot be had, with a thorn. Naked in other respects, they loiter away whole days by the fireside. The rich wear a garment, not, indeed, displayed and flowing, like the Parthians, or the people of Sarmatia, but drawn so tight, that the form of the limbs is palpably expressed. The skins of wild animals are also much in use. Near the Frontier, on the borders of the Rhine, the inhabitants wear them, but with an air of neglect that shows them altogether indifferent about the choice. The people who live more remote, near the northern seas, and have not acquired by commerce a taste for new-fashioned apparel, are more curious in the selection. They choose particular beasts, and, having stripped off the furs, clothe themselves with the spoil, decorated with party-colored spots, or fragments taken from the skins of fish that swim the ocean, as yet unexplored by the Romans. In point of dress there is no distinction between the sexes, except that the garment of the women is frequently made of linen, adorned with purple satin stains, but without sleeves, leaving the arms and part of the bosom uncovered.

Marriage is considered as a strict and sacred institution. In the national character there is nothing so truly commendable. To be contented with one wife is peculiar to the Germans. They differ in this respect from all other savage nations. There are, indeed, a few instances of polygamy; not, however, the effect of loose desire; but occasioned by the ambition of various families, who court the alliance of the chief distinguished by the nobility of his rank and character. The bride brings no portion; she receives a dowry from her husband. In the presence of her parents and relations he makes a tender of part of his wealth; if accepted, the match is approved. In the choice of the presents, female vanity is not consulted. There are no frivolous trinkets to adorn the future bride. The whole fortune consists of oxen, a caparisoned horse, a shield, a spear, and a sword. She in return delivers a present of arms, and, by this exchange of gifts, the marriage is concluded. This is the nuptial ceremony, this is the bond of union, these their hymeneal gods. Lest the wife should think her sex an exemption from the rigors of the severest virtue, and the toils of war, she is informed of her duty by the marriage ceremony, and thence she learns that she is received by her husband to be his partner in toil and danger, to dare with him in war, and suffer with him in peace. The oxen yoked, the horse accoutred, and the arms given on the occasion, inculcate this lesson; and thus she is prepared to live, and thus to die. These are the terms of their union: she receives her armor as a sacred treasure, to be preserved inviolate, and transmitted with honor to her sons, a portion for their wives, and from them descendible to her grandchildren.

In consequence of these manners, the married state is a life of affection and female constancy. The virtue of the woman is guarded from seduction: no public spectacles to seduce her; no banquets to inflame her passions; no baits of pleasure to disarm her virtue. The art of intriguing by clandestine letters is unknown to both sexes. Populous as the country is, adultery is rarely heard of; when detected the punishment is instant, and inflicted by the husband. He cuts off the hair of his guilty wife, and, having assembled her relations, expels her naked from his house, pursuing her with stripes through the village. To public loss of honor no favor is shown. She may possess beauty, youth, and riches; but a husband she can never obtain. Vice is not treated by the Germans as a subject of raillery, nor is the profligacy of corrupting and being corrupted called the fashion of the age. By the practice of some states, female virtue is advanced to still higher perfection; with them none but virgins marry.

When the bride has fixed her choice, her hopes of matrimony have closed for life. With one husband, as with one life, one mind, one body, every woman is satisfied: in him her happiness is centred; her desires extend no further; and the principle is not only an affection for her husband's person, but a reverence for the married state. To set limits to population, by rearing up only a certain number of children, and destroying the rest, is accounted a flagitious crime. Among the savages of Germany, virtuous manners operate more than good laws in other countries.

In every family the children are reared up in filth. They run about naked, and in time grow up to that strength and size of limb which we behold with wonder. The infant is nourished at the mother's breast, not turned over to nurses and to servants. No distinction is made between the future chieftain and the infant son of a common slave. On the same ground, and mixed with the same cattle, they pass their days, till age of manhood draws the line of separation, and early valor shows the person of ingenuous birth. It is generally late before their young men enjoy the pleasures of love; by consequence they are not enfeebled in their prime. Nor are the virgins married too soon. Both parties wait to attain their full growth. In the warm season of mutual vigor the match is made, and the children of the marriage have the constitution of their parents. The uncle by the mother's side regards his nephews with an affection nothing inferior to that of their father. With some, the relation of the sister's children to their maternal uncle is held to be the strongest tie of consanguinity, insomuch that in demanding hostages, that line of kindred is preferred, as the most endearing objects of the family, and, consequently, the most tender pledges. The son is always heir to his father. Last wills and testaments are not in use. In case of failure of issue, the brothers of the deceased are next in succession, or else the paternal and maternal uncles. A numerous train of relations is the comfort and the honor of old age. To live without raising heirs to yourself is no advantage in Germany.

To adopt the quarrels as well as the friendships of your parents and relations is held to be an indispensable duty. In their resentments, however, they are not implacable. Injuries are adjusted by a settled measure of compensation. Atonement is made for homicide by a certain number of cattle, and by that satisfaction the whole family is appeased: a happy regulation, than which

nothing can be more conducive to the public interest, since it serves to curb that spirit of revenge which is the natural result of liberty in the excess. Hospitality and convivial pleasure are nowhere so liberally enjoyed. To refuse admittance to a guest were an outrage against humanity. The master of the house welcomes every stranger, and regales him to the best of his ability. If his stock falls short, he becomes a visitor to his neighbor, and conducts his new acquaintance to a more plentiful table. They do not wait to be invited, nor is it of any consequence, since a cordial reception is always certain. Between an intimate and an entire stranger no distinction is made. The law of hospitality is the same. The departing guest receives as a present whatever he desires, and the host retaliates by asking with the same freedom. A German delights in the gifts which he receives; yet by bestowing he imputes nothing to you as a favor, and for what he receives he acknowledges no obligation.

In this manner the Germans pride themselves upon their frankness and generosity. Their hours of rest are protracted to broad daylight. As soon as they rise, the first thing they do is to bathe, and generally, on account of the intense severity of the climate, in warm water. They then betake themselves to their meal, each on a separate seat, and at his own table. Having finished their repast they proceed completely armed to the dispatch of business, and frequently to a convivial meeting. To devote both day and night to deep drinking is a disgrace to no man. Disputes, as will be the case with people in liquor, frequently arise, and are seldom confined to opprobrious language. The quarrel generally ends in a scene of blood. Important subjects, such as the reconciliation of enemies, the forming of family alliances, the election of chiefs, and even peace and war, are generally canvassed in their carousing festivals. The convivial moment, according to their notion, is the true season for business, when the mind opens itself in plain simplicity, or grows warm with bold and noble ideas. Strangers to artifice, and knowing no refinement, they tell their sentiments without disguise. The pleasure of the table expands their hearts, and calls forth every secret. On the following day the subject of debate is again taken into consideration, and thus two different periods of time have their distinct uses: when warm, they debate; when cool they decide.

Their beverage is a liquor drawn from barley or from wheat, and, like the juice of the grape, fermented to a spirit. The

settlers on the banks of the Rhine provide themselves with wine. Their food is of the simplest kind; wild apples, the flesh of an animal recently killed, or coagulated milk. Without skill in cookery, and without seasoning to stimulate the palate, they eat to satisfy nature. But they do not drink merely to quench their thirst. Indulge their love of liquor to the excess which they require, and you need not employ the terror of your arms: their own vices will subdue them.

Their public spectacles boast of no variety. They have but one sort, and that they repeat at all their meetings. A band of young men make it their pastime to dance entirely naked amidst pointed swords and javelins. By constant exercise this kind of exhibition has become an art, and art has taught them to perform with grace and elegance. Their talents, however, are not let out for hire. Though some danger attends the practice, the pleasure of the spectator is their only recompense. In the character of a German there is nothing so remarkable as his passion for play. Without the excuse of liquor (strange as it may seem!) in their cool and sober moments, they have recourse to dice, as to a serious and regular business, with the most desperate spirit committing their whole substance to chance, and when they have lost their all, putting their liberty and even their persons upon the last hazard of the die. The loser yields himself to slavery. Young, robust, and valiant, he submits to be chained, and even exposed to sale. Such is the effect of a ruinous and inveterate habit. They are victims to folly, and they call themselves men of honor. The winner is always in a hurry to barter away the slaves acquired by success at play: he is ashamed of his victory, and therefore puts away the remembrance of it as soon as possible.

The slaves in general are not arranged at their several employments in the household affairs, as is the practice at Rome. Each has his separate habitation, and his own establishment to manage. The master considers him as an agrarian dependent, who is obliged to furnish a certain quantity of grain, of cattle, or of wearing apparel. The slave obeys, and the state of servitude extends no further. All domestic affairs are managed by the master's wife and children. To punish a slave with stripes, to load him with chains, or condemn him to hard labor, is unusual. It is true that slaves are sometimes put to death, not under color of justice, or of any authority vested in the master; but in a transport of passion, in a fit of rage, as is often the case in a sudden affray; but it is also true that this species of homicide passes with impunity. The freedmen are not of much higher consideration than the actual slaves; they obtain no rank in the master's family, and, if we except the parts of Germany where monarchy is established, they never figure on the stage of public business. In despotic governments they rise above the men of ingenuous birth, and even eclipse the whole body of the nobles. In other states the subordination of the freedmen is a proof of public liberty.

The practice of placing money at interest, and reaping the profits of usury, is unknown in Germany; and that happy ignorance is a better prevention of the evil than a code of prohibitory laws. In cultivating the soil, they do not settle on one spot, but shift from place to place. The state or community takes possession of a certain tract proportioned to its numbers of hands; allotments are afterwards made to individuals according to their rank and dignity. In so extensive a country, where there is no want of land, the partition is easily made. The ground tilled in one year lies fallow the next, and a sufficient quantity always remains, the labor of the people being by no means adequate to the extent or goodness of the soil. Nor have they the skill to make orchard plantations, to inclose the meadow grounds, or to lay out and water gardens. From the earth they demand nothing but corn. Hence their year is not, as with the Romans, divided into four seasons. They have distinct ideas of winter, spring, and summer, and their language has terms for each; but they neither know the blessings nor the name of autumn.

Their funerals have neither pomp nor vain ambition. When the bodies of illustrious men are to be burned, they choose a particular kind of wood for the purpose and have no other attention. The funeral pile is neither strewed with garments, nor enriched with fragrant spices. The arms of the deceased are committed to the flames, and sometimes his horse. A mound of turf is raised to his memory, and this, in their opinion, is a better sepulchre than those structures of labored grandeur, which display the weakness of human vanity, and are, at best, a burden to the dead. Tears and lamentations are soon at an end, but their regret does not so easily wear away. To grieve for the departed is comely in the softer sex. The women weep for their friends; the men remember them.

Of all these various nations the Batavians are the most brave and warlike. Incorporated formerly with the Cattians, but driven out by intestine divisions, they took possession of an island, formed by the Rhine, where without any extent of land on the continent they established a canton in alliance with the Romans. The honor of that ancient friendship they still enjoy, with the addition of peculiar privileges. They are neither insulted with taxes, nor harassed by revenue officers. Free from burdens, imposts, and tributes, they are reserved for the day of battle; a nursery of soldiers. The Mattiaci are in like manner attached to the interest of the Romans. In fact, the limits of the empire have been enlarged, and the terror of our arms has spread beyond the Rhine and the former boundaries. Hence the Mattiaci, still enjoying their own side of the river, are Germans by their situation, yet in sentiment and principle the friends of Rome; submitting, like the Batavians, to the authority of the empire; but, never having been transplanted, they still retain, from their soil and climate, all the fierceness of their native character. The people between the Rhine and the Danube, who occupy a certain tract, subject to an impost of one tenth, and therefore called the Decumate lands, are not to be reckoned among the German nations. The Gauls, from their natural levity prone to change, and rendered desperate by their poverty, were the first adventurers into that vacant region. The Roman frontier, in process of time, being advanced, and garrisons stationed at proper posts, that whole country became part of a province, and the inhabitants of course were reduced to subjection.

Beyond the Mattiaci lies the territory of the Cattians, beginning at the Hercynian forest, but not, like other parts of Germany, a wide and dreary level of fens and marshes. A continued range of hills extends over a prodigious tract, till, growing thinner by degrees, they sink at last into an open country. The Hercynian forest attends its favorite Cattians to their utmost boundary, and there leaves them, as it were, with regret. The people are robust and hardy; their limbs well braced; their countenance fierce, and their minds endowed with vigor beyond the rest of their countrymen. Considered as Germans, their understanding is quick and penetrating. They elect officers fit to command, and obey them implicitly; they keep their ranks, and know how to seize their opportunity; they restrain their natural impetuosity, and wait for the attack; they arrange with judgment the labors

This is the sum of what I have been able to collect touching the origin of the Germans, and the general manners of the people. I now shall enter into a more minute description of the several states, their peculiar rites, and the distinctive character of each; observing at the same time, which were the nations that first passed the Rhine, and transplanted themselves into Gaul. That the Gauls, in ancient times, were superior to the Germans, we have the authority of Julius Cæsar, that illustrious historian of his own affairs. From what is stated by that eminent writer, it is highly probable that colonies from Gaul passed over into Germany; for, in fact, how could a river check the migrations of either nation, when it increased in strength, and multiplied in numbers? So weak an obstacle could not repel them from taking possession of a country, not as yet marked out by power, and of course open to the first occupant. We find, accordingly, that the whole region between the Hercynian forest, the Maine and the Rhine was occupied by the Helvetians, and the tract beyond it by the Boians; both originally Gallic nations. The name of Boiemum, which remains to this day, shows the ancient state of the country, though it has since received a new race of inhabitants. Whether the Araviscians, who settled in Pannonia, were originally a colony from the Osi, a people of Germany; or, on the other hand, whether the Osi overflowed into Germany from the Araviscians, cannot now be ascertained. Thus much is certain, the laws, the manners, and language of both nations are still the same. But which of them first passed the Danube? The same good and evil were to be found on both sides of the river; equal poverty and equal independence. To be thought of German origin is the ambition of the Treverians and the Nervians, both conceiving that the reproach of Gallic softness and effeminacy, which still infect their national manners, may be lost in the splendor of a warlike descent. The Vangiones, the Tribocians, and the Nemetes, who stretch along the banks of the Rhine, are, beyond all doubt, of German extraction. The Ubians, for their services, were made a Roman colony, and, with their own consent, became known by the name of Agriffinians, in honor of their founder; and yet they still look back with pride to their German origin. They issued formerly from that country, and, having given proof of their fidelity, obtained an allotment of territory on the banks of the Rhine, not so much with a view to their security, as to make them a guard to defend the Roman frontier.

of the day, and throw up intrenchments for the night; trusting little to fortune, they depend altogether on their valor; and what is rare in the history of barbarians, and never attained without regular discipline, they place their confidence, not in the strength of their armies, but entirely in their general. The infantry is their main strength. Each soldier carries, besides his arms, his provision and a parcel of military tools. You may see other armies rushing to a battle: the Cattians march to a war. To skirmish in detached parties, or to sally out on a sudden emergence, is not their practice. A victory hastily gained, or a quick retreat, may suit the genius of the cavalry; but all that rapidity, in the opinion of the Cattians, denotes want of resolution: perseverance is the true mark of courage.

A custom, known, indeed, in other parts of Germany, but adopted only by a few individuals of a bold and ardent spirit, is with the Cattians a feature of the national character. From the age of manhood they encourage the growth of their hair and beard; nor will any one, till he has slain an enemy, divest himself of that excrescence, which by a solemn vow he has devoted to heroic virtue. Over the blood and spoils of the vanquished the face of the warrior is for the first time displayed. The Cattian then exults; he has now answered the true end of his being, and has proved himself worthy of his parents and his country. The sluggard continues unshorn, with the uncouth horrors of his visage growing wilder to the close of his days. The men of superior courage and uncommon ferocity wear also an iron ring, in that country a badge of infamy, and with that, as with a chain, they appear self-condemned to slavery, till by the slaughter of an enemy they have redeemed their freedom. With this extraordinary habit the Cattians are in general much delighted. They grow gray under a vow of heroism, and by their voluntary distinctions render themselves conspicuous to their friends and enemies. In every engagement the first attack is made by them: they claim the front of the line as their right, presenting to the enemy an appearance wild and terrible. Even in time of peace they retain the same ferocious aspect; never softened with an air of humanity. They have no house to dwell in, no land to cultivate, no domestic care to employ them. Wherever chance conducts them, they are sure of being maintained. Lavish of their neighbors' substance, and prodigal of their own, they persist in this course, till towards the decline of life their drooping spirit is no longer equal to the exertions of a fierce and rigid virtue.

The Usipians and Tencterians border on the Cattians. Their territory lies on the banks of the Rhine, where that river, still flowing in one regular channel, forms a sufficient boundary. In addition to their military character the Tencterians are famous for the discipline of their cavalry. Their horse is no way inferior to the infantry of the Cattians. The wisdom of their ancestors formed the military system, and their descendants hold it in veneration. Horsemanship is the pride of the whole country, the pastime of their children, the emulation of their youth, and the habit of old age. With their goods and valuable effects their horses pass as part of the succession, not, however, by the general rule of inheritance to the eldest son, but, in a peculiar line, to that son who stands distinguished by his valor and his exploits in war.

In the neighborhood of the last-mentioned states formerly occurred the Bructerians, since that time dispossessed of their territory, and, as fame reports, now no longer a people. The Chanavians and Angrivarians, it is said, with the consent of the adjacent tribes, invaded the country, and pursued the ancient settlers with exterminating fury. The intolerable pride of the Bructerians drew upon them this dreadful catastrophe. The love of plunder was, no doubt, a powerful motive; and perhaps the event was providentially ordained in favor of the Roman people. Certain it is, the gods have of late indulged us with the view of a fierce engagement, and a scene of carnage, in which above sixty thousand of the enemy fell a sacrifice, not to the arms of Rome, but more magnificent still, to the rage of their own internal discord, all cut off, as it were, in a theatre of war, to furnish a spectacle to the Roman army. May this continue to be the fate of foreign nations! If not the friends of Rome, let them be enemies to themselves. For in the present tide of our affairs, what can fortune have in store so devoutly to be wished for as civil dissensions amongst our enemies?

At the back of the states, which I have now described, lie the Dulgibinians, and the Chasuarians, with other nations of inferior note. In front occurs the country of the Frisians, divided into two communities called, on account of their degrees of strength, the Greater and the Lesser Frisia. Both extend along the margin of the Rhine as far as the Ocean, inclosing within their limits

lakes of vast extent, where the fleets of Rome have spread their sails. Through that outlet we have attempted the Northern Ocean, where, if we may believe the account of navigators, the pillars of Hercules are seen still standing on the coast; whether it be that Hercules did in fact visit those parts, or that whatever is great and splendid in all quarters of the globe is by common consent ascribed to that ancient hero. Druses Germanicus was an adventurer in those seas. He did not want a spirit of enterprise; but the navigation was found impracticable in that tempestuous ocean, which seemed to forbid any further discovery of its own element, or the labors of Hercules. Since that time no expedition has been undertaken: men conceived that to respect the mysteries of the gods, and believe without inquiry, would be the best proof of veneration.

We have hitherto traced the western side of Germany. From the point where we stop, it stretches away with a prodigious sweep towards the north. In that vast region the first territory that occurs is that of the Chaucians, beginning on the confines of the Frisians, and though at the extremity bounded by the seashore, yet running at the back of all the nations already described, till, with an immense compass, it reaches the borders of the Cattians. Of this immeasurable tract it is not sufficient to say that the Chaucians possess it: they even people it. Of all the German nations they are, beyond all question, the most respectable. Their grandeur rests upon the surest foundation, the love of justice; wanting no extension of territory, free from avarice and ambition, remote and happy, they provoke no wars, and never seek to enrich themselves by rapine and depredation. Their importance among the nations round them is undoubtedly great; but the best evidence of it is that they have gained nothing but justice. Loving moderation, yet uniting to it a warlike spirit, they are ever ready in a just cause to unsheath the sword. Their armies are soon in the field. In men and horses their resources are great, and even in profound tranquillity their fame is never tarnished.

Bordering on the side of the Chaucians, and also of the Cattians, lies the country of the Cheruscans; a people by a long disuse of arms enervated and sunk in sloth. Unmolested by their neighbors, they enjoyed the sweets of peace, forgetting that amidst powerful and ambitious neighbors the repose which you enjoy serves only to lull you into a calm, always pleasing, but

deceitful in the end. When the sword is drawn, and the power of the strongest is to decide, you talk in vain of equity and moderation: those virtues always belong to the conqueror. Thus it has happened to the Cheruscans: they were formerly just and upright; at present they are called fools and cowards. Victory has transferred every virtue to the Cattians, and oppression takes the name of wisdom. The downfall of the Cheruscans drew after it that of the Fosi, a contiguous nation, in their day of prosperity never equal to their neighbors, but fellow-sufferers in their ruin.

In the same northern part of Germany we find the Cimbrians on the margin of the ocean; a people at present of small consideration, though their glory can never die. Monuments of their former strength and importance are still to be seen on either shore. Their camps and lines of circumvallation are not yet erased. From the extent of ground which they occupied you may even now form an estimate of the force and resources of the state; and the account of their grand army, which consisted of such prodigious numbers, seems to be verified. It was in the year of Rome six hundred and forty, in the consulship of Cæcilius Metellus and Papirius Carbo, that the arms of the Cimbrians first alarmed the world. If from that period we reckon to the second consulship of the Emperor Trajan, we shall find a space of near two hundred and ten years: so long has Germany stood at bay with Rome! In the course of so obstinate a struggle, both sides have felt alternately the severest blows of fortune, and the worse calamities of war. Not the Samnite, nor the republic of Carthage, nor Spain, nor Gaul, nor even the Parthian has given such frequent lessons to the Roman people. The power of the Arascidæ was not so formidable as German liberty. If we except the slaughter of Crassus and his army, what has the East to boast of? Their own commander, Pacorus, was cut off, and the whole nation was humbled by the victory of Ventidius. The Germans can recount their triumphs over Carbo, Cassius, Scaurus Aurelius, Servilius Cæpio, and Cneius Manlius, all defeated, or taken prisoners. With them the republic lost five consular armies; and since that time, in the reign of Augustus, Varus perished with his three legions. Caius Marius, it is true, defeated the Germans in Italy; Julius Cæsar made them retreat from Gaul; and Drusus, Tiberius, and Germanicus overpowered them in their own country: but how much blood did

those victories cost us? The mighty projects of Caligula ended in a ridiculous farce. From that period an interval of peace succeeded, till roused at length by the dissensions of Rome, and the civil wars that followed, they stormed our legions in their winter quarters, and even planned the conquest of Gaul. Indeed we forced them to repass the Rhine; but from that time what has been our advantage? We have triumphed, and Germany is still unconquered.

The Suevians are the next that claim attention. Possessing the largest portion of Germany, they do not, like the Cattians and Tencterians, for one state or community, but have among themselves several subdivisions, or inferior tribes, known by distinct appellations, yet all comprehended under the general name of Suevians. It is the peculiar custom of this people to braid the hair, and tie it up in a knot. Between them and the rest of the Germans this is the mark of distinction. In their own country it serves to discriminate the freeborn from the slave. If the same mode is seen in other states, introduced by ties of consanguinity, or, as often happens, by the propensity of men to imitate foreign manners, the instances are rare, and confined entirely to the season of youth. With the Suevians the custom is continued through life; men far advanced in years are seen with their hoary locks interwoven, and fastened behind, or sometimes gathered into a shaggy knot on the crown of the head. The chiefs are more nicely adjusted: they attend to ornament, but it is a manly attention, not the spirit of intrigue or the affectation of appearing amiable in the eyes of women. When going to engage the enemy, they fancy that from the high structure of their hair they appear taller and gain an air of ferocity. Their dress is a preparation for battle.

The Semnones are ambitious to be thought the most ancient and respectable of the Suevian nation. Their claim they think confirmed by the mysteries of religion. On a stated day a procession is made into a wood consecrated in ancient times, and rendered awful by auguries delivered down from age to age. The several tribes of the same descent appear by their deputies. The rites begin with the slaughter of a man, who is offered as a victim, and thus their barbarous worship is celebrated by an act of horror. The grove is beheld with superstitious terror. No man enters that holy sanctuary without being bound with a chain, thereby denoting his humble sense of his own condition, and the superior attributes of the deity that fills the place. Should he happen to fall, he does not presume to rise, but in that groveling state makes his way out of the wood. The doctrine intended by this bigotry is, that from this spot the whole nation derives its origin, and that here is the sacred mansion of the all-ruling mind, the supreme God of the universe, who holds everything else in a chain of dependence on his will and pleasure. To these tenets much credit arises from the weight and influence of the Semnones, a populous nation, distributed into a hundred cantons, and by the vast extent of their territory entitled to consider themselves as the head of the Suevian nation.

The Langobards exhibit a contrast to the people last described. Their dignity is derived from the paucity of their numbers. Surrounded as they are by great and powerful nations, they live independent, owing their security not to mean compliances, but to that warlike spirit with which they encounter danger. To these succeed in regular order the Reudignians, the Aviones, Angles, and Varinians: the Eudocians, Nuithones, and Suardonians, all defended by rivers, or embosomed in forests. In these several tribes there is nothing that merits attention, except that they all agree to worship the goddess Earth, or, as they call her, Herth, whom they consider as the common mother of all. This divinity, according to their notion, interposes in human affairs, and at times visits the several nations of the globe. A sacred grove on an island in the Northern Ocean is dedicated to her. There stands this sacred chariot, covered with a vestment, to be touched by the priest only. When she takes her seat in this holy vehicle, he becomes immediately conscious of her presence, and in his fit of enthusiasm pursues her progress. The chariot is drawn by cows yoked together. A general festival takes place, and public rejoicings are heard, wherever the goddess directs her way. No war is thought of; arms are laid aside, and the sword is sheathed. The sweets of peace are known, and then only relished. At length the same priest declares the goddess satisfied with her visitation, and reconducts her to her sanctuary. The chariot with the sacred mantle, and if we may believe report, the goddess herself, are purified in a secret lake. In this ablution certain slaves officiate and instantly perish in the water. Hence the terrors of superstition are more widely diffused; a religious horror seizes every mind, and all are content in pious ignorance to venerate that awful mystery which no man

x—232

can see and live. This part of the Suevian nation stretches away to the most remote and unknown recesses of Germany.

On the banks of the Danube (for we shall now pursue that river, in the same manner as we have traced the course of the Rhine), the first and nearest state is that of the Hermundurians, a people in alliance with Rome, acting always with fidelity, and for that reason allowed to trade not only on the frontier, but even within the limits of the empire. They are seen at large in the heart of our splendid colony in the province of Rhætia, without so much as a guard to watch their motions. To the rest of the Germans we display camps and legions, but to the Hermundurians we grant the exclusive privilege of seeing our houses and our elegant villas. They behold the splendor of the Romans but without avarice, or a wish to enjoy it. In the territories of these people the Elbe takes its rise, a celebrated river, and formerly well known to the Romans. At present we only hear of its name.

Contiguous to the last-mentioned people lies the country of the Nariscans, and next in order the Marcomannians and the Quadians. Of these the Marcomannians are the most eminent for their strength and military glory. The very territory now in their possession is the reward of valor, acquired by the expulsion of the Boians. Nor have the Nariscans or Quadians degenerated from their ancestors. As far as Germany is washed by the Danube, these three nations extend along the banks, and form the frontier of the country. The Marcomannians and the Quadians within our own memory obeyed a race of kings, born among themselves, the illustrious issue of Maroboduus and of Tudrus. Foreign princes at present sway the sceptre; but the strength of their monarchy depends upon the countenance and protection of Rome. To our arms they are not often indebted; we choose rather to supply them with money.

At the back of the Marcomannians and Quadians lie several nations of considerable force, such as the Marsignians, the Gothinians, the Osians, and the Burians. In dress and language the last two resemble the Suevians. The Gothinians by their use of the Gallic tongue, and the Osians by the dialect of Pannonia, are evidently not of German origin. A further proof arises from their submitting to the disgrace of paying tribute, imposed upon them as aliens and intruders, partly by the Sarmatians, and partly by the Quadians. The Gothinians have still more reason to

blush; they submit to the drudgery of digging iron in the mines. But a small part of the open and level country is occupied by these several nations: they dwell chiefly in forests, or on the summit of that continued ridge of mountains, by which Suevia is divided and separated from other tribes that lie still more remote. Of these the Lygians are the most powerful, stretching to a great extent, and giving their name to a number of subordinate communities. It will suffice to mention the most considerable; namely, the Arians, the Helvecones, the Manimians, the Elysians, and Naharvalians. The last show a grove famous for the antiquity of its religious rites. The priest appears in a female dress. The gods whom they worship are, in the language of the country, known by the name of Alcis, by Roman interpreters said to be Castor and Pollux. There are, indeed, no idols in their country; no symbolic representations; no traces of foreign superstition. And yet their two deities are adored in the character of young men and brothers. The Arians are not only superior to the other tribes above mentioned, but are also more fierce and savage. Not content with their natural ferocity, they study to make themselves still more grim and horrible by every addition that art can devise. Their shields are black; their bodies painted of a deep color; and the darkest night is their time for rushing to battle. The sudden surprise and funereal gloom of such a band of sable warriors are sure to strike a panic through the adverse army, who fly the field, as if a legion of demons had broken loose to attack them: so true it is that in every engagement the eye is the first conquered. Beyond the Lygians the next state is that of the Gothones, who live under regal government, and are, by consequence, ruled with a degree of power more rigorous than other parts of Germany, yet not unlimited, nor entirely hostile to civil liberty. In the neighborhood of these people we find on the seacoast the Rugians and Lemovians, both subject to royal authority. When their round shields and short swords are mentioned, there are no other particulars worthy of notice.

The people that next occur are the Suiones, who may be said to inhabit the ocean itself. In addition to the strength of their armies, they have a powerful naval force. The form of their ships is peculiar. Every vessel has a prow at each end, and by that contrivance is always ready to make head either way. Sails are not in use, nor is there a range of oars at the sides. The mari-

ners, as often happens in the navigation of rivers, take different stations, and shift from one place to another, as the exigence may require. Riches are by this people held in great esteem; and the public mind, debased by that passion, yields to the government of one, with unconditional, with passive obedience. Despotism is here fully established. The people are not allowed to carry arms in common, like the rest of the German nations. An officer is appointed to keep in a magazine all the military weapons, and for this purpose a slave is always chosen. For this policy the ostensible reason is, that the ocean is their natural fence against foreign invasions, and in time of peace the giddy multitude, with arms ready at hand, soon proceeds from luxury to tumult and commotion. But the truth is, the jealousy of a despotic prince does not think it safe to commit the care of his arsenal to the nobles or the men of ingenuous birth. Even a manumitted slave is not fit to be trusted.

At the further extremity beyond the Suiones there is another sea, whose sluggish waters seem to be in a state of stagnation. By this lazy element the globe is said to be encircled, and the supposition receives some color of probability from an extraordinary phenomenon well known in those regions. The rays of the setting sun continue till the return of day to brighten the hemisphere with so clear a light that the stars are imperceptible. To this it is added by vulgar credulity that when the sun begins to rise, the sound of the emerging luminary is distinctly heard, and the very form of the horses, with the blaze of glory around the head of the god, is palpable to the sight. The boundaries of nature, it is generally believed, terminate here.

On the coast to the right of the Suevian Ocean the Æstyans have fixed their habitations. In their dress and manners they resemble the Suevians, but their language has more affinity to the dialect of Britain. They worship the mother of the gods. The figure of a wild boar is the symbol of their superstition; and he who has that emblem about him thinks himself secure even in the thickest ranks of the enemy, without any need of arms, or any other mode of defense. The use of iron is unknown, and their general weapon is a club. In the cultivation of corn, and other fruits of the earth, they labor with more patience than is consistent with the natural laziness of the Germans. Their industry is exerted in another instance: they explore the sea for amber in their language called Glese, and are the only people who gather that curious substance. It is generally found among the shallows; sometimes on the shore. Concerning the nature or the causes of this concretion, the barbarians, with their usual want of curiosity, make no inquiry. Amongst other superfluities discharged by the sea, this substance lay long neglected, till Roman luxury gave it a name, and brought it into request. To the savages it is of no use. They gather it in rude heaps, and offer it for sale without any form or polish, wondering at the price they receive for it. There is reason to think that amber is a distillation from certain trees, since in the transparent medium we see a variety of insects, and even animals of the wing, which, being caught in the viscous fluid, are afterwards, when it grows hard, incorporated with it. It is probable, therefore, that as the East has its luxuriant plantations, where balm and frankincense perspire through the pores of trees, so the continents and islands of the West have their prolific groves, whose juices, fermented by the heat of the sun, dissolve into a liquid matter, which falls into the sea, and, being there condensed, is afterwards discharged by the winds and waves on the opposite shore. If you make an experiment of amber by the application of fire, it kindles like a torch, emitting a fragrant flame, and, in a little time, taking the tenacious nature of pitch or rosin. Beyond the Suiones we next find the nation of Sitones, differing in nothing from the former except the tameness with which they suffer a woman to reign over them. Of this people it is not enough to say that they have degenerated from civil liberty: they are sunk below slavery itself. At this place ends the territory of the Suevians.

Whether the Peucinians, the Venedians, and Fennians are to be accounted Germans, or classed with the people of Sarmatia, is a point not easy to be determined: though the Peucinians, called by some the Bastarnians, bear a strong resemblance to the Germans. They use the same language: their dress and habitations are the same, and they are equally inured to sloth and filth. Of late, however, in consequence of frequent intermarriages between their leading chieftains and the families of Sarmatia, they have been tainted with the manners of that country. The Venedians are a counterpart of the Sarmatians; like them they lead a wandering life, and support themselves by plunder amidst the woods and mountains that separate the Peucinians and the Fennians. They are, notwithstanding, to be ascribed to Germany, inasmuch as they have settled habitations,

know the use of shields, and travel always on foot, remarkable for their swiftness. The Sarmatians, on the contrary, live altogether on horseback or in wagons. Nothing can equal the ferocity of the Fennians, nor is there anything so disgusting as their filth and poverty. Without arms, without horses, and without a fixed place of abode, they lead a vagrant life; their food the common herbage; the skins of beasts their only clothing; and the bare earth their resting place. For their chief support they depend on their arrows, to which for want of iron, they prefix a pointed bone. The women follow the chase in company with the men, and claim their share of the prey. To protect their infants from the fury of wild beasts, and the inclemency of the weather, they make a kind of cradle amidst the branches of trees interwoven together, and they know no other expedient. The youth of the country have the same habitation, and amidst the trees old age is rocked to rest. Savage as this way of life may seem, they prefer it to the drudgery of the field, the labor of building, and the painful vicissitudes of hope and fear, which always attend the defense and the acquisition of property. Secure against the passions of men, and fearing nothing from the anger of the gods, they have attained that uncommon state of felicity, in which there is no craving left to form a single wish.

The rest of what I have been able to collect is too much involved in fable, of a color with the accounts of the Hellusians and the Oxionians, of whom we are told that they have the human face, with the limbs and bodies of wild beasts. But reports of this kind, unsupported by proof, I shall leave to the pen of others.

Complete. Murphy's translation.

3703

HIPPOLYTE ADOLPHE TAINE

(1828–1893)

HE opening essay of Taine's "History of English Literature" is one of the most important of the nineteenth century and perhaps more characteristic than any other of what has been peculiarly the nineteenth-century method in the study of literature and of history. In order to reach a base for his "History of English Literature," he was not content to study England as he saw it in his lifetime. He went backward over the course of the development of the English character until he found its germ in the Saxons and Angles, men with "huge white bodies, cool blooded, with fierce blue eyes,"—to account for whom he left England to study on the coasts of the North Sea, the morasses and fogs in which two thousand years ago the barbarians whom Rome could not subdue, led "a sad and precarious existence, as it were, face to face with beasts of prey." Literature now has been carried far back towards its origin in human nature itself. Human nature is to be studied as it is affected by soil and climate, by environment in all its manifestations, and by the pressure of men upon each other. Art studied back to the time of the cave man, and is accounted for in everything but the details of its development when the first rude picture is found scratched upon the ivory of a mammoth tusk. Literature, by the same rule, is followed to its beginnings in the "runes" on the staves of the bards or on the sword blades of the warriors of a period almost as remote as the time when the peoples of Europe were still septs of a single tribe, speaking a common language and having a common origin. The action of man upon nature, the reflex action of nature upon man, are considered as the springs of history, in all its phases. This idea, as its controls the literary methods of Taine, is chiefly what made him so remarkable among the great critics of his century, but he is also a master of prose style, as eminent among French writers as Macaulay is among English. He was born at Vouziers, France, April 21st, 1828. His education was careful and thorough, including, as it did, courses in medicine and general science after he had taken the highest honors of the Collège Bourbon in Paris. In 1864 he became professor of Æsthetics at the École des Beaux Arts, and in 1864 and 1865 published the work by which he is best known to readers of Eng-

lish,—the always memorable "History of English Literature,"—with which, whether it be considered as a series of essays or as a critical history of the development of English literature, there is nothing else to compare. It is, however, only one of many works of great brilliancy published by Taine between 1853, when he took his doctor's degree on his "Essay on the Fables of La Fontaine," and 1891, when his "Le Régime Moderne" appeared. He died at Paris, March 5th, 1893.

THE SAXONS AS THE SOURCE OF ENGLISH LITERATURE

I. ENVIRONMENT AND CHARACTER

As you coast the North Sea from the Scheldt to Jutland, you will mark, in the first place, that the characteristic feature is the want of slope; marsh, waste, shoal; the rivers hardly drag themselves along, swollen and sluggish, with long, black-looking waves; the flooding stream oozes over the banks, and appears further on in stagnant pools. In Holland the soil is but a sediment of mud; here and there only does the earth cover it with a crust, shallow and brittle, the mere alluvium of the river, which the river seems ever about to destroy. Thick clouds hover above, being fed by ceaseless exhalations. They lazily turn their violet flanks, grow black, suddenly descend in heavy showers; the vapor like a furnace smoke, crawls forever on the horizon. Thus watered, plants multiply; in the angle between Jutland and the continent, in a fat, muddy soil, "the verdure is as fresh as that of England." Immense forests covered the land even after the eleventh century. The sap of this humid country, thick and potent, circulates in man as in the plants; man's respiration, nutrition, sensations, and habits affect also his faculties and his frame.

The land produced after this fashion has one enemy, to wit, the sea. Holland maintains its existence only by virtue of its dikes. In 1654 those in Jutland burst, and fifteen thousand of the inhabitants were swallowed up. One need only see the blast of the North swirl down upon the low level of the soil, wan and ominous: the vast yellow sea dashes against the narrow belt of flat coast which seems incapable of a moment's resistance; the wind howls and bellows; the sea mews cry; the poor little ships flee as fast as they can, bending almost to the gunwale, and endeavor to find a refuge in the mouth of the river, which seems as hostile as the sea. A sad and precarious existence, as it were, face to face with a beast of prey. The Frisians, in their ancient laws, speak already of the league they have made against "the ferocious ocean." Even in a calm this sea is unsafe. "Before me rolleth a waste of water . . . and above me go rolling the storm clouds, the formless dark-gray daughters of air, which from the sea, in cloudy buckets scoop up the water, ever wearied lifting and lifting, and then pour it again in the sea, a mournful wearisome business. Over the sea, flat on his face, lies the monstrous, terrible North Wind, sighing and sinking his voice as in secret, like an old grumbler; for once in good humor, unto the ocean he talks, and he tells her wonderful stories." Rain, wind, and surge leave room for naught but gloomy and melancholy thoughts. The very joy of the billows has in it an inexplicable restlessness and harshness. From Holland to Jutland, a string of small, deluged islands bears witness to their ravages; the shifting sands which the tide drifts up obstruct and impede the banks and entrance of the rivers. The first Roman fleet, a thousand sail, perished there; to this day ships wait a month or more in sight of port, tossed upon the great white waves, not daring to risk themselves in the shifting, winding channel, notorious for its wrecks. In winter a breastplate of ice covers the two streams; the sea drives back the frozen masses as they descend; they pile themselves with a crash upon the sandbanks, and sway to and fro; now and then you may see a vessel, seized as in a vice, split in two beneath their violence. Picture in this foggy clime amid hoar frost and storm, in these marshes and forests, half-naked savages, a kind of wild beasts, fishers and hunters, but especially hunters of men; these are they, Saxons, Angles, Jutes, Frisians; later on, Danes, who during the fifth and the ninth centuries, with their swords and battle axes, took and kept the island of Britain.

A rude and foggy land, like their own, except in the depth of its sea and the safety of its coasts, which one day will call up real fleets and mighty vessels; green England—the word rises to the lips and expresses all. Here also moisture pervades everything, even in summer the mist rises; even on clear days you perceive it fresh from the great sea girdle, or rising from vast but ever-slushy meadows, undulating with hill and dale, intersected with hedges to the limit of the horizon. Here and there a sunbeam strikes on the higher grasses with burning flash and the splendor of the verdure dazzles and almost blinds

you. The overflowing water straightens the flabby stems; they grow up, rank, weak and filled with sap; a sap ever renewed, for the gray mists creep under a stratum of motionless vapor, and at distant intervals the rim of heaven is drenched by heavy showers. "There are yet commons as at the time of the Conquest, deserted, abandoned, wild, covered with furze and thorny plants, with here and there a horse grazing in solitude. Joyless scene, unproductive soil! What a labor it has been to humanize it! What impression it must have made on the men of the South, the Romans of Cæsar! I thought, when I saw it, of the ancient Saxons, wanderers from West and North, who came to settle in this land of marsh and fogs, on the border of primeval forests, on the banks of these great muddy streams, which roll down their slime to meet the waves. They must have lived as hunters and swineherds, growing, as before, brawny, fierce, gloomy. Take civilization from this soil, and there will remain to the inhabitants only war, the chase, gluttony, drunkenness. Smiling love, sweet poetic dreams, art, refined and nimble thought, are for the happy shores of the Mediterranean. Here the barbarian, ill housed in his mud hovel, who hears the rain pattering whole days among the oak leaves—what dreams can he have, gazing upon his mud pools and his sombre sky?"

II. Traits of the Saxon

HUGE white bodies, cool blooded, with fierce blue eyes, reddish flaxen hair; ravenous stomachs, filled with meat and cheese, heated by strong drinks; of a cold temperament, slow to love, home stayers, prone to brutal drunkenness: these are to this day the features which descent and climate preserve in the race, and these are what the Roman historians discovered in their former country. There is no living, in these lands, without abundance of solid food; bad weather keeps people at home; strong drinks are necessary to cheer them; the senses become blunted, the muscles are braced, the will vigorous. In every country the body of man is rooted deep into the soil of nature; and in this instance still deeper, because, being uncultivated, he is less removed from nature. In Germany, storm-beaten, in wretched boats of hide, amid the hardships and dangers of seafaring life, they were pre-eminently adapted for endurance and

enterprise, inured to misfortune, scorners of danger. Pirates at first,—of all kinds of hunting the man-hunt is most profitable and most noble,—they left the care of the land and flocks to the women and slaves; seafaring, war, and pillage was their whole idea of a freeman's work. They dashed to sea in their two-sailed barks, landed anywhere, killed everything; and having sacrificed in honor of their gods the tithe of their prisoners, and leaving behind them the red light of their burnings, went further on to begin again. "Lord," says a certain litany, "deliver us from the fury of the Jutes." "Of all barbarians these are strongest of body and heart, the most formidable,"—we may add, the most cruelly ferocious. When murder becomes a trade, it becomes a pleasure. About the eighth century, the final decay of the great Roman corpse which Charlemagne had tried to revive, and which was settling down into corruption called them like vultures to the prey. Those who had remained in Denmark with their brothers of Norway, fanatical pagans, incensed against the Christians, made a descent on all the surrounding coasts. Their seakings, "who had never slept under the smoky rafters of a roof, who had never drained the ale horn by an inhabited hearth," laughed at wind and storms, and sang: "The blast of the tempest aids our oars; the bellowing of heaven, the howling of the thunder, hurt us not; the hurricane is our servant, and drives us whither we wish to go." "We hewed with our swords," says a song attributed to Ragnar Lodbrog, "was it not like that hour when my bright bride I seated by me on the couch?" One of them, at the monastery of Peterborough, kills with his own hand all the monks, to the number of eighty-four; others, having taken King Ælla, divided his ribs from the spine, drew his lungs out, and threw salt into his wounds. Harold Harefoot, having seized his rival Alfred, with six hundred men, had them maimed, blinded, hamstrung, scalped, or emboweled. Torture and carnage, greed of danger, fury of destruction, obstinate and frenzied bravery of an over-strong temperament, the unchaining of the butcherly instincts,—such traits meet us at every step in the old Sagas. The daughter of the Danish Jarl, seeing Egil taking his seat near her, repels him with scorn, reproaching him with "seldom having provided the wolves with hot meat, with never having seen for the whole autumn a raven croaking over the carnage." But Egil seized her and pacified her by singing: "I have marched with my bloody sword, and the raven has fol-

lowed me. Furiously we fought, the fire passed over the dwellings of men; we have sent to sleep in blood those who kept the gates." From such table talk, and such maidenly tastes, we may judge of the rest.

Behold them now in England, more settled and wealthier: do you expect to find them much changed? Changed it may be, but for the worse, like the Franks, like all barbarians who pass from action to enjoyment. They are more gluttonous, carving their hogs, filling themselves with flesh, swallowing down deep draughts of mead, ale, spiced wines, all the strong, coarse drinks which they can procure, and so they are cheered and stimulated. Add to this the pleasure of the fight. Not easily with such instincts can they attain to culture; to find a natural and ready culture, we must look amongst the sober and sprightly populations of the South. Here the sluggish and heavy temperament remains long buried in a brutal life; people of the Latin race never at a first glance see in them aught but large gross beasts, clumsy and ridiculous when not dangerous and enraged. Up to the sixteenth century, says an old historian, the great body of the nation were little else than herdsmen, keepers of cattle and sheep; up to the end of the eighteenth drunkenness was the recreation of the higher ranks; it is still that of the lower; and all the refinement and softening influence of civilization have not abolished amongst them the use of the rod and the fist. If the carnivorous, warlike, drinking savage, proof against the climate, still shows beneath the conventions of our modern society and the softness of our modern polish, imagine what he must have been when, landing with his band upon a wasted or desert country, and becoming for the first time a settler, he saw extending to the horizon the common pastures of the border country, and the great primitive forests which furnished stags for the chase and acorns for his pigs. The ancient histories tell us that they had a great and a coarse appetite. Even at the time of the Conquest the custom of drinking to excess was a common vice with men of the highest rank, and they passed in this way whole days and nights without intermission. Henry of Huntingdon, in the twelfth century, lamenting the ancient hospitality, says that the Norman kings provided their courtiers with only one meal a day, while the Saxon kings used to provide four. One day, when Athelstan went with his nobles to visit his relative Ethelfleda, the provision of mead was exhausted at the first salutation, owing to the copiousness of the draughts; but Dunstan, forecasting the extent of the royal appetite, had furnished the house, so that the cupbearers, as is the custom at royal feasts, were able the whole day to serve it out in horns and other vessels, and the liquor was not found to be deficient. When the guests were satisfied, the harp passed from hand to hand, and the rude harmony of their deep voices swelled under the vaulted roof. The monasteries themselves in Edgard's time kept up games, songs, and dances till midnight. To shout, to drink, to gesticulate, to feel their veins heated and swollen with wine, to hear and see around them the riotous orgies, this was the first need of the barbarians. The heavy human brute gluts himself with sensations and with noise.

For such appetites there was a stronger food,—I mean blows and battle. In vain they attached themselves to the soil, became tillers of the ground, in distinct communities and distinct regions, shut up in their march with their kindred and comrades, bound together, separated from the mass, inclosed by sacred landmarks, by primeval oaks on which they cut the figures of birds and beasts, by poles set up in the midst of the marsh, which whosoever removed was punished with cruel tortures. In vain these marches and *gaus* were grouped into states, and finally formed a half-regulated society, with assemblies and laws, under the lead of a single king; its very structure indicates the necessities to supply which it was created. They united in order to maintain peace; treaties of peace occupy their parliaments; provisions for peace are the matter of their laws. War was waged daily and everywhere; the aim of life was, not to be slain, ransomed, mutilated, pillaged, hung, and of course, if it was a woman, violated. Everywhere man was obliged to appear armed, and to be ready, with his burgh or his township, to repel marauders, who went about in bands. The animal was yet too powerful, too impetuous, too untamed. Anger and covetousness in the first place brought him upon his prey. Their history, I mean that of the Heptarchy, is like a history of "kites and crows." They slew the Britons, or reduced them to slavery, fought the remnant of the Welsh, Irish, and Picts, massacred one another, were hewn down and cut to pieces by the Danes. In a hundred years, out of fourteen kings of Northumbria, seven were slain and six deposed. Penda of Mercia killed five kings, and, in order to take the town of Bamborough, demolished all the neighboring villages,

heaped their ruins into an immense pile, sufficient to burn all the inhabitants, undertook to exterminate the Northumbrians, and perished himself by the sword at the age of eighty. Many amongst them were put to death by the thanes; one thane was burned alive; brothers slew one another treacherously. With us civilization has interposed between the desire and its fulfillment, the counteracting and softening preventive of reflection and calculation; here, the impulse is sudden, and murder and every kind of excess spring from it instantaneously. King Edwy having married Elgiva, his relation within the prohibited degrees, quitted the hall where he was drinking on the very day of his coronation, to be with her. The nobles thought themselves insulted, and immediately abbot Dunstan went himself to seek the young man. "He found the adulteress," says the monk Osbern, "her mother, and the king together on the bed of debauch. He dragged the king thence violently, and, setting the crown upon his head, brought him back to the nobles." Afterwards Elgiva sent men to put out Dunstan's eyes, and then, in a revolt, saved herself and the king by hiding in the country; but the men of the North having seized her, "hamstrung her, and then subjected her to the death which she deserved." Barbarity follows barbarity. At Bristol, at the time of the Conquest, as we are told by a historian of the time, it was the custom to buy men and women in all parts of England, and to carry them to Ireland for sale in order to make money. The buyers usually made the young women pregnant, and took them to market in that condition, in order to insure a better price. "You might have seen with sorrow long files of young people of both sexes and of the greatest beauty, bound with ropes, and daily exposed for sale. . . . They sold in this manner as slaves their nearest relatives, and even their own children." And the chronicler adds that, having abandoned this practice, they "thus set an example to all the rest of England." Would you know the manners of the highest ranks, in the family of the last king? At a feast in the king's hall, Harold was serving Edward the Confessor with wine, when Tostig, his brother, moved by envy, seized him by the hair. They were separated. Tostig went to Hereford, where Harold had ordered a royal banquet to be prepared. There he seized his brother's attendants, and cutting off their heads and limbs, he placed them in the vessels of wine, ale, mead, and cider, and sent a message to the king: "If you go to your farm, you will find there plenty

of salt meat, but you will do well to carry some more with you." Harold's other brother, Sweyn, had violated the abbess Elgiva, assassinated Beorn the thane, and, being banished from the country, had turned pirate. When we regard their deeds of violence, their ferocity, their cannibal jests, we see that they were not far removed from the sea kings, or from the followers of Odin, who ate raw flesh, hung men as victims on the sacred trees of Upsala, and killed themselves to make sure of dying as they had lived, in blood. A score of times the old ferocious instinct reappears beneath the thin crust of Christianity. In the eleventh century, Siward, the great Earl of Northumberland, was afflicted with a dysentery; and feeling his death near, exclaimed, "What a shame for me not to have been permitted to die in so many battles, and to end thus by a cow's death! At least put on my breastplate, gird on my sword, set my helmet on my head, my shield in my left hand, my battle-ax in my right, so that a stout warrior, like myself, may die as a warrior." They did as he bade, and thus died he honorably in his armor. They had made one step, and only one, from barbarism.

III. The Origin of the Modern World

UNDER this native barbarism there were noble dispositions unknown to the Roman world, which were destined to produce a better people out of its ruins. In the first place, "a certain earnestness, which leads them out of frivolous sentiments to noble ones." From their origin in Germany this is what we find them, severe in manners, with grave inclinations and a manly dignity. They live solitary, each one near the spring or the wood which has taken his fancy. Even in villages the cottages were detached; they must have independence and free air. They had no taste for voluptuousness; love was tardy, education severe, their food simple; all the recreation they indulged in was the hunting of the aurochs, and a dance amongst naked swords. Violent intoxication and perilous wagers were their weakest points; they sought in preference not mild pleasures, but strong excitement. In everything, even in their rude and masculine instincts, they were men. Each in his own home, on his land and in his hut, was his own master, upright and free, in no wise restrained or shackled. If the commonweal

received anything from him, it was because he gave it. He gave his vote in arms in all great conferences, passed judgment in the assembly, made alliances and wars on his own account, moved from place to place, showed activity and daring. The modern Englishman existed entire in this Saxon. If he bends, it is because he is quite willing to bend; he is no less capable of self-denial than of independence; self-sacrifice is not uncommon, a man cares not for his blood or his life. In Homer the warrior often gives way, and is not blamed if he flees. In the Sagas, in the Edda, he must be over-brave; in Germany the coward is drowned in the mud under a hurdle. Through all outbreaks of primitive brutality gleams obscurely the grand idea of duty, which is, the self-constraint exercised in view of some noble end. Marriage was pure amongst them, chastity instinctive. Amongst the Saxons the adulterer was punished by death; the adulteress was obliged to hang herself, or was stabbed by the knives of her companions. The wives of the Cimbrians, when they could not obtain from Marius assurance of their chastity, slew themselves with their own hands. They thought there was something sacred in a woman; they married but one, and kept faith with her. In fifteen centuries the idea of marriage is unchanged amongst them. The wife on entering her husband's home is aware that she gives herself altogether; "that she will have but one body, one life with him; that she will have no thought, no desire beyond; that she will be the companion of his perils and labors; that she will suffer and dare as much as he, both in peace and war." And he, like her, knows that he gives himself. Having chosen his chief, he forgets himself in him, assigns to him his own glory, serves him to the death. "He is infamous as long as he lives, who returns from the field of battle without his chief." It was on this voluntary subordination that feudal society was based. Man in this race can accept a superior, can be capable of devotion and respect. Thrown back upon himself by the gloom and severity of his climate, he has discovered moral beauty, while others discover sensuous beauty. This kind of naked brute, who lies all day by his fireside, sluggish and dirty, always eating and drinking, whose rusty faculties cannot follow the clear and fine outlines of happily created poetic forms, catches a glimpse of the sublime in his troubled dreams. He does not see it, but simply feels it; his religion is already within, as it will be in the sixteenth century, when he will cast off the sensuous worship imported from Rome, and hallow the faith of the heart. His gods are not inclosed in walls; he has no idols. What he designates by divine names is something invisible and grand, which floats through nature, and is conceived beyond nature, a mysterious infinity which the sense cannot touch, but which "reverence alone can feel"; and when, later on, the legends define and alter this vague divination of natural powers, one idea remains at the bottom of this chaos of giant dreams, namely, that the world is a warfare, and heroism the highest good.

In the beginning, say the old Icelandic legends, there were two worlds, Niflheim the frozen, and Muspell the burning. From the falling snowflakes was born the giant Ymir. "There was in times of old, where Ymir dwelt, nor sand nor sea, nor gelid waves; earth existed not, nor heaven above; 'twas a chaotic chasm, and grass nowhere." There was but Ymir, the horrible frozen Ocean, with his children sprung from his feet and his armpits; then their shapeless progeny, Terrors of the abyss, barren Mountains, Whirlwinds of the North, and other malevolent beings, enemies of the sun and of life; then the cow Andhumbla, born also of melting snow, brings to light, whilst licking the hoarfrost from the rocks, a man Bur, whose grandsons kill the giant Ymir. "From his flesh the earth was formed, and from his bones the hills, the heaven from the skull of that ice-cold giant, and from his blood the sea; but of his brains the heavy clouds are all created." Then arose war between the monsters of winter and the luminous fertile gods, Odin the founder, Baldur the mild and benevolent, Thor the summer thunder, who purifies the air, and nourishes the earth with showers. Long fought the gods against the frozen Jötuns, against the dark bestial powers, the Wolf Fenrir, the great Serpent whom they drown in the sea, the treacherous Loki whom they bind to the rocks, beneath a viper whose venom drops continually on his face. Long will the heroes, who by a bloody death deserve to be placed "in the halls of Odin, and there wage a combat every day," assist the gods in their mighty war. A day will, however, arrive when gods and men will be conquered. Then:—

"Trembles Yggdrasill's ash yet standing; groans that ancient tree, and the Jötun Loki is loosed. The shadows groan on the ways of Hel, until the fire of Surt has consumed the tree. Hrym steers from the east, the waters rise, the mundane snake is coiled in jötun rage.

x—233

The worm beats the water, and the eagle screams; the pale of beak tears carcasses; (the ship) Naglfar is loosed. Surt from the South comes with flickering flame; shines from his sword the Val-god's sun. The stony hills are dashed together, the giantesses totter; men tread the path of Hel, and heaven is cloven. The sun darkens, earth in ocean sinks, fall from heaven the bright stars, fire's breath assails the all-nourishing tree, towering fire plays against heaven itself."

The gods perish, devoured one by one by the monsters; and the celestial legend, sad and grand, now like the life of man, bears witness to the hearts of warriors and heroes.

There is no fear of pain, no care for life; they count it as dross when the idea has seized upon them. The trembling of the nerves, the repugnance of animal instinct which starts back before wounds and death, are all lost in an irresistible determination. See how in their epic the sublime springs up amid the horrible, like a bright purple flower amid a pool of blood. Sigurd has plunged his sword into the dragon Fafnir, and at that very moment they looked on one another; and Fafnir asks, as he dies, "Who art thou? and who is thy father? and what thy kin, that thou wert so hardy as to bear weapons against me?" "A hardy heart urged me on thereto, and a strong hand and this sharp sword. . . . Seldom hath hardy eld a faint-heart youth." After this triumphant eagle's cry Sigurd cuts out the worm's heart; but Regin, brother of Fafnir drinks blood from the wound, and falls asleep. Sigurd, who was roasting the heart, raises his finger thoughtlessly to his lips. Forthwith he understands the language of the birds. The eagles scream above him in the branches. They warn him to mistrust Regin. Sigurd cuts off the latter's head, eats of Fafnir's heart, drinks his blood and his brother's. Amongst all these murders their courage and poetry grew. Sigurd has subdued Brynhild, the untamed maiden, by passing through the flaming fire; they share one couch for three nights, his naked sword betwixt them. "Nor the damsel did he kiss, nor did the Hunnish king to his arm lift her. He the blooming maid to Giuki's son delivered," because, according to his oath, he must send her to her betrothed Gunnar. She, setting her love upon him, "Alone she sat without, at eve of day, began aloud with herself to speak: 'Sigurd must be mine; I must die, or that blooming youth clasp in my arms.'" But seeing him married, she brings about his death. "Laughed then Brynhild Budli's daughter, once only, from her whole soul,

when in her bed she listened to the loud lament of Giuki's daughter." She put on her golden corslet, pierced herself with the sword's point, and as a last request said:—

"Let in the plain be raised a pile so spacious, that for us all like room may be; let them burn the Hun (Sigurd) on the one side of me, on the other side my household slaves, with collars splendid, two at our heads, and two hawks; let also lie between us both the keen-edged sword, as when we both one couch ascended; also five female thralls, eight male slaves of gentle birth fostered with me."

All were burned together; yet Gudrun the widow continued motionless by the corpse, and could not weep. The wives of the jarls came to console her, and each of them told her own sorrows, all the calamities of great devastations and the old life of barbarism.

"Then spoke Giaflang, Giuki's sister: 'Lo, upon earth I live most loveless, who of five mates must see the ending, of daughters twain and three sisters, of brethren eight, and abide behind lonely.' Then spake Herborg, Queen of Hunland: 'Crueller tale have I to tell of my seven sons, down in the Southlands, and the eighth man, my mate, felled in the death mead. Father and mother, and four brothers on the wide sea, the winds and death played with; the billows beat on the bulwark boards. Alone must I sing o'er them, alone must I array them, alone must my hands deal with their departing, and all this was in one season's wearing, and none was left for love or solace. Then was I bound a prey of the battle when that same season wore to its ending; as a tiring maid must I bind the shoon of the duke's high dame, every day at dawning. From her jealous hate gat I heavy mocking, cruel lashes she laid upon me.'"

All was in vain; no word could draw tears from those dry eyes. They were obliged to lay the bloody corpse before her, ere her tears would come. Then tears flowed through the pillow; as "the geese withal that were in the home field, the fair fowls the may owned, fell a-screaming." She would have died, like Sigrun, on the corpse of him whom alone she had loved, if they had not deprived her of memory by a magic potion. Thus affected, she departs in order to marry Atli, king of the Huns; and yet she goes against her will, with gloomy forebodings; for murder begets murder; and her brothers, the murderers of Sigurd, having been drawn to Atli's court, fall in their turn into a snare like that which they had themselves laid. Then Gunnar was

bound, and they tried to make him deliver up the treasure. He answers with a barbarian's laugh:—

"'Högni's heart in my hand shall lie, cut bloody from the breast of the valiant chief, the king's son, with a dull-edged knife.' They the heart cut out from Hialli's breast; on a dish, bleeding, laid it, and it to Gunnar bare. Then said Gunnar, lord of men: 'Here have I the heart of the timid Hialli, unlike the heart of the bold Högni; for much it trembles as in the dish it lies; it trembles more by half while in his breast it lay.' Högni laughed when to his heart they cut the living crest-crasher; no lament uttered he. All bleeding on a dish they laid it, and it to Gunnar bare. Calmly said Gunnar, the warrior Niflung: 'Here have I the heart of the bold Högni, unlike the heart of the timid Hialli; for it little trembles as in the dish it lies: it trembled less while in his breast it lay. So far shalt thou, Atli! be from the eyes of men as thou wilt from the treasures be. In my power alone is all the hidden Niflung's gold, now that Högni lives not. Ever was I wavering while we both lived; now am I so no longer, as I alone survive.'"

It was the last insult of the self-confident man, who values neither his own life nor that of another, so that he can satiate his vengeance. They cast him into the serpent's den, and there he died, striking his harp with his foot. But the inextinguishable flame of vengeance passed from his heart to that of his sister. Corpse after corpse fall on each other; a mighty fury hurls them open eyed to death. She killed the children she had by Atli, and one day on his return from the carnage gave him their hearts to eat, served in honey, and laughed coldly as she told him on what he had fed. "Uproar was on the benches, portentous the cry of men, noise beneath the costly hangings. The children of the Huns wept; all wept save Gudrun, who never wept or for her bear-fierce brothers, or for her dear sons, young, simple." Judge from this heap of ruin and carnage to what excess the will is strung. There were men amongst them, Berserkers, who in battle, seized with a sort of madness, showed a sudden and superhuman strength, and ceased to feel their wounds. This is the conception of a hero as engendered by this race in its infancy. Is it not strange to see them place their happiness in battle, their beauty in death? Is there any people, Hindoo, Persian, Greek, or Gallic, which has formed so tragic a conception of life? Is there any which has peopled its infantine mind with such gloomy dreams? Is there any which has so entirely banished from its dreams the sweetness of enjoyment and the softness of pleasure? Endeavors, tenacious and mournful endeavors, an ecstasy of endeavors — such was their chosen condition. Carlyle said well that in the sombre obstinacy of an English laborer still survives the tacit rage of the Scandinavian warrior. Strife for strife's sake — such is their pleasure. With what sadness, madness, destruction, such a disposition breaks its bonds, we shall see in Shakespeare and Byron; with what vigor and purpose it can limit and employ itself when possessed by moral ideas, we shall see in the case of the Puritans.

Nos. I., II., III. of "The Saxons" complete. From "History of English Literature."

THE CHARACTER AND WORK OF THACKERAY

I. THE NOVEL OF MANNERS

THE novel of manners in England multiplies, and for this there are several reasons: first, it is born there, and every plant thrives well in its own soil; secondly, it is a natural outlet: there is no music in England as in Germany, or conversation as in France; and men who must think and feel find in it a means of feeling and thinking. On the other hand, women take part in it with eagerness; amidst the stagnation of gallantry and the coldness of religion, it gives scope for imagination and dreams. Finally, by its minute details and practical counsels, it opens up a career to the precise and moral mind. The critic thus is, as it were, swamped in this copiousness; he must select in order to grasp the whole, and confine himself to a few in order to embrace all.

In this crowd two men have appeared of superior talent, original and contrasted, popular on the same grounds, ministers to the same cause, moralists in comedy and drama, defenders of natural sentiments against social institutions; who by the precision of their pictures, the depth of their observations, the succession and bitterness of their attacks, have renewed, with other views and in another style, the old combative spirit of Swift and Fielding.

One, more ardent, more expansive, wholly given up to rapture, an impassioned painter of crude and dazzling pictures, a lyric prose writer, omnipotent in laughter and tears, plunged into

fantastic invention, painful sensibility, vehement buffoonery; and by the boldness of his style, the excess of his emotions, the grotesque familiarity of his caricatures, he has displayed all the forces and weaknesses of an artist, all the audacities, all the successes, and all the oddities of the imagination.

The other, more contained, better informed and stronger, a lover of moral dissertations, a counselor of the public, a sort of lay preacher, less bent on defending the poor, more bent on censuring man, has brought to the aid of satire a sustained common sense, a great knowledge of the heart, consummate cleverness, powerful reasoning, a treasure of meditated hatred, and has persecuted vice with all the weapons of reflection. By this contrast the one completes the other; and we may form an exact idea of English taste, by placing the portrait of William Makepeace Thackeray by the side of that of Charles Dickens.

II. THACKERAY'S GREAT SATIRES

NO WONDER if in England a novelist writes satires. A gloomy and reflective man is impelled to it by his character; he is still further impelled by the surrounding manners. He is not permitted to contemplate passions as poetic powers; he is bidden to appreciate them as moral qualities. His pictures become sentences; he is a counselor rather than an observer, a judge rather than an artist. We see by what machinery Thackeray has changed novel into satire.

I open at random his three great works, "Pendennis," "Vanity Fair," "The Newcomes." Every scene sets in relief a moral truth: the author desires that at every page we should form a judgment on vice and virtue; he has blamed or approved beforehand, and the dialogues or portraits are to him only means by which he adds our approbation to his approbation, our blame to his blame. He is giving us lessons; and beneath the sentiments which he describes, as beneath the events which he relates, we continually discover rules for our conduct and the intentions of a reformer.

On the first page of "Pendennis" we see the portrait of an old major, a man of the world, selfish and vain, seated comfortably in his club, at the table by the fire, and near the window, envied by surgeon Glowry, whom nobody ever invites, seeking in

the records of aristocratic entertainments for his own name, gloriously placed amongst those of illustrious guests. A family letter arrives. Naturally he puts it aside and reads it carelessly last of all. He utters an exclamation of horror; his nephew wants to marry an actress. He has places booked in the coach (charging the sum which he disburses for the seats to the account of the widow and the young scapegrace of whom he is guardian), and hastens to save the young fool. If there were a low marriage, what would become of his invitations? The manifest conclusion is: Let us not be selfish, or vain, or fond of good living, like the major.

Chapter the second: Pendennis, the father of the young man in love, had "exercised the profession of apothecary and surgeon," but, being of good birth, his "secret ambition had always been to be a gentleman." He comes into money; is called Doctor, marries the very distant relative of a lord, tries to get acquainted with high families. He boasts to the last day of his life of having been invited by Sir Pepin Ribstone to an entertainment. He buys a small estate, tries to sink the apothecary, and shows off in the new glory of a landed proprietor. Each of these details is a concealed or evident sarcasm, which says to the reader: "My good friend, remain the honest John Tomkins that you are; and for the love of your son and yourself avoid taking the airs of a great nobleman."

Old Pendennis dies. His son, the noble heir of the domain, "Prince of Pendennis and Grand Duke of Fairoaks," begins to reign over his mother, his cousin, and the servants. He sends wretched verses to the county papers, begins an epic poem, a tragedy in which sixteen persons die, a scathing history of the Jesuits, and defends church and king like a loyal Tory. He sighs after the ideal, wishes for an unknown maiden, and falls in love with an actress, a woman of thirty-two, who learns her parts mechanically, as ignorant and stupid as can be. Young folks, my dear friends, you are all affected, pretentious, dupes of yourselves and of others. Wait to judge the world until you have seen it, and do not think you are masters when you are scholars.

The lesson continues and lasts as long as the life of Arthur. Like Le Sage in "Gil Blas," and Balzac in "Le Père Goriot," the author of "Pendennis" depicts a young man having some talent, endowed with good feelings, even generous, desiring to make a name, whilst, at the same time, he falls in with the

maxims of the world; but Le Sage only wished to amuse us, and Balzac only wished to stir our passions: Thackeray, from beginning to end, labors to correct us.

This intention becomes still more evident if we examine in detail one of his dialogues and one of his pictures. We will not find there impartial energy, bent on copying nature, but attentive thoughtfulness, bent on transforming into satire objects, words, and events. All the words of the character are chosen and weighed, so as to be odious or ridiculous. It accuses itself, is studious to display vice, and behind its voice we hear the voice of the writer who judges, unmasks, and punishes it. Miss Crawley, a rich old woman, falls ill. Mrs. Bute Crawley, her relative, hastens to save her, and to save the inheritance. Her aim is to have excluded from the will a nephew, Captain Rawdon, an old favorite, presumptive heir of the old lady. This Rawdon is a stupid guardsman, a frequenter of taverns, a too clever gambler, a duelist, and a roué. Fancy the capital opportunity for Mrs. Bute, the respectable mother of a family, the worthy spouse of a clergyman, accustomed to write her husband's sermons! From sheer virtue she hates Captain Rawdon, and will not suffer that such a good sum of money should fall into such bad hands. Moreover, are we not responsible for our families, and is it not for us to publish the faults of our relatives? It is our strict duty, and Mrs. Bute acquits herself of hers conscientiously. She collects edifying stories of her nephew, and therewith she edifies the aunt. He has ruined so and so; he has wronged such a woman. He has duped this tradesman; he has killed this husband. And above all, unworthy man, he has mocked his aunt! Will that generous lady continue to cherish such a viper? Will she suffer her numberless sacrifices to be repaid by such ingratitude and such ridicule? We can imagine the ecclesiastical eloquence of Mrs. Bute. Seated at the foot of the bed, she keeps the patient in sight, plies her with draughts, enlivens her with terrible sermons, and mounts guard at the door against the probable invasion of the heir. The siege was well conducted, the legacy attacked so obstinately must be yielded up; the virtuous fingers of the matron grasped beforehand and by anticipation the substantial heap of shining sovereigns. And yet a carping spectator might have found some faults in her management. Mrs. Bute managed rather too well. She forgot that a woman persecuted with sermons, handled like a bale of goods, regulated like a clock, might take a dislike to so harassing an authority. What is worse, she forgot that a timid old woman, confined to the house, overwhelmed with preachings, poisoned with pills, might die before having changed her will, and leave all, alas! to her scoundrelly nephew. Instructive and formidable example! Mrs. Bute, the honor of her sex, the consoler of the sick, the counselor of her family, having ruined her health to look after her beloved sister-in-law, and to preserve the inheritance, was just on the point, by her exemplary devotion, of putting the patient in her coffin, and the inheritance in the hands of her nephew.

Apothecary Clump arrives; he trembles for his dear client; she is worth to him two hundred a year; he is resolved to save this precious life, in spite of Mrs. Bute. Mrs. Bute interrupts him, and says: "I am sure, my dear Mr. Clump, no efforts of mine have been wanting to restore our dear invalid, whom the ingratitude of her nephew has laid on the bed of sickness. I never shrink from personal discomfort; I never refuse to sacrifice myself. . . . I would lay down my life for my duty, or for any member of my husband's family." The disinterested apothecary returns to the charge heroically. Immediately she replies in the finest strain; her eloquence flows from her lips as from an over-full pitcher. She cries aloud: "Never, as long as nature supports me, will I desert the post of duty. As the mother of a family and the wife of an English clergyman, I humbly trust that my principles are good. When my poor James was in the smallpox, did I allow any hireling to nurse him? No!" The patient Clump scatters about sugared compliments, and pressing his point amidst interruptions, protestations, offers of sacrifice, railings against the nephew, at last hits the mark. He delicately insinuates that the patient "should have change, fresh air, gayety." "The sight of her horrible nephew casually in the Park, where I am told the wretch drives with the brazen partner of his crimes," Mrs. Bute said (letting the cat of selfishness out of the bag of secrecy), "would cause her such a shock, that we should have to bring her back to bed again. She must not go out, Mr. Clump. She shall not go out as long as I remain to watch over her. And as for my health, what matters it? I give it cheerfully, sir. I sacrifice at the altar of my duty." It is clear that the author attacks Mrs. Bute and all legacy hunters. He gives her ridiculous airs, pompous phrases, a transparent, coarse, and blustering hypocrisy. The reader feels hatred and disgust

for her the more she speaks. He would unmask her; he is pleased to see her assailed, driven into a corner, taken in by the polished manœuvres of her adversary, and rejoices with the author, who tears from her and emphasizes the shameful confession of her tricks and her greed.

Having arrived so far, satirical reflection quits the literary form. In order the better to develop itself, it exhibits itself alone. Thackeray now attacks vice himself, and in his own name. No author is more fertile in dissertations; he constantly enters his story to reprimand or instruct us; he adds theoretical to active morality. We might glean from his novels one or two volumes of essays in the manner of La Bruyère or of Addison. There are essays on love, on vanity, on hypocrisy, on meanness, on all the virtues, all the vices; and turning over a few pages, we shall find one on the comedies of legacies, and on too attentive relatives:—

"What a dignity it gives an old lady, that balance at the banker's! How tenderly we look at her faults, if she is a relative (and may every reader have a score of such), what a kind, good-natured old creature we find her! How the junior partner of Hobbs and Dobbs leads her smiling to the carriage with the lozenge upon it, and the fat wheezy coachman! How, when she comes to pay us a visit, we generally find an opportunity to let our friends know her station in the world! We say (and with perfect truth) 'I wish I had Miss Mac-Whirter's signature to a check for five thousand pounds.' 'She wouldn't miss it,' says your wife. 'She is my aunt,' say you, in an easy careless way, when your friend asks if Miss MacWhirter is any relative. Your wife is perpetually sending her little testimonies of affection; your little girls work endless worsted baskets, cushions, and footstools for her. What a good fire there is in her room when she comes to pay you a visit, although your wife laces her stays without one! The house during her stay assumes a festive, neat, warm, jovial, snug appearance not visible at other seasons. You yourself, dear sir, forget to go to sleep after dinner, and find yourself all of a sudden (though you invariably lose) very fond of a rubber. What good dinners you have—game every day, Malmsey-Madeira, and no end of fish from London! Even the servants in the kitchen share in the general prosperity; and, somehow, during the stay of Miss MacWhirter's fat coachman, the beer is grown much stronger, and the consumption of tea and sugar in the nursery (where her maid takes her meals) is not regarded in the least. Is it so, or is it not so? I appeal to the middle classes. Ah, gracious powers! I wish you would

sent me an old aunt—a maiden aunt—an aunt with a lozenge on her carriage, and a front of light coffee-colored hair—how my children should work workbags for her, and my Julia and I would make her comfortable! Sweet—sweet vision! Foolish—foolish dream!"

There is no disguising it. The reader most resolved not to be warned is warned. When we have an aunt with a good sum to leave, we shall value our attentions and our tenderness at their true worth. The author has taken the place of our conscience, and the novel, transformed by reflection, becomes a school of manners.

MORALIZING IN FICTION

THE lash is laid on very heavily in this school; it is the English taste. About tastes and whips there is no disputing; but without disputing we may understand, and the surest means of understanding the English taste is to compare it with the French taste.

I see in France, in a drawing-room of men of wit, or in an artist's studio, a score of lively people: they must be amused, that is their character. You may speak to them of human wickedness, but on condition of diverting them. If you get angry, they will be shocked; if you teach a lesson, they will yawn. Laugh, it is the rule here—not cruelly, or from manifest enmity, but in good humor and in lightness of spirit. This nimble wit must act; the discovery of a clean piece of folly is a fortunate hap for it. As a light flame, it glides and flickers in sudden outbreaks on the mere surface of things. Satisfy it by imitating it, and to please gay people be gay. Be polite, that is the second commandment, very like the other. You speak to sociable, delicate, vain men, whom you must take care not to offend, but whom you must flatter. You would wound them by trying to carry conviction by force, by dint of solid arguments, by a display of eloquence and indignation. Do them the honor of supposing that they understand you at the first word, that a hinted smile is to them as good as a sound syllogism, that a fine allusion caught on the wing reaches them better than the heavy onset of a dull geometrical satire. Think, lastly (between ourselves), that in politics, as in religion, they have been for a thousand years very well governed, over governed; that when a man is bored he desires

to be so no more; that a coat too tight splits at the elbows and elsewhere. They are critics from choice; from choice they like to insinuate forbidden things; and often, by abuse of logic, by transport, by vivacity, from ill humor, they strike at society through government, at morality through religion. They are scholars who have been too long under the rod; they break the windows in opening the doors. I dare not tell you to please them: I simply remark that, in order to please them, a grain of seditious humor will do no harm.

I cross seven leagues of sea, and here I am in a great unadorned hall, with a multitude of benches, with gas-burners, swept, orderly, a debating club or a preaching house. There are five hundred long faces, gloomy and subdued; and at the first glance it is clear that they are not there to amuse themselves. In this land a grosser mood, overcharged with a heavier and stronger nourishment, has deprived impressions of their swift nobility, and thought, less facile and prompt, has lost its vivacity and its gayety. If we rail before them, we must think that we are speaking to attentive, concentrated men, capable of durable and profound sensations, incapable of changeable and sudden emotion. Those immobile and contracted faces will preserve the same attitude; they resist fleeting and half-formed smiles; they cannot unbend; and their laughter is a convulsion as stiff as their gravity. Let us not skim over our subject, but lay stress upon it; let us not pass over it lightly, but impress it; let us not dally, but strike; be assured that we must vehemently move vehement passions, and that shocks are needed to set these nerves in motion. Let us also not forget that our hearers are practical minds, lovers of the useful; that they come here to be taught; that we owe them solid truths; that their common sense, somewhat contracted, does not fall in with hazardous extemporizations or doubtful hints; that they demand worked-out refutations and complete explanations; and that if they have paid to come in, it was to hear advice which they might apply, and satire founded on proof. Their mood requires strong emotions; their mind asks for precise demonstrations. To satisfy their mood, we must not merely scratch, but torture vice; to satisfy their mind we must not rail in sallies, but by arguments. One word more: down there, in the midst of the assembly, behold that gilded, splendid book, resting royally on a velvet cushion. It is the Bible; around it there are fifty moralists, who a while ago met at the theatre and pelted an actor off the stage with apples, who was guilty of having the wife of a citizen for his mistress. If, with our finger tip, with all the compliments and disguises in the world, we touch a single sacred leaf, or the smallest moral conventionalism, immediately fifty hands will fasten themselves on our coat collar and put us out at the door. With Englishmen we must be English, with their passion and their common sense adopt their leading-strings. Thus confined to recognize truths, satire will become more bitter, and will add the weight of public belief to the pressure of logic and the force of indignation.

From "History of English Literature."

SIR THOMAS NOON TALFOURD

(1795–1854)

THOMAS NOON TALFOURD, author of "Ion" and almost equally celebrated for his oration in defense of Shelley's publisher, was the writer of a number of notable essays and reviews, which belong to the period when English prose style took its tone from the reviews of the "Quarterly" school of anonymous literary dictators. Talfourd, however, is companionable and pleasant rather than assertive in his mode of expression and he deserves to be remembered for this not less than for the subject-matter of his essays. He was born near Stafford, England, January 26th, 1795, and was educated for the bar. He served in Parliament, made a reputation as a forensic orator, sat on the bench of the Court of Common Pleas, wrote essays and plays, and published a "History of Greek Literature" as well as biographies and travels. The tragedy of "Ion" which is his best-known work was put on the stage in 1836. In 1837 he published the "Life and Letters of Charles Lamb," and in 1849–50 "Final Memorials of Charles Lamb." He died at Stafford, March 13th, 1854.

BRITISH NOVELS AND ROMANCES

WE REGARD the authors of the best novels and romances as among the truest benefactors of their species. Their works have often conveyed, in the most attractive form, lessons of the most genial wisdom. But we do not prize them so much in reference to their immediate aim, or any individual traits of nobleness with which they may inform the thoughts, as for their general tendency to break up that cold and debasing selfishness with which the souls of so large a portion of mankind are incrusted. They give to a vast class, who by no means would be carried beyond the most contracted range of emotion, an interest in things out of themselves, and a perception of grandeur and of beauty, of which otherwise they might ever have lived unconscious. Pity for fictitious sufferings is, indeed, very inferior to that sympathy with the universal heart of man which inspires real self-sacrifice; but it is better even to be moved by its ten-

derness than wholly to be ignorant of the joy of natural tears. How many are there for whom poesy has no charm, and who have derived only from romances those glimpses of disinterested heroism and ideal beauty, which alone "make them less forlorn," in their busy career! The good housewife, who is employed all her life in the severest drudgery, has yet some glimmerings of a state and dignity above her station and age, and some dim vision of meek, angelic suffering, when she thinks of the well-thumbed volume of "Clarissa Harlowe," which she found, when a girl, in some old recess, and read, with breathless eagerness, at stolen times and moments of hasty joy. The careworn lawyer or politician, encircled with all kinds of petty anxieties, thinks of the "Arabian Nights Entertainments," which he devoured in his joyful school days, and is once more young, and innocent, and happy. If the sternest puritan were acquainted with Parson Adams, or with Dr. Primrose, he could not hate the clergy. If novels are not the deepest teachers of humanity, they have, at least, the widest range. They lend to genius "lighter wings to fly." They are read where Milton and Shakespeare are only talked of, and where even their names are never heard. They nestle gently beneath the covers of unconscious sofas, are read by fair and glistening eyes in moments snatched from repose, and beneath counters and shopboards minister delights "secret, sweet, and precious." It is possible that, in particular instances, their effects may be baneful; but, on the whole, we are persuaded they are good. The world is not in danger of becoming too romantic. The golden threads of poesy are not too thickly or too closely interwoven with the ordinary web of existence. Sympathy is the first great lesson which man should learn. It will be ill for him if he proceeds no further; if his emotions are but excited to roll back on his heart, and to be fostered in luxurious quiet. But unless he learns to feel for things in which he has no personal interest, he can achieve nothing generous or noble. This lesson is in reality the universal moral of all excellent romances. How mistaken are those miserable reasoners who object to them as giving "false pictures of life — of purity too glossy and ethereal — of friendship too deep and confiding — of love which does not shrink at the approach of ill, but looks on tempests and is never shaken," because with these the world too rarely blossoms! Were these things visionary and unreal, who would break the spell, and bid the delicious enchantment vanish? The soul will not be the

worse for thinking too well of its kind, or believing that the highest excellence is within the reach of its exertions. But these things are not unreal; they are shadows, indeed, in themselves; but they are shadows cast from objects stately and eternal. Man can never imagine that which has no foundation in his nature. The virtues he conceives are not the mere pageantry of his thought. We feel their truth — not their historic or individual truth, but their universal truth — as reflexes of human energy and power. It would be enough for us to prove that the imaginative glories which are shed around our being are far brighter than "the light of common day," which mere vulgar experience in the course of the world diffuses. But, in truth, that radiance is not merely of the fancy, nor are its influences lost when it ceases immediately to shine on our path. It is holy and prophetic. The best joys of childhood — its boundless aspirations and gorgeous dreams — are the sure indications of the nobleness of its final heritage. All the softenings of evil to the moral vision by the gentleness of fancy, are proofs that evil itself shall perish. Our yearnings after ideal beauty show that the home of the soul which feels them is in a lovelier world. And when man describes high virtues, and instances of nobleness, which rarely light on earth, — so sublime that they expand our imaginations beyond their former compass, yet so human that they make our hearts gush with delight, — he discovers feelings in his own breast, and awakens sympathies in ours, which shall assuredly one day have real and stable objects to rest on!

The early times of England — unlike those of Spain — were not rich in chivalrous romances. The imagination seems to have been chilled by the manners of the Norman conquerors. The domestic contests for the disputed throne, with their intrigues, battles, and executions, have none of that rich, poetical interest, which attended the struggles for the Holy Sepulchre. Nor, in the golden age of English genius, were there any very remarkable works of pure fiction. Since that period to the present day, however, there has been a rich succession of novels and romances, each increasing the stores of innocent delight, and shedding on human life some new tint of tender coloring.

The novels of Richardson are at once among the grandest and the most singular creations of human genius. They combine an accurate acquaintance with the freest libertinism, and the sternest professions of virtue — a sporting with vicious casuistry, and the deepest horror of freethinking—the most stately ideas of paternal authority, and the most elaborate display of its abuses. Prim and stiff, almost without parallel, the author perpetually treads on the very borders of indecorum, but with a solemn and assured step, as if certain that he could never fall. "The precise, strait-laced Richardson," says Mr. Lamb in one of the profound and beautiful notes to his specimens, "has strengthened Vice from the mouth of Lovelace, with entangling sophistries, and abstruse pleas against her adversary Virtue, which Sedley, Villiers, and Rochester wanted depth of libertinism sufficient to have invented." He had, in fact, the power of making any set of notions, however fantastical, appear as "truths of holy writ" to his readers. This he did by the authority with which he disposed of all things, and by the infinite minuteness of his details. His gradations are so gentle, that we do not at any one point hesitate to follow him, and should descend with him to any depth before we perceived that our path had been unequal. By the means of this strange magic, we become anxious for the marriage of Pamela with her base master; because the author has so imperceptibly wrought on us the belief of an awful distance between the rights of an esquire and his servant, that our imaginations regard it in the place of all moral distinctions. After all, the general impression made on us by his works is virtuous. Clementina is to the soul a new and majestic image, inspired by virtue and by love, which raises and refines its conceptions. She has all the depth and intensity of the Italian character, with all the purity of an angel. She is at the same time one of the grandest of tragic heroines, and the divinest of religious enthusiasts. Clarissa alone is above her. Clementina steps statelily in her very madness, amidst "the pride, pomp, and circumstance" of Italian nobility; Clarissa is triumphant, though violated, deserted, and encompassed by vice and infamy. Never can we forget that amazing scene, in which, on the effort of her mean seducer to renew his outrages, she appears in all the radiance of mental purity, among the wretches assembled to witness his triumph, where she startles them by her first appearance, as by a vision from above; and holding the penknife to her breast, with her eyes lifted to heaven, prepares to die, if her craven destroyer advances, striking the vilest with deep awe of goodness, and walking placidly, at last, from the circle of her foes, none of them daring to harm her! How pathetic, above all other pathos in the world, are those

x—234

snatches of meditation which she commits to the paper, in the first delirium of her woe! How delicately imagined are her preparations for that grave in which alone she can find repose! Cold must be the hearts of those who can conceive them as too elaborate, or who can venture to criticize them. In this novel all appears most real; we feel enveloped, like Don Quixote, by a thousand threads; and, like him, would we rather remain so forever than break one of their silken fibres. "Clarissa Harlowe" is one of the books which leave us different beings from those which they find us. "Sadder and wiser" do we arise from its perusal.

Yet when we read Fielding's novels after those of Richardson, we feel as if a stupendous pressure were removed from our souls. We seem suddenly to have left a palace of enchantment, where we have passed through long galleries filled with the most gorgeous images, and illumined by a light not quite human nor yet quite divine, into the fresh air, and the common ways of this "bright and breathing world." We travel on the highroad of humanity, yet meet in it pleasanter companions, and catch more delicious snatches of refreshment, than ever we can hope elsewhere to enjoy. The mock heroic of Fielding, when he condescends to that ambiguous style, is scarcely less pleasing than its stately prototype. It is a sort of spirited defiance to fiction, on the behalf of reality, by one who knew full well all the strongholds of that nature which he was defending. There is not in Fielding much of that which can properly be called ideal,—if we except the character of Parson Adams; but his works represent life as more delightful than it seems to common experience, by disclosing those of its dear immunities, which we little think of, even when we enjoy them. How delicious are all his refreshments at all his inns! How vivid are the transient joys of his heroes, in their checkered course—how full and overflowing are their final raptures! His "Tom Jones" is quite unrivaled in plot, and is to be rivaled only in his own works for felicitous delineation of character. The little which we have told us of Allworthy, especially that which relates to his feelings respecting his deceased wife, makes us feel for him, as for one of the best and most revered friends of our childhood. Was ever the "soul of goodness in things evil" better disclosed than in the scruples and the dishonesty of Black George, that tenderest of gamekeepers, and truest of thieves? Did ever health, good-humor, frank-

heartedness, and animal spirits hold out so freshly against vice and fortune as in the hero? Was ever so plausible a hypocrite as Blifil, who buys a Bible of Tom Jones so delightfully, and who, by his admirable imitation of virtue, leaves it almost in doubt, whether, by a counterfeit so dexterous, he did not merit some share of her rewards? Who shall gainsay the cherry lips of Sophia Western? The story of Lady Bellaston we confess to be a blemish. But if there be any vice left in the work, the fresh atmosphere diffused over all its scenes will render it innoxious. "Joseph Andrews" has far less merit as a story, but it depicts Parson Adams, whom it does the heart good to think on. He who drew this character, if he had done nothing else, would not have lived in vain. We fancy we can see him with his torn cassock (in honor of his high profession), his volumes of sermons, which we really wish had been printed, and his "Æschylus," the best of all the editions of that sublime tragedian! Whether he longs after his own sermons against vanity—or is absorbed in the romantic tale of the fair Leonora—or uses his ox-like fists in defense of the fairer Fanny, he equally embodies in his person, "the homely beauty of the good old cause," of high thoughts, pure imaginations, and manners unspotted by the world.

Smollet seems to have had more touches of romance than Fielding, but not so profound and intuitive a knowledge of humanity's hidden treasures. There is nothing in his works comparable to Parson Adams; but then, on the other hand, Fielding has not anything of the kind equal to Strap. Partridge is dry and hard, compared with this poor barber boy, with his generous overflowings of affection. "Roderick Random," indeed, with its varied delineation of life, is almost a romance. Its hero is worthy of his name. He is the sport of fortune rolled about through the "many ways of wretchedness," almost without resistance, but ever catching those tastes of joy which are everywhere to be relished by those who are willing to receive them. We seem to roll on with him, and get delectably giddy in his company.

The humanity of the "Vicar of Wakefield" is less deep than that of "Roderick Random," but sweeter tinges of fancy are cast over it. The sphere in which Goldsmith's powers moved was never very extensive, but within it he discovered all that was good, and shed on it the tenderest lights of his sympathizing genius. No one ever excelled so much as he in depicting amiable follies and endearing weaknesses. His satire makes us at

once smile at and love all that he so tenderly ridicules. The good Vicar's trust in monogamy, his son's purchase of the spectacles, his own sale of his horse to his solemn admirer at the fair, the blameless vanities of his daughters, and his resignation under his accumulated sorrows, are among the best treasures of memory. The pastoral scenes in this exquisite tale are the sweetest in the world. The scents of the hayfield, and of the blossoming hedgerows, seem to come freshly to our senses. The whole romance is a tenderly colored picture, in little, of human nature's most genial qualities.

De Foe is one of the most extraordinary of English authors. His "Robinson Crusoe" is deservedly one of the most popular of novels. It is usually the first read, and always among the last forgotten. The interest of its scenes in the uninhabited island is altogether peculiar; since there is nothing to develop the character but deep solitude. Man, there, is alone in the world, and can hold communion only with nature and nature's God. There is nearly the same situation in "Philoctetes," that sweetest of the Greek tragedies; but there we only see the poor exile as he is about to leave his sad abode, to which he has become attached, even with a childlike cleaving. In "Robinson Crusoe" life is stripped of all its social joys, yet we feel how worthy of cherishing it is, with nothing but silent nature to cheer it. Thus are nature and the soul, left with no other solace, represented in their native grandeur and intense communion. With how fond an interest do we dwell on all the exertions of our fellowman, cut off from his kind; watch his growing plantations as they rise, and seem to water them with our tears! The exceeding vividness of all the descriptions are more delightful when combined with the loneliness and distance of the scene "placed far amid the melancholy main" in which we become dwellers. We have grown so familiar with the solitude, that the print of man's foot seen in the sand seems to appall us as an awful thing!—The Family Instructor of this author, in which he inculcates weightily his own notions of puritanical demeanor and parental authority, is very curious. It is a strange mixture of narrative and dialogue, fanaticism and nature; but all done with such earnestness that the sense of its reality never quits us. Nothing, however, can be more harsh and unpleasing than the impression which it leaves. It does injustice both to religion and the world. It represents the innocent pleasures of the latter as deadly sins, and the former as most gloomy, austere, and exclusive. One lady resolves on poisoning her husband, and another determines to go to the play, and the author treats both offenses with a severity nearly equal!

Far different from this ascetic novel is that best of religious romances, the "Fool of Quality." The piety there is at once most deep and most benign. There is much, indeed, of eloquent mysticism, but all evidently most heartfelt and sincere. The yearnings of the soul after universal good and intimate communion with the divine nature were never more nobly shown. The author is most prodigal of his intellectual wealth — "his bounty is as boundless as the sea, his love as deep." He gives to his chief characters riches endless as the spiritual stores of his own heart. It is, indeed, only the last which gives value to the first in his writings. It is easy to endow men with millions on paper, and to make them willing to scatter them among the wretched; but it is the corresponding bounty and exuberance of the author's soul which here makes the money sterling and the charity divine. The hero of this romance always appears to our imagination like a radiant vision encircled with celestial glories. The stories introduced in it are delightful exceptions to the usual rule by which such incidental tales are properly regarded as impertinent intrusions. That of David Doubtful is of the most romantic interest, and at the same time steeped in feeling the most profound. But that of Clement and his wife is perhaps the finest. The scene in which they are discovered, having placidly lain down to die of hunger together, in gentle submission to heaven, depicts a quiescence the most sublime, yet the most affecting. Nothing can be more delightful than the sweetening ingredients in their cup of sorrow. The heroic act of the lady to free herself from her ravisher's grasp, her trial and her triumphant acquittal, have a grandeur above that of tragedy. The genial spirit of the author's faith leads him to exult especially in the repentance of the wicked. No human writer seems ever to have hailed the contrite with so cordial a welcome. His scenes appear overspread with a rich atmosphere of tenderness, which softens and consecrates all things.

We would not pass over, without a tribute of gratitude, Mrs. Radcliffe's wild and wondrous tales. When we read them, the world seems shut out, and we breathe only in an enchanted region, where lovers' lutes tremble over placid waters, moldering

castles rise conscious of deeds of blood, and the sad voices of the past echo through deep vaults and lonely galleries. There is always majesty in her terrors. She produces more effect by whispers and slender hints that ever was attained by the most vivid display of horrors. Her conclusions are tame and impotent almost without example. But while her spells actually operate, her power is truly magical. Who can ever forget the scene in the "Romance of the Forest," where the marquis, who has long sought to make the heroine the victim of licentious love, after working on her protector, over whom he has a mysterious influence, to steal at night into her chamber, and when his trembling listener expects only a requisition for delivering her into his hands, replies to the question of "then — to-night, my lord!" "Adelaide dies" — or the allusions to the dark veil in the "Mysteries of Udolpho" — or the stupendous scenes in Spalatro's cottage? Of all romance writers Mrs. Radcliffe is the most romantic.

The present age has produced a singular number of authors of delightful prose fiction, on whom we intend to give a series of criticisms. We shall begin with Mackenzie, whom we shall endeavor to compare with Sterne, and for this reason we have passed over the works of the latter in our present cursory view of the novelists of other days.

Complete. From the New Monthly Magazine.

WILLIAM MAKEPEACE THACKERAY

(1811-1863)

T SEEMS to me those verses shine like the stars." Thackeray said of Addison's hymn:—

"The spacious firmament on high
With all the blue ethereal sky,
And spangled heavens, a shining frame,
Their great Original proclaim."

Perhaps nothing else ever said of Addison comes so near doing justice to the calm radiance of his genius. But of Thackeray himself with no less propriety than of Addison, it might be said that his whole life work "shines like the stars." In manliness, in tenderness, in sympathy for all sorts and conditions of men, in freedom from delusions, in hate of cant, in love of truth, he is first among the novelists of England and first without a rival. His "Vanity Fair" is to English fiction what "Hamlet" is to English plays. There is nothing else which resembles it or approaches it. Though, like Shakespeare, Thackeray produced one masterpiece after another, until it seems that his genius had no other limits than that of the universal life of the race, his great novel retains its place of unquestionable eminence among his own works as it does among the works of all other English novelists. In "Vanity Fair" and "Les Miserables" the nineteenth century reached its climaxes of art in prose fiction. They stand with the first part of "Faust," as the highest products of literary art since the "Paradise Lost."

As an essayist Thackeray is always charming for ten minutes at a time. After that, he needs the support of a plot to prevent him from lapsing into the sober sadness of preaching. He was a humorist because human life made him sorrowful. He loved men so well that the suffering of human life filled him with grief too deep for expression, and he became a story teller for the same reason that some silver-haired old man, with his grandchildren on his knees, and the whole sum of the suffering of life in his memory, tells them tales, which they smile to hear, not knowing that the dragons, the giants, and the ogres which the Invincible Prince conquers are to be fought and, it may be, mastered in the struggles between the Divine Soul in them and the Principalities and Powers which oppose it. Such a grandfather is to the children he loves as Thackeray is to all of us.

He knows things unspeakable which it is not lawful for any man to utter except in tale and parable.

He was born July 18th, 1811, at Calcutta, where his father was employed in the civil service of the British imperial government. When about five years old he was sent to England and entered at the Charterhouse School, from which he went (1829) to Trinity College, Cambridge. Leaving Cambridge in 1830 without a degree, he traveled for several years and in 1833 began writing for the National Standard and other periodicals,— including finally Punch, to which he remained a favorite contributor. "The Yellowplush Papers" which contain the most artistic bad spelling in English literature were begun in Fraser's in 1837. They illustrate Thackeray's attitude towards the governing classes in England and suggest the motive for "Vanity Fair," which, when it appeared (1846-48), at once established his place among the greatest writers of England. He was kept busy afterwards until his death, December 24th, 1863. "Pendennis," 1848-50; "Henry Esmond," 1852; "The Newcomes," 1853-55; and "The Virginians," 1857-59, were accompanied by an uninterrupted succession of stories, sketches, essays, and lectures. "The English Humorists" was originally a series of lectures first delivered in 1851, and "The Four Georges" (1860) is made up of the lectures he delivered during his tour in the United States in 1855. His "Roundabout Papers," which appeared in 1862, was his last work published during his lifetime, but his "Early and Late Papers" and his "Ballads" were edited and published after his death.

As a novelist he belongs to the school of Fielding, whom he far surpasses. As a humorist he has learned most from Addison, whom he equals in tenderness and surpasses in breadth, though not comparable with him in delicacy of execution. He is often compared to Dickens, but in their modes of thought and of execution they were wholly different. If Thackeray is to be classed among English men of letters, it must be with Shakespeare, the only English writer who has surpassed him in power to feel and to express the sum total of the pain and pleasure of human life.

W. V. B.

ON A JOKE I ONCE HEARD FROM THE LATE THOMAS HOOD

THE good-natured reader who has perused some of these rambling papers has long since seen (if to see has been worth his trouble) that the writer belongs to the old-fashioned classes of this world, loves to remember very much more than to prophesy, and though he can't help being carried onward, and downward, perhaps, on the hill of life, the swift milestones marking their forties, fifties — how many tens or lustres shall we say?

—he sits under Time, the white-wigged charioteer, with his back to the horses, and his face to the past, looking at the receding landscape and the hills fading into the gray distance. Ah, me! those gray distant hills were green once, and here, and covered with smiling people! As we came up the hill there was difficulty, and here and there a hard pull, to be sure, but strength, and spirits, and all sorts of cheery incident and companionship on the road; there were the tough struggles (by Heaven's merciful will) overcome, the pauses, the faintings, the weakness, the lost way, perhaps, the bitter weather, the dreadful partings, the lonely night, the passionate grief — towards these I turn my thoughts as I sit and think in my hobby-coach under Time, the silver-wigged charioteer. The young folks in the same carriage meanwhile are looking forwards. Nothing escapes their keen eyes — not a flower at the side of a cottage garden, nor a bunch of rosy-faced children at the gate: the landscape is all bright, the air brisk and jolly, the town yonder looks beautiful, and do you think they have learned to be difficult about the dishes at the inn?

Now, suppose Paterfamilias on his journey with his wife and children in the sociable, and he passes an ordinary brick house on the road with an ordinary little garden in the front, we will say, and quite an ordinary knocker to the door, and as many sashed windows as you please, quite common and square, and tiles, windows, chimney pots, quite like others; or suppose, in driving over such and such a common, he sees an ordinary tree, and an ordinary donkey browsing under it, if you like — wife and daughter look at these objects without the slightest particle of curiosity or interest. What is a brass knocker to them but a lion's head, or what not? and a thorn tree with a pool beside it, but a pool in which a thorn and a jackass are reflected?

But you remember how once upon a time your heart used to beat, as you beat on that brass knocker, and whose eyes looked from the window above? You remember how by that thorn tree and pool, where the geese were performing a prodigious evening concert, there might be seen, at a certain hour, somebody in a certain cloak and bonnet, who happened to be coming from a village yonder, and whose image had flickered in that pool? In that pool near the thorn? Yes, in that goose pool, never mind how long ago, when there were reflected the images of the geese — and two geese more. Here, at least, an oldster may have the

advantage of his young fellow-travelers, and so Putney Heath or the New Road may be invested with a halo of brightness invisible to them, because it only beams out of his own soul.

I have been reading the "Memorials" of Hood by his children, and wonder whether the book will have the same interest for others and for younger people, as for persons of my own age and calling. Books of travel to any country become interesting to us who have been there. Men revisit the old school, though hateful to them, with ever so much kindliness and sentimental affection. There was the tree, under which the bully licked you; here the ground where you had to fag out on holidays, and so forth. In a word, my dear sir, You are the most interesting subject to yourself of any that can occupy your worship's thoughts. I have no doubt a Crimean soldier, reading a history of that siege, and how Jones and the gallant 99th were ordered to charge, or what not, thinks, "Ah, yes, we of the 100th were placed so and so, I perfectly remember." So with this "Memorial" of poor Hood, it may have, no doubt, a greater interest for me than for others, for I was fighting, so to speak, in a different part of the field, and engaged, a young subaltern in the battle of Life, in which Hood fell, young still and covered with glory. The "Bridge of Sighs" was his Corunna, his Heights of Abraham — sickly, weak, wounded, he fell in the full blaze and fame of that great victory.

What manner of man was the genius who penned that famous song? What like was Wolfe, who climbed and conquered on those famous Heights of Abraham? We all want to know details regarding men who have achieved famous feats, whether of war, or wit, or eloquence, or endurance, or knowledge. His one or two happy and heroic actions take a man's name and memory out of the crowd of names and memories. Henceforth he stands eminent. We scan him; we want to know all about him; we walk round and examine him, are curious, perhaps, and think are we not as strong and tall and capable as yonder champion; were we not bred as well, and could we not endure the winter's cold as well as he? Or we look up with all our eyes of admiration; will find no fault with our hero; declare his beauty and proportions perfect; his critics envious detractors, and so forth. Yesterday, before he performed his feat, he was nobody. Who cared about his birthplace, his parentage, or the color of his hair? To-day, by some single achievement, or by a series of great actions to

which his genius accustoms us, he is famous, and antiquarians are busy finding out under what schoolmaster's ferule he was educated, where his grandmother was vaccinated, and so forth. If half a dozen washing bills of Goldsmith were to be found to-morrow, would they not inspire a general interest, and be printed in a hundred papers? I lighted upon Oliver, not very long since, in an old Town and Country Magazine, at the Pantheon masquerade "in an old English habit." Straightway my imagination ran out to meet him, to look at him, to follow him about. I forgot the names of scores of fine gentlemen of the past age, who were mentioned besides. We want to see this man who has amused and charmed us; who has been our friend, and given us hours of pleasant companionship and kindly thought. I protest when I came, in the midst of those names of people of fashion, and beaux, and demireps, upon those names, "Sir J. R-yn-lds, in a domino; Mr. Cr-d-ck and Dr. G-ldsm-th, in two old-English dresses," I had, so to speak, my heart in my mouth. What, you here, my dear Sir Joshua? Ah, what an honor and privilege it is to see you! This is Mr. Goldsmith? And very much, sir, the ruff and the slashed doublet become you! O Doctor! what a pleasure I had and have in reading "Animated Nature." How did you learn the secret of writing the decasyllabic line, and whence that sweet wailing note of tenderness that accompanies your song? Was Beau Tibbs a real man, and will you do me the honor of allowing me to sit at your table at supper? Don't you think you know how he would have talked? Would you not have liked to hear him prattle over the champagne?

Now, Hood is passed away — passed off the earth as much as Goldsmith or Horace. The times in which he lived, and in which very many of us lived and were young, are changing or changed. I saw Hood once as a young man, at a dinner which seems almost as ghostly now as that masquerade at the Pantheon (1772), of which we were speaking anon. It was at a dinner of the Literary Fund, in that vast apartment which is hung round with the portraits of very large Royal Freemasons, now unsubstantial ghosts. There at the end of the room was Hood. Some publishers, I think, were our companions. I quite remember his pale face; he was thin and deaf, and very silent; he scarcely opened his lips during the dinner, and he made one pun. Some gentleman missed his snuffbox, and Hood said,—— (the Freemasons' Tavern was kept, you must remember, by Mr. Cuff in those days,

not by its present proprietors). Well, the box being lost, and asked for, and Cuff (remember that name) being the name of the landlord, Hood opened his silent jaws and said. * * * Shall I tell you what he said? It was not a very good pun, which the great punster then made. Choose your favorite pun out of "Whims and Oddities," and fancy that was the joke which he contributed to the hilarity of our little table.

Where those asterisks are drawn on the page, you must know a pause occurred, during which I was engaged with "Hood's Own," having been referred to the book, by this life of the author which I have just been reading. I am not going to dissert on Hood's humor; I am not a fair judge. Have I not said elsewhere that there are one or two wonderfully old gentlemen still alive who used to give me tips when I was a boy? I can't be a fair critic about them. I always think of that sovereign, that rapture of raspberry tarts, which made my young days happy. Those old sovereign contributors may tell stories ever so old, and I shall laugh; they may commit murder, and I shall believe it was justifiable homicide. There is my friend Baggs, who goes about abusing me, and of course our dear mutual friends tell me. Abuse away, mon bon! You were so kind to me when I wanted kindness, that you may take the change out of that gold now, and say I am a cannibal and negro, if you will. Ha, Baggs! Dost thou wince as thou readest this line? Does guilty conscience throbbing at thy breast tell thee of whom the fable is narrated? Puff out thy wrath, and when it has ceased to blow, my Baggs shall be to me as the Baggs of old — the generous, the gentle, the friendly.

No, on second thoughts I am determined I will not repeat that joke which I heard Hood make. He says he wrote these jokes with such ease that he sent manuscripts to the publishers faster than they could acknowledge the receipt thereof. I won't say that they were all good jokes, or that to read a great book full of them is a work at present altogether jocular. Writing to a friend respecting some memoir of him which had been published, Hood says, "You will judge how well the author knows me, when he says my mind is rather serious than comic." At the time when he wrote these words, he evidently undervalued his own serious power, and thought that in punning and broad grinning lay his chief strength. Is not there something touching in that simplicity and humility of faith? "To make laugh is my calling," says he; "I must jump, I must grin, I must tumble, I must turn language head over heels, and leap through grammar"; and he goes to his work humbly and courageously, and what he has to do that does he with all his might, through sickness, through sorrow, through exile, poverty, fever, depression — there he is, always ready to his work, and with a jewel of genius in his pocket! Why, when he laid down his puns and pranks, put the motley off, and spoke out of his heart, all England and America listened in tears and wonder! Other men have delusions of conceit and fancy themselves greater than they are, and that the world slights them. Have we not heard how Liston always thought he ought to play Hamlet? Here is a man with a power to touch the heart almost unequaled, and he passes days and years in writing "Young Ben he was a nice young man," and so forth. To say truth, I have been reading in a book of "Hood's Own" until I am perfectly angry. "You great man, you good man, you true genius and poet," I cry out, as I turn page after page. "Do, do, make no more of these jokes, but be yourself, and take your station."

When Hood was on his deathbed, Sir Robert Peel, who only knew of his illness, not of his imminent danger, wrote to him a noble and touching letter, announcing that a pension was conferred on him:—

"I am more than repaid," writes Peel, "by the personal satisfaction which I have had in doing that for which you return me warm and characteristic acknowledgments.

"You perhaps think that you are known to one with such multifarious occupations as myself merely by general reputation as an author; but I assure you that there can be little which you have written and acknowledged which I have not read; and that there are few who can appreciate and admire more than myself the good sense and good feeling which have taught you to infuse so much fun and merriment into writings correcting folly and exposing absurdities, and yet never trespassing beyond those limits within which wit and facetiousness are not very often confined. You may write on with the consciousness of independence, as free and unfettered as if no communication had ever passed between us. I am not conferring a private obligation upon you, but am fulfilling the intentions of the legislature which has placed at the disposal of the crown a certain sum (miserable, indeed, in amount) to be applied to the recognition of public claims

on the bounty of the crown. If you will review the names of those whose claims have been admitted on account of their literary or scientific eminence, you will find an ample confirmation of the truth of my statement.

"One return, indeed, I shall ask of you,—that you will give me the opportunity of making your personal acquaintance."

And Hood, writing to a friend, inclosing a copy of Peel's letter says: "Sir R. Peel came from Burleigh on Tuesday night, and went down to Brighton on Saturday. If he had written by post, I should not have had it till to-day. So he sent his servant with the inclosed on Saturday night; another mark of considerate attention." He is frightfully unwell, he continues; his wife says he looks quite green; but ill as he is, poor fellow, "his well is not dry. He has pumped out a sheet of Christmas fun, is drawing some cuts, and shall write a sheet more of his novel."

O sad, marvelous picture of courage, of honesty, of patient endurance, of duty struggling against pain! How noble Peel's figure is standing by that sick bed! How generous his words, how dignified and sincere his compassion! And the poor dying man, with a heart full of natural gratitude towards his noble benefactor, must turn to him and say: "If it be well to be remembered by a minister, it is better still not to be forgotten by him in a 'hurly Burleigh!'" Can you laugh? Is not the joke horribly pathetic from the poor dying lips? As dying Robin Hood must fire a last shot with his bow — as one reads of Catholics on their deathbeds putting on a Capuchin dress to go out of the world — here is poor Hood at his last hour putting on his ghastly motley, and uttering one joke more.

He dies, however, in dearest love and peace with his children, wife, and friends; to the former especially his whole life had been devoted, and every day showed his fidelity, simplicity, and affection. In going through the record of his most pure, modest, honorable life, and living along with him, you come to trust him thoroughly, and feel that here is a most loyal, affectionate, and upright soul, with whom you have been brought into communion. Can we say as much for all lives of all men of letters? Here is one at least without guile, without pretension, without scheming, of a pure life, to his family and little modest circle of friends tenderly devoted.

And what a hard work, and what a slender reward! In the little domestic details with which the book abounds, what a sim-

ple life is shown to us! The most simple little pleasures and amusements delight and occupy him. You have revels on shrimps; the good wife making the pie; details about the maid, and criticisms on her conduct; wonderful tricks played with the plum pudding — all the pleasures centring round the little humble home. One of the first men of his time, he is appointed editor of a magazine at a salary of £300 per annum, signs himself exultingly "Ed. N. M. M.," and the family rejoice over the income as over a fortune. He goes to a Greenwich dinner — what a feast and rejoicing afterwards!

"Well, we drank 'the Boz' with a delectable clatter, which drew from him a good warm-hearted speech. . . . He looked very well, and had a younger brother along with him. . . . Then we had songs. Barham chanted a Robin-Hood ballad, and Cruikshank sang a burlesque ballad of Lord H——; and somebody, unknown to me, gave a capital imitation of a French showman. Then we toasted Mrs. Boz, and the Chairman, and Vice, and the Traditional Priest sang the 'Deep, Deep Sea,' in his deep, deep voice; and then we drank to Procter, who wrote the said song; also Sir J. Wilson's good health, and Cruikshank's and Ainsworth's: and a Manchester friend of the latter sang a Manchester ditty, so full of trading stuff, that it really seemed to have been not composed, but manufactured. Jerdan, as Jerdanish as usual on such occasions — you know how paradoxically he is quite at home in dining out. As to myself, I had to make my second maiden speech, for Mr. Monckton Milnes proposed my health in terms my modesty might allow me to repeat to you, but my memory won't. However, I ascribed the toast to my notoriously bad health, and assured them that their wishes had already improved it — that I felt a brisker circulation — a more genial warmth about the heart, and explained that a certain trembling of my hand was not from palsy, or my old ague, but an inclination in my hand to shake itself with every one present. Whereupon I had to go through the friendly ceremony with as many of the company as were within reach, besides a few more who came express from the other end of the table. Very gratifying, wasn't it? Though I cannot go quite so far as Jane, who wants me to have that hand chopped off, bottled, and preserved in spirits. She was sitting up for me, very anxiously, as usual when I go out, because I am so domestic and steady, and was down at the door before I could ring at the gate, to which Boz

kindly sent me in his own carriage. Poor girl! what would she do if she had a wild husband instead of a tame one?"

And the poor anxious wife is sitting up, and fondles the hand which has been shaken by so many illustrious men! The little feast dates back only eighteen years, and yet somehow it seems as distant as a dinner at Mr. Thrale's, or a meeting at Will's.

Poor little gleam of sunshine! very little good cheer enlivens that sad simple life. We have the triumph of the magazine; then a new magazine projected and produced; then illness and the last scene, and the kind Peel by the dying man's bedside, speaking noble words of respect and sympathy, and soothing the last throbs of the tender, honest heart.

I like, I say, Hood's life even better than his books, and I wish, with all my heart, *Monsieur et cher confrère*, the same could be said for both of us, when the ink stream of our life hath ceased to run. Yes: if I drop first, dear Baggs, I trust you may find reason to modify some of the unfavorable views of my character, which you are freely imparting to our mutual friends. What ought to be the literary man's point of honor nowadays? Suppose, friendly reader, you are one of the craft, what legacy would you like to leave your children? First of all (and by Heaven's gracious help) you would pray and strive to give them such an endowment of love as should last certainly for all their lives, and perhaps be transmitted to their children. You would (by the same aid and blessing) keep your honor pure and transmit a name unstained to those who have a right to bear it. You would,—though this faculty of giving is one of the easiest of the literary man's qualities,—you would, out of your earnings, small or great, be able to help a poor brother in need, to dress his wounds, and, if it were but twopence, to give him succor. Is the money which the noble Macaulay gave to the poor lost to his family? God forbid. To the loving hearts of his kindred is it not rather the most precious part of their inheritance? It was invested in love and righteous doing, and it bears interest in heaven. You will, if letters be your vocation, find saving harder than giving or spending. To save, be your endeavor, too, against the night's coming when no man may work; when the arm is weary with the long day's labor; when the brain perhaps grows dark; when the old, who can labor no more, want warmth and rest, and the young ones call for supper.

LIFE IN OLD-TIME LONDON

WE HAVE brought our Georges to London city, and if we would behold its aspect may see it in Hogarth's lively perspective of Cheapside or read of it in a hundred contemporary books which paint the manners of that age. Our dear old Spectator looks smiling upon the streets, with their innumerable signs, and describes them with his charming humor. "Our streets are filled with Blue Boars, Black Swans, and Red Lions, not to mention Flying Pigs and Hogs in Armor, with other creatures more extraordinary than any in the deserts of Africa." A few of these quaint old figures still remain in London town. You may still see there, and over its old hostel in Ludgate Hill, the "Belle Sauvage" to whom the Spectator so pleasantly alludes in that paper; and who was, probably, no other than the sweet American Pocahontas, who rescued from death the daring Capt. Smith. There is the "Lion's Head," down whose jaws the Spectator's own letters were passed; and over a great banker's in Fleet Street, the effigy of the wallet, which the founder of the firm bore when he came into London a country boy. People this street, so ornamented, with crowds of swinging chairmen, with servants bawling to clear the way, with Mr. Dean in his cassock, his lackey marching before him; or Mrs. Dinah in her sack, tripping to chapel, her footboy carrying her ladyship's great prayer book; with itinerant tradesmen, singing their hundred cries (I remember forty years ago, as a boy in London city, a score of cheery, familiar cries that are silent now). Fancy the beaux thronging to the chocolatehouses, tapping their snuffboxes as they issue thence, their periwigs appearing over the red curtains. Fancy Saccharissa, beckoning and smiling from the upper windows, and a crowd of soldiers brawling and bustling at the door — gentlemen of the Life Guards, clad in scarlet, with blue facings, and laced with gold at the seams; gentlemen of the Horse Grenadiers, in their caps of sky-blue cloth, with the garter embroidered on the front in gold and silver; men of the Halberdiers, in their long red coats, as bluff Harry left them, with their ruff and velvet flat caps. Perhaps the King's Majesty himself is going to St. James's as we pass. If he is going to parliament, he is in his coach-and-eight, surrounded by his guards and the high officers of his crown. Otherwise his Majesty only uses a chair, with six footmen walking before, and six yeomen

x—235

of the guard at the sides of the sedan. The officers in waiting follow the king in coaches. It must be rather slow work.

Our Spectator and Tatler are full of delightful glimpses of the town life of those days. In the company of that charming guide, we may go to the opera, the comedy, the puppet show, the auction, even the cockpit; we can take boat at Temple Stairs, and accompany Sir Roger de Coverley and Mr. Spectator to Spring Garden — it will be called Vauxhall a few years hence, when Hogarth will paint for it. Would you not like to step back into the past, and be introduced to Mr. Addison? — not the Right Honorable Joseph Addison, Esq., George the First's Secretary of State, but to the delightful painter of contemporary manners; the man who, when in good humor himself, was the pleasantest companion in all England. I should like to go into Lockit's with him, and drink a bowl along with Sir R. Steele (who has just been knighted by King George, and who does not happen to have any money to pay his share of the reckoning). I should not care to follow Mr. Addison to his secretary's office in Whitehall. There we get into politics. Our business is pleasure, and the town, and the coffeehouse, and the theatre, and the Mall. Delightful Spectator! kind friend of leisure hours! happy companion! true Christian gentleman! How much greater, better, are you than the king Mr. Secretary kneels to!

You can have foreign testimony about old-world London, if you like; and my before-quoted friend, Charles Louis, Baron de Pöllnitz, will conduct us to it. "A man of sense," says he, "or a fine gentleman, is never at a loss for company in London, and this is the way the latter passes his time. He rises late, puts on a frock and, leaving his sword at home, takes his cane, and goes where he pleases. The park is commonly the place where he walks, because 'tis the Exchange for men of quality. 'Tis the same thing as the Tuileries at Paris, only the park has a certain beauty of simplicity which cannot be described. The grand walk is called the Mall; is full of people at every hour of the day, but especially at morning and evening, when their Majesties often walk with the royal family, who are attended only by a half-dozen yeomen of the guard, and permit all persons to walk at the same time with them. The ladies and gentlemen always appear in rich dresses, for the English, who, twenty years ago, did not wear gold lace but in their army, are now embroidered and bedaubed as much as the French. I speak of persons of quality;

for the citizen still contents himself with a suit of fine cloth, a good hat and wig, and fine linen. Everybody is well clothed here, and even the beggars don't make so ragged an appearance as they do elsewhere." After our friend, the man of quality, has had his morning or undress walk in the Mall, he goes home to dress, and then saunters to some coffeehouse or chocolatehouse frequented by the persons he would see. "For 'tis a rule with the English to go once a day at least to houses of this sort, where they talk of business and news, read the papers, and often look at one another without opening their lips. And 'tis very well they are so mute; for were they all as talkative as people of other nations, the coffeehouses would be intolerable, and there would be no hearing what one man said where there are so many. The chocolatehouse in St. James's Street, where I go every morning to pass away the time, is always so full that a man can scarce turn about in it."

Delightful as London city was, King George I. liked to be out of it as much as ever he could; and when there, passed all his time with his Germans. It was with them as with Blucher, one hundred years afterwards, when the bold old Reiter looked down from St. Paul's, and sighed out, "Was für Plunder!" The German women plundered; the German secretaries plundered; the German cooks and intendants plundered; even Mustapha and Mahomet, the German negroes, had a share of the booty. Take what you can get, was the old monarch's maxim. He was not a lofty monarch, certainly; he was not a patron of the fine arts; but he was not a hypocrite, he was not revengeful, he was not extravagant. Though a despot in Hanover, he was a moderate ruler in England. His aim was to leave it to itself as much as possible, and to live out of it as much as he could. His heart was in Hanover. When taken ill on his last journey, as he was passing through Holland, he thrust his livid head out of the coach window, and gasped out, "Osnaburg. Osnaburg!"

From "The Four Georges."

ADDISON

WE LOVE him for his vanities as much as his virtues. What is ridiculous is delightful in him; we are so fond of him because we laugh at him so. And out of that laughter, and out of that sweet weakness, and out of those harmless eccentricities and follies, and out of that touched brain, and out

of that honest manhood and simplicity — we get a result of happiness, goodness, tenderness, pity, piety; such as, if my audience will think their reading and hearing over, doctors and divines but seldom have the fortune to inspire. And why not? Is the glory of heaven to be sung only by gentlemen in black coats? Must the truth be only expounded in gown and surplice, and out of those two vestments can nobody preach it? Commend me to this preacher without orders — this parson in the tiewig. When this man looks from the world, whose weaknesses he describes so benevolently, up to the heaven which shines over us all, I can hardly fancy a human face lighted up with a more serene rapture: a human intellect thrilling with a purer love and adoration than Joseph Addison's. Listen to him: from your childhood you have known the verses; but who can hear their sacred music without love and awe? —

> "Soon as the Evening Shades prevail,
> 　The Moon takes up the wondrous tale,
> And nightly to the listening Earth,
> 　Repeats the story of her birth;
> And all the Stars that round her burn,
> And all the Planets in their turn,
> Confirm the tidings as they roll,
> And spread the truth from pole to pole.
> What though, in solemn silence, all
> Move round this dark terrestrial ball?
> What though no real voice nor sound,
> Among their radiant orbs be found;
> In Reason's ear they all rejoice,
> And utter forth a glorious voice,
> Forever singing as they shine,
> The Hand that made us is Divine."

It seems to me those verses shine like the stars. They shine out of a great, deep calm. When he turns to heaven, a Sabbath comes over that man's mind; and his face lights up from it with a glory of thanks and prayer. His sense of religion stirs through his whole being. In the fields, in the town; looking at the birds in the trees; at the children in the streets; in the morning or in the moonlight; over his books in his own room; in a happy party at a country merrymaking or a town assembly, good-will and peace to God's creatures, and love and awe of him who made them, fill his pure heart and shine from his kind face. If Swift's life was the most wretched, I think Addison's was one of the most enviable. A life prosperous and beautiful — a calm death — an immense fame and affection afterwards for his happy and spotless name.

From "English Humorists."

STEELE

SHORTLY before the Boyne was fought, and young Swift had begun to make acquaintance with English court manners and English servitude, in Sir William Temple's family, another Irish youth was brought to learn his humanities at the old school of Charterhouse, near Smithfield; to which foundation he had been appointed by James, Duke of Ormond, a governor of the House, and a patron of the lad's family. The boy was an orphan, and described, twenty years after, with a sweet pathos and simplicity, some of the earliest recollections of a life which was destined to be checkered by a strange variety of good and evil fortune.

I am afraid no good report could be given by his masters and ushers of that thick-set, square-faced, black-eyed, soft-hearted little Irish boy. He was very idle. He was whipped deservedly a great number of times. Though he had very good parts of his own, he got other boys to do his lessons for him, and only took just as much trouble as should enable him to scuffle through his exercises, and by good fortune escape the flogging block. One hundred and fifty years after, I have myself inspected, but only as an amateur, that instrument of righteous torture still existing, and in occasional use, in a secluded private apartment of the old Charterhouse School; and have no doubt it is the very counterpart, if not the ancient and interesting machine itself, at which poor Dick Steele submitted himself to the tormentors.

Besides being very kind, lazy, and good-natured, this boy went invariably into debt with the tart woman; ran out of bounds, and entered into pecuniary, or rather promissory engagements with the neighboring lollipop vendors and pie men — exhibited an early fondness and capacity for drinking mum and sack, and borrowed from all his comrades who had money to lend. I have no sort

of authority for the statements here made of Steele's early life; but if the child is father of the man, the father of young Steele of Merton, who left Oxford without taking a degree, and entered the Life Guards — the father of Capt. Steele of Lucas's Fusiliers, who got his company through the patronage of my Lord Cutts — the father of Mr. Steele, the Commissioner of Stamps, the editor of the Gazette, the Tatler, and Spectator, the expelled Member of Parliament, and the author of "The Tender Husband" and "The Conscious Lovers"; if man and boy resembled each other, Dick Steele the schoolboy must have been one of the most generous, good-for-nothing, amiable little creatures that ever conjugated the verb *tupto*, I beat; *tuptomai*, I am whipped, in any school in Great Britain.

Almost every gentleman who does me the honor to hear me will remember that the very greatest character which he has seen in the course of his life, and the person to whom he has looked up with the greatest wonder and reverence, was the head boy at his school. The schoolmaster himself hardly inspires such an awe. The head boy construes as well as the schoolmaster himself. When he begins to speak the hall is hushed, and every little boy listens. He writes off copies of Latin verses as melodiously as Virgil. He is good-natured, and, his own masterpieces achieved, pours out other copies of verses for other boys with an astonishing ease and fluency; the idle ones only trembling lest they should be discovered on giving in their exercises, and whipped because their poems were too good. I have seen great men in my time, but never such a great one as that head boy of my childhood; we all thought he must be Prime Minister, and I was disappointed on meeting him in after-life to find he was no more than six feet high.

Dick Steele, the Charterhouse-gown boy, contracted such an admiration in the years of his childhood, and retained it faithfully through his life. Through the school and through the world, whithersoever his strange fortune led this erring, wayward, affectionate creature, Joseph Addison was always his head boy. Addison wrote his exercises. Addison did his best themes. He ran on Addison's messages, fagged for him and blacked his shoes: to be in Joe's company was Dick's greatest pleasure; and he took a sermon or a caning from his monitor with the most boundless reverence, acquiescence, and affection.

From "English Humorists."

GOLDSMITH

A WILD youth, wayward, but full of tenderness and affection, quits the country village where his boyhood has been passed in happy musing, in idle shelter, in fond longing, to see the great world out of doors, and achieve name and fortune; and after years of dire struggle, and neglect and poverty, his heart turning back as fondly to his native place as it had longed eagerly for change when sheltered there, he writes a book and a poem, full of the recollections and feelings of home — he paints the friends and scenes of his youth, and peoples Auburn and Wakefield with remembrances of Lissoy. Wander he must, but he carries away a home relic with him, and dies with it on his breast. His nature is truant; in repose it longs for change: as on the journey it looks back for friends and quiet. He passes to-day in building an air-castle for to-morrow, or in writing yesterday's elegy; and he would fly away this hour, but that a cage and necessity keeps him. What is the charm of his verse, of his style, and humor? His sweet regrets, his delicate compassion, his soft smile, his tremulous sympathy, the weakness which he owns? Your love for him is half pity. You come hot and tired from the day's battle, and this sweet minstrel sings to you. Who could harm the kind vagrant harper? Whom did he ever hurt? He carries no weapon — save the harp on which he plays to you; and with which he delights great and humble, young and old, the captains in the tents, or the soldiers round the fire, or the women and children in the villages, at whose porches he stops and sings his simple songs of love and beauty. With that sweet story of "The Vicar of Wakefield," he has found entry into every castle and every hamlet in Europe. Not one of us, however busy or hard, but once or twice in our lives, has passed an evening with him, and undergone the charm of his delightful music. . . .

Think of him reckless, thriftless, vain if you like — but merciful, gentle, generous, full of love and pity. He passes out of our life, and goes to render his account beyond it. Think of the poor pensioners weeping at his grave; think of the noble spirits that admired and deplored him; think of the righteous pen that wrote his epitaph — and of the wonderful and unanimous response of affection with which the world has paid back the love he gave it. His humor delighting us still; his song fresh and beautiful

as when first he charmed with it; his words in all our mouths; his very weaknesses beloved and familiar — his benevolent spirit seems still to smile upon us; to do gentle kindnesses; to succor with sweet charity; to soothe, caress, and forgive; to plead with the fortunate for the unhappy and the poor.

From "English Humorists."

THEOPHRASTUS

(c. 373–288 B. C.)

S FOR Theophrastus," writes Quintilian, "there is such a divine beauty in his language, that he may be said even to have derived his name* from it." While this "divine beauty" found its vehicle in a melody peculiar to the Greek language and not to be translated, those who read Healey's version of the "Characters" will not be at a loss for· suggestions of Quintilian's reasons for admiring them. As the author of these "Characters," Theophrastus is the founder of a distinct modern school which embraces Sir Thomas Overbury, La Bruyère, John Earle, Owen Felltham, and Thomas Fuller,—each of whom has borrowed and used to advantage methods of character sketching and moralizing which belonged originally to "ethical characters" of the great successor of Aristotle.

The authorities are not agreed on the date of the birth of Theophrastus, but fix it between 373 and 368 B. C. His birthplace was Eresus, on the island of Lesbos, and after studying there under Leuciphus (Alciphus?) he went to Athens and became a disciple of Plato. Becoming an intimate friend of Aristotle who made him the guardian of his children, he was made chief of the Peripatetic school after Aristotle's death and presided over it until his own death in 288 B. C. He was greatly honored by his own generation and was studied by students of science and literature as long as Greek remained a living tongue. Besides his "Characters," Theophrastus wrote extensively on science and philosophy,—notably a "History of Plants" and a "History of Physics," parts of which are still extant.

* Theophrastus, i. e., the Divine Speaker.

THE "CHARACTERS" OF THEOPHRASTUS*

(Translated by Healey. The Complete Text of the Temple Edition)

OF CAVILLING

CAVILLING or cavillation (if we should define it rudely) is a wresting of actions and words to the worse or sadder part. A Caviller is he, who will entertain his enemies with a pretence of love; who applaudeth those publickly, whom secretly he seeketh to supplant. If any man traduce or deprave him, he easily pardoneth him without any expostulation. He passeth by jests broken upon him, and is very affable with those which challenge him of any injury by him to them done. Those which desire hastily to speak with him, he giveth them a Come-again. Whatsoever he doth, he hideth; and is much in deliberation. To those which would borrow money of him, his answere is, 'Tis a dead time; I sell nothing. And when he selleth little, then he braggeth of much. When he heareth any thing he will make shew not to observe it: He will deny he hath seen what he saw. If he bargain for any thing in his own wrong, he will not remember it. Some things he will consider of: some things he knows; some things he knows not; others he wonders at. These words are very usuall with him: I do not believe it; I think not so; I wonder at it ; Of some of these, I was so perswaded before. He will tell you, You mistake him for another: he had no such speech with me. This is beyond belief: find out some other ear for your stories. Shall I believe you, or disable his credit? But take you heed how you give credit to these received sayings, veiled and infolded with so many windings of dissimulation. Men of these manners are to be shunned more than Vipers.

Complete.

OF FLATTERY

FLATTERY may be sayd to be a foul deformed custom in common life, making for the advantage of the Flatterer. A Flatterer is such a one, as if he walk or converse with you, will thus say unto you: Do you observe, how all men's eyes are upon you? I have not noted any in this Town, to be so much beheld. Yesterday in the Gallery you had reason to be proud of

* With Healey's spelling retained throughout.

your reputation. For there being at that time assembled more than thirty persons, and question being made which should be the worthiest Citizen; the company being very impatient it should be disputed, concluded all upon you. These and suchlike he putteth upon him. If there be the least mote upon his clothes, or if there should be none, he maketh a shew to take it off: or if any small straw or feather be gotten into his locks, the Flatterer taketh it away; and smiling saith, you are grown gray ·within these few dayes for want of my company, and yet your hair is naturally as black as any man of your years. If he reply, the Flatterer proclaimeth silence, praiseth him palpably and profusely to his face. When he hath spoken, he breaketh out into an exclamation, with a O well spoken! And if he break a jest upon any, the Flatterer laughs as if he were tickled; muffling himself in his cloak, as if he could not possibly forbear. As he meeteth any, he plaieth the Gentleman-usher, praying them to give way; as if his Patron were a very great person. He buys pears and apples, and bears them home to his children, and gives them (for the most part) in his presence: and kissing them, crieth out, O the worthy Father's lively pieture! If he buy a shoe, if he be present, he swears his foot is far handsomer, and that the shoe mis-shapes it. If at any time he should repair to visit a friend, the Flatterer plays the Herbinger; runs before, and advertiseth them of his coming: and speedily returning back again, telleth him that he hath given them notice thereof. Whatsoever belongeth to the women's Academy, as paintings, preservings, needle-works, and such like, he discourseth of them like my Lady's woman. Of all the guests, he first commends the wine, and always sitting by his Ingle, courts him; asking him how sparingly he feeds, and how he bridles it: and taking some speciall dish from the Table, taketh occasion to commend it. He is busy and full of questions; whether this man be not cold; why he goes so thinne; and why he will not go better cloth'd? Then he whispers in his Patron's ear: and, while others speak, his eye is still upon him. At the Theatre, taking the cushions from the boy, he setteth them up himself: he commendeth the situation and building of the house; the well tilling and husbanding of the ground. In conclusion, you shall always note a Flatterer to speak and do, what he presumeth will be most pleasing and agreeable.

Complete.

OF GARRULITY

GARRULITY is a slippery loosenesse, or a babling of a long inconsiderate speech. A Pratler or Babler is such an one, that unseasonably setting upon any stranger, will commend his wife unto him; or tell his last night's dreams, or what meates, or how many dishes he had at such a feast: and when you listen to him, or that he grows a little encouraged with your attention, he will complain, that modern men are worse than those of elder times: that corn is too cheap, as rents are now improv'd: that there are too many strangers dwelling in the Town: That the Seas, after the Dionysian feasts, will be more smooth, and obedient to the Saylors: and that if there fall good store of raine, there will be greater plenty of those things, which yet are lockt up in the bowels of the earth: and the next year he will till his ground: That 'tis a hard world: and that men have much ado to live: and that when the holy Ceremonies were celebrated, Damippus set up the greatest light: inquireth therefore how many columnes are in the Odeum: and yesterday, he sayth, I was wamble-cropt, and (saving your presence) parbreak't: and what day of the moneth is this? but if any man lend him attention, he shall never be clear of him. He will tell you that the mysteries, "Mense Bœdromione," "Apaturia," "Pyanepsione," "Posideone," the "Dionysia," which now are, were wont to be celebrated. These kind of men are to be shunned, with great wariness and speed, as a man would prevent or outrun an Ague. For 'tis a miserable condition, to continue long with those which cannot distinguish the seasons of business and leisure.

Complete.

OF RUSTICITY OR CLOWNISHNESS

RUSTICITY may seem to be an ignorance of honesty and comliness. A Clown or rude fellow is he, who will go into a crowd or press, when he hath taken a purge: And he that sayth, that Garlick is as sweet as a gilliflower: that wears shoes much larger then his feet: that speaks always very loud: who, distrusting his friends and familiars, in serious affairs adviseth with his servants: who, the things which he heard in the Senate, imparteth to his mercenaries, who do his drudgery in the country:

one that sitteth so with his hose drawn up at his knee as you might see his skin. Upon the way whatsoever strange accident he encountreth, he wondreth at nothing. But if he see an ox, an ass, or a goat, then the man is at a stand, and begins to look about him: proud when he can rob the cupboard or the Cellar, and then snap up a scrap; very carefull that the wench that makes the bread take him not napping. He grinds, caters, drudges, purveighs, and plays the Sutler, for all things belonging to a house provision. When he is at dinner, he casts meat to his beasts; if any body knock at the door, he listens like a Cat for a mouse. Calling his dog to him, and taking him by the snout: This fellow, saith he, keeps my ground, my house, and all that is in it. If he receive money, he rejects it as light; and desireth to have it changed. If he have lent his plough, his scythe, or his sack, he sends for them again at midnight, if he chance to thinke of them in his sleep.

Coming into the City, whomsoever he meeteth, he asketh the price of hides and salt fish, and whether there be any plays this new moon: and so soon as he doth alight, he tells them all that he will be trimmed: And this fellow still sings in the Bath; and clowts his shoes with hob-nails. And because it was the same way to receive his salt meates from Archias, it was his fashion to carry it himself.

Complete.

OF FAIR SPEECH OR SMOOTHNESS

SMOOTHNESS, or fawning, if we should define it, is an encounter containing many allurements to pleasure; and those (for the most part) not more honest than they should be. But a sleekstone or Smooth-boot (as we terme him) is he, that saluteth a man as farre off, as his eye can carry level; stileth him Most worthy; admireth his fortune; and taking him by both the hands, detaineth him, not suffering him to pass. But having a while accompanied him, is very inquisitive when he shall see him again; embroidering and painting out his praise. The same being chosen an Arbitrator, endevoureth not only to content him on whose behalfe he is chosen, but the adverse part likewise, that so he may be held an indifferent friend to them both. He maintaineth, when strangers speak wiser and juster things than his own fellow-Citizens. Being invited to a feast, he

bring a token and would pay nothing, then to wrangle and brabble extremely; fit to keep an Alehouse, or an Inn: to be a Pandar or a Toll-gatherer, a fellow that will forbear no foul or base course: He will be a common Crier, a Cook, a Dicer; he denies his mother food. Being convicted of theft, he shall be drawn and haled by head and shoulders; he shall dwell longer in prison, than in his own house. This is one of those, which ever and anon have a throng about them, calling to them all they meet, to whom they speak in a great broken tone, rayling on them.

And thus they come and go, before they understand what the matter is: whilst he telleth some the beginning; some scantily a word; others he telleth some little part of the whole; affecting to publish and protest his damnable disposition. He is full of suits and actions; both such as he suggesteth against others; and such as are framed against him. He is a common maker of affidavit for other men's absence. He suborneth actions against himself: In his bosom he bears a box, and in his hand a bundle of papers. And such is his impudence, he gives himselfe out to be Generall of the Petti-foggers and Knights of the Post. He puts out money to use: and for a groat, takes daily three farthings. He goes oftentimes into the Fish-market, Taverns, Cooks shops, and Shambles: and the money that he gets by his brocage, he commonly hides in his mouth. These men are very hard to be indured: their tongues are traded in detraction: and when they rail, they do it in such a stormy and tempestuous fashion, as all Courts and Taverns are pestered with their clamors.

Complete.

OF LOQUACITY OR OVERSPEAKING

LOQUACITY is a loosenesse or intemperance of speech. A pratling fellow is he, who saith to him with whom he discourseth, whatsoever he beginneth to say, anticipates him; That he knoweth all already, and that the other saith nothing to purpose; and that if he will apply himselfe to him, he shall understand somewhat. Then interrupting him, Take heed, saith he, that you forget not that you would say, etc. You do well that you have called it to mind, etc. How necessary and usefull a thing confidence is! There's something that I have omitted now, etc. You apprehend it very readily, etc. I did expect that we

entreateth the master of the entertainment to send in for his children: and when they are come, he swears they resemble their father, as near as one figg doth another. Then calling them to him, he kisseth them, and setteth them by him: and jesting with others of the company, saith he, Compare them with the father, they are as like him, as an apple is like an oyster. He will suffer others sleeping to rest in his bosom, when he is loden with a sore burden. He trimmeth himselfe often: he keepeth his teeth clean and white: changeth and Turkizeth his clothes. His walk is commonly in that part, where the Goldsmiths' and Bankers' tables are: and useth those places of activity where young youths do exercise themselves. At shews and in the Theatres, he placeth himself next the Prætors; but in the Courts of Justice he seldom appears. But he buys presents to send to his friend at Byzantium. Little dogges, and Hymettian honey he sends to Rhodes: and he tells his fellow-Citizens that he doth these things. Besides, he keeps an ape at home; buys a Satyr, and Sicilian Doves; and boxes of Treacle, of those which are of a round form; and slaves, those that are somewhat bending and oblique, brought from Lacedæmon; and Tapistry, wherein the Persians are woven and set out. He hath a little yard, graveled, fit for wrestling; and a Tennis Court. And these parts of his house, his manner is to offer your present unto any he meets, whether Philosopher or Sophister, or those which exercise themselves in Arms, or Musick, that they may use their cunning: which while they do, he speaks to one of the lookers on, as if he were but a meer spectator himselfe saith: I pray you, whose wrestling place is this?

Complete.

OF SENSELESSNESS OR DESPERATE BOLDNESS

SENSELESSNESS is that, whereby a man dareth both speak and do against the laws and rules of honesty. The man is he, which readily (or rashly) takes an oath; who is careless of his reputation; reckons little, to be railed upon; is of the garb or disposition of a crafty Imposter; a lewd dirty fellow, daring to do any thing but that is fit. He is not ashamed, being sober, in cool bloud, to dance Country dances and Matachines, as a Zany or Pantalon; and when the Juggelers shew their tricks, to go to every spectator and beg his offering: And if any man

should thus jump together, etc. And seeking the like occasions of pratling and verbosity, permitteth them no truce nor breathing time with whom he discourseth. And when he hath killed these, then he assaulteth fresh men in troops, when they are many assembled together. And those being seriously imployed, he wearies, tires, and puts to flight. Coming into Plays, and wrestling places, he keepeth the boys from learning; pratling with their Masters: and if any offer to go away, he followeth them to their houses. If any thing done publickly be known to him, he will report as private. Then he will tell you of the warre, when Aristophanes that noble Orator lived: or he will tell you a long tedious tale of that battaile which was fought by the Lacedæmonians under Lysander their Generall: and, if ever he spake well publickly himself, that must come in too. And thus speaking, he inveigheth against the giddy multitude; and that so lamely, and with such torment to the hearers; as that one desireth the art of oblivion; another sleeps; a third gives him over in the plain field. In conclusion, whether he sit in judgment (except he sit alone) or if he behold any sports, or if he sit at table; he vexeth his Pew-fellow with his vile, impertinent, importunate prattle: for it is a hell to him to be silent. A secret in his brest is a cole in his mouth. A Swallow in a chimney makes no such noise. And, so his humour be advanced, he's contented to be flouted by his very boyes, which jear him to his face; entreating him, when they go to bed, to talk them asleep.

Complete.

OF NEWS FORGING OR RUMOUR SPREADING

FAME spreading is a devising of deeds and words at the fancy or pleasure of the Inventor. A Newsmonger he is, who meeting with his acquaintance, changing his countenance and smiling, asketh whence come you now? How go the rules now? Is there any news stirring? And still spurring him with questions, tells him there are excellent and happy occurrents abroad. Then, before he answereth, by way of prevention asketh, have you any thing in store? why then I will feast you with my choicest intelligence. Then hath he at hand some cast Captain, or cassierd Souldier, or some Fifes boy lately come from warre, of whom he hath heard some very strange stuff, I warrant you: alwayes producing such authors as no man can control. He will tell him, he heard that Polyspherchon and the King discomfited and overthrew his enemies, and that Cassander was taken prisoner. But if any man say unto him, Do you believe this? Yes marry do I believe it, replieth he: for it is bruited all the Town over by a generall voice. The rumour spreadeth, all generally agree in this report of the warre; and that there was an exceeding great overthrow. And this he gathereth by the very countenance and carriage of these great men which sit at the stern. Then he proceedeth and tells you further, That he heard by one which came lately out of Macedonia, who was present at all which passed, that now these five days he hath bin kept close by them. Then he falleth to terms of commiseration. Alas, good, but unfortunate Cassander! O carefull desolate man! This can misfortune do. Cassander was a very powerfull man in his time, and of a very great commaund: but I would entreat you to keep this to yourselfe; and yet he runneth to every one to tell them of it. I do much wonder what pleasure men should take in devising and dispersing those rumours. The which things, that I mention not the basnesse and deformity of a lie, turne them to many inconveniences.

For, it falls out oftentimes that while these, mountebanklike, draw much company about them, in the Baths and such like places, some good Rogues steal away their clothes, others, sitting in a porch or gallery, while they overcome in a sea, or a landfight, are fined for not appearance. Others, while with their words they valiantly take Cities, loose their suppers. These men lead a very miserable and wretched life. For what Gallery is there, what shop, wherein they waste not whole days, with the penance of those whose eares they set on the Pillory with their tedious unjointed tales?

Complete.

OF IMPUDENCY

IMPUDENCE may be defined, A neglect of reputation for dirty Lucre's sake. An impudent man is he, who will not stick to attempt to borrow money of him, whom he hath already deceived; or from whom he fraudulently somewhat detaineth. When he sacrificeth, and hath season'd it with salt, layeth it up and suppeth abroad: and calling his Page or Lacquey, causing him to take up the scraps, in every man's hearing saith, You honest man, fall to, I pray you, do not spare. When he buyeth any meate he willeth the Butcher to bethink himselfe if in aught he

x—236

bearance; besides usury upon usury, if he continue it. If he invite any, he entertains them so as they rise hungry: and when he goes abroad, if he can scape scottfree, he comes fasting home. He chargeth his wife, that she lend out no salt, oyle, meale, or the like: for you little thinke, saith he, what these come to in a year. In a word, you shall see their Chests mouldy, their keys rusty; for themselves, their habit and diet is alwayes too little for them and out of fashion. Small troughs wherein they anoint themselves: their heads shaven, to save barbing: their shoes they put off at noon days, to save wearing: they deal with the Fullers, when they make clean their clothes, to put in good store of Fullers earth, to keep them from soil and spotting.

Complete.

OF OBSCENITY OR RIBALDRY

IMPURITY or beastliness is not hard to be defined. It is a licentious lewd jest. He is impure or flagitious, who, meeting with modest women, converseth of that which taketh its name of shame or secrecy. Being at a Play in the Theatre, when all are attentively silent, he in a cross conceit applauds, or claps his hands: and when the Spectators are exceedingly pleased, he hisseth: and when all the company is very attentive in hearing and beholding, he lying alone maketh noises, as if Æolus were bustling in his Cave; forcing the Spectators to look another way: and when the Hall or Stage is fullest of company, coming to those which sell nuts and apples, and other fruits standing by them, taketh them away and muncheth them; and wrangleth about their price and such like baubles. He will call to him a stranger he never saw before; and stay one whom he seeth in great haste. If he hear of a man that hath lost a great suit, and is condemn'd in great charges, as he passeth out of the Hall, cometh unto him, and gratulateth, and biddeth God give him joy. And when he hath bought meate, and hired Musicians, he sheweth to all he meeteth and invites them to it. And being at a Barber's shop, or an anointing place, he telleth the company that that night he is absolutely resolved to drink drunk. If he keep a Tavern, he will give his best friends his baptised wine, to keep them in the right way. At plays when they are most worthy the seeing, he suffereth not his children to go to them. Then he sendeth them, when they are to be seen for nothing,

were beholding unto him. Then sitting by the scales, if he can he will throw in some bit of flesh, or (rather than fail) some bone into the scales: the which if he can slily take away againe, he thinkes he hath done an excellent piece of service; if not, then he will steal some scrap from a table, and laughing sneak away. If any strangers which lodge with him desire to see a Play in the Theatre, he bespeaketh a place for them; and under their expence intrudeth himselfe, his children and their pedant. And if he meet any man which hath bought some small commodities, he beggeth part of them of him. And when he goeth to any neighbour's house, to borrow salt, barly, meale, or any the like: such is his impudence he enforceth them to bring any thing, so borrowed, home to his house. Likewise in the Baths, coming to the pans and kettles after he hath filled the bucket, washeth himselfe; not without the storms and clamours of him that keepeth the Bath; and when he hath done, saith, I am bathed; and turning to the Bather or Bath-keeper, saith, Sir, now I thank you for nothing.

Complete.

OF BASE AVARICE OR PARSIMONY

BASE or sordid Parsimony is a desire to save or spare expence without measure of discretion. Basely parsimonious he is, who being with his feast-companions doth exact and stand upon a farthing as strictly as if it were a quarter's rent of his house; and telleth how many drinking cups are taken out, as if he were jealous of some Leger-demain; one of all the company that offereth the leanest sacrifice to Diana. Now what expence soever he is at, he proclaimeth and aggravateth it, as a great disbursement. If any of his servants breake but a pitcher, or an earthen pot, he defalketh it out of their wages. If his wife loose but a Trevet, the Beacons are on fire: he will tosse, turmoil, and ransack every corner in the house; beds, bedsteds, nothing must be spared. He selleth at such rates, that no man can do good upon it. No man may borrow any thing of him; scantly light a stick of fire, for feare of setting his house on fire, not part with so much as a rotten fig, or a withered olive. Every day he surveighs his grounds and the buttals thereof, lest there be any encroaching, or any thing removed. If any debtor miss his day but a minute, he is sure to pay soundly for for-

for the redeemers of the Theatres. When an Ambassador goes abroad, leaving at home his victuall which was publickly given him, he beggeth more of his Camerado's. His manner is to lode his man, which journeys with him, with Cloke-bags and carriages, like a Porter; but taketh an order that his belly be light enough. When he anoints himselfe, he complaines the oyle is rank; and anoints himself with that which he pays not for. If a boy find a brass piece or a counter, he cries half part. These likewise are his. If he buy any thing, he buys it by the Phidonian measure, but he measureth miserably to his servants; shaving, and pinching them to a grain. If he be to pay thirty pound he will be sure it shall want three groats. When he feasteth any of his Allies, his boys that attend, are fed out of the common: and if there scape away but half a raddish or any fragment, he notes it, lest the boys that wait, meete with it.

Complete.

OF UNSEASONABLENESS OR IGNORANCE OF DUE CONVENIENT TIMES

UNSEASONABLENESS is a troublesome bourding and assaulting of those, with whom we have to do. An unseasonable fellow is he, who coming to his friend when he is very busy, interrupts him, and obtrudes his own affairs to be deliberated and debated: or cometh a gossiping to his Sweet-heart, when she is sick of an ague. His manner is likewise to intreat him to solicit or intercede for him, who is already condemn'd for suretyship. He selleth his horse to buy hay: produceth his witnesses, when judgement is given: inveigheth against women, when he is invited to a marriage. Those that are very weary with a long journey, he invites to walk. Oftentimes, rising out of the middest of many, which sit about him, as if he would recount some strange accident, tells them for news an old tedious tale, which they all knew to be trivial before. He is very forward to underrefuse. Those which sacrifice and feast he makes great love to, hoping to get a snatch. If a man beat his servant in his presence, he will tell him that he had a boy that he himselfe beat after that fashion, who hanged himselfe presently after. If he be take those things, which men are unwilling to do, or in modesty chosen Arbitrator betwixt two at difference, which desire earnestly to be accorded, he sets them out further than ever they were before.

Complete.

Of Impertinent Diligence or Over-Officiousness

THAT which we term a foolish sedulity or officiousness is a counterfeiting of our words and actions with a shew or ostentation of love. The manners of such men are these. He vainly undertaketh what he is not able to perform. A matter generally confest to be just, he will with many words, insisting upon some one particular, maintain that it cannot be argued. He causeth the boy or waiter, to mingle more wine by much than all the guests can drink. He urgeth those further, who are already together by the eares. He will lead you the way he knowes not himself: losing himselfe, and him whom he undertaketh to conduct. And coming to a Generall, or a man of great name in Armes, demandeth when he will set a battaile; and what service he will command him the next day after to-morrow. And coming to his father, he telleth him that now his mother is asleep in her chamber. And that the Physician hath forbidden his Patient the use of wine: this fellow perswades him not so much to inthrall himselfe to his Physician's directions; but to put his constitution to it a little. If his wife chance to die, he will write upon her tomb the name of Husband, Father, Mother, and her Country: adding this Inscription, All these people were of very honest life and reputation. And if he be urged to take his oath, turning himselfe to the circumstant multitude: what need I swear now, having sworn oftentimes heretofore?

Complete.

Of Blockishness, Dulness, or Stupidity

YOU may define blockishness to be a dulness or slowness of the mind; where there be question to speak or do. A blockish fellow is he, who after he hath cast up an account, asketh him who stands next him what the sum was; or one, who having a cause to be heard upon a peremptory day, forgets himselfe, and goes into the country: and sitting in the Theatre, falls asleep; and when all are gone, is there left alone. The same, when he hath overgorg'd himselfe, rising in the night to make room for more meate, stumbleth upon his neighbour's dog, and is all to-bewearied. The same, having laid up somewhat very carefully, when he looks for it cannot find it. When he heareth that some friend of his is dead, and that he is intreated

in the common ways, he doth anoint with oyle out of a viall; not departing until he hath worshipped them upon his knees. But if a Mouse hath gnawn his meale bag, he repaireth instantly to his wizards, adviseth with them what were best to be done: who if they answer, that it should be had to the Botchers to mend, our superstitious man, neglecting the Sooth-sayers' direction, shall in honour to his religion emptie his bag and cast it away. He doth also oftentimes perfume, or purify his house: He stayeth not long by any grave or Sepulchre: He goeth not to funeralls, nor to any woman in child-bed. If he chance to have a vision, or any thing that's strange, in his sleep, he goeth to all the Sooth-sayers, Diviners, and Wizards, to know to what god or goddess he should present his vows: and to the end he may be initiated in holy Orders, he goes often unto the Orphetulists, how many moneths with his wife, or if she be not at leisure, with his Nurse, and his daughters. Besides, in corners, before he go from thence, sprinkling water upon his head, he purgeth by sacrifice: and calling for those women which minister, commandeth himselfe to be purged with the sea-onion, or bearing about of a whelp. But if he see any mad man, or one troubled with the falling sickness, all frighted and disquieted, by way of charm, his manner is to spit upon his bosom.

Complete.

Of Causeless Complaining

A CAUSELESS complaint is an expostulation fram'd upon no ground. These are the manners of a querulous wayward man: That if a friend send him a modicum from a banquet, he will say to him that brings it, This is the reason I was not invited: you vouchsafe me not a little pottage and your hedge-wine. And when his mistris kisseth him, I wonder (saith he) if these be not flattering kisses. He's displeased with Jupiter: not only if he do not rain, but if he send it late: And finding a purse upon the way, he complaineth that he never found any great treasure. Likewise when he hath bought a slave for little or nothing, having importuned him that sold him thereunto; I wonder, saith he, if I should ever have bought any thing of worth so cheape. If any man bring him glad tidings, that God hath sent him a son, he answereth: If you had told me I had lost half my wealth, then you had hit it. Having gained a cause

to the funerall, looking sourly, and wringing out a tear or two, sayth; Much good may't do him. When he receiveth money, he calls for witnesses; and winter growing on, he quarrels with his man because he bought him no cucumbers. When he is in the Country, he seethes Lentils himselfe: and so over-salts them, that they cannot be eaten. And when it raineth, How pleasant, saith he, is this Star-water! Being asked how many people were carried out by the holy gate: How many? saith he, I would you and I had so many.

Complete.

Of Stubbornness, Obstinacy, or Fierceness

C ONTUMACY or stubbornness is an hardness or harshness in the passages of common life. A stubborn or harsh fellow is so framed; as if you ask him where such a man is, answereth churlishly: What have I to do with him? trouble me not. Being saluted, he saluteth not againe. When he selleth any thing, if you demand his price, he vouchsafeth not an answer; but rather asketh the buyer what fault he findeth with his wares. Unto religious men, which at solemn feasts present the gods with gifts, he is wont to say, That the gifts which they receive from above are not given them for nothing. If any man casually or unwittingly thrust him, or tread on his foot, it is an immortall quarrell; he is inexorable. And when he refuseth a friend, that demandeth a small sum of money, he cometh after voluntary, and bringeth it himselfe; but with this sting of reproach, Well, come on, hatchet after helve, I'le even lose this too.

Complete.

Of Superstition

S UPERSTITION we may define, A reverend awfull respect to a Sovereignty or divine power. But he is superstitious, which with washt hands, and being besprinkled with holy water out of the Temple, bearing a bay leaf in his mouth, walketh so a whole day together. If that a Weasel cross the way, he will not go forward until another hath past before him, or he hath thrown three stones over the way. If he see any Serpents in an house, there he will build a Chapell. Shining stones which are

by all men's voices, he complains (notwithstanding) of him that pleadeth for him, for that he omitted many things that were due to him. Now if his friends do contribute to supply his wants, and if some one say unto him; Now be cheerful, now be merry: I have great cause, he will say, when I must repay this money back againe, and be beholding for it besides.

Complete.

Of Diffidence or Distrust

D IFFIDENCE or distrust is that which makes us jealous of fraud from all men. A diffident or distrustfull man is he, who if he send one to buy victualls, sends another after him to knowe what he paid. If he beare money about him, he tells it at every furlong. Lying in his bed, he asks his wife if she have lockt her casket; if his chests be fast lockt; if the doors be fast bolted: and although she assure it, notwithstanding, naked, without shoes, he riseth out of his bed, lighteth a candle, surveighs all; and hardly falls asleep againe for distrust. When he comes to his debtors for his use-money, he goes strong with his witnesses. When he is to turne or trim some old gaberdine, he putteth it not to the best Fuller, but to him that doth best secure the return of his commodity. If any man borrow any pots, any pails, or pans, if he lend them it is very rare: but commonly he sends for them instantly againe, before they are well at home with them. He biddeth his boy, not to follow them at the heels, but to go before them, lest they make escape with them. And to those which bid him make a note of any thing they borrow: nay, saith he, lay downe rather· for my men are not at leisure to come and ask it.

Complete.

Of Foulness

F OULNESS is a neglect, or carelessness of the body; a slovenry or beastliness very lothsome to men. A nasty beastly fellow is he, who having a leprosy, or other contagious disease, wearing long and lothsome nails, intrudeth himselfe into company; and saith: Gentlemen of race and antiquity have these diseases; and that his Father and Grandfather were subject to the same. This fellow having ulcers in his legs, nodes or hard tumors in his fingers, seeketh no remedy for them; suffering them to grow incurable; hairy as a Goat; black and worm-eaten teeth, foul breath; with him 'tis frequent and familiar to wipe his nose when he is at meate, to talk with his mouth full, to use rank oyle in his bathings, to come into the Hall or Senate house with Clothes all stained and full of spots. Whosoever went to Sooth-sayers, he would not spare them, but give them foul language. Oftentimes, when supplications and sacrifices were made, he would suffer the bowl to fall out of his hand (as it were casually, but) purposely: then he would take up a great laughter, as if some prodigy or ominous thing had happened. When he heareth any Fidlers he cannot hold but he must keep time, and with a kind of mimicall gesticulation (as it were) applaud and imitate their chords. Then he railes on the Fidler as a trouble-cup; because he made an end no sooner: and while he would spit beyond the table, he all-to-bespawleth him who skinketh at the feast.

Complete.

Of Unpleásantness or Tediousness

IF WE should define Tediousness, it is a troublesome kinde of conversing, without any other damage or prejudice. A tedious fellow is he, who wakeneth one suddenly out of his sleep which went lately to bed; and being entred, troubleth him with impertinent loud prating: and that he who now cometh unto him, is ready to go aboard; and that a little lingring may hurt him: Only I wisht him to forbear, until I had some little conference with you. Likewise, taking the child from the Nurse, he puts meate half chew'd into the mouth, as Nurses are wont; and calling him Pretty, and Lovely, will cull and stroke him. At his meate he tells you, that he tooke *elleborus*, which stuck so that it wrought with him upwards and downwards. Then he tells you that his sieges were blacker than broth, that's set to. He delighteth to enquire of his mother, his friends being present, what day he was born. He will tell that he hath very cold water in his cestern, and complaineth that his house lyeth so open to passengers, as if it were a publick Inn. And when he entertaineth any guests, he brings forth his Parasite, that they may see what manner of brain it is: And in his Feast, turning himselfe to him, he saith; You Parasite, look that you content them well.

Complete.

Of a Base and Frivolous Affectation of Praise

YOU may term this Affectation, a shallow, petty, bastard Ambition, altogether illiberall and degenerous. But the foolish ambitious fellow is he, who, being invited to supper, desireth to sit by the master of the Feast; who brings his sonne from Delphi only that he might cut his haire; who is very desirous to have a Lacquey an Æthiopian; who, if he pay but a pound in silver, affecteth to pay it in money lately coined. And if he sacrifice an ox, his manner is to place the fore-part of his head circled with garlands in the entry of the door, that all men that enter may know that he hath killed an ox. And when he goes in state and pomp with other Knights, all other things being delivered to his boy to bear home, he comes cloked into the market place and there walks his stations. And if a little dog or whippet of his die, O he makes him a tomb, and writes upon a little pillar or Pyramis: Surculus Melitensis, a Melitean Plant. And when he doth consecrate an iron ring to Æsculapius, hanging up still new crownes he shall weare it away. And he himselfe is daily bedawbed with onions. All things which belong to the charge of the Magistrates, whom they call Prytanes, he himselfe is very carefull of: that when they have offered, he may recount the manner to the people. Therefore crowned, and clothed in white, he comes forth into the Assembly and sayeth: We Prytanes, O Athenians, do performe our holy Ceremonies and rites to the mother of the gods, and have sacrificed. Therefore, expect all happy and prosperous events. These things thus related, he returneth home to his house; reporting to his wife, that all things have succeeded beyond expectation.

Complete.

Of Illiberality or Servility

ILLIBERALITY, or Servility, is too great a contempt of glory, proceeding from the like desire to spare expence. An illiberall fellow is he, who if he should gaine the victory in a Tragick encounter, would consecrate to Bacchus a wooden bowl, wherein his name should be inscribed. He is likewise one, who in a needfull distressed season of the Common-wealth, when by the Citizens there is given a very extraordinary contribution, rising up in a full assembly, is either silent or gets him gone. Being

to bestow his daughter, and the sacrifices slaine, he selleth all the flesh, save what is used in holy rites: and he hireth such as are to waite and attend upon the marriage only for that time, which shall diet themselves and eat their own meate. The Captain of the Galley which himselfe set forth, he layes old planks under his Cabin to spare his owne. Coming out of the market place, he puts the flesh he bought in his bosom; and upon any occasion, is forc'd to keep in, till his clothes be made clean. In the Morning, as soon as he riseth, he sweeps the house, and fleas the beds himselfe, and turns the wrong side of his wild cloke outwards.

Complete.

Of Ostentation

OSTENTATION may be sayd to be a vanting or setting out of some good things which are not present. A vanter or forth putter is he that boasts upon the Exchange that he hath store of bank-money: and this he tells to strangers; and is not daunted to discover all his usuring Trade, shewing how high he is grown in gaine. As he travels, if he get a companion, he will tell you he served under Alexander in that noble expedition; and what a number of jewelled drinking pots he brought away. He will maintain, though others dissent, That the Artificers of Asia are better than these of Europe: then, that Arts and Letters came from Antipater; who (they say) ran into Macedonia, scantly accompanied with two more. He, when there was granted a free exportation, when the courtesy was offered him, refused it because he would shun all manner of obloquy. The same man in the dearth of corn gave more than five talents to the poor. But if he sit by those who know him not, he entreateth them to cast accompt and reckon the number of those to whom he hath given: the which if they fall out to be six hundred, his accompt doubled, and their names being added to every one, it will easily be effected; so that anon ten talents will be gathered, the which he affirmeth that he gave to the relief of the poor: And yet in this accompt, I reckon not the Gallies that I did command myselfe; and the other services which I undertook for the good of the Common-wealth. The same man coming to those which sell Barbs, Jennets, and other horses of price, he bears them in hand he would buy them in the Fair *ad Tentoria.* Of those which expose their wares to sale, he calleth to

see a garment of two talents price, and chideth his boy extremely, that he dare follow him without gold. Lastly, dwelling in an hired house, if he have speech with any that knowes it not, he will tell him the house was his Father's; but because it is not of receipt for his train, and entertainment of his friends, he hath an intention to make it away.

Complete.

Of Pride

PRIDE is a contempt of all others save itselfe. A proud man is of this quality: If any man desire to speak with him speedily he will tell him that he will, after supper, walk a turne or two with him. If any man be oblig'd unto him, he will command him to remember the favour; nay, he will urge him to it. He will never come unto any man first. They that buy any thing, or hire any thing of him, he disdains not to admit them, come as early as they list. As he walks bending downe his head, speaks to no man that he meets. If he invites any friends, he sups not with them himselfe; but commits the care of their entertainment unto some one that is at his devotion. When he goes to visit any man, he sends his herbenger before, to signify his approach. When he is to be anointed, or when he feeds, he admits none to his presence. If he clear an accompt with any, he commands his boy to cast away the Compters; and when he casts up the sum, makes the reckoning (as it were) to another. In his letters he never writes, You shall oblige me, but, This I would have done: I have sent one to you that shall receive it. See it be not otherwise, and that speedily.

Complete.

Of Timidity or Fearefulness

FEAREFULNESS may seeme to be a timorous distrustfull dejection of the mind. A fearefull man is of this fashion: if he be at sea, he fears the Promontories to be the enemies' Navy; and at every cross gale or billow, asketh if the Sailors be expert; whether there be not some Novices amongst them, or no. When the Pilot gives the ship but a little clout, he asketh if the ship holde a middle course. He knows not well whether he should fear or hope. He telleth him that sits next him, how he was terrifi'd with a dream not long since; then he puts off his shirt, and gives it the boy; entreats the Sailors to set him on shore. Being in service at land, he calleth his fellow-souldiers unto him, and looking earnestly upon them, saith; 'Tis hard to know whether you be enemies, or no. Hearing a bustling, and seeing some fall, he tells them, That for pure hast he had forgotten his two-hand sword: and so soon as by running he hath recovered his tent, he sendeth the boy to scout warily where the enemy is: Then hideth he his long sword under his pillow: then he spendeth much time in seeking of it. And if by chance he see any wounded brought over toward the tent, he runneth to him, encourageth him, bids him take a man's heart, and be resolute. He's very tender over him, and wipes away the corruption of his wound with a sponge: he drives away the flies. He had rather do any work about the house than fight: He careth not how little blood he looseth himselfe; His two-heel'd sword is his best weapon: When the Trumpet sounds a charge, sitting in his tent: A mischief on him (saith he), he disquieteth the poor wounded man, he can take no rest for him. He loves the blood and glory of another man's wound. He will brag when he comes out of the field, how many friends he brought off with the hazard of his owne life. He brings to the hurt man many of the same band to visit him: and tells them all that he with his owne hand brought him into his tent.

Complete.

OF AN OLIGARCHY, OR THE MANNERS OF THE PRINCIPAL SORT, WHICH SWAY IN A STATE

AN OLIGARCHY may seeme to be a vehement desire of honour, without desire of gaine. Oligarchs, or principal men in a State, have these conditions. When the people consult, whether the Magistrate should have any associate added unto him in the setting out of their shews and pomps, he steppeth forth uncalled for, and pronounceth himselfe worthy of that honour. He hath learned this only verse of Homer: —

«Non multos regnare bonum est, rex unicus esto.»

« The State is at an evil stay, Where more than one the Sceptre sway.»

called him Sosistratus: then from one of the meany he was made an Officer (forsooth). His Mother was noble of Tressa: the which sort of women, say they, are noble when they are at home. And this fellow, for all his pretended gentry, is a very lewd knave. He proceedeth and telleth you, That these are the women which entice men out of their way: He joineth with others which traduce the absent, and saith, I hate the man you blame exceedingly. If you note his face, it discovereth a lewd fellow very worthy of hatred. If you look to his villainies, nothing more flagitious. He gives his wife three farthing tokens to go to market with. In the moneth of January, when the colds are greatest, he compelleth her to wash. His manner is, sitting amongst much company, to rise up and snarl at any; not to spare those that are at rest, and cannot reply.

Complete.

These sayings are frequent with them. 'Tis fit that we assemble ourselves together, deliberate and determine finally: That we free ourselves of the multitude: That we intercept their claim of any place of magistracy or government. If any do them affront or injury, He and I (say they) are not compatible in this city. About noon they go abroad, their beards and haire cut of a midling size, their nails curiously pared, strouting it in the Law-house, saying; There is no dwelling in this City: That they are too much pestered and importuned with multitudes of suitors and causes; That they are very much ashamed, when they see any man in the Assembly beggarly or slovenly; and that all the Orators are an odious profession; and that Theseus was the first, which brought this contagion into Cities and Common-wealths. The like speeches they have with strangers, and such Citizens as are of their own faction.

Complete.

OF LATE LEARNING

LATE, or unseasonable learning, is a desire of getting better furnitures and abilities in the going down of our strength, and the declining of our age. Of those men this is their manner. When such men are threescore years of age, they learn verses out of Poets by heart: and these they begin to sing in their cups and collations. No sooner they have begun, but they forget the rest. Such an one learns of his son, how in service they turn to the right hand and the left. When he goes into the Country, riding upon a borrowed horse, practising how to salute those he meeteth, without a lighting, falling all-to-bemoils himselfe. He dooth practise at the Quintin.

He will learn of one, and teach him againe, as if his Master were unskilfull. He likewise wrestling and bathing doth manage his blind cheeks very wildly.

Complete.

ON DETRACTION OR BACKBITING

DETRACTION is a proneness or swarving of the mind into the worst part in our speech and discourse. A Detractor is thus conditioned: If he be questioned what such an one is, as if he should play the Herald, and set down his pedigree, he begins with the first of his Family. This man's father, saith he, was first called Socias. After he followed the warres, they

HENRY DAVID THOREAU

(1817–1862)

HENRY DAVID THOREAU, one of the most extraordinary men of the nineteenth century, was born in Concord, Massachusetts, July 12th, 1817. His father was a manufacturer of lead pencils and in his later years Thoreau himself occasionally followed the same trade. He studied books with success at Harvard University, but the education which made him remarkable was obtained in the woods and fields. He sympathized strongly with the German Transcendentalists, who were inspired by Goethe, and in translating that cult into the terms of his own thought and the modes of his own disposition, he became an extreme Individualist, in the narrower sense in which that word is sometimes used. He was disposed to deny the necessity and effectiveness of co-operation through government for any purpose, and when he retired to Walden Pond, it was to experiment in living an absolutely independent life. Of course this was not possible, and Thoreau, in attempting to live without help from any one, ended by becoming more helpful to every one than an ordinary education could have made him. In Walden woods, and in the woods generally, he gained a familiarity with all animated nature so exquisite that birds and other wild creatures of the woods lost their fear of him and he recovered what some have supposed to be the original human-condition of inoffensiveness. This deep and subtle knowledge of nature is what gives his works their value, for his habits of thought are not uniform, nor is his philosophy coherent. Indeed, he ought not to be considered as a logician at all, but rather as a poet with intuitions which are often above the best results of the best logic. He died May 6th, 1862, and is buried near his friends Emerson and Hawthorne in the cemetery of Sleepy Hollow. In addition to a considerable number of poems, often admirable in idea, but defective in metre, he wrote «A Week on the Concord and Merrimac Rivers,» 1849; «Walden, or Life in the Woods,» 1854; «Excursions in Field and Forest,» 1863; «The Maine Woods,» 1864; «Cape Cod,» 1865; «Letters to Various Persons,» 1865; and «A Yankee in Canada,» 1866. All these except the first two have appeared since his death. Extracts from his diaries have also been published.

HIGHER LAWS

As I came home through the woods with my string of fish, trailing my pole, it being now quite dark, I caught a glimpse of a woodchuck stealing across my path, and felt a strange thrill of savage delight, and was strongly tempted to seize and devour him raw; not that I was hungry then, except for that wildness which he represented. Once or twice, however, while I lived at the pond, I found myself ranging the woods, like a half-starved hound, with a strange abandonment, seeking some kind of venison which I might devour, and no morsel could have been too savage for me. The wildest scenes had become unaccountably familiar. I found in myself, and still find, an instinct toward a higher, or, as it is named, spiritual life, as do most men, and another toward a primitive, rank, and savage one, and I reverence them both. I love the wild not less than the good. The wildness and adventure that are in fishing still recommended it to me. I like sometimes to take rank hold on life and spend my day more as the animals do. Perhaps I have owed to this employment and to hunting, when quite young, my closest acquaintance with Nature. They early introduce us to and detain us in scenery with which otherwise, at that age, we should have little acquaintance. Fishermen, hunters, woodchoppers, and others, spending their lives in the fields and woods, in a peculiar sense a part of Nature themselves, are often in a more favorable mood for observing her, in the intervals of their pursuits, than philosophers or poets even, who approach her with expectation. She is not afraid to exhibit herself to them. The traveler on the prairie is naturally a hunter, on the head waters of the Missouri and Columbia a trapper, and at the Falls of St. Mary a fisherman. He who is only a traveler learns things at second hand and by the halves, and is poor authority. We are most interested when science reports what those men already know practically or instinctively, for that alone is a true humanity, or account of human experience.

They mistake who assert that the Yankee has few amusements, because he has not so many public holidays, and men and boys do not play so many games as they do in England, for here the more primitive but solitary amusements of hunting, fishing, and the like have not yet given place to the former.

x—237

neglected. This was my answer with respect to those youths who were bent on this pursuit, trusting that they would soon outgrow it. No humane being, past the thoughtless age of boyhood, will wantonly murder any creature, which holds its life by the same tenure that he does. The hare in its extremity cries like a child. I warn you, mothers, that my sympathies do not always make the usual philanthropic distinctions.

Such is oftenest the young man's introduction to the forest, and the most original part of himself. He goes thither at first as a hunter and fisher, until at last, if he has the seeds of a better life in him, he distinguishes his proper objects, as a poet or naturalist it may be, and leaves the gun and fish pole behind. The mass of men are still and always young in this respect. In some countries a hunting parson is no uncommon sight. Such a one might make a good shepherd's dog, but is far from being the Good Shepherd. I have been surprised to consider that the only obvious employment, except wood chopping, ice cutting or the like business, which ever to my knowledge detained at Walden Pond for a whole half day any of my fellow-citizens, whether fathers or children of the town, with just one exception, was fishing. Commonly they did not think that they were lucky, or well paid for their time, unless they got a long string of fish, though they had the opportunity of seeing the pond all the while. They might go there a thousand times before the sediment of fishing would sink to the bottom and leave their purpose pure; but no doubt such a clarifying process would be going on all the while. The governor and his council faintly remember the pond, for they went a-fishing there when they were boys; but now they are too old and dignified to go a-fishing, and so they know it no more forever. Yet even they expect to go to heaven at last. If the legislature regards it, it is chiefly to regulate the number of hooks to be used there; but they know nothing about the hook of hooks with which to angle for the pond itself, impaling the legislature for a bait. Thus, even in civilized communities, the embryo man passes through the hunter stage of development.

I have found repeatedly, of late years, that I cannot fish without falling a little in self-respect. I have tried it again and again. I have skill at it, and like many of my fellows, a certain instinct for it, which revives from time to time, but always when I have done I feel that it would have been better if I had not

Almost every New England boy among my contemporaries shouldered a fowling piece between the ages of ten and fourteen; and his hunting and fishing grounds were not limited like the preserves of an English nobleman, but were more boundless even than those of a savage. No wonder, then, that he did not oftener stay to play on the common. But already a change is taking place, owing, not to an increased humanity, but to an increased scarcity of game, for perhaps the hunter is the greatest friend of the animals hunted, not excepting the Humane Society.

Moreover, when at the pond, I wished sometimes to add fish to my fare for variety. I have actually fished from the same kind of necessity that the first fishers did. Whatever humanity I might conjure up against it was all factitious, and concerned my philosophy more than my feelings. I speak of fishing only now, for I had long felt differently about fowling, and sold my gun before I went to the woods. Not that I am less humane than others, but I did not perceive that my feelings were much affected. I did not pity the fishes nor the worms. This was habit. As for fowling, during the last years that I carried a gun my excuse was that I was studying ornithology, and sought only new or rare birds. But I confess that I am now inclined to think that there is a finer way of studying ornithology than this. It requires so much closer attention to the habits of the birds, that, if for that reason only, I have been willing to omit the gun. Yet notwithstanding the objection on the score of humanity, I am compelled to doubt if equally valuable sports are ever substituted for these; and when some of my friends have asked me anxiously about their boys, whether they should let them hunt, I have answered, yes,—remembering that it was one of the best parts of my education,—make them hunters, though sportsmen only at first, if possible, mighty hunters at last, so that they shall not find game large enough for them in this or any vegetable wilderness,—hunters as well as fishers of men. Thus far I am of the opinion of Chaucer's nun, who

> "yave not of the text a pulled hen
> That saith that hunters ben not holy men."

There is a period in the history of the individual, as of the race, when the hunters are the "best men," as the Algonquins called them. We cannot but pity the boy who has never fired a gun; he is no more humane, while his education has been sadly

fished. I think that I do not mistake. It is a faint intimation, yet so are the first streaks of morning. There is unquestionably this instinct in me which belongs to the lower orders of creation; yet with every year I am less a fisherman, though without more humanity or even wisdom; at present I am no fisherman at all. But I see that if I were to live in a wilderness I should again be tempted to become a fisher and hunter in earnest. Beside, there is something essentially unclean about this diet and all flesh, and I begin to see where housework commences, and whence the endeavor, which costs so much, to wear a tidy and respectable appearance each day, to keep the house sweet and free from all ill odors and sights. Having been my own butcher and scullion and cook, as well as the gentleman for whom the dishes were served up, I can speak from an unusually complete experience. The practical objection to animal food in my case was its uncleanness; and, besides, when I had caught and cleaned and cooked and eaten my fish, they seemed not to have fed me essentially. It was insignificant and unnecessary and cost more than it came to. A little bread or a few potatoes would have done as well, with less trouble and filth. Like many of my contemporaries, I had rarely for many years used animal food, or tea, or coffee, etc.; not so much because of any ill effects which I had traced to them, as because they were not agreeable to my imagination. The repugnance to animal food is not the effect of experience, but is an instinct. It appeared more beautiful to live low and fare hard in many respects; and though I never did so, I went far enough to please my imagination. I believe that every man who has ever been earnest to preserve his higher or poetic faculties in the best condition has been particularly inclined to abstain from animal food, and from much food of any kind. It is a significant fact, stated by entomologists,—I find it in Kirby and Spence,—that "some insects in their perfect state, though furnished with organs of feeding, make no use of them"; and they lay it down as "a general rule, that almost all insects in this state eat much less than in that of larvæ. The voracious caterpillar when transformed into a butterfly," . . . "and the gluttonous maggot when become a fly," content themselves with a drop or two of honey, or some other sweet liquid. The abdomen under the wings of the butterfly still represents the larva. This is the tidbit which tempts his insectivorous fate. The gross feeder is a man in the larva state; and there are whole nations in that condition, nations without fancy or imagination, whose vast abdomens betray them.

It is hard to provide and cook so simple and clean a diet as will not offend the imagination; but this, I think, is to be fed when we feed the body; they should both sit down at the same table. Yet perhaps this may be done. The fruits eaten temperately need not make us ashamed of our appetites, nor interrupt the worthiest pursuits. But put an extra condiment into your dish, and it will poison you. It is not worth the while to live by rich cookery. Most men would feel shame if caught preparing with their own hands precisely such a dinner, whether of animal or vegetable food, as is every day prepared for them by others. Yet till this is otherwise we are not civilized, and, if gentlemen and ladies, are not true men and women. This certainly suggests what change is to be made. It may be vain to ask why the imagination will not be reconciled to flesh and fat. I am satisfied that it is not. Is it not a reproach that man is a carnivorous animal? True, he can and does live, in a great measure, by preying on other animals; but this is a miserable way,—as any one who will go to snaring rabbits, or slaughtering lambs, may learn,—and he will be regarded as a benefactor of his race who shall teach man to confine himself to a more innocent and wholesome diet. Whatever my own practice may be, I have no doubt that it is a part of the destiny of the human race, in its gradual improvement, to leave off eating animals, as surely as the savage tribes have left off eating each other when they came in contact with the more civilized.

If one listens to the faintest but constant suggestions of his genius, which are certainly true, he sees not to what extremes, or even insanity, it may lead him; and yet that way, as he grows more resolute and faithful, his road lies. The faintest assured objection which one healthy man feels will at length prevail over the arguments and customs of mankind. No man ever followed his genius till it misled him. Though the result were bodily weakness, yet perhaps no one can say that the consequences were to be regretted, for these were a life in conformity to higher principles. If the day and the night are such that you greet them with joy, and life emits a fragrance like flowers and sweet-scented herbs, is more elastic, more starry, more immortal, —that is your success. All nature is your congratulation, and you have cause momentarily to bless yourself. The greatest

gains and values are furthest from being appreciated. We easily come to doubt if they exist. We soon forget them. They are the highest reality. Perhaps the facts most astounding and most real are never communicated by man to man. The true harvest of my daily life is somewhat as intangible and indescribable as the tints of morning or evening. It is a little star-dust caught, a segment of the rainbow which I have clutched.

Yet, for my part, I was never unusually squeamish; I could sometimes eat a fried rat with a good relish, if it were necessary. I am glad to have drunk water so long, for the same reason that I prefer the natural sky to an opium-eater's heaven. I would fain keep sober always; and there are infinite degrees of drunkenness. I believe that water is the only drink for a wise man; wine is not so noble a liquor; and think of dashing the hopes of a morning with a cup of warm coffee, or of an evening with a dish of tea! Ah, how low I fall when I am tempted by them! Even music may be intoxicating. Such apparently slight causes destroyed Greece and Rome, and will destroy England and America. Of all ebriosity, who does not prefer to be intoxicated by the air he breathes? I have found it to be the most serious objection to coarse labors long continued, that they compelled me to eat and drink coarsely also. But to tell the truth, I find myself at present somewhat less particular in these respects. I carry less religion to the table,—ask no blessing; not because I am wiser than I was, but, I am obliged to confess, because, however much it is to be regretted, with years I have grown more coarse and indifferent. Perhaps these questions are entertained only in youth, as most believe of poetry. My practice is "nowhere," my opinion is here. Nevertheless I am far from regarding myself as one of those privileged ones to whom the Ved refers when it says, that "he who has true faith in the Omnipresent Supreme Being may eat all that exists," that is, is not bound to inquire what is his food, or who prepares it; and even in their case it is to be observed, as a Hindoo commentator has remarked, that the Vedant limits this privilege to "the time of distress."

Who has not sometimes derived an inexpressible satisfaction from his food in which appetite had no share? I have been thrilled to think that I owed a mental perception to the commonly gross sense of taste, that I have been inspired through the palate, that some berries which I had eaten on a hillside

had fed my genius. "The Soul not being mistress of herself," says Thseng-tseu, "one looks, and one does not see; one listens, and one does not hear; one eats, and one does not know the savor of food." He who distinguishes the true savor of his food can never be a glutton; he who does not cannot be otherwise. A puritan may go to his brown-bread crust with as gross an appetite as ever an alderman to his turtle. Not that food which entereth into the mouth defileth a man, but the appetite with which it is eaten. It is neither the quality nor the quantity, but the devotion to sensual savors; when that which is eaten is not a viand to sustain our animal, or inspire our spiritual life, but food for the worms that possess us. If the hunter has a taste for mud turtles, muskrats, and other such savage tidbits, the fine lady indulges a taste for jelly made of a calf's foot, or for sardines from over the sea, and they are even. He goes to the mill pond, she to her preserve pot. The wonder is how they, how you and I, can live this slimy beastly life, eating and drinking.

Our whole life is startlingly moral. There is never an instant's truce between virtue and vice. Goodness is the only investment that never fails. In the music of the harp which trembles round the world it is the insisting on this which thrills us. The harp is the traveling patterer for the Universe's Insurance Company, recommending its laws, and our little goodness is all the assessment that we pay. Though the youth at last grows indifferent, the laws of the universe are not indifferent, but are forever on the side of the most sensitive. Listen to every zephyr for some reproof, for it is surely there, and he is unfortunate who does not hear it. We cannot touch a string or move a stop, but the charming moral transfixes us. Many an irksome noise, go a long way off, is heard as music, a proud sweet satire on the meanness of our lives.

We are conscious of an animal in us, which awakens in proportion as our higher nature slumbers. It is reptile and sensual, and perhaps cannot be wholly expelled; like the worms which, even in life and health, occupy our bodies. Possibly we may withdraw from it, but never change its nature. I fear that it may enjoy a certain health of its own; that we may be well, yet not pure. The other day I picked up the lower jaw of a hog, with white and sound teeth and tusks, which suggested that there was an animal health and vigor distinct from the spiritual. This

creature succeeded by other means than temperance and purity. "That in which men differ from brute beasts," says Mencius, "is a thing very inconsiderable; the common herd lose it very soon; superior men preserve it carefully." Who knows what sort of life would result if we had attained to purity? If I knew so wise a man as could teach me purity I would go to seek him forthwith. "A command over our passions, and over the external senses of the body, and good acts, are declared by the Ved to be indispensable in the mind's approximation to God." Yet the spirit can for the time pervade and control every member and function of the body, and transmute what in form is the grossest sensuality into purity and devotion. The generative energy, which, when we are loose, dissipates and makes us unclean, when we are continent invigorates and inspires us. Chastity is the flowering of man; and what are called Genius, Heroism, Holiness, and the like, are but various fruits which succeed it. Man flows at once to God when the channel of purity is open. By turns our purity inspires and our impurity casts us down. He is blessed who is assured that the animal is dying out in him day by day, and the divine being established. Perhaps there is none but has cause for shame on account of the inferior and brutish nature to which he is allied. I fear that we are such gods or demigods only as fauns or satyrs, the divine allied to beasts, the creatures of appetite, and that, to some extent, our very life is our disgrace:—

"How happy's he who hath due place assigned
  To his beasts and disaforested his mind!
      .   .   .   .
  Can use his horse, goat, wolf, and ev'ry beast,
  And is not ass himself to all the rest!
  Else man not only is the herd of swine,
  But he's those devils too which did incline
  Them to a headlong rage, and made them worse."

All sensuality is one, though it takes many forms; all purity is one. It is the same whether a man eat, or drink, or cohabit, or sleep sensually. They are but one appetite, and we only need to see a person do any one of these things to know how great a sensualist he is. The impure can neither stand nor sit with purity. When the reptile is attacked at one mouth of his burrow, he shows himself at another. If you would be chaste, you must be temperate. What is chastity? How shall a man know if he is chaste? He shall not know it. We have heard of this virtue, but we know not what it is. We speak comformably to the rumor which we have heard. From exertion come wisdom and purity; from sloth ignorance and sensuality. In the student sensuality is a sluggish habit of mind. An unclean person is universally a slothful one, one who sits by a stove, whom the sun shines on prostrate, who reposes without being fatigued. If you would avoid uncleanness, and all the sins, work earnestly, though it be at cleaning a stable. Nature is hard to be overcome, but she must be overcome. What avails it that you are a Christian, if you are not purer than the heathen, if you deny yourself no more, if you are not more religious? I know of many systems of religion esteemed heathenish whose precepts fill the reader with shame, and provoke him to new endeavors, though it be to the performance of rites merely.

I hesitate to say these things, but it is not because of the subject,—I care not how obscene my words are,—but because I cannot speak of them without betraying my impurity. We discourse freely without shame of one form of sensuality, and are silent about another. We are so degraded that we cannot speak simply of the necessary functions of human nature. In earlier ages, in some countries, every function was reverently spoken of and regulated by law. Nothing was too trivial for the Hindoo lawgiver, however offensive it may be to modern taste. He teaches how to eat, drink, cohabit, void excrement and urine, and the like, elevating what is mean, and does not falsely excuse himself by calling these things trifles.

Every man is the builder of a temple, called his body, to the god he worships, after a style purely his own, nor can he get off by hammering marble instead. We are all sculptors and painters, and our material is our own flesh and blood and bones. Any nobleness begins at once to refine a man's features, any meanness or sensuality to imbrute them.

John Farmer sat at his door one September evening, after a hard day's work, his mind still running on his labor more or less. Having bathed he sat down to recreate his intellectual man. It was a rather cool evening, and some of his neighbors were apprehending a frost. He had not attended to the train of his thoughts long when he heard some one playing on a flute, and that sound harmonized with his mood. Still he thought of

his work; but the burden of his thought was, that though this kept running in his head, and he found himself planning and contriving it against his will, yet it concerned him very little. It was no more than the scurf of his skin, which was constantly shuffled off. But the notes of the flute came home to his ears out of a different sphere from that he worked in, and suggested work for certain faculties which slumbered in him. They gently did away with the street, and the village, and the state in which he lived. A voice said to him,—Why do you stay here and live in this mean, moiling life, when a glorious existence is possible for you? Those same stars twinkle over other fields than these. But how to come out of this condition and actually migrate thither? All that he could think of was to practice some new austerity, to let his mind descend into his body and redeem it, and treat himself with ever-increasing respect.

Complete. From «Walden.»

THOMAS TICKELL

(1686–1740)

THOMAS TICKELL, a friend of Addison and a contributor to the Spectator and Guardian, was born in Cumberland, England, in 1686. He graduated at Oxford in 1708, and nine years later was appointed Undersecretary of State,—a promotion he owed to Addison's friendship. He wrote verse as well as prose. The ballad of «Colin and Lucy» and an elegy on Addison which appeared in the edition of Addison published in 1721 are mentioned as illustrations of his best work in verse. His prose style closely follows that of Addison, but he has genuine feeling for nature and knows how to express it without servile imitation of any one. He died at Bath, April 23d, 1740.

PLEASURES OF SPRING

———Nunc formosissimus annus.
—Virg. Ecl. III. 57.

« Now the gay year in all her charms is drest.»

MEN of my age receive a greater pleasure from fine weather than from any other sensual enjoyment of life. In spite of the auxiliary bottle, or any artificial heat, we are apt to droop under a gloomy sky; and taste no luxury like a blue firmament, and sunshine. I have often, in a splenetic fit, wished myself a dormouse during the winter; and I never see one of those snug animals, wrapped up close in his fur, and compactly happy in himself, but I contemplate him with envy beneath the dignity of a philosopher. If the art of flying were brought to perfection, the use that I should make of it would be to attend the sun round the world, and pursue the spring through every sign of the Zodiac. This love of warmth makes my heart glad at the return of the spring. How amazing is the change in the face of nature; when the earth, from being bound with frost, or covered with snow, begins to put forth her plants and flowers,

to be clothed with green, diversified with ten thousand various dyes; and to exhale such fresh and charming odors, as fill every living creature with delight!

Full of thoughts like these, I make it a rule to lose as little as I can of that blessed season; and accordingly rise with the sun, and wander through the fields, throw myself on the banks of little rivulets, or lose myself in the woods. I spent a day or two this spring at a country gentleman's seat, where I feasted my imagination every morning with the most luxurious prospect I ever saw. I usually took my stand by the wall of an old castle built upon a high hill. A noble river ran at the foot of it, which after being broken by a heap of misshapen stones, glided away in a clear stream, and wandering through two woods on each side of it in many windings, shone here and there at a great distance through the trees. I could trace the mazes for some miles, until my eye was led through two ridges of hills, and terminated by a vast mountain in another county.

I hope the reader will pardon me for taking his eye from our present subject of the spring, by this landscape, since it is at this time of the year only that prospects excel in beauty. But if the eye is delighted, the ear hath likewise its proper entertainment. The music of the birds at this time of the year hath something in it so wildly sweet, as makes me less relish the most elaborate compositions of Italy. The vigor which the warmth of the sun pours afresh into their veins prompts them to renew their species; and thereby puts the male upon wooing his mate with more mellow warblings, and to swell his throat with more violent modulations. It is an amusement by no means below the dignity of a rational soul, to observe the pretty creatures flying in pairs, to mark the different passions in their intrigues, the curious contexture of their nests, and their care and tenderness of their little offspring.

I am particularly acquainted with a wagtail and his spouse, and made many remarks upon the several gallantries he hourly used, before the coy female would consent to make him happy. When I saw in how many airy rings he was forced to pursue her; how sometimes she tripped before him in a pretty pitty-pat step, and scarce seemed to regard the cowering of his wings, and the many awkward and foppish contortions into which he put his body to do her homage, it made me reflect upon my own youth, and the caprices of the fair but fantastic Teraminta.

Often have I wished that I understood the language of birds, when I have heard him exert an eager chuckle at her leaving him; and do not doubt, but that he muttered the same vows and reproaches which I often have vented against that unrelenting maid.

The sight that gave me the most satisfaction was a flight of young birds, under the conduct of the father, and indulgent directions and assistance of the dam. I took particular notice of a beau goldfinch, who was picking his plumes, pruning his wings, and with great diligence adjusting all his gaudy garniture. When he had equipped himself with great trimness and nicety, he stretched his painted neck, which seemed to brighten with new glowings, and strained his throat into many wild notes and natural melody. He then flew about the nest in several circles and windings, and invited his wife and children into the open air. It was very entertaining to see the trembling and the fluttering of the little strangers at their first appearance in the world, and the different care of the male and female parent, so suitable to their several sexes. I could not take my eye quickly from so entertaining an object; nor could I help wishing that creatures of a superior rank would so manifest their mutual affection, and so cheerfully concur in providing for their offspring.

I shall conclude this tattle about the spring, which I usually call "the youth and health of the year," with some verses which I transcribe from a manuscript poem upon hunting. The author gives directions, that hounds should breed in the spring, whence he takes occasion, after the manner of the Ancients, to make a digression in praise of that season. The verses here subjoined are not all upon that subject; but the transitions slide so easily into one another, that I knew not how to leave off until I had writ out the whole digression·—

"In spring let loose thy males. Then all things prove
The stings of pleasure, and the pangs of love:
Ethereal Jove then glads, with genial showers,
Earth's mighty womb, and strews her lap with flow'rs;
Hence juices mount, and buds, embolden'd, try
More kindly breezes, and a softer sky;
Kind Venus revels. Hark! on ev'ry bough,
In lulling strains the feather'd warblers woo.
Fell tigers soften in th' infectious flames,
And lions fawning, court their brindled dames:

Great love pervades the deep; to please his mate,
The whale, in gambols moves his monstrous weight;
Heav'd by his wayward mirth old Ocean roars,
And scatter'd navies bulge on distant shores.

"All Nature smiles: Come now, nor fear, my love,
To taste the odors of the woodbine grove,
To pass the evening glooms in harmless play,
And sweetly swearing, languish life away.
An altar bound with recent flowers, I rear
To thee, best season of the various year.
All hail! such days in beauteous order ran,
So soft, so sweet, when first the world began;
In Eden's bow'rs, when man's great sire assign'd
The names and natures of the brutal kind.
Then lamb and lion friendly walk'd their round,
And hares, undaunted, licked the fondling hound;
Wond'rous to tell! but when with luckless hand,
Our daring mother broke the sole command,
Then want and envy brought their meagre train,
Then wrath came down, and death had leave to reign:
Hence foxes earth'd, and wolves abhorr'd the day,
And hungry churls ensnar'd the nightly prey.
Rude arts at first; but witty want refin'd
The huntsman's wiles, and famine form'd the mind.

"Bold Nimrod first the lion's trophies wore,
The panther bound, and lanc'd the bristling boar;
He taught to turn the hare, to bay the deer,
And wheel the courser in his mid career.
Ah! had he there restrain'd his tyrant hand!
Let me, ye pow'rs, a humbler wreath demand:
No pomps I ask, which crowns and sceptres yield;
Nor dang'rous laurels in the dusty field:
Fast by the forest, and the limpid spring,
Give me the warfare of the woods to sing,
To breed my whelps and healthful press the game,
A mean, inglorious, but a guiltless name."

Complete. From the Guardian.

GEORGE TICKNOR

(1791–1871)

GEORGE TICKNOR, whose "History of Spanish Literature" is one of the best works on that subject, was born at Boston, Massachusetts, August 1st, 1791. After graduating at Dartmouth College he spent two years in Europe and on his return became professor of Spanish, French, and Belles-Lettres at Harvard, where he remained from 1819 to 1835. A second visit to Europe was followed after several years by his "History of Spanish Literature" published in 1849. He wrote also a life of Prescott and a number of miscellaneous papers and essays. He died January 26th, 1871, and his "Life and Letters" was published in 1876.

SPANISH HEROIC BALLADS OF THE CID

THE oldest documents known to exist with ascertained dates in the Spanish language come from the reign of Alfonso VII.

The first of them is a character of Oviedo, in 1145, and the other is the confirmation of a charter of Avilés, in 1155;—neighboring cities in Asturias, and therefore in that part of Spain where we should naturally look for the first intimations of a new dialect. They are important, not only because they exhibit the new dialect just emerging from the corrupted Latin, little or not at all affected by the Arabic infused into it in the southern provinces, but because they are believed to be among the oldest documents ever written in Spanish, since there is no good reason to suppose that language to have existed in a written form even half a century earlier.

How far we can go back towards the first appearance of poetry in the Spanish, or as it was oftener called, Castilian dialect, is not so precisely ascertained. But we know that we can trace Castilian verse to a period surprisingly near the date of the documents of Oviedo and of Avilés. It is, too, a remarkable circumstance, that we can thus trace it by works both long and interesting; for, though ballads, and the other forms of popular poetry, by which we mark indistinctly the beginning of almost every other literature, are abundant in the Spanish, we are not

obliged to resort to them, at the outset of our inquiries, since other obvious and decisive monuments present themselves at once.

The first of these monuments in age, and the first in importance, is the poem commonly called, with primitive simplicity and directness, "The Poem of the Cid." It consists of above three thousand lines, and can hardly have been composed later than the year 1200. Its subject, as its name implies, is taken from among the adventures of the Cid, the great popular hero of the chivalrous age of Spain; and the whole tone of its manners and feelings is in sympathy with the contest between the Moors and Christians, in which the Cid bore so great a part, and which was still going on with undiminished violence at the period when the poem was written. It has, therefore, a national bearing and a national character throughout.

The Cid himself, who is to be found constantly commemorated in Spanish poetry, was born in Burgos about the year 1046, and died in 1099 at Valencia, which he had rescued from the Moors. His original name was Ruy Diaz, or Rodrigo Diaz; and he was by birth one of the considerable barons of his country. The title of "Cid," by which he is almost always known, is often said to have come to him from the remarkable circumstance that five Moorish kings or chiefs acknowledged him in one battle as their "Seid," or their lord and conqueror; and the title of "Campeador," or Champion, by which he is hardly less known, though it is commonly assumed to have been given to him as a leader of the armies of Sancho the Second, has long since been used almost exclusively as a mere popular expression of the admiration of his countrymen for his exploits against the Moors. At any rate, from a very early period he has been called "El Cid Campeador," or the Lord Champion. And in many respects he well deserved the honorable title; for he passed almost the whole of his life in the field against the oppressors of his country, suffering so far as we know, scarcely a single defeat from the common enemy, though, on more than one occasion, he was exiled and sacrificed by the Christian princes to whose interests he had attached himself, and, on more than one occasion, was in alliance with the Mohammedan powers, in order, according to a system then received among the Christian princes of Spain, and thought justifiable, to avenge the wrongs that had been inflicted on him by his own countrymen.

But whatever may have been the real adventures of his life, over which the peculiar darkness of the period when they were achieved has cast a deep shadow, he comes to us in modern times as the great defender of his nation against its Moorish invaders, and seems to have so filled the imagination and satisfied the affections of his countrymen, that centuries after his death, and even down to our own days, poetry and tradition have delighted to attach to his name a long series of fabulous achievements, which connect him with the mythological fictions of the Middle Ages, and remind us almost as often of Amadis and Arthur as they do of the sober heroes of genuine history.

The "Poem of the Cid" partakes of both these characters. It has sometimes been regarded as wholly, or almost wholly, historical. But there is too free and romantic a spirit in it for history. It contains, indeed, few of the bolder fictions found in the subsequent chronicles and in the popular ballads. Still, it is essentially a poem, and in the spirited scenes at the siege of Alcocer and at the Cortes, as well as in those relating to the Counts of Carrion, it is plain that the author felt his license as a poet. In fact, the very marriage of the daughters of the Cid has been shown to be all but impossible; and thus any real historical foundation seems to be taken away from the chief event which the poem records. This, however, does not at all touch the proper value of the work, which is simple, heroic, and national. Unfortunately, the only ancient manuscript of it known to exist is imperfect, and nowhere informs us who was its author. But what has been lost is not much. It is only a few leaves in the beginning, one leaf in the middle, and some scattered lines in other parts. The conclusion is perfect. Of course there can be no doubt about the subject or purpose of the whole. It is the development of the character and glory of the Cid, as shown in his achievements in the kingdoms of Saragossa and Valencia; in his triumph over his unworthy sons-in-law, the Counts of Carrion, and their disgrace before the king and Cortes; and finally, in the second marriage of his two daughters with the Infantes of Navarre and Aragon; the whole ending with a slight allusion to the hero's death, and a notice of the date of the manuscript.

But the story of the poem constitutes the least of its claims to our notice. In truth, we do not read it at all for its mere facts, which are often detailed with the minuteness and formality

x—238

of a monkish chronicle; but for its living pictures of the age it represents, and for the vivacity with which it brings up manners and interests so remote from our own experience, that, where they are attempted in formal history, they come to us as cold as the fables of mythology. We read it because it is a contemporary and spirited exhibition of the chivalrous times of Spain, given occasionally with a Homeric simplicity altogether admirable. For the story it tells is not only that of the most romantic achievements, attributed to the most romantic hero of Spanish tradition, but it is mingled continually with domestic and personal details, that bring the character of the Cid and his age near to our own sympathies and interests. The very language in which it is told is the language he himself spoke, still only half developed; disencumbering itself with difficulty from the characteristics of the Latin; its new construction by no means established; imperfect in its forms, and ill furnished with the connecting particles in which so much of the power and grace of all languages resides; but still breathing the bold, sincere, and original spirit of its times, and showing plainly that it is struggling with success for a place among the other wild elements of the national genius.

And, finally, the metre and the rhyme into which the whole poem is cast are rude and unsettled: the verse claiming to be of fourteen syllables, divided by an abrupt cæsural pause after the eighth, yet often running out to sixteen or twenty; and sometimes falling back to twelve; but always bearing the impress of a free and fearless spirit, which harmonizes alike with the poet's language, subject, and age, and so gives the story a stir and interest, which, though we are separated from it by so many centuries, bring some of its scenes before us like those of a drama.

The first pages of the manuscript being lost, what remains to us begins abruptly, at the moment when the Cid, just exiled by his ungrateful king, looks back upon the towers of his castle at Bivar, as he leaves them. "Thus heavily weeping," the poem goes on, "he turned his head and stood looking at them. He saw his doors open, and his household chests unfastened, the hooks empty and without pelisses and without cloaks, and the mews without falcons and without hawks. My Cid sighed, for he had grievous sorrow; but my Cid spake well and calmly: 'I thank thee, Lord and Father, who art in heaven, that it is my evil enemies who have done this thing unto me.'"

He goes, where all desperate men then went, to the frontiers of the Christian war; and, after establishing his wife and children in a religious house, plunges with three hundred faithful followers into the infidel territories, determined, according to the practice of his time, to win land and fortune from the common enemy, and providing for himself meanwhile, according to another practice of his time, by plundering the Jews as if he were a mere Robin Hood. Among his earliest conquests is Alcocer; but the Moors collect in force, and besiege him in their turn, so that he can save himself only by a bold rally, in which he overthrows their whole array. The rescue of his standard, endangered in the onslaught by the rashness of Bermuez, who bore it, is described in the very spirit of knighthood:—

"Their shields before their breasts, forth at once they go,
  Their lances in their rest, leveled fair and low,
  Their banners and their crests, waving in a row,
  Their heads all stooping down, towards the saddle bow;
  The Cid was in the midst, his shout was heard afar,
  'I am Ruy Diaz, the champion of Bivar;
  Strike amongst them Gentlemen, for sweet Mercy's sake!'
  There where Bermuez fought amidst the foe they brake,
  Three hundred bannered knights, it was a gallant show.
  Three hundred Moors they killed, a man with every blow;
  When they wheeled and turned, as many more lay slain;
  You might see them raise their lances and level them again.
  There you might see the breastplates how they were cleft in twain,
  And many a Moorish shield lie shattered on the plain,
  The pennons that were white marked with a crimson stain,
  The horses running wild whose riders had been slain."

The poem afterwards relates the Cid's contest with the Count of Barcelona; the taking of Valencia; the reconcilement of the Cid to the king, who had treated him so ill; and the marriage of the Cid's two daughters, at the king's request to the two Counts of Carrion, who were among the first nobles of the kingdom. At this point, however, there is a somewhat formal division of the poem, and the remainder is devoted to what is its principal subject, the dissolution of this marriage in consequence of the baseness and brutality of the Counts; the Cid's public triumph over them; their no less public disgrace; and the announcement of the second marriage of the Cid's daughters with the Infantes of Navarre and Aragon, which, of course, raised the Cid himself

to the highest pitch of his honors, by connecting him with the royal houses of Spain. With this, therefore, the poem virtually ends.

The most spirited part of it consists of the scenes at the Cortes, summoned, on demand of the Cid, in consequence of the misconduct of the Counts of Carrion. In one of them, three followers of the Cid challenge three followers of the Counts, and the challenge of Munio Gustioz to Assur Gonzalez is thus characteristically given:—

"Assur Gonzalez was entering at the door,
  With his ermine mantle trailing along the floor;
  With his sauntering pace and his hardy look,
  Of manners or of courtesy little heed he took;
  He was flushed and hot with breakfast and with drink.
  'What ho! my masters, your spirits seem to sink!
  Have we no news stirring from the Cid, Ruy Diaz of Bivar?
  Has he been to Riodivirua, to besiege the windmills there?
  Does he tax the millers for their toll? or is that practice past?
  Will he make a match for his daughters, another like the last?'"

Munio Gustioz rose and made reply:—

"Traitor, wilt thou never cease to slander and to lie?
  You breakfast before mass, you drink before you pray;
  There is no honor in your heart, no truth in what you say;
  You cheat your comrade and your lord, you flatter to betray;
  Your hatred I despise, your friendship I defy!
  False to all mankind and most to God on high,
  I shall force you to confess that what I say is true."

Thus was ended the parley and challenge betwixt these two.
  The opening of the lists for the six combatants, in the presence of the king, is another passage of much spirit and effect:—

"The heralds and the king are foremost in the place.
  They clear away the people from the middle space;
  They measure out the lists, the barriers they fix,
  They point them out in order and explain to all the six:
  'If you are forced beyond the line where they are fixed and traced,
  You shall be held as conquered and beaten and disgraced.'
  Six lances' length on either side an open space is laid,
  They share the field between them, the sunshine and the shade.
  Their office is performed, and from the middle space
  The heralds are withdrawn and leave them face to face.

Here stood the warriors of the Cid, that noble champion;
Opposite, on the other side, the lords of Carrion.
Earnestly their minds are fixed each upon his foe.
Face to face they take their place, anon the trumpets blow;
They stir their horses with the spur, they lay their lances low,
They bend their shields before their breasts, their face to the saddle-
bow,
Earnestly their minds are fixed each upon his foe.
The heavens are overcast above, the earth trembles below;
The people stand in silence, gazing on the show."

These are among the most characteristic passages in the poem. But it is throughout striking and original. It is, too, no less national, Christian, and loyal. It breathes everywhere the true Castilian spirit, such as the old chronicles represent it amidst the achievements and disasters of the Moorish wars; and has very few traces of an Arabic influence in its language, and none at all in its imagery or fancies. The whole of it, therefore, deserves to be read, and to be read in the original; for it is there only that we can obtain the fresh impressions it is fitted to give us of the rude but heroic period it represents: of the simplicity of the governments, and the loyalty and true-heartedness of the people; of the wide force of a primitive religious enthusiasm; of the picturesque state of manners and daily life in an age of trouble and confusion; and of the bold outlines of the national genius, which are often struck out where we should least think to find them. It is indeed a work which, as we read it, stirs us with the spirit of the times which it describes; and as we lay it down and recollect the intellectual condition of Europe when it was written, and for a long period before, it seems certain that, during the thousand years which elapsed from the time of the decay of Greek and Roman culture, down to the appearance of the "Divina Commedia," no poetry was produced so original in its tone, or so full of natural feeling, graphic power, and energy.

From "Spanish Literature."

ALEXIS CHARLES HENRI CLÉREL DE TOCQUEVILLE

(1805–1859)

OCQUEVILLE'S "Democracy in America," (1835–40,) was the first study of American institutions and of the popular tendencies they foster, made by a man great enough to comprehend and impartial enough to state his conclusions fairly. The book was a result of notes made by Tocqueville during a visit to the United States in 1831, when the French government sent him as a special agent to study the American penal system. The report he made on that subject was recognized as having great merit, but it was not until his "Democracy in America" appeared that his genius was recognized. The work secured his admission to the French Academy, and a much more nearly certain assurance of undying reputation than belongs to the majority of French "Immortals." It was at once translated into English and accepted by Americans themselves as a political handbook. Scarcely ever before or since has it happened that a foreign observer should be thus recognized by the people of whom he wrote as one of the highest and best authorities on their own habits and tendencies.

Tocqueville was born at Paris, July 29th, 1805, and educated for the bar. He held a position in the law courts at Versailles for a short time before coming to America, but after the great success of his masterpiece he gave up the law and devoted the rest of his life to literature. He died April 16th, 1859, and his "Complete Works," edited by De Beaumont, appeared between 1860 and 1865.

HISTORY OF THE FEDERAL CONSTITUTION

THE thirteen colonies which simultaneously threw off the yoke of England toward the end of the last century, possessed, as I have already observed, the same religion, the same language, the same customs, and almost the same laws; they were struggling against a common enemy; and these reasons were sufficiently strong to unite them one to another, and to consolidate them into one nation. But as each of them had enjoyed a separate existence, and a government within its own control, the peculiar interests and customs which resulted from this system were opposed to a compact and intimate union,

---

which would have absorbed the individual importance of each in the general importance of all. Hence arose two opposite tendencies, the one prompting the Anglo-Americans to unite, the other to divide their strength. As long as the war with the mother country lasted, the principle of union was kept alive by necessity; and although the laws which constituted it were defective, the common tie subsisted in spite of their imperfections. But no sooner was peace concluded than the faults of the legislation became manifest, and the state seemed to be suddenly dissolved. Each colony became an independent republic, and assumed an absolute sovereignty. The federal government, condemned to impotence by its constitution, and no longer sustained by the presence of a common danger, saw the outrages offered to its flag by the great nations of Europe, while it was scarcely able to maintain its ground against the Indian tribes, and to pay the interest of the debt which had been contracted during the war of independence. It was already on the verge of destruction, when it officially proclaimed its inability to conduct the government, and appealed to the constituent authority of the nation.

If America ever approached (for however brief a time) that lofty pinnacle of glory to which the proud fancy of its inhabitants is wont to point, it was at the solemn moment at which the power of the nation abdicated, as it were, the empire of the land. All ages have furnished the spectacle of a people struggling with energy to win its independence; and the efforts of the Americans in throwing off the English yoke have been considerably exaggerated. Separated from their enemies by three thousand miles of ocean, and backed by a powerful ally, the success of the United States may be more justly attributed to their geographical position than to the valor of their armies, or the patriotism of their citizens. It would be ridiculous to compare the American war to the wars of the French Revolution, or the efforts of the Americans to those of the French, who, when they were attacked by the whole of Europe, without credit, and without allies, were still capable of opposing a twentieth part of their population to their foes, and of bearing the torch of revolution beyond their frontiers while they stifled its devouring flame within the bosom of their country. But it is a novelty in the history of society to see a great people turn a calm and scrutinizing eye upon itself when apprised by the legislature that the wheels of government had stopped; to see it carefully examine the extent

---

of the evil, and patiently wait for two whole years until a remedy was discovered, which it voluntarily adopted without having wrung a tear or a drop of blood from mankind. At the time when the inadequacy of the first constitution was discovered, America possessed the double advantage of that calm which had succeeded the effervescence of the revolution, and of those great men who had led the revolution to a successful issue. The assembly which accepted the task of composing the second constitution was small; but George Washington was its president, and it contained the choicest talents and the noblest hearts which had ever appeared in the New World. This national commission, after long and mature deliberation, offered to the acceptance of the people the body of general laws which still rules the Union. All the states adopted it successively. The new feudal government commenced its functions in 1789, after an interregnum of two years. The revolution of America terminated when that of France began.

From "Democracy in America," Part I.,
Book I., Chap. viii.

THE TYRANNY OF THE MAJORITY

I HOLD it to be an impious and an execrable maxim that, politically speaking, a people has a right to do whatsoever it pleases; and yet I have asserted that all authority originates in the will of the majority. Am I, then, in contradiction with myself?

A general law — which bears the name of justice — has been made and sanctioned, not only by a majority of this or that people, but by a majority of mankind. The rights of every people are consequently confined within the limits of what is just. A nation may be considered in the light of a jury which is empowered to represent society at large, and to apply the great and general law of justice. Ought such a jury, which represents society, to have more power than the society in which the laws it applies originate?

When I refuse to obey an unjust law, I do not contest the right which the majority has of commanding, but I simply appeal from the sovereignty of the people to the sovereignty of mankind. It has been asserted that a people can never entirely outstep the boundaries of justice and of reason in those affairs which are more peculiarly its own; and that consequently full power may fearlessly be given to the majority by which it is represented. But this language is that of a slave.

A majority taken collectively may be regarded as a being whose opinions, and most frequently whose interests, are opposed to those of another being, which is styled a minority. If it be admitted that a man, possessing absolute power, may misuse that power by wronging his adversaries, why should a majority not be liable to the same reproach? Men are not apt to change their characters by agglomeration; nor does their patience in the presence of obstacles increase with the consciousness of their strength. And for these reasons I can never willingly invest any number of my fellow-creatures with that unlimited authority which I should refuse to any one of them.

I do not think that it is possible to combine several principles in the same government, so as at the same time to maintain freedom, and really to oppose them to one another. The form of government which is usually termed mixed has always appeared to me to be a mere chimera. Accurately speaking, there is no such thing as a mixed government (with the meaning usually given to that word), because in all communities some one principle of action may be discovered, which preponderates over the others. England in the last century, which has been more especially cited as an example of this form of government, was in point of fact an essentially aristocratic state, although it comprised very powerful elements of democracy; for the laws and customs of the country were such, that the aristocracy could not but preponderate in the end, and subject the direction of public affairs to its own will. The error arose from too much attention being paid to the actual struggle which was going on between the nobles and the people, without considering the probable issue of the contest, which was in reality the important point. When a community really has a mixed government, that is to say, when it is equally divided between two adverse principles, it must either pass through a revolution, or fall into complete dissolution.

I am therefore of opinion that some one social power must always be made to predominate over the others; but I think that liberty is endangered when this power is checked by no obstacles which may retard its course, and force it to moderate its own vehemence.

Unlimited power is in itself a bad and dangerous thing; human beings are not competent to exercise it with discretion; and God alone can be omnipotent, because his wisdom and his justice are always equal to his power. But no power upon earth is so worthy of honor for itself, or of reverential obedience to the rights which it represents, that I would consent to admit its uncontrolled and all-predominant authority. When I see that the right and the means of absolute command are conferred on a people or upon a king, upon an aristocracy or a democracy, a monarchy or a republic, I recognize the germ of tyranny, and I journey onward to a land of more hopeful institutions.

In my opinion the main evil of the present democratic institutions of the United States does not arise, as is often asserted in Europe, from their weakness, but from their overpowering strength; and I am not so much alarmed at the excessive liberty which reigns in that country as at the very inadequate securities which exist against tyranny.

When an individual or a party is wronged in the United States, to whom can he apply for redress? If to public opinion, public opinion constitutes the majority; if to the legislature, it represents the majority, and implicitly obeys its instructions; if to the executive power, it is appointed by the majority and is a passive tool in its hands; the public troops consist of the majority under arms; the jury is the majority invested with the right of hearing judicial cases; and in certain states even the judges are elected by the majority. However iniquitous or absurd the evil of which you complain may be, you must submit to it as well as you can.

If, on the other hand, a legislative power could be so constituted as to represent the majority without necessarily being the slave of its passions; an executive, so as to retain a certain degree of uncontrolled authority; and a judiciary, so as to remain independent of the two other powers; a government would be formed which would still be democratic, without incurring any risk of tyrannical abuse.

I do not say that tyrannical abuses frequently occur in America at the present day; but I maintain that no sure barrier is established against them, and that the causes which mitigate the government are to be found in the circumstances and the manners of the country more than in its laws.

From «Democracy in America,» Part I., Book I., Chap. xv.

LITERARY CHARACTERISTICS OF DEMOCRATIC AGES

WHEN a traveler goes into a bookseller's shop in the United States, and examines the American books upon the shelves, the number of works appears extremely great; while that of known authors appears, on the contrary, to be extremely small. He will first meet with a number of elementary treatises, destined to teach the rudiments of human knowledge. Most of these books are written in Europe; the Americans reprint them, adapting them to their own country. Next comes an enormous quantity of religious works, Bibles, sermons, edifying anecdotes, controversial divinity, and reports of charitable societies; lastly appears the long catalogue of political pamphlets. In America parties do not write books to combat each other's opinions, but pamphlets which are circulated for a day with incredible rapidity, and then expire.

In the midst of all these obscure productions of the human brain are to be found the more remarkable works of that small number of authors, whose names are, or ought to be, known to Europeans.

Although America is perhaps in our days the civilized country in which literature is least attended to, a large number of persons are nevertheless to be found there who take an interest in the productions of the mind, and who make them, if not the study of their lives, at least the charm of their leisure hours. But England supplies these readers with the larger portion of the books which they require. Almost all important English books are republished in the United States. The literary genius of Great Britain still darts its rays into the recesses of the forests of the New World. There is hardly a pioneer's hut which does not contain a few odd volumes of Shakespeare. I remember that I read the feudal play of «Henry V.» for the first time in a log house.

Not only do the Americans constantly draw upon the treasures of English literature, but it may be said with truth that they find the literature of England growing on their own soil. The larger part of that small number of men in the United States who are engaged in the composition of literary works are English in substance, and still more so in form. Thus they transport into the midst of democracy the ideas and literary

fashion which are current among the aristocratic nations they have taken for their model. They paint with colors borrowed from foreign manners; and as they hardly ever represent the country they were born in as it really is, they are seldom popular there.

The citizens of the United States are themselves so convinced that it is not for them that books are published, that before they can make up their minds upon the merit of one of their authors, they generally wait till his fame has been ratified in England, just as in pictures the author of an original is held to be entitled to judge of the merit of a copy.

The inhabitants of the United States have then at present, properly speaking, no literature. The only authors whom I acknowledge as Americans are the journalists. They, indeed, are not great writers, but they speak the language of their countrymen, and make themselves heard by them. Other authors are aliens; they are to the Americans what the imitators of the Greeks and Romans were to us at the Revival of Learning, an object of curiosity, not of general sympathy. They amuse the mind, but they do not act upon the manners of the people.

I have already said that this state of things is very far from originating in democracy alone, and that the causes of it must be sought for in several peculiar circumstances independent of the democratic principle. If the Americans, retaining the same laws and social condition, had had a different origin, and had been transported into another country, I do not question that they would have had a literature. Even as they now are, I am convinced that they will ultimately have one; but its character will be different from that which marks the American literary productions of our time, and that character will be peculiarly its own. Nor is it impossible to trace this character beforehand.

I suppose an aristocratic people among whom letters are cultivated; the labors of the mind, as well as the affairs of state, are conducted by a ruling class in society. The literary as well as the political career is almost entirely confined to this class, or to those nearest to it in rank. These premises suffice to give me a key to all the rest.

When a small number of the same men are engaged at the same time upon the same objects, they easily concert with one another and agree upon certain leading rules which are to govern them each and all. If the object which attracts the attention of these men is literature, the productions of the mind will soon be subjected by them to precise canons, from which it will no longer be allowable to depart. If these men occupy an hereditary position in the country, they will be naturally inclined, not only to adopt a certain number of fixed rules for themselves, but to follow those which their forefathers laid down for their own guidance; [their code will be at once strict and traditional. As they are not necessarily engrossed by the cares of daily life,—as they have never been so, any more than their fathers were before them,—they have learned to take an interest, for several generations back, in the labors of the mind. They have learned to understand literature as an art, to love it in the end for its own sake, and to feel a scholar-like satisfaction in seeing men conform to its rules. Nor is this all: the men of whom I speak began and will end their lives in easy or in affluent circumstances; hence they have naturally conceived a taste for choice gratifications and a love of refined and delicate pleasures. Nay, more, a kind of indolence of mind and heart, which they frequently contract in the midst of this long and peaceful enjoyment of so much welfare, leads them to put aside, even from their pleasures, whatever might be too startling or too acute. They had rather be amused than intensely excited; they wish to be interested, but not to be carried away.

Now let us fancy a great number of literary performances executed by the men, or for the men, whom I have just described, and we shall readily conceive a style of literature in which everything will be regular and pre-arranged. The slightest work will be carefully touched in its least details; art and labor will be conspicuous in everything; each kind of writing will have rules of its own, from which it will not be allowed to swerve, and which distinguish it from all others. Style will be thought of almost as much importance as thought; and the form will be no less considered than the matter: the diction will be polished, measured, and uniform. The tone of the mind will be always dignified, seldom very animated; and writers will care more to perfect what they produce than to multiply their productions. It will sometimes happen that the members of the literary class, always living among themselves and writing for themselves alone, will lose sight of the rest of the world, which will infect them with a false and labored style; they will lay down minute literary rules for their exclusive use, which will insensibly lead them

to deviate from common sense, and finally to trangress the bounds of nature. By dint of striving after a mode of parlance different from the vulgar, they will arrive at a sort of aristocratic jargon, which is hardly less remote from pure language than is the coarse dialect of the people. Such are the natural perils of literature among aristocracies. Every aristocracy which keeps itself entirely aloof from the people becomes impotent—a fact which is as true in literature as it is in politics.

Let us now turn the picture and consider the other side of it; let us transport ourselves into the midst of a democracy, not unprepared by ancient traditions and present culture to partake in the pleasures of the mind. Ranks are there intermingled and confounded; knowledge and power are both infinitely subdivided, and, if I may use the expression, scattered on every side. Here, then, is a motley multitude, whose intellectual wants are to be supplied. These new votaries of the pleasures of the mind have not all received the same education; they do not possess the same degree of culture as their fathers, nor any resemblance to them—nay, they perpetually differ from themselves, for they live in a state of incessant change of place, feelings, and fortunes. The mind of each member of the community is therefore unattached to that of his fellow-citizens by tradition or by common habits; and they have never had the power, the inclination, nor the time to concert together. It is, however, from the bosom of this heterogeneous and agitated mass that authors spring; and from the same source their profits and their fame are distributed.

I can without difficulty understand that, under these circumstances, I must expect to meet in the literature of such a people with but few of those strict conventional rules which are admitted by readers and by writers in the aristocratic ages. If it should happen that the men of some one period were agreed upon any such rules, that would prove nothing for the following period; for, among democratic nations, each new generation is a new people. Among such nations, then, literature will not easily be subjected to strict rules, and it is impossible that any such rules should ever be permanent.

In democracies it is by no means the case that all the men who cultivate literature have received a literary education; and most of those who have some tinge of belles-lettres, are either engaged in politics, or in a profession which only allows them to taste occasionally and by stealth the pleasures of the mind.

These pleasures, therefore, do not constitute the principal charm of their lives; but they are considered as a transient and necessary recreation amid the serious labors of life. Such men can never acquire a sufficiently intimate knowledge of the art of literature to appreciate its more delicate beauties; and the minor shades of expression must escape them. As the time they can devote to letters is very short, they seek to make the best use of the whole of it. They prefer books which may be easily procured, quickly read, and which require no learned researches to be understood. They ask for beauties, self-proffered, and easily enjoyed; above all, they must have what is unexpected and new. Accustomed to the struggle, the crosses, and the monotony of practical life, they require rapid emotions, startling passages—truths or errors brilliant enough to rouse them up, and to plunge them at once, as if by violence, into the midst of a subject.

Why should I say more? or who does not understand what is about to follow, before I have expressed it? Taken as a whole, literature in democratic ages can never present, as it does in the periods of aristocracy, an aspect of order, regularity, science, and art; its form will, on the contrary, ordinarily be slighted, sometimes despised. Style will frequently be fantastic, incorrect, overburdened, and loose—almost always vehement and bold. Authors will aim at rapidity of execution more than at perfection of detail. Small productions will be more common than bulky books: there will be more wit than erudition, more imagination than profundity; and literary performances will bear marks of an untutored and rude vigor of thought—frequently of great variety and singular fecundity. The object of authors will be to astonish rather than to please, and to stir the passions more than to charm the taste.

Here and there, indeed, writers will doubtless occur who will choose a different track, and who will, if they are gifted with superior abilities, succeed in finding readers, in spite of their defects or their better qualities; but these exceptions will be rare, and even the authors who shall so depart from the received practice in the main subject of their works, will always relapse into it in some lesser details.

I have just depicted two extreme conditions: the transition by which a nation passes from the former to the latter is not sudden but gradual, and marked with shades of very various intensity. In the passage which conducts a lettered people from

the one to the other, there is almost always a moment at which the literary genius of democratic nations has its confluence with that of aristocracies, and both seek to establish their joint sway over the human mind. Such epochs are transient, but very brilliant; they are fertile without exuberance, and animated without confusion. The French literature of the eighteenth century may serve as an example.

I should say more than I mean, if I were to assert that the literature of a nation is always subordinate to its social condition and its political constitution. I am aware that, independently of these causes, there are several others which confer certain characteristics on literary productions; but these appear to me to be the chief. The relations which exist between the social and political condition of a people and the genius of its authors are always very numerous; whoever knows the one is never completely ignorant of the other.

Complete. From «Democracy in America,»
Part II, Book I., Chap. xiii

COUNT LYOFF NIKOLAIEVICH TOLSTOI

(1828–)

LYOFF NIKOLAIEVICH TOLSTOI was born August 28th, 1828 (O. S.) in the province of Tula, Russia. He belonged to the hereditary nobility of Russia and received the education generally given the young nobles of the wealthy provincial families. After leaving the University of Kazan, he entered the Russian army and commanded a battery during the Crimean War, taking part in the storming of Sebastopol. The scenes of carnage and destruction he witnessed during this period of his life affected him deeply and resulted in a strong revulsion against the social, political, and ethical theories of Upper-Class Russia. He finally retired to his estate, renounced his class privileges and began to support himself by manual labor, working at the bench as a shoemaker and using the spade as an agricultural laborer among the peasantry whose dress he had adopted. His real mission, however, was that of a prophet of progress, expressing himself by the modern methods of the essay and the popular novel. With an almost incredible courage, he struck at the foundations of Russian despotism. His protests against the knouting of peasants had more power in them than a pitched battle won by an insurrectionary army, and they so compelled the opinion of the bureaucratic nobility which really governs Russia that Tolstoi was not molested. His views on orthodox Russian religion were equally radical. He proposed for Russia and the world at large what Swift, with great gravity, suggested as certain to be destructive of all social and religious order in England — the actual practice of the Christianity of the Gospels as a rule of life in business, politics, and church management. Having adopted this view, Tolstoi expressed it in a series of celebrated novels and essays, notably in "The Kreutzer Sonata," "My Religion," "What Is Art?" and "Resurrection" books which had great influence in England and America where radical habits of thought were promoted by them. Tolstoi's greatest fault as a novelist is the reflex of his greatest merit. His earnestness makes him so intense that his work gives the reader no relief. The same characteristic appears in his essays also. He is a great man, the greatest Russian of the nineteenth century, and it is doubtful if the Russia of the twentieth will produce any one to equal him. But a great man is not necessarily a great artist, nor is it always necessary that he should be. Horace and Virgil at the court of Augustus;

x—239

Addison and Steele in the age of Queen Anne are great artists. A smith at his anvil, forging sword blades, from white-hot iron, does not lack art, nor does Tolstoi lack it. But it is the art which compels the unwilling — not the divine and immortal art which controls those who do not know they are being controlled until under its influence they grow as a plant grows in the sunshine. W. V. B.

RELIGION, SCIENCE, AND MORALITY

NEITHER philosophy nor science can institute the relation of man to the universe, because such reciprocity must have existence before any kind of science or philosophy can begin; since each investigates phenomena by means of the intellect, and independent of the position or sensations of the investigator; whereas the relation of man to the universe is defined, not by the intellect alone, but by his sensitive perception aided by all his spiritual powers. However much one may assure and instruct a man that all real existence is an idea; that matter is made up of atoms; that the essence of life is corporality or will; that heat, light, movement, electricity are different manifestations of one and the same energy, one cannot thereby explain to a being with pains, pleasures, fears, and hopes, his position in the universe. That position and his consequent relation to the universe is explained only by religion, which says, "The universe exists for thee, and therefore take from life all that thou canst obtain"; or else, "Thou art one of the chosen people of God; serve that people, and accomplish the instructions of that God, and thou and thy people shall be partakers of the highest bliss"; or else, "Thou art the instrument of a supreme will, which has sent thee into the universe to accomplish a work predestined for thee; learn that will, and do it, for that is the sole perfection thou canst achieve."

To understand philosophy and science one needs study and preparation, but neither is required for the understanding of religion: that is at once comprehensible to every man, whatever his ignorance and limitations. A man need acquire neither philosophy nor science to understand his relation to the universe, or to its source; a superfluity of knowledge, encumbering his consciousness, is rather an impediment; but he must renounce, if only for the time, the vanity of the world, and acquire a sense of his material frailty and of truth, which are, as the Gospels tell us,

to be found most often in children and in the simplest, most unlearned, of men. For this reason we see the most simple, ignorant, and untaught men accept clearly, consciously, and easily the highest Christian conception of life, whereas the most learned and cultured linger in crude heathenism. As, for example, we observe men of refinement and education whose conception of existence is the acquirement of personal pleasure or security from pain, as with the shrewd and cultured Schopenhauer, or in the salvation of the soul by sacraments and means of grace, as with learned bishops of the Church; whereas an almost illiterate sectarian peasant in Russia, without the slightest mental effort, achieves the same conception of life as was accomplished by the greatest sages of the world — Epictetus, Marcus Aurelius, Seneca — namely, the consciousness of one's being as the instrument of the will of God — the son of God.

But you may ask me: In what, then, does the essence of this unscientific and unphilosophical knowledge consist? If it be neither scientific nor philosophical, of what sort is it? How is it to be defined? To these questions I can only reply that as religious knowledge is that which precedes, and upon which is founded, every other knowledge, it cannot be defined; there being no essential term of definition in existence. In theological language this knowledge is called revelation. And this word, if we do not give it any mystic meaning, is quite accurate; because this knowledge is not acquired by study, nor by the efforts of individuals, but through the reception by them of the manifestation of the Infinite Mind, which, little by little, discloses itself to men. Why is it that ten thousand years ago men were unable to understand that their sentient existence was not exhausted by the welfare of the individual, and that later came a time when the higher family-social-state-national conception of life was disclosed to mankind? Why is it that, within the limits of historical memory, the Christian conception of life has been disclosed to men? And why has it been disclosed to such a man or men, and precisely at such a time, at such and no other place, in such and no other form? To try to answer these questions by searching for their reasons in the historical circumstances of the time, life, and character and special qualities of those men who first accepted and expressed this conception of life, is as though one were to try to prove why the rising sun first casts his rays on certain objects. The sun of truth, rising higher and higher

upon the world, enlightens it ever further, and is reflected by those forms on which first fall the illumination of its rays and which are most capable of reflecting them. The qualities which give to some the power of receiving the rising truth are no special activities of the mind, but rather passive qualities of the heart, seldom corresponding to a great and inquisitive intellect. Rejection of the vanities of the world, a sense of one's material frailty, truthfulness, are what we observe in every founder of a religion, none of whom have been distinguished by philosophical or scientific acquirement.

In my opinion the chief error, which, more than all else, impedes the true progress of Christian humanity is precisely the fact that the scientific men of our time, who are now in the seat of the teachers, being guided by the heathen conception of life revived at the Renaissance, and having accepted as the essence of Christianity its crudest distortions, and having decided that it is a condition already outworn by mankind (while they consider, on the contrary, that the ancient-social-state conception of heathendom, which is indeed outworn, is the loftiest conception and one that should steadfastly be held by humanity), these men, not only do not understand true Christianity, which comprises that most perfect conception of life toward which all humanity is advancing, but they do not even try to understand it. The chief source of this misunderstanding arises from the fact that men of science, having diverged from Christianity, and seen that their science cannot conform to it, have agreed that Christianity and not science must be at fault: that is, they have assumed, not the fact that science is eighteen hundred years behind Christianity, which embraced the greater part of contemporary society, but that it is Christianity which is eighteen hundred years in arrear. From this distortion of facts arises the curious circumstance that no people have more entangled ideas as to the essence of true knowledge, religion, morality, and existence than men of science, and the yet more curious fact that the science of our time, despite all its successes in examining the phenomena of the material world, appears to be, as to human existence, either unnecessary or productive of merely pernicious results. And hence I hold that it is neither philosophy nor science which can explain the relation of man to the universe, but religion.

From his replies to questions put by the German Ethical Society.

THE ART OF THE FUTURE

PEOPLE talk of the art of the future, understanding by the art of the future a specially refined new art, to be elaborated from the art of one class of society, which is now considered the highest. But such new art of the future cannot and will not exist. Our exclusive art of the upper classes of the Christian world has come to a dead wall. Along the path it has been following it has no further to go. This art once it has failed in the chief condition of art (that it should be led by the religious consciousness), becoming more and more exclusive and therefore more and more corrupt, has become a negative quantity. The art of the future — that which will really come into being — will not be a continuation of the present art, but will arise on perfectly different and new foundations, having nothing in common with those by which our present art of the upper classes is guided.

The art of the future, that is, that part of art which will stand out from the whole of art existing amongst men, will consist not of the transfer of feelings accessible only to some people of the rich classes, as happens now, but will be that art alone which realizes the highest religious consciousness of the people of our time. Only those productions which shall convey the feelings which draw people to brotherly unity, will be counted art; or which convey such feelings, common to all men, as shall have the power to unite all people. Only this art will stand out, be admitted, approved, and spread. And all the rest of art, conveying feelings accessible only to some people, will be considered unimportant, and will be neither condemned nor approved. And the patron of art in general will not be, as happens now, the separate class of rich people, but the whole nation: so that for a production to be considered good, approved, and circulated, it will be necessary for it to satisfy the demands not of a few people, who are in the same often unnatural conditions, but the demands of the whole people, the great masses of the people, who live in the natural conditions of toil.

And artists, who produce art, will not be, as now, only those rare people, selected from a small part of the whole nation, from the rich classes or those close to them, but all those gifted people of the whole nation, who show themselves able and willing for artistic activities.

Artistic activity will then be accessible to the whole people. And this activity will be accessible to individuals from the whole people, because, in the first place, in the art of the future not only will there be no demand for that complex technical skill which disfigures the art of our times, and demands intense effort and great expenditure of time, but on the contrary there will be a demand for clearness, simplicity, and brevity, conditions which are gained not by mechanical effort, but by education of taste. In the second place, artistic activity will become accessible to the whole people, because instead of the present professional schools, accessible only to the few, every one in the preparatory national schools will learn music and painting (singing and drawing) on equal terms with reading, so that every one receiving the first foundations of painting and musical knowledge, and feeling an ability and calling for any of the arts, may be able to perfect himself in it.

People think that if there are no special art schools, technical skill in art will diminish. It will undoubtedly diminish, if by technical skill we understand those complications of art which are now considered valuable; but if by technical skill we understand the clearness, beauty, freedom from great complexity, and conciseness of a production of art, then technical skill will not only not diminish, but will become a hundred times more perfect, even if there are no professional schools, and even if the national schools should not teach the rudiments of drawing and music. It will be perfected because all the artists of genius, now hidden amongst the people, will take part in art, and will give examples of perfection, which will be, as always, the best school of technical skill for artists. Every true artist even now learns not in the school, but in life, from the examples of the great masters; but then, when those who take part in art will be the most gifted people of the whole nation and there will be more examples, and these examples will be more accessible, the teaching in the schools which the future artists lose will be repaid a hundred times by the teaching which the artist will receive from the numerous examples of good art distributed throughout society.

This will be one difference between future and present art. Another difference will be that the art of the future will not be produced by professional artists, who receive a reward for their art, and working at nothing except their art. The art of the

future will be produced by people of the nation, who will work at it when they feel the inner necessity for this activity.

In our society it is thought that an artist will work best and do most if he is materially independent. This opinion would prove once more to demonstration, if it were necessary to prove it, that what is considered art amongst us is not art, but only a semblance of it. It is perfectly true that to produce boots or loaves, division of labor is very advantageous, that the shoemaker or baker who need not prepare his own dinner and firewood makes more boots and loaves than if he were compelled to occupy himself about his dinner and firewood. But art is not a trade, but the transfer of feelings experienced by the artist. And feelings can only have birth in a man when he is at all points living the natural life proper to all men. And therefore the assurance of the material independence of artists is the most destructive condition for the artists' productivity, since it frees the artist from the condition, proper to all men, of struggle with nature for the support of his own life and the life of others, and therefore deprives him of the opportunity and possibility of experiencing the feelings that are most important and proper to human beings. There is no position more destructive to the artist's productivity than the position of complete independence and luxury, in which the artist is generally found in our society.

The artist of the future will live the ordinary life of men, and will earn his living by some form of work. And the fruits of that higher spiritual force, which passes through him, he will try to give to the greatest number of people, because in this transfer to the greatest number of people of the feelings which came to the birth in him is his joy and his reward. The artist of the future will not even understand that an artist, whose chief joy consists in the greatest distribution of his productions, could offer his productions only at a given price.

Until the merchants are cast out of the temple, the temple of art will not be a temple. The art of the future will drive them out.

And therefore the subject-matter of the art of the future, as I represent it to myself, will be quite unlike the present. The substance of the art of the future will not consist in the expression of exclusive feelings: vanity, weariness, satiety, and sensuality in all possible forms, accessible and interesting only to people who have violently separated themselves from that work which is proper to man, but will consist in the expression of feelings

experienced by a man who lives the life that is proper to all people, and flows from the religious consciousness of our time, or feelings accessible to all people without exception.

To people of our circle who do not know, and cannot or will not know the feelings which must constitute the substance of art of the future, it seems that this subject-matter, when compared with the refinements of exclusive feeling, with which they are now occupied, is very poor. "What new thing can be expressed in the field of the Christian feelings of love for our neighbor? And feelings accessible to all men are so insignificant and monotonous," they think. But at the same time the only really new feelings possible in our time are Christian religious feelings, and feelings accessible to all. The feelings flowing from the religious consciousness of our time, Christian feelings, are endlessly new and varied; but not in that one sense, as some think, of depicting Christ and the episodes of the Gospel, or of repeating in a new form the Christian truths of unity, brotherhood, equality, love, but in the sense that all the very oldest manifestations of life, familiar and studied from all sides, evoke the newest, most unexpected and touching feelings, as soon as a person approaches these manifestations from the Christian point of view.

What can be older than the relations of married people, of parents to children, of children to parents, the relations of people to their fellow-countrymen, to people of other races, to aggression, defense, property, the earth, animals? But as soon as a man approaches these manifestations from the Christian point of view, there straightway arise the most endlessly varied, new, complicated, and touching feelings.

In just the same way the field of that art which conveys the very simplest worldly feelings accessible to all, is not contracted, but expanded. In our former art it was considered dignified to convey in art only the expression of feelings belonging to people of a certain exclusive position, and this only when they were conveyed by the most refined means, inaccessible to the majority of people; and all the immense field of popular child art — jokes, proverbs, riddles, songs, dances, children's games, mimicry — was not recognized as a worthy subject of art.

The artist of the future will understand that to write a tale or a little song that touches — an adage or a riddle that entertains — a joke that amuses, or paint a picture that rejoices tens of generations, or millions of children and adults — is incomparably more important and fruitful than to write novels or symphonies, or paint pictures, which for a short time entertain a few people of the rich classes, and are then forgotten forever. And the field of this art of simple feelings accessible to all is immense and still almost untouched.

So that the art of the future will not only not be impoverished, but, on the contrary, will be endlessly enriched in material. And in exactly the same way the form of the art of the future will not only not be lower than the present form of art, but will be beyond all comparison higher than it, higher not in the sense of refined and complicated technical skill, but in the sense of knowing how to convey the feeling which the artist experienced and wishes to convey, briefly, simply, and clearly, without any superfluity.

I remember that once in talking to a famous astronomer, who delivered public lectures on the spectrum analysis of the stars of the Milky Way, I said to him how fine it would be if, with his knowledge and masterly delivery, he should give a public lecture on cosmography, confined to the movement of the earth, as among the auditors of his lecture on the spectrum analysis of the stars of the Milky Way, there were probably very many people, especially women, who do not quite know why day and night exist, or summer and winter. The wise astronomer, smiling, answered me: "Yes, that would be excellent, but it would be very difficult. To lecture on the spectrum analysis of the Milky Way is far easier."

And it is just the same in art: to write a poem in verse of Cleopatra's time, or to paint a picture of Nero burning Rome, or a symphony in the spirit of Brahms and Richard Strauss, or an opera in the spirit of Wagner, is far easier than to tell a simple story without any superfluity, and at the same time in such a way as to convey the feeling of the narrator, or to draw a pencil sketch that will touch or amuse the beholder, or to write four bars of a simple, clear melody, without any accompaniment, which will convey a mood and be remembered by the hearer.

"It is impossible for us now, with our development, to return to the primitive"—say the artists of our times. "It is impossible for us to write stories like the story of Joseph and his Brethren or the 'Odyssey'; or to carve statues like the 'Venus of Milo'; or to compose music like the national songs."

And, in fact, for the artist of our times, this is impossible, but not for the artist of the future, who will be ignorant of all the corruption of technical perfections which conceal the absence of subject-matter, and who, not being a professional artist, and receiving no payment for his work, will only produce art when he feels an irresistible inner necessity to do so.

So completely different from what is now considered art, both in substance and form, will the art of the future be. The subject-matter of the art of the future will be only feelings drawing people to unity, or really uniting them; another form of art will be such as to be accessible to everybody. And therefore the ideal of perfection of the future will not be exclusiveness of feeling, accessible only to some, but, on the contrary, its universality. And not crowdedness, obscurity, and complexity of form, as it is now held to be, but, on the contrary, brevity, clearness, and simplicity of expression. And only when art is like this will it no longer merely amuse and corrupt people, as it does now, demanding the expenditure of their best forces on this, but it will be what it ought to be, an instrument for the transfer of the Christian religious consciousness from the region of intellect and reason to the region of feeling, thus bringing people in reality, in life itself, to that perfection and unity which the religious consciousness points out to them.

Complete. From "What Is Art?" Copyright edition of H. Altemus, Philadelphia. By permission.

THE MARQUIS TSENG

(1839-1890)

THE "Diary of the Marquis Tseng," first translated in 1884, frequently shows the acuteness which characterizes the intellect of the educated Chinaman. It is not intended to be satirical or hypercritical, but the standpoint from which it considers Caucasian customs is so completely extraneous that we have frequent suggestions in it of the satire which Goldsmith puts in the mouth of his imaginary Chinese philosopher in "The Citizen of the World." Tseng, who was born in 1839, spent a good part of his life in the Chinese diplomatic service, residing at St. Petersburg, Paris, and London. His "Diary" was written while he was Chinese minister to England and France. He died April 12th, 1890.

CHARACTERISTICS OF THE FRENCH AND ENGLISH

THE French and English are both fond of lauding their own national customs, and in finding flaws in those of other countries. My French interpreter jeered at the English, and my English interpreter ridiculed the French.

A Chinese going to Europe suffers from two difficulties, to which he finds it very hard to accustom himself: one is the confined nature of the house accommodation, the other the high price of everything. In the West the cost of ground for building purposes is enormous, and the consequence is that people are obliged to live in houses eight or nine stories high. Not only this, but so sparing are they of land in constructing their houses, that there are generally one or two pits underground, which serve as kitchens and wine cellars. Their parks and gardens, however, are laid out on a most extensive scale, and care is taken to copy nature in all its wild simplicity. These resorts of amusement and pleasure vary in size from one to three miles in circumference. Here they show no disposition to stint themselves in the matter of land, and bestow much care upon the neat arrangement of such places, thereby embodying the maxim

transmitted by Mencius, that, "if the people are made to share in the means of enjoyment, they will cherish no feelings of discontent." Both France and England are at one in the above respect.

The English excel in their use of ways and means for the acquisition of wealth; the French delight in extravagance and waste. With the former, the result of the general eagerness to get rich is that everything, however inferior in quality, is high-priced; while with the latter, extravagance has become a national habit, and prices know no bounds. Such is the difference between the two countries, a difference, however, which entails the same inconvenience upon the traveler in either case.

Complete.

WESTERN ARTS AND CIVILIZATION DERIVED FROM CHINA

ONE evening, in conversation with Sung Sheng, he expressed his belief that the systems of government and civilization prevailing in the West bear a close resemblance to the institutions of China in the time of the Chow dynasty. Lao Tsze, he said, after serving as a minister of that dynasty, had gone to the West and transplanted the laws and usages of China into Western soil. The assertion does not, unfortunately, admit of positive proof, but the idea is one of some interest and novelty. I remarked, in reply, that Europe, having been once inhabited by wild tribes, had in all probability derived its literature and political systems from Asia, whence they had gradually spread westward, and this I considered the explanation of the resemblance between European habits and ways and those of China in olden times. I used to tell my French interpreter in jest that China's sacred Emperor descended in an unbroken line through history, and that even as regards Presidents we had Yao and Shun, the best that ever existed. This was of course merely a joke, but still it is plain that all Western institutions have existed in the past in China. For example, in the West articles of household use are invariably carved and engraved with taste and neatness, the idea being derived from the inscriptions found upon goblets, cups, and like utensils of antique date in China. It may be said that steamers, steam engines, and such ingenious contrivances were unknown in past ages. By such an assertion, however, the fact is ignored that mechanical ingenuity depends upon material resources, and varies according to a nation's prosperity or decay. When material resources fail mechanical arts fall into neglect. In olden times China had no lack of mechanical appliances, but as her national prosperity gradually declined, her people fell into idle and thriftless habits, and mechanical arts gradually died out. As, by a glance at what Europe now is, we may see what China once was, so by noting what China now is, we may learn what Europe will one day become. The time will arrive when Western workcraft, now so active and superior, will grow inept, and Western ingenuity give way to homelike simplicity. The fact is, the earth's productions are not sufficient to provide for the manifold wants of its countless people, and deterioration is one of nature's laws.

Complete.

THE EARL OF BEACONSFIELD

ON THE twenty-seventh of March, 1879, I called upon Beaconsfield. He is a man of marvelous attainments and great decision of character, and though over seventy years of age shows no sign of physical decay. The English look upon him as the Great Wall of their country. I have been given to understand that during the struggle between Russia and Turkey, the Turks, conscious of their weakness, were prepared to sue for peace on any terms the Russians might wish to impose. Beaconsfield saw that it was against the interests of England to allow Russia to carry out her designs upon Turkey, and it was entirely owing to him that British troops were employed to assist Turkey and thwart Russia.

The High Ministers and Members of Parliament in England disapproved of the use of force, but Beaconsfield, not heeding their remonstrances, moved the troops and made such a demonstration of war that Russia took fright and finally accepted the English conditions. Beaconsfield's reputation was greatly enhanced by this stroke of policy. When he goes to the House of Parliament, old and young, women and children, flock thither to get a sight of him and hear his words. As they watch his dignified bearing, whispers of approval and respectful deference mark their admiration of the man. Beaconsfield, though far advanced in years, is so pressed with public business that foreign

envoys wishing to see him have to arrange the time of meeting beforehand by letter, and so I followed the same course. His manner was gracious and courteous; his words few and impressive. Our conversation was confined to ordinary topics.

Complete. This and the preceding selections are from the translations of J. N. Jordan for the Nineteenth Century 1884.

HENRY THEODORE TUCKERMAN

(1813–1871)

HENRY THEODORE TUCKERMAN, an entertaining essayist and miscellaneous writer, was born in Boston, Massachusetts, April 20th, 1813. He wrote extensively both in prose and verse. Among his best-known works are "The Italian Sketch-Book," published in 1835; "Rambles and Reveries" in 1841; "Thoughts on the Poets" in 1846; "Characteristics of Literature" in 1849 to 1851; and "Essays" in 1857. He died in New York, December 17th, 1871. His essay on "New England Philosophy" appeared originally in the Democratic Review. It included the "Defense of Enthusiasm," which has been more widely circulated than anything else from his pen.

A DEFENSE OF ENTHUSIASM

LET us recognize the beauty and power of true enthusiasm; and whatever we may do to enlighten ourselves and others, guard against checking or chilling a single earnest sentiment. For what is the human mind, however enriched with acquisitions or strengthened by exercise, unaccompanied by an ardent and sensitive heart? Its light may illumine, but it cannot inspire. It may shed a cold and moonlight radiance upon the path of life, but it warms no flower into bloom; it sets free no icebound fountains. Dr. Johnson used to say that an obstinate rationality prevented him from being a papist. Does not the same cause prevent many of us from unburdening our hearts and breathing our devotions at the shrines of nature? There are influences which environ humanity too subtle for the dissecting knife of reason. In our better moments we are clearly conscious of their presence, and if there is any barrier to their blessed agency, it is a formalized intellect. Enthusiasm, too, is the very life of gifted spirits. Ponder the lives of the glorious in art or literature through all ages. What are they but records of toils and sacrifices supported by the earnest hearts of their votaries? Dante composed his immortal poem amid exile and suffering, prompted by the noble ambition of vindicating himself to posterity; and the sweetest angel of his paradise is the object of his early love. The best countenances the old painters have be-

queathed to us are those of cherished objects intimately associated with their fame. The face of Raphael's mother blends with the angelic beauty of all his madonnas. Titian's daughter and the wife of Corregio again and again meet in their works. Well does Foscolo call the fine arts the children of Love. The deep interest with which the Italians hail gifted men inspires them to the mightiest efforts. National enthusiasm is the great nursery of genius. When Cellini's statue of "Perseus" was first exhibited on the Piazza at Florence, it was surrounded for days by an admiring throng, and hundreds of tributary sonnets were placed upon its pedestal. Petrarch was crowned with laurel at Rome for his poetical labors, and crowds of the unlettered may still be seen on the Mole at Naples, listening to a reader of Tasso. Reason is not the only interpreter of life. The fountain of action is in the feelings. Religion itself is but a state of the affections. I once met a beautiful peasant woman in the valley of the Arno, and asked the number of her children. "I have three here and two in Paradise," she calmly replied, with a tone and manner of touching and grave simplicity. Her faith was of the heart. Constituted as human nature is, it is in the highest degree natural that rare powers should be excited by voluntary and spontaneous appreciation. Who would not feel urged to high achievement, if he knew that every beauty his canvas displayed, or every perfect note he breathed, or every true inspiration of his lyre, would find an instant response in a thousand breasts? Lord Brougham calls the word "impossible" the mother tongue of little souls. What, I ask, can counteract self-distrust, and sustain the higher efforts of our nature but enthusiasm? More of this element would call forth the genius, and gladden the life of New England. While the mere intellectual man speculates, and the mere man of acquisition cites authority, the man of feeling acts, realizes, puts forth his complete energies. His earnest and strong heart will not let his mind rest; he is urged by an inward impulse to embody his thought. He must have sympathy; he must have results. And Nature yields to the magician, acknowledging him as her child. The noble statue comes forth from the marble, the speaking figure stands out from the canvas, the electric chain is struck in the bosoms of his fellows. They receive his ideas, respond to his appeal, and reciprocate his love.

Constant supplies of knowledge to the intellect, and the exclusive culture of reason may, indeed, make a pedant and logician; but the probability is, these benefits, if such they are, will be gained at the expense of the soul. Sentiment, in its broadest acceptation, is as essential to the true enjoyment and grace of life as mind. Technical information, and that quickness of apprehension which New Englanders call smartness, are not so valuable to a human being as sensibility to the beautiful, and a spontaneous appreciation of the divine influences which fill the realms of vision and of sound, and the world of action and feeling. The tastes, affections, and sentiments, are more absolutely the man than his talent or acquirements. And yet it is by and through the latter that we are apt to estimate character, of which they are at best but fragmentary evidences. It is remarkable that in the New Testament allusions to the intellect are so rare, while the "heart" and the "spirit we are of" are ever appealed to. Sympathy is the "golden key" which unlocks the treasures of wisdom; and this depends upon vividness and warmth of feeling. It is therefore that Tranio advises — "In brief, sir, study what you most affect." A code of etiquette may refine the manners, but the "heart of courtesy," which, through the world, stamps the natural gentleman, can never be attained but through instinct; and in the same manner, those enriching and noble sentiments which are the most beautiful and endearing of human qualities, no process of mental training will create. To what end is society, popular education, churches, and all the machinery of culture, if no living truth is elicited which fertilizes as well as enlightens? Shakespeare undoubtedly owed his marvelous insight into the human soul to his profound sympathy with man. He might have conned whole libraries on the philosophy of the passions; he might have coldly observed facts for years, and never have conceived of jealousy like Othello's, the remorse of Macbeth, or love like that of Juliet. When the native sentiments are once interested, new facts spring to light. It was under the excitement of wonder and love, that Byron, tossed on the lake of Geneva, thought that "Jura answered from her misty shroud," responsive to the thunder of the Alps. With no eye of mere curiosity did Bryant follow the lonely flight of the waterfowl. Veneration prompted the inquiry: —

> "Whither 'midst falling dew,
> When glow the heavens with the last steps of day,
> Far through their rosy depths dost thou pursue
> Thy solitary way?"

x—240

Sometimes, in musing upon genius in its simpler manifestations, it seems as if the great art of human culture consisted chiefly in preserving the glow and freshness of the heart. It is certain that in proportion as its merely mental strength and attainment takes the place of natural sentiment, in proportion as we acquire the habit of receiving all impressions through the reason, the teachings of nature grow indistinct and cold, however it may be with those of books. That this is the tendency of the New England philosophy of life and education, I think can scarcely be disputed. I have remarked that some of our most intelligent men speak of mastering a subject, of comprehending a book, of settling a question, as if these processes involved the whole idea of human cultivation. The reverse of all this is chiefly desirable. It is when we are overcome, and the pride of intellect vanished before the truth of nature, when, instead of coming to a logical decision, we are led to bow in profound reverence before the mysteries of life, when we are led back to childhood, or up to God, by some powerful revelation of the sage or minstrel, it is then our natures grow. To this end is all art. Exquisite vocalism, beautiful statuary and painting, and all true literature, have not for their great object to employ the ingenuity of prying critics, or furnish the world with a set of new ideas, but to move the whole nature by the perfection and truthfulness of their appeal. There is a certain atmosphere exhaled from the inspired page of genius, which gives vitality to the sentiments, and through these quickens the mental powers. And this is the chief good of books. Were it otherwise, those of us who have bad memories might despair of advancement. I have heard educated New Englanders boast of the quantity of poetry they have read in a given time, as if rich fancies and elevated thoughts are to be dispatched as are beefsteaks on board our steamboats. Newspapers are estimated by their number of square feet, as if this had anything to do with the quality of their contents. Journeys of pleasure are frequently deemed delightful in proportion to their rapidity, without reference to the new scenery or society they bring into view. Social gatherings are not seldom accounted brilliant in the same degree that they are crowded. Such would not be the case if what the phrenologists call the affective powers were enough considered; if the whole soul, instead of the "meddling intellect" alone, were freely developed; if we realized the truth thus expressed by a powerful writer — "within the en-

tire circle of our intellectual constitution, we value nothing but emotion; it is not the powers, but the fruit of those powers, in so much feeling of a lofty kind as they will yield."

One of the most obvious consequences of these traits appears in social intercourse. Foreigners have ridiculed certain external habits of Americans, but these were always confined to the few, and where most prevalent have yielded readily to censure. There are incongruities of manners still more objectionable, because the direct exponents of character and resulting from the philosophy of life. Delicacy and self-respect are the fruits, not so much of intellect as sensibility. We are considerate towards others in proportion as our own consciousness gives us insight. The sympathies are the best teachers of politeness; and these are ever blunted by an exclusive reliance on perception. Nothing is more common than to find educated New Englanders unconsciously invading the privacy of others, to indulge their idle curiosity, or giving a personal turn to conversation in a way that outrages all moral refinement. This is observable in society professedly intellectual. It is scarcely deemed rude to allude to one's personal appearance, health, dress, circumstances, or even most sacred feelings, although neither intimacy nor confidence lend the slightest authority to the proceeding. Such violation of what is due to others is more frequently met with among the cultivated of this than any other country. It is comparatively rare here to encounter a natural gentleman. A New England philosopher, in a recent work, betrays no little fear of "excess of fellowship." In the region he inhabits there is ground for the apprehension. No standard of manners will correct the evil. The peasantry of Southern Europe and the most ignorant Irishwomen often excel educated New Englanders in genuine courtesy. Their richer feelings teach them how to deal with others. Reverence and tenderness (not self-possession and intelligence) are the hallowed avenues through which alone true souls come together. The cool satisfaction with which character is analyzed and defined in New England is an evidence of the superficial test which observation alone affords. A Yankee dreams not of the world which is revealed only through sentiment. Men, and especially women, shrink from unfolding the depths of their natures to the cold and prying gaze which aims to explore them only as an intellectual diversion. It is the most presumptuous thing in the world for an unadulterated New Englander, however acute and

studious, to pretend to know another human being, if nobly endowed; for he is the last person to elicit latent and cherished emotions. He may read mental capacities and detect moral tendencies, but no familiarity will unveil the inner temple; only in the vestibule will his prying step be endured.

Another effect of this exaggerated estimate of intellect is that talent and character are often regarded as identical. This is a fatal, but very prevalent error. A gift of mind, let it ever be remembered, is not a grace of soul. Training or native skill will enable any one to excel in the machinery of expression. The phrase "artistical," whether in reference to statuary, painting, literature, or manners, implies only aptitude and dexterity. Who is not aware, for instance, of the vast difference between a merely scientific knowledge of music and that enlistment of the sympathies in the art which makes it the eloquent medium of passion, sentiment, and truth? And in literature, how often do we find the most delicate perception of beauty in the writer, combined with a total want of genuine refinement in the man! Art is essentially imitative; and its value, as illustrative of character, depends not upon the mental endowments, but upon the moral integrity of the artist. The idea of talent is associated more or less with the idea of success; and on this account, the lucrative creed of the New Englander recognizes it with indiscriminate admiration; but there is a whole armory of weapons in the human bosom, of more celestial temper. It is a nobler and a happier thing to be capable of self-devotion, loyalty, and generous sympathies, to cherish a quick sense of honor and find absolute comfort only in being lost in another, than to have an eye for color, whereby the rainbow can be transferred to canvas, or a felicity of diction that can embalm the truest pictures in immortal numbers. Not only or chiefly in what he does resides the significance of a human being. His field of action and the availability of his powers depend upon health, education, self-reliance, position, and a thousand other agencies; what he is results from the instincts of his soul, and for these alone he is truly to be loved. It is observable among New Englanders that an individual's qualities are less frequently referred to as a test of character than his performances. It is very common for them to sacrifice social and private to public character, friendship to fame, sympathy to opinion, love to ambition, and sentiment to propriety. There is an obvious disposition among them to appraise men and women at their market rather than their intrinsic value. A lucky speculation, a profitable invention, a salable book, an effective rhetorical effort or a sagacious political ruse — some fact which proves, at best, only adroitness and good fortune, is deemed the best escutcheon to lend dignity to life, or hang as a lasting memorial upon the tomb. Those more intimate revelations and ministries which deal with the inmost gifts of mind, and warmest emotions of the heart, and through which alone love and truth are realized, are but seldom dreamed of in their philosophy.

There is yet another principle which seems to me but faintly recognized in the New England philosophy of life, however it may be occasionally cultivated as a department of literature; and yet it is one which we should deem essentially dear to man, a glorious endowment, a crowning grace of humanity. It is that principle through which we commune with all that is lovely and grand in the universe, which mellows the pictures of memory into pensive beauty, and irradiates the visions of hope with unearthly brightness; which elevates our social experience by the glow of fancy, and exhibits scenes of perfection to the soul that the senses can never realize. It is the poetical principle. If this precious gift could be wholly annihilated amid the commonplace and the actual, we should lose the interest of life. The dull routine of daily experience, the tame reality of things, would weigh like a heavy and permanent cloud upon our hearts. But the office of this divine spirit is to throw a redeeming grace around the objects and the scenes of being. It is the breeze that lifts the weeds on the highway of time and brings to view the violets beneath. It is the holy water which, sprinkled on the Mosaic pavement of life, makes vivid its brilliant tints. It is the mystic harp upon whose strings the confused murmur of toil, gladness, and grief, loses itself in music. But it performs a yet higher function than that of consolation. It is through the poetical principle that we form images of excellence, a notion of progress that quickens every other faculty to rich endeavor. All great men are so, chiefly through unceasing effort to realize in action, or embody in art, sentiments of deep interest or ideas of beauty. As colors exist in rays of light, so does the ideal in the soul, and life is the mighty prism which refracts it. Shelley maintains that it is only through the imagination that we can overleap the barriers of self and become identified with the universal and the distant, and, therefore, that this principle is the

true fountain of benevolent affections and virtue. I know it is sometimes said that the era of romance has passed, that with the pastoral, classic, and chivalrous periods of the world, the poetic element died out. But this is manifestly a great error. The forms of society have greatly changed, and the methods of poetical development are much modified, but the principle itself is essential to humanity. No! mechanical as is the spirit of the age, and wide as is the empire of utility, as long as the stars appear nightly in the firmament, and golden clouds gather around the departing sun; as long as we can greet the innocent smile of infancy and the gentle eye of woman; as long as this earth is visited by visions of glory and dreams of love and hopes of heaven; while life is encircled by mystery, brightened by affection, and solemnized by death, so long will the poetical spirit be abroad, with its fervent aspirations and deep spells of enchantment. Again, it is often urged that the poetical spirit belongs appropriately to a certain epoch of life, and that its influence naturally ceases with youth. But this can only be the case through self-apostasy. The poetical element was evidently intended to mingle with the whole of human experience; not only to glow in the breast of youth, but to dignify the thought of manhood, and make venerable the aspect of age. Its purpose clearly is to relieve the sternness of necessity, to lighten the burden of toil, and throw sacredness and hope even around suffering — as the old painters were wont to depict groups of cherubs above their martyrdoms. Nor can I believe that the agency of this principle is so confined and temporary as many suppose. It is true our contemplation of the beautiful is of short duration, our flights into the ideal world brief and occasional. We can but bend in passing at the altar of beauty, and pluck a flower hastily by the wayside; — but may there not be an instinct which eagerly appropriates even these transitory associations? May they not be unconsciously absorbed into the essence of our life, and gradually refine and exalt the spirit within us? I cannot think that such rich provision for the poetic sympathies is intended for any casual or indifferent end. Rather let us believe there is a mystic language in the flowers, and a deep meaning in the stars, that the transparency of the winter air and the long sweetness of summer twilight pass, with imperceptible power, over the soul; rather let us cherish the thought that the absorbing emotions of love, the sweet excitement of adventure,

and the impassioned solemnity of grief, with a kind of spiritual chemistry, combine and purify the inward elements into nobler action and more perfect results. Of the poetical principle, the philosophy of life in New England makes little account. Emblems of the past do not invite our gaze down the vistas of time. Reverence is seldom awakened by any object, custom, or association. The new, the equal, the attainable, constantly deaden our faith in infinite possibilities. Life rarely seems miraculous, and the commonplace abounds. There is much to excite, and little to chasten and awe. We need to see the blessedness of a rational conservatism, as well as the inspiring call for reform. There are venerable and lovely agencies in this existence of ours which it is sacrilege to scorn. The wisdom of our renowned leaders in all departments is too restless and conscious to be desirable; and it would be better for our boasted "march of mind," if, like the quaint British essayist, a few more "were dragged along in the procession." An extravagant spirit of utility invades every scene of life however sequestered. We attempt not to brighten the grim features of care, or relieve the burdens of responsibility. The daughter of a distinguished law professor in Europe was in the habit of lecturing in her father's absence. To guard against the fascination of her charms, which it was feared would divert the attention of the students, a curtain was drawn before the fair teacher, from behind which she imparted her instructions. Thus do we carefully keep out of sight the poetical and veil the spirit of beauty, that we may worship undisturbed at the shrine of the practical. We ever seek the light of knowledge; but are content that no fertilizing warmth lend vitality to its beams.

When the returning pilgrim approaches the shores of the New World, the first sign of the vicinity of his native land is traced in hues of rare glory on the western sky. The sunsets grow more and more gorgeous as he draws near, and while he leans over the bulwarks of a gallant vessel (whose matchless architecture illustrates the mechanical skill of her birthplace), and watches their shifting brilliancy, it associates itself with the fresh promise and young renown of his native land; and when from the wide solitude of the Atlantic, he plunges once more amid her eager crowds, it is with the earnest and I must think patriotic wish, that with her prosperous activity might mingle more of the poetry of life!

But what the arrangements of society fail to provide, the individual is at liberty to seek. Nowhere are natural beauty and grandeur more lavishly displayed than on this continent. In no part of the world are there such noble rivers, beautiful lakes, and magnificent forests. The ermine robe of winter is, in no land, spread with more dazzling effect, nor can the woodlands of any clime present a more varied array of autumnal tints. Nor need we resort to the glories of the universe alone. Domestic life exists with us in rare perfection; and it requires but the heroism of sincerity and the exercise of taste, to make the fireside as rich in poetical associations as the terrace and veranda of southern lands. Literature, too, opens a rich field. We can wander through Eden to the music of the blind bard's harp, or listen in the orange groves of Verona, beneath the quiet moonlight, to the sweet vows of Juliet. Let us, then, bravely obey our sympathies, and find in candid and devoted relations with others freedom from the constraints of prejudice and form. Let us foster the enthusiasm which exclusive intellectual cultivation would extinguish. Let us detach ourselves sufficiently from the social machinery to realize that we are not integral parts of it; and thus summon into the horizon of destiny those hues of beauty, love, and truth, which are the most glorious reflections of the soul!

From "New England Philosophy."

IVAN SERGEYEVICH TURGENIEFF

(1818–1883)

IVAN SERGEYEVICH TURGENIEFF (written also "Turgeneff") was one of the great novelists whose work made Russian fiction a part of the literature of the world. He was born at Orel, Russia, November 9th, 1818, and educated at the leading colleges of Russia, with a post-graduate course at Berlin. After his return to Russia, he entered the government service in the Department of the Interior and remained thus employed until 1852, when the views he expressed in an obituary of Gogol led to his arrest and imprisonment. After being banished to Orel for several years, he was liberated and allowed to go abroad. From 1854 until his death, September 3d, 1883, most of his time was spent in Baden-Baden, Paris, and other cities of Western Europe, but he visited Russia from time to time, and grew in favor with his countrymen who had at first misunderstood him. In his first notable work, "The Annals of a Sportsman" (1845-57), he gave his influence for the emancipation of the serfs, and showed such talent as a writer, that papers of the series were translated into French, English, and other languages. Among his most noted novels are "Rudin" (1855), "A Nest of Nobles" (1858), "Helene" (1860), "Fathers and Sons" (1862), "Smoke" (1867), and "Virgin Soil" (1876). His "Senilia," which were published in England in 1883, include an extraordinary collection of "Prose Poems" characteristically Russian, and sometimes so original as to call for severe thought before they become intelligible. Perhaps it was because of these very sketches that Tolstoi was first inspired with his strong prejudice against literary "originality" of all kinds.

PROSE POEMS

"ACCEPT THE VERDICT OF FOOLS"

"ACCEPT the verdict of fools."—[Pushkin.] And thou ever speakest truth—thou, our sublime singer—and thou hast spoken it now.

"The verdict of fools and the laughter of the multitude!" . . . Who has not already experienced one or the other?

But this may—and must—be endured; and he to whom strength is given may despise it.

No. He has only devised a slander about one of his friends, and is carefully circulating it abroad. This same slander he heard from the lips of a third one—and believed it himself.

Oh, how content and complacent is this amiable, promising young man!

Complete.

A RULE OF LIFE

"IF you would thoroughly disconcert and irritate your enemy," —this was an old intriguer's advice to me—"accuse him of the same fault, the same vice, that you yourself strive to overcome; reproach him bitterly with it, and heap upon him the severest reproofs.

"First—by these means you will persuade others that this is no vice of yours.

"Second—your indignation is unfeigned. They have the benefit of the reproof of your own conscience.

"Are you perhaps a renegade? Then reproach your adversary with a lack of faith!

"Have you yourself the soul of a lackey? Then upbraid him with his lackey's nature; sneer at him for being a lackey of civilization, of Europe, and of society."

"One can even say that he is a lackey because he is not a lackey!" I remarked.

"Yes, even that" assented the intriguer.

Complete.

THE END OF THE WORLD

I DREAMED that I was in a peasant's hut in some obscure corner of Russia.

It is a large room and low: there are three windows, the walls are painted white, and there is no furniture. Before the hut stretches a desolate plain, which loses itself in the dim distance; above it a gray, monotonous sky hangs like a veil.

I am not alone; there are some ten men in the room. They are ordinary, simple, plainly clad people; they pace up and down in silence; they almost slink. They shun, but still regard each other continually with apprehensive looks.

Not one of them knows how he has come hither, or what manner of men the others are. Disquiet and depression is painted

Still there are blows which wound us more deeply. . . . A man does his utmost; he labors honestly, with all his heart. . . . And yet "honorable souls" turn away from him with disgust; "honest people" redden with indignation at the mere mention of his name. "Depart! Away with thee!" cry young and "honorable" voices. "We need neither thee nor thy works, thou defilest our dwelling—thou canst neither know nor understand us. . . . Thou art our foe!"

What must this man do? . . . He must continue to labor on, making no attempt to vindicate himself—he may not even expect a just verdict.

Once upon a time, the husbandmen cursed the traveler who brought them potatoes as a substitute for bread, the daily food of the poor. . . . The hands at first outstretched to him dashed down the precious gift, flung it in the mire, and trampled on it. And now it is their sustenance—and they do not even know the name of their benefactor.

Be it so! What is a name worth? Though he is nameless, yet he delivered them from death by famine.

So, therefore, let us take heed that what we provide may prove, indeed, wholesome food.

Bitter is the unjust reproof from the lips of those we love. . . . Still we must endure it.

"Strike—but hear me!" cried the Athenian to the Spartan.

"Strike me—but eat and be satisfied!" This is what we must say.

Complete.

A SELF-SATISFIED MAN

A YOUNG man is walking gayly along the Residential Street. His demeanor is careless, cheerful, and self-conscious; his eyes sparkle, a smile is on his lips, and his pleasant face is slightly flushed. He is full of self-confidence and satisfaction.

What has happened to him? Has he made a fortune? Has he attained a higher position in life? Does a loved one await him? Or is it merely—a good breakfast, a feeling of comfort, the fullness of strength, that thus expands his frame? Or may not even the beautiful eight-rayed cross of King Stanislaus of Poland have been hung around his neck?

on every countenance; one after the other they all approach the window, and gaze out anxiously as if they awaited something from without.

And then they wander restlessly up and down once more. A youth who is of the number moans from time to time in a thin, monotonous voice, "Father, I am afraid!" This complaining makes me feel ill—I myself begin to grow frightened. . . . But why? I know not. I only realize that a great, great evil is ever drawing nearer.

The youth continues to moan. Oh, could one but flee from here! This heat! This exhaustion! This oppression! . . . But escape is impossible.

The heaven is like a pall, not a breath of air stirs. . . . Can the breeze also be dead?

Suddenly the youth rushes to the window and cries in mournful accents, "Look! Look! the earth is swallowed up!"

What? . . . Swallowed up? . . . In truth there was a plain before the house—now it stands on the summit of a vast mountain! The horizon has fallen and sunk down, and close by the house yawns a black, deep, gaping abyss!

We all crowd round the window. . . . Our hearts are benumbed with terror. "There—there it is!" . . . whispers my neighbor.

And suddenly, along the whole, wide, unbounded space, something stirs; little rounded hillocks appear to rise and sink on the surface.

The sea! The same idea occurs to us all. It will engulf us all together. . . . But how can that be? How can it scale the heights of this lofty mountain peak?

But it is rising, ever higher, ever higher. . . . And now they are not merely the little hillocks which rippled in the distance. . . . One solitary, dense, monstrous wave encompasses the whole circle of the horizon.

It dashes, dashes toward us! Like an icy whirlwind it approaches, circling round like the gloomy pit of Hell. Everything around is quaking; and there in yonder approaching chaos, a metallic roar of a thousand tongues thunders, crashes, shrieks.

Ha! . . . What howls . . . groans! It is the earth that is crying aloud with fear.

The end of the world is here! . . . The universal end!

The youth moans yet once more. . . . I will cling to my companion—but all of a sudden we are crushed, buried, overwhelmed, carried away by yonder black, icy, roaring wave.

Darkness . . . eternal darkness!

And almost breathless, I awoke.

Complete.

THE BLOCKHEAD

ONCE upon a time there was a blockhead. For a long time he lived happy and content, until at last a report reached him that everybody considered him a brainless fool.

This roused the blockhead and made him sorrowful. He considered what would be the best way to confute this statement.

Suddenly an idea burst upon his wretched mind, and without delay he put it into execution.

One day an acquaintance encountered him in the street, and began to praise a celebrated painter.

"Good God!" cried the blockhead, "do you not know that this man's works have long since been banished to the lumber room? You must be aware of the fact! . . . You are far behind-hand in culture."

The friend was alarmed, and immediately concurred with the blockhead's opinion.

"That is a clever book that I have read to-day!" said another of his acquaintances to him.

"God have mercy!" cried the blockhead. "Are you not ashamed to say so? That book is utterly worthless; there can only be one idea concerning it. And did you not know that? . . . Oh, culture has left you far behind."

And this acquaintance also was alarmed, and he agreed with the blockhead.

"What a splendid fellow my friend, N — N — is!" said a third acquaintance to the blockhead; "he is a truly noble man!"

"Good heavens!" shrieked the blockhead; "N — N — is a notorious scamp! He has already plundered all his relations. Who does not know that? . . . You are sadly wanting in culture!"

And the third acquaintance was also alarmed and instantly accepted the blockhead's opinion. Whatever was praised in the

blockhead's presence, he had always the same answer. And in every case he added, reproachfully, "And you still believe that authority?"

"A spiteful, venomous man!" that was how the blockhead was now known among his acquaintances. "But what a head!"

"And what language!" added others. "What talent!"

And the end of it all was, the editor of a newspaper intrusted the blockhead with the writing of the critiques in his journal.

The blockhead criticized everything, and every one, in his well-known style, and with his customary abuse.

And now, he, the former enemy of every authority, is himself an authority, and the rising generation show him respect, and tremble before him.

And how can the poor youths do otherwise? Certainly, to show him respect is an astonishing notion; but woe to you, if you would take his measure, or try to make him appear as he really was, you would immediately be criticized without mercy.

Blockheads have a brilliant life among cowards.

Complete.

AN EASTERN LEGEND

WHO, in Bagdad, does not know the great Djaffar, the sun of the universe? Once upon a time, many years ago, while Djaffar was still a youth, he was walking in the neighborhood of Bagdad.

Suddenly a hoarse cry fell upon his ear—some one was calling for help.

Djaffar was known among his acquaintance by his lofty mind and wise reflection; he had also a compassionate heart, and could rely upon his strength.

He hastened in the direction of the cry, and discovered a feeble old man, who was being forced toward the city walls by two robbers, who intended plundering him.

Djaffar drew his sabre, and attacked the miscreants; one he slew, and the other fled.

The old man fell at his deliverer's feet, kissed the hem of his garment, and exclaimed, "Brave youth, your generosity shall not remain unrewarded. Apparently, I am only a miserable beggar; but that is a delusion. I am no ordinary man. At daybreak, to-morrow, come to the market place; I will await you by the fountain, and you shall be assured of the truth of my words."

Djaffar hesitated: "This man certainly appears to be nothing but a beggar; however, who can tell? Why should I not make the experiment?" and he answered and said, "It is well, my father, I will come!"

The old man gazed at him, and went away.

At daybreak, the next morning, Djaffar repaired to the market place. The old man was already awaiting him, leaning against the marble basin of the fountain.

He took Djaffar's hand in silence, and led him into a little garden which was surrounded by a high wall.

In the centre of the garden, a tree of an unknown species sprung from the green turf.

It had the appearance of a cypress, but its leaves were of an azure tint.

Three fruits, three apples, hung from the straight and slender twigs; one apple, of medium size, was rather long and milk white; another was large, round, and bright red; the third was small, shriveled, and yellowish.

The tree rustled softly, although no breeze stirred. It sounded soft and sad, as if it were made of glass; it appeared to be conscious of Djaffar's presence.

"Youth!" said the old man, "pluck one of these fruits and take heed: if you pluck and eat the white apple, you will be wiser than all mankind; if you pluck the red apple and eat it, you will become rich as the Jew Rothschild; but if you pluck and eat the yellow apple, then you will be agreeable to the old women. Make up your mind without delay; in an hour the fruit will decay, and the tree will sink deep into the earth."

Djaffar bowed his head and considered. "Which shall I decide upon?" asked he of himself, half aloud. "Were I too wise, life perhaps might disgust me; were I richer than all other men, they would envy me; sooner, therefore, I will pluck and eat the third, withered apple!"

He did so, and the old man laughed with his toothless mouth, and said: "Oh, wisest among all youths! You have chosen aright! Wherefore do you need the white apple? you are already wiser than Solomon. Neither do you want the red apple—you will be rich without it, and no one will envy you your wealth."

"Then tell me, venerable father," said Djaffar, trembling with joy, "where the most honored mother of our Chalise—the beloved of the gods—lives."

The sage bowed to the very earth, and pointed out the way to the youth. . . .

Who in Bagdad does not know the sun of the universe, the great and illustrious Djaffar?

Complete.

THE SPARROW

I RETURNED home from the chase, and wandered through an alley in my garden. My dog bounded before me.

Suddenly he checked himself, and moved forward cautiously, as if he scented game.

I glanced down the alley, and perceived a young sparrow with a yellow beak, and down upon its head. He had fallen out of the nest (the wind was shaking the beeches in the alley violently), and lay motionless and helpless on the ground, with his little, unfledged wings extended.

The dog approached it softly, when suddenly an old sparrow, with a black breast, quitted a neighboring tree, dropped like a stone right before the dog's nose, and, with ruffled plumage, and chirping desperately and pitifully, sprang twice at the open, grinning mouth.

He had come to protect his little one at the cost of his own life. His little body trembled all over, his voice was hoarse, he was in an agony—he offered himself.

The dog must have seemed a gigantic monster to him. But, in spite of that, he had not remained safe on his lofty bough. A Power stronger than his own will has forced him down.

Treasure stood still and turned away. . . . It seemed as if he also felt this Power.

I hastened to call the discomfited dog back, and went away with a feeling of respect.

Yes, smile not! I felt a respect for this heroic little bird, and for the depth of his paternal love.

Love, I reflected, is stronger than death and the fear of death; it is love alone that supports and animates all.

Complete.

THE SKULLS

A MAGNIFICENT, dazzlingly-illuminated hall, a throng of ladies and cavaliers.

All are animated, and join in lively conversation. The conversation turns upon a celebrated singer. They say she is divine, immortal. . . . Ah, how enchanting was that last trill yesterday!

Suddenly, as if by the stroke of a wand, the covering of skin disappeared from every face, from every head, and in an instant the hue of death was on every skull, with its ashy, naked jaw and cheek bones.

I watched the movements of these jaws and cheeks with horror; I saw how the round, bony balls turned round and round, and shone in the glare of the lamps and tapers; saw how smaller balls — the balls of the senseless eyes — revolved in the large ones.

I dare not touch my own face, neither regard it in the mirror.

The skulls, however, moved in just the same way as before; the same sounds that the lips had uttered now proceeded from between jaws that had lost their teeth, and the nimble tongues still prattled of the astonishing melodious lips of the inimitable, immortal — yes, immortal — singer.

Complete. This and the preceding selections were translated for Macmillan's Magazine 1883.

x—241

"MARK TWAIN"
(SAMUEL LANGHORNE CLEMENS)
(1835-)

SAMUEL LANGHORNE CLEMENS, the most popular of all American humorists, was born at Florida, Missouri, November 30th, 1835. At the age of thirteen, he began in a country printing office the course of higher education which he has since continued with such notable results. In 1851, having taken his degree in the printing trade, he began a post-graduate course as a pilot on the Mississippi River, acquiring thus not only the experience which has been invaluable to him as a humorist, but the name he has made so celebrated in America and Europe that, unless it is put upon his monuments, the honorable family name he inherited will scarcely be sufficient to identify him. After several years on the river, he went to Nevada and California, experimenting in mining and journalism, and in 1866 making a visit to the Sandwich Islands. His career as a humorist may be dated more or less inexactly from a series of humorous lectures on Western Life which belong to this period. His first volume, "The Jumping Frog and Other Sketches," was published after his return to the East in 1867. Its success was immediate, but it was greatly surpassed by that of "Innocents Abroad" (1869) and "Roughing It" (1872). "The Adventures of Tom Sawyer," "A Tramp Abroad," "The Prince and the Pauper," "Life on the Mississippi," "Adventures of Huckleberry Finn," "A Connecticut Yankee at King Arthur's Court," and other works, following in rapid succession, have not exhausted his remarkable fertility, and he continues to maintain the quality of his literary output.

The serious purpose which crops out from time to time in nearly everything Mr. Clemens writes is hatred of humbug, — a feeling so genuine and deep seated with him that it nerved him for the impossible task of writing down the love of "Chivalry," which makes a Western cowboy who has read "Ivanhoe" imagine he is a paladin as he races his broncho at full speed down the main street of the town, with all the dogs barking and all the saloon loungers cheering him. Undoubtedly, there are times when Mr. Clemens takes himself seriously as a reformer, but after having educated the public to laugh at everything he does or says, it is of course quite useless for him to attempt seriousness.

ON THE ONE HUNDRED AND THIRTY-SIX VARIETIES OF NEW ENGLAND WEATHER

I REVERENTLY believe that the Maker who made us all makes everything in New England but the weather. I don't know who makes that, but I think it must be raw apprentices in the Weather Clerk's factory, who experiment and learn how in New England, for board and clothes, and then are promoted to make weather for countries that require a good article and will take their custom elsewhere if they don't get it.

There is a sumptuous variety about the New England weather that compels the stranger's admiration — and regret. The weather is always doing something there, always attending strictly to business, always getting up new designs and trying them on the people to see how they will go. But it gets through more business in the spring than in any other season. In the spring I have counted one hundred and thirty-six different kinds of weather inside of four-and-twenty hours. It was I that made the fame and fortune of that man that had that marvelous collection of weather on exhibition at the Centennial that so astounded the foreigners. He was going all over the world and get specimens from all climes. I said, "Don't you do it; you come to New England on a favorable spring day." I told him what we could do in the way of style, variety, and quantity. Well, he came, and he made his collection in four days. As to variety; why, he confessed he got hundreds of kinds of weather that he had never heard of before. And as to quantity; well, after he had picked out and discarded all that were blemished in any way, he not only had weather enough, but weather to spare; weather to hire out; weather to sell; weather to deposit; weather to invest; weather to give to the poor.

The people of New England are by nature patient and forbearing; but there are some things that they will not stand. Every year they kill a lot of poets for writing about "Beautiful Spring." These are generally casual visitors, who bring their notions of spring from somewhere else, and cannot, of course, know how the natives feel about spring. And so, the first thing they know, the opportunity to inquire how they feel has permanently gone by.

Old Probabilities has a mighty reputation for accurate prophecy, and thoroughly well deserves it. You take up the papers and observe how crisply and confidently he checks off what to-day's weather is going to be on the Pacific, down South, in the Middle States, in the Wisconsin region; see him sail along in the joy and pride of his power till he gets to New England, and then see his tail drop. He doesn't know what the weather is to be in New England. He can't any more tell than he can tell how many Presidents of the United States there are going to be. Well, he mulls over it, and by and by he get out something about like this: " Probable northeast to southwest winds, varying to the southward and westward and eastward and points between; high and low barometer, sweeping around from place to place; probable areas of rain, snow, hail, and drought, succeeded or preceded by earthquakes, with thunder and lightning." Then he jots down this postscript from his wandering mind to cover accidents: " But it is possible that the program may be wholly changed in the meantime."

Yes, one of the brightest gems in the New England weather is the dazzling uncertainty of it. There is only one thing certain about it, you are certain there is going to be plenty of weather. A perfect grand review; but you never can tell which end of the procession is going to move first. You fix up for the drought; you leave your umbrella in the house and sally out with your sprinkling-pot, and ten to one you get drowned. You make up your mind that the earthquake is due; you stand from under and take hold of something to steady yourself, and the first thing you know you get struck by lightning. These are great disappointments; but they can't be helped. The lightning there is peculiar; it is so convincing when it strikes a thing it doesn't leave enough of that behind for you to tell whether — well, you'd think it was something valuable and a Congressman had been there.

And the thunder. When the thunder commences merely to tune up, and scrape and saw and key up the instruments for the performance, strangers say, " Why what awful thunder you have here!" But when the baton is raised and the real concert begins, you'll find that stranger down in the cellar with his head in the ash barrel.

Now as to the size of the weather in New England — lengthways I mean. It is utterly disproportionate to the size of that little country. Half the time when it is packed as full as it can stick, you will see that New England weather sticking out beyond the edges, and projecting around hundreds of miles over the neighboring states. She can't hold a tenth part of her weather. You can see cracks all about, where she has strained herself trying to do it.

I could speak volumes about the inhuman perversity of the New England weather, but I will give but a single specimen. I like to hear rain on a tin roof, so I covered part of my roof with tin, with an eye to that luxury. Well, sir, do you think it ever rains on the tin? No, sir, skips it every time.

Mind, I have been trying merely to do honor to the New England weather; no language could do it justice. But, after all, there are one or two things about that weather (or, if you please, effects produced by it), which we residents would not like to part with. If we had not our bewitching autumn foliage, we should still have to credit the weather with one feature which compensates for all its bullying vagaries — the ice storm — when a leafless tree is clothed with ice from the bottom to the top — ice that is as bright and clear as crystal; every bough and twig is strung with ice beads, frozen dewdrops, and the whole tree sparkles, cold and white, like the Shah of Persia's diamond plume! Then the wind waves the branches and the sun comes out and turns all those myriads of beads and drops to prisms, that glow and hum and flash with all manner of colored fires, which change and change again with inconceivable rapidity, from blue to red, from red to green, and green to gold; the tree becomes a sparkling fountain, a very explosion of dazzling jewels, and it stands there the acme, the climax, the supremest possibility in art or nature of bewildering, intoxicating, intolerable magnificence! One cannot make the words too strong.

Month after month I lay up hate and grudge against the New England weather; but when the ice storm comes at last, I say, "There, I forgive you now; the books are square between us; you don't owe me a cent; go and sin no more; your little faults and foibles count for nothing; you are the most enchanting weather in the world."

Complete. Republished by permission of Mr. Clemens.

LINCOLN AND THE CIVIL WAR

(Address by Mr. Clemens at the Lincoln birthday celebration in Carnegie Hall, New York, February 11th, 1901)

THE duties of a presiding officer, upon an occasion like this, are few and simple. Indeed, the duties are but two — one easy, the other difficult: he must introduce the Orator of the evening; then keep still and give him a chance. These duties are about to be strictly fulfilled — even the second one; not out of deference to duty, but to win admiration.

To tell an American audience who and what Col. Watterson is, is not in any way necessary — the utterance of his name is enough; a name which is like one of these electric announcements on the Madison Square tower: the mention of it touches the button in our memory and his history flashes up out of the dark and stands brilliantly revealed and familiar: distinguished soldier, journalist, orator, lecturer, statesman, political leader, rebel, reconstructed rebel; always honest, always honorable, always loyal to his convictions, right or wrong, and not afraid to speak them out; and first, last, and all the time — whether rebel or reconstructed, whether on the wrong side or on the right — a patriot in his heart.

It is a curious circumstance, that without collusion of any kind, but merely in obedience to a strange and pleasant and dramatic freak of destiny, he and I, kinsmen by blood — for we are that — and one-time rebels — for we were that — should be chosen out of a million surviving quondam rebels to come here and bare our heads in reverence and love of that noble soul whom forty years ago we tried with all our hearts and all our strength to defeat and dispossess — Abraham Lincoln! Is not the Rebellion ended and forgotten? Are not the Blue and the Gray one, to-day? By authority of this sign we may answer yes; there was a Rebellion — that incident is closed.

I was born and reared in a slave State, my father was a slave owner; and in the Civil War I was a second lieutenant in the Confederate service — for a while. This second cousin of mine, Col. Watterson, the Orator of this present occasion, was born and reared in a slave State, was a colonel in the Confederate service, and rendered me such assistance as he could in my self-appointed great task of annihilating the Federal armies and break-

ing up the Union. I laid my plans with wisdom and foresight, and if Col. Watterson had obeyed my orders I should have succeeded in my giant undertaking. It was my intention to drive Gen. Grant into the Pacific — if I could get transportation — and I told Col. Watterson to surround the eastern armies and wait till I came. But he was insubordinate, and stood upon a punctilio of military etiquette; he refused to take orders from a second lieutenant — and the Union was saved. This is the first time that this secret has been revealed. Until now, no one outside the family has known the facts. But there they stand: Watterson saved the Union. Yet to this day that man gets no pension.

Those were great days, splendid days. What an uprising it was! For the hearts of the whole nation, North and South, were in the war. We of the South were not ashamed, for like the men of the North we were fighting for what we believed with all our sincere souls to be our rights; on both sides we were fighting for our homes and hearthstones, and for the honor of the flags we loved; and when men fight for these things, and under these convictions, with nothing sordid to tarnish their cause, that cause is holy, the blood spilt in it is sacred, the life that is laid down for it is consecrated. To-day we no longer regret the result; to-day we are glad it came out as it did; but we are not ashamed that we did our endeavor; we did our bravest and best, against desperate odds, for the cause which was precious to us and which our consciences approved: and we are proud — and you are proud — the kindred blood in your veins answers when I say it — you are proud of the record we made in those mighty collisions in the field.

What an uprising it was! We did not have to supplicate for soldiers on either side. "We are coming, Father Abraham, three hundred thousand strong!" That was the music, North and South. The very choicest young blood and brain and brawn rose up, from Maine to the Gulf, and flocked to the standards — just as men always do, when in their eyes their cause is great and fine and their hearts are in it; just as men flocked to the Crusades, sacrificing all they possessed to the cause, and entering cheerfully upon hardships which we cannot even imagine in this age, and upon toilsome and wasting journeys which in our time would be the equivalent of circumnavigating the globe five times over.

North and South we put our hearts into that colossal struggle; and out of it came the blessed fulfillment of the prophecy of the immortal Gettysburg Speech, which said, "We here highly resolve that these dead shall not have died in vain; that this nation, under God, shall have a new birth of freedom; and that government of the people, by the people, for the people, shall not perish from the earth."

We are here to honor the birthday of the greatest citizen, and the noblest and the best, after Washington, that this land or any other has yet produced. The old wounds are healed, you and we are brothers again; you testify it by honoring two of us — once soldiers of the Lost Cause and foes of your great and good leader — with the high privilege of assisting here; and we testify it by laying our honest homage at the feet of Abraham Lincoln, and in forgetting that you of the North and we of the South were ever enemies, and remembering only that we are now indistinguishably fused together, and namable by one common great name — Americans!

Complete. Republished by permission of Mr. Clemens.

JOHN TYNDALL

(1820–1893)

JOHN TYNDALL was born at Leighlin Bridge, Ireland, August 21st, 1820. At the age of twenty-four he began life in the employment of an engineering firm, but a little later he became a teacher at Queenwood College, Hants, and began the course of study and scientific investigation which made him famous. After three years (1848–51) at the University of Marburg, he began making the contributions to the literature of physics which were valued by the learned for their subject-matter and read with pleasure by the general public because of a lucidity of statement which made the difficult things of science seem simple. In 1852 Tyndall was elected a Fellow of the Royal Society, and a year later he became professor of Natural Philosophy in the Royal Institution of London. His investigations of heat, light, and electricity resulted in a series of works of great scientific value, and he wrote besides several volumes of essays specially designed for popular reading. Of these, "Fragments of Science for Unscientific People" (1871) proved so popular that it was followed in 1892 by "New Fragments." Prof. Tyndall died in Surrey, England, December 4th, 1893.

SCIENCE AND SPIRITS

THEIR refusal to investigate "spiritual phenomena" is often urged as a reproach to scientific men. I here propose to give a sketch of an attempt to apply to the "phenomena" those methods of inquiry which are found available in dealing with natural truth.

Some time ago, when the spirits were particularly active in this country, a celebrated philosopher was invited, or rather entreated, by one of his friends to meet and question them. He had, however, already made their acquaintance, and did not wish to renew it. I had not been so privileged, and he therefore kindly arranged a transfer of the invitation to me. The spirits themselves named the time of meeting, and I was conducted to the place at the day and hour appointed.

Absolute unbelief in the facts was by no means my condition of mind. On the contrary, I thought it probable that some physical principle, not evident to the spiritualists themselves, might underlie their manifestations. Extraordinary effects are produced by the accumulation of small impulses. Galileo set a heavy pendulum in motion by the well-timed puffs of his breath. Ellicot set one clock going by the ticks of another, even when the two clocks were separated by a wall. Preconceived notions can, moreover, vitiate, to an extraordinary degree, the testimony of even veracious persons. Hence my desire to witness those extraordinary phenomena, the existence of which seemed placed beyond a doubt by the known veracity of those who had witnessed and described them. The meeting took place at a private residence in the neighborhood of London. My host, his intelligent wife, and a gentleman who may be called X, were in the house when I arrived. I was informed that the "medium" had not yet made her appearance; that she was sensitive, and might resent suspicion. It was therefore requested that the tables and chairs should be examined before her arrival, in order to be assured that there was no trickery in the furniture. This was done; and I then first learned that my hospitable host had arranged that the séance should be a dinner party. This was to me an unusual form of investigation; but I accepted it, as one of the accidents of the occasion.

The "medium" arrived—a delicate-looking young lady, who appeared to have suffered much from ill health. I took her to dinner and sat close beside her. Facts were absent for a considerable time, a series of very wonderful narratives supplying their place. The duty of belief on testimony was frequently insisted on. X appeared to be a chosen spiritual agent, and told us many surprising things. He affirmed that when he took a pen in his hand an influence ran from his shoulder downward, and impelled him to write oracular sentences. I listened for a time, offering no observation. "And now," continued X, "this power has so risen as to reveal to me the thoughts of others. Only this morning I told a friend what he was thinking of, and what he intended to do during the day." Here, I thought, is something that can be at once tested. I said immediately to X: "If you wish to win your cause an apostle, who will proclaim your principles to the world without fear, tell me what I am now thinking of." X reddened, and did not tell me my thought.

Some time previously I had visited Baron Reichenbach, in Vienna, and I now asked the young lady who sat beside me, whether she could see any of the curious things which he describes—the light emitted by crystals, for example? Here is the conversation which followed, as extracted from my notes, written on the day following the séance:—

Medium—Oh, yes; but I see light around all bodies.

I—Even in perfect darkness?

Medium—Yes, I see luminous atmospheres around all people. The atmosphere which surrounds Mr. R. C. would fill this room with light.

I—You are aware of the effects ascribed by Baron Reichenbach to magnets?

Medium—Yes; but a magnet makes me terribly ill.

I—Am I to understand that, if this room were perfectly dark, you could tell whether it contained a magnet, without being informed of the fact?

Medium—I should know of its presence on entering the room.

I—How?

Medium—I should be rendered instantly ill.

I—How do you feel to-day?

Medium—Particularly well; I have not been so well for months.

I—Then, may I ask you whether there is, at the present moment, a magnet in my possession?

The young lady looked at me, blushed, and stammered, "No; I am not *en rapport* with you."

I sat at her right hand, and a left-hand pocket, within six inches of her person, contained a magnet.

Our host here deprecated discussion, as it "exhausted the 'medium.'" The wonderful narratives were resumed; but I had narratives of my own quite as wonderful. These spirits, indeed, seemed clumsy creations compared with those with which my own researches had made me familiar. I therefore began to match the wonders related to me by other wonders. A lady present discoursed on spiritual atmospheres, which she could see as beautiful colors when she closed her eyes. I professed myself able to see similar colors, and, more than that, to be able to see the interior of my own eyes. The medium affirmed that she could see actual waves of light coming from the sun. I retorted that men of science could tell the exact number of waves emitted

in a second, and also their exact length. The "medium" spoke of the performances of the spirits on musical instruments. I said that such performance was gross in comparison with a kind of music which had been discovered some time previously by a scientific man. Standing at a distance of twenty feet from a jet of gas, he could command the flame to emit a melodious note; it would obey, and continue its song for hours. So loud was the music emitted by the gas flame, that it might be heard by an assembly of a thousand people. These were acknowledged to be as great marvels as any of those of spiritdom. The spirits were then consulted, and I was pronounced to be a first-class "medium."

During this conversation a low knocking was heard from time to time under the table. These were the spirits' knocks. I was informed that one knock, in answer to a question, meant "No"; that two knocks meant "Not yet"; and that three knocks meant "Yes." In answer to the question whether I was a "medium," the response was three brisk and vigorous knocks. I noticed that the knocks issued from a particular locality, and therefore requested the spirits to be good enough to answer from another corner of the table. They did not comply; but I was assured that they would do it, and much more, by and by. The knocks continuing, I turned a wine glass upside down, and placed my ear upon it, as upon a stethoscope. The spirits seemed disconcerted by the act; they lost their playfulness, and did not quite recover it for a considerable time.

Somewhat weary of the proceedings, I once threw myself back against my chair, and gazed listlessly out of the window. While thus engaged, the table was rudely pushed. Attention was drawn to the wine, still oscillating in the glasses, and I was asked whether that was not convincing. I readily granted the fact of motion, and began to feel the delicacy of my position. There were several pairs of arms upon the table, and several pairs of legs under it; but how was I, without offense, to express the conviction which I really entertained? To ward off the difficulty, I again turned a wine glass upside down and rested my ear upon it. The rim of the glass was not level, and the hair on touching it caused it to vibrate and produce a peculiar buzzing sound. A perfectly candid and warm-hearted old gentleman at the opposite side of the table, whom I may call A, drew attention to the sound, and expressed his entire belief that it was spiritual. I, however, informed him that it was the moving hair acting on the glass. The explanation was not well received, and X, in a tone of severe pleasantry, demanded whether it was the hair that had moved the table. The promptness of my negative probably satisfied him that my notion was a very different one.

The superhuman power of the spirits was next dwelt upon. The strength of man, it was stated, was unavailing in opposition to theirs. No human power could prevent the table from moving when they pulled it. During the evening this pulling of the table occurred, or rather was attempted, three times. Twice the table moved when my attention was withdrawn from it; on a third occasion, I tried whether the act could be provoked by an assumed air of inattention. Grasping the table firmly between my knees, I threw myself back in the chair, and waited, with eyes fixed on vacancy, for the pull. It came. For some seconds it was pull spirit, hold muscle; the muscle, however, prevailed, and the table remained at rest. Up to the present moment, this interesting fact is known only to the particular spirit in question and myself.

A species of mental scene painting, with which my own pursuits had long rendered me familiar, was employed to figure the changes and distribution of spiritual power. The spirits were provided with atmospheres, which combined with and interpenetrated each other, considerable ingenuity being shown in demonstrating the necessity of time in effecting the adjustment of the atmospheres. In fact, just as in science, the senses, time, and space constituted the conditions of the phenomena. A rearrangement of our positions was proposed and carried out; and soon afterward my attention was drawn to a scarcely sensible vibration on the part of the table. Several persons were leaning on the table at the time, and I asked permission to touch the "medium's" hand. "Oh, I know I tremble," was her reply. Throwing one leg across the other, I accidentally nipped a muscle, and produced thereby an involuntary vibration of the free leg. This vibration, I knew, must be communicated to the floor, and thence to the chairs of all present. I therefore intentionally promoted it. My attention was promptly drawn to the motion, and a gentleman beside me, whose value as a witness I was particularly desirous to test, expressed his belief that it was out of the compass of human power to produce so strange a tremor. "I believe," he added earnestly, "that it is entirely the spirits' work."

"So do I," added, with heat, the candid and warm-hearted old gentleman A. "Why, sir," he continued, "I feel them at this moment shaking my chair." I stopped the motion of the leg. "Now, sir," A exclaimed, "they are gone." I began again, and A once more ejaculated. I could, however, notice that there were doubters present, who did not quite know what to think of the manifestations. I saw their perplexity; and, as there was sufficient reason to believe that the disclosure of the secret would simply provoke anger, I kept it to myself.

Again a period of conversation intervened, during which the spirits became animated. The evening was confessedly a dull one, but matters appeared to brighten towards its close. The spirits were requested to spell the name by which I am known in the heavenly world. Our host commenced repeating the alphabet, and when he reached the letter "P" a knock was heard. He began again, and the spirits knocked at the letter "O." I was puzzled, but waited for the end. The next letter knocked down was "E." I laughed, and remarked that the spirits were going to make a poet of me. Admonished for my levity, I was informed that the frame of mind proper for the occasion ought to have been superinduced by a perusal of the Bible immediately before the séance. The spelling, however, went on, and sure enough I came out a poet. But matters did not end here. Our host continued his repetition of the alphabet, and the next letter of the name proved to be "O." Here was manifestly an unfinished word; and the spirits were apparently in their most communicative mood. The knocks came from under the table, but no person present evinced the slightest desire to look under it. I asked whether I might go underneath; the permission was granted; so I crept under the table. Some tittered; but the candid old A exclaimed, "He has a right to look into the very dregs of it, to convince himself." Having pretty well assured myself that no sound could be produced under the table without its origin being revealed, I requested our host to continue his questions. He did so, but in vain. He adopted a tone of tender entreaty; but the "dear spirits" had become dumb dogs, and refused to be entreated. I continued under that table for at least a quarter of an hour, after which, with a feeling of despair as regards the prospects of humanity never before experienced, I regained my chair. Once there, the spirits resumed their loquacity, and dubbed me "Poet of Science."

This, then, is the result of an attempt made by a scientific man to look into these spiritual phenomena. It is not encouraging; and for this reason: The present promoters of spiritual phenomena divide themselves into two classes, one of which needs no demonstration, while the other is beyond the reach of proof. The victims like to believe, and they do not like to be undeceived. Science is perfectly powerless in the presence of this frame of mind. It is, moreover, a state perfectly compatible with extreme intellectual subtlety and a capacity for devising hypotheses which only require the hardihood engendered by strong conviction, or by callous mendacity, to render them impregnable. The logical feebleness of science is not sufficiently borne in mind. It keeps down the weed of superstition, not by logic, but by slowly rendering the mental soil unfit for its cultivation. When science appeals to uniform experience, the spiritualist will retort, "How do you know that a uniform experience will continue uniform? You tell me that the sun has risen for six thousand years; that is no proof that it will rise to-morrow; within the next twelve hours it may be puffed out by the Almighty." Taking this ground, a man may maintain the story of "Jack and the Bean-Stalk" in the face of all the science in the world. You urge, in vain, that science has given us all the knowledge of the universe which we now possess, while spiritualism has added nothing to that knowledge. The drugged soul is beyond the reach of reason. It is vain that impostors are exposed, and the special demon cast out. He has but slightly to change his shape, return to his house, and find it "empty, swept, and garnished."

From "Fragments of Science."

THE SUN AS THE SOURCE OF EARTHLY FORCES

AS SURELY as the force which moves a clock's hands is derived from the arm which winds up the clock, so surely is all terrestrial power drawn from the sun. Leaving out of account the eruptions of volcanoes, and the ebb and flow of the tides, every mechanical action on the earth's surface, every manifestation of power, organic and inorganic, vital and physical, is produced by the sun. His warmth keeps the sea liquid, and the atmosphere a gas, and all the storms which agitate both are blown by the mechanical force of the sun. He lifts the rivers and the glaciers up to the mountains; and thus the cataract and

the avalanche shoot with an energy derived immediately from him. Thunder and lightning are also his transmitted strength. Every fire that burns and every flame that glows dispenses light and heat which originally belonged to the sun. In these days, unhappily, the news of battle is familiar to us, but every shock, and every charge, is an application, or misapplication, of the mechanical force of the sun. He blows the trumpet, he urges the projectile, he bursts the bomb. And remember, this is not poetry, but rigid mechanical truth. He rears, as I have said, the whole vegetable world, and through it the animal; the lilies of the field are his workmanship, the verdure of the meadows, and the cattle upon a thousand hills. He forms the muscle, he urges the blood, he builds the brain. His fleetness is in the lion's foot; he springs in the panther; he soars in the eagle; he slides in the snake. He builds the forest and hews it down, the power which raised the tree, and which wields the ax, being one and the same. The clover sprouts and blossoms, and the scythe of the mower swings, by the operation of the same force. The sun digs the ore from our mines, he rolls the iron; he rivets the plates, he boils the water; he draws the train. He not only grows the cotton, but he spins the fibre and weaves the web. There is not a hammer raised, a wheel turned, or a shuttle thrown, that is not raised, and turned, and thrown by the sun. His energy is poured freely into space, but our world is a halting place where this energy is conditioned. Here the Proteus works his spells; the self-same essence takes a million shapes and hues, and finally dissolves into its primitive and almost formless form. The sun comes to us as heat; he quits us as heat; and between his entrance and departure the multiform powers of our globe appear. They are all special forms of solar power— the molds into which his strength is temporarily poured, in passing from its source through infinitude.

Presented rightly to the mind, the discoveries and generalizations of modern science constitute a poem more sublime than has ever yet been addressed to the intellect and imagination of man. The natural philosopher of to-day may dwell amid conceptions which beggar those of Milton. So great and grand are they, that, in the contemplation of them, a certain force of character is requisite to preserve us from bewilderment. Look at the integrated energies of our world—the stored power of our coal fields; our winds and rivers; our fleets, armies and guns. What are they? They are all generated by a portion of the sun's energy, which does not amount to an infinitesimal part of the whole. Multiplying our powers by millions of millions, we do not reach the sun's expenditure. And still, notwithstanding this enormous drain, in the lapse of human history we are unable to detect a diminution of his store. Measured by our largest terrestrial standards, such a reservoir of power is infinite; but it is our privilege to rise above these standards, and to regard the sun himself as a speck in infinite extension, —a mere drop in the universal sea. We analyze the space in which he is immersed, and which is the vehicle of his power. We pass to other systems and other suns, each pouring forth energy like our own, but still without infringement of the law, which reveals immutability in the midst of change, which recognizes incessant transference and conversion, but neither final gain nor loss. This law generalizes the aphorism of Solomon, that there is nothing new under the sun, by teaching us to detect everywhere, under its infinite variety of appearances, the same primeval force. To Nature nothing can be added; from Nature nothing can be taken away; the sum of her energies is constant, and the utmost man can do in the pursuit of physical truth, or in the application of physical knowledge, is to shift the constituents of the never-varying total, and out of one of them to form another. The law of conversation rigidly excludes both creation and annihilation. Waves may change to ripples, and ripples to waves,—magnitude may be substituted for number, and number for magnitude,—asteroids may aggregate to suns, suns may resolve themselves into floræ and faunæ, and floræ and faunæ melt in air,—the flux of power is eternally the same. It rolls in music through the ages, and all terrestrial energy,—the manifestations of life, as well as the display of phenomena, are but the modulations of its rhythm.

From "Heat as a Mode of Motion."

x—242

FRANÇOIS MARIE AROUET DE VOLTAIRE

(1694-1778)

VOLTAIRE was born in Paris, November 21th, 1694. His father, François Arouet, was a notary, and the family to which he belonged were middle-class people in good circumstances. The aristocratic "de Voltaire," which François Marie added to the family name for purposes of his own, has obscured the respectable Arouets, but except that they were middle-class people, he had no reason to be ashamed of them. As a result of the friendship of the Abbé de Châteauneuf for his mother, he was carefully educated in what was then the Jesuit Collège Louis-le-Grand. While still at school he showed unmistakable indications of genius. His wit, his verses, and the influence of his Jesuit patrons secured him the favor of court circles in Paris, and he began the remarkable career as a court favorite and iconoclast, poet, dramatist, historian, philosopher, buffoon, and reformer, which has had no parallel in modern times. Often persecuted and sometimes imprisoned for his iconoclastic utterances, he had no more hesitation in recanting his opinion to escape martyrdom than he had in returning to it and reiterating it as soon as he was at a safe distance from his persecutors. His writings in prose and verse, formidable in quantity as in their general tendencies, may not have been directed by a common and well-defined purpose, but they were all the result of the same general impulse—an impulse which moved in him and through him as it did in his generation, impelling France towards the overthrow of feudal aristocracy and absolute monarchy. From July, 1750, to March, 1753, Voltaire lived with Frederick the Great, who had been his warm admirer; but when the two philosophers became better acquainted with each other, they found it impossible to reconcile conflicting details in their plans for a really systematic universe, and as neither of them was accustomed to giving up his own way, they parted in anger, and Frederick was ungrateful and unphilosophical enough to have his instructor in philosophy arrested. The arrest, which occurred while Voltaire was returning to France, was not intended to be anything more than a piece of friendly insult, however, and, after being sufficiently maltreated at Frankfort, Voltaire was released and allowed to proceed to France, where, after several years of unsettled life, he purchased the estate of Ferney. There he lived from 1758 until his death, which

occurred May 30th, 1778, while he was visiting his enthusiastic friends in Paris. It is impossible to estimate the extent of Voltaire's influence, and it would be wearisome to attempt to catalogue his works. In the edition of "Kehl," 1784, and of "Paris," 1829, they make seventy-two volumes. The visit to England which resulted in some of the best of his literary essays ("Letters on England") was made in 1726, and he remained until 1729. Making the acquaintance of Young, Congreve, Pope, and Bolingbroke, he formed his taste by the study of the masters of English literature. Of Voltaire's morals, his admirers are not anxious to speak at unnecessary length. That his influence in forcing changes necessary for progress was great, his worst enemies have long ago conceded. His character as a reformer might have become utterly contemptible if he had not made his influence irresistible. "He could not bring himself to testify in any open and dangerous manner for what he thought to be truth," writes Prof. Saintsbury, with a clear understanding of his vital weakness of character; and we have a valid suggestion of the secret of his strength when Saintsbury adds that he could not "refrain from attacking by every artifice and covert enginery what he thought to be falsehood."

W. V. B.

ON LORD BACON

NOT long since the trite and frivolous question following was debated in a very polite and learned company, viz., Who was the greatest man, Cæsar, Alexander, Tamerlane, Cromwell, etc.?

Somebody answered that Sir Isaac Newton excelled them all. The gentleman's assertion was very just; for if true greatness consists in having received from heaven a mighty genius, and in having employed it to enlighten our own mind and that of others, a man like Sir Isaac Newton, whose equal is hardly found in a thousand years, is the truly great man. And those politicians and conquerors (and all ages produce some) were generally so many illustrious wicked men. That man claims our respect who commands over the minds of the rest of the world by the force of truth, not those who enslave their fellow-creatures; he who is acquainted with the universe, not they who deface it.

Since, therefore, you desire me to give you an account of the famous personages whom England has given birth to, I shall begin with Lord Bacon, Mr. Locke, Sir Isaac Newton, etc. Afterwards the warriors and ministers of state shall come in their order.

I must begin with the celebrated Viscount Verulam, known in Europe by the name of Bacon, which was that of his family. His father had been Lord Keeper, and himself was a great many years Lord Chancellor under King James I. Nevertheless, amidst the intrigues of a court, and the affairs of his exalted employment, which alone were enough to engross his whole time, he yet found so much leisure for study as to make himself a great philosopher, a good historian, and an elegant writer; and a still more surprising circumstance is that he lived in an age in which the art of writing justly and elegantly was little known, much less true philosophy. Lord Bacon, as is the fate of man, was more esteemed after his death than in his lifetime. His enemies were in the British court, and his admirers were foreigners.

When the Marquis d'Effiat attended in England upon the Princess Henrietta Maria, daughter to Henry IV., whom King Charles I. had married, that minister went and visited Lord Bacon, who, being at that time sick in his bed, received him with the curtains shut close. "You resemble the angels," says the Marquis to him; "we hear those beings spoken of perpetually, and we believe them superior to men, but are never allowed the consolation to see them."

You know that this great man was accused of a crime very unbecoming a philosopher,—I mean bribery and extortion. You know that he was sentenced by the House of Lords to pay a fine of about four hundred thousand French livres, to lose his peerage and his dignity of chancellor; but in the present age the English revere his memory to such a degree, that they will scarce allow him to have been guilty. In case you should ask what are my thoughts on this head, I shall answer you in the words which I heard Lord Bolingbroke use on another occasion. Several gentlemen were speaking, in his company, of the avarice with which the late Duke of Marlborough had been charged, some examples whereof being given, Lord Bolingbroke was appealed to (who, having been in the opposite party, might perhaps, without the imputation of indecency, have been allowed to clear up that matter): "He was so great a man," replied his lordship, "that I have forgot his vices."

I shall therefore confine myself to those things which so justly gained Lord Bacon the esteem of all Europe.

The most singular and the best of all his pieces is that which, at this time, is the most useless and the least read.—I mean his

"Novum Scientiarum Organum." This is the scaffold with which the new philosophy was raised; and when the edifice was built, part of it, at least the scaffold was no longer of service.

Lord Bacon was not yet acquainted with nature, but then he knew, and pointed out, the several paths that lead to it. He had despised in his younger years the thing called philosophy in the universities, and did all that lay in his power to prevent those societies of men instituted to improve human reason from depraving it by their quiddities, their horrors of the vacuum, their substantial forms, and all those impertinent terms which not only ignorance had rendered venerable, but which had been made sacred by their being ridiculously blended with religion.

He is the father of experimental philosophy. It must, indeed, be confessed that very surprising secrets had been found out before his time — the sea compass, printing, engraving on copper plates, oil painting, looking-glasses; the art of restoring, in some measure, old men to their sight by spectacles; gunpowder, etc., had been discovered. A new world had been fought for, found, and conquered. Would not one suppose that these sublime discoveries had been made by the greatest philosophers, and in ages much more enlightened than the present? But it was far otherwise; all these great changes happened in the most stupid and barbarous times. Chance only gave birth to most of those inventions; and it is very probable that what is called chance contributed very much to the discovery of America; at least it has been always thought that Christopher Columbus undertook his voyage merely on the relation of a captain of a ship which a storm had driven as far westward as the Caribbean Island. Be this as it will, men had sailed round the world, and could destroy cities by an artificial thunder more dreadful than the real one; but, then, they were not acquainted with the circulation of the blood, the weight of the air, the laws of motion, light, the number of our planets, etc. And a man who maintained a thesis on Aristotle's "Categories," on the universals *a parte rei*, or such-like nonsense, was looked upon as a prodigy.

The most astonishing, the most useful inventions, are not those which reflect the greatest honor on the human mind. It is to a mechanical instinct, which is found in many men, and not to true philosophy, that most arts owe their origin.

The discovery of fire, the art of making bread, of melting and preparing metals, of building houses, and the invention of the shuttle, are infinitely more beneficial to mankind than printing or the sea compass; and yet these arts were invented by uncultivated, savage men.

What a prodigious use the Greeks and Romans made afterwards of mechanics! Nevertheless, they believed that there were crystal heavens, that the stars were small lamps which sometimes fell into the sea, and one of their greatest philosophers, after long researches, found that the stars were so many flints which had been detached from the earth.

In a word, no one before Lord Bacon was acquainted with experimental philosophy, nor with the several physical experiments which have been made since his time. Scarce one of them but is hinted at in his work, and he himself had made several. He made a kind of pneumatic engine, by which he guessed the elasticity of the air. He approached on all sides, as it were, to the discovery of its weight, and had very near attained it, but some time after Torricelli seized upon this truth. In a little time experimental philosophy began to be cultivated on a sudden in most parts of Europe. It was a hidden treasure which Lord Bacon had some notion of, and which all the philosophers, encouraged by his promises, endeavored to dig up.

But that which surprised me most was to read in his work, in express terms, the new attraction, the invention of which is ascribed to Sir Isaac Newton.

We must search, says Lord Bacon, whether there may not be a kind of magnetic power which operates between the earth and heavy bodies, between the moon and the ocean, between the planets, etc. In another place he says, either heavy bodies must be carried towards the centre of the earth, or must be reciprocally attracted by it; and in the latter case it is evident that the nearer bodies, in their falling, draw towards the earth, the stronger they will attract one another. We must, says he, make an experiment to see whether the same clock will go faster on the top of a mountain or at the bottom of a mine; whether the strength of the weights decreases on the mountain and increases in the mine. It is probable that the earth has a true attractive power.

This forerunner in philosophy was also an elegant writer, a historian, and a wit.

His moral essays are greatly esteemed, but they were drawn up in the view of instructing rather than of pleasing; and, as

they are not a satire upon mankind, like Rochefoucauld's "Maxims," nor written upon a skeptical plan, like Montaigne's "Essays," they are not so much read as those two ingenious authors.

His "History of Henry VII." was looked upon as a masterpiece, but how is it possible that some persons can presume to compare so little a work with the history of our illustrious Thuanus?

Speaking about the famous impostor Perkin, son to a converted Jew, who assumed boldly the name and title of Richard IV., King of England, at the instigation of the Duchess of Burgundy, and who disputed the crown with Henry VII., Lord Bacon writes as follows:—

"At this time the King began again to be haunted with sprites, by the magic and curious arts of the Lady Margaret, who raised up the ghost of Richard, Duke of York, second son to King Edward IV., to walk and vex the King.

"After such time as she (Margaret of Burgundy) thought he (Perkin Warbeck) was perfect in his lesson, she began to cast with herself from what coast this blazing star should first appear, and at what time it must be upon the horizon of Ireland; for there had the like meteor strong influence before."

Methinks our sagacious Thuanus does not give in to such fustian, which formerly was looked upon as sublime, but in this age is justly called nonsense.

Complete. Number XII. of "Letters on England."

ON THE REGARD THAT OUGHT TO BE SHOWN TO MEN OF LETTERS

NEITHER the English nor any other people have foundations established in favor of the polite arts like those in France. There are universities in most countries, but it is in France only that we meet with so beneficial an encouragement for astronomy and all parts of the mathematics, for physic, for researches into antiquity, for painting, sculpture, and architecture. Louis XIV. has immortalized his name by these several foundations, and this immortality did not cost him two hundred thousand livres a year.

I must confess that one of the things I very much wonder at is that as the Parliament of Great Britain have promised a reward of £20,000 to any person who may discover the longitude, they should never have once thought to imitate Louis XIV. in his munificence with regard to the arts and sciences.

Merit, indeed, meets in England with rewards of another kind, which redound more to the honor of the nation. The English have so great a veneration for exalted talents, that a man of merit in their country is always sure of making his fortune. Mr. Addison in France would have been elected a member of one of the academies, and, by the credit of some women, might have obtained a yearly pension of twelve hundred livres, or else might have been imprisoned in the Bastile, upon pretense that certain strokes in his tragedy of Cato had been discovered which glanced at the porter of some man in power. Mr. Addison was raised to the post of Secretary of State in England. Sir Isaac Newton was made Master of the Royal Mint. Mr. Congreve had a considerable employment. Mr. Prior was Plenipotentiary. Dr. Swift is Dean of St. Patrick's in Dublin, and is more revered in Ireland than the Primate himself. The religion which Mr. Pope professes excludes him, indeed, from preferments of every kind, but then it did not prevent his gaining two hundred thousand livres by his excellent translation of Homer. I myself saw a long time in France the author of "Rhadamistus" ready to perish for hunger. And the son of one of the greatest men our country ever gave birth to, and who was beginning to run the noble career which his father had set him, would have been reduced to the extremes of misery had he not been patronized by Monsieur Fagon.

But the circumstance which mostly encourages the arts in England is the great veneration which is paid them. The picture of the Prime Minister hangs over the chimney of his own closet, but I have seen that of Mr. Pope in twenty noblemen's houses. Sir Isaac Newton was revered in his lifetime, and had a due respect paid to him after his death,—the greatest men in the nation disputing who should have the honor of holding up his pall. Go into Westminster Abbey, and you will find that what raises the admiration of the spectator is not the mausoleums of the English kings, but the monuments which the gratitude of the nation has erected to perpetuate the memory of those illustrious men who contributed to its glory. We view their statues in that abbey in the same manner as those of Sophocles, Plato, and other immortal personages were viewed in Athens; and I am persuaded that the bare sight of those glorious monuments has fired more than one breast, and been the occasion of their becoming great men.

The English have even been reproached with paying too extravagant honors to mere merit, and censured for interring the celebrated actress Mrs. Oldfield in Westminster Abbey, with almost the same pomp as Sir Isaac Newton. Some pretend that the English had paid her these great funeral honors purposely to make us more strongly sensible of the barbarity and injustice which they object to in us, for having buried Mademoiselle Le Couvreur ignominiously in the fields.

But be assured from me that the English were prompted by no other principle in burying Mrs. Oldfield in Westminster Abbey than their good sense. They are far from being so ridiculous as to brand with infamy an art which has immortalized a Euripides and a Sophocles; or to exclude from the body of their citizens a set of people whose business is to set off with the utmost grace of speech and action those pieces which the nation is proud of.

Under the reign of Charles I. and in the beginning of the civil wars raised by a number of rigid fanatics, who at last were the victims to it, a great many pieces were published against theatrical and other shows, which were attacked with the greater virulence because that monarch and his queen, daughter to Henry I. of France, were passionately fond of them.

One Mr. Prynne, a man of most furiously scrupulous principles, who would have thought himself damned had he worn a cassock instead of a short cloak, and have been glad to see one half of mankind cut the other to pieces for the glory of God, and the *Propaganda Fide*, took it into his head to write a most wretched satire against some pretty good comedies, which were exhibited very innocently every night before their majesties. He quoted the authority of the Rabbis, and some passages from St. Bonaventura, to prove that the "Œdipus" of Sophocles was the work of the evil spirit; that Terence was excommunicated *ipso facto;* and added that doubtless Brutus, who was a very severe Jansenist, assassinated Julius Cæsar for no other reason but because he, who was Pontifex Maximus, presumed to write a tragedy the subject of which was "Œpidus." Lastly, he declared that all who frequented the theatre were excommunicated, as they thereby renounced their baptism. This was casting the highest insult on the king and all the royal family; and as the English loved their prince at that time, they could not bear to hear a

writer talk of excommunicating him, though they themselves afterwards cut his head off. Prynne was summoned to appear before the Star Chamber; his wonderful book, from which Father Lebrun stole his, was sentenced to be burned by the common hangman, and himself to lose his ears. His trial is now extant.

The Italians are far from attempting to cast a blemish on the opera, or to excommunicate Signor Senesino or Signora Cuzzoni. With regard to myself, I could presume to wish that the magistrates would suppress I know not what contemptible pieces written against the stage. For when the English and Italians hear that we brand with the greatest mark of infamy an art in which we excel; that we excommunicate persons who receive salaries from the king; that we condemn as impious a spectacle exhibited in convents and monasteries; that we dishonor sports in which Louis XIV. and Louis XV. performed as actors; that we give the title of the devil's works to pieces which are received by magistrates of the most severe character, and represented before a virtuous queen; when, I say, foreigners are told of this insolent conduct, this contempt for the royal authority, and this Gothic rusticity which some presume to call Christian severity, what idea must they entertain of our nation? And how will it be possible for them to conceive, either that our laws give a sanction to an art which is declared infamous, or that some persons dare to stamp with infamy an art which receives a sanction from the laws, is rewarded by kings, cultivated and encouraged by the greatest men, and admired by whole nations?` And that Father Lebrun's impertinent libel against the stage is seen in a bookseller's shop, standing the very next to the immortal labors of Racine, of Corneille, of Molière, etc.?

Complete. Number XXIII. of "Letters on England." Morley's edition.

RICHARD WAGNER

(1813-1883)

WAGNER's essays and treatises on music, art, literature, and philosophy have been collected into ten thick volumes which have genius enough in them to have made him famous had he been unknown as a musician. They have, too, all the originality and aggressive individuality which those who refuse to admire his music call eccentricity. By no means a great master of prose style, Wagner is at all times a great man who lacks little of being a great thinker. No matter how obscure his sentences may become at times, it is never safe to leave one of them without mastering his meaning, as far as it is possible to do so. His whole life is full of meaning, and everything he writes is full of his life purposes.

Born in Leipsic, May 22d, 1813, he was educated in the University of his native city, where also he began the systematic study of music. In 1833 he became chorus master in the theatre at Würzburg. From 1834 to 1842 he lived and worked successively at Magdeburg, Königsburg, and Paris. In 1843 he was appointed court Kapellmeister at Dresden and remained there until 1849, when he fled to Paris to escape arrest on a charge of complicity in the revolutionary movement of that year. After living in Zurich, London, and Paris until 1861, he returned to Germany and lived a comparatively peaceful life as a composer and musical director in different German cities, until his death, February 13th, 1883. He was twice married, his second wife being Liszt's daughter, Cosima. He took up his residence at Bayreuth in 1872, and in 1876 completed there the theatre which he opened with the performance of the famous "Nibelungen" tetralogy. — composition in which, as in all his works, he seems to have attempted to give expression to the ethnical impulses which have moved the Teutonic race through the whole course of its history.

NATURE, MAN, AND ART

AS MAN stands to Nature, so stands Art to Man. When Nature had developed in herself those attributes which included the conditions for the existence of Man, then Man spontaneously evolved. In like manner, as soon as human life had engendered from itself the conditions for the manifestation of Art-work, this too stepped self-begotten into life.

Nature engenders her myriad forms without caprice or arbitrary aim ("*absichtlos und unwillkurlich*"), according to her need ("*Bedurfniss*"), and therefore of necessity ("*Nothwendigkeit*"). This same necessity is the generative and formative force of human life. Only that which is uncapricious and unarbitrary can spring from a real need; but on need alone is based the very principle of Life.

Man only recognizes Nature's necessity by observing the harmonious connection of all her phenomena; so long as he does not grasp the latter, she seems to him Caprice.

From the moment when man perceived the difference between himself and nature, and thus commenced his own development as man, by breaking loose from the unconsciousness of natural animal life and passing over into conscious life,—when he thus looked Nature in the face and from the first feelings of his dependence on her, thereby aroused, evolved the faculty of thought, —from that moment did error begin, as the earliest utterance of consciousness. But Error is the mother of Knowledge; and the history of the birth of Knowledge out of Error is the history of the human race, from the myths of primal ages down to the present day.

Man erred, from the time when he set the cause of Nature's workings outside the bounds of Nature's self, and for the physical phenomena subsumed a super-physical, anthropomorphic, and arbitrary cause; when he took the endless harmony of her unconscious, instinctive energy for the arbitrary demeanor of disconnected finite forces. Knowledge consists in the hating of this error, in fathoming the necessity of phenomena whose underlying basis had appeared to us Caprice.

Through this knowledge does Nature grow conscious of herself; and verily by man himself, who only through discriminating between himself and Nature has attained that point where he can apprehend her, by making her his "object." But this distinction is merged once more, when man recognizes the essence of nature as his very own, and perceives the same necessity in all the elements and lives around him, and therefore in his own existence no less than in Nature's being; thus not only recognizing the mutual bond of union between all natural phenomena, but also his own community with Nature.

If Nature then, by her solidarity with man, attains in man her consciousness, and if man's life is the very activation of this consciousness,—as it were, the portraiture in brief of Nature,—so does man's life itself gain understanding by means of Science, which makes this human life in turn an object of experience. But the activation of the consciousness attained by Science, the portrayal of the Life that it has learned to know, the impress of this life's necessity and truth, is—Art.

Man will never be that which he can and should be until his life is a true mirror of nature, a conscious following of the only real necessity, the inner natural necessity, and is no longer held in subjugation to an outer artificial counterfeit,—which is thus no necessary, but an arbitrary power. Then first will man become a living man; whereas till now he carries on a mere existence, dictated by the maxims of this or that Religion, Nationality, or State. In like manner will Art not be the thing she can and should be, until she is or can be the true, conscious image and exponent of the real Man, and of man's genuine, nature-bidden life; until she therefore need no longer borrow the conditions of her being from the errors, perversities, and unnatural distortions of our modern life.

The real man will, therefore, never be forthcoming, until true human nature, and not the arbitrary statutes of the state, shall model and ordain his life; while real art will never live, until its embodiments need be subject only to the laws of Nature, and not to the despotic whims of Mode. For as man only then becomes free, when he gains the glad consciousness of his oneness with Nature; so does Art only then gain freedom, when she has no more to blush for her affinity with actual life. But only in the joyous consciousness of his oneness with Nature does man subdue his dependence on her; while Art can only overcome her dependence upon life through her oneness with the life of free and genuine men.

Complete.   "Man and Art," § 1.

LIFE, SCIENCE, AND ART

WHILE man involuntarily molds his life according to the notions he has gathered from his arbitrary views of nature, and embalms their intuitive expression in Religion, these notions become for him in Science the subject of conscious, intentional review and scrutiny.

redemption of the artist; the uprootal of the final trace of busy, purposed choice; the confident determination of what was hitherto a mere imagining; the enfranchisement of thought in sense; the assuagement of the life-need in life itself.

The Art-work, thus conceived as an immediate vital act, is therewith the perfect reconcilement of science with life, the laurel wreath which the vanquished, redeemed by her defeat, reaches in joyous homage to her acknowledged victor.

Complete.   "Man and Art," § 2.

The path of Science lies from error to knowledge, from fancy ("*Vorstellung*") to reality, from Religion to Nature. In the beginning of Science, therefore, Man stands toward life in the same relation as he stood towards the phenomena of Nature when he first commenced to part his life from hers. Science takes over the arbitrary concepts of the human brain, in their totality; while, by her side, life follows in its totality the instinctive evolution of necessity. Science thus bears the burden of the sins of life, and expiates them by her own self-abrogation; she ends in her direct antithesis, in the knowledge of nature, in the recognition of the unconscious, instinctive, and therefore real, inevitable, and physical. The character of science is therefore finite; that of life, unending; just as error is of time, but truth eternal. But that alone is true and living which is sentient, and hearkens to the terms of physicality (*Sinnlichkeit*). Error's crowning folly is the arrogance of Science in renouncing and contemning the world of sense (*Sinnlichkeit*); whereas the highest victory of Science is her self-accomplished crushing of this arrogance, in the acknowledgment of the teaching of the senses.

The end of Science is the justifying of the unconscious, the giving of self-consciousness to life, the reinstatement of the senses in their perceptive rights, the sinking of caprice in the world-will ("*Wollen*") of necessity. Science is therefore the vehicle of knowledge, her procedure mediate, her goal an intermediation; but life is the great ultimate, a law unto itself. As science melts away into the recognition of the ultimate and self-determinate reality of actual life itself, so does this avowal win its frankest, most direct expression in art, or rather in the work of art.

True that the artist does not at first proceed directly; he certainly sets about his work in an arbitrary, selective, and meditating mood. But while he plays the go-between and picks and chooses, the product of his energy is not as yet the work of art; nay, his procedure is the rather that of science, who seeks and probes, and therefore errs in her caprice. Only when his choice is made, when this choice was born from pure necessity,—when thus the artist has found himself again in the subject of his choice, as perfected man finds his true self in Nature,—then steps the Art-work into life, then first is it a real thing, a self-conditioned and immediate entity.

The actual Art-work, that is, its immediate physical portrayal, in the moment of its liveliest embodiment, is therefore the only true

ALFRED RUSSEL WALLACE

(1822–)

ALFRED RUSSEL WALLACE, who ranks with Darwin as an expounder of the theory of Evolution through Natural Selection, was born in Monmouthshire, England, January 8th, 1822. He was an architect by profession, but in 1845 he gave up everything else for the study of natural history, to which he devoted his life. After travel and scientific research in South America and the Malay Archipelago, he prepared a paper "On the Tendency of Varieties to Depart Indefinitely from the Original Type," which was read July 1st, 1858. Darwin's paper on the same subject appeared simultaneously with it. The two naturalists, working under a common impulse and following parallel lines of investigation, reached a similar conclusion and continued thereafter to co-operate in developing their joint theory. Wallace's bent was more towards original investigation than Darwin's, whose greatest successes are due to his genius for co-ordinating and comprehending the material accumulated for him by others. Among Wallace's notable publications are "The Malay Archipelago," 1869; "Contributions to the Theory of Natural Selection," 1870; "Tropical Nature," 1878; and "Land Nationalization," 1882.

THE LIKENESS OF MONKEYS TO MEN

IF THE skeletons of an orang-outang and a chimpanzee be compared with that of a man, there will be the most wonderful resemblance, together with a very marked diversity. Bone for bone, throughout the whole structure, will be found to agree in general form, position, and function, the only absolute differences being that the orang has nine wrist bones, whereas man and the chimpanzee have but eight; and the chimpanzee has thirteen pairs of ribs, whereas the orang, like man, has but twelve. With these two exceptions, the differences are those of shape, proportion, and direction only, though the resulting differences in the external form and motions are very considerable. The greatest of these are, that the feet of the anthropoid or man-like apes, as well as those of all monkeys, are formed like hands, with large opposable thumbs fitted to grasp the branches of trees, but unsuitable for erect walking, while the hands have small small thumbs, but very long and powerful fingers, forming a hook rather than a hand adapted for climbing up trees and suspending the whole weight from horizontal branches. The almost complete identity of the skeleton, however, and the close similarity of the muscles and of all the internal organs, have produced that str.x-ing and ludicrous resemblance to man which every one recogni es in these higher apes and, in a less degree, in the whole mon.ey tribe; the face and features, the motions, attitudes, and gestures being often a strange caricature of humanity. Let us, then, examine a little more closely in what the resemblance consists, and how far, and to what extent, these animals really differ from us.

Besides the face, which is often wonderfully human — although the absence of any protuberant nose gives it often a curiously infantile aspect, monkeys, and especially apes, resemble us most closely in the hand and arm. The hand has well-formed fingers with nails, and the skin of the palm is lined and furrowed like our own. The thumb is, however, smaller and weaker than ours, and is not so much used in taking hold of anything. The monkey's hand is, therefore, not so well adapted as that of man for a variety of purposes, and cannot be applied with such precision in holding small objects, while it is unsuitable for performing delicate operations such as tying a knot or writing with a pen. A monkey does not take hold of a nut with its forefinger and thumb as we do, but grasps it between the fingers and the palm in a clumsy way, just as a baby does before it has acquired the proper use of its hand. Two groups of monkeys — one in Africa and one in South America — have no thumbs on their hands, and yet they do not seem to be in any respect inferior to other kinds which possess it. In most of the American monkeys the thumb bends in the same direction as the fingers, and in none is it so perfectly opposed to the fingers as our thumbs are; and all these circumstances show that the hand of the monkey is, both structurally and functionally, a very different and very inferior organ to that of man, since it is not applied to similar purposes, nor is it capable of being so applied.

When we look at the feet of monkeys we find a still greater difference, for these have much larger and more opposable thumbs and are therefore more like our hands; and this is the case with all monkeys, so that even those which have no thumbs on their

x—243

hands or have them small and weak and parallel to the fingers, have always large and well-formed thumbs on their feet. It was on account of this peculiarity that the great French naturalist, Cuvier, named the whole group of monkeys Quadrumana, or four-handed animals, because, besides the two hands on their fore limbs, they have also two hands in place of feet on their hind limbs. Modern naturalists have given up the use of this term, because they say that the hind extremities of all monkeys are really feet, only these feet are shaped like hands; but this is a point of anatomy, or rather of nomenclature, which we need not here discuss.

Let us, however, before going further, inquire into the purpose and use of this peculiarity, and we shall then see that it is simply an adaptation to the mode of life of the animals which possess it. Monkeys, as a rule, live in trees, and are especially abundant in the great tropical forests. They feed chiefly upon fruits, and occasionally eat insects and birds' eggs, as well as young birds, all of which they find in the trees; and, as they have no occasion to come down to the ground, they travel from tree to tree by jumping or swinging, and thus pass the greater part of their lives entirely among the leafy branches of lofty trees. For such a mode of existence, they require to be able to move with perfect ease upon large or small branches, and to climb up rapidly from one bough to another. As they use their hands for gathering fruit and catching insects or birds, they require some means of holding on with their feet, otherwise they would be liable to continual falls, and they are able to do this by means of their long finger-like toes and large opposable thumbs, which grasp a branch almost as securely as a bird grasps its perch. The true hands, on the contrary, are used chiefly to climb with, and to swing the whole weight of the body from one branch or one tree to another, and for this purpose the fingers are very long and strong, and in many species they are further strengthened by being partially joined together, as if the skin of our fingers grew together as far as the knuckles. This shows that the separate action of the fingers, which is so important to us, is little required by monkeys, whose hand is really an organ for climbing and seizing food, while their foot is required to support them firmly in any position on the branches of trees, and for this purpose it has become modified into a large and powerful grasping hand.

Another striking difference between monkeys and men is that the former never walk with ease in an erect posture, but always use their arms in climbing or in walking on all fours like most quadrupeds. The monkeys that we see in the streets dressed up and walking erect only do so after much drilling and teaching, just as dogs may be taught to walk in the same way; and the posture is almost as unnatural to the one animal as it is to the other. The largest and most manlike of the apes — the gorilla, chimpanzee, and orang-outang — also walk usually on all fours; but in these the arms are so long and the legs so short that the body appears half erect when walking; and they have the habit of resting on the knuckles of the hands, not on the palms like the smaller monkeys, whose arms and legs are more nearly of an equal length, which tends still further to give them a semi-erect position. Still, they are never known to walk of their own accord on their hind legs only, though they can do so for short distances, and the story of their using a stick and walking erect by its help in the wild state is not true. Monkeys, then, are both four-handed and four-footed beasts; they possess four hands formed very much like our hands, and capable of picking up or holding any small object in the same manner; but they are also four-footed, because they use all four limbs for the purpose of walking, running, or climbing; and, being adapted to this double purpose, the hands want the delicacy of touch and the freedom as well as the precision of movement which ours possess. Man alone is so constructed that he walks erect with perfect ease, and has his hands free for any use to which he wishes to apply them; and this is the great and essential bodily distinction between monkeys and men.

From the Contemporary Review.

HORACE WALPOLE

(1717-1797)

HORACE WALPOLE, forgotten as the fourth Earl of Orford, but remembered as the author of "The Castle of Otranto," was born in London, October 5th, 1717. After leaving Cambridge, he traveled on the Continent, accompanied by the poet Gray; and before returning to England, spent a year at Florence. In 1741 he entered Parliament as a Liberal, but his opponents have not neglected to record that he secured lucrative sinecures through his family influence and used the revenues from them to enlarge and adorn his celebrated house on Strawberry Hill. "The Castle of Otranto," by which he is best remembered, appeared in 1765. His "Anecdotes of Painting in England" were published between 1762 and 1771. He died March 2d, 1797. The "Elegant Epistle" intended for posterity, but pretended to be written for the sole benefit of some convenient acquaintance, was a favorite recreation of eighteenth-century "wits." Walpole left a notable collection of such "Letters," an edition of which, edited by Cunningham, appeared in 1857-59.

WILLIAM HOGARTH

HOGARTH was born in the parish of St. Bartholomew, London, the son of a low tradesman, who bound him to a mean engraver of arms* on plate; but before his time was expired he felt the impulse of genius, and felt it directed him to painting, though little apprised at that time of the mode nature had intended he should pursue. His apprenticeship was no sooner expired than he entered into the academy in St. Martin's Lane, and studied drawing from the life, in which he never attained to great excellence. It was character, the passions, the soul, that his genius was given him to copy. In coloring he proved no greater a master; his force lay in expression, not in tints and chiaroscuro. At first he worked for booksellers, and designed and engraved plates for several books; and, which is extraordi-

* This is wrong; it was to Mr. Gamble, an eminent silversmith. Nichol's "Biography."

nary, no symptom of genius dawned in those plates. His "Hudibras" was the first of his works that marked him as a man above the common; yet what made him then noticed now surprises us, to find so little humor in an undertaking so congenial to his talents. On the success, however, of those plates, he commenced painter, a painter of portraits: the most ill-suited employment imaginable to a man whose turn certainly was not flattery, nor his talent adapted to look on vanity without a sneer. Yet his facility in catching a likeness, and the method he chose of painting families and conversations in small, then a novelty, drew him prodigious business for some time. It did not last: either from his applying to the real bent of his disposition, or from his customers apprehending that a satirist was too formidable a confessor for the devotees of self-love. He had already dropped a few of his smaller prints on some reigning follies; but as the dates are wanting on most of them, I cannot ascertain which, though those on the South Sea and "Rabbit Woman" prove that he had early discovered his talent for ridicule, though he did not then think of building his reputation or fortune on its powers.

His "Midnight Modern Conversation" was the first work that showed his command of character; but it was "The Harlot's Progress," published in 1729 or 1730, that established his fame. The pictures were scarce finished, and no sooner exhibited to the public, and the subscription opened, than above twelve hundred names were entered on his book. The familiarity of the subject and the propriety of the execution made it tasted by all ranks of people. Every engraver set himself to copy it, and thousands of imitations were dispersed all over the kingdom. It was made into a pantomime, and performed on the stage. The "Rake's Progress," perhaps superior, had not so much success, from want of novelty; nor, indeed, is the print of "The Arrest" equal in merit to the others.

The curtain was now drawn aside, and his genius stood displayed in its full lustre. From time to time he continued to give those works that should be immortal, if the nature of his art will allow it. Even the receipts for his subscriptions had wit in them. Many of his plates he engraved himself, and often expunged faces etched by his assistants when they had not done justice to his ideas.

Not content with shining in a path untrodden before, he was ambitious of distinguishing himself as a painter of history. But

not only his coloring and drawing rendered him unequal to the task; the genius that had entered so feelingly into the calamities and crimes of familiar life deserted him in a walk that called for dignity and grace. The burlesque turn of his mind mixed itself with the most serious subjects. In his "Danaë," the old nurse tries a coin of the golden shower with her teeth to see if it is true gold; in the "Pool of Bethesda," a servant of a rich ulcerated lady beats back a poor man that sought the same celestial remedy. Both circumstances are justly thought, but rather too ludicrous. It is a much more capital fault that "Danaë" herself is a mere nymph of Drury. He seems to have conceived no higher idea of beauty.

So little had he eyes to his own deficiencies, that he believed he had discovered the principle of grace. With the enthusiasm of a discoverer he cried, "Eureka!" This was his famous line of beauty, the groundwork of his "Analysis," a book that has many sensible hints and observations, but that did not carry the conviction nor meet the universal acquiescence he expected. As he treated his contemporaries with scorn, they triumphed over this publication, and imitated him to expose him. Many wretched burlesque prints came out to ridicule his system. There was a better answer to it in one of the two prints that he gave to illustrate his hypothesis. In "The Ball," had he confined himself to such outlines as compose awkwardness and deformity, he would have proved half his assertion; but he has added two samples of grace in a young lord and lady that are strikingly stiff and affected. They are a Bath beau and a country beauty.

But this was the failing of a visionary. He fell afterwards into a grosser mistake. From a contempt of the ignorant virtuosi of the age, and from indignation at the impudent tricks of picture-dealers, whom he saw continually recommending and vending vile copies to bubble collectors, and from having never studied, indeed having seen, few good pictures of the great Italian masters, he persuaded himself that the praises bestowed on those glorious works were nothing but the effects of prejudice. He talked this language till he believed it; and having heard it often asserted, as is true, that time gives a mellowness to colors and improves them, he not only denied the proposition, but maintained that pictures only grew black and worse by age, not distinguishing between the degrees in which the proposition might

be true or false. He went further; he determined to rival the Ancients, and unfortunately chose one of the finest pictures in England as the object of his competition. This was the celebrated "Sigismonda" of Sir Luke Schaub, now in the possession of the Duke of Newcastle, said to be painted by Correggio, probably by Furino, but no matter by whom. It is impossible to see the picture, or read Dryden's inimitable tale, and not feel that the same soul animated both. After many essays Hogarth at last produced his "Sigismonda," but no more like "Sigismonda" than I to Hercules. Hogarth's performance was more ridiculous than anything he had ever ridiculed. He set the price of £400 on it, and had it returned on his hands by the person for whom it was painted. He took subscriptions for a plate of it, but had the sense at last to suppress it. I make no more apology for this account than for the encomiums I have bestowed on him. Both are dictated by truth, and are the history of a great man's excellencies and errors. Milton, it is said, preferred his "Paradise Regained" to his immortal poem.

The last memorable event of our artist's life was his quarrel with Mr. Wilkes; in which, if Mr. Hogarth did not commence direct hostilities on the latter, he at least obliquely gave the first offense by an attack on the friends and party of that gentleman. This conduct was the more surprising, as he had all his life avoided dipping his pencil in political contests, and had early refused a very lucrative offer that was made to engage him in a set of prints against the head of a court party. Without entering into the merits of the cause, I shall only state the fact. In September, 1762, Mr. Hogarth published his print of "The Times." It was answered by Mr. Wilkes in a severe "North Briton." On this the painter exhibited the caricature of the writer. Mr. Churchill, the poet, then engaged in the war, and wrote his epistle to Hogarth, not the brightest of his works, and in which the severest strokes fell on a defect that the painter had neither caused nor could amend — his age; and which, however, was neither remarkable nor decrepit, much less had it impaired his talents, as appeared by his having composed but six months before one of his most capital works, the satire on the Methodists. In revenge for this epistle, Hogarth caricatured Churchill under the form of a canonical bear, with a club and a pot of porter — *Et vitulâ tu dignus et hic.* Never did two angry men of their abilities throw mud with less dexterity.

Mr. Hogarth, in the year 1730, married the only daughter of Sir James Thornhill, by whom he had no children. He died of a dropsy in his breast at his house in Leicester Fields, October 26th, 1764

From "Anecdotes of Painting
in England."

ON THE AMERICAN WAR

IN SPITE of all my modesty, I cannot help thinking I have a little something of the prophet about me. At least, we have not conquered America yet. I did not send you immediate word of our victory at Boston, because the success not only seemed very equivocal, but because the conquerors lost three to one more than the vanquished. The last do not pique themselves upon modern good breeding, but level only at the officers, of whom they have slain a vast number. We are a little disappointed, indeed, at their fighting at all, which was not in our calculation. We knew we could conquer America in Germany, and I doubt had better have gone thither now for that purpose, as it does not appear hitherto to be quite so feasible in America itself. However, we are determined to know the worst, and are sending away all the men and ammunition we can muster. The Congress, not asleep, neither, have appointed a generalissimo, Washington, allowed a very able officer, who distinguished himself in the last war. Well, we had better have gone on robbing the Indies! it was a more lucrative trade.

STRAWBERRY HILL, August 3d, 1775.

IZAAK WALTON

(1593-1683)

WALTON's "The Complete Angler" demonstrates that in literature as in everything else "love is the fulfilling of the law" of success. It has a charm for thousands who never fish at all, because it was written by a man who so loved fishing that what he wrote of it became a masterpiece,—for the time being the most important thing in the world, capable of distracting the reader's attention from everything else. Who, in reading the peaceful pages of Walton, ever stops to think that they were written in a troublesome world—the world of bloody conflict between Puritan and Cavalier and first published in the very year in which Cromwell drove out the "Rump" Parliament? When the most peaceful of all English books comes from such a time of contention and "babblement," it puts to shame all who complain that their generation denies them the quiet necessary for perfect work.

Walton was born at Stafford, England, August 9th, 1593. For many years he kept a shop in London, but when the civil war began, he gave up business and retired to his birthplace where he bought land and devoted his leisure to fishing and reading. He died December 15th, 1683, aged ninety years. Besides "The Complete Angler," he wrote lives of Donne, Wotton, Hooker, Herbert, and Sanderson.

THE ANGLER'S PHILOSOPHY OF LIFE

WELL, scholar, having now taught you to paint your rod, and we having still a mile to Tottenham High Cross, I will, as we walk towards it in the cool shade of this sweet honeysuckle hedge, mention to you some of the thoughts and joys that have possessed my soul since we met together. And these thoughts shall be told you, that you also may join with me in thankfulness to the Giver of every good and perfect gift for our happiness. And that our present happiness may appear to be the greater, and we the more thankful for it, I will beg you to consider with me how many do, even at this very time, lie under the torment of the stone, the gout, and toothache; and this we are free from. And every misery that I miss is a new mercy;

and therefore let us be thankful. There have been, since we met, others that have met disasters of broken limbs; some have been blasted, others thunderstruck; and we have been freed from these and all those many other miseries that threaten human nature: let us therefore rejoice and be thankful. Nay, which is a far greater mercy, we are free from the insupportable burden of an accusing, tormenting conscience—a misery that none can bear; and therefore let us praise him for his preventing grace, and say, Every misery that I miss is a new mercy. Nay, let me tell you, there be many that have forty times our estates, that would give the greatest part of it to be healthful and cheerful like us, who, with the expense of a little money, have eat, and drank, and laughed, and angled, and sung, and slept securely; and rose next day, and cast away care, and sung, and laughed, and angled again, which are blessings rich men cannot purchase with all their money. Let me tell you, scholar, I have a rich neighbor that is always so busy that he has no leisure to laugh; the whole business of his life is to get money, and more money, that he may still get more and more money; he is still drudging on, and says that Solomon says, "The hand of the diligent maketh rich"; and it is true indeed: but he considers not that it is not in the power of riches to make a man happy: for it was wisely said by a man of great observation, "That there be as many miseries beyond riches as on this side them." And yet God deliver us from pinching poverty, and grant that, having a competency, we may be content and thankful! Let us not repine, or so much as think the gifts of God unequally dealt, if we see another abound with riches, when, as God knows, the cares that are the keys that keep those riches hang often so heavily at the rich man's girdle, that they clog him with weary days and restless nights, even when others sleep quietly. We see but the outside of the rich man's happiness; few consider him to be like the silkworm, that, when she seems to play, is at the very same time spinning her own bowels, and consuming herself; and this many rich men do, loading themselves with corroding cares, to keep what they have, probably unconscionably got. Let us, therefore, be thankful for health and competence, and, above all, for a quiet conscience.

Let me tell you, scholar, that Diogenes walked on a day, with his friend, to see a country fair, where he saw ribbons, and looking-glasses, and nut crackers, and fiddles, and hobbyhorses, and many other gimcracks; and having observed them, and all the

other finnimbruns that make a complete country fair, he said to his friend, "Lord, how many things are there in this world of which Diogenes hath no need!" And truly it is so, or might be so, with very many who vex and toil themselves to get what they have no need of. Can any man charge God that he hath not given him enough to make his life happy? No, doubtless; for nature is content with a little. And yet you shall hardly meet with a man that complains not of some want, though he, indeed, wants nothing but his will; it may be nothing but his will of his poor neighbor, for not worshiping or not flattering him: and thus, when we might be happy and quiet, we create trouble to ourselves. I have heard of a man that was angry with himself because he was no taller; and of a woman that broke her looking-glass because it would not show her face to be as young and handsome as her next neighbor's was. And I knew another to whom God had given health and plenty, but a wife that nature had made peevish, and her husband's riches had made purse-proud, and must, because she was rich, and for no other virtue, sit in the highest pew in the church; which being denied her, she engaged her husband into a contention for it, and at last into a lawsuit with a dogged neighbor, who was as rich as he, and had a wife as peevish and purse-proud as the other; and this lawsuit begot higher oppositions and actionable words, and more vexations and lawsuits; for you must remember that both were rich, and must, therefore, have their wills. Well, this willful purse-proud lawsuit lasted during the life of the first husband, after which his wife vexed and chid, and chid and vexed, till she also chid and vexed herself into her grave; and so the wealth of these poor rich people was cursed into a punishment, because they wanted meek and thankful hearts, for those only can make us happy. I knew a man that had health and riches, and several houses, all beautiful and ready furnished, and would often trouble himself and family to be removing from one house to another; and being asked by a friend why he removed so often from one house to another, replied, "It was to find content in some one of them." But his friend knowing his temper, told him, "If he would find content in any of his houses, he must leave himself behind him; for content will never dwell but in a meek and quiet soul." And this may appear, if we read and consider what our Savior says in St. Matthew's gospel, for he there says, "Blessed be the merciful, for they shall obtain mercy. Blessed

be the pure in heart, for they shall see God. Blessed be the poor in spirit, for theirs is the kingdom of heaven. And blessed be the meek, for they shall possess the earth." Not that the meek shall not also obtain mercy, and see God, and be comforted, and at last come to the kingdom of heaven, but, in the meantime, he, and he only, possesses the earth, as he goes toward that kingdom of heaven, by being humble and cheerful, and content with what his good God has allotted him. He has no turbulent, repining, vexatious thoughts that he deserves better; nor is vexed when he sees others possessed of more honor or more riches than his wise God has allotted for his share; but he possesses what he has with a meek and contented quietness, such a quietness as makes his very dreams pleasing, both to God and himself.

My honest scholar, all this is told you to incline you to thankfulness; and, to incline you the more, let me tell you that though the prophet David was guilty of murder and adultery, and many other of the most deadly sins, yet he was said to be a man after God's own heart, because he abounded more with thankfulness than any other that is mentioned in Holy Scripture, as may appear in his Book of Psalms, where there is such a commixture of his confessing of his sins and unworthiness, and such thankfulness for God's pardon and mercies, as did make him to be accounted, even by God himself, to be a man after his own heart: and let us, in that, labor to be as like him as we can; let not the blessings we receive daily from God make us not to value, or not praise him, because they be common; let not us forget to praise him for the innocent mirth and pleasure we have met with since we met together. What would a blind man give to see the pleasant rivers, and meadows, and flowers, and fountains, that we have met with since we met together? I have been told that if a man that was born blind could obtain to have his sight for but only one hour during his whole life, and should, at the first opening of his eyes, fix his sight upon the sun when it was in his full glory, either at the rising or setting of it, he would be so transported and amazed, and so admire the glory of it, that he would not willingly turn his eyes from that first ravishing object to behold all the other various beauties this world could present to him. And this, and many other like blessings, we enjoy daily. And for most of them, because they be so common, most men forget to pay their praises; but let not us, because it is a sacrifice so pleasing to him that made that sun and us, and still protects us, and gives us flowers, and showers, and stomachs, and meat, and content, and leisure to go a-fishing.

Well, scholar, I have almost tired myself, and, I fear, more than almost tired you. But I now see Tottenham High Cross, and our short walk thither will put a period to my too long discourse, in which my meaning was, and is, to plant that in your mind with which I labor to possess my own soul — that is, a meek and thankful heart. And to that end I have showed you that riches without them (meekness and thankfulness) do not make any man happy. But let me tell you that riches with them remove many fears and cares. And therefore my advice is, that you endeavor to be honestly rich, or contentedly poor; but be sure that your riches be justly got, or you spoil all; for it is well said by Caussin, « He that loses his conscience has nothing left that is worth keeping.» Therefore be sure you look to that. And, in the next place, look to your health, and if you have it, praise God, and value it next to a good conscience; for health is the second blessing that we mortals are capable of — a blessing that money cannot buy — and therefore value it, and be thankful for it. As for money (which may be said to be the third blessing), neglect it not; but note, that there is no necessity of being rich; for I told you there be as many miseries beyond riches as on this side them; and if you have a competence, enjoy it with a meek, cheerful, thankful heart. I will tell you, scholar, I have heard a grave divine say that God has two dwellings, one in heaven, and the other in a meek and thankful heart; which Almighty God grant to me and to my honest scholar! And so you are welcome to Tottenham High Cross.

Venator — Well, master, I thank you for all your good directions, but for none more than this last, of thankfulness, which I hope I shall never forget.

Complete. From «The Complete Angler.»

serious trifling to attempt to prove; but Milton, perhaps, will not so easily resign his claim to equality, if not to superiority. Let it, however, be remembered that if Milton be enabled to dispute the prize with the great champions of antiquity, it is entirely owing to the sublime conceptions he has copied from the Book of God. These, therefore, must be taken away, before we begin to make a just estimate of his genius; and from what remains, it cannot, I presume, be said with candor and impartiality, that he has excelled Homer in the sublimity and variety of his thoughts, or the strength and majesty of his diction.

Shakespeare, Corneille, and Racine are the only modern writers of tragedy that we can venture to oppose to Æschylus, Sophocles, and Euripides. The first is an author so uncommon and eccentric, that we can scarcely try him by dramatic rules. In strokes of nature and character, he yields not to the Greeks; in all other circumstances that constitute the excellence of the drama, he is vastly inferior. Of the three Moderns, the most faultless is the tender and exact Racine: but he was ever ready to acknowledge that his capital beauties were borrowed from his favorite Euripides, — which, indeed, cannot escape the observation of those who read with attention his «Phædra» and «Andromache.» The pompous and truly Roman sentiments of Corneille are chiefly drawn from Lucan and Tacitus; the former of whom, by a strange perversion of taste, he is known to have preferred to Virgil. His diction is not so pure and melifluous, his characters not so various and just, nor his plots so regular, so interesting and simple, as those of his pathetic rival. It is by this simplicity of fable alone, when every single act, and scene, and speech, and sentiment, and word concur to accelerate the intended event, that the Greek tragedies kept the attention of the audience immovably fixed upon one principal object, which must be necessarily lessened, and the ends of the drama defeated by the mazes and intricacies of modern plots.

The assertion of Addison with respect to the first particular, regarding the higher kinds of poetry, will remain unquestionably true, till Nature in some distant age, — for in the present enervated with luxury she seems incapable of such an effort, — shall produce some transcendent genius, of power to eclipse the «Iliad» and the «Œdipus.»

The superiority of the ancient artists in painting is not perhaps so clearly manifest. They were ignorant, it will be said, of light, of shade, and perspective; and they had not the use of oil

JOSEPH WARTON
(1722–1800)

N CLOSING the Adventurer, March 4th, 1754, Hawkesworth wrote that « the pieces signed Z are by the Rev. Mr. Warton, whose translations of Virgil's 'Pastorals' and 'Georgics' would alone sufficiently distinguish him as a genius and a scholar.» The translations thus praised are forgotten, but « the pieces signed Z » will keep Warton's name alive as long as essays in the style of Addison and Steele are valued. He was born in Surrey, England, in 1722. At Winchester School and at Oxford he was intimate with Collins, under whose influence he published verses which attracted the attention of Dr. Johnson. After beginning to write for the Adventurer, he had the hardihood to dissent from the « Great Cham,» and to hold his own against him in an argument on the merits of Pope, Milton, and Shakespeare. The latter years of his life were spent in preparing editions of Pope (1797) and Dryden. He died in London in February, 1800, and his edition of Dryden, completed by his son, was published in 1811.

ANCIENT AND MODERN ART

Veteres ita miratur, laudatque!
— *Horace.*

« The wits of old he praises and admires.»

« IT IS very remarkable,» says Addison, « that notwithstanding we fall short at present of the Ancients, in poetry, painting, oratory, history, architecture, and all the noble arts and sciences which depend more upon genius than experience, we exceed them as much in doggerel, humor, burlesque, and all the trivial arts of ridicule.» As this fine observation stands at present only in the form of a general assertion, it deserves, I think, to be examined by a deduction of particulars and confirmed by an allegation of examples, which may furnish an agreeable entertainment to those who have ability and inclination to remark the revolutions of human wit.

That Tasso, Ariosto, and Camoens, the three most celebrated of modern epic poets, are infinitely excelled in propriety of design, of sentiment and style by Horace and Virgil, it would be

colors, which are happily calculated to blend and unite without harshness and discordance, to give a boldness and relief to the figures, and to form those middle tints which render every well-wrought piece a closer resemblance of nature. Judges of the truest taste do, however, place the merit of coloring far below that of justness of design and force of expression. In these two highest and most important excellences, the ancient painters were eminently skilled, if we trust the testimonies of Pliny, Quintilian, and Lucian; and to credit them we are obliged, if we would form to ourselves any idea of these artists at all; for there is not one Grecian picture remaining; and the Romans, some few of whose works have descended to this age, could never boast of a Parrhasius or Apelles, a Zeuxis, Timanthes, or Protogenes, of whose performances the two accomplished critics above mentioned speak in terms of rapture and admiration. The statues that have escaped the ravages of time, as the « Hercules » and « Laocoon » for instance, are still a stronger demonstration of the power of the Grecian artists in expressing the passions; for what was executed in marble, we have presumptive evidence to think, might also have been executed in colors. Carlo Marat, the last valuable painter of Italy, after copying the head of the « Venus » in the Medicean collection three hundred times, generously confessed that he could not arrive at half the grace and perfection of his model. But to speak my opinion freely on a very disputable point, I must own that if the Moderns approach the Ancients in any of the arts here in question, they approach them nearest in the art of painting. The human mind can with difficulty conceive anything more exalted than « The Last Judgment » of Michael Angelo, and « The Transfiguration » of Raphael. What can be more animated than Raphael's « Paul Preaching at Athens »? What more tender and delicate than Mary holding the child Jesus, in his famous « Holy Family »? What more graceful than « The Aurora » of Guido? What more deeply moving than « The Massacre of the Innocents,» by Lebrun?

But no modern orator can dare to enter the lists with Demosthenes and Tully. We have discourses, indeed, that may be admired for their perspicuity, purity, and elegance; but can produce none that abound in a sublime which whirls away the auditor like a mighty torrent, and pierces the inmost recesses of his heart like a flash of lightning; which irresistibly and instantaneously convinces, without leaving him leisure to weigh the motives of conviction. The sermons of Bourdaloue, the funeral oration of Bossuet, particularly that on the death of Henrietta, and the pleadings of Pelisson for his disgraced patron Fouquet, are the only pieces of eloquence I can recollect that bear any resemblance to the Greek or Roman orator; for in England we have been particularly unfortunate in our attempts to be eloquent, whether in parliament, in the pulpit, or at the bar. If it be urged that the nature of modern politics and laws excludes the pathetic and the sublime, and confines the speaker to a cold argumentative method, and a dull detail of proof and dry matters of fact; yet, surely, the religion of the Moderns abounds in topics so incomparably noble and exalted, as might kindle the flames of genuine oratory in the most frigid and barren genius: much more might this success be reasonably expected from such geniuses as Britain can enumerate; yet no piece of this sort, worthy applause or notice, has ever yet appeared.

The few, even among professed scholars, that are able to read the ancient historians in their inimitable originals, are startled at the paradox of Bolingbroke, who boldly prefers Guicciardini to Thucydides; that is, the most verbose and tedious to the most comprehensive and concise of writers, and a collector of facts to one who was himself an eyewitness and a principal actor in the important story he relates. And, indeed, it may well be presumed that the ancient histories exceed the modern from this single consideration, that the latter are commonly compiled by recluse scholars, unpracticed in business, war, and politics; whilst the former are many of them written by ministers, commanders, and princes themselves. We have, indeed, a few flimsy memoirs, particularly in a neighboring nation, written by persons deeply interested in the transactions they describe; but these, I imagine, will not be compared to " The Retreat of the Ten Thousand," which Xenophon himself conducted and related, nor to "The Gallic War" of Cæsar, nor "the precious fragments" of Polybius, which our modern generals and ministers would not be discredited by diligently perusing, and making them the models of their conduct as well as of their style. Are the reflections of Machiavelli so subtle and refined as those of Tacitus? Are the portraits or Thuanus so strong and expressive as those of Sallust and Plutarch? Are the narrations of Davila so lively and animated, or does his sentiments breathe such a love of liberty and virtue, as those of Livy and Herodotus?

x—244

The supreme excellence of the ancient architecture, the last particular to be touched, I shall not enlarge upon; because it has never once been called in question, and because it is abundantly testified by the awful ruins of amphitheatres, aqueducts, arches, and columns, that are the daily objects of veneration, though not of imitation. This art, it is observable, has never been improved in later ages in one single instance; but every just and legitimate edifice is still formed according to the five old established orders, to which human wit has never been able to add a sixth of equal symmetry and strength.

Such, therefore, are the triumphs of the Ancients, especially the Greeks, over the Moderns. They may, perhaps, be not unjustly ascribed to a genial climate, that gave such a happy temperament of body as was most proper to produce fine sensations; to a language most harmonious, copious, and forcible; to the public encouragements and honors bestowed on the cultivators of literature; to the emulation excited among the generous youth, by exhibitions of their performances at the solemn games; to an inattention to the arts of lucre and commerce, which engross and debase the minds of the Moderns; and, above all, to an exemption from the necessity of overloading their natural faculties with learning and languages, with which we in these later times are obliged to qualify ourselves for writers if we expect to be read.

It is said by Voltaire, with his usual liveliness, "We shall never again behold the time when a Duke de la Rochefoucault might go from the conversation of a Pascal, or Arnauld, to the theatre of Corneille." This reflection may be more justly applied to the Ancients, and it may with much greater truth be said: " The age will never again return when a Pericles, after walking with Plato in a portico built by Phidias, and painted by Apelles, might repair to hear a pleading of Demosthenes, or a tragedy of Sophocles."

Complete. From the Adventurer.

HACHO OF LAPLAND

HACHO, a king of Lapland, was in his youth the most renowned of the Northern warriors. His martial achievements remain engraved on a pillar of flint in the rocks of Hanga, and are to this day solemnly caroled to the harp by the Laplanders, at the fires with which they celebrate their nightly festivi-

ties. Such was his intrepid spirit, that he ventured to pass the lake Vether to the isle of Wizards, where he descended alone into the dreary vault in which a magician had been kept bound for six ages, and read the Gothic characters inscribed on his brazen mace. His eye was so piercing, that, as ancient chronicles report, he could blunt the weapons of his enemies only by looking at them. At twelve years of age, he carried an iron vessel of a prodigious weight, for the length of five furlongs, in the presence of all the chiefs of his father's castle.

Nor was he less celebrated for his prudence and wisdom. Two of his proverbs are yet remembered and repeated among Laplanders. To express the vigilance of the Supreme Being, he was wont to say, " Odin's belt is always buckled." To show that the most prosperous condition of life is often hazardous, his lesson was, " When you slide on the smoothest ice, beware of pits beneath." He consoled his countrymen, when they were once preparing to leave the frozen deserts of Lapland, and resolved to seek some warmer climate, by telling them that the Eastern nations, notwithstanding their boasted fertility, passed every night amidst the horrors of anxious apprehension, and were inexpressibly affrighted, and almost stunned, every morning, with the noise of the sun while he was rising.

His temperance and severity of manner were his chief praise. In his early years he never tasted wine; nor would he drink out of a painted cup. He constantly slept in his armor, with his spear in his hand; nor would he use a battle-ax whose handle was inlaid with brass. He did not, however, persevere in this contempt of luxury; nor did he close his days with honor.

One evening, after hunting the gulos, or wild dog, being bewildered in a solitary forest, and having passed the fatigues of the day without any interval of refreshment, he discovered a large store of honey in the hollow of a pine. This was a dainty which he had never tasted before; and being at once faint and hungry, he fed greedily upon it. From this unusual and delicious repast he received so much satisfaction, that at his return home he commanded honey to be served up at his table every day. His palate, by degrees, became refined and vitiated; he began to lose his native relish for simple fare, and contracted a habit of indulging himself in delicacies; he ordered the delightful gardens of his castle to be thrown open, in which the most luscious fruits had been suffered to ripen and decay, unobserved

and untouched, for many revolving autumns, and gratified his appetite with luxurious desserts. At length he found it expedient to introduce wine, as an agreeable improvement; or a necessary ingredient to his new way of living; and having once tasted it, he was tempted by little and little, to give a loose to the excesses of intoxication. His general simplicity of life was changed; he perfumed his apartments by burning the wood of the most aromatic fir, and commanded his helmet to be ornamented with beautiful rows of the teeth of the reindeer. Indolence and effeminacy stole upon him by pleasing and imperceptible gradations, relaxed the sinews of his resolution, and extinguished his thirst of military glory.

While Hacho was thus immersed in pleasure and in repose, it was reported to him one morning that the preceding night a disastrous omen had been discovered, and that bats and hideous birds had drunk up the oil which nourished the perpetual lamp in the temple of Odin. About the same time, a messenger arrived to tell him that the king of Norway had invaded his kingdom with a formidable army. Hacho, terrified as he was with the omen of the night, and enervated with indulgence, roused himself from his voluptuous lethargy, and, recollecting some faint and few sparks of veteran valor, marched forward to meet him. Both armies joined battle in the forest where Hacho had been lost after hunting; and it so happened that the king of Norway challenged him to single combat, near the place where he had tasted the honey. The Lapland chief, languid and long disused to arms, was soon overpowered; he fell to the ground; and before his insulting adversary struck his head from his body, uttered this exclamation, which the Laplanders still use as an early lesson to their children: " The vicious man should date his destruction from the first temptation. How justly do I fall a sacrifice to sloth and luxury, in the place where I first yielded to those allurements which seduced me to deviate from temperance and innocence! The honey which I tasted in this forest, and not the hand of the king of Norway, conquers Hacho."

Complete. From the Idler.

EDWIN PERCY WHIPPLE

(1819–1886)

EDWIN PERCY WHIPPLE, essayist and critic, was born at Gloucester, Massachusetts, March 8th, 1819. It is said that he began to write for newspapers when only fourteen years old. At eighteen he became "superintendent of the newsroom" in the Boston Merchants' Exchange and several years later he wrote a critique on Macaulay, for which he was thanked by Macaulay himself. The prominence thus given him was well improved. He began a course of lectures on "The Lives of Authors" and continued to lecture successfully, publishing his lectures and essays and meeting with favor from the public. Among his works are "Essays and Reviews," 1848–49; "Literature and Life," 1849; "Character and Characteristic Men," 1866; "Literature of the Age of Elizabeth," 1869; and "Outlooks on Society, Literature, and Politics," posthumous. He died at Boston, June 16th, 1886.

THE LITERATURE OF MIRTH

THE ludicrous side of life, like the serious side, has its literature, and it is a literature of untold wealth. Mirth is a Proteus, changing its shape and manner with the thousand diversities of individual character, from the most superficial gayety, to the deepest, most earnest humor. Thus, the wit of the airy, feather-brained Farquhar glances and gleams like heat lightning; that of Milton blasts and burns like the bolt. Let us glance carelessly over this wide field of comic writers, who have drawn new forms of mirthful being from life's ludicrous side, and note, here and there, a wit or humorist. There is the humor of Goethe like his own summer morning, mirthfully clear; and there is the tough and knotty humor of old Ben Jonson, at times ground down to the edge to a sharp cutting scorn, and occasionally hissing out stinging words, which seem, like his own Mercury's "steeped in the very brine of conceit, and sparkle like salt in fire." There is the incessant brilliancy of Sheridan:—

"Whose humor, as gay as the firefly's light,
    Played round every subject, and shone as it played;
Whose wit in the combat, as gentle as bright,
    Ne'er carried a heart-stain away on its blade."

There is the uncouth mirth, that winds, stutters, wriggles, and screams, dark, scornful, and savage, among the dislocated joints of Carlyle's spavined sentences. There is the lithe, springy sarcasm, the hilarious badinage, the brilliant careless disdain, which sparkle and scorch along the glistening page of Holmes. There is the sleepy smile that sometimes lies so benignly on the sweet and serious diction of old Izaak Walton. There is the mirth of Dickens, twinkling now in some ironical insinuation,—and anon winking at you with pleasant maliciousness, its distended cheeks fat with suppressed glee,—and then, again, coming out in broad gushes of humor, overflowing all banks and bounds of conventional decorum. There is Sydney Smith,—sly, sleek, swift, subtle, —a moment's motion, and the human mouse is in his paw! Mark, in contrast with him, the beautiful heedlessness with which the Ariel-like spirit of Gay pours itself out in benevolent mockeries of human folly. There, in a corner, look at that petulant little man, his features working with thought and pain, his lips wrinkled with a sardonic smile; and, see! the immortal personality has received its last point and polish in that toiling brain, and, in a strait, luminous line, with a twang like Scorn's own arrow, hisses through the air the unerring shaft of Pope to—

"Dash the proud gamester from his gilded car,
    And bare the base heart that lurks beneath a star."

There a little above Pope see Dryden keenly dissecting the inconsistencies of Buckingham's volatile mind, or leisurely crushing out the insect life of Shadwell,—

"——owned, without dispute,
    Throughout the realms of Nonsense, absolute."

There, moving gracefully through that carpeted parlor, mark that dapper, diminutive Irish gentleman. The moment you look at him, your eyes are dazzled with the whizzing rockets and hissing wheels, streaking the air with a million sparks, from the pyrotechnic brain of Anacreon Moore. Again, cast your eyes from that blinding glare and glitter, to the soft and beautiful bril-

liancy, the winning grace, the bland banter, the gliding wit, the diffusive humor, which make you in love with all mankind, in the charming pages of Washington Irving. And now for another change,—glance at the jerks and jets of satire, the mirthful audacities, the fretting and teasing mockeries, of that fat, sharp imp, half Mephistopheles, half Falstaff, that cross between Beelzebub and Rabelais, known in all lands as the matchless Mr. Punch. No English statesman, however great his power, no English nobleman, however high his rank, but knows that every week he may be pointed at by the scoffing finger of that omnipotent buffoon, and consigned to the ridicule of the world. The pride of intellect, the pride of wealth, the power to oppress,—nothing can save the dunce or criminal from being pounced upon by Punch, and held up to a derision or execration which shall ring from London to St. Petersburg, from the Ganges to the Oregon. From the vitriol pleasantries of this arch-fiend of Momus, let us turn to the benevolent mirth of Addison and Steele, whose glory it was to redeem polite literature from moral depravity, by showing that wit could chime merrily in with the voice of virtue, and who smoothly laughed away many a vice of the national character, by that humor which tenderly touches the sensitive point with an evanescent grace and genial glee. And here let us not forget Goldsmith, whose delicious mirth is of that rare quality which lies too deep for laughter; which melts softly into the mind, suffusing it with inexpressible delight, and sending the soul dancing joyously into the eyes to utter its merriment in liquid glances, passing all the expression of tone. And here, though we cannot do him justice, let us remember the name of Nathaniel Hawthorne, deserving a place second to none in that band of humorists, whose beautiful depth of cheerful feeling is the very poetry of mirth. In ease, grace, delicate sharpness of satire, in a felicity of touch which often surpasses the felicity of Addison, in a subtlety of insight which often reaches further than the subtlety of Steele,—the humor of Hawthorne presents traits so fine as to be almost too excellent for popularity, as, to every one who has attempted their criticism, they are too refined for statement. The brilliant atoms flit, hover, and glance before our minds, but the subtle sources of their ethereal light lie beyond our analysis,—

"And no speed of ours avails
    To hunt upon their shining trails."

And now let us breathe a benison on these our mirthful benefactors, these fine revelers among human weaknesses, these stern, keen satirists of human depravity. Wherever humor smiles away the fretting thoughts of care, or supplies that antidote which cleanses

"The stuffed bosom of that perilous stuff
    That weighs upon the heart,"

wherever wit riddles folly, abases pride, or stings iniquity,— there glides the cheerful spirit, or glitters the flashing thought, of these bright enemies of stupidity and gloom. Thanks to them, hearty thanks, for teaching us that the ludicrous side of life is its wicked side, no less than its foolish; that in a lying world there is still no mercy for falsehood; that guilt, however high it may lift its brazen front, is never beyond the lightnings of scorn; and that the lesson they teach agrees with the lesson taught by all experience, that life, in harmony with reason, is the only life safe from laughter—that life, in harmony with virtue, is the only life safe from contempt.

THE POWER OF WORDS

WORDS are most effective when arranged in that order which is called style. The great secret of a good style, we are told, is to have proper words in proper places. To marshal one's verbal battalions in such order that they may bear at once upon all quarters of a subject, is certainly a great art. This is done in different ways. Swift, Temple, Addison, Hume, Gibbon, Johnson, Burke, are all great generals in the discipline of their verbal armies, and the conduct of their paper wars. Each has a system of tactics of his own, and excels in the use of some particular weapon. The tread of Johnson's style is heavy and sonorous, resembling that of an elephant or a mailclad warrior. He is fond of leveling an obstacle by a polysyllabic battering-ram. Burke's words are continually practicing the broadsword exercise, and sweeping down adversaries with every stroke. Arbuthnot "plays his weapon like a tongue of flame." Addison draws up his light infantry in orderly array, and marches through sentence after sentence, without having his ranks disordered or his line broken. Luther is different. His words are "half battle"; "his smiting idiomatic phrases seem to cleave into the very secret of the matter." Gibbon's legions are heavily armed, and march with precision and dignity to the music of their own tramp. They are splendidly equipped, but a nice eye can discern a little rust beneath their fine apparel, and there are suttlers in his camp who lie, cog, and talk gross obscenity. Macaulay, brisk, lively, keen, and energetic, runs his thoughts rapidly through his sentence, and kicks out of the way every word which obstructs his passage. He reins in his steed only when he has reached his goal, and then does it with such celerity that he is nearly thrown backwards by the suddenness of his stoppage. Gifford's words are mosstroopers, that waylay innocent travelers and murder them for hire. Jeffrey is a fine "lance," with a sort of Arab swiftness in his movement, and runs an ironclad horseman through the eye before he has had time to close his helmet. John Wilson's camp is a disorganized mass, who might do effectual service under better discipline, but who under his lead are suffered to carry on a rambling and predatory warfare, and disgrace their general by flagitious excesses. Sometimes they steal, sometimes swear, sometimes drink, and sometimes pray. Swift's words are porcupine's quills, which he throws with unerring aim at whoever approaches his lair. All of Ebenezer Elliot's words are gifted with huge fists, to pummel and bruise. Chatham and Mirabeau throw hot shot into their opponents' magazines. Talfourd's forces are orderly and disciplined, and march to the music of the Dorian flute; those of Keats keep time to the tones of the pipe of Phœbus; and the hard, harsh-featured battalions of Maginn are always preceded by a brass band. Hallam's word infantry can do much execution, when they are not in each other's way. Pope's phrases are either daggers or rapiers. Willis's words are often tipsy with the champaign of the fancy, but even when they reel and stagger they keep the line of grace and beauty, and though scattered at first by a fierce onset from graver cohorts, soon reunite without wound or loss. John Neal's forces are multitudinous and fire briskly at everything. They occupy all the provinces of letters, and are nearly useless from being spread over too much ground. Everett's weapons are ever kept in good order, and shine well in the sun, but they are little calculated for warfare, and rarely kill when they strike. Webster's words are thunderbolts, which sometimes miss the Titans at whom they are hurled, but always leave enduring marks when

they strike. Hazlitt's verbal army is sometimes drunk and surly, sometimes foaming with passion, sometimes cool and malignant, but drunk or sober are ever dangerous to cope with. Some of Tom Moore's words are shining dirt, which he flings with excellent aim. This list might be indefinitely extended, and arranged with more regard to merit and chronology. My own words, in this connection, might be compared to ragged, undisciplined militia, which could be easily rooted by a charge of horse, and which are apt to fire into each other's faces.

From an "Essay on Words."

JOHN GREENLEAF WHITTIER

(1807-1892)

WHITTIER's prose has never competed in popularity with his verse, but he has an easy and flowing style, with frequent picturesque touches which suggest the "image-making power" of the poet. He was born at Haverhill, Massachusetts, December 17th, 1807. His family were Quakers, and he himself remained a member of the "Society" until his death. His early education was defective, as he was obliged to pay for his own tuition by farm work, shoemaking, and school-teaching in his vacations. Among his earliest verses are those published in the Newburyport Free Press, edited by William Lloyd Garrison. From 1828 to 1832 he edited successively the American Manufacturer at Boston, the Gazette at Haverhill, and the New England Weekly Review at Hartford. From 1832 to 1837 he managed the Whittier farm at Haverhill and helped in the Antislavery agitation. In 1838 he went to Philadelphia to edit the Pennsylvania Freeman, having become in the meantime Secretary of the American Antislavery Society. In 1840, however, he returned to Massachusetts and lived there until his death, September 7th, 1892. A complete edition of his poems appeared in 1888-89.

THE YANKEE ZINCALI

HARK! a rap at my door. Welcome anybody, just now. One gains nothing by attempting to shut out the sprites of the weather. They come in at the keyhole; they peer through the dripping panes; they insinuate themselves through the crevices of the casement, or plump down the chimney astride of the raindrops.

I rise and throw open the door. A tall, shambling, loose-jointed figure; a pinched, shrewd face, sunbrown and wind-dried; small, quick-winking black eyes. There he stands, the water dripping from his pulpy hat and ragged elbows.

I speak to him, but he returns no answer. With a dumb show of misery, quite touching, he hands me a soiled piece of parchment, whereon I read what purports to be a melancholy account of shipwreck and disaster, to the particular detriment, loss,

and damnification of one Pietro Frugoni, who is, in consequence, sorely in want of the alms of all charitable Christian persons, and who is, in short, the bearer of this veracious document, duly certified and endorsed by an Italian consul in one of our Atlantic cities, of a high-sounding, but, to Yankee organs, unpronounceable name.

Here commences a struggle. Every man, the Mahometans tell us, has two attendant angels, the good one on his right shoulder, the bad on his left. "Give," says Benevolence, as with some difficulty I fish up a small coin from the depths of my pocket. "Not a cent," says selfish Prudence, and I drop it from my fingers. "Think," says the good angel, "of the poor stranger in a strange land, just escaped from the terrors of the sea storm, in which his little property has perished, thrown half naked and helpless on our shores, ignorant of our language, and unable to find employment suited to his capacity." "A vile impostor!" replies the left-hand sentinel. "His paper, purchased from one of those ready writers in New York, who manufacture beggar credentials at the low price of one dollar per copy, with earthquakes, fires, or shipwrecks, to suit customers."

Amidst this confusion of tongues, I take another survey of my visitant. Ha! a light dawns upon me. That shrewd, old face, with its sharp, winking eyes, is no stranger to me. Pietro Frugoni, I have seen thee before! Sì, Señor, that face of thine has looked at me over a dirty white neckcloth, with the corners of that cunning mouth drawn downwards, and those small eyes turned up in sanctimonious gravity, while thou wast offering to a crowd of half-grown boys an extemporaneous exhortation, in the capacity of a traveling preacher. Have I not seen it peering out from under a blanket, as that of a poor Penobscot Indian, who had lost the use of his hands while trapping on the Madawaska? Is it not the face of the forlorn father of six small children, whom the "marcury doctors" had "pisened" and crippled? Did it not belong to that downcast unfortunate, who had been out to the "Genesee country," and got the "fevern-nager," and whose hand shook so pitifully when held out to receive my poor gift? The same, under all disguises — Stephen Leathers of Barrington — him and none other! Let me conjure him into his own likeness.

"Well, Stephen, what news from old Barrington?"

"Oh, well I thought I knew ye," he answers, not the least disconcerted. "How do you do, and how's your folks? All well

I hope. I took this 'ere paper, you see, to help a poor furriner, who couldn't make himself understood any more than a wild goose. I thought I'd just start him for'ard a little. It seemed a marcy to do it.»

Well and shiftily answered, thou ragged Proteus. One cannot be angry with such a fellow. I will just inquire into the present state of his gospel mission, and about the condition of his tribe on the Penobscot; and it may not be amiss to congratulate him on the success of the steam doctors in sweating the "pisen" of the regular faculty out of him. But he evidently has no wish to enter into idle conversation. Intent upon his benevolent errand, he is already clattering down stairs. Involuntarily I glance out the window just in season to catch a single glimpse of him ere he is swallowed up in the mist.

He has gone; and, knave as he is, I can hardly help exclaiming, "Luck go with him!" He has broken in upon the sombre train of my thoughts, and called up before me pleasant and grateful recollections. The old farmhouse nestling in its valley; hills stretching off to the south, and green meadows to the east; the small stream, which came noisily down its ravine, washing the old garden wall, and softly lapping on fallen stones and mossy roots of beeches and hemlocks; the tall sentinel poplars at the gateway; the oak forest, sweeping unbroken to the northern horizon; the grass-grown carriage path, with its rude and crazy bridge; the dear old landscape of my boyhood lies outstretched before me like a daguerreotype from that picture within, which I have born with me in all my wanderings. I am a boy again; once more conscious of the feeling, half terror, half exultation, with which I used to announce the approach of this very vagabond, and his "kindred after the flesh."

The advent of wandering beggars, or "old stragglers," as we were wont to call them, was an event of no ordinary interest in the generally monotonous quietude of our farm life. Many of them were well known; they had their periodical revolutions and transits; we could calculate them like eclipses or new moons. Some were sturdy knaves, fat and saucy; and, whenever they ascertained that the "men folks" were absent, would order provisions and cider like men who expected to pay for it, seating themselves at the hearth or table with the air of Falstaff — "Shall I not take mine ease in mine own inn?" Others, poor, pale, patient, like Sterne's monk, came creeping up to the door, hat in

hand, standing there in their gray wretchedness with a look of heartbreak and forlornness, which was never without its effect on our juvenile sensibilities. At times, however, we experienced a slight revulsion of feeling, when even these humblest children of sorrow somewhat petulantly rejected our proffered bread and cheese, and demanded instead a glass of cider. Whatever the temperance society might in such cases have done, it was not in our hearts to refuse the poor creatures a draught of their favorite beverage; and wasn't it a satisfaction to see their sad melancholy faces light up as we handed them the full pitcher, and, on receiving it back empty from their brown, wrinkled hands, to hear them, half breathless from their long, delicious draught, thanking us for the favor, as "dear good children"? Not unfrequently these wandering tests of our benevolence made their appearance in interesting groups of man, woman, and child, picturesque in their squalidness, and manifesting a maudlin affection, which would have done honor to the revelers at Poosie-Nansies, —immortal in the cantata of Burns. I remember some who were evidently the victims of monomania, haunted and hunted by some dark thought, possessed by a fixed idea. One, a black-eyed, wild-haired woman, with a whole tragedy of sin, shame, and suffering written in her countenance, used often to visit us, warm herself by our winter fire, and supply herself with a stock of cakes and cold meat, but was never known to answer a question or to ask one. She never smiled; the cold, stony look of her eye never changed; a silent impassive face, frozen rigid by some great wrong or sin. We used to look with awe upon the "still woman," and think of the demoniac of Scripture who had a "dumb spirit."

One — (I think I see him now, grim, gaunt, and ghastly, working his slow way up to our door) — used to gather herbs by the wayside, and call himself Doctor. He was bearded like a hegoat, and used to counterfeit lameness; yet when he supposed himself alone would travel on lustily as if walking for a wager. At length, as if in punishment of his deceit, he met with an accident in his rambles, and became lame in earnest, hobbling ever after with difficulty on his gnarled crutches. Another used to go stooping, like Bunyan's Pilgrim, under a pack made of an old bed-sacking, stuffed out into most plethoric dimensions, tottering on a pair of small meagre legs, and peering out with his wild, hairy face from under his burden like a big-bodied spider. That "man

with the pack" always inspired me with awe and reverence. Huge, almost sublime in its tense rotundity,—the father of all packs,—never laid aside and never opened, what might not be within it? With what flesh-creeping curiosity I used to walk round about it at a safe distance, half expecting to see its striped covering stirred by the motions of a mysterious life, or that some evil monster would leap out of it, like robbers from Ali Baba's jars, or armed men from the Trojan horse.

Often, in the gray of the morning, we used to see one or more of these "gaberlunzie men," pack on shoulder and staff in hand, emerging from the barn or other outbuildings, where they had passed the night. I was once sent to the barn to fodder the cattle late in the evening, and climbing into the mow to pitch down hay for that purpose I was startled by the sudden apparition of a man rising up before me, just discernible in the dim moonlight streaming through the seams of the boards. I made a rapid retreat down the ladder; and was only reassured by hearing the object of my terror calling after me, and recognizing his voice as that of a harmless old pilgrim whom I had known before. Our farmhouse was situated in a lonely valley, half surrounded with woods, with no neighbors in sight. One dark, cloudy night, when our parents chanced to be absent, we were sitting with our aged grandmother in the fading light of the kitchen fire, working ourselves into a very satisfactory state of excitement and terror, by recounting to each other all the dismal stories we could remember of ghosts, witches, haunted houses, and robbers, when we were suddenly startled by a loud rap at the door. A stripling of fourteen, I was very naturally regarded as the head of the household; and with many misgivings I advanced to the door, which I slowly opened, holding the candle tremulously above my head, and peering out into the darkness. The feeble glimmer played upon the apparition of a gigantic horseman, mounted on a steed of a size for such a rider — colossal, motionless, like images cut out of the solid night. The strange visitant gruffly saluted me; and after making several ineffectual efforts to urge his horse in at the door, dismounted, and followed me into the room, evidently enjoying the terror which his huge presence excited. Announcing himself as "Dr. Brown, the great Indian doctor," he drew himself up before the fire, stretched his arms, clenched his fists, struck his broad chest, and invited our attention to what he called his "mortal frame." He

demanded in succession all kinds of intoxicating liquors; and, on being assured that we had none to give him, he grew angry, threatened to swallow my younger brother alive, and seizing me by the hair of my head, as the angel did the prophet at Babylon, he led me about from room to room. After an ineffectual search, in the course of which he mistook a jug of oil for one of brandy, and, contrary to my explanation and remonstrances, insisted upon swallowing a portion of its contents, he released me, fell to crying and sobbing, and confessed that he was so drunk already that his horse was ashamed of him. After bemoaning and pitying himself to his satisfaction, he wiped his eyes, sat down by the side of my grandmother, giving her to understand that he was very much pleased with her appearance; adding that, if agreeable to her, he should like the privilege of paying his addresses to her. While vainly endeavoring to make the excellent old lady comprehend his very flattering proposition, he was interrupted by the return of my father, who, at once understanding the matter, turned him out of doors without ceremony.

On one occasion, a few years ago, on my return from the field at evening, I was told that a foreigner had asked for lodgings during the night; but that influenced by his dark, repulsive appearance, my mother had very reluctantly refused his request. I found her by no means satisfied by her decision. "What if a son of mine were in a strange land?" she inquired self-reproachfully. Greatly to her relief, I volunteered to go in pursuit of the wanderer, and, taking a cross-path over the fields, soon overtook him. He had just been rejected at the house of our nearest neighbor, and was standing in a state of dubious perplexity in the street. His looks quite justified my mother's suspicions. He was an olive-complexioned, black-bearded Italian, with an eye like a live coal — such a face as perchance looks out on the traveler in the passes of the Abruzzo — one of those bandit visages which Salvator has painted. With some difficulty I gave him to understand my errand, when he overwhelmed me with thanks, and joyfully followed me back. He took his seat with us at the supper table; and when we were all seated around the hearth that cold autumnal evening, he told us, partly by words and partly by gestures, the story of his life and misfortunes, amused us with descriptions of his grape gatherings, and festivals of his sunny clime, edified my mother with a recipe for making bread of chestnuts; and in the morning, when, after breakfast, his dark, sullen face lighted up, and his fierce eye moistened with grateful emotion, as in his own silvery Tuscan accent he poured out his thanks, we marveled at the fears which had so nearly closed our door against him; and, as he departed, we all felt that he had left with us the blessing of the poor.

It was not often that, as in the above instance, my mother's prudence got the better of her charity. The regular "old stragglers" regarded her as an unfailing friend; and the sight of her plain cap was to them an assurance of forthcoming creature comforts. There was, indeed, a tribe of lazy strollers, having their place of rendezvous in the town of Barrington, New Hampshire, whose low vices had placed them beyond even the pale of her benevolence. They were not unconscious of their evil reputation, and experience had taught them the necessity of concealing, under well-contrived disguises, their true character. They came to us in all shapes, and with all appearances save the true one, with most miserable stories of mishap and sickness, and all "the ills which flesh is heir to." It was particularly vexatious to discover, when too late, that our sympathies and charities had been expended upon such graceless vagabonds as the "Barrington beggars." An old withered hag, known by the appellation of "Hipping Pat,"—the wise woman of her tribe,—was in the habit of visiting us, with her hopeful grandson who had "a gift for preaching" as well as for many other things not exactly compatible with holy orders. He sometimes brought with him a tame crow, a shrewd, knavish-looking bird, who, when in humor for it, could talk like Barnaby Rudge's raven. He used to say he could "do nothin' at exhortin' without a white handkercher on his neck and money in his pocket,"—a fact going far to confirm the opinions of the Bishop of Exeter and the Puseyites generally, that there can be no priest without tithes and surplice.

These people have for several generations lived distinct from the great mass of the community, like the gipsies of Europe, whom in many respects they closely resemble. They have the same settled aversion to labor, and the same disposition to avail themselves of the fruits of the industry of others. They love a wild, out-of-door life, sing songs, tell fortunes, and have an instinctive hatred of "missionaries and cold water."

x—245

CHRISTOPH MARTIN WIELAND

(1733–1813)

BESIDES translating twenty-two of Shakespeare's plays, translating and annotating Cicero's "Letters," the "Satires" and "Epistles" of Horace, and the "Dialogues" of Lucian, Wieland found time to fill fifty-three volumes with original poems, plays, romances, essays, and philosophical treatises on almost, if not quite, every imaginable subject, from the most spiritual speculation to "Komische Erzählungen," the grossness of which surprised and shocked his admirers.

He was born near Biberach, in Swabia, September 5th, 1733. His father, who was a clergyman, educated him carefully. While still at the University of Tübingen, he wrote his poem on "The Nature of Things," his "Moral Letters" and "Moral Tales," as well as a poem on "Spring" and a work entitled "Anti-Ovid." His writings of this period express an ascetic and repressive view of life, which he afterwards modified, concluding finally that the best philosophy of life is that which promotes self-possession and the temperate realization of all the possibilities of constructive experience. After living at Zurich from 1752 to 1759 and at Biberach as director in Chancery from 1760 to 1769, he was made professor of Philosophy and Literature at Erfurt,—a position he left in 1772 to become tutor to Prince Charles Augustus at Weimar, where he remained until his death, January 20th, 1813.

ON THE RELATION OF THE AGREEABLE AND THE BEAUTIFUL TO THE USEFUL

BALZAC, whose "Letters," once so admired, would furnish an inexhaustible fund of antitheses, concetti, and other witticisms for epigrammatists by profession, was often in the predicament of saying something very flat when he imagined that he had said something very ingenious. Nevertheless, he sometimes made a good hit, as one who spends his whole life in chasing after thoughts necessarily must.

In the following passage I am pleased with the concluding thought, notwithstanding its epigrammatic turn, on account of the

simplicity and luminous truth of the image in which it is clothed. "We must have books," he says, "for recreation and entertainment, as well as books for instruction and for business. The former are agreeable, the latter useful; and the human mind requires both. The canon law and the codes of Justinian shall have due honor, and reign at the universities, but Homer and Virgil need not therefore be banished. We will cultivate the olive and the vine, but without eradicating the myrtle and the rose."

I have two remarks to make, however, respecting this passage. In the first place, Balzac concedes too much to those pedants who turn up their noses at the favorites of the Muses and their works, when he reckons the Homers and the Virgils among the merely agreeable writers. Antiquity, more wise in this respect, thought differently; and Horace maintains with good reason that there is more practical philosophy to be learned from Homer than from Crantor and Chrysippus.

In the next place, it seems to me on the whole to indicate rather a mercantile than a philosophical way of thinking, when people place the agreeable and the useful in opposition to each other, and look upon the former with a kind of contempt in comparison with the latter.

Presuming that what we understand by the agreeable is something that violates neither law nor duty nor sound moral sentiment, I say that the useful, as opposed to the agreeable and the beautiful, is common to us with the lowest brute; and that when we love and honor that which is useful in this sense, we do only what the ox and the ass do likewise. The value of such utility depends on the greater or less degree of indispensableness which attaches to it. So far therefore as a thing is necessary to the preservation of the human species and of civil society, so far it is good indeed, but not on that account excellent. Accordingly, we desire the useful, not on its own account, but only on account of certain advantages which we derive from it. The beautiful, on the other hand, we love by virtue of an intrinsic superiority of our nature over the merely animal. For man alone of all animals is endowed with a delicate feeling for order and beauty and grace. Hence, he is so much the more perfect, so much the more a man, the more extended and intense his love for the beautiful, and the greater the refinement and accuracy with which, by mere sensation, he can distinguish different degrees and kinds of beauty.

And therefore, moreover, it is only the beautiful in art as well as in the mode of life and in morals, that distinguishes social, developed, refined man from savages and barbarians. Nay, all the arts without exception, and the sciences, too, owe their growth almost exclusively to this love for the beautiful and the perfect, inherent in man, and would still be infinitely removed from that degree of perfection to which they have risen in Europe, if men had attempted to confine them within the narrow limits of the necessary and the useful, in the common acceptation of those words.

Socrates did so, and if ever he was mistaken in anything, it was in this. Kepler and Newton would never have discovered the laws of the mundane system,—the noblest product of human thought,—if, in conformity with his precepts, they had confined geometry to mere mensuration, and astronomy to the mere necessities of travel by land and sea, and to the making of almanacs.

Socrates exhorted painters and sculptors to combine the agreeable and the beautiful with the useful; just as he urged mimic dancers to ennoble the pleasure which their art was capable of yielding, and to entertain the heart together with the senses. According to the same principle, he behooved to admonish those laborers who occupy themselves with things essential, to combine the useful as far as possible with the beautiful. But to deny the name of beautiful to everything that is not useful is to confound ideas.

It is true, Nature herself has established a relation between the useful, and the beautiful and graceful. But these are not desirable because they are useful, but because it is the nature of man to enjoy a pure satisfaction in the contemplation of them, a satisfaction altogether similar to that which we derive from the contemplation of moral excellence, and as much a want of rational beings as food, clothing, shelter, are wants of the animal man.

I say of the animal man because they are common to him with all other, or at least, with most other animals. But neither these animal necessities, nor the power and the effort to satisfy them, constitute him a man. In providing food, in building his nest, in choosing a mate, in training his young, in battling with others who would deprive him of his food, or take possession of his dwelling,—in all this he acts, materially considered, as an animal. It is the way and manner in which man —unless reduced to the condition of a brute, and kept therein by cogent, external circumstances— performs these animal functions, that distinguishes him from and raises him above all other orders of animals, and characterizes his humanity. For this animal that calls itself man, and this only, possesses an inborn feeling for beauty and order, possesses a heart disposed to communication of itself, to sympathy with sorrow and with joy, and to an infinite diversity of agreeable and beautiful sentiments. Only this animal possesses a strong propensity to imitate and to create, and labors unceasingly to improve what he has invented and made.

All these qualities together distinguish him essentially from other animals, make him their lord and master, subject land and sea to his dominion, and lead him from step to step so far that, by the almost unlimited extension of his artistic powers, he is enabled to transform Nature herself, and, from the materials which she furnishes, to create for himself a new world, more perfectly adapted to his particular ends.

The first thing in which man displays this his superiority is the refinement and ennobling of all those wants, impulses, and functions which he has in common with other animals. The time which he requires for this purpose is not to be considered. Enough that he finally arrives at that point where he is no longer necessitated to beg his sustenance from mere chance, and where the greater certainty of a richer and better support allows him leisure to think also of perfecting the other necessities of life. He invents one art after another, and each increases the security or the pleasure of his existence. And so he ascends continually from the indispensable to the convenient, from the convenient to the beautiful.

The natural society into which he is born, combined with the necessity of securing himself against the injurious consequences of a too great extension of the human species, leads him at last to civil society and civilized modes of life.

But here, too, no sooner has he provided for the necessary, for the means of internal and external security, than we find him occupied, in thousandfold ways, with beautifying this his new condition. Imperceptibly small villages are transformed into large cities, the abodes of the arts and of commerce, and points of union for the different nations of the earth. Man spreads himself ever further in all senses and in all directions. Naviga-

tion and traffic multiply relations and pursuits by multiplying the wants and the goods of life. Wealth and luxury refine every art whose mother was want and necessity; leisure, ambition, and public encouragement promote the growth of the sciences, which, by the light they diffuse over all the objects of human life, become rich sources of new advantages and enjoyments.

But in the same proportion in which man adorns and improves his external condition, his feeling for the morally beautiful is also unfolded. He renounces the rude and inhuman uses of the savage state, he learns to abhor all violent conduct toward his kind, and accustoms himself to laws of justice and propriety. The manifold relations of the social condition unfold and determine the ideas of politeness and etiquette, and the desire of pleasing others and of gaining their esteem teaches him to restrain his passions, to conceal his faults, to turn his best side out, and to perform whatsoever he does in a decent manner. In a word, his manners improve with the rest of his condition.

Through all these gradations he raises himself at last to the highest perfection of mind possible in this present life, to the great idea of the whole of which he is a part, to the ideal of the fair and good, to wisdom and virtue, and to the worship of the inscrutable, original Power of Nature, the universal Father of Spirits, to know whose laws and to do them is his greatest privilege, his first duty, and his purest pleasure.

All this we denominate, with one word, the progress of Humanity. And now let every one answer for himself the question, whether man would have made this progress if that inborn feeling of the beautiful and the graceful had remained inactive in him? Take from him this, and all the results of his dormant power, all the monuments of his greatness, all the riches of Nature and Art of which he has possessed himself, disappear; he relapses into the brutal condition of the inhabitants of New Holland; and, with him, Nature herself relapses into savage and formless chaos.

What are all these steps by which man gradually approaches perfection but successive embellishments, embellishments of his necessities, his mode of living, his habitation, his apparel, his implements, embellishments of his mind and heart, his sentiments and passions, his language, manners, customs, pleasures?

What a distance from the earliest hovel to a building of Palladio! From the canoe of a Carib to a ship of the line! From

the three blocks by which, in the remotest ages, the Bœotians represented the three Graces, to the Graces of Praxiteles! From a village of Hottentots or wild Indians to a city like London! From the ornaments of a woman of New Zealand to the state dress of a sultana! From the dialect of the natives of Otaheite to the languages of Homer, of Virgil, Tasso, Milton, and Voltaire!

What innumerable gradations of embellishment must men and human things have passed through before they could overcome this almost measureless interval!

The desire to beautify and refine, and the dissatisfaction with the lower grade as soon as a higher was known, are the true, the only, and the very simple forces by which man has been urged onward to the point at which we find him. All nations which have perfected themselves are a proof of this proposition. And if there are any to be found which, without any special impediment, physical or moral, have always remained stationary in the same degree of imperfection, or which betray an entire want of those motives to progress, which have been mentioned, we should have reason to regard them rather as a particular species of manlike animals than as actual men of our own race and kind.

If now, as no one will deny, everything which tends to perfect man and his condition deserves the name of useful, where is there any ground for this hateful antithesis which certain Ostrogoths still make between the useful and the beautiful? Probably these people have never thought what the consequences would be, if a nation, which has reached a high degree of refinement, should banish or let starve its musicians, its actors, its poets, its painters, and other artists; in a word, all who minister in the kingdom of the Muses and the Graces;—or, what would be quite as bad, if it should lose its taste in all these arts.

The loss of things which are incomparably less important would make a great gap in its prosperity. If one should reckon up to you what the consequences would be to the French, if only the two little articles, fans and snuffboxes, were stricken out from the number of European necessities, and if you were to consider that these are but two little twigs of the countless branches of that industry elicited by the love for playthings and trinkets, wherewith all the large children in trousers and long coats around us are affected, and if you were to calculate how

useful to the world even these useless things are, and were to reflect that the departments of the beautiful and the useful are not exclusive departments, but are so manifoldly intertwined with each other that it is impossible ever to define with certainty and precision their respective boundaries,—in short, that there exists such an intimate relation between them that almost all that is useful is or may be made beautiful, and all that is beautiful useful;—if you were to consider all this, you would—

But there are some people who, like the Abderites, grow no wiser by considering. He whose head has, once for all, a crook in it, will never, in his life, be brought to see things as they are seen by all the rest of the world who look straight before them.

And then there is still another class of incorrigible people who have always been avowed contemners of the beautiful, not because their head is placed awry, but because they call nothing useful that does not fill their purse. Now, the trade of a sycophant, a quack, a dealer in charms, a clipper of ducats, a pimp, a Tartuffe, is certainly not beautiful; it is therefore perfectly natural that this gentry should manifest on every occasion a profound contempt for that kind of beauty which yields them nothing. Besides, to how many a blockhead is stupidity useful! How many would lose their whole authority, if those among whom they had won or stolen it had taste enough to distinguish the genuine from the false, the beautiful from the ugly! Such persons, to be sure, have weighty, personal reasons to be enemies of wit and taste. They are in the condition of the honest fellow who had married his homely daughter to a blind man, and was unwilling that his son-in-law should be couched.

But the rest of us, who can only gain by being made wiser,— what Abderites we should be if we suffered ourselves to be persuaded by these gentlemen who are interested in the matter, to become blind or to remain blind, in order that the ugliness of their daughters may not come to light!

From Hedge's translation.

JOHN WILSON

("CHRISTOPHER NORTH")

(1785–1854)

THE "Recreations of Christopher North" and the "Noctes Ambrosianæ" are choice examples of a style which cannot obtain except when the "Republic of Letters" is dominated by an aristocracy which recognizes no one who cannot translate a quotation from Horace at sight. This applies especially to the "Noctes Ambrosianæ," a charming book for all who do not feel under compulsion to share their literary delights with the world at large. The "Recreations of Christopher North" consists of essays published originally in the Reviews and is somewhat more popular in its general style; but, except in his tales and poems, Prof. Wilson writes less to teach the unlearned than for the sake of fellowship with those who do not need to be taught. Born at Paisley, Scotland, May 18th, 1785, he was graduated in 1807 from Magdalen College, Oxford. In 1820 he became professor of Moral Philosophy in the University of Edinburgh, a position he retained for many years. It gave him ample leisure which he employed in contributing to Blackwood's, the Quarterly and other periodicals. Maginn, Hogg, and others were associated with him in the production of the "Noctes Ambrosianæ," a series of papers which ran in Blackwood's from 1822 to 1835. Some of Prof. Wilson's tales were received with great favor and are still to be found in every representative collection of Scottish stories. He died at Edinburgh, April 3d, 1854.

THE WICKEDNESS OF EARLY RISING

I HOPE that you are not an early riser. If you are, throw this into the fire — if not, read it. But I beg your pardon; it is impossible that you can be an early riser; and if I thought so, I must be the most impertinent man in the world; whereas, it is universally known that I am politeness and urbanity themselves. Well then, pray, what is this virtue of early rising that one hears so much about? Let us consider it, in the first place, according to the seasons of the year — secondly, according to people's profession — and thirdly, according to their character.

Let us begin with spring — say the month of March. You rise early in the month of March, about five o'clock. It is somewhat darkish — at least gloomyish — dampish — rawish — coldish — icyish — snowyish. You rub your eyes and look about for your breeches. You find them, and after hopping about on one leg for about five minutes, you get them on. It would be absurd to use a light during that season of the year at such an advanced hour as five minutes past five, so you attempt to shave by the spring dawn. If your nose escapes, you are a lucky man; but dim as it is, you can see the blood trickling down in a hundred streams from your gashed and mutilated chin. I will leave your imagination to conjecture what sort of neckcloth will adorn your gullet, tied under such circumstances. However, grant the possibility of your being dressed — and down you come, not to the parlor, or your study — for you would not be so barbarous — but to enjoy the beauty of the morning, — as Mr. Leigh Hunt would say, "out of doors." The moment you pop your phiz one inch beyond the front wall, a scythe seems to cut you right across the eyes, or a great blash of sleet clogs up your mouth, or a hail shower rattles away at you, till you take up a position behind the door. Why, in goodness' name, did I leave my bed? is the first cry of nature — a question to which no answer can be given, but a long chitter grueing through the frame. You get obstinate and out you go. I give you every possible advantage. You are in the country, and walking with your eyes, I will not say open, but partly so, out of the house of a country gentleman worth five thousand a year. It is now a quarter past five, and a fine sharp blustering morning, just like the season. In going down stairs, the ice not having been altogether melted by the night's rain, whack you come upon your posteriors, with your toes pointing up to heaven, your hands pressed against the globe, and your whole body bob, bob, bobbing, one step after another, till you come to a full stop or period, in a circle of gravel. On getting up and shaking yourself you involuntarily look up to the windows to see if any eye is upon you — and perhaps you dimly discern, through the blind mist of an intolerable headache, the old housekeeper in a flannel nightcap, and her hands clasped in the attitude of prayer, turning up the whites of her eyes at this inexplicable sally of the strange gentleman. Well, my good sir, what is it that you propose to do? Will you take a walk in the garden and eat a little fruit — that is to say, a cabbage leaf, or a Jerusalem

artichoke? But the gardener is not quite so great a goose as yourself and is in bed with his wife and six children. So I leave you knocking with your shoulder against the garden gate — in the intervals of reflection on the virtue of early rising in spring.

March, April, and May are gone, and it is summer — so if you are an early riser, up, you lazy dog, for it is between three and four o'clock. How beautiful is the sunrise! What a truly intellectual employment it is to stand for an hour with your mouth wide open, like a stuck pig, gazing on the great orb of day! Then the choristers of the grove have their mouths open likewise; cattle are also lowing — and if there be a dog kennel at hand, I warrant the pack are enjoying the benefits of early rising as well as the best of you, and yelping away like furies before breakfast. The dew, too, is on the ground, excessively beautiful no doubt — and all the turkeys, how-towdies, ducks, and guinea fowls, are moping, waddling, and strutting about, in a manner equally affecting and picturesque, while the cawing of an adjacent rookery invites you to take a stroll in the grove, from which you return with an epaulet on each shoulder. You look at your watch, and find it is at least five hours till breakfast — so you sit down and write a sonnet to June, or a scene of a tragedy; — you find that the sonnet has seventeen lines — and that the *dramatis personæ*, having once been brought upon the stage, will not budge. While reducing the sonnet to the bakers' dozen, or giving the last kick to your heroine, as she walks off with her arm extended heavenwards, you hear the good old family bell warning the other inmates to doff their nightcaps — and huddling up your papers, you rush into the breakfast parlor. The urn is diffusing its grateful steam in clouds far more beautiful than any that adorned the sky. The squire and his good lady make their entrée with hearty faces, followed by a dozen hoydens and hobble-dehoys — and after the first course of rolls, muffins, dry and butter toast has gone to that bourne from which the fewer travelers that return the better — in come the new-married couple, the young baronet and his blushing bride, who, with that infatuation common to a thinking people, have not seen the sun rise for a month past, and look perfectly incorrigible on the subject of early rising.

It is now that incomprehensible season of the year, — autumn. Nature is now brown, red, yellow, and everything but green. These, I understand, are the autumnal tints so much admired.

Up then and enjoy them. Whichever way a man turns his face early in the morning, from the end of August till that of October, the wind seems to be blowing direct from that quarter. Feeling the rain beating against your back, you wonder what the deuce it can have to do to beat also against your face. Then, what is the rain of autumn in this country — Scotland? Is it rain, or mist, or sleet, or hail, or snow, or what in the name of all that is most abhorrent to a lunged animal is it? You trust to a greatcoat — Scotch plaid — umbrella — clogs, etc., etc., etc.; but of what use would they be to you if you were plopped into the boiler of a steam engine? Just so in a morning of autumn. You go out to look at the reapers. Why the whole corn for twenty miles round is laid flat — ten million runlets are intersecting the country much further than fifty eyes can reach — the roads are rivers, the meadows lakes — the moors seas — nature is drenched, and on your return home, if indeed you ever return (for the chance is that you will be drowned at least a dozen times before that), you are traced up to your bedroom by a stream of mud and gravel, which takes the housemaid an hour to mop up, and when fold after fold of cold, clammy, sweaty, fetid plaids, benjamins, coats, waistcoats, flannels, shirts, breeches, drawers, worsteds, gaiters, clogs, shoes, etc., have been peeled off your saturated body and limbs, and are laid in one misty steaming heap upon an unfortunate chair, there, sir, you are standing in the middle of the floor, in *puris naturalibus*, or, as Dr. Scott would say, in *statu quo*, a memorable and illustrious example of the glory and gain of early rising.

It is winter — six o'clock — you are up — you say so, and as I have never had any reason to doubt your veracity, I believe you. By what instinct, or by what power resembling instinct, acquired by long, painful, and almost despairing practice, you have come at last to be able to find the basin to wash your hands, must forever remain a mystery. Then how the hand must circle round and round the inner region of the wash-hand stand, before, in a blessed moment, it comes in contact with a lump of brown soap. But there are other vessels of china, or porcelain, more difficult to find than the basin: for as the field is larger, so is the search more tedious. Inhuman man! many a bump do the bedposts endure from thy merciless and unrelenting head. Loud is the crash of clothes screen, dressing table, mirror, chairs, stools, and articles of bedroom furniture, seemingly placed for no other purpose than to be overturned. If there is a cat in the room, that cat is the climax of comfort. Hissing and snuffing, it claws your naked legs, and while stooping down to feel if she has fetched blood, smack goes your head through the window, which you have been believing quite on the other side of the room; for geography is gone — the points of the compass are as hidden as at the North Pole — and on madly rushing at a venture out of a glimmer supposed to be the door, you go like a battering-ram against a great vulgar white-painted clothes chest, and fall down exhausted on the uncarpeted and sliddery floor. Now, thou Matutine Rose of Christmas, tell me if there be any exaggeration here? But you find the door — so much the worse, for there is a passage leading to a stair, and head over heels you go, till you collect your senses and your limbs on the bearskin in the lobby.

You are a philosopher, I presume, so you enter your study — and a brown study it is with a vengeance. But you are rather weak than wicked; so you have not ordered poor Grizzy to quit her chaff and kindle your fire. She is snoring undisturbed below. Where is the tinder box? You think you recollect the precise spot where you placed it at ten o'clock the night before, for, being an early riser-up, you are also an early lier-down. You clap your blundering fist upon the inkstand, and you hear it spurting over all your beautiful and invaluable manuscripts — and perhaps over the title-page of some superb book of prints, which Mr. Blackwood, or Mr. Miller, or Mr. Constable, has lent you to look at, and to return unscathed. The tinder box is found, and the fire is kindled — that is to say, it deludes you with a faithless smile; and after puffing and blowing till the breath is nearly out of your body, you heave a pensive sigh for the bellows. You find them on a nail, but the leather is burst and the spout broken, and nothing is emitted but a short asthmatic pluff, beneath which the last faint spark lingeringly expires — and, like Moses when the candle went out, you find yourself once more in the dark. After an hour's execration, you have made good your point, and with hands all covered with tallow (for depend upon it, you have broken and smashed the candle, and had sore to do to prop it up with paper in a socket too full of ancient grease) sit down to peruse or to indite some immortal work, an oration of Cicero or Demosthenes, or an article for Ebony. Where are the snuffers? Upstairs in your bedroom. You snuff the long wick with your fingers, and a dreary streak of black immediately is drawn from

top to bottom of the page of the beautiful Oxford edition of Cicero. You see the words, and stride along the cold dim room in the sulks. Your object has been to improve your mind — your moral and intellectual nature — and along with the rest, no doubt, your temper. You therefore bite your lip, and shake your foot, and knit your brows, and feel yourself to be a most amiable, rational, and intelligent young gentleman.

In the midst of these morning studies, from which the present and all future ages will derive so much benefit, the male and female servants begin to bestir themselves, and a vigorous knocking is heard in the kitchen of a poker brandished by a virago against the great, dull, heaping coal in the grate. Doors begin to bang, and there is heard a clattering of pewter. Then comes the gritty sound of sand, as the stairs and lobby are getting made decent; and, not to be tedious, all the indefinable stir, bustle, uproar, and stramash of a general clearance. Your door is opened every half minute, and formidable faces thrust in, half in curiosity, and half in sheer impertinence, by valets, butlers, grooms, stableboys, cooks, and scullions, each shutting the door with his or her own peculiar bang; while whisperings, and titterings, and hoarse laughter, and loud guffaws, are testifying the opinion formed by these amiable domestics of the conformation of the upper story of the early riser. On rushing into the breakfast parlor, the butt end of a mop or broom is thrust into your mouth, as, heedless of mortal man, the mutched mawsey is what she calls dusting the room; and, stagger where you will, you come upon something surly; for a man who leaves his bed at six of a winter morning is justly reckoned a suspicious character, and thought to be no better than he should be. But, as Mr. Hogg says, I will pursue the parallel no further.

I have so dilated and descanted on the first head of my discourse, that I must be brief on the other two, namely, the connection between early rising and the various professions, and between the same judicious habit and the peculiar character of individuals.

Reader, are you a Scotch advocate? You say you are. Well, are you such a confounded ninny as to leave a good warm bed at four in the morning, to study a case on which you will make a much better speech if you never study it at all, and for which you have already received £2 2s. Do you think Jeffrey hops out of bed at that hour? No, no, catch him doing that. Unless,

therefore, you have more than a fourth part of his business (for, without knowing you, I predict that you have no more than a fourth part of his talents), lie in bed till half-past eight. If you are not in the parliament house till ten, nobody will miss you. Reader, are you a clergyman? A man who has only to preach an old sermon of his old father need not, surely, feel himself called upon by the stern voice of duty to put on his smallclothes before eight in the summer and nine in winter. Reader, are you a half-pay officer? Then sleep till eleven; for well thumbed is your copy of the Army List, and you need not be always studying. Reader, are you an editor? Then dose till dinner; for the devils will be let loose upon thee in the evening, and thou must then correct all thy slips.

But I am getting stupid — somewhat sleepy; for, notwithstanding this philippic against early rising, I was up this morning before ten o'clock; so I must conclude. One argument in favor of early rising, I must, however, notice. We are told that we ought to lie down with the sun, and rise with that luminary. Why, is it not an extremely hard case to be obliged to go to bed whenever the sun chooses to do so? What have I to do with the sun — when he goes down, or when he rises up? When the sun sets at a reasonable hour, as he does during a short period in the middle of summer, I have no objection to set likewise, soon after; and, in like manner, when he takes a rational nap, as in the middle of winter, I don't care if now and then I rise along with him. But I will not admit the general principle; we move in different spheres. But if the sun never fairly sets at all for six months, which they say he does not very far north, are honest people on that account to sit up all that time for him? That will never do.

Finally, it is taken for granted by early risers that early rising is a virtuous habit, and that they are all a most meritorious and prosperous set of people. I object to both clauses of the bill, none but a knave or an idiot — I will not mince the matter — rises early, if he can help it. Early risers are generally milk-sop spoonies, ninnies with broad unmeaning faces and groset eyes, cheeks odiously ruddy, and with great calves to their legs. They slap you on the back, and blow their noses like a mail-coach horn. They seldom give dinners. "Sir, tea is ready." "Shall we join the ladies?" A rubber at whist, and by eleven o'clock the whole house is in a snore. Inquire into his motives for

early rising, and it is, perhaps, to get an appetite for breakfast. Is the great healthy brute not satisfied with three penny-rolls and a pound of ham to breakfast, but he must walk down to the Pierhead at Leith to increase his voracity? Where is the virtue of gobbling up three turkeys' eggs, and demolishing a quartern loaf before his majesty's lieges are awake? But I am now speaking of your red, rosy, greedy idiot. Mark next your pale, sallow early riser. He is your prudent, calculating, selfish, money scrivener. It is not for nothing he rises. It is shocking to think of the hypocrite saying his prayers so early in the morning, before those are awake whom he intends to cheat and swindle before he goes to bed.

I hope that I have sufficiently exposed the folly or wickedness of early rising. Henceforth, then, let no knavish prig purse up his mouth and erect his head with a conscious air of superiority when he meets an acquaintance who goes to bed and rises at a gentlemanly hour.

SACRED POETRY

PEOPLE nowadays will write, because they see so many writing; the impulse comes upon them from without, not from within; loud voices from streets and squares of cities call on them to join the throng, but the still small voice that speaketh in the penetralia of the spirit is mute; and what else can be the result, but, in place of the song of lark, or linnet, or nightingale, at the best a concert of mocking birds, at the worst an oratorio of ganders and bubbleys?

At this particular juncture or crisis, the disease would fain assume the symptoms of religious inspiration. The poetasters are all pious — all smitten with sanctity — Christian all over — and crossing and jostling on the Course of Time — as they think, on the highroad to Heaven and Immortality. Never was seen before such a shameless set of hypocrites. Down on their knees they fall in booksellers' shops, and, crowned with foolscap, repeat to Blue-Stockings prayers addressed in doggerel to the Deity! They bandy about the Bible as if it were an album. They forget that the poorest sinner has a soul to be saved, as well as a set of verses to be damned; they look forward to the First of the month with more fear and trembling than to the Last Day; and beseech a critic to be merciful upon them with far more earnestness than they ever beseeched their Maker. They pray through the press — vainly striving to give some publicity to what must be private forevermore; and are seen wiping away, at tea parties, the tears of contrition and repentance for capital crimes perpetrated but on paper, and perpetrated thereon so paltrily, that so far from being worthy of hell fire, such delinquents, it is felt, would be more suitably punished by being singed like plucked fowls with their own unsalable sheets. They are frequently so singed; yet singeing has not the effect upon them for which singeing is designed; and like chickens in a shower that have got the pip, they keep still gasping and shooting out their tongues, and walking on tiptoe with their tails down, till finally they go to roost in some obscure corner, and are no more seen among bipeds.

Among those, however, who have been unfortunately beguiled by the spirit of imitation and sympathy into religious poetry, one or two — who for the present must be nameless — have shown feeling; and would they but obey their feeling, and prefer walking on the ground with their own free feet, to attempting to fly in the air with borrowed and bound wings, they might produce something really poetical, and acquire a creditable reputation. But they are too aspiring; and have taken into their hands the sacred lyre without due preparation. He who is so familiar with his Bible, that each chapter, open it where he will, teems with household words, may draw thence the theme of many a pleasant and pathetic song. For is not all human nature, and all human life, shadowed forth in those pages? But the heart, to sing well from the Bible, must be embued with religious feelings, as a flower is alternately with dew and sunshine. The study of the book must have been begun in the simplicity of childhood, when it was felt to be indeed divine — and carried on through all those silent intervals in which the soul of manhood is restored, during the din of life, to the purity and peace of its early being. The Bible must be to such a poet even as the sky — with its sun, moon, and stars — its boundless blue with all its cloud mysteries — its peace deeper than the grave, because of realms beyond the grave — its tumult louder than that of life, because heard altogether in all the elements. He who begins the study of the Bible late in life, must, indeed, devote himself to it — night and day — and with a humble and a contrite heart as well as an awakened and soaring spirit, ere he can hope to feel

x—246

what he understands, or to understand what he feels — thoughts and feelings breathing in upon him, as if from a region hanging, in its mystery, between heaven and earth. Nor do we think that he will lightly venture on the composition of poetry drawn from such a source. The very thought of doing so, were it to occur to his mind, would seem irreverent; it would convince him that he was still the slave of vanity, and pride, and the world.

They alone, therefore, to whom God has given genius as well as faith, zeal, and benevolence, will, of their own accord, fix their Pindus either on Lebanon or Calvary — and of these but few. The genius must be high — the faith sure — and human love must coalesce with divine, that the strain may have power to reach the spirits of men, immersed as they are in matter, and with all their apprehensions and conceptions blended with material imagery, and the things of this moving earth and this restless life.

So gifted and so endowed, a great or good poet, having chosen his subject well within religion, is on the sure road to immortal fame. His work, when done, must secure sympathy forever; a sympathy not dependent on creeds, but out of which creeds spring, all of them manifestly molded by imaginative affections of religion. Christian poetry will outlive every other; for the time will come when Christian poetry will be deeper and higher far than any that has ever yet been known among men. Indeed, the sovereign songs hitherto have been either religious or superstitious, and as "the dayspring from on High that has visited us" spreads wider and wider over the earth, "the soul of the world, dreaming of things to come," shall assuredly see more glorified visions than have yet been submitted to her ken. That poetry has so seldom satisfied the utmost longings and aspirations of human nature can only have been because poetry has so seldom dealt in its power with the only mysteries worth knowing — the greater mysteries of religion, into which the Christian is initiated only through faith, an angel sent from heaven to spirits struggling by supplications and sacrifices to escape from sin and death.

These, and many other thoughts and feelings concerning the "vision and the faculty divine," when employed on divine subjects, have arisen within us, on reading — which we have often done with delight — "The Christian Year," so full of Christian poetry of the purest character. Mr. Keble is a poet whom Cow-

per himself would have loved — for in him piety inspires genius, and fancy and feeling are celestialized by religion. We peruse his book in a tone and temper of spirit similar to that which is breathed upon us by some calm day in spring, when all imagery is serene and still — cheerful in the main — yet with a touch and a tinge of melancholy, which makes all the blended bliss and beauty at once more endearing and more profound. We should no more think of criticizing such poetry than of criticizing the clear blue skies — the soft green earth — the "liquid lapse" of an unpolluted stream, that —

"Doth make sweet music with the enamel'd stones,
    Giving a gentle kiss to every flower
It overtaketh on its pilgrimage."

All is purity and peace; as we look and listen, we partake of the universal calm, and feel in nature the presence of him from whom it emanated. Indeed, we do not remember any poetry nearly so beautiful as this, which reminds one so seldom of the poet's art. We read it without ever thinking of the place which its author may hold among poets, just as we behold a "lily of the field" without comparing it with other flowers, but satisfied with its own pure and simple loveliness; or each separate poem may be likened, in its unostentatious — unambitious — unconscious beauty — to

"A violet by a mossy stone,
    Half hidden to the eye."

Of all the flowers that sweeten this fair earth, the violet is indeed the most delightful in itself — form, fragrance, and color — nor less in the humility of its birthplace, and in its haunts in the "sunshiny shade." Therefore, 'tis a meet emblem of those sacred songs that may be said to blossom on Mount Sion. . . .

Poetry in our age has been made too much a thing to talk about — to show off upon — as if the writing and the reading of it were to be reckoned among what are commonly called accomplishments. Thus, poets have too often sacrificed the austere sanctity of the divine art to most unworthy purposes, of which, perhaps, the most unworthy — for it implies much voluntary self-degradation — is mere popularity. Against all such low aims he is preserved, who, with Christian meekness, approaches the muse in the sanctuaries of religion. He seeks not to force his songs

on the public ear; his heart is free from the fever of fame; his poetry is praise and prayer. It meets our ear like the sound of psalms from some unseen dwelling among the woods or hills, at which the wayfarer or wanderer stops on his journey, and feels at every pause a holier solemnity in the silence of nature. Such poetry is indeed got by heart; and memory is then tenacious to the death, for her hold on what she loves is strengthened as much by grief as by joy; and, when even hope itself is dead — if, indeed, hope ever dies — the trust is committed to despair. Words are often as unforgetable as voiceless thoughts; they become very thoughts themselves, and are what they represent. How are many of the simply, rudely, but fervently and beautifully rhymed Psalms of David, very part and parcel of the most spiritual treasures of the Scottish peasant's being!

"The Lord's my shepherd, I'll not want,
    He makes me down to lie
In pastures green: he leadeth me
    The quiet waters by."

These four lines sanctify to the thoughtful shepherd on the braes every stream that glides through the solitary places — they have often given colors to the greensward beyond the brightness of all herbage and of all flowers. Thrice hallowed is that poetry which makes us mortal creatures feel the union that subsists between the Book of Nature and the Book of Life!

From "Recreations of Christopher North."

WILLIAM WIRT

(1772–1834)

IRT'S "Letters of the British Spy," contributed to the Richmond Argus in 1803, proved so popular that they were republished in a volume which passed through many editions. "The Rainbow" and "The Old Bachelor" were series in the style of "The Spectator" contributed by him to the Richmond Enquirer. They met with favor, but did not equal "Letters of the British Spy" in lasting popularity. Wirt was a lawyer, statesman, orator, and historian, as well as an essayist. He was born November 8th, 1772, at Bladensburg, Maryland, but he is completely identified with Virginia where he began the practice of law in 1792, and where he lived until his death, February 18th, 1834. He served as clerk of the Virginia House of Delegates, Chancellor of the Eastern Shore and Member of the House of Delegates. He assisted in the prosecution of Aaron Burr in 1807, and in 1816 was appointed United States District Attorney in Virginia. From 1817 to 1829, he was the Attorney-General of the United States. In 1832 the "Anti-Masons" nominated him for President and "carried" Vermont for him. His "Life of Patrick Henry" is one of the most notable of American biographies, and his oration on the death of Jefferson and Adams (1826) would have made him famous as an orator if he had done nothing else.

A PREACHER OF THE OLD SCHOOL

IT WAS one Sunday, as I traveled through the county of Orange, that my eye was caught by a cluster of horses tied near a ruinous, old, wooden house, in the forest, not far from the roadside. Having frequently seen such objects before, in traveling through these states, I had no difficulty in understanding that this was a place of religious worship.

Devotion alone should have stopped me, to join in the duties of the congregation; but I must confess that curiosity to hear the preacher of such a wilderness was not the least of my motives. On entering, I was struck with his preternatural appearance: he was a tall and very spare old man; his head, which was covered with a white linen cap, his shriveled hands, and his

voice, were all shaking under the influence of a palsy; and a few moments ascertained to me that he was perfectly blind.

The first emotions which touched my breast were those of mingled pity and veneration. But ah! sacred God! how soon were all my feelings changed! The lips of Plato were never more worthy of a prognostic swarm of bees than were the lips of this holy man! It was a day of the administration of the Sacrament; and his subject, of course, was the passion of our Savior. I had heard the subject handled a thousand times; I had thought it exhausted long ago. Little did I suppose that in the wild woods of America I was to meet with a man whose eloquence would give to this topic a new and more sublime pathos than I had ever before witnessed.

As he descended from the pulpit to distribute the mystic symbols, there was a peculiar, a more than human, solemnity in his air and manner which made my blood run cold and my whole frame shiver.

He then drew a picture of the sufferings of our Savior; his trial before Pilate; his ascent up Calvary; his crucifixion, and his death. I knew the whole history; but never, until then, had I heard the circumstances so selected, so arranged, so colored! It was all new: and I seemed to have heard it for the first time in my life. His enunciation was so deliberate that his voice trembled on every syllable; and every heart in the assembly trembled in unison. His peculiar phrases had that force of description that the original scene appeared to be, at that moment, acting before our eyes. We saw the very faces of the Jews: the staring, frightful distortions of malice and rage. We saw the buffet; my soul kindled with a flame of indignation; and my hands were involuntarily and convulsively clinched.

But when he came to touch on the patience, the forgiving meekness of our Savior; when he drew, to the life, his blessed eyes streaming in tears to heaven; his voice breathing to God a soft and gentle prayer of pardon for his enemies, "Father, forgive them, for they know not what they do"—the voice of the preacher, which had all along faltered, grew fainter and fainter, until his utterance being entirely obstructed by the force of his feelings, he raised his handkerchief to his eyes, and burst into a loud and irrepressible flood of grief. The effect is inconceivable. The whole house resounded with the mingled groans and sobs and shrieks of the congregation.

It was some time before the tumult had subsided so far as to permit him to proceed. Indeed, judging by the usual, but fallacious standard of my own weakness, I began to be very uneasy for the situation of the preacher. For I could not conceive how he would be able to let his audience down from the height to which he had wound them, without impairing the solemnity and dignity of his subject, or perhaps shocking them by the abruptness of the fall. But—no; the descent was as beautiful and sublime as the elevation had been rapid and enthusiastic.

The first sentence with which he broke the awful silence was a quotation from Rousseau, "Socrates died like a philosopher, but Jesus Christ like a God!"

I despair of giving you any idea of the effect produced by this short sentence, unless you could perfectly conceive the whole manner of the man, as well as the peculiar crisis in the discourse. Never before did I completely understand what Demosthenes meant by laying such stress on delivery. You are to bring before you the venerable figure of the preacher; his blindness, constantly recalling to your recollection old Homer, Ossian, and Milton, and associating with his performance the melancholy grandeur of their geniuses; you are to imagine that you hear his slow, solemn, well-accented enunciation, and his voice of affecting, trembling melody; you are to remember the pitch of passion and enthusiasm to which the congregation were raised; and then, the few minutes of portentous, deathlike silence which reigned throughout the house; the preacher removing his white handkerchief from his aged face (even yet wet from the recent torrent of his tears), and slowly stretching forth the palsied hand which holds it, begins the sentence, "Socrates died like a philosopher"—then pausing, raising his other hand, pressing them both clasped together, with warmth and energy to his breast, lifting his "sightless balls" to heaven, and pouring his whole soul into his tremulous voice—"but Jesus Christ—like a God!" If he had been, in deed and in truth, an angel of light, the effect could scarcely have been more divine.

Whatever I had been able to conceive of the sublimity of Massillon, or the force of Bourdaloue, had fallen far short of the power which I felt from the delivery of this simple sentence. The blood, which just before had rushed in a hurricane upon my brain, and, in the violence and agony of my feelings, had held my whole system in suspense, now ran back into my heart, with

a sensation which I cannot describe—a kind of shuddering delicious horror! The paroxysm of blended pity and indignation, to which I had been transported, subsided into the deepest self-abasement, humility, and adoration. I had just been lacerated and dissolved by sympathy for our Savior as a fellow-creature; but now, with fear and trembling, I adored him as—"a God!"

If this description gives you the impression that this incomparable minister had anything of shallow, theatrical trick in his manner, it does him great injustice. I have never seen, in any other orator, such a union of simplicity and majesty. He has not a gesture, an attitude, or an accent, to which he does not seem forced, by the sentiment which he is expressing. His mind is too serious, too earnest, too solicitous, and, at the same time, too dignified, to stoop to artifice. Although as far removed from ostentation as a man can be, yet it is clear from the train, the style and substance of his thoughts, that he is not only a very polite scholar, but a man of extensive and profound erudition. I was forcibly struck with a short, yet beautiful character which he drew of our learned and amiable countryman, Sir Robert Boyle. He spoke of him as if "his noble mind had even before death, divested herself of all influence from his frail tabernacle of flesh"; and called him, in his peculiarly emphatic and impressive manner, "a pure intelligence: the link between men and angels."

This man has been before my imagination almost ever since. A thousand times, as I rode along, I dropped the reins of my bridle, stretched forth my hand, and tried to imitate his quotation from Rousseau; a thousand times I abandoned the attempt in despair, and felt persuaded that his peculiar manner and power arose from an energy of soul, which nature could give, but which no human being could justly copy. In short, he seems to be altogether a being of a former age, or of a totally different nature from the rest of men.

From "Letters of the British Spy."

WILLIAM WORDSWORTH

(1770–1850)

WORDSWORTH'S answer to the question "What is a poet?" would be one of the most important pieces of English prose, if it had no other merit than that of suggesting the reasons for the position he assumed when against the general judgment of his contemporaries he attempted to illustrate poetry as the simple and natural expression of what is of all things in man, the most natural, the least artificial—the intuitions and emotions of which, when they are unperverted, reason is properly the servant. As his method was a protest against the artificiality of the school of Pope, a needless quarrel and much bitterness resulted. The solution of the whole difficulty seems to be that verse is not necessarily poetry because it is simple, and that it may easily cease to be poetry by becoming too highly artistic in its forms of expression. Wordsworth himself wrote a good deal of more or less metrical prose, generally of a good literary quality, in illustrating his theories of simplicity, just as disciples of Pope wrote in intolerably good metre much that was neither prose nor poetry, nor in any true sense literature. But over and above all this, poetry is what Wordsworth calls it—"the impassioned expression which is in the countenance of all science," "the first and last of all knowledge"—"as immortal as the heart of man."

Born in Cumberland, England, April 7th, 1770, Wordsworth became Poet Laureate in 1843 and died April 23d, 1850. With Coleridge and Southey, he established the Lake School of English poetry as a protest against the formalism of Pope. The radical revolution in the mode of poetical expression which followed may have been due to such conscious effort as that of the Lake Poets, but no doubt the influence of the intense and wholly unartificial melody of the verse of Robert Burns would have finally brought about the same result even had no theory of opposition to Pope been formulated. It is curious that while the sonnet has the reputation of being a highly artificial form of versification, Wordsworth's theories of simplicity and naturalness are illustrated in his sonnets more pleasingly than in either the "Prelude" or the "Excursion."

W. V. B.

WHAT IS A POET?

TAKING up the subject upon general grounds, I ask what is meant by the word Poet? What is a poet? To whom does he address himself? And what language is to be expected from him? He is a man speaking to men: a man, it is true, endued with more lively sensibility, more enthusiasm and tenderness, who has a greater knowledge of human nature, and a more comprehensive soul, than are supposed to be common among mankind; a man pleased with his own passions and volitions, and who rejoices more than other men in the spirit of life that is in him; delighting to contemplate similar volitions and passions as manifested in the goings on of the universe, and habitually impelled to create them where he does not find them. To these qualities he has added a disposition to be affected more than other men by absent things as if they were present; an ability of conjuring up in himself passions, which are indeed far from being the same as those produced by real events, yet especially in those parts of the general sympathy which are pleasing and delightful) do more nearly resemble the passions produced by real events than anything which, from the motions of their own minds merely, other men are accustomed to feel in themselves; whence, and from practice, he has acquired a greater readiness and power in expressing what he thinks and feels, and especially those thoughts and feelings which, by his own choice, or from the structure of his own mind, arise in him without immediate external excitement.

But whatever portion of this faculty we may suppose even the greatest poet to possess, there cannot be a doubt but that the language which it will suggest to him must, in liveliness and truth, fall far short of that which is uttered by men in real life, under the actual pressure of those passions, certain shadows of which the poet thus produces, or feels to be produced, in himself.

However exalted a notion we would wish to cherish of the character of a poet, it is obvious that, while he describes and imitates passions, his situation is altogether slavish and mechanical, compared with the freedom and power of real and substantial action and suffering. So that it will be the wish of the poet to bring his feelings near to those of the persons whose feelings he

describes, nay, for short spaces of time, perhaps, to let himself slip into an entire delusion, and even confound and identify his own feelings with theirs; modifying only the language which is thus suggested to him by a consideration that he describes for a particular purpose, that of giving pleasure. Here, then, he will apply the principle on which I have so much insisted, namely, that of selection; on this he will depend for removing what would otherwise be painful or disgusting in the passion; he will feel that there is no necessity to trick out or elevate nature; and, the more industriously he applies this principle, the deeper will be his faith that no words which his fancy or imagination can suggest will bear to be compared with those which are the emanations of reality and truth.

But it may be said by those who do not object to the general spirit of these remarks, that, as it is impossible for the poet to produce upon all occasions language as exquisitely fitted for the passion as that which the real passion itself suggests, it is proper that he should consider himself as in the situation of a translator, who deems himself justified when he substitutes excellences of another kind for those which are unattainable by him; and endeavors occasionally to surpass his original, in order to make some amends for the general inferiority to which he feels that he must submit. But this would be to encourage idleness and unmanly despair. Further, it is the language of men who speak of what they do not understand; who talk of poetry as of a matter of amusement and idle pleasure; who will converse with us as gravely about a taste for poetry, as they express it, as if it were a thing as indifferent as a taste for ropedancing, or Frontignac, or Sherry. Aristotle, I have been told, hath said that poetry is the most philosophic of all writing; it is so: its object is truth, not individual and local, but general and operative; not standing upon external testimony, but carried alive into the heart by passion; truth which is its own testimony, which gives strength and divinity to the tribunal to which it appeals, and receives them from the same tribunal. Poetry is the image of man and nature. The obstacles which stand in the way of the fidelity of the biographer and historian, and of their consequent utility, are incalculably greater than those which are to be encountered by the poet who has an adequate notion of the dignity of his art. The poet writes under one restriction only, namely, that of the necessity of giving immediate pleasure to a human being possessed of that

information which may be expected from him, not as a lawyer, a physician, a mariner, an astronomer, or a natural philosopher, but as a man. Except this one restriction, there is no object standing between the poet and the image of things: between this and the biographer and the historian there are a thousand.

Nor let this necessity of producing immediate pleasure be considered as a degradation of the poet's art. It is far otherwise. It is an acknowledgment of the beauty of the universe, an acknowledgment the more sincere because it is not formal, but indirect; it is a task light and easy to him who looks at the world in the spirit of love: further, it is an homage paid to the native and naked dignity of man, to the grand elementary principle of pleasure, by which he knows, and feels, and lives, and moves. We have no sympathy but what is propagated by pleasure. I would not be misunderstood, but wherever we sympathize with pain it will be found that the sympathy is produced and carried on by subtle combinations with pleasure. We have no knowledge, that is, no general principles drawn from the contemplation of particular facts, but what has been built up by pleasure, and exists in us by pleasure alone. The man of science, the chemist, and mathematician, whatever difficulties and disgusts they may have had to struggle with, know and feel this. However painful may be the objects with which the anatomist's knowledge is connected, he feels that his knowledge is pleasure; and where he has no pleasure he has no knowledge. What then does the poet? He considers man and the objects that surround him as acting and reacting upon each other, so as to produce an infinite complexity of pain and pleasure; he considers man in his own nature and in his ordinary life as contemplating this with a certain quantity of immediate knowledge, with certain convictions, intuitions, and deductions, which by habit become of the nature of intuitions; he considers him as looking upon this complex scene of ideas and sensations, and finding everywhere objects that immediately excite in him sympathies which, from the necessities of his nature, are accompanied by an overbalance of enjoyment.

To this knowledge which all men carry about with them, and to these sympathies in which, without any other discipline than that of our daily life, we are fitted to take delight, the poet principally directs his attention. He considers man and nature as essentially adapted to each other, and the mind of man as naturally the mirror of the fairest and most interesting qualities of nature. And thus the poet, prompted by this feeling of pleasure which accompanies him through the whole course of his studies, converses with general nature with affections akin to those which, through labor and length of time, the man of science has raised up in himself, by conversing with those parts of nature which are the objects of his studies. The knowledge both of the poet and the man of science is pleasure; but the knowledge of the one cleaves to us as a necessary part of our existence, our natural and unalienable inheritance; the other is a personal and individual acquisition, slow to come to us, and by no habitual and direct sympathy connecting us with our fellow-beings. The man of science seeks truth as a remote and unknown benefactor; he cherishes and loves it in his solitude; the poet, singing a song in which all human beings join with him, rejoices in the presence of truth as our visible friend and hourly companion. Poetry is the breath and finer spirit of all knowledge; it is the impassioned expression which is in the countenance of all science. Emphatically may be said of the poet, as Shakespeare hath said of man, " that he looks before and after." He is the rock of defense of human nature, an upholder and preserver, carrying everywhere with him relationship and love. In spite of difference of soil and climate, of language and manners, of laws and customs, in spite of things silently gone out of mind, and things violently destroyed, the poet binds together by passion and knowledge the vast empire of human society, as it is spread over the whole earth and over all time. The objects of the poet's thoughts are everywhere; though the eyes and senses of man are, it is true, his favorite guides, yet he will follow wheresoever he can find an atmosphere of sensation in which to move his wings. Poetry is the first and last of all knowledge — it is as immortal as the heart of man. If the labors of men of science should ever create any material revolution, direct or indirect, in our condition, and in the impressions which we habitually receive, the poet will sleep then no more than at present, but he will be ready to follow the steps of the man of science, not only in those general indirect effects, but he will be at his side, carrying sensation into the midst of the science itself. The remotest discoveries of the chemist, the botanist, or mineralogist will be as proper objects of the poet's art as any upon which it can be employed, if the time should ever come when these things shall be familiar to us, and

the relations under which they are contemplated by the followers of these respective sciences shall be manifestly and palpably material to us as enjoying and suffering beings. If the time should ever come when what is now called science, thus familiarized to men, shall be ready to put on, as it were, a form of flesh and blood, the poet will lend his divine spirit to aid the transfiguration, and will welcome the being thus produced as a dear and genuine inmate of the household of man. It is not, then, to be supposed that any one, who holds that sublime notion of poetry which I have attempted to convey, will break in upon the sanctity and truth of his pictures by transitory and accidental ornaments, and endeavor to excite admiration of himself by arts, the necessity of which must manifestly depend upon the assumed meanness of his subject.

EPITAPHS

A VILLAGE churchyard, lying as it does in the lap of nature, may, indeed, be most favorably contrasted with that of a town of crowded population; and sepulture therein combines many of the best tendencies which belong to the mode practiced by the Ancients with others peculiar to itself. The sensations of pious cheerfulness which attend the celebration of the Sabbath Day in rural places are profitably chastised by the sight of the graves of kindred and friends, gathered together in that general home towards which the thoughtful yet happy spectators themselves are journeying. Hence a parish church in the stillness of the country is a visible centre of a community of the living and the dead; a point to which are habitually referred the nearest concerns of both.

As, then, both in cities and in villages, the dead are deposited in close connection with our places of worship, with us the composition of an epitaph naturally turns, still more than among the nations of antiquity, upon the most serious and solemn affections of the human mind upon departed worth — upon personal or social sorrow and admiration — upon religion, individual, and social — upon time, and upon eternity. Accordingly it suffices, in ordinary cases, to secure a composition of this kind from censure, that it contains nothing that shall shock or be inconsistent with this spirit. But to entitle an epitaph to praise more than this is necessary. It ought to contain some thought or feeling belong-

ing to the mortal or immortal part of our nature touchingly expressed; and if that be done, however general or even trite the sentiment may be, every man of pure mind will read the words with sensations of pleasure and gratitude. A husband bewails a wife; a parent breathes a sigh of disappointed hope over a lost child; a son utters a sentiment of filial reverence over a departed father or mother; a friend perhaps inscribes an encomium recording the companionable qualities or the solid virtues of the tenant of the grave, whose departure has left a sadness upon his memory. This, and a pious admonition to the living, and a humble expression of Christian confidence in immortality, is the language of a thousand churchyards; and it does not often happen that anything in a greater degree discriminate or appropriate to the dead or to the living is to be found in them. . . .

The first requisite in an epitaph is that it should speak, in a tone which shall sink into the heart, the general language of humanity as connected with the subject of death — the source from which an epitaph proceeds; of death and of life. To be born and to die are the two points in which all men feel themselves to be in absolute coincidence. This general language may be uttered so strikingly as to entitle an epitaph to high praise: yet it cannot lay claim to the highest unless other excellences be superadded. Passing through all intermediate steps, we will attempt to determine at once what these excellences are, and wherein consists the perfection of this species of composition. It will be found to lie in a due proportion of the common or universal feeling of humanity to sensations excited by a distinct and clear conception conveyed to the reader's mind of the individual whose death is deplored and whose memory is to be preserved; at least of his character as, after death, it appeared to those who loved him, and lament his loss. The general sympathy ought to be quickened, provoked, and diversified by particular thoughts, actions, images — circumstances of age, occupation, manner of life, prosperity which the deceased had known, or adversity to which he had been subject; and these ought to be bound together and solemnized into one harmony by the general sympathy. The two powers should temper, restrain, and exalt each other. The reader ought to know who and what the man was whom he is called upon to think of with interest. A distinct conception should be given (implicitly where it can, rather than explicitly) of the individual lamented. But the writer of an epitaph is not

an anatomist who dissects the internal frame of the mind; he is not even a painter who executes a portrait at leisure and in entire tranquillity: his delineation, we must remember, is performed by the side of the grave; and, what is more, the grave of one whom he loves and admires. What purity and brightness is that virtue clothed in, the image of which must no longer bless our living eyes! The character of a deceased friend or a beloved kinsman is not seen, no — nor ought to be seen, otherwise than as a tree through a tender haze or a luminous mist, that spiritualizes and beautifies it; that takes away indeed, but only to the end that the parts which are not abstracted may appear more dignified and lovely, may impress and affect the more. Shall we say, then, that this is not truth, not a faithful image; and that accordingly the purposes of commemoration cannot be answered? It is truth, and of the highest order! for, though doubtless things are not apparent which did exist, yet, the object being looked at through this medium, parts and proportions are brought into distinct view which before had been only imperfectly or unconsciously seen: it is the truth hallowed by love — the joint offspring of the worth of the dead and the affections of the living! This may easily be brought to the test. Let one whose eyes have been sharpened by personal hostility to discover what was amiss in the character of a good man hear the tidings of his death, and what a change is wrought in a moment! Enmity melts away; and as it disappears, unsightliness, disproportion, and deformity vanish; and through the influence of commiseration a harmony of love and beauty succeeds. Bring such a man to the tombstone on which shall be inscribed an epitaph on his adversary, composed in the spirit which we have recommended. Would he turn from it as from an idle tale? No — the thoughtful look, the sigh, and perhaps the involuntary tear, would testify that it had a sane, a generous, and good meaning; and that on the writer's mind had remained an impression which was a true abstract of the character of the deceased; that his gifts and graces were remembered in the simplicity in which they ought to be remembered. The composition and quality of the mind of a virtuous man, contemplated by the side of the grave where his body is moldering, ought to appear, and be felt, as something midway between what he was on earth walking about with his living frailties, and what he may be presumed to be as a spirit in heaven.

XENOPHON

(c. 430–c. 357 B. C.)

XENOPHON was a disciple of Socrates, on intimate terms with his master, and in his "Memorabilia" we have reports of the conversations of the great philosopher which are less embellished, perhaps, than the similar reports of Plato. This is by no means certain, however, as it was a part of the literary art of the Athens of the time to use the known opinions of a master to the best possible advantage, without any special regard to his own forms of expression. We see the same habit illustrated in the freedom with which the classical historians from Thucydides to Tacitus constructed previously unreported orations to suit the characters and express the views of their statesmen and soldiers, with whom they were dealing.

Xenophon, who was born at Athens about 430 B. C., was a historian and essayist of distinguished merit. His "Anabasis" and "Cyropædia" are always likely to remain favorite text-books because of their pure and simple style, though the latter is evidently a romance in the mode of Sir Thomas More's "Utopia" rather than an authentic account of Persian methods in education. Xenophon died about 357 B. C. Among his minor works are "Symposium," "Hiero," and "Œconomics."

SOCRATES' DISPUTE WITH ARISTIPPUS CONCERNING THE GOOD AND BEAUTIFUL

ONE day Aristippus proposed a captious question to Socrates, meaning to surprise him; and this by way of revenge, for his having before put him to a stand: but Socrates answered him warily, and as a person who has no other design in his conversations than the improvement of his hearers.

The question which Aristippus asked him was whether he knew in the world any good thing, and if Socrates had answered him that meat, or drink, or riches, or health, or strength, or courage are good things, he would forthwith have shown him that it may happen that they are very bad. He therefore gave him such an answer as he ought; and because he knew very well that

x—247

when we feel any indisposition we earnestly desire to find a remedy for it, he said to him: "Do you ask me, for example, whether I know anything that is good for a fever?" "No," said Aristippus. "Or for sore eyes?" said Socrates. "Neither." "Do you mean anything that is good against hunger?" "Not in the least," answered Aristippus. "I promise you," said Socrates, "that if you ask me for a good thing that is good for nothing, I know no such thing, nor have anything to do with it."

Aristippus pressed him yet further, and asked him whether he knew any beautiful thing. "I know a great many," said Socrates. "Are they all like one another?" continued Aristippus. "Not in the least," answered Socrates, "for they are very different from one another." "And how is it possible that two beautiful things should be contrary one to the other?" "This," said Socrates, "is seen every day in men: a beautiful make and disposition of body for running is very different from a beautiful make and disposition for wrestling: the excellence and beauty of a buckler is to cover well him that wears it. On the contrary, the excellence and beauty of a dart is to be light and piercing." "You answer me," said Aristippus, "as you answered me before, when I asked you whether you knew any good thing." "And do you think," replied Socrates, "that the good and the beautiful are different? Know you not that the things that are beautiful are good likewise in the same sense? It would be false to say of virtue that in certain occasions it is beautiful, and in others good. When we speak of men of honor we join the two qualities, and call them excellent and good. In our bodies beauty and goodness relate always to the same end. In a word, all things that are of any use in the world are esteemed beautiful and good, with regard to the subject for which they are proper." "At this rate you might find beauty in a basket to carry dung," said Aristippus. "Yes, if it be well made for that use," answered Socrates; "and, on the contrary, I would say that a buckler of gold was ugly if it were ill made." "Would you say," pursued Aristippus, "that the same thing may be beautiful and ugly at once?" "I would say that it might be good and bad. Often what is good for hunger is bad for a fever; and what is good for a fever is very bad for hunger; often what is beautiful to be done in running is ugly to be done in wrestling; and what is beautiful to do in wrestling is ugly in running. For all things are reputed beautiful and good when they are compared with

those which they suit or become, as they are esteemed ugly and bad when compared with those they do not become."

Thus we see that when Socrates said that beautiful houses were the most convenient, he taught plainly enough in what manner we ought to build them, and he reasoned thus: "Ought not he who builds a house to study chiefly how to make it most pleasant and most convenient?" This proposition being granted, he pursued: "Is it not a pleasure to have a house that is cool in summer and warm in winter? And does not this happen in buildings that front towards the south? For the beams of the sun enter into the apartments in winter, and only pass over the covering in summer. For this reason the houses that front towards the south ought to be very high, that they may receive the sun in winter; and, on the contrary, those that front towards the north ought to be very low, that they may be less exposed to the cold winds of that quarter." In short, he used to say that he had a very beautiful and very agreeable house, who could live there with ease during all the seasons of the year, and keep there in safety all that he has; but that for painting and other ornaments, there was more trouble in them than pleasure.

He said further that retired places, and such as could be seen from afar, were very proper to erect altars and build temples in; for though we are at a distance from them, yet it is a satisfaction to pray in sight of the holy places, and as they are apart from the haunts of men, innocent souls find more devotion in approaching them.

Complete.

IN WHAT MANNER SOCRATES DISSUADED MEN FROM SELF-CONCEIT AND OSTENTATION

LET us now see whether by dissuading his friends from a vain ostentation he did not exhort them to the pursuit of virtue.

He frequently said that there was no readier way to glory than to render oneself excellent, and not to affect to appear so. To prove this he alleged the following example: "Let us suppose," said he, "that any one would be thought a good musician, without being so in reality; what course must he take? He must be careful to imitate the great masters in everything that is not of their art; he must, like them, have fine musical instruments; he must, like them, be followed by a great number of persons

wherever he goes, who must be always talking in his praise. And yet he must not venture to sing in public; for then all men would immediately perceive not only his ignorance, but his presumption and folly likewise. And would it not be ridiculous in him to spend his estate to ruin his reputation? In like manner, if any one would appear a great general, or a good pilot, though he knew nothing of either, what would be the issue of it? If he cannot make others believe it, it troubles him, and if he can persuade them to think so he is yet more unhappy, because, if he be made choice of for the steering of ships, or to command an army, he will acquit himself very ill of his office, and perhaps be the cause of the loss of his best friends. It is not less dangerous to appear to be rich, or brave, or strong, if we are not so indeed, for this opinion of us may procure us employments that are above our capacity, and if we fail to effect what was expected of us there is no remission for our faults. And if it be a great cheat to wheedle one of your neighbors out of any of his ready money or goods, and not restore them to him afterwards, it is a much greater impudence and cheat for a worthless fellow to persuade the world that he is capable to govern a republic." By these and the like arguments he inspired a hatred of vanity and ostentation into the minds of those who frequented him.

Complete.

SEVERAL APOTHEGMS OF SOCRATES

A CERTAIN man being vexed that he had saluted one who did not return his civility, Socrates said to him, "It is ridiculous in you to be unconcerned when you meet a sick man in the way, and to be vexed for having met a rude fellow."

Another was saying that he had lost his appetite and could eat nothing. Socrates, having heard it, told him he could teach him a remedy for that. The man asking what it was, "Fast," said he, "for some time, and I will warrant you will be in better health, spend less money, and eat with more satisfaction afterwards."

Another complained that the water which came into the cistern was warm, and nevertheless he was forced to drink it. "You ought to be glad of it," said Socrates, "for it is a bath ready for you, whenever you have a mind to bathe yourself." "It is too cold to bathe in," replied the other. "Do your servants," said

Socrates, "find any inconvenience in drinking it, or in bathing in it?" "No, but I wonder how they can suffer it." "Is it," continued Socrates, "warmer to drink than that of the temple of Æsculapius?" "It is not near so warm." "You see then," said Socrates, "that you are harder to please than your own servants, or even than the sick themselves."

A master having beaten his servant most cruelly, Socrates asked him why he was so angry with him. The master answered, "Because he is a drunkard, a lazy fellow who loves money, and is always idle." "Suppose he be so," said Socrates: "but be your own judge, and tell me, which of you two deserves rather to be punished for those faults?"

Another made a difficulty of undertaking a journey to Olympia. "What is the reason," said Socrates to him, "that you are so much afraid of walking, you, who walk up and down about your house almost all day long? You ought to look upon this journey to be only a walk, and to think that you will walk away the morning till dinnertime, and the afternoon till supper, and thus you will insensibly find yourself at your journey's end. For it is certain that in five or six days' time you go more ground in walking up and down than you need to do in going from Athens to Olympia. I will tell you one thing more: it is much better to set out a day too soon than a day too late; for it is troublesome to be forced to go long journeys; and on the contrary, it is a great ease to have the advantage of a day beforehand. You were better, therefore, to hasten your departure than be obliged to make haste upon the road."

Another, telling him that he had been on a great journey, and was extremely weary, Socrates asked whether he had carried anything. The other answered that he had carried nothing but his cloak. "Were you alone?" said Socrates. "No; I had a slave with me." "Was not he loaded?" continued Socrates. "Yes, for he carried all my things." "And how did he find himself upon the road?" "Much better than I." "And if you had been to carry what he did, what would have become of you?" "Alas!" said he, "I should never have been able to have done it." "Is it not a shame," added Socrates, "in a man like you, who have gone through all the exercises, not to be able to undergo as much fatigue as his slave?"

Complete. The foregoing selections from the "Memorabilia" are all from translations of Bysshe.

---

equal value; that he could not renounce the pleasures of science; that he had despised riches at a time when he was most in need of them, and it would be shameful to seek them now, when it was more easy for him to do without them; that he should apportion the provision for his journey according to the distance he had to travel; and that having almost reached the end of his course, he ought to think more of his reception at the inn than of his expenses on the road.

A distaste of the manners of a court led Petrarch into solitude when he was only three-and-twenty years of age, although in his outward appearance, in his attention to dress, and even in his constitution, he possessed everything that could be expected from a complete courtier. He was in every respect formed to please; the beauty of his figure caused people to stop in the street, and point him out as he walked along. His eyes were bright, and full of fire; and his lively countenance proclaimed the vivacity of his mind. The freshest color adorned his cheeks; his features were distinct and manly; his shape fine and elegant; his person tall, and his presence noble. The genial climate of Avignon increased the warmth of his constitution. The fire of youth, the beauty of so many women assembled at the court of the Pope from every nation in Europe, and, above all, the dissolute manners of the court, led him, very early in life, into connections with women. A great portion of the day was spent at his toilet in the decorations of dress. His habit was always white, and the least spot or an improper fold gave his mind the greatest uneasiness. Even in the fashion of his shoes he avoided every form that appeared to him inelegant; they were extremely tight, and cramped his feet to such a degree that it would in a short time have been impossible for him to walk, if he had not recollected that it was much better to shock the eyes of the ladies than to make himself a cripple. In walking through the streets, he endeavored to avoid the rudeness of the wind by every possible means; not that he was afraid of taking cold, but because he was fearful that the dress of his hair might be deranged. A love, however, much more elevated and ardent for virtue and belles-lettres always counterbalanced his devotion to the fair sex. In truth, to express his passion for the sex, he wrote all his poetry in Italian, and only used the learned languages upon serious and important subjects. But notwithstanding the warmth of his constitution, he was always chaste. He held

---

JOHANN GEORG ZIMMERMANN

(1728-1795)

ZIMMERMANN was immortalized by his book "On Solitude" ("Über die Einsamkeit"), first published in 1755. Though out of print and somewhat out of fashion at present, it has not ceased, nor will it ever cease, to be read by those who can admire a work of art regardless of its subject. As "The Complete Angler" is now read most by some who fish least, so Zimmermann is read most now by dwellers in cities where any solitude other than that of the crowd is hopeless. He wrote essays "On National Pride," and other subjects, scientific, moral, and philosophical, but as far as the world is concerned he is a man of one book, existing only in his ideal of solitude.

He was born in Aargau, Switzerland, December 8th, 1728. By profession he was a physician, and after serving at Hanover as court physician, he went to Berlin, where he attended Frederick the Great in his last illness. His "Reminiscences" of their acquaintance, published in 1788 and 1790, are characterized as egotistical and unjust to Frederick. Zimmermann was eccentric in many ways; and while his individuality is at times repellent, the fullness with which he has expressed it is the reason, no doubt, he continues to attract readers who ask him only for recreation and are content to look elsewhere for instruction.

THE INFLUENCE OF SOLITUDE

SOLITUDE and the love of liberty rendered all the pleasures of the world odious to the mind of Petrarch. In his old age he was solicited to officiate as secretary to different popes, at whatever salary he thought proper to fix; and, indeed, every inducement that emolument could afford was insidiously made use of to turn his views that way. But Petrarch replied, "Riches acquired at the expense of liberty are the cause of real misery; a yoke made of gold or silver is not less oppressive than if made of wood or lead." He represented to his patrons and friends that he could not persuade himself to give up his liberty and his leisure, because, in his opinion, the world afforded no wealth of

---

all debauchery in the utmost detestation; repentance and disgust immediately seized his mind upon the slightest indulgence with the sex; and he often regretted the sensibility of his feelings; "I should like," said he, "to have a heart as hard as adamant, rather than be so continually tormented by such seducing passions." Among the number of fine women, however, who adorned the court of Avignon, there were some who endeavored to captivate the heart of Petrarch. Seduced by their charms, and drawn aside by the facility with which he obtained the happiness of their company, he became upon closer acquaintance obedient to all their wishes; but the inquietudes and torments of love so much alarmed his mind that he endeavored to shun its toils. Before his acquaintance with Laura, he was wilder than a stag; but, if tradition is to be believed, he had not, at the age of thirty-five, any occasion to reproach himself with misconduct. The fear of God, the idea of death, the love of virtue, the principles of religion, the fruits of the education he received from his mother, preserved him from numerous dangers by which he was surrounded. The practice of the civil law was at this period the only road to eminence at the court of the Pope; but Petrarch held the law in detestation, and reprobated this venal trade. Previous to devoting himself to the church, he exercised for some time the profession of an advocate, and gained many causes; but he reproached himself with it afterwards. "In my youth," says he, "I devoted myself to the trade of selling words, or rather of telling lies; but that which we do against our inclinations is seldom attended with success. My fondness was for solitude, and I therefore attended the practice of the bar with the greater detestation." The secret consciousness which Petrarch entertained of his own merit gave him, it is true, all the vain confidence of youth, and filled his mind with that lofty spirit which begets the presumption of being equal to everything; but his inveterate hatred of the manners of the court impeded his exertions. "I have no hope," said he, in the thirty-fifth year of his age, "of making my fortune in the court of the Vicar of Jesus Christ; to accomplish that I must assiduously visit the palaces of the great; I must flatter, lie, and deceive." Petrarch was not capable of doing this. He neither hated men nor disliked advancement, but he detested the means that he must necessarily use to attain it. He loved glory, and ardently sought it, though not by the ways in which it is generally obtained. He delighted to walk in the most unfrequented paths, and, in consequence, he renounced the world.

The aversion which Petrarch felt to the manners which are peculiar to courts was the particular occasion of his essay "On Solitude." In the year 1346 he was, as usual during Lent, at Vaucluse. The Bishop of Cavailion, anxious to enter into conversation with him, and to taste the fruits of solitude, fixed his residence at the castle, which is situated upon the summit of a high rock, and appears to be constructed more for the habitation of birds than men; at present the ruins of it only remain to be seen. All that the Bishop and Petrarch had seen at Avignon and Naples had inspired them with disgust of residence in cities, and the highest contempt for the manners of a court. They weighed all the unpleasant circumstances they had before experienced, and opposed the situations which produced them to the advantages of solitude. This was the usual subject of their conversation at the castle, and that which gave birth in the mind of Petrarch to the resolution of exploring, and uniting into one work, all his own ideas and those of others upon this delightful subject. This work was begun in Lent and finished at Easter, but he revised and corrected it afterwards, making many alterations, and adding everything which occurred to his mind previous to the publication. It was not till the year 1366 (twenty years afterwards) that he sent it to the Bishop of Cavailion, to whom it was dedicated.

If all that I have said of Petrarch in the course of this work were to be collected into one point of view, it would be seen what very important sacrifices he made to solitude. But his mind and his heart were framed to enjoy the advantages it affords, with a degree of delight superior to that in which any other person could have enjoyed them, and all this happiness he obtained from his disgust to a court, and from his love of liberty.

From « On Solitude. »

NOTED SAYINGS

AND

CELEBRATED PASSAGES

NOTED SAYINGS AND CELEBRATED PASSAGES

FROM THE BEST ESSAYS, ANCIENT AND MODERN.

[While specially striking passages in the text of the WORLD'S BEST ESSAYS are sometimes repeated in this collection, the passages here given are, as a rule, supplementary to the body of the work.]

A'BECKET, GILBERT A. (England, 1811–1856)

The True Principles of Law.— Every gentleman ought to know a little of law, says Coke, and perhaps, say we, the less the better. Servius Sulpicius, a patrician, called on Mucius Scævola, the Roman Pollock (not one of the firm of Castor & Pollux), for a legal opinion, when Mucius Scævola thoroughly flabbergasted Servius Sulpicius with a flood of technicalities, which the latter could not understand. Upon this Mucius Scævola bullied his client for his ignorance; when Sulpicius, in a fit of pique, went home and studied the law with such effect that he wrote one-hundred-and-four-score volumes of law books before he died; which task was, for what we know, the death of him. We should be sorry, on the strength of this little anecdote, to recommend our nobility to go home and write law books; but we advise them to peruse the «Comic Blackstone,» which would have done Servius Sulpicius a great deal of good to have studied. . . . The term Law, in its general sense, signifies a rule of human action, whether animate or inanimate, rational or irrational; and perhaps there is nothing more inhuman or irrational than an action at law. We talk of the law of motion, as when one man springs towards another and knocks him down; or the law of gravitation, in obedience to which the person struck falls to the earth.

If we descend from animal to vegetable life, we shall find the latter acting in conformity with laws of its own. The ordinary cabbage from its first entering an appearance on the bed to its being finally taken in execution and thrust into the pot for boiling, is governed by the common law of nature.

Man, as we are all aware, is a creature endowed with reason and free will; but when he goes to law as plaintiff, his reason seems to have deserted him; while, if he stands in the position of defendant, it is generally against his free will; and thus that «noblest of animals,» man, is in a very ignoble predicament.

Justinian has reduced the principles of law to three;— 1st. That we should live honestly; 2dly, that we should hurt nobody; and 3dly, that we should give every one his due. These principles have, however, been for sometime obsolete in ordinary legal practice. It used to be considered that justice and human felicity were intimately connected, but the partnership seems to have been long ago dissolved; though we cannot say at what particular period. That man should pursue his own true and substantial happiness, is said to be the foundation of ethics or natural law; but if any one plunges into artificial law, with the view of «pursuing his own true and substantial happiness,» he will find himself greatly mistaken.

It is said that no human laws are of any validity if they are contrary to the law of nature; but we do not mean to deny the validity of the poor law, and some others we could mention. The law of nature contributes to the general happiness of men; but it is in the nature of law to contribute only to the happiness of the attorney.— *From the «Comic Blackstone.»*

ADAMS, JOHN QUINCY (America, 1767–1848)

Principles in Politics.— My own deliberate opinion is, that the more of pure moral principle is carried into the policy and conduct of a government, the wiser and more profound will that policy be. If it is not the uniform course of human events that virtue should be crowned with success, it is at least the uniform will of Heaven that virtue should be the duty of man.— *From «Memoirs of John Quincy Adams.»*

Liberty and Eloquence.—With the dissolution of Roman Liberty, and the decline of Roman taste the reputation and the excellency of the oratorical art fell alike into decay. Under the despotism of the Cæsars, the end of eloquence was perverted from persuasion to panegyric, and all her faculties were soon palsied by the touch of corruption, or enervated by the impotence of servitude.— *Lectures on Rhetoric and Oratory.*

ADDISON, JOSEPH (England, 1672–1719)

Conversation in Confidence.— In private Conversation between intimate Friends, the wisest men very often talk like the weakest; for indeed the talking with a Friend is nothing else but thinking aloud. . . .

Conversation in Crowds.— One would think that the larger the Company is in which we are engaged, the greater variety of Thoughts and Subjects would be started into discourse; but instead of this we find that Conversation is never so much straightened and confined as in numerous assemblies.

Love and Ridicule.— Ridicule, perhaps, is a better expedient against Love, than sober advice; and I am of opinion, that Hudibras and Don Quixote may be as effectual to cure the extravagances of this Passion, as any one of the old philosophers.

Courtship.— The pleasantest part of a man's life is generally that which passes in Courtship, provided his Passion be sincere, and the party beloved kind with Discretion. Love, Desire, Hope, all the pleasing motions of the Soul, rise in the pursuit.

Manners and Civilization.— Complaisance renders a Superior amiable, an Equal agreeable, and an Inferior acceptable. It smooths distinction, sweetens conversation, and makes every one in the company pleased with himself. It produces Good Nature and mutual benevolence, encourages the timorous, soothes the turbulent, humanizes the fierce, and distinguishes a society of civilized persons from a confusion of savages.

AIKIN, LUCY (England, 1781–1864)

Queen Elizabeth's Court.— The ceremonial of her court rivaled the servility of the East: no person of whatever rank ventured to address her otherwise than kneeling; and this attitude was preserved by all her ministers during their audiences of business, with the exception of Burleigh, in whose favor, when aged and infirm, she dispensed with its observance. Hentzner, a German traveler who visited England near the conclusion of her reign, relates, that, as she passed through several apartments from the chapel to dinner, wherever she turned her eyes he observed the spectators throw themselves on their knees. The same traveler further relates, that the officers and ladies whose business it was to arrange the dishes and give tastes of them to the yeomen of the guard by whom they were brought in, did not presume to approach the royal table without repeated prostrations and genuflections, and every mark of reverence due to her majesty in person.

The appropriation of her time and the arrangements of her domestic life present several favorable and pleasing traits.

«First in the morning she spent some time at her devotions; then she betook herself to the dispatch of her civil affairs, reading letters, ordering answers, considering what should be brought before the council, and consulting with her ministers. When she had thus wearied herself, she would walk in a shady garden or pleasant gallery, without any other attendance than that of a few learned men. Then she took her coach, and passed in the sight of her people to the neighboring groves and fields; and sometimes would hunt or hawk. There was scarce a day but she employed some part of it in reading and study,— sometimes before she entered upon her state affairs, sometimes after them.»

She slept little, seldom drank wine, was sparing in her diet, and a religious observer of the fasts. She sometimes dined alone, but more commonly had with her some of her friends. «At supper she would divert herself with her friends and attendants; and if they made her no answer would put them upon mirth and pleasant discourse with great civility. She would then also admit Tarleton, a famous comedian and pleasant talker; and other such men, to divert her with stories of the town and the common jests and accidents.»— *From the «Last Days of Queen Elizabeth.»*

ALCOTT, A. BRONSON (America, 1799–1888)

Egotists in Monologue.— Egotists cannot converse, they talk to themselves only.— *«Concord Days,» Part May, Chap. Conversation.*

ALEXANDER, ARCHIBALD (America, 1772–1851)

Natural Scenery.—Whether the scenery with which our senses are conversant in early life has any considerable effect on the character of the mind, is a question not easily determined. It would be easy to theorize on the subject; and formerly I indulged in many lucubrations,— which at the time seemed plausible,— all tending to the conclusion that minds developed under the constant view and impression of grand or picturesque scenery must, in vigor and fertility of imagination, be greatly superior to those who spend their youth in dark alleys, or in the crowded streets of a large city, where the only objects which constantly meet the senses are stone and brick walls, and dirty and offensive gutters.— *From his Works.*

ALFRED THE GREAT (England, 849–901)

The Equal Nobility of Original Human Nature.— God has made all men equally noble in their original nature. True nobility is in the mind not in the flesh. I wish to live honorably while I live, and after my life to leave to the men, who are after me, my memory in good works.— *Longfellow's translation: essay on «Anglo-Saxon Language and Literature.»*

ANTHONY, SUSAN B. (America, 1820–)

Woman and Her Talents.— Woman has been faithful in a few things; now God is going to make her ruler over many things.

ARBUTHNOT, JOHN (Scotland, 1667–1735)

Newton's Place in Science.— Though the industry of former ages had discovered the periods of the great bodies of the universe, and the true system and order of them, and their orbits pretty near; yet was there one thing still reserved for the glory of this age and the honor of the English nation,— the grand secret of the whole machine; which, now it is discovered, proves to be (like the other contrivances of infinite wisdom) simple and natural, depending upon the most known and most common property of matter, *viz.*, gravity. From this the incomparable Mr. Newton has demonstrated the theories of all the bodies of the solar system, of all the primary planets and their secondaries, and among others, the moon, which seemed most averse to numbers; and not only of the planets, the slowest of which completes its period in less than half the age of a man, but likewise of the comets, some of which it is probable spend more than 2,000 years in one revolution about the sun; for whose theory he has laid such a foundation, that after ages, assisted with more observations, may be able to calculate their returns. In a

word, the precession of the equinoctial points, the tides, the unequal vibration of pendulous bodies in different latitudes, etc., are no more a question to those that have geometry enough to understand what he has delivered on those subjects: a perfection in philosophy that the boldest thinker durst hardly have hoped for; and, unless mankind turn barbarous, will continue the reputation of this nation as long as the fabric of nature shall endure. After this, what is it we may not expect from geometry joined to observations and experiments?— *From an essay on the «Usefulness of Mathematical Learning.»*

ARISTOTLE (Greece, 384–322 B.C.)

Education and the State.— It would therefore be best that the state should pay attention to education, and on right principles, and that it should have the power to enforce it; but if it be neglected as a public measure, then it would seem to be the duty of every individual to contribute to the virtue of his children and friends, or at least to make this his deliberate purpose.— *Ethic. x. 10.*

The Training of Children.— Therefore it is necessary to be in a certain degree trained from our very childhood, as Plato says, to feel pleasure and pain at what we ought; for this is education in its true sense.— *Ethic. ii. 2.*

Happiness, the Gift of Heaven.— If, then, there is anything that is a gift of the gods to men, it is surely reasonable to suppose that happiness is a divine gift, and more than anything else of human things, as it is the best.— *Ethic. i. 10.*

One Swallow Does Not Make Spring.— For one swallow does not make spring, nor yet one fine day; so, also, neither does one day, nor a short time, make a man blessed and happy.— *Ethic. i. 6.*

ARNOLD, BENEDICT (America, 1741–1801)

On «True and Permanent Happiness.»— A union of hearts is undoubtedly necessary to happiness; but give me leave to observe that true and permanent happiness is seldom the effect of an alliance founded on a romantic passion; where fancy governs more than judgment. Friendship and esteem, founded on the merit of the object, is the most certain basis to build a lasting happiness upon; and when there is a tender and ardent passion on one side, and friendship and esteem on the other, the heart (unlike yours) must be callous to every tender sentiment, if the taper of love is not lighted up at the flame.— *From a letter to Miss Peggy Shippen. 1778.*

AURELIUS, MARCUS (Rome, 121–180 A.D.)

A Rule for Happiness.— Be simple and modest in thy deportment, and treat with indifference whatever lies between virtue and vice. Love the human race; obey God.— *vii. 31.*

Change in All Things.— Nature, which rules the universe, will soon change all things which thou seest, and out of their substance will make other things, and again other things from the substance of them, that the world may ever be fresh.— *vii. 25.*

The Man Is What He Thinks.— Such as are thy habitual thoughts, such also will be the character of thy mind; for the soul is dyed by the thoughts.— *v. 16.*

AUSTEN, JANE (England, 1775–1817)

«Only a Novel.»— Although our productions have afforded more extensive and unaffected pleasure than those of any other literary corporation in the world, no species of composition has been so much decried. From pride, ignorance, or fashion, our foes are almost as many as our readers; and while the abilities of the nine-hundredth abridger of the «History of England,» or of the man who collects and publishes in a volume some dozen lines of Milton, Pope, and Prior, with a paper from the Spectator, and a chapter from Sterne, are eulogized by a thousand pens, there seems almost a general wish of decrying the capacity and undervaluing the labor of the novelist, and of slighting the performances which have only genius, wit, and taste to recommend them. «I am no novel reader; I seldom look into novels; do not imagine that I often read novels; it is really very well for a novel.» Such is the common cant. «And what are you reading, miss—?» «Oh! it is only a novel!» replies the young lady; while she lays down her book with affected indifference, or momentary shame. It is only «Cecilia,» or «Camilla,» or «Belinda»; or, in short, only some work in which the greatest powers of the mind are displayed, in which the most thorough knowledge of human nature, the happiest delineation of its varieties, the liveliest effusions of wit and humor, are conveyed to the world in the best chosen language. Now, had the same young lady been engaged with a volume of the Spectator, instead of such a work, how proudly would she have produced the book, and told its name! though the chances must be against her being occupied by any part of that voluminous publication of which either the matter or manner would not disgust a young person of taste; the substance of its papers so often consisting in the statement of improbable circumstances, unnatural characters, and topics of conversation, which no longer concern any one living; and their language, too, frequently so coarse as to give no very favorable idea of the age that could endure it.—*From «Northanger Abbey.»*

BACON, FRANCIS (England, 1561–1626)

«Half Way Men.»— The Rabbins note a principle of nature, that putrefaction is more dangerous before maturity than after, and another noteth a position in moral philosophy, that men abandoned to Vice do not so much corrupt manners as those that are half Good and half Evil.

Moroseness and Dignity.— Men possessing minds which are morose, solemn, and inflexible, enjoy, in general, a greater share of Dignity than of Happiness.

BALLOU, HOSEA (America, 1796–1861)

Charity.— How white are the fair robes of Charity, as she walketh amid the lowly habitations of the poor!— *Mss.: Sermons.*

Conscience.— There is one court whose «findings» are incontrovertible, and whose sessions are held in the chambers of our own breast.— *Mss.: Sermons.*

BARRINGTON, SIR J. (Ireland, 1760–1834)

Dress and Address.— Dress has a moral effect upon the conduct of mankind. Let any gentleman find himself with dirty boots, old surtout, soiled neckcloth, and a general negligence of dress, he will, in all probability, find a corresponding disposition by negligence of address.

BARROW, ISAAC (England, 1630–1677)

What Is Wit?— First, it may be demanded what the thing is we speak of, or what this facetiousness doth import? To which question I might reply as Democritus did to him that asked the definition of a man: «'Tis that which we all see and know.» Any one better apprehends what it is by acquaintance than I can inform him by description. It is indeed a thing so versatile and multiform, appearing in so many shapes, so many postures, so many garbs, so variously apprehended by several eyes and judgments, that it seemeth no less hard to settle a clear and certain notion thereof, than to make a portrait of Proteus, or to define the figure of the fleeting air. Sometimes it lieth in pat allusion to a known story, or in seasonable application to a trivial saying, or in forging an apposite tale; sometimes it playeth in words and phrases, taking advantage from the ambiguity of their sense, or the affinity of their sound. Sometimes it is wrapped in a dress of humorous expression; sometimes it lurketh under an odd similitude; sometimes it is lodged in a sly question, in a smart answer, in a quirkish reason, in a shrewd intimation, in cunningly diverting or cleverly retorting an objection; sometimes it is couched in a bold scheme of speech, in a tart irony, in a lusty hyperbole, in a startling metaphor, in a plausible reconciling of contradictions, or in acute nonsense; sometimes a scenical representation of persons or things, a counterfeit speech, a mimical look or gesture passeth for it; sometimes an affected simplicity, sometimes a presumptuous bluntness, giveth it being; sometimes it riseth only from a lucky hitting upon what is strange; sometimes from a crafty wresting obvious matter to the purpose; often it consists in one knows not what, and springeth up one can hardly tell how. Its ways are unaccountable and inexplicable, being answerable to the numberless rovings of fancy and windings of language.

Sin.— Sin is never at a stay; if we do not retreat from it, we shall advance in it; and the further on we go, the more we have to come back.

BARTOL, C. A. (America, 1813–)

Hands and Hearts.— There is a hand that has no heart in it, there is a claw or paw, a flipper or fin, a bit of wet cloth to take of, a piece of unbaked dough on the cook's trencher, a cold clammy thing we recoil from, or greedy clutch with the heat of sin, which we drop as a burning coal. What a scale from the talon to the horn of plenty, is this human palm leaf! Sometimes it is like a knife-shaped, thin-bladed tool we dare not grasp, or like a poisonous thing we shake off, or unclean member, which, white as it may look, we feel polluted by!— *The Rising Faith: Training.*

Enduring and Doing.— Patience is a nobler motion than any deed.— *Radical Problems: Materialism.*

BAXTER, RICHARD (England, 1615–1691)

Modesty a Guard against the Devil.— You little know what you have done, when you have first broke the bounds of modesty; you have set open the door of your fancy to the Devil, so that he can, almost at his pleasure ever after, represent the same sinful pleasure to you anew; he hath now access to your fancy to stir up lustful thoughts and desires, so that when you should think of your calling, or of your God, or of your soul, your thoughts will be worse than swinish, upon the filth that is not fit to be named. If the Devil here get in a foot, he will not easily be got out.

Religion at Your Rope's End.— It is one thing to take God and Heaven for your portion, as believers do; and another thing to be desirous of it, as a reserve when you can keep the World no longer. It is one thing to submit to Heaven, as a lesser evil than Hell; and another thing to desire it as a greater good than Earth. It is one thing to lay up treasures and hopes in Heaven, and seek it first; and another thing to be contented with it in our necessity, and to seek the world before it, and give God that the flesh can spare. Thus differeth the Religion of serious Christians, and carnal worldly Hypocrites.

Sin as Self-Murder.— Use Sin as it will use you; spare it not, for it will not spare you; it is your Murderer, and the Murderer of the World; use it, therefore, as a Murderer should be used. Kill it before it kills you; and though it kill your bodies, it shall not be able to kill your souls; and though it bring you to the grave, as it did your Head, it shall not be able to keep you there. If the thoughts of Death, and the Grave, and Rottenness be not pleasant to you, hearken to every temptation to Sin, as you would hearken to a temptation to Self-Murder, and as you would do if the Devil had brought you a knife, and tempted you to cut your throat with it: so do when he offereth you the bait of Sin. You love not Death; love not the cause of Death.

BEACONSFIELD, LORD (England, 1804–1881)

Greatness in Books and Men.— There are some books, when we close them,— one or two in the course of our life,— difficult as it may be to analyze or ascertain the cause, after which our minds seem to have made a great leap. A thousand obscure things receive light; a multitude of indefinite feelings are determined. Our intellect grasps and grapples with all subjects with a capacity, a flexibility, and a vigor, before unknown to us. It masters questions hitherto perplexing, which are not even touched or referred to in the volume just closed. What is the magic? It is the spirit of the supreme author, by a magnetic influence blending with our sympathizing intelligence that directs and inspires it. By that mysterious sensibility we extend to questions which he has not treated, the same intellectual force which he has exercised over those which he has expounded. His genius for a time remains in us. 'Tis the same with human beings as with books. All of us encounter, at least once in our life, some individual who utters words that make us think forever. There are men whose phrases are oracles; who condense in a sentence the secrets of life; who blurt out an aphorism that forms a character or illustrates an existence. A great thing is a great book; but greater than all is the talk of a great man.

And what is a great man? Is it a minister of state? Is it a victorious general? A gentleman in the Windsor uniform? A field marshal covered with stars? Is it a prelate or a prince? A king, even an emperor? It may be all these; yet these, as we must all daily feel, are not necessarily great men. A great man is one who affects the mind of his generation, whether he be a monk in his cloister agitating Christendom, or a monarch crossing the Granicus, and giving a new character to the Pagan world.— *From « Coningsby.»*

BEDE, THE VENERABLE (England, 673–735)

Anglo-Saxon Origins.— In the year of our Lord 449, Martian being made emperor with Valentinian, and the forty-sixth from Augustus, ruled the empire seven years. Then the nation of the Angles, or Saxons, being invited by the aforesaid king, arrived in Britain with three long ships, and had a place assigned them to reside in by the same king, in the eastern part of the island, that they might thus appear to be fighting for their country, whilst their real intentions were to enslave it. Accordingly they engaged with the enemy, who were come from the north to give battle, and obtained the victory; which, being known at home, in their own country, as also the fertility of the country, and the cowardice of the Britons, a more considerable fleet was quickly sent over, bringing a still greater number of men, which, being added to the former, made up an invincible army. The newcomers received of the Britons a place to inhabit, upon condition that they should wage war against their enemies for the peace and security of the country, whilst the Britons agreed to furnish them with pay. Those who came over were of the three most powerful nations of Germany — Saxons, Angles, and Jutes. From the Jutes are descended the people of Kent, and of the Isle of Wight, and those also in the province of the West-Saxons who are to this day called Jutes, seated opposite to the Isle of Wight. From the Saxons, that is, the country which is now called Old Saxony, came the East-Saxons, the South-Saxons, and the West-Saxons. From the Angles, that is, the country which is called Anglia, and which is said, from that time, to remain desert to this day, between the provinces of the Jutes and the Saxons, are descended the East-Angles, the Midland-Angles, Mercians, all the race of the Northumbrians, that is, of those nations that dwell on the north side of the river Humber, and the other nations of the English. The first two commanders are said to have been Hengist and Horsa. Of whom Horsa, being afterwards slain in battle by the Britons, was buried in the eastern part of Kent, where a monument, bearing his name, is still in existence. They were the sons of Vicgilsus, whose father was Vecta, son of Woden; from whose stock the royal race of many provinces deduce their original. In a short time, swarms of the aforesaid nations came over into the island, and they began to increase so much, that they became terrible to the natives themselves who had invited them. Then, having on a sudden entered into league with the Picts, whom they had by this time repelled by the force of their arms, they began to turn their weapons against their confederates. At first, they obliged them to furnish a greater quantity of provisions; and, seeking an occasion to quarrel, protested, that unless more plentiful supplies were brought them, they would break the confederacy, and ravage all the island; nor were they backward in putting their threats in execution. In short, the fire kindled by the hand of these pagans, proved God's just revenge for the crimes of the people; not unlike that which, being once lighted by the Chaldeans, consumed the walls and the city of Jerusalem. For the barbarous conquerors acting here in the same manner, or rather the just Judge ordaining that they should so act, they plundered all the neighboring cities and country, spread the conflagration from the eastern to the western sea, without any opposition, and covered almost every part of the devoted island. Public as well as private structures were overturned; the priests were everywhere slain before the altars; the prelates and the people, without any respect of persons, were destroyed with fire and sword; nor was there any to bury those who had been thus cruelly slaughtered. Some of the miserable remainder, being taken in the mountains, were butchered in heaps. Others, spent with hunger, came forth and submitted themselves to the enemy for food, being destined to undergo perpetual servitude, if they were not killed even upon the spot. Some, with sorrowful hearts, fled beyond the seas. Others, continuing in their own country, led a miserable life among the woods, rocks, and mountains, with scarcely enough food to support life, and expecting every moment to be their last.— *From the «Ecclesiastical History of England.»*

BEECHER, HENRY WARD (America, 1813–1887)

Character. — Sorrow makes men sincere, and anguish makes them earnest.— *The « Life of Jesus, The Christ,» Chap. XII.*

Joy and Sorrow. — Sorrow is divine; but joy was divine first, and will be after weeping and sorrow are swept out of the universe. Joy is more divine than sorrow; for joy is bread, and sorrow is medicine.— *Sermons: « Plymouth Pulpit,» Second Series: « The Perfect Manhood.»*

Love in Its Fullness.— Love is the river of life in this world. Think not that ye know it who stand at the little tinkling rill — the first small fountain. Not until you have gone through the rocky gorges, and not lost the stream; not until you have gone through the meadow, and the stream has widened and deepened until fleets could ride on its bosom; not until beyond the meadow you have come to the unfathomable ocean, and poured, your treasures into its depths — not until then can you know what love is.— *Sermons: «Plymouth Pulpit,» Second Series: « The Right and the Wrong Way of Giving Pleasure.»*

The Soul Never Sleeps. — We sleep, but the loom of life never stops; and the pattern which was weaving when the sun went down is weaving when it comes up to-morrow.—*« Life Thoughts.»*

BEECHER, LYMAN (America, 1775–1863)

On « American Rudeness. » — Our fathers have been ridiculed as an uncouth and uncourtly generation. And it must be admitted that they were not as expert in the graces of dress, and the etiquette of the drawing-room, as some of their descendants. But neither could these have felled the trees, nor guided the plow, nor spread the sail, which they did; nor braved the dangers of Indian warfare; nor displayed the wisdom in counsel which our fathers displayed; and, had none stepped upon the Plymouth Rock but such effeminate critics as these, the poor natives never would have mourned their wilderness lost, but would have brushed them from the land as they would brush the puny insect from their faces; the Pequods would have slept in safety that night which was their last, and no intrepid Mason had hung upon their rear, and driven into exile the panic-struck fugitives.— *From his Works.*

BELZONI, JOHN BAPTIST (Italy, 1778–1823)

The Ruins at Thebes.— On the 22d, we saw for the first time the ruins of great Thebes, and landed at Luxor. Here I beg the reader to observe, that but very imperfect ideas can be formed of the extensive ruins of Thebes, even from the accounts of the most skillful and accurate travelers. It is absolutely impossible to imagine the scene displayed, without seeing it. The most sublime ideas that can be formed from the most magnificent specimens of our present architecture, would give a very incorrect picture of these ruins; for such is the difference not only in magnitude, but in form, proportion, and construction, that even the pencil can convey but a faint idea of the whole. It appeared to me like entering a city of giants, who, after a long conflict, were all destroyed, leaving the ruins of their various temples as the only proofs of their former existence. The temple of Luxor presents to the traveler at once one of the most splendid groups of Egyptian grandeur. The extensive propylæum, with the two obelisks, and colossal statues in the front; the thick groups of enormous columns; the variety of apartments, and the sanctuary it contains; the beautiful ornaments which adorn every part of the walls and columns, described by Mr. Hamilton — cause in the astonished traveler an oblivion of all that he has seen before. If his attention be attracted to the north side of Thebes by the towering remains that project a great height above the wood of palm trees, he will gradually enter that forest-like assemblage of ruins of temples, columns, obelisks, colossi, sphinxes, portals, and an endless number of other astonishing objects, that will convince him at once of the impossibility of a description. On the west side of the Nile, still the traveler finds himself among wonders. The temples of Gournou, Memnonium, and Medinet Aboo, attest the extent of the great city on this side. The unrivaled colossal figures in the plains of Thebes, the number of tombs excavated in the rocks, those in the great valley of the kings, with their paintings, sculptures, mummies, sarcophagi, figures, etc., are all objects worthy of the admiration of the traveler who will not fail to wonder how a nation which was once so great as to erect these stupendous edifices, could so far fall into oblivion that even their language and writing are totally unknown to us.— *From Belzoni's « Narrative.»*

BIGELOW, JOHN (America, 1817–)

Franklin's Character and Religion.— A considerable familiarity with all the authentic literary remains of Franklin has led me to the following conclusions about his religious opinions: —

1. His highest standard of duty was to do unto others as he would have them do to him.

2. He was rather more of a Unitarian than a Trinitarian, in this respect doubtless sympathizing more completely with Dr. Priestley than with the « good bishop » of St. Asaph's.

3. He accepted the Bible as the safest guide to conduct ever written, but, like many others in our own time, forbore to proclaim his unlimited faith in its entire inspiration, rather from an unwillingness to assert what he had not the learning or ability to prove, than from any conviction that it was not inspired, or that a belief in its inspiration could possibly work any harm.

He believed in all the virtues which were sanctified by the life and death of Christ. If he did not practice them at all times, he simply failed in what no child of Adam has succeeded in doing; to what extent, I leave those to determine who have led less selfish lives; who have done more for their fellow-creatures; who have

more conscientiously expiated their errors; who have been less frequently a stumbling-block to weaker brethren; who in their lives have more successfully illustrated the fidelity with which prosperity and happiness wait on good works, and on that faith in the right of which good works are begotten.—*From a letter to the New York Observer, 1879.*

BOILEAU-DESPRÉAUX (France, 1636–1711)

Who Is the Wisest Man?— The wisest man is generally he who thinks himself the least so.

BOTTA, VINCENZO (Italy, 1818–)

The Character of Cavour.— The grandeur of Cavour's character as a statesman must be estimated by the magnitude of his object, the boldness and the prudence with which he executed his designs, and the extraordinary power which he possessed of foreseeing results and of converting obstacles into means. He combined the originality and depth of a theorist with the practical genius of a true reformer; he understood the character of the age in which he lived, and made it tributary to his great purposes. He made self-government the object of legislation, political economy the source of liberty, and liberty the basis of nationality. Aware that neither revolution or conservatism alone could produce the regeneration of his country, he opposed them in their separate action, while he grasped them both with a firm hand, yoked them together, and led them on to conquest. He saw that Italian independence could only be attained through the aid of foreign alliance; he recognized in Napoleon III. the personification of organized revolution, and the natural ally of the Italian people; and the work, which he foreshadowed, in the union of the Sardinian troops with the armies of England and France in the Crimea, and for which he laid the foundation in the congress of Paris, was achieved with the victories of Magenta and Solferino, and the recognition of the new kingdom of Italy.— *Discourse delivered before the New York Historical Society, 1862.*

BRADFORD, WILLIAM (England and New England, 1590–1657)

On the Death of Elder Brewster.— I am to begin this year with that which was a matter of great sadness and mourning unto them all. About the eighteenth of April died their Reverend Elder, and my dear and loving friend, Mr. William Brewster; a man that had done and suffered much for the Lord Jesus and the Gospel's sake, and had borne his part in weal and woe with this poor persecuted church above thirty-six years in England, Holland, and in this wilderness, and done the Lord and them faithful service in his place and calling. And notwithstanding the many troubles and sorrows he passed through, the Lord upheld him to a great age. He was near fourscore years of age (if not all out) when he died. He had this blessing added by the Lord to all the rest,— to die in his bed, in peace, amongst the midst of his friends, who mourned and wept over him, and ministered what help and comfort they could unto him, and he again recomforted them whilst he could. His sickness was not long, and till the last day thereof he did not wholly keep his bed. His speech continued till somewhat more than half a day, and then failed him; and about nine or ten o'clock that evening he died, without any pangs at all. A few hours before, he drew his breath short, and some few minutes before his last, he drew his breath long, as a man fallen into a sound sleep, without any pangs or gaspings, and so sweetly departed this life unto a better.— *From the « History of the Plymouth Plantation.»*

BROOKS, PHILLIPS (America, 1835–1893)

Friendship.— The place where two friends first met is sacred to them all through their friendship — all the more sacred as their friendship deepens and grows old.— *Sermons: « The Young and Old Christian.»*

Delight in Self-Denial. — Only the soul that with an overwhelming impulse and a perfect trust gives itself up forever to the life of other men, finds the delight and peace which such complete self-surrender has to give.— *Sermons: « The Joy of Self-Sacrifice.»*

BROWN, CHARLES BROCKDEN (America, 1771–1810)

Influence of Foreign Literature.— The ideas annexed to the term peasant are wholly inapplicable to the tiller of ground in America; but our notions are the offspring of the books we read. Our books are almost wholly the productions of Europe, and the prejudices which infect us are derived chiefly from this source. These prejudices may be somewhat rectified by age and by converse with the world, but they flourish in full vigor in youthful minds, reared in seclusion and privacy, and undisciplined by intercourse with various classes of mankind.— *From « Clara Howard.»*

BROWNSON, ORESTES A. (America, 1803–1876)

The Bible. — I remember well the time when the Bible was to me a revolting book, when I could find no meaning in it, and when I could not believe that religious people could honestly regard it as they professed to regard it. Its very style and language were offensive, and if I was called upon to write upon religious topics, I took good care to avoid, as much as possible, the use of its phraseology. But it is not so with me now. Life has developed within me wants which no other book can satisfy. Say nothing now of the divine origin of the Bible; take it merely as an ancient writing which has come down to us, and it is to me a truly wonderful production. I take up the writings of the most admired geniuses of ancient or modern times; I read them, and relish them; and yet there is a depth in my experience they do not fathom. This is much, I say; but I have lived more than is here; I have wants this does not meet; it records only a moiety of my experience. But with the Bible it is not so. Whatever my state, its

anomaly in my experience I note, they seem to have recorded it. What experience these men had, if indeed they spoke from experience! It is well called the Book, for it is the book in which seems to be registered all that the individual or the race ever has lived, or ever can live. It is all here.— *From the Boston Quarterly Review.*

BRYANT, WILLIAM CULLEN (America, 1794–1878)

The Perils of Life.— We hold our existence at the mercy of the elements; the life of man is a state of continual vigilance against their warfare. The heats of noon would wither him like the severed herb; the chills and dews of night would fill his bones with pain; the winter frost would extinguish life in an hour; the hail would smite him to death, did he not seek shelter and protection against them. His clothing is the perpetual armor he wears for his defense, and his dwelling the fortress to which he retreats for safety. Yet, even there the elements attack him; the winds overthrow his habitation; the waters sweep it away. The fire, that warmed and brightened it within, seizes upon its walls, and consumes it, with his wretched family. The earth, where she seems to spread a paradise for his abode sends up death in exhalations from her bosom; and the heavens dart down lightnings to destroy him. The drought consumes the harvests on which he relied for sustenance, or the rains cause the green corn to « rot ere its youth attains a beard.» A sudden blast ingulfs him in the waters of the lake or bay from which he seeks his food; a false step, or a broken twig, precipitates him from the tree which he had climbed for its fruit; oaks falling in the storm, rocks toppling down from the precipices are so many dangers which beset his life. Even his erect attitude is a continual affront to the great law of gravitation, which is sometimes fatally avenged when he loses the balance preserved by constant care, and falls on a hard surface. The very arts on which he relies for protection from the unkindness of the elements betray him to the fate he would avoid, in some moment of negligence, or by some misdirection of skill, and he perishes miserably by his own inventions. Amid these various causes of accidental death, which thus surround us at every moment, it is only wonderful that their proper effect is not oftener produced — so admirably has the Framer of the universe adapted the faculties by which man provides for his safety, to the perils of the condition in which he is placed. — *From « Tales of Glauber-Spa.»*

BUCKMINSTER, JOSEPH STEVENS (America, 1784–1812)

The Quiet Things of Life.— It is not the number of the great, dazzling, affecting, and much talked of pleasures, which makes up the better part of our substantial happiness; but it is the delicate, unseen, quiet, and ordinary comforts, which, all that the world has dignified with the name of pleasure would not compensate us. Let any man inquire, for a single day, what it is which has employed and satisfied him, and which really makes him love life, and he will find that the sources of his happiness lie within a very narrow compass. He will find that he depends almost entirely on the agreeable circumstances which God has made to lie all around him, and which fill no place in the record of public events. Indeed, we may say of human happiness what Paul quotes for a more sacred purpose, « It is not hidden from thee; neither is it far off; it is not in heaven, that thou shouldst say, Who shall go up for us, and bring it unto us? neither is it beyond the sea, that thou shouldst say, Who shall go over the sea for us, and bring it unto us? but is very nigh unto thee in thy mouth, and in thy heart.»—*From his Sermons.*

BURDETTE, ROBERT J. (America, 1844–)

Engaged and Married.— They were very pretty, and there was apparently five or six years' difference in their ages. As the train pulled up at Bussey, the younger girl blushed, flattened her nose nervously against the window, and drew back in joyous smiles as a young man came dashing into the car, shook hands tenderly and cordially, and insisted on carrying her valise, magazine, little paper bundle, and would probably have carried herself had she permitted him. The passengers smiled as she left the car, and the murmur went rippling through the coach, « They're engaged.» The other girl sat looking nervously out of the window, and once or twice gathered her parcels together as though she would leave the car, yet seemed to be expecting some one. At last he came. He bulged in at the door like a house on fire, looked along the seats until his manly gaze fell on her upturned, expectant face, roared, « Come on! I've been waiting for you on the platform for fifteen minutes!» grabbed her basket, and strode out of the car, while she followed with a little valise, a bandbox, a paper bag full of lunch, a birdcage, a glass jar of jelly, and an extra shawl; and a crusty looking old bachelor, in the farther end of the car, croaked out, in unison with the indignant looks of the passengers, « They're married!»

BURKE, EDMUND (Ireland, 1729–1797)

War as the Cause of Corruption.— War suspends the rules of moral obligation, and what is long suspended is in danger of being totally abrogated. Civil Wars strike deepest of all into the manners of the people. They vitiate their Politics; they corrupt their Morals; they pervert even the natural taste and relish of Equity and Justice. By teaching us to consider our fellow-creatures in an hostile light, the whole body of our nation becomes gradually less dear to us. The very names of Affection and Kindred, which were the bond of Charity whilst we agreed, become new incentives to hatred and rage when

BURNET, THOMAS (England, 1635–1715)

«Life But a Circulation of Little Mean Actions.»— What is this Life but a circulation of little mean actions? We lie down and rise again, dress and undress, feed and wax hungry, work or play and are weary, and then we lie down again, and the circle returns. We spend the day in trifles, and when the night comes we throw ourselves into the bed of folly, amongst dreams, and broken thoughts, and wild imaginations. Our reason lies asleep by us, and we are for the time as arrant brutes as those that sleep in the stalls, or in the field. Are not the capacities of man higher than these? And ought not his ambition and expectations to be greater? Let us be adventurers for another world. It is at least a fair and noble chance; and there is nothing in this worth our thoughts or our passions. If we should be disappointed, we are still no worse than the rest of our fellow-mortals; and if we succeed in our expectations, we are eternally happy.

BURTON, ROBERT (England, 1577–1640)

The Devil's Bait.— Worldly Wealth is the Devil's Bait; and those whose minds feed upon Riches, recede, in general, from real Happiness, in proportion as their stores increase; as the Moon when she is fullest is furthest from the Sun.

BUTLER, SAMUEL (England, 1612–1680)

An Opinionater.— An opinionater is his own confidant, that maintains more opinions than he is able to support. They are all bastards commonly and unlawfully begotten; but being his own, he had rather, out of natural affection, take any pains, or beg, than they should want a subsistence. The eagerness and violence he uses to defend them argues they are weak, for if they were true, they would not need it. How false soever they are to him he is true to them; and as all extraordinary affections of love or friendship are usually upon the meanest accounts, he is resolved never to forsake them, how ridiculous soever they render themselves and him to the world. He is a kind of a knight-errant, that is bound by his order to defend the weak and distressed, and deliver enchanted paradoxes, that are bewitched, and held by magicians and conjurors in invisible castles. He affects to have his opinions as unlike other men's as he can, no matter whether better or worse, like those that wear fantastic clothes of their own devising. No force of argument can prevail upon him; for, like a madman, the strength of two men in their wits are not able to hold him down. His obstinacy grows out of his ignorance; for probability has so many ways, that whosoever understands them will not be confident of any one. He holds his opinions as men do their lands, and, though his tenure be litigious, he will spend all he has to maintain it. He does not so much as know what opinion means, which always supposing uncertainty, is not capable of confidence. The more implicit his obstinacy is, the more stubborn it renders him.— *From his «Remains.»*

CÆSAR, CAIUS JULIUS (Rome, 100–44 B. C.)

Prosperity as a Penalty of the Worst Wickedness.— The gods sometimes grant greater prosperity and a longer period of impunity to those whom they wish to punish for their crimes, in order that they may feel more acutely a change of circumstances.— *De Bello Gallico.*

«Rights of War.»— It is the right of war for conquerors to treat those whom they have conquered according to their pleasure.— *B. G. I. 36.*

CALHOUN, JOHN C. (America, 1782–1850)

Inventions and Discoveries.— When the causes now in operation have produced their full effect, and inventions and discoveries shall have been exhausted, if that may ever be, they will give a force to public opinion, and cause changes, political and social, difficult to be anticipated. What will be their final bearing, time only can decide with any certainty.

That they will, however, greatly improve the condition of man ultimately, it would be impious to doubt; it would be to suppose, that the all-wise and beneficient Being, the Creator of all, had so constituted man, as that the employment of the high intellectual faculties with which he has been pleased to endow him, in order that he might develop the laws that control the great agents of the material world, and make them subservient to his use, would prove to him the cause of permanent evil, and not of permanent good.

If, then, such supposition be inadmissible, they must, in their orderly and full development, end in his permanent good. But this cannot be unless the ultimate effect of their action, politically, shall be, to give ascendency to that form of government best calculated to fulfill the ends for which government is ordained. For, so completely does the well-being of our race depend on good government, that it is hardly possible any change, the ultimate effect of which should be otherwise, could prove to be a permanent good.— *From one of his speeches.*

The Danger of Subserviency.— Piracy, robbery, and violence of every description may, as history proves, be followed by virtue, patriotism, and national greatness; but where is the example to be found of a degenerate, corrupt, and subservient people, who have ever recovered their virtue and patriotism? Their doom has ever been the lowest state of wretchedness and misery: scorned, trodden down, and obliterated for ever from the list of nations. May Heaven grant that such may never be our doom!— *From a speech on the «Public Deposits.»*

CAMPISTRON, JEAN GALBERT DE (France, 1656–1723)

«Vox Populi.»— The public! the public! how many fools are required to make up a public!— *Maximes et Pensées.*

Learning and Philosophy.— A small inkling of philosophy leads man to despise learning; much philosophy leads man to esteem it.

CASAUBON, MÉRIC (Switzerland, 1599–1671)

Claiming Divine Right.— It is a common frenzy of the ignorant multitude, to be always engaging Heaven on their side; and indeed it is a successful stratagem of any general to gain authority among his soldiers, if he can persuade them he is the man by Fate appointed for such or such an action, though most impracticable.

Truth the Foundation of All Goodness.— The study of Truth is perpetually joined with the love of Virtue; for there's no Virtue which derives not its original from Truth; as, on the contrary, there is no vice which has not its beginning from a Lie. Truth is the foundation of all knowledge, and the cement of all society.

CATO, MARCUS PORCIUS (Italy, 95–46 B. C.)

Silence the Virtue of the Gods.— I think the first Virtue is to restrain the Tongue: he approaches nearest to the Gods, who knows how to be silent, even though he is in the right.

CERVANTES (Spain, 1547–1616)

Historians.— Historians ought to be precise, truthful, and quite unprejudiced, and neither interest nor fear, hatred nor affection, should cause them to swerve from the path of Truth whose mother is History, the rival of time, the depository of great actions, the witness of what is past, the example and instruction to the present, and monitor to the future.

Scholars Who «Go a Sopping.»— I say, then, that the hardships of the scholar are these: in the first place, poverty (not that they are all poor, but I would put the case in the strongest manner possible), and when I have said that he endures poverty, methinks no more need be said to show his misery. For he who is poor is destitute of every good thing; he endures poverty in all its parts—sometimes in hunger and cold, and sometimes in nakedness, and sometimes in all these together. But, notwithstanding all this, it is not so great but that still he eats, though somewhat later than usual, or of the rich man's scraps and leavings, or, which is the scholar's greatest misery, by what is called among them, going a sopping. Neither do they always want a fireside or chimney-corner of some charitable person, which, if it does not quite warm them, at least abates their extreme cold; and lastly, they sleep somewhere under cover.

«The Multitude of Fools.»— I regard it as true that the number of the unwise is greater than that of the prudent; and though it is better to be praised by the few wise than mocked by a multitude of fools, yet I am unwilling to expose myself to the confused judgment of the giddy vulgar, to whose lot the reading of such books for most part falls.

The Poet and the Historian.— The poet may say or sing, not as things were, but as they ought to have been; but the historian must pen them, not as they ought to have been, but as they really were, without adding to or diminishing anything from the truth.

«Where Truth Is, God Is.»— History is a sacred kind of writing, because truth is essential to it, and where truth is, there God himself is, so far as truth is concerned.

Truth as Oil Upon Water.— Truth may be stretched, but cannot be broken, and always gets above falsehood, as oil does above water.

The Virgin Muse of Poetry.— Poetry, good sir, in my opinion, is like a tender virgin, very young, and extremely beautiful, whom divers other virgins—namely, all the other sciences—make it their business to enrich, polish, and adorn; and to her it belongs to make use of them all, and on her part to give a lustre to them all. But this same virgin is not to be rudely handled, nor dragged through the streets, nor exposed in the turnings of the market place, nor posted on the corners or gates of palaces. She is formed of an alchemy of such virtue, that he who knows how to manage her will convert her into the purest gold of inestimable price. He who possesses her should keep a strict hand over her, not suffering her to make excursions in obscene satires or lifeless sonnets. She must in no way be venal; though she need not reject the profits arising from heroic poems, mournful tragedies, or pleasant and artful comedies. She must not be meddled with by buffoons, or by the ignorant vulgar, incapable of knowing or esteeming the treasures locked up in her.

CHANNING, WILLIAM E. (America, 1780–1842)

The Best Books.— In the best books, great men talk to us, give us their most precious thoughts, and pour their souls into ours. God be thanked for books! They are the voices of the distant and the dead, and make us heirs of the spiritual life of past ages. Books are the true believers. They give to all who will faithfully use them the society, the spiritual presence, of the best and greatest of our race.— *Books.*

Grandeur of Character.— Grandeur of character lies wholly in force of soul,—that is, in the force of thought, moral principle, and love; and this may be found in the humblest condition of life.— *«Every Man Great.»*

The Greatness of Common Men.— The greatest man is he who chooses the Right with invincible resolution; who resists the sorest temptations from within and without, who bears the heaviest burdens cheerfully; who is calmest in storms and most fearless under menace and frowns; whose reliance on truth, on virtue, on God, is most unfaltering. I believe this greatness to be most common among the multitude, whose names are never heard.— *«Every Man Great.»*

Mind Made for Growth.— Every mind was made for growth, for knowledge; and its nature is sinned against when it is doomed to ignorance.— *The Present Age.*

CHARRON, PIERRE (France, 1541–1603)

Pride of Ancestry.— Those who have nothing else to recommend them to the respect of others, but only their Blood, cry it up at a great rate, and have their mouths perpetually full of it. They swell and vapor, and you are sure to hear of their families and relations every third word. By this mark they commonly distinguish themselves; you may depend upon it there is no good bottom, nothing of true worth of their own when they insist on so much, and set their credit upon that of others.

Gratitude.— He who receives a Good Turn should never forget it: he who does one, should never remember it.

CHESTERFIELD, EARL OF (England, 1694–1773)

Blockhead Writers and Readers.— I do by no means advise you to throw away your Time in ransacking, like a dull Antiquarian, the minute and unimportant parts of remote and fabulous times. Let blockheads read, what blockheads wrote.

Ceremony with Fools.— All Ceremonies are in themselves very silly things; but yet a man of the world should know them. They are the outworks of manners and decency, which would be too often broken in upon, if it were not for that defense, which keeps the enemy at a proper distance. It is for that reason that I always treat fools and coxcombs with great Ceremony; true Good-breeding not being a sufficient barrier against them.

CHOATE, RUFUS (America, 1799–1859)

The Starlight of History.— History shows you prospects by starlight, or at best by the waning moon.— *From the «Importance of Illustrating New England History.»*

CICERO, MARCUS TULLIUS (Rome, 106–43 B.C.)

On Poets and Their Inspiration.— I have always learned from the noblest and wisest of men, that a knowledge of other things is acquired by learning, rules, and art; but that a poet derives his power from nature herself,—that the qualities of his mind are given to him, if I may say so, by divine inspiration. Wherefore rightly does Ennius regard poets as under the special protection of heaven, because they seem to be delivered over to us as a beneficent gift by the gods. Let then, judges, this name of poet, which even the very savages respect, be sacred in your eyes, men as you are of the most cultivated mind. Rocks and deserts re-echo to their voice; even the wildest animals turn and listen to the music of their words; and shall we, who have been brought up to the noblest pursuits, not yield to the voice of poets?— *Arch. 8.*

When True Life Begins.— I never, indeed, could persuade myself that souls confined in these mortal bodies can be properly said to live, and that, when they leave them, they die; or that they lose all sense when parted from these vehicles; but, on the contrary, when the mind is wholly freed from all corporeal mixture, and begins to be purified, and recover itself again; then, and then only, it becomes truly knowing and wise.— *Senect. 22.*

CLARKE, JAMES FREEMAN (America, 1810–1888)

Art Born of Religion.— Art itself in all its methods, is the child of religion. The highest and best works in architecture, sculpture and painting, poetry and music, have been born out of the religion of nature.— *«Ten Great Religions,» Part II., Chap. IX.*

CLAUDIAN (CLAUDIANUS) (Egypt, *c.* 365–408 A. D.)

Temperance.— Men live best on moderate means: Nature has dispensed to all men wherewithal to be happy, if Mankind did but understand how to use her gifts.

COLERIDGE, SAMUEL TAYLOR (England, 1772–1834)

Conscience.— Can anything be more dreadful than the Thought that an innocent child has inherited from you a disease, or a weakness, the penalty in yourself of sin, or want of caution.

Enthusiasm and Liberty.— Enlist the interests of stern Morality and religious Enthusiasm in the cause of Political Liberty, as in the time of the old Puritans, and it will be irresistible.

Beast and Angel in Man.— As there is much Beast and some Devil in Man, so is there some Angel and some God in him. The Beast and the Devil may be conquered, but in this life never destroyed.

The Soul.— Either we have an immortal soul, or we have not. If we have not, we are beasts; the first and wisest of beasts, it may be; but still true beasts. We shall only differ in degree, and not in kind; just as the elephant differs from the slug. But by the concession of all the materialists of all the schools, or almost all, we are not of the same kind as beasts; and this also we say from our own consciousness. Therefore, methinks, it must be the possession of a soul within us that makes the difference.

COLUMELLA, LUCIUS JUNIUS MODERATUS (Spain, about *c.* 40 A.D.–?)

What Is Most Important in Any Business.— The most important part in every affair is to know what is to be done.— *De R. R. I. 1.*

The Use of Failure.— Practice and experience are of the greatest moment in arts, and there is no kind of occupation in which men may not learn by their abortive attempts.— *De R. R. I. 1.*

COLVIN, SIDNEY (England, 1845–)

Art and Nature.— Art, in the most extended and most popular sense of the word, means everything which we distinguish from Nature. Art and Nature are the two most comprehensive genera of which the human mind has formed the conception. Under the genus Nature, or the genus Art, we include all the phenomena of the universe. But as our conception of Nature is indeterminate and variable, so in some degree is our conception of Art. Nor does such ambiguity arise only because some modes of thought refer a greater number of the phenomena of the universe to the genus Nature, and others a greater number to the genus Art. It arises also because we do not strictly limit the one genus by the other. The range of the phenomena to which we point when we say Art, is never very exactly determined by the range of the other phenomena which at the same time we tacitly refer to the order of Nature. Everybody understands the general meaning of a phrase like Pope's «Blest with each grace of nature and of art.» In such phrases we intend to designate familiarly as Nature all which exists independently of our study, forethought, and exertion—in other words, those phenomena in ourselves or the world which we do not originate but find; and we intend to designate familiarly as Art, all which we do not find but originate—or in other words, the phenomena which we do add by study, forethought, and exertion to those existing independently of us.— *From an essay on Art.*

CONSTANTINIDES, MICHAEL (Modern Greek, Contemporary)

Modern Greek Love-Songs.— It has been the fate of the Greek nation to be frequently insulted and jeered at by foreigners, but among those who have traveled in Greek countries there are to be found some truthful and impartial men, who not only have admired the good qualities of the Greek people, but have set a high value on their language. Pierre Auguste Guys of Marseilles, writing from Greece in 1750, speaks very favorably of the Greeks of that time and of their language unjustly despised by foreigners. He regards the common language of the people as only transformed on the surface, but as preserving beneath it all the richness and the elegance of ancient Greek. The following observation of his is most useful to those who wish to learn modern Greek: «It is impossible for any one to learn the vernacular Greek,» he says, «without first acquiring a knowledge of the folk-lore and metrical proverbs. The Greeks always speak in apophthegms: they are very fond of the tales and proverbs which tradition has preserved among them in common with their customs. . . .» Speaking of the love-songs of the Greeks he says: «But what shall I say of the language of love employed by the Greeks? Nowhere so much as among them are there found the excessive transports of the passion of love. No other language is capable of supplying such a wealth of expressive epithets as Greek lovers lavish upon their mistresses.— *From «Neohellenica.» Macmillan & Co.*

COOK, JOSEPH (America, 1838–)

Conscience.— God is in the word ought, and therefore it outweighs all but God.— *Boston Monday Lectures: «Unexplored Remainders in Conscience.»*

Our secret thoughts are rarely heard except in secret. No man knows what conscience is until he understands what solitude can teach him concerning it.— *Boston Monday Lectures: «Is the Conscience Infallible?»*

The Unknown is an ocean. What is conscience? The compass of the Unknown.— *Boston Monday Lectures: «The Laughter of the Soul at Itself.»*

Conscience and the Soul.— There is a spectacle grander than the ocean, and that is the conscience. There is a spectacle grander than the sky, and that is the interior of the soul. To write the poem of the human conscience, were the subject only one man, and he the lowest of men, would be reducing all epic poems into one supreme and final epos. . . . It is no more possible to prevent thought from reverting to an ideal than the sea from returning to the shore. With the sailor this is called the tide. With the culprit it is called remorse. God heaves the soul like the ocean.— *Boston Monday Lectures: «The Laughter of the Soul at Itself.»*

COOKE, JOHN ESTEN (America, 1830–1886)

«Stonewall» Jackson at Lexington.— We shall endeavor to lay before the reader a truthful sketch of the form of Jackson, seen moving to and fro in the streets of Lexington, between the years 1851 and 1861. It was the figure of a tall, gaunt, awkward individual, wearing a gray uniform, and apparently moving by separate and distinct acts of volition. The stiff and unbending figure passed over the ground with a sort of stride, as though measuring the distance from one given point to another; and those who followed its curious movements saw it pause at times, apparently from having reached the point desired. The eyes of the individual at such moments were fixed intently upon the ground; his lips moved in soliloquy; the absent and preoccupied gaze, and general expression of the features, plainly showed a profound unconsciousness of time and place.

It was perfectly obvious that the mind of the military-looking personage in the gray coat was busy upon some problem entirely disconnected from his actual surroundings. The fact of his presence at Lexington, in the commonwealth of Virginia, had evidently disappeared from his consciousness; the figures moving around him were mere phantasmagoria; he had traveled in search of some principle of philosophy, or some truth in theology, quite out of the real or workday world, and deep into the land of dreams. If you spoke to him at such times, he awoke, as it were, from a sleep, and looked into your face with an air of simplicity and inquiry, which sufficiently proved the sudden transition which he had made from the world of thought to that of reality.

In lecturing to his class his manner was grave, earnest, full of military brevity, and destitute of all the graces of the speaker. Businesslike, systematic, somewhat stern, with an air of rigid will, as though the matter at issue was of the utmost importance, and he was intrusted with the responsibility of seeing that due attention was paid to it, he did not make a very favorable impression upon the volatile youths who sat at the feet of this military disciplinarian. They listened decorously to the grave professor, but once dismissed from his presence, took their revenge by a thousand jests upon his peculiarities of mind and demeanor.

His oddities were the subject of incessant jokes; his eccentric ways were dwelt upon with all the eloquence and sarcastic gusto which characterize the gay conversation of young men discussing an unpopular teacher. No idiosyncracy of the professor was lost sight of. His stiff, angular figure; the awkard movement of his body; his absent and «grum» demeanor; his exaggerated and apparently absurd devotion to military regularity; his exactions of a similar observance on their part; that general oddity, eccentricity, and singularity in moving, talking, thinking, and acting, peculiar to himself, — all these were described on a thousand occasions, and furnished unfailing food for laughter. They called him «Old Tom Jackson,» and, pointing significantly to their foreheads, said he was « not quite right there.» Some inclined to the belief that he was only a great eccentric; but others declared him «crazy.»

Upon one point, however, there seems to have been a general concurrence — the young teacher's possession of an indomitable fearlessness and integrity in the discharge of every duty. His worst enemies have not ventured to say that he did not walk the straight path of right, and administer his official duties without fear, favor, or affection. They were forced to recognize the fact that this stiff military machine measured out justice to all alike, irrespective of persons, and could not be turned aside from the direct course by any influence around him. The cadets laughed at him, but they were afraid of him.

His great principle of government was, that a general rule should not be violated for any particular good; and his military rule of action was, that a man could always accomplish what he willed to perform. This statement may be paraphrased in the words system, regularity, justice, impartiality, and unconquerable perseverance and determination. — *From his «Biography of Jackson.»*

CORAIS, ADAMANTIUS (Modern Greek, 1748–1833)

An Exhortation to Teachers.— «The learned instructors of the nation should love their children, and consider them as sacred trusts confided to their hands by their parents. The most important lesson for their young minds to learn is to render their dispositions gentle, which instruction in science alone without literature cannot effect. Let them then advise them to acquire a sound knowledge of grammar before they include themselves in the list of students of philosophy, that is to say, to learn first the literature of the Greek language with which Latin should be inseparably united. Science without literature is reduced to the humble level of the mechanical arts. Nearly all the ancient philosophers were also men of letters, and the most distinguished among them were the best grammarians. Our ancestors of imperishable memory well understood that the so-called 'humanities' greatly contribute not only to the art of writing but also to actual gentleness and refinement of manners. On this account our ancestors gave the name of music to general education, because it softens the disposition just as music, properly so called, does, and it was for this reason that the divine Plato advised his disciple Xenocrates to sacrifice frequently to the Graces.» — *From Plutarch's «Parallel Lives.» Translated by Michael Constantinides.*

Equality and Civilization.— «Our ancestors included in their list of proverbs 'Equality is friendship,' that is to say, they regarded this as one of those truths which the examination itself of human nature, and daily experience, which agrees with that examination, render incontestable. But if equality produces friendship among men, inequality necessarily has enmity for her daughter. Nature made us at the beginning all equal, since she gave to all the same feelings, the same desires, and the same wants. But such equality only remains as long as the human frame is in its infancy. As soon as it is matured one man shows himself more intelligent than another, one more highly endowed with natural advantages than another, and therefore inequality is necessarily produced, and this gives rise to disagreement. Such is the condition of all mankind. Inequality then is the work of nature herself, and a cure for it was looked for from the state, but every well-ordered state must of necessity have inequalities. The son is not equal to the father, the pupil to the teacher, the one under trial to the judge, the governed to the master, the hired workman to his employer, the rich to the poor. Whoever seeks to equalize in all respects these superiors with these inferiors, seeks to introduce anarchy in the political community, seeks to make civilized man revert to his original savage condition.» — *From Corais's Introduction to the Second Edition of «Beccaria»* (1823). *Translated by Michael Constantinides.*

The Rhetorical Ability of Socrates.— «Socrates, though he did not profess to be an orator, in the way that the sophists used to boast of their rhetoric, was nevertheless really an orator, and was regarded as such. The rhetoric of Socrates was not like that of the sophists; and this explains what kind of rhetoric Plato means when he ridicules rhetoric and represents his master as despising it. A considerable part of his Gorgias is derision of rhetoric, and yet its bitter denouncer, Plato, showed in the highest degree in this very work that he himself was a great orator. The especial care of the sophists was to please the ear by the harmonious combination of the words, caring little about the value or worthlessness of what was said; and long habit in this kind of combination made them true extempore speakers like the celebrated Italian improvvisatori are at the present day. Just as the latter deliver long extempore orations on whatever subject anyone may propose to them, exactly in the same way the sophists used to speak to them upon every subject without any preparation. Gorgias used to boast that he was ready to reply to every question, and complained that no one any longer asked him anything new: 'No one has ever asked me anything new for many years.' This faculty was regarded as a part of rhetoric, and it so much more easily led astray the inexperienced, and especially the young, inasmuch as in those days one of the great defects of the commonwealth was the love of office, since its ability in speaking was of service, since it gave admission to the assemblies where the popular leadership frequently had occasion for the assistance of extempore public oratory. The worst of it was that the sophists used to boast that their rhetoric had such great power that it made an advantage appear a disadvantage, justice injustice, truth falsehood, and falsehood truth. This was called 'to make the worse appear the better cause,' but, since their conscience told them that such a faculty was a faculty which belonged to rogues, they fastened this too on Socrates; just as they had had the audacity to accuse him of making young men insolent to their own parents, although they themselves brought the young to such a pitch of insolence. The rhetoric of Socrates not only had, as I said, no resemblance whatever to the rhetoric of the sophists, but he did not even teach it as they taught it. The sophists had schools and pupils from whom they received enormous fees. Socrates neither opened a school nor collected pupils: the whole city became his school, and all the citizens were his pupils whom, instead of taking fees from them, he advised themselves also to impart gratis whatever good they had learnt from him, and before the time of Christ taught the precept which Christ announced to His disciples: 'Freely have ye received, freely give.' The rhetoric of Socrates was true rhetoric, that is to say, the power of persuading men in whatever is just, by a reasoning founded on the reality and nature of things, and attested by the speaker's actual sentiments. Although he did not imitate the finished style of the sophists, his words had another kind of eloquence which often convinced those whom the ridiculously elaborate oratory of the sophists had not previously poisoned. If anyone had doubts about this, let him compare the discourses of Socrates in the works of Xenophon with the two extant speeches of Gorgias.» — *From Corais's Introduction to Xenophon's «Memorabilia»* (1825). *Translated by Michael Constantinides.*

Wealth and Education.— «Like wealth, in the same way too, the enlightenment of the mind then only is of service to the state when it is distributed in due proportion among all its members. The accumulation of wealth among a few creates Sybarites and absolute paupers, two sections of the community always at war till they have brought ruin on the commonwealth. From the restriction again of learning to a very small number of the members of the state, there arise the highly learned pedants who prevent the enlightenment of the mass, for fear that the common people may despise them, and in the hope of finding the vulgar of service to them whenever they are inclined to gratify their evil passions.» — *Translated by Michael Constantinides.*

The Education of Women.— «Aristotle says that women comprise one-half of the state; and hence whoever studies the education of men only, leaves half of the state to live as it likes, and not in obedience to the laws. 'Consequently in those states where matters which regard women are of no account, half of the state must be considered as not under legislation;' but when half of it is not subject to the law, the other half soon ceases to respect the laws. From women we derive our birth, and under their control we pass the first years of that time of life which, being more impressionable than any other, is more easily capable of being molded into any form. Whatever disposition women have they impart to us with their very milk.» . . . «A sound education takes its source and receives assistance more from good example than from admonition and instruction. Of what good are lessons to a lad when, wherever he turns his eyes, he sees nothing but lawlessness, men inhuman and slavish, flattering and flattered, wealth esteemed and virtue despised, injustice in luxury and justice starving? Most probably such examples will teach him to adopt that kind of life in which he will find the means of cherishing his animal body and gratifying the passions of his still more animal soul.» — *Translated by Michael Constantinides.*

The Refining Influence of Music.— «The ancient philosophers and legislators considered music a necessary part of education, as having the power to soften the savage qualities of the disposition and give men a sense of propriety; as Plutarch says: 'The ancient Greeks very properly took care above everything to be trained in music; for they considered that it was by means of music that they ought to mold the dispositions of the young and inculcate decorum, inasmuch as music is beyond doubt useful for everything and for every action of importance, and especially in encountering the dangers of war.' Polybius attributes the gentle and benevolent disposition of the Arcadians to the special study of music, which from childhood all of them pursued except the one Arcadian city of the Cynætheans, the cause of whose savage nature, he says, was their utter contempt for music. The thing would rightly appear impracticable if I recommended a complete and expensive course of musical study. But first of all, who does not know that among the poor, and especially in the class of our agriculturists, many of them have each his lute? It suffices for their children to be taught to play it a little more melodiously. Then again the lute players do not confine themselves to the instrument, and not only play the lute but also sing to it. What help would not the teachers of the poor give to them, if, in place of foolish and often unbecoming songs, they composed for poor children hymns to God and such songs as might convey under the cover of pleasant recreation some moral precept! But such benefits we must await from the multiplication of our schools and their more perfect organization: we must wait till we also have established a special school for the education of the poor, on the pattern of the celebrated Fellenberg school, and teachers who have Fellenberg's philanthropy. This Socratic educator of poor children was taught by experience that music for all young children is a powerful means of rendering them civilized and fit for society, an efficient instrument with which to accustom them to regulate their life and work together in peaceful harmony, to moderate their undisciplined inclinations, and purify the feelings of the soul and raise it to lofty thoughts. It is particularly useful for imparting gentleness, for gladdening the heart within due bounds, for softening any natural hardness of character, especially in such children as he received in his school from the class of beggars.» — *Translated by Michael Constantinides.*

CRANMER, THOMAS (England, 1489–1556)

The Benefit of Sound Teaching.— Surely there can be no greater hope of any kind of persons, either to be brought to all honest conversation of living, or to be more apt to set forth and maintain all godliness and true religion, than of such as have been from childhood nourished and fed with the sweet milk, and as it were the pap, of God's holy word, and bridled and kept in awe with His holy commandments. For commonly, as we are in youth brought up, so we continue in age; and savor longest of that thing that we first receive and taste of. — *From a letter to Edward VI.*

CRÈVECŒUR, J. HECTOR ST. JOHN DE (France and America, 1731–1813)

The Harmony of Instinct.— The astonishing art which all birds display in the construction of their nests, ill provided as we may suppose them with proper tools, their neatness, their convenience, always make me ashamed of the slovenliness of our houses; their love to their dame, their incessant careful attention, and the peculiar songs they address to her while she tediously incubates their eggs, remind me of my duty, could I ever forget it. Their affection to their helpless little ones, is a lively precept; and in short the whole economy of what we proudly call the brute creation, is admirable in every circumstance; and vain man, though adorned with the additional gift of reason, might learn from the perfection of instinct, how to regulate the follies, and how to temper the errors which this second gift often makes him commit. — *Letters from an American Farmer. 1782.*

CUMBERLAND, RICHARD (England, 1631–1718)

Making the Best of It.— I do not mean to expose my ideas to ingenious ridicule by maintaining that everything happens to every man for the best; but I will contend, that he, who makes the best use of it, fulfills the part of a wise and good man.

Politeness.— Politeness is nothing more than an elegant and concealed species of Flattery, tending to put the person to whom it is addressed in Good-humor and Respect with himself: but if there is a parade and display affected in the exertion of it, if a man seems to say — Look how condescending and gracious I am! — whilst he has only the common offices of civility to perform, such Politeness seems founded in mistake, and this mistake I have observed frequently to occur in French manners.

CUSHMAN, CHARLOTTE (America, 1816–1876)

Acting as a Fine Art.— No one knows better than myself, after all my association with artists of sculpture and painting, how truly my art comprehends all the others, and surpasses them in so far as the study of mind is more than matter. Victor Hugo makes one of his heroines, an actress say: «My art endows me with a searching eye, a knowledge of the soul and the soul's workings, and spite of all your skill, I read you to the depths.» This is a truth more or less powerful as one is more or less gifted by the good God. — *Extract from a letter to Miss Elizabeth Peabody, of Boston.*

DANA, RICHARD HENRY (America, 1787–1879)

Lear as a Victim of Passion.— In most instances, Shakespeare has given us the gradual growth of a passion, with such little accompaniments as agree with it, and go to make up the whole man. In Lear, his object being to represent the beginning and course of insanity, he has properly enough gone but a little back of it, and introduced to us an old man of good feelings enough, but one who had lived without any true principle of conduct, and whose unruled passions had grown strong with age, and were ready, upon a disappointment, to make shipwreck of an intellect never strong. To bring this about, he begins with an abruptness rather unusual; and the old king rushes in before us, with his passions at their height, and tearing him like fiends. — *From his Works.*

D'AUBIGNÉ, JEAN HENRI MERLE (Switzerland, 1794–1872)

Literature and the Reformation.— The impulse which the Reformation gave to public literature in Germany was immense. Whilst, in the year 1513, only thirty-five publications had appeared, and thirty-seven in 1517, the number of books increased with astonishing rapidity after the appearance of Luther's Thesis. In 1518, we find seventy-one different works; in 1519, one hundred and eleven; in 1520, two hundred and eight; in 1521, two hundred and eleven; in 1522, three hundred and forty-seven; and in 1523, four hundred and ninety-eight. . . . And where were all these published? For the most part at Würtemberg. And who were their authors? Generally Luther and his friends. In 1522, one hundred and thirty of the Reformer's writings were published; and, in the year following, one hundred and eighty-three. In this same year only twenty Roman Catholic publications appeared. The literature of Germany thus saw the light in the midst of struggles, contemporaneously with her religion. Already it appeared, as later times have seen it, learned, profound, full of boldness and activity. The national spirit showed itself for the first time without alloy, and at the very moment of its birth, received the baptism of fire from Christian enthusiasm. — *From «The History of the Reformation.»*

DEMOSTHENES (Greece, 384–322 B. C.)

The Price of Liberty.— Various are the devices for the defense and security of cities, as palisades, walls, ditches, and other such kinds of fortification, all of which are the result of the labors of the hand, and maintained at great expense. But there is one common bulwark, which men of prudence possess within themselves — the protection and guard of all people, especially of free states, against the attacks of tyrants. What is this? Distrust. — *Philip. ii. 23.*

The Quality of Leadership.— For all are willing to unite and to take part with those whom they see ready and willing to put forth their strength as they ought. — *Philip. i. 6.*

DEWEY, ORVILLE (America, 1794–1882)

The Danger of Riches.— Ah! the rust of riches! — not that portion of them which is kept bright in good and holy uses — «and the consuming fire» of the passions which wealth engenders! No rich man — I lay it down as an axiom of all experience — no rich man is safe, who is not a benevolent man. No rich man is safe, but in the imitation of that benevolent God, who is the possessor and dispenser of all the riches of the universe. What else mean the miseries of a selfish, luxurious and fashionable life everywhere? What mean the sighs that come up from the purlieus, and couches, and most secret haunts of all splendid and self-indulgent opulence? Do not tell me that other men are sufferers too. Say not that the poor, and destitute, and forlorn, are miserable also. Ah! just heaven! thou hast in thy mysterious wisdom appointed to them a lot hard, full hard, to bear. Poor houseless wretches! who «eat the bitter bread of penury, and drink the baleful cup of misery»; the winter's wind blow keenly through your «looped and windowed raggedness»; your children wander about unshod, unclothed and untended; I wonder not that ye sigh. But why should those who are surrounded with everything that heart can wish, or imagination conceive — the very crumbs that fall from whose table of prosperity might feed hundreds — why should they sigh amidst their profusion and splendor? They have broken the bond that should connect power usefulness, and opulence with mercy. That is the reason. They have taken up their treasures, and wandered away into a forbidden world of their own, far from the sympathies of suffering humanity; and the heavy night dews are descending upon their splendid revels; and the all-gladdening light of heavenly beneficence is exchanged for the sickly glare of selfish enjoyment; and happiness, the blessed angel that hovers over generous deeds and heroic virtues, has fled away from that world of false gayety and fashionable exclusion. — *From «Moral Views of Society,»* etc.

DICKINSON, JOHN (America, 1732–1808)

The Duty of Freedom.— Honor, justice, and humanity call upon us to hold and to transmit to our posterity, that liberty, which we received from our ancestors. It is not our duty to leave wealth to our children; but it is our duty to leave liberty to them. — *From «The Political Writings of John Dickinson.» 1804.*

DIOGENES, LAERTIUS (Greece, Second Century A. D.)

Heaven Our Fatherland.— To one who said to Anaxagoras, «Hast thou no regard for thy fatherland?» «Softly,» said he, «I have great regard for my fatherland,» pointing to heaven. — *xi. 2, 7.*

DIONYSIUS, OF HALICARNASSUS (Greece, First Century B. C.)

A Nation Improved by Sufferings.— But, above all these, by their form of government, which they improved by learning wisdom from the various misfortunes which happened to them, always extracting something useful from every occurrence. — *i. 9.*

Causes of Good Government.— He was of opinion that the good government of states arose from causes which are always the subject of praise by politicians, but are seldom attended to: first, the aid and favor of the gods, which give success to every human undertaking; next, attention to moderation and justice, by love of which citizens are induced to refrain from injuring each other, and to join in cordial union — making virtue, not shameful pleasures, the measure of their happiness; and, lastly, military courage, which renders even the other virtues to be advantageous to their possessors. — *ii. 18.*

Why Governments Fall.— He requested them to recollect that governments are not put an end to by the poor, and those who have no power, when they are compelled to do justice; but by the rich, and those who have a right by their position to administer public affairs, when they are insulted by their inferiors, and cannot obtain redress. — *v. 66.*

DWIGHT, TIMOTHY (America, 1752–1817)

The Beauty of Nature.— Were all the interesting diversities of color and form to disappear, how unsightly, dull, and wearisome, would be the aspect of the world! The pleasures conveyed to us by the endless varieties with which these sources of beauty are presented to the eye, are so much things of course, and exist so much without intermission, that we scarcely think either of their nature, their number, or the great proportion which they constitute in the whole mass of our enjoyment. But were an inhabitant of this country to be removed from its delightful scenery to the midst of an Arabian desert, a boundless expanse of sand, a waste spread with uniform desolation, enlivened by the murmur of no stream and cheered by the beauty of no verdure, although he might live in a palace and riot in splendor and luxury, he would, I think, find life a dull, wearisome, melancholy round of existence, and amid all his gratifications would sigh for the hills and valleys of his native land, the brooks and rivers, the living lustre of the spring, and the rich glories of the autumn. The ever-varying brilliancy and grandeur of the landscape, and the magnificence of the sky, sun, moon, and stars, enter more extensively into the enjoyment of mankind than we, perhaps, ever think, or can possibly apprehend, without frequent and extensive investigation. This beauty and splendor of the objects around us, it is ever to be remembered, are not necessary to their existence, nor to what we commonly intend by their usefulness. It is therefore to be regarded as a source of pleasure gratuitously superinduced upon the general nature of the objects themselves, and in this light, as a testimony of the divine goodness peculiarly affecting.—*From «Theology Explained and Defended.»*

ELIOTT, STEPHEN (America, 1771–1830)

The Ineffable Sublimity of Nature.—What is there that will not be included in the history of nature? The earth on which we tread, the air we breathe, the waters around the earth, the material forms that inhabit its surface, the mind of man, with all its magical illusions and all its inherent energy, the planets that move around our system, the firmament of heaven—the smallest of the invisible atoms which float around our globe, and the most majestic of the orbs that roll through the immeasurable fields of space—all are parts of one system, productions of one power, creations of one intellect, the offspring of Him, by whom all that is inert and inorganic in creation was formed, and from whom all that have life derive their being.

Of this immense system, all that we can examine, this little globe that we inherit, is full of animation and crowded with forms, organized, glowing with life, and generally sentient. No space is unoccupied—the exposed surface of the rock is incrusted with living substances; plants occupy the bark and decaying limbs of other plants; animals live on the surface and in the bodies of other animals; inhabitants are fashioned and adapted to equatorial heats and polar ice;—air, earth, and ocean teem with life.—*From his Works.*

EMERSON, RALPH WALDO (America, 1803–1882)

«God Is the All-Fair.»—No reason can be asked or given why the soul seeks beauty. Beauty, in its largest and profoundest sense, is one expression for the universe. God is the all-fair. Truth and goodness and beauty are but different faces of the same All. But beauty in nature is not ultimate. It is the herald of inward and internal beauty, and is not alone a solid and satisfactory good. It must stand as a part, and not as yet the last or highest expression of the final cause of nature.—*Prose Works.*

Character.—Character is the habit of action from the permanent vision of truth. It carries a superiority to all the accidents of life. It compels right relation to every other man,—domesticates itself with strangers and enemies.—*Character.*

The Highest Human Quality.—Enthusiasm is the height of man; it is the passing from the human to the divine.—*The Superlative.*

Self the Only Thing Givable.—The only gift is a portion of thyself. . . . Therefore the poet brings his poem; the shepherd, his lamb; the farmer, corn; the miner, a gem; the sailor, coral and shells; the painter, his picture; the girl, a handkerchief of her own sewing.—*Essays: Gifts.*

The Simplicity of Greatness.—Nothing is more simple than greatness; indeed, to be simple is to be great.—*Literary Ethics.*

ERASMUS, DESIDERIUS (Holland, 1465–1536)

Love.—Love, that has nothing but Beauty to keep it in good health, is short-lived.

EVERETT, ALEXANDER H. (America, 1792–1847)

Book Making.—It is remarkable that many of the best books of all sorts have been written by persons who, at the time of writing them, had no intention of becoming authors. Indeed, with a slight inclination to systemize and exaggerate, one might be almost tempted to maintain the position,—however paradoxical it may at first blush appear,—that no good book can be written in any other way; that the only literature of any value is that which grows indirectly out of the real action of society, intended directly to effect some other purpose; and that when a man sits down doggedly in his study, and says to himself, «I mean to write a good book,» it is certain, from the necessity of the case, that the result will be a bad one.

To illustrate this by a few examples: Shakespeare, the Greek Dramatists, Lope and Calderon, Corneille, Racine, and Molière,—in short, all the dramatic poets of much celebrity, prepared their works for actual representation, at times when the drama was the favorite amusement. Their plays, when collected, make excellent books. At a later period, when the drama had in a great measure gone out of fashion, Lord Byron, a man not inferior, perhaps, in poetical genius to any of the persons just mentioned, undertakes, without any view to the stage, to write a book of the same kind. What is the result? Something which, as Ninon de l'Enclos said of the young Marquis de Sévigné, has very much the character of fricasseed snow. Homer, again, or the Homerites, a troop of wandering minstrels, composed, probably without putting them to paper, certain songs and ballads, which they sung at the tables of the warriors and princes of their time. Some centuries afterwards, Pisistratus made them up into a book, which became the bible of Greece. Voltaire, whose genius was perhaps equal to that of any of the Homerites, attempted, in cold blood, to make just such a book; and here, again, the product called the «Henriade» is no book, but another lump of fricasseed snow. What are all your pretended histories? Fables, jest books, satires, apologies, anything but what they profess to be. Bring together the correspondence of a distinguished public character, a Washington, a Wellington, and then, for the first time, you have a real history. Even in so small a matter as a common letter to a friend, if you write one for the sake of writing it, in order to produce a good letter as such, you will probably fail. Who ever read one of Pliny's precious specimens of affectation and formality, without wishing that he had perished in the same eruption of Vesuvius that destroyed his uncle? On the contrary, let one who has anything to say to another at a distance, in the way of either business or friendship, commit his thoughts to paper merely for the purpose of communicating them, and he will not only effect his immediate object, but however humble may be his literary pretensions, will commonly write something that may be read with pleasure by an indifferent third person. In short, experience seems to show that every book, prepared with a view to mere book making, is necessarily a sort of counterfeit, bearing the same relation to a real book which the juggling of the Egyptian magicians did to the miracles of Moses.—*From an article on «Madame de Sévigné.»*

EVERETT, EDWARD (America, 1794–1865)

Literature and Liberty.—Literature is the voice of the age and the state. The character, energy, and resources of the country are reflected and imaged forth in the conceptions of its great minds. They are organs of the time; they speak not their own language; they scarce think their own thoughts; but under an impulse like the prophetic enthusiasm of old, they must feel and utter the sentiments which society inspires. They do not create, they obey the Spirit of the Age,—the serene and beautiful spirit descended from the highest heaven of liberty, who laughs at our preconceptions, and, with the breath of his mouth, sweeps before him the men and the nations that cross his path. By an unconscious instinct, the mind, in the action of its powers, adapts itself to the number and complexion of the other minds with which it is to enter into communion or conflict. As the voice falls into the key which is suited to the space to be filled, the mind, in the various exercises of its creative faculties, strives with curious search for that master-note, which will awaken a vibration from the surrounding community, and which, if it do not find it, is itself too often struck dumb.

For this reason, from the moment in the destiny of nations, that they descend from their culminating point, and begin to decline, from that moment the voice of creative genius is hushed, and at best, the age of criticism, learning, and imitation succeeds. When Greece ceased to be independent, the forum and the stage became mute. The patronage of Macedonian, Alexandrian, and Pergamean princes was lavished in vain. They could not woo the healthy Muses of Hellas, from the cold mountain tops of Greece, to dwell in their gilded halls. Nay, though the fall of greatness, the decay of beauty, the waste of strength, and the wreck of power have ever been among the favorite themes of the pensive muse, yet not a poet arose in Greece to chant her own elegy; and it is after near three centuries, and from Cicero and Sulpicius, that we catch the first notes of pious and pathetic lamentation over the fallen land of the arts. The freedom and genius of a country are invariably gathered into a common tomb, and there

> ——can only strangers breathe
> The name of that which was beneath.

—*From Griswold's Selections.*

FEYJOO, BENITO (Spain, 1676–1764)

That Virtue Alone Is Delightful.—Generally, virtue is imagined to be all asperity, vice all delight; virtue to be placed amid thorns vice to be reclining on a bed of flowers. Yet if we were able to look into the hearts of men, immersed in vicious indulgence, our doubts would speedily vanish. By reflection we shall be able to see them in the mirrors of the soul—that is in the countenance, the speech, and actions. Only look at those unhappy beings, and it will be found that nothing can equal the agitation of their countenance, the frenzy of their actions, and the inconsistency of their speech. You need not be surprised; many are the torments that disturb the enjoyment of their pleasures. Their own conscience, a domestic enemy, an unavoidable guest, though ungrateful, is always there, mingling with the nectar which they are drinking.

With what power does Cicero declare that, the vices of the wicked pictured by the imagination are for them never ending and domestic furies! These are the serpents or vultures which gnaw the entrails of the wicked Typhoeus; these the eagles which tear the heart of the bold Prometheus; these the torments of Cain, a fugitive from all, and even, if it were possible, from himself, wandering over mountains and woods, without even being able to pull out the arrow which pierced his heart.—*Translated by Ramage.*

FICHTE, JOHANN GOTTLIEB (Germany, 1762–1814)

The Test of Worth.—Not alone to know, but to act according to thy knowledge, is thy destination, proclaims the voice of my inmost soul. Not for indolent contemplation and study of thyself, nor for brooding over emotions of piety—no, for action was existence given thee; thy actions, and thy actions alone, determine thy worth.

FONTAINE, JEAN DE LA (France, 1621–1695)

The Danger of Foolish Friends.—Nothing is more dangerous than a friend without discretion; even a prudent enemy is preferable.

FONTENELLE, BERNARD LE BOVIER DE (France, 1657–1757)

All Men of the Same Clay.—Nature has within her hands a certain dough, which is always the same, which she turns this way and that way in a thousand different ways, and out of which she makes men, animals, and plants; and undoubtedly she has not made Plato, Demosthenes, or Homer of a finer or better kind of clay than our philosophers, orators, and poets of the present day. In regard to our minds, which are immaterial, I only look at the connection which they have with the brain, which is material, and which by its different arrangements produces all the varieties that are between them.—*Digression sur les Anciens et les Modernes.*

How to Become Famous.—When we only wish to make a noise in the world, the most prudent and judicious conduct is not the most wise.—*Des Morts Anciens, 1.*

The Passions as Motive Power.—It is the passions which do and undo everything. If reason ruled, nothing would get on. It is said that pilots fear beyond everything those halcyon seas, where the vessel obeys not the helm, and that they prefer wind at the risk of storms. The passions in men are the winds necessary to put everything in motion, though they often cause storms.—*Des Morts Anciens, 1.*

That We May Do Great Things without Knowing How.—Great things are almost always done without our knowing how we have done them, and we are quite surprised that they are done. Ask Cæsar how he made himself master of the world; perhaps he would find it difficult to answer you.—*Des Morts Modernes, 5.*

FRANKLIN, BENJAMIN (America, 1706–1790)

Credit from Trifling Things.—The most trifling actions that affect a man's credit are to be regarded. The sound of your hammer at five in the morning, or nine at night, heard by a creditor, makes him easy six months longer; but if he sees you at a billiard table, or hears your voice at a tavern, when you should be at work, he sends for his money the next day.

Friends and Friendship.—Be slow in choosing a friend, slower in changing.—*From Poor Richard's Almanack for 1735.*

Do good to thy friend to keep him, to thy enemy to gain him.—*From Poor Richard's Almanack for 1734.*

That Money Begets Money.—Remember that money is of a prolific, generating nature. Money can beget money, and its offspring can beget more, and so on. Five shillings turned is six: turned again it is seven and threepence; and so on till it becomes a hundred pounds. The more there is of it, the more it produces every turning, so that the profits rise quicker and quicker. He that kills a breeding sow, destroys all her offspring to the thousandth generation. He that murders a crown, destroys all that it might have produced, even scores of pounds.

FROISSART, JEAN (France, 1337–1410)

The Manners of the Scots.—The Scots are bold, hardy, and much inured to war. When they make their invasions into England, they march from twenty to four and twenty leagues without halting, as well by night as by day; for they are all on horseback, except the camp followers, who are on foot. The knights and esquires are well mounted on large bay horses, the common people on little galloways. They bring no carriages with them, on account of the mountains they have to pass in Northumberland; neither do they carry with them any provisions or bread or wine; for their habits of sobriety are such, in time of war, that they will live for a long time on flesh half sodden, without bread, and drink the river water without wine. They have, therefore, no occasion for pots or pans; for they dress the flesh of their cattle in the skins, after they have taken them off; and, being sure to find plenty of them in the country which they invade, they carry none with them. Under the flaps of his saddle, each man carries a broad plate of metal; behind the saddle, a little bag of oatmeal; when they have eaten too much of the sodden flesh, and their stomachs appears too weak and empty, they place this plate over the fire, mix with water their oatmeal, and when the plate is heated, they put a little of the paste upon it, and make a thin cake, like a cracknel or biscuit, which they eat to warm their stomachs; it is therefore no wonder, that they perform a longer day's march than other soldiers.—*From the Chronicles of England, France, Spain.*

FROTHINGHAM, O. B. (America, 1822–)

Self-Denial.—Whoso lives for humanity must be content to lose himself.—*Life of George Ripley.*

FULLER, THOMAS (England, 1608–1661)

Books as a Nepenthe.—To divert at any time a troublesome fancy, run to thy books: they presently fix thee to them, and drive the other out of thy thoughts. They always receive thee with the same kindness.

Love Is to Be Led.—Affections, like the conscience, are rather to be led than drawn; and 'tis to be feared, they that marry where they do not love, will love where they do not marry.

Behavior to Inferiors.—As the sword of the best tempered metal is most flexible; so the truly generous are most pliant and courteous in their behavior to their inferiors.

Fatted for Destruction.—If the wicked flourish, and thou suffer, be not discouraged. They are fatted for destruction: thou art dieted for health.

GARFIELD, JAMES A. (America, 1831–1881)

Esse Quam Videri.—The possession of great powers no doubt carries with it a contempt for mere external show.—*Oration on Miss Booth.*

The Formation of Character.—Character is the result of two great forces; the initial force which the Creator gave it when he called the man into being;—and the force of all the external influence and culture that mold and modify the development of a life.—*Oration on Congressman Gustave Schleicher.*

If the superior beings of the universe would look down upon the world to find the most interesting object, it would be the unfinished, unformed character of young men, or of young women.—*Hiram College, July, 1880.*

History as a Divine Poem.—The world's history is a divine poem of which the history of every nation is a canto and every man a word. Its strains have been pealing along down the centuries, and though there have been mingled the discords of warring cannon and dying men, yet to the Christian philosopher and historian—the humble listener—there has been a divine melody running through the song which speaks of hope and halcyon days to come.—*«The Province of History.»*

GARRISON, WILLIAM LLOYD (America, 1804–1879)

The Right to Liberty.—The right to enjoy liberty is inalienable. To invade it is to usurp the prerogative of Jehovah. Every man has a right to his own body—to the products of his own labor—to the protection of law—and to the common advantages of society.—*Delivered before the American Antislavery Society, December 6, 1833.*

GAYARRÉ, CHARLES (America, 1805–1895)

The March of De Soto.—On the 31st of May, 1539, the bay of Santo Spiritu, in Florida, presented a curious spectacle. Eleven vessels of quaint shape, bearing the broad banner of Spain, were moored close to the shore; one thousand men of infantry, and three hundred and fifty men of cavalry, fully equipped, were landing in proud array under the command of Hernando De Soto, one of the most illustrious companions of Pizarro in the conquest of Peru, and reputed one of the best lances of Spain! «When he led in the van of battle, so powerful was his charge,» says the old chronicler of his exploits, «so broad was the bloody passage which he carved out in the ranks of the enemy, that ten of his men-at-arms could with ease follow him abreast.» He had acquired enormous wealth in Peru, and might have rested satisfied, a knight of renown, in the government of St. Jago de Cuba, in the sweet enjoyment of youth and power.

But his adventurous mind scorns such inglorious repose, and now he stands erect and full of visions bright, on the sandy shore of Florida, whither he comes, with feudal pride, by leave of the king, to establish nothing less than a marquisate, ninety miles long by forty-five miles wide, and there to rule supreme, a governor for life of all the territory that he can subjugate.

GEORGE, HENRY (America, 1839–1897)

Land Monopoly.—Place one hundred men on an island from which there is no escape, and whether you make one of these men the absolute owner of the other ninety-nine, or the absolute owner of the soil of the island, will make no difference either to him or to them.

In the one case, as the other, the one will be the absolute master of the ninety-nine—his power extending even to life and death, for simply to refuse them permission to live upon the island would be to force them into the sea.

Upon a larger scale, and through more complex relations, the same cause must operate in the same way and to the same end—the ultimate result, the enslavement of laborers, becoming apparent just as the pressure increases which compels them to live on and from land which is treated as the exclusive property of others.

GLADDEN, WASHINGTON (America, 1836–)

The Theologian's Problem.—The priest and the Levite in the parable of the good Samaritan were probably going down to Jericho to attend a convention called to discuss the question, «How shall we reach the masses?»

GOETHE, JOHANN WOLFGANG VON (Germany, 1749–1832)

Conversion and Friendship with Heaven.—As to the value of conversions, God alone can judge; God alone can know how wide are the steps which the soul has to take before it can approach to a community with him, to the dwelling of the perfect, or to the intercourse and friendship of higher natures.

The Burden of Fools.—Of all thieves fools are the worst: they rob you of time and temper.

GOLDONI, CARLO (Italy, 1707–1793)

The Book of the World.—The world is a beautiful book, but of little use to him who cannot read it.—*Pamela, i. 14.*

The Animal that Laughs.—Laughing is peculiar to man; but all men do not laugh for the same reason. There is the Attic salt, which springs from the charm in the words, from the flash of wit, from the spirited and brilliant sally. There is the low joke which arises from scurrility and idle conceit.—*Pamela, i. 16.*

«The Noble Man Does Noble Deeds.»— Noble blood is an accident of fortune; noble actions characterize the great.—*Pamela, i. 6.*

GOLDSMITH, OLIVER (Ireland, 1728–1774)

«Originality.» — People seldom improve, when they have no other model but themselves to copy after.

GRANADA, LUIS DE (Spain, 1504–1588)

The Uncertainty of Things.— This is the great misfortune of life, that it is changeable, and never remains in the same state. «Man,» says Job (xiv. 1), «that is born of woman, is of few days, and full of trouble. He cometh forth like a flower, and is cut down; he fleeth also as a shadow, and continueth not.» What is more changeable? We are told that the chameleon assumes in an hour many colors; the sea of the Euripus has an evil name for its many changes, and the moon takes every day its own peculiar form. But what is all this compared to the changes of man? What Proteus ever assumed so many different forms as man does every hour? Now sick, now in health; now content, now discontent; now sad, now joyous; now timid, now hopeful; now suspicious, now credulous; now peaceful, now recalcitrant; now he wishes, now he wishes not; and many times he knows not what he wants. In short, the changes are as numerous as the accidents in an hour, so that every one of them turns him upside down. The past gives him pain, the present disturbs him, and the future causes him agony.

The Uncertainties of Life.— What will it be if we run over the miseries of all the ages and states of this Life? How full of ignorance is childhood! how light-headed is boyhood! how rash is youth, and how cross is old age! What is a child but a brute animal in the form of a human being? What is youth but a steed with the bit in his mouth and without reins? What the old man, weighed down by years, but a bundle of infirmities and pains? The greatest desire that men have is to reach this age, where man is only more subject to necessities than in the other parts of his life, and even less assisted. For the old is abandoned by the world, by his relations, even his limbs and senses fail him, and himself too; for the use of his reason leaves him, and infirmities alone attend him. This is the goal on which human felicity and the ambition of life fixes its eyes.

The Mystery of Death.— O death, how bitter is the thought of thee! how speedy thy approach! how stealthy thy steps! how uncertain thy hour! how universal thy sway! The powerful cannot escape thee; the wise know not how to avoid thee; the strong have no strength to oppose thee; there is no one rich for thee since none can buy life with treasures. Everywhere thou goest, every place thou besettest, in every spot thou art found. All things have their waxing and waning, but thou remainest ever the same. Thou art a hammer that always strikes — a sword that is never blunt — a net into which all fall — a prison into which all must enter — a sea on which all must venture — a penalty which all must suffer — and a tribute which all must pay. O cruel death! thou carriest off in an hour, in a moment, that which has been acquired with the labor of many years; thou cuttest short the succession of the highborn; thou leavest kingdoms without heirs; thou fillest the world with orphans; thou cuttest short the thread of studies; makest of no use the noblest genius; joinest the end to the beginning without allowing any intermediate space. O death, death! O implacable enemy of the human race! Why hast thou entered into the world?

GREENE, ROBERT (England, 1560–1592)

A Clear Mind and Dignity. — Flesh dipped in the Sea Ægeum, will never be sweet: the herb Trigion being once bit with an asp, never groweth: and conscience once stained with innocent blood, is always tied to a guilty remorse. Prefer thy content before riches, and a clear mind before dignity: so being poor, thou shalt have rich peace, or else rich, thou shalt enjoy disquiet.— *From Pandosto, the Triumph of Time.*

GREVILLE, FULKE (England, 1554–1628)

The Touchstone of Merit. — Ask the man of adversity how other men act towards him: ask those others, how he acts towards them. Adversity is the true touchstone of merit in both; happy if it does not produce the dishonesty of meanness in one, and that of insolence and pride in the other.

Following the Leader. — We laugh heartily to see a whole flock of sheep jump because one did so: might not one imagine that superior beings do the same by us, and for exactly the same reason?

Small Things and Great Results. — Surely no man can reflect, without wonder, upon the vicissitudes of human life, arising from causes in the highest degree accidental and trifling. If you trace the necessary concatenation of human events, a very little way back, you may perhaps discover that a person's very going in or out of a door has been the means of coloring with misery or happiness the remaining current of his life.

The Mote and the Beam.— He that sees ever so accurately, ever so finely into the motives of other people's acting, may possibly be entirely ignorant as to his own: it is by the mental as the corporeal eye, the object may be placed too near the sight to be seen truly, as well as too far off; nay, too near to be seen at all.

Great Souls and Mean Fortunes.— I hardly know a sight that raises one's indignation more, than that of an enlarged soul joined to a contracted fortune; unless it be that so much more common one, of a contracted soul joined to an enlarged fortune.

On the Nature of Women.— Modesty in woman, say some shrewd philosophers, is not

natural; it is artificial and acquired; but what then, and to what end, is that natural taste, that delicate sensation, that approbation of it, in man? . . . I have often thought that the nature of women was inferior to that of men in general, but superior in particular.

GRISWOLD, RUFUS WILMOT (America, 1815–1857)

The Genius of Poe.— His realm was on the shadowy confines of human experience, among the abodes of crime, gloom, and horror, and there he delighted to surround himself with images of beauty and of terror, to raise his solemn palaces and towers and spires in a night upon which should rise no sun. His minuteness of detail, refinement of reasoning, and propriety and power of language — the perfect keeping (to borrow a phrase from another domain of art) and apparent good faith with which he managed the evocation and exhibition of his strange and spectral and revolting creations — gave him an astonishing mastery over his readers, so that his books were closed as one would lay aside the nightmare or the spells of opium. The analytical subtlety evinced in his works has frequently been overestimated, as I have before observed, because it has not been sufficiently considered that his mysteries were composed with the express design of being dissolved. When Poe attempted the illustration of the profounder operations of mind, as displayed in written reason or real action, he frequently failed entirely.— *Memoir of Poe.*

GUICCIARDINI, FRANCIS (Italy, 1483–1540)

Forgiveness and Amendment.— It is more easy to induce a person who has been offended to forgive, than it is to make one who has taken possession of property to make restitution.— *Storia d'Italia.*

Nobility the True Rule of Public Policy.— The counsels of republics ought not to be subject to the influence of low and paltry motives, nor be moved only by selfish advantages, but aim at high and noble ends, thereby adding to their glory, and preserving their reputation, which nothing destroys sooner than the idea that they have not spirit or power to resent injuries, nor preparations sufficient to avenge themselves,— a thing particularly necessary, not so much from the gratification arising from the feeling of vengeance, as that the chastisement of the offender may be a warning to others not to provoke you. Here we have glory united to advantage, and lofty and noble resolutions replete with gain and profit: thus one trouble removes many, and often a single and short effort frees you from many and long toils.— *Storia d'Italia.*

Turbulence and Ignorance in Republics.— As correct decisions cannot be expected from an incapable and ignorant judge, so a people that is turbulent and ignorant cannot be expected, except by chance, to choose magistrates, or deliberate with prudence or according to rational principles.— *Storia d'Italia.*

On Asking Advice.— There is nothing assuredly more necessary in matters of difficulty, and nothing more dangerous, than to ask advice. Advice is less necessary to the wise than to the unwise, and yet the wise are those who derive most advantage from taking counsel with others: for who is so perfect in wisdom as to be able to take everything into account? and in opposing courses of action to discern which is the better? But, then, when advice is asked, how shall we be sure that advice, on which we can depend, will be given? For the counselor, if he be not faithful, or if he be not strongly attached to us, being influenced not only by his own evident advantage, but by every petty object and slight self-gratification, often directs his advice to that end that is most to his own profit, or which pleases him most; and these private ends being for the most part unknown to the person who is asking advice, he does not perceive, unless he be very shrewd, the dishonesty of the advice.— *Storia d'Italia.*

HALL, ROBERT (England, 1764–1831)

The Meaning of Destiny.— The wheels of nature are not made to roll backward: everything presses on towards Eternity: from the birth of Time an impetuous current has set in, which bears all the sons of men towards that interminable ocean. Meanwhile Heaven is attracting to itself whatever is congenial to its nature, is enriching itself by the spoils of earth, and collecting within its capacious bosom whatever is pure, permanent, and divine.

HALLIBURTON, THOMAS CHANDLER (Canada, 1796–1865)

When a Woman Is Always Right.— Every woman is in the wrong until she cries, and then she is in the right instantly.

Hope as a Traveling Companion.— Hope is a pleasant acquaintance, but an unsafe friend. Hope is not the man for your banker, but he may do very well for a traveling companion.

HAMILTON, GAIL (America, 1838–)

The Limit of Responsibility.— Every person is responsible for all the good within the scope of his abilities, and for no more, and none can tell whose sphere is the largest.

Coarse Arts and Fine.— I admire the coarse arts fully as much as I do the fine arts.

HARE, JULIUS CHARLES (England, 1795–1855)

Christianity and Civilization.— Christianity has carried civilization along with it, whithersoever it has gone: and, as if to show that the latter does not depend on physical causes, some of the countries the most civilized in the days of Augustus are now in a state of hopeless barbarism.

What Eloquence Means.— Many are ambitious of saying grand things, that is, of being grandiloquent. Eloquence is speaking out . . . a quality few esteem, and fewer aim at.

HAWTHORNE, NATHANIEL (America, 1804–1864)

Drowned in Their Own Honey.— Bees are sometimes drowned (or suffocated) in the honey which they collect. So some writers are lost in their collected learning.— *American Note Books* (1842).

Happiness as an Incident.— Happiness in this world, when it comes, comes incidentally. Make it the object of pursuit, and it leads us a wild goose chase, and is never attained. Follow some other object, and very possibly we may find that we have caught happiness without dreaming of it, but likely enough it is gone the moment we say to ourselves, «Here it is!» like the chest of gold that treasure seekers find. . . . There is something more awful in happiness than in sorrow,— the latter being earthly and finite, the former composed of the substance and texture of eternity, so that spirits still embodied may well tremble at it.— *American Note Books, July, 1843.*

The Only Reality.— We are but shadows: we are not endowed with real life, and all that seems most real about us is but the thinnest substance of a dream,— till the heart be touched. That touch creates us — then we begin to be — thereby we are beings of reality and inheritors of eternity.— *American Note Books. Salem, October 4, 1840.*

HAZLITT, WILLIAM (England, 1778–1830)

Friendship.— The youth of friendship is better than its old age.

The Religion of Love.— It makes us proud when our love of a mistress is returned; it ought to make us prouder still when we can love her for herself alone, without the aid of any such selfish reflection. This is the religion of love.

HEADLEY, J. T. (America, 1813–)

Naples and Vesuvius. — Tonight we arrived from Castellamare. Our road wound along the bay — near Pompeii, through Torre del Greco, into the city. The sky was darkly overcast — the wind was high and angry, and the usually quiet bay threw its aroused and rapid swell on the beach. Along the horizon, between the sea and sky, hung a storm cloud blacker than the water. Here and there was a small sailing craft or fisherman's boat, pulling for the shore, while those on the beach were dragging their boats still farther up on the sand, in preparation for the rapid-gathering storm. There is always something fearful in this bustling preparation for a tempest. It was peculiarly so here. The roar of the surge was on one side; on the other lay a buried city — a smoking mountain; while our very road was walled with lava that cooled on the spot where it stood. The column of smoke that Vesuvius usually sent so calmly into the sky, now lay on a level with the summit, and rolled rapidly inland, before the fierce sea blast. It might have been fancy; but, amid such elements of strength, and such memories and monuments of their fury, it did seem as if it wanted but a single touch to send valley, towns, mountain, and all, like a fired magazine into the air. Clouds of dust rolled over us, blotting out even the road from our view; while the dull report of cannon from Naples, coming at intervals on our ears, added to the confusion and loneliness of the scene. As we entered the city and rode along the port, the wild tossing of the tall masts as the heavy hulls rocked on the waves, the creaking of the timbers, and the muffled shouts of seamen, as they threw their fastenings, added to the gloom of the evening; and I went to my room, feeling that I should not be surprised to find myself aroused at any moment by the rocking of an earthquake under me. The night did not disappoint the day, and set in with a wildness and fury, that these fire countries alone exhibit. My room overlooked the bay and Vesuvius. The door opened upon a large balcony. As I stood on this, and heard the groaning of the vessels below, reeling in the darkness, and the sullen sound of the surge, as it fell on the beach, while the heavy thunder rolled over the sea, and shook the city on its foundations,— I felt I would not live in Naples. Ever and anon a vivid flash of lightning would throw distant Vesuvius in bold relief against the sky, with his forehead completely wrapped in clouds that moved not to the blast, but clung there, as if in solemn consultation with the mountain upon the night. Overhead the clouds were driven in every direction, and nature seemed bestirring herself for some wild work. At length the heavy raindrops began to fall, one by one, as if pressed from the clouds; and I turned to my room feeling that the storm would weep itself away.— *From «Letters from Italy.»*

HERBERT, EDWARD (England, 1582–1648)

The Miraculous Human Body.— Whoever considers the study of anatomy, I believe, will never be an Atheist; the frame of man's body, and coherence of his parts, being so strange and paradoxical, that I hold it to be the greatest miracle of Nature.

HERDER, JOHANN GOTTFRIED VON (Germany, 1744–1803)

Mother Love and Children.— Last among the characteristics of woman, is that sweet motherly love with which Nature has gifted her; it is almost independent of cold reason, and wholly removed from all selfish hope of reward. Not because it is lovely, does the mother love her child, but because it is a living part of herself,— the child of her heart, a fraction of her own nature. Therefore do her entrails yearn over his wailings; her heart beats quicker at his joy; her blood flows more softly through her veins, when the breast at which he drinks knits him to her. In every uncorrupted nation of the earth, this feeling is the same; climate, which changes everything else, changes not that. It is only the most corrupting forms of society which have power gradually to make luxurious

vice sweeter than the tender cares and toils of maternal love.

HERODOTUS. (Greece, *c.* 484–424 B. C.)

«Mind Your Own Business.»— Many are the precepts recorded by the sages for our instruction, but we ought to listen to none with more attention than that, «It becomes a man to give heed to those things which regard himself.» — *i. 8.*

Comparison the Secret of Knowledge.— Unless a variety of opinions are laid before us, we have no opportunity of selection, but are bound of necessity to adopt the particular view which may have been brought forward. The purity of gold cannot be ascertained by a single specimen; but when we have carefully compared it with others, we are able to fix upon the finest ore.— *vii. 10.*

Cause of the Most Enormous Crimes.— For insolence is the natural result of great prosperity, while envy and jealousy are innate qualities in the mind of man. When these two vices are combined, they lead to the most enormous crimes: some atrocities are committed from insolence, and others from envy. Princes ought to be superior to all such feelings; but, alas! we know that this is not the case. The noble and the worthiest are the object of their jealousy, merely because they feel that their lives are a reproach to them; with the most abandoned they rejoice to spend their time. Calumny they drink in with greedy ears. But what is the most paradoxical of all, if thou showest them merely respectful homage, they take umbrage because thou art not sufficiently humble; whereas, if thou bend the knee with the most submissive looks, thou art kicked away as a flatterer.— *iii. 80.*

Forethought and Failure.— For my own part, I have found from experience that the greatest good is to be got from forethought and deliberation; even if the result is not such as we expected, at all events we have the feeling that we have done all in our power to merit success, and therefore the blame must be attached to fortune alone. The man who is foolish and inconsiderate, even when fortune shines upon him, is not the less to be censured for his want of sense. Dost thou not see how the thunderbolts of heaven lay prostrate the mightiest animals, while they pass over the weak and insignificant? The most splendid palaces and the loftiest trees fall before these weapons of the gods. For God loves to humble the mighty. So also we often see a powerful army melt away before the more contemptible force. For when God in His wrath sends His terror among them, they perish in a way that is little worthy of their former glory. The Supreme Being allows no one to be infinite in wisdom but Himself.— *vii. 10.*

Finis Coronat Opus.— It is the part of wisdom to wait to see the final result of things, for God often tears up by the roots the prosperous, and overwhelms with misery those who have reached the highest pinnacle of worldly happiness.— *i. 32.*

HILDRETH, RICHARD (America, 1807–1865)

Jefferson's Changes.— Between Jefferson as a political theorist, palliating Shay's rebellion by the general remark that a little insurrection now and then is necessary to keep every kind of government in order; between Jefferson as leader of the opposition, denouncing the tax on whiskey as «infernal,» and almost justifying the rebellion against it, and Jefferson as President, dissatisfied with the law of treason as laid down by Chase and Marshall, calling upon Congress for greater stringency, seeking to enforce the embargo by assumptions of power, which, if constitutional, which multitudes questioned, were vastly more arbitrary and meddlesome than anything in the Excise Act, there was, indeed, a striking contrast.— *History of the United States.*

HOLLAND, JOSIAH GILBERT (America, 1819–1881)

Manhood and Its Incidents.— Labor, calling, profession, scholarship, and artificial and arbitrary distinctions of all sorts, are incidents and accidents of life, and pass away. It is only manhood that remains, and it is only by manhood that man is to be measured.— *Talks on Familiar Subjects, 1865.*

Words the Materials of Art.— The temple of art is built of words. Painting and sculpture and music are but the blazon of its windows, borrowing all their significance from the light, and suggestive only of the temple's uses.

«The Choicest Thing in the World.»— The choicest thing this world has for a man is affection — the approval, the sympathy, and the devotion — of true hearts.

Mean Things and Men's «Way.»— Many mean things are done in the family for which moods are put forward as the excuse when the moods themselves are the most inexcusable things of all. A man or woman in tolerable health has no moral right to indulge in an unpleasant mood.

HOLMES, OLIVER WENDELL (America, 1809–1894)

Books Old and New.— Old books, as you well know, are books of the world's youth, and new books are fruits of its age.— *«The Professor at the Breakfast Table,» Chap. IX.*

The Heart's Low Tide.— There are inscriptions on our hearts, which, like that on Dighton Rock, are never to be seen except at dead-low tide.— *The Autocrat of the Breakfast Table.*

Stopping the Strings of the Heart.— Talking is like playing on the harp; there is as much in laying the hands on the strings to stop their vibrations, as in twanging them to bring out their music.— *The Autocrat of the Breakfast Table, Chap. I.*

Seventy Year Clocks.— Our brains are seventy year clocks. The Angel of Life winds them up once for all, then closes the case, and gives the key into the hands of the Angel of the Resurrection.— *The Autocrat of the Breakfast Table.*

HOPKINS, MARK (America, 1802–1887)

«The Picture of Thought.»— Language is the picture and counterpart of thought.— *Address, delivered at the dedication of Williston Seminary, December 1, 1841.*

Virtue as Grace.— Virtue should move easily and gracefully only as it is strong, but it should become strong, that it may move easily and gracefully, and thus become to all men as beautiful as it is obligatory.— *The Connection between Taste and Morals, Lecture II.*

HOPKINSON, FRANCIS (America, 1737–1791)

Eighteenth Century England.— The extreme ignorance of the common people of this civilized country can scarce be credited. In general they know nothing beyond the particular branch of the business which their parents or the parish happened to choose for them. This, indeed, they practice with unremitting diligence; but never think of extending their knowledge farther. A manufacturer has been brought up a maker of pin-heads: he has been at this business forty years and, of course, makes pin-heads with great dexterity; but he cannot make a whole pin for his life. He thinks it is the perfection of human nature to make pin-heads. He leaves other matters to inferior abilities. It is enough for him that he believes in the Athanasian Creed, reverences the splendor of the court, and makes pin-heads. This he conceives to be the sum-total of religion, politics, and trade. He is sure that London is the finest city in the world; Blackfriars Bridge the most superb of all possible bridges; and the river Thames, the largest river in (the) universe. It is in vain to tell him that there are many rivers in America, in comparison of which the Thames is but a ditch; that there are single provinces there larger than all England; and that the colonies, formerly belonging to Great Britain, now independent states, are vastly more extensive than England, Wales, Scotland, and Ireland taken all together—he cannot conceive this. He goes into his best parlor, and looks on a map of England, four feet square; on the other side of the room he sees a map of North and South America, not more than two feet square, and exclaims:—«How can these things be! It is altogether impossible!»—*From the «Translation of a Letter, Written by a Foreigner on His Travels.»*

HYDE, EDWARD, EARL OF CLARENDON (England, 1608–1674)

Good Nature as the Greatest Blessing.— Angry and choleric men are as ungrateful and unsociable as thunder and lightning, being in themselves all storm and tempest; but quiet and easy natures are like fair weather, welcome to all, and acceptable to all men; they gather together what the other disperse, and reconcile all whom the other incense: as they have the good will and the good wishes of all other men, so they have the full possession of themselves, have all their own thoughts at peace, and enjoy quiet and ease in their own fortunes, how straight soever it may be.

Beauty as a Compelling Power.— It was a very proper answer to him who asked, why any man should be delighted with beauty? that it was a question that none but a blind man could ask; since any beautiful object doth so much attract the sight of all men, that it is in no man's power not to be pleased with it.

The World Not to Be Despised.— They take very unprofitable pains who endeavor to persuade men that they are obliged wholly to despise this World and all that is in it, even whilst they themselves live here: God hath not taken all that pains in forming and framing and furnishing and adorning this World, that they who were made by Him to live in it should despise it; it will be well enough if they do not love it so immoderately, to prefer it before Him who made it.

IRVING, WASHINGTON (America, 1783–1859)

Friends That Are Always True.— When all that is worldly turns to dross around us, these books only retain their steady value. When friends grow cold, and the converse of intimates languishes into vapid civility and commonplace, these only continue the unaltered countenance of happier days, and cheer us with that true friendship which never deceived hope, nor deserted sorrow.—*The Sketch Book: «Roscoe.»*

Great Minds in Misfortune.— Little minds are tamed and subdued by misfortune; but great minds rise above it.— *The Sketch Book: «Philip of Pokanoket.»*

«The Almighty Dollar.» — The Almighty Dollar, that great object of universal devotion throughout our land, seems to have no genuine devotees in these particular villages.— *The Creole Village.*

Cultivation and Society.— Society is like a lawn, where every roughness is smoothed, every bramble eradicated, and where the eye is delighted by the smiling verdure of a velvet surface.— *The Sketch Book: «Philip of Pokanoket.»*

«The Truest Thing in the World.»—Who that has languished, even in advanced life, in sickness and despondency; who that has pined on a weary bed in the neglect and loneliness of a foreign land; but has thought on the mother «that looked on his childhood,» that smoothed his pillow and administered to his helplessness? Oh! there is an enduring tenderness in the love of a mother to a son that transcends all other affections of the heart. It is neither to be chilled by selfishness, nor daunted by danger, nor weakened by worthlessness, nor stifled by ingratitude. She will sacrifice every comfort to his convenience; she will surrender every pleasure to his enjoyment; she will glory in his

fame, and exult in his prosperity:—and, if misfortune overtake him, he will be the dearer to her from his misfortunes; and if disgrace settle upon his name, she will still love and cherish him in spite of his disgrace; and if all the world beside cast him off, she will be all the world to him.—*From «The Sketch Book.»*

JACOBI, FRIEDRICH HEINRICH (Germany, 1743–1819)

«Flying Leaves.»— I can live in harmony with everyone who lives in harmony with himself.

What dost thou call a beautiful soul? Thou callest a beautiful soul one that is quick to perceive the good, that gives it due prominence and holds it immovably fast.

It is absurd for a man to say that he hates and despises men, but love and honors Humanity. A general without a particular, a Humanity worthy of honor and love without men who are worthy of honor and love, is a fiction of the brain, a thing that has no existence.

It is the custom of virtue to note the failings of distinguished men not otherwise than with a certain timidity and shame. It is the custom of vice to cover impudence with the appellation of love of truth.

To lay aside all prejudices is to lay aside all principles. He who is destitute of principles is governed, theoretically and practically, by whims.

JAMES I. (Scotland, 1566–1625)

Tobacco as a «Stinking Torment.»—And for the vanities committed by this filthy custom, is it not both great vanity and uncleanness, that at the table, a place of respect, of cleanliness, of modesty, men should not be ashamed, to sit tossing of tobacco pipes and puffing of the smoke of tobacco one to another, making the filthy smoke and stink thereof, to exhale athwart the dishes, and infect the air, when very often men that abhor it are at their repast? Surely smoke becomes a kitchen far better than a dining chamber, and yet it makes a kitchen also oftentimes in the inward parts of men, soiling and infecting them with an unctuous and oily kind of soot, as hath been found in some great tobacco takers, that after their death were opened. And not only meal time, but no other time nor action is exempted from the public use of this uncivil trick: so as if the wives of Dieppe list to contest with this nation for good manners, their worst manners would in all reason be found at least not so dishonest (as ours are) in this point. The public use whereof, at all times, and in all places, hath now so far prevailed, as divers men very sound both in judgment and complexion hath been at last forced to take it also without desire, partly because they were ashamed to seem singular (like the two philosophers that were forced to duck themselves in that rain water and so become fools as well as the rest of the people), and partly to be as one that was content to eat garlic (which he did not love) that he might not be troubled with the smell of it in the breath of his fellows. And is it not a great vanity, that a man cannot heartily welcome his friend now, but straight they must be in hand with tobacco? No, it is become in place of a cure, a point of good fellowship, and he that will refuse to take a pipe of tobacco among his fellows (though by his own election he would rather feel the savor of a sink) is accounted peevish and no good company, even as they do with tippling in the cold eastern countries. Yea the mistress cannot in a more mannerly kind entertain her servant, than by giving him out of her fair hand a pipe of tobacco. But herein is not only a great vanity, but a great contempt of God's good gifts, that the sweetness of man's breath, being a good gift of God, should be willfully corrupted by this stinking smoke, wherein I must confess, it hath too strong a virtue; and so that which is an ornament of nature, and can neither by any artifice be at the first acquired, nor once lost be recovered again, shall be filthily corrupted with an incurable stink, which vile quality is as directly contrary to that wrong opinion which is holden of the wholesomeness thereof, as the venom of putrefaction is contrary to the virtue preservative.

Moreover, which is a great iniquity, and against all humanity, the husband shall not be ashamed to reduce thereby his delicate, wholesome, and clean complexioned wife to that extremity, that either she must also corrupt her sweet breath therewith, or else resolve to live in a perpetual stinking torment.—*From «A Counterblast to Tobacco.»*

JAMES, HENRY (America, 1811–1882)

The Meaning of History.— The very vices and crimes of man place him above Nature, deny his essential finiteness, proclaim his true subjection to be an ideal and infinite object only. And the testimony is undeniable. Consciousness perfectly ratifies it. All history proves that it is man's glory to act without prescription, or from the inspiration of what we call ideas, meaning thereby God. He, and he alone of all things, feels himself subject to an ideal or infinite selfhood, feels himself bound to reproduce or ultimate this infinite or ideal self in every form of action.— *From «Lectures and Miscellanies.»*

JEVONS, W. STANLEY (England, 1835–1882)

«The Money Question.» — It may be safely said that the question of bimetallism is one which does not admit of any precise and simple answer. It is essentially an indeterminate problem. It involves several variable quantities and many constant quantities, the latter being either inaccurately known or in many cases altogether unknown. The present annual supply of gold and silver are ascertained with fair approach of certainty, but the future supplies are matter of doubt. The demand for the metals again involves wholly unknown

quantities, depending partly on the course of trade, but partly also upon the action of foreign peoples and governments, about which we can only form surmises. . . .

Looking at the question, in the first place, as a chronic one, that is, as regarding the constitution of monetary systems during centuries, it is indispensable to remember the fact, too much overlooked by disputants, that the values of gold and silver are ultimately governed, like those of all other commodities, by the cost of production.— *From the Contemporary Review.*

JOHNSON, SAMUEL (England, 1709–1784)

The Greatness of Little Men.— The superiority of some men is merely local. They are great, because their associates are little.

«The Rust of the Soul.» —Sorrow is a kind of rust of the soul, which every new idea contributes in its passage to scour away. It is the putrefaction of stagnant life, and is remedied by exercise and motion.

KAMES, LORD (Scotland, 1696–1782)

Pleasures of the Eye and Ear.— Our first perceptions are of external objects, and our first attachments are to them. Organic pleasures take the lead; but the mind gradually ripening, relisheth more and more the pleasures of the eye and ear, which approach the purely mental without exhausting the spirits, and exceed the purely sensual without danger of satiety. The pleasures of the eye and ear have accordingly a natural aptitude to draw us from the immoderate gratification of sensual appetite; and the mind, once accustomed to enjoy a variety of external objects without being sensible of the organic impression, is prepared for enjoying internal objects where there cannot be an organic impression. Thus the Author of nature, by qualifying the human mind for a succession of enjoyments from low to high, leads it by gentle steps from the most groveling corporeal pleasures, for which only it is fitted in the beginning of life, to those refined and sublime pleasures that are suited to its maturity.

KANT, IMMANUEL (Germany, 1724–1804)

Aims and Duties.— What are the aims, which are at the same time duties? They are, the perfecting of ourselves, the happiness of others.

Doing Good to Others.— Beneficence is a duty. He who frequently practices it, and sees his benevolent intentions realized, at length comes really to love him to whom he has done good.

Serenity and Strength. — Enthusiasm is always connected with the senses, whatever be the object that excites it. The true strength of virtue is serenity of mind, combined with a deliberate and steadfast determination to execute her laws. That is the healthful condition of the moral life; on the other hand, enthusiasm, even when excited by representations of goodness, is a brilliant but feverish glow, which leaves only exhaustion and languor behind.

KENT, JAMES (America, 1763–1847)

Publicity and Bad Politics.— The energy of the press and of popular instruction, and the free and liberal spirit of the age, control or mitigate the evils of a bad administration, or chastise its abuses in every department of government, and they carry their influence to the highest ranks and summits of society.— *A discourse delivered before the N. Y. Historical Society, December 6, 1828.*

KING, THOMAS STARR (America, 1824–1864)

The Miracle of Color.— The fact is, that of all God's gifts to the sight of man, color is the holiest, the most divine, the most solemn. We speak rashly of gay color and sad color, for color cannot at once be good and gay. All good color is in some degree pensive, the loveliest is melancholy, and the purest and most thoughtful minds are those which love color the most.—*The White Hills: The Saco Valley.*

Nature a Hieroglyphic.—Nature is hieroglyphic. Each prominent fact in it is like a type; its final use is to set up one letter of the infinite alphabet, and help us, by its connections to read some statement or statute applicable to the conscious world.— *The White Hills: The Connecticut Valley.*

KINGLAKE, ALEXANDER WILLIAM (England, 1809–1891)

In the Desert.— About this part of my journey, I saw the likeness of a fresh water lake. I saw, as it seemed, a broad sheet of calm water that stretched far and fair toward the south—stretching deep into winding creeks, and hemmed in by jutting promontories, and shelving smooth off toward the shallow side; on its bosom the reflected fire of the sun lay playing, and seeming to float upon waters deep and still.

Though I knew of the cheat, it was not till the spongy foot of my camel had almost trodden in the seeming waters, that I could undeceive my eyes, for the shore line was quite true and natural. I soon saw the cause of the phantasm. A sheet of water heavily impregnated with salts had filled this great hollow, and when dried up by evaporation had left a white saline deposit that exactly marked the space which the waters had covered, and thus sketched a true shore line. The minute crystals of the salt sparkled in the sun, and so looked like the face of a lake that is calm and smooth. . . .

After the fifth day of my journey, I no longer traveled over shifting hills, but came upon a dead level—a dead level bed of sand, quite hard and stubbed with small shining pebbles.

The heat grew fierce; there was no valley nor hollow, no hill, no mound, no shadow of hill nor of mound, by which I could mark the way I was making. Hour by hour I advanced, and saw no change—I was still the very center

of a round horizon; hour by hour I advanced, and still there was the same—and the same, and the same,—the same circle of flaming sky—the same circle of sand still glaring with light and fire. Over all the heaven above—over all the earth beneath, there was no visible power that could balk the fierce will of the sun; «he rejoiced as a strong man to run a race; his going forth was from the end of the heaven, and his circuit unto the ends of it; and there was nothing hid from the heat thereof.» From pole to pole, and from the east to the west, he brandished his fiery sceptre as though he had usurped all heaven and earth. As he bid the soft Persian in ancient times, so now, and fiercely, too, he bid me bow down and worship him; so now in his pride he seemed to command me and say, «Thou shalt have none other gods but me.» I was all alone before him. There were these two pitted together, and face to face—the mighty sun for one, and for the other—this poor, pale, solitary self of mine, that I always carry about with me.

But on the eighth day, and before I had yet turned away from Jehovah for the glittering god of the Persians, there appeared a dark line upon the edge of the forward horizon, and soon the line deepened into a delicate fringe that sparkled here and there, as though it were sown with diamonds. There, then, before me were the gardens and the minarets of Egypt, and the mighty works of the Nile, and I (the eternal Ego that I am!)—I had lived to see, and I saw them.

When evening came I was still within the confines of the desert, and my tent was pitched as usual, but one of my Arabs stalked away rapidly toward the west without telling me of the errand on which he was bent. After a while he returned; he had toiled on a grateful service; he had traveled all the way on to the border of the living world, and brought me back, for token, an ear of rice, full, fresh, and green.

The next day I entered upon Egypt, and floated along (for the delight was as the delight of bathing) through green, wavy fields of rice, and pastures fresh and plentiful, and dived into the cold verdure of groves and gardens, and quenched my hot eyes in shade, as though in deep rushing waters.— *From «Eothen.»*

KNOX, JOHN (Scotland, 1505–1572)

Too Much Honey.— The misfortune is, that when man has found honey, he enters upon the feast with an appetite so voracious, that he usually destroys his own delight by excess and satiety.

The Necessity of Schools.— Seeing that God hath determined that His Church here on earth shall be taught not by angels, but by men, and seeing that men are born ignorant of all godliness, and seeing also now God ceaseth to illuminate men miraculously, suddenly changing them as He did His apostles and others in the primitive Church: of necessity it is that your Honors be most careful for the virtuous education, and godly upbringing of the youth of this realm, if either ye now thirst unfeignedly for the advancement of Christ's glory, or yet desire the continuance of His benefits to the generation following. For as the youth must succeed to us, so ought we to be careful that they have the knowledge and erudition, to profit and comfort that which ought to be most dear to us, to wit, the Church and spouse of the Lord Jesus. —*From «The First Book of Discipline.»*

KRAPOTKIN, PRINCE (Russia, 1842–)

Against Radicals and Socialists.— The modern radical is a centralizer, a State partisan, a Jacobin to the core. And the Socialist walks in his footsteps. Like the Florentines at the end of the fifteenth century, who could only invoke the dictatorship of the State, to save them from the patricians, the Socialists know only how to invoke the same gods, the same dictatorship and the same State, to save us from the abominations of an economic system, created by that very State!—*From «The State—Its Historic Rôle.»*

LA BRUYERE, JEAN DE (France, 1645–1696)

The Slave of Many Masters.— A slave has but one master, the ambitious man has as many masters as there are persons whose aid may contribute to the advancement of his fortune.

«He Is Good That Does Good.»— He is good that does good to others. If he suffers for the good he does, he is better still; and if he suffers from them to whom he did good, he is arrived to that height of goodness, that nothing but an increase of his suffering can add to it: if it proves his death, his virtue is at its summit; it is heroism complete.

The Best Loved Subject. — An egotist will always speak of himself, either in praise or in censure: but a modest man ever shuns making himself the subject of his conversation.

Wild Oats as a Crop. — The generality of men expend the early part of their lives in contributing to render the latter part miserable.

How to Secure Quiet in Cities. — If you suppress the exorbitant love of pleasure and money, idle curiosity, iniquitous pursuits and wanton mirth, what a stillness would there be in the greatest cities! the necessaries of life do not occasion, at most, a third part of the hurry.

The Meaning of Good Taste. — Talent, taste, wit, good sense, are very different things, but by no means incompatible. Between good sense and good taste there exists the same difference as between cause and effect, and between wit and talent there is the same proportion as between a whole and its part.

LAMARTINE, ALPHONSE MARIE LOUIS (France, 1790–1869)

Carlyle's Cromwell.— The name of Cromwell up to the present period has been identified with ambition, craftiness, usurpation, ferocity, and tyranny; we think that his true character is that of a fanatic. History is like the sibyl, and only reveals her secrets to time, leaf by leaf. Hitherto she has not exhibited the real nature and composition of this human enigma. He has been thought a profound politician; he was only an eminent sectarian. Far-sighted historians of deep research, such as Hume, Lingard Bossuet, and Voltaire, have all been mistaken in Cromwell. The fault was not theirs, but belonged to the epoch in which they wrote. Authentic documents had not then seen the light, and the portrait of Cromwell had only been painted by his enemies. His memory and his body have been treated with similar infamy; by the restoration of Charles the Second, by the royalists of both branches, by Catholics and Protestants, by Whigs and Tories, equally interested in degrading the image of the republican Protector.

But error lasts only for a time, while truth endures for ages. Its turn was coming, hastened by an accident.

One of those men of research, who are to history what excavators are to monuments, Thomas Carlyle, a Scotch writer, endowed with the combined qualities of exalted enthusiasm and enduring patience, dissatisfied also with the conventional and superficial portrait hitherto depicted of Cromwell, resolved to search out and restore his true lineaments. The evident contradictions of the historians of his own and other countries who had invariably exhibited him as a fantastic tyrant and a melodramatic hypocrite, induced Mr. Carlyle to think, with justice, that beneath these discordant components there might be found another Cromwell, a being of nature, not of the imagination. Guided by that instinct of truth and logic in which is comprised the genius of erudite discovery, Mr. Carlyle, himself possessing the spirit of a sectary, and delighting in an independent course, undertook to search out and examine all the correspondence buried in the depths of public or private archives, and in which, at the different dates of his domestic, military, and political life, Cromwell, without thinking that he should thus paint himself, has in fact done so for the study of posterity. Supplied with these treasures of truth and revelation, Mr. Carlyle shut himself up for some years in the solitude of the country, that nothing might distract his thoughts from his work. Then having collected, classed, studied, commented on, and rearranged these voluminous letters of his hero, and having resuscitated, as if from the tomb, the spirit of the man and the age, he committed to Europe this hitherto unpublished correspondence, saying, with more reason than Jean Jacques Rousseau, «Receive, and read; behold the true Cromwell!» It is from these new and incontestable documents that we now propose to write the life of this dictator.—*From a Review of Carlyle's «Cromwell.»*

LANDOR, WALTER SAVAGE (England, 1775–1864)

Happiness and Goodness.—Goodness does not more certainly make men happy than happiness makes them good. We must distinguish between felicity and prosperity, for prosperity leads often to ambition, and ambition to disappointment; the course is then over, the wheel turns round but once, while the reaction of goodness and happiness is perpetual.

LAVATER, JOHANN CASPAR (Switzerland, 1741–1801)

The Vinegar and Oil of Human Nature.—Avoid connecting yourself with characters whose good and bad sides are unmixed, and have not fermented together; they resemble vials of vinegar and oil; or palettes set with colors; they are either excellent at home and intolerable abroad, or insufferable within doors and excellent in public; they are unfit for friendship, merely because their stamina, their ingredients of character, are too single, too much apart; let them be finely ground up with each other, and they will be incomparable.

Honesty and Pretense.—The more honesty a man has, the less he affects the air of a saint.

LEDYARD, JOHN (America, 1751–1789)

The Goodness of Women.—I have observed among all nations that the women ornament themselves more than the men; that, wherever found, they are the same kind, civil, obliging, humane, tender beings; that they are ever inclined to be gay and cheerful, timorous, and modest. They do not hesitate, like man, to perform a hospitable or generous action; not haughty, nor arrogant, nor supercilious, but full of courtesy and fond of society; industrious, economical, ingenuous; more liable in general, to err than man, but in general, also, more virtuous, and performing more good actions than he. I never addressed myself, in the language of decency and friendship, to a woman, whether civilized or savage, without receiving a decent and friendly answer. With man it has often been otherwise. In wandering over the barren plains of inhospitable Denmark, through honest Sweden, frozen Lapland, rude and churlish Finland, unprincipled Russia, and the widespread regions of the wandering Tartar, if hungry, dry, cold, wet, or sick, woman has ever been friendly to me, and uniformly so; and to add to this virtue, so worthy of the appellation of benevolence, these actions have been performed in so free and so kind a manner, that, if I was dry, I drank the sweet draught, and, if hungry, ate the coarse morsel with a double relish.—*From the «Life and Travels of John Ledyard.» 1828.*

LEE, ROBERT E. (America, 1807–1870)

The Last Word of the Confederacy.—Remember! we are one country now. Dismiss from your minds all sectional feeling, and bring up your children to be, above all, Americans.

LELAND, CHARLES GODFREY (America, 1824–)

The Rare Old Town of Nuremberg.—I know not how often I have had occasion, during my life, when speaking of Romanesque or Gothic objects, to employ such adjectives as «odd,» «quaint,» «weird,» «strange,» «wild,» «freakish,» «antique,» and «irregular»; but I am very certain that if they could be concentrated or monogrammatized in a single word, it would be exactly the one needed to describe the rare old town of Nuremberg. There is a picturesque disorder—a lyrical confusion—about the entire place, which is perfectly irresistible. Turrets shoot up in all sorts of ways, on all sorts of occasions, upon all sorts of houses; and little boxes, with delicate Gothic windows, cling to their sides and to one another like barnacles to a ship; while the houses themselves are turned around and about in so many positions, that you wonder that a few are not upside down, or lying on their sides, by way of completing the original arrangement of no arrangement at all. It always seemed to me as if the buildings in Nuremberg had, like the furniture in Irving's tale, been indulging over night in a very irregular dance, and suddenly stopped in the most complicated part of a confusion worse confounded. Galleries, quaint staircases, and towers, with projecting upper stories, as well as eccentric chimneys, demented doorways, insane weather vanes, and highly original steeples, form the most commonplace materials in building; and it has more than once occurred to me that the architects of this city, even at the present day, must have imbibed their principles, not from the lecture room, but from the most remarkable inspirations of some romantic scene painter.—*From «Meister Karl's Sketch Book.»*

LESSING, GOTTHOLD EPHRAIM (Germany, 1729–1781)

The Best of All Companions.—The most agreeable of all companions is a simple, frank man, without any high pretensions to an oppressive greatness; one who loves life, and understands the use of it; obliging, alike at all hours; above all, of a golden temper, and steadfast as an anchor. For such an one we gladly exchange the greatest genius, the most brilliant wit, the profoundest thinker.

L'ESTRANGE, SIR ROGER (England, 1616–1704)

Morals from Æsop.—There's hardly any man living that may not be wrought upon more or less by flattery: for we do all of us naturally overween in our own favor: but when it comes to be applied once to a vain fool, it makes him forty times an arranter sot than he was before.

Pragging, lying, and pretending, has cost many a man his life and estate.—*From «Æsop's Fables» translated.*

LE VERT, MADAME OCTAVIA WALTON (America, Nineteenth Century)

The Coliseum.—The Coliseum is crumbling fast away; Rome has fallen from her early grandeur; but the world progresses more proudly than ever, for that fair and glorious land beyond the broad Atlantic has been added to the treasures of time,—that unrivaled land, the birthplace of Washington and of freedom, which seems, «Pallas-like, to have sprung from the head of Jove,» with all the knowledge of departed centuries, and the experience of long-buried nations.

At the end of a soft and balmy day of spring, we first entered the Coliseum. Its immensity and desolation were overpowering. The lips absolutely refused to frame into words the emotions inspired by this grandest of ruins. So, to escape questions from our party concerning the impressions made upon my mind, I stole away from them, and climbing up a mass of stone, I found a little nook, where I seated myself, and, free from interruption, gazed upon the wondrous extent of the majestic Coliseum.

It is of oval form, and when perfect, the walls were one hundred and fifty feet in height. Now, the lofty rim around it is broken in all directions. The deep blue sky seemed to rest like a roof above the arches, which rose up tier above tier to the summit, where once floated an awning, as protection from the midday sun. It is built of travertine rock, whose coarse grain and porous texture afford a safe lodgment for grains of dust. These soon became soil, whence spring myriads of flowers, and tufted bushes of dark-green foliage.

Nature appeared to have seized the ruin from decay, and hidden the ravages of the destroyer beneath a mantle of verdure, sprinkled with glowing blossoms, belonging to a flora unknown elsewhere save in ancient Rome. There were delicate vines clinging around enormous prostrate columns, while long tendrils, like garlands, were waving in the air. Along a terrace which encircled the arena, were still visible ranges of boxes, intended for the emperors and nobles. This was covered as though with a carpet, so various and brilliant-hued were the flowers growing upon it. Far up along the edge of the broken battlements was a fringe of green and shining ivy.

The Coliseum was commenced by Vespasian, and finished by his son Titus in the year 80, a few years after the destruction of Jerusalem. Twelve thousand captured Jews were compelled to labor incessantly in its construction, and when it was completed, for one hundred days gladiatorial combats were held within it, and thousands of Christians were torn to pieces by the wild tigers, lions, and leopards.

During four hundred years, the Coliseum was devoted to these fearful games, where gladiators met, or where savage beasts buried their claws in the quivering flesh of human beings. Seas of blood have washed over the broad arena, and myriads of martyrs to the faith of our holy Redeemer, have yielded up their souls to God

within those circling walls. Hence, with all these memories crowding on the mind, I could readily picture the terrific scenes of those horrible days, when

«The buzz of eager nations ran,
In murmured pity, or loud-roared applause,
As man was slaughtered by his fellow-man.
And wherefore slaughtered? wherefore, but because
Such was the bloody circus' genial laws,
And the imperial pleasure.»

LIEBER, FRANCIS (German American, 1800–1872)

The Meaning of Liberty.—Liberty, in its absolute sense, means the faculty of willing and the power of doing what has been willed, without influence from any other source, or from without. It means self-determination; unrestrainedness of action.

In this absolute meaning, there is but one free being, because there is but one being whose will is absolutely independent upon any influence but that which he wills himself, and whose power is adequate to his absolute will—who is almighty. Liberty, self-determination, unrestrainedness of action, ascribed to any other being, or applied to any other sphere of action, has necessarily a relative and limited, therefore an approximative sense only.

«Vox Populi, Vox Dei.»—The doctrine of *Vox Populi, Vox Dei* is essentially unrepublican, as the doctrine that the people may do what they list under the constitution, above the constitution, and against the constitution, is an open avowal of disbelief in self-government.—*Civil Liberty and Self-Government, 1853.*

LINCOLN, ABRAHAM (America, 1809–1865)

Right Makes Might.—Let us have faith that right makes might, and in that faith, let us to the end, dare to do our duty, as we understand it.—*From an address delivered in New York, February 27th, 1860.*

LIVINGSTON, ROBERT R. (America, 1746–1813)

A Government of Leagued States.—Where a Government is composed of independent States, united not by the power of a sovereign but by their common interest, the Executive Departments form a center of communication between each State and their Chief Council, and are so far links of the chain, which should bind them together, as they render to each similar views of great national objects, and introduce uniformity in their measures for the establishment of general interests.—*From a Circular Letter from the Secretary of Foreign Affairs to the Governors of the Several States, 1830.*

LIVY (TITUS LIVIUS) (Rome, *c.* 59 B.C.–*c.* 17 A.D.)

«Assuaging the Female Mind.»—To these persuasions was added the soothing behavior of their husbands themselves, who urged, in extenuation of the violence they had been tempted to commit, the excess of passion and the force of love; arguments than which there can be none more powerful to assuage the irritation of the female mind.—*i. 9.*

Liberty and Justice.—So difficult is it to preserve moderation in asserting liberty, while, under the pretense of a desire to balance rights, each elevates himself in such a manner as to depress another; for men are apt by the very measures which they adopt to free themselves from fear, to become the objects of fear to others, and to fasten upon them the burden of injustice which they have thrown off from their shoulders, as if there existed in nature a perpetual necessity either of doing or of suffering injury.—*iii. 65.*

Why Politicians are Pleasant.—It results from the nature of the human mind, that he, who addresses the public with a view to his own particular benefit, is studious of rendering himself more generally agreeable than he who has no other object but the advantage of the public.—*iii. 68.*

Familiarity Breeds Contempt.—Being continually in people's sight, which circumstance, by the mere satiety which it creates, diminishes the reverence felt for great characters.—*xxxv. 10.*

LOCKE, JOHN (England, 1632–1704)

The Measure of Science.—Truth, whether in or out of fashion, is the measure of knowledge, and the business of the understanding; whatsoever is besides that, however authorized by consent, is nothing but ignorance, or something worse.

LODGE, THOMAS (England, 1556–1625)

A Choice for Every Man.—Truly, son, it is better to be accounted witty than wealthy, and righteous than rich: praise lasteth for a moment that is grounded on shows, and fame remaineth after death that proceedeth of good substance. Choose whether thou wilt be infamous with Erostratus, or renowned with Aristides; by one thou shalt bear the name of sacrilege, by the other the title of just: the first may flatter thee with similitude, the last will honor thee indeed, and more when thou art dead.—*From «An Alarum against Usurers.»*

LONG, GEORGE (England, 1800–1879)

The Character of a Tyrannicide.—Brutus had moderate abilities, with great industry and much learning: he had no merit as a general, but he had the courage of a soldier; he had the reputation of virtue, and he was free from many of the vices of his contemporaries: he was sober and temperate. Of enlarged political views he had none; there is not a sign of his being superior in this respect to the mass of his contemporaries. When the Civil War broke out, he joined Pompeius, though Pompeius had murdered his father. If he gave up his private enmity, as Plutarch says, for what he believed to be the better cause, the sacrifice was honorable; if there were other motives,

and I believe there were, his choice of his party does him no credit. His conspiracy against Cæsar can only be justified by those, if there are such, who think that a usurper ought to be got rid of in any way. But if a man is to be murdered, one does not expect those to take a part in the act who, after being enemies, have received favors from him, and professed to be friends. The murderers should at least be a man's declared enemies who have just wrongs to avenge. Though Brutus was dissatisfied with things under Cæsar, he was not the first mover in the conspiracy. He was worked upon by others, who knew that his character and personal relation to Cæsar would in a measure sanctify the deed; and by their persuasion, not his own resolve, he became an assassin in the name of freedom, which meant the triumph of his party, and in the name of virtue, which meant nothing.—*From «The Civil Wars of Rome.»*

LONGINUS (Greek, 210–273 A. D.)

The Greatest Thoughts of the Greatest Souls.—For it is impossible for those who have low, mean, and groveling ideas, and who have spent their lives in mercenary employments, to produce anything worthy of admiration, or to be a possession for all times. Grand and dignified expressions must be looked for from those, and those alone, whose thoughts are ever employed on glorious and noble objects.—*De Subl. ix.*

The Genius of Moses.—In the same way the Jewish lawgiver, a man of no ordinary genius, when he had conceived in his mind a just idea of the grandeur of the Supreme Being, has given expression to it in noble language, in the beginning of his work containing His laws:—«And God said,» «What?» «Let there be light: and there was light. Let the earth be: and the earth was.»—*De Subl. ix.*

LOWELL, JAMES RUSSELL (America, 1819–1891)

Truth's Brave Simplicity.—Truth is quite beyond the reach of satire. There is so brave a simplicity in her, that she can no more be made ridiculous than an oak or a pine.—*The Biglow Papers, No. III.*

LYTTELTON, LORD (England, 1709–1773)

Addison and Swift in Hades.—(MR. ADDISON—DR. SWIFT.)

Dr. Swift—Surely, Addison, Fortune was exceedingly inclined to play the fool (a humor her ladyship, as well as most other ladies of very great quality, is frequently in) when she made you a minister of state and me a divine!

Addison—I must confess we were both of us out of our elements; but you don't mean to insinuate that all would have been right if our destinies had been reversed?

Swift—Yes, I do. You would have made an excellent bishop, and I should have governed Great Britain, as I did Ireland, with an absolute sway, while I talked of nothing but liberty, property, and so forth.

Addison—You governed the mob of Ireland; but I never understood that you governed the kingdom. A nation and a mob are very different things.

Swift—Ay, so you fellows that have no genius for politics may suppose; but there are times when, by seasonably putting himself at the head of the mob, an able man may get to the head of the nation. Nay, there are times when the nation itself is a mob, and ought to be treated as such by a skillful observer.

Addison—I don't deny the truth of your proposition; but is there no danger that, from the natural vicissitudes of human affairs, the favorite of the mob should be mobbed in his turn?

Swift—Sometimes there may, but I risked it, and it answered my purpose. Ask the lord-lieutenants, who were forced to pay court to me instead of my courting them, whether they did not feel my superiority.—*From «Dialogues of the Dead.»*

LYTTON, EDWARD GEORGE EARLE LYTTON BULWER, BARON (England, 1803–1873)

Reputation for Small Perfections.—Never get a reputation for a small perfection, if you are trying for fame in a loftier area. The world can only judge by generals, and it sees that those who pay considerable attention to the minutiæ, seldom have their minds occupied with great things. There are, it is true, exceptions; but to exceptions the world does not attend.

MACHIAVELLI, NICOLO (Italy, 1469–1527)

Laws and Manners.—For as laws are necessary that good manners may be preserved, so there is need of good manners that laws may be maintained.—*Dei Discorsi, i. c. 18.*

Religion and Government.—And as the strict observance of religious worship is the cause why states rise to eminence, so contempt for religion brings ruin on them. For where the fear of God is wanting, destruction is sure to follow, or else it must be sustained by the fear felt for their prince, who may thus supply the want of religion in his subjects. Whence it arises that the kingdoms, that depend only on the virtue of a mortal, have a short duration; it is seldom that the virtue of the father survives in the son.—*Dei Discorsi, i. c. 11.*

Liberty Necessary for Good Order.—Those who have given us the wisest and most judicious scheme of a commonwealth, have handed down that some guard must be appointed to watch over liberty, and according to the wisdom of the choice does liberty endure a longer or shorter time. And as in every commonwealth there is a nobility and people of lower rank, the question arises in whose hands liberty may be most safely deposited.—*Dei Discorsi, i. c. 5.*

MAHAFFY, JOHN P. (Ireland, 1839–)

The Future of Education.—The sum of the whole matter is, therefore, this: let us distinguish clearly between technical and liberal instruction, even in the highest forms. To begin with a combination of both at our public schools is perfectly wrong. If they really aim at a liberal education, let that be attended to, and upon the old and well-established principles which have furnished us with cultivated men for many centuries. To allow young boys, or incompetent parents, to select the topics which they fancy useful or entertaining is an absurdity. . . . To make mere technical education as refining as the other is no doubt impossible; but every effort should, nevertheless, be used to let those whose lives compel them to accept this narrower course still feel the truth of the old adage that «manners maketh man.» It is this which affords the strongest argument for having these schools in contact with our old universities, when the very atmosphere breathes a certain kind of refinement not easily attainable elsewhere. But whatever is done in that way, let us not be tempted to muddle the two together, and spoil both, for the sake of making our universities democratic and attractive to the masses.

True cultivation can never be cheap, or hastily acquired. It must always require many years. —*From The Nineteenth Century.*

MALEBRANCHE, NICOLAS (France, 1638-1715)

Making Sacrifices for Fashion.—'Tis related by an ancient author that in Ethiopia the courtiers crippled and deformed themselves, lopped off a limb or two, and sometimes even died, to imitate their princes. 'Twas as scandalous to be seen with a pair of eyes, or to walk upright in the retinue of a crooked and one-eyed king, as it would be ridiculous to appear at court nowadays in ruffs and caps, or in white buskins and gilded spurs. This Ethiopian fashion was as extravagant and incommodious as can well be imagined. But yet it was the fashion. It was cheerfully followed by the court, and the pain to be endured was less thought of than the honor a man purchased by manifesting so generous an affection for his king. In short, this mode, when supported by a pretended reason of friendship, grew up to a custom and a law that obtained a considerable time.

We learn from the relations of those who have traveled in the Levant that this custom is observed in several countries—as also some others as inconsistent with reason and good sense. But there is no necessity of twice cutting the Line to see unreasonable laws and customs religiously observed. We may find the patrons of fantastical and inconvenient fashions nearer home. Our own country will supply us with enough.

MALLOCK, WILLIAM HURRELL (England, 1849-)

The Object of Life.—If you can see nothing in this life worth winning for yourself, and nothing in this life that it would make you miserable to miss, your labors for others will be but the dull round of a treadmill. Our own inner lives and loves must be the light of our world for each of us; and if the light, my friend, that is in us be darkness, oh, how great is that darkness! But I do not yet despair of you. Some day or other, you will learn to love, and then the whole aspect of things will change for you. The old sense of life's worth and solemnity will come back again; you will again be eager, again an enthusiast, and again, perhaps, a poet.—*From* «*A Dialogue on Human Happiness.*»

MANN, HORACE (America, 1796–1859)

Wealth and Generosity.—Great wealth is a misfortune, because it makes generosity impossible. There can be no generosity where there is no sacrifice; and a man who is worth a million of dollars, though he gives half of it away, no more makes a sacrifice, than (if I may make such a supposition) a dropsical man, whose skin holds a hogshead of water, makes a sacrifice when he is tapped for a barrel. He is in a healthier condition after the operation than before it.—*From* «*A Few Thoughts for a Young Man.*»

The Feudalism of English Capital.—The power of money is as imperial as the power of the sword; and I may as well depend upon another for my head, as for my bread. The day is sure to come, when men will look back upon the prerogatives of Capital, at the present time, with as severe and as just a condemnation as we now look back upon the predatory Chieftains of the Dark Ages. Weighed in the balances of the sanctuary, or even in the clumsy scales of human justice, there is no equity in the allotments which assign to one man but a dollar a day, with working, while another has an income of a dollar a minute, without working. Under the reign of Force, or under the reign of Money, there may be here and there a good man who uses his power for blessing and not for oppressing his race; but all their natural tendencies are exclusively bad. In England, we see the feudalism of Capital approaching its catastrophe. In Ireland, we see the catastrophe consummated. Unhappy Ireland! where the objects of human existence and the purposes of human government have all been reversed; where rulers, for centuries, have ruled for the aggrandizement of themselves, and not for the happiness of their subjects; where misgovernment has reigned so long, so supremely, and so atrociously, that at the present time, the «Three Estates» of the realm are Crime, Famine, and Death!—*From* «*A Few Thoughts for a Young Man.*» *1850.*

MARCELLINUS, AMMIANUS (Syria, 330–395 A.D.)

Apothegms from His History.—But in the midst of thorns roses spring up, and amidst savage beasts some are tame.—*Hist. xvi. 7.*

Almost all difficulties may be got the better of by prudent thought, revolving and pondering much in the mind.—*Hist. xvii. 8.*

It is not wonderful that men sometimes are able to discern what is profitable and what is hurtful to them, since we regard their minds to be related to the heavenly beings.—*Hist. xviii. 3.*

Yet the success of plans and the advantage to be derived from them do not at all times agree, seeing the Gods claim to themselves the right to decide as to the final result.—*Hist. xxv. 3.*

MARGARET OF NAVARRE (France, 1492-1549)

Love and Jealousy.—It is said that jealousy is love, but I deny it; for though jealousy be procured by love, as ashes are by fire, yet jealousy extinguishes love as ashes smother the flame.

MARSHALL, JOHN (America, 1755–1835)

The Character of Washington.—No man has ever appeared upon the theater of public action whose integrity was more incorruptible, or whose principles were more perfectly free from the contamination of those selfish and unworthy passions which find their nourishment in the conflicts of party. Having no views which required concealment, his real and avowed motives were the same; and the whole correspondence does not furnish a single case from which even an enemy would infer that he was capable, under any circumstances, of stooping to the employment of duplicity.

No truth can be uttered with more confidence than that his ends were always upright, and his means always pure. He exhibits the rare example of a politician to whom wiles were absolutely unknown, and whose professions to foreign governments and to his own countrymen were always sincere. In him was fully exemplified the real distinction which forever exists between wisdom and cunning, and the importance as well as the truth of the maxim, that «honesty is the best policy.»

If Washington possessed ambition, that passion was, in his bosom, so regulated by principles, or controlled by circumstances, that it was neither vicious nor turbulent. Intrigue was never employed as the means of its gratification, nor was personal aggrandizement its object. The various high and important stations to which he was called by the public voice were unsought by himself; and in consenting to fill them, he seems rather to have yielded to a general conviction that the interests of his country would be thereby promoted, than to his particular inclination.—*From* «*The Life of Washington.*»

MARTINEAU, JAMES (England, 1805–1900)

Life and Immortality.—The corporeal frame is but the mechanism for making thoughts and affections apparent, the signal house with which God has covered us, the electric telegraph by which quickest intimation flies abroad of the spiritual force within us. The instrument may be broken, the dial plate effaced; and, though the hidden artist can make no more signs, he may be rich as ever in the things to be signified. Fever may fire the pulses of the body; but wisdom and sanctity cannot sicken, be inflamed, and die. Neither consumption can waste, nor fracture mutilate, nor gunpowder scatter away, thought, and fidelity, and love, but only that organization which the spirit sequestered therein renders so fair and noble. To suppose such a thing would be to invert the order of rank, which God has visibly established among the forces of our world, and to give a downright ascendency to the brute energies of matter above the vitality of the mind, which, up to that point, discovers, subdues, and rules them; to proclaim the triumph of the sword, the casualty, the pestilence, over virtue, truth, and faith; to set the cross above the crucified; to surrender the holy things of this world to corruption, and shroud its heaven with darkness, and turn its moon into blood.—*From* «*Endeavors After the Christian Life.*»

MARTYN, HENRY (England, 1781–1812)

On the Father of Ten Children.—If the people only make the riches, the father of ten children is a greater benefactor to his country, than he who has added to it ten thousand acres of land, and no people.—*From number 200 of the Spectator.*

MASSILLON, JEAN BAPTISTE (France, 1663-1742)

Marriage.—Every effort is made in forming matrimonial alliances to reconçile matters relating to fortune, but very little is paid to the congeniality of dispositions, or to the accordance of hearts.

MATHER, COTTON (America, 1663–1728)

«An Army of Devils Broke Loose.»—An army of devils is horribly broke in upon the place which is the center, and, after a sort, the firstborn of our English settlements; and the houses of the good people there are filled with the doleful shrieks of their children and servants, tormented by invisible hands, with tortures altogether preternatural. After the mischiefs there endeavored, and since in part conquered, the terrible plague, of evil angels, hath made its progress into some other places, where other persons have been in like manner diabolically handled. These our poor afflicted neighbors, quickly after they become infected and infested with these demons, arrive to a capacity of discerning those which they conceive the shapes of their troubles; and notwithstanding the great and just suspicion, that the demons might impose the shapes of innocent persons in their spectral exhibitions upon the sufferers (which may, perhaps, prove no small part of the witch plot in the issue), yet many of the persons thus represented being examined, several of them have been convicted of a very damnable witchcraft. Yea, more than one, twenty have confessed that they have signed unto a book which the devil showed them, and en-

gaged in his hellish design of bewitching and ruining our land.—*From the* «*Wonders of the Invisible World.*» *1693.*

MATHER, INCREASE (America, 1639–1723)

Bargains with the Devil.—There may have been many in the world who have, upon conviction, confessed themselves guilty of familiarity with the devil. A multitude of instances this way are mentioned by Bodinus, Codronchus, Delrio, Jacquerius, Remigius, and others. Some in this country have affirmed that they knew a man in another part of the world, above fifty years ago, who having an ambitious desire to be thought a wise man, whilst he was tormented with the itch of his wicked ambition, the devil came to him with promises that he should quickly be in great reputation for his wisdom, in case he would make a covenant with him; the conditions whereof were, that when men came to him for his counsel, he should labor to persuade them that there is no God, nor devil, nor heaven, nor hell; and that, such a term of years being expired, the devil should have his soul. The articles were consented to: the man continuing after this to be of a very civil conversation, doing hurt to none, but good to many; and by degrees began to have a name to be a person of extraordinary sagacity, and was sought unto far and near for counsel, his words being esteemed oracles by the vulgar. And he did according to his covenant upon all occasions secretly disseminate principles of atheism, not being suspected for a wizard. But a few weeks before the time indented with the devil was fulfilled, inexpressible horror of conscience surprised him, so that he revealed the secret transactions which had passed betwixt himself and the devil. He would sometimes, with hideous roarings, tell those that came to visit him, that now he knew there was a God, and a devil, and a heaven, and a hell. So did he die a miserable spectacle of the righteous and fearful judgment of God. And every age does produce new examples of those that have by their own confession made the like cursed covenants with the prince of darkness.—*From an essay for the Recording of Illustrious Providences, 1684.*

METASTASIO, PIETRO (Italy, 1698–1782)

Death as a Release.—It is by no means a fact, that death is the worst of all evils; when it comes, it is an alleviation to mortals who are worn out with sufferings.

Secret Grief.—If the internal griefs of every man could be read, written on his forehead, how many who now excite envy, would appear to be the objects of pity?

MIDDLETON, THOMAS FANSHAW (England, 1769–1822)

When Virtue Is Odious.—Virtue itself offends, when coupled with forbidding manners.

MILTON, JOHN (England, 1608–1674)

The Crime of Killing Good Books.—As good almost kill a man as kill a good book. Many a man lives a burden to the earth; but a good book is the precious life-blood of a master spirit, embalmed and treasured up on purpose, to a life beyond life.

The Whole Art of Government.—To make the people fittest to choose, and the chosen fittest to govern, will be to mend our corrupt and faulty education, to teach the people faith, not without virtue, temperance, modesty, sobriety, parsimony, justice; not to admire wealth or honor; to hate turbulence and ambition; to place every one his private welfare and happiness in the public peace, liberty, and safety. They shall not then need to be much mistrustful of their chosen patriots in the grand council; who will be then rightly called the true keepers of our liberty, though the most of their business will be in foreign affairs.—*From* «*A Ready Way to Establish a Free Commonwealth.*»

MONTAIGNE, MICHEL EYQUEM DE (France, 1533–1592)

The Education of Children.—It is a thing worthy of notice that, in that excellent form of civil polity laid down by Lycurgus, which, from its perfection, may be truly called wonderful, while he dwells with much emphasis on the necessity of attending to the education of the young, he makes little mention of learning; as if his noble-minded youth, disdaining to submit to any other yoke except that of virtue, ought to be furnished, instead of our teachers of arts and sciences, with such masters as should train them in valor, prudence, and justice; a precedent followed by Plato in his laws. The method which he suggested was to propound questions relating to men and their actions, and if they condemned or commended this or that person or action, they were to give a reason for so doing; and in this way, while they sharpened their understandings, they became skillful in distinguishing right and wrong.—*From his Essays, i. c. 24.*

The Soul Makes Its Own Fortune.—Fortune does us neither good nor hurt; she only presents us the matter and the seed, which our soul, more powerful than she, turns and applies as she best pleases, being the sole cause and sovereign mistress of her own happy or unhappy condition. All external accessions receive taste and color from the internal constitution, as clothes warm us not with their heat, but our own, which they are adapted to cover and keep in.

MONTESQUIEU, BARON DE (France, 1689-1755)

The Law of Nations.—Men considered as inhabitants of so large a planet, where there must of necessity be many nations, have laws referring to the relation which these nations bear to one another, and this is called «international law.» Considered as living in a society, which must be maintained, they have laws in regard to the relation which the governors bear to the governed, and these are «political

rights.» They have also some in regard to the relation which citizens bear to one another, and these are «civil rights.»—*De l'Esprit, i. c. 3.*

MORE, SIR THOMAS (England, 1478–1535)

Those Who Most Long for Change.—Who quarrel more than beggars? Who does more earnestly long for a change than he that is uneasy in his present circumstances? And who run to create confusions with so desperate a boldness, as those who, having nothing to lose, hope to gain by them?

NEAL, JOHN (America, 1793–1876)

Poetry and Power.—Poetry is the naked expression of power and eloquence. But for many hundred years poetry has been confounded with false music, measure, and cadence; the soul with the body, the thought with the lauguage, the manner of speaking with the mode of thinking. The secondary qualities of poetry have been mistaken for the primary ones.

What I call poetry has nothing to do with art or learning. It is a natural music—the music of woods and waters; not that of the orchestra. It is a fine volatile essence, which cannot be extinguished or confined while there is one drop of blood in the human heart, or any sense of Almighty God among the children of men. I do not mean this irreverently—I mean precisely what I say—that poetry is a religion as well as a music. Nay, it is eloquence. It is whatever affects, touches, or disturbs the animal or moral sense of man. I care not how poetry may be expressed nor in what language, it is still poetry; as the melody of the waters, wherever they may run, in the desert or the wilderness, among the rocks or the grass, will always be melody. It is not artificial music, the music of the head, of learning, or of science, but it is one continual voluntary of the heart; to be heard everywhere at all times, by day and by night, whenever men will stay their hands, for a moment, or lift up their heads and listen. It is not the composition of a master; the language of art, painfully and entirely exact; but is the wild, capricious melody of nature, pathetic or brilliant, like the roundelay of innumerable birds whistling all about you, in the wind and water, sky and air; or the coquetting of a river breeze over the fine strings of an Eolian harp, concealed among green leaves and apple blossoms. *From* «*Randolph.*»

NEPOS, CORNELIUS (Italy, First Century B. C.)

On Ruling by Force.—The power is detested, and miserable is the life, of him who wishes rather to be feared than to be loved.

NEWMAN, JOHN HENRY (England, 1801–1890)

«Vita Militia.»—The whole Church, all elect souls, each in its turn is called to this necessary work. Once it was the turn of others, now it is our turn. Once it was the Apostles' turn. It was St. Paul's turn once. He had all cares on him all at once; covered from head to foot with cares, as Job with sores. And, as if all this were not enough, he had a thorn in the flesh added,—some personal discomfort ever with him. Yet he did his part well,—he was as a strong and bold wrestler in his day, and at the close of it was able to say, «I have fought a good fight, I have finished my course, I have kept the faith.» And, after him, the excellent of the earth, the white-robed army of martyrs, and the cheerful company of confessors, each in his turn, each in his day, have likewise played the man. And so down to this very time, when faith has well-nigh failed, first one and then another have been called out to exhibit before the Great King. It is as though all of us were allowed to stand around His throne at once, and He called on first this man, and then that, to take up the chant by himself, each in his turn having to repeat the melody which his brethren have before gone through.—*From* «*University Sermons.*»

NORTON, ANDREWS (America, 1786–1853)

Van Leaders of Humanity.—It is delightful to remember that there have been men, who, in the cause of truth and virtue, have made no compromises for their own advantage or safety; who have recognized «the hardest duty as the highest»; who, conscious of the possession of great talents, have relinquished all the praise that was within their grasp, all the applause which they might have so liberally received, if they had not thrown themselves in opposition to the errors and vices of their fellow-men, and have been content to take obloquy and insult instead; who have approached to lay on the altar of God «their last infirmity.» They, without doubt, have felt that deep conviction of having acted right, which supported the martyred philosopher of Athens, when he asked, «What disgrace is it to me if others are unable to judge of me, or to treat me as they ought?» There is something very solemn and sublime in the feeling produced by considering how differently these men have been estimated by their contemporaries, from the manner in which they are regarded by God. We perceive the appeal which lies from the ignorance, the folly, and the iniquity of man, to the throne of Eternal Justice. A storm of calumny and reviling has too often pursued them through life, and continued, when they could no longer feel it, to beat upon their graves. But it is no matter. They had gone where all who have suffered, and all who have triumphed in the same noble cause, receive their reward; but where the wreath of the martyr is more glorious than that of the conqueror.—*From* «*Thoughts on True and False Religion.*»

NORTON, JOHN (England, 1606–1663)

The Meaning of Justice.—Relative or moral justice is an external work of God, whereby He proceeds with man according to the law of righteousness freely constituted between Him and them; rendering to every one what is due unto them, thereby, either by way of recompense, in case of obedience, or by way of punishment, in case of disobedience.—*From the Orthodox Evangelist.*

NOVALIS (FRIEDRICH VON HARDENBERG) (Germany, 1772-1801)

Things Too Delicate to Be Thought.—Shame is a feeling of profanation. Friendship, love, and piety ought to be handled with a sort of mysterious secrecy; they ought to be spoken of only in the rare moments of perfect confidence—to be mutually understood in silence. Many things are too delicate to be thought: many more, to be spoken.

OEHLENSCHLÄGER, ADAM GOTTLOB (Denmark, 1779-1850)

Children's Play and Art.—The plays of natural lively children are the infancy of art. Children live in the world of imagination and feeling. They invest the most insignificant object with any form they please, and see in it whatever they wish to see.

OSSOLI, SARAH MARGARET FULLER (America, 1810-1850)

Free Play for Woman's Activities.—We would have every path laid open to woman as freely as to man. Were this done, and a slight temporary fermentation allowed to subside, we should see crystallizations more pure and of more various beauty. We believe the divine energy would pervade nature to a degree unknown in the history of former ages, and that no discordant collision, but a ravishing harmony of the spheres, would ensue.—*Woman in the Nineteenth Century.*

How to Find the Right Friends.—Our friends should be our incentives to right; but not only our guiding, but our prophetic stars. To love by right is much, to love by faith is more; both are the entire love, without which heart, mind, and soul cannot be alike satisfied. We love and ought to love one another, not merely for the absolute worth of each, but on account of a mutual fitness of temporary character.—*Finding a Friend, Chap. V.*

OTIS, JAMES (America, 1725-1783)

A Question of Permanent Interest.—Should the British empire one day be extended round the whole world, would it be reasonable that all mankind should have their concerns managed by the electors of Old Sarum and the «occupants of the Cornish barns and alehouses» we sometimes read of?—*From Considerations on Behalf of the Colonists, 1765.*

OVERBURY, SIR THOMAS (England, 1581-1613)

Wit and Judgment.—Wit is brushwood, judgment timber: the one gives the greatest flame, the other yields the most durable heat; and both meeting make the best fire.

X—250

PARKER, THEODORE (America, 1810-1860)

The American Idea.—There is what I call the American idea. . . . This idea demands, as the proximate organization thereof, a democracy, that is, a government of all the people, by all the people, for all the people; of course, a government of the principles of eternal justice, the unchanging law of God; for shortness' sake I will call it the idea of freedom.—*Speech at the New England anti-Slavery Convention, Boston, May 29th, 1850.*

PARNELL, THOMAS (Ireland, 1679-1718)

On Taking a Man's Measure.—What country linen-draper, or pot-house politician, when the merits of a statesman are discussed, but will undertake to estimate his ability to a T? What young templar, as yet inexperienced in the sensation derived from a touch of a confiding client's handsel-guinea, but will exactly tell you the capabilities and deficiencies of the several judges, assign to each of them his relative merits at law and equity, and supplement his information, if you will, by cataloguing every silk gown according to its worth? We might find examples of this arrogance in every profession. In literature it is offensively prominent; but whether he confesses it or not, almost every human being fancies himself able to measure, if only by rule of thumb, those with whom he is brought in contact, or to whom he thinks it worth while to apply his attention. Every one may be candid enough to own his practical inferiority to him whom he thus unhesitatingly criticizes. He is free to confess he cannot write poems like A, or novels like B, or paint like C, or lead the House of Commons like D; yet, by some peculiar process, inexplicable, I believe, even to himself, he is firmly convinced that whatever judgment he has formed of the intellectual rank of these persons, and consequently of their performances, is invariably and unassailably correct. Indeed, the very readiness with which he recognizes his own inferiority is an incentive to self-esteem, and tends to make him set a higher value on the discrimination he has exhibited in thus discovering their superiority to himself. Strange as it may appear, he possesses a sort of inner judgment which applauds the insight he has displayed in the decision. His favorite axiom is slightly varied from that of the elder Shandy's—«An ounce of one man's judgment is worth a ton of other people's.»

PASCAL, BLAISE (France, 1623-1662)

Against Helping God by the Devil's Methods.—We must not do the least evil even to bring about the greatest good, for «the truth of God requires not the assistance of our untruths,» as the Scripture says.—*From the Provincial Letters.*

The Contradictions of Human Nature.—What a chimera is man! what a confused chaos! what a subject of contradiction!—a professed judge of all things, and yet a feeble worm of the earth! the great depository and guardian of

truth, and yet a mere huddle of uncertainty! the glory and the scandal of the universe!

PAULDING, JAMES KIRKE (America, 1779-1860)

The Character of John Bull.—John Bull was a choleric old fellow, who held a good manor in the middle of a great mill-pond, and which, by reason of its being quite surrounded by water, was generally called Bullock Island. Bull was an ingenious man, an exceedingly good blacksmith, a dexterous cutler, and a notable weaver and pot baker besides. He also brewed capital porter, ale, and small beer, and was in fact a sort of jack of all trades, and good at each. In addition to these, he was a hearty fellow, an excellent bottle-companion, and passably honest, as times go.

But what tarnished all these qualities was a devilish quarrelsome, overbearing disposition, which was always getting him into some scrape or other. The truth is, he never heard of a quarrel going on among his neighbors, but his fingers itched to be in the thickest of them; so that he was hardly ever seen without a broken head, a black eye, or a bloody nose. Such was Squire Bull, as he was commonly called by the country people his neighbors—one of those odd, testy, grumbling, boasting old codgers, that never get credit for what they are, because they are always pretending to be what they are not.—*From «John Bull and Brother Jonathan.»*

PENN, WILLIAM (England, 1644-1718)

The Eternal Law.—There is a Great God and Power, that hath made the world and all things therein, to whom you and I and all people owe their being and well-being; and to whom you and I must one day give an account for all that we do in the world. This Great God hath written his Law in our hearts, by which we are taught and commanded to love and help, and do good to one another, and not to do harm and mischief unto one another.—*From the Select Works of William Penn, 1782.*

PHELPS, AUSTIN (America, 1820-1890)

The Final Test of Success.—The Napoleonic test of character is success, and the final test of success is permanence.

PHILLIPS, WENDELL (America, 1811-1884)

What the Masses Can Do.—Give to the masses nothing to do, and they will topple down thrones and cut throats; give them the government here and they will make pulpits useless, and colleges an impertinence.—*Speech, Boston, October 4, 1859.*

God and His Man.—One on God's side is a majority.—*Speech, Brooklyn, November 1, 1859.*

Revolutions.—Revolutions are not made, they come.—*Speech, Boston, January 28, 1852.*

Revolutions never go backward.—*Speech, Boston, February 17, 1861.*

PINKNEY, WILLIAM (America, 1764-1822)

Oppression.—Oppression is but another name for irresponsible power, if history is to be trusted.—*Speech, «The Missouri Question,» February 15, 1820.*

PLATO (Greece, 429-347 B.C.)

Justice and the Courts.—For a judge sits on the judgment seat, not to administer laws by favor, but to decide with fairness; and he has taken an oath that he will not gratify his friends, but determine with a strict regard to law.—*Apolog. Socr. 24.*

Why Men Hate Each Other.—For misanthropy arises from a man trusting another without having a sufficient knowledge of his character, and, thinking him to be truthful, sincere, and honorable, finds a little afterwards that he is wicked, faithless; and then he meets with another of the same character. When a man experiences this often, and, more particularly, from those whom he considered his most dear and best friends,—at last, having frequently made a slip, he hates the whole world, and thinks that there is nothing sound at all in any of them.—*Phædo. 39.*

«Fear Not Them That Kill the Body.»—For neither Meletus nor Anytus can injure me. It is not in their power; for I do not think that it is possible for a better man to be injured by a worse.—*Apolog. Socr. 18.*

The Cause of All Quarrels.—For nothing else but the body and its desires cause wars, seditions, and fightings.—*Phædo. 11.*

«Return Not Evil for Evil.»—Neither ought a man to return evil for evil, as many think; since at no time ought we to do an injury to our neighbors.—*Crit. 10.*

Truth and Sensuality.—Those wretches who never have experienced the sweets of wisdom and virtue, but spend all their time in revels and debauches, sink downwards day after day, and make their whole life one continued series of errors. They never have the courage to lift the eye upward toward truth, they never feel the least inclination to it. They taste no real or substantial pleasure; but, resembling so many brutes, with eyes always fixed on the earth, and intent upon their loaden tables, they pamper themselves up in luxury and excess.

The Life After Death.—Is it possible, then, that the soul, which is invisible, and proceeding to another place, spotless, pure, and invisible (and, therefore, truly called Hades—*i. e.* invisible), to dwell with the good and wise God (where, if God so wills it, my soul must immediately go),—can this soul of ours, I say, being such and of such an essence, when it is separated from the body, be at once dissipated and utterly destroyed, as many men say? It is impossible to think so, beloved Cebes and Simmias; but it is much rather thus—if it is severed in a state of purity, carrying with it none of the pollutions of the body, inasmuch as

it did not willingly unite with the body in this present life, but fled from it, and gathered itself within itself, as always meditating this—would this be anything else than studying philosophy in a proper spirit, and pondering how one might die easily? would not this be a meditation on death?—*Phædo. 29.*

PLINY THE ELDER (Rome, 23-79 A.D.)

Concerning Religion.—It is advantageous that the gods should be believed to attend to the affairs of man, and the punishment for evil deeds, though sometimes late, is never fruitless.—*H. N. II. 5, 10.*

«Mother Earth.»—The earth receives us at our birth, nourishes and always continues to support us during our life, embracing us at last in her bosom.—*H. N. II. 63.*

The Most Savage Animal.—Other animals live affectionately with their like; we see them crowd together and stand against those that are dissimilar; fierce lions do not fight each other; serpents do not attack serpents, nor do the wild monsters of the deep rage against their like. But, by Hercules, very many calamities arise to man from his fellow-men.—*H. N. VII. 1, 6.*

The Might of Nature.—The power and majesty of the nature of things fail to receive credit at all times, if we merely look at its parts and do not embrace the vast whole in our conceptions.—*H. N. VII. 1, 7.*

PLINY THE YOUNGER (Rome, 62-113 A.D.)

Rectitude in Small Things.—I hold it particularly worthy of a man of honor to be governed by the principles of strict equity in his domestic as well as public conduct; in small, as in great affairs; in his own concerns, as well as in those of others; and if every deviation from rectitude is equally criminal, every approach to it must be equally laudable.—*viii. 2.*

The Highest Virtue.—The highest of characters, in my estimation, is his who is as ready to pardon the moral errors of mankind, as if he were every day guilty of some himself; and at the same time as cautious of committing a fault as if he never forgave one.—*viii. 22.*

PLUTARCH (Greece, *c.* 46 A.D.-?)

An Evil Habit of the Soul.—The continuance and frequent fits of anger produce an evil habit in the soul, called wrathfulness, or a propensity to be angry; which ofttimes ends in choler, bitterness, and morosity; when the mind becomes ulcerated, peevish, and querulous, and like a thin, weak plate of iron, receives impression, and is wounded by the least occurrence.

Our Contempt for Those Who Serve Us.—Often while we are delighted with the work, we regard the workman with contempt. Thus we are pleased with perfumes and purple, while dyers and perfumers are considered by us as low, vulgar mechanics.—*Pericl. 1.*

Principles the Soul of Political Rectitude.—Lycurgus thought that what tended most to secure the happiness and virtue of a people was the interweaving of right principles with their habits and training. These remained firm and steadfast when they were the result of the bent of the disposition, a tie stronger even than necessity; and the habits instilled by education into youth would answer in each the purpose of a lawgiver.—*Lycurg. 13.*

Written Laws Like Spiders' Webs.—When Anacharsis heard what Solon was doing, he laughed at the folly of thinking that he could restrain the unjust proceedings and avarice of his citizens by written laws, which, he said, resembled in every way spiders' webs, and would, like them, catch and hold only the poor and weak, while the rich and powerful would easily break through them.—*Sol. 5.*

POLYBIUS (Greece, 204-125 B.C.)

The Lamp of Experience.—The knowledge of what has gone before affords the best instruction for the direction and guidance of human life.—*i. 1.*

The Lessons of History.—History furnishes the only proper discipline to educate and train the minds of those who wish to take part in public affairs; and the unfortunate events which it hands down for our instruction contain the wisest and most convincing lessons for enabling us to bear our own calamities with dignity and courage.—*i. 1.*

PRENTICE, GEORGE DENISON (America, 1802-1870)

Prenticeana.—You may wish to get a wife without a failing; but what if the lady, after you find her, happens to be in want of a husband of the same character.—*Prenticeana, 1860.*

The editor of the —— Star says that he has never murdered the truth. He never gets near enough to do it any bodily harm.—*Prenticeana.*

About the only person that we ever heard of that wasn't spoiled by being lionized, was a Jew named Daniel.—*Prenticeana.*

A woman always keeps secret what she does not know.—*Exchange.*

It is a pity that all men do not imitate her discretion.—*Prenticeana.*

PRIME, SAMUEL IRENÆUS (America, 1812-1885)

The Simplest Book in the World.—The Bible is the simplest book in the world, and there is no work of its size treating so great a variety of subjects which is more intelligible to the common mind. Errors, heresies, and corruptions in doctrine and practice do not arise from the misconceptions which the «common people» get from reading the Bible, with the Spirit of God alone to guide them. The fundamental truths which all evangelical Christians love to believe are on the surface as well as in the depths of holy Scripture. He who runs may

read. The Bible is a revelation. The author did not employ language to conceal his thoughts. The entrance of his words gives light. They make wise the simple. And that preacher is the best who is the most scriptural, bringing the truth as therein revealed directly to the conscience and the heart.—*Irenæus's Letters. Second Series, 1885.*

PYTHAGORAS (Greece, 582-500 B.C.)

That We Ought to Judge Our Own Actions.—Let not sleep fall upon thy eyes till thou hast thrice reviewed the transactions of the past day. Where have I turned aside from rectitude? What have I been doing? What have I left undone, which I ought to have done? Begin thus from the first act, and proceed; and, in conclusion, at the ill which thou hast done, be troubled, and rejoice for the good.

QUINTILIAN (Rome, 35-95 A.D.)

«Mind of Divine Original.»—As birds are provided by nature with a propensity to fly, horses to run, and wild beasts to be savage, so the working and the sagacity of the brain is peculiar to men; and hence it is that his mind is supposed to be of divine original.—*Lib. i. 1.*

Dullness Not Natural.—The dull and the indocile are in no other sense the productions of nature than are monstrous shapes and extraordinary objects, which are very rare.—*i. 1.*

QUINTUS CURTIUS (First Century A.D.)

On Fortune.—Those whom fortune has induced to trust to her, she makes in a great measure rather desirous of glory than able to seize it.—*iv. 7, 29.*

Superstition of the Uneducated.—Nothing has more power over the multitude than superstition; in other respects powerless, ferocious, fickle, when it is once captivated by superstitious notions, it obeys its priests better than its leaders.—*iv. 10, 7.*

The Country of the Brave.—Wherever the brave man chooses his abode, that is his country.—*vi. 4, 13.*

RABELAIS, FRANÇOIS (France, 1495-1553)

The Dotage of Habit.—Can there be any greater dotage in the world, than for one to guide and direct his courses by the sound of a bell, and not by his own judgment and discretion?

The Cut of the Coat and Character.—It is not the dress that makes the monk. Many are dressed like monks who are inwardly anything but monks: and some wear Spanish caps who have but little of the valor of the Spaniard in them.—*Prologue Livre i.*

Learn Where You Can.—What harm is there in getting knowledge and learning, were it from a sot, a pot, a fool, a winter mitten, or old slipper?—*Pantagruel, iii. 16.*

The Heaven or Hell of Matrimony.—We see many people so fortunate in their marriage that we might say that their life gave some idea or representation of the joys of Paradise. Others again are so unluckily matched, that those devils who tempt the hermits that dwell in the deserts of Thebais and Montserrat are not so wretched as they.—*«Pantagruel,» iii. 5.*

Opportunity's Forelock.—For opportunity has all her hair on her forehead; but when she has passed, you cannot call her back. She has no tuft whereby you can lay hold on her, for she is bald on the back part of her head, and never returns.—*«Gargantua,» i. 37.*

The Country of the Soul.—In this way our soul, when our body is at rest, and the digestion is everywhere accomplished, lacking nothing till it awakes, delights to disport itself, and take a view of its native country, which is heaven. Thence it receives a notable participation of its primeval source and divine origin; and contemplates that infinite and intellectual sphere, whereof the centre is everywhere and the circumference in no place of the universal world.—*«Pantagruel,» iii. 13.*

RALEIGH, SIR WALTER (England, 1552-1618)

On the Keeping of the Mouth.—Jest not openly at those that are simple, but remember how much thou art bound to God, who hath made thee wiser. Defame not any woman publicly, though thou know her to be evil; for those that are faulty cannot endure to be taxed, but will seek to be avenged of thee; and those that are not guilty cannot endure unjust reproach. As there is nothing more shameful and dishonest than to do wrong, so truth itself cutteth his throat that carrieth her publicly in every place. Remember the divine saying, «he that keepeth his mouth, keepeth his life.»

The Worm in the Nut's Kernel.—It were better for a man to be subject to any vice than to drunkenness: for all other vanities and sins are recovered, but a drunkard will never shake off the delight of beastliness; for the longer it possesseth a man, the more he will delight in it, and the elder he groweth the more he shall be subject to it; for it dulleth the spirits, and destroyeth the body as ivy doth the old tree; or as the worm that engendereth in the kernel of the nut.

We Are Judged by Our Friends.—There is nothing more becoming any wise man than to make choice of friends, for by them thou shalt be judged what thou art: let them therefore be wise and virtuous, and none of those that follow thee for gain; but make election rather of thy betters than thy inferiors, shunning always such as are needy; for if thou givest twenty gifts, and refuse to do the like but once, all that thou hast done will be lost, and such men will become thy mortal enemies.

The Test of Love.— Have ever more care that thou be beloved of thy wife, rather than thyself besotted on her; and thou shalt judge of her love by these two observations: First, if thou perceive she have a care of thy estate, and exercise herself therein: the other, if she study to please thee, and be sweet unto thee in conversation, without thy instruction; for Love needs no teaching, nor precept . . .

RANDOLPH, JOHN (America, 1773-1831)

On the Conduct of Life.— This independence, which is so much vaunted, and which young people think consists in doing what they please, when they grow to man's estate (with as much justice as the poor negro thinks liberty consists in being supported in idleness by other people's labor)— this independence is but a name. Place us where you will, along with our rights there must exist correlative duties; and the more exalted the station, the more arduous are these last. . . .

Lay down this as a principle, that truth is to the other virtues what vital air is to the human system. They cannot exist at all without it; and as the body may live under many diseases, if supplied with pure air for its consumption, so may the character survive many defects where there is a rigid attachment to truth. All equivocation and subterfuge belong to falsehood, which consists not in using false words only, but in conveying false impressions, no matter how; and if a person deceive himself, and I, by my silence, suffer him to remain in error, I am implicated in the deception, unless he be one who has no right to rely upon me for information; and in that case it is plain I could not be instrumental in deceiving him. . . .

Remember that labor is necessary to excellence. This is an eternal truth, although vanity cannot be taught to believe or indolence to heed it. I am deeply interested in seeing you turn out a respectable man, in every point of view; and, as far as I could, have endeavored to furnish you with the means of acquiring knowledge, and correct principles and manners at the same time. Self-conceit and indifference are unfriendly, in an equal degree, to the attainment of knowledge, or the forming of an admirable character. The first is more offensive, but does not more completely mar all excellence than the last. . . .

Do not through false shame, through a vicious modesty, entrap yourself into a situation which may dye your cheek with real shame. Say, "No, it will not be in my power—I cannot"; or, if it be a thing which you would willingly do, but doubt your ability, take care to say, "I cannot promise, but if it be in my power, I will do it." Remember, too, that no good man will ever exact a promise of a boy, or a very young person, but for their good; never for his own benefit. In short, a promise

is always a serious evil to him who gives it— often to him who receives it.

When the Persian youths were taught to draw the bow, to speak the truth, and to keep a secret (which, in fact, is nothing but adhering to the truth, the divulger being at once a liar and a traitor), they overran all Western Asia; but when they became corrupt and unfaithful to their word, a handful of Greeks was an overmatch for millions of them. A liar is always a coward.— *From " Letters to a Young Relative," 1834.*

RAWLINSON, GEORGE (England, 1815-)

The Spirit of the Nineteenth Century.— It is the fashion of the day to speculate on the origins of things. Not content with observing the mechanism of the heavens, astronomers discuss the formation of the material universe, and seek in the phenomena which constitute the subject-matter of their science for "Vestiges of Creation." Natural philosophers propound theories of the "Origin of Species " and the primitive condition of man. Comparative philologists are no longer satisfied to dissect languages, compare roots, or contrast systems of grammar, but regard it as incumbent upon them to put forward views respecting the first beginnings of language itself.

To deal with facts is thought to be a humdrum and commonplace employment of the intellect, one fitted for the dull ages when men were content to plod, and when progress, development, "the higher criticism," were unknown. The intellect now takes loftier flights. Conjecture is found to be more amusing than induction, and an ingenious hypothesis to be more attractive than a proved law. Our "advanced thinkers" advance to the furthest limits of human knowledge, sometimes even beyond them; and bewitch us with speculations, which are as beautiful, and as unsubstantial, as the bubbles which a child produces with a little soap and water and a tobacco pipe.— *From "Religions of the Ancient World."*

RECLUS, JEAN JACQUES ÉLISÉE (France, 1830-)

Is Humanity Progressing ?— Has humanity made real progress? It would be absurd to deny it. That which one calls "the democratic tide" is nothing else but this growing sentiment of equality between the representatives of the different castes, until recently hostile one to the other. Under a thousand apparent changes in the surface, the work is being accomplished in the depths of the nations. Thanks to the increasing knowledge men are gaining of themselves and others, they are arriving by degrees at the discovery of the common ground upon which we all resemble each other, and at getting rid of superficial opinions which keep us apart. We are, then, steadily advancing toward future reconciliation, and, by this very fact, toward a form of happiness very different in extent to that which sufficed our forefathers—the animals and the primitive

men. Our material and moral world becomes more vast, and this in itself increases our conception of happiness, which henceforward will only be held to be such on condition of its being shared by all; of its being made conscious and rational, and of its embracing in its scope the earnest researches of science and the possessions of art.

It is, then, with all confidence that we reply to the question which every man asks himself: Yes, humanity has really progressed, from crisis to crisis and from relapse to relapse, since the beginning of those millions of years which constitute the short conscious period of our life.— *From the Contemporary Review.*

RED JACKET (America, 1752-1830)

The Test of Proselyting Zeal.— Brother: The Great Spirit has made us all, but he has made a great difference between his white and red children. He has given us different complexions and different customs. To you he has given the arts. To these he has not opened our eyes. We know these things to be true. Since he has made so great a difference between us in other things, why may we not conclude that he has given us a different religion according to our understanding? The Great Spirit does right. He knows what is best for his children; we are satisfied. . . .

Brother: We are told that you have been preaching to the white people in this place. Those people are our neighbors. We are acquainted with them. We will wait a little while, and see what effect your preaching has upon them. If we find it does them good, makes them honest, and less disposed to cheat Indians, we will then consider again of what you have said.— *Speech against the Foundation of a Mission among the Senecas, 1805.*

REYNOLDS, SIR JOSHUA (England, 1723-1792)

On Genius.— Genius is supposed to be a power of producing excellencies which are out of the reach of the rules of Art; a power which no precepts can teach, and which no industry can acquire.

RICHTER, JEAN PAUL FRIEDRICH (Germany, 1763-1825)

The Last, Best Fruit of Life.— The last, best fruit which comes to late perfection, even in the kindliest soul, is tenderness toward the hard, forbearance toward the unforbearing, warmth of heart toward the cold, philanthropy toward the misanthropic.

Why Poetry Was Invented.— There are so many tender and holy emotions flying about in our inward world, which, like angels, can never assume the body of an outward act; so many rich and lovely flowers spring up which bear no seed, that it is a happiness poetry was invented, which receives into its limbus all these incorporeal spirits, and the perfume of all these flowers.

Fallen Souls.— There are souls which fall from heaven like flowers; but ere the pure and fresh buds can open, they are trodden in the dust of the earth, and lie soiled and crushed under the foul tread of some brutal hoof.

ROCHEFOUCAULD, FRANÇOIS LA (France, 1613-1680)

Why We Seek New Friends.— What makes us like new acquaintances is not so much any weariness of our old ones, or the pleasure of change, as disgust at not being sufficiently admired by those who know us too well, and the hope of being more so by those who do not know so much of us.

Appearances.— In all the professions every one affects a particular look and exterior, in order to appear what he wishes to be thought; so that it may be said the world is made up of appearances.

The Futility of Deceit.— The ordinary employment of artifice is the mark of a petty mind; and it almost always happens that he who uses it to cover himself in one place uncovers himself in another.

Avarice.— Avarice often produces opposite effects: there is an infinite number of people who sacrifice all their property to doubtful and distant expectations; others despise great future advantages to obtain present interests of a trifling nature. . . . Extreme avarice almost always mistakes itself; there is no passion which more often deprives itself of its object, nor on which the present exercises so much power to the prejudice of the future.

Maxims and Reflections.— The generality of men have, like plants, latent properties, which chance brings to light.

The extreme pleasure we take in talking of ourselves should make us fear that we give very little to those who listen to us.

For the credit of virtue it must be admitted that the greatest evils which befall mankind are caused by their crimes.

When our vices quit us, we flatter ourselves with the belief that it is we who quit them.

He who thinks he can find in himself the means of doing without others is much mistaken; but he who thinks that others cannot do without him is still more mistaken.

True eloquence consists in saying all that is necessary, and nothing but what is necessary.

Grace is to the body what good sense is to the mind. . . . Nothing so much prevents our being natural as the desire of appearing so.

We should often have reason to be ashamed of our most brilliant actions, if the world could see the motives from which they spring.

ROCHESTER, EARL OF (England, 1647-1680)

Sacrifices to Moloch.— Mothers who force their daughters into interested marriages are worse than the Ammonites who sacrificed their

children to Moloch—the latter undergoing a speedy death, the former suffering years of torture, but too frequently leading to the same result.

ROUSSEAU, JEAN JACQUES (France, 1712-1778)

Brains as Monuments.— Brains well prepared are the monuments where human knowledge is most surely engraved.—"*Émile,*" i. 3.

Job's Comforters.— Consolation indiscreetly pressed upon us, when we are suffering under affliction, only serves to increase our pain, and to render our grief more poignant.

Taste the Motive for Learning.— The time for acquiring knowledge is so short, it passes away so rapidly, there are so many matters necessary to be acquired, that it is folly to expect it should be sufficient to make a child learned. The question ought not to be to teach it the sciences, but to give it a taste for them, and methods to acquire them when the taste shall be better developed.—"*Émile,*" i. 3.

How a Child Ought to Be Taught to Read and Speak.— Do not give him pieces to recite from tragedies or comedies, nor teach him, as they say, to declaim. Teach him to speak without stammering, distinctly, to articulate clearly, to pronounce with precision and without affectation, to understand and follow grammatical accent and prosody, to speak with sufficient loudness to be heard, but never more than is necessary; a defect generally found in children brought up in schools; in short, nothing too much.—"*Émile,*" i. 2.

Literary Girls as Old Maids.— Every literary girl will remain a maid all her life, as long as there shall be sensible men on the earth: "You ask why I am unwilling to marry you, Galla; you are learned."—"*Émile,*" i. 5.

The Highest Dignity of Womanhood.— Her dignity consists in being unknown to the world; her glory is in the esteem of her husband; her pleasures in the happiness of her family.— "*Émile,*" i. 5.

RUMFORD, BENJAMIN THOMPSON, COUNT (America, 1753-1814)

Happiness for the Vicious.— To make vicious and abandoned people happy, it has generally been supposed necessary, first, to make them virtuous. But why not reverse this order? Why not make them first happy, and then virtuous? If happiness and virtue be inseparable, the end will be as certainly obtained by the one method as by the other; and it is most undoubtedly much easier to contribute to the happiness and comfort of persons in a state of poverty and misery, than, by admonitions and punishments, to reform their morals.— *From "Essays, Political, Economical, and Philosophical." 1796.*

RUSH, BENJAMIN (America, 1745-1813)

Seed that Never Perish.— No one seed of truth or virtue ever perished. Wherever it may

be sowed, or even scattered, it will preserve and carry with it the principle of life. Some of these seeds will produce their fruits in a short time, but the most valuable of them, like the venerable oak, are centuries in growing; but they are unlike the pride of the forest, as well as all other vegetable productions, in being incapable of a decay. They exist and bloom forever.— *From "Biographical Anecdotes of Benjamin Lay." 1798.*

SADI (Persia, 1190-1291 A. D.)

The Blockhead and the Scholar.— The physician Galen saw a blockhead of a fellow who had laid hold of a learned man by the collar, and was treating him most disrespectfully. He said: Had this been a wise man he would never have permitted his concerns with an ignoramus to come to this pass.— " Strife and malignity occur not between two men of sense. A wise man will not dispute with one that is hasty. If an ignoramus is harsh in his rude brutality, a prudent man will soothe him with mild urbanity. A hair can keep two good and holy men together, notwithstanding they are arguing a difference of opinion; but if both sides are contentious and brutal, though it were an iron chain, they would tear it asunder."— *From the " Gulistan."*

Life and Wealth.— Riches are intended for the comfort of life, and not life for the purpose of hoarding riches. I asked a wise man, saying: Who is the fortunate man, and who is the unfortunate? He said: That man was fortunate who spent and gave away, and that man unfortunate who died and left behind:— " Pray not for that good-for-nothing man who did nothing, for he passed his life in hoarding riches, and did not spend them."— *From the " Gulistan."*

Two Who Labored in Vain.— Two persons labored to a vain, and studied to an unprofitable end: he who hoarded wealth and did not spend it, and he who acquired science and did not practice it:— " However much thou art read in theory, if thou hast no practice thou art ignorant. He is neither a sage philosopher nor an acute divine, but a beast of burden with a load of books. How can that brainless head know or comprehend whether he carries on his back a library or a bundle of fagots?"— *From the " Gulistan."*

The Man Who Fired His Harvest.— Learning is intended to fortify religious practice, and not to gratify worldly traffic:— Whoever prostituted his temperance, piety, and science, gathered his harvest into a heap and set fire to it.— *From the "Gulistan."*

The Learned Fool.— An intemperate man of learning is like a blind linkboy: he shows the road to others, but sees it not himself:— " Whoever ventured his life on an unproductive hazard gained nothing by the risk, and lost his own stake."— *From the "Gulistan."*

Against Pardoning Oppressors.— To compassionate the wicked is to tyrannize over the good; and to pardon the oppressor is to deal harshly with the oppressed:— " When thou patronizest and succorest the base born man, he looks to be made the partner of thy fortune." — *From the "Gulistan."*

The Wisdom of Old Time.— Reveal not every secret you have to a friend, for how can you tell but that friend may hereafter become an enemy. And bring not all the mischief you are able to do upon an enemy, for he may one day become your friend. And any private affair that you wish to keep secret, do not divulge to anybody; for, though such a person has your confidence, none can be so true to your secret as yourself:— " Silence is safer than to communicate the thought of thy mind to anybody, and to warn him, saying: Do not divulge it, O silly man! confine the water at the dam-head, for once it has a vent thou canst not stop it. Thou shouldst not utter a word in secret which thou wouldst not have spoken in the face of the public."— *From the "Gulistan."*

SALLUST (Rome, 86-34 B.C.)

Mind and Body.— Our whole strength resides in the powers of the mind and body; while we are willing to submit to the directions of the former, we are anxious to render the body subservient to our will. The one is common to us with the gods; the other with the lower animals.— *Cat. i.*

Be Sure You're Right.— Before one begins, there is need of forethought, and after we have carefully considered, there is need of speedy execution.— *Cat. i.*

Efficiency.— He and he alone seems to me to have the full enjoyment of his existence, who, in whatever employment he may be engaged, seeks for the reputation arising from some praiseworthy deed, or the exercise of some useful talent. But in the great variety of employments, nature points out different paths to different individuals.— *Cat. ii.*

The Intoxication of Prosperity.— The truth is, prosperity unhinges the minds of the wise; much less could they, with their corrupt habits, be expected to refrain from abusing their victory.— *Cat. ii.*

The Low and the High.— Those who pass their lives sunk in obscurity, if they have committed any offense through the impulse of passion, few know of it; their reputation and fortune are alike; those who are in great command and in an exalted station, have their deeds known to all men. Thus, in the highest condition of life, there is the least freedom of action. They ought to show neither partiality nor hatred, but least of all resentment; what in others is called hastiness of temper is in those invested with power styled haughtiness and cruelty.— *Cat. ii.*

SANDERSON, JOHN (America, 1783-1844)

Dining in Paris.— The English are before all nations in bulldogs; perhaps also in mor-

als; but for the art of dressing themselves and their dinners the first honors are due by general acknowledgment to the French. The French are therefore entitled to our first and most serious consideration.

The Revolution having broken up the French clerical nobility, cookery was brought out from the cloisters, and made to breathe the free and ventilated air of common life, and talents no longer engrossed by the few were forced into the service of the community. A taste was spread abroad, and a proper sense of gastronomy impressed upon the public mind. Eating houses, or *restaurans* and *cafés*, multiplied, and skill was brought out by competition to the highest degree of cultivation and development. The number of such houses now in Paris alone exceeds six thousand. But the shortest way to give value to a profession is to bestow honor and reward upon those who administer its duties, and to this policy, nowhere so well understood as in Paris, the French kitchen chiefly owes its celebrity.— *From "The French and English Kitchen."*

SAVONAROLA (Italy, 1452-1498)

Deed and Word.— One only knows that which he practices.

Elegance of language must give way before simplicity in preaching sound doctrine.

SCHAFF, PHILIP (Germany-America, 1819-1893)

Religion and Liberty.— Religion and liberty are inseparable. Religion is voluntary, and cannot and ought not to be forced.

This is a fundamental article of the American creed, without distinction of sect or party. Liberty, both civil and religious, is an American instinct. All natives suck it in with the mother's milk; all immigrants accept it as a happy boon, especially those who flee from oppression and persecution abroad. Even those who reject the modern theory of liberty enjoy the practice, and would defend it in their own interest against any attempt to overthrow it.— "*Church and State in the United States.*" 1888.

SCHURZ, CARL (Germany-America, 1829-)

The Greatest Task for Education.— The great war that education has to carry on in society is a war against the brutal self-assertion of vulgar wealth, with no quarter for the pleasure-hunting idler, and merciless contempt and ridicule for the snob. The prize of this contest is that the rich man shall gain his social position not by the mere fact of his possessing wealth, but by the manner in which he employs his wealth for worthy ends; and when that prize is won by the influence of educational and intellectual superiority, wealth itself will be subjugated for the promotion of true culture and all its elevating influences.

SEDGWICK, CATHERINE M. (America, 1789-1867)

The Sabbath in New England.— The observance of the Sabbath began with the Puritans, as it still does with a great portion of their descendants, on Saturday night. At the going down of the sun on Saturday, all temporal affairs were suspended; and so zealously did our fathers maintain the letter, as well as the spirit of the law, that, according to a vulgar tradition in Connecticut, no beer was brewed in the latter part of the week, lest it should presume to «work» on Sunday.

It must be confessed that the tendency of the age is to laxity; and so rapidly is the wholesome strictness of primitive times abating, that, should some antiquary, fifty years hence, in exploring his garret rubbish, chance to cast his eye on our humble pages, he may be surprised to learn that even now the Sabbath is observed, in the interior of New England, with an almost Judaical severity.

The Sabbath morning is as peaceful as the first hallowed day. Not a human sound is heard without the dwellings, and but for the lowing of the herds, the crowing of the cocks, and the gossiping of the birds, animal life would seem to be extinct, till, at the bidding of the church-going bell, the old and young issue from their habitations, and, with solemn demeanor, bend their measured steps to the meetinghouse; — the families of the minister, the squire, the doctor, the merchant, the modest gentry of the village, and the mechanic and laborer, all arrayed in their best, all meeting on even ground, and all with that consciousness of independence and equality, which breaks down the pride of the rich, and rescues the poor from servility, envy, and discontent. If a morning salutation is reciprocated, it is in a suppressed voice; and if, perchance, nature, in some reckless urchin, burst forth in laughter — «My dear, you forget it's Sunday,» is the ever ready reproof. . . .

Towards the close of the day (or to borrow a phrase descriptive of his feelings, who first used it), «when the Sabbath begins to abate,» the children cluster about the windows. Their eyes wander from their catechism to the western sky, and, though it seems to them as if the sun would never disappear, his broad disk does slowly sink behind the mountain; and, while his last ray still lingers on the eastern summits, merry voices break forth, and the ground resounds with bounding footsteps. The village belle arrays herself for her twilight walk; the boys gather on «the green»; the lads and girls throng to the «singing school»; while some coy maiden lingers at home, awaiting her expected suitor; and all enter upon the pleasures of the evening with as keen a relish as if the day had been a preparatory penance.— *From «Hope Leslie.»*

SELDEN, JOHN (England, 1584–1654)

Ceremony.— Ceremony keeps up things; 'tis like a penny glass to a rich spirit, or some excellent water; without it the water were spilt, and the spirit lost.

Profession and Practice.— They that cry down moral honesty cry down that which is a great part of my religion — my duty toward God and my duty toward man. What care I to see a man run after a sermon, if he cozen and cheat as soon as he comes home? On the other side, morality must not be without religion; for if so, it may change, as I see convenience. Religion must govern it.

SENECA, LUCIUS ANNÆUS (Rome, 4 B. C.–65 A. D.)

Patience with Error.— A physician is not angry at the intemperance of a mad patient, nor does he take it ill to be railed at by a man in a fever. Just so should a wise man treat all mankind, as a physician does his patient, and look upon them only as sick and extravagant.

Joy as Serenity.— True joy is a serene and sober motion: and they are miserably out, that take laughing for rejoicing: the seat of it is within, and there is no cheerfulness like the resolutions of a brave mind.

Self-Control.— I will have a care of being a slave to myself, for it is a perpetual, a shameful, and the heaviest of all servitudes; and this may be done by moderate desires.

Perseverance.— An obstinate resolution gets the better of every obstacle, and shows that there is no difficulty to him who has resolved to be patient.— *De Ira ii. 12.*

The Path to a Happy Life.— The path leading to a happy life is easy; only enter upon it boldly with the favor of the gods.— *De Ira ii. 13.*

The Education of the Young.— Education requires great diligence, which will be very profitable. For it is an easy matter to fashion tender minds; evil habits are with difficulty rooted out, which have grown up with our growth. — *De Ira. ii. 18.*

«We Are All Wicked.»— We are all wicked. Therefore, whatever we blame in another, we shall find in our own bosom. Let us then be forgiving to one another, for, being of evil inclinations ourselves, we live in an evil world. One thing alone can enable us to live at peace, mutual forgiveness.— *De Ira iii. 26.*

The Irrevocable Past.— No one will restore the years gone past, no one will return thee to thyself. Thy days will go on as they have done hitherto, nor canst thou recall nor cause them to halt; they will move on without noise and without warning these of their speed; they will glide on with silent step.— *De Brevit. Vit. 8.*

The Error of One Man Causes Another to Err.— As often happens in a great crowd of men, when the people press against each other, no one falls without drawing another after him, and the foremost are the cause of the ruin of those that follow; so it is in common life; there is no man that erreth to himself, but is the cause and author of other men's error.— *De Vit. Beat. 1.*

SÉVIGNÉ, MARIE DE (France, 1626–1696)

The Blessing of Good Nature.— I cannot tell how much I esteem and admire your good and happy temperament. What folly not to take advantage of circumstances, and enjoy gratefully the consolations which God sends us after the afflictive dispensations which he sometimes sees proper to make us feel! It seems to me to be a proof of great wisdom to submit with resignation to the storm, and enjoy the calm when it pleases him to give it us again: that is, to follow the established order of Providence. Life is too short to rest too long on the same feeling; we must take circumstances as they come, and I feel that I am of this happy temperament: «And I pride myself on it,» as the Italians say.— *Lettre à Bussy, 77.*

Talking of Ourselves. — We like so much to talk of ourselves that we are never weary of those private interviews with a lover during the course of whole years, and for the same reason the devout like to spend much time with their confessor: it is the pleasure of talking of themselves, even though it be to talk ill.— *Lettre à sa fille, 95.*

SEWARD, WILLIAM H. (America, 1801–1872)

War and Democracy. — Democracies are prone to war, and war consumes them. — *Eulogy on John Quincy Adams, Delivered before the Legislature of New York.*

SHAFTESBURY, EARL OF (England, 1671–1713)

Doing Good. — Never did any soul do good, but it became readier to do the same again, with more enjoyment. Never was love, or gratitude, or bounty practiced but with increasing joy, which made the practicer still more in love with the fair act.

One Grain of Honesty Worth the World. — A right mind and generous affection hath more beauty and charms than all other symmetries in the world besides; and a grain of honesty and native worth is of more value than all the adventitious ornaments, estates, or preferments for the sake of which some of the better sort so oft turn knaves.

The Sum of Philosophy.— To philosophize in a just signification is but to carry good breeding a step higher. For the accomplishment of breeding is, to learn what is decent in company, or beautiful in arts; and the sum of philosophy is, to learn what is just in society, and beautiful in nature and the order of the world.

Freedom as the Origin of Politeness.— All politeness is owing to liberty. We polish one another, and rub off our corners and rough sides by a sort of amicable collision. To restrain this is inevitably to bring a rust upon men's understandings.

The Gentleman.— The taste of beauty, and the relish of what is decent, just, and amiable, perfects the character of the gentleman and the philosopher. And the study of such a taste or relish will, as we suppose, be ever the great employment and concern of him who covets as well to be wise and good, as agreeable and polite.

SHENSTONE, WILLIAM (England, 1714–1763)

Envy and Fine Weather.— There is nothing more universally commended than a fine day; the reason is, that people can commend it without envy.

Servants.— The trouble occasioned by want of a servant is so much less than the plague of a bad one, as it is less painful to clean a pair of shoes than undergo an excess of anger.

SIDNEY, SIR PHILIP (England, 1534–1586)

Four Wise Sayings.— The only disadvantage of an honest heart is credulity.

It many times falls out, that we deem ourselves much deceived in others, because we first deceived ourselves.

The lightsome countenance of a friend giveth such an inward decking to the house where it lodgeth, as proudest palaces have cause to envy the gilding.

True love can no more be diminished by showers of evil than flowers are marred by timely rains.

SIMMS, WILLIAM GILMORE (America, 1806–1870)

Reality and Romance.— The world has become monstrous matter-of-fact in latter days. We can no longer get a ghost story either for love or money. The materialists have it all their own way; and even the little urchin, eight years old, instead of deferring with decent reverence to the opinions of his grandmamma, now stands up stoutly for his own. He believes in every «ology» but pneumatology. «Faust» and the «Old Woman of Berkeley» move his derision only, and he would laugh incredulously, if he dared, at the Witch of Endor. The whole armory of modern reasoning is on his side; and, however he may admit at seasons that belief can scarcely be counted a matter of will, he yet puts his veto on all sorts of credulity. That cold-blooded demon called Science has taken the place of all the other demons. He has certainly cast out innumerable devils, however he may still spare the principal. Whether we are the better for his intervention is another question. There is reason to apprehend that in disturbing our human faith in shadows, we have lost some of those wholesome moral restraints which might have kept many of us virtuous, where the laws could not.

The effect, however, is much the more seriously evil in all that concerns the romantic. Our story-tellers are so resolute to deal in the real, the actual only, that they venture on no subjects the details of which are not equally vulgar and susceptible of proof. With this end in view, indeed, they too commonly choose their subjects among convicted felons, in order that they may avail themselves of the evidence which led to their conviction; and, to prove more conclusively their devoted adherence to nature and the truth, they depict the former not only in her condition of nakedness, but long before she has found out the springs of running water. It is to be feared that some of the coarseness of modern taste arises from the too great lack of that veneration which belonged to, and elevated to dignity, even the errors of preceding ages. A love of the marvelous belongs, it appears to me, to all those who love and cultivate either of the fine arts. I very much doubt whether the poet, the painter, the sculptor, or the romancer, ever yet lived, who had not some strong bias,— a leaning, at least,— to a belief in the wonders of the invisible world. Certainly, the higher orders of poets and painters, those who create and invent, must have a strong taint of the superstitious in their composition.— *From «The Wigwam and the Cabin.»*

SMITH, GOLDWIN (England, 1823–)

The Christian Ideal and Science.— Is the Christian Ideal anti-scientific? Why should it be so? What is there in it opposed to the love of any kind of truth? Is not its self-devotion favorable, on the contrary, to earnest and conscientious investigation, and has not this appeared in the characters of eminent discoverers? In Monotheism there can be nothing at variance with the conception or with the study of general law. Mr. Spencer tenders us an equivalent for the Divine Will, the Will of the Power manifested throughout Evolution, and it can make no difference to the scientific inquirer which of the two equivalents is chosen so long as observation is free. That belief in miracle has practically interfered with the formation of the scientific habit of mind, and thus retarded the progress of science, is true; though it need not have done anything of the kind, inasmuch as miracle, instead of denying, assumes the general law, and Newton was a firm believer in miracle; but the Moral Ideal is a thing apart from miracle. In the only prayer dictated by Christ, the physical petition implies no more than that the course of Nature to which we owe our daily bread is sustained by God, as sustained by some power it must be. Prayer for spiritual help, however irrational it may be deemed, cannot possibly interfere with physical investigation. That the character of Christ should be scientific was of course impossible; so it is that the characters of Christians who lived before science or remote from it should be scientific; but surely there are enough men who are scientific and at the same time believers in the Christian Ideal to repel the assumption of an inherent antagonism.— *From the Contemporary Review.*

SMITH, CAPTAIN JOHN (England–Virginia, 1579–1631)

On Colonizing.— What so truly sutes with honour and honestie, as the discovering things unknowne? erecting Townes, peopling Countries, informing the ignorant, reforming things unjust, teaching vertue; and gaine to our Native mother-countrie a kingdom to attend her; finde employment for those that are idle, because they know not what to doe: so farre from wronging any, as to cause Posteritie to remember thee; and remembering thee, ever honour that remembrance with praise? Consider: What were the beginnings and endings of the Monarkies of the Chaldeans, the Syrians, the Grecians, and Romanes, but this one rule; What was it they would not doe, for the good of the common-wealth, or their Mother-citie? For example: Rome, What made her such a Monarchesse, but only the adventures of her youth, not in riots at home; but in dangers abroade? and the justice and judgment out of their experience, when they grewe aged. What was their ruine and hurt, but this; The excesse of idlenesse, the fondnesse of Parents, the want of experience in Magistrates, the admiration of their undeserved honors, the contempt of true merit, their unjust jealousies, their politicke incredulities, their hypocriticall seeming goodnesse, and their deeds of secret lewdnesse? finally, in fine, growing only formall temporists, all that their predecessors got in many years, they lost in few daies. Those by their pains and vertues became Lords of the world; they by their ease and vices became slaves to their servants.— *From a Description of New England.*

«Bagges as a Defence.»— I would be sorry to offend, or that any one should mistake my honest meaning; for I wish good to all, hurt to none. But rich men for the most part are growne to that dotage, through their pride in their wealth, as though there were no accident could end it, or their life. And what hellish care do such take to make it their owne miserie, and their Countries' spoile, especially when there is most neede of their employment? drawing by all manner of inventions, from the Prince and his honest subjects, even the vitall spirits of their powers and estates; as if their Bagges or Bragges were so powerfull a defence, the malicious could not assault them; when they are the only baite, to cause us not to be only assaulted, but betrayed and murdered in our owne security, ere we well perceive it.— *From a Description of New England.*

SMOLLETT, TOBIAS (Scotland, 1721–1771)

The Dullness of Great Wits.— In my last I mentioned my having spent an evening with a society of authors, who seemed to be jealous and afraid of one another. My uncle was not at all surprised to hear me say I was disappointed in their conversation. «A man may be very entertaining and instructive upon paper,» said he, «and exceedingly dull in common discourse. I have observed that those who shine most in private company are but secondary stars in the constellation of genius. A small stock of ideas is more easily managed and sooner displayed than a great quantity

crowded together.»— *From «Humphrey Clinker.»*

SOCRATES (Greece, 470–399 B. C.)

Against Disputing.— If thou continuest to take delight in idle argumentation, thou mayst be qualified to combat with the sophists, but wilt never know how to live with men.

The Reality of Ignorance.— There is no difference between knowledge and temperance; for he who knows what is good and embraces it, who knows what is bad and avoids it, is learned and temperate. But they who know very well what ought to be done, and yet do quite otherwise, are ignorant and stupid.

SOUTH, ROBERT (England, 1633–1716)

The Revenges and Rewards of Conscience. — No man ever offended his own conscience, but first or last it was revenged upon him for it. . . . A palsy may as well shake an oak, or a fever dry up a fountain, as either of them shake, dry up, or impair the delight of conscience. For it lies within, it centres in the heart, it grows into the very substance of the soul, so that it accompanies a man to his grave; he never outlives it, and that for this cause only because he cannot outlive himself.

«An Easy and Portable Pleasure.»— The pleasure of the religious man is an easy and portable pleasure, such an one as he carries about in his bosom, without alarming either the eye or the envy of the world. A man putting all his pleasures into this one is like a traveler's putting all his goods into one jewel; the value is the same, and the convenience greater.

SPARKS, JARED (America, 1789–1866)

Indian Eloquence. — With a strength of character and a reach of intellect, unknown in any other race of absolute savages, the Indian united many traits, some of them honorable and some degrading to humanity, which made him formidable in his enmity, faithless in his friendship, and at all times a dangerous neighbor: cruel, implacable, treacherous, yet not without a few of the better qualities of the heart and the head; a being of contrasts, violent in his passions, hasty in his anger, fixed in his revenge, yet cool in counsel, seldom betraying his plighted honor, hospitable, sometimes generous. A few names have stood out among them, which, with the culture of civilization, might have been shining stars on the lists of recorded fame. Philip, Pontiac, Sassacus, if the genius of another Homer were to embalm their memory, might rival the Hectors and Agamemnons of heroic renown, scarcely less savage, not less sagacious or brave.

Indian eloquence, if it did not flow with the richness of Nestor's wisdom or burn with Achilles' fire, spoke in the deep strong tones of nature, and resounded from the chords of truth. The answer of the Iroquois chief to the French, who wished to purchase his lands, and push him further into the wilderness, Voltaire has pronounced superior to any sayings of the great men commemorated by Plutarch. «We were born on this spot; our fathers were buried here. Shall we say to the bones of our fathers, arise, and go with us into a strange land?»

But more has been said of their figurative language than seems to be justified by modern experience. Writers of fiction have distorted the Indian character, and given us anything but originals. Their fancy has produced sentimental Indians, a kind of beings that never existed in reality; and Indians clothing their ideas in the gorgeous imagery of external nature, which they had neither the refinement to conceive, nor words to express. In truth, when we have lighted the pipe of concord, kindled or extinguished a council fire, buried the bloody hatchet, sat down under the tree of peace with its spreading branches, and brightened the chain of friendship, we have nearly exhausted their flowers of rhetoric. But the imagery prompted by internal emotion, and not by the visible world, the eloquence of condensed thought and pointed expression, the eloquence of a diction extremely limited in its forms, but nervous and direct, the eloquence of truth unadorned and of justice undisguised, these are often found in Indian speeches, and constitute their chief characteristic.

Washington.— Happy was it for America, happy for the world, that a great name, a guardian genius, presided over her destinies in war, combining more than the virtues of the Roman Fabius and the Theban Epaminondas, and compared with whom the conquerors of the world, the Alexanders and Cæsars, are but pageants crimsoned with blood and decked with the trophies of slaughter, objects equally of the wonder and the execration of mankind. The hero of America was the conqueror only of his country's foes, and the hearts of his countrymen. To the one he was a terror, and in the other he gained an ascendency, supreme, unrivaled, the tribute of admiring gratitude, the reward of a nation's love.— *«Remarks on American History.» 1837.*

STANTON, ELIZABETH CADY (America, 1815–)

The Enfranchisement of Woman.— We ask woman's enfranchisement, as the first step toward the recognition of that essential element in government that can only secure the health, strength, and prosperity of the nation. Whatever is done to lift woman to her true position will help to usher in a new day of peace and perfection for the race.— *Address on «Woman Suffrage,» Washington. 1868.*

STEELE, SIR RICHARD (Ireland, 1672–1729)

The Happiest Creature Living. — An healthy old fellow, that is not a fool, is the happiest creature living. It is at that time of life only men enjoy their faculties with pleasure and satisfaction. It is then we have nothing to manage, as the phrase is; we speak the downright truth, and whether the rest of the world will give us the privilege or not, we have so little to ask of them, that we can take it.

What Will Tranquilize the World.—The world will never be in any manner of order or tranquillity, until men are firmly convinced that conscience, honor, and credit are all in one interest; and that without the concurrence of the former, the latter are but impositions upon ourselves and others.

The Man Makes Manners.—I take it for a rule, that the natural, and not the acquired man, is the companion. Learning, wit, gallantry, and good breeding, are all but subordinate qualities in society, and are of no value, but as they are subservient to benevolence, and tend to a certain manner of being or appearing equal to the rest of the company.

STEPHENS, ALEXANDER H. (America, 1812–1883)

The Object of Society.—Many writers maintain that individuals upon entering into society, give up or surrender a portion of their natural rights. This seems to be a manifest error. No person has any natural right whatever to hurt or injure another. The object of society and government is to prevent and redress injuries of this sort; for, in a state of nature, without a restraining power of government, the strong would viciously impose upon the weak.

Another erroneous dogma pretty generally taught is that the object of governments should be to confer the greatest benefit upon the greatest number of its constituent members. The true doctrine is, the object should be to confer the greatest possible good upon every member, without any detriment or injury to a single one.—*From the Introduction to the "History of the United States."*

STERNE, LAURENCE (England, 1713–1768)

Eloquence and Nature.—Great is the power of eloquence: but never is it so great as when it pleads along with nature, and the culprit is a child strayed from his duty, and returned to it again with tears.

The Power of Trifles.—A Word—a Look, which at one time would make no impression—at another time wounds the heart; and like a shaft flying with the wind, pierces deep, which, with its own natural force, would scarce have reached the object aimed at.

Misers of Health.—People who are always taking care of their health are like misers, who are hoarding up a treasure which they have never spirit enough to enjoy.

STEWART, DUGALD (Scotland, 1753–1828)

Imitation as a Governing Power.—The influence of this principle of imitation on the outward appearance is much more extensive than we are commonly disposed to suspect. It operates, indeed, chiefly on the air and movements, without producing any very striking effect on the material form in its quiescent state. So difficult, however, is it to abstract this form from its habitual accompaniments, that the members of the same community, by being accustomed to associate from their infancy in the intercourse of private life, appear, to a careless observer, to bear a much closer resemblance to each other than they do in reality; while, on the other hand, the physical diversities which are characteristical of different nations are in his estimation, proportionally magnified.

The Few Who Think.—There are very few original thinkers in the world, or ever have been; the greatest part of those who are called philosophers, have adopted the opinions of some who went before them.

STORRS, RICHARD SALTER (America, 1821–)

Masterful Courage.—A thorough consent of judgment, conscience, imagination, affection, all vitalized and active, with a certain invincible firmness of will, as the effect of such a consent—this is implied in a really abounding and masterful courage. It is not impatient. It is not imperious. It is not the creature of fractious and vehement will power in man. It is never allied with a passionate selfishness. It is associated with great convictions, has its roots in profound moral experience, is nourished by thoughts of God and the hereafter. It is as sensitive and gentle in spirit as it is persistent and highly resolved.—*Chancellor's Oration delivered at Union College, 1883.*

STORY, JOSEPH (America, 1779–1845)

Indian Summer in New England.—It is now the early advance of autumn. What can be more beautiful or more attractive than this season in New England? The sultry heat of summer has passed away; and a delicious coolness at evening succeeds the genial warmth of the day. The labors of the husbandman approach their natural termination: and he gladdens with the near prospect of his promised reward. The earth swells with the increase of vegetation. The fields wave with their yellow and luxuriant harvests. The trees put forth the darkest foliage, half shading and half revealing their ripened fruits, to tempt the appetite of man, and proclaim the goodness of his Creator Even in scenes of another sort, where nature reigns alone in her own majesty, there is much to awaken religious enthusiasm. As yet, the forests stand clothed in their dress of undecayed magnificence. The winds, that rustle through their tops, scarcely disturb the silence of the shades below. The mountains and the valleys glow in warm green, of lively russet. The rivulets flow on with a noiseless current, reflecting back the images of many a glossy insect, that dips his wings in their cooling waters. The mornings and evenings are still vocal with the notes of a thousand warblers. which plume their wings for a later flight. Above all, the clear blue sky, the long and sunny calms, the scarcely whispering breezes, the brilliant sunsets, lit up with all the wondrous magnificence of light, and shade, and

color, and slowly settling down into a pure and transparent twilight. These, these are days and scenes, which even the cold cannot behold without emotion; but on which the meditative and pious gaze with profound admiration; for they breathe of holier and happier regions beyond the grave.—*From his Centennial Discourse at Salem.*

SUMNER, CHARLES (America, 1811–1874)

Fame and Human Happiness.—Whatever may be the temporary applause of men, or the expressions of public opinion, it may be asserted without fear of contradiction, that no true and permanent fame can be founded, except in labors which promise the happiness of mankind.—*True Glory.*

SWIFT, JONATHAN (Ireland, 1667–1745)

On Repentance in Old Age.—When men grow virtuous in their old age they are merely making a sacrifice to God of the devil's leavings

Politeness in Conversation.—One of the best rules in conversation is, never to say a thing which any of the company can reasonably wish we had rather left unsaid: nor can there anything be well more contrary to the ends for which people meet together, than to part unsatisfied with each other or themselves.

Latent Energy in Ordinary People.—Although men are accused for not knowing their own weakness, yet perhaps as few know their own strength. It is in men as in soils, where sometimes there is a vein of gold, which the owner knows not of.

TACITUS, CORNELIUS (Rome, *c.* 55–117 A.D.)

How Precedent Comes.—All those things which are now held to be of the greatest antiquity, were, at one time, new; and what we to-day hold up by example, will rank hereafter as a precedent.

Pliability and Liberality.—Vitellius possessed all that pliability and liberality, which, when not restrained within due bounds, must ever turn to the ruin of their possessor.

Distempers of the Heart.—Chronic diseases of the body thou canst not cure except by harsh and violent remedies; the heart, too, sick to the very core with vice, corrupted and corrupting, requires an antidote as strong as the poison that inflames our passions.—*Ann. iii. 54.*

When Gratitude Is Possible.—Obligations are only acknowledged when it seems in our power to requite them; if they exceed our ability, gratitude gives way to our hatred.—*Ann. iv. 18.*

The Little Causes of Great Results.—It would not be without advantage to examine these things, slight indeed in appearance, but which are often the secret springs of the most important events.—*Ann. iv. 32.*

Life's Great Reward.—Piles of stones when the judgment of posterity rises to execration are mere charnel houses. I now, therefore, address myself to thy allies of the empire, the citizens of Rome, and the immortal gods; to the gods it is my prayer that, to the end of life, they may grant the blessing of an undisturbed, clear, collected mind, with a due sense of laws, both human and divine. Of mankind I request that, when I am no more, they will do justice to my memory, and with kind acknowledgments, record my name and the actions of my life.—*Ann. iv. 38.*

TALLEYRAND (France, 1754–1838)

The Liar's Idea.—Language is often but a medium for concealing thought.

TAYLOR, BAYARD (America, 1825–1878)

Crossing the Arctic Circle.—We started from Haparanda at noon, on the fifth of January. The day was magnificent; the sky cloudless, and resplendent as polished steel; and the mercury 31° below zero. The sun, scarcely more than the breadth of his disk above the horizon, shed a faint orange light over the broad, level snow plains, and the bluish-white hemisphere of the Bothnian Gulf, visible beyond Tornea. The air was perfectly still, and exquisitely cold and bracing, despite the sharp grip it took upon my nose and ears.

These Arctic days, short as they are, have a majesty of their own—a splendor, subdued though it be; a breadth and permanence of hue, imparted alike to the sky and to the snowy earth, as if tinted glass were held before your eyes. I find myself at a loss how to describe these effects, or the impression they produced upon the traveler's mood. Certainly, it is the very reverse of that depression which accompanies the Polar night, and which even the absence of any real daylight might be considered sufficient to produce.

Our road led up the left bank of the river, both sides of which were studded with neat little villages. The country was well cleared and cultivated, and appeared so populous and flourishing that I could scarcely realize in what part of the world we were. The sun set at a quarter past one, but for two hours the whole southern heaven was superb in its hues of rose and orange. At three o'clock, when we reached Kuckula, the first station, the northern sky was one broad flush of the purest violet, melting into lilac at the zenith, where it met the fiery skirts of sunset. At four o'clock it was bright and moonlight, with the stillest air. We got on bravely over the level, beaten road, and in two hours reached Korpikylä, a large new inn, where we found very tolerable accommodations.

The next day was a day to be remembered: such a glory of twilight splendors for six full hours was beyond all the charms of daylight at any zone. We started at seven, with a temperature of 20° below zero, still keeping up the left bank of the Tornea. The country now rose into bold hills, and the features of the scenery became broad and majestic. The northern sky was again pure violet, and a pale red tinge from

the dawn rested on the tops of the snowy hills. The prevailing color of the sky slowly brightened into lilac, then into pink, then rose color, which again gave way to a flood of splendid orange when the sun appeared. Every change of color affected the tone of the landscape.

The woods, so wrapped in snow that not a single green needle was to be seen, took by turns the hues of the sky, and seemed to give out, rather than to reflect, the opalescent lustre of the morning. The sunshine brightened instead of dispelling these effects. At noon the sun's disk was not more than 1° above the horizon, throwing a level golden light on the hills. The north, before us, was as blue as the Mediterranean, and the vault of heaven overhead canopied us with pink. Every object was glorified and transfigured in the magic glow.

We kept a sharp lookout for the mountain of Avasaxa, one of the stations of Celsius, Maupertius, and the French Academicians, who came here in 1736, to make observations determining the exact form of the earth. Through this mountain, it is said, the Arctic Circle passes, and as Matarengi lies due west of Avasaxa, across the river, we decided to stop there, and take dinner on the Arctic Circle. Here we were, at last, entering the Arctic Zone in the dead of winter—the realization of a dream which had often flashed across my mind, when lounging under the tropical palms; so natural is it for one extreme to suggest the opposite. I took our bearings with a compass ring, as we drove forward, and as the summit of Avasaxa bore due east, we both gave a shout which startled our postilion, and notably quickened the gait of our horses. It was impossible to toss our caps, for they were not only tied upon our heads, but frozen fast to our beards.

Our road now crossed the river and kept up the Russian side to a place with the charming name of Torakankorwa. The afternoon twilight was even more wonderful than that of the forenoon. There were broad bands of purple, pure crimson, and intense yellow, all fusing together into fiery orange at the south, while the north became a semi-vault of pink, then lilac, and the softest violet. The dazzling Arctic hills participated in this play of colors, which did not fade as in the south, but stayed and stayed, as if God wished to compensate by this twilight glory for the loss of the day. Nothing in Italy, nothing in the Tropics, equals the magnificence of the Polar skies. The twilight gave place to a moonlight scarcely less brilliant. Our road was hardly broken, leading through deep snow, sometimes on the river, sometimes through close little glens, hedged in with firs drooping with snow—fairy Arctic solitudes, white, silent, and mysterious.

A Day without a Sun.—Our stay at Muoniovara had given the sun time to increase his altitude somewhat, and I had some doubts whether we should succeed in beholding a day of the Polar winter. The Länsman, however, encouraged us by the assurance that the sun had not yet risen upon his residence; though nearly six weeks had elapsed since his disappearance, but that his return was now looked for every day, since he had already begun to shine upon the northern hills. By ten o'clock it was light enough to read; the southern sky was a broad sea of golden orange, dotted with a few crimson cloud-islands, and we set ourselves to watch, with some anxiety, the gradual approach of the exiled god.

The sky increased in brightness as we watched. The orange flushed into rose, and the pale white hills looked even more ghastly against the bar of glowing carmine which fringed the horizon. A few long purple streaks of cloud hung over the sun's place, and higher up in the vault floated some loose masses, tinged with fiery crimson on their lower edges. About half-past eleven, a pencil of bright-red light shot up—a signal which the sun uplifted to herald his coming. As it slowly moved westward along the hills, increasing in height and brilliancy until it became a long tongue of flame, playing against the streaks of cloud, we were apprehensive that the near disk would rise to view.

When the Länsman's clock pointed to twelve, its face had become so bright as to shine almost like the sun itself; but after a few breathless moments the unwelcome glow began to fade. We took its bearing with a compass, and after making allowance for the variation (which is here very slight), were convinced that it was really past meridian, and the radiance, which was that of morning a few minutes before, belonged to the splendors of evening now. The colors of the firmament began to change in reverse order, and the dawn, which had almost ripened to sunrise now withered away to night without a sunset. We had at last seen a day without a sun.

The snowy hills to the north, it is true, were tinged with a flood of rosy flame, and the very next day would probably bring down the tide mark of sunshine to the tops of the houses. One day, however, was enough to satisfy me. The South is a cup which one may drink to inebriation; but one taste from the icy goblet of the North is enough to allay the curiosity, and quench all further desire.

TAYLOR, JEREMY (England, 1613–1667)

On Marriage.—They that enter into the state of marriage cast a die of the greatest contingency, and yet of the greatest interest in the world, next to the last throw for eternity. Life or death, felicity or a lasting sorrow, are in the power of marriage. A woman, indeed, ventures most, for she hath no sanctuary to retire to from an evil husband; she must dwell upon her sorrow, and hatch the eggs which her own folly or infelicity hath produced; and she is more under it, because her tormentor hath a warrant of prerogative, and the woman may complain to God, as subjects do of tyrant princes; but otherwise she hath no appeal in the causes of unkindness. And though the man can run from many hours of his sadness, yet he must return to it again; and when he sits among his neighbors, he remembers the objection that is in his bosom, and he sighs deeply. The boys, and the peddlers, and the fruiterers, shall tell of this man when he is carried to his grave, that he lived and died a poor wretched person.

The stags in the Greek epigram, whose knees were clogged with frozen snow upon the mountains, came down to the brooks of the valleys, hoping to thaw their joints with the waters of the stream; but there the frost overtook them, and bound them fast in ice, till the young herdsmen took them in their stranger snare. It is the unhappy chance of many men, finding many inconveniences upon the mountains of single life, they descend into the valleys of marriage to refresh their troubles; and there they enter into fetters, and are bound to sorrow by the cords of a man's or woman's peevishness. . . .

Man and wife are equally concerned to avoid all offenses of each other in the beginning of their conversation; every little thing can blast an infant blossom; and the breath of the south can shake the little rings of the vine, when first they begin to curl like the locks of a new-weaned boy; but when by age and consolidation they stiffen into the hardness of a stem, and have, by the warm embraces of the sun and the kisses of heaven, brought forth their clusters, they can endure the storms of the north, and the loud noises of a tempest, and yet never be broken: so are the early unions of an unfixed marriage; watchful and observant, jealous and busy, inquisitive and careful, and apt to take alarm at every unkind word. After the hearts of the man and the wife are endeared and hardened by a mutual confidence and experience, longer than artifice and pretense can last, there are a great many remembrances, and some things present, that dash all little unkindnesses in pieces. . . .

TEMPLE, SIR WILLIAM (England, 1628–1699)

The Worst Curse.—There cannot live a more unhappy creature than an ill-natured old man who is neither capable of receiving pleasures, nor sensible of doing them to others.

The Best Rules for Young Men.—The best rules to form a young man are, to talk little, to hear much, to reflect alone upon what has passed in company, to distrust one's own opinions, and value others that deserve it.

How to Talk Well.—The first ingredient in conversation is truth, the next good sense, the third good humor, and the fourth wit.

THOREAU, HENRY D. (America, 1817–1862)

The Obligation of Duty.—Duty is one and invariable; it requires no impossibilities, nor can it ever be disregarded with impunity; so far as it exists, it is binding so as on no account to be neglected. How can one bind stronger than another?—*Essay, 1837.*

THUCYDIDES (Greece, 471–401 B.C.)

A Great Man's Assurance of Himself.—My history is presented to the public as a possession for all times, and not merely as a rhetorical display to catch the applause of my contemporaries.—*i. 22.*

Expostulation and Accusation.—Expostulation is just toward friends who have failed in their duty; accusation is to be used against enemies guilty of injustice.—*i. 69.*

The Best Security of Power.—For power is more firmly secured by treating our equals with justice than if, elated by present prosperity, we attempt to enlarge it at every risk.—*i. 42.*

TICKNOR, GEORGE (America, 1791–1871)

The Spanish Drama.—Calderon has added to the stage no new form of dramatic composition. Nor has he much modified those forms which had been already arranged and settled by Lope de Vega. But he has shown more technical exactness in combining his incidents, and adjusted everything more skillfully for stage effect. He has given to the whole a new coloring, and, in some respects, a new physiognomy. His drama is more poetical in its tone and tendencies, and has less the air of truth and reality, than that of his great predecessor.—*History of Spanish Literature, 1849.*

TILLOTSON, JOHN (England, 1630–1694)

The Difficulties of Hypocrisy.—It is hard to personate and act a part long; for where truth is not at the bottom, nature will always be endeavoring to return, and will peep out and betray herself one time or another.

A Glorious Victory.—A more glorious victory cannot be gained over another man than this, that when the injury began on his part, the kindness should begin on ours.

Impudence the Sister of Vice.—Shame is a great restraint upon sinners at first; but that soon falls off: and when men have once lost their innocence, their modesty is not like to be long troublesome to them. For impudence comes on with vice, and grows up with it. Lesser vices do not banish all shame and modesty; but great and abominable crimes harden men's foreheads, and make them shameless. When men have the heart to do a very bad thing, they seldom want the face to bear it out.

TSE-SZE (Chinese, *c.* 500 B.C.–?)

The Doctrine of the Mean.—Let the state of equilibrium and harmony exist in perfection, and a happy order will prevail throughout heaven and earth, and all things will be nourished and flourish.

The way of heaven and earth may be completely declared in one sentence. They are without any doubleness, and so they produce things in a manner which is unfathomable.

The way of heaven and earth is large and substantial, high and brilliant, far reaching and long enduring.

The heaven now before us is only this bright shining spot; but when viewed in its inexhaustible extent, the sun, moon, stars, and constellations of the zodiac are suspended in it, and all things are overspread by it. The earth before us is but a handful of soil; but when regarded in its breadth and thickness, it sustains mountains like the Hiva and Yoh, without feeling their weight, and contains the rivers and seas, without their leaking away. The mountain now before us appears only a stone; but when contemplated in all the vastness of its size, we see how the grass and trees are produced on it, and birds and beasts dwell on it, and precious things which men treasure up are found on it. The water now before us appears but a ladleful; yet extending our view to its unfathomable depths, the largest tortoise, iguanas, iguanadons, dragons, fishes, and turtles are produced in them; articles of value and sources of wealth abound in them. . . .

It is only he, possessed of all sagely qualities that can exist under heaven, who shows himself quick in apprehension, clear in discernment, of far-reaching intelligence and all-embracing knowledge, fitted to exercise rule; magnanimous, generous, benign, and mild, fitted to exercise forbearance; impulsive, energetic, firm, and enduring, fitted to maintain a firm hold; self-adjusted, grave, never swerving from the Mean, and correct, fitted to command reverence; accomplished, distinctive, concentrative, and searching, fitted to exercise discrimination.

All-embracing is he and vast, deep and active as a fountain, sending forth in their due seasons his virtue.

All-embracing and vast, he is like heaven. Deep and active as a fountain, he is like the abyss. He is seen, and the people all believe him; he acts, and the people are all pleased with him.

Therefore, his fame overspreads the Middle Kingdom (China), and extends to all barbarous tribes. Wherever ships and carriages reach, wherever the strength of man penetrates; wherever the heavens overshadow and the earth sustains; wherever the sun and moon shine; wherever frost and dews fall — all who have blood and breath unfeignedly honor and love him. Hence it is said — «He is the equal of Heaven.»

TUCKER, NATHANIEL BEVERLEY (America, 1784–1851)

Deception and Abuses in Politics.— It is owing to deception, played off on the unthinking multitude, that in the two freest countries in the world, the most important interests are taxed for the benefit of lesser interests. In England, a country of manufactures, they have been starved that agriculture may thrive. In this, a country of farmers and planters, they have been taxed that manufactures may thrive.— *The Partisan Leader.*

«MARK TWAIN» (SAMUEL L. CLEMENS) (America, 1835–)

On Babies.— «The Babies — as they comfort us in our sorrows, let us not forget them in our festivities.» I like that. We haven't all had the good fortune to be ladies; we haven't all been generals, or poets, or statesmen; but when the toast works down to the babies, we stand on common ground, for we have all been babies. It is a shame that for a thousand years the world's banquets have utterly ignored the baby — as if he didn't amount to anything! If you gentlemen will stop and think a minute,— if you will go back fifty or a hundred years, to your early married life, and recontemplate your first baby, you will remember that he amounted to a good deal, and even something over. You soldiers all know that when that little fellow arrived at the family headquarters you had to hand in your resignation. He took entire command. You became his lackey, his mere bodyservant, and you had to stand around too. He was not a commander who made allowances for time, distance, weather, or anything else. You had to execute his order whether it was possible or not. And there was only one form of marching in his manual of tactics, and that was the doublequick. He treated you with every sort of insolence and disrespect, and the bravest of you didn't say a word. . . . The idea that a baby doesn't amount to anything! Why, one baby is just a house and a front yard full by itself. One baby can furnish more business than you and your whole interior department can attend to. He is enterprising, irrepressible, brimful of lawless activities. Do what you please, you can't make him stay on the reservation. Sufficient unto the day is one baby; as long as you are in your right mind don't you ever pray for twins. Yes, it was high time for a toastmaster to recognize the importance of the babies. Think what is in store for the present crop. Fifty years hence we shall all be dead, I trust, and then this flag, if it still survive,— let us hope it may,— will be floating over a republic numbering two hundred million souls, according to the settled laws of our increase; our present schooner of state will have grown into a political leviathan — a Great Eastern — and the cradled babies of to-day will be on deck. Let them be well trained, for we are going to leave a big contract on their hands. Among the three or four million cradles now rocking in the land are some which this nation would preserve as sacred things, if we could know which ones they are. In one of these cradles the unconscious Farragut of the future is at this moment teething — think of it! — and putting in a world of dead-earnest, unarticulated, but perfectly justifiable profanity over it too; in another the future great historian is lying — and doubtless he will continue to lie until his earthly mission is ended; in another the future President is busying himself with no profounder problem of state than what the mischief has become of his hair so early; and in a mighty array of other cradles there are now some sixty thousand future office-seekers getting ready to furnish him occasion to grapple with that same old problem a second time; and in still one more cradle, somewhere under the flag, the future illustrious commander-in-chief of the American armies is so little burdened with his approaching grandeurs and responsibilities as to be giving his whole strategic mind, at this moment, to trying to find out some way to get his own big toe in his mouth,— an achievement which (meaning no disrespect) the illustrious guest of this evening turned his whole attention to some fifty-six years ago. And if the child is but the prophecy of the man, there are mighty few will doubt that he succeeded.— *From a Speech at the Banquet in Honor of General Grant, by the Army of the Tennessee, at the Palmer House, Chicago, November 14, 1879.*

VAUVENARGUES, MARQUIS DE (France, 1715–1747)

The Law of the Strongest.— Among kings, nations, individuals, the strongest assume rights over the weakest, and the same rule is followed by animate and inanimate beings: so that everything in the universe is ruled by violence: and this system, which we blame with some appearance of justice, is the law the most general, and most unchangeable, and the most important in nature.— «*Réflexions.*»

Discovering Old Things over Again.— When a thought presents itself to our minds as a profound discovery, and when we take the trouble to examine it, we often find it to be a truth that all the world knows.— «*Réflexions.*»

VERPLANCK, GULIAN C. (America, 1786–1870)

The Future of America.— Foreign criticism has contemptuously told us that the national pride of Americans rests more upon the anticipation of the future than on the recollections of the past. Allowing for a little malicious exaggeration, this is not far from the truth. It is so. It ought to be so. Why should it not be so?

Our national existence has been quite long enough, and its events sufficiently various, to prove the value and permanence of our civil and political establishments, to dissipate the doubts of their friends, and to disappoint the hopes of their enemies. Our past history is to us the pledge, the earnest, the type of the greater future. We may read in it the fortunes of our descendants, and with an assured confidence look forward to a long and continued advance in all that can make a people great. — *From an Address on the Fine Arts.*

VOLTAIRE, FRANÇOIS MARIE AROUET DE (France, 1694–1778)

The Secret of Boring People.— The secret of tiring is to say everything that can be said on the subject.

Literary Fame.— The path to literary fame is more difficult than that which leads to fortune. If you are so unfortunate as not to soar above mediocrity, remorse is your portion; if you succeed in your object, a host of enemies spring up around you: thus you find yourself on the brink of an abyss between contempt and hatred.

«WARD, ARTEMUS» (CHARLES F. BROWNE) (America, 1834–1867)

What Preachers Do for Us.— Show me a place where there isn't any Meetin' Houses and where preachers is never seen, and I'll show you a place where old hats air stuffed into broken winders, where the children are dirty and ragged, where gates have no hinges, where the wimmen air slipshod, and where maps of the devil's wild land air painted upon men's shirt bosums with tobacco jooce! That's what I'll show you. Let us consider what the preachers do for us before we aboose 'em.

WASHINGTON, GEORGE (America, 1732–1799)

On Friendship.— A slender acquaintance with the world must convince every man that actions, not words, are the true criterion of the attachment of friends; and that the most liberal professions of good will are very far from being the surest marks of it. . . . True friendship is a plant of slow growth, and must undergo and withstand the shocks of adversity before it is entitled to the appellation.— *Social Maxims: Friendship.*

How to Live Well.— Be courteous to all, but intimate with few; and let those few be well tried before you give them your confidence. True friendship is a plant of slow growth, and must undergo and withstand the shocks of adversity before it is entitled to the appellation. Let your heart feel for the afflictions and distresses of every one, and let your hand give in proportion to your purse; remembering always the estimation of the widow's mite, that it is not every one who asketh that deserveth charity; all, however, are worthy of the inquiry, or the deserving may suffer. Do not conceive that fine clothes make fine men, any more than fine feathers make fine birds. A plain, genteel dress is more admired, and obtains more credit, than lace and embroidery, in the eyes of the judicious and sensible.— *From a Letter to Bushrod Washington, 1783.*

WATTS, ISAAC (England, 1674–1748)

Rules for Convincing Others.— The softest and gentlest address to the erroneous is the best way to convince them of their mistake. Sometimes it is necessary to represent to your opponent that he is not far off from the truth, and that you would fain draw him a little nearer to it. Commend and establish whatever he says that is just and true, as our blessed Savior treated the young scribe when he answered well concerning the two great commandments; «Thou art not far,» says our Lord, «from the kingdom of heaven,» Mark xii. 34. Imitate the mildness and conduct of the blessed Jesus.

Come as near to your opponent as you can in all your propositions, and yield to him as much as you dare in a consistence with truth and justice.

It is a very great and fatal mistake in persons who attempt to convince and reconcile others to their party, when they make the difference appear as wide as possible; this is shocking to any person who is to be convinced; he will choose rather to keep and maintain his own opinions, if he cannot come into yours without renouncing and abandoning everything that he believed before.— *From «The Improvement of the Mind.»*

WEBSTER, DANIEL (America, 1782–1852)

The Sense of Duty.— There is no evil that we cannot either face or fly from, but the consciousness of duty disregarded.

A sense of duty pursues us ever. It is omnipresent, like the Deity.— *Argument on the Trial of John F. Knapp.*

Pride of Ancestry.— There may be, and there often is, indeed, a regard for ancestry, which nourishes only a weak pride; as there is also a care for posterity, which only disguises an habitual avarice, or hides the workings of a low and groveling vanity. But there is also a moral and philosophical respect for our ancestors, which elevates the character and improves the heart. Next to the sense of religious duty and moral feeling, I hardly know what should bear with stronger obligation on a liberal and enlightened mind, than a consciousness of alliance with excellence which is departed; and a consciousness, too, that in its acts and conduct, and even in its sentiments, it may be actively operating on the happiness of those who come after it. Poetry is found to have few stronger conceptions, by which it would affect or overwhelm the mind, than those in which it presents the moving and speaking image of the departed dead to the senses of the living. This belongs to poetry only because it is congenial to our nature. Poetry is, in this respect, but the handmaid of true philosophy and morality. It deals with us as human beings, naturally reverencing those whose visible connection with this state of being is severed, and who may yet exercise we know not what sympathy with ourselves; — and when it carries us forward, also, and shows us the long-continued result of all the good we do in the prosperity of those who follow us, till it bears us from ourselves, and absorbs us in an intense interest for what shall happen to the generations after us, it speaks only in the language of our nature, and affects us with sentiments which belong to us as human beings.— *From a Discourse in Commemoration of the First Settlement of New England.*

WEBSTER, NOAH (America, 1758–1843)

A Dandy Defined.— A dandy, in modern usage, is a male of the human species who dresses himself like a doll and who carries his character on his back.

On Novels for Girls.— With respect to novels so much admired by the young, and so generally condemned by the old, what shall I say? Perhaps it may be said with truth, that some of them are useful, many of them pernicious, and most of them trifling. A hundred volumes of modern novels may be read, without acquiring a new idea. Some of them contain entertaining stories, and where the descriptions are drawn from nature, and from characters and events in themselves innocent, the perusal of them may be harmless.— *Woman's Education in the Last Century.*

WHITMAN, WALT (America, 1819–1892)

The Only Valuable Investments.— Nothing endures but personal qualities; charity and personal force are the only investments worth anything.

WHITTIER, JOHN GREENLEAF (America, 1807–1892)

The Voice of the Pines.— A faint, low murmur, rising and falling on the wind. Now it comes rolling in upon me wave after wave of sweet, solemn music. There was a grand organ swell: and now it dies away as into the infinite distance; but I still hear it — whether with ear or spirit I know not — the very ghost of sound. . . . It is the voice of the pines yonder — a sort of morning song of praise to the Giver of life and Maker of beauty.— *My Summer with Dr. Singletary, Chap. V.*

WILLIAMS, ROGER (England, *c.* 1600–1684)

Bigotry in Religion.— A tenent that fights against the common principles of all civility, and the very civil being and combinations of men in nations, cities, etc., by commixing (explicitly or implicitly) a spiritual and civil state together, and so confounding and overthrowing the purity and strength of both. . . .

A tenent of high blasphemy against the God of Peace, the God of Order, who hath of one blood made all mankind, to dwell upon the face of the earth, now all confounded and destroyed in their civil beings and subsistences by mutual flames of war from their several respective religions and consciences.

A tenent that stunts the growth and flourishing of the most likely and most hopeful commonweals and countries, while consciences, the best, and the best deserving subjects are forced to fly (by enforced or voluntary banishment) from their native countries; the lamentable proof whereof England hath felt in the flight of so many worthy English into the Low Countries and New England, and from New England into old again and other foreign parts.— *From the «Bloody Tenent Made Yet More Bloody.»*

WILLIS, N. P. (America, 1806–1867)

On the Death of Poe.— Our first knowledge of Mr. Poe's removal to this city was by a call which we received from a lady who introduced herself to us as the mother of his wife. She was in search of employment for him, and she excused her errand by mentioning that he was ill, that her daughter was a confirmed invalid, and that their circumstances were such as compelled her taking it upon herself. The countenance of this lady, made beautiful and saintly with an evidently complete giving up of her life to privation and sorrowful tenderness, her gentle and mournful voice urging its plea, her long forgotten but habitually and unconsciously refined manners, and her appealing and yet appreciative mention of the claims and abilities of her son, disclosed at once the presence of one of those angels upon earth that women in adversity can be. It was a hard fate that she was watching over. Mr. Poe wrote with fastidious difficulty, and in a style too much above the popular level to be well paid. He was always in pecuniary difficulty, and, with his sick wife, frequently in want of the merest necessaries of life. Winter after winter, for years, the most touching sight to us, in this whole city, has been that tireless minister to genius, thinly and insufficiently clad, going from office to office with a poem, or an article on some literary subject, to sell — sometimes simply pleading in a broken voice that he was ill, and begging for him — mentioning nothing but that «he was ill,» whatever might be the reason for his writing nothing — and never, amid all her tears and recitals of distress, suffering one syllable to escape her lips that could convey a doubt of him, or a complaint, or a lessening of pride in his genius and good intentions. Her daughter died, a year and a half since, but she did not desert him. She continued his ministering angel — living with him — caring for him — guarding him against exposure, and, when he was carried away by temptation, amid grief and the loneliness of feelings unreplied to, and awoke from his self-abandonment prostrated in destitution and suffering, begging for him still. If woman's devotion, born with a first love and fed with human passion, hallow its object, as it is allowed to do, what does not a devotion like this — pure, disinterested and holy as the watch of an invisible spirit — say for him who inspired it?

WINTER, WILLIAM (America, 1836–)

Character.— It is of little traits that the greatest human character is composed.— «*English Rambles,*» *Part II., Chap. II.*

Noble Friendship.— As often as I came back to his door, his love met me on the threshold, and his noble serenity gave me comfort and peace.— «*English Rambles,*» *Part II., Chap. II.*

The Reserve of Greatness.— There is a better thing than the great man who is always speaking, and that is the great man who only speaks when he has a great word to say.— «*English Rambles,*» *Part I., Chap. V.*

WINTHROP, JOHN (New England, 1587–1649)

The Twofold Liberty.— There is a twofold liberty, natural (I mean as our nature is now corrupt) and civil or federal. The first is common to man with beasts and other creatures. By this, man, as he stands in relation to man simply, hath liberty to do what he lists; it is a liberty to evil as well as to good. This liberty is incompatible and inconsistent with authority, and cannot endure the least restraint of the most just authority. The exercise and maintaining of this liberty makes men grow more evil, and in time to be worse than brute beasts: *omnes sumus licentia deteriores.* This is that great enemy of truth and peace, that wild beast, which all the ordinances of God are bent against, to restrain and subdue it. The other kind of liberty I call civil or federal, it may also be termed moral, in reference to the covenant between God and man, in the moral law, and the politic covenants and constitutions, amongst men themselves. This liberty is the proper end and object of authority, and cannot subsist without it; and it is a liberty you are to stand for, with the hazard (not only of your goods, but) of your lives, if need be. Whatsoever crosseth this is not authority, but a distemper thereof.— *From an Address in the Massachusetts Assembly of 1645.*

XENOPHON (Greece, 430–357 B.C.)

On Trusting the Gods.— Socrates prayed to the gods simply that they would give him what was good, inasmuch as the gods knew best what things are good for man. Those who prayed for gold, or silver, or high power, or anything of that kind, he regarded as doing the same as if they prayed that they might play at dice, or fight, or anything of that kind, of which the result was dependent on chance. — «*Memorabilia,*» *i. 3.*

The Low Minded and the Honorable.— The low minded thou canst not gain otherwise than by giving them something; whereas the honorable and the good thou mayst best attract by treating them in a kindly manner.— «*Memorabilia,*» *ii. 3.*

ZIMMERMANN, JOHANN GEORG (Switzerland, 1728–1795)

Where the Polite Fool Fails.— In the sallies of badinage a polite fool shines; but in gravity he is as awkward as an elephant disporting.

Wit that Perishes.— Many species of wit are quite mechanical: these are the favorites of witlings, whose fame in words scarce outlives the remembrance of their funeral ceremonies.

ZOLA, Émile (France, 1840–)

Life and Labor.— Labor! remember that it is the unique natural law of the world, the regulator which leads organized matter to its unknown goal. Life has no other meaning, no other *raison d'être;* we only appear on this earth in order that we each may contribute our share of labor and disappear. One can only define life by that motion which is communicated to it and which it transmits, and which after all is but so much labor toward the great final work to be accomplished in the depths of the ages. Why, then, should we not be modest, why should we not accept the respective tasks that each of us comes here to fulfill without rebellion, without giving way to the pride of egotism which prompts men to consider themselves centres of gravity, and deters them from falling into the ranks with their fellows? — *From the New Review.*

The General Index should be used in connection with the Chronological and other indexes named below:—

PREFACE TO THE INDEXES

HE text of the WORLD'S BEST ESSAYS extends to 4004 pages; and to make its almost inexhaustible information readily available for the student and general reader, the indexes which follow have been modeled on the modern system used in indexing the great public libraries. The text has been so analyzed that not only the titles of essays, the names of authors, and the names of persons and places mentioned in the text will guide the reader in research, but the subjects treated and the ideas underlying them have been subjected to such analysis that it is hoped the great resources of the work can be focused on the given point on which the indexes are consulted. The cross-references are extensive — perhaps more extensive than have been attempted in any similar index; but the chief usefulness of the General Index will come, no doubt, from its attempt at a severe analysis of the forms of expression taken in different countries and ages by the master ideas which have shaped the course of civilization. In literature, art, religion, science, ethics, and philosophy, law and the science of government, political economy, education, history, music, and musical criticism, the conduct of life and the topics which most nearly affect the home and family, the General Index gives citations with cross-references intended to make the work constantly helpful in the solution of those difficulties, which, though they come to all classes, are apt to be most numerous with the greatest readers. Nine thousand separate slips were used in making the general index alone, while the distinct citations in it will run well over 10,000 and will probably come near averaging with the cross-references in all the indexes three or more to each text page.

A feature of the General Index likely to prove helpful to the reader is the analysis of the essays by subject, which classifies every essay in the work by the idea to which its governing thought belongs. The citations to incidental references to a subject can thus be re-enforced by essays which are wholly or chiefly devoted to it. The Chronological Indexes of Essayists, of Literature, and of Periods and Events will be found specially helpful in the use of the General Index.

GENERAL INDEX OF ESSAYISTS

A'BECKETT — ZOLA

INDEX OF SUBJECTS OF ESSAYS

CHRONOLOGICAL INDEX OF ESSAYISTS AND SUBJECTS

ANCIENT AND CLASSICAL

(582 B. C. to 525 A. D.)

MIDDLE AGES AND RENAISSANCE

(672 A. D. to 1553 A. D.)

CHRONOLOGICAL INDEX OF LITERATURE

2000 B.C. to 1901 A.D.

CHRONOLOGICAL INDEX OF LAW, GOVERNMENT, AND ECONOMICS

c. 1472 B.C. to 1900 A.D.

GENERAL INDEX